OXFORD LIBRARY OF PSYCHOLOGY

AREA EDITORS

Clinical Psychology
David H. Barlow

Cognitive Neuroscience
Kevin N. Ochsner and Stephen M. Kosslyn

Cognitive Psychology
Daniel Reisberg

Counseling Psychology
Elizabeth M. Altmaier and Jo-Ida C. Hansen

Developmental Psychology
Philip David Zelazo

Health Psychology
Howard S. Friedman

History of Psychology
David B. Baker

Methods and Measurement
Todd D. Little

Neuropsychology
Kenneth M. Adams

Organizational Psychology
Steve W. J. Kozlowski

Personality and Social Psychology
Kay Deaux and Mark Snyder

The Oxford Handbook of Evolution and the Emotions

OXFORD LIBRARY OF PSYCHOLOGY

The Oxford Handbook of Evolution and the Emotions

Edited by
Laith Al-Shawaf and Todd K. Shackelford

OXFORD
UNIVERSITY PRESS

Oxford University Press is a department of the University of Oxford. It furthers
the University's objective of excellence in research, scholarship, and education
by publishing worldwide. Oxford is a registered trade mark of Oxford University
Press in the UK and certain other countries.

Published in the United States of America by Oxford University Press
198 Madison Avenue, New York, NY 10016, United States of America.

© Oxford University Press 2024

All rights reserved. No part of this publication may be reproduced, stored in
a retrieval system, or transmitted, in any form or by any means, without the
prior permission in writing of Oxford University Press, or as expressly permitted
by law, by license, or under terms agreed with the appropriate reproduction
rights organization. Inquiries concerning reproduction outside the scope of the
above should be sent to the Rights Department, Oxford University Press, at the
address above.

You must not circulate this work in any other form
and you must impose this same condition on any acquirer.

CIP data is on file at the Library of Congress
ISBN 978–0–19–754475–4

DOI: 10.1093/oxfordhb/9780197544754.001.0001

Printed by Sheridan Books, Inc., United States of America

To my parents

Who fed my love of books and took all my weird childhood questions seriously.

L.A.S.

CONTENTS

Foreword: A Bounty of Riches in Understanding Human Emotions   xiii
  David M. Buss
Contributors   xv
Introduction to *The Oxford Handbook of Evolution and the Emotions*   xxi
  Laith Al-Shawaf

Part I • Understanding Emotions from an Evolutionary Perspective

1. Basic Emotion Theory: A Beginner's Guide   3
    Daniel Cordaro
2. The Past Explains the Present: Emotional Adaptations and the Structure of Ancestral Environments   21
    John Tooby and Leda Cosmides
3. Evolution, Emotion, and Facial Behavior: A 21st-Century View   55
    Alan J. Fridlund and James A. Russell
4. Social Emotions Are Governed by a Common Grammar of Social Valuation: Theoretical Foundations and Applications to Human Personality and the Criminal Justice System   79
    Coltan Scrivner, Daniel Sznycer, Aaron W. Lukaszewski, and Laith Al-Shawaf
5. The Motivational Architecture of Emotions   99
    Marco Del Giudice

Part II • Evolutionary Approaches to Specific Emotions

6. The Recalibrational Theory: Anger as a Bargaining Emotion   135
    Aaron Sell and Daniel Sznycer
7. Shame   145
    Mitchell Landers, Daniel Sznycer, and Laith Al-Shawaf

8. The Neutralization Theory of Hatred   163
   Aaron Sell, Coltan Scrivner, Mitchell Landers, and Anthony C. Lopez
9. Disgust: An Emotion for Pathogen Avoidance   181
   Tara J. Cepon-Robins
10. The Evolved Nature of Pride   203
    Jessica L. Tracy, Eric Mercadante, and Zachary Witkower
11. Romantic Love   219
    Jaclyn K. Doherty and Claudia C. Brumbaugh
12. Neuroendocrine Mechanisms for Human Emotional Attachments   235
    Heather Habecker and Mark V. Flinn
13. Regret   246
    Leif Edward Ottesen Kennair, Trond Viggo Grøntvedt, and Mons Bendixen
14. The Elements of Gratitude   263
    Riley N. Loria, Debra Lieberman, and Eric J. Pedersen
15. Caring and the Evolution of Guilt: A Biopsychosocial Approach to a Pro-Social Emotion   282
    Paul Gilbert
16. Lassitude: A Coordination System to Support Host Immunity   297
    Joshua M. Schrock, Lawrence S. Sugiyama, and J. Josh Snodgrass
17. The Origins of Boredom   317
    Yijun Lin and Erin C. Westgate
18. *Kama Muta*: The Cuteness Emotion   339
    Kamilla Knutsen Steinnes, Johanna Katarina Blomster Lyshol, Janis H. Zickfeld, Thomas Schubert, and Beate Seibt
19. Curiosity: A Behavioral Biology Perspective   357
    Coltan Scrivner
20. An Evolutionary Perspective on Positive Emotions   369
    Amanda P. Kirsch, Erika B. Langley, Carley Vornlocher, and Michelle N. Shiota
21. How Jealousy Works   391
    David M. G. Lewis, Laith Al-Shawaf, and Kortnee C. Evans
22. Chronic Pain, Recuperation, and Care-Eliciting: Evolutionary and Signaling Theory Perspectives   415
    Christopher H. Cantor and Kenneth D. Craig
23. Contentment: The Evolution of Indestructible Well-Being   436
    Daniel Cordaro

24. Happiness   462
    Stefan M. M. Goetz and Glenn E. Weisfeld
25. Grief   483
    Heidi Martin and Carol Cronin Weisfeld
26. Fear: An Evolutionary Perspective on Its Biological, Behavioral, and Communicative Features   500
    Katherine O'Connell, Shawn A. Rhoads, and Abigail A. Marsh
27. The Evolutionary Functions of Sadness: The Cognitive and Social Benefits of Negative Affect   520
    Joseph P. Forgas
28. Humor   543
    Glenn E. Weisfeld and Carol Cronin Weisfeld
29. Compassion: An Evolutionary Account   565
    Jennifer L. Goetz and Emiliana Simon-Thomas

Part III • Emotions in Different Domains of Life

30. Emotions and Status Hierarchies   587
    Patrick K. Durkee
31. Emotions in Politics   607
    Florian van Leeuwen and Michael Bang Petersen
32. A Socio-functional Perspective on Emotion and Cooperation   622
    Diego Guevara Beltran, Michelle N. Shiota, and Athena Aktipis
33. Emotion, Sickness, and Care for the Sick   648
    Leander Steinkopf
34. Emotions and Olfaction   663
    Laura Schäfer and Ilona Croy
35. Emotion and Nonverbal Communication   681
    Elena Svetieva
36. Emotions and Intergroup Conflict   698
    Christian Kotoye and Melissa M. McDonald
37. Emotions and Reconciliation   717
    Yohsuke Ohtsubo and Adam Smith
38. Emotions in Co-Rumination: An Evolutionary Developmental Perspective   737
    Jessica L. Calvi and Jennifer Byrd-Craven
39. An Evolutionary Approach to Emotion Regulation   748
    Michael A. Kisley

40. More than a Feeling: The Comparative Psychology of Emotion   763
    Jennifer Vonk, Lauri Torgerson-White, Jared Edge, and Bridget Benton
41. Emotion and Empathy in Great Apes   791
    Zanna Clay and Diane A. Austry
42. Emotions in Dogs: Neuroscientific, Behavioral, and Comparative Perspectives   809
    Miiamaaria V. Kujala and Juliane Bräuer
43. Comparative Psychology of Frustrative Nonreward   830
    Carmen Torres and Mauricio R. Papini
44. Emotional Vigilance   847
    Guillaume Dezecache and Hugo Mercier
45. More than PMS: The Influence of Hormones on Emotion   861
    Lisa L. M. Welling, Virginia E. Mitchell, Jenna Lunge, and Mercedes Hughes
46. Defect or Design Feature? Toward an Evolutionary Psychology of the Role of Emotion in Motivated Reasoning   885
    Timothy Ketelaar
47. The Emergence of Emotionally Modern Humans: Implications for Language and Learning   910
    Sarah Blaffer Hrdy and Judith M. Burkart
48. Positive Evolutionary Psychology: The New Science of Psychological Growth   929
    Nicole A. Wedberg, Glenn Geher, Brianna McQuade, and Dayna M. Thomas
49. Are There Really So Many Moral Emotions? Carving Morality at Its Functional Joints   944
    Léo Fitouchi, Jean-Baptiste André, and Nicolas Baumard
50. Emotion and Women's Intrasexual Mating Competition   968
    Maryanne L. Fisher
51. Emotions across Cultures   983
    Roza G. Kamiloğlu, YongQi Cong, Rui Sun, and Disa A. Sauter
52. The Role of Emotion in Second- and Third-Party Punishment   997
    Julia Marshall and Katherine McAuliffe
53. Leadership as an Emotional Process: An Evolutionarily Informed Perspective   1021
    Sirio Lonati, Zachary H. Garfield, Nicolas Bastardoz, and Christopher von Rueden

54. The Negative Effect of Ostracism and Other Forms of Social Exclusion on Emotions   1040
    Eric D. Wesselmann, Michaela Pfundmair, Jennifer R. Spoor, and Wesley G. Moons
55. Natural Selection and Human Emotions   1056
    Laura Betzig
56. Evolution, Emotions, and the American Legal System   1067
    Keelah E. G. Williams and Carlton Patrick

Part IV • Emotions in Psychopathology

57. The Harmful Dysfunction Analysis: An Evolutionary Approach to Emotional Disorders   1085
    Jerome C. Wakefield and Jordan A. Conrad
58. Anxiety and Phobias   1109
    Leif Edward Ottesen Kennair, Miriam Lindner, Kristen Hagen, and Simen Mjøen Larsen
59. Credible Sadness, Coercive Sadness: Depression as a Functional Response to Adversity and Strife   1134
    Edward H. Hagen and Kristen L. Syme
60. Evolutionary Perspectives on Eating Disorders   1172
    Riadh Abed
61. Narcissism and Narcissistic Personality Disorder: Evolutionary Roots and Emotional Profiles   1197
    Anna Z. Czarna, Monika Wróbel, Logan F. Folger, Nicholas S. Holtzman, Jennifer R. Daley, and Joshua D. Foster
62. Addiction and Substance Use   1218
    Russil Durrant
63. Rethinking the Neurodiversity Debate from the Harmful Dysfunction Perspective: The Implications of DSM Category Evolutionary Heterogeneity   1238
    Jordan A. Conrad and Jerome C. Wakefield
64. Post-Traumatic Stress Disorder and Post-Combat Reintegration: An Evolutionary Model   1262
    Hector A. Garcia
65. An Evolutionary Approach to Emotional Difficulties in Borderline Personality Disorder   1279
    Lawrence Ian Reed, Cameryn Cooley, and Sara Okun
66. An Evolutionary Perspective on Psychopathy   1298
    Virgil Zeigler-Hill and Gracynn R. Young

67. Obsessive-Compulsive and Related Disorders, Hypochondriasis, and Behavioral Addictions   1317
   Vlasios Brakoulias

Afterword: Evolutionary Emotion Research at the Crossroads   1327
   Marco Del Giudice

Index   1341

FOREWORD: A BOUNTY OF RICHES IN UNDERSTANDING HUMAN EMOTIONS

David M. Buss

A moment of introspection reveals that emotions occupy center stage in human psychological experience. Some are apparent to nearly everyone. We are seized with fear when confronted with a hissing snake within striking distance or an ominous spider silently approaching. Intuition tells us that rage motivates attack. Other emotions more subtly occupy our psychological space: *Schadenfreude*, the pleasure we experience at another's downfall, or *kama muta*, the loving feeling we experience when observing an indescribably cute baby, puppy, or kitten. This important volume heralds tremendous scientific progress in understanding these subjective experiences, theoretical accounts of their origins, the mechanistic and computational nature of their design, their physiological basis, and their expression in manifest behavior.

One signal sign of progress is a prolific expansion of phenomena considered to be proper emotions. Early theorists posited a small list. Ekman, for example, posited six in his original formulation—fear, anger, joy, sadness, disgust, surprise—to which he subsequently added the seventh of contempt. Modern formulations, as instantiated in this volume, explore many more, such as pride, shame, regret, lassitude, grief, gratitude, sexual arousal, and sexual jealousy.

A second sign of progress is both an expansion and a relaxation of theoretical criteria for considering something a "basic emotion." Ekman and his followers tightly yoked emotions to criteria such as having a universal facial expression, helping to solve a problem of survival, presence in nonhuman primates, and states of brief duration. More modern formulations do not require a distinctive or universal facial signature (e.g., jealousy), presence in nonhuman primates (e.g., regret), brevity of experience (e.g., long-lasting lassitude), or linkage to a problem of survival (e.g., romantic love, parental love, sexual arousal).

A third sign of progress centers on a dramatic expansion of the domains of human conduct affected by emotions. These include addiction and substance usage, psychological disorders such as anorexia and post-traumatic stress disorder (PTSD), motivated reasoning and communication, cooperation and intergroup conflict, politics, social status, and even morality. Emotions, consequently, are not isolated psychological phenomena, but permeate many domains of human functioning.

A fourth and related sign of progress centers on the development of more sophisticated theories. As expected in rapidly expanding fields, disagreements and competing accounts flourish. Key axes of disagreement center on whether emotions are "socially constructed" or "functionally specialized," mechanism-rich or mechanism-free, and the biological plausibility of emotional readouts—dimensions well-explored in Del Giudice's excellent Afterword in this volume.

This *Handbook* provides an outstanding landmark, documenting the theoretical and empirical progress in the mushrooming field of evolutionary approaches to emotions. It does not furnish the final word. But it provides abundant documentation of progress made over the past few decades and exciting road maps for future developments in the scientific study of emotions.

CONTRIBUTORS

Riadh Abed
: Retired Psychiatrist, Medical Director and Hon. Senior Clinical Lecturer, University of Sheffield

Athena Aktipis
: Department of Psychology, Arizona State University

Laith Al-Shawaf
: Department of Psychology and Center for Cognitive Archaeology, University of Colorado Colorado Springs, Colorado Springs; Institute for Advanced Study in Toulouse

Jean-Baptiste André
: Département d'études cognitives, Institut Jean Nicod, ENS, EHESS, PSL University, CNRS

Diane A. Austry
: Department of Psychology, Durham University

Nicolas Bastardoz
: Department of Work and Organization Studies, KU Leuven

Nicolas Baumard
: Département d'études cognitives, Institut Jean Nicod, ENS, EHESS, PSL University, CNRS

Diego Guevara Beltran
: Department of Psychology, Arizona State University

Mons Bendixen
: Department of Psychology, Norwegian University of Science and Technology

Bridget Benton
: Department of Psychology, Oakland University

Laura Betzig
: Northwestern University, University of California, and University of Michigan

Vlasios Brakoulias
: School of Medicine, Western Sydney University and Western Sydney Local Health District Mental Health Service, Sydney

Juliane Bräuer
: Department of Linguistic and Cultural Evolution, Max Planck Institute for the Science of Human History, and Department for General Psychology and Cognitive Neuroscience, Friedrich Schiller University of Jena

Claudia C. Brumbaugh
: Department of Psychology, Queens College

Judith M. Burkart
: Department of Anthropology, University of Zurich

Jennifer Byrd-Craven
: Oklahoma Center for Evolutionary Analysis (OCEAN), Oklahoma State University

Jessica L. Calvi
: Salivary Bioscience Laboratory, University of Nebraska-Lincoln

Christopher H. Cantor
　School of Medicine, University of Queensland, Australia

Tara J. Cepon-Robins
　Department of Anthropology, University of Colorado Colorado Springs, Colorado Springs

Zanna Clay
　Department of Psychology, Durham University

YongQi Cong
　Department of Psychology, University of Amsterdam

Jordan A. Conrad
　Department of Social Work, Long Island University and Private Practice, New York City

Cameryn Cooley
　Department of Psychology, The Ohio State University

Daniel Cordaro
　The Contentment Foundation

Leda Cosmides
　Department of Psychological and Brain Sciences, University of California–Santa Barbara

Kenneth D. Craig
　Department of Psychology, University of British Colombia

Ilona Croy
　Department of Psychosomatics, Medical Faculty, Technische Universität Dresden, and Institute of Psychology, Friedrich-Schiller-Universität Jena

Anna Z. Czarna
　Institute of Applied Psychology, Jagiellonian University

Jennifer R. Daley
　Psychology Department, University of Albany

Marco Del Giudice
　Department of Life Sciences, University of Trieste

Guillaume Dezecache
　Université Clermont Auvergne, LAPSCO CNRS

Jaclyn K. Doherty
　Graduate Center, City University of New York

Patrick K. Durkee
　Department of Psychology, California State University, Fresno

Russil Durrant
　Institute of Criminology, School of Social and Cultural Studies, Victoria University of Wellington

Jared Edge
　Department of Psychology, Oakland University

Kortnee C. Evans
　Department of Psychology, Murdoch University

Maryanne L. Fisher
　Department of Psychology, Saint Mary's University; Kinsey Institute, Indiana University; and Psychological Adaptations Research Consortium

Léo Fitouchi
　Département d'études cognitives, Institut Jean Nicod, ENS, EHESS, PSL University, CNRS

Mark V. Flinn
　Department of Anthropology, Baylor University

Logan F. Folger
　Department of Psychology, Oklahoma State University

Joseph P. Forgas
　School of Psychology, University of New South Wales, Sydney

Joshua D. Foster
　Psychology Department, University of South Alabama

Alan J. Fridlund
　Department of Psychological and Brain Sciences, University of California, Santa Barbara

Hector A. Garcia
    Department of Psychology, Texas A&M University, San Antonio; Texas Valley Coastal Bend Veterans Healthcare System

Zachary H. Garfield
    Africa Institute for Research in Economics and Social Sciences, Université Mohammed VI Polytechnique, Rabat, Morocco

Glenn Geher
    Department of Psychology, State University of New York, New Paltz

Paul Gilbert
    College of Health and Social Care Research Centre, University of Derby

Jennifer L. Goetz
    Psychology Program, Centre College

Stefan M. M. Goetz
    Charles Stewart Mott Department of Public Health, College of Human Medicine, Michigan State University, Flint

Trond Viggo Grøntvedt
    Department of Psychology and Department of Public Health and Nursing, HUNT Research Centre, Norwegian University of Science and Technology

Heather Habecker
    Department of Psychology and Neuroscience, Baylor University

Edward H. Hagen
    Department of Anthropology, Washington State University

Kristen Hagen
    Department of Mental Health, Norwegian University of Science and Technology

Nicholas S. Holtzman,
    Department of Psychology, Southeastern Louisiana University

Sarah Blaffer Hrdy
    Department of Anthropology, University of California, Davis

Mercedes Hughes
    Department of Psychology, Oakland University

Roza G. Kamiloğlu
    Department of Psychology, University of Amsterdam

Leif Edward Ottesen Kennair
    Department of Psychology, Norwegian University of Science and Technology

Timothy Ketelaar
    Department of Psychology, New Mexico State University

Amanda P. Kirsch
    Department of Psychology, Arizona State University

Michael A. Kisley
    Department of Psychology, University of Colorado Colorado Springs, Colorado Springs

Christian Kotoye
    Department of Psychology, Oakland University

Miiamaaria V. Kujala
    Department of Psychology, University of Jyväskylä; Faculty of Veterinary Medicine, University of Helsinki; and Department of Neuroscience and Biomedical Engineering, Aalto University School of Science

Mitchell Landers
    Department of Psychology, The University of Chicago

Erika B. Langley
    Department of Psychology, Arizona State University

Simen Mjøen Larsen
    Educational Services

David M. G. Lewis
School of Psychology and Centre for Healthy Ageing, Health Futures Institute, Murdoch University

Debra Lieberman
Department of Psychology, University of Miami

Yijun Lin
Department of Psychology, University of Florida

Miriam Lindner
Department of Psychology, Harvard University

Sirio Lonati
NEOMA Business School—Reims Campus, Reims, France

Anthony C. Lopez
School of Politics, Philosophy and Public Affairs, Washington State University

Riley N. Loria
Department of Psychology and Neuroscience, University of Colorado, Boulder

Aaron W. Lukaszewski
Department of Psychology, California State University, Fullerton

Jenna Lunge
Department of Psychology, Oakland University

Johanna Katarina Blomster Lyshol
Department of Psychology, Oslo New University College

Abigail A. Marsh
Department of Psychology, Georgetown University

Julia Marshall
Department of Psychology and Neuroscience, Boston College

Heidi Martin
Department of Psychology, University of Detroit Mercy

Katherine McAuliffe
Department of Psychology, Boston College

Melissa M. McDonald
Department of Psychology, Oakland University

Brianna McQuade
Department of Psychology, State University of New York, New Paltz

Eric Mercadante
Department of Psychology, University of British Columbia

Hugo Mercier
Département d'études cognitives, Institut Jean Nicod, ENS, EHESS, PSL University, CNRS

Virginia E. Mitchell
Department of Psychology, Oakland University

Wesley G. Moons
Cortex Science

Katherine O'Connell
Interdisciplinary Program in Neuroscience, Georgetown University

Yohsuke Ohtsubo
Department of Social Psychology, University of Tokyo

Sara Okun
Center for Data Science, New York University

Mauricio R. Papini
Department of Psychology, Texas Christian University

Carlton Patrick
Department of Legal Studies, University of Central Florida

Eric J. Pedersen
University of Colorado, Boulder

Michael Bang Petersen
Department of Political Science, Aarhus University

Michaela Pfundmair
  Faculty of Intelligence, Federal University of Administrative Sciences
Lawrence Ian Reed
  Department of Psychology, New York University
Shawn A. Rhoads
  Department of Psychology, Georgetown University
James A. Russell
  Department of Psychology and Neuroscience, Boston College
Disa A. Sauter
  Department of Psychology, University of Amsterdam
Laura Schäfer
  Department of Psychosomatics, Medical Faculty, Technische Universität Dresden
Thomas Schubert
  Department of Psychology, University of Oslo
Joshua M. Schrock
  Institute for Sexual and Gender Minority Health and Wellbeing and Department of Anthropology, Northwestern University
Coltan Scrivner
  Department of Comparative Human Development and Institute for Mind and Biology, The University of Chicago
Beate Seibt
  Department of Psychology, University of Oslo
Aaron Sell
  Departments of Criminology and Psychology, Heidelberg University
Michelle N. Shiota
  Department of Psychology, Arizona State University
Emiliana Simon-Thomas
  Science Director, Greater Good Science Center, University of California, Berkeley
Adam Smith
  Department of Psychology, International Christian University
J. Josh Snodgrass
  Department of Anthropology, University of Oregon
Jennifer R. Spoor
  Business School, La Trobe University
Leander Steinkopf
  Institute of Medical Psychology, Ludwig-Maximilians-Universität München; Department of Education and Psychology, Freie Universität Berlin
Kamilla Knutsen Steinnes
  Consumption Research Norway, Oslo Metropolitan University
Lawrence S. Sugiyama
  Department of Anthropology, University of Oregon
Rui Sun
  Department of Psychology, University of Amsterdam
Elena Svetieva
  Department of Communication, University of Colorado Colorado Springs, Colorado Springs
Kristen L. Syme
  Department of Anthropology, Washington State University, and Department of Applied and Experimental Psychology, Vrije Universiteit Amsterdam
Daniel Sznycer
  Oklahoma Center for Evolutionary Analysis (OCEAN), Department of Psychology, Oklahoma State University

Dayna M. Thomas
Department of Psychology, State University of New York, New Paltz

John Tooby
Department of Anthropology, University of California-Santa Barbara

Lauri Torgerson-White
Farm Sanctuary

Carmen Torres
Department of Psychology, University of Jaén

Jessica L. Tracy
Department of Psychology, University of British Columbia

Florian van Leeuwen
Department of Social Psychology, Tilburg University

Jennifer Vonk
Department of Psychology, Oakland University

Christopher von Rueden
Jepson School of Leadership Studies, University of Richmond

Carley Vornlocher
Department of Psychology, Arizona State University

Jerome C. Wakefield
Center for Bioethics; School of Global Public Health; and Silver School of Social Work, New York University

Nicole A. Wedberg
State University of New York, New Paltz

Carol Cronin Weisfeld
Psychology Department, University of Detroit Mercy

Glenn E. Weisfeld
Department of Psychology, Wayne State University

Lisa L. M. Welling
Department of Psychology, Oakland University

Eric D. Wesselmann
Department of Psychology, Illinois State University

Erin C. Westgate
Department of Psychology, University of Florida

Keelah E. G. Williams
Department of Psychology, Hamilton College

Zachary Witkower
Department of Psychology, University of British Columbia

Monika Wróbel
Institute of Psychology, University of Lodz

Gracynn R. Young
Department of Psychology, Oakland University

Virgil Zeigler-Hill
Department of Psychology, Oakland University

Janis H. Zickfeld
Department of Management, Aarhus University

INTRODUCTION TO *THE OXFORD HANDBOOK OF EVOLUTION AND THE EMOTIONS*

Laith Al-Shawaf

Welcome, dear readers, to *The Oxford Handbook of Evolution and the Emotions* (TOHEE). This book approaches the science of emotion from an evolutionary perspective, collecting key advances from the last few decades in a single volume.

The book is divided into four sections as follows:

Part 1 outlines different ways of approaching emotions from an evolutionary perspective.

Part 2 discusses specific emotions. Chapter topics range from romantic love, pride, and happiness, through shame, anger, and jealousy, to gratitude, kama muta, and compassion.

Part 3 details the role emotions play in many domains of life, including the challenges and opportunities that we encounter on a daily basis – cooperation, intergroup conflict, reconciliation, politics, morality, motivated reasoning, emotion regulation, status hierarchy navigation, illness, the legal system, emotions in nonhuman animals, and more.

Part 4 explores the link between emotions and psychopathology from an evolutionary perspective. This section deals with specific psychological disorders, such as borderline personality disorder, narcissistic personality disorder, post-traumatic stress disorder, and depression. Crucially, it also asks key theoretical questions about how best to conceptualize disorders, and what light evolutionary thinking can shed on this important issue.

Traditionally, the social sciences have been proximate in their focus, largely restricting themselves to "how" questions about mechanism and development while typically ignoring the "why" questions about evolution and biological function. In keeping with this volume's evolutionary approach, its authors give both the proximate and the ultimate levels of analysis their due, addressing both the "hows" and the "whys" of emotion science. This allows for a deeper understanding of emotions and enables us to move toward a more comprehensive science of the mind.

Together, the 67 chapters in this book represent the state of the art in evolutionary approaches to affective science. The chapters offer a stimulating mix of theoretical insights and empirical findings that we hope will inspire new research and prove useful to scholars in a number of fields: psychology, psychiatry, biology, anthropology, sociology, behavioral economics, comparative research, and any discipline whose subject matter touches on emotions in some way.

We put this book together now because the time is ripe for an overview of the field. Emotion research, especially that inspired by evolutionary thinking, has made huge strides over the past few decades. It is gratifying to see how well the scientific method works: we know so much more about emotions in humans and in other species than we did 20 or 30 years ago! At the same time, many questions remain unanswered, and different theoretical perspectives still need to be integrated – or to battle it out in the empirical arena. Emotion research is a young area within a broader science, psychology, that is itself still maturing.

Before we close, I would like to acknowledge that this book is the fruit of a massive collaborative undertaking, and to thank the dozens of authors who contributed their expertise and knowledge to this volume. *The Oxford Handbook of Evolution and the Emotions* boasts close to 70 cutting-edge entries by more than 100 experts in fields ranging from anthropology to zoology. It has been a distinct pleasure to see science and scholarship practiced in such a collaborative, international, and cross-disciplinary manner. This book would not exist without the hard work and perspicacity of these authors.

This volume, then, seeks to accomplish two objectives: document the explosion of new knowledge over the past few decades, and pose key questions about where the field should go next. This is an exciting time for emotion science, and a propitious moment to take stock of our field. We hope you enjoy reading this book as much as we enjoyed putting it together.

PART I

Understanding Emotions from an Evolutionary Perspective

Basic Emotion Theory: A Beginner's Guide

Daniel Cordaro

Abstract

Beginning with the seminal works of Charles Darwin, Basic Emotion Theory (BET) has been one of the cornerstone theoretical frameworks in the study of emotions. Its influence has driven several fields of research in the psychological sciences and continues to provide a foundational road map to exploring the vast, still-uncharted space of human emotion. Basic emotions are discrete, evolutionarily driven processes essential to survival. They are a special subset of discrete emotions that transcend across species, time, and culture. Basic emotions are elementally distinct, genetically determined, and functionally critical. This chapter provides a brief overview of the importance of BET in emotion science, discusses which emotions are basic, and reviews where the science of basic emotions is presently. Based on these current observations, future directions for the study of evolutionarily grounded emotions are discussed.

Key Words: basic emotion theory, evolution, expression, neuroscience, physiology, Darwin

Introduction

The scientific study of emotion is nearly 150 years old. It is a field ripe with zeitgeist-altering empirical advances, and at the same time it is rich with theoretical debate. Herein we briefly review the nature of emotions through the lens of Basic Emotion Theory (BET), the most central narrative in emotion psychology to date. BET has influenced our understanding of the evolutionary underpinnings of emotions and continues to guide empirical advances seeking to decode the universe of emotion experience across species. This chapter briefly reviews the origins of the evolutionary treatment of human emotions, contextualizes the modern understanding of BET, and offers reflections for future directions of the next wave of evolutionary emotion science.

A Brief History of Basic Emotion Theory
Origins

In 1872 Charles Darwin published *The Expression of the Emotions in Man and Animals* (or *Expression*, as Darwin referred to it in shorthand), which quickly became a period bestseller and was widely praised as an accessible introduction to evolutionary theory (Browne, 2002). Darwin's bestselling book by far, *Expression* explored the biological underpinnings of emotions, and examined the evidence regarding how certain features of emotional expression transcended cultures and species (Darwin et al., 1998). *Expression* was a strategically important book, because in Darwin's time, it was unfashionable to discuss similarities between human and nonhuman animals. *Expression* provided a palatable entry point for readers to explore the possibility that humans may share inherited traits with common nonhuman ancestors (Francis, 2007).

Expression pioneered the field of emotion science, and many of Darwin's findings became foundational to modern evolutionary approaches to human emotion. In many ways, *Expression* may be considered the beginning of the science of psychology, as it predated Wundt's pioneering experiments on cognition by nearly a decade (Robinson, 2001).

Darwin's central hypothesis in *Expression* was that emotions and their displays are inherited autonomic tendencies which served individual survival within the context of our ancestors' ancient environment. Emotions, he wrote, are universal across all humans and link us to our primate ancestors. In Darwin's words: "The young and the old of widely different races, both with man and animals, express the same state of mind by the same movements" (1872, p. 351). *Expression* united the fields of psychology and biology for the first time, and also provided a set of three major hypotheses that set the stage for the future of emotion science (Strongman, 1996).

The first of Darwin's hypotheses is that emotions are distinct, neurophysiological events that can be differentiated from one another, and from non-emotion behaviors. The second is that emotions are universal; they are expressed and recognized across cultures, and can be found in nonhuman animals. The third is that emotions either serve or once served a purpose relevant to individual survival (Ekman, 2009). Taken together, these hypotheses birthed the field of emotion science.

A Century Later

While refining Darwin's hypotheses, Tomkins (1962) proposed that there were a limited number of evolutionarily driven basic emotions that are universally expressed and recognized cross-culturally. Later that decade, Ekman and colleagues (1969) conducted one of the most influential pancultural studies in the field of psychology, wherein they found evidence for universal recognition and production of six proposed "basic" emotions: anger, fear, joy, sadness, disgust, and surprise. Together, these six states became the initial candidates of empirical interest in what would later become a burgeoning field of the evolutionary foundations of emotion. The dawn of BET led to hundreds of studies seeking to uncover the origins, causes, and consequences of emotions, as well as multiple new lines of emotion research impacting nearly every branch of the psychological sciences (Keltner et al., 2018).

What Is a Basic Emotion?
Definition and Function

Within the framework of BET, a basic emotion is a distinct, brief, psychophysiological state that enables adaptive solutions to evolutionarily significant problems (Ekman, 1992; Ekman & Cordaro, 2011). Basic emotions are automatic and unbidden, preprogrammed responses to fundamental life situations that are critical to individual survival, from avoiding danger to navigating social hierarchies (Ekman & Davidson, 1994; Keltner et al., 2019; van Kleef, 2016). Across tens of thousands of generations, individuals who responded more effectively to their environment had the greatest chances of reproductive success, and basic emotions are among the most important tools in our environmental response toolkit (Al-Shawaf et al., 2018; Keltner et al., 2019).

Primary Features

Two primary features capture what it means for an emotion to be basic. The first is that basic emotions are *discrete* (see Harmon-Jones et al., 2017). This means that basic emotions are physiologically, neurologically, functionally, and behaviorally distinct from one another, and from non-emotional states. Basic emotions are specific solutions to important environmental problems, and therefore they must have distinct psychophysiological qualities that differentiate one solution from another. The data for discrete emotions incorporate a wide array of measurements, including facial expression, vocal expression, autonomic physiology, affect, behavioral changes, and changes in cognition (Kowalska & Wróbel, 2017). In everyday life, basic emotions blend with one another and with other affective states, producing a rich kaleidoscope of human experience underpinned by inherited action tendencies.

The second feature shared by basic emotions is that they are biologically *evolutionary*. Since time immemorial, humans and our distant primate relatives have fought, loved, succeeded, failed, created, and destroyed—and basic emotions have prompted us to find better, faster, and more efficient solutions to the problems associated with life on earth (Frijda, 2000). As genetic information passed from one generation to the next, genes that coded for automatic, adaptive responses to fundamental life situations resulted in greater reproductive success (Darwin, 1859; Dawkins, 1976; Williams, 1966). After iterating this process many billions of times, the automatic responses that best facilitated genetic transmission became progressively more common and universally shared.

An emotion that is *evolutionary* has a genetic basis that has been iteratively selected for and inherited across countless generations. These hardwired responses are what BET refers to as basic emotions. Evidence for the biological evolution of basic emotions includes the universality of certain emotional expressions, specific autonomic activity, universal appraisals, and neural correlates in regions of the brain that house genetically based, fixed processes, such as the subcortical structures (Panksepp & Watt, 2011). Furthermore, basic emotions can also be found in homologous behaviors of close primate relatives (Parr et al., 2005; Snowdon, 2003).

The *discrete* and *evolutionary* features in BET allow for observation and hypothesis-driven testing of basic emotions. Together, they distinguish basic emotions from other states, such as moods, traits, disorders, and cognitive states. They also differentiate basic emotions from one another, equipping researchers with essential theory to isolate and observe the impact that specific basic emotions have on cognition, behavior, and human well-being (Tracy & Randles, 2011).

Mechanism of Action

Basic emotions depend on the existence of a central organizing mechanism that initiates a cascade of neurological, biochemical, physiological, cognitive, and behavioral changes within an organism (Levenson, 2011). At the root of these central mechanisms are sets of inherited instructions that guide the organism to adaptively interact with the environment in a way that is reflective of our evolutionary and individual history (Tracy & Randles, 2011).

This automatic cascade begins as we receive stimulation through the five senses. These sensory signals are evaluated with a specific appraisal mechanism designed to detect situations that are relevant to the self and the self's goals (Fiske et al., 2010). When key survival-relevant themes are detected, the appraisal mechanism initiates a neuroautonomic response, which evolved to guide our interaction with the environment. Dedicated neurons across multiple regions of the brain signal a release of neurotransmitters, which in turn activate the autonomic nervous system (Vuilleumier, 2005). This catalyzes large-scale system changes in heart rate, perspiration, muscle tension, breathing rate, and hormone levels. These bodily changes arise concurrently with nonverbal signals designed to communicate the sudden shift of our internal states, as we alert others in our environment to what we are feeling (Adolphs, 2002). Here we see sub-second shifts in facial muscle anatomy, vocal utterances, and body positioning, which communicate our appraisal of the situation without the need for symbolic language (Frijda, 2007). There are also concurrent shifts in cognition and behavior to support adaptive action tendencies in response to the original stimulus (Dolan, 2002; Eisenberg, 1986).

These changes are involuntary, automatic, and occur in seconds—but they are nonetheless sensitive to context (Al-Shawaf et al., 2019). The specific mechanism of action for basic emotions can be modified over time and with practice to help us better respond to our individual life experiences and specific environmental pressures (Ekman & Davidson, 1994). This modification process is inseparable from the basic emotion; it is part of the program. Mayr (1974) discussed the evolutionary advantages to what he called "closed" and "open" genetic programs. In a closed genetic program, organisms inherit automatic behaviors that cannot be modified in any way. They are insensitive to environmental input and reflexive. Conversely, in an ontogenetically open program, a particular inherited behavior is susceptible to modification through an organism's life experience. It is editable and becomes more personalized as we navigate the environment of our day-to-day lives.

The mechanisms of action in BET are open programs; as we learn, grow, and develop, modifications to the original basic emotion program will inform action tendencies that allow for successful navigation in the particular environment in which we live (Ekman, 1999). It is important to note that while the mechanisms underlying basic emotions are environmentally modifiable, they do not start out as completely empty systems, devoid of information. Evolution preset the most elemental instructions within our neural circuitry, which initiates primary impulses, autonomic changes, and specific behavioral patterns so that we can experience the world in a way that is consistent with the emotion that has been activated (Ekman & Cordaro, 2011). While the baseline instructions evolved to incorporate additional programming through experience, the baseline instructions themselves likely cannot be reprogrammed without physical injury to the brain (see Damasio et al., 1994). In other words, *anger* is here to stay, but the way we experience anger—and how we deploy it—may change over the course of our lives.

Because basic emotions are open programs, they rarely occur as pure, isolated experiences. Pure basic emotions are more likely to express in very early infancy, or during sudden, extreme situations in adulthood that elicit overwhelmingly singular emotional responses (Plutchik, 1991). Human experience is a rich blend of multiple simultaneous phenomena that combine together from moment to moment, and this experiential complexity makes "pure" basic emotions a rare event in daily life. In addition to emotions, we experience moods, thoughts, physical sensations, memories, affect, meta-affect, and meta-emotions. All of these phenomena are blended together within a rapidly changing environment that additively elicits multiple emotions in succession or simultaneously (Vansteelandt et al., 2005; Zelenski & Larsen, 2000).

To add to the complexity, we also learn new behaviors, rituals, and habits throughout life, which can become associated with the original basic emotion program (Izard, 1992). Cars, airplanes, and commercial space travel are irrelevant to our evolutionary past, but nonetheless within their context we can still experience the fear of a near miss or a rocky landing. The *objects* of fear (e.g., tiger, speeding car, syringe, etc.) have changed dramatically over the course of our evolution—however, the *subject* of fear (the threat of harm) is the same as it was hundreds of thousands of years ago. Specific environments modify our basic emotion responses, and basic emotions are the foundational code on which the modification is possible (Matsumoto, 1989). As we live our lives, new objects become associated with the old subjects of our basic emotions, allowing us to successfully adapt across culture, space, and time.

Combined with the *discrete* and *evolutionary* features of basic emotions, BET's mechanism of action outlines a clear, theory-driven path to understanding emotions. It is within this framework that the science of emotion has developed rich empirical lineages of studies to test these hypotheses across cultures. Detailed theories require equally detailed criteria through which we can test their robustness. Additionally, it is important for the field of emotion science to distinguish between basic emotions and other affective phenomena that may appear similar to emotions but are, in reality, fundamentally different. It is from here that BET answers a critical question: What does it mean for an emotion to be basic?

Empirical Criteria for Basic Emotions

BET provides a clear framework of testable criteria to determine the extent to which an emotion is basic. Ekman (1992) originally proposed nine criteria for the empirical categorization of basic emotions, six of which differentiated basic emotions from other states, and the other three differentiated basic emotions from one another. There have been additions and refinements to this list across the past three decades; however, 13 criteria have largely withstood the test of time and are accepted in most theoretical discussions of BET (for reviews see: Keltner et al., 2019; Scarantino & Griffiths, 2011; Tracy, 2014).

Some theorists merely consider these as characteristics that all basic emotions share, rather than evidence criteria that must be met before considering an emotion basic. Across the field of emotion psychology, there is a wide range of opinions regarding how much evidence is "enough" for an emotion to be basic. This chapter skews on the very conservative side of this range, wherein all 13 criteria must be demonstrated before conclusively calling an emotion basic. This means that emotions will typically lie along a continuum of evidence, where some criteria have been met or failed, while other criteria have yet to be tested. Herein we refer to emotions that have passed some criteria as "candidate basic emotions." Emotions or states which fail to pass any criteria are not considered basic.

Table 1.1 outlines the 13 criteria used to determine whether an emotion is *discrete* and *evolutionary*. The first four criteria are characteristics that all basic emotions share (Ekman 1992). First, basic emotions are immediate responses to fundamental life situations, and therefore must be capable of sub-second **rapid onset** (1) and also sub-minute **brief duration** (2; Esslen et al., 2004; Frijda et al., 1991). Furthermore, the elicitation of basic emotions must be **automatic** (3) and capable of arising without conscious invitation, largely because they are neurologically hardwired and autonomically driven (Ochsner & Gross, 2014). Lastly, a basic emotion must **coordinate multiple bodily systems** (4; e.g., brain,

Table 1.1 The 13 Criteria for the Empirical Study of Basic Emotions

Empirical Criteria for Basic Emotions
I. Shared Criteria

1. Quick onset
    2. Brief duration
    3. Unbidden occurrence
    4. Coherence among response systems

II. Differentiating Criteria

5. Distinct universals in antecedent events
    6. Distinct appraisal mechanism
    7. Distinct subjective experience
    8. Distinct cognition
    9. Distinct behavioral tendencies
    10. **Distinct universal signals**
    11. **Distinct physiology**
    12. **Distinct neurobiology involving subcortical structures**
    13. **Distinct primate homologue**

Note: The first four criteria are shared among all basic emotions, and the remaining nine differentiate basic emotions from one another. **Bold** indicates the criteria which provide the most robust evidence for the evolutionary origins of basic emotions, though all criteria contribute to this to some degree.

nervous system, behavior, cognition, etc.) into a unified, evolutionarily adaptive response (Ekman et al., 1983).

The remaining nine criteria (5–13) differentiate basic emotions from one another, and in particular, the final four provide the most robust evidence for the evolutionary basis of basic emotions. In order for basic emotions to provide adaptive solutions to environmental problems, they must be activated via universally important **self-relevant events** (5). Critical life events, such as realizing personal gain, witnessing injustice, or experiencing a negative evaluation of the self, are prerequisite stimuli that elicit a corresponding basic emotion response—*happiness*, *anger*, and *shame*, respectively, in this case.

The extent to which an event is perceived as critically self-relevant depends on an individual's evaluation of the situation. BET therefore adds to its list of criteria that there must also be a specific **appraisal mechanism** (6) by which we assess life events as fundamental and important to the self. The way in which we evaluate critical moments in our lives determines the emotions we feel during those situations, and each basic emotion has a distinct evaluation system that is shared across cultures. For example, when perceiving a threat in our environment, the basic emotion *fear* is elicited, and when we perceive the irreparable loss of something dear to us, *sadness* arises (Roseman & Smith, 2001). From an evolutionary standpoint, automatic appraisal can be equated with a sudden assumption about our environment. Whether or not the assumption is true is irrelevant, as long as our response helps us to successfully navigate the situation.

Basic emotions elicit distinctive **subjective experiences** (7), measured empirically using affective dimensions of emotion (e.g., pleasantness, activation, perceived control, etc.) and subjective reporting of the direct experience of the emotion (Scherer, 1988, 1997). These subjective experiences must also covary with **distinctive cognitive patterns** (8; Power & Dalgleish, 2015), which can later express as **predictive patterns of behavior** (9; Baumeister et al., 2007; Mauss et al., 2005).

The final four criteria provide the most robust evidence toward the evolutionary origins of basic emotions, though they tend to be the most difficult to ascertain. Basic emotions produce **universal signals** (10) in the face, voice, and body, which were likely functional adaptations in our early evolution and later became a system of nonverbal communication (Keltner et al., 2019). The experience of a basic emotion will therefore covary with specific universal displays that can reliably communicate the emotion across cultures (see encoding and decoding hypotheses, Matsumoto et al., 2008).

When measuring the body's autonomic response to fundamental life situations, there will also be predictive, measurable **physiological patterns** (11; see Kreibig, 2010) associated with basic emotions (e.g., heart rate, skin conductance, heart rate variability, piloerection, blushing, papillary response, etc.). These specific autonomic changes, as well as many of the concurrent patterns in cognition and behavior, will be due to the activation of **dedicated neurons** (12; Dolcos et al., 2011) in the brain that correlate with the experience of specific basic emotions. Furthermore, neural correlates to basic emotions should involve, to some degree, the subcortical structures, because it is from this evolutionarily ancient region of the brain that our fixed neural processes originate (Panksepp & Watt, 2011).

Lastly, both humans and the great apes are among the most social species, and those with the skills to effectively navigate their social world will thrive (J. F. Eisenberg et al., 1972). Nonverbal communication between conspecific nonhuman primates is complex and is expressed multimodally across facial, vocal, and bodily systems. While some primate nonverbal displays are likely intentional and learned, others are involuntary and appear to be **primate homologues** (13) of human basic emotions. This thirteenth criterion crosses the Darwinian threshold from human psychology to evolutionary biology, making the case for basic emotions as both cross-cultural and cross-species universals (Kret et al., 2020).

Taken together, the 13 empirical criteria for the study of basic emotions provide a guiding framework to the science of emotion psychology. They support researchers with a clear road map to design generative lines of research exploring the extent to which human emotions originate evolutionarily, are modified culturally, and impact our lives behaviorally. Perhaps most importantly, they offer testable hypotheses in the scientific pursuit of one of the central questions in psychology today: Which emotions are basic?

The Evidence for Specific Basic Emotions
Evolutionary Origins

According to BET, a basic emotion will fulfill all 13 *discrete* and *evolutionary* empirical criteria; however, the extent to which research has tested each criterion differs widely by emotion. Table 1.2 provides a cursory summary of the state of research for 26 basic emotion candidates that are well studied throughout the emotion literature (see Supplement A at https://osf.io/yth5s for references). A full review across all 13 criteria would be an ambitious task for a short handbook chapter, and so here the focus is on the final four criteria which provide the most robust evidence for the evolutionary origins of emotion: universal signals, physiology, neural correlates, and nonhuman primate homologues (see Keltner et al., 2006).

The other nine criteria tend to be assessed concurrently, though at times indirectly, alongside these final four. For example, studies regarding an emotion's neural correlates simultaneously assess their capability for quick onset, brief duration, and unbidden occurrence (e.g., Etkin et al., 2015). Similarly, studies regarding the physiology and universal signaling of emotions concurrently involve observations of response system coherence, subjective experience, distinct antecedents, and/or distinct appraisal mechanisms (e.g., Cordaro et al., 2020; Gross

Table 1.2 Brief Overview of Evidence for the Evolutionary Origins of 26 Basic Emotion Candidates across Four Critical Empirical Criteria

Emotion	Signal (shade indicates evidence for universality)			Physiology (shade indicates evidence for cross-cultural reliability)	Neural Correlate (shade indicates evidence of subcortical involvement)	Nonhuman Primates (shade indicates homologues in multiple monkey/ape species)	Evidence
	Facial	Vocal	Tactile				
Amusement	✓[1,3,6,7,16,20,22]	✓[36,37,39]	--	✓[46,48,49,50,56,96]	✓[94,95,128]	✓[125,127]	Strong
Anger	✓[1,2,3,4,5,22,25]	✓[36,37,38,39,40]	✓[5,42,43]	✓[18,45,46,56]	✓[92,93,100]	✓[125,127]	Strong
Desire	✓[1,20,21,22]	✓[38,39]	--	✓[46,56,59]	✓[94,102,103]	✓[125,127]	Strong
Fear	✓[1,2,3,4,5,22,25]	✓[36,37,38,39,40]	X[42]	✓[5,44,46,56]	✓[92,100]	✓[125,127]	Strong
Happiness	✓[1,2,3,5,16,20,22,25]	✓[40]	✓[43]	✓[5,44,45,46,56,96]	✓[92,93,100]	✓[125,127]	Strong
Pain	✓[1,20,22,30,31,32,43,79]	✓[39]	--	✓[46,76,77,78,80,91]	✓[92,118,119]	--	Strong
Pride	✓[1,6,16,20,22,25,33,35]	X[36,38,39]	X[42]	✓[56,57,82,83,96]	✓[93,117]	✓[125,126]	Strong
Shame	✓[1,3,22,24,25,35]	X[36,38]	--	✓[84,85,86]	✓[104,117]	✓[125,126]	Strong
Disgust	✓[1,2,3,4,5,22,25]	✓[36,37,38,39,40]	--	✓[5,44,46,56]	✓[92,94,100]	--	Moderate
Sadness	✓[1,2,3,4,5,22,25]	✓[36,37,38,39]	✓[43]	✓[5,44,45,46,47,56]	✓[92,94,95,100]	--	Moderate
Surprise	✓[1,2,3,5,22,25]	✓[36,37,38,39]	X[42]	✓[5,44,46,56]	✓[100,121]	--	Moderate
Awe	✓[3,6,8,16]	✓[36,39]	--	✓[51,52,53,96]	✓[92,93,97,98,99]	--	Emerging
Contempt	✓[2,4,15]	✓[36,38,39,40]	--	--	✓[101]	--	Emerging
Embarrassment	✓[1,3,12,20,22,23,24,25]	✓[36,39]	✓[42,43]	✓[56,60,61,62,63]	✓[104,105,106,107]	--	Emerging
Envy	X[26]	✓[36]	X[42]	✓[51,64]	✓[107,108,109]	--	Emerging
Gratitude	✓[16]	X[36]	✓[42,43]	✓[65,66,96]	✓[110,111,112]	--	Emerging
Guilt	✓[24]	--	✓[42,43]	✓[67,68,69,70]	✓[93,104]	--	Emerging
Love	✓[3,16,20,29]	X[36,38]	✓[42,43]	✓[56,59,73,74,75,96]	✓[113,114,115,116]	--	Emerging
Sympathy	✓[1,20,22]	X[36,39]	✓[42,43]	✓[87,88,89,90]	✓[122,123,124]	--	Emerging
Boredom	✓[1,9,10,11,22]	✓[40]	--	✓[10,11,54,55]	--	--	Nascent
Contentment	✓[1,3,16,22]	✓[38,39,41]	--	✓[46,56,96]	--	--	Nascent
Coyness	✓[1,17,18,22]	--	--	✓[57,58]	--	--	Nascent
Interest	✓[1,16,20,22,27,28]	✓[36,38,39]	--	✓[71,72,96]	--	--	Nascent
Relief	--	✓[36,31,40]	--	✓[56]	✓[120]	--	Nascent
Confusion	✓[1,12,13,14,22]	--	--	--	--	--	Weak
Triumph	--	✓[36,39]	--	--	--	--	Weak

Notes: A checkmark (✓) indicates that the evidence is in favor of the criterion, and an (X) indicates that the evidence is against it. In order for an emotion to be basic, it only needs universal signaling evidence in one modality, though three are listed here (facial, vocal, tactile). This overview is meant as a cursory summary of major studies, rather than a comprehensive review of the emotion literature.

& Levenson, 1993). Nevertheless, a critical next step for the field will be to conduct a rigorous review of all evidence across each of these criteria for all candidate emotions.

For ease of interpretation, Table 1.2 also provides a summary of evidence strength for each emotion. The strength rating is a coarse evaluation of the continuum of evidence across 26 basic emotion candidates, and organizes the emotions into categories based on the breadth and depth of the criterion research to date. It highlights only major reviews or larger studies associated with each emotion and its corresponding criterion; there are many more not listed here that further build on the evidence within each cell, which should be included in a larger review in the future. Table 1.2 also indicates whether or not additional special requirements are met for each criterion (e.g., universality rather than a single-culture demonstration; subcortical involvement rather than the neocortex alone; etc.).

Strong Candidates

At one end of the evidence continuum are the basic emotion candidates backed with the strongest evidence of their evolutionary origins. Eight emotions—*amusement*, *anger*, *desire*, *fear*, *happiness*, *pain*, *pride*, and *shame*—are universally expressed in one or more modalities, correlate with discrete neural activation involving the subcortex, and with the exception of *pain*, exhibit homologous expressions in great apes. Great apes have been found to suppress expressions of *pain*, and so it is yet unclear whether a distinct homologous expression exists in our closest nonhuman relatives (Plesker & Mayer, 2008). However, standing apart from all other strong candidate emotions, the physiology of *pain* is robustly well documented across cultures, due in large part to its immense importance within the medical and biochemical sciences (Dray, 1995). Together, these eight candidates are likely to be basic emotions; however, with the exception of *pain*, more in-depth research into their discrete, universal physiological markers needs to be established. Future studies regarding physiological correlates of these emotions should assess cross-cultural reliability, and also provide rigorous within-emotion and between-emotion comparison data across a wider array of physiological markers than have previously been studied (e.g., combining autonomic, neurotransmitter, hormonal, and biochemical data, etc.). In the same way that the medical field has exhaustively modeled the biomolecular pathways of *pain* (see Steeds, 2009), future investigations in the psychological sciences should conduct similarly extensive research into the underlying physiological and biochemical mechanisms underlying the other emotion candidates.

Moderate Candidates

Moving along the evidence continuum, the basic emotion candidates *disgust*, *sadness*, and *surprise* have been tested with moderate rigor and would otherwise be considered "strong" if not for the absence of nonhuman primate data. To date, there has been little discussion of these emotions in the nonhuman primate psychology literature, although some anecdotal accounts of all three could provide a starting point for future research (Clay et al., 2018; Darwin, 1872). Similar to their "strong" counterparts, several studies have evidenced the physiological markers of "moderate" candidates, but have yet to rigorously test physiological universality, within/between-emotion comparisons, and include a fuller array of biophysiological markers beyond simple autonomic measurements (though these may be sufficient in some cases). Notwithstanding these gaps in the literature, *disgust*, *sadness*, and *surprise* have been tested extensively in the field of emotion communication, with clear and replicable signals universally in the face and voice (e.g., Keltner et al., 2003).

Emerging Candidates

Over the past 30 years, there has been an increasing interest in emotion science to determine whether there are more than just a few universal emotions, or whether there are additional states that are ubiquitously recognized and discretely distinguishable from the more well-studied classic six: *anger, disgust, fear, happiness, sadness,* and *surprise*. A new wave of emotion research has recently expanded upon the original list, and discrete signals have been identified in one or more cultures for the basic emotion candidates *awe, contempt, embarrassment, envy, gratitude, guilt, love,* and *sympathy* (see Keltner & Shiota, 2003). With the exception of *contempt*, there have been multiple studies that provide evidence for discrete physiology of these emerging candidates, though cross-cultural stability has not yet been established. Additionally, *contempt, envy, gratitude, guilt,* and *love* all appear to have neural correlates involving the subcortical regions of the brain, while emerging research on *awe, embarrassment,* and *sympathy* has found initial evidence for discrete neurological activation in the neocortex alone. None of the emerging candidates has been rigorously tested for homologous behaviors in other primates, a clear next step for future research.

Nascent Candidates

Along with the "emerging" candidates, there have also been dozens of "new" emotions that have recently begun to run the gauntlet of the 13 basic emotion criteria, and some of them have shown early promise for candidacy (Keltner & Cordaro, 2017). Noteworthy early-stage research on *boredom, contentment, coyness, interest,* and *relief* has evidenced signal universality in either the face or voice. Especially remarkable is that *contentment* and *interest* appear to have universal expressive patterns in both facial and vocal expressions, and this latter modality has been tested in remote, previously uncontacted populations (Cordaro, Keltner, et al., 2016). None of the "nascent" candidates has been rigorously tested for discrete neurology and primate homology, although some evidence exists for physiological markers in single cultures.

Weak Candidates

At the other end of the evidence continuum are basic emotion candidates for which there is minimal evidence, such as with *confusion* and *triumph*. For both of these states, there is some evidence for expressive universality in a single modality. *Confusion* has been cross-culturally recognized through facial and bodily cues across 10 cultures, while *triumph* has been recognized through nonverbal vocal bursts across 11 cultures, including one uncontacted population (Cordaro et al., 2016; Cordaro et al., 2020). Beyond these initial studies, little evidence exists across the other criteria, though there is theoretical rationale to study these states more rigorously as possible basic emotion candidates (Rozin & Cohen, 2003; Tracy & Robins, 2008).

Which Emotions Are Basic?

The answer to the question "Which emotions are basic?" is not a simple one, and the evidence required to confirm a basic emotion is extensive. However, this is an exciting and promising horizon for the emotion sciences. Understanding the extent to which emotions are basic depends entirely on what the evidence will reveal in the coming years. While eight candidate emotions are backed by strong empirical data regarding their evolutionary origins, no single emotion is conclusively basic. The research has yet to run a candidate through the gauntlet of all 13 empirical criteria, which would provide groundbreaking verification of the existence of basic emotions. Admittedly, the perspective taken in this chapter with regard to the 13 criteria is extremely strict compared to other theorists, however, when the bar is set high, the resulting scientific lineage will stand on a stronger foundation.

It will be critical for future reviews to rigorously map out the extent to which each emotion is basic, and to provide a guiding framework for the next wave of emotion research to fill in the gaps. It is clear that the vast majority of BET research to date has focused on discrete, universal signaling, and the majority of these studies regard facial expressions. Based on the present overview of the literature, it will be important for researchers to shift focus to the areas of physiology, neurology, and primate homology. It will also be essential for the field of emotion science to deepen collaborations across these areas of specialization, because in reality, they are inseparable from one another. With greater collaboration across each criterion domain, the field will be better equipped to efficiently and conclusively fill each gap in the evidence and move collectively toward a universal understanding of human emotions.

When a candidate basic emotion fails any of the 13 basic emotion criteria, it will also be important for the field of emotion science to agree on a categorization structure of states beyond basic emotions. Levenson (2011) makes the case for basic emotions as a special subset of discrete emotions, which may originate via other mechanisms that typically involve cultural learning, individual adaptation, and environmental input over the course of a lifetime. Alternatively, Ekman (1994) has argued that emotions are either basic or some other affective experience (e.g., cognitive state, mood, trait, etc.). In other words, he theorized that all emotions are basic, and that the terms "basic emotion" and "emotion" are functionally equivalent. The resolution to this debate will likely come down to semantics, and so it is critical in future theoretical discussions of human emotions to agree on a unified categorization structure for different types of human affective experiences.

Future research must also increasingly focus on how culture and language play a role in the appraisals, concepts, expressions, and behaviors associated with basic emotions. Basic emotions allow for extensive modifications to suit individual environments, and researching the nature of these modifications will provide a holistic understanding of each emotion's core open program. The topic of culture and experience is perhaps the final frontier of empirical research seeking a complete model of human emotions. If the environment can systematically shape our experience of basic emotions, what is the mechanism behind it, and what are its modification patterns across cultures?

Basic Emotions, Culture, and Experience

A central focus of BET research regards the extent to which a candidate emotion's characteristics vary at the level of culture and the individual. Some discrete emotion theorists have argued that emotions are socially constructed, learned phenomena that have been passed down culturally for generations (Parkinson, 1996). The argument is that our shared ontogeny, not our phylogeny, is responsible for any observable universal features in emotion expression. In light of these criticisms, BET provides a critical empirical framework for understanding how shared culture and evolutionary history have together contributed to our emotional repertoire. The question at the heart of this line of research is: To what extent do evolution and personal experience contribute to how we experience different emotions?

Cultural Variability

In earlier research, a central debate in the emotion sciences regarded whether it was biology or experience that gave rise to our emotions. As with many dualistic battles across our scientific history—nature vs. nurture; particle vs. wave; compassion vs. profit—recent studies have demonstrated that both are present and inseparable from one another. Early work by Ekman

(1993) showed that there may be upward of 60 variants of expressions for a single emotion, and these variants depended on social context (e.g., culture, role, gender, etc.). Other studies across the decades on cultural dialects of emotions (Elfenbein & Ambady, 2003), display rules (Matsumoto, Yoo, et al., 2008), ideal affect (Tsai, 2007), and within-emotion expression variation (Cordaro et al., 2018; Cordaro et al., 2020) together supported BET's assertion that while some key features of emotions are present across cultures, experience can significantly modify their expression in day-to-day life.

Understanding emotions and their patterns requires a rich understanding of the inevitable variability that comes with culture, rituals, and individual life experiences. In this way, a central characteristic of basic emotions is that they are open to modification through personal adaptations to specific environments. It is a misunderstanding of BET that emotions must have a one-to-one correlation with their expression, physiology, behavioral changes, etc. Anyone who has experienced a new culture, even for a short time, knows that this cannot be true. A more nuanced understanding of BET is that while there are universal patterns in basic emotions that can be measured across cultures, these patterns are open to modifications from our environment, shared rituals, experiences, beliefs, and customs.

What we observe as characteristic patterns of basic emotion outcomes are indicative of three sources of input: biology, culture, and individual experience.

1. *Biologically native patterns* in basic emotions are rooted in our evolutionary heritage and are described in the 13 empirical criteria above (e.g., automatic appraisal, universal expression, discrete physiology, etc.). These arise from the core operating program at the root of a basic emotion, which is inherited evolutionarily. In day-to-day observation, these patterns will be exhibited across cultures, and perhaps across species.
2. *Culturally native patterns* are learned through our collective rituals and social norms (Scherer & Wallbott, 1994). For example, every culture has its display rules regarding which expressions are appropriate in certain situations, and which are not. Studies on laughter and smiling have demonstrated that while the upturned lip corners and open-mouthed smile of laughter is universal, some cultures require that the smile is covered with a hand for the sake of politeness (Kraut & Johnston, 1979). Such patterned modifications will arise in single cultures without generalizing universally.
3. *Individually native patterns* arise due to our personal experience in life. These patterns are reliable within one person alone, and cannot be generalized across a population. We all develop our own unique expressions to suit our specific environments. Our personal emotional elicitors, family display rules, and individual reactive tendencies together add a personalized richness to the ways in which we navigate our social world (Gross & John, 2003; Kring et al., 1994).

Several recent studies have captured the extent to which certain characteristics of emotions are both universal and variable across cultures (see Cowen & Keltner, 2020). Typically, these studies involve the emotion elicitation method, where validated stimuli are used to elicit emotional expressions in participants belonging to different cultures. Their expressive reactions are recorded and analyzed for patterns and variants using facial, vocal, and postural analysis methods. For example, in one of the largest studies of its kind to date, Cordaro et al. (2018) used the Facial Action Coding System to analyze over 2,600 facial and body displays of

22 emotions across five cultures. After applying new pattern-recognition techniques, the study identified clear expressive patterns across cultures, as well as systematic cultural variations that were specific to each of the five populations studied. The study estimated that, on average, 50% of what participants expressed across cultures was based on a universal pattern, while 25% of the expression came from a culturally specific dialect. The remaining 25% was due to individual differences and personal experiences.

In moving beyond the original six basic emotion candidates, new research has generated advances in understanding both the universal characteristics that define basic emotions, and also the cultural variability that is part of their open programming. Critical to BET is the assertion that basic emotions have helped us survive, thrive, and reproduce—despite profound variation in individual environments, cultures, and dynamically changing needs across time. Basic emotions' open programming has provided humans with the essential psychological and emotional flexibility required to navigate a dynamic, rapidly changing world.

The Language of Emotions

Humans have a rich symbolic and verbal language used to communicate emotion above and beyond nonverbal body displays. There is wide variability across cultures in the number and meaning of words that are used to connotatively and denotatively describe emotions (Heider, n.d.; Mesquita & Frijda, 1992; Russell, 1991). In fact, when translating emotion words across languages, an exact match can be difficult, and at times, impossible (Jackson et al., 2019).

Words and experiences are independent of one another. There are many times throughout our lives where we will not have the words to capture how we feel; there are also many words that describe feelings we may not yet have experienced. In the high monasteries of Bhutan, the ancient Choekey language is spoken by the most experienced monks, but is largely foreign to the rest of the country—and the world. There is an emotion called *chokkshay* in the Choekey language (Cordaro, Brackett, et al., 2016) which means "the feeling of completeness that comes from the realization that this moment is perfect as it is." The closest single word to *chokkshay* in English is "contentment," but this translation likely does not do it full justice. The good news is that just because the English-speaking world lacks a formal linguistic equivalent to *chokkshay*, we who live outside of the Himalayan monasteries can still enjoy the feeling of completeness in a perfect moment.

Language is socially constructed; over time our cultural collectives agreed upon various abstract symbols and sounds to represent objects, people, places, and experiences (Izard, 1994; Russell & Sato, 1995). Conversely, basic emotions are biologically constructed; over time evolution iteratively crafted responses to important life situations—which we later associated with symbols, words, and phrases. The presence of a unique emotion word in one culture does not imply the presence of unique circuitry or unique phenomenology for a special emotion found only in that culture. Similarly, the absence of a specific basic emotion word in one culture does not imply the absence of analogous basic emotion circuitry. Emotions and language are parallel processes that can inform and provide context about one another, but ultimately cannot guarantee the existence of one another. An example of this is in Robert Levy's (1975) pioneering work in Tahiti, where he found that Tahitians had no words for "grief" and "sadness." Nevertheless, they experienced a "sick, strange" feeling when processing the loss of a loved one.

The framework and methodological toolkit of BET allows researchers to explore the nature of emotions despite linguistic boundaries, as we continue to explore affective phenomena that may be outside our conceptual reach. Research at the intersection of emotion and linguistics has begun to decode the ways that cultures idealize certain emotions, while eschewing others. The language of emotions further empowers the field to better understand cultural display rules, cultural norms, and beliefs about emotions, which play a significant role in our overall experience of and regulation of our inner world.

Conclusion

Emotions are among the most important aspects of life on earth, and in many ways they are the defining feature of what it means to be human. For thousands of years, we have tried to study, control, and train these experiences in order to understand ourselves and our societies on a deeper level. Emotions give our lives flavor and meaning; they are what get us out of bed in the morning, and keep us in bed when we need to be. They inspire creativity, motivation, and are at the heart of all human relationships.

Emotions are a gift from our ancestors, who survived harsher, more uncertain conditions than most of us face today. Each successive generation passed on the genes that coded for action tendencies which promoted survival and reproduction. These action tendencies, the basic emotions, are the core open programs at the center of the human experience. Every basic emotion has similar *discrete* and *evolutionary* qualities that makes them a ripe topic for scientific research.

Since its inception over 80 years ago, BET has provided an elegant and fundamental link between evolutionary biology and psychology. It has supported studies in nearly every branch of the psychological sciences, and it continues to guide empirical research across the emotion sciences. Research inspired by BET reveals over 20 emotions with discrete, universal expressions in the face and voice. Many of these emotions have unique neural correlates involving the subcortical regions of the brain, and over a dozen emotions appear to have discrete physiological correlates, though additional research will be required in this domain to uncover whether there are autonomic markers that can be used to distinguish basic emotions from one another. Lastly, some of the more well-studied emotions have expressive homologues in nonhuman primates, which underlies the profound importance that emotions have had in the evolution of our ancestors across time, culture, and species. While many gaps in our understanding of the nature of emotions still remain, the next wave of research will begin to uncover the ways in which emotions have defined our evolutionary heritage and continue to fundamentally shape the future of humanity.

Acknowledgment

I would like to heartfully acknowledge Paul Ekman for his many years of guidance and support. Ten years ago, Paul trusted his time to an unknown psychology hobbyist, which changed my life forever and opened doors beyond my wildest expectations. I write this piece with humility and gratitude toward a legendary scientist, mentor, and friend.

References

Adolphs, R. (2002). Neural systems for recognizing emotion. *Current Opinion in Neurobiology, 12*(2), 169–177. https://doi.org/10.1016/S0959-4388(02)00301-X

Al-shawaf, L., Lewis, D. M., Webbe, Y. S., & Buss, D. M. (2019). Context, environment, and learning in evolutionary psychology. In T. K. Shackelford & V. A. Weekes-Shackelford (Eds.), *Encyclopedia of evolutionary psychological science*. Springer. https://doi.org/10.1007/978-3-319-16999-6

Al-Shawaf, L., Zreik, K., & Buss, D. M. (2018). Thirteen misunderstandings about natural selection. In *Encyclopedia of evolutionary psychological science* (pp. 1–14). Springer International. https://doi.org/10.1007/978-3-319-16999-6_2158-1

Baumeister, R. F., Vohs, K. D., DeWall, C. N., & Zhang, L. (2007). How emotion shapes behavior: Feedback, anticipation, and reflection, rather than direct causation. *Personality and Social Psychology Review, 11*(2), 167–203. https://doi.org/10.1177/1088868307301033

Browne, J. (2002). *Charles Darwin: The power of place* (Vol. 2 of *A biography*). Princeton University Press.

Clay, Z., Palagi, E., & de Waal, F. B. M. (2018). Ethological approaches to empathy in primates. In K. Z. Meyza & E. Knapska (Eds.), *Neuronal correlates of empathy* (pp. 53–66). Elsevier. https://doi.org/10.1016/B978-0-12-805397-3.00005-X

Cordaro, D. T., Brackett, M., Glass, L., & Anderson, C. L. (2016). Contentment: Perceived completeness across cultures and traditions. *Review of General Psychology, 20*(3), 221–235. https://doi.org/10.1037/gpr0000082

Cordaro, D. T., Keltner, D., Tshering, S., Wangchuk, D., & Flynn, L. M. (2016). The voice conveys emotion in ten globalized cultures and one remote village in Bhutan. *Emotion, 16*(1), 117–128. https://doi.org/10.1037/emo0000100

Cordaro, D. T., Sun, R., Kamble, S., Hodder, N., Monroy, M., Cowen, A., Bai, Y., & Keltner, D. (2020). The recognition of 18 facial-bodily expressions across nine cultures. *Emotion, 20*(7), 1292–1300. https://doi.org/10.1037/emo0000576

Cordaro, D. T., Sun, R., Keltner, D., Kamble, S., Huddar, N., & McNeil, G. (2018). Universals and cultural variations in 22 emotional expressions across five cultures. *Emotion, 18*(1), 75–93. https://doi.org/10.1037/emo0000302

Cowen, A. S., & Keltner, D. (2020). What the face displays: Mapping 28 emotions conveyed by naturalistic expression. *American Psychologist, 75*(3), 349–364. https://doi.org/10.1037/amp0000488

Damasio, H., Grabowski, T., Frank, R., Galaburda, A. M., & Damasio, A. R. (1994). The return of Phineas Gage: Clues about the brain from the skull of a famous patient. *Science, 264*(5162), 1102–1105. https://doi.org/10.1126/science.8178168

Darwin, C. (1872). *The expression of the emotions in man and animals*. Murray.

Darwin, C. (1859). *The origin of species* (6th ed., Vol. 570). Murray.

Darwin, C., Ekman, P. E., & Prodger, P. (1998). *The expression of the emotions in man and animals* (3rd ed.). Oxford University Press.

Dawkins, R. (1976). *The selfish gene*. Oxford University Press.

Dolan, R. J. (2002). Emotion, cognition, and behavior. *Science, 298*(5596), 1191–1194. https://doi.org/10.1126/science.1076358

Dolcos, F., Iordan, A. D., & Dolcos, S. (2011). Neural correlates of emotion–cognition interactions: A review of evidence from brain imaging investigations. *Journal of Cognitive Psychology, 23*(6), 669–694. https://doi.org/10.1080/20445911.2011.594433

Dray, A. (1995). Inflammatory mediators of pain. *British Journal of Anaesthesia, 75*(2), 125–131. https://doi.org/10.1093/bja/75.2.125

Eisenberg, J. F., Muckenhirn, N. A., & Rundran, R. (1972). The relation between ecology a social structure in primates. *Science, 176*(4037), 863–874. https://doi.org/10.1126/science.176.4037.863

Eisenberg, N. (1986). *Altruistic emotion, cognition, and behavior*. Lawrence Erlbaum Associates.

Ekman, P. (1992). An argument for basic emotions. *Cognition and Emotion, 6*(3–4), 169–200. https://doi.org/10.1080/02699939208411068

Ekman, P. (1993). Facial expression and emotion. *American Psychologist, 48*(4), 384–392. https://doi.org/10.1037/0003-066X.48.4.384

Ekman, P. (1994). Strong evidence for universals in facial expressions: A reply to Russell's mistaken critique. *Psychological Bulletin, 115*(2), 268–287. https://doi.org/10.1037/0033-2909.115.2.268

Ekman, P. E. (1999). Basic emotions. In T. Dalgleish & T. Power (Eds.), *Handbook of cognition and emotion* (pp. 45–60). Wiley.

Ekman, P. (2009). Darwin's contributions to our understanding of emotional expressions. *Philosophical Transactions of the Royal Society B: Biological Sciences, 364*(1535), 3449–3451. https://doi.org/10.1098/rstb.2009.0189

Ekman, P., & Cordaro, D. (2011). What is meant by calling emotions basic. *Emotion Review, 3*(4), 364–370. https://doi.org/10.1177/1754073911410740

Ekman, P. E., & Davidson, R. J. (1994). *The nature of emotion: Fundamental questions*. Oxford University Press.

Ekman, P., Levenson, R. W., & Friesen, W. V. (1983). Autonomic nervous system activity distinguishes among emotions. *Science, 221*(4616), 1208–1210. https://doi.org/10.1126/science.6612338

Ekman, P., Sorenson, E. R., & Friesen, W. V. (1969). Pan-cultural elements in facial displays of emotion. *Science, 164*(3875), 86–88. https://doi.org/10.1126/science.164.3875.86

Elfenbein, H. A., & Ambady, N. (2003). Universals and cultural differences in recognizing emotions. *Current Directions in Psychological Science, 12*(5), 159–164. https://doi.org/10.1111/1467-8721.01252

Esslen, M., Pascual-Marqui, R. D., Hell, D., Kochi, K., & Lehmann, D. (2004). Brain areas and time course of emotional processing. *NeuroImage, 21*(4), 1189–1203. https://doi.org/10.1016/j.neuroimage.2003.10.001

Etkin, A., Büchel, C., & Gross, J. J. (2015). The neural bases of emotion regulation. *Nature Reviews Neuroscience, 16*(11), 693–700. https://doi.org/10.1038/nrn4044

Fiske, S. T., Gilbert, D. T., & Lindzey, G. (Eds.). (2010). *Handbook of social psychology* (5th ed.). Wiley.

Francis, K. (2007). *Charles Darwin and the origin of species*. Greenwood Press.
Frijda, N. H. (2000). The psychologist's point of view. In M. Lewis & J. M. Haviland-Jones (Eds.), *Handbook of emotions* (2nd ed., pp. 59–74). Guilford Press.
Frijda, N. H. (2007). What might emotions be? Comments on the comments. *Social Science Information, 46*(3), 433–443. https://doi.org/10.1177/05390184070460030112
Frijda, N. H., Mesquita, B., Sonnenmans, J., & Van Goozen, S. (1991). The duration of affective phenomena or emotions, sentiments and passions. In K. T. Strongman (Ed.), *International review of studies on emotion* (pp. 187–225). Wiley.
Gould, S. J. (2002). *The structure of evolutionary theory*. Harvard University Press.
Gross, J. J., & John, O. P. (2003). Individual differences in two emotion regulation processes: Implications for affect, relationships, and well-being. *Journal of Personality and Social Psychology, 85*(2), 348–362. https://doi.org/10.1037/0022-3514.85.2.348
Gross, J. J., & Levenson, R. W. (1993). Emotional suppression: Physiology, self-report, and expressive behavior. *Journal of Personality and Social Psychology, 64*(6), 970–986. https://doi.org/10.1037/0022-3514.64.6.970
Harmon-Jones, E., Harmon-Jones, C., & Summerell, E. (2017). On the importance of both dimensional and discrete models of emotion. *Behavioral Sciences, 7*, 66. https://doi.org/10.3390/bs7040066
Heider, K. G. (n.d.). *Landscapes of emotion: Mapping three cultures of emotion in Indonesia*. Cambridge University Press.
Izard, C. E. (1992). Basic emotions, relations among emotions, and emotion-cognition relations. *Psychological Review, 99*(3), 561–565. https://doi.org/10.1037/0033-295X.99.3.561
Izard, C. E. (1994). Innate and universal facial expressions: Evidence from developmental and cross-cultural research. *Psychological Bulletin, 115*(2), 288–299. https://doi.org/10.1037/0033-2909.115.2.288
Jackson, J. C., Watts, J., Henry, T. R., List, J.-M., Forkel, R., Mucha, P. J., Greenhill, S. J., Gray, R. D., & Lindquist, K. A. (2019). Emotion semantics show both cultural variation and universal structure. *Science, 366*(6472), 1517–1522. https://doi.org/10.1126/science.aaw8160
Keltner, D., & Cordaro, D. T. (2017). Understanding multimodal emotional expressions: Recent advances in basic emotion theory. In J. M. Fernández-Dols & J. A. Russell (Eds.), *The science of facial expression* (pp. 57–75). Oxford University Press.
Keltner, D., Ekman, P. E., Gonzaga, G. C., & Beer, J. (2003). Facial expression of emotions. In R. J. Davidson, K. R. Scherer, & H. H. Goldsmith (Eds.), *Handbook of affective sciences* (pp. 415–432). Oxford University Press.
Keltner, D., Haidt, J., & Shiota, L. (2006). Social functionalism and the evolution of emotions. In M. Schaller, D. Kenrick, & J. Simpson (Eds.), *Evolution and social psychology* (pp. 115–142). Psychology Press.
Keltner, D., Oatley, K., & Jenkins, J. M. (2018). *Understanding emotions* (4th ed.). Wiley.
Keltner, D., Sauter, D., Tracy, J., & Cowen, A. (2019). Emotional expression: Advances in basic emotion theory. *Journal of Nonverbal Behavior, 43*, 133–160. https://doi.org/10.1007/s10919-019-00293-3
Keltner, D., & Shiota, M. N. (2003). New displays and new emotions: A commentary on Rozin and Cohen (2003). *Emotion, 3*(1), 86–91. https://doi.org/10.1037/1528-3542.3.1.86
Kowalska, M., & Wróbel, M. (2017). Basic emotions. In V. Zeigler-Hill & T. K. Shackelford (Eds.), *Encyclopedia of personality and individual differences* (pp. 1–6). Springer International.
Kraut, R. E., & Johnston, R. E. (1979). Social and emotional messages of smiling: An ethological approach. *Journal of Personality and Social Psychology, 37*(9), 1539–1553. https://doi.org/10.1037/0022-3514.37.9.1539
Kreibig, S. D. (2010). Autonomic nervous system activity in emotion: A review. *Biological Psychology, 84*(3), 394–421. https://doi.org/10.1016/j.biopsycho.2010.03.010
Kret, M. E., Prochazkova, E., Sterck, E. H. M., & Clay, Z. (2020). Emotional expressions in human and non-human great apes. *Neuroscience & Biobehavioral Reviews, 115*, 378–395. https://doi.org/10.1016/j.neubiorev.2020.01.027
Kring, A. M., Smith, D. A., & Neale, J. M. (1994). Individual differences in dispositional expressiveness: Development and validation of the Emotional Expressivity Scale. *Journal of Personality and Social Psychology, 66*(5), 934–949. https://doi.org/10.1037/0022-3514.66.5.934
Levenson, R. W. (2011). Basic emotion questions. *Emotion Review, 3*(4), 379–386. https://doi.org/10.1177/1754073911410743
Levy, R. I. (1975). *Tahitians: Mind and experience in the society islands*. University of Chicago Press.
Matsumoto, D. (1989). Cultural influences on the perception of emotion. *Journal of Cross-Cultural Psychology, 20*(1), 92–105. https://doi.org/10.1177/0022022189201006
Matsumoto, D., Keltner, D., Shiota, M. N., O'Sullivan, M., & Frank, M. (2008). Facial expressions of emotion. In M. Lewis, J. M. Haviland-Jones, & L. F. Barrett (Eds.), *Handbook of emotions* (pp. 211–234). Guilford Press.
Matsumoto, D., Yoo, S. H., & Nakagawa, S. (2008). Culture, emotion regulation, and adjustment. *Journal of Personality and Social Psychology, 94*, 925–937. https://doi.org/10.1037/0022-3514.94.6.925

Mauss, I. B., McCarter, L., Levenson, R. W., Wilhelm, F. H., & Gross, J. J. (2005). The tie that binds? Coherence among emotion experience, behavior, and physiology. *Emotion, 5*(2), 175–190. https://doi.org/10.1037/1528-3542.5.2.175

Mayr, E. (1974). Behavior programs and evolutionary strategies: Natural selection sometimes favors a genetically "closed" behavior program, sometimes an "open" one. *American Scientist, 62*(6), 650–659.

Mesquita, B., & Frijda, N. H. (1992). Cultural variations in emotions: A review. *Psychological Bulletin, 112*(2), 179–204. https://doi.org/10.1037/0033-2909.112.2.179

Ochsner, K. N., & Gross, J. J. (2014). The neural bases of emotion and emotion regulation: A valuation perspective. In J. J. Gross (Ed.), *Handbook of emotion regulation* (pp. 23–42). Guilford Press.

Panksepp, J., & Watt, D. (2011). What is basic about basic emotions? Lasting lessons from affective neuroscience. *Emotion Review, 3*(4), 387–396. https://doi.org/10.1177/1754073911410741

Parkinson, B. (1996). Emotions are social. *British Journal of Psychology, 87*(4), 663–683. https://doi.org/10.1111/j.2044-8295.1996.tb02615.x

Parr, L. A., Waller, B. M., & Fugate, J. (2005). Emotional communication in primates: Implications for neurobiology. *Current Opinion in Neurobiology, 15*(6), 716–720. https://doi.org/10.1016/j.conb.2005.10.017

Plesker, R., & Mayer, V. (2008). Nonhuman primates mask signs of pain. *Laboratory Primate Newsletter, 47*(1), 1–4.

Plutchik, R. (1991). *The emotions: Facts, theories and a new model*. Random House.

Power, M., & Dalgleish, T. (2015). *Cognition and emotion: From order to disorder* (3rd ed.). Psychology Press.

Robinson, D. K. (2001). *Reaction-time experiments in Wundt's Institute and beyond*. https://doi.org/10.1007/978-1-4615-0665-2_6

Roseman, I. J., & Smith, C. A. (2001). Appraisal theory: Overview, assumptions, varieties, controversies. In K. R. Scherer, A. Schorr, & T. Johnstone (Eds.), *Appraisal processes in emotion: Theory, methods, research* (pp. 3–19). Oxford University Press.

Rozin, P., & Cohen, A. B. (2003). High frequency of facial expressions corresponding to confusion, concentration, and worry in an analysis of naturally occurring facial expressions of Americans. *Emotion, 3*(1), 68–75. https://doi.org/10.1037/1528-3542.3.1.68

Russell, J. A. (1991). Culture and the categorization of emotions. *Psychological Bulletin, 110*(3), 426–450. https://doi.org/10.1037/0033-2909.110.3.426

Russell, J. A., & Sato, K. (1995). Comparing emotion words between languages. *Journal of Cross-Cultural Psychology, 26*(4), 384–391. https://doi.org/10.1177/0022022195264004

Scarantino, A., & Griffiths, P. (2011). Don't give up on basic emotions. *Emotion Review, 3*(4), 444–454. https://doi.org/10.1177/1754073911410745

Scherer, K. R. (1988). Criteria for emotion-antecedent appraisal: A review. In Vernon Hamilton, Gordon H. Bower, & Nico H. Frijda (Eds.), *Cognitive perspectives on emotion and motivation* (pp. 89–126). Springer. https://doi.org/10.1007/978-94-009-2792-6_4

Scherer, K. R. (1997). The role of culture in emotion-antecedent appraisal. *Journal of Personality and Social Psychology, 73*(5), 902–922. https://doi.org/10.1037/0022-3514.73.5.902

Scherer, K. R., & Wallbott, H. G. (1994). Evidence for universality and cultural variation of differential emotion response patterning. *Journal of Personality and Social Psychology, 66*(2), 310–328. https://doi.org/10.1037/0022-3514.66.2.310

Snowdon, C. T. (2003). Expression of emotion in nonhuman animals. In R. J. Davidson, H. H. Goldsmith, & K. R. Scherer (Eds.), *Handbook of affective sciences* (pp. 457–480). Oxford University Press.

Sober, E. (1984). *The nature of selection: Evolutionary theory in philosophical focus*. MIT Press.

Steeds, C. E. (2009). The anatomy and physiology of pain. *Surgery (Oxford), 27*(12), 507–511. https://doi.org/10.1016/j.mpsur.2009.10.013

Strongman, K. T. (1996). *The psychology of emotion: Theories of emotion in perspective* (4th ed.). Wiley.

Tomkins, S. S. (1962). *Affect, imagery, consciousness*, Vol. 1: *The positive affects*. Springer. https://doi.org/10.1037/14351-000

Tracy, J. L. (2014). An evolutionary approach to understanding distinct emotions. *Emotion Review, 6*(4), 308–312. https://doi.org/10.1177/1754073914534478

Tracy, J. L., & Randles, D. (2011). Four models of basic emotions: A review of Ekman and Cordaro, Izard, Levenson, and Panksepp and Watt. *Emotion Review, 6*(4), 308–312. https://doi.org/10.1177/1754073911410747

Tracy, J. L., & Robins, R. W. (2008). The nonverbal expression of pride: Evidence for cross-cultural recognition. *Journal of Personality and Social Psychology, 94*(3), 516–530. https://doi.org/10.1037/0022-3514.94.3.516

Tsai, J. L. (2007). Ideal affect: Cultural causes and behavioral consequences. *Perspectives on Psychological Science, 2*(3), 242–259. https://doi.org/10.1111/j.1745-6916.2007.00043.x

van Kleef, G. A. (2016). *The interpersonal dynamics of emotion*. Cambridge University Press. https://doi.org/10.1017/CBO9781107261396

Vansteelandt, K., Van Mechelen, I., & Nezlek, J. B. (2005). The co-occurrence of emotions in daily life: A multilevel approach. *Journal of Research in Personality, 39*(3), 325–335. https://doi.org/10.1016/j.jrp.2004.05.006

Vuilleumier, P. (2005). How brains beware: Neural mechanisms of emotional attention. *Trends in Cognitive Sciences, 9*(12), 585–594. https://doi.org/10.1016/j.tics.2005.10.011

Williams, G. (1966). *Adaptation and natural selection*. Princeton University Press.

Zelenski, J. M., & Larsen, R. J. (2000). The distribution of basic emotions in everyday life: A state and trait perspective from experience sampling data. *Journal of Research in Personality, 34*(2), 178–197. https://doi.org/10.1006/jrpe.1999.2275

CHAPTER 2

The Past Explains the Present: Emotional Adaptations and the Structure of Ancestral Environments

John Tooby and Leda Cosmides

Abstract

Present conditions and selection pressures are irrelevant to the present design of organisms; they do not explain how or why organisms behave adaptively, when they do. To whatever non-chance extent organisms are behaving adaptively, it is (1) because of the operation of underlying adaptations whose present design is the product of selection in the past, and (2) because present conditions resemble past conditions in those specific ways made developmentally and functionally important by the design of those adaptations. All adaptations evolved in response to the repeating elements of past environments, so their design reflects the recurrent properties of those environments. Emotions are adaptations that treat the present as a version of the past. They categorize new situations as instances of evolutionarily recurrent events that posed adaptive problems with large fitness consequences. When activated, an emotion coordinates suites of cognitive and physiological adaptations, in ways well-designed for solving those ancestral problems.

Key Words: emotion, adaptation, adaptationist program, evolutionary psychology, environment of evolutionary adaptedness

Note to the Reader

During the late 1980s, a debate broke out among scientists studying evolution and human behavior. It centered on the nature of evolutionary explanations: Have we provided an evolutionary explanation for an individual's behavior if we demonstrate that behaving in this way promotes that individual's reproduction in modern environments? Or is behavior in the present caused by adaptations that were designed in the past, by natural selection operating over deep time? In 1990, a special issue of Ethology and Sociobiology *(the journal now called* Evolution and Human Behavior*) was devoted to this debate. Its target article, by Paul Turke, presented the argument for the first position, the* adaptiveness or correspondence program. *Our article argued against that view, and in favor of the second position: the* adaptationist program *as applied to psychology. Its title was "The Past Explains the Present: Emotional Adaptations and the Structure of Ancestral Environments"* (Ethology and Sociobiology, 11, *375–424 (1990), copyright by Elsevier).*

Chapter 2 for The Oxford Handbook of Evolution and the Emotions *is an edited version of our 1990 article. We have retained the sections most relevant to understanding the adaptationist program and its relevance to the evolution of emotions. Central to both is the* environment of evolutionary adaptedness, which is defined herein. The sections that we removed are either very specific to the target article by Turke or address technical issues that are difficult to understand without an extensive background in evolutionary biology (e.g., why measuring the fitness of individuals in the present does not explain behavior in the present; why "consciousness" is not an all-purpose inclusive fitness-maximizing device; aggregated and disaggregated fitness). These sections are indicated by ellipses, with the missing section headings in brackets.

> [I]t is very weak methodologically for sociobiology to appeal to past advantages as an explanation of present behavior. . . . Widespread current behaviors have consequences in terms of inclusive fitness at the present time. If they are to be explained on biological grounds at all, they are to be explained in terms of their contribution to inclusive fitness at the present time.
>
> —Austin Hughes (1987, p. 417)

> The variety of social systems and social strategies that we see even within a given species is simply the consequence of the same deep structure rule (say "Maximize the number of offspring you rear to maturity") finding expression in a variety of different forms depending on the particular demographic and environmental context. . . .
>
> [T]hose that concentrate on a search for species-wide universals in behaviour or morphological traits are likely to be disappointed. The number of genuinely universal traits are, I suspect, likely to run to single figures at most and probably correspond to the handful of biological "needs" like warmth, food, and procreation.
>
> —Robin Dunbar (1988, pp. 166–168)

> My main criticism of Medawar's statement is that it focuses attention on the rather trivial problem of the degree to which an organism actually achieves reproductive survival. The central biological problem is not survival as such, but design for survival.
>
> —George Williams (1966, p. 159)

The Adaptationist Program versus the Correspondence Program

There is a deep though largely unexplored schism in modern evolutionary thought over the nature of evolutionary functionalism. Differences reflecting this schism revolve around the question of what role present conditions, as opposed to past conditions, play in the functional explanation of a species' set of adaptations. Those who emphasize the role of ancestral conditions tend to focus on such concepts as design; adaptation; mechanism; fitness, as a property of a design or the genes underlying a design; histories of selection; complexity of functional design; standards of evidence for adaptations (such as efficiency, economy, and precision); the prevalence of species-typicality in complex functional design; the characterization of ancestral conditions or environments of evolutionary adaptedness; and, most of all, the cause-and-effect relationship between ancestral conditions and present adaptations (see, e.g., Barkow, 1984, 1989; Barkow et al., 1992; Cosmides & Tooby, 1987; Daly & Wilson, 1988; Dawkins, 1976, 1982, 1986; Tooby & Cosmides, 1989a, 1989c; Williams, 1966, 1985; see especially Symons, 1987, 1989, 1990). Those who emphasize the role of the present tend to focus on adaptiveness; behavior; fitness, as the property of individuals; the assessment of fitness differentials between individuals; ongoing selection; individuals construed as inclusive fitness maximizers or fitness strivers; claims that contextually appropriate behavioral variation is driven by fitness maximization; an antagonism to characterizing species-typicality (or even stable design) presented as a principled opposition to typological thinking; the present as the environment to which individuals are adapted; the fitness consequences of present behavior; and, most of all, the correspondence between present conditions and present fitness-maximizing behaviors (see, e.g., Alexander, 1979a, 1979b, 1981; Betzig, 1989; most of the articles in Betzig et al., 1988; Borgia, 1989; Caro & Borgerhoff Mulder, 1987; Dunbar, 1988; Hughes, 1987; Smuts, 1989). Although the literature cited deals largely with humans, where the debate is particularly active, it accurately reflects a division that extends throughout the community of behavioral ecologists, and, in fact, throughout biology as a whole. To identify these ideas as a single integrated viewpoint associated with specific individuals as if they were consistent exponents of one side of a binary debate would be a mistake, because nearly everyone in the evolutionary community employs, at one time or another, most of these common concepts for varied purposes. For example, Turke (1990) attempts to produce a hybrid of the two approaches, which starts out arguing for something resembling an adaptationist program, but ends up endorsing and practicing something closer to the second view. Leaving aside the question of within-individual consistency, the ways in which these concepts are systematically used in evolutionary discourse add up to profoundly different visions of the role of the concept of function in evolutionary biology. It is the validity of these alternative approaches to the concept of function, not the views of specific individuals, which is at issue. We will refer to the first approach as the adaptationist program and to the second approach as the correspondence or adaptiveness program (Symons 1990).

As we and others have argued previously (Cosmides & Tooby, 1987; Tooby & Cosmides, 1989a, 1989c; Symons, 1989, 1990, 1992[1]), an evolutionary functionalism that leapfrogs the characterization of adaptations and in its place simply catalogues correspondences between present behavior and present fitness is incomplete and is often guided by serious misinterpretations of Darwinism. We summarize the correspondence (or adaptiveness) view as follows:

> Evolutionary theory states that organisms evolved to be inclusive fitness maximizers and therefore predicts that organisms ought to be behaving adaptively in their present circumstances. This means that functional analysis involves viewing present behavior (or morphology) as the attempt to solve the adaptive problems posed by present circumstances. Darwinism or functional analysis is therefore the investigation of how an individual's present behavior corresponds to or leads to fitness maximization in its present circumstances.

Taken literally, these widely used concepts are incorrect, and they ought to be abandoned as veridical characterizations of Darwinism, functional analysis, and phenotypes. As thought experiments or heuristic devices, however, they can sometimes be useful in guiding thinking, model building, and experimentation, as long as their fundamentally metaphorical nature is not forgotten. Unfortunately, these constructs are now being treated not as heuristic devices, but as uncontroversial factual claims about the character of modern evolutionary and behavioral ecological theory. This process has gone so far that the adaptationist-based evolutionary functionalism that logically derives from the theory of evolution by natural selection has been obscured and in many literatures nearly supplanted by the correspondence program. The difference in views is most striking in how each treats the role of the past.

In *Adaptation and Natural Selection*, Williams criticized (among many other things) the attribution of foresight and anticipation to the evolutionary process, which some claimed created "adaptations designed to meet the demands of geologically future events" (1966, p. 21). This criticism also applies to positing adaptations that evolved to meet the demands of present conditions. An organism's genetic endowment is fixed at conception, and the conditions the developing phenotype faces constitute an unknown future with respect to the evolutionary processes that determined that genetic endowment. Present adaptations were constructed by natural selection in the past, over evolutionary time, without foreknowledge of the conditions they would encounter in the present. Moreover, the effect of present environments on present genetic variability in adaptive designs is the process of ongoing selection, which produces future but not present adaptations. Consequently, the study of ongoing selection is not closely connected to the study of adaptations either, although each may cast some light on the other.

The causal link between past conditions and present biological design is the necessary, logical core of Darwinian explanation. In contrast, the adaptive correspondence between present conditions and present behavior, to the extent that it exists, is contingent, derived, and incidental to Darwinian explanation. It depends solely on how much the present ontogenetic environment of an individual happens to reflect the summed features of the environment during recent evolutionary history, that is, on how different the present environment is from ancestral conditions. In no sense is the correspondence between present conditions and present adaptations a cause of those adaptations, and the current consequences of those adaptations on inclusive fitness is not a cause or an explanation for those adaptations. Present selection pressures or environmentally imposed tasks are causally irrelevant to the present design of organisms and have no role in explaining them. For a Darwinian, the explanation for our present system of adaptations lies completely in the past, starting one generation ago, and extending back across phylogenetic time to include the history of selection that constructed those designs.

Teleology

The human mind seems to love teleology. As human beings, one of the most important things we do is try to understand, explain, and predict the behavior of others, and we have powerful folk theories for doing so. Desires, purposes, strategies, goal seeking, and intentions are teleological concepts that play a powerful role in these folk theories. The appeal of teleological concepts is so strong that even physicists, who have systematically expunged teleology from any formal role, informally discuss concepts and experiments in teleological terms, saying, for example, "the muon wants to decay, but is blocked from doing so because . . ." (Daston, personal communication; Galison, personal communication; Malament, personal communication). Teleological metaphors can make reasoning about certain problems far easier, and there is nothing wrong with this, unless and until one forgets the limitations on their applicability and takes them to be facts.

We suggest that the search for adaptiveness has displaced the search for adaptations[2] because the theoretical logic of adaptationism is expressed in non-teleological causal terms, whereas the correspondence program is expressed primarily in appealing teleological terms such as goal seeking ("the goal of evolution"), purpose ("adaptive purpose"), striving ("fitness striving"), attempts ("the organism's attempt to solve the adaptive problem"), pursuit ("the pursuit of fitness"), strategies ("the organism pursues a fitnesspromoting strategy"), interests ("fitness interests"), motivational characterizations ("selfishness"), and so on. Teleology seems to be far more congenial to spontaneous human thinking,[3] creating the danger that teleological analogy may drive out nonteleological causal reasoning. We suspect this preference for teleology stems from the fact that humans have conscious access to evolved cognitive processes involved with planning, choosing goals, assessing others' motivations, and improvising methods for seeking goals (see Alexander, 1989), but not to many of our innately derived models of physical causality (Proffitt & Gilden, 1989). For this reason, we tend to impose teleological models on the world, sometimes very inappropriately (e.g., the "goal" of evolution was to produce humans), and sometimes because feedback-driven causal processes somewhat resemble teleological processes (e.g., the "goal" of evolution is fitness maximization or gene propagation).

Problems caused by the non-correspondence between the causal processes in evolution and our teleologically expressed intuitive models become especially acute when behavior is at issue. Few are tempted to attribute goal seeking to morphological structures, but some psychological structures do contain goal-seeking subsystems or feedback mechanisms that regulate behavior such that an internally represented state of the world is achieved. The fact that feedback processes in evolution superficially resemble goal seeking mechanisms in organisms leads to the seductive error of believing that the two levels—evolutionary processes and psychological mechanisms—are really one level or refer to the same elements (Tooby & Cosmides, 1989c). This error is the source of claims that evolution's "goal" is the goal of organisms; that because evolution fitness maximizes, organisms are goal-seeking fitness maximizers; that evolution's "purposes" are the organism's purposes, and so on. Once this conflation of evolutionary process with psychological mechanism is made—once organisms are construed as the agents of the evolutionary process, effortfully striving to accomplish the goal of fitness maximization—then the evolutionary study of behavior becomes transformed into the search for the correspondence between observed behavior and fitness maximization in present conditions. Ancestral conditions seem to be logically irrelevant, or at most a "weak" (Hughes 1987) explanation perhaps to be dragged in ad hoc or as a last resort to explain some residue of behavior that is not presently fitness maximizing.

. . . [The Modern Synthesis and the Study of Variation] . . .

From Correspondences to Causal Explanations

There is nothing wrong per se with documenting correspondences, and in fact, such investigations can be very worthwhile. Sciences often begin as the discovery of some pattern of correspondence in the world and are extended by the discovery of others. The east coast of the Americas appears to correspond to the west coast of Europe and Africa. The chemical properties of the elements show recurrent patterns that allow them to be organized into a periodic table. Economists attempt to explain behavioral observations by trying to show how such behavior corresponds to rational utility maximization, a simple axiomatized idealization. In evolutionary biology, the correspondence view frames behavioral investigations as a kind of evolutionary economics, in which one shows how behavior corresponds to "rational fitness maximization" in present conditions (Hughes, 1987). For those who use such correspondence theories, the primary task is taken to be explaining how a set of observations corresponds to the operation of such a principle.

But genuine understanding is found when one not only has rules of correspondence (e.g., continental boundary parallels), but when one also has a causal model of *why* those correspondences are there (e.g., plate tectonics). As a field matures, one set of correspondences is shown to be the causal expression of another more basic set (although, of course, some final level of principles such as quantum mechanics is simply a given). The discovery of such correspondences is one possible starting point in the evolutionary analysis of behavior or morphology (Turke, 1990). But the adaptationist and correspondence programs diverge in how they treat these correspondences and why they are considered important. For the correspondence researcher, the analysis of how behavior corresponds to fitness maximization is the evolutionary explanation, whereas for the adaptationist the discovery of such a correspondence is not an explanation at all, but rather a phenomenon—however much expected—that itself requires explanation.

For an adaptationist, the causal explanation runs as follows. The correspondence between some specified present behavior and what it takes to fitness-maximize (really, fitness-promote) in present conditions is either a coincidence or brought about through systematic causal processes. If an organism is behaving in a certain way in response to a given environmental variable, it is because some set of properties in the organism cause it to do so. To make the claim that behavior is adaptive and that this adaptiveness is not a coincidence is to make the claim that the organism has an adaptation that is solving the adaptive problem. To make the claim that such adaptations exist is to make the claim that they were shaped by a history of selection in ancestral conditions, because natural selection is the only known process (aside from intelligent manufacture) that can create complex functional design over time (Dawkins, 1986). To whatever extent, great or small, a particular present behavior is still adaptive, it is because present conditions still happen to resemble ancestral conditions. Therefore, adaptations are the causal explanation for whatever adaptiveness manifests itself and characterizing adaptations constitutes a necessary part of the explanation of any principle of correspondence, such as why foragers approximately follow the marginal value theorem (Charnov, 1976). The theory that describes the logic of the entire causal process responsible for adaptations is Darwinism.

Darwinism and Adaptations

From a Darwinian perspective, the defining property of life is the reproduction by systems of new and similarly reproducing systems. From this defining property, reproduction, the deductive structure of Darwinism can be built (Dawkins, 1976; Williams, 1985).

The logical core of Darwinism is the theory of natural selection, involving reproduction of design, inheritance of design, variation in design, and differential rates of reproduction caused by differences in design.[4] The fact that the properties of designs have an impact on their rate of reproduction creates a system of positive and negative feedback, called natural selection, that forges an organized relationship between the properties of historically encountered environments, the properties of designs, and their frequency in the world. Usually this leads to fixation of the favored design, although frequency-dependent equilibria sometimes set an upper limit on design frequency in the population. Natural selection is the only known process capable of accounting for complex functional design in living things (Williams, 1985; Dawkins, 1986), and all nonrandom functionality in living systems must be attributed to the action of adaptations. Adaptations are mechanisms or systems of properties "designed" by natural selection to solve the specific problems posed by the regularities of the physical, chemical, ecological, informational, and social environments encountered by the ancestors of a species during the course of its evolution. As a result of the operation of natural selection, organisms (properly described) consist largely of complexly articulated designs. The detailed specification of adaptations is the most appropriate way of describing and organizing our observations about these designs.

The outcomes of the evolutionary process break down into three basic categories: (1) adaptations (often, though not always complex); (2) concomitants or byproducts of adaptations; and (3) random effects. Because concomitants and random flux are usually only identifiable as what is left over after adaptations have been discovered and described, the characterization of a species' adaptations should generally be procedurally prior to investigating claims about random processes or concomitants ("spandrels"). Adaptations are the result of coordination brought about by selection as a feedback process; they are recognizable by "evidence of special design" (Williams, 1966)—that is, by a highly nonrandom coordination between recurring properties of the phenotype and the ancestral environment, which mesh to promote fitness (genetic propagation). Standards for recognizing special design include such factors as economy, efficiency, complexity, precision, specialization, and reliability (Williams, 1966). The demonstration that an aspect of the phenotype is an adaptation is always, at core, a probability argument concerning how nonrandom this coordination is. Concomitants of adaptation are those properties of the phenotype that do not contribute to adaptation per se, but are tied to properties that do, and are therefore incorporated into the organism's design; they are incidental byproducts of adaptations. Any number of concomitants can be "manufactured" at will by the process of describing an organism without reference to its adaptations. There are an infinite number of traits and phenomena one can define and measure, but evolutionarily analyzable order will tend to be found only in those that are causally related to adaptive function.

The study of adaptations can be broken (somewhat arbitrarily) into two halves: evolutionary psychology—the study of the adaptations that regulate behavior—and physiology—the study of morphological structures and processes, whether or not they regulate behavior. To understand the design of human (or any living species') psychology or physiology is usually a problem in reverse engineering: we have working exemplars of the design in front of us, but we need to organize our observations of these exemplars into a systematic functional description of the design. The central tool for organizing these observations is the concept of adaptation. Approximately, an adaptation is:

(1) A cross-generationally recurring set of characteristics of the phenotype developmentally manufactured according to instructions contained in its genetic specification or basis, in interaction with stable and recurring features of the environment (i.e., a design);
(2) whose genetic basis became established and organized in the species (or population) over evolutionary time, because
(3) the set of characteristics systematically interacted with stable and recurring features of the environment (the "adaptive problem"),
(4) in a way that systematically promoted the propagation of the genetic basis of the set of characteristics better than the alternative designs existing in the population during the period of selection. This promotion takes place through enhancing either the reproduction of the individual bearing the set of characteristics or the reproduction of the relatives of that individual, or both.

Adaptationist Analysis

In approaching a given species' behavior from an adaptationist perspective, evolutionary analysis requires several nested but distinct levels (Tooby & Cosmides, 1989c). These are:

1. Models of the evolutionary process, involving definitions of fitness, selection, adaptation, genes, the role of stochastic factors, and general models of such topics as kin-directed altruism, cooperation, sexual recombination, and sexual selection.
2. An analysis of how these principles were manifested as a species-specific array of selection pressures, refracted through the specific ecological, social, genetic, phylogenetic, and informational circumstances experienced along a given species' evolutionary history (Tooby & DeVore, 1987). This is the characterization of ancestral conditions, sometimes referred to as "the environment of evolutionary adaptedness." This involves construction of computational theories (Marr, 1982; Cosmides & Tooby, 1987, 1989), that is, task analyses of what information-processing problems an adaptation must solve.

3. A description of the species' inherited adaptations that evolved to solve the problems posed by the species-specific array of ancestral selection pressures. Steps 1 and 2 are significant because they allow the discovery, investigation, description, and functional analysis of the adaptations. They constitute the ultimate explanation for the design of the adaptations, by specifying the selection pressures and the enduring ancestral conditions in which these selection pressures operated. (It is useful, and often essential, to have a good description of these adaptations as conditional developmental programs that map environmental input into phenotypic output.)
4. A description of the present environment, the environment of ontogeny, in terms of (a) the state of those features that must be stably present for the organism's adaptations to reliably develop, and (b) the state of those features that the organism's adaptive procedures take as input and process into structured phenotypic output, such as environmental cues that regulate facultative adaptations, information processed by cognitive mechanisms, or anything else to which the developmental programs contingently respond.
5. To understand and explain all current behavior, whether adaptive or maladaptive, one needs to integrate the information present in steps 3 and 4 into the particular developmental trajectory of an individual (with other individuals modeled as developmental inputs). The developmental programs that conditionally describe adaptations (and byproducts and noise, if they are of interest) plus the environment of ontogeny together provide a proximate explanation for current behavior ("vertically integrated" explanations [Barkow, 1989]).

Consider, for example, the Westermarck mechanism for promoting incest avoidance (Shepher, 1983; Wolf & Huang, 1980; Lieberman et al., 2007). Analyzing the selection pressures against inbreeding, such as making deleterious recessives homozygous or increasing disease load (Tooby, 1982), constitutes the first stage in the analysis. Analyzing the operation of these forces during our evolutionary history constitutes the second step: What were the statistical properties of the genetic loads and pathogen pressures that our foraging ancestors encountered? What were the demographic risks of inbreeding for various categories of kin, given the range and distribution of experienced social structures? What cues were available for mechanisms to use to assess various kinship relations, and how reliable were they? For humans, like most other long-lived mammals, the genetic loads and pathogen pressures were high enough to create a substantial selection pressure; moreover, given the nature of hunter-gatherer life, social structures were commonly such as to make incest a real possibility, and infant and childhood association provided reliable cues of kinship about potential incest partners. The third step is the discovery, investigation, and characterization of the resulting adaptation or adaptations. In this case, it appears to involve a mechanism that "judges relatedness" for the purpose of incest avoidance (at least) by the duration of mutual intimate exposure in the first several years of life. It uses this cue to dampen sexual interest: familiarity breeds sexual disinterest, a process that lowered the probability of incest between relatives raised together ancestrally. Establishing that something is an adaptation involves showing how it manifests evidence of special design for solving a problem that existed ancestrally and that endured long enough to constitute a selection pressure that could have built a specialized structure as complex as the one observed.

To analyze particular cases of modern behavior, such as within-creche cohort sexual avoidance in Israeli kibbutzim, one needs to describe the relevant ontogenetic environment (step 4): unrelated children of both sexes were raised in small, intimate groups from the earliest ages. The outcome (step 5) was a lack of sexual interest between nonrelatives raised in this fashion. The present behavior—sexual avoidance of reproductively appropriate and accessible nonrelatives—is understood as the operation of underlying adaptations, within a particular ontogenetic environment. There is nothing particularly adaptive about this outcome. But whether avoiding creche-mates happens to be currently adaptive or maladaptive is completely irrelevant to its explanation. Regardless of its present fitness consequences, it remains patterned by underlying adaptations forged in the past.

The research approach is very different for those who see evolutionary functional analysis as the investigation of how an individual's present behavior corresponds to or leads to fitness maximization in his or her present circumstances. The observation that creche-mates avoided each other as sexual partners would prompt the search for how this "strategy" leads to enhanced fitness in the kibbutzim. An endless series of hypotheses could be advanced and even tested (e.g., if one can deceive relative strangers better than those who have known one from infancy, then perhaps strangers should be preferred as more manipulable mates). The fitness of creche-mate avoiders could be compared to the fitness of those (if any) who married creche-mates. "Feasible" alternative strategies (creche-mate avoidance versus creche-mate preferring) could be scrutinized for why each was explained by its fitness consequences, given the particular resources and constraints available to the two sets of strategists. Constructing accounts of why present behaviors lead to positive fitness consequences is always possible, if necessary by invoking additional situational variables and constraints until adaptiveness is demonstrated.

The error in the correspondence program is to finesse steps 2 and 3 and to instead leap directly from general models of evolution (step 1) to current conditions (step 4), in an attempt to "explain" present behavior (step 5) as fitness maximization in present environments. What creates a nonrandom adaptive correspondence between present conditions and present behavior, whenever there is one, is solely the causal structure of steps 2 and 3, plus the contingent fact that the environment of ontogeny resembles the "environment of evolutionary adaptedness" (EEA) with respect to that adaptation.

The Definition of the Environment of Evolutionary Adaptedness

Characterizing an adaptation involves characterizing the ancestral conditions and selection pressures—the adaptive problem—that the adaptation solves. The EEA is not a place or a habitat, or even a time period. Rather, it is a statistical composite of the adaptation-relevant properties of the ancestral environments encountered by members of ancestral populations, weighted by their frequency and fitness-consequences. These properties are selected out of all possible environmental properties as those that actually interacted with the existing design of the organism during the period of evolution. These ancestral conditions must be characterized when functionally analyzing an adaptation. To establish that something is an adaptation, one must establish an improbably close coordination between the adaptive problem constituted by the statistical composite of ancestral conditions and the design features of the adaptation. This description of ancestral conditions is one indispensable aspect of characterizing an adaptation and constitutes part of what we have called the task analysis or computational theory phase of the functional analysis of an adaptation (see Cosmides & Tooby, 1987 [see also 1994a]; Tooby & Cosmides, 1989a; Marr, 1982). Ignoring this logical step does not eliminate it as a necessary part of any evolutionary functional argument—it simply renders functional analysis weak or meaningless.

The concept of the EEA has been criticized under the misapprehension that it refers to a place, or to a typologically characterized habitat, and hence fails to reflect the variability of conditions organisms may have encountered (see Turke, 1990). Humans, for example, undoubtedly encountered a variety of specific habitats during many periods of their evolution and should not be typologically characterized as adapted to living in, for example, the Kalahari desert. Turke and others have complained that to invoke the EEA is to depict the past as a "featureless monolith," or in the human case as a simple constant that only began to change after the rise of agriculture (Turke, 1990). (We found, much to our surprise, that we were described as believing that the Pleistocene was relatively simple and constant and were somewhat justified in thinking so.) There is no basis in the concept of the EEA for any claims of stasis, simplification, or uniform ancestral conditions in the usual sense. As a complex statistical composite of structurally described contingencies of selection, the idea of an EEA involves no oversimplification. Rather the error is to think that a literal place or a habitat, defined by ostension, is a description of the ancestral condition component of the definition of an adaptation. The concept of ancestral conditions or the EEA, as a statistical composite, is necessarily invoked whenever one is making an adaptationist claim, which means whenever one is making an adaptiveness claim, whether researchers are aware of it or not. As a composite, it is necessarily "uniform" in the abstract sense, although that uniform description may involve the detailed characterization of any degree of environmental variability.

To the extent that there is an ambiguity in the concept of the environment of evolutionary adaptedness, it is because of the time-dimension of the problem. Because the history of any evolving lineage extends back several billion years to the origins of life, the characterization of ancestral conditions requires a time-structured approach matching specific statistical environmental regularities against specific instances of evolutionary modification in design. To the extent that the adaptation has assumed an equilibrium design under stabilizing selection, the period of stabilizing selection itself becomes a primary part of the EEA, although for some purposes one may want to distinguish the EEA of stabilizing selection from the EEA during the period of sequential fixations. For this reason, the EEA is adaptation-specific and evolutionary change-specific, with the EEA for the human eye being somewhat distinct from the EEA for the human language faculty. The EEA refers to the statistical composite of environments that were encountered during the period when a design feature changed from one state into another (and was subsequently maintained, if it was). The EEA for the human language faculty consists of the statistical composite of relevant environmental features starting from the incipient appearance of the language faculty until it reached its present structure (although to do a real analysis, this period may need to be partitioned according to particular intermediate steps). Nevertheless, for most ordinary analytic purposes, the EEA for a species (i.e., for its *collection* of adaptations) can be taken to refer to the statistically weighted composite of environmental properties of the most recent segment of a species' evolution that encompasses the period during which its modern collection of adaptations assumed their present form. We have used the word "Pleistocene" in this sense to refer to the human EEA, because its time depth was appropriate for virtually all adaptations of anatomically modern humans, with a few minor exceptions such as the post-weaning persistence of lactase among pastoralist peoples (Tooby, 1985; Tooby & DeVore, 1987; Cosmides & Tooby, 1987; Tooby & Cosmides, 1989a; on lactase, see McCracken, 1971).

The Ontogenetic Environment

The role that present conditions play in the logical structure of Darwinism is highly circumscribed: present conditions participate in the system of causation as the ontogenetic environment (and trivially, as a single increment in the EEA of future adaptations). The individual organism, fixed at conception with a given genetic endowment regulating its developmental programs, encounters its specific ontogenetic environment, which it processes as a set of inputs to these developmental programs. In other words, the organism blindly executes the programs it inherits, and the ontogenetic conditions it encounters serve as parametric inputs to these programs. The putatively species-typical Westermarck incest-avoidance mechanism, presented with the particular set of inputs provided by the ontogenetic environment of the kibbutz, led to the sexual avoidance of otherwise appropriate partners. For the evolved relationship between an animal's genes and its ontogenetic environment to remain coordinated across generations (and hence adaptive), the twin inheritances, genes and environmental invariances (the constellation of environmental features used by development or interacted with by adaptations) must be passed on, intact and relatively unchanged. A single environmental "mutation" (change in an invariance) can be sufficient to make the environment "novel" with respect to many adaptations—that is, can make behavior in many domains maladaptive and "off-track." For example, raising nonrelatives in the same creche is an environmental mutation with respect to the Westermarck mechanisms, which depend for their adaptive expression on an environment in which relatives are creche-mates. This environmental mutation creates potentially maladaptive behavior in mate choice.

Statistical Regularities Define the EEA

The conditions that characterize the EEA are usefully decomposed into a constellation of specific environmental regularities that had impact on fitness and that endured long enough to work evolutionary change on the design of an adaptation. We will call these statistical regularities *invariances*. Invariances need not be conditions that were absolutely unwavering, although many, such as the properties of light or chemical reactions, were. Rather, an invariance is a single descriptive construct, calculated from the point of view of a selected adaptation or design of a given genotype at a given point of time. No matter how variable conditions were, they left a systematically structured average impact on the design, and that systematic impact needs to be coherently characterized in terms of the statistical and structural regularities that constituted the selection pressure responsible. These invariances can be described as sets of conditionals of any degree of complexity, from the very simple (e.g., the temperature was always greater than freezing) to a two-valued statistical construct (e.g., the temperature had a mean of 31.2°C and standard deviation of 8.1), to any degree of conditional and structural complexity that is reflected in the adaptation (e.g., predation on kangaroo rats by shrikes is 17.6% more likely during a cloudless full moon than during a new moon during the first 60 days after the winter solstice if one exhibits adult male ranging patterns). Such descriptions are essential parts of the construction of a task analysis or computational analysis of the adaptive problem that a hypothesized adaptation evolved to solve (Cosmides & Tooby, 1987; Tooby & Cosmides, 1989a).

Adaptations as a Record of the Past

Turke (1990) repeats the common complaint that characterizing the past is impractical because it is not available for direct observation and our present knowledge of it is inadequate. Yet the degree of difficulty in observation is no excuse for logical errors, and substituting present conditions for ancestral conditions in evolutionary functionalism is simply an error. In any case, the task of characterizing the past is not irremediably difficult, but will be easy or difficult depending on the specific issue, the sophistication of the research community, and the power of the methods developed. The essence of Darwin's principled historical framework is that the present world is full of information about the past, as the present consists entirely of outcomes of past causal processes. We do not need a time machine to observe the past. The present, studied with specialized theoretical, inferential, and observational tools, allows observation of the past. Paleontological methods, of course, form one important set of tools, but reliance on them alone, in isolation from other techniques, has contributed unfairly to the idea that our knowledge of the past is "inadequate" for adaptationist analyses. For many purposes the study of present environments as models of past environments is our best window on the past, because an enormous number of factors, from the properties of light to chemical laws to the existence of parasites, have stably endured. Evolutionary theory itself provides a series of powerful inferential tools for characterizing the past which should be integrated with existing paleontological methods of more direct observation (Tooby & DeVore, 1987). For example, validated evolutionary principles also constitute descriptions of constraints operating in the past, from the minimal (finding a mate of the opposite sex is necessary to reproduction in species with two sexes) to the more sophisticated (the possibility of cheating limits the evolution of cooperation).

The discovery and characterization of adaptations is the single most reliable way of discovering the characteristics of the past, because each species' design functions as an instrument that has registered, weighted, and summed enormous numbers of encounters with the properties of past environments. Species are data-recording instruments that have directly "observed" the conditions of the past through direct participation in ancestral environments. A specific complex adaptation constitutes, in the improbability of its specialization of design, a probability test about ancestral conditions based on an enormous and representative sample of the past. Eyes tell one that light was a part of the EEA. Immune systems tell one that disease was both present and an important selective agent. The presence of psychological mechanisms producing male sexual jealousy tells one that female infidelity was part of the human and ring dove EEAs (Daly & Wilson, 1988; Erickson & Zenone, 1977). Observation of the structure of present adaptations and logical deductions from these observations constitute a system for reading back what these ancient but still operational data recorders have to tell us about the past. The study of human cognitive specializations, including human emotional adaptations, may prove to be a surprisingly detailed record of the structure of the past.

... [Adaptations Are the Best Test of Evolutionary Theory] ...

Adaptations Are Usually Population or Species-Typical

The differences between the correspondence and adaptationist programs become clear through considering how each treats the topic of universals versus variability. For someone following the correspondence program, the search for universals is typological and misguided (see Dunbar, 1988; and Borgia's [1989] and Smuts's [1989] criticisms of Buss, 1989). Because the organizing explanatory principle is held to be that organisms do whatever it takes in a situation to maximize fitness, then because circumstances vary, behaviors should and will vary also, and in any way that is appropriate to the goal of fitness maximization in those circumstances. Behavioral (and morphological! [Dunbar, 1988, p. 168]) traits will rarely be universal, and such universals will only be elicited when the same *current* environmental challenge is presented to all members of a species. The universal does not reside in phenotypes or in phenotypic designs, but in principles such as the "deep structure rule," "maximize the number of offspring you rear to maturity" (Dunbar, 1988).

According to evolutionary theory, however, nonaccidental adaptiveness occurs solely because of the operation of adaptations, which in turn entail both a history of selection in ancestral conditions and a genetic basis. Therefore, the distribution of this genetic basis should also be characterized, and in fact commonly falls into only a few alternative patterns (species-typicality, frequency-dependence, population-universality, etc.). Because many or most adaptive problems are complex, they require complex adaptations to solve them. To the extent that the adaptations under discussion are complex adaptations (defined as adaptations that require the coordinated gene action of more than a very small number of genes), then it follows that they will nearly always be universal in the population, and given the population structure of most long-lived species, they will probably be species-typical as well. Their expression may be limited by sex, life-history stage, or circumstance, but at the genetic or design level the adaptation will almost always be speciesuniversal (Tooby & Cosmides, 1990). Complex adaptations necessarily require many genes to regulate their development, and sexual recombination makes it combinatorially improbable that all the necessary genes for a complex adaptation would be together at once in the same individual, if genes coding for complex adaptations varied substantially between individuals.[5] Selection, interacting with sexual recombination, enforces a powerful tendency toward uniformity in the genetic architecture underlying complex functional design at the population level, and usually at the species level as well.[6] Aside from neutral mutations, the bulk of genetic variation is present in populations because it is pathogen-driven frequency-dependent selection for biochemical diversity, rather than because it specifies different functional adaptations between individuals (see Tooby, 1982, for discussion). For these reasons, adaptive design should most often be species-typical design, and may include hundreds to tens of thousands of adaptations (depending on whether one is a lumper or splitter in categorizing them), rather than numbering in the "single figures" (Dunbar, 1988). Human nature is a rich, incredibly intricate articulated structure, and one can expect the evolved informationprocessing mechanisms that regulate social behavior to be no less intricate and complex than the vertebrate eye.

Variability in Expression, Uniformity in Design

Even where the genetic basis of a phenotypic trait is not species- or population-universal, for a structure to qualify as an adaptation it must be recurrent. An adaptation is more than a mere collection of phenotypic properties which, in a particular individual, happen to have the effect of enhancing reproduction—winning the lottery, burning coal, and irrigating fields are not adaptations. An adaptation is a recurrent design that reappears across generations and across individuals. For selection (as opposed to chance) to have manufactured a structure, the evolved design must have had repeated encounters with recurrent properties of the world. Those encounters constitute the history of selection for that design. If characteristics emerge uniquely every generation, or haphazardly from individual to individual, then selection cannot organize them.

This means that the phenotype of an individual organism must be carefully distinguished from the design of the phenotype—fitnesses should be assigned to designs, not to individuals. Natural selection involves design, defined as those properties that are stable across all individuals of the same genotype. As Williams says, "[t]he central biological problem is not survival as such, but design for survival" (1966, p. 159). The individual phenotype manifests innumerable transient properties, which disappear with the death of the phenotype or change idiosyncratically over the life span. Although some of these transient properties may promote reproduction, they are chance-produced beneficial effects, not adaptations (Williams, 1966). Because adaptations are responsible for all non-chance adaptiveness, any claim of adaptiveness must be traced back to underlying adaptations.

The principal confusion of the correspondence program is that most researchers documenting adaptiveness do not distinguish between transient properties, which cannot be adaptations, and design properties, which can. Their reluctance to make this distinction, we suspect, stems from the sense they have that there is far too much transitory adaptiveness to be accidental, and in this they are correct. If they were to exclude from evolutionary analysis everything that apparently varied, there would be scarcely anything left. They point out that organisms frequently vary their behavior adaptively in synchrony with contextual variables (Borgia, 1989; Smuts, 1989). This has led some to define behavioral ecology itself as the study of variation, with such variation held to be explained by the principle of fitness maximization, combined with how contextual variables elicit appropriate variations in behavior. The search for universals is rejected as the typological activity of those who do not really understand evolution (Dunbar, 1988). This approach to behavioral ecology is caught in the paradox that transient phenomena have no position in the logic of Darwinism, and yet such phenomena seem adaptive, rule-governed, and apparently explained by the principle of fitness maximization.

The Role of Phenotypic Description

The solution to this apparent contradiction is found in the task of describing phenotypic design. The logically necessary process of relating adaptiveness to underlying adaptations involves the process of redescribing the variable and the transitory in terms of that which is recurrent and stable. This process of description is key: by choosing the wrong categories, everything about the organism can seem variable and transitory, so that humans appear to have fewer than 10 universal morphological and behavioral traits (Dunbar, 1988, p. 168). By choosing the right categories—adaptationist categories—an immensely intricate species-typical architecture appears, with some limited additional layers of frequency-dependent or population-specific design as well. Discovering the underlying recurrent characteristics that generate the surface phenotypic variability is essential to the discovery of adaptations. Adaptations may be variable in expression, but must be uniform in design (Tooby & Cosmides, 1990).

Because behavior and physiology do vary, underlying design will often be described in terms of conditional rules such as developmental programs or decision rules. This process of description will be obstructed without the recognition that adaptations are the conditional rules of expression of phenotypes, and not phenotypes themselves. One cannot discern adaptations in the variable features of phenotypes, but only in their uniform underlying architecture. Thus, individual phenotypes are instances of designs, but not designs themselves. For example, the cleaner fish, *Labroides dimidiata*, is a protogynous sequential hermaphrodite, which means that an individual typically begins as a female and turns into a male only when it becomes the largest fish in the group (Robertson, 1972). The adaptation is not being male or being female, different for different phenotypes with the same genotype. Rather, the adaptation is the conditional rule "change to male if you are the largest conspecific in the group, remain female if you are not" that regulates which phenotype is expressed, together with the design specification of those organs and properties that make a phenotype a male or female of that species.

Unless genes are different, adaptations are the same. Therefore, to recover adaptive design out of behavioral or morphological observations, one needs to determine what is variable and what is invariant across individuals: only the recurrent is a candidate adaptation. One reason why the avunculate, the English language, cross-cousin marriages, and Tibetan polyandry cannot be adaptations is because they vary from human to human in a way that is not (plausibly) caused by genetic differences between them. These are expressions of adaptations, but not adaptations themselves.

Additional Rules for Functional Analysis

These considerations suggest that several new principles for discussing function and for recognizing or ruling out adaptations can be applied to organize observations about phenotypes.

1. A set of phenotypic properties is not an adaptation if it is transient, varying from individual to individual, and is not part of the recurrent design of individuals of that genotype (in an EEA-standard environment).
2. Therefore, adaptations (as uniform designs) should be distinguished from their expression (which may vary from context to context). Observations about variable behavior need to be sifted for relational invariances to detect underlying adaptations. Any contingent behavioral or physiological phenomenon needs to be related to an underlying recurrent structure.
3. A set of phenotypic properties is not an adaptation if it was absent in the EEA.[7]
4. A set of phenotypic properties is not an adaptation if it did not solve an adaptive problem in the EEA, however fitness-promoting it may be during the present generation.
5. A description of a set of phenotypic properties does not properly characterize an adaptation if that description involves terms and elements for things that did not exist in the EEA.
6. Although population differentiation and frequency-dependent selection may lead to some restricted exceptions, of limited genetic complexity, the designs of most adaptations will be species-typical for species with an open population structure, however condition-limited the expression of those designs may be (Tooby & Cosmides, 1990). Consequently, high heritabilities usually indicate that the heritable component of the phenotypic variation is not an adaptation.
7. Functional analysis should be expressed in adaptationist terms, specifying the selection pressures, recurring environmental elements representing ancestral conditions, and so on. Adaptive or functional outcomes must be linked to underlying uniform adaptations to qualify as a Darwinian account. In contrast, a description of how a culture-specific behavior contributes more to fitness than alternative behaviors does not constitute a functional account of the behavior.
8. Characterizing adaptations requires that one speak in the language of causation rather than teleology. Adaptations are systems of properties that, against a given environmental background, cause the solution to an adaptive problem. Specifying the "goal" of the process, that is, the recurrent fitness-promoting outcome, is only one part of characterizing adaptations. It is further incumbent on the researcher to specify the causal process, method, or procedure that accomplishes the goal. Characterizing the method or procedure that reaches the goal is not an onerous burden, but instead frequently leads to new insights about the nature of the adaptive problem itself. For example, the marginal value theorem (Charnov, 1976) specifies an adaptive problem: how to regulate the behavior of the forager such that it follows the marginal value theorem (e.g., leave patch when gain rate drops to the average in the environment). Attempting to characterize how this goal is achieved raises the question of how the organism could obtain the information necessary to achieve it (what is the average gain rate for the environment; what is the average travel time; how are patch types recognized; and so on). This led to the consideration of additional adaptations that solve these problems (Stephens & Krebs, 1986). Noting a correspondence (e.g., between behavior and the marginal value theorem) does not constitute the characterization of an adaptation; instead it prompts the search for the adaptations responsible for that correspondence.

Behavior versus Mechanism

We have argued elsewhere for the importance of distinguishing adaptive design from its phenotypic expression, but we phrased the argument in terms of the utility of studying the mechanisms regulating behavior rather than simply behavior itself (Cosmides & Tooby, 1987; Tooby & Cosmides, 1989a). Turke argues that behavior can be an adaptation just as much as any other phenotypic property can be (Turke, 1990), and, depending on exactly what is meant by the word "behavior," we agree with him. Dawkins's (1982) discussion of the extended phenotype was perfectly correct in pointing out that any kind of phenotypic consequence is comparable to any other kind in the logic of Darwinism, in its potential for constituting an adaptation. But the issue here turns on what one means by "behavior": behavior as manifest phenotype expression, or behavior as recurrent underlying design. We favor discussing mechanism over behavior because of the usual meaning given to those words: behavior usually refers to any kind of transitory individual phenomenon (she ate spinach; when he became sick he went to the physician and was bled, etc.). When one redescribes behavior in terms of underlying, recurrent design—a requirement for characterizing an adaptation—the resulting description is almost never sufficient unless it uses mechanistic as opposed to behavioral language. Spinach-eating, polygyny, monogamy, agriculture, and the avunculate are no doubt often adaptive behaviors, but are not adaptations. The hypothetical decision rule "eat if blood sugar is below a threshold level and search and handling costs are not too high" is a candidate for an adaptation involved in spinach eating (albeit minimally described), because it could potentially be a universal design feature. To find a human adaptation describable purely in behavioral terms, one would have to fall back on the simple, manifestly universal movements (such as thrusting during copulation) that behavioral ecologists would rather leave to physiologists (see Symons, 1989, 1990, 1992). Behavior is not a useful level for describing adaptations because the language of behavior cannot easily describe design-universals, i.e., the whole structure of environment-procedure-behavioral outcome relationships. Researchers who employ purely behavioral descriptions rarely manage to describe design in a sufficiently precise way to capture what the target of selection was. Moreover, when Turke (1990) invokes neural plasticity to say that mechanisms can vary just as much as behavior can, it is clear that he is using the word "mechanism" in a different sense than we are. By "mechanism" we do not mean "wet" tissues or any aspect of the expressed phenotype. Instead we mean a description of some part of the underlying design of the phenotype. For a given genotype, the description of the underlying design should not vary—if it does, then it has not been described properly. Phenotypes of the same genotype, whether behavioral or physiological, vary. By definition, designs of the same genotype do not.

. . . [Turke's Proposed Program] . . . [Aggregated and Disaggregated Adaptiveness] . . .

Maladaptive Behavior Is Equally Informative

The relevance of Darwinism stems from the fact that every behavior, adaptive or maladaptive, is the product of adaptations (or other linked aspects of underlying design) and hence is patterned by the structure of those adaptations. Its relevance does not depend in the slightest on whether all, most, or no modern behavior is presently adaptive. When framed by adaptationist questions, maladaptive behavior (in the sense of a mechanism's specific disaggregated performance) can be every bit as informative as adaptive behavior. An enormous wealth of modern behavioral phenomena, such as recreational drugs, pornography, films, television, sports, recreational as opposed to procreative sex, gambling, New Age nostrums, horoscopes, anonymous charitable work, blood donation, political dissidence, voting, seeking advice through trance channeling, alcohol use, romance novels, the adoption of nonrelatives, doing evolutionary biology, music, hiking, the sexual abuse of children, and on and on, do not contribute to fitness over known, "feasible" alternatives practiced by others in similar circumstances.[8] Proximate fitness-maximization is not the principle that explains these behaviors, and trying to show (for example) that the purchase of pornography or cocaine enhances the average reproduction of purchasers over nonpurchasers practicing the best "feasible" alternative is sterile, since their present adaptiveness has nothing to do with their existence (see Turke, 1990, on "feasibility").[9] Instead, the purchase of pornography by males must reflect some underlying adaptation, such as the hypothetical and obviously oversimple decision rule: "move toward situations that produce retinal images of naked nubile females and become sexually aroused." Because the EEA lacked artificially created images of females, such a rule would plausibly have been fitness-promoting. Maladaptive behaviors similarly give information about the functional structure of our adaptations and are therefore worth studying. Demographic research (discussed in Vining, 1986; and Turke, 1990) and everyday observation confirm that prosperous individuals in modern industrial nations are having far fewer children than they could and fewer than many poorer families in those same societies. Each of us is familiar with poor and middle-class families with large numbers of healthy children. North American Hutterites *average* more than 10 children per family and have sustained this performance stably for years without exciting much interest from others or prompting any notable tendency for others to imitate the few simple steps that have led to such high reproductive rates. Unusually low cleavage in a famous actress excites more attention than reports that some cultural group has found methods to successfully increase their reproductive rate, and this tells us a great deal about the nature of our adaptations. The fact that large numbers of individuals take drugs, buy pornography, and practice contraception as a means of forgoing reproduction rather than optimally allocating it, rules out large classes of hypotheses about the evolved decision rules in the human psyche. We regard as promising Turke's (1989, 1990) and Draper's (1989) hypothesis that prosperous but socially isolated women in industrial societies may feel poor compared to "poor" women living in extended families, and consequently unnecessarily restrict their reproduction. On this hypothesis, women's resource-assessment mechanisms use cues inappropriate to modern circumstances, but appropriate to the Pleistocene—they monitor how large local kin support networks are, rather than the availability of (more abstract) financial resources.

Hyperadaptiveness as Instantaneous Lamarckianism

The more purely the adaptiveness program is pursued, the more closely it approaches a mutant variant of Lamarckianism. Darwinism is about how the causal action of past conditions causes present designs. Lamarckianism's first principle is about how present conditions cause adaptive changes in structure to be acquired within the life span through the animal's effortful striving to solve the problems the present environment creates. If, as a thought experiment, one imagines as perfect and instantaneous the hypothetical Lamarckian power of the environment to sculpt an organism immediately into the optimal design required by each newly encountered circumstance, one would have a system that resembles what many advocates of an adaptiveness approach describe: "the basic message of evolution for behavioral studies is that behavior always depends on context; individuals tend to behave appropriately in the various and changing circumstances they encounter—with 'appropriately' defined as whatever it takes to survive and reproduce" (Smuts, 1989, p. 32). The structure of present behavior "reflect[s] moment by moment solutions to problems that are particularly pressing in biological terms" (Dunbar, 1988, p. 166). If organisms change instantaneously to incarnate the solutions required by each successive circumstance they enter, the second Lamarckian principle, the inheritance of these acquired characteristics, becomes superfluous, as does Mendelism, because there is no inheritance of traits in such a theory, acquired or not. Offspring are like parents if they face the same conditions, and differ if and when conditions change. What is inherited is solely the trait: "be an all-purpose inclusive fitness maximizer." The principle of fitness maximization, as a kind of allpervading magnetic force, in interaction with specific circumstances, rapidly or instantly impresses itself on the plastic form of organisms to create their present design. Cultures and societies should reflect present selection pressures, unmediated by past-reflecting mechanisms.

Characterized in this way, of course, no one would endorse such a view, but as an implicit set of principles it explains a large number of curious predictions, criticisms, and hypotheses in the literature. Borgia (1989), for example, commenting on Buss's cross-cultural study of human mate preference, criticized Buss's "typological" predictions derived from considerations of hunter-gatherer life—not on the grounds that the human EEA varied, and therefore mechanisms should assess such variation, but on the grounds that selection pressures vary in *modern* cultures. He states, "Buss has failed to do what is necessary in this type of comparison: offer convincing evidence that the observed similarity in cross-cultural patterns of mate preference is due to convergent evolution" (Borgia, 1989, p. 16). If we assume that Borgia is not positing that genetic differences between human cultures explain their differences, these remarks imply a failure to distinguish the logic of cross-specific comparisons (e.g., Clutton-Brock & Harvey, 1984; Tooby, 1982) from the logic of cross-cultural comparisons. Of course there *is* no distinction for those who explain current traits through present fitnessmaximization. Cross-specific comparisons show how patterns of convergent and divergent adaptations are created by parallel and divergent *selection pressures* acting on different species over evolutionary time. They test theories about the long-term effects of selection pressures on species design. Barring investigations of genetic differences between cultures—a relatively minor possibility (Tooby & Cosmides, 1990)—cross-cultural comparisons involve tracking how the same species-typical set of mechanisms performs differently given different environmental inputs over historical time. They test theories about the design of human species-typical adaptations that were created in the human EEA: for example, these adaptations should track ancestral environmental cues that signaled situational variation in the EEA. Finding uniformity of complex adaptive design between different cultures does not require convergent evolution because different cultures are not different species.

All-Purpose Fitness Maximization: The Ultimate ESS

The hyperadaptive Lamarckianism inherent in the claim that current behaviors are "to be explained in terms of their contribution to inclusive fitness at the present time" (Hughes, 1987, p. 417) is generally given a superficially Darwinian gloss, something like this: Because the one constant of evolutionary history has been that success consisted of inclusive fitness promotion, it follows that the best possible adaptation would be a general-purpose inclusive fitness-maximizing device; therefore organisms are equipped with such devices. Such an adaptation would monitor the present action of every selection pressure, calculate what it took to maximize fitness under this particular configuration of forces, and implement that strategy. Thus, "human beings, the product of millions of years of evolution within social groups, have the capacity to read the social environment in which they find themselves in a particular instance, to determine with reasonable certainty the behavioral strategy that will maximize inclusive fitness, and to adopt it. Our biological heritage endows us with the ability to make the best of diverse situations in terms of inclusive fitness" (Hughes, 1987, p. 421). In fact, adaptivist behavioral ecologists attribute this property to organisms generally, by describing organisms as inclusive fitness maximizers, or by saying that they can be expected to behave "as if" they were inclusive fitness maximizers. A phenotypic design that under all possible circumstances always fitness-maximized would be the ultimate ESS, displacing all other designs in the population (indeed, all other life in the universe), because every other "strategy" would on some occasions be inferior. If organisms were equipped with such a device, then of course adaptivist behavioral ecologists would be correct: present circumstances, analyzed according to presently acting selection pressures, would constitute an ontogenetic explanation for behavior. For an adaptationist, present behavior differs between individuals of the same species in the absence of genetic differences because underlying adaptations are monitoring some variable part of the environment as a cue to regulate behavior, as in the decision rule, "attack only if you are larger than your rival." But for an adaptivist, behavior varies in response to whatever selection favors under present circumstances (see Hughes's 1988 analysis of human kinship systems). If organisms are equipped with adaptations that inclusive fitness maximize under all circumstances, then the distinction between selection pressures and cues monitored by adaptations would evaporate, and the current properties of ancestral conditions would become irrelevant. Hyperadaptive Lamarckianism and the theory of modern behavioral ecology would merge in a neo-evolutionary synthesis. The discovery and characterization of how such a miraculous adaptation would operate would be of no small biological interest.

Elsewhere we have discussed at length why we think such a mechanism could not, in principle, exist (Cosmides & Tooby, 1987) . . . [for later treatments of this issue, see Tooby & Cosmides, 1992; Cosmides & Tooby, 1994b].

. . . [Consciousness: The Human Inclusive Fitness Maximizer?] . . .

The Central Role of Ancestral Cues

Cues provide irreplaceable information, and much of psychological architecture is organized around the ancestral cue structure of the world. For example, displays of naked nubile females are a cue in the hypothetical decision rule "move toward situations that produce retinal displays of naked nubile females and become sexually aroused." Pursuing goals such as proximity to nubile females only leads to fitness as long as the cues that define these goals continue to have positive fitness consequences. A change in the cue-decision rule-outcome relationship may break the linkage between the decision rules and adaptive outcomes, and may do so to any degree (Table 2.1).

One process among many that has disturbed these relationships is the accumulation across historical time of technological expertise. As modern culturally generated technical expertise

Table 2.1 The Changing Causal Structure of Environments over Time	
Time 1	*Example: Incest avoidance and the Kibbutz*
$cue_1 \to outcome_1$	(raised with $child_i$ → no sex with a sibling)
$cue_2 \to outcome_2$	(not raised with $child_i$ → sex with a non-sibling)
Time 2	
$cue_1 \to outcome_3$	(raised with $child_i$ → no sex with a non-sibling)
$cue_2 \to outcome_4$	(not raised with $child_i$ → sex with a sibling)

Over time, the relationship between cues, behavioral outcomes, and their fitness consequences changes, making an all-purpose inclusive fitness-maximizing device impossible in principle.

grows, the ability to contrive situations that have the cues that in the past signaled fitness—but that are now dissevered from their prior long-term fitness consequences—has grown in magnitude. People can now easily fabricate situations that concentrate cues that are completely stripped of their ancestrally coupled fitness payoffs: saccharine displays perceptual cues that once reliably signaled nutritional value, without the ancestrally associated nutritional value; magazine erotica displays perceptual cues of opportunities for fertile copulation, without the reality; narcotics can artificially produce highs that once were only stimulated during actual fitness-promoting activities; films, novels, and television provide cues of fitness-relevant information about people whom our mechanisms spuriously judge to be part of our social world, and so on. Because these cues define the goals that figure in human planning, the adaptiveness of planning mechanisms are at the mercy of the structure of the environment. Therefore they do not constitute a system for seeing past the cue-structure of the world into the present structure of selection pressures.

Although it is appealing to think that consciousness or rationality could be free of these constraints, a consideration of what all decision rules need to function indicates that this is not so. Planning requires goals, cues for recognizing goal states, cues for recognizing intermediate states, decision rules, inference procedures, and so on, all of which must ultimately derive from relationships found in the EEA. Although planning mechanisms may function as a high-level executive in the psychological architecture, the detailed conformations of the past are even more obviously reflected in the overarching procedures that make planning possible: emotional adaptations. These tie together the structure of past environments, the cues used to construct interpretations of present conditions, and the psychological mechanisms regulated by such interpretations, including planning mechanisms. As we will discuss, although the emotions do make planning possible, they do so through imposing on the present world an interpretative landscape derived from the covariant structure of the past, and so not even planning offers an escape from the past.

The Emotions as Adaptations to Recurring Situations

> If the mind is viewed as an integrated architecture of different special purpose mechanisms, "designed" to solve various adaptive problems, a functional description of emotion immediately suggests itself. Each mechanism can operate in a number of alternative ways, interacting with other mechanisms. Thus, the system architecture has been shaped by natural selection to structure interactions among different mechanisms so that they function particularly harmoniously when confronting commonly recurrent (across generations) adaptive situations. Fighting, falling in love, escaping predators, confronting sexual infidelity, and so on, each recurred innumerable times in evolutionary history, and each requires that a certain subset of the psyche's behavior-regulating algorithms function together in a particular way to guide behavior adaptively through that type of situation. This structured functioning together of mechanisms is a mode of operation for the psyche, and can be meaningfully interpreted as an emotional state. The characteristic feeling that accompanies each such mode is the signal which activates the specific constellation of mechanisms appropriate to solving that type of adaptive problem. (Tooby, 1985, p. 118)

Animals subsist on information. The single most limiting resource to reproduction is not food or safety or access to mates, but what makes them each possible: the information required for making adaptive behavioral choices. The selection pressure that brings into existence all psychological adaptations (and many nonpsychological ones as well) is the problem of turning encounters with the world into information and using this information to regulate biological processes. Perhaps the greatest adaptive problem facing animals is the decisional opacity of the environment. There are an infinite number of behaviors that an organism could, in principle, engage in; the subset of behaviors that is adaptive in any given situation is, therefore, astronomically small. For this reason, it is not transparent from inspecting the environment which decisions to make—the environment is decisionally "opaque." If there exists no reliable procedure for making a given kind of decision, then performance will be random, and random performance is usually reproductive death—the random firing of each muscle fiber in your body, for example, will lead in short order to death. The present environment poses, but does not solve, the decision-making problem for the organism: it does not compel one decision over another, absent decision rules in the animal.

Moreover, the world is always in flux. It is logically possible to experience it, Zen-like, as an endless series of unique and unprecedented events. Whether events are considered novel or repeated is not just a property of events, but of the system used to categorize them. Every event and circumstance in the world can be considered as unique or as a repetition of an earlier event, depending on the system of categorization used. A system of categorization that experiences each event in the world as unique is useless for making decisions. Natural selection, therefore, will act on the organism's systems of categorization, so that each encounter with the world is perceived and processed in terms of instances of recurring categories. What makes a particular partitioning of events into classes useful to the organism is whether a decision rule based on that categorization leads to adaptive outcomes. For example, deciding between fleeing or not fleeing requires categorizing situations by the cue "predator present"/"predator absent."

Cognitive adaptations must use perceived and categorized events as cues for nonperceivable but recurrent sets of conditions. Alternative fitnesspromoting courses of action define which cues a decision rule will be selected to use: cues are useful to the extent that they can be reliably detected and reliably predict the hidden structure of conditions that determines the success of alternative courses of action. For example, the cue "night" predicts the nonperceivable but recurrent condition "situation in which my ability to detect predatory or enemy ambush far enough in advance to take protective measures is very low," and should therefore regulate decisions about whether to travel, whether to travel alone, how much attention to give to ambiguous stimuli, and so on. The selection pressure that creates adaptations that categorize night as different from day is the need to make these kinds of behavioral decisions. Without cues, animals could not regulate their behavior in adaptive ways. Animals depend on the cue structure of the world.

Cues need not be of uniform sensory characteristics, but can be defined in relation to any recurrently identifiable properties of the world or the animal. For example, rats will eat a novel food if they smell it on the mouth of another rat, but not if they smell it on some other part of another rat's body (Galef, 1990). For the purposes of this decision rule, the category "acceptable to eat" is not defined by any uniform sensory properties in the food itself, but rather by whether its sensory properties match the templates created when the rat encountered and smelled other rats. Similarly, the bundle of stimuli that uniquely identify a greylag goose become recognizable to the decision rules in the hatched offspring through a relational cue that is something like "form a template of the first large mobile entity encountered after hatching that remains close by for greater than a threshold period" (Lorenz, 1970). Many cues that humans use are of this relational kind. Invariances in emotional expression, for example, provide relational cues that allow the assignment of biological meaning to events and stimuli (e.g., the meaning "predator" may be assigned to any large animal that conspecifics express fear toward) (Darwin, 1872; Cosmides, 1983). There is enormous variety in the way objects, situations, and other entities can appear to the senses under different circumstances, but to be reacted to by decision-making algorithms, they must be assigned a meaning in terms that these algorithms use. Representational processes that attach or link the contingent appearance of entities and situations to an evolved algorithm are essential to the operation of any decision rule. If the rule is "flee predators when observed," then there must be an associated algorithm that determines what counts as having observed a predator. Although the cues used may be constant sensory invariances ("is large and has fangs and claws"), relational cues can often improve accuracy ("anything that causes conspecifics to shriek and flee"). Some biological categories have no uniform appearance from generation to generation—for example, one cannot distinguish one's mother from other human females by appearance alone. In such cases, relational cues are essential (e.g., "mother" = "the human female who nursed and took care of me during infancy"). Superficial variability in cultural phenomena masks an underlying uniformity in cues and algorithms.

The requirement that stimuli be sorted into recurrent categories is why "novelty" cannot, in principle, be a discrete selection pressure like temperature. If something is genuinely unprecedented, mechanisms will not assign it to the categories that trigger the correct decision rules, except by chance. Mechanisms that appear able to handle novelty do so only because the apparent novelty resides in one aspect of the phenomenon, while algorithms are operating on other aspects that display subtle or relational cues based on some underlying recurrent uniformity. The ability to handle a certain kind of variation depends on selectively significant encounters with cues probabilistically linked to that type of variation in the evolutionary past.

Situation Cues Elicit Emotions

The human environment of evolutionary adaptedness had a statistically defined structure, which included the association of cues with recurrent conditions. Repeated relationships among conditions constitute evolutionarily recurrent situations. For example, the condition of having a mate plus the condition of one's mate copulating with someone else adds up to a situation of sexual infidelity. To the extent that situations are structured and recurrent over evolutionary time, their statistical properties can be used as the basis for a special kind of psychological adaptation: an emotion. An emotion corresponds to a distinctive system of coordination among the mechanisms that regulate each controllable biological process. That is, "[e]ach emotional state manifests design features 'designed' to solve particular families of adaptive problems, whereby the psychological mechanisms assume a unique configuration. Using this approach, each emotional state can be mapped in terms of its characteristic configuration, and of the particular mode each identifiable mechanism adopts" (Tooby, 1985, p. 120). Thus, each emotion state—fear of predators, guilt, sexual jealousy, rage, grief, and so on—will correspond to an integrated mode of operation that functions as a solution designed to take advantage of the particular structure of the recurrent situation these emotions correspond to. Discovering one's mate in a sexual liaison signals a situation that threatens future reproduction and present investment allocation; this cue should therefore activate sexual jealousy (Daly et al., 1982). The emotion of sexual jealousy constitutes an organized mode of operation specifically designed to deploy the programs governing each psychological mechanism so that each is poised to deal with the exposed infidelity: physiological processes are prepared for violence; the goal of deterring, injuring, or murdering the rival emerges; the goal of punishing or deserting the mate appears; the desire to make oneself more competitively attractive emerges; memory is activated to reanalyze the past; and so on.

How to Characterize an Emotion

To characterize an emotion adaptation, one must identify the following properties of environments and of mechanisms.

1. *A situation*: a recurrent structure of environmental and organismic properties, characterized as a complex statistical composite of how such properties covaried in the environment of evolutionary adaptedness. Examples of situations are being in a depleted nutritional state, competing for maternal attention, being chased by a predator, being about to ambush an enemy, having few friends.
2. *The adaptive problem*: the identification of which organismic states and behavioral sequences will lead to the best average functional outcome, given the situation. For example, what to do given you are being chased by a predator; what to do given you are in a depleted nutritional state.
3. *Cues that signal the presence of the situation*: for example, low blood sugar signals a depleted nutritional state; the looming approach of a large fanged animal signals the presence of a predator; seeing your mate having sex with another signals sexual infidelity; finding yourself alone or avoided by others signals that you have few friends.[10]
4. *Algorithms that monitor for situation-defining cues*: including perceptual mechanisms, proprioceptive mechanisms, and situation-modeling memory.
5. *Algorithms that detect situations*: these mechanisms take the output of the monitoring algorithms in (4) as input, and through integration, probabilistic weighting, and other decision criteria, identify situations as either present or absent (or present with some probability).
6. *Algorithms that assign priorities*: a given world-state may correspond to more than one situation at a time. For example, you may be nutritionally depleted *and* in the presence of a predator. The prioritizing algorithms define which emotion modes are compatible (e.g., hunger and boredom), which are mutually exclusive (e.g., feeding and predator escape). Depending on the relative importance of the situations and the reliability of the cues, the prioritizing algorithms decide which emotion modes to activate and deactivate, and to what degree.
7. *An internal communication system*: given that a situation has been detected, the internal communication system sends a situation-specific signal to all relevant mechanisms; the signal switches them into the appropriate adaptive emotion mode.
8. *A set of algorithms specific to each mechanism that regulates how it responds to each specialized emotion state*: these algorithms determine whether the mechanism should switch on or switch off, and if on, what emotion-specialized performance they will implement.

Any controllable biological process that, by shifting its performance in a specifiable way, would lead to enhanced average fitness outcomes should come to be partially governed by emotional state [see (8) above]. Such processes include the following:

Goals. The cognitive mechanisms that define goal-states and choose among goals in a planning process should be influenced by emotions. For example, vindictiveness—a specialized subcategory of anger—may define "injuring the offending party" as a goal state to be achieved. (Although the functional logic of this process is deterrence, this function need not be represented, either consciously or unconsciously, by the mechanisms that generate the vindictive behavior.)

Motivational priorities. Mechanisms involved in hierarchically ranking goals, or, for non-planning systems, other kinds of motivational and reward systems, should be emotion-dependent. What may be extremely unpleasant in one state, such as harming another, may seem satisfying in another state (e.g., aggressive competition may facilitate counter-empathy).

Information-gathering motivations. Because establishing which situation you are in has enormous consequences for the appropriateness of behavior, the process of detection should involve specialized inference procedures and specialized motivations to discover whether certain suspected facts are true or false. What one is curious about, what one finds interesting, what one is obsessed with discovering should all be emotionspecific.

Imposed conceptual frameworks. Emotions should prompt construals of the world in terms of concepts that are appropriate to the decisions that must be made. If in an angry mood, domain-specific concepts such as social agency, fault, responsibility, and punishment will be assigned to elements in the situation. If hungry, the food-nonfood distinction will seem salient. If endangered, safety-categorization frames will appear. The world will be carved up into categories based partly on what emotional state an individual is in.

Perceptual mechanisms. Perceptual systems may enter emotion-specific modes of operation. When fearful, acuity of hearing may increase. Specialized perceptual inference systems may be mobilized as well; if you've heard rustling in the bushes at night, human and predator figure-detection may be particularly boosted, and not simply visual acuity in general. In fact, non-threat interpretations may be depressed, and the same set of shadows will "look threatening"—that is, given a specific threatening interpretation such as "a man with a knife"—or not, depending on emotion-state.

Memory. The ability to call up particularly appropriate kinds of information out of long-term memory will be influenced. A woman who has just found strong evidence that her husband has been unfaithful may find a torrent of memories about small details that seemed meaningless at the time but that now fit into an interpretation of covert activity. We also expect that what is stored about present experience will be differentially regulated as well, with important or shocking events, for example, stored in great detail.

Attention. The entire structure of attention, from perceptual systems to the contents of high-level reasoning processes, should be regulated by emotional state. If you are worried that your spouse is late and might have been injured, it is hard to concentrate on other ongoing tasks.

Physiology. Each organ system, tissue, or process is a potential candidate for emotion-specific regulation, and "arousal" is doubtless insufficiently specific to capture the detailed coordination involved. Changes in circulatory, respiratory, and gastrointestinal functioning are well-known and documented, as are changes in levels of circulating sex hormones. We expect thresholds regulating the contraction of various muscle groups to change with certain emotional states, reflecting the probability that they will need to be employed. Similarly, immune allocation and targeting may vary with disgust, or with the potential for injury, or with the demands of extreme physical exertion.

Communication processes. What individuals communicate, whether "voluntarily" or "involuntarily," will be influenced by emotion state. The role of emotional expression as a form of functional communication of situation (including intentions) goes back to Darwin, and is widely appreciated (Darwin, 1872; Ekman, 1982). The value of providing information to others, or of obscuring it, will depend on the situation one is in, which is also defined by whom one is with. Expressiveness and the content of expression will be different depending on whether one is alone, with people one trusts, or with social antagonists (where leakage of damaging information will be suppressed). An emotion state of pride should be activated when an individual is in situations in which it will benefit her that certain kinds of information become easily available to others. Body posture, willingness to participate in social activities, and other factors will ease the release of this information through its association with her appearance. The converse is true when someone is ashamed; concealment of information should occur through reticence to speak or be noticed and through avoidance of social situations that would lead others to associate the shameful act with that individual.

Behavior. All psychological mechanisms are involved in the generation and regulation of behavior, so obviously behavior will be regulated by emotion state. More specifically, however, mechanisms proximately involved in the generation of actions (as opposed to processes like face recognition that are only distally regulatory) should be very sensitive to emotion state. Not only may highly stereotyped behaviors of certain kinds be released (as during sexual arousal or rage, or as with species-typical facial expressions and body language), but more complex action-generation mechanisms should be regulated as well. Specific acts and courses of action will be more available as responses in some states than in others, and more likely to be implemented. Emotion mode should govern the construction of organized behavioral sequences that solve adaptive problems.

Specialized inference. Emotion mode should be one factor that governs the activation of specialized inferential systems, such as cheater detection (Cosmides, 1985, 1989; Cosmides & Tooby, 1989), bluff detection, and so on.

Reflexes. Muscular coordination, tendency to blink, threshold for vomiting, shaking, and many other reflexes should be regulated by emotion mode.

Learning. Emotion mode will also regulate learning mechanisms. What someone learns from stimuli will be greatly altered by emotion mode, because of attentional allocation, motivation, situation-specific inferential algorithms, and a host of other factors. Emotion mode will cause the present context to be divided up into situation-specific, functionally appropriate categories, such that the same stimuli and the same environment may be interpreted in radically different ways, depending on emotional state. For example, which stimuli are considered similar should be different in different emotional states, distorting the shape of the individual's psychological "similarity space" (Shepard, 1987).

Affective coloration of events and stimuli. A behavioral sequence is composed of many acts. Each of these acts can be thought of as an intermediate "factor" in the production of a behavioral sequence. Determining which courses of action are worthwhile and which are not is a major informational problem. The payoff of each "factor of production"—of each act in the sequence—must be computed before one can determine whether the whole sequence is worthwhile. Every time there is a change in the world that affects the probable payoff of an act or new information that allows a better evaluation of payoffs, this value needs to be recomputed. Evaluating entire chains as units is not sufficient, because each item in a chain (staying behind from the hunt, making a tool, borrowing materials from a friend, etc.) may be used in another unique sequence at a later time. Therefore, effort, fitness token payoffs (rewards), risks, and many other components of evaluation need to be assigned continually to classes of acts. For this reason, there should be mechanisms that assign hedonic values to acts, tallied as intermediate weights in decision processes. Our stream of actions and daily experiences will be affectively "colored" by the assignment of these hedonic values. If our psychological mechanisms were not using present outcomes to assign hedonic weights to classes of acts, there would be no function to suffering, joy, and so on. Emotion mode obviously impacts the assignment of hedonic values to acts.

Energy level and effort allocation. Overall metabolic budget will, of course, be regulated by emotion, as will specific allocations to various processes and facilitation or inhibition of specific activities. The effort that it takes to perform given tasks will shift accordingly, with things being easier or more effortful depending on how appropriate they are to the situation reflected by the emotion. Thus, fear will make it more difficult to attack an antagonist, while anger will make it easier. The confidence with which a situation has been identified should itself regulate the effortfulness of situation-appropriate activities. Confusion should inhibit the expenditure of energy on costly behavioral responses and should motivate more information gathering and information analysis. Nesse (1991) has suggested that the function of mood is to reflect the propitiousness of the present environment for action, a hypothesis with many merits. We would take his general approach in a somewhat different direction, since the action-reward ratio of the environment is not a function of the environment alone, but an interaction between the structure of the environment and the individual's present understanding of it. (By understanding, we mean the correspondence between the structure of the environment, the structure of the algorithms, and the weightings and other information they use as input parameters.) The phenomenon that should regulate this aspect of mood is a perceived discrepancy between expected and actual payoff. The suspension of activity accompanied by very intense cognitive activity in depressed people looks like an effort to reconstruct models of the world so that future action can lead to payoffs. Depression should be precipitated by a heavy investment in a behavioral enterprise that was expected to lead to a large payoff, but that either failed to materialize, or was not large enough to justify the investment.

Recalibration and imagined experience. Information about outcomes is not equally spread throughout all points in time and all situations. Some situations are information-dense, full of ancestrally stable cues that reliably predicted the fitness consequences of certain decisions and could therefore be used to alter weightings in decision rules. For example, Hamilton's (1964) rule gives the logic for allocating benefits between self and kin, but not the procedures by which a mechanism could estimate the value of, say, a particular piece of food to oneself and one's kin. The payoffs of such acts of assistance vary with circumstances; consequently, each decision about where to allocate assistance depends on inferences about the relative weights of these variables. These inferences are subject to error. Imagine an individual is allocating meat according to Hamilton's rule, using the best information available to her to weigh the relative values of the meat to herself and her sister. The sudden discovery that her sister has become very sick and emaciated may function as an information-dense situation, allowing the recalibration of the algorithms that weighted the relative values of the meat. The sister's sickness functions as a cue that the previous allocation weighting was in error and that the variables need to be reweighted—including all of the weightings embedded in habitual action sequences. Guilt, for example, may function as an emotion mode specialized for recalibration, as may a number of other emotions. Previous courses of action are brought to mind (I could have helped then, why didn't I think to?) to reset choice points in decision rules. The negative valence of depression may be explained similarly; former actions that seemed pleasurable in the past, but which ultimately turned out to lead to bad outcomes, are re-experienced in imagination with a new affective coloration, so that in the future entirely different weightings are called up during choices.

The role of imagery and emotion in planning. Imagery is the representation of perceptual information in a format that resembles actual perceptual input. Being in an environment displaying specific perceptually detectable cues (sweetness, predators, running sores, emotion expressions) triggers certain decision and evaluation rules. Recreating those cues through imagery may trigger the same algorithms (minus their behavioral manifestations), allowing the planning function to evaluate imagined situations by using the same circuits that evaluate real situations. This would allow alternative courses of action to be evaluated in a way similar to the way in which experienced situations are evaluated. In other words, image-based representations may serve to unlock, for the purposes of planning, the same evolved mechanisms that are triggered by an actual encounter with a situation displaying the imagined perceptual and situational cues. For example, imagining the death of your child can call up the emotional state you would experience had this actually happened, activating previously dormant algorithms and making new information available to many different mechanisms. As many have recognized, this simulation process can help in making decisions about future plans. Even though you have never actually experienced the death of a child, for example, an imagined death may activate an image-based representation of extremely negative proprioceptive cues that "tell" the planning function that this is a situation to be avoided. Paradoxically, grief provoked by death may be a byproduct of mechanisms designed to take imagined situations as input: it may be intense so that, if triggered by imagination in advance, it is properly deterrent. Alternatively (or additionally), grief may be intense in order to recalibrate weightings in the decision rules that governed choices prior to the death. If your child died because you make an incorrect choice, then experiencing grief may recalibrate you for subsequent choices. Death may involve guilt, grief, and depression to recalibrate weights on courses of action. One may be haunted by guilt, meaning that courses of action retrospectively judged to be erroneous may be replayed in imagination over and over again, until the reweighting is accomplished. Similarly, joyful experiences may be savored, that is, replayed with attention to all of the details of the experience, so that every step of the course of action can be colored with positive weightings as it is rehearsed, again, until the simulated experience of these pseudo "learning trials" has sufficiently reweighted the decision rules.

People can be expected to respond to ancestral cues whether or not they are still predictively valid, and the imagery and emotion systems induce them to plan the pursuit of proprioceptive goal cues such as pain relief, endorphin-highs, sexual arousal, and sweetness, whether or not these are still valid predictors of inclusive fitness. People plan to steal to get money to take artificial opiates, plan to buy erotica rather than search for a mate, plan to eat injurious but delicious sweets. Indigent people sometimes sell their blood to buy movie tickets. Humans are not fitness maximizers; to the extent they can be characterized as goal-seeking maximizers of any kind, they are ancestral-environment fitness-cue maximizers, a profoundly different thing.

Ever since Darwin (1871, 1872), emotions have been seen as the product of the evolutionary process, and usually, although not always, as functional adaptations (Arnold, 1960, 1968; Chance, 1980; Daly et al., 1982; Darwin, 1872; Eibl-Ebesfeldt, 1971; Ekman, 1982; Frijda, 1986; Hamburg, 1968; Izard, 1977; Otte, 1974; Plutchik, 1980; Tomkins, 1962, 1963; and many others). In fact, much of the best early work in evolutionary psychology stemmed from an evolutionary-functional approach to emotions (e.g., Bowlby, 1969/1982; Daly et al., 1982; Ekman, 1982). The particular interpretive framework advanced here (Tooby, 1985; see also Tooby & Cosmides, 1990) is consistent with much of the vast literature on emotion, and is simply an attempt to integrate into a modern adaptationist framework the idea that the mind consists primarily of a collection of evolved functionspecific information-processing mechanisms (Cosmides & Tooby, 1987; Cosmides, 1985, 1989; Tooby & Cosmides, 1989a; Tooby, 1985) with such views as that emotions are coordinated systems (Arnold, 1960, 1968; Izard, 1977; Frijda, 1986; Lazarus et al., 1980; Plutchik, 1980) that organize action (Frijda, 1986; Lazarus, 1968; Leeper, 1948) appropriate to situations (Arnold, 1960; Frijda, 1986; Lazarus et al., 1980; Tolman, 1923; see especially Neese's excellent discussion, 1991).

Emotions and the Meaning of Situations

The fitness consequences of an act are not a feature of the world that the individual can use to regulate its behavior. Fitness is the expected long-term consequences on genetic propagation of a particular phenotypic design relative to alternative designs. As such, it is inherently unobservable at the time the design alternative actually impacts the world, and therefore cannot function as a cue for a decision rule. The "decision" to allocate 12% rather than 14% of metabolic activity to immune function at six months of age may change every subsequent action in some way, and its impact on reproduction at age 42, for example, is not observable to the infant. Because fitness is relative, the infant would have to have an inventory of all alternative designs to be hypothetically chosen among, cross-tabulated against their expected completed reproduction and inclusive fitness effects. Each course of action (or any hypothetical aspect of phenotypic design) is, from the point of view of an individual, an uncontrolled experiment, providing few grounds for conclusions about alternatives at the time they are undertaken. (Actions repeated sufficiently often over an individual's life can be evaluated by their immediate and observable consequences, according to some decision rule—that is, learning is possible—but the decision rule that evaluates trials and guides learning is itself an ontogenetically uncontrolled and unevaluated experiment.) Instead of the individual computing the course of action with the highest fitness—an impossibility—the world "evaluates" alternative designs cross-generationally and selects the one that propagates, on average and over the long term, most effectively.

The organism cannot directly perceive its present situation according to the actual fitness-contingencies related to alternative courses of action. It cannot follow the cinematic decision rule "do the right thing." Instead, the organism "perceives" its present situation in terms of the recurrent structure of ancestral environments and assigns interpretations to the present environment based on the phylogenetically encountered categories of the past. The ancestrally recurrent structured situation that the organism categorizes itself as being in is the "meaning" of the situation for that organism. It "sees,"—that is, it is organized to respond to—previous fitness contingencies, not present ones. Built into the physiological architecture is the "assumption" that the present parallels the statistical structure of past conditions and fitness contingencies. Thus, part of what emotions make "visible" are the fitness contingencies of actions, but only to the extent that the present recreates the past.

The World as a Computer

According to this analysis of the emotions, the many mechanisms comprising our psychological architecture are deployed according to the "best bet" for how each mechanism should operate in subsequent choices and actions, given the cued situation. This best bet is based on the long-run average of how one specific setting versus alternative settings succeeded over hundreds of thousands of cue-defined ancestral encounters. If potentially lethal violence followed in 24% of the situations in which men discovered infidelity in their mates, then women's mechanisms should be programmed based on that statistical average. No organism's nervous system could possibly model all of the necessary features of the environment or do all the calculations required to figure out what the best arrangement for each mechanism would be, given present stimuli. The "computation" conducted by the evolutionary process requires nothing less than the world itself as an enduring crossgenerational laboratory that measures the frequency of environmental conditions, the reliability of cues, the heritable variations in mechanism-states, the actions taken, and their consequences. The results of this "experiment" or "computation" are stored in the form of evolved phenotypic design. This evolutionary process brings the ancestrally recurrent cue-discriminated and cue-defined situation into a specialized correspondence with the mode of operation of the psychological architecture, so that the algorithms regulating each mechanism are prepared to operate adaptively in those (interpreted as opposed to actual) circumstances. Detailed studies of the cognitive procedures constituting the emotions, representing as they do complex decision rules and statistical weightings, may prove over the next several decades to be our most reliable window into the evolutionary past. Whether (and to what extent) war, paternal care, monogamy, infidelity, food-sharing, and scavenging were major features of our hunter-gatherer past should all be testable by investigating our emotional adaptations. Because emotions reflect the structure of the human past, they constitute a treasure-house of information about the nature of ancestral conditions and about the power of various evolutionary processes.

The cues that the present situation displays function as predictors of a larger encompassing structure of conditions and contingencies that the individual cannot directly observe. Emotions and other component mechanisms lead organisms to act as if certain things were true about their present circumstances, whether or not they are, because they were true of past circumstances. They allow the animal to "go beyond the information given" (Bruner, 1973). In this lies their strength as well as their weakness. They allow organisms to infer on probabilistic grounds the presence of invisible structural features of the world and to navigate among these features. Because many crucial decisions must be made in the absence of sufficient observationally available information, these mechanisms allow adaptive behavior that could not be "rationally" justified based on the information available to one individual accumulated in one lifetime. For the same reason, however, such mechanisms cannot detect when the invariances that held true ancestrally no longer obtain. That is their weakness.

Conclusions

> Acceptance of these conclusions means that some widely used concepts are invalid and must be abandoned. The question inevitably arises as to how such an abundance of misinterpretation has arisen. I believe the major factor is that biologists have no logically sound and generally accepted set of principles and procedures for answering the question: "What is its function?"
>
> —*George Williams (1966, p. 252)*

The last three decades in evolutionary biology have seen enormous advances in the sophistication and power of evolutionary thinking, but the goal of developing "a logically sound and generally accepted set of principles and procedures for answering the question: 'What is its function?'" remains unfinished. Although orthogenesis and inappropriate group selection models have departed, hyperadaptive near-Lamarckianism, the unwarranted neglect of the role of the past, the evasion of the characterization of adaptations, and many other confusions and poor practices have replaced them in various biological literatures.

In this article, we have emphasized how adaptations reflect the configuration of the past. To invert Hughes's (1987) almost Lamarckian dicta on evolutionary explanation (with which we began this article), we have argued that it is illogical for evolutionary biologists to appeal to present advantages as an explanation for present adaptations. Although widespread current behaviors have consequences in terms of inclusive fitness at the present time, these present consequences are entirely irrelevant to explaining the adaptations that produce those behaviors. If these adaptations are to be explained on biological grounds at all, they must be explained in terms of their contribution to inclusive fitness during their past encounters with ancestral conditions, without regard to whether they happen to be fitness-promoting at the present time. Nevertheless, observations about specific patterns of present adaptiveness can provide clues about the structure of specific adaptations. If a set of present behaviors is too fitness-promoting to be coincidence, this suggests the operation of some underlying adaptation, which should be characterized.

For an adaptationist, no large issue hangs on whether modern human behavior is globally described as "adaptive" or not, or on the degree to which the modern world resembles the human EEA. The relevance of Darwinism to human behavior is logically inescapable and would not be in the least diminished if no modern behavior were adaptive. Our inherited design is the same regardless of our circumstances, and it can only be understood with reference to our evolutionary history, whether we are Ache foragers or astronauts orbiting Pluto.

Although humans, as intelligent, cultural, conscious, planning animals, might appear to be fitness-strivers, prospective fitness is not a goal that can be directly observed in a way that can be used to regulate behavior. A general-purpose inclusive fitness maximizer is impossible, and possessing consciousness (or a planning capacity) does not make people fitness-strivers or inclusive fitness maximizers. Describing humans as fitness-strivers is perhaps more appropriate than describing them as, say, ascribed role implementers, vehicles for arbitrary semiotic systems, profit-maximizers, group solidarity-promoters, or other proposed descriptions not inspired by Darwinism. Still, it is an erroneous characterization: humans are adaptation-executers, not fitness-strivers. For this reason, human behavior is not well explained by attempts to show how it corresponds to contextually appropriate fitness pursuit. Instead, it should be explained as the output of adaptations (using present circumstances as input), which are themselves the constructed product of selection under ancestral conditions. Far from being governed by "rational fitness maximization" (Hughes, 1987), the operation of human psychological mechanisms is orchestrated by emotions that frame present circumstances in terms of the evolutionary past. For a Darwinian, there is no escaping the past.

Notes

1. Publications with dates after 1990 were listed as "in press" in our 1990 article.
2. 2023 note: The search for adaptations has grown since this article was written. While the search for adaptiveness still exists, it is much less common now than in 1990.
3. 2023 note: Later developments showed why teleological concepts are so "natural": they are generated by an evolved system specialized for representing mental states, such as goals, desires, beliefs, and intentions—the theory of mind system (e.g., S. Baron-Cohen, *Mindblindness*, MIT Press; 1995).
4. Complications are introduced by the transition from asexual to sexual reproduction because the identity or replicative concordance between genome and gene (or organism's design and transmitted design) was broken, creating the potential for intragenomic conflict (Cosmides & Tooby, 1981; Tooby, 1982). Sexual reproduction breaks the genome into subsets of genes whose reproduction can be, and often is, accomplished under different circumstances, or with different probabilities. Each set (coreplicon) is selected to modify the phenotype of the organism in a way that maximally propagates the genes comprising that set, and hence in ways inconsistent with the other sets that comprise the total genome. Because fitness cannot be maximized for all genes in an individual in the same way, fitness cannot be a property of individuals, but instead can only be assigned to coreplicons, genes, or to inherited designs with a certain specified or assumed kind of genetic basis (cytoplasmic, autosomal, X-chromosomal, generalized Mendelian, etc.). Fitnesses should not be assigned to individuals in any case, because fitnesses are the expected outcomes of certain designs, and not the actual specific reproduction of an individual phenotype. Nevertheless, although the evolution of sex modifies certain elements in Darwinism, the central logic of Darwinism remains essentially intact.
5. The genetic basis for frequency-dependent alternative strategies will tend to be universal also, except for genetic switches (if any) that regulate which strategy an individual will instantiate. Thus, the sexually differentiated

adaptations of males and females—two frequency-dependent alternative strategies—will be coded for by genes that are simultaneously present in both sexes, with the exception of the H-Y antigen, which is a genetic switch. Moreover, selection will tend to restrict the total number of alternative complex strategies through a kind of quasi-senescence process. If there are 50 equally likely alternative evolutionarily stable strategies (ESSs), selection will only have a chance to improve any one of them in one out of 50 generations, while it will be acting on the ESSgeneral aspects of the phenotype every generation. Senescence-like trade-offs between general and expression-limited traits should limit how numerous and how complexly differentiated alternative ESSs can become.

6. Exceptions to the rule of combinatorially enforced design uniformity include single gene adaptations, overdominants, single locus frequency-dependent systems, favorable mutations prior to reaching fixation, genetic switches, and quantitative genetic variation. The argument about the prevalence of species-typicality depends on sufficient gene flow between populations over evolutionary time, a condition that appears to be met by humans. But if populations become isolated enough for long enough periods of time and develop different complex adaptations specified by different sets of alleles, then population-typicality will substitute for species-typicality for many adaptations, creating a situation of incipient speciation. Given length limitations, the slight qualifications in certain arguments about adaptation that may need to be made in the light of certain categories of genetic diversity (e.g., quantitative genetic diversity, single gene adaptations to local conditions) would be too cumbersome to introduce at every appropriate juncture, and so have been left out. They introduce no essential difference into the argument.

7. A drill press is highly nonrandomly organized to perform a function, it is efficient, precise, and specialized, and it may even increase the reproduction of those that use them. Nevertheless, a drill press is not an adaptation because it was not present in the EEA. A second, equally sufficient reason to rule it out as an adaptation is that it is not a recurrent product from individual to individual of the same genotype, in an EEA-resembling environment. Its failure to qualify as an adaptation (or, really, as a part of the description of an adaptation) has nothing to do with the fact that it is an artifact. As part of an extended phenotype, a widely recurring artifact that reappeared across generations and whose developmental rules of expression had been the target of selection would qualify as part of the characterization of an adaptation (for *Homo erectus*, bifacies—so called handaxes—might qualify as such an adaptation).

8. Turke questions our example of the modern initiation of war as obviously maladaptive behavior, given that competition for resources always has winners and losers. We consider such decisions usually maladaptive for another reason: unlike in conditions of primitive warfare, virtually no decision-making elite has been reproductive-resource limited in modern nation-states. Modern economies offer expansive opportunities for the rational discovery of benefitbenefit relations which provide far more resources than conquest can. We argue that zero-sum games were far more prevalent in the relatively unproductive foraging economies that persisted throughout much of human evolution. This leads to a tendency for decision-making elites to frame situations as resource-limited and zero-sum when they are not, leading to dramatic examples of major and unnecessary wastes of resources, labor, and reproduction in costly and often unsuccessful modern warfare.

9. The concept of "adaptation" has a clear-cut definition and a set of standards of evidence for recognizing it. But when closely scrutinized, "adaptiveness" is a far vaguer concept, because adaptiveness is relative to alternative expressions of real or supposed alternative adaptations. "Adaptive" means "relatively more fitness-promoting"; to be meaningful, it requires some preexisting specification of the alternative designs and design-expressions being compared, something rarely provided. The question of whether behavior is adaptive or not, without referring to the relative output of alternative designs, is meaningless. Turke attempts to remedy this by defining adaptiveness as relative to "feasible alternatives," but in so doing invokes a nonexistent theoretical superstructure which would outline in advance all of the forces that would impact on the long-run fitness of a specified strategy as compared to the total set of alternative "feasible" strategies (financial costs of nurses; hypothetical status costs to keeping female children alive in India, etc.). One can only agree with Turke that "it is difficult to know if an imagined behavioral strategy is really more adaptive than actual strategies because it is difficult to also imagine all of the constraints that would apply" (Turke, 1990).

10. The assignment of a situation interpretation to present circumstances is a problem in signal detection theory (Swets et al., 1964; see also Gigerenzer & Murray, 1987)—the animal needs to "detect" what situation it is in on the basis of cues together with specialized interpretation algorithms. Selection will not shape decision rules so that they act solely on the basis of what is most likely to be true, but rather on the basis of the weighted consequences of acts given that something is held to be true. Should you walk under a tree that might conceal a predator? Even if the algorithms assign a 51% (or even 95%) probability to the tree being predator-free, under most circumstances the decision rule should cause you to avoid the tree—to act as if the predator were in it. The benefits of calories saved via a shortcut, scaled by the probability that there is no predator in the tree, must be weighed against the benefits of avoiding becoming cat food, scaled by the probability that there is a predator in the tree. Because the costs and benefits of false alarms, misses, hits, and correct rejections are often unequal, the decision rules may still treat as true situations that are unlikely to be true.

References

Alexander, R. D. (1979a). *Darwinism and human affairs*. University of Washington Press.
Alexander, R. D. (1979b). Evolution and culture. In N. Chagnon & W. Irons (Eds.), *Evolutionary biology and human social behavior* (pp. 59–78). Duxbury Press.
Alexander, R. D. (1981). Evolution, culture, and human behavior: Some general considerations. In R. D. Alexander & D. W. Tinkle (Eds.), *Natural selection and social behavior* (pp. 509–520). Chiron Press.
Alexander, R. D. (1989). Evolution of the human psyche. In P. Mellars & C. Stringer (Eds.), *The human revolution* (pp. 455–513). University of Edinburgh Press.
Arnold, M. B. (1960). *Emotion and personality*. Columbia University Press.
Arnold, M. B. (1968). *The nature of emotion*. Penguin Books.
Barkow, J. H. (1984). The distance between genes and culture. *Journal of Anthropological Research, 37*, 367–379.
Barkow, J. H. (1989). *Darwin, sex, and status: Biological approaches to mind and culture*. University of Toronto Press.
Barkow, J., Cosmides, L., & Tooby, J. (Eds.). (1992). *The adapted mind: Evolutionary psychology and the generation of culture*. Oxford University Press.
Betzig, L. (1989). Rethinking human ethology: A response to some recent critiques. *Ethology and Sociobiology, 19*, 315–324.
Betzig, L., Borgerhoff Mulder, M., & Turke, P. (1988). *Human reproductive behavior*. Cambridge University Press.
Borgia, G. (1989). Typology and human mating preferences. *Behavioral and Brain Sciences, 12*, 16–17.
Bowlby, J. (1969/1982). *Attachment and loss: Vol. 1. Attachment*. Toronto: Penguin Books.
Bruner, J. (1973). *Beyond the information given* (J. M. Anglin, Ed.). W. W. Norton.
Buss, D. M. (1989). Sex differences in human mate preferences: Evolutionary hypotheses tested in 37 cultures. *Behavioral and Brain Sciences, 12*(1), 1–49.
Caro, T. M., & Borgerhoff Mulder, M. (1987). The problem of adaptation in the study of human behavior. *Ethology and Sociobiology, 8*(1), 61–72.
Chance, M. R. A. (1980). An ethological assessment of emotion. In R. Plutchik & H. Kellerman (Eds.), *Emotion: Theory, research, and experience* (pp. 81–111). Academic Press.
Charnov, E. L. (1976). Optimal foraging, the marginal value theorem. *Theoretical Population Biology, 9*(2), 129–136.
Clutton-Brock, T. H., & Harvey, P. H. (1984). Comparative approaches to investigating adaptation. In J. Krebs & N. Davies (Eds.), *Behavioral ecology: An evolutionary approach* (2nd ed., pp. 7–29). Sinauer.
Cosmides, L. (1983). Invariances in the acoustic expression of emotion during speech. *Journal of Experimental Psychology: Human Perception and Performance, 9*, 864–881.
Cosmides, L. (1985). *Deduction or Darwinian Algorithms? An explanation of the "elusive" content effect on the Wason selection task*. Doctoral dissertation, Harvard University. University Microfilms.
Cosmides, L. (1989). The logic of social exchange: Has natural selection shaped how humans reason? Studies with the Wason selection task. *Cognition, 31*, 187–276.
Cosmides, L. & Tooby, J. (1981). Cytoplasmic inheritance and intragenomic conflict. *Journal of Theoretical Biology, 89*, 83–129.
Cosmides, L., & Tooby, J. (1987). From evolution to behavior: Evolutionary psychology as the missing link. In Dupre, J. (Ed.), *The latest on the best: Essays on evolution and optimality* (pp. 276–306). MIT Press.
Cosmides, L., & Tooby, J. (1989). Evolutionary psychology and the generation of culture, Part II. Case study: A computational theory of social exchange. *Ethology and Sociobiology, 10*, 51–97.
Cosmides, L., & Tooby, J. (1994a). Beyond intuition and instinct blindness: The case for an evolutionarily rigorous cognitive science. *Cognition, 50*, 41–77, 1994a.
Cosmides, L., & Tooby, J. (1994b). Origins of domain-specificity: The evolution of functional organization. In L. Hirschfeld & S. Gelman (Eds.), *Mapping the mind: Domain-specificity in cognition and culture* (pp. 85–116). Cambridge University Press.
Daly, M., & Wilson, M. (1988). *Homicide*. Aldine.
Daly, M., Wilson, M., & Weghorst, S. J. (1982). Male sexual jealousy. *Ethology and Sociobiology, 3*, 11–27.
Darwin, C. (1871). *The descent of man and selection in relation to sex*. Murray.
Darwin, C. (1872). *The expression of emotions in man and animals*. Murray.
Dawkins, R. (1976). *The selfish gene*. Oxford University Press.
Dawkins, R. (1982). *The extended phenotype: The gene as the unit of selection*. W. H. Freeman.
Dawkins, R. (1986). *The blind watchmaker*. W. W. Norton.
Draper, P. (1989). African marriage systems: Perspectives from evolutionary ecology. *Ethology and Sociobiology, 10*, 145–169.
Dunbar, R. I. M. (1988). Darwinizing man: A commentary. In L. Betzig, M. Borgerhoff Mulder, & P. Turke (Eds.), *Human reproductive behavior*. Cambridge University Press.

Eibl-Eibesfeldt, I. (1971). *Ethology: The biology of behavior*. Holt, Rinehart, and Winston.
Ekman, P. (Ed.) (1982). *Emotion in the human face* (2nd ed.). Cambridge University Press.
Erickson, C. J., & Zenone, P. G. (1977). Courtship differences in male ring doves: Avoidance of cuckoldry? *Science, 192*, 1353–1354.
Frijda, N. H. (1986). *The emotions*. Cambridge University Press.
Galef, B. G. (1990). An adaptationist perspective on social learning, social feeding, and social foraging in Norway rats. In D. Dewsbury (Ed.), *Contemporary issues in comparative psychology* (pp. 55–79). Sinauer.
Gigerenzer, G., & Murray, D. J. (1987). *Cognition as intuitive statistics*. Lawrence Erlbaum Associates.
Hamburg, D. A. (1968). Emotions in the perspective of human evolution. In S. L. Washburn & P. C. Jay (Eds.), *Perspectives on human evolution* (pp. 246–257). Holt, Rinehart & Winston.
Hamilton, W. D. (1964). The genetical evolution of social behaviour. *Journal of Theoretical Biology, 7*, 1–52.
Hughes, A. L. (1987). Social and antisocial behavior. *Quarterly Review of Biology, 62*(4), 415–421.
Hughes, A. L. (1988). *Evolution and human kinship*. Oxford University Press.
Izard, C. E. (1977). *Human emotions*. Plenum.
Lazarus, R. S. (1968). Emotions and adaptation: Conceptual and empirical relations. In W. J. Arnold (Ed.), *Nebraska symposium on motivation*. University of Nebraska Press.
Lazarus, R. S., Kanner, A. D., & Folkman, S. (1980). Emotions: A cognitive–phenomenological analysis. In R. Plutchik & H. Kellerman (Eds.), *Theories of emotion* (pp. 189–217). Academic Press.
Leeper, R. W. (1948). A motivational theory of emotion to replace "emotion as disorganized response." *Psychological Review, 55*(1), 5.
Lieberman, D., Tooby, J., & Cosmides, L. (2007). The architecture of human kin detection. *Nature, 445*, 727–731.
Lorenz, K. (1970). Companions as factors in the bird's environment. In K. Z. Lorenz (Ed.), *Studies on animal and human behavior*. Vol. I. Harvard University Press.
Marr, D. (1982). *Vision: A computational investigation into the human representation and processing of visual information*. Freeman.
McCracken, R. (1971). Lactase deficiency: An example of dietary evolution. *Current Anthropology, 12*, 479–517.
Nesse, R. M. (1991). What is mood for? *Psycholoquy, 2*(9.2), 4809–4840.
Otte, D. (1974). Effects and functions in the evolution of signaling systems. *Annual Review of Ecology and Systematics, 5*, 385–417.
Plutchik, R. (1980). *Emotion: A psychoevolutionary synthesis*. Harper & Row.
Proffitt, D. R., & Gilden, D. L. (1989). Understanding natural dynamics. *Journal of Experimental Psychology: Human Perception and Performance, 15*, 384–393.
Robertson, D. R. (1972). Social control of sex reversal in a coral-reef fish. *Science, 177*, 1007–1009.
Shepher, J. (1983). *Incest: A biosocial view*. Academic Press.
Shepard, R. N. (1987). Evolution of a mesh between principles of the mind and regularities of the world. In J. Dupre (Ed.), *The latest on the best* (pp. 251–275). MIT Press.
Smuts, R. W. (1987). Behavior depends on context. *Behavioral and Brain Sciences, 12*, 16–17.
Stephens, D. W., & Krebs, J. R. (1986). *Foraging theory* (Vol. 1). Princeton University Press.
Swets, J. A., Tanner, W. D., & Birdsall, T. G. (1964). Decision processes in perception. In J. A. Swets (Ed.), *Signal detection and recognition by human observers* (pp. 3–57). Wiley.
Symons, D. (1979). *The evolution of human sexuality*. Oxford University Press.
Symons, D. (1987). If we're all Darwinians, what's the fuss about? In C. B. Crawford, M. F. Smith, & D. L. Krebs (Eds.), *Sociobiology and psychology* (pp. 121–146). Lawrence Erlbaum Associates.
Symons, D. (1989). A critique of Darwinian anthropology. *Ethology and Sociobiology, 10*, 131–144.
Symons, D. (1990). Adaptiveness and adaptation. *Ethology and Sociobiology, 11*, 427–444.
Symons, D. (1992). On the use and misuse of Darwinism in the study of human behavior. In J. Barkow, L. Cosmides, & J. Tooby (Eds), *The adapted mind: Evolutionary psychology and the generation of culture* (pp. 137–159). Oxford University Press.
Tolman, E. C. (1923). A behavioristic account of the emotions. *Psychological Review*, 30(3), 217.
Tomkins, S. S. (1962). *Affect, imagery, consciousness*, Vol. I. Springer.
Tomkins, S. S. (1963). *Affect, imagery, consciousness*, Vol. II. Springer.
Tooby, J. (1982). Pathogens, polymorphism, and the evolution of sex. *Journal of Theoretical Biology, 97*, 557–576.
Tooby, J. (1985). The emergence of evolutionary psychology. In D. Pines (Ed.), *Emerging Syntheses in Science*. Proceedings of the Founding Workshops of the Santa Fe Institute. The Sante Fe Institute.
Tooby, J., & Cosmides, L. (1989a). Evolutionary psychology and the generation of culture, Part I. Theoretical considerations. *Ethology and Sociobiology, 10*, 29–49.

Tooby, J., & Cosmides, L. (1989b). The innate versus the manifest: How universal does universal have to be? *Behavioral and Brain Sciences, 12*, 36–37.

Tooby, J., & Cosmides, L. (1989c). Evolutionary psychologists need to distinguish between the evolutionary process, ancestral selection pressures, and psychological mechanisms. *Behavioral and Brain Sciences, 12*, 724–725.

Tooby, J., & Cosmides, L. (1990). On the universality of human nature and the uniqueness of the individual: The role of genetics and adaptation. *Journal of Personality, 58*, 17–67.

Tooby, J., & Cosmides, L. (1992). The psychological foundations of culture. In J. Barkow, L. Cosmides, & J. Tooby (Eds.), *The adapted mind: Evolutionary psychology and the generation of culture* (pp. 18–136). Oxford University Press.

Tooby, J., & DeVore, I. (1987). The reconstruction of hominid behavioral evolution through strategic modeling. In W. G. Kinzey (Ed.), *The evolution of human behavior: Primate models* (pp. 183–237). State University of New York Press.

Turke, P. W. (1989). Evolution and the demand for children. *Population and Development Review*, 61–90.

Turke, P. (1990). Which humans behave adaptively, and why does it matter? *Ethology and Sociobiology, 11*, 305–339.

Vining, D. (1986). Social versus reproductive success: The central problem of human sociobiology. *Behavioral and Brain Sciences, 9*, 167–216.

Williams, G. C. (1966). *Adaptation and natural selection: A critique of some current evolutionary thought*. Princeton University Press.

Williams, G. C. (1985). A defense of reductionism in evolutionary biology. *Oxford Surveys in Evolutionary Biology, 2*, 1–27.

Wolf, A. P., & Huang, C. (1980). *Marriage and adoption in China 1845_1945*. Stanford University Press.

CHAPTER 3

Evolution, Emotion, and Facial Behavior: A 21st-Century View

Alan J. Fridlund and James A. Russell

Abstract

Most twentieth-century theories of emotion and behaviors mis-cited Darwin to claim that certain facial behaviors evolved to express emotion. Such theories of "facial expressions of emotion" were: (a) misidentified as evolutionary, and (b) biased toward finding universality in facial behaviors; they were mistaken in (c) holding that such universality implied biology but diversity implied culture, and (d) presenting faces as iconic and acontextual. Based on modern evolutionary theory and data, we offer the Behavioral Ecology View of facial displays as an adaptationist framework based on contemporary ethological conceptions of animal signaling and communication. On this view, faces traditionally attributed to emotion are intention movements which act as contextual "social tools" to modify the trajectories of our social interactions and negotiations. These facial behaviors evolved atomistically with their own instrumentality, rather than as outputs of central emotion mechanisms.

Key Words: Darwin, emotion, evolution, facial expression, nonverbal behavior

This chapter reflects our view that an evolutionary framework remains the most productive one for understanding emotion and those behaviors historically treated as emotion-related (ERBs), but even now, in the third decade of the 21st century, the field is encumbered by outmoded ways of thinking about evolution, and a misconceived view of Darwin's thoughts on ERBs. Our hope here is to provide a reset by which inquiry can be redirected toward more profitable ends, and to suggest a more contemporary evolutionary account.

This chapter focuses on facial behavior, the most discussed and researched topic within the emotion field. We discuss at length Basic Emotion Theory (BET; cf., Kowalska & Wróbel, 2017), whose encapsulation of classical Western presumptions about emotions and faces served as the dominant post–World War II framework (Leys, 2017). Within BET, faces were diagnostic of emotion. "The strongest evidence for distinguishing one emotion from another comes from research on facial expressions" (Ekman, 1992, p. 175).[1] As we detail, BET is sometimes labeled evolutionary, but it is not a viable evolutionary theory.

We then update the Behavioral Ecology View (BECV) of facial displays, which stands as the only modern evolutionary account of facial behavior. Barely 30 years old, BECV has begun to inform research on both public and implicit-audience accounts of responses to social media, smiling in pain, human–computer communication, persuasion, power and dominance, facial displays in rats and chimpanzees, intrapersonal communication in therapeutic narrative writing, and game-theoretic analysis of human deception. Artificial intelligence (AI) researchers have begun using BECV as the basis for modeling human-robot interaction instead of BET-oriented face classification. Finally, José-Miguel Fernández-Dols and his colleagues have conducted masterful studies showing how BECV can account for facial behavior in naturalistic settings. Crivelli and Fridlund (2018) and Fridlund (2017) provided these references, and due to space limitations, we cite reviews in lieu of single articles wherever possible, with apologies to the authors involved.

At the conclusion, we indicate briefly how BECV's evolutionary approach may be especially informative when extended to other ERBs, e.g., perception of *qualia*, autonomic nervous system (ANS) actions, and neural mediation. This more complete treatment is in preparation (Fridlund & Russell, 2025).

Darwin, Expression, and Non-Adaptationism
It is customary to begin with Charles Darwin in discussions of evolution and emotion, but scholars who rely on Darwin's non-adaptationist account in *The Expression of the Emotions in Man and Animals* (Darwin, 1872) must look elsewhere.[2] Darwin (1872) treated emotion as just one of many "states of mind" (not only "passions" like anger, fear, disgust, etc., but also modesty, helplessness, affirmation and negation, patience, obstinacy, and devotion), and did not consider the so-called expressions of the emotions products of natural selection. They were merely remnants of habits that were *once* useful, but had degenerated from disuse atrophy (cf. Darwin's *Principle of Serviceable Associated Habits*) and were passed on via Lamarckian "use-inheritance" (Coleman, 1977).[3] Thus, whereas an ancient ancestor who was provoked might have retaliated by kill-biting the provocateur, civilized people now merely take offense and scowl instead. Weakened states of mind—those "induced, however feebly" (Darwin, 1872, p. 98)—elicited weakened responses. Darwin appropriated his principle nearly *verbatim* from Herbert Spencer's "nascent excitation of psychical state" (Spencer, 1855, p. 231).

Darwin's making most ERBs vestigial rather than functional habits served his main purpose, to depose the Natural Theology account "that certain muscles have been given to man solely that he may reveal to other men his feelings" (C. Darwin, letter to Alfred Russell Wallace, 1867, cited in Fridlund, 1994, p. 18). As Darwin recognized in *Origin of Species* (1859), merely arguing for adaptation was playing into the hands of theologians primed to retort "God made us thus." Instead, Darwin's tactic in *Expression* was to prove "descent with modification" by demonstrating that ERBs were useless baggage from our ancestry, analogous to the "rudimentary, atrophied, or aborted organs" he described in *Origin* (Darwin, 1859, p. 249).[4] Among the structures Darwin (1859, esp. pp. 199–200, 450–458) considered vestigial were pelvic and hind-limb bones in snakes, wings on flightless insects and birds, webbed feet on land birds, and five phalanges in the seal flipper. Among humans, we would add the coccyx and appendix. For Darwin, ERBs suffered the same fate as these once serviceable structures: "the origin of rudimentary organs is simple . . . disuse has been the main agency; that it has led in successive generations to the gradual reduction of various organs, until they have become rudimentary" (Darwin, 1859, p. 251).[5]

Darwin's Anti-Darwinism and Its Persistent Misinterpretation
Darwin's (1872) account was distinctly non-Darwinian (Fridlund, 1992, 1994), in two ways. First was its nonadaptationism, i.e., expressive movements were not selected, they were devolved rudiments. Second was its assumption about inheritance and what it meant for a movement to be "innate." Whereas today it is commonplace to speak of inherited behaviors as coded genetically,[6] Darwin knew nothing of genetics, and it was not until the 1930s that Ronald Fisher,

J. B. S. Haldane, and others reconciled Darwinian adaptationism with Mendelian population genetics to forge the "modern synthesis" of current evolutionary theories.

For Darwin, what was inherited was not expressive behaviors per se, it was *habits*, and he explicitly distinguished innate behaviors (i.e., instincts) from inherited habits (cf., Darwin, 1859, pp. 208–209). This makes Darwin's account not just non-Darwinian, but nonbiological. Darwin's *Expression* was, in fact, a work of associationist psychology born of his British empiricism (Ghiselin, 1969), and today we might restate his take on current ERBs as the transgenerational partial decay of Pavlovian conditional responses.

Despite what Darwin (1872) wrote, today *Expression* is usually miscast as a biological account that aligns with modern Darwinism. The misinterpretations are rife. Keltner and Ekman (2000) gave Darwin the view that "facial expressions evolved to elicit distinct behaviors in conspecifics" (p. 239). That view was not Darwin's. For Shariff and Tracy (2011), "Darwin (1872) proposed that emotion expressions evolved to serve two classes of functions: (a) preparing the organism to respond adaptively . . . and (b) communicating critical social information" (p. 395). He did neither. Tracy, Randles, and Steckler (2015) had Darwin claiming that "emotion expressions evolved in humans from pre-human nonverbal displays" (p. 25),[7] when Darwin held that the expressions had *de*volved, and not from displays but from once-serviceable acts.

Typical is one retelling which has Darwin theorizing that "facial expressions of emotion are universal, not learned differently in each culture; they are biologically determined, the product of man's evolution" (Ekman & Friesen, 1975, p. 23). This influential, persistent view, repeated by many theorists, is wrong on all counts:

1. *Contra* "universality," Darwin (1872) provided many examples of cultural diversity in ERBs. Crying, for example, was a habit "which must have been acquired since the period when man branched off from the common progenitor of the genus *homo* and of the non-weeping anthropomorphous apes" (p. 153). Despite its long history, this habit is readily weakened or strengthened; thus "a frequently repeated effort to restrain weeping . . . does much in checking the habit," but "[o]n the other hand, it appears that the power of weeping can be increased through habit" (p. 155). As evidence, Darwin reported pronounced crying among New Zealand women and "savages" (pp. 155–156), with crying and screaming becoming more restrained "with the advancing culture of the race" (p. 174). Pouting, "which does not seem very common with European children" was nonetheless "characteristic of sulkiness throughout the rest of the world" (p. 233). Sneering was a seeming rarity in Australia, Abyssinia, and China, which Darwin discounts, arguing nonetheless that "this animal-like expression may be more common with savages than with civilized races" (p. 252). All these examples point to Darwin's frank acknowledgment of cultural diversity.
2. On the claim that facial ERBs for Darwin are "not learned differently in each culture," but are "biologically determined," Darwin made clear in his cultural examples that such movements were habits that were malleable within the life span, transmissible within the reproductive life span, with some of these changes paralleling cultural "advancement." This cultural malleability was comparable to Darwin's treatment of morphology in *Descent of Man* (1871), wherein he contended, "Different occupations, habitually followed, lead to changed proportions in various parts of the body," and contrasted English laborers with non-laborers by stating that the hands "are generally smaller in refined or civilized men than in hard-working men or savages, is certain" (pp. 32–33).

The importance Darwin granted to culture was evident in his recognition that "certain powers, such as self-consciousness, abstractions, etc., are peculiar to man," and they were likely incidental to "the continued use of a highly developed language" (Darwin, 1871, p. 105). As a result, "Darwin's ideas appear to have more in common with those of Edward Sapir than those of later reductionist theorists of emotion who claim for themselves Darwin's intellectual legacy regarding the nature of emotions . . ." (Bąk, 2016, p. 29).

3. Finally, Darwin did not consider most ERBs the products of evolution by natural selection, but as degenerate habits. On this final count, one might counter that those movements derived from Lamarckian evolution. But since Lamarckism was progressivist, they would be products of devolution instead, an idea that comported with the title of Darwin's prior book, iconoclastically entitled *Descent of Man* (1871) rather than the theologically more palatable *Ascent*.

In several important respects, Darwin's account was also singularly Western. His view of emotions aligned with Aristotelian and later Cartesian views of the separate "passions." He harbored preconceptions about the movements that supposedly belonged to each emotion from the stylized paintings and engravings of 17th-century French artist and arts doyen Charles LeBrun, and later engravings by Darwin's *Expression* opponent, physician and anatomist Charles Bell. Darwin's knowledge of the ERBs of exotic animals and diverse human cultures was gleaned largely from British correspondents around the world, mostly clergy, missionaries, physicians, and academics, not from natives of those cultures. Consistent with Western traditions, Darwin continued to pit emotion against reason. He did so in terms of actions of the "will" (Darwin, 1872, Ch. 14 and *passim*), the 19th-century term for Aristotle's conation, which could either mitigate the force of habit that would otherwise lead to an expressive movement, or mimic an expressive movement that was typically habitual.[8]

In the end, Darwin's tack in *Expression* to make ERBs simply sets of rudimentary habits was a Pyrrhic victory. In *Expression* he labored, one example after another, to disabuse readers that Natural Theology could explain expressive movements, and he succeeded. But his contemporaries found his principles problematic (Fridlund, 1994), and critically, his tactic left him unable to propose a concurrent adaptationist account of nonverbal behaviors based on natural selection (Burkhardt, 1985).

Was "The Expression of the Emotions" a Misleading Phrase?

One particularly severe criticism of *Expression*, however, was to come from unexpected quarters.[9] Was Darwin's use of "expression" warranted? As we indicated earlier (note 1), the term "expression" is problematic because common usage suggests that an expression must be *of* something. That was the issue pinpointed by American functionalist John Dewey (1894), an evolutionist, who took Darwin to task on this errant implication: "To an onlooker my angry movements are expressions—signs, indications; but surely not to me. To rate such movements as primarily expressive is to fall into the psychologist's fallacy: it is to confuse the standpoint of the observer and explainer with that of the fact observed. . . . In themselves they are movements, acts, and must be treated as such if psychology is to take hold of them right end up" (p. 555). Dewey momentarily fell prey to that same error by referring to "angry movements," but his aim was unswerving. Our faces and other ERBs were functional, he contended, and so they should not be studied as mere indications of something else (excepting paralinguistic gestures with semantic referents, cf. note 20). Later, we follow Dewey's dictum to its obvious conclusion when we describe the Behavioral Ecology View of facial displays.

Face-Reading, and Force-Fitting Faces to Categorical Emotions

Unfortunately, most 20th-century emotion researchers ignored Dewey's criticism and remained in this same paradigm-lock. Today, researchers persist in using "expressions of emotion" and "facial expressions of emotion" as the operative terms for certain sets of facial and sometimes bodily movements. They do so without any acknowledgment that the terms are presuppositions about movements and causes. They continue ancient methods of "face-reading," which began with Aristotle's physiognomic conjectures (Fridlund, 1994), but now believe they can divine emotions from faces instead, in a process they call "emotion recognition."

The first such face-reading study that treated emotion recognition as a foregone conclusion was conducted by Darwin. This was a curious endeavor given his belief that the signal value of most faces was incidental. He had acquired from French physician-physiologist Duchenne de Boulogne a folio of still photos of faces created by faradic (electrical) stimulation of facial muscles. Darwin preselected 11 of "the most characteristic" faces based on a psychiatrist-friend's judgment of their accuracy in "depicting emotions," showed them to his Down House guests—"20 to 30 persons of all kinds," as he described them—and asked the guests to describe the emotion represented by each face.

Unsurprisingly, the houseguests agreed on what the faces "expressed." The preselections almost guaranteed the outcome, given that: (1) the muscles Duchenne stimulated were selected to create, in his words, "the accurate rendering of emotions"; (2) Darwin selected what his consultant believed were "the most characteristic" of the faces; (3) the participants were Darwin's houseguests, a restricted domestic sample; and (4) the guests were instructed to provide emotion terms. The less generous interpretation is that the photographer, experimenter, and participants all held the same preconceptions. (All quotes and detail are from Snyder et al., 2010.)

As Russell (1994) charted experimental psychology's involvement with emotions and faces, most of the early studies treated the premise that emotions could be read in faces as simple common sense. Those studies were soon to defy common sense. Researchers like Herbert Langfeld and his social psychology student Floyd Allport were repeating Darwin's procedures, but found that allowing participants to provide their own emotion words for preselected faces resulted in "correct" (i.e., stipulated) descriptions only about 40%–50% of the time (Allport, 1924, pp. 223–224). The emotion words used for the faces varied across observers, with alterations in response choices and observation contexts, and with actual faces vs. poses. Based on such findings, Allport (1924) modified Darwin's principles, adding the strong proviso that social conditioning could override what was innate, with social context predominating when finding meaning in faces: "When we come upon an individual or a group of people expressing some strong emotion, we immediately attempt to find out what has happened. This knowledge at once gives significance to the otherwise chaotic mass of facial expressions" (p. 226). It appeared that what people—Westerners, as least—did with faces in these studies was ascribe emotion to them, not "recognize" emotion in them, and those ascriptions were not canonical as Darwin, LeBrun, Duchenne, and Bell had supposed. Later empirical work would substantiate these early findings.

Basic Emotion Theory: Seeking Facial Universality and Finding It

Given the weak results of early face-reading studies whose minimal controls exceeded Darwin's, and the ample findings of context-dependency in face interpretation, one might have predicted a turn toward other methods and cultures to examine whether there was diversity in face production, ascriptions to faces, and behavioral responses to faces. This would have been standard, naturalistic science. As we showed, Darwin's examples of cultural diversity in crying, screaming, and sulking suggested ample avenues for research. We might also have hoped for efforts to discern whether William James (1884) and others were right to doubt whether Western emotion concepts constituted a proper or exhaustive framework for describing how other cultures regarded faces and other ERBs (Jackson et al., 2019; Wierzbicka, 1992).

Making Innateness = Uniformity

Unfortunately, none of those avenues of inquiry was pursued. Instead, psychology was seized by an approach that equated evolution with uniformity and sought to prove it, using face-reading as its fundamental evidence. This was the "basic emotions" approach pioneered by clinical and personality psychologist Silvan Tomkins (complete ed. 2008, first volume publ. 1962), who invoked evolution to endorse a set of categorical "primary affects" (see Leys, 2017, for analysis of Tomkins's theorizing). Tomkins and McCarter (1964) named eight, each with labels for its moderate and intense form: interest-excitement, enjoyment-joy, surprise-startle, distress-anguish, fear-terror, shame-humiliation, contempt-disgust, and anger-rage. These primary affects were "controlled by innate affect programs which are inherited as a subcortical structure which can instruct and control a variety of muscles and glands to respond with unique patterns . . . characteristic of a given affect" (p. 120). Those programs had primary outputs to the face, which via evolution "has moved in the direction of increasing expressiveness through greater visibility of the facial musculature and of the patterns of neural innervation. . . . Thus, it seems to have been evolved in part as an organ for the maximal transmission of information" (p. 120).[10]

The return of "face-reading" post–World War II was in great part due to Tomkins's theory and subsequent work by Tomkins's protégé, Paul Ekman.[11] Tomkins and McCarter (1964) provided the explicit rationale: "Because we have identified the face as the primary site of affect and because we have assumed that each of the primary affects is controlled by an innate 'program' which has been inherited, the ability of human beings to recognize these facial responses assumes a more critical theoretical significance than heretofore" (p. 121). One corollary of Tomkins's scheme was that emotions and ERBs were made isomorphic: if emotions were categorical, then there had to be categorical ERBs for each one. If the emotions were universal, then so were the ERBs. Findings about ERBs implied facts about emotions, and vice versa. Ekman (1992) ratified the circularity: the "basic emotions" all had "distinctive universal signals" yet simultaneously, as we quoted at the outset, "The strongest evidence for distinguishing one emotion from another comes from research on facial expressions" (p. 175).

Proving Uniformity

Tomkins and McCarter (1964) sought to prove their claim of categorical "primary affects" with matching faces by convening 24 U.S. "white urban firemen" (p. 122) in small groups and having them view posed face photos. Like Allport and Darwin before them,[12] Tomkins and McCarter preselected the photos; by presupposition, the faces were "posed to exemplify . . . the eight primary affects" (p. 121). But Tomkins and McCarter went even further: they supplied the firemen a short list of response options, a numbered set of categories, each of which contained synonyms for the eight primary affects ("neutral" faces and a neutral response option were included). Perhaps unsurprising was the outcome: a 0.86 correlation of matching choices among the firemen.

Following Tomkins's theorizing and the outlines of the Tomkins-McCarter (1964) study, Paul Ekman, together with associate Wallace Friesen and anthropologist E. R. Sorensen, published highly cited and influential studies of facial expressions of nonliterate indigenous peoples in exotic locales, such as the Fore tribe in Papua New Guinea (Ekman et al., 1969). Just as Allport (1924) found, the initial studies produced disappointing results when participants were asked to label the faces freely. To boost "recognition" rates, Ekman et al. shifted to Tomkins and McCarter's (1964) tactic of having participants pick the closest match from a short list of either emotion labels or emotion-related stories. The list was tailored to fit the six face photos and prescribed emotions which Ekman selected somewhat arbitrarily from Tomkins's eight, with the terms slightly renamed: *happiness, sadness, anger, fear, surprise,* and *disgust* (Colombetti, 2014). Translators asked participants to make the matches, and Sorenson later disclosed his uncertainty about whether the translation included coaching (Sorenson, 1975).

Using these forced-choice, matching-to-sample procedures, people in diverse cultures showed overall statistical significance in matching, even though rates ran as low as 40%–50%. Those rates depended on the level of Westernization of the cultures sampled, and were likely inflated by numerous procedural decisions (Russell, 1994, 2017). In line with the investigators' preconceptions, however, these findings were touted as proving the universal "recognition" of categorical "facial expressions of emotion." Addressing this representation, Crivelli and Fridlund (2018) remarked, "Ironically, the much higher 90% rate of right-handedness worldwide . . . never led to a claim of 'universality of dexterity.' . . . the approximate 10% global rate of sinistrality and ambidexterity constitutes acknowledged, stable, congenital variation" (p. 391). Even BET advocates are now backing away from the early claims. As Keltner, Sauter, Tracy, and Cowen (2019) remarked oxymoronically, "Ekman and Friesen were able to document *some degree of universality* in the production and recognition of a limited set of 'basic emotions'" (p. 134, italics ours).

Based on a highly critical review of previous face-emotion research, and an uncritical interpretation and overextension of his findings, Ekman codified his claims and presented them as his Neurocultural Theory (Ekman, 1972). Ekman originally cast his theory as under Darwin's imprimatur, and so "at some early time in history certain facial movements were acquired to serve some biologically adaptive function," but "are now vestiges . . . which do communicate feelings, but which do not have as their primary purpose the 'expression' of an inner state to another person" (Ekman, 1972, p. 208). But Ekman also claimed that facial movements were nonetheless instigated by a specialized "facial affect program" (FAP), "neurally coded instructions" (p. 216) that were phyletic and universal, as were many of the triggers that activated them.[13] Thus Ekman's Neurocultural Theory simultaneously portrayed our faces as vestigial, but with brain circuitry evolved to produce them.

In its mechanistic approach to face production, Ekman's account of his FAP was strikingly reminiscent of the 1950s–1960s ethology of Konrad Lorenz (1970) and Niko Tinbergen (1953), who observed repetitive, stereotyped animal behaviors and had attributed them to acronymously identical FAPs; these "fixed action patterns" also had triggers, i.e., releasing stimuli. But the Lorenz-Tinbergen FAPs, and the "innate releasing mechanisms" held to produce them, were intended to account for functional instinctual behavior, not rudiments of actions that were "once serviceable" as claimed by Darwin and in Ekman's Neurocultural Theory.

Dismissing Diversity

Ekman's theory offered simple answers to, and ways to answer, thorny questions about faces, emotions, evolution, and culture. It was not a neutral exposition, but an attack on beliefs held by some anthropologists, from fieldwork and other observation, that our facial behavior was a kind of nonverbal language, with some universals but overwhelming cultural dialects.[14] Ekman misrepresented the anthropological position as holding that "facial expressions are specific to culture and that there are no universals" (Ekman, 2006), and he concluded *non sequitur* that "only through a highly unlikely coincidence would a facial expression be found to have the same emotional meaning in two independent cultures" (Ekman, 1972, p. 208). This conclusion was manifestly false, since: (1) all human cultures are the products of one long migration, and habits and customs can migrate with the populations, (2) cultures can develop similar habits and customs via convergent cultural evolution, and (3) some facial movements may be preadapted for cultures to adopt for customary usage.

Nonetheless, by caricaturing anthropologists as univocal "relativists" (Ekman, 1972) and Darwin as a strict universalist, Ekman could insert his theory in-between as one that accommodated both biological universals and cultural variation and modification, when each position had accommodated the other already. By expropriating laboratory-based experimental procedures to the field, Ekman believed he could obtain definitive knowledge beyond what he dismissed as mere anecdotal observations by the "relativists."

Those early cross-cultural studies, some done in what Ekman called "visually isolated" cultures[15] in Papua New Guinea, caught on in academia and the popular press, thanks to an initial publication in *Science* (Ekman et al., 1969). *Universality* was the new buzzword to describe uniformity in both facial ERBs and their corresponding emotions. As Crivelli and Fridlund (2019) contended, the universality claim was an easy sell for the late 1960s, when the world was riven by the Cold War, the United States was mired in the Viet Nam conflict, and the most popular TV ad in history had people from diverse cultures on a hilltop singing, "I'd like to buy the world a Coke." It was consoling and promising to believe that "deep down, we're all the same," already a common belief given most people's limited experience with cultural diversity. There were other reasons to argue for cross-cultural uniformity. Ekman and Friesen both left the U.S. Army with interests in military intelligence, national security, and counterterrorism, and this led to a preoccupation with judging what was "authentic emotion" vs. dissimulation (e.g., Ekman, 1981, 1985; Ekman & Friesen, 1969, 1982). Universality meant that techniques to detect deception would apply cross-culturally.

Cracks in the BET Foundation
The Neurocultural Theory laid the groundwork for a new, widely accepted set of beliefs about emotions and the faces they supposedly expressed, beliefs that took on the status of "settled science" (cf., Russell & Fernández-Dols, 1996, on the "Facial Expression Program"). The 1980s and 1990s, however, saw unprecedented challenges to BET theories generally and the Neurocultural Theory specifically. In a watershed paper, Ortony and Turner (1990) laid bare the inconsistent criteria for determining which emotions were basic, and questioned the essential notion of "basic-ness." In some cases, the challenges represented a resurgence of earlier, pre-BET empirical findings about faces. To wit, Russell and colleagues showed that what observers saw in the Ekman-Friesen poses was not iconic and invariant, but contingent on the culture of the participants, and the context in which the faces appeared; later efforts widened the scope of context effects (reviews by Aviezer & Hassin, 2017; Gendron & Barrett, 2017; Russell, 2017). Russell's dissatisfaction with the ontological soundness of the concept of basic emotions led him to propose a constructionist account instead (Russell, 2003), and we later suggest a biological basis for this account. Items in the English-language emotion lexicon were seen to be heterogeneous clusters or Roschian prototypes rather than essentialist scientific objects or concepts (Fehr & Russell, 1984). Finally, Buss (2014) used sexual jealousy to argue on evolutionary grounds that neither distinctive signals, primate homologues, nor reproductive advantage could be criterial for basic-ness, with other evolutionary cautions elaborated by Al-Shawaf, Conroy-Beam, Asao, and Buss (2016), and Al-Shawaf and Lewis (2017).

Faced with sustained opposition, Ekman (1992) staged a dramatic retrenchment. Emotions were no longer quite so basic or hermetic; echoing Fehr and Russell (1984), each emotion was a "family of related states" (p. 192) that might include multiple facial expressions (p. 176) or no expression at all (p. 177). The to-do about "basic emotions" was recast as too much to-do, because after all, there were many meanings of "basic" (pp. 170–171). Ekman now conceded that universality did not imply biological evolution (p. 170), although he continued to present such causation as either assumed (e.g., Keltner & Ekman, 2000) or extremely probable: "in all likelihood it is by natural selection" (Ekman, 2017, p. 52). In contrast to his earlier embrace of Darwin's vestigial account of faces, Ekman (1992) now allied himself (p. 171) with utilitarian/adaptationist accounts of emotion voiced by Johnson-Laird and Oatley (1989), and Tooby and Cosmides (1990). Whereas in the Neurocultural Theory, emotions were unbidden and their expressions needed social ("display-rule") management, now they had "evolved for their adaptive value in dealing with *fundamental life tasks*" (Ekman, 1992, p. 171, italics in original). Left unclear was what role remained for intermediating cultural display rules when the emotions had evolved for our benefit (further discussion below).

Ekman's (1992) modifications were only the beginning. He and his associates also began offering varying sets of criteria by which to establish basic emotions. Linguist Halszka Bąk (2016) documented the successive revisions:

> The initial number of criteria categorizing an emotion as basic was nine (Ekman 1992), but it shifted to seven (Ekman 1994a), then to eleven (Ekman 1999), only to peak at 13 (Ekman and Cordaro 2011). The criteria changed from simple requirements that each emotion has its dedicated and distinct facial expression to including specific appraisals in emotion perception, and concurrent existence in other primates. (Bąk, 2016, p. 39)

With each change in criteria came new basic emotions:

> As he fought his critics and adapted his theory to the new evidence conflicting it, Ekman shifted his position from a radical denial of the existence of any "non-basic" emotions (Ekman 1992) to one where such emotions existed and fulfilled his categorical criteria only partially (Ekman 1994). As the number of inclusion criteria grew so did the catalog of the basic emotions. It started with six (Ekman et al. 1969), then it doubled (Ekman 1992), then jumped to 15 (Ekman 1999), to culminate implicitly in an even larger number as Ekman (2003) declared the existence of 16 of positive emotions alone. (Bąk, 2016, p. 39)

The dialectic continues. A new generation of Basic Emotion Theorists, some protégés of Ekman, have expanded the list of basic emotions to 20 or more (e.g., Keltner et al., 2019), with critics suggesting that this expansionary thrust owes to both method artifacts and the ad hoc loosening of inclusion criteria, with no consideration of the rationales for the earlier, more restrictive ones (cf., Crivelli & Fridlund, 2019).

The Decline of Universality

The cross-cultural matching studies had been offered as *the* test case for universality, not only of facial expressions but also of their corresponding emotions. Universality would have been easy for BET researchers to reject if false, as Ekman (2017, p. 42) attested, if "the expressions that the majority of people in one country judged as showing one emotion (let us say anger) were judged as showing another emotion (fear) by the majority in another culture. This never happened."

It did, but it took researchers outside the BET tradition to show it. The same faces judged as showing *fear* by the majority of people in one country, the United States, were judged as showing *anger* by the majority in another culture, the Trobriand Islanders of Papua New Guinea. Trobriand Islanders understand BET's supposedly universal "fear" face as an agonistic threat display. This understanding held within and across different islands of their archipelago, regardless of the assessment method (e.g., matching faces to emotion labels vs. stories). Carvings of Trobriand flying witches (*yoyowa*) depicting the use of that putative fear face to threaten villagers extend back more than a century. In addition, this face is used as a threat display not just among one exotic group of people, but also in several African, Amazonian, New Zealand, and other Pacific small-scale, indigenous societies.

Other departures from universality came from efforts of two independent multidisciplinary research teams studying not only Trobrianders from Papua New Guinea, but also three other indigenous peoples. One was Melanesian, and other two were African, the Himba of Namibia and the Mwani of Mozambique. The findings, all gathered after 2012, were obtained using older forced-choice methods as well as newer ones like free-labeling or queries about emotion antecedents (reviews by Crivelli & Gendron, 2017; and Crivelli & Fridlund, 2018).

The presumed concordances between faces and emotion ascriptions may not exist even within Western cultures. A recent meta-analysis of studies of both coded BET-categorized facial expressions and concurrent self-reported emotion showed that covariation between the two was "modest-to-low" (Durán et al., 2017, p. 122). How is this possible when such a connection seems intuitive, at least to Westerners? Two factors undoubtedly contribute: (1) we seldom test our assumptions about what others' faces indicate, or have any ground truth by which to do it; and (2) we are wretched witnesses and historians regarding how we use our own faces—the problems of eyewitness testimony are redoubled when we can't witness ourselves. The low covariations were not just of faces to other ERBs, but among the other ERBs themselves (Durán et al., 2017).

Culture, BET's Great Spoiler of Uniformity

From the start, Ekman's claim of universality had to be reconciled with the imperfect matching rates on the matching-to-sample tasks which he, Sorenson, and Friesen (1969) and later authors employed in their cross-cultural studies. The solution was to invoke a concept that originated with Wilhelm Wundt (1894) but continued with Floyd Allport's ontogenetically acquired "language of the face" (1924) and later observations by Klineberg (1938). It was that enculturation disconnected emotions from their prewired faces. The "emotional expressions," it was held, were "authentic" and "felt" precisely because they were spontaneous and eruptile. This made the disconnects necessary because these faces, Darwinian vestiges all, might erupt in all sorts of unsociable ways, so cultures were forced to develop "cultural display rules" to manage the unbidden eruptions.

Just as he had localized the instigation of facial behavior in his facial affect program, Ekman (1972) extended the neurology by instantiating "display rules" as points somewhere in the brain where neural impulses traveling to the facial affect program, or exiting it to the facial muscles, were intercepted before they could act on the face. This interception might result in throttled or distorted faces, or even the intensification or simulation of facial actions that were not part of the original outflow from the affect program. Such cultural rules might include prescriptions like "big boys don't cry," "look sad at funerals," and "losers shouldn't look angry."

Ekman et al.'s (1969) equation of evolution with universality was evident when display rules were invoked ad hoc to explain only departures from the higher matching rates they obtained, not the higher rates themselves. As Crivelli and Fridlund (2018) emphasized, both diversity and uniformity can result from *either* biology or culture, and they listed the possibilities. Horizontal cultural transmission via migration and assimilation, and convergent cultural evolution from common social selection pressures, can both produce uniformity. Thus, all cultures evolved money, cook with fire, and have wedding ceremonies, and none of these is fundamentally genetic. Conversely, biology can result in marked variations due to adaptive radiation (think *finches*, cf. Darwin, 1859, and Sulloway, 1982), genetic drift, founder effects, and epigenetic marks on subpopulation genomes. Such changes include melanization, blood hemoglobin type, and insulin resistance. None of these variations derives from simple enculturation.

The matching rates that emerged from the cross-cultural studies came from the use of exaggerated poses to represent the "expressions of emotion." With a defiant logic, these stagy poses, reprinted in nearly every psychology and emotion textbook, were held to be the most natural ones; they were "pure" expressions untainted by culture and thus unfettered by display rules. Where would these faces ever be seen? According to the Neurocultural Theory, we are least affected by culture when we are alone, and so our full-blown, prewired "expressions of emotion" would emerge mostly in solitude and rarely in public.[16] Ekman, Davidson, and Friesen (1990) made solitary faces crucial to their BET account and against BECVs: "Facial expressions do occur when people are alone . . . and contradict the theoretical proposals of those who view expressions solely as social signals" (p. 351).

Whereas BET stipulated that facial expressions should be maximal in private and constrained in public, audience-effect studies soon showed the opposite. Facial behavior was maximal in real or imagined interaction and minimal away from it (review by Fernández-Dols & Crivelli, 2013). But what about solitary faces? Fridlund (1992, 1994, 2017; and Crivelli & Fridlund, 2018, 2019) explained them as instances of implicit sociality, and provided numerous examples of commonplace situations in which we are physically alone but "psychologically" social: e.g., when we rehearse a talk before an imaginary audience, yell for help hoping someone is in earshot, pray to God, sexually self-stimulate, talk to houseplants, or bark at intransigent computers. All these instances are accompanied by both words and faces, directed toward people who may or may not be physically present, or animals and objects we transiently grant the ability to grasp our intent (for animistic interpretations, see Fridlund & Duchaine, 1996).

The findings of audience effects, even with implicit and imaginary audiences, forced a startling revision of display rules, probably the most consequential one since the theory's inception. Whereas those rules were devised to account for public faces, Ekman (1997) now extended them to private ones:

> I expect that some display rules are so well established that some people may follow them even when they are alone. And some people when alone may imagine the reactions of others, and then follow the appropriate display rule, as if the others were present. And finally, there may be display rules that specify the management of expression not just with others but when alone. (p. 328; and see Leys, 2017, for discussion)

Although Ekman may have deemed this revision a successful workaround for implicit audience effects, it vitiated key precepts of Neurocultural Theory, perhaps even more than his earlier (1992) round of modifications. By this new formulation, could Ekman now be sure that the "biologically based, evolved, universal facial expressions of emotion" (Ekman, 1984, p. 321), seen in purest form in solitude, weren't actually products of solitary display rules? To whatever extent this might be true, then what did the cross-cultural matching-to-sample studies based on those faces prove? Certainly nothing certain about innateness. Again, from the BET perspective, the higher but still modest matching rates might have simply derived from shared display rules, acquired by convergent learning and/or horizontal transmission from cultural migration and assimilation (Nelson & Russell, 2013).

In the end, the entire display rules concept was untestable, for reasons outlined by Fridlund (1994), Leys (2017), and Crivelli and Fridlund (2019). Briefly, the concept relied on peoples in two different cultures having identical emotions but different faces due to the intermediation of display rules. Thus, male adults grieving the loss of a parent might or might not make cry-faces depending on whether the rule "big boys don't cry" was conventional in their cultures. But then how could the emotions be identical in the respective cultures? A culture which did not sanction crying in adult males would treat a crying male as weak or transgressive. From the BET view, then, the sadness eliciting the grieving would likely be accompanied by guilt and shame, and so the faces would differ as a direct consequence of the different emotions. In cultures without that display rule, the crying would be unstigmatized and the grieving less complicated. In this way, "display rules" are always "emotion rules," a proposition that excludes any possibility of confirming or excluding display rules per se. The single empirical study used to demonstrate display rules, the oft-cited but never-published "Japanese-American" experiment described by Friesen (1972) and incompletely reported by Ekman (1972), was fatally flawed on this count alone. This inability to verify "display rules" independent of the faces they supposedly modified made the Neurocultural Theory's partitioning of faces into non-social/emotional vs. social/conventional ones untestable.

Evolution and the Match Game

Does any of the research we have reviewed speak to evolution? At the very least, an evolutionary account should begin with the real-world uses of facial behaviors, apart from their acknowledged regulation of the facial orifices. Which faces do people make in which settings, and how might that usage confer, or have conferred, reproductive advantage? Do cultures differ in which faces they use, and do those differences accord sensibly with those cultures' social organizations and ecologies? As Darwin recognized, natural selection produces diversity as well as commonality, so do any cultural differences follow a dispersion pattern that might indicate adaptive radiation[17] more than social convention? Do aspects of our ERBs resemble the actions of related species in more than just analogous appearances, i.e., is there evidence of homologies? Are there any cultural invariances in ERBs that do align with the clusters of behaviors and phenomenologies which ostensibly characterize Western emotions?[18]

These questions are complex, and do not admit to easy study or easy answers. Natural and cultural selection intertwine, often inextricably, throughout both phylogeny and ontogeny. Like natural selection, cultural selection relies on variability, ecological selection pressures, and a mode of transmission (trans-generational for both, and for cultural selection, cross-generational as well). Cultural phylogenetics has become a specialty in its own right (Mendoza-Straffon, 2016). Epigenetic mechanisms, which one writer termed "Lamarck's revenge" (Ward, 2018), have blurred the line between what is nature and what is nurture (Lacal & Ventura, 2018; Skvortsova et al., 2018).

If one were to construct even a fledgling evolutionary account of emotion and ERBs, it would have been hard to imagine a greater diversion than to study people's word choices when given photos of facial poses. Poses made to represent *any* psychological state are recognized better than the spontaneous movements associated with those states (cf., Ershadi et al., 2018). Even discounting the flawed early cross-cultural matching studies, "pick the matching emotion" remains a common strategy for studying ERBs. Some investigators attempt to classify emotions by vocal prosody (Laukka & Elfenbein, 2021). Others search for emotion "signatures" in brain activity (but see Touroutoglou et al., 2015). Similar patterns have been sought in the autonomic nervous system, with inconclusive results (Durán et al., 2017; Kreibig, 2010). On facial behavior, despite ample reason for caution (Barrett et al., 2019), massive effort is underway to develop AIs that can reliably identify the "correct" emotion from posed faces as well as faces in the wild (Martinez et al., 2019).

The trend is not promising. Recent BET theorists have vowed to leave the old posed-face matching studies behind, and to study faces instead as part of the "multimodal, dynamic patterns of behavior" comprising "emotional expressions" (e.g., Keltner & Cordaro, 2017, pp. 58–59; and see Keltner et al., 2019). But this is old wine in new bottles. Posed face-reading will be supplanted by "moving face + body reading," when, as Allport (1924) suggested, the social context of ERBs can easily overshadow the ERBs themselves. It also runs afoul of Dewey's dictum, i.e., making our nonverbal behavior an "expression" of something else leads toward intrapsychic conjecture and away from the behavior and its own instrumentality.

Adaptation and Facial Action

That human facial behavior should be studied on its own, as a product of natural selection, was the basis for formulating the leading alternative to BET, the Behavioral Ecology View (BECV). The fullest expositions were provided by Fridlund (1994, 2017) and Crivelli and Fridlund (2018).

The idea that facial behavior and other ERBs might have arisen via natural selection for their signal value would have fit well with Darwin's treatment of sexual selection. He gave precisely that account for ornamental morphologies like colored avian plumage, wattles on carrier pigeons, horns on stags, and manes on lions (all from *Origin of Species*; Darwin, 1859). As we reviewed, Darwin's own tack in *Expression* precluded him from explaining expressive movements as adaptations emerging from natural selection, but other biologists did soon afterward. Fridlund (1994) detailed the key developments, and we abbreviate them here.

The Decline of Mechanistic Ethology

In the early 1900s, ornithologist Oskar Heinroth began studying the social behaviors of various aquatic birds, at the Berlin Zoo, in the South Seas, and in one room of his Berlin flat.[19] He developed a strategy of correlating morphological or behavioral differences among related species to those species' varying niches and social organizations, a strategy that marked the beginning of behavioral ecology (Podos, 1994). Heinroth observed that related graylag geese made one kind of fractionated movement before they broke into flight, but another when setting out to walk. Because the fractionated acts reliably preceded different courses of action, Heinroth termed them *intention movements*, signals of behavioral intentions to other geese (reviewed by Smith, 1977). Heinroth found many such movements, but focused more on their functions (Podos, 1994). How those movements originated, possibly *for* their signal value, required an evolutionary mechanism.

That mechanism was first proposed by another bird-watcher, biologist Julian Huxley, and although it was evolutionary it ran exactly counter to Darwin's treatment of "expressions of the emotions." Whereas Darwin believed that fractionated movements like those Heinroth observed were rudiments of once-complete and once-serviceable acts, Huxley believed that those movements were dramatizations of current complete and now-serviceable acts, or at least parts of them. He drew this conclusion from studies of feeding, nesting, and courting behaviors among egrets and herons in Louisiana, and crested grebes in England (Huxley, 1914; and see retrospective by Brooke, 2014). These behaviors included ornate shows of plumage, loud calls, and repetitive head and neck movements. They all looked derivative of natural behaviors, but were amplified in intensity, duration, or stereotypy in ways that made them energy-consuming distractions from the prosaic matters of feeding, copulating, and nest-building. For Huxley, these behaviors were selected and shaped for their signal value, a process he called *ritualization* (Huxley, 1923). Eventually, the dramatized behaviors, which Huxley (1914) had named "displays," were emitted apart from their origins and freed of their original functions; they had become *emancipated*, a term coined later by Niko Tinbergen (1953). Fridlund (1994) reviewed ritualization accounts for many primate and non-primate behaviors, e.g., dramatized teeth-baring signals possible attack because biting is part of actual attack.

The Ascent of Behavioral Ecology

As we have discussed, the BET view of facial behavior co-opted the 1950s mechanistic ethology of Lorenz and Tinbergen (Lorenz, 1970; Tinbergen, 1953). Instead of red spots on beaks that released appeasement displays and food calls, prototypical emotional events triggered the release ("expression") of emotion that spilled out on our faces and reflected our "true feelings," except if modified by tradition, training, or treachery (deception).

While BET was drawing upon the Lorenz-Tinbergen formulations, modern ethology was abandoning them, severing BET from any continuity with developing models of animal communication. Animal behaviorists began to recognize that most nonhuman signals, even when dramatized from ritualization, didn't look iconic or cartoony but flexible, social, and contextual (Smith, 1977). These revelations led ethologist Robert Hinde to publish provocative twin papers in 1985. The first, "Expression and Negotiation" (1985a), set forth the new view that displays weren't reflexive but strategic, and the second, "Was 'the Expression of the Emotions' a Misleading Phrase?" (1985b) captured the realization that tying animal signals directly to motivational or emotional state was no longer workable. Experiments by Hinde's student Peter Marler proved Hinde's points by showing that the emission of food calls of roosters, considered an appetitive reflex by earlier ethologists, depended upon the presence of hens and the proximity of other roosters. Such audience effects, or the dependence of dyadic interactions on their social context, were soon seen in humans, and as we reviewed above, the effects were observable even when the audiences were implicit or imaginary (Fridlund, 1994, 2017, for reviews).

Behavioral ecologists (cf. Davies et al., 2012; Maynard Smith, 1982) saw animal signaling not as vestigial reflexes, or readouts of internal state, but as adaptations that served the interests of signalers within their social environments. Signals detrimental overall to the signaler would be deselected quickly. Signalers and recipients—even when they were predator and prey (e.g., "pursuit deterrence" signals; see Caro, 2005)—were reconceived as coevolved dyads in which displays indicated the likely behavior of issuers, with recipients using such behavior as cues to the issuers' next moves (Krebs & Dawkins, 1984).

Human Facial Behaviors as Intention Movements: The Behavioral Ecology View

Although Darwin's vestigial reflexology in *Expression* was outdated, modern behavioral ecology's view of expressive behavior as dynamic and contextual suggested a way to preserve Darwin's grander vision of continuity between human and nonhuman signaling. Thus, in the 1990s, Fridlund and colleagues began writing position papers and conducting studies on what became the BECV. In this account, human facial displays, like animal signals, serve the momentary intent of the displayer toward others in social interaction (reviews by Fridlund, 1994, 2017). ("Intent" here is adduced from interactional trajectory; it does not presuppose that people can articulate and/or will disclose what they intend.)

According to BECV, facial displays serve as social tools, and in line with Dewey's injunction, they should be analyzed on their own terms. Just as contemporary ethology had to divest display behaviors of their presumed causal links to animals' motivational states, then a modern evolutionary view of human facial behavior must center on how that behavior was shaped to

Table 3.1 BET vs. BECV Approaches to Facial Behaviors: "Expressions of Emotion" vs. Functional Social Tools

Facial Behavior	Expressions (BET)	Functional social tools (BECV)*
Smiling	Happiness	Influence interactant to play or affiliate
Pouting	Sadness	Recruit interactant's succor or protection
Scowling	Anger	Influence interactant to submit or retreat
Gasping	Fear	Deflect interactant's attack via submission
Nose scrunching	Disgust	Reject current interaction trajectory
Neutral	"Suppressed emotion" (Poker face)	Lead the interactant nowhere in interaction trajectory

BET = Basic Emotions Theory. BECV = Behavioral Ecology View of facial displays.

* Possible facial tool usage, as reflected by behavioral consequence; displays in BECV are dependent on interactants and their social context (adapted from Crivelli & Fridlund, 2018).

influence its receivers. Early on, Fridlund (1992) suggested that the standard tabulation of faces with the emotions they hypothetically expressed be replaced by one showing the "intent" of those faces and the behavioral effects those faces may produce. Table 3.1 (from Crivelli & Fridlund, 2018) does just that.

Table 3.1 lists common faces which BET hypothesizes are hardwired to express specific emotions, but then per BECV reinterprets those faces in terms of some behaviors they are "designed" to produce. These suggestions are not absolute but probabilistic, and they depend upon the interactants' identities, interaction histories, and the current context of interaction. Thus BECV does not stipulate that only the tabulated facial behaviors will produce those responses. A "yuck" face (for BET, "disgust") can deter interaction as much as a scowl (for BET, "anger"), and a sneer (BET's "contempt") can chasten as much as a frown (BET's "sadness"). Furthermore, BECV recognizes that any facial display can accompany any number of emotions while still having the same outcome. A frowny face with tears streaming can accompany news that is tragic ("My child has cancer") or joyous ("My child doesn't have cancer"). Either situation recruits a hug and words of support. Smiles can be issued by proud parents or serial pedophiles, and in each case they can be disarmingly affiliative (e.g., Fridlund, 2021). Scowls may indicate disapproval (being negated), hurt (wounded), impatient (slowed), anger ("screwed"), frustrated (blocked), and constipated (blocked in another way). Regardless of the accompanying internal state, scowls are likely to deter interaction or divert it toward either repair or counter-provocation.[20]

Deception Reinterpreted

BET took face-reading to the moral realm in its stipulation that "facial lies" (Ekman & Friesen, 1982, p. 240) occurred when people made faces in the absence of theoretically prescribed emotions. Smiles in particular were suspect, because they "conceal and distract observers from the clues to true feelings," and can "convey incorrect information that people are happy when they are not" (p. 240). Ekman and Friesen (1982) suggested they could detect inauthenticity in smile morphology. "Felt" smiles issued when we were happy were accompanied by wincing; these supposedly hard-to-fake faces were later called Duchenne smiles (Ekman et al., 1990). Appeasing or ingratiating "social" smiles were "false" because they were "unfelt" (Ekman & Friesen, 1982). Besides discarding the possibility of genuine, felt politeness, the formulation turned everyday courtesy into mendacity (Fridlund, 2017), and its claims have not been supported, since Duchenne smiles are easily faked and occur in situations where they were unexpected (for reviews, see Crivelli & Fridlund, 2019; and Girard et al., 2021).

Much has been made of the notion of "honest signaling," displays that are difficult and costly to hide or fake, and of the BET-related claim by Robert Frank that so-called facial expressions of emotion are honest because they are involuntary and authentic readouts of internal state (Frank, 1988). We refer readers to Ruth Leys's trenchant takedown of Frank's theorizing (Leys, 2013), and to Searcy and Nowicki's (2005) exhaustive cost-benefit analyses of animal signals. Schmidt and Cohn (2001) provided an extended but dated review of adaptationist approaches to facial behaviors that presumed their links to emotion per BET, and they endorsed the "Duchenne smile" as an honest signal because it was supposedly difficult to fake and costly physiologically and attentionally to produce (p. 14).

Such arguments, based in part on Zahavi's handicap principle, strike us as tendentious, since the costs of any facial behavior are incurred for a few seconds at most, and, as Darwin (1872) indicated, most facial behaviors punctuate and highlight speech, with vocalization and articulation being far costlier physiologically and attentionally. With specific regard to the "Duchenne smile," Cohn's later research was part of the undoing of its special status (Girard et al., 2021).

Because BECV proposes no necessary link between display and emotion, it interprets "deception" interactionally and probabilistically, and this carries pragmatic implications. A used-car salesman may be a consummate Duchenne smiler and scam nearly every customer who walks onto his lot. His winning smiles sell cars, and for BET, then, his smiles must be "felt," and what he feels must be "happiness." Is this what we care about, whether he's happy if he scams us? For BECV, the "authenticity" of the salesman's smile lies not in what he feels, but in whether it predicts whether he will treat us fairly if we buy a car from him. We learn whose words and expressions are reliable indicators of their intent, and over time we are likelier to bond with those individuals we find reliable and avoid those who prove otherwise.

In deception, therefore, the "truth" of a display inheres neither in the display nor its displayer, but in the moving average by which a recipient continually calibrates and recalibrates the reliability of the signals issued in *that* context by *that* displayer. Greater predictability of displayers' signals and lower skepticism by recipients toward those signals naturally coevolve with repeated cooperation, else breaches occur that force recalibration, confrontation, or termination of interaction (Mitchell & Thompson, 1991). The "leakage" of "micromomentary expressions" seen by BET theorists as the breakout of "genuine emotion" through an outer mask (Ekman & Friesen, 1969), and used as a telltale cue of "facial lies," is simply a momentary conflict in intentions in social negotiation, like the displacement behavior shown by birds across a territorial boundary (Fridlund, 1994, 2021).

What Evolved, Exactly, and How?

For BECV, displays evolved as social tools directly, not as parts of underlying mechanisms ("facial affect programs") for the production of displays as stipulated by BET. Shared signal systems, especially in small stable groups, facilitate coalition-formation, collective resource procurement, courtship and mating, and the negotiation of agonistic encounters with minimal bloodshed. We believe that such signaling behaviors and sensitivities to them coevolved granularly and incrementally, when the increments resulted in marginally increased reproductive fitness. Natural and cultural selection do not "care about" (specifically select for) the inner workings of behavioral traits (predispositions), only the traits themselves. Facial behaviors that aid individuals in navigating and reproducing within their social terrains will, via their displayers, proliferate horizontally (i.e., culturally and geographically) and vertically (via genetic/epigenetic inheritance), regardless of what neural operations produce them. Accompanying these displays is the coevolution of recipient behavior that is attentive yet skeptical (Krebs & Dawkins, 1984).

Our belief that our facial behaviors evolved in granular fashion, from the outside in, means that our evolutionary account differs from previous ones, which posited some centrally coordinated emotion machinery (e.g., Al-Shawaf et al., 2016; Tooby & Cosmides, 1990). Such machinery, it is said, can be reverse-engineered to reveal evolved Turing-type computational mechanisms that operate algorithmically to solve recurrent life problems (e.g., anger as a function of computed welfare-tradeoff ratios, by Lukaszewski et al., 2020; and prior "life problem" formulation by Plutchik, 1980). From a selectionist standpoint, such inside-out centralist formulations are problematic, and this is why many evolutionary biologists believe that prominent features of hominin evolution (e.g., bipedalism) occurred atomistically, from numerous independent constituents (e.g., centrally placed foramen magnum, altered spine curvature, broadening and shortening of hip bones, convergent big toe), rather than as a suite of features with a central blueprint (e.g., Williams et al., 2010).[21]

Instead, we conceive of our faces and the ways we use them, along with many other ERBs, as products of granular, discrete-trial deep learning, wherein the training trials are the innumerable trials of life, both ancestrally and currently. Co-occurrences of facial behavior with other ERBs (e.g., vocalization, strategic actions) also arose in similar granular fashion, from the outside in. This view is consistent with neural-network approaches and emerging models of evolutionary computing, which use digital analogues to mutation, recombination, selection, and inheritance to achieve optimal solutions without central governance (cf., Aggarwal, 2018; Keller et al., 2016).

BECV is also agnostic about the respective roles played by nature and nurture in the evolution of our current facial behaviors. Along with other evolutionary accounts (e.g., Al-Shawaf et al., 2016), BECV has no interest in presupposing that any facial display might be or should be universal. The outcome is low-stakes, implying neither biological nor cultural origins, nor any specified interaction of the two. Whether certain facial behaviors are cross-cultural bears mostly on issues like travel, trade, and territory, not human nature (Crivelli & Fridlund, 2019).

We repeat our earlier reminder that natural and cultural selection are deeply intertwined. There are both biological and cultural phylogenies to be reconciled, and biology and culture may interact differently in the evolution of various ERBs and among various cultures and peoples. Only quantitative studies comparing display morphologies and usages to molecular taxonomic analyses across extant peoples and nonhuman primates will reveal the extent of the "phylogenetic signal" in our facial behaviors.

Summary

Researchers of human facial displays took wrong turns when they (a) ignored Dewey's dictum that facial "emotional" behavior should be studied on its own terms rather than as an expression of something else; and (b) mistook Darwin's account of "expressions of the emotions" for a selectionist account and stuck with it. Doing so meant that they missed key developments in animal signaling and communication that stressed adaptation and social negotiation. Long after nonhumans were found to be signaling strategically and contextually, human faces were still being regarded as iconic and "triggered" by the kinds of tripwire mechanisms that reigned in 1950s ethology. BECV attempts to establish a modern Darwinian footing for future research, not by extravagant claims, but by arguing simply that the same evolutionary processes that led to animal displays also led to ours. BECV, we suggest, is the most workable view on how our faces evolved and currently function.[22]

Our view of faces and their outside-in granular evolution has implications for other ERBs and emotion itself. Space permits only brief hints: (a) just as we expect no central "affect programs" for faces in the nervous system, we expect no emotion centers in the brain; (b) autonomic nervous system (ANS) ERBs, whose discussion has been tainted by Walter Cannon's "conservative" view of ANS function, are better understood as actions permissive of patterns of exertion enacted during emotional episodes; (c) *qualia*, as James suggested, are fusions of our interoception and proprioception of those patterns given the "exciting fact" that elicited them (James, 1884, p. 189); and (d) with no emotion centers in the brain, "emotions" themselves exist as conceptualizations of those patterns that have evolved across and within cultures, but there is no inherent organization to ERBs, only an apparent one. From this standpoint, a constructionist view of emotion (Russell, 2003) becomes the most defensible evolutionary one. All these issues await further treatment (Fridlund & Russell, 2025).

Acknowledgment

The authors thank Ruth Leys and Blythe Williams for insightful comments and suggestions.

Notes

1. The term "expression" is problematic because its ordinary usage implies a referent, i.e., an expression must be *of* something, such that the face and body are seen as media conveying content. We use "expression" and "expressive" sparsely and advisedly, with no implication that any content or "thing" is expressed. "Emotions" are equally problematic for scientific usage since there are no consensual inclusion or exclusion criteria by which their presence or absence can be ascertained, making their causal role untestable (Fridlund & Russell, 1996). As a result, our use of "emotion" is informal, and the ERB term refers to behaviors, including the perceiving of *qualia*, that are historically, not necessarily essentially, related to emotion. We remain agnostic on whether emotion, and thus "expressions of emotion," will survive as objects of scientific study.
2. We use "*adaptationism*" throughout to refer to a strategy of *considering* whether a behavior or morphology might be an adaptation, not assuming so. George Williams (1966) and many succeeding authors have cautioned against indiscriminate evolutionary teleonomy.
3. Fridlund (1992, 1994) reviewed the three mechanisms by which Darwin attempted to account for ERBs. Apart from the associationist *Principle of Serviceable Associated Habits*, there were principles of *Direct Action of the Nervous System*, which borrowed from physiologist Johannes Müller and especially Spencer to explain "overflows" like graying of the hair and trembling of the muscles; and *Antithesis*, in which an "opposite frame of mind" (Darwin, 1872, p. 56) produced an antithetical ERB that was, like the original, "of the least service" (p. 284), e.g., affirmation vs. negation using vertical vs. lateral head-nods. Such gestures of affirmation and negation, Darwin found, varied across cultures and were not always antithetical in form (Darwin, 1872, pp. 286–292).
4. It was those parts with "trifling physiological importance" to their possessors that, because they reveal ancestry, "are universally admitted as highly serviceable in the definition of whole groups" (Darwin, 1859, p. 416), i.e., in developing taxonomies.
5. By the time he wrote *Expression* (1872), Darwin was recoiling from criticisms that he: (a) overplayed adaptation via natural selection in early versions of *Origin of Species* (e.g., 1859), which gave only about a dozen pages of nearly 300 to rudiments; and (b) insufficiently acknowledged the presence of neutral or even disadvantageous traits. He addressed these criticisms frankly in *Descent of Man* (1871), the research for which spawned *Expression* (Fridlund, 1994, pp. 15–17).
6. Strictly speaking, genes, or at least their coding regions, only code for proteins, and the pathways from protein synthesis to morphological and behavioral phenotypes are enormously complex.
7. This is conjecture from surface appearance in extant primates. Evolutionary biologists recognize the fundamental distinction between *homology*, or common features due to shared ancestry, vs. *homoplasy*, or common features due to parallel or convergent evolution (Rendall & De Fiore, 2007). More precisely, homoplasic features may look similar, but the genes that code for their development can differ. The homoplasy-homology distinction was important enough for a special issue of the *Journal of Human Evolution* (Vol. 52, 2007). Homologies are only

verified when results from molecular taxonomic analysis accord with those from a morphological feature analysis, and consistency indices suggest a "phylogenetic signal" and exclude homoplasy (Williams, 2007). Whether ERBs can ever be verified as homologous is a matter of controversy, with some observers suggesting that behaviors, or patterns of behavior, are too protean and removed from morphology to be amenable to phylogenetic analysis (e.g., Atz, 1970). Notably, changes in morphology may result in the same genetic coding for dissimilar behaviors in disparate species. For example, Fridlund (1994) suggested that brow raising and knitting may be homologous with the pinna retraction and protraction seen in other primates; the actions of the homologous muscles changed with the bulging of the human cranium and the lowered position of the pinnae on the skull (also see Diogo & Santana, 2017). Similarly, smiles optimize the vocal tract for less-threatening high-pitched sounds, and so they may have originated more for their vocal properties than their visual ones (Fridlund, 1994, pp. 305–306). If so, their morphologies may be a function of genes controlling the development of the oropharyngeal cavity as much as those for the relevant facial muscles.

8. Thus, for Darwin, willful ERBs could be *for* communication, and some courtship and mating signals were presented as such in *Expression*. With the majority of (unwilled) innate expressive habits, however, any communication was incidental. A century later, microsociologist Erving Goffman (1959) termed such incidental signal value "given off" (e.g., yawning mainly exhausts CO_2 but others may infer boredom or fatigue), as opposed to that which is "given" (e.g., winks are issued in collusion and flirtation). As we cover later, this distinction presaged the current ethological information-vs.-influence debate (Stegmann, 2013). Although Darwin recognized that "intercommunication is certainly of high service to many animals" and certain ERBs might have been ancestrally "at first intentional" (p. 61) and serviceable, those ERBs became degenerate habits that currently "may not be of the least use" (p. 48). This applied to both current animals and humans.

9. Savvy readers will recognize this section heading as the title of an influential paper by ethologist Robert Hinde (1985b), whose work we mention later.

10. Tomkins and McCarter (1964) seemed unaware that the facial muscles are primarily tractors and sphincters managing the ocular, nasal, and oral orifices of the mammalian face, and the degree of innervation of the human facial muscles matches the precision of control required for ocular protection, light regulation, olfaction, suckling, feeding, and swallowing (Fridlund, 1994). Whether this finely controlled musculature was a preadaptation for *later* modifications for signaling would turn on evidence that the morphology of the muscles and their neural control departed from that required for their sensorimotor functions. No such evidence has been forthcoming. Tomkins and McCarter also believed that the face "expresses affect, both to others and to the self" (p. 120). This claim of facial feedback, whereby we express affect to ourselves, proves elusive experimentally, with successive waves of confirmations vs. disconfirmations, failures to replicate, and multiple interpretations of any positive results.

11. Along with Ekman, Tomkins deputized Carroll Izard to conduct parallel cross-cultural studies, but Izard was not evangelical about his findings (Izard, 1971), and he proceeded to have a long, influential career in infant development.

12. Tomkins mentioned Allport only once in the entire 1200 pages of the four-volume *Affect, Imagery, Consciousness*, and it was not for his face theory or research, but to scold him for proposing an anti-Freudian discontinuity between childhood and adulthood.

13. Continuing this mechanistic view, Ekman and Cordaro (2011, p. 366) referred to the "inescapability" of certain ERBs "when we are in the grip of an emotion" in order to claim the necessity of "central brain mechanisms that are organizing and directing our emotional responses" via "stored sets of instructions." Whereas Ekman's Neurocultural Theory was largely one of behaviors and prewired triggers, the response mechanisms themselves were now "set into action by automatic appraising mechanisms."

14. At the forefront was Ray Birdwhistell, who pioneered the filming and microanalysis of body movements, faces, voices, and postures, and saw them operating as communicative packages interpretable only in the context of the culture and situation. Ekman repeatedly sparred in print with Birdwhistell, whom he claimed "cannot admit the possibility of universals in facial expressions" (Ekman, 1972, p. 209). Not so. Birdwhistell began his kinesics studies "influenced by Darwin's *Expression* . . . and by my own preoccupation with human universals" (1970, p. 29), and while always conceding a biological foundation, he found that cultural variation in nonverbal behavior, faces included, swamped any commonality. Ekman painted another more famous anthropologist, Margaret Mead, with the same broad brush, even though Mead (1975) believed that "human beings may share a core of innate behaviors . . ." (p. 212).

15. Ekman et al.'s (1969) use of "visually isolated" to describe the Fore was hyperbole; they had been in contact with Westerners since the early 1930s, with wider contact throughout the 1950s and 1960s. Among the preceding visitors was pediatrician-virologist Carlton Gadjusek, escorted initially by anthropologist E. R. Sorenson, who introduced Ekman to the Fore roughly a decade later. Following an extensive series of interviews and clinical examinations of Fore volunteers, Gadjusek won the Nobel Prize in Medicine in 1976 for discovering that funerary

endocannibalism among the Fore, especially the ritualistic consumption of deceased relatives' *brains*, was the transmission vector for their endemic, fatal neurodegenerative malady *kuru* (for history of the neurological and anthropological investigations, see Alpers, 2007; for context of Fore endocannibalism and other issues, see review articles in the *Philosophical Transaction of the Royal Society London B Biological Science*, 2008, *363*, Nov. 27).

16. As Leys (2017) stated the premise, these poses "in their very caricatural intensity are among the best examples we have of what we would be like if we were alone" (Leys, 2017, p. 77). Leys related this "problem of the pose" to the classic problem of determining authorial intent in painting.
17. Darwin noted varied proliferations of "our Domestic Races of animals and plants" (1859, p. 43) due to both deliberate and "unconscious" selective breeding by humans, and expected that selection by nature, i.e., *natural selection*, would result in at least as much proliferation (1859, Chapter 1 and 2).
18. Whether there are such clusters we leave open for the moment.
19. Much of Heinroth's data owed to the efforts of his taxidermist spouse, Magdelana, who worked at Berlin's Natural History Museum and hand-reared nearly every available bird species, over 1,000 birds spanning 28 years, in that single room. Schulze-Hagen and Birkhead (2015) provided a detailed and engaging account of their work.
20. In other words, BECV understands faces as influencers and not content providers, excepting those faces that have taken on symbolic value, like razzes ("Bronx cheers"), tongue-in-cheeks, and collusive winks. In the classic ethological "information or influence" debate (cf., discussions in Stegmann, 2013), BECV aligns itself with the latter. This interactional perspective is analogous to pragmatic accounts of language (for parallels, see Fernández-Dols, 2017) and systems models of nonverbal interaction (Patterson, 2019).
21. We thank Blythe Williams for numerous insights regarding the mosaic nature of anthropoid evolution, and for the bipedalism example.
22. An alternative to BECV's ritualization/conventionalization view (Susskind et al., 2008) proposed that "sensory regulation" (p. 843) was the basis of some facial displays. On this account, Susskind et al. contended that the prototypical "expression of fear" was a face that had brows raised and eyes widened, and these changes evolved because they carried "multiple functional benefits" (p. 845), including widening of the visual field, which allowed less-occluded eye scanning, "more effective sampling of the entire visual field" (p. 845), and enhanced "sensory vigilance" (p. 848). Susskind et al. erred, we believe, in (1) assuming that there is such a prototype fear face, and (2) believing that brow-raised eye-widening "enhances detection of the source of potential threat" (p. 847). Contrary to Susskind et al., optometric researchers have long recognized that squinting, which Susskind et al. equated to "sensory rejection to reduce sensory exposure" (p. 847), actually "improves visual acuity for subjects with refractive error and reduces glare in the superior visual field" (Sheedy et al., p. 740). The acuity enhancement most likely results from both glare reduction and aperture effects, just as higher f-stops on camera lenses reduce glare and enhance depth of field in the refracted images. Ecologically, we suggest that a threatened creature may engage in repeated cycles of (1) widening the eyes and raising the brows to permit wider vigilance at the expense of clarity, alternating with (2) squinting to reduce glare and sharpen detection and recognition of the specific threat. The dynamic nature of this visual strategy is inconsistent with any notion of a prototype "fear" face. Whether these behavioral strategies were ritualized *for* signaling would turn on evidence that their amplitudes and/or durations departed from those required for sensorimotor functions.

References

Aggarwal, C. C. (2018). *Neural networks and deep learning*. Springer. doi: 10.1007/978-3-319-94463-0

Allport, F. H. (1924). *Social psychology*. Houghton Mifflin.

Al-Shawaf, L., Conroy-Beam, D., Asao, K., & Buss, D. (2016). Human emotions: An evolutionary psychological perspective. *Emotion Review, 8*, 173–186. doi: 10.1177/1754073914565518

Al-Shawaf, L., & Lewis, D. M. G. (2017). Evolutionary psychology and the emotions. In V. Zeigler-Hill & T. K. Shackelford (Eds.), *Encyclopedia of personality and individual differences*. Springer, Cham. doi: 10.1007/978-3-319-28099-8_516-1

Atz, J. W. (1970). The application of the idea of homology to behavior. In L. R. Aronson, E. Tobach, D. S. Lehrman, & J. S. Rosenblatt (Eds.), *Development and evolution of behavior: Essays in memory of T. C. Schnierla* (pp. 53–74). Freeman.

Aviezer, H., & Hassin, R. R. (2017). Inherently ambiguous: An argument for contextualized emotion perception. In J.-M. Fernández-Dols & J. A. Russell (Eds.), *The science of facial expression* (pp. 333–349). Oxford University Press.

Bąk, H. K. (2016). *Emotional prosody processing for non-native English speakers*. Springer.

Barrett, L. F., Adolphs, R., Marsella, S., Martinez, A. M., & Pollak, S. D. (2019). Emotional expressions reconsidered: Challenges to inferring emotion from human facial movements. *Psychological Science in the Public Interest, 20*, 1–68. doi:10.1177/1529100619832930

Birdwhistell, R. L. (1970). *Kinesics and context*. University of Pennsylvania.

Brooke, M. (2014). In retrospect: The courtship habits of the great crested grebe. *Nature, 513*, 484–485. doi: 10.1038/513484a

Burkhardt, R. W. (1985). Darwin on animal behavior and evolution. In Kohn D. (Ed.), *The Darwinian heritage* (pp. 327–365). Princeton University Press.

Buss, D. (2014). Evolutionary criteria for considering an emotion "basic": Jealousy as an illustration. *Emotion Review, 6*, 313–315. doi: 10.1177/1754073914534481

Caro, T. M. (2005). *Antipredator defenses in birds and mammals.* University of Chicago Press

Coleman, W. L. (1977). *Biology in the nineteenth century: Problems of form, function, and transformation.* Cambridge University Press.

Colombetti, G. (2014). *The feeling body: Affective science meets the enactive mind.* MIT Press.

Crivelli, C., & Fridlund, A. J. (2018). Facial displays are tools for social influence. *Trends in Cognitive Sciences, 22*, 388–399. doi: 10.1016/j.tics.2018.02.006

Crivelli, C., & Fridlund, A. J. (2019). Inside-out: From Basic Emotions Theory to the Behavioral Ecology View. *Journal of Nonverbal Behavior, 43*, 161–194. doi: 10.1007/s10919-019-00294-2

Crivelli, C., & Gendron, M. (2017). Facial expressions and emotions in indigenous societies. In J. M. Fernández-Dols & J. A. Russell (Eds.), *The science of facial expression* (pp. 497–515). Oxford University Press.

Darwin, C. R. (1859). *On the origin of species, or the preservation of favoured races in the struggle for life.* Murray. http://darwin-online.org.uk/converted/pdf/1859_Origin_F373.pdf

Darwin, C. R. (1871). *The descent of man, and selection in relation to sex.* Murray.

Darwin, C. R. (1872). *Expression of the emotions in man and animals.* Albemarle. https://archive.org/details/Darwin1915Emotions/page/n3/mode/2up

Davies, N. B., Krebs, J. R., & West, S. A. (2012). *An introduction to behavioural ecology* (4th ed.). Wiley-Blackwell.

Dewey, J. (1894). The theory of emotion. (I) Emotional attitudes. *Psychological Review, 1*, 553–569.

Diogo, R., & Santana, S. E. (2017). Evolution of facial musculature. In J. M. Fernández-Dols & J. A. Russell (Eds.), *The science of facial expression* (pp. 133–152). Oxford University Press

Durán, J. I., Reisenzein, R., & Fernández-Dols, J. M. (2017). Coherence between emotions and facial expressions. In J. M. Fernández-Dols & J. A. Russell (Eds.), *The science of facial expression* (pp. 107–129). Oxford University Press

Ekman, P. (1972). Universal and cultural differences in facial expressions of emotion. In J. R. Cole (Ed.), *Nebraska Symposium on Motivation, 1971* (Vol. 19, pp. 207–283). Nebraska University Press.

Ekman, P. (1981). Mistakes when deceiving. *Annals of the New York Academy of Sciences, 364*(1), 269–278. doi:10.1111/j.1749-6632.1981.tb34479.x

Ekman, P. (1984). Expression and the nature of emotion. In K. Scherer & P. Ekman (Eds.), *Approaches to emotion* (pp. 319–344). Lawrence Erlbaum Associates.

Ekman, P. (1985). *Telling lies.* Norton.

Ekman, P. (1992). An argument for basic emotions. *Cognition and Emotion, 6*, 169–200. doi:10.1080/02699939208411068

Ekman, P. (1994). All emotions are basic. In P. Ekman and R. J. Davidson (Eds.), *The nature of emotion* (pp. 15–19). Oxford University Press.

Ekman, P. (1997). Expression or communication about emotion. In N. L. Segal, G. E. Weisfeld, & C. C. Weisfeld (Eds.), *Uniting biology and psychology: Integrated perspectives on human development* (pp. 315–338). APA Press.

Ekman, P. (1999). Basic emotions. In T. Dalgleish and M. J. Power (Eds.), *Handbook of cognition and emotion* (pp. 45–60). Wiley.

Ekman, P. (2003). Sixteen enjoyable emotions. *Emotion Researcher, 18*, 6–7.

Ekman, P. (2006). Cross-cultural studies of facial expression. In P. Ekman (Ed.), *Darwin and facial expression* (pp. 228–298). Malor Books.

Ekman, P. (2017). Facial expressions. In J. M. Fernández-Dols & J. A. Russell (Eds.), *The science of facial expression* (pp. 39–56). Oxford University Press

Ekman, P., & Cordaro, D. (2011). What is meant by calling emotions basic? *Emotion Review, 3*(4), 364–370. doi: 10.1177/1754073911410740

Ekman, P., Davidson, R. J., & Friesen, W. V. (1990). The Duchenne smile: Emotional expression and brain physiology: II. *Journal of Personality and Social Psychology, 58*, 342–353. doi: 10.1037/0022-3514.58.2.342

Ekman, P., & Friesen, W. V. (1969). Nonverbal leakage and clues to deception. *Psychiatry: Journal for the Study of Interpersonal Processes, 32*(1), 88–106.

Ekman, P., & Friesen, W. V. (1975). *Unmasking the face: A guide to recognizing emotions from facial clues.* Prentice-Hall.

Ekman, P., & Friesen, W. V. (1982). Felt, false, and miserable smiles. *Journal of Nonverbal Behavior, 6*, 238–252. doi: 10.1007/BF00987191

Ekman, P., Sorenson, E. R., & Friesen, W. V. (1969). Pan-cultural elements in facial displays of emotions. *Science, 164*, 86–88. doi: 10.1126/science.164.3875.86

Ershadi, M., Goldstein, T. R., Pochedly, J., & Russell, J. A. (2018). Facial expressions as performances in mime. *Cognition and Emotion, 32*(3), 494–503. doi: 10.1080/02699931.2017.1317236

Fehr, B., Russell, J. A. (1984). Concept of emotion viewed from a prototype perspective. *Journal of Experimental Psychology: General, 113*, 464–486. doi: 10.1037/0096-3445.113.3.464

Fernández-Dols, J. M. (2017). Natural facial expression. In J. M. Fernández-Dols & J. A. Russell (Eds.), *The science of facial expression* (pp. 457–476). Oxford University Press.

Fernández-Dols, J. M., & Crivelli, C. (2013). Emotion and expression: Naturalistic studies. *Emotion Review, 5*, 24–29. doi: 10.1177/1754073912457229

Frank, R. H. (1988). *Passions within reason: The strategic role of the emotions*. W. W. Norton.

Fridlund, A. J. (1992). Darwin's anti-Darwinism in The Expression of the Emotions in Man and Animals. In K. Strongman (ed.), *International review of emotion* (Vol. 2, pp. 117–137). Wiley.

Fridlund, A. J. (1994). *Human facial expression: An evolutionary view*. Academic Press.

Fridlund, A. J. (2017). The behavioral ecology view of facial displays, 25 years later. In J. M. Fernández-Dols & J. A. Russell (Eds.), *The science of facial expression* (pp. 77–92). Oxford University Press.

Fridlund, A. J. (2021). Do faces lie? Ted Bundy and the smiles of strangers. In C. J. Liberman (Ed.), *Casing nonverbal communication* (pp. 109–125). Kendall-Hunt.

Fridlund, A. J., & Duchaine, B. (1996). "Facial Expressions of Emotion" and the delusion of the hermetic self. In R. Harré & W. G. Parrott (Eds.), *The emotions* (pp. 259–284). Cambridge University Press.

Fridlund, A. J., & Russell, J. A. (1996). The functions of facial expression: What's in a face? In V. Manusov and M. L. Patterson (Eds.), *Sage handbook of nonverbal communication* (pp. 299–319). Sage.

Fridlund, A. J., & Russell, J. A. (2025). The evolution of emotion and its expression: A brief history and a 21st-century view. Manuscript in preparation.

Friesen, W. V. (1972). *Cultural differences in facial expressions in a social situation: An experimental test of the concept of display rules*. Unpublished doctoral dissertation. University of California, San Francisco.

Gendron, M., & Barrett, L. (2017). Facing the past: A history of the face in psychological research on emotion perception. In J. M. Fernández-Dols & J. A. Russell (Eds.), *The science of facial expression* (pp. 15–36). Oxford University Press.

Ghiselin, M. T. (1969). *The triumph of the Darwinian method*. University of California Press.

Girard, J. M., Cohn, J. F., Yin, L., & Morency, L. -P. (2021). Reconsidering the Duchenne smile: Formalizing and testing hypotheses about eye constriction and positive emotion. *Affective Science, 2*, 32–47. doi: 10.1007/s42761-020-00030-w

Goffman, E. (1959). *The presentation of self in everyday life*. Anchor.

Hinde, R. A. (1985a). Expression and negotiation. In G. Zivin (Ed.), *The development of expressive behavior* (pp. 103–116). Academic Press.

Hinde, R. A. (1985b). Was "the Expression of the Emotions" a misleading phrase? *Animal Behaviour, 33*, 985–992. doi: 10.1016/S0003-3472(85)80032-4

Huxley, J. (1914). The courtship habits of the great crested grebe (*Podiceps cristatus*); with an addition to the theory of natural selection. *Proceedings of the Zoological Society of London, 35*, 491–562.

Huxley, J. (1923). Courtship activities in the red-throated diver (*Colymbus stellatus*); together with a discussion of the evolution of courtship in birds. *Journal of the Linnean Society of London, Zoology, 53*, 253–292.

Izard, C. E. (1971). *The face of emotion*. Appleton-Century-Crofts.

Jackson, J. C., Watts, J., Henry, T. R., List, J.-M., Forkel, R., Mucha, P. J., Greenhill, S. J., Gray, R. D., & Lindquist, K. A. (2019). Emotion semantics show both cultural variation and universal structure. *Science, 366*, 1517–1522. doi: 10.1126/science.aaw8160

James, W. (1884). What is an emotion? *Mind, 9*, 188–205.

Johnson-Laird, P. N., & Oatley, K. (1989). The language of emotions: An analysis of a semantic field. *Cognition and Emotion, 3*, 81–123. doi: 10.1080/02699938908408075

Keller, J. M., Liu, D., & Fogel, D. B. (2016). *Fundamentals of computational intelligence: Neural networks, fuzzy systems, and evolutionary computation*. Wiley IEEE Press.

Keltner, D., & Cordaro, D. T. (2017). Understanding multimodal emotional expressions: Recent advancers in Basic Emotion theory. In J. M. Fernández-Dols & J. A. Russell (Eds.), *The science of facial expression* (pp. 57–75). Oxford University Press.

Keltner, D., & Ekman, P. (2000). Facial expression of emotion. In M. Lewis & J. Haviland-Jones (Eds.), *Handbook of emotions* (2nd ed.) (pp. 236–249). Guilford.

Keltner, D., Sauter, D., Tracy, J., & Cowen, A. (2019). Emotional expression: Advances in basic emotion theory. *Journal of Nonverbal behavior, 43*, 133–160. https://doi.org/10.1007/s10919-019-00293-3

Klineberg, O. (1938). Emotional expression in Chinese literature. *Journal of Abnormal and Social Psychology, 33*, 517–520. doi: 10.1037/h0057105

Kowalska, M., & Wróbel. M. (2017). Basic emotions. In V. Zeigler-Hill & T. K. Shackelford (Eds.), *Encyclopedia of personality and individual differences*. Springer, Cham. doi: 10.1007/978-3-319-28099-8_495-1

Krebs, J. R., & Dawkins, R. (1984). Animal signals: Mind-reading and manipulation. In J. R. Krebs & N. B. Davies (Eds.), *Behavioural ecology* (2nd ed., pp. 380–402). Blackwell.

Kreibig, S. D. (2010). Autonomic nervous system activity in emotion: A review. *Biological Psychology, 84*, 394–421. doi:10.1016/j.biopsycho.2010.03.010

Lacal, I., & Ventura, R. (2018). Epigenetic inheritance: Concepts, mechanisms, and perspectives. *Frontiers in Molecular Neuroscience, 11*. doi: 10.3389/fnmol.2018.00292

Laukka, P., & Elfenbein, H. A. (2021). Cross-cultural emotion recognition and in-group advantage in vocal expression: A meta-analysis. *Emotion Review, 13*, 3–11. doi: 10.1177/1754073919897295

Leys, R. (2013). A world without pretense. *Philosophy of Education, 69*, 25–42. doi: 10.47925/2013.025

Leys, R. (2017). *The ascent of affect: Genealogy and critique*. University of Chicago Press.

Lorenz, K. Z. (1970). *Studies on animal and human behavior*, Vols. 1 & 2. Harvard University Press.

Lukaszewski, A. W., Lewis, D. M. G., Durkee, P. K., Sell, A. N., Sznycer, D., & Buss, D. M. (2020). An adaptationist framework for personality science. *European Journal of Personality, 34*(6), 1151–1174. doi:10.1002/per.2292

Martinez, B., Valstar, M. F., Jiang, B., & Pantic, M. (2019). Automatic analysis of facial actions: A survey. *IEEE Transactions on Affective Computing, 10*, 325–347. doi: 10.1109/TAFFC.2017.2731763

Maynard Smith, J. (1982). *Evolution and the theory of games*. Cambridge University Press.

Mead, M. (1975). Review of *Darwin and facial expression*. *Journal of Communication, 25*, 209–213.

Mendoza-Straffon, L. (Ed.). (2016). *Cultural phylogenetics*. Springer.

Mitchell, R. W., & Thompson, N. S. (1991). Projects, routines, and enticements in dog-human play. In P. P. G. Bateson & P. H. Klopfer (Eds.), *Perspectives in ethology*, Vol. 9: *Human understanding and animal awareness* (pp. 189–216). Plenum.

Nelson, N., & Russell, J. A. (2013). Universality revisited. *Emotion Review, 5*, 8–15. doi: 10.1177/1754073912457227

Ortony, A., & Turner, T. J. (1990). What's basic about basic emotions? *Psychological Review, 97*(3), 315–331. doi:10.1037/0033-295X.97.3.315

Patterson, M. L. (2019). A systems model of dyadic nonverbal interaction. *Journal of Nonverbal Behavior, 43*, 111–132. doi: 10.1007/s10919-018-00292-w

Podos, J. (1994). Early perspectives on the evolution of behavior: Charles Otis Whitman and Oskar Heinroth. *Ethology, Ecology & Evolution, 6*(4), 467–480. doi: 10.1080/08927014.1994.9522972

Plutchik, R. (1980). *Emotions: A psychoevolutionary synthesis*. Harper & Row.

Rendall, D., & Di Fiore, A. (2007). Homoplasy, homology, and the perceived special status of behavior in evolution. *Journal of Human Evolution, 52*, 504–521. doi: 10.1016/J.JHEVOL.2006.11.014

Russell, J. A. (1994). Is there universal recognition of emotion from facial expression? A review of the cross-cultural studies. *Psychological Bulletin, 115*, 102–141. doi: 10.1037/0033-2909.115.1.102

Russell, J. A. (2003). Core affect and the psychological construction of emotion. *Psychological Review, 110*, 145–172. doi: 10.1037/0033-295x.110.1.145

Russell, J. A. (2017). Toward a broader perspective on facial expressions. In J. M. Fernández-Dols & J. A. Russell (Eds.), *The science of facial expression* (pp. 93–105). Oxford University Press.

Russell, J. A., & Fernández-Dols, J. M. (1996). What does a facial expression mean? In J. A. Russell & J. M. Fernández-Dols (Eds.), *The psychology of facial expression* (pp. 3–30). Cambridge University Press.

Schmidt, K. L., & Cohn, J. F. (2001). Human facial expressions as adaptations: Evolutionary questions in facial expression research. *Yearbook of Physical Anthropology, 44*, 3–24. doi: 10.1002/ajpa.20001

Schulze-Hagen, K., & Birkhead, T. R. (2015). The ethology and life history of birds: The forgotten contributions of Oskar, Magdalena, and Katharina Heinroth. *Journal of Ornithology, 156*, 9-18. doi: 10.1007/s10336-014-1091-3

Searcy, W. A., & Nowicki, S. (2005). *The evolution of animal communication: Reliability and deception in signaling systems*. Princeton University Press.

Shariff, A. F., & Tracy, J. L. (2011). What are emotion expressions for? *Current Directions in Psychological Science, 20*, 395–399. doi: 10.1177/0963721411424739

Sheedy, J. E., Truong, S. D., & Hayes, J. R. (2003). What are the visual benefits of eyelid squinting? *Optometry and Vision Science, 80*, 740–744.

Skvortsova, K., Iovino, N., & Bogdanović, O. (2018). Functions and mechanisms of epigenetic inheritance in animals. *Nature Reviews Molecular Cell Biology, 19*(12). doi: 10.1038/s41580-018-0074

Smith, W. J. (1977). *The behavior of communicating*. Cambridge University Press.

Snyder, P. J., Kaufman, R., Harrison, J., & Maruf, P. (2010). Charles Darwin's emotional expression "experiment" and his contribution to modern neuropharmacology. *Journal of the History of the Neurosciences, 19*, 158–170. doi: 10.1080/09647040903506679

Sorenson, E. R. (1975). *Culture and the expression of emotion*. Aldine.
Spencer, H. (1855). *Principles of psychology*. Longman, Brown, Green, & Longmans.
Stegmann, U. (Ed.) (2013). *Animal communication theory: Information and influence*. Cambridge University Press.
Sulloway, F. J. (1982). Darwin and his finches: The evolution of a legend. *Journal of the History of Biology, 15*, 1–53.
Susskind, J. M., Lee, D. H., Cusi, A., Feiman, R., Grabski, W., & Anderson, A. K. (2008). Expressing fear enhances sensory acquisition. *Nature Neuroscience, 11*, 843–850. doi: 10.1038/nn.2138
Tinbergen, N. (1953). *Social behaviour in animals*. Chapman and Hall.
Tomkins, S. S. (1962). *Affect, imagery, consciousness*, Vol. I: *The positive affects*. Tavistock.
Tomkins, S. S. (2008). *Affect, imagery, consciousness: The complete edition*. Springer.
Tomkins, S. S., & McCarter, R. (1964). What and where are the primary affects? Some evidence for a theory. *Perceptual and Motor Skills, 18*, 119–158.
Tooby, J., & Cosmides, L. (1990). The past explains the present: Emotional adaptations and the structure of ancestral environments. *Ethology and Sociobiology, 11*, 375–424. doi: 10.1016/0162-3095(90)90017-Z
Touroutoglou, A., Lindquist, K. A., Dickerson, B. C., & Barrett, L. F. (2015). Intrinsic connectivity in the human brain does not reveal networks for "basic" emotions. *Social Cognitive and Affective Neuroscience, 10*, 1257–1265. doi: 10.1093/scan/nsv013
Tracy, J. L., Randles, D., & Steckler, C. M. (2015). The nonverbal communication of emotions. *Current Opinion in Behavioral Sciences, 3*, 25–30. https://doi.org/10.1016/j.cobeha.2015.01.001
Ward, P. (2018). *Lamarck's revenge*. Bloomsbury.
Wierzbicka, A. (1992). Talking about emotions: Semantics, culture, and cognition. *Cognition and Emotion, 6*, 285–319. https://doi.org/10.1080/02699939208411073
Williams, B. A. (2007). Comparing levels of homoplasy in the primate skeleton. *Journal of Human Evolution, 52*, 480–489. doi: 10.1016/j.jhevol.2006.11.011
Williams, B. A., Kay, R. F., & Kirk, E. C. (2010). New perspectives on primate evolution. *Proceedings of the National Academy of Sciences, 107*, 4797–4804. doi: 10.1073/pnas.0908320107
Williams, G. C. (1966). *Adaptation and natural selection*. Princeton University Press.
Wundt, W. (1894). *Lectures on human and animal psychology*. Swan Sonnenschein.

CHAPTER 4

Social Emotions Are Governed by a Common Grammar of Social Valuation: Theoretical Foundations and Applications to Human Personality and the Criminal Justice System

Coltan Scrivner, Daniel Sznycer, Aaron W. Lukaszewski, and Laith Al-Shawaf

Abstract

Social emotions appear to be behavior-regulating programs built by natural selection to solve adaptive problems in the domain of social valuation. For example, shame functions to prevent and mitigate the costs of being socially devalued by others, whereas anger functions to correct those people who attach insufficient weight to the welfare of the self. This chapter reviews theory and evidence suggesting that distinctively functional social emotions such as guilt, gratitude, anger, pride, shame, sadness, and envy are all governed by a shared grammar of social valuation. The authors also provide evidence that social emotions and social valuation operate with a substantial degree of universality across cultures. This emotion-valuation constellation appears to shape human sociality through interpersonal interactions. Expanding upon this, they explore how signatures of this constellation may be evident in two spheres of human sociality: personality and the criminal justice system.

Key Words: social emotions, social valuation, personality, criminal justice, emotion-valuation constellation

Social Valuation and Social Emotions

What underlies social valuation? Evolutionarily, the origin of valuation is closely linked with the degree to which a person positively or negatively impacts the fitness of the valuer. Numerous theories have been proposed to explain the evolution of psychological mechanisms that regulate conspecific valuation, including kin selection (Hamilton, 1964), reciprocation (Trivers, 1971), partner choice (Noë & Hammerstein, 1994), reputation (Nowak & Sigmund, 1998), risk-pooling (Kaplan & Hill, 1985), and externality management (Tooby & Cosmides, 1996). Stemming from these theories are a suite of empirical discoveries that mapped the neurocognitive architecture involved in computing the social value of a target to a valuer. The two key inputs processed by these neurocognitive mechanisms include (1) the target's probable contribution of fitness benefits to the valuer as, for example, kin, mate, trading partner, and fellow coalition member, and (2) the target's probable imposition of fitness costs on the valuer, if not appeased (Barclay & Willer, 2007; Cacioppo et al., 1999; Cuddy et al., 2008; Gilbert, 1997; Hare et al., 2010; Klein et al., 2008; Levy & Glimcher, 2012; Lieberman et al., 2007; Lukaszewski et al., 2015; Sell et al., 2009; Sznycer et al., 2019; Sznycer, De Smet, et al., 2016). The direction and magnitude of these two classes of inputs jointly determine the social value of the target, which influences the degree to which the valuer will sacrifice his or her welfare for a target (Tooby et al., 2008).

Adaptive problems of social valuation include (1) the value of self to others, (2) the value of others to the self, and (3) the loss of valuable others. These adaptive problems would have led to the evolution of neurocognitive programs that efficiently and effectively compute variables relevant to social valuation and lead to on-average adaptive behavioral responses in the situations described above.

Emotions appear to play a central role in how humans solve adaptive problems of social valuation. Emotions have been characterized by evolutionary theorists as neurocognitive adaptations designed by natural selection to orchestrate cognition and behavior in the service of solving complex adaptive problems. The social emotions can be understood as a subset of emotions that solve problems of sociality (Darwin, 1872; Ekman, 1992; Keltner & Haidt, 1999; Nesse, 1990; Tooby, 1985; Tooby & Cosmides, 1990;). These emotions function in part to recalibrate internal variables of the cognitive architecture, including variables that index the social valuations assigned by self and others (Al-Shawaf et al., 2016; Al-Shawaf & Lewis, 2017; Delton & Robertson, 2016; Sell et al., 2009; Sznycer, Cosmides, et al., 2017; Sznycer, Seal, et al., 2017; Sznycer et al., forthcoming; Tooby & Cosmides, 2008). With its emphasis on adaptive problem and adaptive function, this perspective can make sense of many known facts about the social emotions, because natural selection produces close fits between the structure of an adaptive problem and the features of the adaptation that evolved to solve it. For example:

- **Gratitude** appears designed to *enhance cooperation with a social partner* (Algoe et al., 2008; Lim, 2012; Smith et al., 2017). Gratitude is triggered by indications that a conspecific values the focal individual more than expected (Algoe et al., 2008; Lim, 2012; Smith et al., 2017; Tesser et al., 1968; Tsang, 2006a, 2006b). Once activated, gratitude increases the value the individual attaches to the conspecific's welfare (Gordon et al., 2012; Lim, 2012; Smith et al., 2017), which can lead to an escalating cycle of mutual valuation, along with beneficial outcomes for both parties (Algoe et al., 2008; Algoe et al., 2013; Tooby & Cosmides, 1996).
- **Pride** appears to motivate the a*chievement and advertisement of socially valued acts or traits* by someone so that others place more value on that individual's welfare (Cohen et al., 2020; Durkee et al., 2019; Fessler, 1999; Schniter et al., 2020; Sznycer, Al-Shawaf, et al., 2017; Sznycer & Cohen, 2021a; Tracy et al., 2010; Weisfeld, 1999). Pride is triggered in response to achievements—events indicating that an individual has an enhanced capacity to deliver benefits or impose costs on others, along with an associated increase in status (Lewis et al., 1992; Tracy & Matsumoto, 2008). When triggered, the pride system advertises achievements, motivates continued investment in courses of action that bring about achievement, and solicits enhanced valuation from others (Cheng et al., 2013; Riskind & Gotay, 1982; Tracy & Robins, 2008; Weisfeld, 1999; Williams & DeSteno, 2008).
- **Anger** functions to *bargain for better treatment* (Sell, 2011; Sell et al., 2017; Sell & Sznycer, Chapter 6 in this volume). Anger is activated in response to indications that another person places insufficient value on the welfare of the focal individual—less

value than the individual feels entitled to (Sell et al., 2009, 2017). Once triggered, the anger system deploys various tactics to incentivize the other to increase her valuation of the individual: communication of the anger state (Galati et al., 2003; Sell et al., 2014), arguments (Averill, 1982; Sell et al., 2017), and threats of (or actual) withdrawal of assistance or imposition of costs (Daly & Wilson, 1988; Felson, 1982; Sell, 2011).

- **Guilt** appears designed to *remedy situations where one put insufficient weight on the welfare of a valuable other* (often unintentionally), independent of whether the other person knows this (Baumeister et al., 1994; Leith & Baumeister, 1998; McGraw, 1987; Smith et al., 2002; Sznycer, 2010, 2019; Tooby & Cosmides, 2008). Once triggered, the guilt system increases the value that the focal individual attaches to the other's welfare: It interrupts the imposition of costs (Cohen et al., 2013; Cohen et al., 2014) and motivates actions to benefit the victim and repair the relationship through restitutions, amends, apologies, confessions, and acceptance of responsibility (Baumeister et al., 1995; de Hooge et al., 2007; Ketelaar & Au, 2003; Leith & Baumeister, 1998; Ohtsubo & Yagi, 2015; Schniter et al., 2013; Sznycer et al., 2015; Tangney, 1991).

- **Sadness** is activated by the *separation, incapacitation, or death of associates who may otherwise value the individual's welfare and make positive fitness contributions to her* (Keller & Nesse, 2006; Tooby & Cosmides, 1990; see also Hagen, 1999; Hagen & Barrett, 2007). When activated, sadness reduces the motivation to move and to act (Michalak et al., 2009), a response that can prevent behaviors causing further loss (Keller & Nesse, 2006; Welling, 2003). Also, sadness may prompt cognitive activity geared to solve problems related to the loss or to adapt to the loss (Andrews & Thomson, 2009).

- **Shame** functions to *minimize the spread of negative information about the self and the cost of any ensuing devaluation from others* (Durkee et al., 2019; Fessler, 1999; Gilbert, 1997; Landers et al., Chapter 7 in this volume; Sznycer & Cohen, 2021b; Sznycer, Tooby, et al., 2016; Weisfeld & Dillon, 2012). Shame is triggered by indications of probable or actual social devaluation (Dickerson et al., 2008; Robertson et al., 2018; Smith et al., 2002). Shame motivates the individual to inhibit actions that may cause further social devaluation (de Hooge et al., 2008; Fehr & Gächter, 2000), to conceal incriminating information (Leach & Cidam, 2015; Sznycer et al., 2015), and to withdraw from the situation (Wicker et al., 1983). When ashamed, the individual appeases (Keltner et al., 1997) and produces a stereotyped nonverbal display that deters attacks by signaling subordination (Fessler, 1999; Gilbert, 2000; Keltner et al., 1997; Tracy & Matsumoto, 2008; Weisfeld & Dillon, 2012).

- **Envy** is elicited by *indications of competitive superiority in one's positional rivals*. Envy functions to suppress the advantages of one's rivals, a strategy which may be beneficial for the focal individual in zero-sum competitions (Foster, 1965; Gershman, 2015; Hill & Buss, 2008; Lin & Bates, 2020; Schoeck, 1969; Smith & Kim, 2007; Sznycer, Seal, et al., 2017). Envy even motivates the imposition of costs on rivals when the actions are costly to the envious individual himself. Envy combines spite and stealth in the deployment of the spite (Schoeck, 1969). The stealth appears to be a design feature to minimize the cost of spite to the envious individual. Without stealth, the focal individual may face serious costs: spite invites its targets to retaliate against the spiteful individual, the targets of envious spite tend to be (by definition) in a superior position to retaliate, and envy can be understood as an implicit admission of competitive disadvantage that can be used to exploit the envious individual. Envy is associated with schadenfreude—joy in the misfortune of others (Brigham et al., 1997; Sznycer et al., in prep.; van Dijk et al., 2015).

Each of these social emotions—gratitude, pride, anger, guilt, sadness, shame, and envy—are triggered by specific inputs and produce cognitive and behavioral outputs that appear to be functional in solving specific adaptive problems; they have particular information-processing procedures, core-affective properties (Nelson & Russell, 2014; Russell, 1980), physiological signatures (Blascovich & Mendes, 2010; Siegel et al., 2018), and behavioral repertoires.

Here, we argue that despite the functional and structural differences between the different social emotions, they may all be informed by a common set of evaluations. The human mind is expected to aptly appraise the events that trigger these emotions in the local ecology. That is, the mind is expected to accurately estimate the social value that is imputed locally to, for example, being generous, which may form the basis of the activation of pride (if one is generous), the activation of envy (if a rival is generous), and so on. Indeed, it has been hypothesized that the human mind features a generative grammar with universal principles and open parameters that computes the social value of an individual based on that individual's actions (e.g., shares food), traits (e.g., physically formidable), and characteristics (e.g., sibling of chief), and that social emotions consult relevant social values to modulate their operation (Jackendoff, 2006; Sznycer, 2019; Sznycer, Al-Shawaf, et al., 2017; Tooby & Cosmides, 2008).

The Grammar of Valuation

A prediction can be derived from this line of reasoning about social valuation: If performing an action or displaying a trait leads to a positive or negative evaluation of a target individual, then that action or trait may elicit multiple social emotions. For example, wisdom might be a trait that is valued by members of a social group (that is, a positive valuation is attached to those who display wisdom). In this group, *pride* may be activated in a person who displays wisdom; they may feel *anger* if their wisdom is not recognized; the death of a wise person may trigger *sadness*; a person may feel *shame* if they publicly do something that is unwise; *guilt* may be triggered in a person who unintentionally undervalues a wise person; and *envy* may be triggered if one's rival displays wisdom. In each case, the trait (wisdom) is being consulted by the social emotion (pride, anger, sadness, shame, guilt, envy) when the input condition of the emotion is met—having the valued trait in the case of pride; not receiving enough respect for possessing the trait in the case of anger; losing a close other who has the trait in the case of sadness; inadvertently undervaluing someone who possesses the trait in the case of guilt; and others believing that you lack the trait in the case of shame.

A key part of the conceptual framework of the grammar of valuation is that the local value attached to the action or trait (wisdom, in this example) will be—as a first approximation—the same, regardless of which social emotion is accessing the value. For example, the value placed on wisdom in some local ecology would be the same whether it is being accessed by the pride system or the anger system. From this, it may be predicted that the degree to which a trait/action is valued will correspond with the intensity of the social emotion that is triggered by the trait/action. In other words, the more an act causes community members to socially value a target individual who performed that act, the more intense emotions will be mobilized in response to a situation involving that act. Critically, this should be true not only for a single emotion triggered by the action/trait, but also across multiple social emotions that are triggered by the corresponding input situation that involves that action/trait. For example, if athleticism is more highly valued than botanical knowledge in a given social ecology, then, everything else being equal, the intensity of *anger* will be higher when, e.g., someone fails to acknowledge one's athleticism than when someone fails to acknowledge one's botanical knowledge; the intensity of *gratitude* will be higher when someone convinces others that one is athletic than when someone convinces others that one has botanical knowledge; the intensity of *envy* will be higher when one's rival has superior athleticism compared to when one's rival displays superior botanical knowledge, and so on.

Matching the intensity of emotion to the precise value of the elicitor is necessary, because over-activation and under-activation of an emotion relative to the eliciting condition are costly errors. If social emotions are well-engineered adaptations, they should make valuation estimates based on the local social ecology. In some cases, an inaccurate estimate may lead to an emotional display that is not cost-efficient. For example, displaying too much shame for a minor offense means that one accepts steeper devaluation from others than what is warranted by the facts—a maladaptive response. Similarly, displaying too little shame can also result in shunning and the imposition of costs. In some cases, an inaccurate estimate may actually lead to devaluation, such as exhibiting too much pride when it is unwarranted. To guide emotion-activation in a functional manner, social emotions should consult the grammar of valuation to estimate the value that the relevant action or trait affords to local audiences and modulate their activation accordingly.

One of the key functions of emotions is to evaluate future courses of action (Bechara et al., 2000; Schwarz, 2000; Sznycer, Tooby, et al., 2016). However, the ability to evaluate future courses of action only when audience feedback is available would be inefficient, particularly in a species that is equipped with imagination and prospection. Because of this, social emotions should track action/trait valuations even in the absence of communication between the audience and the focal individual. In other words, social emotions are expected to mobilize in anticipation and during the *imagining* of their respective input situation, and not just during the actual situation (Van Der Schalk et al., 2012). From this, we can predict that the anticipated or imagined intensity of social emotions will accurately and precisely track the values afforded to audiences by the relevant acts and traits.

The Grammar of Valuation Appears to Be Universal

The argument so far makes the case that the information-processing structure of social emotions and the grammar of valuation are evolved, species-typical adaptations in humans. If this is the case, the predicted associations between social valuation and the intensities of multiple emotions should be observable within populations worldwide and, in some cases, even between populations. Given the variety of human social ecologies, some actions, traits, and situations bring about evaluative responses and emotions in certain populations but not in others (Haidt, 2012; Sznycer, Tooby, et al., 2016; von Fürer-Haimendorf, 1967). Still, if some universal principles exist within the grammar of valuation, then actions, traits, and situations that tap into these principles may elicit agreement between populations about social valuation and emotions. Moreover, multiple emotions in one population may track the valuations that people hold in a different population.

Previous studies on the emotion of pride have supported these predictions. Studies conducted in 16 industrial countries indicate that the degree to which pride is anticipated following a particular action or trait closely tracks the degree to which audiences value the individual who performs that action or displays that trait (Sznycer, Al-Shawaf, et al., 2017; see also Cohen et al., 2020; Durkee et al., 2019; Leary et al., 1995). Moreover, the anticipated pride in each of the 16 countries tracked the valuations expressed by foreign audiences *in the other 15 countries*. For example, the more South Korean participants valued a target individual for having a certain trait, the more Swiss participants reported pride if they displayed that trait. Furthermore, these findings replicated in 10 traditional small-scale societies (Sznycer, Xygalatas, Alami, et al., 2018). Importantly, it was pride that tracked valuation; other positively valenced emotions did not uniquely track audience valuations (Sznycer, Al-Shawaf, et al., 2017), pointing to the functional specificity of pride.

Similar findings apply to shame. As noted above, the shame system functions to minimize the threat of being devalued by others when negative information about the self might be revealed (or has been revealed) to others. If the shame program is well-calibrated to the evaluations of audiences, one may expect people to feel intense shame regarding personal actions or traits that audiences disvalue greatly, and less intense shame regarding personal actions or traits that audiences devalue mildly. Indeed, studies in industrial societies and traditional small-scale societies show that shame accurately tracks the degree of devaluation expressed by both local audiences and foreign audiences (Cohen et al., 2020; Durkee et al., 2019; Sznycer, Tooby, et al., 2016; Sznycer, Xygalatas, Agey, et al., 2018). These findings are consistent with the hypotheses that the psychology of social valuation and the emotions of pride and shame are evolved, species-wide adaptations.

More recently, Sznycer and Lukaszewski (2019) have reported similar findings regarding other social emotions. Participants from the United States and India rated 25 hypothetical scenarios developed by Sznycer, Al-Shawaf, et al. (2017) in which someone's actions, traits, or circumstances might lead them to be viewed positively by others. The scenarios were designed to elicit reactions in a wide variety of evolutionarily relevant domains, such as social exchange, skills, aggressive contests, mating, parenting, and leadership, and were phrased at a relatively high level of abstraction to make them meaningful across different cultures.

Participants were randomly assigned to one of six conditions: valuation, guilt, sadness, pride, anger, and gratitude. Participants in each condition rated the same basic set of 25 scenarios. What varied across conditions was a prompt, displayed before the scenarios. The prompts were designed to guide the interpretation of the scenarios in a way that would elicit valuation of a target individual or one of five emotions (guilt, sadness, pride, anger, or gratitude). For example, in the valuation condition, the prompt asked participants to imagine that the actions and traits described in the 25 scenarios are true of a target individual: an individual other than the participant who is of the same sex and age as the participant. Participants then rated how they viewed the person from 1 (I wouldn't view them positively at all) to 7 (I'd view them very positively). The five emotion conditions had similar prompts with situation-specific scenarios meant to elicit the respective emotion and a 1–7 rating for the emotion. For example, in the pride condition, the prompt asked participants to imagine that the acts and traits described in the 25 scenarios are true of themselves, and to indicate how much pride they would feel if they were in those situations (1: no pride at all; 7: a lot of pride).

In sum, participants rated, for each of 25 scenarios describing positive acts and traits, either: (1) valuation of another individual, if those things were true of that individual; (2) guilt, if those things were true of another individual on whom the participant has imposed costs—in the absence of any incriminating evidence that publicly reveal this imposition of costs; (3) sadness, if those things were true of a recently deceased neighbor; (4) pride, if those things were true of themselves; (5) anger, if a friend failed to acknowledge those things about them; or (6) gratitude, if a friend convinced others that those things are true of the participant.

Sznycer and Lukaszewski (2019) found that the degree to which local audiences positively value a target individual if various acts or traits are true of the target is positively associated

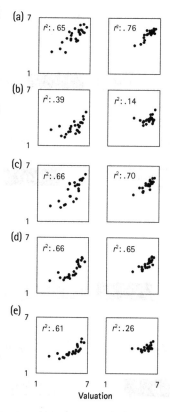

Figure 4.1. Multiple social emotions track social valuation. The extent to which people value each of 25 positive personal characteristics in others (e.g., trustworthiness, bravery, ambitiousness, good table manners) is positively associated with the intensities of: pride (if you had those characteristics), anger (if someone failed to acknowledge that you have those characteristics), gratitude (if someone convinced others that you have those characteristics), sadness (if someone died who had those characteristics), and guilt (if you harmed someone who has those characteristics). Each point in each panel represents the mean valuation rating and mean emotion rating of one personal characteristic. Ratings of valuation, pride, anger, gratitude, sadness, and guilt were given by different participants (between-subjects design). N on which the correlations are based = number of personal characteristics = 25. Effect size: r^2 linear. United States data: panels A–E; India data: panels F–J.

Reprinted with permission from: Sznycer, D. & Lukaszewski, A. W. (2019). The emotion–valuation constellation: Multiple emotions are governed by a common grammar of social valuation. *Evolution and Human Behavior, 40*(4), 395–404.

with the degree to which people feel each of the five different social emotions (Figure 4.1). Not only did the results hold in both the United States and India, but audience valuations in each country were associated with the intensities of the five emotions in the other country (Figure 4.2). This serves as the first empirical evidence that multiple social emotions with highly different functions, computational properties, and phenomenologies are governed in part by a common grammar of social valuation.

In addition to within- and between-culture regularities in emotion, this theoretical framework may also help explain cultural differences in emotion (Sznycer et al., 2012; Sznycer, Al-Shawaf, et al., 2017, Study S1; Sznycer, Tooby, et al., 2016, Study S2; see also Al-Shawaf & Lewis, 2017; Elfenbein & Ambady, 2002; Mesquita & Frijda, 1992; Scherer & Wallbott, 1994). The more an action or trait is valued in culture *A* compared to culture *B*, the more that

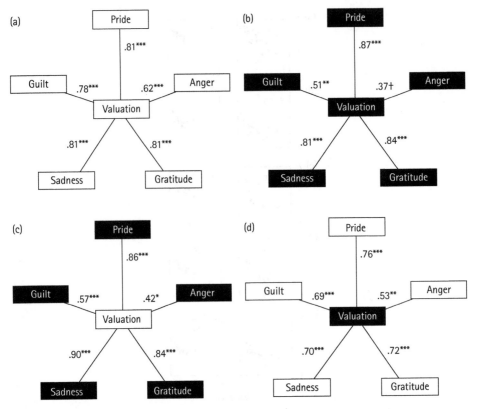

Figure 4.2. Multiple social emotions track social valuation both within and between countries. The valuations expressed by American participants are positively associated with the intensities of pride, anger, gratitude, sadness, and guilt expressed by American participants (panel A) and by Indian participants (panel C). Similarly, the valuations expressed by Indian participants are positively associated with the intensities of pride, anger, gratitude, sadness, and guilt expressed by Indian participants (panel B) and by American participants (panel D). Ratings of valuation, pride, anger, gratitude, sadness, and guilt were given by different participants (between-subjects design). N on which the correlations are based = number of personal characteristics = 25. Numbers represent Pearson's r between valuation and each emotion. *** $p < .001$; ** $p < .01$; * $p < .05$; † $.05 < p < .10$.

Reprinted with permission from: Sznycer, D. & Lukaszewski, A. W. (2019). The emotion-valuation constellation: Multiple emotions are governed by a common grammar of social valuation. *Evolution and Human Behavior, 40*(4), 395–404.

action or trait is expected to elicit various social emotions in culture A compared to culture B. Sznycer and Lukaszewski (2019) found evidence for this prediction as well. This approach can therefore account for—and more importantly, predict in advance—cross-cultural regularities *and* cross-cultural differences in social emotions.

In sum, the human mind-brain appears to be equipped with a complex psychology of social valuation and a suite of emotions that recalibrate internal representations of social value in the minds of self and others. This emotion-valuation constellation shapes the form of interpersonal interactions: with whom we associate, to whom we attend, whom we help, to whom we are grateful, whom we spite, and so on. If the emotion-valuation constellation is a pillar of human sociality, then signatures of this constellation may be evident in various spheres of human behavior and sociality. Next, we briefly review evidence in two such spheres—personality and the criminal justice system—suggesting that this is indeed the case.

Signatures of the Emotion-Valuation Constellation I: Personality

The hypothesis that emotions underlie individual differences in personality—characteristic ways of thinking and behaving—has a long history in psychology (e.g., Allport & Allport, 1921; Mischel & Shoda, 1995; Montag & Panksepp, 2017). This hypothesis is compatible with a recently developed adaptationist framework for discovering the psychological underpinnings of descriptive personality constructs, such as the Big Five (Saucier & Goldberg, 1996) and Big Six (Ashton & Lee, 2007) dimensions (Lukaszewski, 2020; Lukaszewski et al., 2020). This framework holds that, if we are to identify and characterize the psychological mechanisms that generate behavioral variation captured descriptively in nebulous personality dimensions (e.g., "Conscientiousness"), it is essential to begin by building theory-based models of specific behavior-regulating mechanisms. From this perspective, emotions are good candidates to explain personality variation, owing in part to their role in orchestrating functional responses to adaptive problems across many neurocognitive systems (Al-Shawaf et al., 2016; Al-Shawaf & Lewis, 2017; Tooby & Cosmides, 1990). For example, variation in the fear system—whether at the level of individual differences or within people across situations—will orchestrate variation in physiology (e.g., heart rate), attention (e.g., a bias toward detecting threats), and manifest behavior (e.g., fearful facial expression). Once the architecture of fear is provisionally mapped via an adaptationist analysis, the scientist can begin to determine whether variation in fear's activation and outputs are described in the folk parlance of any extant personality constructs (e.g., aspects of Big Five "Neuroticism"; Davis & Panksepp, 2011).

If variation in emotions constitutes (part of) the mechanistic underpinnings of personality, then it is possible that many personality constructs may describe variable behavioral solutions to adaptive problems pertaining to social valuation. For example, as detailed above, anger exhibits strong evidence of special design for solving the adaptive problem of being insufficiently valued by others (Sell et al., 2009, 2017; Tooby et al., 2008). Recently, researchers discovered that both within- and between-person variation in anger's activation and outputs are described in the folk-lexical parlance of the HEXACO (i.e., Big Six) personality dimension labeled "Agreeableness" (Lukaszewski et al., 2020). These findings illustrate (1) the utility of an adaptationist framework for characterizing the mechanisms that give rise to functionally defined dimensions of variation, and (2) the potential superiority of personality taxonomies that are organized around theoretically based dimensions of variation, rather than the largely atheoretical factor-analytical decisions that have historically characterized personality psychology.

A personality taxonomy grounded in the emotion-valuation constellation would capture dimensions of variation that carve the mind at its natural joints, while elucidating the psychological foundations of extant personality dimensions. Much as anger appears to form the mechanistic underpinning of Agreeableness, evidence suggests that variation in the pride (Cheng et al., 2010), shame (Gramzow & Tangey, 1992), envy (Krizan & Johar, 2012), and contempt (Gervais & Fessler, 2017) programs are descriptively captured in aspects of the "Dark Triad" personality dimensions of Narcissism, Machiavellianism, and Psychopathy (Jones & Paulhus, 2014). Further developing theory-based models of within- and between-person variation in the social emotions—as well as the psychometric tools for assessing such variation—may reveal that much of human "personality" is organized around a constellation of adaptive problems pertaining to social valuation. We envision a social-personality science in which researchers don't study lexically based trait factors such as "Conscientiousness" and "Agreeableness," but rather the universal and variable design features of adaptations such as anger, envy, gratitude, pride, shame, and sadness.

The cognitive grammar of social valuation referenced by social emotions to calibrate their operation is likely an important source of both universals in emotions and individual differences. This is true in multiple ways. First, if multiple social emotions consult a common grammar of valuation, then individual differences in how people represent the social value attached to specific acts and traits will lead to individual differences in how those acts or traits trigger emotions. For example, if person A represents eloquence as being more locally valued than person B, then instances of linguistic virtuosity (or incoherence) will correspondingly activate multiple social emotions more intensely in A than B (e.g., pride in response to successfully regaling others; shame in response to public inarticulateness; envy in response to a rival's celebrated speech at the community meeting; etc.). As such, the "common grammar" framework provides the foundation for understanding both universality and individual differences in emotions. It will be crucial for future work in this area to consider not only the substantial uniformity between people in how the emotion-valuation constellation works, but also the systematically predictable differences between cultures and individuals therein.

Variation in the grammar of social valuation is likely key in the decision process by which the activation of a given social emotion leads to specific behavioral outputs. Given the massive set of possible "on-the-ground" contingencies involved in solving a given adaptive problem in a specific circumstance, an emotion program requires access to a decision architecture that can precisely tailor behavioral decisions to the current situational and cultural context (Buss, 1991; Lukaszewski et al., 2020). For example, shame, when activated by potential or actual devaluation, must be able to improvise, or select from among, potentially functional behavioral outputs—should I hide, play dumb, make aggressive threats, cut off one of my fingers, or something else? Buss (1991) proposed a hierarchical structure of tactical output selection wherein specific behavioral outputs are nested within broader act categories. Given that the entire space of specific behavioral outputs that could be deployed in a given situation is nearly infinite—ranging from "rub your tummy" to "make a sexual proposition" to "brandish a weapon"—a decision architecture attempting to select outputs from this space would become paralyzed in the face of combinatorial explosion (Tooby & Cosmides, 1992). Rather, shame, when activated, will circumscribe the decision space to the level of broad act categories (e.g., "prevent others from knowing about disvalued act" vs. "generate compensatory benefits for others") that would have solved the adaptive problem ancestrally, or within one's own ecology. Next, having selected a broad act category (e.g., "prevent others from knowing about disvalued act"), shame must be able to tailor plausibly functional behavioral outputs (e.g., "falsely blame someone else" or "slip away inconspicuously before they see me") to the details of the current situation, taking into account the devaluers' identities and various situational and cultural variables. In this process, within- or between-culture variation in peoples' representation of the extent to which specific acts (or broad act categories) are (dis)valued will play a crucial role in determining which behavioral decisions have the greatest forecasted payoff in the currency of mitigating the costs of social devaluation. For instance, if person A represents being caught in a lie as being more strongly disvalued than person B, then person A will be less likely than B to select the behavioral output [falsely blame someone else]. The same would hold for specific behavioral decisions motivated by any of the social emotions comprising the emotion-valuation constellation.

In sum, the structure of the emotion-valuation constellation, as well as that of its constituent components, may influence a wide range of psychological and behavioral phenomena that have traditionally been studied as aspects of "personality." Mapping the variable parameters of the grammar of social valuation, as well as the social emotions, may therefore help place personality psychology on a new footing—one that carves the mind at its joints, and supplies a framework within which to seamlessly explain within-person, between-person, and cross-cultural variation in behavior.

Signatures of the Emotion-Valuation Constellation II: The Criminal Justice System

Modern skulls house stone-aged minds—the agricultural and industrial revolutions occurred too recently for natural selection to have effected major reorganizations of the human neuro-cognitive architecture (Tooby & Cosmides, 1992). One consequence of this is that modern artifacts and institutions are underlain by ancient adaptations for life in prehistoric small-scale bands of foragers, and signatures of the latter can be seen in the design of the former (Boyer, 2018; Tooby & Cosmides, 1992).

This general hypothesis has been applied to study war (Brown et al., 2021; Manson et al., 1991; Sell et al., 2009; Sell et al., 2017; Tooby & Cosmides, 1988), religion (Barlev et al., 2017; Boyer, 2008; Lang et al., 2019), rituals (Boyer & Liénard, 2006; Xygalatas et al., 2013), politics (Pietraszewski et al., 2015), morality (Alexander, 1987; Curry et al., 2019; DeScioli & Kurzban, 2013; Lieberman & Patrick, 2018; Tooby & Cosmides, 2010), criminal laws (Jones, 2001; Jones & Goldsmith, 2005; Robinson et al., 2007; Stylianou, 2003; Sznycer & Patrick, 2020), redistribution (Lin & Bates, 2020; Petersen et al., 2012, 2013; Sznycer, Seal, et al., 2017; Sznycer, Ermer, et al., 2018), the family (Daly & Wilson, 1995; Lieberman et al., 2007; Salmon & Shackelford, 2007; Sznycer, De Smet, et al., 2016), markets (Boyer & Petersen, 2018; Friedman, 2005; Rubin, 2003), and property rights (Friedman, 2010; Kanngiesser et al., 2020), among other areas of study.

The emotion-valuation constellation regulates how individuals allocate goods and bads (attention, aid, exclusion, exploitation) between themselves and others depending on the characteristics or externalities or contributions of self and others. If societal institutions are created and interpreted (at least in part) through the lens of adaptations for interpersonal interactions (Boyer, 2018; Sznycer, Seal, et al., 2017; Tooby et al., 2006), then the emotion-valuation constellation may shape (at least in part) the institutions that regulate the allocation of goods and bads among people in a society. If so, then signatures of the emotion-valuation constellation will be discernible in those institutions.

Put simply, the rules that regulate some institutions may be traceable to evaluative and emotional-recalibrational processes that evolved as solutions to problems in the domain of interpersonal interactions. Just as individuals condition their help to those individuals who help back, so institutions may condition rewards to those individuals who contribute to the public good or the collective action. Just as individuals devalue and exclude those individuals who are exploitative, so institutions may devalue and punish those individuals who exploit a common resource. And so on. Moreover, if there are commonalities across cultures in the circuit-logic of the emotion-valuation constellation, then (some) institutions in population A may be traceable to the social evaluations and the social emotions of individuals in population B—even when populations A and B exist in different times, geographical spaces, cultural spaces, and ecologies.

As an example of this, consider the institution of the criminal justice system. Humans can create costs for others as a side effect of their actions, and they can benefit at the expense of others in various ways. Given the recurring and consequential nature of conflict to human social life, natural selection would have selected for adaptations to navigate conflict (Cosmides & Tooby, 2006; Jones & Goldsmith, 2005; Patrick, 2016; Robinson et al., 2007; Sell, 2011;

Sell et al., 2009). Some of these adaptations are in the purview of the emotion-valuation constellation: victims' devaluation of offenders, victims' anger directed at offenders, perpetrators' shame and guilt, and so on. Thus, criminal justice systems may bear the stamp of the emotion-valuation constellation.

Consistent with this hypothesis, research suggests that social evaluations and social emotions are important components of people's intuitions of justice as well as criminal laws (where formal criminal laws exist). For example, laypeople agree both within and across countries in how they rank the seriousness of different offenses (Robinson & Kurzban, 2007; Stylianou, 2003) Further, laypeople's justice intuitions generally track the punishments prescribed by the legal codes and judges of their jurisdiction (Kääriäinen, 2018; Robinson et al., 2010).

Recently, Sznycer and Patrick (2020) have shown that laypeople's social evaluations and social emotions closely match the logic and content of laws drawn from ancient Mesopotamian and Chinese legal codes (the Laws of Eshnunna, 1770 BCE; the Tang Code, 635 CE). Study participants with no legal training from the United States and India were shown various ancient offenses as defined in ancient laws. The corresponding punishments provided for those offenses by the ancient laws were not shown to participants. Participants were asked to rate each offense. Participants' responses were positively correlated with the actual punishments provided for those ancient offenses by the ancient laws. This was true for a host of responses, including interpersonal devaluation of offenders, judgments of moral wrongness, mock-legislated punishments (in time in prison and in fines), and perpetrator shame. In addition, the valuation psychology can be seen in the administration of justice, as the mode and intensity of recommended punishment for an offense is more severe when participants perceive offenders to have lower social value, and victims to have higher social value (Lieberman & Linke, 2007; Petersen et al., 2012; see also Williams et al., 2019).

In sum, laypeople can intuitively recreate criminal laws from both familiar and radically unfamiliar cultures, and they can do this in the absence of explicit legal or historical knowledge. They appear to accomplish this through their social evaluations and emotions. This suggests that the emotion-valuation constellation may underlie key aspects of criminal justice systems. We suspect that signatures of the emotion-valuation constellation will be found in other institutions as well.

Concluding Remarks

The emotion-valuation constellation governs whom we value and help, to whom we are indifferent, whom we disvalue and exclude, when we feel anger and demand to be treated better, when we hide in shame, and when we advertise our achievements.

This constellation seems to be a fulcrum of human sociality. Its importance in human affairs is difficult to overstate. For instance, the flow of goods, services, and capital—the economy—is determined to an important extent by who values whom and who values whose assets. The criminal justice system too may be shaped by social valuation, as argued above. Individual differences in personality may also be an outcrop of the emotion-valuation constellation.

Many basic questions remain to be answered about the structure of this common grammar and which aspects of human psychology it underlies. However, the specificity and replicability of the findings outlined here suggest that an evolutionary approach sheds new light on how emotions function and what aspects of behavior and psychology they underpin.

References

Algoe, S. B., Fredrickson, B. L., & Gable, S. L. (2013). The social functions of the emotion of gratitude via expression. *Emotion, 13*(4), 605. https://psycnet.apa.org/doi/10.1037/a0032701

Algoe, S. B., Haidt, J., & Gable, S. L. (2008). Beyond reciprocity: Gratitude and relationships in everyday life. *Emotion, 8*, 425–429. https://psycnet.apa.org/doi/10.1037/1528-3542.8.3.425

Al-Shawaf, L., Conroy-Beam, D., Asao, K., & Buss, D. M. (2016). Human emotions: An evolutionary psychological perspective. *Emotion Review, 8*(2), 173–186. https://doi.org/10.1177%2F1754073914565518

Al-Shawaf, L., & Lewis, D. M. G. (2017). Evolutionary psychology and the emotions. In V. Zeigler-Hill and T. K. Shackelford (Eds.), *Encyclopedia of personality and individual differences* (pp. 1–10). Springer.

Alexander, R. D. (1987). *The biology of moral systems*. Transaction.

Allport, F. H., & Allport, G. W. (1921). Personality traits: Their classification and measurement. *The Journal of Abnormal Psychology and Social Psychology, 16*(1), 6–40. https://psycnet.apa.org/doi/10.1037/h0069790

Andrews, P. W., & Thomson, J. A., Jr. (2009). The bright side of being blue: Depression as an adaptation for analyzing complex problems. *Psychological Review, 116*(3), 620–654. https://doi.apa.org/doi/10.1037/a0016242

Ashton, M. C., & Lee, K. (2007). Empirical, theoretical, and practical advantages of the HEXACO model of personality structure. *Personality and Social Psychology Review, 11*(2), 150–166. https://doi.org/10.1177%2F1088868306294907

Averill, J. R. (1982). *Anger and aggression: An essay on emotion*. Springer.

Barclay, P., & Willer, R. (2007). Partner choice creates competitive altruism in humans. *Proceedings of the Royal Society of London B: Biological Sciences, 274*(1610), 749–753. https://doi.org/10.1098/rspb.2006.0209

Barlev, M., Mermelstein, S., & German, T. C. (2017). Core intuitions about persons coexist and interfere with acquired Christian beliefs about God. *Cognitive Science, 41*, 425–454. https://doi.org/10.1111/cogs.12435

Baumeister, R. F., Stillwell, A. M., & Heatherton, T. F. (1994). Guilt: An interpersonal approach. *Psychological Bulletin, 115*, 243–267. https://psycnet.apa.org/doi/10.1037/0033-2909.115.2.243

Baumeister, R. F., Stillwell, A. M., & Heatherton, T. F. (1995). Personal narratives about guilt: Role in action control and interpersonal relationships. *Basic and Applied Social Psychology, 17*, 173–198. https://psycnet.apa.org/doi/10.1207/s15324834basp1701&2_10

Bechara, A., Damasio, H., & Damasio, A. R. (2000). Emotion, decision making and the orbitofrontal cortex. *Cerebral Cortex, 10*(3), 295–307. https://doi.org/10.1016/j.pscychresns.2015.01.013

Blascovich, J., & Mendes, W. B. (2010). Social psychophysiology and embodiment. In S. T. Fiske, D. T. Gilbert, & G. Lindzey (Eds.), *Handbook of social psychology* (pp. 194–227). Wiley. https://doi.org/10.1002/9780470561119.socpsy001006

Boyer, P. (2008). *Religion explained*. Random House.

Boyer, P. (2018). *Minds make societies: How cognition explains the world humans create*. Yale University Press.

Boyer, P., & Liénard, P. (2006). Why ritualized behavior? Precaution systems and action parsing in developmental, pathological and cultural rituals. *Behavioral and Brain Sciences, 29*(6), 595–613. https://doi.org/10.1017/S0140525X06009332

Boyer, P., & Petersen, M. B. (2018). Folk-economic beliefs: An evolutionary cognitive model. *Behavioral and Brain Sciences, 41*, e158. https://doi.org/10.1017/S0140525X17001960

Brigham, N. L., Kelso, K. A., Jackson, M. A., & Smith, R. H. (1997). The roles of invidious comparisons and deservingness in sympathy and schadenfreude. *Basic and Applied Social Psychology, 19*(3), 363–380. https://doi.org/10.1207/s15324834basp1903_6

Brown, M., Chua, K. J., & Lukaszewski, A. W. (2021). Formidability and socioeconomic status uniquely predict militancy and political moral foundations. *Personality and Individual Differences, 168*, 110284. https://doi.org/10.1016/j.paid.2020.110284

Buss, D. M. (1991). Evolutionary personality psychology. *Annual Review of Psychology, 42*(1), 459–491. https://doi.org/10.1146/annurev.ps.42.020191.002331

Cacioppo, J. T., Gardner, W. L., & Berntson, G. G. (1999). The affect system has parallel and integrative processing components: Form follows function. *Journal of Personality and Social Psychology, 76*(5), 839. https://psycnet.apa.org/doi/10.1037/0022-3514.76.5.839

Cheng, J. T., Tracy, J. L., Foulsham, T., Kingstone, A., & Henrich, J. (2013). Two ways to the top: Evidence that dominance and prestige are distinct yet viable avenues to social rank and influence. *Journal of Personality and Social Psychology, 104*(1), 103–125. https://psycnet.apa.org/doi/10.1037/a0030398

Cheng, J. T., Tracy, J. L., & Henrich, J. (2010). Pride, personality, and the evolutionary foundations of human social status. *Evolution and Human Behavior*, *31*(5), 334–347. https://doi.org/10.1016/j.evolhumbehav.2010.02.004

Cohen, A. S., Chun, R., & Sznycer, D. (2020). Do pride and shame track the evaluative psychology of audiences? Preregistered replications of Sznycer et al. (2016, 2017). *Royal Society Open Science*, *7*, 191922. https://doi.org/10.1098/rsos.191922

Cohen, T. R., Panter, A. T., & Turan, N. (2013). Predicting counterproductive work behavior from guilt proneness. *Journal of Business Ethics*, *114*(1), 45–53. https://doi.org/10.1184/R1/6707429.v1

Cohen, T. R., Panter, A. T., Turan, N., Morse, L., & Kim, Y. (2014). Moral character in the workplace. *Journal of Personality and Social Psychology*, *107*(5), 943. https://doi.apa.org/doi/10.1037/a0037245

Cosmides, L., & Tooby, J. (2006). Evolutionary psychology, moral heuristics, and the law. In G. Gigerenzer & Christoph Engel (Eds.), *Heuristics and the Law* (pp. 175–205). MIT Press.

Cuddy, A. J. C., Fiske, S. T., & Glick, P. (2008). Warmth and competence as universal dimensions of social perception: The stereotype content model and the BIAS map. *Advances in Experimental Social Psychology*, *40*, 61–149. https://doi.org/10.1016/S0065-2601(07)00002-0

Curry, O. S., Mullins, D. A., & Whitehouse, H. (2019). Is it good to cooperate? Testing the theory of Morality-as-Cooperation in 60 Societies. *Current Anthropology*, *60*(1), 47–69. https://doi.org/10.1086/701478

Daly, M., & Wilson, M. (1988). *Homicide*. Aldine de Gruyter.

Daly, M., & Wilson, M. (1995). Discriminative parental solicitude and the relevance of evolutionary models to the analysis of motivational systems. In M. S. Gazzaniga (Ed.), *The cognitive neurosciences* (pp. 1269–1286). MIT Press.

Darwin, C. (1872). *The expression of the emotions in man and animals*. Murray.

Davis, K. L., & Panksepp, J. (2011). The brain's emotional foundations of human personality and the Affective Neuroscience Personality Scales. *Neuroscience & Biobehavioral Reviews*, *35*(9), 1946–1958. https://doi.org/10.1016/j.neubiorev.2011.04.004

de Hooge, I. E., Breugelmans, S. M., & Zeelenberg, M. (2008). Not so ugly after all: When shame acts as a commitment device. *Journal of Personality and Social Psychology*, *95*, 933–943. https://psycnet.apa.org/doi/10.1037/a0011991

de Hooge, I. E., Zeelenberg, M., & Breugelmans, S. M. (2007). Moral sentiments and cooperation: Differential influences of shame and guilt. *Cognition and emotion*, *21*(5), 1025–1042. https://doi.org/10.1080/02699930600980874

Delton, A. W., & Robertson, T. E. (2016). How the mind makes welfare tradeoffs: Evolution, computation, and emotion. *Current Opinion in Psychology*, *7*, 12–16. https://doi.org/10.1016/j.copsyc.2015.06.006

DeScioli, P., & Kurzban, R. (2013). A solution to the mysteries of morality. *Psychological Bulletin*, *139*(2), 477–496. https://psycnet.apa.org/doi/10.1037/a0029065

Dickerson, S. S., Mycek, P. J., & Zaldivar, F. (2008). Negative social evaluation, but not mere social presence, elicits cortisol responses to a laboratory stressor task. *Health Psychology*, *27*, 116–121. https://psycnet.apa.org/doi/10.1037/0278-6133.27.1.116

Durkee, P. K., Lukaszewski, A. W., & Buss, D. M. (2019). Pride and shame: Key components of a culturally universal status management system. *Evolution and Human Behavior*, *40*(5), 470–478. https://doi.org/10.1016/j.evolhumbehav.2019.06.004

Ekman, P. (1992). An argument for basic emotions. *Cognition and Emotion*, *6*, 169–200. https://doi.org/10.1080/02699939208411068

Elfenbein, H. A., & Ambady, N. (2002). On the universality and cultural specificity of emotion recognition: A meta-analysis. *Psychological Bulletin*, *128*(2), 203–235. https://doi.apa.org/doi/10.1037/0033-2909.128.2.203

Fehr, E., & Gächter, S. (2000). Cooperation and punishment in public goods experiments. *American Economic Review*, *90*(4), 980–994. https://doi.org/10.1257/aer.90.4.980

Felson, R. B. (1982). Impression management and the escalation of aggression and violence. *Social Psychology Quarterly*, *45*(4), 245–254. https://doi.org/10.2307/3033920

Fessler, D. M. T. (1999). Toward an understanding of the universality of second order emotions. In A. L. Hinton (Ed.), *Biocultural approaches to the emotions* (pp. 75–116). Cambridge University Press.

Foster, G. M. (1965). Peasant society and the image of limited good. *American Anthropologist*, *67*(2), 293–315. https://doi.org/10.1525/aa.1965.67.2.02a00010

Friedman, D. (2005). Economics and evolutionary psychology. *Advances in Austrian Economics*, *7*, 17–33. https://doi.org/10.1016/S1529-2134(04)07002-4

Friedman, O. (2010). Necessary for possession: How people reason about the acquisition of ownership. *Personality and Social Psychology Bulletin*, *36*(9), 1161–1169. https://doi.org/10.1177%2F0146167210378513

Galati, D., Sini, B., Schmidt, S., & Tinti, C. (2003). Spontaneous facial expressions in congenitally blind and sighted children aged 8–11. *Journal of Visual Impairment and Blindness, 97*(7), 418–428. https://doi.org/10.1177%2F0145482X0309700704

Gershman, B. (2015). The economic origins of the evil eye belief. *Journal of Economic Behavior & Organization, 110,* 119–144. https://doi.org/10.1016/j.jebo.2014.12.002

Gervais, M. M., & Fessler, D. M. (2017). On the deep structure of social affect: Attitudes, emotions, sentiments, and the case of "contempt." *Behavioral and Brain Sciences, 40,* e225. https://doi.org/10.1017/S0140525X16000352

Gilbert, P. (1997). The evolution of social attractiveness and its role in shame, humiliation, guilt and therapy. *British Journal of Medical Psychology, 70,* 113–147. https://doi.org/10.1111/j.2044-8341.1997.tb01893.x

Gilbert, P. (2000). The relationship of shame, social anxiety and depression: The role of the evaluation of social rank. *Clinical Psychology & Psychotherapy, 7,* 174–189. https://doi.org/10.1002/1099-0879(200007)7:3%3C174::AID-CPP236%3E3.0.CO;2-U

Gordon, A. M., Impett, E. A., Kogan, A., Oveis, C., & Keltner, D. (2012). To have and to hold: Gratitude promotes relationship maintenance in intimate bonds. *Journal of Personality and Social Psychology, 103*(2), 257. https://doi.apa.org/doi/10.1037/a0028723

Gramzow, R., & Tangney, J. P. (1992). Proneness to shame and the narcissistic personality. *Personality and Social Psychology Bulletin, 18*(3), 369–376. https://psycnet.apa.org/doi/10.1177/0146167292183014

Hagen, E. H. (1999). The functions of postpartum depression. *Evolution and Human Behavior, 20*(5), 325–359. https://doi.org/10.1016/S1090-5138(99)00016-1

Hagen, E. H., & Barrett, H. C. (2007). Perinatal sadness among Shuar women: Support for an evolutionary theory of psychic pain. *Medical Anthropology Quarterly, 21*(1), 22–40. https://doi.org/10.1525/maq.2007.21.1.22

Haidt, J. (2012). *The righteous mind: Why good people are divided by politics and religion.* Paragon.

Hamilton, W. D. (1964). The genetical evolution of social behaviour. II. *Journal of Theoretical Biology, 7*(1), 17–52. https://doi.org/10.1016/0022-5193(64)90039-6

Hare, T. A., Camerer, C. F., Knoepfle, D. T., O'Doherty, J. P., & Rangel, A. (2010). Value computations in ventral medial prefrontal cortex during charitable decision making incorporate input from regions involved in social cognition. *Journal of Neuroscience, 30*(2), 583–590. https://doi.org/10.1523/JNEUROSCI.4089-09.2010

Hill, S. E., & Buss, D. M. (2008). The evolutionary psychology of envy. In R. Smith (Ed.), *The psychology of envy* (pp. 60–70). Guilford Press.

Jackendoff, R. (2006). The peculiar logic of value. *Journal of Cognition and Culture, 6,* 375–407. https://doi.org/10.1163/156853706778554922

Jones, D. N., & Paulhus, D. L. (2014). Introducing the short dark triad (SD3) a brief measure of dark personality traits. *Assessment, 21*(1), 28–41. https://doi.org/10.1177%2F1073191113514105

Jones, O. D. (2001). Proprioception, non-law, and biolegal history. *Florida Law Review, 53*(5), 831–874.

Jones, O. D., & Goldsmith, T. H. (2005). Law and behavioral biology. *Columbia Law Review, 105*(2), 405–502.

Kääriäinen, J. (2018). Seven criminal cases: Comparing Finnish Punishment policies and Finns' punishment preferences. Helsinki, Finland: University of Helsinki Institute of Criminology and Legal Policy, Research Report 27/2018.

Kanngiesser, P., Rossano, F., Frickel, R., Tomm, A., & Tomasello, M. (2020). Children, but not great apes, respect ownership. *Developmental Science, 23*(1), e12842. https://doi.org/10.1111/desc.12842

Kaplan, H., & Hill, K. (1985). Food sharing among ache foragers: Tests of explanatory hypotheses. *Current Anthropology, 26,* 223–239. https://doi.org/10.1086/203251

Keller, M. C., & Nesse, R. M. (2006). The evolutionary significance of depressive symptoms: Different adverse situations lead to different depressive symptom patterns. *Journal of Personality and Social Psychology, 91,* 316–330. https://doi.apa.org/doi/10.1037/0022-3514.91.2.316

Keltner, D., & Haidt, J. (1999). Social functions of emotions at four levels of analysis. *Cognition & Emotion, 13*(5), 505–521. https://doi.org/10.1080/026999399379168

Keltner, D., Young, R. C., & Buswell, B. N. (1997). Appeasement in human emotion, social practice, and personality. *Aggressive Behavior, 23,* 359–374. https://psycnet.apa.org/doi/10.1002/(SICI)1098-2337(1997)23:5%3C359::AID-AB5%3E3.0.CO;2-D

Ketelaar, T., & Au, W. T. (2003). The effects of feelings of guilt on the behaviour of uncooperative individuals in repeated social bargaining games: An affect-as-in- formation interpretation of the role of emotion in social interaction. *Cognition and Emotion, 17,* 429–453. https://doi.org/10.1080/02699930143000662

Klein, J. T., Deaner, R. O., & Platt, M. L. (2008). Neural correlates of social target value in macaque parietal cortex. *Current Biology, 18*(6), 419–424. https://doi.org/10.1016/j.cub.2008.02.047

Krizan, Z., & Johar, O. (2012). Envy divides the two faces of narcissism. *Journal of Personality, 80*(5), 1415–1451. https://doi.org/10.1111/j.1467-6494.2012.00767.x

Lang, M., Purzycki, B. G., Apicella, C. L., Atkinson, Q. D., Bolyanatz, A., Cohen, E., Handley, C., Kundtová Klocová, E., Lesorogol, C., & Mathew, S. (2019). Moralizing gods, impartiality and religious parochialism across 15 societies. *Proceedings of the Royal Society B, 286*(1898), 20190202. https://doi.org/10.1098/rspb.2019.0202

Leach, C. W., & Cidam, A. (2015). When is shame linked to constructive approach orientation? A meta-analysis. *Journal of Personality and Social Psychology, 109*(6), 983–1002. https://psycnet.apa.org/doi/10.1037/pspa0000037

Leary, M. R., Tambor, E. S., Terdal, S. K., & Downs, D. L. (1995). Self-esteem as an interpersonal monitor: The sociometer hypothesis. *Journal of Personality and Social Psychology, 68,* 518–530. https://psycnet.apa.org/doi/10.1037/0022-3514.68.3.518

Leith, K. P., & Baumeister, R. F. (1998). Empathy, shame, guilt, and narratives of inter-personal conflicts: Guilt-prone people are better at perspective taking. *Journal of Personality, 66*(1), 1–37. https://psycnet.apa.org/doi/10.1111/1467-6494.00001

Levy, D. J., & Glimcher, P. W. (2012). The root of all value: A neural common currency for choice. *Current Opinion in Neurobiology, 22*(6), 1027–1038. https://doi.org/10.1016/j.conb.2012.06.001

Lewis, M., Alessandri, S. M., & Sullivan, M. W. (1992). Differences in shame and pride as a function of children's gender and task difficulty. *Child Development, 63,* 630–638. https://doi.org/10.2307/1131351

Lieberman, D., & Linke, L. (2007). The effect of social category on third party punishment. *Evolutionary Psychology, 5*(2), 289–305. https://doi.org/10.1177%2F147470490700500203

Lieberman, D., & Patrick, C. (2018). *Objection: Disgust, morality, and the law.* Oxford University Press.

Lieberman, D., Tooby, J., & Cosmides, L. (2007). The architecture of human kin detection. *Nature, 445*(7129), 727. https://doi.org/10.1038/nature05510

Lim, J. (2012). *Welfare tradeoff ratios and emotions: Psychological foundations of human reciprocity.* Doctoral dissertation, University of California, Santa Barbara.

Lin, C. A., & Bates, T. C. (2020). Who supports redistribution? Replicating and refining effects of compassion, malicious envy, and self-interest. *Evolution and Human Behavior, 42*(2), 140–147. https://doi.org/10.1016/j.evolhumbehav.2020.08.010

Lukaszewski, A. W. (2020). Evolutionary perspectives on the mechanistic underpinnings of personality. In J. Rauthmann (Ed.), *The handbook of personality dynamics and processes* (pp. 523–550). Elsevier Press.

Lukaszewski, A. W., Lewis, D. M., Durkee, P. K., Sell, A. N., Sznycer, D., & Buss, D. M. (2020). An adaptationist framework for personality science. *European Journal of Personality, 34*(6), 1151–1174. https://doi.org/10.1002/per.2292

Lukaszewski, A. W., Simmons, Z. L., Anderson, C., & Roney, J. R. (2015). The role of physical formidability in human social status allocation. *Journal of Personality and Social Psychology, 110,* 385–406. https://doi.apa.org/doi/10.1037/pspi0000042

Manson, J. H., Wrangham, R. W., Boone, J. L., Chapais, B., Dunbar, R. I. M., Ember, C. R., Irons, W., Marchant, L. F., McGrew, W. C., & Nishida, T. (1991). Intergroup aggression in chimpanzees and humans. *Current Anthropology, 32*(4), 369–390. https://doi.org/10.1007/s12110-012-9132-1

McGraw, K. M. (1987). Guilt following transgression: An attribution of responsibility approach. *Journal of personality and social psychology, 53*(2), 247. https://psycnet.apa.org/doi/10.1037/0022-3514.53.2.247

Mesquita, B., & Frijda, N. H. (1992). Cultural variations in emotions: A review. *Psychological bulletin, 112*(2), 179. https://psycnet.apa.org/doi/10.1037/0033-2909.112.2.179

Michalak, J., Troje, N. F., Fischer, J., Vollmar, P., Heidenreich, T., & Schulte, D. (2009). Embodiment of sadness and depression: Gait patterns associated with dysphoric mood. *Psychosomatic Medicine, 71*(5), 580–587. 10.1097/PSY.0b013e3181a2515c

Mischel, W., & Shoda, Y. (1995). A cognitive-affective system theory of personality: reconceptualizing situations, dispositions, dynamics, and invariance in personality structure. *Psychological Review, 102*(2), 246. https://doi.apa.org/doi/10.1037/0033-295X.102.2.246

Montag, C., & Panksepp, J. (2017). Primary emotional systems and personality: An evolutionary perspective. *Frontiers in Psychology, 8,* 464. https://doi.org/10.3389/fpsyg.2017.00464

Nelson, N. L., & Russell, J. A. (2014). Dynamic facial expressions allow differentiation of displays intended to convey positive and hubristic pride. *Emotion, 14*(5), 857. https://psycnet.apa.org/doi/10.1037/a0036789

Nesse, R. M. (1990). Evolutionary explanations of emotions. *Human Nature, 1,* 261–289. https://doi.org/10.1007/BF02733986

Noë, R., & Hammerstein, P. (1994). Biological markets: supply and demand determine the effect of partner choice in cooperation, mutualism and mating. *Behavioral Ecology and Sociobiology, 35*(1), 1–11. https://psycnet.apa.org/doi/10.1007/BF00167053

Nowak, M. A., & Sigmund, K. (1998). Evolution of indirect reciprocity by image scoring. *Nature, 393*(6685), 573–577. https://doi.org/10.1038/31225

Ohtsubo, Y., & Yagi, A. (2015). Relationship value promotes costly apology-making: Testing the valuable relationships hypothesis from the perpetrator's perspective. *Evolution and Human Behavior, 36*(3), 232–239. https://doi.org/10.1016/j.evolhumbehav.2014.11.008

Patrick, C. J. (2016). The long-term promise of evolutionary psychology for the law. *Arizona State Law Journal, 48*, 995–1012.

Petersen, M. B., Sell, A., Tooby, J., & Cosmides, L. (2012). To punish or repair? Evolutionary psychology and lay intuitions about modern criminal justice. *Evolution and Human Behavior, 33*(6), 682–695. https://doi.org/10.1016/j.evolhumbehav.2012.05.003

Petersen, M. B., Sznycer, D., Cosmides, L., & Tooby, J. (2012). Who deserves help? Evolutionary psychology, social emotions, and public opinion about welfare. *Political Psychology, 33*(3), 395–418. https://doi.org/10.1111/j.1467-9221.2012.00883.x

Petersen, M. B., Sznycer, D., Sell, A., Cosmides, L., & Tooby, J. (2013). The ancestral logic of politics: Upper-body strength regulates men's assertion of self-interest over economic redistribution. *Psychological Science, 24*(7), 1098–1103. https://doi.org/10.1177%2F0956797612466415

Pietraszewski, D., Curry, O. S., Petersen, M. B., Cosmides, L., & Tooby, J. (2015). Constituents of political cognition: Race, party politics, and the alliance detection system. *Cognition, 140*, 24–39. https://doi.org/10.1016/j.cognition.2015.03.007

Riskind, J. H., & Gotay, C. C. (1982). Physical posture: Could it have regulatory or feedback effects on motivation and emotion? *Motivation and Emotion, 6*(3), 273–298. https://doi.org/10.1007/BF00992249

Robertson, T. E., Sznycer, D., Delton, A. W., Tooby, J., & Cosmides, L. (2018). The true trigger of shame: Social devaluation is sufficient, wrongdoing is unnecessary. *Evolution and Human Behavior, 39*, 566–573. https://doi.org/10.1016/j.evolhumbehav.2018.05.010

Robinson, P. H., Goodwin, G. P., & Reisig, M. D. (2010). The disutility of injustice. *New York University Law Review, 85*, 1940–2033.

Robinson, P. H., & Kurzban, R. (2007). Concordance and conflict in intuitions of justice. *Minnesota Law Review, 91*, 1829–1907.

Robinson, P. H., Kurzban, R., & Jones, O. D. (2007). The origins of shared intuitions of justice. *Vanderbilt Law Review, 60*(6), 1633–1688.

Rubin, P. H. (2003). Folk economics. *Southern Economic Journal, 70*(1), 157–171. https://doi.org/10.2307/1061637

Russell, J. A. (1980). A circumplex model of affect. *Journal of Personality and Social Psychology, 39*(6), 1161. https://psycnet.apa.org/doi/10.1037/h0077714

Salmon, C. A., & Shackelford, T. K. (2007). *Family relationships: An evolutionary perspective.* Oxford University Press.

Saucier, G., & Goldberg, L. R. (1996). Evidence for the Big Five in analyses of familiar English personality adjectives. *European Journal of Personality, 10*(1), 61–77. https://psycnet.apa.org/doi/10.1002/(SICI)1099-0984(199603)10:1%3C61::AID-PER246%3E3.0.CO;2-D

Scherer, K. R., & Wallbott, H. G. (1994). Evidence for universality and cultural variation of differential emotion response patterning. *Journal of Personality and Social Psychology, 66*, 310–328. https://doi.apa.org/doi/10.1037/0022-3514.66.2.310

Schniter, E., Sheremeta, R. M., & Sznycer, D. (2013). Building and rebuilding trust with promises and apologies. *Journal of Economic Behavior and Organization, 94*, 242–256. https://doi.org/10.1016/j.jebo.2012.09.011

Schniter, E., Shields, T. W., & Sznycer, D. (2020). Trust in humans and robots: Economically similar but emotionally different. *Journal of Economic Psychology, 78*, 102253. https://doi.org/10.1016/j.joep.2020.102253

Schoeck, H. (1969). *Envy: A theory of social behavior.* Harcourt, Brace, and World.

Schwarz, N. (2000). Emotion, cognition, and decision making. *Cognition & Emotion, 14*(4), 433–440. https://doi.org/10.1080/026999300402745

Sell, A. N. (2011). The recalibrational theory and violent anger. *Aggression and Violent Behavior, 16*(5), 381–389. https://doi.org/10.1016/j.avb.2011.04.013

Sell, A., Cosmides, L., & Tooby, J. (2014). The human anger face evolved to enhance cues of strength. *Evolution and Human Behavior, 35*(5), 425–429. https://doi.org/10.1016/j.evolhumbehav.2014.05.008

Sell, A., Sznycer, D., Cosmides, L., Tooby, J., Krauss, A., Nisu, S., Ceapa, C., & Petersen, M. B. (2017). Physically strong men are more militant: A test across four countries. *Evolution and Human Behavior, 38*(3), 334–340. https://doi.org/10.1016/j.evolhumbehav.2016.11.002

Sell, A., Tooby, J., & Cosmides, L. (2009). Formidability and the logic of human anger. *Proceedings of the National Academy of Sciences, 106*(35), 15073–15078. https://doi.org/10.1073/pnas.0904312106

Siegel, E. H., Sands, M. K., Van den Noortgate, W., Condon, P., Chang, Y., Dy, J., Quigley, K. S., & Barrett, L. F. (2018). Emotion fingerprints or emotion populations? A meta-analytic investigation of autonomic features of emotion categories. *Psychological Bulletin, 144*(4), 343–393. https://doi.apa.org/doi/10.1037/bul0000128

Smith, A., Pedersen, E. J., Forster, D. E., McCullough, M. E., & Lieberman, D. (2017). Cooperation: The roles of interpersonal value and gratitude. *Evolution and Human Behavior, 38*(6), 695–703. http://dx.doi.org/10.1016/j.evolhumbehav.2017.08.003

Smith, R. H., & Kim, S. H. (2007). Comprehending envy. *Psychological Bulletin, 133*(1), 46–64. https://psycnet.apa.org/doi/10.1037/0033-2909.133.1.46

Smith, R. H., Webster, J. M., & Eyre, H. L. (2002). The role of public exposure in moral and nonmoral shame and guilt. *Journal of Personality and Social Psychology, 83*, 138–159. https://psycnet.apa.org/doi/10.1037/0022-3514.83.1.138

Stylianou, S. (2003). Measuring crime seriousness perceptions: What have we learned and what else do we want to know. *Journal of Criminal Justice, 31*(1), 37–56. https://doi.org/10.1016/S0047-2352(02)00198-8

Sznycer, D. (2010). *Cognitive adaptations for calibrating welfare tradeoff motivations, with special reference to the emotion of shame.* Doctoral dissertation, University of California, Santa Barbara.

Sznycer, D. (2019). Forms and functions of the self-conscious emotions. *Trends in Cognitive Sciences, 23*(2), 143–157. https://doi.org/10.1016/j.tics.2018.11.007

Sznycer, D., Al-Shawaf, L., Bereby-Meyer, Y., Curry, O. S., De Smet, D., Ermer, E., Kim, S., Kim, S., Li, M., Lopez Seal, M. F., McClung, J., O, J., Ohtsubo, Y., Quillien, T., Schaub, M., Sell, A., van Leeuwen, F., Cosmides, L., & Tooby, J. (2017). Cross-cultural regularities in the cognitive architecture of pride. *Proceedings of the National Academy of Sciences, 114*(8), 1874–1879. https://doi.org/10.1073/pnas.1614389114

Sznycer, D., Barlev, M., Lopez Seal, M. F., Tooby, J., & Cosmides, L. (in prep.). *The psychology of zero-sum games.*

Sznycer, D., & Cohen, A. S. (2021a). How pride works. *Evolutionary Human Sciences, 3*, e10. https://doi.org/10.1017/ehs.2021.6

Sznycer, D., & Cohen, A. S. (2021b). Are emotions natural kinds after all? Rethinking the issue of response coherence. *Evolutionary Psychology, 19*(2), 14747049211016009. https://doi.org/10.1177/14747049211016009

Sznycer, D., Cosmides, L., & Tooby, J. (2017). Adaptationism carves emotions at their functional joints. *Psychological Inquiry, 28*(1), 56–62. https://psycnet.apa.org/doi/10.1080/1047840X.2017.1256132

Sznycer, D., Delton, A. W., Robertson, T. E., Cosmides, L., & Tooby, J. (2019). The ecological rationality of helping others: Potential helpers integrate cues of recipients' need and willingness to sacrifice. *Evolution and Human Behavior, 40*(1), 34–45. https://doi.org/10.1016/j.evolhumbehav.2018.07.005

Sznycer, D., De Smet, D., Billingsley, J., & Lieberman, D. (2016). Coresidence duration and cues of maternal investment regulate sibling altruism across cultures. *Journal of Personality and Social Psychology, 111*(2), 159–177. https://doi.apa.org/doi/10.1037/pspi0000057

Sznycer, D., Ermer, E., & Tooby, J. (2018). Why do people think that others should earn this or that? *Behavioral and Brain Sciences, 41*, e189. https://doi.org/10.1017/S0140525X18000559

Sznycer, D. & Lukaszewski, A. W. (2019). The emotion-valuation constellation: Multiple emotions are governed by a common grammar of social valuation. *Evolution and Human Behavior, 40*(4), 395–404. https://doi.org/10.1016/j.evolhumbehav.2019.05.002

Sznycer, D., & Patrick, C. (2020). The origins of criminal law. *Nature Human Behaviour, 4*(5), 506–516. https://doi.org/10.1038/s41562-020-0827-8

Sznycer, D., Schniter, E., Tooby, J., & Cosmides, L. (2015). Regulatory adaptations for delivering information: The case of confession. *Evolution and Human Behavior, 36*, 44–51. https://doi.org/10.1016/j.evolhumbehav.2014.08.008

Sznycer, D., Seal, M. F. L., Sell, A., Lim, J., Porat, R., Shalvi, S., Halperin, E., Cosmides, L., & Tooby, J. (2017). Support for redistribution is shaped by compassion, envy, and self-interest, but not a taste for fairness. *Proceedings of the National Academy of Sciences, 114*(31), 8420–8425. https://doi.org/10.1073/pnas.1703801114

Sznycer, D., Sell, A., & Lieberman, D. (2021). Forms and functions of the social emotions. *Current Directions in Psychological Science, 30*(4), 292–299. https://doi.org/10.1177/09637214211007451

Sznycer, D., Takemura, K., Delton, A. W., Sato, K., Robertson, T., Cosmides, L., & Tooby, J. (2012). Cross-cultural differences and similarities in proneness to shame: An adaptationist and ecological approach. *Evolutionary Psychology, 10*, 352–370. https://doi.org/10.1177%2F147470491201000213

Sznycer, D., Tooby, J., Cosmides, L., Porat, R., Shalvi, S., & Halperin, E. (2016). Shame closely tracks the threat of devaluation by others, even across cultures. *Proceedings of the National Academy of Sciences, 113*(10), 2625–2630. https://doi.org/10.1073/pnas.1514699113

Sznycer, D., Xygalatas, D., Agey, E., Alami, S., An, X.-F., Ananyeva, K. I., ... Tooby, J. (2018). Cross-cultural invariances in the architecture of shame. *Proceedings of the National Academy of Sciences, 115*(39), 9702–9707. https://doi.org/10.1073/pnas.1805016115

Sznycer, D., Xygalatas, D., Alami, S., An, X.-F., Ananyeva, K. I., Fukushima, S., & Tooby, J. (2018). Invariances in the architecture of pride across small-scale societies. *Proceedings of the National Academy of Sciences, 115*(33), 8322–8327. https://doi.org/10.1073/pnas.1808418115

Tangney, J. P. (1991). Moral affect: The good, the bad, and the ugly. *Journal of Personality and Social Psychology, 61*, 598–607. https://doi.apa.org/doi/10.1037/0022-3514.61.4.598

Tesser, A., Gatewood, R., & Driver, M. (1968). Some determinants of gratitude. *Journal of Personality and Social Psychology, 9*(3), 233. https://psycnet.apa.org/doi/10.1037/h0025905

Tooby, J. (1985). The emergence of evolutionary psychology. In D. Pines (Ed.), *Emerging syntheses in science* (pp. 67–76). Santa Fe Institute.

Tooby, J., & Cosmides, L. (1988). The evolution of war and its cognitive foundations. *Institute for Evolutionary Studies Technical Report, 88*(1), 1–15.

Tooby, J., & Cosmides, L. (1990). The past explains the present: Emotional adaptations and the structure of ancestral environments. *Ethology and Sociobiology, 11*(4–5), 375–424. https://doi.org/10.1016/0162-3095(90)90017-Z

Tooby, J., & Cosmides, L. (1992). The psychological foundations of culture. In J. Barkow, L. Cosmides, & J. Tooby (Eds.), *The adapted mind: Evolutionary psychology and the generation of culture* (pp. 19–136). Oxford University Press.

Tooby, J., & Cosmides, L. (1996). Friendship and the Banker's Paradox: Other pathways to the evolution of adaptations for altruism. In W. G. Runciman, J. Maynard Smith, & R. I. M. Dunbar (Eds.), *Evolution of social behaviour patterns in primates and man*. Proceedings of the British Academy (Vol. 88, pp. 119–143). Oxford University Press.

Tooby, J., & Cosmides, L. (2008). The evolutionary psychology of the emotions and their relationship to internal regulatory variables. In M. Lewis, J. M. Haviland-Jones, & L. F. Barrett (Eds.), *Handbook of emotions* (pp. 114–137). The Guilford Press.

Tooby, J., & Cosmides, L. (2010). Groups in mind: The coalitional roots of war and morality. In Høgh-Olesen (Ed.), *Human morality and sociality: Evolutionary and comparative perspectives* (pp. 191–234). Palgrave MacMillan.

Tooby, J., Cosmides, L., & Price, M. E. (2006). Cognitive adaptations for n-person exchange: The evolutionary roots of organizational behavior. *Managerial and Decision Economics, 27*(2–3), 103–129. https://doi.org/10.1002/mde.1287

Tooby, J., Cosmides, L., Sell, A., Lieberman, D., & Sznycer, D. (2008). Internal regulatory variables and the design of human motivation: A computational and evolutionary approach. In *Handbook of approach and avoidance motivation* (Vol 15, pp. 251–271). Taylor & Francis.

Tracy, J. L., & Matsumoto, D. (2008). The spontaneous display of pride and shame: Evidence for biologically innate nonverbal displays. *Proceedings of the National Academy of Sciences, 105*, 11655–11660. https://doi.org/10.1073/pnas.0802686105

Tracy, J. L., & Robins, R. W. (2008). The nonverbal expression of pride: Evidence for cross-cultural recognition. *Journal of Personality and Social Psychology, 94*, 516–530. https://doi.apa.org/doi/10.1037/0022-3514.94.3.516

Tracy, J. L., Shariff, A. F., & Cheng, J. T. (2010). A naturalist's view of pride. *Emotion Review, 2*(2), 163–177. https://doi.org/10.1177%2F1754073909354627

Trivers, R. L. (1971). The evolution of reciprocal altruism. *The Quarterly Review of Biology, 46*(1), 35–57. https://doi.org/10.1086/406755

Tsang, J.-A. (2006a). Gratitude and prosocial behaviour: An experimental test of gratitude. *Cognition & Emotion, 20*(1), 138–148. https://psycnet.apa.org/doi/10.1080/02699930500172341

Tsang, J.-A. (2006b). The effects of helper intention on gratitude and indebtedness. *Motivation and Emotion, 30*(3), 198–204. https://psycnet.apa.org/doi/10.1007/s11031-006-9031-z

Van Der Schalk, J., Bruder, M., & Manstead, A. (2012). Regulating emotion in the context of interpersonal decisions: The role of anticipated pride and regret. *Frontiers in Psychology, 3*, 1–9. https://doi.org/10.3389/fpsyg.2012.00513

van Dijk, W. W., Ouwerkerk, J. W., Smith, R. H., & Cikara, M. (2015). The role of self-evaluation and envy in schadenfreude. *European Review of Social Psychology, 26*(1), 247–282. https://psycnet.apa.org/doi/10.1080/10463283.2015.1111600

von Fürer-Haimendorf C. (1967). *Moral and merit: A study of values and social controls in South Asian societies*.

Weidenfeld and Nicolson. (1999). Darwinian analysis of the emotion of pride/shame. In J.M.G. v.d. Dennen & D. Smillie & et al. (Eds.), *The Darwinian heritage and sociobiology* (pp. 319–333). Praeger Publishers/Greenwood Publishing Group.

Weisfeld, G. E., & Dillon, L. M. (2012). Applying the dominance hierarchy model to pride and shame, and related behaviors. *Journal of Evolutionary Psychology, 10*(1), 15–41. https://psycnet.apa.org/doi/10.1556/JEP.10.2012.1.2

Welling, H. (2003). An evolutionary function of the depressive reaction: The cognitive map hypothesis. *New Ideas in Psychology, 21*(2), 147–156. https://psycnet.apa.org/doi/10.1016/S0732-118X(03)00017-5

Wicker, F. W., Payne, G. C., & Morgan, R. D. (1983). Participant descriptions of guilt and shame. *Motivation and Emotion, 7*, 25–39. https://doi.org/10.1007/BF00992963

Williams, K. E., Votruba, A. M., Neuberg, S. L., & Saks, M. J. (2019). Capital and punishment: Resource scarcity increases endorsement of the death penalty. *Evolution and Human Behavior, 40*(1), 65–73. https://doi.org/10.1016/j.evolhumbehav.2018.08.002

Williams, L. A., & DeSteno, D. (2008). Pride and perseverance: The motivational role of pride. *Journal of Personality and Social Psychology, 94*(6), 1007–1017. https://psycnet.apa.org/doi/10.1037/0022-3514.94.6.1007

Xygalatas, D., Mitkidis, P., Fischer, R., Reddish, P., Skewes, J., Geertz, A. W., Roepstorff, A., & Bulbulia, J. (2013). Extreme rituals promote prosociality. *Psychological Science, 24*(8), 1602–1605. https://doi.org/10.1177%2F0956797612472910

CHAPTER 5

The Motivational Architecture of Emotions

Marco Del Giudice

Abstract

Evolutionary research on emotion is increasingly converging on the idea that emotions can be understood as superordinate coordination mechanisms. Despite its plausibility and heuristic power, the coordination approach fails to explicitly address the relations between emotions and motivation. This chapter aims to fill this conceptual gap. The author argues that the current view of emotions as coordination mechanisms should be extended—and partially revised—to include motivational systems as an additional control layer, responsible for the activation and deactivation of specific emotions in the pursuit of domain-specific goals. The extended coordination approach proposed in this chapter facilitates the analysis of folk emotion categories; helps clarify the distinction between emotions and moods; suggests new ways to think about emotion regulation; and provides a more natural interface to model the link between emotions and personality.

Key Words: emotions, emotion regulation, mood, motivational system, personality

Evolutionary research on emotion is increasingly converging on the idea that emotions can be understood as superordinate *coordination mechanisms* or *coordination programs* (Al-Shawaf et al., 2016; Al-Shawaf & Lewis, 2017; Nesse, 1990, 2004; Sznycer, Cosmides, et al., 2017; Tooby & Cosmides, 1990, 2008, Chapter 2 in this volume). In a nutshell, emotions evolved to solve the *coordination problem*—the adaptive problem of how to orchestrate large suites of cognitive, physiological, and behavioral mechanisms so as to produce efficient but flexible responses to recurrent fitness-relevant situations. What we call emotions are organismic modes of operation that fulfill this crucial coordination function; the same applies to other feelings that are not usually categorized as emotions, such as hunger and sexual arousal.

Importantly, coordination mechanisms do not map in a one-to-one fashion on folk categories such as "anger" or "fear," which are often used to refer to multiple mechanisms with somewhat distinct features and functions (Al-Shawaf et al., 2016; Sznycer, Cosmides, et al., 2017; see also Fiske, 2020; Scarantino, 2012). And because emotions have evolved through a complex history of divergence and progressive specialization, they are best described as a multitude of overlapping neurocomputational mechanisms with somewhat fuzzy boundaries (Nesse, 1990, 2004, 2020). Thus, simple taxonomies based on a small number of distinct, sharply differentiated emotions are inevitably limited and artificial; while an adaptationist approach is the best way to "carve emotions at their functional joints" (Sznycer, Cosmides, et al., 2017), there are going to be multiple reasonable ways to do the carving, and inherent uncertainty about the number of mechanisms and their exact boundaries. The coordination approach suggests that the classic distinction between "basic" and "non-basic" emotions is not functionally meaningful (Al-Shawaf et al., 2016; Cosmides & Tooby, 2000); however, it is compatible with some recent updates of basic emotion theory, most notably the reformed version proposed by Scarantino (2015; see also Keltner et al., 2019).

The coordination approach to emotions is biologically plausible, heuristically powerful, and integrative in scope. I believe it has the potential to become the "standard model" in biologically oriented emotion research. However, the model is still incomplete in many respects, and some important issues have remained unaddressed so far. Perhaps the biggest conceptual gap concerns the relations between emotions and motivation. Proponents of the coordination approach have argued that one of the functions of emotion programs is to regulate the individual's motivational priorities (e.g., safety is prioritized when fear is activated; Al-Shawaf et al., 2016; Cosmides & Tooby, 2000; Tooby & Cosmides, 2008). The same authors have invoked the concept of *motivational systems*—computational mechanisms that regulate behavior and decision-making in fitness-relevant domains. For example, Tooby and colleagues (2008) discussed the sexual and altruistic motivational systems as examples of mechanisms that rely on the "kinship index," a hypothetical *internal regulatory variable* (IRV) that tracks the estimated genetic relatedness between the focal individual and other people (e.g., siblings). The sexual system is associated with emotions of lust and disgust, whereas the altruism system is associated with love and closeness. They argued that "[a] high kinship index produces feelings of disgust when accessed by the sexual motivation system at the possibility of sexual contact with the person, and impulses to help when accessed by the system regulating altruistic motivations" (p. 256). This seems to imply that motivational systems activate emotional programs in response to goal-relevant situations. However, the authors also stated that anger orchestrates the activity of "downstream" motivational systems that regulate cooperation and aggression (p. 266). In other papers, emotions such as pride are described as systems that include "motivational subcomponents" (e.g., Sznycer, Cosmides, et al., 2017). While the coordination approach postulates a tight coupling between emotions and motivational systems, the nature of this relation is not clearly specified. As noted by Beall and Tracy (2017), the concept of emotions as coordination mechanisms overlaps substantially with the concept of motivational systems in the literature on motivation (e.g., Kenrick et al., 2010), but the two have not been explicitly connected by evolutionary scholars.

In this chapter, I aim to fill this gap. I argue that the current view of emotions as coordination mechanisms should be extended—and partially revised—to include motivational systems as an additional (second-order) control layer, responsible for the activation and deactivation of specific emotions (Aunger & Curtis, 2013; Beall & Tracy, 2017; Bowlby, 1982; Del Giudice, 2018; Gilbert, 1989, 2005; Lichtenberg et al., 1992; Scott, 1980). Motivational systems regulate the pursuit of key biological goals and coordinate emotions in the service of those goals. From a computational perspective, they take up some of the functions that have been ascribed to emotion mechanisms, including the detection and evaluation of fitness-relevant situations. This reconceptualization has important theoretical implications: just like emotions can solve the basic coordination problem, motivational systems can efficiently solve the higher-order problems that arise in the pursuit of flexible, context-sensitive coordination. Motivational systems contribute to the robustness and evolvability of psychological architectures, by serving as central nodes in a regulatory network with a hierarchical "bow-tie" structure (Csete & Doyle, 2004). A motivational-systems perspective facilitates the analysis of folk emotion categories, and helps clarify the distinction between emotions and moods. At the end of the chapter, I illustrate how the extended coordination approach suggests new ways to think about emotion regulation, and provides a more natural interface to model the link between emotions and personality.

Motivational Systems
Historical Roots of the Concept

The theory of motivational systems originates in the psychology of the early 20th century, most notably in McDougall's concept of *instincts* (1908). McDougall took a strikingly modern approach (Boden, 1965) and described instincts as goal-directed processes that orient attention and perception (cognitive component), give rise to emotional experiences (affective component), and elicit specific action tendencies (conative component). On this view, instincts are not rigid or stereotyped—on the contrary, they motivate learning and enable adaptive behavioral change. McDougall (1908) proposed six "primary" human instincts, each with an associated primary emotion: *flight* (fear), *repulsion* (disgust), *curiosity* (wonder), *pugnacity* (anger), *self-abasement* or *subjection* (negative self-feeling), *self-assertion* or *self-display* (positive self-feeling or elation), and the *parental instinct* (tenderness). Four additional instincts lacked a clearly defined emotional component: *reproduction, gregarious instinct, acquisition,* and *construction*. From a functional perspective, McDougall's cognitive-affective-conative processes can be likened to the emotional coordination mechanisms envisioned by present-day evolutionary scholars.

In his later work, McDougall (1932) switched from "instincts" to "propensities," to avoid the former's connotations of deterministic rigidity. He also expanded the list to include *appeal* or help-seeking, *laughter*, a *migratory* propensity, and some basic physiological motivations (*food-seeking, comfort,* and *rest/sleep*). By that time, however, the popularity of instinct theories in psychology was fading. There were a number of reasons for this reversal of fortune. To begin with, some theorists had started using the concept of instincts in a circular fashion, raising doubts about the explanatory status of this approach. More importantly, behaviorism was on the rise, and its proponents kept attacking instinct theories as old-fashioned and unscientific.[1] On a deeper level, it seemed impossible to reconcile McDougall's "purposive" and goal-oriented view of the mind with a truly "mechanistic" explanation of behavior (see Heckhausen, 2018; Krantz & Allen, 1967; McDougall, 1921, 1924; Scheffer & Heckhausen, 2018). Instinct-like constructs like "needs" and "ergs" would keep resurfacing in the field of personality (e.g., Cattell, 1957; Maslow, 1954; Murray, 1938), but for most psychologists, the concept was going to remain scientifically suspect, if not outright taboo.

At the same time that they were being (prematurely) abandoned in psychology, instincts were taking center stage in the emerging discipline of ethology. Building on Craig's (1918) appetitive-consummatory model, Tinbergen (1951) advanced the notion that instincts can be redefined as hierarchically organized structures of behavior. For example, the stickleback fish's reproductive instinct includes the sub-instincts of fighting, nest building, mating, and offspring care; each of these sub-instincts can trigger a set of appropriate consummatory behaviors (e.g., chasing, biting, threatening as fighting behaviors). Tinbergen's seminal contribution was expanded and recast in the framework of control systems theory (cybernetics), yielding the concept of *behavioral* or *motivational systems*. (In the biological literature, these two labels are essentially synonymous, and I use them interchangeably in this chapter.) Behavioral/motivational systems were conceptualized as hierarchies of feedback-regulated processes, with dedicated goals and subgoals, that control the sequencing of behavior through complex loops of activation and inhibition (Baerends, 1976; McFarland, 1971, 1974; Toates & Archer, 1978).

Conceptual Developments

While behavioral systems theory has informed decades of animal research, ethologists have generally avoided the issue of emotions and affective states (Burghardt, 2019; Burghardt & Bowers, 2017). But as ethological ideas started to filter back into psychology, the connection between the operation of behavioral systems and the experience of emotions became an important topic of investigation. The key contributions in this respect were made by Scott (1980) and Bowlby (1982). In Bowlby's model, feelings are experienced in relation to the activation of a behavioral system, the progress of current behavior in relation to the system's "set goal," and the eventual consequences of behavior (success vs. failure to achieve the set goal).[2] For example, the *attachment system* in infants and children has the set goal of maintaining the proximity and/or availability of the caregiver (and the ultimate function of ensuring the child's survival). The system is activated by perceived dangers or separations (with feelings of anxiety, fear, distress, loneliness), and successfully deactivated by the attainment of proximity and protection (with feelings of relief, comfort, and "felt security"). Lack of progress in reaching proximity (e.g., because of an inconsistent or insensitive caregiver) can elicit anger and protest behaviors (e.g., crying, yelling), whereas protracted failure of the system leads to sadness, despair, and ultimately emotional detachment.

Bowlby's theory of motivation was extended by Gilbert (1989) and Lichtenberg and colleagues (1992). In addition to attachment, Lichtenberg's list of motivational mechanisms includes *defensive*, *exploration/competence*, *sexuality*, *caregiving*, and *affiliative* systems. Gilbert's work is focused on interpersonal relations, with an emphasis on what he calls the "social mentalities" related to *care eliciting* (attachment), *caregiving*, *social ranking* (competition), *formation of alliances* (cooperation, affiliation), and *mating/sexuality* (Gilbert, 2005). Along similar lines, Bugental (2000) argued for the existence of five basic systems that regulate social relationships in our species: *attachment*, *mating*, *reciprocity*, *hierarchical power*, and *coalitional group* (a system that has the goal of acquiring and defending shared group resources, and is involved in intergroup conflict). Bugental also tracked the emergence and development of these systems across the life span and considered their possible neurobiological correlates.

The model of motivation that emerges from this tradition has some notable implications. First, a motivational system can have multiple, thematically related goals, rather than a single overarching goal. For instance, the goals of a system that regulates status/dominance relations may include improving, maintaining, and displaying one's status, as well as deferring or submitting to higher-status individuals (e.g., Gilbert, 1989, 2005). These narrower motivations can be thought of as subsystems within a broader neurocomputational mechanism. Second, motivational systems can embody sophisticated and context-sensitive operation rules, that respond flexibly to the state of the environment and draw on internal representations (including internal regulatory variables) and models of the world (e.g., inferences about the caregiver's intentions and emotions, expectations about the caregiver's likely response, representations of the child's worth and value to the caregiver). Third, motivational systems can reciprocally potentiate and inhibit each other's activity, and thus achieve a degree of collective self-organization without the intervention of other prioritization mechanisms; for example, when the attachment system is activated, it quickly suppresses play and curiosity-driven exploration (Bowlby, 1982). Fourth, a given motivational system is not tied to a single emotion, but to a *set* of characteristic emotions (both "positive" and "negative"). Different emotions are activated depending on contextual factors, internal representations, and the moment-to-moment consequences of the individual's actions. Finally, emotions may be shared by more than one system. For example, anger—or, quite possibly, multiple domain-specific variants of the "anger" program—can be triggered in the context of attachment, but also in those of status competition, aggressive defense, pair bonding, or reciprocal exchange (in response to cheating and betrayal). One implication is that affective labels have low motivational specificity; simply knowing that someone feels "angry" says relatively little about their goals and motivational state.

A distinct and highly influential approach to motivation is Panksepp's research program on "basic emotional systems" (Panksepp, 1998, 2005, 2011; Davis & Panksepp, 2018). Working from a neurobiological and comparative perspective, Panksepp used a broad array of evidence from animal research to describe seven emotional systems shared by all mammals, which give rise to basic emotions or "core emotional feelings." These mechanisms are mainly implemented by subcortical circuits; they are labeled *RAGE* (anger/rage), *FEAR*, *PANIC* (separation panic/sadness), *LUST*, *CARE* (care/nurturance), *PLAY* (joy), and *SEEKING* (a generalized appetitive/exploratory system that regulates reward seeking). More recently, Toronchuk and Ellis (2013) suggested that the model should be expanded to include two additional systems, *DISGUST* and *POWER/dominance*.

One notable contribution of this research program is the attempt to specify in some detail how different systems interact by potentiating or inhibiting one another's activity. For example, Panksepp (1998) drew on neurobiological and pharmacological evidence to argue that RAGE inhibits the activity of FEAR, PANIC, and SEEKING, whereas FEAR potentiates the other three systems. An important limitation of the model—which self-consciously echoes McDougall's instinct theory—is the assumed one-to-one correspondence between each system and one specific emotion, which precludes the strategic flexibility and computational richness of the multi-emotion systems theorized by Bowlby and others. Another limitation is the insistence that, to be truly "basic," emotional systems must be shared across all mammalian species. Each species faces somewhat distinctive adaptive problems, and humans have evolved complex forms of social interaction that make them unique among mammals and primates (e.g., Borgerhoff Mulder & Beheim, 2011; Hrdy & Burkart, 2020, Chapter 47 in this volume; Kaplan et al., 2009; Pinker, 2010; Quinlan, 2008). Thus, humans can be expected to possess species-specific motivations and emotions, as well as many unique variations on pan-mammalian motives (Al-Shawaf et al., 2016; Aunger & Curtis, 2013).

Some Recent Contributions

In the last 10 years or so, there have been several notable contributions based on the concept of behavioral/motivational systems, including integrative works on the systems underlying caregiving (Brown et al., 2012; Schaller, 2018), pair-bonding (Fletcher et al., 2015), dominance and status (Anderson et al., 2015; Johnson et al., 2012), and play (Pellis et al., 2019). Woody and Szechtman (2011) presented a detailed analysis of the *security system* (or *precaution system*; Boyer & Liénard, 2006), a motivational system specialized to prevent rare, potential threats and associated with anxiety and apprehension (in contrast with fear triggered by imminent threats).

In their evolutionary renovation of Maslow's ever-popular "pyramid of needs" (1954), Kenrick and colleagues (2010) described seven fundamental motives—*immediate physiological needs, self-protection, affiliation, status/esteem, mate acquisition, mate retention*, and *parenting*. The ordering of the motives reflects both their cognitive priority (higher to lower precedence) and their timing of emergence during the life course (earlier to later development). Each motive is served by one or more motivational systems, which in turn are composed by "(a) a template for recognizing a particular class of relevant environmental threats or opportunities, (b) inner motivational/physiological states designed to mobilize relevant resources, (c) cognitive decision rules designed to analyze trade-offs inherent in various prepotent responses, and (d) a set of responses designed to respond to threats or opportunities represented by the environmental inputs (i.e., to achieve adaptive goals)" (Kenrick et al., 2010, p. 306). Neel and colleagues (2016) developed the framework by adding *disease avoidance* as distinct from fear-based self-protection, and replacing parenting with a broader motive of *kin care*.

Although Kenrick and colleagues repeatedly implied that evolved responses to threats and opportunities include the experience of feelings, they remained vague about the specific nature and adaptive role of those feelings. Beall and Tracy (2017) set out to complete the framework by linking the activation of each fundamental motivation with the onset of a distinct emotion: fear for self-protection, happiness for affiliation, pride for status/esteem, lust for mate acquisition, romantic love for mate retention, and tenderness for parenting/kin care. In line with the coordination approach, the emotion triggered by a motivational system orchestrates cognition, physiology, and behavior so as to reach the system's adaptive outcome (effectively working as an "effector" of the system). Beall and Tracy made a valuable contribution by explicitly linking the concept of motivational systems with the coordination approach to emotions. As they themselves acknowledged, the idea that complex computational mechanisms like the status/esteem system are associated with just *one* characteristic emotion (instead of multiple emotions, including not only pride but also shame, embarrassment, etc.) is problematic and should be revised. Luckily, more sophisticated models of motivation are readily available (see above) and can be integrated within the same basic framework.

Drawing on a century of literature on this topic, Aunger and Curtis (2013) presented a biologically informed taxonomy of human motivational systems (which they labeled "motives"). Their list comprises *hunger, comfort, fear, disgust, lust, attract* (a system specialized for mating competition), *love* (pair-bonding), *nurture, affiliate, status, justice* (a system that regulates reciprocal exchange), *hoard* (resource acquisition), *create, curiosity,* and *play*. I made a similar attempt to present an organized taxonomy of motivation in a book on psychopathology (Del Giudice, 2018). The admittedly partial list of systems I proposed includes *aggression, fear, security, disgust, status, mating, attachment, caregiving, pair bonding, affiliation, reciprocity, acquisition, play,* and *curiosity*.

A Map of Human Motivational Systems

Even though different scholars have proposed somewhat different taxonomies of motivational systems, there are more commonalities than differences. If one excludes "physiological needs" like hunger, thirst, and thermoregulation, human motivations can be related to five broad categories of adaptive problems: (a) prevention and avoidance of physical hazards; (b) acquisition and enhancement of resources (including "embodied" resources such as knowledge and skills; Kaplan et al., 2000, 2007); (c) mating and reproduction; (d) relations with kin; and (e) relations within and between groups. Each of these categories comprises several specific problems that can be solved by specialized motivational systems, each equipped with domain-relevant goals and algorithms.

Figure 5.1 shows a partial map of human motivational systems, derived from recent syntheses of the literature (mainly Aunger & Curtis, 2013; Del Giudice, 2018; Kenrick et al., 2010). I briefly describe each of the systems later in this section. Note that, while the taxonomy in Figure 5.1 has enough support to serve as a useful starting point, it is also provisional in many respects. Some systems (e.g., fear, attachment) have been studied extensively for decades, and we have detailed information on their adaptive goals, activating cues/situations, operating rules, associated emotions, neurobiological bases, and developmental patterns; other putative systems (e.g., acquisition, creation) are understood only in their generalities, or represent plausible but still largely hypothetical adaptations.

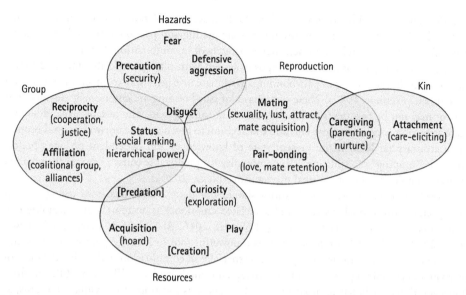

Figure 5.1. A partial map of human motivational systems, grouped into five broad categories of adaptive problems. Some alternative labels used in the literature are shown in parentheses. The systems in square brackets are still mostly hypothetical but warrant further investigation.

How Many Systems?

Questions about the "right" number of constructs are as old as the psychology of motivation; lack of agreement on the number of human instincts was a contributing factor to the waning of instinct theories in the 1920s (Krantz & Allen, 1967; Scheffer & Heckhausen, 2018). A hundred years later, we are much better equipped to deal with this problem, having realized that the evolution of complex biological mechanisms (including the brain) proceeds by reuse, duplication, partial differentiation, and gradual accrual of function (see Barrett, 2012, 2015a). This intricate process of "descent with modification" does not deliver neatly packaged mechanisms with simple, well-specified functions—instead, it produces overlapping mechanisms with somewhat indistinct boundaries, multiple functions, and a great deal of redundancy (Nesse, 2020). Moreover, most computational mechanisms are composed of simpler components or sub-processes, some of which may be shared with other mechanisms. The bottom line is that, as in the case of emotions, it may not be possible to converge on a single, unambiguous taxonomy of motivational systems; there will always be multiple defensible ways to draw boundaries between related systems, and multiple levels of resolution to describe the same computational processes (Kenrick et al., 2010). In fact, the problem of "how many motivational systems there are" is essentially the same problem of "how many emotions there are"—only somewhat more tractable, because there are many fewer motivational systems than distinguishable emotions.

To illustrate, Gilbert (2005) described a single *sexual system* that covers everything from sexual desire to romantic love; Kenrick and colleagues (2010) separated *mate acquisition* (sexual desire and attraction) from *mate retention* (including pair-bonding); while Aunger and Curtis (2013) drew a subtler distinction between systems that regulate sexual desire (*lust*), mate attraction and competition (*attract*), and pair-bonding (*love*). There is no doubt that sexual desire and romantic love share some deep functional connections; however, they can occur independently of one another, have different emotional constellations and evolutionary histories, and serve different goals within the broader task of reproduction (more on this below). I believe there is a strong case for treating mating and pair-bonding as distinct motivational systems that can become activated separately or in combination; but it is also possible to regard them as part of a larger, composite system with phylogenetically older and newer components. In the process of pair-bonding, passionate love gives way to affection and "loving attachment" (Tennov, 1999). These two phases of pair-bonding are emotionally distinct, and may or may not be best described as outputs of the same system. The case of sexual desire vs. mate attraction is even less clear-cut, and the decision to postulate one or two systems becomes more arbitrary (at least in the present state of knowledge) and dependent on one's preferences for "lumping" vs. "splitting." This ambiguity is a predictable consequence of the organic, evolved complexity of motivational mechanisms (Nesse, 2020).

Needless to say, these complications should not deter researchers from trying to map our species' motivational systems (and associated emotions) as accurately and meaningfully as possible. Evolutionary task analysis (Al-Shawaf, 2016; Al-Shawaf & Lewis, 2017; Lewis et al., 2017; Tooby & Cosmides, 2015) is a powerful tool to identify putative systems and draw functional distinctions among them—especially in combination with a rich database of behavioral, neurobiological, and comparative/phylogenetic evidence. This is no different from how evolutionary scholars approach the analysis and classification of individual emotions, as exemplified in many chapters of this volume.

A focus on the adaptive tasks and computational logic of motivational systems is essential to overcome the shortcomings of atheoretical correlational methods, such as factor analysis and principal component analysis (PCA). Patterns of correlations among multiple types of behaviors, emotional experiences, and so forth can be informative and heuristically useful; but when they are used to make inferences about the *mechanisms* that give rise to those behaviors, emotions, etc., correlational analyses are severely limited and can be downright misleading (see also Lukaszewski et al., 2020). The output of a motivational system is not fixed, but conditional on the nature of the current situation (e.g., threat vs. opportunity) and the individual's success or failure relative to the system's goal. These appraisals and the emotional responses they trigger are further modulated by individual differences in the system's working parameters and the value of the relevant regulatory variables. Activation of attachment needs can lead to vigorous crying but also withdrawal and detachment; a challenge to one's status can lead to pride and elevation but also shame, submission, or defeat. In other words, a system can be *functionally* coherent, but this coherence may not translate into simple patterns of correlations among the system's outputs. For example, infants' attachment behaviors in response to separation require at least two dimensions of variation to be adequately summarized (Fraley & Spieker, 2003). Moreover, between-person correlations do not simply reflect the dynamics of individual systems, but also patterns of co-activation and inhibition between multiple systems and individual differences at various timescales. And when the measured indicators include emotions, the use of standard labels makes it impossible to detect functional distinctions *within* folk categories such as "anger" or "anxiety."

Given all the above, it is rather unlikely that the dimensions identified by factor analysis or PCA will correspond to specific mechanisms. In practice, the situation is even worse: first, determining the "correct" number of dimensions to retain is an ill-specified task with no straightforward solution (see Del Giudice, 2021); and second, standard algorithms for rotating factors/components are designed to seek a "simple structure" in the data—a hopelessly unrealistic assumption for many complex biological systems (Lykken, 1971).[3] To illustrate, Brasini and colleagues (2020) performed factor analysis on a pool of behaviors and emotions selected to indicate the activation of seven motivational systems (attachment, caregiving, rank competition, sexuality, cooperation, affiliation, and social play). Unsurprisingly, the analysis failed to clearly identify the hypothesized systems; instead, it returned some composite factors (e.g., a "prosociality" factor mixing caregiving and cooperation; an "insecurity" factor mixing attachment, submission, and shame), as well as a separate factor for dominant and high-status behaviors. Because correlational methods are intrinsically limited in their ability to answer questions about mechanisms and processes (especially in the absence of strong theoretical models), the same problems arise in the study of personality (Baumert et al., 2017; Borsboom et al., 2009; Davis & Panksepp, 2018; Lukaszewski et al., 2020; more on this below).

In the remainder of this section, I outline the motivational systems shown in Figure 5.1. I want to stress that this is only intended as a brief summary, far from an in-depth evolutionary and computational analysis. For more detailed overviews, see Aunger and Curtis (2013); Bugental (2000); Kenrick and colleagues (2010); and Toronchuk and Ellis (2013), in addition to the literature cited in each subsection.[4]

Fear System

The fear system is an ancient defensive mechanism that motivates organisms to avoid or escape immediate threats. This system can be activated by a multitude of cues and situations, and many specific fears are acquired through learning. However, some types of stimuli elicit fear with no need for learning (e.g., sudden loud noises) or after minimal exposure (e.g., snakes, spiders, angry male faces; LoBue & Rakison, 2013; Mallan et al., 2013; Öhman, 2009). *Tonic* and *attentive immobility* are important components of the fear system. Attentive immobility or "freezing" occurs in preparation for escape or fighting; tonic immobility is a kind of paralysis or fainting without loss of consciousness, a last resort defense when harm is inevitable (Hagenaars et al., 2014; Roelofs, 2017). In contrast, successful escape/avoidance triggers feelings of safety and relief.

Defensive Aggression System

Aggression is a basic motivation to harm or threaten other organisms, including—but not limited to—individuals of the same species. Aggression is often deployed as a defensive strategy in response to immediate threats to oneself, one's kin, or one's allies. Defensive aggression has been labeled as *reactive, affective, emotional*, etc.; it is marked by intense arousal, anger, or rage, and can be triggered by high levels of fear (Panksepp, 1998, 2011). For this reason, defensive aggression and fear are sometimes discussed together as part of a unitary "fight-or-flight" or "fight-flight-freeze" system (e.g., Corr et al., 2013; Corr & Krupić, 2017). However, aggressive motivations are not always defensive. A prime example of *proactive, instrumental*, or *predatory* aggression is hunting, which involves extreme aggression toward prey but no anger. In fact, "proactive" aggression can be accompanied by feelings of pleasure and excitement (Chester, 2017; Chichinadze et al., 2011; Panksepp, 1998).

In humans, proactive aggression is also a key component of group conflicts and wars, in the course of which the enemy is dehumanized and effectively treated like prey (Wrangham, 1999, 2018). Proactive aggression can be employed to reinforce dominance hierarchies, take or steal resources, and more generally control the behavior of others. Whereas defensive aggression can be meaningfully treated as a distinct motivational system (in analogy with fear, disgust, etc.), I concur with Aunger and Curtis (2013) that—generally speaking—proactive aggression is best understood as a behavioral tactic in the service of other motivations (e.g., status, acquisition). On the other hand, humans have a long evolutionary history as predators, and a number of cognitive adaptations that seem to be specialized for interactions with prey (Barrett, 2015b). One can tentatively hypothesize the existence of a specialized motivational system for *predation*, which is activated both during hunting/fishing and in intergroup conflicts (Figure 5.1). A predation system would most likely develop in a sex-specific way, and may be only fully expressed in boys and men.

Precaution System

Like the fear system, the precaution system is a mechanism designed to protect organisms from threats. The crucial difference is that fear is triggered by immediate threats, whereas precautionary motivations are activated by *potential* threats—that is, threats that are comparatively rare and hard to detect but may have catastrophic consequences, such as dangerous predators or contaminating pathogens (Boyer & Liénard, 2006; Woody & Szechtman, 2011). Immediate threats evoke fear and escape/fight behaviors; in contrast, activation of the precaution system is marked by anxiety, wariness, and repetitive behaviors such as checking and exploration, which help gather further information about the presence of potential risks. Indeed, the precaution system tends to inhibit fear, preventing flight/panic responses to permit cautious exploration (Graeff, 2004). The precaution system is activated by subtle and indirect cues of danger; but the *absence* of a potential threat is hard or even impossible to determine with certainty, and there are no clear signals indicating whether precautionary behaviors have been successful. Thus, the system is not deactivated by situational cues, but by the precautionary behaviors themselves, provided that they have been correctly executed (Woody & Szechtman, 2011). In my previous work (Del Giudice, 2018), I adopted Woody and Szechtman's label of "security system," but "precaution" (Boyer & Liénard, 2006) is more transparent and less likely to generate confusion with affiliation and attachment.

Disgust System

The disgust system is a defensive mechanism whose original function is preventing contact with pathogens and/or toxins through ingestion of contaminated foods, drinks, or waste products; manipulation of contaminated objects; and contact with infected people or animal pathogen vectors (*pathogen* disgust; Curtis, 2011; Toronchuk & Ellis, 2013). Pathogen disgust promotes physical avoidance, expulsion (e.g., vomiting), and cleaning behaviors. Disgust can also trigger activation of the precaution system, and the two systems often work in synergy. Over evolutionary history, the disgust system has been co-opted and differentiated to deal with other kinds of threats (Tybur et al., 2013). In particular, *sexual* disgust is designed to prevent sexual contact with partners that would be detrimental to fitness, for example because they are too old, too genetically similar (e.g., siblings and other close kin), or prone to sexually transmitted diseases (e.g., highly promiscuous individuals). Finally, disgust in our species is deeply connected to morality: violations of moral norms and taboos can elicit disgust and feelings of uncleanliness and contamination. A likely function of *moral* disgust is to motivate and coordinate social distancing from (and/or condemnation of) individuals who violate moral rules (Tybur et al., 2013). While failure to avoid contact with repulsive objects leads to intense physical discomfort, motivational failures in the sexual and moral domains may also evoke evaluative emotions such as shame and guilt.

Status System

In animals, dominance motivational systems have two complementary functions: (a) enhancing, defending, and displaying one's social rank; and (b) when necessary, submitting to higher-ranking individuals to avoid punishment and retaliation (Toronchuk & Ellis, 2013). In our species, social hierarchies reflect both physical dominance and skill-based *prestige*; the more general concept of a "status system" covers both aspects, emphasizing the complex nature of human competition (see Anderson et al., 2015; Aunger & Curtis, 2013; Cheng et al., 2010; Cheng et al., 2013; Johnson et al., 2012; Maner, 2017). The status system is activated by challenges to one's dominance rank or prestige (from provocations and disrespectful acts to situations that involve social judgments), but also by opportunities to rise in the social hierarchy; depending on the nature of the situation and the person's current rank and capabilities, the associated emotions may include anger, (performance) anxiety, envy, hope, and excitement. The main emotions triggered by success are pride and confidence, whereas failure tends to elicit shame, anger, frustration, and sadness. Importantly, voluntary deference to high-status individuals (leaders, teachers, etc.) can evoke a range of positive emotions such as admiration and awe (Keltner et al., 2006). The concept of a status system absorbs the motivational functions that have been ascribed to the emotional mechanisms of pride and shame, such as promoting and advertising the achievement of socially valued goals/characteristics (Sznycer, 2019; Sznycer, Al-Shawaf, et al., 2017; see also Durkee et al., 2019). Dominance competition often elicits aggression, and the two systems are deeply connected on a functional level (Anderson et al., 2015; Toronchuk & Ellis, 2013).

Mating System

The mating system plays a critical role in reproduction by motivating sexual behavior, from courtship and mate choice to intercourse. The system is activated by the presence or prospect of attractive partners and/or rivals; the emotional constellation of mating is varied, ranging from arousal, desire, excitement, and pleasure to embarrassment, anxiety, and shame (e.g., Al-Shawaf et al., 2016; Toronchuk & Ellis, 2013). In a broader perspective, it is important to note that mating and sexuality can be put in the service of other motivations and goals—for example, reinforcing a long-term bond, enhancing one's social status, exerting dominance, or exchanging sex for gifts and other resources (e.g., Gangestad & Haselton, 2015; Meston & Buss, 2007).

Attachment System

Like most young mammals, infants and children are vulnerable and depend on adults for feeding and protection. The attachment system is designed to monitor and maintain the proximity and availability of caregivers (see above). In infancy and childhood, attachment has high motivational priority, consistent with its critical role in ensuring survival. When activated, the attachment system inhibits play and curiosity; conversely, the presence of an available attachment figure works as a "secure base" for exploration (Cassidy, 2016). In our species, attachment has been co-opted as a building block of close relationships in adulthood, including those with romantic partners and friends (Fletcher et al., 2015; Mikulincer & Shaver, 2016; Zeifman & Hazan, 2016). Specifically, most intimate relationships involve an attachment component, as they provide comfort, reassurance, and safety in times of distress.

Caregiving System

Mirroring the biological function of the attachment system, the caregiving system motivates parents and other caregivers to protect and nurture their dependent young (Brown et al., 2012; Cassidy, 2016; Panksepp, 1998, 2011; Schaller, 2018). As a species, humans show many features of *cooperative breeding*: across societies, care and protection are provided not just by parents, but by multiple individuals including older siblings, grandparents, and friends (Hrdy, 2005; Kramer, 2010). Thus, caregiving motivations need not be restricted to one's biological offspring. Caregiving is primarily activated by displays of immaturity, vulnerability, and/or distress (e.g., crying, cute baby-like features) and can trigger a range of emotions: tenderness, "anxious solicitude," protectiveness, as well as parental love and pride. Failures of the caregiving motivation can trigger powerful negative emotions of sadness and guilt (e.g., Gilbert, Chapter 15 in this volume).

Pair-Bonding System
Pair-bonding is a central feature of human mating. It has plausibly evolved from the integration of sexual attraction with attachment and caregiving—two motivations rooted in parent–child relations—and reused to enable long-term bonding between sexual partners. In part, romantic love can be seen as a blend of emotions associated with these three systems; at the same time, the psychology of love also shows unique features and evidence of functional specialization. For example, being in love temporarily inhibits the desire for alternative sexual partners, thus working as a credible signal of interest and a "commitment device" in view of shared parental investment (Doherty & Brumbaugh, Chapter 11 in this volume; Eastwick, 2009; Fletcher et al., 2015; Gangestad & Thornhill, 2007; Quinlan, 2008). Also, love is powerfully associated with jealousy, an emotional mechanism designed to prevent infidelity by partners (Buss, 2013). For these reasons, it makes sense to postulate a specialized pair-bonding system with the specific goal of forming and maintaining long-term couple relationships (Aunger & Curtis, 2013; Kenrick et al., 2010; see also Barbaro, 2020).

Affiliation System
Affiliation is a key motivational substrate of group living; its function is to enable and sustain long-term relationships with extended kin and other group members, including friends and allies. As with pair bonding, the psychology of affiliation overlaps with that of attachment; at the same time, friendship and group membership are sufficiently distinct from parent–child relations to warrant the idea of a specialized motivational system (Aunger & Curtis, 2013; Bugental, 2000; Kenrick et al., 2010). The affiliation system can be activated not only by the perception of shared interests and goals, but also by threatening situations, lack of social resources (isolation, rejection), and intergroup conflict. Successful affiliation evokes feelings of security and belonging, promotes the formation of a shared group identity, and sustains cooperation and reciprocity.

Reciprocity System
While the affiliation system promotes affective bonding with other group members, the reciprocity system deals with cooperation and with the exchange of favors and resources. Its main tasks are selecting cooperation partners, optimizing joint and personal benefits, and monitoring/enforcing fairness (Bugental, 2000; Keltner et al., 2006). Even though extensive cooperation networks of non-kin are unique to humans, other primates do engage in more limited forms of reciprocity, for example in the context of grooming and food sharing (Engelmann et al., 2015; Jaeggi et al., 2013; Jaeggi & Gurven, 2013). The reciprocity system can be activated by opportunities such as the presence of a capable and trustworthy partner, or by threats such as cheating and unfairness. The corresponding emotions include trust, benevolence, suspiciousness, and moral indignation. In humans, reciprocity is supported by specialized cognitive mechanisms that monitor violations of rules and keep track of partners' contributions and reputations over time (Cosmides & Tooby, 2015). While successful exchanges engender satisfaction and gratitude, failures of reciprocity may arouse intense anger and contempt or guilt, depending on whether one is the victim or the perpetrator.

Acquisition System

An obvious but sometimes overlooked characteristic of our species is the extent to which we store and accumulate resources for future use. Material wealth—in the form of land, cattle, houses, or money—provides immediate adaptive benefits as it improves both mating success (especially in men) and the survival of children (see Borgerhoff Mulder & Beheim, 2011; Nettle & Pollet, 2008). Moreover, stored resources reduce risk by working as a buffer against periods of scarcity and can be passed down from one generation to the next, with cumulative effects on long-term fitness (Borgerhoff Mulder et al., 2009; Winterhalder et al., 1999). Unsurprisingly, humans have strong motivations to acquire resources, accumulate them, and defend them against theft, as well as a distinct psychology of ownership based on emotions such as desire, envy, and greed. The acquisition system likely has its evolutionary roots in the mechanisms that mediate foraging and food hoarding (Aunger & Curtis, 2013; Preston, 2014; Preston & Vickers, 2014). The specific goals of the acquisition system depend on its interaction with other motivations such as mating and pair-bonding. For example, saving resources for future family needs in the context of a long-term relationship is not the same as acquiring costly luxury goods to boost success in courtship and short-term mating (Griskevicius et al., 2007; Sundie et al., 2011).

Aunger and Curtis (2013) argued that humans possess a specific motive to improve and maintain their habitat, making it more conducive to survival and reproduction. The relevant behaviors include building dwellings, removing parasites and other dangers, tidying and repairing habitat, and producing tools and artifacts. While there is little evolutionary work on creation as a motivational system, the construct is plausible enough to be tentatively included in the map of human motivation (Figure 5.1).

Curiosity System

Acquiring knowledge and exploring new environments have long been recognized as fundamental motives in animals (Aunger & Curtis, 2013; Loewenstein, 1994). Information-seeking is essential to building models of the world and improving one's ability to make inferences and predictions (Gottlieb et al., 2013). In humans, knowledge can be used to build prestige or increase one's value as a social partner. Far from being a "cold" cognitive task, the acquisition of information is regulated by a wide range of emotions and feelings, from excitement and surprise to boredom, frustration, and anxiety. Curiosity and exploration are often discussed in association with play, and play is certainly a powerful way to gather information about oneself, other people, and the environment. Even pretend play based on unrealistic scenarios can play a critical role in building sophisticated causal models of the world (Weisberg & Gopnik, 2013). However, there are many ways to acquire knowledge that do not rely on play; moreover, language permits massive transfer of information without the need for firsthand experience. In humans, adaptations for learning seem to be matched by adaptations for *teaching*, the deliberate transmission of knowledge and skills (Csibra & Gergely, 2006; Fogarty et al., 2011).

Play System

Play behaviors are widespread in mammals and absorb a large fraction of juveniles' time and energy. The overarching function of play is to enable self-training in a range of adaptive skills; fighting, parenting, and foraging are prominent recurring themes across species. More specific functions are regulating neuromuscular development, learning how to cope with unexpected events, and testing the limits of one's abilities (Burghardt, 2005; Byers & Walker, 1995; Spinka et al., 2001). While playful motivation in mammals seems to be mediated by a specialized mechanism (Panksepp, 1998, 2005, 2011; Pellis et al., 2019), it always works in synergy with other motivational systems that provide the momentary goals of play and the relevant behavioral/emotional repertoires. For example, rough-and-tumble play stems from the playful coordination of the fear, defensive aggression, predation, and status systems (see Pellis et al., 2019). Cognitive skills are also exercised through play, as when children play games of memory, numbers, and language (e.g., Locke & Bogin, 2006). Finally, play promotes social bonding in synergy with the affiliation system (Toronchuk & Ellis, 2013) and can also be an effective way to *display* skills and other attractive traits (e.g., strength, intelligence) to potential allies and partners.

Extending the Coordination Approach

The standard coordination approach to emotions makes certain assumptions about the computational architecture of emotions. Specifically, emotion mechanisms are thought to comprise two kinds of components: (a) *situation-detecting algorithms* that monitor for situation-defining cues, and perform computations of variable complexity to identify the presence of the activating situation; and (b) *coordination programs* that signal to the downstream mechanisms (e.g., memory, attention, autonomic, and other physiological systems), switching them into the appropriate functioning mode. Because more than one emotion-eliciting situation may occur at the same time (e.g., an animal may be hungry *and* being attacked by a predator), emotion mechanisms are supervised by *prioritizing algorithms* that determine the degree of compatibility between multiple emotion modes, and resolve conflicts by giving priority to the most important or pressing situations (Cosmides & Tooby, 2000; Tooby & Cosmides, 2008, Chapter 2 in this volume). This architecture is sketched in Figure 5.2A. Note that, for clarity, the figure depicts emotions and motivational systems as separate mechanisms with clear-cut boundaries; as I discussed earlier, this is a dramatic simplification of reality.

A motivational-systems perspective suggests some modifications to the standard approach, as illustrated in Figure 5.2B. Most notably, motivational systems take up the task of detecting situations, and subsequently activate different emotions depending on the state of the organism and its environment vis à vis the system's goal(s). This revision has two main consequences. First, emotion mechanisms are effectively reduced to coordination programs. Second, situation-detecting algorithms are decoupled from emotion mechanisms, so that similar situations may give rise to different emotions depending on the motivational state of the individual, while situations pertaining to different motivational domains may trigger the same emotion (possibly with alternative motivation-specific "flavors").

In addition to detecting goal-relevant situations, motivational systems monitor the progress of current behavior in relation to the active goals, evaluate situations in terms of success vs. failure, and strategically deploy emotions in order to increase the chances of success, avoid failure, or deal with failure and mitigate its costs if necessary. In the diagram of Figure 5.2B, these computational tasks are carried out by *goal pursuit/evaluation algorithms*. Note that multiple motivational systems may make use of the same information to perform their computations. For example, information about the possession of socially valued traits such as attractiveness and trustworthiness (see Sznycer & Lukaszewski, 2019) is going to affect evaluations (and the intensity of the corresponding emotions) across a number of distinct motivational domains—from status, reciprocity, and affiliation to mating and pair-bonding (Scrivner et al., Chapter 4 in this volume).

Figure 5.2B makes the additional assumption that control signals flow in one particular direction, that is, from motivational systems to emotion mechanisms but not vice versa (i.e., emotions do not directly coordinate motivational systems). This simplifying assumption is open to revision, as future research unveils the computational logic of various motivational

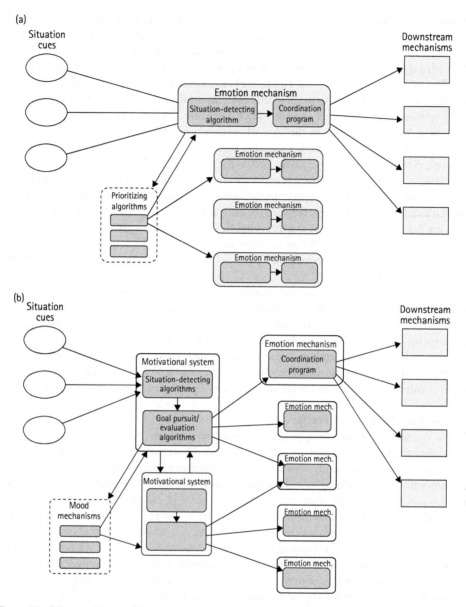

Figure 5.2. Schematic diagram of the computational architectures underlying (A) the standard coordination approach; and (B) the extended coordination approach, in which emotion mechanisms are themselves coordinated by a layer of motivational systems. Each motivational system detects a range of situations, integrates them over time, evaluates them in relation to its specific goals, activates the appropriate emotions, and modulates the activity of other systems. Note that a given emotion may be activated by more than one motivational system, and thus may play a role in the pursuit of more than one adaptive goal. Moods are produced by superordinate mechanisms that use information from motivational systems (and/or other inputs, such as the immune system) to assess/predict the state of the organism and its environment on a more global scale, and to regulate the activity of several motivational systems at once.

systems. To be clear, even if emotions do not directly control motivational systems, they still "motivate behavior" in the sense of activating certain action tendencies. The point is that, according to this model, motivational *goals* are processed upstream of emotions rather than downstream (e.g., pride is triggered by the successful pursuit of status-enhancement goals).

The extended architecture in Figure 5.2B is characterized by a hierarchical "bow-tie" structure, in which a large number of inputs and outputs flow through a small set of common, highly conserved processes that form the "knot" of the tie (Csete & Doyle, 2004). In this case, the central knot corresponds to the layer of motivational systems. Bow-tie architectures are ubiquitous in biological systems, from genetic regulation and immunity to cellular and neural signaling (Doyle & Csete, 2011; Kitano, 2004; Kitano & Oda, 2006). The compact size of the knot (e.g., a small set of regulatory genes or second messenger molecules) permits rapid, efficient control of the entire system in response to challenges and fluctuations. At the same time, the comparatively weak linkages between the central knot and input/output processes increase both the flexibility of the system and its evolvability. For example, a given motivational system can easily evolve to process different situation cues, or trigger additional emotions that were previously specific to other systems, with few or no changes to its set-goals and core algorithms ("plug-and-play modularity").

The Achilles' heel of bow-tie architectures lies in the same features that make them versatile and robust to perturbations—that is, the small size and centralized control function of the knot. If knot processes get damaged or successfully hijacked (for example by parasites), the consequences can be catastrophic. As a result, central processes are more tightly regulated than the ones in the periphery, and tend to evolve at a much slower pace (Csete & Doyle, 2004; Kitano, 2004). These properties of bow-tie architectures could have interesting implications for the study of motivation and emotion from a phylogenetic and comparative perspective.

Higher-Order Coordination Problems

In the standard coordination approach, the need to postulate the existence of prioritizing algorithms (Figure 5.2A) points to what I will call the *second-order* coordination problem. Emotions evolved to efficiently coordinate a large number of psychological and physiological mechanisms, by "centralizing" the detection of situations and the generation of appropriate activity patterns. However, there are not just a handful of emotion mechanisms, but dozens of them—and hence dozens of potential modes of operation for the organism, many of which have mutually contradictory effects;[5] hence, the second-order problem of how to coordinate the activity of this teeming multitude of emotion mechanisms, resolving potential conflicts and maintaining a coherent sequence of behavior. In the standard approach, this role is fulfilled by prioritizing algorithms, whose architecture and functional properties are left unspecified. In the extended approach I am proposing, motivational systems directly control the activation of emotion mechanisms, and thus solve the second-order coordination problem without the need for a dedicated supervisory system.

Although motivational systems solve the second-order coordination problem, they still necessitate ways to resolve conflicts and prioritize certain goals over others, giving rise to a *third-order* coordination problem. This may sound like infinite regress, but it is not: as the number of mechanisms that have to be coordinated shrinks, it becomes possible to use coordination strategies that would be impractical or intractable at lower levels of the control hierarchy. For example, cross-modulation (e.g., reciprocal inhibition between functionally incompatible systems) may allow motivational systems to self-coordinate to a certain degree, and make it possible to "arbitrate" simple priority conflicts without the intervention of superordinate mechanisms. Cross-modulation is feasible within a relatively small set of motivational systems, but would become cumbersome (and potentially unworkable) if scaled up to dozens of emotion mechanisms with thousands of potential connections among them.

Moods as Third-Order Coordination Programs

The concept of higher-order coordination problems shines new light on the old and perplexing question of what differentiates emotions from moods. Phenomenologically, moods are long-lasting and have a diffuse rather than focused quality; unlike emotions, they do not have a specific cause or triggering object, and do not prompt specific behaviors or action tendencies (Beedie et al., 2005; Gendolla, 2000). At the same time, they have a powerful (if nonspecific) impact on motivation, and dispose people to appraise new situations in affect-congruent ways (e.g., attributing hostile intentions to others when one is in an irritable mood; see Siemer, 2009).

Current biological models of mood resonate with Nesse's (1990) suggestion that mood encodes a global estimate of the "propitiousness" of the environment, or the expected rate of reward per unit of effort invested (a plausible internal regulatory variable). Similarly, Morris (1992) framed mood as a system that regulates goal-directed behavior so as to maintain a balance between goal-relevant resources and demands; mood improves when (personal and environmental) resources are more plentiful than necessary to meet demands, and deteriorates when resources are perceived as inadequate. Nettle and Bateson (2012) argued that, as organisms experience rewards and punishments, they revise their estimates of the probability of the two types of outcomes, and adjust the thresholds that determine how easily a new situation is perceived as a potential reward or a potential threat. In this model, the organism's "core" mood reflects the settings of two separate thresholds for detecting/responding to rewards and punishments (e.g., a depressed mood corresponds to high thresholds for both rewards and punishments). Trimmer and colleagues (2013) proposed a somewhat different two-dimensional scheme that distinguishes between the organism's general positive vs. negative expectations and its level of preparedness to act (e.g., a depressed mood corresponds to a combination of negative expectations and low preparedness). In his later work, Nesse (2004) focused on the relation between high vs. low mood and the rate of progress in the pursuit of domain-specific goals. Across domains, reaching one's goals faster than expected elicits positive moods, which in turn facilitate investing more effort; whereas the perception that goals keep getting farther away despite increasing effort is a trigger for low mood and depression, which promote disengagement and effort withdrawal. Eldar and colleagues (2016) echoed these ideas with the notion that mood is especially influenced by prediction errors, and specifically by positive vs. negative discrepancies between expected and actual outcomes (e.g., rewards). In the same paper, they argued that mood encodes the *momentum* of recent outcomes (i.e., their improving or declining trend), and noted that forming global expectations about future rewards based on specific events can be adaptive if different sources of reward (e.g., material resources, social status, sexual partners) tend to be correlated with one another.

From the standpoint of the extended coordination approach, moods are easily understood as the product of third-order coordination mechanisms that (a) receive information from motivational systems about success and failure in the pursuit of domain-specific goals (together with other inputs that encode the state of the organism, for example its immunological condition, energetic balance, and level of fatigue); (b) compute integrative estimates of the present/future state of the organism in relation to its environment, for example based on the momentum of recent outcomes; and (c) strategically modulate the functioning of multiple motivational systems—not just by generically "activating" or "inhibiting" them, but also by selectively influencing their sensitivity to threats vs. opportunities (as in the threshold model by Nettle and Bateson, 2012). Computationally, some of these modulation effects may be construed as changes in the settings of global or motivation-specific regulatory variables. According to this model (Figure 5.2B), moods act as superordinate programs that function to coordinate the activity of motivational systems. They affect cognition, behavior, and physiology on a broad scale, but do so *indirectly* through the action of multiple motivational systems and the corresponding emotions (see also Morris, 1992). To the extent that motivational systems directly modulate one another, some aspects of the phenomenology of moods may reflect self-coordination instead of regulation by superordinate programs; precisely how much top-down regulation is needed to produce moods will become clearer as we learn more about the dynamic interplay between motivational systems.

The extended coordination approach accommodates the main insights of other biological models and accounts for key aspects of the phenomenology of moods, including the combination of high motivational potency and low motivational specificity. It also provides a simple, principled answer to the long-standing question of what the difference is between emotions and moods. Both are coordination adaptations; but emotions are first-order coordination mechanisms activated by motivational systems, whereas moods are third-order coordination mechanisms whose primary function is to modulate the activity of motivational systems. From this vantage point, some putative emotions such as *lassitude* (the feeling of being sick; Schrock et al., 2020, Chapter 16 in this volume) should be classified more precisely as moods. Lassitude does not entail specific goals or action tendencies; but when triggered by cues of infection, it modulates a wide range of motivational systems, including the ones that control mating, parenting, hunger, and thermoregulation (Schrock et al., 2020). The effects on cognition and behavior are profound, and can last for days or even weeks (i.e., until the acute phase of the infection is resolved).

The Sequence Integration Problem

In many cases, the meaning of emotion-eliciting situations is not entirely determined by immediate circumstances, but depends on the preceding sequence of situations, outcomes, and emotions. Winning an unlikely victory after suffering humiliation and shame does not just arouse pride and satisfaction, but intoxicating feelings of triumph. In fact, important situations like revenge, betrayal, and reconciliation are *defined* by their place within thematic sequences of events and emotions, which can be represented as movements toward and away from certain motivational goals. This adds a layer of complexity to the task of detecting and evaluating situations, raising what I will call the *sequence integration problem*. In principle, it would be possible to solve the sequence integration problem with a complex system of regulatory variables whose values are updated and accessed by individual emotion mechanisms. However, a control layer of motivational systems addresses this problem in a more straightforward way. Tracking goals over time and evaluating new events in relation to those goals are crucial functions of motivational systems; sequence integration arises naturally out of these functions, without the need for additional computational machinery.

A Note on Feedback vs. Feedforward Control

Both the classic ethological perspective and contemporary theories of self-regulation (e.g., Carver & Scheier, 2013; DeYoung, 2015; DeYoung & Krueger, 2018; Revelle & Condon, 2015) emphasize the critical role of feedback control in the pursuit of goals. Feedback controllers work by reducing the discrepancy between the current state of the world (as sensed and interpreted by the controller) and a desired state or "set point." The set point can be static (*homeostasis*) but need not be—it is possible for a feedback controller to track a "moving target" that changes based on previous events and/or predictions about the future state of the world (*allostasis*; Sterling & Eyer, 1988).

Here I want to briefly note that feedback regulation is not the only possibility, and suggest that the goal-pursuit algorithms employed by motivational systems will often include both feedback and feedforward processes. Instead of continuously self-correcting based on the consequences of previous actions, feedforward controllers *anticipate* the future state of the system, and execute the appropriate action(s) without further course correction. In the simplest forms of feedforward control, no actual predictions are computed and the response has a fixed and "ballistic" quality, as in the case of rapid protective reflexes (e.g., blinking, pain-induced limb retraction). In more sophisticated instances, the controller computes a model of the system and uses the resulting prediction to generate an action, or a prespecified sequence of actions (see Albertos & Mareels, 2010). A thermostat that turns on and off a heater to maintain the target temperature within a house is a classic example of feedback control. A device that automatically turns on the heater at a certain time in the evening to preempt an (expected) temperature drop during the night would be an example of feedforward control based on a simple model of the system. (For an introduction to the basic concepts of control theory, see Del Giudice, 2015; Del Giudice et al., 2018.)

Feedback and feedforward regulation have complementary strengths and weaknesses. For example, feedforward controllers are more resistant to noise and delays in the system, but are unable to deal with unanticipated events; feedback controllers can function without an accurate model of the system, but can only respond to events "after the fact," without the ability to anticipate them (Albertos & Mareels, 2010; Bechhoefer, 2005). In many situations, combining the two strategies yields dramatically improved performance, and I see no reason why motivational systems should not take advantage of this option (see also Tops et al., 2010; Tops et al., 2021). To give a simple example, encountering a dangerous predator at night activates the fear system and the emotion of fear, which in turn may promote escape behaviors (Tooby & Cosmides, 2008). Like other avoidance goals, escaping from danger can be described as a feedback-regulated process, in which the intensity of fear and the urge to flee diminish as one moves farther away from the threat (Ballard et al., 2017). However, this feedback mechanism is vulnerable to noisy information—e.g., the predator may be closer than it seems, it may be hiding in the dark, or there may be *other* predators lurking in the surroundings. At least initially, the escape response is more likely to operate under feedforward control (just run away as fast as possible); indeed, the optimal strategies for defensive mechanisms that deal with uncertain dangers almost invariably involve an initial feedforward phase (Shudo et al., 2003). Likewise, the (feedback-regulated) goal of increasing the distance from the threat may be supplemented by the (feedforward-regulated) goal of reaching a safe hiding place or some other known refuge. In many cases, a regulatory system that combines the strengths of feedback and feedforward control is going to outcompete a system that relies on just one of these principles.

Other Benefits of an Extended Approach

Throughout this section, I have emphasized the theoretical benefits of extending the coordination approach to include a central role for motivation. Another advantage of an extended approach is that it makes it easier to "carve emotions at their functional joints" (Sznycer, Cosmides, et al., 2017; see also Scarantino, 2015), using motivational systems as a guide to plausible functional distinctions. For example, the folk category of "anger" may be usefully analyzed in view of the distinct adaptive problems posed by reciprocal cooperation, pair-bonding, parent–child attachment, status competition, and defensive aggression. I speculate that, when viewed through this lens, the recalibration theory of anger (Sell et al., 2009; Sell et al., 2017; Sell et al., Chapter 8 in this volume) will turn out to apply only to some domains, or will require modifications to match the specifics of the various motivational systems that deploy "angry" emotions. To illustrate: open defiance by a subordinate may signal a bid for dominance; the implications of this gesture go beyond the fact that the subordinate does not place enough weight on the welfare of the dominant individual, and an adaptive response should take this into account. The anger expressed by infants and children toward unresponsive caregivers is not amplified by self-perceived formidability (Sell et al., 2009), but by self-perceived *vulnerability*—and the associated behaviors also function to display heightened vulnerability and immaturity, rather than strength and competence. Anger and rage in the context of defensive aggression may lack a recalibration function altogether, and terminate when the aggressor is gone or incapacitated. Are these "varieties" of anger produced by the same neurocomputational mechanism, or by distinct mechanisms? Answering this question is going to require sustained research effort, and the task will be much facilitated by a working map of the main motivational systems and their adaptive logic.

Conversely, the conceptual precision and careful analytic style that characterize the coordination approach could greatly improve the current understanding of motivational systems. To begin, the lists of emotions associated with the activation, success, and failure of most motivational systems are plausible but still impressionistic (and most likely incomplete). There is urgent need for a fine-grained, empirically rigorous map of the emotional constellations of human motivations. Similarly, existing attempts at specifying the computational logic of human motivational systems are no more than bare-bones outlines, heuristically useful but lacking in detail and precision (e.g., Bugental, 2000; Kenrick et al., 2010). Needless to say, the computational logic of a motivational system is likely to be more complex than that of a single emotion, as it involves more elaborate decision rules and goal-directed control strategies. Hence, the toolkit of the coordination approach will need to be supplemented, for example with concepts and models from mathematical control theory.

Another problem that would benefit from detailed computational analysis concerns the nature of the interplay between multiple systems. The vague notion that motivational systems "activate" or "inhibit" one another (e.g., Bowlby, 1982; Panksepp, 1998) is rooted in simplistic cybernetic and/or neurobiological models, and should be updated with a modern understanding of psychological adaptations. To illustrate, inhibition of a system may be understood as a change in its general threshold for activation, but also as a change in the evaluation of certain activating cues, a strategic adjustment of the system's goals or criteria for success/failure, a selective suppression of some emotional responses, and so forth. Evolutionary models of emotion and motivation naturally complement one another, and there are no good reasons to maintain a separation between these areas of research (Beall & Tracy, 2017).

Implications for Emotion Regulation
From "Emotion Regulation" to "Motivation Regulation"

After decades of research, emotion regulation remains a scientific puzzle. The slow progress on this topic is largely due to a persistent neglect of function beyond immediate proximate concerns. With few exceptions, work in this area has been guided by the "hedonic assumption" that people are motivated by a desire to feel good and avoid feeling bad, and the related notion that emotion regulation is "adaptive" if it leads to more positive (or less negative) feelings (see Aldao, 2013; Erber & Erber, 2000; Tamir, 2009, 2016). These ingrained assumptions have been challenged by another line of work, showing that people have multiple reasons to change their emotional state in ways that are potentially counter-hedonic (e.g., getting important work done, eliciting help and compassion, displaying empathy, matching the emotions of other group members; see Tamir, 2016). While this more realistic approach has been gaining traction in recent years, the focus is still on immediate goals; so far, there have been very few attempts to understand emotion regulation from an explicitly adaptationist perspective. Kisley (Chapter 39 in this volume) has started to lay the groundwork for this enterprise. Here I adopt the working assumption that, while emotions coordinate the state of the organism to deal with *recurrent* adaptive problems, other cognitive mechanisms have a (limited) ability to second-guess emotional responses based on the *unique* features of a situation (see Kisley, Chapter 39). For example, certain situations may cause detection errors, and trigger emotions that are inappropriate or harmful. (This is especially likely when situation cues are ambiguous, inconsistent, or occur in evolutionarily novel contexts.) In other cases, algorithms correctly detect the current situation, but circumstances make it undesirable to express the relevant emotions or act on them (e.g., because doing so would incur social costs, or interfere with other prioritized goals). In yet other cases, the situation may pose multiple contradictory demands, causing a regulatory conflict that cannot be resolved by low-level arbitration processes.

My goal is not to delve into the details of these scenarios, but to suggest a general shift in perspective that may facilitate their functional and evolutionary analysis. Specifically, many phenomena that are currently studied under the rubric of emotion regulation can be understood more accurately and fruitfully as instances of *motivation* regulation. Consider the social situations in which people prefer to "feel bad" for instrumental reasons. One common example is that people who prepare for competitions and other conflictual interactions (e.g., negotiations with strangers) often want to feel at least somewhat angry (e.g., Tamir & Ford, 2012; Tamir et al., 2008; Tamir et al., 2013). I argue that what people are trying to do is not to feel anger per se, but to strategically upregulate specific motivational systems that include anger as a characteristic emotion. In this case, "feeling angry" likely corresponds to the threat-mode activation of either the status system ("dominance challenge") or the reciprocity system ("unfairness"). Note how a motivational perspective helps one to move beyond the folk concept of anger, and consider alternative functional accounts of the same self-reported emotions. This perspective also suggests new hypotheses about the mechanisms of regulation and their proximate functions. To illustrate: activating the status system before a competitive interaction may work not just for its communicative effects (e.g., van Kleef et al., 2004), but also because it indirectly inhibits the reciprocity and affiliation systems—thus making one less inclined to compromise with the adversary, or less receptive to manipulative cues of affiliation.

Regulation Strategies

It is instructive to apply the same lens to the literature on emotion-regulation strategies (Gross, 2015; McRae & Gross, 2020). Cognitive *reappraisal* involves reinterpreting or re-evaluating the situation to change the way one thinks about it. In some cases, "reinterpreting the situation" means downregulating the motivational system activated by the situation, by re-evaluating the meaning of ambiguous or inconsistent cues ("he didn't mean to disrespect me; he was just in a hurry"). In other cases, it means activating a new system whose activity is incompatible with that of the previous one (e.g., caregiving instead of status: "he didn't mean to disrespect me; he's nervous and depressed because his daughter is sick—poor guy!"). The activation of incompatible motivations may also underlie *distraction* strategies, when the distracting thoughts and/or actions are not merely neutral but engage a different motivational system. Indeed, strategies that belong to different categories according to current taxonomies may share functional commonalities when viewed through a motivational lens.

A motivational perspective could have interesting implications for the efficacy of different self-regulation strategies. For example, strategies that exploit the interplay between different motivational systems may be especially effective, compared with strategies that lack that functional leverage. Also, the success of a certain strategy may depend not just on the specific emotion that one is experiencing, but on the role played by that emotion in the economy of the relevant motivational system. When an emotion is triggered by the *activation* of a system by certain situation cues, it should be relatively easy to deactivate the system through reappraisal, as long as the cues are sufficiently weak or ambiguous. But when a negative emotion marks the *failure* of a system at the end of a sequence of goal-directed actions, reappraisal may become significantly harder, as it demands a complete re-evaluation of the entire course of events and their psychological meaning.

Finally, the model I presented in this chapter may help clarify the differences between the regulation of emotions (or motivations) and that of moods (e.g., Erber & Erber, 2000; Morris, 2000). As third-order coordination programs, moods are not driven by specific events, but by integrative evaluations of the state of the organism in relation to the environment. In this sense, they are harder to regulate than emotions/motivations, and less susceptible to targeted strategies such as reappraisal and suppression. On the other hand, the fact that mood mechanisms integrate over multiple inputs—including the immune system, digestive system, etc.—creates some opportunities for regulation that are not available for lower-order mechanisms. For example, it becomes possible to employ compensatory strategies, so that success in one motivational domain balances out failure in another. Just as importantly, the range of potential regulation mechanisms broadens to include physiological channels such as sleep, eating, and exercise. As Morris (2000) noted, "The most reliable form of mood repair is probably a good night's sleep" (p. 201).

Implications for Personality and Emotion
The Motivational Basis of Personality

The idea that motivations are the basic building blocks of personality has a long history (e.g., Cattell, 1957; Murray, 1938), and is gaining renewed popularity as the field begins to move from the description of individual differences to genuine, process-based explanation (e.g., Corr & Krupić, 2017; Davis & Panksepp, 2018; Dweck, 2017; Read et al., 2010; Read et al., 2017; Schultheiss, 2020). In an influential paper, Denissen and Penke (2008) argued that individual differences in the Big Five traits of the Five Factor Model (Neuroticism/Emotional Stability, Conscientiousness, Agreeableness, Extraversion, and Openness to Experience; McCrae & Costa, 2003) reflect differences in "motivational reaction norms," or response patterns to specific classes of evolutionarily relevant situational cues. Ashton and Lee (2001, 2007) linked the six traits of the HEXACO model to five behavioral domains with a biological interpretation: reciprocal altruism/cooperation (Agreeableness and Honesty-Humility), kin altruism (Emotionality), social engagement (Extraversion), task-related engagement (Conscientiousness), and idea-related engagement (Openness to experience). While these authors did not explicitly discuss motivational systems, the domains they described show some correspondences with more detailed models of human motivation, like the one I have presented in this chapter.

These and similar models (such as DeYoung's [2015] "cybernetic Big Five theory") share a fundamental limitation: because they take factor-analytic traits at face value, they cannot provide a mechanistic, process-focused explanation of personality. Human behavior is not controlled by a handful of general-purpose mechanisms, but by large number of specialized adaptations—certainly much larger than five or six (Michalski & Shackelford, 2010). The traits described by factor-analytic models arise from patterns of *covariation* among multiple mechanisms, including—but not limited to—motivational systems. Covariation between mechanisms can be explained at various levels of analysis, both proximate (e.g., shared genetic and environmental influences, regulation by the same hormones/neuromodulators, reliance on shared regulatory variables, reciprocal activation/inhibition) and ultimate (e.g., synergistic effects on fitness, coordinated expression of life history strategies; see Del Giudice, 2018). Correlated mechanisms produce patterned behaviors, which are then filtered through evolved heuristics for person perception, translated into intuitive person-description concepts, and imperfectly captured by the lexical terms of human languages (Buss, 2011; Lukaszewski, 2020). To be sure, correlations among lexical descriptors can be quite informative; but they provide very little information about the structure, number, and function of the underlying psychological mechanisms (Davis & Panksepp, 2018; Lukaszewski, 2020; Lukaszewski et al., 2020).

The solution to this problem is to invert the direction of analysis, and leverage our knowledge of psychological mechanisms to reconstruct personality from the bottom up ("ground-up adaptationism"; Lukaszewski, 2020). Neel and colleagues (2016) took an initial step in this direction, by assessing Kenrick et al.'s (2010) fundamental motives and correlating them to a host of other individual-difference variables (including the Big Five). However, these authors did not include emotions in the picture. In contrast, Davis and Panksepp (2011, 2018) sought to build an alternative model of personality based on putative basic emotional systems such as RAGE, SEEKING, CARE, and PLAY. This approach to personality puts emotions front and center; unfortunately, it adopts a simplistic conception of the link between motivation and emotion, and covers only a small portion of the human motivational landscape (see above for details). For these reasons, I view Davis and Panksepp's model as an interesting proof of concept, but not a realistic candidate for a general theory of personality.

Even if they do not explicitly include emotions, the computational models of personality developed by Read and colleagues (2010, 2017, 2020) deserve special attention. In these models, personality arises from the behavior of multiple motivational systems that interact with situational affordances and are able to learn from experience. This conception of personality agrees very well with the approach I am proposing, and I see the authors' computational approach as an important step in the right direction (see also Revelle & Condon, 2015). Still, the specifics of the models reveal some notable theoretical limitations. To begin, the lists of motivational systems included in the models are somewhat ad hoc and do not follow a principled taxonomy. Second, the models lack an explicit theory of how different systems interact with one another. Third, all the motivational systems in these models employ the same control algorithm, regardless of their adaptive domain and specific goals. The algorithm is based on a feedback loop, without the possibility of anticipatory feedforward control. Finally, Read and colleagues introduce a separation between "approach motives" such as hunger, dominance, and affiliation; and "avoidance motives" such as avoidance of harm, rejection, and interpersonal conflict. This is a major conceptual problem, because many motivational goals require both approach *and* avoidance, depending on the situation and the state of the organism (e.g., approach food when hungry, avoid it when satiated; approach subordinates if dominant, avoid dominants if subordinate). It is reasonable to postulate that, when emotion programs are activated by motivational systems, the behavioral adaptations they orchestrate include some general-purpose mechanisms that promote approach vs. avoidance of salient stimuli. Stated differently, approach and avoidance mechanisms may function as common behavioral pathways for the action of multiple domain-specific motivations. On the other hand, treating approach and avoidance as distinct *categories* of motivations is a confusing move, and I believe it will prove a theoretical dead end (see also Davis & Panksepp, 2018).[6]

Motivation as the Bridge between Personality and Emotion

If personality is largely the product of individual differences in motivation (in combination with other regulatory processes; e.g., Tops et al., 2010; Tops et al., 2021; Volk & Masicampo, 2020), the extended coordination approach suggests a two-pronged strategy for bridging personality and emotion. First, one should think about personality in explicitly motivational terms, without assuming the functional coherence of standard personality traits. As a rule, factor-analytic traits arise from the (correlated) activity of multiple motivational systems. Second, one should think about emotions not as isolated mechanisms, but as effectors of motivational systems, without assuming the functional coherence of folk emotion labels. A key insight is that emotions do not correspond to motivations in a simple one-to-one fashion; instead, they are deployed *conditionally*, depending on the meaning of a situation in relation to the system's adaptive goals.

As an illustration, consider the broad personality trait of Agreeableness in the Five Factor Model (FFM). People high in Agreeableness are described as kind, trusting, altruistic, and accommodating. Across countries, girls and women score higher than on this trait than boys and men (Lippa, 2010; Mac Giolla & Kajonius, 2019; Murphy et al., 2021; Soto et al., 2011). Agreeableness is associated with low proneness to anger, but high proneness to both guilt and shame (Cohen et al., 2011; Einstein & Lanning, 1998; Reisenzein & Weber, 2009). It correlates negatively with the experience of "hubristic" or dominance-related pride, and positively with "authentic" or prestige-related pride (Beall & Tracy, 2020; Cheng et al., 2010; Tracy & Robins, 2007). From a motivational systems perspective, Agreeableness is a functionally complex trait that reflects individual differences in reciprocity, affiliation, and status (specifically dominance-seeking; see Cheng et al., 2010; DeYoung et al., 2013; Graziano & Tobin, 2017). Beyond this motivational core, Agreeableness is also associated with increased investment in parental and kin care (caregiving system; Buckels et al., 2015; Neel et al., 2016), reduced mate-seeking, lack of interest in short-term mating, and high investment in long-term mating and stable romantic relationships (mating and pair-bonding systems; see Baams et al., 2014; Banai & Pavela, 2015; Bourdage et al., 2007; Holtzman & Strube, 2013; Neel et al., 2016; Schmitt & Buss, 2000).[7]

In functional terms, this pattern of covariation among motivational systems may be explained as a manifestation of individual differences along a "fast-slow continuum" of life-history strategies (see Del Giudice, 2020; Del Giudice et al., 2015; Figueredo et al., 2007; Sela & Barbaro, 2018). From this perspective, the trade-off between mating and parenting—a central aspect of human life-history strategies—drives the observed associations between status, mating, pair-bonding, and caregiving motivations (e.g., Neel et al., 2016); the future-oriented nature of slow strategies promotes increased cooperation and affiliation in addition to lower mating and higher parenting effort (see Del Giudice, 2018).

A motivational analysis of Agreeableness indicates that people high on this trait should experience (and express) less anger in response to violations of reciprocity and affiliation, dominance challenges, and threats to long-term relationships (e.g., romantic jealousy; Lukaszewski et al., 2020). But it also suggests some new hypotheses that run against a simple negative correlation with anger. For example, high-Agreeableness people may react intensely with protective ("parental") anger when their children or other dependents are threatened. And while they tend to get less angry when they experience unfairness and transgressions, things may change when the victims are *other* innocent people (for indirect evidence, see Bizer, 2020). If these hypotheses were supported, they would also raise interesting questions about the existence of functionally distinct variants of anger (e.g., how is "caregiving anger" different from "reciprocity anger" or "dominance anger"? Are these variants expressed differently in males and females?). The same kind of reasoning could be used to develop finer-grained hypotheses about the contexts in which Agreeableness should predict the experience of shame, guilt, and many other less-studied emotions like gratitude and sexual arousal. A more ambitious goal would be not just to refine the concept of Agreeableness, but to develop an alternative, functional model of personality based on a fine-grained understanding of human motivation.

Motivation and Person Perception

The flip side of this view of personality and motivation is that evolved heuristics for person perception ("difference-detecting mechanisms"; Buss, 2011) should be designed to make inferences about people's *motivational* processes, because this is the level of analysis that affords the largest predictive payoffs. An important corollary is that information about people's *emotions* is often going to be interpreted in relation to their (probabilistically inferred) motivational states. This is already implicit in the evolutionary literature on person perception. To illustrate the kinds of problems that person-perception algorithms are designed to solve, Lukaszewski and colleagues (2020) offered a list of questions, including: Who will be a reliable ally or long-term mate? Who is likely to defect on social contracts? Who will rise in the social hierarchy? Who is sexually permissive? To a large extent, these questions concern individual differences in motivational priorities and in the calibration of specific motivational systems.

In the same paper, Lukaszewski and colleagues presented convergent evidence that experiences, facial expressions, and behaviors associated with anger are systematically translated into descriptions that map onto the construct of Agreeableness.[8] I suggest that people employ the outputs of the anger program mainly as cues to the motivational processes of the angry individual. And because motivational systems covary in meaningful patterns, these inferences should often "spill over" to motivational domains that are not directly tapped by the target situation. For example, imagine someone who consistently gets angry and aggressive in the context of cooperative, reciprocal exchanges. That person is also more likely to be driven by dominance concerns, sensitive to behaviors that could be interpreted as dominance challenges, unreliable as a long-term romantic partner, interested in short-term mating opportunities, and so forth. (For evidence that people tend to possess accurate models of the correlations among personality traits, see Stolier et al., 2020.) In general, motivational inferences are so powerful precisely because they allow one to make predictions about people's emotions and behaviors beyond the current situation, including hypothetical events and unlikely yet fitness-critical scenarios ("would he protect me if someone assaulted us?"). Note that, depending on context, observed emotions may convey other kinds of predictive information besides motivation—for example about a person's beliefs, plans, and social alliances.

Based on the motivational analysis presented earlier, one can advance some hypotheses about situations in which anger should *not* trigger inferences of low Agreeableness, or would do so in a much-attenuated fashion. Possible examples are a parent getting angry at someone who is threatening their child, and a witness of blatant injustice getting angry at the perpetrator. Note that, in both scenarios, the emotion labeled as "anger" does not match the recalibration theory of anger (Sell et al., 2009; Sell et al., 2017), except in a loose and indirect sense. This is a nice example of how motivation and emotion can illuminate each other—and why they should be studied together as two sides of the same coin.

Conclusion

As this volume clearly testifies, the evolutionary study of emotion has made tremendous progress over the past few decades. The coordination approach has played a major role by clearing some important conceptual hurdles, emphasizing the computational level of analysis, providing a common language for alternative models, grounding and suggesting productive directions for empirical research. But motivation and emotion are inextricably linked, and it is becoming increasingly apparent that a successful theory of emotion requires an explicit theory of motivation (and vice versa). Here I have taken a step in this direction, by showing how the theory of motivational systems can be used to extend and partially revise the standard coordination approach. I hope that other researchers will find these ideas as exciting as I do, and use the extended framework as a springboard to refine existing theories, explore new hypotheses, and draw fruitful connections within and across disciplines.

Acknowledgments

I am grateful to Laith Al-Shawaf, Romina Angeleri, Steve Gangestad, and Daniel Sznycer for their generous and constructive feedback on this chapter.

Notes

1. On the ideological side, instinct theories were often portrayed as not merely old-fashioned but also politically conservative; in contrast, behaviorism aligned with the tenets of the Progressive movement, including a view of human behavior as radically malleable and an unshakable faith in top-down social engineering (see, e.g., Burnham, 1960).
2. Note that Bowlby (1982) remained agnostic as to whether feelings *cause* behavior, or only serve as intra- and interpersonal signals of the individual's motivational state. In contrast, Scott (1980) argued that the feelings triggered during the operation of behavioral systems contribute to motivate specific goal-relevant behaviors.
3. Intuitively, a simple structure obtains when each of the factors/components shows strong correlations with some indicators, and near-zero correlations with the remaining ones. For technical discussion, see Browne (2001) and Sass & Schmitt (2010).
4. Parts of this section are adapted with permission from Del Giudice (2018).
5. Recent large-scale analyses of emotional expressions and self-reports (see Cowen et al., 2019) suggest at least 25–30 dimensions of variation (extracted with PCA), with denser regions corresponding to "fuzzy" emotion categories. This is almost certainly a lower bound on the numerosity of emotion *mechanisms*, because the resolution of the analysis is limited by the use of folk labels, and the choice of the number of dimensions to retain is somewhat arbitrary. More generally, these results are based on correlational rather than functional analyses, and suffer from the same problems I have discussed in regard to the numerosity of motivational systems.
6. In Gray and McNaughton's (2000) reinforcement sensitivity theory (RST), behavior is regulated by three general-purpose systems that control reward approach (*behavioral activation system* or BAS), punishment avoidance (*fight-flight-freeze system* or FFFS), and approach-avoidance conflicts (*behavioral inhibition system* or BIS). I do not discuss this theory in detail because it provides an extremely partial account of motivation and emotion. For reviews of RST as a model of personality, see Corr et al. (2013) and Corr and Krupić (2017). The recent discussion by Corr & Krupić seems compatible with the idea that approach/avoidance mechanisms function as common pathways for other, domain-specific motivational systems.
7. As a further indication that Agreeableness is not a functionally unitary construct, the HEXACO model defines this trait in a somewhat different way by excluding sentimentality and including (low) irritability, which is a facet of Neuroticism in the FFM (see Ashton & Lee, 2007). Both versions of Agreeableness show a similar motivational profile with respect to reciprocity, affiliation, dominance/status, mating, and pair-bonding; however, the association with caregiving may be more specific to the FFM version (see Ashton & Lee, 2001, 20017; Ashton et al., 2010; Bourdage et al., 2007; Lee et al., 2013). Also, the available data suggest that sex differences on the HEXACO version of Agreeableness are smaller and less consistent than those on the FFM version (Lee & Ashton, 2020).
8. Note that these authors employed the HEXACO version of Agreeableness.

References

Albertos, P., & Mareels, I. (2010). *Feedback and control for everyone*. Springer.

Aldao, A. (2013). The future of emotion regulation research: Capturing context. *Perspectives on Psychological Science, 8*, 155–172.

Al-Shawaf, L. (2016). The evolutionary psychology of hunger. *Appetite, 105*, 591–595.

Al-Shawaf, L., Conroy-Beam, D., Asao, K., & Buss, D. M. (2016). Human emotions: An evolutionary psychological perspective. *Emotion Review, 8*, 173–186.

Al-Shawaf, L., & Lewis, D. M. (2017). Evolutionary psychology and the emotions. In V. Zeigler-Hill & T.K. Shackelford (Eds.), *Encyclopedia of personality and individual differences* (pp. 1452–1461). Springer.

Anderson, C., Hildreth, J. A. D., & Howland, L. (2015). Is the desire for status a fundamental human motive? A review of the empirical literature. *Psychological Bulletin, 141*, 574–601.

Ashton, M. C., & Lee, K. (2001). A theoretical basis for the major dimensions of personality. *European Journal of Personality, 15*, 327–353.

Ashton, M. C., & Lee, K. (2007). Empirical, theoretical, and practical advantages of the HEXACO model of personality structure. *Personality and Social Psychology Review, 11*, 150–166.

Ashton, M. C., Lee, K., Pozzebon, J. A., Visser, B. A., & Worth, N. C. (2010). Status-driven risk taking and the major dimensions of personality. *Journal of Research in Personality, 44*, 734–737.

Aunger, R., & Curtis, V. (2013). The anatomy of motivation: An evolutionary-ecological approach. *Biological Theory, 8*, 49–63.

Baams, L., Overbeek, G., Dubas, J. S., & Van Aken, M. A. (2014). On early starters and late bloomers: The development of sexual behavior in adolescence across personality types. *Journal of Sex Research, 51*, 754–764.

Baerends, G. P. (1976). The functional organization of behaviour. *Animal Behaviour, 24*, 726–738.

Ballard, T., Yeo, G., Vancouver, J. B., & Neal, A. (2017). The dynamics of avoidance goal regulation. *Motivation and Emotion, 41*, 698–707.

Banai, B., & Pavela, I. (2015). Two-dimensional structure of the Sociosexual Orientation Inventory and its personality correlates. *Evolutionary Psychology, 13*, 1474704915604541.

Barbaro, N. (2020). The nature of attachment systems. *Social and Personality Psychology Compass, 14*, e12570.

Barrett, H. C. (2012). A hierarchical model of the evolution of human brain specializations. *Proceedings of the National Academy of Sciences USA, 109*, 10733–10740.

Barrett, H. C. (2015a). *The shape of thought: How mental adaptations evolve.* Oxford University Press.

Barrett, H. C. (2015b). Adaptations to predators and prey. In D. M. Buss (Ed.), *The handbook of evolutionary psychology*, Vol 1: *Foundations* (2nd ed., pp. 246–263). Wiley.

Baumert, A., Schmitt, M., Perugini, M., Johnson, W., Blum, G., Borkenau, P., Costantini, G., Denissen, J. J. A., Fleeson, W., Grafton, B., Jayawickreme, E., Kurzius, E., MacLeod, C., Miller, L. C., Read, S. J., Roberts, B., Robinson, M. D., Wood, D., & Wrzus, C. (2017). Integrating personality structure, personality process, and personality development. *European Journal of Personality, 31*, 503–528.

Beall, A. T., & Tracy, J. L. (2017). Emotivational psychology: How distinct emotions facilitate fundamental motives. *Social and Personality Psychology Compass, 11*, e12303.

Beall, A. T., & Tracy, J. L. (2020). Evolution of pride and shame. In L. Workman, W. Reader, & J. H. Barkow (Eds.), *Cambridge handbook of evolutionary perspectives on human behavior* (pp. 179–193). Cambridge University Press.

Bechhoefer, J. (2005). Feedback for physicists: A tutorial essay on control. *Reviews of Modern Physics, 77*, 783–836.

Beedie, C., Terry, P., & Lane, A. (2005). Distinctions between emotion and mood. *Cognition & Emotion, 19*, 847–878.

Bizer, G. Y. (2020). Who's bothered by an unfair world? The emotional response to unfairness scale. *Personality and Individual Differences, 159*, 109882.

Boden, M. A. (1965). McDougall revisited. *Journal of Personality, 33*, 1–19.

Borgerhoff Mulder, M., & Beheim, B. A. (2011). Understanding the nature of wealth and its effects on human fitness. *Philosophical Transactions of the Royal Society of London B, 366*, 344–356.

Borgerhoff Mulder, M., Bowles, S., Hertz, T., Bell, A., Beise, J., Clark, G., et al. (2009). Intergenerational wealth transmission and the dynamics of inequality in small-scale societies. *Science, 326*, 682–688.

Borsboom, D., Kievit, R. A., Cervone, D., & Hood, S. B. (2009). The two disciplines of scientific psychology, or: The disunity of psychology as a working hypothesis. In J. Valsiner, P. C. Molenaar, M. C. D. P. Lyra, & N. Chaudhary (Eds.), *Dynamic process methodology in the social and developmental sciences* (pp. 67–97). Springer.

Bourdage, J. S., Lee, K., Ashton, M. C., & Perry, A. (2007). Big Five and HEXACO model personality correlates of sexuality. *Personality and Individual Differences, 43*, 1506–1516.

Bowlby, J. (1982). *Attachment and loss*, Vol. I: *Attachment* (rev. ed.). Basic Books.

Boyer, P., & Liénard, P. (2006). Precaution systems and ritualized behavior. *Behavioral and Brain Sciences, 29*, 635–641.

Brasini, M., Tanzilli, A., Pistella, J., Gentile, D., Di Marco, I., Mancini, F., Lingiardi, V., & Baiocco, R. (2020). The social mentalities scale: A new measure for assessing the interpersonal motivations underlying social relationships. *Personality and Individual Differences, 167*, 110236.

Brown, S., Brown, R., & Preston, S. D. (2012). A model of human caregiving motivation. In S. L. Brown, R. M. Brown, & L. A. Penner (Eds.), *Moving beyond self interest: Perspectives from evolutionary biology, neuroscience, and the social sciences* (pp. 75–88). Oxford University Press.

Browne, M. W. (2001). An overview of analytic rotation in exploratory factor analysis. *Multivariate Behavioral Research, 36*, 111–150.

Buckels, E. E., Beall, A. T., Hofer, M. K., Lin, E. Y., Zhou, Z., & Schaller, M. (2015). Individual differences in activation of the parental care motivational system: Assessment, prediction, and implications. *Journal of Personality and Social Psychology, 108*, 497–514.

Bugental, D. B. (2000). Acquisition of the algorithms of social life: A domain-based approach. *Psychological Bulletin, 126*, 187–219.

Burghardt, G. M. (2005). *The genesis of animal play*. MIT Press.

Burghardt, G. M. (2019). A place for emotions in behavior systems research. *Behavioural Processes, 166*, 103881.

Burghardt, G. M., & Bowers, R. I. (2017). From instinct to behavior systems: An integrated approach to ethological psychology. In J. Call, G. M. Burghardt, I. M. Pepperberg, C. T. Snowdon, & T. Zentall (Eds.), *APA handbook of comparative psychology: Basic concepts, methods, neural substrate, and behavior* (p. 333–364). American Psychological Association.

Buss, D. M. (2011). Personality and the adaptive landscape: The role of individual differences in creating and solving social adaptive problems. In D. M. Buss & P. Hawley, *The evolution of personality and individual differences* (pp. 29–57). Oxford University Press.

Buss, D. M. (2013). Sexual jealousy. *Psychological Topics, 22*, 155–182.

Byers, J. A., & Walker, C. (1995). Refining the motor training hypothesis for the evolution of play. *The American Naturalist, 146*, 25–40.

Carver, C. S., & Scheier, M. F. (2013). Goals and emotion. In M. D. Robinson, E. R. Watkins, & E. Harmon-Jones (Eds.), *Guilford handbook of cognition and emotion* (pp. 176–194). Guilford Press.

Cassidy, J. (2016). The nature of the child's ties. In J. Cassidy & P. R. Shaver (Eds.), *Handbook of attachment* (3rd ed., pp. 3–24). Guilford Press.

Cattell, R. B. (1957). *Personality and motivation: Structure and measurement*. World Book.

Cheng, J. T., Tracy, J. L., Foulsham, T., Kingstone, A., & Henrich, J. (2013). Two ways to the top: Evidence that dominance and prestige are distinct yet viable avenues to social rank and influence. *Journal of Personality and Social Psychology, 104*, 103–125.

Cheng, J. T., Tracy, J. L., & Henrich, J. (2010). Pride, personality, and the evolutionary foundations of human social status. *Evolution and Human Behavior, 31*, 334–347.

Chester, D. S. (2017). The role of positive affect in aggression. *Current Directions in Psychological Science, 26*, 366–370.

Chichinadze, K., Chichinadze, N., & Lazarashvili, A. (2011). Hormonal and neurochemical mechanisms of aggression and a new classification of aggressive behavior. *Aggression and Violent Behavior, 16*, 461–471.

Cohen, T. R., Wolf, S. T., Panter, A. T., & Insko, C. A. (2011). Introducing the GASP scale: A new measure of guilt and shame proneness. *Journal of Personality and Social Psychology, 100*, 947–966.

Corr, P. J., DeYoung, C. G., & McNaughton, N. (2013). Motivation and personality: A neuropsychological perspective. *Social and Personality Psychology Compass, 7*, 158–175.

Corr, P. J., & Krupić, D. (2017). Motivating personality: Approach, avoidance, and their conflict. In A. J. Elliot (Ed.), *Advances in motivation science* (Vol. 4, pp. 39–90). Academic Press.

Cosmides, L., & Tooby, J. (2000). Evolutionary psychology and the emotions. In M. Lewis & J. M. Haviland-Jones (Eds.), *Handbook of emotions* (2nd ed., pp. 91–115). Guilford Press.

Cosmides, L., & Tooby, J. (2015). Adaptations for reasoning about social exchange. In D. M. Buss (Ed.), *The handbook of evolutionary psychology* (2nd ed., pp. 625–668). Wiley.

Cowen, A., Sauter, D., Tracy, J. L., & Keltner, D. (2019). Mapping the passions: Toward a high-dimensional taxonomy of emotional experience and expression. *Psychological Science in the Public Interest, 20*, 69–90.

Craig, W. (1918). Appetites and aversions as constituents of instincts. *Biological Bulletin, 34*, 91–107.

Csete, M., & Doyle, J. (2004). Bow ties, metabolism and disease. *Trends in Biotechnology, 22*, 446–450.

Csibra, G., & Gergely, G. (2006). Social learning and social cognition: The case for pedagogy. In Y. Munakata & M. H. Johnson (Eds.), *Processes of change in brain and cognitive development*, Vol. XXI: *Attention and performance* (pp. 249–274). Oxford University Press.

Curtis, V. (2011). Why disgust matters. *Philosophical Transactions of the Royal Society of London B, 366*, 3478–3490.

Davis, K. L., & Panksepp, J. (2018). *The emotional foundations of personality: A neurobiological and evolutionary approach*. W. W. Norton.

Del Giudice, M. (2015). Self-regulation in an evolutionary perspective. In G. H. E. Gendolla, M. Tops, & S. Koole (Eds.), *Handbook of biobehavioral approaches to self-regulation* (pp. 25–42). Springer.

Del Giudice, M. (2018). *Evolutionary psychopathology: A unified approach*. Oxford University Press.

Del Giudice, M. (2020). Rethinking the fast-slow continuum of individual differences. *Evolution and Human Behavior, 41*, 536–549.

Del Giudice, M. (2021). Effective dimensionality: A tutorial. *Multivariate Behavioral Research, 56*, 527–542. https://doi.org/10.1080/00273171.2020.1743631

Del Giudice, M., Buck, C. L., Chaby, L. E., Gormally, B. M., Taff, C. C., Thawley, C. J., Vitousek, M. N., & Wada, H. (2018). What is stress? A systems perspective. *Integrative and Comparative Biology, 58*, 1019–1032.

Del Giudice, M., Gangestad, S. W., & Kaplan, H. S. (2015). Life history theory and evolutionary psychology. In D. M. Buss (Ed.), *The handbook of evolutionary psychology*, Vol 1: *Foundations* (2nd ed., pp. 88–114). Wiley.

Denissen, J. J., & Penke, L. (2008). Motivational individual reaction norms underlying the Five-Factor model of personality: First steps towards a theory-based conceptual framework. *Journal of Research in Personality, 42*, 1285–1302.

DeYoung, C. G. (2015). Cybernetic Big Five theory. *Journal of Research in Personality, 56*, 33–58.

DeYoung, C. G., & Krueger, R. F. (2018). A cybernetic theory of psychopathology. *Psychological Inquiry, 29*, 117–138.

DeYoung, C. G., Weisberg, Y. J., Quilty, L. C., & Peterson, J. B. (2013). Unifying the aspects of the Big Five, the interpersonal circumplex, and trait affiliation. *Journal of Personality, 81*, 465–475.

Doyle, J. C., & Csete, M. (2011). Architecture, constraints, and behavior. *Proceedings of the National Academy of Sciences USA, 108*, 15624–15630.

Durkee, P. K., Lukaszewski, A. W., & Buss, D. M. (2019). Pride and shame: Key components of a culturally universal status management system. *Evolution and Human Behavior, 40*, 470–478.

Dweck, C. S. (2017). From needs to goals and representations: Foundations for a unified theory of motivation, personality, and development. *Psychological Review, 124*, 689–719.

Eastwick, P. W. (2009). Beyond the Pleistocene: Using phylogeny and constraint to inform the evolutionary psychology of human mating. *Psychological Bulletin, 135*, 794–821.

Einstein, D., & Lanning, K. (1998). Shame, guilt, ego development and the five-factor model of personality. *Journal of Personality, 66*, 555–582.

Eldar, E., Rutledge, R. B., Dolan, R. J., & Niv, Y. (2016). Mood as representation of momentum. *Trends in Cognitive Sciences, 20*, 15–24.

Engelmann, J. M., Herrmann, E., & Tomasello, M. (2015). Chimpanzees trust conspecifics to engage in low-cost reciprocity. *Proceedings of the Royal Society of London B, 282*, 20142803.

Erber, R., & Erber, M. W. (2000). The self-regulation of moods: Second thoughts on the importance of happiness in everyday life. *Psychological Inquiry, 11*, 142–148.

Figueredo, A. J., Vásquez, G., Brumbach, B. H., & Schneider, S. M. (2007). The K-factor, covitality, and personality. *Human Nature, 18*, 47–73.

Fiske, A. P. (2020). The lexical fallacy in emotion research: Mistaking vernacular words for psychological entities. *Psychological Review, 127*, 95–113.

Fletcher, G. J. O., Simpson, J. A., Campbell, L., & Overall, N. C. (2015). Pair-Bonding, romantic love, and evolution: The curious case of Homo sapiens. *Perspectives on Psychological Science, 10*, 20–36.

Fogarty, L., Strimling, P., & Laland, K. N. (2011). The evolution of teaching. *Evolution, 65*, 2760–2770.

Fraley, R. C., & Spieker, S. J. (2003). Are infant attachment patterns continuously or categorically distributed? A taxometric analysis of strange situation behavior. *Developmental Psychology, 39*, 387–404.

Gangestad, S. W., & Haselton, M. G. (2015). Human estrus: Implications for relationship science. *Current Opinion in Psychology, 1*, 45–51.

Gangestad, S. W., & Thornhill, R. (2007). The evolution of social inference processes: The importance of signaling theory. In J. P. Forgas, M. G. Haselton, & W. von Hippel (Eds.), *Evolutionary psychology and social cognition* (pp. 33–48). Psychology Press.

Gendolla, G. H. (2000). On the impact of mood on behavior: An integrative theory and a review. *Review of General Psychology, 4*, 378–408.

Gilbert, P. (1989). *Human nature and suffering*. Lawrence Erlbaum Associates.

Gilbert, P. (2005). Compassion and cruelty: A biopsychosocial approach. In P. Gilbert (Ed.), *Compassion: Conceptualisations, research and use in psychotherapy* (pp. 9–74). Routledge.

Gottlieb, J., Oudeyer, P. Y., Lopes, M., & Baranes, A. (2013). Information-seeking, curiosity, and attention: Computational and neural mechanisms. *Trends in Cognitive Sciences, 17*, 585–593.

Graeff, F. G. (2004). Serotonin, the periaqueductal gray and panic. *Neuroscience & Biobehavioral Reviews, 28*, 239–259.

Gray, J. A., & McNaughton, N. (2000). *The neuropsychology of anxiety: An enquiry into the functions of the septo-hippocampal system*. Oxford University Press.

Graziano, W. G., & Tobin, R. M. (2017). Agreeableness and the five factor model. In T. A. Widiger (Ed.), *The Oxford handbook of the five factor model* (pp. 105–132). Oxford University Press.

Griskevicius, V., Tybur, J. M., Sundie, J. M., Cialdini, R. B., Miller, G. F., & Kenrick, D. T. (2007). Blatant benevolence and conspicuous consumption: When romantic motives elicit strategic costly signals. *Journal of Personality and Social Psychology, 93*, 85–102.

Gross, J. J. (2015). The extended process model of emotion regulation: Elaborations, applications, and future directions. *Psychological Inquiry, 26*, 130–137.

Hagenaars, M. A., Oitzl, M., & Roelofs, K. (2014). Updating freeze: Aligning animal and human research. *Neuroscience & Biobehavioral Reviews, 47*, 165–176.

Heckhausen, H. (2018). Historical trends in motivation research. In J. Heckhausen & H. Heckhausen (Eds.), *Motivation and action* (3rd ed., pp. 15–66). Springer.

Holtzman, N. S., & Strube, M. J. (2013). Above and beyond short-term mating, long-term mating is uniquely tied to human personality. *Evolutionary Psychology, 11*, 1101–1129.

Hrdy, S. B. (2005). Comes the child before the man: How cooperative breeding and prolonged postweaning dependence shaped human potentials. In M. E. Lamb & B. S. Hewlett (Eds.), *Hunter-gatherer childhoods: Evolutionary, developmental, and cultural perspectives* (pp. 65–91). Aldine.

Hrdy, S. B., & Burkart, J. M. (2020). The emergence of emotionally modern humans: Implications for language and learning. *Philosophical Transactions of the Royal Society B, 375*, 20190499.

Jaeggi, A. V., De Groot, E., Stevens, J. M., & Van Schaik, C. P. (2013). Mechanisms of reciprocity in primates: Testing for short-term contingency of grooming and food sharing in bonobos and chimpanzees. *Evolution and Human Behavior, 34*, 69–77.

Jaeggi, A. V., & Gurven, M. (2013). Reciprocity explains food sharing in humans and other primates independent of kin selection and tolerated scrounging: A phylogenetic meta-analysis. *Proceedings of the Royal Society of London B, 280*, 20131615.

Johnson, S. L., Leedom, L. J., & Muhtadie, L. (2012). The dominance behavioral system and psychopathology: Evidence from self-report, observational, and biological studies. *Psychological Bulletin, 138*, 692–743.

Kaplan, H. S., Gurven, M., & Lancaster, J. B. (2007). Brain evolution and the human adaptive complex: An ecological and social theory. In S. W. Gangestad & J. A. Simpson (Eds.), *The evolution of mind: Fundamental questions and controversies* (pp. 269–279). Guilford Press.

Kaplan, H. S., Hill, K., Lancaster, J. B., & Hurtado, A. M. (2000). A theory of human life history evolution: Diet, intelligence, and longevity. *Evolutionary Anthropology, 9*, 156–185.

Kaplan, H. S., Hooper, P. L., & Gurven, M. (2009). The evolutionary and ecological roots of human social organization. *Philosophical Transactions of the Royal Society B, 364*, 3289–3299.

Keltner, D., Haidt, J., & Shiota, L. (2006). Social functionalism and the evolution of emotions. In M. Schaller, D. Kenrick, & J. Simpson (Eds.), *Evolution and social psychology* (pp. 115–142). Psychology Press.

Keltner, D., Tracy, J. L., Sauter, D., & Cowen, A. (2019). What basic emotion theory really says for the twenty-first century study of emotion. *Journal of Nonverbal Behavior, 43*, 195–201.

Kenrick, D. T., Griskevicius, V., Neuberg, S. L., & Schaller, M. (2010). Renovating the pyramid of needs: Contemporary extensions built upon ancient foundations. *Perspectives on Psychological Science, 5*, 292–314.

Kitano, H. (2004). Biological robustness. *Nature Reviews Genetics, 5*, 826–837.

Kitano, H., & Oda, K. (2006). Robustness trade-offs and host–microbial symbiosis in the immune system. *Molecular Systems Biology, 2*, 2006.0022.

Kramer, K. L. (2010). Cooperative breeding and its significance to the demographic success of humans. *Annual Review of Anthropology, 39*, 417–436.

Krantz, D. L., & Allen, D. (1967). The rise and fall of McDougall's instinct doctrine. *Journal of the History of the Behavioral Sciences, 3*, 326–338.

Lee, K., & Ashton, M. C. (2020). Sex differences in HEXACO personality characteristics across countries and ethnicities. *Journal of Personality, 88*, 1075–1090.

Lee, K., Ashton, M. C., Wiltshire, J., Bourdage, J. S., Visser, B. A., & Gallucci, A. (2013). Sex, power, and money: Prediction from the Dark Triad and Honesty–Humility. European *Journal of Personality, 27*, 169–184.

Lewis, D. M., Al-Shawaf, L., Conroy-Beam, D., Asao, K., & Buss, D. M. (2017). Evolutionary psychology: A how-to guide. *American Psychologist, 72*, 353–373.

Lichtenberg, J. D., Lachmann, F. M., & Fosshage, J. I. (1992). *Self and motivational systems*. Analytic Press.

Lippa, R. A. (2010). Gender differences in personality and interests: When, where, and why? *Social and Personality Psychology Compass, 4*, 1098–1110.

LoBue, V., & Rakison, D. H. (2013). What we fear most: Developmental advantage for threat-relevant stimuli. *Developmental Review, 33*, 285–303.

Locke, J. L., & Bogin, B. (2006). Language and life history: A new perspective on the development and evolution of human language. *Behavioral and Brain Sciences, 29*, 259–280.

Loewenstein, G. (1994) The psychology of curiosity: A review and reinterpretation. *Psychological Bulletin, 116*, 75–98.

Lukaszewski, A. W. (2020). Evolutionary perspectives on the mechanistic underpinnings of personality. In J. F. Rauthmann (Ed.), *The handbook of personality dynamics and processes* (pp. 523–550). Academic Press.

Lukaszewski, A. W., Lewis, D. M., Durkee, P. K., Sell, A. N., Sznycer, D., & Buss, D. M. (2020). An adaptationist framework for personality science. *European Journal of Personality, 34*, 1151–1174.

Lykken, D. T. (1971). Multiple factor analysis and personality research. *Journal of Experimental Research in Personality, 5*, 161–170.

Mac Giolla, E., & Kajonius, P. J. (2019). Sex differences in personality are larger in gender equal countries: Replicating and extending a surprising finding. *International Journal of Psychology, 54*, 705–711.

Mallan, K. M., Lipp, O. V., & Cochrane, B. (2013). Slithering snakes, angry men and out-group members: What and whom are we evolved to fear? *Cognition and Emotion, 27*, 1168–1180.

Maner, J. K. (2017). Dominance and prestige: A tale of two hierarchies. *Current Directions in Psychological Science, 26*, 526–531.

Maslow, A. H. (1954). *Motivation and personality*. Harper.

McCrae, R. R., & Costa, P. T. (2003). *Personality in adulthood: A five-factor theory perspective* (2nd ed.). Guilford Press.

McDougall, W. (1908). *An introduction to social psychology*. Luce.

McDougall, W. (1921). The use and abuse of instinct in social psychology. *Journal of Abnormal Psychology and Social Psychology, 16*, 285–333.

McDougall, W. (1924). Can sociology and social psychology dispense with instincts? *Journal of Abnormal Psychology and Social Psychology, 19*, 13–41.

McDougall, W. (1932). *The energies of men: A study of the fundamentals of dynamic psychology*. Methuen.

McFarland, D. J. (1971). *Feedback mechanisms in animal behaviour*. Academic Press.

McFarland, D. J. (1974). *Motivational control systems analysis*. Academic Press.

McRae, K., & Gross, J. J. (2020). Emotion regulation. *Emotion, 20*, 1–9.

Meston, C. M., & Buss, D. M. (2007). Why humans have sex. *Archives of Sexual Behavior, 36*, 477–507.

Michalski, R. L., & Shackelford, T. K. (2010). Evolutionary personality psychology: Reconciling human nature and individual differences. *Personality and Individual Differences, 48*, 509–516.

Mikulincer, M., & Shaver, P. R. (2016). *Attachment in adulthood: Structure, dynamics, and change* (2nd ed.). Guilford Press.

Morris, W. N. (1992). A functional analysis of the role of mood in affective systems. *Review of Personality and Social Psychology, 13*, 256–293.

Morris, W. N. (2000). Some thoughts about mood and its regulation. *Psychological Inquiry, 11*, 200–202.

Mulder, M. B., & Beheim, B. A. (2011). Understanding the nature of wealth and its effects on human fitness. *Philosophical Transactions of the Royal Society B, 366*, 344–356.

Murphy, S. A., Fisher, P. A., & Robie, C. (2021). International comparison of gender differences in the five-factor model of personality: An investigation across 105 countries. *Journal of Research in Personality, 90*, 104047.

Murray, H. A. (1938). *Explorations in personality*. Oxford University Press.

Neel, R., Kenrick, D. T., White, A. E., & Neuberg, S. L. (2016). Individual differences in fundamental social motives. *Journal of Personality and Social Psychology, 110*, 887–907.

Nesse, R. M. (1990). Evolutionary explanations of emotions. *Human Nature, 1*, 261–289.

Nesse, R. M. (2004). Natural selection and the elusiveness of happiness. *Philosophical Transactions of the Royal Society of London B, 359*, 1333–1347.

Nesse, R. M. (2020). Tacit creationism in emotion research. In C. Price & E. Walle (Eds.), *Emotion Researcher, ISRE's sourcebook for research on emotion and affect*. International Society for Research on Emotion. https://emotionresearcher.com/tacit-creationism-in-emotion-research

Nettle, D., & Bateson, M. (2012). The evolutionary origins of mood and its disorders. *Current Biology, 22*, R712–R721.

Nettle, D., & Pollet, T. V. (2008). Natural selection on male wealth in humans. *The American Naturalist, 172*, 658–666.

Öhman, A. (2009). Of snakes and faces: An evolutionary perspective on the psychology of fear. *Scandinavian Journal of Psychology, 50*, 543–552.

Panksepp, J. (1998). *Affective neuroscience: The foundations of human and animal emotions*. Oxford University Press.

Panksepp, J. (2005). Affective consciousness: Core emotional feelings in animals and humans. *Consciousness and Cognition, 14*, 30–80.

Panksepp, J. (2011). Cross-species affective neuroscience decoding of the primal affective experiences of humans and related animals. *PLoS ONE, 6*, e21236.

Pellis, S. M., Pellis, V. C., Pelletier, A., & Leca, J. B. (2019). Is play a behavior system, and, if so, what kind? *Behavioural Processes, 160*, 1–9.

Pinker, S. (2010). The cognitive niche: Coevolution of intelligence, sociality, and language. *Proceedings of the National Academy of Sciences USA, 107*, 8993–8999.

Preston, S. D. (2014). Hoarding in animals: The argument for a homology. In R. O. Frost & G. Steketee (Eds.), *The Oxford handbook of hoarding and acquiring* (pp. 187–205). Oxford University Press.

Preston, S. D., & Vickers, B. D. (2014). The psychology of acquisitiveness. In S. D. Preston, M. L. Kringelbach, & B. Knutson (Eds.), *The interdisciplinary science of consumption* (pp. 127–146). MIT Press.

Quinlan, R. J. (2008). Human pair-bonds: Evolutionary functions, ecological variation, and adaptive development. *Evolutionary Anthropology, 17*, 227–238.

Read, S. J., Brown, A. D., Wang, P., & Miller, L. C. (2020). Virtual personalities and neural networks: Capturing the structure and dynamics of personality. In J. F. Rauthmann (Ed.), *The handbook of personality dynamics and processes* (pp. 1037–1057). Academic Press.

Read, S. J., Monroe, B. M., Brownstein, A. L., Yang, Y., Chopra, G., & Miller, L. C. (2010). A neural network model of the structure and dynamics of human personality. *Psychological Review, 117*, 61–92.

Read, S. J., Smith, B. J., Droutman, V., & Miller, L. C. (2017). Virtual personalities: Using computational modeling to understand within-person variability. *Journal of Research in Personality, 69*, 237–249.

Reisenzein, R., & Weber, H. (2009). Personality and emotion. In P. J. Corr & G. Matthews (Eds.), *The Cambridge handbook of personality psychology* (pp. 54–71). Cambridge University Press.

Revelle, W., & Condon, D. M. (2015). A model for personality at three levels. *Journal of Research in Personality, 56*, 70–81.

Roelofs, K. (2017). Freeze for action: Neurobiological mechanisms in animal and human freezing. *Philosophical Transactions of the Royal Society B, 372*, 20160206.

Sass, D. A., & Schmitt, T. A. (2010). A comparative investigation of rotation criteria within exploratory factor analysis. *Multivariate Behavioral Research, 45*, 73–103.

Scarantino, A. (2012). How to define emotions scientifically. *Emotion Review, 4*, 358–368.

Scarantino, A. (2015). Basic emotions, psychological construction, and the problem of variability. In L. F. Barrett & J. A. Russell (Eds.), *The psychological construction of emotion* (pp. 334–376). Guilford Press.

Schaller, M. (2018). The parental care motivational system and why it matters (for everyone). *Current Directions in Psychological Science, 27*, 295–301.

Scheffer, D., & Heckhausen, H. (2018). Trait theories of motivation. In J. Heckhausen & H. Heckhausen (Eds.), *Motivation and action* (3rd ed., pp. 67–112). Springer.

Schmitt, D. P., & Buss, D. M. (2000). Sexual dimensions of person description: Beyond or subsumed by the Big Five? *Journal of Research in Personality, 34*, 141–177.

Schrock, J. M., Snodgrass, J. J., & Sugiyama, L. S. (2020). Lassitude: The emotion of being sick. *Evolution and Human Behavior, 41*, 44–57.

Schultheiss, O.C. (2020). Motives and goals, or: The joys and meanings of life. In J. F. Rauthmann (Ed.), *The handbook of personality dynamics and processes* (pp. 295–322). Academic Press.

Scott, J. P. (1980). The function of emotions in behavioral systems: A systems theory analysis. In R. Plutchick & H. Kellerman (Eds.), *Emotion: Theory, research, and experience*, Vol. 1: *Theories of emotion* (pp. 35–56). Academic Press.

Sela, Y., & Barbaro, N. (2018). Evolutionary perspectives on personality and individual differences. In V. Zeigler-Hill & T. K. Shackelford (Eds.), *The SAGE handbook of personality and individual differences* (Vol. 1, pp. 203–228). SAGE.

Sell, A., Sznycer, D., Al-Shawaf, L., Lim, J., Krauss, A., Feldman, A., Rascanu, R., Sugiyama, L., Cosmides, L., & Tooby, J. (2017). The grammar of anger: Mapping the computational architecture of a recalibrational emotion. *Cognition, 168*, 110–128.

Sell, A., Tooby, J., & Cosmides, L. (2009). Formidability and the logic of human anger. *Proceedings of the National Academy of Sciences USA, 106*, 15073–15078.

Shudo, E., Haccou, P., & Iwasa, Y. (2003). Optimal choice between feedforward and feedback control in gene expression to cope with unpredictable danger. *Journal of Theoretical Biology, 223*, 149–160.

Siemer, M. (2009). Mood experience: Implications of a dispositional theory of moods. *Emotion Review, 1*, 256–263.

Soto, C. J., John, O. P., Gosling, S. D., & Potter, J. (2011). Age differences in personality traits from 10 to 65: Big Five domains and facets in a large cross-sectional sample. *Journal of Personality and Social Psychology, 100*, 330–348.

Spinka, M., Newberry, R. C., & Bekoff, M. (2001). Mammalian play: Training for the unexpected. *Quarterly Review of Biology, 76*, 141–168.

Sterling, P., & Eyer, J. (1988). Allostasis: A new paradigm to explain arousal pathology. In S. Fisher & J. Reason (Eds.), *Handbook of life stress, cognition, and health* (pp. 629–650). Oxford University Press.

Stolier, R. M., Hehman, E., & Freeman, J. B. (2020). Trait knowledge forms a common structure across social cognition. *Nature Human Behaviour, 4*, 361–371.

Sundie, J. M., Kenrick, D. T., Griskevicius, V., Tybur, J. M., Vohs, K. D., & Beal, D. J. (2011). Peacocks, Porsches, and Thorstein Veblen: Conspicuous consumption as a sexual signaling system. *Journal of Personality and Social Psychology, 100*, 664–680.

Sznycer, D. (2019). Forms and functions of the self-conscious emotions. *Trends in Cognitive Sciences, 23*, 143–157.

Sznycer, D., Al-Shawaf, L., Bereby-Meyer, Y., Curry, O. S., De Smet, D., Ermer, E., Kim, S., Kim, S., Li, N. P., Lopez Seal, M. F., McClung, J., O, J., Ohtsubo, Y., Quillien, T., Schaub, M., Sell, A., van Leeuwen, F., Cosmides, L., & Tooby, J. (2017). Cross-cultural regularities in the cognitive architecture of pride. *Proceedings of the National Academy of Sciences USA, 114*, 1874–1879.

Sznycer, D., Cosmides, L., & Tooby, J. (2017). Adaptationism carves emotions at their functional joints. *Psychological Inquiry, 28*, 56–62.

Sznycer, D., & Lukaszewski, A. W. (2019). The emotion-valuation constellation: Multiple emotions are governed by a common grammar of social valuation. *Evolution and Human Behavior, 40*, 395–404.

Tamir, M. (2009). What do people want to feel and why? Pleasure and utility in emotion regulation. *Current Directions in Psychological Science, 18*, 101–105.

Tamir, M. (2016). Why do people regulate their emotions? A taxonomy of motives in emotion regulation. *Personality and Social Psychology Review, 20*, 199–222.

Tamir, M., & Ford, B. Q. (2012). When feeling bad is expected to be good: Emotion regulation and outcome expectancies in social conflicts. *Emotion, 12*, 807–816.

Tamir, M., Ford, B. Q., & Gilliam, M. (2013). Evidence for utilitarian motives in emotion regulation. *Cognition and Emotion, 27*, 483–491.

Tamir, M., Mitchell, C., & Gross, J. J. (2008). Hedonic and instrumental motives in anger regulation. *Psychological Science, 19*, 324–328.

Tennov, D. (1999). *Love and limerence: The experience of being in love*. Scarborough House.

Tinbergen, N. (1951). *The study of instinct*. Clarendon Press.

Toates, F. M., & Archer, J. (1978). A comparative review of motivational systems using classical control theory. *Animal Behaviour, 26*, 368–380.

Tooby, J., & Cosmides, L. (1990). The past explains the present: Emotional adaptations and the structure of ancestral environments. *Ethology and Sociobiology, 11*, 375–424.

Tooby, J., & Cosmides, L. (2008). The evolutionary psychology of the emotions and their relationship to internal regulatory variables. In M. Lewis, J. M. Haviland-Jones, & L. F. Barrett (Eds.), *Handbook of emotions* (3rd ed., pp. 114–137). Guilford Press.

Tooby, J., & Cosmides, L. (2015). The theoretical foundations of evolutionary psychology. In D. M. Buss (Ed.), *The handbook of evolutionary psychology*, Vol 1: *Foundations* (2nd ed., pp. 3–87). Wiley.

Tooby, J., Cosmides, L., Sell, A., Lieberman, D., & Sznycer, D. (2008). Internal regulatory variables and the design of human motivation: A computational and evolutionary approach. In A. J. Elliot (Ed.), *Handbook of approach and avoidance motivation* (pp. 252–271). Taylor & Francis.

Tops, M., Boksem, M. A. S., Luu, P., & Tucker, D. M. (2010). Brain substrates of behavioral programs associated with self-regulation. *Frontiers in Cognition, 1*, 152.

Tops, M., IJzerman, H., & Quirin, M. (2021). Personality dynamics in the brain: Individual differences in updating of representations and their phylogenetic roots. In J. F. Rauthmann (Ed.), *The handbook of personality dynamics and processes* (pp. 126–155). Academic Press.

Toronchuk, J. A., & Ellis, G. F. (2013). Affective neuronal selection: The nature of the primordial emotion systems. *Frontiers in Psychology, 3*, 589.

Tracy, J. L., & Robins, R. W. (2007). The psychological structure of pride: A tale of two facets. *Journal of Personality and Social Psychology, 92*, 506–525.

Trimmer, P. C., Paul, E. S., Mendl, M. T., McNamara, J. M., & Houston, A. I. (2013). On the evolution and optimality of mood states. *Behavioral Sciences, 3*, 501–521.

Tybur, J. M., Lieberman, D., Kurzban, R., & DeScioli, P. (2013). Disgust: Evolved function and structure. *Psychological Review, 120*, 65–84.

van Kleef, G. A., De Dreu, C. K., & Manstead, A. S. (2004). The interpersonal effects of anger and happiness in negotiations. *Journal of Personality and Social Psychology, 86*, 57–76.

Volk, S., & Masicampo, E. J. (2020). Self-regulatory processes and personality. In J. F. Rauthmann (Ed.), *The handbook of personality dynamics and processes* (pp. 345–363). Academic Press.

Weisberg, D. S., & Gopnik, A. (2013). Pretense, counterfactuals, and Bayesian causal models: Why what is not real really matters. *Cognitive Science, 37*, 1368–1381.

Winterhalder, B., Lu, F., & Tucker, B. (1999). Risk-sensitive adaptive tactics: Models and evidence from subsistence studies in biology and anthropology. *Journal of Archaeological Research, 7*, 301–348.

Woody, E. Z., & Szechtman, H. (2011). Adaptation to potential threat: The evolution, neurobiology, and psychopathology of the security motivation system. *Neuroscience & Biobehavioral Reviews, 35*, 1019–1033.

Wrangham, R. W. (1999). Evolution of coalitionary killing. *American Journal of Physical Anthropology, 110*, 1–30.

Wrangham, R. W. (2018). Two types of aggression in human evolution. *Proceedings of the National Academy of Sciences USA, 115*, 245–253.

Zeifman, D. M., & Hazan, C. (2016). Pair bonds as attachments: Mounting evidence in support of Bowlby's hypothesis. In J. Cassidy & P. R. Shaver (Eds.), *Handbook of attachment* (3rd ed., pp. 416–434). Guilford Press.

PART II

Evolutionary Approaches to Specific Emotions

CHAPTER 6

The Recalibrational Theory: Anger as a Bargaining Emotion

Aaron Sell and Daniel Sznycer

> **Abstract**
> This chapter uses the adaptationist program to predict and explain the major features of anger. According to this approach, anger evolved by natural selection to bargain for better treatment. Thus, the major triggers of anger (e.g., cost impositions, cues of disrespect) all indicate an increased willingness (on the part of the offender) to impose costs on the angry individual. Once triggered, the anger system bargains using the two primary incentives: the imposition of costs and the denial of benefits. This simple functional sketch of anger is then supplemented with additional considerations needed to address the resultant selection pressures created by bargaining. This process offers functionally sound and theoretically justified explanations for the following: anger in aggressive and cooperative contexts, the role of apologies and their sincerity, the content of sex-specific insults, the computational structure of "intentionality" in the context of anger, and the origin of the implicit rules of combat.
>
> **Key Words:** welfare trade-off ratio, anger, recalibrational theory, aggression, adaptationism

How should a researcher characterize an emotion like anger? One could list features of the emotion, or describe the behaviors that result from it. One could reference the increased blood pressure, the facial changes, and so on. However, without a description of the emotion's function, this approach will be merely descriptive—a list of facts,[1] understandable only by rote memorization and explained with shallow metaphors or post hoc analogies (e.g., anger is an aggressive response to personal attacks [Lazarus, 1990]; or, anger is a steam engine that releases psychic pressure). Evolutionary psychology offers a better explanation rooted in modern evolutionary biology—the same explanation that is routinely used to characterize every organ of every species on the planet except—oddly—the human brain (Tooby, 2020).

What Is the Evolved Function of Anger?

Emotions are evolved neural programs that govern perceptual, physiological, cognitive, and behavioral responses to important ancestral problems (Al-Shawaf et al., 2016; Tooby & Cosmides, 1990; Tooby et al., 2008). According to the recalibrational theory of anger (Sell, 2011; Sell et al., 2009; Sell et al., 2017), anger evolved to address a particularly potent ancestral selection pressure: the need to bargain for better treatment. In other words, anger increased our ancestors' reproduction by recalibrating the welfare-consideration mechanisms in the skulls of other humans. Thus, to understand how anger works, we have to understand how humans ascribe value to the welfare of other humans (i.e., if you want to understand a key, you must first understand a lock).

How do humans assign social valuation? Again, a functional account offers a more thorough and satisfying explanation. Over evolutionary time, animals would have faced selection pressures to avoid imposing costs on some subset of their conspecifics. For example, because of the shared genetic interests of kin, selection should have designed mechanisms to identify kin (Lieberman et al., 2007) and exploit their interests less ruthlessly than non-kin (Trivers, 1974). Similar selection pressures led to the evolution of mechanisms that valued the welfare of others to avoid costly aggressive contests (Hammersetin & Parker, 1982), to avoid harming those who emit positive externalities (Tooby & Cosmides, 1996), to preserve a reputation for cooperation (Nowak & Sigmund, 1998), and so on. While often studied separately, these selection pressures inevitably would have led to an integrated design so that decisions can be made during actual conflicts of interest, where different factors may point in different directions (e.g., do you take a sandwich from a physically formidable but unintelligent second cousin if no one is looking?).

Such considerations led researchers to posit the evolution of a mechanism for computing the aggregate weight one places on another individual (relative to one's own welfare) when making decisions that affect both. This is called the *welfare trade-off ratio* (WTR), and it is defined as an internal regulatory variable that is consulted when the organism considers a trade-off between their own interests and those of another individual (Sell et al., 2017; Tooby et al., 2008). The WTR acts as a discount variable when comparing the value of a resource (or action or state of affair) for the self versus the value to another. Mathematically, for organism X considering a trade-off with organism Y, organism X's WTR system selects the self-beneficial action whenever: $V_x > WTR_{xy} * V_y$ (where "V" represents the value of the resource). In other words, X will attempt to take the resource (or deny the benefit) whenever they value the outcome more than the other values the outcome, discounted by X's WTR toward Y. For example, if a friend wanted you to help them move (say, a value worth approximately 10 units of welfare to your friend) on your only day off (the loss of which would be worth approximately 6 to you), your WTR toward your friend would determine whether you would say yes or no. A WTR of .5 would discount their interests (estimated to be of value 10 for them) by 50% and result in refusal to help (because 6 > 10 * .5). Thus, the welfare trade-off ratio one has toward another is an index of how much one "cares" about the other individual's welfare when making decisions.

With this simple sketch of the human valuation-setting system, we can then derive from first principles how anger bargains for better treatment. The anger system would need to interface with the WTR calibrating system in the other individual's mind and recalibrate the other person's WTR so that it places greater weight on the interests of the angry person (Sell et al. 2017; Sznycer & Lukaszewski, 2019; Tooby et al., 2008). This analysis leads to specific predictions that can be tested to determine if anger evolved for that function.

The Major Features of Anger Indicate Design to Recalibrate Welfare Trade-Off Ratios

If the recalibrational theory of anger is correct, each of the major features of anger must be well designed to bargain for better treatment—usually by recalibrating the target's WTR in favor of the angry individual.

Feature #1: Anger Activates in Response to Indications of a Low Welfare Trade-Off Ratio
The primary triggers of anger are cues that another has a lower-than-acceptable WTR toward the angry person. Such cues are evident—in theory—from many different behaviors, because the weight one places on another's welfare is likely used by many different cognitive mechanisms (see Sell et al., 2017). For example, we attend more closely to individuals whose interests we value highly (e.g., spouses, children, dangerous high-status individuals, beloved cooperators). Therefore, if person X lacks interest in person Y, this may indicate that X holds a low WTR toward Y, and thus may trigger anger in Y (e.g., walking away while Y is talking, tossing a free copy of Y's book in the trash, responding with "no" when Y asks if X wants to hear a story).

Sell (2017) reports an analysis of naturalistic anger-based arguments that reveal at least 12 computationally distinct triggers of anger. The most common of these is also the most theoretically clear: the target of anger imposes (or indicates a willingness to impose) a hefty cost on the angry person in order to get a relatively small benefit (e.g., refusing to pick up a friend who needs a ride in the rain).

When someone imposes a cost on you, the WTR equation predicts a priori the role of three important variables: the magnitude of the cost imposed on you (i.e., V_x, how bad was it for you?); the magnitude of the benefit the imposer received from harming you (i.e., V_y, what did they get out of it?); and the person the WTR is assigned to (i.e., WTR_{xy}, whom did they think they were doing it to?). The lowest WTR_{xy} is indicated when the target imposes a large cost (high V_x) for a small benefit (low V_y), knowingly on the target (WTR_{xy}). Empirical demonstrations across six cultures (including industrial and foraging peoples) confirmed each prediction for both men and women. Anger is more likely to be triggered as the cost imposed on you *increases*, as the benefit for imposing it on you *decreases*, and when the imposer knew it was specifically *you* that would be hurt by their actions (Sell et al., 2017).

Note that this account of the trigger of anger can also explain the special role of intentionality in anger. A cost imposition indicates a lower WTR most clearly when the target has advance knowledge of the large magnitude of the cost they were imposing, the small magnitude of the benefit, and that the cost would be borne by you in particular. This is why a person can—sometimes—successfully diffuse another's anger by statements such as "I'm sorry, if I thought it would hurt you that badly I wouldn't have done it . . . "; "I'm sorry, I thought if I didn't do this I would lose my house!"; and "I had no idea it was you in the car, I never would have done that to you if I had known." The fact that such statements can diffuse anger suggests that anger is not triggered by harm per se. Anger is triggered by indications of an insufficiently high WTR. Again, the use of these defenses and their effectiveness at defusing anger has been empirically confirmed across cultures (Sell et al., 2017).

Another common trigger of anger involves cues of "insulting beliefs" (Sell, 2017). Because WTRs themselves are calibrated by estimates of traits—e.g., an estimated kinship index regulates WTRs for kin (Lieberman et al., 2007), a relative formidability estimate regulates WTRs among men (Lukaszewski et al., 2016; Sell et al., 2009)—then indications that another person underestimates you on one of these WTR-relevant traits will evidence a lower WTR. If Tony thinks you are stupid, then Tony will hold a lower WTR toward you (assuming your relationship is one in which intelligence is relevant to WTR calibration). This explains why deliberate insults can trigger anger so easily, but also why what counts as an insult differs between different kinds of individuals (e.g., calling a woman sexually promiscuous is more insulting than calling a man such [Preston & Kimberley, 1987], because WTRs toward women are calibrated more by sexual fidelity [Buss et al., 1990]). This explanation also accounts for the fact that unintentional insults are still anger provoking; e.g., if a person does not intend to call you stupid, but nonetheless thinks this, it is still a trigger of anger because the WTR is still impacted by this estimation of your intellect!

Additional triggers of anger include co-opting decisions for the other individual, a lack of empathy, lack of cues of friendship such as self-disclosure and a desire to be in close proximity to the other person, and so on. Each trigger has certain inborn assumptions about the WTR system, e.g., that we feel more empathy toward those whom we have high WTRs toward, which are intuitive but remain potential avenues for future research.

Taken together, these triggers of anger indicate that anger itself responds to cues of an insufficiently high WTR in the other individual. This is—of course—good evidence that the evolved function of anger is to recalibrate those WTRs.

Feature #2: Anger-Based Arguments Follow a Welfare Trade-Off Ratio "Grammar"

The most common behavioral response to anger is rapid communication with the target, i.e., an argument (see Averill, 1982). Indeed, anger activates vocal changes, making one's words louder, more rapid, and generally clearer (i.e., the opposite of mumbling; see Banse & Scherer, 1996), yet more evidence that the function of anger is to influence the mind of the target.

Furthermore, the semantic content of these arguments appears to follow a kind of cognitive grammar of welfare trade-off ratios. When anger is triggered by an act of cost imposition, for example, the subsequent arguments focus on the magnitude of the cost borne by the victim, the magnitude of the benefit gained by the offender, and whether the offender's action was intentional (see Sell, 2017; Sell et al., 2017). Targets of anger, meanwhile, often counter these claims to diffuse anger. This creates a kind of back-and-forth bargaining situation, with the angry person attempting to demonstrate that the target has a deficient WTR, while the target defends themselves by arguing that their WTR is higher than the angry person is claiming.

When triggered by insulting beliefs, the arguments again appear to conform to the grammar of WTRs, specifically whether the target of anger really believes you are deficient on the WTR-calibrating trait and whether or not that trait is relevant to the calibration of their WTR toward you, e.g., "I didn't say you were stupid, I said you made a mistake . . . anyone can make a mistake" and "who cares if you are a bad driver? You are a brilliant and powerful man. . . ."

The mere existence of highly motivated verbal communication between the angry individual and the target of anger suggests that the function of anger is to recalibrate the mind of the target (one can compare this to hatred, wherein communication with the target is anathema; see Sell & Lopez, 2020; also Sell et al., Chapter 8 in this volume). The fact that these arguments appear particularly focused on the WTR-setting machinery of the target indicates that anger functions primarily to upregulate the WTR of the target.

Feature #3: Anger-Based Aggression Functions to Bargain

A living animal is highly ordered matter, and minor alterations to this order (e.g., a bruised aorta, injury to kidney) can bring about dysfunction and death. This fact can be exploited by animals to extract benefits from conspecifics by making the prohibitive cost of disorder (aggression) the price of noncompliance.

Aggression can solve multiple adaptive problems for animals, and thus comes in different forms, e.g., predatory aggression, mate retention, and fear-based aggression (Huntingford, 2013). Anger-based aggression, however, most resembles a kind of bargaining aggression (sometimes called "ritualized aggression" or contests of assessment) that functions to change the mind of the antagonist and trigger submission or retreat (Sell, 2011; Sell & Lopez, 2020).

During ritualized aggression, combatants deploy relatively safe forms of aggression that are designed to determine which combatant would win a more protracted and dangerous bout of aggression. First, the animals typically start with perceptual assessments, e.g., vocal displays, staring contests, and so on. During this stage, animals will often adopt formidability enhancement displays that exaggerate the size of their weaponry (e.g., bare fangs, inflate body size). If both animals persist, the tactics can escalate to more valid and dangerous indicators of fighting ability, e.g., pushing, various kinds of wrestling, and eventually potentially lethal aggression. Crucially, this style of aggression typically terminates when one combatant submits. The function of this aggression is to recalibrate the target's internal representation of the focal actor's aggressive formidability so that they relinquish the contested resource and/or accept their lower position in the dominance hierarchy.

When human anger triggers aggression, it typically takes on the same form as this ritualized aggression, and for the same purpose: to recalibrate the target. Welfare trade-off ratios are calibrated (for some types of relationships) by formidability, i.e., the ability to impose costs on others. This is particularly true of young men (Wilson & Daly, 1985), and explains why it is particularly insulting to a young man to be called weak, cowardly, or otherwise incapable of harming others. In those types of relationships, if one detects that another holds a WTR that is too low, they can be recalibrated by demonstrations of formidability (along with the implicit threat that said formidability can be used against the target) in the form of ritualized aggression.

Just as with many other animals, men typically start a fight with visual and auditory assessments. Previous research has established that humans can accurately estimate the upper body strength (a powerful predictor of individual fighting ability) of adult men from both visual and auditory assessment (Sell, 2012). When combatants do not recalibrate, the aggression can then escalate until one submits or until one is clearly defeated (Felson, 1982; Luckenbill, 1977; Sell, 2011).

These fights are graduated and incremental in the risk involved, and often conform to a kind of logic of "fairness" that functions to preserve the accuracy of the assessment (Romero et al., 2014; Sell et al., 2022; Sell & Lopez, 2020). In other words, the aggression is not designed to inflict injuries directly, but to demonstrate the *ability* to inflict those injuries reliably. This necessitates using combat tactics in situations that preserve the validity of the outcome; i.e., the fight has to be "fair" to prove someone actually "won." If given the option of, for example, hitting someone when they are not prepared, anger-based aggression typically relinquishes this opportunity precisely because a win through this "unfair" route would not be diagnostic of, and would not communicate, one's superior fighting ability. Indeed, anger-based aggression is clearly signaled to the target with loud expressive movements, arguments, and a universal expressive anger face.

Feature #4: The Universal Human Anger Face
Ritualized aggression in nonhuman animals typically starts with formidability enhancement displays that exaggerate cues of fighting ability via modifications to the posture, facial

configuration, piloerections, and/or weapon displays. Since most ancestral human aggression was powered by upper body strength (Sell et al., 2012), one would predict that humans have such displays as well. Additionally, if the recalibrational theory is correct, anger should trigger these displays.

Indeed, human anger is known to generate a universal, closed-mouth anger face by pulling seven distinct facial muscles (see Sell et al., 2014). It is clear that this face is part of our universal nature (e.g., it is produced by six-month-old infants and congenitally blind children). Furthermore, the shape of the face itself is revealed to be a formidability enhancement display. The distinct facial action units that comprise the face each—independently—increase the perceived strength of the face that produces it (Sell et al., 2014). For example, the anger face thins the lips by pressing them firmly together, an effect that increases estimates of the man's strength. The same effects are found for the flared nostrils, the lowered brows, the raised cheeks, and the raised mouth.

This account of the anger face explains not only the existence of the facial configuration (i.e., in order to enhance cues of formidability during early aggressive bargaining), but also the *particular configuration* that it has (i.e., the anger face specifically exaggerates those features that are used to estimate upper body strength; see Sell, 2012; Sell et al. 2014). Such functional explanations highlight the explanatory power of evolutionary theories—especially relative to alternative accounts that merely catalog features without predicting or explaining them.

Feature #5: Anger Coordinates Bargaining in Cooperative Relationships

Enhancing cues of fighting ability can recalibrate WTRs in relationships based on formidability, but there are other types of bargaining. The relationship between adult sisters, for example, is typically not determined by their ability to personally inflict injury on one another. Instead, anger between such individuals should demonstrate the traits that calibrate WTRs in cooperative relationships: specifically, one's ability to *benefit* the other (i.e., cooperative ability).

While not well explored empirically, anger contests in such contexts appear to follow similar "fairness" rules between individuals who benefit from each other. The contest will involve the temporary withdrawal of cooperation such that the angry person treats the other as if they were no longer a valued other. In a bid to recalibrate their WTR, the person lowers their own WTR toward the target; as if to say, "This is how I will treat you if you don't treat me better." Such tactics work—when they work—as implicit threats to terminate mutually cooperative relationships. If the target of anger is willing to end the relationship rather than recalibrate, the cooperative relationship may end and potentially be replaced by one enforced by formidability.

Again, anger appears designed to demonstrate the angry individual's capacity to deliver (or deny) benefits to the target in order to provoke recalibration. This creates the seemingly contradictory behavior of seeking out a person in order to ignore them, or paying close attention to someone to determine if they know you are ignoring them. In both cases, the angry person demonstrates a temporarily lowered WTR to the person, e.g., lowering facial and vocal affect as if talking to a stranger, pretending to not remember person-information, showing a lack of interest in being with the person, and abdicating duties on which the other relies, such as a husband not taking out the trash or a sister not helping her brother with his homework.

As with ritualized aggression, early bouts of cooperative withdrawal typically forgo serious withdrawals, e.g., a mother may "forget" to pay her son's cell phone bill but still remember to pay his college tuition. Moreover, these bouts terminate when the target of the anger recalibrates and apologizes, indicating the temporary nature of these contests and their function to recoup cooperation in mutually beneficial relationships. Indeed, research shows that after such bouts of anger, the dyad typically report a better understanding of each other and a "closer" relationship (Averil, 1982).

These bouts of cooperative withdrawal reveal that the function of anger is to recalibrate the target rather than inflict costs on it. The anger system appears to turn off when the target recalibrates, regardless of whether the individual has been hurt or not. This is particularly illustrated by apologies.

Feature #6: Bargaining Power Calibrates Thresholds for Anger

Anger functions to leverage one's bargaining power to recalibrate the target's WTR. The ability to do this is thus limited by one's bargaining power. Those with more bargaining power can demand better treatment from others and are predicted to become angry over a greater range of offenses, because WTRs are calibrated by the interactants' relative ability to inflict costs and bestow benefits, i.e., by their relative bargaining power. Meanwhile, those with low bargaining power may resort to other strategies to deal with individuals with low WTR (e.g., hatred, avoidance, tolerance; see Sell & Lopez, 2020).

Bargaining power comes in part from the ability to impose costs. For ancestral human males, this would have stemmed in large part from physical strength (upper body strength in particular). Therefore, men with greater upper body strength should set lower thresholds for anger and have a greater history of engaging in aggression. This prediction (and others) have been confirmed in a number of societies, including US college students (Sell et al., 2009), Aka hunter-gatherers (Hess et al., 2010), Swiss adolescents (Sell et al., 2016), and professional athletes (Webster et al., 2020).

Feature #7: Apologies Extinguish Anger

The function of an adaptation can often be understood by noting the conditions that deactivate the adaptation (e.g., the function of hunger is partly revealed when one is satiated and hunger deactivates; Al-Shawaf, 2016). Research suggests that the most effective way to defuse an incident of anger is to offer a sincere apology.

Apologies are verbal indicators of recalibration, typically captured by phrases such as "I was wrong" or "I'm sorry," which contain words that indicate a change of mind, e.g., "regret" or "mistaken." Apologies—if estimated to be sincere—demonstrate that anger has fulfilled its function and the target has recalibrated their WTR. As such, they are astoundingly effective at canceling anger even without tangible restitution (Frantz & Bennigson, 2005). The fact that indicators of mental change are usually sufficient to deactivate anger is a powerful argument that the function of anger is recalibration rather than damage or punishment. The distinction between sincere and insincere apologies remains to be explored from this perspective, but a series of basic predictions can be derived with ease: (i) apologies should become dramatically less effective the second time as they indicate the first apology was not followed by an improved WTR; (ii) effective apologies should be accompanied by statements acknowledging the magnitude of offense (i.e., that the original WTR was indeed too low) rather than a defense that indicates the original

WTR was justified; and (iii) behavior after a sincere apology should be closely monitored for evidence of change.

Conclusions

The features reviewed above are only a fraction of the full complex design of anger. Subroutines in the anger program include remarkably complex adaptations; e.g., anger prepares the body for the possibility of aggression with well-known physiological effects such as increased respiration rate and blood pressure, but there are almost certainly perceptual changes, cognitive search routines (such as a sudden awareness of nearby weapons and allies), risk-evaluation programs (such that one remembers kin that depend on you before accelerating in an act of road rage), memory searches for previous indicators of low WTR from that same target, and so on. The negotiation process of anger also appears to include cognitive searches for information to verify that the target of anger actually holds a low WTR; e.g., angry people interrogate the targets of anger, "why did you do this?" "do you know who you're screwing with?" "what made you think I would agree to this?" and so on (see Sell et al., 2017). Other subroutines in anger would be needed to detect WTRs from comparisons, e.g., a friend wouldn't loan you his car, which didn't provoke anger until he agreed to loan his car to Tony. Given the strength of the selection pressure, it is likely that the anger bargaining system and other connected adaptations are extremely complex and well designed. Much additional work will need to be done in this area.

The advantage of using evolutionary theory to explain human behavior is that hypotheses can be derived from a theory that is known to be true (Dawkins, 1976). Another individual's consideration of one's welfare would have been a powerful selection pressure for our ancestors. This selection would have led to the evolution of an adaptation for upregulating another's concern for your welfare whenever feasible. The engineering requirements for this adaptation would include—at a minimum—the ability to detect cues of devaluation in another, and behavioral responses to that devaluation that leverage bargaining power in a cost-minimizing way (at first) to provoke recalibration, and finally the ability to detect when recalibration is successful. This is a description of anger. More than that, though, this chain of reasoning from first principles is strong enough that if human anger did not exist in our species in roughly the form that it does, it would be a positive mystery in evolutionary theory. No such statement could be truthfully made from non-evolutionary theories.

Note

1. This feature-listing approach may also lead one to conclude that anger lacks biological reality if one finds, as one does, that many anger events lack one or more of the features in the canonical list (cf. Barrett, 2006).

References

Al-Shawaf, L. (2016). The evolutionary psychology of hunger. *Appetite, 105*, 591–595.
Al-Shawaf, L., Conroy-Beam, D., Asao, K., & Buss, D. M. (2016). Human emotions: An evolutionary psychological perspective. *Emotion Review, 8*(2), 173–186.
Averill, J. R. (1982). *Anger and aggression: An essay on emotion*. Springer Science & Business Media.
Banse, R., & Scherer, K. (1996). Acoustic profiles in vocal emotion expression. *Journal of Personality and Social Psychology, 70*(3), 614–636.
Barrett, L. F. (2006). Are emotions natural kinds? *Perspectives on Psychological Science, 1*(1), 28–58.
Buss, D. M., Abbott, M., Angleitner, A., Asherian, A., Biaggio, A., Blanco-Villasenor, A., Bruchon-Schweitzer, M., Ch'U, Y., Czapinski, J., Deraad, B., Ekehammar, B., Lohamy, N. E., Fioravanti, M., Georgas, J., Gjerde, P.,

Guttman, R., Hazan, F., Iwawaki, S., Janakiramaiah, N., . . . Yang, K. (1990). International preferences in selecting mates: A study of 37 cultures. *Journal of Cross-Cultural Psychology, 21*(1), 5–47.

Dawkins, R. (1976). *The selfish gene*. Oxford University Press.

Felson, R. (1982). Impression management and the escalation of aggression and violence. *Social Psychology Quarterly, 45*(4), 245–254.

Frantz, C. M., & Bennigson, C. (2005). Better late than early: The influence of timing on apology effectiveness. *Journal of Experimental Social Psychology, 41*(2), 201–207.

Hess, N., Helfrecht, C., Hagen, E., Sell, A., & Hewlett, B. (2010). Interpersonal aggression among Aka hunter-gatherers of the Central African Republic: Assessing the effects of sex, strength, and anger. *Human Nature, 21*, 330–354.

Huntingford, F. A. (2013). *Animal conflict*. Springer Science & Business Media.

Lazarus, R. S. (1990). *Emotion and adaptation*. Oxford University Press.

Lieberman, D., Tooby, J., & Cosmides, L. (2007). The architecture of human kin detection. *Nature, 445*(7129), 727–731.

Luckenbill, D. (1977). Criminal homicide as a situated transaction. *Social Problems, 25*, 176–186.

Lukaszewski, A. W., Simmons, Z. L., Anderson, C., & Roney, J. R. (2016). The role of physical formidability in human social status allocation. *Journal of Personality and Social Psychology, 110*(3), 385–406.

Nowak, M. A., & Sigmund, K. (1998). Evolution of indirect reciprocity by image scoring. *Nature, 393*(6685), 573–577.

Preston, K., & Kimberley, S. (1987). What's the worst thing . . . ? Gender-directed insults. *Sex Roles, 17*(3), 209–219.

Romero, G. A., Pham, M. N., & Goetz, A. T. (2014). The implicit rules of combat. *Human nature, 25*(4), 496–516.

Sell, A. (2011). The recalibrational theory and violent anger. *Aggression and Violent Behavior, 16*(5), 381–389.

Sell, A. (2012). Evolved cognitive adaptations. In J. Vonk & T. K. Shackelford (Eds.), *The Oxford handbook of comparative evolutionary psychology* (pp. 61–79). Oxford University Press.

Sell, A. (2017). Recalibration theory of anger. In T. K. Shackelford & V. Weekes-Shackelford (Eds.), *Encyclopedia of evolutionary psychological science* (pp. 1–14). Springer. https://doi.org/10.1007/978-3-319-16999-6_1687-1.

Sell, A., Cosmides L., & Tooby, J. (2014). The human anger face evolved to enhance cues of strength. *Evolution and Human Behavior, 35*(5), 425–429.

Sell, A., Eisner, M. P., & Ribeaud, D. (2016). Bargaining power and adolescent aggression: The role of fighting ability, coalitional strength, and mate value. *Evolution and Human Behavior, 37*(2), 105–116.

Sell, A., Hone, L. S., & Pound, N. (2012). The importance of physical strength to human males. *Human Nature, 23*, 30–44.

Sell, A., & Lopez, A. C. (2020). Emotional underpinnings of war: An evolutionary analysis of anger and hatred. In C. Ireland, J. Ireland, M. Lewis, & A. Lopez (Eds.), *The international handbook on collective violence: Current issues and perspectives* (pp. 31–46). Routledge.

Sell, A., Sznycer, D., Al-Shawaf, L., Lim, J., Krauss, A., Feldman, A., Rascanu, R., Sugiyama, L., Tooby, J., & L. Cosmides (2017). The grammar of anger: Mapping the computational architecture of a recalibrational emotion. *Cognition, 168*, 110–128.

Sell, A., Sznycer, D., & Meyers, M. (2022). The implicit rules of combat reflect the evolved function of combat: An evolutionary-psychological analysis of fairness and honor in human aggression. *Evolution and Human Behavior, 43*(4), 304–313.

Sell, A., Tooby, J., & Cosmides, L. (2009). Formidability and the logic of human anger. *Proceedings of the National Academy of Science, 106*(35), 15073–15078.

Sznycer, D., & Lukaszewski, A. W. (2019). The emotion–valuation constellation: Multiple emotions are governed by a common grammar of social valuation. *Evolution and Human Behavior, 40*(4), 395–404.

Tooby, J. (2020). Evolutionary psychology as the crystalizing core of a unified modern social science. *Evolutionary Behavioral Sciences, 14*(4), 390–403.

Tooby, J., & Cosmides, L. (1990). The past explains the present: Emotional adaptations and the structure of ancestral environments. *Ethology and Sociobiology, 11*, 375–424.

Tooby, J., & Cosmides, L. (1996). Friendship and the banker's paradox: Other pathways to the evolution of adaptations for altruism. In *Proceedings-British Academy, 88*, 119–144.

Tooby, J., Cosmides, L., Sell, A., Lieberman, D., & Sznycer, D. (2008). Internal regulatory variables and the design of human motivation: A computational and evolutionary approach. In A. J. Elliot (Ed.), *Handbook of approach and avoidance motivation* (pp. 251–271). Lawrence Erlbaum Associates.

Trivers, R. L. (1974). Parent-offspring conflict. *Integrative and Comparative Biology, 14*(1), 249–264.

Webster, G. D., DeWall, C. N., Xu, Y., Orozco, T., Crosier, B. S., Nezlek, J. B., Bryan, A. D., & Bator, R. J. (2020). Facultative formidability: Physical size shapes men's aggressive traits and behaviors in sports. *Evolutionary Behavioral Sciences, 15*(2), 133–158.

Williams, G. C. (1966). *Adaptation and natural selection: A critique of some current evolutionary thought.* Princeton University Press.

Wilson, M., & Daly, M. (1985). Competitiveness, risk taking, and violence: The young male syndrome. *Ethology and Sociobiology, 6*(1), 59–73.

CHAPTER 7

Shame

Mitchell Landers, Daniel Sznycer, and Laith Al-Shawaf

> **Abstract**
> A central adaptive problem for human ancestors was the potential or actual spread of reputationally damaging information about the self—information that would decrease the inclination of other group members to render assistance. The emotion of shame appears to be the solution engineered by natural selection to defend against this threat. The existing evidence suggests that shame is a neurocomputational program that orchestrates various elements of the cognitive architecture in the service of deterring the individual from making choices wherein the personal benefits are exceeded by the prospective costs of being devalued by others; preventing negative information about the self from reaching others; and minimizing the adverse effects of social devaluation when it occurs. While shame, like pain, causes personal suffering and sometimes leads to hostile behavior, an evolutionary psychological analysis suggests the shame system is elegantly designed to deter injurious choices and make the best of a bad situation.
>
> **Key Words:** shame, emotion, adaptationism, audience effect, social evaluation

Introduction

Shame appears to be a standard feature of human nature, found in all the world's cultures, past and present. But what is shame? And given the pain that shame causes to self and others, why do we have this emotion?

To answer this question, we take an evolutionary approach (Cosmides & Tooby, 2000; Tooby & Cosmides, 1992; Williams, 1966). Central to this approach is the view that humans, like other organisms, evolved via natural selection, a locally anti-entropic process that, through differential reproduction, turns heritable genetic differences into adaptations—design features that are retained because they reliably solved tasks tributary to survival or reproduction in ancestral environments (so-called adaptive problems). Human nature thus consists of the set of adaptations and their byproducts developed over this time span (see, e.g., Al-Shawaf et al., 2020; Tooby & Cosmides, 1992, 2015). Therefore, it is possible to reverse-engineer an adaptation, guided by theories of the adaptive problem that shaped it and information about the structure of the ancestral environments in which it evolved (Tooby & Cosmides, 1992).

Reverse-Engineering Shame: The Adaptive Landscape

Our hunter-gatherer ancestors relied heavily on mutual aid (Burkart et al., 2009; Clutton-Brock, 2009; Kaplan et al., 2000; Tomasello et al., 2012). Research from behavioral ecology, hunter-gatherer archaeology, and contemporary forager societies indicates that our hominin ancestors evolved in environments characterized by high rates of mortality (Burger & Vaupel, 2012), resource scarcity (Hill & Hurtado, 1996), variance in food acquisition (Hill & Hurtado, 1996; Kaplan & Hill, 1985), disease and injury (Sugiyama, 2004), and aggression from predators and conspecifics (Keeley, 1997). Critically, and in contrast to most other animal species, humans have relied and still rely on the other members of their groups—including non-kin—for the assistance necessary for survival and reproduction (Clutton-Brock, 2009; Schrock et al., 2020).

If these selection pressures characterized our species' evolution, then a central adaptive problem shaping human sociality would have been incentivizing one's mates, friends, allies, and fellow group members to render assistance in times of hunger, incapacitation, or interpersonal conflict (Sugiyama, 2004). Indeed, the extent to which other members of one's group valued an individual—and thus helped and refrained from exploiting her—would have had considerable impact on that individual's reproductive success (von Rueden & Jaeggi, 2016). Over the millennia, those individuals who attracted the goodwill and escaped the indifference, censure, and wrath of others would have left behind more copies of their genes. Natural selection would thus have differentially retained those neurocognitive variants (and their underlying genes) that reliably navigated the adaptive problems engendered by the importance of social valuation.

A growing body of evidence suggests that in humans, decisions about whether to deliver or deny help to others are computed by an array of specialized cognitive mechanisms that take in available information about an interaction partner and implement self–other welfare trade-off decisions—decisions that adaptively weigh the costs borne by the actor relative to the benefits received by the beneficiary (Delton & Robertson, 2016; Lieberman et al., 2007; Sznycer et al., 2019; Sznycer, De Smet, et al., 2016; Tooby et al., 2008). Key inputs that humans use to make welfare trade-off decisions include cues of genetic relatedness between self and other, the ability and willingness of the other to confer benefits on the self (e.g., skills, willingness to help), and the ability and willingness of the other to inflict costs on the self (e.g., physical formidability). The mind uses cue-based estimates of these inputs to compute the social value of a target individual to the self (e.g., as sibling, as mate, as friend) and how much weight to attach to the target's welfare when making welfare trade-off decisions.

These estimates of social value are used by internal regulatory mechanisms to guide behavior precisely because they contain useful information (Tooby et al., 2008). For example, self-esteem appears to reflect an internal estimation of the degree to which others acknowledge and include the self (Leary et al., 1995) and can therefore be thought of as barometer for tracking social inclusion. Self-esteem and other internal indices of an individual's value to others (e.g., social status; Mahadevan, 2018) are used by emotional, motivational, and reasoning systems to manage others' impressions of the self, to regain acceptance when one has been excluded, and so on.

Other people value or devalue us on the basis of our behaviors and characteristics. When others detect new information indicating that a target individual is more or less valuable than previously estimated, they recalibrate how much they value the target—upward or downward—with correspondingly positive or negative effects on the target's fitness (Tooby et al., 2008).

The Information Threat Theory of Shame

When new information comes to light that reveals an individual to be less socially valuable to others (or less able to defend their interests) than previously supposed, audiences react by attaching less weight to that person's welfare. Over evolutionary time, individuals devalued in this manner would have been helped less and harmed more, incurring fitness costs. For instance, devalued individuals may be avoided, shunned, denied help, and ostracized (Hales et al., 2016; Kurzban & Leary, 2001). From the perspective of the discredited individual, the adaptive problem of being devalued can be the difference between life and death. This intense selection pressure would have selected for regulatory adaptations to prevent or minimize the spread of negative information about the self and the costs associated with any ensuing devaluation (Fessler, 1999; Gilbert, 1997; Sznycer, 2016; Tooby & Cosmides, 2008; Weisfeld & Dillon, 2012). Preventing social devaluation—and minimizing its costs when it did occur—was thus a major adaptive problem for our species.

This selection pressure is the backdrop for the *information threat theory of shame*: Shame is an adaptation that evolved to defend against information-triggered social devaluation (Sznycer, 2010, 2021; Sznycer, Tooby, et al., 2016; see also Baumeister & Tice, 1990; Fessler, 1999; Gilbert, 1997; Schlenker & Leary, 1982; Weisfeld & Dillon, 2012). If this hypothesis is correct, then we would expect shame to be well-designed to minimize and counteract the threat of devaluation. An adaptation engineered to defeat devaluation would be activated by the prospect of devaluation or by cues of actual devaluation. Once activated, it would coordinate psychology and behavior to: (1) deter the individual from taking courses of action that likely yield more costs from social devaluation than the personal benefits the action would yield; (2) limit the extent to which others learn or spread potentially discrediting information about the self; (3) minimize the degree and scope of any social devaluation that does occur; and, if devaluation occurs, (4) motivate behavior geared toward mitigating its costs.

Existing evidence is consistent with this information threat theory of shame. For instance, when faced with the prospect of devaluation, people feel pain (Eisenberger, 2012; McDonald & Leary, 2005), avoid behaving in ways that could exacerbate devaluation (De Hooge et al., 2008; Fehr & Gächter, 2000), and conceal reputationally damaging information (Rockenbach & Milinski, 2011; Sznycer et al., 2015). When others discover this information, the shamed individual withdraws (Leach & Cidam, 2015), appeases (Keltner et al., 1997), apologizes (Schniter et al., 2013), and produces a phylogenetically ancient nonverbal display (Fessler, 1999; Weisfeld & Dillon, 2012; Landers & Sznycer, 2022) of subordination—signaling that less weight on his or her welfare is expected and acceptable (Gilbert, 2000b). Compared to other displays (e.g., the anger display) or the absence of any display, the shame display effectively mollifies those who observed the transgression (Keltner et al., 1997). Furthermore, the threat of being devalued by others upregulates pro-inflammatory cytokines (Dickerson et al., 2009)—a possible advantage given the increased likelihood of being punished or ostracized and developing an infection, the decreased likelihood of being cared for by others if one gets sick, or both. Importantly, experimentally manipulating (prospective or actual) devaluation reliably elicits shame (Dickerson et al., 2008; Robertson et al., 2018; Smith et al., 2002), even when an individual knows that she hasn't done anything wrong (Robertson et al., 2018). In other words, it is not objective wrongdoing, but rather the *threat of social devaluation*, that is the true trigger of shame (Robertson et al., 2018). As expected if shame is an adaptation designed to limit the threat of (negative) information spread, common knowledge (as opposed to lower levels of knowledge) between the individual and the audience exacerbates shame in the individual (Thomas et al., 2018). Shame sometimes leads to appeasement and enhanced cooperation (De Hooge et al., 2008; Gausel et al., 2016)—an expected response for a system designed to restore one's positive image as a cooperative partner in the minds of others (Leary & Kowalski, 1990). However, shame can also lead to verbal and physical aggression (Fessler, 2001; Tangney et al., 1992; Zhu et al., 2018)—expected if one's cooperative overtures land on deaf ears, if one has limited capacity to generate the benefits that would appease the audience, or if one has the requisite formidability to intimidate the audience.

The information threat theory can also make sense of context effects (see Al-Shawaf et al., 2021). For instance, from the fact that shame is tuned to the devaluative threat from others, it follows that certain acts or traits are likely to elicit devaluation only among specific individuals or groups. For example, an individual's refusal to help a rival of his best friend may cause devaluation by the rival but not by the individual's best friend (see Lukaszewski & Roney, 2010), whereas other acts or traits (e.g., incompetence, dishonesty) may produce fitness costs for broader audiences and thus elicit more widespread reputational harm (and shame). A well-designed shame system—one designed to mitigate these consequences—should therefore be sensitive to partner-choice effects (Baumard & Sperber, 2013; Noë & Hammerstein, 1995; Tooby & Cosmides, 1996) and aim to minimize the total costs of devaluation arising from one's social world. Data assessing the relationship between shame and partner choice are scarce, but the existing evidence is consistent with this argument (Feinberg et al., 2014; Shaw et al., 2014; Sznycer et al., 2012).

The adaptive problem of being devalued is both general (cues of being devalued lead to being helped less) and specific (cues of being devalued are particularly problematic if one has low social support to begin with). Given this, the shame system is expected to incorporate both a general architecture and open parameters that can account for differences in shame across situations, individuals, and populations (Sznycer et al., 2012). For instance, individuals with many socially valued characteristics can impose more costs on others before being devalued and can also more effectively limit the cost of devaluation when it does occur. As expected from this fact, individuals with such characteristics are less prone to shame (Sznycer et al., 2012). Likewise, variation in the characteristics of the audience is expected to elicit variation in the degree of shame activation. A more aggressively formidable audience, for instance, should be more shame-provoking than a weaker audience, all else being equal (see Fessler, 2007). Also, to the extent that devaluation can be mitigated by forming new alliances, the information threat theory predicts that shame-proneness should partly depend on the ease with which one can form new relationships to compensate for those that have been lost. In line with this prediction, when shame responses between Western and Eastern populations[1] were compared, research found that perception of relational mobility—the extent to which people feel they can easily form new relationships—strongly moderated the difference between the two cultures (Sznycer et al., 2012).

Shame is part of a functionally interlinked nexus of social emotions that also includes anger, gratitude, pride, guilt, and perhaps others. Although by hypothesis each of these emotions has a distinct evolved function, each also fundamentally depends on an evolved welfare trade-off psychology (Al-Shawaf et al., 2016; Al-Shawaf & Lewis, 2017; Delton & Robertson, 2012; Schniter et al., 2020; Scrivner et al., Chapter 4 in this volume; Sznycer, Cosmides, & Tooby, 2017; Sznycer & Lukaszewski, 2019; Sznycer et al., 2021; Tooby & Cosmides, 2008; Tooby et al., 2008). For example, the function of anger is to orchestrate bargaining tactics geared toward raising the weight another person places on the welfare of the self when cues indicate that the weight is insufficient; the function of gratitude is to consolidate cooperation with a partner and is activated when the system detects that a target values the welfare of the focal individual; the function of pride is to motivate the individual to capitalize on reputational gains by publicizing (and achieving) traits or acts that enhance valuation by others; the function of shame, or so we argue, is to limit the extent to which an audience reduces the weight placed on one's welfare; and the function of guilt is to prevent (before the fact) or remedy (after the fact) situations in which one placed too little weight on another's welfare (often unintentionally), irrespective of whether the other person will ever find out.

While guilt and shame are somewhat similar to each other, an adaptationist approach can distinguish them functionally while also outlining when they should co-activate. With guilt, the outcome to be avoided is *imposing harm on others we value*; even in cases where our misdeeds are never discovered, the harm we have done remains. In shame, the outcome to be avoided is *being devalued by others*. Thus, while one can simultaneously feel both shame and guilt about the same act, the functions, internal recalibrations, activating cues, and behavioral outputs are distinct. For example, consider the predicament of an unfaithful spouse: One who felt both guilt and shame about infidelity might refrain from it, while one who felt shame but not guilt might continue to be unfaithful but conceal it. We expect that future work will profitably shed light on similarities and differences between shame, guilt, and other social emotions (see Keltner, 1996; Smith et al., 2002; Tangney et al., 1996; Tangney et al., 1992).

Mapping Shame

The information threat theory not only can explain known facts about shame, but also can be used to generate novel, testable hypotheses. Given that the structure of shame reflects the statistical complex of regularities that crafted it over evolutionary time, knowledge of those regularities (and inferences derived from knowing them) can lead to novel a priori predictions about shame's unique design features. We describe an application of this logic next.

As previously discussed, a well-engineered shame system should activate not only reactively but also prospectively, before any devaluation occurs, to minimize the negative fallout that would result from an action likely to bring about social devaluation (Leary, 2015; Sommerville et al., 2013; Sznycer, Tooby, et al., 2016; see also Fehr & Gächter, 2000). In prospective mode, the system must estimate the magnitude of audience devaluation following any socially devalued act (e.g., lying), as well as the likelihood of being detected by an audience, and weigh the resultant expected cost against the payoff of the act to the actor himself (e.g., the benefit derived by the actor's lying). Performing this computation is necessary if the actor is going to forgo net costly courses of action in favor of more profitable ones, irrespective of whether such courses of action are desirable from the perspective of others or not. Furthermore, this calculation must be made *before* one decides to engage in the act itself—the shame system would be severely handicapped indeed if one needed to experience the devaluation of others first in order to know (ex-post) the magnitude of that devaluation. On this account, then, the anticipatory feeling of shame is a reflection of the shame system's internal prediction of the cost of audience devaluation that would occur if one were to engage in a socially disfavored act (Sznycer, Tooby, et al., 2016; see also Crocket et al., 2017). Because it is precisely calibrated to forecast audience devaluation—and in contrast with analyses emphasizing bias in affective forecasting (Wilson & Gilbert, 2005)—such an internal signal of anticipatory shame is predicted to allow an individual to avoid two possible errors: (1) shame under-activation, producing insufficient measures aimed at minimizing devaluation (and thus excessive devaluation from others), and (2) shame over-activation, deterring the individual from taking actions that yield more direct benefits than the costs they'd incur from audience devaluation.

The above analysis suggests that the shame system may be designed (1) to accurately forecast the precise magnitude of devaluation those in one's social ecology would express if one behaved in a way that others disvalue, and (2) to generate an internal signal of anticipatory shame in proportion to that forecast. To test this prediction, Sznycer and colleagues presented participants with an array of potentially devaluative acts or traits and asked them to rate, in a between-subjects design, either the intensity of shame they would feel if the act or trait were true of them, or how negatively they would view another individual if the act or trait were true of the other individual (a measure of audience devaluation). The stimuli included acts and traits such as stinginess, unattractiveness, and poor table manners. Across three industrial societies (United States, India, and Israel), the intensity of anticipatory shame closely tracked the magnitude of devaluation expressed by local audiences in each country (Figure 7.1A–C). Moreover, shame in each country tracked the devaluation ratings in the other two countries, suggesting that both the structure and the content of shame are (in part) universal (Sznycer, Tooby, et al., 2016; see also Cohen et al., 2020; Durkee et al., 2019). Additional studies showed that this effect is specific to shame: other negatively valenced emotions did *not* track audience devaluation (Sznycer, Tooby, et al., 2016). Further, in a replication of this work in 15 traditional small-scale societies, shame was found to track the devaluation expressed by audiences both within and between each of those 15 societies (Sznycer, Xygalatas, Agey, et al., 2018; Figure 7.1D–R). This suggests that shame's tracking of audience devaluation is a pan-human adaptation and not merely a product of cultural contact or convergent cultural evolution.

The Evolved Concept of Audience

The shame system may have co-evolved with, and in its operation may interact with, specialized concepts. One such concept may be *audience*.

A dissection of the *audience* concept with respect to shame has been hampered by several factors. Some researchers doubt that the threat of being devalued by others is causally linked to shame (e.g., Tangney et al., 2007a). Moreover, even among those who do acknowledge the importance of audience in shame, it has rarely been acknowledged that the same event may be viewed as affording negative social value, neutral social value, or positive social value by different observers—that is, that social valuation is individual and relationship-specific (Lukaszewski & Roney, 2010). As Darwin put it, "persons who are exceedingly shy are rarely shy in the presence of those with whom they are quite familiar, and of whose good opinion and sympathy they are perfectly assured—for instance, a girl in the presence of her mother" (1872, p. 331). Indeed, shame mobilizes conditionally as a function of properties of the audience, the focal (ashamed) individual, and the nature of the relationship between them. For example, pulling a blasphemous prank in a church elicits more shame when caught by one's pious mother than by irreligious friends. And when controlling for the audience's piety, the prank elicits more shame when caught by one's pious mother than by an annoying, pious stepmother (Sznycer, Tooby, et al., in prep.).

We distinguish between three subconcepts relevant to the role of audience in the operation of shame: (1) the firsthand audience, (2) the perceived audience, and (3) the effective audience. The firsthand audience is the set of individuals who have (sufficient) firsthand perceptual access to the devaluative situation—regardless of whether the cues they register lead them to devalue the focal individual. These are the people who, for example, see or hear an act of theft firsthand. For instance, three individuals may have witnessed an act of theft committed by person X (they are firsthand audiences), even when person X believes (falsely) that no one saw him. The perceived audience is the set of individuals the focal individual perceives as having (sufficient) firsthand perceptual access to the devaluative situation (regardless of whether the focal individual thinks these observers will devalue him). That is, from the perspective of person X who committed theft, the perceived audience represents *those individuals whom X believes saw or heard what X did firsthand*. The effective audience includes both (a) those individuals in the perceived audience who, in X's estimation, are likely to devalue him, and (b) those individuals outside the perceived audience whom X believes *would* socially devalue

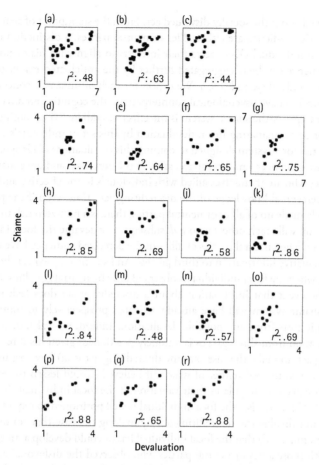

Figure 7.1. The intensity of anticipatory shame tracks the intensity of audience devaluation. Scatterplots A–C: Data from three mass societies (adapted from Sznycer et al., 2016. Shame closely tracks the threat of devaluation by others, even across cultures. *Proceedings of the National Academy of Sciences, 113*(10), 2625–2630). The stimuli were a set of brief hypothetical scenarios describing socially devalued actions and personal characteristics. The scenarios were phrased either from the perspective of the focal individual (e.g., "You are not generous with others"; *shame* condition) or from the perspective of an observer vis-à-vis the focal individual (e.g., "He is not generous with others"; *audience* condition; between-subjects design). For each scenario, participants rated either their feeling of shame if they took those actions or had those characteristics (*shame*), or the degree to which they would negatively view the individual in the scenarios if the individual took those actions or had those characteristics (*audience*). Each point represents the mean shame rating and mean devaluation rating of one scenario.

Data from (N of scenarios): A: United States (29); B: India (29); C: Israel (24). Scatterplots D–R: Data from 15 small-scale societies (adapted from Sznycer et al., 2018. Cross-cultural invariances in the architecture of shame. *Proceedings of the National Academy of Sciences, 115*(39), 9702–9707). Same experimental design, but with a set of 12 scenarios that were different from the ones used in Sznycer et al. (2016). D: Cotopaxi, Ecuador; E: Morona-Santiago, Ecuador; F: Coquimbo, Chile; G: Drâa-Tafilalet, Morocco; H: Enugu, Nigeria; I: Chalkidiki, Greece; J: Ikland, Uganda; K: Le Morne, Mauritius; L: La Gaulette, Mauritius; M: Dhading, Nepal; N: Tuva, Russia; O: Khövsgöl, Mongolia; P: Shaanxi, China; Q: Farming Communities, Japan; R: Fishing Communities, Japan. In all cases, shame ratings and devaluation ratings were given by different participants. Effect sizes: r^2 linear.

him if they learned about the socially disvalued act. From the standpoint of shame, individuals outside the effective audience are either allies or neutral parties, a distinction determined by whether the focal individual (X) expects their interests to align with his or not. Meanwhile, the effective audience can be disaggregated further by the anticipated extent of devaluation, relative status, formidability, and so on. We expect for each of these sub-concepts (except the firsthand audience) to have psychological counterparts in the cognitive architecture of shame.

The proper target of the shame system is the effective audience (i.e., aiming to reduce the likelihood of, or costs emanating from, devaluation by this set of individuals). However, two complications arise for a system designed to counter this devaluation: (1) language enables the transfer of information over time and space, and (2) the perceived audience may include allies or neutral parties who are themselves allied with individuals in the effective audience but who lack firsthand perceptual knowledge of the discrediting act. Thus, even if the perceived audience is exclusively made up of allies or neutral parties, there is a non-zero risk that information about the situation will reach others who *will* subsequently devalue the focal individual. Such a risk persists even when neutral parties or allies in the perceived audience have no incentive to disclose the devaluative information to third parties. And so one may expect the shame system to operate even when the focal individual is observed only by neutrals or allies in the perceived audience: In the event that information about a discrediting act does leak to the effective audience, the shame system will have already activated prospectively to motivate behaviors designed to limit costs from any possible devaluation. Indeed, a focal individual facing the threat of devaluation from third parties is uniquely positioned, given his direct knowledge of the discrediting act, to make the case that the discrediting act is (a) low cost to others and/or (b) of high benefit to the self (either of which, if believed, would lessen the extent to which the effective audience downregulates their valuation of the focal individual (Sell, Sznycer, Al-Shawaf, et al., 2017). Likewise, the focal individual is well positioned to request that allies and neutral parties not divulge the discrediting act by making the case that (c) divulging would not benefit them much, (d) that the focal individual has or could develop a mutually beneficial relationship with those allies or neutral parties who observed the disfavored act, and (e) that divulging the information would harm the focal individual and thus all of their mutually beneficial relationships. Therefore, to prevent discrediting information from spreading, and to maintain control over the narrative applied to any devaluative information leaked, the shame system is expected to aim to silence perceived audiences, even in social configurations that only involve allies and neutral parties.

We note, however, that human alliances shift dynamically: A moral panic may turn those who were once neutrals and allies into members of the effective audience; those in the effective audience today may be bought off or otherwise converted into allies or neutrals—the shame system is expected to be sensitive to these dynamics and to respond accordingly. Lastly, those individuals in the firsthand audience who go unrecognized as part of the perceived audience (that is, those individuals who are aware of the discrediting information but unknown to the focal individual) represent a potential threat. Therefore, we expect the shame system to upregulate attention to exhaustively identify the full extent of the perceived audience. Importantly, however, there is a trade-off between this goal and the goal of avoiding drawing (negative) attention from the firsthand audience (see Rapee & Heimberg, 1997).

Alternative Theories of Shame
According to an alternative theory, shame is an intrapersonal emotion (as opposed to an interpersonal one) that activates in response to how individuals understand, or "attribute," events relevant to their identity goals (i.e., who a person wants to be) (Lewis, 1971; Tangney, 1990;

Tracy & Robins, 2004). The nature of these attributions then specifies which of several emotions is elicited. For instance, when an event occurs that is incongruent with one's identity goals (e.g., failing an exam, when one aspires to be a good student) and one attributes this failure to specific, unstable, or controllable aspects of the self (e.g., not having studied enough), then guilt is activated (Tangney, 1990; Tracy & Robins, 2004). Alternatively, when one makes global, stable, or uncontrollable attributions (e.g., feeling unintelligent), shame is triggered instead (Tangney, 1990; Tracy & Robins, 2004). And when one achieves identity-goal-*congruent* outcomes (e.g., acing an exam, when one aspires to be a good student), achievement-oriented pride or hubris is activated, depending upon whether the attributions are specific and unstable (pride) or global and stable (hubris) (Tracy & Robins, 2004). Because attributional theories consider self-conscious emotions like shame to be intrapersonal emotions, they view the properties of these emotions—everything from how they are elicited to the behavior they induce—to depend critically upon how individuals construe and evaluate their own successes and failures.

However, as discussed above, recent theory and data suggest that shame and other so-called self-conscious emotions have interpersonal adaptive functions (De Hooge et al., 2011; Fessler, 1999; Gilbert, 1997; Leary, 2015; Rodriguez Mosquera, 2018; Sznycer, Tooby, et al., 2016; Sznycer, Xygalatas, Agey, et al., 2018; Weisfeld & Dillon, 2012) and matching neurocognitive architectures that realize those functions (Sznycer, Tooby, et al., 2016; Sznycer, Cosmides, et al., 2017). Self-conscious emotions appear to be information-processing adaptations tailored by natural selection because they helped our human ancestors navigate challenges and opportunities related to social valuation—the disposition to attend to others, associate with others, or trade personal welfare in favor of the welfare of others (Sznycer, 2019). But if this is so, then why are different suites of attributions, as the attributional theories point to, systematically associated with different self-conscious emotions? While this remains an open question, one possibility is that these consciously accessible *intra*personal thoughts are effects of neurocognitive mechanisms with *inter*personal adaptive functions. Consider the case of shame. The information threat theory suggests that when a student fails an exam, his shame system activates if he perceives that he will be devalued for failing and will face costs associated with that devaluation. After such an event, he may consciously experience "feeling dumb" or "feeling like a failure." But these stable, uncontrollable attributions are not the *cause* of his shame—rather, they are merely the consciously accessed outputs of a complex cognitive program that is functionally designed to mitigate reputational damage.

Alternatively, to the extent that self-consciousness is an adaptation, it must somehow have generated the fitness benefits that would have fueled its continued replication over evolutionary time, and interpersonal functions constitute possible causal pathways for these benefits. It is plausible, for instance, that shame's self-consciousness is the result of various recalibrational and decision-making procedures designed to counter devaluation. The following are a few possible candidate procedures. After a potentially devaluing event, the shame system must decide whether to mount a comprehensive response to possible devaluation or to feign normalcy—in some situations, displaying shame may signal culpability when playing dumb would be more cost-effective (Landers & Sznycer, 2022). In either case, the shame system may increase precautions to escape detection in the future, and when mounting a response, may upregulate the weight attached to the welfare of others (at least in public), downgrade estimates of the value of one's own welfare to others (see Leary et al., 1995), and correspondingly downgrade the level of entitlement one displays in future encounters with the effective audience.

These internal recalibrations may underlie the self-conscious phenomenology of shame. The self-blaming of shame (a focus of attributional analyses), too, may support interpersonal functions. For instance, it has been argued that self-blame can be a defensive tactic: a signal of submission that deters attacks (Gilbert, 2016). Consistent with this, women in abusive relationships often blame themselves, but tend to blame their partners after they exit the relationship (Gilbert, 2016). Self-blame may also function to probe for others' assent (or dissent) and thus for changes in others' evaluations of the self, to elicit sympathy or forgiveness, or to feign incompetence so as to exempt oneself from costly future responsibilities (Driscoll, 1989; see Tanaka et al., 2015; Zhu et al., 2017).

An interpersonal approach can also explain differences between the self-conscious experiences associated with shame and guilt—the focus of a great deal of attributional research (Tangney, 1990; Tangney & Dearing, 2002; Tangney et al., 1996; Tracy & Robins, 2004). Recall that according to attributional theories, negative outcomes are attributed to the global, stable, and uncontrollable self in shame, and to specific, unstable, and controllable aspects of the self in guilt. In contrast, an evolutionary perspective suggests that these differences may be rooted in the operation of distinct shame and guilt programs, which in turn reflect the different adaptive problems posed by devaluation (shame) and insufficient valuation of valuable others (guilt). For instance, the feeling that shame is less controllable than guilt may be explained by the fact that countering another's devaluation (shame) is less within an individual's control than upregulating one's valuation of another's welfare (guilt). Second, the fact that guilt follows unintentional expressions of low valuation (McGraw, 1987), whereas shame tracks devaluation from others (e.g., for being a thief, or for being physically unattractive, etc.) may explain why shame-inducing characteristics, more than guilt-inducing actions, are more likely to reflect stable features of an individual. Third, shame-triggering events tend to have broader interpersonal ramifications than guilt-triggering events do—and this may explain the feeling that shame-triggering events are more "global" and less "specific" than guilt-relevant events are. For instance, consider failing to help a friend in need, an omission that may trigger both shame and guilt. The adaptive problem handled by guilt is solved, and guilt's operation interrupted, once the guilty individual upregulates her valuation and behavior toward her friend. In contrast, the failure to help may cause the friend, as well as unaffected third parties, to devalue the shamed individual (Pedersen et al., 2018). That is, the problem that the shame system must tackle *may or may not* be solved once the directly affected party undoes her devaluation. This may explain why shame feels more global and all-encompassing than guilt. Future research will profitably explore the relationship between attributional and adaptationist accounts of shame and other social emotions (see Landers et al., in press).

Attributional theories raise two additional puzzles concerning (1) shame's adaptiveness and (2) its effects. Because shame is sometimes associated with undesirable outcomes such as aggression (Elison et al., 2014; Tangney et al., 1992), attributional researchers view shame as a maladaptive emotion (Tangney, 1991; Tangney et al., 2007b). But this is perplexing, because maladaptive traits are filtered out by natural selection, and yet the shame system persists in the human mind/brain. Furthermore, shame can motivate both aggressive (Elison et al., 2014; Tangney et al., 1992) and cooperative behaviors (De Hooge, 2008; Gausel et al., 2016; Tangney et al., 2014). For example, shame can motivate confessions or denials, approach or avoidance (De Hooge et al., 2018; Gausel et al., 2016), as well as appeasement or externalization of blame (Gilbert, 2000a; Griffin et al., 2016; Tangney, 1990). Why does shame deliver such functionally antithetical behaviors? These puzzles dissolve when considering that social devaluation can be countered through cooperative means or through cunning and force, depending upon the circumstances. When cooperation is a cost-effective means to rehabilitate one's social value in the eyes of others, shame will motivate those behaviors. Otherwise, if such paths are unavailable, the shame system can switch to ignoble methods (Elison et al., 2014;

Tangney et al., 1992)—an expected outcome when social benefits can be secured more cost-effectively through deceit and aggression (Fessler, 1999; Hales et al., 2016; Sell et al., 2016; Weisfeld & Dillon, 2012). Recent findings support this hypothesis. For instance, experimentally inducing shame causes dispositionally selfish people to cooperate more as second players in a sequential Prisoner's Dilemma game (when their decision to defect would be seen by others as unambiguously selfish). By contrast, in a simultaneous Prisoner's Dilemma game, where defection can instead be attributed to a benign fear of being defected on, inducing shame among dispositionally selfish people has no effect on cooperation (Declerk et al., 2014). That is, shame can inhibit defection, but shame can also allow for or promote defection when the situation affords cover. In each case, the behavioral output of shame is tailored to solving the problem of devaluation in that situation.

Or consider another example: When allocators in a money-allocation game offer little money to recipients who are ashamed, those recipients express less anger compared to recipients in a no-shame control condition. However, this is only the case when the recipients know that the low allocators know *why* the recipients are ashamed; when recipients know that the low allocators *do not know* about the shame-causing event, the ashamed recipients express *more* anger (Zhu et al., 2018). In other words, the shame system at once tolerates poor treatment when others are aware of one's low social value, but angrily protests the same poor treatment when it can be plausibly portrayed as undeserved, unjust, or unfair (Sell, Sznycer, Al-Shawaf, et al., 2017). In line with this conditional logic, a recent meta-analysis concluded that "shame had a positive link to constructive approach when failure [. . .] or social image [. . .] was more reparable. In contrast, shame had a negative link to constructive approach when failure was less reparable" (Leach & Cidam, 2015, p. 983). While a comprehensive decision tree detailing shame's behavioral outputs has yet to be fully elucidated, an analysis of the existing evidence suggests that shame functions in an exquisitely cost-effective and context-sensitive manner to diminish social devaluation by deploying tactics that are appropriately tailored to the situation at hand. Attributional researchers have termed shame "ugly" because of its association with externalization of blame and aggression, but that self-same "ugly" experience reflects the transmission of devaluation-relevant information among a set of mental mechanisms operating in a coordinated fashion to minimize the costs of resultant devaluation. For as ugly an experience as shame often is, having no defense against social devaluation is certainly uglier. Moreover, although shame is aversive, it serves an adaptive function, joining the ranks of other aversive-but-adaptive emotions such as disgust (see Lieberman et al., 2007), anger (see Sell, Sznycer, Al-Shawaf, et al., 2017), pain (see Walters & Williams, 2019), and jealousy (see Krems et al., 2020; Lewis et al., Chapter 21 in this volume).

Another alternative theory of shame, an evolutionary theory, views shame through the lens of social norms. For example, it has been argued that violating a norm triggers shame, while acting in accordance with a norm triggers pride (Elster, 1989; Fessler, 1999). Once activated, pride and shame function to reward conformity and punish nonconformity to social norms (Bicchieri, 2005; Fessler, 1999, 2007) to maintain access to the social benefits of cooperation and coordination. Like attributional theories, norm-based accounts of shame tend to be observationally adequate. For example, the statement "Scott feels shame because (people found that) he violated the norm against theft" appears to fit the data and seems to make intuitive sense. Furthermore, we know that punishment can cause any type of behavior to be evolutionarily stable (Boyd & Richerson, 1992), and, consistent with this, people moralize a huge number of vastly different things.

However, the linchpin concept of "norm" begs the question. Common technical definitions of "norm" include, e.g., "cultural understandings concerning the normal, appropriate, or reasonable way to behave" (Fessler, 2007) and "normative standards of behavior that are enforced by informal social sanctions" (Fehr & Fischbacher, 2004). Such definitions are often tautological, vague, or both. Indeed, existing social norms have little in common beyond the fact *that they are normative*. For instance, because of kin selection, it is a cooperation "norm" to help close kin; because of selection against inbreeding depression, it is a sex "norm" to avoid sex with close kin (Lieberman et al., 2007). The word "norm" is ultimately superfluous when more direct causal explanations of the phenomena of interest are available, and where such explanations do not yet exist, it merely serves as a placeholder explanation until they do. Like phlogiston and miasma, "norm" describes and labels a phenomenon, but fails to illuminate it in a causal, explanatory manner. Indeed, it is not an accident that definitions of "norm" are vague and tautological; they are vague and tautological by necessity because we have reduced a wide variety of norms, prescribing and proscribing a wide variety of behaviors, to their lone common denominator: normativeness—the explanandum in the first place.

Norm-based theories of self-conscious emotions face other problems as well. First, lumping all sources of shame (or pride) under the "norm" rubric obscures important differences between them. Consider the shame that arises from, e.g., stinginess vs. low productivity vs. low physical attractiveness vs. eating with the wrong fork. In theory, a well-designed shame system should discriminate functionally among such antecedent conditions—and in practice, it does (De Hooge et al., 2011; Leach & Cidam, 2015). Second, absent any a priori, independently derived, or specific benchmark for determining what is and is not a norm, there is little to prevent one from postulating norms post hoc to explain observed occurrences of shame (or pride). This invites circular reasoning and compromises the falsifiability of norm-based theories. Third, hiding, lying, and worse are part of shame's modus operandi (Declerck et al., 2014; Elison et al., 2014; Fessler, 2001; Sznycer et al., 2015; Tangney, 1990; Tangney et al., 1992; Zhu et al., 2018); in other words, shame often appears to flout norms, not promote conformity with them. Fourth, norms are often thought to be culture-specific. However, there are important cross-cultural commonalities in what people value and disvalue in others and in what elicits pride and shame (Sznycer et al., 2016; Sznycer, Al-Shawaf, et al., 2017; Sznycer & Cohen, 2021; Sznycer & Patrick, 2020; Sznycer, Xygalatas, Alami, et al., 2018; Sznycer, Xygalatas, Agey, et al., 2018). Thus, these emotions seem to be governed less by culture-specific "norms" than by a species-wide architecture of social valuation comprising both invariant principles and open parameters that are filled in with specific, local information during development. Fifth, even if "norm" were provisionally accepted as an adequate explanation, the further question would still remain: Why does that norm exist?

Shame and Criminal Law

Much of human sociality can be understood in terms of the operations of mental procedures that compute, store, recalibrate, and employ internal estimates of social value in decision-making and behavior (Cosmides & Tooby, 2006; Lieberman & Patrick, 2018; Tooby & Cosmides, 1992; see also Boyer, 2018). By hypothesis, the flow of goods (e.g., rewards) and bads (e.g., punishments) in human societies is regulated to an important extent by the interlinked psychologies of social evaluation and shame (as well as other social emotions). If this is so, then signatures of the shame system and the psychology for socially valuing and disvaluing other people should be discernible in, for example, societal institutions (see, e.g., Scrivner et al., Chapter 4 in this volume). This approach has been applied to analyze various phenomena, including war (Hall et al., 2021; Sell et al., 2009; Sell, Sznycer, Cosmides, et al., 2017), resource redistribution (Petersen et al., 2012; Sznycer, Lopez Seal, et al., 2017), and the criminal justice system (Jones & Goldsmith, 2005; Lieberman & Linke, 2007; Robinson & Kurzban, 2007; Sznycer & Patrick, 2020; Williams et al., 2019).

To illustrate how large-scale sociality may arise from "simple" two-person games of social valuation, consider a hypothetical case of a Bayaka forager who steals cassava root from his neighbor. His neighbor, if he were to find out who stole his cassava root, might devalue the thief and want to punish him; and the thief, were he to find out the victim had identified him, might feel shame. Might this two-person model make up the cognitive core not just of interpersonal devaluation and shame, but also of lawmaking in different cultures and historical eras? The answer seems to be "yes." In recent research, participants from the United States and India rated each of various offenses drawn from actual criminal codes: a contemporary criminal code from the United States, an ancient criminal code from China (Tang Code, 1,400 years old), and an ancient criminal code from Mesopotamia (Laws of Eshnunna, 3,800 years ago, one of the most ancient known legal codes) (Sznycer & Patrick, 2020). Participants saw the offenses but not their corresponding legal punishments. The data indicated that participants' ratings of the severity of these offenses (e.g., devaluation of a neighbor who commits the offense, moral wrongness of the offense) correlated positively with the actual punishments dictated for the offenses by the legal codes, both contemporary and ancient. Ratings of perpetrator shame (if participants committed those offenses) also correlated positively with the actual legal punishments (Sznycer & Patrick, 2020). Importantly, participants were excluded from analyses if they reported college training in law or if they could guess the code from which the offenses were drawn. Thus, laypeople with no training in law and no explicit technical knowledge about criminal law—both in general and specifically related to the legal codes evaluated in the study—can nevertheless recreate criminal law using their evaluative intuitions and their feelings of shame. The fact that people can intuitively recreate laws from cultures remote in space and time suggests remarkable universality in the structure and content of social evaluations and shame.

Concluding Remarks

Shame is often portrayed as an ugly and maladaptive emotion. However, if one refocuses the analysis on its adaptive function, shame is a well-designed solution to the much uglier problem of information-triggered social devaluation. Shame, far from being a pathology or a poor substitute for guilt, is an elegantly engineered adaptation packed with features that counter a serious problem endemic to our species' history of sociality. Shame is not the province of East Asian cultures or of people with maladaptive attributional styles. Shame is part and parcel of universal human nature—and we're all the better for it.

Note

1. Japanese and other East Asian populations have been characterized as "shame cultures" (Benedict, 2005).

References

Al-Shawaf, L., Conroy-Beam, D., Asao, K., & Buss, D. M. (2016). Human emotions: An evolutionary psychological perspective. *Emotion Review, 8*(2), 173–186.
Al-Shawaf, L., & Lewis, D. M. (2017). Evolutionary psychology and the emotions. In V. Zeigler-Hill & T. Shackelford (Eds.), *Encyclopedia of personality and individual differences* (pp. 1–10). Springer.
Al-Shawaf, L., Lewis, D. M., Barbaro, N., & Wehbe, Y. S. (2020). The products of evolution: Conceptual distinctions, evidentiary criteria, and empirical examples. In Todd K. Shackelford (Eds.), *The Sage handbook of evolutionary psychology: Foundations of evolutionary psychology* (pp. 70–95). SAGE Publications.
Al-Shawaf, L., Lewis, D. M., Wehbe, Y. S., & Buss, D. M. (2021). Context, environment, and learning in evolutionary psychology. In *Encyclopedia of evolutionary psychological science* (pp. 1330–1341). Springer International Publishing.

Baumard, N., André, J.-B., & Sperber, D. (2013). A mutualistic approach to morality: The evolution of fairness by partner choice. *Behavioral and Brain Sciences, 36*, 59–78.

Baumeister, R. F., & Tice, D. M. (1990). Point-counterpoints: Anxiety and social exclusion. *Journal of Social and Clinical Psychology, 9*, 165–195.

Benedict, R. (2005). *The chrysanthemum and the sword: Patterns of Japanese culture*. Houghton Mifflin Harcourt.

Bicchieri, C. (2005). *The grammar of society: The nature and dynamics of social norms*. Cambridge University Press.

Boyd, R., & Richerson, P. J. (1992). Punishment allows the evolution of cooperation (or anything else) in sizable groups. *Ethology and Sociobiology, 13*, 171–195.

Boyer, P. (2018). *Minds make societies: How cognition explains the world humans create*. Yale University Press.

Burger, O., Baudisch, A., & Vaupel, J. W. (2012). Human mortality improvement in evolutionary context. *Proceedings of the National Academy of Sciences, 109*(44), 18210–18214.

Burkart, J. M., Hrdy, S. B., & Van Schaik, C. P. (2009). Cooperative breeding and human cognitive evolution. *Evolutionary Anthropology: Issues, News, and Reviews, 18*(5), 175–186.

Clutton-Brock, T. (2009). Cooperation between non-kin in animal societies. *Nature, 462*(7269), 51–57.

Cohen, A. S., Chun, R., & Sznycer, D. (2020). Do pride and shame track the evaluative psychology of audiences? Preregistered replications of Sznycer et al. (2016, 2017). *Royal Society Open Science, 7*(5), 191922.

Cosmides, L., & Tooby, J. (2000). Evolutionary psychology and the emotions. In M. Lewis & J. M. Haviland-Jones (Eds.), *Handbook of emotions* (2nd ed., pp. 91–115). New York: Guilford.

Cosmides, L., & Tooby, J. (2006). Evolutionary psychology, moral heuristics, and the law. In G. Gigerenzer & C. Engel (Eds.), *Heuristics and the law* (pp. 175–205). MIT Press; Dahlem University Press.

Crockett, M. J., Siegel, J. Z., Kurth-Nelson, Z., Dayan, P., & Dolan, R. J. (2017). Moral transgressions corrupt neural representations of value. *Nature Neuroscience, 20*(6), 879–885.

Darwin, C. (1872). Self-attention–shame–shyness–modesty: Blushing. In C. Darwin, *The expression of the emotions in man and animals* (pp. 310–347). John Murray. https://doi.org/10.1037/10001-013

De Hooge, I. E., Breugelmans, S. M., & Zeelenberg, M. (2008). Not so ugly after all: When shame acts as a commitment device. *Journal of Personality and Social Psychology, 95*, 933–943.

De Hooge, I. E., Zeelenberg, M., & Breugelmans, S. M. (2011). A functionalist account of shame-induced behaviour. *Cognition & Emotion, 25*(5), 939–946.

De Hooge, I. E., Breugelmans, S. M., Wagemans, F. M., & Zeelenberg, M. (2018). The social side of shame: Approach versus withdrawal. *Cognition and Emotion, 32*(8), 1671–1677.

Declerck, C. H., Boone, C., & Kiyonari, T. (2014). No place to hide: When shame causes proselfs to cooperate. *The Journal of Social Psychology, 154*(1), 74–88.

Delton, A. W., & Robertson, T. E. (2012). The social cognition of social foraging: partner selection by underlying valuation. *Evolution and Human Behavior, 33*(6), 715–725.

Delton, A. W., & Robertson, T. E. (2016). How the mind makes welfare tradeoffs: Evolution, computation, and emotion. *Current Opinion in Psychology, 7*, 12–16.

Dickerson, S. S., Gable, S. L., Irwin, M. R., Aziz, N., & Kemeny, M. E. (2009). Social-evaluative threat and proinflammatory cytokine regulation: An experimental laboratory investigation. *Psychological Science, 20*(10), 1237–1244.

Dickerson, S. S., Mycek, P. J., & Zaldivar, F. (2008). Negative social evaluation, but not mere social presence, elicits cortisol responses to a laboratory stressor task. *Health Psychology, 27*(1), 116.

Driscoll, R. (1989). Self-condemnation: A comprehensive framework for assessment and treatment. *Psychotherapy: Theory, Research, Practice, Training, 26*, 104.

Durkee, P. K., Lukaszewski, A. W., & Buss, D. M. (2019). Pride and shame: Key components of a culturally universal status management system. *Evolution and Human Behavior, 40*(5), 470–478.

Eisenberger, N. I. (2012). The pain of social disconnection: examining the shared neural underpinnings of physical and social pain. *Nature Reviews Neuroscience, 13*(6), 421–434.

Elison, J., Garofalo, C., & Velotti, P. (2014). Shame and aggression: Theoretical considerations. *Aggression and Violent Behavior, 19*(4), 447–453.

Elster, J. (1989). *The cement of society: A survey of social order*. Cambridge University Press.

Fehr, E., & Gächter, S. (2000). Cooperation and punishment in public goods experiments. *American Economic Review, 90*(4), 980–994.

Fehr, E., & Fischbacher, U. (2004). Third-party punishment and social norms. *Evolution and Human Behavior, 25*, 63–87.

Feinberg, M., Willer, R., & Schultz, M. (2014). Gossip and ostracism promote cooperation in groups. *Psychological Science, 25*(3), 656–664.

Fessler, D. M. T. (1999). Toward an understanding of the universality of second-order emotions. In A. L. Hinton (Ed.), *Biocultural approaches to the emotions: Publications of the Society for Psychological Anthropology* (pp. 75–116). Cambridge University Press.

Fessler, D. M. T. (2001). Emotions and cost/benefit assessment: The role of shame and self-esteem in risk taking. In R. Selten & G. Gigerenzer (Eds.), *Bounded rationality: The adaptive toolbox* (pp. 191–214). MIT Press.

Fessler, D. M. T. (2007). From appeasement to conformity: Evolutionary and cultural perspectives on shame, competition, and cooperation. In J. L. Tracy, R. W. Robins, & J. P. Tangney (Eds.), *The Self-Conscious Emotions: Theory and Research* (pp. 174–193). Guilford Press.

Gausel, N., Vignoles, V. L., & Leach, C. W. (2016). Resolving the paradox of shame: Differentiating among specific appraisal-feeling combinations explains pro-social and self-defensive motivation. *Motivation and Emotion, 40*(1), 118–139.

Gilbert, P. (1997.) The evolution of social attractiveness and its role in shame, humiliation, guilt and therapy. *British Journal of Medical Psychology, 70*, 113–147

Gilbert, P. (2000a). The relationship of shame, social anxiety and depression: The role of the evaluation of social rank. *Clinical Psychology and Psychotherapy, 7*, 174–189.

Gilbert, P. (2000b). Varieties of submissive behavior as forms of social defense: Their evolution and role in depression. In L. Sloman & P. Gilbert (Eds.), *Subordination and Defeat* (pp. 3–45). Routledge.

Gilbert, P. (2016). *Depression: The evolution of powerlessness*. Routledge.

Griffin, B. J., Moloney, J. M., Green, J. D., Worthington, Jr, E. L., Cork, B., Tangney, J. P., Van Tongeren, D. R., Davis, D. E., & Hook, J. N. (2016). Perpetrators' reactions to perceived interpersonal wrongdoing: The associations of guilt and shame with forgiving, punishing, and excusing oneself. *Self and Identity, 15*(6), 650–661.

Hales, A. H., Kassner, M. P., Williams, K. D., & Graziano, W. G. (2016). Disagreeableness as a cause and consequence of ostracism. *Personality and Social Psychology Bulletin, 42*, 782–797.

Hall, J., Kahn, D. T., Skoog, E., & Öberg, M. (2021). War exposure, altruism and the recalibration of welfare tradeoffs towards threatening social categories. *Journal of Experimental Social Psychology, 94*, 104101.

Hill, K., & Hurtado, A. M. (1996). *Ache life history: The ecology and demography of a foraging people*. de Gruyter.

Jones, O. D., & Goldsmith, T. H. (2005). Law and behavioral biology. *Columbia Law Review, 105*, 405–502.

Kaplan, H., & Hill, K. (1985). Food sharing among ache foragers: Tests of explanatory hypotheses. *Current Anthropology, 26*, 223–239.

Kaplan, H., Hill, K., Lancaster, J., & Hurtado, A. M. (2000). A theory of human life history evolution: Diet, intelligence, and longevity. *Evolutionary Anthropology, 9*, 156–185.

Keeley, L. H. (1997). *War before civilization*. Oxford University Press.

Keltner, D. (1996). Evidence for the distinctness of embarrassment, shame, and guilt: A study of recalled antecedents and facial expressions of emotion. *Cognition and Emotion, 10*(2), 155–172.

Keltner, D., Young, R. C., & Buswell, B. N. (1997). Appeasement in human emotion, social practice, and personality. *Aggressive Behavior, 23*, 359–374.

Krems, J. A., Williams, K. E., Aktipis, A., & Kenrick, D. T. (2021). Friendship jealousy: One tool for maintaining friendships in the face of third-party threats?. *Journal of Personality and Social Psychology, 120*(4), 977.

Kurzban, R., & Leary, M. R. (2001). Evolutionary origins of stigmatization: The functions of social exclusion. *Psychological Bulletin, 127*(2), 187.

Landers, M., & Sznycer, D. (2022). The evolution of shame and its display. *Evolutionary Human Sciences, 4*, e45.

Landers, M., Sznycer, D., & Durkee, P. K. (in press). Are self-conscious emotions about the self? Testing competing theories of shame and guilt across two disparate cultures. *Emotion*.

Leach, C. W., & Cidam, A. (2015). When is shame linked to constructive approach orientation? A meta-analysis. *Journal of Personality and Social Psychology, 109*(6), 983–1002.

Leary, M. R. (2015). Emotional responses to interpersonal rejection. *Dialogues in Clinical Neuroscience, 17*(4), 435–441.

Leary, M. R., & Kowalski, R. M. (1990). Impression management: A literature review and two-component model. *Psychological Bulletin, 107*, 34–47.

Leary, M. R., Tambor, E. S., Terdal, S. K., & Downs, D. L. (1995). Self-esteem as an interpersonal monitor: The sociometer hypothesis. *Journal of Personality and Social Psychology, 68*(3), 518.

Lewis, H. B. (1971). *Shame and guilt in neurosis*. International Universities Press.

Lieberman, D., & Linke, L. (2007). The effect of social category on third party punishment. *Evolutionary Psychology, 5*(2), 289–305.

Lieberman, D., & Patrick, C. (2018). *Objection: Disgust, morality, and the law*. Oxford University Press.

Lieberman, D., Tooby, J., & Cosmides, L. (2007). The architecture of human kin detection. *Nature, 445*, 727–731.

Lukaszewski, A. W., & Roney, J. R. (2010). Kind toward whom? Mate preferences for personality traits are target specific. *Evolution and Human Behavior*, 31, 29–38.

MacDonald, G., & Leary, M. R. (2005). Why does social exclusion hurt? The relationship between social and physical pain. *Psychological Bulletin*, *131*, 202–223.

Mahadevan, N., Gregg, A. P., & Sedikides, C. (2019). Is self-regard a sociometer or a hierometer? Self-esteem tracks status and inclusion, narcissism tracks status. *Journal of Personality and Social Psychology*, *116*(3), 444.

McGraw, K. M. (1987). Guilt following transgression: An attribution of responsibility approach. *Journal of Personality and Social Psychology*, 53, 247–256.

Noë, R., & Hammerstein, P. (1995). Biological markets. *Trends in Ecology & Evolution*, *10*(8), 336–339.

Pedersen, E. J., McAuliffe, W. H., & McCullough, M. E. (2018). The unresponsive avenger: More evidence that disinterested third parties do not punish altruistically. *Journal of Experimental Psychology: General*, *147*(4), 514.

Petersen, M. B., Sznycer, D., Cosmides, L., & Tooby, J. (2012). Who deserves help? Evolutionary psychology, social emotions, and public opinion about welfare. *Political Psychology*, *33*(3), 395–418.

Rapee, R. M., & Heimberg, R. G. (1997). A cognitive-behavioral model of anxiety in social phobia. *Behaviour Research and Therapy*, *35*(8), 741–756.

Robertson, T. E., Sznycer, D., Delton, A. W., Tooby, J., & Cosmides, L. (2018). The true trigger of shame: Social devaluation is sufficient, wrongdoing is unnecessary. *Evolution and Human Behavior*, *39*(5), 566–573.

Robinson, P. H., & Kurzban, R. (2007). Concordance and conflict in intuitions of justice. *Minnesota Law Review*, *91*, 1829–1907.

Rockenbach, B., & Milinski, M. (2011). To qualify as a social partner, humans hide severe punishment, although their observed cooperativeness is decisive. *Proceedings of the National Academy of Sciences*, *108*, 18307–18312.

Rodriguez Mosquera, P. M. (2018). Cultural concerns: How valuing social-image shapes social emotion. *European Review of Social Psychology*, *29*(1), 1–37.

Schlenker, B. R., & Leary, M. R. (1982). Social anxiety and self-presentation: A conceptualization model. *Psychological Bulletin*, *92*, 641–669.

Schniter, E., Sheremeta, R. M., & Sznycer, D. (2013). Building and rebuilding trust with promises and apologies. *Journal of Economic Behavior and Organization*, *94*, 242–256.

Schniter, E., Shields, T. W., & Sznycer, D. (2020). Trust in humans and robots: Economically similar but emotionally different. *Journal of Economic Psychology*, *78*, 102253.

Schrock, J. M., Snodgrass, J. J., & Sugiyama, L. S. (2020). Lassitude: The emotion of being sick. *Evolution and Human Behavior*, *41*, 44–57.

Sell, A., Eisner, M., & Ribeaud, D. (2016). Bargaining power and adolescent aggression: The role of fighting ability, coalitional strength, and mate value. *Evolution and Human Behavior*, *37*(2), 105–116.

Sell, A., Sznycer, D., Al-Shawaf, L., Lim, J., Krauss, A., Feldman, A., Rascanu, R., Sugiyama, L., Cosmides, L., & Tooby, J. (2017). The grammar of anger: Mapping the computational architecture of a recalibrational emotion. *Cognition*, *168*, 110–128.

Sell, A., Sznycer, D., Cosmides, L., Tooby, J., Krauss, A., Nisu, S., Ceapa, C., & Petersen, M. B. (2017). Physically strong men are more militant: A test across four countries. *Evolution and Human Behavior*, *38*(3), 334–340.

Sell, A., Tooby, J., & Cosmides, L. (2009). Formidability and the logic of human anger. *Proceedings of the National Academy of Sciences*, *106*(35), 15073–15078.

Shaw, A., Montinari, N., Piovesan, M., Olson, K. R., Gino, F., & Norton, M. I. (2014). Children develop a veil of fairness. *Journal of Experimental Psychology: General*, *143*(1), 363–375.

Smith, R. H., Webster, J. M., Parrott, W. G., & Eyre, H. L. (2002). The role of public exposure in moral and non-moral shame and guilt. *Journal of Personality and Social Psychology*, *83*(1), 138–159.

Somerville, L. H., Jones, R. M., Ruberry, E. J., Dyke, J. P., Glover, G., & Casey, B. J. (2013). The medial prefrontal cortex and the emergence of self-conscious emotion in adolescence. *Psychological Science*, *24*(8), 1554–1562.

Sugiyama, L. S. (2004.) Illness, injury, and disability among Shiwiar forager-horticulturists: Implications of health-risk buffering for the evolution of human life history. *American Journal of Physical Anthropology*, *123*, 371–389.

Sznycer, D. (2010). *Cognitive adaptations for calibrating welfare tradeoff motivations, with special reference to the emotion of shame*. Doctoral dissertation, University of California, Santa Barbara.

Sznycer, D. (2019). Forms and functions of the self-conscious emotions. *Trends in Cognitive Sciences*, *23*(2), 143–157.

Sznycer, D. (2021). Foreword. In: Mayer, C.-H., Vanderheiden, E., & Wong, P. (Eds.), *Shame 4.0: Investigating an emotion in digital worlds and the fourth industrial revolution*. Springer.

Sznycer, D., Al-Shawaf, L., Bereby-Meyer, Y., Curry, O. S., De Smet, D., Ermer, E., Kim, S., Kim, S., Li, N. P., Lopez Seal, M. F., McClung, J., O, J., Ohtsubo, Y., Quillien, T., Schaub, M., Sell, A., van Leeuwen, F., Cosmides, L., & Tooby, J. (2017). Cross-cultural regularities in the cognitive architecture of pride. *Proceedings of the National Academy of Sciences*, *114*(8), 1874–1879.

Sznycer, D., & Cohen, A. S. (2021). How pride works. *Evolutionary Human Sciences, 3*, e10.

Sznycer, D., Cosmides, L., & Tooby, J. (2017). Adaptationism carves emotions at their functional joints. Invited commentary in *Psychological Inquiry, 28*(1), 56–62.

Sznycer, D., Delton, A. W., Robertson, T. E., Cosmides, L., & Tooby, J. (2019). The ecological rationality of helping others: Potential helpers integrate cues of recipients' need and willingness to sacrifice. *Evolution and Human Behavior, 40*(1), 34–45.

Sznycer, D., De Smet, D., Billingsley, J., & Lieberman, D. (2016). Coresidence duration and cues of maternal investment regulate sibling altruism across cultures. *Journal of Personality and Social Psychology, 111*(2), 159–177.

Sznycer, D., Lopez Seal, M. F., Sell, A., Lim, J., Porat, R., Shalvi, S., Halperin, E., Cosmides, L., & Tooby, J. (2017). Support for redistribution is shaped by compassion, envy, and self-interest, but not a taste for fairness. *Proceedings of the National Academy of Sciences, 114*(31), 8420–8425.

Sznycer, D., & Lukaszewski, A. W. (2019). The emotion–valuation constellation: Multiple emotions are governed by a common grammar of social valuation. *Evolution and Human Behavior, 40*(4), 395–404.

Sznycer, D., & Patrick, C. (2020). The origins of criminal law. *Nature Human Behavior, 4*, 506–16

Sznycer, D., Schniter, E., Tooby, J., & Cosmides, L. (2015). Regulatory adaptations for delivering information: The case of confession. *Evolution and Human Behavior, 36*, 44–51.

Sznycer, D., Sell, A., & Lieberman, D. (2021). Forms and functions of the social emotions. *Current Directions in Psychological Science, 30*(4), 292–299.

Sznycer, D., Takemura, K., Delton, A. W., Sato, K., Robertson, T., Cosmides, L., & Tooby, J. (2012). Cross-cultural differences and similarities in proneness to shame: An adaptationist and ecological approach. *Evolutionary Psychology, 10*, 352–370.

Sznycer, D., Tooby, J., & Cosmides, L. (in prep.). Shame is modulated by the values that audiences are known to hold.

Sznycer, D., Tooby, J., Cosmides, L., Porat, R., Shalvi, S., & Halperin, E. (2016). Shame closely tracks the threat of devaluation by others, even across cultures. *Proceedings of the National Academy of Sciences, 113*(10), 2625–2630.

Sznycer, D., Xygalatas, D., Agey, E., Alami, S., An, X.-F., Ananyeva, K. I., Atkinson, Q. D., Broitman, B. R., Conte, T. J., Flores, C., Fukushima, S., Hitokoto, H., Kharitonov, A. N., Onyishi, C. N., Onyishi, I. E., Romero, P. P., Schrock, J. M., Snodgrass, J. J., Sugiyama, L. S., Takemura, K., Townsend, C., Zhuang, J.-Y., Aktipis, C. A., Cronk, L., Cosmides, L., & Tooby, J. (2018). Cross-cultural invariances in the architecture of shame. *Proceedings of the National Academy of Sciences, 115*(39), 9702–9707.

Sznycer, D., Xygalatas, D., Alami, S., An, X.-F., Ananyeva, K. I., Fukushima, S., Hitokoto, H., Kharitonov, A. N., Koster, J. M., Onyishi, C. N., Onyishi, I. E., Romero, P. P., Takemura, K., Zhuang, J.-Y., Cosmides, L., & Tooby, J. (2018). Invariances in the architecture of pride across small-scale societies. *Proceedings of the National Academy of Sciences, 115*(33), 8322–8327.

Tanaka, H., Yagi, A., Komiya, A., Mifune, N., & Ohtsubo, Y. (2015). Shame-prone people are more likely to punish themselves: A test of the reputation-maintenance explanation for self-punishment. *Evolutionary Behavioral Sciences, 9*, 1–7.

Tangney, J. P. (1990). Assessing individual differences in proneness to shame and guilt: Development of the Self-Conscious Affect and Attribution Inventory. *Journal of Personality and Social Psychology, 59*, 102–111.

Tangney, J. P. (1991). Moral affect: The good, the bad, and the ugly. *Journal of Personality and Social Psychology, 61*, 598–607.

Tangney, J. P., and Dearing, R. L. (2002). *Shame and guilt*. Guilford Press.

Tangney, J. P., Miller, R. S., Flicker, L., & Barlow, D. H. (1996). Are shame, guilt, and embarrassment distinct emotions? *Journal of Personality and Social Psychology, 70*(6), 1256–1269.

Tangney, J. P., Stuewig, J., & Martinez, A. G. (2014). Two faces of shame: The roles of shame and guilt in predicting recidivism. *Psychological Science, 25*(3), 799–805.

Tangney, J. P., Stuewig, J., & Mashek, D. J. (2007a). Moral emotions and moral behavior. *Annual Review of Psychology, 58*, 345–372.

Tangney, J. P., Stuewig, J., & Mashek, D. J. (2007b). What's moral about the self-conscious emotions. In J. L. Tracy, R. W. Robins, J. P. Tangney (Eds.), *The self-conscious emotions: Theory and research* (pp. 21–37). Guilford Press.

Tangney, J. P., Wagner, P., Fletcher, C., & Gramzow, R. (1992). Shamed into anger? The relation of shame and guilt to anger and self-reported aggression. *Journal of Personality and Social Psychology, 62*, 669–675.

Thomas, K. A., DeScioli, P., & Pinker, S. (2018). Common knowledge, coordination, and the logic of self-conscious emotions. *Evolution and Human Behavior, 39*(2), 179–190.

Tomasello, M., Melis, A. P., Tennie, C., Wyman, E., & Herrmann, E. (2012). Two key steps in the evolution of human cooperation: The interdependence hypothesis. *Current Anthropology, 53*(6), 673–692.

Tooby, J., & Cosmides, L. (1992). The psychological foundations of culture. In J. H. Barkow, L. Cosmides, & J. Tooby (Eds.), *The adapted mind: Evolutionary psychology and the generation of culture* (19–136), Oxford University Press.

Tooby, J., & Cosmides, L. (1996, January). Friendship and the banker's paradox: Other pathways to the evolution of adaptations for altruism. In *Proceedings-British Academy* (Vol. 88, pp. 119–144). Oxford University Press.

Tooby, J., & Cosmides, L. (2008). The evolutionary psychology of the emotions and their relationship to internal regulatory variables. In M. Lewis, J. M. Haviland-Jones, & L. F. Barrett (Eds.), *Handbook of emotions* (3rd ed., pp. 114–137). Guilford Press.

Tooby, J., & Cosmides, L. (2015). The theoretical foundations of evolutionary psychology. In Buss, D. M. (Ed.), The handbook of evolutionary psychology (2nd ed.), Vol. 1: *Foundations* (pp. 3–87). Wiley.

Tooby, J., Cosmides, L., Sell, A., Lieberman, D., & Sznycer, D. (2008). Internal regulatory variables and the design of human motivation: A computational and evolutionary approach. In A. J. Elliot (Eds.), *Handbook of Approach and Avoidance Motivation* (pp. 251–271). Erlbaum.

Tracy, J. L., & Robins, R. W. (2004). Putting the self into self-conscious emotions: A theoretical model. *Psychological Inquiry, 15*, 103–125.

von Rueden, C., & Jaeggi, A. V. (2016). Men's status and reproductive success in 33 nonindustrial societies: Effects of subsistence, marriage system, and reproductive strategy. *Proceedings of the National Academy of Sciences, 113*(39), 10824–10829.

Walters, E. T., & Williams, A. C. C. (2019). Evolution of mechanisms and behaviour important for pain. *Philosophical Transactions of the Royal Society B: Biological Sciences, 374*, 20190275.

Weisfeld, G. E., & Dillon, L. M. (2012). Applying the dominance hierarchy model to pride and shame, and related behaviors. *Journal of Evolutionary Psychology, 10*, 15–41.

Williams, G. C. (1966). Natural selection, the costs of reproduction, and a refinement of Lack's principle. *The American Naturalist, 100*(916), 687–690.

Williams, K. E., Votruba, A. M., Neuberg, S. L., & Saks, M. J. (2019). Capital and punishment: Resource scarcity increases endorsement of the death penalty. *Evolution and Human Behavior, 40*(1), 65–73.

Wilson, T. D., & Gilbert, D. T. (2005). Affective forecasting. *Current Directions in Psychological Science, 14*(3), 131.

Zhu, R., Shen, X., Tang, H., Ye, P., Wang, H., Mai, X., & Liu, C. (2017). Self-punishment promotes forgiveness in the direct and indirect reciprocity contexts. *Psychological Reports, 120*(3), 408–422.

Zhu, R., Xu, Z., Tang, H., Liu, J., Wang, H., An, Y., . . . & Liu, C. (2019). The effect of shame on anger at others: Awareness of the emotion-causing events matters. *Cognition and Emotion, 33*(4), 696–708.

CHAPTER 8

The Neutralization Theory of Hatred

Aaron Sell, Coltan Scrivner, Mitchell Landers, and Anthony C. Lopez

Abstract
This chapter argues that, while often conceptualized as an extreme form of anger, hatred is a distinct emotion, with unique triggers, conceptual orientations, and terminating conditions. This is because hatred evolved to address its own distinct adaptive problem: the existence of individuals who were—on balance—costly to the hater. Because a well-designed system for solving this problem would have been tailored toward neutralizing those costs, the authors call this hypothesis "the neutralization theory of hatred." This theory claims that hatred is triggered by cues that an individual's existence causes fitness decrements for the hater. Cognitively, hatred orients the mind to view costs heaped onto the hated person as benefits to the hater—thus motivating spiteful behavior—and can be characterized as maintaining a negative intrinsic welfare trade-off parameter toward the hated person. Behaviorally, hatred can motivate either avoidance or a predatory cost-infliction strategy that is designed to weaken, incapacitate, or terminate the target.

Key Words: hatred, anger, neutralization theory, recalibrational theory, evolutionary psychology, association value

Introduction

On March 16, 1984, Leon Gary Plauché ambushed and killed Jeff Doucet at the Baton Rouge Metropolitan Airport while Doucet was being transported to jail by the police. Leon spoke on a pay phone in the airport while waiting, and when the handcuffed Doucet was led by, Leon turned and fired one shot into Doucet's head. Local news captured the event on videotape.

Doucet had been taken into custody for kidnapping and molesting Plauché's son. But, strange as it is to say, Plauché did not seem to be angry with Doucet. Notably, Plauché shows no evidence of rage. His face—as best it can be made out from the recording—is calm, his mouth closed. His body is still before he fires. He utters no vocalizations, no yells, no insults, no cries, even after shooting. He does not pace back and forth; indeed, he surrenders calmly and even places the phone receiver he had been talking into back on the hook within a second of having fired a bullet into Doucet's skull. None of these behaviors is consistent with the empirical evidence of anger displays. Rather, we believe Leon Plauché was motivated by hatred—and that his seemingly odd behavior starkly illustrates the functional distinctiveness of hatred and anger.

In this chapter, we describe the neutralization theory of hatred. We propose that this theory can explain the major features of hatred, including its triggering conditions, its effect on internal regulatory variables, and the behavioral strategies it produces as output. The theory holds that hatred evolved via natural selection in order to address a specific selection pressure: the existence of individuals whose well-being imposed a net fitness cost on you. In simple parlance, some people are bad for you. In most species, the evolved solution to this adaptive problem is to heap costs upon the target in an economical way so as to diminish their ability to harm you. This is often done by killing the target (e.g., siblicide in various bird species; see Mock et al., 1990). In humans, however, this lethal response occurs only in a minority of cases. Rather, human hatred appears to make use of a mixed bag of strategies to minimize the costs emanating from the hated target, including: (1) information warfare to diminish the target's social power, (2) low-level surreptitious cost infliction to diminish the target's health, well-being, power, and to incentivize social distance, (3) potentially lethal predatory-style aggression to diminish their power, and (4) avoidance of the target to minimize the costs emanating from them.

It is important to note that this chapter serves as a philosophical examination of the evolution of hatred at the start of a new theory. Very few of the posited design features of this hypothesized adaptation have been subjected to rigorous empirical testing. Enterprising researchers will find many hypotheses worth exploring.

Theoretical Approach: How Can We Know the Function of an Emotion?

This chapter takes an adaptationist approach (Cosmides & Tooby, 2000; Tooby & Cosmides, 1992; Williams, 1966) that argues that natural selection generates phenotypic design that is geared toward solving problems of reproduction. According to this framework, the function of an adaptation is proven to the extent that researchers show a close alignment between the nature of a selection pressure and the design of the hypothesized adaptation. In particular, adaptations must be shown to be efficient, economical, and well-designed to have solved the problems of reproduction faced by our ancestors. Thus, to prove the function of a given emotion, one not only must clearly state the hypothesized selection pressure that gave rise to it (i.e., how did this emotion effectively replicate the genes that gave rise to it in past environments?), but also must demonstrate how each design feature of the adaptation functionally addresses that selection pressure.

Thus, the adaptationist program requires a rigorous exploration of the basic features of any putative adaptation. Unfortunately, basic features are often invisible because of a phenomenon called "instinct blindness" (Cosmides & Tooby, 1994) that leads humans to underestimate their own complicated nature because it is so intuitive to them. This was illustrated most eloquently by the oft-quoted William James in his *Principles of Psychology* (1890):

> To the metaphysician alone can such questions occur as: Why do we smile, when pleased, and not scowl? Why are we unable to talk to a crowd as we talk to a single friend? Why does a particular maiden turn our wits so upside-down? The common man can only say, "Of course we smile, of course our heart palpitates at the sight of the crowd, of course we love the maiden, that beautiful soul clad in that perfect form, so palpably and flagrantly made from all eternity to be loved!"
>
> And so, probably, does each animal feel about the particular things it tends to do in presence of particular objects. They, too, are a priori syntheses. To the lion it is the lioness which is made to be loved; to the bear, the shebear. To the broody hen the notion would probably seem monstrous that there should be a creature in the world to whom a nestful of eggs was not the utterly fascinating and precious and never-to-be-too-much-sat-upon object which it is to her. Thus we may be sure that, however mysterious some animals' instincts may appear to us, our instincts will appear no less mysterious to them. (p. 387)

He goes on to say, "*A priori*, there is no reason to suppose that any sensation might not in some animal cause any emotion and any impulse. To us it seems unnatural that an odor should directly excite anger or fear; or a color, lust" (p. 387). We linger on this point only to establish the importance of explaining what seems obvious about our emotions. If a man were to abuse your child, it seems most obvious that you would feel hatred. But a scientific explanation of this fact is not obvious! In the case of Leon Gary Plauché, such hatred brought no obvious benefit to his son; furthermore, Plauché himself only narrowly avoided spending the rest of his life in prison. If there were—ancestrally—a reproductive benefit to the hatred program that existed in Plauché's brain, it is not obviously evidenced by his shooting Doucet. One is tempted to posit that the "function" of the emotion is the justice it created, but this is exactly the kind of faulty reasoning that William James warned us about. Evolution does not select a gene because of "justice"; nature is simple mathematics—a gene spreads if, on balance, it increases its proportional frequency in the next generation and for no other reason.

One way to avoid instinct blindness is to reason as an engineer: given a problem, what would a well-designed solution look like? For instance, suppose you were a software engineer tasked with designing a robot to avoid physical danger. Would that program look like human fear? By focusing on the selection pressure rather than the adaptation, one can avoid some of the pitfalls of instinct blindness.

Here, we focus on the selection pressure we believe resulted in the emotion of hatred: individuals whose future existence is a net fitness cost to you.

Engineering a Solution to the Existence of Toxic Individuals

The existence of others affects your fitness (Aktipis et al., 2018; Hamilton, 1964; Tooby & Cosmides, 1996; Trivers, 1971). This selection pressure can be illustrated with a simple thought experiment. A given individual—let us call him Leon—will leave a certain finite, quantifiable number of his genes in 100 years. If Leon were to use magic powers to "vanish" another individual from his social group, that number of future genes either increases, decreases, or stays the same. Following others (Petersen et al., 2010; Tooby & Cosmides, 1996), we refer to this delta value measuring the actual change in reproductive success as the "association value" (AV) of the individual such that AV_{xy} represents the impact of x's existence on y's reproductive success. In this formulation, association value is an objective indicator (like Hamilton's *r*) that refers to the actual effect of another's existence on one's fitness. We do not presuppose that individual organisms will have perfect knowledge of association value, just as they do not have perfect knowledge of *r* (Lieberman et al., 2007).

Thus, there exists at any time and for every individual a subset of others whose existence affects their fitness negatively (i.e., individuals with negative association value; for convenience, we refer to such people as "toxic"). Such individuals impose net fitness costs and thus serve as a selection pressure. To the extent that one can mitigate this damage, remove those individuals, or otherwise shape the environment to decrease the fitness costs of the toxic person, one will reproduce more, passing on to future generations the genes that gave rise to mechanisms producing those fitness-enhancing behaviors. Given this logic, we hypothesize that humans possess an adaptation that functions to (1) identify toxic individuals (i.e., those with negative AV to oneself) and (2) act in ways that minimize the fitness costs coming from these individuals.

Identifying Toxic Individuals

How could one know who these toxic individuals are? In the thought experiment above, we eliminated a person and waited 100 years to see the impact. Such an experiment would be impossible, of course. Rather, animals and humans presumably evolved to detect cues that an individual's future AV will be negative and respond to those—admittedly imperfect—cues.

In swallow-tailed kites (a bird native to northern Guatemala), mothers typically lay two eggs. The first hatchling, however, needs to share food and space with their clutch-mate sibling. Therefore, the existence of this second sibling is, presumably, a fitness cost to the first. The solution that evolved was simple—the first hatchling pecks at the skull of its sibling until it cracks and ejects it from the nest (Gerhardt et al., 1997). In this way, the first hatchling secures a monopoly on parental investment and typically proceeds to reproduce more—and this difference was, on average, enough to make up for the copies of its genes in its siblings that can no longer reproduce.

In the swallow-tailed kite, the cue of this toxic individual is relatively straightforward: it is the presence of the other chick in the nest. But for complicated social species such as our own, with debt, mutual dependence, status competition, intergroup conflict, shifting alliances, large-scale group cooperation, mate poaching, and so on, an accurate cue detector will be more difficult to instantiate, and will need to process a greater variety of cues.

The future is difficult to predict in most cases, but we can store evidence from the past. Because the best predictor of future behavior is past behavior (Epstein, 1979; 1980; Ouellette & Wood, 1998), one can reasonably conclude that a person who has imposed very large fitness costs on you will be more likely to impose similar costs in the future. Therefore, if we were to engineer an adaptation that functions to identify toxic individuals, it should at a minimum respond to individuals who have already imposed substantial costs on the individual (without corresponding benefits). Because association value is about the net effect of the person's future existence, small repeated costs would also predict low AV—possibly even more so than one large cost.

Furthermore, humans have—presumably for this sort of reason—evolved the ability to run metacognitive counterfactuals as a form of artificial time travel (Epstude & Roese, 2008). We are capable of estimating what would have happened if we were to change one aspect of a person or situation and predict the future based on that difference. This is key to our ability to blame and credit individuals for outcomes (Martin & Cushman, 2016). This same ability allows us to estimate what our circumstances would be like if a given person did not exist. Such a hypothetical enables us to identify individuals whose existence is bad for us (e.g., if Jessie weren't here, maybe Rick Springfield would have his girl; if Bin Laden hadn't existed, many of our friends and family would still be alive). Note, however, that in the second example, removing a person *after* they have imposed massive fitness costs would not necessarily be selected for (e.g., killing Bin Laden didn't raise the dead, nor did killing Doucet un-molest Leon's son), unless those past behaviors predicted future costs as well. From the point of view of a well-engineered hatred system, toxic individuals should ideally be identified early, before massive fitness consequences occur.

One way to identify toxic individuals before their existence imposes costs is to learn who the toxic individuals are from others—a process akin to mate copying (Gouda-Vossos et al., 2018). Only instead of learning who is a desirable mate, we learn who has negative association value (AV). This strategy relies upon our fellow humans to relay aspects of the toxic individual to us with high fidelity and comes with an additional inaccuracy—a person's association value will differ from one person to the next (e.g., Jessie's girl presumably benefits from Jessie's continued existence even if Rick does not). Therefore, this method of negative AV detection is probably less valid than personal experience unless the person you are learning from is similar to you in ways that predict the target would have similar association values for both of you (e.g., an enemy of my child is usually an enemy of mine as well).

Finally, this AV detection mechanism may make use of other specialized systems that identify targets with negative AV. For example, envy may identify individuals whose continued existence deprives you of a share of resources or stands in the way of your optimal mate choice (DelPriore et al., 2012). Anger identifies individuals who treat your welfare with insufficient respect in ways that will lead to future cost infliction (Sell et al., 2017; Sell & Szyncer, Chapter 4 in this volume). And so forth.

Minimize the Fitness Consequences Coming from the Toxic Individual
Once individuals with negative association value have been identified, the system must implement strategies to reduce the costs imposed by that individual's existence.

The most theoretically clear solution is to cease their existence by killing them. This is a solution readily seen in the animal kingdom. For example, ground squirrels compete for food with prairie dogs, so the prairie dogs kill the ground squirrel's infants and leave them for scavenger birds (Hoogland & Brown, 2016). Prairie dogs have a size and strength advantage over the infants they kill, making this behavior relatively low cost. By contrast, killing conspecifics can be more dangerous because of the costs of fighting, the possibility of retaliation by friends and family of the deceased, and the—often negative—social and reputational consequences that arise by demonstrating a willingness to kill individuals when it is in one's own interest. Furthermore, due to its permanent nature, the killing of toxic individuals makes it impossible to recoup cooperative benefits if one has miscalculated the association value of the person one has killed.

Nonetheless, the fact that killing the target is a permanent and often complete solution to the problem of a negative association value, and that it has been repeatedly selected for in other animals, suggests that killing a toxic individual should be part of human nature's toolkit of evolved responses, even if circumstances frequently make this option injudicious or too costly.

Alternative strategies for dealing with toxic individuals are difficult to predict a priori without an understanding of *how* that individual depresses one's fitness interests. However, generally speaking, if a person's existence is costly to your fitness, the situation would usually have improved to the extent that this person's influence over the social world was diminished. Lessening this person's influence would be a particularly good solution if the negative fitness consequences stemmed from this person actively pursuing their own interests, e.g., in cases of resource competition, mate competition, status blocking, and so on. In those circumstances, lowering the toxic person's health, well-being, reputation, and status would result in improved fitness because the toxic individual would be less capable of pursuing their own interests effectively. In short, toxic individuals should provoke in people a desire to harm them in cost-effective ways. Finally, if the toxic individual is depressing your welfare via interactions with you, then avoiding the toxic individual will be a potentially cost-effective means of reducing the damage done.

In sum, a simple information-processing analysis of the problem of negative association values in past environments leads to the prediction that natural selection should have designed a mechanism that functions to identify individuals whose existence in the future is costly to you, then enacts a suite of cognitive and behavioral procedures designed to minimize the negative fitness consequences of the target's existence. It is our contention that these are the major features of the emotion of hatred. We call this the *neutralization theory of hatred* (see also Sell & Lopez, 2020).

The Neutralization Theory of Hatred

According to the neutralization theory, hatred evolved in order to neutralize the effects of individuals with negative association values, i.e., individuals whose existence is costly to you.

In short, hatred responds to cues that, ancestrally, predicted that a person's continued existence and well-being were a net fitness loss to you. Once triggered by these varied cues, hatred calibrates the individual to treat the target differently. In particular, hatred leads to a negative intrinsic welfare trade-off ratio (iWTR; an internal index that determines when a person will trade off on their own welfare to benefit another;[1] Delton & Robertson, 2016; Sell, 2011; Sell et al., 2017; Tooby et al., 2008). A negative WTR means that a person experiencing hatred will spitefully accept costs in order to impose costs (or avoid benefiting) the target of hate. An intrinsic negative WTR is experienced as a lack of empathy, a desire to see the individual suffer (i.e., sadism when costs are inflicted by the hater, schadenfreude when they are inflicted by other means), and a preoccupation with thoughts of imposing costs on the target. Finally, hatred prudently enacts behavioral strategies that include a predatory style of aggression, information warfare and ally recruitment, and avoidance of the target. Hatred, unlike anger, does not have ready terminating conditions that shut it off (see Sell & Szyncer, Chapter 4 in this volume). It is predicted to maintain itself as an orientation toward the target until they cease to exist or their association value becomes positive, though the behavioral strategies of hatred are not designed to bring about this latter endpoint.

Triggers of Hatred
Our functional analysis suggests four predicted triggers of hatred:

(1) directly experiencing costs from that individual,
(2) hypothetical reasoning about how one's life would be different if that person did not exist or was diminished in power,
(3) socially learning whom others find toxic—with increased certainty put on the opinions of individuals who are similar to us or have shared interests, and
(4) the outputs of other specialized mechanisms that identify individuals with negative association value (e.g., other emotion systems).

Key to each one, and our central prediction, is that hatred is triggered by cues of a negative association value. In short, the existence of the target predicts future costs. Importantly—and as always—we refer to ancestral conditions in which modern genes were selected (Tooby & Cosmides, 1992), not to rational analyses of modern circumstances. For example, it was unlikely that Doucet was going to molest Plauché's child again: Doucet was in police custody and was being led to jail. But police and prison are modern inventions.

Note that cost infliction itself is not a sufficient trigger to know that a person's net future impact will likely be negative. Instead, hatred should be particularly activated by costs that predict large future costs. These include:

(1) Extreme costs that demonstrate a low welfare trade-off ratio (WTR). Recall that WTRs are internal regulatory variables that indicate the extent to which a person will sacrifice their own welfare to benefit yours, or vice versa. They are typically calibrated to .4 to .7 for friends (Delton & Robertson, 2016). A person's WTR is revealed by the kinds of costs they are willing to impose on another in order to benefit themselves (Sell et al., 2017). A low WTR is revealed by imposing large costs on another for relatively trivial benefits (e.g., a colleague using your hand-knit scarf to clean ketchup off his face; burdening your child with painful sexual memories and trauma for a fleeting sexual experience).

Extreme costs alone may be insufficient if they do not reveal a low WTR. For example, if Ted is inattentive and hits your child with his car, it may have devastating effects on your welfare, but this may be insufficient to provoke intense hatred. Now, compare this to Ted seeing your child playing in the street and slamming the gas because he thinks that's funny. This second scenario indicates a much more serious future threat to your fitness, because it reveals his stunningly low WTR toward you and your child. The evolutionary mechanisms needed to distinguish intentional harm from unintentional harm are beginning to be mapped (Martin & Cushman, 2016; Sell et al., 2017), but more work here will be useful for understanding hatred as well. Because intentional harms reveal a much lower WTR toward their target and are thus more predictive of future costs, we predict they will generate more intense hatred. However, it is important to note that hatred does *not* require a low WTR to be triggered. For example, if a woman's husband is sexually attracted to a young flautist, his wife may hate her even if the young woman evinces perfectly acceptable levels of WTR. Indeed, the flautist could lavish respect and care upon the married woman and still be hated by her.

Finally, we should reiterate that repeated small costs can lead to hatred, even in the absence of a low WTR. For example, as argued before (Sell, 2012), cases of elder abuse and child abuse appear to result from the persistent negative effect of having to—at great expense of time, energy, and money—care for another individual's needs.

(2) The ability to reason hypothetically about a person's nonexistence or diminished power should lead to estimates of a negative association value and trigger hatred. Reverse-engineering our ability to engage in counterfactual reasoning is beyond the scope of this chapter (though see Martin & Cushman, 2016), but the fact that we can contemplate how our life would be without a person's existence or well-being is sufficient to provide a cue of another's association value. When we run these hypotheticals and determine that we would be better off without the toxic person, hatred should be triggered. This is particularly clear in cases of envy or jealousy, where the target of hatred has not demonstrated a low WTR or in other ways evinced low moral character or a willingness to harm others. The fact remains, however, that this individual has resources, or a mate, or territory, that might be yours if they were gone.

(3) There would have been a selection pressure to identify toxic individuals as early as possible (e.g., Plauché probably wished he knew that Doucet was a pedophile much earlier than he did). One way of discovering such individuals earlier is to copy the information from others who may have already experienced the costs that emanate from the hated target. For this reason, we expect for hatred to spread socially such that individuals will copy hatred toward targets under some circumstances. Those circumstances likely include the following: (i) you are more likely to copy the hatred of your loved ones and peers because if your loved one hates a person, this person's existence is probably toxic for you as well, given the relationship between love and shared fitness interests;[2] (ii) hatred is more likely to be copied when it is more widespread because this gives some converging evidence that the target is toxic to a large number of people; (iii) you are more likely to copy hatred when the nature of the hated person's toxicity is particularly threatening to you, e.g., parents may be particularly likely to copy Plauché's hatred of Doucet.

Unfortunately, the social learning of hatred suggests that it can become contagious. An error in perception can lead one person to hate another, which is then copied, and can create a snowball effect. Of particular concern is the fact that individuals who defend the hated person are—in perception—preventing the mob from neutralizing this toxic person, and thus are becoming costly themselves. The mob then lowers their estimate of the defender's association value and often hates them as well.

(4) Finally, hatred is predicted to make use of calculations from other emotional systems (and possibly other systems more widely) to identify individuals whose existence is fitness-suppressing. We highlight the following examples:

ANGER

Anger is designed to identify people whose welfare trade-off ratios are below the appropriate negotiated level as perceived by the angry individual (Sell & Szyncer, Chapter 6 in this volume). In short, anger identifies those who do not value you sufficiently. Such a calculation means that the target of the anger is imposing more costs than they otherwise would. Note, however, that in most cases of anger the target is not hated. On the contrary, they are often loved (Averill, 1983; see Sell, 2011). This is because a "lower than it should be" WTR can still translate into an overall beneficial relationship. Indeed, anger is most common between family members or friends who maintain positive association values with each other, but still find room to negotiate over welfare trade-off ratios.

That said, a low WTR will lead someone to impose large costs for relatively trivial benefits and does portend future costs. In short, if someone is willing to knock your ice cream out of your hand for the laughs, what else might they be willing to do? Such a person—if they do not possess other compensating traits—would presumably be a net fitness suppressor for you, and would trigger hatred.

Anger and hatred can both respond to targets who exhibit a low WTR. A full contrast of these emotions is beyond the scope of this chapter, but we note that anger and hatred function distinctly in that anger attempts to recalibrate and bargain with a target, while hatred attempts to neutralize them. These—and other distinctions—are worth more empirical scrutiny.

ENVY

We consider envy an underexplored emotion—at least from the perspective most able to produce clear thinking about its function, namely evolutionary psychology (see Ramachandran & Jalal, 2017; Sznycer et al., 2017). Like Sznycer et al., we take envy to be an adaptation that identifies individuals who hold resources or status that would further our reproductive interests. This gives an incentive to deprive them of that status or power. In short, unless they possess offsetting traits, their existence is a cost to us, and we would be better off if they were to suffer a deprivation of life, status, or resources. Hatred, thus, can be triggered from envy. We consider the long-standing demonization of the wealthy and middle-man minorities to be, in part, a consequence of this emotion (see Sowell, 2016). While this form of envy is generally not functional in modern market economies, envy and hatred evolved in small-scale economies with limited resources shared between small numbers of individuals.

JEALOUSY

Mate competition is arguably as strong a selection pressure as resource competition (Darwin, 1871; Buss, 2005), and because of its competitive nature an individual can benefit by eliminating a toxic rival. Thus, the preconditions are met for hating one's romantic rival in a mate competition scenario—again, presuming no compensating traits. Importantly, this explanation predicts hatred toward one's rival, but not necessarily toward one's mate who may be thinking of straying. We consider Daly and Wilson's arguments that spousal killings are byproducts of a mate-guarding adaptation to be the best explanation of this phenomenon (Daly & Wilson, 1988; Wilson & Daly, 1992). We will note—puzzling though it may be—that spousal killers frequently describe both hatred and love for their victims (Chimbos, 1978). The coexistence of seemingly opposite adaptations that are characterized by self-sacrifice, care, high intrinsic WTR on one hand, and spite, aggression, and negative intrinsic WTR on the other hand, remains to be explored.

FEAR

Individuals capable of imposing great costs on you are—of course—a danger. To the extent that this danger becomes likely, and—importantly—that the source of this danger does not provide useful benefits to you that outweigh this risk, then the feared person or persons are predicted to be hated, i.e., one would be better off without them. The rise in hate crimes toward Muslims after the 9/11 attacks may be an example of this (Disha et al., 2011).

DISGUST

While disgust serves multiple purposes (see Lieberman et al., 2007; Cepon-Robins, Chapter 9 in this volume), one feature of disgust is that it identifies individuals who are potential disease vectors. Disgust triggers avoidance, but it can also establish that the target's existence is a net harm to you. As a result, hatred may be triggered by those who are "disgusting." While removing pathogen vectors could clearly be selected for, we also note that there is a long history of attacks on people who engage in other behavior that can trigger disgust, e.g., individuals engaging in deviant sexual practices, eating unusual foods, and so on. We note, of course, that compensatory factors that upregulate one's intrinsic WTR will counteract this, such that hatred is not reliably activated toward one's child when they get the sniffles. Indeed, introspection suggests that love appears to deactivate disgust.

SHAME

Shame is believed to have evolved in order to slow or stop the spread of negative information about oneself (Sznycer et al., 2012; Landers et al., Chapter 7 in this volume). As such, one feature of shame is to identify the vectors of that negative information—the person who has this information and may spread it to others. Such a person's existence is harmful and would lead to a lower association value as a result. Should that value be negative, we predict that the shamed person should hate the bearer of negative information, even if the person has done nothing with that information.[3]

HATRED

One of the effects of hatred is to heap costs upon the target. If someone hates you, they will lie about you, broadcast your inadequacies, look for costs to put on you, and fantasize about harming you. As a result, your life is likely to be worse off for their existence. Thus, once hatred is revealed, it will likely be reciprocal. This has important implications for how hatred should express itself; specifically, it should be hidden from the target if possible (see below).

Interestingly, this creates a perverse—but empirically verified—prediction (Schopler & Compere, 1971), which is that we should hate those that we have unjustly harmed. If you harm a person—you are presumably triggering hatred in them—which means that they are now an enemy who will likely work against you in the future. Thus, their continued existence is bad for you, triggering hatred.

Finally, we should say that this list is likely not exhaustive. There may be cases where a target is hated merely because they have an incentive to harm you; e.g., a non-offending pedophile is still a person who potentially *wants* to molest your children.

Computational Structure of Hatred

According to the neutralization theory, the most significant effect of hatred is to set a negative intrinsic WTR toward the hated target. The more negative, the more "hated" the target is. Recall that welfare trade-off ratios set the accepted discount rate on another's welfare when making decisions that impact you both. For example, a WTR of .7 toward my friend will cause me to impose costs of 10 on them if I benefit 8 or more, but not if I benefit only 6 or less (i.e., the decision rule is "take the self-beneficial action whenever the benefit to the self is more than the cost to the other times the WTR," or $B_x > C_y * WTR_{xy}$). A negative WTR means that one will take any benefit no matter how much it hurts the target (if B_x is a benefit, it will always be higher than a negative number). For example, an intrinsic WTR of $-.5$ calibrates the individual to exploit the hated target for benefits. She will accept costs in order to hurt the target, if the cost is half the damage to the hated enemy or less. She will also deny herself certain benefits because the target would benefit as well, if the hated target would benefit twice as much or more, and so on. This is the essence of spite.

Herman Melville perfectly illustrated an extreme negative WTR at the conclusion of Moby Dick, when Captain Ahab uses his last breath to spit at the whale. The WTR logic is as follows: Ahab willingly gave up his last breath of air (presumably a weighty benefit as it was all he had left; let's say $B_x = 100$), in order to impose a trivial cost on the whale (spitting on an ocean-soaked mammal with thick skin; let's say $C_y = 1$). Thus Ahab's WTR toward the whale is revealed to be less than or equal to -100, an intense amount of hate that licenses extraordinarily spiteful behavior on Ahab's part.

If you have a negative WTR toward a target, you should be aware and searching for opportunities to impose costs on the target. Such cost infliction is incentivized in the same way that we are incentivized to look for opportunities to help people we value intrinsically. In this way, hatred causes a desire to see that individual hurt whether or not we are causing their hurt (Rempel et al., 2019).

Welfare trade-off ratios are believed to be used in many downstream cognitive systems (see Sell et al., 2017). For example, WTRs appear to govern memory such that higher WTRs lead us to pay more attention to the target and remember more information about them. Forgetting about a person (or an aspect of that person) is thus a trigger of anger because it reveals a low WTR (Sell, 2014). For hatred, the negative WTR presumably causes a similar increase in memory fidelity and for the same reasons. We need to know information about those that we value highly so that we can make choices that benefit them (e.g., I need to remember that my child has an allergy). Similarly, we need to know if our hated enemy has an allergy as well, so that we can make choices that harm them. For this reason, we predict that it is the magnitude of the WTR rather than its valence that increases memory.

Similarly, the recalibrational theory of anger predicts (see Sell & Sznycer, Chapter 6 in this volume) that holding a high WTR toward someone implies that their interests must be considered frequently. For example, when making a decision about whether to move, a woman presumably weighs the likely welfare impact the move will have on those toward whom she has a high WTR (e.g., her husband, her friends, her children, her family). But she will not likely consider the interests of those she has a low intrinsic WTR toward, e.g., her mail carrier, her colleague from HR, her ex-boyfriend. The interests of these individuals are not likely to be considered at all because the low WTR discounts those interests to the point where they would not sway the decision.[4] A highly negative WTR, however, should be considered, just like a highly positive WTR, because it is important to calculate the impact of your decisions on toxic individuals who are imposing costs on you. In this way, a hated person (e.g., WTR = −1.0) is as important as a loved one (e.g., WTR = 1.0) when making one's decisions.

Other effects of high WTRs appear to reverse when the WTR is negative. For example, we enjoy spending time with those that we have high intrinsic WTRs toward, while we tend to avoid those we hate (Aumer & Bahn, 2016). With high intrinsic WTRs, we often experience vicarious enjoyment of happiness (e.g., my wife's smile when she looked at our daughter for the first time still makes me happy) and pain at their pain (e.g., the actual birthing process). With negative intrinsic WTRs, these effects appear reversed such that the pain of our hated enemies is enjoyable (e.g., Thomas Aquinas suspected one of the pleasures of heaven is that we can watch the torture of the damned), and the happiness of our enemies is experienced as suffering.

Behavioral Strategies of Hatred

Our functional analysis of the "toxic individual" selection pressure suggests three kinds of behavioral strategies for neutralizing the target:

(1) killing the target
(2) weakening the target to limit their power and influence
(3) avoiding the target.

Killing a target requires aggression, and aggression is one of the most reliable behavioral tendencies triggered by hatred. However, aggression can be implemented in different ways with different functions (Sell & Lopez, 2020; Wrangham, 2018). For example, anger triggers bargaining-style aggression (see Sell, 2011) designed to force compliance or recalibrate welfare trade-off ratios. According to the neutralization theory, the function of hatred-based aggression is to impose costs efficiently on the target in order to weaken them, diminish their physical or social power, or potentially kill them (Rempel et al., 2019). Thus, the style of aggression activated by hatred is predicted to be "predatory" in nature.

Predatory Aggression

We define predatory-style aggression as aggression used to inflict damage in the most efficient way possible—minimizing risk and maximizing impact, e.g., a lion stalking a gazelle, or a kite killing its sibling. It is characterized mostly by the features that are notably absent: (1) no signaling, (2) no escalation, (3) no monitoring for surrender or submission, (4) continued aggression upon the target's submission, (5) no interrogations of the target's motive or reasoning, and willful violations of the implicit rules of combat (Romero et al., 2014; Sell & Lopez, 2020). Instead, predatory aggression should be characterized by:

(1) Deception in order to minimize the chance for the victim to prepare. This is presumably why hatred does not have a corresponding facial expression, e.g., the anger face exaggerates cues of physical strength to bargain with the target (Marsh et al., 2005; Reed et al., 2014; Sell et al., 2014), but intense hatred appears to have no discernible reliable facial expression for the same reason the lion does not roar at the gazelle.

(2) Rapid deployment of most costly aggression. Predatory aggression is designed to inflict costs, not demonstrate fighting skill, and so the usual pattern of ritualized conspecific aggression wherein two animals fight for dominance has no purpose in predatory aggression. Hatred should motivate the kinds of aggression that are most costly for the victim (constrained by the risks to the attacker, of course). For this reason, hatred-based human aggression should not make use of the usual rituals of threat display (e.g., pushing and shoving, staring contests, threats, and so on; see Sell, 2011).

(3) Aggression should be timed to victim vulnerability. Because hatred-based aggression is often surreptitious, and because retaliation, flight, and self-defense will often inflate the costs of a second attack, a man feeling hatred should choose his first attack judiciously—timed to when it would be most effective. This style of aggression is again evident in the stalking behavior of predators who time their aggression to when prey is most vulnerable.

(4) As a corollary to point (3) above, signs of submission or fear will serve as evidence that the victim is not in a good position to fight back or defend themselves. As such, these responses should have an excited effect on the predatory aggression, as it indicates that this is a judicious time to attack a helpless victim.

(5) Temporary increases in formidability (such as that provided by being in a group of like-minded people) should increase the probability that hatred will give rise to predatory aggression.

(6) Predatory aggression should be more likely than other kinds of aggression to be lethal. While hatred rarely leads to homicide (at least in the modern world; Pinker, 2012), the hatred adaptation was forged in an ancestral world with much more aggression. We cannot know the frequency with which intense hatred led to homicide, but we do note that research on homicidal fantasies shows that they are abundant and common in the modern world (Buss, 2006). The neutralization theory of hatred predicts that most of these fantasies are test runs—i.e., hypotheticals computed to learn the feasibility and practicality of terminating a hated other. Note that the function of the fantasy is to gather information; it is not as a final check before a behavioral strategy is immediately deployed.

Despite its utility, killing those you hate has several potent limitations, including: (1) it can be impractical to carry out given the target's fighting ability or social position; (2) it may invite retaliation; (3) it cannot be undone—errors of judgment are permanent; and (4) it can have harmful reputational costs for the killer. Presumably for these reasons, natural selection has equipped hatred with alternative strategies that can also be effective at limiting the power and influence of a toxic person: information warfare.

Information Warfare

A person's power is often determined by the status, prestige, and concern shown them by others. If such a person uses that power in ways that go against your interests—to the extent that their association value is negative for you—then diminishing their social power can help ameliorate the damage done by the person. In short, one can "damage" a hated other and diminish their power and influence by recalibrating the status-seeking machinery in the minds of other humans in the social group.

We can predict how this is done by understanding the status-setting systems themselves. Borrowing from research on welfare trade-off ratios and the recalibrational theory of anger

(Sell, 2011; Sell et al., 2009; Sell et al., 2017; Tooby et al., 2008) and from direct work on status itself (Durkee et al., 2020), one can postulate that status-setting mechanisms should grant status to those who are capable of defending their own interests (e.g., fighting ability, coalitional strength), producing benefits for others (e.g., hunting skill, holding useful knowledge), and being inclined to benefit those in their group (e.g., loyalty, reciprocity). As such, we can predict that an individual should attempt to spread information about the hated target that minimizes that target's value in the eyes of others: e.g., they are poor cooperators either from effort or ability; they are weak; they are promiscuous backstabbing cowards; and so on. The functional goal of this information warfare is to lower others' WTR toward the target, preferably to the point of engendering hatred toward them. By doing this, a person who hates a target can mobilize other people's hatred mechanisms and deprive the target of allies, friends, social power, and—at times—their life.

Crucially, there is no particular need for this negative information to be truthful (see also Petersen et al., 2020). Given that gossip and character assassination rarely allow for the victim to respond, great gains can be had against a target provided there is no one to counter the negative information. Again, the contagious nature of hatred makes this feature of the adaptation dangerous from a societal perspective. An innocent person, tarred with hateful gossip, will become a bad investment for defenders because those defenders will be seen as helping maintain a toxic individual. The mob will then lower their approximations of the defender's association value, and frequently hate them as well. This can create a perverse incentive for third parties who are now incentivized to hate a target who has no genuine toxic effects, merely to avoid the appearance of defending them.

Attentional Direction and Information Gathering

Emotions frequently direct attention at certain aspects of the environment that predict which of the multiple strategies available to the emotion will be most effective (Cosmides & Tooby, 2000). Of course, hatred directs attention to the target, such that the appearance of a hated other will often distract from other tasks and emotions.

Hatred appears to focus attention on the hated target (Aumer & Bahn, 2016). For example, it would be difficult to concentrate on anything else if you were seated next to your sister's rapist. The hated target is important to attend to for the same reasons that a loved one is: one's decisions need to mold to the welfare of that other. It is therefore important to know what the person does and does not like, who their allies are, what debts they have, what secrets they hold, which individuals they are attracted to, which individuals they hate, and so on. While it is pleasurable to learn about someone you love, there is an odd tendency to feel compelled to learn about someone you hate, despite the fact that doing so is not enjoyable. The phenomena of "hate following" people on social media, for example, involves individuals paying attention to the words and opinions of individuals they hate. Importantly, this phenomenon is not a well-intentioned desire to understand another's perspective, but rather is a hunt for information that can be weaponized against them. Indeed, hatred shows an active aversion to understanding the perspective of the target. It suggests not just a disinterest in the target's defense, but a claim that no defense should be considered. For example, after the 9/11 attacks on the United States by Al Qaeda, the actor Richard Gere spoke in public and suggested that America attempt to "understand" why the terrorists did this, and he was roundly booed for his suggestion. Tactically, understanding the motives of one's enemies may be useful, but curiously hatred (at least intense hatred) appears to negate this—at least over some facets of motivation. We consider the most likely explanation of this phenomena to be that understanding the motives and desires of an enemy will lead to negotiations over those conflicts (see Halperin et al., 2011), and that negotiations are incompatible with the function of hatred, which is to nullify an enemy rather than appease one.

The selection pressure for this feature of hatred—specifically the aversion to learning the motives and explanations for a hated target's behavior—is hypothesized to be this: if a hated target is allowed to offer explanations, caveats, or apologies to the larger social group, this will diminish one's ability to recruit allies against that target. This is because association values will differ from person to person (e.g., Doucet's existence may be less negative to someone who does not have children). The ability to negotiate one's toxicity is one tool a hated person can use to diffuse hatred; e.g., via upregulating WTRs to compensate, as is typically done in apologies—"I know it can't be easy to live with someone like me . . . I'll be more conscientious in the future"—or simply bestowing benefits to countervail their negative effects. A person whose hatred is based on an extremely potent negative association value may not want the target to be able to bargain at all. This final point may explain why when people hate a figure, they often attempt to silence them.

Avoidance

In some cases, the fitness costs of some individuals with negative association values can be blunted by merely not being near them; e.g., a colleague who never lets you get back to work; an ex-boyfriend who tries to shame you with questions. To the extent that avoiding these people reduced their fitness-suppressing effects, natural selection would have selected avoidance as an output of hatred. Indeed, hatred does appear to motivate avoidance of a target, unless—of course—one is intent on aggression (see Aumer & Bahn, 2016).

Terminating Conditions for Hatred

What circumstances should lead hatred to deactivate? According to the selection pressure posited here, hatred should deactivate when the target's association value becomes zero or positive. This can occur for a number of reasons. We speculate on common cases here.

A MISPERCEPTION OF ASSOCIATION VALUE IS CORRECTED

Hatred is activated by internal estimates of a target's association value. Those estimates are necessarily imperfect. If hatred is activated via a misperceived negative association value that is later corrected, hatred should deactivate and guilt should be activated to repair any damage done by hatred (Gilbert, Chapter 15 in this volume). This will sometimes happen upon re-evaluation of a target's actions, e.g., the police arrested the wrong man for killing your mother; the guy who kept pulling your pigtails is actually flirting with you, not bullying you; the stranger who is stalking your Facebook page turns out to be your long-lost brother.

THE TARGET RECALIBRATES THEIR WTR AND THIS RESULTS IN A POSITIVE ASSOCIATION VALUE

To reiterate, WTR is an internal regulatory variable that functions primarily to determine which self-interested actions to take and which altruistic actions to take (Delton & Robertson, 2016; Sell et al., 2017; Tooby et al., 2008). It stores (in colloquial terms) the degree of respect or regard one has for another. Raising another's low WTR is the primary function of anger (Sell, 2011; Sell et al., 2017; Sell & Sznycer, Chapter 6 in this volume), which contains distinct behavioral strategies and triggers. However, a low WTR will lead a person to impose costs on another—and deny them benefits—and as such will (all else being equal) lead to a lower association value. This is presumably why anger and hatred often activate together (i.e., anger bargains for better treatment, while hatred neutralizes the target's power).

If anger successfully bargains for better treatment and the target apologizes and raises their WTR, then it is possible that the estimated association value for that target also becomes positive, and hatred deactivates as well. Note, as mentioned earlier, that hatred can be activated even when the target has a high WTR toward you (e.g., the obsessive ex who is still in love with you has a high WTR toward you; the man who married the woman you were in love with could value you a lot).

SHIFTING ALLIANCE STRUCTURES TURN A HATED ENEMY INTO AN ALLY

Modern politics is replete with examples of enemies becoming allies and vice versa, often with a parallel shift in the minds of the citizenry (e.g., the American movie Rambo 3 awkwardly ends with a tribute to the Taliban). The nature of these shifts is beyond the scope of the current chapter, but given their regular occurrence in our species, we can assume that association value estimators should recalibrate upon new discoveries of alliance; e.g., the bully who teases you nonetheless defends you from a genuinely lethal threat.

NEW AVENUES OF COOPERATION TURN AN ENEMY INTO A POTENTIAL COOPERATOR

Hatred, particularly mutual hatred, is costly. If there exists an opportunity to rekindle a cooperative relationship that would revert negative associations to positive, this would be a potent selection pressure (McCullough, 2008). This will be particularly true when a change in circumstance or social patterns allows for new cooperation. Having a stake in someone else's welfare could be a potent tool for defusing hatred.

THE COSTS OF HATRED OUTWEIGH THE BENEFITS

Hatred is costly. It can motivate spiteful behavior, trigger retaliation, squander attention and resources, and lead others to return hatred on you. If the function of hatred is to neutralize a toxic individual, but hatred fails at doing this because the target cannot be eliminated, cannot be diminished in power, cannot be warred against by coalitions spurred on by information warfare, and cannot be avoided, then the spiteful actions taken by the individual who hates the target will be net costs. Under these circumstances, nature would select for hatred to deactivate, rather than waste the organism's finite budget of energy and resources on ineffective strategies. This conclusion depends on there having been frequent cases (ancestrally) where a hated person could not be cost-effectively neutralized. We are agnostic on this point, but it is a reasonable assumption that the strategies deployed by hatred should self-evaluate their success such that if—for example—an incident of predatory aggression worked effectively, then the aggressive person will be more likely to continue that strategy. Or, if an avoidance strategy fails because the bully seeks out her victim, the victim may be more likely to switch strategies to aggression. If all strategies fail, it is likely that hatred will deactivate or remain dormant until circumstances change. This possibility leads to an interesting prediction: a sudden resurgence of hatred should occur when a powerful hated target demonstrates a new weakness.

Conclusion

In conclusion, the neutralization theory of hatred appears to explain many of the major features of human hatred as the expression of an evolved adaptation that functions to neutralize individuals whose future existence is likely to impose costs on the person experiencing hatred. This adaptation comes online in response to triggers that ancestrally predicted these future costs. These triggers appear to include evidence of a low WTR (a trigger shared with anger), the outcomes of hypotheticals that reveal how one's life would improve without the person, social learning and "hate copying," and outputs from other evolved emotion systems that flag individuals whose continued existence is detrimental. Once activated, hatred coordinates a suite of cognitive responses including: (1) recalibrating one's intrinsic WTR toward the target to be negative, incentivizing spiteful behavior; (2) gathering information on the target, (3) disengaging empathy for the target, and (4) frequent consideration of the target's welfare when making decisions. Hatred also activates a series of behavioral strategies designed to eliminate the target or minimize their power to affect one's welfare. Predatory aggression is the most serious of these strategies, typically deployed after homicidal fantasies test the feasibility and practicality of the behavior. More commonly, a kind of informational warfare is deployed to gather allies against the target and to diminish their social power. Finally, a strategy of avoidance may be pursued.

If correct, future research should be able to map out additional a priori predicted features of this complex adaptation which will further distinguish it from the anger system and other emotional programs. Such research should also be able to identify strategies for diminishing the negative effects of hatred at the societal level.

Notes

1. "Intrinsic" in this context refers to one's WTR in conditions when the target cannot effectively bargain for their own interests. Thus, having a high intrinsic WTR means one cares about the target's welfare even if they will never know about the trade-off. For example, I have a high intrinsic WTR toward my family and care about them even in their absence, but I have a high "monitored" WTR toward my boss, whose opinion and welfare is extremely important to me *when* he is in the room.
2. We consider love to be the opposite of hatred. It identifies individuals whose existence causes positive fitness outcomes for us. It responds to cues that are usually the opposite of those of hatred, and motivates a very high intrinsic WTR. It also triggers fantasies of benefiting and sacrificing for the individual, rather than at their expense.
3. The journalist Christopher Hitchens relates an anecdote about Saddam Hussein killing his translator who was present (and translating) when UN officials spoke down to the dictator. Mr. Hitchens's explanation was that Saddam did not allow anyone to live who had witnessed him feel shame.
4. This results in a delightful trigger of anger in which a person is angry that their interests were not consulted, even if the decision was ultimately satisfactory. For example, a woman was angry at her husband for pulling into a restaurant that she wanted to go to, because he didn't ask her where she wanted to go (Sell, 2014).

References

Aktipis, A., Cronk, L., Alcock, J., Ayers, J. D., Baciu, C., Balliet, D., Boddy, A. M., Curry, O. S., Krems, J. A., Muñoz, A. Sullivan, D., Sznycer, D., Wilkinson, G. S., & Winfrey, P. (2018). Understanding cooperation through fitness interdependence. *Nature Human Behaviour*, 2(7), 429–431.
Aumer, K., & Bahn, A. C. K. (2016). Hate in intimate relationships as a self-protective emotion. In K. Aumer (Eds.), *The psychology of love and hate in intimate relationships* (pp. 131–151). Springer, Cham.
Averill, J. R. (1983). Studies on anger and aggression: Implications for theories of emotion. *American Psychologist*, 38(11), 1145.
Buss, D. M. (2005). *The dangerous passion: Why jealousy is a necessary as love and sex*. Odile Jacob.
Buss, D. M. (2006). *The murderer next door: Why the mind is designed to kill*. Penguin.
Chimbos, P. D. (1978). *Marital violence: A study of interspouse homicide*. R & E Research Associates.
Cosmides, L., & Tooby, J. (1994). Beyond intuition and instinct blindness: Toward an evolutionarily rigorous cognitive science. *Cognition*, 50(1–3), 41–77.
Cosmides, L., & Tooby, J. (2000). Evolutionary psychology and the emotions. In M. Lewis & J. M. Haviland-Jones (Eds.), *Handbook of emotions* (2nd ed., pp. 91–115). Guilford Press.
Daly, M., & Wilson M. (1988). *Homicide*. Transaction Books.
Darwin, C. (1871). *The descent of man, and selection in relation to sex*. Murray.
DelPriore, D. J., Hill, S. E., & Buss, D. M. (2012). Envy: Functional specificity and sex-differentiated design features. *Personality and Individual Differences*, 53(3), 317–322.
Delton, A. W., & Robertson, T. E. (2016). How the mind makes welfare tradeoffs: Evolution, computation, and emotion. *Current Opinion in Psychology*, 7, 12–16.
Disha, I., Cavendish, J. C., & King, R. D. (2011). Historical events and spaces of hate: Hate crimes against Arabs and Muslims in post-9/11 America. *Social problems*, 58(1), 21–46.

Durkee, P. K., Lukaszewski, A. W., & Buss, D. M. (2020). Psychological foundations of human status allocation. *Proceedings of the National Academy of Sciences, 117*(35), 21235–21241.

Epstein, S. (1979). The stability of behavior: I. On predicting most of the people much of the time. *Journal of Personality and Social Psychology, 37*(7), 1097. https://doi.org/10.1037/0022-3514.37.7.1097

Epstein, S. (1980). The stability of behavior: II. Implications for psychological research. *American Psychologist, 35*(9), 790. https://doi.org/10.1037/0003-066X.35.9.790

Epstude, K., & Roese, N. J. (2008). The functional theory of counterfactual thinking. *Personality and Social Psychology Review, 12*(2), 168–192.

Gerhardt, R. P., Gerhardt, D. M., & Vasquez, M. A. (1997). Siblicide in swallow-tailed kites. *The Wilson Bulletin, 109*(1), 112–120.

Gouda-Vossos, A., Nakagawa, S., Dixson, B. J., & Brooks, R. C. (2018). Mate choice copying in humans: A systematic review and meta-analysis. *Adaptive Human Behavior and Physiology, 4*(4), 364–386.

Halperin, E., Russell, A. G., Dweck, C. S., & Gross, J. J. (2011). Anger, hatred, and the quest for peace: Anger can be constructive in the absence of hatred. *Journal of Conflict Resolution, 55*(2), 274–291.

Hamilton, W. D. (1964). The genetical evolution of social behaviour. II. *Journal of Theoretical Biology, 7*(1), 17–52.

Hoogland, J. L., & Brown, C. R. (2016). Prairie dogs increase fitness by killing interspecific competitors. *Proceedings of the Royal Society B: Biological Sciences, 283*(1827), 20160144.

James, W. (1890). *The principles of psychology*, Vol. 1. H. Holt.

Lieberman, D., Tooby, J., & Cosmides, L. (2007). The architecture of human kin detection. *Nature, 445*(7129), 727–731.

Marsh, A. A., Adams, R. B., & Kleck, R. E. (2005) Why do fear and anger look the way they do? Form and social function in facial expressions. *Personality and Social Psychology Bulletin, 31*(1), 73–86.

Martin, J. W., & Cushman, F. (2016). Why we forgive what can't be controlled. *Cognition, 147*, 133–143.

McCullough, M. (2008). *Beyond revenge: The evolution of the forgiveness instinct*. Wiley.

Mock, D. W., Drummond, H., & Stinson, C. H. (1990). Avian siblicide. *American scientist, 78*(5), 438–449.

Ouellette, J. A., & Wood, W. (1998). Habit and intention in everyday life: The multiple processes by which past behavior predicts future behavior. *Psychological Bulletin, 124*(1), 54–74. https://doi.org/10.1037/0033-2909.124.1.54

Petersen, M. B., Osmundsen, M., & Tooby, J. (2020). The evolutionary psychology of conflict and the functions of falsehood. In D. C. Barker & E. Suhay (Eds.), *The politics of truth in polarized America* (pp. 131–150). Oxford University Press.

Petersen, M. B., Sell, A., Tooby, J., and Cosmides, L. (2010). Evolutionary psychology and criminal justice: A recalibrational theory of punishment and reconciliation. In H. Høgh-Olesen (Ed.), *Human morality and sociality* (pp. 72–131). Palgrave Macmillan.

Pinker, S. (2012). *The better angels of our nature: Why violence has declined*. Penguin Group USA.

Ramachandran, V. S., & Jalal, B. (2017). The evolutionary psychology of envy and jealousy. *Frontiers in Psychology, 8*, 1619.

Reed, L. I., DeScioli, P., & Pinker, S. A. (2014). The commitment function of angry facial expressions. *Psychological Science, 25*(8), 1511–1517.

Rempel, J. K., Burris, C. T., & Fathi, D. (2019). Hate: Evidence for a motivational conceptualization. *Motivation and Emotion, 43*(1), 179–190.

Romero, G. A., Pham, M. N., & Goetz, A. T. (2014). The implicit rules of combat. *Human Nature, 25*(4), 496–516.

Schopler, J., & Compere, J. S. (1971). Effects of being kind or harsh to another on liking. *Journal of Personality and Social Psychology, 20*(2), 155.

Sell, A. (2011). The recalibrational theory and violent anger. *Aggression and Violent Behavior, 16*, 381–389.

Sell, A. (2012). Revenge can be more fully understood by making distinctions between anger and hatred: Commentary on McCullough, Kurzan & Tabak's "Cognitive Systems for Revenge and Forgiveness." *Behavioral and Brain Sciences, 36*(1), 36–37.

Sell, A. (2014). Twelve triggers of anger and how they invalidate all major theories of anger and aggression. *International Society for Research on Aggression*, Georgia State University, July 19.

Sell, A., Cosmides L. & Tooby, J. (2014). The human anger face evolved to enhance cues of strength. *Evolution and Human Behavior, 35*(5), 425–429.

Sell, A., & A. C. Lopez (2020). Emotional underpinnings of war: An evolutionary analysis of anger and hatred. In C. Ireland, J. Ireland, M. Lewis, & A. C. Lopez (Eds.), *The international handbook on collective violence: Current issues and perspectives* (pp. 31–46). Routledge.

Sell, A., Sznycer, D., Al-Shawaf, L., Lim, J., Krauss, A., Feldman, A., Rascanu, R., Sugiyama, L., Tooby, J. & L. Cosmides (2017). The grammar of anger: Mapping the computational architecture of a recalibrational emotion. *Cognition, 168*, 110–128.

Sell, A., Tooby, J., & Cosmides, L. (2009). 'Formidability and the logic of human anger', *Proceedings of the National Academy of Science, 106*(35), 15073–78.

Sowell, T. (2016). *Wealth, poverty and politics*. Hachette UK.

Sznycer, D., Seal, M. F. L., Sell, A., Lim, J., Porat, R., Shalvi, S., Halperin, R., Cosmides, L., & Tooby, J. (2017). Support for redistribution is shaped by compassion, envy, and self-interest, but not a taste for fairness. *Proceedings of the National Academy of Sciences, 114*(31), 8420–8425.

Sznycer, D., Takemura, K., Delton, A. W., Sato, K., Robertson, T., Cosmides, L., & Tooby, J. (2012). Cross-cultural differences and similarities in proneness to shame: An adaptationist and ecological approach. *Evolutionary Psychology, 10*(2), 147470491201000213.

Tooby, J., & Cosmides, L. (1992). The psychological foundations of culture. In J. Barkow, L. Cosmides, & J. Tooby (Eds.), *The adapted mind: Evolutionary psychology and the generation of culture* (pp. 19–136). Oxford University Press.

Tooby, J., & L. Cosmides (1996). Friendship and the Banker's Paradox: Other pathways to the evolution of adaptations for altruism. *Proceedings of the British Academy, 88*, 119–43.

Tooby, J., Cosmides, L., Sell, A., Lieberman, D., & Sznycer, D. (2008). Internal regulatory variables and the design of human motivation: A computational and evolutionary approach. In A. J. Elliot (Ed.), *Handbook of approach and avoidance motivation* (pp. 251–271). Psychology Press.

Trivers, R. L. (1971). The evolution of reciprocal altruism. *The Quarterly Review of Biology, 46*(1), 35–57.

Williams, G. C. (1966). *Adaptation and natural selection: A critique of some current evolutionary thought*. Princeton University Press.

Wilson, M. I., & Daly, M. (1992). Who kills whom in spouse killings? On the exceptional sex ratio of spousal homicides in the United States. *Criminology, 30*(2), 189–216.

Wrangham, R. W. (2018). Two types of aggression in human evolution. *Proceedings of the National Academy of Sciences, 115*(2), 245–253.

Disgust: An Emotion for Pathogen Avoidance

Tara J. Cepon-Robins

Abstract

Disgust is a universal human emotion that likely evolved to prevent exposure to substances, people, or activities associated with pathogens. Variation in disgust sensitivity exists based on sex, age, immune status, and other life-history factors. Disgust sensitivity is hypothesized to be flexible, calibrated to local environments based on cost-benefit trade-offs associated with avoidance. Problematically, most disgust research has been focused largely within what have been termed "WEIRD" populations (i.e., Western, educated, industrialized, rich democracies). Consequently, little is known about the disgust response and its downstream effects within populations experiencing high-pathogen environments, subsistence-based lifestyles (e.g., foraging, hunting/fishing, horticulture), and natural fertility. We review what is known about cross-cultural variation in the disgust response and provide testable hypotheses for future research on disgust sensitivity and utility in understudied populations. Collaborations between evolutionary psychology and human biology can fill gaps in the understanding of the disgust emotion through methodological and theoretical synthesis.

Key Words: disgust, pathogen avoidance, evolutionary psychology, human biology, behavioral immune system

Introduction

Our understanding of disgust has increased dramatically since Charles Darwin first described it as a mechanism for avoiding "disagreeable substances" (1872). Today, disgust is understood as a universal human emotion that functions to motivate avoidance of fitness-reducing substances, activities, or individuals generally associated with pathogens in ancestral environments (Cepon-Robins et al., 2021; Curtis & Biran, 2001; Ekman, 1992; Lieberman et al., 2003; Lieberman et al., 2018; Oaten et al., 2009; Rozin et al., 2008; Tybur et al., 2009; Tybur et al., 2013; Tybur et al., 2018; Tybur & Lieberman, 2016). While a growing number of studies are applying evolutionary approaches to understand disgust, there has been limited integration across fields (Tybur et al., 2018), which has resulted in few holistic cross-cultural studies.

Research that combines ideas and methodologies from distinct but overlapping fields, like evolutionary psychology and human population biology, endeavors to increase our understanding of the disgust response (Tybur et al., 2018). For instance, while evolutionary psychology describes how information-processing mechanisms work to generate behavioral responses to environmental cues associated with adaptive problems in ancestral environments (Tooby & Cosmides, 1990, 2015; Tybur & Lieberman, 2016), human population biology examines how physiological, social, and environmental variables (e.g., hygiene or sanitation) affect biological outcomes (e.g., pathogen exposure). Combined, these fields provide a lens through which to test relationships between the evolved nature of disgust and biological/environmental variations, as well as the downstream effects of disgust, to see if they match the hypothesized benefits and patterns.

Most hypotheses related to the evolution of the disgust response center on how disgust functioned in ancestral environments. However, as with most studies related to human health and psychology, research studies focused on disgust have largely occurred in what have been termed "WEIRD" populations[1] (i.e., Western, educated, industrialized, rich, and democratic; Gurven & Lieberman, 2020; Henrich et al., 2010a, 2010b; Rad et al., 2018; Schulz et al., 2018). These populations, while useful for understanding variation in disgust sensitivity within and between certain samples, often vary drastically from the lifestyles, diets, and disease environments that drove the evolution of the disgust response. Humans in many WEIRD populations often consume pre-packaged, processed calorically dense foods, have little interaction with their environment while acquiring nutrients, have elevated sanitation and hygiene that prevents exposure to numerous microorganisms, and often use methods—hormonal or otherwise—to substantially limit number of offspring. These factors can dramatically affect biology, physiology, and psychology (Gurven & Lieberman, 2020) and could lead to very different patterns in disgust sensitivity.

This variation between current lifestyles and our evolved environments creates a mismatch that has resulted in the increase of multiple chronic disorders, including those related to increased hygiene and reduced pathogen exposure, like allergies, autoimmunity, and obsessive-compulsive disorder. These disorders are virtually nonexistent among forager populations and individuals living in low-income countries and regions (Abed & de Pauw, 1998; Blaser & Falkow, 2009; Okada et al., 2010; Stein et al., 2016) due to regular exposure to immune-priming pathogens in conjunction with limited access to hygiene/sanitation education, resources, and infrastructure. Currently, many subsistence-based populations are experiencing lifestyle changes associated with increased participation in market-based economies (i.e., market integration) that are altering environmental interactions, hygiene, and sanitation practices, leading to reduced pathogen exposure (Godoy et al., 2005). Studies on the variability, calibration, and adaptive utility of pathogen-driven emotions like disgust must look beyond WEIRD populations to fully understand evolutionary implications.

Little research on disgust has been conducted among subsistence-based, natural fertility populations with high pathogen burdens (i.e., conditions more similar to environments in which the disgust response is thought to have evolved) (Cepon-Robins et al., 2021; Robins, 2015). This kind of research is needed to accurately test hypotheses regarding variation in disgust sensitivity and whether disgust reduces pathogen exposure. This chapter briefly highlights current hypotheses regarding the adaptive nature, individual variation, and utility of the disgust response. It describes how currently published research may vary from proposed research in understudied populations, emphasizing why more multidisciplinary research is needed in various contexts. Finally, hypotheses about how disgust sensitivity may manifest and function in these contexts are described, and examples are provided to illustrate how these hypotheses can be tested using culturally relevant and minimally invasive methodologies.

The Evolution of Disgust as a Pathogen-Avoidance Mechanism

Disgust researchers generally agree that disgust is a universal human emotion that evolved to elicit avoidance of stimuli recurrently associated with pathogens and other interaction types linked with low expected fitness values (i.e., toxins, low-quality mates) (Ekman, 1992;

Lieberman et al., 2018). Previously, three domains of disgust were proposed: (1) pathogen disgust, associated with avoiding infectious substances; (2) sexual disgust, associated with avoiding fitness-reducing partners or sexual activities; and (3) moral disgust, associated with avoiding dishonest or harmful individuals (Lieberman et al., 2018; Tybur et al., 2009; Tybur et al., 2013). More recent research, however, suggests that all disgust categories may be associated with pathogen avoidance and the associated expected values of consumption or contact (Lieberman et al., 2018; Rozin et al., 2008), culminating in the adaptive problems of "what to touch," "what to eat," and "with whom to have sex" (Lieberman et al., 2018; Rottman, 2014).

While other factors may influence disgust (Lieberman et al., 2018), this chapter focuses on the role of pathogens in shaping the disgust response. Pathogens appear to be the primary selective pressure shaping disgust (Curtis et al., 2004; Curtis et al., 2011; Curtis & Biran, 2001; Fessler & Navarrete, 2003; Schaller, 2016; Schaller & Duncan, 2007; Tybur et al., 2009; Tybur et al., 2013), as well as many other facets of human biology, including the evolution of sexual reproduction, genetic variation, complex immune systems, and other potential adaptations against infection (Karlsson et al., 2014; Lieberman et al., 2018; Robins, 2015; Tooby, 1982). Pathogens have also shaped many aspects of human behavior and personality, including sickness behaviors, mating preferences, social openness, and religiosity (Ackerman et al., 2018; Fincher & Thornhill, 2012; Kavaliers & Choleris, 2018; Schaller & Murray, 2008; Schrock et al., 2020; Shattuck & Muehlenbein, 2015; Thornhill et al., 2010; Winternitz et al., 2017).

The disgust response functions as a "behavioral immune system," motivating avoidance of pathogens and acting as a barrier to infection (Ackerman et al., 2018; Schaller, 2011, 2016; Schaller & Duncan, 2007) by taking in environmental cues, processing potential costs/benefits of contact, and stimulating an avoidance response (Lieberman et al., 2018; Tybur et al., 2009; Tybur et al., 2013; Tybur & Lieberman, 2016). When disgust-eliciting stimuli are encountered and values of consumption or contact are low, the parasympathetic nervous system is activated, resulting in nausea, characteristic facial movements, and avoidance of the stimuli (Lieberman et al., 2018; Rottman, 2014; Tybur et al., 2018). Thus, if an encountered substance has recurrently been associated with pathogens in the past (e.g., bodily fluids, spoiled meats) or gives off cues associated with potential pathogens (e.g., foul odors, signs of infection, sickness behaviors), the disgust response should be triggered and avoidance behaviors should occur (Tybur et al., 2018). Interestingly, the disgust response also appears to stimulate immune function (Stevenson et al., 2012), which creates yet another barrier of protection against pathogens.

Pathogens are a highly variable and constantly adapting collection of organisms. Thus, the proposed disgust domains discussed above may be associated with specific kinds of pathogens and how they are encountered (Curtis & de Barra, 2018). For instance, sexually transmitted diseases (i.e., pathogens transferred through sexual activity) are more likely to be encountered during acts often connected with feelings of sexual disgust (Al-Shawaf et al., 2015). Foodborne illnesses or contagious diseases, on the other hand, are more often encountered in spoiled or contaminated food or through signals of sickness in other individuals, respectively, and would typically lead to avoidance of stimuli associated with pathogen disgust, or more specifically "what to eat" or "what to touch" (Lieberman et al., 2018). Other pathogens are vector-borne or zoonotic and may be associated with disgust toward relevant creatures (e.g., mosquitos, flies, rabid animals; Curtis & Biran, 2001).

In fact, cross-cultural research in Burkina Faso, India, the Netherlands, and the United Kingdom identified five more specific disgust categories: (1) "bodily excretions and body parts"; (2) "decay and spoiled food"; (3) "particular living creatures"; (4) "certain categories of 'other people'"; and (5) "violations of morality or social norms" (Curtis & Biran, 2001).

These categories appear to be associated with specific ways that pathogens are acquired. Thus, how a pathogen is transmitted will shape the kind of disgust elicitor associated with it. In other words, pathogens that spread through person-to-person contact cause cues in the form of bodily excretions (i.e., runny noses, coughing, vomit), while the presence of foodborne pathogens triggers the disgust response in association with foul odors or discolored food. Since pathogens are highly variable and environments differ substantially in which pathogens they contain, disgust sensitivity—both in general and to specific cues—should vary based on likelihood of encountering a particular pathogen in a given environment.

Cross-cultural evidence points to disgust as an evolved emotion that is present in all human populations (Apicella at al., 2018; Cepon-Robins et al., 2021; Curtis & Biran, 2001; Curtis et al., 2004; Ekman et al., 1987; Matsumoto & Ekman, 1989; Rozin et al., 2008; Tybur et al., 2018). For one, nonhuman primates exhibit pathogen-avoidance behaviors consistent with the disgust response (Sarabian et al., 2017), suggesting that the behaviors may have been present in the last common ancestor. In humans, the universality of the disgusted facial expression is the most commonly referenced evidence (Ekman et al., 1987; Matsumoto & Ekman, 1989; Rozin et al., 2008), although some cross-cultural analyses do question this (Jack et al., 2012). Further, the stimuli that trigger the disgust response appear to fall into similar categories regardless of study population (e.g., bodily fluids, contaminants, raw or spoiled foods, insect vectors), even if the exact stimuli vary from culture to culture (Curtis & Biran, 2001; Tybur et al., 2018). A survey of 40,000 internet users from 165 countries found that stimuli recurrently associated with potential disease threats were consistently rated as more disgusting (Curtis et al., 2004). Another study comparing contamination sensitivity between the Hadzabe (Hadza) foragers of Tanzania and the Tannese subsistence-agriculturalists of Vanuatu found that while stimuli associated with contamination varied culturally, there was a universal rejection response to contaminated items in both populations (Apicella et al., 2018). This is one of the few studies to examine disgust-related sensitivities outside WEIRD populations. While there is evidence to suggest that disgust is a universal human emotion that functions to stimulate pathogen avoidance, not enough cross-cultural research has been done in non-WEIRD populations to fully understand the extent of variation that exists and to test its utility in environments more similar to the environments in which the emotion evolved.

Variation in Human Disgust Sensitivity
Individuals vary in their disgust sensitivity, with some being more sensitive than others (Tybur et al., 2018). Disgust sensitivity is defined as an individual's predisposition toward experiencing the disgust emotion in response to relevant cues (Petrowski et al., 2010; Tybur et al., 2018) and ranges from high to low depending on numerous factors. This section highlights factors thought to contribute to variation in disgust sensitivity, including likelihood of environmental exposure to pathogens, age, biological sex, reproductive status, immunosuppression, and nutritional stress (Al-Shawaf & Lewis, 2013; Al-Shawaf et al., 2015; Curtis et al., 2004; Fessler et al., 2005; Fessler & Navarrete, 2003; Fleischman, 2014; Navarrete & Fessler, 2006; Oaten et al., 2009; Sherman & Flaxman, 2002; Tybur et al., 2009; Tybur & Lieberman, 2016).

Pathogens and Environmental Exposures
To be adaptive and beneficial in multiple environmental contexts, psychological mechanisms that confer protections must be flexible and allow for calibration based on context-specific cues (Al-Shawaf, Lewis, Wehbe, et al., 2019). Because disease environments (i.e., the likelihood of encountering pathogens and the types of pathogens encountered) varied throughout

the evolution of the disgust response, it follows that disgust sensitivity should be shaped by an individual's history of infection, learned experience with infective substances, and the current environmental threat associated with pathogen exposure (Schaller, 2011; Tybur et al., 2018). This allows individuals the ability to adapt to specific threats in the immediate environment more rapidly than relying solely on long-term evolutionary change. In support of this idea, research suggests that individuals with a history of illness from infectious diseases may have elevated disgust sensitivity (Stevenson et al., 2009); however, other studies show no connection between infection history and current disgust sensitivity (De Barra et al., 2014; Tybur et al., 2018). Evidence does suggest that evolved learning mechanisms are in place that allow humans and other animals to more readily associate some stimuli with adverse effects over others due to their evolutionary relevance, as is the case with the "Garcia effect" where rats can easily learn to associate nausea with some stimuli (e.g., food), but not others (e.g., lights and sounds; Al-Shawaf, Lewis, Wehbe, et al., 2019; Garcia & Koelling, 1966).

It has also been suggested that disgust sensitivity should be highest among populations living in high-disease environments, since it is in these environments that disgust would be most beneficial (Stevenson et al., 2009). A study comparing undergraduates in Ghana—a country with comparatively higher infectious disease burden—with undergraduates from the United States found that the Ghana sample had significantly higher disgust sensitivity (Skolnick & Dzokoto, 2013). Other studies have attempted to replicate this with larger and more diverse samples and have found no link between high infectious disease burden and elevated disgust sensitivity (Curtis et al., 2011; Tybur et al., 2016; Tybur et al., 2018). In fact, the opposite may be true, and repeat exposure to disgust-eliciting cues could instead result in reduced disgust sensitivity due to habituation (Fessler & Navarrete, 2005).

The lack of consistent support for disgust being highest in high-disease environments may demonstrate the complexity of factors that shape the disgust response. In environments where pathogens are difficult to avoid, for example, increased disgust sensitivity would do little to encourage avoidance and may reduce fitness by decreasing access to subsistence needs like food and sex (Cepon-Robins et al., 2021; Tybur et al., 2018). It is thus hypothesized that mechanisms exist to calibrate disgust sensitivity to the environment to create "functional flexibility" (Ackerman et al., 2018; Al-Shawaf, Lewis, Wehbe, et al., 2019; Tybur & Lieberman, 2016). Specifically, disgust sensitivity should fluctuate based on likelihood of encountering pathogens, the types of pathogens present in the environment, and the fitness-reducing costs associated with both exposure and avoidance (Thornhill et al., 2010; Tybur & Lieberman, 2016).

Evidence of heightened disgust sensitivity in countries with higher pathogen burdens may be related to problems with sampling that targets comparatively affluent individuals. Problematically, multi-country studies have largely targeted higher-income samples, either through internet outreach or through recruitment of university students (Skolnick & Dzokoto, 2013; Tybur et al., 2016). In these cases, when countries are compared, what we see is that countries with higher pathogen burdens have higher disgust sensitivity, but that may be because participants being sampled are those with access to hygienic and infrastructural means that they can use—when motived by their disgust sensitivity—to avoid infection. It is likely that within these countries, individuals of lower socioeconomic status than those typically measured in disgust studies do not have access to these same pathogen-avoidance tools and are consequently exposed to more pathogens. By necessity, these individuals may exhibit lower disgust sensitivity due to pathogen avoidance being more costly or impossible. For instance, without reliable electricity and food refrigeration, individuals will often eat food that has been stored at ambient temperature due to caloric need, even though this food may be close to spoiling and would not generally be consumed by individuals with access to more resources.

Disgust in this context might be reduced because it hinders acquiring needed nutrients, especially if the food shows no obvious signs of spoilage. In these cases, the risks associated with not consuming energy/nutrients may come at a higher cost than encountering pathogens (Tybur & Lieberman, 2016). Thus, high disgust sensitivity is most useful among people living in high-pathogen environments only if they have the means and ability to actively avoid those pathogens without avoidance hindering subsistence and survival (Cepon-Robins et al., 2021). For those who do not have the means of avoidance, high disgust sensitivity would be maladaptive.

This idea is best illustrated in populations living subsistence-based lifestyles in high-pathogen environments. Specifically, research among the Shuar of Ecuador found important relationships between market integration (i.e., production for and consumption from market-based economies) and pathogen disgust sensitivity (Cepon-Robins et al., 2021; Robins, 2015). The Shuar are an Indigenous Amazonian population living in an environment with documented high parasitic and bacterial/viral disease burdens (Cepon-Robins et al., 2014; Cepon-Robins et al., 2021; Gildner et al., 2020; Stagaman et al., 2018; Urlacher et al., 2018). Shuar typically participate in a range of subsistence activities (e.g., foraging, horticulture, hunting, fishing), but are also experiencing rapid and regionally variable integration into market-based economies (Gildner et al., 2020; Liebert et al., 2013; Urlacher et al., 2016). With this shift in subsistence comes a range of lifestyle-related changes, including alterations to housing structure, sanitation infrastructure, and access to medical care. These changes alter exposure to infectious diseases and pathogen-containing stimuli. Research among the Shuar found that higher levels of market integration within households and communities was associated with greater disgust sensitivity (Cepon-Robins et al., 2021; Robins, 2015). In general, market integration has been shown to reduce pathogen exposure through hygiene, sanitation, and infrastructural factors, including access to clean water sources, designated cleanable cooking surfaces, disease-avoidance education, and access to medical care (Campbell et al., 2014; Freeman et al., 2013; Gildner et al., 2020; Godoy et al., 2005).

Because the costs and benefits of pathogen exposure/avoidance shift throughout an individual's life, environmental calibration should be relatively short term. Market integration among the Shuar, for instance, is recent. Many adults living in more market-integrated communities grew up under much less market-integrated circumstances, usually relying entirely on subsistence activities like hunting, fishing, horticulture, and foraging during childhood (Cepon-Robins et al., 2021; Robins, 2015). The relationship between disgust sensitivity and market integration suggests that disgust sensitivity shifts with lifestyle and environmental change. If one must regularly touch dead animals or interact with potentially contaminated soil for subsistence, then it is not beneficial to be disgusted by these stimuli. However, as market integration occurs and lifestyles shift away from these activities, one can afford to upregulate disgust sensitivity and avoid associated stimuli without consequence for survival. More research on relationships between environmental and lifestyle change, infectious disease burden, and disgust in populations living in high-pathogen environments is needed to test these ideas.

Age-Related Variation
Age and associated variation in immune system development and function should also shape the cost/benefit ratio of pathogen avoidance. Disgust sensitivity appears to emerge by middle childhood (Curtis et al., 2004; Oaten et al., 2009; Rottman, 2014). Early in childhood, disgust sensitivity is low; young children are willing to put most objects in their mouths and

respond less robustly to disgust-eliciting stimuli until about 5 to 7 years of age (Rottman, 2014; Stevenson et al., 2010).

The lack of heightened disgust sensitivity in early childhood may be adaptive. During this time, pathogen exposure is extraordinarily important for immune system development (Jackson et al., 2009; Maizels et al., 2014; Okada et al., 2010; Strachan, 1989; von Mutius, 2007). This idea, called the Hygiene Hypothesis or the Old Friends Hypothesis, states that individuals who are exposed to more pathogens and parasites during childhood are less likely to develop disorders associated with immune system dysregulation (e.g., allergies, autoimmunity) later in life (Jackson et al., 2009; Maizels et al., 2014; Okada et al., 2010; Strachan, 1989; von Mutius, 2007). During early childhood, the willingness to interact with most substances and the desire to orally manipulate items in the environment, which older children and adults might find disgusting, may cultivate exposure to the pathogens needed to develop healthy immune systems. Thus, robust disgust responses in early childhood would be maladaptive and lead to health problems later in life, though more research is needed to test this hypothesis.

Some researchers have hypothesized that disgust should increase during older age, because older age tends to be associated with an increase in the perceived risk of infection as well as declines in overall health and immune function (Oaten et al., 2009). Food-related disgust sensitivity has been shown to increase with age (Egolf et al., 2018). Another study on adults in the United Kingdom, the United States, and Canada showed that hygiene disgust also rose with age (Curtis & de Barra, 2018). However, age-related increases in disgust sensitivity have not been observed for other disgust elicitors (Curtis & de Barra, 2018). In fact, most studies suggest that disgust declines with advanced age (Curtis et al., 2004; Fessler & Navarrete, 2005; Oaten et al., 2009). This is thought to be associated with diminishing reproductive value (Curtis et al., 2004), exposure-related desensitization, or energetic trade-offs in which the costs of avoidance no longer outweigh the benefits (Curtis et al., 2004; Fessler & Navarrete, 2005; Oaten et al., 2009).

In support of exposure-related desensitization as a mechanism for age-related variation, a cross-cultural study comparing the United States and rural Costa Rica found that disgust related to death declined with age (Fessler & Navarrete, 2005). The authors suggested that habituation may occur and reduce disgust sensitivity when repeated exposure has not proven hazardous in the past (Fessler & Navarrete, 2005). Though seemingly contradictory, food-related disgust sensitivity increasing with age may provide additional support (Egolf et al., 2018), as older adults may reduce their exposures to new foods (i.e., become less habituated to novel food items) as a way of avoiding potential toxins or pathogens. Food- and hygiene-related disgust sensitivity may both increase with age because these factors can easily be controlled by individuals in WEIRD populations. Future research should assess whether older adults in changing environments (e.g., from relocation, immigration, market integration) experience altered disgust sensitivity with age, to see if the patterns measured to date are associated with habituation or other possible life history trade-offs.

Sex and Reproductive Status-Related Variation

Biological sex and reproductive status/strategies have been associated with variation in disgust sensitivity. For instance, individuals who are more invested in pathogen avoidance tend to favor more monogamous mating strategies and oppose sexual relationships outside of pair bonds (Tybur et al., 2015). Further, individuals with a stronger orientation toward short-term mating exhibit lower sexual and pathogen disgust sensitivities (Al-Shawaf et al., 2015). These studies suggest that disgust sensitivity varies based on an individual's reproductive goals. Because males and females vary in their reproductive goals and overall investment from an evolutionary perspective, it is hypothesized that females should have higher disgust sensitivity due to higher costs of pathogen infection—a hypothesis that has been generally well supported (Al-Shawaf et al., 2015, 2018; Al-Shawaf & Lewis, 2013; Curtis et al., 2004; Curtis & de Barra, 2018; Egolf et al., 2018; Oaten et al., 2009; Tybur et al., 2009).

Variation based on reproductive goals and status may be calibrated by reproductive hormones (Fessler et al., 2005; Fessler & Navarrete, 2003; Fleischman & Fessler, 2011). The Compensatory Behavioral Prophylaxis Hypothesis states that disgust sensitivity should account for alterations in immune function associated with reproductive immunomodulation (Fessler et al., 2005; Fessler & Navarrete, 2003; Fleischman & Fessler, 2011; Miłkowska et al., 2021). For instance, progesterone, which is elevated during the luteal phase of the menstrual cycle and throughout pregnancy, is linked to down-regulated immune responses to promote implantation and support fetal growth and development (Fleischman & Fessler, 2011). It is thus hypothesized that progesterone should be linked to elevated disgust sensitivity. In general, salivary progesterone appears to be positively correlated with disgust sensitivity (Fleischman & Fessler, 2011). Disgust sensitivity has been shown to vary throughout the menstrual cycle (Fessler & Navarrete, 2003; Miłkowska et al., 2021), peaking during the luteal phase in conjunction with progesterone (Żelaźniewicz et al., 2016). In a web-based survey, disgust sensitivity was also shown to be elevated during the first trimester of pregnancy when progesterone rapidly increases (Fessler et al., 2005). However, another study that tracked changes in progesterone throughout the cycle while concomitantly measuring alterations in disgust sensitivity found no relationship between the two (Jones et al., 2018).

Reproductive hormone variation could theoretically also regulate disgust sensitivity in males. In fact, females tend to be more immunocompetent than males and testosterone may have immunosuppressive effects due to the energetic costs associated with maintaining high levels (Al-Shawaf, Lewis, Ghossainy, et al., 2019; Muehlenbein & Bribiescas, 2005; Nunn et al., 2009; Trumble et al., 2016), making males more susceptible to infections. Based on this difference, males with higher testosterone should have higher disgust sensitivity to offset their weaker immune function. While evidence suggests that higher testosterone is associated with a reduced ability to recognize disgust in others (Rukavina et al., 2018), little research exists on relationships between testosterone and disgust sensitivity in men. One study assessing the relationship between disgust sensitivity and testosterone levels in women found no relationship (Jones et al., 2018). This may be because WEIRD populations have more than enough energy to invest in reproduction and immune function and are thus less susceptible to trade-offs. Males with higher testosterone in an urban and suburban Polish sample were able to mount stronger immune responses to influenza vaccines, suggesting that trade-offs between immune function and reproductive hormones in males may be buffered by access to resources (Nowak et al., 2018).

The ideas discussed here point to the need for more research on disgust sensitivity in subsistence-based natural fertility populations. Reproductive hormones vary substantially between natural and non-natural fertility populations as a result of nutritional status, access to medical interventions like birth control, lifetime menstrual cycles and pregnancies, and other factors related to mating strategies. Specifically, females in natural fertility populations tend to have more lifetime pregnancies/births, fewer menstrual cycles, and long periods of intensive breastfeeding (Gurven et al., 2016; Natri et al., 2019). Studies have documented lower levels of reproductive hormone production in both females (Jasienska et al., 2017; Núñez-de la Mora et al., 2007) and males (Bribiescas, 2001; Ellison et al., 2002; Magid et al., 2018; Trumble et al., 2015) in natural fertility populations. These populations may also experience more substantial life history trade-offs associated with lower energy consumption and increased energy devoted to immune function and other parameters over reproductive hormone production (Ellison, 2008). Thus, if disgust sensitivity varies based on sex- and hormone-related immunomodulation, then these relationships should differ between natural and non-natural fertility populations.

Immunosuppression and Nutritional Stress

In general, disgust sensitivity should vary based on immune status. Individuals who are already immunocompromised (i.e., through illness, infection, psychosocial stress, nutritional stress) should have heightened disgust sensitivity (Al-Shawaf & Lewis, 2013; Glaser & Kiecolt-Glaser, 2005; Oaten et al., 2009) and increased motivation to avoid pathogen-containing substances. Yet, aside from during pregnancy (discussed above), little research has been done to see if disgust sensitivity varies among individuals who are immunocompromised. One study conducted among participants in the southwestern United States found that experiencing psychosocial stress (which is associated with immunosuppression) was related to higher disgust sensitivity (Al-Shawaf & Lewis, 2013). Beyond this, few studies have tested relationships between immunosuppression and disgust sensitivity, much less in populations that cannot rely on the buffering effects of medical intervention, sanitation infrastructure, and nutritionally dense foods.

Macroparasitic infections provide a special example to test relationships between infection, immunosuppression, and disgust sensitivity. Populations living in high-pathogen environments are often exposed to macroparasites, like soil-transmitted helminths (i.e., intestinal parasitic worms; Cepon-Robins et al., 2014; Gildner et al., 2020). These kinds of infections trigger a specific branch of the immune system that downregulates the immune system to encourage parasite tolerance (Maizels & McSorley, 2016; Schwartz et al., 2018). Ultimately, this leaves the host susceptible to other infectious disease agents, like bacteria and viruses (Maizels & McSorley, 2016). Limited preliminary research has shown that disgust sensitivity does not appear to be strongly related to soil-transmitted helminth avoidance among a subsistence-based population (Cepon-Robins et al., 2021). However, soil-transmitted helminth infection could theoretically upregulate disgust sensitivity to promote avoidance of bacterial and viral vectors, although this hypothesis needs further testing.

Further, some subsistence-based populations may be more susceptible to experiencing seasonal or chronic nutritional stress (Ellison, 2008; Jasienska & Ellison, 2004), which could calibrate disgust sensitivity based on current and future projections of caloric availability (Tybur et al., 2018). There are two ways that nutritional stress could affect disgust sensitivity. First, because the immediate need to consume calories may outweigh the benefits of avoiding pathogens, nutritional stress could downregulate disgust sensitivity to ensure sufficient caloric/nutrient consumption (Al-Shawaf, 2016). However, by both reducing calories available to mount an immune response and increasing susceptibility to illness, nutritional stress could upregulate disgust to protect against infection (Al-Shawaf, 2016). Studies have shown that participants experiencing hunger while engaging with disgust instruments showed reduced facial disgust expressions or lower disgust-sensitivity scores (Al-Shawaf & Lewis, 2013; Hoefling et al., 2009). These studies, however, examine short-term hunger (as opposed to chronic malnutrition) which, while indicative of perceived nutritional stress, may not capture long-term trade-offs in immune function.

Populations experiencing nutritional stress due to reduced caloric consumption, high energetic output, or elevated immune responses experience trade-offs in growth, development, and fecundity (Ellison, 2008; Jasienska & Ellison, 2004; Urlacher et al., 2018), which affects overall health and well-being. Reduced caloric consumption and/or elevated energy expenditure, even seasonally, produce trade-offs that downregulate reproductive functioning (i.e., halting ovulation and menstruation) in women by suppressing progesterone levels (Ellison, 1990, 2003, 2008; Ellison et al., 1993; Jasienska & Ellison, 2004; Vitzthum, 2009). Fluctuations in ovarian function associated with low energy intake and/or high energy expenditure have been documented in the Lese horticulturalists of Congo, the Tamang agropastoralists of Nepal, and rural Polish farmers (Ellison, 2008; Jasienska & Ellison, 2004). These kinds of trade-offs may send signals that would more intensely calibrate disgust sensitivity. However, whether extreme nutritional stress in these cases would downregulate disgust sensitivity overall to encourage food consumption, upregulate disgust sensitivity to promote pathogen avoidance, or downregulate disgust sensitivity toward some stimuli (e.g., food) while upregulating disgust toward others (e.g., bodily fluids) is unclear and untested (Al-Shawaf, 2016).

Complexity of Individual Variation in Disgust
Disgust sensitivity is complex, with evidence suggesting it is shaped by a combination of environmental calibration, individual experience, social/parental learning, and genetic programming (Davey et al., 1993; Kalyva et al., 2010; Rottman, 2014; Stevenson et al., 2010; Tybur et al., 2020). Disgust sensitivity appears to vary within and between individuals based on numerous overlapping environmental, reproductive, and life-history parameters that help determine the costs and benefits of interacting with certain substances and individuals (Lieberman et al., 2018). In general, disgust sensitivity appears to conform to a broader behavioral prophylaxis hypothesis (Al-Shawaf & Lewis, 2013), in which factors related to sex, satiation, and stress are all intricately connected in calibrating disgust sensitivity. Still, variation in disgust sensitivity in subsistence-based natural fertility populations living in high-pathogen environments (i.e., environments more like those in which disgust is thought to have evolved) remains poorly understood.

Evidence for the Utility of the Disgust Response
While limited research has explored variation in disgust sensitivity outside WEIRD populations, even fewer studies have tested the downstream effects of disgust sensitivity on pathogen avoidance. Multiple studies show that disgust changes with cues of potential pathogen-harboring stimuli (Curtis et al., 2004; Curtis & Biran, 2001; Oaten et al., 2009; Tybur et al., 2009), but only a few preliminary studies exist that test the adaptive benefit of this mechanism for lowering infection prevalence and intensity (Cepon-Robins et al., 2021; de Barra et al., 2014; Robins, 2015; Stevenson et al., 2009). Thus, while it is hypothesized that higher disgust sensitivity should reduce likelihood of infection (Curtis et al., 2004; Tybur & Lieberman, 2016), little is known about whether or not it actually does.

Limited research on the utility of the disgust response for avoiding infection has produced mixed results. In support, a study among university students from Australia found that individuals who had higher disgust sensitivity reported fewer recent infections (Stevenson et al., 2009). A previously discussed study among the Ecuadorian Shuar found that disgust sensitivity was associated with lower levels of biomarkers related to current immune response to bacterial or viral infection (Cepon-Robins et al., 2021). Among the Shuar, higher disgust sensitivity was also associated with reduced exposure to soil-transmitted helminths (Cepon-Robins et al., 2021; Robins, 2015), but that effect was mediated by community-level variation, likely associated with environmental differences and market integration. By contrast, other studies examining the relationship between disgust sensitivity and infection found no connections. For instance, a study in rural Bangladesh found no relationship between childhood infectious disease burden reported in childhood health data and adult levels of disgust sensitivity (de Barra et al., 2014). However, this is not surprising because there were decades between health history information and measured disgust sensitivity.

Beyond exposure to pathogens and parasites, disgust sensitivity could alter exposure to other important symbionts. Because disgust sensitivity is associated with avoidance of substances recurrently associated with pathogens, it is possible that in areas where pathogens are easily avoided due to hygiene/sanitation measures, high disgust sensitivity could be linked to reduced gut microbiota diversity. Evidence suggests that increased market integration is associated with both reduced intestinal microbiota diversity (Blaser & Falkow, 2009; Fragiadakis et al., 2019; Obregon-Tito et al., 2015; Stagaman et al., 2018) and increased disgust sensitivity (Cepon-Robins et al., 2021; Robins, 2015). This warrants further study, as a healthy and diverse intestinal microbiota is critical for proper immune system development and function, as well as digestion (Blaser & Falkow, 2009; Hooper et al., 2012). This is yet another way that heightened disgust sensitivity could be linked to mismatch disorders in WEIRD populations, as gut dysbiosis and a lack of exposure to important microbes and parasites has been linked to disorders related to immune system dysregulation, like allergies, asthma, and autoimmunity (Blaser & Falkow, 2009; Kim et al., 2016). Without testing relationships between disgust and disease avoidance in high-pathogen environments, however, we cannot fully understand how environmental and lifestyle changes have affected these health-related outcomes in WEIRD populations. More research is needed to test the utility of the disgust response in protecting against pathogen exposure, as well as to understand if heightened disgust sensitivity combined with increased ease of avoidance is associated with downstream health problems.

The Need for Multidisciplinary Approaches to Understanding Disgust
With only a handful of exceptions (e.g., Apicella et al., 2018; de Barra et al., 2014; Cepon-Robins et al., 2021; Fessler & Navarrete, 2005; Robins, 2015), the research discussed in this chapter has been conducted among WEIRD or generally high-income populations. More research on disgust is needed among non-WEIRD populations, especially subsistence-based natural fertility populations living in environments characterized by high infectious disease burdens. Importantly, many of these populations are experiencing rapid social and economic change associated with increasing market integration, which creates the opportunity to test hypotheses centered around variation in disgust sensitivity associated with lifestyle change and environmental calibration (Cepon-Robins et al., 2021; Robins, 2015).

Studies on emotion and psychology among these understudied populations are important for a more holistic understanding of human psychology. Studies conducted among Indigenous populations in Paraguay (Ache) and Bolivia (Tsimane) found that models used to measure neuroticism and the other five commonly measured personality traits were a poor fit either because of variation in personality among these populations or because of poor translatability of the instruments (Bailey et al., 2013; Gurven et al., 2013; Smaldino et al., 2019). These studies conclude that personality is likely not structured the same way universally, and instead variation may be based on niche diversity (Smaldino et al., 2019), making tests of evolved emotion and behavior in non-WEIRD populations crucial to a more holistic understanding of the human condition.

Greater methodological and theoretical synthesis, especially between human population biology and evolutionary psychology, can lead to studies that thoroughly explore the cognitive mechanisms, behavioral responses, and downstream effects of disgust sensitivity while accounting for variation within and between human populations. Methods used to measure disgust sensitivity, like free-listing, questionnaires/interviews, and visual and olfactory induction and response, are available (Al-Shawaf, Lewis, Ghossainy, et al., 2019; Culpepper et al.,

2018; Curtis et al., 2004; Haidt et al., 1994; Olatunji et al., 2007). However, because these were first designed and implemented in WEIRD populations, these instruments need to be reworked to be culturally relevant to the sample and translated into the appropriate languages (Cepon-Robins et al., 2021; Robins, 2015).

Measures of lifestyle can be obtained through interviews and may be important for answering questions related to the disgust response. For instance, level of market integration and household structure can be assessed using the Material Style of Life (M-SOL) survey (Bindon et al., 1997), which can be modified for use in multiple population-specific contexts (e.g., Gildner et al., 2020; Leonard et al., 2002; Liebert et al., 2013; Urlacher et al., 2016). Reproductive history questionnaires can be useful for tracking births, breastfeeding duration, and menstrual cycling (e.g., Madimenos et al., 2012). Health history questionnaires can assess past illness, as well as information about immune status and other important contributors to disgust sensitivity (e.g., Stevenson et al., 2009).

Further, finding and validating biomarkers collected using minimally invasive methods that can be used to measure health, hormone levels, stress, and behavior in field settings have become an important pursuit within human population biology (Eick, Cepon-Robins, et al., 2020; Eick, Madimenos, et al., 2020; McDade et al., 2004; McDade et al., 2007; Miller & McDade, 2012; Valeggia, 2007). The sample types that can be collected include whole blood via venipuncture, finger-prick blood spots stored on filter paper (i.e., dried blood spots [DBS]), and urine, saliva, and stool samples, which vary in their invasiveness to participants, biohazard exposure risk, storage needs, and stability. Whole blood samples are the most invasive and carry the highest risk of biohazard exposure, followed by finger-prick blood sampling. Various researchers have detailed the pros and cons of these sample types (e.g., Cepon-Robins, 2021; Gildner, 2021; Vitzthum, 2020).

Example biomarkers that may be relevant to disgust based on the discussion within this chapter include markers of immune function and reproductive hormones. Immune-related biomarkers that may be relevant to disgust and have already been measured in field settings include: (1) markers of innate immune activity and inflammation (e.g., C-reactive protein [CRP], Interleukin-6 [IL-6]); (2) levels of leukocytes (i.e., white blood cells) and lymphocytes (e.g., B-cells and T-cells); and (3) markers of adaptive immune responses to bacterial, viruses, and macroparasites (e.g., immunoglobulins E, G, and M [IgE; IgG; IgM]) (e.g., Blackwell et al., 2016; Cepon-Robins et al., 2021; Sorensen et al., 2006; Urlacher et al., 2018). Relevant reproductive hormones that have been measured in these settings include testosterone, progesterone, and estradiol, among others (e.g., Ellison et al., 2002; Gildner, 2021; Muehlenbein & Bribiescas, 2005; Trumble et al., 2016; Vitzthum, 2020). Markers of infection that have been measured among relevant populations that may be tested in association with disgust sensitivity include soil-transmitted infection status and species-specific infection intensity, as well as intestinal microbiota diversity (e.g., Blackwell et al., 2015; Cepon-Robins et al., 2014; Cepon-Robins et al., 2019; Filippo et al., 2010; Gildner et al., 2020; Obregon-Tito et al., 2015; Stagaman et al., 2018; Tanner et al., 2009). Markers of immune function can also be extended to account for some types of infections (e.g., Cepon-Robins et al., 2021).

Hypotheses Needing Testing Outside WEIRD Environments

Research among subsistence-based natural fertility populations living in high-pathogen environments is needed if we want to fully understand the evolved nature of the disgust response. This section presents relevant hypotheses (and possible ways to test them) that stem from our understanding of the disgust response in WEIRD populations, combined with our knowledge of relevant variations in environment, lifestyle, and health/biology in many non-WEIRD populations.

Hypothesis 1: Disgust Sensitivity Should Be Highest among Individuals Living in High-Pathogen Environments Who Have the Greatest Means to Avoid Pathogens

For some Indigenous and marginalized populations, hygiene measures and infrastructure are less available to prevent infection, and thus disgust sensitivity and avoidance behaviors should theoretically play a larger role in pathogen avoidance (Tybur & Lieberman, 2016). These populations, as discussed above, may also be less able to avoid particular pathogen-containing stimuli, especially if those stimuli must be encountered regularly for subsistence (Tybur & Lieberman, 2016). For these reasons, we would expect to see the highest disgust sensitivity among individuals living in high-pathogen environments who have the greatest ability to avoid disgust-eliciting stimuli. On the other hand, we would expect those without the means of avoidance to have the lowest disgust sensitivity. While these hypotheses have been supported recently in preliminary work among the Shuar of Ecuador (Cepon-Robins et al., 2021), more research is needed to further support these ideas, as well as to understand why this calibration occurs, whether it be through social learning, adaptive psychological responses, systematic desensitization, or some combination of factors.

These hypotheses can be tested using disgust instruments and M-SOL surveys modified for use with the population being researched. Focusing on populations undergoing rapid social and economic change associated with market integration would provide the best opportunity to test environmental calibration of the disgust response within a single population. As populations transition from subsistence based to market integrated, we should see levels of disgust sensitivity increase as means of pathogen avoidance increase.

Hypothesis 2: Disgust Sensitivity in Children Should Start to Increase Once the Adaptive Immune System Begins to Mature

Very young children typically have very low disgust sensitivity (Curtis et al., 2004; Oaten et al., 2009; Rottman, 2014), which may be adaptive to ensure proper pathogen exposure to stimulate immune system development in association with the hygiene/old friends hypotheses (Jackson et al., 2009; Maizels et al., 2014; Okada et al., 2010; Strachan, 1989; von Mutius, 2007). Evidence among the Shuar suggests an age-related transition between innate inflammatory immune responses measured using CRP and adaptive immune responses measured using IgE, with a decrease in CRP throughout childhood and a rapid increase in IgE during the first five years of life (Blackwell et al., 2010). During those early years of immune-system development, children may have low disgust sensitivity to promote necessary exposure to immune-priming pathogens.

Researchers seeking to test this hypothesis in populations with relatively high rates of infectious disease exposure could use disgust instruments combined with age data and CRP/IgE measures to see if elevated disgust sensitivity emerges as the immune system develops. Biomarkers should be measured in conjunction with disgust and age data, as trade-offs in innate/adaptive immunity should vary by population depending on pathogen exposure patterns (Blackwell et al., 2011). Longitudinal studies could also measure these relationships in cohorts of children as their immune systems develop and mature.

Hypothesis 3: As Individuals Age, Disgust Sensitivity Should Decline in Unchanging Environments Based on Habituation; However, It Should Be Elevated Again, at Least Temporarily, as Environments Shift

Despite the general hypothesis that disgust sensitivity should be elevated in older adults, with the exception of food and hygiene disgust, disgust sensitivity has generally been shown to decrease with age in WEIRD populations (Curtis et al., 2004; Egolf et al., 2018; Fessler & Navarrete, 2005; Oaten et al., 2009). Whether disgust declines with age has not been tested in populations experiencing rapid lifestyle change associated with market integration, which could prove useful for understanding whether or not this decline in disgust sensitivity with age is universal and if it is due to habituation, as has been suggested (Fessler & Navarrete, 2005). Studies in populations undergoing rapid market integration could reveal whether disgust remains high or increases among adults experiencing substantial environmental change. This hypothesis could be tested using disgust instruments, M-SOL surveys, and age data. Longitudinal studies could assess age-related changes in disgust sensitivity in cohorts of older adults.

Hypothesis 4: Disgust Sensitivity Should Be Highest (or Lowest) among Individuals Experiencing Immunosuppression or Nutritional Stress

Research in WEIRD populations suggests that disgust sensitivity is increased in association with immunosuppression and nutritional stress (Al-Shawaf & Lewis, 2013; Glaser & Kiecolt-Glaser, 2005; Hoefling et al., 2009; Oaten et al., 2009; Tybur et al., 2018). This idea has not been tested among populations who are immunosuppressed due to high macroparasite loads or who are experiencing levels of nutritional stress that cause substantial life history trade-offs. Testing whether disgust sensitivity is elevated (or lowered) based on these factors is important for understanding how nutritional stress and/or threats to immune function affect disgust sensitivity. Because both factors suppress immune function, pathogen avoidance is important and disgust sensitivity should be increased. However, because they are both also associated with nutritional scarcity, disgust sensitivity may be downregulated to increase access to food. Perhaps in these cases, disgust sensitivity to non-food items should increase while sensitivity to food items decreases to encourage both disease avoidance and nutrient consumption (Al-Shawaf, 2016).

This hypothesis can be tested using disgust instruments combined with markers of infection. Soil-transmitted helminth infection would be ideal to examine in this context because of prevalence and ability to alter immune function. Levels of biomarkers like CRP, IL-6, IgE (and other immunoglobulins), leukocytes, and lymphocytes can be used to assess current or recent infection status and to test relationships between infection, immunosuppression, and disgust sensitivity. Similarly, biomarkers like ghrelin (a hormone associated with increased hunger) and leptin (a hormone associated with satiation) could be measured in association with measures of disgust sensitivity (MacCormack & Muscatell, 2019) to see how short-term and long-term fluctuations in experiencing hunger affect the disgust response. Further, disgust sensitivity could also be measured in populations that experience seasonal nutritional stress to determine if disgust sensitivity increases, decreases, or remains the same during periods of resource scarcity or increased energy output. Measures associated with malnutrition could also be observed, including anthropometric evidence of slowed growth (Urlacher et al., 2018) and stunting/wasting in children (Briend et al., 2015), as well as levels of biomarkers of nutritional status and renal functioning (e.g., hemoglobin, vitamin D25, calcium, urea; Felder et al., 2016; Thakur et al., 2014).

Hypothesis 5: Higher Disgust Sensitivity Should Be Associated with Reduced Evidence of Pathogen Infection

Disgust sensitivity likely evolved to protect against pathogen exposure by motivating avoidance of pathogen-containing substances (Curtis et al., 2004; Curtis & Biran, 2001; Oaten et al., 2009; Tybur et al., 2009) and, to some degree, stimulating immune responses to fight off infections (Stevenson et al., 2012). However, whether higher disgust sensitivity reduces infection risk has been understudied, especially in populations living in environments with high pathogen burdens. To date, the only research to test this in a subsistence population documented markers of parasite infection (e.g., soil-transmitted helminth infection presence, species-specific intensity, and the biomarker IgE) and biomarkers of immune responses to bacterial/viral infections (e.g., CRP, IL-6) in conjunction with disgust questionnaires (Cepon-Robins et al., 2021; Robins, 2015). Results were promising, with elevated disgust sensitivity associated with lower levels of inflammatory biomarkers related to infection. Studies focused on testing this hypothesis could use similar methods and could also explore other biomarkers of infection (e.g., IgG, IgM) as well as microbiota diversity to determine if these markers of pathogen/microbe exposure are reduced in individuals with higher disgust sensitivity.

Conclusions

This chapter has highlighted ways that disgust sensitivity varies within WEIRD populations. It revealed how and why these factors may further vary outside WEIRD contexts and provided examples of methods that can be used to test disgust-related hypotheses in subsistence-based natural fertility populations living in high-pathogen environments. Studies that examine disgust sensitivity in these environments (i.e., environments more similar to those in which disgust evolved) are needed now more than ever, as many populations transition to more market-integrated lifestyles that will alter disgust sensitivity. Understanding how reproductive hormone and fertility patterns, seasonal or chronic nutritional stress, and high-pathogen environments shape the human disgust response is crucial for understanding the evolved nature of the emotion. Comparing disgust data from these populations to data already gathered in WEIRD populations could reveal which elements of the disgust response are universal and whether the disgust response functions as hypothesized (i.e., to reduce exposure to fitness-reducing substances or individuals recurrently associated with pathogens throughout human evolution). Further, this work promises to reveal important evolutionary implications about changes in human lifestyle that may be contributing to immune-related (i.e., allergy and autoimmunity) and psychological (i.e., obsessive-compulsive disorder) disorders observed in WEIRD populations. This research may make important connections between evolved psychological mechanisms and human health outcomes.

Note

1. It is important to note that the "WEIRD" and "non-WEIRD" designations potentially create a false dichotomy, and each contains highly variable and often overlapping combinations of lifestyles and behaviors. This chapter focuses on the aspects of so-called WEIRD lifestyles associated with calorie-rich diets, reduced infectious disease exposure, elevated reproductive hormone levels, and contraceptive-altered fertility. Not all WEIRD populations are characterized by these factors, and many non-WEIRD populations are experiencing some or all of these factors. The inaccuracy and limitations of this label, especially "Western," has been recognized elsewhere (Fuentes, 2022).

References

Abed, R. T., & de Pauw, K. W. (1998). An evolutionary hypothesis for obsessive compulsive disorder: A psychological immune system? *Behavioural Neurology*, *11*(4), 245–250.
Ackerman, J. M., Hill, S. E., & Murray, D. R. (2018). The behavioral immune system: Current concerns and future directions. *Social and Personality Psychology Compass*, *12*(2), e12371. https://doi.org/10.1111/spc3.12371
Al-Shawaf, L. (2016). The evolutionary psychology of hunger. *Appetite*, *105*, 591–595. https://doi.org/10.1016/j.appet.2016.06.021
Al-Shawaf, L., & Lewis, D. M. G. (2013). Exposed intestines and contaminated cooks: Sex, stress, & satiation predict disgust sensitivity. *Personality and Individual Differences*, *54*(6), 698–702. https://doi.org/10.1016/j.paid.2012.11.016

Al-Shawaf, L., Lewis, D. M. G., & Buss, D. M. (2015). Disgust and mating strategy. *Evolution and Human Behavior, 36*(3), 199–205. https://doi.org/10.1016/j.evolhumbehav.2014.11.003

Al-Shawaf, L., Lewis, D. M. G., & Buss, D. M. (2018). Sex differences in disgust: Why are women more easily disgusted than men? *Emotion Review, 10*(2), 149–160. https://doi.org/10.1177/1754073917709940

Al-Shawaf, L., Lewis, D. M. G., Ghossainy, M., & Buss, D. (2019). Experimentally inducing disgust reduces desire for short-term mating. *Evolutionary Psychology Science, 5*, 267–275. https://doi.org/10.1007/S40806-018-0179-Z

Al-Shawaf, L., Lewis, D. M. G., Wehbe, Y. S., & Buss, D. M. (2019). Context, environment, and learning in evolutionary psychology. In T. K. Shackelford & V. A. Weekes-Shackelford (Eds.), *Encyclopedia of evolutionary psychological science* (pp. 1–12). Springer International. https://doi.org/10.1007/978-3-319-16999-6_227-1

Apicella, C. L., Rozin, P., Busch, J. T. A., Watson-Jones, R. E., & Legare, C. H. (2018). Evidence from hunter-gatherer and subsistence agricultural populations for the universality of contagion sensitivity. *Evolution and Human Behavior, 39*(3), 355–363. https://doi.org/10.1016/j.evolhumbehav.2018.03.003

Bailey, D. H., Walker, R. S., Blomquist, G. E., Hill, K. R., Hurtado, A. M., & Geary, D. C. (2013). Heritability and fitness correlates of personality in the Ache, a natural-fertility population in Paraguay. *PLoS ONE, 8*(3), e59325. https://doi.org/10.1371/journal.pone.0059325

Bindon, J. R., Knight, A., Dressler, W. W., & Crews, D. E. (1997). Social context and psychosocial influences on blood pressure among American Samoans. *American Journal of Physical Anthropology, 103*(1), 7–18. https://doi.org/10.1002/(SICI)1096-8644(199705)103:1<7::AID-AJPA2>3.0.CO;2-U

Blackwell, A. D., Gurven, M. D., Sugiyama, L. S., Madimenos, F. C., Liebert, M. A., Martin, M. A., Kaplan, H. S., & Snodgrass, J. J. (2011). Evidence for a peak shift in a humoral response to helminths: Age profiles of IgE in the Shuar of Ecuador, the Tsimane of Bolivia, and the U.S. NHANES. *PLOS Neglected Tropical Diseases, 5*(6), e1218. https://doi.org/10.1371/journal.pntd.0001218

Blackwell, A. D., Snodgrass, J. J., Madimenos, F. C., & Sugiyama, L. S. (2010). Life history, immune function, and intestinal helminths: Trade-offs among immunoglobulin E, C-reactive protein, and growth in an Amazonian population. *American Journal of Human Biology, 22*(6), 836–848. https://doi.org/10.1002/ajhb.21092

Blackwell, A. D., Tamayo, M. A., Beheim, B., Trumble, B. C., Stieglitz, J., Hooper, P. L., Martin, M., Kaplan, H., & Gurven, M. (2015). Helminth infection, fecundity, and age of first pregnancy in women. *Science, 350*(6263), 970–972. https://doi.org/10.1126/science.aac7902

Blackwell, A. D., Trumble, B. C., Suarez, I. M., Stieglitz, J., Beheim, B., Snodgrass, J. J., Kaplan, H., & Gurven, M. (2016). Immune function in Amazonian horticulturalists. *Annals of Human Biology, 43*(4), 1–45. https://doi.org/10.1080/03014460.2016.1189963

Blaser, M. J., & Falkow, S. (2009). What are the consequences of the disappearing human microbiota? *Nature Reviews Microbiology, 7*(12), 887–894. https://doi.org/10.1038/nrmicro2245

Bribiescas, R. G. (2001). Reproductive ecology and life history of the human male. *American Journal of Physical Anthropology, 116*(S33), 148–176. https://doi.org/10.1002/ajpa.10025

Briend, A., Khara, T., & Dolan, C. (2015). Wasting and stunting—similarities and differences: Policy and programmatic implications. *Food and Nutrition Bulletin, 36*(Suppl 1), S15–S23. https://doi.org/10.1177/15648265150361S103

Campbell, S. J., Savage, G. B., Gray, D. J., Atkinson, J.-A. M., Magalhães, R. J. S., Nery, S. V., McCarthy, J. S., Velleman, Y., Wicken, J. H., Traub, R. J., Williams, G. M., Andrews, R. M., & Clements, A. C. A. (2014). Water, sanitation, and hygiene (WASH): A critical component for sustainable soil-transmitted helminth and schistosomiasis control. *PLOS Neglected Tropical Diseases, 8*(4), e2651. https://doi.org/10.1371/journal.pntd.0002651

Cepon-Robins, T. J. (2021). Measuring attack on self: The need for field-friendly methods development and research on autoimmunity in human biology. *American Journal of Human Biology, 33*(1), e23544. https://doi.org/10.1002/ajhb.23544

Cepon-Robins, T. J., Blackwell, A. D., Gildner, T. E., Liebert, M. A., Urlacher, S. S., Madimenos, F. C., Eick, G. N., Snodgrass, J. J., & Sugiyama, L. S. (2021). Pathogen disgust sensitivity protects against infection in a high pathogen environment. *Proceedings of the National Academy of Sciences, 118*(8), e2018552118. https://doi.org/10.1073/pnas.2018552118

Cepon-Robins, T. J., Gildner, T. E., Schrock, J., Eick, G., Bedbury, A., Liebert, M. A., Urlacher, S. S., Madimenos, F. C., Harrington, C. J., Amir, D., Bribiescas, R. G., Sugiyama, L. S., & Snodgrass, J. J. (2019). Soil-transmitted helminth infection and intestinal inflammation among the Shuar of Amazonian Ecuador. *American Journal of Physical Anthropology, 170*(1), 65–74. https://doi.org/10.1002/ajpa.23897

Cepon-Robins, T. J., Liebert, M. A., Gildner, T. E., Urlacher, S. S., Colehour, A. M., Snodgrass, J. J., Madimenos, F. C., & Sugiyama, L. S. (2014). Soil-transmitted helminth prevalence and infection intensity among geographically and economically distinct Shuar communities in the Ecuadorian Amazon. *Journal of Parasitology, 100*(5), 598–607. https://doi.org/10.1645/13-383.1

Culpepper, P. D., Havlíček, J., Leongómez, J. D., & Roberts, S. C. (2018). Visually activating pathogen disgust: A new instrument for studying the behavioral immune system. *Frontiers in Psychology, 9*, e1397. https://doi.org/10.3389/fpsyg.2018.01397

Curtis, V., Aunger, R., & Rabie, T. (2004). Evidence that disgust evolved to protect from risk of disease. *Proceedings of the Royal Society B: Biological Sciences, 271*(Suppl 4), S131–S133.

Curtis, V., & Biran, A. (2001). Dirt, disgust, and disease: Is hygiene in our genes? *Perspectives in Biology and Medicine, 44*(1), 17–31. https://doi.org/10.1353/pbm.2001.0001

Curtis, V., & de Barra, M. (2018). The structure and function of pathogen disgust. *Philosophical Transactions of the Royal Society B: Biological Sciences, 373*(1751), e20170208. https://doi.org/10.1098/rstb.2017.0208

Curtis, V., de Barra, M., & Aunger, R. (2011). Disgust as an adaptive system for disease avoidance behaviour. *Philosophical Transactions of the Royal Society B: Biological Sciences, 366*(1568), 1320. https://doi.org/10.1098/rstb.2011.0002

Darwin, C. (1872). *Expression of emotion in man and animals*. D. Appleton. http://www.online-literature.com/darwin/expression-of-emotion/11/

Davey, G. C. L., Forster, L., & Mayhew, G. (1993). Familial resemblances in disgust sensitivity and animal phobias. *Behaviour Research and Therapy, 31*(1), 41–50. https://doi.org/10.1016/0005-7967(93)90041-R

de Barra, M., Islam, M. S., & Curtis, V. (2014). Disgust sensitivity is not associated with health in a rural Bangladeshi sample. *PLoS ONE, 9*(6), e100444. https://doi.org/10.1371/journal.pone.0100444

Egolf, A., Siegrist, M., & Hartmann, C. (2018). How people's food disgust sensitivity shapes their eating and food behaviour. *Appetite, 127*, 28–36. https://doi.org/10.1016/j.appet.2018.04.014

Eick, G. N., Cepon-Robins, T. J., Devlin, M. J., Kowal, P., Sugiyama, L. S., & Snodgrass, J. J. (2020). Development and validation of an ELISA for a biomarker of thyroid dysfunction, thyroid peroxidase autoantibodies (TPO-Ab), in dried blood spots. *Journal of Physiological Anthropology, 39*(1), 16. https://doi.org/10.1186/s40101-020-00228-8

Eick, G. N., Madimenos, F. C., Cepon-Robins, T. J., Devlin, M. J., Kowal, P., Sugiyama, L. S., & Snodgrass, J. J. (2020). Validation of an enzyme-linked immunoassay assay for osteocalcin, a marker of bone formation, in dried blood spots. *American Journal of Human Biology, 32*(5), e23394. https://doi.org/10.1002/ajhb.23394

Ekman, P. (1992). Are there basic emotions? *Psychological Review, 99*(3), 550. https://doi.org/10.1037/0033-295X.99.3.550

Ekman, P., Friesen, W. V., O'Sullivan, M., Chan, A., Diacoyanni-Tarlatzis, I., Heider, K., Krause, R., LeCompte, W. A., Pitcairn, T., & Ricci-Bitti, P. E. (1987). Universals and cultural differences in the judgments of facial expressions of emotion. *Journal of Personality and Social Psychology, 53*(4), 712–717. https://doi.org/10.1037//0022-3514.53.4.712

Ellison, P. (2008). Energetics, reproductive ecology, and human evolution. *PaleoAnthropology, 2008*, 172–200. https://dash.harvard.edu/handle/1/2643116

Ellison, P. T. (1990). Human ovarian function and reproductive ecology: New hypotheses. *American Anthropologist, 92*(4), 933–952. https://doi.org/10.1525/aa.1990.92.4.02a00050

Ellison, P. T. (2003). Energetics and reproductive effort. *American Journal of Human Biology, 15*(3), 342–351. https://doi.org/10.1002/ajhb.10152

Ellison, P. T., Bribiescas, R. G., Bentley, G. R., Campbell, B. C., Lipson, S. F., Panter-Brick, C., & Hill, K. (2002). Population variation in age-related decline in male salivary testosterone. *Human Reproduction (Oxford, England), 17*(12), 3251–3253. https://doi.org/10.1093/humrep/17.12.3251

Ellison, P. T., Panter-Brick, C., Lipson, S. F., & O'Rourke, M. T. (1993). The ecological context of human ovarian function. *Human Reproduction (Oxford, England), 8*(12), 2248–2258. https://doi.org/10.1093/oxfordjournals.humrep.a138015

Felder, S., Braun, N., Stanga, Z., Kulkarni, P., Faessler, L., Kutz, A., Steiner, D., Laukemann, S., Haubitz, S., Huber, A., Mueller, B., & Schuetz, P. (2016). Unraveling the link between malnutrition and adverse clinical outcomes: Association of acute and chronic malnutrition measures with blood biomarkers from different pathophysiological states. *Annals of Nutrition and Metabolism, 68*(3), 164–172. https://doi.org/10.1159/000444096

Fessler, D. M. T., Eng, S. J., & Navarrete, C. D. (2005). Elevated disgust sensitivity in the first trimester of pregnancy. *Evolution and Human Behavior, 26*(4), 344–351. https://doi.org/10.1016/j.evolhumbehav.2004.12.001

Fessler, D. M. T., & Navarrete, C. D. (2003). Domain-specific variation in disgust sensitivity across the menstrual cycle. *Evolution and Human Behavior, 24*(6), 406–417. https://doi.org/10.1016/S1090-5138(03)00054-0

Fessler, D. M. T., & Navarrete, C. D. (2005). The effect of age on death disgust: Challenges to terror management perspectives. *Evolutionary Psychology, 3*(1), 147470490500300130. https://doi.org/10.1177/147470490500300120

Filippo, C. D., Cavalieri, D., Paola, M. D., Ramazzotti, M., Poullet, J. B., Massart, S., Collini, S., Pieraccini, G., & Lionetti, P. (2010). Impact of diet in shaping gut microbiota revealed by a comparative study in children from

Europe and rural Africa. *Proceedings of the National Academy of Sciences, 107*(33), 14691–14696. https://doi.org/10.1073/pnas.1005963107

Fincher, C. L., & Thornhill, R. (2012). Parasite-stress promotes in-group assortative sociality: The cases of strong family ties and heightened religiosity. *The Behavioral and Brain Sciences, 35*(2), 61–79. https://doi.org/10.1017/S0140525X11000021

Fleischman, D. S. (2014). Women's disgust adaptations. In Viviana A. Weekes-Shackelford & Todd K. Shackelford (Eds.), *Evolutionary perspectives on human sexual psychology and behavior* (pp. 277–296). Springer Science + Business Media. https://doi.org/10.1007/978-1-4939-0314-6_15

Fleischman, D. S., & Fessler, D. M. T. (2011). Progesterone's effects on the psychology of disease avoidance: Support for the compensatory behavioral prophylaxis hypothesis. *Hormones and Behavior, 59*(2), 271–275. https://doi.org/10.1016/j.yhbeh.2010.11.014

Fragiadakis, G. K., Smits, S. A., Sonnenburg, E. D., Van Treuren, W., Reid, G., Knight, R., Manjurano, A., Changalucha, J., Dominguez-Bello, M. G., Leach, J., & Sonnenburg, J. L. (2019). Links between environment, diet, and the hunter-gatherer microbiome. *Gut Microbes, 10*(2), 216–227. https://doi.org/10.1080/19490976.2018.1494103

Freeman, M. C., Clasen, T., Brooker, S. J., Akoko, D. O., & Rheingans, R. (2013). The impact of a school-based hygiene, water quality and sanitation intervention on soil-transmitted helminth reinfection: A cluster-randomized trial. *The American Journal of Tropical Medicine and Hygiene, 89*(5), 875–883. https://doi.org/10.4269/ajtmh.13-0237

Fuentes, A. (2022). WEIRD Indeed, but there is more to the story: anthropological reflections on Henrich's "The Weirdest people in the world." *Religion, Brain, & Behavior, 12*(3), 284–290. https://doi.org/10.1080/2153599X.2021.1991458

Garcia, J., & Koelling, R. A. (1966). Relation of cue to consequence in avoidance learning. *Psychonomic Science, 4*(1), 123–124. https://doi.org/10.3758/BF03342209

Gildner, T. E. (2021). Reproductive hormone measurement from minimally invasive sample types: Methodological considerations and anthropological importance. *American Journal of Human Biology, 33*(1), e23535. https://doi.org/10.1002/ajhb.23535

Gildner, T. E., Cepon-Robins, T. J., Liebert, M. A., Urlacher, S. S., Schrock, J. M., Harrington, C. J., Madimenos, F. C., Snodgrass, J. J., & Sugiyama, L. S. (2020). Market integration and soil-transmitted helminth infection among the Shuar of Amazonian Ecuador. *PLoS ONE, 15*(7), e0236924. https://doi.org/10.1371/journal.pone.0236924

Glaser, R., & Kiecolt-Glaser, J. K. (2005). Stress-induced immune dysfunction: Implications for health. *Nature Reviews Immunology, 5*(3), 243–251. https://doi.org/10.1038/nri1571

Godoy, R., Reyes-García, V., Byron, E., Leonard, W. R., & Vadez, V. (2005). The effect of market economies on the well-being of indigenous peoples and on their use of renewable natural resources. *Annual Review of Anthropology, 34*(1), 121–138. https://doi.org/10.1146/annurev.anthro.34.081804.120412

Gurven, M., Costa, M., Ben Trumble, Stieglitz, J., Beheim, B., Eid Rodriguez, D., Hooper, P. L., & Kaplan, H. (2016). Health costs of reproduction are minimal despite high fertility, mortality and subsistence lifestyle. *Scientific Reports, 6*, 30056. https://doi.org/10.1038/srep30056

Gurven, M. D., & Lieberman, D. E. (2020). WEIRD bodies: Mismatch, medicine and missing diversity. *Evolution and Human Behavior, 41*(5), 330–340. https://doi.org/10.1016/j.evolhumbehav.2020.04.001

Gurven, M., von Rueden, C., Massenkoff, M., Kaplan, H., & Vie, M. L. (2013). How universal is the Big Five? Testing the Five-Factor Model of personality variation among forager-farmers in the Bolivian Amazon. *Journal of Personality and Social Psychology, 104*(2), 354–370. https://doi.org/10.1037/a0030841

Haidt, J., McCauley, C., & Rozin, P. (1994). Individual differences in sensitivity to disgust: A scale sampling seven domains of disgust elicitors. *Personality and Individual Differences, 16*(5), 701–713. https://doi.org/10.1016/0191-8869(94)90212-7

Henrich, J., Heine, S. J., & Norenzayan, A. (2010a). Most people are not WEIRD. *Nature, 466*(7302), 29–29. https://doi.org/10.1038/466029a

Henrich, J., Heine, S. J., & Norenzayan, A. (2010b). The weirdest people in the world? *Behavioral and Brain Sciences, 33*, 61–135. doi: 10.1017/S0140525X0999152X.

Hoefling, A., Likowski, K. U., Deutsch, R., Häfner, M., Seibt, B., Mühlberger, A., Weyers, P., & Strack, F. (2009). When hunger finds no fault with moldy corn: Food deprivation reduces food-related disgust. *Emotion (Washington, D.C.), 9*(1), 50–58. https://doi.org/10.1037/a0014449

Hooper, L. V., Littman, D. R., & Macpherson, A. J. (2012). Interactions between the microbiota and the immune system. *Science (New York, N.Y.), 336*(6086), 1268–1273. https://doi.org/10.1126/science.1223490

Jack, R. E., Garrod, O. G. B., Yu, H., Caldara, R., & Schyns, P. G. (2012). Facial expressions of emotion are not culturally universal. *Proceedings of the National Academy of Sciences, 109*(19), 7241–7244. https://doi.org/10.1073/pnas.1200155109

Jackson, J. A., Friberg, I. M., Little, S., & Bradley, J. E. (2009). Review series on helminths, immune modulation and the hygiene hypothesis: Immunity against helminths and immunological phenomena in modern human populations: coevolutionary legacies? *Immunology, 126*(1), 18–27. https://doi.org/10.1111/j.1365-2567.2008.03010.x

Jasienska, G., Bribiescas, R. G., Furberg, A.-S., Helle, S., & Núñez-de la Mora, A. (2017). Human reproduction and health: An evolutionary perspective. *Lancet (London, England), 390*(10093), 510–520. https://doi.org/10.1016/S0140-6736(17)30573-1

Jasienska, G., & Ellison, P. T. (2004). Energetic factors and seasonal changes in ovarian function in women from rural Poland. *American Journal of Human Biology, 16*(5), 563–580. https://doi.org/10.1002/ajhb.20063

Jones, B. C., Hahn, A. C., Fisher, C. I., Wang, H., Kandrik, M., Lee, A. J., Tybur, J. M., & DeBruine, L. M. (2018). Hormonal correlates of pathogen disgust: Testing the compensatory prophylaxis hypothesis. *Evolution and Human Behavior, 39*(2), 166–169. https://doi.org/10.1016/j.evolhumbehav.2017.12.004

Kalyva, E., Pellizzoni, S., Tavano, A., Iannello, P., & Siegal, M. (2010). Contamination sensitivity in autism, Down syndrome, and typical development. *Research in Autism Spectrum Disorders, 4*(1), 43–50. https://doi.org/10.1016/j.rasd.2009.07.005

Karlsson, E. K., Kwiatkowski, D. P., & Sabeti, P. C. (2014). Natural selection and infectious disease in human populations. *Nature Reviews. Genetics, 15*(6), 379–393. https://doi.org/10.1038/nrg3734

Kavaliers, M., & Choleris, E. (2018). The role of social cognition in parasite and pathogen avoidance. *Philosophical Transactions of the Royal Society B: Biological Sciences, 373*(1751), 20170206. https://doi.org/10.1098/rstb.2017.0206

Kim, D., Yoo, S.-A., & Kim, W.-U. (2016). Gut microbiota in autoimmunity: Potential for clinical applications. *Archives of Pharmacal Research, 39*(11), 1565–1576. https://doi.org/10.1007/s12272-016-0796-7

Leonard, W. R., Galloway, V. A., Ivakine, E., Osipova, L., & Kazakovtseva, M. (2002). Ecology, health and lifestyle change among the Evenki herders of Siberia. In William R. Leonard, Victoria A. Galloway, & Evgueni Ivakine (Eds.), *Human biology of pastoral populations* (206–235). Cambridge University Press.

Lieberman, D., Billingsley, J., & Patrick, C. (2018). Consumption, contact and copulation: How pathogens have shaped human psychological adaptations. *Philosophical Transactions of the Royal Society B: Biological Sciences, 373*(1751), 20170203. https://doi.org/10.1098/rstb.2017.0203

Lieberman, D., Tooby, J., & Cosmides, L. (2003). Does morality have a biological basis? An empirical test of the factors governing moral sentiments relating to incest. *Proceedings of the Royal Society B: Biological Sciences, 270*(1517), 819–826.

Liebert, M. A., Snodgrass, J. J., Madimenos, F. C., Cepon, T. J., Blackwell, A. D., & Sugiyama, L. S. (2013). Implications of market integration for cardiovascular and metabolic health among an indigenous Amazonian Ecuadorian population. *Annals of Human Biology, 40*(3), 228–242. https://doi.org/10.3109/03014460.2012.759621

MacCormack, J. K., & Muscatell, K. A. (2019). The metabolic mind: A role for leptin and ghrelin in affect and social cognition. *Social and Personality Psychology Compass, 13*(9), e12496. https://doi.org/10.1111/spc3.12496

Madimenos, F. C., Snodgrass, J. J., Liebert, M. A., Cepon, T. J., & Sugiyama, L. S. (2012). Reproductive effects on skeletal health in Shuar women of Amazonian Ecuador: A life history perspective. *American Journal of Human Biology, 24*(6), 841–852. https://doi.org/10.1002/ajhb.22329

Magid, K., Chatterton, R. T., Ahamed, F. U., & Bentley, G. R. (2018). Childhood ecology influences salivary testosterone, pubertal age and stature of Bangladeshi UK migrant men. *Nature Ecology & Evolution, 2*(7), 1146–1154. https://doi.org/10.1038/s41559-018-0567-6

Maizels, R. M., & McSorley, H. J. (2016). Regulation of the host immune system by helminth parasites. *Journal of Allergy and Clinical Immunology, 138*(3), 666–675. https://doi.org/10.1016/j.jaci.2016.07.007

Maizels, R. M., McSorley, H. J., & Smyth, D. J. (2014). Helminths in the hygiene hypothesis: Sooner or later? *Clinical and Experimental Immunology, 177*(1), 38–46. https://doi.org/10.1111/cei.12353

Matsumoto, D., & Ekman, P. (1989). American-Japanese cultural differences in intensity ratings of facial expressions of emotion. *Motivation and Emotion, 13*(2), 143–157. https://doi.org/10.1007/BF00992959

McDade, T. W., Burhop, J., & Dohnal, J. (2004). High-sensitivity enzyme immunoassay for C-reactive protein in dried blood spots. *Clinical Chemistry, 50*(3), 652–654. https://doi.org/10.1373/clinchem.2003.029488

McDade, T. W., Williams, S., & Snodgrass, J. J. (2007). What a drop can do: Dried blood spots as a minimally invasive method for integrating biomarkers into population-based research. *Demography, 44*(4), 899–925. https://doi.org/10.1353/dem.2007.0038

Miłkowska, K., Galbarczyk, A., Klimek, M., Zabłocka-Słowińska, K., & Jasienska, G. (2021). Pathogen disgust, but not moral disgust, changes across the menstrual cycle. *Evolution and Human Behavior, 42*(5), 402–408. https://doi.org/10.1016/j.evolhumbehav.2021.03.002.

Miller, E. M., & McDade, T. W. (2012). A highly sensitive immunoassay for interleukin-6 in dried blood spots. *American Journal of Human Biology, 24*(6), 863–865. https://doi.org/10.1002/ajhb.22324

Muehlenbein, M. P., & Bribiescas, R. G. (2005). Testosterone-mediated immune functions and male life histories. *American Journal of Human Biology, 17*(5), 527–558. https://doi.org/10.1002/ajhb.20419

Natri, H., Garcia, A. R., Buetow, K. H., Trumble, B. C., & Wilson, M. A. (2019). The pregnancy pickle: Evolved immune compensation due to pregnancy underlies sex differences in human diseases. *Trends in Genetics, 35*(7), 478–488. https://doi.org/10.1016/j.tig.2019.04.008

Navarrete, C. D., & Fessler, D. M. T. (2006). Disease avoidance and ethnocentrism: The effects of disease vulnerability and disgust sensitivity on intergroup attitudes. *Evolution and Human Behavior, 27*(4), 270–282. https://doi.org/10.1016/j.evolhumbehav.2005.12.001

Nowak, J., Pawłowski, B., Borkowska, B., Augustyniak, D., & Drulis-Kawa, Z. (2018). No evidence for the immunocompetence handicap hypothesis in male humans. *Scientific Reports, 8*(1), 7392. https://doi.org/10.1038/s41598-018-25694-0

Núñez-de la Mora, A., Chatterton, R. T., Choudhury, O. A., Napolitano, D. A., & Bentley, G. R. (2007). Childhood conditions influence adult progesterone levels. *PLoS Medicine, 4*(5), e167. https://doi.org/10.1371/journal.pmed.0040167

Nunn, C. L., Lindenfors, P., Pursall, E. R., & Rolff, J. (2009). On sexual dimorphism in immune function. *Philosophical Transactions of the Royal Society B: Biological Sciences, 364*(1513), 61–69. https://doi.org/10.1098/rstb.2008.0148

Oaten, M., Stevenson, R. J., & Case, T. I. (2009). Disgust as a disease-avoidance mechanism. *Psychological Bulletin, 135*(2), 303–321. https://doi.org/10.1037/a0014823

Obregon-Tito, A. J., Tito, R. Y., Metcalf, J., Sankaranarayanan, K., Clemente, J. C., Ursell, L. K., Zech Xu, Z., Van Treuren, W., Knight, R., Gaffney, P. M., Spicer, P., Lawson, P., Marin-Reyes, L., Trujillo-Villarroel, O., Foster, M., Guija-Poma, E., Troncoso-Corzo, L., Warinner, C., Ozga, A. T., & Lewis, C. M. (2015). Subsistence strategies in traditional societies distinguish gut microbiomes. *Nature Communications, 6*(1), 6505. https://doi.org/10.1038/ncomms7505

Okada, H., Kuhn, C., Feillet, H., & Bach, J.-F. (2010). The "hygiene hypothesis" for autoimmune and allergic diseases: An update. *Clinical & Experimental Immunology, 160*(1), 1–9. https://doi.org/10.1111/j.1365-2249.2010.04139.x

Olatunji, B. O., Williams, N. L., Tolin, D. F., Abramowitz, J. S., Sawchuk, C. N., Lohr, J. M., & Elwood, L. S. (2007). The disgust scale: Item analysis, factor structure, and suggestions for refinement. *Psychological Assessment, 19*(3), 281–297.

Petrowski, K., Paul, S., Schmutzer, G., Roth, M., Brähler, E., & Albani, C. (2010). Domains of disgust sensitivity: Revisited factor structure of the questionnaire for the assessment of disgust sensitivity (QADS) in a cross-sectional, representative German survey. *BMC Medical Research Methodology, 10*, 95. https://doi.org/10.1186/1471-2288-10-95

Rad, M. S., Martingano, A. J., & Ginges, J. (2018). Toward a psychology of *Homo sapiens*: Making psychological science more representative of the human population. *Proceedings of the National Academy of Sciences, 115*(45), 11401–11405. https://doi.org/10.1073/pnas.1721165115

Robins, T. C. (2015). *Social change, parasite exposure, and immune dysregulation among shuar forager-horticulturalists of Amazonia: A biocultural case-study in evolutionary medicine* [PhD dissertation, University of Oregon]. http://hdl.handle.net/1794/19317.

Rottman, J. (2014). Evolution, development, and the emergence of disgust. *Evolutionary Psychology, 12*(2), 427–433. https://doi.org/10.1177/147470491401200209

Rozin, P., Haidt, J., & McCauley, C. R. (2008). Disgust. In Lisa Feldman Barrett, Michael Lewis, & Jeannette M. Haviland-Jones (Eds.), *Handbook of emotions* (3rd ed, pp. 757–776). Guilford Press.

Rukavina, S., Sachsenweger, F., Jerg-Bretzke, L., Daucher, A. E., Traue, H. C., Walter, S., & Hoffmann, H. (2018). Testosterone and its influence on emotion recognition in young, healthy males. *Psychology, 9*(7), 1814. https://doi.org/10.4236/psych.2018.97106

Sarabian, C., Ngoubangoye, B., & MacIntosh, A. J. J. (2017). Avoidance of biological contaminants through sight, smell and touch in chimpanzees. *Royal Society Open Science, 4*(11), e170968. https://doi.org/10.1098/rsos.170968

Schaller, M. (2011). The behavioural immune system and the psychology of human sociality. *Philosophical Transactions of the Royal Society B: Biological Sciences, 366*(1583), 3418–3426. https://doi.org/10.1098/rstb.2011.0029

Schaller, M. (2016). The behavioral immune system. In David M. Buss (Ed.),. *The handbook of evolutionary psychology*, Vol. 1: *Foundations* (2nd ed., pp. 206–224). Wiley.

Schaller, M., & Duncan, L. A. (2007). The behavioral immune system: Its evolution and social psychological implications. In Joseph P. Forgas, Martie G. Haselton, & William von Hippel (Eds.), *Evolution and the social mind: Evolutionary psychology and social cognition* (pp. 293–307). Routledge/Taylor & Francis Group.

Schaller, M., & Murray, D. R. (2008). Pathogens, personality, and culture: Disease prevalence predicts worldwide variability in sociosexuality, extraversion, and openness to experience. *Journal of Personality and Social Psychology*, *95*(1), 212–221. https://doi.org/10.1037/0022-3514.95.1.212

Schrock, J. M., Snodgrass, J. J., & Sugiyama, L. S. (2020). Lassitude: The emotion of being sick. *Evolution and Human Behavior*, *41*(1), 44–57. https://doi.org/10.1016/j.evolhumbehav.2019.09.002

Schulz, J., Bahrami-Rad, D., Beauchamp, J., & Henrich, J. (2018). The origins of WEIRD psychology (SSRN Scholarly Paper ID 3201031). *Social Science Research Network*. https://doi.org/10.2139/ssrn.3201031

Schwartz, C., Hams, E., & Fallon, P. G. (2018). Helminth modulation of lung inflammation. *Trends in Parasitology*, *34*(5), 388–403. https://doi.org/10.1016/j.pt.2017.12.007

Shattuck, E. C., & Muehlenbein, M. P. (2015). Human sickness behavior: Ultimate and proximate explanations. *American Journal of Physical Anthropology*, *157*(1), 1–18. https://doi.org/10.1002/ajpa.22698

Sherman, P. W., & Flaxman, S. M. (2002). Nausea and vomiting of pregnancy in an evolutionary perspective. *American Journal of Obstetrics and Gynecology*, *186*(Suppl 5), S190–S197. https://doi.org/10.1067/mob.2002.122593

Skolnick, A. J., & Dzokoto, V. A. (2013). Disgust and contamination: A cross-national comparison of Ghana and the United States. *Frontiers in Psychology*, *4*, e91. https://doi.org/10.3389/fpsyg.2013.00091

Smaldino, P. E., Lukaszewski, A., von Rueden, C., & Gurven, M. (2019). Niche diversity can explain cross-cultural differences in personality structure. *Nature Human Behaviour*, *3*(12), 1276–1283. https://doi.org/10.1038/s41562-019-0730-3

Sorensen, M. V., Leonard, W. R., Tarskaya, L. A., Ivanov, K. I., Snodgrass, J. J., Alekseev, V. P., Krivoshapkin, V. G., & Rifai, N. (2006). High-sensitivity C-reactive protein, adiposity, and blood pressure in the Yakut of Siberia. *American Journal of Human Biology*, *18*(6), 766–775. https://doi.org/10.1002/ajhb.20547

Stagaman, K., Cepon-Robins, T. J., Liebert, M. A., Gildner, T. E., Urlacher, S. S., Madimenos, F. C., Guillemin, K., Snodgrass, J. J., Sugiyama, L. S., & Bohannan, B. J. M. (2018). Market integration predicts human gut microbiome attributes across a gradient of economic development. *MSystems*, *3*(1), e00122–17. https://doi.org/10.1128/mSystems.00122-17

Stein, D. J., Hermesh, H., Eilam, D., Segalas, C., Zohar, J., Menchon, J., & Nesse, R. M. (2016). Human compulsivity: A perspective from evolutionary medicine. *European Neuropsychopharmacology*, *26*(5), 869–876. https://doi.org/10.1016/j.euroneuro.2015.12.004

Stevenson, R. J., Case, T. I., & Oaten, M. J. (2009). Frequency and recency of infection and their relationship with disgust and contamination sensitivity. *Evolution and Human Behavior*, *30*(5), 363–368. https://doi.org/10.1016/j.evolhumbehav.2009.02.005

Stevenson, R. J., Hodgson, D., Oaten, M. J., Moussavi, M., Langberg, R., Case, T. I., & Barouei, J. (2012). Disgust elevates core body temperature and up-regulates certain oral immune markers. *Brain, Behavior, and Immunity*, *26*(7), 1160–1168. https://doi.org/10.1016/j.bbi.2012.07.010

Stevenson, R. J., Oaten, M. J., Case, T. I., Repacholi, B. M., & Wagland, P. (2010). Children's response to adult disgust elicitors: Development and acquisition. *Developmental Psychology*, *46*(1), 165. https://doi.org/10.1037/a0016692

Strachan, D. P. (1989). Hay fever, hygiene, and household size. *BMJ: British Medical Journal*, *299*(6710), 1259–1260.

Tanner, S., Leonard, W. R., Mcdade, T. W., Reyes-Garcia, V., Godoy, R., & Huanca, T. (2009). Influence of helminth infections on childhood nutritional status in lowland Bolivia. *American Journal of Human Biology*, *21*(5), 651–656. https://doi.org/10.1002/ajhb.20944

Thakur, N., Chandra, J., Pemde, H., & Singh, V. (2014). Anemia in severe acute malnutrition. *Nutrition*, *30*(4), 440–442. https://doi.org/10.1016/j.nut.2013.09.011

Thornhill, R., Fincher, C. L., Murray, D. R., & Schaller, M. (2010). Zoonotic and non-zoonotic diseases in relation to human personality and societal values: Support for the Parasite-Stress Model. *Evolutionary Psychology*, *8*(2), 151–169. https://doi.org/10.1177/147470491000800201

Tooby, J. (1982). Pathogens, polymorphism, and the evolution of sex. *Journal of Theoretical Biology*, *97*(4), 557–576. https://doi.org/10.1016/0022-5193(82)90358-7

Tooby, J., & Cosmides, L. (1990). The past explains the present: Emotional adaptations and the structure of ancestral environments. *Ethology and Sociobiology*, *11*(4), 375–424. https://doi.org/10.1016/0162-3095(90)90017-Z

Tooby, J., & Cosmides, L. (2015). Conceptual foundations of evolutionary psychology. In D. M. Buss (Ed.), *The handbook of evolutionary psychology* (pp. 5–67). Wiley. https://doi.org/10.1002/9780470939376.ch1

Trumble, B. C., Blackwell, A. D., Stieglitz, J., Thompson, M. E., Suarez, I. M., Kaplan, H., & Gurven, M. (2016). Associations between male testosterone and immune function in a pathogenically stressed forager-horticultural population. *American Journal of Physical Anthropology, 161*(3), 494–505. https://doi.org/10.1002/ajpa.23054

Trumble, B. C., Stieglitz, J., Eid Rodriguez, D., Cortez Linares, E., Kaplan, H. S., & Gurven, M. D. (2015). Challenging the inevitability of prostate enlargement: Low levels of benign prostatic hyperplasia among Tsimane forager-horticulturalists. *The Journals of Gerontology: Series A, Biological Sciences and Medical Sciences, 70*(10), 1262–1268. https://doi.org/10.1093/gerona/glv051

Tybur, J. M., Çınar, Ç., Karinen, A. K., & Perone, P. (2018). Why do people vary in disgust? *Philosophical Transactions of the Royal Society B: Biological Sciences, 373*(1751), e20170204. https://doi.org/10.1098/rstb.2017.0204

Tybur, J. M., Inbar, Y., Aarøe, L., Barclay, P., Barlow, F. K., Barra, M. de, Becker, D. V., Borovoi, L., Choi, I., Choi, J. A., Consedine, N. S., Conway, A., Conway, J. R., Conway, P., Adoric, V. C., Demirci, D. E., Fernández, A. M., Ferreira, D. C. S., Ishii, K., . . . Žeželj, I. (2016). Parasite stress and pathogen avoidance relate to distinct dimensions of political ideology across 30 nations. *Proceedings of the National Academy of Sciences, 113*(44), 12408–12413. https://doi.org/10.1073/pnas.1607398113

Tybur, J. M., Inbar, Y., Güler, E., & Molho, C. (2015). Is the relationship between pathogen avoidance and ideological conservatism explained by sexual strategies? *Evolution and Human Behavior, 36*(6), 489–497. https://doi.org/10.1016/j.evolhumbehav.2015.01.006

Tybur, J. M., & Lieberman, D. (2016). Human pathogen avoidance adaptations. *Current Opinion in Psychology, 7*, 6–11. https://doi.org/10.1016/j.copsyc.2015.06.005

Tybur, J. M., Lieberman, D., & Griskevicius, V. (2009). Microbes, mating, and morality: Individual differences in three functional domains of disgust. *Journal of Personality and Social Psychology, 97*(1), 103–122. https://doi.org/10.1037/a0015474

Tybur, J. M., Lieberman, D., Kurzban, R., & DeScioli, P. (2013). Disgust: Evolved function and structure. *Psychological Review, 120*(1), 65–84. https://doi.org/10.1037/a0030778

Tybur, J. M., Wesseldijk, L. W., & Jern, P. (2020). Genetic and environmental influences on disgust proneness, contamination sensitivity, and their covariance. *Clinical Psychological Science, 8*(6), 1054–1061. https://doi.org/10.1177/2167702620951510

Urlacher, S. S., Ellison, P. T., Sugiyama, L. S., Pontzer, H., Eick, G., Liebert, M. A., Cepon-Robins, T. J., Gildner, T. E., & Snodgrass, J. J. (2018). Tradeoffs between immune function and childhood growth among Amazonian forager-horticulturalists. *Proceedings of the National Academy of Sciences, 115*(17), e3914–e3921. https://doi.org/10.1073/pnas.1717522115

Urlacher, S. S., Liebert, M. A., Snodgrass, J. J., Blackwell, A. D., Cepon-Robins, T. J., Gildner, T. E., Madimenos, F. C., Amir, D., Bribiescas, R. G., & Sugiyama, L. S. (2016). Heterogeneous effects of market integration on subadult body size and nutritional status among the Shuar of Amazonian Ecuador. *Annals of Human Biology, 43*(4), 316–329. https://doi.org/10.1080/03014460.2016.1192219

Valeggia, C. R. (2007). Taking the lab to the field: Monitoring reproductive hormones in population research. *Population and Development Review, 33*(3), 525–542.

Vitzthum, V. J. (2020). Field methods and strategies for assessing female reproductive functioning. *American Journal of Human Biology, 33*(5), e23513. https://doi.org/10.1002/ajhb.23513

Vitzthum, V. J. (2009). The ecology and evolutionary endocrinology of reproduction in the human female. *American Journal of Physical Anthropology, 140*(S49), 95–136. https://doi.org/10.1002/ajpa.21195

von Mutius, E. (2007). Allergies, infections and the hygiene hypothesis: The epidemiological evidence. *Immunobiology, 212*(6), 433–439. https://doi.org/10.1016/j.imbio.2007.03.002

Winternitz, J., Abbate, J. L., Huchard, E., Havlíček, J., & Garamszegi, L. Z. (2017). Patterns of MHC-dependent mate selection in humans and nonhuman primates: A meta-analysis. *Molecular Ecology, 26*(2), 668–688. https://doi.org/10.1111/mec.13920

Żelaźniewicz, A., Borkowska, B., Nowak, J., & Pawłowski, B. (2016). The progesterone level, leukocyte count and disgust sensitivity across the menstrual cycle. *Physiology & Behavior, 161*, 60–65. https://doi.org/10.1016/j.physbeh.2016.04.002

CHAPTER 10

The Evolved Nature of Pride

Jessica L. Tracy, Eric Mercadante, and Zachary Witkower

Abstract

A large body of research suggests that the self-conscious emotion of pride is a universal and evolved part of human nature, which functions to help individuals navigate their social hierarchies, motivating them to engage in behaviors that allow them to attain and maintain social rank, and communicating to others which group members are deserving of rank attainment and should be targets of social learning. Studies also suggest that there are two distinct facets of pride: authentic and hubristic, associated with distinct forms of self-favorability—self-esteem and narcissism, respectively. Furthermore, each pride facet may function to facilitate the attainment of a distinct form of social rank—prestige or dominance—both of which are viable and likely evolved pathways to rank, power, and social influence.

Key Words: pride, evolution, prestige, dominance, hierarchy

Pride is one of the most central emotions shaping human social behavior and group dynamics. It is *the* emotion that motivates people to do what it takes to get ahead and attain social rank. Higher rank promotes greater adaptive fitness than low rank, and a large body of evidence attests to a strong relation between social rank and fitness or well-being across species (e.g., Barkow, 1975; Hill & Hurtado, 1989; von Rueden et al., 2011). By facilitating the attainment of social rank, pride thus serves a critical adaptive function. A large body of evidence suggests that humans evolved to experience pride, and that pride is an adaptive part of our affective and behavioral repertoire (Tracy, 2016; Tracy et al., 2010).

Yet pride is different from many other adaptive emotions, like anger, fear, and happiness. In contrast to these "basic" emotions, pride is a "self-conscious" emotion, meaning that its experience requires the activation of self-awareness, and an ability to use that self-awareness to focus on one's self-representations. To experience a self-conscious emotion—be it pride, shame, guilt, or embarrassment—a person must use their self-conscious "I"-self to focus on their self-concept or identity—the "me" self, according to James's (1890) distinction. They must then make a self-evaluation—an appraisal of whether their self-concept is currently meeting, exceeding, or failing to meet their goals for their identity, or the kind of person they want to be. For pride, the self-evaluation needs to be in the affirmative; pride occurs when people appraise themselves as meeting or exceeding identity goals.

Pride can thus be understood as an emotional tracking device—an internal mechanism that tells the self when its current behaviors, or external events, put the individual on track to becoming the kind of person they want to become. Correspondingly, an absence of pride tells the self that something is missing, and action must be taken to attain pride and restore self-esteem (Weidman et al., 2016). The person we want to be—our identity—is in turn shaped by cultural and societal rules and norms; we want to become the kind of person who is valued by our societies (Robins et al., 2010; Tracy, 2016; Tracy & Robins, 2004a). These people are the ones who hold social status, meaning that they are admired and receive deference, and have power and influence over others. Pride is therefore the emotion that tells us when our behaviors, actions, and our global self are as we most want them to be—on track to helping us attain status. A desire for pride, in turn, prompts us to engage in those behaviors that will earn us status. For this reason, pride is functional.

What Is Pride?
The Pride Nonverbal Expression

Traditionally, a prominent gold-standard criteria used to determine whether a particular emotion is likely to be evolved is whether it has a distinct, cross-culturally recognized nonverbal expression (e.g., Ekman, 1992b; Tracy & Randles, 2011). Studies conducted over the past 15 years provide strong evidence for a cross-cultural, reliably recognized pride expression (see Figure 10.1; Tracy & Robins, 2004b, 2007a, 2008a).

The prototypical pride expression involves the body (i.e., expanded posture, head tilted slightly back, arms akimbo with hands on hips or raised above the head with hands in fists) as well as the face (i.e., small smile; Tracy & Robins, 2004b, 2007a), and is reliably recognized and distinguished from similar emotions (e.g., happiness, excitement) by individuals across cultures, including highly isolated, largely preliterate traditional small-scale societies in Burkina Faso and Fiji, where participants had almost no exposure to Western cultural knowledge (Tracy & Robins, 2008a; Tracy et al., 2013). Pride-recognition rates in educated U.S. samples range around 80%–90%, and pride can be recognized quickly and efficiently from a single snapshot image (Tracy & Robins, 2008b). High levels of recognition for the pride expression have been documented by several different labs (Cordaro et al., 2019; Beck et al., 2010; Brosi et al., 2016; see Witkower & Tracy, 2019a, for a review).

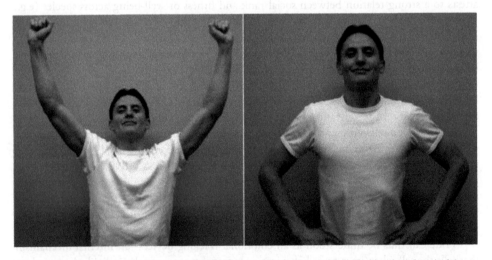

Figure 10.1. Prototypical pride expressions, with arms raised (left), and arms akimbo and hands on hips (right). Both displays are reliably recognized at high rates in educated Western samples and by members of isolated small-scale traditional societies.

The recognizable pride expression is also spontaneously *displayed* in pride-eliciting situations (i.e., success) by children as young as three years (Belsky & Domitrovich, 1997; Lewis et al., 1992; Stipek et al., 1992), high school students who have performed well on a class exam (Weisfeld & Beresford, 1982), and adult athletes from a wide range of cultures, as well as congenitally blind athletes who could not have learned to show pride through visual modeling (Tracy & Matsumoto, 2008). These findings suggest that the pride expression is a universal human response to success. It is unlikely that the expression would (a) be recognized so consistently, (b) generalize to individuals who could not have learned it through cross-cultural transmission (i.e., films, television, magazines), or (c) be reliably and spontaneously displayed in pride-eliciting situations by those who have never seen others display it, if it were not an innate human universal.

However, the pride expression differs from other highly recognizable and universal emotion expressions in that accurate recognition of pride requires bodily and head components, as well as facial muscle movements. Pride can be recognized at fairly high rates of accuracy from the face and head alone, but accurate recognition does require the presence of an upward head tilt, which is not the case for other universally recognized expressions (Cordaro et al., 2019; Tracy & Robins, 2004b). This distinction, which also characterizes the shame expression (Izard, 1971; Keltner, 1995; Tracy, Robins, et al., 2009), may be indicative of the unique early evolutionary origins of these two self-conscious emotion expressions; they may be homologous with nonhuman dominance and submission displays, which involve similar bodily and head movements and less facial behavior (see Tracy, 2016; Tracy & Randles, 2011).

The Psychological Structure of Pride

Scholars have long noted that pride is also unusual in the way it is experienced and conceptualized: it appears to be *not just one thing*. While most contemporary psychological scientists have considered pride to be a positive and socially useful emotion that underlies self-esteem and achievement motivation, religious scholars and philosophers—from Aristotle and Lao Tzu to Thomas Aquinas and the Dalai Lama—have long cautioned against pride's dark or "sinful" side (see Tracy, 2016; Tracy et al., 2010). Partly on the basis of these accounts, researchers have postulated distinct "authentic" and "hubristic" components of the emotion (Lewis, 2000; Tracy & Robins, 2004a, 2007b; Tangney et al., 1989), and several lines of research support this account.

First, when asked to think about and list words relevant to pride, research participants consistently generate two different categories of concepts, which, based on similarity ratings, empirically form two separate clusters of semantic meaning; see Figure 10.2. The first cluster (authentic pride) includes words like "accomplished" and "confident," and fits with a prosocial, achievement-oriented conceptualization of pride. The second cluster (hubristic pride) includes words like "arrogant" and "conceited," and fits with a self-aggrandizing, egotistical conceptualization (Tracy & Robins, 2007b). A similar two-cluster pattern also emerged in a study examining semantic conceptualizations of pride in mainland China, among university students who generated pride words indigenously in Chinese (Shi et al., 2015). This cross-cultural replication suggests that the tendency to make conceptual distinctions between authentic and hubristic pride is unlikely to be an artifact of Western culture, and may reflect pride's universal structure.

The second piece of evidence supporting the dual-faceted structure of pride comes from studies asking participants to rate their subjective feelings during a pride experience and studies asking for the feelings that describe their dispositional tendency to feel pride (i.e., trait pride). Factor analyses of these ratings consistently reveal two relatively independent factors,

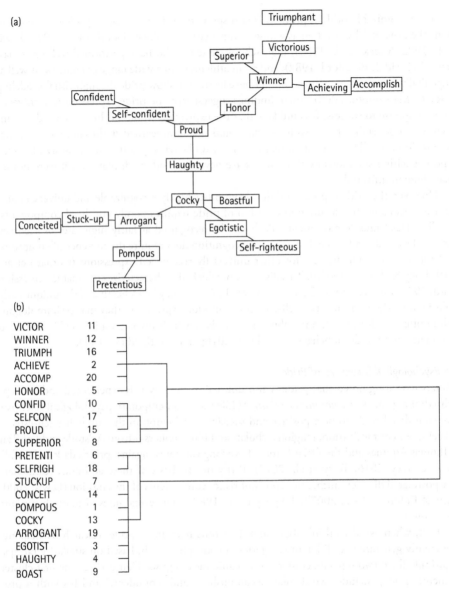

Figure 10.2. A: Visual map of links among pride-related constructs produced by pathfinder analysis. B: Dendrogram of hierarchical structure of pride-related constructs, produced by cluster analysis.

which closely parallel the two semantic clusters. Subsequent analyses demonstrated that the two pride factors are not artifacts of a tendency to group together good vs. bad, activated vs. deactivated, or trait vs. state words (Tracy & Robins, 2007b). These factor analytic findings have been replicated in mainland China and South Korea, using both indigenously derived pride-related words (in Chinese and Korean) and translated versions of English words found to represent authentic and hubristic pride in the United States (Shi et al., 2015).

The distinction between these two facets of pride is further supported by studies examining the personality correlates of each facet, as findings suggest that they diverge in

Table 10.1 Correlations of Authentic and Hubristic Pride with Theoretically Related Traits and Behaviors

Domain	Authentic Pride	Hubristic Pride
Self-evaluation		
Explicit self-esteem[f]	.50*	−.14*
Implicit self-esteem[g]	.26*	−.10
Self-efficacy[e]	.62***	−.06
Narcissism[f]	.32*	.22*
Shame-proneness[f]	−.28*	.09*
Big Five Personality Factors		
Extraversion[f]	.39*	.11
Agreeableness[f]	.19*	−.26*
Conscientiousness[f]	.38*	−.25*
Emotional Stability[f]	.28*	−.05
Openness[f]	.29*	.01
Attributions for success		
Effort attributions[f]	.17*	−.10*
Ability attributions[f]	.02	.09*
Interpersonal emotions and functioning		
Authenticity[g]	.46*	−.11*
Envy[e]	.05	.27***
Fear of negative evaluation[e]	−.33***	.17***
Petty crimes and misbehaviors[g]	−.05	.20*
Aggression[g]	−.20*	.26*
Dyadic adjustment[g]	.24*	−.11*
Prejudice[a]	−.12***	.29***
Peer-rated dominance[c]	.01	.36**
Peer-rated prestige[c]	.33*	−.01
Goal pursuit		
Reward sensitivity[b]	.27***	.21***
Punishment sensitivity[b]	−.15***	−.14***
Self-control[b]	.31***	−.24***
Perseverance[b]	.41***	−.18***
Intrinsic motivation[d]	.37***	−.11*
Extrinsic motivation[d]	.05	.10*

Note. References for each effect are indicated with superscripts, as follows: [a] Ashton-James & Tracy, 2012; [b] Carver et al., 2010; [c] Cheng et al., 2010; [d] Damian & Robins, 2013; [e] Dickens & Robins, 2022; [f] Tracy & Robins, 2007a; [g] Tracy, Cheng, et al., 2009.

*$p < .05$

**$p < .01$

***$p < .001$

numerous ways (see Table 10.1). At both the trait and state levels, authentic pride is positively related to the socially desirable and psychologically adaptive Big Five traits of Extraversion, Agreeableness, Conscientiousness, Emotional Stability, and Openness to Experience, whereas hubristic pride is consistently negatively related to the two pro-social traits of Agreeableness and Conscientiousness (Tracy & Robins, 2007b). These distinct personality profiles have been replicated in a Chinese sample (Shi et al., 2015). People high in authentic pride tend to have high explicit and implicit self-esteem, whereas those high in hubristic pride tend to have low implicit and explicit self-esteem, yet score high in narcissism and shame-proneness (Tracy, Cheng, et al., 2009), consistent with a theoretical distinction between the two prides as correspondent to the distinction between genuine self-esteem and narcissism (Tracy et al., 2011).

The facets also differ in their associations with a range of social behaviors and mental health outcomes; each facet of pride seems to underlie a different way of engaging with the social world and approaching one's goals, and, perhaps as a result, is linked to divergent mental health outcomes. Individuals high in dispositional authentic pride tend to be low in depression, trait anxiety, social phobia, aggression, hostility, and rejection sensitivity; and high in life satisfaction, relationship satisfaction, dyadic adjustment, and social support; and they report being securely attached to their relationship partners. In addition, lab experiments manipulating authentic pride have found that such experiences increase delay of gratification (Ho et al., 2016). In contrast, individuals high in dispositional hubristic pride are more likely to experience chronic anxiety; be hostile, aggressive, and un-empathic toward those who are different from them; exhibit a tendency toward interpersonal conflict as well as a range of other antisocial misbehaviors (e.g., drug use, petty crimes); and report lower dyadic adjustment and social support (Ashton-James & Tracy, 2012; Orth et al., 2010; Tracy, Cheng, et al., 2009).

Given their divergent personality profiles, it is not surprising that the pride facets are located in different quadrants of the Interpersonal Circumplex (i.e., the independent dimensions of agency and communion; Kiesler, 1983). Although agency is positively linked to both facets, individuals high in communion are prone to authentic pride only; hubristic pride shows a negative relationship with communal traits (Cheng et al., 2010). This distinction is revealed in goal striving as well; both facets are positively related to an approach orientation, but individuals high in dispositional authentic pride vigorously engage in their major life goals and put failures in perspective, whereas those high in dispositional hubristic pride set unrealistically high goals for fame and success, and interpret any positive event as indicative of their own greatness (Carver et al., 2010).

Consistent with these distinct approaches to interpreting one's achievements, studies suggest that the two pride facets are elicited by distinct cognitive appraisals. Pride occurs when individuals appraise a positive event as relevant to their identity and their goals, and as internally caused (i.e., due to the self; Ellsworth & Smith, 1988; Roseman, 1991; Tracy & Robins, 2004a; Weiner, 1985); the finding that success elicits self-reported pride experiences has been replicated in American and Japanese samples (Imada & Ellsworth, 2011; Tracy & Robins, 2007b). Yet authentic and hubristic pride are further distinguished by subsequent attributions; authentic pride may result from attributions to internal but unstable, specific, and controllable causes, such as effort (e.g., "I won because I practiced"), whereas hubristic pride is more likely to occur from attributions to internal but stable, global, and uncontrollable causes, such as ability (e.g., "I won because I'm great"; Tracy & Robins, 2007b). Studies in China produced findings that replicate these patterns. Based on content coding of Chinese participants' pride descriptions, those who experienced hubristic pride tended to attribute their successes to internal and stable abilities, but *not* to unstable behaviors. Nonetheless, although the effort/ability attribution distinction is one factor determining whether an individual experiences authentic or hubristic pride in response to a success, other factors such as personality and social comparisons are likely to play a role as well, and research is needed to address this issue—to disentangle the cognitive, emotional, and dispositional processes that determine which facet of pride an individual will experience in response to the same success event.

In more recent work, we found that the two facets of pride also show divergent relations with another supposedly deadly sin: greed. Individuals high in dispositional greed were found to experience elevated levels of both authentic and hubristic pride in response to new acquisitions, but shortly after making these purchases, their feelings of authentic pride faded while their feelings of hubristic pride remained relatively stable (Mercadante & Tracy, 2023). This pattern emerged across several studies, including longitudinal research that assessed participants' feelings about new acquisitions soon after they were purchased and then tracked changes in these feelings over subsequent weeks. The sharp rise and subsequent decline in pride observed among greedy individuals following acquisitions was largely specific to authentic pride, and held when controlling for shared variance with generalized positive affect. Although one might expect the more antisocial, hubristic pride to underlie the constant acquisitiveness seen among those high in greed, these results suggest that greedy individuals use acquisitions as a way of regulating their often-low self-esteem. This pattern was pronounced among greedy individuals with low self-esteem, suggesting that these individuals are dependent on the bursts of authentic pride that new acquisitions bring.

Why Did Humans Evolve to Experience Pride?
Adaptive Benefits of the Pride Experience

Pride may have evolved to serve the distal function of enhancing social rank—an outcome with clear adaptive benefits—through several distinct paths (see also Tracy et al., 2010). First, the pride experience motivates individuals to strive for achievements in socially valued domains. Pride feelings are pleasurable and thus reinforcing; there is no other emotion that makes individuals feel not only good, but also good about *themselves*. Through socialization, children come to experience pride in response to praise for socially valued achievements, first by parents and later by teachers and peers. Eventually, individuals experience pride in response to these accomplishments even without others' evaluations (although positive feedback from others can enhance a pride experience, by making the social value of a given achievement more salient). The reinforcing properties of pride then motivate individuals to seek future achievements; so, without any need for external evaluations or rewards, individuals strive to develop an identity that coheres with social norms. Those who are successful in this pursuit are rewarded with social approval, acceptance, and increased social status, all of which promote adaptive fitness.

Supporting this account, high levels of generalized pride (i.e., not specifically assessed as authentic or hubristic) cause individuals to demonstrate increased effort and persistence at challenging activities (Sigall & Gould, 1977), and the effects of pride on increased effort cannot be explained by positive mood (Williams & DeSteno, 2008). Similarly, pride experienced after successfully exercising self-control by avoiding temptation predicts viewing self-control goals as more important, and resisting future temptations (Hofmann & Fisher, 2012). There is also evidence that pride promotes pro-social behaviors toward others. In responding to social dilemmas, individuals who were asked to think about pride-eliciting events reported that cooperation was more important, and cooperated more, compared to those asked to think about enjoyment-eliciting events (Dorfman et al., 2014). Moreover, when people anticipate feeling proud after making fair decisions about resource allocation in an economic decision-making game, they become more likely to make fair decisions when subsequently interacting with a stranger (van der Schalk et al., 2012). Pride thus motivates a range of behaviors important for becoming a valued group member who abides by social norms and is successful in their most important pursuits: self-regulation, hard work and persistence, cooperation, and an orientation toward fairness and generosity.

In addition to *motivating* socially valued achievements and behaviors, pride promotes high rank through its intrapsychic *informational* properties. According to the "affect as information" hypothesis (Schwarz & Clore, 1983), emotional feelings function, in part, to inform individuals of changes in their environment, and thereby allow them to respond flexibly to significant events. Building on this account, pride may inform individuals that they merit increased status and group acceptance, thus allowing them to respond accordingly. Given that trait pride (along with shame) is the emotional disposition most strongly related to self-esteem (Brown & Marshall, 2001), pride may serve this informational function through its influence on self-esteem. Researchers have suggested that self-esteem functions as a social barometer, or "sociometer," informing individuals of their social status and thereby ensuring that they behave in ways that maintain their status and others' acceptance, and avoid rejection (Leary et al., 1995). Pride may be the affective mechanism that leads to increases in self-esteem, which feed into the sociometer.

Supporting this account, long-distance runners who achieved greater training success over the course of a month, and undergraduate students who performed well on an exam, reported greater pride (in this case, authentic pride) in their performance compared to those who had achieved less success in both domains (Weidman et al., 2016). Furthermore, participants who felt less authentic pride regarding their progress reported stronger intentions to adjust their behavior over the subsequent month, presumably in an attempt to increase their likelihood of making progress toward their goals and increasing their pride feelings. Perhaps most important, among those students who felt low pride from a poor exam performance and were consequently motivated to study harder for the next exam, feelings of low pride predicted an improvement on the following exam. This effect held controlling for past exam performance, indicating that the informational effect of pride on achievement goes beyond the information provided by knowledge of one's prior performance.

Yet if pride evolved to serve the distal function of promoting high rank, and authentic pride appears to serve that function by encouraging hard work and persistence following setbacks, one question that arises is what the function of hubristic pride might be. Why would humans have evolved to experience this antisocial, psychologically dysfunctional kind of pride? The answer to this question likely resides in the dominance-prestige account of rank attainment. According to this theory, humans evolved to seek and attain status through two distinct strategies, *dominance* and *prestige*, where dominance is a form of status attained through force, threat, and intimidation; and prestige is a form of status attained through the display of knowledge, valuable skills, and earned respect (Henrich & Gil-White, 2001). Dominant individuals wield power by controlling costs and benefits in many domains, including access to resources, mates, and well-being. They incite fear in subordinates by withholding resources, and subordinates submit by complying with demands or providing deference to avoid further bodily harm or loss of resources. Prestige, in contrast, likely arose in evolutionary history when humans acquired the ability to obtain cultural information from other group members, making it adaptive to selectively attend and defer to the most knowledgeable or skilled others. Prestigious individuals thus acquire power by virtue of their competence and knowledge, and by permitting followers to copy them. Lab studies support this account, showing that among groups of individuals working together, both strategies are spontaneously adopted, and both are strongly associated with emergent social influence in the group (Cheng et al., 2013).

Building on this account, we have argued that the two facets of pride may have separately evolved as the affective mechanisms that, respectively, underpin the dominance and prestige systems (see Cheng et al., 2010; Tracy et al., 2010; Tracy et al., 2020). Specifically, hubristic pride may facilitate the attainment of dominance by motivating individuals to behave in an aggressive and intimidating manner; these behaviors are, in turn, associated with peer perceptions of dominance (Cheng et al., 2010). Hubristic pride also provides a sense of grandiosity and entitlement that may allow individuals to do what is required to take power rather than earn it, and to feel little empathy for those who get in the way. When individuals experience hubristic pride, they evaluate themselves as better than others, and experience a subjective sense of dominance and superiority. Furthermore, individuals high in hubristic pride tend to be hostile, aggressive, un-empathic toward those who are different from them, and exhibit a tendency toward interpersonal conflict (Ashton-James & Tracy, 2012; Tracy, Cheng, et al., 2009). A recent series of studies provide direct behavioral evidence for this account: individuals high in hubristic pride become willing to lie to exaggerate their performance on task when doing so might help them attain higher status. Importantly, these individuals did not simply lie anytime they had the opportunity to show off or impress others. Instead, they did so only when facing a direct threat to their status, in the form of collaborating on a task with a partner who had just outperformed them. In contrast, when they expected to work with a partner who had previously underperformed, or when they were unaware of their partner's prior performance (i.e., when their status was not threatened), hubristically proud participants were no more likely to lie about their own performance than were those low in hubristic pride (Mercadante & Tracy, 2022). These findings suggest that hubristic pride may motivate antisocial and even immoral behavior, but not indiscriminately—only when such acts might allow for the acquisition of increased rank. These effects were specific to hubristic pride; the same pattern did not emerge for authentic pride, suggesting that only the former is related to engaging in dishonest behavior for the sake of status enhancement.

Authentic pride, in contrast, may facilitate the attainment of prestige by motivating and reinforcing achievements and other indicators of competence, and providing individuals with feelings of genuine self-confidence that may allow them to comfortably demonstrate social attractiveness and generosity, both of which are associated with peer perceptions of prestige (Cheng et al., 2010). In order to retain subordinates' respect, prestigious individuals must avoid succumbing to feelings of power and superiority. Feelings of authentic pride may be part of what leads these individuals to focus on their achievements without demonstrating a sense of superiority; studies show that authentic pride is positively associated with a graceful form of humility based on appreciating others' value and contributions without feeling badly about oneself (Weidman et al., 2018), and also with the inhibition of aggression and hostility (Cheng et al., 2010). The evidence that both state and trait authentic pride are associated with pro-social behavior, agreeableness, conscientiousness, and voluntary moral action (Hart & Matsuba, 2007; Tracy, Cheng, et al., 2009; Tracy & Robins, 2007b; Verbeke et al., 2004) is consistent with this account.

Several studies provide direct support for these theorized associations between each facet of pride and each status strategy (e.g., Cheng et al., 2010). First, in a study assessing dispositional levels of the two pride facets and dominance and prestige, individuals prone to authentic pride were found to rate themselves as highly prestigious, whereas those prone to hubristic pride rated themselves as higher in dominance. In a second study, this pattern was replicated using peer ratings of dominance and prestige; varsity athletes rated the extent to which team members used each strategy. Individuals high in self-reported authentic pride were viewed by their teammates as prestigious (but not dominant), whereas those high in self-reported hubristic pride were viewed as dominant (but not prestigious).

It also makes sense that an affective mechanism like pride would be a functional means for individuals to determine (unconsciously or consciously) which strategy to use. Although both dominance and prestige are viable strategies for acquiring high rank, the effectiveness of each varies with individual attributes (e.g., physical size, skills) and the situation in which it is used. However, as is the case for many psychological processes, conscious, deliberate analysis about which strategy to pursue in a given situation is likely to be costly, as such mental computations are inefficient, error-prone, and potentially hampered by metacognitive awareness (e.g., doubts about one's competence at, or the social appropriateness of, performing the fitness-maximizing behavior). An automatic affective mechanism propelling the appropriate response in each context, occurring under the radar of any metacognition, would free up valuable mental resources (Plutchik, 1980). Affect programs guided by automatic analyses of the relative costs and benefits of potential responses to events are thought to have evolved to promote quick behavioral and cognitive responses to recurrent, evolutionarily significant events (Cosmides & Tooby, 2000). Pride thus may be the automatic affect program that allows individuals to cope most effectively with opportunities for rank attainment, and the two facets of pride may have separately evolved to guide behaviors oriented toward the attainment of dominance or prestige specifically (Cheng et al., 2010; Tracy et al., 2010; Witkower et al., 2022).

Adaptive Benefits of the Pride Nonverbal Expression

Across species, a variety of adaptive benefits are accrued by those who effectively send and receive signals of high rank through readily identified nonverbal displays. Individuals who can successfully communicate their own deservedness of social rank are likely to receive increased social influence and attention (Cashdan, 1998; Cheng et al., 2013; Foulsham et al., 2010), a greater allocation of potentially scarce resources (Brown & Maurer, 1986), higher-quality mates (e.g., Apicella et al., 2007; von Rueden & Jaeggi, 2016), and deference (Sell et al., 2014). Conversely, an ability to recognize high rank in others can help avoid potentially costly agonistic encounters (Ellyson & Dovidio, 1985; Stirrat et al., 2012) as well as facilitate social learning opportunities (Birch et al., 2010; Chudek et al., 2012; Martens et al., 2012), the identification of desirable mates (Fink et al., 2007; Havlicek et al., 2005), and power maneuvering (Muller & Mazur, 1997). It is therefore likely that humans evolved specific ways of communicating their deservedness of high rank to others, possibly through nonverbal signaling.

Given the evidence reviewed above suggesting that the pride experience functions to promote and facilitate increases in social rank, as well as evidence that the pride expression is spontaneously displayed after successes in valued domains, which are likely to promote rank (Tracy & Matsumoto, 2008; Witkower et al., 2022), the nonverbal expression of pride may have evolved, in part, to communicate information about an individual's increasing social rank to others (Fessler, 1999; Tracy & Robins, 2007a; Tracy et al., 2010; Witkower et al., 2020).

The pride expression is likely to have phylogenetic origins in more ancient nonhuman dominance displays, which often involve bodily and head movements that are similar to human displays of pride. For example, high-ranking chimpanzees have been observed to show "inflated" or "bluff" displays after defeating a rival and prior to an agonistic encounter; these include behaviors such as arms raised and body expanded (de Waal, 1989; Martens et al., 2010). The chest-beating intimidation displays of mountain gorillas (Schaller, 1963) and the "strutting confident air" characteristic of dominant catarrhine monkeys (Maslow, 1936) also share behavioral similarities with the expansive components of the human pride expression. In addition to these mammals, expansive nonverbal behaviors are used to signal high rank in birds (Ballentine et al., 2008), arachnids (deCarvalho et al.,, 2004), reptiles (Greenberg & MacLean, 1978; Jara & Pincheira-Donoso, 2015; Jones, 2017), and fish (Forsatkar et al., 2016).

Furthermore, studies suggest that pride expressions serve a similar signaling function in humans, as they are reliably perceived as communicating high rank (Shariff & Tracy, 2009; Shariff et al., 2012; Tracy et al., 2013). A series of studies using implicit measures found that observers demonstrated an automatic and unavoidable tendency to perceive pride displays as conveying high status, both when pride was compared with low-status emotions and when it was compared with emotions less theoretically relevant to status (Shariff & Tracy, 2009). This association also emerged when pride was compared with happiness and anger expressions, suggesting that the association between pride and high status cannot be attributed to the positive valence of the pride expression, nor to a tendency to view certain emotions (like anger) as particularly powerful. In an additional study, the implicit association between high status and pride emerged even when pride displays were compared with displays in which the actor's face was neutral but his arms were extended from his body, making him appear larger. This result demonstrates that the association between pride and high status is not due merely to the increased size or amount of space taken up by those showing pride.

The automaticity of the association between pride displays and high-status concepts is relevant to our evolutionary account of pride displays; if the expression evolved as a pre-linguistic, pre-conscious form of communication, then its perception is a task that animal brains have been completing for millions of years, and likely occurs through low-level cognitive processes that can elicit adaptive behavioral responses without any need for conscious reflection (Bargh & Pietromonaco, 1982). Furthermore, if understanding pride's functional message required conscious deliberation, the expression would be less effective as a rapid source of information. More practically, these findings suggest that the human ability to rapidly and involuntarily assess the social status of others may be due, in part, to humans' ability to automatically recognize and interpret displays of pride.

Perhaps most important for our account of pride as an evolved status signal is evidence that the automatic association between pride displays and high-status concepts generalizes across diverse populations. We replicated several of the studies measuring implicit associations between pride and status, reviewed above, in a population of villagers living in a small-scale traditional society on a remote island in Fiji, essentially cut off from the rest of the global population (Tracy et al., 2013). These studies found that the pride expression is strongly implicitly associated with high status among both highly educated North American university students and Fijian villagers, despite the fact that Fijians hold a set of cultural practices and rituals that suppress personal status displays by individuals of both high and low ascribed statuses. That is, Fijian cultural rules prohibit any nonverbal behaviors that communicate an individual's belief that he or she deserves increased status, making Fiji a "tough test" of the question of whether pride is a universal status signal. If the pride display did not evolve as a status signal, there are few cultural explanations as to why status and pride would have become tightly interconnected in Fiji. As a result, the finding that pride displays are strongly and automatically associated with high status in Fiji provides compelling support for the evolutionary account.

Which Kind of Status Does Pride Signal?
The pride expression communicates both authentic and hubristic pride, and observers have a difficult time disentangling the two expressions from a single static display, unless contextual information is included (Tracy & Prehn, 2012), or the expresser is observed in motion, showing the display in a dynamic manner (Lange & Crusius, 2015; Nelson & Russel, 2014). Given that the two facets of pride appear to have divergent associations with prestige and dominance, respectively, one might therefore expect the pride display to communicate both forms of social

rank. However, recent evidence suggests that the pride expression is more strongly associated with prestige than dominance (Witkower et al., 2019).

First, the pride expression triggers automatic associations with concepts related to the possession of knowledge and expertise (Birch et al., 2010; Martens, 2014), suggesting that the form of status associated with these displays is the more prestigious variety. More direct evidence comes from studies testing whether the critical nonverbal behaviors associated with the pride expression are judged as conveying prestige versus dominance (Witkower et al., 2019). Across a wide range of targets posing various nonverbal expressions, and a variety of participants judging them, displays that included expansive posture, a slight smile, and an upward head tilt—that is, all components of the prototypical pride expression—were perceived as highly prestigious, but *not* as highly dominant.

Further supporting this account, Witkower and colleagues (2019) coded the nonverbal behaviors spontaneously displayed by individuals engaging in a collaborative group task, among which hierarchies had naturally emerged. Individuals who were perceived by their peers in the group as prestigious tended to display expressions that included an upward head tilt, slight smile, and expansiveness. In contrast, those perceived as dominant displayed expansiveness but no smile or upward head tilt. Furthermore, displaying the pride expression behaviors was associated with the attainment of social rank in the group—based on peer ratings and ratings made by outside observers—and the effect of pride displays on increased rank was mediated by perceptions of prestige but not dominance. These findings thus suggest that the pride expression communicates an individual's prestige, which in turn results in conferrals of social rank—but that this same display does not promote perceptions of dominance. This same research found that there is a distinct nonverbal display that does reliably communicate dominance, across cultures, and this display shares certain features with pride (i.e., expansive posture) but not others (i.e., in the dominance display there is no smile, and the head is tilted downward rather than upward; see Witkower et al., 2019; Witkower & Tracy, 2019b; Witkower et al., in press).

Conclusions and Future Directions

The research reviewed in this chapter suggests that pride is likely to be an evolved and adaptive emotion in humans, which functions to help individuals navigate their social hierarchies, by motivating them to engage in behaviors that allow them to attain and maintain social rank, and by communicating to others which group members are deserving of higher rank and should be targets of social learning. Furthermore, because there are two distinct ways to experience pride, this emotion is related to both evolved strategies for rank attainment: dominance and prestige.

Although numerous directions for future work lay ahead, we hope that this review has laid the groundwork for such endeavors. The past several decades have seen a major shift in researchers' understanding of and attention toward this emotion; prior to the 1990s (e.g., Tangney & Fischer, 1995), pride was only rarely included in psychological research, and only in the first decade of the twenty-first century did scholars begin to consider it an emotion of equal importance and biological foundation as the basic emotions of anger, fear, and sadness (e.g., Tracy & Robins, 2004a, 2004b). Today, however, psychological scientists regularly study pride and include it in a wide range of research endeavors (see Weidman et al., 2017), making it likely that our understanding of this emotion will only increase. We expect to see continued growth in both of these areas moving forward, along with a more complete elucidation of the affective pathways underlying the attainment of social rank and the various ways in which individuals navigate their hierarchies.

References

Apicella, C., Feinberg, D., & Marlowe, F. (2007). Voice pitch predicts reproductive success in male hunter-gatherers. *Biology Letters, 3*(6), 682–684.

Ashton-James, C. E., & Tracy, J. L. (2012). Pride and prejudice: How feelings about the self influence judgments of others. *Personality and Social Psychology Bulletin, 38*(4), 466–476.

Ballentine, B., Searcy, W. A., & Nowicki, S. (2008). Reliable aggressive signalling in swamp sparrows. *Animal Behaviour, 75*(2), 693–703.

Bargh, J. A., & Pietromonaco, P. (1982). Automatic information processing and social perception: The influence of trait information presented outside of conscious awareness on impression formation. *Journal of Personality and Social Psychology, 43*, 437–449.

Barkow, J. H. (1975). Prestige and culture: A biosocial interpretation. *Current Anthropology, 16*, 553–572.

Beck, A., Cañamero, L., & Bard, K. A. (2010). Towards an affect space for robots to display emotional body language. *19th International Symposium in Robot and Human Interactive Communication*, Viareggio, Italy, 464–469.

Belsky, J., & Domitrovich, C. (1997). Temperament and parenting antecedents of individual difference in three-year-old boys' pride and shame reactions. *Child Development, 68*, 456–466.

Birch, S. A., Akmal, N., & Frampton, K. L. (2010). Two-year-olds are vigilant of others' non- verbal cues to credibility. *Developmental Science, 13*(2), 363–369.

Brosi, P., Spörrle, M., Welpe, I. M., & Heilman, M. E. (2016). Expressing pride: Effects on perceived agency, communality, and stereotype-based gender disparities. *Journal of Applied Psychology, 101*(9), 1319.

Brown, J. D., & Marshall, M. A. (2001). Self-esteem and emotion: Some thoughts about feelings. *Personality and Social Psychology Bulletin, 27*, 575–584.

Brown, J. H., & Maurer, B. A. (1986). Body size, ecological dominance and Cope's rule. *Nature, 324*(6094), 248–250.

Carver, C. S., Sinclair, S., & Johnson, S. L. (2010). Authentic and hubristic pride: Differential relations to aspects of goal regulation, affect, and self-control. *Journal of Research in Personality, 44*, 698–703.

Cashdan, E. (1998). Smiles, speech, and body posture: How women and men display sociometric status and power. *Journal of Nonverbal Behavior, 22*(4), 209–228.

Cheng, J. T., Tracy, J. L., Foulsham, T., Kingstone, A., & Henrich, J. (2013). Two ways to the top: Evidence that dominance and prestige are distinct yet viable avenues to social rank and influence. *Journal of Personality and Social Psychology, 104*, 103–125.

Cheng, J. T., Tracy, J. L., & Henrich, J. (2010). Pride, personality, and the evolutionary foundations of human social status. *Evolution and Human Behavior, 31*(5), 334–347.

Chudek, M., Heller, S., Birch, S., & Henrich J. (2012). Prestige-biased cultural learning: Bystander's differential attention to potential models influences children's learning. *Evolution and Human Behavior, 33*(1), 46–56.

Cordaro, D. T., Sun, R., Kamble, S., Hodder, N., Monroy, M., Cowen, A., Bai, Y., & Keltner, D. (2019). The recognition of 18 facial-bodily expressions across nine cultures. *Emotion, 20*(7), 1292–1300.

Cosmides, L., & Tooby, J. (2000). Evolutionary psychology and the emotions. In M. Lewis & J. M. Haviland-Joes (Eds.), *Handbook of Emotions* (2nd ed., pp. 91–115). New York: Guilford Press.

Damian, R. I., & Robins, R. W. (2013). Aristotle's virtue or Dante's deadliest sin? The influence of authentic and hubristic pride on creative achievement. *Learning and Individual Differences, 26*, 156–160.

deCarvalho, T. N., Watson, P. J., & Field, S. A. (2004). Costs increase as ritualized fighting progresses within and between phases in the sierra dome spider, *Neriene litigiosa*. *Animal Behaviour, 68*(3), 473–482.

de Waal, F. (1989). *Chimpanzee politics: Power and sex among apes*. Johns Hopkins University Press.

Dickens, L. R., & Robins, R. W. (2022). Pride: A meta-analytic project. *Emotion, 22*(5), 1071–1087.

Dorfman, A., Eyal, T., & Bereby-Meyer, Y. (2014). Proud to cooperate: The consideration of pride promotes cooperation in a social dilemma. *Journal of Experimental Social Psychology, 55*, 105–109.

Ekman, P. (1992b). Are there basic emotions? *Psychological Review, 99*, 550–553.

Ellsworth, P. C., & Smith, C. A. (1988). Shades of joy: Patterns of appraisal differentiating pleasant emotions. *Cognition and Emotion, 2*, 301–331.

Ellyson, S. L., & Dovidio, J. F. (1985). Power, dominance, and nonverbal behavior: Basic concepts and issues. In S. L. Ellyson & J. F. Dovidio (Eds.), *Power, dominance, and nonverbal behavior* (pp. 1–27). Springer.

Fessler, D. M. T. (1999) Toward an understanding of the universality of second order emotions. In A. Hinton (Ed.), *Beyond nature or nurture: Biocultural approaches to the emotions* (pp. 75–116). Cambridge University Press.

Fink, B., Neave, N., & Seydel, H. (2007). Male facial appearance signals physical strength to women. *American Journal of Human Biology, 19*(1), 82–87.

Forsatkar, M. N., Nematollahi, M. A., & Brown, C. (2016). The toxicological effect of Ruta graveolens extract in Siamese fighting fish: A behavioral and histopathological approach. *Ecotoxicology, 25*(4), 824–834.

Foulsham, T., Cheng, J. T., Tracy, J. L., Henrich, J., & Kingstone, A. (2010). Gaze allocation in a dynamic situation: Effects of social status and speaking. *Cognition, 117*(3), 319–331.

Greenberg, N., & MacLean, P. D. (1978). Ritualistic social behaviors in lizards. In N. Greenberg & P. MacLean (Eds.), *Behavior and neurology of lizards: An interdisciplinary colloquium* (Vol. 77, p. 253). Department of Health, Education, and Welfare, Public Health Service, Alcohol, Drug Abuse, and Mental Health Administration, National Institute of Mental Health.

Hart, D., & Matsuba, M. K. (2007). The development of pride and moral life. In J. L. Tracy, R. W. Robins, & J. P. Tangney (Eds.), *The self-conscious emotions: Theory and research* (pp. 114–133). Guilford Press.

Havlicek, J., Roberts, S. C., & Flegr, J. (2005). Women's preference for dominant male odour: Effects of menstrual cycle and relationship status. *Biology Letters, 1*(3), 256–259.

Henrich, J., & Gil-White, F. J. (2001). The evolution of prestige: Freely conferred deference as a mechanism for enhancing the benefits of cultural transmission. *Evolution and Human Behavior, 22*, 165–196.

Hill, K., & Hurtado, A. M. (1989). Hunter-gatherers of the New World. *American Scientist, 77*, 436–443.

Ho, S.-Y., Tong, E. M. W., & Jia, L. (2016). Authentic and hubristic pride: Differential effects on delay of gratification. *Emotion, 16*(8), 1147–1156.

Hofmann, W., & Fisher, R. R. (2012). How guilt and pride shape subsequent self-control. *Social Psychological and Personality Science, 3*(6), 682–690.

Imada, T., & Ellsworth, P. C. (2011). Proud Americans and lucky Japanese: Cultural differences in appraisal and corresponding emotion. *Emotion, 11*(2), 329–345.

Izard, C. E. (1971). *The face of emotion*. Appleton-Century-Crofts.

James, W. (1890). *The principles of psychology*. Harvard University Press.

Jara, M., & Pincheira-Donoso, D. (2015). The neck flattening defensive behaviour in snakes: First record of hooding in the South American colubrid genus Philodryas. *Animal Biology, 65*(1), 73–79.

Jones, B. (2017). *The evolution of defensive strategies in Cobras*. Doctoral dissertation, Bangor University.

Keltner, D. (1995). Signs of appeasement: Evidence for the distinct displays of embarrassment, amusement, and shame. *Journal of Personality and Social Psychology, 68*, 441–454.

Kiesler, D. J. (1983). The 1982 interpersonal circle: A taxonomy for complementarity in human transactions. *Psychological Review, 90*(3), 185–214.

Lange, J., & Crusius, J. (2015). The tango of two deadly sins: The social-functional relation of envy and pride. *Journal of Personality and Social Psychology, 109*(3), 453–472.

Leary, M. R., Tambor, E. S., Terdal, S. K., & Downs, D. L. (1995). Self-esteem as an interpersonal monitor: The sociometer hypothesis. *Journal of Personality and Social Psychology, 68*(3), 518–530.

Lewis, M. (2000). Self-conscious emotions: Embarrassment, pride, shame, and guilt. In M. Lewis & J. M. Haviland-Jones (Eds.), *Handbook of emotions* (2nd ed., pp. 623–636). Guilford Press.

Lewis, M., Alessandri, S. M., & Sullivan, M. W. (1992). Differences in shame and pride as a function of children's gender and task difficulty. *Child Development, 63*, 630–638.

Martens, J. P. (2014). *The pride learning bias: Evidence that pride displays cue knowledge and guide social learning.* Thesis, University of British Columbia. Retrieved from https://open.library.ubc.ca/collections/ubctheses/24/items/1.0166990

Martens, J. P., Tracy, J. L., Cheng, J., Parr, L. A., & Price, S. (2010, January). *Do the chimpanzee bluff display and human pride expression share evolutionary origins?* Poster presented at the annual meeting for the Society for Personality and Social Psychology. Las Vegas, NV.

Martens, J. P., Tracy, J. L., & Shariff, A. F. (2012). Status signals: Adaptive benefits of displaying and observing the nonverbal expressions of pride and shame. *Cognition and Emotion, 26*(3), 390–406.

Maslow, A. H. (1936). The role of dominance in the social and sexual behavior of infrahuman primates: I. Observations at Vilas Park Zoo. *The Pedagogical Seminary and Journal of Genetic Psychology, 48*, 261–277.

Mercadante, E. J., & Tracy, J. L. (2022). A paradox of pride: Hubristic pride predicts strategic dishonesty in response to status threats. *Journal of Experimental Psychology: General, 151*(7), 1681–1706.

Mercadante, E. J., & Tracy, J. L. (2023). How does it feel to be greedy? The role of pride in avaricious acquisition. *Journal of Personality*. Advanced Online Publication. https://onlinelibrary.wiley.com/doi/abs/10.1111/jopy.12852

Muller, U., & Mazur, A. (1997). Facial dominance in *Homo sapiens* as honest signaling of male quality. *Behavioral Ecology, 8*(5), 569–579.

Nelson, N. L., & Russell, J. A. (2014). Dynamic facial expressions allow differentiation of displays intended to convey positive and hubristic pride. *Emotion, 14*(5), 857–864.

Orth, U., Robins, R. W., & Soto, C. J. (2010). Tracking the trajectory of shame, guilt, and pride across the life span. *Journal of Personality and Social Psychology, 99*(6), 1061–1071.

Plutchik, R. (1980). *Emotion: A psychoevolutionary synthesis*. Harper and Row.

Robins, R. W., Tracy, J. L., & Trzesniewski, K. (2010). Naturalizing the self. In O. P. John, R. W. Robins, & L. A. Pervin (Eds.), *Handbook of personality* (3rd ed., pp. 421–447). Guilford Press.

Roseman, I. J. (1991). Appraisal determinants of discrete emotions. *Cognition and Emotion, 5*, 161–200.

Schaller, G. B. (1963). *The mountain gorilla: Ecology and behavior.* University of Chicago Press.

Schwarz, N., & Clore, G. L. (1983). Mood, misattribution, and judgments of well-being: Informative and directive functions of affective states. *Journal of Personality and Social Psychology, 45*, 513.

Sell, A., Cosmides, L., & Tooby, J. (2014). The human anger face evolved to enhance cues of strength. *Evolution and Human Behavior, 35*(5), 425–429.

Shariff, A. F., & Tracy, J. L. (2009). Knowing who's boss: Implicit perceptions of status from the nonverbal expression of pride. *Emotion, 9*, 631–639.

Shariff, A. F., Tracy, J. L., & Markusoff, J. L. (2012). (Implicitly) judging a book by its cover: The power of pride and shame expressions in shaping judgments of social status. *Personality and Social Psychology Bulletin, 38*(9), 1178–1193.

Shi, Y., Chung, J. M., Cheng, J. T., Tracy, J. L., Robins, R. W., Chen, X., & Zheng, Y. (2015). Cross-cultural evidence for the two-facet structure of pride. *Journal of Research in Personality, 55*, 61–74.

Sigall, H., & Gould, R. (1977). The effects of self-esteem and evaluator demandingness on effort expenditure. *Journal of Personality and Social Psychology, 35*, 12–20.

Stipek, D., Recchia, S., & McClintic, S. (1992). Self-evaluation in young children. *Monographs of the Society for Research in Child Development, 57*(1), 100.

Stirrat, M., Stulp, G., & Pollet, T. V. (2012). Male facial width is associated with death by contact violence: Narrow-faced males are more likely to die from contact violence. *Evolution and Human Behavior, 33*(5), 551–556.

Tangney, J. P., & Fischer, K. W. (Eds.). (1995). *Self-conscious emotions: The psychology of shame, guilt, embarrassment, and pride.* Guilford Press.

Tangney, J. P., Wagner, P., & Gramzow, R. (1989). *The Test of Self-Conscious Affect (TOSCA).* George Mason University.

Tracy, J. L. (2016). *Take pride: Why the deadliest sin holds the secret to human success.* Houghton Mifflin Harcourt.

Tracy, J. L., Cheng, J. T., Martens, J., & Robins, R. (2011). The affective core of narcissism: Inflated by pride, deflated by shame. In W. K. Campbell & J. D. Miller (Eds.), *Handbook of narcissism and narcissistic personality disorder* (pp. 330–343). John Wiley & Sons.

Tracy, J. L., Cheng, J. T., Robins, R. W., & Trzesniewski, K. H. (2009). Authentic and hubristic pride: The affective core of self-esteem and narcissism. *Self and Identity, 8*(2–3), 196–213.

Tracy, J. L., & Matsumoto, D. (2008). The spontaneous expression of pride and shame: Evidence for biologically innate nonverbal displays. *Proceedings of the National Academy of Sciences, 105*(33), 11655–11660.

Tracy, J. L., Mercadante, E., Witkower, Z., & Cheng, J. T. (2020). The evolution of pride and social hierarchy. In B. Gawronski (Ed.), *Advances in experimental social psychology* (Vol. 62, pp. 51–114). Academic Press.

Tracy, J. L., & Prehn, C. (2012). Arrogant or self-confident? The use of contextual knowledge to differentiate hubristic and authentic pride from a single nonverbal expression. *Cognition and Emotion, 26*(1), 14–24.

Tracy, J. L., & Randles, D. (2011). Four models of basic emotions: A review of Ekman and Cordaro, Izard, Levenson, and Panksepp and Watt. *Emotion Review, 3*(4), 397–405.

Tracy, J. L., & Robins, R. W. (2004a). Putting the self into self-conscious emotions: A theoretical model. *Psychological Inquiry, 15*, 103–125.

Tracy, J. L., & Robins, R. W. (2004b). Show your pride: Evidence for a discrete emotion expression. *Psychological Science, 15*(3), 194–197.

Tracy, J. L., & Robins, R. W. (2007a). The psychological structure of pride: A tale of two facets. *Journal of Personality and Social Psychology, 92*(3), 506.

Tracy, J. L., & Robins, R. W. (2007b). The prototypical pride expression: Development of a nonverbal behavior coding system. *Emotion, 7*(4), 789–801.

Tracy, J. L., & Robins, R. W. (2008a). The nonverbal expression of pride: Evidence for cross-cultural recognition. *Journal of Personality and Social Psychology, 94*(3), 516–530.

Tracy, J. L., & Robins, R. W. (2008b). The automaticity of emotion recognition. *Emotion, 8*(1), 81–95.

Tracy, J. L., Robins, R. W., & Schriber, R. A. (2009). Development of a FACS-verified set of basic and self-conscious emotion expressions. *Emotion, 9*, 554–559.

Tracy, J. L., Shariff, A. F., & Cheng, J. T. (2010). A naturalist's view of pride. *Emotion Review, 2*, 163–177.

Tracy, J. L., Shariff, A. F., Zhao, W., & Henrich, J. (2013). Cross-cultural evidence that the nonverbal expression of pride is an automatic status signal. *Journal of Experimental Psychology: General, 142*(1), 163–180.

Van Der Schalk, J., Bruder, M., & Manstead, A. (2012). Regulating emotion in the context of interpersonal decisions: The role of anticipated pride and regret. *Frontiers in Psychology, 3*, 513.

Verbeke, W., Belschak, F., & Bagozzi, R. P. (2004). The adaptive consequences of pride in personal selling. *Journal of the Academy of Marketing Science, 32*(4), 386–402.

von Rueden, C., Gurven, M., & Kaplan, H. (2011). Why do men seek status? Fitness payoffs to Dominance and Prestige. *Proceedings of the Royal Society B: Biological Sciences, 278,* 2223.

von Rueden, C. R., & Jaeggi, A. V. (2016). Men's status and reproductive success in 33 nonindustrial societies: Effects of subsistence, marriage system, and reproductive strategy. *Proceedings of the National Academy of Sciences, 113*(39), 10824–10829.

Weidman, A. C., Cheng, J. T., & Tracy, J. L. (2018). The psychological structure of humility. *Journal of Personality and Social Psychology, 114*(1), 153–178.

Weidman, A. C., Steckler, C. M., & Tracy, J. L. (2017). The jingle and jangle of emotion assessment: Imprecise measurement, casual scale usage, and conceptual fuzziness in emotion research. *Emotion (Washington, D.C.), 17*(2), 267–295.

Weidman, A. C., Tracy, J. L., & Elliot, A. J. (2016). The benefits of following your pride: Authentic pride promotes achievement. *Journal of Personality, 84*(5), 607–622.

Weiner, B. (1985). An attributional theory of achievement motivation and emotion. *Psychological Review, 92,* 548–573.

Weisfeld, G. E., & Beresford, J. M. (1982). Erectness of posture as an indicator of dominance or success in humans. *Motivation and Emotion, 6,* 113–131.

Williams, L. A., & DeSteno, D. (2008). Pride and perseverance: The motivational role of pride. *Journal of Personality and Social Psychology, 94,* 1007–1017.

Witkower, Z., Hill, A. K., Koster, J., Pun, A., & Baron, A., & Tracy, J. L. (in press). Nonverbal displays of dominance and prestige: Evidence for cross-cultural and earlyemerging recognition. *Journal of Experimental Psychology: General.*

Witkower, Z., Mercadante, E. J., & Tracy, J. L. (2020). How affect shapes status: Distinct emotional experiences and expressions facilitate social hierarchy navigation. *Current Opinion in Psychology, 33,* 18–22.

Witkower, Z., Mercadante, E., & Tracy, J. L. (2022). The chicken and egg of pride and social rank. *Social Psychological and Personality Science, 13*(2), 382–389.

Witkower, Z., & Tracy, J. L. (2019a). Bodily communication of emotion: Evidence for extrafacial behavioral expressions and available coding systems. *Emotion Review, 11*(2), 184–193.

Witkower, Z., & Tracy, J. L. (2019b). A facial-action imposter: How head tilt influences perceptions of dominance from a neutral face. *Psychological Science, 30*(6), 893–906.

Witkower, Z., Tracy, J. L., Cheng, J. T., & Henrich, J. (2019). Two signals of social rank: Prestige and dominance are associated with distinct nonverbal displays. *Journal of Personality and Social Psychology, 118*(1), 89–120.

CHAPTER 11

Romantic Love

Jaclyn K. Doherty and Claudia C. Brumbaugh

Abstract

Humans are uniquely designed to be affected in numerous ways by romantic love. Romantic love is an intense feeling that attracts people to one another and keeps them together for some length of time. Thus, romantic love is thought to serve the purpose of relationship maintenance and the biological function of passing on the genes of the two individuals involved when offspring result. This chapter discusses the universality and ultimate functions of romantic love, as well as how romantic love is reflected in human biology (e.g., via brain and hormonal processes). Considering both psychological and physiological outcomes, the authors then weigh the benefits (e.g., elation and energy) and drawbacks (e.g., obsession and suicide) of romantic love. The chapter ends with a discussion of the life-span trajectory of romantic love and what happens after romantic love has "done its job."

Key Words: pair-bonding, reproduction, neurotransmitter, hormone, benefits of love, drawbacks of love, mental health

> *I crave your mouth, your voice, your hair.*
> *Silent and starving, I prowl through the streets.*
> *Bread does not nourish me, dawn disrupts me, all day*
> *I hunt for the liquid measure of your steps. . .*
>
> —*Love Sonnet XI, Pablo Neruda*

Romantic love permeates the human experience and is one of the most pervasive phenomena in our species. Questions surrounding the intense cravings, sleepless nights, and appetite loss associated with romantic love, as described above by Neruda, have been explored through poetry, literature, art, and music. In fact, between 1960 and 2010, approximately 67% of the songs on the U.S. Billboard top-40 singles list included references to love relationships—this percentage soared above that of any other topic (Christenson et al., 2019). Beyond popular culture and art, romantic love is also investigated in more systematic fields of study. In anthropology, love has been identified as a universal experience, which can unexpectedly befall even the starkest cynic (Lindholm, 2006). Although sociologists previously avoided the study of love, perhaps questioning its larger social significance, Jackson (1993) endorsed its sociological study by asserting that "love cannot be treated as if it has an existence independent of the social and cultural context within which it is experienced" (p. 202). The present chapter will delve into the topic of romantic love from an evolutionary perspective, drawing primarily from psychological, biological, and anthropological studies. We review romantic love's universality, functionality, and biological underpinnings. Then, we explore the everyday benefits and drawbacks of romantic love, as well as how it unfolds over time.

Universality and Cultural Differences

Consensus exists that romantic love has the potential to be present around the world in all people, though its manifestations may rest on cultural norms and mores. For instance, couples in South Korea wear matching outfits to express that they are in love, and men in Fiji present their hopeful future father-in-law with a polished whale tooth (Solomon, 2017). Humans are essentially born equipped with a biological makeup to someday love others romantically. The processes underlying love are linked to human biology; thus it follows that romantic love is universal and can touch anyone's life.

A substantial amount of research by a variety of social scientists finds that romantic love can be clearly identified cross-culturally. One of the most impactful efforts was by Jankowiak and Fischer (1992), who examined ethnographies, folklore, and songs in 166 cultures and found evidence of romantic love in 89% of them. The authors' approach was conservative; although they could not find direct proof of romantic love in some ethnographies, that does not necessarily rule out its existence in the remaining 11% of the cultures. Others similarly determined that feelings of romantic passion are equivalent across cultures (Doherty et al., 1994). For example, comparing Eastern European countries and the United States, De Munck et al. (2011) found strong consensus across individuals that romantic love makes people want to be together. These universal patterns provide good evidence that romantic love serves the function of bringing people together for some period of time in which they could potentially reproduce.

Given the research evidence, romantic love is acknowledged to exist on a universal scale. However, just as emotional experience and expression can vary depending on culture (Fischer et al., 2004; Koopmann-Holm & Tsai, 2014), romantic love manifests somewhat differently ideologically, emotionally, and behaviorally in different parts of the world. People in some parts of the world see romantic love in a somewhat negative light. For instance, in China some people associate romantic love with obligation and potential energy wasted (Murstein, 1974; Wu & Shaver, 1993). Meanwhile, Eastern Europeans perceive romantic love as momentary and unrealistic (Karandashev, 2015). In spite of the tendency for Western cultures to idealize romantic love, to believe it is enduring, and to associate love with positive emotional states (e.g., Shaver et al., 1991; Wu & Shaver, 1993), people in individualistic cultures are less likely to experience passionate love (Doherty et al., 1994), to be in love currently (Doherty et al., 1994), or to report ever having been in love (De Munck et al., 2011), compared to people from collectivist cultures. One might think that people should fall in love *more* frequently if a culture holds positive attitudes toward romantic love, but it seems the opposite is true. Perhaps idealization leads to a more impossible standard, and people in Western cultures are left feeling that their personal experience of this thing called romantic love has fallen short. In line with this thinking, people in individualistic cultures experience less affection and gratification when they are in love (Dion & Dion, 1991). Thus, the let-down of actual experience and the unattainability of what Westerners believe is "true" romantic love is likely a function of unrealistic expectations.

Whether romantic love is perceived as fleeting seems to depend on culture, but it's worth reviewing cross-cultural differences in a more prolonged state of romantic love as well. Much of this work addresses "love styles" including *eros, ludus, pragma, storge, mania,* and *agape* (Lee, 1988). In brief, *eros* captures the sexually charged passionate part of love; *ludus* involves fun and play; *pragma* is practical and realistic; *storge* concerns commitment and friendship; *mania* is an obsessive, co-dependent brand of love; and *agape* is characterized by selflessness and altruism. Comparing Mexican Americans and European Americans, Contreras et al. (1996) found that Mexican Americans were higher on *ludus* and *pragma* than European Americans. Goodwin and Findlay (1997) compared Chinese and British college students. The Chinese students scored higher on *pragma* and *agape*, and lower on eros than the British students. Murstein et al. (1991) compared French and American people, finding that Americans were higher on *storge* and *mania*, and the French were higher on *agape*. Finally, work outside of love styles finds differences between the United States and Eastern Europe. Individuals in the United States conceptualize romantic love as involving sacrifice, commitment, comfort, and friendship, whereas Eastern Europeans disagree and care very little about the friendship component of love (De Munck et al., 2011), possibly due to their disbelief that romantic love endures.

In sum, despite the vastness of culture and geographical space between humans, people nevertheless agree that romantic love results in a strong desire to be together, which would serve the evolutionary and biological drives to reproduce and care for offspring. Yet, there are cross-cultural differences in how people conceptualize romantic love, the traditions surrounding it, and what people expect from it. Regardless of the specific notions of love, it appears to be ubiquitous, with some fine-grained differences that align with the mores of the particular culture. However, the features that vary according to culture probably have negligible impact on more significant, evolutionarily relevant outcomes and mechanisms surrounding pair-bonding and reproduction.

Ultimate Functions

Despite cultural differences in the expression of romantic love, its evolutionary functions are thought to be consistent throughout humanity. Ultimately, romantic love serves as a mechanism to trigger pair-bonding in humans (Fisher, 1994; Fletcher et al., 2015), and it is considered to be evolutionarily advantageous in the following ways: it encourages individuals to seek mates with preferred genetic traits (Fisher et al., 2005; Fisher et al., 2006), increases commitment between partners (Fletcher et al., 2015; Gonzaga et al., 2008), and may even increase the success of reproduction (Sorokowski et al., 2017).

Helen Fisher, a prominent researcher of evolution and romantic love, asserts that mating and reproduction are influenced by three major processes: lust/sex drive, attraction/romantic love, and attachment (Fisher & Brown, 2002). Lust promotes sexual relationships between an individual and others of the same species through an innate desire for sexual pleasure. In contrast, romantic love promotes pair-bonding with particular individuals, optimizing the genetic potential of offspring. Finally, the attachment system fosters a committed relationship between bonded couples, in which individuals offer support for their partner, primarily via protection and parenting. The attachment system encourages both parents to invest time and resources into their offspring, increasing children's likelihood of survival (Brumbaugh & Fraley, 2006; Fletcher et al., 2015). Although the three systems are highly interrelated, biologically they operate independently (Fisher, 2000; Fisher et al., 2006).

While those in romantic love usually experience sexual desire for their partners, the emotional aspects of their relationships tend to take precedence, indicating that romantic love serves a function beyond sexual pleasure and conceiving offspring (Fisher et al., 2005; Fisher et al., 2006). Gonzaga et al. (2008) found that romantic love for a partner was associated with increased commitment to the relationship, while sexual desire was not related to this outcome. Further support for the differentiation between romantic love and sex drive has been established by neuroscientific studies. For example, Aron et al. (2005) found that the brain regions activated in individuals experiencing love differ from the regions typically activated in those experiencing sexual desire. They concluded that romantic love must be a separate system than sex drive, and it likely evolved, in part, to aid in the selection of an appropriate mate through a courtship system.

Romantic love results in attraction toward certain individuals with whom successful reproduction and child rearing is most likely (Fisher et al., 2006). Romantic love may be favored by natural selection because it conserves energy and time when identifying a good reproductive mate—otherwise, individuals may waste energy and time seeking inappropriate mates. Human offspring, as compared to those of other mammals, take longer to develop and are more likely to thrive when both parents contribute to their rearing (Pilakouta et al., 2018), so pair-bonds between human parents tend to be more exclusive and last longer than those of other mammalian species (Brumbaugh & Fraley, 2006). Since courtship and mate selection are taxing processes, romantic love facilitates reproduction by motivating individuals to focus their resources on specific individuals with whom they have a greater likelihood of producing and preserving offspring. In this way, romantic love is thought to be a motivational system, encouraging individuals to distinguish which traits in a potential mate are most advantageous to successful transmission of genes to future generations (de Boer et al., 2012; Fisher et al., 2006).

In addition to motivating individuals to focus their energy on desired genetic traits, romantic love seems to serve as a mechanism to suppress the search for another partner (Fletcher et al., 2015; Gonzaga et al., 2008; Maner et al., 2009). Gonzaga and colleagues (2008) conducted a study to explore romantic love's function in establishing relational commitment and suppressing thoughts of other attractive individuals. They found that participants reporting greater levels of love for their partners felt more committed to them and were less likely to think about and remember details about an attractive person who was presented earlier in the study. These effects were further demonstrated experimentally; those who completed a writing task about love for their romantic partner, as opposed to writing tasks about sexual desire or an unrelated topic, were also less likely to think about the attractive other. Gonzaga et al.'s findings support the evolutionary hypothesis of romantic love as a device to commit people to existing pair-bonds and suppress thoughts about other potential partners. This device likely aids in solidifying the bond between individuals, so they can more successfully reproduce and support offspring with fewer distractions (Fletcher et al., 2015).

For romantic love to be considered an evolved mechanism, it must also contribute to successful conception and transmission of genetic information via offspring (Al-Shawaf et al., 2018). A more direct link between romantic love and reproduction was investigated by Sorokowski et al. (2017), utilizing Sternberg's (1986) model of love, which identifies three primary dimensions of love: intimacy, passion, and commitment. For both men and women, the commitment dimension of romantic love was positively correlated with reproductive success, as defined by the number of children born in their current marriage. They concluded that the commitment aspect of romantic love in particular may increase the stability and success of romantic relationships, which would explain associations between committed love and reproductive success.

Evidence from Biology
Not only is the functional basis for romantic love supported by evolutionary theory and psychological evidence, but biological and neuroscientific research has further defined love and its evolution. This work establishes neurochemicals involved in brain activation when one

is in love: dopamine, serotonin, norepinephrine, and oxytocin. Cortisol and oxytocin hormones, involved in biological processes outside of the brain, have also been implicated in these biological processes. These substrates are associated with long-term mating and reproductive strategies (Acevedo et al., 2020), and the neural correlates of intense romantic love are closely tied to reward and motivation (Aron et al., 2005). It is probable that these biological processes function bidirectionally in relation to romantic love, such that the presence of love may trigger biological responses, but neurotransmitter and hormone activity likely underlie and further influence the experience of love.

Dopamine

Increased dopamine levels in the brain's ventral tegmental area (VTA), nucleus accumbens, prefrontal cortex, and ventral pallidum while in love explain the motivational and reward processes associated with romantic love and pair-bonding (Young & Wang, 2004). Several neuroscientific studies have linked thoughts about a beloved romantic partner to increased activity in dopamine-rich brain areas through functional magnetic resonance imaging (fMRI) (Acevedo et al., 2020; Aron et al., 2005) and event-related potential (ERP) (Langeslag et al., 2007) studies. These findings are consistent with the general functions of dopamine (including attention, motivation, and focus) which are also typically reported in love relationships.

An fMRI study investigating these brain activations found that when participants looked at photos of their beloved romantic partner during an early stage of intense love, as compared to photos of an acquaintance, there were increased activations in the reward and motivation centers (Aron et al., 2005). This aligns with the hypothesis that romantic love is associated with euphoric responses and increases in attention through dopamine-rich brain activations. Acevedo et al. (2020) conducted another fMRI study, recruiting couples within a few months of their weddings, to further assess the brain regions associated with romantic love. They found that when participants viewed photos of their spouse, as opposed to photos of neutral acquaintances, there was increased brain activation in the substantia nigra and VTA. The activation of these dopamine-rich areas rewards individuals for behaviors that promote the endurance of their love (Acevedo et al., 2020).

In addition to fMRI findings, ERP studies find similar support for the association between romantic love and dopamine levels. For example, participants viewed photos of their romantic partner, their friend (to control for familiarity), and a beautiful stranger (to control for attractiveness) as ERPs were measured (Langeslag et al., 2007). While people viewed photos of their romantic partners, they experienced larger late positive potentials (LPPs) than when they viewed the control photos. Since LPPs are associated with stimuli that evoke emotion and/or involve task completion, increased motivated attention has been linked to these activations. Therefore, Langeslag et al. (2007) concluded that when participants viewed photos of their beloved romantic partners, they experienced increases in attention, and this attention to their partner may serve to enhance survival and reproductive processes.

Serotonin

Three primary theories have been outlined to explain the negative relationship between romantic love and serotonin (Meyer, 2007). Two of these theories stem from patient outcomes associated with selective serotonin reuptake inhibitors (SSRIs), which are psychoactive medications that increase serotonin levels, typically in the treatment of anxiety or depression. SSRIs have been linked to sexual dysfunction and dulled emotions, and it is argued that these effects may be detrimental to the formation of romantic love connections (Meyer, 2007; Tocco & Brumbaugh, 2019). Further, increases in dopamine (discussed above as a possible effect of romantic love) are associated with lower levels of serotonin. Together, these effects lend theoretical support for the relationship between romantic love and lower serotonin levels (Meyer, 2007).

Marazziti et al. (1999) aimed to find empirical evidence for the involvement of the serotonin neurochemical system in romantic love. They recruited participants who recently fell in love, participants with unmedicated obsessive-compulsive disorder (OCD), and control participants. OCD patients are typically responsive to SSRI treatments, which suggests that those with unmedicated OCD have relatively low levels of serotonin. The density of serotonin receptors was compared among the three groups to indirectly compare serotonin levels. They found that those who were in love had more similar serotonin receptor densities to those with OCD than to the controls. This suggests that the neurochemical state of falling in love is similar to that of OCD in that it likely involves decreases in serotonin levels (Marazziti et al., 1999). The parallels between romantic love and OCD demonstrate just one of the potential undesirable effects that love can have.

Norepinephrine

Increased levels of norepinephrine have also been associated with romantic love (Fisher, 2004; Seshadri, 2016). Effects associated with increases in norepinephrine may seem familiar to those who have been in love, including sleeplessness and loss of appetite, as well as increased heart rate, energy, and excitement. Norepinephrine also improves memory, and it is common for individuals to experience increased memory of the person whom they love (Fisher, 2004).

Oxytocin

Oxytocin, both as a neurotransmitter in the brain and a hormone outside of the brain, has been associated with romantic love (Young, 2009). Much of the research concerning the biological underpinnings of romantic love, especially those investigating hormones, has been conducted using prairie vole animal models. The prairie vole is a monogamous species of rodent that exhibits pair-bonding behaviors similar to those of humans. These studies showed that increases in oxytocin and vasopressin hormone levels were associated with romantic love, and they interacted with the dopamine system to offer reward for these love behaviors (Young, 2009; Young & Wang, 2004). Similarly, human studies reveal that oxytocin hormone activity tends to increase during periods of early-stage romantic relationships and is associated with positive interaction reciprocity between partners (Fletcher et al., 2015; Schneiderman et al., 2012). Human experimental studies have furthered these findings by introducing oxytocin to the brain via nasal sprays (Fletcher et al., 2015). One experiment found that positive communication during conflict resolution was more likely among romantic couples exposed to intranasal oxytocin than those who were exposed to a placebo, demonstrating the potential relationship between oxytocin and human pair-bonding (Ditzen et al., 2009). This exposure to oxytocin was also associated with decreases in salivary cortisol levels, which may indicate lower stress levels following conflict.

Cortisol

The hypothalamic–pituitary–adrenal axis (HPA axis), which is associated with increases in stress, has been shown to increase in activity during the very early stages of love relationships; meanwhile, decreased HPA axis activity is found in the later stages of love relationships (Esch & Stefano, 2005a). However, based on measurements of cortisol release from the HPA axis, the effects of love may be more nuanced than originally thought (Weisman et al., 2015). After collecting saliva samples from single individuals and from couples in recently formed non-cohabitating romantic relationships, Weisman and colleagues found that single individuals secreted more cortisol on a daily basis than those in love. Among people in romantic relationships, those with lower levels of daily cortisol were engaged in more goal-oriented, reciprocal, and committed partnerships. These individuals also reported higher levels of "being-in-love." It is possible that feelings of commitment lead to a sense of calm, which further explains the lower cortisol levels (Weisman et al., 2015).

Brain Activations over Time
The intensity of love relationships tends to diminish over time as couples settle into long-term relationships (Fisher et al., 2005). However, there is neural evidence to suggest that although it feels less intense, the motivational processes of romantic love do not necessarily disappear as relationships endure. Aron et al. (2005) found that the brain regions activated and deactivated by short-term intense romantic love were similar to those affected by long-term romantic love, despite long-term love's relative lack of intensity. Similarly, Acevedo et al. (2012) found in their fMRI study that participants who reported intense love relationships with their long-term partners experienced increased activation in their brain's dopamine systems, involving the VTA and caudate nucleus, which supported their hypothesis that long-term relationship neural activity is similar to that of new relationships. However, long-term relationships may rely more on brain areas containing higher levels of opioids and serotonin, which is not typically found in new relationships, and this may explain behavioral differences between the stages.

Reward and motivation systems are not only essential to the process of initial romantic love, but they can remain active throughout the relationship (Acevedo et al., 2012; Aron et al., 2005). These findings support the idea that romantic love, which is experienced early in relationships, may be maintained in long-term relationships as well. While other brain activations are different between short- and long-term love, indicating some variances between the two stages, the persistence of the reward and motivational systems emphasizes their importance in forming and maintaining pair-bonds. Importantly, the hardwired, biological bases of these findings support the notion that romantic love serves an important function in humans.

Benefits of Romantic Love
Positive Feelings
Being in love is an experience that stands out over one's lifetime, mainly due to the overwhelming feelings and motivations that accompany romantic love. Romantic love is characterized by intense positive feelings such as elation and euphoria. Cross-culturally, passionate love is a strong predictor of positive emotions (Kim & Hatfield, 2004). These emotional highs correspond to strong, pleasant feelings toward the beloved (Guerra et al., 2011; Stanton et al., 2014) and feelings resembling hypomania, a mood state characterized by persistent disinhibition and mood elevation (Brand et al., 2007). Aside from intense emotions, people generally feel more positive about themselves and their lives when they are in love. For instance, romantic love has a beneficial impact on positive identity development in adolescence (Kroger, 2006), and it correlates with greater self-confidence and self-efficacy (Brand et al., 2007). Although directionality is unclear, there is also a strong positive relationship between passionate love and the belief in free will (Boudesseul et al., 2016), demonstrating an association between romantic love and a sense of autonomy and determination. Coupled young adults generally report higher well-being than singles (Brumbaugh, 2017, 2019; Gómez-López et al., 2019), and being married corresponds to less psychological distress (Braithwaite et al., 2010; Simon, 2002). Granted, some of this work pertains to simply being in a relationship versus being single, rather than being in romantic love versus some other relational phase. However, much

of the research on unmarried (single versus coupled) adults uses young adults as participants; young, coupled adults are typically in an early relational stage, during which they experience heightened feelings of romantic love. Finally, passionate love toward a romantic partner seems to trickle into other domains of life, corresponding to broader feelings of compassionate love and caring toward humanity (Singh et al., 2018).

Physical Outcomes
Although romantic love is mostly registered as an intense positive feeling and a desire to be with the loved one, romantic love also has subtler effects on physiology and cognition, as well as broader effects on neural reward systems that correspond to increased energy, attention, and motivation (Fisher et al., 2016). Thus, romantic love may be a coordinating mechanism that regulates various aspects of psychology and physiology, similar to the coordinating functions that have been proposed for emotions (Al-Shawaf & Lewis, 2017). As for physical health, romantic love appears to be beneficial. Those who are in love are more physically active, energetic, and sexually active (Brand et al., 2007). When passionate love is reciprocated from one's love interest, at least in late adolescence, this interchange has positive effects on general health and the immune system (Smith & Hokland, 1988). Ironically, people who are in the throes of romantic love sleep less nightly but report better sleep quality (Smith & Hokland, 1988). Young adults in committed relationships are less likely to have weight problems (Braithwaite et al., 2010), and compared to unmarried people, married individuals have fewer issues with alcohol abuse (Leonard & Rothbard, 1999). Romantic love has also been shown to lower stress, which is a well-known contributor to illness and disease (Esch & Stefano, 2005a). The presence and touch of the beloved has additional benefits, such as increased physical pain tolerance (Floyd et al., 2018). Even simply reflecting on a romantic partner raises blood glucose levels (Stanton et al., 2014), which map onto positive, energizing processes and the ability to self-regulate (Gailliot et al., 2007). Importantly, romantic love's positive effects on health could be a boon to individuals as they procreate and raise young children. Physical health motivates one to engage in sexual activity and increases energy for the burdensome activities related to bringing up highly altricial offspring (e.g., Jiannine, 2018). In a similar vein, a generally positive demeanor that corresponds to romantic love could be protective and adaptive when dealing with the challenges of raising offspring.

Cognition
Having constant intrusive thoughts about a partner during the majority of waking hours (Tennov, 1979) seems like it could become a distracting mental impediment. But indeed, cognition is another psychological arena that can be improved by romantic love. For instance, people who are deeply in love with their partners have heightened abilities to understand others' intentions and emotions (Wlodarski & Dunbar, 2014). This ability to "mentalize" can be helpful in coordinated parenting, relational efforts, and in upkeep of the pair-bond which ultimately promotes survival of offspring. Being sensitive to the feelings of those in one's family unit is adaptive, but this ability can also transfer more widely. For example, Wlodarski and Dunbar (2014) found that men in particular had a heightened ability to understand strangers' psychological states when a romantic partner representation was activated. Because mental activation of the beloved increases men's ability to understand others outside of the romantic relationship, this process could additionally assist in other adaptive problems, increasing men's capacity to detect and guard from potential outside social threats, such as mate poachers. Other beneficial cognitive effects include findings that people have better concentration when

they report being in love (Brand et al., 2007), and that being in love leads to faster word detection in lexical decision tasks, suggesting improved decision-making as an effect of romantic love (Bianchi-Demicheli et al., 2006).

Partner Benefits
So far, benefits to oneself as a function of romantic love have been discussed, but the target of one's fascination—the romantic partner—can also be the recipient of beneficial effects. First, people are motivated to make their partner happy when they are in love (Clark & Mills, 1979), and this is usually reflected in increased altruism toward one's partner. However, it should be noted that the increase in altruism is not universal (e.g., this effect does not hold true for East Asian women; Nelson & Yon, 2019). Second, both partners who are in love benefit via the process of partner idealization (e.g., Murray, 1999). Women who are in passionate love with their partner literally see their partner differently; they perceive more favorable qualities in their partner's face, such as being more physically attractive and looking more trustworthy (Gunaydin et al., 2015). The person who idealizes has a sense of validation that they chose an excellent partner, the partner being idealized comes off better than they are in reality, and these positive illusions ultimately promote relationship satisfaction and relational stability. Partner idealization could thus be a mediator between romantic love and the desire to remain in the relationship, as it encourages continued investment in the relationship. Finally, a partner can benefit from romantic love via fidelity. Research finds that people are only able to feel intense romantic love for one person at a time (Berscheid & Meyers, 1996). Being unable to passionately love two people simultaneously allows for the monopolization of positive feelings, so that all of one's romantic attention can be directed toward the object of love. In sum, all of the positives associated with romantic love, whether they be psychological, physical, cognitive, or motivational, encourage beneficial biological behaviors like reproduction and relationship maintenance to the advantage of offspring survival.

Drawbacks of Romantic Love

While humans have evolved to increase the likelihood of successful genetic transmission, some of the day-to-day effects of these processes may have negative implications on their lives and relationships. These outcomes are not objectively negative because they evolved to enhance relationship stability and benefit offspring, but they may still impact life in ways that *feel* negative. In other words, just as there are positive day-to-day effects associated with romantic love, as previously discussed, there are also negative effects. These negative manifestations can happen during, or as a consequence of, the formation of romantic love relationships. Especially during the initial intense stages of love, physiological changes, stress, dependence, and obsession can have adverse effects. Additionally, negative emotions such as jealousy may be experienced during ongoing romantic relationships, which can result in powerful feelings of distress and anxiety. Finally, negative outcomes, even suicide, may occur when a love relationship is terminated. Through these negative aspects of romantic love, we may witness an evolutionary trade-off. Ultimately, the function of romantic love as an evolved mechanism—to encourage committed pair-bonds and to enhance the production and survival of offspring—outweighs the discomfort, pain, distress, and other negative "side effects" of love.

Physiology and Stress
Physiological changes that occur alongside intense romantic love tend to involve the sympathetic nervous system (Fisher et al., 2005; Mercado & Hibel, 2017) and include increased sweating, increased heart rate, loss of appetite, trouble sleeping, and abnormal bowel movements

(Brand et al., 2007; Esch & Stefano, 2005b; Stefano et al., 2008). Physiological symptoms of romantic love are often accompanied by stress, perhaps due to the relationship's uncertainty, and these alerts can be evolutionarily protective (Stefano et al., 2008). However, as love solidifies and uncertainty diminishes, the relationship itself may help to quell stress and negative physiological experiences, and lovers can relax (Mercado & Hibel, 2017; Stefano et al., 2008).

Addiction

Initially, romantic love feels intensely euphoric. Over time, as people settle into love, they feel calm and content, but this shift is accompanied by feelings of longing, which can be painful if unsatisfied. Upon dissolution of a romantic relationship, there are often severe feelings of depression and grief. An abusive relationship with drugs often follows a similar trajectory. Additional behavioral parallels between romantic love and addiction include increases in risk-taking, dependence, and mood swings, as well as decreases in self-control (Fisher et al., 2010). Evolutionarily, this behavioral addiction to love promotes an individual's commitment to a specific partner and to reproduction, while conserving the time and energy that they may otherwise be exerting to find other mates (Fisher et al., 2016).

Not only can romantic love feel like an addiction, but there is emerging evidence that it biologically resembles addiction in humans and other monogamous mammals (Burkett & Young, 2012; Fisher et al., 2010). It has been argued that romantic love is a "behavioral addiction" due to the similarities between the neurochemical activity when experiencing love and when abusing drugs (Burkett & Young, 2012). For example, dopamine is released both during drug use and during the experience of romantic love (Burkett & Young, 2012; Fisher et al., 2010), rewarding individuals and leading to plastic changes in neurochemistry (Aragona et al., 2006; Burkett & Young, 2012). Additionally, opioid system activity, which is associated with pair-bonding and mating behaviors in prairie voles (Burkett et al., 2011), works to further reward animals for their experiences with drugs and condition their expectations for drug use (Burkett & Young, 2012).

Researchers from multiple disciplines have discovered parallels between the neurochemistry of drug addiction and that of romantic love. Feelings of longing and pain associated with the tolerance- and withdrawal-like stages of love relationships comprise just one potential negative outcome associated with the state. However, Fisher et al. (2016) argue that addiction to romantic love, while it can be difficult and painful, ultimately allows for "personal growth and positive emotions" (p. 7).

Mental Health

OCD is, in part, characterized by "intrusive thinking" (Fisher & Brown, 2002), which is similar to characteristics of romantic love, albeit on a smaller scale (de Boer et al., 2012; Feygin et al., 2006; Fisher, 2004; Fisher et al., 2010). Of course, being in love is not a mental disorder, but understanding the similarities between these two states, both in terms of behavior and neurochemistry, may offer new ways to understand love and new paradigms by which to study it. For example, remember that Marazziti et al. (1999) found that those who were in love had more similar serotonin receptor densities to those with OCD than to those in the control group. This suggests that the state of falling in love is similar to the state of having OCD, in that it involves decreased serotonin levels, and these effects may be felt through an obsession-like focus on a romantic partner. In addition to OCD-like symptoms, romantic love has also been associated with increased symptoms of state anxiety, depression, and hypomania (Bajoghli et al., 2014; Brand et al., 2015).

Jealousy
From an evolutionary perspective, romantic jealousy serves as an adaptive evolutionary mechanism to increase the likelihood of romantic relationship endurance (Buss & Haselton, 2005). While this mechanism may benefit relationship maintenance, it is driven by unpleasant feelings of distress. Both men and women share the emotional mechanism of jealousy in three primary ways: (1) jealousy signals potential threats to their relationship; (2) it is triggered by other viable mates for their partners; and (3) it functions as a "motivational mechanism" which prevents their partner from committing infidelity (Buss & Haselton, 2005). It is thought that distressful romantic jealousy is triggered to prevent relationship indiscretions by recognizing suspicions of partner infidelity and unconsciously assessing mate value (Brown, 2003). Evolutionarily, infidelity is incompatible with the preferred pair-bonded relationship because it diverts resources away from the partnership, decreases the likelihood of successful reproduction, and may cause the loss of reproductively relevant resources. While studies suggest that men tend to be more sensitive to sexual jealousy and women tend to be more sensitive to emotional jealousy (Buss et al., 1992; Ward & Voracek, 2004; Wiederman & Kendall, 1999), both genders seem to have similarly distressful experiences when faced with threats to their love relationships.

Suicide
People may experience suicidal ideations in response to infidelity, the termination of a romantic relationship, or the obstruction of a desired love relationship (Lindholm, 2006). Perhaps especially when the loss of a partner is abrupt or when there is betrayal or neglect, feelings of distress or depression can magnify and increase the likelihood of suicidal behaviors (O'Connor, 2016). Romantic love in relation to suicide has been studied by analyzing suicide notes. The topics addressed in suicide notes have not been found to differ between genders or across several cultures, including Germany, Hong Kong, the United Kingdom, and the United States (Canetto & Lester, 2002). In both men's and women's suicide notes, romantic relationships were the most commonly mentioned topic, even as compared to topics like work and school (Canetto & Lester, 2002). Further, Fisher et al. (2005) suggest that suicidal tendencies demonstrate the intensity of romantic love, as compared to sex drive, because people are more likely to commit suicide due to unrequited love than unsatisfied sexual urges. In sum, when relationships are thwarted, romantic love may contribute to suicidal ideation, which aligns with its negative mental health outcomes in an extreme sense and demonstrates the profound importance of love in the human species.

Falling out of Love
Timeline and Process
There are two sides to this relationship story—whether romantic love inevitably declines, or it if can endure. It has been argued that, if you factor out the obsessive or infatuation part of romantic love and focus only on the romantic component, then romantic love can survive over a long-term period (Graham, 2011; O'Leary et al., 2012). Evolutionary claims have been made that sustained romantic love maintains pair-bonds in the face of relationship stress or attractive alternatives (Buss, 2006). Romantic love, when it continues to exist, can help long-term couples stay interested in their partner and vivacious (Fisher, 2006). If the energy provided by romantic love at later ages can maintain health and improve longevity, then inclusive fitness benefits to grandchildren and other kin could also result. Sheets (2014) found that romantic love tended to decrease for the first 20 years of a relationship but then bounced back over longer periods, such that those who were together for 40 years or more said they had just

as much romantic love for their partner as in the early years. However, this could be an effect of retrospective bias, or it may be an element of the general positivity effect that accompanies age (Carstensen & Mikels 2005). Life transitions such as children leaving the home or retirement may be responsible as well. In other words, later-life couples may have more time for each other and learn to love each other again in the way they did in the early days.

There may also be ways to actively rally against romantic love's decline. Some claim that shared participation in novel tasks (Aron et al., 2000) and interruptions to relationship routines (Berscheid, 1983) can deter declines in romantic love. It seems that tackling new activities and experiences may be one way to keep romantic love from decreasing (Langeslag & van Strien, 2016). Those who argue for sustained romantic love tend to imply that it is exceptional but possible, and over longer periods romantic love needs to be actively cultivated, rather than passively maintained as it is in early phases of relationships. Overall, research suggests that romantic love is not universal in long-term relationships as it is in burgeoning relationships, but it does persist for some. It is strongly associated with relationship satisfaction in both short- and long-term relationships, as well as with general life satisfaction (Acevedo & Aron, 2009), which suggests it has the ability to keep people together in either relational situation. It may also be helpful to survival to have a partner who feels strongly about you in your later years as your own health deteriorates (Brumbaugh & Wood, 2013).

Many have argued that love can go on, but that it morphs from romantic love to companionate love. Companionate love involves ongoing attachment to one's partner and a life intertwined, but it is less intense emotionally, and more similar to friendship (Hatfield & Rapson, 1993). Some say that romantic love transforms in a linear fashion over time into companionate love (e.g., Hatfield & Walster, 1978; Sternberg, 1986). Companionate love is thought to keep people together over a sustained duration, unlike the temporary "hot glue" that romantic love brings. However, relationships may also sometimes encompass both types of love (Sprecher & Regan, 1998).

Conclusions

It has been noted that humans are one of the very few mammals that pair-bond (Brumbaugh & Fraley, 2006). Unlike most other mammals, biparental care is a crucial condition to successfully raising offspring. In these ways, humans are unique. Humans are also uniquely designed to be touched in various ways by romantic love. Romantic love is accompanied by strong positive emotions and motivations to be by the loved one's side. Overall, research on the evolved mechanism of romantic love suggests that its function is to work as a commitment device and solidify pair-bonded relationships through increased focus on compatible mates. The phenomenon of romantic love seems to be universal and has manifestations in the brain and body. While romantic love functions unconsciously to result in sustained pair-bonds and reproduction, there are both benefits and drawbacks that people subjectively experience as a result of romantic love. Whether romantic love can last is up for debate. Regardless, romantic love can be thought of as a mechanism that facilitates pair-bonding and ultimately successful reproduction.

References

Acevedo, B. P., & Aron, A. (2009). Does a long-term relationship kill romantic love? *Review of General Psychology*, *13*(1), 59–65.

Acevedo, B. P., Aron, A., Fisher, H. E., & Brown, L. L. (2012). Neural correlates of long-term intense romantic love. *Social Cognitive and Affective Neuroscience*, *7*(2), 145–159.

Acevedo, B. P., Poulin, M. J., Collins, N. L., & Brown, L. L. (2020). After the honeymoon: Neural and genetic correlates of romantic love in newlywed marriages. *Frontiers in Psychology*, *11*, 634.

Al-Shawaf, L., & Lewis, D. (2017). Evolutionary psychology and the emotions. In V. Zeigler-Hill & T. K. Shackelford (Eds.) *Encyclopedia of personality and individual differences* (pp. 1–10). Springer.

Al-Shawaf, L., Zreik, K., & Buss, D. M. (2018). Thirteen misunderstandings about natural selection. In T. K. Shackelford, & V. Weekes-Shackelford (Eds.), *Encyclopedia of evolutionary psychological science* (pp. 1–14). Springer.

Aragona, B. J., Liu, Y., Yu, Y. J., Curtis, J. T., Detwiler, J. M., Insel, T. R., & Wang, Z. (2006). Nucleus accumbens dopamine differentially mediates the formation and maintenance of monogamous pair bonds. *Nature Neuroscience, 9*(1), 133–139.

Aron, A., Fisher, H., Mashek, D. J., Strong, G., Li, H., & Brown, L. L. (2005). Reward, motivation, and emotion systems associated with early-stage intense romantic love. *Journal of Neurophysiology, 94*(1), 327–337.

Aron, A., Norman, C. C., Aron, E. N., McKenna, C., & Heyman, R. E. (2000). Couples' shared participation in novel and arousing activities and experienced relationship quality. *Journal of Personality and Social Psychology, 78*(2), 273–284.

Bajoghli, H., Keshavarzi, Z., Mohammadi, M.-R., Schmidt, N. B., Norton, P. J., Holsboer-Trachsler, E., & Brand, S. (2014). "I love you more than I can stand!": Romantic love, symptoms of depression and anxiety, and sleep complaints are related among young adults. *International Journal of Psychiatry in Clinical Practice, 18*(3), 169–174.

Berscheid, E. (1983). Emotion. In H. H. Kelley, E. Berscheid, A. Christensen, J. H. Harvey, T. L. Huston, G. Levinger, E. McClintock, L. A. Peplau, & D. R. Peterson (Eds.), *Close relationships* (pp. 110–168). Freeman.

Berscheid, E., & Meyers, S. A. (1996). A social categorical approach to a question about love. *Personal Relationships, 3*(1), 19–43.

Bianchi-Demicheli, F., Grafton, S. T., & Ortigue, S. (2006). The power of love on the human brain. *Social Neuroscience, 1*(2), 90–103.

Boudesseul, J., Lantian, A., Cova, F., & Bègue, L. (2016). Free love? On the relation between belief in free will, determinism, and passionate love. *Consciousness and Cognition, 46*, 47–59.

Braithwaite, S. R., Delevi, R., & Fincham, F. D. (2010). Romantic relationships and the physical and mental health of college students. *Personal Relationships, 17*(1), 1–12.

Brand, S., Foell, S., Bajoghli, H., Keshavarzi, Z., Kalak, N., Gerber, M., Schmidt, N. B., Norton, P. J., & Holsboer-Trachsler, E. (2015). "Tell me, how bright your hypomania is, and I tell you, if you are happily in love!": Among young adults in love, bright side hypomania is related to reduced depression and anxiety, and better sleep quality. *International Journal of Psychiatry in Clinical Practice, 19*(1), 24–31.

Brand, S., Luethi, M., von Planta, A., Hatzinger, M., & Holsboer-Trachsler, E. (2007). Romantic love, hypomania, and sleep pattern in adolescents. *Journal of Adolescent Health, 41*(1), 69–76.

Brown, W. (2003). Fluctuating asymmetry and romantic jealousy. *Evolution and Human Behavior, 24*(2), 113–117.

Brumbaugh, C. C. (2017). Transferring connections: Friend and sibling attachments' importance in the lives of singles. *Personal Relationships, 24*, 534–549.

Brumbaugh, C. C. (2019). Well-being of partnered versus single people. In C. T. Hill (Ed.), *Intimate relationships across cultures: A comparative study* (pp. 164–166). Cambridge University Press.

Brumbaugh, C. C., & Fraley, R. C. (2006). The evolution of attachment in romantic relationships. In M. Mikulincer & G.S. Goodman (Eds.), *Dynamics of romantic love: Attachment, caregiving, and sex* (pp. 71–101). Guilford Press.

Brumbaugh, C. C., & Wood, D. (2013). Mate preferences across life and across the world. *Social Psychological and Personality Science, 4*(1), 100–107.

Burkett, J. P., & Young, L. J. (2012). The behavioral, anatomical and pharmacological parallels between social attachment, love and addiction. *Psychopharmacology, 224*(1), 1–26.

Burkett, J. P., Spiegel, L. L., Inoue, K., Murphy, A. Z., & Young, L. J. (2011). Activation of μ-opioid receptors in the dorsal striatum is necessary for adult social attachment in monogamous prairie voles. *Neuropsychopharmacology, 36*(11), 2200–2210.

Buss, D. M. (2006). The evolution of love. In R. Sternberg & K Weis (Eds.), *The new psychology of love* (pp. 65–86). Yale University Press.

Buss, D. M., & Haselton, M. (2005). The evolution of jealousy: Comment. *Trends in Cognitive Sciences, 9*(11), 506–507.

Buss, D. M., Larsen, R. J., Westen, D., & Semmelroth, J. (1992). Sex differences in jealousy: Evolution, physiology, and psychology. *Psychological Science, 3*(4), 251–255.

Canetto, S. S., & Lester, D. (2002). Love and achievement motives in women's and men's suicide notes. *The Journal of Psychology: Interdisciplinary and Applied, 136*(5), 573–576.

Carstensen, L. L., & Mikels, J. A. (2005). At the intersection of emotion and cognition: Aging and the positivity effect. *Current Directions in Psychological Science, 14*(3), 117–121.

Christenson, P. G., de Haan-Rietdijk, S., Roberts, D. F., & ter Bogt, T. F. M. (2019). What has America been singing about? Trends in themes in the U.S. top-40 songs: 1960–2010. *Psychology of Music, 47*(2), 194–212.

Clark, M. S., & Mills, J. (1979). Interpersonal attraction in exchange and communal relationships. *Journal of Personality and Social Psychology, 37*(1), 12–24.

Contreras, R., Hendrick, S. S., & Hendrick, C. (1996). Perspectives on marital love and satisfaction in Mexican American and Anglo-American couples. *Journal of Counseling & Development, 74*(4), 408–415.

de Boer, A., van Buel, E. M., & Ter Horst, G. J. (2012). Love is more than just a kiss: A neurobiological perspective on love and affection. *Neuroscience, 201*, 114–124.

De Munck, V. C., Korotayev, A., de Munck, J., & Khaltourina, D. (2011). Cross-cultural analysis of models of romantic love among US residents, Russians, and Lithuanians. *Cross-Cultural Research, 45*(2), 128–154.

Dion, K. K., & Dion, K. L. (1991). Psychological individualism and romantic love. *Journal of Social Behavior and Personality, 6*(1), 17.

Ditzen, B., Schaer, M., Gabriel, B., Bodenmann, G., Ehlert, U., & Heinrichs, M. (2009). Intranasal oxytocin increases positive communication and reduces cortisol levels during couple conflict. *Biological Psychiatry, 65*(9), 728–731.

Doherty, R. W., Hatfield, E., Thompson, K., & Choo, P. (1994). Cultural and ethnic influences on love and attachment. *Personal Relationships, 1*(4), 391–398.

Esch, T., & Stefano, G. B. (2005a). Love promotes health. *Neuroendocrinology Letters, 26*(3), 264–267.

Esch, T., & Stefano, G. B. (2005b). The neurobiology of love. *Neuroendocrinology Letters, 26*(3), 175–192.

Feygin, D. L., Swain, J. E., & Leckman, J. F. (2006). The normalcy of neurosis: Evolutionary origins of obsessive–compulsive disorder and related behaviors. *Progress in Neuro-Psychopharmacology and Biological Psychiatry, 30*(5), 854–864.

Fischer, A. H., Rodriguez Mosquera, P. M., Van Vianen, A. E., & Manstead, A. S. (2004). Gender and culture differences in emotion. *Emotion, 4*(1), 87.

Fisher, H. (1994). The nature of romantic love. *The Journal of NIH Research, 6*, 59–64.

Fisher, H. (2000). Lust, attraction, attachment: Biology and evolution of the three primary emotion systems for mating, reproduction, and parenting. *Journal of Sex Education and Therapy, 25*(1), 96–104.

Fisher, H. (2004). *Why we love: The nature and chemistry of romantic love*. Macmillan.

Fisher, H. (2006). The drive to love. In R. Sternberg & K Weis (Eds.), *The new psychology of love* (pp. 87–115). Yale University Press.

Fisher, H., Aron, A., & Brown, L. L. (2005). Romantic love: An fMRI study of a neural mechanism for mate choice. *Journal of Comparative Neurology, 493*(1), 58–62.

Fisher, H. E., Aron, A., & Brown, L. L. (2006). Romantic love: A mammalian brain system for mate choice. *Philosophical Transactions of the Royal Society B: Biological Sciences, 361*(1476), 2173–2186.

Fisher, H. E., & Brown, L. L. (2002). Defining the brain systems of lust, romantic attraction, and attachment. *Archives of Sexual Behavior, 31*, 413–419.

Fisher, H. E., Brown, L. L., Aron, A., Strong, G., & Mashek, D. (2010). Reward, addiction, and emotion regulation systems associated with rejection in love. *Journal of Neurophysiology, 104*(1), 51–60.

Fisher, H. E., Xu, X., Aron, A., & Brown, L. L. (2016). Intense, passionate, romantic love: A natural addiction? How the fields that investigate romance and substance abuse can inform each other. *Frontiers in Psychology, 7*, 687.

Fletcher, G. J. O., Simpson, J. A., Campbell, L., & Overall, N. C. (2015). Pair-bonding, romantic love, and evolution: The curious case of homo sapiens. *Perspectives on Psychological Science, 10*(1), 20–36.

Floyd, K., Ray, C. D., van Raalte, L. J., Stein, J. B., & Generous, M. A. (2018). Interpersonal touch buffers pain sensitivity in romantic relationships but heightens sensitivity between strangers and friends. *Research in Psychology and Behavioral Sciences, 6*(1), 27–34.

Gailliot, M. T., Baumeister, R. F., DeWall, C. N., Maner, J. K., Plant, E. A., Tice, D. M., Brewer, L. E., & Schmeichel, B. J. (2007). Self-control relies on glucose as a limited energy source: Willpower is more than a metaphor. *Journal of Personality and Social Psychology, 92*(2), 325.

Gómez-López, M., Viejo, C., & Ortega-Ruiz, R. (2019). Well-being and romantic relationships: A systematic review in adolescence and emerging adulthood. *International Journal of Environmental Research and Public Health, 16*(13), 2415.

Gonzaga, G. C., Haselton, M. G., Smurda, J., Davies, M. S., & Poore, J. C. (2008). Love, desire, and the suppression of thoughts of romantic alternatives. *Evolution and Human Behavior, 29*(2), 119–126.

Goodwin, R. & Findlay, C. (1997). "We were just fated together"... Chinese love and the concept of yuan in England and Hong Kong. *Personal Relationships, 4*, 85–92.

Graham, J. M. (2011). Measuring love in romantic relationships: A meta-analysis. *Journal of Social and Personal Relationships, 28*(6), 748–771.

Guerra, P., Campagnoli, R. R., Vico, C., Volchan, E., Anllo-Vento, L., & Vila, J. (2011). Filial versus romantic love: Contributions from peripheral and central electrophysiology. *Biological Psychology, 88*(2–3), 196–203.

Gunaydin, G., & DeLong, J. E. (2015). Reverse correlating love: Highly passionate women idealize their partner's facial appearance. *PLoS ONE, 10*(3). doi: https://doi.org/10.1371/journal.pone.0121094

Hatfield, E., & Rapson, R. (1993). Love and attachment processes. In M. Lewis & J. M. Halaviland (Eds.), *Handbook of emotions* (pp. 595–604). Guilford Press.

Hatfield, E., & Walster, G. W. (1978). *A new look at love: A revealing report on the most elusive of all emotions*. University Press of America.

Jackson, S. (1993). Even sociologists fall in love: An exploration in the sociology of emotions. *Sociology, 27*(2), 201–220.

Jankowiak, W. R., & Fischer, E. F. (1992). A cross-cultural perspective on romantic love. *Ethnology, 31*(2), 149–155.

Jiannine, L. M. (2018). An investigation of the relationship between physical fitness, self-concept, and sexual functioning. *Journal of Education and Health Promotion, 7*, 57.

Karandashev, V. (2015). A cultural perspective on romantic love. *Online Readings in Psychology and Culture, 5*(4), 2.

Kim, J., & Hatfield, E. (2004). Love types and subjective well-being: A cross-cultural study. *Social Behavior & Personality: An International Journal, 32*(2), 173–182.

Koopmann-Holm, B., & Tsai, J. L. (2014). Focusing on the negative: Cultural differences in expressions of sympathy. *Journal of Personality and Social Psychology, 107*, 1092–1115.

Kroger, J. (2006). *Identity development: Adolescence through adulthood*. Sage Publications.

Langeslag, S. J., & van Strien, J. W. (2016). Regulation of romantic love feelings: Preconceptions, strategies, and feasibility. *PloS ONE, 11*(8), e0161087.

Langeslag, S. J. E., Jansma, B. M., Franken, I. H. A., & Van Strien, J. W. (2007). Event-related potential responses to love-related facial stimuli. *Biological Psychology, 76*(1), 109–115.

Lee, J. A. (1988). Love-styles. In Sternberg, R. J. & Barnes, M. L. (Eds.) *The psychology of love* (pp. 38–67). Yale University Press.

Leonard, K. E., & Rothbard, J. C. (1999). Alcohol and the marriage effect. *Journal of Studies on Alcohol* (Suppl 13), 139–146.

Lindholm, C. (2006). Romantic love and anthropology. *Etnofoor, 19*(1), 5–21.

Maner, J. K., Gailliot, M. T., & Miller, S. L. (2009). The implicit cognition of relationship maintenance: Inattention to attractive alternatives. *Journal of Experimental Social Psychology, 45*(1), 174–179.

Marazziti, D., Akiskal, H. S., Rossi, A., & Cassano, G. B. (1999). Alteration of the platelet serotonin transporter in romantic love. *Psychological Medicine, 29*(3), 741–745.

Mercado, E., & Hibel, L. C. (2017). I love you from the bottom of my hypothalamus: The role of stress physiology in romantic pair bond formation and maintenance. *Social and Personality Psychology Compass, 11*(2) 1–12.

Meyer, D. (2007). Selective serotonin reuptake inhibitors and their effects on relationship satisfaction. *The Family Journal, 15*(4), 392–397.

Murray, S. L. (1999). The quest for conviction: Motivated cognition in romantic relationships. *Psychological Inquiry, 10*(1), 23–34.

Murstein, B. I. (1974). *Love, sex, and marriage through the ages*. Springer.

Murstein, B. I., Merighi, J. R., & Vyse, S. A. (1991). Love styles in the United States and France: A cross-cultural comparison. *Journal of Social and Clinical Psychology, 10*(1), 37–46.

Nelson, A. J., & Yon, K. J. (2019). Core and peripheral features of the cross-cultural model of romantic love. *Cross-Cultural Research, 53*(5), 447–482.

O'Connor, J. (2016). The evolution of love and suicide. *Quadrant Magazine, 60*(5), 46–49.

O'Leary, K. D., Acevedo, B. P., Aron, A., Huddy, L., & Mashek, D. (2012). Is long-term love more than a rare phenomenon? If so, what are its correlates? *Social Psychological and Personality Science, 3*(2), 241–249.

Pilakouta, N., Hanlon, E. J., & Smiseth, P. T. (2018). Biparental care is more than the sum of its parts: Experimental evidence for synergistic effects on offspring fitness. *Proceedings of the Royal Society B: Biological Sciences, 285*(1884), 1–7.

Schneiderman, I., Zagoory-Sharon, O., Leckman, J. F., & Feldman, R. (2012). Oxytocin during the initial stages of romantic attachment: Relations to couples' interactive reciprocity. *Psychoneuroendocrinology, 37*(8), 1277–1285.

Seshadri, K. G. (2016). The neuroendocrinology of love. *Indian Journal of Endocrinology and Metabolism, 20*(4), 558–563.

Shaver, P. R., Wu, S., & Schwartz, J. C. (1991). Cross-cultural similarities and differences in emotion and its representation: A prototype approach. In M. S. Clark (Ed.), *Review of personality and social psychology* (Vol. 13, pp. 175–212). Sage.

Sheets, V. L. (2014). Passion for life: Self-expansion and passionate love across the life span. *Journal of Social and Personal Relationships, 31*(7), 958–974.

Simon, R. W. (2002). Revisiting the relationships among gender, marital status, and mental health. *American Journal of Sociology, 107*(4), 1065–1096.

Singh, B., Salve, S., & Mhaske, R. S. (2018). Does personality, gratitude and passionate love makes youth compassionate? *Journal of Psychosocial Research, 13*(1), 245–254.

Smith, D. F., & Hokland, M. (1988). Love and salutogenesis in late adolescence: A preliminary investigation. *Psychology: A Journal of Human Behavior, 25*, 44–49.

Solomon, S. (2017, April 11). In Fiji, nothing says "I love you" like a sperm whale tooth. *New York Times.* https://www.nytimes.com/2017/04/11/world/asia/suva-fiji-tabua.html

Sorokowski, P., Sorokowska, A., Butovskaya, M., Karwowski, M., Groyecka, A., Wojciszke, B., & Pawlowski, B. (2017). Love influences reproductive success in humans. *Frontiers in Psychology, 8*, 1922.

Sprecher, S., & Regan, P. C. (1998). Passionate and companionate love in courting and young married couples. *Sociological Inquiry, 68*(2), 163–185.

Stanton, S. C., Campbell, L., & Loving, T. J. (2014). Energized by love: Thinking about romantic relationships increases positive affect and blood glucose levels. *Psychophysiology, 51*(10), 990–995.

Stefano, G., Stefano, J., & Esch, T. (2008). Anticipatory stress response: A significant commonality in stress, relaxation, pleasure and love responses. *Medical Science Monitor: International Medical Journal of Experimental and Clinical Research, 14*(2), RA17–21.

Sternberg, R. J. (1986). A triangular theory of love. *Psychological Review, 93*(2), 119–135.

Tennov, D. (1979). *Love and limerence: The experience of being in love.* Stein & Day.

Tocco, C., & Brumbaugh, C. C. (2019, March). Antidepressants may not be the most "attractive" way to treat depression. [Conference presentation]. EPA 2019 Convention, New York, NY.

Ward, J., & Voracek, M. (2004). Evolutionary and social cognitive explanations of sex differences in romantic jealousy. *Australian Journal of Psychology, 56*(3), 165–171.

Wiederman, M. W., & Kendall, E. (1999). Evolution, sex, and jealousy: Investigation with a sample from Sweden. *Evolution and Human Behavior, 20*(2), 121–128.

Weisman, O., Schneiderman, I., Zagoory-Sharon, O., & Feldman, R. (2015). Early stage romantic love is associated with reduced daily cortisol production. *Adaptive Human Behavior and Physiology, 1*(1), 41–53.

Wlodarski, R., & Dunbar, R. I. (2014). The effects of romantic love on mentalizing abilities. *Review of General Psychology, 18*(4), 313–321.

Wu, S., & Shaver, P. R. (1993, August). American and Chinese love conceptions: Variations on a theme. 101st meeting of the American Psychological Association Convention, Toronto.

Young, L. J. (2009). Love: Neuroscience reveals all. *Nature, 457*(7226), 148–148.

Young, L. J., & Wang, Z. (2004). The neurobiology of pair bonding. *Nature Neuroscience, 7*(10), 1048–1054.

CHAPTER 12
Neuroendocrine Mechanisms for Human Emotional Attachments

Heather Habecker and Mark V. Flinn

Abstract

Family relationships are a key component of human sociality. Here we integrate information from genetics and neuroendocrinology with cross-cultural analyses of family behavior and evolutionary logic. Hormonal and neural mechanisms provide clues to the evolution of the emotional and cognitive systems that influence human family psychology. Evolved changes in affiliative neuropeptide (oxytocin, arginine vasopressin) and associated neurobiological mechanisms primarily in the medial frontal lobe, the ventral forebrain, the ventral basal ganglia, and the hypothalamus enable attachment and bonding emotions that underpin the extended kin relationships characteristic of humans. These adaptive changes in family and kinship psychology are critical for the development of other major aspects of human sociality, including inter-group cooperation and cumulative culture. The extended family facilitates tolerance and connections among groups. Bilateral, multigenerational, and affinal kinship links are critical. The emotional systems that underpin this unique human pattern of kinship networks are key to understanding how human intelligence, culture, and sociality coevolved.

Key Words: emotion, attachment, hormone, oxytocin, family

Evolution of Emotions

Objective analysis of emotions and feelings is elusive. Most studies are based on description of behavior, including "expressions" inferred to reflect internal states (Darwin, 1872; Ekman & Davidson, 1994). Steroid and peptide hormones, associated neurotransmitters, and other chemical messengers influence emotional states and guide the behaviors of mammals in many important ways (Ellison, 2009; Lee et al., 2009; Panksepp, 2009). Here we use a Tinbergen (1963) approach, integrating evolutionary logic, phylogeny, developmental influences (ontogeny), and neuroendocrinological mechanisms (Pfaff et al., 2019; Weisfeld & Goetz, 2013) to understand the emotions that influence human family relationships.

Some of our most potent human emotions are associated with close social relationships: a mother holding her newborn infant; siblings reunited after a long absence; lovers embracing (Adolphs, 2003). Natural selection has designed our neurobiological mechanisms, in concert with our endocrine systems, to generate sensations that guide interactions with these evolutionarily important individuals (Amodio & Frith, 2006; Bartels & Zeki, 2004). Humans have much in common with our primate relatives, including the same basic hormones and neurotransmitters that underlie our emotional responses (Babb et al., 2015). But our unique human evolutionary history has modified us to respond to different circumstances and situations; we experience reward and punishment for somewhat different stimuli than our phylogenetic cousins. Chimpanzees and humans share the same emotional delight—the sensational reward—when biting into a ripe, juicy mango. The endocrine, neurological, and associated emotional responses of a human father to interactions with his child (e.g., Gray et al., 2002; Storey et al., 2000; Wynne-Edwards, 2001), however, are quite different from those of a chimpanzee male (Fernandez-Duque et al., 2009; Rilling & Mascaro, 2017). Happiness for a human (Buss, 2000) has many unique designs, such as romantic love (Fisher et al., 2006), that involve modification of the neurological receptors and processors of shared endogenous messengers from our phylogenetic heritage (Allman et al., 2001). Many of the characteristics of humans' unique sociality, especially attachment and bonding, are modulated by these shared neuroendocrine systems (e.g., Flinn, Duncan, et al., 2012; Gray & Anderson, 2010).

The Neuroscience of Emotions

The emotions we experience arise from a complex interplay of multiple systems in the body and brain (Dalgleish, 2004). Emotions can be broken into three interconnected components: physiology, behavior, and subjective experience. Physiologically, emotional responses arise from activity in the motor cortex, the brainstem, and the autonomic nervous system (ANS). The visceral component of this response arises from projections from the medial frontal lobe, the ventral forebrain, the ventral basal ganglia, and the hypothalamus that terminate on the visceral motor centers in the brainstem and the preganglionic autonomic neurons, as seen in Figure 12.1 (Purves et al., 2017). Projections from the medial frontal lobe, the ventral forebrain, the ventral basal ganglia, and the hypothalamus, in addition to projections from the posterior frontal lobe, also terminate on the somatic premotor and motor neuron pools, resulting in voluntary motor responses related to emotion. The somatic premotor and motor neuron pools also receive input from the brainstem and volitional motor centers in the motor

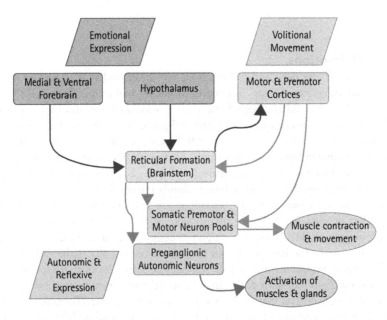

Figure 12.1. Connections from emotions to volitional movement.

and premotor cortex (which itself receives input from the posterior frontal lobe), the basal ganglia, and the cerebellum (Purves et al., 2017).

Specifically, descending pyramidal and extrapyramidal projections from the motor cortex and brainstem to the reticular formation, motor neurons of the cranial nerve nuclei, and the ventral horn result in volitional movement associated with emotion. Emotional expression (including both reflexes, such as reflexive facial expressions, and emotional behaviors, such as voluntary facial expression), on the other hand, arises from pyramidal and extrapyramidal projections from the limbic center of the ventromedial forebrain and the hypothalamus, terminating on reticular formation and the autonomic preganglionic neurons in the brainstem and spinal cord (Purves et al., 2017). The reticular formation, possessing several integrative centers, is especially important in both volitional and autonomic emotional responses. Because it feeds into areas of the brainstem and spinal cord, it can produce widespread visceral and somatic motor responses that can override reflexes and can involve almost every organ in the body. This integration in the reticular formation is critical for the coordination of expression of emotional behavior because the systems underlying volitional movement and autonomic emotional expression are separate motor components. This can be evidenced by different types of facial paresis; for example, voluntary facial paresis arises from a disruption to the volitional movement system (i.e., projections from the motor cortex and brainstem), whereas emotional facial paresis arises from a disruption in the emotional expression system (i.e., medial forebrain and hypothalamus) (Purves et al., 2017).

The subjective experience of emotion, while not necessary for the coordinated expression of emotional behaviors, can still influence autonomic emotional responses. For example, thinking about emotional topics (i.e., activation of the forebrain) or specific movements of facial muscles associated with emotion can activate visceral emotional responses in the muscles and internal organs (Purves et al., 2017).

Subjective "feelings" of emotion originate in the cerebral cortex, where some lateralization of emotional function is observed. The supra-sylvian region of the posterior frontal and anterior parietal lobes of the right hemisphere is important for expression and comprehension of affective aspects of speech. Damage to this region results in aprosodia, which is the inability to express emotion in speech (i.e., speaking in monotone) (Purves et al., 2017). The right hemisphere of the cerebral cortex also processes negative emotions and governs the left lower face, leading to emotional facial expressions being more quickly and fully expressed by the left side. The left hemisphere processes positive emotion and, to a lesser degree than the right side, the perception and expression of emotions. Both sides process language-related emotion (Purves et al., 2017).

Early research by Paul Broca (1878), James Papez (1937), and Paul D. MacLean (1952, 1958) identified regions of the limbic system as crucial to processing emotion. More recent research has identified areas outside of the limbic system as important for emotion as well (Purves et al., 2017). Figure 12.2 summarizes relations among the most important regions associated with emotion.

The amygdala is especially important for processing and remembering both positive and negative affective experiences (Salinas & McGaugh, 1996). Located near the hippocampus, in the anterior/medial temporal lobe, the amygdalae are responsible for detecting, discriminating, and learning what cues in our environment are emotionally salient, particularly which cues might be a threat (Purves et al., 2017). Using past memories to judge whether or not something may be a threat, the amygdala is crucial for fear (threat) or approach (non-threat) responses. It is composed of three structures, the medial, basolateral, and central areas. The medial amygdala receives input from the olfactory bulb and olfactory cortex. The basolateral

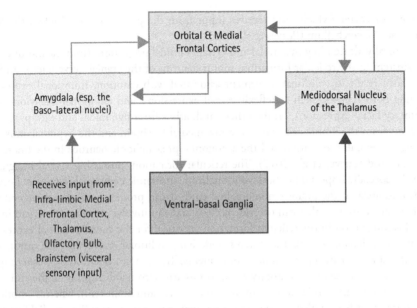

Figure 12.2. Important brain regions associated with emotion.

amygdala, which is larger in humans, has connections to the cerebral cortex, especially the orbital and medial prefrontal cortices, as well as to the anterior temporal lobe. The central amygdala shares connections to the hypothalamus and brainstem, particularly areas associated with visceral emotional responses. Due to these connections to cortical regions that process sensory information and effector systems such as the hypothalamus and brainstem, the amygdala is able to process new stimuli, use past information to determine threat, coordinate autonomic responses based on this judgment, and then remember the interaction for future use (Adolphs et al., 1994; Purves et al., 2017).

Long-term potentiation (LTP) and long-term depression (LTD) have been extensively researched in the amygdala, using fear-conditioning in rodents. LTP is the persistent strengthening of synapses based on temporally linked patterns of activity and is considered a major underlying mechanism in synaptic plasticity, learning and memory, and post-traumatic stress disorder. LTD, essentially the opposite of LTP, is the long-lasting decrease in synaptic strength between neurons. Because primates have de-emphasized olfactory bulbs, relying more on visual cues to process social information, the enlarged basolateral area of the amygdala in humans suggests that this region is likely crucial to the development and maintenance of emotional attachment with family members. It also provides insight into how positive or negative interactions with these individuals can shape socioemotional and mental health outcomes more broadly. The following section discusses the mechanisms underlying how emotional attachments to family members, via affiliative neuropeptides like oxytocin (OXT), are related to emotional processing in the amygdala.

The Neuroendocrinology of Attachment

OXT is synthesized primarily in the supraoptic (SON) and paraventricular nuclei (PVN) of the hypothalamus (Burbach et al., 1992). The hypothalamus is located beneath the thalamus and is an integral component of the limbic system. Regulating metabolic, reproductive, and sociobehavioral processes via its projections to central nervous system (CNS) structures as well as its projections to the pituitary gland, axon terminals from hypothalamic neurons release OXT directly into the bloodstream via capillaries in the posterior pituitary. OXT released into the bloodstream then acts on targets in the CNS and peripheral nervous system (PNS), where it is important for social cognition and behavior, attachment, and other major functions.

OXT is crucial for the development of social bonds and emotional attachment, especially with family members (Feldman, 2007; Heinrichs & Domes, 2008; Heinrichs et al., 2009). Among mammals, hormonal activation initially stimulates maternal behavior among new mothers. Once she has begun to care for her offspring, however, hormones are not required for maternal behavior to continue (Fleming et al., 1997). Olfactory and somatosensory stimulation from interactions between offspring and mother are, however, usually required for the parental care to continue (e.g., Fleming et al, 1999). The stimulation from suckling raises OXT levels in rodents and breastfeeding women, which then results in not only milk letdown but also a decrease in limbic hypothalamic-anterior pituitary-adrenal cortex system (HPA) activity and a shift in the autonomic nervous system (ANS) from a sympathetic tone to a parasympathetic tone. This results in a calmness seen as conducive to remaining in contact with the infant. It also results in a shift from external-directed energy toward the internal activity of nutrient storage and growth (Uvnas-Moberg, 1998).

Given the adaptive value of extensive biparental care and prolonged attachment found in the mating pair and larger family network, particularly siblings, it is not surprising that similar neurohormonal mechanisms active in the maternal-offspring bond would also be selected to underlie these other attachments (Bales et al., 2004; Gordon et al., 2007). Though there is some variation among species and between males and females (Berg & Wynne-Edwards, 2002; Swain et al., 2014), the same general neurohormonal systems active in bonding and attachment in other species are found in humans (Carter, 2002; Fleming et al., 2002; Lee et al., 2009; Panksepp, 2004; Wynne-Edwards, 2003). For example, androgen response to pair-bonding appears complex (e.g., van der Meij et al., 2008), but similar to parent-offspring attachment in that pair-bonded males tend to have lower testosterone levels in non-challenging conditions (Alvergne et al., 2009; Flinn, Ponzi, et al., 2012; Gettler et al., 2019; Gray & Campbell, 2009; Kuzawa et al., 2009). Moreover, males actively involved in caretaking behavior appear to have temporarily diminished testosterone levels (Gray et al., 2007). Furthermore, the dopamine D2 receptors in the nucleus accumbens appear to link the affiliative OXT and AVP pair-bonding mechanisms with positive rewarding mental states (Aragona et al., 2003; Curtis & Wang, 2003). This neurochemical cascade in reward circuits in the brain results in the powerful addiction that parents have for their offspring as well as other individuals whose relationships are critical for survival and reproduction. One particularly important mechanism for establishing and maintaining emotional attachments to family members may be OXTergic activity in the amygdala.

Data from functional magnetic resonance imaging (fMRI), immunohistochemistry, and radioligand assays suggest a complex relationship between OXTergic activity and the amygdala, showing that under some conditions OXT is associated with a decrease in amygdala activity, but other times is associated with an increase (for review, see Habecker & Flinn, 2019). These findings may be partially explained by OXTergic activity in the infra-limbic medial prefrontal cortex (IL-mPFC) and the basolateral region of the amygdala. Specifically, *OXT* can influence glutamatergic (Glu) transmission at the terminals of the IL-mPFC pyramidal neurons that project to the basolateral nucleus of the amygdala (Ninan, 2011). The IL-mPFC-basolateral amygdala circuit is regulated primarily by Glu and GABA activity, such that, under normal circumstances, the glutamatergic activity of the IL-mPFC neurons result in LTD of activity in the amygdala. More precisely, the enhancement of glutamatergic IL-mPFC output facilitates inhibition of the central amygdala via mediation by the intercalated cell masses (ITC) of the amygdala. This occurs because high levels of glutamate, as an excitatory neurotransmitter projected from the IL-mPFC to the ITC masses, results in ITC GABA projections inhibiting activity in the central nucleus. This circuit is considered critical to a "top-down" fear response (Ninan, 2011).

"Bottom-up" fear responses arise in the thalamus, temporal lobe, hippocampus, and/or primary auditory cortex, terminating on the lateral nucleus, which functions in the coordination and planning of movements, which itself projects to the basolateral region of the amygdala (Ninan, 2011). Like the "top-down" fear circuit, the basolateral amygdala also projects to the central nucleus of the amygdala, which functions as the major output nucleus of the amygdala and facilitates both conscious perception of emotion and autonomic emotional responses (Ninan, 2011).

As seen in Figure 12.3, OXTergic projections from the IL-mPFC effectuate endocannabinoid (CB) release from the presynaptic regions of ITC neurons, which travels in a retrograde fashion to the postsynaptic IL-mPFC neuron terminals, reducing Glu release from the IL-mPFC. Reduction in Glu release in the IL-mPFC results in a reduction of GABA from the ITC neurons to the central nucleus of the amygdala, which increases activity in the central nucleus (Ninan, 2011). Using rodent brain slices that were pretreated with OXT, Ninan (2011) demonstrated that OXT converted the LTD into LTP in the central nucleus via activity-dependent plasticity of glutamatergic synapses in the IL-mPFC via two mechanisms: synaptic insertion of calcium-permeable AMPA receptors and depression of basal Glu. The author concluded that OT may modulate social behavior in a top-down fashion by influencing glutamatergic activity at the IL-mPFC and the amygdala in a CB-dependent manner.

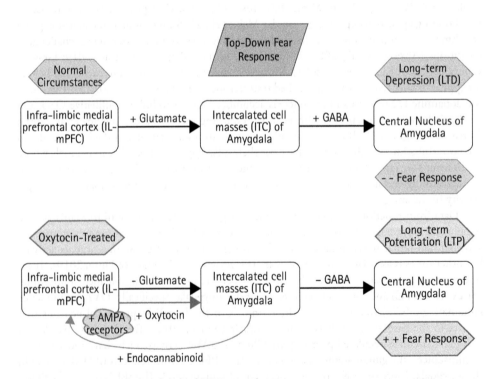

Figure 12.3. Potential mechanism for role of OXT on attachment.

As this study used rodent brain slices, the results should be viewed less as a definitive mechanism underlying human emotional attachments to family members and more of a potential mechanism. As a facilitator of LTP in the amygdala, OXTergic activity may broadly moderate emotional attachments in humans by enabling approach behaviors and feelings of calm, allowing attachments to be established and maintained. Aside from the more general interpretations of activity in these regions, such as approach or avoid, this circuit is part of larger circuits that underlie more complex emotional responses to individuals with whom we interact, none more pivotal for positive or negative socioemotional development than family members.

In order for emotional attachment to occur, interactions with someone need to be rewarding. One of the most important circuits for reward is the mesocorticolimbic reward circuit. A dopaminergic (DA) pathway, the reward circuit connects the ventral tegmental area (VTA) to the nucleus accumbens (NAcc) and the olfactory tubercle in the ventral striatum (VS), of which DAergic activity in the NAcc is especially crucial (Purves et al., 2017). In addition to DA released from the VTA, the NAcc also receives Glu-ergic input from the hippocampus, amygdala, and the medial prefrontal cortex (mPFC). When activated by these regions, the NAcc releases GABA onto the ventral pallidum (VP) (Purves et al., 2017). The NAcc and the anterior cingulate cortex (ACC) mediate reward processing, critical for attachment behavior (Harlé et al., 2012). Neural networks of the NAcc can become associated with different stimuli based on immediately experienced, as well as expected (i.e., future) reward contingencies (Deadwylera et al., 2004), whereas the subcallosal ACC is thought to be involved in emotional processing or internal states (Reid et al., 2010). Together, the frontal regions that mediate reward, motivation, and affect regulation project primarily to the rostral striatum, including the NAcc, the medial caudate nucleus, and the medial and ventral rostral putamen; these areas are collectively referred to as the VS (Haber, 2011). While the VS and the VTA DA neurons are the regions most commonly associated with reward, reward-responsive activation is not restricted to these, but is found throughout the striatum and substantia nigra, pars compacta (SNc) (Haber, 2011). This striatal region is also involved in various aspects of reward evaluation and incentive-based learning and is associated with pathological risk-taking and addictive behaviors (Haber, 2011). The VS projects to the VP and substantia nigra and from there is transferred to the ACC and orbitofrontal cortex (OFC) via the mediodorsal nucleus of thalamus (Haber, 2011). The VP is necessary for normal reward and motivation, specifically encoding reward and motivation signals. Furthermore, stimulation of the VP is sufficient to cause reward and motivation enhancements (Smith et al., 2009).

In addition to DA in the reward centers of the brain, OXT is also an important neurotransmitter in these regions contributing to emotional attachment. While most neuropeptide receptor distributions are fairly conserved across mammals, OXT receptor (OXTR) distribution is an exception and can vary even among closely related species (Insel, 2010; Insel & Shapiro, 1992). For example, in many monogamous or pair-bonding species, such as the marmoset, the California mouse, and the prairie vole, OXTR sites in the (VP), especially the NAcc, are critical for reward-related behaviors (Insel, 2010; Insel & Shapiro, 1992). Non-monogamous, closely related species, such as the montane vole, have little to no OXTR in these regions (Insel, 2010; Insel & Shapiro, 1992). Thus, the emotional attachments underlying pair-bonding and parental behavior have an intrinsic reward potential in the prairie vole that is absent or reduced in the montane vole (Aragona et al, 2006). In order to understand the mechanisms underlying human emotional attachments to family members, it is important to determine where OXT receptors are in the human brain, which has been difficult to do conclusively (Habecker & Flinn, 2019). While there is no evidence of OTR binding in the human NAcc, there is evidence of OTergic activity in reward-related regions of the human brain (Boccia et al., 2013; Gimpl & Fahrenholz, 2001; Grace et al., 2018; Quintana et al., 2019). As such, OTergic processing of social input, reinforcement, and memory are likely crucial in the acquisition and maintenance of emotional attachments within the human family (Bakermans-Kranenburg & van IJzendoorn, 2008; Feldman et al., 2012), such as the pair-bond, parent-offspring bond, sibling bonds, and bonds between grandparents and grandchildren (Flinn & Ward, 2015).

Key Transitions in the Evolution of Emotional Response in Human Family Relationships

The genetic pathway that, step by step, mutation by mutation, resulted in our distinctive neuroendocrine system described in previous sections likely has a deep evolutionary history. A critical precondition for the evolution of the extraordinary social and cultural aptitudes of humans was emotional tolerance (Hare, 2017; Rilling et al., 2002) that enabled interactions with individuals from other communities. This is a major difference between humans and the other hominoids, a unique aspect of human sociality that intensified selection for culture and concomitant intelligence: the development of intergroup relationships based on kinship and reciprocity (e.g., Chagnon et al., 2017; MacFarlan et al., 2014). Human band-level societies are characterized by fluid, open composition and movement (Walker et al., 2011). Relationships, and hence ideas, are free to roam.

Information can move among communities of humans much, much more rapidly than for other hominoids. At some point our ancestors evolved emotional systems that allowed them to "get along" amicably with individuals from other communities, and the potential for the flow of information—for memes to go "viral"—was opened, and hence greatly intensified selection for cognitive and linguistic abilities to use culture. This is in contrast to chimps and gorillas, who are siloed into their mutually hostile communities, with minimal opportunity for information diffusion, and hence minimal culture. The extended family—including especially lifelong brother-sister relationships and multigenerational relationships—facilitated tolerance and connections among groups. Bilateral, multigenerational kinship and affinal links are critical (Chapais, 2008; Flinn, 2017). The emotional systems that underpin this unique human pattern of kinship networks are key to understanding how human intelligence, culture, and sociality coevolved.

References

Adolphs, R. (2003). Cognitive neuroscience of human social behavior. *Nature Reviews, Neuroscience, 4*(3), 165–178.

Adolphs, R., Tranel, D., Damasio, H., & Damasio, A. (1994). Impaired recognition of emotion in facial expressions following bilateral damage to the human amygdala. *Nature, 372,* 669.

Allman, J. M., Hakeem, A., Erwin, J. M., Nimchinsky, E., & Hof, P. (2001). The anterior cingulate cortex: The evolution of an interface between emotion and cognition. *Annals of the New York Academy of Sciences, 935*(1), 107–117.

Alvergne, A., Faurie, C., & Raymond, M. (2009). Variation in testosterone levels and male reproductive effort: Insight from a polygynous human population. *Hormones and Behavior, 56*(5), 491–497.

Amodio, D. M., & Frith, C. D. (2006). Meeting of minds: The medial frontal cortex and social cognition. *Nature Reviews Neuroscience, 7*(4), 268–277.

Aragona, B. J., Liu, Y., Curtis, J. T., Stephan, F. K. & Wang, Z. (2003). A critical role for nucleus accumbens dopamine in partner-preference formation in male prairie voles. *Journal of Neuroscience 23,* 3483–3490.

Aragona, B. J., Liu, Y., Yu, Y. J., Curtis, J. T., Detwiler, J. M., Insel, T. R., & Wang, Z. (2006). Nucleus accumbens dopamine differentially mediates the formation and maintenance of monogamous pair bonds. *Nature Neuroscience, 9,* 133–139.

Babb, P., Fernandez-Duque, E., & Schurr, T. (2015). Oxytocin receptor gene sequences in owl monkeys and other primates show remarkable interspecific regulatory and protein coding variation. *Molecular Phylogenetics and Evolution, 91,* 160–177.

Bakermans-Kranenburg, M. J., & van IJzendoorn, M. H. (2008). Oxytocin receptor (OXTR) and serotonin transporter (5-HTT) genes associated with observed parenting. *Social Cognitive and Affective Neuroscience, 3*(2), 128–134..

Bales, K. L., Kim, A. J., Lewis-Reese, A. D., & Carter, C. S. (2004). Both oxytocin and vasopressin may influence alloparental behavior in male prairie voles. *Hormones and Behavior, 45*(5), 354–361.

Bartels, A., & Zeki, S. (2004). The neural correlates of maternal and romantic love. *NeuroImage, 21*, 1155–1166.

Berg, S. J., & Wynne-Edwards, K. E. (2002). Salivary hormone concentrations in mothers and fathers becoming parents are not correlated. *Hormones and Behavior, 42*(4), 424–436.

Boccia, M. L., Petrusz, P., Suzuki, K., Marson, L., & Pedersen, C. A. (2013). Immunohistochemical localization of oxytocin receptors in human brain. *Neuroscience, 253*, 155–164.

Broca, P. (1878). Anatomie comparée des circonvolutions cérébrales: Le grande lobe limbique et la scissure limbique dans la série des mammifères. *Revue d'Anthropologie, 1*, 385–498.

Burbach, J. P. H., Adan, R. A., & de Bree, F. M. (1992). Regulation of oxytocin gene expression and forms of oxytocin in the brain. *Annals of the New York Academy of Sciences, 652*(1), 1–13.

Buss, D. M. (2000). The evolution of happiness. *American Psychologist, 55*, 15–23.

Carter, C. S. (2002). Neuroendocrine perspectives on social attachment and love. In J. T. Cacioppo, G. G. Berntson, R. Adolphs, C. S. Carter, R. J. Davidson, M. K. McClintock, et al. (eds.), *Foundations in social neuroscience* (pp. 853–890). MIT Press.

Chagnon, N. A., Lynch, R. F., Shenk, M. S., Hames, R. & Flinn, M. V. (2017). Cross cousin marriage among the Yanomamö shows evidence of parent-offspring conflict and mate competition between siblings. *Proceedings of the National Academy of Sciences, 114*(13), E2590–E2607. doi: 10.1073/pnas.1618655114

Chapais, B. (2008). *Primeval kinship: How pair-bonding gave birth to human society*. Harvard University Press.

Curtis, T. J., & Wang, Z. (2003). The neurochemistry of pair bonding. *Current Directions in Psychological Science, 12*(2), 49–53.

Dalgleish, T. (2004). The emotional brain. *Nature Reviews Neuroscience, 5*(7), 583–589.

Darwin, C. (1872). *The expression of the emotions in man and animals*. Murray. https://doi.org/10.1037/10001-000

Deadwyler, S. A., Hayashizaki, S., Cheer, J., & Hampson, R. E. (2004). Reward, memory and substance abuse: Functional neuronal circuits in the nucleus accumbens. *Neuroscience & Biobehavioral Reviews, 27*(8), 703–711.

Ekman, P., & Davidson, R. J. (Eds.). (1994). *Series in affective science. The nature of emotion: Fundamental questions*. Oxford University Press.

Ellison, P. T. (2009). *On fertile ground: A natural history of human reproduction*. Harvard University Press.

Feldman, R. (2007). Oxytocin and social affiliation in humans. *Hormones and Behavior, 61*(3), 380–391.

Feldman, R., Zagoory-Sharon, O., Weisman, O., Schneiderman, I., Gordon, I., Maoz, R., & Ebstein, R. P. (2012). Sensitive parenting is associated with plasma oxytocin and polymorphisms in the OTR and CD38 genes. *Biological Psychiatry, 72*(3), 175–181.

Fernandez-Duque, E., Valeggia, C. R., & Mendoza, S. P. (2009). The biology of paternal care in non-human primates. *Annual Review of Anthropology, 38*, 115–130.

Fisher, H., Aron, A., & Brown, L. L. (2006). Romantic love: A mammalian system for mate choice. *Philosophical Transactions of the Royal Society B, 361*, 2173–2186.

Fleming, A. S., Corter, C., Stallings, J., & Steiner, M. (2002). Testosterone and prolactin are associated with emotional responses to infant cries in new fathers. *Hormones and Behavior, 42*, 399–413.

Fleming, A. S., O'Day, D. H., & Kraemer, G. W. (1999). Neurobiology of mother-infant interactions: Experience and central nervous system plasticity across development and generations. *Neuroscience and Biobehavioral Reviews, 23*, 673–685.

Fleming, A. S., Ruble, D., Krieger, H., & Wong, P. Y. (1997). Hormonal and experiential correlates of maternal responsiveness during pregnancy and the puerperium in human mothers. *Hormones and Behavior, 31*(2), 145–158.

Flinn, M. V. (2017). The human family: Evolutionary origins and adaptive significance. In M. Teyberanc & F. Ayala (Eds.), *On Human Nature* (pp. 251–262). National Academy of Sciences. Elsevier.

Flinn, M. V., Duncan, C., Quinlan, R. L., Leone, D. V., Decker, S. A. & Ponzi, D. (2012). Hormones in the wild: Monitoring the endocrinology of family relationships. *Parenting: Science and Practice, 12*(2), 124–133. doi: 10.1080/15295192.2012.683338

Flinn, M.V., Ponzi, D., and Muehlenbein, M. P. (2012). Hormonal mechanisms for regulation of aggression in human coalitions. *Human Nature, 22*(1), 68–88. doi: 10.1007/s12110-012-9135-y

Flinn, M. V., & Ward, C.V. (2015). The role of hormones in the evolution of the human family. In D. Buss (Ed.), *Handbook of evolutionary psychology* (2nd ed., pp. 598–622). Wiley.

Gettler, L. T., Sarma, M. S., Lew-Levy, S., Bond, A., Trumble, B. C., & Boyette, A. H. (2019). Mothers' and fathers' joint profiles for testosterone and oxytocin in a small-scale fishing-farming community: Variation based on marital conflict and paternal contributions. *Brain and Behavior, 9*, e01367. https://doi.org/10.1002/brb3.1367

Gimpl, G., & Fahrenholz, F. (2001). The oxytocin receptor system: Structure, function, and regulation. *Physiological Reviews, 81*(2), 629–683.

Gordon, I., Zagoory-Sharon, O., Leckman, J. F., & Feldman, R. (2007). Oxytocin and the development of parenting in humans. *Biological Psychiatry, 68*(4), 377–382.

Grace, S. A., Rossell, S. L., Heinrichs, M., Kordsachia, C., & Labuschagne, I. (2018). Oxytocin and brain activity in humans: A systematic review and coordinate-based meta-analysis of functional MRI studies. *Psychoneuroendocrinology, 96*, 2–64.

Gray, P. B., & Anderson, K. G. (2010). *Fatherhood: Evolution and human paternal behavior*. Harvard University Press.

Gray, P. B., & Campbell, B. C. (2009). Human male testosterone, pair bonding and fatherhood. In P. T. Ellison & P. B. Gray (Eds.), *Endocrinology of social relationships* (pp. 270–293). Harvard University Press.

Gray, P. B., Kahlenberg, S., Barrett, E., Lipson, S., & Ellison, P. T. (2002). Marriage and fatherhood are associated with lower testosterone in males. *Evolution and Human Behavior, 23*, 193–201.

Gray, P. B., Parkin, J. C., & Samms-Vaughan, M. E. (2007). Hormonal correlates of human paternal interactions: A hospital-based investigation in urban Jamaica. *Hormones and Behavior, 52*, 499–507.

Habecker, H., & Flinn, M. V. (2019). Evolution of hormonal mechanisms for human family relationships. In T. Henley, M. Rossano, & E. Kardas (Eds.), *Handbook of cognitive archaeology: Psychology in pre-history* (pp. 58–75). Routledge.

Haber, S. N. (2011). Neuroanatomy of reward: A view from the ventral striatum. In Gottfried, J. (Ed.), *Neurobiology of sensation and reward* (Chap. 11). CRC Press. doi: 10.1201/b10776-15.

Hare, B. (2017). Survival of the friendliest: *Homo sapiens* evolved via selection for prosociality. *Annual Review Psychology, 68*, 155–186. doi: 10.1146/annurev-psych-010416-044201

Harlé, K. M., Chang, L. J., van't Wout, M., & Sanfey, A. G. (2012). The neural mechanisms of affect infusion in social economic decision-making: A mediating role of the anterior insula. *Neuroimage, 61*(1), 32–40.

Heinrichs, M., Dawans, B. V., & Domes, G. (2009). Oxytocin, vasopressin, and human social behavior. *Frontiers in Neuroendocrinology, 30*(4), 548–557.

Heinrichs, M., & Domes, G. (2008). Neuropeptides and social behaviour: Effects of oxytocin and vasopressin in humans. *Progress in Brain Research, 170*, 337–350.

Insel, T. R. (2010). The challenge of translation in social neuroscience: A review of oxytocin, vasopressin, and affiliative behavior. *Neuron, 65*(6), 768–779.

Insel, T. R., & Shapiro, L. E. (1992). Oxytocin receptor distribution reflects social organization in monogamous and polygamous voles. *Proceedings of the National Academy of Sciences, 89*(13), 5981–5985.

Kuzawa, C. W., Gettler, L. T., Muller, M. N., McDade, T. W., & Feranil, A. B. (2009). Fatherhood, pairbonding and testosterone in the Philippines. *Hormones and Behavior, 56*(4), 429–435.

Lee, H.-J., Macbeth, A. H., Pagani, J., & Young, W. S. (2009). Oxytocin: The great facilitator of life. *Progress in Neurobiology, 88*(2), 127–151.

Macfarlan, S. J., Walker, R. S., Flinn, M. V., & Chagnon, N. A. (2014). Lethal coalitionary aggression and long-term alliances among Yanomamö men. *Proceedings of the National Academy of Sciences, 111*(47), 16662–16669. doi: 10.1073/pnas.1418639111

Maclean, P. D. (1952). Some psychiatric implications of physiological studies on frontotemporal portion of limbic system (visceral brain). *Electroencephalography & Clinical Neurophysiology, 4*, 407–418. https://doi.org/10.1016/0013-4694(52)90073-4

MacLean, P. D. (1958). Contrasting functions of limbic and neocortical systems of the brain and their relevance to psychophysiological aspects of medicine. *The American Journal of Medicine, 25*(4), 611–626. https://doi.org/10.1016/0002-9343(58)90050-0

Ninan, I. (2011). Oxytocin suppresses basal glutamatergic transmission but facilitates activity-dependent synaptic potentiation in the medial prefrontal cortex. *Journal of Neurochemistry, 119*(2), 324–331.

Panksepp, J. (2004). *Affective neuroscience: The foundations of human and animal emotions*. Oxford University Press.

Panksepp, J. (2009). Carving "natural" emotions: "Kindly" from bottom-up but not top-down. *Journal of Theoretical and Philosophical Psychology, 28*(2), 395–422.

Papez, J. W. (1937). A proposed mechanism of emotion. *Archives of Neurology & Psychiatry, 38*(4), 725–743. doi:10.1001/archneurpsyc.1937.02260220069003

Pfaff, D., Tabansky, I., & Haubensak, W. (2019). Tinbergen's challenge for the neuroscience of behavior. *Proceedings of the National Academy of Sciences, 116*(20), 9704–9710.

Purves, D., Augustine, G. J., Fitzpatrick, D., Hall, W. C., LaMantia, A., Mooney, R. D., Platt, M. L., & White, L. E. (2017). *Neuroscience* (6th ed.). Oxford University Press.

Quintana, D. S., Rokicki, J., van der Meer, D., Alnæs, D., Kaufmann, T., Córdova-Palomera, A., Dieset, I., Andreassen, O. A., & Westlye, L. T. (2019). Oxytocin pathway gene networks in the human brain. *Nature Communications, 10*(1), 1–12.

Reid, M. A., Stoeckel, L. E., White, D. M., Avsar, K. B., Bolding, M. S., Akella, N. S., Knowlton, R. C., den Hollander, J. A., & Lahti, A. C. (2010). Assessments of function and biochemistry of the anterior cingulate cortex in schizophrenia. *Biological Psychiatry, 68*(7), 625–633.

Rilling, J., Gutman, D., Zeh, T., Pagnoni, G., Berns, G., and Kilts, C. (2002). A neural basis for social cooperation. *Neuron, 35*(2), 395–405

Rilling, J. K., & Mascaro, J. S. (2017). The neurobiology of fatherhood. *Current Opinion in Psychology, 15*, 26–32.

Salinas, J. A., & McGaugh, J. L. (1996). The amygdala modulates memory for changes in reward magnitude: involvement of the amygdaloid GABAergic system. *Behavioural Brain Research, 80*(1–2), 87–98.

Smith, K. S., Tindell, A. J., Aldridge, J. W., & Berridge, K. C. (2009). Ventral pallidum roles in reward and motivation. *Behavioural Brain Research, 196*(2), 155–167.

Storey, A. E., Walsh, C. J., Quinton, R. L., & Wynne-Edwards, K. E. (2000). Hormonal correlates of paternal responsiveness in new and expectant fathers. *Evolution and Human Behavior, 21*, 79–95.

Swain, J. E., Kim, P., Spicer, J., Ho, S. S., Dayton, C. J., Elmadih, A., & Abel, K. M. (2014). Approaching the biology of human parental attachment: Brain imaging, oxytocin and coordinated assessments of mothers and fathers. *Brain Research, 1580*, 78–101.

Tinbergen, N. (1963). On aims and methods of ethology. *Zeitschrift für Tierpsychologie, 20*, 410–433.

Uvnas-Moberg, K. (1998). Oxytocin may mediate the benefits of positive social interaction and emotions, *Psychoneuroendocrinology, 23*, 819–835.

van der Meij, L., Buunk, A. P., van de Sande, J. P., & Salvador, A. (2008). The presence of a woman increases testosterone in aggressive dominant men. *Hormones and Behavior, 54*, 640–644.

Walker, R. S., Hill, K., Flinn, M. V., & Ellsworth, R. (2011). Evolutionary history of hunter-gatherer marriage practices. *PLoS ONE, 6*(4), e19066. doi: 10.1371/ journal.pone.0019066

Weisfeld, G. E., & Goetz, S. M. M. (2013). Applying evolutionary thinking to the study of emotion. *Behavioral Sciences, 3*, 388–407.

Wynne-Edwards, K. E. (2001). Hormonal changes in mammalian fathers. *Hormones and Behavior, 40*, 139–145.

Wynne-Edwards, K. E. (2003). From dwarf hamster to daddy: The intersection of ecology, evolution, and physiology that produces paternal behavior. In P. J. B. Slater, J. S. Rosenblatt, C. T. Snowden, & T. J. Roper (Eds.), *Advances in the study of behavior* (Vol. 32, 207–261). Academic Press.

CHAPTER 13

Regret

Leif Edward Ottesen Kennair, Trond Viggo Grøntvedt, and Mons Bendixen

Abstract

Regret is a counterfactual cognitive-emotional response to choices one has made in the past. In hindsight, when considering one's behavior, one feels aversive emotion and wishes one had made a different choice. There are few sex differences in regret; however, the mating domain does show sex differences. Especially, sex differences in regret for having had or having passed up casual sex has been studied. The suggested adaptive function is that regret about past sexual experiences may reduce future maladaptive sexual behaviors. However, this has only recently been subjected to empirical testing using a predictive, longitudinal design. This chapter considers regret, in general, and evolutionary research into casual sex regret. The discussion focuses on how it may be necessary to reformulate the current understanding of the function of regret, as well as how evolutionary approaches may inform other areas where there may be robust sex differences in regret.

Key Words: regret, short-term sex, action regret, inaction regret, function

Introduction

Regret is a "counterfactual cognitive-emotional processing of past events where one in hindsight wishes the past had been different" (Kennair & Bendixen, 2018, p. 1). One considers what one did do—the choice one made—and contemplates how doing differently would have been more desirable in hindsight. We seem to be able to imagine both alternative positive outcomes, which probably are both biased and relatively realistic, and to consider the negative effects of our behavior in greater detail in hindsight than we were able to when acting in the moment. However, that is to a large degree the human condition. And this ability need not be an adaptation.

The current chapter will provide a short introduction to the general research into regret, which often is more about anticipatory regret: imagine how you would feel if you did this? We will then consider how robust sex differences (Galperin et al., 2013; Kennair et al., 2018; Roese et al., 2006) are predicted by Sexual Strategies Theory (Buss & Schmitt, 1993), and review the research into proximate mechanisms that may explain individual and sex differences in sexual action and inaction regret. We conclude by critically discussing the evidence of an evolutionary function of regret, and what possible alternative functions this emotional-cognitive process may have.

Regret Research in Psychology

Regret research in psychology not only has focused on regret as an affective reaction to bad outcomes of decisions or processes, but also has addressed regret as a motivation of future behavior. This suggestion is not that regret is functional in the evolutionary sense. From an evolutionary perspective, regret might have had a function throughout the evolutionary history of humans, for instance motivating us to change behaviors in the future in order to not feel regret, and hence it is a universal feeling that has evolutionary consequences. In the general psychology approach, regret is instead about using information from earlier situations for better decisions in the future and to reduce regret, as it is suggested to cause negative health outcomes (Roese et al., 2009), and hence is best avoided. However, this changing behavior aspect from theories of regret fits well with an evolutionary approach of how our emotions are functional in motivating behaviors (e.g., Al-Shawaf et al., 2016; Nesse, 1990). Behavioral implications of regret have also been suggested earlier by, for instance, Festinger (1964), and more recent theories that attempt to explain regret also include a focus on how regret is expected to change future behaviors.

One theory of regret regulation has been proposed by Zeelenberg and Pieters (2007) which defines regret and addresses how and when regret is predicted (e.g., retrospective regret or anticipated regret), how regret is dependent on justification of the decision, and suggests a battery of regret-regulation strategies for managing current regret and preventing future regret. Zeelenberg and Pieters's theory is not an evolutionary approach to regret; it doesn't explicitly suggest that regret is a feeling and mental process that has evolved to help us change our behavior in future situations. But in line with a functional approach to regret and the link with how regret predicts change in future behavior, the theory suggests that regret influences behavioral decisions (Zeelenberg & Pieters, 2007). In order to prevent future regret, three different strategies are suggested: decision-focused, alternative-focused, and feeling-focused, with various subcategories (Zeelenberg & Pieters, 2007).

The distinction between managing current regret and preventing future regret is clearest in the decision-focused category. For reducing future regret, but not for managing current regret, Zeelenberg and Pieters (2007) suggest that individuals improve their decisions in the future. There is a myriad of situations which can cause regret and that will repeat in the future (e.g., buying a faulty product, deciding not to go to the gym today, not investing in certain stocks). By being aware of the situation that leads to regret, one strategy of preventing future regret is to change future behavior to increase the decision quality. As a comment to the regret regulation proposed by Zeelenberg and Pieters, Roese and colleagues (2007) went further in suggesting "that the overall arc of any regret theory must be situated within an understanding of behavior regulation" (p. 27). As such, the primary function of feelings of regret is to change action and improve decision-making. Regret regulation theory is thus based on the feeling-is-for-doing approach to emotions (Pieters & Zeelenberg, 2007), yet again taking for granted that the emotion of regret leads to adaptive changes in future behaviors. People also seem to believe that regret has a psychological function (Saffrey et al., 2008). People not only believe that regret is beneficial to gain insight into their own behavior and current dispositions, but also seem to believe that regretting previous incidents prepares us to avoid such behaviors in the future. So, while theory suggests it, and we seem to believe it, do feelings of regret cause changes in future behaviors?

Several studies have investigated how regret could lead to changes in behaviors (for reviews, see Zeelenberg, 1999; Zeelenberg et al., 2001). In a meta-analysis of health behavior and anticipated regret, Brewer, DeFrank, and Gilkey (2016) found associations between the two. However, apart from studies investigating follow-up on vaccination or cancer screenings, which have high potential health risks, the majority of studies included in the meta-analysis measured intentions of changes in health behaviors, such as intention to quit smoking, drinking, or speeding, or intentions to start exercising. So while it would seem that the empirical evidence is in line with the feeling-is-for-doing approach and with the regret-changes-behavior approach (e.g., Zeelenberg et al., 2001), the majority of studies investigating regret have focused on anticipated regret, regret related to hypothetical situations or anticipated or intended changes in behavior, or have been retrospective. For instance, in consumer behavior, individuals are asked about regret from personal experiences (e.g., Zeelenberg & Pieters, 2004) or anticipated regret in hypothetical scenarios (e.g., Simonson, 1992).

Nevertheless, there are exceptions that also are in support of regret leading to behavioral changes, for instance in a study by O'Connor, McCormack, and Feeney (2014) who investigated regret and change in behavior in three groups of young children (5-, 7-, and 9-year-olds). Based on the hypothesis that regret would improve subsequent decision-making, O'Connor and colleagues predicted that when regret emerged developmentally in children, it would also be accompanied with improvements in what they termed "adaptive choice switching"—making a different decision when faced with the same or similar choice again. Children were faced with a choice at time 1, discovered the outcome of their decision, and were asked to complete the same task at time 2. The researchers used differences in happiness ratings before and after the time 1 decision as a measurement of experienced regret. If children regretted their choice at time 1, by showing a lower happiness rating after their first choice, they were expected to have a higher rate of adaptive choice switching at time 2. Interestingly, there was little reported sadness in the youngest children who made the poorer choice at time 1, whereas almost all children in the two older groups who made the poorer choice did report feeling sadder. Regret (or at least sadness over not making a better choice) therefore appears to develop between the ages of 5 and 7, as suggested in other studies (e.g. Burns et al., 2012; Weisberg & Beck, 2010). The overall results from these experiments were that the majority of children reported more sadness following a poor choice at time 1 and changed their choice at time 2. Some children who made the better choice the first time also switched choices at time 2; nevertheless, overall, there were fewer children changing their strategy (making a different choice at time 2) when selecting the better choice at time 1. According to the authors, this is initial evidence that experienced regret can influence decision-making. This might be true, but the definition of regret was not quite the same as the one used among adults (reduction in happiness), these were relatively small groups, and the changes in behaviors rated as adaptive choices were not reflected by all participants experiencing regret. If experienced regret changes people's behavior, we would see the effects of regret in behaviors related to the situation in which regret was experienced in their future. To our knowledge, there have been very few studies that have investigated whether experiencing regret, not just anticipated regret, changes people's behavior, not just intention to change, in the real world, and not just in hypothetic scenarios. As such, there is very little direct evidence of a function of regret in the literature.

A different area has been the focus of most of the evolutionary research on regret: Are there any sex differences in regret? And, if so, where might these have been hypothesized? While regret has been subjected to investigations across various domains, sex differences seem to be rare. Roese and colleagues (2006) noted this lack of replicated differences between women and men. And while there have been a few studies investigating sex differences in regret, these are individual studies that find sex differences in specific behaviors. For instance, Li, Li, Cao, and Niu (2018) examined how regret and disappointment impacted women and men when repurchasing stocks, and found a sex difference only when individuals repurchased a sold stock that increased in price, but not when the stocks decreased in price. To our knowledge, the studies that find sex differences in areas other than the sexual domain have not been replicated and thus need to be examined further. We will address this question from an evolutionary perspective, as the sexual domain is expected to show sex differences due to the sexes facing different adaptive problems throughout human evolutionary history.

Empirical Studies of Casual Sex Regret: An Evolutionary Approach
Sexual Strategies Theory

Over human history, biparental care and extensive parental cooperation has increased the survival of offspring. The prolonged childhood would have been particularly challenging in our ancestors, and selection pressures are likely to have designed adaptations for attachment, commitment, and affection, along with other adaptations related to mating and mate preferences. Trivers (1972) proposed that asymmetries in minimal parental investment would select for sex-differentiated mating psychologies, resulting in more choosiness and reluctance to mate in the higher-investing sex, and greater intrasexual competition among the less-investing sex. As for all mammals, minimum obligatory investment in offspring is markedly higher for human females in terms of pregnancy, birth, breastfeeding, and nurturing. The cost of mating and having sex, particularly casual sex, without any commitment or bond would be particularly high in our ancestral mothers, and casual sex would be selected against. Still, casual sex is prevalent, particularly among young adults (Monto & Carey, 2014), and for each time a man has uncommitted sex with a woman, the reverse necessarily follows, although men's and women's motivations, feelings, and aftermath reflections may differ.

Sexual Strategies Theory (SST; Buss, 1998; Buss & Schmitt, 1993, 2017) can be considered an expansion and elaboration of Trivers's (1972) theory of parental investment and sexual selection. SST provides a framework for understanding sex differences in sexual psychology and identifies two major strategies in human mating: the more prevalent long-term strategy that involves seeking a committed relationship marked by dependability and mutual feelings of love; and the less prevalent short-term strategy that is primarily sexual and that does not involve any commitment or emotional bonding. Short-term strategies include one-night stands and casual sex, but also repeated sexual encounters over time without any expectations of future romantic bonding (Bendixen et al., 2018). Although both women and men have evolved to form long-term relationships that support biparental care, SST suggests that each sex may pursue short-term matings opportunistically. But the costs and benefits of short-term mating strategies are not symmetrical for the two sexes, and women who engage in short-term mating may partly do so for different reasons than men, and perhaps as a strategy to acquire a long-term partner (Haselton & Buss, 2000). While men could enhance their reproductive success without much effort and concern once they have succeeded mating, women should be more apprehensive about her partner's investment in the relationship before, during, and after any short-term sexual encounter. Throughout evolutionary history, the fitness bottleneck for men has been sexual access to fertile women (Buss, 2017), and one of the adaptations evolved for preventing missed opportunities include men's over-perception of ambivalent sexual signals from women, known as sexual over-perception bias (Haselton & Buss, 2000).

It follows from the above that men will invest in, and pursue, short-term mating more than women and will do so without consideration of commitment and investment. Regarding emotions following short-term sexual encounters, men and women are expected to differ; men should report stronger needs to detach from their one-night stand partners, while women should report stronger needs for attachment and closeness, and they will worry more about being abandoned. Finally, men will tend to regret missed opportunities for mating more than women, while women will tend to regret one-night stands and any casual sex that is devoid of commitment more than men.

Emotional Reactions after Sex

A number of studies have examined emotional reactions, both positive and negative, after casual sex. Below, we present the main findings from these studies in short. We note that although emotional reactions are conceptually overlapping with regret, they reflect partially distinct features of processing. While emotional reactions are more online and readily available subjective feelings with physical correlates, the counterfactual cognitive-emotional response to past events that signifies regret involves some hindsight mental processing.

Haselton and Buss (2001) hypothesized that women may sometimes use short-term mating to acquire a long-term partner. If so, then an affective shift from a short-term mode to increased feelings of commitment and love after sex needs to occur. For men, the hypothesized affective shift for short-term mating strategies would involve more negative perceptions of one's partner's attractiveness following casual sex. This shift would help disconnecting and prevent the casual sex encounter developing into a long-term sexual relationship. Haselton and Buss (2001) examined this in two studies, and in Study 2 ($n = 203$) they specifically asked about six feelings immediately before and after having sex for the first time with their current (or a prior) partner. The feelings were grouped into two factors: sexual attractiveness and commitment. Men found their partner slightly less sexually attractive after having had intercourse and felt slightly more committed. Women did not change their perceptions of attractiveness, but they reported moderately stronger commitment after intercourse. For both sexes, higher number of prior sex partners was associated with feeling of less commitment. Hence, unrestricted sociosexuality may influence changes in feelings toward a new sex partner.

In a qualitative explorative study of feelings after a typical casual sex encounter (a "hookup") among college students (Paul & Hayes, 2002), the most commonly reported feelings were "regretful or disappointed" (35%), and women were more likely than men to report this feeling. Women were also more likely than men to ruminate about a hookup and feel greater shame and self-doubt in the aftermath of the experience. In contrast, men were more likely to report feeling satisfied.

In a large online study of 1,743 people who had experienced one-night stands, Campbell (2008) asked the participants to report on their "morning-after" feelings using a 12-item scale (6 positive and 6 negative evaluations). Women reported less positive ($d = 0.54$) and more negative ($d = 0.45$) feelings. Far more women than men reported feelings of being used ($d = 0.70$) and worried moderately more about loss of their reputation ($d = 0.40$). The majority of the participants were not currently in a relationship, but most comparisons of reasons for unmated and mated participants showed no significant differences (loss of reputation being an exception). Subtracting the negative evaluations from the positive (i.e., net gain score), Campbell reported that women's net gain scores were just above zero (on a ±18 scale) and that men's score was a mere 4.5. She observed that casual sex was not all positive for either sex, and that casual sex clearly had its downsides.

In a study of 500 college students, Owen and Fincham (2011) found that both men and women reported more positive than negative emotional reactions to hooking up. However, men reported more positive and less negative emotions than women. Relative to women, men reported fewer negative emotional responses to encounters that involved intercourse. The authors also found that negative emotions were associated with symptoms of depression, while positive emotions were related to hope for, and discussion of, a committed relationship.

Townsend and Wasserman (2011) found in a study of 696 college students that even when women deliberately engaged in casual sex, greater number of partners was associated with more feelings of concern and vulnerability. For men the opposite relationship was found. The author's prediction that casual sex should be more strongly associated with more marital thoughts in women than in men was not supported. For both men and women, a greater number of partners was associated with less thinking about marriage.

Finally, in a cross-cultural study of four samples from three nations, Fernandes, Kennair, Hutz, Natividade, and Kruger (2016) examined the frequency and intensity of negative postcoital emotions. Fernandes et al. (2016) found that negative postcoital emotions were prevalent and followed sex-specific predictions from SST. Across all samples, women reported more intense negative emotions reflecting need for bonding (e.g., need to be comforted, sadness, loneliness) than negative feeling related to avoidance of bonding (e.g., need to be alone, irritability, anger). Men reported opposite patterns. The authors concluded that negative postcoital emotions were functional, rather than expressions of psychopathology.

Casual Sex Regret

In the following, we present an overview of the studies that have specifically measured regret related to sexual encounters.

Oswalt, Cameron, and Koob (2005) studied sexual regret in sexually active college students ($n = 270$). When they asked how often they had regretted their decision to engage in sexual activity during their life, only one in four said they "never" had any regrets. Ten percent reported regrets "often" or "always," while "sometimes" was most prevalent response (37%). There was no sex difference in how often men and women had regretted sexual activity, and the reasons for regretting were similar, except for feeling pressured by their partner (more prevalent for women). Moral concern was the most prevalent reason for regretting (37%), followed by being under the influence of alcohol (32%). Number of sex partners was associated with more frequent regret in this sample.

In a study of 152 sexually active college women, Eshbaugh and Gute (2008) found, similar to Oswalt et al. (2005), that "no regrets" following past sexual decisions was uncommon (23%). The asked specifically about sexual encounters with someone the participants knew for less than 24 hours or had sex with only once. Their findings suggest that only reproductively relevant sexual behavior (i.e., sexual intercourse) elicited more frequent regret. Performing or receiving oral sex was not associated with regret.

Feelings of regret was also common after uncommitted sex in a study of 200 Canadian university students (Fisher et al., 2012). Women regretted their casual sex experiences moderately more frequently than men ($d = 0.39$). When they listed specific reasons for their regret, men more than women mentioned they were not physically attracted to their partner, that they had unprotected sex, and that their partner wanted a future relationship. Women mentioned cheating on their current partner and that they hardly knew their sex partner as reasons for regret more than men.

Across three studies and diverse methodologies and data sources, Galperin et al. (2013) examined sex differences in regret following short-term sexual encounters. Their first study, covering 200 students, examined anticipated regret intensity in men and women when responding to hypothetical scenarios describing a one-night stand or a missed one-night stand opportunity. The scenarios were presented with male and female actors, and the participants also rated their anticipated regrets if they found themselves in such a situation. The findings suggest that the participants anticipated markedly more regret in women than in men following a one-night stand ($d = 1.19$) and markedly more regret in men than in women following a missed one-night stand ($d = 0.80$). These sex differences were even stronger for the self-ratings (with women reporting more action regret: $d = 1.47$, and men reporting more inaction regret: $d = 1.82$). In their second study, which included a sample of 395 adult men and women using an online recruitment approach, each participant marked on an 88-item checklist what regrets they had experienced. Across the 39 items, women reported moderately higher overall number of action regrets than men ($d = 0.48$). Comparably, across the 30 inaction regrets, men reported markedly higher overall number than women ($d = 0.90$). Galperin and colleagues' third study covered a large online sample of more than 24,000 respondents. Level of education, sexual orientation, and relationship status were recorded. Participants were asked to think of their most recent experience that involved having had sex with someone, or that they had passed up a chance to have casual sex. Four response options were given: "I'm glad I did it"; "Neutral: neither glad nor have regrets"; "I regret it somewhat"; and "I regret it very much." Galperin and colleagues (2013) found that the sex differences in regret were more distinct for heterosexual respondents than for bisexuals and gays/lesbians. For the heterosexual sample, women ($M = 1.40$) regretted more than men ($M = 0.78$) the last time they had casual sex ($d = 0.60$). Men ($M = 1.20$) regretted passing up more than women ($M = 0.57$; $d = 0.73$).

The first replication of Galperin et al. (2013) was done by Kennair, Bendixen, and Buss (2016). They analyzed a sample of 263 Norwegian students using the outcome measure from Study 3. They also included a number of proximal factors that Galperin et al. (2013) hypothesized would be associated with level of regret, such as worries about pregnancy, sexually transmitted infections (STIs), and reputation, and lack of sexual gratification. They also examined the effect of individual differences in sociosexual orientation (SOI-R). The results were strongly supportive of the original study. Although the overall level of action and inaction regret in the Norwegian sample was lower than in the large online US sample, the level of action regret was moderately higher for women than for men ($d = 0.47$) and that level of inaction regret was markedly higher for men than for women ($d = 0.82$). The analyses of factors associated with action and inaction regret suggest that reputational worries significantly increased the level of action regret (primarily for women), while there was no additional effect of worry about pregnancy and STIs. In addition, both less sexual gratification and more restricted sociosexuality were associated with higher levels of action regret. More inaction regret was associated with less worry about reputation and higher levels of sexual gratification the last time they had casual sex. Those with higher levels of sociosexuality (primarily the attitude dimension) regretted passing up more.

As a follow-up to the first replication, Bendixen, Asao, Wyckoff, Buss, and Kennair (2017) did a direct comparison of student samples for Norway ($n = 853$) and the United States ($n = 466$)[1] on level of action and inaction regret. In this study, the effect of religiosity and sociosexuality was examined, and in a separate paper using the same samples and data sources, the effects of additional proximate factors were examined (Kennair et al., 2018). Despite large differences in level of religiosity between the Norwegian and the US samples ($d = 1.19$), and the higher gender equality and sexual liberalisms in Norway, the sex differences in action and inaction regret were comparable across nations and in line with the findings reported above. Women showed more action regret in both Norway ($d = 0.41$) and the United States ($d = 0.32$), while men indicated more inaction regret in the Norwegian sample ($d = 0.71$) and the US sample ($d = 0.86$). Higher level of religiosity was moderate-to-strongly associated with more restricted sociosexual attitudes in both cultures. However, religiosity was only marginally associated with action and inaction regret in both cultures. On the other hand, less restricted sociosexual attitudes were clearly associated with less action regret and more inaction regret (the effect of sociosexual desires was significant, but weaker).

The analyses of proximate factors from the above samples were restricted to action regret (Kennair et al., 2018). These factors included measures of worry and sexual gratification from the first replication, and additional measures of sexual disgust, feeling pressured to have sex, partner's sexual competence, and taking the initiative to have casual sex. Each of the proximate factors was significantly associated with level of regret for having had casual sex the last time. These associations were present for both men and women and in both cultures, and moderation (interaction) analyses including sex and culture revealed only one effect: the effect of taking sexual initiative on action regret was stronger for women than for men. The multivariate regression analyses including all six predictors showed that the strongest and most consistent predictor was sexual disgust (and particularly the moral aspect of it), followed by lack of sexual gratification (in combination with lack of competence), and initiative. When the effect of the above predictors was accounted for, there was no additional effect of feeling pressured or worry on action regret.

In their most recent study, Kennair, Grøntvedt, and Bendixen (2021) examined both concurrent proximate predictors and longitudinal effects of casual sex regret. The first wave (T1) included 399 Norwegian students, and complete data from both waves were secured for 222 students at the follow-up approximately 4.5 months later (T2). The predictors of most recent casual sex encounter included sociosexuality (SOI-Attitudes) and positive and negative metacognitions as stable individual factors, and also regret processing, sexual disgust, sexual gratification, being intoxicated, sexual initiative, and the perceived short-term mate-value of the partner. At T1, restricted sociosexual attitudes and regret processing were both positive and moderately associated with action regret. More sexual disgust, less sexual gratification, and perceiving the mate-value of one's casual sex partner as low were all strongly associated with more action regret. Finally, those who reported higher levels of sexual initiative also reported less action regret, while being intoxicated or not showed no relationship with level of action regret.

Is Regret a Mechanism to Prevent Future Maladaptive Behavior?

As noted in the introduction to the chapter, most researchers who study regret take for granted that there must be behavioral consequences of regret, even though it is often by proxy and hypothetical (e.g., Pieters & Zeelenberg, 2007; Roese et al., 2007). There is a clear function, albeit not described in evolutionary terms, that there must be "feeling for doing." Further, people also hold beliefs about the benefits or functions of regret (Saffrey et al., 2008). Despite being considered a negative emotion, regret is considered to be beneficial in achieving five different social and intrapsychic tasks, including: preserving social harmony, making sense of past experiences, facilitating approach behaviors, facilitating avoidance behaviors, and finally, gaining insights into the self (Saffrey et al., 2008). These beliefs about regret could be conceptualized as metacognitions about regret, and we will compare these to metacognitions about rumination below. However, let us start by pointing out that both researchers and laypersons share beliefs that the aversive experience of regret helps us guide future behavior in a more adaptive manner.

Galperin et al. (2013) suggested that the evolved function of specific action and inaction sexual regret would be to improve future sexual choices and behavior so that these became more adaptive because of the negative emotional experience of the regret. This is based on the presumption that regret changes future behavior and that regret provides a negative emotional experience that one will wish to avoid in the future. This is problematic, given that regret is, as stated above, not perceived as being that emotionally aversive (Saffrey et al., 2008). Nevertheless, no emotional or cognitive process that does not influence behavior in some way—in other words, that influences reality—may be subject to selection. Therefore, it is reasonable to assume that are specific behavioral outcomes of regret, especially given the systematic and robust sex difference, which is in line with SST. Thus, the questions are: What is the evolutionary benefit for men (especially) to regret passing up an extra reproductive possibility? And what are the possible evolutionary benefits for women (especially) to regret having had a one-night stand? In other words, what behavioral changes would regret bring about? Galperin and colleagues did not specify these behaviors.

In an attempt at operationalizing what the behavioral outcomes of casual sex action and inaction regret, Kennair et al. (2021) suggested the following: inaction regret should increase the number of casual sex partners in the near future. This seems pretty obvious, if you regret not having had a one-night stand when opportunity presented itself, you should increase your casual sex behavior; that is, unless the reason you did not have sex is because you really are quite sociosexually restricted, of course. For action regret, however, it is less obvious. Kennair and colleagues suggested that casual sex action regret could result in three different behaviors: fewer one-night stands, changing mating strategy and entering long-term relationships, or choosing to have sex with more attractive partners.

As most of the research on regret addresses anticipated regret and hypothetical scenarios, rather than longitudinal behavioral change, it is not clear that the regret process does influence behavior—as both researchers and laypersons believe. This may be surprising; however, that is the state of most emotions, apart from fear, where we have known, accepted, and understood the function of fear ever since Darwin (1872), including the fight and flight response (Cannon, 1915) and how different species have species-specific defense responses (Bolles, 1970). We also have good functional understanding of disgust and know how this emotion may protect against contamination (Al-Shawaf et al., 2018; Tybur et al., 2009) (see Chapter 9 and Chapter 58 in the present volume). Thus, no concrete behaviors have been studied in a longitudinal design, where past measured regret predicts future behaviors.

In the first regret study to use such a design, Kennair et al. (2021) tested these possible adaptive functions of casual sex regret using longitudinal data from 222 students. They found no support for the hypotheses that men who more regretted passing up their most recent casual sex opportunity at time 1 increased their casual sex behavior at time 2, approximately 4.5 months later, or that women who regretted more their most recent casual sex encounter reduced their casual sex behavior at time 2. Also, they did not find that regretting casual sex at time 1 increased the likelihood of entering a more committed relationship at time 2 (the likelihood was in fact lower; people who regretted one-night stands were less likely to find and commit to a long-term partner in the near future). Finally, there was no effect of regret on changes in short-term attractiveness of their most recent partner among those who reported a new casual sex partner between time 1 and time 2. While it is far from certain that the operationalizations from this specific study are exactly what Galperin and colleagues had in mind, or even the correct, adaptive changes in future behavior following regret, this first test of the evolutionary function of action and inaction casual sex regret seems to suggest that there is no expected behavioral change following regret. The one change to behavior, fewer long-term partners, is not consistent with either the specific predictions or metacognition that regret facilitates or improves social behavior.

The problem here is that while both researchers (Galperin et al., 2013; Zeelenberg & Pieters, 2007) and people in general (Saffrey et al., 2008) believe that regret is adaptive, this may not necessarily be so. Examples of other emotional-cognitive processes that are similar to regret, but where clinical findings suggest that they are not functional, are depressive rumination and worry. Depressed patients, for example, hold both positive and negative metacognitions about depressive rumination (Papageorgiou & Wells, 2001a, 2001b). Negative metacognitions about rumination are beliefs such as that once one has started ruminating one cannot stop (uncontrollability), while positive metacognitions are beliefs such as that rumination will solve problems or provide insights into how to change future behavior and avoid making mistakes. As such, depressive rumination seems to include many functions similar to regret, in people's minds. Metacognitions about worry are paradoxically believed to "make me safe"—however, even people who have developed a generalized anxiety disorder due to excessive worry believe this about worry, despite worry causing them to be chronically anxious. An evolutionary approach to depression—the Adaptive Rumination Hypothesis (Andrews & Thomson, 2009; Bartoskova et al., 2018)—is founded on the veracity of these metacognitions about depressive rumination being true, and thus of rumination being helpful and unavoidable for depressed patients. In other words, researchers and patients share the functional beliefs about rumination, too, not only about regret—and to a large degree these overlap. Nevertheless, metacognitive therapy of worry (generalized anxiety disorder) and depression (Wells, 2009) targets these metacognitions that maintain depressive rumination and worry, and aids the patients in discontinuing their rumination or worry. This is an efficient therapy for these disorders (Hagen et al., 2017; Hjemdal et al., 2019; Nordahl et al., 2018). Three-year follow-up data suggest that not only are the treatment effects of discontinuing rumination better than competing treatment methods, one also finds improved quality of life and better workforce or study participation (Solem et al., 2019). In conclusion, clinical studies suggest that commonly held beliefs about certain types of mental processing that increases aversive emotional states are not true, and that these are not adaptive—not in the here and now, and not from an evolutionary perspective (Kennair et al., 2017).

Kennair et al. (2021) found that concurrent metacognitions and regret processing (inspired by rumination processing) predicted regret in the here and now. Common experiences among depressed patients suggests that they have not solved any problems. Worrying, by imagining worst-case scenarios, is not problem-solving behavior, despite the definition of worry as verbal problem-solving behavior—rather, it is a problem-focused cognitive process (Kennair, 2007) (and discontinuing worry is an effective treatment; Nordahl et al., 2018). The same may be true for regret. We regret a whole range of different behaviors. And when we ask for forgiveness, we promise to change and never do it again. And yet we sin, err, and transgress, time and time again. We break our own rules and promises. We eat that last piece of cake, we skip our physical exercise, we drink too much, we say something we should not have, we spend too much before payday, we invest too little for a rainy day, we regret it this last time, but likely we do these things because of who we are, our human nature and our personality—and therefore there is a high probability that we have done this before. These are generally behaviors that are problematic only if they are lifestyle behaviors—in other words, repeated and habitual or trait-like behaviors. Another set of problematic behaviors, addictions, also are predicted by faulty metacognitions and unhelpful cognitive processing (Janssen et al., 2020; Solem et al., 2020). At a larger level, we vote for politicians that do not serve our interests, we exterminate species, we go to war, we deplete resources, we bring too many children into the world, and we contaminate our environment. We might regret our choices in these areas, too, but few governments or individuals make behavioral changes that really matter.

What May the Function of Regret Be?

This leads us to the surprising tentative conclusion that the function of regret might not be to change and improve the adaptive consequences of behavior. It may be that regret and rumination both work to some degree in assessing past experiences, behavior, and choices from a fitness-relevant perspective; thus women will be more skeptical of short-term sexual encounters, given the cost-benefit analysis of short-term sex for women, and men will provide differential behavioral predictions (Buss, 1998; Buss & Schmitt, 1993, 2017). Note that most people do not regret most of their short-term sex encounters or even regret passing up sex. Many predictors of these two types of regret are identified, making each situation complex and multifaceted (Bendixen et al., 2017; Kennair & Bendixen, 2018; Kennair et al., 2016; Kennair et al., 2021; Kennair et al., 2018). People might therefore not generalize much to next potential short-term sexual situation, either. However, in the here and now, SST will predict who makes an emotional-cognitive assessment of the situation as desirable or regrettable post hoc.

From an evolutionary perspective, one would need to understand the function of regret as a process that changes behavior. Barring evidence of this, there is no reason to continue to speculate that intuitive beliefs about regret as a reason for behavior change are more than what Nisbett and Wilson (1977) refer to as utilization of a priori causal theories, explanations that may originate from cultural transmission or even subjective empirical observations that link certain stimuli to certain responses (covariation). In other words, we often cannot and do not know the true reasons of our behavior; there are many mental processes we do not have verbal access to (Kurzban, 2010). Casual sex regret may be akin to relationship satisfaction, an online implicit gauge of whether one's many differing fitness goals are being met by the partner at any given time (Conroy-Beam et al., 2015, 2016). However, relationship satisfaction might be as predictive of behavior as people imagine (Machia & Ogolsky, 2020). There are probably many areas with emotions and motivation where we do not have insights into how cognitive processing, emotions, and behavior are connected. Within this area there are bound to be counterintuitive explanations and mechanisms.

Gauging behavior in the "here and now" may be the result of several mental mechanisms overlapping with guilt, shame, rumination, and disappointment. The overlap of guilt and regret in Saffrey et al. (2008) probably ought to have received more attention. There is also evidence of disgust and lack of sexual gratification in casual sex regret (Kennair et al., 2016; Kennair et al., 2018). Attributions, aims of behavior, and emotional valence of the situation, in addition to hindsight bias, may influence regret—in the specific situation as well as after the event. All of these aspects have some fitness consequence, and emotionally will elicit more or less satisfaction and more or less aversion.

Our ability to produce counterfactual scenarios in our imagination is also probably a crucial as well as defining feature of the emotional and cognitive processing of regret. Yet again, in hindsight we may evaluate what happened against a legion of different, more desirable outcomes. These will probably also, when desired, be scenarios that left us with more pleasure, more status and social standing, more resources, and increased fitness. However, just like worrying to stay safe does not make us safe, only anxious, or ruminating to solve problems rarely helps us, only makes us blue, it is possible that regret only makes us dissatisfied, not better at attaining our goals. However, emotional integration and conscious processing of our thoughts, desires, experiences, and emotional states are part of our nature. Maybe regret is merely a nonfunctional aspect of this conscious integration of our many states and cognitions. There is little evidence of any other specific function. Research needs to study actual regret in a longitudinal framework and show systematic predictive effect on concrete behavioral outcomes. The first attempt at that was regrettably not able to find any effect of regret on changes in behaviors (Kennair et al., 2021).

Other Domains of Regret That Might Show Sex Differentiation
Roese and colleagues (2006) investigated regret in the social domain, where sex differences in regret within romantic relationships and other interpersonal relationships were investigated.

From an evolutionary perspective, they hypothesized that women and men would differ in inaction and action regret, specifically within the romantic relationship settings. There were no sex differences in regret in the interpersonal aspects (parental, sibling, and friendship interactions) apart from the romantic relationship domain. Men emphasized inaction regrets more than action regrets in the romantic relationship setting, whereas women reported equally on action and inaction regrets in the same setting. No such sex difference was evident in regrets on parental or friendship interactions. Within the romantic domain, the most striking sex difference emerged in the inaction regret of sexual possibilities (e.g., wished I could have more sex with different people, and kicked myself for missing out on a chance to have sex with [her/him]). Men showed significantly more inaction regret than women, and no sex difference was seen in action regret. In addition, men more than women regretted not dating more people, possibly also related to the inaction regret of sexual behavior, as dating more people might entail more sexual partners, but this is our speculation. These results suggest that it was only in the sexual-romantic domain that one found sex differences. This finding was not surprising from an SST perspective, which inspired Galperin and colleagues' (2013) work, which again has fueled several investigations of proximate mechanisms involved in casual sex action and inaction regret, with a special focus on sex differences (Bendixen et al., 2017; Kennair & Bendixen, 2018; Kennair et al., 2016; Kennair et al., 2021; Kennair et al., 2018). However, will an evolutionary approach to regret be able to inform us of other domains that might be predicted to show sex differences (Al-Shawaf et al., 2016)?

Emotional consideration of fitness-reducing behaviors should be the eliciting precursor for regret. In addition, to discover sex differences in regret, one needs to consider behavioral domains where sexual conflict theory may provide insights into sex differences (Buss, 2017). There need to be differential adaptive outcomes for men and women throughout evolutionary history, for similar behavior to elicit different levels or patterns of regret.

One area where evolutionary analyses provided insight into sex differentiation of emotions is the study of jealousy (Buss et al., 1992). Using continuous and forced-choice measures in the same sample population provides similar sex differences of a robust finding for heterosexual samples: Women more than men will be distressed by emotional infidelity, while men more than women will be distressed by sexual infidelity (Bendixen et al., 2015), although women do report more jealousy on the continuous measures (Bendixen et al., 2015). Combining jealousy scenarios and theory on error management, Bendixen and colleagues (2018) investigated to what extent individuals believed in expressed forgiveness after infidelity within couples. Using infidelity scenarios and romantically involved couples, they investigated whether there was an expected underestimation of belief in expressed forgiveness within couples. Not fully believing a partner's forgiveness after infidelity is suggested to have the function of securing that the transgression is fully mended with reparative behavior from the transgressor's side. (You tell me that you forgive me after being unfaithful to you, but I would rather try even harder to make amends to show that I realize that this transgression was extremely severe and that I will fight for our relationship.) As expected, both men and women showed negative forgiveness bias in both sexual and emotional infidelity scenarios; however, this bias was less pronounced for men in the emotional infidelity scenarios. Men also reported women's' emotional infidelity as less of a threat to the relationship, in addition to expressing more forgiveness for such infidelity compared to a sexual infidelity scenario. Men don't really seem to understand the severity of emotional infidelity, or at least don't consider being emotionally involved with a woman outside of a relationship as much of a problem as women consider it to be.

Let us consider and speculate about two possible domains where we might predict sex differences in regret. First, we would from an evolutionary perspective expect more regret in men because of choices that either lead to status loss or lack of status gain, either regarding occupational choices or poor financial choices and failed investments. Men will in general have greater fitness costs in this domain compared to women, due to female partner preferences (Walter et al., 2020) and intrasexual conflict within this area. Thus, there should be more distress, disappointment, and consequence for men who make poor choices that affect their future status.

Another area, where a direct comparison might be less forthcoming because of menopause, but that nonetheless might be relevant, is regret about not having had children. Women more than men reproduce in modern societies (Jensen, 2013). Women also are more distressed by not having children than men (Rotkirch, 2007). Female sexual psychology is influenced by nearing menopause, resulting in what is called reproduction expediting: the shift in behavior and emotional priorities to increase likelihood of pregnancy before it is too late (Easton et al., 2010). While all men who do not have children certainly are not childless by choice, we still expect that at a certain age, women more than men will regret not having had (more) children.

Future Research on Sex Differences and Function of Regret

To be clear, in most psychological domains there are small sex differences (Archer, 2019; Ellis et al., 2008). The largest and most relevant are exactly in the areas of sexual psychology (predicted by parental investment SST and sexual conflict theory) and negative emotional processing. Therefore, it might be that the findings of Roese et al. (2006) reflect the most relevant sex-differentiated regret domain. However, we would suggest that future regret research employ the Al-Shawaf et al. (2016) approach to an evolutionary analysis of the function of emotions. In doing so, one needs to not only approach domains where sexual conflict theory might inform us of sex differences, but also consider what future behavior would be considered adaptive after regret in specific situations. The first attempts at defining more adaptive behavior following action and inaction regret did not pan out (Kennair et al., 2021); however, there might be several reasons for this: the time period between the two data-collection waves might have been too short; the operationalization of adaptive behavior might not have been correct; the regret scale used might not provide enough variance, and maybe regret processing suggested in the paper is more relevant than the retrospective measure. While it is unclear how increased casual sex behavior should not be the most obvious behavioral change after regretting passing up a one-night stand opportunity, such opportunities may not be that frequent. Therefore, establishing the association between regret and future behavior might be difficult. In any case, one study is not decisive—the field needs more research. However, it also needs to critically assess the intuitive beliefs about how cognitive-emotional processes influence behavior and mood. We probably engage in many different behaviors without understanding why or how they affect us.

Conclusions

Regret is a counterfactual cognitive-emotional process, where we consider our past behavior and choices and imagine how we would be better off if only we had acted differently. It is commonly believed that the aversive force of regret will affect future behavior, in order to avoid future regret or the consequences one is currently regretting. While such time travel probably happens to some extent, it is clear that other similar mental processes are not efficient in achieving similar aims. Further, there are almost no longitudinal predictive studies considering what would be the relevant adaptive shift in behavior. Finally, the only such study to date drew a blank on predictive, longitudinal effects of regret on behavior change, despite the effect of many previously discovered concurrent predictors of regret. There seems to be reason to question whether we fully understand the function of regret, although we do know that we can predict regret in a specific situation based on an evolutionary understanding of factors that might describe the specific context as less satisfactory and adaptive and more undesirable, distressing and disappointing. At this point, regret seems to function more as an integration of emotional valences surrounding discrete experiences, rather than a process that guides future behavior. This conservative conclusion is probably not the last word in this discussion, though, as it warrants more and thorough research attempting to demonstrate the predictive value of regret on future adaptive behavior.

Note

1. For the analyses of action and inaction regret, only those who reported having had casual sex or having passed up casual sex opportunities were included.

References

Al-Shawaf, L., Conroy-Beam, D., Asao, K., & Buss, D. M. (2016). Human emotions: An evolutionary psychological perspective. *Emotion Review, 8*(2), 173–186. doi: 10.1177/1754073914565518

Al-Shawaf, L., Lewis, D. M. G., & Buss, D. M. (2018). Sex differences in disgust: Why are women more easily disgusted than men? *Emotion Review, 10*(2), 149–160. doi: 10.1177/1754073917709940

Andrews, P. W., & Thomson, J. A., Jr. (2009). The bright side of being blue: Depression as an adaptation for analyzing complex problems. *Psychological Review, 116*(3), 620–654. doi: 10.1037/a0016242

Archer, J. (2019). The reality and evolutionary significance of human psychological sex differences. *Biological Reviews, 94*(4), 1381–1415. doi: 10.1111/brv.12507

Bartoskova, M., Sevcikova, M., Durisko, Z., Maslej, M. M., Barbic, S. P., Preiss, M., & Andrews, P. W. (2018). The form and function of depressive rumination. *Evolution and Human Behavior, 39*(3), 277–289. https://doi.org/10.1016/j.evolhumbehav.2018.01.005

Bendixen, M., Asao, K., Wyckoff, J. P., Buss, D. M., & Kennair, L. E. O. (2017). Sexual regret in US and Norway: Effects of culture and individual differences in religiosity and mating strategy. *Personality and Individual Differences, 116*, 246–251. https://doi.org/10.1016/j.paid.2017.04.054

Bendixen, M., Kennair, L. E. O., & Buss, D. M. (2015). Jealousy: Evidence of strong sex differences using both forced choice and continuous measure paradigms. *Personality and Individual Differences, 86*(0), 212–216. http://dx.doi.org/10.1016/j.paid.2015.05.035

Bendixen, M., Kennair, L. E. O., & Grøntvedt, T. V. (2018). Casual sex. In T. K. Shackelford & V. A. Weekes-Shackelford (Eds.), *Encyclopedia of evolutionary psychological science* (pp. 1–8). Springer International.

Bolles, R. C. (1970). Species-specific defense reactions and avoidance learning. *Psychological Review, 77*(1), 32–48. doi: 10.1037/h0028589

Brewer, N. T., DeFrank, J. T., & Gilkey, M. B. (2016). Anticipated regret and health behavior: A meta-analysis. *Health Psychology, 35*(11), 1264–1275. doi: 10.1037/hea0000294

Burns, P., Riggs, K. J., & Beck, S. R. (2012). Executive control and the experience of regret. *Journal of Experimental Child Psychology, 111*(3), 501–515. doi: 10.1016/j.jecp.2011.10.003

Buss, D. M. (1998). Sexual strategies theory: Historical origins and current status. *The Journal of Sex Research, 35*(1), 19–31. doi: 10.1080/00224499809551914

Buss, D. M. (2017). Sexual conflict in human mating. *Current Directions in Psychological Science, 26*(4), 307–313. doi: 10.1177/0963721417695559

Buss, D. M., Larsen, R. J., Westen, D., & Semmelroth, J. (1992). Sex differences in jealousy: Evolution, physiology, and psychology. *Psychological Science, 3*, 251–255. doi: 10.1111/j.1467-9280.1992.tb00038.x

Buss, D. M., & Schmitt, D. P. (1993). Sexual Strategy Theory: An evolutionary perspective on human mating. *Psychological Review, 100*(2), 204–232. doi: 10.1037/0033-295X.100.2.204

Buss, D. M., & Schmitt, D. P. (2017). Sexual Strategies Theory. In T. K. Shackelford & V. A. Weekes-Shackelford (Eds.), *Encyclopedia of evolutionary psychological science* (pp. 1–5). Springer International.

Campbell, A. (2008). The morning after the night before: Affective reactions to one-night stands among mated and unmated women and men. *Human Nature, 19*, 157–173. doi: 10.1007s12110-008-9036-2

Cannon, W. B. (1915). *Bodily changes in pain, hunger, fear and rage: An account of recent researches into the function of emotional excitement.* D. Appleton.

Conroy-Beam, D., Goetz, C. D., & Buss, D. M. (2015). Why do humans form long-term mateships? An evolutionary game-theoretic model. In J. M. Olson & M. P. Zanna (Eds.), *Advances in experimental social psychology* (Vol. 51, pp. 1–39). Academic Press.

Conroy-Beam, D., Goetz, C. D., & Buss, D. M. (2016). What predicts romantic relationship satisfaction and mate retention intensity: Mate preference fulfillment or mate value discrepancies? *Evolution and Human Behavior, 37*(6), 440–448. https://doi.org/10.1016/j.evolhumbehav.2016.04.003

Darwin, C. (1872). *The expression of the emotions in man and animals*. Murray.

Easton, J. A., Confer, J. C., Goetz, C. D., & Buss, D. M. (2010). Reproduction expediting: Sexual motivations, fantasies, and the ticking biological clock. *Personality and Individual Differences, 49*(5), 516–520. https://doi.org/10.1016/j.paid.2010.05.018

Ellis, L., Hershberger, S., Field, E., Wersinger, S., Pellis, S., Geary, D., Palmer, C., Hoyenga, K., Hetsroni, A., & Karadi, K. (2008). *Sex differences: Summarizing more than a century of scientific research*. Psychology Press.

Eshbaugh, E. M., & Gute, G. (2008). Hookups and sexual regret among college women. *The Journal of Social Psychology, 148*(1), 77–90. doi: 10.3200/SOCP.148.1.77-90

Fernandes, H. B. F., Kennair, L. E. O., Hutz, C. S., Natividade, J. C., & Kruger, D. J. (2016). Are negative postcoital emotions a product of evolutionary adaptation? Multinational relationships with sexual strategies, reputation, and mate quality. *Evolutionary Behavioral Sciences, 10*(4), 219–244. http://dx.doi.org/10.1037/ebs0000050

Festinger, L. (1964). The post-decision process. In L. Festinger (Ed.), *Conflict, decision, and dissonance* (pp. 97–100). Stanford University Press.

Fisher, M. L., Worth, K., Garcia, J. R., & Meredith, T. (2012). Feelings of regret following uncommitted sexual encounters in Canadian university students. *Culture, Health & Sexuality, 14*(1), 45–57. doi: 10.1080/13691058.2011.619579

Galperin, A., Haselton, M. G., Frederick, D. A., Poore, J., von Hippel, W., Buss, D. M., & Gonzaga, G. C. (2013). Sexual regret: Evidence for evolved sex differences. *Archives of Sexual Behavior, 42*(7), 1145–1161. doi: 10.1007/s10508-012-0019-3

Hagen, R., Hjemdal, O., Solem, S., Kennair, L. E. O., Nordahl, H. M., Fisher, P., & Wells, A. (2017). Metacognitive therapy for depression in adults: A waiting list randomized controlled trial with six months follow-up. *Frontiers in Psychology, 8*(31). doi: 10.3389/fpsyg.2017.00031

Haselton, M. G., & Buss, D. M. (2000). Error management theory: A new perspective on biases in cross-sex mind reading. *Journal of Personality and Social Psychology, 78*(1), 81–91. doi:10.1037/0022-3514.78.1.81

Haselton, M. G., & Buss, D. M. (2001). The affective shift hypothesis: The functions of emotional changes following sexual intercourse. *Personal Relationships, 8*(4), 357–369. doi: 10.1111/j.1475-6811.2001.tb00045.x

Hjemdal, O., Solem, S., Hagen, R., Kennair, L. E. O., Nordahl, H. M., & Wells, A. (2019). A randomized controlled trial of metacognitive therapy for depression: Analysis of 1-year follow-up. *Frontiers in Psychology, 10*(1842). doi: 10.3389/fpsyg.2019.01842

Janssen, A. G., Kennair, L. E. O., Hagen, R., Hjemdal, O., Havnen, A., & Solem, S. (2020). Positive and negative metacognitions about alcohol: Validity of the Norwegian PAMS and NAMS. *Addictive Behaviors, 108*, 106466. https://doi.org/10.1016/j.addbeh.2020.106466

Jensen, A.-M. (2013). Rising fertility, fewer fathers: Crossroads of network, gender and class. In A. L. Ellingsæter, A.-M. Jensen, & M. Lie (Eds.), *The social meaning of children and fertility change in Europe* (pp. 120–135): Routledge.

Kennair, L. E. O. (2007). Fear and fitness revisited. *Journal of Evolutionary Psychology, 5*(1), 105–117. doi: 10.1556/JEP.2007.1020

Kennair, L. E. O., & Bendixen, M. (2018). Sexual regret. In T. K. Shackelford & V. A. Weekes-Shackelford (Eds.), *Encyclopedia of evolutionary psychological science* (pp. 1–5). Springer International.

Kennair, L. E. O., Bendixen, M., & Buss, D. M. (2016). Sexual regret: Tests of competing explanations of sex differences. *Evolutionary Psychology, 14*(4), 1–9. doi: 10.1177/1474704916682903

Kennair, L. E. O., Grøntvedt, T. V., & Bendixen, M. (2021). The function of casual sex action and inaction regret: A longitudinal investigation. *Evolutionary Psychology, 19*(1). doi: 10.1177/1474704921998333

Kennair, L. E. O., Kleppestø, T. H., Larsen, S. M., & Jørgensen, B. E. G. (2017). Depression: Is rumination really adaptive? In T. K. Shackelford & V. Zeigler-Hill (Eds.), *Evolution and psychopathology* (pp. 73–92). Springer.

Kennair, L. E. O., Wyckoff, J. P., Asao, K., Buss, D. M., & Bendixen, M. (2018). Why do women regret casual sex more than men do? *Personality and Individual Differences, 127*, 61–67. https://doi.org/10.1016/j.paid.2018.01.044

Kurzban, R. (2010). *Why everyone (else) is a hypocrite: Evolution and the modular mind*. Princeton University Press.

Li, J., Li, D., Cao, Q., & Niu, X. (2018). The role of regret and disappointment in the repurchase effect: Does gender matter? *Journal of Behavioral and Experimental Economics, 75*, 134–140. doi: 10.1016/j.socec.2018.06.005

Machia, L. V., & Ogolsky, B. G. (2020). The reasons people think about staying and leaving their romantic relationships: A mixed-method analysis. *Personality and Social Psychology Bulletin, 47*(8), 1279–1293. doi:10.1177/0146167220966903

Monto, M. A., & Carey, A. G. (2014). A new standard of sexual behavior? Are claims associated with the "hookup culture" supported by General Social Survey Data? *The Journal of Sex Research, 51*(6), 605–615. doi: 10.1080/00224499.2014.906031

Nesse, R. M. (1990). Evolutionary explanations of emotions. *Human Nature, 1*(3), 261–289. doi: 10.1007/BF02733986

Nisbett, R. E., & Wilson, T. D. (1977). Telling more than we can know: Verbal reports on mental processes. *Psychological Review, 84*(3), 231–259. doi: 10.1037/0033-295X.84.3.231

Nordahl, H. M., Borkovec, T. D., Hagen, R., Kennair, L. E. O., Hjemdal, O., Solem, S., Hansen, B., Haseth, S., & Wells, A. (2018). Metacognitive therapy versus cognitive–behavioural therapy in adults with generalised anxiety disorder. *British Journal of Psychiatry Open, 4*(5), 393–400. doi: 10.1192/bjo.2018.54

O'Connor, E., McCormack, T., & Feeney, A. (2014). Do children who experience regret make better decisions? A developmental study of the behavioral consequences of regret. *Child Development, 85*(5), 1995–2010. doi: 10.1111/cdev.12253

Oswalt, S. B., Cameron, K. A., & Koob, J. J. (2005). Sexual regret in college students. *Archives of Sexual Behavior, 34*(6), 663–669. doi: 10.1007/s10508-005-7920-y

Owen, J., & Fincham, F. D. (2011). Young adults' emotional reactions after hooking up encounters. *Archives of Sexual Behavior, 40*(2), 321–330. doi: 10.1007/s10508-010-9652-x

Papageorgiou, C., & Wells, A. (2001a). Metacognitive beliefs about rumination in recurrent major depression. *Cognitive and Behavioral Practice, 8*(2), 160–164. https://doi.org/10.1016/S1077-7229(01)80021-3

Papageorgiou, C., & Wells, A. (2001b). Positive beliefs about depressive rumination: Development and preliminary validation of a self-report scale. *Behavior Therapy, 32*(1), 13–26. https://doi.org/10.1016/S0005-7894(01)80041-1

Paul, E. L., & Hayes, K. A. (2002). The casualties of "casual" sex: A qualitative exploration of the phenomenology of college students' hookups. *Journal of Social and Personal Relationships, 19*(5), 639–661. doi: 10.1177/0265407502195006

Pieters, R., & Zeelenberg, M. (2007). A theory of regret regulation 1.1. *Journal of Consumer Psychology, 17*(1), 29–35. doi: 10.1207/s15327663jcp1701_6

Roese, N. J., Epstude, K., Fessel, F., Morrison, M., Smallman, R., Summerville, A., Galinsky, A. D., & Segerstrom, S. (2009). Repetitive regret, depression, and anxiety: Findings from a nationally representative survey. *Journal of Social and Clinical Psychology, 28*(6), 671–688. doi: 10.1521/jscp.2009.28.6.671

Roese, N. J., Pennington, G. L., Coleman, J., Janicki, M., Li, N. P., & Kenrick, D. T. (2006). Sex differences in regret: All for love or some for lust? *Personality & Social Psychology Bulletin, 32*(6), 770–780. doi: 10.1177/0146167206286709

Roese, N. J., Summerville, A., & Fessel, F. (2007). Regret and behavior: Comment on Zeelenberg and Pieters. *Journal of Consumer Psychology, 17*(1), 25–28. doi: 10.1207/s15327663jcp1701_5

Rotkirch, A. (2007). All that she wants is a(nother) baby? Longing for children as a fertility incentive of growing importance. *Journal of Evolutionary Psychology, 5*(1), 89–104. doi: 10.1556/JEP.2007.1010

Saffrey, C., Summerville, A., & Roese, N. J. (2008). Praise for regret: People value regret above other negative emotions. *Motivation and Emotion, 32*(1), 46–54. doi: 10.1007/s11031-008-9082-4

Simonson, I. (1992). The influence of anticipating regret and responsibility on purchase decisions. *Journal of Consumer Research, 19*(1), 105–118. doi: 10.1086/209290

Solem, S., Kennair, L. E. O., Hagen, R., Havnen, A., Nordahl, H. M., Wells, A., & Hjemdal, O. (2019). Metacognitive therapy for depression: A 3-year follow-up study assessing recovery, relapse, work force participation, and quality of life. *Frontiers in Psychology, 10*(2908). doi: 10.3389/fpsyg.2019.02908

Solem, S., Pedersen, H., Nesse, F., Garvik Janssen, A., Ottesen Kennair, L. E., Hagen, R., Havnen, A., Hjemdal, O., Caselli, G., & Spada, M. M. (2020). Validity of a Norwegian version of the Desire Thinking Questionnaire (DTQ): Associations with problem drinking, nicotine dependence and problematic social media use. *Clinical Psychology & Psychotherapy, 28*(3), 615–622. doi: 10.1002/cpp.2524

Townsend, J. M., & Wasserman, T. H. (2011). Sexual hookups among college students: Sex differences in emotional reactions. *Archives of Sexual Behavior, 40*(6), 1173–1181. doi: 10.1007/s10508-011-9841-2

Trivers, R. (1972). Parental investment and sexual selection. In B. Campbell (Ed.), *Sexual selection and the descent of man, 1871–1971* (pp. 136–179). Aldine.

Tybur, J. M., Lieberman, D., & Griskevicius, V. (2009). Microbes, mating, and morality: Individual differences in three functional domains of disgust. *Journal of Personality and Social Psychology, 97*(1), 103–122. doi: 10.1037/a0015474

Walter, K. V., Conroy-Beam, D., Buss, D. M., Asao, K., Sorokowska, A., Sorokowski, P., Aavik, T., Akello, G., Alhabahba, M. M., Alm, C., Amjad, N., Anjum, A., Atama, C. S., Duyar, D. A., Ayebare, R., Batres, C., Bendixen, M., Bensafia, A., Bizumic, B., . . . Zupančič, M. (2020). Sex differences in mate preferences across 45 countries: A large-scale replication. *Psychological Science, 31*(4), 408–423. doi: 10.1177/0956797620904154

Weisberg, D. P., & Beck, S. R. (2010). Children's thinking about their own and others' regret and relief. *Journal of Experimental Child Psychology, 106*(2), 184–191. doi: 10.1016/j.jecp.2010.02.005

Wells, A. (2009). *Metacognitive therapy for anxiety and depression.* Guilford Press.

Zeelenberg, M. (1999). The use of crying over spilled milk: A note on the rationality and functionality of regret. *Philosophical Psychology, 12*(3), 325–340. doi: 10.1080/095150899105800

Zeelenberg, M., Inman, J. J., & Pieters, R. G. M. (2001). What we do when decisions go awry: Behavioral consequences of experienced regret. In E. U. Weber, J. Baron, & G. Loomes (Eds.), *Conflict and tradeoffs in decision making* (pp. 136–155). Cambridge University Press.

Zeelenberg, M., & Pieters, R. (2004). Beyond valence in customer dissatisfaction: A review and new findings on behavioral responses to regret and disappointment in failed services. *Journal of Business Research, 57*(4), 445–455. doi: 10.1016/S0148-2963(02)00278-3

Zeelenberg, M., & Pieters, R. (2007). A theory of regret regulation 1.0. *Journal of Consumer Psychology, 17*(1), 3–18. doi: 10.1207/s15327663jcp1701_3

CHAPTER 14

The Elements of Gratitude

Riley N. Loria, Debra Lieberman, and Eric J. Pedersen

Abstract

Gratitude is a key emotion motivating the initiation and maintenance of cooperative relationships. However, it has received relatively little attention from evolutionarily minded social scientists. We have learned much about gratitude in the past two decades that sheds light on gratitude's purported evolved functions, but several questions remain: Does gratitude rely on benefit delivery? Does it require that a cost be incurred? Does gratitude correspond to a change in another's value of the self, the self's value of another, or both? And how do expressions of gratitude influence perceptions of the expressor? This chapter begins with an overview of the science of gratitude by reviewing research from positive and social psychology, highlighting the cross-cultural similarities and differences in the experience and expression of gratitude. The authors then focus on evolutionary perspectives on gratitude, discuss experimental results that adjudicate between them, and suggest profitable lines of future research.

Key Words: gratitude, cooperation, evolution, pro-sociality, welfare trade-off ratio

Introduction

In daily life, we consistently recognize the importance of gratitude for the sake of both our relationships and our well-being. We send each other "thank you" notes in response to gifts, we thank strangers for holding a door open, and it is often a faux pas to forget to express thanks, even in cases where it is clearly a formality rather than a genuine expression of gratitude. We teach children from an early age the importance of expressing gratitude in these types of instances. Countless words have been written on the importance of counting blessings and cultivating a grateful disposition for one's mental health, and research generally supports these notions (Davis et al., 2016). The significance and prevalence of feelings and expressions of gratitude in human social life suggests that gratitude may serve important functions to facilitate cooperative behavior (e.g., Keltner & Haidt, 1999; Van Kleef, 2009). But where did gratitude and its related social conventions arise from? What might be gratitude's evolved functional structure? The scientific study of gratitude has to date largely taken place in the realms of positive and social psychology, and it has only relatively recently received much attention. As such, research on gratitude remains largely in its infancy. And despite likely playing a key role in the development of cooperative relationships, gratitude has not received much attention from evolutionarily minded scholars. In this chapter, we review some of the social psychological research on gratitude, explore existing evolutionary accounts of the emotion, detail some of our recent work on an information-processing model of gratitude, and highlight some of the open questions about gratitude that we find most interesting.

A Brief Review of the Science of Gratitude

Gratitude is a positive emotion that is evoked when one receives costly, unexpected, and intentionally rendered benefits, and is thought to play a key role in regulating the initiation and maintenance of numerous kinds of cooperative relationships (Algoe et al., 2010; Bartlett et al., 2012; DeSteno et al., 2010; McCullough et al., 2001, McCullough et al., 2008; Trivers, 1971). Researchers have typically distinguished between "trait" gratitude and "state" gratitude. Trait gratitude is one's relatively stable propensity to feel gratitude and has been linked to numerous behaviors (e.g., readily forgiving a transgressor) and tendencies (e.g., experiencing low levels of envy; McCullough et al., 2002b). In contrast, state gratitude refers to the experience of gratitude at a given time, often in response to a specific event. Functional accounts of gratitude have largely focused on state gratitude, and hence that is our primary focus here. Initially, however, we review some of the relevant research findings on trait gratitude and, later, discuss their possible implications for a complete evolutionary account of gratitude. We focus our brief review of the extant gratitude literature on four areas: (1) trait gratitude's connection with positive affect, (2) gratitude interventions and well-being, (3) gratitude's role in pro-sociality, and 4) cross-cultural commonalities and differences in gratitude.

Trait Gratitude

Trait gratitude has been linked to numerous well-being outcomes. For example, researchers have found that higher trait gratitude is correlated with the ability to cope with stress (Wood et al., 2007), less depression and higher levels of social support (Wood, Maltby, et al., 2008), reports of higher life satisfaction (Wood, Joseph, et al., 2008), better performance in school (Froh et al., 2008), better quality sleep (Wood et al., 2009), and decreased development of psychopathology (Rosmarin et al., 2008). In addition to these relationships with well-being, trait gratitude has also been shown to predict various kinds of positive pro-social attitudes and outcomes (McCullough et al., 2002b; McCullough et al., 2004). For example, a study from McCullough and colleagues asked participants to rate themselves on (trait) gratitude, pro-sociality (such as empathetic concern and perspective taking), and reports of pro-social behavior. In addition to rating themselves, participants were asked to pick four peers who knew them well to answer the same questions. Greater self-reported and peer-reported gratitude was correlated with higher scores on a measure of trait empathy, and peer informants also rated more grateful participants as being more pro-social overall (McCullough et al., 2002b). In another study, children's expected gratitude for being picked in a team sport was positively correlated with their expectations of reciprocating the gesture with a gift for the selecting team member (Graham, 1988).

Trait gratitude also correlates with typically pro-social personality traits. In particular, people rated as more grateful in both self-report and peer-report surveys scored higher in agreeableness, which, as measured in the Big Five personality traits, encompasses other largely pro-social traits like empathy (Graziano et al., 1996; Saucier & Goldberg, 1998). McCullough and colleagues (2004) conducted study in which participants completed a battery of personality measures including measures of life satisfaction, the Big Five personality inventory, spirituality, optimism, and depressive symptoms. Gratitude was measured via responses in diary entries over 21 days. Participants reported to what extent they were feeling each of several emotions; those included as a measure of gratitude on each day were "grateful," "thankful," and "appreciative." Across two studies, greater experience of gratitude over this 21-day period correlated with higher life satisfaction/well-being, optimism, and lower depression. Gratitude was also correlated with extraversion and, again, agreeableness, both pro-social traits within the Big Five. Notably, correlational findings on the opposite side of the pro-social personality trait spectrum have showed that, following false positive feedback regarding completion of a partnered task, narcissism negatively correlated with gratitude ratings toward one's assigned partner (Farwell & Wohlwend-Lloyd, 1998). These numerous correlational findings surrounding trait gratitude offer insight into its potential value as a predictor of individual differences in pro-social motivation.

Gratitude Interventions and Well-Being

As the experience of gratitude is often associated with positive outcomes, cultivating gratitude has been explored as a mental health intervention. If gratitude can be successfully induced, then participants may experience the affective benefits of gratitude. A common gratitude manipulation instructs participants to reflect on the people in their lives that make them grateful. For example, Watkins and colleagues (2003) induced gratitude by having participants either write a letter to, write a short essay about, or reflect on someone to whom they felt grateful. Following this gratitude manipulation, the researchers found increases in positive affect in every condition, with the greatest increase in the letter-writing condition (see also Toepfer & Walker, 2009). Using a similar writing reflection task, Emmons and McCullough (2003) found that recalling and listing the sources of one's gratitude also increases positive affect. In one study design, which was also conceptually replicated, participants completed a weekly diary for two and a half months, in which they either listed the sources of their gratitude, the sources of their hassles, or mundane life events. Participants in the gratitude condition reported increased optimism and life satisfaction, as well as a reduction in complaints about physical pain and discomfort. Further, the researchers hypothesized that the observed increase in positive affect at the end of all three studies was not simply the result of the diary intervention per se (i.e., the result of general positive affect generated from the diary exercise), but rather was specifically the result of the gratitude elicited during the exercise. They found evidence for complete mediation such that the diary intervention increased positive affect only to the degree that the manipulation was able to elicit gratitude.

This kind of intervention has been tested in a variety of settings. For example, one intervention focused on reducing burnout among healthcare professionals (Cheng et al., 2015). Much like the aforementioned studies, participants were randomly assigned to a gratitude condition, a comparison condition, or a no treatment condition. Participants in the gratitude condition wrote diary entries twice a week for four weeks about moments in their jobs for which they were thankful. Participants in the hassle condition wrote about aversive events at work for the four weeks. The gratitude intervention group reported significantly lower stress and depressive symptoms than either the hassle or control groups. Similar interventions have been conducted in a variety of professions—for example, studies with athletes and teachers yield similar results. Gratitude interventions often yield greater well-being and more positive mental states (Chan, 2011; Gabana et al., 2019).

Gratitude and Pro-sociality

Gratitude's general role as a means of facilitating pro-social behavior is one of the key features of its importance in cooperative relationships. Decisions surrounding interpersonal interactions are a high priority to social creatures; for humans, successful navigation of the social world is key for survival. Based on the importance of social choices, researchers argue that emotions likely serve the functionally adaptive purpose of directing humans' behavior in social exchanges (Keltner & Haidt, 1999). More generally, evolutionary psychologists have posited that emotions coordinate a host of mechanisms (e.g., attention, reflexes, motivation) which function together to solve complex adaptive problems (Tooby & Cosmides, 2008). Since any given adaptive problem is multifaceted (e.g., aiming to form a cooperative partnership but being vigilant for the possibility of exploitation or disease threats), the psychological systems involved in solving them involve complex mental accounting and thereby likely rely on emotions to serve a coordinator role to guide decision-making and behavior (Al-Shawaf et al., 2016; West et al., 2011).

Social relationships present one key area in which emotions are likely well-adapted, important coordinators. A variety of evidence favors the idea that emotions can impact social behaviors, particularly helping behaviors (Carlson et al., 1988). Gratitude researchers in social psychology offer an account of gratitude as an affective state which can facilitate helping behavior beyond mere adherence to social norms (as older work had suggested; Bartlett & DeSteno, 2006; Gouldner, 1960; Walster et al., 1973). McCullough and colleagues (2001) proposed an account of gratitude as a kind of social exchange "barometer" measuring and expressing changes of individual valuation of cooperative partners. This is a useful analogy when considering the pro-social impacts of gratitude as both a transient emotional state and as an enduring trait.

A substantial body of work has offered experimental evidence of gratitude as a driving force for helping behaviors. For example, research from Bartlett and DeSteno (2006) established a causal link between the experience of gratitude and helping behaviors. In this study, confederates in the gratitude condition assisted participants with contrived computer issues, preventing them from losing their work. Later, the confederate asked if the participant would help them out by completing a somewhat time-consuming survey. The researchers found that participants in this condition both expressed more gratitude and were more likely to help the confederate with her task. Also of note, in a follow-up iteration of the experiment, a different confederate than the original helper asked for assistance with the same survey task, and results remained virtually the same; by varying the beneficiary, this finding accounts for reciprocity norms as another potential cause of this behavior (Bartlett & DeSteno, 2006).

Another experimental manipulation of gratitude also tested the effect of anonymity on helping behavior in response to a favor versus a chance positive outcome. Participants received or distributed raffle tickets depending on the task round. In round one, participants were told they randomly received 3 of 10 possible tickets. In round two, a contrived partner gave them 9 tickets, keeping only 1 for themself. In the third round, the participant was the distributor of the tickets and could offer the other person any number of tickets. In one condition, their role as distributor was anonymous and in the other it was not. This experiment revealed no negative effect of anonymity on sending tickets; the gratitude condition was again a significant predictor of pro-social behavior (Tsang & Martin, 2019). This finding offers experimental evidence suggesting that the social desirability motivation of engaging in a helping act cannot entirely account for such behavior.

Many of the previously described findings focus on interactions with short-term cooperative partners whom the participant may or may not encounter again. Based on such work, we might conclude that gratitude can play a role in helping to initiate relationships in short-term contexts that, due to their mutually beneficial value, have the potential to solidify into long-term bonds. Gratitude is also important for ongoing relationships. Those with whom we have enduring relationships are most likely to be the ones offering aid and are most valuable in our social networks. Close relationships, wherein continual cooperation occurs and rapport has already been established, often operate based upon communal norms; that is to say, helping and benefits are provided by one partner to another based upon current need rather than explicit tit-for-tat tracking of exchanges (Mills et al., 2004). Gratitude in such relationships can indicate an intention to maintain this dynamic and help the benefactor when need roles are reversed. These effects have been examined in several ways.

For example, Algoe and colleagues (2008) examined the correlation between feelings of gratitude and relationship closeness among pairs of sorority sisters during a week of ritual gift-giving. At the beginning of the week, Big Sisters (older members) were anonymously paired with Little Sisters (new members). Each day throughout the week, Little Sisters received a personalized gift from their Big Sister. At the end of the week, identities were revealed. As might be expected based upon gratitude's theorized role as a facilitator of initiating close relationships, the gratitude of the Little Sisters toward Big Sisters predicted relationship closeness of each pair, including beyond the gift-giving week, and this effect was bolstered to the extent that the gifts were perceived to be costly and effortful.

Building on these findings, a number of researchers working with couples in romantic relationships have used the generation of partner-specific gratitude as an intervention for improving satisfaction within romantic relationships. Using a manipulation in which couples are made to think about and subsequently transcribe the detailed ways in which they feel gratitude toward each other, researchers have found that gratitude acts as a romantic "booster shot" (Algoe et al., 2010), and helps maintain "intimate bonds" (Gordon et al., 2012). Long-term romantic partners are often the individuals with whom people cooperate most frequently. Thereby, if gratitude plays a key role in cooperation, it should impact romantic relationships. Algoe and colleagues (2010) explored this by asking cohabiting couples a variety of questions about their relationship and daily interactions. Over a 14-day period, each person reported whether they had done something nice for their partner, whether their partner had done something nice for them, their emotional response to their partner's behavior (including indebtedness and gratefulness), and relationship quality (measured as satisfaction and connectedness). As predicted, experiencing more gratitude predicted more positive outcomes on relationship quality measures.

A wide array of findings over the past several decades indicate that the experience of gratitude encourages pro-social behavior. However, questions about the details of gratitude's influence remain somewhat open. A common critique of work on gratitude and pro-social behavior suggests that pro-social effects of the emotion are merely due to the positive affect associated with receiving something, rather than gratitude per se. One experiment differentiated gratitude from general positive affect by including one condition in a resource-distribution task in which participants randomly received a resource reward; they were led to believe they received greater payment than they had in the previous round due to chance. In the other condition the monetary reward was a favor from another person; the confederate stated that they noticed the participant not getting as much money in the previous round, so they wanted to give them the money this time. Participants received the same amount of money in both conditions. Despite both conditions inducing a measured positive affect, the favor/gratitude condition still elicited more cooperative behavior; subjects in this condition gave more money to their partner in the third round (the round following the one in which they had earned the reward; Tsang, 2006). Thus, although gratitude is accompanied by positive affect generally, this work suggests that the impact of gratitude goes above and beyond the results of a good mood.

Cross-Cultural Commonalities and Differences
Much of the work discussed up until this point has focused on gratitude research in Western societies. How well do these results generalize across cultures? If gratitude is, as many researchers have posited, an adaptive social emotion, there should be substantial overlap in the effects and relationships we observe across cultures—of course, there should also be some variation due to cultural emotional "accents" and display rules. Here we briefly review some of the (relatively sparse) existing cross-cultural work on gratitude, as well as note some important questions that have yet to be examined.

Most cross-cultural studies on gratitude have been conducted in the last decade and very few have compared more than two societies. Until recently, almost all compared two WEIRD (Western, educated, industrialized, rich, democratic) societies, such as the United States and the United Kingdom (Sommers & Kosmitzki, 1988). Studies like these reveal that gratitude has many similar key features among individualistic countries but is still subject to a degree of cultural variation. For example, between the US and UK samples from Morgan and colleagues (2014), both generated similar positive features associated with gratitude (e.g., happiness, hugging, etc.) but the UK sample generated more negative features of gratitude (e.g., more guilt if the favor was too great).

A few recent studies have also compared individualistic versus collectivist societies. Multiple studies compared gratitude expression and well-being interventions in the United States with South Korea (Layous et al., 2013) and Japan (Lee et al., 2012; Robustelli & Whisman, 2018), as well as between Anglo Americans and Asian Americans (Boehm et al., 2011). One study also compared the effectiveness of gratitude interventions in three cultural groups: Anglo American, Asian American, and Indian (Titova et al., 2017). Yet another recent study investigated gratitude expression in eight languages in societies around the world (Floyd et al., 2018). Another included seven societies and compared the development of gratitude expression in children and adolescents (Mendonça et al., 2018). Some key cultural differences in the understanding of gratitude were revealed by these studies, including that collectivist cultures tended to have a greater incidence of a negative side of gratitude (e.g., guilt). Although gratitude interventions often still had a positive effect on well-being in collectivist cultures, the effects were weaker than in individualistic cultures (Layous et al., 2013). Researchers comparing optimism interventions to gratitude interventions make the argument that this difference is likely accounted for by the tendency in collectivist cultures to view indebtedness as a facet of gratitude, an explanation further evidenced by the tendency for collectivists' requests for favors to include more apologies in addition to thanks (Lee et al., 2012; Titova et al., 2017).

Some work has also compared non-WEIRD countries to each other. One paper compared university students in Japan and Thailand (Naito et al., 2005), another compared Iranian and Malay university students (Farnia & Sattar, 2015), and a third compared Hausa-, Chinese-, and Arabic-speaking students (Isyaku et al., 2016). Much like the other cross-cultural work discussed thus far, this body of literature suggests that some of gratitude's effects and details of its expression vary by culture. For example, while Malaysian and Iranian students both reported they would exhibit more respect in expressing gratitude in response to a favor from a teacher than from a friend, Iranians focused more on positive emotions associated with gratitude as compared to Malaysians. Malaysians emphasized the feeling of indebtedness associated with gratitude instead of feelings like appreciation, indicating that gratitude has a more negative emotional connotation within Malaysian culture (Farnia & Sattar, 2015).

Though far from offering a comprehensive account of gratitude around the world, cross-cultural research on the topic to date has addressed a number of relevant questions. One of the most frequently investigated issues in cross-cultural gratitude work is how people in different societies express gratitude. For example, the two largest cross-cultural studies on gratitude each investigated gratitude expression (Floyd et al., 2018; Mendonça et al., 2018). The aim of these studies has been to separate gratitude as a feeling from gratitude as a linguistic practice, which in the United States are closely related (i.e., saying "thank you" is an indicator of gratitude felt for another person), but in non-English-speaking societies may be less related. Work in this area indicates that although levels of reciprocity for favors are quite similar cross-culturally (in both Western and non-Western comparisons) the actual verbal expression of gratitude is fairly different (Mendonça et al., 2018). Gratitude is less often expressed verbally in countries other than the United States; notably, some cultures are less likely than others to express gratitude to those who would be expected to be benefactors (e.g., family members) as such favors are considered part of their duties (Floyd et al., 2018). In sum, expressions of gratitude may be quite different across cultures despite the underlying psychological similarities.

In addition to cross-cultural work centered around gratitude expression, other work has focused on gratitude interventions and the emotion's impact on well-being. Such studies have tested whether interventions such as expressing optimism, conveying gratitude, and practicing kindness increase happiness in people in non-WEIRD societies in the same way such practices do for people in WEIRD societies (Boehm et al., 2011; Layous et al., 2013). As touched upon earlier, though gratitude interventions were more effective than control conditions at improving happiness, the interventions were more effective in individualistic cultures. Other studies have investigated how gratitude affects life satisfaction in Japan (Robustelli & Whisman, 2018) and China (Kong et al., 2015). Such work finds similar positive effects of gratitude on life satisfaction, though the strength of the effect still varies with cultural and individual differences.

Some other recent work examining the relationship between gratitude and other emotions has been conducted cross-culturally. As cited earlier, gratitude and indebtedness have been investigated in papers that compare the United States to societies in East Asia, particularly Japan and Korea, where gratitude is often expressed by saying "I'm sorry" and the terms for gratitude and indebtedness are used almost interchangeably (Lee et al., 2012; Oishi et al., 2019). Such studies exemplify that cultural differences in verbal expressions may yield a different understanding of certain emotions. Additionally, the relationship between gratitude and forgiveness has been studied in India (Kumar & Dixit, 2014), Cape Verde, and Portugal (Wilks et al., 2015). In both cases, trait gratitude was positively related to forgiveness. Gratitude's relationship with envy has been studied in Guatemala; researchers found that perspective taking and empathy related to increased gratitude and decreased envy (Poelker et al., 2019).

It is also worth noting that efforts have been made to validate trait gratitude measures cross-culturally. The Gratitude Questionnaire-Six Item Form (GQ-6) developed by McCullough and colleagues (2002a) in the United States has been the focus of validation efforts in a number of countries. The measure includes six items, such as "I have so much in my life to be thankful for," and focuses mainly on the emotional component of gratitude. Validation efforts have been made in countries including Germany, Spain, and Ecuador (Cabrera-Vélez et al., 2019; Hudecek et al., 2020; Magallares et al., 2018). After translation, the GQ-6 demonstrated validity in each country, though some researchers removed one question to improve reliability based on factor analysis. Though further validation globally would be beneficial, these consistent findings in several different cultures are promising.

In sum, although there are some examples of cross-cultural gratitude research, a great deal remains unexamined. Research to date has shown that the particularities of gratitude expression and interpretation are subject to contextual variation, but evidence so far indicates that the underlying psychological structure of gratitude appears to be relatively invariant across cultures. Indeed, if gratitude has been shaped by natural selection to solve adaptive problems surrounding relationship formation and maintenance, we should find that the information-processing structure of gratitude is invariant across cultures, and its effects on expressions and behavior are modified by the cultural context in which they are realized.

Evolutionary Accounts of Gratitude

As illustrated with our review of the literature, the past 20 years of research on gratitude has focused on its causes and consequences, its potential mental and physical health benefits, and its role in relationships. Despite this impressive body of research, only recently have researchers begun to describe functional accounts of gratitude from an evolutionary perspective. This is an interesting oversight considering how central work on cooperation has been among evolutionary social scientists. Indeed, the robust evidence suggesting a link between gratitude and pro-sociality suggests that gratitude plays a key role in the adaptive systems that regulate cooperation. In this section of the chapter, we address some of functional accounts of gratitude and its role in benefit exchange.

Finding partners with whom to form mutually beneficial cooperative relationships has been a constant selection pressure throughout human evolutionary history (Barclay, 2013; Delton et al., 2011; Trivers, 1971). Biologists have developed robust theories to explain *why* cooperation can occur among genetic relatives and within social exchange relationships (i.e., they identify the routes by which cooperation increases inclusive fitness and thereby can evolve via natural selection; Hamilton, 2017; Trivers, 1971). However, relatively little attention has been focused on *how* social exchange relationships are formed (i.e., the proximate factors that motivate relationship formation) and, in some cases, strengthened to the point of being considered "deep engagement" relationships (Tooby & Cosmides, 1996). That is, *humans have friends* (as do, perhaps, a small number of other nonhuman animal species; Seyfarth & Cheney, 2011; Silk, 2002). Despite decades of research on the factors that drive benefit delivery between family members and reciprocal exchange partners, far less work has examined the systems that motivate the development and maintenance of friendships (Hruschka, 2010). Several researchers have proposed that gratitude might play a key role in the establishment and maintenance of relationships by both (a) motivating those who experience gratitude toward another to reciprocate cooperation and (b) signaling to another that he or she is valued (Forster et al., 2017; McCullough et al., 2008; Smith et al., 2017; Tooby & Cosmides, 2008; Trivers, 1971).

Here we primarily focus on what might be called the information-processing structure of gratitude: what specific inputs and internal representations are involved in feeling gratitude, which can then inform our understanding of the functions that gratitude is designed to serve.

Gratitude and Welfare Trade-Off Ratios

In social species, including humans, actions taken by one individual often have fitness consequences for others—food eaten by one person is not available to another; a friend benefits from help that is costly to the helper; a mate courted by one person is, potentially, unavailable to another (Tooby et al., 2008). To the extent that those fitness consequences for others impact an actor's own inclusive fitness, a selection pressure arises for taking into account others' welfare and estimating the extent to which the actor's own welfare is interdependent with theirs. Hence, sociality likely gives rise to computational systems that are capable of estimating welfare interdependence on the basis of multiple fitness-relevant inputs such that social behavior can be adaptively regulated.

A proposed output of such a system is called a welfare trade-off ratio (WTR; Delton, 2010; Delton & Robertson, 2016; Tooby et al., 2008; Tooby & Cosmides, 2008), which is hypothesized to be an internal regulatory variable that weights the welfare of another individual relative to the self—that is, the WTR person i holds for person j ($WTR_{i \to j}$) is the ratio of person i's valuation of person j's welfare relative to person i's own welfare (Aktipis et al., 2018; Balliet et al., 2017; Brown & Brown, 2006; Hofmann et al., 2018; Rachlin, 2015; Roberts, 2005). Thus, when $WTR_{i \to j}$ is 0, i has no regard for j's welfare (i.e., i would not incur any cost to benefit to j); when $WTR_{i \to j}$ is 1, i regards j's welfare as equivalent to i's own (i.e., i would incur any cost outweighed by the benefit to j). All else equal, the higher $WTR_{i \to j}$, the more willing i is to incur costs to benefit j. Theoretically, $WTR_{i \to j}$ could also be negative (i.e., i would incur a cost to impose a cost on j) or greater than 1 (i.e., i values j's welfare greater than i's own).

WTR-generating mechanisms might compute WTR estimates for particular social partners on the basis of several inputs that are relevant to welfare interdependence. These might include ancestrally valid cues of genetic relatedness (e.g., siblingship; Lieberman et al., 2007), past experiences of cooperative or exploitive interaction with the partners (Krasnow et al., 2012), estimates of the future interaction opportunities with the partners (Delton et al., 2011; McCullough et al., 2014), shared parental investments with the partners (Clutton-Brock, 1989), and traits that increase partners' bargaining power, such as fighting ability and mate value (Sell et al., 2009). Once a WTR estimate is established for an individual, that estimate can be used to adaptively regulate social behavior via motivational systems (Tooby et al., 2008; Tooby & Cosmides, 2008). Importantly, WTRs will be updated whenever new, relevant inputs are processed. WTR estimates likely originate in the form of diffuse probability distributions, weighted by whatever WTR-relevant cues are available (e.g., mate value, perceived fighting ability, any available reputation information), and then are refined through an updating process, with some cues (e.g., relatedness) having stronger impacts than others (e.g., a single interaction).

A person who confers a benefit has revealed that he or she might care for the beneficiary's welfare and, all else being equal, represents a good candidate in which to invest (Tooby & Cosmides, 1996). Cognitively, the process of increasing the social value for a partner who confers benefits could be described as an increase in one's internal WTR toward the benefactor, which manifests as an increased willingness to return benefits downstream. Strategically, it would also benefit recipients to communicate their increased social valuation (and inclination to cooperate) so that benefactors could be positively reinforced to dispense benefits into the future (McCullough et al., 2001). Some scholars hypothesize that gratitude evolved to motivate beneficiaries to reciprocate and communicate their increased social valuation of benefactors (Lim, 2012; Smith et al., 2017).

Tooby and Cosmides (2008) proposed a model of gratitude that is based on the notion that the observed costs and benefits associated with an act should be indicative of one's WTR for another. According to Tooby and Cosmides, "Gratitude is triggered by new information indicating that another places a higher value on one's welfare than one's system had previously estimated . . ." (2008, p. 135) and that gratitude functions to increase one's WTR toward benefactors. In other words, gratitude is a consequence of *perceived* changes in the benefactor's WTR for the recipient (*perceived $\Delta WTR_{other \to self}$*) and is antecedent to, or perhaps concurrent with, the recipient's own changes in WTR for the benefactor (*experienced $\Delta WTR_{self \to other}$*).

One plausible alternative model is that changes in recipients' WTRs for benefactors (*experienced $\Delta WTR_{self \to other}$*) precede recipients' emotional responses. Some scholars have argued and found evidence that gratitude functions to communicate the positive change in experienced social value and motivations to cooperate (Forster et al., 2022; Peng et al., 2018; Smith et al., 2017). Indeed, evidence from research examining the effects of receiving thanks on benefactors' pro-sociality suggests that recipients' expressions of gratitude are sufficient to facilitate continued cooperation from benefactors (Grant & Gino, 2010). This is telling, as cooperation can ensue without the need for the recipient to infer what, if any, change occurred in the benefactor's mind, *perceived* $\Delta WTR_{other \rightarrow self}$. It is therefore possible that changes in $WTR_{self \rightarrow other}$ suffice to account for reports of gratitude, with one's gratitude functioning to promote communication of increased value and one's WTR functioning to motivate cooperative versus exploitative behavior, as WTRs are purported to do across all social interactions (Tooby et al., 2008; Tooby & Cosmides, 2008).

In a recent experiment (Smith et al., 2017), we used a modified version of the game Cyberball (Williams et al., 2000) to test how WTRs and gratitude responded to benefit delivery. We told participants that they would be playing a computer game of catch with three other "participants," all of whom were actually part of the research team. After the participant met the other three players, they were taken to a separate room and completed a survey using hypothetical monetary trade-offs to assess their WTR toward each of the other three players. Consistent with the fact that the other players were strangers, WTRs started off quite low. After assessing the participants' WTRs of the other three players, a computerized game of catch began. In this particular game, every time a player threw the ball to the player designated as the "Treasurer," the player earned 50 cents. Thus, participants' goal was to get the ball and then have the opportunity to throw it to the Treasurer.

In one condition, the Treasurer excluded the participant from the game, never throwing the ball to them. After the other players played catch with the Treasurer for a number of rounds, one of the other players began to throw the ball to the participant. That is, instead of throwing the ball to the Treasurer to increase their own winnings, this helpful player threw the ball to the participant so that they could earn some money—this benefactor went out of their way, and paid a cost, to benefit the subject.

After the game, participants again completed a WTR measure for each of the three players to see how much they valued the other players. We also asked participants to rate how they felt about the players on several dimensions—most notably, how grateful they were toward the others. Finally, participants played a multi-person dictator game. In this one-move game, participants were given $10 and told to allocate as much or as little as they wanted to each of the other players.

We found three important patterns. First, participants valued the helpful player more after the game. That is, WTRs increased for the player who helped the participant—and only this player. The WTRs for all remaining players either stayed the same or decreased. Second, we found that increases in WTR predicted the level of gratitude the participant felt toward the benefactor—the greater the increase in how much participants valued the benefactor, the more gratitude they reported in response to that help. Third, we found that participants allocated far larger percentages of money in the dictator game to the player who helped them than to the other players who did not. But, unlike with gratitude, the increase in WTR did not predict the amount of money sent in the dictator game. Instead, it was the post-game level of reported WTR (how much participants currently valued the welfare of the person) that predicted dictator game behavior.

This is a subtle but important distinction: *positive changes* in WTRs predicted gratitude, whereas *current* WTR values predicted giving (above and beyond the effects of gratitude). Gratitude seems to correspond to positive changes in how much we value others, and thus suggests that when we express gratitude to someone, we are effectively signaling that, by virtue of their actions, we value them more than we did before—and that we might be more likely to provide benefits to them in the future.

Though we found a strong link between how much recipients increased their WTRs toward benefactors and their reported feelings of gratitude in this study, we did not measure recipients' perceptions of benefactors' WTRs toward themselves, nor did we vary the magnitude of costs and benefits. Thus, it is possible that these results are explainable instead as a result of changes in perceived $WTR_{other \rightarrow self}$, the specific $WTR_{other \rightarrow self}$ implied by the benefactor's behavior, the perceived costs and benefits, or some other unmeasured variable that impacted recipients' WTR for their benefactors.

Thus, we conducted two follow-up experiments (Forster et al., 2022) in which we tested this "WTR change" model against nine other possible causal models of gratitude. To do so, we created a procedure in which participants were led to believe they were interacting with a partner in an economic game in which the partner donated money to the subject at a cost to themselves. We manipulated the size of the benefit, the cost to the partner, and the implied WTR the partner had for the subject as a function of the decision. We also measured both subjects' WTR for their partner and their estimate of their partner's WTR toward them before and after the interaction. In both experiments, only the subject's change in their WTR toward their partner consistently predicted gratitude, replicating the results of Smith et al. (2017).

Across four alternative conceptualizations of WTR-based models, we found no evidence in favor of the expectation violation model (i.e., that gratitude occurs when a benefactor is perceived to value the recipient more than expected) put forth by Tooby and Cosmides (2008). Nevertheless, our favored model is consistent with the major aspect of Tooby and Cosmides's model that gratitude is related to an increase in value for benefactors. Whereas the Tooby and Cosmides model suggests that expectation violations lead to (either in sequence or concurrently) gratitude and increases in the recipient's value for the benefactor, our model is equally consistent with the reverse: that increases in the recipient's value for the benefactor lead to gratitude. Hence, the direction of causality remains an open question, and we are aware of no extant data that can tease the two possibilities apart.

The Communicative Function of Gratitude

To date, gratitude research has primarily focused on the factors that lead a beneficiary to experience gratitude, and on the ways in which the beneficiary reacts to experiencing gratitude. A related but less studied aspect of gratitude, however, concerns its potential to communicate information between the beneficiary who experiences gratitude and others around them. Gratitude is generally accompanied by characteristic expressions, which play an important role in how people perceive and communicate with one another. Because grateful individuals are especially likely to cooperate in future interactions, the extent to which a person appears grateful may inform others about that person's potential as a good future cooperator. Here we focus on the possible functional role that expressions of gratitude play in forming and solidifying mutually beneficial relationships by communicating the value a beneficiary places upon their benefactor. If feelings of gratitude do indeed indicate increases in the expresser's valuation of their benefactor as well as an increased propensity to engage in cooperative behavior, gratitude expressions should be a valid cue to others of the experiencer's cooperative potential. That is, an expression of gratitude should serve to communicate that one's WTR toward their benefactor has increased either in place of, or in conjunction with, one's propensity of returning benefits to the benefactor. In this way, the relationship could be reinforced without necessarily involving an immediate return benefit, which could invite even further benefits from the benefactor or simply solidify the relationship. In other words, a gratitude expression could potentially help boost the formation of a relationship by effectively serving as a stand-in for immediate reciprocity.

We posit that one of gratitude's evolved functions is to motivate individuals to communicate to their benefactors that, as a consequence of their actions, there has been an increase in the value that the beneficiary ascribes to the benefactor's welfare. This signal of gratitude should, in turn, update the benefactor's view of the beneficiary as "someone who cares about my welfare" and can motivate cognitive processes and behaviors that increase the likelihood that the two will develop and maintain a mutually beneficial association. Thus, our view is that there are two separate yet interconnected computational systems associated with gratitude: (1) systems that, upon detecting an act perceived as beneficial, motivate the signaling of gratitude; and (2) gratitude-detection systems that take as input expressions of gratitude and motivate subsequent pro-social and affiliative behaviors.

Specifically, expressions of gratitude communicate to a benefactor that the recipient acknowledges the benefits and can strategically foreshadow the beneficiary's intent to return benefits (i.e., the beneficiary's WTR for the benefactor has either remained high or has increased). In this way, gratitude is a communicative device that attempts to reinforce the benefactor's positive behaviors by maintaining or increasing the benefactor's WTR for the beneficiary.

It is important to note that there are cases in which expressions of gratitude may fail to elicit cooperative behavior from the perceiver. First, because expressions of gratitude are cheap talk—in other words, they are not costly—people could in theory express gratitude deceitfully (or in response to social norms) without actually feeling grateful. Gratitude expressions may only elicit cooperative behavior to the extent that they are perceived to genuinely reflect the underlying emotion of gratitude. Additionally, gratitude may be used to make inferences about the minimum amount of cooperation the gratitude expresser expects in order to continue a cooperative relationship, which can later allow the perceiver to behave exploitatively. Some have suggested that, in the context of negotiations, people may be more likely to "lowball" others whom they perceive as generally grateful because they believe that such others would have generally lower expectations for others' cooperative behavior (Yip et al., 2018). However, because humans often compete with others for the favor of good cooperators (Barclay, 2013), people should often be incentivized to please, rather than exploit, grateful others. It is worth noting that contextual factors likely increase or decrease the likelihood of an individual to behave exploitatively, such as the degree of fitness interdependence between the actors, whether the interaction is observed by others and thus has reputational consequences, and whether the current interaction has implications for future interactions.

In some recent work (Ramos et al., in preparation), we tested whether gratitude expressions would increase people's willingness to cooperate with the expresser and whether it would lead to exploitation. One study began with subjects being paired initially with one other real subject for a one-minute chat before completing baseline measures of WTR, and all interactions following the chat were staged. The interaction took place in a chat room and served the dual purpose of convincing subjects they would be interacting with a real person and to create variability in baseline WTRs by having subjects learn some things about their partner. Following the measure of WTR, subjects were introduced to a puzzle task that consisted of a grid of smiley faces, with each face being either white, gray, green, yellow, or orange. Using this information, subjects were prompted to generate a specific three-digit number within five minutes and were told that they would receive a $1 bonus if they correctly solved the puzzle. Given the lack of specific clues and the possible combinations of numbers to correspond with features of the image, correctly solving the puzzle without any aid would be highly improbable. We told subjects that one person in each dyad would be given a hint to help solve the puzzle, and that the other person would have to attempt to solve the puzzle on their own—in fact, the subject was always given the hint, which made solving the puzzle trivial.

After subjects entered the correct solution, they were given the choice to share the hint with the partner at no cost to themselves, which virtually all subjects elected to do. After subjects shared the hint, they were advanced to a screen to indicate that they were waiting for the other subject to solve the puzzle before moving on. After several seconds, the other subject "solved" the task and subjects were notified. In the "no message" condition, subjects advanced to the section to respond to self-report emotion items and follow-up WTR measures. In all other conditions, subjects were told that they could send a message to the other subject and that the other subject would return a message in response. After subjects sent their message, they waited for a brief period before receiving one of the following messages: In the "aggravating" condition, subjects received, "I didn't need your help." In the "neutral" condition, subjects received, "Interested to see what the next task is." In the "grateful" condition, subjects received, "Thanks for the help! Interested to see what the next task is." In the "very grateful" condition, subjects received, "Thanks for the help! I was really stuck and couldn't get through that on my own, I really appreciate it! Interested to see what the next task is."

Consistent with our hypothesis, participants who received a gratitude expression were more likely to choose to interact with the same partner for another cooperative task than those who received a neutral or aggravating message. Willingness to cooperate with this partner was associated with participants' WTR for the partner. Additionally, participants who received a grateful message also showed increases in WTR for their partners. Results from a structural equation model suggested that the effect of gratitude expressions on pro-social behavior was fully mediated by changes in $WTR_{self \rightarrow other}$. Overall, these results support our hypothesis that expressions of gratitude are effective at reinforcing cooperation. The results are also consistent with the notion that these effects of gratitude expressions are driven by changes in the perceiver's valuations of the welfare of the gratitude expresser.

In two follow-up studies using the same general design, we examined the effect of expressions of gratitude on perceiver's cooperative behavior by either having participants (a) interact with a partner or (b) witness two other people interact, and subsequently play an economic game with the beneficiary. Across these studies, expressions of gratitude from the beneficiary increased subjects' views of the beneficiary as "grateful" and viewing the expresser as grateful was positively associated with cooperative behavior (i.e., sending money to the partner in either a dictator game or an ultimatum game). The results are consistent with the view that people have higher valuations for, and are more willing to cooperate with, grateful partners than ungrateful partners. Importantly, this positive relationship between perceptions of a beneficiary's gratitude and cooperative behavior toward the beneficiary was present even when participants played a strategic bargaining game (the ultimatum game) rather than the dictator game. Furthermore, subjects' proposals in the game were in line with typical results in both games, indicating that expressions of gratitude did not lead to any exploitation. Finally, the positive relationship between perceived gratitude and cooperative behavior was also present (though to a smaller extent) when the beneficiary's gratitude expression was directed at a person other than the participant themselves. Hence, expressions of gratitude may be used as a cue in partner-choice decisions even when one does not have a personal history with the expresser.

Indirect Reciprocity
Another proposal for the function of gratitude is in the context of indirect reciprocity. Nowak and Roch (2007) used a mathematical model to show how gratitude could motivate beneficiaries to provide benefits to people other than their benefactors. In this model, rather than obtaining benefits through direct reciprocation, benefactors eventually are rewarded through an indirect chain of benefit delivery through others—so-called upstream indirect reciprocity. Some studies do show people behaving in a manner consistent with this model after a gratitude induction. For example, Emmons and McCullough (2003) found that grateful participants were more likely to report extending either emotional or physical assistance to someone in need during the 13 days the participants reported on their mood and behaviors. Bartlett and DeSteno (2006) showed that a manipulation of gratitude caused participants to be more likely to subsequently help a stranger with a costly and time-consuming task. Finally, DeSteno and colleagues (2010) found that a gratitude manipulation caused participants to be more likely to offer money to a community pot in a subsequent economic game, which, importantly, did not involve the participant's benefactor.

However, some important caveats for these findings are needed. In the DeSteno et al. (2010) experiment, the benefactor immediately left the beneficiary's immediate environment following the gratitude-inducing interaction, and hence was not a possible target for reciprocation. Had the benefactor been a player in the economic game, it seems likely that the beneficiary would have preferentially rewarded the benefactor at the expense of the community pot, similar to our previously discussed result from our Cyberball experiment (Smith et al., 2017). Additionally, in the Bartlett and DeSteno (2006) experiment, when the researchers stopped the participant just prior to meeting the stranger in need of help with a questionnaire, and reminded the participant about the source of their gratitude (i.e., the benefactors who helped them fix their computer at outset of the experiment), upstream-reciprocal behavior (i.e., electing to help the stranger) disappeared. Thus, though the indirect reciprocity proposal is plausible, we suspect that most of the existing empirical results supporting it are explainable as byproducts of the experimental contexts that have altered how the operation of gratitude can take place—that is, by altering the participant's ability to direct their gratitude toward their benefactor.

Open Questions
Though the body of work on gratitude has greatly increased in recent years, many open questions remain. Here we briefly mention some that stand out as particularly interesting.

What Are the Specific Roles of Costs and Benefits?
Tesser et al. (1968) were among the first to develop a causal model of gratitude based on the benefits to the receiver, the costs to the benefactor, and the benefactor's intentions—findings which have been reinforced by several subsequent investigations (McCullough et al., 2001, 2004; Smith et al., 2017; Tsang, 2006; Yu et al., 2018). At this point, it is taken for granted that the size of the costs and benefits in an interaction will impact gratitude felt in response. However, in our previously mentioned experiments in which we parametrically manipulated costs and benefits (Forster et al., 2022), we found no compelling evidence to suggest that the magnitude of costs or benefits associated with an act directly predict gratitude, findings which run counter to prior research (DeSteno et al., 2010; Emmons & McCullough, 2003; Forster et al., 2017; Tesser et al., 1968). However, it should be noted that our design included costly benefit delivery in all cases, which we systematically varied. Thus, these null results do not imply that the *presence* of a cost and/or benefit is not an important prerequisite of gratitude,

but rather we found no evidence in our design that the *magnitude* of costs and benefits predict the *magnitude* of gratitude felt. The vast majority of previous research manipulating benefits has either used hypothetical scenarios or simply manipulated *whether* there was a cost and/or benefit. Hence, to us the evidence suggests that costs and benefits are necessary but not sufficient to induce gratitude, and how those costs and benefits impact one's WTR for a benefactor (i.e., what information they carry that causes one to update, or not, their WTR) is likely a vital piece to the puzzle.

Is Gratitude a Discrete Emotion/Natural Kind?

Emotions remain a subject of contention in the psychological literature. Some models propose a number of discrete emotions, and some propose that all emotions can be described by two or more dimensions (e.g., valence and arousal; Lench et al., 2011; Sreeja & Mahalakshmi, 2017). Gratitude's categorization as a natural kind, an emotion which is intrinsically distinct from others, is debatable and difficult to test. As noted earlier in the chapter, some researchers have attempted to distinguish the effects of gratitude from general positive affect (Tsang, 2006); however, this does not necessarily answer the question of whether the emotion itself is distinct from others. It might simply be explained as the positive affect induced by positive change in one's valuation of others' welfare and thereby only be distinct in its cause. Continuing to refine our understanding of what specific adaptive problems gratitude evolved to solve and, if possible, demonstrating that its information-processing structure is distinct from that of other emotions, will be vital in answering this question (Al-Shawaf et al., 2016; Tooby et al., 2008).

Qualia

What, if anything, is the purpose of the actual feeling state, or qualia, of gratitude? Tooby and colleagues (2008) have argued that emotional qualia might be the consciously accessible output of computational systems whose operations are not accessible—that is, that felt emotions are a readable format that can be acted upon. We have speculated that the feeling state of gratitude might motivate the signaling to the benefactor that WTR has increased (or perhaps reinforce that one's high WTR has been maintained). It is also possible that the feeling state helps to communicate genuine gratitude rather than just socially obligatory, norm-abiding displays. That is, feelings of gratitude might lead to hard-to-fake expressions of gratitude, much like Duchenne smiles, that can be interpreted as more reliable signals of how much one values another.

What Do the Positive Well-Being Outcomes Imply about the Functional Structure of Gratitude?

As reviewed above, there are well-documented positive mental and physical health outcomes associated with the experience of gratitude. A 2016 meta-analysis found that gratitude interventions overall preformed at least as well as other psychological interventions and better than various controls (Davis et al., 2016). Beyond the conclusion that gratitude may serve a useful applied function as a therapeutic tool, this raises the question of whether these positive outcomes offer any insight into the functional structure of gratitude. Cultivating gratitude might serve to reinforce one's existing social network and reduce stress related to uncertainty in one's social standing. We think this area is ripe for exploration considering how most of the literature on the positive effects of gratitude has to date been relatively divorced from more functional accounts.

Conclusion

Despite significant progress over the past two decades, research on gratitude, particularly from an evolutionary perspective, remains in its infancy. Given the prominent role that research on cooperation has among evolutionarily minded social scientists, we think an increased focus on the systems involved in relationship formation and maintenance, such as gratitude, will help advance the field with a more comprehensive understanding of the complex dynamics involved in cooperation. Gratitude is likely to play a key role here.

References

Aktipis, A., Cronk, L., Alcock, J., Ayers, J. D., Baciu, C., Balliet, D., Boddy, A. M., Curry, O. S., Krems, J. A., & Muñoz, A. (2018). Understanding cooperation through fitness interdependence. *Nature Human Behaviour*, *2*(7), 429.

Algoe, S. B., Gable, S. L., & Maisel, N. C. (2010). It's the little things: Everyday gratitude as a booster shot for romantic relationships. *Personal Relationships*, *17*(2), 217–233. https://doi.org/10.1111/j.1475-6811.2010.01273.x

Algoe, S. B., Haidt, J., & Gable, S. L. (2008). Beyond reciprocity: Gratitude and relationships in everyday life. *Emotion*, *8*(3), 425–429. https://doi.org/10.1037/1528-3542.8.3.425

Al-Shawaf, L., Conroy-Beam, D., Asao, K., & Buss, D. M. (2016). Human emotions: An evolutionary psychological perspective. *Emotion Review*, *8*(2), 173–186. https://doi.org/10.1177/1754073914565518

Balliet, D., Tybur, J. M., & Van Lange, P. A. M. (2017). Functional interdependence theory: An evolutionary account of social situations. *Personality and Social Psychology Review*, *21*(4), 361–388.

Barclay, P. (2013). Strategies for cooperation in biological markets, especially for humans. *Evolution and Human Behavior*, *34*(3), 164–175. https://doi.org/10.1016/j.evolhumbehav.2013.02.002

Bartlett, M., Condon, P., Bauman, J., & Destano, D. (2012). Gratitude: Prompting behaviours that build relationships. *Cognition and Emotion*, *26*(1), 2–13.

Bartlett, M. Y., & DeSteno, D. (2006). Gratitude and prosocial behavior: Helping when it costs you. *Psychological Science*, *17*(4), 319–325. https://doi.org/10.1111/j.1467-9280.2006.01705.x

Boehm, J. K., Lyubomirsky, S., & Sheldon, K. M. (2011). A longitudinal experimental study comparing the effectiveness of happiness-enhancing strategies in Anglo Americans and Asian Americans. *Cognition and Emotion*, *25*(7), 1263–1272. https://doi.org/10.1080/02699931.2010.541227

Brown, S. L., & Brown, R. M. (2006). Selective investment theory: Recasting the functional significance of close relationships. *Psychological Inquiry*, *17*(1), 1–29.

Cabrera-Vélez, M., Lima-Castro, S., Peña-Contreras, E., Aguilar-Sizer, M., Bueno-Pacheco, A., & Arias-Medina, P. (2019). Adaptation and validation of the gratitude questionnaire GQ-6 for the Ecuadorian context. *Avaliacao Psicologica*, *18*(2), 129–137. https://doi.org/10.15689/ap.2019.1802.16215.03

Carlson, M., Charlin, V., & Miller, N. (1988). Positive mood and helping behavior: A test of six hypotheses. *Journal of Personality and Social Psychology*, *55*(2), 211–229. https://doi.org/10.1037/0022-3514.55.2.211

Chan, D. W. (2011). Burnout and life satisfaction: Does gratitude intervention make a difference among Chinese school teachers in Hong Kong? *Educational Psychology*, *31*(7), 809–823 https://doi.org/10.1080/01443410.2011.608525

Cheng, S.-T., Tsui, P. K., & Lam, J. H. M. (2015). Improving mental health in health care practitioners: randomized controlled trial of a gratitude intervention. *Journal of Consulting and Clinical Psychology*, *83*(1), 177–186. https://doi.org/10.1037/a0037895

Clutton-Brock, T. H. (1989). Mammalian mating systems. *Proceedings of the Royal Society B*, *236*, 339–372.

Davis, D. E., Choe, E., Meyers, J., Wade, N., Varjas, K., Gifford, A., Quinn, A., Hook, J. N., Van Tongeren, D. R., Griffin, B. J., & Worthington, E. L. (2016). Thankful for the little things: A meta-analysis of gratitude interventions. *Journal of Counseling Psychology*, *63*(1), 20–31. https://doi.org/10.1037/cou0000107

Delton, A. W. (2010). *A psychological calculus for welfare tradeoffs*. Doctoral dissertation, University of California.

Delton, A. W., Krasnow, M. M., Cosmides, L., & Tooby, J. (2011). Evolution of direct reciprocity under uncertainty can explain human generosity in one-shot encounters. *Proceedings of the National Academy of Sciences*, *108*, 13335–13340.

Delton, A. W., & Robertson, T. E. (2016). How the mind makes welfare tradeoffs: Evolution, computation, and emotion. *Current Opinion in Psychology*, *7*, 12–16.

DeSteno, D., Bartlett, M. Y., Baumann, J., Williams, L. A., & Dickens, L. (2010). Gratitude as moral sentiment: Emotion-guided cooperation in economic exchange. *Emotion*, *10*(2), 289–293. https://doi.org/10.1037/a0017883

Emmons, R. A., & McCullough, M. E. (2003). Counting blessings versus burdens: An experimental investigation of gratitude and subjective well-being in daily life. *Journal of Personality and Social Psychology*, *84*(2), 377–389. https://doi.org/10.1037/0022-3514.84.2.377

Farnia, M., & Sattar, H. Q. A. (2015). A cross-cultural study of Iranians' and Malays' expressions of gratitude. *Journal of Intercultural Communication, 37*, 1–20.

Farwell, L., & Wohlwend-Lloyd, R. (1998). Narcissistic processes: Optimistic expectations, favorable self-evaluations, and self-enhancing attributions. *Journal of Personality, 66*(1), 65–83. https://doi.org/10.1111/1467-6494.00003

Floyd, S., Rossi, G., Baranova, J., Blythe, J., Dingemanse, M., Kendrick, K. H., Zinken, J., & Enfield, N. J. (2018). Universals and cultural diversity in the expression of gratitude. *Royal Society Open Science, 5*(5), 180391. https://doi.org/10.1098/rsos.180391

Forster, D. E., Pedersen, E. J., McCullough, M. E., & Lieberman, D. (2022). Evaluating benefits, costs, and social value as predictors of gratitude. *Psychological Science, 33*(4), 538–549.

Forster, D. E., Pedersen, E. J., Smith, A., McCullough, M. E., & Lieberman, D. (2017). Benefit valuation predicts gratitude. *Evolution and Human Behavior, 38*(1), 18–26. https://doi.org/10.1016/j.evolhumbehav.2016.06.003

Froh, J. J., Sefick, W. J., & Emmons, R. A. (2008). Counting blessings in early adolescents: An experimental study of gratitude and subjective well-being. *Journal of School Psychology, 46*(2), 213–233. https://doi.org/10.1016/j.jsp.2007.03.005

Gabana, N. T., Steinfeldt, J., Wong, Y. J., & Chung, Y. B. (2019). Attitude of gratitude: Exploring the implementation of a gratitude intervention with college athletes. *Journal of Applied Sport Psychology, 31*(3), 273–284. https://doi.org/10.1080/10413200.2018.1498956

Gordon, A. M., Impett, E. A., Kogan, A., Oveis, C., & Keltner, D. (2012). To have and to hold: Gratitude promotes relationship maintenance in intimate bonds. *Journal of Personality and Social Psychology, 103*(2), 257–274. https://doi.org/10.1037/a0028723

Gouldner, A. W. (1960). The norm of reciprocity: A preliminary statement. *American Sociological Review, 25*(2), 161–178. https://doi.org/10.2307/2092623

Graham, S. (1988). Children's developing understanding of the motivational role of affect: An attributional analysis. *Cognitive Development, 3*(1), 71–88. https://doi.org/10.1016/0885-2014(88)90031-7

Grant, A. M., & Gino, F. (2010). A little thanks goes a long way: Explaining why gratitude expressions motivate prosocial behavior. *Journal of Personality and Social Psychology, 98*(6), 946–955. https://doi.org/10.1037/a0017935

Graziano, W. G., Jensen-Campbell, L. A., & Hair, E. C. (1996). Perceiving interpersonal conflict and reacting to it: The case for agreeableness. *Journal of Personality and Social Psychology, 70*(4), 820–835. https://doi.org/10.1037/0022-3514.70.4.820

Hamilton, W. D. (1964). The genetical evolution of social behavior. II. *Journal of Theoretical Biology, 7*(1), 44–89. https://doi.org/10.4324/9780203790427-5

Hofmann, W., Brandt, M. J., Wisneski, D. C., Rockenbach, B., & Skitka, L. J. (2018). Moral punishment in everyday life. *Personality and Social Psychology Bulletin, 44*(12), 1697–1711. https://doi.org/10.1177/0146167218775075

Hruschka, D. J. (2010). The development of friendships. In *Friendship: development, ecology, and evolution of a relationship* (pp. 146–167). University of California Press. https://doi.org/doi:10.1525/9780520947887-010

Hudecek, M. F. C., Blabst, N., Morgan, B., & Lermer, E. (2020). Measuring gratitude in Germany: Validation study of the German version of the Gratitude Questionnaire-Six Item Form (GQ-6-G) and the Multi-Component Gratitude Measure (MCGM-G). *Frontiers in Psychology, 11*, 590108. https://doi.org/10.3389/FPSYG.2020.590108

Isyaku, H., Yuepeng, M., Mahdi, Q., Sarhan, G., Salih, N., & Paramasivan, S. (2016). A comparative study of cross-cultural gratitude strategies among Hausa, the case of Arab and Chinese students. *Advances in Language and Literary Studies, 7*(6), 137–156. https://doi.org/10.7575/aiac.alls.v.7n.6p.137

Keltner, D., & Haidt, J. (1999). Social functions of emotions at four levels of analysis. *Cognition and Emotion, 13*(5), 505–521.

Kong, F., Ding, K., & Zhao, J. (2015). The relationships among gratitude, self-esteem, social support and life satisfaction among undergraduate students. *Journal of Happiness Studies, 16*(2), 477–489. https://doi.org/10.1007/s10902-014-9519-2

Krasnow, M. M., Cosmides, L., Pedersen, E. J., & Tooby, J. (2012). What are punishment and reputation for? *PLoS One, 7*(9), e45662.

Kumar, A., & Dixit, V. (2014). Forgiveness, gratitude and resilience among Indian youth. *Indian Journal of Health & Wellbeing, 5*(12), 1414–1419. https://login.ezproxy.net.ucf.edu/login?auth=shibb&url=http://search.ebscohost.com/login.aspx?direct=true&db=edb&AN=100548039&site=eds-live&scope=site

Layous, K., Lee, H., Choi, I., & Lyubomirsky, S. (2013). Culture matters when designing a successful happiness-increasing activity: A comparison of the United States and South Korea. *Journal of Cross-Cultural Psychology, 44*(8), 1294–1303. https://doi.org/10.1177/0022022113487591

Lee, H. E., Park, H. S., Imai, T., & Dolan, D. (2012). Cultural differences between Japan and the United States in uses of "apology" and "thank you" in favor asking messages. *Journal of Language and Social Psychology, 31*(3), 263–289. https://doi.org/10.1177/0261927X12446595

Lench, H. C., Flores, S. A., & Bench, S. W. (2011). Discrete emotions predict changes in cognition, judgment, experience, behavior, and physiology: A meta-analysis of experimental emotion elicitations. *Psychological Bulletin, 137*(5), 834–855. https://doi.org/10.1037/a0024244

Lieberman, D., Tooby, J., & Cosmides, L. (2007). The architecture of human kin detection. *Nature, 445*, 727–731.

Lim, K.-H. (2012). The effects of gratitude enrichment program on school adjustment, life satisfaction & emotional-behavioral problems of children. *The Korean Journal of Elementary Counseling, 11*(1), 107–122.

Magallares, A., Recio, P., & Sanjuán, P. (2018). Factor structure of the gratitude questionnaire in a Spanish sample. *The Spanish Journal of Psychology, 21*, E53. https://doi.org/10.1017/sjp.2018.55

McCullough, M. E., Emmons, R. A., Kilpatrick, S. D., & Larson, D. B. (2001). Is gratitude a moral affect? *Psychological Bulletin, 127*(2), 249–266. https://doi.org/10.1037/0033-2909.127.2.249

McCullough, M. E., Emmons, R. A., & Tsang, J. (2002a). The Gratitude Questionnaire-Six Item Form (GQ-6). *Journal of Personality, 2001*, 80, 112–117.

McCullough, M. E., Emmons, R. A., & Tsang, J. A. (2002b). The grateful disposition: A conceptual and empirical topography. *Journal of Personality and Social Psychology, 82*(1), 112–127. https://doi.org/10.1037/0022-3514.82.1.112

McCullough, M. E., Kimeldorf, M. B., & Cohen, A. D. (2008). An adaptation for altruism. *Current Directions in Psychological Science, 17*(4), 281–285. https://doi.org/10.1111/j.1467-8721.2008.00590.x

McCullough, M. E., Pedersen, E. J., Tabak, B. A., & Carter, E. C. (2014). Conciliatory gestures promote forgiveness and reduce anger in humans. *Proceedings of the National Academy of Sciences, 111*(30), 11211–11216.

McCullough, M. E., Tsang, J. A., & Emmons, R. A. (2004). Gratitude in intermediate affective terrain: Links of grateful moods to individual differences and daily emotional experience. *Journal of Personality and Social Psychology, 86*(2), 295–309. https://doi.org/10.1037/0022-3514.86.2.295

Mendonça, S. E., Merçon-Vargas, E. A., Payir, A., & Tudge, J. R. H. (2018). The development of gratitude in seven societies: Cross-cultural highlights. *Cross-Cultural Research, 52*(1), 135–150. https://doi.org/10.1177/1069397117737245

Mills, J., Clark, M. S., & Ford, T. E. (2004). Measurement of communal strength. *Personal Relationships, 11*, 213–230.

Morgan, B., Gulliford, L., & Kristjánsson, K. (2014). Gratitude in the UK: A new prototype analysis and a cross-cultural comparison. *Journal of Positive Psychology, 9*(4), 281–294. https://doi.org/10.1080/17439760.2014.898321

Naito, T., Wangwan, J., & Tani, M. (2005). Gratitude in university students in Japan and Thailand. *Journal of Cross-Cultural Psychology, 36*(2), 247–263. https://doi.org/10.1177/0022022104272904

Nowak, M. A., & Roch, S. (2007). Upstream reciprocity and the evolution of gratitude. *Proceedings of the Royal Society B: Biological Sciences, 274*(1610), 605–610. https://doi.org/10.1098/rspb.2006.0125

Oishi, S., Koo, M., Lim, N., & Suh, E. M. (2019). When gratitude evokes indebtedness. *Applied Psychology: Health and Well-Being, 11*(2), 286–303. https://doi.org/10.1111/aphw.12155

Peng, C., Nelissen, R. M. A., & Zeelenberg, M. (2018). Reconsidering the roles of gratitude and indebtedness in social exchange. *Cognition and Emotion, 32*(4), 760–772. https://doi.org/10.1080/02699931.2017.1353484

Poelker, K. E., Gibbons, J. L., & Maxwell, C. A. (2019). The relation of perspective-taking to gratitude and envy among Guatemalan adolescents. *International Perspectives in Psychology: Research, Practice, Consultation, 8*(1), 20–37. https://doi.org/10.1037/ipp0000103

Rachlin, H. (2015). Social cooperation and self-control. *Managerial and Decision Economics, 37*(4), 249–260. https://doi.org/10.1002/mde.2714

Ramos, J., Wadsworth, L., Reilly, S., Forster, D. E. & Pedersen, E. J. (in prep.). *On the reputational function of gratitude: People prefer to cooperate with grateful partners*.

Roberts, G. (2005). Cooperation through interdependence. *Animal Behaviour, 70*(4), 901–908.

Robustelli, B. L., & Whisman, M. A. (2018). Gratitude and life satisfaction in the United States and Japan. *Journal of Happiness Studies, 19*(1), 41–55. https://doi.org/10.1007/s10902-016-9802-5

Rosmarin, D. H., Krumrei, E. J., & Pargament, K. I. (2008). Are gratitude and spirituality protective factors against psychopathology. *International Journal, 2*(2), 1–8.

Saucier, G., & Goldberg, L. R. (1998). What is beyond the Big Five? Plenty! *Journal of Personality, 68*(5), 821–835. https://doi.org/10.1111/1467-6494.00117

Sell, A., Tooby, J., & Cosmides, L. (2009). Formidability and the logic of human anger. *Proceedings of the National Academy of Sciences, 106*, 15073–15078.

Seyfarth, R. M., & Cheney, D. L. (2011). The evolutionary origins of friendship. *Annual Review of Psychology, 63*(1), 153–177. https://doi.org/10.1146/annurev-psych-120710-100337

Silk, J. B. (2002). Females, food, family, and friendship. *Evolutionary Anthropology, 11*(3), 85–87. https://doi.org/10.1002/evan.10011

Smith, A., Pedersen, E. J., Forster, D. E., McCullough, M. E., & Lieberman, D. (2017). Cooperation: The roles of interpersonal value and gratitude. *Evolution and Human Behavior, 38*(6), 695–703. https://doi.org/10.1016/j.evolhumbehav.2017.08.003

Sommers, S., & Kosmitzki, C. (1988). Emotion and social context: An American–German comparison. *British Journal of Social Psychology, 27*(1), 35–49. https://doi.org/https://doi.org/10.1111/j.2044-8309.1988.tb00803.x

Sreeja, P. S., & Mahalakshmi, G. (2017). Emotion models: A review. *International Journal of Control Theory and Applications, 10*(8), 651–657.

Tesser, A., Gatewood, R., & Driver, M. (1968). Some determinants of gratitude. *Journal of Personality and Social Psychology, 9*(3), 233–236. https://doi.org/10.1037/h0025905

Titova, L., Wagstaff, A. E., & Parks, A. C. (2017). Disentangling the effects of gratitude and optimism: A cross-cultural investigation. *Journal of Cross-Cultural Psychology, 48*(5), 754–770. https://doi.org/10.1177/0022022117699278

Toepfer, S., & Walker, K. (2009). Letters of gratitude: Improving well-being through expressive writing. *The Journal of Writing Research, 1*, 181–198.

Tooby, J., & Cosmides, L. (1996). Friendship and the banker's paradox: Other pathways to the evolution of adaptations for altruism. *Proceedings of the British Academy, 10*(5), 681–683. https://doi.org/10.1002/(sici)1520-6300(1998)10:5<681::aid-ajhb16>3.3.co;2-i

Tooby, J., & Cosmides, L. (2008). The evolutionary psychology of the emotions and their relationship to internal regulatory variables. In M. Lewis, J. M. Haviland-Jones, & L. F. Barrett (Eds.), *Handbook of emotions* (3rd ed., pp. 114–137). Guilford Press.

Tooby, J., Cosmides, L., Sell, A. N., Lieberman, D., & Sznycer, D. (2008). Internal regulatory variables and the design of human motivation: A computational and evolutionary approach. In A. J. Elliott (Ed.), *Handbook of approach and avoidance motivation* (pp. 251–271). Lawrence Erlbaum Associates.

Trivers, R. L. (1971). The evolution of reciprocal altruism. *The Quarterly Review of Biology, 46*(1), 35–57. https://doi.org/10.1086/406755

Tsang, J. A. (2006). Gratitude and prosocial behaviour: An experimental test of gratitude. *Cognition and Emotion, 20*(1), 138–148. https://doi.org/10.1080/02699930500172341

Tsang, J. A., & Martin, S. R. (2019). Four experiments on the relational dynamics and prosocial consequences of gratitude. *Journal of Positive Psychology, 14*(2), 188–205. https://doi.org/10.1080/17439760.2017.1388435

Van Kleef, G. A. (2009). How emotions regulate social life: The emotions as social information (EASI) model. *Current Directions in Psychological Science, 18*(3), 184–188. https://doi.org/10.1111/j.1467-8721.2009.01633.x

Walster, E., Walster, G. W., Piliavin, J., & Schmidt, L. (1973). "Playing hard to get": Understanding an elusive phenomenon. *Journal of Personality and Social Psychology, 26*(1), 113–121. https://doi.org/10.1037/h0034234

Watkins, P. C., Khathrane Woddward, Stone, T., & Kolts, R. L. (2003). Gratitude and happiness: Development of a measure of gratitude, and relationships with subjective well-being. *Social Behavior and Personality, 31*(5), 431–452.

West, S. A., El Mouden, C., & Gardner, A. (2011). Sixteen common misconceptions about the evolution of cooperation in humans. *Evolution and Human Behavior, 32*(4), 231–262. https://doi.org/10.1016/j.evolhumbehav.2010.08.001

Wilks, D. C., Neto, F., & Mavroveli, S. (2015). Trait emotional intelligence, forgiveness, and gratitude in Cape Verdean and Portuguese students. *South African Journal of Psychology, 45*(1), 93–101. https://doi.org/10.1177/0081246314546347

Williams, K. D., Cheung, C. K. T., & Choi, W. (2000). Cyberostracism: Effects of being ignored over the internet. *Journal of Personality and Social Psychology, 79*(5), 748–762. https://doi.org/10.1037//0022-3514.79.5.748

Wood, A. M., Joseph, S., & Linley, P. A. (2007). Coping style as a psychological resource of grateful people. *Journal of Social and Clinical Psychology, 26*(9), 1076–1093. https://doi.org/10.1521/jscp.2007.26.9.1076

Wood, A. M., Joseph, S., Lloyd, J., & Atkins, S. (2009). Gratitude influences sleep through the mechanism of pre-sleep cognitions. *Journal of Psychosomatic Research, 66*(1), 43–48. https://doi.org/10.1016/j.jpsychores.2008.09.002

Wood, A. M., Joseph, S., & Maltby, J. (2008). Gratitude uniquely predicts satisfaction with life: Incremental validity above the domains and facets of the five factor model. *Personality and Individual Differences, 45*(1), 49–54. https://doi.org/https://doi.org/10.1016/j.paid.2008.02.019

Wood, A. M., Maltby, J., Gillett, R., Linley, P. A., & Joseph, S. (2008). The role of gratitude in the development of social support, stress, and depression: Two longitudinal studies. *Journal of Research in Personality, 42*(4), 854–871. https://doi.org/10.1016/j.jrp.2007.11.003

Yip, J. A., Schweitzer, M. E., & Nurmohamed, S. (2018). Trash-talking: Competitive incivility motivates rivalry, performance, and unethical behavior. *Organizational Behavior and Human Decision Processes, 144*, 125–144. https://doi.org/10.1016/j.obhdp.2017.06.002

Yu, H., Gao, X., Zhou, Y., & Zhou, X. (2018). Decomposing gratitude: Representation and integration of cognitive antecedents of gratitude in the brain. *Journal of Neuroscience, 38*(21), 4886–4898. https://doi.org/10.1523/JNEUROSCI.2944-17.2018

CHAPTER 15

Caring and the Evolution of Guilt: A Biopsychosocial Approach to a Pro-Social Emotion

Paul Gilbert

Abstract

Mammals are confronted with a number of life tasks to support their survival and reproduction. A core reproductive task is care of offspring. This requires competencies for detecting offspring needs, distress protecting from harm. Later evolved motives to care and support allies and in-group members. Guilt evolved with caring motives and alerts to the possibility of causing harm or not preventing it (for example by not meeting needs). It triggers urgent action if harm could or has occurred. Guilt can therefore arise when one has caused unintended harm or allowed harm to occur that one could have prevented. It is very different to shame. The chapter also discusses how some forms of antisocial behavior are associated with diminished care and compassion motives and an absence of guilt. Here the therapeutic task is to facilitate care and compassion motives and hence capacities to experience the remorse and sadness of guilt.

Key Words: compassion, guilt, harm, prevention, shame

Caring and the Need to Avoid Causing Harm

From predation to social dominance fights and tribal conflict, harming others is endemic to the evolutionary process. Guilt, however, seems to have evolved for the *avoidance of causing harm and reparation*. In humans, guilt can be associated with aversive emotions (e.g., alarm, sadness, and remorse) that generate reparative behaviors and avoidance of such behaviors in the future (Gilbert, 2019). The evolutionary question, then, is why (its evolved function) and how (its phylogeny) we have evolved "an aversive reaction to causing some forms of harm in some contexts." One obvious reason for not causing harm to others is that they will retaliate or disengage from a desired relationship. Another is that having a reputation as helpful and not harmful supports the development of trust and advantageous relationships. Guilt is an aversive experience to warn that our behavior endangers such mutually beneficial relationships. A third reason is where harming others, either by acts of commission or omission, affects one's own genetic self-interests (e.g., offspring).

Harm avoidance can have different sources, some of which can be fear or shame based. Although there are cognitive ways of distinguishing between shame and guilt (for example, guilt involves negative judgments about behavior, whereas shame involves negative judgments about

With thanks to Tommy Plowright for help in the preparation of this chapter.

the self (Gilbert, 2007; Tangney & Dearing, 2003), these do not illuminate the underlying differences in their basic evolved motivational systems and functions. As noted elsewhere, shame is primarily linked with the evolution of competitive behavior (Gilbert, 1998, 2007, 2019) and reputation maintenance (Sznycer et al., 2016; Sznycer et al., 2018). The psychology of shame tends to focus on a sense of social diminishment, inferior social comparison linked with loss of standing in the eyes of others, anxiety, and social withdrawal (Gilbert 2007). Guilt, in contrast, has none of these. Rather the focus is an empathic bridge to the harm done with a sense of sorrow and remorse that triggers reparative efforts. Issues of social standing, social comparison, and social reputation are irrelevant. Whereas shame emerges out of competitive motives linked to a demotion in status, guilt evolves and emerges out of caring behavior (Gilbert, 2019).

The Evolution of Caring as the Basis for Guilt

To explore the function and phylogeny of guilt, we can start by noting that all organic life is faced with two life tasks, to survive and reproduce (Buss, 2019). In species that are mobile (unlike plants) and reproduce sexually, there are two basic strategies. For many non-avian egg-laying species, the earliest reproductive strategies are called r-selection. They produce hundreds of eggs, of which only a few will survive to adulthood. Many species that lay multiple eggs have little, if any, parental investment, although, as noted below, some species of fish do. A very major change came with what is called k-selection of reproductive strategies. These species move toward having fewer offspring but invest time and resources in feeding and protecting them until they are mature enough to become self-sufficient. These strategies, which involve heavier parental investment, are called k-selected strategies (Geary, 2000). The archetype for caring would appear to be a reproductive strategy involving parental investment. Later, mammals evolved to have live birth and have infants who are not static in a nest but move with the parent. One of the parental tasks is therefore to maintain proximity (keep an eye open for the infant) to avoid it becoming lost or vulnerable to predation (Bowlby, 1969). A second key parental task was to develop feature detectors for infant distress and need and to be able to take actions to address them. These actions are not only to help the infant flourish, but also to prevent harm; an unfed or poorly thermoregulated infant dies.

This gradual emergence of k-reproductive strategies was to have major consequences for subsequent evolution of the central and autonomic nervous system (Brown & Brown, 2015; Carter et al., 2017; Gilbert, 1989, 2020; Mayseless, 2016; Porges, 2007; Wang 2005). Although we tend to focus on caring in mammals, McGhee and Bell (2014) studied three-spined sticklebacks, where fathers provide the care and protection. They note that:

> During the approximately two weeks that fathers provide care, they defend their nest from predators, fan the nest with their pectoral fins to provide fresh oxygen to the embryos and once the embryos hatch, retrieve fry that stray from the nest. During this period, offspring rely on yolk reserves provisioned by their mother prior to fertilization. Fathers do not feed offspring, but there is evidence that offspring antipredator behaviour . . . mate preference . . . and morphology . . . can be sensitive to the effects of fathers. (p. 2)

They go on to discuss how paternal caring influences the epigenetics of their offspring, including for traits like anxiety. Indeed, it is now known that across many different species, the quality of parental caring impacts epigenetics and can attenuate or amplify vulnerabilities to threat sensitivity (Cowan et al., 2016; Kumsta, 2019). Given that caring has such profoundly important impacts, mechanisms will evolve to keep it on course. An obvious question, then, is: What keeps our sticklebacks maintaining their caring behaviors in the face of other motives, such as pursuing food or sex? At this stage of evolution, the answer is not yet guilt, but those mechanisms may well be the forerunners of what will become *mechanisms for guilt*. Stated differently, we can expect parents to be equipped with mechanisms for monitoring what should be provided against what is actually being provided. When that mechanism detects a mismatch between what is provided compared to what is required, the stickleback will have to change its behavior to improve the care that it offers its offspring if there is a mismatch.

Many species hunt and provide food for their offspring. From an evolutionary point of view, parents must not be tempted to eat it all themselves. Therefore, parents must also be equipped with mechanisms for inhibiting their own desires in favor of attending to the needs of the infant. Indeed, the issue of putting "the other" first and giving up something to benefit the other is central to the concept of altruism (Buss. 2019; Colqhoun et al., 2020; Preston, 2013; Ricard, 2015). In a review, Preston (2013) offered the following definitions for altruism:

> Altruistic responding is defined as any form of helping that applies when the giver is motivated to assist a specific target *after perceiving their distress or need*. . . . Altruistic responding implies an active behavioral response initiated by the perception of need, which is differentiated from cooperative, diffuse, or unintentional forms of altruism that likely derive from other evolutionary and mechanistic origins. . . . Altruistic responding further narrows these classifications to only include cases where the motivation to respond is fomented by direct or indirect perception of the other's distress or need. . . . This excludes cases that emerged later in time or include diverse processes, such as cooperation or helping influenced by strategic goals, social norms, display rules, or mate signaling. (p. 1307; italics added)

For Preston (2013), the origins of altruistic responding are in the evolution of detecting and responding to distress calls in infants—coming to their aid. This raises the possibility that one aspect of guilt might pertain to situations in which we understand that others will benefit from things that we have, but we do not want to share them. Guilt, and the anticipation of guilt, may entice us to act against our reservations.

Caring and the Awareness and Inhibition of Harming

Parents do not just provide resources to their offspring; they also avoid harming them, another example of care. For example, MacLean et al. (1985) highlighted the evolution of cannibalism-inhibiting mechanisms. In various species, parental fish will eat fry if they get too close; they become just another meal. Thus, kin recognition and a rule that specifies "don't eat the kids" provide another mechanism for inhibiting harm. In addition, with the advent of live birth and parental investment, infant and parent will live in close proximity. This was facilitated by a variety of changes to the autonomic nervous system, particularly the vagus nerve and frontal cortex (Porges, 2007, 2017). These changes regulate the threat system (particularly fight and flight) so that the parent is not inclined to harm the infant and the infant is not inclined to take flight. If parents do inadvertently harm or injure their infants, then they are disposed to try to repair the harm they have caused. Indeed, in many species, sick, dying, and dead infants are not immediately abandoned. Instead, the parent will try to resuscitate them, for a short while at least. This is particularly true in many primates (Watts, 2020). For the most part, then, parents put the needs of the offspring first and usually do not engage in hurtful behavior such as challenging, biting, or injuring their offspring (as they might a competitor). Inadvertently doing so prompts remedial action. Hence, some sort of recognition that one has caused harm and needs to make amends appears to have emerged quite early in the evolutionary process.

There is now considerable evidence that a wide range of species, from avian to rodent to primate, have been observed behaving in ways that prevent harm to others. An early study by Church (1959) found that rodents will not pull a lever to obtain food if doing so causes a conspecific to receive an electric shock at the same time. De Waal and Preston (2017) reviewed the evidence of why different species, and in particular primates, choose not to be harmful to others in some contexts. Questions remain as to whether the distress animals feel in response to causing harm is best conceptualized as guilt or anxiety.

A Violence Inhibition Mechanism

Working with people who do cause harm, and in particular people with psychopathic personalities, Blair (1995, 2007, 2017) noted that several ethologists had proposed that various mechanisms had evolved to regulate or inhibit aggression. He suggested the evolution of what he called a *violence inhibition mechanism* (VIM). Submissive behavior is certainly one common behavior that can downregulate aggressive behavior from a more dominant individual (Gilbert, 2000), but he suggested that signals of distress, particularly fearful and sad expressions and vocalizations, have also evolved as signals that inhibit hostile intent and actions.

Over a number of years, there has been considerable research on how we respond psychologically and physiologically to cues of distress (Morey et al., 2012). One characteristic of psychopaths, Blair's focus of study, is that they do not psychologically or physiologically respond to distress signals (Blair, 2017). However, having developmental and personality traits that orientate to nonresponsiveness to distress is only part of the story. Clearly, in many species, aggression is a very powerful strategy to get what the animal wants, and tragically for humans, guilt is a fragile inhibitor and is often contextual. The history of the past 10,000 years, following the emergence of agriculture, male-dominated hierarchical groups, and the nature of tribal conflict, have shown that humans can go out of their way to be violent and cause suffering (Black, 2016). This can be seen on a massive scale, as witnessed in the tribal wars, genocides, tortures, forms of execution (e.g., burnings and crucifixion), exploitation via slavery, and more. Clearly, guilt is not an inhibitor in these contexts, raising the question of what facilitates *and inhibit*s guilt in tribal contexts.

Callousness versus Cruelty

Violence inhibition is only one of many aspects of harm inhibition because there are many different types of harm that do not involve violence. Here, it is important to make a distinction between callousness and cruelty. Callousness is an indifference to the pain and suffering of others, including that which we cause to others (and at times oneself). Our behavior is purely self-interest. We neither enjoy nor are concerned with the harmfulness of our actions. These actions include many forms of criminal behavior, such as breaking into people's houses or bank accounts, scamming, or pursuing business aims (e.g., fossil fuels) that are known to be harmful, but perpetrators are indifferent to pain they cause. Pain and damage are not the focus of the action; self-benefit is. Interestingly, these kinds of criminal and harmful behaviors may respond to distress cues if they are physically confronted by them. One of the ideas behind restorative justice is that by bringing perpetrator and victim together, the perpetrator has to confront the nonverbal and physical cues of distress from the victim. This may break through empathic disengagement, which callousness tends to be, and generate feelings of guilt (Clark, 2008; Van Ness & Strong, 2014). Recently Vu et al., 2023 report on a series of studies, which they call wig for ignorance, where people *deliberately* choose not to pay attention to the harmful consequences of their action in order to pursue selfish motives.

Cruelty differs from callousness, which involves indifference or turning a blind eye to the harmfulness we cause, because in cruelty the whole point of the behavior *is to be harmful* and cause pain and suffering. Neither are we empathically disengaged, as we can be in callousness. Indeed, it is precisely *because we know* how to cause pain and suffering, or we know how to humiliate people, that we do it. Here it is not just that we are unresponsive to signals of distress; we actually enjoy them. The German word *schadenfreude* comes from *Schaden*, which means to harm or damage, and *Freude*, which means "joy." By definition then, *schadenfreude* means enjoying someone else's misfortune or suffering. It is also referred to as malicious pleasure (Leach et al., 2003). Hence, cruelty inhibits guilt in different ways from callousness. It is possible that this evolved from mechanisms that are associated with pleasure from power and being energized by stimulating subordinate fear. After all, that is what dominant behavior is evolved to do: to frighten others to back off and give up resources. Callousness, in contrast, has no interest in whether people are frightened or not. Better distinctions between callous behavior and cruel behavior would help us develop better therapeutic interventions, but compassion focused therapy has shown some promise (Riberio da Silva et al., 2020).

Remorse and Repair
Another key behavior associated with guilt is reparation. Here much depends upon on the nature of the harm caused, intentional or unintentional, callous or cruel. For example, we might feel guilty about forgetting a friend's birthday because it indicates that we haven't held them in mind, or we might feel guilty because we borrowed something of value from them and broke it, or because of a far more intentional behavior such as having an affair with the partner of one's best friend. People might steal from the office or big department stores but not from individuals because they minimized harm of the former. Clearly, intentional versus unintentional harmful behavior is important here as to the degree to which we feel remorse and wish to compensate or repair. We might replace our friend's possession, and we might apologize for forgetting the birthday and buy an extra special present as compensation. Yu, Hu, Hu, and Zhou (2014) have shown that the same neurophysiological mechanisms that underpin feelings of guilt also underpinned desires for compensation and reparation. Although reparative behaviors can be to try to "save face" with the other or avoid shame, which would not involve sadness, sadness-generated desires to compensate to repair would be linked to guilt. Hence, it is possible to distinguish the guilt associated with an act, a failure to act, the emotions associated with the desire for reparation, and the emotions that might follow if reparation is unsuccessful. Hence, another distinguishing feature of psychopathic or "guiltless" behavior is showing little interest in *reparation* for harm caused.

Altruism Inhibition
Altruism, the giving to, or sharing with, others resources we might need ourselves, can be costly. So evolution has evolved mechanisms for dispensing care and sharing judiciously; it is not offered equally to all, and for some (e.g., outgroup members) they can be deliberately withheld (Colqhoun et al., 2020). Altruistic behavior is much more likely to be focused on kin and friends than non-kin and strangers (Burnstein et al., 1994). Children show caring and helping behavior by their second year, such as picking up pegs fallen on the floor and handing them to a person who needs them or opening doors for others (Dunfield & Kuhlmeier, 2013; Warneken & Tomasello, 2006). For the most part, the child is pleased to do it, and the behavior creates positive feelings between the child and the receiver. However, in much of this research there was no cost to the child. Genuine altruism requires helping-caring in the face of cost to the actor. Green et al. (2018) investigated how distress-sensitive and helpful, young children would be if there were a cost to their helping. They found that children would help a hand puppet achieve a goal of completing a task (e.g., puzzle) if there was no cost to them, but helping fell significantly when they had to give up something they wanted to help the puppet. Even when the puppet made appeals and behaved as if distressed, the child still did not give

up their own resources or rewards to help the distressed puppet. Sometimes they appeared distressed themselves and possibly felt "guilt," but it did not affect helping behavior (Kirby, personal communication). In other words, even though the child felt bad about not helping, they still did not help.

Altruism—but to Whom?

Once the template for caring behavior was established, with various neurophysiological systems such as oxytocin (Carter et al., 2017), evolution was able to expand the motivation to be caring beyond immediate kin relationships. Whereas caring for kin is regarded as kin altruism, caring for those who may reciprocate in the future is called reciprocal altruism (Colqhoun et al., 2020). Dimensions linked to reciprocal altruism are liking, trust, and identification. We are far more likely to want to care for those we like, trust, and know than those we do not. This shows up in studies of empathy, too. For example, Hein et al. (2010) found that empathy neurocircuits (relating to mirror neurons) are activated if one watches somebody one knows, or with whom one identifies, having their hand pricked with a pin. However, these effects were significantly diminished if the person having their hand pricked was a member of an opposing sports team or a stranger. In addition, although the hormone oxytocin underpins caring behavior, it is contextual in its effects. In some contexts, oxytocin makes us more aggressive and distrusting (De Dreu et al., 2011). The essence of the story is that caring for others—and inhibiting harming them—is very much linked to how they are conceptualized in people's field of relating. If they are perceived as the enemy, we may have very little guilt in harming them.

Given the importance of reciprocal alliances and cooperation, there is reason to believe that guilt would have played a role in helping individuals maintain cooperative relations. In these contexts, guilt relates to a breaking of trust or letting others down in reciprocal agreements that could damage the relationship.

Caring, Guilt, and Social Responsibility

For various and complex reasons, humans are one of the few species that allows, encourages, and even needs other individuals (besides the parents) to be involved with infant care. This is called alloparenting, and it is defined by parental functions (care, protection, provision of comfort, play) being provided by an individual other than parents (Hrdy, 2009). Indeed, it is possible for children to seek out these others in preference to their own parents if the parent-offspring relationship is not such a good one. Alloparenting became highly adaptive for small group–living humans (Narvaez, 2017). Not only did it provide the infant with multiple interactions that facilitate complex social learning and a sense of social safeness and social engagement, but it provided resources to the parents, particularly the mother. The implication is that this extended network would take responsibility for childcare and for each other. This means that the extension of care in these networks also provides capacities for feeling guilty if one does not play one's role, or if a child is injured or a mother suffers in a way that one could have prevented.

There are many other avenues by which early humans developed a sense of responsibility in caring for each other (Camilleri et al., 2023; Dunbar, 2014). Whatever those roots are, it is the caring motivation that carries the capacity for guilt, primarily in the context of either having harmed someone unintentionally or failing in one's responsibilities, obligations, or promises.

Some years ago, we developed a scale to look at different types of guilt, including guilt that involved hurting people in comparison to cheating or breaking a cooperative deal. Unfortunately, we never published the data, but there was some indication that these guilt domains can differ with function and focus. There is, for example, the possibility of a special type of "cooperative guilt" (feeling bad) when we cheat on a deal or break a trust, although further work could explore the degree to which fear of retaliation may also be involved. Julle-Danière, Whitehouse, Vrij, Gustafsson, and Waller (2020) highlight that guilt has a number of different functions, including the fact that guilt can mitigate punishment from a victim. After harming somebody, an individual who shows little guilt is more likely to be punished than one who expresses genuine guilt. The relationship between displays of guilt and forgiveness is especially important in close relationship and also where people are in regular contact. In forensics too, distinctions are made between the role of guilt verses shame between restorative versus retributive justice. Restorative justice that, is focused on acknowledging and expressing guilt, is more likely to be associated with victim forgiveness (Clark, 2008; Witvliet et al., 2008). In other words, humans are able to discern subtle differences in the motivational expressions of people as being related to genuine remorse as opposed to faked remorse, shame-linked apology, or simple forgiveness-seeking.

Caring for the Sick
As discussed above, the evolution of early mechanisms underpinning caring are associated with the infant-parent relationship (Mayseless, 2016). Beyond the infant-parent dyad, Kessler (2020) highlights that many species care for their sick and injured. She explored the evolution of what she calls "healthcare"—caring for sick individuals—reviewing work on ants (*Megaponera Analis*) who are prone to injury such as losing legs. However, if nest mates carry them back to the nest, their chances of recovery are 80%, compared to 10% for those who are not carried back. Kessler also highlights a range of evolved caring behaviors (e.g., grooming) whose function appears to be parasite and infection control. She suggests that such caring can be partly driven by concerns for the health of genetically related others. In addition, this should be more important for species living in close confinement with each other, as opposed to those that disperse after birth. Spikins (2015, 2017) also points out that care has multiple functions, such as protecting, providing food and shelter, as well as caring for individuals when they are sick. This seems to have been a fundamental part of human evolution. This is evidenced by the archaeological record showing that individuals lived with diseases and serious injuries that they could not have survived unless they had been cared for (Spikins, 2017).

New Evolved Human Brain Functions Are Necessary for Guilt
While some of the early mechanisms underpinning guilt can be tracked through phylogenetic time, full-blown guilt may require a certain kind of psychological insight and self-awareness. This requires complex cognitive abilities and competencies of various forms. It is now understood that around a million years ago, our ancestors began to evolve a series of new cognitive competencies (Byrne, 1995). There are at least three different types of competency that are of interest. The first is our capacity for types of reasoning that allow us to think in time (Suddendorf, 2018) and also to see the patterns in things, develop language, and use symbols for thinking (Baron-Cohen, 2020). We might call this a "reasoning brain," which enabled us to go from eating seeds to planting them, building flint axes to wheels to vaccines. The role of reasoning by itself in guilt is unclear. It is relevant because it enables us to understand harm that we have inflicted in the past or could inflict in the future.

A second set of competencies enable empathy and the *mentalization* of the minds of others (Luyten et al., 2020). While other animals certainly show degrees of empathy (Preston, 2013), empathy is very advanced in humans. Empathic concern for others seems to occur very early in life (Zahn-Waxler et al., 1992). This is key to the analysis of guilt because it is our ability to have insight and *understand* that others can suffer and the nature of that suffering, and that we may be the cause of it, that is a root of guilt. Without an empathic connection to a sense of self as a causal agent of suffering to another, guilt cannot exist. It raises the question of the degree to which guilt requires us to be aware of others as conscious beings who can suffer. We might think we have a sense of guilt with non-sentient objects, such as "feeling guilty about not looking after the car or garden." However, it is uncertain if we actually feel guilt toward "damaged objects" or if we simply regret the consequences of our (in)action. For the moment, then, we can suggest that guilt is only experienced when we anticipate living "entities" suffering and more so if we think they have conscious awareness. Shame in only felt in connection to other human minds where status/reputation matters.

Linked to this idea is the work of O'Connor, Berry, Lewis, and Stiver (2011), who suggest that guilt acts to maintain altruistic behavior via (1) stimulating empathic connectedness and (2) generating concern for the suffering and needs of others. They, too, note that there must first be some empathic connection and awareness of suffering that stimulates helping behavior. If indeed guilt depends on empathic connection, then humans will be more guilt-prone because they are more empathically sophisticated (Luyten et al., 2020).

How we develop that empathic connection to harm is complex, however, and seems to depend upon our experiences of other people being empathic toward us in the past. For example, individuals who come from non-caring backgrounds can struggle to mature the necessary competencies for this awareness. In a major review of the neurophysiology of empathy, Shirtcliff, Vitacco, Graf, Gostisha, Merz, and Zahn-Waxler (2009) found evidence to support this view. They summarize their findings saying:

> The review proposes neurobiological impairments in individuals who display little empathy are not necessarily due to a reduced ability to understand the emotions of others. Instead, evidence suggests individuals who show little arousal to the distress of others likewise show decreased physiological arousal to their own distress; one manifestation of reduced stress reactivity may be a dysfunction in empathy which supports psychopathic-like constructs (e.g., callousness). (p. 137)

So if one cannot process one's own distress, then the mechanisms for empathy appear not to work well. This is important to guilt because empathy seems to require a functioning mirror neuron system (de Waal & Preston, 2017). This is also important with individuals who have psychopathic traits. In an electro-physiological study, Decety, Lewis, and Cowell (2015) showed that people with psychopathic traits exhibited less empathic concern and less affect-sharing in response to distressed individuals than those with lower scores on psychopathy. These individuals are also noted for their lack of caring motives, guilt, and remorse. Some may be helped by deliberately stimulating and practicing caring motives through compassion training that helps people work through their own (early) emotional pain (Ribeiro da Silva et al., 2019; Ribeiro da Silva et al., 2020). People who cannot process sadness and guilt can be at risk of harming others partly because guilt depends upon the ability to tolerate and experience these emotions. This has huge implications for forensic services because while some believe shaming and retribution are important for prevention, others suggest that understanding how to facilitate the capacity to experience guilt is more important. This in turn requires therapeutic work on the client's own grief-based processes that may have emerged out of abusive backgrounds (Gilbert, 2018; Ribeiro da Silva et al., 2020).

Another way to conceptualize this is that the maturation of the caring system requires extensive, early experiences of being cared for, and without this, individuals engage in a different maturational trajectory which is more oriented toward self-protective and competitive behavior rather than caring behavior (Gilbert 2017, 2020). For example, there is evidence that receiving care can offset callous behavior in later life, even in individuals with callous traits (Wright et al., 2018). Combinations of poor early attachment/care and callous traits are a particularly potent combination for the inhibition of guilt.

Along with our new brain competencies that enable us reason with conceptual thinking and a sense of self, to have a capacity for empathic insight, there is a third new neurophysiological competency for being *conscious of being conscious* (Gilbert, 2019, 2020)—what Thích Nhất Hạnh (1975) called *the miracle of mindfulness* in recognition of this special and mysterious quality and competency of self-awareness. Conscious self-awareness, our ability to have awareness that we exist as an "individual self" and to be able to *purposely observe* the contents of our own minds, and to have *knowing intentionality*, is an evolutionary game changer. For example, as Goodall (1990) points out, many chimpanzees engage in conflicts where they inflict pain on others, but it is unlikely they knowingly wish to cause pain and work out how to do it to create the most suffering. Their fights are generally functional. By contrast, human cruelty is the knowing, purposeful, and intentional infliction of pain and suffering. Like callousness, it requires a turning off of the potential for guilt by inhibiting the motive to care. Compassion is in a sense the opposite: *caring with a knowing awareness* of why caring is important, combined with and working out what to do to care for the other individual. Without these high-level competencies, caring is similar to the basic forms of caring that many other animals express (Gilbert, 2017, 2020).

Defining Guilt

Everyday use of the word *guilt* implies an attribution of causality, as in a court being "found responsible" for a harmful act or outcome. The psychological understanding is different and involves a number of different psychological processes that all relate to the *motive to care*.

1. Here, guilt relates to an internal process linked to certain types of evaluation, emotional experience, and motivation that can include an attribution of blame. Baumeister, Stillwell, and Heartheon (1994, 2001) suggest that the prototypical meaning of "guilt" is behaving in a way that results in harm, either through acts of commission or omission.
2. A second dimension of guilt is that the harm was unintended. In a court of law, whether you intended or did not intend to cause harm would not be relevant to being found "guilty" or not, but it might influence one's sentence. Psychologically it is a fundamental distinction. One may feel guilty for vengeful behaviors later, but not at the time. So guilt must be *unintended harm*.
3. Baumeister et al. (1994, 2001) note that guilt requires some kind of empathic connection to the harm one has done that causes *distress* in the guilty individual. To unintentionally cause harm but not be distressed by it would be regarded as callousness (Gilbert, 2018). Empathic connection by itself is not enough for guilt because, as noted above, it can also lead to cruelty. In war contexts (empathic) recognition that one has caused harm is a cause for celebration, not distress.
4. Many authors point out that guilt motivates reparative behavior and the desire to make amends and set things right. Causing harm from self-interest (for example, criminal behavior such as hacking into people's bank accounts or business practices such as driving wages down and impoverishing people) and not feeling any desire for reparation when that harm becomes obvious is callousness. This has major implications for the social injustices and unequal resource distribution in the world today.

5. Callousness can be distinguished from *cruelty* in that callousness involves a certain empathic disengagement from distress, whereas cruelty is based upon an insight into what causes suffering and the enjoyment of distress cues. One of the great tragedies of humans is that we can work out how to torture people to intensify terror and prolong their suffering. Clearly guilt is well and truly turned off.
6. The emotions associated with guilt tend to be ones of sadness and remorse. This suggests that it is tapping into evolved systems linked to loss.
7. Guilt, and the anticipation of guilt, can promote caring and prosocial behavior (Xu et al., 2012; Tangney & Dearing 2003).
8. Guilt might promote courage—for example, it may lead people to refuse to comply with harmful requests by authorities (Ent & Baumeister, 2015).
9. Important too is the concept of survivor guilt (Hutson et al., 2015; O'Connor et al., 2000; O'Connor et al., 2002), where individuals can feel a painful sense of loss because they have survived and others have not, or they have suffered less than others. In these days of COVID-19, this is likely to be an ongoing rising problem, particularly in the face of the epidemic of grief.
10. This also fits with the guilt we can feel of "failing to rescue," e.g., leaving somebody behind whom we might have been able to help. The film *The Martian* was centered around the importance of the feelings that arose when the crew realized they had left one of their colleagues behind (who they thought had died but had not). The distress was partly linked to the guilt they would feel if they didn't turn back and try to rescue him, even if this meant putting themselves at risk. In hunter-gatherer societies, it is likely that our ability to recognize that if we got lost others would come to find us would have created strong bonds and security to explore. You can contrast that with the belief that if lost, no one would bother to look for you. Hence, we can anticipate that people will come to look for us or try to help us partly because of the negative affect of guilt they would feel if they didn't. This is why we worry about those with psychopathic traits because they wouldn't feel guilt and thus wouldn't be motivated to help. Guilt then can support bonds and trust.
11. A source of guilt that's very prominent today is from the tragedies of COVID-19. Not being able to hold the hands of a dying loved one or say goodbye to them, even when people *know it is not their fault*, can leave people with enormous sadness and sense of guilt. This is linked to the guilt that "I wasn't able to get to you or be there for you."
12. These forms of guilt also attest to another core aspect of guilt—its relation to moral principles. For those who are not motivated by, or have little concern or care for others, they are unlikely to feel guilt in response to exploiting or harming others. Psychopathic individuals who lack care-focused motivational orientation also appear to lack the morals, concerns, and issues of guilt that emanate from these care-based motivational systems.

Shame and Guilt

Before finishing this chapter, it is important to note the distinctions between shame and guilt (Gilbert, 2007, 2019). This is important because most distinctions do not consider the evolutionary origins and underpinnings that differentiate the two. They focus more on cognitive processes such as attributions and distinctions, behavioral evaluation, and global self-evaluation. As noted briefly above, shame is not rooted in the caring system, but rather in the social rank and competitive system. When shame is activated, it stimulates concerns with social presentation and a sense of personal exposure and diminishment (Gilbert, 1998; Landers et al., Chapter 7 in this volume; Lewis 1992). To offer a practical way to contrast these very different responses to causing harm, consider two men, Tom and Harry, who have affairs and are discovered by their partners. Tom has a shame-focused response. He has a sense of personal diminishment in the eyes of others who may now look down on him, and he worries about how his partner sees him and his lost status or attractiveness in his/her eyes. He worries whether his partner will forgive him and how to rebuild the relationship so he can feel better and wanted again. He becomes self-critical. He desperately wants to make amends but *mainly to prevent reputational and status losses, to seek forgiveness of his partner and be loved/wanted again*. These are all *self* repair. Shame is "I feel bad about me, and I think you feel bad about me, and if people hear about this they will think ill of me." It is all about (bad) "me, me, me."

Harry, on the other hand, has a guilt response. He is able to recognize that his partner is hurt and likely sees this as a betrayal. He mentalizes the mind of his partner, rather than just focusing on his own feeling. Harry might not even feel that bad about his behavior, but instead focuses on its impact on his partner. He is less concerned with his reputation and more concerned for the upset he has caused his partner. He has a genuine desire to help his partner feel better and to repair the damage. Harry will try to be honest about his behavior and work it through from there. Besides guilt, his primary emotions are sorrow and remorse *for the pain his partner is going through*.

Toward a Model

This chapter suggests that the emergence of guilt is rooted in caring motives that (excluding ant recovery) may initially evolved in the context of the parent-offspring attachment system to ensure the survival of infants. To care efficiently, the carer needs to be sensitive to the distress and needs of the infant, and also must know how best to address them. This suggests mechanisms for identifying the behaviors that *should* occur against those that are not occurring and producing behavioral corrections to close the gap. These mechanisms provide possible evolutionary underpinnings of guilt, with its associated emotions of sadness and remorse. Sadness evolved as a part of coping with interpersonal loss of people we care for and about (Arias et al., 2020).

Figure 15.1 suggests therefore that the motivational root of guilt is located in *caring motivation*. For many animals this motivational system orients their attention to their infants' distress and needs, and motivates behaviors to address these. A second key is the ability to

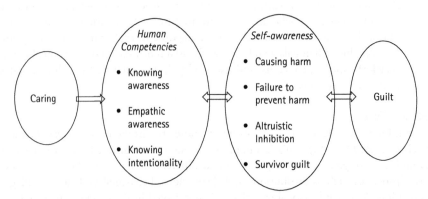

Figure 15.1. Caring motivation and the evolution of guilt. Adapted from Gilbert, P. (2018). *Living Like Crazy* with permission Annwyn House.

make judgments about the needs of the other against what we are actually providing, with our new brain competencies, complex understanding about the needs of others, and our ability to help, neglect or hurt. So guilt can be triggered in the context of forms of harmful or unhelpful behavior. First, is causing unintentional harm. Second, is the recognition that we have failed to prevent harm, whether by inaction or some other means. Third, we can experience guilt as a form of altruistic inhibition (Green et al., 2018). Such data suggest the possibility that competitive cultures and worldviews, particularly neoliberalism, with its focus on striving, having, and winning, can undermine altruistic guilt. We gradually become less concerned with the struggles of others around us, wanting neither to help them nor rescue them as we pursue our own self-interest. A related aspect of this can be survivor guilt, in which we recognize we are much better off than the vast majority of people on this planet, and justice requires us to share our resources. However, this guilt is either not felt in those who could make changes or if they are, not translated into behavior to address inequalities. Feeling guilt does not always mean we will act wisely and compassionately to address the source of our guilt. Indeed, out of self-interest, guilt is unfortunately fairly easy to override.

Therapy
Given the evolutionary background to guilt, and its important role in maintaining pro social behavior, guilt can be an important therapeutic target. Individuals who struggle with empathy and are prone to be inconsiderate, hurtful, or harmful to self and/or others may require "guilt work." This is one of the targets in CFT to increase people's sensitivity to their own contribution to harm and suffering (Riberio da Silva, et al., 2020). That process, however, is complex because it often requires individuals to develop processing systems that may have been inhibited due to childhood trauma (Gilbert & Simos, 2022). Hence therapy for guilt can be to help those who seem unable to feel it and also to those who perhaps experience it too much and inappropriately, and become trapped in relationships, for guilt-linked fear of assertiveness or change. Important too are those who deliberately choose to deny "turn a blind eye" to the harm they cause in order to pursue self-interest (Vu et al., 2023). Here is a deliberate act not to feel guilt.

Conclusion
This chapter argued that the psychological and behavioral infrastructures for maintaining caring behavior, and preventing harm to others, has a long phylogeny. Violations to those outcomes would have alerted the parents, usually the mother, to re-attend to caring. The origins of guilt may therefore be signals that we have not provided what is necessary for a close other, even though we had the resources to, and/or that we have inadvertently caused harm to another. While we can see some of the forerunners for guilt—such as empathy—in other animals, human experiences of guilt require self-awareness and knowing intentionality.

This chapter also argued that guilt has facilitators and inhibitors. One of the great tragedies for human beings is that caring compassion and guilt have many inhibitors (Gilbert & Mascaro, 2017; Gilbert & Simos 2022). It is the inhibition of the care motive (by various routes) that make us one of the cruelest species. Hence, we are paradoxically a species of extremes: capable of great compassion and intense guilt, but also horrific violence and cruelty. Although we can suffer from feelings of guilt, and there are some mental health problems where guilt is accentuated, guilt is clearly part of caring and the avoidance of harming motivation. It would have played a fundamental role in the evolution of a range of caring, compassionate and cooperative behaviors, particularly during our hunter-gatherer evolution. Because we can be distressed by causing harm or failing to address suffering, guilt is a very important constituent of pro-social behavior, if at time easily tuned off.

References

Arias, J. A., Williams, C., Raghvani, R., Aghajani, M., Baez, S., Belzung, C., Booij, L., Busatto, J., HY Fu, C., Ibamez, A., Lidell, B. J., Lowe, L., Pemminx, B.W.J.H., Rosa, P., & Kenp, S. H. (2020). The neuroscience of sadness: A multidisciplinary synthesis and collaborative review. *Neuroscience & Biobehavioral Reviews, 111*, 199–228.

Baron-Cohen, S. (2020). *The pattern seekers: A new theory of human invention.* Allen Lane.

Baumeister, R. F., Stillwell, A. M., & Heatherton, T. F. (1994). Guilt: An interpersonal approach. *Psychological Bulletin, 115*(2), 243.

Baumeister, R. F., Stillwell, A. M., Heatherton, T. F., & Parrott, W. G. (2001). Interpersonal aspects of guilt: Evidence from narrative studies. In W. G. Parrot (Ed.), *Emotions in social psychology: Essential readings* (pp. 295–305). Psychology Press.

Black, W. (2016). *Psychopathic cultures and toxic empires.* Frontline Noir.

Blair, R. J. R. (1995) . A cognitive developmental approach to morality: Investigating the psychopath. *Cognition, 57*, 1–29.

Blair R. J. R. (2007). The amygdala and ventromedial prefrontal cortex in morality and psychopathy. *Trends in Cognitive Sciences, 11*, 387–392.

Blair, R. J. R. (2017). Emotion-based learning systems and the development of morality. *Cognition, 167*, 38–45.

Bowlby, J. (1969). *Attachment and loss, Vol. 1: Attachment.* Basic Books.

Brown, S. L., & Brown, R. M. (2015). Connecting prosocial behavior to improved physical health: Contributions from the neurobiology of parenting. *Neuroscience and Biobehavioral Reviews, 55*, 1–17.

Brown, S. L., & Brown, R. M. (2017). Compassionate neurobiology and health. *The Oxford Handbook of Compassion Science, 159*–172.

Burnstein, E., Crandall, C., & Kitayama, S. (1994). Some neo-Darwinian rules for altruism: Weighing cues for inclusive fitness as a function of biological importance of the decision. *Journal of Personality and Social Psychology, 67*, 773–807.

Buss, D. M. (2019). *Evolutionary psychology: The new science of the mind* (6th edition). London Psychology Press: UK.

Byrne, R. W. (1995). *The thinking ape: Evolutionary origins of intelligence.* Oxford University Press on Demand.

Camilleri, T., Rockey S., & Dunbar, R. (2023). *The social brain: The psychology of successful groups.* Cornerstone Press.

Carter, S., Bartal, I. B., & Porges, E. (2017). The roots of compassion: An evolutionary and neurobiological perspective. In E. M. Seppälä, E. Simon-Thomas, S. I. Brown, M. C. Worline, C. D. Cameron, & J. R. Doty (Eds.), *The Oxford handbook of compassion science* (pp. 178–188). Oxford University Press.

Church, R. M. (1959). Emotional reactions of rats to the pain of others. *Journal of Comparative & Physiological Psychology, 52*, 132–134.

Clark, J. N. (2008). The three Rs: Retributive justice, restorative justice, and reconciliation. *Contemporary Justice Review, 11*(4), 331–350.

Colqhoun, L., Workman, L., & Fowler, J. (2020). The problem of altruism and future directions. In L. Workman, W. Reader, & J. H. Barkow (Eds.), *Cambridge handbook of evolutionary perspectives on human behavior* (pp. 125–138). Cambridge University Press.

Cowan, C. S. M., Callaghan, B. L., Kan, J. M., & Richardson, R. (2016). The lasting impact of early-life adversity on individuals and their descendants: Potential mechanisms and hope for intervention. *Genes, Brain and Behavior, 15*(1), 155–168.

Decety, J., Lewis, K. L., & Cowell, J. M. (2015). Specific electrophysiological components disentangle affective sharing and empathic concern in psychopathy. *Journal of Neurophysiology, 114*(1), 493–504.

De Dreu, C. K., Greer, L. L., Van Kleef, G. A., Shalvi, S., & Handgraaf, M. J. (2011). Oxytocin promotes human ethnocentrism. *Proceedings of the National Academy of Sciences, 108*(4), 1262–1266.

de Waal, F. B. M., & Preston, S. D. (2017). Mammalian empathy: Behavioural manifestations and neural basis. *Nature Reviews Neuroscience, 18*, 498–509.

Dunbar, R. (2014). *Human evolution: A Pelican introduction.* Penguin.

Dunfield, K. A., & Kuhlmeier, V. A. (2013). Classifying prosocial behavior: Children's responses to instrumental need, emotional distress, and material desire. *Child Development, 84*, 1766–1776. https://doi.org/10.1111/cdev.12075

Ent, M. R., & Baumeister, R. F. (2015). Individual differences in guilt proneness affect how people respond to moral tradeoffs between harm avoidance and obedience to authority. *Personality and Individual Differences, 74*, 231–234.

Geary, D. C. (2000). Evolution and proximate expression of human paternal investment. *Psychological Bulletin, 126*(1), 55.

Gilbert, P. (1989). *Human nature and suffering.* Routledge.

Gilbert, P. (1998). What is shame? Some core issues and controversies. In P. Gilbert & B. Andrews (Eds.), *Shame: Interpersonal behavior, psychopathology and culture* (pp. 3–36). Oxford University Press.

Gilbert, P. (2000). Varieties of submissive behaviour: Their evolution and role in depression. In L. Sloman & P. Gilbert (Eds.), *Subordination and defeat: An evolutionary approach to mood disorders* (pp. 3–46). Lawrence Erlbaum Associates.

Gilbert, P. (2007). The evolution of shame as a marker for relationship security. In J. L. Tracy, R.W. Robins, & J. P Tangney (Eds.), *The self-conscious emotions: Theory and research* (pp. 283–309). Guilford Press.

Gilbert, P. (2017). Compassion as a social mentality: An evolutionary approach. In P. Gilbert (Ed.), *Compassion: Concepts, research and applications* (pp. 31–68). Routledge.

Gilbert. P. (2018). *Living like crazy* (2nd ed.). Annwyn House.

Gilbert, P. (2019). Distinguishing shame, humiliation and guilt: An evolutionary functional analysis and compassion focused Interventions. In C.-H. Mayer & E. Vanderheiden (Eds), *The bright side of shame* (pp. 413–432). Springer.

Gilbert, P. (2020). The evolution of prosocial behavior: From caring to compassion. In L. Workman, W. Reader, & J. H. Barkow (Eds.), *Cambridge handbook of evolutionary perspectives on human behavior* (pp. 419–435). Cambridge University Press.

Gilbert, P., & Mascaro, J. (2017). Compassion: Fears, blocks, and resistances: An evolutionary investigation. In E. M. Seppälä, E. Simon-Thomas, S. L. Brown, M. C. Worline, L. Cameron, & J. R. Doty (Eds.), *The Oxford handbook of compassion science* (pp. 399–420). Oxford University Press.

Goodall, J. (1990). *Through a window: Thirty years with the chimpanzees of Gnome*. Penguin.

Green, M., Kirby, J. N., & Nielsen, M. (2018). The cost of helping: An exploration of compassionate responding in children. *British Journal of Developmental Psychology, 36*, 673–678. doi: 10.1111/bjdp.12252

Hein, G., Silani, G., Preuschoff, K., Batson, C. D., & Singer, T. (2010). Neural responses to ingroup and outgroup members' suffering predict individual differences in costly helping. *Neuron, 68*, 149–160.

Hrdy, S. B. (2009). *Mothers and others: The evolutionary origins of mutual understanding*. Harvard University Press.

Hutson, S. P., Hall, J. M., & Pack, F. L. (2015). Survivor guilt. *Advances in Nursing Science, 38*(1), 20–33.

Julle-Danière, E., Whitehouse, J., Vrij, A., Gustafsson, E., & Waller, B. M. (2020). The social function of the feeling and expression of guilt. *Royal Society Open Science, 7*(12), 1–10, 200617.

Kessler, S. E. (2020). Why care: Complex evolutionary history of human healthcare networks. *Frontiers in Psychology, 11*, 199. doi:10.3389/fpsyg.2020.00199

Kumsta, R. (2019). The role of epigenetics for understanding mental health difficulties and its implications for psychotherapy research. *Psychology and Psychotherapy: Theory, Research and Practice, 92*(2), 190–207. doi: 10.1111/papt.12227

Leach, C. W., Spears, R., Branscombe, N. R., & Dossje, B. (2003). Malicious pleasure: Schadenfreude at the suffering of another group. *Journal of Personality and Social Psychology, 84*, 932–943.

Luyten, P., Campbell, C., Allison, E., & Fonagy, P. (2020). The mentalizing approach to psychopathology: State of the art and future directions. *Annual Review of Clinical Psychology, 16*, 297–325.

MacLean, R. B., Griffith, J. S., & McGee, M. V. (1985). Threadfin shad, Dorosoma petenense Günther, mortality: Causes and ecological implications in a south-eastern United States reservoir. *Journal of Fish Biology, 27*(1), 1–12.

Mayseless, O. (2016). *The caring motivation: An integrated theory*. Oxford University Press.

McGhee, K. E., & Bell, A. M. (2014). Paternal care in a fish: Epigenetics and fitness enhancing effects on offspring anxiety. *Proceedings of the Royal Society B: Biological Sciences, 281*(1794), 20141146.

Morey, R. A., McCarthy, G., Selgrade, E. S., Seth, S., Nasser, J. D., & LaBar, K. S. (2012). Neural systems for guilt from actions affecting self versus others. *Neuroimage, 60*, 683–692.

Narvaez. D. (2017). Evolution, child raising and compassionate morality. In P. Gilbert (Ed.), *Compassion: Concepts, research and applications* (pp. 31–68). Routledge.

O'Connor, L. E., Berry, J. W., Lewis, T. B., & Stiver, D. J. (2011). Empathy-based pathogenic guilt, pathological altruism, and psychopathology. In B. Oakley, A. Knafo, G. Madhavan, & D. S. Wilson (Eds.), *Pathological altruism* (pp. 10–30). Oxford University Press.

O'Connor, L. E, Berry, J. W., Weiss, J., & Gilbert, P. (2002). Guilt, fear, submission, and empathy in depression. *Journal of Affective Disorders, 71*, 19–27.

O'Connor, L. E., Berry, J. W., Weiss, J., Schweitzer, D., & Sevier, M. (2000). Survivor guilt, submissive behaviour and evolutionary theory: The down-side of winning in social competition. *British Journal of Medical Psychology, 73*, 519–530.

Porges, S. W. (2007). The polyvagal perspective. *Biological Psychology, 74*(2), 116–143.

Porges S. W. (2017). Vagal pathways: Portals to compassion. In E. M. Seppälä, E. Simon-Thomas, S. L. Brown, & M. C. Worline, (Eds.), *The Oxford handbook of compassion science* (pp. 189–202). Oxford University Press.

Preston, S. D. (2013). The origins of altruism in offspring care. *Psychological Bulletin, 139*, 1305–1341.

Ribeiro da Silva, D., Rijo, D., Castilho, P., & Gilbert, P. (2019). The efficacy of a compassion-focused therapy–based intervention in reducing psychopathic traits and disruptive behavior: A clinical case study with a juvenile detainee. *Clinical Case Studies*, *18*(5), 323–343.

Riberio da Silva, D. R., Rijo, D., Salekin, R. T., Paulo, M., Miguel, R., & Gilbert, P. (2020). Clinical change in psychopathic traits after the PSYCHOPATHY. COMP program: Preliminary findings of a controlled trial with male detained youth. *Journal of Experimental Criminology*, *17*(3), 397–421.

Ricard, M. (2015). *Altruism: The power of compassion to change yourself and the world*. Atlantic Books.

Shirtcliff, E. A., Vitacco, M. J., Graf, A. R., Gostisha, A. J., Merz, J. L., & Zahn-Waxler, C. (2009). Neurobiology of empathy and callousness: Implications for the development of antisocial behavior. *Behavioral Sciences and the Law*, *27*, 137–171. doi: 10.1002/bsl.862

Spikins, P. (2015). *How compassion made us human: The evolutionary origins of tenderness, trust and morality*. Spear and Sword Books.

Spikins, P. (2017). Prehistoric origins the compassion of far distant strangers. In P. Gilbert (Ed.), *Compassion: Concepts, research and applications* (pp. 16–30). Routledge.

Suddendorf, T. (2018). Two key features created the human mind: Inside our heads. *Scientific American*, *319*(3), 42–47.

Sznycer, D., Tooby, J., Cosmides, L., Porat, R., Shalvi, S., & Halperin, E. (2016). Shame closely tracks the threat of devaluation by others, even across cultures. *Proceedings of the National Academy of Sciences*, *113*(10), 2625–2630.

Sznycer, D., Xygalatas, D., Agey, E., Alami, S., An, X. F., Ananyeva, K. I., Atkinson, Q. D., Broitman, B. R., Conte, T. J., Flores, C., Fukushima, S., Hitokoto, H., Kharitonov, A. N., Onyishi, C. N., Onyishi, I. E., Romero, P. P., Schrock, J. M., Snodgrass, J. J., Sugiyama, L. S, . . . Tooby, J. (2018). Cross-cultural invariances in the architecture of shame. *Proceedings of the National Academy of Sciences*, *115*(39), 9702–9707.

Tangney, J. P., & Dearing, R. L. (2003). *Shame and guilt*. Guilford Press.

Van Ness, D. W., & Strong, K. H. (2014). *Restoring justice: An introduction to restorative justice*. Routledge.

Vu, L., Soraperra, I., Leib, M., van der Weele, J., & Shalvi, S. (2023). Ignorance by choice: A meta-analytic review of the underlying motives of willful ignorance and its consequences. *Psychological Bulletin*, *149* (9-10), 611–635.

Wang, S. (2005). A conceptual framework for integrating research related to the physiology of compassion and the wisdom of Buddhist teachings. *Compassion: Conceptualisations, Research and Use in Psychotherapy*, *75*, 120.

Warneken, F., & Tomasello, M. (2006). Altruistic helping in human infants and young chimpanzees. *Science*, *311*, 1301. https://doi.org/10.1126/science.1121448

Watts, D. P. (2020). Responses to dead and dying conspecifics and heterospecifics by wild mountain gorillas (*Gorilla beringei beringei*) and chimpanzees (*Pan troglodytes schweinfurthii*). *Primates*, *61*(1), 55–68.

Witvliet, C. V. O., Worthington, E. L., Jr., Root, L. M., Sato, A. F., Ludwig, T. E., & Exline, J. J. (2008). Retributive justice, restorative justice, and forgiveness: An experimental psychophysiology analysis. *Journal of Experimental Social Psychology*, *44*, 10–25.

Wright, N., Hill, J., Sharp, H., & Pickles, A. (2018). Maternal sensitivity to distress, attachment and the development of callous-unemotional traits in young children. *Journal of Child Psychology and Psychiatry*, *59*(7), 790–800.

Xu, H., Bègue, L., & Bushman, B. J. (2012). Too fatigued to care: Ego depletion, guilt, and prosocial behavior. *Journal of Experimental Social Psychology*, *48*(5), 1183–1186.

Yu, H., Hu, J., Hu, L., & Zhou, X. (2014). The voice of conscience: neural bases of interpersonal guilt and compensation. *Social Cognitive and Affective Neuroscience*, *9*(8), 1150–1158.

Zahn-Waxler, C., Radke-Yarrow, M., Wagner, E., & Chapman, M. (1992). Development of concern for others. *Developmental Psychology*, *28*, 126–136.

CHAPTER 16

Lassitude: A Coordination System to Support Host Immunity

Joshua M. Schrock, Lawrence S. Sugiyama, and J. Josh Snodgrass

> **Abstract**
> Infectious disease is a powerful force of selection. Perpetual exposure to pathogens throughout evolutionary history has driven the evolution of multiple mechanisms that promote host survival in the face of disease. The highly conserved innate immune system is deployed in response to a wide variety of pathologies, including infection, injury, and toxin exposure. Activation of the innate immune system triggers a coordinated set of neuropsychological changes that help the host mount an effective immune response. These regulatory changes generate the experience of feeling sick. The authors of this chapter use the term *lassitude* to describe the superordinate coordinating program (i.e., emotion) that coordinates motivational and behavioral responses to disease. Lassitude is triggered by a reliably occurring situation (i.e., disease) and it orchestrates other mechanisms (e.g., appetite, fatigue, nausea, pain, and thermoregulatory motivation) to help solve the adaptive problems that arise when the innate immune response is activated to fight disease.
>
> **Key Words:** evolutionary medicine, disease, survival, immunity, motivation

Infectious disease is a major cause of morbidity and mortality for most complex organisms, including humans (Hart, 1990; Hill et al., 2007; Knoll & Carroll, 1999; Sugiyama, 2004; Vos et al., 2020). The perpetual threat of infectious disease exerts a powerful selection pressure favoring host adaptations for avoiding, tolerating, or resisting infection (Cepon-Robins et al., 2021; Horns & Hood, 2012; Lieberman et al., 2018). The human immune system is a collection of evolved mechanisms for detecting, neutralizing, and eliminating pathogens (Akira et al., 2006; Cooper & Alder, 2006; McDade et al., 2016). Many aspects of vertebrate immune function are highly conserved (Adelman & Martin, 2009; Boehm, 2012), and human immune systems are remarkably similar to those of nonhuman primates and other mammals (Plaza et al., 2020; Shay et al., 2013).

A substantial body of literature suggests that animals, including humans, behave in ways that support immune function when sick (Adelman & Martin, 2009; Dantzer & Kelley, 2007; Hart, 1990; Shattuck & Muehlenbein, 2015). A variety of factors (e.g., host metabolic state, diet, developmental pathogen exposure, ambient temperature, environmental stressors) can influence the efficacy of the immune response (Kluger et al., 1975; Lopes et al., 2014; Murray & Murray, 1979; Schrock et al., 2019). Host behavior plays a key role in optimizing conditions for immune function (Adelman & Martin, 2009; Dantzer & Kelley, 2007; Hart, 1990; Shattuck & Muehlenbein, 2015). For example, some animals seek out warmer microclimates during infection (Hetem et al., 2008; Kluger, 1979), and inhabiting warmer microclimates when sick improves survival rates in experimental studies (Boltana et al., 2013; Kluger et al., 1975). Multiple species, including humans, eat less when sick (MacDonald et al., 2014; Shattuck & Muehlenbein, 2015), and an experiment with mice demonstrated that eating less when fighting infection improves survival rates (Murray & Murray, 1979).

The availability of immunity-promoting behaviors presents a coordination problem. On one hand, these behaviors might reduce the risk of dying from infectious disease. On the other hand, these behaviors can impose substantial opportunity costs. For example, indiscriminate resting behavior could cause the resting individual to unnecessarily miss critical cues of predation risk. Indiscriminate warmth-seeking could cause the warmth-seeker to unnecessarily miss out on resource-rich foraging patches.

The mind comprises many different adaptations, each functionally specialized to solve a particular adaptive problem. As Cosmides and Tooby (2000, p. 92) explain, this in itself poses an additional kind of adaptive problem: "Programs that are individually designed to solve specific adaptive problems could, if simultaneously activated, deliver outputs that conflict with one another, interfering with or nullifying each other's functional products." Continuing to focus on digging up tubers to satisfy hunger, for example, could be disastrous in the face of a stalking lion. Lack of a superordinate system to prioritize and coordinate responses to the stalking lion instead of continuing to forage for tubers could well be fatal. In fact, many adaptive problems are best solved via coordination of many different subprograms, including, in the case of a stalking lion, orientation and attention to the predator, rapid assessment of its distance, direction of travel, whether it has spotted one, decreased or elevated heart rate depending on the imminence of the threat, and downregulation of hunger, digestion, and other less immediately fitness-consequential processes (Al-Shawaf, 2016). As in this instance of vigilance and preparedness for fight or flight (Stein & Nesse, 2011), superordinate regulatory adaptations are required to coordinate different suites of mechanisms in response to particular adaptive problems, including their activation and deactivation in response to particular cues that the relevant adaptive problem is present. On this view, emotions are superordinate programs that coordinate subordinate adaptations, and deactivate alternate emotions that organize competing responses. They include subroutines that monitor for ancestrally relevant cues indicating the target adaptive problem is present, that activate when they detect the defining cues of their target adaptive problem above a problem-specific threshold, and that coordinate activation of subordinate physiological, psychological, and behavioral mechanisms, while deactivating or downregulating others (Al-Shawaf et al., 2016; Al-Shawaf & Lewis, 2017; Cosmides & Tooby, 2000; Nesse, 1990; Tooby & Cosmides, 1990, 2008) (see Tooby & Cosmides, Chapter 2 in this volume).

In previous work, we described a superordinate program that coordinates multiple adaptations in response to infection (Schrock et al., 2019). We call this program "lassitude" and we show it has the defining characteristics of an emotion (see Box 16.1). Lassitude scans for cues indicating immune activation. When it detects cues of immune activation, it upregulates motivational variables that are useful for supporting immunity (e.g., warmth-seeking, resting) and downregulates motivations that are detrimental to immunity (hunger, sexual motivation).

Here we introduce the situation-defining cues that trigger lassitude and provide examples of motivational variables that are modulated by lassitude. Many of the motivational changes that occur in response to immune activation are phylogenetically conserved (Adelman & Martin, 2009; Schrock et al., 2019; Shattuck & Muehlenbein, 2016), and many of the empirical examples in this chapter are drawn from studies of animal models. When available, we also

> **Box 16.1** A Note on Terminology
>
> In this chapter, and in previous work, we use the term "lassitude" to refer to the superordinate program that scans for cues of immune activation and orchestrates regulatory changes to support immunity when cues of immune activation are detected (Schrock et al., 2019). Lassitude is closely related to "sickness behavior," which is a term used to describe the behavioral changes that animals (including humans) frequently exhibit during infection (Adelman & Martin, 2009; Dantzer & Kelley, 2007; Hart, 1990; Shattuck & Muehlenbein, 2015). We choose a different term in order to distinguish the superordinate program "lassitude" from its behavioral outputs in sickness behavior. This is, in some ways, parallel to the difference in meaning between the terms "hunger" (a coordinating mechanism) and "feeding behavior" (one of its behavioral outputs) (Al-Shawaf, 2016; Pelot & Grill, 2018). We elected not to call the superordinate program "sickness" because this term is often used as a synonym for illness or disease, which may lead readers to confuse the underlying pathology with host's regulatory response to that pathology. We also wanted to avoid naming the superordinate program after any term that is commonly used in contemporary medicine to describe a symptom (e.g., fatigue, malaise). In using the term "lassitude," we do not intend to diminish the importance of the groundbreaking research that has been conducted on sickness behavior. Indeed, we draw heavily on the sickness behavior literature throughout this chapter, because in many ways it defines or describes some of the key behavioral outputs of lassitude. "Lassitude" is a term no longer in everyday use, defined as: "(1) a condition of weariness or debility; (2) a condition characterized by lack of interest, energy, or spirit" (Merriam-Webster Online Dictionary, 2021). The term "lassitude" has occasionally been used in the medical literature to refer to persistent fatigue or tiredness, although this use of the term is now rare (Solberg, 1984). Our use of the term "lassitude" goes beyond these definitions. Using an archaic term provides us greater freedom to describe the superordinate regulatory program to the reader, without having to carry the conceptual baggage of other commonly used terms (e.g., "sickness").

give examples from human studies. Along the way, we consider how the motivational changes induced by immune activation can give rise to the subjective experience of being sick.

Situation-Defining Cues That Activate Lassitude

The vertebrate immune system includes generalized mechanisms that are effective against a wide variety of pathogens (i.e., the "innate" immune system) (Akira et al., 2006). It also includes cellular memory-based responses that are tailored to specific pathogens (i.e., the "acquired" immune system) (Cooper & Alder, 2006). While this division of the immune system into innate and acquired domains is an oversimplification, it is nonetheless useful for introducing the costs and benefits of different immune mechanisms (McDade et al., 2016). Innate immune responses (e.g., fever, inflammation) can activate quickly but are more calorically costly and tend to cause greater collateral damage to the host (Akira et al., 2006; McDade et al., 2016). Acquired immune responses are less calorically costly and cause less damage to the host, but immunological memory takes time to develop (Cooper & Alder, 2006; McDade et al., 2016).

The initial response to an invading pathogen (i.e., the acute phase response) is dominated by innate immune mechanisms, including systemic inflammation (Akira et al., 2006; Dantzer & Kelley, 2007). Inflammation facilitates the destruction and removal of invading entities that damage cells, as well as the removal of damaged and necrotic cells themselves (Medzhitov, 2008). A key function of the acute phase response is to keep the host alive long enough for acquired immunity to develop. The motivational changes induced by immune activation are most prominent during the acute phase response. The acute phase response typically subsides following an immune challenge. However, sustained activation of acute phase mechanisms (e.g., chronic systemic inflammation) is involved in the pathogenesis of various chronic conditions such as cardiovascular disease, rheumatoid arthritis, and some cancers (Kotas & Medzhitov, 2015). Chronic lassitude, driven by sustained activation of the acute phase response, may play a role in some of the psychiatric comorbidities of chronic disease, such as persistent fatigue and depression (Swain, 2000; Wells et al., 1988).

Many of our cells are equipped with pattern recognition receptors that evolved to detect molecular cues indicating the invasion of pathogenic entities (e.g., infectious microbes, toxins, damaged cells) (Akira et al., 2006). These molecular cues of pathology include pathogen-associated molecular patterns (PAMPs) and damage-associated molecular patterns (DAMPs) (El Chamy et al., 2008; Roh & Sohn, 2018). When cell pattern-recognition receptors detect the presence of PAMPs or DAMPs, they trigger the production and dispersal of pro-inflammatory cytokines from the cell (Oberholzer et al., 2000). These pro-inflammatory cytokines function as signaling peptides that carry activation signals to other cells in the body, which leads to a rapid systemic immune response when pro-inflammatory cytokines are produced at sufficient levels (McCusker & Kelley, 2013).

One type of PAMP that is recognized by our immune system is found on lipopolysaccharide (LPS), a molecule that forms part of the outer membrane of gram-negative bacteria (e.g., *E. coli*) (Raetz & Whitfield, 2002). Treatment with LPS, even without a live pathogen attached, triggers systemic pro-inflammatory cytokine production, which leads to classic signs of acute infection, including elevated body temperature, reduced food intake, and increased lethargy (Dantzer & Kelley, 2007; McCusker & Kelley, 2013). Treatment with LPS is the most common method of experimentally inducing the acute phase response, which includes systemic inflammation and the classic symptoms and behavioral changes associated with sickness (Lasselin, Lekander, et al., 2020). Many of the empirical studies cited in this chapter use LPS administration to experimentally induce sickness behavior.

Inflammation is a key mechanism involved in destroying and clearing invading pathogens, but inflammatory immune responses also produce a certain level of "friendly fire" that leads to collateral damage in host cells (Pawelec et al., 2014). The brain is largely shielded from pathogens and inflammatory damage by the blood-brain barrier, a wall of endothelial cells separating the blood supply from the brain (Abbott et al., 2010). Nevertheless, the central nervous system monitors signals of pro-inflammatory activity in peripheral tissues (McCusker & Kelley, 2013). These pro-inflammatory signals can reach the brain through multiple pathways, including afferent signaling via the vagus nerve (Pavlov & Tracey, 2012), selective diffusion of signaling molecules across the blood-brain barrier (Erickson et al., 2020), and active transport of signaling molecules across the blood-brain barrier (Pan et al., 2011). The pro-inflammatory signals that reach the brain provide a set of situation-defining cues that trigger the motivational, perceptual, and behavioral changes characteristic of lassitude (Adelman & Martin, 2009; McCusker & Kelley, 2013; Schrock et al., 2019). These cues operate in a dose-dependent manner. Above a certain threshold, greater pro-inflammatory signaling leads to greater changes in motivation and behavior (Grigoleit et al., 2011).

Motivational Variables Regulated by Lassitude

When the lassitude program detects cues of immune activation, it triggers a series of shifts in a variety of key motivational systems. In the sections below, we describe how lassitude changes the expected values of the following motivations and behaviors: *movement/rest, warmth-seeking, consumption, mating, parental effort, threat avoidance, care-seeking*, and *signaling vulnerability* (Figure 16.1). To achieve context-sensitive regulation, each motivational system that receives input from the lassitude program must weigh the immunological benefits of the motivational change against its opportunity costs.

One of the key challenges in the fight against infection is to devote enough energetic resources to fund energetically costly acute phase immune response, while still maintaining other somatic functions that are critical for survival (McDade et al., 2016). Every 1°C increase in body temperature during febrile infection increases resting metabolic rate (RMR, the energy consumed by the body at rest) by about 13% (Del Bene, 1990). Even non-febrile

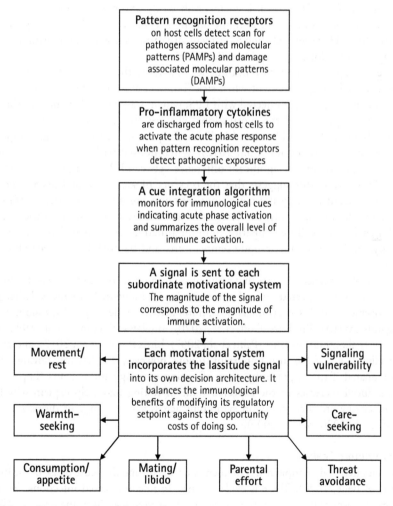

Figure 16.1. A schematic overview of the lassitude system.

upper respiratory tract infection can increase RMR by 8%–14% (Muehlenbein et al., 2010). These figures likely underestimate the actual energy costs of immune activation, as they do not account for energetic savings from temporary reductions in other energetically expensive domains of somatic effort, such as the production and maintenance of skeletal muscle (Blackwell et al., 2010; Garcia et al., 2020; Urlacher et al., 2018; van Heeckeren et al., 2000). Many of the motivational changes that occur during infection contribute, directly or indirectly, to the overarching goal of funding the high energy costs of the acute phase immune response (Shattuck & Muehlenbein, 2015).

Effects on Movement and Rest

Movement is a key part of everyday life for all vertebrates, including humans. Movement is required to carry out key life activities, including subsistence, exploration, parental investment, mating, and other social interactions (Munroe et al., 1983; Pollard & Blumstein, 2008). Vertebrates, including humans, tend to move less and rest more when sick (i.e., when the immune system is activated to fight infection) (Lasselin, Karshikoff, et al., 2020; Shattuck & Muehlenbein, 2015). Movement is energetically costly, and reducing movement increases the energetic resources available for immune function (Pontzer et al., 2016; Snodgrass, 2012; Westerterp, 2017). However, reducing movement also carries substantial opportunity costs, as movement is required for a variety of key life activities.

A series of experiments with zebra finches illustrated the trade-off between the costs and benefits of reducing movement when sick (Lopes et al., 2012; Lopes et al., 2014). In these experiments, birds were injected with LPS, which is a powerful inducer of the acute-phase immune response and the motivational changes that accompany immune activation. When housed alone, LPS-treated individuals spent more time resting compared to placebo-treated controls (Lopes et al., 2012). When housed with social competitors and potential mates, there was no significant difference between LPS- and placebo-treated animals in activity levels. This suggests that the presence of social competitors and potential mates was a sufficiently strong alternative motivation to counteract the lethargy of immune activation. In a follow-up study, the birds who spent more time resting in the aftermath of the LPS challenge exhibited superior immune function, as measured by bacterial killing capacity, ability to modulate body temperature, and haptoglobin-like activity (Lopes et al., 2014).

The available evidence suggests that acute phase immune activation is energetically costly and that it reduces the expected value of movement in sick individuals. Increased lethargy (i.e., reduced movement) in sick individuals is common across a wide range of taxonomic groups including humans (Lasselin, Karshikoff, et al., 2020), monkeys (Friedman et al., 1996), ungulates (Hetem et al., 2008), rodents (Palin et al., 2007), birds (Lopes et al., 2012), and amphibians (Llewellyn et al., 2011). It is important to note, however, that lethargy during infection can be attenuated if the opportunity costs of resting outweigh the benefits (Lopes, 2014). Lassitude-induced increases in the expected value of resting may help explain why fatigue and loss of energy are such common symptoms across a wide range of diseases (Lasselin, Karshikoff, et al., 2020; Swain, 2000).

Effects on Warmth-Seeking

Fever (i.e., elevated body temperature) frequently occurs during the acute phase of the immune response (Del Bene, 1990). There is evidence that, in uncomplicated infections, fever is an adaptive mechanism that improves the efficacy of the acute phase immune response (Boltana et al., 2013; Kluger et al., 1975). Though the mechanisms that explain the immune benefits of fever are not fully understood, recent research suggests that fever may promote immunity in part by helping T-cells (critical mediators of the acute phase response) move toward the locations of invading pathogens (Lin et al., 2019).

One study illustrated the protective effects of fever by exposing rabbits to the potentially lethal pathogen *Pasteurella multocida* (Vaughn et al., 1980). Rabbits in one group were treated with an antipyretic (i.e., fever-suppressing) drug infused directly into the preoptic-anterior hypothalamus (to minimize interference with non-fever immune processes in the periphery) and rabbits in the other group were treated with a control solution at the same site. Animals in both groups exhibited fever, but fever in the antipyretic group was substantially reduced in the first few hours of acute infection. All of the rabbits in the antipyretic group died, whereas only 29% of the rabbits in the control group died, suggesting that the ability to mount a fever during the early stages of infection may promote survival. Importantly, none of the rabbits died that were treated with the antipyretic alone (without pathogen exposure).

One limitation of the rabbit study described above is that drugs that reduce fever may also interfere with non-fever aspects of the acute phase immune response. It is difficult to determine whether the observed survival benefit is attributable to blockade of fever or interference with some other unmeasured aspect of immune function.

Another informative line of evidence on fever and survival during infection comes from studies of ectothermic lizards, whose body temperature is largely determined by ambient temperature (Kluger, 1979). In lizards, body temperature can be experimentally manipulated by changing ambient temperature, thereby avoiding the unintended collateral effects on immune function that may occur with pharmacological methods of manipulating fever. Sick lizards exhibit "behavioral fever"—preferentially seeking out warmer environments when sick, leading to elevated body temperatures. In one experiment, researchers inoculated lizards with a potentially lethal pathogen (*Aeromonas hydrophila*) and housed lizards in low, neutral, or warm ambient temperatures (Kluger et al., 1975). The lizards housed in warmer conditions exhibited substantially higher survival rates.

Behavioral fever is not exclusive to ectotherms. For example, one study using remote tracking devices found that free-ranging greater kudu preferentially inhabit warmer microclimates when infected with an opportunistic infection (Hetem et al., 2008). Chills (i.e., subjective feelings of coldness, often accompanied by shaking) are a common symptom of infectious disease in humans (Holmqvist et al., 2020). Chills may motivate the host to seek a warmer environment/warmer microclimate in order to raise body temperature. Human cultural innovations, such as clothing (Toups et al., 2011) and control of fire (Hlubik et al., 2019), may have played an important role in reducing infectious disease mortality by reducing the energy cost of mounting a fever to fight infection.

Effects on Consumption

Food intake leads to net energy gain in the long term, but the upfront energy costs for digesting food are substantial (5%–15% of total energy expenditure, depending on diet composition) (Westerterp, 2004). Food intake temporarily increases resting metabolic rate by 20%–30%, returning to baseline 4–6 hours following a meal (Secor, 2009). If this period of high digestive cost overlaps with the acute-phase immune response to an invading pathogen, it could siphon a substantial quantity of energetic resources away from immune function during a critical phase of the fight against infection.

Reduced calorie intake and weight loss occur frequently during infection and have been described in a variety of species (Shattuck & Muehlenbein, 2015; van Heeckeren et al., 2000). To test the functional immune benefits of calorie restriction during infection, one study infected mice with a potentially lethal infectious pathogen (*Listeria monocytogenes*) (Murray & Murray, 1979). Mice in one experimental condition were intubated and force-fed to normal levels of calorie intake, while mice in the other experimental condition were sham-intubated without force-feeding and allowed to self-regulate their calorie intake. As expected, mice in the self-regulating condition reduced their calorie intake with the onset of infection and exhibited substantially lower mortality rates and shorter duration of illness than the force-fed group, suggesting that reduced calorie intake during illness plays an important role in supporting immunity.

Reduced calorie intake during infection is a double-edged sword—it appears to reduce the risk of mortality from potentially lethal infections, but it also increases the risk of death from starvation in hosts who are energetically depleted. An effective motivational system that regulates feeding must integrate information about both active immune challenges and the host's underlying metabolic state in order to balance these two risks.

One study provided an experimental example demonstrating that this integration of host metabolic information does indeed occur (MacDonald et al., 2014). They assigned rats to 28 days of 50% calorie restriction, 21 days of 50% calorie restriction, 14 days of 50% calorie restriction, or no calorie restriction. They then treated the animals with LPS to elicit an acute immune response and allowed animals in all conditions to self-regulate calorie intake. Rats who had not been calorie restricted exhibited substantial reductions in food intake when treated with LPS. Rats who experienced 28 days of calorie restriction exhibited no reductions in ad libitum food intake when treated with LPS, which likely reflected an elevated starvation risk. Rats who had faced calorie restriction for 21 or 14 days exhibited moderate reductions in ad libitum food intake when treated with LPS. This suggests that the motivational system that regulates feeding integrates information about both active immune challenges and the host's metabolic state when computing the expected value of calorie intake.

Calorie intake is not the only consumption parameter that changes during infection. Aka hunter-gatherer men of the Central African Republic experience endemic infection with soil-transmitted helminths (intestinal worms) (Roulette et al., 2014). Aka men also engage in high rates of tobacco smoking. A clinical trial found that treatment with anti-parasite medication led to reduced tobacco intake relative to placebo as indexed by levels of cotinine measured in saliva, suggesting that interoceptive cues arising from parasite infection play a role in motivating tobacco consumption in Aka men (Roulette et al., 2014). This may be due to the anti-parasitic properties of nicotine (Kohler, 2001). Along the same lines, selective consumption of plants with antiparasitic properties has been observed in multiple nonhuman primate species (Barelli & Huffman, 2017; Ghai et al., 2015; Huffman, 1997).

Another study found that Efe hunter-gatherer men spend less time hunting when sick, but actually spend more time in pursuit of honey (Bailey, 1991), which has known antimicrobial properties (Mandal & Mandal, 2011). The increased preference for honey when sick may also reflect sugar's low digestion costs (compared to proteins) and rapid availability as an energy source following ingestion (compared to both fats and proteins).

Some foods are more energetically costly to digest than others (Westerterp, 2004), and some foods are converted to available calories (i.e., blood glucose) more quickly than others (Franz, 1997). The metabolic cost of digestion is an "overhead" cost that reduces the energetic resources that are immediately available for immune function (Snodgrass, 2012). In fact, this overhead cost may be one reason why calorie intake reduces immune effectiveness. If an acutely sick host has available fat reserves, it is more efficient to fund the energy costs of immune function by mobilizing fat reserves instead of incurring the short-term metabolic costs of digesting food. In terms of the primary dietary macronutrients, fats have the lowest digestion costs, carbohydrates have intermediate digestion costs, and proteins have the highest digestion costs (Westerterp, 2004). Carbohydrates provide available energy (in the form of blood glucose) more quickly than do proteins or fats (Franz, 1997).

The ideal foods, if any, to eat when sick would be those that have low digestion costs and rapidly convert to available calories. In one experiment, rats were allowed to feed ad libitum on high-protein, high-carbohydrate, and high-fat foods. Rats treated with LPS or with a dose of pro-inflammatory cytokines reduced their overall calorie intake, but they increased relative consumption of carbohydrates and decreased relative consumption of proteins (Aubert et al., 1995). This study suggests that lassitude can induce not only changes in calorie intake but also changes in specific nutrient preferences. The increased relative preference for carbohydrates when sick may reflect carbohydrates' low digestion costs (compared to proteins) and rapid availability as an energy source following ingestion (compared to both fats and proteins).

This inflammation-induced relative preference for easily digestible carbohydrates may lead to a vicious self-perpetuating cycle in the context of chronic cardiometabolic conditions (e.g., diabetes, hypertension). Chronic activation of the acute-phase response (i.e., systemic inflammation) due to chronic conditions may lead to long-term increases in relative preferences for carbohydrate intake, which may further exacerbate the underlying chronic cardiometabolic conditions (Kotas & Medzhitov, 2015).

Another benefit of reducing food intake during infection is that it reduces the risk of acquiring a secondary foodborne infection at a time when the immune system is already facing a challenge. We hypothesize that sick individuals are even more avoidant of foods with cues indicating higher pathogen risk (e.g., meat, uncooked foods) compared to healthy individuals (Sherman & Flaxman, 2002). This sickness-induced change in the expected value of ingesting higher-risk foods may be one reason why nausea is such a common symptom in a variety of infectious diseases (Scorza et al., 2007).

Pathogen disgust is an emotion that motivates us to minimize unnecessary contact with potentially pathogenic substrates in the environment (Cepon-Robins et al., 2021; Lieberman et al., 2018; Tybur et al., 2009) (see Cepon-Robins, Chapter 9 in this volume). Given the high risks of contracting a secondary infection when our energetic resources are already occupied fighting a primary infection, we hypothesize that the activation of lassitude during illness also leads to temporary increases in disgust sensitivity (Al-Shawaf & Lewis, 2013; Cepon-Robins et al., 2021; Lieberman et al., 2018).

Effects on Mating

Differential reproduction is the core determinant of evolutionary fitness. Mating behavior, in sexually reproducing species, is an important determinant of differential reproduction. Life history theory examines the evolution of strategies that navigate trade-offs between current reproduction, survival, and future reproduction (Stearns, 1989). Investing in immune function, in order to increase the host's chances of surviving infection, is an investment in survival and future reproduction from a life history standpoint (Adelman & Martin, 2009; Clutton-Brock, 1984; Snodgrass, 2012; Sugiyama, 2004; Trivers, 1972). Lassitude is a mechanism that prioritizes immune function at the cost of current productive and reproductive behavior (e.g., foraging, exploration, mating) (Schrock et al., 2019).

Deploying behaviors to prioritize immune function at the cost of current reproduction is likely to provide the greatest payoff in species where individuals who survive a given bout of infection have strong possibilities of future reproduction. We therefore hypothesize that infection-related motivational changes are more pronounced in species (and life history stages) where the average residual reproductive value, contingent on surviving infection, is greater

(Adelman & Martin, 2009). Residual reproductive value is a function of current age, the probability of surviving to age x, the average number of offspring produced by an individual of age x, and the long-term population growth rate (Fisher, 1930).

The obligate energy costs of reproduction are greater for females, especially in mammals, where gestation and lactation consume a substantial proportion of the maternal energy budget for an extended period of time (Butte & King, 2005). Given the high energy costs and extended duration of the mammalian reproductive cycle, female reproductive function is particularly prone to disruption by energetic stressors (Ellison, 2009). The sex-differentiated energy costs of reproduction may have contributed to sex-differentiated selection pressures on the motivational systems that regulate sexual behavior.

Initiating a pregnancy when the prospective parent's metabolic resources are already strained (e.g., during active infection) may be, on average, riskier for females, who experience higher obligate energy costs of reproduction. Following this logic, we hypothesize that, during infection, female mammals exhibit greater reductions in sexual interest than do males. Potential sex differences in mating-related aspects of lassitude may have far-reaching clinical implications in contemporary societies where chronic inflammatory conditions are relatively common (Kotas & Medzhitov, 2015).

Sex differences in sexual motivation during immune activation were demonstrated in a study that treated male and female rats with a pro-inflammatory stimulus (LPS or a dose of pro-inflammatory cytokines) or a control solution prior to exposing them to a potential mate (Avitsur & Yirmiya, 1999). The pro-inflammatory stimuli caused females to exhibit substantial reductions in behaviors indicating sexual interest in the potential mate but did not attenuate these behaviors in males.

We are unaware of any studies that systematically investigate human sex differences in infection-induced libido changes. However, a study of patients with inflammatory bowel disease, which produces similar immunological cues to gastrointestinal infection, found that a greater proportion of female patients reported reduced sexual activity and reduced libido compared to male patients (Muller et al., 2010).

Effects on Parental Effort

The vigilance and movement involved in parental behavior is calorically costly. Reducing parental behavior during infection would make more energy available to support immune function, but it may also be detrimental to offspring survival. In general, we expect the level of parental effort during infection to balance the immune benefits of resting against the costs imposed by resting on offspring health, development, and survival.

Humans evolved to be cooperative breeders, with multiple people other than biological parents investing in juveniles (Burkart et al., 2009; Kramer & Otarola-Castillo, 2015; Lukas & Clutton-Brock, 2012). In subsistence forager and forager-horticulturalist societies, injury and illness have significant negative effects on productivity (Gurven et al., 2012; Sugiyama & Chacon, 2000). Provisioning to sick and injured bandmates is an important feature underwriting human life history (Gurven et al., 2000; Gurven et al., 2012; Sugiyama, 2004; Sugiyama & Scalise Sugiyama, 2003), with prehistoric archaeological evidence (Dickel & Doran, 1989; Tilley, 2015; Tilley & Oxenham, 2011; Trinkaus & Zimmerman, 1982) augmenting the observation in extant forager and forager-horticulturalist societies noted above. This leads to another prediction: that parental lassitude will also be sensitive to child need, own support, and the probable investments of alloparents. Children too are expected to be responsive to these sources of parental and alloparental care, and their ability to forage for themselves or obtain aid from others is thus expected to moderate the parental investment decisions (Sugiyama & Chacon 2000).

While providing parental care entails costs to the parent, it can also promote offspring survival and development (Klug & Bonsall, 2014). This trade-off between the fitness costs and benefits of parental investment has led to the evolution of complex motivational systems for regulating parental behavior in species, like humans, that provide parental care (Burkart et al., 2009; Kramer & Otarola-Castillo, 2015; Schaller, 2018; Trivers, 1972).

An experiment with mice illustrated the trade-off between the costs and benefits of providing parental care when sick (Aubert et al., 1997). Mouse dams who were caring for litters of newborn pups were treated with LPS or control and the ambient temperature was manipulated by the experimenter. At neutral ambient temperatures, LPS treatment led to reduced rates of nest-building behavior in the mouse dams. At colder temperatures, which represent a survival threat to mouse pups, who are practically ectothermic, the LPS-treated dams engaged in nearly the same level of nest-building behavior as the control dams. This suggests that the survival threat posed by cold temperatures was a sufficiently compelling alternative motivation to overcome the lethargy from being sick.

Anecdotally, it appears common for human parents to feel sick but to "power through" those feelings of sickness in order to continue providing parental care. This may be particularly likely in contexts where alloparents are unavailable or when there is a clear danger to the offspring. The degree to which sick individuals reduce parental behavior likely depends on the severity of the parent's illness, as well the potential costs of reducing parent effort. The costs of reducing parental effort are shaped by factors such as the child's degree of dependence, the presence and severity of environmental hazards, and the availability of social allies who can provide care.

Effects on Threat Avoidance
Threat detection and avoidance are critical for promoting survival (Stein & Nesse, 2011). However, threat avoidance can also be costly, potentially leading to missed opportunities for social interaction, mating, foraging, and other fitness-relevant behaviors. A motivational system whose function is to detect and avoid threats must balance the costs and benefits of threat avoidance. The importance of avoiding threat exposure may be greater than usual during infection. Acquiring a physical injury may carry an even higher mortality risk when the body's energetic resources are already diverted toward fighting infection.

This hypothesis has been supported by studies showing that sick individuals find threatening stimuli more aversive than do healthy individuals. For example, one study showed that rhesus monkeys treated with a dose of pro-inflammatory cytokines (which induces sickness) exhibit more agitated behavior in response to threatening behavior from a human experimenter compared to rhesus monkeys treated with a control solution (Friedman et al., 1996). Another study treated human participants with LPS (and a control solution) and performed neuroimaging while showing the participants images that varied in threat content (Inagaki et al., 2012). The LPS-treated individuals exhibited greater amygdala reactivity to images of social threats compared to the control-treated individuals.

These studies suggest that the expected value of threat avoidance is greater in sick individuals compared to healthy individuals, all else being equal. This may explain, at least in part, why humans often report stronger feelings of anxiety when sick (Lasselin et al., 2016).

Effects on Care-Seeking
Receiving care during illness is an important determinant of survival in humans. For example, the bioarchaeological record provides multiple examples of healed skeletal pathologies that would almost certainly have been fatal in the absence of care from someone else (Dickel & Doran, 1989; Tilley, 2015; Tilley & Oxenham, 2011; Trinkaus & Zimmerman, 1982).

A study of Shiwiar forager-horticulturalists found that most living individuals had experienced at least one health crisis that would likely have been fatal in the absence of aid from a conspecific (Sugiyama, 2004). Other studies in subsistence societies report similar findings (Gurven et al., 2000; Gurven et al., 2012).

Given the importance of receiving care when sick, we hypothesize that lassitude shifts the balance of relative social preferences to favor being in proximity to social allies, who are the most likely providers of care. In support of this hypothesis, a neuroimaging study found that LPS-treated individuals (vs. controls) reported greater desire to be with their loved ones and exhibited greater reward-related neural activity when looking at images of their loved ones (Inagaki et al., 2015).

Outward signs of illness (e.g., reduced locomotion, changes in facial expressions, changes in body language) may play a role in communicating to social allies that the host is in a vulnerable state and needs care (Axelsson et al., 2018; Schrock et al., 2019; Sundelin et al., 2015). It has been hypothesized that the placebo effect (e.g., improvement in symptoms simply from receiving care) may be explained by our motivation to receive care when sick (Steinkopf, 2015; Tiokhin, 2016). Improvement in symptoms after receiving care may provide a form of rewarding feedback that motivates continued care-seeking behavior from the sick individual and encourages continued effort from the caregiver.

The activation of lassitude may be an important input for other emotion programs that keep track of how much other people value us (pride, shame, guilt) (Sznycer, 2019) (Landers et al., Chapter 7 in this volume). Given that we often need care when we are sick, it would be especially costly when we are sick to engage in behaviors that cause other people to devalue us. We therefore hypothesize that sick individuals are even more attuned than usual to scenarios that would cause social allies to change their valuation of the sick person. Consistent with this hypothesis, a neuroimaging study found that participants who were treated with LPS (vs. a control solution) exhibited greater neural reactivity to both positive and negative social feedback (Muscatell et al., 2016).

Hagen and Syme (Chapter 59 in this volume) argue that depressive symptoms function to elicit greater investment from social allies. Eliciting investment from social allies during illness has been an important determinant of survival throughout human evolutionary history (Dickel & Doran, 1989; Gurven et al., 2012; Sugiyama, 2004; Tilley, 2015; Tilley & Oxenham, 2011; Trinkaus & Zimmerman, 1982). This may explain why the acute phase immune response has the capacity to trigger depressive symptoms (Lasselin, Schedlowski, et al., 2020; Stieglitz et al., 2015).

Effects on Signaling Vulnerability

Advertising outward signs of illness may be a double-edged sword. When directed at social allies, outward signs of illness may help us elicit care. But displaying outward signs of illness in the presence of a rival may prompt the rival to exploit the sick individual's vulnerable state (e.g., increased efforts to steal food/mates/territory or to undermine the sick individual's social standing). We hypothesize that sick individuals are motivated to mask outward signs of illness in situations where displaying vulnerability is costly (see also Cosmides & Tooby, 2000; Svetieva, Chapter 35 in this volume).

This principle has been illustrated by an experiment with male mice, where dominant and subordinate individuals were housed in pairs (Cohn & de Sa-Rocha, 2006). In this scenario, the dominant mouse represents a greater threat to the subordinate mouse than vice versa. When the dominant mice were made sick via LPS administration, they exhibited reduced movement, reflecting a motivational change that occurs frequently during infection. In contrast, when the subordinate mice were made sick via LPS administration, they did not reduce movement. The subordinate mice appear to have suppressed behavioral signs of illness, perhaps motivated by the high costs of displaying vulnerability in the presence of a dominant competitor.

Conclusions and Future Directions

In this chapter, we have proposed that lassitude is a coordinating mechanism (i.e., an "emotion") that scans for cues of immune activation. When cues of immune activation are detected, lassitude regulates key motivational systems, upregulating motivations that promote immune function and downregulating motivations that undermine immune function. When lassitude sends a signal to initiate a motivational adjustment, the motivational system integrates the input signal in a context-sensitive manner, balancing the benefits of making the motivational adjustment against its costs. Theoretical work on the evolution of the emotions has proposed that the emotions are superordinate programs that solve reliably occurring coordination problems (Al-Shawaf et al., 2016; Cosmides & Tooby, 2000; Nesse, 1990; Tooby & Cosmides, 1990, 2008) (see Tooby & Cosmides, Chapter 2 in this volume). Drawing on this theoretical perspective, we proposed in prior work that lassitude is an emotion (Schrock et al., 2019).

The evidence reviewed in this chapter suggests that lassitude is an evolved mechanism, but we are not arguing that lassitude always has adaptive consequences in every instance of its deployment. Some human adaptations that yielded net fitness benefits throughout most of our evolutionary history (e.g., metabolic systems that rapidly deposit body fat, effort systems that minimize unnecessary physical activity) have led to high rates of chronic cardiometabolic disease in contemporary environments where highly processed foods are readily available and demands for physical work are minimal (Corbett et al., 2018; Eaton & Eaton III, 2003; Eaton et al., 1988; Kuzawa, 1998; Lieberman, 2015). Lassitude may be subject to similar problems stemming from evolutionary mismatch. For example, chronic cardiometabolic diseases (e.g., diabetes, hypertension) may contribute to sustained low-grade activation of the acute phase immune response (i.e., systemic inflammation) (Kotas & Medzhitov, 2015). Sustained inflammation may lead to chronic lassitude, which includes fatigue and depressive symptoms (Swain, 2000; Wells et al., 1988). Chronic fatigue and depression may reduce physical activity and social engagement, which may further exacerbate the underlying chronic condition and contribute to the development of additional comorbidities (Ong et al., 2016; Warburton & Bredin, 2017). This vicious self-perpetuating cycle may contribute to the emergence of chronic disease epidemics in contemporary societies (Schrock, 2020).

It is worth noting that Del Giudice (Chapter 5 in this volume) extends theoretical perspectives on superordinate programs to distinguish between different classes of coordinating programs. In his classification system, emotions are first-order coordinating programs, motivational systems are second-order coordination programs that coordinate multiple emotions, and moods are third-order coordination programs that coordinate multiple motivational systems. He proposes that lassitude is best characterized as a third-order superordinate program, or mood, that coordinates multiple motivational systems in response to cues of immune activation. It is beyond the scope of this chapter to situate lassitude within Del Giudice's extended framework, but we believe his theoretical refinement provides promising directions for future research on superordinate programs.

Systematic comparative studies are needed to determine which aspects of lassitude are broadly conserved across species and which aspects of lassitude are derived features. One study compared responses to LPS treatment between rodents and humans and reported broadly similar patterns, but rodent studies assessed the effects of LPS using behavioral paradigms, and human studies largely used subjective reports (Lasselin, Schedlowski, et al., 2020). Standardized behavioral measures are needed to facilitate the comparison of lassitude across species.

The clearest evidence for many of the motivational changes induced by lassitude comes from experimental studies using animal models. However, it is worth noting that using safe doses of LPS to experimentally induce lassitude and sickness behavior has become increasingly well established as a research paradigm in humans (Lasselin, Lekander, et al., 2020). Furthermore, a psychometric instrument for measuring the motivational changes that occur during immune activation has been developed that is sufficiently sensitive to capture the effects of low-dose LPS treatment, at least in the limited range of samples where it has been tested (Andreasson et al., 2018). These developments have contributed to a growing field of experimental research on lassitude and sickness behavior in humans. The geographic bias in study samples for human behavioral and biological research has been well documented (Gurven & Lieberman, 2020; Henrich et al., 2010). Research on lassitude and sickness behavior is no exception to this pattern. Research is needed to characterize human lassitude and sickness behavior in a broader range of cultures and ecologies.

The evidence reviewed in this chapter suggests that lassitude is a superordinate program that scans for cues of immune activation, and when these cues are detected, selectively modulates motivational variables in ways that promote immunity. Lassitude has coevolved with pathogens, and some pathogen lineages may evolve strategies to circumvent lassitude or even manipulate lassitude for their own ends. For example, some pathogens initially parasitize a prey species and then complete their life cycle in a predator that consumes the initial host (Lafferty & Shaw, 2013). In this scenario, infection-induced lethargy in the prey species may increase the risk of predation, thereby providing a benefit to the pathogen that comes at a cost to the lethargic host.

Lassitude has also coevolved with cognitive mechanisms for responding to sick individuals (Steinkopf, 2015; Tiokhin, 2016). Detecting signs of illness in a conspecific can trigger pathogen-avoidance disgust (Lieberman et al., 2018) (see Cepon-Robins, Chapter 9 in this volume; Steinkopf, Chapter 33 in this volume), but these signs of illness can also trigger a motivation to provide care. This introduces a potential motivational conflict (Al-Shawaf et al., 2016) in which pathogen-avoidance disgust promotes avoidance of the sick person, while the motivation to provide care promotes approaching the sick person. The cognitive mechanisms that navigate this approach–avoidance conflict have yet to be elaborated. This conflict between approaching and avoiding a sick person highlights a broader point—evolved coordination mechanisms (i.e., emotions) must be exquisitely context sensitive in order to generate coherent functional outputs (Al-Shawaf et al., 2019).

Lassitude is the product of a long history of coevolution between hosts, pathogens, and social conspecifics. Developing a comprehensive picture of lassitude and its evolution will require a combination of mathematical/computational modeling, mechanistic experiments, field research, and comparative studies. This will require collaboration between scholars in different fields, including evolutionary biology, psychology, anthropology, behavioral ecology, and neuroscience. The literature on lassitude and sickness behavior is already moving toward an integrated approach (Lasselin, Schedlowski, et al., 2020; Schrock et al., 2019; Shattuck & Muehlenbein, 2016). We believe that this field of study provides an important opportunity to demonstrate how evolutionary approaches to the emotions can add value to research on human psychology, biology, and behavior.

References

Abbott, N. J., Patabendige, A. A., Dolman, D. E., Yusof, S. R., & Begley, D. J. (2010). Structure and function of the blood-brain barrier. *Neurobiology of Disease, 37*(1), 13–25. doi: 10.1016/j.nbd.2009.07.030

Adelman, J. S., & Martin, L. B. (2009). Vertebrate sickness behaviors: Adaptive and integrated neuroendocrine immune responses. *Integrative and Comparative Biology, 49*(3), 202–214.

Akira, S., Uematsu, S., & Takeuchi, O. (2006). Pathogen recognition and innate immunity. *Cell, 124*(4), 783–801.

Al-Shawaf, L. (2016). The evolutionary psychology of hunger. *Appetite, 105*, 591–595.

Al-Shawaf, L., Conroy-Beam, D., Asao, K., & Buss, D. M. (2016). Human emotions: An evolutionary psychological perspective. *Emotion Review, 8*(2), 173–186. doi: 10.1177/1754073914565518

Al-Shawaf, L., & Lewis, D. M. (2017). Evolutionary psychology and the emotions. In Virgil Zeigler-Hill & Todd K. Shackelford (Eds.), *Encyclopedia of personality and individual differences* (pp. 1–10). Springer Nature Switzerland AG.

Al-Shawaf, L., & Lewis, D. M. G. (2013). Exposed intestines and contaminated cooks: Sex, stress, & satiation predict disgust sensitivity. *Personality and Individual Differences, 54*(6), 698–702. doi: 10.1016/j.paid.2012.11.016

Al-Shawaf, L., Lewis, D. M. G., Wehbe, Y. S., & Buss, D. M. (2019). Context, environment, and learning in evolutionary psychology. In Todd K Shackelford & Viviana A. Weekes-Shackelford (Eds.), *Encyclopedia of evolutionary psychological science* (pp. 1–12). Springer Nature Switzerland AG.

Andreasson, A., Wicksell, R. K., Lodin, K., Karshikoff, B., Axelsson, J., & Lekander, M. (2018). A global measure of sickness behaviour: Development of the Sickness Questionnaire. *Journal of Health Psychology, 23*(11), 1452–1463. doi: 10.1177/1359105316659917

Aubert, A., Goodall, G., & Dantzer, R. (1995). Compared effects of cold ambient temperature and cytokines on macronutrient intake in rats. *Physiology and Behavior, 57*(5), 869–873.

Aubert, A., Goodall, G., Dantzer, R., & Gheusi, G. (1997). Differential effects of lipopolysaccharide on pup retrieving and nest building in lactating mice. *Brain, Behavior, and Immunity, 11*(2), 107–118.

Avitsur, R., & Yirmiya, R. (1999). The immunobiology of sexual behavior: Gender differences in the suppression of sexual activity during illness. *Pharmacology, Biochemistry and Behavior, 64*(4), 787–796.

Axelsson, J., Sundelin, T., Olsson, M. J., Sorjonen, K., Axelsson, C., Lasselin, J., & Lekander, M. (2018). Identification of acutely sick people and facial cues of sickness. *Proceedings of the Royal Society B: Biological Sciences, 285*(1870), 20172430. doi: 10.1098/rspb.2017.2430

Bailey, R. C. (1991). *The behavioral ecology of Efe Pygmy men in the Ituri Forest, Zaire*. University of Michigan Museum.

Barelli, C., & Huffman, M. A. (2017). Leaf swallowing and parasite expulsion in Khao Yai white-handed gibbons (Hylobates lar), the first report in an Asian ape species. *American Journal of Primatology, 79*(3), 1–7.

Blackwell, A. D., Snodgrass, J. J., Madimenos, F. C., & Sugiyama, L. S. (2010). Life history, immune function, and intestinal helminths: Trade-offs among immunoglobulin E, C-reactive protein, and growth in an Amazonian population. *American Journal of Human Biology, 22*(6), 836–848.

Boehm, T. (2012). Evolution of vertebrate immunity. *Current Biology, 22*(17), R722–R732.

Boltana, S., Rey, S., Roher, N., Vargas, R., Huerta, M., Huntingford, F. A., Goetz, F. W., Moore, J., Garcia-Valtanen, P., Estepa, A., & MacKenzie, S. (2013). Behavioural fever is a synergic signal amplifying the innate immune response. *Proceedings of the Royal Society of London B: Biological Sciences, 280*(1766), 20131381.

Burkart, J. M., Hrdy, S. B., & Van Schaik, C. P. (2009). Cooperative breeding and human cognitive evolution. *Evolutionary Anthropology: Issues, News, and Reviews, 18*(5), 175–186. doi: https://doi.org/10.1002/evan.20222

Butte, N. F., & King, J. C. (2005). Energy requirements during pregnancy and lactation. *Public Health Nutrition, 8*(7A), 1010–1027.

Cepon-Robins, T. J., Blackwell, A. D., Gildner, T. E., Liebert, M. A., Urlacher, S. S., Madimenos, F. C., Eick, G. N., Snodgrass, J. J., & Sugiyama, L. S. (2021). Pathogen disgust sensitivity protects against infection in a high pathogen environment. *PNAS Proceedings of the National Academy of Sciences of the United States of America, 118*(8). doi: 10.1073/pnas.2018552118

Clutton-Brock, T. H. (1984). Reproductive effort and terminal investment in iteroparous animals. *The American Naturalist, 123*(2), 212–229. doi: 10.1086/284198

Cohn, D. W., & de Sa-Rocha, L. C. (2006). Differential effects of lipopolysaccharide in the social behavior of dominant and submissive mice. *Physiology and Behavior, 87*(5), 932–937.

Cooper, M. D., & Alder, M. N. (2006). The evolution of adaptive immune systems. *Cell, 124*(4), 815–822.

Corbett, S., Courtiol, A., Lummaa, V., Moorad, J., & Stearns, S. (2018). The transition to modernity and chronic disease: Mismatch and natural selection. *Nature Reviews Genetics, 19*(7), 419–430.

Cosmides, L., & Tooby, J. (2000). Evolutionary psychology and the emotions. *Handbook of emotions, 2*(2), 91–115.

Dantzer, R., & Kelley, K. W. (2007). Twenty years of research on cytokine-induced sickness behavior. *Brain, Behavior, and Immunity, 21*(2), 153–160.

Del Bene, V. E. (1990). Temperature. In H. K. Walker, W. D. Hall, & J. W. Hurst (Eds.), *Clinical methods: The history, physical, and laboratory examinations*. Butterworths. https://www.ncbi.nlm.nih.gov/books/NBK201/

Dickel, D. N., & Doran, G. H. (1989). Severe neural tube defect syndrome from the Early Archaic of Florida. *American Journal of Physical Anthropology, 80*(3), 325–334.

Eaton, S. B., & Eaton III, S. B. (2003). An evolutionary perspective on human physical activity: Implications for health. *Comparative Biochemistry & Physiology. Part A, Molecular & Integrative Physiology, 136*(1), 153–159.

Eaton, S. B., Konner, M., & Shostak, M. (1988). Stone agers in the fast lane: Chronic degenerative diseases in evolutionary perspective. *American Journal of Medicine, 84*(4), 739–749.

El Chamy, L., Leclerc, V., Caldelari, I., & Reichhart, J. M. (2008). Sensing of "danger signals" and pathogen-associated molecular patterns defines binary signaling pathways "upstream" of Toll. *Nature Immunology, 9*(10), 1165–1170.

Ellison, P. T. (2009). *On fertile ground: A natural history of human reproduction*: Harvard University Press.

Erickson, M. A., Wilson, M. L., & Banks, W. A. (2020). In vitro modeling of blood–brain barrier and interface functions in neuroimmune communication. *Fluids and Barriers of the CNS, 17*(1), 26. doi: 10.1186/s12987-020-00187-3

Fisher, R. A. (1930). *The genetical theory of natural selection*. Clarendon Press.

Franz, M. J. (1997). Protein: Metabolism and effect on blood glucose levels. *Diabetes Educator, 23*(6), 643–646.

Friedman, E. M., Reyes, T. M., & Coe, C. L. (1996). Context-dependent behavioral effects of interleukin-1 in the rhesus monkey (Macaca mulatta). *Psychoneuroendocrinology, 21*(5), 455–468. doi: 10.1016/0306-4530(96)00010-8

Garcia, A. R., Blackwell, A. D., Trumble, B. C., Stieglitz, J., Kaplan, H., & Gurven, M. D. (2020). Evidence for height and immune function trade-offs among preadolescents in a high pathogen population. *Evolution, Medicine, and Public Health, 2020*(1), 86–99. doi: 10.1093/emph/eoaa017

Ghai, R. R., Fugere, V., Chapman, C. A., Goldberg, T. L., & Davies, T. J. (2015). Sickness behaviour associated with non-lethal infections in wild primates. *Proceedings of the Royal Society of London B: Biological Sciences, 282*(1814), 20151436.

Grigoleit, J. S., Kullmann, J. S., Wolf, O. T., Hammes, F., Wegner, A., Jablonowski, S., Engler, H., Gizewski, E., Oberbeck, R., & Schedlowski, M. (2011). Dose-dependent effects of endotoxin on neurobehavioral functions in humans. *PLoS ONE [Electronic Resource], 6*(12), e28330.

Gurven, M. D., Allen-Arave, W., Hill, K., & Hurtado, M. (2000). "It's a wonderful life": Signaling generosity among the Ache of Paraguay. *Evolution and Human Behavior, 21*(4), 263–282. doi: 10.1016/s1090-5138(00)00032-5

Gurven, M. D., & Lieberman, D. E. (2020). Weird bodies: Mismatch, medicine and missing diversity. *Evolution and Human Behavior, 41*(5), 330–340. doi: 10.1016/j.evolhumbehav.2020.04.001

Gurven, M. D., Stieglitz, J., Hooper, P. L., Gomes, C., & Kaplan, H. (2012). From the womb to the tomb: The role of transfers in shaping the evolved human life history. *Experimental Gerontology, 47*(10), 807–813.

Hart, B. L. (1990). Behavioral adaptations to pathogens and parasites: Five strategies. *Neuroscience & Biobehavioral Reviews, 14*(3), 273–294.

Henrich, J., Heine, S. J., & Norenzayan, A. (2010). The weirdest people in the world? *Behavioral and Brain Sciences, 33*(2-3), 61–83. doi: 10.1017/s0140525x0999152x

Hetem, R. S., Mitchell, D., Maloney, S. K., Meyer, L. C., Fick, L. G., Kerley, G. I., & Fuller, A. (2008). Fever and sickness behavior during an opportunistic infection in a free-living antelope, the greater kudu (Tragelaphus strepsiceros). *American Journal of Physiology - Regulatory Integrative & Comparative Physiology, 294*(1), R246–R254.

Hill, K., Hurtado, A. M., & Walker, R. S. (2007). High adult mortality among Hiwi hunter-gatherers: Implications for human evolution. *Journal of Human Evolution, 52*(4), 443–454.

Hlubik, S., Cutts, R., Braun, D. R., Berna, F., Feibel, C. S., & Harris, J. W. K. (2019). Hominin fire use in the Okote member at Koobi Fora, Kenya: New evidence for the old debate. *Journal of Human Evolution, 133*, 214–229.

Holmqvist, M., Inghammar, M., Pahlman, L. I., Boyd, J., Akesson, P., Linder, A., & Kahn, F. (2020). Risk of bacteremia in patients presenting with shaking chills and vomiting: A prospective cohort study. *Epidemiology and Infection, 148*, e86.

Horns, F., & Hood, M. E. (2012). The evolution of disease resistance and tolerance in spatially structured populations. *Ecology and Evolution, 2*(7), 1705–1711.

Huffman, M. A. (1997). Current evidence for self-medication in primates: A multidisciplinary perspective. *American Journal of Physical Anthropology, 104*(S25), 171–200. doi: https://doi.org/10.1002/(SICI)1096-8644(1997)25+<171::AID-AJPA7>3.0.CO;2-7

Inagaki, T. K., Muscatell, K. A., Irwin, M. R., Cole, S. W., & Eisenberger, N. I. (2012). Inflammation selectively enhances amygdala activity to socially threatening images. *NeuroImage, 59*(4), 3222–3226.

Inagaki, T. K., Muscatell, K. A., Irwin, M. R., Moieni, M., Dutcher, J. M., Jevtic, I., Breen, E. C., & Eisenberger, N. I. (2015). The role of the ventral striatum in inflammatory-induced approach toward support figures. *Brain, Behavior, and Immunity, 44*, 247–252.

Klug, H., & Bonsall, M. B. (2014). What are the benefits of parental care? The importance of parental effects on developmental rate. *Ecology and Evolution, 4*(12), 2330–2351. doi: https://doi.org/10.1002/ece3.1083

Kluger, M. J. (1979). Fever in ectotherms: Evolutionary implications. *American Zoologist, 19*(1), 295–304. doi: 10.1093/icb/19.1.295

Kluger, M. J., Ringler, D. H., & Anver, M. R. (1975). Fever and survival. *Science, 188*(4184), 166–168.

Knoll, A. H., & Carroll, S. B. (1999). Early animal evolution: Emerging views from comparative biology and geology. *Science, 284*(5423), 2129–2137.

Kohler, P. (2001). The biochemical basis of anthelmintic action and resistance. *International Journal for Parasitology*, *31*(4), 336–345.

Kotas, M. E., & Medzhitov, R. (2015). Homeostasis, inflammation, and disease susceptibility. *Cell*, *160*(5), 816–827.

Kramer, K. L., & Otarola-Castillo, E. (2015). When mothers need others: The impact of hominin life history evolution on cooperative breeding. *Journal of Human Evolution*, *84*, 16–24.

Kuzawa, C. W. (1998). Adipose tissue in human infancy and childhood: an evolutionary perspective. *American Journal of Physical Anthropology*, *107*(Suppl 27), 177–209.

Lafferty, K. D., & Shaw, J. C. (2013). Comparing mechanisms of host manipulation across host and parasite taxa. *Journal of Experimental Biology*, *216*(Pt 1), 56–66.

Lasselin, J., Elsenbruch, S., Lekander, M., Axelsson, J., Karshikoff, B., Grigoleit, J. S., Engler, H., Schedlowski, M., & Benson, S. (2016). Mood disturbance during experimental endotoxemia: Predictors of state anxiety as a psychological component of sickness behavior. *Brain, Behavior, and Immunity*, *57*, 30–37. doi: 10.1016/j.bbi.2016.01.003

Lasselin, J., Karshikoff, B., Axelsson, J., Åkerstedt, T., Benson, S., Engler, H., Schedlowski, M., Jones, M., Lekander, M., & Andreasson, A. (2020). Fatigue and sleepiness responses to experimental inflammation and exploratory analysis of the effect of baseline inflammation in healthy humans. *Brain, Behavior, and Immunity*, *83*, 309–314. doi: 10.1016/j.bbi.2019.10.020

Lasselin, J., Lekander, M., Benson, S., Schedlowski, M., & Engler, H. (2020). Sick for science: Experimental endotoxemia as a translational tool to develop and test new therapies for inflammation-associated depression. *Molecular Psychiatry*, *26*(8), 3672–3683. doi: 10.1038/s41380-020-00869-2

Lasselin, J., Schedlowski, M., Karshikoff, B., Engler, H., Lekander, M., & Konsman, J. P. (2020). Comparison of bacterial lipopolysaccharide-induced sickness behavior in rodents and humans: Relevance for symptoms of anxiety and depression. *Neuroscience and Biobehavioral Reviews*, *115*, 15–24. doi: 10.1016/j.neubiorev.2020.05.001

Lieberman, D., Billingsley, J., & Patrick, C. (2018). Consumption, contact and copulation: How pathogens have shaped human psychological adaptations. *Philosophical Transactions of the Royal Society of London B: Biological Sciences*, *373*(1751), 20170203.

Lieberman, D. E. (2015). Is exercise really medicine? An evolutionary perspective. *Current Sports Medicine Reports*, *14*(4), 313–319.

Lin, C., Zhang, Y., Zhang, K., Zheng, Y., Lu, L., Chang, H., Yang, H., Yang, Y., Wan, Y., Wang, S., & Yuan, M. (2019). Fever promotes T lymphocyte trafficking via a thermal sensory pathway involving heat shock protein 90 and α4 integrins. *Immunity*, *50*(1), 137–151. doi: https://doi.org/10.1016/j.immuni.2018.11.013

Llewellyn, D., Brown, G. P., Thompson, M. B., & Shine, R. (2011). Behavioral responses to immune-system activation in an anuran (the cane toad, *Bufo marinus*): Field and laboratory studies. *Physiological and Biochemical Zoology*, *84*(1), 77–86. doi:10.1086/657609

Lopes, P. C. (2014). When is it socially acceptable to feel sick? *Proceedings of the Royal Society of London B: Biological Sciences*, *281*(1788), 20140218.

Lopes, P. C., Adelman, J., Wingfield, J. C., & Bentley, G. E. (2012). Social context modulates sickness behavior. *Behavioral Ecology and Sociobiology*, *66*(10), 1421–1428. doi: 10.1007/s00265-012-1397-1

Lopes, P. C., Springthorpe, D., & Bentley, G. E. (2014). Increased activity correlates with reduced ability to mount immune defenses to endotoxin in zebra finches. *Journal of Experimental Zoology Part A- Ecological Genetics & Physiology*, *321*(8), 422–431.

Lukas, D., & Clutton-Brock, T. (2012). Cooperative breeding and monogamy in mammalian societies. *Proceedings of the Royal Society of London B: Biological Sciences*, *279*(1736), 2151–2156.

MacDonald, L., Hazi, A., Paolini, A. G., & Kent, S. (2014). Calorie restriction dose-dependently abates lipopolysaccharide-induced fever, sickness behavior, and circulating interleukin-6 while increasing corticosterone. *Brain, Behavior, and Immunity*, *40*, 18–26.

Mandal, M. D., & Mandal, S. (2011). Honey: Its medicinal property and antibacterial activity. *Asian Pacific Journal of Tropical Biomedicine*, *1*(2), 154–160.

McCusker, R. H., & Kelley, K. W. (2013). Immune-neural connections: How the immune system's response to infectious agents influences behavior. *Journal of Experimental Biology*, *216*(Pt 1), 84–98.

McDade, T. W., Georgiev, A. V., & Kuzawa, C. W. (2016). Trade-offs between acquired and innate immune defenses in humans. *Evolution, Medicine, and Public Health*, *2016*(1), 1–16.

Medzhitov, R. (2008). Origin and physiological roles of inflammation. *Nature*, *454*(7203), 428–435.

Merriam-Webster Online Dictionary. (2021). Definition of lassitude. Retrieved from https://www.merriam-webster.com/dictionary/lassitude

Muehlenbein, M. P., Hirschtick, J. L., Bonner, J. Z., & Swartz, A. M. (2010). Toward quantifying the usage costs of human immunity: Altered metabolic rates and hormone levels during acute immune activation in men. *American Journal of Human Biology*, *22*(4), 546–556.

Muller, K. R., Prosser, R., Bampton, P., Mountifield, R., & Andrews, J. M. (2010). Female gender and surgery impair relationships, body image, and sexuality in inflammatory bowel disease: patient perceptions. *Inflammatory Bowel Diseases, 16*(4), 657–663.

Munroe, R. H., Munroe, R. L., Michelson, C., Koel, A., Bolton, R., & Bolton, C. (1983). Time allocation in four societies. *Ethnology, 22*(4), 355–370.

Murray, M. J., & Murray, A. B. (1979). Anorexia of infection as a mechanism of host defense. *American Journal of Clinical Nutrition, 32*(3), 593–596.

Muscatell, K. A., Moieni, M., Inagaki, T. K., Dutcher, J. M., Jevtic, I., Breen, E. C., . . . Eisenberger, N. I. (2016). Exposure to an inflammatory challenge enhances neural sensitivity to negative and positive social feedback. *Brain, Behavior, and Immunity, 57*, 21–29.

Nesse, R. M. (1990). Evolutionary explanations of emotions. *Human Nature, 1*(3), 261–289. doi: 10.1007/bf02733986

Oberholzer, A., Oberholzer, C., & Moldawer, L. L. (2000). Cytokine signaling: Regulation of the immune response in normal and critically ill states. *Critical Care Medicine, 28*(4 Suppl), N3–12.

Ong, A. D., Uchino, B. N., & Wethington, E. (2016). Loneliness and health in older adults: A mini-review and synthesis. *Gerontology, 62*(4), 443–449.

Palin, K., Bluthe, R.-M., McCusker, R. H., Moos, F., Dantzer, R., & Kelley, K. W. (2007). TNF alpha-induced sickness behavior in mice with functional 55 kD TNF receptors is blocked by central IGF-I. *Journal of Neuroimmunology, 187*(1–2), 55–60. doi: 10.1016/j.jneuroim.2007.04.011

Pan, W., Stone, K. P., Hsuchou, H., Manda, V. K., Zhang, Y., & Kastin, A. J. (2011). Cytokine signaling modulates blood-brain barrier function. *Current Pharmaceutical Design, 17*(33), 3729–3740.

Pavlov, V. A., & Tracey, K. J. (2012). The vagus nerve and the inflammatory reflex: Linking immunity and metabolism. *Nature Reviews Endocrinology, 8*(12), 743–754.

Pawelec, G., Goldeck, D., & Derhovanessian, E. (2014). Inflammation, ageing and chronic disease. *Current Opinion in Immunology, 29*, 23–28.

Pelot, N. A., & Grill, W. M. (2018). Effects of vagal neuromodulation on feeding behavior. *Brain Research, 1693*(Pt B), 180–187.

Plaza, D. F., Gomez, M. F., & Patarroyo, M. A. (2020). NHP-immunome: A translational research-oriented database of non-human primate immune system proteins. *Cellular Immunology, 347*, 103999.

Pollard, K. A., & Blumstein, D. T. (2008). Time allocation and the evolution of group size. *Animal Behaviour, 76*(5), 1683–1699. doi: 10.1016/j.anbehav.2008.08.006

Pontzer, H., Durazo-Arvizu, R., Dugas, L. R., Plange-Rhule, J., Bovet, P., Forrester, T. E., Lambert, E. V., Cooper, R. S., Schoeller, D. A., & Luke, A. (2016). Constrained total energy expenditure and metabolic adaptation to physical activity in adult humans. *Current Biology, 26*(3), 410–417. doi: 10.1016/j.cub.2015.12.046

Raetz, C. R., & Whitfield, C. (2002). Lipopolysaccharide endotoxins. *Annual Review of Biochemistry, 71*, 635–700.

Roh, J. S., & Sohn, D. H. (2018). Damage-associated molecular patterns in inflammatory diseases. *Immune Network, 18*(4), e27. doi: 10.4110/in.2018.18.e27

Roulette, C. J., Mann, H., Kemp, B. M., Remiker, M., Roulette, J. W., Hewlett, B. S., Kazanji, M., Breurec, S., Monchy, D., Sullivan, R. J., & Hagen, E. H. (2014). Tobacco use vs. helminths in Congo basin hunter-gatherers: self-medication in humans? *Evolution and Human Behavior, 35*(5), 397–407. doi: 10.1016/j.evolhumbehav.2014.05.005

Schaller, M. (2018). The parental care motivational system and why it matters (for everyone). *Current Directions in Psychological Science, 27*(5), 295–301. doi: 10.1177/0963721418767873

Schrock, J. M. (2020). *Why our immune systems make us feel sick: Pathologies, adaptations, and evolutionarily novel conditions.* Doctoral dissertation, University of Oregon, Eugene.

Schrock, J. M., Snodgrass, J. J., & Sugiyama, L. S. (2019). Lassitude: The emotion of being sick. *Evolution and Human Behavior, 41*(1), 44–57. doi: 10.1016/j.evolhumbehav.2019.09.002

Scorza, K., Williams, A., Phillips, J. D., & Shaw, J. (2007). Evaluation of nausea and vomiting. *American Family Physician, 76*(1), 76–84.

Secor, S. M. (2009). Specific dynamic action: A review of the postprandial metabolic response. *Journal of Comparative Physiology - B, Biochemical, Systemic, & Environmental Physiology, 179*(1), 1–56.

Shattuck, E. C., & Muehlenbein, M. P. (2015). Human sickness behavior: Ultimate and proximate explanations. *American Journal of Physical Anthropology, 157*(1), 1–18.

Shattuck, E. C., & Muehlenbein, M. P. (2016). Towards an integrative picture of human sickness behavior. *Brain, Behavior, and Immunity, 57*, 255–262.

Shay, T., Jojic, V., Zuk, O., Rothamel, K., Puyraimond-Zemmour, D., Feng, T., Wakamatsu, E., Benoist, C., Koller, D., Regev, A., & ImmGen Consortium. (2013). Conservation and divergence in the transcriptional programs of the human and mouse immune systems. *Proceedings of the National Academy of Sciences of the United States of America, 110*(8), 2946–2951.

Sherman, P. W., & Flaxman, S. M. (2002). Nausea and vomiting of pregnancy in an evolutionary perspective. *American Journal of Obstetrics and Gynecology, 186*(5 Suppl Understanding), S190–S197.

Snodgrass, J. J. (2012). Human energetics. In S. Stinson, B. Bogin, & D. O'Rourke (Eds.), *Human Biology* (pp. 325–384). John Wiley & Sons.

Solberg, L. I. (1984). Lassitude: A primary care evaluation. *JAMA, 251*(24), 3272–3276.

Stearns, S. C. (1989). Trade-offs in life-history evolution. *Functional Ecology, 3*(3), 259–268.

Stein, D. J., & Nesse, R. M. (2011). Threat detection, precautionary responses, and anxiety disorders. *Neuroscience and Biobehavioral Reviews, 35*(4), 1075–1079. doi: 10.1016/j.neubiorev.2010.11.012

Steinkopf, L. (2015). The signaling theory of symptoms: An evolutionary explanation of the placebo effect. *Evolutionary Psychology, 13*(3), 1474704915600559. doi: 10.1177/1474704915600559

Stieglitz, J., Trumble, B. C., Thompson, M. E., Blackwell, A. D., Kaplan, H. S., & Gurven, M. D. (2015). Depression as sickness behavior? A test of the host defense hypothesis in a high pathogen population. *Brain, Behavior, and Immunity, 49*, 130–139. doi: 10.1016/j.bbi.2015.05.008

Sugiyama, L. S. (2004). Illness, injury, and disability among Shiwiar forager-horticulturalists: Implications of health-risk buffering for the evolution of human life history. *American Journal of Physical Anthropology, 123*(4), 371–389.

Sugiyama, L. S., & Chacon, R. (2000). Effects of illness and injury on foraging among the Yora and Shiwiar: Pathology risk as adaptive problem. In L. Cronk, N. Chagnon, & W. Irons (Eds.), *Adaptation and human behavior: An anthropological perspective* (pp. 371–395). Routledge.

Sugiyama, L. S., & Scalise Sugiyama, M. (2003). Social roles, prestige, and health risk. *Human Nature, 14*(2), 165–190. doi: 10.1007/s12110-003-100-4

Sundelin, T., Karshikoff, B., Axelsson, E., Hoglund, C. O., Lekander, M., & Axelsson, J. (2015). Sick man walking: Perception of health status from body motion. *Brain, Behavior, and Immunity, 48*, 53–56. doi: 10.1016/j.bbi.2015.03.007

Swain, M. G. (2000). Fatigue in chronic disease. *Clinical Science, 99*(1), 1–8.

Sznycer, D. (2019). Forms and functions of the self-conscious emotions. *Trends in Cognitive Sciences, 23*(2). doi: 10.1016/j.tics.2018.11.007

Tilley, L. (2015). *Theory and practice in the bioarchaeology of care*. Springer.

Tilley, L., & Oxenham, M. F. (2011). Survival against the odds: Modeling the social implications of care provision to seriously disabled individuals. *International Journal of Paleopathology, 1*(1), 35–42. https://doi.org/10.1016/j.ijpp.2011.02.003

Tiokhin, L. (2016). Do symptoms of illness serve signaling functions? (hint: Yes). *The Quarterly Review of Biology, 91*(2), 177–195. doi: 10.1086/686811

Tooby, J., & Cosmides, L. (1990). The past explains the present: Emotional adaptations and the structure of ancestral environments. *Ethology & Sociobiology, 11*(4–5), 375–424. doi: 10.1016/0162-3095(90)90017-z

Tooby, J., & Cosmides, L. (2008). The evolutionary psychology of the emotions and their relationship to internal regulatory variables. In M. Lewis, J. M. Haviland-Jones, & L. F. Barrett (Eds.), *Handbook of emotions* (3rd ed., pp. 114–137). Guilford Press.

Toups, M. A., Kitchen, A., Light, J. E., & Reed, D. L. (2011). Origin of clothing lice indicates early clothing use by anatomically modern humans in Africa. *Molecular Biology and Evolution, 28*(1), 29–32.

Trinkaus, E., & Zimmerman, M. R. (1982). Trauma among the Shanidar Neandertals. *American Journal of Physical Anthropology, 57*(1), 61–76.

Trivers, R. (1972). Parental investment and sexual selection. In B. G. Campbell (Eds.), *Sexual Selection and the Descent of Man* (pp. 136–179). Aldine de Gruyter.

Tybur, J. M., Lieberman, D., & Griskevicius, V. (2009). Microbes, mating, and morality: Individual differences in three functional domains of disgust. *Journal of Personality and Social Psychology, 97*(1), 103–122.

Urlacher, S. S., Ellison, P. T., Sugiyama, L. S., Pontzer, H., Eick, G., Liebert, M. A., Cepon-Robins, T. J., Gildner, T. E., & Snodgrass, J. J. (2018). Tradeoffs between immune function and childhood growth among Amazonian forager-horticulturalists. *Proceedings of the National Academy of Sciences, 115*(17), E3914–E3921.

Van Heeckeren, A. M., Tscheikuna, J., Walenga, R. W., Konstan, M. W., Davis, P. B., Erokwu, B., Haxhiu, M. A., & Ferkol, T. W. (2000). Effect of *Pseudomonas* infection on weight loss, lung mechanics, and cytokines in mice. *American Journal of Respiratory and Critical Care Medicine, 161*(1), 271–279.

Vaughn, L. K., Veale, W. L., & Cooper, K. E. (1980). Antipyresis: Its effect on mortality rate of bacterially infected rabbits. *Brain Research Bulletin, 5*(1), 69–73.

Vos, T., Lim, S. S., Abbafati, C., Abbas, K. M., Abbasi, M., Abbasifard, M., Abbasi-Kangevari, M., Abbastabar, H., Abd-Allah, F., Abdelalim, A., & Abdollahi, M. (2020). Global burden of 369 diseases and injuries in 204 countries and territories, 1990–2019: A systematic analysis for the Global Burden of Disease Study 2019. *Lancet*, *396*(10258), 1204–1222.

Warburton, D. E. R., & Bredin, S. S. D. (2017). Health benefits of physical activity: A systematic review of current systematic reviews. *Current Opinion in Cardiology*, *32*(5), 541–556.

Wells, K. B., Golding, J. M., & Burnam, M. A. (1988). Psychiatric disorder in a sample of the general population with and without chronic medical conditions. *American Journal of Psychiatry*, *145*(8), 976–981.

Westerterp, K. R. (2004). Diet induced thermogenesis. *Nutrition & Metabolism*, *1*(1), 5. doi: 10.1186/1743-7075-1-5

Westerterp, K. R. (2017). Control of energy expenditure in humans. *European Journal of Clinical Nutrition*, *71*(3), 340–344.

CHAPTER 17

The Origins of Boredom

Yijun Lin and Erin C. Westgate

Abstract

This chapter argues that boredom provides an evolutionary solution to minimizing prediction error by incentivizing learning. While reducing prediction error is crucial for cognitive processes, the potential solution of isolating oneself in extremely predictable environments raises the "Dark Room Problem." Boredom evolved to prevent this problem, making it affectively undesirable by signaling a lack of successful attentional engagement in a valued goal-congruent activity. This aversive state motivates individuals to re-engage in meaningful activities and reallocate attentional resources. The chapter reviews behavioral science and computational modeling evidence supporting boredom's role in maximizing learning and reducing prediction error. Additionally, the authors propose that boredom's functions extend beyond modern humans to various species, presenting evidence of boredom-like states in nonhuman animals (e.g., stereotyped behavior). This chapter emphasizes the adaptive value of boredom, addressing its origins and prevalence across human and nonhuman contexts, and discusses the relationship between boredom and technology in modern society.

Key Words: boredom, evolution, meaning, attention, adaptive

《约客》赵师秀 黄梅时节家家雨，青草池塘处处蛙。
有约不来过夜半，闲敲棋子落灯花。

In Summer rain comes a-knocking at homes here and there;
In the green grass and ponds croaking frogs are everywhere.
Past midnight, my friend who says he would come is not here;
I rap on the chess pieces in leisure, And knock off the lamp's burnt wick with pleasure.
—Zhao Shixiu (1170–1219), "Appointment with a Friend"

More than a thousand years ago, boredom surfaced in the works of ancient Chinese poets. Zhao Shixiu, from the Southern Song dynasty, described his efforts to "while away" boredom as he waited up at night for a friend. Bored, he occupied himself fiddling with a chess set

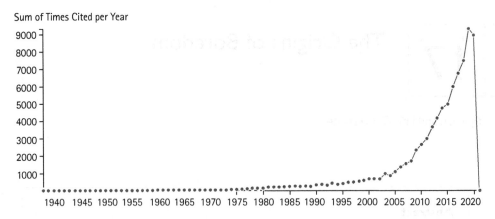

Figure 17.1. Scholarly citations for boredom-related publications from 1864 to 2020.

and lamp wick. Tapping out soft sounds to break the silence of the night may have been the ancients' solution to boredom. However, more than a thousand years later, how does boredom present itself?

Although many of us couldn't be more familiar with it, boredom is one of the most understudied negative emotions in psychology. According to the Web of Science, researchers published only 4,751 articles on boredom from 1864 to 2020 (Clarivate Analytics, 2020; see Figure 17.1), compared to fear (with 181,560 publications) or anger (41,616 publications). Despite this historical lack of scholarly interest, boredom is extremely common (Chin et al., 2017). In a sample of 3,867 American adults, 63% of participants experienced boredom at least once during a 10-day span, with rates highest among men and teenagers, unmarried adults, and low-income households (Chin et al., 2017).

Surprisingly, boredom occurs even during situations when it might seem counterproductive. At the beginning of the U.S. coronavirus outbreak, Google Trends saw a spike in searches for "boredom topic" (an aggregate of search terms classified internally by Google as relating to boredom) in March 2020 (see Figure 17.2). At the time, most restaurants and movie theaters were closed; many states required residents to stay home to reduce infection. Surely it would be adaptive, in such a situation, to do so happily and enjoy the extra time afforded by freedom from commuting and overwork. Yet, instead, newspapers filled with anecdotal reports of people in lockdown feeling bored (e.g., Friedman, 2020; McAlinden, 2020; Rosenwald, 2020), some of whom felt tempted to violate social distancing restrictions (Boylan et al., 2021; cf. Lin et al., 2023; Westgate et al., 2023). That boredom can lead to negative outcomes has been widely documented: experimental studies show that boredom increases willingness to harm one's self (Havermans et al., 2015; Nederkoorn et al., 2016; Wilson et al., 2014) as well as others (Pfattheicher et al., 2021). And correlational data link boredom to a wide range of negative public outcomes, including substance use and drug-related mortality (e.g., Baldwin & Westgate, 2020; Iso-Ahola & Crowley, 1991).

In short, boredom does not seem adaptive. People tolerate, and often respond to it, poorly, despite its prevalence. But why would we continue to experience boredom if it perpetuates maladaptive behaviors? To understand this paradox requires exploring the evolutionary origins of boredom, and the adaptive function of negative emotions more generally. In this chapter, we propose that although boredom is an aversive, unpleasant state that often produces seemingly maladaptive behaviors, it provides an important evolutionary solution to minimizing

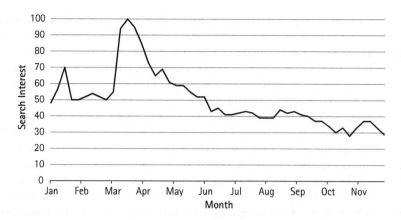

Figure 17.2. Google searches for "boredom topic" in the United States (2020). Note: Numbers represent search interest relative to the highest point on the chart for the given region and time. 100 = peak popularity, 50 = half as popular, 0 = insufficient data available.

prediction error and facilitating learning. People and nonhuman animals alike are motivated to re-engage in meaningful activities and reallocate attentional resources to reduce boredom. In doing so, boredom maximizes strategies favoring exploration and discovery, and fosters pursuit of long-term goals and learning.

Boredom as Information

Affect, behavior, and cognition exist today because of their adaptive value in the past (e.g., Darwin, 1964; Dawkins, 1976). Many theories posit that emotion plays an important role in helping organisms adapt to and survive in their environments (Plutchik, 1980). For instance, when confronted by basic needs for safety and sustenance in the face of danger, fear can be an important defensive tool. Without fear, organisms are hampered in appropriately evaluating or navigating the dangers of their environment, greatly reducing odds of survival (e.g., Lebel, 2017; Misslin, 2003). According to prominent theories, fear and other forms of negative affect thus act as a "stop" signal, alerting us to problems in the environment, while forms of positive affect act as a "go" signal, alerting us that all is well (Clore & Huntsinger, 2007; Huntsinger et al., 2014; Storbeck & Clore, 2008).

Specifically, theories of affect-as-information propose that automatic appraisals of situations provide conscious information in the form of affect and emotions, processes shaped by our subjective experience and attributions (Clore et al., 2001). Such informative affective states help us survive, reproduce, and flourish. Boredom, like all emotions, is thus a source of important information about whether we are productively engaged with our environment. However, this interpretation of boredom requires a rethinking of many traditional models of emotion. According to the "classic view of emotion" (Bliss-Moreau, 2018), basic emotions reflect underlying biological units and adaptive values; each basic emotion has its own corresponding unique pattern of facial expressions, physiological processes, and behavioral reactions (e.g., Darwin, 1872; Ekman, 1992; Izard, 1992). One consequence of this theoretical framework is the assumption that we should be able to measure and identify specific emotions using nonverbal markers, such as facial expression, and physiological and neural markers. The classic view of emotion generally assumes that emotion has been consistently shaped by evolutionary adaptation and thus is consistent across species and cultures.

However, extensive empirical evidence questions these assumptions. First, modern evolutionary approaches to emotions do not fully endorse the distinction between basic and non-basic emotions (Al-Shawaf et al., 2016; Al-Shawaf & Lewis, 2017) because many emotions, such as envy (e.g., DelPriore et al., 2012), embarrassment (e.g., Keltner & Buswell, 1996), and romantic love (e.g., Hazan & Shaver, 1987), are applicable to a wide range of adaptive problems related to mating, reproduction, and childrearing. Second, while many studies have suggested that certain emotions should be universal, empirical counterexamples are easily found. For instance, when asked to sort images of posed and unposed facial expressions, participants from the Himba ethnic group do not show the "universal" pattern exhibited by Americans because they hold different antecedent knowledge of emotional concepts. Because culture and language shape emotion concepts, people in different cultures thus categorize and express emotions in different ways (Gendron et al., 2014). Third, while many researchers have argued that emotions have discrete facial expressions and physiological markers (Cordaro, Chapter 1 in this volume; Cowen et al., 2021; Keltner et al., 2006), recent meta-analyses call these findings into question. Aggregated across many such individual studies, these meta-analyses find that specific emotions cannot be reliably differentiated by physiological responses (Siegel et al., 2018), facial expressions (Barrett et al., 2019; Gendron et al., 2014), or neural dynamics (Lindquist et al., 2012). That is, researchers cannot accurately predict which specific emotion a person is experiencing simply by observing seemingly "objective" characteristics, such as their heart rate, smile, or amygdala activity. Rather, differences *within* an emotion (e.g., expressions of anger) are often as great as the differences *between* emotions (e.g., expressions of anger vs. sadness; Barrett, 2009).

What is the crucial factor in emotion formation, if not specific differences in physiological or neural features? Theories of constructed emotion (Bliss-Moreau, 2018), including appraisal theories, argue that instead we must look to the situations that elicit emotions, and—specifically—to people's construals (e.g., Barrett, 2006; Clore & Ortony, 2013). Thus, while basic affect (e.g., valence, arousal) may be physiological in nature, it is how we categorize and interpret that affect which determines the specific emotions we feel (e.g., Dutton & Aron, 1974; Schachter & Singer, 1962). And because construal mediates the journey from affect to emotion, emotions vary across individuals, situations, and cultures (Cannon, 1927; Potthoff et al., 2016).

The Key Ingredients of Boredom: Meaning and Attention

The *Merriam-Webster Dictionary* defines boredom as the state of being weary and restless through lack of interest (Merriam-Webster, 2020). However, psychological definitions focus instead on the *causes* of boredom, rather than its prototypical symptoms or experiential components. In short, people feel bored when unable to engage their attention in valued-goal congruent activity (Westgate & Wilson, 2018). According to the Meaning and Attentional Components (MAC) model, boredom thus has two components—meaning and attention.

ATTENTION DEFICITS

Boredom is caused, in part, by attention deficits. When attention and meaning are both entered as simultaneous predictors of boredom, attention independently predicts boredom ($b = .34$), even after controlling for meaning (Westgate & Wilson, 2018). External distractions reduce boredom on simple but not complicated tasks (Damrad-Frye & Laird, 1989; Fisher, 1998), and when attention is manipulated experimentally, participants find an overly easy version of an air traffic control task (i.e., inattention) more boring ($M = 7.77$, $SD = 1.46$) than a challenging version ($M = 7.27$, $SD = 1.57$). Nor is boredom due solely to under-stimulation

(Csikszentmihalyi, 2000; Eastwood et al., 2012). Both under- and overstimulation create a mismatch between cognitive demands and mental resources that makes it difficult to maintain attention (Berlyne, 1960; Westgate & Wilson, 2018; Wickens, 1991). For instance, people feel *more* bored when an air traffic control task is either too easy or too hard (and *less* bored when it is "just right"), and experimental manipulation of cognitive demands replicate this effect (Westgate & Wilson, 2018; Westgate et al., 2017).

MEANING DEFICITS

At the same time, meaning deficits can also cause boredom. When entered as simultaneous predictors in correlational studies, meaning significantly predicts boredom (b = −.35), even after controlling for attention (Westgate & Wilson, 2018). Likewise, meaningless repetitive tasks lead to boredom (van Tilburg & Igou, 2012, 2017), and experimentally endowing otherwise monotonous tasks with meaning (via charitable contributions or utility value interventions) reliably reduces boredom (Hulleman et al., 2010; Schmeitzky & Freund, 2013; Westgate & Wilson, 2018).

DIFFERENT INGREDIENTS, DIFFERENT EXPERIENCES

Although it might seem reasonable that meaning and attention would interact, empirical evidence to date suggests this is not the case. For instance, in a meta-analysis of 14 correlational studies (Westgate & Wilson, 2018), while both meaning (b = −.35) and attention (b = .34) predicted boredom when entered as simultaneous predictors of boredom in a regression, they were not highly correlated (r = −.12), and did not interact (b = .005, 95% CI [−.03, .04]); experimental results simultaneously manipulating attention and meaning replicate this lack of interaction (η_p^2 = .004, p = .37).

These qualitatively different causes of boredom may also result in qualitatively different *experiences* of boredom. For instance, inducing boredom via attentional deficits results in greater inattention (but not greater disengagement, agitated affect, dysphoric affect, or distorted time perceptions; Westgate & Wilson, 2018), which mediated its effect. Likewise, inducing boredom via meaning deficits results in greater disengagement, agitated affect, dysphoric affect, and distorted time perception (but not inattention), all of which in turn mediated the effect of the meaning manipulation.

BOREDOM AS INFORMATION

In short, boredom, like fear and other emotions, behaves as an affective alarm that signals us to a lack of meaningful engagement in the environment. This can occur when activities are not personally meaningful or do not offer a good fit for current resources. Moreover, these causes can inspire different strategies for reducing boredom. If we are bored due to a lack of meaning, then we can reappraise activities in ways that make it more valuable or goal-consistent (or, disengage and pursue a more meaningful activity). If, however, we believe we are bored because it is hard to pay attention, then we can adjust either the task's difficulty or our own cognitive capacity (or, disengage and pursue a more optimally challenging activity). In this sense, boredom offers a powerful source of information about our lives, guiding us toward activities that are appropriately challenging and meaningful, and steering us away from activities that are not. In doing so, boredom maximizes opportunities for optimal learning.

The Boredom Paradox

Yet, if boredom is so useful, why is it implicated in such a broad range of problematic societal and individual outcomes? Below we briefly review this formidable challenge to our argument for boredom's adaptive nature, before introducing several possible explanations that reconcile both the benefits and risks of boredom to explain why it has persisted.

Mental Health Risks

Boredom coexists with other negative emotions, including loneliness, anger, sadness, and worry (Chin et al., 2017), and both trait and state boredom are positively associated with anxiety and depression (e.g., Chao et al., 2020; Sommers & Vodanovich, 2000). In the workplace, boredom is associated with fatigue and dissatisfaction (Skowronski, 2012), and people are willing to voluntarily hurt themselves to reduce boredom. For instance, 67% of men and 25% of women gave themselves at least one shock rather than be bored with their own thoughts for 15 minutes (Wilson et al., 2014). Such harm may also be directed outward. Trait boredom is associated with higher levels of anger and aggression (Dahlen et al., 2004), and across 15 studies and over 7,000 participants, researchers found that boredom causes sadistic behavior (Pfattheicher et al., 2021). People high in trait boredom reported more online trolling and fantasies of shooting people, robbing banks, and revenge. Bored soldiers behaved more sadistically toward coworkers, and bored parents behaved more sadistically toward their children.

Physical Health Risks

In addition to mental health, boredom is associated with a number of health risk behaviors and outcomes. For instance, both trait and state boredom have been associated with binge eating (Moynihan et al., 2015) as well as substance use, including alcohol (Orcutt, 1984; Westgate & Fairbairn, 2020) and marijuana (Willging et al., 2014; but see Block et al., 1998; Wegner et al., 2008). In big data from Google search and government records, regional increases in boredom are associated with maladaptive public health across all 50 US states. Boredom searches are associated with higher drug-related mortality and more frequent drug abuse searches, as well as more frequent self-harm searches (Baldwin & Westgate, 2020). Boredom has also been associated with worse sleep quality, due to inattention and bedtime procrastination (Teoh et al., 2020).

Self-Regulation Failure

Boredom may also form an important link in self-regulation and explain behaviors such as procrastination (Blunt & Pychyl, 1998; Vodanovich & Rupp, 1999; Wan et al., 2014). Procrastination shares many of the same sources as boredom, according to the MAC model. For instance, people are more likely to procrastinate on a task when it feels meaningless (Lee, 2005); feelings which are also likely to increase boredom. Likewise, the mismatch of attentional resources makes it more difficult to concentrate on important tasks, which increases boredom and makes distraction more likely (Ferrari, 2000).

Is It Causal?

Much of the above research is correlational, or reflects differences in boredom-proneness or trait boredom (which might be explained by confounds or third variables; see Westgate & Steidle, 2020). However, experimental studies suggest that boredom plays a causal role in many of these outcomes. For instance, experimentally induced boredom increases pursuit of novel experiences, even if those experiences are negative (Bench & Lench, 2019). The same is true of physically painful experiences. For instance, Havermans and colleagues (2015) found that participants delivered more electric shocks to themselves over the course of an hour spent watching an 85-second documentary clip on repeat (vs. watching the full documentary). Likewise, participants randomly assigned to a boredom induction administered more electric shocks to themselves than those assigned to sadness or control conditions (Nederkoorn et al., 2016). Across a series of experiments (Pfattheicher et al., 2021), participants assigned to watch a boring video were more likely to kill helpless worms and deduct monetary payments from other participants for no personal gain, compared to those assigned to watch a fun video. They were also more likely to monetarily punish wrongdoers for past bad behavior. Finally, experimentally inducing boredom increased people's consumption of chocolate (Havermans et al., 2015), and desire to eat (especially unhealthy) snacks (Moynihan et al., 2015).

In short, boredom is associated with a wide array of negative outcomes, from individual mental to societal health risk behavior. This presents a troubling paradox: if boredom is adaptive, why is it so often associated with maladaptive behaviors and outcomes?

The Origin of Boredom

Drawing on the above, we propose five explanations for why boredom persists despite its apparent drawbacks. In short, we theorize that the potential costs of boredom (e.g., in environments with limited opportunity or constrained choice) are outweighed by the potential benefits that boredom confers. Importantly, we argue that boredom maximizes strategies favoring exploration and discovery, and promotes learning. In doing so, boredom offers an important evolutionary solution to minimizing prediction error and achieving homeostasis. We outline the ways in which it does so below.

Emotions as Feedback

Traditional theories suggest that emotions "trigger" behavior, reliably and directly. But recent work suggests that instead of directly causing behavior, emotion provides feedback regarding our behaviors' consequences (Baumeister et al., 2007). Acting kindly feels good (encouraging future kindness), while acting meanly may feel good in the moment, but later makes us feel bad (discouraging future meanness). Boredom "punishes" behavior lacking in meaning or optimal attentional engagement, encouraging people to disengage from those behaviors in the present, and making such behavior less likely in the future. In other words, the negative affect that accompanies boredom negatively reinforces an individual's decision to engage (or disengage) in it.

Stimuli gain positive and negative affective value when they break homeostasis (Barrett & Simmons, 2015), or the delicate physiological balance between a person's internal physiological resources and external environmental demands (Lerner, 1954). Affect is thus an easy and "cheap" way for the body to inform the conscious mind that homeostasis is under threat, while specific emotions (such as boredom) help us pinpoint the causes of negative affect and restore homeostasis. For instance, when people respond to boredom with sadistic behavior, they do so to remedy deficits in attention by seeking stimulation, rather than restoring meaning (Pfattheicher et al., 2021). Without specific emotions, we might feel "bad" but without a clear sense of why; and without knowledge of the underlying problem, the causes of negative affect become harder to address.

This feedback not only shapes behavior in the moment, but changes predictions for how future behavior will make us feel. Learning from current emotion-behavior patterns allows people to generalize to future events. Upon encountering similar situations, such evaluations occur automatically, allowing for optimal decisions with minimal cognitive effort. For instance, a graduate student who suffers through boring statistics courses may inadvertently learn to avoid statistics. Boredom, like other emotions, thus serves as an intrinsic motivational system, rewarding and encouraging certain activities, while discouraging others.

Minimizing Opportunity Costs
One consequence of such feedback is that boredom minimizes opportunity costs, the loss of potential gain from other alternatives when a person chooses one particular alternative (Kurzban et al., 2013). Many theorists argue that boredom's primary purpose is to signal such opportunity costs and is primarily triggered by the perception that such costs are occurring (or are imminent; e.g., Wojtowicz et al., 2019). Thus, boredom is theorized to occur when benefits do not offset costs, motivating us to recompute the benefit-cost ratio, disengage from the current task, and reallocate our resources (Agrawal et al., 2022; Kurzban et al., 2013). For instance, when placed in a room with alluring alternatives (e.g., a laptop, puzzle), participants report greater boredom while thinking than when stuck in an empty room (Struk et al., 2020), because opportunity costs are more salient.

Because boredom signals that we are engaged in a meaningless activity, or unsuccessfully engaged in a target activity, or both, boredom serves as a dynamic evaluation of such motivational and cognitive costs. Persisting at activities when we have neither the motivation nor ability to do so puts us in the position of forgoing better alternatives—ones that may be more meaningful, or which we would be more successful at.

Maximizing Learning
By motivating people to seek out optimally challenging and meaningful activities, boredom maximizes opportunities for learning. Evidence from behavioral science and computational modeling supports this role. For instance, people who take challenging coursework in college, or who study abroad, report their lives are psychologically richer (and less boring; Oishi & Westgate, 2022) as a result, and think about the world in more complex ways (Oishi et al., 2021). In an experimental setting, bored participants were more inclined to choose novel images, even a novel image that was more negative (Bench & Lench, 2019).

Evidence from reinforcement learning more directly demonstrates the role of boredom in promoting learning. Curiosity drives learning progress, yet as an independent driver has its limitation—curiosity blocks learning agents from certain outcomes and can produce obsessive habitual actions because curiosity alone cannot inform agents about prior exposure to similar situations. Unlike curiosity, boredom *can* detect repetitive exposure and devaluate known outcomes. Thus, both curiosity and boredom as internal rewards make knowledge acquisition a dynamic, goal-directed process and maximize learning outcomes and minimize opportunity costs (see Schmidhuber, 1991; Yu et al., 2019). Experiments show that, compared to conventional reinforcement learning, models adding curiosity and boredom as dual internal rewards yield better performance on maze navigation tasks by reducing prediction error and increasing external rewards (Yamamoto & Ishikawa, 2010).

Fostering Exploration
One way that boredom maximizes learning is by fostering exploration. Other animals (such as chipmunks) navigate the fundamental trade-off between exploitation and exploration by, for instance, spending more time exploiting high-quality food patches, but more time exploring alternatives when patch quality is low (Kramer & Weary, 1991; Krebs et al., 1978; Mehlhorn et al., 2015). Such strategies are also common among humans. For instance, the abnormally prolonged period of human childhood is thought to offer an evolutionarily advantageous extended period of exploration (Gopnik, 2020).

Boredom may play a similar role for adults, by increasing novelty seeking (Bench & Lench, 2019) and willingness to take risks (e.g., Wegner & Flisher, 2009). People report greater boredom in environments with little information, which in turn increases exploratory behavior (Geana et al., 2016). Experimentally induced boredom increases pursuit of novel experiences, even if those experiences are negative (Bench & Lench, 2019). Participants who viewed a neutral image set 10 times (vs. 0 times or 3 times) were more inclined to subsequently request to view a novel negative (vs. neutral) image. Evidence from reinforcement learning likewise suggests that boredom elicits exploration to reduce boredom (Gomez-Ramirez & Costa, 2017). Boredom thus signals a need to switch between exploration and exploitation, thereby minimizing opportunity costs (Danckert, 2019). For instance, people are less satisfied with their relationships when they perceive their partners are bored (Dobson et al., 2023), which may prompt them to end the relationship and explore alternatives.

Reducing Prediction Error
One consequence of the above processes is that boredom may be an important feedback mechanism for optimally reducing prediction error. Reducing prediction error, it has been argued, is a core organizing principle underlying cognition. However, one way to reduce error is to isolate oneself in extremely predictable environments (i.e., the "Dark Room Problem"; Sun & Firestone, 2020), where there's no way to learn and explore. We argue that boredom evolved, at least in part, to prevent this. Specifically, boredom makes such a solution affectively undesirable, by aversively signaling a lack of successful attentional engagement in a valued goal-congruent activity. To reduce this aversive state, people are motivated to re-engage in meaningful activities and reallocate attentional resources, which maximizes learning.

In particular, boredom may act as a brake on strategies that reduce prediction error primarily via reducing environmental complexity. Such under-stimulation produces boredom, which prompts people to regulate their environments by seeking out greater complexity—forestalling the problem of the "dark room" (e.g., Gomez-Ramirez & Costa, 2017). At the same time, such increases in complexity spur greater opportunities for learning. For instance, when reinforcement-learning models are programmed to use curiosity and boredom as internal rewards, boredom outperforms curiosity, leading to greater gains in learning and ability to predict the environment (Schmidhuber, 1991; Yamamoto & Ishikawa, 2010; Yu et al., 2019). Boredom thus creates a state of homeostasis that optimizes the reduction of *global* prediction error, by forestalling strategies that rely on reducing *local* error (e.g., via under-stimulation) as well as those that result in environmental complexity too great to effectively process (e.g., overstimulation).

Beasts of Boredom

Boredom and its precursors, we argue, may serve as a basic motivational mechanism not only for humans, but among many nonhuman animals as well. Below, we review evidence for boredom-like states in nonhuman animals, and argue that animals may experience boredom due to sharing many of the same psychological and physiological components of emotion as humans.

Whether nonhuman animals experience emotion is hotly debated. One obvious difficulty is that we cannot simply ask a dog or a fish (or an octopus) what they are feeling. Cosmides and Tooby (2000) suggest that we can characterize an emotion, in both humans and nonhuman animals, according to its situations and cues, because emotion is a superordinate program that detects, coordinates, and solves adaptive problems. And yet, extensive research in human populations suggests that the best and most accurate method of measuring emotion is direct self-report (Robinson & Clore, 2002). This is also a problem for the classic view of emotion; although such approaches view emotions as specific physiological and behavioral reactions, these interpretations cannot be verified without animals' self-reported emotions

(Bliss-Moreau, 2017). For instance, a mouse may freeze because it is afraid—or because it is happy, bored, or simply contemplating its next actions. Instead, theories of constructed emotion provide an alternative approach to deconstructing animals' emotions, by suggesting that affect (i.e., the experience of valence and arousal that forms the basis of emotions) *is* conserved across species (Russel, 2003). Affect is the product of disequilibrium between organisms and their environment, which serves the purpose of signaling stimuli that are harmful or beneficial for survival. With this approach in mind, while we may not be able to ask an octopus what it is feeling, we can measure the ingredients that make up emotion (e.g., core affect, attention, and predictive coding; Bliss-Moreau, 2017; Bliss-Moreau et al., 2021) through physiological and behavioral means. In particular, we can examine whether nonhuman animals share the psychological prerequisites for emotional experience in humans: affect, conceptual knowledge, social context, and (possibly) language.

Do animals share the same emotional experiences as humans? Possibly. Since many emotions serve as predictive signals to evaluate the relationship between organisms and their environment, some emotions (and their corresponding consequences) should be consistent across species. One way to examine this question is to observe whether certain situations elicit behavioral responses in nonhuman animals that are analogous to those observed in bored humans in similar situations. For instance, under-stimulation has been widely documented as a cause of self-reported boredom in humans (Csikzentmihalyi, 2000; Eastwood et al., 2012). Likewise, animals in under-stimulated environments, such as cages or zoos, exhibit responses analogous to boredom in humans, including stereotyped behavior, novelty seeking, and play behavior (Burn, 2017). Likewise, boredom-like states in animals may cause maladaptive behaviors similar to that in humans. For instance, pigs housed in non-enriched conditions for five months showed reduced behavioral diversity compared to those housed in enriched conditions (Wemelsfelder et al., 2000). Stereotypic behavior has been observed in caged animals such as mink and mice, although its relationship with boredom remains unclear (Meagher et al., 2017).

If boredom is adaptive in human adults, then we should see it (or its precursors) in both human children and nonhuman animals. That nonhuman animals are sensitive to under- and overstimulation has been widely documented, suggesting a mechanism parallel to that of the attention component in humans. Furthermore, evidence for a meaning-like component comes, perhaps somewhat unexpectedly, from the long history of animal research on learning and operant conditioning (Skinner, 1963). Such research clearly shows that nonhuman animals, including pigeons, cats, and the great apes, respond with more interest and engagement to high-value rewards (e.g., M&Ms) than low-value rewards (e.g., cucumber), and that such engagement produces greater learning (e.g., Egan et al., 2007). In humans, construing current activity as congruent with valued goals is felt as a heightened sense of meaning, and increasing value in analogous ways (e.g., monetary contribution to a charity) creates parallel effects (Westgate & Wilson, 2018). And like in humans, these states appear adaptive: just as humans seek cognitive engagement and meaning to get rid of boredom, animals experiencing boredom-like states also seek out novel stimuli and enriched environments. For instance, non-enriched mink showed stronger interest in stimuli (consistent with boredom-like states) compared to enriched mink (Meagher et al., 2017; Meagher & Mason, 2012). And boredom, argues Burns (2017), motivates animals to explore their environment and learn new things, which facilitates the identification of environmental resources and dangers.

In sum, boredom-like states appear common in animals, and appear to be elicited by the same situational factors that cause boredom in adult humans, with similar behavioral consequences. This may also be true of young human children. One-year-old infants exhibit a boredom-like state when presented with uninteresting stimuli (Kagan & Lewis, 1965); and evidence from linguistic studies suggests that by the age of seven, children understand the meaning of boredom (although only half of children do so at age four; Nook et al., 2020). This trend becomes even more robust by adolescence and pre-adolescence; for instance, leisure boredom in German children modestly increased from the ages of 10 to 14 (Spaeth et al., 2015). The above evidence suggests that boredom-like states may be common in children and nonhuman species; yet whether they share the same experiential features, much less causes and consequences as in human adults, is a topic of much-needed research.

Making Boredom Adaptive

We argue emotions are adaptive, but boredom has been predominantly linked to *negative* outcomes. Generally speaking, features that hamper the odds of survival and reproduction are less likely to be retained and thus gradually disappear (Darwin, 1964). From this perspective, the capacity to experience boredom should have been heavily selected against. Why then is boredom so common? We suggest two possibilities: (1) that while boredom is often the source of many negative outcomes, its negative effects may depend on people's lay beliefs, and (2) that whether boredom is positive or negative is a function of the environment. In particular, we explore the role of environmental mismatches between ancestral and modern environments.

Bringing the Person Back to the Situation

Believing boredom to be bad may be a self-fulfilling prophecy (Rosenthal, 1974). In a meta-analysis of over 19,950 adults, negative attitudes toward depressive affect had a particularly strong association with depression (Yoon et al., 2018); that is, believing that depression was bad made the actual experience of depression worse. Similarly, negative beliefs about boredom may aggravate its experience. Evidence from cognitive-behavioral therapy suggests that changing maladaptive beliefs about emotion can beneficially impact well-being (Corstorphine, 2006; De Castella et al., 2015), and believing emotions to be malleable may diminish the maladaptive outcomes brought by negative emotions (Kneeland et al., 2016; Tamir et al, 2007).

A growing body of evidence suggests that boredom promotes meaning-seeking activity (e.g., van Tilburg & Igou, 2017). Feeling bored is linked to better performance on tasks accessing associative thought, a key component of creativity (Gasper & Middlewood, 2014), and boredom is related to mind-wandering, a kind of attention deficit conducive to creative problem-solving (Mooneyham & Schooler, 2013). For instance, people who completed a boredom induction (followed by a creative task) came up with a higher number of uses for a pair of polystyrene cups than participants who completed the creative task first (Mann & Cadman, 2014). Although many of these studies rely on small sample sizes, they suggest that positive outcomes of boredom may be possible.

Thus, we predict that if people believe boredom is bad, they are more likely to behave badly when bored; if people believe in the beneficial value of boredom, they are more likely to behave constructively. Finally, as a cautionary note, we observe that if researchers are predisposed to believe that boredom leads to negative outcomes, they may be more likely to look for such associations, leading to a cycle of research that may inadvertently skew the apparent distribution of the boredom-behavior relationship.

The Person-Environment Fit

Environments powerfully shape people's experiences of boredom, as well as their range of possible reactions. Different environments may thus elicit different types of boredom—with different consequences. And good choices require good options; the very environments that make boredom most likely may also be those least likely to afford positive solutions. Thus, in environments with impoverished options, boredom may cease to be a useful adaptive signal.

DIFFERENT CAUSES, DIFFERENT CONSEQUENCES

Different types of boredom confer different information—and may be accompanied by different consequences. For instance, boredom due to under-stimulation may encourage people to seek out interesting activities, while boredom due to overstimulation may encourage enjoyable activities instead. Interest requires cognitive resources to make sense of novel complex stimuli (Berlyne, 1971; Silvia, 2006); thus, interesting activities may be more appealing when people are bored due to under-stimulation, because such boredom informs people they have sufficient cognitive resources to experience interest. For instance, among 79 students assigned to an under-stimulating (vs. overstimulating) version of a letter-detection task, participants who completed the easy version subsequently preferred to play an interesting game, whereas those assigned to the difficult version preferred an enjoyable one instead (Westgate, 2018). Thus, one simple reason for why boredom sometimes results in negative (versus positive) outcomes may simply be a function of the type of boredom experienced, and the information it provides.

ACTION OVER INACTION

Emotions punish (and reward) behaviors. If boredom increases people's baseline preferences for action (over inaction), then inducing boredom experimentally should increase any action available. Overall, people prefer action over inaction (Albarracin et al., 2019); this tendency may be exaggerated when bored. Boredom increases novelty-seeking (Bench & Lench, 2019) and reward sensitivity (Milyavskaya et al., 2019). Thus, we predict that in situations that offer only a single available course of action, boredom will increase pro-social behavior if that available action is positive, but increase antisocial behavior if that action is negative (Yucel & Westgate, 2022). These results would account for previous findings that when only pro-social actions are available, people become more pro-social when bored, and that when only antisocial actions are available, people become more antisocial when bored; that is, previous findings may be a byproduct of experimental designs that confound pro-sociality/antisociality with action/inaction.

CHOICE AVAILABILITY

This general push toward action means that environments constrain people's ability to make good choices when bored. For instance, in experiments conducted by Pfattheicher et al. (2021), bored people tend to deduct rewards from other participants. However, when provided another option—boosting others' pay or deducting it—almost 90% of participants chose to boost others' pay, and boredom no longer predicted sadistic behavior among those low in trait sadism. Likewise, across 50 US states, regions lower in opportunity for meaning-making exhibited more boredom, as indexed by Google search activities. And regional boredom, in turn, predicted problematic public health outcomes, even after controlling for overall well-being. This suggests not only that people are more likely to experience boredom in areas devoid of opportunity, but also that lack of opportunity limits options that might enable people to escape from boredom, creating a vicious cycle.

For instance, a meta-analysis suggests a modest negative relationship between boredom and academic outcomes, = −.24 (Tze et al., 2016). We argue that this relationship is due to teaching strategies that do not foster meaning and optimal attention, and students' lack of control and autonomy in responding to such environments; that is, with few opportunities to respond constructively to school boredom, students find other alternatives (such as bullying and antisocial behavior; e.g., Pfattheicher et al., 2023). For instance, compared to students who criticize the teacher or distract themselves to cope with boredom, students who reappraise the situation and augment the value of the current class were less frequently bored and fared more positively emotionally, motivationally, and cognitively (Nett et al., 2011).

ENVIRONMENTAL MISMATCHES

Malfunctioning adaptations, evolutionary conflicts, adaptively biased mechanisms, and other constraints on natural selection may make behaviors and emotions that were once adaptive in the evolutionary past maladaptive in modern environments (Al-Shawaf et al., 2021). For instance, our predilection for high-sugar foods, once scarce and beneficial to survival, is less advantageous today when overconsumption of widely available sugar can contribute to the development of diabetes and other health risks (Symons, 1992). Such environmental mismatch between ancestral and modern society may alter the prevalence and form of the presence of boredom and also undermine the adaptive value of boredom in modern society. Technological progress in the form of automation has greatly increased productivity and safety, but has also been implicated in increasing boredom across a wide variety of professions, including air traffic control, firewatch teams, factory manufacturing (e.g., assembly lines), and anesthesiology. Likewise, new technology in the form of social media and cell phones offers easy and quick "solutions" to feelings of boredom (Kale, 2020). However, social media may not be the best solution to boredom in the long run and may even lead to maladaptive outcomes (Elhai et al., 2018).

In a hunting-gathering society, humans live in groups and spend most of the time looking for food, so they don't have a lot of idle time to feel bored. But modern society is different. The development of agriculture and industry liberated us from heavy physical labor, and we live in a small family instead of large groups, so we have more leisure time and thus have more opportunity to feel bored. Also, think about meaning and attention, two components of boredom. In an ancestral setting, meaning for humans is just survival and reproduction. Our ancestors paid attention just to find food sources or to keep themselves safe from attack by beasts. But the meaning for humans has richer implications in modern society. We have other pursuits, like being committed to advocating for minorities and building an egalitarian society, besides making a living, and thus we must pay attention to a variety of tasks to pursue our goals, instead of simply approaching food and avoiding threats.

In summary, while boredom can lead to negative behaviors, it doesn't have to. The usefulness of boredom as a signal depends in part on the environment in which it is experienced. In environments with many good alternatives, boredom may be helpful in steering people toward better options; in contrast, in environments with limited options, or where a person's choices are highly constrained, boredom may cease to serve such adaptive functions. Limited autonomy may thus weaken interest and lead to boredom in situations that are already unpleasant to begin with (Deci & Ryan, 1985; Harackiewicz et al., 1987; Lepper & Greene, 1978). What people do about boredom thus depends on their own beliefs about its causes and benefits. In addition, while boredom may have been adaptive in our evolutionary past, not all such behaviors are necessarily adaptive today (Neuberg et al., 2010). We explore the consequences of this below.

Boredom Today

Emotions and behaviors may lose their adaptive value due to change in the environment, and formerly adaptive tendencies may (in the present context) actually lead to maladaptive outcomes. Although the word "boredom" has only existed in English for a little over 200 years (Merriam-Webster, 2020), its connotation has already changed considerably. In the Western world, "bore" [1768], the predecessor of boredom, referred to the act of being "tiresome or dull"; boredom appeared as early as the 1760s as an English expression to describe the supposedly "French" experience of having a dull time (Westgate & Steidle, 2020). This does not mean that people in the past did not feel bored; for instance, boredom appears in ancient Chinese poetry, largely in the context of leisure boredom. More recently, however, boredom has been deemed a problem of modernity, or even of technology.

Boredom and Technology

Smartphones and other modern technology provide continual stimulation; social media, in particular, provides continually shifting variety (e.g., images, text, video) carefully calibrated to capture attention in short "chunks." For instance, Twitter imposes a 280-character limit on its posts, and videos on TikTok (a video-sharing social media platform) average only 15 seconds. Most importantly, social media content is personalized via algorithms designed to retain users. Obviously, social media itself is not boring; it is specifically designed for optimal attentional engagement, stimulating users with a stream of familiar tropes punctuated by novel content, providing intermittent reinforcement for scrolling and refreshing.

For instance, TikTok downloads spiked during the beginning of the COVID-19 outbreak. Compared to the week prior to lockdown, UK TikTok downloads increased by 34% the week the lockdown was announced (Kale, 2020). Is this a bad thing? Several studies find that using smartphones as a strategy to reduce boredom ultimately results in many negative outcomes such as anxiety and depression (Elhai et al., 2018). But not all studies paint a similarly bleak picture—for instance, although excessive use of smartphones and the internet was associated with anxiety and depression in a sample of 375 undergraduates, there was no relationship between these outcomes and using smartphones and the internet specifically as a method to reduce boredom (Panova & Lleras, 2016).

However, while social media may offer a temporary harbor from boredom, it may not be an effective long-term solution. Despite maximizing attention, technology varies considerably in the extent to which it aligns with valued goals—and thus, its meaningfulness. According to the *displacement-interference-complementary* framework of smartphone use (Kushlev & Leitao, 2020), for instance, smartphone use influences subjective well-being via three mechanisms: (1) replacing other activities, (2) interfering with concurrent activities, and (3) affording information and activities not otherwise available. The first two mechanisms negatively impact well-being by replacing (or interfering with) activities essential for well-being (i.e., via opportunity costs). Relying on smartphones can impair our social connection to the real world (Dwyer et al., 2018; Kushlev et al., 2017; Kushlev et al., 2019); and social media scrolling, especially, has been associated with decreased social connection and loneliness (Burke et al, 2010). A recent study (Allcott et al., 2020) found causal evidence for this link: paying people to deactivate their Facebook account for four weeks led to decreased political polarization and increased subjective well-being.

However, social media use can increase well-being when it complements real-world experience by offering information or access to activities one might not otherwise have. For instance, information-seeking on social media predicts meaningful engagement, while sociability does not (Leung, 2020). Likewise, active use (directly interacting with users on a platform) has been associated with increased subjective well-being, while passive use (i.e., observing but not interacting) has been associated with decreased subjective well-being (Verduyn et al., 2017). These findings echo our own predictions—when using social media to escape from boredom, meaningful use (i.e., active use, intentional information-seeking) may decrease boredom, but meaningless use (i.e., aimless "doom scrolling") may be ineffective or even increase boredom.

Another concern is that social media and technology may make us more susceptible to boredom over time. In one news article from *The Guardian*, people complained that TikTok rendered them unable to engage in longer content, such as that offered on YouTube or Netflix (Haigney, 2020), and heavy smartphone users do report more severe attention problems (Hadar et al., 2017). Thus, one concern is that prolonged exposure to technology might result in cognitive and motivational changes that impair attentional capacity and hurt the ability to delay gratification. If TikTok rewards users every 15–30 seconds, users might become accustomed to this rate and shift their time-discounting preferences from long-term to short-term rewards. Such short-term orientation has been implicated in many problems, including lower financial savings (Ersner-Hershfield et al., 2009), more procrastination (O'Donoghue & Rabin, 2001), and general failure in goal pursuit.

In sum, more experimental research is needed to determine the causal relationship between boredom and technology (i.e., whether boredom makes us spend more time on smartphones, or whether excessive smartphone use aggravates boredom, or both), and the outcome of boredom-driven smartphone use (i.e., whether it reduces vs. amplifies boredom).

Socioecological Views of Boredom

Finally, we want to consider boredom in the context of modern socioecological structures, such as structural inequality. Experience sampling data suggests that boredom is higher among individuals with lower household income (Chin et al., 2017), and cross-national data suggest that boredom during the 2020 coronavirus pandemic was higher among countries with lower GDP, even after controlling for a host of other variables (Westgate et al., 2023). Likewise, boredom is quite common among people experiencing homelessness (Marshall et al., 2020), due to limited opportunity and financial ability to procure services and products to fill time with meaningful activities.

We predict boredom will be especially common in environmental contexts that are highly constrained, yet offer few outlets for meaning or optimal challenge. The US prison system, for example, may be one such example. Boredom pervades the life of incarcerated youth (Bengtsson, 2012). Likewise, educational settings that stifle opportunities for meaningful challenge may foster boredom; classroom boredom has been associated with attentional problems and low intrinsic motivation (Pekrun et al., 2010).

We propose that policies, such as universal basic income and housing-first policies, that guarantee access to resources and opportunities may buffer against boredom and its associated societal costs. Likewise, reducing income inequality may offer an important path forward to reducing societal boredom, and can be addressed by resource-reallocation policies such as progressive taxation. Research has shown progressive taxation to be positively associated with subjective well-being, largely because it reduces income inequality (Oishi et al., 2012; Oishi et al., 2018). Furthermore, having positive outlets available may reduce maladaptive responses to boredom and improve public health.

In short, boredom evolved to provide information about people's current motivational and cognitive capacities and to redirect them toward more meaningful or beneficial activities. However, that signal can go awry in the modern environment, when opportunities for meaningful optimal challenges are unavailable, or when competing outlets (e.g., social media) offer temporary solutions that feel good, but come at a long-term cost. Thus, shifting boredom in modern society may require shifting society itself to foster equity in opportunities for meaning-making and challenge.

Conclusion

Although boredom can produce maladaptive outcomes, it serves an important adaptive function in providing feedback about our behavior and environments, fostering exploration, minimizing opportunity costs, maximizing learning, and finally, reducing prediction error. Boredom signals that we are either unable or unwilling to continue our current activity successfully due to deficits in attention and/or meaning, and motivates us to change it. Although it may not feel good, we argue that the world would be worse without boredom. After all, without boredom, Zhao Shixiu might have waited forever (in vain) for his feckless friend to appear, and never have left his dark room to pen the poem he shared with us, and by extension, with you.

Author Note

We thank Daniel Norman for his assistance in preparing this chapter.

References

Agrawal, M., Mattar, M. G., Cohen, J. D., & Daw, N. D. (2020). The temporal dynamics of opportunity costs: A normative account of cognitive fatigue and boredom. *Psychological Review, 129*(3), 564–585. https://doi.org/10.1037/rev0000309

Albarracín, D., Sunderrajan, A., Dai, W., & White, B. X. (2019). The social creation of action and inaction: From concepts to goals to behaviors. *Advances in Experimental Social Psychology, 60*, 223–271. https://doi.org/10.1016/bs.aesp.2019.04.001

Allcott, H., Braghieri, L., Eichmeyer, S., & Gentzkow, M. (2020). The welfare effects of social media. *American Economic Review, 110*(3), 629–676. https://doi.org/10.1257/aer.20190658

Al-Shawaf, L., Conroy-Beam, D., Asao, K., & Buss, D. M. (2016). Human emotions: An evolutionary psychological perspective. *Emotion Review, 8*(2), 173–186.

Al-Shawaf, L., & Lewis, D. M. (2017). Evolutionary psychology and the emotions. In Virgil Zeigler-Hill & Todd K. Shackelford (Eds.), *Encyclopedia of personality and individual differences* (pp. 1–10). Springer International Publishing.

Al-Shawaf, L., Lewis, D. M. G., Barbaro, N., & Wehbe, Y. S. (2021). The products of evolution: Conceptual distinctions, evidentiary criteria, and empirical examples. In T. K. Shackleford (Ed.), *The SAGE handbook of evolutionary psychology: Foundations of evolutionary psychology* (pp. 70–95). Sage.

Baldwin, M., & Westgate, E. C. (2020). States of boredom: Downsides to being bored in the USA. Unpublished manuscript.

Barrett, L. F. (2006). Solving the emotion paradox: Categorization and the experience of emotion. *Personality and Social Psychology Review, 10*, 20–46. https://doi.org/10.1207%2Fs15327957pspr1001_2

Barrett, L. F. (2009). Variety is the spice of life: A psychological construction approach to understanding variability in emotion. *Cognition and Emotion, 23*(7), 1284–1306. https://doi.org/10.1080/02699930902985894

Barrett, L. F., Adolphs, R., Marsella, S., Martinez, A. M., & Pollak, S. D. (2019). Emotional expressions reconsidered: Challenges to inferring emotion from human facial movements. *Psychological Science in the Public Interest, 20*, 1–68. https://doi.org/10.1177%2F1529100619832930

Barrett, L. F., & Simmons, W. K. (2015). Interoceptive predictions in the brain. *Nature Reviews Neuroscience, 16*(7), 419–429.

Baumeister, R. F., Vohs, K. D., Nathan DeWall, C., & Zhang, L. (2007). How emotion shapes behavior: Feedback, anticipation, and reflection, rather than direct causation. *Personality and Social Psychology Review, 11*(2), 167–203.

Bench, S. W., & Lench, H. C. (2019). Boredom as a seeking state: Boredom prompts the pursuit of novel (even negative) experiences. *Emotion, 19*(2), 242–254. https://doi.org/10.1037/emo0000433

Bengtsson, T. T. (2012). Boredom and action: Experiences from youth confinement. *Journal of Contemporary Ethnography, 41*(5), 526–553.

Berlyne, D. E. (1960). *Conflict, arousal, and curiosity*. McGraw-Hill.

Berlyne, D. E. (1971). *Aesthetics and psychobiology*. Appleton-Century Crofts.

Bliss-Moreau, E. (2017). Constructing nonhuman animal emotion. *Current Opinion in Psychology, 17*, 184–188. https://doi.org/10.1016/j.copsyc.2017.07.011

Bliss-Moreau, E. (2018, October 16). Discrete versus dimensional models of emotion? *Emotion News*. http://emotionnews.org/discrete-versus-dimensional-models-of-emotion/

Bliss-Moreau, E., Williams, L. A., & Karaskiewicz, C. L. (2021). Evolution of emotion in social context. *Encyclopedia of Evolutionary Psychological Science*, 2487–2499.

Block, R. I., Erwin, W. J., Farinpour, R., & Braverman, K. (1998). Sedative, stimulant, and other subjective effects of marijuana: Relationships to smoking techniques. *Pharmacology Biochemistry and Behavior*, *59*(2), 405–412.

Blunt, A., & Pychyl, T. A. (1998). Volitional action and inaction in the lives of undergraduate students: State orientation, procrastination and proneness to boredom. *Personality and Individual Differences*, *24*(6), 837–846. https://doi.org/10.1016/S0191-8869(98)00018-X

Boylan, J., Seli, P., Scholer, A. A., & Danckert, J. (2020). Boredom in the COVID-19 pandemic: Trait boredom proneness, the desire to act, and rule-breaking. *Personality and Individual Differences*, *171*, 110387. https://doi.org/10.1016/j.paid.2020.110387

Burke, M., Marlow, C., & Lento, T. (2010). Social network activity and social well-being. *Proceedings of the SIGCHI Conference on Human Factors in Computing Systems*, 1909–1912. https://doi.org/10.1145/1753326.1753613

Burn, C. C. (2017). Bestial boredom: A biological perspective on animal boredom and suggestions for its scientific investigation. *Animal Behaviour*, *130*, 141–151.

Cannon, W. B. (1927). The James-Lange theory of emotions: A critical examination and an alternative theory. *The American Journal of Psychology*, *39*(1–4), 106–124. https://doi.org/10.2307/1415404

Chao, M., Chen, X., Liu, T., Yang, H., & Hall, B. J. (2020). Psychological distress and state boredom during the COVID-19 outbreak in China: The role of meaning in life and media use. *European Journal of Psychotraumatology*, *11*(1), 1769379. https://doi.org/10.1080/20008198.2020.1769379

Chin, A., Markey, A., Bhargava, S., Kassam, K. S., & Loewenstein, G. (2017). Bored in the USA: Experience sampling and boredom in everyday life. *Emotion*, *17*, 359–368. https://doi.org/10.1037/emo0000232

Clarivate Analytics. (2020, October 21). *Boredom topic*. Web of Science. Retrieved October 21, 2020, from www.webofknowledge.com.

Clore, G. L., Gasper, K., & Garvin, E. (2001). Affect as information. In J. P. Forgas (Ed.), *Handbook of affect and social cognition* (pp. 121–144). Lawrence Erlbaum Associates.

Clore, G. L., & Huntsinger, J. R. (2007). How emotions inform judgment and regulate thought. *Trends in Cognitive Sciences*, *11*(9), 393–399. https://doi.org/10.1016/j.tics.2007.08.005

Clore, G. L., & Ortony, A. (2013). Psychological construction in the OCC model of emotion. *Emotion Review*, *5*, 335–343. https://doi.org/10.1177%2F1754073913489751

Corstorphine, E. (2006). Cognitive–emotional–behavioural therapy for the eating disorders: Working with beliefs about emotions. *European Eating Disorders Review*, *14*(6), 448–461. https://doi.org/10.1002/erv.747

Cosmides, L., & Tooby, J. (2000). Evolutionary psychology and the emotions. In M. Lewis & J. M. Haviland-Jones (Eds.), *Handbook of emotions* (2nd ed., pp. 91–115). Guilford.

Cowen, A. S., Keltner, D., Schroff, F., Jou, B., Adam, H., & Prasad, G. (2021). Sixteen facial expressions occur in similar contexts worldwide. *Nature*, *589*(7841), 251–257. https://doi.org/10.1038/s41586-020-3037-7

Csikszentmihalyi, M. (2000). *Beyond boredom and anxiety: Experiencing flow in work and play*. Jossey-Bass.

Dahlen, E. R., Martin, R. C., Ragan, K., & Kuhlman, M. M. (2004). Boredom proneness in anger and aggression: Effects of impulsiveness and sensation seeking. *Personality and Individual Differences*, *37*(8), 1615–1627. https://doi.org/10.1016/j.paid.2004.02.016

Damrad-Frye, R., & Laird, J. D. (1989). The experience of boredom: The role of the self-perception of attention. *Journal of Personality and Social Psychology*, *57*, 315–320. http://dx.doi.org/10.1037/0022-3514.57.2.315

Danckert, J. (2019). Boredom: Managing the delicate balance between exploration and exploitation. In J. Ros Velasco (Ed.), *Boredom is in your mind* (pp. 37–53). Springer.

Darwin, C. (1872). *The expression of emotions in animals and man*. Murray.

Darwin, C. (1964). *On the origin of species: A facsimile of the first edition*. Harvard University Press.

Dawkins, R. (1976). *The selfish gene*. Oxford University Press.

De Castella, K., Goldin, P., Jazaieri, H., Heimberg, R. G., Dweck, C. S., & Gross, J. J. (2015). Emotion beliefs and cognitive behavioural therapy for social anxiety disorder. *Cognitive Behaviour Therapy*, *44*(2), 128–141. https://doi.org/10.1080/16506073.2014.974465

Deci, E. L., & Ryan, R. M. (1985). *Intrinsic motivation and self-determination in human behavior*. Plenum Press. http://dx.doi.org/10.1007/978-1-4899-2271-7

DelPriore, D. J., Hill, S. E, & Buss, D. M. (2012). Envy: Functional specificity and sex-differentiated design features. *Personality and Individual Differences*, *53*, 317–322.

Dobson, K., Stanton, S. C., Balzarini, R. N., & Campbell, L. (2023). Are you tired of "us?" Accuracy and bias in couples' perceptions of relational boredom. *Journal of Social and Personal Relationships*, *40*(10), 3091–3120. https://doi.org/10.1177/02654075231168141

Dutton, D. G., & Aron, A. P. (1974). Some evidence for heightened sexual attraction under conditions of high anxiety. *Journal of Personality and Social Psychology, 30*(4), 510–517. https://doi.org/10.1037/h0037031

Dwyer, R. J., Kushlev, K., & Dunn, E. W. (2018). Smartphone use undermines enjoyment of face-to-face social interactions. *Journal of Experimental Social Psychology, 78*, 233–239. https://doi.org/10.1016/j.jesp.2017.10.007

Eastwood, J. D., Frischen, A., Fenske, M. J., & Smilek, D. (2012). The unengaged mind: Defining boredom in terms of attention. *Perspectives on Psychological Science, 7*, 482–495. http://dx.doi.org/10.1177/1745691612456044

Egan, L. C., Santos, L. R., & Bloom, P. (2007). The origins of cognitive dissonance: Evidence from children and monkeys. *Psychological Science, 18*, 978–983.

Ekman, P. (1992). An argument for basic emotions. *Cognition and Emotion, 6*(3–4), 169–200. https://doi.org/10.1080/02699939208411068

Elhai, J. D., Vasquez, J. K., Lustgarten, S. D., Levine, J. C., & Hall, B. J. (2018). Proneness to boredom mediates relationships between problematic smartphone use with depression and anxiety severity. *Social Science Computer Review, 36*(6), 707–720. https://doi.org/10.1177/0894439317741087

Ersner-Hershfield, H., Garton, M., Ballard, K., Samanez-Larkin, G., & Knutson, B. (2009). Don't stop thinking about tomorrow: Individual differences in future self-continuity account for saving. *Judgment and Decision Making, 4*(4), 280–286. doi: 10.1017/S1930297500003855

Ferrari, J. R. (2000). Procrastination and attention: Factor analysis of attention deficit, boredomness, intelligence, self-esteem, and task delay frequencies. *Journal of Social Behavior and Personality, 15*(5; SPI), 185–196.

Fisher, C. D. (1998). Effects of external and internal interruptions on boredom at work: Two studies. *Journal of Organizational Behavior, 19*, 503–522. https://doi.org/10.1002/(SICI)1099-1379(199809)19:5%3C503::AID-JOB854%3E3.0.CO;2-9

Friedman, R. A. (2020, August 21). Is the lockdown making you depressed, or are you just bored? *New York Times.* https://www.nytimes.com/2020/08/21/opinion/sunday/covid-depression-boredom.html?auth=login-google.

Gasper, K., & Middlewood, B. L. (2014). Approaching novel thoughts: Understanding why elation and boredom promote associative thought more than distress and relaxation. *Journal of Experimental Social Psychology, 52*, 50–57. https://doi.org/10.1016/j.jesp.2013.12.007

Geana, A., Wilson, R., Daw, N. D., & Cohen, J. D. (2016). Boredom, information-seeking and exploration. *Cognitive Science.*

Gendron, M., Roberson, D., van der Vyver, J. M., & Barrett, L. F. (2014). Perceptions of emotion from facial expressions are not culturally universal: Evidence from a remote culture. *Emotion, 14*(2), 251–262. https://doi.org/10.1037/a0036052

Gomez-Ramirez, J., & Costa, T. (2017). Boredom begets creativity: A solution to the exploitation-exploration tradeoff in predictive coding. *Biosystems, 162*, 168–176. https://doi.org/10.1016/j.biosystems.2017.04.006

Gopnik, A. (2020). Childhood as a solution to explore–exploit tensions. *Philosophical Transactions of the Royal Society B, 375*(1803), 20190502. https://doi.org/10.1098/rstb.2019.0502

Hadar, A., Hadas, I., Lazarovits, A., Alyagon, U., Eliraz, D., & Zangen, A. (2017). Answering the missed call: Initial exploration of cognitive and electrophysiological changes associated with smartphone use and abuse. *PLoS One, 12*(7), e0180094. https://doi.org/10.1371/journal.pone.0180094.

Haigney, S. (2020, May 16). TikTok is the perfect medium for the splintered attention spans of lockdown. *The Guardian.* https://www.theguardian.com/commentisfree/2020/may/16/tiktok-perfect-medium-splintered-attention-spans-coronavirus-lockdown

Harackiewicz, J. M., Abrahams, S., & Wageman, R. (1987). Performance evaluation and intrinsic motivation: The effects of evaluative focus, rewards, and achievement orientation. *Journal of Personality and Social Psychology, 53*, 1015–1023. http://dx.doi.org/10.1037/0022-3514.53.6.1015

Havermans, R. C., Vancleef, L., Kalamatianos, A., & Nederkoorn, C. (2015). Eating and inflicting pain out of boredom. *Appetite, 85*, 52–57. https://doi.org/10.1016/j.appet.2014.11.007

Hazan, C., & Shaver, P. (1987). Romantic love conceptualized as an attachment process. *Journal of Personality and Social Psychology, 52*(3), 511–524.

Hulleman, C. S., Godes, O., Hendricks, B. L., & Harackiewicz, J. M. (2010). Enhancing interest and performance with a utility value intervention. *Journal of Educational Psychology, 102*(4), 880–895. http://dx.doi.org/10.1037/a0019506

Huntsinger, J. R., Isbell, L. M., & Clore, G. L. (2014). The affective control of thought: Malleable, not fixed. *Psychological Review, 121*(4), 600–618. https://doi.org/10.1037/a0037669

Iso-Ahola, S. E., & Crowley, E. D. (1991). Adolescent substance abuse and leisure boredom. *Journal of Leisure Research, 23*(3), 260–271. https://doi.org/10.1080/00222216.1991.11969857

Izard, C. E. (1992). Basic emotions, relations among emotions, and emotion-cognition relations. *Psychological Review, 99*(3), 561–565. https://doi.org/10.1037/0033-295X.99.3.561

Kagan, J., & Lewis, M. (1965). Studies of attention in the human infant. *Merrill-Palmer Quarterly of Behavior and Development, 11*(2), 95–127.

Kale, S. (2020, April 26). How coronavirus helped TikTok find its voice. *The Observer.* https://www.theguardian.com/technology/2020/apr/26/how-coronavirus-helped-tiktok-find-its-voice

Keltner, D., & Buswell, B. N. (1996). Evidence for the distinctness of embarrassment, shame, and guilt: A study of recalled antecedents and facial expressions of emotion. *Cognition and Emotion, 10*(2), 155–172.

Keltner, D., Haidt, J., & Shiota, L. (2006). Social functionalism and the evolution of emotions. In M. Schaller, D. Kenrick, & J. Simpson (Eds.), *Evolution and social psychology* (pp. 115–142). Psychology Press.

Kneeland, E. T., Dovidio, J. F., Joormann, J., & Clark, M. S. (2016). Emotion malleability beliefs, emotion regulation, and psychopathology: Integrating affective and clinical science. *Clinical Psychology Review, 45*, 81–88. https://doi.org/10.1016/j.cpr.2016.03.008

Kramer, D. L., & Weary, D. M. (1991). Exploration versus exploitation: A field study of time allocation to environmental tracking by foraging chipmunks. *Animal Behaviour, 41*(3), 443–449.

Krebs, J. R., Kacelnik, A., & Taylor, P. (1978). Test of optimal sampling by foraging great tits. *Nature, 275*(5675), 27–31.

Kurzban, R., Duckworth, A., Kable, J., & Myers, J. (2013). An opportunity cost model of subjective effort and task performance. *Behavioral and Brain Sciences, 36*(6), 661–679. doi: 10.1017/S0140525X12003196

Kushlev, K., Hunter, J. F., Proulx, J., Pressman, S. D., & Dunn, E. (2019). Smartphones reduce smiles between strangers. *Computers in Human Behavior, 91*, 12–16. https://doi.org/10.1016/j.chb.2018.09.023

Kushlev, K., & Leitao, M. R. (2020). The effects of smartphones on well-being: Theoretical integration and research agenda. *Current Opinion in Psychology, 36*, 77–82. doi: 10.1016/j.copsyc.2020.05.001.

Kushlev, K., Proulx, J. D. E., & Dunn, E. W. (2017). Digitally connected, socially disconnected: The effects of relying on technology rather than other people. *Computers in Human Behavior, 76*, 68–74. https://doi.org/10.1016/j.chb.2017.07.001

Lebel, R. D. (2017). Moving beyond fight and flight: A contingent model of how the emotional regulation of anger and fear sparks proactivity. *Academy of Management Review, 42*(2), 190–206.

Lee, E. (2005). The relationship of motivation and flow experience to academic procrastination in university students. *The Journal of Genetic Psychology, 166*(1), 5–15. https://doi.org/10.3200/GNTP.166.1.5-15

Lepper, M. R., & Greene, D. E. (1978). *The hidden costs of reward: New perspectives on the psychology of human motivation.* Lawrence Erlbaum Associates.

Lerner, I. M. (1954). *Genetic homeostasis.* Wiley.

Leung, L. (2020). Exploring the relationship between smartphone activities, flow experience, and boredom in free time. *Computers in Human Behavior, 103*, 130–139. https://doi.org/10.1016/j.chb.2019.09.030

Lin, Y., LePine, S. E., Krause, A. N., & Westgate, E. C. (2023). A little help from my friends: Lack of social interaction predicts greater boredom during the COVID-19 pandemic. *Social and Personality Psychology Compass*, e12871.

Lindquist, K. A., Wager, T. D., Kober, H., Bliss-Moreau, E., & Barrett, L. F. (2012). The brain basis of emotion: A meta-analytic review. *Behavioral and Brain Sciences, 35*, 121–143. http://dx.doi.org/10.1017/s0140525x11000446.

Mann, S., & Cadman, R. (2014). Does being bored make us more creative? *Creativity Research Journal, 26*(2), 165–173. https://doi.org/10.1080/10400419.2014.901073

Marshall, C. A., Roy, L., Becker, A., Nguyen, M., Barbic, S., Tjörnstrand, C., Gewurtz, R., & Wickett, S. (2020). Boredom and homelessness: A scoping review. *Journal of Occupational Science, 27*(1), 107–124. https://doi.org/10.1080/14427591.2019.1595095

McAlinden, M. (2020, May 29). Lockdown boredom led me to smoke more weed. *BBC.* https://www.bbc.com/news/uk-scotland-52849794.

Meagher, R. K., & Mason, G. J. (2012). Environmental enrichment reduces signs of boredom in caged mink. *PLOS ONE, 7*(11), e49180. https://doi.org/10.1371/journal.pone.0049180

Meagher, R. K., Campbell, D. L. M., & Mason, G. J. (2017). Boredom-like states in mink and their behavioural correlates: A replicate study. *Applied Animal Behaviour Science, 197*, 112–119. https://doi.org/10.1016/j.applanim.2017.08.001

Mehlhorn, K., Newell, B. R., Todd, P. M., Lee, M. D., Morgan, K., Braithwaite, V. A., Hausmann, D., Fiedler, K., & Gonzalez, C. (2015). Unpacking the exploration–exploitation tradeoff: A synthesis of human and animal literatures. *Decision, 2*(3), 191–215. http://dx.doi.org/10.1037/dec0000033

Merriam-Webster. (2020). Boredom. *Merriam-Webster.com dictionary.* Retrieved October 13, 2020, from https://www.merriam-webster.com/dictionary/boredom.

Milyavskaya, M., Inzlicht, M., Johnson, T., & Larson, M. J. (2019). Reward sensitivity following boredom and cognitive effort: A high-powered neurophysiological investigation. *Neuropsychologia, 123*, 159–168. https://doi.org/10.1016/j.neuropsychologia.2018.03.033

Misslin, R. (2003). The defense system of fear: Behavior and neurocircuitry. *Neurophysiologie Clinique/Clinical Neurophysiology, 33*(2), 55–66. https://doi.org/10.1016/S0987-7053(03)00009-1

Mooneyham, B. W., & Schooler, J. W. (2013). The costs and benefits of mind-wandering: A review. *Canadian Journal of Experimental Psychology/Revue canadienne de psychologie expérimentale, 67*(1), 11–18. https://doi.org/10.1037/a0031569

Moynihan, A. B., Tilburg, W. A. P. van, Igou, E. R., Wisman, A., Donnelly, A. E., & Mulcaire, J. B. (2015). Eaten up by boredom: Consuming food to escape awareness of the bored self. *Frontiers in Psychology, 6*, Article 369. https://doi.org/10.3389/fpsyg.2015.00369

Nederkoorn, C., Vancleef, L., Wilkenhöner, A., Claes, L., & Havermans, R. C. (2016). Self-inflicted pain out of boredom. *Psychiatry Research, 237*, 127–132. https://doi.org/10.1016/j.psychres.2016.01.063

Nett, U. E., Goetz, T., & Hall, N. C. (2011). Coping with boredom in school: An experience sampling perspective. *Contemporary Educational Psychology, 36*(1), 49–59.

Neuberg, S. L., Kenrick, D. T., & Schaller, M. (2010). Evolutionary social psychology. In S. T. Fiske, D. T. Gilbert, & G. Lindzey (Eds.), *Handbook of social psychology* (pp. 761–796). Wiley. https://doi.org/10.1002/9780470561119.socpsy002021

Nook, E. C., Stavish, C. M., Sasse, S. F., Lambert, H. K., Mair, P., McLaughlin, K. A., & Somerville, L. H. (2020). Charting the development of emotion comprehension and abstraction from childhood to adulthood using observer-rated and linguistic measures. *Emotion, 20*(5), 773–792. http://dx.doi.org/10.1037/emo0000609

O'Donoghue, T., & Rabin, M. (2001). Choice and procrastination. *The Quarterly Journal of Economics, 116*(1), 121–160. https://doi.org/10.1162/003355301556365

Oishi, S., Kushlev, K., & Schimmack, U. (2018). Progressive taxation, income inequality, and happiness. *American Psychologist, 73*(2), 157–168. https://doi.org/10.1037/amp0000166

Oishi, S., Schimmack, U., & Diener, E. (2012). Progressive taxation and the subjective well-being of nations. *Psychological Science, 23*(1), 86–92. https://doi.org/10.1177/0956797611420882

Oishi, S., & Westgate, E. C. (2022). A psychologically rich life: Beyond happiness and meaning. *Psychological Review, 129*(4), 790–811. https://doi.org/10.1037/rev0000317

Oishi, S., Westgate, E., Cha, Y., Heintzelman, S. J., Buttrick, N., & Choi, H. (2021). The politics, curiosity, and complexity of a happy life, a meaningful life, and a psychologically rich life. Unpublished manuscript, University of Virginia.

Orcutt, J. D. (1984). Contrasting effects of two kinds of boredom on alcohol use. *Journal of Drug Issues, 14*(1), 161–173. https://doi.org/10.1177/002204268401400112

Panova, T., & Lleras, A. (2016). Avoidance or boredom: Negative mental health outcomes associated with use of information and communication technologies depend on users' motivations. *Computers in Human Behavior, 58*, 249–258. https://doi.org/10.1016/j.chb.2015.12.062

Pekrun, R., Goetz, T., Daniels, L. M., Stupnisky, R. H., & Perry, R. P. (2010). Boredom in achievement settings: Exploring control–value antecedents and performance outcomes of a neglected emotion. *Journal of Educational Psychology, 102*(3), 531–549. doi:10.1037/a0019243

Pfattheicher, S., Lazarević, L. B., Nielsen, Y. A., Westgate, E. C., Krstić, K., & Schindler, S. (2023). I enjoy hurting my classmates: On the relation of boredom and sadism in schools. *Journal of School Psychology, 96*, 41–56. https://doi.org/10.1016/j.jsp.2022.10.008.

Pfattheicher, S., Lazarevic, L. B., Westgate, E. C., & Schindler, S. (2021). On the relation of boredom and sadistic aggression. *Journal of Personality and Social Psychology, 121*(3), 573–600. https://doi.org/10.1037/pspi0000335

Plutchik, R. (1980). A general psychoevolutionary theory of emotion. In R. Plutchik & H. Kellerman (Eds.), *Emotion: Theory, research, and experience* (pp. 3–33). Academic Press.

Potthoff, S., Garnefski, N., Miklósi, M., Ubbiali, A., Domínguez-Sánchez, F. J., Martins, E. C., Witthöft, M., & Kraaij, V. (2016). Cognitive emotion regulation and psychopathology across cultures: A comparison between six European countries. *Personality and Individual Differences, 98*, 218–224. https://doi.org/10.1016/j.paid.2016.04.022

Robinson, M. D., & Clore, G. L. (2002). Belief and feeling: Evidence for an accessibility model of emotional self-report. *Psychological Bulletin, 128*, 934–960. http://dx.doi.org/10.1037/0033-2909.128.6.934

Rosenthal, R. (1974). *On the social psychology of the self-fulfilling prophecy: Further evidence for Pygmalion effects and their mediating mechanisms*. MSS Modular Publications.

Rosenwald, M. (2020, March 28). These are boom times for boredom and the researchers who study it. *Washington Post*. https://www.washingtonpost.com/local/these-are-boom-times-for-boredom-and-the-researchers-who-study-it/2020/03/27/0e62983a-706f-11ea-b148-e4ce3fbd85b5_story.html.

Russell, J. A. (2003). Core affect and the psychological construction of emotion. *Psychological Review, 110*(1), 145–172. https://doi.org/10.1037/0033-295X.110.1.145

Schachter, S., & Singer, J. (1962). Cognitive, social, and physiological determinants of emotional state. *Psychological Review, 69*, 379–399. https://psycnet.apa.org/doi/10.1037/h0046234

Schmeitzky, J. R., & Freund, A. M. (2013). Goal focus and the experience of boredom. *Poster presented at the Max Planck Institute on the LIFE Course*, Ann Arbor, Michigan.

Schmidhuber, J. (1991). A possibility for implementing curiosity and boredom in model-building neural controllers. In *Proceedings of the international conference on simulation of adaptive behavior: From animals to animats* (pp. 222–227).

Siegel, E. H., Sands, M. K., Van den Noortgate, W., Condon, P., Chang, Y., Dy, J., Quigley, K. S., & Barrett, L. F. (2018). Emotion fingerprints or emotion populations? A meta-analytic investigation of autonomic features of emotion categories. *Psychological Bulletin, 144*(4), 343–393. http://doi.org/10.1037/bul0000128

Silvia, P. J. (2006). *Exploring the psychology of interest*. Oxford University Press. http://dx.doi.org/10.1093/acprof:oso/9780195158557.001.0001

Skinner, B. F. (1963). Operant behavior. *American Psychologist, 18*, 503.

Skowronski, M. (2012), When the bored behave badly (or exceptionally). *Personnel Review, 41*(2), 143–159. https://doi.org/10.1108/00483481211200006

Sommers, J., & Vodanovich, S. J. (2000). Boredom proneness: Its relationship to psychological-and physical-health symptoms. *Journal of Clinical Psychology, 56*(1), 149–155. https://psycnet.apa.org/doi/10.1002/(SICI)1097-4679(200001)56:1%3C149::AID-JCLP14%3E3.0.CO;2-Y

Spaeth, M., Weichold, K., & Silbereisen, R. K. (2015). The development of leisure boredom in early adolescence: Predictors and longitudinal associations with delinquency and depression. *Developmental Psychology, 51*, 1380–1394.

Storbeck, J., & Clore, G. L. (2008). Affective arousal as information: How affective arousal influences judgments, learning, and memory. *Social and Personality Psychology Compass, 2*(5), 1824–1843. https://doi.org/10.1111/j.1751-9004.2008.00136.x

Struk, A. A., Scholer, A. A., Danckert, J., & Seli, P. (2020). Rich environments, dull experiences: How environment can exacerbate the effect of constraint on the experience of boredom. *Cognition and Emotion, 34*(7), 1517–1523. https://doi.org/10.1080/02699931.2020.1763919

Sun, Z., & Firestone, C. (2020). The dark room problem. *Trends in Cognitive Sciences, 24*(5), 346–348. https://doi.org/10.1016/j.tics.2020.02.006

Symons, D. (1992). On the use and misuse of Darwinism in the study of human behavior. In J. H. Barkow, L. Cosmides, & J. Tooby (Eds), *The adapted mind: Evolutionary psychology and the generation of culture* (pp. 137–159). Oxford University Press.

Tamir, M., John, O. P., Srivastava, S., & Gross, J. J. (2007). Implicit theories of emotion: Affective and social outcomes across a major life transition. *Journal of Personality and Social Psychology, 92*(4), 731–744. https://doi.org/10.1037/0022-3514.92.4.731

Teoh, A. N., Ooi, E. Y. E., & Chan, A. Y. (2020). Boredom affects sleep quality: The serial mediation effect of inattention and bedtime procrastination. *Personality and Individual Differences, 171*, 110460. https://doi.org/10.1016/j.paid.2020.110460

Tze, V. M., Daniels, L. M., & Klassen, R. M. (2016). Evaluating the relationship between boredom and academic outcomes: A meta-analysis. *Educational Psychology Review, 28*(1), 119–144.

van Tilburg, W. A. P., & Igou, E. R. (2012). On boredom: Lack of challenge and meaning as distinct boredom experiences. *Motivation and Emotion, 36*(2), 181–194. https://doi.org/10.1007/s11031-011-9234-9

van Tilburg, W. A., & Igou, E. R. (2017). Can boredom help? Increased prosocial intentions in response to boredom. *Self and Identity, 16*(1), 82–96. https://psycnet.apa.org/doi/10.1080/15298868.2016.1218925

Verduyn, P., Ybarra, O., Résibois, M., Jonides, J., & Kross, E. (2017). Do social network sites enhance or undermine subjective well-being? A critical review. *Social Issues and Policy Review, 11*(1), 274–302. https://doi.org/10.1111/sipr.12033

Vodanovich, S. J., & Rupp, D. E. (1999). Are procrastinators prone to boredom? *Social Behavior and Personality, 27*(1), 11. http://dx.doi.org/10.2224/sbp.1999.27.1.11

Wan, H. C., Downey, L. A., & Stough, C. (2014). Understanding non-work presenteeism: Relationships between emotional intelligence, boredom, procrastination and job stress. *Personality and Individual Differences, 65*, 86–90. https://doi.org/10.1016/j.paid.2014.01.018

Wegner, L., & Flisher, A. J. (2009). Leisure boredom and adolescent risk behaviour: A systematic literature review. *Journal of Child and Adolescent Mental Health, 21*(1), 1–28.

Wegner, L., Flisher, A. J., Chikobvu, P., Lombard, C., & King, G. (2008). Leisure boredom and high school dropout in Cape Town, South Africa. *Journal of Adolescence, 31*(3), 421–431. https://doi.org/10.1016/j.adolescence.2007.09.004

Wemelsfelder, F., Hunter, E. A., Mendl, M. T., & Lawrence, A. B. (2000). The spontaneous qualitative assessment of behavioural expressions in pigs: First explorations of a novel methodology for integrative animal welfare measurement. *Applied Animal Behaviour Science, 67*(3), 193–215. https://doi.org/10.1016/S0168-1591(99)00093-3

Westgate, E. C. (2018). *Why boredom is interesting*. Unpublished doctoral dissertation, University of Virginia.

Westgate, E. C., Buttrick, N. R., Lin, Y., El Helou, G., Agostini, M., Bélanger, J. J., Gützkow, B., Kreienkamp, J., Abakoumkin, G., Abdul Khaiyom, J. H., Ahmedi, V., Akkas, H., Almenara, C. A., Atta, M., Bagci, S. C., Basel, S., Berisha Kida, E., Bernardo, A. B. I., Chobthamkit, P., . . . Pontus Leander, N., et al. (2023). Pandemic boredom: Little evidence that lockdown-related boredom affects risky public health behaviors across 116 countries. *Emotion*. Advance online publication: https://doi.org/10.1037/emo0001118

Westgate, E. C., & Fairbairn, C. A. (2020). Buzzed, but not bored: How boredom leads to "bad" behavior. Unpublished manuscript.

Westgate, E. C., & Steidle, B. (2020). Lost by definition: Why boredom matters for psychology and society. *Social and Personality Psychology Compass, 14*(11), e12562. https://doi.org/10.1111/spc3.12562

Westgate, E. C., & Wilson, T. D. (2018). Boring thoughts and bored minds: The MAC model of boredom and cognitive engagement. *Psychological Review, 125*(5), 689–713. https://doi.org/10.1037/rev0000097

Westgate, E. C., Wilson, T. D., & Gilbert, D. T. (2017). With a little help for our thoughts: Making it easier to think for pleasure. *Emotion, 17*(5), 828–839. https://doi.org/10.1037/emo0000278

Wickens, C. D. (1991). Processing resources and attention. In D. L. Damos (Ed.), *Multiple-task performance* (pp. 3–34). Taylor & Francis.

Wilson, T. D., Reinhard, D. A., Westgate, E. C., Gilbert, D. T., Ellerbeck, N., Hahn, C., Brown, C. L., & Shaked, A. (2014). Just think: The challenges of the disengaged mind. *Science, 345*(6192), 75–77. https://doi.org/10.1126/science.1250830

Wojtowicz, Z., Chater, N., & Loewenstein, G. (2019). Boredom and flow: An opportunity cost theory of motivational attention. Available at SSRN: http://dx.doi.org/10.2139/ssrn.3339123

Yamamoto, N., & Ishikawa, M. (2010). Curiosity and boredom based on prediction error as novel internal rewards. In Akitoshi Hanazawa, Tsutom Miki, & Keiichi Horio (Eds.), *Brain-inspired information technology* (pp. 51–55). Springer.

Yoon, S., Dang, V., Mertz, J., & Rottenberg, J. (2018). Are attitudes towards emotions associated with depression? A conceptual and meta-analytic review. *Journal of Affective Disorders, 232*, 329–340. https://doi.org/10.1016/j.jad.2018.02.009

Yu, Y., Chang, A. Y. C., & Kanai, R. (2019). Boredom-driven curious learning by homeo-heterostatic value gradients. *Frontiers in Neurorobotics, 12*, 88. https://doi.org/10.3389/fnbot.2018.00088

Yucel, M., & Westgate, E. C. (2022). From electric shocks to the electoral college: How boredom guides moral behavior. In A. Elpidorou (Ed.), *The moral psychology of boredom* (pp. 35–56). Rowman & Littlefield.

CHAPTER 18

Kama Muta: The Cuteness Emotion

Kamilla Knutsen Steinnes, Johanna Katarina Blomster Lyshol, Janis H. Zickfeld, Thomas Schubert, and Beate Seibt

> **Abstract**
>
> Cuteness, as described through Konrad Lorenz's *Kindchenschema*, refers to a youthful and fragile appearance through a set of physical features such as large eyes, a round head, and a small nose. Such features elicit careful behavior in the perceiver, capture attention, and motivate approach. This chapter describes various responses to cuteness and discusses how these are culturally unifying yet affected by cultural salience and personal differences. Despite the long line of empirical studies suggesting that cuteness has an evolutionary function, recent advances indicate that responses to cuteness go beyond maternal caregiving to offspring. According to different theories, cuteness may evoke compassion, tenderness, empathic concern, nurturant love, *kawaii*, or dimorphous emotional expressions, facilitating pro-social behavior, social engagement, and humanization. The chapter suggests that evolutionary and cultural aspects of these emotional states can be united through the common core of devotion to communal relationships—at the heart of the *kama muta* emotion.
>
> **Key Words:** kama muta, cuteness, communal sharing, baby schema, being moved

Introduction

Adorable features such as big round eyes and a small nose are usually found in infants and baby animals, and they attract and sustain our attention, motivate approach, and affect our behavior. And while there is a large consensus among scholars of cuteness that cute objects tend to evoke positive feelings in the beholder, the exact nature of this emotional response remains unclear. Marketing, charity campaigns, product design, and entertainment industries have long acknowledged and exploited the appeal of cuteness and the emotion it evokes (Buckley, 2016; Nittono, 2016; Nittono et al., 2012). Hence, this emotion is a widespread phenomenon that is commonly felt, yet rarely investigated. At first glance, cuteness may appear too trivial and undeserving of academic attention, but the way we respond to cuteness is one of the most powerful determinants of human behavior (Dale et al., 2017; Kringelbach et al., 2016; May, 2019). "Cute" typically refers to someone or something small, fragile, and pleasant, and is often associated with the infantile visual features of the baby schema described below. Cuteness is not restricted to visual infant features only, but may also include the sound of babbling babies (Seifritz et al., 2003; van Riem et al., 2012; Young et al., 2018), the baby smell of infants' clothing (Porter et al., 1983), and even soft colors and round shapes of product design (Nenkov & Scott, 2014). This chapter focuses on the visual features of *Kindchenschema* cuteness (Lorenz, 1943, 1971), rather than broader approaches to cuteness like *whimsical* cuteness of product design (Nenkov & Scott, 2014), or cute sounds and smells (Kringelbach et al., 2016). According to Dale et al. (2017), studies of cuteness can be divided into two main focus areas: cuteness as an aesthetic, and cuteness as a psychological response. This chapter will focus on the latter by first reviewing literature linking cuteness to evolutionary fitness and adaptive caretaking behavior. Second, evidence implying that the emotional response to cuteness is cultural-general, yet modified by cultural and individual variance, will be presented. Third, several emotional perspectives on cuteness will be reviewed through the common lens of evoking more than parental caretaking, and interpreted as a complex response affected by cognition and emotion. Finally, the authors propose that these various theories of the cuteness emotion may be unified through the common core of communal sharing (CS), which represents the main elicitor of the social-relational *kama muta* emotion, often labeled as being *moved* or *touched*.

Survival of the Cutest

Cuteness is associated with evolutionary fitness. Charles Darwin (1872) noted that infants possess a quality that attracts attention and encourages caregiving from adults, which leads to increased chances of reproductive success. Parents' and caregivers' relation with infants is critical for the latter's survival and development (Kringelbach et al., 2016). Cute infant features have evolved and endured through Darwinian selection, as a cute offspring was more likely to receive attention and caregiving from adults and was thus more likely to survive and reproduce (Dydynski, 2020). Similar "cutifying" effects are seen in the evolution of pets (Dale, 2017; Kaminski et al., 2019), toys (Hinde & Barden, 1985), and cartoon characters (Gould, 1982).

The science behind cuteness, through systematic biological inquiry, was introduced by ethologist Konrad Lorenz in 1943. He proposed the idea of the "baby schema"—a set of facial and bodily characteristics that make someone or something appear cute and that releases innate mechanisms that motivate caregiving in the perceiver (Lorenz, 1971). The baby schema, or *Kindchenschema*, includes features such as a large head relative to body size, large eyes, chubby cheeks, a high and protruding forehead, a small nose and chin, and small ears. These childlike features are neotenous, i.e., only found in children and youth, and gradually abate as the offspring ages. Beyond signaling youth, cute features also tend to communicate helplessness, innocence, physical weakness and smallness, vulnerability, dependence, and naïveté (Batson et al., 2005; Berry & McArthur, 1985; Dijker, 2014; May, 2019; Zebrowitz, 2006). Because cute features are retained in childhood, Lorenz suggested that an affinity for cuteness was a result of natural selection, increasing individuals' chances for survival through caring for offspring (Lorenz, 1943). Hence, a built-in cuteness response would lead adults and even adolescents to want to care for infants, regardless of whether they had children themselves (i.e., alloparenting). Lorenz extended this hypothesis of the caretaking response to cuteness to apply both *within* and *across* species. Specifically, he observed that parents took care of their young, and that humans displayed a similar response to cute infants as to animals resembling these across species. Contemporary research supports this extension of the cuteness response to animals (e.g., Archer & Monton, 2011; Borgi & Cirulli, 2016; Borgi et al., 2014; Little, 2012). Borgi et al. (2014), for instance, found that both children (as young as three years) and adults perceived photos of babies, puppies, and kittens with high adherence to the baby schema to be cuter than photos of the same species with low baby schema. Hence, the cuteness response is not merely evoked by infants from our own species, but also and incidentally from other animals displaying features of the baby schema.

The evolutionary caretaking hypothesis of cuteness proposed by Lorenz has undergone substantial empirical testing. Overall, findings show that cuteness can evoke behavioral tendencies related to protection and care. Research has demonstrated that infants and animals with features of the baby schema capture the attention of adults and children alike, are perceived as cute, are preferentially treated compared to the less cute, and that cute infants are more likely to be adopted and receive attention, toys, baby talk, and caregiving from adults (Borgi et al., 2014; Brosch et al., 2007; Glocker, Langleben, Ruparel, Loughead, Gur, et al., 2009; Glocker, Langleben, Ruparel, Loughead, Valdez, et al., 2009; Golle et al., 2013; Golle et al., 2015; Hildebrandt & Fitzgerald, 1979, 1981; Little, 2012; Volk et al., 2007; Wolfensohn, 2020). Kruger (2015), for example, tested Lorenz's hypothesis by showing participants photos of semi-precocial baby animals (that require caretaking) and super-precocial baby animals (that do not require caretaking) and asking them to rate the animals. The semi-precocial baby animals were judged as cuter, more attractive, helpless, and youthful, and less mature and independent compared to the super-precocial baby animals. Moreover, the semi-precocial baby animals evoked stronger caregiving-related behaviors in the participants, such as wanting to pet and adopt them. Thus, cuteness is historically presumed to evoke an innate, instinctual, mainly maternal, caregiving response. Several experimental research studies have demonstrated that Lorenz's baby schema accurately defines what and whom we perceive to be cute. This is further corroborated by neuroimaging studies of cuteness, demonstrating that baby schema stimuli trigger rapid and unique brain activity in areas associated with attention, focus, emotion, and reward, such as the precuneus, orbitofrontal cortex, and nucleus accumbens (Glocker, Langleben, Ruparel, Loughead, Valdez, et al., 2009; Kringelbach et al., 2008; Kringelbach et al., 2016). That is, cuteness taps into our reward system in the brain, which stimulates our emotions and motivates our intention to nurture human and animal infants displaying features of the baby schema—resulting in increased chances of survival of the cutest.

Despite the long line of empirical studies suggesting that cuteness has an evolutionary component, contemporary research indicates that responses to cuteness go beyond maternal caregiving to offspring. A series of psychological studies identified that the cuteness response also encompasses empathy, humanization, and sharing. The individual response to the baby schema may not be as instinctual and spontaneous as first believed, but is mediated through cognition and emotion and is influenced by personality and other individual differences, as well as by cultural factors and their salience.

The Cuteness Response is Culturally Universal, yet Individually Different

This chapter proposes that cuteness—along with the emotion it evokes—is not culture-specific or discriminating, but rather culture-general and universal. In fact, the baby schema in infants captures the attention of adults, regardless of the infants' race or ethnicity (Proverbio et al., 2011; Zebrowitz et al., 1993). Furthermore, Esposito et al. (2014) found that physiological arousal measured through facial temperature increased in response to infant faces, regardless of whether the infant belonged to the perceiver's cultural in-group or out-group. While the absence of significant difference is not proof of equivalence, these results suggest that cuteness responses often disregard both in- and out-group divisions and cultural familiarity.

Despite cuteness and the emotional response to it appearing to be underpinned by a universal core across cultures (Esposito et al., 2014; Nittono, 2016), this global phenomenon is more salient and appreciated in certain cultures. Consider the availability of labels. For many emotions, languages have both terms that describe one's inner state ("I am fearful") and the quality of the evoking stimuli ("This dog is frightening"). There is, for example, no inner-state term for the emotion evoked by cuteness in certain cultures (e.g., English, Norwegian, German), while other cultures do have a corresponding label for this emotion (e.g., Hungarian, Estonian, Finnish; Steinnes et al., 2019). East Asian countries are perhaps the most notable examples of cultures where cuteness is highly prevalent and pervasive. The concept of *kawaii*, for example, has long been acknowledged and celebrated in Japan and is considered a central aspect of the country's contemporary culture (Nittono, 2016). East Asian cuteness cultures are accredited as one of the key influences to the global rise of cuteness in mainstream culture (Dale, 2016), and cuteness plays a significant role in modern consumer (Ngai, 2012) and digital cultures (Wittkower, 2012).

Besides cultural variations in salience, responses to cuteness are influenced by individual factors such as age, gender, and stage in life. Both children and adults respond to cuteness. Children aged 3–6 years show a preference for the baby schema in both human and animal faces, measured by gaze allocation and cuteness ratings (Borgi et al., 2014). Several studies show a similar preference in adults (e.g., Archer & Monton, 2011; Brosch et al., 2007; Glocker, Langleben, Ruparel, Loughead, Gur, et al., 2009). Moreover, empirical evidence of individual differences suggest that women respond more strongly to baby schema than men. Women are better at accurately picking out the cutest infant faces, as indexed by the faces' correspondence to Lorenz's baby schema (Lobmaier et al., 2010). Moreover, pro-socially oriented women (but not pro-socially oriented men) respond to cuteness through increased physical carefulness, as a proxy for the embodiment of caregiving (Sherman et al., 2013). Hormonal effects may also influence cuteness perception. High levels of reproductive hormones in women can increase their sensitivity to cuteness compared to low levels of reproductive hormones (Sprengelmeyer et al., 2009), and women are most sensitive to cuteness cues during the ovulation phase of their menstrual cycle (Lobmaier et al., 2015). There are, however, no gender differences when it comes to motivation to view cute babies. Both men and women will exert themselves in order to look longer at infant faces (Hahn et al., 2013; Parsons et al., 2011). Although no differences *between* genders emerge in motivation to view infant faces, there appear to be differences *within* genders. Specifically, women who report being more interested in interacting with babies expend more effort to look longer at infant faces (Hahn et al., 2015). When participants are asked to rate the cuteness of babies through self-reports, women tend to rate babies as cuter compared to men. Conversely, neuroimaging studies indicate that the cuteness response triggers the same brain area activation in both genders (Kringelbach et al., 2008). This apparent discrepancy between self-reports and brain scans of the cuteness response might be associated with societal gender expectations and norms surrounding childrearing and emotional expressions. Taken together, these findings indicate that responding to cuteness is influenced by age, culture, and biological sex, as well as changes in life circumstances such as pregnancy and parenting (Schaller, 2018).

Beyond Caretaking: Cuteness Fosters Socialization, Humanization, and Emotion Regulation

Contemporary research on cuteness understands responses to cuteness to a larger extent as socialization and emotion, and to a lesser extent as parental caretaking. The broadened psychological conceptualization of cuteness finds that exposure to cute objects typically induces a positive emotional response involving feelings of tenderness, affection, caregiving, socialization, compassion, empathy, and love (e.g., Nittono et al., 2012; Schaller, 2018; Sherman & Haidt, 2011; Shiota et al., 2014).

Social Engagement and Morality
Challenging the classical theory of cuteness as an innate release mechanism of parental caregiving, Sherman and Haidt (2011) argued that cute objects motivate social engagement, playfulness, and affiliation. The difference is the assumption that emotional and cognitive factors mediate between stimulus and response. Specifically, they proposed a "cuteness response" as an evolved moral emotion that facilitates social relations and humanizes the targets. They placed *disgust* as an opposing moral emotion to the cuteness response, both of which are posited as highly cognitive emotions. While cute objects are humanized, pleasant, and highly approachable, disgusting objects are dehumanized, unpleasant, and highly aversive. Cuteness is proposed to have evolved as a trigger of social motivations related to parental care, such as cuddling and embracing, suggesting a relationship between social engagement and caretaking (Sherman & Haidt, 2011).

Evaluating a baby's potential sociability is suggested as an explanation for why cuteness evokes caretaking in nonparents (Sherman & Haidt, 2011). In support of this view, infants are not rated as most cute when they are the most vulnerable and most in need of care, but rather when they are between the age of 10 months and three years (Hildebrandt & Fitzgerald, 1979; Sanefuji et al., 2007; Sherman & Haidt, 2011). At this age, they begin expressing greater awareness of other infants and adults, as well as paying more attention to social interactions. Moreover, infants are perceived as cuter when they are happy and smiling than when they are crying and in distress (Hildebrandt, 1983). In a similar experiment, Parsons et al. (2014) found that happy infants were rated as cuter than infants displaying a less positive temperament, and adults were more motivated to view the happy infants. Furthermore, Langlois, Ritter, Casey, and Sawin (1995), found that mothers of cute infants were more affectionate and playful around their babies than mothers of less-cute infants. Hence, Sherman and Haidt (2011) argued that smiling babies invite socialization, and that when infants are at their cutest they are beginning to socialize and engage with others. For this reason, cuteness is proposed to be a contributor to the socialization of children (including those of others), and thus a contributing factor in humans' development of community and cooperation (Sherman & Haidt, 2011).

The socialization perspective is further supported by evidence of embodied physical care in response to cuteness. In addition, viewing pictures of cute baby animals (such as kittens and puppies), compared to their adult and less-cute counterparts, increases carefulness in the perceiver when performing a fine motor dexterity task as a proxy for caregiving (Sherman et al., 2009). The fine motor dexterity task involved the participant playing a doctor in the operation game, trying to help a patient by carefully removing harmful objects from the patient's body with a pair of tweezers. Sherman et al. (2009) explain their results through embodied cognition. Viewing cute pictures can elicit tenderness in terms of both a positive emotional state and tender physical behavior. Nittono et al. (2012) further elaborate these findings through three experiments demonstrating that looking at pictures of cute animals improves carefulness in performing tasks that require focused attention, enhancing carefulness in both the motor and perceptual domains. Based on these results, Nittono et al. (2012) argue that the power of cuteness goes beyond social engagement and caregiving. They postulate that the emotional response evoked by cuteness leads to attentional focus and careful behavior and may have broad effects on both cognition and behavior.

Empathic Concern
Several other scholars support the socialization and moral perspective of cuteness. For example, Dale (2017) also argues that the emotional response to cute objects prompts engagement, companionship, communication, and interactive play. He suggests that cuteness functions as

an adaptive cooperative survival strategy that fosters pro-sociality. Kringelbach et al. (2016) further support this view by proposing that, beyond caretaking, cuteness evokes empathy, sympathy, and compassion, and consequently facilitates complex social relations. They suggest that anthropomorphizing of cute objects through humanizing them extends human morality and reduces dehumanization and discrimination against out-groups. Dijker (2014) notes that cuteness is tied to vulnerability and suggests that vulnerable objects evoke various moral emotions such as tenderness and sympathy. Sympathy, for example, is recognized across several cultures by the exclamation "aww" (Cordaro et al., 2016). Compatible findings show that baby schema features are perceived as warm and sociable (Zebrowitz et al., 2007), and that both signs of cuteness and vulnerability in faces evoke pro-social behavior (Keating et al., 2003). Additionally, Wang, Mukhopadhyay, and Patrick (2017) found that consumers experienced feelings of tenderness in response to conservation appeals showing baby schema cuteness. Zhang and Zhou (2020) second the moral understanding of cuteness and propose that the pro-social benefits of cuteness can be used to educate children about morality, altruism, and empathy. Indeed, several studies demonstrate that cuteness evokes empathic concern in the perceiver (e.g., Levin et al., 2017; Steinnes et al., 2019). Tenderness and compassion (or sympathy) are suggested to be part of the broader term *empathic concern* (Lishner et al., 2011; Lishner et al., 2008; Niezink et al., 2012). Tenderness seems to be more prominently related to cute stimuli (Lishner et al., 2011), and is characterized by reduced aspects of sadness in comparison to compassion (Kalawski, 2010). Similarly, the concept of *nurturant love*, an affectionate response to cute stimuli that motivates caregiving (Shaver et al., 1996; Shiota et al., 2014), has also been related to compassion or empathic concern (Weidman & Tracy, 2020a). Empathic concern is typically defined as a response to others in need, and may be described as feeling sympathetic, compassionate, tender, softhearted, warm, and moved (Batson et al., 1987; Steinnes et al., 2019). Cuteness does, in fact, evoke empathic concern in the perceiver. Levin et al. (2017), for example, found that cute objects in distress, such as a child or a puppy, evoke more empathic concern than human adults in distress. Similarly, infants and baby animals evoke more empathic concern compared to adult humans and animals (Lishner et al., 2008; Zickfeld et al., 2018).

Kawaii

Like Sherman and Haidt (2011), Nittono (2016) argues that cuteness evokes caregiving in a broader sense, such as being more careful and encouraging socialization in children. He conceptualizes cuteness and the response to it as the Japanese term kawaii. Historically, kawaii has been used to refer to something or someone small, weak, and in need of protection (Berque et al., 2020). Recently, the term has expanded to refer to an entire culture of *kawaii*, which permeates virtually all aspects of Japanese society and can be anything charming, adorable, childish, and lovable (Lieber-Milo & Nittono, 2019). Dale (2016) notes that *kawaii*, or "East Asian cute," is one of the most significant factors influencing cuteness worldwide. *Kawaii* can refer to objects both *with* and *without* baby schema (Nittono & Ihara, 2017) and may include humans, robots, animals, anime characters, movies, handwriting, clothing, food, mannerism, and so on. *Kawaii* has a unique meaning in Japanese and is considered to not be fully translatable to other languages (Nittono, 2016). Nevertheless, *kawaii* may be roughly translated to "lovely," "pretty," "adorable," and similar terms (Nittono, 2016), although the closest equivalent English word for *kawaii* is "cute" (Marcus et al., 2018; Nittono & Ihara, 2017). Nittono (2016) puts forward a behavioral "two-layer model" of *kawaii*-cuteness. The two-layer model understands cuteness as both a biologically based emotion and as a culturally determined social value. The response to *kawaii* is a highly positive, moderately arousing, and socially motivated emotion that is typically evoked by (but not limited to) cute babies and children. *Kawaii* encourages both parental care of needy offspring and promotes socialization as the offspring ages and starts to interact with others. Other studies of *kawaii* have shown that *kawaii* pictures (both with and without baby schema) can elicit facial muscles associated with smiling, suggesting that stimuli evoking *kawaii* motivate socialization and approach-motivation and evoke a positive emotional state (Nittono & Ihara, 2017).

Cute Aggression

Other scholars argue for a more nuanced view of the argument that cuteness evokes a predominantly positive emotional response. In "The cuteness of the avant-garde," Ngai (2005) suggests that cuteness in consumerism evokes conflicting and simultaneous feelings of tenderness and aggression. That is, parallels are drawn between cuteness and affectionate and nurturing responses, as well as aggressive and violent responses. According to Ngai (2012), cuteness as an aesthetic evokes an emotional response that is characterized by an unbalanced power dynamic, wherein the perceiver feels superior and dominant over the cute object through the latter's vulnerability and powerlessness. Such experienced dominance may, on one hand, lead the perceiver to want to protect and care for the cute object. On another hand, it may promote some form of aggression toward the cute object.

In a related line of experimental research, emotional responses to cuteness are considered to be "dimorphous" expressions of both caregiving and behaviors that resemble aggression, such as pinching, squeezing, biting, and teeth clenching (Aragón & Bargh, 2018; Aragón et al., 2015). The latter is termed "cute aggression" and defines the impulse to squeeze, pinch, and bite cute objects, albeit importantly *without* any intention to hurt (Aragón et al., 2015). Hence, cute aggression may be understood as an example of dimorphous emotional expressions, which may be defined as the expression of an emotion when experiencing another emotion, such as laughing when feeling sad (Stavropoulos & Alba, 2018). Aragón et al. (2015) studied emotional responses to cute stimuli (i.e., photos of baby animals and human infants) through self-reports in an online survey. Their results suggested that cute objects displaying features of the baby schema evoked both caretaking and cute aggression in participants. Specifically, their findings revealed a mediation of self-reports of feeling overwhelmed by positive emotion on the correlation between cuteness ratings and cute aggression (Aragón et al., 2015). From an evolutionary perspective, the authors postulate that being overwhelmed by emotion and hence somewhat debilitated in response to cute babies in need of protection is not adaptive behavior. Thus, these dimorphous expressions are argued to have evolved to regulate intense and overwhelming positive emotions (Aragón et al., 2015; Stavropoulos & Alba, 2018). Dale (2016, 2017) argues that cute aggression is regulated through channeling aggressive behavioral tendencies through social engagement. That is, instead of causing harm to a cute object, the perceiver rather engages in playful linguistic and behavioral outburst in response to its cuteness, such as squealing, exclaiming "aww," cooing, clenching fists, and gritting teeth. In this way, the perceiver directs the overwhelmingly positive emotion evoked by cuteness away from the cute target by embracing playful and childlike behavior. Dale argues that such channeling of cute aggression protects the cute object from potential harm, as well as encouraging continued social engagement with it.

Kama Muta as the Common Denominator

Relative to other emotions, the published research on the cuteness emotion is remarkably scarce (Buckley, 2016). We speculate that one reason for this is the lack of a common emotional conceptual understanding and corresponding name of the emotion in

English. Language and terminology are important drivers of attitudes and behaviors, and precisely defined psychological concepts are crucial when studying the constructs they denote—especially for emotions (Fiske, 2020). We argue that the various cuteness emotion theories can be unified through two concepts: The various relational aspects evoked by cuteness share the core of CS, and the actual emotional reactions can be understood with the emotion concept of *kama muta*, which is evoked if CS suddenly intensifies. CS refers to social interactions where people feel they share a common identity that focuses on sharing according to need and ability, and is communicated by means of aspects such as synchrony, touch, or commensalism (Fiske, 2004b). *Kama muta* (Sanskrit for "moved by love") represents a positive social emotion evoked by a sudden intensification of such CS relations (Fiske et al., 2019). If intense, *kama muta* is typically accompanied by moist eyes or tears, chills or goosebumps, and a warm feeling in the chest (Zickfeld et al., 2020; Zickfeld, Schubert, Seibt, Blomster, et al., 2019). A touching father-daughter reunion at an airport, a heartwarming wedding speech from the groom to the bride, and a mother's first embrace of her newborn child are typical examples of *kama muta* (Fiske, 2019). Importantly, observing and interacting with cute animals also evokes *kama muta* (Steinnes et al., 2019). In order to characterize the relationship between cuteness and *kama muta*, we will focus on the biological and cultural evolution of *kama muta*, its relation to other emotions, its motivational functions, and finally consider empirical evidence related to cute animals and infants.

Kama Muta and Its Biological and Cultural Evolution

Reviewing the evidence presented so far, it seems clear that Lorenz's initial idea of a direct link between perceiving a *Kindchenschema* stimulus and caretaking behavior should be modified. In its stead, we can assume that baby schema stimuli evoke an emotional response that in turn motivates caretaking behavior (Sherman & Haidt, 2011). Whether and what caretaking behavior ensues depends on the situation, similar to the way in which fear can lead to fight, freeze, or flight depending on the situation.

Can this emotion be identified clearly? Any theoretical proposal would need to accommodate the basic findings identified earlier in the chapter: The emotion motivates approach and caretaking; the emotion is experienced as positive; the emotion is accompanied by a set of nonverbal behaviors including smiling, vocalizations such as "aww"; and finally, the emotion is universal at its core but still is modified by cultural peculiarities. All the emotional states outlined above motivate approach and care for the cute elicitor. Several labels for the emotion evoked by cuteness have been suggested, including *cuteness response*, *kawaii*, *cute-affect*, *aww*, *tenderness*, *nurturant love*, and *cute-emotion* (Buckley, 2016; Dale, 2017; Kalawski, 2010; Nittono, 2016; Sherman & Haidt, 2011; Shiota et al., 2014). Inherent in these proposals is that the emotion is unique for cute stimuli.

The authors of this chapter believe that the emotion these labels refer to is *kama muta*, an emotion that is defined and observed more broadly than just in response to cute stimuli. *Kama muta* theory grew out of observations on experiences that English speakers label as *being moved* or *touched*, and the theoretical framework offered by Relational Models Theory (Fiske, 1992) and its sister theories Complementarity Theory and Conformation Theory (Fiske, 2000, 2004a). The basic assumptions of *kama muta* theory are the following.

Emotions in general and *kama muta* in particular are understood as a combination of a biologically prepared blueprint and culturally transmitted complements. This view is rooted in *dual inheritance theories*, which assume that humans have been shaped in parallel by biological and cultural evolution (Boyd, 2018; Boyd & Richerson, 1985; Fiske, 2000;

Henrich, 2016), and is coherent with arguments in developmental and embodied cognition (Lee & Schwarz, 2020; Schubert & Grüning, 2021). Cultures can be understood as providing *implementations* of the basic emotional blueprints and making them unique in various ways: They can emphasize and ritualize situations in which the emotion should be felt strongly. They can teach specific ways to express the emotion. They can emphasize some prepared ways to express the emotion and suppress others. Through labeling, they can differentiate from or assimilate the emotion to other emotions. What cultures do for emotions can be likened to what they do for color perception. Both emotions and color perception are determined by a universal biological basis, but different cultures have developed different color spaces and concepts that are adapted to the local environment and differ substantially in their complexity and structure. This structure in turn influences cognitive processes and to some extent perception, especially at the borders between color concepts (Roberson et al., 2000).

Dual inheritance theories propose an interplay between biological and cultural evolution. Cultural evolution creates concepts, skills, and behaviors that are adapted to the environment, which includes the human body itself. In that sense, the cultural components of emotions are adaptations to the biologically evolved blueprints—for instance, some rudimentary facial expressions, the ability to cry, etc. But the outcomes of cultural evolution in turn create an environment for the biological evolution to adapt to. For instance, our surprisingly short guts and small jaws are adaptations to a long history of cooking our food and thereby reducing the need for chewing and detoxifying in the gut. Similarly, it seems well possible, although speculative at this time, that some aspects of our biology of emotions are in fact adaptations to early cultural adaptations.

Kama muta theory further argues that the domain for which *kama muta* evolved biologically and culturally is the relational building block of CS, as defined by Relational Models Theory (Fiske, 1992). Social relations that build on top of the blueprint for CS are relations where people feel that they share some important essence and are interchangeable in some way. In such relations, people typically share resources and burdens according to need and ability. Such relations are communicated and regulated through behaviors that index the connection of bodies through sharing of real or virtual essences, touch, synchronous behavior, imitation, shared clothing, or body markings, etc. Communal sharing relations often underlie parental caretaking (Fiske, 2004b).

Kama muta is evoked when people experience a sudden intensification of a CS relation. This can be the start of a new relation, the modification of an existing relation that was previously following a different model, or the intensification of an already existing communal relation. Marriage proposals and marriages, surprise reunions, being given a new pet, becoming a parent, and being praised by a parent are all situations where people often feel *kama muta*. Interestingly, we can also feel *kama muta* when observing others in such situations (in real life or even in fiction), presumably because we identify with those involved.

When people feel *kama muta*, they tend to experience bodily warmth, goosebumps, and to tear up. They often express the emotion with vocalizations such as "aww" and moving a hand to their heart. They report that they experience positive affect and often want to share the experience with others. They also report motivation of being socially close to the agent which evoked *kama muta* (Blomster Lyshol et al., 2022; Blomster Lyshol et al., 2023). These effects have been observed in several cultures (Schubert, Zickfeld, Seibt et al., 2018; Seibt, Zickfeld, Zhu et al., 2018; Zickfeld, Schubert, Seibt, Blomster, et al., 2019) and are consistent with the larger literature on *being moved* (Zickfeld, Schubert, Seibt, & Fiske, 2019).

Kama Muta and Its Relation to Other Concepts
Kama muta has been theoretically and empirically linked to several other emotion concepts including *awe, empathic concern, compassion, admiration, sadness,* and *gratitude* (Fiske et al., 2019; Zickfeld et al., 2020; Zickfeld, Schubert, Seibt, Blomster, et al., 2019; Zickfeld, Schubert, Seibt, & Fiske, 2019). For example, awe, an emotion elicited by perceptions of vastness and a need for accommodation (Keltner & Haidt, 2003), has been successfully differentiated from *kama muta* with regard to its physiological responses, subjective feelings, or action tendencies (Zickfeld et al., 2020; 2019). On the other hand, the concept of empathic concern, often referred to as *empathy* (Zickfeld et al., 2020), and including aspects of *compassion* (or *sympathy*) and *tenderness* (Kalawski, 2010; Lishner et al., 2011; Niezink et al., 2012), has been argued to represent a specific subtype of *kama muta* responses (Zickfeld et al., 2017). Studies focusing on the relation between trait empathic concern and state *kama muta* have provided a consistent association (Zickfeld, Schubert, Seibt, Blomster, et al., 2019; Zickfeld et al., 2017), while both concepts employ the same or similar measurements at the state level. The concept of empathic concern has been associated with cuteness responses (Batson et al., 2005; Lishner et al., 2008; Niezink et al., 2012), specifically the aspect referred to as *tenderness*, which has been considered a prototypical response to cute targets (Kalawski, 2010). All of these concepts include a caregiving function, whether in response to others in need, vulnerability, or cuteness (Niezink et al., 2012). In addition, the concepts of compassion and tenderness have been linked to *nurturant love* (Shaver et al., 1996; Weidman & Tracy, 2020a), which is elicited by "physical and behavioral cuteness" (Shiota et al., 2014, p. 108). We argue that all of these concepts—empathic concern, tenderness, compassion, sympathy, and nurturant love—represent an emotional reaction in response to intensifications in CS and in turn motivate attending to CS relationships in the form of altruistic (Batson, 2010) or caregiving behavior (Shiota et al., 2014). While studies found that these concepts show a high theoretical and methodological overlap to the point of being indistinguishable (Weidman et al., 2017; Weidman & Tracy, 2020a, 2020b), we think that CS and thereby *kama muta* represent the common denominator in merging all these concepts.

Kama Muta and Its Motivational Aspects
Relational Models Theory posits that people are fundamentally motivated to socially interact with others (Fiske, 1992). Due to the importance of social relationships, it is further posited that specific emotions are evoked by the state of one's relationship, which motivates behaviors aimed at fulfilling one's relational needs (Fiske, 2002). Thus, *kama muta*, which is evoked by a sudden intensification of a CS relationship, motivates devotion to the CS relation that evoked *kama muta* (Fiske et al., 2019). As outlined above, CS relationships are characterized by members of the CS relationship focusing on what they have in common, thus making them socially interchangeable. The specific common aspect which is in focus depends on the situation: in some situations, kinship is the main focus; in other situations, the focus is on a common humanity (Fiske, 2004b; Haslam, 2006). By focusing on this communality, people respond to the needs of their CS partners (Fiske, 1992). Thus, the motivational effect of *kama muta* is viewing the agent eliciting *kama muta* and oneself as the same, and to respond to the needs of the agent. Studies have shown that *kama muta* is related with increased ratings of communality, operationalized for instance through viewing oppositional partisans belonging to a common American in-group (Blomster Lyshol, Seibt, et al., 2020), viewing out-groups as humans (Blomster Lyshol, Thomsen, et al., 2020), and motivation to adopt Norwegian culture (Blomster Lyshol, 2020; Blomster Lyshol, Pich, et al., 2022; Blomster Lyshol, Thomsen, et al., 2020). Supporting the notion that *kama muta* motivates people to respond to the needs

of their CS partners, studies have shown that *kama muta* is related with increased motivation to vote for a political candidate (Seibt et al., 2019), and motivation to behave communally in general (Zickfeld, Schubert, Seibt, Blomster, et al., 2019; Zickfeld, Schubert, Seibt, & Fiske, 2019). We argue that the motivational effects described in the cuteness response (Sherman & Haidt, 2011), *kawaii* (Nittono, 2016), baby schema (Lorenz, 1943; 1971), and cute aggression (Aragón et al., 2015) accounts can fit into our *kama muta* account. Our arguments are presented in the following paragraphs.

Sherman and Haidt (2011) argue that viewing cute children results in a cuteness response, which is an emotional response that motivates people to socially engage with cute agents, by playing and talking with the agent. Furthermore, Sherman and Haidt (2011) propose that a mentalizing process (i.e., viewing the agent as having human properties) is then activated in order to strengthen the social bond. Steinnes et al. (2009) found that cute animals cuddling with each other, compared to cute animals not cuddling, evoked more *kama muta*, and were rated as cuter and more human. Furthermore, *kama muta* has been shown to increase humanization of out-group protagonists (Blomster Lyshol, Thomsen, et al., 2020; Sherman & Haidt, 2011; Steinnes et al., 2019). This corroborates the argument that feeling *kama muta* aligns with Sherman and Haidt's (2011) account that cuteness prompts a socializing response. However, we argue that humanization of cute agents is a process of viewing the cute agents as potential CS partners; having a CS relationship with an agent entails focusing on what one has in common with the agent (Fiske, 1992). Viewing the agent as human entails that one is sharing a common human essence with the agent (Demoulin et al., 2009), thus perceiving the agent as a potential partner of CS. With the focus of commonalities in mind, we predict that this motivates one to respond to the needs of their CS partner, which includes play and talk.

Responding to the needs of a CS partner also involves taking care of her, especially if the CS partner is a child. Thus, our *kama muta* account also aligns with the motivational effects of cuteness described by Lorenz (1943, 1971) and Nittono (2016). They argue that cute agents motivate tender caretaking and protection of one's vulnerable offspring. Indeed, Relational Models Theory postulates that human CS relationships evolved from mammalian mother-child bonds (Fiske, 2004b). The *kama muta* account explains how cute agents are humanized, motivating people to socially engage with, and take care of, the cute agent: the motivational effect of *kama muta* is focusing on commonalities and responding to the needs of the CS partner. When one feels *kama muta* from a cute agent, one perceives the agent and oneself as having a shared essence, thus humanizing them. Furthermore, when focusing on this shared essence, one is motivated to respond to the needs of the cute agent, where the needs depend on the agent and the situation. Lastly, Aragón et al. (2015) argue that displays of aggressive behavior are common in response to cute stimuli. This aggressive behavior includes squeezing, pinching, and biting the cute agents without the intention to hurt them. As the intention of the "aggressive" behavior is not to hurt the cute agent, we argue that this behavior should rather be thought of as a highly intense way of communicating one's CS devotion to the cute agent, such as impassioned cuddling and play (Fiske, 2004b).

In sum, the motivational effect of *kama muta* is to enhance the CS relationship that evoked *kama muta*. This enhancement takes the form of cognitively focusing on what one has in common with the agent, i.e., implementing the relational model of CS. Further, the enhancement of a CS relationship also takes the form of coordinating according to the CS relational model, which is to respond to the needs of the CS relational partner, or connecting one's body with the CS relational partner (Fiske, 1992, 2004a). This fits with the motivational effects described in the cuteness response (Sherman & Haidt, 2011), *kawaii* (Nittono, 2016), baby schema (Lorenz, 1943, 1971), and cute aggression (Aragón et al., 2015) accounts; motivation to socially engage, humanize, take care of, and display impassioned cuddling are all examples of CS devotion.

Kama Muta *and Its Empirical Evidence as the Cuteness Emotion*

Cuteness has been shown to evoke emotional responses that, as argued above, are all part of *kama muta*, such as *empathic concern, compassion, tenderness,* and *nurturant love*. Apparently common to all responses, despite cultural background, is that cute objects evoke a distinctive emotion. This chapter proposes *kama muta* as the typical cuteness emotion. Evidence, both direct and indirect, supporting this proposition comes from both quantitative and qualitative data featuring babies and animals as stimuli, through a combination of experiments, semi-structured interviews, and diary studies.

In a set of two experiments, Steinnes et al. (2019) found that videos of cute animals, compared to less-cute animals, elicited stronger responses of *kama muta*, and videos of two animals playing together were rated as cuter, humanized, and resulted in more *kama muta*. *Kama muta* was measured across four emotional components: vernacular labels; motivation to form or strengthen CS relations; emotional valence; and sensations and signs. Specifically, the first study found that videos of animals high in cuteness evoked stronger *kama muta* than animals low in cuteness, particularly among participants high in trait empathic concern. The second study showed that observing two cute animals in an affectionate interaction (as a proxy for high CS) evoked stronger cuteness ratings, humanization, and *kama muta* than observing animals with low CS interaction. Study 2 also found that trait empathic concern positively predicted cuteness ratings. These studies provide some initial direct evidence that cute animals trigger the emotion of *kama muta* and that intensifications of CS trigger perceptions of cuteness. This experimental evidence implies that experiencing *kama muta* is positive, rewarding, and encourages us to seek out triggers, such as puppies and babies, that can evoke the emotion over and over. *Kama muta* motivates bonding and solidarity between the elicitor and perceiver, and strengthens communal feelings and social relationships. Thus, sharing cute videos or photos with others represents social connection through wanting to share a positive emotional experience with other people. It is also important to note the differences in the *kama muta* intensity experienced by the individual participants. For example, individual self-reports of the *kama muta* components showed variance in experiencing the sensations and signs of *kama muta*. Some participants reported tearing up and having moist eyes, whereas others reported not feeling any sensations of tears at all in response to the cute animal videos. While it is imperative to point out that responses to cuteness are individually different, the findings in Steinnes et al. (2019) suggest that *the typical response* to cuteness is *kama muta*.

Further indirect evidence comes from a qualitative study analyzing diaries of and interviews with parents of newborn babies over the first six weeks. Hoëm and Lunnan-Reitan (2020) found that they experienced being moved in two different ways: as a fleeting moment and as a brief experience of calm. Both experiences seemed to have distinct functions. The fleeting moments were characterized by a realization of the new reality of the presence of the baby in the family, along with a sense of wonder, joy, and gratitude. It motivated participants to prioritize devoting time, energy, and attention to the baby and the family by directing their attention toward the preciousness of the moment. The experiences of calm were characterized by being completely absorbed and present in the moment, by being open and focusing on the baby, and by losing track of time. It helped participants be attentive to the needs of the baby, e.g., by feeding it, talking to it, holding it, and looking at it. Both forms of being moved were characterized by tears and a feeling of warmth in the chest. They both were experienced as an increase in CS, and thus could be different variants of *kama muta*. Moved as fleeting moment seems to be more important for the parent to form an attachment to the baby and to represent the new relationship, while moved as calm seems to be more important for being attentive to, understanding, and fulfilling the needs of the newborn. Both fathers and mothers reported such moments. These results are preliminary, and we do not yet know how they relate to the cuteness of the baby specifically. However, in light of the findings on cuteness, it seems plausible that the cuteness of the baby is an important cue for eliciting both types of being moved, and that these moments, in turn, boost the perception of one's own baby as particularly cute.

Conclusion

Ever since Konrad Lorenz introduced cuteness as an academic interest field and proposed the baby schema as an instinctual elicitor of parental caretaking, there has been increasing research on the emotional and motivational mediators between the cute stimulus and the resulting behavior. This accumulating work has provided evidence for a unique cuteness response that appears both complex and informed by cultural salience, yet universally linked through an underlying common denominator. Numerous emotional concepts have been proposed in response, although most remain insular to cuteness. The authors of this chapter propose to tie this work, both theoretically and empirically, to communal relations and *kama muta* theory. The biological and cultural evolution of *kama muta*, how it relates to other proposed cuteness emotions, its motivational components, and empirical evidence link cuteness to *kama muta*. This approach can unify the various emotional perspectives of the cuteness response described in this chapter through the common conceptual core of suddenly intensified *communal sharing* and the *kama muta* emotion it evokes.

References

Aragón, O. R., & Bargh, J. A. (2018). "So happy I could shout!" and "So happy I could cry!" Dimorphous expressions represent and communicate motivational aspects of positive emotions. *Cognition and Emotion*, *32*(2), 286–302. doi: 10.1080/02699931.2017.1301388

Aragón, O. R., Clark, M. S., Dyer, R. L., & Bargh, J. A. (2015). Dimorphous expressions of positive emotion: Displays of both care and aggression in response to cute stimuli. *Psychological Science*, *26*(3), 259–273. doi: 10.1177/0956797614561044

Archer, J., & Monton, S. (2011). Preferences for infant facial features in pet dogs and cats. *Ethology*, *117*(3), 217–226. doi: 10.1111/j.1439-0310.2010.01863.x

Batson, C. D. (2010). Empathy-induced altruistic motivation. In M. Mikulincer & P. R. Shaver (Eds.), *Prosocial motives, emotions, and behavior: The better angels of our nature*. (pp. 15–34). American Psychological Association.

Batson, C. D., Fultz, J., & Schoenrade, P. A. (1987). Distress and empathy: Two qualitatively distinct vicarious emotions with different motivational consequences. *Journal of Personality*, *55*(1), 19–39. doi: 10.1111/j.1467-6494.1987.tb00426.x

Batson, C. D., Lishner, D. A., Cook, J., & Sawyer, S. (2005). Similarity and nurturance: Two possible sources of empathy for strangers. *Basic and Applied Social Psychology*, *27*(1), 15–25. doi: 10.1207/s15324834basp2701_2

Berque, D., Chiba, H., Ohkura, M., Sripian, P., & Sugaya, M. (2020). Fostering cross-cultural research by cross-cultural student teams: A case study related to kawaii (cute) robot design. In P-L. P. Rau (Ed.), *Cross-cultural design. User experience of products, services, and intelligent environments: 22nd HCI International Conference* (pp. 553–563). Springer.

Berry, D. S., & McArthur, L. Z. (1985). Some components and consequences of a babyface. *Journal of Personality and Social Psychology*, *48*(2), 312–323. doi: 10.1037/0022-3514.48.2.312

Blomster Lyshol, J. K. (2020). *Moving out-groups closer: Kama muta evoked during intergroup contact forms common in-groups and improves intergroup relations*. Doctoral dissertation, Department of Psychology, University of Oslo. https://www.sv.uio.no/psi/forskning/aktuelt/arrangementer/disputaser/2020/Lyshol/johanna_blomsterlyshol.pdf.

Blomster Lyshol, J. K., Pich, O., & Seibt, B. (2022). Moved to Norway, then moved by Norway: How moments of kama muta is related with immigrants' acculturation. *Journal of Cross-Cultural Psychology, 53*(9), 1117–1144. https://doi.org/10.1177/00220221221104944

Blomster Lyshol, J. K., Seibt, B., Oliver, M. B., & Thomsen, L. (2023). Moving out-partisans closer: How kama muta can contribute to closing the partisan divide in the US. *Group Processes & Intergroup Relations, 26*(2), 493–511. https://doi.org/10.1177/13684302211067152

Blomster Lyshol, J. K., Thomsen, L., & Seibt, B. (2020). Moved by observing the love of others: Kama muta evoked through media fosters humanization of out-groups. *Frontiers in Psychology, 11*(1240). doi: 10.3389/fpsyg.2020.01240

Borgi, M., & Cirulli, F. (2016). Pet face: Mechanisms underlying human-animal relationships. *Frontiers in Psychology, 7*, 298. doi: 10.3389/fpsyg.2016.00298

Borgi, M., Cogliati-Dezza, I., Brelsford, V., Meints, K., & Cirulli, F. (2014). Baby schema in human and animal faces induces cuteness perception and gaze allocation in children. *Frontiers in Psychology, 5*, 411. doi: 10.3389/fpsyg.2014.00411

Boyd, R. (2018). *A different kind of animal: how culture transformed our species*. Princeton University Press.

Boyd, R., & Richerson, P. J. (1985). *Culture and the evolutionary process*. University of Chicago Press.

Brosch, T., Sander, D., & Scherer, K. R. (2007). That baby caught my eye . . . attention capture by infant faces. *Emotion, 7*(3), 685–689. doi: 10.1037/1528-3542.7.3.685

Buckley, R. C. (2016). Aww: The emotion of perceiving cuteness. *Frontiers in Psychology, 7*(1740). doi: 10.3389/fpsyg.2016.01740

Cordaro, D. T., Keltner, D., Tshering, S., Wangchuk, D., & Flynn, L. M. (2016). The voice conveys emotion in ten globalized cultures and one remote village in Bhutan. *Emotion, 16*(1), 117–128. doi: 10.1037/emo0000100

Dale, J. P. (2016). Cute studies: An emerging field. *East Asian Journal of Popular Culture, 2*(1), 5–13. doi: 10.1386/eapc.2.1.5_2

Dale, J. P. (2017). The appeal of the cute object: Desire, domestication, and agency. In J. P. Dale, J. Goggin, J. Leyda, A. McIntyre, P., & D. Negra (Eds.), *The aesthetics and affects of cuteness* (pp. 35–55). Routledge.

Dale, J. P., Goggin, J., Leyda, J., McIntyre, A. P., & Negra, D. (2017). *The aesthetics and affects of cuteness*. Routledge.

Darwin, C. (1872). *The expression of the emotions in man and animals*. J. Murray.

Demoulin, S., Cortes, B. P., Viki, T. G., Rodriguez, A. P., Rodriguez, R. T., Paladino, M. P., & Leyens, J.-P. (2009). The role of in-group identification in infra-humanization. *International Journal of Psychology, 44*(1), 4–11. doi: 10.1080/00207590802057654

Dijker, A. J. M. (2014). A theory of vulnerability-based morality. *Emotion Review, 6*(2), 175–183. doi: 10.1177/1754073913514120

Dydynski, J. M. (2020). Modeling cuteness: Moving towards a biosemiotic model for understanding the perception of cuteness and Kindchenschema. *Biosemiotics, 13*(2), 223–240. doi: 10.1007/s12304-020-09386-9

Esposito, G., Nakazawa, J., Ogawa, S., Stival, R., Kawashima, A., Putnick, D. L., & Bornstein, M. H. (2014). Baby, you light-up my face: Culture-general physiological responses to infants and culture-specific cognitive judgements of adults. *PLoS ONE, 9*(10), e106705. doi: 10.1371/journal.pone.0106705

Fiske, A. P. (1992). The four elementary forms of sociality: Framework for a unified theory of social relations. *Psychological Review, 99*(4), 689–723. doi: 10.1037/0033-295x.99.4.689

Fiske, A. P. (2000). Complementarity theory: Why human social capacities evolved to require cultural complements. *Personality and Social Psychology Review, 4*(1), 76–94. doi: 10.1207/s15327957pspr0401_7

Fiske, A. P. (2002). Socio-moral emotions motivate action to sustain relationships. *Self and Identity, 1*(2), 169–175. doi: 10.1080/152988602317319357

Fiske, A. P. (2004a). Four modes of constituting relationships: Consubstantial assimilation; space, magnitude, time, and force; concrete procedures; abstract symbolism. In N. Haslam (Ed.), *Relational models theory: A contemporary overview* (pp. 61–146). Lawrence Erlbaum Associates.

Fiske, A. P. (2004b). Relational models theory 2.0. In N. Haslam (Ed.), *Relational models theory: A contemporary overview* (pp. 3–25). Lawrence Erlbaum Associates.

Fiske, A. P. (2019). *Kama muta: Discovering the connection emotion*. Routledge.

Fiske, A. P. (2020). The lexical fallacy in emotion research: Mistaking vernacular words for psychological entities. *Psychological Review, 127*(1), 95–113. doi: 10.1037/rev0000174

Fiske, A. P., Seibt, B., & Schubert, T. (2019). The sudden devotion emotion: Kama muta and the cultural practices whose function is to evoke it. *Emotion Review, 11*(1), 74–86. doi: 10.1177/1754073917723167

Glocker, M. L., Langleben, D. D., Ruparel, K., Loughead, J. W., Gur, R. C., & Sachser, N. (2009). Baby schema in infant faces induces cuteness perception and motivation for caretaking in adults. *Ethology, 115*(3), 257–263. doi: 10.1111/j.1439-0310.2008.01603.x

Glocker, M. L., Langleben, D. D., Ruparel, K., Loughead, J. W., Valdez, J. N., Griffin, M. D., Sachser, N., & Gur, R. C. (2009). Baby schema modulates the brain reward system in nulliparous women. *Proceedings of the National Academy of Sciences, 106*(22), 9115. doi: 10.1073/pnas.0811620106

Golle, J., Lisibach, S., Mast, F. W., & Lobmaier, J. S. (2013). Sweet puppies and cute babies: perceptual adaptation to babyfacedness transfers across species. *PLoS ONE, 8*(3), e58248–e58248. doi: 10.1371/journal.pone.0058248

Golle, J., Probst, F., Mast, F. W., & Lobmaier, J. S. (2015). Preference for cute infants does not depend on their ethnicity or species: Evidence from hypothetical adoption and donation paradigms. *PLoS ONE, 10*(4), e0121554. doi: 10.1371/journal.pone.0121554

Gould, S. J. (1982). *The panda's thumb: More reflections in natural history.* W. W. Norton.

Hahn, A. C., DeBruine, L. M., & Jones, B. C. (2015). Reported maternal tendencies predict the reward value of infant facial cuteness, but not cuteness detection. *Biology Letters, 11*(3), 20140978. doi: 10.1098/rsbl.2014.0978

Hahn, A. C., Xiao, D., Sprengelmeyer, R., & Perrett, D. I. (2013). Gender differences in the incentive salience of adult and infant faces. *Quarterly Journal of Experimental Psychology (Hove), 66*(1), 200–208. doi: 10.1080/17470218.2012.705860

Haslam, N. (2006). Dehumanization: An integrative review. *Personality and Social Psychology Review, 10*(3), 252–264. doi: 10.1207/s15327957pspr1003_4

Henrich, J. (2016). *The Secret of our success: How culture is driving human evolution, domesticating our species, and making us smarter.* Princeton University Press.

Hildebrandt, K. A. (1983). Effect of facial expression variations on ratings of infants' physical attractiveness. *Developmental Psychology, 19*(3), 414–417. doi: 10.1037/0012-1649.19.3.414

Hildebrandt, K. A., & Fitzgerald, H. E. (1979). Facial feature determinants of perceived infant attractiveness. *Infant Behavior & Development, 2*(4), 329–339. doi: 10.1016/S0163-6383(79)80043-0

Hildebrandt, K. A., & Fitzgerald, H. E. (1981). Mothers' responses to infant physical appearance. *Infant Mental Health Journal, 2*(1), 56–61. doi: 10.1002/1097-0355(198121)2:1<56::Aid-imhj2280020109>3.0.Co;2-g

Hinde, R. A., & Barden, L. A. (1985). The evolution of the teddy bear. *Animal Behaviour, 33*(4), 1371–1373. doi: 10.1016/S0003-3472(85)80205-0

Hoëm, H., & Lunnan-Reitan, A. (2020). *Foreldres erfaringer med å bli rørt i tiden rundt fødsel.* (Master Thesis). Department of Psychology, University of Oslo. http://urn.nb.no/URN:NBN:no-82006

Kalawski, J. P. (2010). Is tenderness a basic emotion? *Motivation and Emotion, 34*(2), 158–167. doi:10.1007/s11031-010-9164-y

Kaminski, J., Waller, B. M., Diogo, R., Hartstone-Rose, A., & Burrows, A. M. (2019). Evolution of facial muscle anatomy in dogs. *Proceedings of the National Academy of Sciences, 116*(29), 14677. doi: 10.1073/pnas.1820653116

Keating, C. F., Randall, D. W., Kendrick, T., & Gutshall, K. A. (2003). Do babyfaced adults receive more help? The (cross-cultural) case of the lost resume. *Journal of Nonverbal Behavior, 27*(2), 89–109. doi: 10.1023/A:1023962425692

Keltner, D., & Haidt, J. (2003). Approaching awe, a moral, spiritual, and aesthetic emotion. *Cognition and Emotion, 17*(2), 297–314. doi: 10.1080/02699930302297

Kringelbach, M. L., Lehtonen, A., Squire, S., Harvey, A. G., Craske, M. G., Holliday, I. E., Green, A. L., Aziz, T. Z., Hansen, P. C., Cornelissen, P. L., & Stein, A. (2008). A specific and rapid neural signature for parental instinct. *PLoS ONE, 3*(2), e1664. doi: 10.1371/journal.pone.0001664

Kringelbach, M. L., Stark, E. A., Alexander, C., Bornstein, M. H., & Stein, A. (2016). On cuteness: Unlocking the parental brain and beyond. *Trends in Cognitive Sciences, 20*(7), 545–558. doi: 10.1016/j.tics.2016.05.003

Kruger, D. J. (2015). Non-mammalian infants requiring parental care elicit greater human caregiving reactions than superprecocial infants do. *Ethology, 121*(8), 769–774. doi: 10.1111/eth.12391

Langlois, J. H., Ritter, J. M., Casey, R. J., & Sawin, D. B. (1995). Infant attractiveness predicts maternal behaviors and attitudes. *Developmental Psychology, 31*(3), 464–472. doi: 10.1037/0012-1649.31.3.464

Lee, S. W. S., & Schwarz, N. (2020). Grounded procedures: A proximate mechanism for the psychology of cleansing and other physical actions. *Behavioral and Brain Sciences,* 1–78. doi:10.1017/s0140525x20000308

Levin, J., Arluke, A., & Irvine, L. (2017). Are people more disturbed by dog or human suffering? Influence of victim's species and age. *Society & Animals: Journal of Human-Animal Studies, 25*(1), 1–16.

Lieber-Milo, S., & Nittono, H. (2019). From a word to a commercial power: A brief introduction to the kawaii aesthetic in contemporary Japan. *Innovative Research in Japanese Studies, 3,* 13–32. doi: 10.18910/73599

Lishner, D. A., Batson, C. D., & Huss, E. (2011). Tenderness and sympathy: Distinct empathic emotions elicited by different forms of need. *Personality and Social Psychology Bulletin, 37*(5), 614–625. doi: 10.1177/0146167211403157

Lishner, D. A., Oceja, L. V., Stocks, E. L., & Zaspel, K. (2008). The effect of infant-like characteristics on empathic concern for adults in need. *Motivation and Emotion, 32*(4), 270–277. doi: 10.1007/s11031-008-9101-5

Little, A. C. (2012). Manipulation of infant-like traits affects perceived cuteness of infant, adult and cat faces. *Ethology, 118*(8), 775–782. doi: 10.1111/j.1439-0310.2012.02068.x

Lobmaier, J. S., Probst, F., Perrett, D. I., & Heinrichs, M. (2015). Menstrual cycle phase affects discrimination of infant cuteness. *Hormones and Behavior, 70,* 1–6. doi: 10.1016/j.yhbeh.2015.02.001

Lobmaier, J. S., Sprengelmeyer, R., Wiffen, B., & Perrett, D. I. (2010). Female and male responses to cuteness, age and emotion in infant faces. *Evolution and Human Behavior, 31*(1), 16–21. doi: 10.1016/j.evolhumbehav.2009.05.004

Lorenz, K. (1943). Die angeborenen Formen möglicher Erfahrung. *Zeitschrift für Tierpsychologie, 5*(2), 235–409. doi: 10.1111/j.1439-0310.1943.tb00655.x

Lorenz, K. (1971). Studies in animal and human behaviour, Vol. 2. Methuen. *Psychological Medicine, 2*(3), 325–325. doi: 10.1017/S0033291700042756

Marcus, A., Kurosu, M., & Ma, X. (2018). *Cuteness engineering: Designing adorable products and services*: Springer.

May, S. (2019). *The power of cute*. Princeton University Press.

Nenkov, G. Y., & Scott, M. L. (2014). "So cute I could eat it up": Priming effects of cute products on indulgent consumption. *Journal of Consumer Research, 41*(2), 326–341. doi: 10.1086/676581

Ngai, S. (2005). The cuteness of the avant-garde. *Critical Inquiry, 31*(4), 811–847. doi: 10.1086/444516

Ngai, S. (2012). *Our aesthetic categories: Zany, cute, interesting* (6th ed.). Harvard University Press.

Niezink, L. W., Siero, F. W., Dijkstra, P., Buunk, A. P., & Barelds, D. P. H. (2012). Empathic concern: Distinguishing between tenderness and sympathy. *Motivation and Emotion, 36*(4), 544–549. doi: 10.1007/s11031-011-9276-z

Nittono, H. (2016). The two-layer model of "kawaii": A behavioural science framework for understanding kawaii and cuteness. *East Asian Journal of Popular Culture, 2*(1), 79–95. doi: 10.1386/eapc.2.1.79_1

Nittono, H., Fukushima, M., Yano, A., & Moriya, H. (2012). The power of kawaii: Viewing cute images promotes a careful behavior and narrows attentional focus. *PLoS ONE, 7*(9), e46362. doi: 10.1371/journal.pone.0046362

Nittono, H., & Ihara, N. (2017). Psychophysiological responses to kawaii pictures with or without baby schema. *SAGE Open, 7*(2), 2158244017709321. doi: 10.1177/2158244017709321

Parsons, C. E., Young, K. S., Bhandari, R., van Ijzendoorn, M. H., Bakermans-Kranenburg, M. J., Stein, A., & Kringelbach, M. L. (2014). The bonnie baby: Experimentally manipulated temperament affects perceived cuteness and motivation to view infant faces. *Developmental Science, 17*(2), 257–269. doi: 10.1111/desc.12112

Parsons, C. E., Young, K. S., Kumari, N., Stein, A., & Kringelbach, M. L. (2011). The motivational salience of infant faces is similar for men and women. *PLoS ONE, 6*(5), e20632–e20632. doi: 10.1371/journal.pone.0020632

Porter, R. H., Cernoch, J. M., & McLaughlin, F. J. (1983). Maternal recognition of neonates through olfactory cues. *Physiology and Behavior, 30*(1), 151–154. doi: 10.1016/0031-9384(83)90051-3

Proverbio, A. M., De Gabriele, V., Manfredi, M., & Adorni, R. (2011). No race effect (ORE) in the automatic orienting toward baby faces: When ethnic group does not matter. *Psychology, 2*(9), 931–935. doi: 10.4236/psych.2011.29140

Roberson, D., Davies, I., & Davidoff, J. (2000). Color categories are not universal: Replications and new evidence from a stone-age culture. *Journal of Experimental Psychology: General, 129*(3), 369–398. doi: 10.1037/0096-3445.129.3.369

Sanefuji, W., Ohgami, H., & Hashiya, K. (2007). Development of preference for baby faces across species in humans (*Homo sapiens*). *Journal of Ethology, 25*(3), 249–254. doi: 10.1007/s10164-006-0018-8

Schaller, M. (2018). The parental care motivational system and why it matters (for everyone). *Current Directions in Psychological Science, 27*(5), 295–301. doi: 10.1177/0963721418767873

Schubert, T. W., & Grüning, D. J. (2021). Proper understanding of grounded procedures of separation needs a dual inheritance approach. *Behavioral and Brain Sciences, 44*. doi: 10.1017/S0140525X20000394

Schubert, T. W., Zickfeld, J. H., Seibt, B., & Fiske, A. P. (2018). Moment-to-moment changes in feeling moved match changes in closeness, tears, goosebumps, and warmth: Time series analyses. *Cognition and Emotion, 32*(1), 174–184. doi: 10.1080/02699931.2016.1268998

Seibt, B., Schubert, T. W., Zickfeld, J. H., & Fiske, A. P. (2019). Touching the base: Heart-warming ads from the 2016 U.S. election moved viewers to partisan tears. *Cognition and Emotion, 33*(2), 197–212. doi: 10.1080/02699931.2018.1441128

Seibt, B., Schubert, T. W., Zickfeld, J. H., Zhu, L., Arriaga, P., Simão, C., Nussinson, R., & Fiske, A. P. (2018). Kama Muta: Similar emotional responses to touching videos across the United States, Norway, China, Israel, and Portugal. *Journal of Cross-Cultural Psychology, 49*(3), 418–435. doi: 10.1177/0022022117746240

Seifritz, E., Esposito, F., Neuhoff, J. G., Lüthi, A., Mustovic, H., Dammann, G., von Bardeleben, U., Radue, E. W., Cirillo, S., Tedeschi, G., & Di Salle, F. (2003). Differential sex-independent amygdala response to infant crying and laughing in parents versus nonparents. *Biological Psychiatry, 54*(12), 1367–1375. https://doi.org/10.1016/S0006-3223(03)00697-8

Shaver, P. R., Morgan, H. J., & Wu, S. (1996). Is love a "basic" emotion? *Personal Relationships, 3*(1), 81–96. https://doi.org/10.1111/j.1475-6811.1996.tb00105.x

Sherman, G. D., & Haidt, J. (2011). Cuteness and disgust: The humanizing and dehumanizing effects of emotion. *Emotion Review, 3*(3), 245–251. doi: 10.1177/1754073911402396

Sherman, G. D., Haidt, J., & Coan, J. A. (2009). Viewing cute images increases behavioral carefulness. *Emotion, 9*(2), 282–286. doi: 10.1037/a0014904

Sherman, G. D., Haidt, J., Iyer, R., & Coan, J. A. (2013). Individual differences in the physical embodiment of care: Prosocially oriented women respond to cuteness by becoming more physically careful. *Emotion, 13*(1), 151–158. doi: 10.1037/a0029259

Shiota, M. N., Neufeld, S. L., Danvers, A. F., Osborne, E. A., Sng, O., & Yee, C. I. (2014). Positive emotion differentiation: A functional approach. *Social and Personality Psychology Compass, 8*(3), 104–117. https://doi.org/10.1111/spc3.12092

Sprengelmeyer, R., Perrett, D. I., Fagan, E. C., Cornwell, R. E., Lobmaier, J. S., Sprengelmeyer, A., Aasheim, H. B. M., Black, I. M., Cameron, L. M., Crow, S., Milne, N., Rhodes, E. C., & Young, A. W. (2009). The cutest little baby face: A hormonal link to sensitivity to cuteness in infant faces. *Psychological Science, 20*(2), 149–154. doi: 10.1111/j.1467-9280.2009.02272.x

Stavropoulos, K. K. M., & Alba, L. A. (2018). "It's so cute I could crush it!": Understanding neural mechanisms of cute aggression. *Frontiers in Behavioral Neuroscience, 12*(300). doi: 10.3389/fnbeh.2018.00300

Steinnes, K. K., Blomster, J. K., Seibt, B., Zickfeld, J. H., & Fiske, A. P. (2019). Too cute for words: Cuteness evokes the heartwarming emotion of kama muta. *Frontiers in Psychology, 10*(387). doi: 10.3389/fpsyg.2019.00387

van Riem, M. M., I. M. H., Tops, M., Boksem, M. A., Rombouts, S. A., & Bakermans-Kranenburg, M. J. (2012). No laughing matter: Intranasal oxytocin administration changes functional brain connectivity during exposure to infant laughter. *Neuropsychopharmacology, 37*(5), 1257–1266. doi:10.1038/npp.2011.313

Volk, A. A., Lukjanczuk, J. L., & Quinsey, V. L. (2007). Perceptions of child facial cues as a function of child age. *Evolutionary Psychology, 5*(4), 801–814. doi: 10.1177/147470490700500409

Wang, T., Mukhopadhyay, A., & Patrick, V. M. (2017). Getting consumers to recycle NOW! When and why cuteness appeals influence prosocial and sustainable behavior. *Journal of Public Policy & Marketing, 36*(2), 269–283. doi: 10.1509/jppm.16.089

Weidman, A. C., Steckler, C. M., & Tracy, J. L. (2017). The jingle and jangle of emotion assessment: Imprecise measurement, casual scale usage, and conceptual fuzziness in emotion research. *Emotion, 17*(2), 267–295. doi: 10.1037/emo0000226

Weidman, A. C., & Tracy, J. L. (2020a). Picking up good vibrations: Uncovering the content of distinct positive emotion subjective experience. *Emotion, 20*(8), 1311–1331. doi: 10.1037/emo0000677

Weidman, A. C., & Tracy, J. L. (2020b). A provisional taxonomy of subjectively experienced positive emotions. *Affective Science, 1*(2), 57–86. doi: 10.1007/s42761-020-00009-7

Wittkower, D. E. (2012). On the origins of the cute as a dominant aesthetic category in digital culture. In T. W. Luke & J. Hunsinger (Eds.), *Putting knowledge to work and letting information play* (pp. 167–175). Sense.

Wolfensohn, S. (2020). Too cute to kill? The need for objective measurements of quality of life. *Animals (Basel), 10*(6). doi: 10.3390/ani10061054

Young, K. S., Parsons, C. E., Stein, A., Vuust, P., Craske, M. G., & Kringelbach, M. L. (2018). Neural responses to infant vocalizations in adult listener. In S. Frühholz & P. Belin (Eds.), *The Oxford handbook of voice perception* (pp 251–276). Oxford University Press.

Zebrowitz, L. A. (2006). Finally, faces find favor. *Social Cognition, 24*(5), 657–701. doi: 10.1521/soco.2006.24.5.657

Zebrowitz, L. A., Kikuchi, M., & Fellous, J.-M. (2007). Are effects of emotion expression on trait impressions mediated by babyfaceness? Evidence from connectionist modeling. *Personality and Social Psychology Bulletin, 33*(5), 648–662. doi: 10.1177/0146167206297399

Zebrowitz, L. A., Montepare, J. M., & Lee, H. K. (1993). They don't all look alike: Individuated impressions of other racial groups. *Journal of Personality and Social Psychology, 65*(1), 85–101. doi: 10.1037//0022-3514.65.1.85

Zhang, Z., & Zhou, J. (2020). Cognitive and neurological mechanisms of cuteness perception: A new perspective on moral education. *Mind, Brain, and Education, 14*(3), 209–219.

Zickfeld, J. H., Arriaga, P., Santos, S. V., Schubert, T. W., & Seibt, B. (2020). Tears of joy, aesthetic chills and heartwarming feelings: Physiological correlates of kama muta. *Psychophysiology, 57*(12), e13662. https://doi.org/10.1111/psyp.13662

Zickfeld, J. H., Kunst, J. R., & Hohle, S. M. (2018). Too sweet to eat: Exploring the effects of cuteness on meat consumption. *Appetite, 120*, 181–195. doi: 10.1016/j.appet.2017.08.038

Zickfeld, J. H., Schubert, T. W., Seibt, B., Blomster, J. K., Arriaga, P., Basabe, N., Blaut, A., Caballero, A., Carrera, P., Dalgar, I., Ding, Y., Dumont, K., Gaulhofer, V., Gračanin, A., Gyenis, R., Hu, C-P., Kardum, I., Lazarević, L. B., Mathew, L., . . . Fiske, A. P. (2019). Kama muta: Conceptualizing and measuring the experience often labelled being moved across 19 nations and 15 languages. *Emotion, 19*(3), 402–424. doi: 10.1037/emo0000450

Zickfeld, J. H., Schubert, T. W., Seibt, B., & Fiske, A. P. (2017). Empathic concern is part of a more general communal emotion. *Frontiers in Psychology, 8*(723). doi: 10.3389/fpsyg.2017.00723

Zickfeld, J. H., Schubert, T. W., Seibt, B., & Fiske, A. P. (2019). Moving through the literature: What is the emotion often denoted being moved? *Emotion Review, 11*(2), 123–139. doi: 10.1177/1754073918820126

Curiosity: A Behavioral Biology Perspective

Coltan Scrivner

Abstract

Despite a rich history of research, scientists have not been able to agree upon a single definition or taxonomy of curiosity. These diverging perspectives have led to a breadth of research that has yet to be integrated under one framework. The author of this chapter proposes that research on curiosity can benefit from an evolutionary perspective, and more broadly from a biological perspective on information-gathering behavior. The author synthesizes the literature on curiosity from the perspective of behavioral biology—i.e., Tinbergen's four questions. The behavioral biology framework provides a powerful lens through which questions about behavior can be asked and iterative empirical work and theoretical construction can take place. In particular, the author argues that evolutionary perspectives on curiosity can help identify the "joints" of nature at which curiosity may be carved.

Key Words: curiosity, ethology, evolution, behavioral biology, Tinbergen

Overview of Perspectives on Curiosity

Like many aspects of human psychology that seem too obvious to require a definition and rigorous scientific explanation, curiosity has been difficult to define and explain. William James (1890) proposed that there are two types of curiosity. The first involves seeking information about novel objects. This type of curiosity, James contends, is present in most animals. The second type, which James suggested has almost nothing to do with the first and is specific to humans, is scientific curiosity or metaphysical wonder. James argued that this type of curiosity is more concerned with ways of conceptualizing objects, rather than the objects themselves. Scientific curiosity responds not to novel stimuli per se, but rather to gaps in knowledge. Still, James only briefly mused about curiosity, and did not offer empirical evidence for his conceptual distinction. Daniel Berlyne (1954) was the first experimental psychologist to investigate curiosity in detail. He also broke down curiosity into two major types, resulting in a distinction that resembled James's. The first type of curiosity he called "perceptual curiosity," referring to the drive to gather information about novel stimuli until they are no longer so novel. Berlyne gave the example of a rat that exhibits increased exploratory activity around a new stimulus. He distinguished this novelty-seeking form of curiosity from "epistemic curiosity," which he suggests is more about acquiring knowledge and is largely unique to humans.

Berlyne (1966) later divided curiosity along a second axis: specific vs. diversive. Specific curiosity occurs when there is a gap in information about some phenomenon. This gap produces discomfort, which motivates one to seek out additional information about that specific phenomenon. An example of this can be seen if you briefly show a participant a complex image. Given the chance, the participant will most likely want to reinvestigate the image, reducing the gap in knowledge that was produced from the momentary look. On the other hand, diversive curiosity arises when an organism is under-stimulated and seeks novel stimulation to satisfy the feeling of deprivation. An example of this can be seen if a participant is placed in a dark room with the option to press buttons to make lights appear. The human participant will press buttons in a sequence that produces variety in the light patterns (Berlyne, 1966).

Decades later, Loewenstein (1994) offered a reinterpretation of the psychology of curiosity. He criticized the concept of diversive curiosity, arguing that it was more akin to sensation-seeking and more related to boredom than it was to scientific curiosity. He noted that previous theories of curiosity fail to answer why people like to feel curious and, if they do indeed like it, why they try to end it through information-seeking. Loewenstein offers a new perspective on curiosity in an attempt to reconcile these issues with previous theories. His information-gap theory of curiosity, which deals only with internally motivated, specific state curiosity (as opposed to externally motivated, diversive, or trait curiosity), predicts that curiosity arises to resolve uncertainty about a specific topic. The logical conclusion of this prediction is that curiosity will have an inverted-U shape relationship with knowledge such that curiosity rises as an individual learns about a topic, peaks when an individual possesses a moderate degree of knowledge or confidence in a topic, and declines thereafter.

Several other theoretical frameworks have been offered, such as curiosity as a "knowledge emotion" (Silvia, 2010) or curiosity functioning to maximize the ability to make good decisions in the future (Dubey & Griffiths, 2020a; Silvia, 2010). Each of these frameworks has its own set of empirical studies that support the main theory, making it difficult to ascertain which framework is most useful. One aspect that is missing from most previous theoretical frameworks of curiosity is an evolutionary perspective. While some do offer "functional" explanations for curiosity, these functional explanations still raise the question: Why does this state or trait exist? A proposed answer to this "why" question is important for guiding research on the psychology of curiosity.

The Behavioral Biology Framework

I propose in this chapter that research on curiosity can benefit from an evolutionary perspective, and more broadly from a biological perspective on information-gathering behavior. One framework that is likely to be illuminating for research on curiosity is the framework proposed by ethologist Nikolaas Tinbergen for investigating behavior from a biological perspective. Tinbergen (1963) proposed that to fully understand a behavior, four types of questions must be asked. The first question is about the proximate causation or mechanism underlying the behavior. In other words, what is the most immediate cause of the behavior? This can be in terms of either the stimulus that evokes the behavior or in the information processing that occurs in the brain (though a comprehensive mechanistic explanation will address both). The second question asks how the behavior changes over time during the life span of the organism—i.e., the developmental or ontogenetic question. The third question relates to the adaptive value of the behavior. What is the function of the behavior, and how does this relate to survival and/or reproduction? The fourth question is the phylogenetic question. How did this behavior evolve over time? Is it present in closely related species in one form or another?

These four questions split behavioral explanations into two kinds: proximate and ultimate. Mechanistic explanations and developmental explanations are proximate explanations. Proximate explanations focus on "how"—how a behavior works and how it changes throughout the life course. Adaptive (or functional) and phylogenetic explanations are ultimate explanations. These explanations focus on "why"—why does a behavior manifest the way that it does, and why does it exist in the species? These four questions are meant to offer a guide for a robust biological investigation of a particular behavior. While others have suggested that curiosity be investigated from an ethological perspective (Kidd & Hayden, 2015), this perspective has not been widely adopted in research on the psychology of curiosity. Moreover, research and theoretical accounts on the adaptive significance of curiosity are severely lacking from the psychological literature.

There appears to be no agreed-upon definition for curiosity, and this chapter will not argue for one definition over another. Some definitions include all exploratory behavior (e.g., specific and diversive curiosity) and some exclude extrinsically motivated behavior. Using a more specific definition of curiosity that only includes internally motivated behavior can provide direction and a necessary narrowing of research, but it comes with its own problems. In particular, it is difficult to identify the motives behind particular curiosity-like behaviors in nonhuman animals (Kidd & Hayden, 2015). Rather than circumscribe curiosity more stringently, this chapter will take a broad look at information-seeking behavior as at least analogous to curiosity. This is a useful approach under the evolutionary paradigm because it allows connections to be drawn between human curiosity and its analogs in other animals. This perspective is especially important for the phylogenetic and functional explanations of curiosity. Thus, the general ethological definition of curiosity as a drive state for information will be used here, as it was in Kidd and Hayden's (2015) analysis of curiosity from the ethological paradigm. A robust analysis of information-seeking utilizing Tinbergen's four questions may allow for an evolutionarily informed taxonomy of curiosity to be created and tested in future research.

Phylogenetic Level

Anyone with a pet at home is likely to agree that animals can exhibit curiosity. Dogs are insatiably curious about new toys that are brought home, and cats will thoroughly inspect all grocery bags if given the opportunity. Glickman and Sroges (1966) conducted the seminal experimental investigation of animal curiosity in over 200 animals at two zoos in Chicago and New York City. In particular, the study assessed the degree to which different animals would investigate novel objects. Glickman and Sroges introduced to the cages where the animals were housed a pair of wooden blocks, two lengths of steel chain, two pieces of wooden dowel, two pieces of rubber tubing, and a paper ball. Where possible, males and females of the same species were tested, and items were either not reused or were thoroughly washed before reuse. Each item was placed in the cage for six minutes, with the session divided into five-second intervals. Within each interval, orienting behavior (looking) and contact were assessed. Glickman and Sroges found that primates and carnivores were the most curious animals in the sample, while rodents, "primitive mammals," and reptiles appeared significantly less curious about the novel objects. Juveniles across species were also more curious than adults.

It is clear from the zoo study that most mammals exhibited something like curiosity. Glickman and Sroges interpreted their findings in light of the feeding patterns and predators in the animals' natural habitats. In other words, animals whose natural habitats offer more refuge from danger and require more complex behaviors for food acquisition might display greater specific curiosity in response to novel objects.

The increased neophilic behavior and genetic similarity of nonhuman primates to humans make them a prime point of comparison for questions about the phylogenetic roots of human-like curiosity. Like humans, monkeys demonstrate specific curiosity about information when solving puzzles, even in the absence of clear extrinsic motivation (Harlow, 1950; Harlow et al., 1950). Even in accordance with a stricter definition of curiosity, monkeys demonstrate curiosity about counterfactuals by sacrificing reward to learn information with no strategic benefit (Wang & Hayden, 2019). Even though species-typical tendencies toward curiosity-like traits exist, individuals within a species also vary with respect to curiosity due to a combination of genetic predispositions and environmental cues (Sih et al., 2004). For example, squirrel monkeys who experience mild stress early in their lives are more likely to exhibit increased novelty-seeking behaviors (Parker et al., 2007). Differences between conspecifics in exploratory behavior can be large, and have been linked to reproductive fitness (Reader, 2015).

It is currently unclear how similar curiosity in humans is to curiosity in nonhuman animals. Certainly novelty-seeking and exploratory behavior can be closely compared both theoretically and empirically. However, curiosity about things like causation may be more difficult to compare for a phylogenetic analysis. Still, various kinds of curiosity-like behavior, broadly speaking, have been documented in nonhuman animals and may be mappable onto human traits (Gosling & John, 1999). Likewise, these various aspects of curiosity may be connected through an evolutionarily ancient neurocircuitry system that is largely conserved in mammals (Montag & Panksepp, 2017; Wright & Panksepp, 2012). A more complete cataloging of curiosity-like behaviors in nonhuman animals may help shine a light on what is unique about human curiosity (if anything). A functional evolutionary analysis of curiosity may help guide phylogenetic analyses in an iterative manner.

Functional (Adaptive) Level
Berlyne offered one of the first functional accounts of curiosity in the psychological literature when he argued that part of the function of the curiosity drive was to resolve uncertainty (Berlyne, 1960). Curiosity as uncertainty reduction has remained a popular idea and has been an important part of many curiosity research programs (Kashdan et al., 2018; Litman & Jimerson, 2004; Loewenstein, 1994). While it seems reasonable that reducing uncertainty about the world is a key feature of curiosity, surely this is not the only feature of curiosity. If this were the case, it would be difficult for organisms to focus their curiosity in a useful fashion. After all, uncertainty exists about nearly every phenomenon. In some cases, curiosity may be driven by extreme uncertainty, while in others it is driven by moderate uncertainty (Dubey & Griffiths, 2020a). At best, the argument that the function of curiosity is to reduce uncertainty is incomplete and leaves much to be desired.

Dubey and Griffiths (2020b) have posited that the function of curiosity is to increase the usefulness of one's own knowledge. Under this hypothesis, the value of knowledge is a function of the organism's current knowledge about the environment and the probability of encountering some stimulus in the future. In positing this function, Dubey and Griffiths have attempted to reconcile the uncertainty-reduction perspective and the novelty-seeking perspective on curiosity. When an organism is faced with a novel stimulus, it should investigate it only if that stimulus is likely to occur again. Still, this raises the question of how some stimulus in the environment might be perceived and integrated in the mind. For example, the current value of some piece of information may be at odds with the value of that information over the course of human evolution. Most people in the United States do not encounter wild snakes in their lifetime. However, most people in the United States still display an attentive bias toward snakes (LoBue & DeLoache, 2008; Öhman & Mineka, 2003). If this attentive bias falls under the purview of curiosity, then the "value" of the knowledge appears to be influenced by a deep evolutionary history with the stimulus. To account for this type of curiosity, "current knowledge" in the Dubey and Griffiths hypothesis must include some calculation of the attentive predispositions that humans have inherited from their ancestors. Likewise, most people do not encounter serial killers in their lifetime, yet true crime is a wildly popular form of entertainment. Many people are genuinely curious about serial killers, despite the fact that the probability of encountering a serial killer is exceedingly low. Thus, something other than just current knowledge about the environment and the probability of encountering some stimulus in the future is influencing curiosity.

Part of the reason why a taxonomy of curiosity has not been agreed upon is that the function of curiosity is not agreed upon. Of course, it can be difficult to give a function to a concept that is ill-defined. One way to approach this is to try to identify the functions of the various behaviors that constitute the umbrella construct of curiosity. Many of these behaviors may well be related to individual success and reproductive fitness. Because of this, the psychological mechanisms that mediate curiosity have probably been shaped by natural selection. Consequently, these psychological mechanisms will be well-suited for dealing with particular socio-ecological problems. Identifying these socio-ecological problems in conjunction with a comparative psychological analysis (i.e., the phylogenetic analysis) may shed light on an appropriate taxonomy for curiosity.

Curiosity has been classified in many different ways. For example, James classified curiosity as either novelty-seeking or scientific curiosity, while Berlyne split curiosity along the specific/diversive axis and the perceptual/epistemic axis. Litman (2008) split epistemic curiosity into interest and deprivation based on whether it stimulated positive affect and diversive exploration (interest) or reduced uncertainty and stimulated specific exploration (deprivation). More recently, Kashdan et al. (2018) constructed the five-dimensional curiosity scale to try to capture the bandwidth of curiosity. Through a series of studies that began with over 100 curiosity-related items, Kashdan et al. identified five major dimensions of curiosity: joyous exploration, deprivation sensitivity, stress tolerance, social curiosity, and thrill seeking. A more recent iteration of the scale splits social curiosity into overt and covert social curiosity (Kashdan et al., 2020). While the new scale from Kashdan et al. provides a data-driven approach to identifying dimensions of curiosity, it leaves some important theoretical questions about curiosity unanswered. For example, are these different dimensions caused by the same underlying suite of psychological mechanisms? What is the function of curiosity in each of these dimensions, and why might they be divided this way?

Evolutionary psychologists have argued that emotions can be understood as coordinating mechanisms that process particular kinds of information and regulate other aspects of physiology, behavior, and cognition (Al-Shawaf et al., 2015; Cosmides & Tooby, 2000). Under this view, "emotions" include emotions as they have been traditionally understood (e.g., fear, disgust, anger), as well as motivational states and drives such as lassitude (Schrock et al., 2020) and hunger (Al-Shawaf, 2016). Viewing emotions, motivational states, and drives as coordinating mechanisms has several advantages. It offers a form of non-arbitrary emotion classification, increased heuristic value for identifying emotions that should be studied, and a systematic method for a priori hypothesis generation and testing through evolutionary task analysis (Al-Shawaf et al., 2015; Marr, 1982). Evolutionary task analysis involves asking four key questions: (1) What adaptive problem, if any, did this mechanism evolve to solve? (2) Which subtasks must be solved in the solution of this adaptive problem? (3) Which information-processing programs are capable of solving these subtasks? (4) How should these programs be coordinated to deliver a well-designed solution to this adaptive problem? (Al-Shawaf et al., 2015). Studying curiosity through this functional lens may offer several avenues for future research and may help create a more effective and functionally accurate taxonomy of curiosity.

One type of curiosity that does not seem to be captured in previous work is morbid curiosity. Morbid curiosity has been defined as a motivation to seek out information about threatening or dangerous phenomena (Scrivner, 2021a). People high in morbid curiosity may be more likely to expose themselves to simulations of danger through fiction and may learn particular emotional or behavioral strategies from exposure to real or fictionalized dangerous situations (Scrivner et al., 2021; Scrivner et al., 2022). Moreover, morbid curiosity seems to be an individual difference that is distinct from the five dimensions of curiosity, disgust sensitivity, and sensation-seeking (Oosterwijk, 2017; Scrivner, 2021a, 2021b).

A clear function of morbid curiosity also appears to be emerging. Dangerous situations have been and continue to be present in everyday life for humans. In general, an organism should try to avoid dangerous situations. However, there is some value in knowing about danger, as this could lead to a better ability to avoid or deal with these situations in the future. Due to the unique ability to simulate experiences through fiction, humans can create low-cost learning "experiences" with danger. These situations can be quite immersive, activating physiological, behavioral, and emotional responses that correspond to what would occur if the situation were real (Andersen et al., 2020). This allows those engaging with recreational fear to learn more about the situation, how they would respond, and how they can improve that response for a better outcome. Some preliminary evidence suggests that engagement with frightening fiction could correspond to psychological resilience in the face of situations that induce anxiety or feelings of uncertainty (Scrivner et al., 2021). However, because these situations can be scary, disgusting, or otherwise off-putting, they require some motivation to simulate. Morbid curiosity provides the motivational boost that shifts the perceived cost/benefit ratio to encourage approach behavior that leads to engagement with morbid fictional material.

My own research on the psychology of morbid curiosity was inspired by the fact that dangerous situations are common, that these situations can have fitness consequences, that humans can simulate these dangerous situations, and that learning about these situations can lead to more efficient responses. In other words, a functional approach was taken in the development of this research program. Similar arguments were made for the inclusion of a social curiosity dimension in the five-dimensional curiosity scale. Kashdan et al. (2018) argued that being curious about people warranted further investigation as a separate dimension due to the primacy of interpersonal relationships in human life. These kinds of functional approaches to curiosity can offer specific areas in which to investigate behavior in humans and other animals and may help produce a reliable taxonomy of curiosity.

Developmental Level
As is the case with pet owners noticing the curiosity of their animals, parents would most likely agree that children display a great deal of curiosity. Human infants in particular have a profound proclivity for exploring and learning about their environment. Infants possess particular attention biases that facilitate learning. Some of these include biases that promote motion detection (Agyei et al., 2016), shape or object learning (Yee et al., 2012), and attention to faces (Farroni et al., 2005). Similar to predispositions in language acquisition, these simple biases guide infant perception so that they can more efficiently learn about the important aspects of a world with a nearly infinite number of stimuli.

Some research on infant learning supports both complexity-based preferences proposed by Berlyne (1960) and information-gap motives proposed by Loewenstein (1994). According to these models, learners should prefer intermediate levels of complexity or moderate information gaps. Material in this range would fall into an optimal level of understanding for productive and efficient learning. Indeed, infants do seem to prefer both visual and auditory stimuli that present a moderate level of complexity (Kidd et al., 2012, 2014). This finding is in line with Piaget's (1945) argument that play serves to construct knowledge through interactions with the environment. In this model, curiosity is the motivation that drives the behavior (play). This also corresponds with Csikszenthmihalyi's (1990) notion of flow, wherein an inverted U-shaped relationship exists between perceived challenge of some task and intrinsic motivation. As with play and curiosity, moderately challenging tasks offer an opportunity for optimal performance.

In addition to children being voracious learners, the juvenile period in humans is exceptionally long and costly. Children require extensive care and may not be self-sufficient until well into their teenage years. Humans in forager societies consume nearly 25% of their lifetime energy consumption by age 15, yet only produce about 5% of their anticipated energy acquisition by the same age (Kaplan et al., 2000). This incredible imbalance in energy consumption and acquisition suggests that the extended juvenile period in humans is probably adaptive in some ways. Given the complex nature of human societies and human psychology, human childhood likely needs to be extended in order to allow humans time to develop and prepare for the uniquely complex adult human life.

Thus, extended childhood appears to be a human life-history adaptation. Alison Gopnik (2020) has argued that extended childhood in humans is a solution to the explore-exploit problem. The explore-exploit problem refers to the decisions that organisms have to make when they are faced with the opportunity to either exploit known aspects of their environment for resources or rewards, or to explore unknown aspects of their environment for a payoff that could be large, small, or nonexistent. Moreover, the explore decision may not provide current payoff, but may instead provide future payoff. Because natural environments are so complex and time and energy are limited, organisms cannot possibly try all solutions for the best one. Most solutions to the explore-exploit dilemma begin with exploration and gradually move toward exploitation. Once enough is known about the environment, it becomes more efficient and productive to exploit for current benefits rather than to explore for unknown benefits or future benefits.

Gopnik and her colleagues have argued that this solution is also represented in the developmental trajectory of humans (Gopnik et al., 2015; Gopnik et al., 2017; Lucas et al., 2014). Humans have an unusually long juvenile period in which exploration and learning are prioritized over exploitation. Although the human juvenile period is particularly well-adapted for exploration, the juvenile period of other animals, and certainly other primates, may also suit this purpose. Comparative evidence suggests that juveniles of many species learn better, explore more options, and are often more innovative than adults, a finding that holds in mice (Johnson & Wilbrecht, 2011), birds (O'Hara & Auersperg, 2017), hyenas (Benson-Amram & Holekamp, 2012), and monkeys (Bergman & Kitchen, 2009; Perry et al., 2017). Even among adults, increased innovation and diverse exploration of hypotheses are associated with younger age. For example, theoretical scientists, whose work focuses on re-envisioning how something works, tend to produce their best and most innovative work earlier in their career (Scrivner & Maestripieri, 2018). Indeed, similarities between the cognition of children and theoretical scientists have been noted elsewhere (Gopnik, 1996). Thus, the juvenile period as a period of exploration is a general principle that applies especially strongly to humans. Given the complexity of human social life and the ability to forecast and imagine hypothetical and counterfactual scenarios, it is no surprise that human children are exceptionally curious and motivated learners.

Mechanistic Level

The most proximate cause, or the mechanism, of all human behavior is rooted in the brain. Dopamine plays a key role in the mechanistic basis of curiosity. Dopamine is a neurotransmitter that modulates motivational behavior, in particular learning and reward-related motivation. Dopaminergic activity, particularly in the midbrain dopaminergic neurons, appears to be relevant for curiosity. For example, participants in one study answered trivia questions and rated their curiosity for each answer while their brain activity was assessed via functional magnetic resonance imaging (fMRI). When participants reported higher curiosity about answers to trivia questions, fMRI analyses revealed greater activity in the midbrain dopaminergic neurons (Gruber et al., 2014).

Though the exact relationship between dopamine and reward-related motivation is not entirely clear, one popular hypothesis is that dopaminergic neurons encode predictions errors in expected reward (Arias-Carrión et al., 2010). This neuroscientific hypothesis lines up well with the psychological hypothesis that curiosity functions to minimize uncertainty. By encoding prediction errors through dopaminergic activity, animals will be able to improve future predictions relating to the outcome of a particular reward-relevant stimulus. In turn, this leads to better decisions about how to act toward this reward stimulus in the future. Thus, dopamine's role in moderating behavior by encoding prediction error may be one neurological mechanism underlying curiosity.

Some researchers have hypothesized that the brain normalizes and encodes information from a variety of sources into a common currency by which action decisions can be made (Levy & Glimcher, 2012). By normalizing the value of information into a common currency, increasingly complex decisions can be made that include information from a variety of qualitatively different sources. If, per Dubey and Griffiths, the function of curiosity is to increase the value of knowledge, and value is neurologically normalized into a common currency, then information that is perceived as more important may be more likely to provoke curiosity. Dubey and colleagues (2022) tested this hypothesis in a study where they presented participants with scientific facts and manipulated how valuable information about those facts would be. As they predicted, participants rated their curiosity about a fact as higher when that fact was perceived to be more valuable. These findings correspond with the hypothesis that the function of curiosity is to learn useful information about the world and improve the value of knowledge that one holds.

However, humans are often curious about information that has no instrumental value (as are monkeys; e.g., Wang & Hayden, 2019). Interestingly, the common neural code for information-representation appears to encode both instrumental and non-instrumental information, casting doubt on the distinction that is sometimes made in curiosity between intrinsic and extrinsic motivation for information-seeking (Kobayashi & Hsu, 2019). The common neurological activation for information-seeking also corroborates Panksepp's SEEKING system among mammals (Panksepp & Moskal, 2008). Moreover, these studies suggest that information may be neurologically valued in the same manner as other goods, a finding that has been previously demonstrated in monkeys (Bromberg-Martin & Hikosaka, 2011).

While much research has been conducted on midbrain dopaminergic neurons, less work has looked at where curiosity "begins" in the brain. Curiosity-related input from the sensory organs may first be processed in the orbitofrontal cortex (OFC). Blanchard et al. (2015) conducted a study where monkeys could sacrifice a primary reward such as water for information about a gamble. Blanchard and colleagues found that while OFC neurons appeared to encode variables like water amount and value of the information about the gamble, integration of these variables into a common currency did not occur in the OFC. Instead, the researchers concluded that the OFC encoded the relevant variables before sending the signal downstream to the midbrain, where signals are integrated into the common currency for rewards.

Conclusions

Curiosity continues to be one of the most important and widely valued psychological traits. However, research on curiosity has been focused on narrowly defined definitions or taxonomies. In this chapter, I argue that one productive way for researchers to approach the study of curiosity is to utilize the behavioral biology framework. Tinbergen's four questions—mechanism, development, evolutionary function, and phylogeny—allow for a broad, comprehensive analysis of animal behavior. Notably, Kidd and Hayden (2015) have argued for the same approach to curiosity. By stepping back and incorporating a larger perspective on curiosity, psychologists can avoid the trap noted by Tinbergen in his 1963 paper, where he stated:

> It has been said that, in its haste to step into the twentieth century and to become a respectable science, Psychology skipped the preliminary descriptive stage that other natural sciences had gone through, and so was soon losing touch with the natural phenomena. (p. 411)

Science has come a long way since Tinbergen first made this claim, and psychologists, neuroscientists, biologists, and other researchers interested in studying curiosity have a wealth of new knowledge, tasks, instruments, and technology at their fingertips. Researchers studying curiosity should avoid being overly narrow in their description of curiosity and aim instead for an integration of perspectives and empirical data. To do this will require a broader perspective on curiosity, like the one offered by Tinbergen's four questions.

Analyzing curiosity through this perspective may also help produce a taxonomy for curiosity that carves nature at its joints. Curiosity has been split in several different ways, including novelty-seeking and scientific (James, 1890), perceptual and epistemic (Berlyne, 1954) specific and diversive (Berlyne, 1966), interest and deprivation (Litman, 2008), forward and backward (Shin & Kim, 2019), bottom-up and top-down (Kashdan, 2012), and along several other dimensions (e.g., Kashdan et al., 2020). One reason why so much diversity exists in classifying and defining curiosity is because functional accounts of curiosity have yet to be rigorously investigated. While some work has been done in robotics and artificial intelligence on the function of curiosity, these studies would benefit from a functional evolutionary analysis of human and animal curiosity.

Evolutionary perspectives may help identify the "joints" of nature at which curiosity may be carved (Sznycer et al., 2017). This can be assisted by comparative evidence from a variety of organisms, from simple creatures like *C. elegans* to phylogenetically similar primates like chimpanzees and bonobos. Identifying curiosity-like behaviors in other animals and understanding their development across the animal's life span can also shed light on the evolutionary function of these behaviors. The identification of curiosity-like behaviors and their development can lead to more informed mechanistic analyses. These mechanistic analyses can, in turn, be carefully manipulated in the laboratory to test various hypotheses about curiosity and its function.

While these four questions can in principle be considered in isolation, it is often productive to consider them in groups. For example, one could look at how the neurobiological mechanisms that underlie some curiosity-like behavior change throughout the life course. Change in curiosity-like behavior throughout the life course could be compared in phylogenetic analysis, which could in turn provide information about the function of that particular behavior. Functional accounts of curiosity can be pitted against each other through mechanistic manipulations in the laboratory. Thus, the behavioral biology framework provides a powerful lens through which questions about behavior can be asked and iterative empirical work and theoretical construction can take place.

References

Agyei, S. B., van der Weel, F. R. R., & van der Meer, A. L. H. (2016). Development of visual motion perception for prospective control: Brain and behavioral studies in infants. *Frontiers in Psychology, 7*, 100.

Al-Shawaf, L. (2016). The evolutionary psychology of hunger. *Appetite, 105*, 591–595. https://doi.org/10.1016/j.appet.2016.06.021

Al-Shawaf, L., Conroy-Beam, D., Asao, K., & Buss, D. M. (2015). Human emotions: An evolutionary psychological perspective. *Emotion Review, 8*(2), 173–186. https://doi.org/10.1177/1754073914565518

Andersen, M. M., Schjoedt, U., Price, H., Rosas, F. E., Scrivner, C., & Clasen, M. (2020). Playing with fear: A field study in recreational horror. *Psychological Science, 31*(12), 1497–1510.

Arias-Carrión, O., Stamelou, M., Murillo-Rodríguez, E., Menéndez-González, M., & Pöppel, E. (2010). Dopaminergic reward system: A short integrative review. *International Archives of Medicine, 3*(1), 1–6. https://doi.org/10.1186/1755-7682-3-24

Benson-Amram, S., & Holekamp, K. E. (2012). Innovative problem solving by wild spotted hyenas. *Proceedings of the Royal Society B: Biological Sciences, 279*(1744), 4087–4095.

Bergman, T. J., & Kitchen, D. M. (2009). Comparing responses to novel objects in wild baboons (*Papio ursinus*) and geladas (*Theropithecus gelada*). *Animal Cognition, 12*(1), 63–73.

Berlyne, D. E. (1954). A theory of human curiosity. *British Journal of Psychology, 45*(3), 180–191.

Berlyne, D. E. (1960). *Conflict, arousal, and curiosity*. McGraw-Hill.

Berlyne, D. E. (1966). Curiosity and exploration. *Science, 153*(3731), 25–33.

Blanchard, T. C., Hayden, B. Y., & Bromberg-Martin, E. S. (2015). Orbitofrontal cortex uses distinct codes for different choice attributes in decisions motivated by curiosity. *Neuron, 85*(3), 602–614.

Bromberg-Martin, E. S., & Hikosaka, O. (2011). Lateral habenula neurons signal errors in the prediction of reward information. *Nature Neuroscience, 14*(9), 1209–1216.

Cosmides, L., & Tooby, J. (2000). Evolutionary psychology and the emotions. In M. Lewis & J. M. Haviland-Jones (Eds.), *Handbook of emotions* (2nd ed., pp. 91–115). Guilford Press.

Csikszentmihalyi, M. (1990). *Flow: The psychology of optimal experience*. Harper Collins.

Dubey, R., & Griffiths, T. L. (2020a). Reconciling novelty and complexity through a rational analysis of curiosity. *Psychological Review, 127*(3), 455–476.

Dubey, R., & Griffiths, T. L. (2020b). Understanding exploration in humans and machines by formalizing the function of curiosity. *Current Opinion in Behavioral Sciences, 35*, 118–124.

Dubey, R., Griffiths, T., & Lombrozo, T. (2022). If it's important, then I'm curious: Increasing perceived usefulness stimulates curiosity. *Cognition, 226*, 105193. https://doi.org/10.1016/j.cognition.2022.105193

Farroni, T., Johnson, M. H., Menon, E., Zulian, L., Faraguna, D., & Csibra, G. (2005). Newborns' preference for face-relevant stimuli: Effects of contrast polarity. *Proceedings of the National Academy of Sciences, 102*(47), 17245–17250.

Glickman, S. E., & Sroges, R. W. (1966). Curiosity in zoo animals. *Behaviour, 26*(1), 151–188.

Gopnik, A. (1996). The scientist as child. *Philosophy of Science, 63*(4), 485–514. https://doi.org/10.1086/289970

Gopnik, A. (2020). Childhood as a solution to explore–exploit tensions. *Philosophical Transactions of the Royal Society B, 375*(1803), 20190502.

Gopnik, A., Griffiths, T. L., & Lucas, C. G. (2015). When younger learners can be better (or at least more open-minded) than older ones. *Current Directions in Psychological Science, 24*(2), 87–92. https://doi.org/10.1177/0963721414556653

Gopnik, A., O'Grady, S., Lucas, C. G., Griffiths, T. L., Wente, A., Bridgers, S., Aboody, R., Fung, H., & Dahl, R. E. (2017). Changes in cognitive flexibility and hypothesis search across human life history from childhood to adolescence to adulthood. *Proceedings of the National Academy of Sciences, 114*(30), 7892–7899.

Gosling, S. D., & John, O. P. (1999). Personality dimensions in nonhuman animals: A cross-species review. *Current Directions in Psychological Science, 8*(3), 69–75.

Gruber, M. J., Gelman, B. D., & Ranganath, C. (2014). States of curiosity modulate hippocampus-dependent learning via the dopaminergic circuit. *Neuron, 84*(2), 486–496.

Harlow, H. F. (1950). Learning and satiation of response in intrinsically motivated complex puzzle performance by monkeys. *Journal of Comparative and Physiological Psychology, 43*(4), 289. https://doi.org/10.1037/h0058114

Harlow, H. F., Harlow, M. K., & Meyer, D. R. (1950). Learning motivated by a manipulation drive. *Journal of Experimental Psychology, 40*(2), 228–234.

James, W. (1890). *The principles of psychology*, Vol. 1. Henry Holt.

Johnson, C., & Wilbrecht, L. (2011). Juvenile mice show greater flexibility in multiple choice reversal learning than adults. *Developmental CognitiveNneuroscience, 1*(4), 540–551. https://doi.org/10.1016/j.dcn.2011.05.008

Kaplan, H., Hill, K., Lancaster, J., & Hurtado, A. M. (2000). A theory of human life history evolution: Diet, intelligence, and longevity. *Evolutionary Anthropology, 9*(4), 156–185.

Kashdan, T. B. (2012). Reconsidering the neuroevolutionary framework of the SEEKING system: Emphasizing context instead of positivity. *Neuropsychoanalysis, 14*(1), 46–50. https://doi.org/10.1080/15294145.2012.10773686

Kashdan, T. B., Disabato, D. J., Goodman, F. R., & McKnight, P. E. (2020). The Five-Dimensional Curiosity Scale Revised (5DCR): Briefer subscales while separating overt and covert social curiosity. *Personality and Individual Differences, 157*, 109836. https://doi.org/10.1016/j.paid.2020.109836

Kashdan, T. B., Stiksma, M. C., Disabato, D. J., McKnight, P. E., Bekier, J., Kaji, J., & Lazarus, R. (2018). The five-dimensional curiosity scale: Capturing the bandwidth of curiosity and identifying four unique subgroups of curious people. *Journal of Research in Personality, 73*, 130–149. https://doi.org/10.1016/j.jrp.2017.11.011

Kidd, C., & Hayden, B. Y. (2015). The psychology and neuroscience of curiosity. *Neuron, 88*(3), 449–460.

Kidd, C., Piantadosi, S. T., & Aslin, R. N. (2012). The Goldilocks effect: Human infants allocate attention to visual sequences that are neither too simple nor too complex. *PloS One, 7*(5), e36399.

Kidd, C., Piantadosi, S. T., & Aslin, R. N. (2014). The Goldilocks effect in infant auditory attention. *Child Development, 85*(5), 1795–1804.

Kobayashi, K., & Hsu, M. (2019). Common neural code for reward and information value. *Proceedings of the National Academy of Sciences, 116*(26), 13061–13066.

Levy, D. J., & Glimcher, P. W. (2012). The root of all value: A neural common currency for choice. *Current Opinion in Neurobiology, 22*(6), 1027–1038.

Litman, J. A. (2008). Interest and deprivation factors of epistemic curiosity. *Personality and Individual Differences, 44*(7), 1585–1595. https://doi.org/10.1016/j.paid.2008.01.014

Litman, J. A., & Jimerson, T. L. (2004). The measurement of curiosity as a feeling of deprivation. *Journal of Personality Assessment, 82*(2), 147–157. https://doi.org/10.1207/s15327752jpa8202_3

LoBue, V., & DeLoache, J. S. (2008). Detecting the snake in the grass: Attention to fear-relevant stimuli by adults and young children. *Psychological Science, 19*(3), 284–289. https://doi.org/10.1111%2Fj.1467-9280.2008.02081.x

Loewenstein, G. (1994). The psychology of curiosity: A review and reinterpretation. *Psychological Bulletin, 116*(1), 75. https://doi.org/10.1037/0033-2909.116.1.75

Lucas, C. G., Bridgers, S., Griffiths, T. L., & Gopnik, A. (2014). When children are better (or at least more open-minded) learners than adults: developmental differences in learning the forms of causal relationships. *Cognition, 131*(2), 284–299.

Marr, D. (1982). *Vision: A computational investigation into the human representation and processing of visual information.* Freeman.

Montag, C., & Panksepp, J. (2017). Primary emotional systems and personality: An evolutionary perspective. *Frontiers in Psychology, 8*, 464.

O'Hara, M., & Auersperg, A. M. (2017). Object play in parrots and corvids. *Current Opinion in Behavioral Sciences, 16*, 119–125. https://doi.org/10.1016/j.cobeha.2017.05.008

Öhman, A., & Mineka, S. (2003). The malicious serpent: Snakes as a prototypical stimulus for an evolved module of fear. *Current Directions in Psychological Science, 12*(1), 5–9. https://doi.org/10.1111%2F1467-8721.01211

Oosterwijk, S. (2017). Choosing the negative: A behavioral demonstration of morbid curiosity. *PloS One, 12*(7), e0178399.

Panksepp, J., & Moskal, J. (2008). Dopamine and SEEKING: Subcortical "reward" systems and appetitive urges. In A. J. Elliot (Ed.), *Handbook of approach and avoidance motivation* (pp. 67–87). Psychology Press. https://doi.org/10.4324/9780203888148.ch5

Parker, K. J., Rainwater, K. L., Buckmaster, C. L., Schatzberg, A. F., Lindley, S. E., & Lyons, D. M. (2007). Early life stress and novelty seeking behavior in adolescent monkeys. *Psychoneuroendocrinology, 32*(7), 785–792.

Perry, S. E., Barrett, B. J., & Godoy, I. (2017). Older, sociable capuchins (*Cebus capucinus*) invent more social behaviors, but younger monkeys innovate more in other contexts. *Proceedings of the National Academy of Sciences, 114*(30), 7806–7813. https://doi.org/10.1073/pnas.1620739114

Piaget, J. (1945). Play, Dreams and Imitation in Childhood. Psychology Press.

Reader, S. M. (2015). Causes of individual differences in animal exploration and search. *Topics in Cognitive Science, 7*(3), 451–468.

Schrock, J. M., Snodgrass, J. J., & Sugiyama, L. S. (2020). Lassitude: The emotion of being sick. *Evolution and Human Behavior, 41*(1), 44–57. https://doi.org/10.1016/j.evolhumbehav.2019.09.002

Scrivner, C. (2021a). The psychology of morbid curiosity: Development and initial validation of the morbid curiosity scale. *Personality and Individual Differences, 183*, 111139. https://doi.org/10.1016/j.paid.2021.111139

Scrivner, C. (2021b). An infectious curiosity: Morbid curiosity and media preferences during a pandemic. *Evolutionary Studies in Imaginative Culture, 5*(1), 1–12.

Scrivner, C., Johnson, J. A., Kjeldgaard-Christiansen, J., & Clasen, M. (2021). Pandemic practice: Horror fans and morbidly curious individuals are more psychologically resilient during the COVID-19 pandemic. *Personality and Individual Differences, 168*, 110397.

Scrivner, C., & Maestripieri, D. (2018). Creativity patterns in the production of scientific theories and literary fiction. *KNOW: A Journal on the Formation of Knowledge, 2*(1), 137–154. https://doi.org/10.1086/696984

Scrivner, C., Andersen, M. M., Schjødt, U., & Clasen, M. (2022). The psychological benefits of scary play in three types of horror fans. *Journal of Media Psychology*. https://doi.org/10.1027/1864-1105/a000354

Shin, D. D., & Kim, S. I. (2019). Homo curious: Curious or interested? *Educational Psychology Review, 31*, 853–874. https://doi.org/10.1007/s10648-019-09497-x

Sih, A., Bell, A. M., Johnson, J. C., & Ziemba, R. E. (2004). Behavioral syndromes: An integrative overview. *The Quarterly Review of Biology, 79*(3), 241–277. https://doi.org/10.1086/422893

Silvia, P. J. (2010). Confusion and interest: The role of knowledge emotions in aesthetic experience. *Psychology of Aesthetics, Creativity, and the Arts, 4*(2), 75. https://doi.org/10.1037/a0017081

Sznycer, D., Cosmides, L., & Tooby, J. (2017). Adaptationism carves emotions at their functional joints. *Psychological Inquiry, 28*(1), 56–62. https://doi.org/10.1080/1047840X.2017.1256132

Tinbergen, N. (1963). On aims and methods of ethology. *Zeitschrift für tierpsychologie, 20*(4), 410–433. https://doi.org/10.1111/j.1439-0310.1963.tb01161.x

Wang, M. Z., & Hayden, B. Y. (2019). Monkeys are curious about counterfactual outcomes. *Cognition, 189*, 1–10.

Wright, J. S., & Panksepp, J. (2012). An evolutionary framework to understand foraging, wanting, and desire: The neuropsychology of the SEEKING system. *Neuropsychoanalysis, 14*(1), 5–39. https://doi.org/10.1080/15294145.2012.10773683

Yee, M., Jones, S. S., & Smith, L. B. (2012). Changes in visual object recognition precede the shape bias in early noun learning. *Frontiers in Psychology, 3*, 533.

CHAPTER 20

An Evolutionary Perspective on Positive Emotions

Amanda P. Kirsch, Erika B. Langley, Carley Vornlocher, and Michelle N. Shiota

Abstract

What does it mean to apply an evolutionary perspective to the study of positive emotions? This chapter addresses this question, both looking back at research informed by evolutionary theorizing and looking toward future advances. Although an evolutionary perspective is most explicitly invoked in theory and research on specific emotions, it also plays an important role in emphasizing dimensions of core affect and emotion-eliciting appraisals. The authors discuss why most early research focused on the adaptive value of negative emotions, and the changes that have led to growing interest in positive emotions. They provide an overview of the research addressing the adaptive functions of positive emotions, including examples from multiple emotion theories. Finally, they offer several suggestions for applying an evolutionary perspective to research on the positive emotions, considering advances in evolutionary biology, ethology, and neuroscience for what emotions are, how they work, and their implications in the modern world.

Key Words: positive emotion, emotion, evolutionary psychology, cognition, interpersonal relations

The proposal that aspects of human cognition and behavior have evolutionary origins, and are therefore part of "human nature," has often been controversial (Confer et al., 2010). During the mid-20th century this was the case for emotion as well; the dominant view in the social sciences was that pretty much everything about human emotion was socially constructed, and varied from culture to culture (Ekman, 1972). Since the 1970s, however, this has changed. Although an evolutionary framework is most explicitly adopted in theory and research on specific emotion states (including "basic" or "discrete" emotions), all major modern theories of emotion presume that human affective experience has some evolved origins and serves adaptive functions. Various theories disagree on what emotions are, what *aspects* of emotions are adaptations, and what functions emotions serve, but the notion that emotions have some evolutionary foundation is widely accepted and has proved a powerful engine for empirical research (Shiota, 2014).

In this chapter we begin by asking what is involved in adopting an evolutionary perspective on positive emotions, disentangling adaptive function from other ways in which positive emotions might be described as functional, and articulating links between positive emotion states and broader evolved fundamental motivations. We then offer a rich survey of empirical research addressing the adaptive functions of positive affect, mood, and emotions—both those conferring direct benefit for individual fitness, and those in which fitness benefits are mediated by healthy, interdependent relationships with other humans. We conclude with some words of caution for those seeking to rigorously apply an evolutionary perspective in their own research on positive emotions, and with some suggested directions for future research.

What Does It Mean to Take an Evolutionary Approach to Emotion?

An evolutionary perspective on emotions takes as its foundation the assumption that mechanisms of emotional responding are species-typical traits, inherited from ancient ancestors for whom emotions served important functions. Put simply, we have emotions because they conferred important benefits upon those whose generations of offspring became our species. Functional analysis has become increasingly prominent in emotion theory and research, but what does it even mean for a psychological mechanism, such as emotion, to have a *function*?

From a sociocultural perspective, one might propose that emotions are functional primarily in guiding culturally appropriate behavior and facilitating social cohesion (e.g., Averill, 1980; Mesquita & Boiger, 2014). Researchers working from this perspective often emphasize ways in which emotion concepts are culturally constructed, with emotional feelings, language, expression, and behavior shaped by one's social environment (e.g., Barrett, 2017). Alternatively, one might propose that positive emotions in particular are functional in the sense that they are a key component of psychological well-being (Diener, 2000). In contrast, an evolutionary perspective emphasizes *adaptive* function, defined as the extent to which a genetically influenced trait tended to enhance our ancestors' reproductive success, thereby growing more prevalent over generations. In the case of emotions, the genetic characteristics in question are thought to have promoted psychological and physiological aspects of emotional responses to crucial situations, which facilitated behavioral reactions to those situations resulting in differential rates of successful reproduction.

In explaining evolutionary perspectives on emotions it is useful to differentiate proximate versus ultimate cause (Dewsbury, 1999; Scott-Phillips et al., 2011). In the context of emotion, proximate causes refer to temporally near reasons for having some present-day emotional response, and can explain the immediate mechanism of the response. For example, someone might feel a burst of sexual desire because they are chatting with an attractive person of the desired sex, because they are experiencing a surge of testosterone, because they are in a romantic setting, and/or because they've been exposed to a lot of popular media highlighting the value of sex as a source of enjoyment and self-esteem. In contrast, ultimate causes are those rooted in the species' ancestral history, explaining why the capacity to have the emotional response exists at all, rather than why a particular individual has that response at a particular moment in time. In this case, an ultimate explanation would highlight the crucial role of sexual reproduction in producing offspring for future generations, and the biological and motivational properties of mammalian desire that facilitate reproductive behavior. In this way, ultimate explanations are closely aligned with the meaning of function in the evolutionary sense.

Proximate and ultimate explanations can both be correct, and proximate causes often point to mechanisms by which ultimate causes are carried out. For example, much research has found that physical characteristics correlated with fertility and genetic health are perceived as sexually attractive (e.g., Jokela, 2009; Singh et al., 2010), and that hormonal fluctuations help heighten both men's and women's sexual interest when conception is most likely (e.g., Miller & Maner, 2010; Shirazi et al., 2018), linking proximate causes of sexual desire to the ultimate function of successful reproduction. Not only are proximate and ultimate causes both accurate, but having both explanations is crucial to complete understanding of a behavioral phenomenon.

Similarly, analyses emphasizing sociocultural, well-being, and adaptive functions of emotion are not mutually exclusive, and these aspects of functionality are intertwined in complex ways. However, an evolutionary perspective entails distinctive propositions and constraints relative to the alternatives. The evolved mechanisms of emotions and capacities for emotional experiences are expected to be universal among neurotypical humans (Ekman, 1992; Plutchik, 1984; Tomkins, 1984). This proposition in no way precludes a strong influence of learning and culture on the exact situations that evoke emotions, or on observable emotional behavior (Al-Shawaf et al., 2019; Shiota, 2024). However, an evolutionary view suggests that emotions should be triggered by eliciting situations interpreted as presenting a certain kind of threat or opportunity that was critical for our ancestors' reproductive success; that emotional responses should involve reliably occurring cognitive, physiological, and motivational features; and that these features facilitate overt behaviors that, while varying based on learned experience and situational context, still share and promote a common goal (e.g., fighting, fleeing, or "playing dead" in order to escape; Bracha, 2004; Cosmides & Tooby, 2000; Ekman, 1992).

Because many situations that served as selection pressures driving emotions' evolution greatly pre-date the human species (e.g., predator threat, need to acquire food and territory, pathogen threat, competition for status, mate seeking and retention, offspring and kin care), the mechanisms for the corresponding emotions are likely shared with some nonhuman animals. For this reason, research reflecting an evolutionary perspective on emotion may emphasize and examine continuities linking humans to other primates and mammals (Ekman, 1992; Scarantino, 2018). Other evolved emotional responses—including some positive emotions—may be specific to humans (Al-Shawaf et al., 2016; Shiota et al., 2017).

It is important to note that all major modern theories of emotion—including the basic/discrete/specific emotion family of theories (e.g., Ekman, 1992; Shiota, 2024; Tracy & Randles, 2011), the core affect and psychological construction family of theories (e.g., Barrett, 2017; Russell, 2003), and the appraisal dimension-focused component process model (Scherer, 2009)—agree that some aspects of human emotional responding are products of our evolutionary heritage. Moreover, theories generally agree that evolved mechanisms of emotion interact in rich and complex ways with learning, context, and lived experience to produce the tapestry of human emotion (e.g., Al-Shawaf et al., 2019; Barrett, 2017; Ekman & Coradro, 2011; Scherer, 2009; Shiota, 2017). Where they diverge is in the specific mechanisms that are thought to have evolved, and how they connect to the more readily observable proximal causes of behavior. Nonetheless, the evolutionary perspective is most clearly articulated in theories emphasizing specific emotions such as fear, anger, and pride, which entail further constraints on functional analyses beyond those described above (Shiota, 2024). First, emotions are expected to have evolved as domain-specific responses to qualitatively different types of eliciting situations, rather than to goal-conducive versus -obstructive situations in general (Ekman, 1992). Second, these theories typically predict that the mechanism generating complex, functional emotional responses is some kind of dedicated, "superordinate" neural circuit that coordinates otherwise divergent cognitive, physiological, and motivational processes (e.g., Al-Shawaf et al., 2016; Cosmides & Tooby, 2000; Ekman, 1992). Third, many theorists predict that activation of this circuit should produce a "coherent" observable response, in which different aspects of emotional responding, such as visceral change, nonverbal expression, and subjective feeling, reliably co-occur during strong emotion (Mauss et al., 2005; though see Al-Shawaf et al., 2016, for discussion of why coherence might *not* necessarily be expected).

For decades, most research on emotion through an evolutionary lens focused on negative emotions—particularly those of fear, anger, sadness, and disgust. This may be because these emotions have fairly obvious links to threats to adaptive fitness (e.g., pathogen threat for disgust; threat to status and/or resources for anger). Identifying the adaptive functions of pleasant/positive emotions proved more challenging. However, in the 21st century this view has shifted dramatically. This is due in part to growing recognition that behavioral adaptations are conserved not only based on helping ancestors survive immediate, mortal threats, but also based on the "total lifetime fitness consequences" of behavior (Cosmides & Tooby, 2000). Barbara Fredrickson's (2001) Broaden-and-Build Theory of positive emotions has played a crucial role in the field, highlighting subtler effects of positive emotions on attention and cognitive processing that have downstream implications for social, psychological, and material resource acquisition and reproductive success. Shiota and colleagues (2017) have further emphasized the diversity of recurring opportunities to enhance one's fitness presented by the mammalian environment, and the corresponding variety of potentially discrete positive emotions.

To a greater extent than for the negative emotions, the key opportunities evoking positive emotions are often social in nature, supporting the complex, interdependent relationships that are a hallmark of the human species and that characterize many other primates as well (Shiota et al., 2004). For example, caring for offspring and other young kin is essential to ensuring successful mammalian reproductive success. Sexual activity resulting in a baby is not enough to secure this success; ongoing, active nurturance is necessary for the young to survive and ultimately reproduce as well. Yet only recently have researchers devoted serious effort to studying the emotion state that has been called tenderness or nurturant love, proposed as a response to cuteness and vulnerability (e.g., Lishner et al., 2011; O'Neil et al., 2018). In addition, earlier approaches emphasized emotions' roles in promoting survival (Ekman, 1992), but largely ignored reproduction, kin care, and other selection pressures indirectly related to survival and fitness. Modern approaches take these aspects into consideration (Al-Shawaf et al., 2016; Cosmides & Tooby, 2000). Because of advances such as these, researchers now acknowledge that positive emotions may play just as crucial roles as negative emotions in promoting adaptive behavior.

Positive Emotions and the Fundamental Social Motives
Emotions are commonly defined as relatively brief, short-lived phenomena evoked by real or imagined events in the environment (Ekman, 1992; Shiota et al., 2017). From an evolutionary perspective, one might expect that short-lived, situationally evoked emotions are tied functionally to the individual's broader fitness-relevant goals. Fundamental social motives have been defined as universal psychological goals reflecting central fitness-related life tasks, and promoting essential, adaptive social behaviors (Neel et al., 2016). These goals include self-protection, affiliation, status acquisition, mate acquisition, mate retention, and kin/offspring care (Kenrick et al., 2010). Whereas emotions last for a short period of time and are evoked by the environment, fundamental motives are long-term, underlying goals (Kenrick et al., 2010). When fundamental motives are activated by an environmental cue, an emotional response is often the result. Examining the links between fundamental social motives and positive emotions can help illustrate how emotions are tied to basic evolutionary tasks and give rise to behaviors that are essential for survival and reproduction (see Table 20.1).

An example of a relationship between a fundamental motive and a specific emotion is status-seeking and pride. Among primates and many other group-dwelling mammals, higher social status confers increased access to important material and social resources, leading to a better chance of flourishing for oneself and one's offspring—especially when resources are scarce (Pérusse, 1993; Von Rueden et al., 2008). Pride has been defined as the emotion felt after completing a personally and socially valued achievement, which is a pathway to attaining higher status (Tracy

Table 20.1 Examples of Linked Fundamental Social Motives and Positive Emotions

Fundamental Motive	Emotion	Adaptive Function
Status enhancement	Pride	Display eligibility for high status; gain increased access to material and social resources accompanying high status
Kin care	Nurturant love	Invest time, effort, resources in nurturing offspring and other kin to maturity
Mate acquisition	Sexual desire	Identify promising reproductive partner; communicate interest; prepare body for mating
Mate retention	Attachment love	Secure and maintain mate's commitment to co-parenting shared offspring
Affiliation	Attachment love	Maintain secure, mutually beneficial relationships with group members beyond kin

& Robins, 2007a, 2007b, 2007c). Pride functions as an immediate motivator to seek and achieve status (Tracy & Robins, 2007b, 2007c; Williams & DeSteno, 2008). In this way, pride and status-seeking are linked, with status-seeking as the ongoing fundamental motive, and pride as the shorter-lived emotional experience that is evoked by momentary opportunities to increase one's status, and that helps to facilitate concrete status-seeking behavior.

Another example is the relationship of the fundamental motive of kin care with the positive emotion of nurturant love (sometimes referred to as tenderness; e.g., Lishner et al., 2011). The kin care motive reflects the need to support and care for one's offspring and other kin, as one's inclusive fitness is tied to the survival and reproductive success of one's genetic relatives (Burnstein et al., 1994; Van den Berghe & Barah, 1977; West & Gardner, 2013), thereby helping to maximize the inclusion of one's genes in future generations. Mammals invest strongly in offspring until they reach self-sufficiency and reproductive age (Zeveloff & Boyce, 1980), and primates in particular have lengthy juvenile periods in which offspring fitness depends heavily on investment from parents and other adult kin (Joffe, 1997; Walker et al., 2006). Nurturant love has been described as a discrete emotion evoked by a social partner's physical and behavioral cuteness, vulnerability, and expression of need (O'Neil et al., 2018). Notably, both anecdotal and empirical evidence show that intense human nurturant love can be elicited by cute and/or vulnerable non-kin individuals, and even by the young of other species—a generalization of the emotional response that may reflect the context of human shared caregiving norms (O'Neil et al., 2018; see also Steinnes et al., this volume). Linking the human emotional experience of nurturant love to the fundamental motive of kin care has facilitated theory development for both constructs. Further examples of linked fundamental motives and positive emotions are offered in Table 20.1.

An evolutionary perspective on positive emotions provides new avenues for theorizing, offering a way to integrate evidence about modern emotional responses into a larger, coherent framework that considers ultimate functions. In addition, an evolutionary approach to research on human emotions can and should guide rigorous, innovative hypothesis generation, with theoretical analyses of adaptive function suggesting non-obvious predictions for effects or aspects of a given emotion state. The next sections of this chapter offer a number of examples of the functions of positive affect and emotions, as supported by empirical affective science.

Intrapersonal Functions of Positive Affect and Emotions

In this section we focus on aspects of positive emotions that play out within the individual experiencing the emotion, and have direct implications for that individual's fitness. The great majority of the work to be discussed has emphasized the effects of positive mood, affect, and emotion on attention and information processing; more overt behavioral implications will be discussed in the following section on interpersonal/social functions of positive emotions. In addition, because rigorous theorizing about the adaptive functions of specific/discrete positive emotions did not begin until the 21st century, at which point social functions were a more prominent research focus (Shiota et al., 2004), much of the work to be discussed in this section focuses on the effects of experimentally evoked pleasant mood, and on positive emotion as a broad category. Where there is additional work on specific positive emotions, it will be discussed. Work on physiological aspects of positive emotions (both short- and long-term) and on the roles positive emotion can play in regulating stress and distress is reviewed as well.

Positive Mood/Emotion and Cognition

A rich, established body of research has examined how pleasant affect, positive mood, and positive emotion influence attention and information processing. Within affective science, *affect* is commonly defined in terms of the valence and arousal level of subjective feelings; *mood* is defined as a broad, lingering affect state that may not be linked to a particular stimulus; and *emotion* is often reserved for relatively brief responses to emotion-eliciting stimuli (Fernández-Dols & Russell, 2003). Although the body of work reviewed below reflects multiple distinct theoretical perspectives, emphasizing different aspects of emotional responding as primary (e.g., conscious subjective feeling; motivational direction; activation of cognitive biases), these findings can still be synthesized to provide a rich understanding of how positive emotions influence the way individuals perceive and interpret the world.

Theories emphasizing the cognitive effects of overall pleasant affect or mood—including Core Affect Theory, the Affect Infusion Model, and Affect as Information Hypothesis—share the proposal that the valence of an individual's internal feeling state carries a signal value that influences how information is processed (Forgas, 1995; Russell, 2003; Schwarz & Clore, 1983). Negative affect is thought to signal to the person experiencing it that something is wrong, the environment may contain threats, and it would be best to proceed with caution. Positive affect, in contrast, signals that things are going well, the environment may contain opportunities, and it is safe to continue along one's current path and explore. In this theoretical approach, internal feeling states serve as a lens through which the environment is interpreted.

One robust finding is that positive states lead us to view the world through "rose-colored glasses," such that positive mood results in less critical judgment than does negative mood (Pham, 2007). For example, experimentally elicited positive mood has been found to result in more positive judgments of political candidates (Isbell & Wyer, 1999), consumer products (Gorn et al., 1993), and weak persuasive arguments (Bless et al., 1990). Positive mood can also influence the way in which information is processed, promoting greater reliance on cognitive heuristics or stereotypes (Bodenhausen et al., 1994). For example, Park and Banaji (2000) found that relative to participants in neutral and negative moods, those in a positive mood were more likely to assign race-connoting names (African American vs. European American) to fictitious individuals from stereotype-consistent social categories (politician, basketball player, or criminal). Another study used a mock juror paradigm in which participants were presented with brief summaries of hypothetical crimes, and then asked to rate the likelihood that an accused person with either a male-connoting name (Nicholas) or female-connoting name (Nicole) had committed that crime. Those induced to feel a positive mood rated male defendants as more likely to be guilty, relative to those in a neutral state, consistent with the stereotype that men commit more crimes than women (Curtis, 2013).

Recent evidence suggests that positive affect leads us to endorse and continue using whatever processing mode is currently most accessible, rather than questioning and potentially changing that style. For example, when counter-stereotypic processing is already primed, positive affect will instead *reduce* stereotype-consistent responding in tasks such as those above (Huntsinger et al., 2010; Huntsinger et al., 2014). Taken together, the findings above suggest that positive mood facilitates a cognitive "go" mode in which active engagement with the environment and continuation of one's current or default information-processing style are promoted, at the expense of cognitive and behavioral caution.

By emphasizing the implications of positive mood for cognition, rather than nonverbal expression or overt behavior, these early theories set the stage for models of positive emotion more explicitly infused with principles of evolutionary theory. Barbara Fredrickson's (2001) Broaden-and-Build Theory built further on the idea of information-processing effects to address the mechanics of how positive emotions are relevant to adaptive fitness. Broaden-and-Build Theory focuses on positive *emotions* rather than mood, placing greater emphasis on brief, adaptive responses to emotion-eliciting situations. The key tenets of Broaden-and-Build Theory are: (1) the momentary effects of positive emotions on cognition center on broadening the scope of attention and promoting a more flexible, creative mindset; and (2) this mindset opens the door to accumulation of personal resources that can be drawn upon in times of challenge, boosting the individual's chance of survival and achievement of reproductive success.

The "broadening" hypothesis proposes that positive emotions lead to expanded awareness of possible options and outcomes, which promotes novel, exploratory, and diverse ways of thinking and behaving (Fredrickson, 2001). Support for the broadening hypothesis has been demonstrated most frequently through the use of visual perception tasks, such as the Navon Letter Task and Kimchi-Palmer Task. Navon figures include a larger recognizable letter (referred to as the "global" component) composed of smaller copies of a different letter (referred to as the "local" component), such as a large F made from small Hs. The Kimchi-Palmer Task is similar, but task figures are composed of shapes such as circles and triangles, rather than letters. In each case, the participant is asked which of two figures is most similar to a target, with one option similar to the target in the global component and the other similar in the local component. Experimentally elicited positive affect has been shown to evoke higher tendency to choose based on global similarity, suggesting preferential attention to visual wholes rather than specific elements (e.g., Fredrickson & Branigan, 2005; Wadlinger & Isaacowitz, 2006). Positive affect has also been linked to increased creativity and cognitive flexibility (Baas et al., 2008; Lyubomirsky et al., 2005), as well as heightened detection of similarities among people or objects, which allows for more inclusive categorization (Isen, 1987; Ellsworth & Smith, 1988; Isen & Daubman, 1984; Bolte et al., 2003).

Broaden-and-Build Theory has had tremendous impact, launching a wave of empirical research on positive emotions per se. Further research has built on this foundation, examining effects of different varieties of positive emotion in order to refine our understanding of the relationship between emotion and cognition. One strong body of research has distinguished the effects of positive emotion involving high behavioral approach motivation from that characterized by low approach motivation (Harmon-Jones et al., 2013). Gray's (1970) influential theory of mammalian behavior posits that two neural systems regulate our responses to environmental cues. Whereas the Behavioral Inhibition System (BIS) is sensitive to signals of danger, punishment, and novelty, and motivates the individual to withdraw and avoid harm, the Behavioral Activation System (BAS) is sensitive to reward, and drives action forward to approach and attain something desirable (Carver & White, 1994). Positive emotion is often characterized by high approach motivation, linked to BAS activation, and reward is typically associated with positive feelings, yet there are exceptions. For example, contentment is high on pleasantness, but low on approach motivation (Gable & Harmon-Jones, 2010).

Research differentiating high- versus low-approach-motivation positive emotion suggests that the latter promotes attentional broadening, as predicted by Broaden-and-Build Theory; but that the former often results in *narrowed* scope of attention, typically targeting a desired reward. In one study, Gable and Harmon-Jones (2008) used funny videos of cats to induce low-approach positive emotion, and videos of desserts to induce high-approach positive emotion; participants then completed the Kimchi-Palmer Task described above. Participants viewing the desserts videos selected local-similar options at higher rates than those seeing the cat videos, suggesting that appetitive drive results in narrowed attention. Another study elicited approach motivation by having participants lean forward in their chair, whereas low approach motivation was elicited by asking participants to recline; all participants were asked to smile, eliciting pleasant affect. Participants were then asked to rate 10 items on the degree to which they fit a given category (e.g. fruit), with some items clearly fitting the category (e.g., apple), while others were weaker exemplars of the given category (e.g., tomato). Leaning forward led to more narrowed, less inclusive categorization of the weak exemplar than reclining (Price & Harmon-Jones, 2010).

In a third technique, researchers manipulated approach motivation by using anticipation of a monetary reward (Gable & Harmon-Jones, 2011). Participants were presented with either "pre-goal" visual cues indicating the possibility of winning money on the current trial of a computer-based memory task, or "post-goal" cues indicating money would only be won after all trials were complete. Memory task targets were visual stimuli presented either in the screen's center or on its periphery. Pre-goal cues resulted in better memory for centrally presented stimuli rather than peripheral stimuli, but the opposite effect was observed for post-goal cues. These effects were replicated using photos of desserts as primes to evoke heightened approach motivation; like the pre-goal cues, these led to better memory for centrally presented stimuli than for peripheral stimuli, whereas neutral photos (rocks) had the opposite effect. Taken together, these findings further support the notion that high-approach positive emotion facilitates cognitive narrowing, which helps drive action forward to attain a target of appetitive motivation such as food, money, or a potential mate.

Beyond the implications of high versus low approach motivation, might there be other differences among positive emotions in terms of cognition? If discrete positive emotions evolved as means of addressing qualitatively distinct fitness-relevant opportunities, we should expect this to be the case. Few studies have addressed this possibility thus far, but these indicate a promising avenue for future research. Earlier we described the evidence that positive mood tends to promote heuristic-based information processing and less critical judgment. Awe—a positive emotion evoked by vast, extraordinary stimuli not readily processed in terms of the stored knowledge on which heuristics and cognitive shortcuts are often based—appears to be a distinct exception to the heuristic-facilitation effect. For example, Griskevicius, Shiota, and Neufeld (2010) found that experimentally evoked awe led to more critical responses to weak persuasive arguments, and persuasion only by strong arguments, whereas most other positive emotions led to ready persuasion by both weak and strong arguments as seen in prior research. Danvers and Shiota (2017) found that unlike other positive emotions, awe reduced the tendency to impute false, but schema-consistent short story details into memory for the story. These studies provide evidence that, far from encouraging the cognitive "go" mode seen in many positive affect states, awe may interrupt ongoing cognitive processes, hinder reliance on heuristics, and encourage information processing that is less filtered through prior knowledge and experience (Shiota, Thrash, et al., 2014).

Positive Emotion, Autonomic Physiology, and Physical Health
Although less research has addressed physiological relative to cognitive aspects of positive emotions, short-term visceral and long-term health consequences of positive emotion are now well documented in the literature. Most positive emotions are characterized by heightened peripheral arousal caused by an increase in sympathetic nervous system activation, which is presumably linked to the approach/appetitive motivation discussed earlier (Kreibig, 2010). There is some empirical evidence of differences among discrete positive emotions as well. In one study comparing physiological reactivity to visual images evoking appetitive enthusiasm, awe, attachment love, nurturant love, and contentment, significantly distinct autonomic profiles were identified for different emotions (Shiota et al., 2011). Enthusiasm, for example, was found to facilitate a broad increase in sympathetic activation, consistent with the arousal needed to pursue and attain a desirable reward. Attachment and nurturant love were characterized by increased cardiac arousal, but not increased blood pressure or heightened sweat gland activity. Awe was characterized by *withdrawal* of sympathetic influence on the heart, consistent with a soothed physiological state promoting stillness rather than arousal (Shiota et al., 2011). As might be expected, contentment also seems to involve reduced rather than heightened "fight-flight" sympathetic arousal (Kreibig, 2010). Although this work has begun to unpack some physiological differences among discrete positive emotions, additional research is greatly needed in this area to expand our understanding (Kreibig, 2010).

Beyond the immediate visceral responses associated with positive emotions, other research has identified robust relationships between positive emotions and broader, long-term health outcomes. Positive affect is consistently associated with decreased morbidity and lower mortality rates, though the positive affect-mortality link appears to be strongest for older individuals (see Pressman & Cohen, 2005, for review). Positive affect has also been linked to better quality and efficiency of sleep, though these effects appear to vary among specific positive states (Cross & Pressman, 2017). Positive affect also predicts enhanced immune function, with findings generally pointing to an upregulation of immune response to pathogens, though these effects may also be parsed out according to levels of activation (Pressman & Black, 2012). Though these studies have looked specifically at positive affect predicting health outcomes, the relationship between positive affect and health can often be reciprocal.

Regulatory Functions of Positive Emotion
So far, this section has highlighted ways in which positive emotions influence cognition and physiology, emphasizing processes that typically occur outside of our conscious awareness. However, other lines of research suggest that we can harness the power of positive emotions and consciously use them to our benefit. Early work examining the *undoing effect* provided early experimental evidence for positive emotions' ability to help people bounce back from stress and distress. Fredrickson and colleagues (2000) found that contentment and amusement elicited by short film clips resulted in faster cardiovascular recovery after an anxiety-inducing task, as compared to film clips evoking sad or neutral states. Other research has examined the implications of emotion-regulation techniques that leverage positive emotions for well-being. A study of AIDS patients' caregivers (typically their romantic partners) found that those who were able to create positive meaning in their interactions with sick partners reported boosted morale and sustained well-being, despite the fatigue and psychological distress they experienced (Folkman et al., 1994). Other work has demonstrated that emotion-regulation

strategies involving positive emotion generation, such as positive reappraisal and savoring pleasant sensory events, are distinctly associated with higher psychological well-being (Shiota, 2006). In another study comparing experimentally instructed positive reappraisal to detached reappraisal while viewing distressing film clips, those in the positive reappraisal condition reported more positive thoughts and more positive emotional valence, and showed preserved overall emotional responding rather than disengagement (Shiota & Levenson, 2012). Together these findings suggest that positive emotions can play a unique role in curbing negative effects of stress, if used skillfully.

Social Functions of Positive Emotions

In this section we turn to the social functions of positive emotions—ways in which positive emotions facilitate the formation, maintenance, and effective navigation of interpersonal relationships. As an "ultrasocial" species, humans rely heavily on cooperation with others to complete fundamental life tasks: gathering food, reciprocal exchange of goods, caring for kin, protection against predators, and so forth (Campbell, 1983). Thus, individual humans are crucial fitness-relevant features of each other's environments, so much so that loneliness is associated with increased risk for morbidity and mortality (Hawkley & Cacioppo, 2010). Unlike other ultrasocial species, which rely upon genetically identical or closely related individuals for cooperation, coordination, and division of labor, human societies are forged over long periods of time through extensive cooperation among unrelated or loosely related group members. In this context, selection pressures toward the cooperation and selflessness required to reap society-level benefits compete with pressures for individual reproductive success (Richerson & Boyd, 1998). While humans benefit from cooperation, there is also potential for conflict and competition among group members, so humans need dynamic mechanisms for navigating the complex social environment and achieving social-relational goals (Van Vugt & Schaller, 2008). Emotions are ideal for this purpose, their social functions highlighted by the fact that emotions are expressed more in social settings than alone (Clark et al., 2004; Provine, 2016).

Positive emotions play important roles in building the highly interconnected, interdependent networks of relationships on which humans rely. For example, some positive emotions are central in identifying new cooperative social partners. How can we determine who intends to cooperate with us and who might exploit us? Researchers have posited that expressing positive emotion through a smile evolved as a reliable solution to this problem, communicating trustworthiness and the intent to cooperate (Centorrino et al., 2015; Niedenthal et al., 2019; Owren & Bachorowski, 2001; Ravaja et al., 2004; Schmidt et al., 2012). Studies of interactions between unfamiliar partners have found that smiling individuals are often assumed to be socially trustworthy (Brown et al., 2003; Scharlemann, et al., 2001). Smiling creates a positive feedback loop between individuals, leading to reciprocal felt and expressed happiness (Surakka & Hietanen, 1998); this shared positive affect is thought to engender reciprocal cooperative behavior (Boone & Buck, 2003). Moreover, Danvers and Shiota (2018) demonstrated that we are sensitive to this reciprocity, finding that participants whose partners dynamically matched their own smiles during a conversation were more likely to cooperate with that partner in a subsequent prisoners' dilemma task, presumably taking smile reciprocity as an indicator of trustworthiness. Although smiles are vulnerable to false signaling as cues of cooperative intent, people are sensitive to the difference between a genuine (Duchenne) smile and a faked smile (Johnston et al., 2010; Krumhuber et al., 2007).

Unlike the research on cognitive features of positive affect and emotion, research on social behavior has often addressed theorized differences in the adaptive functions of specific positive emotion states. One important adaptive opportunity surrounds the identification and acquisition of a high-quality mate. *Sexual desire* draws our attention to promising potential sexual partners, promotes flirtatious behavior that communicates interest (e.g., lip licks, lip wipes, and tongue protrusions), and initiates a physiological response that prepares the body for mating as arousal increases (Gonzaga et al., 2006; Haj-Mohamadi et al., 2020; Rowland, 2006). Sexual desire also activates subtler, gender-specific behaviors related to attracting mates, including increased conspicuous material consumption, increased risk-taking, and decreased loss aversion in men (Baker & Maner, 2008; Griskevicius et al., 2007), and broadcasting helping behavior, agreeableness, and social support in women (Griskevicius et al., 2007). Generally, sexual desire has been found to decrease for both men and women as age increases, which speaks to its link to mating motivation (Levine, 2003; Osborn et al., 1988; Schiavi, 1999).

Other positive emotions bind us to relationship partners for the long term. Human beings are born especially vulnerable, requiring caregivers on whom they depend for several years for their every need, and have evolved to seek proximity to and protection by these caregivers (Bowlby, 1969). A proposed solution to this immense vulnerability is *attachment love*, an emotional response that promotes approach toward a reliable caregiver, as well as elicitation and acceptance of nurturance from attachment figures when in need (Shiota, Neufeld, et al., 2014). Although attachment is often discussed in terms of a parent-child relationship, attachment is also experienced in close adult relationships (Ainsworth, 1989; Doherty & Brumbaugh, Chapter 11 in this volume). The neuropeptide oxytocin is thought to facilitate attachment and social attunement in both humans and nonhuman mammals (Carter, 1998; Insel & Young, 2001), is released during affectionate touch (Cascio et al., 2019), and intranasal administration of oxytocin has been found to increase trust and acceptance of interpersonal risk (Kosfeld et al., 2005). Both oxytocin and the presence of a trusted social partner are associated with decreased stress reactivity, perhaps accounting for the health benefits related to positive social interactions (Heinrichs et al., 2003; Hennessy, 1997).

On the other side of the parent-offspring relationship lies an emotion felt by the caregiver, *nurturant love*. Protecting one's offspring has direct implications for adaptive fitness of both parent and child (Hrdy, 2009). Parental care and responsiveness are consistently shown to have an effect on the offspring's cognitive and social development, further impacting fitness (Stein et al., 2013). Research has demonstrated the strong attentional pull of infant faces and cries, as compared to those of adults (Brosch et al., 2008; Young et al., 2017). Although some studies using eye-tracking and experimental manipulation of cuteness have shown that this attentional pull is stronger for women than for men (Cárdenas et al., 2013; Lobmaier et al., 2010), an infant's helplessness and need for caregiving are similarly motivationally salient for both sexes (Parsons et al., 2011). Effective nurturance requires vigilance against threat and active caregiving, both of which are promoted by nurturant love (Goetz et al., 2010; O'Neil et al., 2018). As an experimentally evoked state, nurturant love is associated with a bias toward both physical carefulness and caution in processing new information (e.g., Griskevicius, Shiota, & Neufeld, 2010; Sherman et al., 2013).

Humor and shared *amusement* support affiliative connections as well (Knight, 2013), so much so that shared laughter can promote social bonding, even among strangers (Graham, 1995). When asked to rank the importance of various qualities in potential mates, teenagers (Hansen, 1977; Regan and Joshi, 2003), undergraduates (Goodwin, 1990; Sprecher & Regan, 2002), and married couples (Buss & Barnes, 1986) all report a strong preference for funny partners, demonstrating the high mate value conferred by humor. Amusement and laughter are common occurrences between social partners; most couples laugh together at least once daily (Lauer et al., 1990). This shared humor serves to support pair-bonding, and is strongly associated with relationship satisfaction (Hall, 2013; Ziv, 1988).

Once a bond is formed, positive emotions aid in maintaining ongoing relationships. *Gratitude* has been defined as the positive emotion felt by the recipient of kindness or unexpected support or aid from some benefactor (Trivers, 1971). Expressions of gratitude communicate appreciation for the kind act and a willingness to reciprocate kindness toward the benefactor in the future (Bartlett & DeSteno, 2006). This strengthens the relationship between the recipient and the benefactor, and encourages behaviors that continue to bring the individuals closer, including further commitment by the benefactor to help again in the future; this process builds both parties' social and psychological resources (Algoe et al., 2013; Wood et al., 2008). Gratitude centers around the exchange of benefits and may have been instrumental in advancing humans' tendencies to cooperate with unrelated others in a reciprocal fashion (McCullough et al., 2008). These cooperative tendencies are theorized to emerge via estimates of welfare valuation, or internal representations of interpersonal value, which overlap with many other conceptualizations of fitness valuations (Roberts, 2005; Smith et al., 2017). Gratitude then can be seen as signaling receptivity to benefits, appreciation, and the intent to continue the valuable, cooperative relationship.

Humans are cooperative, but also hierarchical. This presents another key fitness opportunity: the chance to achieve higher social status. As noted earlier, high social status confers a host of fitness-relevant benefits, including greater access to high-quality mates, cooperative conspecifics, and material resources (Keltner et al., 2003; Kemper, 1991; Pérusse, 1993; Smith, 2004). When we accomplish some socially valued task, such as mastering a skill or receiving an award, we experience *pride* (Williams & DeSteno, 2009). Through the display of pride, people advertise their accomplishment and display dominance, claiming an advance in their social hierarchy (Tracy & Robins, 2007b). Behaviorally, pride is accompanied by distinct and cross-culturally recognized postural changes (arms akimbo, head lifted, expanded posture) and material displays (e.g., expensive watches) that draw attention to one's success (Tracy & Robins, 2007a; Tracy & Robins, 2007b; Griskevicius, Shiota, & Nowlis, 2010). In both humans and laboratory animals, dominance promotes increased reward consumption, greater risk taking, and a general increase in behavioral activation (Davis et al., 2009). Together, these behaviors would have evoked positive evaluations of the person displaying pride, leading to further respect and assistance from others in the ancestral environment of evolutionary adaptedness (Sznycer et al., 2017). In a sample of participants from 16 nations, Sznycer and colleagues (2017) found that intensity of felt pride was closely associated with the magnitude of positive evaluations from others, suggesting that pride serves as a universal valuation system which anticipates social approval and guides behavior to evoke respect and deference from others.

Whereas pride is linked to the opportunity to attain higher status, *embarrassment* is felt after a social gaffe that draws others' attention and might reduce one's status (Keltner & Buswell, 1997). Although in Western culture embarrassment is typically experienced as unpleasant, this is not the case across all cultures. For example, in Bedouin society the emotion *hasham* is closely linked to the Western concepts of shame and embarrassment, and involves a similar nonverbal display; yet it can be pleasant and is socially desirable, indicating modesty and acceptance of one's proper place (Abu-Lughod, 1985). Behaviorally, embarrassment is accompanied by blushing, gaze aversion, and face touching as well as a controlled smile (Keltner, 1995). This expression has been found to appease social partners, acknowledging the transgression, reducing the likelihood of punishment or retaliation, and helping to protect one's social status (Keltner, 1995; Keltner & Anderson 2000).

Recommendations for a Future of Rigorous Evolutionary Affective Science

Although the broad proposal that human affective experience has some roots in our evolutionary heritage is generally accepted, particular applications of the evolutionary perspective in emotion research have been the subject of much heated debate (e.g., Barrett, 2017). Critiques of evolutionary psychology may be tied in part to political and disciplinary ideologies (Jonason & Schmitt, 2016), and criticisms often reflect misunderstanding of the perspective and associated research (Al-Shawaf et al., 2019; Al-Shawaf et al., 2018). However, fair concerns can be raised regarding limitations of theorizing and methodology in some affective science research framed as representing an evolutionary perspective. A commitment to rigorous evolutionary theorizing and methods not only improves the quality of the research, but also points toward exciting new directions for future affective science to take. In this final section of the chapter we offer some recommendations for conducting high-quality evolutionary affective science, and highlight the opportunities these recommendations present.

Build on Strong Theoretical Foundations

An accusation sometimes made against evolutionary psychology is that of "post hoc" theorizing (Confer et al., 2010), in which a commonly observed phenomenon is identified, a theory of the phenomenon's adaptive function is generated, and then evidence (perhaps involving raw frequencies or simple correlations; Simpson & Campbell, 2015) is provided to support the theory. Because research on emotion so often begins with readily observable behavior and emotion constructs embedded in the lexicon, it can sometimes be vulnerable to this charge. As a hypothetical example within affective science, one might propose that the human propensity for responding to infant nonhuman animals with a tenderness/nurturant love response must have served an adaptive function—perhaps ensuring that livestock survived infancy—and then go on to demonstrate the universality of this phenomenon as evidence of its evolved origin (while ignoring the possibility that the trait is a byproduct of mechanisms supporting cooperative child care; O'Neil et al., 2018).

Rigorous research from an evolutionary perspective carefully avoids post hoc theorizing, developing theories not by working backward from easily seen features of a given emotion or aspect of emotional responding, but by working forward from careful analysis of the eliciting situation and selection pressures expected to have shaped that response (Al-Shawaf et al., 2018; Shiota et al., 2017). This approach not only avoids the "post hoc" problem, but also leads to a rich array of novel, falsifiable, and consequential hypotheses that would not be predicted by alternative theories (Al-Shawaf et al., 2018; Cosmides & Tooby, 2000). Beyond predicting universality, strong theorizing emphasizes psychological and physiological mechanisms by which adaptive functions are carried out, leading to hypotheses that demonstrate those mechanisms in action (Lewis et al., 2017; Shiota, 2017) and also to a priori predictions about context and individual differences (Al-Shawaf & Lewis, 2017; Al-Shawaf et al., 2018). What turns the mechanism on and off? When should the mechanism "misfire," or be displayed in a nonadaptive context, given the way that it works? Can competing hypotheses about mechanism be identified, one emphasizing evolutionary origin and another emphasizing sociocultural origin, and then pitted against each other empirically? In emotion research such mechanisms may include situational appraisals thought to activate the emotional response, and subtle cognitive, physiological, nonverbal, and behavioral aspects of the response to emotion stimuli, allowing researchers to move beyond self-reported feelings. Claims that some mechanism distinctly reflects the function of a particular emotion should be tested by pitting the target emotion condition against multiple alternative emotion states, chosen to rule out plausible alternative explanations.

Don't Rely on English-Language Emotion Constructs

As is the case for psychology in general (Henrich et al., 2010), the great majority of research on emotion has been conducted in Western nations, using English-speaking participants and English-language materials. More concerns about this are discussed below, but a key issue in affective science is the heavy reliance on English-language emotion vocabulary as a major starting point for selecting constructs to investigate, and developing theories about those constructs. The bulk of emotion research has addressed states for which a word is readily available—fear, anger, sadness, disgust—leading in part to the relative dearth of research on specific positive emotions (two notable exceptions, pride and gratitude, also show strong convergence between the English-language concept and the theorized emotion construct; Cheng et al., 2010; Trivers, 1971).

Three types of errors emerge from over-reliance on a single language's vocabulary. The first is failure to study states lacking a commonly used English term. For example, in the 1980s and 1990s theorists debated whether "love" should be included in their growing taxonomies of "basic" or functionally distinct emotions. The conclusion was usually no. Ekman (1984) concluded that love is a "plot" involving a scripted sequence of events, feelings, and behaviors that play out between two or more people over time, rather than a momentary emotional experience. Frijda and colleagues (1991) described love as a "sentiment" or lasting attitude toward a target, rather than an emotion. Shaver and colleagues (1996) noted that one might experience surges of love that correspond more closely to emotion states, and suggested the distinction among attachment-related, caregiving-related, and sexual variants of love that has influenced some research described in this chapter. However, empirical research on these states has largely faltered, in part for want of terminology that can be used in research. Grounding theories of love in the functional analyses proposed by Shaver and colleagues (1996), and elaborated by Shiota and colleagues (2017), can be an alternative starting point for research.

The second error involves ignoring emotional experiences that are common in other cultures and named in their languages, but not in English. For example, Japanese has a term for a state closely corresponding to the construct of attachment love, *amae* (Doi & Bester, 1973). It is hard to imagine affective scientists in Japan leaving *amae* out of a taxonomy of basic emotions, but English-language researchers missed the opportunity. The third error is that of conflating the lay lexical concept with the scientific construct for research purposes. For example, "awe" is derived from the Old English term for fear, and philosophy dating back to Edmund Burke in the 18th century has assumed our response to the extraordinary or "sublime" includes both reverence and terror. However, a growing body of evidence shows that while awe may at times be accompanied by fear, given a stimulus that is threatening as well as vast, the observable features of core awe are clearly distinct from those of fear, and it is typically experienced as a positive-valence state (e.g., Cowen et al., 2019; Shiota et al., 2011).

Emotions Are Not Fixed Action Patterns

Because an evolutionary view of emotions implies universality of emotion-generating mechanisms, some wrongly infer that observable emotional *responses* should manifest in the exact same way, every time, given the necessary situation or stimulus. On the contrary, emotional mechanisms' flexibility and responsiveness to prior learning and current context are central to their functionality (Anderson & Adolphs, 2014). Rather than fixed-action patterns, emotion mechanisms should look more like if-then algorithms that can update and adjust to new situations (Al-Shawaf et al., 2016; Al-Shawaf et al., 2017; Al-Shawaf et al., 2019). Real fitness-critical situations are variable, so an algorithm that can quickly obtain the necessary information and calculate the behavioral option most likely to succeed (e.g., run from a predator, or stand and fight?) would prove most adaptive. The exact situations that evoke an emotional response, and the behaviors that result, should be strongly influenced by learning and experience, although it should be possible to predict some of the variability a priori (Al-Shawaf & Lewis, 2017; Al-Shawaf et al., 2018) and also to identify the underlying adaptive problem and solution across this variability (Ekman, 1992). For example, the specific behaviors and skills that are valued by a society, and therefore merit an increase in social status, depend on that group's ecology and economic structure. Because of this, what counts as an "achievement" and thus evokes a feeling of pride should be mutable based on what is valued by one's group. Although pride expressions share a common postural signature across cultures (Tracy & Matsumoto, 2008), these may be modulated based on cultural norms as well (e.g., Hwang & Matsumoto, 2014).

Researchers studying emotion often treat variability at the individual and cultural levels as noise, but this variability itself offers rich opportunities for theory-driven, process-oriented research. For example, we might predict that men and women will show different propensities for experiencing nurturant love. Women typically have more at stake in the success of each individual child, because women are more restricted in total potential number of offspring, and pay a much larger physical toll in birthing and raising them, than is true for men (Møller & Thornhill, 1998). Because of this differential parental investment, we should expect women on average to demonstrate greater nurturant love reactivity than men (e.g., in nonverbal expression, physiology, and cognitive effects)—an effect that would likely extend to non-kin and even nonhuman infant stimuli as well.

Although evolutionary affective scientists often aim to demonstrate the cross-cultural universality of some phenomenon, cultural differences can also be predicted based on proposed adaptive functions (Al-Shawaf et al., 2017). For example, both individuals and cultural groups vary in their impulse control. Although low impulse control is often presumed to be a deficit in the relatively predictable, resource-rich ecologies in which academic researchers live, evidence suggests that impulsivity tends to be higher, and may even be beneficial, in unpredictable, resource-scarce environments (e.g., Copping et al., 2013; Fenneman & Frankenhuis, 2020; Gelfand et al., 2011). Studies asking how universal emotion mechanisms interact with such features of ecology and culture are currently uncommon, yet can play a highly valuable role in demonstrating how these mechanisms fulfill their functions (Confer et al., 2010; Lewis et al., 2017; Sell et al., 2017; Sznycer et al., 2017; Sznycer et al., 2012; Sznycer et al., 2016; Sznycer et al., 2018; for two strong examples, see Elfenbein et al., 2007; and Kim et al., 2011). Needless to say, this will require increased investment in research beyond the WEIRD (Western, educated, industrialized, rich, democratic) societies most commonly studied in affective science (Henrich et al., 2010).

Conclusion

The evolutionary perspective has played an important role in the development of affective science as a field, and is increasingly adopted in research on positive emotions. Conceptualizing emotions as adaptations provides a valuable framework for both theoretical integration and the generation of fresh, novel hypotheses. To this point, application of the evolutionary perspective to emotion has often involved demonstrating "universal" aspects of English-language emotion constructs, and specific emotion features that are consistent with proposed functions. However, there is enormous potential for future research to investigate "new" emotions defined in terms of adaptive problem rather than emotion vocabulary; the mechanisms by which theorized functions are carried out; the emotion- and context-specificity of these mechanisms; and the ways in which universal mechanisms interact with culture, ecology, and individual differences to produce the vivid array of human emotional experience (Al-Shawaf et al., 2016; Al-Shawaf & Lewis, 2017; Al-Shawaf et al., 2019; Cosmides & Tooby, 2000; Tooby & Cosmides, 2008).

References

Abu-Lughod, L. (1985). Honor and the sentiments of loss in a Bedouin society. *American Ethnologist, 12*(2), 245–261.
Ainsworth, M. D. S. (1989). Attachments beyond infancy. *American Psychologist, 44*, 709–716.
Algoe, S. B., Fredrickson, B. L., & Gable, S. L. (2013). The social functions of the emotion of gratitude via expression. *Emotion, 13*(4), 605–609.
Al-Shawaf, L., Conroy-Beam, D., Asao, K., & Buss, D. M. (2016). Human emotions: An evolutionary psychological perspective. *Emotion Review, 8*(2), 173–186.
Al-Shawaf, L., & Lewis, D. M. (2017). Evolutionary psychology and the emotions. In V. Zeigler-Hill & T.K. Shackelford (Eds.), *Encyclopedia of personality and individual differences* (pp. 1452–1461). Springer International Publishing.
Al-Shawaf, L., Lewis, D. M., Wehbe, Y. S., & Buss, D. M. (2019). Context, environment, and learning in evolutionary psychology. In T. K. Shackelford & V. A. Weekes-Shackelford (Eds.), *Encyclopedia of evolutionary psychological science* (pp. 1330–1341). Springer Nature Switzerland.
Al-Shawaf, L., Zreik, K., & Buss, D. M. (2018). Thirteen misunderstandings about natural selection. In T. K. Shackelford, V.A. Weekes-Shackelford (Eds.), *Encyclopedia of evolutionary psychological science* (pp. 8162–8174). Springer International Publishing.
Anderson, D. J., & Adolphs, R. (2014). A framework for studying emotions across species. *Cell, 157*(1), 187–200.
Averill, J. R. (1980). A constructivist view of emotion. In R. Plutchik & H. Kellerman (Eds.), *Emotion: Theory, research, and experience*, Vol. 1: *Theories of emotion* (pp. 305–339). Academic Press.
Baas, M., De Dreu, C. K. W., & Nijstad, B. A. (2008). A meta-analysis of 25 years of mood-creativity research: Hedonic tone, activation, or regulatory focus? *Psychological Bulletin, 134*(6), 779–806.
Baker, M. D., Jr., & Maner, J. K. (2008). Risk-taking as a situationally sensitive male mating strategy. *Evolution and Human Behavior, 29*(6), 391–395
Barrett, L. F. (2017). *How emotions are made: The secret life of the brain*. Houghton Mifflin Harcourt.
Bartlett, M. Y., & DeSteno, D. (2006). Gratitude and prosocial behavior: Helping when it costs you. *Psychological Science, 17*(4), 319–325.
Bless, H., Bohner, G., Schwarz, N., & Strack, F. (1990). Mood and persuasion: A cognitive response analysis. *Personality and Social Psychology Bulletin, 16*(2), 331–345.
Bodenhausen, G. V., Kramer, G. P., & Süsser, K. (1994). Happiness and stereotypic thinking in social judgment. *Journal of Personality and Social Psychology, 66*(4), 621–632.
Bolte, A., Goschke, T., & Kuhl, J. (2003). Emotion and intuition: Effects of positive and negative mood on implicit judgments of semantic coherence. *Psychological Science, 14*(5), 416–421.
Boone, R. T., & Buck, R. (2003). Emotional expressivity and trustworthiness: The role of nonverbal behavior in the evolution of cooperation. *Journal of Nonverbal Behavior, 27*(3), 163–182.
Bowlby, J. (1969). *Attachment and loss*, Vol. 1: *Attachment*. Hogarth Press.
Bracha, H. S. (2004). Freeze, flight, fight, fright, faint: Adaptationist perspectives on the acute stress response spectrum. *CNS Spectrums, 9*(9), 679–685.
Brosch, T., Sander, D., Pourtois, G., & Scherer, K. R. (2008). Beyond fear: Rapid spatial orienting toward positive emotional stimuli. *Psychological Science, 19*(4), 362–370.
Brown, W. M., Palameta, B., & Moore, C. (2003). Are there nonverbal cues to commitment? An exploratory study using the zero-acquaintance video presentation paradigm. *Evolutionary Psychology, 1*(1), 42–69.
Burnstein, E., Crandall, C., & Kitayama, S. (1994). Some neo-Darwinian decision rules for altruism: Weighing cues for inclusive fitness as a function of the biological importance of the decision. *Journal of Personality and Social Psychology, 67*(5), 773–789.
Buss, D. M., & Barnes, M. (1986). Preferences in human mate selection. *Journal of Personality and Social Psychology, 50*(2), 559–570.
Campbell, D. T. (1983). The two distinct routes beyond kin selection to ultrasociality: Implications for the humanities and social sciences. In Diane Bridgeman (Ed.), *The nature of prosocial development: Theories and strategies* (pp. 11–41). Academic Press.

Cárdenas, R. A., Harris, L. J., & Becker, M. W. (2013). Sex differences in visual attention toward infant faces. *Evolution and Human Behavior, 34*(4), 280–287.

Carter, C. S. (1998). Neuroendocrine perspectives on social attachment and love. *Psychoneuroendocrinology, 23*(8), 779–818.

Carver, C. S., & White, T. L. (1994). Behavioral inhibition, behavioral activation, and affective responses to impending reward and punishment: The BIS/BAS scales. *Journal of Personality and Social Psychology, 67*(2), 319.

Cascio, C. J., Moore, D., & McGlone, F. (2019). Social touch and human development. *Developmental Cognitive Neuroscience, 35*, 5–11.

Centorrino, S., Djemai, E., Hopfensitz, A., Milinski, M., & Seabright, P. (2015). Honest signaling in trust interactions: Smiles rated as genuine induce trust and signal higher earning opportunities. *Evolution and Human Behavior, 36*(1), 8–16.

Cheng, J. T., Tracy, J. L., & Henrich, J. (2010). Pride, personality, and the evolutionary foundations of human social status. *Evolution and Human Behavior, 31*(5), 334–347.

Clark, M. S., Fitness, J., & Brissette, I. (2004). Understanding people's perceptions of relationships is crucial to understanding their emotional lives. In M. B. Brewer & M. Hewstone (Eds.), *Perspectives on social psychology. Emotion and motivation* (pp. 21–46). Blackwell.

Confer, J. C., Easton, J. A., Fleischman, D. S., Goetz, C. D., Lewis, D. M., Perilloux, C., & Buss, D. M. (2010). Evolutionary psychology: Controversies, questions, prospects, and limitations. *American Psychologist, 65*(2), 110.

Copping, L. T., Campbell, A., & Muncer, S. (2013). Violence, teenage pregnancy, and life history. *Human Nature, 24*(2), 137–157.

Cosmides, L., & Tooby, J. (2000). Evolutionary psychology and the emotions. In M. Lewis & J. M. Haviland-Jones (Eds.), *Handbook of emotions* (2nd ed., pp. 91–115). Guilford Press.

Cowen, A. S., Laukka, P., Elfenbein, H. A., Liu, R., & Keltner, D. (2019). The primacy of categories in the recognition of 12 emotions in speech prosody across two cultures. *Nature Human Behaviour, 3*(4), 369–382.

Cross, M. P., & Pressman, S. D. (2017). Understanding the connections between positive affect and health. In C. L. Cooper & J. C. Quick (Eds.), *The handbook of stress and health: A guide to research and practice* (pp. 75–95). John Wiley & Sons.

Curtis, G. J. (2013) Don't be happy, worry: Positive mood, but not anxiety, increases stereotyping in a mock-juror decision-making task. *Psychiatry, Psychology and Law, 20*(5), 686–699.

Danvers A. F., & Shiota, M. N. (2017). Going off script: Effects of awe on memory for script-typical and irrelevant narrative detail. *Emotion, 17*(6), 938–952.

Danvers, A. F., & Shiota, M. N. (2018). Dynamically engaged smiling predicts cooperation above and beyond average smiling levels. *Evolution and Human Behavior, 39*(1), 112–119.

Davis, J. F., Krause, E. G., Melhorn, S. J., Sakai, R. R., & Benoit, S. C. (2009). Dominant rats are natural risk takers and display increased motivation for food reward. *Neuroscience, 162*(1), 23–30.

Dewsbury, D. A. (1999). The proximate and the ultimate: Past, present, and future. *Behavioural Processes, 46*(3), 189–199.

Diener, E. (2000). Subjective well-being: The science of happiness and a proposal for a national index. *American Psychologist, 55*(1), 34–43.

Doi, T., & Bester, J. (1973). *The anatomy of dependence*. Kodansha International.

Ekman, P. (1972). Universals and cultural differences in facial expressions of emotions. In J. K. Cole (Ed.), *Nebraska Symposium on Motivation, 1971* (Vol. 19, pp. 207–283). University of Nebraska Press.

Ekman, P. (1984). Expressions and the nature of emotion. In K. R. Scherer & P. Ekman (Eds.), *Approaches to emotion* (pp. 319–343). Lawrence Erlbaum Associates.

Ekman, P. (1992). An argument for basic emotions. *Cognition & Emotion, 6*(3–4), 169–200.

Ekman, P., & Cordaro, D. (2011). What is meant by calling emotions basic. *Emotion Review, 3*(4), 364–370.

Elfenbein, H. A., Beaupré, M., Lévesque, M., & Hess, U. (2007). Toward a dialect theory: Cultural differences in the expression and recognition of posed facial expressions. *Emotion, 7*(1), 131–146.

Ellsworth, P. C., & Smith, C. A. (1988). Shades of joy: Patterns of appraisal differentiating pleasant emotions. *Cognition and Emotion, 2*(4), 301–331.

Fenneman, J., & Frankenhuis, W. E. (2020). Is impulsive behavior adaptive in harsh and unpredictable environments? A formal model. *Evolution and Human Behavior, 41*(4), 261–273.

Fernández-Dols, J. M., & Russell, J. A. (2003). Emotion, affect, and mood in social judgments. In I. B. Wiener (Ed.), *Handbook of psychology* (pp. 283–298). Wiley.

Folkman, S., Chesney, M. A., & Christopher-Richards, A. (1994). Stress and coping in caregiving partners of men with AIDS. *Psychiatric Clinics of North America, 17*(1), 35–53.

Forgas, J. P. (1995). Mood and judgment: The affect infusion model (AIM). *Psychological Bulletin, 117*(1), 39–66.

Fredrickson, B. L. (2001). The role of positive emotions in positive psychology: The broaden-and-build theory of positive emotions. *American Psychologist, 56*(3), 218–226.

Fredrickson, B. L., & Branigan, C. (2005). Positive emotions broaden the scope of attention and thought-action repertoires. *Cognition and Emotion, 19*(3), 313–332.

Fredrickson, B. L., Mancuso, R. A., Branigan, C., & Tugade, M. M. (2000). The undoing effect of positive emotions. *Motivation and Emotion, 24*(4), 237–258.

Frijda, N. H., Mesquita, B., Sonnemans, J., & van Goozen, S. (1991). The duration of affective phenomena or emotions, sentiments and passions. In K. T. Strongman (Ed.), *International Review of Studies on Emotion* (Vol. 1, pp. 187–225). Wiley.

Gable, P. A., & Harmon-Jones, E. (2008). Approach-motivated positive affect reduces breadth of attention. *Psychological Science, 19*(5), 476–482.

Gable, P., & Harmon-Jones, E. (2010). The motivational dimensional model of affect: Implications for breadth of attention, memory, and cognitive categorisation. *Cognition and Emotion, 24*(2), 322–337.

Gable, P. A., & Harmon-Jones, E. (2011). Attentional consequences of pregoal and postgoal positive affects. *Emotion, 11*(6), 1358–1367.

Gelfand, M. J., Raver, J. L., Nishii, L., Leslie, L. M., Lun, J., Lim, B. C., Duan, L., Almaliach, A., Ang, S., Arnadottir, J., Aycan, Z., Boehnke, K., Boski, P., Cabecinhas, R., Chan, D., Chhokar, J., D'Amato, A., Subirats, M., Fischlmayr, I. C., . . . Yamaguchi, S. (2011). Differences between tight and loose cultures: A 33-nation study. *Science, 332*(6033), 1100–1104.

Goetz, J. L., Keltner, D., & Simon-Thomas, E. (2010). Compassion: An evolutionary analysis and empirical review. *Psychological Bulletin, 136*(3), 351–374.

Gonzaga, G. C., Turner, R. A., Keltner, D., Campos, B., & Altemus, M. (2006). Romantic love and sexual desire in close relationships. *Emotion, 6*(2), 163–179.

Goodwin, R. (1990). Sex differences among partner preferences: Are the sexes really very similar? *Sex Roles, 23*(9–10), 501–513.

Gorn, G. J., Goldberg, M. E., & Basu, K. (1993). Mood, awareness, and product evaluation. *Journal of Consumer Psychology, 2*(3), 237–256.

Graham, E. E. (1995). The involvement of sense of humor in the development of social relationships. *Communication Reports, 8*(2), 158–169.

Gray, J. A. (1970). The psychophysiological basis of introversion-extraversion. *Behavior Research and Therapy, 8*, 249–266.

Griskevicius, V., Shiota, M. N., & Neufeld, S. L. (2010). Influence of different positive emotions on persuasion processing: A functional evolutionary approach. *Emotion, 10*(2), 190–206.

Griskevicius, V., Shiota, M. N., & Nowlis, S. M. (2010). The many shades of rose-colored glasses: An evolutionary approach to the influence of different positive emotions. *Journal of Consumer Research, 37*(2), 238–250.

Griskevicius, V., Tybur, J. M., Sundie, J. M., Cialdini, R. B., Miller, G. F., & Kenrick, D. T. (2007). Blatant benevolence and conspicuous consumption: When romantic motives elicit strategic costly signals. *Journal of Personality and Social Psychology, 93*(1), 85–102.

Haj-Mohamadi, P., Gillath, O., & Rosenberg, E. L. (2020). Identifying a facial expression of flirtation and its effect on men. *The Journal of Sex Research, 58*(2), 137–145.

Hall, J. A. (2013). Humor in long-term romantic relationships: The association of general humor styles and relationship-specific functions with relationship satisfaction. *Western Journal of Communication, 77*(3), 272–292.

Hansen, S. L. (1977). Dating choices of high school students. *Family Coordinator, 26*, 133–138.

Harmon-Jones, E., Gable, P. A., & Price, T. F. (2013). Does negative affect always narrow and positive affect always broaden the mind? Considering the influence of motivational intensity on cognitive scope. *Current Directions in Psychological Science, 22*(4), 301–307.

Hawkley, L. C., & Cacioppo, J. T. (2010). Loneliness matters: A theoretical and empirical review of consequences and mechanisms. *Annals of Behavioral Medicine, 40*(2), 218–227.

Heinrichs, M., Baumgartner, T., Kirschbaum, C., & Ehlert, U. (2003). Social support and oxytocin interact to suppress cortisol and subjective responses to psychosocial stress. *Biological Psychiatry, 54*(12), 1389–1398.

Hennessy, M. B. (1997). Hypothalamic-pituitary-adrenal responses to brief social separation. *Neuroscience & Biobehavioral Reviews, 21*(1), 11–29.

Henrich, J., Heine, S. J., & Norenzayan, A. (2010). Most people are not WEIRD. *Nature, 466*(7302), 29–29.

Hrdy, S. B. (2009). *The woman that never evolved*. Harvard University Press.

Huntsinger, J. R., Isbell, L. M., & Clore, G. L. (2014). The affective control of thought: Malleable, not fixed. *Psychological Review, 121*(4), 600–618.

Huntsinger, J. R., Sinclair, S., Dunn, E., & Clore, G. L. (2010). Affective regulation of stereotype activation: It's the (accessible) thought that counts. *Personality & Social Psychology Bulletin, 36*(4), 564–577.

Hwang, H. C., & Matsumoto, D. (2014). Cultural differences in victory signals of triumph. *Cross-Cultural Research*, *48*(2), 177–191.

Isbell, L. M., & Wyer, R. S. (1999). Correcting for mood-induced bias in the evaluation of political candidates: The roles of intrinsic and extrinsic motivation. *Personality and Social Psychology Bulletin*, *25*(2), 237–249.

Isen, A. M. (1987). Positive affect, cognitive processes, and social behavior. In L. Berkowitz (Ed.), *Advances in experimental social psychology* (Vol. 20, pp. 203–253). Academic Press.

Isen, A. M., & Daubman, K. A. (1984). The influence of affect on categorization. *Journal of Personality and Social Psychology*, *47*(6), 1206–1217.

Joffe, T. H. (1997). Social pressures have selected for an extended juvenile period in primates. *Journal of Human Evolution*, *32*(6), 593–605.

Johnston, L., Miles, L., & Macrae, C. N. (2010). Why are you smiling at me? Social functions of enjoyment and non-enjoyment smiles. *British Journal of Social Psychology*, *49*(1), 107–127.

Jokela, M. (2009). Physical attractiveness and reproductive success in humans: Evidence from the late 20th century United States. *Evolution and Human Behavior*, *30*(5), 342–350.

Jonason, P. K., & Schmitt, D. P. (2016). Quantifying common criticisms of evolutionary psychology. *Evolutionary Psychological Science*, *2*(3), 177–188.

Keltner, D. (1995). Signs of appeasement: Evidence for the distinct displays of embarrassment, amusement, and shame. *Journal of Personality and Social Psychology*, *68*(3), 441–454.

Keltner, D., & Anderson, C. (2000). Saving face for Darwin: The functions and uses of embarrassment. *Current Directions in Psychological Science*, *9*(6), 187–192.

Keltner, D., & Buswell, B. N. (1997). Embarrassment: Its distinct form and appeasement functions. *Psychological Bulletin*, *122*(3), 250–270.

Keltner, D., Gruenfeld, D. H., & Anderson, C. (2003). Power, approach, and inhibition. *Psychological Review*, *110*, 265–284.

Kemper, T. D. (1991). Predicting emotions from social relations. *Social Psychology Quarterly*, *54*(4), 330–342.

Kenrick, D. T., Griskevicius, V., Neuberg, S. L., & Schaller, M. (2010). Renovating the pyramid of needs: Contemporary extensions built upon ancient foundations. *Perspectives on Psychological Science*, *5*(3), 292–314.

Kim, H. S., Sherman, D. K., Mojaverian, T., Sasaki, J. Y., Park, J., Suh, E. M., & Taylor, S. E. (2011). Gene–culture interaction: Oxytocin receptor polymorphism (OXTR) and emotion regulation. *Social Psychological and Personality Science*, *2*(6), 665–672.

Knight, N. K. (2013). Evaluating experience in funny ways: How friends bond through conversational hum. *Text & Talk*, *33*(4–5), 553–574.

Kosfeld, M., Heinrichs, M., Zak, P. J., Fischbacher, U., & Fehr, E. (2005). Oxytocin increases trust in humans. *Nature*, *435*(7042), 673–676.

Kreibig, S. D. (2010). Autonomic nervous system activity in emotion: a review. *Biological Psychology*, *84*(3), 394–421.

Krumhuber, E., Manstead, A. S., Cosker, D., Marshall, D., Rosin, P. L., & Kappas, A. (2007). Facial dynamics as indicators of trustworthiness and cooperative behavior. *Emotion*, *7*(4), 730–735.

Lauer, R. H., Lauer, J. C., & Kerr, S. T. (1990). The long-term marriage: Perceptions of stability and satisfaction. *The International Journal of Aging and Human Development*, *31*(3), 189–195.

Levine, S. B. (2003). The nature of sexual desire: A clinician's perspective. *Archives of Sexual Behavior*, *32*(3), 279–285.

Lewis, D. M., Al-Shawaf, L., Conroy-Beam, D., Asao, K., & Buss, D. M. (2017). Evolutionary psychology: A how-to guide. *American Psychologist*, *72*(4), 353–373.

Lishner, D. A., Batson, C. D., & Huss, E. (2011). Tenderness and sympathy: Distinct empathic emotions elicited by different forms of need. *Personality and Social Psychology Bulletin*, *37*(5), 614–625.

Lobmaier, J. S., Sprengelmeyer, R., Wiffen, B., & Perrett, D. I. (2010). Female and male responses to cuteness, age and emotion in infant faces. *Evolution and Human Behavior*, *31*(1), 16–21.

Lyubomirsky, S., King, L., & Diener, E. (2005). The benefits of frequent positive affect: does happiness lead to success? *Psychological Bulletin*, *131*(6), 803–855.

Mauss, I. B., Levenson, R. W., McCarter, L., Wilhelm, F. H., & Gross, J. J. (2005). The tie that binds? Coherence among emotion experience, behavior, and physiology. *Emotion*, *5*(2), 175–190.

McCullough, M. E., Kimeldorf, M. B., & Cohen, A. D. (2008). An adaptation for altruism: The social causes, social effects, and social evolution of gratitude. *Current Directions in Psychological Science*, *17*(4), 281–285.

Mesquita, B., & Boiger, M. (2014). Emotions in context: A sociodynamic model of emotions. *Emotion Review*, *6*(4), 298–302.

Miller, S. L., & Maner, J. K. (2010). Scent of a woman: Men's testosterone responses to olfactory ovulation cues. *Psychological Science*, *21*(2), 276–283.

Møller, A. P., & Thornhill, R. (1998). Male parental care, differential parental investment by females and sexual selection. *Animal Behaviour, 55*(6), 1507–1515.

Neel, R., Kenrick, D. T., White, A. E., & Neuberg, S. L. (2016). Individual differences in fundamental social motives. *Journal of Personality and Social Psychology, 110*(6), 887–907.

Niedenthal, P. M., Rychlowska, M., Zhao, F., & Wood, A. (2019). Historical migration patterns shape contemporary cultures of emotion. *Perspectives on Psychological Science, 14*(4), 560–573.

O'Neil, M. J., Danvers, A. F., & Shiota, M. N. (2018). Nurturant love and caregiving emotions. In H. C. Lench (Ed.), *Functions of emotion* (pp. 175–193). Springer.

Osborn, M., Hawton, K., & Gath, D. (1988). Sexual dysfunction among middle aged women in the community. *British Medical Journal (Clinical Research Ed), 296*(6627), 959–962.

Owren, M. J., & Bachorowski, J.-A. (2001). The evolution of emotional expression: A "selfish-gene" account of smiling and laughter in early hominids and humans. In T. J. Mayne & G. A. Bonanno (Eds.), *Emotions: Current issues and future directions* (pp. 152–191). Guilford Press.

Park, J., & Banaji, M. R. (2000). Mood and heuristics: The influence of happy and sad states on sensitivity and bias in stereotyping. *Journal of Personality and Social Psychology, 78*, 1005–1023.

Parsons, C. E., Young, K. S., Kumari, N., Stein, A., & Kringelbach, M. L. (2011). The motivational salience of infant faces is similar for men and women. *PloS ONE, 6*(5), e20632.

Pérusse, D. (1993). Cultural and reproductive success in industrial societies: Testing the relationship at the proximate. *Behavioral and Brain Sciences, 16*(2), 267–322.

Pham, M. T. (2007). Emotion and rationality: A critical review and interpretation of empirical evidence. *Review of General Psychology, 11*(2), 155–178.

Plutchik, R. (1984). Emotions: A general psychoevolutionary theory. In K. R. Scherer & P. Ekman (Eds.), *Approaches to emotion* (pp. 197–219). Lawrence Erlbaum Associates.

Pressman, S. D., & Black, L. L. (2012). Positive emotions and immunity. In S. C. Segerstrom (Ed.), *The Oxford handbook of psychoneuroimmunology* (pp. 92–104). Oxford Univeristy Press.

Pressman, S. D., & Cohen, S. (2005). Does positive affect influence health? *Psychological Bulletin, 131*(6), 925–971.

Price, T. F., & Harmon-Jones, E. (2010). The effect of embodied emotive states on cognitive categorization. *Emotion, 10*(6), 934–938.

Provine, R. R. (2016). Laughter as a scientific problem: An adventure in sidewalk neuroscience. *Journal of Comparative Neurology, 524*(8), 1532–1539.

Ravaja, N., Kallinen, K., Saari, T., & Keltikangas-Jarvinen, L. (2004). Suboptimal exposure to facial expressions when viewing video messages from a small screen: Effects on emotion, attention, and memory. *Journal of Experimental Psychology: Applied, 10*(2), 120–131.

Regan, P. C., & Joshi, A. (2003). Ideal partner preferences among adolescents. *Social Behavior and Personality, 31*(1), 13–20.

Richerson, P. J., & Boyd, R. (1998). The evolution of human ultra-sociality. In I. Eibl-Eibisfeldt & F. Salter (Eds.), *Indoctrinability, ideology, and warfare: Evolutionary perspectives* (pp. 71–95). Berghahn Books.

Roberts, G. (2005). Cooperation through interdependence. *Animal Behaviour, 70*(4), 901–908.

Rowland, D. L. (2006). The psychobiology of sexual arousal and response: Physical and psychological factors that control our sexual response. *Sex and Sexuality, 2*, 37–66.

Russell, J. A. (2003). Core affect and the psychological construction of emotion. *Psychological Review, 110*(1), 145–172.

Scarantino, A. (2018). Are LeDoux's survival circuits basic emotions under a different name? *Current Opinion in Behavioral Sciences, 24*, 75–82.

Scharlemann, J. P., Eckel, C. C., Kacelnik, A., & Wilson, R. K. (2001). The value of a smile: Game theory with a human face. *Journal of Economic Psychology, 22*(5), 617–640.

Scherer, K. R. (2009). The dynamic architecture of emotion: Evidence for the component process model. *Cognition and Emotion, 23*(7), 1307–1351.

Schiavi, R. C. (1999). *Aging and male sexuality*. Cambridge University Press.

Schmidt, K., Levenstein, R., & Ambadar, Z. (2012). Intensity of smiling and attractiveness as facial signals of trustworthiness in women. *Perceptual and Motor Skills, 114*(3), 964–978.

Schwarz, N., & Clore, G. L. (1983). Mood, misattribution, and judgments of well-being: Informative and directive functions of affective states. *Journal of Personality and Social Psychology, 45*(3), 513–523.

Scott-Phillips, T. C., Dickins, T. E., & West, S. A. (2011). Evolutionary theory and the ultimate–proximate distinction in the human behavioral sciences. *Perspectives on Psychological Science, 6*(1), 38–47.

Sell, A., Sznycer, D., Al-Shawaf, L., Lim, J., Krauss, A., Feldman, A., Rascanu, R., Sugiyama, L., Cosmides, L., & Tooby, J. (2017). The grammar of anger: Mapping the computational architecture of a recalibrational emotion. *Cognition, 168*, 110–128.

Sherman, G. D., Haidt, J., Iyer, R., & Coan, J. A. (2013). Individual differences in the physical embodiment of care: Prosocially oriented women respond to cuteness by becoming more physically careful. *Emotion, 13*(1), 151–158.

Shaver, P. R., Morgan, H. J., & Wu, S. (1996). Is love a "basic" emotion? *Personal Relationships, 3*(1), 81–96.

Shiota, M. N. (2006). Silver linings and candles in the dark: Differences among positive coping strategies in predicting subjective well-being. *Emotion, 6*(2), 335–339.

Shiota, M. N. (2014). Evolutionary approaches to positive emotion. In M. Tugade, M. N. Shiota, & L. Kirby (Eds.), *Handbook of positive emotion* (pp. 44–59). Guilford Press.

Shiota, M. N. (2017). Comment: The science of positive emotion: You've come a long way, baby/There's still a long way to go. *Emotion Review, 9*(3), 235–237.

Shiota, M. N. (2024, forthcoming). Basic and discrete emotion theories. In A. Scarantino (Ed.), *Emotion theory: The Routledge comprehensive guide: Volume I: History, contemporary theories, and key elements*. Taylor & Francis.

Shiota, M. N., Campos, B., Keltner, D., & Hertenstein, M. J. (2004). Positive emotion and the regulation of interpersonal relationships. In P. Philippot & R. S. Feldman (Eds.), *The regulation of emotion* (pp. 129–157). Lawrence Erlbaum Associates.

Shiota, M. N., Campos, B., Oveis, C., Hertenstein, M. J., Simon-Thomas, E., & Keltner, D. (2017). Beyond happiness: Building a science of discrete positive emotions. *American Psychologist, 72*(7), 617–643.

Shiota, M. N., & Levenson, R. W. (2012). Turn down the volume or change the channel? Emotional effects of detached versus positive reappraisal. *Journal of Personality and Social Psychology, 103*(3), 416–429.

Shiota, M. N., Neufeld, S. L., Danvers, A. F., Osborne, E. A., Sng, O., & Yee, C. I. (2014). Positive emotion differentiation: A functional approach. *Social and Personality Psychology Compass, 8*(3), 104–117.

Shiota, M. N., Neufeld, S. L., Yeung, W. H., Moser, S. E., & Perea, E. F. (2011), Feeling good: Autonomic nervous system responding in five positive emotions. *Emotion, 11*, 1368–1378.

Shiota, M. N., Thrash, T., Danvers, A. F., & Dombrowski, J. T. (2014). Transcending the self: Awe, elevation, and inspiration. In M. Tugade, M. N. Shiota, & L. Kirby (Eds.), *Handbook of positive emotion* (pp. 362–395). Guilford Press.

Shirazi, T. N., Bossio, J. A., Puts, D. A., & Chivers, M. L. (2018). Menstrual cycle phase predicts women's hormonal responses to sexual stimuli. *Hormones and Behavior, 103*, 45–53.

Simpson, J. A., & Campbell, L. (2015). Methods of evolutionary sciences. In D. Buss (Ed.), *The handbook of evolutionary psychology* (pp. 1–21). Wiley.

Singh, D., Dixson, B. J., Jessop, T. S., Morgan, B., & Dixson, A. F. (2010). Cross-cultural consensus for waist–hip ratio and women's attractiveness. *Evolution and Human Behavior, 31*(3), 176–181.

Smith, A., Pedersen, E. J., Forster, D. E., McCullough, M. E., & Lieberman, D. (2017). Cooperation: The roles of interpersonal value and gratitude. *Evolution and Human Behavior, 38*(6), 695–703.

Smith, E. A. (2004). Why do good hunters have higher reproductive success? *Human Nature, 15*(4), 343–364.

Sprecher, S., & Regan, P. C. (2002). Liking some things (in some people) more than others: Partner preferences in romantic relationships and friendships. *Journal of Social and Personal Relationships, 19*(4), 463–481.

Stein, A., Malmberg, L. E., Leach, P., Barnes, J., Sylva, K., & FCCC team. (2013). The influence of different forms of early childcare on children's emotional and behavioural development at school entry. *Child: Care, Health and Development, 39*(5), 676–687.

Surakka, V., & Hietanen, J. K. (1998). Facial and emotional reactions to Duchenne and non-Duchenne smiles. *International Journal of Psychophysiology, 29*(1), 23–33.

Sznycer, D., Al-Shawaf, L., Bereby-Meyer, Y., Curry, O. S., De Smet, D., Ermer, E., Kim, S., Kim, S., Li, N. P., Seal, M. F. L., McClung, J., O, J., Ohtsubo, Y., Quillien, T., Schaub, M., Sell, A., van Leeuwen, F., Cosmides, L., Tooby, J. (2017). Cross-cultural regularities in the cognitive architecture of pride. *Proceedings of the National Academy of Sciences, 114*(8), 1874–1879.

Sznycer, D., Takemura, K., Delton, A. W., Sato, K., Robertson, T., Cosmides, L., & Tooby, J. (2012). Cross-cultural differences and similarities in proneness to shame: An adaptationist and ecological approach. *Evolutionary Psychology, 10*(2), 147470491201000213.

Sznycer, D., Tooby, J., Cosmides, L., Porat, R., Shalvi, S., & Halperin, E. (2016). Shame closely tracks the threat of devaluation by others, even across cultures. *Proceedings of the National Academy of Sciences, 113*(10), 2625–2630.

Sznycer, D., Xygalatas, D., Agey, E., Alami, S., An, X. F., Ananyeva, K. I., Atkinson, Q. D., Broitman, B. R., Conte, T. J, Flores, C., Fukushima, S., Hitokoto, H., Kharitonov, A. N., Onyishi, C. N., Onyishi, I. E., Romero, P. P.,

Schrock, J. M., Snodgrass, J. J., Sugiyama, L. S., . . . Tooby, J. (2018). Cross-cultural invariances in the architecture of shame. *Proceedings of the National Academy of Sciences, 115*(39), 9702–9707.

Tomkins, S. S. (1984). Affect theory. In K. R. Scherer & P. Ekman (Eds.), *Approaches to emotion* (pp. 163–195). Lawrence Erlbaum Associates.

Tooby, J., & Cosmides, L. (2008). The evolutionary psychology of the emotions and their relationship to internal regulatory variables. In M. Lewis, J. M. Haviland-Jones, & L. F. Barrett (Eds.), *Handbook of emotions* (pp. 114–137). Guilford Press.

Tracy, J. L., & Matsumoto, D. (2008). The spontaneous expression of pride and shame: Evidence for biologically innate nonverbal displays. *Proceedings of the National Academy of Sciences, 105*(33), 11655–11660.

Tracy, J. L., & Randles, D. (2011). Four models of basic emotions: A review of Ekman and Cordaro, Izard, Levenson, and Panksepp and Watt. *Emotion Review, 3*(4), 397–405.

Tracy, J. L., & Robins, R. W. (2007a). Emerging insights into the nature and function of pride. *Current Directions in Psychological Science, 16*(3), 147–150.

Tracy, J. L., & Robins, R. W. (2007b). The nature of pride. In J. L. Tracy, R. W. Robins, & J. P. Tangney (Eds.), *The self-conscious emotions: Theory and research* (pp. 263–282). Guilford Press.

Tracy, J. L., & Robins, R. W. (2007c). The psychological structure of pride: A tale of two facets. *Journal of Personality and Social Psychology, 92*(3), 506–525.

Trivers, R. L. (1971). The evolution of reciprocal altruism. *The Quarterly Review of Biology, 46*(1), 35–57.

Van den Berghe, P. L., & Barash, D. P. (1977). Inclusive fitness and human family structure. *American Anthropologist, 79*(4), 809–823.

Van Vugt, M., & Schaller, M. (2008). Evolutionary approaches to group dynamics: An introduction. *Group Dynamics: Theory, Research, and Practice, 12*(1), 1–6.

Von Rueden, C., Gurven, M., & Kaplan, H. (2008). The multiple dimensions of male social status in an Amazonian society. *Evolution and Human Behavior, 29*(6), 402–415.

Wadlinger, H. A., & Isaacowitz, D. M. (2006). Positive mood broadens visual attention to positive stimuli. *Motivation and Emotion, 30*(1), 87–99.

Walker, R., Burger, O., Wagner, J., & Von Rueden, C. R. (2006). Evolution of brain size and juvenile periods in primates. *Journal of Human Evolution, 51*(5), 480–489.

West, S. A., & Gardner, A. (2013). Adaptation and inclusive fitness. *Current Biology, 23*(13), R577–R584.

Williams, L. A., & DeSteno, D. (2008). Pride and perseverance: The motivational role of pride. *Journal of Personality and Social Psychology, 94*(6), 1007–1017.

Williams, L. A., & DeSteno, D. (2009). Pride: Adaptive social emotion or seventh sin? *Psychological Science, 20*(3), 284–288.

Wood, A. M., Maltby, J., Gillett, R., Linley, P. A., & Joseph, S. (2008). The role of gratitude in the development of social support, stress, and depression: Two longitudinal studies. *Journal of Research in Personality, 42*(4), 854–871.

Young, K. S., Parsons, C. E., Stein, A., Vuust, P., Craske, M. G., & Kringelbach, M. L. (2017). The neural basis of responsive caregiving behaviour: Investigating temporal dynamics within the parental brain. *Behavioural Brain Research, 325*(Part B), 105–116.

Zeveloff, S. I., & Boyce, M. S. (1980). Parental investment and mating systems in mammals. *Evolution, 34*(5), 973–982.

Ziv, A. (1988). Humor's role in married life. *Humor: International Journal of Humor Research, 1*(3), 223–229.

CHAPTER 21

How Jealousy Works

David M. G. Lewis, Laith Al-Shawaf, and Kortnee C. Evans

Abstract

This chapter seeks to invigorate work at the boundary of knowledge about jealousy. First, the chapter conducts a task analysis of the adaptive problem that jealousy is hypothesized to solve. This task analysis reveals key gaps in current knowledge about jealousy. Second, the chapter presents an array of new, testable hypotheses about this important human emotion. These include hypotheses about within-sex individual differences (in contrast to the historical emphasis on between-sex differences), hypotheses about within-individual shifts in jealousy over time, and hypotheses about the distinct tactics the jealousy system should deploy in response to different forms of relationship threat. Finally, the chapter emphasizes the need for more research on jealousy in relationships other than monogamous mating relationships, including consensually non-monogamous relationships as well as non-mating relationships. This chapter contributes novel theoretical insights and suggests future directions that can help generate new empirical discoveries about this important human emotion.

Key Words: sexual jealousy, human mating, mate retention, infidelity, individual differences, sex differences, friendship jealousy

Introduction

Recently, major strides have been made toward mapping the design features of emotions such as anger (Sell, 2005, 2011; Sell, Sznycer, et al., 2017), shame (Sznycer, 2010; Sznycer et al., 2012; Sznycer et al., 2016), pride (Sznycer et al., 2017; Sznycer et al., 2018; Sznycer & Cohen, 2021b), and many others (this volume). Few emotions, however, have received as much theoretical and empirical attention as jealousy (see Buss, 2013, for review). Precisely because jealousy is already one of the best-characterized emotional adaptations, at this stage it may be most productive not to ask what the design features of jealousy are, but rather what design features of jealousy have not yet been investigated and identified. We hope that this chapter usefully orients researchers in this manner; although a great deal is known about the design of the jealousy program, there is still much exciting work to do.

This chapter takes two steps toward invigorating work at the boundary of knowledge about jealousy. First, other resources (e.g., Buss, 2013) provide thorough descriptions of known design features of jealousy. However, these resources tend to follow an organization (e.g., centered on sex differences) that does not readily reveal where gaps in knowledge remain. By contrast, organizing an emotion program's design features chronologically, using a task analysis—from the initial inputs that activate the program; through the operation of cognitive, affective, and behavioral design features that the program coordinates to solve the relevant problem; to the program's deactivation once cues indicate that the problem has been resolved—may be a more systematic means of revealing which features of the emotion remain unmapped. In this chapter, we take this approach: we conduct a task analysis of the problem that jealousy is hypothesized to have evolved to solve, and, in doing so, draw attention to key aspects of the jealousy program that remain unknown.

Second, we advance numerous new hypotheses about the operation of jealousy. These include hypotheses about within-sex individual differences (in contrast to the historical emphasis on between-sex differences), within-individual shifts in jealousy over time, and the specific behavioral outputs that jealousy deploys in response to distinct contextual factors. Some of these new hypotheses appear naturally as we organize already-known features of jealousy chronologically (around a task analysis), whereas others appear in a dedicated "Future Directions" section at the end of the chapter.

We focus on jealousy in the context of mating relationships. Although important strides have recently been made toward an understanding of "friendship jealousy" (e.g., Krems et al., 2021; see also Schützwohl et al., 2019), and intriguing adaptationist hypotheses have been advanced about jealousy in the context of kin relations (e.g., sibling jealousy; Hart, 2018), it is unclear whether these represent different psychological mechanisms (Schützwohl et al., 2019) or the operation of the same information-processing system across different relationship types. Given these issues and uncertainties—to which we return in the "Future Directions" section below—we focus on the well-characterized design and operation of jealousy in mating relationships.

The Adaptive Problem

The key first step in a priori, theory-driven evolutionary research is to identify the selection pressures—the adaptive problem—thought to have driven the evolution of the hypothesized adaptation under investigation (Tooby & Cosmides, 1990, 1992; Williams, 1966; see also Lewis et al., 2017; Lukaszewski et al., 2020). Ancestrally, infidelity or abandonment by one's romantic partner would have posed substantial costs to both males and females (Buss, 2000; Buss et al., 1992; Wilson & Daly, 1996). This recurrent adaptive problem is hypothesized to have caused the evolution of an information-processing program—*jealousy*—that detects and appraises threats to a valued relationship, and coordinates behavior to thwart those threats (Buss, 1988; Buss & Shackelford, 1997; Daly et al., 1982).

The Solution

The second step in adaptationist research should be to conduct a task analysis of that problem: to elucidate the exact nature of the problem and articulate the features that a system is expected to have if it is an adaptation that evolved to solve that problem.

At one level of abstraction, the historical research on jealousy could be regarded as being based on such a task analysis. Broadly, research has shown that the jealousy program activates in response to cues to a partner's possible infidelity or defection, and that it motivates behaviors that plausibly function to thwart the threat. At a more precise level, research has shown that jealousy activates in response to numerous specific situational inputs probabilistically indicative of infidelity (e.g., see Shackelford & Buss, 1997b) and identified a diverse suite of behavioral outputs that the jealousy program mobilizes to ward off threats to the valued relationship (Buss, 1988). Indeed, whereas the tactical behavioral outputs of other emotion programs are yet unknown, research on jealousy established an inventory of the program's behavioral outputs over 30 years ago (see Buss, 1988).

Jealousy: At the Forefront, but Important Work Remains

Initial research on jealousy was ahead of its time, perhaps both for better and worse. It was at the front line of introducing an evolutionary meta-theoretical framework to the study of human emotion—one could argue that, for many years, it was one of the only emotions being earnestly investigated through an adaptationist lens. A potentially negative consequence of jealousy being at the vanguard of adaptationist research on human emotion, though, is that important investigations of jealousy took place prior to the publication of several formative papers in evolutionary psychology and therefore could not take full advantage of important conceptual tools that appeared in those papers. In particular, early work on jealousy focused more on sex differences and less on the sequence of information-processing and behavioral coordination steps necessary to solve the adaptive problem. Consequently, although the highly productive program of research on jealousy made many discoveries, it may not have mapped the emotion's underlying cognitive architecture as systematically as it would have if it had been driven by a chronological task analysis.

More recent work on other emotions, such as Sell and colleagues' work on anger (e.g., Sell, 2005, 2011; Sell, Sznycer, et al., 2017), has been more closely guided by such a task analysis. This has enabled it to illuminate key features of the emotion's information-processing and behavioral coordination design. First, anger activates when ego perceives that someone else has placed too little value on ego's welfare. Second, the program mobilizes cognitive systems to determine whether this initial perception is accurate, including motivating behaviors to acquire further information to confirm or disconfirm the original assessment. Third, if the initial assessment was correct—if the target indeed placed too little value on ego's welfare—the anger program organizes behaviors that interface with cognitive systems in the target's mind to increase the value that the target places on ego's welfare. Finally, anger deactivates when the costs of its continued operation exceed the benefits (for example, when it receives inputs indicating that the value that the target places on ego has been upregulated) (see Sell, 2005, 2011; Sell, Sznycer, et al., 2017; see also Al-Shawaf & Lewis, 2017; Lukaszewski et al., 2020).

Although research on jealousy has documented an extensive catalog of inputs that activate the program, and a diverse taxonomy of tactical behavioral outputs that the emotion mobilizes, a more systematic and detailed task analysis may better organize these features of jealousy and may also lead to the discovery of previously unknown components of jealousy's behavior-coordinating architecture. For example, the Mate Retention Inventory (MRI; Buss, 1988; Buss & Shackelford, 1997; Shackelford et al., 2005) is perhaps the most extensive taxonomy of behavioral outputs coordinated by an emotion program, with over 100 acts organized into 19 different act clusters or "tactics." Similarly, Shackelford and Buss (1997b) identified over 100 cues to infidelity (i.e., inputs to the jealousy program), and organized these cues into 14 distinct factors. Despite the comprehensiveness and many other merits of these taxonomies, they do not address two important features of jealousy's information-processing design.

First, the MRI does not elucidate the *sequential* nature of the task of detecting, appraising, and warding off infidelity threats. For example, behaviors such as "He read her personal mail" and "He hit the guy who made a pass at her" are found in categories of behavior that, in the hierarchy of the MRI, are parallel. This parallel categorization does not effectively capture that these tactics tend to be deployed at different stages of solving the relevant adaptive problem. The former behavior may be an initial output of jealousy to monitor for or acquire further information about a potential threat. The latter behavior, on the other hand, is more characteristically an output mobilized at a later stage (e.g., in response to a confirmed threat). This is not to say that the MRI explicitly advances the idea that these behaviors are alternatives to one another at a single stage. Rather, because the MRI is principally organized by the *target* of the behavior (i.e., *intersexual manipulations* directed at ego's mate vs. *intrasexual manipulations* directed at potential mate poachers), rather than by a task analysis of the adaptive problem, the MRI does not effectively capture the sequence of information-processing and behavioral coordination steps necessary to solve the relevant adaptive problem.

Second, the MRI is a taxonomy of outputs that is largely independent of the inputs that activate jealousy, and Shackelford and Buss's (1997b) "Cues to Infidelity" is a taxonomy of inputs that is largely independent of the behavioral outputs in response to them. In other words, existing research does not clearly specify input-output mappings for this emotion. As Buss (2013) notes, there are many distinct instantiations or subclasses of the broad adaptive problem of infidelity: one of ego's same-sex rivals could show an interest in ego's mate; ego's mate could give off cues of interest in another party—or merely of sexual disinterest in ego; or, if ego's mate is significantly higher in mate value than ego, this enduring feature of the relationship could pose a looming threat of infidelity or abandonment (Buss, 2000). Each of these distinct scenarios falls into the abstract class of cues that are expected to be inputs that activate jealousy. However, these distinct scenarios require different cognitive, affective, and behavioral solutions. To take just one example, inflicting costs on an intrasexual rival may be an effective strategy for deterring a potential mate poacher, but is not an effective tactic for solving the problem of a mate who has fallen out of love with ego.

These limitations represent an opportunity for jealousy research—one that is particularly ripe precisely because scholars have already established these valuable taxonomies of inputs and outputs. Coupled with these resources, a systematic task analysis—including distinct analyses of the different problems posed by distinct instantiations of infidelity threat (e.g., a rival is attempting to poach one's mate vs. one's mate has wandering eyes)—should enable researchers to organize jealousy's outputs according to the functional sequences in which they are deployed, and to make progress toward *specific* input-output mappings (see Sznycer & Cohen, 2021a; see also Al-Shawaf et al., 2016).

Jealousy: A Task Analysis
Step 1: Detect and Activate in Response to Cues of Relationship Threat

The first step in solving the adaptive problem of a mate's potential infidelity or defection is to detect cues to that threat and activate in response to them. This is exactly what the jealousy system does. Jealousy "lie[s] dormant until [it is] activated by cues signaling that [the] adaptive problem is being confronted" (Buss & Shackelford, 1997, p. 348). Empirical research has demonstrated that jealousy activates in response to dozens of distinct cues to infidelity (Shackelford & Buss, 1997b), and that this activation is associated with the mobilization of physiological, psychological, and behavioral resources (Buss et al., 1992; Pietrzak et al., 2002).

However, jealousy's mobilization of behavioral outputs can carry significant costs, including time, energy, and opportunity costs. These costs will often be outweighed when there is a veritable infidelity threat. However, false positives—anti-infidelity behaviors when there is no real infidelity threat—not only entail wasted effort, but also may jeopardize the very relationship that the jealousy program is trying to protect (Barelds & Barelds-Dijkstra, 2007). Consequently, we should expect jealousy to be designed to avoid the dual errors of over-activation (i.e., mobilization of further resources in the absence of real infidelity threat) and under-activation (i.e., the failure to mobilize resources in the presence of true infidelity threat) (see Sznycer, 2019, for a discussion of this "just right" Goldilocks principle in the design and operation of psychological adaptations, including emotions).

Schützwohl's (2006) data are consistent with this Goldilocks principle. Schützwohl presented males and females with a description of one of two scenarios, both of which depicted their partner meeting a potential interloper. However, the two scenarios differed in their infidelity likelihood. In one scenario, the partner voluntarily disclosed meeting the other person. In the other scenario, the meeting was not openly disclosed, and the partner came home late on multiple occasions. Consistent with the Goldilocks design principle, participants in the lower infidelity likelihood condition exhibited significantly lower activation of the jealousy program, whereas participants in the higher infidelity likelihood condition exhibited greater activation of jealousy (see also Lewis, Lukaszewski, et al., 2023).

Step 2: Appraise the Threat

After activating, jealousy should continue to exhibit the Goldilocks principle. This means that even after it activates in response to probabilistic cues to infidelity, it should not automatically mobilize its full arsenal of anti-infidelity outputs. Instead, we should expect jealousy to first deploy less costly tactics, such as information search, to determine whether the initial perception of a threat was accurate (see Sell, Sznycer, et al., 2017, for evidence of this design principle in the context of anger), identify the principal cause of the threat (e.g., a cause exogenous to the relationship such as an interested mate poacher or an endogenous cause such as an unsatisfied mate), and ascertain the type of threat (i.e., emotional infidelity versus sexual infidelity). At present, some of these features of jealousy have been thoroughly investigated, whereas others have not.

THE TYPE OF THREAT: SEXUAL INFIDELITY VS. EMOTIONAL INFIDELITY

In monogamous relationships, extra-pair emotional intimacy and extra-pair sexual relations are both considered forms of infidelity (Kruger et al., 2013; Thornton & Nagurney, 2011). However, sexual infidelity and emotional infidelity are distinct adaptive problems, and the consequences of those problems differ for males and females.

Because fertilization occurs internally in human females, they can always be assured of the maternity of their offspring, whereas males can never be 100% certain of their paternity. As a result, males (but not females) risk unknowingly investing valuable time and resources in offspring that are not biologically their own. Consequently, across deep evolutionary time, a mate's *sexual infidelity* would have been costlier to males than to females (on average). We should therefore expect the jealousy program to exhibit sex-differentiated design features in response to the threat of sexual infidelity (see Symons, 1979).

Although it does not jeopardize a female's maternity when her male partner engages in extra-pair affairs, such affairs can still carry large costs for the female, in particular if they are accompanied by a diversion of her mate's time, effort, attention, and investment away from her and her offspring (Buss, 2013). This *emotional infidelity* would have posed an acute adaptive problem for females for multiple reasons, including decreased offspring survival in the absence of an investing mate (Hurtado & Hill, 1992). We should therefore expect the jealousy program to exhibit sex-differentiated design features in response to a mate's emotional infidelity as well (Symons, 1979).

Consistent with these hypotheses, Buss and colleagues (1992) showed that males exhibited more pronounced physiological, psychological, and behavioral responses to sexual infidelity than to emotional infidelity, whereas the opposite pattern was observed among females. Males' responses to sexual infidelity, compared to their responses to emotional infidelity, were associated with greater upset, increased skin conductance, increased heart rate, and greater contraction of the corrugator supercilii ("frowning") muscle. Females, on the other hand, exhibited greater electrodermal activity, heart rate, and electromyographic activity in response to emotional than sexual infidelity (Buss et al., 1992). These observed sex differences in response to sexual versus emotional infidelity have been robustly replicated using both forced-choice and continuous-rating measures, as well as both hypothetical and actual infidelity experiences, and have been extended to include changes in skin temperature and neurophysiological activation as assessed by functional magnetic resonance imaging (see Becker et al., 2004; Edlund et al., 2006; Pietrzak et al., 2002; Shackelford et al., 2000; Takahashi et al., 2006). Sex differences in the operation of jealousy have also been replicated across diverse cultures, including multiple non-WEIRD cultures and traditional societies (Scelza et al., 2020).

These findings demonstrate that jealousy operates in a sex-differentiated fashion, in line with a priori hypotheses based on sex-differentiated selection pressures. However, it is not clear at exactly which stage(s) of information processing and behavioral coordination these psychological and physiological features of jealousy (e.g., upset, increased heart rate) contribute to solving the adaptive problem of infidelity threat. This issue is compounded by the fact that these responses have been documented primarily in response to *confirmed* infidelity rather than in response to cues indicating *possible* infidelity. Consequently, the research documenting these responses to confirmed infidelity may not reveal exactly what people do when they detect *ambiguous* cues to infidelity threat. We are unaware of any lab or group of researchers programmatically investigating the operation of jealousy during this key stage of threat appraisal. However, distinct findings from independent laboratories begin to paint a picture of some of jealousy's design features at this initial stage of addressing the adaptive problem.

INFORMATION ACQUISITION: DIRECTLY QUESTIONING ONE'S PARTNER ABOUT THE TYPE OF INFIDELITY THREAT

One way to obtain further information about a potential threat is to directly question one's partner. Several studies suggest that such direct interrogation may be an important feature of jealousy. Buss (1988), for example, found that the mate retention tactics deployed by American undergraduates included behaviors such as "questioned my partner about what she did when we were apart." However, this and other interrogative behaviors were not differentiated with respect to whether information was being sought about sexual versus emotional infidelity. Because of sex differences in the costs of sexual versus emotional infidelity, we should expect males to be more focused on acquiring information about the threat of sexual infidelity, and females to be more focused on acquiring information about emotional infidelity.

This appears to be precisely what they do. Schützwohl (2006) found that, when males and females were asked what they would do if they learned that their partner had spent time with a potential mate poacher, males were more likely than females to indicate that they would seek information about possible sexual aspects of the encounter, whereas females were more likely than males to indicate that they would seek information about their partner's emotional closeness to the potential interloper. Kuhle and colleagues (Kuhle, 2011; Kuhle et al., 2009) found similar sex differences, although they were not investigating people's responses at the initial stage of assessing and appraising a threat—rather, they investigated how people interrogate their partners *after certain infidelity* had already occurred. When they learned about their partner's extra-pair relationship, females were more likely than males to seek information about whether their partner was in love with the interloper, whereas males were more likely than females to ask questions about sexual infidelity.

These findings make important contributions toward understanding the design and function of direct interrogation tactics. However, we should expect jealousy to motivate subtler behaviors than blunt questions such as "Have you slept with him?" (Schützwohl, 2006, p. 287) or "Do you love her?" (p. 288). It can be very costly to the unfaithful partner to reveal that they have been unfaithful, so directly interrogating a partner about their fidelity will often yield inaccurate information (see Andrews et al., 2008; Cole, 2001; Kuhle et al., 2009). Additionally, we should expect direct interrogation to have more nuanced functions than simply to determine whether sexual or emotional infidelity has already occurred. If a key function of jealousy is to *prevent* infidelity, then it should motivate people to acquire information about the likelihood of *future* infidelity. Based on these considerations, jealousy should motivate people to seek information about much more than just their partner's past behavior and the type of infidelity, and to acquire that information through subtle as well as furtive means.

INFORMATION ACQUISITION: SUBTLE INTERROGATION TACTICS ABOUT THE CAUSE

A system that evolved to prevent infidelity should seek information about the cause of infidelity threat (e.g., an endogenous cause such as a mate who is actively engaging in extra-pair mating effort, versus an exogenous cause such as a rival showing interest in one's mate).

Identifying the precise cause of the threat is crucial. The jealousy program can deploy many different behavioral outputs, but the usefulness of any given output will be tightly linked to the cause of the problem. For example, behaviors such as "Threatened to hit a man who was making moves on my partner" (Buss, 1988) may be successful for dealing with an encroaching mate poacher but futile for solving the problem of a mate who has fallen out of love with ego. We should therefore expect the jealousy program to motivate interrogation tactics that are designed to acquire detailed information about the cause of the threat.

Schützwohl's (2006) data are consistent not only with the hypothesis that the jealousy program searches for information about the occurrence and type of infidelity, but also with the hypothesis that jealousy specifically seeks information about the *cause* of infidelity. For example, when people inquired about their partners' emotional involvement with an interloper, they asked not only about whether their partner was in love with the interloper, but also about whether their partner still loved them (the participants). This makes sense because a partner being in love with someone else and a partner falling out of love with ego are two different problems with distinct behavioral solutions. People also sought information from 10 categories that were *not* directly about whether emotional or sexual infidelity had occurred. For example, people asked about the *circumstances* in which their mate met the rival as well as about *aspects of the rival*.

These questions about *circumstances* and *aspects of the rival* may reflect important features of the jealousy program. For example, acquiring information about the circumstances in which one's mate met the interloper could alert one to the specific environments (e.g., work), individuals (e.g., one's mate's new boss, who likes to take his employees out for drinks), times (e.g., after work), and other situational variables linked to an increased likelihood of subsequent encounters with the current interloper or other potential future interlopers. The purpose of asking questions about *aspects of the rival* may be to gather information about the physical phenotype of the rival, including the rival's physical attractiveness. Because males, on average, place greater value on a potential mate's physical attractiveness than females do (e.g., Buss, 1989; Li et al., 2002; see also Lewis et al., 2011; Lewis et al., 2012), we might expect female jealousy to be more sensitive to a rival's physical attractiveness. Consistent with this, evidence suggests that, on average, rival attractiveness has stronger effects on female than male jealousy (e.g., Dijkstra & Buunk, 1998, 2002; replicated by Pollet & Saxton, 2020).

Although existing research sheds light on some of these facets of jealousy, there are several key design features that remain unaddressed. For example, broadly defined categories such as *aspects of the rival* do not differentiate between characteristics such as physical attractiveness and social status. Because females, on average, place greater value on a potential mate's social status than males do (e.g., Buss, 1989; Li et al., 2002), male jealousy may be more sensitive to a rival's status (Dijkstra & Buunk, 1998, 2002; but see Pollet & Saxton, 2020). Collapsing rival characteristics into a single category prevents more nuanced analyses to determine whether males and females seek different information about their rivals.

Similarly, questions such as "May I see him/her?" (Schützwohl, 2006) are not sufficiently specified to determine whether males and females are seeking *different* information when they engage in information search about the physical phenotype of rivals. For example, because physical formidability likely has a greater impact on male intrasexual competition (Sell et al., 2012) *and* female mate choice (e.g., see Frederick & Haselton, 2007; for review, see Lewis, Evans, & Al-Shawaf, 2023), males may be more motivated than females to seek information about the rival's physical formidability. Similarly, we might expect information search to be tied to an individual's specific weaknesses or worries—for example, individuals who perceive their careers or material resources to be lacking might be more motivated to seek information about these specific attributes in the rival. These hypotheses about the operation of jealousy at the threat appraisal stage await future testing.

INFORMATION ACQUISITION: SURREPTITIOUS BEHAVIORS

An unfaithful mate may suffer severe costs if they reveal their infidelity to their partner, even if only via indirect cues. Such costs could include their partner attempting to thwart the affair, engaging in a retaliatory affair, or terminating the relationship. Consequently, unfaithful mates may lie or actively mislead their partners (Cole, 2001; Kuhle et al., 2009). We should therefore expect the jealousy program to seek information without relying on the direct testimony of the mate. Consistent with this, Buss (1988) found that mate retention tactics include behaviors to acquire information about infidelity threat without relying on information from one's partner. Moreover, these behaviors appear designed to avoid revealing one's own suspicions. This may be strategic: if one's mate becomes aware of one's suspicions, one's mate might make a greater effort to conceal information about their infidelity, or, if they are actually faithful, such unjustified suspicions could jeopardize the relationship (Barelds & Barelds-Dijkstra, 2007). These tactics to surreptitiously acquire information about infidelity threat include behaviors ranging from "Dropped by unexpectedly to see what my partner was doing" to "Read my partner's personal mail." They also include information-acquisition behaviors that involve third parties, such as "Had my friends check up on my partner" (see Buss, 1988). The recruitment of third parties may serve several potential functions. These include acquiring information when one is unable to be present (but see Russell et al., 2017; Russell et al., 2018), as well as more easily hiding one's suspicions from one's partner (for a broader discussion of "coalitional" mate retention tactics, see Pham, Barbaro, & Shackelford, 2015). These hypotheses about the distinct functions of such indirect means of information acquisition and the specific contexts in which they are deployed remain to be rigorously tested (see also Barbaro et al., 2015; Pham, Barbaro, Mogilski, & Shackelford, 2015).

INFERENCES UNDER UNCERTAINTY: THREAT APPRAISAL BIASES

An ideal information-processing system would make accurate inferences about the presence or absence of infidelity threat 100% of the time. However, in the real world, inferences about infidelity must almost always be made under conditions of uncertainty—especially if unfaithful mates actively conceal cues to infidelity. In such a world, inferential errors are inevitable. The two possible inferential errors—false positives (inferring the presence of infidelity threat when it is absent) and false negatives (inferring the absence of infidelity threat when there is a real threat)—have asymmetrical costs, which can select for cognitive biases (see Haselton &

Buss, 2000), including sex-differentiated biases when the cost asymmetry differs between the sexes (see also Al-Shawaf, 2016a; Lewis, Al-Shawaf, Semchenko, & Evans, 2022).

The false negative of erroneously inferring that a partner has been *sexually* faithful is costly for both males and females, but it is costlier for males than females because only males can unwittingly raise somebody else's child. We might therefore expect any cognitive biases toward false positives about a mate's sexual infidelity to be more pronounced among males. Consistent with this hypothesis, Andrews and colleagues (2008) found that males, relative to females, had a higher ratio of false positive errors to false negative errors when making inferences about whether their partner had been unfaithful (see also Goetz & Causey, 2009). We are not aware of any research testing for sex-differentiated biases in inferences about *emotional* infidelity. However, to the extent that a partner's emotional infidelity was costlier, on average, to females than to males—and a false negative about a partner's emotional infidelity was therefore costlier to females—we might expect a sex difference in the opposite direction. We await future research testing this hypothesis.

Step 3: Defend against the Threat

If the jealousy program infers that there is indeed an infidelity threat—as a consequence of any combination of initial cues, subsequent acquisition of new information, and inferences under uncertainty—we should expect it to mobilize behaviors to prevent the perceived threat from translating into actual infidelity. Reducing the likelihood of infidelity can be achieved through a variety of means, reflected by the diverse tactics in the Mate Retention Inventory.

Although these distinct tactics all share the same abstract function of defending against infidelity threat, they operate at a more specific level. Some tactics, such as *concealment of mate* and *monopolization of mate's time*, achieve their function by keeping one's mate away from environments associated with infidelity threat. Other tactics interface with cognitive systems in the mind of a potential mate poacher. For example, tactics such as *intrasexual threats* and *violence* use actual or threatened aggression to dissuade interlopers from mate-poaching attempts. Yet other tactics are directed toward one's mate. Some of these inflict costs (e.g., "she hit him when she caught him flirting with someone else"), whereas others bestow benefits ("he was helpful when she really needed it").

Some of these benefit-bestowing tactics may be more successful for decreasing the threat of emotional than sexual infidelity, or vice versa. For example, if male provisioning of resources was an important benefit that shaped female long-term mating strategies (e.g., see Marlowe, 2003) and the emotional attachment associated with such pair-bonds (see Belk & Coon, 1993; Lawler et al., 1994; see also Balconi & Fronda, 2020), then tactics that deliver material resources may be an effective means for males to address concerns about the threat of *emotional* infidelity. On the other hand, if a principal function of extra-pair copulations for females is to obtain "good genes" for their offspring (Gangestad & Simpson, 2000), then behaviors by the female's partner that deliver material resources (but not genetic resources) may be less effective for thwarting the threat of *sexual* infidelity. Whether males are more likely to provision resources in response to the threat of emotional infidelity than in response to the threat of sexual infidelity, and whether resource provisioning is more effective at thwarting the threat of a female's emotional (relative to sexual) infidelity are two research questions that have yet to be investigated.

The efficacy of some of these tactics also depends on characteristics of the rival. For example, behaviors such as "Threatened to hit a man who was making moves on my partner" or "Picked a fight with a man who was interested in my partner" may extinguish a mate poaching threat when one is more physically formidable than the interloper. However, if the opposite is true, then such behaviors may be ineffective and may even exacerbate the threat: a public defeat in intrasexual competition may decrease perceptions of one's desirability as a mate, and the interloper's victory may increase perceptions of their desirability (Sell, Lukaszewski, & Townsley, 2017).

These considerations reflect a key principle: a behavioral response to a problem will only be successful to the extent that the response is tailored to the specific instantiation of the problem (for in-depth discussions of why context is crucial in evolutionary psychology, see Al-Shawaf et al., 2019; Lewis, Al-Shawaf, Thompson, & Buss, 2021; Lewis & Buss, 2021). This principle reinforces the overarching hypothesis that the jealousy program should seek information about the specific features of the infidelity threat that it faces (e.g., rival characteristics, circumstances): it needs this information in order to effectively solve the relevant problem.

This principle also underscores the point that jealousy must operate according to *specific* input-output mappings. Abundant research has addressed the *general and abstract* processing structure of jealousy: it activates in response to a broad class of situational inputs (i.e., cues to infidelity). However, for jealousy to effectively thwart the threat of infidelity—which, as discussed above, comes in many different forms, with diverse causes and sources—it must selectively deploy its different behavioral outputs in precise functional alignment with specific inputs.

A key next step will therefore be to use existing resources, such as taxonomies of jealousy's inputs (e.g., "Cues to Infidelity" from Shackelford & Buss, 1997b) and outputs (e.g., the MRI; Buss, 1988), to investigate how jealousy maps *specific* outputs onto *specific* inputs. One way to translate these existing resources into these specific mappings is through detailed task analyses of different forms of the broad adaptive problem of infidelity threat. Researchers should consider how the efficacy of different mate retention tactics depends on the specific form of the infidelity threat, such as its source (e.g., endogenous vs. exogenous to the relationship), the surrounding circumstances (e.g., if the source is exogenous, the specific environments in which a would-be mate poacher is likely to pose a threat), and the characteristics of the rival. These contextual features, which can vary widely across different instantiations of infidelity threat, can profoundly impact the efficacy of distinct mate retention tactics. We should therefore expect the jealousy program to deploy specific tactics in functional alignment with these specific features of the threat.

Although a growing body of research has examined the differential deployment of mate retention tactics as a function of individual differences such as sex (e.g., Buss & Shackelford, 1997; see also Atari, Barbaro, Shackelford, & Chegeni, 2017; Chaudhary et al., 2018), personality (e.g., Atari, Barbaro, Sela, et al., 2017; McKibbin et al., 2014), attachment orientation (Barbaro et al., 2021; Nascimento et al., 2021; see also Barbaro et al., 2016; Barbaro et al., 2019), and mate value (Miner, Starratt, & Shackelford, 2009; see also Miner, Shackelford, & Starratt, 2009), as well as the "type" of jealousy experienced (see Davis et al., 2018) and sperm competition risk (Goetz et al., 2005), we are aware of only one study—an unpublished dissertation by Lewis (2013)—that has examined the differential deployment of mate retention tactics specifically as a function of distinct forms of infidelity threat.

Reiterating some of Buss and Shackelford's (1997) logic, Lewis argued that a male being mated to a female who is higher in mate value than he is poses a looming infidelity threat. Lewis (2013) also reasoned that being low in mate value poses an *independent* source of infidelity threat above and beyond any such mate value discrepancy (see also Miner, Shackelford, & Starratt, 2009; Miner, Starratt, & Shackelford, 2009). More precisely, these two cues—(1) a male's mate value and (2) the discrepancy between his mate value and that of his partner—predict distinct forms of relationship threat. The genetic benefits that a female could reap from a sexual affair with a male of high mate value depend on the mate value of her current partner, *independent* of any mate value discrepancy between her and her current partner. However, the female's ability to secure a different long-term partner who is higher in mate value than her current partner likely *does* depend on this mate value discrepancy; if a female is mated to a male lower in mate value than she is, it should be easier for her to secure a new long-term partner higher in mate value than her current partner. Consequently, her partner's mate value may more strongly predict the threat of her sexual infidelity than the threat of her long-term defection, whereas the discrepancy between her mate value and her partner's mate value may be a stronger predictor (than his mate value alone) of the threat of her long-term defection.

Lewis (2013) found distinct patterns of mate retention behavior among men that appear functionally tailored to these different threats. When a male is mated to a female who is higher in mate value than he is, provisioning (non-genetic) resources could be effective for increasing her perceptions of the value of the present relationship, and thereby reduce her likelihood of her terminating the long-term relationship or defecting to another long-term mate. Consistent with this, Lewis (2013) found that males mated to females higher in mate value than themselves were more likely to deploy benefit-provisioning mate retention tactics, such as *love and care* and *resource display* (e.g., "spent a lot of money on my partner").

However, if an important function of extra-pair copulations for females is to secure genetic benefits, then males' provisioning of non-genetic resources may not successfully thwart the threat of sexual infidelity. To the extent that men's (low) mate value is a predictor specifically of his partner's sexual infidelity (and less so of her long-term abandonment), then we might expect low-mate-value men to engage in a subset of mate retention tactics that appear designed specifically to thwart infidelity threat. Consistent with this hypothesis, Lewis (2013) found that men of lower mate value more frequently engaged in tactics such as *punish mate's infidelity threat* as well as *vigilance* and *monopolization of mate's time*—tactics that may reduce or eliminate a mate's ability to consort with potential affair partners. These findings point to the conclusions that, among men, the jealousy system (a) processes, as distinct cues, both low mate value and mate value discrepancies, and (b) differentially responds to these predictors of infidelity and abandonment threat through functionally tailored tactics. Overall, mate value discrepancies predicted the deployment of 12 distinct tactics (11 of which were *not* predicted by low mate value among men), and low mate value among men predicted their deployment of 4 anti-infidelity tactics (only 1 of which was predicted by mate value discrepancies).

This example illustrates the utility of (1) considering how different cues may predict distinct forms of relationship threat, (2) conducting task analyses of these distinct forms of threat, and (3) carrying out cost-benefit analyses of jealousy's distinct behavioral outputs *in the context of those different forms of threat* in order to identify the specific tactics that we should expect the jealousy program to deploy. We hope that research is soon characterized by this greater specificity about jealousy's information-processing and behavioral coordination architecture; the identification of specific input-output mappings is a key part of a mature and comprehensive understanding of an emotion program (see Sznycer & Cohen, 2021a; see also Al-Shawaf et al., 2016). We anticipate that researchers will be able to make rapid progress toward identifying these input-output mappings by carrying out these analyses of specific forms of threat and making good use of the extensive inventories of specific inputs and outputs already available, such as Shackelford and Buss's (1997b) "Cues to Infidelity," Buss's (1988) Mate Retention Inventory, and Pham, Barbaro, and Shackelford's (2015) complementary Coalitional Mate Retention Inventory.

Future Directions
Step 4: Deactivate When the Threat Has Been Resolved

We should expect jealousy to be characterized by design features that interrupt its operation after the threat of infidelity has been resolved (see Sznycer, 2019; see also Al-Shawaf, 2016b; Al-Shawaf et al., 2016; for a parallel set of deactivation or "offlining" hypotheses about hunger and sexual arousal, respectively). These "switching off" design features have been documented for emotions such as anger (Sell, Sznycer, et al., 2017), but little is known about what turns the jealousy program off—rendering this a key future research direction.

There are two very different ways in which infidelity threat can resolve: the threat may be successfully thwarted, or the threat may translate into actual infidelity. We should expect jealousy to respond differently to these distinct outcomes, including in ways that might not initially be obvious.

WHEN THE THREAT IS SUCCESSFULLY THWARTED

When the threat is successfully thwarted, the jealousy program may cease its operation. This "turning off" may manifest in multiple ways. One way is ceased information search. Another is the decreased deployment of mate retention tactics designed specifically to address infidelity threat (e.g., *punish mate's infidelity threat*). Yet another way is the reduction of some of the negative subjective states that jealousy mobilizes.

Consistent with the last hypothesis that the deactivation of jealousy may manifest in a reduction of negative affect, Schützwohl (2008) found that both males and females indicated being relieved to learn that their partners had not been unfaithful. Moreover, consistent with known sex differences in the operation of jealousy, Schützwohl found that (1) males, compared to females, indicated greater relief in response to learning that their mate had not been sexually unfaithful, whereas (2) females indicated greater relief in response to learning that their mate had not been emotionally unfaithful than in response to learning that their partner had not been sexually unfaithful.

Schützwohl (2008) did not find support, however, for the prediction that the magnitude of relief experienced would track the degree of infidelity threat, which was based on the idea that the activation of jealousy is proportional to the degree of threat. We think this unexpected finding might reflect an overlooked design feature of jealousy: at least under some circumstances, the jealousy program *may actually be designed to turn off when infidelity becomes certain*.

WHEN INFIDELITY IS CERTAIN

If the jealousy program is designed to prevent infidelity, then when infidelity becomes certain, we might expect jealousy to operate differently between (1) people who intend to terminate the relationship in response to their partner's infidelity and (2) those who seek to maintain the relationship despite their partner's infidelity. This is because the threat of the partner's further unfaithful behavior remains an adaptive problem for those who seek to maintain the relationship, but not for those who seek to break up.

Among those who seek to stay in the relationship, the jealousy program may increase its sensitivity to infidelity cues. This increased sensitivity could include activating in response to a larger range of cues, including those with low predictive validities, as well as producing stronger responses to cues that have moderate predictive validities. The jealousy program may also deploy more mate retention tactics, in particular tactics geared toward thwarting (further) infidelity, such as *vigilance* and *monopolization of mate's time*.

On the other hand, when infidelity is certain and the individual intends to terminate the relationship, the continued operation of jealousy is likely to carry costs but no compensatory benefits—and may therefore be designed to turn off. This may help explain an unpredicted finding in Schützwohl (2008): people indicate *greater* relief when their partner's "merely suspected" infidelity is disconfirmed than when "virtually certain" infidelity is disconfirmed. In other words, being uncertain about—but suspecting—a partner's infidelity may be associated with greater activation of the jealousy program than when one is almost certain that infidelity has occurred. This is consistent with the hypothesis that the jealousy program is (1) designed to remain active when the benefits of doing so (i.e., *preventing* infidelity) exceed the costs of its operation, and (2) designed to turn off when those costs exceed the benefits, which is precisely what occurs when one intends to terminate the relationship and the partner's further infidelity is thus no longer an adaptive problem.

Lewis and colleagues (Lewis, 2013; Lewis, Lukaszewski, et al., 2023) also found evidence consistent with this hypothesis. Lewis (2013) presented participants with five scenarios of increasing infidelity threat and asked them to describe what they would think, feel, say, and do in response to each scenario. Lewis and colleagues then presented these written responses to third parties, who rated the level of jealousy exhibited in each response. Across the first four scenarios, people's jealousy increased in proportion to the likelihood of infidelity. However, this increasing activation of the jealousy program in proportion to the likelihood of infidelity *disappeared when infidelity became certain* in the fifth scenario (Lewis, Lukaszewski, et al., 2023).

When Infidelity Is Certain: Terminate the Relationship, or Attempt to Restore It?
Although Schützwohl (2008) and Lewis and colleagues (Lewis, 2013; Lewis, Lukaszewski, et al., 2023; see also Lukaszewski et al., 2020) provide preliminary evidence suggesting that jealousy may deactivate when infidelity becomes certain, a key shortcoming of their work is that they do not have any measures of participants' intentions to maintain versus terminate the relationship. Capturing this information is important for testing the hypothesized design features of jealousy discussed here. Among people who intend to terminate the relationship, we might expect decreased activation of jealousy, whereas we might expect the opposite among people who seek to restore the relationship.

Moreover, the algorithms by which the jealousy program makes this decision—to terminate the relationship or attempt to reinstate it after a partner's infidelity—are an important but relatively unexplored facet of jealousy's information-processing architecture. Shackelford and colleagues (e.g., Shackelford & Buss, 1997a; Shackelford et al., 2002) made important initial strides two decades ago, but work has been sparse since then (e.g., 16 years later, Bendixen et al., 2018, attempted a replication study). Shackelford et al. (2002) provided evidence suggesting that the inputs the jealousy program uses to make the "terminate or reinstate" decision include the *type* of infidelity committed, in interaction with the sex of the decision-maker. Consistent with study hypotheses, Shackelford and colleagues (2002) found that more men (65%) than women (52%) reported that sexual infidelity would be more difficult to forgive than emotional infidelity, and more men (55%) than women (42%) reported a greater likelihood of terminating the relationship after sexual than emotional infidelity. The authors also found that, if the partner had been *both* sexually and emotionally unfaithful, more men (58%) than women (41%) reported that the sexual aspect of the infidelity would be more difficult to forgive.

We also might expect the cognitive architecture responsible for the decision to terminate or attempt to restore the relationship to process the relative mate values of the decision-maker and their unfaithful partner. When one is the lower-mate-value partner in the relationship, one has a lower likelihood of being able to secure another partner as high in mate value as the current partner, compared to when one is the higher-mate-value partner. Consequently, we might expect the jealousy program to process the mate value discrepancy within the dyad as input when determining whether to terminate the relationship or attempt to reinstate it. If this hypothesis is correct, then people should be less likely to terminate a relationship with an unfaithful partner when that partner is higher in mate value than they are, compared to when the partner is equal or lower in mate value. Consistent with this, women married to men who are lower in mate value than themselves report being more likely to seek divorce in response to their husband's unfaithfulness (Shackelford & Buss, 1997a).

Research by Phillips (2010) provides evidence that (1) further suggests that mate value discrepancies are an important input into the algorithms responsible for the terminate-or-reinstate decision, and (2) is consistent with the hypothesis that the jealousy program deactivates when the decision to terminate is made. Phillips (2010) asked people to indicate the extent to which they would experience anxiety and insecurity if they discovered that their partner had been sexually unfaithful. If the hypotheses discussed here are correct—that jealousy is designed to (1) take, as input, mate value discrepancies when making the terminate-or-reinstate decision, and (2) deactivate when the choice is made to terminate—then we should expect jealousy to be more likely to deactivate among people who are higher in mate value than their unfaithful partners. Phillips's (2010) observations are consistent with this hypothesis: people who perceived themselves as higher in mate value than their partner scored lower on a composite measure of anxiety and insecurity in response to their partner's infidelity.

Collectively, these findings suggest that mate value discrepancies and the type of infidelity, in interaction with the sex of the decision-maker, are inputs that the jealousy program processes in the context of the decision to terminate or restore the relationship after a partner's infidelity. We anticipate that jealousy is sensitive to numerous other inputs linked to the costs and benefits of terminating versus reinstating the relationship. These include one's perceptions of the likelihood of violent retaliatory aggression if one terminates the relationship; one's access to allies who could offer protection against such aggression; the availability and mate values of potential mates in the local mating pool; and whether one shares offspring with the unfaithful partner (e.g., see Betzig, 1989; Buckle et al., 1996).

Jealousy versus Anger
Phillips (2010) also indirectly points toward the importance of more clearly differentiating between the distinct psychological architectures of jealousy and anger, which frequently co-activate. The jealousy program is a hypothesized adaptation designed to activate in response to infidelity threat, whereas the anger program is a hypothesized adaptation designed to activate in response to another person placing too little value on one's welfare. On this view, jealousy and anger are distinct programs designed to deal with different adaptive problems. However, the cues that trigger the jealousy program should frequently trigger the anger program as well. For example, behaviors by one's mate that suggest that one's mate is seeking extra-pair mating opportunities are cues to infidelity threat—which should activate the jealousy program—*and* they indicate that one's mate places too little value on one's welfare—which should activate the anger program (see Sell, 2005, 2011; Sell, Sznycer, et al., 2017; see also Lewis, Lukaszewski, et al., 2023; Lukaszewski et al., 2020). Consequently, we should expect jealousy and anger to frequently co-activate.

This frequent co-activation makes it difficult to determine how best to classify behavioral responses to such scenarios. For example, it is not entirely clear whether behaviors such as "She became angry when her partner flirted too much" (see Buss, 1988) are best classified as outputs of jealousy or anger. Moreover, it is plausible that one of the broad classes of output from the jealousy program is *to activate the anger program*. These and other complications can make it challenging to disentangle these emotion programs under certain circumstances.

Nonetheless, we think this is an important task for future research, and one that will pay off. Phillips (2010) had participants report how much anxiety, insecurity, hostility, and anger they would experience in response to their partner's sexual infidelity. Phillips composited participants' responses to these questions to create measures of "insecurity" (anxiety, insecurity) and "indignation" (anger, hostility). "Insecurity" appears to capture the outputs of the jealousy program, whereas "indignation" appears to reflect the outputs of the anger program. People higher in mate value than their unfaithful partners reported *lower* levels of insecurity, consistent with the ideas that (1) such mate value discrepancies predict the decision to terminate the relationship, and (2) once the terminate decision is made, this turns off the jealousy program. However, and by contrast, people higher in mate value indicated that they would experience *more* indignation. This is consistent with the hypothesis that individuals who have higher bargaining power expect their welfare to be valued more, thereby have a lower threshold for the activation of the anger program, and, consequently, experience more anger (Sell et al., 2009). In short, Phillips's (2010) work provides preliminary evidence that the (de)activation of the jealousy program is not inextricably tied to the (de)activation of the anger program. This suggests that, despite the frequent co-activation of jealousy and anger, these two emotions have distinct information-processing architectures that differentially respond to distinct inputs.

Lewis and colleagues (Lewis, 2013; Lewis, Lukaszewski, et al., 2023; see also Lukaszewski et al., 2020) found further evidence suggesting that jealousy and anger are distinct emotion programs that are activated by at least partially non-overlapping classes of inputs. In their research, Lewis and colleagues presented mated individuals with five different scenarios that exhibited progressively increasing levels of infidelity threat. The fifth scenario, which described certain infidelity, provided a key test of the discriminant activation of anger and jealousy. Because certain infidelity unequivocally reveals the devaluation of ego by ego's mate, the fifth scenario should have resulted in the *greatest* anger. However, if as hypothesized in this chapter, certain infidelity *deactivates* the jealousy program (at least in some individuals in some contexts; see above), then jealousy should have increased progressively across the scenarios *until* the fifth scenario. In precise alignment with this reasoning, people's anger increased across the scenarios and was highest in the certain infidelity condition, whereas jealousy increased across the infidelity scenarios *until* the fifth scenario—at which point it did not increase. Although these findings are a minority in a broader literature that has frequently documented the co-activation of jealousy and anger, they highlight the important future endeavor of disentangling the information-processing architectures of these different emotions.

Jealousy across Relationship Types: Distinct Adaptive Problems and Functions

Much of this chapter has emphasized "zooming in" on jealousy in mating relationships: important progress can be made through future work that is *more specific*—about the instantiation of infidelity threat, including its type and source; about the probabilistic costs and benefits of distinct mate-retention tactics, including variation in these costs and benefits across different instantiations of infidelity threat; about individual difference and contextual variables likely to influence the decision to terminate or attempt to restore a relationship upon discovering infidelity; and so on. Indeed, greater specificity will be fundamental to a more sophisticated and comprehensive understanding of how jealousy works.

Another key future direction will be to "zoom out" and consider jealousy at a level of *greater abstraction*—as an emotion program that responds to "a threat to a valued social relationship" (Buss, 2013, p. 155, citing Daly et al., 1982). This high level of abstraction usefully highlights that jealousy should not be restricted to mating; it should also operate in other types of relationships. Indeed, there is evidence of jealousy in friendships (e.g., Krems et al., 2021) and other relationship types (e.g., among siblings; see Hart, 2018).

Although this "zooming out" from mating relationships usefully guides attention to jealousy in other relationship types, characterizing jealousy at this high level of abstraction could also carry pitfalls that should be avoided. For example, this way of characterizing jealousy implicitly suggests that the same emotion program operates in both mating and non-mating relationships. It might therefore be tempting to attempt to empirically address questions such as "Are friendship jealousy and mating jealousy the same or different adaptations?"

We suggest that such questions may not be well-formulated, and that researchers should direct their attention in a different manner. Because mechanisms (like jealousy) are defined by their function, functions are defined by the problem they solve, and problems can be described at varying levels of abstraction, questions about the *number* of mechanisms are often unhelpful, because the answer depends on the level of abstraction or specificity at which adaptive problems are being described (for a general discussion of this issue, see Pietraszewski & Wertz, 2021; see also Shackelford, 2003). Rather, as we have emphasized throughout this chapter, researchers should focus on precisely characterizing specific adaptive problems; identifying, a priori, information-processing and behavior-coordinating design features capable of economically and efficiently solving those problems (Al-Shawaf et al., 2021); and testing for evidence of these hypothesized design features.

On this view, the relevant and most interesting question in the context of jealousy in mating relationships versus jealousy in friendships is not whether they are different adaptations. Rather, it is: What important differences exist between the adaptive problems of *threat to a mateship* and *threat to a friendship*? And how might cognitive and behavioral solutions to these distinct problems differ?

Answering these questions requires attending more deeply to the concept of *infidelity*. This concept is central to the literature on jealousy in mating relationships, but is virtually absent from discussions of friendship jealousy. On the one hand, it is possible that the concept of infidelity does not pertain to friendships. Indeed, if a necessary precondition for invoking the concept of infidelity is an implicit social contract involving *exclusive* access to the other person and their resources—and one of the defining features of a friendship is *non*-exclusivity—then the concept of infidelity might simply not apply to friendships. On the other hand, people can have very pronounced emotional responses when a friend's resources are diverted to a third party (e.g., see Krems et al., 2021). This suggests that although the implicit social contract associated with friendship may not involve "infidelity" in the sense above, there *is* an implicit social contract, and violations of that contract activate jealousy. If jealousy is designed to operate across multiple relationship types, but its operation varies as a function of the implicit social contracts entailed by different relationship types, then more precisely characterizing these implicit social contracts is a key future direction for research on jealousy.

Little appears to be known about the implicit social contract of friendship, and even less is known about whether there are distinct social contracts associated with different types of friendship. For example, a "best" friend may not simply be the friend to whom someone is closest. Instead, a "best" friendship may be characterized by an implicit social contract that is qualitatively different from other friendships. For example, if ego's friend shared their resources with others but did not also share them with ego, that might violate a best friendship but not necessarily other friendship types. That is, best friendship might be characterized by an implicit rule of *obligatory inclusion* that is absent from the implicit contracts of other friendship types. Another rule that might categorically differentiate best friendship from other friendships is the implicit stipulation that ego's best friend will ally with ego in any antagonistic encounter between ego and a third party (see DeScioli & Kurzban, 2009; Shaw et al., 2017). Researchers can pit these alternative views—(1) a best friend is merely the friend to whom one is closest, and (2) best friendship is a categorically different and special relationship type—against each other by identifying and testing their divergent predictions. For example, if best friendship is *not* a categorically different relationship type, then all individuals with friends should have report having a best friend. However, if best friendship is defined by a distinct social contract, then only those individuals who have a friend who meets the terms of that contract should report having a best friend. This is a key distinction to be tested in future research.

If the implicit terms of the social contract of best friendship differ from those of other friendships, then we might expect jealousy to operate categorically differently in the context of best friendship compared to other friendships. For example, if the first author of this chapter got married and invited the third author to his wedding—but did not invite the second author—that could violate the implicit social contract between the first and second authors, thereby activating the latter's jealousy program—whereas if the first author invited the second author to his wedding but not the third author, that might *not* violate the implicit social contract between the first and third authors and consequently *not* activate the third author's jealousy program. Future research on friendship jealousy could profit from identifying precisely what terms are included in the implicit social contracts of friendships, including determining whether the terms implicit to friendship and best friendship differ. This will enable researchers to more precisely test how jealousy works in the context of friendship.

Similarly, research is needed to better establish precisely what terms are stipulated by different kinds of *mating* relationships, as the jealousy program may operate differently across these relationship types. For example, what constitutes infidelity in long-term monogamous relationships differs from what qualifies as infidelity in consensually non-monogamous (CNM) relationships. Contrary to misconceptions, "cheating" can and does occur in CNM relationships. It may not be defined by exclusivity, but rather by whether the partner was informed of the third party, the degree of emotional connection with the third party, or other terms, some of which may be implicit and others of which may be explicit (see Moors et al., 2017; see also Mogilski et al., 2019). Research on differences in jealousy between monogamous and CNM relationships is relatively new (e.g., Mogilski et al., 2019; Valentova et al., 2020), and we eagerly await new research into how jealousy might operate differently across these different types of long-term mating relationships.

Similarly, relatively little is known about the operation of jealousy in short-term, uncommitted relationships. Again, the definition of "infidelity" in the context of long-term monogamous relationships presumably does not apply to these relationships. However, given that many important fitness-relevant benefits can be derived from short-term relationships, we should expect jealousy to operate to protect such relationships when they are threatened by third parties. For example, the resources that one derives from a "friend with benefits" (FWB) relationship would be threatened if one's FWB formed a new long-term, monogamous relationship; the FWB may cease to provide those "benefits" (e.g., sex) because doing so would violate their new, sexually exclusive relationship (see Lewis et al., 2012, for a discussion of the relationship between people's relationship status and their openness to mating with their friends; see also Lewis et al., 2011). Consequently, people may attempt to impede the formation of long-term relationships between their FWBs and third parties. This may include the deployment of mate-retention tactics such as *derogation of competitors* (Buss, 1988). However, some mate-retention tactics, such as *physical signals of possession*, might actively violate the FWB relationship. Consequently, we might expect the operation of jealousy in FWB relationships to be characterized by a distinct profile of mate-retention tactics compared to long-term relationships. Future research should be able to address these questions through a combination of qualitative approaches (e.g., act nomination procedures in which people describe what they do to maintain and protect their FWB relationships) and quantitative analyses (e.g., testing for differences in the relative frequencies at which distinct mate-retention tactics are deployed in FWB relationships versus long-term, monogamous mateships).

More broadly, we eagerly await further research testing how jealousy activates and manifests in uncommitted mating relationships. The lack of commitment that defines these relationships changes the costs and benefits of jealousy in several ways. First, on average, the loss of a short-term mate is less costly than the loss of a long-term mate. Second, by definition, short-term mateships are not characterized by long-term investment, so the risk of unwittingly investing in somebody else's offspring is largely nullified. Because this adaptive problem of being cuckolded is specific to males, the absence of this adaptive problem from short-term relationships may attenuate some of the sex differences in jealousy observed in long-term, monogamous relationships. Third, the activation of jealousy to protect against relationship threats consumes time and resources. Jealousy therefore entails costs, including opportunity costs. These costs may be higher among short-term-oriented individuals, as they could instead allocate those resources toward alternative short-term mating efforts. The benefits of protecting against third-party threats may also be minimal, given the often transient nature of the relationship in the first place. In short, the costs of jealousy in uncommitted mating may be higher, and the benefits lower, than in exclusive long-term mateships. Based on this, we might expect to observe lower levels of jealousy (1) in uncommitted relationships relative to committed monogamous relationships, and (2) among people oriented toward short-term mating. As an alternative to the latter hypothesis, people oriented toward uncommitted mating may not exhibit less jealousy overall, but may instead exhibit a distinct profile of mate-retention behavior. Specifically, they may be less likely to engage in mate-retention tactics that require their time and physical presence, and more likely to engage in tactics that can thwart threats without requiring much investment, such as sexual inducements (Buss, 1988).

We are not aware of much research testing these or other theoretically anchored hypotheses about the differential operation of the jealousy program as a function of mating strategy. Of the work that has investigated the relationship between jealousy and sociosexual orientation, much of its focus has been on demonstrating that sex differences in jealousy are robust after controlling for this individual difference variable (e.g., Brase et al., 2014; Bendixen et al., 2015). Moreover, existing studies have produced inconsistent results with respect to the relationship between mating strategy and jealousy. Treger and Sprecher (2011) found that an orientation toward short-term mating was associated with *greater* distress to infidelity, whereas Russell and Harton (2005) found no relationship between sociosexual orientation and jealousy. We hope to see future hypothesis-driven investigations into the relationship between mating strategy and the operation of the jealousy program, including research that tests for individual differences in the deployment of specific mate-retention tactics as a function of sociosexual orientation (see also Al-Shawaf, Lewis, et al., 2015; Al-Shawaf, Lewis, & Buss, 2015, for examples of mating strategy-linked differences in the operation of an emotion). More broadly, we think a key future direction for jealousy research is a growth in focus on the myriad types of mating relationships—not just long-term, monogamous relationships.

Quantitative Variation in the Jealousy Program

The idea that jealousy may operate differently across individuals as a function of their mating strategy points toward the broader question of variation in the parameterization of the jealousy program. Potential proximate causes for such variation include genetic variation, stable situational evocation, and developmental calibration, the latter two of which may produce both between-individual differences and within-individual shifts (see Lewis et al., 2020; see also Lewis, 2015; Lewis et al., 2018; Lukaszewski et al., 2020). For example, people in environments characterized by many mating rivals (e.g., females in an environment with a female-biased operational sex ratio) may have lower thresholds for the activation of jealousy, compared to their counterparts in environments with an abundance of available mates (e.g., females in an environment with a male-biased operational sex ratio). There are also several reasons that individuals may exhibit shifts in the parameterization of the jealousy program. For example, when a person's mate commits infidelity, the program may respond by lowering its threshold for activation, and this effect may even persist into future relationships with other partners (see Burchell & Ward, 2011; Tagler, 2010; Zandbergen & Brown, 2015). Additionally, when one partner is more dependent on the other than usual (e.g., he is ill or injured, she is pregnant or has just given birth) (see Marlowe, 2003), they may exhibit heightened sensitivity (e.g., lower thresholds for jealousy activation). We eagerly await future research testing these and other hypotheses about between- and within-individual variation in jealousy.

Conclusion

Much is already known about jealousy, but a great deal of work remains in order to achieve a comprehensive understanding of this emotion. An important goal should be to identify jealousy's information-processing and behavior-coordinating design features at different stages of addressing the problem of relationship threat. Gaps in current knowledge exist with respect to (1) the information-acquisition features of jealousy in the early stages of detecting and appraising the threat, (2) the differential deployment of distinct mate-retention tactics as a function of distinct forms of threat, and (3) the information-processing architecture of the algorithms involved in the decision to terminate or attempt to restore a relationship after infidelity is discovered.

Major strides have been made toward understanding how jealousy works in *long-term monogamous mateships*, but much less is known about jealousy in other mating relationships (e.g., "friends with benefits" relationships, CNM relationships). Even more broadly, future work is needed to better understand how jealousy operates across other relationship types beyond mating, including friendships and family relationships (e.g., competition among siblings over parental resources).

Finally, there is robust evidence of sex differences in jealousy, but sex differences are just a small subset of between-individual differences. Many individual difference variables, such as sociosexual orientation, may shift the costs and benefits of jealousy. If so, then we might expect to observe variation in the jealousy program's parameterization (e.g., activation threshold) and behavioral outputs (e.g., specific mate-retention tactics) as a function of these individual difference variables. The same logic applies to *within*-individual changes in jealousy over time. Changing environments, critical life events, and changes in the adaptive problems that individuals face at different stages of the lifespan may be associated with ongoing developmental calibration of the jealousy system.

In short, much is known about jealousy, and much remains to be discovered. We hope this chapter makes a modest contribution toward the continued progress of research on this important human emotion. If the progress made in the first decades of its investigation is any indication of the progress that will be made in the forthcoming years, then we can expect many exciting new developments and discoveries to come.

References

Al-Shawaf, L. (2016a). Could there be a male commitment skepticism bias and a female sexual overperception bias? Novel hypotheses based on Error Management Theory. *Evolutionary Psychological Science*, 2(3), 237–240.

Al-Shawaf, L. (2016b). The evolutionary psychology of hunger. *Appetite*, 105, 591–595.

Al-Shawaf, L., Conroy-Beam, D., Asao, K., & Buss, D. M. (2016). Human emotions: An evolutionary psychological perspective. *Emotion Review*, 8(2), 173–186.

Al-Shawaf, L., & Lewis, D. M. G. (2017). Evolutionary psychology and the emotions. In V. Zeigler-Hill, & T. K. Shackelford (Eds.), *Encyclopedia of personality and individual differences* (pp. 1452–1461). Springer.

Al-Shawaf, L., Lewis, D. M. G., Alley, T. R., & Buss, D. M. (2015). Mating strategy, disgust, and food neophobia. *Appetite*, 85, 30–35.

Al-Shawaf, L., Lewis, D. M. G., Barbaro, N., & Wehbe, Y. S. (2021). The products of evolution: conceptual distinctions, evidentiary criteria, and empirical examples. In T. K. Shackelford (Ed.), *SAGE Handbook of Evolutionary Psychology* (pp. 70–95). Sage.

Al-Shawaf, L., Lewis, D. M. G., & Buss, D. M. (2015). Disgust and mating strategy. *Evolution and Human Behavior*, 36(3), 199–205.

Al-Shawaf, L., Lewis, D. M. G., Wehbe, Y. S., & Buss, D. M. (2019). Context, environment, and learning in evolutionary psychology. In T. K. Shackelford, & V. A. Weekes-Shackelford (Eds.), *Encyclopedia of evolutionary psychological science* (pp. 1–12). Springer.

Andrews, P. W., Gangestad, S. W., Miller, G. F., Haselton, M. G., Thornhill, R., & Neale, M. C. (2008). Sex differences in detecting sexual infidelity. *Human Nature*, 19(4), 347–373.

Atari, M., Barbaro, N., Sela, Y., Shackelford, T. K., & Chegeni, R. (2017). The Big Five personality dimensions and mate retention behaviors in Iran. *Personality and Individual Differences*, 104, 286–290.

Atari, M., Barbaro, N., Shackelford, T. K., & Chegeni, R. (2017). Psychometric evaluation and cultural correlates of the Mate Retention Inventory–short form (MRI-SF) in Iran. *Evolutionary Psychology*, 15(1), 1–11.

Balconi, M., & Fronda, G. (2020). The "gift effect" on functional brain connectivity: Inter-brain synchronization when prosocial behavior is in action. *Scientific Reports*, 10(1), 1–10.

Barbaro, N., Pham, M. N., & Shackelford, T. K. (2015). Solving the problem of partner infidelity: Individual mate retention, coalitional mate retention, and in-pair copulation frequency. *Personality and Individual Differences*, 82, 67–71.

Barbaro, N., Pham, M. N., Shackelford, T. K., & Zeigler-Hill, V. (2016). Insecure romantic attachment dimensions and frequency of mate retention behaviors. *Personal Relationships*, 23(3), 605–618.

Barbaro, N., Sela, Y., Atari, M., Shackelford, T. K., & Zeigler-Hill, V. (2019). Romantic attachment and mate retention behavior: The mediating role of perceived risk of partner infidelity. *Journal of Social and Personal Relationships*, 36(3), 940–956.

Barbaro, N., Weidmann, R., Burriss, R. P., Wünsche, J., Bühler, J. L., Shackelford, T. K., & Grob, A. (2021). The (bidirectional) associations between romantic attachment orientations and mate retention behavior in male-female romantic couples. *Evolution and Human Behavior*, 42(6), 497–506.

Barelds, D. P., & Barelds-Dijkstra, P. (2007). Relations between different types of jealousy and self and partner perceptions of relationship quality. *Clinical Psychology & Psychotherapy*, 14(3), 176–188.

Becker, D. V., Sagarin, B. J., Guadagno, R. E., Millevoi, A., & Nicastle, L. D. (2004). When the sexes need not differ: Emotional responses to the sexual and emotional aspects of infidelity. *Personal Relationships*, 11(4), 529–538.

Belk, R. W., & Coon, G. S. (1993). Gift giving as agapic love: An alternative to the exchange paradigm based on dating experiences. *Journal of Consumer Research*, 20(3), 393–417.

Bendixen, M., Kennair, L. E. O., & Buss, D. M. (2015). Jealousy: Evidence of strong sex differences using both forced choice and continuous measure paradigms. *Personality and Individual Differences*, 86, 212–216.

Bendixen, M., Kennair, L. E. O., & Grøntvedt, T. V. (2018). Forgiving the unforgivable: Couples' forgiveness and expected forgiveness of emotional and sexual infidelity from an error management theory perspective. *Evolutionary Behavioral Sciences*, 12(4), 322–335.

Betzig, L. (1989). Causes of conjugal dissolution: A cross-cultural study. *Current Anthropology*, 30(5), 654–676.

Brase, G. L., Adair, L., & Monk, K. (2014). Explaining sex differences in reactions to relationship infidelities: Comparisons of the roles of sex, gender, beliefs, attachment, and sociosexual orientation. *Evolutionary Psychology*, 12(1), 73–96.

Buckle, L., Gallup, G. G., Jr., & Rodd, Z. A. (1996). Marriage as a reproductive contract: Patterns of marriage, divorce, and remarriage. *Ethology & Sociobiology*, 17(6), 363–377.

Burchell, J. L., & Ward, J. (2011). Sex drive, attachment style, relationship status and previous infidelity as predictors of sex differences in romantic jealousy. *Personality and Individual Differences*, 51(5), 657–661.

Buss, D. M. (1988). From vigilance to violence: Tactics of mate retention in American undergraduates. *Ethology and Sociobiology, 9*(5), 291–317.

Buss, D. M. (1989). Sex differences in human mate preferences: Evolutionary hypotheses tested in 37 cultures. *Behavioral and Brain Sciences, 12*(1), 1–14.

Buss, D. M. (2000). *The dangerous passion: Why jealousy is as necessary as love and sex*. Bloomsbury.

Buss, D. M. (2013). Sexual jealousy. *Psychological Topics, 22*(2), 155–182.

Buss, D. M., Larsen, R. J., Westen, D., & Semmelroth, J. (1992). Sex differences in jealousy: Evolution, physiology, and psychology. *Psychological Science, 3*(4), 251–256.

Buss, D. M., & Shackelford, T.K. (1997). From vigilance to violence: Mate retention tactics in married couples. *Journal of Personality and Social Psychology, 72*(2), 346–361.

Chaudhary, N., Al-Shawaf, L., & Buss, D. M. (2018). Mate competition in Pakistan: Mate value, mate retention, and competitor derogation. *Personality and Individual Differences, 130,* 141–146.

Cole, T. (2001). Lying to the one you love: The use of deception in romantic relationships. *Journal of Social and Personal Relationships, 18*(1), 107–129.

Daly, M., Wilson, M., & Weghorst, S. J. (1982). Male sexual jealousy. *Ethology and Sociobiology, 3*(1), 11–27.

Davis, A. C., Desrochers, J., DiFilippo, A., Vaillancourt, T., Arnocky, S. (2018). Type of jealousy differentially predicts cost-inflicting and benefit-provisioning mate retention. *Personal Relationships, 25*(4), 596–610.

DeScioli, P., & Kurzban, R. (2009). The alliance hypothesis for human friendship. *PloS ONE, 4*(6), e5802.

Dijkstra, P., & Buunk, B. P. (1998). Jealousy as a function of rival characteristics: An evolutionary perspective. *Personality and Social Psychology Bulletin, 24*(11), 1158–1166.

Dijkstra, P., & Buunk, B. P. (2002). Sex differences in the jealousy-evoking effect of rival characteristics. *European Journal of Social Psychology, 32*(6), 829–852.

Edlund, J. E., Heider, J. D., Scherer, C. R., Farc, M. M., & Sagarin, B. J. (2006). Sex differences in jealousy in response to actual infidelity. *Evolutionary Psychology, 4*(1), 462–470.

Frederick, D. A., & Haselton, M. G. (2007). Why is muscularity sexy? Tests of the fitness indicator hypothesis. *Personality & Social Psychology Bulletin, 33*(8), 1167–1183.

Gangestad, S. W., & Simpson, J. A. (2000). The evolution of human mating: Trade-offs and strategic pluralism. *Behavioral and Brain Sciences, 23*(4), 573–587.

Goetz, A. T., & Causey, K. (2009). Sex differences in perceptions of infidelity: Men often assume the worst. *Evolutionary Psychology, 7*(2), 253–263.

Goetz, A. T., Shackelford, T. K., Weekes-Shackelford, V. A., Euler, H. A., Hoier, S., Schmitt, D. P., & LaMunyon, C. W. (2005). Mate retention, semen displacement, and human sperm competition: A preliminary investigation of tactics to prevent and correct female infidelity. *Personality and Individual Differences, 38*(4), 749–763.

Hart, S. L. (2018). Jealousy and attachment: Adaptations to threat posed by the birth of a sibling. *Evolutionary Behavioral Sciences, 12*(4), 263–275.

Haselton, M. G., & Buss, D. M. (2000). Error Management Theory: A new perspective on biases in cross-sex mind reading. *Journal of Personality and Social Psychology, 78*(1), 81–91.

Hurtado, A. M., & Hill, K. R. (1992). Paternal effect on offspring survivorship among Ache and Hiwi hunter-gatherers: Implications for modeling pair-bond stability. In B. S. Hewlett (Ed.), *Father-child relations: Cultural and biosocial contexts* (pp. 31–55). Aldine de Gruyter.

Krems, J. A., Williams, K. E., Aktipis, A., & Kenrick, D. T. (2021). Friendship jealousy: One tool for maintaining friendships in the face of third-party threats? *Journal of Personality and Social Psychology, 120*(4), 977–1012.

Kruger, D. J., Fisher, M. L., Edelstein, R. S., Chopik, W. J., Fitzgerald, C. J., & Strout, S. L. (2013). Was that cheating? Perceptions vary by sex, attachment anxiety, and behavior. *Evolutionary Psychology, 11*(1), 159–171.

Kuhle, B. X. (2011). Did you have sex with him? Do you love her? An in vivo test of sex differences in jealous interrogations. *Personality and Individual Differences, 51*(8), 1044–1047.

Kuhle, B. X., Smedley, K. D., & Schmitt, D. P. (2009). Sex differences in the motivation and mitigation of jealousy-induced interrogations. *Personality and Individual Differences, 46*(4), 499–502.

Lawler, E. J., Koon, J., Baker, M. R., & Large, M. D. (1994). Mutual dependence and gift giving in exchange relations. In B. Markovsky, K. Heimer, & J. O'Brien (Eds.), *Advances in group processes* (Vol. 12, pp. 271–298). JAI Press.

Lewis, D. M. G. (2013). *Individual differences and universal condition-dependent mechanisms*. Doctoral dissertation, University of Texas at Austin. UT Electronic Theses and Dissertations. http://hdl.handle.net/2152/21305

Lewis, D. M. G. (2015). Evolved individual differences: Advancing a condition-dependent model of personality. *Personality and Individual Differences, 84,* 63–72.

Lewis, D. M. G., Al-Shawaf, L., & Buss, D. M. (2020). Evolutionary personality psychology. In P. Corr & G. Matthews (Eds.), *The Cambridge handbook of personality psychology* (2nd ed., pp. 223–234). Cambridge University Press.

Lewis, D. M. G., Al-Shawaf, L., Conroy-Beam, D., Asao, K., & Buss, D. M. (2012). Friends with benefits II: Mating activation in opposite-sex friendships as a function of sociosexual orientation and relationship status. *Personality and Individual Differences, 53*, 622–628.

Lewis, D. M. G., Al-Shawaf, L., Conroy-Beam, D., Asao, K., & Buss, D. M. (2017). Evolutionary psychology: A how-to guide. *American Psychologist, 72*(4), 353–373.

Lewis, D. M. G., Al-Shawaf, L., Janiak, M. C., & Akunebu, S. P. (2018). Integrating molecular genetics and evolutionary psychology: Sexual jealousy and the androgen receptor (AR) gene. *Personality and Individual Differences, 120*, 276–282.

Lewis, D. M. G., Al-Shawaf, L., Semchenko, A. Y., & Evans, K. C. (2022). Error management theory and biased first impressions: How do people perceive potential mates under conditions of uncertainty? *Evolution and Human Behavior, 43*(2), 87–96.

Lewis, D. M. G., Al-Shawaf, L., Thompson, M. B., & Buss, D. M. (2021). Evolved psychological mechanisms. In T. K. Shackleford (Ed.), *The SAGE handbook of evolutionary psychology: Foundations of evolutionary psychology* (pp. 96–119). Sage Reference.

Lewis, D. M. G., & Buss, D. M. (2021). The evolution of human personality. In O. P. John & R. W. Robins (Eds.), *Handbook of personality: Theory and Research* (pp. 3–34). Guilford Press.

Lewis, D. M. G., Conroy-Beam, D., Al-Shawaf, L., Raja, A., DeKay, T., & Buss, D. M. (2011). Friends with benefits: The evolved psychology of same- and opposite-sex friendship. *Evolutionary Psychology, 9*, 543–563.

Lewis, D. M. G., Evans, K. C., & Al-Shawaf, L. (2023). The logic of physical attractiveness: What people find attractive, when, and why. In D. M. Buss (Ed.), *The Oxford handbook of human mating* (pp. 178–205). Oxford University Press.

Lewis, D. M. G., Lukaszewski, A. W., Durkee, P. K., Sell, A. N., Sznycer, D., Buss, D. M., & Al-Shawaf, L. (2023). An adaptationist framework for personality science: Jealousy as a worked example. [Manuscript in preparation]. School of Psychology, Murdoch University.

Li, N. P., Bailey, J. M., Kenrick, D. T., & Linsenmeier, J. A. (2002). The necessities and luxuries of mate preferences: Testing the tradeoffs. *Journal of Personality and Social Psychology, 82*(6), 947–955.

Lukaszewski, A. W., Lewis, D. M. G., Durkee, P. K., Sell, A. N., Sznycer, D., & Buss, D. M. (2020). An adaptationist framework for personality science. *European Journal of Personality, 34*(6), 1151–1174.

Marlowe, F. W. (2003). A critical period for provisioning by Hadza men: Implications for pair bonding. *Evolution and Human Behavior, 24*(3), 217–229.

McKibbin, W. F., Miner, E. J., Shackelford, T. K., Ehrke, A. D., & Weekes-Shackelford, V. A. (2014). Men's mate retention varies with men's personality and their partner's personality. *Personality and Individual Differences, 56*, 62–67.

Miner, E. J., Shackelford, T. K., & Starratt, V. G. (2009). Mate value of romantic partners predicts men's partner-directed verbal insults. *Personality and Individual Differences, 46*(2), 135–139.

Miner, E. J., Starratt, V. G., & Shackelford, T. K. (2009). It's not all about her: Men's mate value and mate retention. *Personality and Individual Differences, 47*(3), 214–218.

Mogilski, J. K., Reeve, S. D., Nicolas, S. C., Donaldson, S. H., Mitchell, V. E., & Welling, L. L. (2019). Jealousy, consent, and compersion within monogamous and consensually non-monogamous romantic relationships. *Archives of Sexual Behavior, 48*(6), 1811–1828.

Moors, A. C., Matsick, J. L., & Schechinger, H. A. (2017). Unique and shared relationship benefits of consensually non-monogamous and monogamous relationships. *European Psychologist, 22*(1), 55–71.

Nascimento, B. S., Little, A. C., Monteiro, R. P., Hanel, P. H., & Vione, K. C. (2021). Attachment styles and mate-retention: Exploring the mediating role of relationship satisfaction. *Evolutionary Behavioral Sciences, 16*(4), 362–370.

Pham, M. N., Barbaro, N., Mogilski, J. K., & Shackelford, T. K. (2015). Coalitional mate retention is correlated positively with friendship quality involving women, but negatively with male-male friendship quality. *Personality and Individual Differences, 79*, 87–90.

Pham, M. N., Barbaro, N., & Shackelford, T. K. (2015). Development and initial validation of the coalitional mate retention inventory. *Evolutionary Psychological Science, 1*(1), 4–12.

Phillips, A. (2010). Indignation or insecurity: The influence of mate value on distress in response to infidelity. *Evolutionary Psychology, 8*(4), 736–750.

Pietraszewski, D., & Wertz, A. E. (2022). Why evolutionary psychology should abandon modularity. *Perspectives on Psychological Science, 17*(2), 465–490.

Pietrzak, R. H., Laird, J. D., Stevens, D. A., & Thompson, N. S. (2002). Sex differences in human jealousy: A coordinated study of forced-choice, continuous rating-scale, and physiological responses on the same subjects. *Evolution and Human Behavior, 23*(2), 83–94.

Pollet, T. V., & Saxton, T. K. (2020). Jealousy as a function of rival characteristics: Two large replication studies and meta-analyses support gender differences in reactions to rival attractiveness but not dominance. *Personality and Social Psychology Bulletin, 46*(10), 1428–1443.

Russell, E. M., Babcock, M. J., Lewis, D. M. G, Ta, V. P., & Ickes, W. (2018). Why attractive women want gay male friends: A previously undiscovered strategy to prevent mating deception and sexual exploitation. *Personality and Individual Differences, 120*, 283–287.

Russell, E. B., & Harton, H. C. (2005). The "other factors": Using individual and relationship characteristics to predict sexual and emotional jealousy. *Current Psychology, 24*(4), 242–257.

Russell, E. M., Ta, V. P., Lewis, D. M. G., Babcock, M. J., & Ickes, W. (2017). Why (and when) straight women trust gay men: Ulterior mating motives and female competition. *Archives of Sexual Behavior, 46*(3), 763–773.

Scelza, B. A., Prall, S. P., Blumenfield, T., Crittenden, A. N., Gurven, M., Kline, M., Koster, J., Kushnick, G., Mattison, S. M., Pillsworth, E., Shenk, M. K., Starkweather, K., Stieglitz, J., Sum, C., Yamaguchi, K., & McElreath, R. (2020). Patterns of paternal investment predict cross-cultural variation in jealous response. *Nature Human Behaviour, 4*(1), 20–26.

Schützwohl, A. (2006). Sex differences in jealousy: Information search and cognitive preoccupation. *Personality and Individual Differences, 40*(2), 285–292.

Schützwohl, A. (2008). Relief over the disconfirmation of the prospect of sexual and emotional infidelity. *Personality and Individual Differences, 44*(3), 668–678.

Schützwohl, A., Joshi, N., & Abdur-Razak, F. (2019). Competitor derogation in romantic jealousy and friendship rivalry. *Evolutionary Behavioral Sciences, 16*(1), 14–22.

Sell, A. N. (2005). *Regulating welfare tradeoff ratios: Three tests of an evolutionary-computational model of human anger*. Doctoral dissertation, University of California. Publication No. 3186820. Proquest Dissertations.

Sell, A. N. (2011). The recalibrational theory and violent anger. *Aggression and Violent Behavior, 16*(5), 381–389.

Sell, A., Hone, L. S., & Pound, N. (2012). The importance of physical strength to human males. *Human Nature, 23*(1), 30–44.

Sell, A., Lukazsweski, A. W., & Townsley, M. (2017). Cues of upper body strength account for most of the variance in men's bodily attractiveness. *Proceedings of the Royal Society B: Biological Sciences, 284*(1869), 20171819.

Sell, A., Sznycer, D., Al-Shawaf, L., Lim, J., Krauss, A., Feldman, A., Rascanu, R., Sugiyama, L., Cosmides, L., & Tooby, J. (2017). The grammar of anger: Mapping the computational architecture of a recalibrational emotion. *Cognition, 168*, 110–128.

Sell, A., Tooby, J., & Cosmides, L. (2009). Formidability and the logic of human anger. *Proceedings of the National Academy of Science, 106*(35), 15073–15078.

Shackelford, T. (2003). Preventing, correcting, and anticipating female infidelity: Three adaptive problems of sperm competition. *Evolution and Cognition, 9*(1), 90–96.

Shackelford, T. K., & Buss, D. M. (1997a). Anticipation of marital dissolution as a consequence of spousal infidelity. *Journal of Social and Personal Relationships, 14*(6), 793–808.

Shackelford, T. K., & Buss, D. M. (1997b). Cues to infidelity. *Personality and Social Psychology Bulletin, 23*(10), 1034–1045.

Shackelford, T. K., Buss, D. M., & Bennett, K. (2002). Forgiveness or breakup: Sex differences in responses to a partner's infidelity. *Cognition & Emotion, 16*(2), 299–307.

Shackelford, T. K., Goetz, A. T., & Buss, D. M. (2005). Mate retention and marriage: Further evidence of the reliability of the Mate Retention Inventory. *Personality and Individual Differences, 39*, 415–426.

Shackelford, T. K., LeBlanc, G. J., & Drass, E. (2000). Emotional reactions to infidelity. *Cognition & Emotion, 14*(5), 643–659.

Shaw, A., DeScioli, P., Barakzai, A., & Kurzban, R. (2017). Whoever is not with me is against me: The costs of neutrality among friends. *Journal of Experimental Social Psychology, 71*, 96–104.

Symons, D. (1979). *The evolution of human sexuality*. Oxford University Press.

Sznycer, D. (2010). *Cognitive adaptations for calibrating welfare tradeoff motivations, with special reference to the emotion of shame*. Doctoral dissertation, University of California, Santa Barbara. Publication No. 3439655. Proquest Dissertations.

Sznycer, D. (2019). Forms and functions of the self-conscious emotions. *Trends in Cognitive Sciences, 23*(2), 143–157.

Sznycer, D., Al-Shawaf, L., Bereby-Meyer, Y., Curry, O. S., De Smet, D., Ermer, E., Kim, S., Kim, S., Li, N. P., Seal, M. F. L, McClung, J., Jiaqing, O., Ohtsubo, Y., Quillien, T., Schaub, M., Sell, A., van Leeuwen, F., Cosmides, L., & Tooby, J. (2017). Cross-cultural regularities in the cognitive architecture of pride. *Proceedings of the National Academy of Sciences, 114*(8), 1874–1879.

Sznycer, D., & Cohen, A. S. (2021a). Are emotions natural kinds after all? Rethinking the issue of response coherence. *Evolutionary Psychology, 19*(2), 1–17.

Sznycer, D., & Cohen, A. S. (2021b). How pride works. *Evolutionary Human Sciences, 3*, e10.

Sznycer, D., Takemura, K., Delton, A. W., Sato, K., Robertson, T., Cosmides, L., & Tooby, J. (2012). Cross-cultural differences and similarities in proneness to shame: An adaptationist and ecological approach. *Evolutionary Psychology, 10*(2), 352–370.

Sznycer, D., Tooby, J., Cosmides, L., Porat, R., Shalvi, S., & Halperin, E. (2016). Shame closely tracks the threat of devaluation by others, even across cultures. *Proceedings of the National Academy of Sciences, 113*(10), 2625–2630.

Sznycer, D., Xygalatas, D., Alami, S., An, X. F., Ananyeva, K. I., Fukushima, S., Hitokoro, H., Kharitonov, A. N., Koster, J. M., Onyishi, C. N., Onyishi, I. E., Romero, P. P., Takemura, K., Zhuang, J., Cosmides, L., & Tooby, J. (2018). Invariances in the architecture of pride across small-scale societies. *Proceedings of the National Academy of Sciences, 115*(33), 8322–8327.

Tagler, M. J. (2010). Sex differences in jealousy: Comparing the influence of previous infidelity among college students and adults. *Social Psychological and Personality Science, 1*(4), 353–360.

Takahashi, H., Matsuura, M., Yahata, N., Koeda, M., Suhara, T., & Okubo, Y. (2006). Men and women show distinct brain activations during imagery of sexual and emotional infidelity. *NeuroImage, 32*(3), 1299–1307.

Thornton, V., & Nagurney, A. (2011). What is infidelity? Perceptions based on biological sex and personality. *Psychology Research and Behavior Management, 4*, 51–58.

Tooby, J., & Cosmides, L. (1990). The past explains the present: Emotional adaptations and the structure of ancestral environments. *Ethology and Sociobiology, 11*, 375–424.

Tooby, J., & Cosmides, L. (1992). The psychological foundations of culture. In J. Barkow, L. Cosmides, & J. Tooby (Eds.), *The adapted mind: Evolutionary psychology and the generation of culture* (pp. 1–72). Oxford University Press.

Treger, S., & Sprecher, S. (2011). The influences of sociosexuality and attachment style on reactions to emotional versus sexual infidelity. *Journal of Sex Research, 48*(5), 413–422.

Valentova, J. V., de Moraes, A. C., & Varella, M. A. C. (2020). Gender, sexual orientation and type of relationship influence individual differences in jealousy: A large Brazilian sample. *Personality and Individual Differences, 157*, 109805.

Williams, G. C. (1966). *Adaptation and natural selection: A critique of some current evolutionary thought*. Princeton University Press.

Wilson, M. I., & Daly, M. (1996). Male sexual proprietariness and violence against wives. *Current Directions in Psychological Science, 5*(1), 2–7.

Zandbergen, D. L., & Brown, S. G. (2015). Culture and gender differences in romantic jealousy. *Personality and Individual Differences, 72*, 122–127.

CHAPTER 22

Chronic Pain, Recuperation, and Care-Eliciting: Evolutionary and Signaling Theory Perspectives

Christopher H. Cantor and Kenneth D. Craig

> **Abstract**
> This chapter explores evidence suggesting an adaptive basis for chronic pain and the conceptual implications. A literature review included: human pain, animal pain across species, caregiving, cooperation, evolutionary theory, and signaling theory. Traditional models of chronic pain focus on proximal features rather than distal origins. Evolutionary perspectives emphasize pain's late recuperative stage involving interactions between helpers and sufferers. Species vary in care-eliciting/caregiving behaviors, with some being biologically prepared to help, while others ignore injured conspecifics. Cooperation, the foundation of caregiving, evolved through diverse mechanisms. Research highlights communication and coping aspects of pain behavior, with signaling theory and cost-benefit perspectives adding new dimensions. If chronic pain evolved promoting care-elicitation to facilitate recuperation it may have been ancestrally adaptive. Understanding chronic pain in the social contexts of patients' lives provides greater understanding than viewing patients as displaying abnormal pain behaviors.
>
> **Key Words:** chronic pain, evolution, across species, signaling theory, cooperation, caregiving

Introduction

It is widely accepted that acute pain serves adaptive functions, despite relative ignorance about its evolution (Walters & Williams, 2019). Acute pain typically is rapidly responsive to tissue damage, has a relatively short time course, ranging from seconds and hours to perhaps days and weeks before waning, and supports escape and future avoidance of bodily danger. There are evolved continuities between invertebrates and vertebrates, and contemporary mammalian nociceptive systems are remarkably similar to those of fish, with whom they share distant common ancestry (Sneddon, 2019). (Nociception refers to neural structures and responses to noxious stimuli.) In both fish and mammals, noxious events result in behavioral and physiological changes, including changed activity levels, guarding, suspension of normal behaviors, and increased abnormal behaviors, all of which are prevented by administering analgesics.

Pain is closely associated with nociception and is defined by the International Association for the Study of Pain (Raja et al., 2020) as "[a]n unpleasant sensory and emotional experience associated with, or resembling that associated with, actual or potential tissue damage" (p. 1976). Both verbal reports and nonverbal expression are endorsed as assessment approaches; the latter is of particular benefit in recognizing the behavioral changes observed in people with communication limitations (Hadjistavropoulos et al., 2011) and in animal studies (Walters & Williams, 2019).

Pain's emotional component is our focus, emotions being action patterns with functional advantages shaped by natural selection (Marks & Nesse, 1994). Emotions organize and motivate behaviors appropriate to environmental challenges (de Waal, 2011) and promote survival and reproduction (Al-Shawaf et al., 2015; Auvray et al., 2010; Fanselow & Lester 1988). In humans and closely related mammals, emotions complement cognitive capabilities as they correspond to appraisals of the physical and social environments.

Only recently have researchers considered the possibility of chronic pain being adaptive, as to clinicians it appears to provide no apparent protective or recuperative benefits (Walters & Williams, 2019; Williams, 2016). Persistent high levels of suffering and disability would be expected to be eliminated or minimized by natural selection, unless the observed costs were offset by less obvious benefits or were the unavoidable byproducts of other beneficial adaptations.

Consideration of this topic is further confused by pain potentially serving different adaptive functions concurrently—protective and communicative. Even these functions are not singular; for example, communication may warn conspecifics of hazards or may elicit care, the latter being this chapter's focus.

One protective function has been conceptualized by Nesse and Schulkin (2019) in terms of the "smoke detector principle," where the costs of responding unnecessarily may be far less than the cost of not responding when seriously needed. By analogy, the principle dictates both more fire evacuations and more pain will be experienced than are strictly necessary. Similarly, Error Management Theory predicts that if judgments are made under uncertainty, and the costs of false positive and false negative errors have been asymmetric over evolutionary history, selection should have favored a bias toward making the least costly error (e.g., fleeing on hearing an unseen potential predator wastes a little energy, whereas not fleeing may be fatal).

Repeated experiences of pain may also be adaptive by heightening sensitivity, promoting hypervigilance for predators and hostile conspecifics in a hazardous environment (Nesse & Schulkin, 2019; Walters & Williams, 2019). This mirrors Cantor's model of post-traumatic stress disorder representing heightened hypervigilance and activation of mammalian defenses in response to severe threats or actual harm in a perceived hazardous environment (Cantor, 2005, 2009; Cantor & Price, 2007).

Chronic pain may also represent a maladaptive mismatch between pain programming for the ancestral environment and its persistence in a different contemporary environment (Nesse & Schulkin, 2019).

In early simple organisms the sensory and emotional components of pain motivated reflexive and automated survival behaviors, whereas in organisms with more complex nervous systems higher-order cognitive and social capabilities have permitted more complex sociobehavioral adaptations (Williams & Craig, 2016).

While many continuities in pain behaviors are observed across species, dissimilarities suggest species-specific adaptations (Broom, 1998, 2001). Human pain behavior often occurs in social contexts characterized by cooperation, empathy, care-eliciting, and caregiving, especially among kin. However, pain may also bring loss of status and exploitation. Interpersonal aspects of pain behavior originally were conceptualized in operant conditioning terms (Main et al., 2014; Williams, 2002), but subsequently have been substantially elaborated. Communication (Craig, 2015; Hadjistavropoulos et al., 2011; Krahe et al., 2103) and coping aspects of pain have received increased attention (Lumley et al., 2011; Sullivan et al., 2001). Communication requires pain signaling and receiving, but biological signaling theory, which we discuss in detail, has rarely been applied to pain. First, we will turn to pain's phases and their functions.

Phases and Functions of Pain

Episodes of pain unfold over time, beginning with tissue insult in a biologically prepared organism. This is followed by the pain experience, comprising sensations, feelings and thoughts, and behavioral expression of distress with reactions from others (Craig, 2015). With continuing exposure to pain or its persistence, both pain experience and expression may be transformed by sensitization or habituation. Later, complex recuperative efforts will be associated with changes in emotional and behavioral activity (Bolles & Fanselow, 1980; Wall, 1979, 1989).

Historically, most attention has been devoted to the transition from acute to chronic pain (e.g., Glare et al., 2019). Here, pain fails to resolve and dissipate over time, and there typically is continuing pain and suffering, behavioral and social disabilities, and transformations in how the individual interacts with others (Katz & Seltzer, 2014). The understanding of persistence and lack of recovery will benefit from a focus on the late recuperative phase, a stage necessitating protracted transactions with others.

The complexity of a painful event is evident in the initial reaction. Pain is a conscious experience involving perception and interpretation of noxious input, including sensory, emotional, and cognitive features in an immediate social context, as determined by genetic, ancestral, interpersonal, and experiential life history influences. Hence, diverse behavioral and physiological responses can be expected in individual efforts to establish control of pain (Craig et al., 2011; Hadjistavropoulos & Craig 2002).

Along with pain, unexpected tissue insults may evoke fear, the most rapid emotion promoting survival behaviors (Broom, 1998). Pain is not necessarily an immediate consequence of physical trauma. Conscious trauma patients may initially be unaware of potentially fatal injuries and pain (Melzack et al., 1982). Such pain inhibition may be primarily driven by fear (Bolles & Fanselow, 1980). Overt reactions may have both protective and communicative functions, with escaping and obtaining aid the priorities of this acute phase.

Vocalizations—communication with group members—may evoke protection of the injured animal or alert conspecifics to danger (Craig et al., 2010), but carry risks of alerting predators. Darwin (1890) noted that cattle and horses suffered great pain in silence, but when this was excessive or associated with terror, they uttered fearful sounds. Wounded deer may initially run indistinguishably from the unwounded, as the priority is escape, so pain is inhibited (Wall, 1989).

In the ensuing days, injured deer may remain immobile for hours and isolate themselves from the herd (Wall, 1979). Their threshold for disturbance may be raised and they can be approached more closely before moving off, conserving energy despite increased vulnerability to predators and conspecifics.

Though adaptive, protective behaviors carry costs (Walters, 1994). In nonhuman animals they include diversion from hunting/foraging and reproductive behavior, as well as increased vulnerability to predation. As soon as healing suffices, wound monitoring and resumption of normal behavior become key. The costs of immobility would have been greater in ancestral environments where the threats of starvation and predation were greater.

Chronic Pain and Recuperation

While acute pain usually ends with recovery, chronic pain appears associated with an indefinite extension of the protective mechanisms of the recuperative phase. Recuperation involves an adaptive reorganization of the host's homeostatic and behavioral priorities to facilitate immune responses, protective mechanisms, and survival.

Recuperation facilitates healing and involves illness behavior, including cognitive, affective, and behavioral features. Lassitude, psychomotor retardation, impaired memory, confusion, decreased motivation, anxiety and depression, loss of libido, menstrual disturbances, disturbed sleep patterns, and altered social relationships may occur (Brydon et al., 2008; Schrock et al., 2020; Wall, 1979). Similarly, recuperating injured macaque monkeys rest and groom more, forage less, and initiate fewer aggressive interactions (Dittus & Ratnayeke, 1989).

Hyperalgesia (heightened pain perception and focus) during the recuperative phase may inhibit fear (Walters, 1994) and is often accompanied by allodynia (pain provoked by a stimulus that does not normally provoke pain). Both of these features often develop well after the injury and facilitate wound protection.

Sickness behavior involves an immune system–to-brain communication (Vollmer-Conna, 2001). Malaise during chronic pain serves the immunological response, as lethargy conserves energy for fighting pathogens and tissue repair (Broom, 1998). Resting also is adaptive because sleep deprivation and excess activity can reduce immunological responses and waste energy needed for other biological processes.

The impacts of these biological mechanisms and pain behaviors on social functioning are important, but have received less attention. Social support from conspecifics may facilitate recuperative mechanisms (Broom, 2006), but incapacity and sick role behavior reduce the animal's hierarchical social status (de Waal, 1998). This reduced capacity may increase vulnerability and dependency on others. Animals may disguise debilitation, as vulnerability increases risks of predation and exploitation by conspecifics. Vulnerability does not automatically elicit support and care from others.

Humans manifesting chronic pain may be subjected to systematic stigma and debilitating consequences (De Ruddere & Craig, 2016). The reduced costs of chronic pain in caring modern human communities, compared with the ancestral environment, may paradoxically fuel its continuation in what has been described as "the pain of altruism" (Finlay 2019). The reduced likelihood of starvation, predation, and serious exploitation in modern communities may permit and/or drive more intense pain experiences.

Species-Specific Pain Behavior
How similar are human and nonhuman pain experiences? If humans and nonhuman animals respond similarly to comparable situations, parsimony suggests that their emotional and other experiences may be similar (de Waal, 2011). Dissimilar responses suggest the reverse. While words are convenient for pain communication, they are not essential, and pain in animals can be inferred from shared nonverbal behavioral responses (Mogil & Crager, 2004), as is accepted for human infant research (Grunau & Craig, 1987).

Nociception is widely represented throughout the animal world, with its antecedents likely reflected in the tropisms of unicellular organisms (Broom, 1998). Bateson (1991) noted many similarities in nociceptive systems between nonhuman animals and humans. Physiological similarities include: receptors sensitive to noxious stimuli located in functionally useful positions; neural pathways connecting nociceptive receptors to the brain; central nervous system (CNS) opioid receptors; brain structures analogous to those in the human cerebrum; and analgesics modifying responses to noxious stimuli. Broom (1998) described nociception as occurring in all vertebrates studied, including fish (which possess nociceptive processing systems similar to those of terrestrial vertebrates), as well as nervous systems displaying the capacity for fear and suffering (Broom, 2007; Chervova, 2000) and long-term memory (Braithwaite & Boulcott, 2007).

Injury-related behavior remains subject to strong selection pressures that have been present since the dawn of animal life (Walters, 1994). Adaptative genotypes and phenotypes tend to be conserved over evolutionary time. Survival behaviors that protect from physical harm would have been essential even in the earliest, least complex organisms. New patterns of responses would be added to those already available, depending upon functional success. Thus, commonalities are expected in the course of phylogenetic evolution, along with dissimilarities reflecting specific environmental demands. Automatic reaction patterns would be expected in simple animals, whereas a flexible capacity for inhibition and control of responses would be expected in more complex organisms.

Walters (1991) described three pain phases in *Aplysia* (marine snails) of injury detection, escape, and recuperation—similar to human phasic responses. With severe injuries, *Aplysia* may show little activity for several days, but if touched during this time, especially near the wounds, they have low thresholds for escape. Hypersensitivity around the injury is important for survival, as wounds may leak substances attracting predators and parasites. Persistent sensitization of nociceptors in *Aplysia* displays many similarities to nociceptive changes in chronic pain in mammals (Walters & Moroz, 2009).

Behavioral similarities across taxa are readily evident (Dawkins, 1990; Mogil, 2015; Mogil & Crager, 2004). Common responses to noxious stimuli include nociceptive withdrawal reflexes, vocalization, facial expressions, posturing (e.g., cowering), locomotion (e.g., flight) and affective responses (e.g., depression) (Mellor et al., 2000). These support escape and avoidance, or efforts to minimize damage to the body; inhibition of behaviors incompatible with escape (e.g., feeding); and a capacity to associate neutral contextual events with noxious stimuli via learning. Active defense typically is followed by prolonged immobility and enhanced vigilance (Walters & Moroz, 2009). Some actions extend beyond intrapersonal functions to signal danger and/or the need for help from conspecifics. Facial expressions demonstrate substantial continuity in pain display across species, from mice (Langford, Bailey, et al., 2010) to horses (Chambers & Mogil, 2015; Mogil et al., 2020; van Rysewyk, 2016).

Discontinuities within and across species in behavioral expression during pain typically represent adaptations to unique environmental niches. Different species display different survival strategies for dealing with injuries. Mellor et al. (2000) concluded that there were greater interspecies than intraspecies variations in pain behaviors. The dominance of medical/laboratory settings in pain research in the absence of evolutionarily relevant contexts has been a major shortcoming of pain expression research (Schmidt, 2002).

The social contexts of animals' lives are often reflected in unique adaptations. Humans, like other large primates and many mammalian species, live socially and often help conspecifics when attacked by predators or conspecifics (Broom & Fraser, 2007). However, many species do not help injured conspecifics. Further, there has been a dearth of research into rescue behavior in the wild, and such behavior is likely to be far more prevalent than current reports suggest (Nowbahari & Hollis, 2010). Pain behaviors will differ depending on contextual characteristics, such as whether observers are predators, conspecific strangers, social group members or family, or human pain researchers. Pain vocalization and other pain communication behaviors seem advantageous for social species in eliciting care from helpful conspecifics, but disadvantageous (e.g., attracting predators) for prey species that do not help injured conspecifics, such as sheep and antelope.

Small cats are vulnerable not only to predators but to conspecific rivals that may exploit any incapacity to protect their territory, so their capacity to conceal injury appears to be an evolved strategy, unlike more socially gregarious dogs, who may be assisted by their packs (Dwyer, 2004).

Dogs with abdominal pains may arch their backs; sheep with foot rot may kneel (Broom, 2006); and guinea pigs squeal urgently and repetitively, but rarely show aggression, while rats squeal but also become aggressive (Mench & Mason, 1997). Young pigs, dogs, and humans make considerable noise when hurt, but young sheep do not (Broom, 1998). Wild sheep rarely vocalize during acute injuries, and vocalization appears particularly inhibited in situations with high predation risk (Dwyer, 2004).

Domestic sheep show little or no response to mulesing surgery to reduce fly-strike, in which sheep are held upside down in holding frames and large areas of perianal skin are excised. They often remain silent and walk away, yet sheep physiological and nonverbal behavioral responses to tissue damage are similar to other mammals, and subsequently they may avoid situations in which the damage occurred. It is extremely likely that they feel pain, even though they show little behavioral response (Broom, 1998).

Although less inclined to signal injury than many other farm animals, domesticated sheep are more vocal than wild sheep (Stilwell et al., 2007), possibly as the predatorial selection pressure against vocalization has been reduced in domestic sheep. Domestic sheep may vocalize when socially isolated and at feeding time, but not in the presence of a tethered dog, mirroring the behavior of wild sheep in the presence of predators. Lambs tend to be less recumbent after genital/ring tailing when near dogs (potential predators) (Mellor et al., 2000).

Cattle also conceal vulnerability (Stilwell et al., 2007). Ungulates in loosely organized herds tend to respond indifferently to or avoid sick conspecifics (Hart, 1990). A horse with a broken leg may graze normally (Broom, 1998), although facial expressions may disclose pain experiences (Chambers & Mogil, 2015).

Cost-benefit scenarios differ when injuries occur after a prey animal has been detected by a predator. During ongoing attacks, when silence is no longer helpful, vocalization may martial assistance. Horses, often silent when injured, uttered loud and peculiar vocalizations when attacked by wolves (Broom, 1998). Even in species that do not help conspecifics, loud vocalization when attacked by predators may be adaptive by scaring predators into aborting attacks or for warning kin.

Monkeys, normally noisy, are mostly quiet giving birth, when they are at increased risk from predators (Bateson, 1991). This contrasts with human labor pain vocalization, possibly because helpers improve maternal and infant survival (Finlay, 2019). Many primates often show remarkably little reaction to surgical procedures or to trauma. Indeed, primates often mask signs of pain, to avoid becoming targets for predators and to reduce loss of social rank associated with injury (Plesk & Mayer, 2008).

Humans experiencing abrupt, acute pain appear strongly motivated to vocalize, even with knowledge that no one is nearby, suggesting an involuntary component to the response. However, such alarm signals may be suppressed in the presence of strangers and accompanied by embarrassment, suggesting status concerns (Badali, 2008).

These observations suggest that modern human capacities evolved from those of ancient hominids and earlier, less complex species. The greater the survival function of sensory/emotional/behavioral modules, the more ancient will be their evolved foundations. Pain, with species-specific strategic variations, serves vital physiological and behavioral survival functions and is reliant on biologically prepared (readily activated) foundations as opposed to blank slates. Over evolutionary time and especially in humans, capacities evolved for reflection and deliberation, permitting personal agency. Human cognitive, linguistic, and social competencies render them more capable of acquiring skills that help them elicit care from their peers.

The Evolution of Cooperation

Cooperation appears fundamental for understanding species-specific pain communication and associated helping, from one animal providing care for another, through to multi-person social systems (e.g., hospitals).

The existing literature on cooperation and its evolution led Nowak and Highfield in 2011 to state, "Previously, there were only two basic principles of evolution—mutation and selection . . . we must now accept that cooperation is the third principle" (p. 36). Similarly, Wilson (2012) suggested that the extraordinary human capacity for cooperation underpins their social conquest of the Earth.

Cooperation can be defined as "costly behavior performed by one individual that increases the payoff of others" (Silk, 2007, p. 118). Altruism—closely related to cooperation, but not synonymous, as cooperation can be enlisted to harm others—can be defined as a proclivity to benefit others involving a cost to oneself (Van Vugt et al., 2007). Cooperative and affiliative behaviors are much more common than aggression in all primates, even chimpanzees, which are more frequently aggressive than humans (Sussman et al., 2005). Altruistic cooperation has been observed between unrelated individuals and even across species (Nowak, 2006), and there are many anecdotes involving cross-species interventions to help threatened or injured members of other species.

Earlier ideas of evolutionary foundations of cooperation based exclusively on self-interest have been challenged (Fehr et al, 2002; Sussman et al., 2005). The evolution of cooperation could have involved a variety of precursor mechanisms. The simplest and commonest is mutualism, where both parties directly benefit (Rutte & Taborsky, 2007). Direct reciprocity (A helps B because B has helped A) is based on a partner's previous behavior to a donor. Indirect reciprocity involves A helping B because B has helped C; i.e., B has developed a reputation for helping. This partly explains cooperation often surpassing family boundaries and direct relationships. A helpful reputation may bring a range of social network rewards (Nowak & Sigmund, 2005; Van Vugt et al., 2007). While direct reciprocity relies on repeated encounters between the same two individuals, indirect reciprocity does not, but it probably requires substantial cognition, including memory for interactions and environments and monitoring of ever-changing social networks (Nowak, 2006). It also is dependent on a greater likelihood of eventual benefits than costs to the helper. These may include future encounters with others knowing the helper's reputation. Altruistic cooperation may be further promoted by network reciprocity, in which cooperators can prevail by forming cooperative network clusters (e.g., human clubs and religious groups). Indirect reciprocity may require a theory of mind and may have been a driving force in human cerebral evolution (Nowak & Sigmund, 2005) and the development of civilization (Wilson, 2012).

Inclusive fitness involving individual fitness benefiting from the reproductive success of kin in proportion to their relatedness (Hamilton, 1964a, 1964b) provides an obvious basis for cooperation between closely related individuals. More controversial has been the recrudescence of group selection. The notion that individual reproductive success was paramount did not hold up to Wilson and colleagues' studies on eusociality, a characteristic of certain *Hymenoptera* (e.g., ants, bees, and wasps) (Nowak et al., 2010). In eusociality, some individuals reduce their own reproductive potential to raise the offspring of others. This underlies the most advanced forms of social organization (Wilson, 2012). Group selection processes in eusocial communities may allow whole populations of individuals to prevail and thereby achieve genetic success despite relatively small degrees of individual relatedness. Group selection does not negate the importance of individual selection, but for some species, including humans, multilevel selection—genetic, individual, and group—appears important (Boyd,

2006). Multilevel selection also embraces cultural evolution, which involves transgenerational transmission of knowledge and social skills, without which our technological achievements and social organizations would have amounted to little.

We referred earlier to species-specific pain behavior and how some mammals help injured others, while others do not. If there is one mammal possessing the genotype and phenotype to take pain-related caregiving to a new level, it would be *Homo sapiens*, whose almost eusocial division of labor results in extreme social complexity (Wilson, 2012). Human healthcare, educational, political, and cultural institutions illustrate this complexity.

Altruistic Cooperation and Empathy

Altruistic cooperation and empathy are key components to helping pain sufferers at both individual and societal levels. Cooperation may be extensive in animals lacking capacity for awareness, as in *Hymenoptera*. Nevertheless, cognitive sophistication enhances the development and complexity of cooperation.

Morality has been defined as a suite of interrelated other-regarding behaviors that cultivate and regulate complex interactions within social groups that relate to well-being and harm, and norms of right and wrong (Bekoff & Pierce, 2009). Harm and benefit are basic units of moral currency. Morality has species-specific features. Across species, there is compelling evidence for moral behavior in primates, social carnivores (e.g., wolves), cetaceans, elephants, and some rodents, although human values and priorities need not be the rule.

Morality comprises three clusters of personal qualities (Bekoff & Pierce, 2009): cooperation (including altruism, reciprocity, honesty, and trust); empathy (supporting sympathy, compassion, grief, and consolation); and justice (sharing, equity, fair play, and forgiveness). Morality is not our focus, but this scheme is of interest as it replicates some of the qualities related to cooperation, and prompts consideration of cheating, trust, and justice in the pain context.

Empathy comprises the capacity to understand personal experiences of another. The inferred experiences may comprise thoughts, feelings, sensations, or motives, and may involve automatic/implicit or intentional/explicit use of cognitions and affect (Goubert et al., 2005) associated with neuroregulatory systems (Hadjistavropoulos & Craig, 2002). Pain expression may elicit complex reactions in observers, including self-oriented apprehension of danger, but it also may elicit other-orientated concern and aid. Functional imaging has revealed that observations of pain in others involve brain areas implicated in processing the affective and motivational aspects of one's own pain, including the anterior cingulate cortex, the anterior insula, and the right temporo-parietal regions (Decety & Jackson, 2006; Simon et al., 2006; Singer et al., 2004). Empathy largely involves affective and cognitive features of pain, rather than its sensory components. Motor areas are also involved, reflecting the function of preparing pain observers for action (Avenanti et al., 2005).

De Waal (2008) proposed a spectrum of empathy, the simplest being emotional contagion (self-centered distress from empathy with another's distress). Next is sympathetic concern that might fuel consoling behaviors—common in humans and apes, but not in monkeys. Finally, perspective-taking (understanding the needs of others), combined with the emotional aspects of empathy, results in targeted help (seen in apes, whales, dolphins, and elephants). In humans, all three levels of empathy exist, with evidence appearing early in life. Nonhuman primates and children often display emotional contagion to strong emotional displays of others (de Waal, 2011; Fabrega, 1997). An infant's crying may result in another following suit.

Chimpanzees, our closest relatives, frequently show concern for injured or sick others (Goodall, 1986), may care for a sick female's offspring (Huffman & Seifu, 1989), and may endanger their lives to rescue others (Preston & de Waal, 2002).

Evidence is accumulating that the mechanism underlying empathy is phylogenetically ancient, probably as old as mammals and birds (de Waal, 2008). Perception of the emotional state of another automatically activates shared representations (Decety & Jackson, 2006), causing a matching of the observer's emotional state with that of the observed. Empathy evolved in social animals, promoting altruism dispensed in accordance with predictions from kin-selection and reciprocal altruism theory (de Waal, 2008). Infants activate caregiving in parents through distress vocalization, facial expression, and other behaviors. That such mechanisms persist into and throughout adulthood illustrates the survival value of empathy-inducing signals.

While *Hymenoptera* cooperate, they lack capacity for empathy. Elements of empathy are evident in birds: hens showed alert attention to their chicks (even without distress calls) when their chicks were subjected to unpleasant stimuli, and similar physiological responses to when they themselves experienced the stimuli (Edgar et al., 2011).

Langford et al. (2006) succeeded in demonstrating pain empathy in mice pairs: in some pairs both individuals were injected with a noxious substance ("both writhing"), but in others only one of the two were injected. They found greater pain behavior in an individual mouse in "both writhing" conditions than in "one writhing" (one injected), suggesting pain communication and empathy in mice, at least at the level of emotional contagion. Manipulation of visual, auditory, olfactory, and tactile communication revealed only visual blockade altered the results, suggesting that the communication of pain was predominantly visual. Langford, Bailey, et al. (2010) subsequently performed the first study of facial expressions of pain in a nonhuman species. Female mice preferred to stay closer to familiar mice in pain, suggesting something more than emotional contagion. Their demonstration of an expressive "pain face" in mice and subsequent work with other animals (Chambers & Mogil, 2015) mirrors that of human pain communication.

Langford, Tuttle, et al. (2010) found that social proximity of the observer mice reduced pain behavior, but separation of observer mice from pain-affected cage mates by transparent glass barriers eliminated this "analgesic" response, suggesting physical contact was important in this communication. These studies strongly suggest that the behavioral correlates of mice in pain serve the function of soliciting aid.

In summary, both cooperation and empathy appear relevant to the evolution of pain-related caregiving in cognitively sophisticated species.

From Cooperation and Empathy to Caregiving

An ecological perspective on pain dictates consideration of the responses of conspecifics to pain behaviors. Ancestral environments were much more dangerous than are contemporary ones, and the potential consequences of injuries and painful diseases were correspondingly greater. Injuries are common among nonhuman primates, and compensatory care is considered an important trait in many primate species (Chapman & Chapman, 1987). Human caregiving relationships vary from caregiving typical of familiar/trustworthy conspecifics, to exploitation, more likely with unfamiliar/untrustworthy others (Vigil & Strenth, 2014).

Caregiving has been observed in social carnivores, cetaceans, and some primates, especially chimpanzees (Fabrega, 1997). Groups facing hostility from neighboring conspecifics may benefit from maintaining a critical mass of members, even if caregivers do not receive future reciprocity for their help. Fabrega (1997) argues that human care-eliciting sick role behavior reflects an evolved "sickness healing adaptation" with an underlying neural basis further elaborated by learning. The adaptation is founded on natural selection (involving genetic mechanisms) and is elaborated by social selection (involving social and observational learning). Given genotypic and phenotypic continuity, successive generations do not have to rediscover socially transmitted units of information.

Recapping, evidence suggests that cooperation and empathy are not limited to humans, have evolved substantially through natural selection, and are relevant to helping others in pain. While similarities and dissimilarities in pain-helping responses across species exist, cooperation and empathy provide more complex pain-related caregiving in cognitively sophisticated species—humans in particular.

Psychological Support and Pain Communication
Key roles for cooperation and empathy are evident in human studies of social support. Patients with chronic illnesses almost universally display better adaptation to disability when supported (Turk et al., 1992), although exceptions have been reported, with social support not diminishing pain intensity (Kerns & Turk 1984). Paradoxically, chronic pain patients (CPPs) tend to report greater pain in the presence of solicitous supports, again demonstrating the importance of the audience in pain communications (e.g., Block et al., 1980; Flor et al., 1987; Fordyce et al., 1973; Romano et al., 1992; Romano et al., 1995; Turk et al., 1992).

Social reinforcement explains almost one-third of the variance in pain reporting and activity levels (Flor et al., 1987). Vulnerability and dependency seem important, as chronic back pain patients were more easily influenced by operant conditioning factors than healthy controls (Flor et al., 2002). Research has demonstrated greater expression of pain to safe/trustworthy others and reduced expression to less familiar/trustworthy others, serving vulnerability and empowerment functions, respectively (Vigil & Strenth, 2014). Menstrual cycle variations have experimentally been found to influence different pain expression to male and female experimenters (Vigil et al., 2015). An extensive literature review (Leonard et al., 2006) of 74 studies during 1978–2005 identified complex relationships among chronic pain, marital functioning, and psychological distress. While having a solicitous spouse predicted greater pain expression, this was moderated by marital satisfaction, with high positive relationships predicting less patient distress.

Family system and cognitive behavioral perspectives also have been used to explain how chronic pain impacts families and how family responses influence pain problems (Leonard et al., 2006; Lewandowski et al., 2007; Turk et al., 1992). Cognitive behavioral transactional models involve family beliefs about illness, pain, disability, and coping, and their impacts on patients. Schwartz et al. (2005) concluded that studies of negative spouse responses to pain have yielded inconsistent findings, but are mostly associated with greater patient psychosocial distress and depression. Empathetic spouse communications appear distinct from solicitous responses. The former convey understanding and may serve to distract or punish the person in pain, whereas the latter are more simply attentive with greater capacity to serve as reinforcement (Cano et al., 2008). Satisfaction with spouse responses to pain may serve as a coping resource, reducing patients' cognitive and emotional distress reactions (Holtzman & DeLongis, 2007). Both physical and emotional dependency may change relationship dynamics. Pain may both attract and repel family members. Social support may foster pain, disability, and dependency.

The impact of social context is also important in understanding interpersonal communications about pain (Craig, 2015; Hadjistavropoulos et al., 2011; Prkachin & Craig, 1995; Sullivan et al., 2000; Thorn et al., 2003). While candor about pain would seem the best strategy in obtaining optimal care, people tend to be careful about when and with whom they communicate painful distress (Craig, 2015; Vigil & Strenth, 2014). Frank expressions of pain are more likely with trusted family members, but misrepresentations can be expected when these could lead to adverse consequences (Craig et al., 1999), with suppression of signs of pain in the presence of those likely to exploit or humiliate the injured person. This suppression may reflect an adaptive ancestral tendency to hide signs of injury from predators and exploitative conspecifics. The increase in pain expression in the presence of solicitous others also may reflect the fact that the injured are no longer suppressing their pain communication, as opposed to the possibility that they are amplifying or exaggerating their pain expression (Kunz et al., 2009).

Motor responses, particularly those involving key survival behaviors, involve both automatic/reflexive and voluntary/controlled neuroregulatory systems (Craig et al., 2010; Hadjistavropoulos & Craig, 2002). Both nonverbal and vocal behaviors are widely employed in the animal world for communication. Particularly important in humans and some mammals is facial expression (Williams, 2002). Verbal reports engage higher cerebral centers, but facial responses are largely involuntary. Human neonates have innate pain communication abilities. They communicate painful distress with relatively specific facial expressions (Grunau & Craig, 1987). Behavioral coding systems for capturing facial pain expression in mice, rats, rabbits, and horses are now available (Chambers & Mogil, 2015).

Pain communication involves both pain expression by the individual and an interaction in which the signaled message is received; to be of benefit, the signal must affect the receiver's behavior in some way (Hadjistavropoulos et al., 2011). These capacities would have coevolved. Help-giving carries costs, so it is conditional on genuine need, with caregivers being alert to cheating (Cosmides & Tooby, 1992). Cultural influences such as the acceptability or unacceptability of displays of vulnerability are also relevant, along with interpersonal and situational factors. Both pain signaling and decoding (receiving) are influenced by contextual and environmental factors.

Signaling Theory

Only recently has pain research considered the science of signaling theory (Steinkopf, 2016a), despite its important role in biology and economics. We offer selected observations from this field to encourage consideration of its applications to understanding pain communications.

Biological signaling theory examines signals as fundamental components of communication using evolutionary currencies (Hasson, 2009). It examines different types of signals based on their evolutionary mechanisms, considering costs, benefits, modes of perception, modes of reliability (or deception), and the nature of the information provided. Cues are differentiated from signals. Large male size may indicate good reproductive potential, as does the male peacock's use of its ornate tail. The former is a cue, the latter a signal. Cues transmit unchanging reality and are permanently "on," whereas signals (advertisements) may be switched "on" and "off."

Signals primarily function to change behaviors of others and per se do not *directly* benefit the signaler. Costs are involved. The peacock's tail provides no direct/immediate benefit—it does not facilitate flight, stabilization, or defense. Its indirect function is to signal good health and reproductive potential. Another illustration of biological signaling is stotting in gazelles—leaping off the ground with all four legs stiffly straight. Gazelles are far more likely to stot in response to coursing predators (chases over long distances, e.g., wild dogs) than to stalkers (surprise predators, e.g., cheetahs) (Al-Shawaf & Lewis, 2017; Fitzgibbon & Fanshaw, 1988). Stotting signals the animal's fitness, its potential for outrunning the predator, and the futility of the chase. Dogs were found to select gazelles stotting at lower rates. Those gazelles that successfully outran hunters had stotted more than those that were killed. Gazelles only stot when the risk of capture is high, suggesting energy costs. Stotting is an *honest* signal of fitness.

Maynard-Smith and Harper (2003) define signals as "any act or structure which alters the behavior of other organisms, which evolved because of that effect, and which is effective because the receiver's response has also evolved" (p. 17). Receivers must on average benefit by responding in ways favorable to the signalers. Four key properties are involved: signals transmit information; signals elicit recipient responses; signalers and/or recipients benefit; signals are usually costly (Hasson, 1994). Pain expression satisfies these criteria by transmitting a state of distressing need, to a receiver, with one or both benefiting from the transaction, but at the price of the painful experience with its associated impairments. Neonatal crying and facial grimaces during invasive procedures provide an illustration (Grunau & Craig, 1987). Many other symptoms of illnesses serve signaling functions (Steinkopf, 2016a; Tiokhin, 2016).

Zahavi (1975) coined the "handicap principle," which describes a mechanism promoting honest signaling that limits cheating. The reliability of the communication is increased in proportion to the costs of the advertisement. The quality of the peacock's tail is costly in terms of energetic requirements for the development and maintenance of this ornate cumbersome advertisement and is a liability for hiding or flight from predators. Similarly, in modern life a Ferrari is a useful signal of high male status. Why don't more males use them? Because the signal is so costly. If Ferraris were readily affordable, they would lose their resource-signaling utility. The evolutionary stability of persuasive signaling necessitates honesty, which incurs costs (Grafen, 1990), and receivers should pay more attention to, and respond more readily to, costly signals (Maynard Smith & Harper, 1995).

Chronic pain is very costly both in terms of its aversiveness and its impacts on the psychosocial functioning of CPPs and their associates. Efforts to suppress pain are likely to be frequent in the presence of unfamiliar/untrustworthy others, but suppression of pain expression/signaling is not easily managed (Hill & Craig, 2002) and is less likely in medical care contexts. It is paradoxical that chronic pain-related disabilities are so often viewed as dishonest signaling by medical caregivers (De Ruddere & Craig, 2016), perhaps reflecting the emphasis on self-report rather than broader assessment of the behavioral and social impact of pain on the person's life. However, distinguishing genuine from faked or more commonly exaggerated pain is difficult (Hill & Craig, 2002), although advances have been made focusing on nonverbal expression (Bartlett et al., 2014). These challenges contribute to the focus by observers on overt causes, such as gaping wounds (Steinkopf, 2016a, 2016b). Provided both signalers and receivers similarly benefit, the signaling system is stable (Tiokhin, 2016).

Zahavi's handicap principle has been highly influential, but early modeling produced negative results (Grose, 2011). Grafen's (1990) models of honest signaling mechanisms contributed to a resurgence of interest in the handicap principle. Grafen noted that the mechanism must provide for greater capacity for higher-quality individuals to absorb increased signal costs. Substantial costs may not be necessary where both parties experience similar benefits (Lachmann et al., 2001).

Signaling theory is broad in its scope, operating outside biology (e.g., economics) and within biology, both within and across species, and even crossing the plant–animal divide. Autumn yellow-green coloration of trees' leaves has been found to aid defense against aphids because coloration signals unpalatability. Autumn coloration was stronger in tree species facing a high diversity of damaging specialist aphids (Hamilton & Brown, 2001). The selective resorption of leaf pigments depletes access to energy, the strategy's costs. Such studies demonstrate not only coevolution of signaler and responder, but also coevolution across diverse species, illustrating the breadth and ecological importance of signaling theory.

Signals of need require cooperation and usually involve costs to prevent runaway cheating. Signals of need include pain behaviors as signals of injury or illness (Craig et al., 1991). Curiously, the pain-signaling process itself may have some analgesic effect. Swearing compared with not swearing has been found experimentally to increase cold-pressor pain tolerance (Stephens et al., 2009), probably satisfying a signaling function.

Conclusions

Acute pain has clearly been evolutionarily adaptive, with its emotional component driving survival behaviors through protective and communicative functions. Clinically, chronic pain has been viewed as maladaptive, but evolutionary perspectives suggest both maladaptive and adaptive explanations. For example, the smoke detector principle suggests it is better to have a warning system sound too frequently than the reverse (Nesse, 2005; Nesse & Schulkin, 2019). What may be adaptive on average may come with numerous instances that are individually maladaptive.

If chronic pain has been adaptive in ancestral environments and at times with contemporary individuals, the late recuperative phase of the pain response appears most relevant. It involves longer-term responses serving diverse physiological and behavioral functions ranging from the immunological benefits of resting to care-eliciting from conspecifics (Wall, 1979, 1989). The *emotional* features of chronic pain appear to subserve recuperation by driving care-eliciting behavior and other longer-term physiological, immunological, and behavioral influences, including resting (Wall 1979, 1989).

Sick role behavior, of which pain behavior is a subset, functions as an expression of a centrally mediated motivational state that reorganizes priorities to promote survival (Brydon et al., 2008). This includes selective communication of needs to others, who vary in their likelihood to help, neglect, or exploit the injured/sick individual. The complexities of pain as a social transaction cannot be underestimated.

Traditional biomedical and psychological approaches to understanding and treating pain largely failed to recognize sufferers' social contexts and their potential for promoting or diminishing chronic pain strategic responses. For example, athletes have subordinates eager to replace them in competitive hierarchies, so chronic pain-enhancing care-eliciting strategies would carry greater costs than for non-athletes. Conversely, not being an athlete and having a solicitous partner would make a care-eliciting strategy less costly/more valuable.

Caregiving is a subset of cooperation. Various evolutionary mechanisms underlying cooperation are relevant to understanding and helping individuals with persistent pain. Inclusive fitness theory suggests that caregiving will be more freely provided by closely related individuals (Rutte & Taborsky 2007), and this remains apparent in contemporary humans. However, this adaptation may be a factor accounting for observations of increased pain perception and pain-related disability—contemporary maladaptations—in chronic pain patients (CPPs) with solicitous partners.

Indirect reciprocity relies more on reputation, which partly depends on cognitive ability to remember and track helpers (Nowak & Sigmund 2005). For this cooperative mechanism to evolve stably, soliciting unwarranted aid is limited by recognition and punishment of cheats. Strong motivations by contemporary clinicians to exclude malingerers from medico-legal benefits reflect this ancient orientation. Stigmatic attitudes toward sufferers of chronic pain may arise from both the loss of social status associated with chronic pain-related disabilities and from potential helpers, protective of their resources, being primed to suspect cheating (DeRuddere et al., 2013).

Morality involves cooperation, empathy, and justice (Bekoff & Pierce 2009). The innate morality of pain behavior involves preparedness to cooperate under a system of rules. Empathy helps people identify need and motivates caregiving. Concern for others is more developed in humans than in most other species, although this partly reflects benign civilized environments, as compassion may be more circumscribed in less privileged environments. However, empathy at least in its most basic form—emotional contagion—has been observed in chimpanzees (Goodall, 1986), some other primates, social carnivores (Bekoff & Pierce, 2009), cetaceans (Fabrega, 1997), elephants (Bradshaw, 2009), and experimental mice observing conspecifics in pain (Langford, Bailey, et al., 2010). It remains to be clarified to what extent the higher forms of empathy, particularly empathic perspective action-taking, exist beyond *Homo* (de Waal, 2016).

Most contemporary clinical approaches to pain fail to adequately recognize pain's communicational element, yet parents of infants are highly attentive to it, and from an early age infants display pain behavior by signaling distress in response to even minor pains. Humans employ a range of sick role behaviors to elicit care, reflecting an evolved "sickness healing adaptation" with an underlying neural basis that is elaborated by cultural learning (Fabrega, 1997). Sickness and healing have been founded on natural selection and elaborated by cultural selection.

Ancestral costs of enduring pain involved disadvantages during hunting, gathering, mate attraction, and defense against hostile conspecifics and predators, as well as within-group exploitation and status loss. Such costs are consistent with Zahavi's (1975) handicap principle of biological signaling theory. The greater the benefits to the signaler/care-elicitor and the greater the costs to the signal recipient/caregiver, the greater the pain experience (signal cost) would need to be to maintain an evolutionarily stable equation (Maynard Smith & Harper 1995). Stoic responses preserve autonomy and status at the cost of reduced care. Needy responses elicit more generous care but carry the costs of loss of autonomy and status. Responder/caregiver benefits include the preservation of the family or other group unit, with costs including diversion from other activities and sharing of resources. Signaling theory is compatible with this coevolved scenario. Pain perception and disability might be expected to be weaker in communities where hunger is more acute and the costs to both caregivers and injured individuals deter the care-eliciting strategy. This is a potential explanation for the observation that pain and disability associated with back complaints are less common in developing countries (Waddell 2004).

This distal explanatory model potentially complements the proximal gate control and pain neuromatrix models, whereby pain and other sensory inputs to the central nervous system undergo processing, heightening or moderating pain experiences (Melzack 1999; Melzack & Wall 1965). Both are dependent on contextual inputs, and possibly in chronic pain these contextual and strategic issues, including signal cost, contribute to central pain sensitization (Walters & Williams, 2019).

Signals are honest on average, and the level of cheating will be limited accordingly. Attending to the cost of the signal may distinguish cheats from non-cheats. Consciousness in the assessment of signaled quality is neither assumed nor excluded—it is irrelevant (Grafen, 1990). Altruistic punishment, the punishment of free-riders (cheats), is an essential feature of communal cooperation, without which the system could not reach stable equilibrium (Fehr & Gachter, 2002).

Further attention to the application of signaling theory to understanding chronic pain is warranted, from both research and clinical perspectives. Clinicians, insurers, and disability compensation systems tend to be alert to the possibility of CPPs seeking support without adequate impairment, but rarely attend to suppression of medical complaints and symptoms. Clinicians' reputations are not helped by treating malingerers (cheats), perhaps contributing to high levels of false positives (unwarranted suspicion of honest pain patients). Yet estimates suggest that fraudulent misrepresentation of pain is relatively rare (Craig & Badali, 2004).

This evolutionary theory supports the communication (e.g., Hadjistavropoulos et al., 2011) and communal coping models (Sullivan et al., 2000), suggesting that pain may be more understandable, predictable, and potentially treatable when interpersonal and other contextual issues (e.g., job viability given the pain complaint) are understood. If chronic pain was sometimes ancestrally adaptive, understanding its evolved mechanisms may point the way to new research and treatment directions that may help alleviate the suffering and disabilities of those with chronic pain.

This evolutionary care-eliciting model canvasses new directions for pain research, but requires evidence to assess the validity of its individual and collective components. Williams (2019) has rightly noted that beyond humans, farm animals (receiving human care), and rodent models there is no evidence of chronic pain in other mammals. However, sometimes lack of evidence results from lack of relevant research. Until relatively recently, many researchers doubted that nonhuman animals experienced even acute pain. Now it is increasingly accepted that many fish (early species of which were distant ancestors of humans) (Sneddon, 2019), probably all mammals, and some invertebrates (annelids, arthropods, and mollusks) experience both nociception and pain (Walters & Williams, 2019).

Studies of different species-specific pain behaviors and conspecific interactions, particularly in their natural environments, may shed light on the essential phenomenology of human pain responses. The theory predicts that chronic pain displays will be greater in more cooperative care-providing social species than in less cooperative, less social, and non-care-providing species.

Chronic pain research challenges in wild animals are considerable and are not aided by subjective as opposed to functional approaches to pain research. Wild animals pursuing reclusive chronic pain behavior may be difficult to study over extended periods. Furthermore, while the evolved protective aspects of pain may be relevant to all mammals, the communicative care-eliciting strategy we have highlighted for chronic pain may be irrelevant to non-social species, and even within social mammal species it may only be found in the minority of care-eliciting/care-providing species. Elephants in particular may be worthy of study, being large (easily tracked and more ready research funds), highly social, and generally highly caring (Bradshaw, 2009). Further, injured elephants housed in sanctuaries would be readily available for study.

Pain research in animals has been appropriately limited by the ethics of inflicting injuries. This can be partially circumvented by comparing recovery times of different species following standardized surgical procedures, or naturalistic recovery times of untreated similar injuries in the wild. Domestic animals and pets also provide research opportunities. Biologically, dogs are caring of in-group others, and cats considerably less so. Even with human caregiving to pets, our theory predicts that cats would recover function and return to self-sufficiency more quickly than dogs following major surgery (e.g., amputations following road trauma). Anecdotally, domestic animal owners may be surprised at how quickly their animals resume activities following fractures or surgery.

While animal research is facilitated by the functional approach to pain, animal studies may yet shed light on subjective pain. An important question is whether the injured of less caregiving species hide pain of similar intensity to that of helping species, or actually experience less severe pain, perhaps suppressed by endorphins or other mechanisms? Might a recuperating domestic cat while outdoors hide pain from the exploitative neighboring cats, only to display greater pain behavior when it has safely returned indoors?

Acknowledgments
Our thanks to Amanda C. de C. Williams for her helpful early suggestions on content.

Funding
This research received no specific grant from any funding agency in the public, commercial, or not-for-profit sectors.

References
Al-Shawaf, L., Conroy-Beam, D., Asao, K. & Buss, D. M. (2015). Human emotions: An evolutionary psychological perspective. *Emotion Review*, 8(2), 173–186. doi: 10.1177/1754073914565518

Al-Shawaf, L., & Lewis, D. M. G. (2017). The handicap principle. In T.K. Shackleford & V.A. Shackleford-Weekes (Eds.), *Encylopedia of evolutionary psychological science*. Springer International. https://doi.org/10.1007/978-3-319-16999-6_2100-2101

Auvray, M., Myin, E., & Spence, C. (2010) The sensory-discriminative and affective-motivational aspect of pain. *Neuroscience and Biobehavioral Reviews*, 34(2), 214–223. http://dx.doi.org/10.1016/j.neubiorev.2008.07.008

Avenanti, A., Bueti, D., Galati, G. & Aglioti, S.M. (2005) Transcranial magnetic stimulation higlights the sensorimotor side of empathy for pain. *Nature Neuroscience*, 8, 955–960. https://doi.org/10.1038/nn1481

Badali, M. (2008). *Experimenter audience effects on young adults' facial expressions during pain*. Unpublished doctoral dissertation, University of British Columbia.

Bartlett, M. S., Littlewort, G. C., Frank, M. G. & Lee, K. (2014). Automatic decoding of facial movements reveals deceptive pain expressions. *Current Biology*, 24(7), 738–743. http://doi:10.1016/j.cub.2014.02.009

Bateson, P. (1991). Assessment of pain in animals. *Animal Behaviour*, 42(5), 827–839. http://doi:10.1016/S0003-3472(05)80127-7

Bekoff, M., & Pierce, J. (2009). *Wild justice: The moral lives of animals*. University of Chicago Press.

Block, A. R., Kremer, E. F., & Gaylor, M. (1980). Behavioral treatment of chronic pain: The spouse as a discriminative cue for pain behavior. *Pain*, 9(2), 243–252. http://doi: 10.1016/0304-3959(80)90011-1

Bolles, R. C., & Fanselow, M. S. (1980). A perceptual-defensive-recuperative model of fear and pain. *Behavioral and Brain Sciences*, 3(2), 291–323. http://dx.doi.org/10.1017/S0140525X0000491X

Boyd, R. (2006). The puzzle of human sociality. *Science*, 314(5805), 1555–1556. https://doi.org/10.1126/SCIENCE.1136841

Bradshaw, G. A. (2009). *Elephants on the edge: What animals teach us about humanity*. Yale University Press.

Braithwaite, V. A., & Boulcott, P. (2007). Pain perception, aversion and fear in fish. *Diseases in Aquatic Organisms*, 75(2), 131–138. http://doi: 10.3354/dao075131

Broom, D. M. (1998). Welfare stress, and the evolution of feelings. *Advances in the Study of Behavior*, 27, 371–404.

Broom, D. M. (2001). Coping, stress and welfare. In D. M. Broom (Ed.), *Coping with challenge: Welfare in animals including humans*. Proceedings of Dahlem Conference (pp. 1–9). Dahlem University Press.

Broom, D. M. (2006). Behavior and welfare in relation to pathology. *Applied Animal Behavior Science*, 97(1), 73–83. http://dx.doi.org/10.1016/j.applanim.2005.11.019

Broom, D. M. (2007). Cognitive ability and sentience: Which aquatic animals should be protected? *Diseases of Aquatic Organisms*, 75(2), 99–108.

Broom, D. M., & Fraser, A. F. (2007). Behaviour towards predators and social attackers. In D. M. Broom & A. F. Fraser (Eds.), *Domestic animal behaviour and welfare* (4th ed., pp. 73–76). CAB International. http://www.cabi.org/cabebooks/ebook/20083100841

Brydon, L., Harrison, N. A., Walker, C., Steptoe, A., & Critchley, H. D. (2008). Peripheral inflammation is associated with altered substantia nigra activity and psychomotor slowing in humans. *Biological Psychiatry*, 63(11), 1022–1029. http://dx.doi.org/10.1016/j.biopsych.2007.12.007

Cano, A., Barterian, J. A., & Heller, J. B. (2008). Empathic and non-empathic interaction in chronic pain couples. *Clinical Journal of Pain, 24*(8), 678–684. http://dx.doi.org/10.1097%2FAJP.0b013e31816753d8

Cantor, C. (2005). *Evolution and posttraumatic stress: Disorders of vigilance and defence*. Routledge.

Cantor, C. (2009). Post-traumatic stress disorder: Evolutionary perspectives. *Australian and New Zealand Journal of Psychiatry, 43*(11), 1038–1048. http://:doi10.3109/00048670903270407

Cantor, C. H., & Price, J. (2007). Traumatic entrapment, appeasement and complex post-traumatic stress disorder: Evolutionary perspectives of hostage reactions, domestic abuse and the Stockholm Syndrome. *Australian and New Zealand Journal of Psychiatry, 41*(5), 377–384. http://doi:10.1080/00048670701261178

Chambers, C. T., & Mogil, J. S. (2015). Ontogeny and phylogeny of facial expression of pain. *Pain, 156*(5), 798–799. http://doi: 10.1097/j.pain.0000000000000133

Chapman, C. A., & Chapman, L. J. (1987). Social responses to the traumatic injury of a juvenile spider monkey (*Ateles geoffroyi*). *Primates, 28*(2), 271–275.

Chervova, L. S. (2000). Behavioural responses of fish to pain stimuli. *Journal of Ichthyology, 40*(8; Suppl 2), S287–S290.

Cosmides, L., & Tooby, J. (1992). Cognitive adaptations for social exchange. In J. H. Barkow, L. Cosmides, & J. Tooby (Eds.), *The adapted mind: Evolutionary psychology and the generation of culture* (pp. 163–228). Oxford University Press.

Craig, K. D. (2015). The social communication model of pain. *Pain, 156*(7), 1198–1199. https://doi.org/10.1097/j.pain.0000000000000185

Craig, K. D., & Badali, M. A. I. (2004). Introduction to the special series on the detection of pain deception and malingering. *Clinical Journal of Pain, 20*(6), 377–382. http://doi: 10.1097/00002508-200411000-00001.

Craig, K. D., Hill, M. L., & McMurtry, B. (1999). Detecting deception and malingering. In A. R. Block, E. F. Kramer, & E. Fernandez (Eds.), *Handbook of chronic pain syndromes: Biopsychosocial perspectives* (pp. 41–58). Lawrence Erlbaum Associates.

Craig, K. D., Hyde, S. A., & Patrick, C. J. (1991). Genuine, suppressed, and faked facial behaviour during exacerbation of chronic low back pain. *Pain, 46*(2), 161–172. https://doi.org/10.1016/0304-3959(91)90071-5

Craig, K. D., Prkachin, K. M., & Grunau, R. V. E. (2011). The facial expression of pain. In D. C. Turk & R. Melzack (Eds.), *Handbook of pain assessment* (3rd ed., pp. 117–133). Guilford.

Craig, K. D., Versloot, J., Goubert, L., Vervoort, T., & Crombez, G. (2010). Perceiving others in pain: Automatic and controlled mechanisms. *Journal of Pain, 11*(2), 101–108. http://dx.doi.org/10.1016/j.jpain.2009.08.008

Darwin, C. ([1890] 2009). *The expression of the emotions in man and the animals* (2nd ed., pp. 84–110). Penguin Books.

Dawkins, M. S. (1990). From an animal's point of view: Motivation, fitness and animal welfare. *Behavioral and Brain Sciences, 13*(1), 1–61. http://dx.doi.org/10.1017/S0140525X00077104

Decety, J., & Jackson, P. L. (2006). A social-neuroscience perspective on empathy. *Current Directions in Psychological Science, 15*(2), 54–58. http://doi: 10.1111/j.0963-7214.2006.00406.x

De Ruddere, L., & Craig, K. D. (2016). Understanding stigma and chronic pain: A state of the art review. *Pain, 157*(8), 1607–1610. http://doi: 10.1097/j.pain.0000000000000512

De Ruddere, L., Goubert, L., Vervoort, T., Kappesser, J., & Crombez, G. (2013). Impact of being primed with social deception upon observer responses to others' pain. *Pain, 154*(2), 221–226. http://doi: 10.1016/J.pain.2012.10.002

de Waal, F. B. M. (1998). *Chimpanzee politics: Power and sex among apes*. Johns Hopkins University Press.

de Waal, F. B. M. (2008). Putting the altruism back into altruism: The evolution of empathy. *Annual Reviews in Psychology, 59*, 279–300. http://doi:10.1146/annurev.psych.59.103006.093625

de Waal, F. B. M. (2011). What is an animal emotion? *Annals of the New York Academy of Sciences, 1224*(1), 191–206. http://doi: 10.1111/j.1749-6632.2010.05912.x

de Waal, F. B. M. (2016). *Are we smart enough to know how smart animals are?* W. W. Norton.

Dittus, W. P. J., & Ratnayeke, S. M. (1989). Individual and social behavioural responses to injury in wild toque macaques (*Macaco sinica*). *International Journal of Primatology, 10*(3), 215–234.

Dwyer, C. M. (2004). How has the risk of predation shaped the behavioural responses of sheep to fear and distress? *Animal Welfare, 13*(3), 269–281.

Edgar, J. L., Lowe, J. C., Paul, E. S., & Nicol, C. J. (2011). Avian maternal response to chick distress. *Proceedings of the Royal Society B, 278*(1721), 3129–3134. http://doi: 10.1098/rspb.2010.2701

Fabrega, H. (1997). *Evolution of sickness and healing*. University of California Press.

Fanselow, M. S., & Lester, L. S. (1988). A functional behavioristic approach to aggressively motivated behavior: Predatory imminence as a determinant of the topography of defensive behaviour. In R. C. Bolles & M. D. Beecher (Eds.), *Evolution and learning* (pp. 185–212). Laurence Erlbaum Associates.

Fehr, E., Fischbacher, U., & Gachter, S. (2002). Strong reciprocity, human cooperation, and the enforcement of social norms. *Human Nature, 13*(1), 1–25. https://doi.org/10.1007/s12110-002-1012-7

Fehr, E. & Gachter, S. (2002). Altruistic punishment in humans. *Nature, 415*, 137–40. http://doi:10.1038/415137a

Finlay, B. L. (2019). The neuroscience of vision and pain: Evolution of two disciplines. *Philosophical Transactions of the Royal Society B, 374*(1785), 20190292. http://dx.doi.org/10.1098/rstb.2019.0292

Fitzgibbon, C. D., & Fanshaw, J. H. (1988). Stotting in Thomson's gazelles: An honest signal of condition. *Behavioral Ecology and Sociobiology, 23*, 69–74. https://doi.org/10.1007/BF00299889

Flor, H., Kerns, R. D., & Turk, D. C. (1987). The role of spouse reinforcement, perceived pain, and activity levels of chronic pain patients. *Journal of Psychosomatic Research, 31*(2), 251–259. http://dx.doi.org/10.1016/0022-3999(87)90082-1

Flor, H., Knost, B., & Birbaumer, N. (2002). The role of operant conditioning in chronic pain: An experimental investigation. *Pain, 95*(1–2), 111–118. http://dx.doi.org/10.1016/S0304-3959(01)00385-2

Fordyce, W., Fowler, R., Lehmann, J., Delateur, P. J., Sand, P. L., & Trieschmann, R. B. (1973). Operant conditioning in the treatment of chronic pain. *Archives of Physical and Medical Rehabilitation, 54*(9), 399–408.

Glare, P., Aubrey, K. R., & Myles, P. S. (2019). Transition from acute to chronic pain after surgery. *Lancet, 393*(10180), 1537–1546. doi: https://doi.org/10.1016/S0140-6736(19)30352-6.

Goodall, J. (1986). *The chimpanzees of Gombe: Patterns of behavior*. Harvard University Press.

Goubert, L., Craig, K. D., Vervoort, T., Morely, S., Sullivan, M. J. L., Williams, A. C. de C., Cano, A., & Crombez, G. (2005). Facing others in pain: The effects of empathy. *Pain, 118*, 285–288. http://doi: 10.1016/j.pain.2005.10.025

Grafen, A. (1990). Biological signals as handicaps. *Journal of Theoretical Biology, 144*(4), 517–546. http://dx.doi.org/10.1016/S0022-5193(05)80088-8

Grose, J. (2011). Modelling and the fall and the rise of the handicap principle. *Biology and Philosophy, 26*(5), 677–696. https://doi.org/10.1007/s10539-011-9275-1

Grunau, R. V. E., & Craig, K. D. (1987). Pain expression in neonates: Facial action and cry. *Pain, 28*(3), 395–410. https://doi.org/10.1016/0304-3959(87)90073-x

Hadjistavropoulos, T., Breau, L., & Craig, K. D. (2011). Pain assessment in adults and children with limited ability to communicate. In D. C. Turk & R. Melzack (Eds.), *Handbook of pain assessment* (3rd ed., pp. 260–282). Guilford Press.

Hadjistavropoulos, T., & Craig, K. D. (2002). A theoretical framework for understanding self-report and observational measures of pain: A communications model. *Behavior Research and Therapy, 40*(5), 551–570. http://dx.doi.org/10.1016/S0005-7967(01)00072-9

Hadjistavropoulos, T., Craig, K. D., Duck, S., Cano, A., Goubert, L., Jackson, P. L., Mogil, J. S., Rainville, P., Sullivan, M. J. L., Williams, A. C. de C., Vervoort, T., & Fitzgerald, T. D. (2011). A biopsychosocial formulation of pain communication. *Psychological Bulletin, 137*(6), 910–939. http://psycnet.apa.org/doi/10.1037/a0023876

Hamilton, W. D. (1964a). The genetical evolution of social behaviour I. *Journal of Theoretical Biology, 7*(1), 1–16. https://doi.org/10.1016/0022-5193(64)90038-4

Hamilton, W. D. (1964b). The genetical evolution of social behaviour II. *Journal of Theoretical Biology, 7*(1), 17–52. https://doi.org/10.1016/0022-5193(64)90039-6

Hamilton, W. D., & Brown, S. P. (2001). Autumn tree colours as a handicap signal. *Proceedings of the Royal Society of London B, 268*(1475), 1489–1493. doi: 10.1098/rspb.2001.1672

Hart, B. L. (1990). Behavioral adaptations to pathogens and parasites: Five strategies. *Neuroscience and Biobehavioral Reviews, 14*(3), 273–294. http://dx.doi.org/10.1016/S0149-7634(05)80038-7

Hasson, O. (1994). Cheating signals. *Journal of Theoretical Biology, 167*, 223–238.

Hasson, O. (2009). Emotional tears as biological signals. *Evolutionary Psychology, 7*(3), 363–370. https://doi.org/10.1177%2F147470490900700302

Hill, M. L., & Craig, K. D. (2002). Detecting deception in pain expressions: The structure of genuine and deceptive facial displays. *Pain, 98*(1–2), 135–144. https://psycnet.apa.org/doi/10.1016/S0304-3959(02)00037-4

Holtzman, S., & DeLongis, A. (2007). One day at a time: The impact of daily satisfaction with spouse responses on pain, negative affect and catastrophizing among individuals with rheumatoid arthritis. *Pain, 131*(1–2), 202–213. https://doi.org/10.1016/j.pain.2007.04.005

Huffman, M. A., & Seifu, M. (1989). Observations on the illness and consumption of possible medicinal plant *Vermonia amygdalina* (Del.), by a wild chimpanzee in the Mahale Mountains National Park, Tanzania. *Primates, 30*, 51–63. http://link.springer.com/article/10.1007/BF02381210

Katz, J., & Seltzer, Z. (2014). Transition from acute to chronic postsurgical pain: Risk factors and protective factors. *Expert Review of Neurotherapeutics, 9*, 723–744. https://doi.org/10.1586/ern.09.20

Kerns, R. D., & Turk, D. C. (1984). Depression and chronic pain: The mediating role for the spouse. *Journal of Marriage and Family Therapy, 46*(4), 845–852. http://www.jstor.org/stable/352532

Krahe, C., Springer, A., Weinman, J. A., & Fotopoulou, A. (2013). The social modulation of pain: Others as predictive signals of salience—a systematic review. *Frontiers of Human Neuroscience, 7*, 386. http://doi:10.3389/fnhum.2013.00386

Kunz, M., Mylius, V., Schepelmann, K., & Lautenbacher, S. (2009). Effects of age and mild cognitive impairment on the pain response system. *Gerontology, 55*, 674–682. https://doi.org/10.1159/000235719

Lachmann, M., Szamado, S., & Bergstrom, C. T. (2001). Cost and conflict in animal signals and human language. *Proceedings of the National Academy of Sciences, 98*(23), 13189–13194. https://dx.doi.org/10.1073%2Fpnas.231216498

Langford, D. J., Bailey, A. L., Chanda, M. L., Clarke, S. E., Drummond, T. E., Echols, S., Glick, S., Ingrao, J., Klassen-Ross, T., LaCroix-Fralish, M. L., Matsumiya, L., Sorge, R. E., Sotocinal, S. G., Tabaka, J. M., Wong, D., van den Maagdenberg, A. M. J. M., Ferrari, M. D., Craig, K. D., & Mogil, J. S. (2010). Coding of facial expressions of pain in the laboratory mouse. *Nature Methods, 7*, 447–449. doi:10.1038/nmeth.1455

Langford, D. J., Crager, S. E., Shehzad, Z., Smith, S. B., Sotocinal, S. G., Levenstat, J. S., Chanda, M. L., Levetin, D. J., & Mogil, J. S. (2006). Social modulation of pain as evidence for empathy in mice. *Science, 312*(5782), 1967–1970. http://doi:10.1126/science.1128322

Langford, D. J., Tuttle, A. H., Brown, K., Deschenes, S., Fischer, D. B., Mutso, A., Root, K. C., Sotocinal, S. G., Stern, M. A., Mogil, J. S., & Sternberg, W. F. (2010). Social approach to pain in laboratory mice. *Social Neuroscience, 5*(2), 163–70. http://doi: 10.1080/17470910903216609

Leonard, M. T., Cano, A., & Johansen, A. B. (2006). Chronic pain in a couples context: A review and integration of theoretical models and empirical evidence. *Journal of Pain, 7*(6), 377–90. http://dx.doi.org/10.1016/j.jpain.2006.01.442

Lewandowski, W., Morris, R., Drauker, C. B., & Risko, J. (2007). Chronic pain and the family: Theory-driven approaches. *Issues in Mental Health Nursing, 28*(9), 1019–1044. doi: 10.1080/01612840701522200

Lumley, M. A., Cohen, J. L., Borszcz, G. S., Cano, A., Radcliffe, A. M., Porter, L. S., Schubiner, H., & Keefe F. J. (2011). Pain and emotion: A biopsychosocial review of recent research. *Journal of Clinical Psychology, 67*(9), 942–968. http://doi: 10.1002/jclp.20816

Main, C. J., Keefe, F. J., Jensen, M. P., Vlaeyen, J. W. S., & Vowles, K. E. (Eds.) (2014). *Fordyce's behavioral methods for chronic pain and illness*. IASP Press.

Marks, I. M., & Nesse, R. M. (1994). Fear and fitness: An evolutionary analysis of anxiety disorders. *Ethology and Sociobiology, 15*(5–6), 247–261. http://dx.doi.org/10.1016/0162-3095(94)90002-7

Maynard Smith, J., & Harper, D. G. C. (1995). Animal signals: Models and terminology. *Journal of Theoretical Biology, 177*(3), 305–311. http://dx.doi.org/10.1006/jtbi.1995.0248

Maynard Smith, J., & Harper, D. (2003). *Animal signals* (pp. 1–15). Oxford University Press.

Mellor, D. J., Cook, C. J., & Stafford, K. J. (2000). Quantifying some responses to pain as a stressor. In G. P. Moberg & J. A. Mench (Eds.), *The biology of animal stress: Basic principles and implications for animal welfare* (pp. 171–198). CAB International.

Melzack, R. (1999). From the gate to the neuromatrix. *Pain*, Suppl. 6, S121–S126. http://doi: 10.1016/s0304-3959(99)00145-1.

Melzack, R., & Wall, P. D. (1965). Pain mechanisms: A new theory. *Science, 150*(3699), 971–979. http://doi: 10.1126/science.150.3699.971

Melzack, R., Wall, P. D., & Ty, T. C. (1982). Acute pain in an emergency clinic: Latency of onset and descriptor patterns related to different injuries. *Pain, 14*(1), 33–43.

Mench, J. A., & Mason, G. J. (1997). Behaviour. In M .C. Appleby & B. O. Hughes (Eds.), *Animal welfare* (pp. 127–141). CAB International.

Mogil, J. S. (2015). Social modulation by and of pain in humans and rodents. *Pain*, 156(Suppl 1), S35–S41. http://doi: 10.1097/01.j.pain.0000460341.62094.77

Mogil, J. S., & Crager, D. E. (2004). What should we be measuring in behavioral studies of chronic pain in animals? *Pain, 112*(1–2), 12–15. http://doi: 10.1016/j.pain.2004.09.028

Mogil, J., Pang, D., Dutra, G., & Chambers, C. (2020). The development and use of facial grimace scales for pain measurement in animals. *Neuroscience and Biobehavioral Reviews, 116*, 480–493. https://doi.org/10.1016/j.neubiorev.2020.07.013

Nesse, R. (2005). Natural selection and the regulation of defences: A signal detector analysis of the smoke detector principle. *Evolution and Human Behavior, 26*(1), 88–105. http://dx.doi.org/10.1016/j.evolhumbehav.2004.08.002

Nesse, R. M., & Schulkin, J. (2019). An evolutionary medicine perspective of pain and its disorders. *Philosophic Transactions of the Royal Society B, 374*(1785). https://doi.org/10.1098/rstb.2019.0288

Nowak, M. A. (2006). Five rules for the evolution of cooperation. *Science, 314*(5805), 1560–1563. http://: 10.1126/science.1133755

Nowak, M. A., & Highfield, R. (2011). *Supercooperators: Altruism, evolution, and why we need each other to succeed.* Free Press.

Nowak, M. A., & Sigmund, K. (2005). Evolution of indirect reciprocity. *Nature, 437,* 1291–1298. http://doi:10.1038/nature04131

Nowak, M. A., Tarnita, C. E., & Wilson, E. O. (2010). The evolution of eusociality. *Nature, 466,* 1057–1062. http://doi:10.1038/nature09205

Nowbahari, E., & Hollis, K. L. (2010). Rescue behavior: Distinguishing between rescue, cooperation and other forms of altruistic behavior. *Communicative and Integrative Biology, 3*(2), 77–79. doi: 10.4161/cib.3.2.10018

Plesk, R., & Mayer, V. (2008). Nonhuman primates mask signs of pain. *Laboratory Primate Newsletter, 47,* 1–3.

Preston, S. D., & de Waal, F. B. M. (2002). Empathy: Its ultimate and proximate bases. *Behavioral and Brain Sciences, 25*(1), 1–72. http://dx.doi.org/10.1017/S0140525X02000018

Prkachin, K. M., & Craig, K. D. (1995). Expressing pain: The communication and interpretation of facial pain signals. *Journal of Nonverbal Behavior, 19,* 191–205. http://doi:10.1007/BF02173080

Raja, S. N., Carr, D. B., Cohen, M., Finnerup, N. B., Flor, H., Gibson, S., Keefe, F. J., Mogil, J. S., Ringkamp, M., Sluka, K. A., Song, X. J., Stevens, B., Sullivan, M. D., Tutelman, P. R., Ushida, T., & Vader, K. (2020). The revised International Association for the Study of Pain definition of pain: Concepts, challenges, and compromises. *Pain, 161*(9), 1976–1982. doi: 10.1097/j.pain.0000000000001939

Romano, J. M., Turner, J. A., Friedman, L. S., Bulcroft, R. A., Jensen, M. P., Hops, H., & Wright, S. F. (1992). Sequential analysis of chronic pain behaviors and spouse responses. *Journal of Consulting and Clinical Psychology, 60*(5), 777–782. http://psycnet.apa.org/doi/10.1037/0022-006X.60.5.777

Romano, J. M., Turner, J. A., Jensen, M. P., Friedman, L. S., Bulcroft, R. A., Hops, H., & Wright, S. F. (1995). Chronic pain patient-spouse behavioral interactions predict patient disability. *Pain, 63*(3), 353–360. http://dx.doi.org/10.1016/0304-3959(95)00062-3

Rutte, C., & Taborsky, M. (2007). Generalized reciprocity in rats. *Public Library of Science Biology, 5*(7), e196. http://doi: 10.1371/journal.pbio.0050196

Schmidt, K. L. (2002). The evolutionary novel context of clinical caregiving and facial displays of pain. *Behavioral and Brain Sciences, 25*(4), 471–472. http://dx.doi.org/10.1017/S0140525X02390083

Schrock, J. M., Snodgrass, J. J., & Sugiyama, L. S. (2020). Lassitude: The emotion of being sick. *Evolution and Human Behavior, 41*(1), 44–57. https://doi.org/10.1016/j.evolhumbehav.2019.09.002

Schwartz, L., Jensen, M. P., & Romano, J. M. (2005). The development and psychometric evaluation of an instrument to assess spouse responses to pain and well behavior in patients with chronic pain: The spouse response inventory. *Journal of Pain, 6*(4), 243–252. http://dx.doi.org/10.1016/j.jpain.2004.12.010

Shackelford, T. K., & Weekes-Shackelford, V. A. (Eds.) (2021). *Encyclopedia of evolutionary psychological science.* Springer International. https://doi.org/10.1007/978-3-319-16999-6_2100-1

Silk, J. (2007). Empathy, sympathy and prosocial preferences in primates. In R. I. M. Dunbar & L. Barrett (Eds.), *Oxford handbook of evolutionary psychology* (pp. 115–126). Oxford University Press.

Simon, D., Craig, K. D., Miltner, W. H. R., & Rainville, P. (2006). Brain responses to dynamic facial expressions of pain. *Pain, 126,* 309–318. http://dx.doi.org/10.1016/j.pain.2006.08.033

Singer, T., Seymour, B., O'Doherty, J., Kaube, H., Dolan, R. J., & Frith, C. D. (2004). Empathy for pain involves the affective but not sensory components of pain. *Science, 303*(5661), 1157–1162. http://doi: 10.1126/science.1093535

Sneddon, L. U. (2019). Evolution of nociception and pain: Evidence from fish models. *Philosophical Transactions of the Royal Society B, 374*(1785), 20190290. http://dx.doi.org/10.1098/rstb.2019.0290

Steinkopf, L. (2016a). An evolutionary perspective on pain communication. *Evolutionary Psychology, 14*(2), 1–7. https://doi.org/10.1177%2F1474704915600559

Steinkopf, L. (2016b). Disgust, empathy, and care of the sick: An evolutionary perspective. *Evolutionary Psychological Science, 3,* 149–158. http://doi: 10.1007/s40806-016-0078-0

Stephens, R., Atkins, J., & Kingston, A. (2009). Swearing as a response to pain. *NeuroReport, 20*(12), 1056–1060. http://doi: 10.1097/WNR.0b013e32832e64b1

Stilwell, G., Lema, M. S., & Broom, D. M. (2007). Comparing the effect of three different disbudding methods on behaviour and plasma cortisol of calves. *Revista Portuguesa de Ciências Veterinárias, 102,* 281–288.

Sullivan, M. J. L., Thorn, B., Haythornthwaite, J. A., Keefe, F., Martin, M., Bradley, L. A., & Leffebvre, J. C. (2001). Theoretical perspectives on the relation between catastrophizing and pain. *Clinical Journal of Pain, 17*(1), 52–64. https://doi.org/10.1097/00002508-200103000-00008

Sullivan, M. J. L., Tripp, D. A., & Santor, D. (2000). Gender differences in pain and pain behaviour: The role of catastrophizing. *Cognitive Therapy Research, 24,* 121–134. http://link.springer.com/article/10.1023/A:1005459110063 - page-1

Sussman, R. W., Garber, P. A., & Cheverud, J. M. (2005). Importance of cooperation and affiliation in the evolution of primate sociality. *American Journal of Physical Anthropology, 128*(1), 84–97. http://doi: 10.1002/ajpa.20196

Thorn, B. E., Ward, L. C., Sullivan, M. J. L., & Boothby, J. L. (2003). Communal coping model of catastrophizing: conceptual model building. *Pain, 106*(1–2), 1–2. http://doi: 10.1016/S0304-3959(03)00228-8

Tiokhin, L. (2106). Do symptoms of illness serve signaling functions? (Hint: Yes). *Quarterly Review of Biology, 91*(2),177–195. http://doi: 10.1086/686811

Turk, D. C., Kerns, R. D., & Rosenberg, R. (1992). Effects of marital interaction on chronic pain and disability: Examining the down side of social support. *Rehabilitation Psychology, 37*(4), 259–274. http://psycnet.apa.org/doi/10.1037/h0079108

Van Rysewyk, S. (2016). Nonverbal indicators of pain. *Animal Sentience: An Interdisciplinary Journal on Animal Feeling, 3*(30), n.p.

Van Vugt, M., Roberts, G., & Hardy, C. (2007). Competitive altruism: A theory of reputation-based cooperation in groups. In R. I. M. Dunbar & L. Barrett (Eds.), *The Oxford handbook of evolutionary psychology* (pp. 531–540). Oxford University Press.

Vigil, J. M., & Strenth, C. (2014). No pain, no social gains: A social-signaling perspective of human pain behaviours. *World Journal of Anesthesiology, 3*(1),18–30 http://doi:10.5313/wja.v3.i118

Vigil, J. M., Di Domenico, J., Strenth, C., Coulombe, P., Kruger, E., Mueller, A. A., Beltran, D. G., & Adams, I. (2015*).* Experimenter effects on pain reporting in women vary across the menstrual cycle. *International Journal of Endocrinology, 2015*, 1–8. http://dx.doi.org/10.1155/2015/520719

Vollmer-Conna, U. (2001). Acute sickness behaviour: An immune system-to-brain communication? *Psychological Medicine, 31*(5), 761–767. https://doi.org/10.1017/S0033291701003841

Waddell, G. (2004). *The back pain revolution* (2nd ed.). Churchill-Livingstone Press.

Wall, P. D. (1979). On the relation of injury to pain: The John J. Bonica lecture. *Pain, 6*(3), 253–264. https://doi.org/10.1016/0304-3959(79)90047-2

Wall, P. D. (1989). Introduction. In P.D. Wall & R. Melzack (Eds.), *Textbook of pain* (pp. 1–18). Churchill-Livingstone Press.

Walters, E. T. (1991). A functional, cellular and evolutionary model of nociceptive plasticity in Aplysia. *Biological Bulletin, 180*, 241–251. http://www.biolbull.org/content/180/2/241.full.pdf+html

Walters, E. T. (1994). Injury-related behavior and neuronal plasticity: An evolutionary perspective on sensitisation, hyperalgaesia and analgaesia. *International Review of Neurobiology, 36*, 327–427. http://doi: 10.1016/S0074-7742(08)60307-4

Walters, E. T., & Moroz, L. L. (2009). Molluscan memory of injury: Evolutionary insights into chronic pain and neurological disorders. *Brain Behavior and Evolution, 74*(3), 206–218. https://doi.org/10.1159/000258667

Walters, E. T., & Williams, A. C. de C. (2019). Evolution of mechanisms and behaviour important for pain. *Philosophical Transactions of the Royal Society B, 374*, 20190275. https://dx.doi.org/10.1098/rstb.2019.0275

Williams, A. C. de C. (2016). What can evolutionary theory tell us about chronic pain? *Pain, 157*(4), 788–790. https://doi.org/10.1097/j.pain.0000000000000464

Williams, A. C. de C. (2002). Facial expression of pain: An evolutionary account. *Behavioral and Brain Sciences, 25*(4), 439–488. http://doi: 10.1017/S0140525X02000080

Williams, A. C. de C. (2019). Persistence of pain in humans and other mammals. *Philosophical Transactions of the Royal Society B, 374*, 20190276. http://dx.doi.org/10.1098/rstb.2019.0276

Williams, A. C. de C., & Craig, K. D. (2016). Updating the definition of pain. *Pain, 157*(11), 2420–2423. https://doi.org/10.1097/j.pain.0000000000000613

Wilson, E. O. (2012). *The social conquest of earth*. Liveright.

Zahavi, A. (1975). Mate selection: A selection for a handicap. *Journal of Theoretical Biology, 53*, 205–214. http://dx.doi.org/10.1016/0022-5193(75)90111-3

CHAPTER 23

Contentment: The Evolution of Indestructible Well-Being

Daniel Cordaro

Abstract

Contentment is felt when one's present experience is perceived to be complete as it is. There is a growing literature which, when taken together, establishes contentment as a discrete, universally recognized emotion that is distinct from happiness and other related pleasant states. Contentment serves several evolutionarily important functions critical to individual survival, and it supports the sustainability of larger ecosystems. It buffers against resource overconsumption and serves as a barometer for unconditional acceptance of self and others. Contentment is highly valued across philosophical traditions spanning 4,000 years, and its facial and vocal expressions are recognized and displayed across cultures. This chapter takes an evolutionary approach to contentment and reviews the historical and empirical literatures giving rise to its importance for emotion psychology. Based on these observations, future directions for the continued study of this empirically rich and philosophically important basic emotion are discussed.

Key Words: contentment, happiness, positive psychology, expression, physiology, evolution

Introduction

Humanity's search for true happiness and well-being is older than the written word. The foundation of many major philosophical traditions and the origins of psychology itself come from a deep desire to find greater meaning, purpose, and joy in life (Hergenhahn & Henley, 2014). At the root of these explorations is an emotion that underscores what it means to flourish as a human being. Despite being colloquially overshadowed by *happiness* for the past century, it has been a central theme in discussions on human wellness for over 4,000 years (Saunders, 1966).

Contentment is a low-intensity, pleasant emotion that arises when we perceive our environment to be complete as it is, without the need for modifications or additions (Cordaro, Brackett, et al., 2016). It is elicited by an unconditional acceptance of the present moment, and it has served a critical reproductive function throughout our evolutionary lineage (Bjørn Grinde, 2012). True to its humble and unobtrusive nature, contentment is the gentle, homeostatic hum of pleasantness that signals "all is well" biologically, psychologically, and environmentally. It is the affective space that human experience reliably returns to in the absence of more intense stimuli and emotions, such as fear, disgust, anger, and elation. This chapter highlights how contentment serves as a barometer for allostatic load—more commonly known as stress—and provides a brief review of the theoretical, evolutionary, and philosophical treatments of contentment across culture, tradition, and time. Decades of evidence across disciplines provide robust evidence for contentment as a basic emotion, and this chapter discusses these studies, as well as future empirical directions required to conclusively determine the extent to which this emotion is discrete and evolutionary.

Basic Emotion Criteria

For millions of years, all sentient life on earth struggled, gained, lost, fought, fled, and triumphed throughout the ages. During these struggles, emotions have helped us find efficient solutions to fundamental life situations related to reproduction and survival (Keltner, Tracy, et al., 2019). The emotions elicited by these situations—frustration, joy, sadness, anger, fear, and pride, respectively—initiated elegantly crafted psychophysiological changes that suited the adaptive needs of the problem at hand (Ekman & Cordaro, 2011). Over the past 150 years, emotion science has sought to understand the causes, consequences, and biological origins of emotions, and has established a list of empirical criteria that, when met, provide robust evidence of an emotion's evolutionary origins (Table 23.1; see also Cordaro, 2021).

Early work on the evolutionary origins of emotions focused primarily on a small subset of basic emotions: *anger*, *joy*, *fear*, *disgust*, *surprise*, and *sadness* (Ekman, 1992). However, after the turn of the century, the field of emotion psychology saw burgeoning interest in "new" emotions above and beyond the original six (see Keltner, Sauter, et al., 2019),. Despite this expanding interest in emotions, there is a paucity of studies on low-intensity pleasant emotions, which arise during life's more peaceful moments. The high-activation bias in the emotion sciences is due, at least in part, to the fact that Darwin himself focused on autonomically activating pleasant states (e.g., joy, delight, determination, etc.), and said very little about their low-activation counterparts, with the exception of "calm," which he considered the absence of high-intensity negative states like fear and rage (Darwin, 1872, p. 293). Throughout the development of the field of emotion psychology, the high-activation bias was further reinforced by

Table 23.1 The 13 Criteria for the Empirical Study of Basic Emotions
Empirical Criteria for Basic Emotions
I. Shared Criteria
1. Quick onset 2. Brief duration 3. Unbidden occurrence 4. Coherence among response systems
II. Differentiating Criteria
5. Distinct universals in antecedent events 6. Distinct appraisal mechanism 7. Distinct subjective experience 8. Distinct cognition 9. Distinct behavioral tendencies **10. Distinct universal signals** **11. Distinct physiology** **12. Distinct neurobiology involving subcortical structures** **13. Distinct primate homologue**

Note: The first four criteria are shared among all basic emotions, and the remaining nine differentiate basic emotions from one another. **Bold** indicates the criteria which provide the most robust evidence for the evolutionary origins of basic emotions, though all criteria contribute to this to some degree.

Replicated from Chapter 1 of this *Handbook*.

the fact that high-activation emotions have, by nature, more obvious signals, outcomes, and autonomic impact than their low-activation counterparts (Kensinger & Corkin, 2004).

Cordaro and colleagues (2016) were the first to propose a theoretical framework for contentment as a basic emotion. After conducting a cross-cultural assessment and analysis of antecedent conditions for contentment, they determined that its main appraisal involves a sense of wholeness or completeness in the present moment. According to Cordaro and colleagues (2016), contentment arises whenever we feel unconditional acceptance of our present experience, and they suspected that further research and review of the literature would uncover evidence suggesting that contentment is a basic emotion. Since then, the field of emotion psychology has delivered further support for this theory, and herein it is proposed that contentment fulfills at least 8 of the 13 basic emotion criteria (see Table 23.1).

The central question of the present chapter is thus: To what extent is contentment a basic emotion? Basic emotions must serve a universally adaptive function that supported the reproductive goals of our ancestors and helped with survival-relevant situations (Levenson, 2011). This chapter reviews the evidence that contentment has been found to fulfill the following criteria (numbered per Table 23.1): quick onset (1), brief duration (2), unbidden occurrence (3), and coherence among response systems (4). Contentment also has a universal antecedent (5), a distinct appraisal mechanism (6), and distinct universal signals (10). There is also a growing evidence basis that experiences of contentment covary with distinct autonomic responses, and that the individual differences in these responses can be predicted genetically (11). This brief review takes into account four millennia of contentment philosophy across dozens of cultures, and based on this evidence proposes that contentment arises as a result of our sense of unconditional completeness in the present moment. In many ways, contentment is a journey across time, space, and tradition; we therefore begin by unraveling this foundational component of our shared philosophical legacy.

History of Contentment
Santosha Lineage

VEDIC PHILOSOPHY

All great stories begin with love, and the ancient lineage of contentment philosophy is no exception. Uruvashi, a celestial Apsara (angel), and King Pururavas, a mortal, had fallen helplessly and unexpectedly for one another. Uruvashi, the dawn goddess, was the most beautiful of all the Apsaras, and was unlike any other woman Pururavas had ever met before. She was the embodiment of her name—in Sanskrit, *Uras* means "heart" and *Vashi* is "one who controls." A profoundly unlikely pair, the two started their courtship where most successful relationships begin—by negotiating terms. What could celestial goddess Uruvashi, "one who controls the heart," possibly ask for? Very simply, she requested one drop of pure butter each day for her mealtime, along with two other small preferences. After many years of living together, one day Uruvashi's requests were forgotten. The terms broken, she began to depart for the heavens as Pururavas tried desperately to convince her to stay. Tragically for him, Uruvashi had made up her mind:

> When changed in form, wandering with mortals, I lived with them for many delightful years. I ate once a day a small quantity of butter (ghee), and with contentment (*Santosha*) in this I now depart. (Griffith, 2013; r.ve. 10.95.16; ca. 2000 BCE)

Uruvashi, the dawn goddess, the one who controls the heart, is self-fulfilled with her experience in the human realm, and so she moves on to the heavens without looking back.

While heartbreaking (to us mortals), this 4,000-year-old hymn is also profound. The one who controls the heart can be contented with a simple drop of butter each day, and when the situation requires Uruvashi to move on, she does so with grace, peace, and self-assurance. The story inspires the question: When it is time for us to return to the heavens, how can we, like Uruvashi, do so with contentment in our hearts?

Philosophical discussions of contentment pre-date the written word. The celestial hymns of the Vedas were transmitted verbally for countless centuries, long before systems of writing became widely available. When discussing the meaning of "true" happiness and sustainable well-being, the Vedas expansively discuss *santosha* and its many synonyms (e.g, *purna*, *akama*, etc.)—a deep sense of permanent, inner wholeness that nothing can take away from us (Aurobindo, 1951):

> That is wholeness. Creation is wholeness. From that wholeness flows the world's wholeness. This wholeness flows out from that wholeness, yet that wholeness remains whole. (Isha Upanishad, Yajur Veda; ca. 1100 BCE)

Thousands of years of philosophy are condensed into a single word; *santosha* is a combination of two Sanskrit terms. The first is *saṃ*, which means "complete," "whole," and "together." It describes something that is without any lack or missing component whatsoever. It is a union of all parts into one whole. The second is *tosha*, which means "satisfied" and "enough." It is the fundamental acceptance of something as it is, without requiring any additional modifications (Burrow, 2001). Bringing these words together, *santosha* describes a state of unconditional acceptance of one's experience in the present moment. It is a feeling of wholeness and completeness with regard to one's self, one's life, and everything in it—both pleasant and unpleasant.

Around 500 BCE, the Yoga Sutras (lit. "threads of unity") of Patañjali became one of the most influential philosophical teachings in the practice of *yoga*. Patañjali taught that in order to attain enlightenment, one must engage in eight prerequisite practices that clear the mind and prepare the body for the ultimate attainment of permanent, inner completeness. These eight limbs became the foundations of the Ashtanga Yoga (lit. "eight limbs of unity") philosophy, one of the most well-known disciplines still widely practiced today. The eight limbs are divided into two major categories: the *yamas* (personal ethics) and *niyamas* (virtuous habits). Patañjali clearly and concisely describes the unparalleled importance of cultivating the *niyama santosha*:

> From contentment alone comes true happiness. (II VR II; ca. 500 BCE)

While brief in words, Patañjali was profound in concept. This was one of the first philosophical treatments of contentment as a fundamentally discrete state distinct from happiness (Bryant, 2015). Even more interesting is his clear distinction between true happiness, which arises from contentment, and false happiness—which is everything else. A bold hypothesis, Patañjali set the stage for the widespread adoption of practices that could lead to a sense of contentment in life.

Around a century after Patañjali, the *niyama santosha* is echoed throughout the entire Mahabarata, one of the two major Sanskrit epics of ancient India (Buck, 2019). According to the legend, two warring families wage battle over control over the Kingdom of Kurukshetra. The epic highlights the intricate details of the 18-day battle, including weapons used, battle formations, parties involved, and—perhaps most importantly—spiritual crises solved. This latter topic serves as the foundation for the more philosophical chapters of the Mahabarata, the most notable of which is the Bhagavad Gita (Prabhupada & Bhaktivedanta, 1972, Chapter 6).

The Gita describes the day of battle, focusing on our hero Arjuna, who stands with bow in hand and arrows in quiver. Before leading his troops into battle, Arjuna is paralyzed by the senselessness of war, and the confusion of setting out to kill those he considers family on the opposing side. Upon asking the heavens for guidance, Krishna, a form of the god Vishnu, intervenes by teaching Arjuna the path to enlightenment, and how to break the chains of Karmic bondage (the cycle of rebirth):

> One who remains the same towards friend or foe, in honor or disgrace, in heat or cold, in pleasure or pain; who is free from attachment; who is indifferent to censure or praise; quiet, content with whatever one has, unattached to country or house, contented and devoted, that person is dearest to me [Krishna]. (IV.21.158; ca. 400 BCE)

After the dust settles from the great battle, the subsequent chapters of the Mahabarata focus on rebuilding society and re-establishing peace. The *Shanti Parva* (Chapter of Peace) continues to elaborate on the importance of contentment (Buck, 2019):

> Contentment is the highest heaven, contentment is the highest bliss. There is no higher experience than contentment. When one draws away all craving desires like a tortoise drawing in all limbs, then the natural resplendence of his soul soon manifests itself. (s.p. Chapter 21; ca. 400 BCE)

As yogic philosophy progressed throughout the millennia, the focus on contentment became more apparent. Many later works, such as the Shiva Sutras and Vaṣistha's Yoga, provide details on how to access contentment, and its critical importance along the journey to enlightenment. The Shiva Sutras (Hughes, 2007) clearly identify that contentment can simply be found inside without needing to do anything in particular. According to this second-century BCE text, the path to contentment can be summarized in a single line:

> Simply sit and be absorbed by the contentment of your heart. (VII; 3.17)

Can contentment really be found by simply directing one's attention inward to a sense of peace that is already inside? If so, how can we access it? Vaṣistha's Yoga, a seventh-century CE masterpiece describing the concentrated essence of all ancient Yogic philosophy, identifies four categories of practices that reliably lead to a sense of indestructible wellness within (Venkatesananda, 2010):

> There are four gatekeepers who guard the path to inner liberation. They are *shanti* (quietness of the mind), *satsanga* (wise and virtuous company), *vichara* (inquiry into the nature of self), and *santosha* (contentment). . . . Befriend at least one of them even at the expense of your own life, because by securing one as a friend, the other three will follow. (v.y. XI, 59–61)

Vaṣistha's Yoga continues to elaborate on core philosophical requirements that elicit a sense of wholeness that is already inside us. It is a radical and at times paradoxical departure from the notion that we need to "do" or "achieve" happiness. In fact, it argues that by seeking to achieve something, we move farther away from the true happiness of contentment altogether.

BUDDHIST PHILOSOPHY

One of the most influential figures interested in the nature of true happiness was Siddhartha Gautama, who lived his life in what is now Nepal (Kelen, 2014). Born to a wealthy aristocratic family, Siddhartha was the heir-apparent of the Shakya clan, the leaders of a small republic at the border of India. According to early sources, an insatiable curiosity to understand the nature of reality began to haunt Siddhartha, and after finding some yogic ascetics in the forest, he decided to leave his luxurious life in pursuit of inner truth. A student of the Vedic texts, Siddhartha quickly mastered meditation and began teaching across the subcontinent. After explicitly forbidding his followers from creating a religion around his life and teachings, Buddhism nonetheless began to spread shortly after Siddhartha's death around the fourth century BCE. On contentment, Siddhartha famously taught:

> Health is the greatest gift, contentment is the greatest wealth, a trusted friend is the best relative, enlightenment is the greatest bliss. (Byrom, 2010, v. 204)

DAOIST PHILOSOPHY

Around the same time Siddhartha Gautama was learning to meditate, Laozi had already completed the Tao Te Ching, and Daoism was growing its cultural roots in China (Waley, 2013). Influenced by both Vedic philosophy and Confucianism, the Tao Te Ching centered its teachings on the "Tao" or the natural way and order of the universe. The Tao Te Ching's short yet deeply impactful 81 sections focus on aligning one's mind, virtues, and actions with the natural order of the universe. One of the cornerstone philosophies is 知足 (*zhīzú*, contentment), and Laozi echoes similar wisdom to that which had preceded these writings for thousands of years:

> Knowing others is cleverness;
> Knowing the self is enlightenment.
> Mastering others requires effort;
> Mastering the self requires real strength.
>
> He who knows contentment is rich.
> Perseverance is a sign of willpower.
> He who stays where he is endures.
> To die but not to perish is to be eternally present. (Laozi & English, 1972, Chapter 33)

LATER TRADITIONS

The lineage of *santosha* across the ages was one of the most influential emotion-based philosophies in history, underpinning several major world religions, many of which cannot be reviewed here due to the limitations of a short chapter. Nevertheless, contentment inspired central philosophical themes across Confucianism, Zen, Jainism, Sikhism, and Shinto—all of which are rooted in the simple concept of realizing the wholeness that is already inside us (Smith & Marranca, 2009).

S-L-M Lineage

JUDAIC PHILOSOPHY

The sixth through fourth centuries BCE were extraordinarily generative years from a philosophical perspective. As the Vedas were flourishing across South Asia, and Siddhartha Gautama and Laozi were teaching the art of living with *santosha* and *zhīzú*, another world-altering lineage of philosophy was emerging from Western Asia in Babylon. After thousands of years of being passed down through oral tradition, the Torah was compiled as systems of writing became more commonplace across the known world. Describing the monotheistic philosophies, stories, and values of the Jewish faith, the Torah has been a foundation of Western thinking for millennia.

Originally written in Hebrew, one of the oldest languages next to Sanskrit, the Torah expounds on one of the most important Semitic root words in the entire language system: S-L-M (*shalam*; *Shin-Lamedh-Mem*). Literally translated, S-L-M means being whole, intact, and complete. Speaking to the importance of this concept, the Torah features it 300 times across multiple parables and discussions.

Stemming from the Semitic root S-L-M is the Hebrew word *shalom*, a ubiquitous greeting for Hebrew speakers that means much more than "peace," as it is often translated. *Shalom* is a deep sense of inner wholeness, a connection to God and the universe, and a sense of unshakable equanimity despite whatever pleasure or pain life is offering at the moment. The "peace" referred to in translations of *shalom* is more than just the absence of conflict; it is a deep, personal sense of completeness on multiple levels—physical, mental, and spiritual. According to several Jewish sages, *shalom* is the very purpose of the Torah itself:

> All that is written in the Torah was written for the sake of Shalom. (Steinsaltz, 2009; Talmud, Gittin, 59b)

CHRISTIAN PHILOSOPHY

From the Torah, the Hebrew word *shalom* later became *shlam* in Aramaic, which was the language spoken by one of the greatest revolutionaries and compassionate leaders of his time. Jesus of Nazareth was a Hebrew scholar, who grew up with humble beginnings as the son of a woodcarver in what is now Israel. Much as Siddhartha Gautama mastered and taught the practices expounded in the Vedas, Jesus had mastered and began teaching the core practices of the Torah—among them love, devotion, compassion, equality, and freedom. One of the most important concepts that Jesus taught was *shlam*, the sense of inner completeness. As the Old and New Testaments of the Christian Bible were being compiled in ancient Greek, *shlam* and *shalom* became *eiréné*, which comes from the Greek root *eirō*, meaning "to join together into a whole." *Eiréné* is so important that it appears over 100 times throughout the Bible, and in the New Testament alone, 62 of the 260 chapters feature at least one reference to it—not least of which was when Jesus famously said:

> Peace (*Eiréné*) I leave with you; my peace (*eiréné*) I give to you. I do not give you as the world gives. Do not let your hearts be troubled and do not be afraid. (Aland et al., 1993; John 14:27)

ISLAMIC AND SUFI PHILOSOPHY

After ancient Greek *eiréné*, The S-L-M lineage makes one final stop before meeting us at the present time. S-L-M is also the root of the Arabic words *salām* (similar to *shalom*) and also *Islam* (surrender to God), and forms one of the foundational principals of the entire Islamic and Sufi philosophical systems. The trilateral Arabic root (س ل م; *sīn-lām-mīm*) occurs 140 times in 16 derivations throughout the Qur'an. We also see the emotion word synonym *Rida* (divine contentment) when describing the relationship between God and God's creations:

> God has contentment (*Rida*) with them, and they have contentment with God. (Shihab, 2007; Qur'an 5:119; 9:100; 98:8)

This passage appears three times throughout the Qur'an, evidence of the vital importance of the concept of contentment between God and all of creation. In fact, the S-L-M lineage of contentment is so prevalent across the Abrahamic line of philosophies, that it is one of only a few foundational teachings that unify the main monotheistic religions. Although modern linguistic translations have leaned heavily on the word "peace" when describing S-L-M based words, their true meaning goes far deeper.

Contentare Lineage

The modern English word "contentment" is derived from Latin *contentare*, meaning "to hold together" or "that which is contained." Similar to its Greek counterpart, the root of *contentare* describes something whole and complete, the entire contents of something. *Contentare* later evolved into *contentus*, meaning a person who felt whole and complete. Someone who feels *contentus* has no desires beyond what exists in the present moment; they are whole, fully contained (Klein, 1966; Weekley, 2012). This later evolved into English *contentment*, bringing together *content* (that which is contained) and *-ment* (a resulting state), meaning a state of perceived completeness. While the colloquial use of the word *contentment* is often conflated with concepts like laziness, complacency, and indifference—the true meaning could not be farther from these. For over 4,000 years of human writing, contentment has been, and still remains, one of the most prevalent and philosophically significant emotions related to the nature of happiness. For ease of reference, Table 23.2 describes all major translations and etymological roots of the word *contentment* across 11 languages.

The Evolution of Contentment

The prevalence of contentment in its many forms across most major philosophical traditions is a testament to its importance to the human experience. More recently, research in biology and psychology has begun to reveal the evolutionary significance of contentment and its critical function for survival and reproduction (Grinde, 2002). It is through the lens of human evolution that we can begin to understand why contentment appears so universally across culture, language, and time.

The survival of all organisms hinges on homeostasis, the process by which we maintain physical, mental, and biochemical balance. Our lifelong struggle for biological permanence is shared by every life system on earth as we constantly navigate rapidly changing forces both internally and externally (Schulkin, 2004). Luckily for us, this process requires very little conscious input on our part. A bit of food and water here and there and avoiding danger are generally all that is required to maintain homeostasis, while the rest is completely automated by the millions of biochemical background processes running from moment to moment.

One of the primary functions of emotions is that they support the regulation of homeostasis through *allostasis*, the process by which organisms return to homeostasis after a significant challenge is experienced in the environment (McEwen, 1998). Through our perception of the environment, emotions allow us to quickly assess and react to critical situations which may disrupt our delicate homeostatic balance. This occurs as a cascade of neurological, biochemical, physiological, cognitive, and behavioral changes, whose combined subjective experience gives rise to the "feeling" that accompanies each discrete emotion (Cacioppo et al., 2000). However, as helpful as emotions are, too much emotional intensity has long-term consequences. Allostatic load—more commonly called *stress*—has a cumulative effect on the body and mind and can eventually lead to physical illness and psychopathology (McEwen, 2004). This is perhaps why Blaise Pascale, 17th-century philosopher and mathematician, wrote of the urgency of finding time to calm the nervous system:

> All of humanity's problems stem from a person's inability to sit quietly in a room alone. (Pascal, 1888)

What, then, elicits the onset of contentment? Cummins (2010, 2018) proposed that contentment arises when we perceive our allostatic load to be minimal, when no other intense emotions or stimuli are present. Contentment, in turn, is a barometer of our psychophysiological proximity to our baseline homeostatic state. When homeostasis fails due to a perception of overwhelming allostatic load, we lose contact with the feelings of contentment due to more dominant negative or positive emotions that are immediately survival-relevant. Contentment, therefore, is homeostatically protective in that allostatic deviations from baseline

Table 23.2 Contentment Linguistic Traditions across 11 Philosophically Significant Cultures

Language	Native Word	English Approximation	Etymology	Meaning	Featured Prominently by
Sanskrit	संतोष	santōṣha	*Sam* (completeness) + *tosha* (acceptance)	Complete acceptance of the present moment	The Vedas
Pali	सन्तोसो	santoso	*Sam* (completeness) + *tutthi* (satisfaction, delight)	Complete satisfaction with the present moment	Pali Canons
Tibetan	ཆོག་ཤེས	Chog shes	*Chog* (to know) + *shes* (enough, completeness)	Knowledge of enough	Dhammapada
Chinese	知足	zhīzú	知 (to know) + 足 (enough, completeness)	Knowledge of enough	Tao Te Ching
Japanese	知足	chisoku	知 (to know) + (enough, completeness)	Knowledge of enough	Zen scriptures
Hebrew	שלום	shalom	Š-L-M (join together into a whole)	To be enough, complete	The Torah
Aramaic	ܫܠܡ	shlam	Š-L-M (join together into a whole)	To be enough, complete	Jesus of Nazareth
Arabic	سلام	salām	S-L-M (join together into a whole)	To be enough, complete	The Qur'an
Greek	Εἰρήνη	Eirēnē	*Eirō* (join together into a whole)	To be enough, complete	The Bible (original)
Latin	Contentare	contentare	*Con* (with, together) + *tenere* (to hold)	To be held together, complete	The Bible (later translations)
English	Contentment	contentment	*Content* (that which is contained, complete) + *ment* (resulting state)	State of completeness, wholeness	Present-day speakers

are immediately and clearly felt as the absence of contentment. Grinde (2013) referred to this phenomenon as the *default state of contentment*, meaning that contentment is the emotion that humans reliably return to after other, more intense experiences subside. This initiates a positive feedback cycle wherein contentment arises when we engage in activities, mindsets, and social relationships that best facilitate a healthy return to homeostasis.

It is important to note here that it is the *perception* of allostatic load that promotes deviations from contentment, rather than the objective presence of allostatically significant stimuli. In other words, the *object* of stress may differ from person to person, so it is our *appraisal* of a stressful event that gives rise to emotions of discontent. Conversely, it is the *appraisal* of the situation as complete—not the situation itself—that gives rise to contentment (see Frijda et al., 1989). Stress appraisal and management are a well-studied phenomenon, wherein individuals with greater stress tolerance and more effective self-care practices can manage significantly more allostatic load than those with lower tolerance and poorer care practices (Boyce & Ellis, 2005).

Empirical evidence reveals that contentment in the absence of perceived allostatic load is ubiquitous across cultures, despite profound differences in socioeconomic status, access to resources, health concerns, and personal challenges. Cacioppo and Berntson (1994) coined the term *positivity offset* to describe the phenomenon wherein study participants consistently rated neutral stimuli as eliciting a slightly pleasant, contented feeling. Taken in the context of their experiments, when participants were simply sitting in the experiment room with no immediate task at hand, they reliably reported feeling pleasant, content, and mildly happy (Norris et al., 2011). The positivity offset has been further replicated in dozens of studies around the world (Ito & Cacioppo, 2005). For example, when studying the cross-cultural implications of this phenomenon, Diener and Diener (1996) conducted one of the largest studies in the history of positivity offset, and found that in 86% of the 43 nations that they surveyed, most people reported above-average levels of life satisfaction a majority of the time. Diener and colleagues (2015) further provided an evolutionary rationale for why humans experience contentment during more mundane or low-stimulation activities. They proposed that the positivity offset increases chances of reproductive and survival success due to three primary adaptive advantages:

(1) *Broaden and build.* It is well-established in the field of emotion psychology that positive emotions expand creative thinking, encourage new relationships, and motivate us to activate and develop resources to solve problems and innovate (Fredrickson & Branigan, 2005). It is therefore advantageous for humans to repeatedly return to a mildly pleasant, contented state during low-stimulus events. Research has shown that contentment specifically encourages us to consider new priorities and focus on new views of the self (Fredrickson, 2013).

(2) *Social bonding.* Happy humans develop pro-social relationships more quickly, make more friends, and develop more skills and resources for taking care of offspring as compared to unhappy humans. A baseline state of contentment is advantageous to attract more friends and potential mates, and to raise healthier, more well-adapted progeny. Conversely, the absence of positive affect is associated with unsociability, boredom, and lack of energy to explore and relate to others.

(3) *Physical and psychological health.* Contentment is a barometer for one's perceived allostatic load. The more effective an organism is at detecting and solving allostasis issues, the less it will experience stress and its concomitant psychophysiological health problems. This promotes general longevity and fitness, and subsequently, greater chances

of reproduction and offspring survival. Contentment is also a type of inner barometer which, over time, teaches us which activities, mindsets, and social relationships best facilitate autonomic health and wellness.

The positivity offset is not only ubiquitous and critical to survival, it also has a genetic marker. Ashare and colleagues (2013) studied the extent to which two single nucleotide polymorphisms coding for serotonin receptor function predicted positivity offset intensity in males and females. Genetic testing determined that males with a 102T allele and females with a 1019C allele both experienced greater positivity offset than those with the 102C and 1019G alleles, respectively. This study demonstrated that positivity in the absence of intense stimuli has a genetic basis, and that it is likely mediated by serotonin production and reception in the brain.

Taken together, there is a clear biological, evolutionary, and genetic rationale for the importance of contentment in human reproduction, survival, and well-being. It is in these universal situations where allostatic load is minimized that contentment is elicited as a biological signal that "all is well." In order to conclusively establish contentment as a basic emotion, however, there must be a distinct and measurable autonomic response associated with experiences of contentment. Furthermore, these physiological markers should be related to the downstream biochemical systems related to serotonin reception, nervous system regulation, and general parasympathetic activation.

Contentment Physiology

Over the past several decades, the field of psychophysiology has expanded the list of well-studied emotions (e.g., happiness, sadness, fear, anger, etc.) to include more states with suspected evolutionary origins (see Keltner, Sauter, et al., 2019). Interestingly, the majority of "new" emotions brought into the autonomic spotlight all have one feature in common—they activate the sympathetic nervous system and downregulate the parasympathetic nervous system (Levenson, 2011). This imbalanced focus on sympathetically activating pleasant emotions has opened a critical empirical gap in the field, which inspires the question: Are there evolutionarily grounded emotions that activate parasympathetic responses, promoting rest and regeneration?

One of the most direct methods of assessing an emotion's impact on human bodily systems is through psychophysiological analysis (Mauss et al., 2005). In this line of research, emotion elicitation is facilitated either via external stimuli or internal generation, and the impact of the emotion on various bodily systems is simultaneously measured (Coan & Allen, 2007). The most common systems studied are relatively simple autonomic data including heart rate (HR), electrodermal activity (EDA), respiratory rate (RR), and systolic/diastolic blood pressure (SBP/DBP). Recent studies have also begun to use more robust measurements of the cardiorespiratory response, such as heart rate variability (HRV), left ventricular ejection time (LVET), respiratory tidal volume (V_t), and blood CO_2 partial pressure (pCO_2). Lastly, a smaller number of studies have focused on hormonal changes (e.g., cortisol, DHEA) related to the stress response, as well as neuro-electrical responses through electroencephalograph (EEG) measurement (for a review of physiological methodologies see Luecken & Gallo, 2008). Together, this collection of methods provides a useful toolkit for understanding the discrete physiological changes that covary with the experience of specific emotions.

Psychophysiological studies of contentment typically rely on the emotion induction method, wherein study participants are exposed to contentment-inducing stimuli, such as film clips of relaxing nature scenes, fireplaces, instrumental music, tranquil scenery, etc. (Siedlecka & Denson, 2019). Other studies use emotion-recall methodology, wherein participants are prompted to remember a time when they felt content, or to write about a time when they felt unconditionally whole, which allows participants to consciously generate the experience of contentment (Westermann et al., 1996). As the emotion is induced, concurrent physiological data are collected and analyzed to ascertain the extent to which autonomic changes covary with the felt experience of the target emotion.

Kreibig (2010) conducted one of the most comprehensive reviews on the psychophysiology of 16 emotions, wherein specific autonomic markers that differentiated each of these 16 states were systematically evaluated and compared. Contentment was distinct from all other states in that it tended to downregulate the sympathetic nervous response, while at the same time activating the parasympathetic nervous system. In other words, feelings of contentment tended to covary with decreased α and β-andrenergic and cholinergic-mediated sympathetic systems, and it increased vagally mediated systems. When comparing these outcomes with other pleasant emotions like happiness, amusement, and pride, these high-intensity emotions tended to activate the sympathetic nervous system, a clear differentiator from contentment.

The physiological outcomes of contentment-mediated responses are summarized, along with their corresponding references, in Table 23.3. One of the most well-studied effects of contentment on the autonomic nervous system is a reliable decrease in both heart rate and respiratory rate (Christie & Friedman, 2004; Van Diest et al., 2001). Consistent with these results, additional studies identified decreases in mean arterial pressure, which early research found in both systolic and diastolic readings (Schwartz et al., 1981). Taken together, these effects imply activation of parasympathetic nerves, which control heart rate, involuntary respiration rate, and arterial pressure.

Looking further into contentment's impact on cardiopulmonary activity, Ritz and colleagues (2005) presented emotionally evocative images to participants and observed the extent to which discrete emotions covaried with changes in heart rate variability, a key indicator of vagus nerve activation. HRV has been an important biomarker in the medical literature for the past few decades, because higher HRV readings correlate with global autonomic nervous system health (Westermann et al., 1996), disease resistance (Thayer et al., 2010), and longevity (Zulfiqar et al., 2010). Contentment inductions elicited increases in HRV and simultaneous decreases in heart rate and respiratory rate, indicating that contentment likely attenuates the vagal response, leading to its hallmark reduction in sympathetic activity and upregulation of parasympathetic activity.

Van Diest and colleagues (2001) presented participants with emotionally evocative imagery, and found significant decreases in respiratory tidal volume and increases in the partial pressure of blood CO_2 for those viewing contentment-inducing photographs. These findings indicate that contented participants had shallower breathing concurrent with slight increases in CO_2 saturation in the blood. This finding is generally consistent with other findings regarding reduced respiratory rate and heart rate for those experiencing contentment. Additionally, Nyklíček and colleagues (1997) used music to induce contentment in participants, and noted a significant increase in left ventricular ejection time (LVET), which is defined by the ejection time between the opening and closing of the aortic valve. LVET has been an important biomarker of general cardiovascular health, where lower LVET scores have been found to be predictive of heart failure, myocardial infarction, and death (Biering-Sørensen et al., 2018).

Lastly, only one study to date has measured the biochemical underpinnings of contentment. Cortisol is a steroid hormone with several critical functions in the human body, including glucogenesis, metabolism regulation, immune function, and the inhibition of the inflammatory response to stress (Oakley & Cidlowski, 2013). It is a gold-standard biomarker whose upregulation in the body is a reliable indicator of psychophysiological stress, including anxiety and depression (Staufenbiel et al., 2013). Bershadsky and colleagues (2014) found that participants who learned and practiced Hatha Yoga reported significantly elevated levels of contentment across a five-month period as compared to a control group. Most importantly, those who experienced greater levels of contentment also had significantly lower concentrations of salivary cortisol across the entire study period. Table 23.3 provides a summary of findings across all psychophysiological studies of contentment, along with relevant references.

Taking all of these studies into consideration, this early work on the physiological correlates of contentment provides preliminary evidence that contentment is likely a discrete emotion at the level of the autonomic nervous system. The onset of contentment invites a unique, distinguishable cascade of physiological changes that differentiates it from other high-intensity positive emotions like happiness, amusement, pride, and excitement. Perhaps most importantly, contentment may also play a critical biological role in human health as it promotes autonomic rest, regeneration, and healing. This offers the field of emotion psychology an exciting horizon to explore the extent to which contentment plays a role in longevity and well-being.

Future studies regarding physiological correlates of contentment should assess cross-cultural reliability of these autonomic responses. Additionally, further research must also provide rigorous within-emotion and between-emotion comparison data across a wider array of physiological markers than have been reported here (e.g., combining autonomic, neurotransmitter, hormonal, and biochemical data, etc.). Of greatest interest to future investigations of contentment will be the biochemical underpinnings of contentment's parasympathetic response. Although it is relatively new in the field of medical diagnostics, salivary testing for acetylcholinesterase activity may provide a biochemical target indicator of trait emotions that mediate parasympathetic activation. Additionally, in light of Ashare and colleagues' (2013) findings on the genetic markers of the positivity offset, the serotonin production and biochemical signaling pathway is another clear target of investigation in the biochemistry of contentment.

Universal Expressions of Contentment

One of the most generative and enduring branches of emotion research is the study of nonverbal expressions in the face, voice, posture, and touch (see Keltner et al., 2003). Downstream from the body's autonomic activation, the expression of emotions provides an outward signal of our inward experiences. Expressive universality serves as a key basis of evidence when determining the evolutionary origins of emotions (see Al-Shawaf et al., 2016; Al-Shawaf & Lewis, 2017), and understanding cross-cultural differentiation of emotion expression can highlight how the state is perceived and idealized in different traditions around the world (Matsumoto, 1989). The study of emotional expression typically involves two main hypothesis tests (see Matsumoto et al., 2008). The *decoding hypothesis* tests the extent to which people from different cultures agree on the interpretation of nonverbal signals. The decoding hypothesis is usually one of the first lines of research when studying a candidate basic emotion. The *encoding hypothesis* tests the extent to which people from different cultures around the world will produce the same type of signal when communicating a specific emotion. The encoding hypothesis seeks to understand the facial muscles, vocal tones, postural changes, and tactile patterns involved in cross-cultural emotion communication. In general, when an emotion can be *decoded* and *encoded* reliably across cultures, including remote, previously uncontacted societies, the emotion is a more robust candidate for a basic emotion.

Ekman and colleagues (1990) sought to understand the nature of "Duchenne smiles," or "genuine" smiles, as they are often referred to in the literature. They hypothesized that Duchenne smiles involved zygomatic major contractions along with action of the orbicularis oculi (crow's feet wrinkles, eye squint). Conversely, non-genuine or "polite" smiles involved only zygomatic major with no action around the eyes. The authors hypothesized that all spontaneous expressions of pleasant, approach-directed emotions would involve Duchenne activity to some degree, and they set out to test this by observing the facial actions of participants experiencing amusement, happiness, excitement, interest, contentment, and several unpleasant emotions. In support of their hypothesis, all of the pleasant emotions produced Duchenne-typical facial actions—except for contentment. They concluded that perhaps their contentment stimuli did not produce genuine feelings of contentment, or maybe contentment had no reliable facial expression at all. Future research, they concluded, would need to more rigorously unpack the expression of contentment. It would take nearly 30 years of stepwise research to do so.

After nearly a decade of empirical obscurity, contentment resurfaced in a fashion true to its origins. Hejmadi and colleagues (2000) published the first study of its kind regarding the ancient Hindu theory of emotion and its expression through theater and dance. The authors mined the *Nayasastra*, a rich first-century Sanskrit treatise on the performing arts, which proposes in great detail the specific muscle movements, postures, and sounds that performers can use to accurately convey over 40 different emotions (Ghosh, 1967). One of the most well-described states in the *Nayasastra* is *dhṛti* (contentment), which is clearly defined in Chapter VII, sections 56–57:

> Dhṛti is caused by heroism, spiritual knowledge, learning, wealth, purity, good conduct, devotion to one's superiors, getting an excessive amount of money, enjoying sports, and the like. It is to be represented on the stage by actions such as enjoyment of objects gained, while not grumbling over objects unattained, not dwelling on the past, and not dwelling on objects partially enjoyed or lost. Contentment arising from spiritual knowledge, purity, wealth, and power is always to be represented on the stage by an absence of fear, sorrow, and sadness. When one enjoys attained objects such as sweet sound, touch, taste, form, and smell—and is not sorry over their non-attainment, one is said to have contentment.

Hejmadi and colleagues (2000) presented participants from India and the United States with videotaped portrayals of the *Nayasastra*'s emotions, and participants were asked to determine which emotion was being expressed through either forced-choice or free-response methodology. In both conditions and across both cultures, contentment was identified with above-chance ratings ranging from 50% to 80%. These data demonstrated that a 2,000-year-old depiction of emotion theatrics can withstand the test of time and culture, and provide initial evidence for a possible universal expression of contentment.

After the turn of the century, the field of acoustic recognition of emotions received increasing attention from researchers around the world (Simon-Thomas et al., 2009). A radical departure from a centuries-old focus on facial expressions, the study of nonverbal vocal bursts offered new empirical insights into emotions that are conveyed through mechanisms other than the face. Sauter and Scott (2007) collected samples of nonverbal acoustic sounds conveying achievement, amusement, contentment, pleasure, and relief—and presented them to British and Swedish participants, who were asked to sort the sounds into their respective emotion categories. Contentment vocalizations were recognized at above-chance rates in both cultures, and were distinguishable from the other related positive emotion vocal bursts.

Table 23.3 Overall Findings for 10 Psychophysiological Measurements of Autonomic Responses to Contentment (References for Each Finding Are in Supplement A)

	HR	EDA	RR	SBP	DBP	HRV	LVET	V_t	pCO_2	Cort.
Christie & Friedman, (2004)	↓	↓		↓	↓					
Hess et al. (1992)	↓	↓								
Nyklíček et al. (1997)	↓						↑			
Palomba & Stegagno (1993)	↓	↓								
Ritz et al. (2005)	↓		↓			↑		↓		
Schwartz et al. (1981)	↓			↓	↓					
Van Diest et al. (2001)	↓							↓	↑	
Bershadsky et al. (2014)			↓						↑	↓

Note: HR = heart rate; EDA = electrodermal activity; RR = respiratory rate; SBP = systolic blood pressure; DBP = diastolic blood pressure; HRV = heart rate variability; LVET = left ventricular ejection time; V_t = tidal respiratory volume; pCO_2 = partial pressure of blood CO_2; Cort. = cortisol.

Laukka and colleagues (2013) sought to expand the list of acoustically differentiable emotions by studying the decoding rates of nine positive and nine negative emotions across five cultures. In this study, participants from India, Kenya, Singapore, and the United States were asked to generate nonverbal vocalizations for each emotion, and raters in Sweden were asked to determine which emotion was being expressed by choosing one from the list of 18 emotions studied. Serenity/contentment was again recognized at above-chance rates in all four cultures, demonstrating for the second time—in a wider subset of cultures—that contentment can be expressed and recognized through nonverbal vocal bursts.

One of the most conclusive tests of the evolutionary origins of an emotion regards its ability to be recognized by remote, uncontacted cultures. In 2016, Cordaro and colleagues (2016) traveled to the high Himalayas of Eastern Bhutan, where they presented culturally isolated villagers with nonverbal acoustic bursts of 16 emotions as the final data set among 10 additional studies conducted in China, Germany, India, Japan, South Korea, New Zealand, Pakistan, Poland, Turkey, and the United States. Contentment vocalizations were perceived at above-chance rates across all 11 cultures, and they were distinguished from other similar pleasant states like happiness, desire, relief, and interest. This study marked the first major demonstration of the fact that contentment vocalizations are discernible even among culturally isolated peoples.

While Hejmadi and colleagues (2000) and Laukka and colleagues (2013) provided initial evidence for a cross-cultural expression of contentment in posture and voice, a gap remained in the facial expression literature. One of the reasons why a contentment facial expression had been difficult to ascertain was that its hypothesized archetype was so similar to related positive states like happiness and joy (see Keltner & Cordaro, 2017). Further research was required to determine whether contentment was a discrete emotion or simply part of the happiness family of emotions. In 2018, Cordaro and colleagues published one of the largest studies to date on the encoding of 22 emotion expressions across five cultures. It was an ambitious study, which collected 2,600 free-response facial and body expressions of 22 emotions across participants native to China, India, Japan, Korea, and the United States. Cordaro and colleagues (2018) coded each expression muscle by muscle using the Facial Action Coding System (FACS; Ekman & Roseberg, 1997), and used a novel methodology for identifying expressive patterns within and across cultures for over 25,000 action units collected for the 22 emotions. When the dust settled, three facial/bodily actions found across all five cultures reliably distinguished contentment from other related positive emotions, and these included a slight smile, relaxed eyelids, and a deep inhalation followed by slow exhalation (FACS codes 12 & 43 with deep breath).

This study, while extensive, only addressed the encoding hypothesis. A critical question remained: Will participants from around the world *recognize* the contentment archetype, and will cross-cultural populations reliably *distinguish* it from similar emotions? In a follow-up study, Cordaro and colleagues (2020) published the largest data set to date on the decoding of 18 emotional facial expressions across nine cultures (see also Keltner & Cordaro, 2017). Participants from China, Japan, Korea, New Zealand, Germany, Poland, Pakistan, Turkey, and the United States rated a library of facial expressions featuring actors diverse in gender, ethnicity, and age. In this study, the authors hypothesized that contentment would be reliably distinguished from happiness based on a few subtle, yet meaningful morphological changes in the face. The facial actions of archetypical happiness were well established at the time and included inner- and outer-orbicularis oculi contraction, open-mouthed contraction of zygomaticus major, and a slight jaw drop (Frank et al., 1993). In this study, the archetypal contentment expression included two simple facial actions: a slight relaxation of the eyelids and a slight contraction of zygomaticus major with the mouth closed. While morphologically similar to many other positive emotions in the series, contentment was reliably distinguished from all of them, and it was accurately decoded at above-chance rates (nearly 70% accuracy) across all nine cultures.

Lastly, Cowen and colleagues (2019) conducted a study in which over 2,000 vocal bursts produced in a laboratory setting and generated in real life were presented to English-speaking US participants. Using a mixed design model, they collected over 24,000 forced-choice judgments of vocal burst stimuli as well as over 24,000 free-response judgments of the same stimuli. The results indicated that both forced-choice and free-response methodologies led to above-chance ratings and categorization of all but five emotions, and contentment was among those categorized accurately.

Across multiple replications, cultures, and modalities of expression, contentment is robustly and reliably communicated through facial and vocal signals. From its humble beginnings as an abnormality of Duchenne smile data to a promising candidate as a basic emotion, the morphology and acoustic properties of contentment have demonstrated recognition in even the remotest places on Earth. Since the establishment of the contentment expression in the face and voice, new research on the behavioral outcomes of contentment had begun to receive increased interest. In light of this, several scales of state and trait contentment have appeared throughout the literature as tools for future work on contentment in the behavioral sciences.

Measuring Contentment

Before the dawn of the positive psychology movement, emotion research had focused almost exclusively on one positive emotion—*happiness* (Argyle, 2013). Dozens of psychometric scales had been designed to treat different aspects of happiness, but it was not until just after the turn of the century that interest grew in the study of "new" candidate basic emotions. In light of this growing interest in positive emotions, Shiota and colleagues (2006) provided the first treatment of contentment as a measurable emotional trait. The Dispositional Positive Emotion Scale (DPES) was designed as a comprehensive psychometric battery of seven positive emotion trait measurements—*amusement, awe, compassion, contentment, joy, love,* and *pride*. While the entire battery is 32 items, each emotion subscale is relatively short, typically five or six items long, and subscales typically have an acceptable internal reliability (Cronbach's α ranges from 0.75 to 0.92). Also noteworthy in this study is that dispositional contentment was a significant predictor of a secure adult attachment style, and also the strongest negative predictor of anxious and preoccupied attachment.

Four months after the DPES was published, Lavallee and colleagues (2007) developed a scale which focused specifically on general feelings of contentment, which they called the Contentment with Life Assessment Scale (CLAS). Similar to the Satisfaction with Life Scale (SWLS), the CLAS targeted concepts related to life fulfillment, meeting aspirations, and dissatisfaction with what one is doing with one's life. It had acceptable internal reliability (Mean Cronbach's α = 0.87), was positively associated with subjective well-being, and negatively correlated with anxiety and stress. The CLAS was developed as an improvement on the SWLS, and so it focused on items related to one's perception of one's life, rather than the experience of contentment itself. In general, the CLAS may be an appropriate metric when measuring perceptions of accomplishment, fulfillment, and achievement of life goals, whereas the DPES was designed to directly assess trait contentment.

While the DPES and CLAS provided early tools for measuring state and life contentment, respectively, one's experience of contentment may vary on a moment-to-moment basis.

In light of the need for state assessment of contentment, Taylor and colleagues (2017) created the State Contentment Measure. This 13-item assessment focuses on somatic components thought to be related to contentment (e.g., "my shoulders are relaxed"; "my body feels tense"), as well as various life perceptions (e.g., "at this time I feel in control of my life"; "I feel unfulfilled with what I am achieving in life"). The SCM's internal reliability was acceptable (Cronbach's α = 0.89), and it correlated negatively with expected divergent measures (anxiety, depression, stress), and positively with convergent measures (happiness, SWLS, and mindfulness). While the initial results of the SCM appeared promising, future studies are required to determine whether this scale can be generalized beyond a collegiate sample, and for the clinical populations for which it was intended.

These measures of state and trait contentment offered a starting point for measuring unconditional completeness, but they were nonetheless all developed in a Western context with little or no foundations in the philosophy of contentment. In 2019, two new trait measures of contentment emerged to fill this gap, and both were developed from an Indian context, comprising items derived from a rich history of contentment in ancient wisdom (*santosha*). Published only months apart, the Comprehensive Satisfaction Index (ComSI) and the Scale of Positive Temperament in Indian Context (PTI) offered a more historically resourced item database and aimed to more formally address the nature and importance of contentment in society and culture.

Even though the ComSI's English translation refers to "satisfaction" as its primary empirical target, the authors make it clear that the items are derived from ancient concepts of *santosha*. The practical purpose of the ComSI was to measure satisfaction with life in aging populations, and with this in mind, Singh and colleagues (2019) developed a 26-item scale requesting ratings of satisfaction along various dimensions of one's life and activities (e.g., satisfaction with security, family, accomplishments, finances, quality time, etc.). Unlike the previous measures of contentment, the ComSI's factor analysis revealed a three-factor model, which clustered items into categories relating to satisfaction with living environment, satisfaction with economic and personal freedom, and satisfaction with leisure activities. While the ComSI demonstrated convergent validity when compared to similar measures, internal reliability was either not tested or not reported.

In contrast to the ComSI's items, which focus on perceptions of the external world, the PTI's items almost exclusively assess internal experiences of contentment (e.g., feeling confident, peaceful, enthusiastic) as well as personal behaviors related to contentment (e.g., I accept help, have reasonable expectations, do not compare myself to others, etc.). Item construction relied on collecting statements from existing positive temperament scales, and analyzing them via exploratory factor analysis to ascertain how many distinct positive temperament categories would emerge. Bedi and Verma's (2019) resulting four-factor structure included trait dimensions of Adaptability, Optimism, Perseverance, and Self-Contentment—the latter of which can be used separately from the rest as its own measure of contentment temperament. The internal consistency of the items was generally acceptable (Cronbach's α ranged from 0.72 to 0.91), and the 4-week test-retest reliability was strong (0.79–0.96).

In light of the previous studies aiming to measure different aspects of contentment, Cordaro, Bradley, and colleagues (2020) assessed the strengths and limitations of these approaches with their Positive Emotion Assessment of Contentment Experience (PEACE) scale. The PEACE scale aimed to accomplish four main goals: (1) develop a stable measure of trait contentment; (2) create simple, diverse items representing both internal and external experiences of contentment; (3) select items in the context of universal concepts in contentment philosophy; and (4) demonstrate improved predictive power compared to other standard measures of contentment. The PEACE scale analysis resulted in a single-factor, 15-item assessment with very high internal consistency (Cronbach's α = .93) as well as high 90-day test-retest reliability (r = .86). Additionally, the PEACE scale demonstrated acceptable convergent and divergent validity with respect to other related constructs (e.g., SWL, PWB, anxiety, depression, stress, and personality metrics), and in a comparative analysis, the PEACE scale predicted key well-being and mental health outcomes above and beyond the DPES.

More importantly, Cordaro, Bradley, and colleagues (2020) used the PEACE scale to predict behavior during a resource dilemma game. Participants played "The Timber Game," wherein they acted as the owners of a logging company who had to decide how much of the forest they would bid to cut down. The Timber Game places its participants into a dilemma—they must choose between personal financial gain and collective environmental impact. Prior to playing The Timber Game, participants responded to a battery of assessments, including the PEACE. Not only did higher PEACE scores predict greater concern for the environment, those who scored + 1 SD on the PEACE scale opted to cut down 20% fewer trees on average than those with –1 SD scores on the PEACE scale. The study found that trait contentment could be an important factor in decision-making as it relates to personal profit versus collective gain. Specifically, the authors emphasized future research on the relationship between cultivating contentment and concern for the environmental crisis, which is one of the greatest challenges faced by humanity today.

Supplement A (https://osf.io/628bv) provides a summary of all psychometric scales measuring either state or trait contentment, and scale items are provided for convenience. The past several decades of research on contentment have yielded several useful psychometric tools for the study of state and trait acceptance of the present moment. This made it possible for behavioral researchers to better understand the appraisals, behaviors, and life outcomes of people with differing levels of contentment.

Contentment Appraisal, Behaviors, and Well-Being Outcomes

While studies on the behavioral and life outcomes of dispositionally content individuals are relatively sparse compared to more well-studied emotions, research over the past few decades has laid the foundations in support of contentment as a discrete emotion with important implications for health, wellness, and prosocial behavior. In line with the evolutionary theory of contentment, one of the most reliable outcomes of cultivating contentment is a reduction in stress and anxiety (Witoonchart & Bartlet, 2002), and it may also play an important moderating role in addiction recovery (Poage et al., 2004). Several studies have also identified contentment as a predictor of psychological resilience in the face of critical, life-threatening health issues (Balthip et al., 2013) as well as significant social inequity and marginalization (Choudhry et al., 2017), and aging (Halaweh et al., 2018).

Another promising line of research on the cultivation of contentment is the impact of mindfulness on the physical and mental health of its practitioners (Grossman et al., 2004). A recent meta-analysis by Dussault and colleagues (2020) found that engaging in a mindfulness practice elicits significant increases in connection with others and contentment with one's life and self. Pandya (2019) conducted a two-year longitudinal study of the impact of mindfulness meditation on a group of 166 adults. The practice significantly reduced loneliness, and increased personal well-being and daily experiences of contentment across the population. Additionally, Gull and Rana (2013) found that a forgiveness practice significantly correlated to increases in both contentment and well-being for their male participants.

In a similar line of work, Bradley and colleagues (2018) provided a school intervention program called "The Four Pillars of Well-Being," wherein mindfulness and contentment philosophy were taught directly to teachers and students across a 12-month intervention period. After one year of using the program, the teacher population reported increases in self-compassion, teaching efficacy, and daily experiences contentment. Student populations reported more positive overall moods and increases in emotion granularity, a key factor in the development of emotional intelligence (Salovey & Pizarro, 2003). Overall, the program correlated positively with well-being and contentment, and negatively with stress. An additional follow-up study concluded that the effects of the intervention held across three years, and that teacher burnout was significantly reduced, along with increases in contentment across the population (Bradley & Cordaro, 2020).

Ng and Hou (2017) conducted a series of studies to explore the relationship between adult attachment styles and psychological illness. After collecting attachment style and emotion disposition data from 284 adults, the researchers found that dispositional contentment mediated the positive relationship between anxious attachment style and symptoms of anxiety and depression. In other words, participants with greater anxious attachment styles tended to experience lower dispositional contentment, which in part explained why they exhibited greater symptoms of anxiety and depression. This was one of the first ever reports of a positive emotion disposition specifically mediating the relationship between an anxious attachment style and psychological illness, underscoring the importance of contentment in the promotion of mental wellness.

A recent series of studies by Cordaro and colleagues (2021) were the first to provide broad evidence for *contentment* as a discrete emotion, differentiable from related positive states like *happiness*, *pride*, and *relief*. They provided a series of six studies that aimed to test contentment's similarities to other states, affective qualities, covariance with well-being, and underlying appraisal mechanism. Using a novel affective mapping methodology involving 29 different emotions, the first study in the series asked participants to rate the similarities between each of the 29 emotions in the series (e.g., happiness and contentment; gratitude and anger). They collected similarity rating data for all 406 permutations of emotion pairs, and after calculating mean similarities between each emotion, they produced a three-dimensional visual representation of emotion space for the 29 different English emotion concepts (Figure 23.1, reproduced from the original). A cluster analysis revealed four distinct emotion categories within the emotion space, and contentment belonged in a cluster containing other low-activation pleasant states (e.g., *gratitude*, *relief*, *peace*, etc.). Most pertinent to the investigation, *contentment* and *happiness* occupied distinct clusters, providing initial evidence that happiness—the most well-studied emotion in the field of psychology—is conceptually discrete from *contentment*, a new candidate basic emotion.

The subsequent two studies in the series tested the extent to which four comparison emotions, *contentment*, *happiness*, *joy*, and *relief*, were differentiable along various affective dimensions. After collecting rating data from hundreds of participants along four affective dimensions, analyses revealed that contentment differentiated from the other three comparison states as a *pleasant, low arousal, low acquisition-orientation emotion focused on the present moment* (rather than the past or future). These results were replicated in a third study using a more rigorous methodology—ratings of free-response emotion stories of participants' experiences of the four comparison emotions. After collecting 140 free-response narratives, coders naïve to the hypotheses and the emotions being studied rated the stories along the same four dimensions. In a significant replication of the previous study, contentment again differentiated from the three comparison states along the same affective dimensions.

The series of studies by Cordaro and colleagues (2021) also tested the well-being of dispositionally contented individuals. The study measured dispositional contentment as a predictor

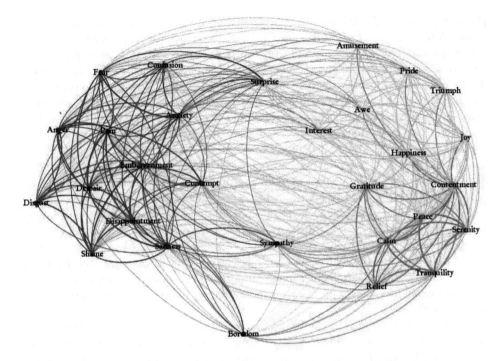

Figure 23.1. Affective space map of 29 discrete emotions. Each color represents a statistically differentiated family cluster of emotions, demonstrating that contentment is likely discretely different from happiness and other related positive states.

of psychological well-being, subjective well-being, and unconditional self-acceptance, and tested whether trait contentment would predict these key well-being outcomes above and beyond related positive emotion traits such as *amusement, awe, compassion, joy, love,* and *pride*. After controlling for age, gender, and all other comparison emotion traits, contentment significantly predicted all well-being outcomes. Furthermore, contentment was the single greatest predictor of unconditional self-acceptance (USA), and in a subsequent experimental manipulation of contentment, USA uniquely mediated the relationship between contentment and life satisfaction. This provided the first demonstration of contentment's unique impact on well-being outcomes, and provided evidence for the appraisal of self-completeness as an antecedent condition for contentment to arise.

Conclusion

For more than 4,000 years, the nature of indestructible wellness has been a core feature of human philosophy and scientific direction. At the core of what it means to flourish as a human being is *contentment*, an emotion that arises as a result of our perception of life as complete and whole as it is. Across tens of thousands of generations of our ancestors, contentment afforded reproductive and survival benefits as it promoted creativity, exploration, prosocial bonding, and well-being. Studies show that its low-intensity, pleasant affect is ubiquitous across cultures, especially when there are no other intense stimuli present, and that it has a genetic basis. While psychophysiological research on contentment is still in early stages, there appears to be reliable autonomic changes that covary with experiences of contentment. Downstream from the autonomic nervous system, the facial and vocal expressions of contentment are well studied; they are discrete, universal, and are recognizable even in remote, previously uncontacted populations. Lastly, there appear to be discrete and reliable behavioral outcomes associated with increases in contentment, and many of these relate to decreases in stress, anxiety, and depression—and increases in overall mental health and wellness.

Taken together, this brief review establishes the strong likelihood of contentment as a basic emotion, as it fulfills at least 8 of the 13 empirical criteria for evolutionarily grounded basic emotions. Further research must establish the universality of contentment's psychophysiological patterns and its reliable impact on human behavior and cognition, establish neurological correlates, and provide discrete primate homologues of its expression. While there is still much work to be done, we may nonetheless take a moment to sit quietly and enjoy the completeness and effortless pleasure that is our natural state.

References

Al-Shawaf, L., Conroy-Beam, D., Asao, K., & Buss, D. M. (2016). Human emotions: An evolutionary psychological perspective. *Emotion Review*, *8*(2), 173–186. https://doi.org/10.1177/1754073914565518

Al-Shawaf, L., & Lewis, D. M. G. (2017). Evolutionary psychology and the emotions. In *Encyclopedia of personality and individual differences* (pp. 1–10). Springer International. https://doi.org/10.1007/978-3-319-28099-8_516-1

Aland, B., Aland, K., Karavidopoulos, J., Martini, C. M., & Metzger, B. M. (Eds.). (1993). *The Greek new testament* (4th ed.). Deutsche Bibelgesellschaft.

Argyle, M. (2013). *The psychology of happiness* (2nd ed.). Routledge. https://doi.org/10.4324/9781315812212

Ashare, R. L., Norris, C. J., Wileyto, E. P., Cacioppo, J. T., & Strasser, A. A. (2013). Individual differences in positivity offset and negativity bias: Gender-specific associations with two serotonin receptor genes. *Personality and Individual Differences*, *55*(5), 469–473. https://doi.org/10.1016/j.paid.2013.04.009

Aurobindo, S. (1951). *Isha upanishad*. Aurobindo Ashram Press.

Balthip, Q., Petchruschatachart, U., Piriyakoontorn, S., & Boddy, J. (2013). Achieving peace and harmony in life: Thai Buddhists living with HIV/AIDS. *International Journal of Nursing Practice*, *19*, 7–14. https://doi.org/10.1111/ijn.12039

Bedi, J., & Verma, T. (2019). Development of a scale of positive temperament in Indian context. *Indian Journal of Psychological Medicine*, *41*(6), 569–577. https://doi.org/10.4103/IJPSYM.IJPSYM_498_18

Bershadsky, S., Trumpfheller, L., Kimble, H. B., Pipaloff, D., & Yim, I. S. (2014). The effect of prenatal Hatha yoga on affect, cortisol and depressive symptoms. *Complementary Therapies in Clinical Practice*, *20*(2), 106–113. https://doi.org/10.1016/j.ctcp.2014.01.002

Biering-Sørensen, T., Querejeta Roca, G., Hegde, S. M., Shah, A. M., Claggett, B., Mosley, T. H., Butler, K. R., & Solomon, S. D. (2018). Left ventricular ejection time is an independent predictor of incident heart failure in a community-based cohort. *European Journal of Heart Failure*, *20*(7), 1106–1114. https://doi.org/10.1002/ejhf.928

Boyce, W. T., & Ellis, B. J. (2005). Biological sensitivity to context: I. An evolutionary-developmental theory of the origins and functions of stress reactivity. *Development and Psychopathology*, *17*(2). https://doi.org/10.1017/S0954579405050145

Bradley, C., & Cordaro, D. T. (2020). Impacts of the four pillars of wellbeing curriculum: A 3-year pilot study. *Translational Issues in Psychological Science*, *6*(4), 404–411. https://doi.org/10.1037/tps0000275

Bradley, C., Cordaro, D. T., Zhu, F., Vildostegui, M., Han, R. J., Brackett, M., & Jones, J. (2018). Supporting improvements in classroom climate for students and teachers with the four pillars of wellbeing curriculum. *Translational Issues in Psychological Science*, *4*(3), 245–264. https://doi.org/10.1037/tps0000162

Bryant, E. F. (2015). *The yoga sutras of Patanjali: A new edition, translation, and commentary*. North Point Press.

Buck, W. (2019). *Mahabharata*. University of California Press.

Burrow, T. (2001). *The sanskrit language*. Motilal Banarsidass.

Byrom, T. (2010). *The Dhammapada: The sayings of the Buddha*. Random House.

Cacioppo, J. T., & Berntson, G. G. (1994). Relationship between attitudes and evaluative space: A critical review, with emphasis on the separability of positive and negative substrates. *Psychological Bulletin*, *115*(3), 401–423. https://doi.org/10.1037/0033-2909.115.3.401

Cacioppo, J. T., Berntson, G. G., Larsen, J. T., Poehlmann, K. M., & Ito, T. A. (2000). The psychophysiology of emotion. In *Handbook of emotions* (2nd ed., pp. 173–191). Guilford Press.

Choudhry, F. R., Park, M. S.-A., Golden, K., & Bokharey, I. Z. (2017). "We are the soul, pearl and beauty of Hindu Kush Mountains": Exploring resilience and psychological wellbeing of Kalasha, an ethnic and religious minority group in Pakistan. *International Journal of Qualitative Studies on Health and Well-Being, 12*(1), 1267344. https://doi.org/10.1080/17482631.2016.1267344

Christie, I. C., & Friedman, B. H. (2004). Autonomic specificity of discrete emotion and dimensions of affective space: A multivariate approach. *International Journal of Psychophysiology, 51*(2), 143–153. https://doi.org/10.1016/j.ijpsycho.2003.08.002

Coan, J. A., & Allen, J. J. B. (Eds.). (2007). *Handbook of emotion elicitation and assessment.* Oxford University Press.

Cordaro, D., Bai, Y., Bradley, C., Zhu, F., Han, R., & Keltner, D. (2021). Contentment and unconditional self-acceptance: Wellbeing beyond happiness. *Cognition and Emotion.*

Cordaro, D. T., Brackett, M., Glass, L., & Anderson, C. L. (2016). Contentment: Perceived completeness across cultures and traditions. *Review of General Psychology, 20*(3), 221–235. https://doi.org/10.1037/gpr0000082

Cordaro, D. T., Bradley, C., Zhang, J. W., Zhu, F., & Han, R. (2020). The development of the Positive Emotion Assessment of Contentment Experience (PEACE) Scale. *Journal of Happiness Studies,* 1–22. https://doi.org/10.1007/s10902-020-00295-9

Cordaro, D. T., Keltner, D., Tshering, S., Wangchuk, D., & Flynn, L. M. (2016). The voice conveys emotion in ten globalized cultures and one remote village in Bhutan. *Emotion, 16*(1), 117–128. https://doi.org/10.1037/emo0000100

Cordaro, D. T., Sun, R., Kamble, S., Hodder, N., Monroy, M., Cowen, A., Bai, Y., & Keltner, D. (2020). The recognition of 18 facial-bodily expressions across nine cultures. *Emotion.* https://doi.org/10.1037/emo0000576

Cordaro, D. T., Sun, R., Keltner, D., Kamble, S., Huddar, N., & McNeil, G. (2018). Universals and cultural variations in 22 emotional expressions across five cultures. *Emotion, 18*(1), 75–93. https://doi.org/10.1037/emo0000302

Cowen, A. S., Elfenbein, H. A., Laukka, P., & Keltner, D. (2019). Mapping 24 emotions conveyed by brief human vocalization. *American Psychologist, 74*(6), 698–712. https://doi.org/10.1037/amp0000399

Cummins, R. A. (2010). Subjective wellbeing, homeostatically protected mood and depression: A synthesis. *Journal of Happiness Studies, 11*(1), 1–17. https://doi.org/10.1007/s10902-009-9167-0

Cummins, R. A. (2018). The golden triangle of happiness: Essential resources for a happy family. *International Journal of Child, Youth and Family Studies, 9*(4), 12–39. https://doi.org/10.18357/ijcyfs94201818638

Darwin, C. (1872). *The expression of the emotions in man and animals.* Murray.

Diener, E., & Diener, C. (1996). Most people are happy. *Psychological Science, 7*(3), 181–185. https://doi.org/10.1111/j.1467-9280.1996.tb00354.x

Diener, E., Kanazawa, S., Suh, E. M., & Oishi, S. (2015). Why people are in a generally good mood. *Personality and Social Psychology Review, 19*(3), 235–256. https://doi.org/10.1177/1088868314544467

Dussault, É., Fernet, M., & Godbout, N. (2020). A metasynthesis of qualitative studies on mindfulness, sexuality, and relationality. *Mindfulness, 11*(12), 2682–2694. https://doi.org/10.1007/s12671-020-01463-x

Ekman, P. (1992). An argument for basic emotions. *Cognition and Emotion, 6*(3–4), 169–200. https://doi.org/10.1080/02699939208411068

Ekman, P., & Cordaro, D. (2011). What is meant by calling emotions basic. *Emotion Review, 3*(4), 364–370. https://doi.org/10.1177/1754073911410740

Ekman, P., Davidson, R. J., & Friesen, W. V. (1990). The Duchenne smile: Emotional expression and brain physiology: II. *Journal of Personality and Social Psychology, 58*(2), 342–353. https://doi.org/10.1037/0022-3514.58.2.342

Ekman, P., & Roseberg, E. L. (Eds.). (1997). *What the face reveals: Basic and applied studies of spontaneous expression using the Facial Action Coding System.* Oxford University Press.

Frank, M. G., Ekman, P., & Friesen, W. V. (1993). Behavioral markers and recognizability of the smile of enjoyment. *Journal of Personality and Social Psychology, 64*(1), 83–93. https://doi.org/10.1037/0022-3514.64.1.83

Fredrickson, B. L. (2013). Positive emotions broaden and build. In *Advances in experimental social psychology* (pp. 1–53). https://doi.org/10.1016/B978-0-12-407236-7.00001-2

Fredrickson, B. L., & Branigan, C. (2005). Positive emotions broaden the scope of attention and thought-action repertoires. *Cognition & Emotion, 19*(3), 313–332. https://doi.org/10.1080/02699930441000238

Frijda, N. H., Kuipers, P., & ter Schure, E. (1989). Relations among emotion, appraisal, and emotional action readiness. *Journal of Personality and Social Psychology, 57*(2), 212–228. https://doi.org/10.1037/0022-3514.57.2.212

Ghosh, M. (1967). *The Nātyasāstra ascribed to Bharata-Muni.* Asiatic Society.

Griffith, R. T. (2013). *The Rig Veda.* Library of Alexandria.

Grinde, B. (2002). Happiness in the perspective of evolutionary psychology. *Journal of Happiness Studies, 3*(4), 331–354. https://doi.org/10.1023/A:1021894227295

Grinde, B. (2012). An evolutionary perspective on happiness and mental health. *Journal of Mind and Behavior, 33*(1–2), 49–67. https://www.jstor.org/stable/43854323

Grinde, B. (2013). Happiness and mental health as understood in a biological perspective. *Homo Oeconomicus, 29*(4), 535–556.

Grossman, P., Niemann, L., Schmidt, S., & Walach, H. (2004). Mindfulness-based stress reduction and health benefits. *Journal of Psychosomatic Research*, *57*(1), 35–43. https://doi.org/10.1016/S0022-3999(03)00573-7

Gull, M., & Rana, S. (2013). Manifestation of forgiveness, subjective well being and quality of life. *Journal of Behavioural Sciences*, *23*(2), 17–36. https://doi.org/10.13140/RG.2.2.16923.05929

Halaweh, H., Dahlin-Ivanoff, S., Svantesson, U., & Willén, C. (2018). Perspectives of older adults on aging well: A focus group study. *Journal of Aging Research*, *2018*, 1–9. https://doi.org/10.1155/2018/9858252

Hejmadi, A., Davidson, R. J., & Rozin, P. (2000). Exploring Hindu Indian emotion expressions: Evidence for accurate recognition by Americans and Indians. *Psychological Science*, *11*(3), 183–187. https://doi.org/10.1111/1467-9280.00239

Hergenhahn, B. R., & Henley, T. B. (2014). *An introduction to the history of psychology* (7th ed.). Cengage Learning.

Hess, U., Kappas, A., McHugo, G. J., Lanzetta, J. T., & Kleck, R. E. (1992). The facilitative effect of facial expression on the self-generation of emotion. *International Journal of Psychophysiology*, *12*(3), 251–265. https://doi.org/10.1016/0167-8760(92)90064-I

Hughes, J. (2007). *Shiva Sutras: The supreme awakening* (2nd ed.). Munshiram Manoharlal.

Ito, T., & Cacioppo, J. (2005). Variations on a human universal: Individual differences in positivity offset and negativity bias. *Cognition & Emotion*, *19*(1), 1–26. https://doi.org/10.1080/02699930441000120

Kelen, B. (2014). *Gautama Buddha: In life and legend*. Open Road Media.

Keltner, D., & Cordaro, D. T. (2017). Understanding multimodal emotional expressions: Recent advances in basic emotion theory. In J. M. Fernández-Dols & J. A. Russell (Eds.), *The science of facial expression* (pp. 57–75). Oxford University Press.

Keltner, D., Ekman, P. E., Gonzaga, G. C., & Beer, J. (2003). Facial expression of emotions. In R. J. Davidson, K. R. Scherer, & H. H. Goldsmith (Eds.), *Handbook of affective sciences* (pp. 415–432). Oxford University Press.

Keltner, D., Sauter, D., Tracy, J., & Cowen, A. (2019). Emotional expression: Advances in basic emotion theory. *Journal of Nonverbal Behavior*, *43*, 133–160. https://doi.org/10.1007/s10919-019-00293-3

Keltner, D., Tracy, J. L., Sauter, D., & Cowen, A. (2019). What basic emotion theory really says for the twenty-first century study of emotion. *Journal of Nonverbal Behavior*, *43*(2), 195–201. https://doi.org/10.1007/s10919-019-00298-y

Kensinger, E. A., & Corkin, S. (2004). Two routes to emotional memory: Distinct neural processes for valence and arousal. *Proceedings of the National Academy of Sciences*, *101*(9), 3310–3315. https://doi.org/10.1073/pnas.0306408101

Klein, E. (1966). *A comprehensive etymological dictionary of the English language*, Vol. 1. Elsevier.

Kreibig, S. D. (2010). Autonomic nervous system activity in emotion: A review. *Biological Psychology*, *84*(3), 394–421. https://doi.org/10.1016/j.biopsycho.2010.03.010

Laozi, F. G., & English, J. (1972). *Tao te ching* (1st ed.). Vintage Books.

Laukka, P., Elfenbein, H. A., Söder, N., Nordström, H., Althoff, J., Chui, W., Iraki, F. K., Rockstuhl, T., & Thingujam, N. S. (2013). Cross-cultural decoding of positive and negative non-linguistic emotion vocalizations. *Frontiers in Psychology*, *4*, 353. https://doi.org/10.3389/fpsyg.2013.00353

Lavallee, L. F., Hatch, P. M., Michalos, A. C., & McKinley, T. (2007). Development of the Contentment with Life Assessment Scale (CLAS): Using daily life experiences to verify levels of self-reported life satisfaction. *Social Indicators Research*, *83*(2), 201–244. https://doi.org/10.1007/s11205-006-9054-6

Levenson, R. W. (2011). Basic emotion questions. *Emotion Review*, *3*(4), 379–386. https://doi.org/10.1177/1754073911410743

Luecken, L. J., & Gallo, L. C. (Eds.). (2008). *Handbook of physiological research methods in health psychology*. SAGE Publications. https://doi.org/10.4135/9781412976244

Matsumoto, D., Keltner, D., Shiota, M. N., O'Sullivan, M., & Frank, M. (2008). Facial expressions of emotion. In M. Lewis, J. M. Haviland-Jones, & L. F. Barrett (Eds.), *Handbook of emotions* (pp. 211–234). Guilford Press.

Mauss, I. B., McCarter, L., Levenson, R. W., Wilhelm, F. H., & Gross, J. J. (2005). The tie that binds? Coherence among emotion experience, behavior, and physiology. *Emotion*, *5*(2), 175–190. https://doi.org/10.1037/1528-3542.5.2.175

McEwen, B. S. (1998). Stress, adaptation, and disease: Allostasis and allostatic load. *Annals of the New York Academy of Sciences*, *840*(1), 33–44. https://doi.org/10.1111/j.1749-6632.1998.tb09546.x

McEwen, B. S. (2004). Protection and damage from acute and chronic stress: Allostasis and allostatic overload and relevance to the pathophysiology of psychiatric disorders. *Annals of the New York Academy of Sciences*, *1032*(1), 1–7. https://doi.org/10.1196/annals.1314.001

Ng, S. M., & Hou, W. K. (2017). Contentment duration mediates the associations between anxious attachment style and psychological distress. *Frontiers in Psychology*, *8*, 258. https://doi.org/10.3389/fpsyg.2017.00258

Norris, C. J., Larsen, J. T., Crawford, L. E., & Cacioppo, J. T. (2011). Better (or worse) for some than others: Individual differences in the positivity offset and negativity bias. *Journal of Research in Personality, 45*(1), 100–111. https://doi.org/10.1016/j.jrp.2010.12.001

Nyklíček, I., Thayer, J. F., & Van Doornen, L. J. P. (1997). Cardiorespiratory differentiation of musically-induced emotions. *Journal of Psychophysiology, 11*, 304–321.

Oakley, R. H., & Cidlowski, J. A. (2013). The biology of the glucocorticoid receptor: New signaling mechanisms in health and disease. *Journal of Allergy and Clinical Immunology, 132*(5), 1033–1044. https://doi.org/10.1016/j.jaci.2013.09.007

Palomba, D., & Stegagno, L. (1993). Physiology, perceived emotion, and memory: Responding to film sequences. In *The structure of emotion* (pp. 156–167). Hogrefe & Huber.

Pandya, S. P. (2019). Meditation program mitigates loneliness and promotes wellbeing, life satisfaction and contentment among retired older adults: A two-year follow-up study in four South Asian cities. *Aging & Mental Health*, 1–13. https://doi.org/10.1080/13607863.2019.1691143

Pascal, B. (1888). *The thoughts of Blaise Pascal*. Kegan Paul, Trench.

Poage, E. D., Ketzenberger, K. E., & Olson, J. (2004). Spirituality, contentment, and stress in recovering alcoholics. *Addictive Behaviors, 29*(9), 1857–1862. https://doi.org/10.1016/j.addbeh.2004.03.038

Prabhupada, S., & Bhaktivedanta, A. C. (1972). *Bhagavad-Gita as it is*. Bhaktivedanta Book Trust.

Ritz, T., Thöns, M., Fahrenkrug, S., & Dahme, B. (2005). Airways, respiration, and respiratory sinus arrhythmia during picture viewing. *Psychophysiology, 42*, 568–578. https://doi.org/10.1111/j.1469-8986.2005.00312.x

Salovey, P., & Pizarro, D. A. (2003). The value of emotional intelligence. In R. J. Sternberg, J. Lautrey, & T. I. Lubart (Eds.), *Models of intelligence* (pp. 263–278). American Psychological Association.

Saunders, J. (1966). *Greek and Roman philosophy after Aristotle*, Vol. 8. Simon & Schuster.

Sauter, D. A., & Scott, S. K. (2007). More than one kind of happiness: Can we recognize vocal expressions of different positive states? *Motivation and Emotion, 31*(3), 192–199. https://doi.org/10.1007/s11031-007-9065-x

Schulkin, J. (Ed.). (2004). *Allostasis, homeostasis, and the costs of physiological adaptation*. Cambridge University Press.

Schwartz, G. E., Weinberger, D. A., & Singer, J. A. (1981). Cardiovascular differentiation of happiness, sadness, anger, and fear following imagery and exercise. *Psychosomatic Medicine*. https://doi.org/10.1097/00006842-198108000-00007

Shihab, M. Q. (2007). *"Membumikan" Al-Quran: Fungsi dan peran wahyu dalam kehidupan masyarakat*. Mizan.

Shiota, M. N., Keltner, D., & John, O. P. (2006). Positive emotion dispositions differentially associated with Big Five personality and attachment style. *The Journal of Positive Psychology, 1*(2), 61–71. https://doi.org/10.1080/17439760500510833

Siedlecka, E., & Denson, T. F. (2019). Experimental methods for inducing basic emotions: A qualitative review. *Emotion Review, 11*(1), 87–97. https://doi.org/10.1177/1754073917749016

Simon-Thomas, E. R., Keltner, D. J., Sauter, D., Sinicropi-Yao, L., & Abramson, A. (2009). The voice conveys specific emotions: Evidence from vocal burst displays. *Emotion, 9*(6), 838–846. https://doi.org/10.1037/a0017810

Singh, B., Pandey, N. M., Mehrotra, B., Srivastava, A., Chowdhury, A. K., & Tiwari, S. C. (2019). Development of Comprehensive Satisfaction Index (ComSI) and its association with WHOQOL-BREF. *Indian Journal of Psychological Medicine, 41*(6), 562–568. https://doi.org/10.4103/IJPSYM.IJPSYM_295_18

Smith, H., & Marranca, R. (2009). *The world's religions*. HarperOne.

Staufenbiel, S. M., Penninx, B. W. J. H., Spijker, A. T., Elzinga, B. M., & van Rossum, E. F. C. (2013). Hair cortisol, stress exposure, and mental health in humans: A systematic review. *Psychoneuroendocrinology, 38*(8), 1220–1235. https://doi.org/10.1016/j.psyneuen.2012.11.015

Steinsaltz, A. (2009). *The essential Talmud* (13th ed.). Basic Books.

Taylor, T. A., Medvedev, O. N., Owens, R. G., & Siegert, R. J. (2017). Development and validation of the State Contentment Measure. *Personality and Individual Differences, 119*, 152–159. https://doi.org/10.1016/j.paid.2017.07.010

Thayer, J. F., Yamamoto, S. S., & Brosschot, J. F. (2010). The relationship of autonomic imbalance, heart rate variability and cardiovascular disease risk factors. *International Journal of Cardiology, 141*(2), 122–131. https://doi.org/10.1016/j.ijcard.2009.09.543

Van Diest, I., Proot, P., Van De Woestijne, K. P., Han, J. N., Devriese, S., Winters, W., & Van Den Bergh, O. (2001). Critical conditions for hyperventilation responses: The role of autonomic response propositions during emotional imagery. *Behavior Modification, 25*(4), 621–639. https://doi.org/10.1177/0145445501254008

Venkatesananda, S. (2010). *Vasistha's yoga*. State University of New York Press.

Waley, A. (2013). *The way and its power: A study of the Tao Te Ching and its place in Chinese thought*. Routledge.

Weekley, E. (2012). *An etymological dictionary of modern English*, Vol. 2. Courier Dover Publications.

Westermann, R., Spies, K., Stahl, G., & Hesse, F. W. (1996). Relative effectiveness and validity of mood induction procedures: A meta-analysis. *European Journal of Social Psychology, 26*(4), 557–580. https://doi.org/10.1002/(SICI)1099-0992(199607)26:4<557::AID-EJSP769>3.0.CO;2-4

Witoonchart, C., & Bartlet, L. (2002). The use of a meditation programme for institutionalized juvenile delinquents. *Journal of the Medical Association of Thailand, 85*, S790–S793.

Zulfiqar, U., Jurivich, D. A., Gao, W., & Singer, D. H. (2010). Relation of high heart rate variability to healthy longevity. *The American Journal of Cardiology, 105*(8), 1181–1185. https://doi.org/10.1016/j.amjcard.2009.12.022

CHAPTER 24

Happiness

Stefan M. M. Goetz and Glenn E. Weisfeld

Abstract
This chapter proposes a model of happiness from a discrete emotions theory perspective. It takes a materialistic view of happiness, arguing that happiness is a nonspecific catch-all category of positive emotions that evolved to promote the repetition of fitness-enhancing behaviors. The chapter begins by laying out the view of the evolutionary significance of happiness, arguing that positive affects represent proximate mechanisms that reinforce and guide adaptive behaviors but are not direct targets of selection. Rather, the resultant adaptive behaviors are the targets. It then discusses potential signaling functions of the expression of happiness and presents the neural bases of positive emotions. It also addresses why happiness is ephemeral, concluding that were it not, the behaviors that initially engendered happiness would be less likely to be repeated. Finally, it discusses contemporary measurement approaches before concluding with a brief discussion of some of the correlates of happiness and pathology.

Key Words: discrete emotion theory, affect, happiness, hedonic adaptation, emotional expression

The study of happiness raises many interesting scientific, sociopolitical, and philosophical questions. This chapter will discuss the evolutionary significance of happiness, global happiness vs. specific emotions, developmental and sex differences, facial expressions, neural bases, the evolution of affect, various adaptive emotional phenomena, and the measurement of happiness. The chapter will next review research on some correlates of personal happiness: personality, marriage, children, friendship, work, leisure, religion, age and sex, and nationality. The last section will briefly discuss happiness pathology.

Evolutionary Significance

A common evolutionary view of happiness is that pleasurable states reward adaptive behaviors, promoting their repetition (e.g., Buss, 2000). Unhappy experiences are punitive and promote avoidance of the preceding behavior. An organism that is happy presumably is succeeding in addressing its fitness needs. However, selection occurs not for happiness but for adaptive behaviors that yield happiness; happiness is natural selection's way of inducing adaptive behaviors.

Emotions prompt particular adaptive behaviors. They are often unpleasant, conveying a need to take active measures. Examples include hunger, drowsiness, thirst, and sexual urges.

The most urgent needs, such as for oxygen and fluid, take priority over less-pressing ones. But priorities shift as needs are met and opportunities come and go.

An evolutionary viewpoint that considers the adaptive value of normal behavioral and physiological traits contrasts with a view of traditional medicine. Doctors seek to minimize pain and other aversive states, as well as to promote survival. But sometimes the goals of pain relief and biological fitness conflict. An example is the use of antipyretic medicines to treat fever. Research on poikilothermic reptiles and on humans has shown that infection raises body temperature, harming pathogens and speeding recovery (Kluger, 1991). Fever alters the environment of pathogens that thrive at normal human body temperature, and enhances immune function. Knowledge of the adaptive value of fever allows the physician to consider withholding the drug.

Another ethical dilemma concerning an evolutionary perspective on happiness is this: What matters more, individual happiness or collective happiness (Buss, 2000)? Individual fitness considerations are paramount in evolutionary thinking, as most human adaptations can be explained from an individual selection framework (e.g., Kay et al., 2020). For example, aggressive behaviors evolved to enhance the fitness of the aggressor. But, by definition, aggression harms the victim. Would an evolutionary clinician try merely to maximize the happiness of the patient, even at the expense of others? One possible resolution of this problem might be to invoke principles of reciprocal altruism, and point out to the patient that enhancing one's reputation for honesty, fairness, and compassion usually redounds to one's overall benefit.

The Importance of Specific Emotions

In the ethological tradition, it is essential to recognize the importance and specificity of emotions. Animals have specific needs, and natural selection has favored specificity in identifying these needs and addressing each appropriately. It would not do for an animal to have a desire for happiness, in general. Every animal—every cell—needs to feed, hydrate itself, protect itself, eliminate bodily waste, and reproduce. A general desire for happiness would leave it suspended in confusion. This is not to deny that people can experience a general affect of happiness, and express this state with a specific facial expression. This complication is discussed below. But more specific guidance is necessary to meet our many specific ancient tissue needs. The view that emotions are ancient and specific is referred to as discrete emotions theory, and contrasts with the claim that emotions are human artifices based on cognitive constructs.

The same is true for evolved emotional expressions: the more specific they are, the more useful they are in influencing the behavior of the receiver. The ability to send and receive universal facial expressions emerges in the first months of life. This allows the parent to cater to the infant's specific needs, and the infant to convey them accurately, before verbal communication develops.

If we grant that specific emotions evolved, the problem remains of agreeing on emotion categories. What are the universal human emotions? Psychologists disagree on this question. And yet evolutionary theorists agree on the existence of many emotions, including hunger, disgust, sexual feelings, tactile feelings, loneliness or grief, interest, pride and shame, fear, and anger (Weisfeld, 2019). Less agreement obtains for thirst, drowsiness, humor, fatigue, and others. These disagreements concern how to characterize these latter states. Are they emotions or motives or biological drives or sensations or something else? But these are terminological disagreements. If these putative candidates are psychological complexes with identifiable elicitors, affects, and behaviors, why not recognize them as emotions?

Note that most terms for emotions refer to their respective affects, which are arguably the most distinguishing feature of an emotion. Perhaps affects deserve more attention by emotions theorists, especially with regard to happiness. Psychology has often avoided studying affects because of their subjectivity. How do we know what another person is feeling? Can we trust self-reports? Can we trust introspection (Nisbett & Wilson, 1977; Schachter & Singer, 1962)? Well, we trust them in many other domains of psychology—sensation, perception, attitudes, beliefs, etc.—why not affects? Can we doubt that a starving person is hungry, or that a knife wound causes pain? Perhaps we can reach some agreement on the basic emotions if we ask: What are the universal affects?

If we can agree on universal human emotions, or affects, we can better understand why a person does something. Why did this person vote that way? Why did he say that? Why does a racist or homophobe act as she does—out of fear, anger, disgust, or what? If we had a list of the emotional possibilities, we could consider each, and arrive at plausible, testable answers. Armed with such a list and an understanding of the function, elicitors, expressions, and behavior of each emotion, we might be able to identify the emotion operating. We would also avoid the psychoanalytic notion of displacement: that one emotional need can be met by addressing another need. This makes no adaptive sense; for example, no amount of love song crooning or poetry writing can satisfy the sex drive.

Once we identify a universal emotion, we need to understand how it functions. Understanding how an emotion addresses a fitness need would prevent confusion. Psychology still does not agree on how some emotions enhance fitness, such as anger. Catharsis explanations of anger still appear, and other explanations refer only to the communicative value of the expression of anger (Reed et al., 2014; Sell, 2011). Trivers (1971) may have been right: anger prompts moralistic aggression that punishes cheaters. Anger arises in response to a perceived misdeed, whether committed by an adversary or observed by a third party (Weisfeld, 1972). Anger need not arise from a personal injury or insult; we can be angered by, say, mistreatment of another person's child or even disrespect of a flag. To the extent that the misdeed is corrected by retaliation (by the victim or a bystander) or by offering a plausible excuse, anger is dissipated (Weisfeld, 2019). Actions such as attacking an innocent third party are ineffective. Misdeeds trigger anger, and only correction of the misdeed reduces anger. The adaptive response is precise and appropriate.

Evolution of Affect

Speculation abounds concerning whether animals experience affects. One of the functions of affects seems to be to prioritize responses. Feelings of hunger, say, are weighed against feelings of danger (Al-Shawaf, 2016). Somehow our brains quantify and compare these qualitatively different feelings. Even insects seem to be able to prioritize their responses to stimuli. Fruit flies will flee rather than eat if they see a shadow overhead indicating the presence of a predator (Gibson et al., 2015). But we can imagine this occurring without positing the existence of affects; the flight tendency might simply inhibit feeding.

Insects can exhibit habituation effects, suggesting some quantitative variation in the intensity of motivation, and perhaps also of affects. In the case of the fruit fly, cessation of fleeing occurs only after repeated exposure to shadows, indicating some quantitative register. Habituation and sensitization occur in the sea slug *Aplysia* through modifications in the amount of neurotransmitter released (Beatty, 1995). So graded responses can occur in many ways aside from affects, including varying the number of neurons recruited.

Behaviorally, insects and other metazoans seem to experience pleasure and displeasure. They will seek escape from stimuli that people find noxious, such as objects causing bodily injury. Rats clearly like or dislike electrical stimulation of particular limbic system sites. Since affectively sensitive sites in the human brain are found mainly in the limbic system, one might argue that possession of these structures by an animal indicates a capacity for affect. A recent study demonstrated that, under different behavioral conditions, mice exhibited different and corresponding facial expressions mediated by the anterior insula (Dolensek et al., 2020). These expressions were graded, depending upon the intensity of the stimulus.

However, that expressions are mediated by the limbic system in mammals has long been known, and the idea that this indicates the existence of affects is questionable. Neural structures in mammals, such as the insula, have antecedents in the invertebrate brain. Even echinoderms and mollusks have nervous systems. So this reasoning begs the question of when the brain evolved affect. Dolensek et al. (2020) seemed to assume that facial expressions indicate the existence of affects, but affects can exist without specific expressions, and displays in animals might occur without being prompted by affects. Is a bee performing a waggle dance feeling anything? In short, neural mechanisms mediate whatever emotional responses occur in animals, whether affects or not. The emergence of affect from these mechanisms at some point in phylogeny may remain a philosophical mystery.

It seems well established that newborns, and even fetuses at seven months, can experience pain. Sensation of pain would seem to be essential in the postnatal world, although reflexive withdrawal from a painful stimulus occurs at the spinal cord level. However, even in infants, pain stimuli are passed up the spinal cord to the brain so that escape movements and avoidance conditioning can occur. Further, the limbic system of the newborn mediates the pain cry, which is distinct from other cries of distress. That too suggests the experience of affect.

Affects are involved in the major forms of learning. They function in operant conditioning, in constituting rewards and punishments. If affects are necessary for operant conditioning, then affects are found in even the simplest organisms with nervous systems. Emotional responses, including visceral changes such as salivation as exhibited by Pavlov's dogs, can be classically conditioned. The dogs also showed eagerness when signs of feeding appeared, indicating conditioning of the hunger affect. Even androgen secretion responses have been demonstrated to respond to conditioning (Antunes & Oliveira, 2009; Graham & Desjardins, 1980).

The process of learning is guided by the pursuit of happiness (Pugh, 1977). The effort that we expend toward reaching a goal can be affected by our prospects for reaching the goal, and the resulting benefits. Our curiosity motivates us to begin an investigation. As we make progress, our interest grows; if we are stymied by problems that are too difficult, we become bored or even angered at whoever is responsible for our perplexity. In fact, perplexity or confusion may have an evolved expression featuring furrowed brows, perhaps an appeal for help. Additionally, such expressions are prominent in the face of incredulity, perhaps signaling a failed attempt to be persuaded, consistent with views of epistemic vigilance and argumentative theory (Mercier & Sperber, 2011; Sperber et al., 2010). If we solve the problem, we experience elation at our insight—a sharp satisfaction of our curiosity. These emotions heighten effort when we are making cognitive progress, and incline us to shift our strategies or give up when we are failing.

A related phenomenon is *fatigue*. We do not merely become tired from caloric expenditure. We almost never exhaust our energy stores (Hockey, 2013). Rather, we become tired when our efforts are unavailing or pointless. However, fatigue is adaptive in that it conserves metabolic energy and shifts attention to more propitious activities (Kurzban et al., 2013). The tendency to do so is called the law of economy (Weisfeld, 1999). It explains why animals do not jog, as behaviors that do not serve fitness are weeded out of the gene pool. Metabolically costly behaviors, but useless from the perspective of fitness, are not evolutionarily viable forms of behavior.

Developmental, Individual, and Sex Differences

A list of human emotions would provide a framework for understanding individual, developmental, and sex differences. Most emotions theorists are social psychologists who study adults. Accordingly, most lists of basic emotions apply only to adults. But emotions change through development, just as cognitive abilities do. There is less consensus about the emotional life of infants, children, and adolescents than about adults. For purposes of illustration of the extent of these developmental differences, we might characterize the emotions at each major stage of the life span as follows.

Infancy includes hunger, a separate sucking drive (Pugh, 1977), drowsiness, fear, and contact comfort. Enjoyment of being rocked also exists, perhaps to ensure that a young primate boards the mother when she moves off (Pugh, 1977). In childhood, fear declines with increasing competence, and curiosity rises to motivate play. Starting at two years of age, children become responsive emotionally to praise and criticism; in other words, pride and shame emerge. This allows parents to reward and punish a child by a mere frown or smile. Language ability allows children to specify their needs, and to receive verbal guidance. Adolescents experience the onset of libidinous and related amorous motivation (Weisfeld, 1999). Competitiveness and nurturance rise, and sex differences are magnified as the sexes develop their respective reproductive roles. Hormonal changes underlie these sex differences, just as they do cognitive sex differences (Kimura, 1999). Adulthood sees the consequences of the emotional changes of adolescence play out. Most people marry, thereby satisfying the particular social bonding motive of amorousness. The production of children mobilizes nurturance tendencies, which include a capacity for empathy. In the elderly, sexual desire and marital satisfaction decline along with fertility. Nurturance toward grandchildren emerges. Fear increases in tandem with vulnerability to injury and disease.

Individual differences exist in emotional experience. People vary in their thresholds for different emotions (Davidson, 1998; Lukaszewski et al., 2020). Individual differences can grade into pathology (Nesse & Ellsworth, 2009); some people may have too low a threshold for, say, anxiety, and others a threshold that is too high. Many personality or temperamental concepts can be understood in these terms (Lukaszewski et al., 2020). Individuals differ in their timidity, irritability, libido, self-esteem, curiosity, empathy, drowsiness—on each of the emotions. The Big Five maps only incompletely on these differences in emotional thresholds. The sexes may differ too in their average thresholds for, say, fear, disgust, and sexual motivation (Al-Shawaf et al., 2018; Baumeister, Catanese, et al., 2001; Maeng & Milad, 2015).

Evolved Expressions

The smile, the facial expression of happiness, raises some puzzling theoretical questions. Unlike most other universal expressions, happiness does not seem to reflect a single affect or fitness-enhancing behavior. Rather, the happiness expression serves as a catch-all, to reflect satisfaction of any number of biological needs. We can express happiness as a result of feelings of safety, entertainment, positive social contact, pain relief, pride, retribution, cognitive insight, sexual fulfillment, good news—any pleasure at all. So why did we evolve such a vague signal?

Pugh (1977) suggested that more specific positive affects and expressions grade into nonspecific happiness at high levels of intensity. The positive affects seem to make use of the same neural mechanism for registering pleasure. When pleasure is intense, the causes of this happiness are usually apparent and need not be specified by our expressions, Pugh asserted. Aside from considerations of economy, it is hard to see why general happiness would have evolved, why the specific mechanisms would not have sufficed, why they would have merged at high intensities.

Another possibility is that happiness serves as a nonspecific indicator to others that the status quo is satisfactory. Such a mechanism could apply to any situation that benefited a child, for example. An all-purpose signal of this sort would apply even to situations that had never arisen in prehistory, and for which there was no evolved response. For example, a child might be amused by a set of Legos. The happiness display would serve as an all-clear signal, reassuring the parent that all is well. A happy child would merely need to be supervised for any adverse change, or assisted in maintaining or re-establishing favorable conditions.

By the same token, the general sadness expression, also universal, signals distress of nearly any type. It motivates the parent or other potential altruist of some adverse condition to be corrected. Identification of the specific problem would require further probing. Presumably, nonspecificity of signals is more of a problem for negative emotions requiring active intervention than for positive ones requiring no corrective action. Perhaps for this reason, we have evolved expressions of disgust, anger, fear, shame, and pain. We seem to have clear expressions for fewer positive emotions, such as pride, sexual satisfaction, and mirth.

Our species, with its highly variable and artificially constructed environments, may have favored evolution of general signals for beneficial and adverse conditions. The question of why happiness and sadness evolved as general emotions in humans, perhaps exclusively, seems seldom to be asked. For that matter, it is also puzzling why sadness does not receive nearly the same attention as happiness, a point made by Forgas (Chapter 27 in this volume).

Another evolutionary question is why a particular expression takes the form that it does. Darwin developed three principles in this attempt: those of direct action of the nervous system, serviceable associated habits, and antithesis. In modern parlance, these refer, respectively, to observable autonomic changes, intention movements, and opposite expressions conveying opposite meaning (Weisfeld, 2019). These principles go a long way toward explaining why the expression of fear, for example, takes the form that it does. Trembling reflects activation of the sympathetic system, turning away from an adversary is a flight intention movement, and raised eyebrows are antithetical to the lowered eyebrows of anger. Sometimes, we can understand why the particular form of an expression was effective in eliciting a desirable behavior in the receiver for the sender. Perhaps the expression began as an incidental, or accidental behavior, and then was ritualized by natural selection into a stereotypic display via genetic assimilation (e.g., Renn & Schumer, 2013).

What about the origin of the sadness expression of crying? The best explanation may be that offered by Roes (1990). He proposed that crying mimics the appearance of a newborn. A crying newborn must elicit care immediately and intensively—from a complete stranger! Most people react strongly to this signal, even bystanders. According to Roes, natural selection recruited this infantile expression and applied it to other persons and situations that require helpful intervention. Indeed, crying after infancy, like that of neonates, entails a face suffused with moisture (tears rather than birth fluids), contortion of the face (from crying rather than passage through the birth canal), wailing, and sobbing for breath. Even adults cry when bereaved, depressed, or are otherwise overcome by adversity, and the signal often elicits empathy and attempts at assistance.

Yet another puzzling phenomenon is tears of joy, a trait Darwin considered "purposeless" (Darwin, [1872] 1965). A six-year-old recently learned that she was getting a puppy and burst into tears, which she explained by saying, "I'm crying because I'm happy." Why do people sometimes cry precisely when they are happy? Our suggestion is that crying can occur when a person receives or perceives an act of altruism. Acts of kindness are especially affecting, as in this example. We sometimes cry when we hear "moving" music or other art forms (perhaps a byproduct of a culturally constructed supernormal stimulus), and when someone does something heroic or unselfish. By crying, we express our appreciation for this good deed or accomplishment. Crying with joy utilizes the same expression that evolved to elicit care from parents. Since volitional crying is relatively difficult, the production of tears adds credibility to the honesty of the signal (Reed et al., 2019). Appreciative crying may induce the altruist to offer some favor to us later. In other words, tears of joy may serve as an expression of gratitude, inviting others to offer us favors in the expectation that we will reciprocate. Crying evokes assistance for the appreciative. Note that we say we "appreciate" a favor as well as a work of art. A person who fails to appreciate a favor or musical composition does not merit further offerings. So it is essential to express one's appreciation verbally or nonverbally. The six-year-old was crying from gratitude, to express her appreciation for the puppy. Her parents may be inclined to offer her additional favors as a result. Milder, more routine favors may elicit gratitude that prompts reciprocation (Trivers, 1971) but not be extraordinary enough to elicit tears.

Neural Bases
In recent years much attention has been devoted to the neurochemical basis of happiness. Research has distinguished between liking and wanting. Pleasure itself, also referred to as consummation, seems to be mediated by endorphins and, for social pleasures, oxytocin (Panksepp, 1998; Toates, 1986). For example, endorphins mediate stress-induced analgesia. Euphoriant drugs induce pleasure by mimicking natural neurotransmitters and neurohumors. Wanting, or seeking, formerly referred to as appetitive behavior or conation (from *conari*, to try), is mediated by dopamine. Avoidance behavior is also mediated by dopamine (Berridge & Kringelbach, 2016).

The distinction between liking and wanting is incomplete; dopamine mediates not only wanting, but also anticipation of rewards and liking them (Rolls, 1999). It is hard to imaging seeking a reward without anticipating and imagining gaining it. Nevertheless, the distinction may be valid. Stark et al. (2020) provide evidence that anhedonia is characterized by a deficit in wanting, or reward seeking, rather than in liking. Dopamine antagonists evoke reports of blunted happiness (Rosenzweig et al., 2005). Tomkins (1962) observed that, while we are eating, we are hungry and satisfied at the same time. For example, we experience satiety for one food and switch to another. Pugh (1977) called the affective feedback that guides our consummatory behavior concurrent values.

Anatomically, pleasure centers of the brain are found almost exclusively in the limbic system, including the hypothalamus, midbrain, amygdala, insula, orbitofrontal cortex, and anterior cingulate cortex (Stark et al., 2020). The medial forebrain bundle is particularly active in reports of pleasure; it connects the midbrain through the hypothalamus to the nucleus accumbens. Animals and people seek out stimulation of these limbic structures, which commonly contain opiate receptors (e.g., Mansour et al., 1988; Nummenmaa & Tuominen, 2018). Likewise, displeasure and avoidance of stimulation are elicited by stimulation of limbic sites (Olds & Milner, 1954). The hypothalamus seems to be rich in its versatility; virtually any affect can be elicited by its activation. Most affects are mediated by limbic structures, including pleasure from psychoactive drugs.

It makes sense in terms of economy for the same neural structure and neurotransmitters to mediate seeking, liking, and other common properties of emotions. However, the organism also needs specific mechanisms to mediate different emotional behaviors such as feeding, defense, and reproduction. This seems to be why we possess numerous distinct affects. Indeed, particular limbic structures specialize in particular affects, e.g., the insula for disgust (Husted et al., 2006), the orbitofrontal cortex for pride and shame (Fuster, 1997), the septum for sex (Heath, 1972), and the amygdala for fear (LeDoux, 1996). Many researchers have concluded that different affects are mediated by different limbic structures (Hamann, 2012; Murphy et al., 2003; Phan et al., 2002; Saaarimaki et al., 2015). This evidence supports discrete emotions theory.

On the other hand, some of these limbic structures mediate a variety of affects. These include the hypothalamus, midbrain, insula, nucleus accumbens, and orbitofrontal cortex (Stark et al., 2020). The paradox may be resolved by finer anatomical analysis. Structures such as the hypothalamus and amygdala have multiple nuclei with distinct functions. The anterior insula, for example, mediates a range of bodily feelings, but different affects are represented in different regions (Wood et al., 2014). Similarly, different regions of orbitofrontal cortex mediate taste, olfaction, and aversive emotions—although, as is often the case, the results of these investigations are somewhat contradictory (Kringelbach et al., 2008; Stark et al., 2020).

Of course, the neocortex also plays a role in emotion. Emotional behavior is suppressed by the cerebral cortex. A decorticated animal shows disinhibited emotional responses. However, detailed analysis suggests that the cortex fine-tunes responses to stimuli that might elicit an emotional response (LeDoux, 1996). The cortex analyzes the stimulus for its emotional salience, and may suppress emotional responding or facilitate it. Similarly, the amygdala attaches specific positive or negative emotional connotation to previously neutral stimuli—fear, sexual associations, etc.

Emotions can be experienced vicariously, in our imagination. When we recall a previous event, the memory is colored by the original accompanying affect. We do not just recall that we visited a zoo, for example; we also re-experience the sounds, sights, and smells of the episode. This is true of patients with psychomotor epilepsy; they have learned that their seizures are not "real" events, but only imaginary ones, yet they still relive the original affects each time.

The ability to recall the affects of previous experiences helps us to plan our actions (Kahneman, 2011). The prospect of a reward activates limbic reward areas, as we vicariously anticipate repeating the past pleasure (McClure et al., 2007). We seek to repeat pleasurable experiences, and avoid repeating unpleasant ones. The capacity for vicarious emotion also allows us to identify with other people and their experiences, the basis for observational learning. This may help explain the appeal of the theater, literature, storytelling, and film; these portrayals offer vivid instruction for how to handle various situations (e.g., Bietti et al., 2017; Sugiyama, 2001; 2005).

The ability to empathize with others presumably motivates us to help them. We "feel their pain," as well as their pleasure. The anterior insula and the cingulate cortex seem to be involved in empathy (Hein et al., 2016; Wondra & Ellsworth, 2015). Empathy may be especially pronounced in parental care; empathy may be experienced intensely in the case of our own children. The capacity for vicarious emotion also allows us to imagine how our enemies might be helped or harmed, allowing us to manipulate them accordingly. Substances that directly and intensely activate these emotions, while temporarily bringing joy, leave the user dissatisfied because they may lead to disregard of other emotional needs.

Various Adaptive Emotional Phenomena of Happiness

Happiness and goal-setting vary quantitatively with many factors. In most cases, the adaptive value of these phenomena is discernible. Some examples follow. Happiness is fleeting. Pugh (1977) suggested that our feelings gravitate toward the negative pole of the happiness spectrum. Pride at an accomplishment fades, loneliness builds with solitude, and boredom supplants interest. This grim tendency might be adaptive in preventing complacency. Individuals who lapsed into contentment might be disadvantaged compared with more relentlessly ambitious rivals. As we satisfy one need, another arises. Various terms have been applied to a related phenomenon. "Adaptation" or "habituation" usually refers to sensory stimuli. Terms more specific to affect include *hedonic adaptation* and *relativity of rewards*. These terms are applied to phenomena such as enjoying a cold shower when we are hot, but disliking one when we are already cool (Craig, 2016). Similarly, someone who habitually eats steak will be unhappy with a hamburger. Quadriplegics eventually adjust to their handicap, and have good and bad days like everyone else (Schulz & Decker, 1985). However, they usually remain somewhat less happy than other people. This tendency might prevent us from becoming discouraged by repeated failure to reach difficult goals, and from becoming complacent from repeated success. It keeps our goal-setting realistic.

Now consider goal-setting in competitive situations. Our happiness varies with the circumstances of our success. Defeating a child at tennis offers no pride, but defeating a champion is exhilarating. It makes adaptive sense to choose a goal that is appropriate for one's abilities, for which there is a reasonable chance of success. For example, animals in a hierarchy challenge individuals similar in rank (Hobson & DeDeo, 2015). There is little point in challenging an opponent that is certain to be defeated or certain to defeat oneself. Social comparison research shows that people compare their performances with those of acquaintances and others in similar circumstances, rather than applying some absolute standard that may be unrealistic. Similarly, people are most curious about the performances of those close to them in rank and ability. Realistic goal-setting keeps our hopes up, so we don't despair as a result of failure. For example, the superior student can be told that she can still do better, and the weak student can be encouraged to keep trying, to seek to improve.

McClelland (1958) demonstrated that we raise our aspirations with success, and lower them with failure, so that we set realistic goals. People throwing darts aim for a score just above their previous performance—a realistic one, given that people improve their scores with practice. Setting moderately attainable goals, which most people do, would maximize effort by minimizing uncertainty of the outcome, thus increasing the challenge (Atkinson & Litwin, 1960). By contrast, people who have low self-esteem and self-confidence avoid competition, either by withdrawing from the contest or by setting very easy or very hard goals, thus minimizing uncertainty of outcome. For example, US college students with high self-confidence choose realistic major subjects (Isaacson, 1964). Those with low self-confidence select easy or hard major subjects.

Other "biases" in emotional responding that would have been adaptive in prehistory have been documented (Hazelton et al., 2009). The "negativity bias" in interpreting neutral facial expressions as threatening sensitizes us to potential danger (Baumeister, Bratslavsky, et al., 2001). Men overperceive women's sexual interest, so as not to miss out on mating opportunities (Abbey, 1982). Young children, especially boys, overestimate their dominance rank (Omark & Edelman, 1976). Adults tend to be overconfident about their prospects in war and interpersonal competition, giving them the advantage of perseverance and projected confidence (Johnson & Fowler, 2011; Murphy et al., 2015; von Hippel & Trivers, 2011).

Also, we have a bias toward immediate gratification (Frederick et al., 2002). We prioritize recent events in our responding. Events that are soon to occur are more predictable and controllable than events far into the future. The philosopher Jeremy Bentham (1907) identified "propinquity," or immediacy, as one factor enhancing the pleasure of a reward. Imminent rewards are more certain (another virtue of a reward cited by Bentham). Likewise, the "goal gradient effect" of heightened effort as the reward is approached makes adaptive sense.

Partly because of immaturity of the prefrontal cortex, children are less able to predict future outcomes than are adolescents with more life experience, and so children "live in the present" more than adolescents, who in turn are more impulsive than adults. Having had more experience in life and being better able to predict outcomes may allow one to defer an immediate pleasure for a later and greater one. So, why do we often respond impulsively? In most cases, this is because of urgency. We do not have the luxury of time to escape imminent danger. Speed of response imposes the cost of deliberating about how to respond best. However, speed of response is adaptive under many circumstances. For example, spontaneity seems to be endearing in a friend, perhaps because it indicates sincerity rather than calculation.

Measurement of Happiness

The study of global happiness has not been entirely successful. The term "subjective well-being" has been proposed as a substitute. However, this term means precisely the same as happiness (Argyle, 2001). Happiness has sometimes been split into life satisfaction, positive affect, and negative affect. Scales measuring each have shown some statistical independence, perhaps because each assesses a different set of emotions (Argyle, 2001).

Brock (1993) distinguished between hedonistic conceptions of happiness; preference satisfaction theories, assessing success in meeting personal goals; and ideal theories, crediting personal autonomy, for example. Of the three, hedonism seems the least culturally relative. Presumably, human emotions are the same across cultures. Barkow (1999) suggested that happiness in the modern world might be enhanced by adopting some practices, such as strong nurturance of children, that characterized prehistoric life and are retained by extant forager peoples. These ancient practices might be more attuned to our evolved emotional needs than contemporary urban life. For example, Lyubomirsky and Boehm (2010) suggested that modern childrearing is less satisfying than it was in prehistory, possibly accounting for the paradox that it seems to be stressful for parents, even if it yields long-term rewards.

Research on happiness is a growing field, partly due to dissatisfaction with economic measures such as personal or household income or gross domestic product (GDP—although some economic instruments are sophisticated mathematically and evolutionarily (e.g., Rayo & Becker, 2007). Some instruments measure the happiness of the individual, whereas others assess collective well-being, such as rates of child poverty. Annas (1993) suggested that inventories should be different for the sexes. The Swedish level-of-living surveys assess employment, education, social connections, leisure, and political participation (Erikson, 1993). The Swedes value "normalization" for their citizens, seeking to provide complete life satisfaction, a view consistent with discrete emotions theory.

Health measures are objective measures of well-being, and reflect psychological factors such as social support. Health relates directly to biological fitness, since it influences survival and also fertility. Health and longevity are correlated with happiness in cross-cultural research (Okun et al., 1984). Medical quality-of-life inventories include factors such as physical mobility, self-reliance, and social support. However, mental health is much more strongly related to happiness than is physical health (Clark et al., 2018).

Clark et al. (2018) developed a methodology for quantifying self-reported life satisfaction due to factors such as social support and health. They argued that social policy should be governed not by economic indicators, but by endeavoring to maximize life satisfaction in a population. Many of their cross-national data on factors in life satisfaction will be cited below.

However, few of these measures examine specific emotions. From a utilitarian perspective, happiness reflects the sum total of the various affects, and nothing else. Why not try to identify the universal affects and define happiness as including them all? Granted, weighting the various affects would be difficult, but perhaps some consensus could be reached with regard to the prioritization of the emotions, as Maslow (1959) proposed. In addition, people could be surveyed as to how important the various emotions are to them. If people's attitudes and beliefs can be measured, why not the intensity of their affects? A more systematic use of instruments measuring emotional intensity may be helpful in this respect (e.g., Larsen, 1985).

Some inventories have referred to specific sources of pleasure. A European survey found that the most commonly named pleasures were those of friendship, pride, food, drink, and sex (Argyle, 2001). "Time use" studies have asked about happiness associated with watching TV, commuting, cooking, exercising, worshiping, and childcare, among other activities, but other forms of leisure and vacation time are usually omitted (Krueger et al., 2009).

As an example of a list of the universal affects in adults, Weisfeld (2019) proposed: cutaneous sensations, thirst, hunger, tasting, smelling, disgust, fear, interest and related cognitive feelings (see above), fatigue, drowsiness, sexual feelings, love/loneliness, anger, pride/shame, and appreciation of humor and the arts. This list rests on many debatable assumptions, but it might serve as a basis for discussion and improvement.

One objection to defining happiness in emotional terms is that certain moral dilemmas would not be satisfactorily addressed. For example, most respondents balk at the moral choice of killing one person to secure organs to transplant into five other people, thereby saving their lives. But if we posit the existence of the emotion of empathy for the victim, we might be deterred from favoring sacrificing him. Furthermore, some inchoate recognition of Rawls's "veil of ignorance" may produce apprehension at such a system. Researchers have identified an *identifiable victim effect* to account for this "irrational" sympathy for a specific victim (Small & Loewenstein, 2003). Our feelings for others, not just for ourselves, are "real." Also, we might credit Kant's categorical imperative, the claim that moral actions must pass muster as general principles for human behavior. If hospitals were allowed to sacrifice some patients for the sake of others, chaos would reign.

One current societal concern is with economic inequality, which is associated with inequality in health, diet, political power, and other factors. Humans may be inherently angered by inequity (Benabou & Tirole, 2006) and "envy is inversely related to happiness (Belk, 1984). Theodore Roosevelt called comparison "the thief of joy," particularly if perceived to be the result of unfair processes (Starmans et al., 2017). Even simians may "go on strike" if short-changed in the rewards they receive for performing a task (Brosnan & de Waal, 2014). The expectation that rewards be proportional to accomplishments may underlie dominance behavior, in which prerogatives are proportional to rank (Weisfeld & Dillon, 2012).

Some additional moral principles may have evolved bases that would protect us from unwise or extreme application of utilitarianism. We seem to possess beliefs in equity, reciprocity, empathy, mating possessiveness, in-group loyalty, and inbreeding avoidance, for example. People also value personal freedom, protection from crime, honest government, and other societal ideals. Violations of these ideals presumably evoke anger, which could be taken into account in any inventory of satisfaction of universal emotions. This would avoid the problem of cultural and political relativism in social values.

Personality Factors

People tend to be happier when with other people (Kahneman et al., 2004). Nesse (1989) characterized happy people as sociable and self-confident. Similarly, high self-esteem, low anxiety, and physical attractiveness are correlated with happiness (Hills & Argyle, 2001). All these traits are characteristic of dominant individuals. Happiness has heritability around 0.50 or more (Lybomirsky, 2007). Attractive, entertaining, pro-social people are rewarding. Happy people laugh a lot (Ruch & Carrell, 1998). Their frequent smiles indicate that things are going well.

What are we to make of the apparent stability in happiness? One approach is to recognize that our appraisal system may have evolved to quickly reach adaptation to prompt continuing striving (as discussed above). The consequence of an ever rising "level of aspiration" is a stable level of happiness (Luhmann & Intelisano, 2018). Additionally, stability might be a function of stable conditions (e.g., Clark, 2015). Nes and colleagues found that genetics could explain a hefty portion of the variance in the population's happiness; nonetheless, time-specific effects were tied to situational factors, consistent with what we call a "consumptive model" of inclusive fitness correlates (Nes et al., 2006).

Marriage

Social support is strongly correlated with happiness. It lowers cortisol levels and improves longevity (Kielcolt-Glaser & Glaser, 1999). Marriage tends to increase sexual satisfaction, provide economies of scale, reduce social stress, and raise social status. In a British study, marital satisfaction was the strongest correlate of happiness identified (Russell & Wells, 1994). Married people are happier and healthier than other people. This is only partly due to the fact that people who marry are better off in the first place; people benefit when they marry, and are worse off if they divorce. Separation is often traumatic, and happiness seldom returns to baseline (reviewed by Clark et al., 2018). Divorced women are less happy than widows (Field, 2011; Joshanloo, 2018).

Children

Happiness tends to rise with the birth of a child, but returns to baseline in two years (Clark et al., 2018). Happiness is not related to the number of children, only to having them—except that happiness declines around the world after three children (Stanca, 2016). Evolutionary theorists have been puzzled by the widely reported claim that happiness falls with the birth of a child. Why should happiness decline with successful reproduction? One possible explanation is that selection merely needs to reward sex, and procreation is simply the consequence. Alternatively, the paradox may be resolved if life satisfaction rises due to the pleasures of parenthood even if marital satisfaction does not. Also, a fall in marital satisfaction after reproduction may be atypical when considering the environment of evolutionary adaptedness. Marital satisfaction may decline, slightly, in Western societies without grandparents to aid in childcare; it does not fall in societies with the extended family (Dillon & Beechler, 2010).

Children especially bring happiness to the parent if they are well cared for. If economic factors make it difficult to raise them, having children can result in hardship and misery for parents. A cross-national study found that negative economic conditions can counteract the positive effects of parenthood (Stanca, 2012). A country's family policies have a large impact on how well children and parents do. Policies that help children to be cared for by their biological parents and other relatives yield the best results. The extended family is virtually universal in tribal societies (Stephens, 1963).

Friendship

Aristotle's notion of "friendship of the good" characterized friendship as shared knowledge that each will act for the sake of the other's well-being, but these features are not per se the goals of the relationship (Aristotle, 1985). Although these mutual material benefits do ultimately explain why friendship formation evolved, acting deliberately in self-interest indicates weak friendships, not strong ones likely to bring happiness. Nonetheless, some data support the notion that trust and friendship are first built more narrowly on reciprocal exchanges before transmuting into communal friendships in which "cooperation without counting" prevails (Silk, 2003).

Consistent with the "banker's paradox"—reciprocal altruism in which "investment" in cooperative relationships is contingent on the beneficiary's ability to reciprocate—happy people attract others as friends, and gain benefits from these friends (Lewis et al., 2015; Tooby & Cosmides, 1996). This may be one of the signal functions of expressed happiness. Good friends are helpful and trustworthy. They ask personal questions, keep secrets, and disclose personal information (Wheeler et al., 1983). They show concern for others, and are open and honest, making them appear trustworthy. In other words, they are good candidates for the benefits of reciprocal altruism. Indeed, the sociologist Georg Simmel posited that the emotions of faithfulness and gratitude are operant in the production of strong ties between individuals (Greco et al., 2015), However, the role of reciprocity as a mediator between the relationship of happiness and friendship can at times be overstated (cf. Lewis et al., 2015).

Like spouses, friends resemble each other on any number of traits. Homophily probably reflects the tendency toward kin altruism (e.g., Christakis & Fowler, 2014), though mutual empathy also enhances the quality of friendships (Chow et al., 2013) and may be more readily achieved as a function of similarity (e.g., Preston & de Waal, 2002). However, Clark and Ayers (1992) found that female friend dyads were more similar than male friend dyads, which one would not expect if empathy was operative in producing homophily, as women tend to be more empathetic then men (e.g., Baron-Cohen & Wheelwright, 2004; Derntl et al., 2010; but see Baez et al., 2017). Additionally, similarity may reduce envy, especially in the domain of mate value, and therefore engender greater happiness in friendships (Lewis et al., 2015). Regardless of mechanism, similarity enhances feelings of solidarity.

In addition to gender differences in homophily, women's friendships tend to be more intimate than men's. Women tend to be more compassionate than men, and to be more rewarding as friends. A British study revealed that having male friends did not reduce people's loneliness; only female friends did (Argyle & Henderson, 1985). A naturalistic experiment found that adolescent boys offered practical help when someone had a bicycle accident; the girls consoled the victim instead (Savin-Williams, 1987).

Work

Unemployment in those seeking to work is associated with great unhappiness, and no adaptation or social comparison effect was observed in a study in the United Kingdom, Germany, and Australia (Clark et al., 2018). Chronic unemployment is associated with crime, and criminals tend to be unhappy. They also distress the public by the threat that they pose. In Germany, high unemployment is tempered by shortening work hours rather than imposing layoffs (Kurzarbeit). Yet people report greater unhappiness when at work than for almost any other activity (Clark et al., 2018). Companies with satisfied employees prosper financially from expenditures on their workers. Aiding in work-family balance, as by shorter work hours, is especially remunerative.

Many American men choose to stay home rather than take a miserable job. Many of these poorly educated men suffer from "diseases of despair"—depression, accidents, and drug abuse including alcoholism. Jobs have become increasingly stressful in the United States in recent years, partly because of the decline in labor union membership. Many US women too prefer to stay home to raise their children, because balancing work and family is difficult without paid parental leave and affordable day care.

Historically, men are more likely than women to take factory jobs, which can be hot, dangerous, fatiguing, dirty, and noisy. Partly because of these adverse conditions, men are paid more than women, who are drawn more to indoor service jobs (Farrell, 2005). But the main reason why women are paid less is that they spend less time on the job and more time caring for children (Becker, 1991). Childless women earn almost as much as men. Countries that provide more support for families, such as the Scandinavian ones (Partanen, 2017), have higher rates of female employment than, say, Japan, Italy, and the United States.

A satisfying job offers autonomy, meaningful work, task variety, evidence of success, and good pay (van der Doef & Maes, 1999). European workers report that they find group tasks and positive relations with coworkers especially gratifying (West et al., 1998). Workers in the helping professions are prone to burnout, risking feelings of ineffectiveness, suicide, and alcoholism (Maslach, 2003).

Income within a developed society is moderately correlated with happiness, but personal happiness rises only temporarily with an increase in income (Clark et al., 2018). Because of social comparison effects, average happiness does not rise as a wealthy, industrialized country becomes more prosperous, the Easterlin paradox (Easterlin, 1974). Income makes more of an impact on personal happiness in poorer countries (Diener & Biswas-Diener, 2000). Educational level is correlated with happiness, but mainly because it contributes to income.

As for income inequality, an extra dollar earned by a rich person brings less of a gain in happiness than it would for a poor person. This "diminishing marginal utility effect" argues for income equalization. Income inequality in a country is also associated with low life expectancy. Yet individual happiness continues to rise even at high income levels; there is no ceiling effect (Pinker, 2018). People want to be paid fairly. A British study found that workers preferred being paid 1£ more than other workers over being paid 2£ but less than fellow workers (Leicht & Shepelak, 1994). But most workers do not object to being overpaid! Lottery winners are not particularly happy, perhaps because they do not deserve their bounty (Smith & Razzell, 1975). Testosterone rises with success in men, but not as a result of good fortune (Mazur & Lamb, 1980).

Leisure

Socializing, pets, the arts, travel, education, and charity work can be very gratifying (Garrity & Stallones, 1998). An Australian study reported that psychosomatic symptoms declined after several days of vacation (Pearce, 1982). Man does not live by bread alone. Watching TV tends not to be very satisfying (Csikszentmihayli & Larsen, 1984). TV watching in the United States is associated with less newspaper reading, participation in social organizations, voting, and trust in others (Putnam, 1996). Consistent with the importance of leisure on happiness, a recent large international study found that paying for time-saving services promoted greater happiness than material purchases (Whillans et al. 2017).

Religion

Religion seems to offer moderate benefits to Europeans, mainly because of social contacts and social pressure to practice healthy behaviors (Clark & Lelkes, 2009). Church-goers live longer because of better health practices (Comstock & Partridge, 1972). Religiosity does not make people feel that life is more meaningful, although belief in an afterlife can be consoling (Osarchuk & Tate, 1973). Developed countries with the best economies and highest personal happiness are the relatively secular, Protestant ones (Clark et al., 2018). The poor, uneducated, and oppressed are more religious—Marx's opium of the people (Beit-Hallahmi & Argyle, 1997). Many evolutionary theories of religion include the idea that anticipation of eternal rewards or punishment by an all-knowing, all-powerful deity keeps people behaving themselves, thereby benefiting society. Many religions feature belief in a hereafter, such as all pre-contact North American Indigenous tribes (Catlin, 1973).

Age and Sex
Clark et al. (2018) examined factors involved in children's happiness and in raising a contented, well-behaved, emotionally healthy child. Critical for the development of happiness into adulthood is the mother's mental health; cognitive development is much less important. Men's happiness is closely related to income. Women's happiness is more closely tied to the health and happiness of their children (Clark et al., 1996). Widows especially benefit from having children (Stanca, 2016). Data from developed countries indicate that happiness rises from the 50s and peaks in the early 70s. Retirement is usually beneficial, especially for laborers, but not for those with interesting work (Ross & Mirowski, 1995). Participation in organizations and cultural activities is associated with happiness in retirees, as are physical and mental health and partner's health. Reductions in hearing, vision, and mobility have negative effects.

National Differences
The Scandinavians, Swiss, and Dutch consistently rank high in happiness. Poor countries, such as the Central African Republic, Burundi, and Tanzania, score lowest (Veenhoven, 2012). Latin American countries score higher than expected from their widespread poverty, perhaps because of strong family ties. The United States, Canada, and Australia expect their citizens to say they are happy, so scores there may be inflated (Diener et al., 1995).

Happiness is high in countries where people are trustworthy, as evidenced by "lost wallet" experiments, and where the government is democratic and respected (Clark et al., 2018). Good government is highly correlated with personal happiness. Personal freedom and income equality help. In China, happiness is less closely tied to personal factors than to the well-being of one's family (Suh et al., 1997). Economic development and family planning services raise happiness (Diener et al., 1995). Immigrants to developed countries rise in happiness to the level of natives (Helliwell et al., 2018). Despite claims of personal happiness, the United States has high rates of poverty, illiteracy, illness, obesity, crime, teen pregnancy, divorce, violence, student debt, and drug use. Immigrants to the United States tend to have lower rates of these problems, but suffer more from them with each generation. This is the immigrant paradox— we expect people to do better as they assimilate to US culture, but instead they do worse.

Pathology
Many, if not most, mental illnesses entail some disorder of affect. Depression is a common diagnosis in developed countries, and antidepressants are widely prescribed. Depression often leads to debilitation and even suicide, but may be over-diagnosed; pathological individuals tend to be selected out. Manic-depression may be a qualitatively different condition, since it can be effectively treated differently, with lithium.

DeCatanzaro (1987) offered an evolutionary explanation for depression. He concluded that many suicides had low inclusive fitness. Depressed or suicidal people often have no family ties, have disgraced their family, or see themselves as a burden on their family, though some have questioned these factors on the grounds that leaving one's group would be effective and preserves the possibility of future fitness. Of course, deCatanzaro did not propose the existence of a gene for self-destruction. But if happiness reflects success in meeting fitness needs, then unhappiness might reflect failure to do so, with the inevitable result in some cases of depression and suicide, especially if lethal weapons are at hand.

Another disorder of happiness is anhedonia, mentioned above. It is hard to imagine anyone lacking all emotion and motivation, as opposed to being overwhelmed by fatigue, as in chronic fatigue syndrome, or depression. In Parkinsonism, initiative for voluntary action is reduced. Complete lack of motivation would be a death sentence, and a condition strongly selected against. Less-energetic individuals would also be at a selective disadvantage compared with go-getters.

Concluding Comments

In conclusion, an evolutionary approach to the study of happiness has served as a useful organizing framework and generative approach. Many of the peculiarities of this emotion, e.g., its ephemeral nature, have been profitably explained. Nonetheless, further insights may be gained by broadening our search within this framework. Much of the literature, functional analyses included, has narrowly focused on happiness at the expense of overlooking other discrete positive emotions, trading off ease with granularity. Reorienting to a discrete emotions functional analysis may shed new light on the pathways through which the correlates of happiness contributed to inclusive fitness ancestrally. Furthermore, such an approach broadens the set of proximate mechanisms that together contribute to an individual's happiness and may elucidate the trait processes inherent to individual, gender, and age differences in the experience of happiness. Overall, the discrete emotions model provides an additional heuristic for theorizing how any particular correlate of happiness might have enhanced inclusive fitness in the environment of evolutionary adaptedness.

References

Abbey, A. (1982). Sex differences in attributions for friendly behavior: Do males misperceive female's friendliness? *Journal of Personality and Social Psychology, 42*, 830–838.

Al-Shawaf, L. (2016). The evolutionary psychology of hunger. *Appetite, 105*, 591–595.

Al-Shawaf, L., Lewis, D. M. G., & Buss, D. M. (2018). Sex differences in disgust: Why are women more easily disgusted than men? *Emotion Review, 10*, 149–160.

Annas, J. (1993). Women and the quality of life: Two norms or one? In M. C. Nussbaum & A. Sen (Eds.), *The quality of life* (pp. 279–296). Oxford University Press.

Antunes, R. A., & Oliveira, R. F. (2009). Hormonal anticipation of territorial challenges in cichlid fish. *Proceedings of the National Academy of Sciences, 106*, 15985–15989.

Argyle, M. (2001). *The psychology of happiness* (2nd ed.). Routledge.

Argyle, M., & Henderson, M. (1985). *The anatomy of relationships*. Penguin.

Aristotle. (1985). Nicomachean ethics. In J. Barnes (Ed.), *The complete works of Aristotle* (pp. 120–136). Bollingen Series LXXI, 2. Princeton University Press.

Atkinson, J. W., & Litwin, G. H. (1960), Achievement motive and test anxiety conceive as motive to approach success and motive to avoid failure. *Journal of Abnormal and Social Psychology, 60*, 52–63.

Baez, S., Flichtentrei, D., Prats, M., Mastandueno, R., García, A. M., Cetkovich, M., & Ibáñez, A. (2017). Men, women . . . who cares? A population-based study on sex differences and gender roles in empathy and moral cognition. *PloS ONE, 12*(6), e0179336.

Barkow, J. H. 1999). Happiness in evolutionary perspective. In N. L. Segal, G. E. Weisfeld, & C. C. Weisfeld (Eds.), *Uniting psychology and biology: Integrative perspectives on human development* (pp. 397–418). American Psychological Association.

Baron-Cohen, S., & Wheelwright, S. (2004). The empathy quotient: An investigation of adults with Asperger syndrome or high functioning autism, and normal sex differences. *Journal of Autism and Developmental Disorders, 34*, 163–175.

Baumeister, R. F., Bratslavsky E., Finkenauer, C., & Vohs, K. D (2001). Bad is stronger than good. *Review of General Psychology, 5*, 323–370.

Baumeister, R. F., Catanese, K. R., & Vohs, K. D. (2001). Is there a gender difference in strength of sex drive? Theoretical views, conceptual distinctions, and a review of relevant evidence. *Personality and Social Psychology Review, 5*, 242–273.

Beatty, J. (1995). *Principles of behavioral neuroscience*. Brown & Benchmark.

Becker, G. S. (1991). *A treatise on the family* (2nd ed.). Harvard University Press.
Beit-Hallahmi, G., & Argyle, M. (1997). *The psychology of religious behavior, belief and experience*. Routledge.
Belk, R. W. (1984). Three scales to measure constructs related to materialism: Reliability, validity, and relationships to measures of happiness. In T. C. Kinnear (Ed.), *Advances in consumer research* (Vol. 11, pp. 291–297). Association for Consumer Research.
Benabou, R., & Tirole, J. (2006). Belief in a just world and redistributive politics. *Quarterly Review of Economics, 121*, 699–746.
Bentham, J. (1907). *An introduction to the principles of morals and legislation*. Clarendon Press.
Berridge, K. C., & Kringelbach, M. L. (2016). From pleasure to happiness: "Liking" and "wanting" in mind and brain. In L. Feldman Barrett, M. Lewis, & J. M. Haviland-Jones (Eds.), *Handbook of emotions* (4th ed., pp. 133–145). Guilford Press.
Bietti, L. M., Tilston, O., & Bangerter, A. (2017). Storytelling as adaptive collective sensemaking. *Topics in Cognitive Science, 11*, 710–732.
Brock, D. (1993). Quality of life measures in health care and medical ethics. In M. C. Nussbaum & A. Sen (Eds.), *The quality of life* (pp. 95–132). Oxford University Press.
Brosnan, S. F., & de Waal, F. B. M. (2014). Evolution of responses to (un)fairness. *Science, 346*, 1251776.
Buss, D. M. (2000). The evolution of happiness. *American Psychologist, 53*, 5–23.
Catlin, G. (1973). *Letters and notes on the manners, customs, and conditions of North American Indians*, Vol. 1. Dover.
Chow, C. M., Ruhl, H., & Buhrmester, D. (2013). The mediating role of interpersonal competence between adolescents' empathy and friendship quality: A dyadic approach. *Journal of Adolescence, 36*(1), 191–200.
Christakis, N. A., & Fowler, J. H. (2014). Friendship and natural selection. *Proceedings of the National Academy of Sciences, 111*, 10796–10801.
Clark, A., Oswald A., & Warr, P. (1996). Is job satisfaction U-shaped in age? *Journal of Occupational and Organizational Psychology, 69*, 57–81.
Clark, A. E., Flèche, S., Layard, R., Powdthavee, N., & Ward, G. (2018). *The origins of happiness: the science of wellbeing over the life course*. Princeton University Press.
Clark, A. E., & Lelkes, O., 2009. Let us pray: Religious interactions in life satisfaction. Working Papers. Paris School of Economics, Paris.
Clark, G. (2015). *The son also rises: Surnames and the history of social mobility*. Princeton University Press.
Clark, M. L., & Ayers, M. (1992). Friendship similarity during early adolescence: Gender and racial patterns. *The Journal of Psychology, 126*(4), 393–405.
Comstock, G. W., & Partridge, K. B. (1972). Church attendance and health. *Journal of Chronic Diseases, 25*, 665–672.
Craig, A. D. (2016). Interoception and emotion: A neuroanatomical perspective. In L. Feldman Barrett, M. Lewis, & J. M. Haviland-Jones (Eds.), *Handbook of emotion* (4th ed., pp. 215–234). Guilford Press.
Csikszentmihayli, M., & Larsen, R. (1984). *Being adolescent*. Basic Books.
Darwin, C. ([1872] 1965). *The expression of the emotions in man and animals*. University of Chicago Press.
Davidson, R. J. (1998). Affective style and affective disorders: Perspectives from affective neuroscience. *Cognition and Emotion, 12*, 307–330.
deCatanzaro, D. (1987). Evolutionary pressures and limits to self-preservation. In C. Crawford, M. Smith, & D. Krebs (Eds.), *Sociobiology and psychology: Ideas, issues and applications* (pp. 311–351). Lawrence Erlbaum Associates.
Derntl, B., Finkelmeyer, A., Eickhoff, S., Kellermann, T., Falkenberg, D. I., Schneider, F., & Habel, U. (2010). Multidimensional assessment of empathic abilities: Neural correlates and gender differences. *Psychoneuroendocrinology, 35*(1), 67–82.
Diener, E., & Biswas-Diener, R. (2000). Income and subjective well-being: Will money make us happy? University of Illinois, unpublished manuscript.
Diener, E., Diener, M., & Diener, C. (1995). Factors predicting the subjective well-being of nations. *Journal of Personality and Social Psychology, 69*, 851–864.
Dillon, L. M., & Beechler, M. P. (2010). Marital satisfaction and the impact of children in collectivist cultures: A meta-analysis. *Journal of Evolutionary Psychology, 8*, 7–22.
Dolesek, N., Gehrlach, D. A., Klein, A. S., & Gogolla, N. (2020). Facial expressions of emotion states and their neuronal correlates in mice. *Science, 368*, 89–94.
Easterlin, R. (1974). Does economic growth improve the human lot? In P. A. David & W. B. Melvin (Eds.), *Nations and households in economic growth* (pp. 89–125). Stanford University Press.
Erikson, R. (1993). Descriptions of inequality: The Swedish approach to welfare research. In M. C. Nussbaum & A. Sen (Eds.), *The quality of life* (pp. 67–83). Oxford University Press.
Farrell, W. (2005). *Why men earn more: The startling truth behind the pay gap—and what women can do about it*. New York American Management Association.

Frederick, S., Loewenstein,G., & O'Donoghue, T. (2002). Time discounting and time preference: a critical review. *Journal of Economic Literature, 40*, 351–401.

Fuster, J. M. (1997). *The prefrontal cortex: Anatomy, physiology, and neuropsychology of the frontal lobe*. Raven Press.

Garrity, E., & Stallones, L. (1998). Effects of pet contact on human well-being. In C. C. Wilson & D. C. Turner (Eds.), *Companion animals in human health* (pp. 3–22). Sage.

Gibson, W. T., Gonzalez, C. R., Fernandez, C., Ramasamy, L., Tabachnik, T., Du, R. R., Felsen, P. D., Maire, M. R., Perona, P., & Anderson, D. J. (2015). Behavioral responses to a repetitive visual threat stimulus express a persistent state of defensive arousal in Drosophila. *Current Biology, 25*, 1401–1415.

Graham, J. M., & Desjardins, C. (1980). Classical conditioning: Induction of luteinizing and testosterone secretion in anticipation of sexual activity. *Science, 210*, 1039–1041.

Greco, S., Holmes, M., & McKenzie, J. (2015). Friendship and happiness from a sociological perspective. In M. Demir (Ed.), *Friendship and happiness* (pp. 19–35). Springer.

Hamann, S. (2012). Mapping discrete and dimensional emotions onto the brain: Controversy and consensus. *Trends in Cognitive Science, 16*, 458–466.

Hazelton, M. G., et al. (2009). Adaptive rationality: An evolutionary perspective on cognitive bias. *Social Cognition, 27*, 733–763.

Heath, R. G. (1972). Pleasure and brain activity in man. *Journal of Nervous and Mental Disease, 154*, 3–18.

Hein, G., Engelmann, J. B., Vollberg, M. C., & Tobler, P. N. (2016). How learning shapes the empathic brain. *Proceedings of the National Academy of Sciences, 113*, 80–85.

Helliwell, J. F, Layard, R., & Sachs, J. (Eds.). (2018). *World happiness report*. United Nations Sustainable Development Network.

Hills, P., & Argyle, M. (2001). Happiness, introversion-extraversion and happy introverts. *Personality and Individual Differences, 230*, 595–608.

Hobson, E. A., & DeDeo, S. (2015). Social feedback and the emergence of rank in animal society. *PLoS Computational Biology, 11*(9), e1004411.

Hockey, G. R. J. (2013). *The psychology of fatigue: Work, effort and control*. Cambridge University Press.

Husted, D., Shapira, N. A., & Goodman, W. K. (2006). The neurocircuitry of obsessive-compulsive disorder and disgust. *Progress in Neuro-Psychopharmacology & Biological Psychiatry, 30*, 389–399.

Isaacson, R. I. (1964). Relations between N-achievement, test anxiety, and curricular choices. *Journal of Abnormal and Social Psychology, 68*, 447–452.

Johnson, D. D. P., & Fowler, J. H. (2011). The evolution of overconfidence. *Nature, 477*, 317–320.

Joshanloo, M. (2018). Gender differences in the predictors of life satisfaction across 150 nations. *Personality and Individual Differences, 135*, 312–315.

Kahneman, D., Krueger, A. B., Schkade, D. A., Schwarz, N., & Stone, A. A. (2004). A survey method for characterizing daily life experience: The day reconstruction method. *Science, 306*, 1776–1780.

Kahneman, D. (2011). *Thinking, fast and slow*. Macmillan.

Kay, T., Keller, L., & Lehmann, L. (2020). The evolution of altruism and the serial rediscovery of the role of relatedness. *Proceedings of the National Academy of Sciences, 117*, 28894–28898.

Kielcolt-Glaser, J., K., & Glaser, R. (1999). Chronic stress and mortality among older adults. *Journal of the American Medical Association, 282*, 2259–2260.

Kimura, D. (1999). *Sex and cognition*. MIT Press.

Kluger, M. J. (1991). Fever: Role of pyrogens and cryogens. *Physiological Review, 91*, 93–127.

Kringelbach, M. L., Lehtonen, A., Squire, S., Harvey, A. G., Craske, M. G., Holliday, I. E., Green, A. L., Aziz, T. Z., Hansen, P. C., Cornelissen, P. L., & Stein, A. (2008). A specific and rapid neural signature for parental instinct. *PloS one, 3*(2), e1664. doi:10.1371/journal.pone.0001664

Krueger, A. B., et al. (2009). Comparing time use and subjective well-being in France and the US. *Social Indicators Research, 93*, 7–18.

Kurzban, R., Duckworth, A., Kable, J. W., & Myers, J. (2013). An opportunity cost model of subjective effort and task performance. *Behavioral and Brain Sciences, 36*, 661–679.

Larsen, R. J. (1985). *Theory and measurement of affect intensity as an individual difference characteristic*. Doctoral dissertation, University of Illinois at Urbana-Champaign, ProQuest Information & Learning.

LeDoux, J. (1996). *The emotional brain: The mysterious underpinnings of emotional life*. Simon & Schuster.

Leicht, K. T., & Shepelack, N. (1994). Organizational justice and satisfaction with economic rewards. *Research in Social Stratification and Mobility, 13*, 175–202.

Lewis, D. M., Al-Shawaf, L., Russell, E. M., & Buss, D. M. (2015). Friends and happiness: An evolutionary perspective on friendship. In M. Demir (Ed.), *Friendship and happiness* (pp. 37–57). Springer.

Luhmann, M., & Intelisano, S. (2018). Hedonic adaptation and the set point for subjective well-being. In E. Diener, S. Oishi, & L. Tay (Eds.), *Handbook of well-being* (pp. 219–243). DEF.

Lukaszewski, A. W., Lewis, D. M., Durkee, P. K., Sell, A. N., Sznycer, D., & Buss, D. M. (2020). An adaptationist framework for personality science. *European Journal of Personality, 34*, 1151–1174.

Lyubomirsky, S., (2007). *The how of happiness: A new approach to getting the life you want*. Penguin.

Lyubomirsky, S., & Boehm, J. K. (2010). Human motives, happiness, and the puzzle of parenthood: Commentary on Kenrick et al., (2010). *Perspectives on Psychological Science, 5*, 327–334.

Maeng, L. Y., & Milad, M. R. (2015). Sex differences in anxiety disorders: Interactions between fear, stress, and gonadal hormones. *Hormones and Behavior, 76*, 106–117.

Mansour, A., Khachaturian, H., Lewis, M. E., Akil, H., & Watson, S. J. (1988). Anatomy of CNS opioid receptors. *Trends in Neurosciences, 11*, 308–314.

Maslach, C. (2003). *Burnout: The cost of caring*. Malor Books.

Maslow, A. H. (1959). *New knowledge in human values*. Harper & Row.

Mazur, A., & Lamb, T. (1980). Testosterone, status and mood in human males. *Hormones and Behavior, 14*, 236–246.

McClelland, D. C. (1958). Methods of measuring human motivation. In J. W. Atkinson (Ed.), *Motives in fantasy, action, and society* (pp. 7–42). Van Nostrand Reinhold.

McClure, S. M., et al (2007). Time discounting for primary rewards. *Journal of Neuroscience, 27*, 5796–5804.

Mercier, H. & Sperber, D. (2011) Why do humans reason? Arguments for an argumentative theory. *Behavioral and Brain Sciences, 34*(2), 57–74.

Murphy, G. C., Nimmo-Smith, L., & Lawrence, A. D. (2003). Functional neuroanatomy of emotions: A meta-analysis. *Cognitive and Affective Behavioral Neuroscience, 3*, 207–233.

Murphy, S. C., von Hippel, W., Dubbs, S. L., Angilletta Jr., M. J., Wilson, R. S., Trivers, R., & Barlow, F. K. (2015). The role of overconfidence in romantic desirability and competition. *Personality and Social Psychology Bulletin, 41*, 1036–1052.

Nes, R. B., Røysamb, E., Tambs, K., Harris, J. R., & Reichborn-Kjennerud, T. (2006). Subjective well-being: Genetic and environmental contributions to stability and change. *Psychological Medicine, 36*, 1033–1042.

Nesse, R. M. (1989). Evolutionary explanations of emotions. *Human Nature, 1*, 261–289.

Nesse, R. M., & Ellsworth, P. C. (2009). Evolution, emotions, and emotional disorders. *American Psychologist, 64*, 129–139.

Nisbett, R. E., & Wilson, T. D. (1977). Telling more than we can know: Verbal reports on mental processes. *Psychological Review, 84*, 231–259.

Nummenmaa, L., & Tuominen, L. (2018). Opioid system and human emotions. *British Journal of Pharmacology, 175*(14), 2737–2749.

Okun, M. A., Stock, W. A.., Haring, M. J., & Witten, R. A. (1984). Health and subjective well-being: A meta-analysis. *International Journal of Aging and Human Development, 19*, 11–132.

Olds, J., & Milner, P. (1954). Positive reinforcement produced by electrical stimulation of septal area and other regions of the rat brain. *Journal of Comparative and Physiological Psychology, 47*, 419–427.

Omark, D. R., & Edelman, M. S. (1976). The development of attention structures in young children. In M. R. A Chance & R. R. Larsen (Eds.), *The social structure of attention* (pp. 119–151). Wiley.

Osarchuk, M., & Tate, S. J. (1973). Effect of induced fear of death on belief in afterlife. *Journal of Personality and Social Psychology, 27*, 225–240.

Panksepp, J. (1998). *Affective neuroscience: The foundations of human and animal emotions*. Oxford University Press.

Partanen, A. (2017). *The Nordic theory of everything: In search of a better life*. Prelude Books.

Pearce, P. L. (1982). *The social psychology of tourist behaviour*. Pergamon.

Phan, K. L., Wager, T., Taylor, S. F., & Liverzon, I. (2002). Functional neuroanatomy of emotion: A meta-analysis of emotion activation studies in PE and fMRI. *NeuroImage, 16*, 331–348.

Pinker, S. (2018). *Enlightenment now: The case for reason, science, humanism, and* progress. Viking.

Preston, S. D., & de Waal, F. B. M. (2002). Empathy: Its ultimate and proximate bases. *Behavioral and Brain Sciences, 25*, 1–72.

Pugh, G. E. (1977). *The biological origin of human values*. Basic Books.

Putnam, R. D. (1996). The strange disappearance of civic American. *Policy: A Journal of Public Policy and Ideas, 12*, 3–15.

Rayo, L., & Becker, G. S. (2007). Habits, peers, and happiness: An evolutionary perspective. *American Economic Review, 97*, 487–491.

Reed, L. I., DeScioli, P., & Pinker, S. A. (2014). The commitment function of angry facial expressions. *Psychological Science, 25*, 1511–1517.

Reed, L. I., Matari, Y., Wu, M., & Janaswamy, R. (2019). Emotional tears: An honest signal of trustworthiness increasing prosocial behavior? *Evolutionary Psychology, 17*, 1–8. doi.org/10.1177/1474704919872421

Renn, S. C. P., & Schumer, M. E. (2013). Genetic accommodation and behavioural evolution: insights from genomic studies. *Animal Behavior, 85*, 1012–1022.

Roes, F. L. (1990). Waraom huilen mensen? [Why do people cry?] *Psychologie, 10*, 44–45.

Rolls, E. T. (1999). *The brain and emotion*. Oxford University Press.

Rosenzweig, M. R., Breedlove, S. M., & Watson, N. V. (2005). *Biological psychology: An introduction to behavioral and cognitive neuroscience* (4th ed.). Sinauer.

Ross, C. E., & Mirowsky, J. (1995). Explaining the social patterns of depression: Control and problem-solving or support and talking. *Journal of Health and Social Behavior, 39*, 206–219.

Ruch, W., & Carrell, A. (1998). Trait cheerfulness and the sense of humour. *Personality and Individual Differences, 24*, 329–333.

Russell, R. J. H., & Wells, P. A. (1994). Predictors of happiness in married couples. *Personality and Individual Differences, 17*, 313–321.

Saarimaki, H., et al. (2015). Discrete neural signatures of basic emotions. *Cerebral Cortex, 26*, 2563–2573.

Savin-Williams, R. C. (1987). *Adolescence: An ethological perspective*. Springer-Verlag.

Schachter, S., & Singer, J. (1962). Cognitive, social, and physiological determinants of emotional state. *Psychological Review, 69*, 379–399.

Schulz, R., & Decker, S. (1985). Long-term adjustment to physical disability: The role of social support, perceived control, and self-blame. *Journal of Personality and Social Psychology, 48*, 1162–1172.

Sell, A. N. (2011). The recalibrational theory and violent anger. *Aggression and Violent Behavior, 16*, 381–389.

Small, D. A., & Loewenstein, G. (2003). Helping a victim or helping the victim: Altruism and identifiability. *Journal of Risk and Uncertainty, 26*, 5–16.

Silk, J. B. (2003). Cooperation without counting: The puzzle of friendship. In P. Hammerstein (Ed.), *Dahlem workshop report: Genetic and cultural evolution of cooperation* (pp. 37–54). MIT Press.

Smith, S., & Razzell, P. (1975). *The pools winners*. Caliban Books.

Sperber, D., Clément, F., Heintz, C., Mascaro, O., Mercier, H., Origgi, G., & Wilson, D. (2010). Epistemic vigilance. *Mind and Language, 25*, 359–393.

Stanca, L. (2012). Suffer the little children: Measuring the effects of parenthood on well-being worldwide. *Journal of Economic Behavior and Organization, 81*, 742–750.

Stanca, L. (2016). The geography of parenthood and well-being: Do children make us happy, where and why? *World Happiness Report, 2*, 88–102.

Stark, E., Berridge, K. C., & Kringelbach, M. L. (2020). Are we designed to be happy? The neuroscience of making sense of pleasure. In L. Workman, W. Reader, & J. H. Barkow (Eds.), *The Cambridge handbook of evolutionary perspectives on human behavior* (pp. 91–96). Cambridge University Press.

Starmans, C., Sheskin, M., & Bloom, P. (2017). Why people prefer unequal societies. *Nature Human Behaviour, 1*, 1–7.

Stephens, W N. (1963). *The family in cross-cultural perspective*. Holt, Rinehart & Winston.

Sugiyama, M. S. (2001). Food, foragers, and folklore: The role of narrative in human subsistence. *Evolution and Human Behavior, 22*, 221–240.

Sugiyama, M. S. (2005). Narrative theory and function: Why evolution matters. *Philosophy and Literature, 25*, 233–250.

Suh, E., Diener, E., Oishi, s., & Triandis, H. (1997). The shifting basis of life satisfaction, judgments across cultures: Emotions versus norms. *Journal of Personality and Social Psychology, 74*, 482–493.

Toates, R. (1986). *Motivational systems*. Cambridge University Press.

Tomkins, S. S. (1962). *Affect, imagery, and consciousness*, Vol 1: *The positive affects*. Springer.

Tooby, J., & Cosmides, L. (1996). Friendship and the banker's paradox: Other pathways to the evolution of adaptations for altruism. In W. G. Runciman, J. M. Smith, & R. I. M. Dunbar (Eds.), *Evolution of social behavior patterns in primates and man* (Vol. 88, pp. 119–143). Oxford University Press.

Trivers, R.L. (1971). The evolution of reciprocal altruism. *Quarterly Review of Biology, 46*, 35–57.

van der Doef, M., & Maes, S. (1999). The job demands-control (-support) model and psychological well-being: A review of 20 years of empirical research. *Work and Stress, 13*, 87–115.

Veenhoven, R. (2012). Cross-cultural differences in happiness: Cultural measurement bias or effect of culture? *International Journal of Wellbeing, 2*, 333–353.

von Hippel, W., & Trivers, R. (2011). The evolution and psychology of self-deception. *Behavioral and Brain Sciences, 34*, 1–56.

Weisfeld, G. E. (1972). Violations of social norms as inducers of aggression. *International Journal of Group Tensions, 2*, 53–69.

Weisfeld, G. E. (1999). *Evolutionary principles of human adolescence.* Basic Books.

Weisfeld, G. E. (2019). *Evolved emotions: An interdisciplinary and functional analysis.* Lexington Books.

Weisfeld, G. E., & Dillon, L. M. (2012). Applying the dominance hierarchy model to pride and shame and related behaviors. *Journal of Evolutionary Psychology, 10*, 15–41.

West, M. A., Borrill, C. S., & Unsworth, K. L. (1998). Team effectiveness in organizations. In C. Cooper & I. T. Robertson (Eds), *International review of industrial and organizational psychology* (Vol 13, pp. 1–48). Wiley.

Wheeler, L., Reis, J., & Nezlek, J. (1983). Loneliness, social interaction, and social roles. *Journal of Personality and Social Psychology, 45*, 943–953.

Whillans, A. V., Dunn, E. W., Smeets, P., Bekkers, R., & Norton, M. I. (2017). Buying time promotes happiness. *Proceedings of the National Academy of Sciences, 114*, 8523–8527. doi.org/10.1073/pnas.1706541114

Wondra, J. D., & Ellsworth, P. C. (2015). An appraisal theory of empathy and other vicarious emotional experiences. *Psychological Review, 122*, 411–428.

Wood, K. H., Ver Hoef, L. W., & Knight, D. C. (2014). The amygdala mediates the emotional modulation of threat-elicited skin conductance response. *Emotion, 14*, 693–700.

CHAPTER 25

Grief

Heidi Martin and Carol Cronin Weisfeld

Abstract
Theories about grief include the stage theory of Kübler-Ross and the Parkes-Bowlby theory (based on attachment theory). While the former is not well supported by research, cross-cultural research affirms the latter. This chapter uses Tinbergen's Four Questions to understand grief. Tinbergen's questions explore two levels of proximate causation: ontogeny and immediate mechanisms such as learning; two additional levels describe evolutionary or more distal explanations: phylogenetic and evolutionary (functional) causation. Developmentally, behavioral characteristics of grief change over the human life span. Immediate causation for feeling grief is found in heightened autonomic nervous system arousal, and environmental inputs, such as degree of relatedness with the one lost. Phylogenetically, grief likely evolved in social species, such as humans and other primates, elephants, and domesticated dogs. Functionally, grief may be a byproduct of attachment; however, grief may serve other functions, such as encouraging protective parenting and compelling relatives to comfort the bereaved. Clinical applications are discussed.

Key Words: attachment, grief, loss, pathological grief, Parkes-Bowlby Theory, Tinbergen's Four Questions

Stop all the clocks, cut off the telephone,
Prevent the dog from barking with a juicy bone,
Silence the pianos and with muffled drum
Bring out the coffin, let the mourners come.

Let aeroplanes circle moaning overhead
Scribbling on the sky the message "He is Dead."
Put crepe bows round the white necks of the public doves,
Let the traffic policemen wear black cotton gloves.

He was my North, my South, my East and West,
My working week and my Sunday rest,
My noon, my midnight, my talk, my song;
I thought that love would last forever: I was wrong.

The stars are not wanted now; put out every one,
Pack up the moon and dismantle the sun,
Pour away the ocean and sweep up the wood;
For nothing now can ever come to any good.

—W. H. Auden, *"Funeral Blues"*

Grief, being too profound to be captured easily by scholarly tomes, is often described through poetry or art. In much the same way, we try to describe love through poetry or art, because love, also, is profound and difficult to treat in scholarly writing. Grief is a universal experience, and all cultures seek to manage it (Kalish, 1981). Investigations into the phenomenon and experience of grief have proceeded out of theoretical and practical motivations. Psychologists, who are particularly interested in helping individuals cope with grief, have provided several frameworks for understanding the phenomenon, and these frameworks have assisted healthcare providers and counselors with approaches that vary in their utility. This chapter will begin with definitions, review theoretical frameworks for conceptualizing grief, and point out the most promising directions for future research.

Hall (2014) reviewed the major theories of grief and evaluated their empirical support. Several stage or phase theories have been proposed, the most well-known of which is the stage theory of Kübler-Ross (1969). These theories assert that particular pathways are experienced by most individuals experiencing loss. It is important to credit Kübler-Ross with breaking new ground because she asked healthcare providers to pay attention to the importance of caring for terminally ill patients, including attending to their psychological needs, rather than focusing solely on curing them (Sigelman & Rider, 2015). Kübler-Ross proposed that grief follows five stages: denial, anger, bargaining, depression, and acceptance. The theory continues to be embraced enthusiastically by many practitioners who present it in training programs for nurses and family counselors, despite a lack of empirical support for the proposed stages (Hall, 2014). Attempting to account for individual and cultural differences (which cannot be accounted for in the Kübler-Ross theory), Stroebe and Schut (1999) presented a Dual Process Model of Grief. Their theory describes an oscillation between emotional processing in grief and cognitive functioning that allows one to engage in problem-solving. Worden (2008) also emphasized both the emotional and the cognitive aspects of the grief process, stressing the differences in people's experiences that likely create idiosyncratic grief experiences. These latter two theories address the issue of individual differences much more capably, but still there are challenges. Even the question of "letting go" of the lost person has become a matter of debate. While Freud ([1917] 1957) wrote of the importance of breaking ties to the loved one and moving on to other relationships, modern theorists (Klass et al., 1996) suggest that there may be healthy ways to maintain the relationship to the loved one, perhaps as a spiritual, if not a physical, relationship. As Hall (2014, p. 9) put it, "there exists the possibility of the deceased being both present and absent." This kind of thinking is in keeping with Native American traditions of visiting with ancestors in dreams, and non-Western traditions of lingering spirits of lost loved ones (e.g., Talayesva, 1942).

If one is to make sense of grief, one must look to theories that go beyond simplistic stage theories and present empirical support for their assertions. According to the thinking of John Bowlby, who wrote the classic work on attachment and loss (1980), love and grief may be understood as aspects of the same human experience. This chapter will center its exploration of grief in Bowlby's attachment theory, as extended in the work of C. M. Parkes (2006). Evidence for particular aspects of grief will be explored further by means of the Four Questions framework of Nobel Prize winner and founder of ethology, Niko Tinbergen (1963). He suggested studying behavior by looking at different levels of causation. Levels of causation include ultimate levels (phylogeny and survival value, or function) of the behavior and proximate levels (ontogeny and immediate or mechanistic causes) of the behavior. These are commonly called Tinbergen's Four Questions, and they encourage us to look across disciplines to clarify our understanding of behavior (Medicus, 2005). Notably, these are complementary, not conflicting, explanations of behavior, allowing us to analyze behavior on multiple levels simultaneously (Al-Shawaf et al., 2018). Another exploration of grief through an evolutionary lens is found in the work of Nesse (2005), who offers a framework for further research. After consideration of normal and pathological grief, the chapter will conclude by returning to the Parkes-Bowlby theory as a way of better understanding grief, including pathological grief, through its relationship with attachment, particularly as elucidated in the work of Kosminsky and Jordan (2016).

Definitions and Theoretical Approach of Parkes (Parkes-Bowlby Theory)

Grief has been defined as "a particular case of the general feeling of separation from a loved one" (Weisfeld, 2019, p. 209). Nesse (2005) has suggested that grief may be a "specialized form of useful sadness" (p. 214). Though the term *bereavement* has been used interchangeably with the term *grief*, the terms have different connotations. While *bereavement* is defined as the condition of having lost a loved one ("bereavement," n.d.), this chapter uses and focuses on the concept of grief as the psychological response to the loss of a loved one. In keeping with this differentiation, Hall (2014) wrote "Grief can be defined as the response to the loss in all of its totality—including its physical, emotional, cognitive, behavioural and spiritual manifestations—and as a natural and normal reaction to loss. Put simply, grief is the price we pay for love, and a natural consequence of forming emotional bonds to people" (p. 7). Weisfeld (2019) noted Darwin's observation that grief is often characterized by sobbing, a particularly intense form of crying (Darwin, 1998). In human and nonhuman infants, the first phase of reaction to separation is the active distress phase, in which crying functions, in most cases, to bring the parent back to the abandoned infant. In human adults who have experienced loss, crying (and perhaps sobbing even more so) function to attract sympathy from caregivers, family, and friends who might be motivated to provide support for the bereaved adult (Weisfeld, 2019). In cases where the parent does not return, infants typically move into a second phase that looks like depression (Bowlby, 1988). Bowlby wrote that this subdued phase probably protects an infant from predators in the absence of the mother. Abandoned infants are not likely to survive, particularly in altricial species, where the infant is relatively helpless and highly dependent on the mother after birth (Freedman, 1974). An infant is more likely to survive if the infant is rescued or adopted by a conspecific with whom the infant can form a new attachment (reorganizing its world of relationships, as Bowlby and others have described the process). An example of this reorganization was seen in the case of two captive infant baboons who were orphaned by an encephalitis infection that swept through their troop and killed their mothers. Both infants made obvious expressions of distress, to which older female relatives responded with care amounting to functional adoption (Weisfeld et al., 1983).

C. M. Parkes (2006) formulated a model of grief based on the theoretical and empirical work of Bowlby (1980) and Ainsworth (Ainsworth et al., 1978). The model begins with the assumption that attachment is the precursor; it is loss of an attachment figure that leads to grief. It follows, then, that the attachment style an individual experienced early on will give shape and form to their grief later on. Parkes engaged in a major research project, the Harvard Bereavement Study, to test this idea. Ainsworth's classic Strange Situation protocol, with infants one year of age, had established three major styles of attachment between mother and infant: secure, insecure anxious/ambivalent, and insecure avoidant. Later work by Main (Main & Solomon, 1986) confirmed a fourth style, disorganized attachment. Each attachment style is described in Table 25.1. Infants' behaviors provided the basis for categorizing their attachment styles as secure or insecure, with the variations seen in the latter. Notably, the Strange Situation protocol provided information about relating to the mother, a stranger, and a new environment. Parkes reasoned that each attachment style, because of its lasting imprint

Table 25.1 Attachment Styles and Correlated Grief Characteristics

Attachment Style	Childhood Behaviors (at one year of age)	Percentage of Infants in United States	Behaviors in Adult Bereavement
Secure	Child explores confidently, interacts with stranger when Mom is present. Child protests Mom's departure, responds positively when Mom returns.	60%–65%	Adult may experience overlapping phases of numbness, crying, yearning for lost person, moving between disorganization and reorganization toward healing.
Insecure: Anxious/Ambivalent	Child is clingy with Mom and fearful toward both stranger and environment. Child is very upset when Mom leaves but ambivalent, perhaps angry, upon her return.	10%	Because of being overly dependent, adult may be clingy, experiencing intense grief that becomes chronic. Loneliness is great and persistent. Possible history of marital disagreement.
Insecure: Avoidant	Child explores environment, but in a less organized way, and may be indifferent to stranger. Child shows little reaction to Mom's departure or return.	10%–15%	Due to difficulties with expressing affection, grief may be delayed or inhibited. This may eventually lead to increasing disability and illness. Possible history of distrust and disagreement in marital relationship.
Insecure: Disorganized	Child does not explore, seems confused by stranger. No consistent response to Mom's departure; may approach/avoid Mom upon her return.	10%–15%	Adult shows a "mixture of unsatisfactory attachment strategies" (Parkes, 2006, p. 109). Increased risk of helplessness, panic, depression, anxiety, alcohol use, suicide.

Notes: Ainsworth and colleagues originally documented behavioral characteristics of three attachment styles; this work was later augmented by the documenting of a fourth style, Insecure/Disorganized, by Main. Percentages are based on subsequent studies by many authors. Adult bereavement correlates were documented by Parkes (2006) and colleagues in the Harvard Bereavement Study.

Sources: Ainsworth et al., 1978; Parkes, 2006; Sigelman & Rider, 2015.

on an individual, would lead to particular characteristics of relating to others, and also lead to particular reactions upon the loss of a significant other.

The fourth column of Table 25.1 summarizes what Parkes found in the Harvard Bereavement Study, by assessing attachment style using the Retrospective Attachment Questionnaire (RAQ; Parkes, 2006), and obtaining extensive information about recent bereavements and how participants handled those bereavements. Parkes utilized path analysis to confirm links between attachment score on the RAQ and various behaviors in bereavement. Parkes hypothesized that secure childhood attachment would lead to secure adult attachment; and, furthermore, the loss of a secure adult loved one would be less distressing than the loss of an insecure relationship. (This may seem counterintuitive to the reader, and, as described below, Nesse reported some contradictory evidence in work that he and his colleagues reported in 2001.) Parkes documented painful grief, to be sure, after the loss of a secure partnership, but the trajectory of grief was smoother and shorter in duration than it was after the loss of an insecure partnership. For example, in both clinical and nonclinical subsamples, participants with high secure attachment reported low marital disharmony, better coping skills, and less overall distress as they lived through the difficult time of bereavement. Parkes wrote that these individuals experienced overlapping phases of numbness, crying, and yearning for the lost loved one; they also experienced periods of disorganization and reorganization of their lives, but their path to recovering from loss caused them less suffering than was seen in people with insecure attachment histories of all types. Parkes emphasized that numbness, disorganization, and the other reported behaviors were not to be understood as developmental stages such as those proposed by Kübler-Ross. Parkes also emphasized that the experience of grief is made even more idiosyncratic by other variables such as the age, gender, cultural background, and traumatic history of the individual who experiences the loss of a loved one, as well as the circumstances of the loss. As shown in Table 25.1, it is the insecurely attached individual who is more likely to experience troubled grief, delayed grief, or chronic grief. These profiles will be discussed further in the section on Pathology and Clinical Applications, below.

One of the cautions emphasized in the work of Parkes is that the grief experience is idiosyncratic. Carr et al. (2001) reported on findings from another large-scale prospective study of grief showing that in some cases where the relationship has been ambivalent, grief can be a relatively easy experience. Nesse (2005) suggests that an evolutionary framework can be enormously helpful here, pointing researchers in the direction of examining more closely, among other things, the roles of genetic relatedness and level of committed exchange between spousal partners when exploring the experience of grief in those left behind.

Tinbergen's Four Questions

The ethologist Niko Tinbergen proposed in a 1963 paper that, in order to really understand a behavior, it is helpful to analyze the behavior on four levels: phylogenetic causation (how the behavior evolved through and across different species), ontogenetic causation (how the behavior develops over time), immediate causation (or mechanism, including psychological and physiological mechanisms), and functional causation in evolution (the possible survival or reproductive value of the behavior). The next sections examine grief on each of those levels.

Distal Level of Analysis: Phylogeny

Several observers have reported examples of expressions in nonhuman animals that appear to be expressions of grief, and the circumstances in which the expressions occur support this interpretation (Bekoff, 2000). Nonetheless, these observations are often greeted with skepticism by those who argue that grief cannot be possible without higher cognitive functioning (and we shall return to this issue in the discussion of human infants' reactions, in the Ontogeny section below). In a 2013 review of grief in animals, Brooks Pribac (2013) argues, "The primary parameter of consideration in claims about animal grief should instead be the animals' capacity to experience attachment and loss, a subject which rarely ever receives adequate attention" (p. 70). The author, citing Schore (2005) and others, argues that early attachments allow for the maturation of homeostatic mechanisms in the young animal, through bidirectional influences with the body of the caretaking adult (usually the mother). Neuro-endocrinological maturation and self-regulation depend on this early mutual dependence; consequently, when the body of the parent is removed from the infant's world, the infant's body becomes dysregulated and stressed, and cries of distress signal the danger of "collapse" that the infant is experiencing. (These neuro-endocrinological mechanisms are discussed more in the section on Mechanisms below.)

Brooks Pribac (2013) documents many examples of animal grief found in the ethological literature. Elephants provide a striking example of engaging in ritualized behavior after the death of another elephant, covering the body of the deceased with dirt and returning to it later (Bradshaw, 2009). Several species of birds are mentioned in this review as well. In Goodall's famous accounts of chimpanzee behavior (1986, 1990), she provided several examples of "depression" seen in orphaned chimpanzees. Importantly, Goodall's descriptions come from years of careful ethological observation of family groupings of chimpanzees in their natural habitat, in Gombe game reserve and later Gombe National Park in Tanzania (central Africa). Goodall provided detailed accounts of 13 infant chimpanzees who were orphaned due to a variety of lethal illnesses in their mothers. Goodall saw a general pattern of reactions in these orphans: "All initially showed signs of clinical depression; they became listless, and frequency of play dropped" (Goodall, 1986, p. 101). Some developed abnormal behaviors like pulling out their own hair and rocking back and forth. One particularly well-known example is that of Flint, a young male who was very dependent on his mother; when she died, the son exhibited changed posture, lack of appetite, lethargy, and illness, and he died when he was quite young. Orphaned gorillas are reported to waste away in a similar fashion (McRae, 2000). Goodall (1986), however, observed that there were fewer symptoms of depression in orphaned chimpanzees whose mothers had been "somewhat rejecting and lacking in affection" (1986, p. 101); these orphans eventually recovered and showed behaviors that appeared to be normal. Even in nonhuman animals, there are signs that the attachment history between the individuals may play a role in the path taken by an animal left behind.

There have been anecdotal reports of nonhuman primate mothers carrying around the body of a stillborn infant for days, but Altmann (1980) described similar behavior in baboon mothers in the wild, and attributed it to instinctive holding and carrying, rather than imputing a new emotional state to the mothers. As Nesse (2005, pp. 214–215) put it in his discussion of such behaviors, "it is difficult to tell if this is a special response or just a continuation of previous attachment behavior." Lorenz (1991) described the depressed appearance typically seen in a greylag goose that loses its partner. Bekoff (2000) described expressions that appear to reflect depression after loss, in elephants, dolphins, killer whales, and sea lions. Even given the difficulties interpreting these behaviors, they certainly deserve more serious consideration as possible signs of grief.

Following our earlier argument, in order for these nonhuman animals to experience grief, must it be necessary that the animals have experienced love? Panksepp (1998) made that exact case, arguing that homologies are seen in human and nonhuman animals in terms of neurochemical mechanisms involved in love. Bekoff (2000, p. 866) argued, "It is unlikely that romantic love (or any emotion) first appeared in humans with no evolutionary precursors in animals." King, who cites many examples of the expression of grief in nonhuman primates, argues that animal grief must be preceded by signs of attachment between the animals, beyond association necessary for survival (as, for example, when a troop member has lost the protection of a troop leader). She suggests further that evidence for grief must be found in both observational and physiological data (King, 2017). These important questions deserve more research, building on the existing accounts provided by a variety of observers of animal behavior in their natural environments. This research needs to be supported by substantial funding, as the research is so difficult to accomplish and many species of interest are currently endangered.

Proximate Level of Analysis: Ontogeny

This section, covering ontogenetic aspects of grief, will draw on several sources that heretofore have not received sufficient attention in discussions of grief. In order to consider the development of grief over the human life span, one must take into account the development of cognitive capacities, beginning with infancy and childhood. Jean Piaget revolutionized developmental psychology with his stage theory as presented in 1936. This developmental theory has been used in a variety of contexts to explain children's behaviors, cognitive processes, and more. Piaget's theory has been applied to how children deal with certain life events, including loss, based on how they process loss at different stages. Children in each stage will respond to a loss differently, and thus parents may need to explain the event differently. Silverman et al. (1992) describe the application of Piaget's theory to loss in that "the nature of the construction of the deceased is connected to the child's developmental level, with particular reference to children's changing ability to know themselves and to know others (Kegan, 1982; Piaget, 1954)" (p. 496). In order to understand the child's construction of loss, we must first understand each of the developmental levels described by Piaget.

Piagetian Theory

The first stage, the sensorimotor stage, occurs during roughly the first 18 months of an infant's life. During this stage, children begin to understand their world through their senses and motor operations before language has been acquired. In this stage, infants learn via reflexes, imitation, assimilation, and accommodation, and begin to coordinate and differentiate schemas.

The second stage, the preoperational stage, is said to occur between ages two and seven. The hallmark of this stage is symbolic reasoning. Children's schemas have developed to the point that they are able to hold representations in their mind without seeing them. This also indicates a further shift in identifying other people as figures outside of and different from the self. Olin (2016) aptly comments that "it is common for children in this stage to think that others are experiencing the same feelings or having the same reasons for behavior as they do" (p. 4). These children are unable to comprehend reversibility, or that objects can be changed and return to their original state of being, which is acquired later in development.

Next comes the concrete operational stage, lasting from about age 7 to age 12. Hunter and Smith (2008) detail that "at this stage, children demonstrate logical thought through the use of mental operations to solve concrete problems" (p. 145). This period organizes the concrete thinking to prepare for the next stage of formal thinking (Symons-Bradbury, 2004). Schemas become even more differentiated as more are obtained.

The formal operational stage, which is said to emerge around age 12 or adolescence, is Piaget's final stage. Piaget and Inhelder (2000) describe that this stage is characterized by the cognitive ability to differentiate between form and content and to reason correctly about ideas one may not yet fully understand. Even when adolescents encounter an idea for the first time, they are able to conceptualize it through their preexisting schemas. The adolescent is able to understand more complex—even abstract—schemas and better coordinate them together.

The Concept of Loss

Loss, as previously conceptualized, can comprise many different experiences of separation. Unexpected and multiple losses can alter our perception and assumptions of the world and affect those with even the most secure attachments (Parkes, 2006). Relating Piaget's stages to Bowlby's attachment styles, we can think about the effect of loss on children's attachment styles at the different stages of development. Brennan and Shaver (1998), for example, found that childhood parental loss was associated with an insecure-dismissive adult attachment style. They become rejecting of the parental figure, likely perceiving the loss as abandonment, yet they idealize the lost parent at the same time.

Parkes (2006) similarly finds that separations from parents—including death, divorce, and war—were significantly associated with insecure attachments, specifically disorganized and avoidant type attachments. The more insecure the attachment to the parent was prior to the separation, the more likely the separation would lead to distress following the bereavement; those who have more secure attachments with the parent would likely better tolerate the separation. Additionally, separations from the mother are more highly correlated with insecure attachment patterns than are separations from the father.

Krepia et al. (2017) comment accordingly, "The perception of death relates with and depends primarily on a child's age" (p. 1717); as we have learned through Piaget's stages, age corresponds with developmental level and cognitive ability. A child's perception of loss will therefore depend upon which developmental stage they are in. To understand the differences in the stages, let us begin with the sensorimotor stage.

Loss for Children in the Sensorimotor Stage

Nagy (1959) and Speece and Brent (1984) (as cited in Krepia et al., 2017) have developed structural theories in determining age differences in how children deal with loss. In terms of the sensorimotor stage, Speece and Brent (1984) find that the concepts of finality and irreversibility are important for children to understand the meaning of death. Hopkins (2014), in describing Nagy's (1959) research, states that "children under five do not recognise death as irreversible, and instead view death as a departure or sleep" (p. 12). Regarding the concept of reversibility, children of this age may not understand that when a person dies, they do not come back—it is irreversible. In response to death, children of this age may often believe that "if he or she shouts loudly enough he or she can awaken the deceased person" (Symons-Bradbury, 2004, p. 20).

Children of this age may imitate the reactions of those with whom they are bonded, as imitation is largely relevant in this age group. For example, if they see a loved one cry, they may also cry. Sometimes, because of the perception that children of this age would not fully understand the concept of loss, parents fail to acknowledge the loss to these children. However, this results in what Hall (2014) describes as disenfranchised grief, wherein the grieving child is excluded because the loss is not openly acknowledged. This failure to address the grief and the loss can lead to children's further misunderstanding of loss.

Loss for Children in the Preoperational Stage

Nagy (1959) found that children between the ages of five and nine understand the general concept of loss and that death means the end of a life, but they believe there could be a way out of it (Krepia et al., 2017). These children struggle to differentiate death from life, and often personify death (Hopkins, 2014). The child symbolizes death with the personification of it, and as they begin to understand death, they may hold the mental representation of the deceased in their mind. When asked a question of how to make dead things come back to life, these children may respond with a comment such as, "'By thinking about them; then they can live in our mind, but you can't really make them come alive again'" (Koocher, 1974, p. 408).

Children of this age may understand what loss is in a general sense and understand its finality, but may not fully understand that it is irreversible. Thus, they try to copy the deceased by pretending they are dead to understand this abstract principle and assimilate it into their schemas. Koocher (1974) comments, "Since he has had no personal experience with death (i.e., he himself has never died), the child at this level might not be expected to regard death as permanent" (p. 408). As children progress from the preoperational stage to the concrete operational stage, much of their thinking becomes more logical, and this is when research shows that children are better able to understand many of the concepts associated with death.

Hunter and Smith (2008) cite a few studies describing the differences between preoperational and concrete operational stages: "Thirty-five percent of six to eight-year-olds comprehended the universality of death compared to 95% of children nine years and older" (p. 146). With regard to three main components of death (universality, irreversibility, and nonfunctionality), Speece and Brent (1992) [in Hunter and Smith, 2008] found that although children in the preoperational stage demonstrated understanding of at least one of these components, a mature understanding of all three components did not develop until closer to the age of 10. The concept of universality refers to the idea that death is inevitable and will happen to everyone, even themselves. As children grow in their ability to accommodate and begin to conceptualize concrete problems (i.e. death), they are better able to understand this concept of universality.

Loss for Children in the Concrete Operational Stage
Much of the research regarding children's perception of loss has been conducted with children of this stage. Symons-Bradbury (2004) details that as a child in this stage begins to understand the irreversibility and finality of loss and death, "the child realizes that it cannot be accounted for by magical explanations" (p. 22). In discussing the concept of irreversibility, a child of the concrete operational stage has not only confronted the fact that everyone—including themselves—will die, but also that dying is irreversible. Children understand that the deceased's death is different from their own, as well as that the loss of a loved one through divorce or war is not because of their own doing, but because of some external power. In reference to this development, suicide may be a difficult concept for the child to learn, but the feelings of the deceased are now able to be differentiated from their own. A younger child could think that because the deceased was sad and took their own life, and now the child is sad, that maybe they should follow suit. A child in the concrete operational stage understands that others have their own views, different from their own, and is able to accept that the self is different from other.

With the understanding of finality comes intense emotional reactions. Symons-Bradbury (2004) comments that "school-going children may have deep emotional reactions of sadness and depression upon the death of a loved one" (p. 23). It may therefore be especially important to explain the death to children of this age, help them to understand it, and help them to deal with the emotional implications of it. Heath et al. (2008) offer many suggestions for how to assist children in grieving, including that "younger students benefit from basic information and concrete details" (p. 261). This information is accurate and helpful in relating to these children's needs to have the basic understanding to be able to conceptualize the loss.

A study by Mireault et al. (2002) looked at adult women who lost their mother under the age of 18. The mean age of these women at the time of the mother's death was 11.8 years old, which would be categorized under the Concrete Operational stage. Compared to a group of women who did not lose their mothers at a young age, the "motherless" women reported increased anxiety and avoidance in their adult attachments. This supports the aforementioned findings that childhood loss is associated with adult attachment styles, and age of loss can have an impact on the child's development.

Loss for Children in the Formal Operational Stage
In the final stage of development, adolescents are able to conceptualize loss much like adults do. This helps to understand how attachment style formed in childhood relates to the way that loss is handled by both children and adults and can affect attachment style in adult relationships. Slaughter (2005) comments that "[i]n the final stage (Formal Operational), children hold an adult view of death as an inevitable, universal final stage in the life cycle of all living things" (p. 181). Adolescents better understand the cause of death and the universality of it, an understanding that comes with important emotional implications. They are also able to use their preexisting schemas to conceptualize notions they have not encountered before, so they can accommodate different types of death into their perception of loss.

Furthermore, an adolescent can use their abstract thought and logic to understand the effect that the loss may have on their life. Silverman et al. (1992) write that "the child seeks to gain not only an understanding of the meaning of death, but a sense of the meaning of this now-dead parent in his or her life" (p. 502). Thus, an adolescent grapples with the knowledge that has been gained thus far—that not only is death universal, irreversible, sad, and can happen in many different ways, but also that it can affect them without actually happening to them. While the acquisition of the concept of universality has been discussed in previous stages, the abstract concept of understanding the effect that loss may have on one's life is more pertinent in this formal operational stage. Heath et al. (2008) comment that in consoling an adolescent, it is necessary to realize that adolescents understand others' perspectives and are more aware of the reasons surrounding the loss.

Proximate Level of Analysis: Mechanisms
In Tinbergen's framework, mechanisms or immediate causes can include environmental influences (which might result in learned responses) and biological influences (such as neurochemical changes associated with the loss of a loved one). Recent work on Evolved Psychological Mechanisms is summarized in a chapter by Lewis, Al-Shawaf, Thompson and Buss (2020), and this concept is an important expansion of Tinbergen's thinking. Briefly, an Evolved Psychological Mechanism is an information-processing mechanism whereby the individual is sensitive to environmental inputs and, based on the individual's history or circumstances, the individual will produce one in a range of possible responses (an output). In the case of grief, humans are inclined to grieve a loss, but the particular expression of grief depends on the particular circumstances, such as whether the loss of a loved one was more difficult because it was unexpected or violent. There is considerable evidence that grief can be more intense and prolonged if a family member was lost unexpectedly (e.g., losing a young child) or if the loss involved violence or suicide (Parkes, 2006). Nesse (2005) suggested that degree of genetic relatedness is an important predictor of the intensity of grief, arguing that "it seems likely that natural selection differentiated generic sadness into a special pattern to deal with the special aspects of loss of kin" (p. 216); Nesse provided additional evidence in pointing out how severe is the loss of a child who has just reached his or her own reproductive potential. Segal (2019)

found that the loss of an identical twin is more difficult to endure than the loss of a fraternal twin or a non-twin sibling, reflecting the greater genetic relatedness and relatively greater loss in terms of reproductive fitness.

Spousal loss may be another special case of grief. Although one's spouse is not a genetic relative, spouses often have accumulated years of committed exchange of valuable instrumental and emotional resources, and these relationships are very hard to duplicate (Nesse, 2005). The findings of Parkes (2006) are somewhat surprising in this context, in that he found that reactions are more intense in the case of a relationship strained by insecure attachment (Parkes, 2006). As discussed above, Parkes found that a secure relationship seems to predict grief that is less likely to be an overwhelming burden and is more likely to be resolved before becoming chronic for the survivor. More research is needed to clarify these patterns of grief involving spousal loss later in life.

Biochemical correlates of loss have been documented in birds and nonhuman primates, by researchers examining mother-infant attachment and separation. Archer (1992) reviewed the attachment research, commenting on the rigidity of imprinting as seen in young geese, as contrasted with the flexibility seen in human infants. Archer summarized the differences he saw between attachment and separation by concluding, "There is far greater cross-species generality in separation reactions than in the way attachments are formed" (1992, p. 42). Archer cited Bowlby (1973) who described short-term effects of separation in many species as seen in three phases: active distress; a less active phase called despair; and behavioral reorganization that might involve attaching to a new (surrogate) mother. Elevated cortisol has been seen in the young of various species during the first two phases (Hofer, 1984; Levine et al., 1987). Levine and colleagues (1987) saw distress calling and elevated cortisol in young separated squirrel monkeys and rhesus macaque monkeys. When calling failed to bring reunion with the mother, vocalizing tapered off as the infant moved on to despair; but, surprisingly, cortisol levels continued to rise. The infants' emergency response systems continued to be mobilized in response to the urgent challenge, even though the infants appeared subdued. Cessation of calling can be seen as functional in that a quiet infant is less likely to attract predators; however, elevated cortisol will do long-term damage to various body tissues in the infant's body, including the immune system. In separated infants, thermoregulation and sleep cycles are also disturbed (Osterweis, 1984). These responses are somewhat dependent on whether it was the mother or the infant who was removed from the location. Osterweis further cautions that, based on nonhuman primate research, there can be discontinuities between the behavioral and physiological measures of the loss response; that is, one type of measure can reveal a dysregulated response, while the other appears to be normal. Clearly more research on physiological mechanisms is needed, with special attention to age-related changes (thus this research would address both proximal levels of causation simultaneously).

Research on humans has also focused on cortisol changes. An early study of grief in parents whose children had died of leukemia (Hofer et al., 1972) documented elevated cortisol levels in parents, levels that remained high for years after these tragic losses. There are also hints of involvement of prolactin, growth hormone, and ACTH. It is likely that circadian rhythms are disturbed, as manifested in sleep difficulties; such disturbances are known to interfere with the functioning of T-lymphocytes, thereby leading to immune system compromise or failure. In addition, it is suspected that changes in epinephrine/norepinephrine result in cardiac arrhythmias, elevating the risk of cardiovascular incidents (Buckley et al., 2012).

Osterweis (1984), acknowledging that primate research shows that infants' bodily regulation is disrupted by maternal loss, suggested that even for human adults, grief may disrupt regulation of bodily function in the survivor:

> The death of someone with whom a person has lived in close proximity involves the loss of social entraining stimuli for circadian systems, and may therefore disrupt normal biological timing. In fact, there is evidence that social interactions for human beings may be the cues regulating human biological rhythms, rather than light or temperature as in other species. (1984, p. 18)

Hofer suggested that physiological regulation could be disturbed even in the loss of some distant beloved person, because even the internal representation may serve a regulatory function (Hofer, 1984). This latter case might be an example of an Evolved Psychological Mechanism generating, as an output, a chain reaction of physiological responses.

Distal Level of Analysis: Function in Terms of Survival or Reproduction

Tinbergen's fourth level of analysis of causation is the functional question: How does the behavior increase chances of survival or reproduction? This chapter has already cited Bowlby's insights concerning the function of a separated infant's cry of protest (which may cause the mother to return to the infant), and the ensuing lapse into subdued depression if she does not return (which may protect the infant from predators that are within earshot); both behavioral tendencies will increase the likelihood that the infant will survive.

Extrapolating those behaviors to adulthood, as Roes (1990) did, one sees the sobbing of a bereaved person as compelling caregivers to tend to the person. Similarly, the depressed posture and sad expression of a grieving person may cause others to attend to the bereaved and try to provide emotional support. Meanwhile, the depressed person may use the possible social withdrawal as a time to take stock and reorganize his or her social world, in the face of a major restructuring of that world (Kosminsky & Jordan, 2016).

Several authors have suggested that the developing mammalian nervous system might require occasional stressors to allow the infant's nervous system to go through cycles of arousal and return to resting state, in order to prime the system, as it were, and calibrate optimal settings for that individual in that environment. Blum, describing Levine's (1956) research with rats, wrote, ". . . some challenging experience—as long as it's not an overwhelming traumatic experience—may be helpful, even necessary, in building the kind of body response system that will serve us best" (Blum, 2002, p. 182). Similarly, Porges (2011) has suggested that the polyvagal system, which seems to be involved in achieving balance between the two branches of the autonomic nervous system, needs to be calibrated through experience in a world of real threats and genuinely helpful resources like parents (resulting in what Porges calls vagal tone). Thus naturally occurring separations from parents (as might happen during foraging for food), followed by comforting reunions, may serve the function of creating a mature stress-response system that will later serve the mature organism.

In suggesting that grief is a specialized form of sadness, Nesse (2005) offered that human grief often includes many useful behaviors. These behaviors include searching for what was lost (compare that to what has been described above in young children's reactions to loss); making corrections or escaping from the situation to avoid further loss; warning kin about the danger and coming together with them to avoid further loss; experiencing mental pain to reflect on how the loss happened; and searching for a replacement or a new life configuration. Nesse is not arguing that grief evolved as a distinct emotion with its own function, but he is suggesting that grief may serve some purposes. He suggests, further, that the extent of grief should be somewhat predictable, based on some testable ideas which deserve further research:

> Grief intensity should be a function of characteristics of the person lost, including the coefficient of relationship (percentage of genes in common), reproductive value, nonreplaceable instrumental

value, and strength of an irreplaceable committed relationship. All of these will be influenced by individual, group and cultural variations. (2005, p. 217)

In both the section on Phylogeny and the section on Mechanisms, above, the importance of social attachment as a neuro-endocrinological regulatory mechanism was introduced. This concept emerges again and again in multilevel behavioral studies, precisely because it is so important to survival in the evolution of so many different classes of animals, from birds to mammals. While readers may accept the idea that attachment disruption would be physiologically disrupting for infants, they may be less inclined to expect a similar physiological disruption in adults experiencing loss. That disruption of bodily regulation, necessary for survival, is exactly what is proposed in the work of Porges (2011), Osterweis (1984), and Hofer (1984), among others, as described above. Grief may be the cry of a body that has lost its mooring and is adrift in space and time.

Pathology and Clinical Applications

Much research has been completed regarding complicated grief at a clinical level, yet we did not see a complicated grief or prolonged grief disorder added to the fifth edition of the *Diagnostic and Statistical Manual of Mental Disorders* (DSM-5; APA, 2013). In 1997, Horowitz et al. (as cited in Parkes, 2006) used the self-report rating scales and studied subjects following bereavement. They produced a model set of criteria for a complicated grief disorder (CGD). Though a history of depression and anxiety disorder was associated with an increased risk of CGD, it was noted that both major depressive disorder and adjustment disorder do not fully cover the extent of the symptoms associated with CGD. Additionally, Prigerson et al. developed an Inventory of Complicated Grief in 1995 (as cited in Parkes, 2006), which assessed criteria for CGD, and further updated Horowitz's findings for a set of criteria for CGD in 2001. It was thought that this disorder would be added to the new DSM-5 in a new category of "Attachment Disorders," as Hall (2014) discusses; however, neither the new disorder nor the new category was added.

Hall (2014) comments that both Horowitz's and Prigerson's work on complicated grief were combined, and CGD was renamed as prolonged grief disorder (PGD). This disorder is characterized by distress due to separation and "cognitive, emotional and behavioural symptoms that can develop after the death of a significant other. The symptoms must last for at least six months and cause significant impairment in social, occupational and other important areas of functioning" (Hall, 2014, p. 11). Though there was significant support for the inclusion of this disorder in the DSM-5, and though the symptoms associated with PGD have been shown to differ from other disorders and normal grief reaction, PGD was not included in the DSM-5. However, persistent complex bereavement disorder was included as a condition for further study.

Hall (2014) further discusses interventions that are beneficial for bereaved clients. Though intervention is not effective for those with uncomplicated grief, it is effective for those at higher risk for complicated grief. Schut and Stroebe (2005; as cited in Hall, 2014) point out that intervention in the case of routine grief can interfere with the "natural" grieving process. Additionally, antidepressants have been found to have little effect on symptoms of complicated grief. Instead, Hall (2014) suggests, specialized complicated grief therapy would be more helpful for clients with complicated grief. This treatment should be individualized, just as grief is.

When attempting to differentiate between complicated and uncomplicated grief, aspects to be taken into account include the circumstances of loss, the age of the bereaved person at the time of loss, and other elements. But the attachment history of the bereaved person is likely to be at the heart of their ability to experience grief without being overwhelmed by it. Thus, Kosminsky and Jordan (2016), rather than focusing on other elements that differentiate between complicated and noncomplicated grief, have taken what we have learned from research based in attachment theory and have made thoughtful application to psychotherapeutic work with bereaved clients. (The reader is asked to refer to Table 25.1 again, especially the column labeled Behaviors in Adult Bereavement, which summarizes the findings of Parkes.) Kosminsky and Jordan (2016) provide the following broad definition of grief therapy:

> Grief therapy is a concentrated form of empathically attuned and skillfully applied social support, in which the therapist helps the bereaved person reregulate after a significant loss by serving as a transitional attachment figure. This includes addressing deficits in affect regulation and mentalizing related to both the loss at hand, and early neglect or trauma, as needed. In an environment that encourages exploration and growth, the bereavement therapist supports the bereaved in experiencing and tolerating feelings relating to grief, integrating new information and skills, and developing a new self-narrative that incorporates the impact of the loss. The goal of grief therapy is integration of the loss on a psychological and neurological level. Successful grief therapy encourages a state of flexible attention to the loss, and to the relationships, roles, and experiences that are still available to the bereaved individual, in order that they may reengage in life, without relinquishing their attachment to the deceased. (2016, p. 100)

The authors assume that loss of an attachment figure is always dysregulating; they write that the extreme distress of the abandoned child is "mirrored" in the distress of the adult who loses a loved one. This dysregulation will be even more problematic for survivors of early abuse or neglect, or for those whose loss occurs violently. If the bereaved adult is to find a pathway to healthy re-regulation of psychological and neurological processes, it will likely be through a "dyadic and transactional process that is facilitated by, if not dependent on, the engaged, attuned presence of one or more other people" (Kosminsky & Jordan, 2016, p. 101). The role of the grief therapist is clear here. While there is broad empirical support for the importance of the therapeutic alliance in general (Norcross, 2011), there is growing evidence that an attuned therapeutic relationship may be fundamentally essential in the context of grief therapy. Kosminsky and Jordan went on to assert, "An attuned grief therapist works with clients to create a balance between too much and too little engagement with their emotional reactions to the death" thus expanding "the client's affective flexibility" (2016, p. 103). Eventually, the hope is, the client who is able to re-regulate his or her emotions will be able to integrate the loss and move on to a restructured universe of relationships.

Conclusions

This chapter has explored the emotion of grief primarily through the lens of Tinbergen's four levels of analysis: phylogeny, ontogeny, proximal mechanisms of causation, and functional causation (Tinbergen, 1963). Grief seems to have evolved in many species, with related neurophysiological elements, in tandem with attachment; and both attachment and grief seem to benefit survival in multiple ways. The developing child presents special challenges in terms of dealing with loss; the cognitive changes described by Piaget provide a framework to assist adults attempting to assist children who are bereaved. Grief therapy may benefit from a firm basis in attachment theory, through which the bereaved person's personal history of secure or insecure attachment provides a context in which a solid therapeutic alliance can provide a path forward for the client. There is much to be learned through research from an evolutionary viewpoint, focused on genetic relatedness, reproductive potential, and strength of commitment to a lost partner (Nesse, 2005).

At the time of this writing, the world was entering year three of the COVID-19 pandemic. The virus had claimed over 800,000 American lives, and more than 5 million lives around the globe. It was common for victims to die in hospital with no family present; nurses and doctors offered the last human comfort to strangers, by the hundreds. Even for people who died of causes unrelated to COVID-19, there might be no wake, no shiva, no graveside funeral ceremony, no communal singing to bring comfort. Those of us who experienced Zoom funerals during the COVID-19 pandemic describe ceremonies that brought us impoverished contact with bereaved family members and friends, and left us with heightened feelings of helplessness and loss and little closure. This chapter concludes with a call for researchers to attend to the great personal losses of this pandemic and learn as much as possible about how to better understand grief and better understand how to help our fellow living beings cope with loss.

References

Ainsworth, M. D. S., Blehar, M., Waters, E., & Wall, S. (1978). *Patterns of attachment*. Lawrence Erlbaum Associates.

Al-Shawaf, L., Lewis, D. M. G., Wehbe, Y. S., & Buss, D. M. (2018). Context, environment, and learning in evolutionary psychology. In T. K. Shackelford & V. A. Weekes-Shackelford (Eds.), *Encyclopedia of evolutionary psychological science* (pp. 1–12). Springer.

Altmann, J. (1980). *Baboon mothers and infants*. Harvard University Press.

APA (2013). *Diagnostic and statistical manual of mental disorders* (5th ed.). American Psychological Association.

Archer, J. (1992). *Ethology and human development*. Barnes & Noble.

Bekoff, M. (2000). Animal emotions: Exploring passionate natures: Current interdisciplinary research provides compelling evidence that many animals experience such emotions as joy, fear, love, despair and grief—we are not alone. *Bioscience, 50*(10), 861–870.

Bereavement. (n.d.). In *American Psychological Association dictionary of psychology*. Retrieved from https://dictionary.apa.org/bereavement.

Blum, D. (2002). *Love at Goon Park: Harry Harlow and the science of affection*. Berkley.

Bowlby, J. (1973). *Attachment and loss*, Vol. 2: *Separation: Anxiety and anger*. Hogarth Press.

Bowlby, J. (1980). *Attachment and loss*, Vol. 3: *Loss: Sadness and depression*. Basic Books.

Bowlby, J. (1988). *A secure base: Parent-child attachment and healthy human development*. Basic Books.

Bradshaw, G. A. (2009). *Elephants on the edge: What animals teach us about humanity*. Yale University Press.

Brennan, K. A., & Shaver, P. R. (1998). Attachment styles and personality disorders: Their connections to each other and to parental divorce, parental death, and perceptions of parental caregiving. *Journal of Personality, 66*, 835–878.

Brooks Pribac, T. (2013). Animal grief. *Animal Studies Journal, 2*(2), 67–90.

Buckley, T., Sunari, D., Marshall, A., Bartrop, R., McKinley, S., & Tofler, G. (2012). Physiological correlates of bereavement and the impact of bereavement interventions. *Dialogues in Clinical Neuroscience, 14*(2), 129–148.

Carr, D., House, J. S., Wortman, C., Nesse, R. M., & Kessler, R. C. (2001). Psychological adjustment to sudden and anticipated spousal death among the older widowed. *Journal of Gerontology: Social Sciences, 56B*, S237–248.

Darwin, C. (1998). *The expression of the emotions in man and animals* (3rd ed.). Oxford University Press.

Freedman, D. G. (1974). *Human infancy: An evolutionary perspective*. Halsted Press.

Freud, S. ([1917] 1957). Mourning and melancholia. In J. Strachey (Ed. and Trans.), *The Standard edition of the complete psychological works of Sigmund Freud* (Vol. 14, pp. 152–170). Hogarth Press.

Fry, M. (1978). Images of death in children. In K. Yamamoto (Ed.), *Death in the life of children* (pp. 33–55). Kappa Delta Pi Press.

Goodall, J. (1986). *The chimpanzees of Gombe: Patterns of behavior*. Belknap Press.

Goodall, J. (1990). *Through a window*. Houghton-Miflin.

Hall, C. (2014). Bereavement theory: Recent developments in our understanding of grief and bereavement. *InPsych, 33*(1), 7–12.

Heath, M. A., Leavy, D., Hansen, K., Ryan, K., Lawrence, L. & Sonntag, A. G. (2008). Coping with grief: Guidelines and resources for assisting children. *Intervention in School and Clinic, 43*(5), 259–269.

Hofer, M. A. (1984). Relationships as regulators: A psychobiologic perspective on bereavement. *Psychosomatic Medicine, 46*, 183–197.

Hofer, M. A., Wolff, C. T., Friedman, S. B., & Mason, J. W. (1972). A psychoendocrine study of bereavement: I. 17-hydroxycorticosteroid excretion rates of parents following death of their children from leukemia. *Psychosomatic Medicine, 34*(6), 481–491.

Hopkins, M. (2014). *The development of children's understanding of death*. University of East Anglia.

Hunter, S. B., & Smith, D. E. (2008). Predictors of children's understandings of death: age, cognitive ability, death experience and maternal communicative competence. *OMEGA, 57*(2), 143–162.

Kalish, R. (1981). *Death, grief, and caring relationships*. Brooks Cole.

King, B. (2017). The expression of grief in monkeys, apes, and other animals. In A. C. G. M. Robben (Ed.), *Death, mourning, and burial: A cross-cultural reader* (pp. 202–208). Wiley.

Klass, D., Silverman, P. R., & Nickman, S. L. (Eds.). (1996). *Continuing bonds: New understandings of grief*. Taylor and Francis.

Koocher, G. P. (1974). Talking with children about death. *American Journal of Orthopsychiatry, 44*(3), 404–411.

Kosminsky, P. S., & Jordan, J. R. (2016). *Attachment-informed grief therapy*. Routledge.

Krepia, M., Krepia, V., & Tsilingiri, M. (2017). School children's perception of the concept of death. *International Journal of Caring Sciences, 10*(3), 1717–1722.

Kübler-Ross, E. (1969). *On death and dying*. Macmillan.

Levine, S. (1956). A further study of infantile handling and adult avoidance learning. *Journal of Personality, 25*, 70–80.

Levine, S., Wiener, S. G., Coe, C. L., Bayart, F. E. S., & Hayashi, K. T. (1987). Primate vocalization: A psychobiological approach. *Child Development, 58*, 1409–1419.

Lewis, D. M. G., Al-Shawaf, L., Thompson, M. B., & Buss, D. M. (2020). Evolved psychological mechanisms. In T. K. Shackelford (Ed.), *The SAGE Handbook of Evolutionary Psychology* (pp. 96–119). Sage.

Lorenz, K. Z. (1991). *Here I am—Where are you?* Harcourt Brace Jovanovich.

Main, M., & Solomon, J. (1986). Discovery of a new, insecure disorganized/disoriented attachment pattern. In T. B. Brazelton & M. Yogman (Eds.), *Affective development in infancy* (pp. 95–124). Ablex.

McRae, M. (2000). Central Africa's orphaned gorillas: Will they survive the wild? *National Geographic, 197*(2), 84–97.

Medicus, G. M. (2005). Mapping transdisciplinarity in human sciences. In J. W. Lee (Ed.), *Focus on gender identity* (pp. 95–114). Nova Science.

Mireault, G., Bearor, K., & Thomas, T. (2002) Adult romantic attachment among women who experienced childhood maternal loss. *OMEGA, 44*(1), 97–104.

Nagy, M. (1959). The child's view of death. In H. Feifel (Ed.), *The meaning of death* (pp. 79–98). McGraw Hill.

Nesse, R. M. (2005). An evolutionary framework for understanding grief. In D. Carr, R. M. Nesse, & C. B. Wortman (Eds.), *Spousal bereavement in late life* (pp. 195–226). Springer.

Norcross, J. C. (2011). *Psychotherapy relationships that work: Evidence-based responsiveness* (2nd ed.). Oxford.

Olin, T. C. (2016). *Discussing death with young children*. [Unpublished master's thesis]. California State University—San Bernardino.

Osterweis, M. (1984). Toward a biology of grieving. In M. Osterweis, F. Solomon, & M. Green (Eds.), *Bereavement: Reactions, consequences, and care* (pp. 145–176). National Academies Press.

Panksepp, J. (1998). *Affective neuroscience: The foundations of animal and human emotions*. Oxford.

Parkes, C. M. (2006). *Love and loss: The roots of grief and its complications*. Routledge.

Parkes, C. M., & Prigerson, H. G. (2010). *Bereavement: Studies of grief in adult life, Fourth edition* (4th ed.). Routledge.

Piaget, J., & Inhelder, B. (2000). *The psychology of the child*. Basic Books.

Porges, S. W. (2011). *The polyvagal theory: Neurophysiological foundations of emotions, attachment, communication, and self regulation*. W. W. Norton.

Roes, F. L. (1990). Waarom huilen mensen? (Why do people cry?). *Psychologie, 10*, 44–45.

Schore, A. N. (2005). Attachment, affect regulation, and the developing right brain: Linking developmental neuroscience to pediatrics. *Pediatrics in Review, 26*, 204–217.

Segal, N. L. (2019). Evolutionary perspectives on the loss of a twin. In T. K. Shackelford & V. Ziegler-Hill (Eds.), *Evolutionary perspectives on death* (pp. 25–36). Springer Nature.

Sigelman, C. K., & Rider, E. A. (2015). *Life-span human development* (8th ed.). Cengage Learning.

Silverman, P. R., Nickman, S., & Worden, J. W. (1992). Detachment revisited: The child's reconstruction of a dead parent. *American Journal of Orthopsychiatry, 62*(4), 494–503.

Slaughter, V. (2005). Young children's understanding of death. *Australian Psychologist, 40*(3), 179–186.

Speece, M. W., & Brent, S. B. (1984). Children's understanding of death: A review of three components of a death concept. *Child Development, 55*(5), 1671–1686.

Speece, M. W., & Brent, S. B. (1992). The acquisition of a mature understanding of three components of the concept of death. *Death Studies, 16*(3), 211–229.

Stroebe, M. S., & Schut, H. (1999). The dual process model of coping with bereavement: rationale and description. *Death Studies, 23*(3), 197–224.

Symons-Bradbury, J. (2004). *Children's perceptions of death: A Piagetian perspective*. [Unpublished master's thesis]. University of the Witwatersrand Johannesburg.

Talayesva, D. C. (1942). *Sun chief: The autobiography of a Hopi Indian* (L. Simmons, Ed.). Yale University Press.
Tinbergen, N. (1963). On the aims and methods of ethology. *Zeitschrift für Tierpsychologie, 20*, 410–433. http://www.worldcat.org/title/zeitschrift-für-tierpsychologie/oclc/643500275.
Weisfeld, C. C., Buschmohle, S., & Steinberg, S. (1983). Adoption in captive baboons (*Papio papio*): A comparative case study of mother-infant interaction. Paper presented at the Society for Research in Child Development convention, Detroit, MI.
Weisfeld, G. E. (2019). *Evolved emotions: An interdisciplinary and functional analysis*. Lexington.
Worden, J. W. (2008). *Grief counseling and grief therapy: Handbook for the mental health practitioner* (4th ed.). Springer.

CHAPTER 26

Fear: An Evolutionary Perspective on Its Biological, Behavioral, and Communicative Features

Katherine O'Connell, Shawn A. Rhoads, and Abigail A. Marsh

Abstract

Fear is the multimodal state that accompanies the anticipation of an imminent or predictable aversive outcome. This state promotes adaptive autonomic, behavioral, and cognitive responses such as avoidance, escape, and learning. Fear is essential to animal species' survival, and as such is highly conserved, with the emergence of basic fear learning and responding dating back at least 700 million years. The adaptive significance of fear reflects its effects not only on physiology and behavior, but also on social outcomes. Across a wide range of species, fear can be socially communicated via visual, auditory, and chemical signals, which promote avoidance of threat and social learning in observers. In some social species, the communication of fear can also benefit expressers by inhibiting aggression and eliciting care from observers. This chapter reviews the evolutionary functions and neural circuitry of fear and its autonomic, behavioral, and communicative features.

Key Words: fear, amygdala, fear learning, fear expression, social communication

Introduction

In 2018, 31-year-old climber Alex Honnold made history as the first person to complete a "free solo" climb up the face of El Capitan, a dizzying 3,000-foot vertical granite wall that looms over California's Yosemite National Park. No ropes or safety gear are used during a free solo climb, such that for most of the four hours Honnold spent scaling the wall he was one missed hold, slipped foot, or falling rock away from falling hundreds or thousands of feet to his death. Although the risks his climbs entail and his calm demeanor during and after them have led many observers to assume Honnold must be entirely without fear, his own descriptions reveal otherwise. In one recent 12-minute talk (Honnold, 2018), Honnold uses some variation of the word "scared" to describe his climbing experiences over a dozen times.

It is unlikely a climber like Honnold would have survived long enough to scale El Capitan were he truly fearless. Fear, like pain, is an aversive state that is so crucial to survival in risky contexts that few organisms seem to be without it. Experimental evidence suggests moths even retain their fear of aversive stimuli they encountered as caterpillars, despite the fact that during metamorphosis they dissolve into little more than a mass of undifferentiated caterpillar soup. Almost nothing of the original caterpillar remains when the moth emerges except a few organized groups of cells—and fear (Blackiston et al., 2008).

Defining Fear

Fear can be best described as the multimodal state that accompanies the anticipation of an aversive outcome and that promotes adaptive autonomic, behavioral, and cognitive responses, including avoidance, escape, appeasement, and learning (Adolphs, 2013; LeDoux, 2003; Marsh, 2013; Tovote et al., 2015). In the hierarchy of emotions, fear and its mirror-image, seeking (the anticipation of an appetitive outcome, sometimes called anticipation or curiosity), are among the most evolutionarily ancient, well-conserved, culturally universal, early to emerge in childhood, and well-articulated in terms of the neural pathways that support them (Adolphs, 2013; Elfenbein & Ambady, 2002; Gross & Canteras, 2012; LeDoux, 2003; Leppänen & Nelson, 2012; Papini et al., 2019; Tovote et al., 2015).

Fear can be distinguished from other evolutionarily conserved aversive states, like sadness and anger, by its anticipatory nature. Fear is observed when an aversive outcome has not yet occurred and can potentially be avoided or escaped, for example, when a predator is nearby or another person has uttered a threat. When the aversive event has already taken place—or cannot be escaped or avoided and so is all but certain, such as when the individual is cornered and cannot escape an attacker—anger or sadness, which reflect distress following an unwanted outcome, is more likely to result (Lench et al., 2016; Roseman, 1984). To the extent the outcome is interpreted (either consciously or unconsciously) as reversible, it will typically result in anger, a high-activation emotion that promotes effortful activities aimed at reversing the outcome, such as aggression (Blair, 2012). If the outcome is interpreted as irreversible, it will more typically result in sadness, a low-activation emotion that promotes coping, conservation of resources, and solicitation of social comfort (Arias et al., 2020) (Figure 26.1).

Fear can also be distinguished from anxiety in that it occurs in response to a clearly identifiable stimulus and prepares the organism to cope with that threat. By contrast, anxiety occurs in response to an unclear, distant, or unpredictable threat; lingers for sustained periods; and, unlike fear, does not always have clear adaptive significance (Davis et al., 1997). Defining fear (and other emotions) this way—in terms of eliciting contexts and functions within those contexts—may be more useful than definitions based on any single autonomic, behavioral, or subjective change that the emotion yields (Lench et al., 2015).

Early conceptualizations proposed that each emotion had a peripheral signature that could be used to deduce the associated state. However, subsequent research has not found a clear peripheral "signature" that reliably distinguishes any given emotion from other states (Levenson, 2014; Siegel et al., 2018). This is in part because emotions are marked by their flexibility relative to other phenomena that link discrete responses to external stimuli (for example, reflexes). Fear, by contrast, potentiates a gradient of responses depending on the probability and/or magnitude of the threat (Adolphs, 2013; Davis, 1986). As discussed below, the anticipation of an aversive outcome that is remote or mild usually results in parasympathetic activation accompanied by orienting or freezing; only if the threat is closer and more threatening will sympathetic activation emerge, accompanied by active escape (Adolphs, 2013; Blair, 2012).

Some typologies of emotion have attempted to classify and define the major emotions based on nonverbal cues, such as facial expressions, that are associated with them. Perhaps most famously, Ekman and colleagues (Ekman, 2002) developed a well-articulated dictionary of facial action units (AUs), combinations of which were described as reliable indicators of specific emotions like fear (AUs 1 [inner brow raiser] + 2 [outer brow raiser] + 4 [brow lowerer] + 5 [eye widener] + 20 [lip stretcher] + 26 [jaw drop]). This research provided early compelling evidence that certain human communicative cues are recognized and displayed across cultures (Ekman et al., 1969). Although fear and its nonverbal expressions can serve essential social

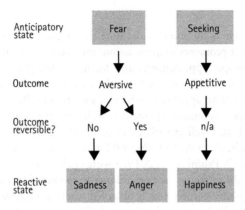

Figure 26.1. A functional model of five emotions. A functionalist perspective on fear and other emotions predicts the emergence of at least five emotions in anticipation or response to appetitive or aversive outcomes. Thus, for example, fear is distinguished from seeking by the aversive versus appetitive nature of the anticipated stimulus. Fear can be distinguished from sadness and anger in that fear is anticipatory, whereas sadness and anger typically occur in response to events that have occurred or are inescapable. Sadness and anger can be further distinguished according to the degree the aversive outcome is perceived as reversible. (Because appetitive outcomes do not require reversal, no such distinction occurs following appetitive events.) In that all organisms can learn to anticipate and respond to appetitive or aversive events, this model predicts that analogues of at least these five emotions will be observed across species, and helps to explain their near-universal inclusion as so-called basic emotions. These emotions are likely positioned at the top of a hierarchy that gives rise to more complex emotional states not discussed here.

functions (Marsh, 2016; Sacco & Hugenberg, 2011), the hypothesis that human emotions correspond one-to-one with facial expressions, such that the expression can be reliably used to deduce an expresser's specific internal state, is not well supported (Crivelli & Fridlund, 2018).

In light of the evidence that emotions like fear cannot be defined in terms of clear physiological or behavioral signatures, some have argued that emotions should instead be defined solely in terms of their subjectively experienced outcomes. According to this conceptualization, fear can only be inferred if a person can report that they are feeling fear (LeDoux & Hofmann, 2018). In other words, fear is defined in terms of the consciously experienced state that a person interprets and labels as fear or a close synonym. This conceptualization of emotion makes fear and other emotions easy to assess using self-report measures—at least in awake, linguistic, neurotypical human adults. But there are disadvantages of conflating the experience of emotions with self-reported linguistic descriptions of them (Anand & Craig, 1996). For one, self-reports can be inaccurate (Paulhus & Vazire, 2007). In addition, much cognition is nonlinguistic (Fedorenko & Varley, 2016). Patients who lose language abilities following a stroke can still perform arithmetic (Varley et al., 2005), working memory tasks (Paulraj et al., 2018), and indicate understanding of others' intentions in theory of mind tasks (Willems et al., 2011). One case study of a man who suffered from fluctuating loss of language due to a brain tumor reported his experiences of the world were largely unchanged by the inability to verbalize them (Lubbock, 2010). This conceptualization nonetheless proposes that nonlinguistic adults and children, human infants, and nonhuman animals cannot be assumed to have any subjective experience of fear (LeDoux & Pine, 2016; Fanselow & Pennington, 2017). The presumption that the ability to reflect on and describe one's own internal states is required to feel emotion led to atrocities as recently as the 1980s, when human infants routinely underwent major surgery without anesthesia (they were only administered paralyzing agents to keep them from moving) in accordance with the belief that without language or self-awareness, infants could not feel fear or pain (Anand & Craig, 1996; Boffey, 1987). (Similar assumptions also held for nonhuman animals, who also routinely were denied surgical pain relief; Rollin, 1986.)

It is now accepted that fear and some other emotions are shared across ages and species and do not depend on language or self-awareness; hence the modern consensus that to perform surgery on an infant or nonhuman animal without anesthesia or analgesia—the purpose of which is to temporarily eliminate felt pain and fear—is monstrous. By contrast, self-awareness—being able to reflect on one's own experiences—is likely fully present only in certain species and humans older than about two years (Moore et al., 2007) and is required to be able to identify and verbally label one's own internal states (de Waal, 2019).

Due to limitations in defining emotion in terms of a single external outcome (be it physiology, behavior, or self-reported experience), we concur with the view that an emotion is best understood as a central nervous system state evoked by particular stimuli or contexts and which gives rise to observable behaviors and relevant cognitive, somatic, and physiological responses (Adolphs, 2013; Adolphs & Anderson, 2018). Fear, according to this conceptualization, is the central state that results from the anticipation of an aversive outcome (or threat) and that potentiates adaptive changes in physiology, behaviors, and experiences.

Evolutionary Origins of Fear

The capacity to avoid, escape, and learn from threats is shared across many animal species, consistent with the adaptive significance of fear (Haaker et al., 2019). Vertebrates and invertebrates alike—among them ants, fruit flies, moths, nautiluses, and sea slugs (Carew & Sahley, 1986)—demonstrate prepared avoidance and escape responses to unconditioned threats such as electric shock and the ability to learn associations with stimuli that accompany these threats (fear learning), suggesting the emergence of fear responding dates back at least 700 million years (Hedges et al., 2006).

Conserved features of fear responding can be assessed using paradigms that assess responses to universal unconditioned threats. One such threat is hypercapnia, or suffocation (real or simulated) induced by the inhalation of high concentrations of carbon dioxide (CO_2). Hypercapnia can elicit fear responses and fear learning across species ranging from roundworms (Azzam et al., 2010) to fruit flies—which rapidly alter their flight patterns in response to detecting a high CO_2 environment (Suh et al., 2004)—to mice, rats, and humans. Mice freeze in chambers where they are exposed to 10% CO_2 concentrations, and will subsequently learn to avoid such chambers (Ziemann et al., 2009). Rats exposed to 10%–20% CO_2 concentrations may rear up, scratch, and push on the lids of their tanks, or emit distress vocalizations, with behaviors varying with the study procedures (Améndola & Weary, 2020). After inhaling similar concentrations, humans show increased heart rate and respiratory rate (Balderston et al., 2017) and report feeling paralyzed, panicky, and wanting to escape (Balderston et al., 2017; Quagliato et al., 2018; Schruers et al., 2004).

These responses are governed in species-dependent ways by neurons with receptors sensitive to CO_2. In mammals, these receptors are distributed in a network of brain regions that include the amygdala, bed nucleus of the stria terminalis (BNST), and brainstem nuclei that evoke behavioral fear responses to hypercapnia (Niel & Weary, 2006; Taugher et al., 2014; Ziemann et al., 2009). Supporting the conserved, distributed nature of the network, even humans lacking an amygdala, who typically fail to exhibit fear in response to conditioned and unconditioned threats, nonetheless report subjective fear in response to hypercapnia (Feinstein et al., 2013), suggesting fail-safe-like mechanisms for responding to unconditioned threats of extreme evolutionary importance. But the flexible nature of fear responding, even to ancient threats, is also evident. The specific response observed to hypercapnia depends on the context and on species-specific attributes. Responses range from active escape from CO_2-rich air to reduction of bodily movement and vocalization (rodents; Chisholm et al., 2013) or chemosensory signaling (fruit flies; Suh et al., 2004) to warn conspecifics of the threat. If the threat becomes insurmountable (for example, pre-euthanasia), behavioral quiescence may arise (Blackshaw et al., 1988; Smith & Harrap, 1997) consistent with a coping response.

Electric shock is another reliably aversive stimulus across invertebrate and vertebrate species. Following aversive conditioning (pairing a neutral stimulus with electric shock), the threat of anticipated shock induces fear-relevant responses. Dogs learn to jump over a barrier to escape a chamber when a light previously paired with shock turns on (Solomon & Wynne, 1953). Octopus learn not to attack crabs with a painted square on their shell that had been linked previously with shock (Boycott & Young, 1955). Zebrafish quickly learn to swim to escape locations associated with shock (Aoki et al., 2015), and crabs learn to avoid a chamber associated with a shock (Magee & Elwood, 2013). Even sea slugs, which have only 10,000 neurons, learn to associate a conditioned stimulus with a shock (Hawkins et al., 1983; Walters et al., 1981), showing behavioral responses including siphon withdrawal, escape locomotion, and decreased feeding when anticipating shock. And caterpillars conditioned to associate shock with an odor retain learned avoidance of the odor even after metamorphosis (Blackiston et al., 2008).

Why shock so reliably elicits fear across species is not as obvious as for hypercapnia, but may be a prepared form of predator avoidance (Gallant et al., 2014), or may simply reflect the physical effects of shock on neurons and the tissue they innervate, including aversive sensations, muscle spasms, thermal injury, and other damage (Bryan et al., 2009). This makes the threat of shock a valuable study tool due to its translational potential and controllability in the laboratory.

Given the wide variation in nervous systems across species that show common forms of fear responding to threatening physical events like hypercapnia and shock, it is clear that no single neural process or system supports fear responding and fear learning across all species. However, investigations of vertebrate species demonstrate remarkable conservation of the subcortical brain circuits that support fear responding and fear conditioning in teleosts (finned fishes), birds, amphibians, reptiles, and mammals (O'Connell & Hofmann, 2012).

The Neural Circuitry and Chemical Processes That Support Fear

The detection of threat initiates a rapid cascade of central changes that collectively result in fear. In mammals, visual, chemosensory, and auditory threats reach the brain's central fear system through different routes, but converge in the amygdala. The amygdala is a subcortical structure composed of approximately 12 subnuclei, five of which play essential roles in fear detection, fear learning, and/or the coordination of fear responses (Adolphs & Anderson, 2018). The basal and lateral amygdala (BLA) are the primary input nuclei and receive signals from diverse brain areas including cortex, thalamus, and midbrain (McDonald & Mascagni, 1996; Pitkänen et al., 1997; van Vulpen & Verwer, 1989). The BLA projects medially to the central nucleus of the amygdala (CeA), the primary output nucleus, which mediates fear expression by coordinating downstream autonomic, endocrine, and behavioral targets (Davis, 1992; Keifer et al., 2015).

Autonomic and Endocrine Responses

The autonomic nervous system (ANS) controls muscles essential to body function, such as the heart and diaphragm, and is responsible for animals being able to maintain normal body functions like ensuring circulation of oxygenated blood. Fear robustly affects activity of the ANS, for example, causing an increase in heart rate, respiratory rate, and pupil dilation (Adolphs & Anderson, 2018; Davis, 1992; Levenson, 2014). In response to a threat, the CeA coordinates ANS responses in part through efferent projections to the lateral hypothalamus (LeDoux et al., 1988), nucleus ambiguus, and parabrachial nucleus (Davis, 1992; Lang & Davis, 2006).

Activity of the sympathetic nervous system—the ANS subdivision that activates in response to fear (the "fight or flight system")—is primarily initiated by projections from CeA to lateral hypothalamus. Lateral hypothalamus mobilizes a range of sympathetic responses, including increasing heart rate and blood vessel constriction (LeDoux et al., 1988). CeA also affects functioning of the parasympathetic nervous system—the ANS subdivision that is dominant at rest—primarily through inhibitory projections to nucleus ambiguus and dorsal motor nucleus of the vagus in the medulla, which control resting activity of the heart through the vagus nerve (Price & Amaral, 1981; Thayer & Lane, 2009). Due to this inhibitory influence on activity of the vagus nerve, fear can reduce heart rate variability, which serves as a common noninvasive measurement of physiological fear and anxiety in humans (Chalmers et al., 2014). Increases in respiratory rate are also associated with fear, and specifically with CeA projections to the parabrachial nucleus of the pons (Kapp et al., 1989), which sends synapses to phrenic motor neurons that affect the diaphragm.

The effects of fear on the body occur both through neuronal projections directly to peripheral muscles, as described above, and through systemic changes to circulating hormones via the endocrine system. The CeA projects to the paraventricular nucleus of the hypothalamus (PVN) to stimulate long-lasting, endocrine responses to fear and other stressors. The PVN is one of three regions that together form the hypothalamus-pituitary-adrenal (HPA) axis, which controls peripheral, hormone-mediated responses to stress. The HPA axis consists of a series of connections beginning with PVN neurons releasing a peptide, corticotropin-releasing factor (CRF), that binds to receptors in the anterior pituitary (Vale et al., 1981). Binding of CRF in the anterior pituitary stimulates adrenocorticotropic hormone (ACTH) release into the bloodstream. In turn, circulating ACTH binds to receptors in the adrenal glands near the kidneys, resulting in glucocorticoid release, which initiates a cascade of body-wide endocrine effects.

Glucocorticoids (primarily cortisol in primates and corticosterone in rodents) affect peripheral organs and central receptors, as nearly every cell in the body expresses glucocorticoid receptors (Nicolaides et al., 2010). Despite often complex interactions between glucocorticoids and other cell-signaling pathways, in most cases, glucocorticoid release leads to increased sympathetic activity, including vasoconstriction and increased cardiac output, which allows more glucose to be available to cells (Sapolsky et al., 2000).

The direct control of CeA (or a homologue) over autonomic function and activation of the HPA axis is highly conserved across vertebrates (Martínez-García & Lanuza, 2018; Moreno & González, 2007), underscoring the evolutionary importance of fear.

In humans, fear responding is often measured using noninvasive measures of autonomic effects, including increased skin-conductance response, pupil dilation, increased heart rate, and reduced heart rate variability (Adolphs & Anderson, 2018; Cacioppo et al., 2007). These outcomes are also measured in other species, although a weakness of such measures is their nonspecific nature (in that they indicate general autonomic arousal rather than fear specifically). Perhaps as a consequence, behavioral measures are more commonly used to study fear in animal models.

Low-Level Behavioral Responses

The adaptive significance of fear reflects both its effects on autonomic activity and the survival-related behaviors it potentiates. Whereas autonomic changes prepare the body for energy expenditure, a hierarchy of behavioral defensive strategies must be selected from to optimize survival. In preparation for this, a first step of defense relies on a vigilant, typically immobile positioning (Gray & McNaughton, 2000; Lang et al., 2000) as well as potentiation of the startle response.

Abrupt sensory inputs (e.g., a loud noise) elicit reflexive movements aimed at protecting the body. In mammals, these can involve a whole-body curling motion to protect abdominal organs or an eyeblink to avoid eye injury. Fear reliably potentiates these responses due to connections from CeA affecting the nucleus reticularis pontis caudalis (Hitchcock & Davis, 1991; Rosen et al., 1991) (this pathway may also be modulated by the superior colliculus; Zhao & Davis, 2004).

Primary defensive behavioral responses to fear additionally involve connections from CeA to periaqueductal gray, a key midbrain structure composed of multiple subregions that coordinates behavioral responses to proximal threats (Davis, 1992; LeDoux et al., 1988). While known for initiating freezing, periaqueductal gray additionally coordinates flight-or-fight behaviors, vocalizations, and analgesia (Depaulis & Bandler, 2012; Gray & McNaughton, 2000). Information from periaqueductal gray travels to lower brainstem nuclei to drive individual motor components of the fear response.

Behavioral response to a threat largely depends on proximity and context. A "quick and dirty" route carrying sensory information from brainstem directly to thalamus then to amygdala bypasses cortical processing (Elorette et al., 2018; Gray & McNaughton, 2000; LeDoux, 1996) and can initiate coarse behavioral responses, such as undirected escape, through periaqueductal gray (causing animals to sometimes run into environmental obstacles). More sophisticated escape actions depend on additional brain areas such as cingulate and hippocampus (Fanselow, 1994; Graeff, 1994; Gray & McNaughton, 2000; Halladay & Blair, 2015).

Flight initiation distance is an ecologically valid metric of fear, and indexes the distance at which an organism flees from an approaching threat. Flight initiation relies on coordinated activity between medial prefrontal cortex, CeA, and periaqueductal gray (Branco & Redgrave, 2020). Birds in rural areas or that live near many predators show longer flight initiation distance—that is, they flee a threat more distant relative to city birds—indicating environmental adaptation. Similar brain regions are activated in humans during approaching threat, for example when a tarantula is placed near their feet versus further away during brain imaging (Mobbs et al., 2010).

The CeA is densely interconnected with (and partly contiguous with) a small region of the basal forebrain, the BNST. The CeA and BNST share many downstream targets, and combined, make up the primary nodes of the central extended amygdala (De Olmos & Heimer, 1999; Oler et al., 2017; Shackman & Fox, 2016). The BNST is involved during states of sustained anxiety in humans (Alvarez et al., 2011; Davis et al., 2010; Somerville et al., 2010) and rodents (Davis et al., 1997), and with anxious temperament in macaques (Fox et al., 2018). Specifically, the *lateral* subdivision of CeA, which receives only sparse input from other amygdala nuclei, sends efferent connections almost entirely to BNST, which then has widespread projections that can initiate a state of sustained anxiety (Fudge & Tucker, 2009; Walker & Davis, 2008). The *medial* subdivision of CeA, however, projects broadly throughout the brain to initiate phasic fear responses (Walker & Davis, 2008). These sustained anxious versus phasic fear circuits—involving lateral CeA/BNST and medial CeA regions, respectively—are complicated by evidence of each region downregulating the other (Gungor et al., 2015; Meloni et al.,

2006). These remain important topics of study because of their relevance to psychopathology and involvement of unique neurotransmitter systems that open a door for targeted psychopharmacological manipulation.

Inactivation of rodent BNST, but not amygdala, blocks freezing induced by the presence of a predator odor (Endres et al., 2005), during which heightened vigilance (i.e., sustained anxiety) is likely preferable to a phasic fear fight-or-flight response. Similarly, enhanced startle reflexes are observed in rats exposed to a bright light (an innately aversive stimulus), an effect again blocked by inactivation of BNST, but not amygdala (Davis et al., 1997). Thus, cues signaling an unpredictable or remote threat engage anxiety-linked BNST-mediated responses rather than classically defined CeA fear responses associated with an imminent threat.

The biological and behavioral relevance of amygdala projections to downstream effector regions, including lateral and periventricular hypothalamus, BNST, vagal brainstem regions, and nucleus reticularis pontis caudalis, have been identified through work in rodent models (Davis, 1992; LeDoux et al., 1988). However, in primates and humans, CeA robustly projects to areas of cortex such as mPFC and insula that in turn also project to overlapping downstream targets. How these cortical layover signals may shape fear responses is poorly understood (Fox et al., 2010; Janak & Tye, 2015; Pajolla et al., 2001; Reppucci & Petrovich, 2016). But in humans and other species with a large neocortex, connections from CeA to effector regions are likely additionally modulated by activity in cortical areas.

Social Communicative Responses

In addition to the autonomic, escape, and avoidance responses observed in response to threat, social communicative fear behaviors are also often observed. These behaviors include the emission of odors (chemosensory/olfactory), vocalizations (acoustic/auditory), and facial and body expressions (visual), that vary across species.

As discussed earlier, both invertebrates and vertebrates emit odors in response to threatening stimuli. Fruit flies emit CO_2 when encountering an electric shock (Suh et al., 2004); fish release other chemicals (alarm substances) in response to predatory fish stimuli (Pfeiffer, 1977; Speedie & Gerlai, 2008); and cattle produce olfactory cues in their urine (Boissy et al., 1998). Although humans are often viewed as less dependent on olfactory signaling than other species, fear is also encoded in human body odor and sweat (de Groot et al., 2020; Smeets et al., 2020) in a way that can be correctly detected by other human observers (de Groot & Smeets, 2017)

Fear is also signaled via auditory alarm calls, which can be vocal or nonvocal. Nonvocal alarm calls include the sounds produced by the wings of pigeons when fleeing danger, which have a distinctively higher tempo and elicit vigilance or flight in nearby conspecifics (Murray et al., 2017). Fear vocalizations are produced by many species. For example, birds (Gyger et al., 1987), squirrels (Davis, 1984), and monkeys (Seyfarth et al., 1980) produce audible alarm calls in the presence of predators, the features of which may signal the nature of the threat (raptors versus snakes versus felines) (Seyfarth et al., 1980; Templeton et al., 2005). Rats and mice emit ultrasonic vocalizations in the 22-kHz range when approached by predators, which are undetectable to common predators but are detectable to conspecifics (Brudzynski, 2005, 2015; Litvin et al., 2007; Sangiamo et al., 2020). Neurostimulation studies have determined that dorsal and medial periaqueductal gray, in concert with their reciprocal connections to thalamic and hypothalamic nuclei, are involved in the production of ultrasonic alarm calls (Depaulis et al., 1992; Yajima et al., 1980). These vocalizations—for example, during conditioning—are impaired among rodents with lesions to CeA/BLA or hippocampus (Antoniadis & McDonald, 2000) as well as nucleus accumbens, medial prefrontal cortex, and medial dorsal thalamic nucleus (Antoniadis & McDonald, 2006; Frysztak & Neafsey, 1994). Humans also produce characteristic fear vocalizations such as screams, the meaning of which are interpretable across cultures (Elfenbein & Ambady, 2002; Sauter et al., 2010) and which are characterized by a high mean pitch (Sauter et al., 2010) and a perceptually "rough" acoustic quality (Arnal et al., 2015).

Finally, many species signal fear with visual displays of the body. Common mammalian postural expressions of fear include piloerection, crouching, and hunching of the back in rodents (Blanchard & Blanchard, 1969; Carstens & Moberg, 2000; Cavigelli & McClintock, 2003; Iwata & LeDoux, 1988) as well as crouching and trembling in dogs (Beerda et al., 1998), cats, and nonhuman primates (Carstens & Moberg, 2000). Humans' visual fearful expressions include facial cues such as widened eyes, grimaces (contraction of the risorius muscle), and raised and drawn together eyebrows (contraction of the medial frontalis and corrugator supercilii muscle). Elements of the human fearful expression can be observed in other nonhuman primates in analogous contexts, particularly the grimace, supporting the conserved nature of aspects of this expression (Parr et al., 2007).

Behaviors that signal fear carry both risks and potential rewards. Some of these behaviors, such as alarm calls, increase susceptibility to threat by drawing attention to the expresser and signaling their potential vulnerability. However, these costs may be outweighed by other adaptive functions. In some cases, these include signaling danger to conspecifics and increasing their survival odds, which may yield inclusive fitness benefits (such signals are most likely to occur in the presence of kin) (Litvin et al., 2007). A second social function that fear cues may serve is soliciting care or inhibiting aggression from perceivers. In social species, including humans, characteristic fear behaviors, such as crouching and low posture, widened eyes, or high-pitched vocalizations, simulate features of small or juvenile conspecifics (Atkinson et al., 2007; Beerda et al., 1998; Schenkel, 1967). It might appear counterintuitive that an organism facing an attacker would want to look more vulnerable and infantile, but juveniles are often the beneficiaries of care and reduced aggression (Kringelbach et al., 2016), suggesting that such features of fear cues may be adaptive. Fear cues that mimic infantile appearance features inhibit attack in canine species (Schenkel, 1967). And in humans, the wide eyes, raised brows, and rounded appearance of the prototypical fearful facial expression cause the expresser to appear more physically babyish (Marsh, Adams, et al., 2005), elicit behavioral approach (Hammer & Marsh, 2015; Marsh, Ambady, et al., 2005), and potentiate caring motivation—even when the fearful expression is presented subliminally (Brethel-Haurwitz et al., 2017; Marsh & Ambady, 2007). These advantages are in addition to potential sensory and physiological advantages that these expressions may serve, including creating subjectively larger visual fields, allowing faster eye movements, or increasing nasal airflow during inhalation (Susskind et al., 2008).

To serve these functions, fear communication signals must first be perceived and accurately decoded. Perception of fear cues is mediated by the relevant sensory cortices and integrated in subcortical regions implicated in the experience of fear (see Figure 26.2), which facilitates the social transmission of fear information. For instance, the odorant released by fruit flies prompts olfactory neuron-mediated avoidance behavior in other flies (Suh et al., 2004). In mammals such as mice, the amygdala serves as a primary chemosensor through activation of a specific ion channel (the acid-sensing ion channel 1a), which is required for normal experienced fear behaviors (Coryell et al., 2007; Coryell et al., 2008) and detects changes in pH from chemosignals (Ziemann et al., 2009). The amygdala also responds to vocal alarm signals, information from which follows a similar pathway as other auditory threat signals: the information is first integrated in the inferior colliculus and then filtered by the

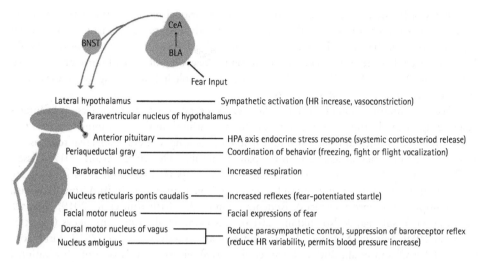

Figure 26.2. Efferent connections from the amygdala associated with the fear response. BLA = basolateral amygdala; CeA = central nucleus of amygdala; BNST = bed nucleus of the stria terminalis; HPA Axis = hypothalamus-pituitary-adrenal axis; HR = heart rate.

Figure adapted from Davis (1992).

medial geniculate nucleus (MGN) of the auditory thalamus (Pereira et al., 2020; Portfors, 2018) before it is relayed to the amygdala. Simultaneously, this information is processed by the auditory cortex before being fed forward to various subcortical regions, such as the lateral amygdala, CeA, perirhinal cortex, periaqueductal gray, and hypothalamus (Parsana et al., 2012; Sadananda et al., 2008), whereupon it triggers defensive behaviors in perceivers (Parsana et al., 2012; Pereira et al., 2020).

Information about visual fear signals is thought to be relayed to the amygdala via both a "quick and dirty" pathway (described above) and a "slow and sophisticated" pathway (Gray & McNaughton, 2000; LeDoux, 1996). The "slow and sophisticated" pathway includes visual cortex and the inferior temporal cortex (including fusiform face gyrus), which are involved in further processing of face information, and which share reciprocal connections with the amygdala. Although early evidence suggested these were the only two pathways by which visual fear cues reached the amygdala, recent studies in nonhuman and human primates have suggested that fear cues may arrive in the amygdala via multiple streams through association cortex (Pessoa & Adolphs, 2010), including a stream specialized for social perception (Pitcher & Ungerleider, 2021)

The central role of the amygdala in coordinating responses to social fear cues across sensory modalities—including chemosensory signals (de Groot et al., 2012; Mujica-Parodi et al., 2009), vocal expressions, (Aubé et al., 2013; Fecteau et al., 2007; Phillips et al., 1998), visual facial expressions (Adolphs et al., 1994; Fusar-Poli et al., 2009; Luo et al., 2007), and body postures (Sprengelmeyer et al., 1999)—is well-established. Lesions to the human amygdala consistently result in deficits in recognizing and responding to fear cues across modalities (Adolphs et al., 1994; Anderson & Phelps, 2000; Geissberger et al., 2020; Sprengelmeyer et al., 1999), and even making predictions about others' fear using purely semantic information (Cardinale et al., 2021). Together, these data suggest that the amygdala plays a key role in coordinating a multimodal internal representation of fear that incorporates episodic, sensory, and interoceptive information and aids in the interpretation of social fear cues (Marsh, 2016).

In other words, the amygdala is essential to a basic form of empathy: translating between others' experience of fear and one's own states by activating personal, neural, and mental representations of that state (De Waal & Preston, 2017; Decety & Jackson, 2006). It should be emphasized that the amygdala is active during the decoding of a broad range of emotional expressions (Wang et al., 2017), but plays a more central role in interpreting social fear than it does other emotional cues (Marsh, 2016).

Accurate interpretation of social fear cues serves several important roles. First, it facilitates responding to and learning about potentially harmful stimuli in the environment. Social fear cues may serve as unconditioned stimuli capable of eliciting a relevant affective response in observers that becomes associated with the paired stimulus (Debiec & Olsson, 2017; Olsson & Phelps, 2007). In fact, the neural mechanisms that support observational fear learning are similar to those that support non-social fear learning (e.g., convergence in BLA from thalamus, hippocampus, and sensory cortices). Rodents (Jeon et al., 2010; Kim et al., 2019; Knapska et al., 2006; Yusufishaq & Rosenkranz, 2013), cats (John et al., 1968), monkeys (Cook & Mineka, 1989; Mineka & Cook, 1984), and humans (Lindström et al., 2018; Lindström et al., 2019; Olsson et al., 2007; Olsson et al., 2016) all exhibit this type of observational learning about harmful stimuli from observing social fear cues. Rhesus monkeys can even learn about threatening stimuli from observing human fear behaviors (Mineka & Cook, 1984).

Accurate interpretation of social fear cues also plays an important role in regulating social interactions. In signaling distress and vulnerability, and aided by their resemblance to infantile features (Marsh, Adams, et al., 2005), fearful expressions appear to be robust elicitors of caring motivation in perceivers and inhibitors of aggression (Brethel-Haurwitz et al., 2017; Marsh & Ambady, 2007). Evidence that fearful facial expressions are perceived as affiliative (Hess et al., 2000) and elicit behavioral approach rather than avoidance from perceivers makes clear that these expressions should not be interpreted simply as "threat cues," which primarily elicit avoidance (Hammer & Marsh, 2015; Marsh, Ambady, et al., 2005). Rather, in a social context, fearful expressions may serve as appeasement cues, similar to the fear and submission displays of other social species (Schenkel, 1967; Smith & Price, 1973), which serve to defuse agonistic or aggressive encounters by eliciting care. Consistent with this, the detection and accurate interpretation of fearful expressions is consistently associated with increased prosocial and altruistic motivations and behaviors (Marsh et al., 2014; Marsh & Ambady, 2007; Rajhans et al., 2016), whereas deficits in the ability to recognize others' fear are associated with increased aggression and callousness (Marsh & Blair, 2008). Individual variation in sensitivity to social fear cues has been linked to the volume and responsiveness of the amygdala (Lozier et al., 2014; Marsh et al., 2014), consistent with the idea that the integrity of this structure is essential for generating empathic representations of others' fear. Cultural factors also likely play a role in influencing sensitivity to social fear cues, in light of evidence of cultural variation in the specific forms that fearful expressions take, and which can affect cross-cultural accuracy of fear recognition (Elfenbein, 2013; Elfenbein & Ambady, 2002).

Conclusions
Fear responding, learning, and communication support essential adaptive functions and promote survival and fitness. The adaptive power of fear derives in part from its aversive nature, which typically motivates avoidance and escape from stimuli that elicit it. This is not to say that fear is purely beneficial. For one, its aversive qualities can make fear subjectively unpleasant. The distressing quality of fear—and similarly, anxiety—are among the most common reasons that people seek clinical treatment (Finley et al., 2018; Stinson et al., 2007). Although the prevalence of common disorders of fear and anxiety may reflect the evolutionary benefits

of these states (Adolphs & Anderson, 2018; Marks & Nesse, 1994), excessive or sustained activation of fear or anxiety networks can cause adverse health effects, including metabolic, hormonal, and cardiovascular changes (Radley et al., 2015). Considering fear and anxiety from an evolutionary perspective may aid in understanding psychiatric disorders of fear and anxiety (Nesse, 2001), and perhaps illuminate why these disorders appear to be increasing in frequency (Goodwin, 2003; Goodwin et al., 2020). One possibility that has been proposed is that exposure to threats is required for the development of mature fear and anxiety regulatory networks (Luna et al., 2004). The dramatic reduction in threats to safety experienced by modern humans may generate insufficient fear learning experiences to tune the development of anxiety.

This brings us back to the case of climber Alex Honnold, whose capacity for fear appears to be intact, but whose training involves repeatedly confronting sources of threat and risk under carefully scaffolded conditions, providing him the ability to successfully learn to regulate this emotion and thus ensure his fear is serving not only deep adaptive goals, but his proximal personal goals as well.

References

Adolphs, R. (2013). The biology of fear. *Current Biology, 23*(2), R79–R93. https://doi.org/10.1016/j.cub.2012.11.055

Adolphs, R., & Anderson, D. J. (2018). *The neuroscience of emotion: A new synthesis*. Princeton University Press.

Adolphs, R., Tranel, D., Damasio, H., & Damasio, A. (1994). Impaired recognition of emotion in facial expressions following bilateral damage to the human amygdala. *Nature, 372*(6507), 669–672. https://doi.org/10.1093/neucas/3.4.267-a

Alvarez, R. P., Chen, G., Bodurka, J., Kaplan, R., & Grillon, C. (2011). Phasic and sustained fear in humans elicits distinct patterns of brain activity. *NeuroImage, 55*(1), 389–400. https://doi.org/10.1016/j.neuroimage.2010.11.057

Améndola, L., & Weary, D. M. (2020). Understanding rat emotional responses to CO_2. *Translational Psychiatry, 10*(1), 253. https://doi.org/10.1038/s41398-020-00936-w

Anand, K. J. S., & Craig, K. D. (1996). New perspectives on the definition of pain. *Pain, 67*, 3–6. https://doi.org/10.1016/0304-3959(96)03135-1

Anderson, A. K., & Phelps, E. A. (2000). Expression without recognition: Contributions of the human amygdala to emotional communication. *Psychological Science, 11*(2), 106–111. https://doi.org/10.1111/1467-9280.00224

Antoniadis, E. A., & McDonald, R. J. (2000). Amygdala, hippocampus and discriminative fear conditioning to context. *Behavioural Brain Research, 108*(1), 1–19. https://doi.org/10.1016/S0166-4328(99)00121-7

Antoniadis, E. A., & McDonald, R. J. (2006). Fornix, medial prefrontal cortex, nucleus accumbens, and mediodorsal thalamic nucleus: Roles in a fear-based context discrimination task. *Neurobiology of Learning and Memory, 85*(1), 71–85. https://doi.org/10.1016/j.nlm.2005.08.011

Aoki, R., Tsuboi, T., & Okamoto, H. (2015). Y-maze avoidance: An automated and rapid associative learning paradigm in zebrafish. *Neuroscience Research, 91*, 69–72. https://doi.org/10.1016/j.neures.2014.10.012

Arias, J. A., Williams, C., Raghvani, R., Aghajani, M., Baez, S., Belzung, C., Booij, L., Busatto, G., Chiarella, J., Fu, C. H., Ibanez, A., Liddell, B. J., Lowe, L., Penninx, B. W. J. H., Rosa, P., & Kemp, A. H. (2020). The neuroscience of sadness: A multidisciplinary synthesis and collaborative review. *Neuroscience and Biobehavioral Reviews, 111*(October 2018), 199–228. https://doi.org/10.1016/j.neubiorev.2020.01.006

Arnal, L. H., Flinker, A., Kleinschmidt, A., Giraud, A. L., & Poeppel, D. (2015). Human screams occupy a privileged niche in the communication soundscape. *Current Biology, 25*(15), 2051–2056. https://doi.org/10.1016/j.cub.2015.06.043

Atkinson, A. P., Heberlein, A. S., & Adolphs, R. (2007). Spared ability to recognise fear from static and moving whole-body cues following bilateral amygdala damage. *Neuropsychologia, 45*(12), 2772–2782. https://doi.org/10.1016/j.neuropsychologia.2007.04.019

Aubé, W., Angulo-Perkins, A., Peretz, I., Concha, L., & Armony, J. L. (2013). Fear across the senses: Brain responses to music, vocalizations and facial expressions. *Social Cognitive and Affective Neuroscience, 10*(3), 399–407. https://doi.org/10.1093/scan/nsu067

Azzam, Z. S., Sharabi, K., Guetta, J., Bank, E. M., & Gruenbaum, Y. (2010). The physiological and molecular effects of elevated CO_2 levels. *Cell Cycle, 9*(8), 1528–1532. https://doi.org/10.4161/cc.9.8.11196

Balderston, N. L., Liu, J., Roberson-Nay, R., Ernst, M., & Grillon, C. (2017). The relationship between dlPFC activity during unpredictable threat and CO2-induced panic symptoms. *Translational Psychiatry, 7*(12), 1266. https://doi.org/10.1038/s41398-017-0006-5

Beerda, B., Schilder, M. B. H., Van Hooff, J. A., De Vries, H. W., & Mol, J. A. (1998). Behavioural, saliva cortisol and heart rate responses to different types of stimuli in dogs. *Applied Animal Behaviour Science, 58*(3–4), 365–381. https://doi.org/10.1016/S0168-1591(97)00145-7

Blackiston, D. J., Casey, E. S., & Weiss, M. R. (2008). Retention of memory through metamorphosis: Can a moth remember what it learned as a caterpillar? *PLoS ONE, 3*(3), e1736. https://doi.org/10.1371/journal.pone.0001736

Blackshaw, J. K., Beattie, A. W., Fenwick, D. C., & Allan, D. J. (1988). The behaviour of chickens, mice and rats during euthanasia with chloroform, carbon dioxide and ether. *Laboratory Animals, 22*(1), 67–75. https://doi.org/10.1258/002367788780746674

Blair, R. J. R. (2012). Considering anger from a cognitive neuroscience perspective. *Wiley Interdisciplinary Reviews: Cognitive Science, 3*(1), 65–74. https://doi.org/10.1002/wcs.154

Blanchard, R. J., & Blanchard, D. C. (1969). Crouching as an index of fear. *Journal of Comparative and Physiological Psychology, 67*(3), 370–375. https://doi.org/10.1037/h0026779

Boffey, P. M. (1987, November 24). Infants' sense of pain is recognized, finally. *New York Times*, 3.

Boissy, A., Terlouw, C., & Le Neindre, P. (1998). Presence of cues from stressed conspecifics increases reactivity to aversive events in cattle: Evidence for the existence of alarm substances in urine. *Physiology and Behavior, 63*(4), 489–495. https://doi.org/10.1016/S0031-9384(97)00466-6

Boycott, B. B., & Young, J. Z. (1955). A memory system in Octopus vulgaris Lamarck. *Proceedings of the Royal Society B: Biological Sciences, 143*(913), 449–480. https://doi.org/10.1098/rspb.1955.0024

Branco, T., & Redgrave, P. (2020). The neural basis of escape behavior in vertebrates. *Annual Review of Neuroscience, 43*, 417–439. https://doi.org/10.1146/annurev-neuro-100219-122527

Brethel-Haurwitz, K. M., O'Connell, K., Cardinale, E. M., Stoycos, S. A., Lozier, L. M., Vanmeter, J. W., & Marsh, A. A. (2017). Amygdala-midbrain connectivity indicates a role for the mammalian parental care system in extraordinary altruism. *Proceedings of the Royal Society B: Biological Sciences, 284*(1865), 20171731. https://doi.org/10.1098/rspb.2017.1731

Brudzynski, S. M. (2005). Principles of rat communication: Quantitative parameters of ultrasonic calls in rats. *Behavior Genetics, 35*(1), 85–92. https://doi.org/10.1007/s10519-004-0858-3

Brudzynski, S. M. (2015). Pharmacology of ultrasonic vocalizations in adult rats: Significance, call classification and neural substrate. *Current Neuropharmacology, 13*(2), 180–192. https://doi.org/10.2174/1570159x13999150210141444

Bryan, B. C., Hurley, R. A., Taber, K. H., & Andrew, C. J. (2009). Electrical injury, Part I: Mechanism. *The Journal of Neuropsychiatry and Clinical Neurosciences, 21*(3), 240–244.

Cacioppo, J. T., Tassinary, L. G., & Berntson, G. G. (2007). Psychophysiological science: Interdisciplinary approaches to classic questions about the mind. In J. T. Cacioppo, L. G. Tassinary, & G. G. Berntson (Eds.), *Handbook of psychophysiology* (pp. 1–16). Cambridge University Press.

Cardinale, E. M., Reber, J., O'Connell, K., Turkeltaub, P. E., Tranel, D., Buchanan, T. W., & Marsh, A. A. (2021). Bilateral amygdala damage linked to impaired ability to predict others' fear but preserved moral judgements about causing others fear. *Proceedings of the Royal Society B: Biological Sciences, 288*(1943), 20202651. https://doi.org/10.1098/rspb.2020.2651

Carew, T. J., & Sahley, C. L. (1986). Invertebrate learning and memory: From behavior to molecules. *Annual Review of Neuroscience, 9*, 435–487. https://doi.org/10.1146/annurev.ne.09.030186.002251

Carstens, E., & Moberg, G. P. (2000). Recognizing pain and distress in laboratory animals. *ILAR Journal, 41*(2), 62–71. https://doi.org/10.1093/ilar.41.2.62

Cavigelli, S. A., & McClintock, M. K. (2003). Fear of novelty in infant rats predicts adult corticosterone dynamics and an early death. *Proceedings of the National Academy of Sciences, 100*(26), 16131–16136. https://doi.org/10.1073/pnas.2535721100

Chalmers, J. A., Quintana, D. S., Abbott, M. J. A., & Kemp, A. H. (2014). Anxiety disorders are associated with reduced heart rate variability: A meta-analysis. *Frontiers in Psychiatry, 5*(80). https://doi.org/10.3389/fpsyt.2014.00080

Chisholm, J., De Rantere, D., Fernandez, N. J., Krajacic, A., & Pang, D. S. J. (2013). Carbon dioxide, but not isoflurane, elicits ultrasonic vocalizations in female rats. *Laboratory Animals, 47*(4), 324–327. https://doi.org/10.1177/0023677213493410

Cook, M., & Mineka, S. (1989). Observational conditioning of fear to fear-relevant versus fear-irrelevant stimuli in rhesus monkeys. *Journal of Abnormal Psychology, 98*(4), 448–459. https://doi.org/10.1037/0021-843X.98.4.448

Coryell, M. W., Wunsch, A. M., Haenfler, J. M., Allen, J. E., McBride, J. L., Davidson, B. L., & Wemmie, J. A. (2008). Restoring acid-sensing ion channel-1a in the amygdala of knock-out mice rescues fear memory but not unconditioned fear responses. *Journal of Neuroscience, 28*(51), 13738–13741. https://doi.org/10.1523/JNEUROSCI.3907-08.2008

Coryell, M. W., Ziemann, A. E., Westmoreland, P. J., Haenfler, J. M., Kurjakovic, Z., Zha, X. ming, Price, M., Schnizler, M. K., & Wemmie, J. A. (2007). Targeting ASIC1a reduces innate fear and alters neuronal activity in the fear circuit. *Biological Psychiatry, 62*(10), 1140–1148. https://doi.org/10.1016/j.biopsych.2007.05.008

Crivelli, C., & Fridlund, A. J. (2018). Facial displays are tools for social influence. *Trends in Cognitive Sciences, 22*(5), 388–399. https://doi.org/10.1016/j.tics.2018.02.006

Davis, L. S. (1984). Alarm calling in Richardson's ground squirrels (*Spermophilus richardsonii*). *Zeitschrift Für Tierpsychologie, 66*(2), 152–164. https://doi.org/10.1111/j.1439-0310.1984.tb01362.x

Davis, M. (1986). Pharmacological and anatomical analysis of fear conditioning using the fear-potentiated startle paradigm. *Behavioral Neuroscience, 100*(6), 814–824.

Davis, M. (1992). The role of the amygdala in fear and anxiety. *Annual Review of Neuroscience, 15*, 353–375. https://doi.org/10.1146/annurev.ne.15.030192.002033

Davis, M., Walker, D. L., & Lee, Y. (1997). Amygdala and bed nucleus of the stria terminalis: Differential roles in fear and anxiety measured with the acoustic startle reflex. *Philosophical Transactions of the Royal Society B: Biological Sciences, 352*(1362), 1675–1687. https://doi.org/10.1098/rstb.1997.0149

Davis, M., Walker, D. L., Miles, L., & Grillon, C. (2010). Phasic vs sustained fear in rats and humans: Role of the extended amygdala in fear vs anxiety. *Neuropsychopharmacology, 35*(1), 105–135. https://doi.org/10.1038/npp.2009.109

de Groot, J. H. B., Kirk, P. A., & Gottfried, J. A. (2020). Encoding fear intensity in human sweat. *Philosophical Transactions of the Royal Society B: Biological Sciences, 375*(1800), 20190271. https://doi.org/10.1098/rstb.2019.0271

de Groot, J. H. B., & Smeets, M. A. M. (2017). Human fear chemosignaling: Evidence from a meta-analysis. *Chemical Senses, 42*(8), 663–673. https://doi.org/10.1093/chemse/bjx049

de Groot, J. H. B., Smeets, M. A. M., Kaldewaij, A., Duijndam, M. J. A., & Semin, G. R. (2012). Chemosignals communicate human emotions. *Psychological Science, 23*(11), 1417–1424. https://doi.org/10.1177/0956797612445317

De Olmos, J. S., & Heimer, L. (1999). The concepts of the ventral striatopallidal system and extended amygdala. *Annals of the New York Academy of Sciences, 877*(1), 1–32. https://doi.org/10.1111/j.1749-6632.1999.tb09258.x

de Waal, F. B. M. (2019). Fish, mirrors, and a gradualist perspective on self-awareness. *PLoS Biology, 17*(2), e3000112. https://doi.org/10.1371/journal.pbio.3000112

de Waal, F. B. M., & Preston, S. D. (2017). Mammalian empathy: Behavioural manifestations and neural basis. *Nature Reviews Neuroscience, 18*(8), 498–509. https://doi.org/10.1038/nrn.2017.72

Debiec, J., & Olsson, A. (2017). Social fear learning: From animal models to human function. *Trends in Cognitive Sciences, 21*(7), 546–565. https://doi.org/10.1016/j.tics.2017.04.010

Decety, J., & Jackson, P. L. (2006). A social-neuroscience perspective on empathy. *Current Directions in Psychological Science, 15*(2), 54–58.

Depaulis, A., & Bandler, R. (Eds.). (2012). *The midbrain periaqueductal gray matter: Functional, anatomical, and neurochemical organization*. Springer Science & Business Media.

Depaulis, A., Keay, K. A., & Bandler, R. (1992). Longitudinal neuronal organization of defensive reactions in the midbrain periaqueductal gray region of the rat. *Experimental Brain Research, 90*(2), 307–318. https://doi.org/10.1007/BF00227243

Ekman, P. (2002). *Facial action coding system (FACS)*. Consulting Psychologists Press.

Ekman, P., Sorenson, E. R., & Friesen, W. V. (1969). Pan-cultural elements in facial displays of emotion. *Science, 164*(3875), 86–88.

Elfenbein, H. A. (2013). Nonverbal dialects and accents in facial expressions of emotion. *Emotion Review, 5*(1), 90–96. https://doi.org/10.1177/1754073912451332

Elfenbein, H. A., & Ambady, N. (2002). On the universality and cultural specificity of emotion recognition: A meta-analysis. *Psychological Bulletin, 128*(2), 203–235. https://doi.org/10.1037/0033-2909.128.2.203

Elorette, C., Forcelli, P. A., Saunders, R. C., & Malkova, L. (2018). Colocalization of tectal inputs with amygdala-projecting neurons in the macaque pulvinar. *Frontiers in Neural Circuits, 12*(October), 1–12. https://doi.org/10.3389/fncir.2018.00091

Endres, T., Apfelbach, R., & Fendt, M. (2005). Behavioral changes induced in rats by exposure to trimethylthiazoline, a component of fox odor. *Behavioral Neuroscience, 119*(4), 1004–1010. https://doi.org/10.1037/0735-7044.119.4.1004

Fanselow, M. S. (1994). Neural organization of the defensive behavior system responsible for fear. *Psychonomic Bulletin & Review, 1*(4), 429–438. https://doi.org/10.3758/BF03210947

Fanselow, M. S., & Pennington, Z. T. (2017). The danger of LeDoux and Pine's two-system framework for fear. *American Journal of Psychiatry, 174*(11), 1120. https://doi.org/10.1176/appi.ajp.2017.17070818

Fecteau, S., Belin, P., Joanette, Y., & Armony, J. L. (2007). Amygdala responses to nonlinguistic emotional vocalizations. *NeuroImage, 36*(2), 480–487. https://doi.org/10.1016/j.neuroimage.2007.02.043

Fedorenko, E., & Varley, R. (2016). Language and thought are not the same thing: evidence from neuroimaging and neurological patients. *Annals of the New York Academy of Sciences, 1369*(1), 132–153. https://doi.org/10.1111/nyas.13046.Language

Feinstein, J. S., Buzza, C., Hurlemann, R., Follmer, R. L., Dahdaleh, N. S., Coryell, W. H., Welsh, M. J., Tranel, D., & Wemmie, J. A. (2013). Fear and panic in humans with bilateral amygdala damage Justin. *Nature Neuroscience, 16*(3), 270–272. https://doi.org/10.1038/nn.3323.Fear

Finley, C. R., Chan, D. S., Scott, M. B. A., & Ccfp, G. (2018). What are the most common conditions in primary care? Une revue systématique: Les problèmes de santé les plus fréquents dans les soins primaires. *Canadian Family Physician, 64*(11), 832–840.

Fox, A. S., Oler, J. A., Birn, R. M., Shackman, A. J., Alexander, A. L., & Kalin, N. H. (2018). Functional connectivity within the primate extended amygdala is heritable and associated with early-life anxious temperament. *Journal of Neuroscience, 38*(35), 7611–7621. https://doi.org/10.1523/JNEUROSCI.0102-18.2018

Fox, A. S., Shelton, S. E., Oakes, T. R., Converse, A. K., Davidson, R. J., & Kalin, N. H. (2010). Orbitofrontal cortex lesions alter anxiety-related activity in the primate bed nucleus of stria terminalis. *Journal of Neuroscience, 30*(20), 7023–7027. https://doi.org/10.1523/JNEUROSCI.5952-09.2010

Frysztak, R. J., & Neafsey, E. J. (1994). The effect of medial frontal cortex lesions on cardiovascular conditioned emotional responses in the rat. *Brain Research, 643*(1–2), 181–193. https://doi.org/10.1016/0006-8993(94)90024-8

Fudge, J. L., & Tucker, T. (2009). Amygdala projections to central amygdaloid nucleus subdivisions and transition zones in the primate. *Neuroscience, 159*(2), 819–841. https://doi.org/10.1016/j.neuroscience.2009.01.013

Fusar-Poli, P., Placentino, A., Carletti, F., Landi, P., Allen, P., Surguladze, S., Benedetti, F., Abbamonte, M., Gasparotti, R., Barale, F., Perez, J., Mcguire, P., & Politi, P. (2009). Functional atlas of emotional faces processing: A voxel-based meta-analysis of 105 functional magnetic resonance imaging studies. *Journal of Psychiatry & Neuroscience, 34*(6), 418–432.

Gallant, J. R., Traeger, L. L., Volkening, J. D., Moffett, H., Chen, P., Novina, C. D., Jr., G. N. P., Anand, R., Wells, G. B., Pinch, M., Güth, R., Unguez, G. A., & Albert, J. S. (2014). Evolution of electric organs. *Science, 344*(6191), 1522–1525.

Geissberger, N., Tik, M., Sladky, R., Woletz, M., Schuler, A. L., Willinger, D., & Windischberger, C. (2020). Reproducibility of amygdala activation in facial emotion processing at 7T. *NeuroImage, 211*, 116585. https://doi.org/10.1016/j.neuroimage.2020.116585

Goodwin, R. D. (2003). The prevalence of panic attacks in the United States: 1980 to 1995. *Journal of Clinical Epidemiology, 56*(9), 914–916. https://doi.org/10.1016/S0895-4356(03)00126-4

Goodwin, R. D., Weinberger, A. H., Kim, J. H., Wu, M., & Galea, S. (2020). Trends in anxiety among adults in the United States, 2008–2018: Rapid increases among young adults. *Journal of Psychiatric Research, 130*, 441–446. https://doi.org/10.1016/j.jpsychires.2020.08.014

Graeff, F. G. (1994). Neuroanatomy and neurotransmitter regulation of defensive behaviors and related emotions in mammals. *Brazilian Journal of Medical and Biological Research, 27*, 811–829.

Gray, J. A., & McNaughton, N. (2000). *The neuropsychology of anxiety: An enquiry into the functions of the septo-hippocampal system* (2nd ed.). Oxford University Press.

Gross, C. T., & Canteras, N. S. (2012). The many paths to fear. *Nature Reviews Neuroscience, 13*(9), 651–658. https://doi.org/10.1038/nrn3301

Gungor, N. Z., Yamamoto, R., & Paré, D. (2015). Optogenetic study of the projections from the bed nucleus of the stria terminalis to the central amygdala. *Journal of Neurophysiology, 114*(5), 2903–2911. https://doi.org/10.1152/jn.00677.2015

Gyger, M., Marler, P., & Pickert, R. (1987). Semantics of an avian alarm call system: The male domestic fowl, *Gallus domesticus*. *Behaviour, 102*(1–2), 15–40. http://www.jstor.org/stable/4534610

Haaker, J., Maren, S., Andreatta, M., Merz, C. J., Richter, J., Richter, S. H., Meir Drexler, S., Lange, M. D., Jüngling, K., Nees, F., Seidenbecher, T., Fullana, M. A., Wotjak, C. T., & Lonsdorf, T. B. (2019). Making translation work: Harmonizing cross-species methodology in the behavioural neuroscience of Pavlovian fear conditioning. *Neuroscience and Biobehavioral Reviews, 107*, 329–345. https://doi.org/10.1016/j.neubiorev.2019.09.020

Halladay, L. R., & Blair, H. T. (2015). Distinct ensembles of medial prefrontal cortex neurons are activated by threatening stimuli that elicit excitation vs. inhibition of movement. *Journal of Neurophysiology, 114*(2), 793–807. https://doi.org/10.1152/jn.00656.2014

Hammer, J. L., & Marsh, A. A. (2015). Why do fearful facial expressions elicit behavioral approach? Evidence from a combined approach-avoidance implicit association test. *Emotion, 15*(2), 3047–3054. https://doi.org/10.1037/emo0000054.

Hawkins, R. D., Abrams, T. W., Carew, T. J., & Kandel, E. R. (1983). A cellular mechanism of classical conditioning in Aplysia: Activity-dependent amplification of presynaptic facilitation. *Science, 219*(4583), 400–405.

Hedges, S. B., Dudley, J., & Kumar, S. (2006). TimeTree: A public knowledge-base of divergence times among organisms. *Bioinformatics, 22*(23), 2971–2972. https://doi.org/10.1093/bioinformatics/btl505

Hess, U., Senecal, S., Kirouac, G., Herrera, P., Philippot, P., & Kleck, R. E. (2000). Emotional expressivity in men and women: Stereotypes and self-perceptions. *Cognition and Emotion, 14*(5), 609–642. https://doi.org/10.1080/02699930050117648

Hitchcock, J. M., & Davis, M. (1991). Efferent pathway of the amygdala involved in conditioned fear as measured with the fear-potentiated startle paradigm. *Behavioral Neuroscience, 105*(6), 826–842.

Honnold, A. (2018). *How I climbed a 3,000-foot vertical cliff—without ropes.* TED. https://www.ted.com/talks/alex_honnold_how_i_climbed_a_3_000_foot_vertical_cliff_without_ropes

Iwata, J., & LeDoux, J. E. (1988). Dissociation of associative and nonassociative concommitants of classical fear conditioning in the freely behaving rat. *Behavioral Neuroscience, 102*(1), 66–76. https://doi.org/10.1037/0735-7044.102.1.66

Janak, P. H., & Tye, K. M. (2015). From circuits to behaviour in the amygdala. *Nature, 517*, 284–292. https://doi.org/10.1038/nature14188

Jeon, D., Kim, S., Chetana, M., Jo, D., Ruley, H. E., Lin, S. Y., Rabah, D., Kinet, J. P., & Shin, H. S. (2010). Observational fear learning involves affective pain system and Ca v 1.2 Ca 2+ channels in ACC. *Nature Neuroscience, 13*(4), 482–488. https://doi.org/10.1038/nn.2504

John, E. R., Chesler, P., Bartlett, F., & Victor, I. (1968). Observation learning in cats. *Science, 159*(3822), 1489–1491.

Kapp, B. S., Markgraf, C. G., Schwaber, J. S., & Bilyk-Spafford, T. (1989). The organization of dorsal medullary projections to the central amygdaloid nucleus and parabrachial nuclei in the rabbit. *Neuroscience, 30*(3), 717–732. https://doi.org/10.1016/0306-4522(89)90164-4

Keifer, O. P., Hurt, R. C., Ressler, K. J., & Marvar, P. J. (2015). The physiology of fear: Reconceptualizing the role of the central amygdala in fear learning. *Physiology, 30*(5), 389–401. https://doi.org/10.1152/physiol.00058.2014

Kim, A., Keum, S., & Shin, H. S. (2019). Observational fear behavior in rodents as a model for empathy. *Genes, Brain and Behavior, 18*(1), 8–10. https://doi.org/10.1111/gbb.12521

Knapska, E., Nikolaev, E., Boguszewski, P., Walasek, G., Blaszczyk, J., Kaczmarek, L., & Werka, T. (2006). Between-subject transfer of emotional information evokes specific pattern of amygdala activation. *Proceedings of the National Academy of Sciences, 103*(10), 3858–3862. https://doi.org/10.1073/pnas.0511302103

Kringelbach, M. L., Stark, E. A., Alexander, C., Bornstein, M. H., & Stein, A. (2016). On cuteness: Unlocking the parental brain and beyond. *Trends in Cognitive Sciences, 20*(7), 545–558. https://doi.org/10.1016/j.tics.2016.05.003

Lang, P. J., & Davis, M. (2006). Emotion, motivation, and the brain: Reflex foundations in animal and human research. *Progress in Brain Research, 156*, 3–29. https://doi.org/10.1016/S0079-6123(06)56001-7

Lang, P. J., Davis, M., & Öhman, A. (2000). Fear and anxiety: Animal models and human cognitive psychophysiology. *Journal of Affective Disorders, 61*(3), 137–159. https://doi.org/10.1016/S0165-0327(00)00343-8

LeDoux, J. E. (1996). *The emotional brain.* Simon & Schuster.

LeDoux, J. E. (2003). The emotional brain, fear, and the amygdala. *Cellular and Molecular Neurobiology, 23*(4–5), 727–738. https://doi.org/10.1023/A:1025048802629

LeDoux, J. E., & Hofmann, S. G. (2018). The subjective experience of emotion: A fearful view. *Current Opinion in Behavioral Sciences, 19*, 67–72. https://doi.org/10.1016/j.cobeha.2017.09.011

LeDoux, J. E., Iwata, J., Cicchetti, P., & Reis, D. J. (1988). Different projections of the central amygdaloid nucleus mediate autonomic and behavioral correlates of conditioned fear. *Journal of Neuroscience, 8*(7), 2517–2529. https://doi.org/10.1523/jneurosci.08-07-02517.1988

LeDoux, J. E., & Pine, D. S. (2016). Using neuroscience to help understand fear and anxiety: A two-system framework. *American Journal of Psychiatry, 173*(11), 1083–1093. https://doi.org/10.1176/appi.ajp.2016.16030353

Lench, H. C., Bench, S. W., Darbor, K. E., & Moore, M. (2015). A functionalist manifesto: Goal-related emotions from an evolutionary perspective. *Emotion Review, 7*(1), 90–98. https://doi.org/10.1177/1754073914553001

Lench, H. C., Tibbett, T. P., & Bench, S. W. (2016). Exploring the toolkit of emotion: What do sadness and anger do for us? *Social and Personality Psychology Compass, 10*(1), 11–25. https://doi.org/10.1111/spc3.12229

Leppänen, J. M., & Nelson, C. A. (2012). Early development of fear processing. *Current Directions in Psychological Science, 21*(3), 200–204. https://doi.org/10.1177/0963721411435841

Levenson, R. W. (2014). The autonomic nervous system and emotion. *Emotion Review, 6*(2), 100–112. https://doi.org/10.1177/1754073913512003

Lindström, B., Golkar, A., Jangard, S., Tobler, P. N., & Olsson, A. (2019). Social threat learning transfers to decision making in humans. *Proceedings of the National Academy of Sciences, 116*(10), 4732–4737. https://doi.org/10.1073/pnas.1810180116

Lindström, B., Haaker, J., & Olsson, A. (2018). A common neural network differentially mediates direct and social fear learning. *NeuroImage, 167*, 121–129. https://doi.org/10.1016/j.neuroimage.2017.11.039

Litvin, Y., Blanchard, D. C., & Blanchard, R. J. (2007). Rat 22 kHz ultrasonic vocalizations as alarm cries. *Behavioural Brain Research, 182*(2), 166–172. https://doi.org/10.1016/j.bbr.2006.11.038

Lozier, L. M., Cardinale, E. M., Vanmeter, J. W., & Marsh, A. A. (2014). Mediation of the relationship between callous-unemotional traits and proactive aggression by amygdala response to fear among children with conduct problems. *JAMA Psychiatry, 71*(6), 627–636. https://doi.org/10.1001/jamapsychiatry.2013.4540

Lubbock, T. (2010). *Tom Lubbock: A memoir of living with a brain tumour*. The Guardian. https://www.theguardian.com/books/2010/nov/07/tom-lubbock-brain-tumour-language

Luna, B., Garver, K. E., Urban, T. A., Lazar, N. A., & Sweeney, J. A. (2004). Maturation of cognitive processes from late childhood to adulthood. *Child Development, 75*(5), 1357–1372. https://doi.org/10.1111/j.1467-8624.2004.00745.x

Luo, Q., Holroyd, T., Jones, M., Hendler, T., & Blair, J. (2007). Neural dynamics for facial threat processing as revealed by gamma band synchronization using MEG. *NeuroImage, 34*(2), 839–847. https://doi.org/10.1016/j.neuroimage.2006.09.023

Magee, B., & Elwood, R. W. (2013). Shock avoidance by discrimination learning in the shore crab (*Carcinus maenas*) is consistent with a key criterion for pain. *Journal of Experimental Biology, 216*(3), 353–358. https://doi.org/10.1242/jeb.072041

Marks, I. f. M., & Nesse, R. M. (1994). Fear and fitness: An evolutionary analysis of anxiety disorders. *Ethology and Sociobiology, 15*(5–6), 247–261. https://doi.org/10.1016/0162-3095(94)90002-7

Marsh, A. A. (2013). What can we learn about emotion by studying psychopathy? *Frontiers in Human Neuroscience, 7*, 181. https://doi.org/10.3389/fnhum.2013.00181

Marsh, A. A. (2016). Understanding amygdala responsiveness to fearful expressions through the lens of psychopathy and altruism. *Journal of Neuroscience Research, 94*(6), 513–525. https://doi.org/10.1002/jnr.23668

Marsh, A. A., Adams, R. B., & Kleck, R. E. (2005). Why do fear and anger look the way they do? Form and social function in facial expressions. *Personality and Social Psychology Bulletin, 31*(1), 73–86. https://doi.org/10.1177/0146167204271306

Marsh, A. A., & Ambady, N. (2007). The influence of the fear facial expression on prosocial responding. *Cognition and Emotion, 21*(2), 225–247. https://doi.org/10.1080/02699930600652234

Marsh, A. A., Ambady, N., & Kleck, R. E. (2005). The effects of fear and anger facial expressions on approach- and avoidance-related behaviors. *Emotion, 5*(1), 119–124. https://doi.org/10.1037/1528-3542.5.1.119

Marsh, A. A., & Blair, R. J. R. (2008). Deficits in facial affect recognition among antisocial populations: A meta-analysis. *Neuroscience and Biobehavioral Reviews, 32*(3), 454–465. https://doi.org/10.1016/j.neubiorev.2007.08.003

Marsh, A. A., Stoycos, S. A., Brethel-Haurwitz, K. M., Robinson, P., VanMeter, J. W., & Cardinale, E. M. (2014). Neural and cognitive characteristics of extraordinary altruists. *Proceedings of the National Academy of Sciences, 111*(42), 15036–15041. https://doi.org/10.1073/pnas.1408440111

Martínez-García, F., & Lanuza, E. (2018). Evolution of vertebrate survival circuits. *Current Opinion in Behavioral Sciences, 24*, 113–123. https://doi.org/10.1016/j.cobeha.2018.06.012

McDonald, A. J., & Mascagni, F. (1996). Cortico-cortical and cortico-amygdaloid projections of the rat occipital cortex: A Phaseolus vulgaris leucoagglutinin study. *Neuroscience, 71*(1), 37–54. https://doi.org/10.1016/0306-4522(95)00416-5

Meloni, E. G., Jackson, A., Gerety, L. P., Cohen, B. M., & Carlezon, W. A. (2006). Role of the bed nucleus of the stria terminalis (BST) in the expression of conditioned fear. *Annals of the New York Academy of Sciences, 1071*, 538–541. https://doi.org/10.1196/annals.1364.059

Mineka, S., & Cook, M. (1984). Observational conditioning of snake fear in rhesus monkeys. *Journal of Abnormal Psychology, 93*(4), 355–372. https://doi.org/10.1037/0021-843X.95.4.307

Mobbs, D., Yu, R., Rowe, J. B., Eich, H., FeldmanHall, O., & Dalgleish, T. (2010). Neural activity associated with monitoring the oscillating threat value of a tarantula. *Proceedings of the National Academy of Sciences, 107*(47), 20582–20586. https://doi.org/10.1073/pnas.1009076107

Moore, C., Mealiea, J., Garon, N., & Povinelli, D. J. (2007). The development of body self-awareness. *Infancy, 11*(2), 157–174. https://doi.org/10.1111/j.1532-7078.2007.tb00220.x

Moreno, N., & González, A. (2007). Evolution of the amygdaloid complex in vertebrates, with special reference to the anamnio-amniotic transition. *Journal of Anatomy, 211*(2), 151–163. https://doi.org/10.1111/j.1469-7580.2007.00780.x

Mujica-Parodi, L. R., Strey, H. H., Frederick, B., Savoy, R., Cox, D., Botanov, Y., Tolkunov, D., Rubin, D., & Weber, J. (2009). Chemosensory cues to conspecific emotional stress activate amygdala in humans. *PLoS ONE, 4*(7), e6415. https://doi.org/10.1371/journal.pone.0006415

Murray, T. G., Zeil, J., & Magrath, R. D. (2017). Sounds of modified flight feathers reliably signal danger in a pigeon. *Current Biology, 27*(22), 3520–3525.e4. https://doi.org/10.1016/j.cub.2017.09.068

Nesse, R. M. (2001). On the difficulty of defining disease: A Darwinian perspective. *Medicine, Health Care, and Philosophy, 4*(1), 37–46. https://doi.org/10.1023/A:1009938513897

Nicolaides, N. C., Galata, Z., Kino, T., Chrousos, G. P., & Charmandari, E. (2010). The human glucocorticoid receptor: Molecular basis of biologic function. *Steroids, 75*(1), 1–12. https://doi.org/10.1016/j.steroids.2009.09.002

Niel, L., & Weary, D. M. (2006). Behavioural responses of rats to gradual-fill carbon dioxide euthanasia and reduced oxygen concentrations. *Applied Animal Behaviour Science, 100*(3–4), 295–308. https://doi.org/10.1016/j.applanim.2005.12.001

O'Connell, L. A., & Hofmann, H. A. (2012). Evolution of a vertebrate social decision-making network. *Science, 336*(6085), 1154–1157. https://doi.org/10.1126/science.1218889

Oler, J. A., Tromp, D. P. M., Fox, A. S., Kovner, R., Davidson, R. J., Alexander, A. L., McFarlin, D. R., Birn, R. M., Berg, B. E., DeCampo, D. M., Kalin, N. H., & Fudge, J. L. (2017). Connectivity between the central nucleus of the amygdala and the bed nucleus of the stria terminalis in the non-human primate: Neuronal tract tracing and developmental neuroimaging studies. *Brain Structure and Function, 222*(1), 21–39. https://doi.org/10.1007/s00429-016-1198-9

Olsson, A., McMahon, K., Papenberg, G., Zaki, J., Bolger, N., & Ochsner, K. N. (2016). Vicarious fear learning depends on empathic appraisals and trait empathy. *Psychological Science, 27*(1), 25–33. https://doi.org/10.1177/0956797615604124

Olsson, A., Nearing, K. I., & Phelps, E. A. (2007). Learning fears by observing others: The neural systems of social fear transmission. *Social Cognitive and Affective Neuroscience, 2*(1), 3–11. https://doi.org/10.1093/scan/nsm005

Olsson, A., & Phelps, E. A. (2007). Social learning of fear. *Nature Neuroscience, 10*(9), 1095–1102. https://doi.org/10.1038/nn1968

Pajolla, G. P., Crippa, G. E., Corrêa, S. A. L., Moreira, K. B., Tavares, R. F., & Corrêa, F. M. A. (2001). The lateral hypothalamus is involved in the pathway mediating the hypotensive response to cingulate cortex-cholinergic stimulation. *Cellular and Molecular Neurobiology, 21*(4), 341–356. https://doi.org/10.1023/A:1012650021137

Papini, M. R., Penagos-Corzo, J. C., & Pérez-Acosta, A. M. (2019). Avian emotions: Comparative perspectives on fear and frustration. *Frontiers in Psychology, 9*(Jan), 433390. https://doi.org/10.3389/fpsyg.2018.02707

Parr, L. A., Waller, B. M., Vick, S. J., & Bard, K. A. (2007). Classifying chimpanzee facial expressions using muscle action. *Emotion, 7*(1), 172–181. https://doi.org/10.1037/1528-3542.7.1.172

Parsana, A. J., Li, N., & Brown, T. H. (2012). Positive and negative ultrasonic social signals elicit opposing firing patterns in rat amygdala. *Behavioural Brain Research, 226*(1), 77–86. https://doi.org/10.1016/j.bbr.2011.08.040

Paulhus, D. L., & Vazire, S. (2007). The self-report method. In R. W. Robins, R. C. Fraley, & R. F. Krueger (Eds.), *Handbook of research methods in personality psychology* (pp. 224–239). Guilford Press. https://doi.org/10.1002/0470013435.ch6

Paulraj, S. R., Schendel, K., Curran, B., Dronkers, N. F., & Baldo, J. V. (2018). Role of the left hemisphere in visuospatial working memory. *Journal of Neurolinguistics, 48*, 133–141. https://doi.org/10.1016/j.jneuroling.2018.04.006

Pereira, A. G., Farias, M., & Moita, M. A. (2020). Thalamic, cortical, and amygdala involvement in the processing of a natural sound cue of danger. *PLoS Biology, 18*(5), 1–15. https://doi.org/10.1371/journal.pbio.3000674

Pessoa, L., & Adolphs, R. (2010). Emotion processing and the amygdala: From a "low road" to "many roads" of evaluating biological significance. *Nature Reviews Neuroscience, 11*(11), 773–782. https://doi.org/10.1038/nrn2920

Pfeiffer, W. (1977). The distribution of fright reaction and alarm substance cells in fishes. *Copeia, 1977*(4), 653–665.

Phillips, M. L., Young, A. W., Scott, S. K., Calder, A. J., Andrew, C., Giampietro, V., Williams, S. C. R., Bullmore, E. T., Brammer, M., & Gray, J. A. (1998). Neural responses to facial and vocal expressions of fear and disgust. *Proceedings of the Royal Society B: Biological Sciences, 265*(1408), 1809–1817. https://doi.org/10.1098/rspb.1998.0506

Pitcher, D. J., & Ungerleider, L. G. (2021). Evidence for a third visual pathway specialized for social perception. *Trends in Cognitive Sciences, 25*(2), 100–110. https://doi.org/10.1016/j.tics.2020.11.006

Pitkänen, A., Savander, V., & LeDoux, J. E. (1997). Organization of intra-amygdaloid circuitries in the rat: An emerging framework for understanding functions of the amygdala. *Trends in Neurosciences, 20*(11), 517–523. https://doi.org/10.1016/S0166-2236(97)01125-9

Portfors, C. V. (2018). Processing of ultrasonic vocalizations in the auditory midbrain of mice. In Brudzynski, S. M. (Ed.), *Handbook of ultrasonic vocalization* (pp. 73–82). Elsevier.

Price, J. L., & Amaral, D. G. (1981). An autoradiographic study of the projections of the central nucleus of the monkey amygdala. *Journal of Neuroscience, 1*(11), 1242–1259. https://doi.org/10.1523/jneurosci.01-11-01242.1981

Quagliato, L. A., Freire, R. C., & Nardi, A. E. (2018). The role of acid-sensitive ion channels in panic disorder: A systematic review of animal studies and meta-analysis of human studies. *Translational Psychiatry, 8*(1), 185. https://doi.org/10.1038/s41398-018-0238-z

Radley, J., Morilak, D., Viau, V., & Campeau, S. (2015). Chronic stress and brain plasticity: Mechanisms underlying adaptive and maladaptive changes and implications for stress-related CNS disorders. *Neuroscience and Biobehavioral Reviews, 58*, 79–91. https://doi.org/10.1016/j.neubiorev.2015.06.018

Rajhans, P., Altvater-Mackensen, N., Vaish, A., & Grossmann, T. (2016). Children's altruistic behavior in context: The role of emotional responsiveness and culture. *Scientific Reports, 6*(1), 24089. https://doi.org/10.1038/srep24089

Reppucci, C. J., & Petrovich, G. D. (2016). Organization of connections between the amygdala, medial prefrontal cortex, and lateral hypothalamus: A single and double retrograde tracing study in rats. *Brain Structure and Function, 221*(6), 2937–2962. https://doi.org/10.1007/s00429-015-1081-0

Rollin, B. E. (1986). Animal pain. In M. W. Fox & L. D. Mickley (Eds.), *Advances in animal welfare science* (2nd ed., pp. 91–106). Springer.

Roseman, I. J. (1984). Cognitive determinants of emotion: A structural theory. In P. Shaver (Ed.), *Review of personality in social psychology* (pp. 11–36). Sage Publications.

Rosen, J. B., Hitchcock, J. M., Sananes, C. B., Miserendino, M. J. D., & Davis, M. (1991). A direct projection from the central nucleus of the amygdala to the acoustic startle pathway: Anterograde and retrograde tracing studies. *Behavioral Neuroscience, 105*(6), 817–825. https://doi.org/10.1037/0735-7044.105.6.817

Sacco, D. F., & Hugenberg, K. (2011). Fear expressions: Function and form. In A. D. Gervaise (Ed.), *Psychology of fear: New research* (pp. 69–82). Nova Science.

Sadananda, M., Wöhr, M., & Schwarting, R. K. W. (2008). Playback of 22-kHz and 50-kHz ultrasonic vocalizations induces differential c-fos expression in rat brain. *Neuroscience Letters, 435*(1), 17–23. https://doi.org/10.1016/j.neulet.2008.02.002

Sangiamo, D. T., Warren, M. R., & Neunuebel, J. P. (2020). Ultrasonic signals associated with different types of social behavior of mice. *Nature Neuroscience, 23*(3), 411–422. https://doi.org/10.1038/s41593-020-0584-z

Sapolsky, R. M., Romero, L. M., & Munck, A. U. (2000). How do glucocorticoids influence stress responses? Integrating permissive, suppressive, stimulatory, and preparative actions. *Endocrine Reviews, 21*(1), 55–89. https://doi.org/10.1210/er.21.1.55

Sauter, D. A., Eisner, F., Ekman, P., & Scott, S. K. (2010). Cross-cultural recognition of basic emotions through nonverbal emotional vocalizations. *Proceedings of the National Academy of Sciences, 107*(6), 2408–2412. https://doi.org/10.1073/pnas.1508604112

Schenkel, R. (1967). Submission: Its features and function in the wolf and dog. *American Zoologist, 7*(2), 319–329.

Schruers, K. R. J., Van De Mortel, H., Overbeek, T., & Griez, E. (2004). Symptom profiles of natural and laboratory panic attacks. *Acta Neuropsychiatrica, 16*(2), 101–106. https://doi.org/10.1111/j.0924-2708.2004.0084.x

Seyfarth, R. M., Cheney, D. L., & Marler, P. (1980). Monkey responses to three different alarm calls: Evidence of predator classification and semantic communication. *Science, 210*(4471), 801–803. https://doi.org/10.1126/science.7433999

Shackman, A. J., & Fox, A. S. (2016). Contributions of the central extended amygdala to fear and anxiety. *Journal of Neuroscience, 36*(31), 8050–8063. https://doi.org/10.1523/JNEUROSCI.0982-16.2016

Siegel, E. H., Sands, M. K., Van den Noortgate, W., Condon, P., Chang, Y., Dy, J., Quigley, K. S., & Feldman Barrett, L. (2018). Emotion fingerprints or emotion populations? A meta-analytic investigation of autonomic features of emotion categories. *Psychological Bulletin, 144*(4), 343–393.

Smeets, M. A. M., Rosing, E. A. E., Jacobs, D. M., van Velzen, E., Koek, J. H., Blonk, C., Gortemaker, I., Eidhof, M. B., Markovitch, B., de Groot, J., & Semin, G. R. (2020). Chemical fingerprints of emotional body odor. *Metabolites, 10*(3), 84. https://doi.org/10.3390/metabo10030084

Smith, & Price, G. R. (1973). The logic of animal conflict. *Nature, 246*(5427), 15–18. https://doi.org/10.1038/246015a0

Smith, W., & Harrap, S. B. (1997). Behavioural and cardiovascular responses of rats to euthanasia using carbon dioxide gas. *Laboratory Animals, 31*(4), 337–346. https://doi.org/10.1258/002367797780596130

Solomon, R. L., & Wynne, L. C. (1953). Traumatic avoidance learning: Acquisition in normal dogs. *Psychological Monographs: General and Applied, 67*(4), 1–19. https://doi.org/10.1037/h0093649

Somerville, L. H., Whalen, P. J., & Kelley, W. M. (2010). Human bed nucleus of the stria terminalis indexes hypervigilant threat monitoring. *Biological Psychiatry, 68*(5), 416–424. https://doi.org/10.1016/j.biopsych.2010.04.002.Human

Speedie, N., & Gerlai, R. (2008). Alarm substance induced behavioral responses in zebrafish (*Danio rerio*). *Behavioural Brain Research, 188*(1), 168–177. https://doi.org/10.1016/j.bbr.2007.10.031

Sprengelmeyer, R., Young, A. W., Schroeder, U., Grossenbacher, P. G., Federlein, J., Büttner, T., & Przuntek, H. (1999). Knowing no fear. *Proceedings of the Royal Society B: Biological Sciences, 266*(1437), 2451–2456. https://doi.org/10.1098/rspb.1999.0945

Stinson, F. S., Dawson, D. S., Chou, S. P., Smith, S., Goldtein, R. B., Ruan, W. J., & Grant, B. F. (2007). The epidemiology of DSM-IV specific phobia in the USA: Results from the National Epidemiologic Survey on Alcohol and Related Conditions. *Psychological Medicine, 37*(7), 1047–1059. https://doi.org/10.1017/S0033291707000086

Suh, G. S. B., Wong, A. M., Hergarden, A. C., Wang, J. W., Simon, A. F., Benzer, S., Axel, R., & Anderson, D. J. (2004). A single population of olfactory sensory neurons mediates an innate avoidance behaviour in Drosophila. *Nature, 431*(7010), 854–859. https://doi.org/10.1038/nature02980

Susskind, J. M., Lee, D. H., Cusi, A., Feiman, R., Grabski, W., & Anderson, A. K. (2008). Expressing fear enhances sensory acquisition. *Nature Neuroscience, 11*(7), 843–850. https://doi.org/10.1038/nn.2138

Taugher, R. J., Lu, Y., Wang, Y., Kreple, C. J., Ghobbeh, A., Fan, R., Sowers, L. P., & Wemmie, J. a. (2014). The bed nucleus of the stria terminalis is critical for anxiety-related behavior evoked by CO_2 and acidosis. *The Journal of Neuroscience, 34*(31), 10247–10255. https://doi.org/10.1523/JNEUROSCI.1680-14.2014

Templeton, C. N., Greene, E., & Davis, K. (2005). Behavior: Allometry of alarm calls: Black-capped chickadees encode information about predator size. *Science, 308*(5730), 1934–1937. https://doi.org/10.1126/science.1108841

Thayer, J. F., & Lane, R. D. (2009). Claude Bernard and the heart-brain connection: Further elaboration of a model of neurovisceral integration. *Neuroscience and Biobehavioral Reviews, 33*(2), 81–88. https://doi.org/10.1016/j.neubiorev.2008.08.004

Tovote, P., Fadok, J. P., & Luthi, A. (2015). Neuronal circuits for fear and anxiety. *Nature Reviews Neuroscience, 16*(6), 317–331. https://doi.org/10.1038/nrn3945

Vale, W., Spiess, J., Rivier, C., & Rivier, J. (1981). Characterization of a 41-residue ovine hypothalamic peptide that stimulates secretion of corticotropin and β-endorphin. *Science, 213*(4514), 1394–1397. https://doi.org/10.1097/00006254-198205000-00013

van Vulpen, E. H. S., & Verwer, R. W. H. (1989). Organization of projections from the mediodorsal nucleus of the thalamus to the basolateral complex of the amygdala in the rat. *Brain Research, 500*, 389–394. https://doi.org/10.1016/0006-8993(89)90337-5

Varley, R. A., Klessinger, N. J. C., Romanowski, C. A. J., & Siegal, M. (2005). Agrammatic but numerate. *Proceedings of the National Academy of Sciences, 102*(9), 3519–3524. https://doi.org/10.1073/pnas.0407470102

Walker, D. L., & Davis, M. (2008). Role of the extended amygdala in short-duration versus sustained fear: A tribute to Dr. Lennart Heimer. *Brain Structure and Function, 213*(1–2), 29–42. https://doi.org/10.1007/s00429-008-0183-3

Walters, E. T., Carew, T. J., & Kandel, E. R. (1981). Associative learning in Aplysia: Evidence for conditioned fear. *Science, 211*(4481), 504–506.

Wang, S., Yu, R., Tyszka, J. M., Zhen, S., Kovach, C., Sun, S., Huang, Y., Hurlemann, R., Ross, I. B., Chung, J. M., Mamelak, A. N., Adolphs, R., & Rutishauser, U. (2017). The human amygdala parametrically encodes the intensity of specific facial emotions and their categorical ambiguity. *Nature Communications, 8*, 1–13. https://doi.org/10.1038/ncomms14821

Willems, R. M., Benn, Y., Hagoort, P., Toni, I., & Varley, R. (2011). Communicating without a functioning language system: Implications for the role of language in mentalizing. *Neuropsychologia, 49*(11), 3130–3135. https://doi.org/10.1016/j.neuropsychologia.2011.07.023

Yajima, Y., Hayashi, Y., & Yoshi, N. (1980). The midbrain central gray substance as a highly sensitive neural structure for the production of ultrasonic vocalization in the rat. *Brain Research, 198*(2), 446–452. https://doi.org/10.1016/0006-8993(80)90759-3

Yusufishaq, S., & Rosenkranz, J. A. (2013). Post-weaning social isolation impairs observational fear conditioning. *Behavioural Brain Research, 242*(1), 142–149. https://doi.org/10.1016/j.bbr.2012.12.050

Zhao, Z., & Davis, M. (2004). Fear-potentiated startle in rats is mediated by neurons in the deep layers of the superior colliculus/deep mesencephalic nucleus of the rostral midbrain through the glutamate non-NMDA receptors. *Journal of Neuroscience, 24*(46), 10326–10334. https://doi.org/10.1523/JNEUROSCI.2758-04.2004

Ziemann, A. E., Allen, J. E., Dahdaleh, N. S., Drebot, I. I., Coryell, M. W., Wunsch, A. M., Lynch, C. M., Faraci, F. M., Howard, M. A., Welsh, M. J., & Wemmie, J. A. (2009). The amygdala is a chemosensor that detects carbon dioxide and acidosis to elicit fear behavior. *Cell, 139*(5), 1012–1021. https://doi.org/10.1016/j.cell.2009.10.029

CHAPTER 27

The Evolutionary Functions of Sadness: The Cognitive and Social Benefits of Negative Affect

Joseph P. Forgas

Abstract

What is the point of sadness? The adaptive benefits of other negative emotions such as anger, disgust, and fear have long been recognized, yet the evolutionary functions of sadness remain poorly understood, even though many practicing psychologists deal with sadness and depression. This chapter offers an evolutionary explanation for the adaptive benefits of sadness, as an important signal that influences our thinking and judgments. Extensive experimental research now suggests that induced sadness can promote improved functioning on various cognitive and social tasks, including memory performance, judgments, inferences, the detection of deception, social perception, interpersonal communication, and strategic communication and interactions. These results support theoretical models that predict that negative affect promotes a more accommodative, vigilant, and externally focused thinking strategy. The relevance of these findings for affect-cognition theories will be discussed, and the practical implications of this research for improving social thinking and performance in applied fields will be considered.

Key Words: sadness, affect and cognition, affect infusion, mood effect, social behavior infusion

Introduction

Fluctuating affective states are ever-present in our lives, and they color and filter everything we think and do during our waking hours (Zajonc, 2000). This chapter deals with the adaptive, evolutionary role of negative affective states in guiding our reactions to the manifold challenges of everyday life, and in particular, the functional benefits that flow from the temporary experience of sadness. In our discussion we will be guided by evolutionary theorizing that assumes that affective reactions serve important adaptive functions, operating like functional "mind modules" that spring into action in response to environmental contingencies (Al-Shawaf & Lewis, 2017; Buss, 2019; Forgas et al., 2007; Frijda, 1986; Tooby & Cosmides, 1992). In particular, the chapter will survey a range of experimental studies offering convergent, and somewhat counterintuitive, evidence for the often useful and adaptive consequences of mild sadness for social cognition, judgments, motivation, and interpersonal behavior.

It is remarkable that in empirical psychology, affect has long remained the least understood aspect of the traditional historical tripartite division of the human mind into cognition, affect, and conation (Hilgard, 1980). For millenia, affect was considered a primitive, archaic, and dangerous force that has an invasive quality capable of compromising rational thinking and behavior (Harari, 2014; Koestler, 1967). In Western philosophy the view that affect is dangerous and primitive can be traced to the works of Plato. This principle also informed Freud's psychoanalytic speculations, which also emphasized the view of affect as a primeval invasive force that requires considerable psychological energy to be effectively controlled.

Thanks to advances in neurophysiology and evolutionary psychology, this view has undergone a fundamental revision in recent decades. As a result of advances in neuroanatomy, we now know that affect often serves as an essential and adaptive input determining how we respond to social situations (Adolphs & Damasio, 2001; Forgas, 1995, 2002; Frijda, 1986; Zajonc, 2000). After decades of neglect, renewed psychological interest in the empirical study of affective phenomena emerged in the early 1980s. Frijda (1986), Adolphs and Damasio (2001), and Zajonc (1980) were among the first to recognize that affective reactions often constitute the primary and dominant dimension of responding to social situations (Unkelbach et al., 2008), operating as an adaptive signal that guides subsequent reactions. Affect also plays a critical role in organizing how people cognitively represent and respond to everyday social experiences (Forgas, 1979). Instead of mentally representing social situations in terms of their objective, descriptive features, implicit representations of the social world are primarily organized in terms of how people feel about them: many social "stimuli can cohere as a category even when they have nothing in common other than the emotional responses they elicit" (Niedenthal & Halberstadt, 2000, p. 381).

Negative Affect

Negative affect and sadness in particular have long represented a major challenge for evolutionary theorizing (Andrews & Thompson, 2009). Since positive affective states are hedonistically desirable and often provide obvious positive feedback when engaging in adaptive behaviors, their evolutionary functions could be relatively easily discerned. The incessant search for happiness has been a recurring theme for philosophers for centuries (Haidt, 2007). The "hedonic principle" of seeking pleasure and avoiding pain was long considered the quintessential "simple and sovereign principle" to explain all human behavior (Allport, 1985). A more sophisticated version of the hedonic principle was developed by utilitarian philosophers like Jeremy Bentham and David Hume, who thought that rational humans may use a "hedonistic calculus" to calibrate the likely positive and negative consequences of alternative courses of action (Haidt, 2007). Our own age is characterized by perhaps the most unrelenting individual and cultural pursuit of happiness. As any visit to a bookstore will confirm, there are shelves full of self-help books offering strategies to achieve happiness and avoid pain and sadness. There appears to be a strange obsession in modern Western cultures with the emphasis on the benefits of positive affective states, and the rejection of negative affect as undesirable and dispensable. One consequence is that the adaptive evolutionary functions of negative affective states, and sadness in particular, remain poorly understood and often denied. Partly to redress this imbalance, this chapter will focus on the evolutionary functions and benefits of one of the most common, yet elusive negative affective states: sadness.

The Benefits of Sadness

Despite the enduring human quest for happiness, it is intriguing that the emotional repertoire of *Homo sapiens* is heavily skewed toward negative emotions. Four of the six basic emotions are negative—fear, anger, disgust, and sadness (Ekman & Cordaro, 2011). Some of the adaptive functions of these negative emotions in our ancestral environment are now relatively well understood (Al-Shawaf et al., 2015). Fear is instrumental to avoiding dangerous situations, anger helps to focus attention and energy on overcoming obstacles, and disgust plays a key role in avoiding contamination and illness.

But what is the adaptive function of sadness, perhaps the most common, ubiquitous, and problematic of our negative emotions? Dealing with sadness is probably the major challenge for most professional psychologists and counselors, and much of the psychology profession is employed in managing and alleviating sadness. But can sadness be controlled or eliminated, and even if this was possible, is it desirable to remove all sadness from our lives? Without the experience of sadness, the meaning of happiness would not be quite the same. More to the point, the important adaptive functions of sadness remain puzzling and poorly understood (Andrews & Thompson, 2009; Ciarrochi et al., 2006). Should we view sadness as a "problem emotion" that must be controlled and managed, when other more intense negative emotions such as fear, anger, and disgust are accepted as having some adaptive function?

The Cultural Context

In previous periods of human history, experiences of sadness and melancholia were considered legitimate and even useful affective states that deserved to be cultivated (Sedikides et al., 2006). Many great works of art in Western civilization depict experiences of sadness, loss, and tragedy as instructive and worthy of rehearsal. Sadness and loss are central themes from the classic Greek tragedies through Shakespeare's works and the dramas of Chekhov, Ibsen, and the great novels of the 19th century, including Tolstoy, Flaubert, Dostoyevsky, Dumas, Dickens, and Balzac. Such overarching concern with the exploration of the landscape of sadness, loss, and melancholia cannot be coincidental. Rehearsing and familiarizing ourselves with tales of tragedy and misadventure have been considered instructive and ennobling in previous epochs. These great works tell us something fundamental about the inevitability of unhappiness, and the need to prepare for it and learn to cope with it. It is only in the modern era that the legitimacy of dwelling on misfortune has become questionable, and a veritable industry often driven by marketing and advertising objectives has grown up promoting the cult of positivity. Arguably, the elimination of the earlier and more balanced view of the landscape of human affectivity in our culture has not been universally beneficial.

Evolutionary Functions

Like all affective states, sadness functions as a built-in evolutionary signal that promotes adaptive changes in the behavior of the organism, and can also directly trigger communicative displays that are instantly recognized by others (Ekman & O'Sullivan, 1991). There is now some evidence that most affective states, and sadness in particular, directly activate facial expressions that are universal and recognized in all human cultures (Frijda, 1986), suggesting the possibility of a direct and bidirectional neural link between affective experiences and corresponding facial expressions.

Accordingly, in a highly social species such as humans, the experience and display of sadness likely function as a powerful signal to others, communicating a withdrawal from competitive and potentially costly activities (Andrews & Thomson, 2009; Buss, 2019). In addition, sadness displays also invite and elicit empathy, support, and care from the immediate network of those around us (Buss, 2019; Watson & Andrews, 2002).

Even more important for our purposes is the internal signaling function of sadness. Experiencing and displaying sadness operate as an internal cue to disengage from and abandon costly and potentially hopeless activities that might consume considerable resources without much hope of a positive outcome. In a related manner, the onset of sadness may be an important corrective signal to counteract the habitual human tendency for optimism and overconfidence that characterizes many human social endeavors (von Hippel, 2018). By producing a more realistic and less optimistic assessment of situational contingencies, sadness helps to promote a more objective and realistic assessment, redirecting our efforts into potentially more promising endeavors (Nesse & Williams, 1994; Stevens & Price, 1996).

It is only in the past couple of decades that experimental research has demonstrated the specific mechanisms that link sadness to cognitive and behavioral outcomes. Two distinct kinds of effects have been identified. The affective experience of sadness reliably triggers preferential access to more negative and pessimistic contents from memory, typically resulting in a more downbeat and cautious cognitive and judgmental style. We may identify this pattern of affect infusion into thinking as the adaptive consequence of sadness on the *content* of cognition. The second spontaneous effect of sadness is its influence on the *process* of cognition, automatically triggering a more externally attentive, accommodating, concrete, and detail-oriented information-processing style (Bless & Fiedler, 2006; Schwarz, 1990). We can refer to this second evolutionary effect of sadness as a *processing* or *cognitive tuning* function—subtly shifting the information-processing strategies employed along a processing continuum (Schwarz, 1990).

We will review empirical evidence to document both kinds of adaptive functions here. Consistent with evolutionary theorizing, the experiments described will illustrate that the temporary experience of sadness can produce important adaptive benefits by promoting selective access to more negative information, promoting more cautious and pessimistic reactions on a variety of tasks.

Further, the evidence will also show that the adaptive benefits of negative affect, and sadness in particular, can be linked to specific changes in information-processing strategies. Several experiments found that sadness produces important functional consequences by spontaneously triggering cognitive, motivational, and behavioral strategies that are well suited to dealing with the requirements of more demanding social situations (Buss, 2019; Frijda, 1986).

Of course, this is not to suggest that negative affect is always beneficial and that positive affect has no adaptive consequences. We know that positive affect often promotes creativity, flexibility, and cooperation, and improves life satisfaction (Forgas, 1994, 1998a, 1998b; 2002; Forgas & George, 2001; Frederickson, 2009). The point is that different affective states, by spontaneously triggering different information-processing strategies, recruit a thinking style that is most appropriate in a given situation (Al-Shawaf et al., 2019; Bless & Fiedler, 2006; Forgas & Eich, 2013), consistent with the view that affective states "exist for the sake of signalling states of the world that have to be responded to" (Frijda, 1988, p. 354).

Many of the evolutionary consequences of sadness are subtle, automatic, and unconscious. It is the influence of moods rather than distinct emotions that will be of greatest interest here, as sad moods are more common, more enduring, and typically produce more uniform and reliable cognitive and behavioral consequences than do more intense, conscious, and context-specific emotions (Forgas, 2002, 2006). Moods are low-intensity, diffuse, and relatively enduring affective states without a salient antecedent cause and therefore little conscious cognitive content. In contrast, emotions are more intense, short-lived, and usually have a definite cause and conscious cognitive content (Forgas, 1995, 2002). We will next briefly consider the most recent theoretical approaches linking sad affect to cognition and behavior, and review a number of experiments demonstrating the beneficial effects of negative affective states for cognition, motivation, and interpersonal behavior. The role of different information-processing strategies in mediating these effects will receive special attention. Contemporary theories linking affect to cognition and behavior identify two kinds of affective influences: (1)

informational or content effects, when an affective state directly influences the valence of information people access and use; and (2) *processing effects*, when affect influences the way information is processed.

Informational and Content Effects

Sad affect has an adaptive informational effect on thinking and behavior by selectively triggering more negative thoughts, memories, and associations, and so producing a more hesitant and cautious response style. It is unfortunate that few early experiments directly explored affective influences on cognition and behavior. In one early study, Feshbach and Singer (1957) found that attempts to suppress fear paradoxically increased the tendency to perceive "another person as fearful and anxious" (p. 286), suggesting that the "suppression of fear facilitates the tendency to project fear onto another social object" (p. 286). Using a conditioning framework, Razran (1940) found that people made more positive judgments about the same political messages when feeling good (after a free lunch!) rather than feeling bad (exposed to unpleasant stimuli), something politicians have long suspected. Clore and Byrne (1974) also used a classical conditioning approach to show that affective states can influence unrelated interpersonal judgments and behaviors. More recently, information-processing theories have been proposed to explain how affective states can have an adaptive, evolutionary influence on coloring the way people perceive and respond to social situations. Two complementary theories have been proposed to explain this process of *affect infusion*, a memory-based *affect priming* mechanism, and the inferential *affect-as-information* model.

Affect Priming

The affect-priming account (Bower, 1981) argues that affective experiences are embedded in an associative network of memory representations. The experience of an affective state such as sadness will thus selectively prime associated memory contents previously linked to that affect, and such activated constructs are more likely to be spontaneously retrieved and used in subsequent constructive cognitive tasks. Several early studies confirmed that people induced to feel good or bad tended to selectively remember more mood-congruent details from their childhood as well as their recent past (Bower, 1981). Such affect infusion can also influence how people interpret social behaviors (Forgas et al., 1984) and form impressions of others (Forgas & Bower, 1987). This memory-based affect infusion caused by affect-priming mechanisms occurs most reliably when a task requires open, constructive processing promoting more extensive retrieval processes, as is the case with many judgments, inferences, associations, impression formation, and interpersonal behaviors (e.g., Bower & Forgas, 2001; Forgas, 2002; Forgas & Eich, 2013).

The Inferential/Misattribution Model

The complementary *affect-as-information* model proposed by Schwarz and Clore (1988; Clore et al., 2001) suggests instead that "rather than computing a judgment on the basis of recalled features of a target, individuals may . . . ask themselves: 'how do I feel about it? [and] in doing so, they may mistake feelings due to a pre-existing state as a reaction to the target" (Schwarz, 1990, p. 529). Thus, affect congruence is caused by a simple inferential error, as people misattribute a preexisting affective state as indicating an evaluative reaction to an unrelated social stimulus. This model, like previous affect-conditioning theories (Clore & Byrne, 1974), predicts a simple, blind temporal association between prevailing affect and an unrelated experience. Such affective misattribution is most likely when "the task is of little personal relevance, when little other information is available, when problems are too complex to be solved systematically, and when time or attentional resources are limited" (Fiedler, 2001, p. 175). This happens, for example, when people are unexpectedly asked to perform personally uninvolving off-the-cuff judgments (Forgas & Moylan, 1987; Schwarz & Clore, 1988).

Integrative Theories
Adaptive affect infusion into thinking, judgments, and behavior depends on whether a person needs to engage in constructive, open thinking that requires the use of new information to construct a response. The Affect Infusion Model (AIM; Forgas, 1995, 2002) argues affective influences on cognition depend on the processing styles adopted in different situations. When a person already has a preexisting response to a familiar situation that can be directly accessed without any online evaluation, or when a response is predetermined by a salient motivational objective (e.g., try to look good at a job interview), according to the AIM we should not expect any affect infusion to occur. Affect infusion into thinking and behavior is only likely when some constructive processing is required. Affective states such as sadness should only bias the valence of thinking when either elaborative (substantive) or heuristic processing occurs. The AIM also makes a counterintuitive prediction, now confirmed in numerous experiments: affect infusion should be increased when more lengthy, extensive, and constructive thinking is required to deal with a more complex, unusual, or unfamiliar target or situation (Forgas & Eich, 2013).

The Benefits of Negative Affect Infusion
Sadness—typically a spontaneous reaction to challenging or difficult situations—may thus have important beneficial effects in many situations by automatically promoting access to more negative, pessimistic, and adverse information. Experiments showing such an effect typically employ a two-stage procedure. Participants are first induced to experience a sad, negative affective state (for example, exposure to sad vs. happy movies, music, autobiographic memories, or positive or negative feedback). Once affect is induced, responses to a subsequent memory, or judgmental or behavioral task, are evaluated. Results showed that people spend longer reading and encoding mood-congruent material, linking it into a richer network of primed associations, and, as a result, they are better able to remember such information (see Bower & Forgas, 2001). These effects occur because "concepts, words, themes, and rules of inference that are associated with that emotion will become primed and highly available" and function as "interpretive filters of reality" (Bower, 1981, p. 395).

Affect Infusion in Memory and Judgments
The negativity bias associated with sad mood promotes a more pessimistic and careful assessment of the ongoing situation. The fundamental finding is that people in a sad mood are better at selectively remembering negative information and information first encoded in a negative mood (Bower, 1981; Fiedler, 2001; Forgas, 1995). Implicit tests confirm a similar bias; for example, people in a sad mood are more likely to complete word stems (e.g., *can . . .*) with negative than with positive words (e.g., *cancer* versus *candy*; Ruiz-Caballero, & Gonzalez, 1994). Selective negative affect infusion also influences the valence of associations. When asked to free associate to words such as *life*, sad subjects generate more negative associations, and also produce more negative stories in the Thematic Apperception Test (Bower, 1981).

Sad affect also triggers more negative and pessimistic social judgments about social stimuli such as human faces (Schiffenbauer, 1974), more guarded impressions of people (Forgas & Bower, 1987), as well as more critical self-judgments (Forgas et al., 1984; Sedikides, 1995). These effects are greater when more open, constructive thinking is required to deal with complex or unfamiliar stimuli (Forgas, 1994, 1995). For example, students induced into a sad mood were more likely to accept responsibility and blame themselves for failure in an exam, compared to those in a happy mood (Forgas et al., 1990). Thus, sad mood may have an adaptive influence on self-assessment, promoting greater internal attributions and taking greater responsibility for outcomes, which should promote coping. Sad mood also resulted in the more negative, pessimistic, and cautious assessment of others, including people's own personal relationships, and this effect was greatest when judging complex, problematic issues that called for more extensive processing (Forgas, 1993, 1994).

Affect Infusion in Social Behaviors

When social behaviors require a degree of substantive, generative processing, negative affect infusion may produce more pessimistic, avoidant, and less confident interpersonal strategies that have adaptive advantages in more uncertain and challenging situations.

REQUESTING

In situations calling for more cautious behavior and greater attention to possible adverse consequences, negative affect may produce adaptive benefits by selectively priming more negative, pessimistic information and more cautious behavior. One such common strategic task is requesting, a complex communicative move that is characterized by uncertainty and the risk of being refused or giving offense. Requests must be formulated with just the right degree of politeness vs. assertiveness so as to maximize compliance without risking giving offense. In such situations, sad mood may produce distinct adaptive benefits by promoting access to more negative information that should lead to more cautious, polite, and considerate requests (Forgas, 1999a). In several experiments we found that when happy or sad persons were asked to select among more or less polite request formulation they would use in easy or difficult social situations (Forgas, 1999a), sad persons preferred more polite and considerate requests, whereas happy participants preferred more assertive and impolite requests. Remarkably, as predicted by the Affect Infusion Model, sad mood effects on requesting were stronger in a difficult rather than in an easy interpersonal situation that required more elaborate, substantive processing.

Similar mood effects on requesting were also demonstrated in real-life situations (Forgas, 1999b, Exp. 2), when happy or sad participants were unexpectedly asked to "get a file from a neighboring office." Their requests were recorded and analyzed, showing that sad mood participants again used significantly more polite, elaborate, and hedging requests (Figure 27.1).

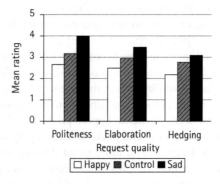

Figure 27.1. Mood effects on naturally produced requests: Sad mood increased the degree of politeness, elaboration, and hedging in the request formulations used. After Forgas (1999b).

SELF-DISCLOSURE

An even clearer example of the potential adaptive functions of sad mood is provided by experiments that compared the self-disclosure strategies adopted by sad vs. happy participants. Self-disclosure is again an important, but risky interpersonal strategy, and so greater caution induced by sad mood can produce an adaptive effect in restraining too much intimate or inappropriate disclosure. In these experiments, participants were induced either into a happy or a sad mood, and then exchanged self-disclosing e-mails with a "partner." Sad persons disclosed less intimate, less varied, and less abstract information, confirming that affect infusion can significantly impact strategic interpersonal behaviors (Forgas, 2011c; Figure 27.2).

These studies show that people perceive themselves, others, and the world around them in a manner that is congruent with their current mood. Sadness and negative affect produce a more pessimistic, cautious, and avoidant cognitive and behavioral style, consistent with the evolutionary idea that sadness functions as an adaptive, evolutionary warning signal (Andrews & Thompson, 2009; Buss, 2019). As predicted by the Affect Infusion Model (Forgas, 1995), numerous experiments show that affect infusion effects are greater in situations when the task is more difficult and demanding and so requires a greater degree of open, generative processing, in turn increasing the likelihood that affectively primed contents are retrieved from memory and preferentially used in constructing a response.

Adaptive Information-Processing Effects

Affect may also have an adaptive influence on the *process* of cognition, that is, *how* people think (Clark & Isen, 1982; Forgas, 2002). It has long been suspected that negative mood may function as an alarm signal, promoting a more effortful and vigilant processing style (Schwarz, 1990; Schwarz & Bless, 1991; Sinclair & Mark, 1992). Evolutionary explanations highlighted *functional principles* suggesting that affective states exist for the purpose of modulating the degree of effort and care required to deal with more or less demanding situations (Forgas et al., 2007). This cognitive tuning principle has recently been developed into a comprehensive theory by Bless and Fiedler (2006), who explicitly argue that different moods have the evolutionary function of recruiting qualitatively different processing *styles*. Following the processing dichotomy introduced by Piaget, Bless and Fiedler (2006) argue that sadness and negative moods call for *accommodative, bottom-up* processing, directed at discovering new, relevant details in the external world in a challenging situation. In contrast, positive moods recruit *assimilative, top-down* processing, signaling that reliance on existing schematic knowledge and heuristics is adequate (Bless, 2000; Bless & Fiedler, 2006; Fiedler, 2001). In an adaptive pattern, *accommodation* in sad mood thus involves increased attention to new information, greater sensitivity to external norms and social expectations, and a more concrete, piecemeal, and bottom-up processing style.

Numerous experiments now confirm that negative affect, by facilitating the processing of new external information, can improve memory performance, reduce judgmental mistakes (Forgas, 1998a; Forgas, 2011a, 2011b), and also improve the effectiveness of social behaviors such as persuasive communication (Forgas, 2007). Experimental evidence for the adaptive benefits of negative affect will be summarized next, highlighting the benefits of sadness for social attention, memory, judgments, motivation, as well as strategic interpersonal behaviors.

Attention and Memory Benefits

The ability to notice and remember incidentally encountered information in our daily environment is one of the most fundamental cognitive faculties (Forgas & Eich, 2013). Such incidental memories can be of crucial importance in everyday life, as well as in forensic and

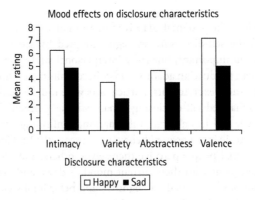

Figure 27.2. Affective influence on self-disclosure: sad mood promotes a more pessimistic and cautious self-disclosure style, resulting in less intimacy, variety, abstraction and greater negativity in what is disclosed.

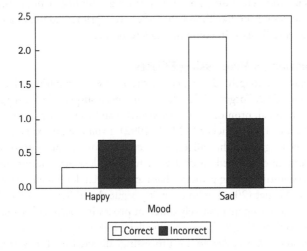

Figure 27.3. Shoppers in a sad mood (induced by bad weather) show better memory for incidental objects encountered in a news agency, with more correct, and fewer incorrect items recalled compared to those in a happy mood (good weather). Source: Forgas, Goldenberg, & Unkelbach (2009).

legal practice (Loftus, 1979; Neisser, 1982). In an adaptive sense, sad mood, by recruiting a more accommodative and externally focused processing style, should result in improved memory performance. In situations when people experience negative affect, as a consequence of more accommodative processing, their attention and memory for details should spontaneously improve. This principle was confirmed in a field experiment. Shoppers in a local news agency were asked about their memory for small details inside the shop on cold, rainy days (sad mood), and bright, sunny days (good mood; Forgas et al., 2009). Those in a sad mood (on rainy days) recalled and also recognized significantly more details they had seen (Figure 27.3). These mood-induced processing effects, consistent with evolutionary theorizing, are fast, spontaneous, automatic, and subconscious. We found that people are unable to control these mood effects, even when explicitly instructed to do so.

Can sad mood also protect against the common tendency for people to incorporate later, incorrect details into their *eyewitness memories* (Fiedler et al., 1991; Loftus, 1979;

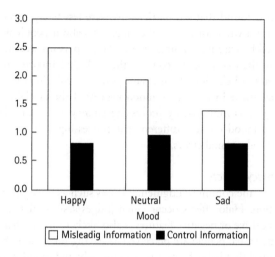

Figure 27.4. Sad mood reduces the effects of misleading information on distorting eyewitness memory accuracy compared to happy or neutral mood. Source: Forgas, Vargas, & Laham (2005), Experiment 2.

Wells & Loftus, 2003)? Despite earlier suggestions that we need to examine "the mediating role of mood in eyewitness testimony" (Fiedler et al., 1991, p. 376), this task was not undertaken until recently. In a series of experiments, we exposed participants to complex scenes (photos of a traffic accident, observing an altercation in a lecture; Forgas et al., 2005). Sometime later, they were induced into happy or sad moods before receiving questions about the scenes that either did, or did not contain misleading, false information (e.g., "Did you see the woman in the brown coat force her way into the lecture?" [the woman wore a black coat]). After a further interval of up to one week, eyewitness memory for the original target events was tested. In all experiments, negative mood reduced, and positive mood increased the tendency to incorporate misleading information into eyewitness memories (Figure 27.4). A signal detection analysis confirmed that negative mood indeed improved the ability to accurately discriminate between correct and false details. These results suggest the counterintuitive effect that negative mood can improve memory performance, and protect against subsequent eyewitness distortions, consistent with a more assimilative-accommodative processing style it promotes (Bless, 2000; Fiedler & Bless, 2001; Forgas, 1995, 2002).

Judgmental Benefits

Many common judgmental errors in everyday life occur because people are imperfect and often inattentive information processors (Forgas, 2011b). Can sad mood, through its influence on triggering a more thorough and accommodating processing strategy, reduce some of the common judgmental errors?

The *fundamental attribution error* (FAE) or *correspondence bias* refers to a pervasive tendency by people to infer intentionality and internal causation and underestimate the impact of situational forces in their social judgments when observing others (Jones & Davis, 1965). This error occurs because perceivers pay disproportionate attention to salient information such as the actor and neglect information about situational constraints). If sad mood facilitates accommodative processing, it should reduce the incidence of the FAE by directing greater attention to situational information (Forgas, 1998b).

Several experiments found that sad participants were less likely to succumb to the fundamental attribution error when asked to make judgments about people whose behavior was, or was not, constrained by external circumstances. Happy persons were more likely, and sad people were less likely than controls to commit the FAE and incorrectly attribute internal causes to externally caused behaviors. Consistent with the evolutionary, adaptive processing influence of sad affect, those in a negative mood processed the available information more carefully and thoroughly, as indicated by processing latency and recall data. A mediational analysis also found that mood-induced differences in processing style was a significant mediator of mood effects on judgmental errors.

Halo Effects and Primacy Effects

Sad affect also reduces some common judgmental biases such as *halo effects* and *primacy effects* in impression formation. Halo effects occur when judges assume that a person with some visible but irrelevant positive or negative features is also likely to have other positive characteristics. For example, attractive people are perceived as having more desirable personalities. In one experiment we found that halo effects can be reduced by sad mood: the appearance of the writer had less of an influence on the evaluation of their competence when judges experienced sad mood rather than happy mood (Forgas, 2011b; Figure 27.5).

The adaptive benefits of sad mood on judgmental accuracy were also confirmed by other studies looking at the influence of mood on the primacy effect—the tendency by judges to place disproportionate emphasis on early information when forming impressions (Asch, 1946; Luchins, 1958). Primacy effects often disappear when judges process every detail equally carefully. Since negative mood can reliably trigger more accommodative processing strategies (Bless & Fiedler, 2006; Forgas, 2002, 2007), primacy effects should also be reduced by a sad mood, as confirmed by several experiments (Forgas, 2011a).

Stereotyping

Another common judgmental bias occurs when people rely on their preexisting stereotypes rather than valid individual information in responding to others. Sad mood may also reduce

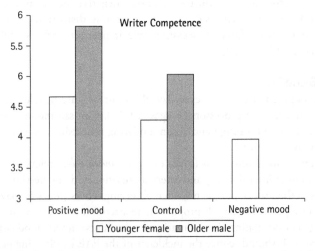

Figure 27.5. Sad mood reduces the halo effect: judgments of a writer's competence were less influenced by their physical appearance when in a negative rather than in a positive mood After Forgas (2011b).

people's tendency to rely on stereotypes. In one experiment, happy or sad people were asked to play a video game using the "shooter's bias" paradigm where participants had to rapidly fire at a person only when he was holding a gun (Correll et al., 2002; Correll et al., 2007). In addition, the appearance of the targets was also manipulated so they did, or did not, appear to be Muslims (wearing a turban). Negative stereotypes about out-groups, such as Muslims, influence such responses. However, we found that induced positive mood increased, and negative mood reduced, the implicit bias to fire more at Muslim targets, again consistent with the adaptive functions of negative mood triggering more accommodative processing and reduced reliance on stereotyped information (Unkelbach et al., 2008).

Detecting Deception

Negative affect may well function as an evolutionary defense against excessive gullibility, also improving the ability to detect deception (Forgas, 2019; Lane & de Paulo, 1999). In one experiment, we asked happy or sad participants to detect deception in the videotaped statements of people accused of theft, who were either lying, or telling the truth (Forgas & East, 2008b). As expected, we found that those in a negative mood were more dubious, and also better able to correctly identify deceptive targets, confirming the adaptive cognitive benefits of negative mood (Figure 27.6).

Sad mood also increases skepticism about the observed communications of others. For example, the interpretation of facial expressions also showed a significant mood bias. When we asked happy or sad participants to judge the genuineness of positive, neutral, and negative facial expressions, those in a negative mood were significantly less likely to accept facial expressions as genuine. In a follow-up experiment, we also asked happy or sad judges to determine the genuineness of facial expressions of the six basic emotions (i.e., anger, fear, disgust, happiness, surprise, and sadness) as displayed by trained actors. Once again, negative mood reduced, and positive mood increased people's tendency to accept the facial displays as genuine, consistent with sad mood triggering a more accommodative and attentive processing style (Figure 27.7).

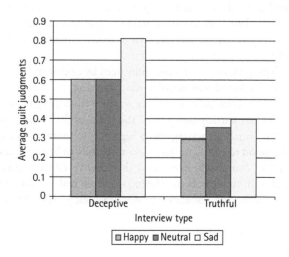

Figure 27.6. Sad mood improved judges' ability to discriminate between truthful and deceptive targets. After Forgas and East (2008b).

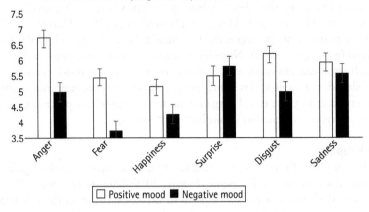

Figure 27.7. Sad mood judges are significantly more skeptical and are less likely to accept facial expressions of basic emotions as genuine compared to happy judges (except for the "surprise" expression where differences due to mood were nonsignificant). After Forgas & East (2008b).

Reduced Gullibility

Other experiments suggest that negative affect has an overall beneficial influence on reducing gullibility and increasing skepticism (Forgas, 2019). For example, in one study we asked happy or sad judges to estimate the likely truth of a number of urban legends and fake news, such as "power lines cause leukemia" or "the CIA murdered Kennedy" (Forgas & East, 2008a). Negative mood increased skepticism and reduced gullibility, but only for new and unfamiliar claims that required online processing to evaluate new information. In another experiment, participants rated the likely truth of 25 true and 25 false knowledge trivia statements, and were also informed whether each claim was actually true. Two weeks later, after a positive or negative mood induction, only participants in a negative mood were able to correctly distinguish between the true and false claims they had seen previously. Those in a positive mood tended to rate all previously seen claims as true, showing a familiarity effect, confirming that happy mood increased and sad mood reduced judges' tendency to simply rely on the "what is familiar is true" heuristic. Thus, sad mood conferred a clear adaptive advantage by promoting a more accommodative, systematic processing style and better memory for factual information (Fiedler & Bless, 2001).

Sometimes, truth judgments may also be influenced by irrelevant cues, such as the cognitive fluency of a claim. We found that negative affect can decrease the extent to which people rely on irrelevant heuristic cues, such as fluency in their truth judgments (Koch & Forgas, 2012). When happy or sad participants judged the truth of 30 ambiguous statements presented with high or low visual fluency (against a high or low contrast background), judges in a neutral and positive mood rated fluent claims as more likely to be true than disfluent claims. However, negative affect completely eliminated this fluency effect (Figure 27.8). Affective influences on inferred truth judgments may be important in real-life situations, as many such judgments (such as believing or disbelieving fake news, etc.) typically occur in affect-rich contexts.

Bullshit Receptivity

Humans are inclined to search for, and often find meaning in, intentionally random or meaningless information. This tendency is surprisingly common even among some academics,

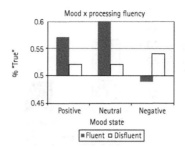

Figure 27.8. When in a sad mood, judges were less likely to be influenced by irrelevant cues such as the cognitive fluency and visibility of different messages in evaluating their truthfulness. After Koch & Forgas (2012).

especially those interested in postmodernist theorizing (Sokal & Bricmont, 1998). In an intriguing study, Pennycook et al. (2015) found that people are inclined to perceive some meaning and depth even in vacuous, pseudo-profound computer-generated text. Can sad or happy mood have a significant influence on people's receptivity to see meaning even in meaningless, "bullshit" text? In one study we asked participants in a happy or sad mood (after viewing cheerful or sad videotapes) to rate the meaningfulness of two kinds of verbal "bullshit" text, including vacuous computer-generated random New Age pronouncements (e.g. "Good health imparts reality to subtle creativity"; see http://wisdomofchopra.com/), as well as meaningless psychological jargon phrases (e.g. "subjective instrumental sublimations"; Forgas et al., 2018).

As expected, those in a positive mood perceived more "meaning" compared to those in a sad mood in these gibberish texts. Sad mood judges were not only less gullible, but also took more time to arrive at a judgment, and also had better recall and recognition memory for the phrases than did those in a positive mood, consistent with the predicted mood-induced processing differences. In a related study, we used uninterpretable, abstract visual rather than verbal stimuli (abstract expressionist paintings). Participants were recruited in public places and received a mood induction (reminiscing about happy or sad life episodes) before judging the meaningfulness of four abstract expressionist images (Forgas et al., 2018). Once again, sad mood reduced the tendency to perceive meaning in these uninterpretable images compared to positive mood (Figure 27.9).

Motivational Benefits
Improved Perseverance
Sad affective states may also have a counterintuitive effect on perseverance when performing difficult and demanding tasks. If sad mood functions as an evolutionary alarm signal indicating problematic situations, then trying harder to solve difficult problems may be one of its adaptive consequences. There is some prior evidence that affect can have a profound influence on effortful activity. For example, positive often promotes less effortful strategies in order to safeguard a more pleasant current affective state (*mood maintenance*; Clark & Isen, 1982). In contrast, negative affect can serve as an evolutionary warning signal, automatically recruiting more effortful, attentive, and vigilant information processing and behavior, as a means to improve an unpleasant affective state—the *mood repair* hypothesis (Frijda, 1986; Schwarz, 1990).

In one experiment we (Goldenberg & Forgas, 2013) found that negative affect produced greater perseverance when happy or sad participants worked on a demanding cognitive abilities task. Those in a negative mood spent more *time* on the task, attempted more *questions*, and *answered* more correctly (Figure 27.9). A mediational analysis confirmed that it was

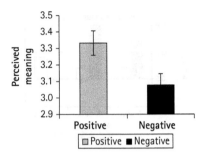

Figure 27.9. Mood effects on visual bullshit receptivity: sad mood reduced the tendency to perceive meaning in abstract expressionist paintings compared to positive mood.

mood-induced differences in believing in the value of effort that mediated these effects. We should note that sadness is only likely to produce increased perseverance in circumstances when the task is clearly achievable. When the task is hopeless, the adaptive functions of sadness may be to help the organism to disengage and terminate a fruitless effort.

Reduced Self-Handicapping
Negative affect may also produce more adaptive and realistic self-judgments by reducing counterproductive strategies such as defensive self-handicapping (Jones & Berglas, 1978). Self-handicapping occurs when people crate artificial handicaps for themselves as a means of protecting the self from damaging attributions due to expected failure. In one experiment we investigated mood effects on people's tendency to *self-handicap* and create artificial hindrances for themselves (Alter & Forgas, 2007). We expected and found that positive mood increased, and negative mood decreased self-handicapping when participants were led to doubt their ability to do well on a cognitive task, by choosing to drink either a performance-enhancing or a performance-inhibiting tea. The beneficial consequences of negative affect on promoting realistic self-assessments may be particularly important in organizational settings, where until now the presumed universal benefits of positive affect received almost exclusive emphasis (Forgas & George, 2001).

Improved Verbal Communication
Conversational Competence
Several experiments also indicate that the adaptive functions of mild sadness also extend to improving verbal communication strategies. In a series of three experiments (Koch et al., 2013), we predicted and found that participants in a sad mood communicated significantly more effectively and complied significantly better with Grice's (1975) normative maxims in conversational situations than did participants in a positive mood when using natural language to describe previously observed social events (Figure 27.10). Negative mood actually improved the quality of language production, as sad participants adopted more careful and effective conversational strategies when asked to describe observed situations to an audience. This effect was not merely due to improvements in their ability to encode and remember the observed details, but also extended to a more effective verbal communication style consistent with a more attentive and accommodative processing mode.

Language Processing
The beneficial effects of mild sad mood apply not only to language *production*, but also can improve people's ability to *monitor and understand* problematic linguistic expressions. In

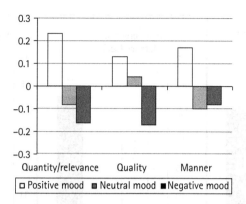

Figure 27.10. Mood effects on conversational competence and adherence to Grice's (1975) conversational maxims (Z-scores): sad mood produced fewer violations of the maxims of quantity, quality cooperative principle in spoken language compared with positive mood. After Koch, Forgas & Matovic (2013), Experiment 1.

two experiments (Matovic et al., 2014) we demonstrated that mild sad mood significantly improved people's ability to correctly identify imperfect and potentially ambiguous "bad" sentences that could not be interpreted properly (ambiguous anaphora; Figure 27.11). An analysis of response latencies further confirmed that consistent with the adaptive, evolutionary hypothesis, sad mood actually produced more attentive processing, which mediated mood effects on improved language comprehension. These results are conceptually consistent with negative affect selectively promoting a more concrete and externally focused processing style.

Persuasion

The adaptive consequences of sad mood in triggering more accommodative processing and greater attention to external information may also produce benefits for difficult interpersonal strategies that require careful focus on the outside world. For example, one of the most common influence strategies used to get what we want from others in everyday life is verbal persuasion. People rely on language to present the best possible case for a proposed view or action. Although there has been long-standing interest in how persuasive messages are interpreted and processed by *recipients*, the question of how affect influences the *production* of persuasive messages received little attention (but see Bohner & Schwarz, 1993). In several experiments, we predicted that accommodative processing promoted by sad mood should result in more concrete and factual thinking and produce more effective persuasive messages (Forgas, 2007). In these studies, we asked happy or sad participants to write persuasive arguments for or against topical issues, such as an increase in student fees, or Aboriginal land rights. Their arguments were rated by two raters for overall quality, persuasiveness, concreteness, and valence. We found that those in a sad mood produced higher quality, more concrete, and more persuasive arguments than happy participants (Figure 27.12).

The real test of persuasive argument quality is whether naïve recipients are persuaded by them. In a follow-up experiment, naïve participants were presented with the arguments written by sad or happy negative mood persuaders. Arguments written in a sad mood were significantly more effective in producing real attitude change than were arguments produced by happy persuaders (Forgas, 2007). In another realistic study, participants were asked to persuade a partner to volunteer for an experiment. Again, negative mood resulted in higher quality persuasive arguments, and a mediational analysis confirmed that sad mood actually induced slower and more accommodative thinking, and more concrete and specific arguments. These results show that sad mood can have an adaptive influence and can improve

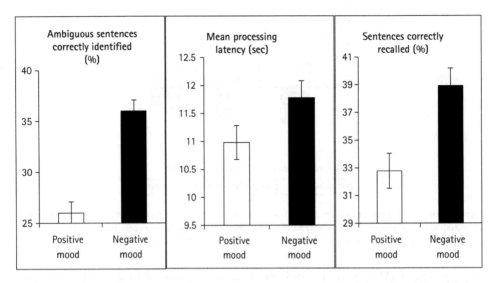

Figure 27.11. Sad mood improved the ability to detect ambiguous communication (left panel), and also resulted in longer and more elaborate processing (middle panel), and better memory for the target information compared to positive mood. After Matovic, Koch & Forgas (2014).

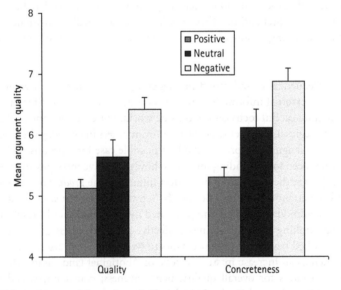

Figure 27.12. Sad mood improved the quality and effectiveness of persuasive messages, consistent with sad mood participants using more concrete and specific formulations After Forgas (2007), Experiment 2.

the quality and effectiveness of persuasive arguments, consistent with negative affect promoting a more concrete, accommodative, externally focused information-processing style (Forgas, 1998a, 1998b; Forgas et al., 2005).

Ingratiation

One of the most difficult strategic interpersonal tasks requiring considerable verbal sophistication is ingratiation: trying to create a positive impression about ourselves in a partner, without appearing to do so (Jones, 1964). In several experiments, we explored the possibility that mild sad mood may also produce benefits in performing such a challenging task (Matovic & Forgas, 2018). We found for the first time that mild sad mood actually improved communicators' ability to effectively use ingratiatory tactics such as flattery, conformity, and self-promotion. Ingratiatory messages written in a sad mood were actually more effective in creating a positive impression than messages written in a positive mood (Figure 27.13). An analysis of response latencies (processing strategies) and memory data also showed that these improvements were due to sad mood promoting a more extensive and attentive style.

Improving Fairness

Evolutionary psychologists have long wondered about the possibility that negative affect may provide hidden social benefits by arousing and promoting interpersonal sympathy and fairness (Buss, 2019; Forgas et al., 2007; Tooby & Cosmides, 1992). Whereas positive affect may selectively trigger more optimistic, confident, assertive, and selfish behaviors, sadness and negativity may prime more cautious, pessimistic assessment and more accommodative processing, resulting in greater attention to external expectations and norms. A series of experiments looked at mood effects on the level of selfishness vs. fairness in strategic interactions such as the dictator game and the ultimatum game. In the *dictator game*, allocators have the power to distribute resources (e.g., money, raffle tickets, etc.) between themselves and a partner in any way they like. In the *ultimatum game*, allocators face a partner who has a veto power. If a distribution is rejected, neither side gets anything. According to classical economic theories, rational actors should maximize benefits to the self; yet research suggests that allocators are influenced by norms of fairness and often offer a fair distribution (Güth et al., 1982). Affect may influence such decisions by triggering different processing strategies: those in a negative mood might adopt more accommodative, careful, and externally attentive strategies than those in a positive affective state, and come to pay greater attention to external norms of fairness, rather than internal desires to be selfish.

In several experiments we (Tan & Forgas, 2010) explored the effects of happy or sad mood on the behavior of allocators in the dictator game. Results showed that happy players were significantly more selfish and kept more resources (e.g., raffle tickets) to themselves, while sad allocators were fairer. Similar mood effects on fairness were also found in the more complex decisional environment in the ultimatum game, where partners may reject offers. Again, as hypothesized, those in a sad mood allocated significantly more resources to others than did

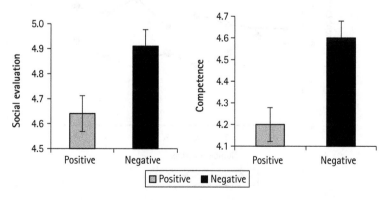

Figure 27.13. Ingratiating messages produced by communicators experiencing a sad mood were significantly more effective and resulted in more favorable ratings of the communicators by recipients on measures of *social evaluation* and *competence* compared to messages written by happy ingratiators. After Matovic & Forgas (2018).

happy individuals. This pattern was also confirmed when rather than using a single allocation task, a series of eight allocations were used to different partners. Overall, those in a sad mood were fairer and less selfish, and as the trials progressed, sad individuals actually became fairer (Figure 27.14). In other words, sad mood functioned as an adaptive input, promoting attention to external norms of fairness.

These mood effects could also be directly linked to differences in processing style, as sad individuals took longer to make allocation decisions than did happy individuals, consistent with their expected more accommodative and attentive processing style. We also found that *responders* were also more concerned with fairness when induced into a sad mood, and were more likely to reject unfair offers (Forgas & Tan, 2013). Overall, 57% of those in sad mood rejected unfair offers compared to only 45% in the positive mood condition, consistent with processing theories that predict that sad mood should increase accommodative attention to external fairness norms. These results further support the evolutionary idea that sad mood has important functional and adaptive consequences in situations where greater attention to external information is required.

Summary and Conclusion

Overall, the series of experiments reviewed here provide compelling evidence for the important evolutionary benefits of mild dysphoria—sadness—in many everyday situations (Andrews & Thompson, 2009; Buss, 2019). These results are broadly consistent with recent evolutionary theories that suggest that the human affective repertoire has been largely shaped by processes of natural selection, and mood states function as evolutionary algorithms that promote appropriate responses in particular situations (von Hippel, 2018). In other words, all of our affective states—including the unpleasant ones—can function as efficient and pre-programmed "mind modules" or "coordinating mechanisms" that produce tangible benefits in some circumstances (Al-Shawaf & Lewis, 2017; Al-Shawaf et al., 2015; Tooby & Cosmides, 1992).

These studies show that we ought to understand and accept temporary states of dysphoria as a normal part of the human affective repertoire (Frijda, 1986). These findings are in stark contrast with the emphasis on the benefits of positive affect in the recent literature, as well as

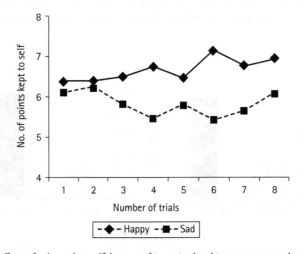

Figure 27.14. The effects of sad mood on selfishness vs. fairness in the ultimatum game: sad participants kept fewer rewards to themselves and gave more to their partners, consistent with their greater attention to external fairness norms. After Forgas & Tan (2013).

in much of our popular culture (Forgas & Eich, 2013; Forgas & George, 2001). A more realistic view should accept that positive affect is *not* universally desirable, and the elimination of dysphoria from our lives is neither desirable nor possible. The evidence shows that people in a mild sad mood are less prone to judgmental errors (Forgas, 2011a, 2011b, 2011c), are more resistant to eyewitness distortions (Forgas et al., 2005), are fairer and more sensitive to social norms (Forgas, 1999a,b), and are better at a variety of verbal communication tasks requiring attention to situational details (Forgas, 2007; Koch et al., 2013; Matovic et al., 2014).

This is not to say that negative affect is *always* beneficial. Negative affective states that are intense, enduring, and debilitating, such as depression, clearly produce negative consequences and require clinical intervention. However, mild, temporary mood states of the kind that we all regularly experience in everyday life do have important adaptive consequences, suggesting that over evolutionary time, affective states became adaptive, functional triggers that automatically promote motivational and information-processing strategies that are appropriate in a given situation. Mild sadness is typically an affective response that occurs in problematic, difficult, or unfamiliar situations, and by triggering more cautious, pessimistic, and attentive reactions, it promotes a more appropriate response. The main implication of this line of research is that accepting the entire range of our affective reactions, including the negative ones, may be more conducive to human well-being than single-mindedly focusing on the pursuit of positive affective states alone.

Author's Note

Support from the Australian Research Council is gratefully acknowledged.
For further information on this research program, see also websites at: http://forgas.socialpsychology.org and http://www2.psy.unsw.edu.au/Users/JForgas .

References

Adolphs, R. & Damasio, A. (2001). The interaction of affect and cognition: A neurobiological perspective. In J. P. Forgas (Ed.), *The handbook of affect and social cognition* (pp. 27–49). Lawrence Erlbaum Associates.
Allport, G. W (1985). The historical background of social psychology. In G. Lindzey & E. Aronson (Eds.), *The handbook of social psychology* (2nd ed., Vol. 1, pp. 1–46). McGraw Hill.
Al-Shawaf, L., Conroy-Beam, D., Asao, K., & Buss, D. (2015). Human emotions: An evolutionary psychological perspective. *Emotion Review*, 8(2), 173–186. https://doi.org/10.1177/1754073914565518
Al-Shawaf, L., & Lewis, D. (2017). Evolutionary psychology and the emotions. In V. Zeigler-Hill & T. K. Shackelford (Eds.), *Encyclopedia of personality and individual differences*. Springer. https://doi.org/10.1007/978-3-319-28099-8_516-1
Al-Shawaf, L., Lewis, D., Wehbe, Y., & Buss, D. (2019). *Context, environment, and learning in evolutionary psychology*. Springer. https://doi.org/10.1007/978-3-319-16999-6_227-1
Alter, A. L. & Forgas, J. P. (2007). On being happy but fearing failure: The effects of mood on self-handicapping strategies. *Journal of Experimental Social Psychology*, 43, 947–954.
Andrews, P. W., & Thompson, J. A. (2009). The bright side of being blue: Depression as an adaptation for analyzing complex problems. *Psychological Review*, 116(3), 620–654.
Asch, S. E. (1946). Forming impressions of personality. *Journal of Abnormal and Social Psychology*, 41, 258–290.
Bless, H. (2000). The interplay of affect and cognition: The mediating role of general knowledge structures. In J. P. Forgas (Ed.), *Feeling and thinking: The role of affect in social cognition*. (pp. 201–222). Cambridge University Press.
Bless, H., & Fiedler, K. (2006). Mood and the regulation of information processing and behavior. In J. P. Forgas (Ed.), *Affect in social thinking and behavior* (pp. 65–84). Psychology Press.
Bohner, G., & Schwarz, N. (1993). Mood states influence the production of persuasive arguments. *Communication Research*, 20, 696–722.
Buss, D. (2019). *Evolutionary psychology: The new science of the mind*. Routledge.
Bower, G. H. (1981). Mood and memory. *The American Psychologist*, 36, 129–148.
Bower, G. H., & Forgas, J. P. (2001). Mood and social memory. In J. P. Forgas (Ed.), *The handbook of affect and social cognition* (pp. 95–120). Lawrence Erlbaum Associates.

Ciarrochi, J. V., Forgas, J. P., & Mayer, J. D. (Eds.). (2006). *Emotional intelligence in everyday life* (2nd ed.). Psychology Press.

Clark, M. S., & Isen, A. M. (1982). Towards understanding the relationship between feeling states and social behavior. In A. H. Hastorf & A. M. Isen (Eds.), *Cognitive social psychology* (pp. 73–108). Elsevier-North Holland.

Clore, G. L., & Byrne, D. (1974). The reinforcement affect model of attraction. In T. L. Huston (Ed.), *Foundations of interpersonal attraction* (pp. 143–170). Academic Press.

Clore, G. L., Gasper, K., & Garvin, E. (2001). Affect as information. In J. P. Forgas (Ed.), *The handbook of affect and social cognition* (pp. 121–144). Lawrence Erlbaum Associates.

Correll, J., Park, B., Judd, C. M., & Wittenbrink, B. (2002). The police officer's dilemma: Using ethnicity to disambiguate potentially threatening individuals. *Journal of Personality and Social Psychology, 83*(6), 1314–1329.

Correll, J., Park, B., Judd, C. M., Wittenbrink, B., Sadler, M. S., & Keesee, T. (2007). Across the thin blue line: Police officers and racial bias in the decision to shoot. *Journal of Personality and Social Psychology, 92*(6), 1006–1023.

Ekman, P., & Cordaro, D. (2011). What is meant by calling emotions basic. *Emotion Review, 3,* 364–370

Ekman, P., & O'Sullivan, M. (1991). Who can catch a liar? *American Psychologist, 46,* 913–920.

Feshbach, S., & Singer, R. D. (1957). The effects of fear arousal and suppression of fear upon social perception. *Journal of Abnormal and Social Psychology, 55,* 283–288.

Fiedler, K. (2001). Affective influences on social information processing. In J. P. Forgas (Ed.), *The handbook of affect and social cognition* (pp. 163–185). Lawrence Erlbaum Associates.

Fiedler, K., Asbeck, J., & Nickel, S. (1991). Mood and constructive memory effects on social judgment. *Cognition and Emotion, 5,* 363–378.

Fiedler, K. & Bless, H. (2001). The formation of beliefs in the interface of affective and cognitive processes. In N. Frijda, A. Manstead, & S. Bem (Eds.), *The influence of emotions on beliefs* (pp. 144–170). Cambridge University Press.

Forgas, J. P. (1979). *Social episodes: The study of interaction routines.* Academic Press.

Forgas, J. P. (1993). On making sense of odd couples: Mood effects on the perception of mismatched relationships. *Personality and Social Psychology Bulletin, 19,* 59–71.

Forgas, J. P. (1994). Sad and guilty? Affective influences on explanations of conflict episodes. *Journal of Personality and Social Psychology, 66,* 56–68.

Forgas, J. P. (1995). Mood and judgment: The Affect Infusion Model (AIM). *Psychological Bulletin, 116,* 39–66.

Forgas, J. P. (1998a). On feeling good and getting your way: Mood effects on negotiation strategies and outcomes. *Journal of Personality and Social Psychology, 74,* 565–577.

Forgas, J. P. (1998b). Happy and mistaken? Mood effects on the fundamental attribution error. *Journal of Personality and Social Psychology, 75,* 318–331.

Forgas, J. P. (1999a). On feeling good and being rude: Affective influences on language use and requests. *Journal of Personality and Social Psychology, 76,* 928–939.

Forgas, J. P. (1999b). Feeling and speaking: Mood effects on verbal communication strategies. *Personality and Social Psychology Bulletin, 25,* 850–863.

Forgas, J. P. (2002). Feeling and doing: Affective influences on interpersonal behavior. *Psychological Inquiry, 13,* 1–28.

Forgas, J. P. (Ed.). (2006). *Affect in social thinking and behavior.* Psychology Press.

Forgas, J. P. (2007). When sad is better than happy: Negative affect can improve the quality and effectiveness of persuasive messages and social influence strategies. *Journal of Experimental Social Psychology, 43,* 513–528.

Forgas, J. P. (2011a). Can negative affect eliminate the power of first impressions? Affective influences on primacy and recency effects in impression formation. *Journal of Experimental Social Psychology, 47,* 425–429.

Forgas, J. P. (2011b). She just doesn't look like a philosopher . . . ? Affective influences on the halo effect in impression formation. *European Journal of Social Psychology, 41,* 812–817.

Forgas, J. P. (2011c). Affective influences on self-disclosure strategies. *Journal of Personality and Social Psychology. 100*(3), 449–461.

Forgas, J. P. (2019). Happy believers and sad skeptics? Affective influences on gullibility. *Current Directions in Psychological Science, 28*(3), 306–313.

Forgas, J. P., & Bower, G. H. (1987). Mood effects on person perception judgements. *Journal of Personality and Social Psychology, 53,* 53–60.

Forgas, J. P., Bower, G. H., & Krantz, S. (1984). The influence of mood on perceptions of social interactions. *Journal of Experimental Social Psychology, 20,* 497–513.

Forgas, J. P., Bower, G. H., & Moylan, S. J. (1990). Praise or blame? Affective influences on attributions for achievement. *Journal of Personality and Social Psychology, 59,* 809–818.

Forgas, J. P., & East, R. (2008a). How real is that smile? Mood effects on accepting or rejecting the veracity of emotional facial expressions. *Journal of Nonverbal Behavior, 32,* 157–170.

Forgas, J. P., & East, R. (2008b). On being happy and gullible: Mood effects on scepticism and the detection of deception. *Journal of Experimental Social Psychology, 44,* 1362–1367.

Forgas, J. P., & Eich, E. E. (2013). Affective influences on cognition: Mood congruence, mood dependence, and mood effects on processing strategies. In A. F. Healy & R. W. Proctor (Eds.), *Experimental psychology.* Volume 4 in I. B. Weiner (Ed.), *Handbook of psychology* (pp. 61–82). Wiley.

Forgas, J. P., & George, J. M. (2001). Affective influences on judgments and behavior in organizations: An information processing perspective. *Organizational Behavior and Human Decision Processes, 86,* 3–34.

Forgas, J. P., Goldenberg, L., & Unkelbach, C. (2009). Can bad weather improve your memory? A field study of mood effects on memory in a real-life setting. *Journal of Experimental Social Psychology, 54,* 254–257.

Forgas, J. P., Haselton, M. G., & von Hippel, W. (Eds.). (2007). *Evolution and the social mind.* Psychology Press.

Forgas, J. P., Matovic, D., & Slater, I. (2018). *Mood effects on bullshit receptivity.* Manuscript, University of New South Wales, Sydney.

Forgas, J. P., & Moylan, S. (1987) After the movies: The effects of transient mood states on social judgments. *Personality and Social Psychology Bulletin, 13,* 478–489.

Forgas, J. P., & Tan, H. B. (2013). To give or to keep? Affective influences on selfishness and fairness in computer-mediated interactions in the dictator game and the ultimatum game. *Computers and Human Behavior, 29,* 64–74.

Forgas, J. P., Vargas, P., & Laham, S. (2005). Mood effects on eyewitness memory: Affective influences on susceptibility to misinformation. *Journal of Experimental Social Psychology, 41,* 574–588.

Fredrickson, B. L. (2009). *Positivity.* Crown.

Frijda, N. (1986). *The emotions.* Cambridge University Press.

Frijda, N. (1988). The laws of emotion. *American Psychologist, 43,* 349–358.

Goldenberg, L., & Forgas, J. P. (2013). *Mood effects on perseverance: Positive mood reduces motivation according to the hedonistic discounting hypothesis.* Manuscript, University of New South Wales, Sydney.

Grice, H. P. (1975). Logic and conversation. In P. Cole & J. Morgan (Eds.) *Syntax and Semantics* (Vol. 3, pp. 41–58). Academic Press.

Güth, W., Schmittberger, R. & Schwarze, B. (1982) An experimental analysis of ultimatum bargaining. *Journal of Economic Behavior & Organization, 3,* 367–388

Haidt, J. (2007). *The happiness hypothesis.* Basic Books.

Harari, Y. N. (2014). *Sapiens: A brief history of humankind.* Vintage.

Hilgard, E. R. (1980). The trilogy of mind: Cognition, affection, and conation. *Journal of the History of the Behavioral Sciences, 16,* 107–117.

Jones, E. E. (1964). *Ingratiation.* Appleton-Century-Crofts.

Jones, E. E., & Berglas, S. (1978). Control of attributions about the self through self-handicapping strategies: The appeal of alcohol and the role of underachievement. *Personality and Social Psychology Bulletin, 4,* 200–206.

Jones, E. E., & Davis, K. E. (1965). From acts to dispositions. In L. Berkowitz (Ed.), *Advances in experimental social psychology* (pp. 219–266). Academic Press.

Koch, A. S., & Forgas, J. P. (2012). Feeling good and feeling truth: The interactive effects of mood and processing fluency on truth judgments. *Journal of Experimental Social Psychology, 48,* 481–485.

Koch, A. S., Forgas, J. P. & Matovic, D. (2013). Can negative mood improve your conversation? Affective influences on conforming to Grice's communication norms. *European Journal of Social Psychology, 43,* 326–334.

Koestler, A. (1967). *The ghost in the machine.* Penguin.

Lane, J. D., & DePaulo, B. M. (1999). Completing Coyne's cycle: Dysphorics' ability to detect deception. *Journal of Research in Personality, 33,* 311–329.

Loftus, E. F. (1979). *Eyewitness testimony.* Harvard University Press.

Luchins, A. H. (1958). Definitiveness of impressions and primacy-recency in communications. *Journal of Social Psychology, 48,* 275–290.

Matovic, D., & Forgas, J. P. (2018). Mood effects on ingratiation: Affective influences on producing and responding to ingratiating messages. *Journal of Experimental Social Psychology, 76,* 186–197.

Matovic, D., & Forgas, J. P. (2018). The answer is in the question? Mood effects on processing verbal information and impression formation. *Journal of Language and Social Psychology, 37,* 578–590.

Matovic, D., Koch, A., & Forgas, J. P. (2014). Can negative mood improve language understanding? Affective influences on the ability to detect ambiguous communication. *Journal of Experimental Social Psychology, 52,* 44–49.

Neisser, U. (1982). *Memory observed: Remembering in natural contexts.* Freeman.

Nesse, R. M., & Williams, G. C. (1994). *Why we get sick: The new science of Darwinian medicine.* Times Books.

Niedenthal, P., & Halberstadt, J. (2000). Grounding categories in emotional response. In J. P. Forgas (Ed.), *Feeling and thinking: The role of affect in social cognition* (pp. 357–386). Cambridge University Press.

Pennycook, G., Cheyne, J. A., Barr, N., Koehler, D. J., & Fugelsang, A. (2015). On the reception and detection of pseudo-profound bullshit. *Judgment and Decision Making, 10,* 549–563.

Razran, G. H. S. (1940). Conditioned response changes in rating and appraising sociopolitical slogans. *Psychological Bulletin, 37*, 481.
Ruiz-Caballero, J. A., & Gonzalez, P. (1994). Implicit and explicit memory bias in depressed and non-depressed subjects. *Cognition and Emotion, 8*, 555–570.
Schiffenbauer, A. I. (1974). Effect of observer's emotional state on judgments of the emotional state of others. *Journal of Personality and Social Psychology, 30*, 31–35.
Schwarz, N. (1990). Feelings as information: Informational and motivational functions of affective states. In E. T. Higgins & R. Sorrentino (Eds.), *Handbook of motivation and cognition* (Vol. 2, pp. 527–561). Guildford Press.
Schwarz, N., & Bless, H. (1991). Happy and mindless, but sad and smart? The impact of affective states on analytic reasoning. In J. P. Forgas (Ed.), *Emotion and social judgments* (pp. 55–71). Pergamon Press.
Schwarz, N., & Clore, G. L. (1988). How do I feel about it? The informative function of affective states. In K. Fiedler & J. P. Forgas (Eds.), *Affect, cognition, and social behavior* (pp. 44–62). Hogrefe.
Sedikides, C. (1995). Central and peripheral self-conceptions are differentially influenced by mood: Tests of the differential sensitivity hypothesis. *Journal of Personality and Social Psychology, 69*, 759–777. doi: 10.1037/0022-3514.69.4.759
Sedikides, C., Wildschut, T., Arndt, J., & Routledge, C. (2006). Affect and the self. In J. P. Forgas (Ed.), *Affect in social thinking and behavior*. (pp. 197–216). Psychology Press.
Sinclair, R. C., & Mark, M. M. (1992). The influence of mood state on judgment and action. In L. L. Martin & A. Tesser (Eds.), *The construction of social judgments* (pp. 165–193). Lawrence Erlbaum Associates.
Sokal, A., & Bricmont, J. (1998). *Intellectual impostures*. Profile Books.
Stevens, A., & Price, J. (1996). *Evolutionary psychiatry: A new beginning*. Routledge.
Tan, H. B., & Forgas, J. P. (2010). When happiness makes us selfish, but sadness makes us fair: Affective influences on interpersonal strategies in the dictator game. *Journal of Experimental Social Psychology, 46*, 571–576.
Tooby, J., & Cosmides, L. (1992). The psychological foundations of culture. In J. H. Barkow & L. Cosmides (Eds.), *The adapted mind: Evolutionary psychology and the generation of culture* (pp. 19–136). Oxford University Press.
Unkelbach, C., Forgas, J. P., & Denson, T. F. (2008). The turban effect: The influence of Muslim headgear and induced affect on aggressive responses in the shooter bias paradigm. *Journal of Experimental Social Psychology, 44*, 1409–1413.
Von Hippel, W. (2018). *The social leap*. Harper.
Watson, P. J., & Andrews, P. W. (2002). Toward a revised evolutionary adaptationist analysis of depression: the social navigation hypothesis. *Journal of Affective Disorders, 72*, 1–14.
Wells, G. L., & Loftus, E. F. (2003). Eyewitness memory for people and events. In A. M. Goldstein (Ed.), *Handbook of psychology: Forensic psychology* (Vol. 11, pp. 149–160). John Wiley & Sons, Inc.
Zajonc, R. B. (1980). Feeling and thinking: Preferences need no inferences. *The American Psychologist, 35*, 151–175.
Zajonc, R. B. (2000). Feeling and thinking: Closing the debate over the independence of affect. In J. P. Forgas (Ed.), *Feeling and thinking: The role of affect in social cognition* (pp. 31–58). Cambridge University Press.

CHAPTER 28

Humor

Glenn E. Weisfeld and Carol Cronin Weisfeld

> **Abstract**
> Humor has been studied from an evolutionary point of view beginning with Darwin. Some evolutionary theorists have regarded humor as a universal emotion. With its distinct affect and expression, humor meets most criteria for having an evolved basis. The expression of laughter has homologues in other primates and, as in children, is observed during tickling and other social play. This chapter proposes a functional theory of laughter that attempts to account for the fitness benefits for recipient and producer of humor. The recipient gains information and practice that are of later utility in social encounters. Alternative functional explanations for humor are reviewed, but these often feature group selection ideas and fail to account for the fitness value for the humorist. Humor appreciation is correlated with health, but mainly because healthy people are less anxious and hence disposed to appreciate jokes.
>
> **Key Words:** humor, laughter, mirth, evolution, dominance, courtship, marriage

Introduction

Psychology in recent years has come to be interested in pleasurable behaviors such as humor; this line of inquiry has been called positive psychology. Humor is one of the rare emotions with no negative affect—except that puns can be painful! Studies of humor have been published for many decades. Courses on the subject are offered in numerous universities, and a textbook, *Psychology of Humor*, is in its second edition (Martin & Ford, 2018). This chapter will begin by considering the evolutionary perspective of humor. This will be followed by a section on humor as a basic emotion. Next will come sections on humor's evolved basis, expressions, possible functions, development, individual differences, relation to play, neural bases, and pathology.

Humor in Evolutionary Perspective

Humor seems eminently suitable for treatment by evolutionary scholars, particularly ethologists employing observational methods. It is a universal behavior with a characteristic expression. Darwin (1998) himself studied laughter. A case can be made (see below) for regarding humor appreciation as a basic emotion, and emotions are a main topic of study by ethologists, again starting with Darwin.

Research has been conducted on all of Tinbergen's (1963) four questions as applied to humor and laughter. Possible homologues of human laughter are found in other mammals. The development of humor has been analyzed. The neural mediation of humor and laughter have been examined, and the heritability of humor production has been explored. Lastly, the adaptive value of humor has been probed. Although most research on humor has been conducted by psychologists, many of these findings can be incorporated into an evolutionary framework.

Humor as an Emotion

Emotions theorists have sometimes recognized humor as a distinct emotion, e.g., McDougall (1923), Ekman (1994), and Pugh (1977). Theorists disagree about the properties of an emotion. There is a consensus that an emotion has several facets, but which facets to include remain controversial (Weisfeld, 2019). Some theorists assert that a human emotion must have counterparts in other primates; others make no attempt at comparative analysis. Many theorists claim that an emotion must have a distinct expression, but even Ekman (1994), who omitted laughter from his list of six universal expressions, acknowledged that some emotions lack an expression.

Surprisingly, many theorists omit inclusion of a distinct affect in defining a basic emotion, even though the most distinguishing feature of an emotion is probably its affect. Moreover, most emotions are identified by affective terms such as hunger and fear (Zajonc, 1980). Affects occupy a pivotal role in emotional reactions to stimuli: an internal or external stimulus elicits a particular affect, which then triggers a behavioral response and any expression or physiological adjustments (LeDoux, 1996).

How does humor fare as a basic emotion by these various criteria? Panksepp (2005) asserted that the basic properties of an emotion comprise its affect, behavior, elicitors, expression, and physiological adjustments. Humor has a distinctive expression and a distinctive affect, sometimes referred to as mirth (e.g., Martin & Ford, 2018). However, the elicitors, behavior, and physiological changes of humor are not very clear-cut.

Evolved Basis

Humor, or mirth, clearly has an evolved basis, so if it qualifies as an emotion, it constitutes a basic (not blended) human emotion. Evidence that a human behavior has an evolved basis includes its universality, early developmental onset, presence in related species, stereotypy of form, and specific neural basis (Weisfeld, 1982). Laughter occurs in all cultures (Aldis, 1975). It appears early, at two to four months of age (McGhee 1979), even in congenitally blind and deaf infants (Goodenough, 1932)

The phylogenetic origins of human laughter are well established. The stereotypic human laughter expression occurs in many simians too. Chimpanzees vocalize when tickled in a manner similar to that of children (Darwin, 1998), and seek out being tickled. Vocalizations resembling human laughter can accompany social play in the great apes, entellus langurs, various baboons, and rhesus macaques (Aldis, 1975). Even young rats vocalize in a distinctive way when tickled on the back of the neck by a human handler or another rat (Panksepp & Burgdorf, 2003). This only occurs when the rat is relaxed and not, say, when a cat's odor is present, just as humor appreciation is inhibited by anxiety. Rats seek out handlers who have ticked them before, as well as cage mates that provide similar stimulation. Anecdotal evidence suggests that other young mammals also enjoy being tickled, especially about the neck.

Captive and even wild chimpanzees and gorillas have sometimes exhibited an appreciation for humor that goes beyond enjoyment of tickling and play fighting (reviewed by McGhee, 1979). A chimpanzee in a zoo would walk around with a brick on its back and then throw dirt at spectators attracted to the stunt. One gorilla that knew sign language once put his thumb in his ear and signed "drink," and then "funny." Wild chimpanzees sometimes torture small animals and "laugh" at the victim's antics (de Waal, 2019). On one occasion, a researcher put on a panther mask, which, as expected, evoked threatening behavior from the nearby wild chimpanzees. When he removed the mask, one of the chimpanzees broke into sustained laughter. A functional link between tickling and humor is suggested by the fact that individuals who laugh a lot when tickled also laugh readily at jokes (Fridlund & Loftus, 1990).

Expressions

Laughter and smiling show continuity in form between humans and other higher primates (Goodall, 1968). The facial muscles involved in human laughter are roughly homologous to those of monkeys and apes when tickled (van Hooff, 1972). The human smile evolved from an appeasement display in simians, called the silent, bared-teeth display (van Hooff, 1972). Human laughter evolved from the primate play face, a relaxed, open-mouth display. Although the smile and laughter have different evolutionary origins, both expressions involve the same muscle, the zygomatic major. The contractions are generally stronger and longer lasting in laughter than in smiling (Ruch, 1993), and additional muscles are recruited (Ruch & Ekman, 2001). The sound properties of this expression likewise are similar in humans and other primates. However, laughter is quieter in simians, consistent with their greater danger from predators (de Waal, 2019). As primate amusement intensifies, smiles grade into laughter, and the vocal element is added (Pollio et al., 1972). Then laughter fades in volume and subsides, followed by the same for smiling. Laughter is both a visual and an auditory signal, which makes it especially effective—in the dark, around obstacles, while facing away, and at a distance. It also varies in intensity and veracity, unlike most simian signals.

Although laughter is correlated with subjective funniness (Chapman, 1983), it occurs in a variety of social contexts, not all of them humorous. A diary study revealed that most incidents of laughter arose incidentally during social interactions that evoked a humorous remark, and seldom in response to joke telling (Martin & Kuiper, 1999). Laughter also is precipitated by gaffes. People may laugh from anxiety or to appease others, as a friendly display (Munro, 1951). The human smile and laughter have different evolutionary origins but similar functions in appeasement and in displaying amusement.

Genuine, or Duchenne, laughter is more effective behaviorally than feigned laughter, presumably because it is more veridical (Lavan et al., 2016). Faking smiles and laughter is difficult to do convincingly, largely because contracting the muscles around the eyes (orbicularis oculi) is usually omitted, and the muscles around the mouth (orbicularis oris) may not contract (Ruch & Ekman, 2001). Duchenne laughter tends to be higher pitched than feigned laughter (Gervais & Wilson, 2005). Laughter is a good example of the generally greater validity of nonverbal expressions than verbal ones; we often say "that's funny" but not feel it.

Laughter is contagious. Comedians often employ a "laugh track" of recorded group laughter because it stimulates laughter by a live audience. Laughter puts people in a relaxed mood that makes them receptive to humor. Hearing laughter seems to prime people not only to laugh but also to appreciate the proffered jokes. Similarly, when about to tell a joke, people often announce their intention to do so.

A Possible Functional Explanation
The Mystery of Humor

Unlike most emotions, the essence of humor remains puzzling to scholars. In this, we are in good company: An acquaintance of Abraham Lincoln, Joseph Gillespie, reported that "He [Lincoln] used to say that the attempt to ascertain wherein wit consisted baffled him more than any other undertaking of the kind[.] That the first impression would be that the thing was of easy solution but the varieties of wit were so great that what would explain one case would be wholly inapplicable to another" (Wilson & Davis, 1998, p. 506). Like Lincoln, some theorists have addressed the question of what makes something funny—the proximate question, not the distal one, of functional value.

Other theorists have proposed unitary functional explanations of humor, but these have largely failed to account for laughter at tickling, for word play, or for other forms and features of humor. Some of the common theories fail to account for laughter in nonhuman primates. Many theories are based on dubious group selection ideas. Most theories consider the possible benefit for the audience, but not for the humorist. The principle of individual selection requires that both the recipient of humor and the producer of humor must gain some fitness benefit. Joke telling is a voluntary social behavior that each party must engage in willingly. An evolutionary theory proposed by Weisfeld (1993) attempted to address these deficiencies and will now be described.

Benefits to the Recipient

Functional analysis of enjoyment of tickling has challenged many theorists, including Darwin. Back in 1897, Hall and Allin observed that laughter at tickling is most readily evoked if targeted at the armpits, soles, neck, cheeks, waist, and ribs. Koestler (1964) noted that these are spots especially vulnerable to attack. He proposed that being tickled provides practice at eluding attacks aimed at these areas. Indeed, successful tickling consists of a sudden aggressive thrust at the body, often evoking a defensive flexion of the trunk or other protective or evasive action. Darwin (1998) noted that, to be effective, the target must not anticipate the site of the thrust; thus, we cannot tickle ourselves (McDougall, 1923). Learning to ward off attacks would be advantageous from a young age; accordingly, even infants enjoy being tickled (Plooj, 1979), starting in the first year of life (Sroufe & Wunsch, 1972). Also consistent with this functional explanation, enjoyment of being tickled wanes after early childhood; presumably, an older child has learned how to parry such attacks, and has little need for further practice. Being tickled is often aversive in adulthood (Harris & Alvarado, 2005)—a possible instance of a negative affect of this emotion.

Laughter at being tickled seems to function to encourage such beneficial stimulation. The sound of laughter is generally pleasurable and hence rewarding (Bachorowski & Owren, 2003). Laughter has been described as musical, and this may be especially true of the delightful laughter of a baby (Apte, 1985). This feedback may gratify the parent, who continues to tickle or play with the child, who gains motoric skills that enhance survivability.

Similarly, children's laughter at play with peers seems to reward and perpetuate play, to their mutual benefit. These forms of social play are often agonistic, and may function to facilitate mutual practice in attack, flight, defense, and evasion. Laughter at social play encourages further play. Children's social play with laughter lasted longer than play without it (Davila-Ross et al., 2011). Following the biogenetic law, the earlier onset of laughter at tickling, in the first year of life, suggests that this behavior evolved before it was extended to peer play, which begins at around two or three years of age.

What about other forms of humor, such as jokes? What does the recipient of humor gain? Most theorists agree that jokes convey information that is of later utility. Across cultures, many jokes feature a trickster's clumsy, antisocial, futile attempts to satisfy his biological needs (Apte, 1985). The recipient presumably learns to avoid committing these gaffes, much as a person learns to avoid slipping on a banana peel by seeing a clown do so. Information about social conduct may be effectively conveyed by illustrating the foibles of a butt, fool, or clown, who commits some foolish faux pas (false step). The audience—and sometimes the butt himself—learns to avoid making these blunders. Committing a minor gaffe, such as farting or being seen naked, often amuses observers and evokes embarrassment in the victim (Weisfeld & Weisfeld, 2014). Jokes often highlight subtle social errors. These social subtleties are hard to master, and many jokes pertain to minor social missteps. But if the victim depicted is seriously injured, humorousness is precluded, perhaps because the mood of playfulness is undercut by sympathy for the victim.

Various factors intensify the edifying effect of a joke. If there is fitness relevance to the content of the joke, that makes it funnier. Many jokes pertain to sex, aggression, and dominance, for example. Similarly, people like true stories more than fables (Pugh, 1977). Funniness makes jokes more memorable and repeated, enhancing their impact (Cline & Kellaris, 2007). We can think of jokes as undergoing selection for their effectiveness and utility. These facts are consistent with an informational explanation for the function of hearing jokes.

Being the recipient of humor is emotionally satisfying in various ways. Understanding a punch line provides satisfying cognitive insight, and perhaps also feelings of pride at getting the joke. If the recipient later benefits from utilizing the information imparted by the joke, additional affective gains are realized.

Harder to explain are jokes based on linguistic oddities, such as puns and double meanings. For example, a person is asked to pronounce this series of spelled-out words: MacMillan, MacTavish, MacInerny, MacDonald, Machinery. As Pugh (1977) pointed out, the exceptional case is the most informative one, and linguistic and logic jokes often are based on idiosyncrasies. These jokes may protect us from saying embarrassing things or strengthen our powers of reasoning; jokes get us to consider all possibilities, a feature of formal operational thinking. Similarly, Vaid (1999) suggested that humor disrupts habitual reasoning that might not apply to the current case. Pugh (1977) noted that incongruity, a common feature of jokes, arises from counterexamples, which are especially informative because they help to define categories. He referred to humor as "nature's way of motivating the social sharing of counter examples" (p. 329).

Benefits to the Humorist

But what is the benefit of telling jokes? Weisfeld (1993) proposed that the humorist gains social credit, or social capital. People gain approval for telling good jokes, and for telling them well. Setting up a joke with just the right information and delivering the punch line at just the right time are crucial. This is a skill, like other art forms, and like other forms it earns credit and expressions of appreciation and obligation (Weisfeld, 2006). Since a person gains credit by being funny, we dislike laughing at a joke from an enemy; we hate to give the person credit. But employees often feign laughter at the boss's jokes, presumably in order to gain favor (Kane et al., 1977).

Affectively, the humorist experiences pride as a result of the laughter and other expressions of appreciation. Pride results from a rise in social status and entails feeling entitled to claim prerogatives of rank (Weisfeld & Dillon, 2012). Telling a joke that falls flat can be embarrassing. It can lead others to perceive the jokester as being more aggressive and less friendly than someone whose jokes succeed (Derks et al., 1995). Telling jokes is a competitive, risky behavior that can result in a loss of status.

Funny people are generally well liked, and are favored in various ways. They may be invited to parties and not be expected to reciprocate. They may advance in their occupations because of their ability to amuse others and put them at their ease. Men and women use humor to initiate and maintain various social connections (Bressler et al., 2006). Humor tends to make people feel closer to each other, and enhances liking (Treger et al., 2013). Even just working on humorous tasks enhanced feelings of closeness (Fraley & Aron, 2004). Thus, abundant evidence suggests that telling jokes tends to pay dividends, most obviously money paid to a comedian or cartoonist.

One obvious way of repaying the humorist is by telling jokes in return. Because humor is highly contagious, joke-telling sessions are a common social phenomenon. Each joke seems to serve as a meta-communication, lightening mood and encouraging reciprocity and promoting solidarity.

Gervais and Wilson (2005) dismissed Weisfeld's theory on the grounds that it fails to show how humor evolved from existing traits. To the contrary, Weisfeld traced humor in our species from simian laughter during tickling and other forms of social play, cited examples of sight gags and linguistic humor in captive apes, and described similarities between social play and humor that indicate a common evolutionary origin. Gervais and Wilson speculate about when in hominin evolution humor and non-Duchenne laughter emerged, but laughter is not the only human expression with a feigned version, so non-Duchenne laughter does not seem to require a specific evolutionary explanation.

Gervais and Wilson assert that humor and laughter evolved to signal safe conditions. Why would laughter have been needed to signal safety when humans and many other species employ appeasement displays to accomplish the same thing? Furthermore, laughter seems mainly to reflect amusement, not feelings of security. Gervais and Wilson fail to explain why incongruity is often a feature of jokes, beyond saying that playful incongruity is a sign of safety. Gervais and Wilson ignore the fact that most jokes have a butt or fool whose antics are amusing. This seems to indicate some function that is more specific than signaling safety. They do view humor as aiding creativity by engendering playful emotional contagion, but many creative acts are solitary, and it is hard to see why they must occur in a group setting. Their explanation also relies on positing group selection, yet the benefits to the humorist and recipient seem to be distinct.

One of the complications in trying to explain the function of humor is that humor takes various forms. Martin et al. (2003) developed a humor styles questionnaire, and identified four styles: affiliative, self-enhancing, self-defeating, and aggressive. These different styles can be understood in part as reflecting differences in dominance, or social standing. Using affiliative humor builds social relationships, and is associated with extraversion and openness to experience (Vernon et al., 2008). Self-enhancing humor elevates one's social standing, and is positively correlated with extraversion and negatively with neuroticism. Both of these prosocial styles suggest a dominant personality; dominant individuals tend to be sociable and low in anxiety. Aggressive humor is positively correlated with neuroticism and negatively correlated with conscientiousness and agreeableness. Consistent with this pattern, aggressive individuals tend to be low-ranking. In self-defeating or self-deprecating humor, the humorist makes fun of himself, to the amusement of the audience. Individuals using this style tend to be neurotic, anxious, and depressed (Schermer et al., 2013); their use of humor reflects their low social standing but may be ingratiating. The Weisfeld theory seems to fit the affiliative and self-enhancing humor styles best. But the relevance of all four styles to dominance status is consistent with the idea that telling jokes can raise one's rank. Some other theories will now be described.

Other Functional Explanations of Humor
Correction of Deviant Behavior
This explanation most closely fits the aggressive style of humor. Bergson (1911) proposed that humor can be used to correct misbehavior by a group member. This group selection explanation can be recast in terms of individual selection by observing that one person can correct another through ridicule. Of course, third parties may observe one person ridiculing another, spreading the corrective benefit to the group.

Many forms of humor, including ridicule, mockery, mimicry, satire, parody, sarcasm, and caricature, possess this corrective potential. Ridicule or mockery seems to be more painful to receive and remember than simple criticism; this function may have added selection pressure in favor of the evolution of humor. Eibl-Eibesfeldt (1989) observed that the staccato phonation of laughter resembles the mobbing calls of birds summoning allies to harass a predator—although this may be a case of convergent evolution.

Laughter is indeed capable of correcting deviant behavior (Bryant et al., 1983). Criticism applied with the balm of humor may be easier to accept (Haig, 1988). Ridicule can be poignant and effective if done delicately; teasing a friend can be endearing as well as informative. On the other hand, nasty mockery can be excessively embarrassing or insulting, and can weaken the relationship. Observers too may be embarrassed or offended by the ridicule, to the detriment of the humorist's social standing. Ridicule may amuse some people present but alienate others, and thus is of dubious net fitness benefit.

Simple tactful criticism or shunning can be equally effective in correcting misbehavior. Clever criticism should be as effective as ridicule (Kane et al., 1977). McDougall (1923) expressed doubt that the complex emotion of humor evolved for this possibly superfluous purpose. Perhaps ridicule is simply a special application of the general form of many jokes: someone does something foolish, and revealing the foolishness is amusing and informative for the audience. If the butt is present and is aware of being mocked, his or her misbehavior may be corrected in the process. This corrective lesson may later benefit the butt and the audience.

Competition
A related theory of humor, and one that likewise fits the aggressive humor category well (Schermer et al., 2013), is that we revel in the failure or embarrassment of the butt. Aristotle (1895) pointed out that personal defects are a common source of the ludicrous, and Hobbes (1651) offered a "sudden glory" interpretation of humor. Similar ideas have been advanced by Alexander (1986), Lorenz (1963), and Plato (1871).

Indeed, many jokes can be described as put-down humor. Joke telling is often competitive, as in adolescents' "doing the dozens." Across cultures, adolescents, especially males, frequently engage in bouts of ridiculing, or "ranking," each other (Apte, 1985). For example, Greenland Eskimos traditionally resolved disputes through public contests of ridiculing each other (Levine, 1977).

Consistent with this explanation, ridicule tends to flow down the dominance hierarchy (Chapman, 1983). Similarly, evaluative comments flowed from the better volleyball players in a middle school toward the poorer ones (Weisfeld & Weisfeld, 1984). In this respect, humor can be seen as being corrective (see above).

It is difficult to see how one's fitness is enhanced by laughing at another's failure; the failure itself is usually apparent. Another problem is that "serious" misfortune is not funny, except perhaps when the victim is disliked (Schadenfreude) (Bateson, 1969). McDougall (1923) proposed that humor relieves us of the burden of excessive sympathy for the fool. However, this effect seems to be part of the reciprocal altruism system (Trivers, 1971); we feel less sympathy for people whose misfortune is their own fault (Lerner & Simmons, 1966). Sympathy for the butt reduces humorousness, rather than humorousness reducing sympathy.

This theory has been criticized on various additional grounds. It does not explain laughter at tickling or word play, laughter in simians and infants, or the incongruity element. It is unlikely that humor evolved in order to provide a basis for competition; people, especially boys, will compete over most any skill. In a spelling bee, boys (but not girls) competed to be first to press the buzzer to try to spell a word—even if they did not know how to spell it (Weisfeld et al., 1983)!

Perhaps our pleasure at the butt of a joke is simply a byproduct of the fact that seeing someone else look foolish makes us feel good in comparison. Along these lines, it seems there is no reason to assert that humor provides a catharsis of aggression. In fact, exposure to aggressive humor tends to heighten aggression, not reduce it (Berkowitz, 1970). Aggressive people seem to like aggressive humor simply because aggression interests them.

Group Solidarity

Another functional theory of humor proposes that it promotes group solidarity (Alexander, 1986). This explanation seems to fit the affiliative humor style most closely. Humor can indeed increase self-reported cohesion among group members (Flamson & Barrett, 2008). For example, mutual ribbing seemed to enhance solidarity in a Chippewa tribal council (Miller, 1967). In a longitudinal study at a Canadian police academy, group cohesion increased through the use of aggressive humor, directed first at oneself and then at out-group members and finally at in-group members (Terrion & Ashforth, 2002). The contagiousness of laughter and the fact that the amount of laughter increases with group size suggest the operation of "an automatic social synchronization process that predates language" (Provine, 1992, p. 2). This group selection explanation might be recast in terms of dyads.

However, it is unclear why the emotion of humor, with its word play, tickling of children as young as four months, and incongruity would have evolved for this purpose. Why would it be necessary to share jokes in order to engender solidarity when sharing rituals, dress, values, language, and experiences carries the same benefit? The socially cohesive effect of humor might merely be a byproduct. The solidarity explanation grades into the competitiveness theory. Group solidarity can come at the expense of hostility to the out-group, resulting in no net fitness benefit. Humor is often used to mock and stigmatize outgroup members, and can increase acceptance of disparagement of targeted groups such as women and minorities (Ford et al., 2014).

Health

The idea that humor is healthful was bolstered in the public mind by a testimonial by Norman Cousins (1979) on its supposed analgesic effects. No data were presented, but the theory gained wide acceptance.

Hearing jokes does not seem to have any clear health benefits (Svebak et al., 2004). Healthy people enjoy jokes mainly because they have few health worries and therefore are receptive to humor. This probably explains the correlation sometimes found between enjoying humor and heart health, for example. Similarly, enjoying humor is associated with sensing less pain, evidently because people in pain are less receptive to humor (Zweyer et al., 2004). When exposure to humor is correlated with lower reports of pain, a placebo effect seems to be operating (Mahony et al., 2001). Effects of humor on the immune system are mixed (reviewed by Martin & Ford, 2018).

The evolutionists Greengross and Miller (2008) reasoned that, if humor is salubrious, professional comics might be healthier. They found, to the contrary, that improv artists were less healthy than the control group. Another study showed that funnier comedians died younger than less funny ones, and straight men outlived their comical partners (Stewart & Thompson, 2015).

Hearing jokes is thought to be an effective way of relaxing, but sympathetic arousal increases when the punch line is delivered (Chapman, 1976), and in proportion to the degree of amusement (Langevin & Day, 1972). Furthermore, it would not be adaptive if we could "laugh our troubles away," because the source of our troubles would remain to harm us. Suppression of the immune system or symptoms of disease is generally hazardous.

Various emotional factors may complicate health effects of humor. Romundstad, Svebak, Holen, and Hofmen (2016) found that the cognitive component of sense of humor—being able to understand jokes and perhaps being neurologically healthy—was positively correlated with longevity, but the affective component was negatively correlated. Using affiliative humor is associated with better health, but self-defeating humor with poorer health (Richards & Kruger, 2017). Affiliative humor might enhance social support, which is known to be healthful.

Psychological Benefits

Hearing jokes and laughing are pleasurable, although it is difficult to tease apart the effects of humor from other factors that enhance feelings of well-being (Kim et al., 2015). Affiliative and self-enhancing humor seem to be especially beneficial (Ford et al., 2016), and aggressive humor detrimental (Cann, Davis, et al., 2011). Exposure to self-enhancing humor appears to be beneficial in tamping down stressors (Ford et al., 2017), perhaps by reframing stressors in a positive way (Cann, Stilwell, et al., 2011). Martin and Lefcourt (1983) showed that ability to generate humor was related to stress reduction.

One possibility is that laughter signals to kin and allies that the situation is safe enough to permit joking, as Gervais and Wilson proposed (2005). The contagion effect of humor is consistent with this explanation. However, this seems to be a byproduct or application of humor. And, like the effect on health, if humor mitigates adaptive stressors, it might be counterproductive in fitness terms. Similarly, optimistic people who think everything will work out are inclined to ignore hazards such as smoking and poor diet (Friedman et al., 1993).

Humor has been employed in various practical settings. McGhee (2010) developed an instructional program for increasing people's experience of humor. Little research has been conducted on the use of humor in psychotherapy. Marcus (1990) described certain patients who minimize the seriousness of their conditions by using humor to dismiss them as "one big joke." Different humor styles can have opposite effects. Affiliative and self-enhancing humor have been shown to increase cooperation, performance, and satisfaction in the workplace (Meyer et al., 1993). Workplace humor can relieve monotony, express resentment of managers or regulations, or mask the authority of managers (Dwyer, 1991). One study found that leaders' positive humor enhanced creativity; negative humor reduced it (Lee, 2015). On the other hand, aggressive humor is a common form of sexual harassment in the workplace (Pryor, 1995).

Humor seems to enhance retention of material in the classroom, but evidently at the expense of retention of non-humorous material (Schmidt & Williams, 1971). Providing humor before a math exam seemed to improve performance by lowering anxiety (Ford et al., 2012). Students prefer humorous textbooks and instructors, but improvements in learning are hard to demonstrate (Klein et al., 1982). Using ridicule in the classroom can upset children (Bryant et al., 1983).

Courtship

The evolutionary psychologist Geoffrey Miller (1998, 2000) proposed that women are attracted to funny men because ability to tell jokes is a sign of intelligence; that is, he asserted that a good sense of humor is sexually selected. People seeking a mate often cite good sense of humor (GSOH) as high on their list of desirable attributes (Sprecher & Regan, 2002). Personals ads, especially those placed by women, often specify GSOH (Buunk et al., 2008). Men and women do tend to use humor to attract a mate (Li et al., 2009); however, women but not men have shown a tendency to find a humorous suitor attractive (Bressler & Balshine, 2000).

A degree of intelligence does seem to be required to invent or tell good jokes (see below), but research shows that people do not seek a particularly intelligent mate. Rather, they seek a mate similar to them in intelligence. Spouses are very highly correlated on IQ (Richardson, 1939). This can only occur if people prefer to marry someone matched to them on intelligence, not someone smarter. If all women sought to marry an intelligent man and women did all the choosing, couples would not be highly correlated on intelligence. The wife's intelligence would not be particularly correlated with her husband's; perhaps attractive wives would gain the smartest husbands, as Miller imagined. A high correlation between spouses on intelligence—as is actually the case—could come about if women did all the choosing and selected a man of similar intelligence, or if both sexes chose as intelligent a mate as they could win over. But Miller's theory is that the wife does most of the choosing; if so, a smart man could not refuse to marry a dumb woman who chose him, and couples would not be matched on intelligence. Another possibility is that people are matched on types of humor enjoyed, such as political jokes or puns. Couples do tend to resemble each other on many variables.

Li et al. (2009) suggested that people do not use humorousness as an important basis for choosing a mate. Instead, they found that both sexes interpret humor production and appreciation as a sign of romantic interest. Indeed, teasing is a common form of flirtation, and may be a sign of interest (Keltner et al., 1998). Walle (1976) suggested that a man can use risqué humor to amuse a woman, and if she rejects him, he can save face by declaring that she is a prude or lacks a sense of humor.

An important ethological study examined humor and laughter between a man and woman introduced to each other (Grammer, 1990). Women reported liking a man who had made them laugh, but men did not particularly like a woman who had made them laugh. Instead, men liked a woman who laughed at their jokes! This does suggest an element of sexual selection. However, it is equally plausible that women merely indicated their preference for a man by laughing at his jokes. Her laughter did indeed seem to have the effect of indicating interest, in that the man responded by liking the woman. A study by Lundy, Tan, and Cunningham (1998) indicated that the humorousness of a man increased his appeal to a woman only if she thought he was physically attractive.

Marriage

Humor may be important in strengthening marriages. Couples report that humor contributed to their marital satisfaction (Lauer et al., 1990). Ziv and Gadish (1989) found that having a funny spouse was correlated with marital satisfaction for husbands and wives. An observational study revealed that couples who laughed and joked a lot had happier marriages (Carstensen et al., 1995). Having a funny spouse seems to be more beneficial than one's own use of humor (de Koning & Weiss, 2002).

A cross-cultural study confirmed that people are happier with a spouse who makes them laugh (Weisfeld et al., 2011). This effect was stronger for wives than for husbands, in the United States, the United Kingdom, and Turkey—although the opposite was true in Russia.

An observational study showed that US wives laughed more than husbands (Weisfeld & Stack, 2002).

However, people whose spouse made them laugh did not regard the spouse as being particularly intelligent (Weisfeld et al., 2011). Rather, having a funny spouse may be satisfying because it indicates a willingness to amuse and entertain one's spouse. Joke telling may be a sign of commitment, kindness, and reassurance. In return, laughing at the spouse's jokes may serve as a sign of acceptance, respect, and contentment, a granting of status. Not laughing at the spouse's jokes may indicate rejection or hostility. Humor reveals the tenor of the marriage for both parties. Consistent with the principle of female choice, husbands joke more than wives. Like courtship, marital humor in some ways is a floor show put on for the woman.

But humor in marriage can have negative effects. Joking in marriage can be nasty mockery, or it can be a way of "laughing off" confrontation of serious issues (Cohan & Bradbury, 1997). Affiliative humor is associated with marital satisfaction, but self-deprecating and aggressive humor negatively relate to it (Cann et al., 2011).

Humor surely did not evolve specifically to enhance courtship or marriages. It functions in many kinds of relationships, not just reproductive ones. It begins in childhood, well before romantic motivation appears, and extends to same-sex friendships and work settings, too. Yet spousal humor was an important factor in marital satisfaction for both sexes in the United States, the United Kingdom, Turkey, and Russia, although not among the Chinese (Weisfeld et al., in prep.). It seems that the intimacy and duration of marriages can be better sustained with a funny companion who seeks to amuse the spouse.

Development

Various developmental trends are consistent with an informational, or cognitive, explanation for the function of hearing jokes. In order to be funny, a joke needs to be appropriate for a child's degree of cognitive development: the cognitive consistency, or cognitive congruity, principle (Zigler et al., 1966). Content that is too simple provides no new information, and content that is too perplexing likewise provides no opportunity for insight. Children prefer jokes that illustrate cognitive concepts that they are beginning to understand. For example, infants are typically amused by peek-a-boo and Jack-in-the-box. Appreciating these phenomena seems to depend on a capacity for understanding object permanence (McGhee, 1979). In order to be receptive to a joke, it helps if the child is relaxed; fear can interfere with comprehension, and fear is engendered by extreme novelty. One-year-olds laughed at peek-a-boo more with their mothers than with a stranger (MacDonald & Silverman, 1978).

As children get older and more cognitively mature, their tastes in humor become more complex. For example, consider this joke: Johnny is asked if he wants his pizza divided into four or six pieces. He replies, better make it four; I could never eat six. Appreciating this joke depends on mastery of the Piagetian concept of conservation (McGhee, 1976). Children who are too young to understand this concept do not find the joke funny; those who are in the throes of mastering it do find it funny. Those who are much older again do not find it funny. For adults too, jokes that are too simple for our tastes strike us as silly and not amusing; we have little to learn from them (Athey, 1977). Senile adults may again find simple jokes amusing (Schaier & Cicirelli, 1976), specifically jokes based on violations of conservation (Mak & Carpenter, 2007).

Across cultures, many jokes have an element of incongruity (Schultz, 1977). Often this derives from exaggeration, understatement, or ambiguity, all of which entail some incongruity or paradox. Infants often laugh at incongruous stimuli. However, in order to be amused, the child must comprehend the incongruity. If not, the stimulus is regarded as puzzling or even frightening (Parrott & Gleitman, 1989). For example, in order to be amused, an infant who is shown a Jack-in-the-box must understand that Jack still exists when hidden (Sroufe & Wunsch, 1972). Cognitive resolution of such incongruities is presumably informative, confirming the validity and application of the relevant cognitive principle.

How can this incongruity element be reconciled with the proposition that hearing jokes provides information about social gaffes to be avoided? Jokes tend to pertain to "ticklish" social situations that are unusual and perplexing. Typically, the clown or butt fails to appreciate the incongruity of the situation, and as a result behaves maladroitly. Often the incongruity takes the form of a verbal inconsistency or paradox that bewilders or embarrasses the butt. Only a comparatively few jokes, such as word play, seem to feature incongruity resolution without a social context.

Ironic humor seems to entail incongruity. Gibbs (1986) asserted that irony can refer to a statement contrary to the intended meaning. The incongruity lies in the contrast between the literal and implied meanings of a statement (Dews et al., 1996). Sarcasm is a special case of irony in which someone is disparaged by a positive comment that cloaks an insult. Irony without sarcasm and a butt is not particularly funny, as in calling a rainy day beautiful.

Appreciation of irony seems to depend upon development of sufficient theory of mind, around age six, entailing the ability to imagine the motivation of the ironist (Sullivan et al., 1995). At this age children also begin to avoid behaviors for which other children have been ridiculed (Bryant et al., 1983). However, not until age eight or nine did children find ironic insults (or sarcasm) funnier than literal insults (Dews et al., 1996). Adults found subtler examples of irony funnier than more obvious ones.

Other developmental processes are also consistent with a cognitive interpretation of the function of humor. When young children begin to understand symbols, they engage in pretend play, including silliness such as an adult pretending to be a child or using a tool for the wrong purpose. Pretend play expands the child's opportunities for conjuring up incongruous scenarios.

Adolescence is a stage of heightened competitiveness, since reproductive fitness comes into play (Weisfeld, 1999). Across cultures, adolescents frequently ridicule each other (Apte, 1985). Adolescents' humor often pertains to sex, peer norms, and relations with authorities (reviewed by Weisfeld, 1993).

Cultural differences can shape the content of jokes. In US adults, jokes commonly pertain to sex, ethnicity, politics, and alcohol (Winick, 1976). In the United Kingdom, jokes frequently relate to subtle social class distinctions. The Chinese tend to use humor sparingly; it is sometimes regarded as a sign of not being a serious, dependable person (Weisfeld et al., in prep.). For other examples, see Ziv (1988).

With experience, we learn what sorts of jokes will be understood, accepted, and appreciated by particular audiences. A joke can fail if it is not understood, if it is considered improper, or if it does not appeal to the person's particular sense of humor. Being an art form, humor is distinctly a matter of taste (Weisfeld, 2006). Commonality in tastes in humor can engender group solidarity (Flamson & Barrett, 2008). The salience of the content for the individual renders it more humorous; angered subjects preferred aggressive jokes, and sexually aroused ones preferred sexual humor (Strickland, 1959). Aggressive people tend to like aggressive humor (Holmes, 1969), and those in a violent country (the US) liked hostile jokes more than did Japanese and Senegalese subjects (Goldstein, 1977).

In the elderly, humor comprehension is related to working memory, which may decline in old age (Shammi & Stuss, 2003). However, elderly people in the United Kingdom rated humorous material as funnier than did younger individuals. The same was found to be true of elderly Germans with respect to incongruity humor (Ruch et al., 1990).

Individual Differences

Behavioral genetics studies on appreciation of humor have been inconclusive (reviewed by Martin & Ford, 2018). Whether genetic, shared environmental, or nonshared environmental influences predominate depends partly on how sense of humor is measured, e.g., which humor style is examined. Many studies do not tease apart the effects of gene-environment interaction.

Humor production and comprehension are related to IQ and academic achievement scores (Pellegrini et al., 1987). Humor production is also related to creativity and divergent thinking (Brodzinsky, 1977).

The ability to produce jokes is somewhat separate from the ability to understand them. Children who are regarded as funny tend to be popular, outgoing, self-confident leaders (Warners-Kleverlaan et al., 1996). These are attributes of dominant individuals (Weisfeld & Dillon, 2012), and studies of children of various ages confirm that humor is associated with dominance (McGhee, 1980a, 1980b). This conclusion is consistent with the idea that producing humor can gain social credit. Children who sought attention from adults, as well as being dominant among their peers, later had better senses of humor (McGhee, 1980a). Professional comics tend to be dominant (McGhee, 1986).

Sex differences in humor are consistent with the idea that joke telling is motivated by a desire for social recognition. Joke telling is more common in males across cultures (Goldstein & McGhee, 1972), Boys are more humorous than girls starting well before puberty, implying that this reflects the sex difference in competitive motivation rather than sexual selection. Men prefer put-down jokes more than women, who favor self-deprecating humor more (Zillman, 1977). And men compete more than women to show that they have gotten the joke (Alexander, 1986). Women seem to appreciate humor more than men do (Ziv, 1984), but perhaps because women are more willing to grant credit to the jokester than are men.

Humor and Play

This element of incongruity and its resolution distinguish humor from social play. In humor, insight into resolving the incongruity occurs suddenly, with the punch line, whereas the pleasure of social play is protracted. Proper timing of the punch line is essential (Fry, 1963). The content of humor is mainly social, and especially concerns social foibles (Bergson, 1911), whereas play can be asocial, including object play and motoric play. Humor seems specifically to provide information about delicate social situations, at least in adulthood.

But these two behaviors have much in common (Mannell & McMahon, 1982). Both provide information or skills of later utility (Boulton & Smith, 1992). Play and tickling are common in the primates and generally have deferred benefits, appropriate for species practicing a slow life-history strategy. Across mammals, play predominates during immaturity. In humans, too, play is prominent in childhood, during the growth plateau (Weisfeld, 1999). However, play in humans lasts through the life span, inspiring the appellation *Homo ludens*.

In both humor and play, pleasure is maximal if the content is appropriate in difficulty for the individual. Fear can inhibit both play and humor; moderate tickling produced the most laughter in chimpanzees (Plooij, 1979). Anxiety and depression can interfere with enjoyment of humor as well as of play (Haig, 1988). Novelty is another essential element for a joke or game. Games can become boring with repetition, and the same is true of "stale" jokes (Gelb & Zinkhan, 1986). Novelty is needed to impart new information. Both play and humor are enhanced if the content is relevant to biological fitness (Boulton & Smith, 1992).

Other similarities have been identified between play and humor that suggest a common evolutionary origin. Smiling and laughter serve as meta-communication to set a mood of frivolity in both cases (Fry, 1963). The play face and laughter emerge at about the same time in humans (L. J. Stettner, personal communication, 1992) and chimpanzees (Plooij, 1979). Being in a playful mood enhances enjoyment of humor (Bariaud, 1988). Children's ratings of sense of humor correlate with measures of playfulness (Barnett, 1991). Nursery school children who played a lot scored high on humor initiation and laughter (McGhee & Lloyd, 1982). Linguistically, play and humor seem to show some overlap: ludicrous (from *ludere*, to play), joke (from *jocus*, a joke or game), horseplay, word play, trick, etc. These many similarities befit two behaviors with common expressions and evolutionary origins.

Neural Bases
Humor Comprehension
Patients with right hemisphere damage can show deficits in humor comprehension. Involvement of the right hemisphere is consistent with the importance of incongruity in humor comprehension; this hemisphere predominates in mediating spatial relations; cf. congruent triangles. Right hemisphere damage was associated with difficulty in identifying an ending that would resolve the incongruity in a joke (Bihrle et al., 1986). This and other research has led to the conclusion that the left hemisphere is involved in recognizing incongruity, and the right hemisphere in resolving it (Gillikin & Derks, 1991). Of course, the left hemisphere mainly mediates comprehension of the verbal content of jokes. Left hemisphere damage can eliminate appreciation of cartoons with captions but spares comprehension of cartoons without captions (Kolb & Wishaw, 1985).

In the right hemisphere, the frontal lobe seems to be particularly involved in humor comprehension (Shammi & Stuss, 1999). This is consistent with findings that comprehension is related to theory of mind functioning (Happé, et al., 1999). Brownell and Stringfellow (2000) reconciled this information about the role of the frontal lobe and right hemisphere by suggesting that incongruity resolution in humor often involves theory of mind—correctly attributing beliefs to particular individuals.

Later studies have attempted to provide more specific anatomical information. One functional magnetic resonance imaging (fMRI) study found that exposure to incongruity-resolution cartoons bilaterally activated the inferior frontal gyrus and the temporoparietal junctions (Samson et al., 2008). Another such inquiry revealed that incongruity-resolution jokes activated the left inferior frontal gyrus, superior frontal gyrus, and left inferior parietal lobule (Chan et al., 2013). The differences in laterality between these two studies may reflect the greater verbal content in the latter. It seems that both hemispheres mediate incongruity resolution of jokes. A blood-oxygen-level-dependent (BOLD) study implicated inferior frontal gyrus, temporal pole gyrus, and temporoparietal junction bilaterally (Campbell et al., 2015). As a general rule, both hemispheres cooperate in higher cognitive tasks. These inconsistent results are consistent with the fact that humor comprehension involves many parts of the brain, as well as with the frequent inconsistency of neuroimaging research results.

Humor Appreciation
Mirth involves the mesolimbic reward system and other limbic structures that are activated during emotional responding (Shibata et al., 2014). These structures include the thalamus, ventral striatum, nucleus accumbens, ventral tegmental area, hypothalamus, and amygdala. One study implicated the orbitofrontal cortex, another limbic structure (Iwase et al., 2002). This evidence supports the argument for humor being an emotion.

Electrical stimulation of various brain structures in conscious surgical patients can evoke reports of mirth (e.g., Fried et al., 1998). Patients typically confabulate, inventing some explanation for perceiving humorousness. For example, in this study the patient attributed humorousness to a picture of a horse in the room. In another striking example, a surgeon swabbed the floor of the third ventricle, touching the hypothalamus. The patient burst out laughing, told jokes, uttered obscene remarks, and alluded to the supposedly hilarious antics of a surgeon present (Martin, 1950).

Laughter

Many neuropathological conditions include spontaneous laughter. In most cases, the laughter is "sham," with no affective element. However, mirth usually results if the damage includes limbic structures, such as the anterior cingulate cortex (Szameitat et al., 2010). Laughter can also be triggered by nitrous oxide.

Duchenne expressions, including laughter, involve various limbic system structures and the brainstem areas innervating cranial nerves leading to the facial muscles and larynx (Frank & Ekman, 1993). Posed expressions bypass the limbic system; they originate in the motor areas of the frontal lobe and proceed directly through the pyramidal tract to the brainstem and cranial nerves. Patients with extensive cortical damage typically exhibit Duchenne laughter but not voluntary laughter. Limbic lesions can spare posed expressions.

The perception of evolved emotional expressions also involves various limbic structures such as the insula and amygdala, again depending on the particular emotion. Perception of laughter entails the temporal lobe and amygdala (Fusar-Poli et al., 2009). Imitation of the laughter expression activates the frontal lobe, which contains mirror neurons (Caruana et al., 2015). The contagion effect of laughter is mediated by (mirror?) neurons in the premotor area of the frontal lobe and insula (Gervais & Wilson, 2005).

Humor Pathology

The conditions involved in sham laughter include bulbar palsy; pseudobulbar palsy (the most common); and basal ganglia, hypothalamic, and temporal lobe pathology (Bannister, 1973). Other neurological conditions, such as Parkinson's and multiple sclerosis, can cause excessive laughter accompanied by mirth. Laughing can be excessive in mania, dementia (Duchowny, 1983), and Angelman syndrome, a condition involving genomic imprinting (Williams, 2010). Various forms of brain damage can disinhibit laughter (Wild et al., 2003). The patient is unable to modulate or inhibit laughter normally. Often these bouts of sustained laughter are signs of an impending stroke, as, for example, in *fou rire prodromique* (ominous crazy laughter). Comprehension of jokes tends to be impaired in schizophrenia (Polimeni & Reiss, 2006).

In gelastic (laughing) epilepsy, convulsions are accompanied by bouts of laughter that last less than a minute; most patients are rendered unconscious (Arroyo et al., 1993). Some patients have literally laughed themselves to death. Most cases begin in childhood, but can begin in newborns (Sher & Brown, 1976). Patients who remain conscious report having experienced mirth, so this is an example of psychomotor, or temporal lobe, epilepsy involving the limbic system (Wild et al., 2003).

Lesions to the limbic orbitofrontal cortex can result in Witzelsucht, facetiousness. The patient makes inappropriate or excessive jokes (Lishman, 1978). The orbitofrontal cortex seems to mediate feelings of pride and shame (Fuster, 1997). Patients typically have an excessive notion of their own worth, and evidently think they are hilarious. Patients typically show reduced activation of this area, especially on the right side (Tranel et al., 2007). Since the right hemisphere tends to mediate negative affects, it makes sense that patients have elevated self-esteem.

Laughter is contagious, and epidemics of hysterical laughter have been documented (Izard, 1979). One episode that began at a convent school in Africa spread to 14 other schools, forcing their closure, then to the girls' relatives, and then to neighboring villages (Bean, 1967). The schools were closed, and some girls were hospitalized for exhaustion.

Ruch and Proyer (2009) have identified a condition called gelotophobia. This refers to people who are highly sensitive to being ridiculed. Doubtless, all normal people are embarrassed by ridicule to some degree. Perhaps excessive sensitivity to ridicule warrants a special pathological term. However, it may be better simply to recognize that any emotion can have too low or too high a threshold, but that most people are in the normal range due to stabilizing selection. Likewise, their term for insufficient sensitivity to ridicule, gelotophilia, seems superfluous.

Conclusions

The theory of the function of humor as proposed here has been extended to account for effects of humor on group solidarity, dominance status, and deviant behavior, and its use in friendship, courtship, marriage, and various group settings. Simply put, jokes are amusing, enlightening, and memorable. Humor can correct perceived misbehavior by illustrating foibles, and can be used to disparage a competitor. Often these misbehaviors arise in delicate social situations, and require the subtlety of the incongruity resolution of humor to resolve. Jokes of fitness relevance and salience to the recipient tend to be funnier. The ability to produce and appreciate jokes depends on cognitive capacity being congruent with the content.

The humorist gains status from offering these benefits; joke telling is something of a competitive sport enhanced by intelligence. Appreciative laughter at a good joke is rewarding, encouraging further such offerings. Competitive people seek the status that comes with successful joke telling. The more competitive gender jokes more. The artful humorist may be rewarded with friendship, popularity, and other social dividends.

Humor can take different forms; the affiliative style is pro-social, and the self-enhancing style raises one's status. Aggressive humor is also competitive, but in a negative way. Self-defeating humor expresses low status and can be ingratiating. All these forms can raise the dominance status of the successful humorist.

Because the benefits of hearing jokes tend to be deferred, humor is a low-priority emotion. But a basic emotion it is, and one worthy of attention by evolutionary scholars and mainstream psychologists. The prominence of humor in our daily lives suggests that dominance-seeking colors our existence to such a degree that we have evolved a specific emotion to guide us through the thickets of delicate social commerce, to entertain and inform others, and also to defeat rivals through ridicule. Far from being an inconsequential byproduct of natural selection, humor epitomizes our most complex and subtlest cognitive and social capacities as a species. It draws on the entire human brain.

Much remains to be learned about humor. It is still difficult to explain what makes a given joke funny, let alone how to fashion a good joke or amusing retort. Our bafflement at humor, like Lincoln's, may be nature's biggest joke of all.

References

Aldis, O. (1975). *Play fighting*. Academic Press.
Alexander, R. D. (1986). Ostracism and indirect reciprocity: The reproductive significance of humor. *Ethology and Sociobiology, 7*, 253–270.
Apte, M. L. (1985). *Humor and laughter: An anthropological approach*. Cornell University Press.
Aristotle (1895). The politics. In S. H. Butcher (Ed.), *Aristotle's theory of poetry and fine art*. Macmillan.

Arroyo, S., Lesser, R. P., Gordon, B., Uematsu, S., Art, J., Schwerdt, P., Hart, J., Schwerdt, P., Andreasson, K., & Fisher, R. S. (1993). Mirth, laughter and gelastic seizures. *Brain, 116*, 757–780.

Athey, C. (1977). Humour in children related to Piaget's theory of intellectual development. In A. J. Chapma & H. C. Foot (Eds.), *It's a funny thing, humour* (pp. 215–218). Pergamon Press.

Bachorowski, J.-A., & Owren, M. J. (2003). Sounds of emotion: Production and perception of affect-related vocal acoustics. *Annals of the New York Academy of Sciences, 1000*, 244–265.

Bannister, R. (1973). *Brain's clinical neurology* (4th ed.). Oxford University Press.

Bariaud, F. (1988). Age differences in children's humor. *Journal of Children in Contemporary Society, 20*, 15–45.

Barnett, J. A. (1991). The playful child: Measurement of a disposition to play. *Play and Culture, 4*, 51–74.

Bateson, G. (1969). The position of humor in human communication. In J. Levine (Ed.), *Motivation in humor* (pp. 159–166). Atherton.

Bean, W. G. (1967). *Rare diseases and lesions: Their contributions to clinical medicine*. Charles C. Thomas.

Bergson, H. (1911). *Laughter: An essay on the meaning of the comic*. Macmillan.

Berkowitz, L. (1970). Aggressive humor as a stimulus to aggressive responses. *Journal of Personality and Social Psychology, 16*, 710–717.

Bihrle, A. M., Brownell, H. H., & Powelson, J. A. (1986). Comprehension of humorous and nonhumorous materials by left and right brain-damaged patients. *Brain and Cognition, 5*, 399–411.

Bressler, E. R., & Balshine, S. (2000). The influence of humor on desirability. *Evolution and Human Behavior, 27*, 29–39.

Boulton, M., & Smith, P. K. (1992). The social nature of play fighting and play chasing: Mechanisms and strategies underlying cooperation and compromise. In J. Barkow, L. Cosmides & J. Tooby (Eds.), *The adapted mind: Evolutionary psychology and the generation of culture* (pp. 429–450). Oxford University Press.

Bressler, E. R., Martin, R. A., & Balshine, S. (2006). Production and appreciation of humor as sexually selected traits. *Evolution and Human Behavior, 27*, 121–130.

Brodzinsky, D. M. (1977). Children's comprehension and appreciation of verbal jokes in relation to conceptual tempo. *Child Development, 48*, 960–967.

Brownell, H. H., & Stringfellow, A. (2000). Cognitive perspectives on humor comprehension after brain injury. In L. T. Conner & L. K. Obler (Eds.), *Neurobehavior of language and cognition: Studies of neural imaging and brain damage* (pp. 241–258). Kluwer Academic.

Bryant, J., Brown, D., Parks, S. L., & Zillmann, D. (1983). Children's imitation of a ridiculed model. *Human Communication Research, 10*, 243–255.

Buunk, A. P., Park, J. H., & Dubbs, S. L. (2008). Parent-offspring conflict in mate preferences. *Review of General Psychology, 12*, 47–62.

Campbell, D. W., Wallace, M. G., Modirrousta, M., Polimeni, J. O., McKeen, N. A., & Reiss, J. P. (2015). The neural basis of humour comprehension and humour appreciation: The roles of the temporoparietal junction and superior frontal gyrus. *Neuropsychologia, 79*, 10–20.

Cann, A., Davis, H. B., & Zapata, C. L. (2011). Humor styles and relationship satisfaction in dating couples: Perceived versus self-reported humor styles as predictors of satisfaction. *Humor, 24*, 1–20.

Cann, A., Stilwell, K., & Taku, K. (2011). Humor styles, positive personality and health. *Europe's Journal of Psychology, 3*, 213–235.

Carstensen, L. L., Gottman, J. M., & Levenson, R. W. (1995). Emotional behavior in long-term marriage. *Psychology and Aging, 10*, 140–149.

Caruana, F., Avanzini, P., Gozzo, F., Francione, S., Cardinale, F., & Rizzolatti, G. (2015). Mirth and laughter elicited by electrical stimulation of the human anterior cingulate cortex. *Cortex, 71*, 323–331.

Chan, Y. C., Chen, H.-C., & Lavalee, J. P. (2013). The impact of gelotophobia, gelatophilia, and katagelasticism on creativity. *Humor, 26*, 609–628.

Chapman, A. J. (1976). Social aspects of humorous laughter. In A. J. Chapman & H. C. Foot (Eds.), *Humour and laughter: Theory research, and applications* (pp. 155–185). Wiley.

Chapman, A. J. (1983). Humor and laughter in social interaction and some implications for humor research. In P. E. McGhee & J. H. Goldstein (Eds.), *Handbook of humor research* (pp. 135–157). Springer-Verlag.

Cline, T. W., & Kellaris, J. J. (2007). The influence of humor strength and humor-message relatedness on ad memorability: A dual process model. *Journal of Advertising, 36*, 55–67.

Cohan, C. L., & Bradbury, T. N. (1997). Negative life events, marital interaction and the longitudinal course if newlywed marriage. *Journal of Personality and Social Psychology, 73*, 114–128.

Cousins, N. (1979). *Anatomy of an illness as perceived by the patient: Reflections on healing and regeneration*. W. W. Norton.

Darwin, C. (1998). *The expression of the emotions in man ad animals* (3rd ed.). Oxford University Press.

Davila-Ross, M., Allcock, B., Thomas, C. D., & Bird, A. (2011). Aping expressions? Chimpanzees produce distinct laugh styles when responding to laughter of others. *Emotion, 11*, 1013–1020.

de Koning, F., & Weiss, R. O. (2002). The relational humor inventory: Functions of humor in close relationships. *American Journal of Family Therapy, 30*, 1–18.

de Waal, F. (2019). *Mama's last hug: Animal emotions and what they tell us about ourselves*. W. W. Norton.

Derks, P., Kalland, S., & Etgen, M. (1995). The effect of joke type and audience response on the reaction to a joke: Replication and extension. *Humor, 8*, 327–337.

Dews, S., Winner, E., Kaplan, F., Rosenblatt, E., Hunt, M., Lim, K., McGovern, A., Qualter, A., & Smarsh, B. (1996). Children's understanding of the meaning and functions of verbal irony. *Child Development, 67*, 3071–3085.

Duchowny, M. S. (1983). Pathological disorders of laughter. In P. E. McGhee & J. H. Goldstein (Eds.), *Handbook of humor research*, Vol. 2: *Applied studies* (pp. 89–108). Springer-Verlag.

Dwyer, T. (1991). Humor, power, and change in organizations. *Human Relations, 44*, 1–19.

Eibl-Eibesfeldt, I. (1989). *Human ethology*. Aldine de Gruyter.

Ekman, P. (1994). All emotions are basic. In P. Ekman & R. J. Davidson (Eds.), *The nature of emotions: Fundamental questions* (pp. 15–19). Oxford University Press.

Flamson, T., & Barrett, H. C. (2008). The encryption theory of humor: A knowledge-based mechanism of honest signaling. *Evolution, Mind and Behaviour, 6*, 261–281.

Ford, T. E., Ford, B. L., Boxer, C. F., & Armstrong, J. (2012) Effect of humor on state anxiety and math performance. *Humor, 25*, 59–74.

Ford, T. E., Lappi, S. K., & Holden, C. J. (2016). Personality, humor styles, and happiness. *Europe's Journal of Psychology, 12*, 320–337.

Ford, T. E., Lappi, S. K., O'Connor, E. C., & Banos, N. C. (2017). Manipulating humor styles: Engaging in self-enhancing humor reduces state anxiety. *Humor, 30*, 169–191.

Ford, T. E., Woodzicka, J. A., Triplett, S. R., & Kochersberger, A. O. (2014). Not all groups are equal: Differential societal sexism. *Current Research in Social Psychology*, September, 64–81.

Fraley, B., & Aron, A. (2004). The effect of a shared humorous experience on closeness in initial encounters. *Personal Relationships, 11*, 61–78.

Frank, M. G., & Ekman, P. (1993). Not all smiles are created equal: The differences between enjoyment and nonenjoyment smiles. *Humor, 6*, 9–26.

Fridlund, A. M.., & Loftus, J. M. (1990). Relations between tickling and humorous laughter: Preliminary support for the Darwin-Hecker hypothesis. *Biological Psychology, 30*, 141–150.

Fried, I., Wilson, C. L., MacDonald, K. A., & Behnke, E. J. (1988). Electric current stimulates laughter. *Nature, 391*, 650.

Friedman, H. S., Tucker, J. S. Tomlinson-Keasey, C., Schwartz, J. E., Wingard, D. L., & Criqui, M. H. (1993). Does childhood personality predict longevity? *Journal of Personality and Social Psychology, 65*, 176–185.

Fry, W. G. (1963). *Sweet madness*. Pacific Books.

Fusar-Poli, P., Placentino, A., Carletti, F., Landi, P., Allen, P., Surguladze, S., Benedetti, F., Abbamonte, M., Gasparotti, R., Barale, F., Perez, J., McGuire, & Politi, P. (2009). Functional atlas of emotional faces processing: A vowel-based meta-analysis of 105 functional magnetic resonance imaging studies. *Journal of Psychiatry and Neuroscience, 34*, 418–432.

Fuster, J. M. (1997). *The prefrontal cortex: Anatomy, physiology, and neuropsychology of the frontal lobe*. Raven Press.

Gelb, B. D., & Zinkhan, G. M. (1986). Humor and advertising effectiveness after repeated exposures to a radio commercial. *Journal of Advertising, 15*, 15–20.

Gervais, M., & Wilson, D. S. (2005). The evolution and functions of laughter and humor: A systematic approach. *Quarterly Review of Biology, 80*, 395–430.

Gibbs, R. W. (1986). On the psycholinguistics of sarcasm. *Journal of Experimental Psychology: General, 115*, 3–15.

Gillikin, L. S., & Derks, P. L. (1991). Humor appreciation and mood in stroke patients. *Cognitive Rehabilitation, 9*, 30–35.

Goldstein, J. H. (1977). Cross-cultural research: Humor here and there. In A. J. Chapman & H. C. Foot (Eds.), *It's a funny thing, humour* (pp. 167–174). Pergamon.

Goldstein, J. H., & McGhee, P. E. (Eds.) (1972). *The psychology of humor: Theoretical perspectives and empirical issues*. Academic Press.

Goodall, J. (1968). The behavior of free-living chimpanzees in the Gombe Stream Reserve. *Animal Behaviour Monographs, 1*, 165–311.

Goodenough, F. L. (1932). Expression of the emotions in a blind-deaf child. *Journal of Abnormal & Social Psychology, 27*, 328–333.

Grammer, K. (1990). Strangers meet: Laughter and nonverbal signs of interest in opposite-sex encounters. *Journal of Nonverbal Behavior, 14*, 209–236.

Greengross, G., & Miller, G. F. (2008). Dissing oneself versus dissing rivals: Effects of status, personality and sex on the short-term and long-term attractiveness of self-deprecating and other-deprecating humor. *Evolutionary Psychology, 6*, 393–408.

Haig, R. A. (1988). *The anatomy of humor: Biopsychosocial and therapeutic perspectives*. Charles C. Thomas.

Hall, G. S., & Allin, A. (1897). The psychology of tickling, laughing, and the comic. *American Journal of Psychology, 9*, 1–44.

Happé, F., Brownell, H., & Winner, E. (1999). Acquired "theory of mind": Impairments following stroke. *Cognition, 70*, 211–240.

Harris, C. R., & Alvarado, N. (2005). Facial expressions, smile types, and self-report during humour, tickle, and pain. *Cognition and Emotion, 19*, 655–669.

Holmes, D. S. (1969). Sensing humor: Latency and amplitude of responses related to MMPI profiles. *Journal of Consulting and Clinical Psychology, 33*, 296–301.

Izard, C. E. (1979). *Emotions in personality and psychopathology*. Plenum.

Iwase, M., Ouchi, Y., Okada, H., Yokoyama, C., Nobezawa, S., Yoshikawa, F., Hideo Tsukada, H., Takeda, M., Yamashita, K., Taked, M., Yamaguti, K., Kuratsune, H., Shimizu, A., & Watanabe, Y. (2002). Neural substrates of human facial expression of pleasant emotion induced by comic films: A PET study. *NeuroImage, 17*, 758–768.

Kane, T. R., Suls, J., & Tedeschi, J. T. (1977). Humour as a tool of social interaction. In A. J. Chapman & H. C. Foot (Eds.), It's a funny thing, humour (pp. 13–16). Pergamon Press.

Keltner, D., Young, R. C., Heerey, E. A., Oernig, C., & Monarch, N. D. (1998). Teasing in hierarchical and intimate relations. *Journal of Personality and Social Psychology, 75*, 1231–1247.

Kim, H., Lee, S., Uysal, M., Kim, J., & Ahn, K. (2015). Nature-based tourism: Motivation and subjective well-being. *Journal of Travel & Tourism Marketing, 32*(suppl. 1), S76–S96.

Klein, D. M., Bryant, J., & Zillmann, D. (1982). Relationship between humor in introductory textbooks and students' evaluations of the texts' appeal and effectiveness. *Psychological Reports, 50*, 235–241.

Koestler, A. (1964). *The act of creation*. Hutchinson.

Kolb, G., & Whishaw, I. Q. (1985). *Fundamentals of human neuropsychology*. Freeman.

Langevin, R., & Day, H. I. (1972). Physiological correlates of humor. In J. H. Goldstein & P. E. McGhee (Eds.), *The psychology of humor: Theoretical perspectives and empirical issues* (pp. 129–142). Academic.

Lauer, R. H., Lauer, J. C., & Kerr, S. T. (1990). The long-term marriage: Perceptions of stability and satisfaction. *International Journal of Aging and Human Development, 31*, 181–195.

Lavan, N., Scott, S. K., & McGettigan C. (2016). Laugh like you mean it: Authenticity modulates acoustic, physiological and perceptual properties of laughter. *Journal of Nonverbal Behavior, 40*, 133–149.

LeDoux, J. (1996). *The emotional brain: The mysterious underpinnings of emotional life*. Simon & Schuster.

Lee, D.-R. (2015). The impact of leader's humor on employees' creativity: The moderating role of trust in leader. *Seoul Journal of Business, 21*, 59–86.

Lerner, M. J., & Simmons, C. H. (1966). Observers' reaction to the "innocent victim": Compassion or rejection? *Journal of Personality and Social Psychology, 4*, 203–210.

Levine, J. (1977). Humour as a form of therapy: Introduction to symposium. In A. J. Chapman & H. C. Foot (Eds.), *It's a funny thing, humour* (pp. 127–137). Pergamon Press.

Li, N. P., Griskevicius, V., Durante, K. M., Jonason, P. K., Pasisz, D. J., & Aumer, K. (2009). An evolutionary perspective on humor: Sexual selection or interest indication? *Personality and Social Psychology Bulletin, 35*, 923–936.

Lishman, W. A. (1978). *Organic psychiatry*. Blackwell.

Lorenz, K. (1963). *On aggression*. Bantam.

Lundy, D. E., Tan, J., & Cunningham, M. R. (1998). Heterosexual romantic preferences: The importance of humor and physical attractiveness. *Personal Relationships, 5*, 311–325.

MacDonald, N. E., & Silverman, I. W. (1978). Smiling and laughter in infants as a function of level of arousal and cognitive devaluation. *Developmental Psychology, 14*, 235–241.

Mahony, D. L., Burroughs, W. J., & Hieatt, A. C. (2001). The effects of laughter on discomfort thresholds: Does expectation become reality? *Journal of General Psychology, 12*, 161–175.

Mark, W., & Carpenter, B. D. (2007). Humor comprehension in older adults. *Journal of the International Neuropsychological Society, 13*, 606–614.

Mannell, R. C., & McMahon, L. (1982). Humor as play: Its relationship to psychological well-being during the course of a day. *Leisure Sciences, 5*, 143–155.

Marcus, N. N. (1990). Treating those who fail to take themselves seriously: Pathological aspects of humor. *American Journal of Psychotherapy, 44*, 423–432.

Martin, J. P. (1950). Fits of laughter (sham mirth) in organic cerebral disease. *Brain, 73*, 453–464.
Martin, R. A., & Ford, T. E. (2018). *Psychology of humor: An integrative approach* (2nd ed.). Academic Press.
Martin, R. A.., & Kuiper, N. A. (1999). Daily occurrence of laugher: Relationships with age, gender, and Type A personality. *Humor: International Journal of Humor Research, 12*, 355-384.
Martin, R. A., & Lefcourt, H. M. (1983). Sense of humor as a moderator of the relation between stressors and moods. *Journal of Personality and Social Psychology, 45*, 1313–1324.
Martin, R. A., Puhlik-Doris, P., Larsen, G., Gray, J., & Weir, K. (2003). Individual differences in uses of humor and their relation to psychological well-being: Development of the humor styles questionnaire. *Journal of Research in Personality, 37*, 48–75.
McDougall, W. (1923.) *Outline of psychology*. Scribner's.
McGhee, P. E. (1976). Humor across the life span: Sources of developmental change and individual differences. In L. Nahemow, K. A. McCluskey-Fawcett, & P. E. McGhee (Eds.), *Humor and aging* (pp. 27–51). Academic.
McGhee, P. E. (1979). *Humor: Its origins and development*. Freeman.
McGhee, P. E. (1980a). Development of the sense of humour in childhood: A longitudinal study. In P. E. McGhee & A. J. Chapman (Eds.), *Children's humor* (pp. 213–223). Wiley.
McGhee, P. E. (1980b). Development of the creative aspects of humour. In P. E. McGhee & A J. Chapman (Eds.), *Children's humour* (pp. 119–139). Wiley.
McGhee, P. E., & Lloyd, S. A. (1982). Behavioral characteristics associated with the development of humor in young children. *Journal of Genetic Psychology, 14*, 253–259.
McGhee, P. E. (1986). Humor across the life span: Sources of developmental change and individual differences. In L. Nahemow, K. A. McCluskey-Fawcett, & P. E. McGhee (Eds.), *Humor and aging* (pp. 37–51). Academic Press.
McGhee, P. E. (2010). *Humor: The lighter path to resilience and health*. American Psychological Association.
Meyer, J. P., Allen, N. J., & Smith, C. A. (1993). Commitment to organizations and occupations: Extension and test of a three-component conceptualization. *Journal of Applied Psychology, 78*, 538–551.
Miller, F. C. (1967. Humor in a Chippewa tribal council. *Ethnology, 6*, 264–271.
Miller, G. F. (1998). Mate choice turns cognitive. *Trends in Cognitive Sciences, 2*, 190–198.
Miller, G. F. (2000). *The mating mind: How sexual choice shaped the evolution of human nature*. Doubleday.
Monro, D. H. (1951). *Argument of laughter*. Melbourne University Press.
Panksepp, J. (2005). Affective consciousness: Core emotional feelings in animals and humans *Consciousness and Cognition, 14*, 30–80.
Panksepp, J., & Bergdorf, J. (2003). "Laughing" rats and the evolutionary antecedents of human joy? *Physiology and Behavior, 79*, 533–547.
Parrot, W. G., & Gleitman, H. (1989). Infants' expectations in play: The joy of peek-a-boo. *Cognition and Emotion, 3*, 291–311.
Pellegrini, D. S., Masten, A. S., Garmezy, N., & Ferrarese, M. J. (1987). Correlates of social and academic competence in middle childhood. *Journal of Child Psychology and Psychiatry and Allied Disciplines, 28*, 699–714.
Plato. (1871). Philebus. In B. Jowett (Ed. and Trans.), *The dialogues of Plato*. Oxford University Press.
Plooij, F. (1979). How wild chimpanzee babies trigger the onset of other-infant play—and what the mother makes of it. In M. Bullowa (Ed.), *Before speech: The beginning of interpersonal communication* (pp. 223–243). Cambridge University Press.
Polimeni, J., & Reiss, J. P. (2006). Humor perception deficits in schizophrenia. *Psychiatry Research, 141*, 229–232.
Pollio, H. R., Mers, R. W., & Lucchesi, W. (1972). Humor, laugher, and smiling: Some preliminary observations of funny behaviors In J. H. Goldstein & P. E. McGhee (Eds.), *The psychology of humor: Theoretical perspectives and empirical issues* (pp. 211–239). Academic.
Provine, R. (1992). Contagious laughter: Laughter is a sufficient stimulus for laughs and smiles. *Bulletin of the Psychonomic Society, 30*, 1–4.
Pryor, J. B. (1995). The psychological impact of sexual harassment on women in the US military. *Basic and Applied Social Psychology, 17*, 581–603.
Pugh, G. E. (1977). *The biological basis of human values*. Basic Books.
Richards, K., & Kruger, G. (2017). Humor styles as moderators in the relationship between perceived stress and physical health. *SAGE Open, 7*, 2158244017711485.
Richardson, H. M. (1939). Studies of mental resemblance between husbands and wives and between friends. *Psychological Bulletin, 36*, 104–120.
Romundstad, S., Sebak, S., Holen, A., & Holmen, J. (2016). A 15-year follow-up study of sense of humor and causes of mortality: The Nord-Trøndelag Health Study. *Psychosomatic Medicine, 78*, 345–353.
Ruch, W. (1993). Exhilaration and humor. In M. Lewis & J. M. Haviland (Eds.), *Handbook of emotions* (pp. 605–614). Guilford Press.

Ruch, W., & Ekman, P. (2001). The expressive pattern of laughter. In A. Kaszniak (Ed.), *Emotion, qualia and consciousness* (pp. 426–430). Word Scientific.

Ruch, W., McGhee, P. E., & Hehl, F.-J. (1990). Age differences in the enjoyment of incongruity-resolution and nonsense humor during adulthood. *Psychology and Aging, 5*, 348–355.

Ruch, W., & Proyer, R. T. (2009). Extending the study of gelotophobia: On gelotophiles and katagelasticists. *Humor, 22*, 183–212.

Samson, A. C., Zysset, S., & Huber, O. (2008). Cognitive humor processing: Different logical mechanisms in nonverbal cartoons—an fMRI study. *Social Neuroscience, 3*, 125–140.

Schaier, A. H., & Cicirelli, V. G. (1976), Age differences in humor comprehension and appreciation in old age. *Journal of Gerontology, 3*, 577–582.

Schermer, J. A., Martin, R. A., Martin, N. G., Lynskey, M., & Vernon, P. A. (2013). The general factor of personality and humor styles. *Personality and Individual Differences, 54*, 890–893.

Schmidt, H. E., & Williams, D. I. (1971). The evolution of theories of humour. *Journal of Behavioral Science, 1*, 95–106.

Schultz T. R. (1977). A cross-cultural study of the structure of humour. In A. J. Chapman & H. C. Foot (Eds.), *It's a funny thing, humour* (pp. 176–179). Pergamon Press.

Shammi, P., & Stuss, D. T. (1999). Humour appreciation: A role of the right frontal lobe. *Brain, 122*, 657–666.

Shammi, P., & Stuss, D. T. (2003). The effects of normal aging on humor appreciation. *Journal of the International Neuropsychological Society, 9*, 855–863.

Sher, P. K., & Brown, S. B. (1976). Gelastic epilepsy: Onset in neonatal period. *American Journal of Diseases of Childhood, 130*, 1126–1131.

Shibata, M., Terasawa, Y. & Umeda, S. (2014). Integration of cognitive and affective networks in humor comprehension. *Neuropsychologia, 65*, 137–145.

Sprecher, S., & Regan, P. C. (2002). Liking some things (in some people) more than others: Partner preferences in romantic relationships and friendships. *Journal of Social and Personal Relationships, 19*, 463–481.

Sroufe, L. A., & Wunsch, J. P. (1972). The development of laughter in the first year of life. *Child Development, 43*(4), 1326–1344.

Stewart, S., & Thompson, D. R. (2015). Does comedy kill? A retrospective, longitudinal cohort, nested case-control study of humour and longevity in 53 British comedians. *International Journal of Cardiology, 180*, 258–261.

Strickland, J. F. (1959). The effect of motivational arousal on humor preferences. *Journal of Abnormal and Social Psychology, 59*, 278–281.

Sullivan, K., Winner, E., & Hopfield, N. (1995). How children tell a lie from a joke: The role of second-order mental state attributions. *British Journal of Developmental Psychology, 13*, 191–204.

Svebak, S., Martin, R. A., & Holmen, J. (2004). The prevalence of sense of humor in a large, unselected county population in Norway: Relations with age sex, and some health indicators. *Humor, 17*, 121–134.

Szameitat, D. P., Kreifelts, B., Alter, K., Szameitat, A. J., Sterr, A., Grodd, W., & Wildgruber, D. (2010). It is not always tickling: Distinct cerebral responses during perception of different laughter types. *NeuroImage, 53*, 1264–1271.

Terrion, J. L., & Ashforth, B. E. (2002). From "I" to "we": The role of putdown humor and identity in the development of a temporary group. *Human Relations, 55*, 55–88.

Tinbergen, N. (1963). On the aims and methods of ethology. *Zeitgeist für Tierpsychologie, 20*, 410–433.

Tranel, D., Hathaway-Nepple, J., & Anderson, S. W. (2007). Impaired behavior in real-world tasks following damage to the ventromedial prefrontal cortex. *Journal of Clinical and Experimental Neuropsychology, 29*, 319–332.

Treger, S., Sprecher, S., & Erber, R. (2013). Laughing and liking: Exploring the interpersonal effects of humor use in initial social interactions. *European Journal of Social Psychology, 43*, 532–543.

Trivers, R. L. (1971). The evolution of reciprocal altruism. *Quarterly Review of Biology, 46*, 35–57.

Vaid, J. (1999). The evolution of humor: Do those who laugh last? In D. H. Rosen & M. C. Luebbert (Eds.), *Evolution of the psyche* (pp. 123–138). Praeger/Greenwood.

van Hooff, J. A. R. A. M. (1972). A comparative approach to the phylogeny of laughter and smiling. In R. A. Hinde (Ed.), *Nonverbal communication* (pp. 209–238). Cambridge University Press.

Vernon, P. A., Martin, R. A., Schermer, J. A., & Mackie, A. (2008). A behavioral genetic investigation of humor styles and their correlations with the big-5 personality dimensions. *Personality and Individual Differences, 44*, 1116–1125.

Walle, A. (1976). Getting picked up without being put down: Jokes and the bar rush. *Journal of the Folklore Institute, 13*, 201–217.

Warners-Kleverlaan, N., Oppenheimer, L., & Sherman, L. (1996). To be or not to be humorous: Does it make a difference? *Humor, 9*, 117–141.

Weisfeld, C. C., Dowgwillo, E. A., Butovskaya, M. L., Imamoğlu, E. O., Wang, J., Weisfeld, G. E., & Hill, E. M. (in prep.). Which spousal behaviors predict marital satisfaction when couples have children? A multi-level modeling analysis in five cultures.

Weisfeld, C. C., & Stack, M. A. (2002). When I look into your eyes. *Psychology, Evolution and Gender, 4*, 125–147.

Weisfeld, C. C., Weisfeld, G. E., Warren, R. A., & Freedman, D. G. (1983). The spelling bee: A naturalistic study of female inhibition in mixed-sex competition. *Adolescence, 18*, 695–708.

Weisfeld, G. E. (1982). The nature-nurture issue and the integrating concept of function. In B. B. Wolman and G. Stricker (Eds.), *Handbook of developmental psychology* (pp. 208–229). Prentice-Hall.

Weisfeld, G. E. (1993). The adaptive value of humor and laughter. *Ethology and Sociobiology, 14*, 141–169.

Weisfeld, G. E. (1999). *Evolutionary principles of human adolescence*. Basic Books.

Weisfeld, G. E. (2006). Humor appreciation as an adaptive esthetic emotion. *Humor, 19*, 1–26.

Weisfeld, G. E. (2019). *Evolved emotions: An interdisciplinary and functional* analysis. Lexington Books.

Weisfeld, G. E., & Dillon, L. M. (2012). Applying the dominance hierarchy model to pride and shame and related behaviors. *Journal of Evolutionary Psychology, 10*, 15–41.

Weisfeld, G. E., & Weisfeld, C. C. (1984). An observational study of social evaluation: An application of the dominance hierarchy model. *Journal of Genetic Psychology, 145*, 89–99.

Weisfeld, G. E., & Weisfeld, M. B. (2014). Does a humorous element characterize embarrassment? *Humor, 27*, 65–85.

Weisfeld, G. E., Nowak, N. T., Lucas, T., Weisfeld, C. C., Imamoğlu, E. O., Butovskaya, M., Shen, J., & Parkhill, M. R. (2011). Do women seek humorousness in men because it signals intelligence? A cross-cultural test. *Humor, 24*, 435–462.

Wild, B., Rodden, F. A., Grodd, W., & Ruch, W. (2003). Neural correlates of laughter and humour. *Brain, 126*, 2121–2138.

Williams, C. A. (2010). The behavior phenotype of the Angelman syndrome. *American Journal of Medical Genetics Part C: Seminars in Medical Genetics, 154*, 432–437.

Wilson, D. L., & Davis, R. O. (Eds.), *Herndon's informants: Letters, interviews, and statements about Abraham Lincoln*. University of Illinois Press, 1998.

Winick, C. (1976). The social contents of humor. *Journal of Communication, 26*, 124–128.

Zajonc, R. B. (1980). Feeling and thinking: Preferences need no inferences. *Psychological Bulletin, 35*, 151–175.

Zigler, E., Levine, J., & Gould, L. (1966). Cognitive processes in the development of children's appreciation of humor. *Child Development, 37*, 507–518.

Zillmann, D. (1977). Humour and communication: Introduction. In A. J. Chapman & H. C. Foot (Eds.), *It's a funny thing, humour* (pp. 291–301). Pergamon.

Ziv, A. (1984). *Personality and sense of humor*. Springer.

Ziv, A. (1988). Teaching and learning with humor: Experiment and replication. *Journal of Experimental Education, 57*, 5–15.

Ziv, A., & Gadish, O. (1989). Humor and marital satisfaction. *Journal of Social Psychology, 129*, 759–768.

Zweyer, K., Velker, B., & Ruch, W. (2004). Do cheerfulness, exhilaration, and humor production moderate pain tolerance? A FACS study. *Humor, 17*, 85–119.

CHAPTER 29

Compassion: An Evolutionary Account

Jennifer L. Goetz and Emiliana Simon-Thomas

Abstract

This chapter presents compassion as an emotion evolved to promote nurturance and cooperation. What does an evolutionary approach bring to the understanding of compassion? An evolutionary approach brings particular questions to the fore, including the origins and functions of compassion, which then lead directly to questions about the antecedents and situations in which compassion occurs, the biological structures and mental processes by which compassion emerges, the behavioral expression and outcomes of compassion, and the degree to which compassion is universal or variable across cultures. The authors review research on these questions while also providing an update of their predictions and model of compassion.

Key Words: compassion, emotion, sympathy, empathy, evolution, cooperation

What Is Compassion?

One of the most difficult aspects of research on compassion has been identifying the "thing" we are studying. Is it an emotion, a motive, a dispositional trait, or a cultivated attitude? Furthermore, what do we call it? Compassion? Empathy? Sympathy? As someone recently noted (Cuff et al., 2016), there are as many definitions of empathy as there are researchers working on it, and we venture to say that compassion is similar. In our original work (Goetz et al. 2010), we presented an argument for compassion as a discrete and evolved emotional experience. In that review, we defined compassion as a state of concern for the suffering or unmet need of another, coupled with a desire to alleviate that suffering (Goetz et al., 2010). Our goal was to link disparate work and bring an evolutionary approach to the study of compassion. Since our 2010 article, the field has exploded (see Figure 29.1). We do not see our review as the source of this explosion, but rather as part of a wave of interest in pro-sociality. Work on compassion and empathy has advanced dramatically to settle on some agreed-upon distinctions and theoretical clarification, which we summarize next.

While we use the term *compassion* to label this emotional state (Goetz et al., 2010; Goetz & Simon-Thomas, 2017), others refer to it as *empathic concern* (Batson, 2011; Zaki, 2014) and *sympathy* (Eisenberg & Eggum, 2009; Weiner, 1995). To a degree, the labels are less important than the recognition of the subjective emotional experience of concern for the other's welfare and a desire to see their suffering alleviated. Research suggests that this compassionate feeling state and its constituent affect, cognitions, motivations, and behaviors are distinct from sadness, love, and pain (Goetz & Peng, 2019). Compassion is also distinct from more self-focused responses like personal distress (i.e., "empathic distress") which, though often the result of

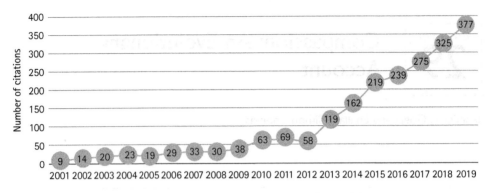

Figure 29.1. Citations of "compassion" as keyword by year in peer-reviewed psycINFO.

exposure to others' suffering, predicts less altruistic helping and more avoidant behavior (see Batson, 2011, for a review). Our experience suggests that the term *compassion* may be used less often in everyday English than *empathy* and *sympathy*. And research suggests that lay conceptions of the term *compassion* may not be distinct, but instead overlap with *sympathy*, *empathy*, and *tenderness* (Shaver et al., 1987; Weidman & Tracy, 2020).

For conceptual clarity, we offer some rationale for distinguishing between these interrelated constructs. *Empathy* is an umbrella term that encompasses many processes in which an observer may come to understand, share, or feel "moved" by another's emotional or physical state (Batson, 2011). Empathy is not specific to unmet need, pain, or suffering, but also occurs in contexts that involve pleasant (e.g., empathic laughter), hostile (e.g., escalating interpersonal anger), and other felt and expressed states. Among empathic processes, researchers have found support for the distinction between affective empathy and cognitive empathy.

In affective empathy (also called *experience sharing*; Zaki, 2014) and emotional empathy (Klimecki & Singer, 2017), a person experiences elements of feeling that are similar to another's emotions. Affective empathy is a relatively automatic process that originates in part from mimicry, in which a person mirrors another's expression or physical demeanor. Terms such as emotion contagion, vicarious experience, or empathic sharing have been used to describe adopting some aspect of another's emotional state.

In comparison, cognitive empathy is a more cognitively complex and effortful process in which an individual consciously adopts another person's perspective and tries to understand how that person is feeling or thinking. Cognitive empathy is sometimes referred to as mentalizing (Klimecki & Singer, 2017; Zaki, 2014, 2020) or perspective-taking (Batson, 2011; Davis, 1983), and it can be measured by one's empathic accuracy, or ability to accurately identify the other's emotions (Ickes, 1993; Zaki et al., 2009). Although either cognitive or affective empathy in response to another's suffering may be a catalyst to feeling compassion, neither guarantee compassion. Research on individual differences in affective empathy and experience of compassion show they are only weakly correlated (Jordan et al., 2016), and affective empathy can initiate self-focused responses like personal distress (i.e., "empathic distress"). Finally, we do not see cause for distinction between compassion and sympathy. Although some have described sympathy as fellow-feeling without intention to act (Gilbert, 2017), neither lay use (e.g., Weidman & Tracy, 2020) nor biological evidence aligns with this distinction.

Compassion as an Emotion

We continue to define and approach the study of compassion as an emotion. Other researchers have studied compassion as a core motive (Brown & Brown, 2017; Gilbert, 2017), a dispositional trait (Davis, 1983), and as a cultivated attitude (Lavelle, 2017). We do not disagree with these approaches and see them as complementary rather than opposing. We agree that humans have likely evolved a broad caregiving motivational system, that there are individual differences in the tendency to experience compassion, and that compassion can be cultivated and encouraged—or inhibited and discouraged—by social and cultural context or interventions. Rather than debate whether compassion is an emotion or a motive, we take a dialectical approach. Researchers can study compassion fruitfully from each of these theoretical frames.

In this chapter, however, we conceptualize compassion as an evolved emotional response to recurring survival and reproductive challenges. This evolved emotion framework makes certain predictions, including that compassion is a multi-componential and short-lived experience that responds to distinct antecedents and includes specific patterns of subjective psychological experience, cognitive appraisals, physiological changes, and motivational and behavioral tendencies, including nonverbal signals (Ekman, 1992). It should also involve distinct activity in physiological systems and patterns of activation in neural pathways. Finally, compassion and its component processes should be universal across cultures, so we make an effort in the chapter to incorporate research that includes non-WEIRD (Western, educated, industrialized, rich, and democratic) cultural samples.

Evolutionary Origins of Compassion

For compassion and concomitant costly helping behavior to evolve, there must be mechanisms by which to gain long-term benefits. Evolutionary theorizing has shown that the long-term benefits of helping genetic relatives rely on different factors than helping non-kin (see Kurzban et al., 2015 for a review). Individuals incur direct fitness costs when helping genetic relatives, but reap inclusive fitness benefits because those relatives share genes (Hamilton, 1964). As suggested by inclusive fitness theory (Hamilton, 1964), resource sharing and help vary with relatedness across cultures (e.g., Nolin, 2010; Wiessner, 2002; Xue, 2013). Also consistent with Hamilton's theory, close kin are more likely to receive help when it is biologically significant, such as in life-and-death situations (Burnstein et al., 1994) and when the cost of helping is very high (Korchmaros & Kenny, 2006; Stewart-Williams, 2007).

On the other hand, helping non-kin is riskier. Theories of direct and indirect reciprocity suggest that psychological systems should be sensitive to potential exploitation and cheating and to whether people in need are likely to return help in the future (Nowak, 2006; Nowak & Sigmund, 2005). Consistent with this argument, people are more likely to help unrelated individuals with whom they have a close and ongoing relationship (Stewart-Williams, 2007, 2008), with whom they have previously cooperated (Axelrod & Hamilton, 1981), as well as strangers who have good reputations (Nowak & Sigmund, 2005), and people who are members of their in-group over members of an out-group (Stürmer et al., 2005).

Biologically, explanations for costly helping behavior have been rooted in the care of vulnerable offspring (see Batson, 2011; Kurzban et al., 2015; Preston & de Waal, 2000, for reviews). Human offspring require heavy parental investment (Hrdy, 1999), which relies on dedicated biological systems. In the past decade, evidence increasingly grounds compassion in biological systems that evolved to motivate interpersonal caregiving, from parent-to-infant to heroic rescue between strangers. Spikins and colleagues mapped out a timeline that spans 6 mya (million years ago) to the present day, documenting the emergence of compassionate acts, from fleeting consolation behaviors toward victims of harm to extended care of diseased or disabled conspecifics to collective mourning rituals and symbolic emblems of care (Spikins et al., 2010). Furthermore, as we summarize below, researchers have identified connections among the systems involved in offspring care, empathy, compassion, and altruism (Preston, 2013; Swain et al., 2012). In a recent perspective, Condon and Makransky (2020) suggest that an individual's relational stability, established through warm attentive early life caregiving, is foundational to the potential for experiencing compassion. However, this analysis does not support a wholesale analogy between the biology of offspring care and compassion; other component processes involved in experiences of compassion engage additional, interconnected, bidirectionally influential biological systems.

Antecedents and Appraisals

When will people feel compassion? Based on an evolutionary approach, we argued (Goetz et al., 2010) that compassion should respond to distinct antecedent events that center upon the evolutionary challenge it evolved to address: the reduction of suffering. In addition, a key result of a functional approach is that compassion is not unconditional but instead is shaped by cost–benefit ratios. In more specific terms, we argued, compassion should be more likely when the other person is related—genetically or in terms of shared values and interests—to oneself, is a good candidate for subsequent cooperative behavior or reciprocal altruism, and when the potential benefits of helping outweigh the potential costs (Goetz et al., 2010). Based on this, we articulated an appraisal model of compassion that was shaped by (a) relevance of the suffering person to the self, (b) the suffering person's deservingness of help, and (c) one's own ability to cope with the situation at hand. In formulating this appraisal model, we distinguished compassion from empathic distress, sadness, and love, all of which had been proposed as alternative accounts for compassion.

Research continues to support our position that compassion is distinct from sadness and love and that its key antecedent is unmet need or suffering (Preston, 2013; Stellar et al., 2020; Sznycer et al., 2019). Research in non-Western cultures has shown that other people's need or suffering are the primary antecedents of compassion and sympathy in China and Singapore (Goetz & Peng, 2019; Tong, 2015). For example, when asked to describe times in their own life when they felt *sympathy* or its counterpart *tóngqíng* (同情), Americans and Chinese almost uniformly described situations in which other people were in physical or emotional pain or need (Goetz & Peng, 2019). Events that elicited sympathy were different from those that elicited sadness, which were primarily about personal loss, misfortune, or failure, and those that elicited love, which were primarily about feeling secure or affection with a close other.

Studies have also continued to generate results consistent with our predicted appraisal model, with some welcome refinements. Next, we summarize research that has expanded our understanding of the multiple component processes that we argue are inherent to feeling and acting on compassion.

Appraisals of Costs and Benefits

One breakthrough for our functional account of compassion is the recognition that compassion is more than a reflexive emotional experience that people cannot control. Instead, like other emotions, compassion involves motivational processes, guided by conceptual knowledge, formed habits, and in-the-moment reasoning, that can dial up or down the experience. Rather than automatically and involuntarily feeling a particular intensity of compassion, research suggests that people weigh multiple contextual factors, such as: Can I afford to feel compassion in this situation? Is it worthwhile to extend compassion to this person? Must I act on my feelings of compassion, how can I do that, and will it make any difference? Below, we organize the factors that play a role in compassion's calculation, including predictions about the costs of feeling compassion, perceptions of potential benefits of feeling and acting on compassion, and judgments of one's own ability to provide meaningful help.

The Costs of Compassion

Appraisals of the costliness of compassion can occur at different stages, mainly centered around the perceived cost to personal safety or emotional ease, and the cost of providing support or help. Despite initial approaches to compassion categorized as a positive emotion (Shaver et al., 1987), compassion is often experienced as unpleasant (Condon & Feldman Barrett, 2013; Goetz & Peng, 2019) and effortful to such an extent that people avoid situations in which they might feel compassion (Cameron et al., 2019). When people know that they will be asked to donate or help, they are more likely to avoid compassion-eliciting situations (Shaw et al., 1994), and people who tend to feel more personally distressed by others' pain or suffering are drawn to avoid situations in which they might feel empathy or compassion (Davis et. al., 1999).

Believing that compassion will lead to outsized costs (measured with items like "I worry that if I am compassionate, vulnerable people can be drawn toward me") is tied to lower scores on measures of both dispositional compassion and willingness to help, as well as lower compassion in response to sad faces (Kirby et al., 2019). In contrast, people who more readily endorse compassion satisfaction ("I get satisfaction from being able to help people") score higher in dispositional compassion and altruistic behavior. People also report less compassion in response to situations that may be more difficult to address, like another person's pain from a physical injury, compared to situations that people feel more capable of supporting, like another person's emotional upset (Stellar et al., 2020). And finally, work on "compassion collapse" describes how people temper their compassion in response to greater magnitude of mass or group suffering, compared to smaller-scale pain and suffering (Cameron & Payne, 2011). If compassion were strictly responsive to the magnitude of suffering or need, then it should increase in intensity with increased suffering. Instead, people reliably report feeling more compassion in response to an identifiable individual's suffering than when confronted with the suffering of many (e.g., Small et al., 2007).

In sum, the greater the costs that one is likely to incur in connection with the feeling of compassion or the action it inspires, the more likely people are to avoid feeling it or to downregulate it. This conclusion may seem contradictory to the well-established fact that compassion responds directly to need and suffering—and the expectation that more need would predict more compassion rather than less. However, the degree of need can serve as an indicator of both potential costs of helping and the potential benefits of acting on compassion, a subject to which we now turn.

Perception of Benefits of Help

The higher the potential benefits of helping, the more likely one is to feel compassion and act on it (Goetz et al., 2010). In our early work, we focused on two indicators of potential benefits: (a) relevance of the sufferer to the self, and (b) beliefs about the sufferer's deservingness of help. Furthermore, evolutionary theory suggests that the potential benefits of helping an individual vary with relationship type—whether they are kin, a mate, or a potential cooperation partner. Here we expand our review beyond characteristics of the suffering individual to also include the broader context.

One form of self-relevance is genetic relationship. Consistent with inclusive fitness theory (Hamilton, 1964), anthropological and psychological evidence show that genetic relatedness predicts resource sharing and help across cultures. Interestingly, however, there is a hint that compassion may not be the primary motivator of helping genetic relatives. Some researchers have found that closer genetic relatives do not necessarily evoke more compassion, but that emotional closeness or sense of obligation may be stronger predictors of help for relatives than compassion (Cialdini et al., 1997; Goetz & Halgren, 2020; Korchmaros & Kenny, 2006). Furthermore, kin often receive help above and beyond that suggested by emotional connection (Curry et al., 2013; Hackman et al., 2015) and felt compassion (Goetz & Halgren, 2020). As a result, some theorists have argued that compassion motivates less costly help, while other psychological factors motivate the more costly help that kin often receive (Maner et al., 2002; Neuberg et al., 1997). Still others have argued (and found) that the effect of empathy on helping may be stronger in the context of kin than non-kin relationships (Maner & Gailliot, 2007). That is, people may empathize and feel compassion for non-kin, but be less likely to act on it. In our own research, we found that closer relatives were helped more—and received more costly forms of help—even though they did not elicit more compassion than less closely related individuals (Goetz & Halgren, 2020). Thus, it is unclear whether compassion is felt more for kin, whether compassion is acted on more often for kin, or whether compassion plays no special role in caring for kin.

In the case of non-kin, compassion should be sensitive not only to the degree of interdependence with the other, but also to the likelihood of reciprocation versus exploitation and cheating. Thus, people are more likely to empathize and feel compassion for strangers who appear similar to them (DeSteno, 2015; Maner et al., 2002), for racial ingroup members (Stürmer et al., 2005; Stürmer et al., 2006), and for people who are known cooperators rather than known egoists (Stellar et al., 2014). A recent study showed that, despite feeling compassion, participants were less willing to help a needy person who did not sacrifice for them than for one who did (Sznycer et al., 2019). Because of this, some theorists have argued that the function of compassion may not be about caring for suffering individuals per se, but more about creating and maintaining cooperative ties (Sznycer et al., 2019).

Consistent with a focus on targets' pro-social tendencies, compassion is strongly predicted by attributions of responsibility, control, and effort (Rudolph et al., 2004). Individuals who are deemed responsible for their need—for example, losing their job due to laziness—are unlikely to be good cooperators and therefore elicit less compassion and helping. On the other hand, individuals who are not responsible for their need—for example, losing their job due to illness—are deemed more likely to be good cooperators and elicit more compassion and helping. More recent research suggests that compassion is universally concerned with these factors. For example, compassion was associated with appraisals of situational agency and control in Singapore (Tong, 2015) and with perceptions of suffering as undeserved in China (Goetz & Peng, 2019).

Estimating the benefits of compassion also includes appraisals of the broader context, such as the actor's own need for cooperative ties. When individuals believe they are in need of cooperative ties, they will be more likely to feel compassion. In contrast, when individuals feel self-sufficient, they will be less likely to feel compassion. This argument is consistent with research showing that individuals and communities become more cooperative and pro-social in the face of disasters (Kaniasty & Norris, 1995). It also helps to explain the well-established but counterintuitive "class-compassion gap" in which people with more material resources feel less compassion and are less pro-social than people with fewer material resources (see Piff & Moskowitz, 2017, for a review). For example, Stellar et al. (2012) found that individuals lower in social class reported higher levels of trait compassion. In another study (also Stellar et al., 2012), lower-class participants felt more compassion and also showed greater heart rate deceleration, an index of interpersonal attunement, in response to a compassion-inducing video than did upper-class participants.

An evolutionary approach generates many hypotheses around the potential benefits of compassion. First, it remains unclear whether and how relationship type and closeness influence the links in the attribution-compassion-helping pathway, as one would expect based on the functional differences of kin, mates, and other cooperative relationships (Clark et al., 2015). For example, when family members have brought suffering upon themselves, do people shift attributions to be more "benevolent" and see them as less responsible than they would for strangers, thus facilitating compassion and help? Alternatively, do people disregard responsibility attributions, feel, and act on compassion despite blaming close kin for their suffering? Our own research in this area (Goetz & Halgren, 2020) suggests a third possibility—that the link between attribution and compassion is robust across relationship type. In two studies, closer relatives were seen as equally responsible for their actions and elicited no more compassion, yet closely related individuals received more costly help. These findings suggest that compassion is sensitive to others' potential pro-sociality (in this case, via responsibility attributions), regardless of relatedness.

Second, work on appraisals suggests that individual differences in compassion may be related to dispositional appraisal patterns in which one tends to see others as blameworthy, as in liberal versus conservative responses to welfare (Delton et al., 2018; Petersen et al., 2012). It also suggests that inducing compassion may shift appraisals of others to be less blameworthy or more vulnerable (Lerner & Keltner, 2000; Oveis et al., 2010). Furthermore, there are open questions about the mechanisms by which training to increase the scope and magnitude of compassion works (Skwara et al., 2017; Weisz & Zaki, 2017). In addition to shifting emotion regulation patterns to reduce personal distress, compassion training may lead people to blame others less for their suffering, or may remove blame as a barrier to helping. This is consistent with a Buddhist perspective, in which all beings are seen as suffering and deserving of compassion (Lavelle, 2017) .

Perception of Ability to Help

In addition to weighing potential costs and benefits of helping, research suggests that people weigh their ability to meet the demands of the situation. If an actor feels they are able to help, they are more likely to feel compassion and act on it. However, if an actor feels unable to help, or that their emotional or physical resources are not sufficient, then they are less likely to feel compassion or act on it. Instead, they avoid or suppress feeling compassion for fear of becoming overwhelmed and distressed. Perception of one's own abilities have been operationalized in a few ways: self-efficacy, individual differences in emotion regulation, and individual differences in sensitivity to distress.

Individuals vary in how effective they feel at empathizing with others' emotions (Caprara et al., 2012), as well as how impactful they feel they can be at helping others (Caprara et al., 2012). People who feel ineffective at empathizing are more likely to avoid empathy-inducing situations than those who feel effective at empathizing (Cameron et al., 2019). Similarly, feeling capable of helping increases compassion. People who have overcome past adversity show more compassion and pro-social behavior than people who have not experienced adversity (Lim & DeSteno, 2016). Past adversity also predicts less susceptibility to the numeracy bias, in which people feel less compassion for larger numbers of suffering people than for individuals (Lim & DeSteno, 2020). Mediation analyses suggest that this is because people who have overcome adversity feel more capable of helping, and consequently, feel more compassion. Indeed, researchers were able to eliminate the numeracy bias amongst people who had not experienced adversity by experimentally boosting their feelings of effectiveness at helping (Lim & Desteno, 2020).

Emotion regulation likely also contributes to a person's perception of their own ability to meet the demands of a situation. Theorists have long argued that the ability to manage one's affective arousal is important to feeling compassion and exhibiting pro-social behavior

(Batson et al., 1987; Eisenberg et al., 1996). People who experience intense or persistent personal distress in response to others' suffering avoid situations in which they might be exposed to suffering—for example, they are less likely to volunteer (Davis et al., 1999) or more likely to engage in egoistic behavior that will reduce their distress (Batson, 2011). However, the relationships between emotion regulation, empathy, and compassion are likely more complex. Emotion regulation involves a variety of processes and strategies that contribute to an individual's ability to accentuate, reduce, or shift the emotions they are feeling, including choosing or modifying situations and contexts encountered, redirecting attention, reappraising or shifting thoughts and beliefs, and suppressing emotional experience (Gross, 2015; Thompson et al., 2019). Researchers have begun to study how these particular emotion-regulation strategies may intersect with empathy and compassion. Thus far, it appears that reappraisal is positively related to factors that may contribute to compassion, such as cognitive empathy and perspective-taking (Lockwood et al., 2014; Powell, 2018) while suppression is tied to reduced perspective-taking and sharing of others' emotions (Lockwood et al., 2014; Powell, 2018). Further, when faced with a stranger who had experienced mental health issues, the tendency to suppress emotion predicted less compassion and helping, as well as more desire for physical distance (Lebowitz & Dovidio, 2015). In contrast, the tendency to reappraise is related to greater likelihood and incidence of compassion.

Expression of Compassion
An approach to compassion as an emotion suggests that compassion should be reliably expressed (encoded) and perceived (decoded). Emotion theorists have argued that if emotions evolved, then they should have distinct signals that are recognized for all humans regardless of language or culture. Early on, Ekman and colleagues' groundbreaking work (Ekman et al., 1969) showed that six prototypical facial expressions were consistently labeled as happiness, sadness, anger, fear, surprise, and disgust in a range of cultures. Since Ekman's early work, expansions of the emotions studied and innovations in research methodology have shown that upward of 20 emotions are potentially communicable and recognizable (Cowen & Keltner, 2020). In line with this research, study of sympathy and compassion expression has expanded over the past decade. This work has focused on three modes of communication: (1) nonverbal facial and body expression (e.g., gestures, posture), (2) vocal intonation and nonlinguistic bursts, and (3) physical touch. Overall, the evidence for distinctly identifiable facial and bodily expression of compassion is less strong, but suggests that voice and touch may be channels of communication that effectively convey compassion (App et al., 2011; Hertenstein et al., 2006). Still, further research is needed to test whether this holds across cultures. Below we describe the evidence for expression of compassion in further detail and conclude by highlighting areas of opportunity for future research.

Work on naturalistic expressions has shown that—at least for English-speaking Americans—people consistently perceive sympathy in facial expressions (Cowen & Keltner, 2020) and brief vocal bursts (Cowen et al., 2019) that differ from those of distress, sadness, pain, and love expressions. Early on, the compassion facial expression was proposed to have elements of sadness combined with approach signals (Haidt & Keltner, 1999), such as inner eyebrows raised, lips pressed, and head leaned slightly forward. Although initial tests were not encouraging (Haidt & Keltner, 1999), recent studies of this prototypical facial expression found that it was labeled as sympathy at above-chance levels by participants from nine different cultures (Cordaro et al., 2020). Thus, it seems that at least one prototypical facial expression may be reliably perceived as compassion across cultures. Whether it is the most common or the most comprehensible way in which compassion is expressed, however, remains to be seen.

Some research has begun to examine how compassion is expressed spontaneously in the face and body. One study found that participants were more likely to express compassion in response to photographs of emotional suffering, but more likely to express distress and pain in response to photographs of physical suffering (Stellar et al., 2020). To examine how compassion is naturally encoded in facial expression across cultures, Cordaro and colleagues (Cordaro et al., 2018) collected facial expressions from participants in China, Japan, South Korea, India, and the United States. They prompted participants to imagine "you see someone with an injury and you feel sympathy for them" and to show how this would be expressed. The expressions were then coded according to the Facial Affect Coding System (FACS). Across the five cultures, the sympathy-for-injury expression included lips parted, jaw dropped, and head leaned forward, and was distinct from expressions of sadness (which included a frown, furrowed brow, and head down) and physical pain (which included eyes closed, and teeth clenched). The head leaned forward distinguished sympathy expressions from all other emotional expressions. This suggests that compassion/sympathy is communicated in facial expression within these cultures, although it did not provide support for the expression originally tested by Haidt and Keltner (1999).

Study of vocal expression has found low levels of absolute accuracy for recognition of compassion in nonverbal vocalizations, albeit higher than chance (Cordaro et al., 2016; Simon-Thomas et al., 2009). However, early research suggests that compassion can be signaled through touch, in particular through consoling patting and stroking movements (recognized as compassion in the US and Spain in Hertenstein et al., 2006). When asked how they would prefer to communicate compassion, participants opted for touch over face and body (App et al., 2011). Observers were also more accurate in identifying compassion from observed touch as compared to facial and bodily displays. However, much more research is needed in the areas of voice and touch as expression channels for compassion.

In summary, the evidence for a distinct expression of compassion is mixed (as it was in 2010). At the very least, decontextualized facial expressions are not spontaneously labeled as compassion or sympathy at the same rates as other emotions like anger or fear. However, studies do suggest there is consistency within cultures in how sympathy is expressed in the face and that the head leaning forward and lips parted may be parts of an expression across cultures. This evidence, coupled with limited research on voice and touch modalities, is consistent with the argument we made in 2010 that "the interpretation of the expression of compassion may prove to be more context dependent than that of other emotions" (Goetz et al., 2010, p. 361). Unlike many other prototypical emotions that have been studied (e.g., anger, fear, amusement), compassion is functional in close physical proximity, and we would expect its expression to be understood in this context, both to needy individuals and to third-party observers. It is our hope that researchers will continue to pursue these avenues of research.

In addition, there are many potential avenues of research that might examine the function and outcomes of expressing compassion. Compassion should be reliably encoded and decoded because the expression signals that the person cares about and wants to help the needy individual. Therefore, in addition to being reliably encoded and decoded, we would also expect that compassion expressions can be judged for authenticity and intensity of feeling, that they evoke a feeling of being consoled and supported and may even reduce pain and suffering, and that expressions of compassion are perceived as signals of pro-sociality and commitment to the suffering person by third-party observers. To our knowledge, there is little work on the interpersonal effects of compassion expressions (though see Falconer et al., 2019).

Broader Outcomes of Compassion

An evolutionary approach to compassion provides a focus on function. Our analysis here, as well as that of others, argues that compassion helps offspring and kin survive and creates and maintains cooperative relationships with non-kin. Put another way, the function of compassion ". . . is to enhance the welfare of a needy other, either because their welfare is inherently valuable to the individual . . . or as a cost-effective overture to a mutually-beneficial relationship" (Sznycer et al., 2019).

Thus far, research on the outcomes of compassion has focused on the person experiencing compassion—their behavior, expression, and desirability as a relationship partner. A well-established body of research shows that compassion motivates people to help (see Batson, 2011; Goetz et al., 2010, for reviews). Research shows that compassion can even motivate people to lie if they feel it will reduce or prevent harm (Lupoli et al., 2017). As we have shown here, an evolutionary approach to compassion as an emotion also predicts that it should be communicable via nonverbal signals. Finally, compassionate individuals should be more desirable and successful as relationship partners (Davis, 2017).

However, we also expect that compassion will have outcomes for targets—that is, compassion should enhance the welfare of needy others. This is an area that is open for research. Do individuals feel better when someone expresses compassion? Do they perceive compassion expressions as soothing and comforting? Furthermore, do individuals who have received compassionate care feel gratitude, and are they more likely to cooperate in the future with the person who expressed compassion for them, or another third party?

It is also likely that compassion's signal has a broader audience. That is, compassion likely signals to third-party witnesses that the actor is a compassionate person and that they value other peoples' welfare. In support of this, Barasch et al. (2014) found that people believe compassion is an authentic signal that the actor feels concern for others (at least in the US). For example, the more a person is believed to feel sympathy or distress in response to a video about hungry children, the more participants perceive their donation to be motivated by altruism (Barasch et al., 2014). Interestingly, research by Lupoli and colleagues (2020) shows that people who are believed to be compassionate are seen as more benevolent, but not always more trustworthy and honest. For example, compassionate managers were seen as less likely to allocate a bonus fairly among employees when one of the employees was suffering.

Distinct Biological Profile and Structures

We opened this chapter with theoretical advances that ground compassion in nurturance and caregiving demands, which suggests that biological systems that drive offspring care play a formative role in the experience of compassion. We then reviewed distinctions between compassion and related states like empathy, sadness, and love, and discussed how appraisals shape compassion. In this section, we survey the evidence from biological studies that measure underlying activity or correlated or causal changes in the body and brain related to compassion and its underlying component processes.

Several teams have outlined parallels between the biological systems involved in compassion and those that drive offspring care (Preston, 2013) and parental nurturance (Kohl et al., 2017; Swain et al., 2012). Research suggests that the human brain has caregiving pathways that are homologous to those necessary for rodent maternal behaviors like licking, nursing, and retrieving pups, including the medial preoptic area of the hypothalamus (MPOA), bed nucleus of the stria terminalis (BNST), and the periaqueductal gray (PAG). Several studies have reported activation in these regions in humans while feeling compassion in laboratory settings (Simon-Thomas et al., 2012; Singer & Engert, 2019). Conversely, studies have documented diminished activation in these regions in response to pain and suffering in individuals diagnosed with clinical psychopathy—for which the central defining characteristic is absence of compassion (Decety et al., 2013).

Anatomically, neural caregiving pathways are highly interconnected with reward circuits that signal pleasure and reinforce pleasurable experiences, including the ventral striatum and orbitofrontal cortex (OFC) regions. Activation in reward circuits has been linked to affectionate urges, interpersonal warmth, soothing touch behaviors, and reassuring "parenteese" vocalizations in parents presented with images of or sounds from infants (Kringelbach et al., 2016; Li et al., 2018). Reward signal has also been reported in people reflecting upon the supportive social bonds that uphold their sense of secure interpersonal attachment (Mikulincer & Shaver, 2020) or their feelings of romantic love (Acevedo et al., 2012). Given our ultra-social nature as a species, these caregiving pathways and interconnected reward circuits are posited to play a prominent role in the full scope of human mental experience and behavior, including compassion (Tomasello, 2014).

Consistent with this connection between compassion and caregiving biology, evidence implicates the neuropeptide oxytocin—the hallmark parenting and pair-bonding hormone—in experiences of compassion. Anatomically, oxytocin is manufactured in a key node of the caregiving pathway, the hypothalamus, and passed to the bloodstream and widely throughout the brain. Compassion is associated with greater production of oxytocin, as well as higher density of oxytocin receptors in the human nervous system (Carter et al., 2017). Aside from its established role in physical aspects of childbirth and nursing, oxytocin soothes stress in response to threats, increases the salience of social information (Shamay-Tsoory & Lamm, 2018), and strengthens long-term romantic bonds (Isgett et al., 2016). Intranasal administration of oxytocin increases interpersonal trust, cooperativeness, and charitable giving—as well as more restorative approaches to upholding moral norms like fairness and justice (Krueger et al., 2013). Genetic studies connect genotypes that enable more robust oxytocin signaling with receptivity to pro-social traits (Christ et al., 2016) and psychological resilience (Saphire-Bernstein et al., 2011). Further work suggests that early life social adversity can alter oxytocin-related gene expression in ways that reduce oxytocin function and predict attachment avoidance (Ein-Dor et al., 2018) impaired social functioning, and greater risk of mental disorders (Schwaiger et al., 2019).

The idea that compassion emerges from caregiving complements an increasingly justified biological model of compassion built upon Polyvagal Theory (Porges, 2017). Here, the argument is that compassion is intrinsically tied to parasympathetic influence on the autonomic nervous system, largely imposed by the ventral, myelinated portion of the 10th cranial nerve: the vagus nerve (Di Bello et al., 2020). Vagal tone, an index of generalized influence of the vagus nerve on peripheral physiology, is tied to overall cardiovascular health, better recovery from stressors, enhanced feelings of social closeness (Kok & Fredrickson, 2010), and increased pro-social states and behaviors in general (Kirby et al., 2017). People with higher vagal tone score higher on measures of felt and expressed compassion, and evoked experiences of compassion are associated with increased vagal influence on peripheral physiology (Stellar et al., 2015). Several studies have shown that compassion-training regimens lead to increased vagal tone, which both lowers stress-related arousal and channels mental resources toward affiliative states and behaviors (Bornemann et al., 2016).

Atop these prosocial systems, we turn to neural pathways and systems that influence and modulate the experience of compassion. As we elaborate in the next few paragraphs, compassion typically involves biological activation related to empathy, both the affective mirroring and the cognitive perspective-taking varieties, which each have distinct neural signatures.

Compassion also engages brain regions and pathways involved in cost–benefit analysis—including appraisals of the self and other people, interpretations of the setting and context, and predictions about possible outcomes, all of which configure the range of possible responses to unmet need, pain, or suffering (Ashar et al., 2017).

Studies continue to clarify how empathy can, though does not always, inspire compassion. Trying to share or simulate others' felt pain, for example, activates the anterior insula (which signals one's own visceral arousal) and anterior cingulate cortex (which adjusts how and where attention is allocated and directed). These areas are known for representing non-sensory aspects of painful experience (e.g., worry, fear; Fallon et al., 2020; Singer & Engert, 2019), often respond to ambiguous circumstances with multiple response options, and stimulate physiological arousal in the service of a protective or defensive response. Perceiving others in distress is initially activating and roughly coded as the presence of a potential threat. This redirects attention toward situation-relevant information like the suffering person and the immediate challenge at hand. In order for an emotional experience of compassion to arise, this early affective response must be channeled in a pro-social direction, rather than a self-focused state like empathic distress. Affective empathy in response to other's pain and suffering serves as a salience signal—indicating that the situation warrants attentional focus and that neural resources should be directed to other component processes (e.g., appraisal, cost–benefit analysis) that can either enhance or inhibit the experience of compassion.

Another neural system that processes social information in compassion-eliciting situations and impacts the likelihood of it occurring is most important for perspective taking. Specifically, the superior temporal sulcus (STS) and temporal parietal junction (TPJ), which enable people to recognize and understand the meaning of other people's emotional expressions and take another person's point of view, play a key role in compassion. Studies show that the anatomical volume and magnitude of activation in STS and TPJ regions predict altruistic giving, a prototypical behavioral outcome of compassion (David et al., 2017; Morishima et al., 2012). Compassion-based training has been shown to enhance activation in these regions in response to compassion-eliciting stimuli (Calderon et al., 2018). Inhibition of STS/TPJ regions via transcranial magnetic stimulation (TMS) increases personal distress in response to compassion elicitors, suggesting that lack of STS/TPJ involvement steers neural resources toward self-defensive processes and away from pro-social processes (Miller et al., 2020). The neural systems that support cognitive empathy contribute to the calculus of whether or how strong a person's experience of compassion might be.

A third neural system that is more self-focused and involves the ventral and dorsal aspects of the medial prefrontal and dorsolateral prefrontal cortex regions (mPFC and DLPFC, respectively) is also routinely implicated in compassion. The mPFC and DLPFC are known for synthesizing information perceived in real time with personal knowledge and goals, taking existing beliefs and self-interest into account, and regulating emotional experience to guide responses accordingly (Herold et al., 2016). To satisfy these objectives, mPFC/DLPFC circuits can both upregulate and downregulate aspects of experience, which in research on compassion can make the pattern of findings seem paradoxical. On the one hand, compassion-focused training can increase activation in the DLPFC and correspondingly decrease activation in the amygdala (the brain's salience detector), a pattern which suggests that the training increases the ability to regulate personal distress and deploy resources toward pro-social responding in response to compassion-evoking stimuli (Weng et al., 2018). On the other hand, given the choice to be generous or act in self-interest, greater cortical thickness and activation in the DLPFC has been associated with more strategic, self-serving choices, suggesting greater capacity to stifle the urge to behave fairly (Müller-Leinß et al., 2018). The apparent contradiction of the influence of these pathways on compassion suggests that their impact depends on the particular appraisals that individuals make in the face of compassion-eliciting situations.

Another initially counterintuitive pattern of activation that has emerged in studies of compassion elicited in laboratory settings involves reward circuitry, typically implicated in signaling personal pleasure. Specifically, both brief and extended compassion training have led to increased activation in reward-signaling structures such as the middle insula and the striatum (including the caudate, putamen, globus pallidus, and nucleus accumbens) in response to compassion-eliciting stimuli (Klimecki et al., 2013). At first glance, it seems odd that the brain would signal pleasure in response to images of pain and suffering. Further consideration, however, has led to two sensible explanations.

First, drawing from compassion-training scholars, the experience of extending compassion toward suffering is pleasurable. It includes feelings of closeness and affection, the intention to do good, and the "warm glow" of knowing one is doing good in the world (Ricard, 2013). In fact, in addition to signaling pleasure in well-characterized dopaminergic reward pathways, the striatum also possesses a high density of oxytocin receptors, which reinforce affectionate and affiliative experiences. Thus, consistent with studies of the neural correlates of romantic love, compassion training may activate and strengthen a cascade of biological processes that counteract distress in response to seeing others' pain and suffering by producing feelings of safety, connection, and pleasure. Second, as part of having an intention to help and considering options for helping a suffering person, one may anticipate relief or other positive emotions like inspiration and gratitude in the suffering person. One may also anticipate vicarious pleasure through positive empathy with the other person's improved state, which reliably enlists reward circuits (Kawamichi et al., 2013; Morelli et al., 2018).

While the neuroscience of compassion has progressed considerably in the past decade, it has not led to a perfect distillation of a simple neural marker or reliably consistent pattern of activation across multiple systems for compassion. Rather, we have learned that there are many moving parts that employ intersecting biological systems during an experience of compassion. These pathways work in concert, supporting multiple component processes that can influence whether or not a person experiences compassion in response to pain and suffering. The complexity of the biological machinations underlying compassion does, however, present a wide range of opportunity for ongoing research on mechanisms of compassion. How, for instance, do different neural systems influence each other? Which neural systems are impacted by interventions that aim to boost compassion, and how? From exercises that focus on potentiating offspring care pathways, to training aimed at sensitizing vicarious pleasure responses, to practices that weigh the long-term benefit of helping over the short-term boon of avoiding compassion-eliciting situations, there are many touchpoints along the trajectory from perceived suffering to compassion that could be leveraged.

Conclusion

We began this chapter by asking what an evolutionary approach brings to our understanding of compassion. By de-romanticizing compassion and approaching it from a functional perspective, the research reviewed here has expanded our conceptual, behavioral, and biological knowledge of the experience. We are grateful that our appraisal model for the emotional experience of compassion served as a preliminary guiding resource for this body of work. Today, it still seems to be the case that people can follow several paths upon encountering another person's pain and suffering, and that both internal and external context contribute to which path they take. In addition, an evolutionary approach to compassion has expanded conceptualizations and study of emotions. Finally, an evolutionary approach to compassion contributes to broader research on human cooperation. We hope the research continues to reveal the dynamics of these processes in ways that enable people to optimize compassion for the betterment of themselves and the greater good.

References

Acevedo, B. P., Aron, A., Fisher, H. E., & Brown, L. L. (2012). Neural correlates of long-term intense romantic love. *Social Cognitive and Affective Neuroscience, 7*(2), 145–159. http://dx.doi.org.libproxy.berkeley.edu/10.1093/scan/nsq092

App, B., McIntosh, D. N., Reed, C. L., & Hertenstein, M. J. (2011). Nonverbal channel use in communication of emotion: How may depend on why. *Emotion, 11*(3), 603–617. https://doi.org/10.1037/a0023164

Ashar, Y. K., Andrews-Hanna, J. R., Dimidjian, S., & Wager, T. D. (2017). Empathic care and distress: Predictive brain markers and dissociable brain systems. *Neuron, 94*(6), 1263–1273. doi: S0896-6273(17)30415-4 [pii]

Axelrod, R., & Hamilton, W. (1981). The evolution of cooperation. *Science, 211*(4489), 1390–1396. https://doi.org/10.1126/science.7466396

Barasch, A., Levine, E. E., Berman, J. Z., & Small, D. A. (2014). Selfish or selfless? On the signal value of emotion in altruistic behavior. *Journal of Personality and Social Psychology, 107*(3), 393–413. https://doi.org/10.1037/a0037207

Batson, C. D. (2011). *Altruism in humans.* Oxford University Press.

Batson, C. D., Fultz, J., & Schoenrade, P. A. (1987). Distress and empathy: Two qualitatively distinct vicarious emotions with different motivational consequences. *Journal of Personality, 55*(1), 19–39. https://doi.org/10.1111/j.1467-6494.1987.tb00426.x

Bornemann, B., Kok, B. E., Böckler, A., & Singer, T. (2016). Helping from the heart: Voluntary upregulation of heart rate variability predicts altruistic behavior. *Biological Psychology, 119*, 54–63. http://dx.doi.org.libproxy.berkeley.edu/10.1016/j.biopsycho.2016.07.004

Brown, S., & Brown, M. (2017). Compassionate neurobiology and health. In E. M. Seppälä, E. Simon-Thomas, S. L. Brown, M. C. Worline, C. D. Cameron, & J. R. Doty (Eds.), *The Oxford handbook of compassion science.* (pp. 159–172). Oxford University Press.

Burnstein, E., Crandall, C., & Kitayama, S. (1994). Some neo-Darwinian decision rules for altruism: Weighing cues for inclusive fitness as a function of the biological importance of the decision. *Journal of Personality and Social Psychology, 67*(5), 773–789. https://doi.org/10.1037/0022-3514.67.5.773

Calderon, A., Ahern, T., & Pruzinsky, T. (2018). Can we change our mind about caring for others? the neuroscience of systematic compassion training. In L. Stevens & C. C. Woodruff (Eds.), *The neuroscience of empathy, compassion, and self-compassion* (pp. 213–234). Elsevier Academic Press.

Cameron, C. D., & Payne, B. K. (2011). Escaping affect: How motivated emotion regulation creates insensitivity to mass suffering. *Journal of Personality and Social Psychology, 100*(1), 1–15. https://doi.org/10.1037/a0021643

Cameron, C. D., Scheffer, J. A., Hadjiandreou, E., Hutcherson, C. A., Ferguson, A. M., & Inzlicht, M. (2019). Empathy is hard work: People choose to avoid empathy because of its cognitive costs. *Journal of Experimental Psychology: General, 148*(6), 962–976. http://dx.doi.org/10.1037/xge0000595

Caprara, G. V., Alessandri, G., & Eisenberg, N. (2012). Prosociality: The contribution of traits, values, and self-efficacy beliefs. *Journal of Personality and Social Psychology, 102*(6), 1289–1303. https://doi.org/10.1037/a0025626

Carter, C. S., Bartal, I. B., & Porges, E. C. (2017). The roots of compassion: An evolutionary and neurobiological perspective. In E. M. Seppälä, E. Simon-Thomas, S. L. Brown, M. C. Worline, C. D. Cameron, & J. R. Doty (Eds.), *The Oxford handbook of compassion science* (pp. 173–187). Oxford University Press.

Christ, C. C., Carlo, G., & Stoltenberg, S. F. (2016). Oxytocin receptor (OXTR) single nucleotide polymorphisms indirectly predict prosocial behavior through perspective taking and empathic concern. *Journal of Personality, 84*(2), 204–213. doi:10.1111/jopy.12152

Cialdini, R. B., Brown, S. L., Lewis, B. P., Luce, C., & Neuberg, S. L. (1997). Reinterpreting the empathy–altruism relationship: When one into one equals oneness. *Journal of Personality and Social Psychology, 73*(3), 481–494. https://doi.org/10.1037/0022-3514.73.3.481

Clark, M. S., Boothby, E. J., Clark-Polner, E., & Reis, H. T. (2015). Understanding prosocial behavior requires understanding relational context. In D. A. Schroeder & W. G. Graziano (Eds.), *The Oxford handbook of prosocial behavior* (pp. 329–345). Oxford University Press.

Condon, P., & Feldman Barrett, L. (2013). Conceptualizing and experiencing compassion. *Emotion, 13*(5), 817–821. https://doi.org/10.1037/a0033747

Condon, P., & Makransky, J. (2020). Recovering the relational starting point of compassion training: A foundation for sustainable and inclusive care. *Perspectives on Psychological Science, 15*(6), 1346–1362. doi: 10.1177/1745691620922200

Cordaro, D. T., Keltner, D., Tshering, S., Wangchuk, D., & Flynn, L. M. (2016). The voice conveys emotion in ten globalized cultures and one remote village in Bhutan. *Emotion, 16*(1), 117–128. https://doi.org/10.1037/emo0000100

Cordaro, D. T., Sun, R., Kamble, S., Hodder, N., Monroy, M., Cowen, A., Bai, Y., & Keltner, D. (2020). The recognition of 18 facial-bodily expressions across nine cultures. *Emotion, 20*(7), 1292–1300. https://doi.org/10.1037/emo0000576

Cordaro, D. T., Sun, R., Keltner, D., Kamble, S., Huddar, N., & McNeil, G. (2018). Universals and cultural variations in 22 emotional expressions across five cultures. *Emotion, 18*(1), 75–93. https://doi.org/10.1037/emo0000302

Cowen, A. S., Elfenbein, H. A., Laukka, P., & Keltner, D. (2019). Mapping 24 emotions conveyed by brief human vocalization. *American Psychologist, 74*(6), 698–712. https://doi.org/10.1037/amp0000399

Cowen, A. S., & Keltner, D. (2020). What the face displays: Mapping 28 emotions conveyed by naturalistic expression. *American Psychologist, 75*(3), 349–364. https://doi.org/10.1037/amp0000488

Cuff, B. M. P., Brown, S. J., Taylor, L., & Howat, D. J. (2016). Empathy: A review of the concept. *Emotion Review, 8*(2), 144–153. https://doi.org/10.1177/1754073914558466

Curry, O., Roberts, S. G. B., & Dunbar, R. I. M. (2013). Altruism in social networks: Evidence for a "kinship premium." *British Journal of Psychology, 104*(2), 283–295. https://doi.org/10.1111/j.2044-8295.2012.02119.x

David, B., Hu, Y., Krüger, F., & Weber, B. (2017). Other-regarding attention focus modulates third-party altruistic choice: An fMRI study. *Scientific Reports, 7*, 43024. https://doi.org/10.1038/srep43024

Davis, M. H. (1983). Measuring individual differences in empathy: Evidence for a multidimensional approach. *Journal of Personality and Social Psychology, 44*(1), 113–126. https://doi.org/10.1037/0022-3514.44.1.113

Davis, M. H. (2017). Empathy, compassion, and social relationships. In E. M. Seppälä, E. Simon-Thomas, S. L. Brown, M. C. Worline, C. D. Cameron, & J. R. Doty (Eds.), *The Oxford handbook of compassion science.* (pp. 299–315). Oxford University Press.

Davis, M. H., Mitchell, K. V., Hall, J. A., Lothert, J., Snapp, T., & Meyer, M. (1999). Empathy, expectations, and situational preferences: Personality influences on the decision to participate in volunteer helping behaviors. *Journal of Personality, 67*(3), 469–503. https://doi.org/10.1111/1467-6494.00062

Decety, J., Skelly, L. R., & Kiehl, K. A. (2013). Brain response to empathy-eliciting scenarios involving pain in incarcerated individuals with psychopathy. *JAMA Psychiatry, 70*(6), 638–645. doi: 10.1001/jamapsychiatry.2013.27

Delton, A. W., Petersen, M. B., DeScioli, P., & Robertson, T. E. (2018). Need, compassion, and support for social welfare. *Political Psychology, 39*(4), 907–924. https://doi.org/10.1111/pops.12450

DeSteno, D. (2015). Compassion and altruism: How our minds determine who is worthy of help. *Current Opinion in Behavioral Sciences, 3*, 80–83. https://doi.org/10.1016/j.cobeha.2015.02.002

Di Bello, M., Carnevali, L., Petrocchi, N., Thayer, J. F., Gilbert, P., & Ottaviani, C. (2020). The compassionate vagus: A meta-analysis on the connection between compassion and heart rate variability. *Neuroscience and Biobehavioral Reviews, 116*, 21–30. doi: S0149-7634(20)30443-7

Ein-Dor, T., Verbeke, W. J. M. I., Mokry, M., & Vrticka, P. (2018). Epigenetic modification of the oxytocin and glucocorticoid receptor genes is linked to attachment avoidance in young adults. *Attachment & Human Development, 20*(4), 439–454. doi: https://pubmed.ncbi.nlm.nih.gov/29513137/

Eisenberg, N., & Eggum, N. D. (2009). Empathic responding: Sympathy and personal distress. In J. Decety & W. Ickes (Eds.), *The social neuroscience of empathy* (pp. 71–83). MIT Press. https://doi.org/10.7551/mitpress/9780262012973.003.0007

Eisenberg, N., Fabes, R. A., Murphy, B., Karbon, M., Smith, M., & Maszk, P. (1996). The relations of children's dispositional empathy-related responding to their emotionality, regulation, and social functioning. *Developmental Psychology, 32*(2), 195–209. https://doi.org/10.1037/0012-1649.32.2.195

Ekman, P. (1992). An argument for basic emotions. *Cognition and Emotion, 6*(3–4), 169–200. https://doi.org/10.1080/02699939208411068

Ekman, P., Sorenson, E. R., & Friesen, W. V. (1969). Pan-cultural elements in facial displays of emotion. *Science, 164*(3875), 86–88. https://doi.org/10.1126/science.164.3875.86

Falconer, C. J., Lobmaier, J. S., Christoforou, M., Kamboj, S. K., King, J. A., Gilbert, P., & Brewin, C. R. (2019). Compassionate faces: Evidence for distinctive facial expressions associated with specific prosocial motivations. *PLOS ONE, 14*(1), e0210283. https://doi.org/10.1371/journal.pone.0210283

Fallon, N., Roberts, C., & Stancak, A. (2020). Shared and distinct functional networks for empathy and pain processing: A systematic review and meta-analysis of fMRI studies. *Social Cognitive and Affective Neuroscience, 15*(7), 709–723. doi: 10.1093/scan/nsaa090

Gilbert, P. (2017). *Compassion: Concepts, Research and Applications*. Routledge.

Goetz, J. L., & Halgren, S. (2020). Closeness or compassion? Relatedness and causal control influence helping via distinct pathways. *The Journal of Social Psychology, 160*(4), 479–495. https://doi.org/10.1080/00224545.2019.1681352

Goetz, J. L., Keltner, D., & Simon-Thomas, E. (2010). Compassion: An evolutionary analysis and empirical review. *Psychological Bulletin, 136*(3), 351–374. https://doi.org/10.1037/a0018807

Goetz, J. L., & Peng, K. (2019). Sympathy and responses to suffering: Similarity and variation in China and the United States. *Emotion, 19*(2), 320–333. https://doi.org/10.1037/emo0000443

Goetz, J. L., & Simon-Thomas, E. (2017). The landscape of compassion: Definitions and scientific approaches. In E. Seppälä, E. Simon-Thomas, S. L. Brown, M. C. Worline, C. D. Cameron, & J. Doty (Eds.), *The Oxford handbook of compassion science* (pp. 3–16). Oxford University Press.

Gross, J. (2015). Emotion regulation: Current status and future prospects. *Psychological Inquiry, 26*(1), 1–26.

Hackman, J., Danvers, A., & Hruschka, D. J. (2015). Closeness is enough for friends, but not mates or kin: Mate and kinship premiums in India and U.S. *Evolution and Human Behavior, 36*(2), 137–145. https://doi.org/10.1016/j.evolhumbehav.2014.10.002

Haidt, J., & Keltner, D. (1999). Culture and facial expression: Open-ended methods find more expressions and a gradient of recognition. *Cognition and Emotion, 13*(3), 225–266. https://doi.org/10.1080/026999399379267

Hamilton, W. D. (1964). The genetical evolution of social behaviour. II. *Journal of Theoretical Biology, 7*(1), 17–52. https://doi.org/10.1016/0022-5193(64)90039-6

Herold, D., Spengler, S., Sajonz, B., Usnich, T., & Bermpohl, F. (2016). Common and distinct networks for self-referential and social stimulus processing in the human brain. *Brain Structure & Function, 221*(7), 3475–3485. doi: 10.1007/s00429-015-1113-9

Hertenstein, M. J., Keltner, D., App, B., Bulleit, B. A., & Jaskolka, A. R. (2006). Touch communicates distinct emotions. *Emotion, 6*(3), 528–533. https://doi.org/10.1037/1528-3542.6.3.528

Hrdy, S. B. (1999). *Mother nature: A History of mothers, infants, and natural selection*. Pantheon. https://repository.library.georgetown.edu/handle/10822/546389

Ickes, W. (1993). Empathic accuracy. *Journal of Personality, 61*(4), 587–610. https://doi.org/10.1111/j.1467-6494.1993.tb00783.x

Isgett, S. F., Algoe, S. B., Boulton, A. J., Way, B. M., & Fredrickson, B. L. (2016). Common variant in OXTR predicts growth in positive emotions from loving-kindness training. *Psychoneuroendocrinology, 73*, 244–251. doi: S0306-4530(16)30556-X

Jordan, M. R., Amir, D., & Bloom, P. (2016). Are empathy and concern psychologically distinct? *Emotion, 16*(8), 1107–1116. https://doi.org/10.1037/emo0000228

Kaniasty, K., & Norris, F. H. (1995). Mobilization and deterioration of social support following natural disasters. *Current Directions in Psychological Science, 4*(3), 94–98. https://doi.org/10.1111/1467-8721.ep10772341

Kawamichi, H., Tanabe, H. C., Takahashi, H. K., & Sadato, N. (2013). Activation of the reward system during sympathetic concern is mediated by two types of empathy in a familiarity-dependent manner. *Social Neuroscience, 8*(1), 90–100. doi: 10.1080/17470919.2012.744349 [doi]

Kirby, J. N., Doty, J. R., Petrocchi, N., & Gilbert, P. (2017). The current and future role of heart rate variability for assessing and training compassion. *Frontiers in Public Health, 5*, 40. doi: 10.3389/fpubh.2017.00040

Kirby, J. N., Seppälä, E., Wilks, M., Cameron, C. D., Tellegen, C. L., Nguyen, D. T. H., Misra, S., Simon-Thomas, E., Feinberg, M., Martin, D., & Doty, J. (2019). Positive and negative attitudes towards compassion predict compassionate outcomes. *Current Psychology, 40*, 4884–4894. https://doi.org/10.1007/s12144-019-00405-8

Klimecki, O. M., Leiberg, S., Lamm, C., & Singer, T. (2013). Functional neural plasticity and associated changes in positive affect after compassion training. *Cerebral Cortex, 23*(7), 1552–1561. http://dx.doi.org.libproxy.berkeley.edu/10.1093/cercor/bhs142

Klimecki, O. M., & Singer, T. (2017). The compassionate brain. In E. Seppälä, E. Simon-Thomas, S. L. Brown, M. C. Worline, C. D. Cameron, & J. Doty (Eds.), *The Oxford handbook of compassion science* (pp. 109–120). Oxford University Press. https://doi.org/10.1093/oxfordhb/9780190464684.013.9

Kohl, J., Autry, A. E., & Dulac, C. (2017). The neurobiology of parenting: A neural circuit perspective. *BioEssays: News and Reviews in Molecular, Cellular and Developmental Biology, 39*(1), 1–11. doi: 10.1002/bies.201600159

Kok, B. E., & Fredrickson, B. L. (2010). Upward spirals of the heart: Autonomic flexibility, as indexed by vagal tone, reciprocally and prospectively predicts positive emotions and social connectedness. *Biological Psychology, 85*(3), 432–436. doi: 10.1016/j.biopsycho.2010.09.005 [doi]

Korchmaros, J. D., & Kenny, D. A. (2006). An evolutionary and close-relationship model of helping. *Journal of Social and Personal Relationships, 23*(1), 21–43. https://doi.org/10.1177/0265407506060176

Kringelbach, M. L., Stark, E. A., Alexander, C., Bornstein, M. H., & Stein, A. (2016). On cuteness: Unlocking the parental brain and beyond. *Trends in Cognitive Sciences, 20*(7), 545–558.

Krueger, F., Parasuraman, R., Moody, L., Twieg, P., de Visser, E., McCabe, K., O'Hara, M., & Lee, M. R. (2013). Oxytocin selectively increases perceptions of harm for victims but not the desire to punish offenders of criminal offenses. *Social Cognitive and Affective Neuroscience, 8*(5), 494–498.

Kurzban, R., Burton-Chellew, M. N., & West, S. A. (2015). The evolution of altruism in humans. *Annual Review of Psychology, 66*(1), 575–599. https://doi.org/10.1146/annurev-psych-010814-015355

Lavelle, B. D. (2017). Compassion in context: Tracing the Buddhist roots of secular, compassion-based contemplative programs. In E. Seppälä, E. Simon-Thomas, S. L. Brown, M. C. Worline, C. D. Cameron, & J. Doty (Eds.), *The Oxford handbook of compassion science* (pp. 17–26). Oxford University Press. https://doi.org/10.1093/oxfordhb/9780190464684.013.2

Lebowitz, M. S., & Dovidio, J. F. (2015). Implications of emotion regulation strategies for empathic concern, social attitudes, and helping behavior. *Emotion, 15*(2), 187–194.

Lerner, J. S., & Keltner, D. (2000). Beyond valence: Toward a model of emotion-specific influences on judgement and choice. *Cognition and Emotion, 14*(4), 473–493. https://doi.org/10.1080/026999300402763

Li, T., Horta, M., Mascaro, J. S., Bijanki, K., Arnal, L. H., Adams, M., Barr, R. G., & Rilling, J. K. (2018). Explaining individual variation in paternal brain responses to infant cries. *Physiology & Behavior, 193*(Part A), 43–54.

Lim, D., & DeSteno, D. (2016). Suffering and compassion: The links among adverse life experiences, empathy, compassion, and prosocial behavior. *Emotion, 16*(2), 175–182. https://doi.org/10.1037/emo0000144

Lim, D., & DeSteno, D. (2020). Past adversity protects against the numeracy bias in compassion. *Emotion, 20*(8), 1344–1356. https://doi.org/10.1037/emo0000655

Lockwood, P. L., Seara-Cardoso, A., & Viding, E. (2014). Emotion regulation moderates the association between empathy and prosocial behavior. *PLOS ONE, 9*(5), 6.

Lupoli, M. J., Jampol, L., & Oveis, C. (2017). Lying because we care: Compassion increases prosocial lying. *Journal of Experimental Psychology: General, 146*(7), 1026–1042. https://doi.org/10.1037/xge0000315

Lupoli, M. J., Zhang, M., Yin, Y., & Oveis, C. (2020). A conflict of values: When perceived compassion decreases trust. *Journal of Experimental Social Psychology, 91*, 104049. https://doi.org/10.1016/j.jesp.2020.104049

Maner, J. K., & Gailliot, M. T. (2007). Altruism and egoism: Prosocial motivations for helping depend on relationship context. *European Journal of Social Psychology, 37*(2), 347–358. https://doi.org/10.1002/ejsp.364

Maner, J. K., Luce, C. L., Neuberg, S. L., Cialdini, R. B., Brown, S., & Sagarin, B. J. (2002). The effects of perspective taking on motivations for helping: Still no evidence for altruism. *Personality and Social Psychology Bulletin, 28*(11), 1601–1610. https://doi.org/10.1177/014616702237586

Mikulincer, M., & Shaver, P. R. (2020). Broaden-and-build effects of contextually boosting the sense of attachment security in adulthood. *Current Directions in Psychological Science, 29*(1), 22–26. http://dx.doi.org.libproxy.berkeley.edu/10.1177/0963721419885997

Miller, J. G., Xia, G., & Hastings, P. D. (2020). Right temporoparietal junction involvement in autonomic responses to the suffering of others: A preliminary transcranial magnetic stimulation study. *Frontiers in Human Neuroscience, 14*, http://dx.doi.org.libproxy.berkeley.edu/10.3389/fnhum.2020.00007

Morelli, S. A., Knutson, B., & Zaki, J. (2018). Neural sensitivity to personal and vicarious reward differentially relates to prosociality and well-being. *Social Cognitive and Affective Neuroscience, 13*(8), 831–839. doi: 10.1093/scan/nsy056

Morishima, Y., Schunk, D., Bruhin, A., Ruff, C. C., & Fehr, E. (2012). Linking brain structure and activation in temporoparietal junction to explain the neurobiology of human altruism. *Neuron, 75*(1), 73–79. doi: 10.1016/j.neuron.2012.05.021

Morelli, S. A., Knutson, B., & Zaki, J. (2018). Neural sensitivity to personal and vicarious reward differentially relates to prosociality and well-being. *Social Cognitive and Affective Neuroscience, 13*(8), 831–839. doi: 10.1093/scan/nsy056

Müller-Leinß, J., Enzi, B., Flasbeck, V., & Brüne, M. (2018). Retaliation or selfishness? An rTMS investigation of the role of the dorsolateral prefrontal cortex in prosocial motives. *Social Neuroscience, 13*(6), 701–709. http://dx.doi.org.libproxy.berkeley.edu/10.1080/17470919.2017.1411828

Neuberg, S. L., Cialdini, R. B., Brown, S. L., Luce, C., Sagarin, B. J., & Lewis, B. P. (1997). Does empathy lead to anything more than superficial helping? Comment on Batson et al. (1997). *Journal of Personality and Social Psychology, 73*(3), 510–516. https://doi.org/10.1037/0022-3514.73.3.510

Nolin, D. A. (2010). Food-sharing networks in Lamalera, Indonesia: Reciprocity, kinship, and distance. *Human Nature (Hawthorne, N.Y.), 21*(3), 243–268. https://doi.org/10.1007/s12110-010-9091-3

Nowak, M. A. (2006). Five rules for the evolution of cooperation. *Science (New York, N.Y.), 314*(5805), 1560–1563. https://doi.org/10.1126/science.1133755

Nowak, M. A., & Sigmund, K. (2005). Evolution of indirect reciprocity. *Nature, 437*(7063), 1291–1298. https://doi.org/10.1038/nature04131

Oveis, C., Horberg, E. J., & Keltner, D. (2010). Compassion, pride, and social intuitions of self-other similarity. *Journal of Personality and Social Psychology, 98*(4), 618–630. https://doi.org/10.1037/a0017628

Petersen, M. B., Sznycer, D., Cosmides, L., & Tooby, J. (2012). Who deserves help? Evolutionary psychology, social emotions, and public opinion about welfare. *Political Psychology, 33*(3), 395–418. https://doi.org/10.1111/j.1467-9221.2012.00883.x

Piff, P. K., & Moskowitz, J. P. (2017, September 28). The class–compassion gap. In E. Seppälä, E. Simon-Thomas, S. L. Brown, M. C. Worline, C. D. Cameron, & J. Doty (Eds.), *The Oxford handbook of compassion science* (pp. 317–330). Oxford University Press. https://doi.org/10.1093/oxfordhb/9780190464684.013.24

Porges, S. W. (2017). Vagal pathways: Portals to compassion. In E. M. Seppälä, E. Simon-Thomas, S. L. Brown, M. C. Worline, C. D. Cameron, & J. R. Doty (Eds.), *The Oxford handbook of compassion science* (pp. 189–202). Oxford University Press.

Powell, P. A. (2018). Individual differences in emotion regulation moderate the associations between empathy and affective distress. *Motivation and Emotion, 42*(4), 602–613. https://doi.org/10.1007/s11031-018-9684-4

Preston, S. D. (2013). The origins of altruism in offspring care. *Psychological Bulletin, 139*(6), 1305–1341. http://dx.doi.org.libproxy.berkeley.edu/10.1037/a0031755

Preston, S., & de Waal, F. (2002). Empathy: Its ultimate and proximate bases. *Behavioral and Brain Sciences, 25*(1), 1–20. doi:10.1017/S0140525X02000018

Ricard, M. (2013). A Buddhist view of happiness. In S. A. David, I. Boniwell, & A. Conley Ayers (Eds.), *The Oxford handbook of happiness* (pp. 344–356). Oxford University Press.

Rudolph, U., Roesch, S., Greitemeyer, T., & Weiner, B. (2004). A meta-analytic review of help giving and aggression from an attributional perspective: Contributions to a general theory of motivation. *Cognition & Emotion, 18*(6), 815–848. https://doi.org/10.1080/02699930341000248

Saphire-Bernstein, S., Way, B. M., Kim, H. S., Sherman, D. K., & Taylor, S. E. (2011). Oxytocin receptor gene (OXTR) is related to psychological resources. *Proceedings of the National Academy of Sciences, 108*(37), 15118–15122. doi: 10.1073/pnas.1113137108

Schwaiger, M., Heinrichs, M., & Kumsta, R. (2019). Oxytocin administration and emotion recognition abilities in adults with a history of childhood adversity. *Psychoneuroendocrinology, 99*, 66–71. doi: S0306-4530(18)30149-5 [pii]

Shamay-Tsoory, S., & Lamm, C. (2018). The neuroscience of empathy: From past to present and future. *Neuropsychologia, 116*(Pt A), 1–4. doi: S0028-3932(18)30183-0 [pii]

Shaver, P., Schwartz, J., Kirson, D., & O'Connor, C. (1987). Emotion knowledge: Further exploration of a prototype approach. *Journal of Personality and Social Psychology, 52*(6), 1061–1086. https://doi.org/10.1037//0022-3514.52.6.1061

Shaw, L. L., Batson, C. D., & Todd, R. M. (1994). Empathy avoidance: Forestalling feeling for another in order to escape the motivational consequences. *Journal of Personality and Social Psychology, 67*(5), 879–887. https://doi.org/10.1037/0022-3514.67.5.879

Simon-Thomas, E. R., Godzik, J., Castle, E., Antonenko, O., Ponz, A., Kogan, A., & Keltner, D. J. (2012). An fMRI study of caring vs self-focus during induced compassion and pride. *Social Cognitive and Affective Neuroscience, 7*(6), 635–648. http://dx.doi.org.libproxy.berkeley.edu/10.1093/scan/nsr045

Simon-Thomas, E. R., Keltner, D. J., Sauter, D., Sinicropi-Yao, L., & Abramson, A. (2009). The voice conveys specific emotions: Evidence from vocal burst displays. *Emotion (Washington, D.C.), 9*(6), 838–846. https://doi.org/10.1037/a0017810

Singer, T., & Engert, V. (2019). It matters what you practice: Differential training effects on subjective experience, behavior, brain and body in the ReSource project. *Current Opinion in Psychology, 28*, 151–158. doi: S2352-250X(18)30141-6 [pii]

Skwara, A. C., King, B. G., & Saron, C. D. (2017). Studies of training compassion: What have we learned; what remains unknown. In E. M. Seppälä, E. Simon-Thomas, S. L. Brown, M. C. Worline, C. D. Cameron, & J. R. Doty (Eds.), *The Oxford handbook of compassion science* (pp. 219–236). Oxford University Press.

Small, D. A., Loewenstein, G., & Slovic, P. (2007). Sympathy and callousness: The impact of deliberative thought on donations to identifiable and statistical victims. *Organizational Behavior and Human Decision Processes, 102*(2), 143–153. https://doi.org/10.1016/j.obhdp.2006.01.005

Spikins, P. A., Rutherford, H. E., & Needham, A. P. (2010). From homininity to humanity: Compassion from the earliest archaics to modern humans. *Time and Mind, 3*(3), 303–325. https://doi.org/10.2752/175169610X12754030955977

Stellar, J., Feinberg, M., & Keltner, D. (2014). When the selfish suffer: Evidence for selective prosocial emotional and physiological responses to suffering egoists. *Evolution and Human Behavior, 35*(2), 140–147. https://doi.org/10.1016/j.evolhumbehav.2013.12.001

Stellar, J. E., Anderson, C. L., & Gatchpazian, A. (2020). Profiles in empathy: Different empathic responses to emotional and physical suffering. *Journal of Experimental Psychology: General, 149*(7), 1398–1416. https://doi.org/10.1037/xge0000718

Stellar, J. E., Cohen, A., Oveis, C., & Keltner, D. (2015). Affective and physiological responses to the suffering of others: Compassion and vagal activity. *Journal of Personality and Social Psychology, 108*(4), 572–585. doi: 10.1037/pspi0000010

Stellar, J. E., Manzo, V. M., Kraus, M. W., & Keltner, D. (2012). Class and compassion: Socioeconomic factors predict responses to suffering. *Emotion, 12*(3), 449–459. https://doi.org/10.1037/a0026508

Stewart-Williams, S. (2007). Altruism among kin vs. nonkin: Effects of cost of help and reciprocal exchange. *Evolution and Human Behavior, 28*(3), 193–198. https://doi.org/10.1016/j.evolhumbehav.2007.01.002

Stewart-Williams, S. (2008). Human beings as evolved nepotists: Exceptions to the rule and effects of cost of help. *Human Nature, 19*(4), 414–425. https://doi.org/10.1007/s12110-008-9048-y

Stürmer, S., Snyder, M., Kropp, A., & Siem, B. (2006). Empathy-motivated helping: The moderating role of group membership. *Personality and Social Psychology Bulletin, 32*(7), 943–956. https://doi.org/10.1177/0146167206287363

Stürmer, S., Snyder, M., & Omoto, A. M. (2005). Prosocial emotions and helping: The moderating role of group membership. *Journal of Personality and Social Psychology, 88*(3), 532–546. https://doi.org/10.1037/0022-3514.88.3.532

Swain, J. E., Konrath, S., Brown, S. L., Finegood, E. D., Akce, L. B., Dayton, C. J., & Ho, S. S. (2012). Parenting and beyond: Common neurocircuits underlying parental and altruistic caregiving. *Parenting: Science and Practice, 12*(2–3), 115–123. http://dx.doi.org.libproxy.berkeley.edu/10.1080/15295192.2012.680409

Sznycer, D., Delton, A. W., Robertson, T. E., Cosmides, L., & Tooby, J. (2019). The ecological rationality of helping others: Potential helpers integrate cues of recipients' need and willingness to sacrifice. *Evolution and Human Behavior, 40*(1), 34–45. https://doi.org/10.1016/j.evolhumbehav.2018.07.005

Thompson, N. M., Uusberg, A., Gross, J. J., & Chakrabarti, B. (2019). Empathy and emotion regulation: An integrative account. In N. Srinivasan (Ed.), *Progress in brain research* (Vol. 247, pp. 273–304). Elsevier. https://doi.org/10.1016/bs.pbr.2019.03.024

Tomasello, M. (2014). The ultra-social animal. *European Journal of Social Psychology, 44*(3), 187–194. doi: 10.1002/ejsp.2015

Tong, E. M. W. (2015). Differentiation of 13 positive emotions by appraisals. *Cognition & Emotion, 29*(3), 484–503. https://doi.org/10.1080/02699931.2014.922056

Weidman, A. C., & Tracy, J. L. (2020). Picking up good vibrations: Uncovering the content of distinct positive emotion subjective experience. *Emotion, 20*(8), 1311–1331. https://doi.org/10.1037/emo0000677

Weiner, B. (1995). *Judgments of responsibility: A foundation for a theory of social conduct.* Guilford Press.

Weisz, E., & Zaki, J. (2017). Empathy-building interventions. In E. Seppälä, E. Simon-Thomas, S. L. Brown, M. C. Worline, C. D. Cameron, & J. Doty (Eds.), *The Oxford handbook of compassion science* (pp. 205–217). Oxford University Press. https://doi.org/10.1093/oxfordhb/9780190464684.013.16

Weng, H. Y., Lapate, R. C., Stodola, D. E., Rogers, G. M., & Davidson, R. J. (2018). Visual attention to suffering after compassion training is associated with decreased amygdala responses. *Frontiers in Psychology, 9* http://dx.doi.org.libproxy.berkeley.edu/10.3389/fpsyg.2018.00771

Wiessner, P. (2002). Hunting, healing, and hxaro exchange. A long-term perspective on !Kung (Ju/'hoansi) large-game hunting. *Evolution and Human Behavior, 23*(6), 407–436. https://doi.org/10.1016/S1090-5138(02)00096-X

Xue, M. (2013). Altruism and reciprocity among friends and kin in a Tibetan village. *Evolution and Human Behavior, 34*(5), 323–329. https://doi.org/10.1016/j.evolhumbehav.2013.05.002

Zaki, J. (2014). Empathy: A motivated account. *Psychological Bulletin, 140*(6), 1608–1647. https://doi.org/10.1037/a0037679

Zaki, J. (2020). Integrating empathy and interpersonal emotion regulation. *Annual Review of Psychology, 71*(1), 517–540. https://doi.org/10.1146/annurev-psych-010419-050830

Zaki, J., Weber, J., Bolger, N., & Ochsner, K. (2009). The neural bases of empathic accuracy. *Proceedings of the National Academy of Sciences, 106*(27), 11382–11387. https://doi.org/10.1073/pnas.0902666106

PART III

Emotions in Different Domains of Life

CHAPTER 30

Emotions and Status Hierarchies

Patrick K. Durkee

Abstract

Emotions define and are defined by status hierarchies. This chapter examines human emotions in relation to hierarchy navigation. Because emotional adaptations evolve in response to selective pressures, the chapter first presents evidence supporting the ubiquity of hierarchies and the fitness-relevance of status in the ancestral past. Next, the author provides a sketch of the recurrent adaptive challenges likely posed by life within hierarchically organized groups to circumscribe the hierarchy-navigation tasks that emotional adaptations are expected to address. The chapter then highlights several emotions—pride, shame, envy, admiration, respect, contempt, anger, and fear—that appear to facilitate hierarchy navigation, reviews the evidence for their functional design, and explores ways in which relative differences in status may modulate recurring emotional experiences. Finally, the author discusses how understanding the interplay between emotions and hierarchy navigation can inform understanding of broad individual differences.

Key Words: hierarchy, status, emotion, individual difference, personality

Emotions and Status Hierarchies

Emotions and status hierarchies are deeply intertwined. In a proximate sense, several emotions—such as those labeled pride, shame, admiration, respect, envy, and contempt in our lexicon—demarcate relative differences in status and the resulting hierarchical structure of human social groups (Steckler & Tracy, 2014; Van Vugt & Tybur, 2015; Witkower et al., 2020). Status-relevant information and relative differences in status, in turn, activate and modulate patterns of different emotional experiences in everyday life (van Kleef & Lange, 2020). The evolution of emotions can be expected to have been partially directed and refined by the recurrent adaptive problems posed by hierarchies throughout our ancestral past (Tooby & Cosmides, 1990). Moreover, the constellation of human emotions and their influences on group dynamics likely contributed to the evolution of prestige-processes that are unique to human status hierarchies (Gervais & Fessler, 2017; Henrich & Gil-White, 2001). Status hierarchies therefore partially define—and are largely defined by—emotions at multiple levels of analysis.

In this chapter, I aim to build upon the growing literature on the evolved functions of emotions and their roles in human status hierarchies (e.g., Steckler & Tracy, 2014; Van Vugt & Tybur, 2015; Witkower et al., 2020). As does much of the work in this edited volume, I will explore the interplay between status hierarchies and emotions through an adaptationist lens

(Al-Shawaf et al., 2016; Cosmides & Tooby, 2000; Nesse, 1990; Sznycer, Cosmides, et al., 2017; Tooby & Cosmides, 1990). On this view, emotions are superordinate functional mechanisms instantiated in our neurobiology. These emotion adaptations are activated by cues of adaptive problems to coordinate thoughts, motivations, and behaviors in ways that would have led to net fitness gains for our ancestors over deep time.

The functions of emotional adaptations are shaped by ancestrally recurrent challenges (Tooby & Cosmides, 1990). If status hierarchies reliably exhibited selection pressures on our ancestors throughout human evolution, we should expect that at least some of our emotions function to aid in solving the challenges posed by life in hierarchically organized social groups. Thus, we can reverse-engineer the design features of our emotions by reasoning about the specific adaptive challenges posed by hierarchies. Before outlining specific adaptive challenges, examining relevant emotions, and exploring implications for broad individual differences, I will set up the rationale for expecting hierarchy navigation adaptations by summarizing the evidence for the ubiquity of hierarchies and fitness-relevance of status.

The Ubiquity of Hierarchies and Ancestral Importance of Status

Two conditions must be met for adaptations designed to facilitate hierarchy navigation to evolve. First, hierarchies and the adaptive challenges they pose must have been recurrent throughout our evolutionary history. Second, relative position within the hierarchy must have been reliably linked to ancestral fitness. In this section, I present an overview of the evidence supporting these prerequisites.

Hierarchies are ubiquitous across the animal kingdom. Group-living species inevitably form hierarchical social groups of varying steepness and complexity, wherein rank is characterized by predictable behavioral patterns of deference, influence, and attention (Boehm, 1999; Chase, 1974; Franz et al., 2015; Issa et al., 1999; Meese & Ewbank, 1973). Status hierarchies are a universal feature of human social groups in both modern industrialized and small-scale societies (Anderson et al., 2015; Brown, 1991; von Rueden et al., 2008). They likely were throughout our ancestral past as well. In many species, including nonhuman primates, hierarchical rank (i.e., status) is defined largely by patterns of agonistic aggression, coercion, and threat displays, such that physically formidable individuals who can more effectively inflict costs on group members and withhold resources attain higher status (de Waal, 1982; Franz et al., 2015). Because humans possess the cognitive architecture to assort hierarchically based on aggressive formidability (Durkee et al., 2018; Sell et al., 2009; Toscano et al., 2016), threatened or actualized cost inflict could play an analogous role in human status hierarchies in some contexts (Cheng, 2020; Cheng et al., 2013; Durkee et al., 2021). However, theoretical considerations suggest that pure, in-group-directed cost inflict is unlikely to lead to status over time because humans can form leveling coalitions to depose overly aggressive, undeserving individuals with relative ease (Boehm, 1999, 2012; Cheng, 2020; Gintis et al., 2015; Lukaszewski et al., 2016; Wrangham, 2021). The logic of human status allocation instead appears to be driven primarily by social valuation, competence, and prestige-related processes whereby individuals tentatively tolerate others having greater relative access to resources, influence over group outcomes, and attention to the extent that they directly or indirectly generate benefits for others in the group (Chapais, 2015; Durkee et al., 2020; Durkee et al., 2021; Garfield & Hagen, 2020; Garfield et al., 2019; Garfield et al., 2020; Henrich & Gil-White, 2001; Redhead et al., 2019). Thus, while human status hierarchies may function somewhat differently than those of nonhuman animals, they are pervasive—and as I detail below, consequential—features of human groups.

Evidence suggests that status was linked to fitness-relevant outcomes throughout our evolutionary past. In many nonhuman primate species, status—measured by patterns of grooming and deference—predicts higher fertility and mating success in males, as well as greater offspring survival for females (Cowlishaw & Dunbar, 1991; Majolo et al., 2012). In humans, men's status—as indexed by wealth and political influence—is positively associated with several reproductively relevant outcomes, including surviving offspring, fertility rates, and mating success across 33 non-industrial societies (von Rueden & Jaeggi, 2016). Men's status is also associated with other fitness-relevant benefits in small-scale societies, such as privileged access to resources (Patton, 2000), and more allies and cooperative partners (von Rueden et al., 2011; von Rueden et al., 2019). In studies of Tsimane forager-horticulturalists in the Bolivian Amazon, higher relative wealth was associated with fewer negative health outcomes (Jaeggi et al., 2020), and women with more political influence tended to have healthier children on average (Alami et al., 2020). Even in modern industrialized societies,[1] where natural fertility is atypical and birthrates are lower than in non-industrialized societies, social status is positively related to proxies of ancestral reproductive success, such as greater mating success, especially for men (de Bruyn et al., 2012; Fieder et al., 2011; Hopcroft, 2006, 2015, 2021). Taken together, this research demonstrating links between status and fitness across diverse cultures is suggestive that high status bolstered ancestral fitness.

In sum, status hierarchies were likely recurrent and pervasive features of the ancestral social landscape, and relative status within these hierarchies likely contributed to fitness throughout our evolutionary past. Given these recurrent selection pressures, we should expect that humans possess psychological adaptations to navigate hierarchies. Consideration of the range of adaptive problems posed by life in hierarchies throughout human evolution may elucidate some of these adaptations.

Adaptive Problems Posed by Life in Hierarchically Organized Social Groups

Because emotions evolved to solve adaptive challenges, it is necessary to detail the array of recurrent adaptive challenges posed by life in hierarchically organized social groups to fully map the constellation of emotions that are functionally intertwined with status hierarchies. In this section, I provide a rough task analysis of the challenges posed by hierarchical social groups that our ancestors would have had to solve to successfully navigate status hierarchies. We can then examine how the characteristics of different emotions might reveal signatures of functional design corresponding to the adaptive challenges of hierarchy navigation.

Defining the adaptive problems associated with hierarchy navigation necessarily involves abstraction and generalization. Just as the boundaries between many psychological entities are "fuzzy" (Del Giudice, Chapter 5 in this volume; Nesse, 1990), the adaptive challenges of hierarchy navigation are overlapping and cannot be neatly categorized into discrete units. Further, the specific challenges posed by hierarchies cannot be specified for every possible cultural context and every human group. But there are regularities in the types of challenges posed by hierarchies that could be targets for selection to shape functional mechanisms, such as emotions, that overcome them. I aim to detail partially distinct adaptive challenges at a level of abstraction applicable to most contexts in which humans have lived throughout evolutionary history. We should not expect that every adaptive challenge will be faced by every individual living in a hierarchy, but rather that they likely had to be overcome with enough regularity in the ancestral past such that functional mechanisms designed to solve them should be part of the human species-typical cognitive architecture. Additionally, not every adaptive challenge posed by hierarchies necessitates an evolved emotional response to address it: some may be adequately solved by other classes of adaptations, such as internal regulatory variables or perceptual mechanisms (Tooby et al., 2008). Finally, emotions—let alone their folk labels (cf. Fiske, 2020)—may not map onto adaptive challenges in a one-to-one manner.

Still, conducting a task analysis of the adaptive challenges posed by hierarchies can guide consolidation of existing evidence for the role of emotions in hierarchy navigation and generate new predictions about their design features. Below, I detail several classes of adaptive challenges posed by hierarchies: pursuing and attaining status, leveraging acquired status for fitness gains, maintaining one's acquired status, mitigating status loss when it occurs, allocating status to others, tracking others' status, interacting with higher-status individuals, and hierarchy restructuring or leveling.

Pursuing Status

One of the central adaptive problems of hierarchy navigation is pursuing status. This broad challenge encompasses many other, more concrete sub-challenges. These sub-challenges include identification and cultivation of status-enhancing characteristics, advertisement of these characteristics, avoidance or concealment of status-decreasing characteristics, and appropriate calibration of motivations for status pursuit.

To pursue status, individuals must identify—consciously or not—the myriad local status criteria to assess which tactics and strategies can be used to gain status within their local environment (Buss et al., 2020). Individuals must then determine which criteria, tactics, and strategies they can effectively implement in the pursuit of status (Kyl-Heku & Buss, 1996). This likely requires some degree of self-assessment and comparison to others on status-relevant criteria. Some status criteria are relatively unalterable characteristics (e.g., age, height, being the child of a high-status individual), but many others are less immutable and must be cultivated (e.g., hunting skills, being a reliable group member) or accentuated (e.g., attractiveness). For status criteria that involve social learning (e.g., culturally specific skills), individuals must identify skilled models to learn from or emulate (Henrich & Gil-White, 2001). Given that the combinations of status criteria that could be pursued are essentially infinite, individuals must determine how to allocate their limited time and energy in the service of maximizing the qualities they can leverage for status pursuit within the cultural milieu.

Although many acts, characteristics, and events that could enhance status will be readily apparent to others in the group (e.g., physical attractiveness), others may be less apparent (e.g., humor, bravery, pro-sociality). Individuals may need to advertise status-enhancing personal characteristics to receive commensurate status boosts. In contrast, any of the myriad acts, characteristics, or events that could decrease status may need to be concealed or compensated for to prevent status loss—or, if status loss has already occurred, individuals might need to mitigate further damages (e.g., through appeasement or bargaining; Sznycer, 2019). Moreover, individuals must identify and encode status gains or losses to track their relative position in the hierarchy (Durkee et al., 2019).

Another sub-problem of status pursuit is that individuals must appropriately calibrate *motivations* for status pursuit. These motivations need not be consciously represented as desiring status per se[2]—they could be represented as motivations to carry out behaviors and pursue goals that were reliably associated with status attainment in the ancestral past (Buss, 1997; Tooby et al., 2008). Because status pursuit is just one of many fundamental motives (Kenrick et al., 2010), status striving must be calibrated to balance the trade-offs that accompany effort spent pursuing status with the time and effort needed to address other important adaptive problems, such as maintaining shelter, finding food, acquiring mates, parenting, and mate retention. Although status attainment may further other fundamental motives (e.g., acquiring mates) and status pursuit may be furthered by successfully solving other adaptive problems (e.g., being good at finding food), the appropriate ratio of status-striving relative to other activities must be judiciously allocated, given finite time and energy budgets (Durkee et al., 2023). The ideal calibration may differ predictably between individuals as a function of individual difference variables (e.g., sex, age, physical attractiveness) and socio-ecologies (e.g., hierarchy steepness, mating system, food abundance), as well as across development as costs and benefits of pursuing different goals change.

Leveraging Status

In tandem with status pursuit and attainment, individuals living in hierarchically organized groups face the challenge of efficiently leveraging acquired status to harvest the associated benefits, such as increased access to resources or control over group decisions. This adaptive challenge may solve itself to the extent that one's status is derived from others' perceptions of value as a generator of positive externalities or as a skilled cultural model (Henrich & Gil-White, 2001; Henrich et al., 2015). In such cases, lower-status individuals might be motivated to bestow benefits on higher-status, skilled models or producers as an investment in greater future returns on valuable resources, to foster a relationship in which they can efficiently learn status-relevant skills, or to receive other incidental benefits. Still, each individual within the group could benefit by free-riding on positive externalities without providing respect, deference, or allowing higher-status individuals priority access to resources (Price & Van Vugt, 2014). Consequently, higher-status individuals may sometimes need to solve the challenge of incentivizing deference from others—possibly by threatening or actuating benefit withdrawal or cost infliction. To facilitate bargaining for the benefits associated with higher status, status gains may require upregulating internal estimates of the respect, deference, and entitlement, as well as recruitment of allies to further increase one's coalitional bargaining power.

Maintaining Status

In addition to pursuing and leveraging status, maintaining status is also a partially distinct adaptive challenge. At minimum, solving this adaptive challenge likely requires continuing to develop and display any skills or qualities necessary to continue to generate the benefits that are relevant to one's status attainment. The maintenance of status also likely requires the continued avoidance or concealment of acts, characteristics, and events that would diminish one's status (Sznycer, 2019). The challenge of maintaining status is complicated by the challenge of leveraging status, since withholding benefits, hoarding resources, being too controlling, or inflicting costs in too self-interested a manner may damage one's status in the long run (Gintis et al., 2015; Wrangham, 2021). Moreover, because others in the group are likely to be competitors for the same status niche, maintaining one's status requires identifying potential rivals and finding ways to outcompete them, when necessary (Hill & Buss, 2008). This adaptive challenge is likely more salient if one's status is derived from generating benefits for only a minority of group members, rather than the entire group—unless the group of coalitional allies one is generating benefits for is so formidable that they can stave off leveling attempts from the larger group (Durkee et al., 2021; Mead & Maner, 2012). In either case, maintaining status without generating commensurate benefits likely requires greater energy and time expenditures to deal with competitors and leveling coalitions.

Mitigating Status Loss

An inevitable challenge faced by individuals living in hierarchically organized groups is status loss. History is replete with high-status individuals suffering devastating falls from grace.

While the vast majority of people are not likely to experience such extreme status swings, the status of most individuals is in constant negotiation, resulting in frequent ups and downs, so some degree of at least temporary status loss over one's lifetime is likely.

Many factors can bring about status loss (Buss et al., 2020). Individuals can experience status loss when previously concealed status-damaging characteristics come to light, when they fail to generate benefits that their status depends on, when rivals outcompete them in status-relevant domains, when moving to a new group changes their relative value in status-relevant domains, when they are deposed by a leveling coalition for hoarding too many resources or inflicting too many costs, and when a mating relationship or friendship that provided status via the mate's or friend's status ends.

Status loss triggers a cascade of adaptive challenges, the scale and specifics of which will often depend on the particular reason for status loss and the amount of status loss. At a minimum, status loss is likely to entail a commensurate loss of influence and access to resources, which may need to be supplemented. Status damage may also lead to loss of coalitional allies, friends, mates, and even kin support (von Rueden et al., 2019). In the extreme, complete loss of respect can result in being exiled from one's community, which would likely be detrimental to survival and reproductive success in most contexts throughout human evolution (Buss, 1990). When status is lost, individuals must recalibrate internal estimates of entitlement downward in accordance with the degree of status loss to appropriately interact with others. Internal estimates of one's standing on socially relevant traits that partially depend on status—such as mate value—may need to be recalibrated as well. Alternatively, if individuals attempt to mitigate status loss by bargaining or making consolations to regain their relative standing, they must determine effective negotiation strategies (Kyl-Heku & Buss, 1996).

Allocating and Tracking Status
Another set of challenges associated with life in hierarchically organized groups is allocating status to others and tracking others' relative status. Status allocation is an adaptive challenge because the relative differences in respect, attention, and influence that emerge from status distribution will partially define one's own relative access to resources, as well as group outcomes (Buss et al., 2020; Henrich & Gil-White, 2001). Individuals must then allocate status sparingly, directing it toward individuals who would generate benefits with their greater relative influence, and withholding it from those who would fail to do so. As with status pursuit, status allocation subsumes the challenge of identifying personal characteristics that are valuable within the local ecology; however, in this case, individuals must apply (implicit or explicit) knowledge of these criteria to determine to whom to allocate status, and to track the status of others. Tracking others' status likely also depends on tracking indicators of the extent to which others in the group have allocated status to everyone else, using cues such as patterns of deference and emulation, coalitional networks, and apparent access to resources.

Knowing where others stand in the hierarchy relative to oneself—as well as how strong their status motivations are—is necessary to coordinate interactions with others and behavioral tactics in ways that are appropriate based on relative differences in hierarchical rank (Kyl-Heku & Buss, 1996) and to avoid the costs of overestimating one's own status (Anderson et al., 2006). What constitutes situationally appropriate behaviors, however, depends on a wealth of contextual information (Lukaszewski et al., 2020). Thus, in addition to tracking current status rankings and motivations, individuals may need to store and reference past rankings and reasons for changes in status, as well as make forecasts of the likely status trajectories of others in the group—such as younger individuals who may become competitors or potential allies.

Interacting with Higher-Status Individuals

As hinted above, appropriately interacting with others based on their relative status is another partially distinct adaptive challenge associated with life in hierarchically organized groups. Higher-status individuals, in consequence of their greater influence and respect within the group, will possess greater relative control over the flow of benefits and costs within the group (Cheng et al., 2013; Lukaszewski et al., 2016; Maner & Mead, 2010; von Rueden, 2014). It could therefore pay to interact with high-status individuals in ways that could lead to benefits being directed to the self—or to cooperative partners and kin—to improve one's inclusive fitness. Conversely, it could be detrimental to one's fitness if an interaction with a higher-status other made it more likely that benefits would be directed away from—or costs inflicted on—the self or those within one's sphere of inclusive fitness. It is therefore sometimes necessary to produce deference to higher-status individuals, even in conflicts of interest, to avoid cost infliction or benefit withdrawal and to maximize net fitness in the long term. Moreover, to the extent that higher-status individuals attained their status by acquiring learnable or practicable traits and skills, they could be a cultural model to learn from to enhance one's own status, but deference or ingratiation may be necessary to gain and maintain access to the model (Henrich & Gil-White, 2001). Coordinating thoughts, attention, and behaviors to take advantage of potential learning opportunities, curry favor with higher-status individuals, and avoid cost infliction is therefore an important adaptive challenge.

Hierarchy Restructuring and Leveling

Because status hierarchies partially define access to resources within a group, humans living in such groups also face the adaptive challenge of structuring the hierarchy in self-beneficial ways when possible—or at least restructuring the hierarchy when necessary, to avoid detrimental fitness outcomes (Cheng, 2020; Gintis et al., 2015; Lukaszewski et al., 2016). Specifically, if the ratio of costs inflicted to benefits generated flowing downward from higher-status individuals to lower-status individuals is tipped too far in the cost-infliction direction, it would no longer benefit individuals in the group to allow the higher-status individuals to influence group outcomes. This adaptive problem could be solved by lower-status individuals if they form a leveling coalition that has collectively greater formidability than the cost-inflicting higher-status individuals. To solve the challenge of restructuring the hierarchy, it is necessary to solve the sub-challenges posed by alliance formation and associated collective action problems (van Schaik et al., 2006; Wiessner, 2019). Moreover, because higher-status individuals may place barriers to restructuring or leveling in order to maintain their status (Case & Maner, 2014), individuals seeking to subvert or reform the hierarchy would have to overcome these barriers as well.

Emotions Associated with Adaptive Problems Posed by Hierarchies

Because of the fitness-consequences of status and the array of recurrent adaptive challenges posed by hierarchies, the human mind should be equipped with a collection of functional mechanisms, designed through selection, to aid in hierarchy navigation (Kyl-Heku & Buss, 1996; Tooby & Cosmides, 1990). In this section, I single out several emotions that appear to either directly support hierarchy navigation or, more simply, are likely to be activated by the adaptive challenges associated with hierarchies: pride, shame, envy, admiration, respect, contempt, anger, and fear. These are by no means the only emotions that can be expected to be related to hierarchy navigation, but they provide enough breadth to explore the functional interconnectedness of hierarchies and emotions for the purposes of this chapter.[3] Table 30.1 provides an overview of how each emotion may facilitate hierarchy navigation.

Table 30.1 Overview of the Ways in Which Focal Emotions May Aid in Solving Adaptive Challenges Posed by Hierarchy Navigation

	Pride	Shame	Envy	Admiration	Respect	Contempt	Anger	Fear
Pursuing status	Motivate and reward pursuit of status-enhancing skills and characteristics	Avoid and conceal status-decreasing events and characteristics	Identify competitors and motivate competition	Identify models and valued skills, motivate imitation and emulation	Identify status criteria	NA	NA	Prevent overly risky status pursuit
Leveraging status	Upregulate entitlement, signal status to others	NA	NA	NA	NA	Downregulate cooperation with low value others	Bargain for better treatment, more benefits	Prevent behaviors that could lead to leveling attempts
Maintaining status	Motivate maintenance and improvement of status criteria	Conceal and avoid status-decreasing characteristics	Facilitate continued competition	Facilitate continued emulation and imitation	Avoid cost-infliction from higher-status others	Avoid cooperation with low-value partners	Punish challengers, recalibrate devaluers	Prevent behaviors that could lead to leveling attempts
Mitigating status loss	NA	Coordinate avoidance, appeasement	Derogate or undermine rivals	NA	NA	NA	NA	Prevent behaviors that could lead to further costs
Tracking and allocating status	NA	NA	Recognize potential status differential	Recognize and allocate status to useful models	Recognize social value and facilitate status conferral	Recognize low social value traits or individuals	NA	NA
Interacting with higher-status others	NA	NA	Facilitate competition	Facilitate ingratiation, learning, and emulation	Produce deference	NA	NA	Recognize and prevent costs that could be imposed
Hierarchy restructuring and leveling	NA	NA	Motivation to tear down others	NA	NA	Recognize high-status others' low personal cooperative value	Motivate and coordinate aggressive bargaining	NA

Note: See main text for relevant references. NA = emotion not expected to be reliably activated by cues of the given adaptive challenge.

After examining the potential roles of each emotion in hierarchy navigation, I will also explore predictions about individual differences in each emotion as a function of relative status and vice versa, given their design features. To do so, it will be useful to distinguish predictions about *thresholds* and *frequencies* of emotion activation. I will use *thresholds* to refer to the minimal value of an eliciting-cue that can activate a given emotion. I will use *frequencies* (or average levels) to refer specifically to the extent to which an emotion is activated or experienced across situations. Although these parameters can be expected to covary, there is utility in distinguishing between them because they can produce different—sometimes conflicting—predictions about individual differences in emotional experience as a function of relative status within a hierarchy.

Pride
The features of pride appear well designed to aid in solving several problems of status pursuit. Across cultures, pride is activated in response to various personal characteristics in near perfect correspondence with the degree to which those personal characteristics are valued in ego's culture (Cohen et al., 2020; Sznycer, Al-Shawaf, et al., 2017; Sznycer & Lukaszewski, 2019; Sznycer, Xygalatas, Alami, et al., 2018), as well as the status impacts of those personal characteristics (Durkee et al., 2019). Thus, pride can aid in solving the problem of identifying and encoding status-enhancing acts, characteristics, and events. The activation of pride is often accompanied by a species-typical nonverbal display that is characterized by an expansive posture upward-tilted head, and audience-directed gaze (Tracy & Matsumoto, 2008; Tracy & Robins, 2007). This nonverbal display is recognized cross-culturally and is interpreted as a cue of higher status (Shariff & Tracy, 2009; Shariff et al., 2012; Tracy & Robins, 2008b; Tracy et al., 2013), suggesting that the pride display may be designed specifically to signal status increases to others. The pleasurable experience of pride—and the forecasting of this experience—may also serve to motivate the attainment or pursuit of status-enhancing characteristics. Finally, pride appears to make behaviors that would facilitate status pursuit and maintenance—such as demanding better treatment, spreading information about the pride-inducing event, investing further in pride-inducing skills—more likely (Sznycer & Cohen, 2021).

Given these design features, several predictions can be generated regarding the impact of relative differences in status on individual differences in pride experiences. Most clearly, high-status individuals can be expected to have higher frequencies or average levels of pride experiences than lower-status individuals. This more frequent pride may partially explain higher-status individuals' relatively stronger status motive (Anderson et al., 2020). Moreover, to the extent that elevated pride levels are accompanied by more frequent or conspicuous pride displays, higher status may be associated with increased signaling of hierarchical rank to reinforce status differentials. Conversely, pride thresholds may be lower at lower levels of the hierarchy to facilitate pursuing status and advertising status gains, to the extent that these behaviors are more crucial for lower-ranking individuals.

Shame
In many ways, the design features of shame the mirror image of those of pride—but they are functionally suited to solve different adaptive problems. The amount of shame people across cultures expect to feel in response to different personal characteristics being true of them increases in close proportion to the degree to which those personal characteristics decrease their social value and status in the eyes of others in their local communities (Cohen et al., 2020; Durkee et al., 2019; Sznycer & Lukaszewski, 2019; Sznycer et al., 2016; Sznycer, Xygalatas, Agey, et al., 2018). This suggests that shame may aid in hierarchy navigation by forecasting

negative consequences of personal characteristics to facilitate preemptive avoidance or concealment of those traits. Interestingly, shame is even activated by devaluation that is not due to any explicit wrongdoing, demonstrating that shame is principally concerned with peer valuations, rather than the valuation one may feel is deserved (Robertson et al., 2018). Shame experiences are often accompanied by a nonverbal postural display characterized by a downward gaze and slumped posture (Tracy & Matsumoto, 2008). Viewers of shame displays automatically interpret it as a cue to the displayer's low status (Shariff et al., 2012). Displaying shame also functions to elicit forgiveness and submission, as is interpreted by viewers as conveying remorse, withdrawal, and willingness to placate, which may help to mitigate further costs of status loss (Keltner 1995; Keltner & Harker, 1998; Keltner et al., 1997; Martens et al., 2012).

Because the features of shame are relevant for solving adaptive challenges at all levels of the hierarchy—namely those related to preventing and mitigating status loss—the expectations about how relative rank is related to shame are somewhat complicated. Lower-status individuals may be more likely to experience shame more frequently, because they are more likely to experience devaluation by others in the group. However, since avoiding or concealing status-decreasing events and characteristics is crucial for maintaining status as well, higher-status individuals may experience more preemptive, forecasted shame to facilitate status maintenance. Moreover, it is possible that individuals with lower thresholds for shame activation are better able to navigate status hierarchies and attain higher status, which would also suggest that higher-status individuals would (preemptively) experience shame more frequently by virtue of lower thresholds for shame activation, which facilitates forecasting the status impacts of behaviors or the concealment of status-decreasing characteristics. On the other hand, one of the benefits of higher status may be increased buffering from the costs of devaluation; if shame thresholds can change as a function of current status, then this buffering from devaluation may reduce shame sensitivity and make shame experiences less common at higher status levels. Likewise, if people with fewer devalued characteristics are simply more likely to gain status, then higher-status individuals may experience shame less frequently, regardless of their shame thresholds.

Envy
The characteristics of envy appear to facilitate comparison and direct competition with others in the service of increasing ego's relative status (Hill & Buss, 2006). Envy[4] is aroused in response to the perceived advantage of a competitor relative to the self (Miceli & Castelfranchi, 2007; Parrott & Smith, 1993; Smith & Kim, 2007). The experience of envy is associated with brain-activation patterns similar to those seen when experiencing physical pain (Takahashi et al., 2009), and with motivations to alleviate the painful envious feelings (Cohen-Charash & Larson, 2017). These motivations are accompanied by thoughts of inferiority, as well as hostile and spiteful intentions (Miceli & Castelfranchi, 2007; Smith & Kim, 2007), which do not necessarily translate into hostile, spiteful actions (Hill & Buss, 2008). The outputs of envy fall into strategies of competitor-derogation and self-promotion (Crusius et al., 2020). Unfortunately, most empirical work on the outputs of envy is focused on professional workplace contexts (e.g., Moran & Schweitzer, 2008; Schaubroeck & Lam, 2004), so it is unclear how variable and effective the specific outputs of envy are across contexts. The outputs of envy, like all emotions, should be sensitive to contextual cues relevant for determining the effectiveness of tactical outputs (Lukaszewski et al., 2020). There does not appear to be nonverbal displays reliably associated with envy (Witkower et al., 2020). The absence of an envy display may be a design feature of envy because displayed envy would be an indication of a perceived status differential, and that a leveling attempt may occur (Hill & Buss, 2008). Concealing

the presence of envy may facilitate success in closing the perceived status gap by not alerting the competitor and by concealing the perceived status differential from others who may not perceive it.

These design features lead to several predictions about the relationship between relative status and individual differences in envy. First, all else being equal, higher-status individuals can be predicted to experience less envy than lower-status individuals, given that lower-status individuals should have more higher-status targets to direct envy toward. If the salience or frequency of direct competition increases at higher rungs of the hierarchy, however, it may be that higher-status individuals feel envy more frequently or more strongly than lower-status individuals. Relatedly, the threshold for envy may change depending on relative status and the number of competitors with similar status levels, such that envy is triggered more easily if there are more potential competitors.

Admiration and Respect

Several challenges of hierarchy navigation may jointly or independently be solved by admiration and respect. Admiration and respect are elicited by perceptions of another's competence and warmth (Fiske, 2015; Li & Fischer, 2007; Wojciszke et al., 2009). Because competence and pro-sociality are both determinants of status (Durkee et al., 2020), the activation of admiration and respect can facilitate the recognition of status-enhancing characteristics, and upregulation of their status within ego's mind. Respect can also aid in solving the challenge of deferring to higher-status others in conflicts of interest, because respect entails a willingness to defer (Wojciszke et al., 2009). Although admiration may share many of the basic features of respect, admiration appears to also specifically involve ingratiation with competent, skilled others in a way that could facilitate learning of the status-relevant skill (Onu et al., 2016); this feature may aid in meeting the challenge of acquiring culturally valued competencies and characteristics. Thus, while the terms *admiration* and *respect* are often used interchangeably in the folk lexicon, they may describe multiple emotion programs that solve distinct challenges of hierarchy navigation. Additional empirical research is needed to further investigate these distinct psychological entities.

Admiration and respect experiences can also be predicted to vary in frequency and intensity as a function of relative status. Respect, for instance, may be activated more frequently in individuals lower in the hierarchy, to facilitate deference in return for any benefits generated by higher-status individuals. Higher-status individuals may less frequently feel respect toward lower-status individuals—aside from perhaps baseline recognition of others' intrinsic value. To the extent that admiration differs from respect in being geared specifically toward emulating and learning from skilled culture models, it can be expected to be felt more frequently by lower-status individuals toward higher-status individuals. Likewise, admiration experiences should be more common as one is pursuing status through the development of culturally relevant skills—becoming less common once high skill, and putatively higher status, has been attained. Further, frequencies of admiration should also depend more on individual differences in status motivations and be more narrowly targeted at higher-status individuals who possess skills or characteristics that are relevant to the niche in which the admirer is pursuing status, whereas respect should not necessarily depend on status motivations but rather on recognition of others' higher status or valuable qualities.

Contempt

The characteristics of contempt appear to facilitate hierarchy navigation via distancing from others of low relational value, exclusion of contemptuous individuals from social networks, and reinforcement of status differentials. Contemptuous feelings are elicited by incompetence (Hutcherson & Gross, 2011) and violations of social or moral obligations (Fischer & Giner-Sorolla, 2016; Rozin et al., 1999), which decrease status across cultures (Buss et al., 2020; Durkee et al., 2020). When people feel contempt, they tend to derogate and socially exclude the targeted individual, which contributes to the deterioration of any relationship between the involved parties (Fischer & Roseman, 2007). A nonverbal facial expression defined by the raising of one corner of the upper lip (i.e., the unilateral lip curl) often accompanies contemptuous feelings (Ekman & Friesen, 1986; Fischer & Giner-Sorolla, 2016; Matsumoto & Ekman, 2004). But the unilateral lip curl is often perceived as anger or disgust by viewers cross-culturally,[5] which casts some doubt on the specific communicative function of contempt expressions (for review, see Fischer & Giner-Sorolla, 2016; Matsumoto & Ekman, 2004).

Given the apparent functional characteristics of contempt, individual differences in manifest contempt can be expected to be defined by relative differences in hierarchical rank. Because contempt is targeted at individuals who are perceived to be low in social value (Gervais & Fessler, 2017), higher-status individuals can be predicted to experience contempt more frequently than lower-status individuals to the extent that they perceive low-status individuals to be low in cooperative value. Similarly, higher relative status may be associated with lower contempt thresholds in order to facilitate cold indifference to, or avoidance of, individuals who are lower status, to facilitate the reservation of time and energy budgets for cooperative endeavors with higher status. On the other hand, lower-status individuals could also be predicted to frequently experience contempt toward higher-status others in contexts where higher-status individuals are failing to generate the benefits that their status is derived from—or worse, using their greater relative control to directly inflict costs on lower-status individuals in a self-interested manner.

Anger

Although anger is unlikely to be designed specifically to facilitate hierarchy navigation, it can be expected to be elicited by many adaptive challenges posed by hierarchies. According to the recalibrational theory of anger (Sell et al. 2009), anger is designed to motivate bargaining for better treatment from conspecifics. In support of this theoretical account, anger is reliably activated by cues that ego is being undervalued (Sznycer & Lukaszewski, 2019). The intensity of anger in a given situation is sensitive to a variety of relevant contextual details, such as the intent and motivations of the transgressor (Sell et al., 2017), and the relative bargaining power between ego and the transgressor (Sell et al., 2009). The facial expression that often accompanies anger is recognized cross-culturally, communicates the angered individual's intent to bargain for better treatment, and may be designed to signal one's ability to effectively bargain using aggression (i.e., physical formidability; Sell et al., 2014).

An appreciation of the anger program's design features leads to the expectation that anger will be reliably activated by several aspects of hierarchy navigation—and may play a role in solving them. For instance, anger could be expected to play a role in extracting the benefits of status, such as preferential treatment and priority access to contested resources. If one's treatment by another individual is below what might be entitled by one's relative status, the outputs of anger can play a role in recalibrating the target's self-directed welfare trade-off ratio in the future—allowing higher-status individuals to maximize the benefits of status going forward. In contrast, recognition that another individual perceives themselves to be entitled to more favorable treatment or access to resources than is commensurate with their status, the activation of anger can serve to downwardly calibrate the target's perceptions of entitlement to more closely match ego's estimation of the individual's entitlement. These anger-based negotiations between individuals may function to partially define and regulate relative differences in status. On the more extreme end, the advertisement and recognition of collective anger among multiple members of a group is likely a crucial component of forming leveling coalitions.

Several interesting relationships between individual differences in anger and relative status can be predicted. For one, because any given higher-status individual will tend to have greater relative bargaining power than any given lower-status individual—by virtue of greater control over resources, access to resources, or coalitional allies—they can be expected to more effectively leverage anger to recalibrate perceived undervaluation (Sell et al., 2009). Thus, it could be predicted that, all else being equal, higher-status individuals will have lower thresholds for anger and will be less likely to inhibit their anger than lower-status individuals. To the extent that higher-status individuals are genuinely valued by group members, however, lower-status individuals may less frequently engage in actions that would anger higher-status individuals (e.g., challenging them for a greater share of resources) such that the observable association between relative status and anger frequency across situations is negative or null. The relationship between status and average anger levels or frequencies of anger experiences could also be negative if lower-status individuals are (implicitly or explicitly) aware of the greater anger-proneness of higher-status individuals—as well as the greater costs they could inflict—and thus avoid doing things that could anger them. To complicate matters further, the expression of anger may depend on status, such that higher-status individuals have greater freedom to express anger than lower-status individuals (van Kleefe & Lange, 2020), and relationship is likely to be somewhat dependent on cultural norms about expression (Park et al., 2013)—this discrepancy between anger experience and anger expression highlights the need to more closely examine anger thresholds in order to understand how status differences interact with the design features of anger.

Fear

The design features of fear may be involved in hierarchy navigation by guiding interactions to avoid cost-infliction from higher-status others. Fear is activated by many cues of ancestrally relevant threats to survival, ranging from snakes, spiders, and heights to social exclusion, foreboding strangers, and out-group members (Cosmides & Tooby, 2000; Öhman & Mineka, 2001, 2003). The activation of fear, in turn, promotes contextually sensitive behaviors designed to alleviate the harm potentiated by the survival threat, such as increased vigilance, avoidance, escape, and freezing behaviors (Lerner & Keltner, 2001; Maner et al., 2005). Fear in social situations is also related to conformity to avoid costs (Griskevicius et al., 2006). The species-typical fear expression is universally recognized (Boucher & Carlson, 1980; Tracy & Robins, 2008a). The fearful face appears to be functionally designed to enhance visual perception (Susskind et al., 2008), and may also function to alert others to impending danger (Reed & DeScioli, 2017; Whalen et al., 2001) and elicit social support (Marsh et al., 2005; Marsh & Ambady, 2007). To the extent that fear expressions are interpreted by others as signals of subordination, fear may also aid in solving the adaptive challenge of submitting to higher-status others and ceding in agnostic status contests (Steckler & Tracy, 2014; Witkower et al., 2020).

Relative differences in rank can be expected to define a great deal of variance in fear experiences within groups. For instance, because higher-status individuals can withdraw benefits and inflict costs on lower-status individuals with a greater degree of impunity, lower-status individuals can be predicted to experience more fear of higher-status individuals than vice versa. This could be driven by lower fear thresholds in lower-status individuals or by more frequently experiencing threatened cost infliction. In most cases, however, fear in hierarchies may not look like the paralyzing fear associated with immediate survival threats. Instead, fear toward higher-status others may tend to manifest as perceptions of the higher-status other as intimidating, a hesitancy to approach higher-status others without good reason, and heightened caution when interacting with higher-status others—especially in direct conflicts of interest. Contrasting with these predictions, higher-status individuals can be expected to experience fear that is caused by same- and lower-status individuals as well. For example, higher-status individuals may experience (preemptive) fear when considering the probability of a leveling coalition, or when spotting envy in competitors, in order to avoid the cost infliction that may be directed their way.

Hierarchy Navigation, Emotions, and Broad Individual Differences

Thus far, I have outlined an array of adaptive challenges that are posed by hierarchies and the network of emotions that may be designed to overcome them—or more simply, be reliably activated by them. It is clear that hierarchies and the adaptive challenges they pose can be expected to define much of individuals' emotional experience and content in everyday life. Here, I will briefly consider how further study of the interplay between hierarchy navigation and emotions may also inform our understanding of broad individual differences, such as personality traits.

Thoughts, feelings, and behaviors are the basic elements of personality (Mischel & Shoda, 1995). Thus, if we want to understand and explain the psychological underpinnings of personality traits and their development over time, it would be helpful to understand the design of emotion programs and how their input-output structure can produce reliably varying individual differences in thoughts, feelings, and behavior (Lukaszewski, 2021; Lukaszewski et al., 2020). Given that hierarchy navigation and relative differences in status can be expected to explain much of the manifest variation in emotional expression, both inter-individually and intra-individually across time, the patterns of variation captured by broad personality taxonomies—such as the Big Five (Digman, 1990; McCrae & Costa, 1987) and the HEXACO (Lee & Ashton, 2004)—can be expected to be partially defined by the outputs of emotions that are activated by the adaptive challenges of hierarchy navigation.

Understanding whether and how individual differences in emotional experiences arise from hierarchy navigation and relative differences in status may therefore be useful in explaining personality variation. For instance, the personality trait Agreeableness appears to be capturing outputs of the anger program such that people more prone to anger are perceived as less Agreeable (Lukaszewski et al., 2020). Thus, understanding how relative status may alter anger thresholds and frequency of anger experiences can help to explain manifest differences in Agreeableness between individuals, as well as within individuals as they change in status. Similarly, the inter-individual variation in shame, pride, and envy thresholds and frequencies—which can arise from many factors, such as genetic mutations that add noise to emotion systems, varying (mis)perceptions of the status impacts of behaviors, different calibrations of status-striving motivations, and existing relative status differences—may help to explain variation along other broad, emergent personality dimensions, such as Honesty-Humility, Extraversion, and Conscientiousness. Although emotions guide hierarchy navigation, manifest differences in personality also influence the status that individuals attain (Anderson et al., 2001; Cheng et al., 2010; Grosz et al., 2020), so there likely exist feedback loops between hierarchical rank, emotion parameters, and personality. At an even broader level, the variety of status niches—and the unique combinations of traits that are most status-relevant within them—may partially define the patterns of trait covariation at the population level and manifest differences in personality structure across populations (see Durkee et al., 2022; Gurven et al., 2013; Lukaszewski et al., 2017; Smaldino et al., 2019). Finally, further exploration of how hierarchical structure modulates emotions can also facilitate the explanation of cross-cultural differences in emotional qualia and folk-affective concepts (Gervais & Fessler, 2017).

Conclusion

This chapter has explored the inextricable links between emotions and status hierarchies. The ubiquity of status hierarchies and fitness-relevance of status suggest that humans should possess psychological adaptations—such as emotions—for navigating hierarchies. To identify and understand these emotional adaptations, it will be helpful to fully map the numerous and specific adaptive challenges posed by life in hierarchically organized social groups and detail the subtasks required to overcome them. This endeavor has the potential not only to improve our understanding of emotions, but also to reveal how broad patterns of individual and cultural variation may arise from species-typical adaptations for navigating the adaptive challenges posed by status hierarchies.

Acknowledgments

I thank David Buss, Courtney Crosby, Anna Sedlacek, Rebecka Hahnel-Peeters, Kendall Baker, and members of the Center for the Study of Human Nature (CSHN) for constructive feedback.

Notes

1. But note that because the mechanisms that comprise our mind were designed by selection pressures operating over deep time throughout our evolutionary history, status-fitness links need not be present in the modern environment for these mechanisms to be activated (Tooby & Cosmides, 1990)—only ancestrally relevant cues to challenges associated with hierarchy navigation need be present.
2. While evidence suggests that desiring status and striving for status are fundamental human motives which are consciously represented to some extent (Anderson et al., 2015; Kenrick et al., 2010; Ko et al., 2020), many more motives that are not represented as status motives may ultimately serve status pursuit.
3. For alternative perspectives and additional discussion pertaining to the hierarchy-relevance of these and other emotions (e.g., social anxiety, sadness, disgust), see: Buss, 1990; Gilbert, 2001; Steckler & Tracy, 2014; van Kleefe & Lange, 2020; Witkower et al., 2020.
4. I note that some theories of envy distinguish *benign* and *malicious* envy. But the degree to which these distinctions represent different manifestations of a singular envy program or distinct emotional programs selected for by natural selection to solve different adaptive problems remains unclear. For a thorough review of differences unitary versus dual models of envy, see Crusius et al., 2020.
5. These inconsistencies in how contempt manifests may suggest that the psychological phenomena captured by "contempt" and its synonymous folk labels (e.g., scorn, disdain, disregard) could be more accurately characterized as a sentiment (i.e., a network of emotions connected by an attitude; Gervais & Fessler, 2017). More research is needed to pinpoint what type (or types) of psychological entities are captured by lexical labels of contempt and detail their design features.

References

Alami, S., Von Rueden, C., Seabright, E., Kraft, T. S., Blackwell, A. D., Stieglitz, J., Kaplan, H., Gurven, M. (2020). Mother's social status is associated with child health in a horticulturalist population. *Proceedings of the Royal Society B: Biological Sciences, 287*(1922), 1–9.

Al-Shawaf, L., Conroy-Beam, D., Asao, K., & Buss, D. M. (2016). Human emotions: An evolutionary psychological perspective. *Emotion Review, 8*(2), 173–186.

Anderson, C., Hildreth, J. A. D., & Howland, L. (2015). Is the desire for status a fundamental human motive? A review of the empirical literature. *Psychological Bulletin, 141*(3), 574.

Anderson, C., Hildreth, J. A. D., & Sharps, D. L. (2020). The possession of high status strengthens the status motive. *Personality and Social Psychology Bulletin, 46*(12), 1712–1723.

Anderson, C., John, O. P., Keltner, D., & Kring, A. M. (2001). Who attains social status? Effects of personality and physical attractiveness in social groups. *Journal of Personality and Social Psychology, 81*(1), 116.

Anderson, C., Srivastava, S., Beer, J. S., Spataro, S. E., & Chatman, J. A. (2006). Knowing your place: Self-perceptions of status in face-to-face groups. *Journal of Personality and Social Psychology, 91*(6), 1094.

Boehm, C. (1999). *Hierarchy in the forest: The evolution of egalitarian behavior.* Harvard University Press.

Boehm, C. (2012). Ancestral hierarchy and conflict. *Science, 336*(6083), 844–847.

Boucher, J. D., & Carlson, G. E. (1980). Recognition of facial expression in three cultures. *Journal of Cross-Cultural Psychology, 11*(3), 263–280.

Brown, D. E. (1991). *Human universals.* McGraw-Hill.

Buss, D. M. (1990). The evolution of anxiety and social exclusion. *Journal of Social and Clinical Psychology, 9*(2), 196–201.

Buss, D. M. (1997). Human social motivation in evolutionary perspective: Grounding terror management theory. *Psychological Inquiry, 8*(1), 22–26.

Buss, D. M., Durkee, P. K., Shackelford, T. K., Bowdle, B. F., Schmitt, D. P., Brase, G. L., Choe J. C., & Trofimova, I. (2020). Human status criteria: Sex differences and similarities across 14 nations. *Journal of Personality and Social Psychology, 119*(5), 979–998.

Case, C. R., & Maner, J. K. (2014). Divide and conquer: When and why leaders undermine the cohesive fabric of their group. *Journal of Personality and Social Psychology, 107*(6), 1033.

Chapais, B. (2015). Competence and the evolutionary origins of status and power in humans. *Human Nature, 26*(2), 161–183.

Chase, I. D. (1974). Models of hierarchy formation in animal societies. *Behavioral Science, 19*(6), 374–382.

Cheng, J. T. (2020). Dominance, prestige, and the role of leveling in human social hierarchy and equality. *Current Opinion in Psychology, 33*, 238–244.

Cheng, J. T., Tracy, J. L., Foulsham, T., Kingstone, A., & Henrich, J. (2013). Two ways to the top: evidence that dominance and prestige are distinct yet viable avenues to social rank and influence. *Journal of Personality and Social Psychology, 104*(1), 103.

Cheng, J. T., Tracy, J. L., & Henrich, J. (2010). Pride, personality, and the evolutionary foundations of human social status. *Evolution and Human Behavior, 31*(5), 334–347.

Cohen, A. S., Chun, R., & Sznycer, D. (2020). Do pride and shame track the evaluative psychology of audiences? Preregistered replications of Sznycer et al. (2016, 2017). *Royal Society Open Science, 7*(5), 1–12.

Cohen-Charash, Y., & Larson, E. C. (2017). What is the nature of envy? In R. H. Smith, U. Merlone, & M. K. Duffy (Eds.), *Envy at work and in organizations* (pp. 1–37). Oxford University Press.

Cosmides, L., & Tooby, J. (2000). Evolutionary psychology and the emotions. In M. Lewis & J. M. Haviland-Jones (Eds.), *Handbook of emotions* (2nd ed., pp. 91–115). Guilford.

Cowlishaw, G., & Dunbar, R. I. (1991). Dominance rank and mating success in male primates. *Animal Behaviour, 41*(6), 1045–1056.

Crusius, J., Gonzalez, M. F., Lange, J., & Cohen-Charash, Y. (2020). Envy: An adversarial review and comparison of two competing views. *Emotion Review, 12*(1), 3–21.

de Bruyn, E. H., Cillessen, A. H., & Weisfeld, G. E. (2012). Dominance-popularity status, behavior, and the emergence of sexual activity in young adolescents. *Evolutionary Psychology, 10*(2), 1–24.

de Waal, F. (1982). *Chimpanzee politics: Sex and power among apes.* Jonathan Cape.

Digman, J. M. (1990). Personality structure: Emergence of the five-factor model. *Annual Review of Psychology, 41*(1), 417–440.

Durkee, P. K., Goetz, A. T., & Lukaszewski, A. W. (2018). Formidability assessment mechanisms: Examining their speed and automaticity. *Evolution and Human Behavior, 39*(2), 170–178.

Durkee, P. K., Lukaszewski, A. W., & Buss, D. M. (2019). Pride and shame: Key components of a culturally universal status management system. *Evolution and Human Behavior, 40*(5), 470–478.

Durkee, P. K., Lukaszewski, A. W., & Buss, D. M. (2020). Psychological foundations of human status allocation. *Proceedings of the National Academy of Sciences, 117*(35), 21235–21241.

Durkee, P., Lukaszewski, A., & Buss, D. M. (2021, April 20). Status foundations: Further consideration of the role of "dominance" and the relative importance of cost infliction and benefit generation. *PsyArXiv*, 1–21. https://doi.org/10.31234/osf.io/4gvt5

Durkee, P. K., Lukaszewski, A. W., & Buss, D. M. (2023). Status-impact assessment: Is accuracy linked with status motivations? *Evolutionary Human Sciences, 5*, e17.

Durkee, P., Lukaszewski, A., von Rueden, C., Gurven, M., Buss, D. M., & Tucker-Drob, E. M. (2022). Niche diversity predicts personality structure across 115 nations. *Psychological Science, 33*(2), 285–298.

Ekman, P., & Friesen, W. V. (1986). A new pan-cultural facial expression of emotion. *Motivation and Emotion, 10*(2), 159–168.

Fieder, M., Huber, S., & Bookstein, F. L. (2011). Socioeconomic status, marital status and childlessness in men and women: an analysis of census data from six countries. *Journal of Biosocial Science, 43*(5), 619.

Fischer, A., & Giner-Sorolla, R. (2016). Contempt: Derogating others while keeping calm. *Emotion Review, 8*(4), 346–357.

Fischer, A. H., & Roseman, I. J. (2007). Beat them or ban them: The characteristics and social functions of anger and contempt. *Journal of Personality and Social Psychology, 93*(1), 103.

Fiske, A. P. (2020). The lexical fallacy in emotion research: Mistaking vernacular words for psychological entities. *Psychological Review, 127*(1), 95.

Fiske, S. T. (2015). Intergroup biases: A focus on stereotype content. *Current Opinion in Behavioral Sciences, 3*, 45–50.

Franz, M., McLean, E., Tung, J., Altmann, J., & Alberts, S. C. (2015). Self-organizing dominance hierarchies in a wild primate population. *Proceedings of the Royal Society B: Biological Sciences, 282*(1814), 1–9.

Garfield, Z. H., & Hagen, E. H. (2020). Investigating evolutionary models of leadership among recently settled Ethiopian hunter-gatherers. *The Leadership Quarterly, 31*(1), 1–18.

Garfield, Z. H., Hubbard, R. L., & Hagen, E. H. (2019). Evolutionary models of leadership. *Human Nature, 30*(1), 23–58.

Garfield, Z. H., Syme, K. L., & Hagen, E. H. (2020). Universal and variable leadership dimensions across human societies. *Evolution and Human Behavior, 41*(5), 397–414.

Gervais, M. M., & Fessler, D. M. (2017). On the deep structure of social affect: Attitudes, emotions, sentiments, and the case of "contempt." *Behavioral and Brain Sciences, 40*, 1–63.

Gilbert, P. (2001). Evolution and social anxiety: The role of attraction, social competition, and social hierarchies. *Psychiatric Clinics, 24*(4), 723–751.

Gintis, H., van Schaik, C., & Boehm, C. (2015). Zoon politikon: The evolutionary origins of human political systems. *Current Anthropology, 56*(3), 340–341.

Griskevicius, V., Goldstein, N. J., Mortensen, C. R., Cialdini, R. B., & Kenrick, D. T. (2006). Going along versus going alone: When fundamental motives facilitate strategic (non) conformity. *Journal of Personality and Social Psychology, 91*(2), 281.

Grosz, M. P., Leckelt, M., & Back, M. D. (2020). Personality predictors of social status attainment. *Current Opinion in Psychology, 33*, 52–56.

Gurven, M., Von Rueden, C., Massenkoff, M., Kaplan, H., & Lero Vie, M. (2013). How universal is the Big Five? Testing the five-factor model of personality variation among forager-farmers in the Bolivian Amazon. *Journal of Personality and Social Psychology, 104*(2), 354.

Henrich, J., Chudek, M., & Boyd, R. (2015). The Big Man Mechanism: How prestige fosters cooperation and creates prosocial leaders. *Philosophical Transactions of the Royal Society B: Biological Sciences, 370*(1683), 1–13.

Henrich, J., & Gil-White, F. J. (2001). The evolution of prestige: Freely conferred deference as a mechanism for enhancing the benefits of cultural transmission. *Evolution and Human Behavior, 22*(3), 165–196.

Hill, S. E., & Buss, D. M. (2006). Envy and positional bias in the evolutionary psychology of management. *Managerial and Decision Economics, 27*(2–3), 131–143.

Hill, S. E., & Buss, D.M. (2008). The evolutionary psychology of envy. In R. Smith (Ed.), *The psychology of envy* (pp. 60–70). Guilford Press.

Hopcroft, R. L. (2006). Sex, status, and reproductive success in the contemporary United States. *Evolution and Human Behavior, 27*(2), 104–120.

Hopcroft, R. L. (2015). Sex differences in the relationship between status and number of offspring in the contemporary US. *Evolution and Human Behavior, 36*(2), 146–151.

Hopcroft, R. L. (2021). High income men have high value as long-term mates in the US: Personal income and the probability of marriage, divorce, and childbearing in the US. *Evolution and Human Behavior, 42*(5), 409–417.

Hutcherson, C. A., & Gross, J. J. (2011). The moral emotions: A social-functionalist account of anger, disgust, and contempt. *Journal of Personality and Social Psychology, 100*(4), 719.

Issa, F. A., Adamson, D. J., & Edwards, D. H. (1999). Dominance hierarchy formation in juvenile crayfish *Procambarus clarkii*. *Journal of Experimental Biology, 202*(24), 3497–3506.

Jaeggi, A. V., Blackwell, A. D., von Rueden, C., Trumble, B., Stieglitz, J., Garcia, A., Kraft, T. S., Kaplan, H., Gurven, M. (2020). Relative wealth and inequality associate with health in a small-scale subsistence society. *medRxiv*, 1–48.

Keltner, D. (1995). Signs of appeasement: Evidence for the distinct displays of embarrassment, amusement, and shame. *Journal of Personality and Social Psychology, 68*(3), 441.

Keltner, D., & Harker, L. (1998). The forms and functions of the non-verbal signal of shame. In P. Gilbert & B. Andrews (Eds.), *Shame: Interpersonal behavior, psychopathology, and culture* (pp. 78–98). Oxford University Press.

Keltner, D., Young, R. C., & Buswell, B. N. (1997). Appeasement in human emotion, social practice, and personality. *Aggressive Behavior, 23*(5), 359–374.

Kenrick, D. T., Neuberg, S. L., Griskevicius, V., Becker, D. V., & Schaller, M. (2010). Goal-driven cognition and functional behavior: The fundamental-motives framework. *Current Directions in Psychological Science, 19*(1), 63–67.

Ko, A., Pick, C. M., Kwon, J. Y., Barlev, M., Krems, J. A., Varnum, M. E., Neel, R., Peysha, M., Watcharaporn, B., Brandstatter, E., Crispim, A. C., Cruz, J. E., David, D., David, O. A., De Felipe, R. P., Fetvadjiev, V. H., Fischer, R., Galdi, S., Galindo, O., . . . Kenrick, D. T. (2020). Family matters: Rethinking the psychology of human social motivation. *Perspectives on Psychological Science, 15*(1), 173–201.

Kyl-Heku, L. M., & Buss, D. M. (1996). Tactics as units of analysis in personality psychology: An illustration using tactics of hierarchy negotiation. *Personality and Individual Differences, 21*(4), 497–517.

Lee, K., & Ashton, M. C. (2004). Psychometric properties of the HEXACO personality inventory. *Multivariate Behavioral Research, 39*(2), 329–358.

Lerner, J. S., & Keltner, D. (2001). Fear, anger, and risk. *Journal of Personality and Social Psychology, 81*(1), 146.

Li, J., & Fischer, K. W. (2007). Respect as a positive self-conscious emotion in European Americans and Chinese. In J. L. Tracy, R. W. Robins & J. P. Tangney (Eds.), *The self-conscious emotions: Theory and research* (pp. 224–242). Guilford Press.

Lukaszewski, A. W. (2021). Evolutionary perspectives on the mechanistic underpinnings of personality. In J. F. Rauthmann (Ed.), *The handbook of personality dynamics and processes* (pp. 523–550). Academic Press.

Lukaszewski, A. W., Gurven, M., von Rueden, C. R., & Schmitt, D. P. (2017). What explains personality covariation? A test of the socioecological complexity hypothesis. *Social Psychological and Personality Science, 8*(8), 943–952.

Lukaszewski, A. W., Lewis, D. M., Durkee, P. K., Sell, A. N., Sznycer, D., & Buss, D. M. (2020). An adaptationist framework for personality science. *European Journal of Personality, 34*(6), 1151–1174.

Lukaszewski, A. W., Simmons, Z. L., Anderson, C., & Roney, J. R. (2016). The role of physical formidability in human social status allocation. *Journal of Personality and Social Psychology, 110*(3), 385.

Majolo, B., Lehmann, J., de Bortoli Vizioli, A., & Schino, G. (2012). Fitness-related benefits of dominance in primates. *American Journal of Physical Anthropology, 147*(4), 652–660.

Maner, J. K., Kenrick, D. T., Becker, D. V., Robertson, T. E., Hofer, B., Neuberg, S. L., Delton, A., Butner, J., & Schaller, M. (2005). Functional projection: How fundamental social motives can bias interpersonal perception. *Journal of Personality and Social Psychology, 88*(1), 63.

Maner, J. K., & Mead, N. L. (2010). The essential tension between leadership and power: When leaders sacrifice group goals for the sake of self-interest. *Journal of Personality and Social Psychology, 99*(3), 482.

Marsh, A. A., & Ambady, N. (2007). The influence of the fear facial expression on prosocial responding. *Cognition and Emotion, 21*(2), 225–247.

Marsh, A. A., Ambady, N., & Kleck, R. E. (2005). The effects of fear and anger facial expressions on approach-and avoidance-related behaviors. *Emotion, 5*(1), 119.

Martens, J. P., Tracy, J. L., & Shariff, A. F. (2012). Status signals: Adaptive benefits of displaying and observing the nonverbal expressions of pride and shame. *Cognition and Emotion, 26*(3), 390–406.

Matsumoto, D., & Ekman, P. (2004). The relationship among expressions, labels, and descriptions of contempt. *Journal of Personality and Social Psychology, 87*(4), 529.

McCrae, R. R., & Costa, P. T. (1987). Validation of the five-factor model of personality across instruments and observers. *Journal of Personality and Social Psychology, 52*(1), 81.

Mead, N. L., & Maner, J. K. (2012). On keeping your enemies close: Powerful leaders seek proximity to ingroup power threats. *Journal of Personality and Social Psychology, 102*(3), 576.

Meese, G. B., & Ewbank, R. (1973). The establishment and nature of the dominance hierarchy in the domesticated pig. *Animal Behaviour, 21*(2), 326–334.

Miceli, M., & Castelfranchi, C. (2007). The envious mind. *Cognition and Emotion, 21*(3), 449–479.

Mischel, W., & Shoda, Y. (1995). A cognitive-affective system theory of personality: Reconceptualizing situations, dispositions, dynamics, and invariance in personality structure. *Psychological Review, 102*(2), 246.

Moran, S., & Schweitzer, M. E. (2008). When better is worse: Envy and the use of deception. *Negotiation and Conflict Management Research, 1*(1), 3–29.

Nesse, R. M. (1990). Evolutionary explanations of emotions. *Human Nature, 1*(3), 261–289.

Öhman, A., & Mineka, S. (2001). Fears, phobias, and preparedness: Toward an evolved module of fear and fear learning. *Psychological Review, 108*(3), 483.

Öhman, A., & Mineka, S. (2003). The malicious serpent: Snakes as a prototypical stimulus for an evolved module of fear. *Current Directions in Psychological Science, 12*(1), 5–9.

Onu, D., Kessler, T., & Smith, J. R. (2016). Admiration: A conceptual review. *Emotion Review, 8*(3), 218–230.

Park, J., Kitayama, S., Markus, H. R., Coe, C. L., Miyamoto, Y., Karasawa, M., Love, G., Kawakami, N., Boylan, J. M., & Ryff, C. D. (2013). Social status and anger expression: The cultural moderation hypothesis. *Emotion, 13*(6), 1122.

Parrott, W. G., & Smith, R. H. (1993). Distinguishing the experiences of envy and jealousy. *Journal of Personality and Social Psychology, 64*(6), 906.

Patton, J. (2000). Reciprocal altruism and warfare. In L. Cronk, W. Irons, & N. Chagnon (Eds.), *Adaptation and human behavior: An anthropological perspective* (pp. 417–436). Aldine de Gruyter.

Price, M. E., & Van Vugt, M. (2014). The evolution of leader–follower reciprocity: The theory of service-for-prestige. *Frontiers in Human Neuroscience, 8*, 363.

Redhead, D. J., Cheng, J. T., Driver, C., Foulsham, T., & O'Gorman, R. (2019). On the dynamics of social hierarchy: A longitudinal investigation of the rise and fall of prestige, dominance, and social rank in naturalistic task groups. *Evolution and Human Behavior, 40*(2), 222–234.

Reed, L. I., & DeScioli, P. (2017). Watch out! How a fearful face adds credibility to warnings of danger. *Evolution and Human Behavior, 38*(4), 490–495.

Robertson, T. E., Sznycer, D., Delton, A. W., Tooby, J., & Cosmides, L. (2018). The true trigger of shame: Social devaluation is sufficient, wrongdoing is unnecessary. *Evolution and Human Behavior, 39*(5), 566–573.

Rozin, P., Lowery, L., Imada, S., & Haidt, J. (1999). The CAD triad hypothesis: A mapping between three moral emotions (contempt, anger, disgust) and three moral codes (community, autonomy, divinity). *Journal of Personality and Social Psychology, 76*(4), 574.

Schaubroeck, J., & Lam, S. S. (2004). Comparing lots before and after: Promotion rejectees' invidious reactions to promotees. *Organizational Behavior and Human Decision Processes, 94*(1), 33–47.

Sell, A., Cosmides, L., & Tooby, J. (2014). The human anger face evolved to enhance cues of strength. *Evolution and Human Behavior, 35*(5), 425–429.

Sell, A., Cosmides, L., Tooby, J., Sznycer, D., Von Rueden, C., & Gurven, M. (2009). Human adaptations for the visual assessment of strength and fighting ability from the body and face. *Proceedings of the Royal Society B: Biological Sciences, 276*(1656), 575–584.

Sell, A., Sznycer, D., Al-Shawaf, L., Lim, J., Krauss, A., Feldman, A., Rascanu, R., Sugiyama, L., Cosmides, L., Tooby, J. (2017). The grammar of anger: Mapping the computational architecture of a recalibrational emotion. *Cognition, 168*, 110–128.

Shariff, A. F., & Tracy, J. L. (2009). Knowing who's boss: Implicit perceptions of status from the nonverbal expression of pride. *Emotion, 9*(5), 631.

Shariff, A. F., Tracy, J. L., & Markusoff, J. L. (2012). (Implicitly) judging a book by its cover: The power of pride and shame expressions in shaping judgments of social status. *Personality and Social Psychology Bulletin, 38*(9), 1178–1193.

Smaldino, P. E., Lukaszewski, A., von Rueden, C., & Gurven, M. (2019). Niche diversity can explain cross-cultural differences in personality structure. *Nature Human Behaviour, 3*(12), 1276–1283.

Smith, R. H., & Kim, S. H. (2007). Comprehending envy. *Psychological Bulletin, 133*(1), 46.

Steckler, C., & Tracy, J. L. (2014). The emotional underpinnings of social status. In J. T. Cheng, J. L. Tracy, & C. Anderson (Eds.), *The psychology of social status* (pp. 201–224). Springer.

Susskind, J. M., Lee, D. H., Cusi, A., Feiman, R., Grabski, W., & Anderson, A. K. (2008). Expressing fear enhances sensory acquisition. *Nature Neuroscience, 11*(7), 843.

Sznycer, D. (2019). Forms and functions of the self-conscious emotions. *Trends in Cognitive Sciences, 23*(2), 143–157.

Sznycer, D., Al-Shawaf, L., Bereby-Meyer, Y., Curry, O. S., De Smet, D., Ermer, E., Kim, S., Kim, S., Li, N., Lopez, M. F. S., McClung, J., Jiaqing, O., Ohtsubo, Y., Quillien, T., Schuab, M., Sell, A., van Leeuwen, F., Cosmides, L., & Tooby, J. (2017). Cross-cultural regularities in the cognitive architecture of pride. *Proceedings of the National Academy of Sciences, 114*(8), 1874–1879.

Sznycer, D., & Cohen, A. S. (2021). How pride works. *Evolutionary Human Sciences, 3*, 1–6.

Sznycer, D., Cosmides, L., & Tooby, J. (2017). Adaptationism carves emotions at their functional joints. *Psychological Inquiry, 28*(1), 56–62.

Sznycer, D., & Lukaszewski, A. W. (2019). The emotion–valuation constellation: Multiple emotions are governed by a common grammar of social valuation. *Evolution and Human Behavior, 40*(4), 395–404.

Sznycer, D., Tooby, J., Cosmides, L., Porat, R., Shalvi, S., & Halperin, E. (2016). Shame closely tracks the threat of devaluation by others, even across cultures. *Proceedings of the National Academy of Sciences, 113*(10), 2625–2630.

Sznycer, D., Xygalatas, D., Agey, E., Alami, S., An, X. F., Ananyeva, K. I., Atkinson, Q., Broitman, B., Conte, T., Flores, C., Fukishima, S., Hitokoto, H., Kharitinov, A., Onyishi, C., Romero, P., Schrok, J., Sugiyama, L., . . . Tooby, J. (2018). Cross-cultural invariances in the architecture of shame. *Proceedings of the National Academy of Sciences, 115*(39), 9702–9707.

Sznycer, D., Xygalatas, D., Alami, S., An, X. F., Ananyeva, K. I., Fukushima, S., Hitokoto, H., Kharitinov, A., Koster, J., Onyishi, C., Onyishi, I., Romero, P., Zhuang, J., Cosmides, L., & Tooby, J. (2018). Invariances in the architecture of pride across small-scale societies. *Proceedings of the National Academy of Sciences, 115*(33), 8322–8327.

Takahashi, H., Kato, M., Matsuura, M., Mobbs, D., Suhara, T., & Okubo, Y. (2009). When your gain is my pain and your pain is my gain: Neural correlates of envy and schadenfreude. *Science, 323*(5916), 937–939.

Tooby, J., & Cosmides, L. (1990). The past explains the present: Emotional adaptations and the structure of ancestral environments. *Ethology and Sociobiology, 11*(4–5), 375–424.

Tooby, J., Cosmides, L., Sell, A., Lieberman, D. & Sznycer, D. (2008) Internal regulatory variables and the design of human motivation: A computational and evolutionary approach. In A. J. Elliot (Ed.), *Handbook of approach and avoidance motivation* (pp. 251–271). Lawrence Erlbaum Associates.

Toscano, H., Schubert, T. W., Dotsch, R., Falvello, V., & Todorov, A. (2016). Physical strength as a cue to dominance: A data-driven approach. *Personality and Social Psychology Bulletin, 42*(12), 1603–1616.

Tracy, J. L., & Matsumoto, D. (2008). The spontaneous expression of pride and shame: Evidence for biologically innate nonverbal displays. *Proceedings of the National Academy of Sciences, 105*(33), 11655–11660.

Tracy, J. L., & Robins, R. W. (2007). The prototypical pride expression: Development of a nonverbal behavior coding system. *Emotion, 7*(4), 789.

Tracy, J. L., & Robins, R. W. (2008a). The automaticity of emotion recognition. *Emotion, 8*(1), 81.

Tracy, J. L., & Robins, R. W. (2008b). The nonverbal expression of pride: Evidence for cross-cultural recognition. *Journal of Personality and Social Psychology, 94*(3), 516.

Tracy, J. L., Shariff, A. F., Zhao, W., & Henrich, J. (2013). Cross-cultural evidence that the nonverbal expression of pride is an automatic status signal. *Journal of Experimental Psychology: General, 142*(1), 163.

van Kleef, G. A., & Lange, J. (2020). How hierarchy shapes our emotional lives: Effects of power and status on emotional experience, expression, and responsiveness. *Current Opinion in Psychology, 33*, 148–153.

van Schaik, Carel P., S. A. Pandit, & E. R. Vogel. 2006. Toward a general model for male-male coalitions in primate groups. In P. M. Kappeler and Carel P. van Schaik (Eds.), *Cooperation in primates and humans: Mechanisms and evolution* (pp. 151–171). Springer.

Van Vugt, M., & Tybur, J. M. (2015). The evolutionary foundations of hierarchy: Status, dominance, prestige, and leadership. In D. M. Buss (Ed.), *The handbook of evolutionary psychology* (2nd ed., pp. 788–809). Wiley.

von Rueden, C. (2014). The roots and fruits of social status in small-scale human societies. In J. T. Cheng, J. L. Tracy, & C. Anderson (Eds.), *The psychology of social status* (pp. 179–200). Springer.

von Rueden, C., Gurven, M., & Kaplan, H. (2008). The multiple dimensions of male social status in an Amazonian society. *Evolution and Human Behavior, 29*(6), 402–415.

von Rueden, C., Gurven, M., & Kaplan, H. (2011). Why do men seek status? Fitness payoffs to dominance and prestige. *Proceedings of the Royal Society B: Biological Sciences, 278*(1715), 2223–2232.

von Rueden, C., & Jaeggi, A. V. (2016). Men's status and reproductive success in 33 nonindustrial societies: Effects of subsistence, marriage system, and reproductive strategy. *Proceedings of the National Academy of Sciences, 113*(39), 10824–10829.

von Rueden, C., Redhead, D., O'Gorman, R., Kaplan, H., & Gurven, M. (2019). The dynamics of men's cooperation and social status in a small-scale society. *Proceedings of the Royal Society B: Biological Sciences, 286*(1908), 1–9.

Whalen, P. J., Shin, L. M., McInerney, S. C., Fischer, H., Wright, C. I., & Rauch, S. L. (2001). A functional MRI study of human amygdala responses to facial expressions of fear versus anger. *Emotion, 1*(1), 70.

Wiessner, P. (2019). Collective action for war and for peace. Current *Anthropology, 60*(2), 224–244.

Witkower, Z., Mercadante, E. J., & Tracy, J. L. (2020). How affect shapes status: Distinct emotional experiences and expressions facilitate social hierarchy navigation. *Current Opinion in Psychology, 33*, 18–22.

Wojciszke, B., Abele, A. E., & Baryla, W. (2009). Two dimensions of interpersonal attitudes: Liking depends on communion, respect depends on agency. *European Journal of Social Psychology, 39*(6), 973–990.

Wrangham, R. W. (2021). Targeted conspiratorial killing, human self-domestication and the evolution of groupishness. *Evolutionary Human Sciences, 3*, 1–21.

CHAPTER 31

Emotions in Politics

Florian van Leeuwen and Michael Bang Petersen

Abstract

Politics is the process of negotiating resources, both in the here-and-now and in the future, by establishing rules about resource allocation. Previous work has argued that adaptations for politics include capacities for political judgment and behavior. The chapter reviews the key role played by emotions for both political judgment and behavior. First, the authors detail how emotions that specifically evolved for negotiation (e.g., anger and envy) influence political judgment and behavior. Second, they review how a number of emotions that were not designed for negotiation also influence political judgment and behavior. Specifically, they review work on the relation between disgust and political attitudes for illustration. Overall, the authors argue for the view that emotions are inherent to politics. Politics—including persuasion, ideology, social coordination, and the pursuit of long-term political goals—cannot be disentangled from emotions. Hence, the classical opposition between emotion and rationality in politics is misleading.

Key Words: emotion, politics, goal, negotiation, political behavior

Emotions in Politics

Emotions are likely to subvert our reasoning and decision-making. At least, that is the classic view on the matter in the Western history of ideas (e.g., Keltner & Lerner, 2010). If emotions subvert our ability to deliberate and make good decisions, then emotions would be detrimental to democratic politics, and it would be desirable to reduce the influence of emotions on political judgment and behavior. However, an analysis of what emotions and politics are, and recent empirical work on these topics, points to at least three reasons for optimism. First, concerns that easily manipulated emotions will subvert rational politics might be exaggerated, because people are also equipped with evolved defenses against emotion-based persuasion. Second, worries that increased threats (and the associated experience of negative emotions) result in shifts toward social conservatism might be based on a mistaken view of the relation between negative emotions and problem-solving abilities. Third, concerns that emotions push politics toward solving short-term rather than long-term problems might be unwarranted, because emotions might play a role in the pursuit of long-term goals.

Politics Is Negotiating about Entitlement

Politics is the process of negotiating about resources, both in the here-and-now and in the future, by establishing rules about resource allocation: who gets what, when, and how (Lasswell, 1950). In other words, political behavior involves creating or revising shared expectations about entitlement. Politics is the manifestation of psychological adaptations designed to solve the conflict and coordination problems that emerge from group living. Work in political psychology (e.g., Jost & Sidanius, 2004) and especially evolutionary political psychology (Petersen, 2016) provides a starting point for thinking about the psychological mechanisms involved in politics. Evolutionary political psychology is the study of human politics by applying the theoretical toolkit offered by evolutionary psychology (Tooby & Cosmides, 2015).

Evolutionary political psychology can be summarized with four principles (for details, see Petersen, 2016):

1. The psychological mechanisms that humans evolved for politics (our evolved political psychology) were crafted by natural selection to operate adaptively in small-scale societies. Mass societies have emerged too recently to have shaped our evolved political psychology.
2. Evolved political psychology provides an underlying default structure for mass politics. That is, our evolved psychology provides default intuitions and preferences. Political arrangements that fit with these intuitions are likely to be perceived as appealing or compelling, which predicts that across societies political institutions will have particular features and will be oriented toward solving similar problems (Boyer & Petersen, 2012).
3. Politics is an arms race about information, and our evolved political psychology was shaped by the coevolution of strategies and counter-strategies to manipulate information. Because politics is about shared expectations about entitlement, selection pressures favored both *offensive* strategies that sought to decrease the sense of entitlement in the minds of others and *defensive* counter-strategies to resist such manipulation.
4. In mass societies, our evolved political psychology often responds to events and groups without direct experience, but rather on the basis of information provided by others (e.g., rumors, gossip, news) and mental simulations (i.e., imagination and other forms of forecasting; Petersen & Aarøe, 2013).

The offensive strategies and defensive counter-strategies described above must include adaptations for political judgment and political behavior (Petersen, 2016). Adaptations for political judgment involve abilities to evaluate rules about resource distributions. Without abilities to make such evaluations, individuals would not be able to strive for increased entitlement, or to further their own political interests. These adaptations for political judgment include a sense of self-interest, a sense of the interests of close others, and a sense of the distribution of interests within the greater collective (i.e., some form of public opinion assessment). These senses are designed to answer three questions: *How does this rule affect me? How does this rule affect others who are valuable to me? How do others evaluate this rule?* A key assumption is that the psychological mechanisms that make these judgments use decision rules that were fitness-enhancing under ancestral conditions (Tooby & Cosmides, 1990).

Adaptations for political behavior involve behavioral strategies that seek to target and change shared mental models about who is entitled to what. These adaptations include capacities for acquiring status, coalitional rivalry, persuasion, and informational vigilance (Petersen, 2016). These kinds of activities may involve a variety of emotional experiences, such as pride triggered by a gain in status, sadness over a lost election, or anger toward an exploitative elite. Indeed, recent work suggests that humans have evolved a suite of emotions for negotiating about entitlement, including anger, envy, compassion, pride, and shame (e.g., Sell et al., 2017; Sznycer, 2019). While political scientists have long recognized the role of emotions in political judgment and behavior (e.g., Marcus, 2000; Valentino et al., 2011), we here assess this role from an adaptationist perspective.

Emotions Coordinate Thinking and Action for Goal Pursuit

There is no discipline-wide consensus among psychologists about how to define emotions—for example, a chapter in the *Handbook of Social Psychology* (Keltner & Lerner, 2010) lists eight viable definitions. Most definitions indicate that emotions involve a physiological response and orient the person to respond to ongoing events in their environment. Theoretical work in evolutionary psychology has proposed and developed a precise definition of what emotions are: "superordinate mechanisms that evolved to coordinate the activity of other programs in the solution of adaptive problems" (Al-Shawaf et al., 2015, p. 173; Cosmides & Tooby, 2000; Tooby & Cosmides, 1990, 2008). The suite of other mechanisms controlled by emotions is broad and includes mechanisms for attention, perception, memory, categorization, learning, energy allocation, physiology, and behavior. In other words, the proposal is that "emotions are mechanisms that set the brain's highest-level goals. Once triggered by a propitious moment, an emotion triggers a cascade of subgoals and sub-subgoals that we call thinking and acting" (Pinker, 1997, p. 373). Of course, this definition is a working hypothesis, a conjecture that serves as a middle-level theory (Buss, 1995), from which specific and testable hypotheses can be derived.

This superordinate mechanism view of emotions has at least two advantages compared to alternative definitions. First, compared to definitions that exclude function (e.g., defining emotion as "positive or negative experience that is associated with a particular pattern of physiological activity"; Schachter et al., 2020, p. 410), it includes an explanation for why emotions influence so many other psychological and physiological processes. Approaches that ignore evolved function make it difficult or impossible to explain why emotions would have such broad influences. In contrast, the superordinate mechanism view explains the broad effects of emotions on other processes in terms of the evolved function of emotions. Functional goal-directed behavior requires that there is a high degree of coordination between numerous psychological and physiological processes. Solving a particular adaptive problem requires a particular kind of coordination between attention, memory, physiology, movement, etc. The conjecture is that each emotion evolved to solve this coordinating function for a particular adaptive problem (Al-Shawaf et al., 2015; Tooby & Cosmides, 1990, 2015).

Second, the superordinate mechanism view has an advantage when compared to definitions that characterize basic emotions as having three features: distinctive universal signals (i.e., a communicative signal such as a facial expression), distinctive physiology, and distinct antecedents (Ekman, 1992). While this proposal has inspired much fruitful work on emotions, the proposal that emotions with distinct signals are more basic than those without distinct signals remains arbitrary. It is not clear what is gained or explained by adding (or removing) the label *basic*, nor is it clear why this must be predicated on whether or not the emotion has an associated signal. The superordinate mechanism view suggests that there may be emotions—such as envy (Smith & Kim, 2007) and sexual jealousy (Tooby & Cosmides, 1990)—that evolved to solve crucial adaptive problems, but that lack a distinct facial expression, simply because a distinct facial expression did not help solving the adaptive problem (Al-Shawaf et al., 2015).

Emotions for Negotiation Influence Political Judgment and Behavior

Given this understanding of emotions, we believe that emotions influence political judgment and behavior in at least two ways. As politics involves negotiating rules about entitlement, emotions that evolved for negotiating with others are likely to play a key role in politics. In addition, the view that emotions are superordinate mechanisms suggests that multiple emotions may influence political judgment and behavior, even though these emotions have not evolved specifically for negotiating entitlement, but rather because these emotions regulate some processes that influence or feed into political judgment or behavior. Below we review examples of recent work on both such processes.

Recent work suggests that humans have evolved a suite of emotions for negotiating about entitlement, including anger (Sell et al., 2009), pride (Sznycer, Al-Shawaf, et al., 2017), shame (Sznycer et al., 2016), envy, and compassion (Sznycer, Seal, et al., 2017). Each of these emotions seems to be a distinct strategy for increasing what one is entitled to in the minds of others.

Anger is the emotion that was selected for resolving conflicts of interest in favor of the self by convincing (e.g., persuading or threatening) others to place greater weight on the welfare of the self (Sell, 2011; Sell et al., 2009). The recalibrational theory of anger posits that individuals have mental representations of welfare trade-off ratios, i.e., the relative weight placed on the welfare of others compared to welfare of the self (Tooby et al., 2008; Delton & Robertson, 2016). The higher someone's welfare trade-off ratio toward you, the more they weigh your welfare in making decisions, and the more likely they are to choose options that benefit you. When the ratio equals 1, the other person values your welfare as much as their own welfare. When the ratio is 0.5, they value their own welfare twice as much as yours. When the ratio is 0.25, they value their own welfare four times as much as yours. This means that they might opt for actions that give them a benefit of 1 unit, but cost you nearly 4 units (of reproductively relevant resources). If someone reveals such a low welfare trade-off ratio toward you, you might be motivated to convince them to treat you better. The system that activates and executes this attempt to raise their welfare trade-off ratio toward you is anger.

Anger coordinates psychological and physiological programs to implement two negotiation strategies: imposing costs on others, and withholding benefits from others. In some situations, you might be able to impose costs on others, for example when you are physically stronger or have lots of allies. In other situations, you might not be able to impose costs, and can only withhold benefits (e.g., not engage in cooperative endeavors with the other). Both of these strategies are incentives for the other to place greater weight on your welfare. Based on these considerations, Sell et al. (2009) hypothesized that increased abilities to impose costs (operationalized as physical strength) and withhold benefits (operationalized as attractiveness) would relate to greater success in resolving conflicts in one's favor, feeling more entitled, and being angered more easily. The findings showed that among men, physical strength predicted anger-proneness, history of fighting, perceived utility of aggression, entitlement, and success in conflict, and that attractiveness predicted entitlement and success in conflict. Among women, attractiveness predicted anger-proneness, perceived utility of aggression, entitlement, and success in conflict.

As mentioned above, a key idea in evolutionary political psychology is that people make political judgments by using decision rules that were adaptive under ancestral conditions. When negotiating under ancestral conditions, physical strength and attractiveness were relevant variables because they affected one's ability to impose costs and confer benefits. However, these variables are irrelevant when forming attitudes about modern mass politics, such as whether to support the military invasion of another country, or whether a nation's politics should be geared toward more equality or inequality. Hence, from a normative perspective, physical strength and attractiveness should not influence judgments about modern politics. Yet, in studies conducted by Sell et al. (2009), stronger men and more attractive women were also more supportive of war. This illustrates how evolutionary approaches predict findings that may seem puzzling but are supported by the data, and that cannot be explained by theories of humans as rational actors. The relation between physical strength and support for war has now been replicated in samples from Argentina, Denmark, and Romania—though not in a sample from Israel (Sell et al., 2017). Recent work suggests that this relationship generalizes to support for and participation in intra-state political violence (e.g., anti-government protests; Bartusevicius, 2021). The relation between physical strength and entitlement also extends to attitudes about inequality: across 12 samples with over 6,000 participants, stronger men were more supportive of political and economic inequality (Petersen & Laustsen, 2019).

Anger is not the only emotion that influences political judgments about inequality. Modern societies have extensive social welfare policies for reducing inequality and providing support for those in need. Compassion and envy are emotions that influence political attitudes about redistribution (Sznycer, Seal, et al., 2017; Delton, Petersen, DeScioli, et al., 2018). Under ancestral conditions, humans faced uncertainty about the supply of food. On some days, you might not find enough food to feed your family. But someone else may be lucky and find more than they can eat on that day. By sharing food, individuals who are lucky pay a small cost, but provide a large benefit to those who are unlucky. Individuals who share when they are lucky are appreciated and are likely to receive shared food in the future when they are unlucky. Based on these and other considerations, it was hypothesized that compassion serves as a form of social insurance, and therefore is sensitive not only to absolute needs (such as lacking resources or being poor or ill) but also to instances of being unlucky and of sudden increases in hardship (Delton, Petersen, DeScioli, et al., 2018). A series of studies that measured compassion toward people in different situations showed that participants felt more compassion *both* toward individuals who had few resources *and* individuals who had suddenly been unlucky. Crucially, these feelings of compassion influenced judgments about social welfare: individuals who evoked more compassion were judged to be more entitled to receive social welfare, a finding replicated in both Denmark and the United States (Petersen et al., 2012).

Inequality is omnipresent. This creates a selection pressure for strategies for interacting with those who are better off than oneself. Envy may be a key emotion for this adaptive problem. Sznycer, Seal, et al. (2017) hypothesized that envy motivates and coordinates strategies for reducing the welfare of individuals who are better off than oneself. Envy is different from self-interest, in that self-interest motivates the pursuit of improving one's situation regardless of the resources of others, but envy specifically motivates the decrease of relative differences in resources or status. Based on this reasoning, they predicted that feelings of envy should relate to support for redistribution, a prediction that was supported in samples from the United States, the United Kingdom, India, and Israel.

Evidence is accumulating that pride and shame are key emotions for influencing expectations about entitlement, by recalibrating welfare trade-off ratios in the minds of others. Such emotions are likely relevant to political negotiation. In short, the proposal is that pride coordinates the pursuit and advertising of socially valued, status-boosting actions (Sznycer, Al-Shawaf, et al., 2017; Sznycer, Xygalatas, Alami, et al., 2018). Shame is its counterpart: it motivates the avoidance of status-lowering actions and limits the spread of information that may damage one's status (Sznycer et al., 2016; Szncyer, Xygalatas, Agey, et al., 2018). Guilt (Sznycer, 2019) and gratitude (Smith et al., 2017) may also regulate welfare trade-off ratios—perhaps both in one's own mind and in that of others—and appear designed to keep valuable relationships alive. While there is much work about the relation between national pride and politics (e.g., Solt, 2011; Ray, 2018), the influences of pride, shame, guilt, and gratitude on political judgment and behavior (e.g., Delton, Petersen, & Robertson, 2018), are promising avenues for further research.

Emotions as the Object of Negotiation

Do other emotions—those not designed for negotiating about entitlement, but for other adaptive problems—influence politics? A wealth of evidence suggests that they do. These other emotions seem to influence political judgment and behavior in at least two ways. One path of influence is direct and involves mental simulation of relevant events. For example, when a person is asked whether they favor or oppose a law forbidding sex between opposite-sex siblings, they might imagine such an event, feel disgust toward it, and conclude that the law aligns with their preferences (the disgust indicates that the self does not want to engage in such actions), which increases the likelihood that they will favor the law (cf. Tybur et al., 2013).

The second path builds on the existence of the first path and involves persuasion by others. As mentioned above, humans have evolved abilities for persuasion, and one strategy for persuading others is activating their emotions (e.g., Brader, 2005). The existence of emotions in the minds of others has selected for capacities to use emotions in order to strategically manipulate others. Fear appeals are a common form of such emotion-based persuasion; these are persuasive communications that attempt to arouse fear by "emphasizing the potential danger and harm that will befall individuals if they do not adopt the messages' recommendations" (Tannenbaum et al., 2015, p. 1178). Some fear appeals may also aim to evoke other emotions than fear. For example, anti-smoking campaigns around the world try to discourage people from smoking by printing disgusting images on cigarette packaging.

However, individuals are not easily manipulated by emotion-based persuasion. As mentioned above, adaptations for political judgment and behavior include mechanisms for *informational vigilance*. Any form of communication makes an individual vulnerable to manipulation, because the goal of communication is to change the mental state of the organism receiving information (Krebs & Dawkins, 1984). However, when a particular form of communication is manipulative to such an extent that the costs to receivers are (on average) larger than the benefits, then there is selection for receivers to become insensitive to the signals (e.g., by ignoring such signals or being unable to process them; Al-Shawaf et al., 2015).

Humans have evolved such mechanisms for informational vigilance (also called epistemic vigilance; Sperber et al., 2010). Work in psychology, anthropology, political science, and marketing suggests that humans are not gullible, but vigilant toward implausible information, and tend to hold on to their prior beliefs (Mercier, 2017). Humans are not easily convinced by attempts at persuasion. Work in psychology and political science shows that humans can engage in motivated reasoning, ignoring or discounting information that counters their prior beliefs (Kunda, 1990). Such motivated reasoning might be one form of informational vigilance, protecting individuals from acquiring implausible ideas or ideas that are detrimental to their fitness interests (Petersen, 2016). A striking example of resistance to well-intended persuasion comes from work in the 1970s and 1980s on intentions to use seat belts. When seat belts were introduced, intentions to use them were generally low. The idea was that fear appeals would convince people of the risks involved and boost intentions to use them. But videos showing the danger posed by not using seat belts had so little influence on people's intentions to use them that the risk researcher Paul Slovic concluded that people are incapable of accurately perceiving the risks involved and thus argued for laws mandating seat-belt use (Slovic, 1985).

Are Tendencies to Feel Emotions Related to Political Attitudes?

Research on the influence of emotions (others than those for negotiation) on politics can be tied to at least two questions. One question is: *Are individual differences in tendencies to feel particular emotions related to political attitudes?* The second question results from the fact that the stimuli or situations that typically trigger negative emotions are associated with threats or worries (e.g., Keltner & Lerner, 2010) and asks: *Does perceiving threats influence political attitudes?* Below we review recent work relating to each of these questions.

The idea that individuals who are prone to negative emotions such as fear and anger are likely to have more conservative political attitudes has a long history in political psychology (e.g., Jost et al., 2003). Over the past decade, a large number of studies has asked whether another negative emotion, disgust, also relates to conservative political attitudes. This work demonstrates that an emotion that did not evolve for negotiating about entitlement can have a substantial influence on political judgment and behavior.

First, it turns out that disgust is not one emotion, but probably three: pathogen disgust, sexual disgust, and moral disgust (Tybur et al., 2009; Tybur et al., 2013). The function of pathogen disgust is to motivate and coordinate the avoidance of pathogenic infection (Tybur et al., 2013). The function of sexual disgust is to motivate avoidance of costly sexual interactions with unwise mate choices, whereas the function of moral disgust is to coordinate condemnation with other people in situations of conflict.[1] There is substantial evidence that pathogen disgust coordinates the avoidance of pathogenic infection (Oaten et al., 2009). For example, objects or people associated with cues of pathogens reliably evoke disgust (e.g., Curtis et al., 2004). This suggests that individuals who are more motivated to avoid pathogens—i.e., are more pathogen disgust sensitive—are more likely to have negative attitudes toward policies that activate pathogen disgust.

A key feature of pathogen disgust is that it works in a "better safe than sorry" manner. The system can make two kinds of mistakes: failing to detect and avoid pathogens (i.e., a false negative) or incorrectly inferring the presence of pathogens and motivating avoidance of pathogens that do not actually exist (i.e., a false positive). The former kind of error tends to be more costly than the latter. Hence, the system is calibrated toward making false positive errors (Schaller, 2015; Tybur & Lieberman, 2016; see also Haselton & Buss, 2000; Haselton & Nettle, 2006; Nesse, 2005). Ethnic out-groups and foreign immigrants are often associated with infectious disease (Oaten et al., 2011), sometimes because they come from areas with a high prevalence of infectious disease (and thus may be infectious), and other times because of rumors and propaganda. Based on such considerations, it was hypothesized that motivations to avoid pathogens should relate to anti-immigration attitudes (Faulkner et al., 2004). Recent work has borne out this prediction: in samples from both the United States and Denmark, individuals who were more sensitive to pathogen disgust were more opposed to immigration (Aarøe et al., 2017; Ji et al., 2019).

There appears to be a large set of objects, entities, or practices that through persuasion can become associated with infection or contamination, such as homeless people, genetically modified foods, vaccines, and nuclear power. Individuals who are more disgust sensitive will tend to favor policies that remove these objects or entities (Clay, 2017; Clifford & Piston, 2017; Clifford & Wendell, 2016; Hacquin et al., 2022; Kam & Estes, 2016). Pathogen disgust sensitivity not only relates to narrow measures of policy attitudes, but reliably correlates with measures of socially conservative ideology (Terrizzi et al., 2013; Tybur et al., 2016), identification with conservative parties, and voting for conservative parties (Aarøe et al., 2020).[2]

Does Perceiving Threats Influence Political Attitudes?

As mentioned above, a large amount of work in political psychology has examined whether and how emotional responses to threats—fears, anxiety, worries, etc.—relate to political attitudes. Indeed, an influential standard view is that perceptions of threat (and the worries they activate) influence political ideology by making people more favorable toward conservative right-wing policies (Jost et al., 2003). This view was supported by a meta-analysis (including 22,818 participants from 12 countries) that showed that individuals with more fears and worries were more supportive of conservative ideology. However, recent empirical work examining the relationships between specific threats and attitudes toward specific political issues across a larger variety of cultures suggests that there is no straightforward relation between feeling threatened and political ideology. An analysis of data from the World Values Survey from more than 60,000 participants from 56 countries showed that while being worried about war was associated with identifying with right-wing ideology, being worried about crime in one's neighborhood was associated with identifying with left-wing ideology (Brandt et al., 2020). In addition, facing the threat of poverty was associated with both support for left-wing economic beliefs (e.g., opposing economic inequality) and right-wing cultural beliefs (e.g., supporting status-based discrimination on the job market).

The complex relation between perceiving threats and political attitudes is partly a result of the fact that both threat and ideology are broad constructs, each consisting of multiple dimensions. It is possible that when each of these underlying dimensions is accurately measured, then measures of specific threats will relate specifically to support for policies, parties, and ideologies that are associated with reducing those threats (Brandt et al., 2020; Eadeh & Chang, 2019). But what policies (and parties and ideologies) will people perceive as reducing particular threats? An adaptationist perspective suggests that people will form such judgments using heuristics that worked well in ancestral small-scale societies (see the first principle of evolutionary political psychology mentioned above). We think that a first step in unraveling the relation between threats and ideology is to find the mistaken assumptions that underlie the standard view that right-wing ideology is an anxiety-reducing response to threats.

While the standard view might be tenable in the narrow sense that some conservative policies and beliefs have palliative effects and momentarily reduce feelings of anxiety (e.g., Osmundsen & Petersen, 2017), we think that as a broad generalization, it rest on two untenable assumptions. First, it assumes that individuals with a right-wing ideology have more or more intense worries (i.e., perceive more problems or threats). Second, it assumes that adherence to tradition is a viable means of reducing problems (i.e., neutralizing a threat or reducing a source of worry).

Regarding the first assumption, while right-wing ideology is associated with worries about social cohesion, security and physical violence, and changing norms about sexuality and religion (Duckitt et al., 2010), this does not mean those on the left worry less. One major element that distinguishes left-wing and right-wing ideology is views about inequality and redistribution (e.g., Jost et al., 2003). In other words, those on the left tend to worry more about there being too much inequality, while those on the right tend to worry more about there being not enough inequality (e.g., Pratto et al., 1994). Indeed, work on the relation between moral values and political ideology supports the broad notion that liberals are more concerned with violations of norms of equality and fairness (Graham et al., 2009; Kivikangas et al., 2021). This suggests that the difference between those on the left and those on the right is not in *how much* they worry, but rather in *what* they worry about. Zooming in on political hot-buttons supports this view: those on the right tend to be more concerned about immigration, law and order, and taxes, while those on the left tend to be more concerned about the environment, social security, and healthcare (Seeberg, 2017).

Second, the standard view proposed that conservative ideology relates to traits that tend to lower anxieties and worries, such as resistance to change, conformity to traditions, and low openness to experience (Jost et al., 2003; Sibley & Duckitt, 2008). The assumption that these broad conservative traits reduce or neutralize threats and uncertainties (e.g., Duckitt et al., 2010; Jost et al., 2003) does not align with an adaptationist perspective. Traditions probably only help address a narrow range of problems. Consider the basic problem of nutrition. Eating involves the problem of getting poisoned or infected by eating contaminated food, and this risk may be reduced by following traditions about what to eat (Murray et al., 2011). However, the problem of having insufficient food can be reduced with different behaviors, such as appealing to egalitarian norms (Petersen et al., 2013) and breaking habits and eating novel foods (Al-Shawaf, 2016; Perone et al., 2021). Analyses of how humans solve problems suggests that conservative traits like resistance to change, conformity to traditions, and low openness to experience are not effective strategies for dealing with problems (Cosmides & Tooby, 2002; Deutsch, 2011). Traditions will also often not provide a solution to novel problems, because traditions (other than those that characterize science, such as rational criticism) do not typically contain the knowledge or procedures that are needed to solve novel problems (Deutsch, 2011).

For example, the personality trait of *openness to experience* reflects predispositions to be creative, unconventional, and innovative (Ashton & Lee, 2007). Low openness to experience is thus associated with reduced tendencies for creativity and innovation. Humans appear to have evolved a unique set of mental abilities for solving problems, involving improvisational intelligence (Cosmides & Tooby, 2002) and creativity (Deutsch, 2011). Hence, there seems a mismatch between the broad set of stimuli that trigger negative emotions (e.g., predators, hunger, infectious disease, job loss, public speaking) and the presumed function of conservative ideology. It seems poor design to have emotions that are triggered by cues that an adaptive problem is present, but then reduce the probability that the organism can solve the problem by reducing creativity and adjusting attitudes so that conventions seem appealing and innovations aversive. Humans have adapted to life in the cognitive niche, where information about how to solve problems is the most valuable resource (Pinker, 2010; Tooby & Devore, 1987). As humans are an intensely social species, it is likely that when an individual faced a novel problem, there were some others who had faced similar problems in the past and who had found ways to make (minimal) improvements. In such an environment, individuals who were more open to adopting useful innovations would likely have fared better than those ignoring innovations. Hence, each emotion may include design to activate a *particular kind* of openness or creativity when faced with an adaptive problem. As the proverb goes, necessity is the mother of invention.

More generally, an adaptationist perspective suggests that the way in which threats influence political judgment and behavior depends on what kinds of judgments and behaviors typically helped resolve that particular threat in the ancestral environment. The mechanisms that regulate these judgments should not take into account whether the policies involved are currently associated with left-wing or right-wing politics. For example, for those who have less, the problem of large inequality is not addressed by endorsing the status quo (cf. Brandt, 2013), but rather by reducing the welfare of those who are better off—a complex goal, the pursuit of which may be coordinated by envy (Sznycer, Seal, et al., 2017).

Emotions Are Inherent to Politics

Following the classic view that emotions are likely to subvert our reasoning and decision-making, one might call for making politics more rational by removing the pernicious influence of emotions. The above discussion may seem to follow the classic view by focusing on how emotions influence political judgment and behavior. This may give the impression that it would be possible to remove emotions from politics, in the sense that emotions are epiphenomena that can distort political judgments and behaviors. In contrast, we propose that this view is neither fruitful nor tenable, as emotions and politics are inherently related.

The view that humans are political animals (Petersen, 2016) suggests that adaptations for politics have a pervasive influence on human behavior. The notion that some emotions are for politics (see above), entails that emotions and politics cannot be separated. An agent without emotions for negotiating would simply not engage in politics when confronted with a rule that reduces their entitlement. Without emotional systems, there would be no systems for generating the valuations that are key for political judgments and no systems for propelling the actions that are key to political negotiation. Rather than maintaining a division between emotions on the one hand and adaptations for politics on the other hand, we think that it might be fruitful to consider politics as inherently related to emotions. In other words, the emotions that evolved for negotiating entitlement (anger, compassion, envy, pride, shame, and perhaps others) are at the core of our evolved political psychology.

Does this mean that politics is reduced to heated irrational debates about short-term projects? Standard definitions that characterize emotions as short-lived responses to current events (Keltner & Lerner, 2010) suggest an affirmative answer. In contrast, the superordinate mechanism view suggests that emotions enable politics, including social coordination for political projects, both normatively desirable and undesirable, and both in the short and long term.

Emotions Enable Coordination with Others

Darwin's ([1872] 2009) work on the expression of emotions has inspired the bulk of evolutionary-minded research of emotions. Indeed, there has been extensive debate about the facial expressions associated with basic emotions (e.g., Ekman, 1992). A widespread assumption is that the expression of one's emotional state has some communicative value (e.g., Ekman, 1992; McCullough & Reed, 2016). However, biological theories of communication show this assumption to be unwarranted (Al-Shawaf et al., 2015; Al-Shawaf & Lewis, 2020; McCullough & Reed, 2016). Sometimes it might be beneficial to conceal an emotional state from others (i.e., hold a poker face). Some emotions, like envy and sexual jealousy, appear to lack a distinct facial expression.

The superordinate mechanism view suggests that expressions of emotions are not an inherent feature of a small set of basic emotions, but rather that the expression of emotions should be strategic and should serve the pursuit of one's goals. Emotion expression might play a pivotal role in achieving some self-serving political goals, such as acquiring status via coalitional rivalry (including collective violence; see Horowitz, 2001). However, not all emotional coordination must be that destructive: expressing disgust at moral violations can also be used to coordinate condemnation of norm violations (Lieberman et al., 2018; Molho et al., 2017), and for example might be used to reduce exploitation and corruption.

A closer look at how and why emotional signals (and in particular facial expressions) enable political coordination suggests that emotions might help coordinate against authoritarian leaders. Recent work on how people solve coordination problems suggests that some communicative behaviors (such as facial expressions, blushing, and laughing) may be especially useful for creating common knowledge (De Freitas et al., 2019; Thomas et al., 2014). Facial expressions create common knowledge because they are salient to both the expresser and the perceivers and are rapidly and easily decoded: "The perceiver not only knows the intended mental state of the expresser but knows that the expresser knows it, that the expresser knows that the perceiver knows it, and so on" (Thomas et al., 2014, p. 672). This points to the possibility that there may be a set of emotional signals that serve social coordination by generating common knowledge. Studies of how minority groups respond to repression suggest that humor is sometimes used as a form of resistance (Vollhardt et al., 2020). In addition, in some societies there are professions dedicated to making fun of authorities: comedians and late-night talk-show hosts. One function of laughter might be to coordinate opposition toward undeserved claims of authority (Pinker, 1997). Humor at the expense of inept leaders might reduce the shared sense of what the authority figure is entitled to.

Emotions Enable the Pursuit of Long-Term Goals

Characterizing emotions as short-lived affective responses to ongoing events makes *mental time travel* difficult to explain (Boyer, 2008). Memories often have a vivid emotional component (e.g., re-experiencing the shame of saying something foolish during a job interview) and imagining the future can involve strong emotional experiences (e.g., intense happiness when imagining that you will finally meet a distant loved one). If our emotions are reactions to ongoing events, then why do we also feel them when recalling the past and imagining the future?

Studies of mental time travel suggest that the affective aspects of memories and imagination are crucial for self-control in two ways (Boyer, 2008). First, episodic memory of emotional events seems to help inhibit impulsive behavior. Second, forecasting of emotional events seems to reduce time discounting (i.e., discounting rewards in the future). The emotional aspects of mental time travel seem to fit with the view that emotions are superordinate mechanisms. From this perspective, the phenomenon of mental time travel reveals that emotions are not necessarily designed for regulating short-term goal pursuit, but may include design for regulating behavior across longer time spans. Some emotions, such as fear of snakes, may be systems dedicated to short-term responses (Öhman & Mineka, 2003). But other emotions may be designed for the pursuit of long-term goals.

For example, pride is characterized as motivating socially valued behavior and so relates to acquiring status. But is the pride system only active in the moment that we feel proud? Status is hard to acquire and often involves highly coordinated behaviors over long stretches of time. For social organisms, acquiring and maintaining status are of primary importance. If achieving this goal requires the coordination of behaviors across long periods of time, then the superordinate mechanism view of emotions entails the prediction that the pride system includes design for such long-term behavioral control—including remembering past achievements and imagining future proud achievements. It is not very helpful to assign emotions the role of regulating behavior in the short term and to explain long-term coordination by virtue of self-control. Self-control is a linguistic shorthand for the inhibition of short-term-oriented responses, which facilitates the pursuit of long-term goals; it is not a mechanism. It is a label, rather than an explanation.

By associating emotions with short-term affective responses, researchers may have overlooked a number of longer-lasting influences of emotions on judgment and behavior. From an applied perspective, this is unfortunate. If emotions regulate the pursuit of our highest-level goals, then understanding how the emotions work is crucial for knowing how to achieve long-term political goals. Achieving long-term political goals such as democracy, wealth, and good healthcare requires extensive coordination between individuals. We should prepare for the *next* pandemic, which may be in the distant future. We will be in a better position to achieve such coordination if we understand better how emotions guide us toward or away from particular long-term goals.

Notes

1. There is currently some debate as to whether this division is accurate, in particular about whether pathogen disgust also includes design for avoiding consumption of plant toxins and whether moral disgust is a distinct emotion (Lieberman et al., 2018; Rozin & Falon, 1987). In addition, disgust is often described as an output of the behavioral immune system (the set of psychological mechanisms that evolved for avoiding infection; Schaller, 2015), rather than as a superordinate system controlling pathogen avoidance. This is simply a matter of terminology. Most audiences will expect that the word *disgust* refers to the affective state, rather than the entire motivational system. Hence, for the sake of communication, *disgust* is sometimes used to refer to the affective state, and the motivational system is called the *behavioral immune system*. When defined as a superordinate mechanism, the emotion pathogen disgust is equivalent to the behavioral immune system (Lieberman & Patrick, 2014).
2. Sexual disgust also relates to socially conservative attitudes (Kurzban et al., 2010). Whether the relation between pathogen disgust and socially conservative ideology can be attributed to sexual disgust is currently unclear (Aarøe et al., 2020; Billingsley et al., 2018; Tybur et al., 2015).

References

Aarøe, L., Petersen, M. B., & Arceneaux, K. (2017). The behavioral immune system shapes political intuitions: Why and how individual differences in disgust sensitivity underlie opposition to immigration. *American Political Science Review, 111*(2), 277–294. doi: 10.1017/S0003055416000770

Aarøe, L., Petersen, M. B., & Arceneaux, K. (2020), The behavioral immune system shapes partisan preferences in modern democracies: Disgust sensitivity predicts voting for socially conservative parties. *Political Psychology, 41*, 1073–1091. doi: 10.1111/pops.12665

Al-Shawaf, L. (2016). The evolutionary psychology of hunger. *Appetite, 105*, 591–595.

Al-Shawaf, L., Conroy-Beam, D., Asao, K., & Buss, D. M. (2015). Human emotions: An evolutionary psychological perspective. *Emotion Review, 8*, 173–186.

Al-Shawaf, L., & Lewis, D. M. G. (2020). Evolutionary psychology and the emotions. In V. Zeigler-Hill and T.K. Shackelford (Eds.). *Encyclopedia of personality and individual differences* (pp. 1452–1461). Springer. https://doi.org/10.1007/978-3-319-24612-3_516

Ashton, M. C., & Lee, K. (2007). Empirical, theoretical, and practical advantages of the HEXACO model of personality structure. *Personality and Social Psychology Review, 11*(2), 150–166.

Bartusevicius, H. (2021). Physical strength predicts political violence. *Evolution and Human Behavior, 42*(5), 423–430.

Billingsley, J., Lieberman, D., & Tybur, J. M. (2018). Sexual disgust trumps pathogen disgust in predicting voter behavior during the 2016 US presidential election. *Evolutionary Psychology, 16*(2), 1–15. https://doi.org/10.1177/1474704918764170

Boyer, P. (2008). Evolutionary economics of mental time travel? *Trends in Cognitive Sciences, 12*(6), 219–224.

Boyer, P., & Petersen, M.B. (2012). The naturalness of (many) social institutions: Evolved cognition as their foundation. *Journal of Institutional Economics, 8*(01), 1–25.

Brader, T. (2005), Striking a responsive chord: How political ads motivate and persuade voters by appealing to emotions. *American Journal of Political Science, 49*, 388–405. https://doi.org/10.1111/j.0092-5853.2005.00130.x

Brandt, M. (2013). Do the disadvantaged legitimize the social system? A large-scale test of the status–legitimacy hypothesis. *Journal of Personality and Social Psychology, 104*(5), 765–785.

Brandt, M. J., Turner-Zwinkels, F. M., Karapirinler, B., van Leeuwen, F., Bender, M., van Osch, Y., & Adams, B. G. (2020). The association between threat and politics depends on the type of threat, the political domain, and the country. *Personality and Social Psychology Bulletin, 47*(2), 324–343. https://doi.org/10.1177/0146167220946187

Buss, D. M. (1995). Evolutionary psychology: A new paradigm for psychological science. *Psychological Inquiry, 6*(1), 1–30.

Clay, R. (2017). The behavioral immune system and attitudes about vaccines: Germ aversion predicts more negative vaccine attitudes. *Social Psychological and Personality Science, 8*, 162–172.

Clifford, S., & Piston, S. (2017). Explaining public support for counterproductive homelessness policy: The role of disgust. *Political Behavior, 39*, 503–525. https://doi.org/10.1007/s11109-016-9366-4

Clifford, S., & Wendell, D. G. (2016). How disgust influences health purity attitudes. *Political Behavior, 38*(1), 155–178.

Cosmides, L., & Tooby, J. (2000). Evolutionary psychology and the emotions. In M. Lewis & J. M. Haviland-Jones (Eds.), *Handbook of emotions* (2nd ed., pp. 91–115). Guilford Press.

Cosmides, L., & Tooby, J. (2002). Unraveling the enigma of human intelligence: Evolutionary psychology and the multimodular mind. In R. J. Sternberg & J. C. Kaufman (Eds.), *The evolution of intelligence* (pp. 145–198). Lawrence Erlbaum Associates Publishers.

Curtis, V., Aunger, R., & Rabie, T. (2004). Evidence that disgust evolved to protect from risk of disease. *Proceedings of the Royal Society B: Biological Sciences, 271*(Suppl 4), S131–S133.

Darwin, C. ([1872] 2009). *The expression of the emotions in man and animals*. Penguin Classics.
De Freitas, J., Thomas, K., DeScioli, P., & Pinker, S. (2019). Common knowledge, coordination, and strategic mentalizing in human social life. *Proceedings of the National Academy of Sciences, 116*(28), 13751–13758.
Delton, A. W., Petersen, M. B., DeScioli, P., & Robertson, T. E. (2018). Need, compassion, and support for social welfare. *Political Psychology, 39*(4), 907–924.
Delton, A. W., Petersen, M. B., & Robertson, T. E. (2018). Partisan goals, emotions, and political mobilization: The role of motivated reasoning in pressuring others to vote. *The Journal of Politics, 80*(3), 890–902.
Delton, A. W., & Robertson, T. E. (2016). How the mind makes welfare tradeoffs: Evolution, computation, and emotion. *Current Opinion in Psychology, 7*, 12–16.
Deutsch, D. (2011). *The beginning of infinity: Explanations that transform the world*. Allen Lane.
Duckitt, J., Bizumic, B., Krauss, S. W., & Heled, E. (2010). A tripartite approach to right-wing authoritarianism: The authoritarianism-conservatism-traditionalism model. *Political Psychology, 31*(5), 685–715.
Eadeh, F. R., & Chang, K. K. (2019). Can threat increase support for liberalism? New insights into the relationship between threat and political attitudes. *Social Psychological and Personality Science, 11*, 88–96. https://doi.org/10.1177/1948550618815919
Ekman, P. (1992). An argument for basic emotions. *Cognition and Emotion, 6*, 169–200.
Faulkner, J., Schaller, M., Park, J. H., & Duncan, L. A. (2004). Evolved disease-avoidance mechanisms and contemporary xenophobic attitudes. *Group Processes & Intergroup Relations, 7*(4), 333–353.
Graham, J., Haidt, J., & Nosek, B. (2009). Liberals and conservatives rely on different sets of moral foundations. *Journal of Personality and Social Psychology, 96*(5), 1029–1046.
Hacquin, A., Altay, S., Aarøe, L., & Mercier, H. (2022). Disgust sensitivity and public opinion on nuclear energy. *Journal of Environmental Psychology, 80*, 1–13. https://doi.org/10.1016/j.jenvp.2021.101749
Haselton, M. G., & Buss, D. M. (2000). Error management theory: A new perspective on biases in cross-sex mind reading. *Journal of Personality and Social Psychology, 78*, 81–91.
Haselton, M. G., & Nettle, D. (2006). The paranoid optimist: An integrative evolutionary model of cognitive biases. *Personality and Social Psychology Review, 10*, 47–66.
Horowitz, D. L. (2001). *The deadly ethnic riot*. University of California Press.
Ji, T., Tybur, J. M., & van Vugt, M. (2019). Generalized or origin-specific out-group prejudice? The role of temporary and chronic pathogen-avoidance motivation in intergroup relations. *Evolutionary Psychology, 17*(1), 1–14. doi: 10.1177/1474704919826851.
Jost, J. T., Glaser, J., Kruglanski, A. W., & Sulloway, F. J. (2003). Political conservatism as motivated social cognition. *Psychological Bulletin, 129*(3), 339–375.
Jost, J. T., & Sidanius, J. (Eds.). (2004). *Political psychology: Key readings*. Psychology Press.
Kam, C. D., & Estes, B. A. (2016). Disgust sensitivity and public demand for protection. *The Journal of Politics, 78*, 481–496. https://doi.org/10.1086/684611
Keltner, D., & Lerner, J. (2010). Emotion. In S. Fiske & D. Gilbert (Eds.), *The handbook of social psychology* (pp. 312–347). McGraw Hill.
Kivikangas, J. M., Fernández-Castilla, B., Järvelä, S., Ravaja, N., & Lönnqvist, J. E. (2021). Moral foundations and political orientation: Systematic review and meta-analysis. *Psychological Bulletin, 147*, 55–94.
Krebs, J. R., & Dawkins, R. (1984). Animal signals: Mind-reading and manipulation. In J. R. Krebs & N. B. Davies (Eds.), *Behavioural ecology: An evolutionary approach* (2nd ed., pp. 380–402). Blackwell Scientific.
Kunda, Z. (1990). The case for motivated reasoning. *Psychological Bulletin, 8*, 480–498.
Kurzban, R., Dukes, A., & Weeden, J. (2010). Sex, drugs and moral goals: Reproductive strategies and views about recreational drugs. *Proceedings of the Royal Society B: Biological Sciences, 277*(1699), 3501–3508.
Lasswell, H. D. (1950). *Politics: Who gets what, when, how*. P. Smith.
Lieberman, D., & Patrick, C. (2014). Are the behavioral immune system and pathogen disgust identical? *Evolutionary Behavioral Sciences, 8*(4), 244–250.
Lieberman, D., Billingsley, J., & Patrick, C. (2018). Consumption, contact and copulation: How pathogens have shaped human psychological adaptations. *Philosophical Transactions of the Royal Society B: Biological Sciences, 373*(1751), 1–12. http://dx.doi.org/10.1098/rstb.2017.0203
Marcus, G. E. (2000). Emotions in politics. *Annual Review of Political Science, 3*(1), 221–250.
McCullough, M. E., & Reed, L. I. (2016). What the face communicates: Clearing the conceptual ground. *Current Opinion in Psychology, 7*, 110–114.
Mercier, H. (2017). How gullible are we? A review of the evidence from psychology and social science. *Review of General Psychology, 21*(2), 103–122.
Molho, C., Tybur, J. M., Güler, E., Balliet, D., & Hofmann, W. (2017). Disgust and anger relate to different aggressive responses to moral violations. *Psychological Science, 28*(5), 609–619.

Murray, D. R., Trudeau, R., & Schaller, M. (2011). On the origins of cultural differences in conformity: Four tests of the pathogen prevalence hypothesis. *Personality and Social Psychology Bulletin, 37*(3), 318–329.

Nesse, R. M. (2005). Natural selection and the regulation of defenses: A signal detection analysis of the smoke detector principle. *Evolution and Human Behavior, 26*(1), 88–105.

Oaten, M., Stevenson, R. J., & Case, T. I. (2009). Disgust as a disease-avoidance mechanism. *Psychological Bulletin, 135*(2), 303–321.

Oaten, M., Stevenson, R. J., & Case, T. I. (2011). Disease avoidance as a functional basis for stigmatization. *Philosophical Transactions of the Royal Society B: Biological Sciences, 366*(1583), 3433–3452.

Öhman, A., & Mineka, S. (2003). The malicious serpent: Snakes as a prototypical stimulus for an evolved module of fear. *Current Directions in Psychological Science, 12*(1), 5–9.

Osmundsen, M., & Petersen, M. B. (2017). Political ideology and precautionary reasoning: Testing the palliative function of right-wing ideology on obsessive-compulsive symptoms. *Social Cognition, 35*(4), 450–474.

Perone, P., Çınar, Ç., D'ursi, P., Durmuşoğlu, L. R., Lal, V., & Tybur, J. (2021). Examining the effect of hunger on responses to pathogen cues and novel foods. *Evolution and Human Behavior, 42,* 371–378. https://doi.org/10.1016/j.evolhumbehav.2021.02.004

Petersen, M. B. (2016). Evolutionary political psychology. In D. M. Buss (Ed.), *Handbook of evolutionary psychology* (2nd ed., Vol. 2, pp. 1084–1102). Wiley.

Petersen, M.B., & Aarøe, L. (2013). Politics in the mind's eye: Imagination as a link between social and political cognition. *American Political Science Review, 107*(02), 275–293.

Petersen, M. B., & Laustsen, L. (2019). Upper-body strength and political egalitarianism: Twelve conceptual replications. *Political Psychology, 40*(2), 375–394.

Petersen, M. B., Sznycer, D., Cosmides, L., & Tooby, J. (2012). Who deserves help? Evolutionary psychology, social emotions, and public opinion about welfare. *Political Psychology, 33*(3), 395–418.

Pinker, S. (1997). *How the mind works*. W. W. Norton.

Pinker, S. (2010). The cognitive niche: Coevolution of intelligence, sociality, and language. *Proceedings of the National Academy of Sciences, 107*(Suppl 2), 8993–8999.

Pratto, F., Sidanius, J., Stallworth, L., & Malle, B. (1994). Social dominance orientation: A personality variable predicting social and political attitudes. *Journal of Personality and Social Psychology, 67*(4), 741–763.

Ray, S. (2018). Ethnic inequality and national pride. *Political Psychology, 39,* 263–280. doi: 10.1111/pops.12406

Rozin, P., & Falon, A. E. (1987). A perspective on disgust. *Psychological Review, 94*(1), 23–41.

Schachter, D., Gilbert, D., Wegner, D., & Hood, B. (2020). *Psychology* (3rd European ed.). Red Globe Press.

Schaller, M. (2015). The behavioral immune system. In D.M. Buss (Ed.), *Handbook of evolutionary psychology* (2nd ed., pp. 206–224). Wiley.

Seeberg, H. B. (2017). How stable is political parties' issue ownership? A cross-time, cross-national analysis. *Political Studies, 65*(2), 475–492. https://doi.org/10.1177/0032321716650224

Sell, A. N. (2011). The recalibrational theory and violent anger. *Aggression and Violent Behavior, 16*(5), 381–389.

Sell, A., Sznycer, D., Al-Shawaf, L., Lim, J., Krauss, A., Feldman, A., Rascanu, R., Sugiyama, L., Cosmides, L., & Tooby, J. (2017). The grammar of anger: Mapping the computational architecture of a recalibrational emotion. *Cognition, 168,* 110–128.

Sell, A., Tooby, J., & Cosmides, L. (2009). Formidability and the logic of human anger. *Proceedings of the National Academy of Sciences, 106*(35), 15073–15078.

Sibley, C. G., & Duckitt, J. (2008). Personality and prejudice: A meta-analysis and theoretical review. *Personality and Social Psychology Review, 12*(3), 248–279.

Slovic, P. (1985, January 30). Only new laws will spur seat-belt use [Editorial]. *Wall Street Journal.* http://hdl.handle.net/1794/22517

Smith, A., Pedersen, E. J., Forster, D. E., McCullough, M. E., & Lieberman, D. (2017). Cooperation: The roles of interpersonal value and gratitude. *Evolution and Human Behavior, 38*(6), 695–703.

Smith, R. H., & Kim, S. H. (2007). Comprehending envy. *Psychological Bulletin, 133*(1), 46–64.

Solt, F. (2011). Diversionary nationalism: Economic inequality and the formation of national pride. *The Journal of Politics, 73*(3), 821–830.

Sperber, D., Clément, F., Heintz, C., Mascaro, O., Mercier, H., Origgi, G., & Wilson, D. (2010). Epistemic vigilance. *Mind & Language, 25,* 359–393. http://dx.doi.org/10.1111/j.1468-0017.2010.01394.x

Sznycer, D. (2019). Forms and functions of the self-conscious emotions. *Trends in Cognitive Sciences, 23*(2), 143–157.

Sznycer, D., Al-Shawaf, L., Bereby-Meyer, Y., Curry, O. S., De Smet, D., Ermer, E., Kim, S., Kim, S., Li, N. P., Lopez Seal, M. F., McClung, J., O, J., Ohtsubo, Y., Quillien, T., Schaub, M., Sell, A., van Leeuwen, F., Cosmides, L., & Tooby, J. (2017). Cross-cultural regularities in the cognitive architecture of pride. *Proceedings of the National Academy of Sciences, 114*(8), 1874–1879.

Sznycer, D., Lopez Seal, M. F., Sell, A., Lim, J., Porat, R., Shalvi, S., Halperin, E., Cosmides, L., & Tooby, J. (2017). Support for redistribution is shaped by compassion, envy, and self-interest, but not a taste for fairness. *Proceedings of the National Academy of Sciences, 114*(31), 8420–8425.

Sznycer, D., Tooby, J., Cosmides, L., Porat, R., Shalvi, S., & Halperin, E. (2016). Shame closely tracks the threat of devaluation by others, even across cultures. *Proceedings of the National Academy of Sciences, 113*(10), 2625–2630.

Sznycer, D., Xygalatas, D., Agey, E., Alami, S., An, X. F., Ananyeva, K. I., Atkinson, Q. D., Broitman, B. R., Conte, T. J., Flores, C., Fukushima, S., Hitokoto, H., Kharitonov, A. N., Onyishi, C. N., Onyishi, I. E., Romero, P. P., Schrock, J. M., Snodgrass, J. J., Sugiyama, L. S., Takemura, K., . . . Tooby, J. (2018). Cross-cultural invariances in the architecture of shame. *Proceedings of the National Academy of Sciences, 115*(39), 9702–9707.

Sznycer, D., Xygalatas, D., Alami, S., An, X. F., Ananyeva, K. I., Fukushima, S., Hitokoto, H., Kharitonov, A. N., Koster, J. M., Onyishi, C. N., Onyishi, I. E., Romero, P. P., Takemura, K., Zhuang, J. Y., Cosmides, L., & Tooby, J. (2018). Invariances in the architecture of pride across small-scale societies. *Proceedings of the National Academy of Sciences, 115*(33), 8322–8327.

Tannenbaum, M. B., Hepler, J., Zimmerman, R. S., Saul, L., Jacobs, S., Wilson, K., & Albarracín, D. (2015). Appealing to fear: A meta-analysis of fear appeal effectiveness and theories. *Psychological Bulletin, 141*(6), 1178–1204.

Terrizzi, J. A., Jr., Shook, N. J., & McDaniel, M. A. (2013). The behavioral immune system and social conservatism: A meta-analysis. *Evolution and Human Behavior, 34*(2), 99–108.

Thomas, K., DeScioli, P., Haque, O., & Pinker, S. (2014). The psychology of coordination and common knowledge. *Journal of Personality and Social Psychology, 107*(4), 657–676.

Tooby, J., & Cosmides, L. (1990). The past explains the present: Emotional adaptations and the structure of ancestral environments. *Ethology and Sociobiology, 11*(4), 375–424.

Tooby, J., & Cosmides, L. (2008). The evolutionary psychology of the emotions and their relationship to internal regulatory variables. In M. Lewis, J. M. Haviland-Jones, & L. F. Barrett (Eds.), *Handbook of emotions* (3rd ed., pp. 114–137). Guilford.

Tooby, J. & Cosmides, L. (2015). The theoretical foundations of evolutionary psychology. In D. M. Buss (Ed.), *The handbook of evolutionary psychology*, Vol. 1: *Foundations* (2nd ed., pp. 3–87). Wiley.

Tooby, J., Cosmides, L., Sell, A., Lieberman, D., & Sznycer, D. (2008). Internal regulatory variables and the design of human motivation: A computational and evolutionary approach. In A. Elliot (Ed.), *Handbook of approach and avoidance motivation* (pp. 251–271). Lawrence Erlbaum Associates.

Tooby J., & DeVore, I. (1987). The reconstruction of hominid behavioral evolution through strategic modeling. In W. Kinzey (Ed.), *Primate models of hominid behavior* (pp. 183–237). State University of New York Press.

Tybur, J. M., Inbar, Y., Aarøe, L., Barclay, P., Barlow, F. K., de Barra, M., Becker, D. V., Borovoi, L., Choi, I., Choi, J. A., Consedine, N. S., Conway, A., Conway, J. R., Conway, P., Adoric, V. C., Demirci, D. E., Fernández, A. M., Ferreira, D. C., Ishii, K., Jakšić, I., . . . Žeželj, I. (2016). Parasite stress and pathogen avoidance relate to distinct dimensions of political ideology across 30 nations. *Proceedings of the National Academy of Sciences, 113*, 12408–12413. doi: 10.1073/pnas.1607398113

Tybur, J. M., Inbar, Y., Güler, E., & Molho, C. (2015). Is the relationship between pathogen avoidance and ideological conservatism explained by sexual strategies? *Evolution and Human Behavior, 36*(6), 489–497.

Tybur, J. M., & Lieberman, D. (2016). Human pathogen avoidance adaptations. *Current Opinion in Psychology, 7*, 6–11.

Tybur, J. M., Lieberman, D., & Griskevicius, V. (2009). Microbes, mating, and morality: Individual differences in three functional domains of disgust. *Journal of Personality and Social Psychology, 97*(1), 103–122.

Tybur, J., Lieberman, D., Kurzban, R., & DeScioli, P. (2013). Disgust: Evolved function and structure. *Psychological Review, 120*(1), 65–84.

Valentino, N. A., Brader, T., Groenendyk, E. W., Gregorowicz, K., & Hutchings, V. L. (2011). Election night's alright for fighting: The role of emotions in political participation. *The Journal of Politics, 73*(1), 156–170.

Vollhardt, J. R., Okuyan, M., & Ünal, H. (2020). Resistance to collective victimization and oppression. *Current Opinion in Psychology, 35*, 92–97.

CHAPTER 32

A Socio-functional Perspective on Emotion and Cooperation

Diego Guevara Beltran, Michelle N. Shiota, and Athena Aktipis

Abstract

Humans sociality is inextricably linked to cooperation. The human life history required cooperation in the form of pair-bonding, alloparenting, intergenerational transfers of calories, and extensive food sharing among kin and non-kin. Cooperating to achieve mutual goals often led to better outcomes compared to uncoordinated individual efforts. However, avoiding exploitation was critical to managing the challenges of sociality. Building on a socio-functional perspective, this chapter summarizes evidence showcasing the role that emotion plays in guiding *proximate* mechanisms that facilitate cooperation or hinder competition through their effect on partner choice and relationship management. The authors further organize these emotions (e.g., compassion, sadness, gratitude, anger, shame, guilt) by their proposed interpersonal *ultimate* functions based on the ways in which they promote cooperation via (1) distinguishing high-value from low-value partners; (2) building and maintaining lasting cooperative relationships with valuable partners; and (3) identifying when to de-invest from or terminate existing relationships.

Key Words: social emotion, interpersonal function, fitness interdependence, cooperation, evolution

Among human ancestors, cooperating to achieve mutual goals often led to better outcomes compared to individual efforts. While cooperation can be advantageous, cooperation also invites opportunities for exploitation. Throughout evolutionary history, humans have had to manage the challenges of sociality in order to enjoy the benefits. Ancestral humans had to cooperate with partners who were both willing and capable of generating benefits; avoid incapable or cost-inflicting partners; maintain long-lasting cooperative relationships; and decide when to terminate existing relationships.

We begin this chapter by summarizing theory and research on the human adaptive complex—the distinctly human collection of evolved physiological and behavioral traits linking life-span developmental trajectory, dietary needs, complex social living, and extensive cooperation with both kin and non-kin. We then discuss how emotions can function as social valuation regulatory mechanisms. Within this framework, emotions are thought to play an important role in guiding cooperative decisions, helping humans form and maintain strong interdependent relationships while managing the potential threats of social partners' cheating and/or defection. We then review the rich body of evidence about specific ways that emotions can support humans in building new positively interdependent relationships; investing in the maintenance of existing positively interdependent relationships; and terminating negatively interdependent or non-beneficial relationships. Table 32.1 shows a summary of the social emotions covered in this chapter, and their effects on relational valuation and cooperation, organized by their proposed interpersonal function.

Sources of Fitness Interdependence: The Human Adaptive Complex

Humans are highly interdependent organisms, relying on one another for survival and reproduction (Aktipis et al. 2018). Compared to nonhuman primates, humans reach reproductive maturity later, with far longer juvenile periods. During this juvenile period, children are dependent on others to subsidize their energy needs (Kaplan et al., 2000; Kaplan et al., 2007). In contrast, with the acquisition of knowledge and specialized skills, human adults eventually produce more calories than they consume, creating energy surpluses that are invested in juveniles.

The demands associated with the long period of juvenile dependency are managed in large part through cooperative resource provisioning and caregiving. Food production among hunter-gatherers is characterized by a division of labor by sex, with men primarily investing in hunting (and provisioning excess calories), and women primarily investing in gathering and high-quality childcare (Kaplan et al., 2000; Kaplan et al., 2007). Humans also engage in highly cooperative breeding, with juveniles receiving care from adults other than their mother, as well as older juveniles (Hrdy, 2007; Kramer, 2011), especially under harsher environments (Martin et al. 2020). Humans have remarkably long life spans as well, spending over one-third of their lives in the post-reproductive stage—a period in which they can continue to provide surplus food and caregiving support (Kaplan et al., 2000).

This unique human life history is thought to be an adaptation to the distinct ecological feeding niche exploited by humans (Del Giudice et al., 2016; Kaplan et al., 2000; Kaplan et al., 2007). The human diet consists of skill-intensive, nutrient-rich foods that demand extensive cooperation between kin and non-kin to forage effectively. On average, the hunter-gatherer diet consists of 60% hunted foods, 32% difficult to extract foods (e.g., food that is underground, or with hard shells), and only 8% easily collected foods (e.g., fruit) (Kaplan et al., 2000). A consequence of relying on nutrient-rich foods, such as large animals, is that the return rate is highly variable. For example, Hill and Hurtado (2009) observed that hunters can expect to be successful as little as 4% or as much as 60% of the time, depending on the ecology. In addition, illness and injuries often prevent individuals from foraging altogether.

A solution to this problem, observed across all hunter-gatherer groups, is to engage in cooperative food-sharing (Cronk et al., 2019). Food-sharing reduces variance in daily consumption, subsidizing caloric needs when one is sick, injured, or just unlucky (Kaplan et al., 2000). For example, Ache hunter-gatherers who share can consume up to 80% more calories than those who do not share (Kaplan et al., 1985; Kaplan & Hill, 1985). Similarly, Ache men who share larger amounts of food, in proportion to what they produce, typically receive more food from others when they are sick or injured (Gurven et al., 2000). Thus, humans pool calories by transferring to group members surpluses from large-game hunting and acquisition of other nutrient-rich foods—tasks that are themselves most effectively accomplished through cooperative efforts.

In addition to pooling calories, cooperation allows humans to mitigate a variety of other risks to fitness, such as injuries, illness, loss of valuable partners or objects, and conflicts such as aggression and exploitation. Among Tsimane horticulturalists, for example, people who experience these problems report receiving help in the form of food, medicine, money, or childcare—primarily from kin and spouses, although non-kin are also valuable sources of

Table 32.1 Summary of the Impact of Emotion on Partner Valuation and Cooperation

Interpersonal Function	Trigger	Emotion	Partner Valuation	Outcome (Direction)	Citation
Choosing partners to cooperate with	Distraught target	Compassion	Raises valuation assigned to target	Prisoner's Dilemma (+)	Batson & Moran, 1999; Batson & Ahmad, 2001; Rumble et al., 2009
				Dictator Game (+)	Edele et al., 2013
				Welfare Trade-off (+)	Sznycer et al., 2019
			Lowers valuation third-parties assign the self when empathizing with negative groups	Like & respect (−)	Wang & Todd, 2021
	Loss of valuable target, goal, or object	Sadness (loss aversion)	NA	Public & Common Good Game (+)	Polman & Kim, 2013
				Ultimatum Game (−)	Harlé & Sanfey, 2007
				Trust Game (mixed)	Kirchsteiger et al., 2006
		Sadness (elicit support)	Raises valuation others assign the self if they feel compassion	Negotiation (+)	Sinaceur & Tiedens, 2006
	Receiving larger than expected benefits	Gratitude	Raises valuation assigned to target	Give Some Dilemma (+)	DeSteno et al., 2010
				Dictator Game (+)	Tsang & Martin, 2019

			Pick up pencils (+) Allocate onerous tasks (−)	Behler et al., 2020
			Cheating (−)	DeSteno et al., 2019
			Dictator Game (+) Welfare Trade-off (+)	Smith et al., 2017
	Trivial social transgression	Embarrassment	Raises valuation others assign the self	Feinberg et al., 2012
	Information conveys capacity to provide/withhold benefits	Pride (status conferral)	Raises valuation others assign self	Wubben et al., 2012
			Donations (−)	Tracy et al., 2018
		Pride (inauthentic)	Lowers valuation others assign the self	Wubben et al., 2012
		Pride (goal pursuit)	NA	Dorfman et al., 2014
	Receiving lower than expected benefits	Anger (self expects amends)	Raises valuation others assign the self	Polman & Kim, 2013
			Ultimatum Game (−)	Fabiansson & Denson, 2012

(continued)

Table 32.1 Continued

Interpersonal Function	Trigger	Emotion	Partner Valuation	Outcome (Direction)	Citation
	Delivering lower than expected benefits	Target conveys anger (self makes amends)	Raises valuation assigned to target	Negotiation (+)	Sinaceur & Tiedens, 2006
				Ultimatum Game (+)	van Dijk et al., 2008
	Target has something of value that one lacks	Envy	Lowers valuation assigned to target	Prisoner's Dilemma (−)	Parks et al., 2002
	Receiving poorer treatment than target			Betting Game (−)	Zizzo & Oswald, 2001
				Pick up pencils (−) Allocate onerous tasks (+)	Behler et al., 2020
				Meta-analysis of trait envy & social dilemmas (−)	Thielmann et al., 2020
	Moral transgression	Disgust	Lowers valuation assigned to target	Ultimatum Game (−)	Chapman et al., 2009
				Ultimatum Game (−)	Moretti & di Pellegrino, 2010
				Damage reputation & avoidance (+)	Molho et al., 2017
				Prejudice (+)	Dasgupta et al., 2009

Building and maintaining cooperative relationships	Sharing positive information	Positive empathy	Raises valuation assigned to target	Dehumanization (+)	Buckels & Trapnell, 2013
				Connectedness (+)	Morelli et al., 2015
				Relationship dissatisfaction & dissolution (−)	Gable et al., 2004; 2006; Otto et al., 2015
	Receiving benefits from interdependent target	Gratitude	Raises valuation assigned to target	Closeness & belongingness (+)	Algoe et al., 2008
				Shared fate (+)	Lambert et al., 2010
	Delivering lower than expected benefits to interdependent target	Guilt (self makes mends)	Repairs losses of valuation others assign the self	Intention to cooperate (+)	Robertson et al., 2014
				Prisoner's Dilemma & Ultimatum Game (+)	Ketelaar & Tung Au, 2003
				Give Some Dilemma (+)	de Hooge et al., 2007; Nelissen et al., 2007
				Meta-analysis of guilt-proneness in social dilemmas (+)	Thielmann et al., 2020
	Receiving lower than expected benefits from interdependent target	Target conveys guilt (self expects amends)	Repairs losses of valuation assigned to target	Negotiation (−)	Van Kleef et al., 2006

(*continued*)

Table 32.1 Continued

Interpersonal Function	Trigger	Emotion	Partner Valuation	Outcome (Direction)	Citation
	Information conveys incompetency Nontrivial social transgression	Shame	Attenuates losses of valuation others assign the self	Give Some Dilemma (+)	de Hooge et al., 2008
	Receiving lower than expected benefits from interdependent target	Anger (self expects amends)	Raises valuation target assigns the self	Aggression & reconciliation (+)	Fischer & Roseman, 2007
				Remind of interdependence (+)	Robertson et al., 2014
				Public Goods Game (+)	Fehr & Fischbacher, 2004; Fehr & Gächter, 2002; Gächter et al., 2008
				Ultimatum Game (−)	Henrich et al., 2006; Pillutla & Murnighan, 1996; Van Kleef et al., 2008
				Negotiation (−)	Ramirez-Fernandez et al. 2018
	Delivering lower than expected benefits to interdependent target	Target conveys anger (self makes amends)	Raises valuation assigned to target	Negotiation (+)	Lelieveld et al. 2011

Terminating costly relationships	Chronically receiving lower than expected benefits	Anger	Target fails to recalibrate valuation towards self	Work effort (−) Intention to quit job (+)	Kiefer, 2005
				Relationship satisfaction (−) Aggression (+)	Guerrero et al., 2008
		Sadness	Target fails to recalibrate valuation towards self	Avoidance (+) Relationship satisfaction (−)	Guerrero et al., 2008
				Relationship satisfaction (−) Relationship dissolution (+)	Røsand et al., 2014; Sweeney & Horwitz, 2001
	Chronically receiving lower than expected benefits Information conveys target is incompetent	Contempt	Long-lasting loss of valuation towards target	Reconciliation (−) Derogation (+) Exclusion (+)	Fischer & Roseman, 2007
				Relationship satisfaction (−) Relationship dissolution (+)	Gottman et al., 1998

Note: Except when specified (i.e., "Target conveys anger," and "Target conveys guilt"), emotion always refers to the self experiencing/conveying the emotion, process, or sentiment.

support (Gurven et al., 2012). Beyond food-sharing, other forms of risk-pooling have also been observed across all types of subsistence groups. For example, Maasai herders transfer livestock to risk-pooling partners after droughts; Fijian fisher-horticulturalists provide aid after cyclones; and ranchers in the American Southwest help neighboring ranchers in response to unforeseeable labor challenges (Cronk et al., 2019). Whether it's in terms of calories, childcare, or labor, risk-pooling over time makes social partners intrinsically valuable, because partners share a stake in each other's fates (Aktipis et al., 2018; Ayers et al., 2023; Balliet et al., 2017; Roberts, 2005).

While they are crucial elements of the human adaptive complex, the cooperative behaviors above inherently involve social dilemmas, each with multiple potential solutions in which the best outcome for the *individual* is sometimes at odds with the most *mutually* beneficial outcome. One example involves the trade-off between investment in current offspring versus future reproduction (Del Giudice et al., 2016). The extended juvenile period during which children are calorically dependent requires heavy biparental investment. However, men may have the opportunity to increase their fitness by acquiring multiple mates (Courtiol et al., 2012), which can result in reduced investment in existing offspring and thereby imposes a cost on the mothers' fitness. Thus, men can increase their fitness by defecting on universally recognized rules of pair-bonded biparental investment (i.e., marriage).

Another example is in the domain of food-sharing. Hunting is risky, energetically costly, and presents opportunity costs (Kaplan et al., 2000). One could potentially maximize individual gains by exploiting others' generosity or defecting from the risk-sharing contract—if one can do so without suffering penalties. For example, experimental studies show that people are more likely to act greedy (i.e., request help when not in need), and stingy (i.e., refuse helping even when able to) when resources can be hidden, because people cannot know whether risk-pooling partners are faking need or are genuinely unable to help (Claessens et al., 2020).

Because the potential for "free-riding" invariably arises in cooperative relationships, humans have evolved cheater-detection mechanisms that help identify and sanction those who violate the rules of cooperation (Cosmides et al., 2010). While cheater-detection mechanisms are computationally complex, and punishing defectors can be individually costly, an alternative solution to the free-rider problem is to simply choose which partners to interact with (Noë & Hammerstein, 1994, 1995). Partner choice can involve selecting partners carefully, but also can simply be a matter of leaving uncooperative partners and groups (Aktipis 2004, 2011).

The need to differentiate high-quality cooperative partners from low-quality partners presented an important adaptive problem for ancestral humans. Individual variation in both ability and willingness to deliver benefits gave rise to biological markets for cooperators, in which high-quality individuals chose the best available partners, and individuals had to compete to be chosen by those with the most benefits to share (Barclay, 2016; Barclay & Willer, 2007). This competition for being chosen as a cooperative partner influenced our social evolution in myriad ways (Nesse, 2007). Humans who possessed psychological mechanisms that allowed them to both show that they were good partners and ascertain whether others were good partners would have an evolutionary advantage over those who didn't (Tooby & Cosmides 1996). This shaped selection pressures for the ability to identify high-quality prospective partners, sustain lasting, positive fitness-interdependent relationships, and decide when to de-invest from or terminate relationships that were costly or no longer beneficial.

Emotions and the Problem of Cooperation: Theoretical Perspectives

If the need to differentiate high- from low-quality cooperative partners presents an adaptive problem, what is the solution? Emotions may have evolved to help humans (and our mammalian and primate relatives) navigate this complex terrain (e.g., Fischer & Manstead, 2016; Keltner & Haidt, 1999; Shiota et al., 2004). Emotions can be defined as complex responses to recurring, fitness-relevant situations, consisting of cognitive, physiological, motivational, and nonverbal expressive elements that, taken together, tend to orchestrate a behavioral response that proved adaptive more often than not for us and our mammalian ancestors (Adolphs & Andler, 2018; Cosmides & Tooby, 2000; Ekman, 1992; Hommel et al., 2017; Keltner & Gross, 1999; Tracy, 2014).

Twentieth-century research on emotions typically emphasized intrapersonal adaptive functions, in which emotionally motivated behavior directly enhances the organism's fitness. For example, fear can help an organism escape from a predator (Cosmides & Tooby, 2000; Ohman & Mineka, 2001); and emotions surrounding hunger, such as appetitive enthusiasm, support the organism's actions to acquire food (Levenson, 1999). In contrast, 21st-century research has more strongly emphasized interpersonal or social adaptive functions, in which emotions facilitate relationships with other conspecifics, with the relationships serving as the fitness-enhancing factor (Fischer & Manstead, 2008; Keltner et al., 2006; Keltner & Haidt, 1999). In the following sections we highlight examples of social/interpersonal functions, paying special attention to the proximal roles that emotional responses can play in supporting cooperative behavior.

Emotions as Valuation Regulatory Mechanisms

While most emotional responses likely include some elements that influence individual fitness by way of relationships with others, the "social emotions" are thought to have evolved specifically to solve distinct adaptive problems inherent in complex, cooperative social living. Social emotions are thought to track relationship partners' actual and probable impact on one's own fitness; to assign relational value to each partner corresponding to their expected fitness impact; and to update valuations based on partners' contributions to one's welfare (Al-Shawaf et al., 2016; Sznycer & Lukaszewski, 2019; Tooby et al., 2008). Expected fitness implications are evaluated in terms of conspecifics' attributes (e.g., skill) and behavior (e.g., sharing). All else being equal, one should assign higher value to conspecifics who possess benefit-generating attributes in relevant domains, such as skill in acquiring food. However, relationship partners with greater ability to generate benefits may also have greater ability to impose costs (e.g., strength), and partners who impose costs are assigned lower relational value. Thus, valuation is also calibrated by partners' *willingness* to deliver benefits and, to some extent, willingness to make sacrifices to avoid imposing costs.

Within this framework, social emotions serve a dual signaling function. First, emotions convey that one has the capacity to deliver or withhold benefits. For example, pride advertises one's status-elevating attributes and access to valuable resources. Second, emotions such as gratitude draw our attention to potential partners who appear willing to deliver benefits. Because pride can convey the ability to generate benefits, displays of pride can potentially influence others to value you more highly. Gratitude is thought to track others' willingness to sacrifice, and therefore elevates the valuation that the self assigns to benefactors (Sznycer & Lukaszewski, 2019).

How Social Emotions Guide Cooperative Behavior

We begin this section by briefly describing how emotional expressivity supports cooperative action and allows people to differentiate cooperators from non-cooperators. The examples of cooperation that will follow include giving (i.e., unidirectional transfers of resources); direct, indirect, and generalized forms of reciprocity (i.e., bidirectional and third-party transfers of resources); negotiation (i.e., bidirectional demands and concessions of resources); punishment (i.e., unidirectional and third-party reductions in another's resources); as well as avoidance and exclusion (i.e., preventing others from gaining access to resources). We recognize that these examples reflect distinct ways in which people engage in and manage resources and resource transfers. However, we make use of the term *cooperation* throughout this chapter in reference to any one of the examples described above, with the unifying framework that these various types of cooperation are *proximately* guided by distinct emotional responses in the service of three basic *ultimate* interpersonal functions: promoting cooperation toward valuable partners, and defection toward low-value partners; shaping existing interdependent relationships to promote commitment to long-term cooperation; and allowing people to recognize when to de-invest from or terminate existing relationships. Wherever appropriate, we highlight the dual roles of emotions in conveying information regarding relational value: first, by conveying information to the self about a target's relational value; and second, by conveying one's own relational value to targets.

With Whom Should I Cooperate? Emotions' Role in Choosing Cooperative Partners
EMOTIONAL EXPRESSIVITY

Among mammals, nonverbal expressions of emotion generally help to coordinate behavior across individuals. For example, fear vocalizations communicate the presence of danger to other group members (e.g., Anderson et al. 2018), and crying evokes others' intent to provide support (e.g., Zickfeld et al., 2021). Laughter is particularly contagious, and shared amused laughter in particular has been found to promote cooperative behavior (Gervais & Wilson, 2005).

Emotional expressivity plays an important role in helping people distinguish likely cooperators from cheaters. People rate targets who smile as more likable and trustworthy, and consequently expect smiling targets to be more cooperative (Krumhuber et al., 2007). Emotional expressivity promotes cooperation in part because people believe that those who act on emotion, compared to people who act on reason, are more likely to make cooperative choices based on pro-social emotions such as guilt and empathy (Levine et al., 2018). This expectation is not unfounded. For example, cooperators tend to express more positive emotion prior to making fair offers; and more negative emotion after receiving unfair offers (Kaltwasser et al., 2017; Schug et al., 2010).

Although people can often distinguish real from feigned cooperative cues, such as smiles (Gunnery & Ruben, 2016) and laughter (Bryant & Aktipis, 2014; Bryant et al., 2018), these cues can be faked (Gunnery et al., 2013), and therefore have the potential to be false signals. For example, Danvers and Shiota (2018) found that partners who displayed dynamically engaged smiles—smiling that occurs in response to a partner's smiling—tended to evoke higher rates of partner cooperation in a subsequent prisoner's dilemma task, even though dynamically engaged smiles did not significantly predict one's own cooperative behavior. This suggests that smiling may sometimes be a manipulative cue rather than an honest signal of cooperative intent.

COMPASSION AND EMPATHY

Goetz and colleagues (2010) propose that states such as sympathy, pity, and empathy belong to a cluster of compassion-related states whose primary motivational and behavioral output is alleviating the distress of a target in need. People are more likely to experience empathy for kin and close others (de Waal & Preston, 2017; Preston & de Waal, 2002), but often experience empathy toward strangers as well (Depow et al., 2021; McAuliffe et al., 2018).

Compassionate states motivate people to alleviate a target's distress, expending energy on in-the-moment cooperation. For example, trait affective empathy (i.e., feeling emotion in response to a target's emotions, as distinct from simply recognizing them) is associated with greater generosity (Edele et al., 2013). Inducing empathic concern increases cooperation in the prisoner's dilemma as well (Batson & Moran, 1999), even after learning that partners had previously defected (Batson & Ahmad, 2001), and sometimes even when partners defect more than once (Rumble et al., 2009).

Empathy is often manipulated by asking participants to take the emotional (i.e., affective) perspective of a distraught target. A meta-analysis on the effect of perspective-taking on empathy finds that people report similar levels of concern when they engage in affective perspective-taking and when no explicit instructions to empathize are given. In contrast, people report less concern when they engage in detached perspective-taking, relative to affective perspective-taking or no instructions to empathize. These findings suggest that empathic concern may be the default response to another's distress because taking a detached perspective dampens otherwise naturally emerging concern (McAuliffe et al., 2020).

Compassion-related states reflect and are modulated by our expectations regarding a target's potential value as a relationship partner. Another study found that participants who empathized with a target in need perceived the target as a valuable partner, and in turn were more inclined to help the distressed target when need was the only available cue. However, empathic concern did *not* motivate helping if participants were told that the distressed target did not value the participant highly. Thus, while empathic concern is activated by need, empathic concern seems to only motivate helping partners who also value you, and therefore have high future potential as cooperative partners (Sznycer et al., 2019).

Highly empathetic people are more likely to provide assistance to others in need, and may therefore be better equipped to recruit new cooperative partners. For example, empathic concern predicts willingness to help when people perceive low interependence in their relationships, but not when they perceive high interdependence with others, presumably as a means to build new cooperative relationships (Guevara Beltran, Shiota & Aktipis, 2023). Empathetic people also benefit from greater network centrality among groups of friends, if those friends rely heavily on trust and sharing negative experiences (Morelli et al., 2017).

However, being highly empathetic can come with costs as well. For example, people who empathize with antagonizing groups are *less* liked and respected than those who reject those groups (Wang & Todd, 2021). Thus, while there are relational benefits to feeling empathy, doing so indiscriminately can be costly. This suggests that selection pressures likely pulled for emotional systems that could modulate empathy strategically, suppressing or enhancing it depending on the context and the potential costs or benefits associated with it (Ferguson et al. 2020; Zaki 2014).

SADNESS

People often feel sad after losing a valued partner or being unable to achieve a goal (Keller & Nesse, 2006). Sadness elicits compassion from others, and therefore social support (Bonanno et al., 2008). Notably, expressions of sadness met by chronically unresponsive partners may lead people to feel sustained lower moods (e.g., depression; Guerrero et al., 2008). This can lead people to value unresponsive partners less, ultimately increasing the likelihood of relationship dissolution (see section "Recognizing When to De-invest or Dissolve Existing Relationships").

Sadness affects cooperation in experimental games. People in sad states are more likely to reject unfair offers in ultimatum games (Harlé & Sanfey, 2007), and to reciprocate (both positively and negatively) in trust games (Kirchsteiger et al., 2006). Sadness promotes cooperation especially when targets are empathetic. Dyads who engaged in a negotiation task in which one person was instructed to express sadness earned higher payoffs when the counterpart expressed other-oriented concern, and believed the opportunity for future cooperation was high (Sinaceur & Tiedens, 2006).

Sadness also tends to promote loss aversion (Andrews & Thomson, 2009). Sadness induces a cognitive state that enables people to analyze complex problems, allowing people to reflect on and understand the loss of valuable partners or goals (Andrews & Thomson, 2009). Loss aversion may, in turn, promote cooperative behavior. People in sad states make larger contributions to and take less from common pools. While yielding lower payoffs, taking too much or contributing too little could result in zero earnings. Presumably, sad participants make more conservative choices in order to ensure greater-than-zero payoffs (Polman & Kim, 2013).

GRATITUDE
People feel gratitude upon receiving a larger than expected benefit, and this feeling of gratitude makes people value the benefactor more (Sznycer & Lukaszewski, 2019). Gratitude is thought to be an important emotion in sustaining reciprocal altruism (Trivers, 1971)—a type of cooperation in which resource transfers flow back and forth in a tit-for-tat fashion. However, gratitude also promotes other types of cooperation that are not fully accounted for by reciprocal altruism. For example, Nowak and Roch (2007) argue that gratitude promotes indirect reciprocity—cooperation that occurs among three or more individuals, in which being the recipient of help motivates helping someone other than the benefactor. Employing agent-based modeling, they found that agents who engage in indirect reciprocity can outcompete cheaters over evolutionary time. Although Nowak and Roch (2007) did not directly model gratitude in their agent-based models, they argued that gratitude is a candidate proximate mechanism that allowed humans to sustain the evolution of indirect reciprocity.

Experimental work shows that gratitude toward a stranger motivates cooperation, even when individually costly, when the recipient is anonymous, when the target is dissimilar in moral values, and when the potential for future cooperation is low (DeSteno et al., 2010; Tsang & Martin, 2019). Gratitude also promotes pro-sociality and reduces antisociality. For example, in one study participants who were made to recall a time in which they felt gratitude subsequently helped a confederate more, and avoided assigning tasks that would have made it more difficult for the confederate to earn credits (Behler et al., 2020). Gratitude inhibits cheating as well. In one study, participants in a grateful state were less likely to lie about the result of a coin flip, even though lying would have allowed them to avoid an onerous task by having it assigned to another participant (DeSteno et al., 2019).

When people feel gratitude, they are more likely to assign higher valuation to those who gave to them, and to act more generously toward them in the future. In a cyberball game in which people could earn money by passing the ball to only one person (i.e., a "treasurer" who could pass the ball to multiple players), participants felt more gratitude when the treasurer excluded them from the first half of the game, but then passed the ball to participants in the second half. Presumably, participants who were excluded in the first half of the game perceived being included in the second half as an unexpected gesture of generosity. Participants who felt gratitude more strongly valued the treasurer more highly, and behaved more generously toward her (Smith et al., 2017).

EMBARRASSMENT

Showing embarrassment is thought to serve an appeasement function that leads to greater liking, trust, and overall greater affiliation (Feinberg et al., 2012; Keltner & Anderson, 2000). People experience embarrassment in response to trivial transgressions that are often humorous rather than derogating, and when the audience consists of distant rather than close others (Tangney et al., 1996). Embarrassment might signal cooperative intent. Feinberg and colleagues (2012) found that people who expressed stronger embarrassment tended to behave more generously. Moreover, people who express embarrassing stories are perceived as more pro-social (e.g., generous), and less antisocial (e.g., manipulative). Consequently, people are more trusting and cooperative toward targets who display high levels of embarrassment (Feinberg et al., 2012). Because people are more likely to experience embarrassment in the presence of distant rather than close others (Tangney et al., 1996), embarrassment might play a more prominent role earlier in relationships when people are signaling cooperative intent.

PRIDE

People feel authentic pride (i.e., pride that emerges from honest cues of capacity) when their ability to provide (or withhold) benefits from others is enhanced. Showing pride can elevate one's status, and prompt audiences to assign greater valuation toward the person exhibiting pride (Martens et al., 2012; Sznycer & Lukaszewski, 2019). Pride is thought to increase relational value through two routes. First, experiencing pride can motivate people to achieve relevant goals, increasing their ability to generate or withhold benefits in the future. Second, people who express pride are reliably perceived by others as possessing higher status (Martens et al., 2012; Sznycer & Lukaszewski, 2019).

Across several studies, participants who were shown targets displaying prototypical expressions of pride (i.e., raised chin, arms akimbo, expanded chest) were perceived to possess higher status than targets displaying no emotion (Shariff et al., 2012). Tracy et al. (2013) also found that both US undergraduates and Fijian villagers rate targets expressing nonverbal displays of pride as possessing higher status than targets expressing shame, happiness, or no affect. Thus, the nonverbal signals associated with feelings of pride are likely universally recognized. Similarly, people across industrialized countries and small-scale societies report that they would feel pride if others learned that they possess status-conferring attributes such as attractiveness and expertise (Sznycer, Al-Shawaf, et al., 2017; Sznycer, Xygalatas, Alami, et al., 2018; Durkee et al., 2019).

Because expressions of pride are reliably recognized as conveying skills, status, and expertise, pride expressions are expected to evoke cooperation from perceivers. Consistent with this idea, people are more likely to imitate those who convey nonverbal displays of genuine pride (Martens & Tracy, 2013). In another study, participants who received a pride-conveying message from their partner made more positive attributions about those partners (e.g., sympathetic), expected partners to take less from a common pool, and were themselves more cooperative (Wubben et al., 2012).

It appears that expression of pride can be perceived as a cue of cooperative intent. Perceived hubris, on the other hand, is associated with *lower* perceived cooperative intent. Hubris is defined as an inauthentic display of pride in that it does not emerge from honest cues of capacity. Because people anticipate less cooperation from hubristic partners, people who display inauthentic pride motivate defection from their partners (Wubben et al., 2012).

In addition, because expressions of pride signal greater ability to provide and withhold benefits, those expressions may also dampen perceived need. This may inhibit some forms of cooperation. A study examining donations toward start-ups in developing nations found that men who display pride in their profile pictures received less donations because they were perceived to be in less need than men who did not display pride (Tracy et al., 2018). Lastly, experiencing pride promotes goal attainment, and thus may promote cooperation when the goal to cooperate is salient (Martens et al., 2012). For example, participants who recalled a time when they felt pride agreed more strongly that cooperation was important, and were more cooperative in a common goods game (Dorfman et al., 2014).

ANGER

One proposed function of anger is to let others know they are not valuing you as highly as you expect them to. Thus, anger can be thought of as a tool for compelling others to raise the benefits they provide to you, and/or to reduce the costs they impose (Sell et al., 2017; Sznycer & Lukaszewski, 2019). In either case, anger tends to hinder in-the-moment cooperation. For example, in one study participants in an angry state took more money from, and contributed less to, a common resource pool (Polman & Kim, 2013). Similarly, people who feel anger after receiving negative feedback make smaller offers in ultimatum games (Fabiansson & Denson, 2012).

Although anger may inhibit cooperation by the person feeling the anger, anger displays may *evoke* cooperative behavior from others. People make larger concessions to negotiation partners who express anger, therefore taking smaller gains (Sinaceur & Tiedens, 2006). In a related experiment, participants who learned that their partner was angry made larger offers in ultimatum games. These studies show that people are sensitive to displays of anger, and make larger offers/concessions to avoid retaliation (van Dijk et al., 2008). Anger also plays an important role in relationship resolution, relationship dissolution, and third-party punishment, which we discuss in later sections.

ENVY

People feel envy toward those who receive better treatment, or have something of value that the envier lacks. Feelings of envy can sometimes motivate people to spitefully harm others—the opposite of generosity. Ultimately, envy enhances one's relative standing by promoting behaviors that reduce the target's welfare (Sznycer, Lopez Seal et al., 2017). Reducing another's welfare decreases their ability to generate or impose costs, consequently lowering the valuation that others may assign to targets; and by extension, improving the relative valuation that others may assign to the self.

Work from behavioral economics shows that people high in dispositional envy are more likely to defect in prisoners' dilemmas when they receive smaller endowments than others, even when receiving additional resources later that would objectively attenuate inequality (Parks et al., 2002). In a related experiment, participants received unequal endowments and could see others' cumulative earnings. At the end of the study, 62% of participants chose to spend a portion of their money to reduce others' earnings, spending an average of 48% of their own funds to decrease other participants' accounts. Notably, people most frequently paid to reduce the funds of the highest-earning player (Zizzo & Oswald, 2001).

Incidental envy also inhibits cooperation more generally. In one series of studies participants instructed to feel envy picked up fewer pencils to help a confederate; reported greater intentions to harm a confederate; and assigned more onerous tasks to a confederate, making it more difficult for the confederate to earn research credits (Behler et al., 2020). A meta-analysis linking personality variables and cooperation found that dispositional envy is among the most reliable negative predictors of cooperation across social dilemmas (Thielmann et al., 2020).

DISGUST

The model of disgust proposed by Tybur and colleagues (2013; Tybur & Lieberman, 2016), suggests that disgust serves three functions: pathogen avoidance, avoidance of fitness-jeopardizing mates, and coordinating disgust-evoking moral behavior. When people feel disgust, they value the targets of disgust less, and feel less positively interdependent towards them (Guevara Beltran, Whisner et al., 2023), in some cases hindering cooperation. In ultimatum games, participants are likely to experience disgust when receiving increasingly unfair offers (Chapman et al., 2009). People in experimentally evoked disgust states are also more likely to reject unfair offers in ultimatum games: participants who were shown disgust-inducing images (e.g., bodily waste) rejected 84% of unfair offers, whereas participants in sad and neutral states rejected 46% and 41% of unfair offers, respectively. In addition, participants made to feel disgust rated unfair offers as being more unfair, relative to participants in sad or neutral states (Moretti & di Pellegrino, 2010).

Beyond the effect of disgust on relational valuation, feeling disgust may also lead people to devalue other social groups. In some research, participants in a minimal group paradigm who were shown disgust-inducing images developed stronger prejudices toward out-groups, and disgust exacerbated existing prejudices against marginalized groups compared to the in-group (Dasgupta et al., 2009). In a related experiment, participants in an induced disgust state developed greater implicit dehumanization against out-groups relative to the in-group (Buckels & Trapnell, 2013).

Consistent with the view that disgust coordinates moral behavior, participants in one study who read vignettes of moral transgressions reported feeling angrier when they themselves were the victim, compared to when the victim was a third party. There was also suggestive evidence that people felt more disgust than anger when the victim was a third party. Lastly, while anger motivated willingness to engage in direct aggression (e.g., motivation to hit), disgust motivated willingness to engage in indirect aggression such as damaging the target's reputation, or ignoring the person (Molho et al., 2017).

Building and Maintaining Cooperative Relationships

Beyond the initial stage of selecting partners for cooperative effort, emotions play important roles in coordinating, navigating, and strengthening ongoing cooperative relationships. We discuss several specific mechanisms in this section.

COMPASSION, EMPATHY, AND CAPITALIZING ON POSITIVE EXPERIENCES

Experiencing compassion motivates pro-sociality, which may give rise to gratitude and thereby promote future cooperation. However, a suffering target can also motivate an empathizer's avoidance (Grynberg & López-Pérez, 2018; López-Pérez et al., 2014). Although empathy toward individuals who are displaying distress can sometimes lead to avoidance, positive empathy—the process of understanding and vicariously sharing others' positive emotions—can strengthen bonds (Morelli et al., 2015). Positive empathy is correlated with social connectedness (Morelli et al., 2015). In addition, sharing positive events strengthens close relationships above and beyond the effect of the event itself. Among couples, talking about positive events in one's life, especially when met by an enthusiastic partner, predicts greater relationship satisfaction and lower relationship dissolution (Gable et al. 2004; Gable et al. 2006; Otto et al. 2015).

GRATITUDE

As discussed earlier, gratitude promotes in-the-moment cooperation when people receive larger than expected benefits—often early in relationship initiation. Gratitude has bidirectional effects in developing relationships as well, helping to foster growing interdependence and strengthen bonds. In one study of a sorority initiation event, women reported feeling gratitude after receiving a series of gifts from more senior members. In turn, gratitude predicted greater closeness between junior and senior members, and a greater sense of community toward the sorority one month after the event (Algoe et al., 2008). In another study, participants instructed to recall a time in which they felt grateful toward a close other reported a greater sense of mutual responsibility for the target's welfare six weeks later (Lambert et al., 2010). Taken together, studies of the effects of gratitude on cooperation demonstrate that gratitude raises the valuation people place on benefactors, increases the probability of future cooperation, facilitates the formation of new relationships, and strengthens existing bonds.

GUILT

People experience guilt when they deliver lower than expected benefits to, or impose costs on, positively interdependent others. In response, guilt motivates people to make amends or repair losses of valuation (Sznycer & Lukaszewski, 2019). For example, people who were excluded because they were ostensibly caught free-riding reported more guilt than anger, and were willing to engage in greater cooperative behaviors to regain inclusion (Robertson et al., 2014). In iterated prisoner's dilemmas, people who were instructed to feel guilt acted more cooperatively if they had behaved uncooperatively during the first half of the study. In another study, people who made unfair offers in ultimatum games reported feeling guilt, and as hypothesized, this guilt predicted making more generous offers in the games one week later (Ketelaar & Tung Au, 2003).

The effect of guilt on cooperation appears to be moderated by a person's general tendency to cooperate. Pro-socials—people who seek to maximize joint outcomes—behave cooperatively whether or not they feel guilty. In contrast, pro-selfs—people who typically seek to maximize individual gains—are more cooperative only after remembering a time in which they felt guilt (Ketelaar & Tung Au, 2003). In another study, participants who recalled a previous time when they had felt guilt (e.g., breaking another's valuable objects) were more cooperative in a give some dilemma (i.e., giving to a common pool), but again the effects of guilt on cooperation were qualified by cooperative personality type. Whereas pro-socials were unaffected by the manipulation, guilt motivated pro-selfs to behave as cooperatively as pro-socials (de Hooge et al., 2007; Nelissen et al., 2007).

Guilt also promotes cooperation in negotiations. In a study where people performed a negotiation task, participants demanded larger concessions from partners who conveyed guilt (e.g., *I feel guilty for not having conceded more*; Van Kleef et al., 2006). These results highlight that people expect opponents who convey guilt to make amends. Lastly, a meta-analysis found that guilt-proneness was among the strongest trait-level predictors of cooperation across social dilemmas (Thielmann et al., 2020). In sum, guilt promotes cooperation because it allows people to amend wrongdoings in order to regain losses of valuation from interdependent others, thereby repairing existing valuable relationships.

SHAME

People typically feel shame if they have committed a transgression, such as violations of fairness, or show incompetence in a situation. Shame is activated in situations that might lead others to lower their valuation of you. In response, shame motivates withdrawal or avoidance to ameliorate or prevent further devaluation (Martens et al., 2012; Sznycer & Lukaszewski, 2019). People across subsistence groups report that they would feel the most shame if others learned that they possessed devaluing attributes such as being known as a thief (Durkee et al.,

2019; Sznycer et al., 2016; Sznycer, Xygalatas, Agey, et al., 2018). Notably, people feel shame when they expect others to devalue them, even when *no* transgressions have been committed. For example, people experienced shame when they were ostensibly excluded from a public goods game because of their presumed low contributions, even when their contributions were actually high (Robertson et al., 2018). Shame can also influence cooperation more directly. In two studies, pro-selfs, but not pro-socials, in an experimentally induced shame state were more cooperative in a give some dilemma (i.e., giving to a shared pool); in another study, participants who experienced shame after receiving feedback that they were of low intelligence were more cooperative in a give some dilemma (de Hooge et al., 2008).

ANGER

Although anger can hinder cooperation, people also recruit anger in service of re-balancing and resolving inequities in ongoing relationships. When one partner responds to a partner's anger appropriately, anger is diminished, allowing for reconciliation (Fischer & Giner-Sorolla, 2016). In negotiation tasks, participants who receive an anger-conveying message from partners make higher concessions in the following round, presumably in order to prevent further disagreement (Lelieveld et al. 2011). People expect more generous offers when negotiating with close friends than with acquaintances, and feel more anger when close friends, relative to acquaintances, make lower than expected offers. People who feel anger when receiving lower than expected offers from close friends are also less likely to accept such offers (Ramirez-Fernandez et al. 2018).

The function of increasing one's value to other relationship partners appears specific to anger, in contrast to other negative emotions. In recall studies, participants who remembered a time in which they felt anger reported less derogation and rejection, greater short-term verbal attacks, and higher reconciliation toward the target than those instructed to remember an experience of contempt. In addition, participants did not feel sustained anger after days (Fischer & Roseman, 2007). In another study, participants who were ostensibly excluded from a group because they posed a pathogen threat (a reason outside of their control) reported feeling more anger than guilt. Angrier participants were more likely to remind others of their existing interdependence to regain inclusion (Robertson et al., 2014).

Anger can deter others from taking advantage or exploiting you. People feel anger when others treat them unfairly, and consequently feel motivated to retaliate. In order for cooperation to be evolutionarily viable, individuals must be able to detect and deter free-riders (Cosmides et al. 2010; Fehr & Fischbacher 2004; Fehr & Gächter 2002). Across all types of subsistence groups, people punish unfair offers in ultimatum games (Henrich et al., 2006), and anger motivates third-party punishment in public goods tasks, even when it is individually costly (Fehr & Fischbacher, 2004; Fehr & Gächter, 2002). Those who punish are more generous in dictator games (Henrich et al., 2006), suggesting that punishment and generosity are mechanisms that go hand in hand in the long-term successful maintenance of cooperation. A review on the role of anger in ultimatum games shows that anger reliably predicts rejections of unfair offers (Van Kleef et al., 2008). Moreover, anger is actually a better predictor of rejecting unfair offers than the perceived unfairness of such offers (Pillutla & Murnighan, 1996).

Beyond in-the-moment effects, the threat of anger and punishment might also increase cooperation over the long term. Fehr and Gächter (2000) have demonstrated that people make more stable contributions in public goods tasks when others can punish. Moreover, third-party punishment results in higher collective earnings over longer periods of time, indicating that punishing free-riders, even though individually costly, is a viable strategy for sustaining long-term cooperation (Gächter et al., 2008).

A prevailing view is that altruistic punishment is the primary mechanism via which defection is deterred, and thus cooperation maintained in groups over time. However, recent investigations challenge this view. In a study investigating over 300 formal and customary court cases of a horticultural society in Papua New Guinea, third-party individuals readily served as witnesses to provide information in service of restorative retributions. Conflicts arose primarily as a result of marital, land, or assault allegations. More often than not, third-party witnesses provided crucial information that helped to solve cases such that the wrongdoer was made to make amends toward the victim, instead of excluding or imposing a nonrestorative punishment on the wrongdoer. In this alternative to punishment, third-party witnesses gain standing in their community, victims see direct reparations, and wrongdoers are able to regain inclusion in the community if they make amends (Wiessner, 2020). Thus, restorative justice provides an alternative avenue through which defection can be managed, and cooperation sustained over time. However, whether or how social emotions differ in this context compared to punishment needs to be evaluated in future studies.

Recognizing When to De-invest or Dissolve Existing Relationships

Time and energy are limited, and thus investments toward one partner are accompanied by opportunity costs, such as reduced ability to invest in new and potentially more rewarding relationships (Tooby & Cosmides, 1996). Leaving relationships can be a viable strategy whenever better alternatives are available (Aktipis 2004, 2011). Failing to recognize when partners no longer provide benefits (i.e., absence of interdependence), or failing to recognize when others impose greater costs than benefits (i.e., negative interdependence) would have resulted in significant losses of fitness for ancestral humans. Social emotions play important roles in helping us navigate relationship dissolution.

ANGER AND SADNESS

What are the consequences of failing to respond appropriately to a valued partner's anger, or expressions of sadness? Work from industrial psychology shows that anger leads to de-investment toward organizations. Specifically, poor working conditions (e.g., low respect, unfairness) elicit feelings of anger toward employers, and anger in turn predicts lower work-related effort and higher intentions to quit (Kiefer, 2005).

Anger and sadness are also associated with de-investment within the context of close relationships. Married couples report more anger and sadness when they feel like they are getting less from the relationship than they are investing in it. People in under-benefiting relationships are more likely to experience sadness that promotes avoidant behaviors (e.g., spending time alone) than sadness that elicits social support (e.g., discussing problems). Similarly, people in under-benefiting relationships are more likely to experience anger that motivates disruptive behavior (e.g., criticizing), rather than relationship resolution. In turn, both sadness and anger between couples in under-benefiting relationships predict greater relationship dissatisfaction (Guerrero et al., 2008).

Relationship dissatisfaction was the strongest predictor of relationship dissolution among a large sample of European adults ($N > 18,000$). Specifically, women who reported the most relationship dissatisfaction were 3.26 times more likely to report divorce or separation than women reporting low relationship dissatisfaction. Moreover, men and women with depressive symptoms were 40%–50% more likely to report relationship dissolution than people reporting no depressive symptoms (Røsand et al., 2014). In a related study, Sweeney and Horwitz (2001) find that 20%–25% of people who initiate divorce report depressive symptoms, compared to only 10% for people who do not initiate divorce. Functional accounts of depression propose that depression may lead to extensive rumination in order to allow people to arrive at the best solution to a complex problem (e.g., whether or not to divorce). An alternative functional account of depression is that it elicits support from people who have a stake in the depressed individual (e.g., a spouse; Hagen, 2011). Taken together, these studies highlight the role of sadness and anger as potential mediators between the perception of receiving lower than expected benefits over time (e.g., being in an under-benefiting relationship), to relationship dissatisfaction, and ultimately to relationship dissolution.

CONTEMPT

Contempt can be described as a sentiment consisting of basic emotions such as anger and disgust, as well as attitudes and cognitions toward specific people or groups (Fischer & Giner-Sorolla, 2016; Gervais & Fessler, 2017). People feel contempt when targets behave incompetently, or when targets are perceived to be incompetent, and therefore low in relational value. Consequently, contempt is accompanied by diminished pro-social emotions such as compassion, and motivates avoidance or exclusion rather than short-term aggression aimed at resolving the relationship (Fischer & Giner-Sorolla, 2016; Gervais & Fessler, 2017).

Experimental results support the idea that contempt tracks incompetency and low valuation. Participants who read vignettes of people behaving incompetently (e.g., a man tries to impress a woman by fixing her car, but makes it worse), or who were asked to recall a time in which another behaved incompetently, reported feeling more contempt than anger or disgust (Hutcherson & Gross, 2011). Participants also reported less motivation for reconciliation, more derogation, and greater rejection toward the target. In addition, people reported feeling sustained contempt after days, but not sustained anger. Because anger is thought to promote in-the-moment reparations, such as when people demand that others treat them more fairly, anger can promote reconciliation. In contrast, contempt is accompanied by a long-lasting devaluation of another and does not promote in-the-moment reparations. Thus, feeling sustained contempt indicates relationship dissolution rather than reparation (Fischer & Roseman, 2007). Contempt is also associated with relationship dissatisfaction and divorce. Married couples who made verbal and nonverbal displays of contempt during video-recorded interactions, accompanied by belligerence and defensiveness, were more likely to express relationship dissatisfaction and ultimately divorce compared to couples who did not show contempt (Gottman et al., 1998).

Although anger and sadness can be activated in service of relationship resolution, frequent, repeated feelings of these emotions toward a target may eventually lead to contempt. Repeated experiences of sadness in response to an interdependent partner's failure to provide support may translate into contempt for the partner. Similarly, repeated experiences of anger in response to an interdependent partner's failure to increase the benefits afforded toward the self may over time develop into feelings of contempt toward the partner. Unlike anger and sadness, which are typically short-lived, contempt is accompanied by long-lasting devaluation of the target (Fischer & Giner-Sorolla, 2016; Gervais & Fessler, 2017).

Conclusion

Drawing from the feeding-niche hypothesis (Kaplan et al., 2000), we have argued that the need to pool calories, and other sources of risks (Cronk et al., 2019), renders conspecifics intrinsically valuable because partners who pool risks share a stake in each other's fates (Aktipis et al., 2018; Roberts, 2005). In turn, fitness interdependence facilitates the extensive cooperative behavior that is characteristic of the human life history. Cooperation often yields greater collective benefits than uncoordinated individual efforts, but the temptation to defect can undermine these cooperative relationships, and changing landscapes of costs and benefits can lead previously beneficial relationships to become costly. To reap the benefits of cooperation while avoiding exploitation, ancestral humans had to exert careful partner choice, giving preference to partners who were both able and willing to deliver benefits; build and maintain long-lasting relationships with valuable partners, and de-invest from or terminate relationships that were no longer beneficial. The social emotions, which are theorized to track expected contributions of fitness others will impose on the self (Al-Shawaf et al., 2016; Sznycer & Lukaszewski, 2019; Tooby et al., 2008), guide cooperation in service of these basic interpersonal functions.

References

Adolphs, R., & Andler, D. (2018). Investigating emotions as functional states distinct from feelings. *Emotion Review*, *10*(3), 191–201.

Aktipis, A., Cronk, L., Alcock, J., Ayers, J. D., Baciu, C., Balliet, D., Boddy, A. M., Curry, O. S., Krems, J. A., Muñoz, A., Sullivan, D., Sznycer, D., Wilkinson, G. S., & Winfrey, P. (2018). Understanding cooperation through fitness interdependence. *Nature Human Behaviour*, *2*(7), 429–431.

Aktipis, C. A. (2004). Know when to walk away: Contingent movement and the evolution of cooperation. *Journal of Theoretical Biology*, *231*(2), 249–260.

Aktipis, C. A. (2011). Is cooperation viable in mobile organisms? Simple Walk Away rule favors the evolution of cooperation in groups. *Evolution and Human Behavior*, *32*(4), 263–276.

Algoe, S. B., Haidt, J., & Gable, S. L. (2008). Beyond reciprocity: Gratitude and relationships in everyday life. *Emotion*, *8*(3), 425–429.

Al-Shawaf, L., Conroy-Beam, D., Asao, K., & Buss, D. M. (2016). Human emotions: An evolutionary psychological perspective. *Emotion Review*, *8*(2), 173–186.

Anderson, C. L., Monroy, M., & Keltner, D. (2018). Emotion in the wilds of nature: The coherence and contagion of fear during threatening group-based outdoors experiences. *Emotion*, *18*(3), 355–368.

Andrews, P. W., & Thomson, J. A., Jr. (2009). The bright side of being blue: Depression as an adaptation for analyzing complex problems. *Psychological Review*, *116*(3), 620–654.

Ayers, J. D., Sznycer, D., Sullivan, D., Guevara Beltrán, D., van den Akker, O. R., Muñoz, A. E., Hruschka, D. J., Cronk, L., & Aktipis, A. (2022). Fitness interdependence as indexed by shared fate: Factor structure and validity of a new measure. *Evolutionary Behavioral Sciences*. https://doi.org/10.1037/ebs0000300.

Balliet, D., Tybur, J. M., & Van Lange, P. A. M. (2017). Functional Interdependence Theory: An evolutionary account of social situations. *Personality and Social Psychology Review*, *21*(4), 361–388.

Barclay, P. (2016). Biological markets and the effects of partner choice on cooperation and friendship. *Current Opinion in Psychology*, *7*, 33–38.

Barclay, P., & Willer, R. (2007). Partner choice creates competitive altruism in humans. *Proceedings of the Royal Society B: Biological Sciences*, *274*(1610), 749–753.

Batson, C. D., & Ahmad, N. (2001). Empathy-induced altruism in a prisoner's dilemma II: What if the target of empathy has defected? *European Journal of Social Psychology*, *31*(1), 25–36.

Batson, C. D., & Moran, T. (1999). Empathy-induced altruism in a prisoner's dilemma. *European Journal of Social Psychology*, *29*(7), 909–924.

Behler, A. M. C., Wall, C. S. J., Bos, A., & Green, J. D. (2020). To help or to harm? Assessing the impact of envy on prosocial and antisocial behaviors. *Personality and Social Psychology Bulletin*, *46*(7), 1156–1168.

Bonanno, G. A., Goorin, L., & Coifman, K. G. (2008). Sadness and grief. In Lewis, M., Haviland-Jones, J. M., & Barrett, L. F. (Ed.), *Handbook of emotions* (pp. 797–806). Guildford Press.

Bryant, G. A., & Aktipis, C. A. (2014). The animal nature of spontaneous human laughter. *Evolution and Human Behavior*, *35*(4), 327–335.

Bryant, G. A., Fessler, D. M. T., Fusaroli, R., Clint, E., Amir, D., Chávez, B., Denton, K. K., Díaz, C., Duran, L. T., Fančovićová, J., Fux, M., Ginting, E. F., Hasan, Y., Hu, A., Kamble, S. V., Kameda, T., Kuroda, K., Li, N. P., Luberti, F. R., . . . Zhou, Y. (2018). The perception of spontaneous and volitional laughter across 21 societies. *Psychological Science*, *29*(9), 1515–1525.

Buckels, E. E., & Trapnell, P. D. (2013). Disgust facilitates outgroup dehumanization. *Group Processes & Intergroup Relations: GPIR*, *16*(6), 771–780.

Chapman, H. A., Kim, D. A., Susskind, J. M., & Anderson, A. K. (2009). In bad taste: Evidence for the oral origins of moral disgust. *Science*, *323*(5918), 1222–1226.

Claessens, S., Ayers, J. D., Cronk, L., & Aktipis, A. (2020). Need-based transfer systems are more vulnerable to cheating when resources are hidden. *Evolution and Human Behavior, 42*(2), 104–112.

Cosmides, L., & Tooby, J. (2000). Evolutionary psychology and the emotions. In M. Lewis & J. M. Haviland-Jones (Eds.), *Handbook of emotions* (2nd ed., pp. 91–115). Guilford Press.

Cosmides, L., Barrett, H. C., & Tooby, J. (2010). Colloquium paper: Adaptive specializations, social exchange, and the evolution of human intelligence. *Proceedings of the National Academy of Sciences, 107*(Suppl 2), 9007–9014.

Courtiol, A., Pettay, J. E., Jokela, M., Rotkirch, A., & Lummaa, V. (2012). Natural and sexual selection in a monogamous historical human population. *Proceedings of the National Academy of Sciences, 109*(21), 8044–8049.

Cronk, L., Berbesque, C., Conte, T., Gervais, M., Iyer, P., McCarthy, B., Sonkoi, D., Townsend, C., & Aktipis, A. (2019). Managing risk through cooperation: Need-based transfers and risk pooling among the societies of the Human Generosity Project. In L. R. Lozny & T. H. McGovern (Eds.), *Global perspectives on long term community resource management* (pp. 41–75). Springer International.

Danvers, A. F., & Shiota, M. N. (2018). Dynamically engaged smiling predicts cooperation above and beyond average smiling levels. *Evolution and Human Behavior, 39*(1), 112–119.

Dasgupta, N., DeSteno, D., Williams, L. A., & Hunsinger, M. (2009). Fanning the flames of prejudice: The influence of specific incidental emotions on implicit prejudice. *Emotion, 9*(4), 585–591.

de Hooge, I. E., Breugelmans, S. M., & Zeelenberg, M. (2008). Not so ugly after all: When shame acts as a commitment device. *Journal of Personality and Social Psychology, 95*(4), 933–943.

de Hooge, I. E., Zeelenberg, M., & Breugelmans, S. M. (2007). Moral sentiments and cooperation: Differential influences of shame and guilt. *Cognition and Emotion, 21*(5), 1025–1042.

Del Giudice, M., Gangestad, S. W., & Kaplan, H. S. (2016). Life history theory and evolutionary psychology. In D. M. Buss (Ed.), *The handbook of evolutionary psychology*, Vol. 1: *Foundations* (pp. 88–114). Wiley & Sons.

Depow, G. J., Francis, Z., & Inzlicht, M. (2021). The Experience of Empathy in Everyday Life. *Psychological Science, 32*(8), 1198–1213. https://doi.org/10.31234/osf.io/hjuab

DeSteno, D., Bartlett, M. Y., Baumann, J., Williams, L. A., & Dickens, L. (2010). Gratitude as moral sentiment: Emotion-guided cooperation in economic exchange. *Emotion, 10*(2), 289–293.

DeSteno, D., Duong, F., Lim, D., & Kates, S. (2019). The grateful don't cheat: Gratitude as a fount of virtue. *Psychological Science, 30*(7), 979–988.

de Waal, F. B. M., & Preston, S. D. (2017). Mammalian empathy: Behavioural manifestations and neural basis. *Nature Reviews. Neuroscience, 18*(8), 498–509.

Dorfman, A., Eyal, T., & Bereby-Meyer, Y. (2014). Proud to cooperate: The consideration of pride promotes cooperation in a social dilemma. *Journal of Experimental Social Psychology, 55*, 105–109.

Durkee, P. K., Lukaszewski, A. W., & Buss, D. M. (2019). Pride and shame: Key components of a culturally universal status management system. *Evolution and Human Behavior, 40*(5), 470–478.

Edele, A., Dziobek, I., & Keller, M. (2013). Explaining altruistic sharing in the Dictator-Game: The role of affective empathy, cognitive empathy, and justice sensitivity. *Learning and Individual Differences, 24*, 96–102.

Ekman, P. (1992). An argument for basic emotions. *Cognition and Emotion, 6*(3–4), 169–200.

Fabiansson, E. C., & Denson, T. F. (2012). The effects of intrapersonal anger and its regulation in economic bargaining. *PloS One, 7*(12), e51595.

Fehr, E., & Fischbacher, U. (2004). Third-party punishment and social norms. *Evolution and Human Behavior, 25*(2), 63–87.

Fehr, E., & Gachter, S. (2000). Cooperation and punishment in public goods experiments. *The American Economic Review, 90*(4), 980–994.

Fehr, E., & Gächter, S. (2002). Altruistic punishment in humans. *Nature, 415*(6868), 137–140.

Feinberg, M., Willer, R., & Keltner, D. (2012). Flustered and faithful: Embarrassment as a signal of prosociality. *Journal of Personality and Social Psychology, 102*(1), 81–97.

Ferguson, A. M., Cameron, C. D., & Inzlicht, M. (2020). Motivational effects on empathic choices. *Journal of Experimental Social Psychology, 90*, 104010. https://doi.org/10.1016/j.jesp.2020.104010

Fischer, A., & Giner-Sorolla, R. (2016). Contempt: Derogating others while keeping calm. *Emotion Review, 8*(4), 346–357.

Fischer, A. H., & Manstead, A. S. R. (2008). Social functions of emotion. In M. Lewis, J. M. Haviland-Jones, & L. F. Barret (Eds.), *Handbook of emotions* (3rd ed., pp. 456–468). Guilford Press.

Fischer, A. H., & Manstead, A. S. (2016). Social functions of emotion and emotion regulation. In L. Feldman Barret, M. Lewis, & J. M. Haviland-Jones (Eds.), *Handbook of emotions* (4th ed., pp. 424–439). Guilford Press.

Fischer, A. H., & Roseman, I. J. (2007). Beat them or ban them: The characteristics and social functions of anger and contempt. *Journal of Personality and Social Psychology, 93*(1), 103–115.

Gable, S. L., Gonzaga, G. C., & Strachman, A. (2006). Will you be there for me when things go right? Supportive responses to positive event disclosures. *Journal of Personality and Social Psychology, 91*(5), 904–917.

Gable, S. L., Reis, H. T., Impett, E. A., & Asher, E. R. (2004). What do you do when things go right? The intrapersonal and interpersonal benefits of sharing positive events. *Journal of Personality and Social Psychology, 87*(2), 228–245.

Gächter, S., Renner, E., & Sefton, M. (2008). The long-run benefits of punishment. *Science, 322*(5907), 1510.

Gervais, M., & Wilson, D. S. (2005). The evolution and functions of laughter and humor: A synthetic approach. *The Quarterly Review of Biology, 80*(4), 395–430.

Gervais, M. M., & Fessler, D. M. T. (2017). On the deep structure of social affect: Attitudes, emotions, sentiments, and the case of "contempt." *The Behavioral and Brain Sciences, 40*, e225.

Goetz, J. L., Keltner, D., & Simon-Thomas, E. (2010). Compassion: An evolutionary analysis and empirical review. *Psychological Bulletin, 136*(3), 351–374.

Gottman, J. M., Coan, J., Carrere, S., & Swanson, C. (1998). Predicting marital happiness and stability from newlywed interactions. *Journal of Marriage and the Family, 60*(1), 5.

Grynberg, D., & López-Pérez, B. (2018). Facing others' misfortune: Personal distress mediates the association between maladaptive emotion regulation and social avoidance. *PloS ONE, 13*(3), e0194248.

Guerrero, L. K., La Valley, A. G., & Farinelli, L. (2008). The experience and expression of anger, guilt, and sadness in marriage: An equity theory explanation. *Journal of Social and Personal Relationships, 25*(5), 699–724.

Guevara Beltran, D., Shiota, M. N., & Aktipis, A. (2023). Empathic concern motivates willingness to help in the absence of interdependence. *Emotion* . https://doi.org/10.1037/emo0001288

Guevara Beltran, D., Whisner, C. M., Krems, J. A., Todd, P. M., & Aktipis, A. (2023). Food scarcity and disease concern reduce interdependence when people eat together. *European Journal of Social Psychology*. https://doi.org/10.1002/ejsp.2972

Gunnery, S. D., Hall, J. A., & Ruben, M. A. (2013). The deliberate Duchenne smile: Individual differences in expressive control. *Journal of Nonverbal Behavior, 37*(1), 29–41.

Gunnery, S. D., & Ruben, M. A. (2016). Perceptions of Duchenne and non-Duchenne smiles: A meta-analysis. *Cognition and Emotion, 30*(3), 501–515.

Gurven, M., Allen-Arave, W., Hill, K., & Hurtado, M. (2000). "It's a wonderful life": Signaling generosity among the Ache of Paraguay. *Evolution and Human Behavior, 21*(4), 263–282.

Gurven, M., Stieglitz, J., Hooper, P. L., Gomes, C., & Kaplan, H. (2012). From the womb to the tomb: The role of transfers in shaping the evolved human life history. *Experimental Gerontology, 47*(10), 807–813.

Hagen, E. H. (2011). Evolutionary theories of depression: A critical review. *Canadian Journal of Psychiatry / Revue Canadienne de Psychiatrie, 56*(12), 716–726.

Harlé, K. M., & Sanfey, A. G. (2007). Incidental sadness biases social economic decisions in the ultimatum-game. *Emotion, 7*(4), 876–881.

Henrich, J., McElreath, R., Barr, A., Ensminger, J., Barrett, C., Bolyanatz, A., Cardenas, J. C., Gurven, M., Gwako, E., Henrich, N., Lesorogol, C., Marlowe, F., Tracer, D., & Ziker, J. (2006). Costly punishment across human societies. *Science, 312*(5781), 1767–1770.

Hill, K., & Hurtado, A. M. (2009). Cooperative breeding in South American hunter-gatherers. *Proceedings of the Royal Society B: Biological Sciences, 276*(1674), 3863–3870.

Hommel, B., Moors, A., Sander, D., & Deonna, J. (2017). Emotion meets action: Towards an integration of research and theory. *Emotion Review, 9*(4), 295–298.

Hrdy, S. B. (2007). Evolutionary context of human development: The cooperative breeding model. In C. A. Salmon & T. K. Shackelford (Eds.), *Family relationships: An evolutionary perspective* (pp. 39–68). Oxford University Press.

Hutcherson, C. A., & Gross, J. J. (2011). The moral emotions: A social-functionalist account of anger, disgust, and contempt. *Journal of Personality and Social Psychology, 100*(4), 719–737.

Kaltwasser, L., Hildebrandt, A., Wilhelm, O., & Sommer, W. (2017). On the relationship of emotional abilities and prosocial behavior. *Evolution and Human Behavior, 38*(3), 298–308.

Kaplan, H., & Hill, K. (1985). Hunting ability and reproductive success among male Ache foragers: Preliminary results. *Current Anthropology, 26*(1), 131–133.

Kaplan, H., Hill, K., Cadeliña, R. V., Hayden, B., Hyndman, D. C., Preston, R. J., Smith, E. A., Stuart, D. E., & Yesner, D. R. (1985). Food sharing among Ache Foragers: Tests of explanatory hypotheses [and comments and reply]. *Current Anthropology, 26*(2), 223–246.

Kaplan, H., Hill, K., Lancaster, J., & Hurtado, A. M. (2000). A theory of human life history evolution: Diet, intelligence, and longevity. *Evolutionary Anthropology, 9*(4), 156–185.

Kaplan, H. S., Gurven, M., & Lancaster, J. B. (2007). Brain evolution and the human adaptive complex: An ecological and social theory. In S. W. Gangestad & J. A. Simpson (Eds.), *The evolution of mind: Fundamental questions and controversies* (pp. 259–269). Guilford Press.

Keller, M. C., & Nesse, R. M. (2006). The evolutionary significance of depressive symptoms: Different adverse situations lead to different depressive symptom patterns. *Journal of Personality and Social Psychology, 91*(2), 316–330.

Keltner, D., & Anderson, C. (2000). Saving face for Darwin: The functions and uses of embarrassment. *Current Directions in Psychological Science, 9*(6), 187–192.

Keltner, D., & Gross, J. J. (1999). Functional accounts of emotions. *Cognition and Emotion, 13*(5), 467–480.

Keltner, D., & Haidt, J. (1999). Social functions of emotions at four levels of analysis. *Cognition and Emotion, 13*(5), 505–521.

Keltner, D., Haidt, J., & Shiota, M. N. (2006). Social functionalism and the evolution of emotions. In M. Schaller (Ed.), *Evolution and social psychology* (Vol. 390, pp. 115–142). Psychosocial Press.

Ketelaar, T., & Tung Au, W. (2003). The effects of feelings of guilt on the behaviour of uncooperative individuals in repeated social bargaining games: An affect-as-information interpretation of the role of emotion in social interaction. *Cognition & Emotion, 17*(3), 429–453.

Kiefer, T. (2005). Feeling bad: Antecedents and consequences of negative emotions in ongoing change. *Journal of Organizational Behavior, 26*(8), 875–897.

Kirchsteiger, G., Rigotti, L., & Rustichini, A. (2006). Your morals might be your moods. *Journal of Economic Behavior & Organization, 59*(2), 155–172.

Kramer, K. L. (2011). The evolution of human parental care and recruitment of juvenile help. *Trends in Ecology & Evolution, 26*(10), 533–540.

Krumhuber, E., Manstead, A. S. R., Cosker, D., Marshall, D., Rosin, P. L., & Kappas, A. (2007). Facial dynamics as indicators of trustworthiness and cooperative behavior. *Emotion, 7*(4), 730–735.

Lambert, N. M., Clark, M. S., Durtschi, J., Fincham, F. D., & Graham, S. M. (2010). Benefits of expressing gratitude: Expressing gratitude to a partner changes one's view of the relationship. *Psychological Science, 21*(4), 574–580.

Lelieveld, G.-J., Van Dijk, E., Van Beest, I., Steinel, W., & Van Kleef, G. A. (2011). Disappointed in you, angry about your offer: Distinct negative emotions induce concessions via different mechanisms. *Journal of Experimental Social Psychology, 47*(3), 635–641.

Levenson, R. W. (1999). The intrapersonal functions of emotion. *Cognition and Emotion, 13*(5), 481–504.

Levine, E. E., Barasch, A., Rand, D., Berman, J. Z., & Small, D. A. (2018). Signaling emotion and reason in cooperation. *Journal of Experimental Psychology: General, 147*(5), 702–719.

López-Pérez, B., Carrera, P., Ambrona, T., & Oceja, L. (2014). Testing the qualitative differences between empathy and personal distress: Measuring core affect and self-orientation. *The Social Science Journal, 51*(4), 676–680.

Martens, J. P., & Tracy, J. L. (2013). The emotional origins of a social learning bias: Does the pride expression cue copying? *Social Psychological and Personality Science, 4*(4), 492–499.

Martens, J. P., Tracy, J. L., & Shariff, A. F. (2012). Status signals: Adaptive benefits of displaying and observing the nonverbal expressions of pride and shame. *Cognition & Emotion, 26*(3), 390–406.

Martin, J. S., Ringen, E. J., Duda, P., & Jaeggi, A. V. (2020). Harsh environments promote alloparental care across human societies. *Proceedings of the Royal Society B: Biological Sciences, 287*, 20200758. https://doi.org/10.1098/rspb.2020.0758

McAuliffe, W. H. B., Carter, E. C., Berhane, J., Snihur, A. C., & McCullough, M. E. (2020). Is empathy the default response to suffering? A meta-analytic evaluation of perspective taking's effect on empathic concern. *Personality and Social Psychology Review, 24*(2), 141–162.

McAuliffe, W. H. B., Forster, D. E., Philippe, J., & McCullough, M. E. (2018). Digital altruists: Resolving key questions about the empathy-altruism hypothesis in an internet sample. *Emotion, 18*(4), 493–506.

Molho, C., Tybur, J. M., Güler, E., Balliet, D., & Hofmann, W. (2017). Disgust and anger relate to different aggressive responses to moral violations. *Psychological Science, 28*(5), 609–619.

Morelli, S. A., Lieberman, M. D., & Zaki, J. (2015). The emerging study of positive empathy: Positive empathy. *Social and Personality Psychology Compass, 9*(2), 57–68.

Morelli, S. A., Ong, D. C., Makati, R., Jackson, M. O., & Zaki, J. (2017). Empathy and well-being correlate with centrality in different social networks. *Proceedings of the National Academy of Sciences, 114*(37), 9843–9847.

Moretti, L., & di Pellegrino, G. (2010). Disgust selectively modulates reciprocal fairness in economic interactions. *Emotion, 10*(2), 169–180.

Nelissen, R. M. A., Dijker, A. J. M., & deVries, N. K. (2007). How to turn a hawk into a dove and vice versa: Interactions between emotions and goals in a give-some dilemma game. *Journal of Experimental Social Psychology, 43*(2), 280–286.

Nesse, R. M. (2007). Runaway social selection for displays of partner value and altruism. *Biological Theory, 2*(2), 143–155.

Noë, R., & Hammerstein, P. (1994). Biological markets: Supply and demand determine the effect of partner choice in cooperation, mutualism and mating. *Behavioral Ecology and Sociobiology, 35*(1), 1–11.

Noë, R., & Hammerstein, P. (1995). Biological markets. *Trends in Ecology & Evolution, 10*(8), 336–339.

Nowak, M. A., & Roch, S. (2007). Upstream reciprocity and the evolution of gratitude. *Proceedings of the Royal Society B: Biological Sciences, 274*(1610), 605–609.

Ohman, A., & Mineka, S. (2001). Fears, phobias, and preparedness: Toward an evolved module of fear and fear learning. *Psychological Review, 108*(3), 483–522.

Otto, A. K., Laurenceau, J.-P., Siegel, S. D., & Belcher, A. J. (2015). Capitalizing on everyday positive events uniquely predicts daily intimacy and well-being in couples coping with breast cancer. *Journal of Family Psychology, 29*(1), 69–79.

Parks, C. D., Rumble, A. C., & Posey, D. C. (2002). The effects of envy on reciprocation in a social dilemma. *Personality & Social Psychology Bulletin, 28*(4), 509–520.

Pillutla, M. M., & Murnighan, J. K. (1996). Unfairness, anger, and spite: Emotional rejections of ultimatum offers. *Organizational Behavior and Human Decision Processes, 68*(3), 208–224.

Polman, E., & Kim, S. H. (2013). Effects of anger, disgust, and sadness on sharing with others. *Personality & Social Psychology Bulletin, 39*(12), 1683–1692.

Preston, S. D., & de Waal, F. B. M. (2002). Empathy: Its ultimate and proximate bases. *The Behavioral and Brain Sciences, 25*(1), 1–20; discussion 20–71.

Ramirez-Fernandez, J., Ramirez-Marin, J. Y., & Munduate, L. (2018). I expected more from you: The influence of close relationships and perspective taking on negotiation offers. *Group Decision and Negotiation, 27*(1), 85–105.

Roberts, G. (2005). Cooperation through interdependence. *Animal Behaviour, 70*(4), 901–908.

Robertson, T. E., Delton, A. W., Klein, S. B., Cosmides, L., & Tooby, J. (2014). Keeping the benefits of group cooperation: Domain-specific responses to distinct causes of social exclusion. *Evolution and Human Behavior, 35*(6), 472–480.

Robertson, T. E., Sznycer, D., Delton, A. W., Tooby, J., & Cosmides, L. (2018). The true trigger of shame: Social devaluation is sufficient, wrongdoing is unnecessary. *Evolution and Human Behavior, 39*(5), 566–573.

Røsand, G.-M. B., Slinning, K., Røysamb, E., & Tambs, K. (2014). Relationship dissatisfaction and other risk factors for future relationship dissolution: A population-based study of 18,523 couples. *Social Psychiatry and Psychiatric Epidemiology, 49*(1), 109–119.

Rumble, A. C., Van Lange, P. A. M., & Parks, C. D. (2009). The benefits of empathy: When empathy may sustain cooperation in social dilemmas. *European Journal of Social Psychology, 40*(5), 856–866.

Schug, J., Matsumoto, D., Horita, Y., Yamagishi, T., & Bonnet, K. (2010). Emotional expressivity as a signal of cooperation. *Evolution and Human Behavior, 31*(2), 87–94.

Sell, A., Sznycer, D., Al-Shawaf, L., Lim, J., Krauss, A., Feldman, A., Rascanu, R., Sugiyama, L., Cosmides, L., & Tooby, J. (2017). The grammar of anger: Mapping the computational architecture of a recalibrational emotion. *Cognition, 168*, 110–128.

Shariff, A. F., Tracy, J. L., & Markusoff, J. L. (2012). (Implicitly) judging a book by its cover: The power of pride and shame expressions in shaping judgments of social status. *Personality & Social Psychology Bulletin, 38*(9), 1178–1193.

Shiota, M. N., Campos, B., Keltner, D., & Hertenstein, M. J. (2004). Positive emotion and the regulation of interpersonal relationships. In P. Philippot & R.S. Feldman (Eds.), *The regulation of emotion* (pp. 127–155). Lawrence Erlbaum Associates.

Sinaceur, M., & Tiedens, L. Z. (2006). Get mad and get more than even: When and why anger expression is effective in negotiations. *Journal of Experimental Social Psychology, 42*(3), 314–322.

Smith, A., Pedersen, E. J., Forster, D. E., McCullough, M. E., & Lieberman, D. (2017). Cooperation: The roles of interpersonal value and gratitude. *Evolution and Human Behavior, 38*(6), 695–703.

Sweeney, M. M., & Horwitz, A. V. (2001). Infidelity, initiation, and the emotional climate of divorce: are there implications for mental health? *Journal of Health and Social Behavior, 42*(3), 295–309.

Sznycer, D., Al-Shawaf, L., Bereby-Meyer, Y., Curry, O. S., De Smet, D., Ermer, E., Kim, S., Kim, S., Li, N. P., Lopez Seal, M. F., McClung, J., O, J., Ohtsubo, Y., Quillien, T., Schaub, M., Sell, A., van Leeuwen, F., Cosmides, L., & Tooby, J. (2017). Cross-cultural regularities in the cognitive architecture of pride. *Proceedings of the National Academy of Sciences, 114*(8), 1874–1879.

Sznycer, D., Delton, A. W., Robertson, T. E., Cosmides, L., & Tooby, J. (2019). The ecological rationality of helping others: Potential helpers integrate cues of recipients' need and willingness to sacrifice. *Evolution and Human Behavior, 40*(1), 34–45.

Sznycer, D., Lopez Seal, M. F., Sell, A., Lim, J., Porat, R., Shalvi, S., Halperin, E., Cosmides, L., & Tooby, J. (2017). Support for redistribution is shaped by compassion, envy, and self-interest, but not a taste for fairness. *Proceedings of the National Academy of Sciences, 114*(31), 8420–8425.

Sznycer, D., & Lukaszewski, A. W. (2019). The emotion–valuation constellation: Multiple emotions are governed by a common grammar of social valuation. *Evolution and Human Behavior, 40*(4), 395–404.

Sznycer, D., Tooby, J., Cosmides, L., Porat, R., Shalvi, S., & Halperin, E. (2016). Shame closely tracks the threat of devaluation by others, even across cultures. *Proceedings of the National Academy of Sciences, 113*(10), 2625–2630.

Sznycer, D., Xygalatas, D., Agey, E., Alami, S., An, X.-F., Ananyeva, K. I., Atkinson, Q. D., Broitman, B. R., Conte, T. J., Flores, C., Fukushima, S., Hitokoto, H., Kharitonov, A. N., Onyishi, C. N., Onyishi, I. E., Romero, P. P., Schrock, J. M., Snodgrass, J. J., Sugiyama, L. S., . . . Tooby, J. (2018). Cross-cultural invariances in the architecture of shame. *Proceedings of the National Academy of Sciences, 115*(39), 9702–9707.

Sznycer, D., Xygalatas, D., Alami, S., An, X.-F., Ananyeva, K. I., Fukushima, S., Hitokoto, H., Kharitonov, A. N., Koster, J. M., Onyishi, C. N., Onyishi, I. E., Romero, P. P., Takemura, K., Zhuang, J.-Y., Cosmides, L., & Tooby, J. (2018). Invariances in the architecture of pride across small-scale societies. *Proceedings of the National Academy of Sciences, 115*(33), 8322–8327.

Tangney, J. P., Miller, R. S., Flicker, L., & Barlow, D. H. (1996). Are shame, guilt, and embarrassment distinct emotions? *Journal of Personality and Social Psychology, 70*(6), 1256–1269.

Thielmann, I., Spadaro, G., & Balliet, D. (2020). Personality and prosocial behavior: A theoretical framework and meta-analysis. *Psychological Bulletin, 146*(1), 30–90.

Tooby, J., & Cosmides, L. (1996). Friendship and the banker's paradox: Other pathways to the evolution of adaptations for altruism. In W. G. Runciman, J. M. Smith, & R. I. M. Dunbar (Eds.), *Evolution of social behaviour patterns in primates and man* (pp. 119–143). Oxford University Press.

Tooby, J., Cosmides, L., Sell, A., Lieberman, D., & Sznycer, D. (2008). Internal regulatory variables and the design of human motivation: A computational and evolutionary approach. In A. J. Elliot (Ed.), *Handbook of approach and avoidance motivation, 15,* 251–271. Taylor & Francis.

Tracy, J. L. (2014). An evolutionary approach to understanding distinct emotions. *Emotion Review, 6*(4), 308–312.

Tracy, J. L., Shariff, A. F., Zhao, W., & Henrich, J. (2013). Cross-cultural evidence that the nonverbal expression of pride is an automatic status signal. *Journal of Experimental Psychology: General, 142*(1), 163–180.

Tracy, J. L., Steckler, C. M., Randles, D., & Mercadante, E. (2018). The financial cost of status signaling: Expansive postural displays are associated with a reduction in the receipt of altruistic donations. *Evolution and Human Behavior, 39*(5), 520–528.

Trivers, R. L. (1971). The evolution of reciprocal altruism. *The Quarterly Review of Biology, 46*(1), 35–57.

Tsang, J.-A., & Martin, S. R. (2019). Four experiments on the relational dynamics and prosocial consequences of gratitude. *The Journal of Positive Psychology, 14*(2), 188–205.

Tybur, J. M., & Lieberman, D. (2016). Human pathogen avoidance adaptations. *Current Opinion in Psychology, 7,* 6–11.

Tybur, J. M., Lieberman, D., Kurzban, R., & DeScioli, P. (2013). Disgust: Evolved function and structure. *Psychological Review, 120*(1), 65–84.

van Dijk, E., van Kleef, G. A., Steinel, W., & van Beest, I. (2008). A social functional approach to emotions in bargaining: When communicating anger pays and when it backfires. *Journal of Personality and Social Psychology, 94*(4), 600–614.

Van Kleef, G. A., De Dreu, C. K. W., & Manstead, A. S. R. (2006). Supplication and appeasement in conflict and negotiation: The interpersonal effects of disappointment, worry, guilt, and regret. *Journal of Personality and Social Psychology, 91*(1), 124–142.

Van Kleef, G. A., van Dijk, E., Steinel, W., Harinck, F., & van Beest, I. (2008). Anger in social conflict: Cross-situational comparisons and suggestions for the future. *Group Decision and Negotiation, 17*(1), 13–30.

Wang, Y. A., & Todd, A. R. (2021). Evaluations of empathizers depend on the target of empathy. *Journal of Personality and Social Psychology, 121*(5), 1005–1028.

Wiessner, P. (2020). The role of third parties in norm enforcement in customary courts among the Enga of Papua New Guinea. *Proceedings of the National Academy of Sciences, 117*(51), 32320–32328.

Wubben, M. J. J., De Cremer, D., & van Dijk, E. (2012). Is pride a prosocial emotion? Interpersonal effects of authentic and hubristic pride. *Cognition & Emotion, 26*(6), 1084–1097.

Zaki, J. (2014). Empathy: A motivated account. *Psychological Bulletin, 140*(6), 1608–1647.

Zickfeld, J. H., van de Ven, N., Pich, O., Schubert, T. W., Berkessel, J. B., Pizarro, J. J., Bhushan, B., Mateo, N. J., Barbosa, S., Sharman, L., Kökönyei, G., Schrover, E., Kardum, I., Aruta, J. J. B., Lazarevic, L. B., Escobar, M. J., Stadel, M., Arriaga, P., Dodaj, A., . . . Vingerhoets, A. (2021). Tears evoke the intention to offer social support: A systematic investigation of the interpersonal effects of emotional crying across 41 countries. *Journal of Experimental Social Psychology, 95,* 104137.

Zizzo, D. J., & Oswald, A. J. (2001). Are people willing to pay to reduce others' incomes? *Annales d'Économie et de Statistique, 63/64,* 39–65.

CHAPTER 33

Emotion, Sickness, and Care for the Sick

Leander Steinkopf

> **Abstract**
> Humans usually are not left alone when they are ill or injured, and this makes a big difference in survival and healing: for instance, with the caring support of the group, a broken bone can heal when it would otherwise hinder survival. Being sick or injured in humans is inherently social and is based on emotional communication and negotiation. On the one hand, emotions of pain and malaise bring about adaptive behavior changes in the sick individual and communicate the sick status to others by displaying emotional expressions of suffering. On the other hand, potential helpers may offer care based on emotions of compassion, or may avoid the coughing and sneezing individual because they are disgusted or afraid of infection. This chapter argues that emotional aspects of sickness and healing are deeply rooted in the evolutionary past and play an important though underappreciated role in healthcare in the modern day.
>
> **Key Words:** pain, sickness, disgust, empathy, care

Introduction

Illness and injury have been vital adaptive problems throughout the evolutionary history of humans and their predecessors. Hence, respective selection pressures have shaped adaptations to address these problems, including the immune system with its complex set of defense mechanisms. However, usually the individual human is not left to her own means when sick or injured, but may receive support, care, and treatment from other individuals (e.g. Kessler, 2020; Spikins et al., 2019; Steinkopf, 2015). Pro-social responses toward sick conspecifics can also be found in other species, but extensive and elaborate support, care, and treatment are unique to humans and are a human universal (Hart, 2011; Kessler et al., 2017; Kessler et al., 2018).

To get a sense of how social support in case of sickness and injury can make a big difference for survival, one can imagine an individual animal with a broken leg left to its own means. It would be unable to (effectively) hunt or forage, to follow the group, to escape predators, and ultimately would be unable to survive. If, however, the same animal in the same situation were to receive support in terms of food and water, if the group would carry or wait for the individual, offer protection from predators, and even promote healing, the injured animal would be much more likely to survive. In spite of the difficulty of finding archaeological evidence for such behaviors, several fossils are documented that show cases of continued survival after (bone) injuries that would have led to death without others' help (Spikins et al., 2019; Tilley, 2015). In contemporary hunter-gatherer societies, illness and injury are common and mutual helping widespread (Gurven et al., 2012; Sugiyama, 2004). Helping in case of sickness is even regarded as an early form of health insurance, as extensive pro-social behavior of an individual heightens the chance that the individual will receive extensive care if he or she later becomes sick or injured (Gurven et al., 2000; K. Hill & Hurtado, 2009; Navarrete & Fessler, 2006).

Mounting an immune response to infection is highly costly in terms of energy. Being absolved from other duties such as childcare or foraging allows one to devote a greater share of bodily resources to defense against the infection. Otherwise, if keeping up normal functioning is necessary, fewer resources can be devoted to immune activity, and these trade-offs between normal functioning and immune responses hinder recovery. These examples suggest the hypothesis that humans could only evolve their long life span under the condition of social support in case of sickness and injury (Gurven et al., 2012; Sugiyama, 2004).

In sum, illness and injury are crucial adaptive problems for humans (and certainly not only humans) and one adaptive answer to these selection pressures is support, care, and treatment granted by healthy individuals to the sick or injured individual. Hence, what we refer to today as a therapeutic encounter is not a phenomenon of modern times but a recurrent social situation throughout human evolution. Fabrega (1997) recognized that the sick role and the helper role are two sides of a medical coin: "The sickness side announces, communicates, and expresses the suffering of conditions of disease and injury; the healing side is but the response aimed at comforting, undoing, relieving, fixing, minimizing" (p. 290). In other words, there is a coevolution between two social roles that yielded respective adaptations, analogous to the relationship between adaptations for cheating on the one hand and cheater detection on the other hand, for infidelity on the one hand and mate-retention behaviors and dealing with paternity uncertainty on the other hand, for signaling partner value and scrutinizing partner value. Adaptations for these recurrent social situations often take the shape of emotions (Tooby & Cosmides, 2008). In the case of sickness and care for the sick, we are mostly dealing with emotions of pain and malaise on the suffering side, while the most important emotions on the helping side are compassion, but also disgust and fear (see Steinkopf, 2017a, 2017b). In essence, the sick side has to convince the helping side of granting support, while the helping side has to regulate helping behavior in a way that promises the biggest payoff in terms of inclusive fitness (Steinkopf, 2017b). In both cases, emotions play an important part. On the sick side, emotions like pain and malaise regulate behavior and physiological processes in a way that promotes recovery plus (and here more important) sending convincing signals of need; on the helping side, emotions like compassion and disgust regulate helping behavior in a way that benefits the helper the most in terms of inclusive fitness, reputation, and future reciprocity (Steinkopf 2017a).

This chapter focuses on the emotions associated with injury and somatic illness, while explanations of the mechanisms behind mental illness and respective treatment and care can be found elsewhere (Brüne, 2008; Kohrt et al., 2020; Nesse, 2019). However, the basic ideas are similar. Just as pain and malaise can be regarded as emotional mechanisms to address the problems of injury and infection, depression and anxiety can be regarded as (malfunctioning) emotional mechanisms to address problems in the social sphere. Furthermore, if we concentrate on the communicative functions of these emotions, pain, malaise, depression, and anxiety are merely different channels through which need is communicated (Steinkopf, 2017b). The parallels go even further when we take into account that all these aversive emotions can persist beyond underlying somatic or social conditions and become chronic diseases with no apparent underlying reason (e.g., Williams, 2016). Further parallels will be mentioned throughout the chapter, though mental disease is not its focus.

Emotions of Pain and Sickness

Sickness and pain are commonly seen as strictly somatic phenomena with emotions merely considered as epiphenomena. This is partly based on our modern medical model, which concentrates on underlying physiological malfunctions or physical damage in order to explain and treat symptoms of pain and sickness. The model is certainly successful. However, infection and injury in humans usually take place within a social context, they can have strong social consequences, and, most importantly, helpful others can address the problem of the sufferer. Hence, emotional responses to infection and injury are not very likely to be mere epiphenomena of underlying somatic problems, but rather adaptive responses shaped by natural selection to yield adaptive behavior in the sufferer and, consequentially, in surrounding others to a particular situation highly important for survival.

Pain

At first view, pain is regarded as mere sensation, as an alarm bell that rings when tissue is damaged. But there are two senses in which this is inaccurate: first, pain is much more than that, namely an emotion with important motivational aspects. Second, pain is not even a sensation of tissue damage in the strict sense, as tissue damage does not necessarily trigger pain and, conversely, tissue damage is not necessary to sense pain (Craig, 2018; Wall, 1999). The quale of pain is so attention grabbing that we often miss its motivational aspects: We immediately withdraw from the painful situation (e.g., hot stove), we spare the injured body part to allow healing (e.g., use the other hand for cooking), we learn for the future (e.g., not to touch hot stoves), we communicate our problem (e.g., "Ouch!"), we inspect the injured body part and might seek care treatment (Wall, 1999). Obviously, these motivational mechanisms prevent further injury and enable healing. Withdrawing and avoiding the painful stimulus are key to limiting injury, while sparing and caring are prerequisites of healing (Wall, 1999).

However, what mostly interests us in the present chapter are the communicative aspects of pain (see Williams, 2002; Williams & Kappesser, 2018), which serve the function of convincing potential helpers (Finlay & Syal, 2014; Steinkopf, 2016). To give an illustrative example, Finlay and Syal (2014) proposed conceptualizing labor pain from a communicative perspective. Though pain during childbirth reflects the problems of a small birth canal combined with a large skull of the baby (obstetric dilemma), the presence of potential helpers that have to be mobilized for assistance may be another (not mutually exclusive) explanation for unbearable labor pain. In fact, assistance at birth is a human universal and probably makes a big difference in terms of evolutionary fitness, as both the life of the mother and the life of the baby to be born are at stake. Thus, labor pain when surrounded by potentially helpful others may have a fitness advantage. In contrast, many other species give birth silently, perhaps because they do not receive assistance when expressing pain and might even attract predators by communicating their vulnerability (Finlay & Syal, 2014).

Beyond childbirth, pain communication goes far beyond a mumbled "Ouch!" and facial expressions. Sparing an injured body part usually makes the injury visible to others, withdrawal from rewarding social endeavors may attract attention, and low mood might motivate consolation. Especially in the context of stable social groups, these behavior changes are easily observable and at the same time act as costly and therefore credible signals of need (Steinkopf, 2016). Sparing body parts limits behavioral options, and withdrawal from social opportunities is inherently costly in fitness terms. It would therefore be highly costly to convincingly fake pain in order to benefit from being supported and absolved from duties (Steinkopf, 2016). As opposed to this, in modern medical contexts pain judgments are made based on brief therapeutic encounters where long-lasting and thus costly behavior changes cannot be observed. So in the modern medical contest, there is a risk of pain being faked, so-called malingering, but also the much more detrimental risk of doubt, pain underestimation, and pain undertreatment (Steinkopf, 2016; Williams & Kappesser, 2018). Especially when an underlying pathology cannot be found, pain is often not taken seriously (e.g. Chibnall & Tait, 1995; Twigg & Byrne, 2015). In contrast, in the context of ancient group life, emotional reactions of the sufferer were the only sources of information (short of observable anatomical damage) and there were no magnetic resonance imaging (MRIs), ultrasounds, or endoscopes that could cast doubt on a person's subjective suffering.

The sensation and expression of pain is highly dependent on the social aspects of the surrounding, as demonstrated by research on the social modulation of pain (Krahé et al., 2013). For example, from an evolutionary perspective, one would assume that pain should be displayed in the presence of potentially supporting others, while it should be suppressed in presence of adversaries who might take advantage of the vulnerability (Cosmides & Tooby, 2000; Kappesser, 2019; see Williams et al., 2016), but empirical results are inconsistent (Kappesser, 2019). Heterogeneous outcomes might be based on the use of different definitions of "social context" and thus different operationalizations and also on a lack of theory (Kappesser, 2019). Furthermore, as communication and social interaction are based on meaning and interpretation and thus sensitive to subtle differences, heterogeneity of outcomes may be an inherent problem and challenge of the field. For example, the presence of supporting others can either be regarded as an indication that help is already underway or it can be interpreted as a worthwhile opportunity for pain expression as receptive others are around (see Steinkopf, 2016, 2017b).

Though several lines of research have led to contradictory results (e.g. Karos, 2020), the studies conducted in the field yield interesting findings on the social plasticity of pain. Healthcare providers that appear more familiar to the patient may lead to lower pain ratings (Mattarozzi et al., 2020). Confederates that either appear threatening or benevolent, based on experimental manipulation, influence pain sensation and expression, in the sense that threat reduced facial expression of pain while intensifying the sensation of pain (Karos et al., 2020). Empathetic comments can reduce pain ratings during the application of painful thermal heat stimuli (Fauchon et al., 2019); similarly, affective touch from one's partner can soothe pain (von Mohr et al., 2018). Again, thinking of pain as an emotion like sadness as opposed to a bodily sensation makes intuitively understandable the idea that the presence and behavior of others has a strong impact on suffering.

Sickness Behavior/Malaise/Lassitude/Feeling Sick
When we are sick, we feel a certain way, behave a certain way, have certain motivations (or rather a lack of them), and our sickness is clearly recognizable from our behavior and facial expression. However, contrary to common belief, these symptoms are not caused by the infection itself, but are instead a defense of the body against the infection. Lethargy and muscle aches, for example, are thought to serve as energy-saving devices to free resources for immune functioning, loss of appetite may help sequestrate infectious agents from necessary nutrients and may again free energy that would otherwise be devoted to digestion. In psychoneuroimmunology and related disciplines, this particular state is called *sickness behavior* (Aubert, 1999; Dantzer & Kelley, 2007; Hart, 1988) and is usually defined by typical behavior, a particular mode of physiological functioning, and the regulation through pro-inflammatory cytokines. As these disciplines deal with different species, not only humans, they tend to ignore qualia associated with this state, as these cannot be observed from the outside, and nonhuman species are not able to answer self-report questionnaires. From a more human-centered or

psychological perspective, the qualia associated with being sick attract more attention, so sickness behavior can be regarded as an emotion referred to as malaise (Tooby & Cosmides, 2008), lassitude (Schrock et al., 2020), or simply "feeling sick" (e.g., Shakhar & Shakhar, 2015). We are weak, weary, and lose appetite, we feel anxious, bleak, and vulnerable, we like to withdraw from social interaction and avoid activity. The description of lassitude or malaise might remind some of the symptoms of depression, which is not a coincidence, as there might be phylogenetic and physiological links between depression and sickness behavior (Andrews & Durisko, 2017; Eisenberger & Moieni, 2020). Again, we concentrate on the communicative function of the emotion.

Signs and symptoms of sickness could be mere cues without communicative intent, and recognizing them could be a nontrivial endeavor that needs highly sensitive social cognition. In fact, even subtle cues of sickness can be recognized from facial photographs or body odor samples (Olsson et al., 2014; Regenbogen et al., 2017; Sarolidou et al., 2020), and social cognition may be specially adapted for recognizing sick conspecifics (Kessler et al., 2017). However, signs and symptoms of sickness, including facial expression, may not only be cues, but may have been shaped by natural selection to signal the need for aid (Steinkopf, 2015; Steinkopf & de Barra, 2018; Tiokhin, 2016; Tooby & Cosmides, 2008) and signal infection to prevent community spread (Shakhar & Shakhar, 2015). On the other hand, cues of sickness could be suppressed to allow affiliation. This is the case, for example, in male zebra finches—they show symptoms of sickness when they are alone, but their symptoms are suppressed when they are in a group context or introduced to a novel female (Lopes et al., 2012; Lopes et al., 2013). For them, unlike humans, there is nothing to gain in terms of care and treatment from having and showing symptoms to conspecifics, but they miss out on opportunities for mating, caring for offspring, or competing for territory and social status (see Lopes, 2014).

It contradicts our everyday understanding of pain and sickness to regard them as mechanisms that are to some degree independent of underlying somatic pathologies. That is why the results of placebo research are such a challenge for most of academic medicine and for our everyday understanding of health and disease. Research on placebo effects shows that even a treatment without any active ingredient, like a saline injection introduced as morphine, sham surgery introduced as a valid surgical intervention, or, most prominently, a sugar pill introduced as a painkiller, can reduce symptoms such as pain, irritable bowel syndrome, swelling, and depression (e.g., Colloca, 2019; Enck & Klosterhalfen, 2020; Howe et al., 2017; Kirsch, 2019). Certainly, it is not the "ineffective" treatment itself that causes amelioration, but the meaning of medical contexts and rituals, as well as the belief of being adequately treated and respective positive expectations (e.g., Kaptchuk, 2011; Moerman & Jonas, 2002; Steinkopf, 2015).

What appears puzzling in the usual understanding of symptoms makes much more sense when we regard symptoms of sickness not only as internal defense mechanisms, but also as signals of need that are selected for a communicative purpose (Steinkopf, 2015). From this perspective, discernible symptoms act as signals to others that support, care, and treatment are needed. When support, care, and treatment are granted, the signaling function is fulfilled and the symptoms can decrease, even if the underlying pathology has not been completely resolved. Again, taking an emotional perspective on sickness creates an intuitive understanding of how social factors have the potential to alleviate suffering. When a friend is deeply sad about a breakup, we might offer consolation rather than actively trying to bring back the girlfriend that left, and although the breakup is the underlying cause of his sadness, we are not surprised that he feels better after he talked to us about what happened. When we take into account the emotional aspects of sickness, the healing effects of placebos or compassionate care immediately make sense.

Further Emotional Considerations
Sickness can also be regarded as an unintended test of social status. Falling ill reduces one's current value as a group member (see Karos et al., 2018) and even imposes costs on others in terms of interruption of cooperation and exchange (Hagen et al., 2008), consumption of altruistic acts like food sharing and care, and possible infection. Thus, the neediness of a sick person may bring her insights about her social value within the group, with stark consequences for her mood and self-esteem (see Kirkpatrick & Ellis, 2003; Leary et al., 1995; Leary & Baumeister, 2000; Leary & Downs, 1995). This is reflected by heightened neural sensitivity for social threats and social rewards after an inflammatory challenge (see Eisenberger et al., 2017; Moieni & Eisenberger, 2018; Muscatell et al., 2016). Being left alone when sick not only is bad news regarding the problem at hand, but also indicates a low social value more generally, and may thus induce low mood and low self-esteem beyond sickness. In this sense, falling ill within a generally pro-social environment is a special case of the general mechanism of testing social bonds through imposing costs on alleged social allies, as proposed by Zahavi (1977).

Therefore, patient satisfaction may not only be based on competent treatment of the ailment, but also on the subjective outcome of the aforementioned test. Further, healing or the conviction of being healed may require a positive outcome of the social test. Healing in this sense is not only the restoration of health, but also the affirmation of one's value for the group. This could partly explain why shamanic healing rituals can involve the whole family or the whole group and last for days (e.g., Kaptchuk, 2011; Ongaro, 2020; Winkelman, 2010)—they may be effective through giving extensive positive social feedback, thereby evoking patient satisfaction through a costly signal of group cohesion (see also Winkelman, 2010, p. 225). Similarly, in modern contexts, a warm bedside manner, patient-centered care, and striving for patient autonomy may act as credible signals that the patient is socially valued despite his incapacities. In contrast, lack of warmth, patience, and communicative skills in a doctor, as well as a bad doctor-patient relationship, raises the likelihood of patients suing their doctor, even in the absence of actual malpractice (Hickson et al., 1994; Levinson et al., 1997; Roter, 2006), implying that patients may sense "emotional malpractice" when their doctor doesn't show them enough care. Regarding sickness episodes as tests of social value further emphasizes the role of emotional experience and emotional communication for healing outcomes and patient satisfaction.

Emotions and Care for the Sick
Our behavior toward sick others is crucially guided by the emotions of empathy and disgust, disgust being the emotion that motivates avoidance and self-protection, whereas empathy motivates approach and pro-social behavior. Obviously, these emotions are contradictory in their consequences, but they draw on similar information, can complement each other, and, from the perspective of evolutionary history, without disgust, extensive empathetic responding probably would not be possible.

Empathy and Compassion
Empathy is "the ability and tendency to share and understand others' internal states" (Zaki & Ochsner, 2018, p. 871). Thus empathy does not *necessarily* entail the motivation to act in a pro-social manner when one shares and understands others' suffering, whereas the motivation to help and alleviate suffering is an integral part of the definition of compassion (DeSteno

et al., 2018). However, as the terms *empathy* and *compassion* are often used interchangeably, we do not differentiate here, but assume that empathetic responding leads to compassion, pro-social motivation, and helping. Still, it is certainly possible that empathy allows an onlooker to understand the internal state of an incapacitated sufferer without developing pro-social motivation and then, instead of helping, simply to pass by or even take advantage of it. In fact, exploitation and predation probably have been important factors in the evolution of displays of weakness (Steinkopf, 2016; Tiokhin, 2016; Williams et al., 2016; Williams & Kappesser, 2018); however, this is not the focus of the present chapter as empathic concern and compassion are the aspects of empathy most relevant for healthcare (Decety, 2020).

Benefits of Empathy
Empathy with the sick can only be an evolutionarily stable strategy when the benefits outweigh the costs for the actor. There are three types of payoffs one can expect from helping a sick individual: (1) care for kin heightens inclusive fitness (kin selection); (2) caring for non-kin that is part of the same social group may entail reciprocal altruism; (3) caring for others may improve reputation, which translates into higher value as social partner or mate and indirect reciprocity.

Caring for kin, especially offspring, is often regarded as the phylogenetic origin of empathy and compassion (de Waal, 2008; Decety et al., 2016; Preston, 2013) and thus the most basic form of care (for the sick). Caring for other members of one's group has been conceptualized as a social buffer against illness and injury (Sugiyama, 2004). Every individual member of the group bears a certain risk of becoming temporarily incapable of foraging, moving, or caring for offspring. However, if members of the group can rely on support and care from the group, the costs for the individual are distributed and the risk buffered—if the whole group does not fall ill at the same time, that is. This risk-buffering strategy is theorized to be the basis for the evolution of human longevity (Gurven et al., 2012; Sugiyama, 2004). Finally, generous helping can contribute to reputation and status (Hardy & Van Vugt, 2006; Zahavi, 1995), which is reflected by the high social status of healers in ancient societies (Singh, 2017) and by the occupational prestige of healthcare workers today.

Regarding reputation, it is important to note that in order to improve reputation through pro-social behavior, one must be observed by others. Accordingly, people are more likely to behave in a pro-social way when others watch (see Bradley et al., 2018). However, because this may appear like selfish impression management, let us change perspective: burnout is more likely when care work is not rewarded with gratitude and recognition (Bennett et al., 1996). In contrast, care for a sick individual based on kin altruism or direct reciprocity does not need observers to benefit the helper. All in all, empathy, compassion, and care are more likely when there is kinship, familiarity, and observers (Steinkopf, 2017a, 2017b).

The Environment of Empathic Adaptedness
During most of their history, humans did not live in big anonymous societies without direct dependence on each other, but in groups of a size that allowed direct relationships between all members (Dunbar, 1995; Wilson, 1978). Kinship relations, strong social ties, mutual acquaintance, and interdependence in these ancient groups have been prerequisites for the evolution of "human healthcare networks" and their underlying emotions (Kessler, 2020; Kessler et al., 2018; Steinkopf, 2017a; Williams & Kappesser, 2018). Social structure in industrialized nations has changed tremendously since its hunter-gatherer roots, but the extraordinary human capacity for empathy, compassion, and care has persisted.

The combination of a changed social structure with virtually unchanged emotional mechanisms may be an explanation for why actual human behavior does not neatly fit the above hypotheses on benefits of helping the sick. In an ancient group with mutual acquaintance, stable membership, and strong interdependence, the likelihood was high that helping a random other member who was in pain would have promoted inclusive fitness, invited future reciprocity, and improved reputation, as other group members would have known about this caring act. Under such circumstances, mechanisms of empathy and compassion could evolve that presumably persisted although circumstances changed. Today, buying groceries for the sick elderly woman next door does not promote inclusive fitness, is not likely to be reciprocated, and does not improve reputation as no one on the same floor will notice—and still we probably will not refuse when our neighbor asks for the favor. However, the roots of empathy and compassion in group life do not have solely rosy consequences, as in-group favoritism often comes with out-group discrimination (Steinkopf, 2017a; see also Bressan, 2020), as is for example reflected by racial discrimination in healthcare (e.g., Alsan et al., 2019; Drwecki et al., 2011; Green et al., 2003; A. Hill et al., 2018).

Care Motivation beyond Emotion
Empathy and compassion are not the only sources of motivation to help sick individuals, though they may be the only emotional sources. Social norms and social pressure may cause helping as well, and so might rational thoughts or calculations about future reciprocity. Today it is obvious that physicians, nurses, and other healthcare professionals are not driven by compassion all the time, but rather by the structures of social institutions. While we generally regard these institutions as new and not applicable to ancestral environments, shamanism is probably quite old (Singh, 2017). Hence, there was likely the occupation and social position of the healer who was not necessarily driven by compassion but simply did his job. Also, he orchestrated collaborative helping efforts as well as healing rituals by the group, procedures that may not be primarily motivated by compassion.

Furthermore, in certain situations the dominant motivation for helping is not compassion with the suffering but rather the motivation to affiliate with the attractive and appealing (Hauser et al., 2014). Combining both, the beneficial type of pro-social behavior might be directed toward a desirable social partner who is in dire need, e.g., a high-status person who is sick or in pain. In fact, research on hunter-gatherer societies shows that those individuals that contributed the most to the group when healthy received the most support when they fell sick (Gurven et al., 2000; Sugiyama, 2004; Sugiyama & Chacon, 2000).

Disgust
Disgust is "an evolved psychological system for protecting organisms from infection through disease avoidant behavior" (Curtis et al., 2011, p. 389) and it is commonly regarded as part of the so-called behavioral immune system, "a motivational system that evolved as a means of inhibiting contact with disease-causing parasites" (Murray & Schaller, 2016, p. 76), but as the definitions suggest, the two concepts overlap considerably. In any case, the behavioral immune system and its vital emotion disgust are preventive mechanisms that trigger avoidance of sources of infection—in our case, sick individuals. Just like empathy and compassion should motivate one to approach a sick individual, disgust should motivate avoidance, potentially resulting in a motivational conflict (Steinkopf, 2017a). Thereby, it is important to note that psychological mechanisms like emotions are highly context-sensitive (Al-Shawaf et al., 2019). For example, disgust can be suppressed in mating contexts, or its display might be more pronounced in the presence of children when observational learning is important (Al-Shawaf

et al., 2016). And disgust may even cause approach instead of avoidance, for example when the source of a disgusting odor has to be found, or when the source of disgust needs to be killed or removed (Al-Shawaf et al., 2016). However, in the present chapter we focus on the avoidance function of disgust and, for the sake of simplicity, leave contextual factors aside.

REGULATION OF DISGUST
The main function of disgust is to avoid sources of infection; thus risk of contagion should be the main information feeding into the regulation of the disgust response, suggesting that symptoms of infectious disease in a sick person should activate a strong disgust response, while bleeding wounds (blood being a potentially infectious body fluid) should result in a weaker response, and unbloody bone injuries or depression should not elicit disgust at all. However, infectiousness and risk of contagion cannot be reliably judged by onlookers; there is always the risk of mistaking an allergic sneezing for the symptom of a flu, or sickness behavior for a minor depressive episode. As errors can occur, perception in general should be biased in order to avoid the more costly errors at the expense of erring in a less costly way more often— better safe than sorry (Haselton & Nettle, 2006; Nesse, 2005). In our case, the behavioral immune system should be oversensitive, as underestimating the risk of contagion has high costs (Neuberg et al., 2011). Therefore, not only actual signs of infection but also deviations from arbitrary norms, such as obesity, sexual orientation, ugliness, and facial disfigurements can activate the behavioral immune system (e.g., de Zavala et al., 2014; Klebl et al., 2020; Master et al., 2009; Ryan et al., 2012; but see Vartanian et al., 2017). So, instead of actual infectiousness, the severity of the condition or deviation might be the crucial input information for the behavioral immune system. However, a serious condition might not only trigger a strong response of disgust and avoidance, but the same stimulus is a strong signal of need for help, thus eliciting compassion and approach and possibly resulting in an approach-avoidance conflict (Steinkopf, 2017a).

ALTRUISTIC DISGUST
Empathy and compassion can lead to altruistic behavior, while disgust can preclude care. However, disgust and avoidance are not necessarily the "selfish" response to the sight of a sick individual, as our practice of "social distancing" during the COVID-19 pandemic made us aware. Kessler (2020) differentiates between two kinds of healthcare behaviors: social care and community health behaviors. While social care, which we here refer to as care for the sick, takes place when disgust is either weak or overcome, community health behaviors usually do not help the sick individual but the health of the group. Avoiding a sick conspecific may thus not only benefit the avoiding individual but also the rest of the group through preventing further spread of the infectious agent. So, the emotion of disgust not only can be regarded as part of the individual behavioral immune system, as an individual defense, but also can contribute to protection of the larger group.

Integrating Empathy and Disgust
Compassion can cause approach, and disgust is usually associated with avoidance. In this sense the two emotions are opposed to each other, but when we take a closer look at our behavior toward sick individuals we can recognize that both emotions can be at work at the same time and can shape our behavior adaptively (Steinkopf, 2017a). While compassion may lead us to help a person in need, disgust may motivate us to wash our hands afterward. Disgust may motivate us to take safety measures like putting on gloves and a face mask before approaching someone. Conversely, while disgust may drive us away from the option of helping through

close contact, compassion may still motivate us to take indirect measures like organizing help or support. Thus, compassion and disgust may act in concert to yield helping behavior that minimizes the risk of infection for the helping side and perhaps even the risk of secondary infections on the receiving end (Steinkopf, 2017a). To put it paradoxically, sickness disgust makes sickness compassion possible, because disgust shapes helping behavior in a way that minimizes potential costs and thus makes compassion an evolutionarily stable strategy.

Conclusion

The modern medical paradigm traces human suffering back to underlying physiological or mechanical malfunctions or disorders. Accordingly, healthcare means addressing these underlying malfunctions. To use a common metaphor, the body is regarded as machinery and medicine as a repair service. In this paradigm, phenomena such as somatization, physiologically unexplained symptoms, effects of placebos, and compassionate care fit uneasily in the standard metatheory. However, the human body is adapted not only to the risks of infection and injury, but also to the fact of group social life, to the chance of receiving support, care, and treatment from others, as well as to the opportunity to support, treat, and care for others in need. Therefore, the emotions that constitute our response to infection and injury, as well as the emotions that regulate support and care, namely pain and lassitude, empathy and disgust, are not merely soft factors that might be considered after physical and physiological interventions are done; these emotions are at the heart of sickness and healing.

Medical interventions have become more and more effective, but the emotional needs of patients probably have not changed since Paleolithic times. They still need the same things: a convincing rationale, healing rituals, compassionate care, long-lasting support, and social integration. Their emotional reactions to infection and injury, namely lassitude and pain, have been shaped not only to motivate behavior that facilitates healing and immune activity, but also to convince others of the sufferer's neediness. Suffering is not a straightforward consequence of injury and infection, but an emotional mechanism of the body to address injury and infection and to mobilize others for assistance. These elaborate emotional mechanisms are ignored when medicine concentrates exclusively on underlying physiological pathologies (e.g., Craig, 2018; Steinkopf, 2015).

Certainly, it is easier said than done to demand compassionate care and enduring support. Not only are our emotional mechanisms of suffering not adapted to modern contexts, but neither are the emotional mechanisms constituting compassionate care. Mutual healthcare in the group setting always took place between familiar group members, whereas today often complete strangers meet for therapeutic encounters. As we have contemplated above, this is neither the best condition for patient satisfaction nor for the development of empathy and compassion. However, to bring the current situation a little closer to stable group life, health policy should aim for long-lasting therapeutic relationships that may promote trust and reliance as needed by the patients, as well as gratitude and acknowledgment for the practitioner.

References

Alsan, M., Garrick, O., & Graziani, G. (2019). Does diversity matter for health? Experimental evidence from Oakland. *American Economic Review, 109*(12), 4071–4111. https://doi.org/10.1257/aer.20181446

Al-Shawaf, L., Conroy-Beam, D., Asao, K., & Buss, D. M. (2016). Human emotions: An evolutionary psychological perspective. *Emotion Review, 8*(2), 173–186. https://doi.org/10.1177/1754073914565518

Al-Shawaf, L., Lewis, D. M. G., Wehbe, Y. S., & Buss, D. M. (2019). Context, environment, and learning in evolutionary psychology. In T. K. Shackelford & V. A. Weekes-Shackelford (Eds.), *Encyclopedia of evolutionary psychological science* (pp. 1–12). Springer International. https://doi.org/10.1007/978-3-319-16999-6_227-1

Andrews, P. W., & Durisko, Z. (2017). The evolution of depressive phenotypes. In R. J. DeRubeis & D. R. Strunk (Eds.), *The Oxford handbook of mood disorders* (pp. 24–36). Oxford University Press.

Aubert, A. (1999). Sickness and behaviour in animals: A motivational perspective. *Neuroscience and Biobehavioral Reviews, 23*(7), 1029–1036.

Bennett, L., Ross, M. W., & Sunderland, R. (1996). The relationship between recognition, rewards and burnout in AIDS caring. *AIDS Care, 8*(2), 145–153. https://doi.org/10.1080/09540129650125830

Bradley, A., Lawrence, C., & Ferguson, E. (2018). Does observability affect prosociality? *Proceedings of the Royal Society B: Biological Sciences, 285*(1875), 20180116. https://doi.org/10.1098/rspb.2018.0116

Bressan, P. (2020). Strangers look sicker (with implications in times of COVID-19). *BioEssays: News and Reviews in Molecular, Cellular and Developmental Biology, 43*(3), e2000158. https://doi.org/10.1002/bies.202000158

Brüne, M. (2008). *Textbook of evolutionary psychiatry: The origins of psychopathology*. Oxford University Press.

Chibnall, J. T., & Tait, R. C. (1995). Observer perceptions of low back pain: Effects of pain report and other contextual factors. *Journal of Applied Social Psychology, 25*(5), 418–439. https://doi.org/10.1111/j.1559-1816.1995.tb01597.x

Colloca, L. (2019). The placebo effect in pain therapies. *Annual Review of Pharmacology and Toxicology, 59*(1), 191–211. https://doi.org/10.1146/annurev-pharmtox-010818-021542

Cosmides, L., & Tooby, J. (2000). Evolutionary psychology and the emotions. In M. Lewis & Haviland-Jones (Eds.), *Handbook of emotions* (2nd ed., pp. 91–115). Guilford Press.

Craig, K. (2018). Toward the social communication model of pain. In T. Hervort, K. Karos, Z. Trost, & K. M. Prkachin (Eds.), *Social and interpersonal dynamics in pain: We don't suffer alone* (pp. 23–41). Springer. https://doi.org/10.1007/978-3-319-78340-6_2

Curtis, V., de Barra, M., & Aunger, R. (2011). Disgust as an adaptive system for disease avoidance behaviour. *Philosophical Transactions of the Royal Society B: Biological Sciences, 366*(1563), 389–401. https://doi.org/10.1098/rstb.2010.0117

Dantzer, R., & Kelley, K. W. (2007). Twenty years of research on cytokine-induced sickness behavior. *Brain, Behavior, and Immunity, 21*(2), 153–160. https://doi.org/10.1016/j.bbi.2006.09.006

de Waal, F. B. M. (2008). Putting the altruism back into altruism: The evolution of empathy. *Annual Review of Psychology, 59*, 279–300. https://doi.org/10.1146/annurev.psych.59.103006.093625

de Zavala, A. G., Waldzus, S., & Cypryanska, M. (2014). Prejudice towards gay men and a need for physical cleansing. *Journal of Experimental Social Psychology, 54*, 1–10. https://doi.org/10.1016/j.jesp.2014.04.001

Decety, J. (2020). Empathy in medicine: What it is, and how much we really need it. *The American Journal of Medicine, 133*(5), 561–566. https://doi.org/10.1016/j.amjmed.2019.12.012

Decety, J., Bartal, I. B.-A., Uzefovsky, F., & Knafo-Noam, A. (2016). Empathy as a driver of prosocial behaviour: Highly conserved neurobehavioural mechanisms across species. *Philosophical Transactions of the Royal Society B: Biological Sciences, 371*(1686), 20150077. https://doi.org/10.1098/rstb.2015.0077

DeSteno, D., Condon, P., & Dickens, L. (2018). Gratitude and compassion. In L. F. Barrett, M. Lewis, & J. M. Haviland-Jones (Eds.), *Handbook of emotions* (4th ed., pp. 835–846). Taylor & Francis.

Drwecki, B. B., Moore, C. F., Ward, S. E., & Prkachin, K. M. (2011). Reducing racial disparities in pain treatment: The role of empathy and perspective-taking. *Pain, 152*(5), 1001–1006. https://doi.org/10.1016/j.pain.2010.12.005

Dunbar, R. (1995). Neocortex size and group size in primates: A test of the hypothesis. *Journal of Human Evolution, 28*(3), 287–296. https://doi.org/10.1006/jhev.1995.1021

Eisenberger, N. I., & Moieni, M. (2020). Inflammation affects social experience: Implications for mental health. *World Psychiatry, 19*(1), 109–110. https://doi.org/10.1002/wps.20724

Eisenberger, N. I., Moieni, M., Inagaki, T. K., Muscatell, K. A., & Irwin, M. R. (2017). In sickness and in health: The co-regulation of inflammation and social behavior. *Neuropsychopharmacology, 42*(1), 242–253. https://doi.org/10.1038/npp.2016.141

Enck, P., & Klosterhalfen, S. (2020). Placebo responses and placebo effects in functional gastrointestinal disorders. *Frontiers in Psychiatry, 11*, 797. https://doi.org/10.3389/fpsyt.2020.00797

Fabrega, H. (1997). *Evolution of sickness and healing*. University of California Press.

Fauchon, C., Faillenot, I., Quesada, C., Meunier, D., Chouchou, F., Garcia-Larrea, L., & Peyron, R. (2019). Brain activity sustaining the modulation of pain by empathetic comments. *Scientific Reports, 9*, 8398. https://doi.org/10.1038/s41598-019-44879-9

Finlay, B. L., & Syal, S. (2014). The pain of altruism. *Trends in Cognitive Sciences, 18*(12), 615–617. https://doi.org/10.1016/j.tics.2014.08.002

Green, C. R., Anderson, K. O., Baker, T. A., Campbell, L. C., Decker, S., Fillingim, R. B., Kalauokalani, D. A., Kaloukalani, D. A., Lasch, K. E., Myers, C., Tait, R. C., Todd, K. H., & Vallerand, A. H. (2003). The unequal burden of pain: Confronting racial and ethnic disparities in pain. *Pain Medicine (Malden, Mass.), 4*(3), 277–294. https://doi.org/10.1046/j.1526-4637.2003.03034.x

Gurven, M., Allen-Arave, W., Hill, K., & Hurtado, M. (2000). "It's a wonderful life": Signaling generosity among the Ache of Paraguay. *Evolution and Human Behavior, 21*(4), 263–282. https://doi.org/10.1016/S1090-5138(00)00032-5

Gurven, M., Stieglitz, J., Hooper, P. L., Gomes, C., & Kaplan, H. (2012). From the womb to the tomb: The role of transfers in shaping the evolved human life history. *Experimental Gerontology, 47*(10), 807–813. https://doi.org/10.1016/j.exger.2012.05.006

Hagen, E. H., Watson, P. J., & Hammerstein, P. (2008). Gestures of despair and hope: A view on deliberate self-harm from economics and evolutionary biology. *Biological Theory, 3*(2), 123–138. https://doi.org/10.1162/biot.2008.3.2.123

Hardy, C. L., & Van Vugt, M. (2006). Nice guys finish first: The competitive altruism hypothesis. *Personality and Social Psychology Bulletin, 32*(10), 1402–1413. https://doi.org/10.1177/0146167206291006

Hart, B. L. (1988). Biological basis of the behavior of sick animals. *Neuroscience and Biobehavioral Reviews, 12*(2), 123–137. https://doi.org/10.1016/S0149-7634(88)80004-6

Hart, B. L. (2011). Behavioural defences in animals against pathogens and parasites: Parallels with the pillars of medicine in humans. *Philosophical Transactions of the Royal Society B: Biological Sciences, 366*(1583), 3406–3417. https://doi.org/10.1098/rstb.2011.0092

Haselton, M. G., & Nettle, D. (2006). The paranoid optimist: An integrative evolutionary model of cognitive biases. *Personality and Social Psychology Review, 10*(1), 47–66. https://doi.org/10.1207/s15327957pspr1001_3

Hauser, D. J., Preston, S. D., & Stansfield, R. B. (2014). Altruism in the wild: When affiliative motives to help positive people overtake empathic motives to help the distressed. *Journal of Experimental Psychology: General, 143*(3), 1295–1305. https://doi.org/10.1037/a0035464

Hickson, G. B., Clayton, E. W., Entman, S. S., Miller, C. S., Githens, P. B., Whetten-Goldstein, K., & Sloan, F. A. (1994). Obstetricians' prior malpractice experience and patients' satisfaction with care. *JAMA, 272*(20), 1583–1587. https://doi.org/10.1001/jama.1994.03520200039032

Hill, A., Jones, D., & Woodworth, L. (2018). A doctor like me: Physician-patient race-match and patient outcomes. *SSRN Electronic Journal*, 3211276. https://doi.org/10.2139/ssrn.3211276

Hill, K., & Hurtado, A. M. (2009). Cooperative breeding in South American hunter-gatherers. *Proceedings of the Royal Society B: Biological Sciences, 276*(1674), 3863–3870. https://doi.org/10.1098/rspb.2009.1061

Howe, L. C., Goyer, J. P., & Crum, A. J. (2017). Harnessing the placebo effect: Exploring the influence of physician characteristics on placebo response. *Health Psychology, 36*(11), 1074–1082. https://doi.org/10.1037/hea0000499

Kappesser, J. (2019). The facial expression of pain in humans considered from a social perspective. *Philosophical Transactions of the Royal Society B: Biological Sciences, 374*(1785), 20190284. https://doi.org/10.1098/rstb.2019.0284

Kaptchuk, T. J. (2011). Placebo studies and ritual theory: A comparative analysis of Navajo, acupuncture and biomedical healing. *Philosophical Transactions of the Royal Society B: Biological Sciences, 366*(1572), 1849–1858. https://doi.org/10.1098/rstb.2010.0385

Karos, K. (2020). The enduring mystery of pain in a social context. *Journal of Adolescent Health, 66*(5), 524–525. https://doi.org/10.1016/j.jadohealth.2020.02.005

Karos, K., Meulders, A., Goubert, L., & Vlaeyen, J. W. S. (2020). Hide your pain: Social threat increases pain reports and aggression, but reduces facial pain expression and empathy. *The Journal of Pain, 21*(3), 334–346. https://doi.org/10.1016/j.jpain.2019.06.014

Karos, K., Williams, A. C. de C., Meulders, A., & Vlaeyen, J. W. S. (2018). Pain as a threat to the social self: A motivational account. *PAIN, 159*(9), 1690–1695. https://doi.org/10.1097/j.pain.0000000000001257

Kessler, S. E. (2020). Why care: Complex evolutionary history of human healthcare networks. *Frontiers in Psychology, 11*, 199. https://doi.org/10.3389/fpsyg.2020.00199

Kessler, S. E., Bonnell, T. R., Byrne, R. W., & Chapman, C. A. (2017). Selection to outsmart the germs: The evolution of disease recognition and social cognition. *Journal of Human Evolution, 108*, 92–109. https://doi.org/10.1016/j.jhevol.2017.02.009

Kessler, S. E., Bonnell, T. R., Setchell, J. M., & Chapman, C. A. (2018). Social structure facilitated the evolution of care-giving as a strategy for disease control in the human lineage. *Scientific Reports*, 13997. https://doi.org/10.1038/s41598-018-31568-2

Kirkpatrick, L. A., & Ellis, B. J. (2003). An evolutionary-psychological approach to self-esteem: Multiple domains and multiple functions. In G. J. O. Fletcher & M. S. Clark (Eds.), *Blackwell handbook of social psychology: Interpersonal processes* (pp. 409–436). Wiley. https://doi.org/10.1002/9780470998557.ch16

Kirsch, I. (2019). Placebo effect in the treatment of depression and anxiety. *Frontiers in Psychiatry, 10*, 407. https://doi.org/10.3389/fpsyt.2019.00407

Klebl, C., Greenaway, K., Rhee, J., & Bastian, B. (2020). Ugliness judgments alert us to cues of pathogen presence. *Social Psychological and Personality Science, 12*(5), 617–628. 194855062093165. https://doi.org/10.1177/19485 50620931655

Kohrt, B. A., Ottman, K., Panter-Brick, C., Konner, M., & Patel, V. (2020). Why we heal: The evolution of psychological healing and implications for global mental health. *Clinical Psychology Review, 82*, 101920. https://doi.org/10.1016/j.cpr.2020.101920

Krahé, C., Springer, A., Weinman, J. A., & Fotopoulou, A. (2013). The social modulation of pain: Others as predictive signals of salience—a systematic review. *Frontiers in Human Neuroscience, 7*, 386. https://doi.org/10.3389/fnhum.2013.00386

Leary, M. R., & Baumeister, R. F. (2000). The nature and function of self-esteem: Sociometer theory. In M. P. Zanna (Ed.), *Advances in experimental social psychology* (Vol. 32, pp. 1–62). Academic Press. https://doi.org/10.1016/S0065-2601(00)80003-9

Leary, M. R., & Downs, D. L. (1995). Interpersonal functions of the self-esteem motive. In M. H. Kernis (Eds.), *Efficacy, agency, and self-esteem* (pp. 123–144). Springer. https://doi.org/10.1007/978-1-4899-1280-0_7

Leary, M. R., Tambor, E., Terdal, S. K., & Downs, D. L. (1995). Self-esteem as an interpersonal monitor: The sociometer hypothesis. *Journal of Personality and Social Psychology, 68*(3), 518–530. https://doi.org/10.1037/0022-3514.68.3.518

Levinson, W., Roter, D. L., Mullooly, J. P., Dull, V. T., & Frankel, R. M. (1997). Physician-patient communication: The relationship with malpractice claims among primary care physicians and surgeons. *JAMA, 277*(7), 553–559. https://doi.org/10.1001/jama.1997.03540310051034

Lopes, P. C. (2014). When is it socially acceptable to feel sick? *Proceedings of the Royal Society B: Biological Sciences, 281*(1788), 20140218. https://doi.org/10.1098/rspb.2014.0218

Lopes, P. C., Adelman, J., Wingfield, J. C., & Bentley, G. E. (2012). Social context modulates sickness behavior. *Behavioral Ecology and Sociobiology, 66*(10), 1421–1428. https://doi.org/10.1007/s00265-012-1397-1

Lopes, P. C., Chan, H., Demathieu, S., González-Gómez, P. L., Wingfield, J. C., & Bentley, G. E. (2013). The impact of exposure to a novel female on symptoms of infection and on the reproductive axis. *Neuroimmunomodulation, 20*(6), 348–360. https://doi.org/10.1159/000353779

Master, S. L., Eisenberger, N. I., Taylor, S. E., Naliboff, B. D., Shirinyan, D., & Lieberman, M. D. (2009). A picture's worth: Partner photographs reduce experimentally induced pain. *Psychological Science, 20*(11), 1316–1318. https://doi.org/10.1111/j.1467-9280.2009.02444.x

Mattarozzi, K., Caponera, E., Russo, P. M., Colonnello, V., Bassetti, M., Farolfi, E., & Todorov, A. (2020). Pain and satisfaction: Healthcare providers' facial appearance matters. *Psychological Research, 85*, 1706–1712. https://doi.org/10.1007/s00426-020-01330-3

Moerman, D. E., & Jonas, W. B. (2002). Deconstructing the placebo effect and finding the meaning response. *Annals of Internal Medicine, 136*(6), 471–476.

Moieni, M., & Eisenberger, N. I. (2018). Effects of inflammation on social processes and implications for health. *Annals of the New York Academy of Sciences, 1428*(1), 5–13. https://doi.org/10.1111/nyas.13864

Murray, D. R., & Schaller, M. (2016). The behavioral immune system: Implications for social cognition, social interaction, and social influence. In J. M. Olson & M. P. Zanna (Eds.), *Advances in experimental social psychology* (pp. 75–129). Elsevier Academic Press.

Muscatell, K. A., Moieni, M., Inagaki, T. K., Dutcher, J. M., Jevtic, I., Breen, E. C., Irwin, M. R., & Eisenberger, N. I. (2016). Exposure to an inflammatory challenge enhances neural sensitivity to negative and positive social feedback. *Brain, Behavior, and Immunity, 57*, 21–29. https://doi.org/10.1016/j.bbi.2016.03.022

Navarrete, C. D., & Fessler, D. M. T. (2006). Disease avoidance and ethnocentrism: The effects of disease vulnerability and disgust sensitivity on intergroup attitudes. *Evolution and Human Behavior, 27*(4), 270–282. https://doi.org/10.1016/j.evolhumbehav.2005.12.001

Nesse, R. M. (2005). Natural selection and the regulation of defenses: A signal detection analysis of the smoke detector principle. *Evolution and Human Behavior, 26*(1), 88–105. https://doi.org/10.1016/j.evolhumbehav.2004.08.002

Nesse, R. M. (2019). *Good reasons for bad feelings: Insights from the frontier of evolutionary psychiatry*. Dutton.

Neuberg, S. L., Kenrick, D. T., & Schaller, M. (2011). Human threat management systems: self-protection and disease avoidance. *Neuroscience and Biobehavioral Reviews, 35*(4), 1042–1051. https://doi.org/10.1016/j.neubiorev.2010.08.011

Olsson, M. J., Lundström, J. N., Kimball, B. A., Gordon, A. R., Karshikoff, B., Hosseini, N., Sorjonen, K., Olgart Höglund, C., Solares, C., Soop, A., Axelsson, J., & Lekander, M. (2014). The scent of disease: Human body odor contains an early chemosensory cue of sickness. *Psychological Science, 25*(3), 817–823. https://doi.org/10.1177/0956797613515681

Ongaro, G. (2020). *The "placebo effect" in highland Laos: Insights from Akha medicine and shamanism into the problem of ritual efficacy*. London School of Economics.

Preston, S. D. (2013). The origins of altruism in offspring care. *Psychological Bulletin, 139*(6), 1305–1341. https://doi.org/10.1037/a0031755

Regenbogen, C., Axelsson, J., Lasselin, J., Porada, D. K., Sundelin, T., Peter, M. G., Lekander, M., Lundström, J. N., & Olsson, M. J. (2017). Behavioral and neural correlates to multisensory detection of sick humans. *Proceedings of the National Academy of Sciences, 114*(24), 6400–6405. https://doi.org/10.1073/pnas.1617357114

Roter, D. (2006). The patient-physician relationship and its implications for malpractice litigation. *Journal of Health Care Law & Policy, 9*, 304.

Ryan, S., Oaten, M., Stevenson, R. J., & Case, T. I. (2012). Facial disfigurement is treated like an infectious disease. *Evolution and Human Behavior, 33*(6), 639–646. https://doi.org/10.1016/j.evolhumbehav.2012.04.001

Sarolidou, G., Axelsson, J., Kimball, B. A., Sundelin, T., Regenbogen, C., Lundström, J. N., Lekander, M., & Olsson, M. J. (2020). People expressing olfactory and visual cues of disease are less liked. *Philosophical Transactions of the Royal Society B: Biological Sciences, 375*(1800), 20190272. https://doi.org/10.1098/rstb.2019.0272

Schrock, J. M., Snodgrass, J. J., & Sugiyama, L. S. (2020). Lassitude: The emotion of being sick. *Evolution and Human Behavior, 41*(1), 44–57. https://doi.org/10.1016/j.evolhumbehav.2019.09.002

Shakhar, K., & Shakhar, G. (2015). Why do we feel sick when infected—can altruism play a role? *PLoS Biology, 13*(10), e1002276. https://doi.org/10.1371/journal.pbio.1002276

Singh, M. (2017). The cultural evolution of shamanism. *The Behavioral and Brain Sciences, 41*, e66. https://doi.org/10.1017/S0140525X17001893

Spikins, P., Needham, A., Wright, B., Dytham, C., Gatta, M., & Hitchens, G. (2019). Living to fight another day: The ecological and evolutionary significance of Neanderthal healthcare. *Quaternary Science Reviews, 217*, 98–118. https://doi.org/10.1016/j.quascirev.2018.08.011

Steinkopf, L. (2015). The signaling theory of symptoms: An evolutionary explanation of the placebo effect. *Evolutionary Psychology, 13*(3), 1474704915600559. https://doi.org/10.1177/1474704915600559

Steinkopf, L. (2016). An evolutionary perspective on pain communication. *Evolutionary Psychology, 14*(2), 1474704916653964. https://doi.org/10.1177/1474704916653964

Steinkopf, L. (2017a). Disgust, empathy, and care of the sick: An evolutionary perspective. *Evolutionary Psychological Science, 3*(2), 149–158. https://doi.org/10.1007/s40806-016-0078-0

Steinkopf, L. (2017b). The social situation of sickness: An evolutionary perspective on therapeutic encounters. *Evolutionary Psychological Science, 3*(3), 270–286. https://doi.org/10.1007/s40806-017-0086-8

Steinkopf, L., & de Barra, M. (2018). Therapeutic encounters and the elicitation of community care. *Behavioral and Brain Sciences, 41*, 35–36. https://doi.org/10.1017/S0140525X17002175

Sugiyama, L. S. (2004). Illness, injury, and disability among Shiwiar forager-horticulturalists: Implications of health-risk buffering for the evolution of human life history. *American Journal of Physical Anthropology, 123*(4), 371–389. https://doi.org/10.1002/ajpa.10325

Sugiyama, L. S., & Chacon, R. (2000). Effects of illness and injury on foraging among the Yora and Shiwiar: Pathology risk as adaptive problem. In L. Cronk, N. Chagnon, & W. Irons (Eds.), *Adaptation and human behavior* (pp. 371–395). Routledge.

Tilley, L. (2015). *Theory and practice in the bioarchaeology of care*. Springer International.

Tiokhin, L. (2016). Do symptoms of illness serve signaling functions? (hint: yes). *The Quarterly Review of Biology, 91*(2), 177–195.

Tooby, J., & Cosmides, L. (2008). The evolutionary psychology of the emotions and their relationship to internal regulatory variables. In M. Lewis, J. M. Haviland-Jones, & L. F. Barrett (Eds.), *Handbook of emotions* (3rd ed., pp. 114–137). Guilford Press.

Twigg, O. C., & Byrne, D. G. (2015). The influence of contextual variables on judgments about patients and their pain. *Pain Medicine (Malden, Mass.), 16*(1), 88–98. https://doi.org/10.1111/pme.12587

Vartanian, L., Trewartha, T., Beames, J., Azevedo, S., & Vanman, E. (2017). Physiological and self-reported disgust reactions to obesity. *Cognition and Emotion, 32*, 1–14. https://doi.org/10.1080/02699931.2017.1325728

von Mohr, M., Krahé, C., Beck, B., & Fotopoulou, A. (2018). The social buffering of pain by affective touch: A laser-evoked potential study in romantic couples. *Social Cognitive and Affective Neuroscience, 13*(11), 1121–1130. https://doi.org/10.1093/scan/nsy085

Wall, P. (1999). *Pain: The science of suffering*. Weidenfeld and Nicolson.

Williams, A. C. de C. (2002). Facial expression of pain: An evolutionary account. *The Behavioral and Brain Sciences, 25*(4), 439–455; discussion 455-488.

Williams, A. C. de C. (2016). What can evolutionary theory tell us about chronic pain? *Pain, 157*(4), 788–790. https://doi.org/10.1097/j.pain.0000000000000464

Williams, A. C. de C., Gallagher, E., Fidalgo, A. R., & Bentley, P. J. (2016). Pain expressiveness and altruistic behavior: An exploration using agent-based modeling. *PAIN, 157*(3), 759–768. https://doi.org/10.1097/j.pain.0000000000000443

Williams, A. C. de C., & Kappesser, J. (2018). Why do we care? Evolutionary mechanisms in the social dimension of pain. In T. Hervort, K. Karos, Z. Trost, & K. M. Prkachin (Eds.), *Social and interpersonal dynamics in pain: We don't suffer alone* (pp. 3–22). Springer. https://doi.org/10.1007/978-3-319-78340-6_1

Wilson, E. (1978). *On human nature*. Harvard University Press.

Winkelman, M. (2010). *Shamanism: A biopsychosocial paradigm of consciousness and healing* (2nd ed.). Praeger.

Zahavi, A. (1977). The testing of a bond. *Animal Behavior, 25*, 246–247. https://doi.org/10.1016/0003-3472(77)90089-6

Zahavi, A. (1995). Altruism as a handicap: The limitations of kin selection and reciprocity. *Journal of Avian Biology, 26*(1), 1–3. https://doi.org/10.2307/3677205

Zaki, J., & Ochsner, K. (2018). Empathy. In L. F. Barrett, M. Lewis, & J. M. Haviland-Jones (Eds.), *Handbook of emotions* (4th ed., pp. 871–884). Taylor & Francis.

CHAPTER 34

Emotions and Olfaction

Laura Schäfer and Ilona Croy

Abstract

This chapter provides a comprehensive overview linking the sense of smell to the field of emotion. The authors focus on the evolution of the olfactory system and its anatomical pathways, including overlapping structures with emotional processing circuits. The chapter proceeds with a detailed analysis of the functional relationship between olfaction and emotion based on the following topics: odors and leading emotional reactions; odors as chemosignals within social communication (focusing on a definition of chemosignals; chemosignals and emotional contagion; and chemosignals within intimate relationships); and odors as a basis for multisensory integration in the context of emotional processing. Throughout the chapter, the authors present a broad range of experimental studies including behavioral and neuroimaging investigations, as well as implications of research on patients with olfactory deficits.

Key Words: olfaction, emotion, sensory system, smell disorder, limbic system, evolution, sense of smell, chemosignals, chemosensory communication, body odor

Introduction

The sense of smell affects human behavior independent from its recognition (Sela & Sobel, 2010). This influence is based on a strong coupling of olfactory and affective perception. Pleasant odors enhance well-being and mood (Lehrner et al., 2000); unpleasant odors evoke disgust (Croy, Olgun, et al., 2011); familiar odors provide comfort (McBurney et al., 2006); and body odors convey attractiveness (Sorokowska et al., 2018), anxiety (Prehn-Kristensen et al., 2009), or aggression states (Mutic et al., 2016). This chapter explores how the sense of smell impacts feelings and emotional states. We address how odors differ from other sensory stimuli, bridging the gap from the evolutionary importance of odors to recent neuroscience on associations between olfaction and emotions.

Despite initial neglect in research of human perception, with vision and hearing being more prominent targets (Hutmacher, 2019), olfaction is an ancient sense (Stoddart, 2012). Odors initiate emotional and behavioral responses, which enhance survival—e.g., by allowing detection of rotten food or by guiding the infant to find the maternal breast (Stevenson, 2010). Ehrlichman and Bastone (1992) reviewed previous available findings and formulated the idea of "olfaction as an emotional sense," including defining several propositions supporting this concept. These included, e.g., that *hedonicity* is the leading percept of olfactory perception and that hedonic tone is likewise part of affective reactions, the *anatomical overlap* between emotional and olfactory neural circuits, or evidence on *direct effects of odors on emotions and memory.* Although we will not examine every proposition in detail, single aspects will be presented throughout the chapter.

To derive commonalities and connections between olfaction and emotion, it is first necessary to clarify these terms. Olfaction is "the function whereby odors are perceived," and odors, in turn, are "particular sensations elicited by the action of certain chemical substances on the olfactory system" (Soudry et al., 2011, p. 18). When it comes to emotion, clarification of terms is more complicated, as there is no consistent definition. A classical description has been established by Schachter and Singer (1962, p. 380), who labeled emotions as "a state of physiological arousal and of cognition appropriate to this state of arousal." A common feature of most definitions refers to emotion as a "mental state" which occurs, e.g., on the basis of a physiological sensation (Cabanac, 2002).

According to Soudry et al. (2011), similarities between olfaction and emotion can be categorized in terms of anatomical and functional aspects. *Anatomical similarities* refer to the fact that the emergence of olfactory processing structures paralleled the development of the ancient brain (for an overview, see Pribram & Kruger, 1954) and occurred in areas such as the limbic system (Gottfried, 2006), which is an old, essential system encoding affective and olfactory stimuli (Soudry et al., 2011). *Functional similarities* are observed by studies investigating smell disordered patients. These patients show not only reduced neural processing of emotional stimuli such as pictures (Han et al., 2019), but also a reduction in overall well-being, quality of life (Croy, Nordin, et al., 2014), and enhanced vulnerability to depression (Croy & Hummel, 2017). Considering the main functions of olfaction, which consist of guidance of nutrition, hazard avoidance, and social communication (Stevenson, 2010), this link is not astonishing. However, it is necessary to analyze carefully how olfactory perception influences emotional states to derive broader conclusions.

In the first part of the chapter, we elucidate the *anatomical relationship* between olfaction and emotion based on (1) a short overview of evolution and olfaction, followed by (2) a detailed description of the anatomical pathways of olfactory processing, including its links to emotional neural circuits. The second part of the chapter deals with the *functional liaison* between olfaction and emotion, whereby we (1) present major emotions related to the olfactory percept; (2) reveal insights in the function of chemosignals (e.g., how body odors can affect emotional states); and (3) summarize the interplay of olfaction and the other sensory systems when it comes to emotional perception. For each section, recent evidence from behavioral as well as neuroimaging studies is presented, followed by presentation of findings in patients with impaired olfactory abilities.

A Short Evolutionary and Anatomical Perspective on Olfactory Processing

Olfaction has been characterized as the "most elementary and most fleeting of all senses" (Mombaerts, in Wilhelm, 2009, p. 33). It is one of the oldest, as well as one of the subtlest, sensory domains. Humans can detect and discriminate thousands of odors (Bushdid et al., 2014) and this ability is of crucial evolutionary relevance.

Phylogenetically, chemosensation is the oldest form of communication, originating 500 million years ago (Stoddart, 2012). Thus, olfaction was established before the onset of myelinated processing, which occurred about 100 million years later (Zalc et al., 2008), and olfactory stimuli are still processed primarily through unmyelinated fibers. The forebrain of subreptilian vertebrates is dominated by olfactory processing, and the same conserved structures apply to humans, although newer structures have also emerged during evolution (Northcutt, 2002; for an overview, see Pribram & Kruger, 1954). Chemosensory input enables environmental assessment and thus hazard avoidance, as well as identification of suitable food and sexual partners. Hence, olfactory stimuli provide information that is critical to the survival. To utilize such information, an avoidance or approaching motivation with the appropriate behavioral consequences is necessary. Such motivation is enabled by emotional processing of olfaction. Even more, as olfaction was one of the first senses to evolve, it may have been the driver for the onset of emotional processing, and structures that process emotions and odors are thought to have coevolved (Northcutt, 2002). Therefore, the same olfactory brain structures that underlie survival functions in invertebrates and subreptiles also monitor basic human emotions and behaviors (LeDoux, 2012).

The processing of olfactory information in humans differs from that of the other senses by a relatively long time for receptor activation, bypassing of the thalamus, short signaling pathways to the limbic system, and by poor spatial and temporal resolution. Odors reach the olfactory epithelium, which is located in the upper part of the olfactory mucosa, and bind to the cell bodies of olfactory receptor neurons. This chemical binding procedure is slow compared to visual input. The first chemosensory peripheral potentials occur after 70 to 100 ms (Kobal, 1981) as compared to 35 ms for visual stimulation of the retina (Holder et al., 2007). Derivations from the human olfactory epithelium show that the pleasantness and unpleasantness of odors are already encoded at a peripheral level (Lapid et al., 2011). The olfactory receptor neurons terminate in the olfactory bulb, where activation patterns of olfactory glomeruli represent different odor qualities (Firestein, 2001). From the olfactory bulb, information propagates to a number of structures, including the entorhinal and piriform cortex, which are parts of the primary olfactory cortex (Gottfried, 2006; Wilson et al., 2015). The secondary and tertiary olfactory cortices, including the amygdaloid complex (Zald & Pardo, 1997), the hippocampus, the orbitofrontal cortex, the prefrontal cortex, the nucleus accumbens, parahippocampal gyrus, insula (Lascano et al., 2010), and ventral striatum (Gottfried, 2006), are indirectly connected to the olfactory bulb. Olfactory fibers reaching the amygdala and hippocampus bypass the thalamus (Keller, 2011) (see Figure 34.1).

Due to the slow chemical binding and central information processing via unmyelinated—hence slow-conducting fibers—behavioral responses to odors are delayed and occur with latencies of 600–1,200 ms (Cain, 1976). Again, this is slower than the 200 ms response time for visual stimuli (Spence & Driver, 1997). Moreover, olfactory information is not spatially coded. Neither the first central olfactory processing structure—the olfactory bulb—nor the subsequent structures show a clear odotopic organization (Wilson et al., 2014). Hence, humans cannot localize whether an odor was presented to the left or the right nostril—at least if the odor does not simultaneously activate the trigeminal system (Croy, Schulz, et al., 2014; Skramlik, 1924). This results in a poor ability to detect changes in the olfactory environment (Menzel et al., 2019), which results in a "constant state of change-blindness" toward olfactory stimuli (Sela & Sobel, 2010, p. 12).

Disorders of Olfaction

Approximately one in four people in Western society has an impaired sense of smell (e.g., Vennemann et al., 2008), referred to as hyposmia, or—in the complete absence of an olfactory perception—anosmia. As with other senses, olfactory impairment is more prevalent in older than younger people (Doty et al., 1984) and the decline occurs around the fifth decade (Hummel et al., 2007).

Olfactory disorders can be divided into acquired and congenital, with acquired disorders making up the majority, and isolated congenital anosmia occurring in only about 1 in 10,000 people (Bojanowski et al., 2013).

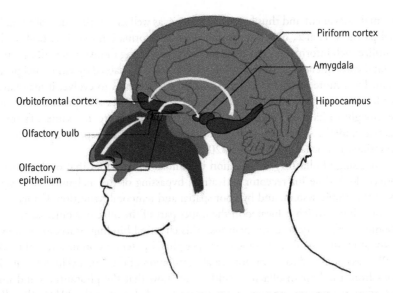

Figure 34.1. Anatomical areas of olfactory processing. In the olfactory epithelium, located in the upper part of the nasal tract, molecules bind to the olfactory receptor neurons, the axons of which reach the olfactory bulb. From there, olfactory fibers project to the piriform cortex, entorhinal cortex (not shown), amygdala, and hippocampus before reaching secondary and tertiary olfactory processing areas, such as the orbitofrontal gyrus. Most olfactory processing neurons bypass the thalamus, which serves as a relay for processing of other senses.

Acquired hyposmia and anosmia occur mainly in sinunasal diseases and postviral, but also after traumatic cranial injuries, such as after motorcycle accidents, or as a concomitant symptom in neurodegenerative diseases such as Parkinson's or Alzheimer's disease (Doty, 2012; C. Marin et al., 2018; Temmel et al., 2002).

In addition to the quantitative olfactory disorders of hyposmia and anosmia, which affect the magnitude of the olfactory impression, qualitative disorders occur less frequently (Croy, Nordin, et al., 2014). These phenomena, called parosmia, phantosmia, or olfactory hallucination, are characterized by unpleasant odor impressions and occur partly as transitory phenomenon during the regeneration of the sense of smell.

Emotion and Olfaction

Olfaction serves as a cue to beneficial objects, such as food, and as a defense mechanism that allows the individual to move away from prospective hazards (Stevenson, 2010) and to prepare for the appropriate regurgitating or avoidance response (Croy, Laqua, et al., 2013; Ruser et al., 2021). However, although visual stimuli can communicate a wide array of emotions, olfactory cues mainly relate to disgust and happiness (Croy, Olgun, et al., 2011). Hence, people describe an odor as pleasant or unpleasant, or as disgusting or "nice," but the richness of subtle emotional experiences is underrepresented for olfaction (Bensafi et al., 2002).

The induction of adaptive behavioral responses by odors has been targeted in experimental studies. While pleasant odors (e.g., chocolate) increase subjects' looking duration for presented visual stimuli (Knasko, 1995), olfactory exposure to putrescine, a chemical substance released from dead and decaying bodies, enhances vigilance reactions, increases flight behavior, threat-related cognition, and hostility toward an out-group (Wisman & Shrira, 2015).

There is inter- and intra-individual variability in the perception of olfactory stimuli that depends on cultural background, genetics, associative learning, and physiological conditions (Mantel et al., 2019) and which is facilitated by the ambiguity of olfactory information (Croy et al., 2015). Therefore, the environmental context has an impact on olfactory evaluation (De Araujo et al., 2005). The same feces-like odor, obtained from the anal gland of cats, for instance, is perceived either as extremely unpleasant or as a nice, farm-like fragrance, depending on life experiences (Croy et al., 2016).

Body Odors as a Means of Social Sommunication
What Are Pheromones and Chemosignals?

Body odors contribute to communication in many species. In animals, olfactory cues guide mate choice (Roberts & Gosling, 2004), kin recognition (Henkel & Setchell, 2018), and increase the probability of survival (Asahina et al., 2008). Those chemical agents involved in interactions between organisms are called semiochemicals; a large part of semiochemicals are pheromones, which are the responsible signals for within-species communication (Wyatt, 2014). Pheromones are "molecules that are evolved signals [. . .] which are emitted by an individual and received by a second individual of the same species, in which they cause a specific reaction, for example, a stereotyped behaviour or a developmental process" (Wyatt, 2010, p. 687, modified from Karlson & Lüscher, 1959). From an evolutionary point of view, this exchange has to be "beneficial [. . .] to both sender and receiver" (Meredith, 2001, p. 440). Chemosensory reception and processing occurs in the accessory olfactory system via the vomeronasal organ (VNO; Jacobson organ; Meredith, 2001). For instance, vomeronasal perception of olfactory signals from female mice leads to steroid hormone secretion in males (Pfeiffer & Johnston, 1994). The difference between pheromones and other semiochemicals is that while pheromones are signals, other semiochemicals "can be used for information but did not evolve for that function" (Wyatt, 2014, p. 6). This includes molecule combinations, referred to as signature mixtures, characterizing an individual odor profile, which are learned and used to recognize kinship (for details, see Wyatt, 2014).

In humans, the chemical agents responsible for communication are termed *chemosignals*. Evidence of human pheromones historically and currently is debated (Meredith, 2001; Suhle & Croy, 2019). The only established human pheromone occurs within the mother-child relationship and refers to the maternally released breast odor, which elicits directed infant's movements toward the odor (Varendi & Porter, 2001). Not only in the context of parents and children, but also within romantic relationships, body odors provide information for perception (e.g., attractiveness; Sorokowska et al., 2018) and behavior (e.g., sexuality; Cerda-Molina et al., 2013). Besides intimate relationships, chemosignals guide communication in various social situations, in which they transfer information about the releaser, including physical status (i.e., health or nutrition status; Havlicek & Lenochova, 2006; Olsson et al., 2014) or the releaser's emotional state, which can lead to emotional contagion in the receiver (de Groot et al., 2015). In the following, the major research areas referring to (1) emotional status and contagion and (2) intimate relationships are considered in detail.

Emotional Status and Contagion

The exchange of emotional information is a frequently studied phenomenon related to perception of human chemosignals. The sender's emotional state is communicated via body odors as emotional involvement alters the composition of human sweat (Smeets et al., 2020). In addition, odor profile varies as a dose-response function of emotional intensity: De Groot et al. (2020) demonstrated that intensity of induced fear in the odor donor related to enhanced axillary sweat, and higher numbers of volatile compounds in sweat.

Humans are able to classify odors indicating happiness vs. fear based on the emotional situation during sampling and mediated by the releaser's sex (Chen & Haviland-Jones, 2000). Besides allowing classification of emotional states, chemosignals carry the potential for emotional contagion from sender to receiver: body odors sampled in a happy mood evoke electrophysiological facial reactions related to happiness in the perceiver (de Groot et al., 2015). Likewise, negative emotions, such as aggression (Mutic et al., 2016), disgust, or fear (de Groot et al., 2012) are communicated by human body odors and evoke emotion-specific responses in the receiver. These findings on subjective and electrophysiological assessments are supported by imaging data: emotional odors activate different neural patterns when originating from sweat sampled in an anxiety (exam) vs. in a sport condition (Prehn-Kristensen et al., 2009). While anxiety signals activate brain regions responsible for empathy and social behavior, those activations are not observable after exposure to sweat odor originating from physical exercise. Physical competition nevertheless seems to be communicated by sweat; Fialová et al. (2020) investigated body odor perception in response to competition. They sampled odors from mixed martial arts fighters after a competition and explored perceived quality in relationship to competition outcome. Their results showed reduction in perceived quality after a competition irrespective of the outcome, but the odors of losers were rated less attractive when the rater was in a negative emotional state. Supporting this finding, Adolph et al. (2010) revealed elevated skin conductance responses in subjects after exposure to sweat sampled in a competition vs. a neutral condition.

Emotional contagion has been assumed to serve the evolutionary purpose of survival by enhancing alertness to fearful stimuli to detect potential threat and allow flight reactions (Susskind et al., 2008; Wisman & Shrira, 2015), by downregulating perception to decrease exposure to disgust-associated stimuli (Scherer et al., 2001; Susskind et al., 2008), and by induction of approach behavior in response to pleasant stimuli (Gomez & Gomez, 2002).

Intimate Relationships
Romantic Relationships
When it comes to partner choice, different physiological and social factors come into play to find the right mate, and olfaction plays a subtle but recognizable role (see Mahmut & Croy, 2019, for overview). While men name good looks as the most important attractiveness criterion, women report it is body odor that is most important. And for both sexes, liking of a potential partner's natural body odor is most decisive for sexual interest (Herz & Inzlicht, 2002). Experimental studies have investigated attractiveness perception by means of body odor. Human body odor is produced through secretion of lacrimal, urogenital, apocrine, and mammary glands. A high concentration of volatile odorants is found in the axilla area with densely distributed apocrine sweat glands (Natsch & Emter, 2020), which are present from birth, but become active at puberty (Grammer et al., 2005). Those secretions are scentless but bacterial decomposition of the single components leads to the perceived smell of sweat (Brennan & Zufall, 2006). Body odors consist of stable (genetic) and dynamic (hormonal, environmental) compounds. While environmental variables, such as culture (e.g., differences in hygiene-related behavior; Soo & Stevenson, 2007) or nutrition (e.g., garlic, Fialová et al., 2016), are variable and thus difficult to target in experimental studies, previous research has focused on the stable genetic and low-dynamic, hormonal components to explore the influence of body odors on mate choice and sexual behavior.

Among the *genetic* components, the human leucocyte antigen (HLA) profile has been a focus of previous research. The HLA system is an important player in the immune response, and its alleles are co-dominantly inherited as a combination of paternal and maternal haplotype (Kromer, 2015). Mating with an HLA-dissimilar partner may beneficial from an evolutionary point of view, as this enhances the offspring's immune variability and thus healthiness. HLA-similar odors evoke other neural reactivity patterns in the human brain than HLA-dissimilar odors (Milinski et al., 2013) and Wedekind et al. (1995) were the first to show that body odors of HLA-dissimilar donors were perceived as more pleasant. This initiated a number of studies on HLA effects as mediators of attractiveness perception in human mate choice, and the heterogeneous findings resulted in debate (for a review, see Havlicek & Roberts, 2009). A recent meta-analysis does not find evidence for HLA-mediated body odor perception or for its influence on mate choice (Havlíček et al., 2020). The relevance of HLA for human mating remains unclear (see also Croy et al., 2020).

Regarding the constituents of body odor, steroid hormones and their metabolites affect olfactory perception. Among these, androstanol, androstadienone (primary components of male sweat; Gower et al., 1994), and estradiol (reflecting estrogen levels in sweat; Gower & Ruparelia, 1993) elicit sex-specific neural responses in the hypothalamus (Savic et al., 2001; Savic & Berglund, 2010), which links to the release of hormones relevant for sexual behavior (Meethal & Atwood, 2005). Exposure to androstadienone mediates mood in a sex-differential manner—namely, lower mood in men and higher mood in women after smelling the odorant (Jacob et al., 2001). Men perceive female body odors as most attractive during ovulation, which is reflected in elevated testosterone levels after exposure to female body odors sampled throughout that ovulatory cycle phase. Beyond that, male attractiveness ratings of women's body odors relate to the donors' reproductive state in terms of estradiol and progesterone levels (Lobmaier et al., 2018).

Body odors are not only mediators of attractiveness perception, but also a source of comfort and well-being. Asking healthy adults for sources of comfort during separation periods, a majority seek contentment in the smell of the partner, by smelling or even sleeping in a worn garment (McBurney et al., 2006). Granqvist et al. (2019) showed that subjective and physiological discomfort during stress are diminished when participants could smell their partner's odor. Women in partnerships prefer their own partner's body odor compared to the odors of other men, and this preference relates to familiarity of the odor (Mahmut et al., 2019). Another study points toward an olfactory deflection phenomenon within passionate relationships—women with greater romantic love perform worse in identification of a male friend's body odor, which might contribute to deflected attention toward potential new mates (Lundström & Jones-Gotman, 2009).

Sexuality

The sense of smell influences sexual behavior. Perception of female ovulatory axilla and vulva scents, for example, are associated with heightened sexual interest, paralleled by elevated testosterone and decreased cortisol levels (Cerda-Molina et al., 2013), which relate to greater engagement in flirting, but also facilitation of affiliation and intimacy (Ditzen et al., 2008; van der Meij et al., 2012). In line with that, the hypothalamic response to exposure of androstadienone may reflect a neural correlate for sexual motivation (Burke et al., 2012; Sewards & Sewards, 2003). Hedonic quality of specific odorants varies as a function of sexual experience: women with sexual experience perceive the odor of androstenone as more pleasant than women without sexual experience (Knaapila et al., 2012), which implies that an associative learning mechanism shapes perceived odor quality. In view of findings demonstrating a relationship between disgust and lower sexual arousal (Andrews et al., 2015), as well as reduced pleasantness of touch during smelling an unpleasant odor (Croy, Angelo, et al., 2014), perceived pleasantness of intimate odors might be crucial for sexual experience. Not only the quality of olfactory perception but also the level of olfactory abilities is linked to sexual experience: healthy students exhibiting more sensitive odor thresholds report greater pleasure during intercourse, and in women, olfactory sensitivity correlates with more frequent orgasms (Bendas et al., 2018). Although in that healthy sample olfactory performance did not affect sexual desire, which is important to initiate sexual behavior, or sexual performance (duration/frequency of intercourse), these results suggest an impact of odor perception on sexual satisfaction during sexual activities.

Findings in Patients with Anosmia/Hyposmia
Congenital and acquired olfactory dysfunction are associated with quantitative and qualitative impairments in sexuality. Male patients with isolated congenital anosmia report fewer sexual partners, while affected women state heightened partnership insecurity (Croy, Bojanowski, et al., 2013); and about one-third of patients with acquired smell loss describe a decrement in their sexual desire after disease onset, which is predicted by severity of olfactory impairment and symptoms of depression (Schäfer, Mehler, et al., 2019). This finding is supported by qualitative reports, in which those affected state to feel a lack of intimacy and sexual attraction caused by body odors prior to the olfactory loss (Schäfer, Mehler, et al., 2019).

Mother-Child Relationship
The affective bond between a mother and her infant is shaped by mutual biological cues, which facilitate the formation of attachment in the first year of life (Bowlby, 1958; Swain, 2008). Chemosignals play a pronounced role in that process, as the olfactory system is well-developed already *in utero* and helps in orienting toward the environment immediately after birth (Schaal et al., 2004; Schaal & Orgeur, 1992). The newborn has to rely on the tactile and olfactory domain, as vision and audition are poorly developed at birth and need several months to mature to full functioning (Graven, 2004). Infants are able to detect familiar odors, such as the odor of amniotic fluid (Schaal et al., 1995), which is why olfactory recognition abilities are assumed to be transferred from pre- to postnatal state. Also, infants show odor preferences after birth for odors they had been acquainted to by their mother's diet during pregnancy (Schaal et al., 2000).

The areolar region of the breast is important as it releases a characteristic pattern of volatile odors which allows the infant to find the nipple (Doucet et al., 2009). The secretion is a mixture of sweat, sebum, and milk, and this combination boosts motivation to drink (Doucet et al., 2009). In addition, breast odor enhances multisensory integration in the infant. A study by Doucet, Soussignan, Sagot, and Schaal (2007) revealed that babies gaze longer into their mother's eyes and search more strongly for eye contact when they are exposed to maternal breast odor than when they do not have olfactory stimulation. Even infants fed with formula milk show stronger oral reactions when they are exposed to the odor of maternal milk (Marlier & Schaal, 2005). Preterm infants exhibit enhanced sucking rates and milk ingestion when they are exposed to the maternal milk odor during feeding periods with formula (Yildiz et al., 2011).

These innate reactions facilitate survival of the newborn. Beyond that, familiar odors exert stress-relieving effects at early infant age. Maternal body odor thus has been the most prominent source of comfort, and has been shown to reduce physiological stress during a routine heel-stick procedure or separation periods (Neshat et al., 2016; Nishitani et al., 2009). To experience such soothing effects, the infant needs to recognize that odor as familiar. Newborns are able to distinguish their mother from other women by axillary odor, already two days postpartum (M. M. Marin et al., 2015).

Mothers are able to reliably recognize their own infant based on body odor within the first days postpartum (Porter et al., 1983), and even after less than one hour of exposure postpartum (Kaitz et al., 1987). Olfactory-mediated kin recognition is assumed to facilitate attachment formation by allowing a targeted investment of altruistic resources (Park et al., 2008). Beyond informing about belonging to one's own family, the infant odor is an important source of instrumental and affective communication (Okamoto et al., 2016). As young parents often describe, the scent of their own baby is immensely pleasing and its hedonic signature is assumed to function as a biological signal promoting affection toward the infant (Croy et al., 2017). Supporting this observation, questionnaire studies revealed that this pleasant evaluation (1) is especially true for the odor of the infant head, which is used as a source for affective experience (Okamoto et al., 2016); and (2) is highest in infants, and decreases with the child's age (Croy et al., 2017). Behavioral studies provide further evidence for these reports. When presented with body odors of own child and unfamiliar children, mothers prefer their own child's odor (Croy et al., 2019; Schäfer et al., 2020). That mechanism seems to be related to bonding quality: the olfactory preference for own child's odor applies to healthy mothers, but is absent in mothers with postpartum bonding disorders—in comparison to the healthy controls, the patients group neither preferred nor identified their own baby's body odor among unfamiliar odor samples (Croy et al., 2019). In a similar vein, Fleming et al. (1993) found the quality of olfactory experience, namely a positive hedonic evaluation of one's own baby's odor, to be associated with positive feelings and closer contact between mother and infant. This is not only true for babies, but also can be transferred to children of primary school age; Dubas et al. (2009) reported that mothers show lower punishment behavior toward their child when they evaluate their child's odor as more pleasant.

Additional hints about the hedonic value carried by children's odors come from neuroimaging studies. When presented with unfamiliar baby body odors, mothers show greater neural reactions than non-mothers in the global prefrontal cortex (Nishitani et al., 2014), as well as in specific regions associated with reward processing (Lundström et al., 2013). A recent functional magnetic resonance imaging (fMRI) study targeted maternal brain responses to own baby's odor to develop an optimal fMRI paradigm detecting neural correlates of baby body odors (Schäfer, Hummel, et al., 2019). The results revealed that the own baby's body odor activates primary and secondary olfactory, as well as social processing, structures (superior temporal gyrus, STG) and hence may represent a relevant social cue for relationship formation.

Findings in Patients with Anosmia/Hyposmia

A survey of Bojanowski et al. (2013) points to the fact that patients with congenital anosmia suffer from missing the olfactory experience in close family relationships. About one-quarter of the sample stated regretting not being able to smell the own child's or the partner's body odor. Empirical evidence from olfactory disordered patients, however, has been insufficient, and this requires further investigation.

Odors as Background for Other Senses: Sensory Integration When It Comes to Emotional Reactions

Olfactory perception depends on context and integration with other sensory impressions. Due to the poor spatial and temporal resolution of olfactory information (Sela & Sobel, 2010), the sense of smell needs further information, for example as provided by the visual system, to locate the odorant in space, or as provided by the language system, to recognize the odor (Olofsson & Gottfried, 2015). G. Zhou et al. (2019) recently discovered that interaction between olfactory and auditory stimuli is reflected by phase-synchrony of neural oscillations in the respective processing cortices. The integration of different modalities mutually shapes and boosts sensory processing (Thesen et al., 2004). This could be applied to strengthen outcomes of clinical interventions, such as in the context of parent-child relationships. Here, the interaction between olfactory and tactile perception is of special relevance—from animal studies, it is known that this interaction is essential for early attachment formation (Fleming et al., 1999). Both senses mature earlier than other sensory systems (Graven, 2004) and human studies also demonstrate their importance for early childhood development (Modrcin-Talbott et al., 2003; Yildiz et al., 2011). The combination of olfactory and tactile stimuli is used, e.g., in the kangaroo mother care technique and has a pain-reducing effect on premature infants (Johnston et al., 2009). Multisensory enhancement is also assumed to shape infantile perceptual development in a specific manner; four-month-old infants exhibit augmented neural responses of selective facial categorization but not general visual processing when exposed to maternal odor (Leleu et al., 2020). In a similar vein, pleasant odor perception has been associated with increased look duration toward smiling vs. disgusted face in infants (Godard et al., 2016). In adults, similar mechanisms are observed: when presented to emotional visual stimuli, emotional recognition performance is improved during simultaneous odor exposure, which is paralleled by enhanced connectivity between the respective crossmodal cortical areas (Novak et al., 2015). Such a mechanism accounts for synergy in ambiguous situations, to support stimulus encoding by "inverse effectiveness" (Stein & Meredith, 1993), thus leading to enhanced survival reactions. In line with that, W. Zhou and Chen (2009) demonstrated that fearful odors bias emotional attribution to ambiguous faces, resulting in more fearful interpretation. Social processing of faces is thus prone to subtle influences of cross-modal olfactory input: Li et al. (2007) revealed that unconscious odor perception shapes likability ratings of facial expressions with regard to the odor valence, and Seubert et al. (2014) demonstrated that attractiveness perception varies with concomitant odor stimulation and appraisal.

Findings in Patients with Anosmia/Hyposmia
The encoding of emotional information is a key factor in social communication to allow empathy and appropriate reactions toward a communication partner (Lawrence et al., 2004). In healthy individuals, olfactory performance is related to empathy (Mahmut & Stevenson, 2012, 2016), and heightened olfactory sensitivity is found in individuals with greater social agreeableness (Croy, Springborn, et al., 2011). In turn, patients after traumatic brain injury (Neumann et al., 2012) exhibit lower performances in affect recognition and lower scores of empathy measures in relation to olfactory dysfunction. Reports of patients with olfactory loss further reveal problems with social life and a range of insecurities, including worries about social relations and concerns about their personal hygiene in social situations (e.g., the fear of smelling bad; Blomqvist et al., 2004; Croy, Nordin, et al., 2014). However, many hyposmic or anosmic patients are able to cope with their impairment and often do not notice their deficit (Oleszkiewicz et al., 2020). This again points to the importance of sensory integration, in which the sense of smell serves as an important, but not indispensable, background on which other senses are perceived.

Conclusion
The sense of smell and emotions are functionally related to each other. Olfactory and emotional processing pathways share anatomical structures, and odors play a crucial role in social

Olfactory Communication

Emotional Contagion
- Aggression
- Anxiety
- Happiness

Romantic Relationship
- Sexuality
- Mate Choice

Parent Child Relationship
- Kin Recognition
- Affection

Figure 34.2. Different functions of human olfactory communication relating to emotional contagion and intimate relationships (romantic relationships and parent-child relationships).

communication. Chemosignals transport emotional information and evoke emotional contagion in the receiver. Furthermore, they contribute to kin recognition and affection in intimate relationships (see Figure 34.2). Olfaction is on the one hand an important sensory channel for social communication and emotional perception, but also particularly significant in the interaction with other senses to increase multimodal perception.

References

Adolph, D., Schlösser, S., Hawighorst, M., & Pause, B. M. (2010). Chemosensory signals of competition increase the skin conductance response in humans. *Physiology & Behavior, 101*(5), 666–671. https://doi.org/10.1016/j.physbeh.2010.08.004

Andrews, A. R., Crone, T., Cholka, C. B., Cooper, T. V., & Bridges, A. J. (2015). Correlational and experimental analyses of the relation between disgust and sexual arousal. *Motivation and Emotion, 39*(5), 766–779. https://doi.org/10.1007/s11031-015-9485-y

Asahina, K., Pavlenkovich, V., & Vosshall, L. B. (2008). The survival advantage of olfaction in a competitive environment. *Current Biology, 18*(15), 1153–1155. https://doi.org/10.1016/j.cub.2008.06.075

Bendas, J., Hummel, T., & Croy, I. (2018). Olfactory function relates to sexual experience in adults. *Archives of Sexual Behavior, 47*(5), 1333–1339. https://doi.org/10.1007/s10508-018-1203-x

Bensafi, M., Rouby, C., Farget, V., Bertrand, B., Vigouroux, M., & Holley, A. (2002). Psychophysiological correlates of affects in human olfaction. *Neurophysiologie Clinique = Clinical Neurophysiology, 32*(5), 326–332. https://doi.org/10.1016/s0987-7053(02)00339-8

Blomqvist, E. H., Brämerson, A., Stjärne, P., & Nordin, S. (2004). Consequences of olfactory loss and adopted coping strategies. *Rhinology, 42*(4), 189–194.

Bojanowski, V., Hummel, T., & Croy, I. (2013). [Isolated congenital anosmia: Clinical and daily life aspects of a life without a sense of smell]. *Laryngo-Rhino-Otologie, 92*(1), 30–33. https://doi.org/10.1055/s-0032-1329949

Bowlby, J. (1958). The nature of the child's tie to his mother. *International Journal of Psychoanalysis, 39*, 350–373.

Brennan, P. A., & Zufall, F. (2006). Pheromonal communication in vertebrates. *Nature, 444*(7117), 308–315. https://doi.org/10.1038/nature05404

Burke, S. M., Veltman, D. J., Gerber, J., Hummel, T., & Bakker, J. (2012). Heterosexual men and women both show a hypothalamic response to the chemo-signal androstadienone. *PLoS ONE, 7*(7), e40993. https://doi.org/10.1371/journal.pone.0040993

Bushdid, C., Magnasco, M. O., Vosshall, L. B., & Keller, A. (2014). Humans can discriminate more than 1 trillion olfactory stimuli. *Science, 343*(6177), 1370–1372.

Cabanac, M. (2002). What is emotion? *Behavioural Processes, 60*(2), 69–83.

Cain, W. S. (1976). Olfaction and the common chemical sense: Some psychophysical contrasts. *Sensory Processes, 1*(1), 57–67.

Cerda-Molina, A. L., Hernández-López, L., de la O, C. E., Chavira-Ramírez, R., & Mondragón-Ceballos, R. (2013). Changes in men's salivary testosterone and cortisol levels, and in sexual desire after smelling female axillary and vulvar scents. *Frontiers in Endocrinology, 4*, 1–9. https://doi.org/10.3389/fendo.2013.00159

Chen, D., & Haviland-Jones, J. (2000). Human olfactory communication of emotion. *Perceptual and Motor Skills, 91*(3), 771–781. https://doi.org/10.2466/pms.2000.91.3.771

Croy, I., Angelo, S. D., & Olausson, H. (2014). Reduced pleasant touch appraisal in the presence of a disgusting odor. *PLoS ONE, 9*(3), e92975. https://doi.org/10.1371/journal.pone.0092975

Croy, I., Bojanowski, V., & Hummel, T. (2013). Men without a sense of smell exhibit a strongly reduced number of sexual relationships, women exhibit reduced partnership security: A reanalysis of previously published data. *Biological Psychology, 92*(2), 292–294. https://doi.org/10.1016/j.biopsycho.2012.11.008

Croy, I., Drechsler, E., Hamilton, P., Hummel, T., & Olausson, H. (2016). Olfactory modulation of affective touch processing: A neurophysiological investigation. *NeuroImage, 135*, 135–141. https://doi.org/10.1016/j.neuroimage.2016.04.046

Croy, I., Frackowiak, T., Hummel, T., & Sorokowska, A. (2017). Babies smell wonderful to their parents, teenagers do not: An exploratory questionnaire study on children's age and personal odor ratings in a Polish sample. *Chemosensory Perception, 10*(3), 81–87. https://doi.org/10.1007/s12078-017-9230-x

Croy, I., & Hummel, T. (2017). Olfaction as a marker for depression. *Journal of Neurology, 264*(4), 631–638. https://doi.org/10.1007/s00415-016-8227-8

Croy, I., Laqua, K., Suess, F., Joraschky, P., Ziemssen, T., & Hummel, T. (2013). The sensory channel of presentation alters subjective ratings and autonomic responses toward disgusting stimuli: Blood pressure, heart rate and skin conductance in response to visual, auditory, haptic and olfactory presented disgusting stimuli. *Frontiers in Human Neuroscience, 7*, 1–10. https://doi.org/10.3389/fnhum.2013.00510

Croy, I., Mohr, T., Weidner, K., Hummel, T., & Junge-Hoffmeister, J. (2019). Mother-child bonding is associated with the maternal perception of the child's body odor. *Physiology & Behavior, 198*, 151–157. https://doi.org/10.1016/j.physbeh.2018.09.014

Croy, I., Nordin, S., & Hummel, T. (2014). Olfactory disorders and quality of life: An updated review. *Chemical Senses, 39*(3), 185–194.

Croy, I., Olgun, S., & Joraschky, P. (2011). Basic emotions elicited by odors and pictures. *Emotion (Washington, D.C.), 11*(6), 1331–1335. https://doi.org/10.1037/a0024437

Croy, I., Ritschel, G., Kreßner-Kiel, D., Schäfer, L., Hummel, T., Havlíček, J., Sauter, J., Ehninger, G., & Schmidt, A. H. (2020). Marriage does not relate to major histocompatibility complex: A genetic analysis based on 3691 couples. *Proceedings of the Royal Society B: Biological Sciences, 287*(1936), 20201800. https://doi.org/10.1098/rspb.2020.1800

Croy, I., Schulz, M., Blumrich, A., Hummel, C., Gerber, J., & Hummel, T. (2014). Human olfactory lateralization requires trigeminal activation. *Neuroimage, 98*, 289–295.

Croy, I., Springborn, M., Lötsch, J., Johnston, A. N. B., & Hummel, T. (2011). Agreeable smellers and sensitive neurotics: Correlations among personality traits and sensory thresholds. *PLoS ONE, 6*(4), e18701. https://doi.org/10.1371/journal.pone.0018701

Croy, I., Zehner, C., Larsson, M., Zucco, G. M., & Hummel, T. (2015). Test–retest reliability and validity of the Sniffin' TOM Odor Memory Test. *Chemical Senses, 40*(3), 173–179. https://doi.org/10.1093/chemse/bju069

De Araujo, I. E., Rolls, E. T., Velazco, M. I., Margot, C., & Cayeux, I. (2005). Cognitive modulation of olfactory processing. *Neuron, 46*(4), 671–679.

de Groot, J. H. B., Kirk, P. A., & Gottfried, J. A. (2020). Encoding fear intensity in human sweat. *Philosophical Transactions of the Royal Society B: Biological Sciences, 375*(1800), 20190271. https://doi.org/10.1098/rstb.2019.0271

de Groot, J. H. B., Smeets, M. A. M., Kaldewaij, A., Duijndam, M. J. A., & Semin, G. R. (2012). Chemosignals communicate human emotions. *Psychological Science, 23*(11), 1417–1424. https://doi.org/10.1177/0956797612445317

de Groot, J. H. B., Smeets, M. A. M., Rowson, M. J., Bulsing, P. J., Blonk, C. G., Wilkinson, J. E., & Semin, G. R. (2015). A sniff of happiness. *Psychological Science, 26*(6), 684–700. https://doi.org/10.1177/0956797614566318

Ditzen, B., Hoppmann, C., & Klumb, P. (2008). Positive couple interactions and daily cortisol: On the stress-protecting role of intimacy. *Psychosomatic Medicine, 70*(8), 883–889. https://doi.org/10.1097/PSY.0b013e318185c4fc

Doty, R. L. (2012). Olfactory dysfunction in Parkinson disease. *Nature Reviews Neurology, 8*(6), 329–339. https://doi.org/10.1038/nrneurol.2012.80

Doty, R. L., Shaman, P., Applebaum, S. L., Giberson, R., Siksorski, L., & Rosenberg, L. (1984). Smell identification ability: Changes with age. *Science, 226*(4681), 1441–1443.

Doucet, S., Soussignan, R., Sagot, P., & Schaal, B. (2007). The "smellscape" of mother's breast: Effects of odor masking and selective unmasking on neonatal arousal, oral, and visual responses. *Developmental Psychobiology, 49*(2), 129–138. https://doi.org/10.1002/dev.20210

Doucet, S., Soussignan, R., Sagot, P., & Schaal, B. (2009). The secretion of areolar (Montgomery's) glands from lactating women elicits selective, unconditional responses in neonates. *PLoS ONE, 4*(10), e7579.

Dubas, J. S., Heijkoop, M., & van Aken, M. A. G. (2009). A preliminary investigation of parent–progeny olfactory recognition and parental investment. *Human Nature, 20*(1), 80–92.

Ehrlichman, H., & Bastone, L. (1992). Olfaction and emotion. In M. J. Serby & K. L. Chobor (Eds.), *Science of olfaction* (pp. 410–438). Springer. https://doi.org/10.1007/978-1-4612-2836-3_15

Fialová, J., Roberts, S. C., & Havlíček, J. (2016). Consumption of garlic positively affects hedonic perception of axillary body odour. *Appetite, 97*, 8–15. https://doi.org/10.1016/j.appet.2015.11.001

Fialová, J., Třebický, V., Kuba, R., Stella, D., Binter, J., & Havlíček, J. (2020). Losing stinks! The effect of competition outcome on body odour quality. *Philosophical Transactions of the Royal Society B: Biological Sciences, 375*(1800), 20190267. https://doi.org/10.1098/rstb.2019.0267

Firestein, S. (2001). How the olfactory system makes sense of scents. *Nature, 413*(6852), 211–218. https://doi.org/10.1038/35093026

Fleming, A. S., Corter, C., Franks, P., Surbey, M., Schneider, B., & Steiner, M. (1993). Postpartum factors related to mother's attraction to newborn infant odors. *Developmental Psychobiology, 26*(2), 115–132.

Fleming, A. S., O'Day, D. H., & Kraemer, G. W. (1999). Neurobiology of mother–infant interactions: Experience and central nervous system plasticity across development and generations. *Neuroscience and Biobehavioral Reviews, 23*(5), 673–685.

Godard, O., Baudouin, J.-Y., Schaal, B., & Durand, K. (2016). Affective matching of odors and facial expressions in infants: Shifting patterns between 3 and 7 months. *Developmental Science, 19*(1), 155–163. https://doi.org/10.1111/desc.12292

Gomez, A., & Gomez, R. (2002). Personality traits of the behavioural approach and inhibition systems: Associations with processing of emotional stimuli. *Personality and Individual Differences, 32*(8), 1299–1316. https://doi.org/10.1016/S0191-8869(01)00119-2

Gottfried, J. A. (2006). Smell: Central nervous processing. *Taste and Smell, 63*, 44–69.

Gower, D. B., Holland, K. T., Mallet, A. I., Rennie, P. J., & Watkins, W. J. (1994). Comparison of 16-androstene steroid concentrations in sterile apocrine sweat and axillary secretions: Interconversions of 16-androstenes by the axillary microflora—a mechanism for axillary odour production in man? *The Journal of Steroid Biochemistry and Molecular Biology, 48*(4), 409–418. https://doi.org/10.1016/0960-0760(94)90082-5

Gower, D. B., & Ruparelia, B. A. (1993). Olfaction in humans with special reference to odorous 16-androstenes: Their occurrence, perception and possible social, psychological and sexual impact. *The Journal of Endocrinology, 137*(2), 167–187. https://doi.org/10.1677/joe.0.1370167

Grammer, K., Fink, B., & Neave, N. (2005). Human pheromones and sexual attraction. *European Journal of Obstetrics and Gynecology and Reproductive Biology, 118*(2), 135–142. https://doi.org/10.1016/j.ejogrb.2004.08.010

Granqvist, P., Döllinger, L., Vestbrand, K., Tullio Liuzza, M., Olsson, M. J., Blomqvist, A., & Lundström, J. N. (2019). The scent of security: Odor of romantic partner alters subjective discomfort and autonomic stress responses in an adult attachment-dependent manner. *Physiology & Behavior, 198*, 144–150. https://doi.org/10.1016/j.physbeh.2018.08.024

Graven, S. N. (2004). Early neurosensory visual development of the fetus and newborn. *Clinics in Perinatology, 31*(2), 199–216.

Han, P., Hummel, T., Raue, C., & Croy, I. (2019). Olfactory loss is associated with reduced hippocampal activation in response to emotional pictures. *NeuroImage, 188*, 84–91. https://doi.org/10.1016/j.neuroimage.2018.12.004

Havlicek, J., & Lenochova, P. (2006). The effect of meat consumption on body odor attractiveness. *Chemical Senses, 31*(8), 747–752. https://doi.org/10.1093/chemse/bjl017

Havlicek, J., & Roberts, S. C. (2009). MHC-correlated mate choice in humans: A review. *Psychoneuroendocrinology, 34*(4), 497–512. https://doi.org/10.1016/j.psyneuen.2008.10.007

Havlíček, J., Winternitz, J., & Roberts, S. C. (2020). Major histocompatibility complex-associated odour preferences and human mate choice: Near and far horizons. *Philosophical Transactions of the Royal Society B: Biological Sciences, 375*(1800), 20190260. https://doi.org/10.1098/rstb.2019.0260

Henkel, S., & Setchell, J. M. (2018). Group and kin recognition via olfactory cues in chimpanzees (Pan troglodytes). *Proceedings of the Royal Society B: Biological Sciences, 285*(1889), 20181527. https://doi.org/10.1098/rspb.2018.1527

Herz, R. S., & Inzlicht, M. (2002). Sex differences in response to physical and social factors involved in human mate selection. *Evolution and Human Behavior, 23*(5), 359–364. https://doi.org/10.1016/S1090-5138(02)00095-8

Holder, G. E., Brigell, M. G., Hawlina, M., Meigen, T., Vaegan, & Bach, M. (2007). ISCEV standard for clinical pattern electroretinography: 2007 update. *Documenta Ophthalmologica, 114*(3), 111–116. https://doi.org/10.1007/s10633-007-9053-1

Hummel, T., Kobal, G., Gudziol, H., & Mackay-Sim, A. (2007). Normative data for the "Sniffin' Sticks" including tests of odor identification, odor discrimination, and olfactory thresholds: An upgrade based on a group of more than 3,000 subjects. *European Archives of Oto-Rhino-Laryngology, 264*(3), 237–243.

Hutmacher, F. (2019). Why is there so much more research on vision than on any other sensory modality? *Frontiers in Psychology, 10*, 1–12. https://doi.org/10.3389/fpsyg.2019.02246

Jacob, S., Hayreh, D. J. S., & McClintock, M. K. (2001). Context-dependent effects of steroid chemosignals on human physiology and mood. *Physiology & Behavior, 74*(1), 15–27. https://doi.org/10.1016/S0031-9384(01)00537-6

Johnston, C. C., Filion, F., Campbell-Yeo, M., Goulet, C., Bell, L., McNaughton, K., & Byron, J. (2009). Enhanced kangaroo mother care for heel lance in preterm neonates: A crossover trial. *Journal of Perinatology, 29*(1), 51–56.

Kaitz, M., Good, A., Rokem, A. M., & Eidelman, A. I. (1987). Mothers' recognition of their newborns by olfactory cues. *Developmental Psychobiology, 20*(6), 587–591. https://doi.org/10.1002/dev.420200604

Karlson, P., & Lüscher, M. (1959). "Pheromones": A new term for a class of biologically active substances. *Nature, 183*(4653), 55–56.

Keller, A. (2011). Attention and olfactory consciousness. *Frontiers in Psychology, 2*, 1–13. https://doi.org/10.3389/fpsyg.2011.00380

Knaapila, A., Tuorila, H., Vuoksimaa, E., Keskitalo-Vuokko, K., Rose, R. J., Kaprio, J., & Silventoinen, K. (2012). Pleasantness of the odor of androstenone as a function of sexual intercourse experience in women and men. *Archives of Sexual Behavior, 41*(6), 1403–1408. https://doi.org/10.1007/s10508-011-9804-7

Knasko, S. C. (1995). Pleasant odors and congruency: Effects on approach behavior. *Chemical Senses, 20*(5), 479–487. https://doi.org/10.1093/chemse/20.5.479

Kobal, G. (1981). *Elektrophysiologische untersuchungen des menschlichen Geruchssinns*. Thieme. https://scholar.google.com/scholar_lookup?title=Elektrophysiologische%20Untersuchungen%20des%20menschlichen%20Geruchssinns&publication_year=1981&author=G.%20Kobal

Kromer, J. R. (2015). *Einfluss von HLA-Allelen auf Körpergeruch und Partnerschaft*. Technische Universität Dresden. file://med/zfs/users/SCHAEFELA/Downloads/Jana_Kromer_2015.pdf

Lapid, H., Shushan, S., Plotkin, A., Voet, H., Roth, Y., Hummel, T., Schneidman, E., & Sobel, N. (2011). Neural activity at the human olfactory epithelium reflects olfactory perception. *Nature Neuroscience, 14*(11), 1455–1461. https://doi.org/10.1038/nn.2926

Lascano, A. M., Hummel, T., Lacroix, J.-S., Landis, B. N., & Michel, C. (2010). Spatio-temporal dynamics of olfactory processing in the human brain: An event-related source imaging study. *Neuroscience, 167*(3), 700. https://doi.org/10.1016/j.neuroscience.2010.02.013

Lawrence, E. J., Shaw, P., Baker, D., Baron-Cohen, S., & David, A. S. (2004). Measuring empathy: Reliability and validity of the Empathy Quotient. *Psychological Medicine, 34*(5), 911–920. https://doi.org/10.1017/S0033291703001624

LeDoux, J. (2012). Rethinking the emotional brain. *Neuron, 73*(4), 653–676.

Lehrner, J., Eckersberger, C., Walla, P., Pötsch, G., & Deecke, L. (2000). Ambient odor of orange in a dental office reduces anxiety and improves mood in female patients. *Physiology & Behavior, 71*(1), 83–86. https://doi.org/10.1016/S0031-9384(00)00308-5

Leleu, A., Rekow, D., Poncet, F., Schaal, B., Durand, K., Rossion, B., & Baudouin, J.-Y. (2020). Maternal odor shapes rapid face categorization in the infant brain. *Developmental Science, 23*(2), e12877. https://doi.org/10.1111/desc.12877

Li, W., Moallem, I., Paller, K. A., & Gottfried, J. A. (2007). Subliminal smells can guide social preferences. *Psychological Science, 18*(12), 1044–1049. https://doi.org/10.1111/j.1467-9280.2007.02023.x

Lobmaier, J. S., Fischbacher, U., Wirthmüller, U., & Knoch, D. (2018). The scent of attractiveness: Levels of reproductive hormones explain individual differences in women's body odour. *Proceedings of the Royal Society B: Biological Sciences, 285*(1886), 20181520. https://doi.org/10.1098/rspb.2018.1520

Lundström, J., Mathe, A., Schaal, B., Frasnelli, J., Nitzsche, K., Gerber, J., & Hummel, T. (2013). Maternal status regulates cortical responses to the body odor of newborns. *Frontiers in Psychology, 4*, 597. https://doi.org/10.3389/fpsyg.2013.00597

Lundström, J. N., & Jones-Gotman, M. (2009). Romantic love modulates women's identification of men's body odors. *Hormones and Behavior, 55*(2), 280–284. https://doi.org/10.1016/j.yhbeh.2008.11.009

Mahmut, M. K., & Croy, I. (2019). The role of body odors and olfactory ability in the initiation, maintenance and breakdown of romantic relationships: A review. *Physiology & Behavior, 207*, 179–184. https://doi.org/10.1016/j.physbeh.2019.05.003

Mahmut, M. K., & Stevenson, R. J. (2012). Olfactory abilities and psychopathy: Higher psychopathy scores are associated with poorer odor discrimination and identification. *Chemosensory Perception, 5*(3), 300–307. https://doi.org/10.1007/s12078-012-9135-7

Mahmut, M. K., & Stevenson, R. J. (2016). Investigating left- and right-nostril olfactory abilities with respect to psychopathy. *Chemosensory Perception, 9*(3), 131–140. https://doi.org/10.1007/s12078-016-9210-6

Mahmut, M. K., Stevenson, R. J., & Stephen, I. (2019). Do women love their partner's smell? Exploring women's preferences for and identification of male partner and non-partner body odor. *Physiology & Behavior, 210*, 112517. https://doi.org/10.1016/j.physbeh.2019.04.006

Mantel, M., Ferdenzi, C., Roy, J.-M., & Bensafi, M. (2019). Individual differences as a key factor to uncover the neural underpinnings of hedonic and social functions of human olfaction: Current findings from PET and fMRI studies and future considerations. *Brain Topography, 32*(6), 977–986.

Marin, C., Vilas, D., Langdon, C., Alobid, I., López-Chacón, M., Haehner, A., Hummel, T., & Mullol, J. (2018). Olfactory dysfunction in neurodegenerative diseases. *Current Allergy and Asthma Reports, 18*(8), 42. https://doi.org/10.1007/s11882-018-0796-4

Marin, M. M., Rapisardi, G., & Tani, F. (2015). Two-day-old newborn infants recognise their mother by her axillary odour. *Acta Paediatrica, 104*(3), 237–240. https://doi.org/10.1111/apa.12905

Marlier, L., & Schaal, B. (2005). Human newborns prefer human milk: Conspecific milk odor is attractive without postnatal exposure. *Child Development, 76*(1), 155–168.

McBurney, D. H., Shoup, M. L., & Streeter, S. A. (2006). Olfactory comfort: Smelling a partner's clothing during periods of separation. *Journal of Applied Social Psychology, 36*(9), 2325–2335. https://doi.org/10.1111/j.0021-9029.2006.00105.x

Meethal, S., & Atwood, C. (2005). The role of hypothalamic-pituitary-gonadal hormones in the normal structure and functioning of the brain. *Cellular and Molecular Life Sciences, 62*, 257–270. https://doi.org/10.1007/s00018-004-4381-3

Menzel, S., Hummel, T., Schäfer, L., Hummel, C., & Croy, I. (2019). Olfactory change detection. *Biological Psychology, 140*, 75–80. https://doi.org/10.1016/j.biopsycho.2018.11.010

Meredith, M. (2001). Human vomeronasal organ function: A critical review of best and worst cases. *Chemical Senses, 26*(4), 433–445.

Milinski, M., Croy, I., Hummel, T., & Boehm, T. (2013). Major histocompatibility complex peptide ligands as olfactory cues in human body odour assessment. *Proceedings of the Royal Society B: Biological Sciences, 280*(1755), 20122889. https://doi.org/10.1098/rspb.2012.2889

Modrcin-Talbott, M. A., Harrison, L. L., Groer, M. W., & Younger, M. S. (2003). The biobehavioral effects of gentle human touch on preterm infants. *Nursing Science Quarterly, 16*(1), 60–67.

Mutic, S., Parma, V., Brünner, Y. F., & Freiherr, J. (2016). You smell dangerous: Communicating fight responses through human chemosignals of aggression. *Chemical Senses, 41*(1), 35–43.

Natsch, A., & Emter, R. (2020). The specific biochemistry of human axilla odour formation viewed in an evolutionary context. *Philosophical Transactions of the Royal Society B: Biological Sciences, 375*(1800), 20190269. https://doi.org/10.1098/rstb.2019.0269

Neshat, H., Jebreili, M., Seyyedrasouli, A., Ghojazade, M., Hosseini, M. B., & Hamishehkar, H. (2016). Effects of breast milk and vanilla odors on premature neonate's heart rate and blood oxygen saturation during and after venipuncture. *Pediatrics and Neonatology, 57*(3), 225–231.

Neumann, D., Zupan, B., Babbage, D. R., Radnovich, A. J., Tomita, M., Hammond, F., & Willer, B. (2012). Affect recognition, empathy, and dysosmia after traumatic brain injury. *Archives of Physical Medicine and Rehabilitation, 93*(8), 1414–1420. https://doi.org/10.1016/j.apmr.2012.03.009

Nishitani, S., Kuwamoto, S., Takahira, A., Miyamura, T., & Shinohara, K. (2014). Maternal prefrontal cortex activation by newborn infant odors. *Chemical Senses, 39*(3), 195–202.

Nishitani, S., Miyamura, T., Tagawa, M., Sumi, M., Takase, R., Doi, H., Moriuchi, H., & Shinohara, K. (2009). The calming effect of a maternal breast milk odor on the human newborn infant. *Neuroscience Research, 63*(1), 66–71.

Northcutt, R. G. (2002). Understanding vertebrate brain evolution. *Integrative and Comparative Biology, 42*(4), 743–756.

Novak, L. R., Gitelman, D. R., Schuyler, B., & Li, W. (2015). Olfactory-visual integration facilitates perception of subthreshold negative emotion. *Neuropsychologia, 77*, 288–297. https://doi.org/10.1016/j.neuropsychologia.2015.09.005

Okamoto, M., Shirasu, M., Fujita, R., Hirasawa, Y., & Touhara, K. (2016). Child odors and parenting: A survey examination of the role of odor in child-rearing. *PLoS ONE, 11*(5): e0154392. https://doi.org/10.1371/journal.pone.0154392

Oleszkiewicz, A., Kunkel, F., Larsson, M., & Hummel, T. (2020). Consequences of undetected olfactory loss for human chemosensory communication and well-being. *Philosophical Transactions of the Royal Society B: Biological Sciences, 375*(1800), 20190265. https://doi.org/10.1098/rstb.2019.0265

Olofsson, J. K., & Gottfried, J. A. (2015). The muted sense: Neurocognitive limitations of olfactory language. *Trends in Cognitive Sciences, 19*(6), 314–321. https://doi.org/10.1016/j.tics.2015.04.007

Olsson, M. J., Lundström, J. N., Kimball, B. A., Gordon, A. R., Karshikoff, B., Hosseini, N., Sorjonen, K., Olgart Höglund, C., Solares, C., Soop, A., Axelsson, J., & Lekander, M. (2014). The scent of disease: Human body odor contains an early chemosensory cue of sickness. *Psychological Science, 25*(3), 817–823. https://doi.org/10.1177/0956797613515681

Park, J. H., Schaller, M., & Van Vugt, M. (2008). Psychology of human kin recognition: heuristic cues, erroneous inferences, and their implications. *Review of General Psychology, 12*(3), 215–235. https://doi.org/10.1037/1089-2680.12.3.215

Pfeiffer, C. A., & Johnston, R. E. (1994). Hormonal and behavioral responses of male hamsters to females and female odors: Roles of olfaction, the vomeronasal system, and sexual experience. *Physiology & Behavior, 55*(1), 129–138. https://doi.org/10.1016/0031-9384(94)90020-5

Porter, R. H., Cernoch, J. M., & McLaughlin, F. J. (1983). Maternal recognition of neonates through olfactory cues. *Physiology & Behavior, 30*(1), 151–154. https://doi.org/10.1016/0031-9384(83)90051-3

Prehn-Kristensen, A., Wiesner, C., Bergmann, T. O., Wolff, S., Jansen, O., Mehdorn, H. M., Ferstl, R., & Pause, B. M. (2009). Induction of empathy by the smell of anxiety. *PloS ONE, 4*(6), e5987.

Pribram, K. H., & Kruger, L. (1954). Functions of the olfacfory brain. *Annals of the New York Academy of Sciences, 58*, 109–138.

Roberts, S. C., & Gosling, L. M. (2004). Manipulation of olfactory signaling and mate choice for conservation breeding: A case study of harvest mice. *Conservation Biology, 18*(2), 548–556. https://doi.org/10.1111/j.1523-1739.2004.00514.x

Ruser, P., Koeppel, C. J., Kitzler, H. H., Hummel, T., & Croy, I. (2021). Individual odor hedonic perception is coded in temporal joint network activity. *NeuroImage, 229*, 117782. https://doi.org/10.1016/j.neuroimage.2021.117782

Savic, I., & Berglund, H. (2010). Androstenol: A steroid derived odor activates the hypothalamus in women. *PLoS ONE, 5*(2), e8651. https://doi.org/10.1371/journal.pone.0008651

Savic, I., Berglund, H., Gulyas, B., & Roland, P. (2001). Smelling of odorous sex hormone-like compounds causes sex-differentiated hypothalamic activations in humans. *Neuron, 31*(4), 661–668. https://doi.org/10.1016/S0896-6273(01)00390-7

Schaal, B., Hummel, T., & Soussignan, R. (2004). Olfaction in the fetal and premature infant: Functional status and clinical implications. *Clinics in Perinatology, 31*, 261–285. https://doi.org/10.1016/j.clp.2004.04.003

Schaal, B., Marlier, L., & Soussignan, R. (1995). Responsiveness to the odour of amniotic fluid in the human neonate. *Neonatology, 67*(6), 397–406.

Schaal, B., Marlier, L., & Soussignan, R. (2000). Human foetuses learn odours from their pregnant mother's diet. *Chemical Senses, 25*(6), 729–737.

Schaal, B., & Orgeur, P. (1992). Olfaction in utero: Can the rodent model be generalized? *Quarterly Journal of Experimental Psychology: Section B, 44*(3–4), 245–278.

Schachter, S., & Singer, J. (1962). Cognitive, social, and physiological determinants of emotional state. *Psychological Review, 69*(5), 379.

Schäfer, L., Hummel, T., & Croy, I. (2019). The design matters: How to detect neural correlates of baby body odors. *Frontiers in Neurology, 9*. https://doi.org/10.3389/fneur.2018.01182

Schäfer, L., Mehler, L., Hähner, A., Walliczek, U., Hummel, T., & Croy, I. (2019). Sexual desire after olfactory loss: Quantitative and qualitative reports of patients with smell disorders. *Physiology & Behavior, 201*, 64–69. https://doi.org/10.1016/j.physbeh.2018.12.020

Schäfer, L., Sorokowska, A., Sauter, J., Schmidt, A. H., & Croy, I. (2020). Body odours as a chemosignal in the mother–child relationship: New insights based on an human leucocyte antigen-genotyped family cohort. *Philosophical Transactions of the Royal Society B: Biological Sciences, 375*(1800), 20190266. https://doi.org/10.1098/rstb.2019.0266

Scherer, K. R., Schorr, A., & Johnstone, T. (2001). *Appraisal processes in emotion: Theory, methods, research*. Oxford University Press.

Sela, L., & Sobel, N. (2010). Human olfaction: A constant state of change-blindness. *Experimental Brain Research, 205*(1), 13–29. https://doi.org/10.1007/s00221-010-2348-6

Seubert, J., Gregory, K. M., Chamberland, J., Dessirier, J.-M., & Lundström, J. N. (2014). Odor valence linearly modulates attractiveness, but not age assessment, of invariant facial features in a memory-based rating task. *PLoS ONE, 9*(5), e98347. https://doi.org/10.1371/journal.pone.0098347

Sewards, T. V., & Sewards, M. A. (2003). Representations of motivational drives in mesial cortex, medial thalamus, hypothalamus and midbrain. *Brain Research Bulletin, 61*(1), 25–49. https://doi.org/10.1016/S0361-9230(03)00069-8

Skramlik, E. v. (1924). Die physiologische Charakteristik von riechenden Stoffen. *The Science of Nature, 12*(40), 813–824.

Smeets, M. A. M., Rosing, E. A. E., Jacobs, D. M., van Velzen, E., Koek, J. H., Blonk, C., Gortemaker, I., Eidhof, M. B., Markovitch, B., de Groot, J., & Semin, G. R. (2020). Chemical fingerprints of emotional body odor. *Metabolites*, *10*(3), 84. https://doi.org/10.3390/metabo10030084

Soo, M. L. M., & Stevenson, R. J. (2007). The moralisation of body odor. *Mankind Quarterly*, *47*(3), 25–56.

Sorokowska, A., Pietrowski, D., Schäfer, L., Kromer, J., Schmidt, A. H., Sauter, J., Hummel, T., & Croy, I. (2018). Human Leukocyte Antigen similarity decreases partners' and strangers' body odor attractiveness for women not using hormonal contraception. *Hormones and Behavior*, *106*, 144–149. https://doi.org/10.1016/j.yhbeh.2018.10.007

Soudry, Y., Lemogne, C., Malinvaud, D., Consoli, S.-M., & Bonfils, P. (2011). Olfactory system and emotion: Common substrates. *European Annals of Otorhinolaryngology, Head and Neck Diseases*, *128*(1), 18–23.

Spence, C., & Driver, J. (1997). Audiovisual links in exogenous covert spatial orienting. *Perception & Psychophysics*, *59*(1), 1–22.

Stein, B. E., & Meredith, M. A. (1993). *The merging of the senses*. MIT Press.

Stevenson, R. J. (2010). An initial evaluation of the functions of human olfaction. *Chemical Senses*, *35*(1), 3–20. https://doi.org/10.1093/chemse/bjp083

Stoddart, D. M. (2012). *The ecology of vertebrate olfaction*. Springer Science & Business Media.

Suhle, P., & Croy, I. (2019). Pheromones and social chemo signals. In A. Lykins (Ed.), *Encyclopedia of sexuality and gender*. Springer. https://doi.org/10.1007/978-3-319-59531-3_8-1

Susskind, J. M., Lee, D. H., Cusi, A., Feiman, R., Grabski, W., & Anderson, A. K. (2008). Expressing fear enhances sensory acquisition. *Nature Neuroscience*, *11*(7), 843–850. https://doi.org/10.1038/nn.2138

Swain, J. E. (2008). Baby stimuli and the parent brain: functional neuroimaging of the neural substrates of parent-infant attachment. *Psychiatry (Edgmont)*, *5*(8), 28–36.

Temmel, A. F., Quint, C., Schickinger-Fischer, B., Klimek, L., Stoller, E., & Hummel, T. (2002). Characteristics of olfactory disorders in relation to major causes of olfactory loss. *Archives of Otolaryngology–Head & Neck Surgery*, *128*(6), 635–641.

Thesen, T., Vibell, J. F., Calvert, G. A., & Österbauer, R. A. (2004). Neuroimaging of multisensory processing in vision, audition, touch, and olfaction. *Cognitive Processing*, *5*(2), 84–93. https://doi.org/10.1007/s10339-004-0012-4

van der Meij, L., Almela, M., Buunk, A. P., Fawcett, T. W., & Salvador, A. (2012). Men with elevated testosterone levels show more affiliative behaviours during interactions with women. *Proceedings of the Royal Society B: Biological Sciences*, *279*(1726), 202–208. https://doi.org/10.1098/rspb.2011.0764

Varendi, H., & Porter, R. H. (2001). Breast odour as the only maternal stimulus elicits crawling towards the odour source. *Acta Paediatrica*, *90*(4), 372–375. https://doi.org/10.1111/j.1651-2227.2001.tb00434.x

Vennemann, M. M., Hummel, T., & Berger, K. (2008). The association between smoking and smell and taste impairment in the general population. *Journal of Neurology*, *255*(8), 1121–1126.

Wedekind, C., Seebeck, T., Bettens, F., & Paepke, A. J. (1995). MHC-dependent mate preferences in humans. *Proceedings of the Royal Society of London B: Biological Sciences*, *260*(1359), 245–249. https://doi.org/10.1098/rspb.1995.0087

Wilhelm, K. (2009). The genetic story behind a good nose. *MaxPlanckResearch Science*, *3*(09), 33–39.

Wilson, D. A., Chapuis, J., & Sullivan, R. M. (2015). Cortical olfactory anatomy and physiology. In R. Doly (Ed.), *Handbook of olfaction and gustation* (3rd ed., pp. 209–225). John Wiley & Sons.

Wilson, D. A., Xu, W., Sadrian, B., Courtiol, E., Cohen, Y., & Barnes, D. C. (2014). Cortical odor processing in health and disease. *Progress in Brain Research*, *208*, 275–305.

Wisman, A., & Shrira, I. (2015). The smell of death: Evidence that putrescine elicits threat management mechanisms. *Frontiers in Psychology*, *6*, 1–11. https://doi.org/10.3389/fpsyg.2015.01274

Wyatt, T. D. (2010). Pheromones and signature mixtures: Defining species-wide signals and variable cues for identity in both invertebrates and vertebrates. *Journal of Comparative Physiology A*, *196*(10), 685–700. https://doi.org/10.1007/s00359-010-0564-y

Wyatt, T. D. (2014). *Pheromones and animal behavior: Chemical signals and signatures*. Cambridge University Press.

Yildiz, A., Arikan, D., Gözüm, S., Taştekın, A., & Budancamanak, İ. (2011). The effect of the odor of breast milk on the time needed for transition from gavage to total oral feeding in preterm infants. *Journal of Nursing Scholarship*, *43*(3), 265–273.

Zalc, B., Goujet, D., & Colman, D. (2008). The origin of the myelination program in vertebrates. *Current Biology*, *18*(12), R511–R512.

Zald, D. H., & Pardo, J. V. (1997). Emotion, olfaction, and the human amygdala: Amygdala activation during aversive olfactory stimulation. *Proceedings of the National Academy of Sciences*, *94*(8), 4119–4124. https://doi.org/10.1073/pnas.94.8.4119

Zhou, G., Lane, G., Noto, T., Arabkheradmand, G., Gottfried, J. A., Schuele, S. U., Rosenow, J. M., Olofsson, J. K., Wilson, D. A., & Zelano, C. (2019). Human olfactory-auditory integration requires phase synchrony between sensory cortices. *Nature Communications, 10*(1), 1–12.

Zhou, W., & Chen, D. (2009). Fear-related chemosignals modulate recognition of fear in ambiguous facial expressions. *Psychological Science, 20*(2), 177–183. https://doi.org/10.1111/j.1467-9280.2009.02263.x

CHAPTER 35

Emotion and Nonverbal Communication

Elena Svetieva

Abstract

In this chapter, the author reviews how an evolutionary perspective has influenced the earliest theory and research on the nonverbal communication of emotion, including subsequent debate as to whether there are basic emotions, the concordance of felt emotion to expressed emotion, and the extent to which the nonverbal communication of emotion is biologically innate or socially constructed. This chapter considers some of the assumptions that have fueled these debates and outlines how an evolutionary view of emotion expression is commensurate with multiple theoretical perspectives and the empirical findings that have shaped them. The chapter also outlines under-researched areas in the nonverbal communication of emotion, existing opportunities for deepening the understanding of how evolutionary pressures shape why, when, and how humans communicate emotion, and finally, promising directions for study in this field.

Key Words: nonverbal communication, emotion expression, evolution, communication, emotion

In thinking about examples of nonverbal communication, the sighs, hugs, scowls, winks, and guffaws that are part of the daily human experience, it is not difficult to see how the nonverbal system makes possible our social-emotional lives. When this capacity is taken away from us, such as when we are communicating via email, we are left grasping for ways to make sure that we are communicating the right tone, that our sarcasm is taken in jest, that the person can tell we care about them. We soon see how impoverished social life would be if we had to rely on words alone. The importance of this communication capacity, both in humans and nonhuman animals, has captured the attention of many scientists across multiple disciplines: psychology, biology, anthropology, neuroscience, history, sociology, just to name a few. It has also consistently attracted the attention of evolutionary scientists, and an evolutionary perspective has informed some of the most productive areas of research in emotion and nonverbal communication. In fact, the nonverbal communication of emotion was a specific area of interest for the father of evolutionary theory, Charles Darwin ([1872] 2009). At the same time, it has also animated considerable debate, especially around the key ideas of basic emotions, the links between felt emotion to expressed emotion, and the extent to which expression of emotion is a biologically innate or socially constructed mode of communication. The primary purpose of this chapter is to provide an integrative overview, informed by an evolutionary perspective, of the basic ideas on emotion and nonverbal communication: (1) how and why we evolved the capacity to communicate emotion nonverbally, (2) key theories on the nonverbal communication of emotion, and (3) the ways in which an evolutionary perspective, when understood and applied properly, can inform and guide research in the field.

Why Would We Evolve the Capacity and Propensity for the Nonverbal Communication of Emotion?

To understand why we evolved the capacity for the nonverbal communication of emotion, we must consider why it is adaptive. An adaptation is a solution to a problem of survival or reproduction that has been shaped by natural selection (Tooby & Cosmides, 1992). For something to be evolutionarily adaptive, we ask whether it helps deal with threats or opportunities to survival or reproduction. The theory of natural selection applies not only to physical traits, but also to psychological mechanisms that allow us to meet environmental challenges and survive to reproduction (Floyd, 2006). The question then becomes: Does the nonverbal communication of emotion help us deal with threats or opportunities to survival or reproduction?

First we consider the related but separate issue of how the human (and nonhuman animal) capacity to *experience* emotion is adaptive. Evolutionary psychologists think of emotions as "superordinate programs" or "evolved psychological mechanisms," or a toolbox for dealing with problems that allows us to survive and reproduce (Al-Shawaf et al., 2016; Cosmides & Tooby, 2000). Emotions coordinate physiology and cognition in a way that moves the individual and guides their behavior in a functionally organized way (Tooby & Cosmides, 2008). Specifically, the activation of emotion can set in motion a set of changes to physiology, attention, and cognition that are useful (e.g., Frijda, 1986), allowing us to quickly recognize and learn about situations, and equally quickly coordinate our responses (physiological, cognitive, behavioral) to what the situation demands. In an often-used example, the fear that we experience when perceiving a predator is what allows us to mobilize energy and cognition to evade this threat (perhaps to run or to hide). However, in addition to the changes in physiology and cognition that allow us to identify and escape a threat, we might also vocalize, or show an expression of fear—lips stretched, eyes wide. What is the *purpose* of this expression?

The first thing that we must consider is that not all emotions are expressed or communicated to others. For example, the component process model (CPM; Scherer, 1984) characterizes an emotional state as having multiple components—cognitive assessment, motivation, physiological processes (such as changes to respiration or heart rate), and expression (smiling, shrieks, or other vocalizations). When a situation is appraised as being new or relevant to the individual's goals, it can set in motion the other components, all of which can then exert dynamic influence on each other. Affective expression or vocalization is therefore a component of the "emotion program," but this component neither defines nor characterizes emotional experience. There are human emotions for which there is no prototypical or recognizable expression, either in terms of facial displays or vocalizations, but for which nevertheless the experience of the emotion helps to organize the response (e.g., sexual jealousy; see Al-Shawaf et al., 2016). There are also emotions that we express but do not feel, a useful tendency to which we will return later in the chapter.

From an evolutionary perspective, we ask the question: Why do we express and communicate (certain) emotions that we feel? If the benefit of the "emotion psychological toolkit" is adaptive for the individual organism, why not leave it at that? Any of us who have been inadvertently betrayed by our own emotion expression, whether blushing, tears, or laughter we could not suppress, might ask why we would evolve such a system, which is at best inconvenient, and at worst, a liability. Even when considering human and nonhuman animals alike, we can wonder whether it is not more beneficial to the individual animal that it does not signal its inner state, perceptions, or motivations, by not giving away excitement at finding a stash of food or other prized resource, or giving enemies an advantage by revealing weakness during moments of sadness or fear.

The answer to this question has several components. The first relates to the human tendency to live in close groups. Sociality, as a primate adaptation, enhances survival to reproduction by providing access to key resources like food and mates, as well as protection from threats. Aside from these benefits, group living comes with costs, including not only competition for mates, but also the need to establish, defend, and/or defer to the status and dominance hierarchies along which key resources (food, mates) flow (Buss, 1991; Van Vugt & Tybur, 2015). The success of group living depends on the effectiveness with which individuals can coordinate, exchange information, apologize/retreat, and take care of one another. The capacity to communicate emotion and immediately recognize emotion signals in others serves as a key piece of information about the situation, reactions, and/or intentions in the moment, allowing the behavior of both observer and source to be successfully coordinated (Matsumoto et al., 2008; Van Kleef 2009). For example, the human tendency to express distress may have coevolved with the human willingness to look after those who are sick, hurt, or otherwise helpless (Balsters et al., 2013). Showing distress, sadness, or pain leads others to engage in prosocial behavior (Marsh & Ambady, 2007), to show care and social support (Balsters et al., 2013); showing anger leads others to retreat or concede, including during negotiation (Sinaceur & Tiedens, 2006). The tendency to express emotion (and recognize the expressions of those around us) therefore is an adaptive benefit produced by the selection pressures of group living.

The adaptiveness of expressing emotion becomes more apparent when we consider the expression of fear as a form of reciprocal altruism. Trivers (1971) considers the example of the "fear call," a loud vocalization common among animals that indicates a predator or threat. Though this call may be initially "costly" to the expressor/sender as it essentially reveals the location of the sender to the predator(s), it is beneficial if and when it is reciprocated (Trivers, 1971). Emotion expression is evolutionarily adaptive in contexts where there are multiple and equal opportunities for reciprocity, such as when living in social groups of closely related conspecifics, as well as other situations involving non-kin. Moreover, the honest signaling of our emotion may be costly, but honestly expressing emotions to our close kin provides information, including information as to how they may increase our welfare (Tooby & Cosmides, 2020). In animal communication, however, the experience of fear (e.g., in response to the presence of a predator) may result in a vocalization, but the animal neither "intends" to inform nor create fear in a receiver, and the receiver makes no inferences about the mental state of the sender—nonetheless, it is adaptive for both the sender to vocalize and for the receiver to use this vocalization as information about their environment (Seyfarth & Cheney, 2003). Over time, provided that the tendency toward honest emotion signaling is more beneficial than not, we would expect a greater preponderance of this tendency among the population.

While we might see the adaptiveness of the nonverbal communication of emotion in the context of group living among kin, there is another manner in which it may have evolved. Boone and Buck (2003) outline how nonverbal communication of emotion may have played a role in the development of trust and cooperation among *strangers*. The human tendency to collaborate with non-kin is unique even when compared with our closest primate relatives (Høgh-Olesen, 2010). If we imagine human interactions in the context of the prisoner's dilemma wherein each party has the option to leave or exit after the initial encounter, there is a resultant pressure to identify cooperators from the outset. Nonverbal expressivity is a "first impressions" signal used to discriminate, in zero-history situations, between those who are likely to cooperate with us and those who are likely to exploit us (Boone & Buck, 2003). Among nonverbal communication signals, the smile in particular has been linked to establishing trust and cooperative intent (Scharlemann et al., 2001). The nonverbal communication of emotion, by signaling motivations and intentions, facilitates trust, whereas a lack of expressivity inhibits it.

In sum, our evolved capacity for the nonverbal communication of emotion allows us to meet the challenges and reap the benefits of group living and social exchange for enhancing human survival to reproduction. However, in addition to understanding the adaptive benefits of the nonverbal communication of emotion, an evolutionary account can help us understand how this adaptation came about, including why certain expressions take the form that they do. To do so, we take a step away from considering the social function and we now consider how the expression of emotion may be beneficial to the individual.

The Origins of the Nonverbal Communication of Emotion: Why We Communicate Emotion the Way That We Do

If we accept the argument that the communication of emotion enhances the success of group living (which increases our survival to reproduction), then we might still be left wondering why we communicate emotion the way that we do. The first observation that we must make is that the communication of emotion exists primarily in the nonverbal domain. While our capacity for language has allowed us to talk, even at great length, about the emotions we are experiencing, the primary channel through which we communicate emotion is the nonverbal one. Emotion can be communicated in a number of modalities: facial display, gaze (Adams & Kleck 2005), vocalization (Bryant, 2020), touch (Hertenstein et al., 2009), posture, body movement, as well as physiological changes such as blushing (Dijk et al., 2009) or crying (Vingerhoets & Bylsma, 2016). Despite the multiple avenues and modalities for the nonverbal expression of emotion, much of the research on how emotion is expressed has focused on the face. It is only within the past decade that more systematic research has emerged on the expression of emotion in the body (Dael et al., 2012) and voice (see Laukka et al., 2016, for verbal emotional vocalization; Cordaro et al., 2016, and Sauter et al., 2010, for studies of nonverbal emotion vocalization such as screams and laughs).

One way we can see that our capacities for emotion communication evolved earlier than verbal language capacity is the ontology/development within our species, which is simply to observe that human infants can communicate their needs to their mothers and interact nonverbally with their world long before they develop the capacity for verbal language (Fox & Davidson, 1988; Sroufe, 1996). The idea that the communication of emotion exists outside of language is further supported by evidence that our nonverbal communication of emotion can affect complementary emotion reactions in others, outside of awareness (Dimberg & Ohman, 1996). Emotion communication via the nonverbal domain allows us to readily signal inner states, motivations, needs, and intended behaviors to others (Matsumoto et al., 2008), and we can do so without using language, and without even awareness. Research in human perception outlines the fast and efficient way that human facial expressions are decoded, suggesting that the ability to recognize these signals coevolved with the tendency to send them (Schyns et al., 2009).

We can, however, also ask the more specific questions of why certain expressions take the form that they do, and what it is that they communicate to others. Why do we associate smiles with happiness, rather than pulling our eyebrows up and down, or some other movement altogether, and what does the smile signal to others? This question has engaged many scientists, especially during the past 50 years, and has led to the development of a number of theories about the communication of emotion.

Theories about the Nonverbal Communication of Emotion
Basic Emotion Theory
Basic Emotion Theory is founded on the idea there is a small set of emotions, such as fear, anger, disgust, sadness, and joy, that enable us to navigate and respond to the majority of challenges in the social and physical world, and for which we inherit a tendency to experience, express, and recognize their occurrence (Keltner et al., 2019). Each expression of these emotions is believed to have originally evolved to regulate internal affective physiology and modulate sensory acquisition. In *The Expression of the Emotions in Man and Animals*, Charles Darwin ([1872] 2009) wrote about emotion expression as a "serviceable habit," seeding the idea of emotion expression as a functional adaptation. If we consider the expression of anger—the lowered brows, curled-in lips, and glaring eyes, we see how this expression functions to enhance focus on a target and prepare for attack. Recent evidence for Darwin's ideas comes from Susskind et al. (2008), in which computational analyses based on mapping vectors in the human face could empirically establish that fear and disgust are "antithetical" expressions in terms of their function for the sender. The configuration of the fear face increases the amount of sensory information by increasing the size of the visual field and sensory vigilance, whereas disgust allows the individual to "cut off" sensory information, or expel offending substances (Lee et al., 2013; Susskind et al., 2008; Susskind & Anderson, 2008). These findings provide a coherent account of why certain expressions take the form that they do and provide a path from mutation to adaptation.

Evidence of continuity in expressive forms between humans, nonhuman primates, and other animals supports the idea that the initial adaptation served a sensory regulation function for the individual organism. There are numerous examples of nonhuman and mammalian precursors to human expression of emotion. Primate expressions of anger involve lowered brows and mouth configurations that communicate increased anger, but primates are also capable of subtle expressions of emotion, including those that can vary on a continuum between two emotions such as fear and anger (Chevalier-Skolnikoff, 1973). The continuities extend beyond facial expressions. Vocal bursts exist outside of language (shrieks, growls) and are readily observed to be used by nonhuman animals (Seyfarth & Cheney 2003; Snowdon 2003).

Some theorists believe that in its "second wave" of evolution, the expression of emotion evolved higher-order social functions (Chapman et al., 2009; Eibl-Eibesfeldt, 2017; Ekman, 1992; Shariff & Tracy, 2011). Through a process of ritualization and exaggeration, these expressions came to function as communicative signals that play an important role in the coordination of social life (Eibl-Eibesfeldt, 2017). For example, while the expression of disgust may have initially functioned to "cut off" the offending object from the perceiver, it has evolved to gain sociocultural meaning, so much so that it can be expressed in reaction to offensive ideas, conduct, or groups of people (Chapman et al., 2009). Darwin even considered that whatever intra-individual functions emotion expressions may have originally served, extreme ritualization over time meant that their original function is no longer relevant.

Supporting evidence for the idea that the nonverbal (facial) communication of emotion is an adaptation comes from the similarity in how emotion is communicated across different cultures. The classic work of Ekman, Sorenson, and Friesen (1969) found that remote and preliterate cultures recognize and similarly express emotions like anger and fear, with impressive effect sizes given unfamiliarity with the task, testing effects, and other problems that can plague cross-cultural research. Ekman (1993) reached the conclusion that the expression of emotion is part of the experience of that emotion—that expressions are involuntary and that therefore they can be trusted as an indicator of felt emotion. Biological support for this idea comes from understanding of neuropsychological origins of emotion experience and the direct pathways, unmediated by language or motor control, that connect emotion regions in the brain with facial musculature (Rinn, 1984). From this research came the idea that there is a basic set of emotions, universally produced and recognized, that we can think of as programs or packages (with physiological, cognitive correlates) that are adaptive insofar as they help us to address problems of survival to reproduction, whether that be to escape from threats or fend off rivals.

The extent to which the human nonverbal expression of emotion is universal across cultures or culturally specific has generated debate, with questions about how much artifactual agreement is created by the nature of the research paradigm and evidence that the amount of agreement may be overestimated (Russell, 1994). Ekman's findings raise interesting questions, such as why recognition accuracy varies for different emotion categories, why some emotion pairs are frequently mistaken for each other, and what specifically is behind subtle cultural variations. Nonetheless, together with evidence of recognizable nonverbal emotion communication in congenitally blind and deaf infants (Eibl-Eibesfeldt, 1973) and adults (Matsumoto & Willingham, 2009), we can be confident that there are expressive patterns in the face that are part of our genetic inheritance, and that these expressions are not arbitrary (in the way verbal signifiers are), but that they contain emotion-relevant information, and that this information functions to communicate and coordinate social interaction.

More recent research has sought to expand the idea of emotion expression beyond the original categories. For example, research on multimodal expression of emotion found that for 22 emotions, there were patterns of expression across multiple modalities found across cultures (Cordardo et al., 2018). Keltner et al. (2019) reported that the number of emotions that can be readily recognized increases when multiple modalities are considered rather than just the face. Most recently, computational analysis of facial expressions using 6 million publicly available videos across 144 different countries found considerable consistency in human facial expressions in similar contexts, whether they be weddings, watching fireworks, or attending sporting competitions (Cowen et al., 2020). The results of this study found 70% shared variance across all 12 world regions between context and facial expression (e.g., sport with expressions of triumph), all without the use of surveys, but rather through the analysis of naturalistic settings. The authors concluded that the nonverbal communication of emotion is a "universal language of social life" (Cowen et al., 2020, p. 6).

Behavioral Ecology
The latter half of the 20th century also saw the emergence of ethology and the science of observing behavioral patterns in the animal world. Tinbergen (1952) originated the modern ethological study of animal signals, including those that are physical (such as antlers that are used in service of sexual selection) and those that are behavioral in nature, such as emotion displays. From the ethological perspective, whether an expression of emotion contains information about the expressor's inner state is irrelevant, and the term "expression" may be a misnomer. Animals respond to the emotions of other animals without mentalizing as to what emotion is being represented.

The behavioral ecology view of human emotion display, introduced by Fridlund (1991a), emphasized that displaying emotion evolved to signal social motives and intentions, opposing the idea that emotion displays express emotional states. Fridlund (1991b) situated his findings in the ethological view of animal signals and emphasized the social communication function of human emotion displays. What informed this model was a number of findings that an implied audience can enhance smiling, and further findings of social facilitation effects of the expression of seemingly spontaneous emotion (Fridlund, 1991b). The behavioral ecology view of emotion emphasized the social dimension of how and when emotions are displayed, rather than a view of emotion as simply an expressive reflex. From this perspective, the forms that expressions take are less revelatory and relevant than the functions they serve.

Dawkins and Krebs (1978) outline how animal signals that express emotion are a tool by which animals predict and influence each other's behavior. Rather than emphasizing the value of animal communication in terms of cooperation and information exchange, they state that "natural selection favors individuals who successfully manipulate the behavior of other individuals, whether or not this is to the advantage of manipulated individuals" (Dawkins & Krebs, 1978, p. 309). An expression like anger initially benefits the expressor (e.g., bared teeth in preparation for attack), but it also offers the receiver a learning opportunity that bared teeth in others mean an attack is likely imminent. To the extent that bared teeth reliably result in the retreat of another, there is a subsequent selection pressure to display anger strategically to intimidate rivals and avert fatal conflict. The key words here are "likely" and "reliably" in that they express the probabilistic nature of the value of these signals. The signals nonetheless function to influence, rather than "express."

Parkinson (2005) provides a review of the emotion-as-expression and emotion-as-social-motive communication models, comparing the claims of both Basic Emotion Theory and the behavioral ecology view. For any facial display (or expression) to be functional, there must be links between the display and the underlying emotion. If the expression of anger was not probabilistically associated with the feeling of anger (readiness for attack plus the physiological and hormonal changes that enable and activate the aggressor to attack), then the value of the signal would be lost. If anyone might feign an expression of anger, then this expression would no longer be valuable in predicting consequences, and the relevance or value of the display would disappear. Dawkins and Krebs (1978) use similar reasoning to outline why deception cannot become a dominant communication strategy; in other words, why there must be some concomitance between the (emotion) signal and (emotional) reality.

Behavioral ecology, with its simultaneous integration of evolutionary theory and an appreciation of how nonverbal emotion displays are affected by aspects of the (social) environment, provided the impetus to understand and describe the social dimension and functionality of human emotion expression.

The Social Construction of Emotion Expression

At the same time as the emergence of the behavioral ecology view, there was growing evidence that there is human emotion experience without expression, expression without emotion experience, and numerous factors aside from emotionality that impact the extent to which an emotion is expressed (Fernández-Dols & Ruiz-Belda, 1995; Parkinson, 2005). While Ekman tried to account for these phenomena by invoking the concept of display rules (Ekman, 1972; Ekman & Friesen, 2003), they appeared insufficient as explanatory concepts to account for the subtle effects of context on the communication of emotion. Findings that the social context seemed more influential in determining emotion expressions like smiling (Kraut & Johnson, 1979) put in question the basic emotion view that we simply communicate what we feel. More recently, there is evidence that humans do not consistently express prototypical emotions as a signal of experienced emotion and that cross-cultural recognizability of emotion can vary (see Barrett, 2011).

Averill (1980) instead saw the emotions we display as part of enacting a "role" within a larger "social drama." Local norms and cultures influence our emotions, not simply by controlling or suppressing the emotions we display, but by constructing the nature of our emotional experience. Social constructionist views of emotion expression emphasize the extent to which emotion is not something that one has, but rather something that one *does*, and that is not so much expressed as it is *performed*.

Constructionist views emphasize the substantial body of research which puts into question the extent to which the nonverbal communication of emotion correlates with any experience of emotion. For example, Ekman's distinction between Duchenne smiles (as an expressive correlate of felt happiness) and non-Duchenne smiles (as polite, or false smile expressions) is challenged by evidence that individuals can produce Duchenne smiles voluntarily (Gunnery et al., 2013; Krumhuber & Manstead, 2009). Despite convincing evidence of the recognizability of basic/prototypical emotion expressions, we can also see that we rarely observe these expressions spontaneously and in real life. Feldman Barrett (2011) offers a further counterpoint to Basic Emotion Theory: the nonverbal communication of emotion is not adaptive, but a byproduct of an adaptation to ascribe psychological meaning and intention to moving objects.

Constructionist theories that consider how the emotions we experience and express are a product of social forces are pitted at the other end of the spectrum from Basic Emotion Theory, and are also seen as a counterpoint to the evolutionary view of emotion expression. However, this is misleading. What the constructionist view highlights is the profound *sociality* of emotion. We can see animal communication as a form of manipulation, with Høgh-Olesen's (2010) observation that "[w]arning and food calls left aside, apes and monkeys communicate almost exclusively with the purpose of getting others to do what they want" (p. 70). Humans, on the other hand, often express emotion simply to share. This "unprompted information sharing reveals a helpful, interested other-directedness that seems natural to humans, but almost absent in other species" (Høgh-Olesen, 2010, p. 70). Sharing emotion helps to build and maintain group identity and group bonds, over and above the mere exchange of information and coordination (Spoor & Kelly, 2004). Mechanisms of emotion contagion (Hatfield et al., 2014) mean that expressed emotion can quickly impact felt emotion in groups, which can have downstream effects on group members (Barsade & Gibson, 1998). Expressing emotion thus increases group cohesiveness, attachment, and rapport, which consequently enhances the efficacy with which groups can pursue goals and can exert influence over each other as members (Spoor & Kelly, 2004).

Social Functional Account
Researchers who retain the core assumptions of Basic Emotion Theory but place emphasis on its social functions have broadened the methodological approach of this research and its empirical focus to understanding how the communication of emotion influences and coordinates social perception and interaction (see Keltner et al., 2019, for a review). Blushing, for example, is an unintentional display of emotion that is beneficial to the expressor insofar as they are treated more sympathetically by observers (van Dijk et al., 2009). Smiling, given its marked susceptibility to social context effects, may have evolved to communicate social intent and negotiate social relationships (Parkinson, 2005). For example, Parr and Waller (2006) summarize how the primate silent bared teeth display, often thought to be a homologue to the human smile, seems to serve different social functions, depending on whether the social organization of the species is based on dominance hierarchies (in which case it functions as a submissive signal), or whether it is more egalitarian (in which case it is more affiliative). It does not mean that there is no variation in this signal, and that it is not used in other contexts, but understanding its function means observing the contexts in which it occurs most frequently, and then observing the most common effect it has on the receiver. More recently, researchers have focused on how human smiles are communication tools that serve different

social functions (Rychlowska et al., 2019). Distinct smile expressions have been identified that communicate positive experiences or intentions (reward smile); forming and maintaining social bonds (affiliation smile); and negotiating status within and across social hierarchies (dominance smile) (Martin et al., 2017; Rychlowska et al., 2017).

An Evolutionary Perspective on Nonverbal Communication of Emotion: Integrating Theory and Guiding Research

I have outlined how several theoretical perspectives on the nonverbal communication of emotion are commensurate with an evolutionary view, each highlighting a different aspect that can build the scientific understanding of the whole. However, to more appropriately integrate an evolutionary perspective into the study of emotion and nonverbal communication, we need to get a clearer understanding of what an evolutionary perspective does and does not imply.

One Cause Does Not Negate Another

An evolutionary view of the expression of emotion requires us to divest ourselves of dichotomous thinking. Brill and Schwab (2020) suggest that we move away from the Popperian paradigm, with its dichotomous approach to making sense of data as either supporting or falsifying a theory. Based on Tinbergen (1963), evolutionary scientists emphasize the difference between proximal causes (the immediate circumstances that result in a behavior) and ultimate causes (which refer to higher-order causes for a behavior) (Floyd, 2006; Lewis et al., 2017). There are therefore multiple ways in which a behavior may be caused, and identifying one cause does not negate the existence of another. Part of incorporating evolutionary theory into the study of emotion communication is to accept that an explanation of the specific, immediate cause of a nonverbal behavior (the proximate cause) can be commensurate with an account of the function of the behavior in our evolutionary history (ultimate cause). If we know about a proximal cause, then the evolutionary account will *complement* this explanation, rather than compete with it (Al-Shawaf et al., 2020). If we take the example of some nonverbally communicated emotion, say laughing at a friend's joke, the proximate cause might be the unexpected paradox at the core of humor, our internally experienced mirth finding a cortical path to motor movement and facial expression, but the ultimate cause may be the benefit of expressing positive emotion in forming and maintaining affiliative bonds.

Let us consider an example, the consistent finding that women smile more than men during social interaction (LaFrance & Hecht, 2000). Though many explanations have been offered for this effect, Andersen (2006) states that the field of communication has remained resistant to considering the influence of evolutionary factors in the existence of sex differences in nonverbal communication. Observed sex differences are typically discussed in terms of cultural expectations that women smile more, that they are expected to perform more "social connection" functions (Hall & Halberstadt, 1986), and that women smiling more is a sociological function of their less powerful position in society (Henley, 1995). In highlighting the necessity of socialization as an explanation for this effect, Parkinson (2005) considers that "it is hard to imagine an innate mechanism that attunes facial movements to culturally specific gender roles" (p. 303). Part of gaining a more complete understanding of the "whys" behind this effect is to consider how culture and biology may be working in parallel.

Chaplin (2015)'s biopsychosocial model of sex differences in emotion expression considers both innate/biological factors and socialization factors, and shows us what scientific inquiry might look like when we consider culture, biology, and immediate context at the same time. In boys, biological factors (such as in utero exposure to testosterone) result in neurocognitive and physiological differences, such as more limited language capacity and higher arousal, that can make them more likely to physically express negative, externalizing emotion. Socialization comes into play as both boys and girls observe sex-differentiated behaviors, including the kind of emotion expression that is associated with being a boy or a girl, developing cognitive schemas which function to guide their own behavior. Biopsychosocial models provide an analysis at the proximal level (Lewis et al., 2017) in that they emphasize aspects of both the immediate context/situation (including individuals present), as well as the broader environment and culture that will influence the nature and extent of sex differences in emotion expression that we might observe.

An evolutionary perspective then considers the *ultimate* cause of this difference, and specifically what selection pressures might have produced such a difference. The accounts that are produced from a distal level of analysis do not need to disprove or contradict those obtained by a proximal level of analysis (Lewis et al., 2017). In accounting for the robust sex differences in social skills, including the encoding and decoding of nonverbal communication, Andersen (2006) highlights that an evolutionary environment was largely matrilineal, with men existing along the periphery, and women responsible for maintaining affiliative bonds broadly, as well as nurturing and caring for children, specifically. The social role of women therefore coevolved with expressivity and, in particular, expressivity of positive, affiliative emotion. A related account is offered by Ellis (2006), where the focus is on the pressures that inhibited social smiling by men—resource acquisition and competition, which prioritized dominant, competitive displays (such as expressions of anger) over signals of weakness or friendliness (such as smiling, or expressions of fear and sadness).

These are not innate or hard-wired behavioral differences, and they may not be observed in certain cultures or contexts. To the extent that we use evolutionary theory to guide and inform research in nonverbal communication of emotion, we must consider that certain traits that are the outcomes of natural selection may only be manifested in relevant contexts, and not visible at an overly generalized or simplistic level of inquiry (Al-Shawaf & Lewis, 2017; Floyd, 2006). An evolutionary perspective means that we (1) articulate the evolutionary advantage of more positive emotion expression by women relative to men (or alternatively stated, less smiling by men relative to women); (2) make predictions about when we might and might not observe such sex differences; and (3) create research designs that allow us to test our predictions.

Social Situations, Culture, and Context Matter
An evolutionary perspective on the nonverbal communication of emotion does not presuppose that there are only a limited number of basic emotions, or that patterns of expression are invariably associated with certain emotion elicitors (Al-Shawaf et al., 2016). An evolutionary view does not imply genetic determinism in the expression of emotion, that emotions are a set of natural kinds, that there is direct concordance between the experience of (any) emotion and the expression of that emotion, or that there is universality in how and when emotions are communicated nonverbally.

An evolutionary perspective instead highlights the universality of psychological *mechanisms* rather than behavior (Lewis et al., 2017). Evidence of universality in how certain prototypical emotions are perceived and expressed *does* indicate the existence of a universal psychological mechanism around perception and cognition of facial movements, postures, and vocalizations. Just as we are born with the neurocognitive architecture that allows us to rapidly acquire language, whose form and dialect are shaped by our environment, so do humans possess neurocognitive capacities for the multimodal expression of emotion, capacities which then are shaped by the contexts, environment, and culture (Elfenbein et al., 2007).

It is commensurate with the existence of basic emotion-expression categories, as well as the influence of contextual factors that modulate the function of these expressions both across and within species.

For emotion expressions to be useful in coordinating social interactions, they must be able to be utilized flexibly, and with context dependence. From an evolutionary perspective, context, time, and culture matter. For example, consider how context might influence the "honesty" of our emotion signals. A purely honest, inflexible system of emotion expression as a direct and unambiguous readout of our inner state might be costly, especially in dealing with rivals, out-groups, or even when negotiating social hierarchies within our own groups. Showing weakness via an expression of fear toward a rival might encourage attack and imperil survival, whereas a bluffed expression of anger might be more likely to discourage attack and avert a fatal conflict. Showing sadness and pain would only be adaptive when in the context of our own kin/close group members, who, according to the theory of inclusive fitness (Hamilton, 1964), would be those who are most motivated to help. In essence, context modulates when our emotion communication is more directly related to our emotion experience.

If we accept that emotion communication evolved in the context of group living with individuals we are related to and can trust, then it is reasonable to assume that we would be able to flexibly modulate our expressions so that we are not engaging in as much "honest signaling" when we are with strangers and out-group members. Evidence for this prediction comes from Buck et al. (1992), who found that both the nature of the emotion and the social context (e.g., the relationship between the sender and receiver) modulates emotion expression. Strangers inhibit our expressiveness, while friends augment it. Consider that we can observe such social context effects even among nonhuman animals. Chevalier-Skolnikoff (1973) describes how stumptail monkeys can exhibit four types of threat displays, which depend on the position between two animals in the dominance hierarchy. Karakashian et al. (1988) used hawk silhouettes to find that the alarm call behavior of domestic roosters was influenced by the audience—a rooster would emit alarm calls when in the presence of their own species (regardless of sex), but not another species. By contrast, food calling was modulated by the sex of the "audience"; the presence of a hen enhanced it, while the presence of another rooster inhibited it. More importantly, roosters who were alone may not emit alarm calls, but appeared to still show behavior indicative of fear (visual fixation on the "predator," freezing, etc.).

Understanding cultural differences in nonverbal communication can also be illuminated with an evolutionary perspective. Rychlowska et al. (2015) accounted for cultural differences in emotion expressivity with the concept of historical heterogeneity, namely the extent to which migration data indicate that the present-day population of a nation historically descends from few or many source countries. Their analysis indicates that countries with high historical heterogeneity endorse more emotional expressivity, supporting their hypothesis that "amplified emotional expressivity in the face and body would be a likely adaptation to diversity in original emotion practices, rules and language" (Rychlowska et al., 2015, p. E2430). The term "adaptation" in this context does not refer to an evolutionary adaptation, which occurs over a much longer period and which enhanced survival to reproduction during the evolution of our species. It does, however, describe how environmental factors can activate or inhibit our tendency to display emotion and can over time lead to the development of marked cultural differences around the nonverbal communication of emotion. Their research also specifically examined smiling and presented a plausible account for how more exaggerated and prototypical emotion displays around affiliative-social smiling emerged as a mechanism for building trust and enhancing cooperation in contexts where there are no preexisting relational bonds or kinship ties (e.g., as in Boone & Buck, 2003).

Cultural differences and group membership can also affect how we perceive the emotion communication of others. The evidence for some of these ideas can be found when observing differences in how quickly we recognize certain emotion expressions as a function of whether they are displayed by an in-group or an out-group member. Chiao et al. (2008), for example, found more accurate recognition and greater amygdala activation to own-culture fear faces, concluding that limbic activation is modulated by the culture of the perceiver and emotion target. Evolutionarily speaking, fear faces of in-group members more accurately signal potential threats to ourselves, and so we would expect them to be more salient to the perceiver.

Finally, the flexibility of the human emotion display can also be observed when considering socioeconomic context. When in the Alto de Cruzeiro in Brazil, Scheper-Hughes (1992) observed a distinct lack of grief display among young mothers who had lost an infant. We may think of losing an infant as one of the most universal and powerful elicitors of sadness and grief. However, harsh economic factors in the Alto de Cruzeiro resulted in the reinterpretation by the group of the loss of an infant as a blessing. In this situation, the task for scientists, including those working from an evolutionary perspective, is not to explain away deviations from universality, but to investigate the flexibility of the human emotion response and the adaptations that enhance or inhibit the experience and expression of powerful emotions. The flexibility with which we use, perceive, and react to nonverbal communication of emotion reflects design features of adaptation that allow humans to survive, reproduce, and thrive in many social contexts and groups (Tooby & Cosmides, 1992).

An evolutionary perspective therefore does not imply that the work of nonverbal emotion communication investigators be limited to identifying and defending the existence of prototypical expression types elicited by defined emotion states and consistent across different cultures. An expression may share a similar evolutionary history (even across species) but may have evolved to serve different functions because of environmental influences. Adopting an evolutionary perspective instead asks us to consider how evolutionary pressures may have shaped nonverbal emotion communication. Schmidt and Cohn (2001), for example, identify a number of "socioecological contexts"—such as infant/caregiver interactions, cooperative interactions, and competitive interactions—each with their own set of demands on the nature and consequences of different facial communication of emotion, and which must be examined separately.

Future Directions

Evolutionary psychologists often consider the "lag" between the capacities, preferences, and behavioral repertoires we have evolved, and the environments we find ourselves living in. Most of our (evolutionary) history has been in the context of hunter-gatherer societies, so the adaptations that evolved to meet the environmental challenges of those times are not always useful for modern living (Floyd, 2006). Consider the often-used example of the evolved preference for sweet and fatty food, which may have been adaptive in the Pleistocene period, but which in the current environment presents a health hazard.

Evolutionary adaptations for the nonverbal communication of emotion also need not be beneficial for the individual, their success and well-being, or the broader group or society in which they reside. Modern technology has changed how we work and interact with others. Nonverbal communication of emotion as a tool to coordinate, develop trust, and "smooth over" social interactions (often without conscious awareness) is an evolutionary adaptation which presents modern challenges and barriers to accurately communicating interpersonal motivations when we appreciate the ubiquity of text-based communication technology (such as email and text). Those who find themselves working with distributed and remote teams might soon realize the difficulty of creating working relationships and interpersonal trust through the primarily task-oriented nature of email communication.

It also means we are driven to find other means to share our emotions, such as can be seen by the proliferated use of emojis (Troiano & Nante, 2018) and GIFs (Miltner & Highfield, 2017) to communicate emotional meaning. Modern communication technologies also mean that communicating and sharing our emotional reactions can reach and influence a larger group of people, as the (in)famous Facebook experiment on emotion contagion demonstrated (Kramer et al., 2014), which may have outsize effects on civic society and political polarization, and even intergroup conflict and aggression (Matsumoto et al., 2014). The lag between modern communication technology affordances and our evolved system of emotion communication is an under-researched yet critical area for further inquiry.

Conclusion

In this chapter I have shown how an evolutionary perspective can be a connecting thread through several theoretical accounts of the nature, origin, and function of the nonverbal communication of emotion. Evolutionary thinking encourages us to consider the multiple ways in which human behavior is caused and the importance both of innate and environmental/cultural factors in shaping why, how, and when we express emotion. An evolutionary perspective is commensurate with the idea that nonverbal communication of emotion is dynamic, integrated into the people and places that surround us, and colored by our cognitive biases, personal predisposition, and social learning history. We can begin to appreciate that different theoretical perspectives are not as at odds with one another as it may seem, but rather that they illuminate different components of this evolved system for sharing with others our feelings, reactions, and intentions. A more complete understanding of the evolutionary forces that have shaped why and how we communicate emotion is not just a path to advancing communication science and a call for thoughtful, carefully designed research; it also holds the key to understanding how our evolutionary history at times collides with modern life and the ways in which we might (re)design how we work, play, and interact.

Author's Note

https://orcid.org/0000-0001-9632-4728

References

Adams, R. B., Jr. & Kleck, R. E. (2005). Effects of direct and averted gaze on the perception of facially communicated emotion. *Emotion, 5*(1), 3–11. https://doi.org/10.1037/1528-3542.5.1.3

Al-Shawaf, L., Conroy-Beam, D., Asao, K., & Buss, D. M. (2016). Human emotions: An evolutionary psychological perspective. *Emotion Review, 8*(2), 173–186. https://doi.org/10.1177/1754073914565518

Al-Shawaf, L., & Lewis, D. M. G. (2017). Evolutionary psychology and the emotions. In V. Zeigler-Hill & T. K. Shackelford (Eds.), *Encyclopedia of personality and individual differences* (pp. 1–10). Springer International. https://doi.org/10.1007/978-3-319-28099-8_516-1

Al-Shawaf, L., Lewis, D. M., Barbaro, N., & Wehbe, Y. S. (2020). The products of evolution: Conceptual distinctions, evidentiary criteria, and empirical examples. In T Shackelford (Ed.), *The Sage handbook of evolutionary psychology: Foundations of evolutionary psychology* (pp. 70–95). Sage.

Andersen, P. A. (2006). The evolution of biological sex differences in communication. In K. Dindia & D. J. Canary (Eds.), *Sex differences and similarities in communication* (pp. 114–130). Psychology Press.

Averill, J. R. (1980). A constructivist view of emotion. In R. Plutchik & H. Kellermann (Eds.), *Emotion: Theory, research, and experience* (pp. 305–339). Academic Press.

Balsters, M. J. H., Krahmer, E. J., Swerts, M. G. J., & Vingerhoets, Ad J. J. M. (2013). Emotional tears facilitate the recognition of sadness and the perceived need for social support. *Evolutionary Psychology, 11*(1), 148–158. https://doi.org/10.1177/147470491301100114

Barrett, L. F. (2011). Was Darwin wrong about emotional expressions? *Current Directions in Psychological Science*, *20*(6), 400–406. https://doi.org/10.1177/0963721411429125

Barsade, S. G., & Gibson, D. E. (1998). Group emotion: A view from top and bottom. In *Composition* (pp. 81–102). Elsevier Science/JAI Press.

Boone, R. T., & Buck, R. (2003). Emotional expressivity and trustworthiness: The role of nonverbal behavior in the evolution of cooperation. *Journal of Nonverbal Behavior*, *27*(3), 163–182. https://doi.org/10.1023/A:1025341931128

Brill, M., & Schwab, F. (2020). Evolutionary reasoning in communication scholarship: Generating and testing sound hypotheses. In K. Floyd & R. Weber (Eds.), *The handbook of communication science and biology* (pp. 93–106). Routledge. https://doi.org/10.4324/9781351235587-9

Bryant, G. A. (2020). The evolution of human vocal emotion. *Emotion Review*, *13*(1), 25–33. https://doi.org/10.1177/1754073920930791

Buck, R., Losow, J. I., Murphy, M. M., & Costanzo, P. (1992). Social facilitation and inhibition of emotional expression and communication. *Journal of Personality and Social Psychology*, *63*(6), 962–968. https://doi.org/10.1037/0022-3514.63.6.962

Buss, D. M. (1991). Evolutionary personality psychology. *Annual Review of Psychology*, *42*(1), 459–491. https://doi.org/10.1146/annurev.ps.42.020191.002331

Chaplin, T. M. (2015). Gender and emotion expression: A developmental contextual perspective. *Emotion Review*, *7*(1), 14–21. https://doi.org/10.1177/1754073914544408

Chapman, H. A., Kim, D. A., Susskind, J. M., & Anderson, A. K. (2009). In bad taste: Evidence for the oral origins of moral disgust. *Science*, *323*(5918), 1222–1226. https://doi.org/10.1126/science.1165565

Chevalier-Skolnikoff, S. (1973). Facial expression of emotion in nonhuman primates. In P. Ekman (Ed.), *Darwin and facial expression: A century of research in review* (pp. 11–89). Academic Press.

Chiao, J. Y., Iidaka, T., Gordon, H. L., Nogawa, J., Bar, M., Aminoff, E., Sadato, N., & Ambady, N. (2008). Cultural specificity in amygdala response to fear faces. *Journal of Cognitive Neuroscience*, *20*(12), 2167–2174. https://doi.org/10.1162/jocn.2008.20151

Cordaro, D. T., Keltner, D., Tshering, S., Wangchuk, D., & Flynn, L. M. (2016). The voice conveys emotion in ten globalized cultures and one remote village in Bhutan. *Emotion*, *16*(1), 117–128. https://doi.org/10.1037/emo0000100

Cowen, A. S., Keltner, D., Schroff, F., Jou, B., Adam, H., & Prasad, G. (2020). Sixteen facial expressions occur in similar contexts worldwide. *Nature*, *589*, 251–257. https://doi.org/10.1038/s41586-020-3037-7

Dael, N., Mortillaro, M., & Scherer, K. R. (2012). Emotion expression in body action and posture. *Emotion*, *12*(5), 1085–1101. https://doi.org/10.1037/a0025737

Darwin, C. ([1872] 2009). *The expression of the emotions in man and animals* (F. Darwin, Ed.; 2nd ed.). Cambridge University Press. https://doi.org/10.1017/CBO9780511694110

Dawkins, R., & Krebs, J. R. (1978). Animal signals: Information or manipulation. *Behavioural Ecology: An Evolutionary Approach*, *2*, 282–309.

Dijk, C., de Jong, P. J., & Peters, M. L. (2009). The remedial value of blushing in the context of transgressions and mishaps. *Emotion*, *9*(2), 287. https://doi.org/10.1037/a0015081

Dimberg, U., & Öhman, A. (1996). Behold the wrath: Psychophysiological responses to facial stimuli. *Motivation and Emotion*, *20*(2), 149–182. https://doi.org/10.1007/BF02253869

Eibl-Eibesfeldt, I. (1973). The expressive behavior of the deaf-and-blind born. In M. von Cranach & I. Vine (Eds.), *Social communication and movement* (pp. 163–194). Academic Press.

Eibl-Eibesfeldt, I. (2017). *Human ethology*. Routledge.

Ekman, P. (1972). Universals and cultural differences in facial expressions of emotion. In J. K. Cole (Ed.), *Nebraska Symposium on Motivation* (Vol. 19, pp. 207–283). University of Nebraska Press.

Ekman, P. (1992). An argument for basic emotions. *Cognition and Emotion*, *6*(3–4), 169–200. https://doi.org/10.1080/02699939208411068

Ekman, P. (1993). Facial expression and emotion. *American Psychologist*, *48*(4), 384. https://doi.org/10.1037/0003-066X.48.4.384

Ekman, P., & Friesen, W. V. (2003). *Unmasking the face: A guide to recognizing emotions from facial clues*. ISHK.

Ekman, P., Sorenson, E. R., & Friesen, W. V. (1969). Pan-cultural elements in facial displays of emotion. *Science*, *164*(3875), 86–88. https://doi.org/10.1126/science.164.3875.86

Elfenbein, H. A., Beaupré, M., Lévesque, M., & Hess, U. (2007). Toward a dialect theory: Cultural differences in the expression and recognition of posed facial expressions. *Emotion*, *7*(1), 131–146. https://doi.org/10.1037/1528-3542.7.1.131

Ellis, L. (2006). Gender differences in smiling: An evolutionary neuroandrogenic theory. *Physiology & Behavior, 88*(4), 303–308. https://doi.org/10.1016/j.physbeh.2006.03.034

Fernández-Dols, J.-M., & Ruiz-Belda, M.-A. (1995). Are smiles a sign of happiness? Gold medal winners at the Olympic Games. *Journal of Personality and Social Psychology, 69*(6), 1113–1119. https://doi.org/10.1037/0022-3514.69.6.1113

Floyd, K. (2006). An evolutionary approach to understanding nonverbal communication. In V. Manusov & M. L. Patterson (Eds.), *The Sage handbook of nonverbal communication* (pp. 139–157). Sage Publications. https://doi.org/10.4135/9781412976152.n8

Fox, N. A., & Davidson, R. J. (1988). Patterns of brain electrical activity during facial signs of emotion in 10-month-old infants. *Developmental Psychology, 24*(2), 230–236. https://doi.org/10.1037/0012-1649.24.2.230

Fridlund, A. J. (1991a). Evolution and facial action in reflex, social motive, and paralanguage. *Biological Psychology, 32*(1), 3–100. https://doi.org/10.1016/0301-0511(91)90003-Y

Fridlund, A. J. (1991b). Sociality of solitary smiling: Potentiation by an implicit audience. *Journal of Personality and Social Psychology, 60*(2), 229. https://doi.org/10.1037/0022-3514.60.2.229

Frijda, N. H. (1986). *The emotions*. Cambridge University Press.

Gunnery, S. D., Hall, J. A., & Ruben, M. A. (2013). The deliberate Duchenne smile: Individual differences in expressive control. *Journal of Nonverbal Behavior, 37*(1), 29–41. https://doi.org/10.1007/s10919-012-0139-4

Hall, J. A., & Halberstadt, A. G. (1986). Smiling and gazing. In J. S. Hyde & M. C. Linn (Eds.), *The psychology of gender: Advances through meta-analysis* (pp. 136–158). Johns Hopkins University Press.

Hamilton, W. D. (1964). The genetical evolution of social behaviour. I. *Journal of Theoretical Biology, 7*(1), 1–16. https://doi.org/10.1016/0022-5193(64)90038-4

Hatfield, E., Bensman, L., Thornton, P. D., & Rapson, R. L. (2014). New perspectives on emotional contagion: A review of classic and recent research on facial mimicry and contagion. *Interpersona: An International Journal on Personal Relationships, 8*(2), 159–179. https://doi.org/10.5964/ijpr.v8i2.162

Henley, N. M. (1995). Body politics revisited: What do we know today. In P. J. Kalbfleisch & M. J. Cody (Eds.), *Gender, power, and communication in human relationships* (pp. 27–61). Routledge.

Hertenstein, M. J., Holmes, R., McCullough, M., & Keltner, D. (2009). The communication of emotion via touch. *Emotion, 9*(4), 566–573. https://doi.org/10.1037/a0016108

Høgh-Olesen, H. (2010). Human nature: A comparative overview. *Journal of Cognition and Culture, 10*(1–2), 59–84. https://doi.org/10.1163/156853710X497176

Karakashian, S. J., Gyger, M., & Marler, P. (1988). Audience effects on alarm calling in chickens (*Gallus gallus*). *Journal of Comparative Psychology, 102*(2), 129–135. https://doi.org/10.1037/0735-7036.102.2.129

Keltner, D., Sauter, D., Tracy, J., & Cowen, A. (2019). Emotional expression: Advances in Basic Emotion Theory. *Journal of Nonverbal Behavior, 43*(2), 133–160. https://doi.org/10.1007/s10919-019-00293-3

Kramer, A. D. I., Guillory, J. E., & Hancock, J. T. (2014). Experimental evidence of massive-scale emotional contagion through social networks. *Proceedings of the National Academy of Sciences, 111*(24), 8788–8790. https://doi.org/10.1073/pnas.1320040111

Kraut, R. E., & Johnston, R. E. (1979). Social and emotional messages of smiling: An ethological approach. *Journal of Personality and Social Psychology, 37*(9), 1539–1553. https://doi.org/10.1037/0022-3514.37.9.1539

Krumhuber, E. G., & Manstead, A. S. R. (2009). Can Duchenne smiles be feigned? New evidence on felt and false smiles. *Emotion, 9*(6), 807–820. https://doi.org/10.1037/a0017844

LaFrance, M., & Hecht, M. A. (2000). Gender and smiling: A meta-analysis. In A. H. Fischer (Ed.), *Gender and emotion: Social psychological perspectives* (pp. 118–142). Cambridge University Press. https://doi.org/10.1017/CBO9780511628191.007

Laukka, P., Elfenbein, H. A., Thingujam, N. S., Rockstuhl, T., Iraki, F. K., Chui, W., & Althoff, J. (2016). The expression and recognition of emotions in the voice across five nations: A lens model analysis based on acoustic features. *Journal of Personality and Social Psychology, 111*(5), 686–705. https://doi.org/10.1037/pspi0000066

Lee, D. H., Susskind, J. M., & Anderson, A. K. (2013). Social transmission of the sensory benefits of eye widening in fear expressions. *Psychological Science, 24*(6), 957–965. https://doi.org/10.1177/0956797612464500

Lewis, D. M. G., Al-Shawaf, L., Conroy-Beam, D., Asao, K., & Buss, D. M. (2017). Evolutionary psychology: A how-to guide. *American Psychologist, 72*(4), 353–373. https://doi.org/10.1037/a0040409

Marsh, A. A., & Ambady, N. (2007). The influence of the fear facial expression on prosocial responding. *Cognition and Emotion, 21*(2), 225–247. https://doi.org/10.1080/02699930600652234

Martin, J., Rychlowska, M., Wood, A., & Niedenthal, P. (2017). Smiles as multipurpose social signals. *Trends in Cognitive Sciences, 21*(11), 864–877. https://doi.org/10.1016/j.tics.2017.08.007

Matsumoto, D., Hwang, H. C., & Frank, M. G. (2014). Emotions expressed by leaders in videos predict political aggression. *Behavioral Sciences of Terrorism and Political Aggression, 6*(3), 212–218. https://doi.org/10.1080/19434 472.2013.769116

Matsumoto, D., Keltner, D., Shiota, M. N., O'Sullivan, M., & Frank, M. (2008). Facial expressions of emotion. In M. Lewis, J. M. Haviland-Jones, & L. F. Barrett (Eds.), *Handbook of emotions* (3rd ed., pp. 211–234). Guilford Press.

Matsumoto, D., & Willingham, B. (2009). Spontaneous facial expressions of emotion of congenitally and noncongenitally blind individuals. *Journal of Personality and Social Psychology, 96*(1), 1–10. https://doi.org/10.1037/a0014037

Miltner, K. M., & Highfield, T. (2017). Never gonna GIF you up: Analyzing the cultural significance of the animated GIF. *Social Media + Society, 3*(3), 1–11. https://doi.org/10.1177/2056305117725223

Parkinson, B. (2005). Do facial movements express emotions or communicate motives? *Personality and Social Psychology Review, 9*(4), 278–311. https://doi.org/10.1207/s15327957pspr0904_1

Parr, L. A., & Waller, B. M. (2006). Understanding chimpanzee facial expression: Insights into the evolution of communication. *Social Cognitive and Affective Neuroscience, 1*(3), 221–228. https://doi.org/10.1093/scan/nsl031

Rinn, W. E. (1984). The neuropsychology of facial expression: A review of the neurological and psychological mechanisms for producing facial expressions. *Psychological Bulletin, 95*(1), 52–77. https://doi.org/10.1037/0033-2909.95.1.52

Russell, J. A. (1994). Is there universal recognition of emotion from facial expression? A review of the cross-cultural studies. *Psychological Bulletin, 115*(1), 102. https://doi.org/10.1037/0033-2909.115.1.102

Rychlowska, M., Jack, R. E., Garrod, O. G. B., Schyns, P. G., Martin, J. D., & Niedenthal, P. M. (2017). Functional smiles: Tools for love, sympathy, and war. *Psychological Science, 28*(9), 1259–1270. https://doi.org/10.1177/0956797617706082

Rychlowska, M., Manstead, A. S. R., & van der Schalk, J. (2019). The many faces of smiles. In U. Hess & S. Hareli (Eds.), *The social nature of emotion expression: What emotions can tell us about the world* (pp. 227–245). Springer International. https://doi.org/10.1007/978-3-030-32968-6_13

Rychlowska, M., Miyamoto, Y., Matsumoto, D., Hess, U., Gilboa-Schechtman, E., Kamble, S., Muluk, H., Masuda, T., & Niedenthal, P. M. (2015). Heterogeneity of long-history migration explains cultural differences in reports of emotional expressivity and the functions of smiles. *Proceedings of the National Academy of Sciences, 112*(19), E2429–E2436.

Sauter, D. A., Eisner, F., Ekman, P., & Scott, S. K. (2010). Cross-cultural recognition of basic emotions through nonverbal emotional vocalizations. *Proceedings of the National Academy of Sciences, 107*(6), 2408–2412. https://doi.org/10.1073/pnas.0908239106

Scharlemann, J. P. W., Eckel, C. C., Kacelnik, A., & Wilson, R. K. (2001). The value of a smile: Game theory with a human face. *Journal of Economic Psychology, 22*(5), 617–640. https://doi.org/10.1016/S0167-4870(01)00059-9

Scheper-Hughes, N. (1992). *Death without weeping: The violence of everyday life in Brazil*. University of California Press.

Scherer, K. R. (1984). On the nature and function of emotion: A component process approach. In K. R. Scherer & P. Ekman (Eds.), *Approaches to emotion* (pp. 293–398). Psychology Press.

Schmidt, K. L., & Cohn, J. F. (2001). Human facial expressions as adaptations: Evolutionary questions in facial expression research. *American Journal of Physical Anthropology, 116*(S33), 3–24. https://doi.org/10.1002/ajpa.20001

Schyns, P. G., Petro, L. S., & Smith, M. L. (2009). Transmission of facial expressions of emotion co-evolved with their efficient decoding in the brain: Behavioral and brain evidence. *PLoS ONE, 4*(5), e5625. https://doi.org/10.1371/journal.pone.0005625

Seyfarth, R. M., & Cheney, D. L. (2003). Signalers and receivers in animal communication. *Annual Review of Psychology, 54*(1), 145–173. https://doi.org/10.1146/annurev.psych.54.101601.145121

Shariff, A. F., & Tracy, J. L. (2011). What are emotion expressions for? *Current Directions in Psychological Science, 20*(6), 395–399. https://doi.org/10.1177/0963721411424739

Sinaceur, M., & Tiedens, L. Z. (2006). Get mad and get more than even: When and why anger expression is effective in negotiations. *Journal of Experimental Social Psychology, 42*(3), 314–322. https://doi.org/10.1016/j.jesp.2005.05.002

Snowdon, C. T. (2003). Expression of emotion in nonhuman animals. In R. J. Davidson, K. R. Scherer, & H. Hill Goldsmith (Eds.), *Handbook of affective sciences* (pp. 457–480). Oxford University Press.

Spoor, J. R., & Kelly, J. R. (2004). The evolutionary significance of affect in groups: Communication and group bonding. *Group Processes & Intergroup Relations, 7*(4), 398–412. https://doi.org/10.1177/1368430204046145

Sroufe, L. A. (1996). *Emotional development: The organization of emotional life in the early years*. Cambridge University Press. https://doi.org/10.1017/CBO9780511527661

Susskind, J. M., & Anderson, A. K. (2008). Facial expression form and function. *Communicative & Integrative Biology, 1*(2), 148–149. https://doi.org/10.4161/cib.1.2.6999

Susskind, J. M., Lee, D. H., Cusi, A., Feiman, R., Grabski, W., & Anderson, A. K. (2008). Expressing fear enhances sensory acquisition. *Nature Neuroscience, 11*(7), 843–850. https://doi.org/10.1038/nn.2138

Tinbergen, N. (1952). "Derived" activities; their causation, biological significance, origin, and emancipation during evolution. *The Quarterly Review of Biology, 27*(1), 1–32.

Tinbergen, N. (1963). On aims and methods of ethology. *Zeitschrift Für Tierpsychologie, 20*(4), 410–433.

Tooby, J., & Cosmides, L. (1992). The psychological foundations of culture. In J. H. Barkow, L. Cosmides, & J. Tooby (Eds.), *The adapted mind: Evolutionary psychology and the generation of culture* (pp. 19–136). Oxford University Press.

Tooby, J., & Cosmides, L. (2008). The evolutionary psychology of the emotions and their relationship to internal regulatory variables. In M. Lewis, J. M. Haviland-Jones, & L. F. Barrett (Eds.), *Handbook of emotions* (3rd ed., pp. 114–137). Guilford Press.

Tooby, J., & Cosmides, L. (2020). Natural selection and the nature of communication. In K. Floyd & R. Weber (Eds.), *The handbook of communication science and biology* (pp. 21–49). Routledge.

Trivers, R. L. (1971). The evolution of reciprocal altruism. *The Quarterly Review of Biology, 46*(1), 35–57. https://doi.org/10.1086/406755

Troiano, G., & Nante, N. (2018). Emoji: What does the scientific literature say about them? A new way to communicate in the 21th century. *Journal of Human Behavior in the Social Environment, 28*(4), 528–533. https://doi.org/10.1080/10911359.2018.1437103

Van Kleef, G. A. (2009). How emotions regulate social life: The emotions as social information (EASI) model. *Current Directions in Psychological Science, 18*(3), 184–188.

Van Vugt, M., & Tybur, J. M. (2015). The evolutionary foundations of status hierarchy. In D. M. Buss (Ed.), *The handbook of evolutionary psychology* (Vol. 2, pp. 788–809). Wiley.

Vingerhoets, A. J. J. M., & Bylsma, L. M. (2016). The riddle of human emotional crying: A challenge for emotion researchers. *Emotion Review, 8*(3), 207–217. https://doi.org/10.1177/1754073915586226

CHAPTER 36
Emotions and Intergroup Conflict

Christian Kotoye and Melissa M. McDonald

Abstract

Historically, humans have lived in groups to promote survival and reproduction. However, group-based living has stimulated conflict between groups over various resources. These conflicts present a threat to the reproductive fitness, which is categorized and managed with appropriate behavioral responses. This chapter examines the role of emotions in this process. Emotions promote an adaptive response, by which their category and magnitude are calibrated to match the perceived threat. The self-protection and disease-avoidance threat-management systems use social-based emotional responses and their resulting behaviors to detect and respond to potential harm from conspecifics. This chapter also discusses the differences in responses to threats from out-group members and individual variation (e.g., strength, sex, health) which shapes the adaptive response. This model is integrated with research that has identified emotional interventions to reduce intergroup prejudice and discrimination.

Key Words: emotions, emotion regulation, intergroup, conflict, threat management

Introduction

Conflicts between groups have been recurrent throughout human existence; starting with early humans in small bands of hunter-gatherers (Bowels, 2009; Choi & Bowles, 2007; Gat, 2015; Keeley, 1996; Martin & Frayer, 1997) and extending to current conflicts between racial and ethnic groups, nations, and a large collection of other arbitrary group distinctions. This conflict poses a serious threat to the reproductive fitness of those involved. Contests over status, territory, resources, and mating opportunities present the risk of injury and death; the loss of allies, kin, and mates; diminished dominance and prestige; and the forfeiture of resources necessary for survival and reproduction. These risks may have selected for an adaptive system capable of detecting potential threats to one's reproductive fitness in the domain of intergroup conflict, estimating the likelihood and severity of the threat, and calibrating an emotional response that generates a cascade of cognitive and behavioral outputs that promote adaptive action.

In this chapter, we emphasize the importance and specificity of the emotional response in producing functional behavior. Emotions are modes of functioning that coordinate a collection of related adaptive responses in physiology, cognition, and behavior (Nesse, 1990). These modes of functioning were shaped by recurrent threats to early humans' fitness that called for a quick and near-automatic response to survive. Importantly, to be adaptive, emotions must produce a pattern of activation that is functional in a particular context. Intergroup conflict can present a variety of different threats (e.g., physical harm, disease transmission, circumvention of reproductive choice) that require different solutions (e.g., avoidance vs. aggression). The interpretation of threat is likely to vary as a function of individual characteristics (dominance motivations, physical strength, sex, etc.) (Schaller & Neuberg, 2012) and the affordances of the environment (presence of allies, access to weapons, means of escape, etc.). Emotions play a key role in motivating the adaptive action that the appraisal of a particular threat calls for. For example, fear promotes avoidance of interpersonal and intergroup conflict, whereas anger promotes approach and an escalation of hostilities. The present review aims to integrate a threat-management system perspective (Neuberg et al., 2011) with the theory of cognitive appraisals of emotions (Arnold, 1960; reviewed in Ellsworth & Scherer, 2003) to provide a framework for considering how a temporal process of threat detection and management unfolds to produce intergroup bias and conflict. Additionally, we will discuss research on interventions that take advantage of this temporal process to disrupt its output—that is, interventions that function to alter emotional experiences in the hopes of reducing intergroup bias and conflict.

Intergroup Conflict

Conflict between groups is a pervasive feature of human interaction. At the beginning of January 2021, the people of the United States were gripped by news that a mob of President Trump's supporters stormed and breached the walls of the US Capitol in an attempt to prevent certification of the election of President-elect Joe Biden. This follows in the footsteps of a summer of worldwide protests demanding racial justice following the death of George Floyd, and countless other Black people, at the hands of police; a spike in xenophobia expressed against Asian people owing to the racist labeling of the novel coronavirus COVID-19 as the "China virus" (Tessler et al., 2020); outrage over the inhumane treatment of immigrants and asylum seekers at the US-Mexico border; and a cyber-security attack on the US government believed to have been instigated by the Russian government. Conflicts such as these exact a heavy toll—emotionally, financially, politically, and in terms of lives lost. According to the Uppsala Conflict Data Program (2021), there were a total of 76,480 deaths from various types of large-scale conflict in 2019. Importantly, intergroup conflict is not a unique feature of modern human societies, but instead is deeply ingrained in our evolutionary past.

Early human groups were composed mostly of small bands of hunter-gatherers within familial groups, usually ranging from 25 to 100 members, or larger tribes of multiple kin groups, or more rarely, large groups of people (300–1,000) who shared cultural systems and language (Wrangham & Glowacki, 2012). These tribes/bands of hunter-gathers engaged in conflict with other groups at similar or higher rates compared to modern humans (Bowles, 2009; Ember & Ember, 1992; Pinker, 2012). Evidence for the frequency and character of early human intergroup conflict is gleaned from ethnographic, archaeological, and genetic records. Collectively, this research characterizes intergroup conflict as a persistent feature of early human life (though see Fry, 2006; Fry & Söderberg, 2013). For example, a census of 551 individuals over five generations of the Ecuadorian Waorani society found that the highest death rate by violence within the society was 54% in men and 39% among women—an extreme example (Larrick et al., 1979). Similarly, research by Chagnon (1988) found that through 23 years of observing the Yanomamö, approximately 30% of the deaths among adult males were due to violence. Additional evidence comes from the documentation of (predominantly male) skeletons preserved from the Nataruk people of the late Pleistocene/Early Holocene period that show evidence of violent death (Lahr et al., 2016). Additional archaeological evidence is reviewed by Gat (2015), highlighting the discovery of fortified settlements in the

American Northwest, hypothesized to have been there for at least 4,000 years, as well as body armor thought to have been used in battle prior to European colonialism. Similarly, evidence of early humans preparing for defense is found in the Çatal-Huyuk in Anatolia, where defensive, pueblo-style houses were arranged to facilitate defense from invaders (Mellart, 1967).

Early conflict among hunter-gatherers was characterized by skirmishes over land, resources, and mating opportunities, as well as by raids and ambushes that used the element of surprise to the group's advantage (Gat, 2015; Turney-High, 1991; van der Dennen, 1995). Less common among hunter-gatherers, but frequent in modern industrialized society, are protracted conflicts, in which the goals of each group are incompatible with one another (Bar-Tal et al., 1989; Mitchell, 1989; Rubin et al., 1994). Some such conflicts are described as intractable. These conflicts are protracted and violent; they are perceived as zero-sum and all-encompassing, and are resistant to compromise and attempts at resolution (Bar-Tal, 2007). Because of the violent and lengthy nature of these conflicts, they inspire hatred and deep animosity toward the other group, and consume a large portion of the resources and focus of the group (Kriesberg, 1998).

Although modern conflict differs from early conflict in scale, strategy, and tool usage, it is commonly motivated by the same underlying forces, such as the desire to acquire and control valuable resources and territory, to gain status via prestige or dominance, and to retaliate for past transgressions. The motivation for conflict is expected to correspond closely with the emotions experienced by groups in conflict. Revenge (or blood revenge) is a particularly emotional motivation for intergroup conflict. It refers to the killing (or harming) of another in retaliation for violence or some other type of transgression against an individual, ally, or kin (Chagnon, 1988; Schumann & Ross, 2010). The urge to seek retribution stems from feelings of anger or hatred directed at the perpetrator (Feinberg, 1970; Threadgill & Gable, 2020). Often, the conflict is related to sexual transgressions. As observed in the Yanomamö, a collection of hunter-gatherer tribes in the Amazon, quarrels over sexual access to women can lead to homicide, causing a rift in the group and resulting in the tribe splitting into two new groups engaged in conflict (Chagnon, 1988). Along similar lines, Rozée (1993) summarized ethnographic data indicating that 63% of nonindustrial societies, randomly selected from the Standard Cross Cultural Sample (Murdock & White, 1969), engage in *theft rape*. This occurs when a woman is involuntarily abducted and kept captive as a slave, concubine, prostitute, wife, or spoil of war. Along similar lines, Sanday (1981) reports that two key predictors of rape among small-scale societies are warfare and raiding other groups for wives (Chang et al., 2011). These actions are likely to motivate angry retaliatory violence.

Conflicts instigated by revenge may not seem adaptive; however, the contrary may be theorized, especially when looking at this phenomenon more closely in hunter-gatherer societies. The occurrence of revenge raids and retaliatory killings is found in multiple hunter-gatherer societies, for instance, the Waorani and the Yanomamö (Beckerman et al., 2009; Chagnon, 1988). For example, despite the differences in the rates of warfare and aggression among the Waorani and the Yanomamö, both societies expressed the importance of retaliation in the case of kin victims (albeit at different levels of importance). Revenge, especially when inflicted swiftly and successfully, can be a deterrent to future raids (Chagnon, 1988; McCullough et al., 2013). This is accomplished by reducing the perception of fitness benefits from raids against a vengeful group. Swift and successful revenge raids may give a group a reputation of being aggressive and vengeful and may ward off attempts from males of other groups to engage in intergroup killings, abductions, or rapes. As a result, this reputational deterrent may increase the fitness of the members of the group.

Conflicts are instigated not only by revenge, but also by disputes over resources. Commonly resources that instigate conflict are women from either the in-group or the out-group (Chagnon, 1988). For example, skirmishes over infidelity or competition for access to women can start as simple violent competitions in the Yanomamö, characterized by duels. However, these can become violent enough that lethal aggression breaks out between individuals and, subsequently, between groups. Additionally, raids and battles were instigated by struggles over access to finite resources such as hunting grounds, fishing territories, and watering holes (Gat, 2015).

Sex Differences in Intergroup Conflict

The descriptions above highlight a persistent feature of intergroup conflict, namely that it is predominantly instigated by men and targeted at men (McDonald et al., 2012). This is not to suggest that women do not suffer (or gain) as a consequence of intergroup conflict; indeed, they often do. Although women are rarely involved as combatants or warriors of conflict, they are often treated as the driving motivation and spoils of war (Chagnon, 1988; Fison & Howitt, 1991; Gat, 2015; Meggit, 1962; Sanday, 1981; Walker & Bailey 2013). To understand why men and women occupy different roles in intergroup conflict, the reproductive costs and benefits that accrue to each sex as a function of conflict must be examined.

THE FEMALE PSYCHOLOGY OF INTERGROUP CONFLICT

The benefits of intergroup conflict, if successfully waged, include increased access to resources, territory, mates, and elevated status as a warrior. Among men, these benefits can be translated into reproductive success, either directly in the abduction or rape of women from an out-group, or indirectly via the increase in status and resources that make one appealing as a potential mate. These same benefits are not so easily translated into reproductive success for women, in large part owing to lower lifetime reproductive capacity (Glutton-Brock & Vincent, 1991). That is, increased access to resources and elevated status may enable women to more effectively compete for higher-quality mates, but given the large obligatory parental investment required of women (Trivers, 1972), such benefits would likely have a small impact on overall reproductive success. A more obvious deterrent to women's participation in physical conflict is sex differences in physical stature and strength, particularly among hunter-gatherers, for whom much of the fighting relies on upper-body strength (Sell et al., 2012). Consequently, women would be more likely than men to suffer injury or death while fighting. Moreover, given the important role that women play in ensuring the health and survival of their offspring (Campbell, 1999; Sear & Mace, 2008), any injury sustained or time away from offspring could negatively affect the livelihood of their children. Overall, the cost-benefit trade-off for warfare among women does not favor their participation.

This has consequences for the threat posed by intergroup conflict to women. Out-group men are not a competitive threat, and approach-oriented motivations and emotions that foster aggressive action will not benefit women the way they do men. Rather, women face a different set of threats in the context of intergroup conflict, namely their own abduction and rape and the murder of their dependent children. The costs of filicide to reproductive fitness are severe, but so too are those of abduction and rape. Women who are raped may incur physical injury, making it difficult for them to provision food for themselves and their offspring; they may suffer reputational harm within their group, making it difficult to acquire or retain a long-term mate; and most severely, rape circumvents women's ability to select a mate (McKibbin & Shackelford, 2011; Thornhill & Thornhill, 1983). Women who are abducted face similar costs, as they are often subjected to group rape, prostitution, slavery, and service as a concubine (Rozée, 1993). Given the asymmetry in size and strength between men and women, defending against sexual aggression from out-group raiders is likely to risk injury with a low rate of success. Consequently, women are more likely to favor an avoidance-based strategy to reduce the risk of becoming the victim of a sexual assault (Archer, 2009), one that is likely to be governed by a fear-based emotional response.

THE MALE PSYCHOLOGY OF INTERGROUP CONFLICT

In both modern and early warfare, the primary participants have been men. Adams (1983) examined rates of female participation in warfare in stateless societies and found that only 9 of 67 cultures mention women's involvement as warriors. In the United States, men accounted for 95% of the enlisted service people in the military as of 2015 (Council on Foreign Relations, 2020) and 97.6% of all reported casualties across two recent conflicts involving the United States (Operation Enduring Freedom and Operation Iraqi Freedom; Cross et al., 2011).

Men's involvement in intergroup conflict can be understood via an analysis of the potential costs and benefits to their participation. The most glaring costs are the potential for physical injury or death. Yet the risk of death was not as high among hunter-gatherers as it might seem when extrapolating from modern warfare, at least among the initiators of conflict. The situations in which a group is willing to attack another group are such that the chances of victory are nearly assured (e.g., surprise ambushes, attacking a weaker group, and outnumbering the target group; Johnson & MacKay, 2015; Manson & Wrangham, 1991; Tooby & Cosmides, 1988; Wrangham, 1999; Wrangham & Glowacki, 2012). As noted previously, the reproductive fitness benefits of warfare for men include access to resources captured from the opponent, including their women, as well as an elevation in status associated with one's reputation as a successful warrior (reviewed in McDonald et al., 2012; van Vugt, 2009; van Vugt et al., 2007). These benefits stand a good chance of being converted into large gains in reproductive fitness. In addition to these benefits, refusal to participate in warfare may result in punishment, including ostracism from one's group (Boyd et al. 2003; Mathew & Boyd 2014). Indeed, it may be the fear and shame of being labeled a coward that pushes reluctant men into battle.

The potential reproductive rewards of intergroup conflict have led researchers to propose that men are equipped with a *male-warrior psychology* (McDonald et al., 2012; van Vugt et al., 2007). The male-warrior hypothesis states that men's intergroup bias is motivated by the desire to establish and maintain dominance over other groups. As a consequence, this motivation is characterized by aggressive inclinations and is fueled by approach-oriented emotions such as anger and excitement. Given this, it is not surprising that men express more intergroup prejudice and discrimination than women across a wide range of domains and contexts (reviewed in McDonald et al., 2011). However, because the risks of warfare are non-zero, aggressive intergroup inclinations are likely to be moderated by men's physical strength and stature. Consistent with this, physically stronger men report greater support for the use of military force in international affairs (Sell et al. 2009; Sell et al., 2012) and more strongly endorse anti-egalitarian attitudes, including group-based hierarchy (Price et al., 2011).

The above describes contexts in which men are the instigators of conflict, yet men are also the primary targets of this violence, and the psychology governing defense of one's group during a surprise ambush or raid is likely to differ from that which governs attack. Although the risk of casualties is low for the attacking group, that is not the case for those on the defensive. In the context of an attack in which one's group's likelihood of successful defense is low, the adaptive response may be to flee if escape is possible, bolstered by an emotional response of fear. The variation in threats (and opportunities) that intergroup conflict presents to men, as well as women, highlights the potential complexities of managing one's response to social threats. Failure to manage the threats adaptively could result in grave consequences to one's reproductive fitness. Below we consider how a threat-management perspective (Neuberg et al., 2011) provides a lens through which to understand how men and women manage the adaptive challenges presented by intergroup conflict.

Threat-Management Systems for Intergroup Conflict

Recurrent challenges to fitness from the threat of intergroup conflict likely generated selection pressure for adaptive responses. These responses would have to be sensitive to various cues in the environment, calibrated to one's own strengths and weaknesses, and capable of quickly producing cognitive and behavioral responses, coordinated by the activation of an emotional state. Neuberg, Kenrick, and Schaller (2011) proposed such an adaptive system, arguing that humans are equipped with precautionary threat-management systems that mitigate the threats posed by the social lifestyle of humans. In particular, two systems were proposed: one for self-protection (i.e., to manage threats of violence and physical harm), and one for disease avoidance (i.e., to manage threats of infection and disease). Each of these systems connects with a threat posed by interactions with out-groups—as agents of intergroup conflict, and as potential vectors of disease transmission. Below we provide an overview of how threat-management systems operate, and then examine their relevance to understanding intergroup conflict and bias.

Basic Principles of Threat-Management Systems

Despite the divergence in the types of threats addressed by these two systems, there are common features associated with their operation (Neuberg et al., 2011). Because of the need to quickly diagnosis whether a threat is present, they are prone to mistakes. These mistakes should err toward an oversensitivity to the detection of threat. This is because the cost of making a mistake in which a real threat is ignored is higher than the cost of assuming a non-threat is real. For example, if an individual ignores cues indicating that another seeks to harm them or is infected with a pathogen, they may suffer serious injury, illness, or death. Thus, it is more adaptive for threat-management systems to err toward false alarms (Haselton & Nettle, 2006).

Threat-management systems are also expected to be sensitive to circumstances and individual traits associated with increased vulnerability. In an environment associated with danger (e.g., run-down buildings and graffiti; Kahn & Davies, 2017), the self-protection threat-management system is likely to be vigilant in scanning for threats, and labeling ambiguous stimuli as threatening. Similarly, individuals who perceive that they are especially vulnerable to threat are likely to express greater sensitivity to threat. For example, people who have high levels of chronic anxiety, see the world as a dangerous place, or are physically weak, may perceive greater vulnerability to harm from out-groups, and those with a greater susceptibility to infection may perceive greater vulnerabilities to disease transmission (e.g., Faulkner et al., 2004; Maner et al., 2005; Murray et al., 2019; Park et al., 2003; Park et al., 2007; Schaller et al., 2003).

A key feature of a threat-management system is the ability to produce coordinated perceptual, affective, cognitive, and behavioral responses—all functioning in concert to mitigate the consequences of the perceived threat. Once the perceptual system identifies a threat, an emotional response is elicited that activates a particular mode of functioning, which can then coordinate a collection of adaptive responses in physiology, cognition, and behavior (Nesse, 1990; Nesse & Ellsworth, 2009; Neuberg et al., 2011). Given the role of emotion as a precursor to action, it is important that the emotion activated is specific to the threat posed, or the response will not aid in adaptive behavior. In other words, each threat system is argued to be domain specific—different systems scan for different threats, and different threats require different responses. Although disgust and fear are both likely to promote avoidance, the mode of functioning is sufficiently distinct that experiencing disgust as a group of angry men ambush your group is not likely to coordinate the proper behavioral response. Below we describe the role of emotions in coordinating adaptive responses in greater detail.

Emotional Appraisals of Threat

The emotions elicited by threat-management systems coordinate a cascade of responses in the body (Cosmides & Tooby, 2000; Nesse, 1990; Nesse & Ellsworth, 2009; reviewed by Neuberg et al., 2011). In the context of intergroup conflict, physically aggressive actions are typically linked to anger, hatred, contempt, and occasionally, disgust (Bar-Tal, 2007; Chagnon, 1988; Cosmides & Tooby, 2000; Matsumoto et al., 2016; reviewed by Tratner & McDonald, 2019). Avoidance of a stimulus via fleeing or freezing is promoted by fear and disgust in the intergroup context (Cosmides & Tooby, 2000; Crandall & Moriarty, 1995; Nesse, 1990; Nesse & Ellsworth, 2009; Neuberg et al., 2011).

The emotional appraisal theory (Arnold, 1960; reviewed by Ellsworth & Scherer, 2003) fits most closely with the role that emotions play in a threat-management system. This theoretical perspective describes emotions as specialized states shaped by natural selection that increase the fitness of an individual in specific situations by coordinating a suite of behavioral, physiological, and cognitive responses (Nesse, 1990). Emotions serve as a shortcut to activate a cascade of responses, much like a program on a computer that, when activated, activates many other subprograms that work in concert to achieve a goal (e.g., flee, avoid, fight; Cosmides & Tooby, 2000). These emotional programs would have evolved through recurrent pressures that required multiple responses in a short amount of time (Cosmides & Tooby, 2000; Nesse, 1990; Nesse & Ellsworth, 2009).

Emotional appraisals of the situation (the initial focus of the threat-management systems) focus on novelty and environmental changes, intrinsic pleasantness or unpleasantness, goal obstacles or facilitators, unpredictability, agency (the situation is caused by the subject, another person, or circumstances), controllability, and compatibility with social norms or personal values (Ellsworth & Scherer, 2003). These appraisals are used to determine the appropriate emotion for that situation. For instance, the sum of appraisals when perceiving an out-group male may suggest that the man is a new stimulus, obstructs survival goals, is an unpredictable actor, and expresses qualities (e.g., physical formidability) that indicate that fear is an appropriate response, and thus the best course of action is to flee rather than fight. However, perhaps another individual perceives this man as predictable and within control (less physically formidable); in this case, the appropriate emotion may be anger, and thus fighting may be a better behavioral response. Goal obstacles may alter which responses are possible, such that even if an individual desires to flee, that may not be a viable option. In an example of this, people primed with an out-group male exhibited different action tendencies as a function of the constraints of their local environment (Cesario et al., 2010). Those in a confined space displayed increased accessibility of fight-related words, whereas those in an open space (without goal obstacles) displayed an increase in accessibility of words related to flight (Cesario et al., 2010). Much like a group surrounded by an ambush of out-group warriors, not all situations afford the desired behavioral response. Future research should examine how emotions change in these contexts. Do people experiencing the threat of harm, who feel fear and desire to flee, shift toward an approach-oriented emotional response, such as anger, when flight is not an option?

Self-Protection Threat Management and Intergroup Conflict

Due to the recurrent threats posed by other people over evolutionary history, a threat-management system for self-protection would likely be equipped with mechanisms for detecting threat in the context of interpersonal interactions. This system prioritizes traits in others that signal the desire to enact harm, and these cues would assist in the decision to escape, or to stay and attack the aggressor (Neuberg et al., 2011). A strong cue of impending physical harm is derived from others' faces—angry facial expressions in particular, which would usually precede physical altercations (Ekman & Friesen, 2003; Goetz et al., 2013; Zebrowitz et al., 2010; Zebrowitz & Montepare, 2006; Zhang, 2018)—along with nonverbal cues like body posture (De Meijer et al., 1991; Sinke et al., 2010).

These cues to threats of physical harm discerned from angry facial expressions are especially relevant when observed in out-group men. As described above, men—especially out-group men—are common perpetrators of physical harm to both men and women. As a result of this recurrent threat of harm, cues of potential threat from out-group men are likely to be processed with a lower threshold for alarm. Evidence of this is found in a study that assessed differences in facial recognition for in-group men compared to out-group men. Participants were found to have greater memory for the faces of in-group men when facial expressions were neutral. However, this effect was erased or reversed when the male faces displayed anger. That is, angry out-group male faces were remembered as well or better than in-group male faces (Ackerman et al., 2006).

In addition to the faces of out-group men, the self-protective system is activated when other cues in the environment that are associated with threat are paired with the presence of out-group men. For example, the setting of a dangerous neighborhood influenced participants to make more errors in perceiving Black men versus White men as dangerous in a task to "shoot" or "not shoot" targets armed with a gun or a harmless object (Kahn & Davies, 2017). Further, the activation of the self-protection system can increase sensitivity in the categorization of group membership, as found in a study in which White participants who were primed with a threat to their self-protection were more likely to later categorize pictures of men by their racial group (Maner et al., 2012). This activation of the self-protection system that promotes the categorization of out-group men and attributing them to threats extends to existing groups (e.g., Blacks and Arabs) and to those that are newly constructed (i.e., minimal groups; Maner et al., 2012; Miller et al., 2010, 2012).

Further, these attributions of danger to out-group men, and the sensitivity to categorize men by their group membership, is more pronounced among those who express greater self-perceived vulnerability to threats. For instance, those who have a strong belief that the world is a dangerous place are more likely to associate out-group men with "danger"-relevant stereotypes and are more likely to categorize men by their racial group membership; similar results were found for those who believe they are vulnerable to interpersonal threats (Maner et al., 2012; Miller et al., 2010; Schaller, Park, & Faulkner, 2003; Schaller, Park, & Mueller, 2003). Overall, results are consistent with a self-protection threat-management system, but more research is needed to test the mediating role of emotions in producing cognitive and behavioral responses to threat cues.

A Threat-Management System for Protecting Reproductive Choice

The threat of intergroup conflict poses distinct adaptive challenges to women, relative to men, suggesting that women may be equipped with specialized mechanisms for protecting reproductive choice—particularly in an intergroup conflict context, owing to the elevated risk of rape and abduction (McDonald et al., 2015). Evidence consistent with this perspective includes results demonstrating that women's prejudice toward out-group men is greatest when the risk of sexual coercion and assault are higher. For example, research on dating preferences has shown that women have stronger endogamous mating preferences than men (Fisman et al., 2008; Sprecher et al., 1994). In an analysis of online dating profiles, 42% of women (vs. 17% of men) preferred a partner of their same ethnic background (Hitsch et al., 2010). Moreover, this effect appears to be an underestimate of the true magnitude of women's bias given that even when women indicated they had no race/ethnic dating preference, they nevertheless displayed a strong same-race preference in their actual dating decisions on the site. Thus, women express greater bias in intimate dating domains that afford more opportunities for men to circumvent reproductive choice. This is notable given that men typically express greater intergroup prejudice than women in nearly every other domain (reviewed in McDonald et al., 2011).

Consistent with a threat-management perspective, women's bias against out-group men is expected to be greatest among women who perceive themselves to be particularly vulnerable to sexual coercion. Along these lines, women who reported greater vulnerability to sexual coercion (e.g., "I am afraid of being sexually assaulted") also expressed greater bias against out-group men but not out-group women, or in-group men or women (Navarrete et al., 2010). A similar pattern was observed in a study examining an implicit measure of bias: women who reported more vulnerability to sexual coercion took longer to extinguish a conditioned fear of out-group men, but not of out-group women, in-group men, or in-group women (Navarrete et al., 2010). These findings provide evidence for the specificity of women's bias toward the agents who likely posed the greatest threat to reproductive choice over evolutionary history, namely out-group *men*.

An important moderator of the reproductive costs of rape is conception risk. Many of the fitness consequences of rape are only realized if the rape results in pregnancy. As a result, women may be equipped with mechanisms designed to be particularly vigilant to threats to reproductive choice when conception risk is elevated. This risk peaks in the days preceding ovulation (Wilcox et al., 2001). Given the recurrent sexual threat posed by *out-group* men, women may be equipped with specialized mechanisms promoting intergroup bias and the avoidance of out-group men at peak conception risk. Consistent with this prediction, women's intergroup bias was positively associated with conception risk, particularly among women who appraised themselves as vulnerable to sexual coercion (Navarrete et al., 2009). Laboratory research has linked these same mechanisms to behavioral outcomes in a dating context (McDonald et al., 2015), demonstrating that women near ovulation and who appraised themselves as vulnerable to sexual coercion were least likely to accept a date request from an out-group man. These findings suggest that women's threat-management system promotes avoidance of out-group men in contexts that present a greater risk of sexual assault, and that the expression of this bias is moderated by factors associated with the likelihood of assault and the reproductive costs of assault were it to occur.

Women's bias against out-group men is also expected to vary as a function of assessments of the likely threat posed by those out-group men. Men who are more physically formidable may be a greater threat to women's reproductive choice, owing to their greater ability to effectively overpower a woman, and a greater proclivity for aggression (Sell et al., 2009). Consistent with this prediction, women who implicitly associated the out-group with physicality evinced greater implicit bias against out-group men as a function of conception risk (McDonald et al., 2011; McDonald & Navarrete, 2015). In other words, women's bias against out-group men was greater when those men were perceived to be especially physically formidable, and when the reproductive consequences of sexual assault were heightened due to elevated conception risk.

Overall, these findings suggest that women possess unique psychological mechanisms for managing the threat posed by out-group men, and that these mechanisms are sensitive to factors that increase the likelihood and reproductive costs of the relevant threat, as predicted by a threat-management perspective. Moreover, given the tendency for the outcomes of this system to center on intergroup bias and avoidance, it is likely that the emotional impetus driving such behavior is based in fear, though additional research is needed to identify the temporal cascade of emotional, cognitive, and behavioral output.

Disease Avoidance Threat Management and Intergroup Conflict

The disease avoidance threat-management system is theorized to be vigilant against pathogen threats to an individual's physical health, but it also has implications for intergroup bias and conflict. The disease avoidance system, often referred to as the behavioral immune system (Schaller, 2015; Schaller & Duncan, 2007; Schaller & Park, 2011) is designed to help the immune system by avoiding people and environments with potential pathogen risks. The risk of contracting a disease or infection would have been high among early humans (Dobson & Carper, 1996; McNeill, 1976; Ridley, 1994; Zuk, 2008; reviewed by Schaller & Murray, 2010), and much more difficult to treat without modern medicine. Contact with out-group members, particularly among early humans, presents a serious threat of disease transmission, as out-group members may carry pathogens to which another group has not yet developed immunity. As a result, cues of out-group membership activate the disease avoidance system in a similar manner as would skin lesions and rashes.

In response to the perception of a disease threat, the system elicits the emotion of disgust to promote behavior to avoid contact with or exposure to pathogens (Nesse, 1990; Nesse & Ellsworth, 2009; Neuberg et al., 2011). In an intergroup context, disgust is elicited by those perceived as associated with disease risk, including foreigners and gay men (Cottrell et al., 2010; Curtis et al., 2004; Stevenson & Repacholi, 2005). Disgust reactions promote behaviors to avoid subjects of the potential disease risk and transmission. In some cases, however, avoidance is not possible, and thus aggressive action may be used to remove the threat of disease transmission (Neuberg et al., 2011).

The broad range of cues used to assess the risk of pathogen transmission, as well as the tendency to err on the side of assuming a threat is present, can lead to avoidance of people who pose no threat of infection (Kurzban & Leary, 2001; Neuberg et al., 2011). This mispairing of disease cues connects with intergroup bias as well. Individuals who appraise themselves as more vulnerable to disease transmission are more likely to associate out-group members (e.g., immigrants and foreigners) with danger and to express less positive attitudes toward them (Faulkner et al., 2004; Navarrete et al., 2007; Park et al., 2003; Park et al., 2007). In an interesting example of this, bias has been shown to vary within individuals as a function of changes in immune system vulnerability (Navarrete et al., 2007). In the first trimester of pregnancy, women are more vulnerable to infection due to their bodies' mechanisms that lower their immune system's defenses temporarily to accommodate the developing fetus. Women in this stage of pregnancy show more disgust responses (Fessler et al., 2005) as well as a stronger preference for in-group members (Navarrete et al., 2007).

These prejudices promote preferences for intergroup separation and distance. This can be seen in the staunch support for the deportation of or prevention of entry to certain immigrant groups and refugees. These disgust responses may also promote aggression between groups. Disgust is associated with dehumanization of out-groups, particularly in the tendency to see out-groups as animalistic (Buckels & Trapnell, 2013). This tendency to dehumanize the out-group has been connected with violence against them. The Nazis, for example, depicted Jews as analogous to swine, vermin, and insects (Bytwerk, 1983). These dehumanizing and disgust-inducing metaphors are a common narrative for genocide, in which out-groups targeted by genocidal campaigns are associated with animals and the defiance of ideal, civilized cultural norms, thereby justifying eradication of the group (Savage, 2007). Evidence of this is found in the assessment of the writings that people who perpetrated or supported "hate crimes" recorded on websites in reference to the targeted group. These perpetrators and supporters used emotive language suggesting disgust (along with other emotions, such as hate) more frequently than when compared to normal communication (Taylor, 2007). Overall, the association of out-group members with disgust may make it easier to justify their exclusion from one's society, and even to promote aggression against them.

Emotion-Focused Interventions

Although emotions are argued to play a crucial role in coordinating adaptive responses to intergroup conflict, the tendency of threat-management systems to err toward false positives suggests that our emotional responses to out-groups are not always warranted, particularly as intergroup conflict has declined over time (Pinker, 2012). In an effort to reduce intergroup conflict and bias, extensive work has investigated how emotional appraisals and emotion regulation can be utilized to ameliorate intergroup conflict and bias. Research on emotion regulation has focused on when and how emotions can be influenced or changed, especially in interpersonal contexts (Gross, 2008), but has more recently been expanded to intergroup contexts as well (Halperin et al., 2011).

A Model for Appraisals and Emotional Regulation in Intergroup Conflict

Halperin and Sharvit (2011) developed an appraisal-based framework for emotions and the regulation of emotions. According to the framework, the standard sequence of processing for emotional responses starts with the cue of the occurrence of an event and an appraisal of the event, which then leads to an emotional reaction, and ends with attitude and behavioral outputs. This process is influenced by three main factors. The first factor is the framing, or the perceived context of the event (e.g., whether a punch thrown by another is seen as a defensive reaction or unprovoked may inspire fear vs. anger, respectfully). Second, nonaffective and individual factors (e.g., socioeconomic status, moral values, need for structure) have an impact on the appraisal of an event or group by having individuals evaluate situations based on their preexisting worldviews or contexts (Halperin, 2008, 2011; Halperin, Sharvit, et al., 2011). Lastly, the amount of previous exposure and experience dealing with emotional reactions to similar events can promote emotional sentiments which bias an individual in the emotional appraisal process (Arnold, 1960; Frijda, 1986; Halperin, 2013; Halperin, Sharvit, et al., 2011), especially if the emotional sentiment has been cultured for a long period of time (e.g., bias assuming threat from Muslims among Jews, or Blacks as perceived by White Americans).

This model recognizes the opportunity for reappraisal at three potential time points. Reappraisals are as simple as the act of reconsidering the event or one's interpretation of the event for alternative explanations for the cause or its implications (Ochsner & Gross, 2008). Thus, the model proposes that the first opportunity for reappraisal occurs during the event or via recall of information about the event, referred to as "online reappraisals." Online reappraisals can be shifted by collecting new information. For example, in the context of a failed peace summit, to promote guilty emotional responses instead of the initial anger-related emotions (i.e., anger or resentment toward the other party for the failure to invoke peace), reports of the event may highlight the in-group's role in the failure, rather than highlighting the out-group's faults, thus increasing the group's experience of guilt (Wohl et al., 2006). This experience of guilt instead of anger can motivate an individual to seek reconciliation instead of further violence (Doosje et al., 1998; Iyer et al., 2003).

As another example, online reappraisals may be helpful when in a potentially dangerous situation. Imagine that a person notices an approaching man who is scowling and, therefore, potentially dangerous. An online reappraisal wherein the collection of more information, perhaps from a friendly other, reveals that the man was squinting while looking at his watch, thereby altering the initial evaluation perceiving him to be angry and threatening. This may change one's emotional response to one of curiosity or another non-threat-related emotional response instead of the initial fearful or angry response (Wohl et al., 2006). These reappraisals aim to change the perception of the event so that the emotional reaction is less severe; however, this is more effective when the online emotion regulation occurs in the initial stage of the cognitive appraisal process (Sheppes & Merian, 2007).

The second and third opportunities for reappraisal occur via prospective reappraisal either before or during the initial emotional appraisal. Prospective reappraisals utilize cognitive change to one's beliefs and sentiments toward a group. Adjusting one's ideologies and/or their emotional sentiments about a group before the emotion-triggering events occur has been documented by Gross and Levenson (1997) to be effective in promoting emotion regulation. In their work, participants watched sad and amusing films and were preemptively told to either suppress their emotional response or to simply watch the films. Those who inhibited their emotional experience decreased their emotional responses to the films. In a real-world example, dialogue groups between Israeli Jews and Palestinians in which individuals from each group hear stories about the other group, sit down and confront people from the other group, and other methods that promote a narrative about the other group are helpful in regulating the conflict-prompting emotions (e.g., hatred and anger) in favor of more conciliatory emotions (e.g., empathy; Maoz, 2011).

This model has been theorized to be effective in the process of limiting the occurrence of intergroup conflicts by adjusting one's long-term or recently developed emotions and attitudes toward a group or individual. The model is applied by its authors to intervene in the cognitive appraisals by individuals at the outbreak and escalation of conflict, at the de-escalation of conflict, and at the reconciliation between conflicted parties.

In efforts to encourage de-escalation of conflict, adjusting the dynamic between fear and hope can be useful (Jarymowicz & Bar-Tal, 2006). Fear can be involved in the prevention of conflict, but can also be involved in the perpetuation of already existing conflicts. Fear that is maintained over time can perpetuate conflict in that the individuals involved will be more suspicious of and paranoid about the out-group, which could discourage attempts to negotiate or compromise (Duckitt & Fisher, 2003; Feldman & Stenner, 1997; Jost et al., 2003; Stephan & Stephan, 2000). In contrast, hope can inspire thoughts of achievement and a belief in a more stable future, which can inspire more willingness to engage in efforts to end the conflict (Jarymowicz & Bar-Tal, 2006). To promote de-escalation of conflict, the model suggests that promoting hope should engage individuals in setting goals toward reconciliation or other more realistic goals in the future (Halperin, 2008).

Finally, the model focuses on increasing empathy and decreasing hatred to facilitate the reconciliation stage. The best route to facilitate this process is through prospective regulation in which the recurrently expressed hatred is decreased and, as a result, empathy is adopted. The strategy for inducing this effect is much like the one used to reduce hatred's effect on the outbreak of conflict; to encourage perspective-taking and to compel individuals in the conflicting groups to think of the feelings of each other (Batson et al., 1997; Davis, 2018). The effect of empathy on reconciliation was demonstrated in a study among Catholics and Protestants in

Northern Ireland—the mere opportunity of contact and the potential for friendship between the two groups preceded expressions of empathy (Tam et al., 2008).

More work focused on increasing the prevalence of positive emotions is needed to inform interventions to intergroup conflict. As stated above, research has found that fostering emotions that inspire perspective-taking, such as empathy (Batson et al., 2002), result in downstream effects for helping others and is associated with decreasing aggression in individuals even when engaged in intractable conflicts (Rosler et al., 2017; Shechtman & Basheer, 2005). Additionally, decreasing Schadenfreude—the proclivity to feel amusement and joy when observing or being informed of the negative experience of another from an out-group (Cikara et al., 2011)—in response to out-group members' suffering may be an effective way to improve relations and decrease or eliminate conflict and discrimination between groups (Cikara & Fiske, 2011).

Gateway Groups
Another route to altering emotions that foster or perpetuate intergroup conflict is via gateway groups. Gateway groups include people who belong to both the in-group and the out-group, for example, someone who is biracial, and identifies as both Black and White. Gateway group members hold a unique position that has the potential to be influential on the psychologies of those around them who belong to at least one of the groups that the gateway group member embodies. Interactions with those embodying both the in-group and the out-group are theorized to have an effect on multiple emotions that perpetuate intergroup conflict (Levy et al., 2017). Due to the dual identities that gateway groups inhabit, they are in a position to influence conflicting group members' appraisals of the other group, along with other attributes they associate with the out-group, for instance, attitudes and behaviors toward the out-group (Levy et al., 2017).

Gateway groups may have an effect on the emotions experienced by groups engaged in conflict, and the ability to engage in emotional regulation. Research on social categorization highlights the effect that clear social categories between groups can have on the emotional responses experienced between them (Crisp & Hewstone, 1999; Dovidio et al., 2009; Nguyen & Benet-Martínez, 2013; Levy et al., 2017). Research by Cikara and colleagues (2014) has shown that blurring boundaries between groups—that is, by altering the perception of definitive differences between groups—can increase the ability to feel empathy for out-groups by decreasing empathy bias toward one's in-group (i.e., the preference to show empathy toward one group over another). Levy et al. (2017) predicts that this effect of social blurring can be achieved by the interaction between group members with those in gateway groups. Additionally, gateway groups can reduce negative emotions between groups, such as anger, hatred, and shame.

Hatred also relies on the distance between groups and the distinctiveness of social categories (Halperin, 2008, 2011; Halperin, Russell, et al., 2011). Therefore, Levy and colleagues (2017) similarly predict that the presence of gateway groups will blur these distinctions and thus decrease the expression of hatred. Levy and colleagues additionally predict that gateway groups can influence the appraisal process. Primarily, they predict the ability for gateway groups to influence online regulation by adjusting individuals' beliefs about a group before the interaction occurs, through an increase in positive emotions toward those group members. Prospective emotional regulation also is influenced by gateway groups by impacting the beliefs and attitudes toward an out-group through the blurred social categories that are promoted by interacting with gateway groups. Lastly, gateway groups can promote the reframing of individuals' initial outlooks on the information or the nature of the events in encounters with relevant out-groups due to increased perspective-taking and the ability to identify with the other group's motivations or intentions for a potential conflict-inducing event.

Conclusion

The pervasiveness of intergroup conflict across modern and ancestral environments has produced recurrent costs and benefits to reproductive fitness. Adaptive responses to the challenges and affordances of intergroup conflict depend on the ability to quickly assess features of the environment, the physical capabilities and expressed mental and emotional states of others, and an internal cataloguing of one's own vulnerabilities and capabilities. Threat-management systems for pathogens and violence may play an important role in synthesizing this input and translating it into a coordinated emotional, cognitive, and behavioral response. Here we have placed an emphasis on the important role that emotions play in directing this response. Although we view emotions as functional in bringing about adaptive responses, it is important to consider that threat-management systems are prone to false positives, and that we live in a modern society in which threats to our physical safety and health are much less frequent and severe than those faced by our ancestors. We also come into contact with people whom our ancestral brain perceives as out-groups on the basis of arbitrary features (e.g., skin color, language, style of dress) far more frequently. The result may be the activation of threat-management systems when other modes of operating would be more beneficial, both for the individual and the society as a whole. The emerging work on emotion-based interventions to lower tensions and promote reconciliation between groups in conflict capitalizes on the utility of emotions by altering that emotional experience, thereby altering the cognitive and behavioral consequences. We encourage researchers to continue to map the mechanisms that translate perceptual input into emotions, cognitions, and behaviors that perpetuate conflict, and as our understanding of these processes improves, to use that knowledge to intervene in conflicts that do not serve the welfare of society.

References

Ackerman, J. M., Shapiro, J. R., Neuberg, S. L., Kenrick, D. T., Becker, D. V., Griskevicius, V., & Schaller, M. (2006). They all look the same to me (unless they're angry). *Psychological Science*, *17*(10), 836–840. doi: 10.1111/j.1467-9280.2006.01790.x

Adams, D. B. (1983). Why there are so few women warriors. *Behavior Science Research*, *18*(3), 196–212. doi: 10.1177/106939718301800302

Archer, J. (2009). Does sexual selection explain human sex differences in aggression? *Behavioral and Brain Sciences*, *32*(3-4), 249–266. doi:10.1017/s0140525x09990951

Arnold, M. B. (1960). *Emotion and personality*. Columbia University Press.

Bar-Tal, D. (2007). Sociopsychological foundations of intractable conflicts. *American Behavioral Scientist*, *50*(11), 1430–1453. doi: 10.1177/0002764207302462

Bar-Tal, D., Kruglanski, A. W., & Klar, Y. (1989). Conflict termination: An epistemological analysis of international cases. *Political Psychology*, *10*(2), 233. https://doi.org/10.2307/3791646

Batson, C. D., Chang, J., Orr, R., & Rowland, J. (2002). Empathy, attitudes, and action: Can feeling for a member of a stigmatized group motivate one to help the group? *Personality and Social Psychology Bulletin*, *28*(12), 1656–1666. doi: 10.1177/014616702237647

Batson, C. D., Early, S., & Salvarani, G. (1997). Perspective taking: Imagining how another feels versus imaging how you would feel. *Personality and Social Psychology Bulletin*, *23*(7), 751–758. doi: 10.1177/0146167297237008

Beckerman, S., Erickson, P. I., Yost, J., Regalado, J., Jaramillo, L., Sparks, C., Iromenga, M., & Long, K. (2009). Life histories, blood revenge, and reproductive success among the Waorani of Ecuador. *Proceedings of the National Academy of Sciences*, *106*(20), 8134–8139. doi: 10.1073/pnas.0901431106

Bowles, S. (2009). Did warfare among ancestral hunter-gatherers affect the evolution of human behaviors? *Science*, *324*(5932), 1293–1298. doi: 10.1126/science.1168112

Boyd, R., Gintis, H., Bowles, S., & Richerson, P. J. (2003). The evolution of altruistic punishment. *Proceedings of the National Academy of Sciences*, *100*, 3531–3535.

Buckels, E. E., & Trapnell, P. D. (2013). Disgust facilitates outgroup dehumanization. *Group Processes & Intergroup Relations, 16*(6), 771–780. doi: 10.1177/1368430212471738

Bytwerk, R. L. (1983). *Julius Streicher: The man who persuaded a nation to hate Jews*. Stein and Day.

Campbell, A. (1999). Staying alive: Evolution, culture, and women's intrasexual aggression. *Behavioral and Brain Sciences, 22*(2), 203–214. doi: 10.1017/s0140525x99001818

Cesario, J., Plaks, J. E., Hagiwara, N., Navarrete, C. D., & Higgins, E. T. (2010). The ecology of automaticity. *Psychological Science, 21*(9), 1311–1317. doi: 10.1177/0956797610378685

Chagnon, N. A. (1988). Life histories, blood revenge, and warfare in a tribal population. *Science, 239*(4843), 985–992. doi: 10.1126/science.239.4843.985

Chang, L., Lu, H. J., Li, H., & Li, T. (2011). The face that launched a thousand ships: The mating-warring association in men. *Personality and Social Psychology Bulletin, 37*(7), 976–984. doi: 10.1177/0146167211402216

Choi, J., & Bowles, S. (2007). The coevolution of parochial altruism and war. *Science, 318*(5850), 636–640. doi: 10.1126/science.1144237

Cikara, M., Bruneau, E., Bavel, J. V., & Saxe, R. (2014). Their pain gives us pleasure: How intergroup dynamics shape empathic failures and counter-empathic responses. *Journal of Experimental Social Psychology, 55*, 110–125. doi: 10.1016/j.jesp.2014.06.007

Cikara, M., Bruneau, E. G., & Saxe, R. R. (2011). Us and them: Intergroup failures of empathy. *Current Directions in Psychological Science, 20*(3), 149–153. doi: 10.1177/0963721411408713

Cikara, M., & Fiske, S. T. (2011). Stereotypes and Schadenfreude. *Social Psychological and Personality Science, 3*(1), 63–71. doi: 10.1177/1948550611409245

Cosmides, L., & Tooby, J. (2000). Evolutionary psychology and the emotions. In M. Lewis & J. M. Haviland-Jones (Eds.), *Handbook of Emotions*, (2nd edn, pp. 91–115). Guilford Press.

Cottrell, C. A., Richards, D. A., & Nichols, A. L. (2010). Predicting policy attitudes from general prejudice versus specific intergroup emotions. *Journal of Experimental Social Psychology, 46*(2), 247–254.

Council on Foreign Relations Editors (Ed.). (2020, July 13). Demographics of the U.S. military. Council on Foreign Relations. https://www.cfr.org/backgrounder/demographics-us-military

Crandall, C. S., & Moriarty, D. (1995). Physical Illness stigma and social rejection. *British Journal of Social Psychology, 34*(1), 67–83.

Crisp, R. J., & Hewstone, M. (1999). Differential evaluation of crossed category groups: Patterns, processes, and reducing intergroup bias. *Group Processes & Intergroup Relations, 2*(4), 307–333.

Cross, J. D., Johnson, A. E., Wenke, J. C., Bosse, M. J., & Ficke, J. R. (2011). Mortality in female war veterans of Operations Enduring Freedom and Iraqi Freedom. *Clinical Orthopaedics & Related Research, 469*(7), 1956–1961. doi: 10.1007/s11999-011-1840-z

Curtis, V., Aunger, R., & Rabie, T. (2004). Evidence that disgust evolved to protect from risk of disease. *Proceedings of the Royal Society B: Biological Sciences, 271*, S131–S133.

Davis, M. H. (2018). *Empathy: A social psychological approach*. Routledge.

De Meijer, M. (1991). The attribution of aggression and grief to body movements: The effect of sex-stereotypes. *European Journal of Social Psychology, 21*(3), 249–259. doi: 10.1002/ejsp.2420210307

Dobson, A. P., & Carper, E. R. (1996). Infectious diseases and human population history. *Bioscience, 46*(2), 115–126.

Doosje, B., Branscombe, N. R., Spears, R., & Manstead, A. S. (1998). Guilty by association: When one's group has a negative history. *Journal of Personality and Social Psychology, 75*(4), 872.

Dovidio, J. F., Gaertner, S. L., & Saguy, T. (2009). Commonality and the complexity of "we": Social attitudes and social change. *Personality and Social Psychology Review, 13*(1), 3–20.

Duckitt, J., & Fisher, K. (2003). The impact of social threat on worldview and ideological attitudes. *Political Psychology, 24*(1), 199–222.

Ekman, P., & Friesen, W. V. (2003). *Unmasking the face: A guide to recognizing emotions from facial clues*. Prentice-Hall.

Ellsworth, P. C., & Scherer, K. R. (2003). *Appraisal processes in emotion*. Oxford University Press.

Ember, C. R., & Ember, M. (1992). Resource unpredictability, mistrust, and war: A cross-cultural study. *Journal of Conflict Resolution, 36*(2), 242–262.

Faulkner, J., Schaller, M., Park, J. H., & Duncan, L. A. (2004). Evolved disease-avoidance mechanisms and contemporary xenophobic attitudes. *Group Processes & Intergroup Relations, 7*(4), 333–353.

Feinberg, J. (1970). *Doing and deserving: Essays in the theory of responsibility*. Princeton University Press.

Feldman, S., & Stenner, K. (1997). Perceived threat and authoritarianism. *Political Psychology, 18*(4), 741–770.

Fessler, D. M., Eng, S. J., & Navarrete, C. D. (2005). Elevated disgust sensitivity in the first trimester of pregnancy. *Evolution and Human Behavior, 26*(4), 344–351. https://doi.org/10.1016/j.evolhumbehav.2004.12.001

Fisman, R., Iyengar, S. S., Kamenica, E., & Simonson, I. (2008). Racial preferences in dating. *The Review of Economic Studies, 75*, 117–132. doi: 10.1111/j.1467-937X.2007.00465.x

Fison, L., & Howitt, A. (1991). *Kamilaroi and Kurnai: Group-marriage and relationship, and marriage by elopement, drawn chiefly from the usage of the Australian Aborigines also the Kurnai tribe, their customs in peace and war*. Aboriginal Studies Press.

Frijda, N. H. (1986). *The emotions*. Cambridge University Press.

Fry, D. P. (2006). *The human potential for peace: An anthropological challenge to assumptions about war and violence*. Oxford University Press.

Fry, D. P., & Söderberg, P. (2013). Lethal aggression in mobile forager bands and implications for the origins of war. *Science, 341*, 270–273. doi: 10.1126/science.1235675

Gat, A. (2015). Proving communal warfare among hunter-gatherers: The quasi-Rousseauan error. *Evolutionary Anthropology, 24*, 111–126.

Glutton-Brock, T. H., & Vincent, A. C. (1991). Sexual selection and the potential reproductive rates of males and females. *Nature, 351*(6321), 58–60.

Goetz, S. M., Shattuck, K. S., Miller, R. M., Campbell, J. A., Lozoya, E., Weisfeld, G. E., & Carré, J. M. (2013). Social status moderates the relationship between facial structure and aggression. *Psychological Science, 24*(11), 2329–2334.

Gross, J. J. (2008). Emotion regulation. In M. Lewis, J. M. Haviland-Jones, & L. F. Barrett (Eds.), *Handbook of emotions* (pp. 497–512). Guilford Press.

Gross, J. J., & Levenson, R. W. (1997). Hiding feelings: The acute effects of inhibiting negative and positive emotion. *Journal of Abnormal Psychology, 106*(1), 95.

Halperin, E. (2008). Group-based hatred in intractable conflict in Israel. *Journal of Conflict Resolution, 52*(5), 713–736.

Halperin, E. (2011). Emotional barriers to peace: Emotions and public opinion of Jewish Israelis about the peace process in the Middle East. *Peace and Conflict: Journal of Peace Psychology, 17*(1), 22–45. https://doi.org/10.1080/10781919.2010.487862

Halperin, E., Russell, A. G., Dweck, C. S., & Gross, J. J. (2011). Anger, hatred, and the quest for peace: Anger can be constructive in the absence of hatred. *Journal of Conflict Resolution, 55*, 274–291.

Halperin, E., Sharvit, K., & Gross, J. J. (2011). Emotion and emotion regulation in intergroup conflict: An appraisal-based framework. In D. Bar-Tal (Ed.), *Intergroup conflicts and their resolution: A social psychological perspective* (pp. 83–103). Taylor & Francis.

Haselton, M. G., & Nettle, D. (2006). The paranoid optimist: An integrative evolutionary model of cognitive biases. *Personality and Social Psychology Review, 10*(1), 47–66.

Hitsch, G. J., Hortaçsu, A., & Ariely, D. (2010). What makes you click? Mate preferences in online dating. *Quantitative Marketing and Economics, 8*, 393–427. doi: 10.1007/s11129-010-9088-6

Iyer, A., Leach, C. W., & Crosby, F. J. (2003). White guilt and racial compensation: The benefits and limits of self-focus. *Personality and Social Psychology Bulletin, 29*(1), 117–129.

Jarymowicz, M., & Bar-Tal, D. (2006). The dominance of fear over hope in the life of individuals and collectives. *European Journal of Social Psychology, 36*(3), 367–392.

Johnson, D. D. P., & MacKay, N. J. (2015). Fight the power: Lanchester's laws of combat in human evolution. *Evolution and Human Behavior, 36*(2), 152–163.

Jost, J. T., Glaser, J., Kruglanski, A. W., & Sulloway, F. J. (2003). Political conservatism as motivated social cognition. *Psychological Bulletin, 129*(3), 339.

Kahn, K. B., & Davies, P. G. (2017). What influences shooter bias? The effects of suspect race, neighborhood, and clothing on decisions to shoot. *Journal of Social Issues, 73*(4), 723–743.

Keeley, L. H. (1996). *War before civilization*. Oxford University Press.

Kriesberg, L. (1998). Intractable conflicts. In E. Weiner (Ed.), *The handbook of interethnic coexistence* (pp. 332–342). Continuum.

Kurzban, R., & Leary, M. R. (2001). Evolutionary origins of stigmatization: The functions of social exclusion. *Psychological Bulletin, 127*(2), 187.

Lahr, M. M., Rivera, F., Power, R. K., Mounier, A., Copsey, B., Crivellaro, F., & Leakey, A. (2016). Inter-group violence among early Holocene hunter-gatherers of West Turkana, Kenya. *Nature, 529*(7586), 394–398.

Larrick, J. W., Yost, J. A., Kaplan, J., King, G., & Mayhall, J. (1979). Part one: Patterns of health and disease among the Waorani Indians of eastern Ecuador. *Medical Anthropology, 3*(2), 147–189.

Levy, A., van Zomeren, M., Saguy, T., & Halperin, E. (2017). Intergroup emotions and gateway groups: Introducing multiple social identities into the study of emotions in conflict. *Social and Personality Psychology Compass, 11*(6), e12320.

Maner, J. K., Kenrick, D. T., Becker, D. V., Robertson, T. E., Hofer, B., Neuberg, S. L., & Schaller, M. (2005). Functional projection: How fundamental social motives can bias interpersonal perception. *Journal of Personality and Social Psychology, 88*(1), 63.

Maner, J. K., Miller, S. L., Moss, J. H., Leo, J. L., & Plant, E. A. (2012). Motivated social categorization: Fundamental motives enhance people's sensitivity to basic social categories. *Journal of Personality and Social Psychology, 103*(1), 70–83. https://doi.org/10.1037/a0028172

Manson, J. H., & Wrangham, R. W. (1991). Intergroup aggression in chimpanzees and humans. *Current Anthropology, 32*, 369–390. doi: 10.1086/203974.

Maoz, I. (2011). Does contact work in protracted asymmetrical conflict? Appraising 20 years of reconciliation-aimed encounters between Israeli Jews and Palestinians. *Journal of Peace Research, 48*(1), 115–125.

Martin, D. L., & Frayer, D. W. (Eds.). (1997). *Troubled times: Violence and warfare in the past* (Vol. 4). Psychology Press.

Mathew, S., & Boyd, R. (2014). The cost of cowardice: Punitive sentiments towards free riders in Turkana raids. *Evolution and Human Behavior, 35*, 58–64.

Matsumoto, D., Hwang, H. C., & Frank, M. G. (2016). The effects of incidental anger, contempt, and disgust on hostile language and implicit behaviors. *Journal of Applied Social Psychology, 46*(8), 437–452.

McCullough, M., Kurzban, R., & Tabak, B. (2013). Cognitive systems for revenge and forgiveness. *Behavioral and Brain Sciences, 36*(1), 1–15. doi: 10.1017/S0140525X11002160

McDonald, M. M., Asher, B. D., Kerr, N. L. & Navarrete, C. D. (2011). Fertility and intergroup bias in racial and minimal-group contexts: Evidence for shared architecture. *Psychological Science, 22*, 860–865. doi: 10.1177/0956797611410985

McDonald, M. M., Donnellan, M. B., Cesario, J., & Navarrete, C. D. (2015). Mate choice preferences in an intergroup context: Evidence for a sexual coercion threat-management system among women. *Evolution and Human Behavior, 36*, 438–445. doi: 10.1016/j.evolhumbehav.2015.04.002

McDonald, M.M., & Navarrete, C.D. (2015). Examining the link between conception risk and intergroup bias: The importance of conceptual coherence. Commentary on: In search of an association between conception risk and prejudice, by C. Hawkins, C. Fitzgerald, & B. Nosek. *Psychological Science, 26*, 253–255.

McDonald, M. M., Navarrete, C. D., & Van Vugt, M. (2012). Evolution and the psychology of intergroup conflict: The male warrior hypothesis. *Philosophical Transactions of the Royal Society B: Biological Sciences, 367*(1589), 670–679.

McKibbin, W. F., Shackelford, T. K., Miner, E. J., Bates, V. M., & Liddle, J. R. (2011). Individual differences in women's rape avoidance behaviors. *Archives of Sexual Behavior, 40*, 343–349.

McNeill, W. H. (1976). *Plagues and peoples*. Penguin.

Meggitt, M. (1962). *Desert people: A study of the Walbiri Aborigines of central Australia*. University of Chicago Press.

Mellaart, J. (1967). *Çatal Hüyük, a neolithic town in Anatolia*. Thames & Hudson.

Miller, S. L., Maner, J. K., & Becker, D. V. (2010). Self-protective biases in group categorization: Threat cues shape the psychological boundary between "us" and "them." *Journal of Personality and Social Psychology, 99*(1), 62.

Miller, S. L., Zielaskowski, K., & Plant, E. A. (2012). The basis of shooter biases. *Personality and Social Psychology Bulletin, 38*(10), 1358–1366. https://doi.org/10.1177/0146167212450516

Mitani, J. C., Watts, D. P., & Amsler, S. J. (2010). Lethal intergroup aggression leads to territorial expansion in wild chimpanzees. *Current Biology, 20*(12), R507–R508.

Mitchell, C. R. (1989). *The structure of international conflict*. Springer.

Murdock, G. P., & White, D. R. (1969). Standard cross-cultural sample. *Ethnology, 8*(4), 329. doi: 10.2307/3772907

Murray, D. R., Kerry, N., & Gervais, W. M. (2019). On disease and deontology: Multiple tests of the influence of disease threat on moral vigilance. *Social Psychological and Personality Science, 10*(1), 44–52.

Navarrete, C. D., Fessler, D. M., & Eng, S. J. (2007). Elevated ethnocentrism in the first trimester of pregnancy. *Evolution and Human Behavior, 28*(1), 60–65.

Navarrete, C. D., Fessler, D. M., Fleischman, D. S., & Geyer, J. (2009). Race bias tracks conception risk across the menstrual cycle. *Psychological Science, 20*, 661–665. doi: 10.1111/j.1467-9280.2009.02352.x

Navarrete, C. D., McDonald, M. M., Molina, L. E., & Sidanius, J. (2010). Prejudice at the nexus of race and gender: An outgroup male target hypothesis. *Journal of Personality and Social Psychology, 98*, 933–945. doi: 10.1037/a0017931

Nesse, R. M. (1990). Evolutionary explanations of emotions. *Human Nature, 1*(3), 261–289.

Nesse, R. M., & Ellsworth, P. C. (2009). Evolution, emotions, and emotional disorders. *American Psychologist, 64*(2), 129.

Neuberg, S. L., Kenrick, D. T., & Schaller, M. (2011). Human threat management systems: Self-protection and disease avoidance. *Neuroscience & Biobehavioral Reviews, 35*(4), 1042–1051.

Nguyen, A. M. D., & Benet-Martínez, V. (2013). Biculturalism and adjustment: A meta-analysis. *Journal of Cross-Cultural Psychology, 44*(1), 122–159.

Ochsner, K. N., & Gross, J. J. (2008). Cognitive emotion regulation: Insights from social cognitive and affective neuroscience. *Current Directions in Psychological Science, 17*(2), 153–158.

Park, J. H., Faulkner, J., & Schaller, M. (2003). Evolved disease-avoidance processes and contemporary anti-social behavior: Prejudicial attitudes and avoidance of people with physical disabilities. *Journal of Nonverbal Behavior, 27*(2), 65–87.

Park, J. H., Schaller, M., & Crandall, C. S. (2007). Pathogen-avoidance mechanisms and the stigmatization of obese people. *Evolution and Human Behavior, 28*(6), 410–414.

Pinker, S. (2012). *The better angels of our nature: Why violence has declined*. Penguin Group USA.

Price, M. E., Kang, J., Dunn, J., & Hopkins, S. (2011). Muscularity and attractiveness as predictors of human egalitarianism. *Personality and Individual Differences, 50*(5), 636–640.

Ridley, M. (1994). *The red queen: Sex and the evolution of human nature*. Harper Perennial.

Rosler, N., Cohen-Chen, S., & Halperin, E. (2017). The distinctive effects of empathy and hope in intractable conflicts. *Journal of Conflict Resolution, 61*(1), 114–139.

Rozée, P. D. (1993). Forbidden or forgiven? *Psychology of Women Quarterly, 17*(4), 499–514. doi: 10.1111/j.1471-6402.1993.tb00658.x

Rubin, J. Z., Pruitt, D. G., & Kim, S. H. (1994). *Social conflict: Escalation, stalemate, and settlement*. McGraw-Hill.

Sanday, P. R. (1981). The socio-cultural context of rape: A cross-cultural study. *Journal of Social Issues, 37*(4), 5–27. doi: 10.1111/j.1540-4560.1981.tb01068.x.

Savage, R. (2007). "Disease incarnate": Biopolitical discourse and genocidal dehumanisation in the age of modernity. *Journal of Historical Sociology, 20*(3), 404–440.

Schaller, M. (2015). The behavioral immune system. In D. M. Buss (Ed.), *The handbook of evolutionary psychology* (pp. 1–19). Wiley.

Schaller, M., & Duncan, L. A. (2007). The behavioral immune system: Its evolution and social psychological implications In J. P. Forgas, M. G. Haselton, & W. von Hippel (Eds.), *Evolution and the social mind: Evolutionary psychology and social cognition* (pp. 293–307). Taylor & Francis.

Schaller, M., & Murray, D. R. (2010). Infectious disease and the creation of culture. In M. J. Gelfand, C. Chiu, & Y. Hong (Eds.), *Advances in culture and psychology* (Vol. 1, pp. 99–151). Oxford University Press.

Schaller, M., & Neuberg, S. L. (2012). Danger, disease, and the nature of prejudice (s). In M. Zanna & J. Olson (Eds.), *Advances in experimental social psychology* (Vol. 46, pp. 1–54). Academic Press.

Schaller, M., & Park, J. H. (2011). The behavioral immune system (and why it matters). *Current Directions in Psychological Science, 20*(2), 99–103.

Schaller, M., Park, J. H., & Mueller, A. (2003). Fear of the dark: Interactive effects of beliefs about danger and ambient darkness on ethnic stereotypes. *Personality and Social Psychology Bulletin, 29*(5), 637–649.

Schumann, K., & Ross, M. (2010). The benefits, costs, and paradox of revenge. *Social and Personality Psychology Compass, 4*(12), 1193–1205.

Sear, R., & Mace, R. (2008). Who keeps children alive? A review of the effects of kin on child survival. *Evolution and Human Behavior, 29*(1), 1–18.

Sell, A., Hone, L. S., & Pound, N. (2012). The importance of physical strength to human males. *Human Nature, 23*(1), 30–44.

Sell, A., Tooby, J., & Cosmides, L. (2009). Formidability and the logic of human anger. *Proceedings of the National Academy of Sciences, 106*(35), 15073–15078.

Shechtman, Z., & Basheer, O. (2005). Normative beliefs supporting aggression of Arab children in an intergroup conflict. *Aggressive Behavior, 31*(4), 324–335.

Sheppes, G., & Meiran, N. (2007). Better late than never? On the dynamics of online regulation of sadness using distraction and cognitive reappraisal. *Personality and Social Psychology Bulletin, 33*(11), 1518–1532.

Sinke, C. B., Sorger, B., Goebel, R., & de Gelder, B. (2010). Tease or threat? Judging social interactions from bodily expressions. *Neuroimage, 49*(2), 1717–1727.

Sprecher, S., Sullivan, Q., & Hatfield, E. (1994). Mate selection preferences: Gender differences examined in a national sample. *Journal of Personality and Social Psychology, 66*, 1074–1080. doi: 10.1037/0022-3514.66.6.1074

Stephan, W. G., & Stephan, C. W. (2000). An integrated threat theory of prejudice. In S. Oskamp (Ed.), *Reducing prejudice and discrimination* (pp. 23–45). Lawrence Erlbaum Associates.

Tam, T., Hewstone, M., Kenworthy, J. B., Cairns, E., Marinetti, C., Geddes, L., & Parkinson, B. (2008). Postconflict reconciliation: Intergroup forgiveness and implicit biases in Northern Ireland. *Journal of Social Issues, 64*(2), 303–320.

Taylor, K. (2007). Disgust is a factor in extreme prejudice. *British Journal of Social Psychology, 46*(3), 597–617.

Tessler, H., Choi, M., & Kao, G. (2020). The anxiety of being Asian American: Hate crimes and negative biases during the COVID-19 pandemic. *American Journal of Criminal Justice, 45*(4), 636–646. https://doi.org/10.1007/s12103-020-09541-5

Thornhill, R., & Thornhill, N. W. (1983). Human rape: An evolutionary analysis. *Ethology and Sociobiology, 4*(3), 137–173.

Threadgill, A. H., & Gable, P. A. (2020). Revenge is sweet: Investigation of the effects of approach-motivated anger on the RewP in the motivated anger delay (MAD) paradigm. *Human Brain Mapping, 41*(17), 5032–5056.

Tooby, J., & Cosmides, L. (1988). The evolution of war and its cognitive foundations. *Institute for Evolutionary Studies Technical Report, 88*(1), 1–15.

Tratner, A. E., & McDonald, M. M. (2020). Genocide and the male warrior psychology. In L. Newman (Ed.), *Confronting humanity at its worst: Social psychological perspectives on genocide* (pp. 3–28). Oxford University Press. doi: 10.1093/oso/9780190685942.003.0001

Trivers, R. L. (1972). Parental investment and sexual selection. In B. Campbell (Ed.), *Sexual selection and the descent of man* (pp. 136–179). Aldine-Atherton.

Turney-High, H. H. (1991). *Primitive war: Its practices and concepts.* University of South Carolina Press.

Uppsala Conflict Data Program (2021). *UCDP conflict encyclopedia.* Retrieved on March 1, 2021, from https://ucdp.uu.se/encyclopedia

van der Dennen, J. M. G. (1995). *The origin of war: The evolution of a male-coalitional reproductive strategy* (Vol. 1–2). Origin Press.

Van Vugt, M. (2009). Sex differences in intergroup competition, aggression, and warfare. *Annals of the New York Academy of Sciences, 1167,* 124–134. doi: 10.1111/j.1749-6632.2009.04539.x

Van Vugt, M., Cremer, D. D., & Janssen, D. P. (2007). Gender differences in cooperation and competition: The male-warrior hypothesis. *Psychological Science, 18*(1), 19–23.

Walker, R. S., & Bailey, D. H. (2013). Body counts in lowland South American violence. *Evolution and Human Behavior, 34,* 29–34. doi: 10.1016/j.evolhumbehav.2012.08.003

Wilcox, A. J., Dunson, D. B., Weinberg, C. R., Trussell, J., & Baird, D. D. (2001). Likelihood of conception with a single act of intercourse: providing benchmark rates for assessment of post-coital contraceptives. *Contraception, 63*(4), 211–215.

Wohl, M. J. A., Branscombe, N. R., & Klar, Y. (2006). Collective guilt: Emotional reactions when one's group has done wrong or been wronged. *European Review of Social Psychology, 17*(1), 1–37. https://doi.org/10.1080/10463280600574815

Wrangham, R. W. (1999). Evolution of coalitionary killing. *American Journal of Physical Anthropology, 110,* 1–30.

Wrangham, R. W., & Glowacki, L. (2012). Intergroup aggression in chimpanzees and war in nomadic hunter-gatherers: Evaluating the chimpanzee model. *Human Nature, 23,* 5–29. doi: 10.1007/s12110-012-9132-1

Zebrowitz, L. A., Kikuchi, M., & Fellous, J. M. (2010). Facial resemblance to emotions: Group differences, impression effects, and race stereotypes. *Journal of Personality and Social Psychology, 98*(2), 175.

Zebrowitz, L. A., & Montepare, J. (2006). The ecological approach to person perception: Evolutionary roots and contemporary offshoots. In M. Schaller, J. A. Simpson, & D. T. Kenrick (Eds.), *Evolution and social psychology* (pp. 81–113). Psychosocial Press.

Zhang J. (2018). The human anger face likely carries a dual-signaling function. *Frontiers in Behavioral Neuroscience, 12,* 26. https://doi.org/10.3389/fnbeh.2018.00026

Zuk, M. (2008). *Riddled with life: Friendly worms, ladybug sex, and the parasites that make us who we are.* Harcourt.

CHAPTER 37

Emotions and Reconciliation

Yohsuke Ohtsubo and Adam Smith

Abstract

This chapter provides an overview of the evolution of reconciliatory tendencies and relevant proximate emotions. First, evolutionary game analyses reveal that individuals in long-term relationships are better off maintaining mutual cooperation, and the long-term nature of relationships makes forgiveness adaptive. However, possibilities of erroneous defection make forgiving strategies (generous tit-for-tat) and conciliatory gestures (contrite tit-for-tat) even more advantageous than the simple tit-for-tat strategy. Second, the animal reconciliation literature provides empirical evidence for the presence of reconciliatory tendencies in various species. Third, the human reconciliation literature largely confirms the insights from evolutionary game analyses and the animal reconciliation literature. It also reveals some proximate emotions of human reconciliation processes: empathy and relational anxiety facilitate forgiveness, while guilt promotes sincere apologies. More importantly, relationship value, which is implicated as an ultimate explanation of reconciliation, is positively associated with the abovementioned proximate emotions in reconciliation processes.

Key Words: forgiveness, apology, evolutionary game theory, empathy, guilt, relational anxiety

Group living confers on animals various types of adaptive benefits, such as protection from predators and efficient territory defense, but also imposes adaptive costs due to competition over resources (Markham & Gesquiere, 2017; Silk, 2007). If two or more individuals share the same habitat that contains only a limited amount of resources, some conflicts are inevitable. However, animals are unlikely to acquire the adaptive benefits of group living if such conflicts lead to the dissolution of relationships (especially long-standing ones). Fortunately, natural selection has also led to the evolution of mechanisms to resolve these conflicts—psychological mechanisms for reconciling with one's current opponent. A basic expectation is that reconciliatory tendencies can evolve if the adaptive benefits of maintaining a peaceful relationship with one's current opponent exceed the costs of dissolution of the partnership. However, it is not obvious when this condition is met. Therefore, in this chapter, we (1) review some prominent theoretical studies in evolutionary game theory to clarify the conditions under which reconciliatory tendencies evolve; (2) we then look for evidence for evolved tendencies of reconciliation in animal behaviors; and finally (3) we review the human reconciliation literature focusing on the two aspects of human reconciliation processes (i.e., forgiveness and apology-making) and their proximate emotions.

Evolvability of Reconciliation
The Iterated Prisoner's Dilemma and Tit-for-Tat

The minimum unit of group living is a dyad, that is, a pair of two individuals. Whether two individuals are better off cooperating (as opposed to competing) has been intensely investigated in the context of the prisoner's dilemma (e.g., Axelrod, 1984; Rapoport & Chammah, 1965), a game wherein two players must choose whether to cooperate or defect against each other. Importantly, the payoffs (from largest to smallest) are as follows: defection against a cooperative player (the payoff of "temptation," T) > mutual cooperation ("reward," R) > mutual defection ("punishment," P) > cooperation with a player who defects ("sucker," S). If two players engage in the prisoner's dilemma a single time, defection is the dominant strategy, meaning that each player is better off defecting, regardless of their partner's choice. However, as Axelrod (1984) nicely demonstrated, if the same players engage in an *iterated* (i.e., repeated) prisoner's dilemma, a simple and fundamentally cooperative strategy, the so-called *tit-for-tat* strategy (TFT), outperforms many other uncooperative strategies.

TFT is nice, retaliatory, and forgiving (Axelrod, 1984). It is "nice" in the sense that it never chooses defection unless the other player chooses it first; TFT does not attempt to exploit a cooperative player. TFT is "retaliatory" in the sense that it will respond with defection if its partner chose defection in the previous round. In other words, TFT does not allow its partner to exploit it more than once. Despite such a retaliatory tendency, TFT is also "forgiving." It does not hold grudges and resumes cooperating as soon as its partner does so.

Axelrod and Hamilton (1981) examined whether TFT can be an evolutionarily stable strategy against an "unconditionally uncooperative strategy" (typically called "ALLD"), which always chooses defection. Their analysis showed that TFT is indeed evolutionarily stable against ALLD as long as the same pair keeps interacting with each other for a sufficient period of time. It is easy to verify this conclusion. In a population where all individuals play TFT, they repeatedly earn R for mutual cooperation. Imagine that a rare unconditionally uncooperative mutant, ALLD, emerges in this population. Although ALLD succumbs to the temptation of earning the larger payoff (T) from unilateral exploitation in the initial round, it is stuck with the punishment of earning the smaller payoff (P) of mutual defection in subsequent rounds. Therefore, if the interaction lasts sufficiently long, ALLD's initial advantage (earning T, which is larger than R) is offset by the subsequent disadvantage of repeatedly earning P, which is smaller than R. This analysis not only provides a tremendous insight into the evolution of cooperation, it also reveals a minimum condition for forgiveness to be adaptive: *repeated interaction*.

Noise and Generosity

Although TFT is a forgiving strategy, it may not be sufficiently forgiving to thrive in "noisy" real-world environments where individuals sometimes fail to act in the way they intended (e.g., failing to cooperate despite intending to do so). In such noisy environments, even a pair of initially cooperative TFT players are liable to fall into an uncooperative spiral—if one TFT player erroneously chooses defection in the n-th round, its partner will choose defection in the $(n + 1)$th round, and so on. Only if one of the TFT players is willing to forgive the partner's previous defection can the pair revert to mutual cooperation. Thus, it appears that TFT could benefit by being more "generous" with its forgiveness policy.

Nowak and Sigmund (1992) ran a computer simulation with a population of strategies that varied in terms of the probability of cooperating after a partner's cooperation (p) and the probability of cooperating after a partner's defection (q). Notice that TFT is defined as $(p, q) = (1, 0)$, while ALLD is defined as $(0, 0)$. At the beginning of the simulation, each individual had randomly set p and q values (the possible range of p and q was set as between .01 and .99). They were then randomly paired with another individual, played the prisoner's dilemma for an indefinite period of time, and their cumulative payoffs were computed. After each generation, strategies associated with greater cumulative payoffs increased in frequency (akin to natural selection), while strategies associated with smaller payoffs decreased. ALLD-like strategies (i.e., $p \approx 0$, $q \approx 0$) initially increased because they were able to exploit generous strategies (i.e., $q > 0$). However, once the population was mostly dominated by ALLD-like strategies, TFT-like strategies (i.e., $p \approx 1$ and $q \approx 0$) were able to invade the population. TFT-like strategies, if they were paired with another TFT-like player, were able to reap the benefit of mutual cooperation (R), while ALLD-like strategies were no longer able to exploit generous strategies (remember that the population now mostly consists of ALLD-like strategies). Once the population was dominated by TFT-like strategies, however, now slightly more generous strategies, such as $(p, q) \approx (1, 1/3)$ increased in frequency (the exact value of $q \approx 1/3$ is not particularly important because the optimal q value depends on other parameters such as the amounts of the four payoffs in the prisoner's dilemma). As long as there is some degree of noise in an environment, generous TFT (GTFT; $p = 1$, $q > 0$) outperforms the standard TFT strategy due to its willingness to forgive some degree of error. Without any errors, GTFT may neutrally drift in the population of TFT, but should not be actively selected for. Therefore, *some degree of error* in implementing a cooperative strategy appears to be a precondition for generosity (i.e., forgiving some of a partner's misdeeds without retaliation) to evolve.

The Role of Contrition

In the real world, when people fail to cooperate even though their strategy (or decision policy) calls for cooperation, it is typical for them to actively seek forgiveness from their victims by expressing some sign of contrition (e.g., an apology) instead of passively waiting for the partner's forgiveness. Such a strategy is known as *contrite tit-for-tat* (CTFT), and is proven to be evolutionarily stable under noisy environments (Boyd, 1989). CTFT decides whether to cooperate based on "standing"—cooperate with a partner whose standing is "good" but defect against a partner whose standing is "bad." One's standing is good at the outset and remains good as long as it behaves as the strategy calls for. However, it becomes bad if one defects against a partner whose standing is good. To restore its standing, CTFT cooperates when its own standing is bad. Boyd related this strategy to "contrition" because it cooperates after its own error, thereby allowing its partner to enjoy the greater payoff of T. This then makes the contrite individual's standing revert to "good" while keeping the partner's standing "good" because the partner's defection after the erroneous defection is exactly what CTFT calls for.

The presence of "noise" again plays a key role in what evolves. Notice that if there are no errors, a pair of TFT and CTFT, for example, keep cooperating and there will be no differences in the payoffs of these two strategies. This implies that TFT can drift in a population of CTFT. However, in a noisy environment, TFT's erroneous defection will be met by CTFT's defection. Unfortunately, TFT is not equipped with the generosity to forgive CTFT's defection, and thus cannot restore mutual cooperation. Consequently, TFT in a noisy environment earns a smaller amount of payoff than would a pair of CTFT strategies. Therefore, it can be argued that Boyd showed that the presence of noise predisposes the evolution of yet another means of reconciliation—costly displays of contrition to seek forgiveness.

In sum, evolutionary game theoretic analyses show that repeated interaction is the fundamental requirement for a minimal form of forgiveness to evolve, and the presence of noise (i.e., the possibility of errors) is a key factor driving the evolution of additional conciliatory tendencies: forgiving without retaliation (GTFT) and displaying a costly sign of contrition (CTFT).

Although in this section we have focused on a set of seminal works associated with three representative strategies, other studies directly or indirectly support this conclusion—reconciliatory tendencies are evolvable in the presence of repeated interaction and noise (e.g., Boerlijst et al., 1997; Martinez-Vaquero et al., 2015; Molander, 1985; Wu & Axelrod, 1995). Moreover, empirical studies with human participants revealed that conciliatory strategies outperformed non-conciliatory strategies, such as TFT, when the experimenter artificially introduced some noise regarding the partner's choices (e.g., Kollock, 1993; Van Lange et al., 2002).

Reconciliation in Nonhuman Animals

A series of evolutionary game analyses showed that reconciliation is evolvable in theory. The next question is an empirical one: Do animals other than humans in fact reconcile with their current opponent? The answer is, perhaps to the surprise of some readers, quite often "yes." In this section, we first review empirical evidence for animal reconciliation, and then review three hypotheses about animal reconciliation. In our view, the first hypothesis regards the ultimate cause of reconciliation, while the second is about the proximate cause. The third hypothesis regards the evolution of conciliatory signals (see Mayr, 1961, for the distinction between the ultimate vs. proximate causes; see also Al-Shawaf et al., 2021; Laland et al., 2011).

Evidence for Animal Reconciliation

A systematic method of research on animal reconciliation was initiated by a primatologist, de Waal (1989). In a seminal study, de Waal and van Roosmalen (1979) showed that chimpanzees (*Pan troglodytes*) were more likely to engage in nonviolent bodily contact, such as kissing and grooming, after agonistic interactions. A similar pattern (post-conflict reunion) was later confirmed among a macaque species: de Waal and Yoshihara (1983) showed that rhesus macaques (*Macaca mulatta*) more quickly approached their former opponents after agonistic interactions (post-conflict) than during the same time period on a different observation day (i.e., a matched control). This method, the comparison of the frequency of reunions between the post-conflict and matched-control phases (the PC-MC method) became the standard tool to assess animal reconciliation, and later studies revealed that various primate species engage in post-conflict reunion with their former opponents (see de Waal, 1993, for a review, and Appendix A of Aureli & de Waal, 2000, for a list of primate species that engage in post-conflict reunion; see also Table 1 in Arnold et al., 2010, for a similar list).

Reconciliation is not restricted to primates, however. The same pattern has been observed in various other animal species, such as spotted hyenas (*Crocuta crocuta*), domestic goats (*Capra hircus*), wolves (*Canis lupus*), bottlenose dolphins (*Tursiops truncatus*), red-necked wallabies (*Macropus rufogriseus*), and even some bird species (see Romero & Aureli, 2017; Schino, 2000, for reviews). Given the evidence of reconciliation in such phylogenetically distant species, Romero and Aureli (2017) state, "this conflict resolution mechanism must have evolved independently several times in association with the rise of group living" (p. 883). This conclusion resonates with the results of the previously discussed evolutionary game analyses suggesting that reconciliatory tendencies are evolvable in most social species: (1) repeated interaction is a precondition for group living, and (2) it is implausible to assume that all members of a group can cooperate (when mutual cooperation is called for) in absence of error all the time. Such conditions are likely to hold for most group-living species, and thus it is natural to observe reconciliation in a wide array of group-living animals.

VALUABLE RELATIONSHIP HYPOTHESIS: ULTIMATE EXPLANATION

Although reconciliation has been observed in many species, this does not mean that every conflict is followed by a friendly reunion. In any studied species, the likelihood of reconciliation varies across dyads. Accordingly, researchers have attempted to explain this variation. For example, de Waal and Yoshihara (1983) suspected that kinship might explain reconciliation among rhesus macaques. Although they indeed found a significant effect of kinship (i.e., kin dyads were more likely to reconcile with each other than non-kin dyads), the effect became nonsignificant after controlling for the effect of relationship quality. In other words, rhesus macaques were more likely to reconcile with valuable partners, but not necessarily with kin members. Although valuable partners are often kin, adaptive benefits of high-quality relationships are not limited to indirect fitness benefits via genetic relatedness. Among nonhuman primate species, adaptive benefits of high-quality relationships may accrue, for example, from "the tendencies to tolerate others near resources, to support them in aggressive encounters with third parties, to protect them against external threats, and to facilitate access to food or social resources, and to be a willing mate" (Cords & Aureli, 2000, p. 181). Empirical evidence from other primate species corroborates de Waal and Yoshihara's (1983) result: dyads with high-quality relationships are more likely to reconcile than dyads with low-quality relationships (see Cords & Aureli, 2000, for a review).

Based on such empirical evidence, de Waal and Aureli (1997) proposed the *valuable relationship hypothesis* that posits "reconciliation aims at restoring valuable relationships" (p. 320). This is an ultimate explanation of reconciliation: the adaptive function of reconciliation is to maintain a long-term cooperative relationship, especially when the relationship value exceeds the value of the resource over which the two individuals are competing. The valuable relationship hypothesis thus predicts that the frequency of reconciliation within dyads would increase when both dyad members come to value each other more than before. This prediction was confirmed by an ingenious experiment by Cords and Thurnheer (1993), who trained seven dyads of long-tailed macaques (*Macaca fascicularis*) to perform a simple cooperative task to obtain attractive foods—designed to increase the relationship value of the dyads. Following the training, the dyads were subjected to experimentally induced conflicts by the researchers. As predicted, six out of the seven dyads increased their frequency of reconciliation as compared to their base level of reconciliation (which was measured prior to the training). Interestingly, this result could not be explained by increased friendliness; the dyads were equally friendly both before and after the experiment. The researchers suggest that the dyads may have *felt* more friendly, but the only immediately observable result was a partner-specific predilection for reconciliation.

This basic idea of the valuable relationship hypothesis is consistent with the central insight of the prisoner's dilemma. If a particular dyad cooperates with each other for a long period of time, yet they sometimes engage in agonistic interactions over resources of relatively small value, it is beneficial for them to reconcile. The valuable relationship hypothesis is therefore an ultimate explanation of reconciliation; relationship repair confers adaptive benefits on a given set of opponents.

Uncertainty-Reduction Hypothesis: Proximate Explanation

After conflicts, primates exhibit behavioral signs of stress—self-directed behaviors, such as self-scratching, self-grooming, body-shaking, and yawning (e.g., Aureli & van Schaik, 1991; Castels & Whiten, 1998). This has been confirmed by physiological measures such as increased heart rate, salivary cortisol concentration, and plasma corticosterone levels (Maestripieri et al., 1992). Peaceful post-conflict reunions effectively reduce these stress measures to the baseline (pre-conflict) level (see Romero & Aureli, 2017, Table 42.1, for a summary of the results from a wide range of primate species). For the victims, peaceful post-conflict reunions inform them that the conflicts are over, and their former aggressors are no longer likely to attack them again (Silk, 1996). However, it has been shown that aggressors also experience stress after conflicts due to uncertainty about future cooperation—the victim may stop grooming the aggressor or supporting them when the aggressor is involved in agonistic interactions with other individuals (Aureli, 1997). Therefore, the *uncertainty-reduction hypothesis* maintains that the proximate cause of reconciliation is a particular aversive emotion caused by conflicts known as *post-conflict anxiety* (Aureli, 1997). We hereafter refer to this proximate emotion as *relational anxiety*.

Because the valuable relationship hypothesis is an ultimate explanation and the uncertainty-reduction hypothesis is a proximate explanation, the two hypotheses are not mutually exclusive, but complementary in nature (Mayr, 1961). Therefore, they can be easily integrated. If the adaptive function of reconciliation is to restore valuable relationships, and the proximate cause of reconciliation is the reduction of relational anxiety, it is expected that animals would experience greater stress after conflicts with valuable partners than less valuable partners. This prediction has been confirmed: long-tailed macaques showed more self-scratching when they had conflicts with partners of high relationship quality compared to those of relatively lower relationship quality (Aureli, 1997). Likewise, the same pattern has been replicated in studies of several other primate species (Romero & Aureli, 2017). This pattern that relational anxiety (an aversive emotion caused by conflict) is well tuned to relationship value is evinced by the following behavioral tendency that is widely observed among primates—conflict with valuable partners causes *both* relational anxiety and an increased motivation to reconcile.

Parenthetically, although the uncertainty-reduction hypothesis tends to emphasize the motivating role of negative emotions in conflict resolution, Aureli and Smucny (2000) noted that positive emotions may likewise play some role in animal conflict resolution. For example, Aureli and Smucny refer to the possible role of endogenous opioids, which are related to mother-infant bonding, affection, and affiliative touch. In addition to the eradication of aversive emotions, opiates generated by friendly restored contact with former opponents conceivably provide an additional drive for reconciliation.

Benign Intent Hypothesis

Silk (1996) criticized the valuable relationship hypothesis (in her article, she refers to it as the "relationship-repair hypothesis") arguing that the benefits of post-conflict friendly reunions are associated with more immediate ends: "tolerance among former opponents is restored to baseline levels, aggression is inhibited, affiliation is facilitated, and victims' concern about future aggression is alleviated" (p. 39). Therefore, Silk (1996, 2002) argues that long-term relationship repair is not necessary to explain why former opponents reconcile. However, Cords and Aureli (1996) pointed out that the distinction between long-term relationship repair and immediate re-establishment of friendly contact is elusive. For example, the immediate restoration to the baseline level of interaction might appear to be a short-term effect; yet if two individuals fail to reconcile immediately after a hostile interaction, their relationship quality might be undermined indefinitely.

Rather than delve into the debate over the long- and short-term benefits of reconciliation, it is noteworthy that Silk's (1996, 2002) hypothesis, so-called *benign intent hypothesis*, gives conciliatory signals (e.g., mere proximity, certain types of vocalization) a special status in reconciliation. This interpretation of peaceful post-conflict contact (in this case, in research on primates) as a signal may be relevant to CTFT. If a "contrite" aggressor exhibits a sign of benign intent, dyads can effectively resume a friendly interaction. Although the evolutionary stability of CTFT requires a long-term interaction, Silk (1996, 2002) does not emphasize the role of long-term relationships in the evolution of signals of benign intentions. Rather, Silk emphasizes the shared interest of the aggressors and the victims—both parties desire to end the conflict and would be better off immediately settling it (e.g., aggressors might benefit from being groomed by their victims and victims can alleviate their anxiety about renewed aggression). In other words, Silk (1996, 2002) conceptualizes the post-conflict situation as a coordination game, in which two players' interests align with each other and the players only need a non-costly signal to coordinate their behaviors (Crawford & Sobel, 1982; Maynard Smith, 1991; Skyrms, 2010). Accordingly, Silk (1996) argues that signals of benign intent can be non-costly.

There is evidence that non-costly signals of benign intent serve to facilitate reconciliation. A series of studies on female baboons (*Papio cynocephalus ursinus*) revealed that higher-ranking aggressors were less likely to supplant their subordinate victims when they grunted to the victims than when they did not (Cheney et al., 1995), and victims were more likely to let the former aggressors handle their infants when the aggressors grunted to them (Silk et al., 1996). Moreover, Cheney and Seyfarth (1997) conducted an ingenious playback experiment in which the victims of prior conflicts heard either the recorded grunt of their aggressor, the grunt of another higher-ranking female, or no grunt at all. The results showed that former victims who heard their aggressors' grunt were more likely to approach their aggressors, and tolerated the presence of their aggressors' proximity. These results imply that energetically low-cost vocalization facilitates friendly post-conflict interaction. The effectiveness of the low-cost signal is amenable to a coordination game interpretation. However, according to Silk, Kaldor, and Boyd (2000), such a low-cost signal is also evolutionarily stable if the aggressor and victim are embedded in a long-term relationship and the victim believes the aggressor has not used false signals in the past. This model invokes the potential (future) cost of false signals. Regardless of which model (coordination game vs. long-term relationship) adequately explains the low-cost conciliatory signals in some nonhuman primate species, it is in stark contrast to CTFT, which is a form of *immediately* costly signal because the former defector needs to accept a one-time exploitation by their partner. With these distinctions in mind, we will discuss the issue of whether conciliatory signals need to be immediately costly when reviewing the human reconciliation literature.

Human Reconciliation from an Evolutionary Perspective

Evolutionary game theory clarified the necessary conditions for forgiveness and contrition to evolve, while the research on nonhuman animal (mostly primate) reconciliation not only confirmed a central game theoretic insight (i.e., relationship repair is the adaptive function of reconciliation) but also revealed an important proximate emotion of reconciliation (i.e., relational anxiety). It is only natural to ask whether the same pattern holds for humans.

In fact, the PC-MC method has been applied to reconciliation among human children of various ages in different cultures, and the results are consistent with studies on nonhuman primates. Children are more likely to engage in peacemaking behaviors after conflicts than during matched control periods: to resolve conflicts, they may apologize, offer to share disputed objects, hug, invite their partner to resume play, and engage in ritualized practices such as peacemaking rhymes (see Butovskaya et al., 2000, for a review). Stress, measured by both self-directed behaviors among 3–4-year-old children (Fujisawa et al., 2005) and salivary cortisol among 7–15-year-old boys (Butovskaya, 2008), increases after conflicts and decreases after reconciliation. However, these developmental studies, which were based on the PC-MC method, are not clear about the factor of relationship quality. For example, some studies predicted that friends, as compared to acquaintances, engage in post-conflict reunion more frequently. However, the prediction was not confirmed; post-conflict reunion was equally likely in both types of relationships in a study conducted in the United States, and acquaintances in fact engaged in post-conflict reunion more frequently than friends in a study conducted in Russia (cited in Butovskaya et al., 2000). This may be due to the fact that friends and acquaintances engage in different kinds of activities, and acquaintances tend to be involved in more intense conflicts, which require immediate conflict resolution (Butovskaya et al., 2000). Moreover, the extent to which apologies (one of the most widely used reconciliatory signals in humans) need to be costly is not clear in developmental studies. In this section, we will review the forgiveness and apology literature relevant to these questions. In doing so, we will also review possible emotional mediators of human reconciliation processes.

Forgiveness

Definitions of forgiveness differ slightly among researchers (Worthington, 2005). Importantly, however, definitions of forgiveness have obvious similarities with the behavioral definition of animal reconciliation. For example, Rusbult, Hannon, Stocker, and Finkel (2005) defined forgiveness as "the victim's willingness to resume pretransgression interaction tendencies—the willingness to forego grudge and vengeance, instead coming to behave toward the perpetrator in a positive and constructive manner" (p. 186). McCullough, Worthington, and Rachal (1997) likewise defined interpersonal forgiveness as "the set of motivational changes whereby one becomes (a) decreasingly motivated to retaliate against an offending relationship partner, (b) decreasingly motivated to maintain estrangement from the offender, and (c) increasingly motivated by conciliation and goodwill for the offender, despite the offender's hurtful actions" (pp. 321–322). Parenthetically, although these definitions may convey the impression that forgiveness is a multidimensional construct, a recent psychometric study revealed that forgiveness is a single-dimensional construct varying from hostility to friendliness (Forster et al., 2020). More relevant to the current review, given the similarity between human forgiveness and animal reconciliation, de Waal and Pokorny (2005) speculated that both processes share an emotional switch that "moves the attitude toward another individual from aggressive and/or fearful to friendly, perhaps even affectionate" (p. 18). Therefore, it is reasonable to expect some degree of continuity between the studies on human forgiveness and animal reconciliation (McCullough, 2008; McCullough et al., 2013).

VALUABLE RELATIONSHIP HYPOTHESIS AND FORGIVENESS

McCullough and his colleagues conducted a series of empirical studies that tested the validity of the valuable relationship hypothesis in the human forgiveness process. For example, McCullough, Luna, Berry, Tabak, and Bono (2010) repeatedly assessed forgiveness—over the course of several months—of participants who had recently encountered interpersonal transgressions prior to the outset of the study. This repeated-measures procedure allowed the researchers to examine the trajectory of each participant's forgiveness process. McCullough et al. found that relationship value accelerated the forgiveness process—the more valuable their offenders, the more quickly participants forgave their offenders. Autobiographical recall studies also confirmed that in the United States and Japan, people were more likely to forgive their offender when the pre-transgression relationship value of the offender was high (Burnette et al., 2012; McCullough et al., 2014; Smith et al., 2020).

There is substantial convergent evidence for the valuable relationship hypothesis in humans, with many studies revealing that variables conceptually related to relationship value promote forgiveness. A comprehensive meta-analytic review on antecedents of interpersonal forgiveness revealed that relationship closeness, relationship commitment, and relationship satisfaction were all positively associated with forgiveness (Fehr et al., 2010; the mean correlations between these three variables and forgiveness were .27, .19, and .36, respectively). The positive effect of relationship closeness on forgiveness has been confirmed in six countries (China, Italy, Japan, the Netherlands, Turkey, and the US; Karremans et al., 2011). Reviewing neuroimaging studies on forgiveness, Fourie, Hortensius, and Decety (2020) identified three psychological mechanisms of forgiveness: (1) *cognitive control*; (2) *perspective-taking*, which we will take up in the subsequent section; and (3) *social valuation*, which is directly relevant to the valuable relationship hypothesis. The brain's "valuation region," which is referred to as either the ventromedial prefrontal cortex (vmPFC) or the orbitofrontal cortex (OFC), was likewise engaged when participants made a decision to forgive their offenders (e.g., Farrow et al., 2001; Ohtsubo et al., 2018; see also Ohtsubo et al., 2020, for the evidence of the vmPFC/OFC's involvement in relationship valuation).

As in the case of primate conflicts, human conflicts cause stress (see Worthington et al., 2007, for a review; see also Riek & Mania, 2012, for a meta-analysis on the negative association between forgiveness and stress/anxiety), and forgiveness seems to return physiological arousal to baseline levels (Lawler et al., 2003). A recent meta-analytic review indicated that forgiveness was strongly correlated with psychological health measures and two specific physical health outcomes (i.e., heart rate and blood pressure), and thus suggested that forgiveness would promote psychological health by reducing stress responses to interpersonal conflicts (Rasmussen et al., 2019). More relevant to the valuable relationship hypothesis, Karremans, Van Lange, Ouwerkerk, and Kluwer (2003) showed that commitment moderates the level of stress elicited by unforgiveness: not forgiving a committed relationship partner causes higher psychological tension than not forgiving an uncommitted relationship partner.

The findings we reviewed in this section parallel the findings in the animal reconciliation literature. People are inclined to forgive more valuable relationship partners than less valuable partners. This pattern confirms the primary prediction of the valuable relationship hypothesis. Furthermore, interpersonal conflicts cause stress, and this stress seems to be tuned to the relationship value of the current opponent. By reconciling with one's opponent, relational uncertainty and its associated stress are mitigated. This result is consistent with the uncertainty-reduction hypothesis.

MEDIATION BY PROXIMATE EMOTIONS

Although we confirmed that relationship value predicts forgiveness, one might suspect that this association is mediated by conscious and deliberate cost-benefit analysis. In fact, some scholars define forgiveness as consisting of both emotional and decisional components (Worthington, 2005), and self-control has been identified as a robust predictor of forgiveness (Burnette et al., 2014). If people can deliberately decide to ignore a valuable partner's transgression to ensure prospective benefits accruing from the relationship, it does not appear appropriate to argue that the human forgiveness process primarily relies on an evolved psychological mechanism whose function is relationship repair.

However, we already reviewed the finding that the intensity of psychological tension due to interpersonal conflict is highly tuned to relationship value (Karremans et al., 2003), which suggests that the forgiveness process can only be partially accounted for by conscious deliberation. Furthermore, there is another important proximate emotion. It has been well-established that *empathy* leads to forgiveness. According to Fehr et al.'s (2010) meta-analysis, the mean correlation between state empathy toward an offender and forgiveness was .53. At first glance, this might appear perplexing—why on earth should victims feel empathy for their offenders?

However, victims might empathize with their offenders who are experiencing aversive emotions, such as guilt and interpersonal regret (McCullough et al., 1997). It is reasonable to expect that such affective empathy with the offenders' psychological suffering leads to forgiveness. Cognitive empathy (or perspective-taking) might also be relevant (Fourie et al., 2020). As attributions of malignant intent and responsibility for the transgression to offenders typically hinders forgiveness (the mean correlations were -.50 and -.39, respectively, in Fehr et al.'s meta-analysis), taking the offender's perspective might help victims to notice external reasons for the transgression, and such external attributions might increase victims' forgiveness.

If empathy is an integral part of the human forgiveness process, the next question is whether it is modulated by relationship value. Smith et al. (2020) asked their participants to report an interpersonal transgression that they had recently experienced. Participants also reported empathy they felt for their offenders, along with the offender's pre-transgression relationship value and the current level of forgiveness. Smith et al. found that empathy partially—yet significantly—mediated the association between relationship value and forgiveness in American and Japanese samples. There is also suggestive evidence for the perspective-taking interpretation. Kearns and Fincham (2005) showed that the relationship quality–forgiveness association in romantic couples was mediated by motivated cognition that prevents the victim from exaggerating the seriousness of their partner's transgression. Among other elements, external attribution of the offenders' behaviors, which might have been promoted by perspective-taking, was responsible for this motivated cognitive process. In sum, these studies suggest that both affective empathy and cognitive empathy (i.e., perspective-taking), which are proximate causes of forgiveness, seem to be well tuned to relationship value.

Although not directly relevant to proximate emotions, it is worth mentioning an interesting finding regarding the automaticity of the relationship value–forgiveness association. Karremans and Aarts (2007) presented their participants a series of hypothetical offenses (e.g., lying, cheating) and asked participants to report their willingness to forgive each of the offenses. Before presenting each offense scenario, participants were subliminally primed with either the name of a close other, the name of a non-close other, or a nonsense syllable. Although the identity of the offenders was not explicitly presented in the scenario, participants were moderately more willing to forgive the hypothetical offenses in the close-other condition than in the other two control conditions. Taken together, the studies reviewed in this section suggest that although the relationship value–forgiveness association may be partly attributable to deliberative processes (i.e., conscious cost-benefit analysis), proximate emotions (i.e., heightened psychological tension, empathy) play a vital role at an unconscious level, which suggests that we have a natural inclination to forgive valuable partners.

PERCEIVED EXPLOITATION RISK

An evolutionary perspective on forgiveness highlights the importance of relationship value. However, the evolved decision rule to forgive valuable partners needs to be accompanied by a complementary decision rule to prevent future exploitation because forgiveness entails lowering one's guard (by reducing avoidance and revenge motivations; McCullough et al., 2013). The effect of perceived exploitation risk parallels concerns about renewed aggression (i.e., relational anxiety) among primates. Burnette et al. (2012) asked participants in the United States to rate the likelihood that a transgressor will offend them again, as well as the transgressor's relationship value. Although participants were more forgiving of their valuable relationship partners, this effect was reduced when they perceived the likelihood of further exploitation as being high. Smith et al. (2020) conducted a conceptual replication in the United States and Japan. Among the US sample, they observed the interaction effect between relationship

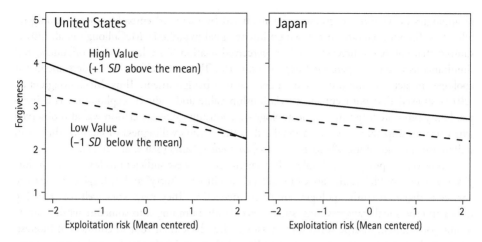

Figure 37.1. The effects of relationship value and perceived exploitation risk on forgiveness in the United States (left) and Japan (right). Adapted from Smith et al. (2020).

value and exploitation risk on forgiveness, which Burnette et al. originally found in the United States. However, among the Japanese sample only the main effects of relationship value and exploitation risk, but not their interaction, were significant: perceived exploitation risk reduced forgiveness to the same extent, regardless of the level of relationship value of one's partner (see Figure 37.1). Although we do not have a decisive explanation for this cultural difference at this point, the bottom line is that if offenders want to be forgiven, they need to effectively communicate that they do not intend to harm their victims again. Therefore, among humans, it is typical that offenders offer sincere apologies to mitigate their victims' perception of exploitation risk.

Apology-Making

An apology in its simplest form is a statement of "I'm sorry." However, researchers have defined it as a complex of separable components (Blatz & Philpot, 2010; Goffman, 1971; Lazare, 2004; Ohbuchi et al., 1989; Schlenker & Darby, 1981). Although there are some variations in these definitions, most authors seem to agree that apologies often include expressions of remorse, acceptance of responsibility, admission of the victims' suffering, promise of forbearance, and offers of repairs. Compared to the stylized benign intent signals of nonhuman animals, such as grunts, there seems to be a litany of human benign intent signals, from simply saying "sorry" to elaborate apologies that include all of the abovementioned elements. In this section, we consider whether a signaling model can add parsimony to research on human apology-making, and then discuss which proximate emotions promote apology-making.

APOLOGY AS A SIGNAL OF BENIGN INTENT

If human apologies have something in common with animal conciliatory gestures, we expect that apologies induce forgiveness from their victims. This has been empirically confirmed. The mean correlation between apology and forgiveness is estimated as .40 and .33 in Fehr et al.'s (2010) and Riek and Mania's (2012) meta-analyses, respectively. There are some plausible proximate mechanisms for how apologies induce forgiveness. First, as apologies tend to involve offenders' expression of remorse, victims might empathize with their offenders' experience of contrition. Indeed, McCullough et al. (1997) showed that the positive effect of apologies on victims' forgiveness was mediated by increased empathy toward apologetic offenders. Second, relevant to the benign intent signal hypothesis, McCullough et al. (2014) showed that apologies increased victims' perceived relationship value of their offenders, and simultaneously reduced perceived exploitation risk. These two effects are understandable if apologies in fact communicate the offender's current benign intent. Thus, McCullough et al. (2014) showed that both enhanced relationship value and reduced exploitation risk independently promote forgiveness. The apology–relationship value association was also observed when relationship value was operationalized as the victim's willingness to sacrifice their own welfare for the sake of the offender—the *welfare trade-off ratio* (Sell et al., 2017).

However, if apologies as simple as just saying "sorry" were sufficient to lead to victim forgiveness, why wouldn't exploitative offenders always just say "sorry" and be forgiven? The basic answer is that non-costly apologies are often ineffective. They may work well for resolving minor interpersonal transgressions, such as accidently bumping into someone while waiting in line. But human interpersonal transgressions often have their root in conflicts of interest, which makes many situations more complicated than straightforward coordination games. Recall that in nonhuman primate examples, both aggressors and victims were better off resuming a friendly interaction, and they only needed a non-costly signal to confirm that they were in fact playing a coordination game. Likewise, a long-term relationship among a pair of primates curtails the incentive of dishonest signals (Silk et al., 2000). However, unlike most primate species who do not migrate from one group to another very often, humans form societies characterized by extensive fission-fusion—verbal disputes and fighting can result in individuals switching groups (Couzin & Laidre, 2009). Accordingly, in the case of humans, exploitative partners may attempt to repeatedly exploit or free-ride on their gullible victims. The possible presence of exploiters undermines the ability of cost-free signals to act as honest signals of benign intent (Laidre & Johnstone, 2013). This consideration leads to a prediction that when victims estimate high exploitation risk by a certain offender, they will not accept cost-free statements of apology (e.g., just saying, "Sorry, I won't do that again"). By contrast, such cost-free apologies may be sufficient for victims who believe that there is little risk of being exploited by the same offender again (e.g., the stranger who bumped into them while waiting in line). We will review preliminary evidence for this prediction shortly.

Ohtsubo and Watanabe (2009) proposed a model of costly apology, which assumes that offenders who highly value the relationship with their victim and sincerely intend not to commit the same transgression again have a larger incentive to reconcile with their victim than offenders who do not value the relationship. This is basically a flipside application of the valuable relationship hypothesis, this time from the perspective of the offender. Because of the asymmetric incentive for reconciliation between sincere and insincere offenders, there can be a separating equilibrium where sincere offenders offer costly apologies (because the cost can be offset by restoring a more valuable relationship), while insincere offenders offer non-costly apologies (see also Martinez-Vaquero et al., 2015; O'Connor, 2016; Okamoto & Matsumura, 2001, for other models of costly apology). If victims are equipped with a psychological mechanism designed to distinguish the two types of apologies, it is expected that costly apologies (e.g., apologies entailing offers of repairs; apologies entailing cancellations of a favorite activity or important business meeting to prioritize time with the victim) will be perceived as being more sincere than non-costly apologies (i.e., just saying "sorry").

EMPIRICAL TESTS OF THE COSTLY APOLOGY MODEL

Several social psychological studies, not explicitly informed by the costly apology model, nonetheless provide evidence consistent with this model. For example, in Bottom, Gibson,

Daniels, and Murnighan's (2002) iterated prisoner's dilemma experiment, after a partner's uncooperative choice (i.e., defection), some players were explicitly invited to exploit that partner's cooperative choices for the next few rounds (recall that CTFT does something similar). Participants who received such a costly form of apologetic message, as compared with those who received only a verbal expression of apology, were more cooperative as the rounds of the prisoner's dilemma game progressed, suggesting that they had forgiven the partner's previous defection (see also Tabak et al., 2012, for the effectiveness of a CTFT-like conciliatory gesture). In line with this finding, it has been shown that overcompensating a victim makes them more likely to trust their transgressor than when they receive exact or partial compensation (Desmet et al., 2010, 2011). In addition, a fascinating field experiment confirmed the external validity of these laboratory results. Bolkan, Goodboy, and Daly (2010) requested their participants to send a genuine letter of complaint to real organizations that had recently failed them. Some participants received responses from the organizations, while others did not. Organizations that offered apologies coupled with amends, versus those that offered apologies alone, significantly enhanced participants' intention to do future business with said organizations.

Although these findings seem to support the costly apology model, these results cannot be considered full-fledged support because of the following two limitations. First, according to the model, costly forms of apology function as a signal of benign intent (i.e., an offender's honest intention to restore the relationship). Thus, the most relevant measure should be *perceived sincerity*, not forgiveness itself, although perceived sincerity should in turn facilitate forgiveness. However, none of the above studies directly measured perceived sincerity or its theorized mediational role. Second, costly apologies do not necessarily take the form of compensation or amends. The logic behind the costly apology model is that offenders who value the endangered relationship have a larger incentive to restore it than offenders who do not. Accordingly, the amount of the cost that the offender incurs—not the amount of benefit the victim receives—determines the honesty of the signal. Ohtsubo and Watanabe (2009) tested whether the cost that offenders *unilaterally incur* would enhance perceived sincerity in a vignette study and a behavioral experiment. Both studies confirmed the prediction. Costly apologies increased perceived sincerity, and this effect was replicated in seven countries: Chile, China, Indonesia, Japan, the Netherlands, South Korea, and the United States (Ohtsubo et al., 2012). Parenthetically, this cross-cultural study also measured willingness to forgive and found the effect of costly apologies failed to reach the conventional significance level in two countries (Indonesia and South Korea), suggesting a closer association of costly apologies with perceived sincerity than with forgiveness.

A more theory-driven dissociation between costly apologies and forgiveness can be found when victims do not suspect exploitative intent (e.g., continued free-riding, repeated offenses) from their offenders. In other words, when it is transparent that offenders do not have exploitative intent, we predict that non-costly apologies are sufficient to induce forgiveness. A vignette study confirmed this prediction (see Appendix of Ohtsubo & Watanabe, 2009). When the scenarios explicitly described the unintentional nature of an original transgression, participants in both the costly apology and non-costly apology conditions were equally willing to forgive the offender. Nonetheless, interestingly, participants still perceived a costly apology as more sincere than a non-costly apology. A flipside of this finding is that apologies, if perceived as insincere, do not promote forgiveness, and sometimes even backfire (e.g., Risen & Gilovich, 2007; Skarlicki et al., 2004).

A recent functional magnetic resonance imaging (fMRI) study also confirmed the central presumption of the costly apology model—the primary function of costly apologies is to communicate benign intent. In this study (Ohtsubo et al., 2018), participants were exposed to a series of hypothetical transgressions and the offender's reactions (either costly apology, non-costly apology, or no apology). They imagined that one of their real friends in fact had acted in the way each scenario described, and rated the forgivability of their offender. Although the researchers did not ask their participants to evaluate the sincerity of the offender's reactions, the costly apology scenarios, as compared with the non-costly apology and no apology scenarios, strongly engaged the theory-of-mind network (i.e., the medial prefrontal cortex [mPFC], bilateral temporoparietal junction [TPJ], and precuneus) of participants' brains—a network involved in taking others' perspectives. This result suggests that in response to the costly apology scenarios, participants spontaneously became cognizant of the offender's intention (see Ohtsubo et al., 2020, for a similar finding in the context of group apology). Parenthetically, in this study, as we already noted, the social valuation region (i.e., vmPFC/OFC) also responded more strongly to the costly apology scenarios than the non-costly apology and no apology scenarios.

PROXIMATE EMOTIONS OF APOLOGY-MAKING

It is well-established that *guilt* promotes apology-making (e.g., Baumeister et al., 1994, 1995; Leith & Baumeister, 1998; Tangney & Dearing, 2002). In a similar vein, guilt also promotes forgiveness-seeking (Riek et al., 2014). The more central question to this review is whether the intensity of guilt is tuned to relationship value. The answer seems to be "yes." Nelissen (2014) conducted a set of three experiments, wherein he employed different manipulations of relationship value, and consistently found that relationship value modulates the intensity of guilt. For example, in one study, Nelissen experimentally led participants to commit a mild form of transgression against their experimental partner (e.g., assigning a boring task to the partner while assigning a more enjoyable task to themselves). As expected, participants reported greater levels of guilt when the relationship value of the partner was high (e.g., the partner was assigned to play the dictator role in a dictator game wherein a large amount of money would be at stake) than when it was low (e.g., when a small amount of money would be at stake). Bridging the guilt literature and the costly apology model, Ohtsubo and Yagi (2015) revealed that participants were more likely to make costly apologies toward more valuable victims than less valuable victims. Moreover, the association between relationship value and costly apologies was partially mediated by guilt.

There is another line of research suggesting that guilt promotes a costly display of contrition—self-punishment (e.g., Bastian et al., 2011; Griffin et al., 2016; Inbar et al., 2013; Nelissen, 2012; Watanabe & Ohtsubo, 2012). For example, guilt promotes costly altruistic behaviors, such as blood donation (Darlington & Macker, 1966). Nelissen (2012) maintains that self-punishment is meant to appease the victim of transgression because participants in his experiment exhibited self-punishment when—and only when—their victim was observing their self-punitive behavior. However, in other studies (Bastian et al., 2011; Inbar et al., 2013), guilt was induced by having participants recall their past transgressions. Although their past victim was not present in the laboratory, guilt still facilitated self-punishment. This finding makes sense if self-punishment communicates one's intention to comply with social norms; it is not necessarily directed only to victims. In fact, a self-punitive cooperative signal is evolvable in the indirect reciprocity context (Tanaka et al., 2016). However, the true function of self-punishment is still not clear and needs to be further investigated from an evolutionary perspective (see Syme et al., 2016, for an evolutionary hypothesis on the function of an extreme form of self-punishment, suicide attempts).

It is noteworthy that some researchers consider that shame and embarrassment could also serve the function of victim appeasement after transgressions (e.g., Keltner et al., 1997).

Tangney and Dearing (2002), however, argue that shame does not promote apology-making, but rather hinders it because shame is associated with a lowered sense of self-worth and thus motivates withdrawal from social interactions. Nevertheless, shame as well as guilt might promote self-punishment (Tanaka et al., 2015). The effect of shame on self-punishment makes sense if shame is tuned to one's reputation or negative evaluations by others (Robertson et al., 2018; Sznycer et al., 2018) and the function of self-punishment is to communicate one's willingness to comply with social norms, and thus one's value as a community member. However, the associations between shame, self-punishment, and potential reputation-restoring effects have yet to be examined.

Embarrassment seems to serve the appeasement function after relatively minor mishaps (Keltner, 1995). Interestingly, Keltner noted that although guilt does not have characteristic emotional expressions, embarrassment does: "embarrassment is marked by gaze aversion, shifty eyes, speech disturbances, face touches, and a nervous, silly smile" (Keltner, 1995, p. 441). It is noteworthy that these embarrassment expressions are all non-costly signals of the actor's internal state. We speculate that embarrassment expressions are effective in appeasement because embarrasement is typically expressed after minor transgressions, whereafter victims typically do not worry about further exploitation.

Conclusion

In this chapter we first confirmed that reconciliatory tendencies are evolvable—repeated interaction makes TFT evolutionarily stable against an uncooperative strategy (ALLD); repeated interaction plus "noise" allow two forms of reconciliatory tendencies to evolve: GTFT that forgoes some (but not all) of a partner's transgressions, and CTFT that invites a partner to punish its errors. Repeated interaction and behavioral errors (i.e., noise) are ubiquitous in most group-living species, increasing the likelihood that psychological mechanisms for reconciliation will evolve. The animal reconciliation literature in fact provides empirical evidence for reconciliation in a wide range of taxa (e.g., primates, other mammals, birds). The animal reconciliation literature also provides evolutionary hypotheses about reconciliation: the valuable relationship hypothesis maintains that the ultimate cause of reconciliation is relationship repair. The benign intent signal hypothesis argues that some signal of current benign intent is required for former opponents to safely resume a friendly interaction. It is also suggested that a proximate cause of reconciliation is reduction of uncertainty and relational anxiety.

The human reconciliation literature largely confirms the insights from the animal reconciliation literature. Relationship value promotes both forgiveness and costly apology-making, which can be conceptualized as a human counterpart of benign intent signaling. Relational anxiety and stress also facilitated human reconciliation, and forgiveness relieved such aversive emotions. However, empathy was the most important proximate emotion for forgiveness. If victims empathize with their offenders, who might exhibit some suffering due to guilt, they are more likely to forgive their offenders. Thus, guilt appears to be the proximate emotion driving costly apology-making. More importantly, both victim empathy and offender guilt are modulated by relationship value: victims tend to empathize with more valuable offenders, and offenders tend to experience more intense guilt when they harm a more valuable partner.

The two-sided effects of relationship value merit some discussion because reconciliation cannot be achieved unilaterally. For example, no matter how strongly the offender desired to repair the relationship, it would dissolve if the victim had no willingness to forgive the offender. It is also noteworthy that in typical interpersonal conflicts, both victims and offenders tend to blame each other (Baumeister et al., 1990). Therefore, it is not sufficient to seek methods that appease either victims or offenders alone—any effective cause of reconciliation should appease both sides simultaneously. To our knowledge, however, there are no such variables, other than relationship value, that have been known to elicit conciliatory emotions from both sides. We can thus conclude that while there is ample room for future investigations, the reconciliation literature illustrates the utility of the evolutionary perspective in deepening our understanding of reconciliation, and the relevance of social emotions in the reconciliation process.

References

Al-Shawaf, L., Lewis, D. M. G., Barbaro, N., & Wehbe, Y. S. (2021). The products of evolution: Conceptual distinctions, evidentiary criteria, and empirical examples. In T. K. Shackelford (Ed.), *The SAGE handbook of evolutionary psychology* (pp. 70–95). SAGE. https://doi.org/10.4135/9781529739442.n5

Arnold, K., Fraser, O. N., & Aureli, F. (2010). Postconflict reconciliation. In C. J. Campbell, A. Fuentes, K. C. MacKinnon, S. K. Bearder, & R. M. Stumpf (Eds.), *Primates in perspective* (pp. 608–625). Oxford University Press.

Aureli, F. (1997). Post-conflict anxiety in nonhuman primates: The mediating role of emotion in conflict resolution. *Aggressive Behavior*, *23*(5), 315–328. https://doi.org/10.1002/(SICI)1098-2337(1997)23:5<315::AID-AB2>3.0.CO;2-H

Aureli, F., & de Waal, F. B. M. (Eds.). (2000). *Natural conflict resolution*. University of California Press.

Aureli, F., & Smucny, D. (2000). The role of emotion in conflict and conflict resolution. In F. Aureli & F. B. M. de Waal (Eds.), *Natural conflict resolution* (pp. 199–224). University of California Press.

Aureli, F., & van Schaik, C. P. (1991). Post-conflict behaviour in long-tailed macaques (*Macaca fascicularis*): II. Coping with the uncertainty. *Ethology*, *89*(2), 101–114. https://doi.org/10.1111/j.1439-0310.1991.tb00297.x

Axelrod, R. (1984). *The evolution of cooperation*. Basic Books.

Axelrod, R., & Hamilton, W. D. (1981). The evolution of cooperation. *Science*, *211*(4489), 1390–1396. https://doi.org/10.1126/science.7466396

Bastian, B., Jetten, J., & Fasoli, F. (2011). Cleansing the soul by hurting the flesh: The guilt-reducing effect of pain. *Psychological Science*, *22*(3), 334–335. https://doi.org/10.1177/0956797610397058

Baumeister, R. F., Stillwell, A. M., & Heatherton, T. F. (1994). Guilt: An interpersonal approach. *Psychological Bulletin*, *115*(2), 243–267. https://doi.org/10.1037/0033-2909.115.2.243

Baumeister, R. F., Stillwell, A. M., & Heatherton, T. F. (1995). Personal narratives about guilt: Role in action control and interpersonal relationships. *Basic and Applied Social Psychology*, *17*(1–2), 173–198. https://doi.org/10.1207/s15324834basp1701&2_10

Baumeister, R. F., Stillwell, A., & Wotman, S. R. (1990). Victim and perpetrator accounts of interpersonal conflict: Autobiographical narratives about anger. *Journal of Personality and Social Psychology*, *59*(5), 994–1005. https://doi.org/10.1037/0022-3514.59.5.994

Blatz, C. W., & Philpot, C. (2010). On the outcomes of intergroup apologies: A review. *Social and Personality Psychology Compass*, *4*(11), 995–1007. https://doi.org/10.1111/j.1751-9004.2010.00318.x

Boerlijst, M. C., Nowak, M. A., & Sigmund, K. (1997). The logic of contrition. *Journal of Theoretical Biology*, *185*(3), 281–293. https://doi.org/10.1006/jtbi.1996.0326

Bolkan, S., Goodboy, A. K., & Daly, J. A. (2010). Consumer satisfaction and repatronage intentions following a business failure: The importance of perceived control with an organizational complaint. *Communication Reports*, *23*(1), 14–25. https://doi.org/10.1080/08934211003598767

Bottom, W. P., Gibson, K., Daniels, S. E., & Murnighan, J. K. (2002). When talk is not cheap: Substantive penance and expressions of intent in rebuilding cooperation. *Organization Science*, *13*(5), 497–513. https://doi.org/10.1287/orsc.13.5.497.7816

Boyd, R. (1989). Mistakes allow evolutionary stability in the repeated prisoner's dilemma game. *Journal of Theoretical Biology*, *136*(1), 47–56. https://doi.org/10.1016/S0022-5193(89)80188-2

Burnette, J. L., Davisson, E. K., Finkel, E. J., Van Tongeren, D. R., Hui, C. M., & Hoyle, R. H. (2014). Self-control and forgiveness: A meta-analytic review. *Social Psychological and Personality Science*, *5*(4), 443–450. https://doi.org/10.1177/1948550613502991

Burnette, J. L., McCullough, M. E., Van Tongeren, D. R., & Davis, D. E. (2012). Forgiveness results from integrating information about relationship value and exploitation risk. *Personality and Social Psychology Bulletin*, *38*(3), 345–356. https://doi.org/10.1177/0146167211424582

Butovskaya, M. L. (2008). Reconciliation, dominance and cortisol levels in children and adolescents (7–15-year-old boys). *Behaviour*, *145*(11), 1557–1576. https://doi.org/10.1163/156853908786131342

Butovskaya, M., Verbeek, P., Ljungberg, T., & Lunardini, A. (2000). A multicultural view of peacemaking among young children. In F. Aureli & F. B. M. de Waal (Eds.), *Natural conflict resolution* (pp. 243–258). University of California Press.

Castels, D. L., & Whiten, A. (1998). Post-conflict behaviour of wild olive baboons. II. Stress and self-directed behaviour. *Ethology, 104*(2), 148–160. https://doi.org/10.1111/j.1439-0310.1998.tb00058.x

Cheney, D. L., & Seyfarth, R. M. (1997). Reconciliatory grunts by dominant female baboons influence victims' behaviour. *Animal Behaviour, 54*(2), 409–418. https://doi.org/10.1006/anbe.1996.0438

Cheney, D. L., Seyfarth, R. M., & Silk, J. B. (1995). The role of grunts in reconciling opponents and facilitating interactions among adult female baboons. *Animal Behaviour, 50*(1), 249–257. https://doi.org/10.1006/anbe.1995.0237

Cords, M., & Aureli, F. (1996). Reasons for reconciling. *Evolutionary Anthropology, 5*(2), 43–45. https://doi.org/10.1002/(SICI)1520-6505(1996)5:2<42::AID-EVAN3>3.0.CO;2-Y

Cords, M., & Aureli, F. (2000). Reconciliation and relationship qualities. In F. Aureli & F. B. M. de Waal (Eds.), *Natural conflict resolution* (pp. 177–198). University of California Press.

Cords, M., & Thurnheer, S. (1993). Reconciling with valuable partners by long-tailed macaques. *Ethology, 93*(4), 315–325. https://doi.org/10.1111/j.1439-0310.1993.tb01212.x

Couzin, I. D., & Laidre, M. E. (2009). Fission–fusion populations. *Current Biology, 19*(15), R633–R635. https://doi.org/10.1016/j.cub.2009.05.034

Crawford, V. P., & Sobel, J. (1982). Strategic information transmission. *Econometrica, 50*(6), 1431–1451. https://doi.org/10.2307/1913390

Darlington, R. B., & Macker, C. E. (1966). Displacement of guilt-produced altruistic behavior. *Journal of Personality and Social Psychology, 4*(4), 442–443. https://doi.org/10.1037/h0023743

Desmet, P. T. M., De Cremer, D., & van Dijk, E. (2010). On the psychology of financial compensation to restore fairness transgression: When intentions determine value. *Journal of Business Ethics, 95*(S1), 105–115. https://doi.org/10.1007/s10551-011-0791-3

Desmet, P. T. M., De Cremer, D., & van Dijk, E. (2011). In money we trust? The use of financial compensations to repair trust in the aftermath of distributive harm. *Organizational Behavior and Human Decision Processes, 114*(2), 75–86. https://doi.org/10.1016/j.obhdp.2010.10.006

de Waal, F. B. M. (1989). *Peacemaking among primates*. Harvard University Press.

de Waal, F. B. M. (1993). Reconciliation among primates: A review of empirical evidence and unresolved issues. In W. A. Mason & S. P. Mendoza (Eds.), *Primate social conflict* (pp. 111–144). State University of New York Press.

de Waal, F. B. M., & Aureli, F. (1997). Conflict resolution and distress alleviation in monkeys and apes. In C. S. Carter, I. I. Lederhendler, & B. Kirkpatrick (Eds.), *Annals of the New York Academy of Sciences*, Vol. 807: *The integrative neurobiology of affiliation* (pp. 317–328). New York Academy of Sciences. https://doi.org/10.1111/j.1749-6632.1997.tb51919.x

de Waal, F. B. M., & Pokorny, J. J. (2005). Primate conflict and its relation to human forgiveness. In E. L. Worthington (Ed.), *Handbook of forgiveness* (pp. 17–32). Brunner-Routledge.

de Waal, F. B. M., & van Roosmalen, A. (1979). Reconciliation and consolation among chimpanzees. *Behavioral Ecology and Sociobiology, 5*(1), 55–66. https://doi.org/10.1007/BF00302695

de Waal, F. B. M., & Yoshihara, D. (1983). Reconciliation and redirected affection in rhesus monkeys. *Behaviour, 85*(3/4), 224–241. http://dx.doi.org/10.1163/156853983X00237

Farrow, T. F. D., Zheng, Y., Wilkinson, I. D., Spence, S. A., Deakin, J. F. W., Tarrier, N., Griffiths, P. D., & Woodrull, P. W. R. (2001). Investigating the functional anatomy of empathy and forgiveness. *NeuroReport, 12*(11), 2433–2438. http://dx.doi.org/10.1097/00001756-200108080-00029

Fehr, R., Gelfand, M. J., & Nag, M. (2010). The road to forgiveness: A meta-analytic synthesis of its situational and dispositional correlates. *Psychological Bulletin, 136*(5), 894–914. http://dx.doi.org/10.1037/a0019993

Forster, D. E., Billingsley, V. J., Russell, M., McCauley, T. G., Smith, A., Burnette, J. L., Ohtsubo, Y., Schug, J., Lieberman, D., & McCullough, M. E. (2020). Forgiveness takes place on an attitudinal continuum from hostility to friendliness: Toward a closer union of forgiveness theory and measurement. *Journal of Personality and Social Psychology, 119*(4), 861–880. https://10.1037/pspi0000227

Fourie, M. M., Hortensius, R., & Decety, J. (2020). Parsing the components of forgiveness: Psychological and neural mechanisms. *Neuroscience and Biobehavioral Reviews, 112*, 437–451. https://doi.org/10.1016/j.neubiorev.2020.02.020

Fujisawa, K. K., Kutsukake, N., & Hasegawa, T. (2005). Reconciliation pattern after aggression among Japanese preschool children. *Aggressive Behavior, 31*(2), 138–152. https://doi.org/10.1002/ab.20076

Goffman, E. (1971). *Relations in public: Microstudies of the public order*. Basic Books.

Griffin, B. J., Moloney, J. M., Green, J. D., Worthington, E. L., Jr., Cork, B., Tangney, J. P., Van Tongeren, D. R., Davis, D. E., & Hook, J. N. (2016). Perpetrators' reactions to perceived interpersonal wrongdoing: The associations of guilt and shame with forgiving, punishing, and excusing oneself. *Self and Identity, 15*(6), 650–661. http://dx.doi.org/10.1080/15298868.2016.1187669

Inbar, Y., Pizzaro, D. A., Gilovich, T., & Ariely, D. (2013). Moral masochism: On the connection between guilt and self-punishment. *Emotion, 13*(1), 14–18. http://dx.doi.org/10.1037/a0029749

Karremans, J. C., & Aarts, H. (2007). The role of automaticity in determining the inclination to forgive close others. *Journal of Experimental Social Psychology, 43*(6), 902–917. https://doi.org/10.1016/j.jesp.2006.10.012

Karremans, J. C., Regalia, C., Paleari, F. G., Fincham, F. D., Cui, M., Takada, N., Ohbuchi, K., Terzino, K., Cross, S. E., & Uskul, A. K. (2011). Maintaining harmony across the globe: The cross-cultural association between closeness and interpersonal forgiveness. *Social Psychological and Personality Science, 2*(5), 443–451. https://doi.org/10.1177/1948550610396957

Karremans, J. C., Van Lange, P. A. M., Ouwerkerk, J. W., & Kluwer, E. S. (2003). When forgiving enhances psychological well-being: The role of interpersonal commitment. *Journal of Personality and Social Psychology, 84*(5), 1011–1026. https://doi.org/10.1037/0022-3514.84.5.1011

Kearns, J. N., & Fincham, F. D. (2005). Victim and perpetrator accounts of interpersonal transgressions: Self-serving or relationship-serving biases? *Personality and Social Psychology Bulletin, 31*(3), 321–333. https://doi.org/10.1177/0146167204271594

Keltner, D. (1995). Signs of appeasement: Evidence for the distinct displays of embarrassment, amusement, and shame. *Journal of Personality and Social Psychology, 68*(3), 441–454. https://doi.org/10.1037/0022-3514.68.3.441

Keltner, D., Young, R. C., & Buswell, B. N. (1997). Appeasement in human emotion, social practice, and personality. *Aggressive Behavior, 23*(5), 359–374. https://doi.org/10.1002/(SICI)1098-2337(1997)23:5<359::AID-AB5>3.0.CO;2-D

Kollock, P. (1993). Cooperation in an uncertain world: An experimental study. *Sociological Theory and Methods, 8*(1), 3–18. https://doi.org/10.11218/ojjams.8.3

Laidre, M. E., & Johnstone, R. A. (2013). Animal signals. *Current Biology, 23*(18), R829–R833. http://dx.doi.org/10.1016/j.cub.2013.07.070

Laland, K. N., Sterelny, K., Odling-Smee, J., Hoppitt, W., & Uller, T. (2011). Cause and effect in biology revisited: In Mayr's proximate-ultimate dichotomy still useful? *Science, 334*(6062), 1512–1516. http://dx.doi.org/10.1126/science.1210879

Lawler, K. A., Younger, J. W., Piferi, R. L., Billington, E., Jobe, R., Edmondson, K., & Jones, W. H. (2003). A change of heart: Cardiovascular correlates of forgiveness in response to interpersonal conflict. *Journal of Behavioral Medicine, 26*(5), 373–393. https://doi.org/10.1023/A:1025771716686

Lazare, A. (2004). *On apology.* Oxford University Press.

Leith, K. P., & Baumeister, R. F. (1998). Empathy, shame, guilt, and narratives of interpersonal conflicts: Guilt-prone people are better at perspective taking. *Journal of Personality, 66*(1), 1–37. https://doi.org/10.1111/1467-6494.00001

Maestripieri, D., Schino, G., Aureli, F., & Troisi, A. (1992). A modest proposal: Displacement activities as an indicator of emotions in primates. *Animal Behaviour, 44*(5), 967–979. https://doi.org/10.1016/S0003-3472(05)80592-5

Markham, A. C., & Gesquiere, L. R. (2017). Costs and benefits of group living in primates: An energetic perspective. *Philosophical Transactions of the Royal Society B: Biological Sciences, 372*(1727), 20160239. http://dx.doi.org/10.1098/rstb.2016.0239

Martinez-Vaquero, L. A., Han, T. A., Pereira, L. M., & Lenaerts, T. (2015). Apology and forgiveness evolve to resolve failures in cooperative agreements. *Scientific Reports, 5,* 10639. https://doi.org/10.1038/srep10639

Maynard Smith, J. (1991). Honest signalling: The Philip Sidney game. *Animal Behaviour, 42*(6), 1034–1035. https://doi.org/10.1016/S0003-3472(05)80161-7

Mayr, E. (1961). Cause and effect in biology. *Science, 134*(3489), 1501–1506. https://doi.org/10.1126/science.134.3489.1501

McCullough, M. E. (2008). *Beyond revenge: The evolution of the forgiveness instinct.* Jossey-Bass.

McCullough, M. E., Kurzban, R., & Tabak, B. A. (2013). Cognitive systems for revenge and forgiveness. *Behavioral and Brain Sciences, 36*(1), 1–15. https://doi.org/10.1017/S0140525X11002160

McCullough, M. E., Luna, L. R., Berry, J. W., Tabak, B. A., & Bono, G. (2010). On the form and function of forgiving: Modeling the time-forgiveness relationship and testing the valuable relationships hypothesis. *Emotion, 10*(3), 358–376. https://doi.org/10.1037/a0019349

McCullough, M. E., Pedersen, E. J., Tabak, B. A., & Carter, E. C. (2014). Conciliatory gestures promote forgiveness and reduce anger in humans. *Proceedings of the National Academy of Sciences, 111*(30), 11211–11216. https://doi.org/10.1073/pnas.1405072111

McCullough, M. E., Worthington, E. L., Jr., & Rachal, K. C. (1997). Interpersonal forgiving in close relationships. *Journal of Personality and Social Psychology, 73*(2), 321–336. https://doi.org/10.1037/0022-3514.73.2.321

Molander, P. (1985). The optimal level of generosity in a selfish, uncertain environment. *Journal of Conflict Resolution, 29*(4), 611–618. https://doi.org/10.1177/0022002785029004004

Nelissen, R. M. A. (2012). Guilt-induced self-punishment as a sign of remorse. *Social Psychological and Personality Science, 3*(2), 139–144. https://doi.org/10.1177/1948550611411520

Nelissen, R. M. A. (2014). Relational utility as a moderator of guilt in social interactions. *Journal of Personality and Social Psychology, 106*(2), 257–271. https://doi.org/10.1037/a0034711

Nowak, M. A., & Sigmund, K. (1992). Tit for tat in heterogeneous populations. *Nature, 355*(6357), 250–253. https://doi.org/10.1038/355250a0

O'Connor, C. (2016). The evolution of guilt: A model-based approach. *Philosophy of Science, 83*(5), 897–908. https://doi.org/10.1086/687873

Ohbuchi, K., Kameda, M., & Agarie, N. (1989). Apology as aggression control: Its role in mediating appraisal of and response to harm. *Journal of Personality and Social Psychology, 56*(2), 219–227. https://doi.org/10.1037/0022-3514.56.2.219

Ohtsubo, Y., Matsunaga, M., Himichi, T., Suzuki, K., Shibata, E., Hori, R., Umemura, T., & Ohira, H. (2020). Role of the orbitofrontal cortex in the computation of relationship value. *Social Neuroscience, 15*(5), 600–612. https://doi.org/10.1080/17470919.2020.1828164

Ohtsubo, Y., Matsunaga, M., Tanaka, H., Suzuki, K., Kobayashi, F., Shibata, E., Hori, R., Umemura, T., & Ohira, H. (2018). Costly apologies communicate conciliatory intention: An fMRI study on forgiveness in response to costly apologies. *Evolution and Human Behavior, 39*(2), 249–256. https://doi.org/10.1016/j.evolhumbehav.2018.01.004

Ohtsubo, Y., & Watanabe, E. (2009). Do sincere apologies need to be costly? Test of a costly signaling model of apology. *Evolution and Human Behavior, 30*(2), 114–123. https://doi.org/10.1016/j.evolhumbehav.2008.09.004

Ohtsubo, Y., Watanabe, E., Kim, J., Kulas, J. T., Muluk, H., Nazar, G., Wang, F., & Zhang, J. (2012). Are costly apologies universally perceived as being sincere? A test of the costly apology-perceived sincerity relationship in seven countries. *Journal of Evolutionary Psychology, 10*(4), 187–204. https://doi.org/10.1556/JEP.10.2012.4.3

Ohtsubo, Y., & Yagi, A. (2015). Relationship value promotes costly apology-making: Testing the valuable relationships hypothesis from the perpetrator's perspective. *Evolution and Human Behavior, 36*(3), 232–239. https://doi.org/10.1016/j.evolhumbehav.2014.11.008

Okamoto, K., & Matsumura, S. (2001). The evolution of punishment and apology: An iterated prisoner's dilemma model. *Evolutionary Ecology, 14*(8), 703–720. https://doi.org/10.1023/A:1011612522206

Rapoport, A., & Chammah, A. M. (1965). *Prisoner's dilemma*. University of Michigan Press.

Rasmussen, K. R., Stackhouse, M., Boon, S. D., Comstock, K., & Ross, R. (2019). Meta-analytic connections between forgiveness and health: The moderating effects of forgiveness-related distinctions. *Psychology & Health, 34*(5), 515–534. https://doi.org/10.1080/08870446.2018.1545906

Riek, B. M., Luna, L. M. R., & Schnabelrauch, C. A. (2014). Transgressors' guilt and shame: A longitudinal examination of forgiveness seeking. *Journal of Social and Personal Relationships, 31*(6), 751–772. https://doi.org/10.1177/0265407513503595

Riek, B. M., & Mania, E. W. (2012). The antecedents and consequences of interpersonal forgiveness: A meta-analytic review. *Personal Relationships, 19*(2), 304–325. https://doi.org/10.1111/j.1475-6811.2011.01363.x

Risen, J. L., & Gilovich, T. (2007). Target and observer differences in the acceptance of questionable apologies. *Journal of Personality and Social Psychology, 92*(3), 418–433. https://doi.org/10.1037/0022-3514.92.3.418

Robertson, T. E., Sznycer, D., Delton, A. W., Tooby, J., & Cosmides (2018). The true trigger of shame: Social devaluation is sufficient, wrongdoing is unnecessary. *Evolution and Human Behavior, 39*(5), 566–573. https://doi.org/10.1016/j.evolhumbehav.2018.05.010

Romero, T., & Aureli, F. (2017). Conflict resolution. In J. Call, G. M. Burghardt, I. M. Pepperberg, C. T. Snowdon, & T. Zentall (Eds.), *APA handbook of comparative psychology: Basic concepts, methods, neural substrate, and behavior* (pp. 877–897). American Psychological Association. https://doi.org/10.1037/0000011-042

Rusbult, C. E., Hannon, P. A., Stocker, S. L., & Finkel, E. J. (2005). Forgiveness and relational repair. In E. L. Worthington, Jr. (Ed.), *Handbook of forgiveness* (pp. 185–205). Routledge.

Schino, G. (2000). Beyond the primates: Expanding the reconciliation horizon. In F. Aureli & F. B. M. de Waal (Eds.), *Natural conflict resolution* (pp. 225–242). University of California Press.

Schlenker, B. R., & Darby, B. W. (1981). The use of apologies in social predicaments. *Social Psychology Quarterly, 44*(3), 271–278. https://doi.org/10.2307/3033840

Sell, A., Sznycer, D., Al-Shawaf, L., Lim, J., Krauss, A., Feldman, A., Rascanu, R., Sugiyama, L., Cosmides, L., & Tooby, J. (2017). The grammar of anger: Mapping the computational architecture of a recalibrational emotion. *Cognition, 168*(), 110–128. https://doi.org/10.1016/j.cognition.2017.06.002.

Silk, J. B. (1996). Why do primates reconcile? *Evolutionary Anthropology, 5*(2), 39–42. https://doi.org/10.1002/(SICI)1520-6505(1996)5:2<39::AID-EVAN2>3.0.CO;2-R

Silk, J. B. (2002). The form and function of reconciliation in primates. *Annual Review of Anthropology, 31*, 21–44. https://doi.org/10.1 146/annurev.anthro.31.032902.101743

Silk, J. B. (2007). The adaptive value of sociality in mammalian groups. *Philosophical Transactions of the Royal Society B: Biological Sciences, 362*(1480), 539–559. https://doi.org/10.1098/rstb.2006.1994

Silk, J. B., Cheney, D. L., & Seyfarth, R. M. (1996). The form and function of post-conflict interactions between female baboons. *Animal Behaviour, 52*(2), 259–268. https://doi.org/10.1006/anbe.1996.0171

Silk, J. B., Kaldor, E., & Boyd, R. (2000). Cheap talk when interests conflict. *Animal Behaviour, 59*(2), 423–432. https://doi.org/10.1006/anbe.1999.1312

Skarlicki, D. P., Folger, R., & Gee, J. (2004). When social accounts backfire: The exacerbating effects of a polite message or an apology on reactions to an unfair outcome. *Journal of Applied Social Psychology, 34*(2), 322–341. https://doi.org/10.1111/j.1559-1816.2004.tb02550.x

Skyrms, B. (2010). *Signals: Evolution, learning, and information*. Oxford University Press.

Smith, A., McCauley, T. G., Yagi, A., Yamaura, K., Shimizu, H., McCullough, M. E., & Ohtsubo, Y. (2020). Perceived goal instrumentality is associated with forgiveness: A test of the valuable relationships hypothesis. *Evolution and Human Behavior, 41*(1), 58–68. https://doi.org/10.1016/j.evolhumbehav.2019.09.003

Syme, K. L., Garfield, Z. H., & Hagen, E. H. (2016). Testing the bargaining vs. inclusive fitness models of suicidal behavior against the ethnographic record. *Evolution and Human Behavior, 37*(3), 179–192. https://doi.org/10.1016/j.evolhumbehav.2015.10.005

Sznycer, D., Xygalatas, D., Agey, E., Alami, S., An, X.-F., Ananyeva, K. I., Atkinson, Q. D., Broitman, B. R., Conte, T. J., Flores, C., Fukushima, S., Hitokoto, H., Kharitonov, A. N., Onyishi, C. N., Onyishi, I. E., Romero, P. P., Schrock, J. M., Snodgrass, J. J., Sugiyama, L. S., Takemura, K., Townsend, C., Zhuang, J.-Y., Aktipis, C. A., Cronk, L., Cosmides, L., & Tooby, J. (2018). Cross-cultural invariances in the architecture of shame. *Proceedings of the National Academy of Sciences, 115*(39), 9702–9707. https://doi.org/10.1073/pnas.1805016115

Tabak, B. A., McCullough, M. E., Luna, L. R., Bono, G., & Berry, J. W. (2012). Conciliatory gestures facilitate forgiveness and feelings of friendship by making transgressors appear more agreeable. *Journal of Personality, 80*(2), 503–536. https://10.1111/j.1467-6494.2011.00728.x

Tanaka, H., Ohtsuki, H., & Ohtsubo, Y. (2016). The price of being seen to be just: An intention signalling strategy for indirect reciprocity. *Proceedings of the Royal Society B: Biological Sciences, 283*(1835), 20160694. https://doi.org/10.1098/rspb.2016.0694

Tanaka, H., Yagi, A., Komiya, A., Mifune, N., & Ohtsubo, Y. (2015). Shame-prone people are more likely to punish themselves: A test of the reputation-maintenance explanation for self-punishment. *Evolutionary Behavioral Sciences, 9*(1), 1—7. https://doi.org/10.1037/ebs0000016

Tangney, J. P., & Dearing, R. L. (2002). *Shame and guilt*. Guilford Press.

Van Lange, P. A. M., Ouwerkerk, J. W., & Tazelaar, M. J. A. (2002). How to overcome the detrimental effects of noise in social interaction: The benefits of generosity. *Journal of Personality and Social Psychology, 82*(5), 768–780. https://doi.org/10.1037//0022-3514.82.5.768

Watanabe, E., & Ohtsubo, Y. (2012). Costly apology and self-punishment after an unintentional transgression. *Journal of Evolutionary Psychology, 10*(3), 87–105. https://doi.org/10.1556/JEP.10.2012.3.1

Worthington, E. L., Jr. (2005). Initial questions about the art and science of forgiving. In E. L. Worthington, Jr. (Ed.), *Handbook of forgiveness* (pp. 1–13). Routledge.

Worthington, E. L., Jr., Witvliet, C. V. O., Pietrini, P., & Miller, A. J. (2007). Forgiveness, health, and well-being: A review of evidence for emotional versus decisional forgiveness, dispositional forgiveness, and reduced unforgiveness. *Journal of Behavioral Medicine, 30*(4), 291–302. https://doi.org/10.1007/s10865-007-9105-8

Wu, J., & Axelrod, R. (1995). How to cope with noise in the iterated prisoner's dilemma. *Journal of Conflict Resolution, 39*(1), 183–189. https://doi.org/10.1177/0022002795039001008

CHAPTER 38

Emotions in Co-Rumination: An Evolutionary Developmental Perspective

Jessica L. Calvi and Jennifer Byrd-Craven

Abstract

Co-rumination is a developmental psychology concept that encompasses the social process of rehashing, speculation, mutual encouragement, and negative affect about a problem, originally described in Rose's (2002) observation in youths' same-sex friendships. The negative valence of the emotional content and verbal processing of a social problem are both integral to the construct, such that co-rumination facilitates trade-offs between intimacy and internalizing symptoms in same-sex friendships. Emotional contagion facilitates nonverbal communication in humans and has biological underpinnings that communicate emotional content and encourage synchrony between conspecifics. Co-rumination and associated processes may represent part of a suite of adaptations that facilitate alliance formation with non-kin. This chapter summarizes the recent literature on co-rumination, emotional contagion, empathy, and their biological underpinnings, and places these processes in the broader context of human sociality.

Key Words: friendship, co-rumination, empathy, emotional contagion, developmental psychology, human sociality

Co-rumination is a construct whose origin is in youth and adolescent friendship research—its name is derived from the phenomenon in which two friends discuss a negatively valenced event or interaction ad nauseum, such that both individuals ruminate (or rather, obsess) over the problem together (Rose, 2002). This gave rise to the term *co-rumination*, which has four defining features: (1) *focus on negative affect*; (2) *mutual encouragement* of problem discussion; (3) *rehashing* (repeatedly discussing the problem or details of the problem with high frequency); and (4) *speculation* about the causes and consequences of the problem. Thus, it was conceptualized as a combination of self-disclosure (sharing personal thoughts and feelings with another) and rumination (focusing on internal negative affect).

The friendship literature had, to that point, identified a paradoxical relationship in which adolescent female same-sex friendships exhibited high levels of intimacy, self-disclosure, and support, while concurrently exhibiting high levels of internalizing (depression and anxiety) symptoms and problematic emotional adjustment (Rose, 2002; Rose & Rudolph, 2006). In subsequent studies, some researchers further subdivided co-rumination into co-brooding and co-reflection (Bastin et al., 2014; Bastin et al., 2018), and much research has examined the context of other emotion-related skills in relation to co-rumination (Borowski & Zeman, 2018; Spendelow et al., 2017).

Research in the past two decades on friendships has shown that co-rumination is a specific type of interaction that is more prevalent in female same-sex friendships. Developmental studies of sex differences in several social-emotional domains may contribute to understanding the prevalence of negative self-disclosure and problem discussion within these same-sex friendships, differences which become more prominent during and after adolescence (Schwartz-Mette & Rose, 2012). Co-rumination research has expanded to other types of social relationships (romantic, parent-child, and even coworker relationships; see Haggard et al., 2011; Rose et al., 2014; Waller & Rose, 2013). This indicates that co-rumination is a lifelong social dynamic in which individuals engage with their close others, with both positive and negative interpersonal and physiological consequences (Byrd-Craven et al., 2008; Byrd-Craven et al., 2011). In the following sections, we discuss the friendship literature that gave rise to the concept of co-rumination, the physiological consequences of co-rumination, and the role of emotions and emotion-related constructs that contribute to the process of co-rumination (namely emotional contagion, empathy, and physiological synchrony).

Current Findings on Friendship Dynamics and Co-Rumination

Sex differences in intrasexual competition and parental investment set the stage for associated behavioral differences in the context of close relationships (Byrd-Craven & Geary, 2013). Same-sex friendships serve as sources of social support for both sexes, but in different ways. Relative to girls and women, boys and men form larger same-sex coalitions, often with differentiated roles, and establish intimacy through shared activities. Girls and women are more likely than boys and men to focus on an ethos of equality in their friendship groups and establish intimacy through dyadic self-disclosure. These differences begin early in childhood, around age 2–3 years, are observed cross-culturally, and are mediated through the organizational effects of prenatal hormone exposure (Byrd-Craven & Geary, 2013; Collaer & Hines, 1995). For a more extensive review of sex differences in early childhood, see Geary and colleagues (2003) and Geary (2010, 2020).

Sex differences in the social dynamics of friendships that began in childhood continue in adolescence and early adulthood. Young females age 10–15 years report shorter durations of friendships and greater distress at the dissolution of friendships than young males (Benenson & Christakos, 2003). Despite this experience of greater distress, females report less tolerance for violations in peer relationships and report higher levels of anger and longer time periods to reconcile conflict (Benenson et al., 2014). However, Benenson and colleagues (2011) conclude that these one-to-one relationships are "inherently more fragile than a relationship situated within a larger group containing temporary substitute partners, allies, and mediators" (p. 1). Research on sex differences in adult friendships and social interactions has found that males have more friends, whereas females report higher levels of intimacy in fewer friendships (Bank & Hansford, 2000; Vigil, 2007).

Self-disclosure is also common in friendships, such that males and females share personal information with their confidants, albeit typically in different contexts (Caldwell & Peplau, 1982). As stated above, for girls and women, dyadic self-disclosure is the primary means by which intimacy is established (Rose & Rudolph, 2006). Unlike normative self-disclosure, Rose (2002) specifically outlines that co-rumination constitutes an extreme form of self-disclosure and shared rumination behaviors (taken together). Co-rumination refers to "negative affect" (which implies a suite of negatively valenced emotions). Developmental research typically examines the effects of co-rumination as a feature of friendships that contributes to negative outcomes, including symptoms of depression, anxiety, and related interpersonally focused constructs (e.g., Barstead et al., 2013; Rose et al., 2014) found mostly in young female samples. Research has also shown that a paradoxical relationship exists with co-rumination, such that females report feeling greater intimacy in their same-sex friendships but also display higher levels of internalizing symptoms (Rose & Rudolph, 2006) and experience greater empathic distress as a result of others' distress (Smith & Rose, 2011).

The study of co-rumination in middle childhood, adolescence, and various stages of adulthood has contributed to the understanding of self-disclosure and its important role in many social relationships, ranging from friendships (Rose et al., 2014), to familial relationships (Waller & Rose, 2013), and professional/work relationships (Haggard et al., 2011). A meta-analysis of self-reported co-rumination identified a significant effect of co-rumination partner (same-sex best friend vs. other partner; Spendelow et al., 2017), but additional work is needed to understand better the individual benefits and behavioral processes that underlie friendship maintenance and co-rumination sessions.

In addition, the physiological consequences of co-rumination have been explored such that many studies of laboratory-based tasks show that females experience physiological stress reactions to problem discussions (Byrd-Craven et al., 2011; Rankin et al., 2018). Females who self-report high levels of co-rumination report feeling closer after co-ruminating with their best/closest friend (Byrd-Craven et al., 2011). Common problems in observed discussions between female same-sex best friends were breakups of romantic relationships and analyzing others' behaviors in interpersonal relationships and social situations (Byrd-Craven et al., 2008). However, others have found an effect of "depression contagion," such that adolescents are more likely to develop depressive symptoms if exposed to a person who is depressed (Schwartz-Mette & Rose, 2012; Schwartz-Mette & Smith, 2018). In addition, further research is needed to understand male same-sex friendships, including identifying which topics are covered during co-rumination sessions for males, and whether and which benefits are conferred to participants during these discussions.

Some research has examined the give-and-take nature of intimate relationships and the processes that facilitate emotional closeness, from biological bases to mental health outcomes. Co-rumination may be an interpersonal phenomenon that allows humans to process their negative emotional states as a means to self-regulate and socialize their negative emotions (Borowski & Zeman, 2018). For example, an individual may want to discuss with a friend the anger they feel after a family member's comment. In this scenario, the friend may validate feelings of anger at the family member's comment, or they may discuss how and why they would feel a different negative emotion instead (e.g., sadness) or a nuanced gradient of anger (e.g., annoyance), which refines the emotional experience within a suite of negative emotions for the other individual. Given co-rumination's association with internalizing symptoms, many treat co-rumination as more detrimental than beneficial, seeking to address the negative aspects of this social process (e.g., Carlucci et al., 2018; Spendelow et al., 2017; Stone et al., 2019). However, the nature of underlying processes that facilitate intimacy in same-sex friendships over the life span is still poorly understood, often due to the analysis of friendship factors not considering sex (Rose, 2002).

Given the frequency of co-rumination, particularly in same-sex female friendships, co-rumination may represent a social process that functions to establish empathetic responding and bonding. Underlying sex differences, favoring females, in the ability to attend to and decode both verbal and nonverbal information, along with associated physiological processes (e.g., cortisol reactivity), likely facilitate this as a method of establishing and maintaining alliances (Rankin et al., 2018). Though it is not without costs, rather than representing a pathological process, this social process may be viewed better and studied as a protective factor against other negative social outcomes, like social rejection or exclusion. Biological and physiological processes such as empathy and emotional contagion may facilitate friendship-maintenance behaviors such as co-rumination and protect the self and others against social rejection or exclusion. In addition, empathy and emotional contagion are related constructs that show sex differences and would be best understood from an adaptive perspective. In the following section, we discuss these emotion-related processes both as independently defined by the research literature, as well as within the context of co-rumination.

Empathy and Emotional Contagion
One area of social behavior research that has shown sex differences is empathy, or the ability to understand and share the emotional experience of another individual (Baron-Cohen & Wheelwright, 2004; Davis, 1983). Most researchers agree that there are two central components of empathy: cognitive empathy and emotional empathy (Davis et al., 1999; Decety & Jackson, 2006; Preston & de Waal, 2002; Watt, 2007). *Cognitive empathy* refers to the ability of an individual to understand the beliefs, attitudes, thoughts, and motivations of others (Decety & Jackson, 2004; Hoffman, 1977, 2000), whereas *emotional empathy* is often conceptualized as emotional contagion (Hatfield et al., 1993), or the ability to feel the same emotion by witnessing another's emotional experience. Some researchers argue that these two types of empathy are separate (Davis, 1983), whereas others argue that they are independent but overlapping types of empathy (Baron-Cohen & Wheelwright, 2004).

Emotional contagion is thought to be the precursor to several socially related abilities; e.g., it is considered to be part of, or a precursor to, empathy (de Waal, 2008; Iacoboni, 2009; Kimura et al., 2008). Emotional contagion is defined as the tendency of an individual to unconsciously imitate the emotions of others around him/her (Hatfield et al., 1993); it is closely related to our innate imitative ability, which is likely an adaptation to navigate complex social networks (Iacoboni, 2009; Lakin et al., 2003). Emotional contagion is subdivided into two components: mimicry and affective resonance. The behavioral mimicry of emotion expression, sometimes referred to as the "chameleon effect," is the "non-conscious mimicry of the postures, mannerisms, facial expressions, and other behaviors of one's interaction partners, such that one's behavior passively and unintentionally changes to match that of others" (Chartrand & Bargh, 1999, p. 1). Thus, like chameleons, we as humans cannot always control these tendencies to imitate those around us. This effect is part of emotional contagion, in that individuals mirror the emotional states of others automatically. Affective resonance is the process by which an emotion expressed by another affects not only the motor behavior of an observer, but also the mood state of the observer (Doherty, 1997; Hatfield et al., 1993). Emotional contagion is often equated with affective empathy in theoretical definitions of empathy (Davis, 1983; Hoffman, 1975; Smith, 2006), whereas others posit that emotional empathy entails a different emotional response to a target individual than the target is feeling (e.g., feeling anger when the target feels sadness; Nakahashi & Ohtsuki, 2015).

In contrast, cognitive empathy encompasses or equates to cognitive perspective-taking skills and is the ability to imagine, with intention, the feelings and motivations of others (de Waal, 2008; Eisenberg, 1991; Smith, 2006). There are similarities between this definition and the definition of theory of mind (ToM; Premack & Woodruff, 1978), or the idea that individuals attribute thoughts, motivations, beliefs, and desires to another person that are separate from their own cognitions (Flavell, 1999; Humphrey, 1976; Oberman & Ramachandran, 2007), but an added component is appreciating the affective perspective of another (Harwood

& Farrar, 2006). Many theorists equate ToM to the cognitive aspect of empathy (e.g., Baron-Cohen & Wheelwright, 2004; Singer, 2006).

Historically, research on empathy measures have indicated a female advantage, with adult females scoring higher than adult males on self-report (Baron-Cohen & Wheelwright, 2004; Davis, 1983) and behavioral measures (Baron-Cohen et al., 2001) of empathy. However, these self-report questionnaires use questions that focus on direct face-to-face interactions (e.g., "I am quick to spot when someone in a group is feeling awkward or uncomfortable") or individuals interacting within a group (Baron-Cohen & Wheelwright, 2004) rather than overall group behavior (e.g., "I am quick to spot the overall mood of a room full of people"). Females pay closer attention to the eyes in facial decoding (Hall et al., 2010; Shen & Itti, 2012). The "Reading the Mind in the Eyes" Test Revised (Baron-Cohen et al., 2001) uses pictures of the eye region to test ability to read facial expressions, with a focus on decoding emotional expressions and "empathic accuracy." Thus, like co-rumination, it is possible that females have an advantage in that they have socialization experiences that allow them to practice these skills more often, which can contribute to sex differences found in these measures later in life (Byrd-Craven & Geary, 2013).

Although researchers have criticized some emotion-based self-report measures as female-biased (e.g., Eisenberg & Fabes, 1998; Eisenberg et al., 1987; Eisenberg & Lennon, 1983; Zarbatany et al., 1985), sex differences in socialization and exposures during development likely contribute to sex differences found in both the co-rumination literature and the empathy literature (Maccoby, 1998; Maccoby & Jacklin, 1987). Thus, it is possible that females have additional practice at emotion-focused skills through both socialization and exposure to situations that invoke problem-based conversation (i.e., co-rumination) in face-to-face conversations, facilitating the sex difference findings in emotion-related processes later in life.

An additional layer of empathy and empathy-related concepts address physiological synchrony, concordance, or attunement as mechanisms for coordinated behaviors in humans (Butler & Randall, 2013). Research on physiological measures of attunement has produced mixed results; however, this may be due to varying definitions of these related terms, the pairs/groups examined, and/or the measurement of the biological system (see Palumbo et al., 2017). Various studies have examined the effects of inducing physiological synchrony in parent-child dyads (Byrd-Craven et al., 2020), friends (Byrd-Craven et al., 2011; Cook, 2020; Rankin et al., 2018), romantic couples (Bizzego et al., 2020; Golland et al., 2015), and strangers (Bizzego et al., 2020). Studies have also investigated both autonomic synchrony (Butler & Randall, 2013; Palumbo et al., 2017) and HPA-axis synchrony (Rankin et al., 2018; Rankin et al., 2021). Although these measures of synchrony may help to elucidate which biological systems underlie the connections between empathy and co-rumination sessions in real time, others have pointed out that the long-term effects of synchrony must examine timescale and/or investigate how these effects are sustained over time. These avenues of research have given rise to other concepts. For example, researchers have posited that, as an extension of emotional contagion (which is fleeting, by definition), mood contagion (Block & Burnett Heyes, 2020; Neumann & Strack, 2000), depression contagion (Joiner, 1994; Schwartz-Mette & Smith, 2018), and/or peer contagion (Dishion & Tipsord, 2011) may be forms of influence that facilitate negative aspects of close interpersonal relationships in friendship dyads or groups, such as deviancy, body image, or self-injury. In addition, researchers have discussed co-regulation, a concept adapted from emotion-regulation research and synchrony research for application to close relationships as a means of understanding the long-term effects of shared emotions over time (Butler & Randall, 2013), as well as the nature of support offered to individuals in close relationships (e.g., instrumental vs. emotional support; Cohen et al., 2000) to elucidate relationships between social support and internalizing symptoms. Thus, understanding both the underlying mechanisms (e.g., physiological attunement, empathy) and the behavioral manifestations (e.g., co-rumination) will help researchers direct interventions to decrease the occurrences of depression and anxiety, particularly among young women.

Taken together, co-rumination and associated psychosocial processes like emotional contagion, empathy, and attunement represent a suite of characteristics designed to facilitate the kind of information tracking and exchange that is representative of long-term non-kin alliances. The willingness to invest time, energetic resources (as indexed by a stress response), and to experience negative affect on behalf of a social partner likely serves as a signal of relationship value. Thus, these processes may be best understood when placed in the context of the selection pressures surrounding same-sex friendships.

Evolutionary Theories

One unresolved issue outlined in the above research is "why?" From an evolutionary perspective, there is a functional organization in the mechanisms that produce emotions that reflect adaptive solutions to recurrent problems our ancestors faced (Tooby & Cosmides, 2008). This perspective can be extended to the study of emotions evidenced in important (i.e., deep engagement) relationships, like parental or romantic love, but also in non-kin or non-mating relationships like friendship (Crawford & Krebs, 1998; Tooby & Cosmides, 1992). Emotions serve as coordinating mechanisms to guide behavior toward adaptive solutions (Al-Shawaf & Lewis, 2020).

Much of the past evolutionary approaches to the study of emotion have used a comparative approach and have focused on emotions shared with other species. Examining the social emotions, relatively unique to humans, allows us to better understand the key adaptive problems faced by our uniquely social ancestors. The existence of social emotions underscores the utility of continuously recalibrating one's welfare trade-off ratio to maximize long-term social payoffs (Al-Shawaf et al., 2016). The social emotions function to influence internal representations of the self and others (Sznycer et al., 2021). For example, anger is triggered when one perceives themselves to not be valued as highly as one should be. Shared anger, as is often the case in co-rumination, may function to communicate that one shares this perception and is motivated to act accordingly on the friend/ally's behalf. Similarly, emotions like guilt help us maintain cooperative relationships with others (Trivers, 1971), and is closely tied to the monitoring of reciprocal exchange, such as the exchange of information and emotional valence in co-rumination sessions. Relatedly, gratitude, a complementary emotion to guilt, is likely a "recalibrational emotion program" that is triggered when one receives information that one is a valued social partner (Tooby & Cosmides, 1996). Even unpleasant emotions that are experienced in the context of friendships, like jealousy, function to motivate us to maintain valued relationships (Krems et al., 2021). It is likely that expressions of emotions like empathy, within the context of co-rumination, can also function to maintain the relationship by signaling comradery.

In addition, evolutionary theories offer predictions as to how and why peers and friends benefit us. For example, peers can provide unique benefits in navigating developmentally contingent concerns. There are several evolutionary theories that contribute to our understanding of same-sex friendships. The Tend-and-Befriend Theory (Taylor et al., 2000) of female stress response posits that females (more than males) are prone to "tending" (i.e., checking or protecting their offspring) and "befriending" (i.e., seeking out and giving social support during stressful times to their friends and family) when stressed. There is some support for the theory, although some researchers (Geary & Flinn, 2002) have asserted that males also show tend-and-befriend behaviors under stress. Thus, it is possible that under stress or strain, the emotional support offered by allies/friends allows females (and males) to cope with the challenges.

Some theorists have proposed that friendships serve the function of benefiting individuals' competitiveness as mates, such that males should seek same-sex friendships that increase these benefits (Lewis et al., 2011). Benefits for males, in the context of sex-specific selection pressures, include having allies within a coalition; thus, males are predicted to (and have been found to) value characteristics in friends that enhance their own fitness as mates, such as access to resources and abilities related to competition (e.g., physical prowess, leadership) over the emotional benefits more typical of female friendships (Lewis et al., 2011; Vigil, 2007).

In contrast, evolutionary theories have proposed that personal information disclosed can be weaponized for reputation management (Hess, 2006). Self-disclosure is particularly risky in female friendships, and violations of trust or perceived betrayals can be especially harmful to female friendships (Hess, 2017; Hess & Hagen, 2006, 2019). In addition, empathy should be considered within a subset of specific social abilities that enable the individual to better navigate relationships and to maximize the utility of certain types of relationships in which he/she is empathizing. Stated another way, the skills related to empathy are not always used for feel-good purposes as is often conceptualized in the literature; these same skills can also be used to manipulative ends (Shirtcliff et al., 2009). Therefore, co-rumination sessions may serve not only to benefit the target (i.e., a friend understands and facilitates discussion of a difficult social problem for clarity and increased closeness in the friendship), but also may allow the empathizer to understand their friend's motivations, emotional responses, and problems, which they can later exploit if needed. In terms of empathy's conceptualization, empathizing may be especially beneficial to the empathizer (not just the target), particularly in a co-rumination session. For example, the empathizer will encourage further problem discussion by invoking emotion-based language. A statement which encourages the target to respond with their own emotional response to the situation under discussion, like "That would be so annoying to me," invokes both the negative affect and provides encouragement to continue discussing the problem. The costs associated with co-rumination in the developmental literature (e.g., depression and anxiety symptoms) may represent signals of this investment. This emotion-laden process then results in increases in social support and, optimally, social status. For example, the bonding process and content associated with co-rumination enhances the perception of support against a shared rival, and likely increases willingness to leverage reputational attacks against that rival (Reynolds, 2022).

In conclusion, we argue that co-rumination and associated processes like empathy and emotional contagion establish same-sex alliances by evoking investment and information disclosure. The trade-offs associated with co-rumination may be best understood from an evolutionary perspective, as co-rumination appears to be part of a collection of processes that women use for navigating the nuances of same-sex relationships. Thus, a nuanced approach to co-rumination (Smith & Rose, 2011) and related biological and physiological processes should continue to motivate research, with evolutionary-based theories informing the conceptual bases for these findings, such that evolutionary theories of friendship (Hess, 2006, 2017) and stress (Geary & Flinn, 2002; Taylor et al., 2000) can generate new hypotheses to elucidate our understanding of friendships and potentially intervene when the negative effects of co-rumination manifest in social relationships.

References

Al-Shawaf, L., Conroy-Beam, D., Asao, K., & Buss, D. M. (2016). Human emotions: An evolutionary psychological perspective. In *Emotion Review, 8*(2), 173–186. https://doi.org/10.1177/1754073914565518

Al-Shawaf, L., & Lewis, D. M. G. (2020). Evolutionary psychology and the emotions. In V. Zeigler-Hill, & T. K. Shackelford (Eds.), *Encyclopedia of personality and individual differences*. Springer, Cham. https://doi.org/10.1007/978-3-319-24612-3_516

Bank, B. J., & Hansford, S. L. (2000). Gender and friendship: Why are men's best same-sex friendships less intimate and supportive? *Personal Relationships, 7*(1), 63–78. https://doi.org/10.1111/j.1475-6811.2000.tb00004.x

Baron-Cohen, S., & Wheelwright, S. (2004). The empathy quotient: An investigation of adults with asperger syndrome or high functioning autism, and normal sex differences. *Journal of Autism and Developmental Disorders, 34*(2), 163–175. https://doi.org/10.1023/B:JADD.0000022607.19833.00

Baron-Cohen, S., Wheelwright, S., Hill, J., Raste, Y., & Plumb, I. (2001). The "Reading the Mind in the Eyes" test revised version: A study with normal adults, and adults with asperger syndrome or high-functioning autism. *Journal of Child Psychology and Psychiatry, 42*(2), 241–251. https://doi.org/10.1111/1469-7610.00715

Barstead, M. G., Bouchard, L. C., & Shih, J. H. (2013). Understanding gender differences in co-rumination and confidant choice in young adults. *Journal of Social and Clinical Psychology, 32*(7), 791–808. https://doi.org/10.1521/jscp.2013.32.7.791

Bastin, M., Bijttebier, P., Raes, F., & Vasey, M. W. (2014). Brooding and reflecting in an interpersonal context. *Personality and Individual Differences, 63*, 100–105. https://doi.org/10.1016/j.paid.2014.01.062

Bastin, M., Vanhalst, J., Raes, F., & Bijttebier, P. (2018). Co-brooding and co-reflection as differential predictors of depressive symptoms and friendship quality in adolescents: investigating the moderating role of gender. *Journal of Youth and Adolescence, 47*(5), 1037–1051. https://doi.org/10.1007/s10964-017-0746-9

Benenson, J. F., & Christakos, A. (2003). The greater fragility of females' versus males' closest same-sex friendships. *Child Development, 74*(4), 1123–1129. https://doi.org/10.1111/1467-8624.00596

Benenson, J. F., Kuhn, M. N., Ryan, P. J., Ferranti, A. J., Blondin, R., Shea, M., Charpentier, C., Thompson, M. E., & Wrangham, R. W. (2014). Human males appear more prepared than females to resolve conflicts with same-sex peers. *Human Nature, 25*(2), 251–268. https://doi.org/10.1007/s12110-014-9198-z

Benenson, J. F., Markovits, H., Thompson, M. E., & Wrangham, R. W. (2011). Under threat of social exclusion, females exclude more than males. *Psychological Science, 22*(4), 538–544. https://doi.org/10.1177/0956797611402511

Bizzego, A., Azhari, A., Campostrini, N., Truzzi, A., Ng, L. Y., Gabrieli, G., Bornstein, M. H., Setoh, P., & Esposito, G. (2020). Strangers, friends, and lovers show different physiological synchrony in different emotional states. *Behavioral Sciences, 10*(1), 11. https://doi.org/10.3390/bs10010011

Block, P., & Burnett Heyes, S. (2020). Sharing the load: Contagion and tolerance of mood in social networks. *Emotion, 22*(6), 1193–1207. https://doi.org/10.1037/emo0000952

Borowski, S. K., & Zeman, J. (2018). Emotional competencies relate to co-rumination: Implications for emotion socialization within adolescent friendships. *Social Development, 27*(4), 808–825. https://doi.org/10.1111/sode.12293

Butler, E. A., & Randall, A. K. (2013). Emotional coregulation in close relationships. *Emotion Review, 5*(2), 202–210. https://doi.org/10.1177/1754073912451630

Byrd-Craven, J., Criss, M. M., Calvi, J. L., Cui, L., Baraldi, A., & Sheffield Morris, A. (2020). Adrenocortical attunement, reactivity, and potential genetic correlates among parent–daughter dyads from low-income families. *Developmental Psychobiology, 62*(8), 1035–1045. https://doi.org/10.1002/dev.21970

Byrd-Craven, J., & Geary, D. C. (2013). An evolutionary understanding of sex differences. In M. K. Ryan & N. R. Branscombe (Eds.), *The Sage handbook of gender and psychology* (pp. 100–114). Sage. https://doi.org/10.4135/9781446269930.n7

Byrd-Craven, J., Geary, D. C., Rose, A. J., & Ponzi, D. (2008). Co-ruminating increases stress hormone levels in women. *Hormones and Behavior, 53*(3), 489–492. https://doi.org/10.1016/https://doi.org/10.1016/j.yhbeh.2007.12.002

Byrd-Craven, J., Granger, D. A., & Auer, B. J. (2011). Stress reactivity to co-rumination in young women's friendships: Cortisol, alpha-amylase, and negative affect focus. *Journal of Social and Personal Relationships, 28*(4), 469–487. https://doi.org/10.1177/0265407510382319

Caldwell, M. A., & Peplau, L. A. (1982). Sex differences in same-sex friendship. *Sex Roles, 8*(7), 721–732. https://doi.org/10.1007/BF00287568

Carlucci, L., D'Ambrosio, I., Innamorati, M., Saggino, A., & Balsamo, M. (2018). Co-rumination, anxiety, and maladaptive cognitive schemas: When friendship can hurt. *Psychology Research and Behavior Management, 11*, 133–144. https://doi.org/10.2147/PRBM.S144907

Chartrand, T. L., & Bargh, J. A. (1999). The chameleon effect: The perception-behavior link and social interaction. *Journal of Personality and Social Psychology, 76*(6), 893–910. https://doi.org/10.1037/0022-3514.76.6.893

Cohen, S., Underwood, L. G., & Gottlieb, B. H. (Eds.). (2000). *Social support measurement and intervention: A guide for health and social scientists*. Oxford University Press. https://doi.org/10.1093/med:psych/9780195126709.001.0001

Collaer, M. L., & Hines, M. (1995). Human behavioral sex differences: A role for gonadal hormones during early development? *Psychological Bulletin, 118*(1), 55–107. https://doi.org/10.1037/0033-2909.118.1.55

Cook, E. C. (2020). Affective and physiological synchrony in friendships during late adolescence. *Journal of Social and Personal Relationships, 37*(4), 1296–1316. https://doi.org/10.1177/0265407519895106

Crawford, C. B., & Krebs, D. L. (Eds.). (1998). *Handbook of evolutionary psychology: Ideas, issues, and applications*. Lawrence Erlbaum Associates.

Davis, M. H. (1983). Measuring individual differences in empathy: Evidence for a multidimensional approach. *Journal of Personality and Social Psychology, 44*(1), 113–126. https://doi.org/10.1037/0022-3514.44.1.113

Davis, M. H., Mitchell, K. V., Hall, J. A., Lothert, J., Snapp, T., & Meyer, M. (1999). Empathy, expectations, and situational preferences: Personality influences on the decision to participate in volunteer helping behaviors. *Journal of Personality, 67*(3), 469–503. https://doi.org/10.1111/1467-6494.00062

Decety, J., & Jackson, P. L. (2004). The functional architecture of human empathy. *Behavioral and Cognitive Neuroscience Reviews, 3*(2), 71–100. https://doi.org/10.1177/1534582304267187

Decety, J., & Jackson, P. L. (2006). A social-neuroscience perspective on empathy. *Current Directions in Psychological Science, 15*(2), 54–58. https://doi.org/10.1111/j.0963-7214.2006.00406.x

de Waal, F. B. M. (2008). Putting the altruism back into altruism: The evolution of empathy. *Annual Review of Psychology, 59*(1), 279–300. https://doi.org/10.1146/annurev.psych.59.103006.093625

Dishion, T. J., & Tipsord, J. M. (2011). Peer contagion in child and adolescent social and emotional development. *Annual Review of Psychology, 62*(1), 189–214. https://doi.org/10.1146/annurev.psych.093008.100412

Doherty, R. W. (1997). The emotional contagion scale: A measure of individual differences. *Journal of Nonverbal Behavior, 21*(2), 131–154. https://doi.org/10.1023/A:1024956003661

Eisenberg, N. (1991). Values, sympathy, and individual differences: Toward a pluralism of factors influencing altruism and empathy. *Psychological Inquiry, 2*(2), 128–131. https://doi.org/10.1207/s15327965pli0202_5

Eisenberg, N., & Fabes, R. A. (1998). Prosocial development. In W. Damon & N. Eisenberg (Ed.), *Handbook of child psychology: Social, emotional, and personality development* (5th ed., Vol. 3, pp. 701–778). John Wiley & Sons.

Eisenberg, N., Fabes, R. A., Bustamante, D., & Mathy, R. M. (1987). Physiological indices of empathy. In N. Eisenberg & J. Strayer (Eds.), *Empathy and its development*. (pp. 380–385). Cambridge University Press.

Eisenberg, N., & Lennon, R. (1983). Sex differences in empathy and related capacities. *Psychological Bulletin, 94*(1), 100–131. https://doi.org/10.1037/0033-2909.94.1.100

Flavell, J. H. (1999). Cognitive development: Children's knowledge about the mind. *Annual Review of Psychology, 50*, 21–45. https://doi.org/10.1146/annurev.psych.50.1.21

Geary, D. C. (2010). *Male, female: The evolution of human sex differences* (2nd ed.). American Psychological Association.

Geary, D. C., Byrd-Craven, J., Hoard, M. K., Vigil, J., & Numtee, C. (2003). Evolution and development of boys' social behavior. *Developmental Review, 23*(4), 444–470. https://doi.org/10.1016/j.dr.2003.08.001

Geary, D. C., & Flinn, M. V. (2002). Sex differences in behavioral and hormonal response to social threat: Commentary on Taylor et al. (2000). *Psychological Review, 109*(4), 745–753. https://doi.org/10.1037/0033-295X.109.4.745

Golland, Y., Arzouan, Y., & Levit-Binnun, N. (2015). The mere co-presence: Synchronization of autonomic signals and emotional responses across co-present individuals not engaged in direct interaction. *PLoS ONE, 10*(5), e0125804. https://doi.org/10.1371/journal.pone.0125804

Haggard, D. L., Robert, C., & Rose, A. J. (2011). Co-rumination in the workplace: Adjustment trade-offs for men and women who engage in excessive discussions of workplace problems. *Journal of Business and Psychology, 26*(1), 27–40. https://doi.org/10.1007/s10869-010-9169-2

Hall, J. K., Hutton, S. B., & Morgan, M. J. (2010). Sex differences in scanning faces: Does attention to the eyes explain female superiority in facial expression recognition? *Cognition and Emotion, 24*(4), 629–637. https://doi.org/10.1080/02699930902906882

Harwood, M. D., & Farrar, M. J. (2006). Conflicting emotions: The connection between affective perspective taking and theory of mind. *British Journal of Developmental Psychology, 24*(2), 401–418. https://doi.org/10.1348/026151005X50302

Hatfield, E., Cacioppo, J. T., & Rapson, R. L. (1993). Emotional contagion. *Current Directions in Psychological Science, 2*(3), 96–100. https://doi.org/10.1111/1467-8721.ep10770953

Hess, N. H. (2006). *Informational warfare: Female friendship and the coalitional manipulation of reputation* (Publication No. 3206400) [Doctoral dissertation, University of California Santa Barbara]. ProQuest Dissertations and Theses.

Hess, N. H. (2017). Informational warfare: Coalitional gossiping as a strategy for within-group aggression. In M. L. Fisher (Ed.), *The Oxford handbook of women and competition*. (pp. 223–246). Oxford University Press.

Hess, N. H., & Hagen, E. H. (2006). Psychological adaptations for assessing gossip veracity. *Human Nature, 17*(3), 337–354. https://doi.org/10.1007/s12110-006-1013-z

Hess, N. H., & Hagen, E. H. (2019). Gossip, reputation, and friendship in within-group competition. In F. Giardini & R. Wittek (Eds.), *The Oxford handbook of gossip and reputation* (pp. 274–302). Oxford University Press. https://doi.org/10.1093/oxfordhb/9780190494087.013.15

Hoffman, M. L. (1975). Altruistic behavior and the parent-child relationship. *Journal of Personality and Social Psychology, 31*(5), 937–943. https://doi.org/10.1037/h0076825

Hoffman, M. L. (1977). Sex differences in empathy and related behaviors. *Psychological Bulletin, 84*(4), 712–722. https://doi.org/10.1037/0033-2909.84.4.712

Hoffman, M. L. (2000). *Empathy and moral development*. Cambridge University Press. https://doi.org/10.1017/cbo9780511805851

Humphrey, N. K. (1976). The social function of intellect. In P. P. G. Bateson & R. A. Hinde (Eds.), *Growing points in ethology* (pp. 303–317). Cambridge University Press.

Iacoboni, M. (2009). Imitation, empathy, and mirror neurons. *Annual Review of Psychology, 60*(1), 653–670. https://doi.org/10.1146/annurev.psych.60.110707.163604

Joiner, T. E. (1994). Contagious depression: Existence, specificity to depressed symptoms, and the role of reassurance seeking. *Journal of Personality and Social Psychology, 67*(2), 287–296. https://doi.org/10.1037/0022-3514.67.2.287

Kimura, M., Daibo, I., & Yogo, M. (2008). The study of emotional contagion from the perspective of interpersonal relationships. *Social Behavior and Personality, 36*(1), 27–42. https://doi.org/10.2224/sbp.2008.36.1.27

Krems, J. A., Williams, K. E. G., Aktipis, A., & Kenrick, D. T. (2021). Friendship jealousy: One tool for maintaining friendships in the face of third-party threats? *Journal of Personality and Social Psychology, 120*(4), 977–1012. https://doi.org/10.1037/pspi0000311

Lakin, J. L., Jefferis, V. E., Cheng, C. M., & Chartrand, T. L. (2003). The chameleon effect as social glue: Evidence for the evolutionary significance of nonconscious mimicry. *Journal of Nonverbal Behavior, 27*(3), 145–162. https://doi.org/10.1023/A:1025389814290

Lewis, D. M. G., Conroy-Beam, D., Al-Shawaf, L., Raja, A., DeKay, T., & Buss, D. M. (2011). Friends with benefits: The evolved psychology of same- and opposite-sex friendship. *Evolutionary Psychology, 9*(4), 543–563. https://doi.org/10.1177/147470491100900407

Maccoby, E. E. (1998). *The two sexes: Growing up apart, coming together*. Harvard University Press.

Maccoby, E. E., & Jacklin, C. N. (1987). Gender segregation in childhood. *Advances in Child Development and Behavior, 20*(C), 239–287. https://doi.org/10.1016/S0065-2407(08)60404-8

Nakahashi, W., & Ohtsuki, H. (2015). When is emotional contagion adaptive? *Journal of Theoretical Biology, 380*, 480–488. https://doi.org/10.1016/j.jtbi.2015.06.014

Neumann, R., & Strack, F. (2000). "Mood contagion": The automatic transfer of mood between persons. *Journal of Personality and Social Psychology, 79*(2), 211–223. https://doi.org/10.1037/0022-3514.79.2.211

Oberman, L. M., & Ramachandran, V. S. (2007). The simulating social mind: The role of the mirror neuron system and simulation in the social and communicative deficits of autism spectrum disorders. *Psychological Bulletin, 133*(2), 310–327. https://doi.org/10.1037/0033-2909.133.2.310

Palumbo, R. V., Marraccini, M. E., Weyandt, L. L., Wilder-Smith, O., McGee, H. A., Liu, S., & Goodwin, M. S. (2017). Interpersonal autonomic physiology: A systematic review of the literature. *Personality and Social Psychology Review, 21*(2), 99–141. https://doi.org/10.1177/1088868316628405

Premack, D., & Woodruff, G. (1978). Does the chimpanzee have a theory of mind? *Behavioral and Brain Sciences, 1*(4), 515–526. https://doi.org/10.1017/S0140525X00076512

Preston, S. D., & de Waal, F. B. M. (2002). Empathy: Its ultimate and proximate bases. *Behavioral and Brain Sciences, 25*(1), 1–20. https://doi.org/10.1017/S0140525X02000018

Rankin, A., Garza, R., & Byrd-Craven, J. (2021). The endocrinology of female friendships: Cortisol and progesterone attunement after separation. *Biological Psychology, 161*, 108059. https://doi.org/10.1016/j.biopsycho.2021.108059

Rankin, A., Swearingen-Stanborough, C. S., Granger, D. A., & Byrd-Craven, J. (2018). The role of co-rumination and adrenocortical attunement in young women's close friendships. *Psychoneuroendocrinology, 98*, 61–66. https://doi.org/10.1016/j.psyneuen.2018.07.027

Reynolds, T. A. (2022). Our grandmothers' legacy: Challenges faced by female ancestors leave traces in modern women's same-sex relationships. *Archives of Sexual Behavior, 51*(7), 3225–3256.

Rose, A. J. (2002). Co-rumination in the friendships of girls and boys. *Child Development, 73*(6), 1830–1843. https://doi.org/10.1111/1467-8624.00509

Rose, A. J., & Rudolph, K. D. (2006). A review of sex differences in peer relationship processes: Potential trade-offs for the emotional and behavioral development of girls and boys. *Psychological Bulletin, 132*(1), 98–131. https://doi.org/10.1037/0033-2909.132.1.98

Rose, A. J., Schwartz-Mette, R. A., Glick, G. C., Smith, R. L., & Luebbe, A. M. (2014). An observational study of co-rumination in adolescent friendships. *Developmental Psychology, 50*(9), 2199–2209. https://doi.org/10.1037/a0037465

Schwartz-Mette, R. A., & Rose, A. J. (2012). Co-rumination mediates contagion of internalizing symptoms within youths' friendships. *Developmental Psychology, 48*(5), 1355–1365. https://doi.org/10.1037/a0027484

Schwartz-Mette, R. A., & Smith, R. L. (2018). When does co-rumination facilitate depression contagion in adolescent friendships? Investigating intrapersonal and interpersonal factors. *Journal of Clinical Child and Adolescent Psychology, 47*(6), 912–924. https://doi.org/10.1080/15374416.2016.1197837

Shen, J., & Itti, L. (2012). Top-down influences on visual attention during listening are modulated by observer sex. *Vision Research, 65*, 62–76. https://doi.org/10.1016/j.visres.2012.06.001

Shirtcliff, E. A., Vitacco, M. J., Graf, A. R., Gostisha, A. J., Merz, J. L., & Zahn-Waxler, C. (2009). Neurobiology of empathy and callousness: Implications for the development of antisocial behavior. *Behavioral Sciences and the Law, 27*(2), 137–171. https://doi.org/10.1002/bsl.862

Singer, T. (2006). The neuronal basis and ontogeny of empathy and mind reading: Review of literature and implications for future research. *Neuroscience and Biobehavioral Reviews, 30*(6), 855–863. https://doi.org/10.1016/j.neubiorev.2006.06.011

Smith, A. (2006). Cognitive empathy and emotional empathy in human behavior and evolution. *Psychological Record, 56*(1), 3–21. https://doi.org/10.1007/BF03395534

Smith, R. L., & Rose, A. J. (2011). The "cost of caring" in youths' friendships: Considering associations among social perspective taking, co-rumination, and empathetic distress. *Developmental Psychology, 47*(6), 1792–1803. https://doi.org/10.1037/a0025309

Spendelow, J. S., Simonds, L. M., & Avery, R. E. (2017). The relationship between co-rumination and internalizing problems: A systematic review and meta-analysis. *Clinical Psychology and Psychotherapy, 24*(2), 512–527. https://doi.org/10.1002/cpp.2023

Stone, L. B., Mennies, R. J., Waller, J. M., Ladouceur, C. D., Forbes, E. E., Ryan, N. D., Dahl, R. E., & Silk, J. S. (2019). Help me feel better! Ecological momentary assessment of anxious youths' emotion regulation with parents and peers. *Journal of Abnormal Child Psychology, 47*(2), 313–324. https://doi.org/10.1007/s10802-018-0454-2

Sznycer, D., Sell, A., & Lieberman, D. (2021). Forms and functions of the social emotions. *Current Directions in Psychological Science, 30*(4), 292–299. https://doi.org/10.1177/09637214211007451

Taylor, S. E., Klein, L. C., Lewis, B. P., Gruenewald, T. L., Gurung, R. A., & Updegraff, J. A. (2000). Biobehavioral responses to stress in females: tend-and-befriend, not fight-or-flight. *Psychological Review, 107*(3), 411–429. https://doi.org/10.1037/0033-295X.107.3.411

Tooby, J., & Cosmides, L. (1992). The psychological foundations of culture. In J. H. Barkow, L. Cosmides, & J. Tooby (Eds.), *The adapted mind: Evolutionary psychology and the generation of culture* (pp. 19–136). Oxford University Press.

Tooby, J., & Cosmides, L. (1996). Friendship and the banker's paradox: Other pathways to the evolution of adaptations for altruism. In W. G. Runciman, J. M. Smith, & R. I. M. Dunbar (Eds.), *Evolution of social behaviour patterns in primates and man* (pp. 119–143). Oxford University Press.

Tooby, J., & Cosmides, L. (2008). The evolutionary psychology of the emotions and their relationship to internal regulatory variables. In M. Lewis, J. M. Haviland-Jones, & L. F. Barrett (Eds.) *Handbook of emotions* (3rd ed., pp. 114–137). Guilford Press.

Trivers, R. L. (1971). The evolution of reciprocal altruism. *The Quarterly Review of Biology, 46*(1), 35–57. https://doi.org/10.1086/406755

Vigil, J. M. (2007). Asymmetries in the friendship preferences and social styles of men and women. *Human Nature, 18*(2), 143–161. https://doi.org/10.1007/s12110-007-9003-3

Waller, E. M., & Rose, A. J. (2013). Brief report: Adolescents' co-rumination with mothers, co-rumination with friends, and internalizing symptoms. *Journal of Adolescence, 36*(2), 429–433. https://doi.org/10.1016/j.adolescence.2012.12.006

Watt, D. (2007). Toward a neuroscience of empathy: Integrating affective and cognitive perspectives. *Neuropsychoanalysis, 9*(2), 146–151. https://doi.org/10.1080/15294145.2007.10773550

Zarbatany, L., Hartmann, D. P., Gelfand, D. M., & Vinciguerra, P. (1985). Gender differences in altruistic reputation: Are they artifactual? *Developmental Psychology, 21*(1), 97–101. https://doi.org/10.1037/0012-1649.21.1.97

CHAPTER 39

An Evolutionary Approach to Emotion Regulation

Michael A. Kisley

> **Abstract**
> Emotion regulation includes a broad and diverse array of cognitive and behavioral phenomena, the common underlying feature being the explicit, voluntary alteration of one's emotions. Given the critical adaptive and system-coordinating functions that emotional responses provide, it is not immediately clear why the ability to modify one's emotions would have evolved. But, as argued here, emotion regulation can increase reproductive success through a number of mechanisms including improved management of threats and competitive situations, flexible adjustment to social environments, and the advantageous expenditure of limited physiological, cognitive, and behavioral resources. So-called maladaptive emotion regulation is also considered from an evolutionary perspective. Sex differences, sexual selection, cultural relativity, and certain behaviors in non-human animals are also discussed, given their relevance to an evolutionary understanding of emotion regulation. This review is anticipated to be of relevance to emotion regulation researchers, as well as to evolutionary psychologists who study emotion function.
>
> **Key Words:** emotion regulation, evolution, self-control, self-regulation, emotional suppression

Emotion regulation refers to attempts by an individual to modify their emotions. This includes but is not limited to influencing which emotion is present in a given situation, the intensity or duration of an emotional response to a particular stimulus, and the behavioral expression of an emotion (Gross, 1998, 2014). Typically, one employs several different approaches to modifying their emotions throughout each day (English et al., 2017). For example, the strategy of *attentional deployment* might involve directing one's attention away from a stimulus that would otherwise elicit an uncomfortable emotion, such as ignoring another person's flagrant behavior in order to avoid becoming upset. By contrast, *cognitive reappraisal* involves attempting to reinterpret a situation to modify one's emotional response, for example telling oneself that the individual behaving flagrantly may have just experienced a trauma, and their behavior is therefore excusable.

Despite a vast research literature on emotion regulation (a search for the terms "emotion regulation" and "regulation of emotion" at the time of writing revealed over 14,000 entries in SCOPUS), very few researchers have considered the potential adaptive nature of emotion regulation from an evolutionary perspective. Given that emotions are inherently adaptive functions (Izard, 1972) and of fundamental importance (Plutchik, 1980), it will be important to understand why emotion regulation, that is, the ability to modify one's emotions, would have evolved at all. By coordinating the activity of physiological, cognitive, and behavioral systems, emotions help organisms solve *adaptive problems* (Tooby & Cosmides, 2008). For example, by increasing the body's readiness for action through both sympathetic nervous system and hormonal activation, focusing attention and perceptual processing on threat-related cues in the immediate environment, and impelling one to take self-protective action such as running or hiding, fear helps an animal solve the adaptive problem of predator avoidance (Al-Shawaf et al., 2016). This is adaptive because it increases the likelihood that the animal will survive to reproduce, and thus contribute its genetic material to future generations (Tooby & Cosmides, 1990). Given this, what would be the adaptive value of purposefully changing one's emotions, and consequently modifying the associated functional outcomes? Put another way, what adaptive problem does emotion regulation solve?

Although emotion regulation has been argued to be *adaptive*, to date such arguments have been limited primarily to *proximate* as opposed to *ultimate* considerations, the latter being the common currency of evolutionary biology and evolutionary psychology. For example, *pro-hedonic goals*, specifically to experience pleasure and avoid pain, will tend to motivate one to upregulate pleasant emotions such as happiness and downregulate unpleasant emotions such as fear (Bloore et al., 2020; Gross, 2014; Larsen, 2000). But even if one succeeds in experiencing more emotional comfort, it is not clear why this by itself would necessarily be "adaptive." In fact, as argued below, it may often be *maladaptive* from an evolutionary perspective. *Instrumental goals* motivate one to regulate emotions in a manner that leads to the achievement of longer-term objectives, even when those emotions are considered largely *contra-hedonic*. For example, it has been shown that individuals who engage in activities that upregulate their anger, such as listening to anger-consonant music, subsequently perform better in a confrontation-based game (Tamir et al., 2008). Other so-called adaptive outcomes of emotion regulation have been argued to include greater feelings of well-being, fewer symptoms of psychopathology, higher academic achievement, and more social connections (reviewed by McRae & Gross, 2020). But by limiting consideration to only proximate outcomes, *adaptiveness* remains subjectively dependent upon the unique long-term goals of each individual person (Mauss & Tamir, 2014), and the values of the culture in which they reside (Mesquita et al., 2014). This limited viewpoint has contributed to the "disorganized" state of the emotion regulation literature (Bloore et al., 2020).

The term *maladaptive* has also been applied inconsistently in the emotion regulation literature. Some consider emotion regulation maladaptive when the proximate outcomes of modifying one's emotions are essentially the opposite of those listed above, including for example increased symptoms of psychopathology (Gross & Jazaieri, 2014). Others consider certain forms of emotion regulation, such as *rumination, expressive suppression*, and *experiential avoidance*, to always be maladaptive regardless of the context in which they are employed (Aldao & Nolen-Hoeksema, 2012). This relativism and lack of consistency in the emotion regulation literature stems from two broader problems. First, as discussed above, there is not consensus on what makes for *adaptive* emotion regulation. Second, and related to this, there is no widely accepted theoretical framework for understanding emotion regulation that can account for the pattern of findings across the literature (Naragon-Gainey et al., 2017). Conceptualizing emotion regulation from an evolutionary perspective, specifically by investigating its contribution to *reproductive success*, shows promise for helping to remedy these issues.

What Is Emotion Regulation?

The influential Process Model provides a framework for understanding how (as opposed to why) different emotion regulation strategies are deployed at different stages of the emotion generation process, in order to modify the emotion that results (Gross, 1998, 2014; McRae & Gross, 2020). *Antecedent-focused* strategies, including attentional deployment and cognitive reappraisal, mentioned above, change the way that incoming information is initially appraised, and consequently the specific emotion and/or emotional intensity that is subsequently evoked. In *situation selection*, one voluntarily selects a situation in order to regulate their emotions, such as deciding not to attend a party with strangers in order to avoid the emotional discomfort one is likely to experience. By contrast, a *situation modification* approach to the same party might involve bringing a friend to hopefully avoid the emotional awkwardness associated with not knowing anyone. *Expressive suppression* is a *response-focused* approach because it involves trying to modify the emotional response that has already been elicited; typically hiding, to the extent possible, outward behavioral signs of an emotion, including but not limited to facial expressions. Additional strategies of emotion regulation not originally presented in the process model have been described (reviewed by Naragon-Gainey et al., 2017), including mindfulness-based approaches that emphasize awareness and acceptance of the physiological, cognitive, and subjective aspects of emotion, which lead to less intense and shorter duration emotional responses (Roemer et al., 2015).

Emotion can be regulated by both *explicit* (voluntary, controlled) and *implicit* (involuntary, automatic) factors. Dampening, or habituation, of an emotional response due to repeated exposure to a stimulus is an example of implicit regulation, because it tends to occur automatically (Gyurak & Etkin, 2014). Other implicit regulation examples include changes in one's immune capacity and overall physical health that modify emotional responses without voluntary control (Miller et al., 2005). But such implicit factors overlap substantially with what has been described as the "contextual dependence" of an emotional response (Al-Shawaf et al., 2016). Put another way, it can be difficult to disentangle implicit regulation of emotion from the emotional response itself (Gyurak & Etkin, 2014). As such, the focus of the present chapter will be on voluntary emotion regulation.

Emotion regulation researchers have also been careful to distinguish between *intrinsic* regulation, or self-regulation, and *extrinsic* regulation for which emotions are modified by the influence of another (recently reviewed by Lindsey, 2020). For example, a toddler's emotional response to the appearance of a stranger will differ depending upon—that it, will be regulated by—the presence/absence of their primary caregiver, as well as the quality of their relationship with that caregiver (Ainsworth et al., 1978). The function and importance of this form of relational regulation has previously been argued for from an evolutionary perspective (Bowlby, 1969). By contrast, and as discussed above, the evolutionary adaptiveness of intrinsic emotion regulation has received relatively little consideration, and will therefore receive greater attention here. The present review thus concerns the potential adaptive nature of voluntary self-regulation of emotion from an evolutionary perspective.

Before considering the potential adaptive value of emotion regulation, it is important to address the following question: Is it possible to disentangle voluntary emotion regulation from the emotional response itself? Given that emotions are conceptualized here as *superordinate mechanisms* that coordinate multiple aspects of the emotional response, including importantly cognitive and behavioral aspects (Al-Shawaf et al., 2016; Tooby & Cosmides, 2008), one could argue that the forms of explicit emotion regulation described above are simply a sub-part of an emotional response (Gross & Feldman Barrett, 2011; Kappas, 2011). And further, a behavioral response caused by an emotional reaction will tend to modify that emotion, but there is no reason to consider that to represent a separate process from the emotional response per se. Reconsideration of a classic example can help clarify this issue and address these concerns: a lone individual outside their camp at night detects a sound that suggests a nearby predator

(Tooby & Cosmides, 2008). This leads to the emotion of fear, which coordinates multiple processes, including a change in immediate goals from food-gathering to self-protection, physiological arousal of the body, increased vigilance and attention directed toward the source of the sound, engagement of additional cognitive resources including quickly scanning memory for possible nearby hiding locations, and ultimately a behavioral response of running and hiding. Once out of danger from the predator, as a direct result of the behavioral response, the emotion of fear will be modified; more specifically, it will be reduced. Wouldn't this be considered emotion regulation in the current conceptualization? No, explicit emotion regulation would involve an attempt to *directly modify one's emotion without necessarily undertaking an action in response to, and congruent with, that emotion.* Such regulation in this example might take the form of cognitive reappraisal, attempting to dampen fear by telling oneself, "It's probably just the wind." In addition to illustrating the difference between an emotion response and emotion regulation, this particular example highlights the critical need for explaining the evolution of emotion regulation. Utilized in this particular way, emotion regulation appears to be potentially maladaptive, because it could decrease one's reproductive success by increasing the risk of predation. Given this, why did humans evolve the capacity to change their emotions? Relatedly, in which situations is emotion regulation adaptive in an ultimate sense?

Why Regulate Emotions?

Explaining emotion regulation from an evolutionary perspective requires consideration of the adaptive problems that this function solves. More specifically, the outcomes of emotion regulation need ultimately to be related back to reproductive success, that is, the likelihood that an animal will convey genes into future generations. The chances of doing so can be improved in multiple ways, including, for example, mate acquisition, sexual reproduction, as well as the survival of offspring to reproductive maturity through successful parenting and/or the provision of critical resources (Tooby & Cosmides, 1990). By contrast, the vast majority of emotion regulation research to date has been framed from functionalist theories of emotion regulation emphasizing proximate outcomes such as attainment of personal or culturally specified goals, subjective well-being, and apparent success as defined by contemporary society. Of course, attainment of some of these goals can also contribute to reproductive success. Indeed, because relatively little research on emotion regulation has been framed from an evolutionary perspective to date, this review also draws from literature framed around such proximate goals in order to assemble a body of evidence to support the adaptive nature of emotion regulation from the perspective of improved reproductive success. Recommendations for more targeted evolutionary-framed research going forward are provided here as well.

Instrumental Outcomes

Emotion regulation has been shown to improve the outcome of emotionally laden situations for individuals in ways that could contribute to their reproductive success. Of immediate relevance, a mindfulness-based emotion regulation intervention has been shown to nearly double the rate of successful pregnancy induction in women undergoing in vitro fertilization (Li et al., 2016; for a review of additional studies, see Frederiksen et al., 2015). Direct connections like this between a psychological function and reproductive outcomes are exceptional, both in the context of emotion regulation and throughout evolutionary psychology more broadly. Indirect evidence for improved reproductive success is often provided by demonstrations of outcomes that increase access to potential mating opportunities, such as competitive advantages in contests and improved resource acquisition (Puts, 2010; Stockley & Campbell, 2013). Indeed, emotion regulation can increase the likelihood of such outcomes. For example, it has been shown that voluntarily upregulating anger leads to improved performance in a confrontational video game (Tamir et al., 2008). In another study, upregulation of anger also improved outcomes for individuals engaged in contentious social negotiations over limited resources (Tamir & Ford, 2012). This general effect is apparently not limited to confrontational behaviors. Tamir and Ford (2012) also showed that individuals assigned to upregulate happiness performed better during a "collaborative" negotiation involving limited resources.

Resource acquisition is also improved by emotion regulation during the ultimatum game (van't Wout et al., 2010). In this game, one participant offers a share of $10 to another participant, such as "I keep $8, you get $2." The participant who receives the offer can turn it down, in which case neither participant receives anything. In most versions of this game, especially when the players do not know each other and are only playing a single round, it is unreasonable for the second participant to turn down *any* non-zero offer, because they do not gain any resources by doing so. Yet participants reliably turn down offers perceived as unfair, especially in the $8/$2 and $9/$1 range, apparently to punish the other player who made the offer (reviewed by Debove et al., 2016). However, the cognitive reappraisal instructions "adopt a neutral attitude . . . view the offers with detached interest or try to come up with possible reasons why someone might give you a certain offer," led the second participant to accept such imbalanced offers significantly more often (van't Wout et al., 2010). Whereas the other studies described above provide evidence that upregulating emotion that is congruent with a situation can improve outcomes, this last example demonstrates that emotion regulation can also be employed to reduce the interference of emotion in the pursuit of adaptive goals. Taken together, these findings suggest that emotion regulation can increase one's evolutionary fitness through flexible adaptation to the unique circumstances presented by each situation.

Flexible Adjustment to Social Environmental Conditions

Although emotions evolved to solve adaptive problems that recur throughout the evolutionary past of humans and our ancestor species, it has been argued that *effortful control* of those emotions may also be adaptive because it allows one to better align their emotional responses to rapidly changing and novel environmental contexts (MacDonald, 2008). Although this might include the physical environment, the behavioral flexibility conferred through voluntary emotion regulation is anticipated to be especially relevant to social environments. For example, killing a rival in response to the emotion of sexual jealousy may be adaptive in a narrow sense because it reduces sexual competition, but maladaptive within social contexts for which such action will lead to ostracism or punishment, and/or when the likelihood of retaliation by the victim's kin is high (MacDonald, 2008). Emotion regulation may also play a role in *developmental plasticity*, whereby an organism's behavior develops to fit adaptively within the physical and social parameters of their immediate environment, including such variables as access to food and mates, level of parental investment, and frequency and forms of social competition (Ellis & Del Giudice, 2019). One way in which individuals flexibly adapt to such circumstances is through the formation of different relationship attachment *styles* that fit best within the social environment in which one developed, and that have been argued to increase one's reproductive success within that environment (Belsky, 1997; Del Giudice, 2009). These styles of relating to others, including the ways children relate to their caregivers, and the ways sexual partners relate to each other, are each associated with very different patterns of emotion regulation: whereas *anxiously attached* individuals tend to engage in behaviors and cognitions that *up*regulate emotions associated with close relationships, *avoidantly attached* individuals tend to do the opposite, engaging in behaviors and cognitions that lead to emotion *down*regulation (Cassidy, 1994; Kisley et al., 2019).

Belonging to a social group provides adaptive benefits, including shared labor, resources, and information, cooperative food gathering and hunting, diffusion of exposure to risk and cooperative defense against threats, increased access to reproductive opportunities, and help with care for offspring (reviewed by Baumeister & Leary, 1995). Thus, if emotion regulation improves one's ability to navigate social environments, it could thereby improve reproductive success. Indeed, at least in modern contexts, people frequently and regularly engage in emotion regulation in order to address socially relevant goals such as impression management, which contributes to perceived status and mate acquisition, as well as avoiding conflicts and "making others feel better," both of which can strengthen social bonds (English et al., 2017). Expressive suppression in particular can be useful for "keeping up appearances," by not revealing one's current emotional state to others (English et al., 2017; Soto et al., 2011). In addition to broadly improving one's social function and connectedness, emotion regulation contributes to the successful navigation of the unique and varied social norms and practices that characterize the social environment within which an individual functions (Mesquita et al., 2014; Tamir et al., 2016).

It has been argued that the adaptive benefits of social belonging have exerted selective pressures specifically on emotional processes throughout the evolution of the human ancestral lineage. For example, it has been suggested that humans were selected for *pro-sociality* (Hare, 2017), and an important part of this is process was the improved cooperative communication that resulted from reductions in "emotional reactivity" (Hare & Tomasello, 2005; see also Koch et al., 2018). Similarly, MacLean (2016) has argued that "self-control" and the ability to "inhibit" aggression can lead to the formation of more stable social groups. Although these researchers do not specifically make reference to voluntary emotion regulation in their arguments, such a mechanism may be an especially adaptive one for modulating emotion because it would allow for flexible modification of emotional processes in order to better navigate novel and changing social conditions, without a generalized dampening of emotional reactivity that could weaken the coordinating function of emotions in solving other adaptive problems.

Energy Economics

Emotional responses are expensive from an energy consumption standpoint: an emotion coordinates and mobilizes multiple physiological, cognitive, and behavioral systems in response to a given situation (Tooby & Cosmides, 1990). As such, being able to flexibly modify emotional responses, downregulating them in particular, could allow an individual to save valuable energy and resources that could be redirected toward other functions in direct support of reproductive success. Of course, this will not be adaptive in all situations. The example provided above in which one reappraises the sounds of a predator as something non-threatening will save energy, but will also increase the likelihood of being injured or killed. By contrast, refusing to gather food after dark in order to avoid the emotion fear (an example of situation selection) will save energy without compromising immediate safety. Additional examples provided below highlight the potential for saving cognitive, behavioral, and physiological resources typically expended by an emotion through explicit regulation.

SAVING ATTENTIONAL RESOURCES

Emotions are distracting in the sense that they redirect one's attention, a cognitive resource, toward the stimulus which evoked the emotion, and away from one's intended attentional target (Öhman et al., 2001; Pratto & John, 1991). Although such distractions can alert one to a real threat, or redirect one's attention to an unexpected adaptive opportunity, more often than not such emotional distractions tend to be disruptive. This is consistent with a study that assessed the reasons why individuals engage in emotion regulation during daily life (English et al., 2017). Among the reasons commonly endorsed for routinely regulating emotions was to allow one to "get work done." This supports the idea that people are motivated to regulate their emotions in order to regulate their attention. Additional studies, described immediately below, more directly demonstrate that people are able to strategically save attentional resources through such efforts.

Measurements of brain electrical activity provide evidence that emotion regulation can save attentional and associated neural processing resources. By cognitively reappraising the meaning of emotional pictures, one can downregulate the amplitude of a specific scalp-recorded event-related potential associated with attention allocation (reviewed by Hajcak et al., 2010). For example, some of these studies have involved "reframing" the emotional significance of images through language: instead of targeting "negative" images, asking participants to watch for images that are "not positive" led to decreases in brain response amplitudes to emotionally unpleasant images (Kisley et al., 2011). In a related study, categorizing images as "less positive" rather than "more negative" had a similar effect (though only in a sample of young adults; Rehmert & Kisley, 2013). Of more direct relevance to reproductive success, it has been shown that reappraising one's own mating market value (e.g., telling oneself, "I am hot") changes the allocation of attention toward potential mates based on their attractiveness in a manner consistent with the strategic saving of attentional resources (Morgan & Kisley, 2014). Specifically, when their self-rated market value was appraised to be higher, male participants showed smaller scalp-recorded event-related potential responses to images of women rated as less attractive, despite large, sustained responses to images of women rated as more attractive. Put another way, by upregulating their confidence, these men were effectively ignoring less desirable potential mates.

SAVING BEHAVIORAL RESOURCES

Emotion downregulation has also been shown to reduce behavioral expenditures associated with emotional responses. To date, this has primarily been shown with electromyographic measurements of facial muscle activity. Inducing unpleasant emotions tends to increase the amplitude of facial muscle contractions that result from presentation of a startling sensory stimulus such as a loud sound (Lang et al., 1990). But voluntary emotion downregulation leads to reductions in such startle responses, reliably demonstrated with large effect sizes (Zaehringer et al., 2020). Downregulation also reduces the contraction of facial muscles involved in emotional facial expression more generally, with medium effect sizes (Zaehringer et al., 2020). But the energy savings provided by emotion regulation on facial muscle contractions seem relatively minor. Although not yet quantified in the literature, presumably more substantial savings would result from the broader influence of emotion regulation on an individual's overall behavior. For example, an individual who successfully downregulates their anger may avoid an unnecessary confrontational contest with a rival, saving themselves both the energy expended during the confrontation, as well as the energy needed to repair any injuries that might result. Additional research will be required to verify this type of commonsense prediction.

SAVING PHYSIOLOGICAL RESOURCES

Studies of energy savings resulting from emotion regulation based on acute physiological measures have been mixed. Contrary to energy savings, the emotion regulation strategy of expression suppression actually *increases* sympathetic tone in the body (Levenson, 2003) which implies the expenditure of additional energy over and above the otherwise unaltered behavioral expression of the emotion. Cognitive reappraisal does not appear to reliably reduce sympathetic nervous system activation of the body based on measurements of skin conductance and pupil dilation (Zaehringer et al., 2020). Effects on cardiovascular variables, including heart rate and blood pressure, have been more reliably demonstrated, but they are generally small effects (Chen & Miller, 2014; Zaehringer et al., 2020). However, it is important to keep in mind that cognitive reappraisal can involve either downregulating emotion intensity or, alternatively, attempting to change the specific emotion experienced, and few studies have carefully dissociated these forms of reappraisal. Only the former would be expected to produce physiological savings. Indeed, it has been shown that skin conductance levels are significantly reduced in women by *detached reappraisal* where participants are instructed specifically to cognitively distance themselves from the emotional stimulus presented (Shiota & Levenson, 2012). Despite the relative lack of clear energy savings associated with acute sympathetic activation associated with emotion regulation, people who commonly use cognitive reappraisal strategies tend to have better health overall, and to be buffered from chronic stressors including, for example, low socioeconomic status (Chen & Miller, 2014). This suggests that potential physiological savings afforded by emotion regulation may be more demonstrable by considering one's long-standing practices as opposed to acute situations.

Are There Sex Differences in Emotion Regulation?

Because energy investment in sexual reproduction differs between female and male animals (Trivers, 1972), observation of sex differences in emotion regulation would provide additional evidence that this function can contribute to reproductive success. Female humans must invest substantially more energy into the biological reproductive process and, in general, also invest more energy in subsequent parenting of offspring than males (Geary, 2000). As such, women would have more reason than men to avoid engaging in every potential mating opportunity that arises (Buss & Schmitt, 1993), which may be predicted to correspond to a higher incidence of attempts to downregulate their emotions of attraction and desire associated with sexual encounters (MacDonald, 2008). On average, women do engage in emotion regulation more often than men (Nolen-Hoeksema & Aldao, 2011), and tend to be better able to voluntarily inhibit arousal associated with emotional responses (Bjorklund & Kipp, 1996), but this has not yet been directly studied within the context of mating opportunities. One study showed that training in emotion regulation techniques can delay first-time engagement in vaginal sex in adolescents, but sex differences were not assessed (Houck et al., 2018).

There is preliminary evidence that emotion regulation can impact sexual selection. In one study, women's faces expressing sadness were rated by men as less attractive than faces showing neutral or happy expressions (Mueser et al., 1984). Although not directly studied, this finding implies that downregulating sadness or upregulating happiness could increase perceived attractiveness of women, even if the regulation is only directed toward the behavioral facial expression component of each emotion. By contrast, the findings of another study imply that upregulating prideful expressions is more likely to increase the perceived attractiveness of men's faces. Tracy and Beall (2011) showed that men's expressions of happiness were rated by women as less attractive than prideful expressions, presumably consistent with pride's signal of status. Otherwise, more generally dampening emotional displays through emotion regulation may especially increase men's perceived desirability. A cross-cultural study of factors considered important in a potential mate found that women rated "emotional stability and maturity" to be of greater importance than men, although this was one of the smaller significant sex differences detected, and men also rated this factor as being relevant (Buss et al., 1990). A study of emotion regulation *motives* uncovered sex differences that could contribute to reproductive success. Timmers et al. (1998) found that men were more motivated to engage in regulation of emotional expression in order to demonstrate power and control, whereas women were more motivated to regulate emotional expression for the purposes of relationship maintenance.

Changes in emotion regulation occur in parallel with changes in female fertility, consistent with a role for emotion regulation in sex and reproduction. For example, the overall effectiveness of experimentally introduced emotion regulation strategies in modifying emotional experience varies over the course of the menstrual cycle (Olatunji et al., 2020). However, it is unknown whether women actually engage in emotion regulation more often during different phases of the cycle, for example during peak fertility. Further, this and other related studies to date have not directly investigated the impact and prevalence of emotion regulation specifically within reproductively relevant situations, such as sexual encounters. For example, whereas it has been shown that bodily physiological responses associated specifically with the emotion of *fear* are more strongly downregulated by cognitive reappraisal when levels of endogenous estradiol are at peak levels during the menstrual cycle (Graham et al., 2017), the impact of emotion regulation on *desire* during different phases of the cycle has not been assessed. Nevertheless, the consistently demonstrated relationship between the menstrual cycle and emotion regulation processes supports the idea that sex hormones are an "endogenous contextual factor" associated with emotion regulation in women (Graham et al., 2018).

Additional Important Questions
What Is Maladaptive Emotion Regulation?
It is important to distinguish "maladaptive" emotion regulation as defined from an evolutionary perspective from that based on more proximate considerations. Whereas the former can be defined as emotion regulation practices that negatively impact reproductive success, the latter is typically considered to be emotion regulation practices that are associated with increased rates of psychopathology and correspondingly reduced experiences of well-being, broadly defined (Gross & Jazaieri, 2014). Reproductive success and a sense of well-being often co-occur, but the one is not necessary for the other. Indeed, it has been argued that some forms of psychopathology can increase reproductive success within certain contexts (Ribeiro da Silva et al., 2015). For example, and as discussed above, the development of anxious and avoidant attachment styles, both considered to include pathological forms of emotion regulation, may nevertheless increase reproductive success within one's developmental social context (Belsky, 1997; Del Giudice, 2009). This certainly does not imply that any given emotion regulation practice that increases reproductive success is "right," or in any other sense desirable from the standpoint of an individual's values, including the values of the culture to which they belong. But understanding that emotion regulation practices which negatively impact one's sense of well-being may nevertheless increase their reproductive success could potentially help explain the relatively high prevalence of so-called emotion *misregulation* described in the literature.

On the other hand, given the mismatch between the modern environment and that which predominated during the vast majority of human evolution, it might be the case that the majority of emotion regulation practiced by modern humans does not clearly solve adaptive problems that would have been more prevalent and critical in the past. For example, contrary to the so-called instrumental motives for emotion regulation described above, where individuals regulate their emotions in order to obtain certain situational outcomes, most attempts to regulate emotions in modern contexts stem from pro-hedonic motivations (Bloore et al., 2020; Gross, 2014; Tamir, 2015). In other words, most of the time, people engage in purposeful attempts to upregulate pleasant emotions and downregulate unpleasant ones, regardless of their immediate physical and social environments. Although doing so may increase one's subjective sense of well-being, it will not necessarily contribute to reproductive success. An example comes from the study of *disgust avoidance*, a form of situation selection. Although disgust is an emotion that helps solve the adaptive problem of pathogen avoidance (Oaten et al., 2009), *overuse* of premeditated actions to avoid experiencing this uncomfortable emotion is expected to reduce reproductive success by preventing one from trying unfamiliar foods (i.e., potential sources of nutrition) and possibly even engaging in sexual opportunities (von Spreckelsen et al., 2020). As another example, purposefully upregulating happiness despite a lack of access to resources and mating opportunities ("Don't worry, be happy") could negatively impact one's physical health and reduce the likelihood of passing on genetic material. This does not imply that pro-hedonic emotion regulation is inappropriate or should not be practiced, simply that the increased emotional comfort it promotes is not necessarily adaptive in an evolutionary sense.

Is Emotion Regulation Universally Present across Cultures?

The frequency and form of emotion regulation practices have been hypothesized to vary across cultures in a manner that reflects the corresponding emotion *values* and *end-goals* of those differing cultures (Mesquita et al., 2014; Tamir et al., 2016). For example, expressive suppression is associated with negative social and physical health outcomes in Western, *independent* cultural contexts, but not in the Eastern, *interdependent* cultures that have been tested (reviewed by Ford & Mauss, 2015). In fact, there is evidence that expressive suppression can increase a sense of well-being for interdependent people in certain contexts (Le & Impett, 2013). These effects are believed to relate to a culturally informed desire to avoid disrupting social harmony and burdening others with emotional displays. Employing emotion regulation practices in a manner that allows one to adhere to culturally defined norms in this way has been described as "adaptive" because of associated social rewards, as well as a greater sense of interpersonal harmony with others that results (Ford & Mauss, 2015). Such outcomes may indeed be adaptive in an evolutionary sense as well, because they will tend to increase one's social interconnectivity, which will confer numerous benefits discussed above, including but not limited to access to resources, protection from risks, access to mating opportunities, and help with raising offspring (Baumeister & Leary, 1995).

The demonstration of differences in specific emotion regulation practices across cultures does not necessarily imply that emotion regulation is a strictly cultural phenomenon, i.e., not evolved through natural selection. To address this issue, it will be important to investigate whether or not voluntary emotion regulation, broadly defined, can be found across all human cultures, despite the cultural relativity in the specific pattern of emotion regulation practices. Such a demonstration of emotion regulation universality would provide additional evidence for the potential adaptive value of this function in an evolutionary sense. In particular, it will be especially informative to study the prevalence and pattern of emotion regulation practices within hunter-gatherer cultures that are likely to be more similar to those common within the environment of evolutionary adaptedness for our species.

Do Nonhuman Animals Engage in Emotion Regulation?

If emotion regulation evolved to solve adaptive problems, it is reasonable to ask whether it did so before the human lineage split off from other species. Certainly, the emotions of nonhuman animals are regulated in implicit, or automatic, ways. For example, repeated exposure to a potentially threatening novel stimulus will lead to dampened emotional responses, or habituation, as long as no deleterious consequences are associated with that stimulus, and this has been interpreted as a form of implicit emotion regulation (Gyurak & Etkin, 2014). But do nonhuman animals attempt to *explicitly* modify their emotional responses? Although it is challenging to answer this question definitively without a direct means for assessing animals' internal intentions and motives, there is suggestive evidence.

Nonhuman animal research of emotion regulation has focused primarily on *self-control,* a broad construct that includes but is not limited to the ability to "exercise control over one's own emotions," and that has been hypothesized to arise from cognitive precursors including inhibition and the ability to regulate emotions (Green & Spikins, 2020). Many species of animals exhibit behavioral signs of self-control, which is believed to be especially adaptive for successfully navigating complex social structures and also avoiding frustration associated with delayed access to food. For example, chimpanzees have been observed to employ *self-distraction*, a form of the emotion regulation strategy of attentional deployment, in order to inhibit the temptation to accept a small candy reward immediately so that they can receive a larger candy reward eventually (Evans & Beran, 2007). In related research, rhesus monkeys have been shown to inhibit fearful expressions and to downregulate aggressive behavior within certain social contexts (Suomi, 2009). Although it has been argued that young monkeys learn these forms of emotion regulation through interactions with their mothers and peers, this does not necessarily mean that such regulation is explicit, as opposed to implicit, once it has been learned.

Perhaps the most convincing evidence for explicit regulation of emotion in nonhuman animals comes from ethological observation. Frans de Waal describes chimpanzees who appear to purposefully hide facial expressions, a form of expressive suppression, that may be perceived as socially inappropriate. This includes hiding an expression by turning away from another animal, blocking the view of their face with a hand, trying to "wipe it off their face," and forcefully pushing their lips over their teeth in order to hide a sign of aggression (de Waal, 2019). Regardless of whether these and the other behaviors mentioned above arise from voluntary or involuntary processes, their presence in nonhuman animals supports the adaptive value of emotion regulation in general.

Summary and Conclusion

Despite some disagreements in the formal definition of emotion, researchers who study emotion from an evolutionary perspective agree that emotions convey critical and adaptive functionality to an animal, contribute ultimately to survival and reproductive functions, and represent the outcome of millions of years of selection (Al-Shawaf et al., 2016). Therefore, at first glance, voluntarily changing one's emotions appears to be maladaptive in an evolutionary framework. However, as reviewed here, emotion regulation can contribute to reproductive success in a number of ways, including but not limited to improved instrumental outcomes in specific contexts, flexibility in the navigation of social structures important for survival and reproduction, and more efficient use of energy and resources that may otherwise be deployed by emotional responses. Further research designed explicitly from an evolutionary perspective will be required to provide more direct evidence for a possible fit between emotion regulation and the adaptive problems it may have evolved to solve (see also Del Giudice, Chapter 5 in the present volume), sex differences in emotion regulation that could contribute to sexual selection and reproductive success, as well as the potential universality of emotion regulation, broadly defined, across cultures and across species.

Acknowledgments

The author gratefully acknowledges constructive suggestions provided by Laith Al-Shawaf, Marco Del Giudice, Margarita Meza-Whitlatch, Rhea Pedler, and Joshua Shulkin.

References

Ainsworth, M. D. S., Blehar, M. C., Waters, E., & Wall, S. (1978). *Patterns of attachment: A psychological study of the strange situation.* Lawrence Erlbaum Associates.

Aldao, A., & Nolen-Hoeksema, S. (2012). The influence of context on the implementation of adaptive emotion regulation strategies. *Behaviour Research and Therapy, 50*(7–8), 493–501. doi: 10.1016/j.brat.2012.04.004

Al-Shawaf, L., Conroy-Beam, D., Asao, K., & Buss, D. M. (2016). Human emotions: An evolutionary psychological perspective. *Emotion Review, 8*(2), 173–186. doi: 10.1177/1754073914565518

Baumeister, R. F., & Leary, M. R. (1995). The need to belong. *Psychological Bulletin, 117*(3), 497–529. doi: 10.1037/0033-2909.117.3.497

Belsky, J. (1997). Attachment, mating, and parenting: An evolutionary interpretation. *Human Nature, 8*(4), 361–381.

Bjorklund, D. F., & Kipp, K. (1996). Parental investment theory and gender differences in the evolution of inhibition mechanisms. *Psychological Bulletin, 120*(2), 163–188. doi: 10.1037/0033-2909.120.2.163

Bloore, R. A., Jose, P. E., & Roseman, I. J. (2020). General emotion regulation measure (GERM): Individual differences in motives of trying to experience and trying to avoid experiencing positive and negative emotions. *Personality and Individual Differences, 166*, 1–10, 110174. doi: 10.1016/j.paid.2020.110174

Bowlby, J. (1969). *Attachment and loss.* Basic Books.

Buss, D. M., & Schmitt, D. P. (1993). Sexual strategies theory: An evolutionary perspective on human mating. *Psychological Review, 100*(2), 204–232. doi: 10.1037//0033-295X.100.2.204

Buss, D. M., Abbott, M., Angleitner, A., Asherian, A., Biaggio, A., Blanco-Villasenor, A., Bruchon-Schweitzer, M., Ch'U, H., Czapinski, J., Deraad, B., Ekehammar, B., El Lohamy, N., Fioravanti, M., Georgas, J., Gjerde, P., Guttman, R., Hazan, F., Iwawaki, S., Janakiramaiah, N., . . . Yang, K. (1990). International preferences in selecting mates. *Journal of Cross-Cultural Psychology, 21*(1), 5–47. doi: 10.1177/0022022190211001

Cassidy, J. (1994). Emotion regulation: Influences of attachment relationships. *Monographs of the Society for Research in Child Development, 59*(2–3), 228–249. doi: 10.1111/j.1540-5834.1994.tb01287.x

Chen, E., & Miller, G. E. (2014). Early-life socioeconomic status, emotion regulation, and the biological mechanisms of disease across the lifespan. In J. J. Gross (Ed.), *Handbook of emotion regulation* (2nd ed., pp. 586–595). Guilford Press.

Debove, S., Baumard, N., & André, J. (2016). Models of the evolution of fairness in the ultimatum game: A review and classification. *Evolution and Human Behavior, 37*(3), 245–254. doi: 10.1016/j.evolhumbehav.2016.01.001

Del Giudice, M. (2009). Sex, attachment, and the development of reproductive strategies. *Behavioral and Brain Sciences, 32*(1), 1–67. doi: 10.1017/S0140525X09000016

de Waal, F. (2019). *Mama's last hug: Animal emotions and what they tell us about ourselves.* W. W. Norton.

Ellis, B. J., & Del Giudice, M. (2019). Developmental adaptation to stress: An evolutionary perspective. *Annual Review of Psychology, 70*(1), 111–139. doi: 10.1146/annurev-psych-122216-011732

English, T., Lee, I. A., John, O. P., & Gross, J. J. (2017). Emotion regulation strategy selection in daily life: The role of social context and goals. *Motivation and Emotion, 41*(2), 230–242. doi: 10.1007/s11031-016-9597-z

Evans, T. A., & Beran, M. J. (2007). Chimpanzees use self-distraction to cope with impulsivity. *Biology Letters, 3*(6), 599–602. doi: 10.1098/rsbl.2007.0399

Ford, B. Q., & Mauss, I. B. (2015). Culture and emotion regulation. *Current Opinion in Psychology, 3*, 1–5. doi: 10.1016/j.copsyc.2014.12.004

Frederiksen, Y., Farver-Vestergaard, I., Skovgård, N. G., Ingerslev, H. J., & Zachariae, R. (2015). Efficacy of psychosocial interventions for psychological and pregnancy outcomes in infertile women and men: A systematic review and meta-analysis. *BMJ Open, 5*(1), e006592. doi: 10.1136/bmjopen-2014-006592

Geary, D. C. (2000). Evolution and proximate expression of human paternal investment. *Psychological Bulletin, 126*(1), 55–77. doi: 10.1037/0033-2909.126.1.55

Graham, B. M., Ash, C., & Den, M. L. (2017). High endogenous estradiol is associated with enhanced cognitive emotion regulation of physiological conditioned fear responses in women. *Psychoneuroendocrinology, 80*, 7–14. doi: 10.1016/j.psyneuen.2017.02.023

Graham, B. M., Denson, T. F., Barnett, J., Calderwood, C., & Grisham, J. R. (2018). Sex hormones are associated with rumination and interact with emotion regulation strategy choice to predict negative affect in women following a sad mood induction. *Frontiers in Psychology, 9*, 937. doi: 10.3389/fpsyg.2018.00937

Green, J., & Spikins, P. (2020). Not just a virtue: The evolution of self-control. *Time and Mind, 13*(2), 117–139. doi: 10.1080/1751696X.2020.1747246

Gross, J. J. (2014). Emotion regulation: Conceptual and empirical foundations. In J. J. Gross (Ed.), *Handbook of emotion regulation* (2nd ed., pp. 3–20). New York: Guilford Press.

Gross, J. J. (1998). The emerging field of emotion regulation. *Review of General Psychology, 2*(3), 271–299. doi: 10.1037/1089-2680.2.3.271

Gross, J. J., & Feldman Barrett, L. (2011). Emotion generation and emotion regulation: One or two depends on your point of view. *Emotion Review, 3*(1), 8–16. doi: 10.1177/1754073910380974

Gross, J. J., & Jazaieri, H. (2014). Emotion, emotion regulation, and psychopathology. *Clinical Psychological Science, 2*(4), 387–401. doi: 10.1177/2167702614536164

Gyurak, A., & Etkin, A. (2014). A neurobiological model of implicit and explicit emotion regulation. In J. J. Gross (Ed.), *Handbook of emotion regulation* (2nd ed., pp. 76–90). Guilford Press.

Hajcak, G., MacNamara, A., & Olvet, D. M. (2010). Event-related potentials, emotion, and emotion regulation: An integrative review. *Developmental Neuropsychology, 35*(2), 129–155. doi: 10.1080/87565640903526504

Hare, B. (2017). Survival of the friendliest: *Homo sapiens* evolved via selection for prosociality. *Annual Review of Psychology, 68*(1), 155–186. doi: 10.1146/annurev-psych-010416-044201

Hare, B., & Tomasello, M. (2005). Human-like social skills in dogs? *Trends in Cognitive Sciences, 9*(9), 439–444. doi: 10.1016/j.tics.2005.07.003

Houck, C. D., Barker, D. H., Hadley, W., Menefee, M., & Brown, L. K. (2018). Sexual risk outcomes of an emotion regulation intervention for at-risk early adolescents. *Pediatrics (Evanston), 141*(6), e20172525. doi: 10.1542/peds.2017-2525

Izard, C. E. (1972). *Patterns of emotions: A new analysis of anxiety and depression*. Academic Press.

Kappas, A. (2011). Emotion and regulation are one. *Emotion Review, 3*(1), 17–25. doi: 10.1177/1754073910380971

Kisley, M. A., Campbell, A. M., Larson, J. M., Naftz, A. E., Regnier, J. T., & Davalos, D. B. (2011). The impact of verbal framing on brain activity evoked by emotional images. *Journal of Integrative Neuroscience, 10*(4), 513–524. doi: 10.1142/S0219635211002816

Kisley, M., Caudle, C. S., & Harvey, A. M. (2019). Affect intolerance is associated with insecure attachment and reduced self-esteem in adults. *Archives of Psychology, 3*(8), 1–21. doi: 10.31296/aop.v3i8.121

Koch, S. B. J., Mars, R. B., Toni, I., & Roelofs, K. (2018). Emotional control, reappraised. *Neuroscience and Biobehavioral Reviews, 95*, 528–534. doi: 10.1016/j.neubiorev.2018.11.003

Lang, P. J., Bradley, M. M., & Cuthbert, B. N. (1990). Emotion, attention, and the startle reflex. *Psychological Review, 97*(3), 377–395. doi: 10.1037/0033-295X.97.3.377

Larsen, R. J. (2000). Toward a science of mood regulation. *Psychological Inquiry, 11*(3), 129–141. doi: 10.1207/s15327965pli1103_01

Le, B. M., & Impett, E. A. (2013). When holding back helps: Suppressing negative emotions during sacrifice feels authentic and is beneficial for highly interdependent people. *Psychological Science, 24*(9), 1809–1815. doi: 10.1177/0956797613475365

Levenson, R. W. (2003). Blood, sweat, and fears: the autonomic architecture of emotion. *Annals of the New York Academy of Sciences, 1000*, 348–366. doi: 10.1196/annals.1280.016

Li, J., Long, L., Liu, Y., He, W., & Li, M. (2016). Effects of a mindfulness-based intervention on fertility quality of life and pregnancy rates among women subjected to first in vitro fertilization treatment. *Behaviour Research and Therapy, 77*, 96–104. doi: 10.1016/j.brat.2015.12.010

Lindsey, E. W. (2020). Relationship context and emotion regulation across the life span. *Emotion, 20*(1), 59–62. doi: 10.1037/emo0000666

MacDonald, K. B. (2008). Effortful control, explicit processing, and the regulation of human evolved predispositions. *Psychological Review, 115*(4), 1012–1031. doi: 10.1037/a0013327

MacLean, E. L. (2016). Unraveling the evolution of uniquely human cognition. *Proceedings of the National Academy of Sciences, 113*(23), 6348–6354. doi: 10.1073/pnas.1521270113

Mauss, I. B., & Tamir, M. (2014). Emotion goals: How their content, structure, and operation shape emotion regulation. In J. J. Gross (Ed.), *Handbook of emotion regulation* (2nd ed., pp. 376–389). Guilford Press.

McRae, K., & Gross, J. J. (2020). Emotion regulation. *Emotion, 20*(1), 1–9.

Mesquita, B., De Leersnyder, J., & Albert, D. (2014). The cultural regulation of emotions. In J. J. Gross (Ed.), *Handbook of emotion regulation* (2nd ed., pp. 284–301). Guilford Press.

Miller, A. H., Capuron, L., & Raison, C. L. (2005). Immunologic influences on emotion regulation. *Clinical Neuroscience Research, 4*(5), 325–333. doi: 10.1016/j.cnr.2005.03.010

Morgan, L. K., & Kisley, M. A. (2014). The effects of facial attractiveness and perceiver's mate value on adaptive allocation of central processing resources. *Evolution and Human Behavior, 35*(2), 96–102. doi: 10.1016/j.evolhumbehav.2013.11.002

Mueser, K. T., Grau, B. W., Sussman, S., & Rosen, A. J. (1984). You're only as pretty as you feel: Facial expression as a determinant of physical attractiveness. *Journal of Personality and Social Psychology, 46*(2), 469–478. doi: 10.1037/0022-3514.46.2.469

Naragon-Gainey, K., McMahon, T. P., & Chacko, T. P. (2017). The structure of common emotion regulation strategies: A meta-analytic examination. *Psychological Bulletin, 143*(4), 384–427. doi: 10.1037/bul0000093

Nolen-Hoeksema, S., & Aldao, A. (2011). Gender and age differences in emotion regulation strategies and their relationship to depressive symptoms. *Personality and Individual Differences, 51*(6), 704–708. doi: 10.1016/j.paid.2011.06.012

Oaten, M., Stevenson, R. J., & Case, T. I. (2009). Disgust as a disease-avoidance mechanism. *Psychological Bulletin, 135*(2), 303–321. doi: 10.1037/a0014823

Öhman, A., Flykt, A., & Esteves, F. (2001). Emotion drives attention. *Journal of Experimental Psychology. General, 130*(3), 466–478. doi: 10.1037/0096-3445.130.3.466

Olatunji, B. O., Cox, R. C., & Li, I. (2020). Disgust regulation between menstrual cycle phases: Differential effects of emotional suppression and reappraisal. *Journal of Behavior Therapy and Experimental Psychiatry, 68*, 101543. doi: 10.1016/j.jbtep.2019.101543

Plutchik, R. (1980). *Emotion: A psychoevolutionary synthesis.* Harper & Row.

Pratto, F., & John, O. P. (1991). Automatic vigilance: The attention-grabbing power of negative social information. *Journal of Personality and Social Psychology, 61*(3), 380–391. doi: 10.1037//0022-3514.61.3.380

Puts, D. A. (2010). Beauty and the beast: Mechanisms of sexual selection in humans. *Evolution and Human Behavior, 31*(3), 157–175. doi: 10.1016/j.evolhumbehav.2010.02.005

Rehmert, A. E., & Kisley, M. A. (2013). Can older adults resist the positivity effect in neural responding? The impact of verbal framing on event-related brain potentials elicited by emotional images. *Emotion, 13*(5), 949–959. doi: 10.1037/a0032771

Ribeiro da Silva, D., Rijo, D., & Salekin, R. T. (2015). The evolutionary roots of psychopathy. *Aggression and Violent Behavior, 21*, 85–96. doi: 10.1016/j.avb.2015.01.006

Roemer, L., Williston, S. K., & Rollins, L. G. (2015). Mindfulness and emotion regulation. *Current Opinion in Psychology, 3*, 52–57. doi: 10.1016/j.copsyc.2015.02.006

Shiota, M. N., & Levenson, R. W. (2012). Turn down the volume or change the channel? Emotional effects of detached versus positive reappraisal. *Journal of Personality and Social Psychology, 103*(3), 416–429. doi: 10.1037/a0029208

Soto, J. A., Perez, C. R., Kim, Y., Lee, E. A., & Minnick, M. R. (2011). Is expressive suppression always associated with poorer psychological functioning? A cross-cultural comparison between European Americans and Hong Kong Chinese. *Emotion, 11*(6), 1450–1455. doi: 10.1037/a0023340

Stockley, P., & Campbell, A. (2013). Female competition and aggression: interdisciplinary perspectives. *Philosophical Transactions. Biological Sciences, 368*(1631), 20130073. doi:10.1098/rstb.2013.0073

Suomi, S. J. (2009). How gene-environment interactions can influence the development of emotion regulation in rhesus monkeys. In S. L. Olson & A. J. Sameroff (Eds.), *Biopsychosocial regulatory processes in the development of childhood behavioral problems* (pp. 19–37). Cambridge University Press.

Tamir, M., Mitchell, C., & Gross, J. J. (2008). Hedonic and instrumental motives in anger regulation. *Psychological Science, 19*(4), 324–328. doi: 10.1111/j.1467-9280.2008.02088.x

Tamir, M. (2015). Why do people regulate their emotions? A taxonomy of motives in emotion regulation. *Personality and Social Psychology Review, 20*(3), 199–222. doi: 10.1177/1088868315586325

Tamir, M., & Ford, B. Q. (2012). When feeling bad is expected to be good: Emotion regulation and outcome expectancies in social conflicts. *Emotion, 12*(4), 807–816. doi: 10.1037/a0024443

Tamir, M., Schwartz, S. H., Cieciuch, J., Riediger, M., Torres, C., Scollon, C., Dzokoto, V., Zhou, X., & Vishkin, A. (2016). Desired emotions across cultures: A value-based account. *Journal of Personality and Social Psychology, 111*(1), 67–82. doi: 10.1037/pspp0000072

Timmers, M., Fischer, A. H., & Manstead, A. S. R. (1998). Gender differences in motives for regulating emotions. *Personality and Social Psychology Bulletin, 24*(9), 974–985.

Tooby, J., & Cosmides, L. (1990). The past explains the present: Emotional adaptations and the structure of ancestral environments. *Ethology and Sociobiology, 11*(4–5), 375–424. doi: 10.1016/0162-3095(90)90017-Z

Tooby, J., & Cosmides, L. (2008). The evolutionary psychology of the emotions and their relationship to internal regulatory variables. In J. M. Lewis & L. F. Haviland-Jones (Eds.), *Handbook of emotions* (3rd ed., pp. 114–137). Guilford Press.

Tracy, J. L., & Beall, A. T. (2011). Happy guys finish last: The impact of emotion expressions on sexual attraction. *Emotion, 11*(6), 1379–1387. doi: 10.1037/a0022902

Trivers, R. L. (1972). Parental investment and sexual selection. In B. Campbell (Ed.), *Sexual selection and the descent of man: 1871–1971* (pp. 136–179). Aldine.

van't Wout, M., Chang, L. J., & Sanfey, A. G. (2010). The influence of emotion regulation on social interactive decision-making. *Emotion, 10*(6), 815–821. doi: 10.1037/a0020069 von Spreckelsen, P., Jonker, N., Vugteveen, J., Wessel, I., Glashouwer, K. A., & de Jong, P. J. (2020). Individual differences in avoiding feelings of disgust: Development and construct validity of the disgust avoidance questionnaire. *PLOS ONE, 16*(3), e0248219. doi: 10.1371/journal.pone.0248219

Zaehringer, J., Jennen-Steinmetz, C., Schmahl, C., Ende, G., & Paret, C. (2020). Psychophysiological effects of downregulating negative emotions: Insights from a meta-analysis of healthy adults. *Frontiers in Psychology, 11*, 470. doi: 10.3389/fpsyg.2020.00470

CHAPTER 40

More than a Feeling: The Comparative Psychology of Emotion

Jennifer Vonk, Lauri Torgerson-White, Jared Edge, and Bridget Benton

Abstract

This chapter reviews the available methods for assessing components of emotion, with emphasis on positive and negative emotional experiences in nonhuman animals (NHAs). The authors consider the ability of NHAs to receive and interpret signals of emotion from conspecifics and allospecifics and address the possible impacts of domestication in addition to natural selection pressures on the expression of emotion. The authors find little evidence for the hypothesis that group-living species exhibit greater emotional complexity compared to non-group-living species. They discuss challenges while emphasizing the importance of developing more objective methods for assessing emotional experiences in NHAs. They conclude that emotion is still poorly understood in NHAs. Improving this understanding will be critical for informing acceptable welfare standards and practices for captive and domestic species.

Key Words: nonhuman animal, emotion expression, signal, selection pressure, welfare

Even the most mundane events elicit an emotional experience for humans. Watching a sunrise, something that happens tens of thousands of times in the average human's life, might reduce heart rate and create a subjective feeling of calm and awe (Bowler et al., 2010). Yet, despite a long-standing claim for the special status of humans (Chapman & Huffman, 2018), humans are not the only species to experience emotion. Scientists have been concerned with the evolution of human emotion at least since Darwin's 1872 treatise, *Emotions in Man and Animals*. The consensus today is that there is continuity in the experience and expression of emotion in species as diverse as insects, fish, and chimpanzees. The comparative study of emotion can inform an understanding of why humans experience emotion as we do and instill a sense of obligation that humans treat other species with compassion.

Emotions are intense but brief affective responses to an event, and include an expressive component, a physiological component, and the subjective experience termed "feeling" (Désiré et al., 2002). In nonhuman animals (NHAs), we must infer the existence of the subjective component based on behavioral and physiological responses to an event (Burghardt, 2019; Wiepkema, 1987). For example, the physiological response of a rabbit to a fox sighting includes elevated heart rate and glucocorticoid levels, which might trigger a response of running from the fox. Scientists can measure physiological and expressive responses to the eliciting event, and based on analogy to human experience, attribute the presence of a fear state in the rabbit. Neural biology and activation in NHAs approximate those in humans in response to similar eliciting events or stimuli (Désiré et al., 2002). The adaptive value of emotion and its functional role in processes from reproduction to learning make it likely that emotional experiences are widespread within the animal kingdom—a prospect we will evaluate in light of current methodological tools.

Appraisal Theories

For a full comparative analysis of NHA emotion, it is necessary to understand the frameworks used in human emotion studies. Panksepp's (1998) model of affective neuroscience recognized that defining NHA emotions is subjective and, as such, mapped seven regions of the brain associated with seven emotion states (COMMAND SYSTEM/emotion): SEEKING/expectancy; RAGE/anger; FEAR/anxiety; LUST; CARE/nurturing; PANIC/sadness; and PLAY/social joy. Command systems were identified by electrically or chemically stimulating regions of the brain, observing behaviors and vocalizations, and allowing study subjects to self-stimulate. For instance, electrical stimulation of the extended lateral hypothalamic corridor activated the SEEKING system in rats, resulting in exploratory and search behaviors, and self-stimulation of this region, indicating a positive emotion state. Each of these command systems maps to a different region of the brain, results in a unique release of neurochemicals and hormones, leads to a different behavioral expression, and is either positive or negative, corroborating that these are distinct states (Panksepp, 2011). These command systems are found in all mammals (Davis & Montag, 2019; Panksepp, 2011). Unlike other models (e.g., Ekman, 1972), Panksepp's model connected to motivation and did not rely on facial expressions (Burghardt, 2019). Despite his compelling work, Panksepp's framework has not been widely adopted, likely due to the reliance on neuroscientific methods to differentiate similar emotions.

Although there have been models identifying more than four, the most commonly accepted primary emotions identified in humans are happiness, sadness, fear/surprise, and anger/disgust (Jack et al., 2014). However, researchers have also identified secondary emotions, including the self-conscious emotions (shame, embarrassment, guilt, pride, and envy). The lack of attention to more nuanced emotions in NHAs may not be because correlates for these emotions are absent, but because of the subjectivity involved in such determinations and the continued reluctance of the scientific community to attribute what were previously perceived to be uniquely human traits to NHAs (Lazarus, 1991). We explore the science that challenges this bias.

Whereas psychologists have utilized a wide range of models to categorize the subjective component of emotion, the dimensional approach is most commonly applied to NHAs. In this approach, the subjective component of emotion involves two interacting dimensions: valence (positive/negative) and arousal or excitation (weak/strong or low/high; Désiré et al., 2002; Schlosberg, 1954). For instance, cows stroked by humans experience a positively valenced, low arousal state whereby their nasal temperatures and heart rates drop, and they fall asleep (Proctor & Carder, 2015a). The positive valence induced by stroking is supported by reduced heart rate and cortisol in cows exposed to stressful procedures (which have the opposite effects), as well as reduced flight distances in the presence of humans. Cows experience positively valenced, high arousal states when they make achievements in learning, in concert with increased heart rates, jumps, bucks, and kicks (Hagen & Broom, 2004). Conversely, they experience a negatively valenced, high arousal state communicated via vocalization and visible eye whites when separated from their calves (Sandem & Braastad, 2005). Although assignment of emotion states to dimensions is subjective, relying on analogy and corroborating evidence validates the model to some degree.

Understanding that positive emotions signal events that promote survival and reproduction and that negative emotions signal events that impair survival and reproduction, we can explore the evolutionary origins of emotion using a comparative approach (Panksepp, 2011). Emotion is adaptive in that it promotes social bonding (pleasure, happiness, sadness), alerts self and others to possible threats (disgust, fear), and allows an organism to respond to threat (anger) (Darwin, 1872; Ekman, 1972; Lazarus, 1991). The resulting motivated behaviors are thus shaped by natural selection (Weisfeld & Goetz, 2013). Secondary emotions (e.g., guilt, shame, envy) help individuals mediate their responses to others and modify their social behaviors to protect their social selves (Gruenewald et al., 2007). Thus, it is reasonable to assume that many other species share the ability to experience and regulate emotion, but abilities related to the communication and comprehension of emotion may be especially pronounced in group-living species or species that form pair-bonds and/or engage in parental care. Furthermore, the expression and understanding of emotion in NHAs may have been shaped by human intervention, such as through domestication and captivity. Before we can assess environmental and anthropogenic influences on the evolution of capacities related to emotion, we must first consider how these traits can be assessed in NHAs.

Assessing Emotion Capacities

Studying emotions in NHAs relies on indirect measures, such as observing correlates of emotions (Kirkden & Pajor, 2006). Methodologies can be categorized as physiological, behavioral (Dawkins, 2006), and—more recently—cognitive.

Physiological Variables

Physiological variables reflect changes in biological functions in response to external events. These changes in biological function can then be compared to similar adjustments observed in humans to draw parallels in the likely emotion states that NHAs experience. Changes in functions such as heart rate, brain activity, and respiration rate can indicate an emotional reaction following a potentially emotion-inducing situation (Dawkins, 2006). However, determining the emotion that is experienced based solely on physiological data can be difficult, as changes in functions (e.g., rise in heart rate) are associated with various emotional reactions, potentially indicating level of arousal but not valence (Paul et al., 2005). For example, increases in heart rate within cattle can indicate a positively or negatively valenced emotion (Hagen & Broom, 2004; Neave et al., 2013). Despite these difficulties in interpretation, researchers rely on the argument by analogy, assuming that events aversive to humans are also aversive to NHAs by way of shared physiological (including brain activation) and behavioral responses. It will be important to use corroborating information to better understand if these analogies hold true.

Hormones

Hormone analyses, specifically examinations of glucocorticoids, can indicate level of arousal and the specific valence of an emotional reaction due to association with stressful or negative situations (Gartland et al., 2014). Increases in glucocorticoids, urination, and defecation appear to be more clearly linked to negative valence rather than a change in valence or arousal (Boissy et al., 1998; Kanitz et al., 2019; Neave et al., 2013; Reimert et al., 2013; Reimert et al., 2015; van der Staay et al., 2017; von Eugen et al., 2019). These analyses can provide an estimate of the level of stress an animal is experiencing, potentially indicating fear. Elevated cortisol levels have been associated with increases in fear in humans (Jovanovic et al., 2011). Because cortisol concentrations can be assessed through collection of blood, saliva, or urine samples (Turpeinen & Hämäläinen, 2013), cortisol levels can be examined in captive and wild populations. However, gathering samples from wild populations involves risks and confounds. The process through which an individual is captured, and the time taken to gather samples, can increase blood parameters including cortisol levels (Pavlova et al., 2018), which can complicate interpretation of emotion. Less invasive measures, such as measuring cortisol concentration in hair follicles, can be used to examine long-term effects of stress (Macbeth et al., 2010). However, considering the relatively short-term nature of emotions (Désiré et al., 2002; Panksepp, 1994; Verduyn et al., 2011), it is debatable whether these methods can be used to examine emotional reactions.

Infrared Thermography
Infrared thermography (IRT) involves a camera that detects infrared energy emitted by a subject and converts it to temperature, resulting in an image that maps temperatures across the surface of the subject. IRT is a noninvasive method to extract peripheral temperature data that can be linked to emotion without disrupting the subject. It has been used with nonhuman primates (Chotard et al., 2018; Heintz et al., 2019), dogs (Travain et al., 2016), pigs (Boileau et al., 2019), sheep (Stubsjøen et al., 2009), cows (Stewart et al., 2007), horses (Dai et al., 2015; Sanchez et al., 2016), mice (Faraji & Metz, 2020; Gjendal et al., 2018), and chickens (Edgar et al., 2013; Herborn et al., 2018; Moe et al., 2017). Many animals exhibit emotional fever, whereby an increase in body temperature and change in heart rate have been linked to emotion states (Cabanac & Aizawa, 2000; Cabanac & Bernieri, 2000; Cabanac & Cabanac, 2000; Oka, 2015). A change in peripheral temperatures measured through IRT is indicative of a shift in valence rather than a particular emotion state (Hussein, 2019; Proctor & Carder, 2015a; Sandem, Braastad, et al., 2006). For example, drops in nasal temperatures in cattle have been associated with shifts in emotional valence, although both positively and negatively valenced stimuli produce this effect (Proctor & Carder, 2015a, 2016). Changes in body temperature or heart rate may indicate emotional arousal rather than valence (Briefer et al., 2015; Moe et al., 2012). When these methods are better understood, changes in body temperature associated with emotional reactions could be observed in wild populations without the need to disturb subjects.

Neurological Underpinnings of Emotion
Regions within the human brain have been identified as important components of the emotional system. The amygdala and orbitofrontal cortex have been implicated in emotional behavior for many mammals (Man et al., 2012). Many parallels have been drawn between the brain structures active during emotional reactions in humans and other mammals, including Panksepp's (1998) model of affective neuroscience, as mammals share the same brain structures, including some form of neocortex (Kaas, 2011). However, the enhanced neocortex of humans has been linked to potentially unique aspects of emotional experience (i.e., knowledge of internal states; Rose, 2002). Lesion studies involving rodents, cats, and nonhuman primates have found alterations in social behavior that match those found in humans with brain damage to similar regions (Kolb & Taylor, 1990).

Despite numerous anatomical differences between mammalian and non-mammalian brains, emotion processes have been evidenced in the brains of birds and fish (Kittilsen, 2013). Within birds, structures homologous to the mammalian amygdala have been identified, with regions in the arcopallium related to the fear response (Hanics et al., 2017). Damage to specific regions can increase or decrease the fear response (Saint-Dizier et al., 2009) and damage to the right hemisphere generates stronger effects than similar damage to the left hemisphere (Philips & Youngren, 1986). Regions in the telencephalon of fish are homologous with the mammalian amygdala, with damage to these regions altering the fear response (Portavella et al., 2004). Structures with similar functions in animals as phylogenetically distant from humans as fish suggests that the basic circuitry associated with emotional processes may be very old on an evolutionary timescale (Chandroo et al., 2004).

LATERALIZATION
Evidence of emotional lateralization in vertebrates supports the "emotional-valence hypothesis," which suggests that emotional processing is split between the hemispheres, with negatively valenced emotions primarily processed in the right hemisphere and positively valenced emotions primarily processed in the left hemisphere (Silberman & Weingartner, 1986). For example, responses to food rewards have been linked to left hemisphere activity (Reefmann et al., 2009). This lateralization has been further supported via lesion studies, with a greater reduction of distress calls following damage to the archistriatum in the right but not left hemisphere in chicks (Phillips & Youngren, 1986). Associations between fear, anxiety, and aggression and left hemisphere lateralization have been demonstrated through behavioral measures (e.g., eye preference when examining a predator; Koboroff et al., 2008) and physiological measures (e.g., EEG; Kalin et al., 1998). Evidence for lateralization in fish and amphibians has been weaker than for mammals, birds, and reptiles (Leliveld et al., 2013). Continuity of hemispheric specialization of emotion processing suggests a long evolutionary history of lateralization, contrary to claims that this neural organization is unique to humans. At the least, lateralization appears conserved throughout the primate order (Lindell, 2013).

Chemical Signals

The expressive component of emotion can include pheromones, chemical cues that can be spread over long distances and outlast the duration of the emotion that initiated its release (Fujisawa et al., 2008; Karlson & Lüscher, 1959). Research on the expression of emotions has almost exclusively examined tactile, visual, and auditory modalities, despite pheromones being a significant component of communication for many species. This narrow focus may be due to the limited understanding of pheromone use or social chemosignaling among humans (Frumin et al., 2015), potentially limiting our ability to understand the importance of these cues for NHAs (Wyatt, 2020).

An exception to this oversight is the long history of research on the use of pheromones as alarm signals (Blum, 1969). Chemical alarm signals are commonly used by social insects and fish, taxa that may have a reduced capacity for auditory signals to communicate distress due to physiological/environmental limitations (Døving & Lastein, 2009; Verheggen et al., 2010). Chemical alarm signals can alter the behavior of nearby individuals, with fish displaying an increase in fear behaviors (Døving & Lastein, 2009; Mathuru et al., 2012). Chemical alarm signals may also permit interspecific communication of emotions with some fish species (Pollock et al., 2003). Mammals also respond to chemical cues of stress. Fear responses have been induced in rats and cattle using odors from stressed conspecifics (Boissy et al., 1998; Rottman & Snowdon, 1973). Although the relation between chemical signals and emotions other than fear is largely unknown, penmates of pigs given intranasal oxytocin behaved in ways associated with positive affect, even though the exposed pigs did not alter their behavior (Reimert et al., 2015). Chemical signals such as sex pheromones may also be associated with positive emotions, but such a connection has yet to be examined. Although many animals respond to chemical cues, this response does not imply that they represent the emotional state of the signaler.

Behavioral Variables
Negative Behaviors
Researchers are reliant on overt behaviors occurring during or after an emotional event to draw inferences about internal states in NHAs (Paul et al., 2005). Research on NHA emotion has focused on behaviors associated with negative emotions, due to the ease with which these behaviors can be elicited, as well as attempts to improve the welfare of captive animals by reducing the occurrence of events or conditions that elicit negative behaviors (Désiré et al., 2002). Behaviors associated with fear, frustration, anger, and aversion are associated with stressful or aversive events (DeCatanzaro, 1999). Fear, for example, is associated with freezing, defecation, urination, crouched posture, escape attempts, and vocalizations (Reimert et al., 2013).

Vocalizations in response to emotional stimuli are common. In rats, 22-kHz and 50-kHz vocalizations correlate with avoidance and approach behaviors, respectively (Makowska & Weary, 2013). Tree shrews have demonstrated the ability to differentiate affect intensity expressed through vocalizations of conspecifics and display increased or decreased levels of stress in response (Schehka & Zimmermann, 2012). Female red deer vocalized calls of longer duration and higher frequency as social discomfort, measured as frequency of bites from female conspecifics, increased (Volodin et al., 2018). Such signals can communicate information about social rank and prevent overt aggression.

Much of the literature concerning posturing in NHAs focuses on threat displays. Threat can be linked to the experience of fear as well as anger. Some behaviors, such as opening the mouth, are an evolutionarily homologous element of aggressive threat displays. For example, opossums engage in a well-known expression called the open-mouth threat display (Hara & Myers, 1973). Some birds engage in this same behavior by opening their beaks and orienting them in a particular way to intimidate conspecifics (Waller & Micheletta, 2013). Organisms may engage in submissive posturing to demonstrate recognition of signals of threat. For example, rainbow skinks attempting to court a mate or establish territory may engage in head-bobbing (Waller & Micheletta, 2013). These submissive postures are commonly linked to fear or the experience of aversive emotion. Attention to posture is important in identifying when an animal is experiencing psychological as well as physical discomfort.

Many of these negative behaviors have been observed in captivity, highlighting the potential for captive environments to produce deleterious effects on the subjective experience of emotions in NHAs. In addition, behaviors such as self-injury and coprophagy among nonhuman primates and injury due to over-grooming in rodents and over-preening in captive birds may be unlikely to occur in wild populations, with most observations coming from captive populations (Dellinge-Ness & Handler, 2006; Hopper et al., 2016; Khoo et al., 2020). However, this is not to imply that negative emotions do not occur in natural populations. Grief, for example, has been inferred among wild populations of nonhuman primates based on physical interactions with the corpse of a group member, as well as secondary interactions such as guarding behavior, some of which have been likened to death rituals (Gonçalves & Carvalho, 2019), although there are other interpretations of these behaviors (Brosnan & Vonk, 2019). The study of grief has been bolstered due to the abundance of evidence from wild populations across many species (King, 2017; Pribac, 2013).

EMOTIONAL REACTIVITY
Tests of emotional reactivity have commonly been used with domesticated species to examine the effects of human behavior and management procedures on fear responses (Brajon et al., 2015). The most common variants are the arena (open field), novel object, approach, intruder, and restraint tests (Forkman et al., 2007). In the arena test, an individual is placed

in the middle of an open area and the frequency of behaviors, including those associated with positive emotions, such as exploratory behavior, and those associated with negative emotions, such as fear responses (e.g., freezing; Laurence et al., 2012), are measured. Novel object tests introduce a novel object into an area that the subject has habituated to, with latency to approach the object and exploratory behavior examined (Boissy & Bouissou, 1995). During human approach tests, the subject is confronted by an unknown human who slowly moves toward the subject, measuring latency to approach the human or fear responses such as flight (Leliveld et al., 2017). Restraint tests involve the use of specialized restraints or a human holding the subject and observing their reactions; some subjects may display fear responses, while others may find the close contact comforting (Lyons & Price, 1987; Price & Thos, 1980). Tonic immobility tests are a variation of the restraint test performed with poultry due to their tendency to freeze in response to potential threat of predation (Favreau-Peigné et al., 2016). The back test involves placing smaller mammals on their backs and holding them loosely to see how quickly and how frequently they attempt to escape (Hessing et al., 1993). These tests are often used in conjunction to assess stability of reactivity over time (Hessing et al., 1993) or connections with specific events such as handling during development (e.g., Hemsworth et al., 1986). Domestic species are universally capable of experiencing and conveying negative emotions in response to events that humans recognize as aversive.

EMOTIONAL CONTAGION

Not only do NHAs experience negative emotion, but they can internalize the emotions of conspecifics through emotional contagion, which is evidenced when an emotion is induced in individuals and the emotional response rapidly spreads to other members of the group that have not experienced the eliciting event (Reimert et al., 2017). Emotional contagion has been considered a basic building block for empathy. Some studies show contagion of negative but not positive emotions (Adrianse et al., 2019; Huber et al., 2017). Yong and Ruffman (2014) reported that dogs showed submissive behaviors, vigilance, and increased cortisol after listening to humans crying, compared to baseline white noise. The authors inferred a form of cross-species empathy likely due to domestication processes or ontogenetic experiences. Dogs have also shown increased stressed behavior when caregivers are distressed and trapped (Van Bourg et al., 2020). Huber et al. (2017) found that dogs responded to negative emotional sounds from dogs and humans, but responded with more freezing to the dog sounds. Research is beginning to uncover positive emotional contagion in NHAs, specifically pigs, that not only exhibited more negative behaviors when their penmates had previously been exposed to negative events, but also engaged in more nosing behavior, body contact, and play with penmates that had previously benefited from peat and straw peppered with chocolate-covered raisins (Reimert et al., 2017). Facial mimicry has also been connected to emotional contagion (Palagi et al., 2019). What the experience of emotional contagion means for an explicit understanding of the emotions of conspecifics is, like most topics we have discussed, still under debate (Adriaense et al., 2019; Vonk, 2019).

Positive Behaviors

Although attempts to improve welfare have focused on reducing the occurrence of behaviors associated with negative emotions, animal welfare efforts have moved beyond alleviation of negative states to the provisioning of conditions conducive to positive states and, hence, "a life worth living" or a "good life" (Boissy et al., 2007; Edgar et al., 2013; Mellor, 2016). Assessments of positive emotions in captive settings focus on specific behaviors: reproduction, foraging and feeding, affiliative behavior, grooming, and vocalizations (Boissy et al., 2007).

Play behavior, which can encompass a variety of behaviors, is considered a sign of positive emotion among captive animals (Held & Špinka, 2011), and has been observed among many mammals, and less commonly in birds (Diamond & Bond, 2003), reptiles (Burghardt et al., 1996), and fish (Burghardt et al., 2015). Play is more often observed in captive than wild animals, including companion animals, although this could reflect biases in opportunities to observe. It is also observed more often when resources are plentiful (Baldwin & Baldwin, 1976; del Toro et al., 2020), supporting the idea that it could reflect positive welfare. Play behavior strengthens social bonds with conspecifics and is therefore adaptive for group-living species or species in which offspring are raised with siblings.

Play is not the only potentially pleasurable behavior that has been observed. Cassill et al. (2016) observed fire ants engaged in abdominal wagging for no apparent purpose. This abdominal wagging (horizontal posturing) is differentiated from abdominal flagging (vertical posturing) outside the nest as a response to threats, or abdominal stridulating (downward posturing) if buried and in distress. Abdominal wagging was most often displayed inside the nest while consuming nutrients from sugar water or from brood grooming. Conspecifics did not meaningfully react to ants when wagging their abdomens. As a result, Cassill et al. (2016) speculated that abdominal wagging is a display of pleasure from consuming nutrients.

Affiliative behaviors, such as maintaining proximity, grooming, or providing food or protection, can build or strengthen group bonds (Boissy et al., 2007). Self-grooming, rather than being a direct sign of positive emotions, may be performed to achieve a relaxation effect, reducing arousal during a stressful situation, and thus is often observed in captive situations (Manning & Dawkins, 1992; Spruijt et al., 1992). Indeed, studies investigating the welfare of laying hens in battery cages found that comfort behaviors such as dustbathing and ground scratching, which cannot be performed by caged hens, are behaviors that hens need and will work for (Bubier, 1996; Weeks & Nicol, 2006), and hence are likely related to positive emotion.

Vocalizations can be an indicator of positive or negative emotions. The short chirping sounds produced by rats may signal positive emotions (Manteuffel et al., 2004; Panksepp & Burgdorf, 2003, whereas pigs produce shorter barks and grunts in positive situations (Briefer et al. 2019; Friel et al., 2019; Reimert et al., 2013). Some vocalizations are not linked to valence, such as purring in cats, which occurs in response to pleasurable or distressing experiences (Cannas et al., 2020). Given that the experience of positive emotions would reinforce the behavior associated with such feelings, there is reason to believe the subjective experience of happiness is widespread in the animal kingdom.

Facial Expressions

Facial expressions, which can convey both positive and negative emotions, are an important component of emotional experience and are well studied, especially among mammals. The Facial Action Coding System (FACS; Ekman & Friesen, 1978) was developed to code the movement of different muscles in the face and different movements of the head as Action Units (Ekman et al., 2002). The FACS has been modified to identify emotions using facial cues in chimpanzees (Vick et al., 2007), macaques (Parr et al., 2010), gibbons (Waller et al., 2012), orangutans (Caeiro et al., 2013), cats (Caeiro et al., 2017), dogs (Waller et al., 2013), and horses (Wathan et al., 2015).

In mammals, especially primates and canids, facial expressions share some characteristics that humans recognize as expressions of specific emotions. The baring of teeth varies in its meaning based on the position of surrounding mouthparts. Wrinkling of the muzzle and full display of the teeth reflect elements of anger, whereas a more horizontal stretching of the mouth with a partial display of teeth reflects a relaxed or submissive expression (Waller & Micheletta, 2013). Reading facial expressions that appear threatening may reduce aggression, as macaques that displayed neutral expressions participated in more aggressive interactions than those that displayed agonistic expressions (Waller et al., 2016). Fear and frustration can be apparent based on increased presentation of the whites of the eyes (Proctor & Carder, 2015b; Sandem et al., 2002; Sandem & Braastad, 2005; Sandem, Braastad, et al., 2006; Sandem, Janczak, et al., 2006). Relaxed open mouth (ROM), an expression that manifests in a variety of mammalian species, signals engagement in play behavior, which promotes social bonding between conspecifics (Palagi et al., 2019). There is some evidence that chimpanzees exhibit flexibility in the use of facial expressions, such as laughter. This work, using ChimpFACS, hints at the evolutionary origins of human laughter—suggesting that it evolved from open-mouth faces of ancestral apes (Davila-Ross et al., 2015). Although one might assume these signals to be present only in social mammals, researchers have suggested that typically solitary sun bears can engage in facial mimicry—matching the play signals of conspecifics (Taylor et al., 2019). This finding suggests that even solitary species recognize emotional expressions in conspecifics.

Domestic dogs and cats evolved features and dispositions that enhance interactions with humans. Eyebrow movement is thought to be unique to domestic dogs and conveys expressions, such as fear and sadness, that elicit sympathy and compassion in humans (Bloom & Friedman, 2013; Kaminski et al., 2019). In cats, expressions and behaviors can be categorized as frustration, fear, and relaxed engagement. The intensity of each emotional expression is heightened while interacting with humans, suggesting that cats' domestication process selected for adaptive emotional expression (Bennet et al., 2017).

Ear movement can often express an animal's emotional state. For example, the ear positions of mice may correlate with emotional reactivity and threat assessment (Lecorps & Féron, 2015). Mice displayed more forward-facing ear positions when approaching a novel odor at a fast pace (indicating less fear and caution) and more backward-facing ear positions when approaching a novel odor at a slow pace (indicating more fear and caution). Pigs and cows also exhibit forward-facing ears when experiencing positive emotions (Czycholl et al., 2020; Proctor & Carder, 2014). Submissive states are characterized by ears that are pulled back against the head, while aggressive or attentive states are characterized by ears that face forward and stand erect (Waller & Micheletta, 2013). There is homology in the expression of mammalian ear positions, although this is not a cue available to humans. Facial and body features interact to convey specific emotions. In rats, orbital tightening, nose/cheek flattening, ear changes, and whisker changes are components of a pain grimace that communicates distress (Sotocinal et al., 2011). Thus, it is important that researchers studying emotions in NHAs consider the animal as a whole and are aware of inter-species differences.

DISCRIMINATION OF FACIAL EXPRESSIONS

In addition to measuring NHAs' subjective experience of emotion, researchers have investigated what NHAs understand about others' emotions. Individuals of various species recognize and respond appropriately to signals of emotion in conspecifics, and sometimes even allospecifics. For example, individuals respond to community alarm calls, discriminate between threatening and non-threatening potential predators (Carlson et al., 2020; Palmer & Gross, 2018), and avoid sites linked to an aversive experience for others (e.g., McKillup & McKillup, 1995). However, the ability to discriminate outward cues of distinct internal states does little to inform an individual's underlying representation of those cues. Do NHAs perceive the cues as merely predictive of different behavioral outcomes, or can they, like humans, represent emotion as an internal psychological state? Researchers currently do not have the tools to answer this question conclusively because the inference of internal states depends on their outward correlates, making it impossible to disentangle reasoning about the outward cues from representing the internal states.

This challenge notwithstanding, understanding the cues used clarifies the modality and mechanisms used by different species to interpret behavior related to emotion. The ability to discriminate emotion in other species is a highly researched skill in humans, but there is sparse research describing NHAs' abilities to discriminate emotions in species other than humans. Such studies have so far been limited to species that interact regularly with humans. Experimental studies of emotion discrimination commonly use a hidden object task whereby human experimenters direct an emotional expression (e.g., happiness, fear, disgust, neutral) to an object. Buttelmann and Tomasello found that dogs (2013) and chimpanzees (Buttelmann et al., 2009) discriminated containers associated with positive from negative (disgust) but not neutral emotions. Capuchin monkeys used the emotions of conspecifics, rather than humans, to evaluate the positive or negative valence of objects (Morimoto & Fujita, 2012). Merola and colleagues (2014) showed that dogs preferentially investigated a box to which caregivers directed happy over fearful or neutral expressions but did not differentiate boxes to which caregivers directed fearful versus neutral expressions. These researchers suggested that dogs learned to associate positive expressions of their caregivers with rewards. This research team has also shown that dogs and cats engage in social referencing when they are confronted with a novel or ambiguous object or situation (Merola et al., 2015), suggesting that they recognize that caregivers can provide cues as to whether a situation is safe or potentially dangerous. Both species adjusted their behavior depending on whether their caregivers provided positive or negative facial and vocal messages. Dogs mirrored their caregivers' behavior to positive and negative objects, suggesting a role for observational conditioning (Merola et al., 2012). Whether they recognized those cues as representative of their caregivers' underlying emotion is undetermined. Indeed, Yong and Ruffman (2015) tested dogs in a similar paradigm where dogs were more attentive to the experimenter when fearful or confused compared to when happy expressions were presented. They suggested that dogs do not understand the cues but seek more information under conditions of ambiguity.

Other paradigms assessing whether NHAs discriminate and represent emotions involve matching-to-sample tasks where the subject must match an image of a conspecific or human expressing a particular emotion to an image of a scenario that presents either a positive or negative valence. Chimpanzees matched such images accurately in a pioneering study by Parr (1998), but successful performance may reflect little more than associations between familiar events and objects and expressions that conspecifics displayed in concert with these events. Cross-modal matching experiments have examined whether dogs and cats can match a happy or angry vocalization with the corresponding facial expression. Dogs looked longer at happy or angry dog and human faces that were congruent with the vocalization valence. Cats showed a similar pattern except for positive cat emotions. The authors interpreted these findings to mean that dogs (Albuquerque et al., 2016) and cats (Quaranta et al., 2020) recognize emotional expressions in both conspecifics and humans. However, in violation of expectation paradigms, researchers typically interpret longer looking times to incongruent, rather than congruent, stimuli as a sign of comprehension, highlighting inconsistencies in how subjective measures such as looking time are interpreted. Furthermore, Quaranta et al.'s study (2020) suffered from a number of methodological limitations in addition to the inconsistent results. Contradictory results have also been obtained. Yong and Ruffman (2016) found that dogs did not look longer at matching emotional stimuli, although dogs preferred to look at angry or happy faces compared to sad faces, indicating that they did differentiate visual expressions.

In another study presenting dogs with faces of human emotion, dogs' viewing time, in contrast to humans, did not vary as a function of emotion expression. Dogs' visual scanning appeared more rigid than that of humans (Correia-Caerio et al., 2020). Therefore, whereas some companion dogs and cats may be sensitive to caregivers' expressions, they may not process this information in the same manner that humans do and may fail to generalize to unfamiliar humans, suggesting limited use of these cues. Horses also discriminate photographs of happy and angry human facial expressions, showing a left-gaze bias and increased heart rate to angry faces, which is a lateralized response associated with negative stimuli (Smith et al., 2016), and which was also demonstrated in dogs (Siniscalchi et al., 2018). However, no evidence for such differentiation emerged when the data of Smith et al. (2016) were reanalyzed using more sensitive measures (Schmoll, 2016). Functional asymmetries in the processing of facial emotions have also been evidenced in chimpanzees (Fernández-Carriba et al., 2002). Further work is needed to determine the representations that underlie performance in such tasks.

In a more naturalistic task, cats were observed for spontaneous reactions to familiar and unfamiliar humans expressing anger versus happiness (Galvan & Vonk, 2016). Cats displayed more positive behaviors and spent more time with their caregiver when the caregiver appeared happy compared to when she appeared angry. They also looked more to their caregiver than a stranger during a negative conversation, although this preference was not statistically significant for positive conversations. Horses, which have undergone greater selection pressure for sociality and interactions with humans compared to cats, respond differentially to human vocalizations of laughter and growling, showing increased freezing and vigilance to negative vocalizations compared to positive vocalizations (Smith et al., 2018). Although cats (Chijiiwa et al., 2021; Leete et al., 2020) have not demonstrated the ability to assign reputation to humans, horses appear to remember humans and respond differentially to them based on their previous facial expressions (Proops et al., 2018, although see Amici, 2019).

Humans have difficulty recognizing emotion in other species—an ability that may depend on experience and a positive attitude toward the species in question. Amici and colleagues (2019) found that humans could accurately recognize anger and happiness in dogs from an early age regardless of experience, but further experiences were necessary for more nuanced discriminations, as adults, on average, had difficulty recognizing fear in dogs. The same participants struggled to recognize emotions in chimpanzees. Despite close phylogenetic relatedness, chimpanzee expressions are markedly different from humans, with chimpanzees relying more on ear and head movements to convey emotion. Facial expressions appear to have evolved to be species-specific (Correia-Caerio et al., 2020). Thus, experience is critical for understanding emotions in other species, and it is likely that these abilities reflect associations between observable cues (either visual or auditory) and outcomes, rather than an abstract representation of emotion states in others.

Cognitive Measures
Cognitive Bias Tests
Observations of overt behaviors in response to valenced stimuli are valuable but may be subject to human error/bias (Mendl et al., 2010). Therefore, tests of cognitive bias have been developed to allow arguably more objective and standardized assessments of subjects' current positive or negative affective states. During the judgment bias test, a subject is trained to distinguish between a stimulus that is positive (associated with reward) and one that is negative (associated with aversive outcome or lack of reward) and is then presented with ambiguous stimuli that typically fall between the positive and negative stimuli on a perceptual or spatial continuum (Mendl et al., 2009). Subjects that respond to the ambiguous stimuli as they did to

the positive stimulus are defined as optimistic (positive affect), whereas those that respond to the ambiguous stimuli as they did to the negative stimulus are defined as pessimistic (negative affect; Düpjan et al., 2013). Cognitive bias tests have been used to examine affect after an emotional event (Baracchi et al., 2017). If an animal has been placed under stressful conditions, it is more likely to be pessimistic (Schlüns et al., 2017). The judgment bias test has also been presented following positive events, like added enrichment (Douglas et al., 2012; Keen et al., 2013; McGuire, Vonk, Fuller, & Allard, 2017) or to assess changes in affect based on seasonal or environmental changes (McGuire & Vonk, 2018; Vonk et al., 2021). These tests have demonstrated positive and negative affective states in many species, including insects (Adriaense et al., 2019; Asher et al., 2016; Daros et al., 2014; Deakin et al., 2016; d'Ettorre et al., 2017; Keen et al., 2013; McGuire et al., 2018). However, researchers have noted that judgments may reflect cognitive rather than emotional judgments (Perdue, 2017).

Variants of the cognitive bias test have been developed. The ambiguous cue paradigm has been modified to present subjects with novel ambiguous stimuli that do not simply reflect midpoints on a perceptual continuum between positive and negative stimuli. Subjects are presented with pairs of stimuli in a training phase that consisted of a stimulus that was always rewarded (P), a stimulus that was never rewarded (N), and an ambiguous stimulus (A) that was rewarded when paired with N but not rewarded when paired with P. At test, A was paired with a novel stimulus. Choices of A were considered to reflect optimistic responses. In addition to responses at test, responses in PA versus NA trials during training can reveal biases to focus on reward or lack of reward, which may be correlated with affect (McGuire, Vonk, Fuller, & Allard, 2017; McGuire, Vonk, & Johnson-Ulrich, 2017). A downside of all cognitive bias tests is the requirement of a criterion level of performance during a typically extensive training phase, and only a limited number of exposures to ambiguous stimuli are possible before they are no longer ambiguous. Furthermore, responses to the ambiguous stimuli are somewhat open to interpretation, with animals sometimes showing purportedly optimistic responses after negative events, thus sometimes leading researchers to re-evaluate test conditions rather than evaluating the validity of the paradigm (Perdue, 2017). Speeded response tests (Bethell et al., 2019; Cronin et al., 2018; McGuire & Vonk, 2020), as well as NHA applications of the emotional Stroop test (Allritz et al., 2016; Laméris et al., 2022; Vonk et al., 2022), have been developed to circumvent these concerns, but these have their own methodological limitations. Cognitive testing of emotional well-being is still under refinement, although the rapid proliferation of studies using such methods emphasizes the importance of assessing animals' emotional well-being without relying on inferences from external behaviors that can have different underlying causes.

Secondary Emotions

Humans recognize a range of emotions beyond the primary emotions of fear, anger, sadness, joy, and disgust, often referred to as secondary emotions (Ekman, 1992). For example, the self-conscious emotions, including shame, embarrassment, guilt, and pride (Miller & Leary, 1992; Tangney & Fischer, 1995), are hypothesized to emerge after self-awareness develops, at 18–24 months of age in humans (Lewis et al., 1989). Because these emotions are tied to self-awareness in humans, and there is not yet compelling evidence for self-awareness in NHAs, it is sometimes assumed that these emotions are absent in NHAs (Keltner & Buswell, 1997; although see Bekoff, 2002; Buck, 1999; Masson & McCarthy, 1995). Jealousy and envy are distinguished from these other self-conscious emotions in that they do not involve the evaluative component that includes an internalized rule (Morris et al., 2008), and may emerge earlier, perhaps as early as nine months in humans (Hart, 2016). If jealousy and envy appeared earlier in our evolutionary history, they may be widespread in NHAs. These emotions may be adaptive in allowing organisms to compete successfully for scarce resources.

There has been little empirical work investigating these emotions in NHAs. In the absence of validated psychological tools for exploring complex emotions in nonverbal organisms, one approach is to examine factors that underlie such emotions in humans and search for evidence of these predictors in other species. For example, if theory of mind (ToM), which allows organisms to reflect on how they are perceived by others, is necessary to experience self-conscious emotions, researchers can examine the subjective experience and expression of these emotions in individuals with ToM impairments, such as individuals with autism. Although the absence of such emotions in these individuals would not allow a definitive conclusion that these emotions must also be lacking in NHAs for whom there is little evidence of ToM, positive evidence would suggest that ToM is not necessary for the experience and expression of these emotions. Similarly, if empathy is presumed a prerequisite for shame and guilt due to the ability to internalize the feelings we may have caused in others, then we should not expect these emotions to be experienced in NHAs for whom there is little evidence of empathy. Note that the absence of evidence does not necessitate that the capacities are absent in NHAs, because the same challenges that confound experiments designed to uncover the subjective experience of emotion also overwhelm our capacity to effectively test for ToM or empathy in nonverbal organisms (see Povinelli, 2020). Furthermore, humans have difficulty distinguishing expressions of these complex secondary emotions, even in humans (Ekman, 1993). These challenges aside, below we briefly reflect on what is known about secondary emotions in NHAs.

Shame/Guilt/Embarrassment

In humans, self-conscious emotions likely emerge from socialization to human communal norms (Miller & Leary, 1992). Although it has been argued that these emotions may serve social goals rather than biological functions (Keltner & Buswell, 1997), social goals should be conceived of as supporting biological functions rather than as mutually exclusive motives. Embarrassment, shame, and guilt are distinguished in that they are evoked by attributions of different emotions; shame is linked to others' anger and disgust, guilt is linked to others' pain, and embarrassment is linked to others' amusement (Keltner & Buswell, 1997). Thus, if humans alone attribute emotion to others (ToM), they may be unique in the capacity to distinguish these emotions (Bennett & Gillingham, 1991; Tangney et al., 1996). Children with autism differ from neurotypical controls in narratives of embarrassment, but not sadness or happiness (Capps et al., 1992). Furthermore, ToM may allow humans to experience vicarious emotions, such as embarrassment for another. There is some evidence for emotional contagion in NHAs; however, this work has focused on contagion of emotions like distress, rather than contagion of secondary emotions.

If secondary emotions promote peaceful coexistence by encouraging community members to follow group norms to avoid aversive emotional experiences, other group-living species may experience similar emotions. However, as these emotions seem to be based on a sense of shared norms and values, their emergence would depend on the capacity for the rudimentary elements of a sense of morality. It is unlikely that asocial species would experience these emotions as they serve little purpose other than to encourage adherence to social norms and values. Dog owners routinely report dogs behaving in ways consistent with shame when they have misbehaved (Hecht et al., 2012) and researchers have examined whether dogs feel shame or guilt for committing a forbidden act (Horowitz, 2009). However, the behaviors could also be interpreted as anticipating punishment from the caregiver based on past experiences. If companion animals show these emotions only in the presence of a human, and especially a scolding or otherwise apparently angry human, it is likely that they are responding to the threat of this negative outcome rather than to an internal state of shame or guilt (Horowitz, 2009; Ostojić et al., 2015).

Researchers have examined appeasement displays in NHAs as a corollary to embarrassment (e.g., de Waal 1986, 1988). The displays, which appear in diverse species including rodents, birds, and nonhuman primates, share some similarities such as gaze aversion, downward head movements revealing the neck—resulting in a reduction in apparent size—and self-touching or grooming (summarized in Table 5 in Keltner & Buswell, 1997). It is possible that embarrassment serves a similar function in humans and other species—to reduce aggression or retaliation after a social transgression. By this account, embarrassment and appeasement displays function to restore social relations, which promotes group stability. As Keltner and Buswell (1997) acknowledge, appeasement in NHAs seems evoked primarily by tangible events, rather than the sorts of abstract representations of social rules that dictate the experience of these emotions in humans.

Of the self-conscious emotions, shame and embarrassment were reported at the lowest rates in a survey of companion animal caregivers (Morris et al., 2008). Whereas there were few species differences in the reporting of primary emotions, there was a large range in the reporting of secondary emotions, with these emotions being ascribed with the greatest frequency to dogs, except for pride and empathy, which were most frequently reported for horses.

Envy/Jealousy

Theorists propose that jealousy may serve an adaptive function and exist in a basic form in infants and NHAs, while a more elaborated form may be unique to humans. This more elaborated form develops with age in concert with increasing cognitive sophistication (Chung & Harris, 2018). The core motivational state may be rooted in the need to prevent others from interfering with important social relationships. The basic form of jealousy can be described as motivating an urge to regain attention that a close associate is paying to a rival (Chung & Harris, 2018). Jealousy is sometimes treated as synonymous with envy, although envy may be used when one desires what another possesses (Cohen-Charash, 2009), rather than resulting from the loss of a personal relationship. As with the self-conscious emotions, jealousy is presumed adaptive for animals that may experience conflict among siblings for access to resources and parental attention (Harris & Prouvost, 2014) or conflict among competitors for access to mates. Thus, although one might expect a greater likelihood of jealousy in group-living species, group-living is not a necessary condition so long as the animal relies on some form of social interaction for resources that are critical for survival and reproduction.

Of secondary emotions, people ascribed jealousy to their with companion animals at the highest rate (Morris et al., 2008). Su et al. (2018) also found that caregivers attributed jealousy to both dogs and cats at very high levels. Higher levels of attachment were strongly associated with attribution of emotions to pets. Morris et al. conducted a follow-up interview with 40 caregivers to identify the contexts and behaviors that indicate jealousy in their dogs. The most common context involved the lavishing of affection or attention on another (often the caregiver's partner). Descriptions of jealousy were limited to cases of immediate precipitating factors and not the kind of persistent abstractions of personal relations that provoke jealous feelings in humans. Anecdotally, people with companion animals often ascribe jealousy to their animals (Hötzel et al., 2019; Mathes & Deuger, 1982; Mitchell & Hamm, 1997; Morris et al., 2008), but it is possible to explain their behavior without referring to an underlying state of jealousy. Animals respond to loss of resources in a way that is adaptive. If the behavior has been selected for over generations or trained in a constrained series of circumstances, as is the case for guarding behavior, it is difficult to consider it as analogous to human jealousy.

Recently, some empirical attention has been given to whether other species experience jealousy. However, even when NHAs act aggressively toward potential rivals, it is difficult to determine whether NHAs experience jealousy or are responding directly to the threatened loss of desired objects or resources. A dog that bites a new puppy that is receiving affection from his caregivers could just as readily be angry or fearful of the new puppy as it is jealous that his caregivers are giving the puppy so much attention. To begin to tease these motivations apart, researchers might contrast the dog's response to the puppy when the puppy is receiving attention from the dog's caregivers versus from a stranger. One influential study examined domestic dogs' response to their caregivers' attention to three different objects. Consistent with jealousy, dogs displayed more attention-seeking and aggressive behaviors when the caregiver directed attention to a moving, barking toy dog, compared to an inanimate object or a book (Harris & Prouvost, 2014). Notably, jealous behaviors are indicated when attention and affection is redirected to a third party, not simply withdrawn. However, it is unclear the extent to which dogs are "fooled" by the fake dogs used in these studies (Prato-Previde, Nicotra, Fusar Poli, et al., 2018; Prato-Previde, Nicotra, Pelosi, et al., 2018). Instead, fake dogs may be merely strange and confusing, eliciting greater attention than the control objects. In another study with dogs (Cook et al., 2018), the availability of the food was not controlled and there was no control condition where the dog was present but not receiving food. Furthermore, because this study involved food rather than affection, it may not meet the criteria for evoking jealousy rather than envy (Vonk, 2018). Abdai et al. (2018) found that dogs showed more jealous behavior with social partners versus objects as targets of attention. Lastly, some researchers using similar protocols have failed to find evidence of jealousy in dogs (Prato-Previde, Nicotra, Fusar Poli, et al., 2018; Prato-Previde, Nicotra, Pelosi, et al., 2018). For example, dogs did not actively try to regain the owner's attention or intervene between the owner and the fake dog, nor did they differentiate the caregiver from an unfamiliar person interacting with the same objects (Prato-Previde, Nicotra, Pelosi, et al., 2018).

When the neurobiology of an emotion is well understood, it might be possible to examine brain activation in NHAs for similar responses to analogous events. In humans, jealousy is linked to activation in subcortical regions including the amygdala and hippocampus, as well as in the insula and regions of the posterior temporal sulcus (Harmon-Jones et al., 2009). There are sex differences in the pattern of activation as well, further complicating the picture. Rilling and colleagues (2004) showed increased activation in the same brain areas in male rhesus macaques watching a mate interact with another male, which is suggestive that there are similar subjective experiences when watching events that might invoke jealousy. Cook et al. (2018) found amygdala activation to be greater for dogs observing caregivers providing food to a fake dog compared to placing food in a bucket. However, it is possible that the dogs were simply responding to the receipt of reward by a conspecific without attending to the role the caregiver played in offering the food.

Although most experimental research has focused on the human-animal bond rather than exploring jealousy between conspecifics, one notable exception examined the response of socially monogamous male coppery Titi monkeys to conditions in which their female mate or an unfamiliar female was next to a stranger male (Maninger et al., 2017). Functional imaging was used to examine cerebral glucose metabolism. Testosterone, cortisol, oxytocin, and vasopressin—hormones involved in mate guarding—were also measured in each condition. Neural and physiological changes in the jealousy condition coincided with greater looking at the mate versus the pair involving strangers. Maninger and colleagues suggested that these changes may underpin the experience of jealousy in nonhuman primates to maintain the reproductive pair unit. However, Webb et al. (2020) observed that chimpanzees directed negative reactions at dyads containing new group members when social conditions for jealousy were met (Webb et al., 2020). Negative reactions to social closeness among groupmates increased during a period of introductions of novel members to the group and were more pronounced when the actor had a strong personal tie to one of the members of the dyad, consistent with a jealousy-based explanation. Males were more likely to intervene in male-male dyads, suggesting that rivalry over mates was not the primary mechanism. These authors argue for the adaptive nature of jealous reactions in protecting fitness-enhancing relationships, including those of a coalitionary nature.

As it becomes more acceptable to view the study of secondary emotions in NHAs as viable, researchers will continue to profit from technological and methodological advances in these areas.

Selection Pressures

In the above sections we have incorporated speculation about selection pressures that likely gave rise to particular emotion capacities in different species. Our necessarily shallow review of the broad literature suggests that humans have yet to reach a clear understanding of how emotion is experienced and expressed in NHAs. This knowledge is hampered by insufficient methodology, ethical concerns, and human bias. Yet, even complex emotions like jealousy are clearly not unique to humans. The expression of emotion is unlikely restricted to group-living species and is adaptive for animals that engage in any form of social interaction, whether affiliative or agonistic. Thus far, there is greater evidence for discrimination of others' emotions in social species such as primates and dogs, but this is likely affected by biases to study emotion in social species. We have touched on the modalities in which emotion can be expressed, yet it is likely that there are means by which animals convey emotion states that are inaccessible to humans, who are limited by our own subjective experiences and sensory capacities. Despite these weaknesses, however, humans may be unique in our ability to reason about the emotions of other species as underlying psychological experiences. Given this privileged ability, humans should use this capacity and knowledge to inform their practices in managing the lives of captive animals.

Artificial Selection

The evolution and experience of emotion in a significant proportion of NHAs are driven by both purposeful and accidental artificial selection. Humans select for or against emotional experiences in other species that contribute to the farmed, companion animal, and laboratory animal industries. Different emotions are adaptive or maladaptive in these artificial environments.

The experience of fear is widespread in NHAs. In the mid-trophic levels of a natural ecosystem, fear of predators is essential to ecosystem balance, whereby animals reduce their foraging efforts to avoid predation. Removing the need for fear of predators in those species changes the foraging behavior of mid-trophic species, thus allowing lower trophic species to increase in abundance (Suraci et al., 2016). Fear is critical to maximizing fitness and increasing survival for prey species. However, chronic fear is linked to reduced survival, often through downstream effects of chronically elevated glucocorticoids (Clinchy et al., 2013). The implications of this "ecology of fear" for domestication of NHAs are wide-ranging (Brown et al., 1999). The best candidates for domestication are species that do not have a natural fear of humans, or species in which that fear can be reduced through artificial selection. The experience of fear in farmed species is likely the result of multiple factors including (1) the selection (either natural or human-directed) of less fearful species to domesticate; (2) natural selection for less fearful individuals through impacts of fear on fitness in captive environments; and (3) artificial selection of traits linked to fear.

Domestication began 12,000 years ago via three potential pathways: commensal, prey, or directed (Teletchea, 2016). Commensal domestication was largely driven by animals like chickens, cats, and dogs themselves, that moved into human environments and developed a relationship of mutual benefit. In the prey pathway, humans were the primary drivers of domestication, choosing species similar to those they had depleted through hunting (e.g., sheep, goats, cattle) and beginning to manage their wild populations until eventually they managed their reproduction. The directed pathway was also driven by humans and was a quicker, more purposeful attempt to control the reproduction of wild species, resulting in artificial selection to meet human needs (e.g., horses, donkeys, camels).

Regardless of the pathway to domestication, one of the most notable evolutionary changes to domesticated species is the reduction or elimination of fear of humans (Driscoll et al., 2009; Teletchea, 2016). During commensal domestication, less fearful (and potentially bolder) individuals moved into human environments, where they experienced increased fitness relative to their wild counterparts and, hence, resulted in future generations that were less fearful. Indeed, birds in urban areas are less fearful of humans than their rural counterparts (Møller, 2010). During prey domestication, humans were more likely to choose species that exhibited a tolerance to human approach and, hence, were also less fearful. During directed domestication, humans likely chose first less fearful species, and then, less fearful individuals.

Fear is arguably the most well-studied emotion in farmed animals, likely because a reduction in fear allows NHAs to be in close enough contact with a potential predator (i.e., humans) that they can be subjected to stressful industry standard practices such as tail docking, castration, beak trimming, and disbudding. Humans have artificially selected for production, in the case of animals used as food, traits like growth rate and body weight (Haskell et al., 2014; Tallentire et al., 2016). Coincidentally, a growing body of research finds that many of the traits favored by the chicken industry occur in concert with reduced fearfulness (Agnvall et al., 2012; Agnvall et al., 2015; Agnvall et al., 2018; Kops et al., 2013) and that behavioral reactions in a human approach test are heritable (Agnvall et al., 2012; Katajamaa et al., 2018). Whereas there is no evidence that modern-day artificial selection efforts have purposely selected against fear responses in chickens, fear is linked to traits that are desired in chickens raised for food.

In cattle, recent research highlights the need to incorporate personality traits that impact the ease of handling animals, including fearfulness, into selection indexes. This could increase welfare while also increasing productivity, as calmer animals grow faster, have better feed conversion rates, and have improved meat quality (Haskell et al., 2014).

The animal agriculture and aquaculture industries can use this knowledge to further reduce fear, and potentially increase traits that result in positive emotion under farming conditions (Agnvall et al., 2018; Boissy et al., 2005). However, caution is warranted when integrating behavioral traits, including personality and emotion, into selection indices, as selection for desirable traits may result in unintended selection of undesirable traits (Boissy et al., 2005). Aggression and behavior during handling in pigs (i.e., fear) are heritable, and aggressive pigs are harder to handle (d'Eath et al., 2009). Chen and others (1994) eliminated fear in mice through introduction of knock-out genes, and without fear, the mice fought so hard against a conspecific that they often injured themselves.

Conclusion

A variety of species experience both positively and negatively valenced emotions, and the environments humans put NHAs in impact those emotions (Douglas et al., 2012). Humans have a moral obligation to provide "a life worth living" for the billions of animals in our care (Mellor, 2016). Many emotions are either heritable or linked to heritable traits, which suggests the possibility of genetic selection to improve welfare. A vast body of animal welfare research can inform the provision of animals with environments conducive to a positive welfare state in which the proportion of positively valenced emotion states outweighs negatively valenced states. Because of the potential pitfalls in genetic selection for NHAs that are more likely to experience positively valenced emotions (Chen et al., 1994; d'Eath et al., 2009), we urge those responsible for the care of NHAs to utilize animal welfare science to improve environmental conditions, to exploit the variety of methods available to measure emotion, and where that knowledge does not exist, to encourage and support those research efforts while considering the possibility that not all species can experience positive emotions in captivity. Furthermore, we recognize that research on emotion in NHAs is conceived of and designed through a human lens. If we consider that there may be some emotions unique to humans, we must also consider that there may be others that are unique to NHAs, and that our human perspective may be insufficient to uncover these emotions.

References

Abdai, J., Baño Terencio, C., Pérez Fraga, P., & Miklósi, Á. (2018). Investigating jealous behaviour in dogs. *Scientific Reports*, *8*(1), 8911. doi: 10.1038/s41598-018-27251-1

Adriaense, J. E. C., Martin, J. S., Schiestl, M., Lamm, C., & Bugnyar, T. (2019). Negative emotional contagion and cognitive bias in common ravens (*corvus corax*). *Proceedings of the National Academy of Sciences*, *116*(23), 11547–11552. http://dx.doi.org/10.1073/pnas.1817066116

Agnvall, B., Bélteky, J., Katajamaa, R., & Jensen, P. (2018). Is evolution of domestication driven by tameness? A selective review with focus on chickens. *Applied Animal Behaviour Science*, *205*, 227–233. https://doi.org/10.1016/j.applanim.2017.09.006

Agnvall, B., Jöngren, M., Strandberg, E., & Jensen, P. (2012). Heritability and genetic correlations of fear-related behaviour in red junglefowl-possible implications for early domestication. *PLoS ONE*, *7*(4). https://doi.org/10.1371/journal.pone.0035162

Agnvall, B., Katajamaa, R., Altimiras, J., & Jensen, P. (2015). Is domestication driven by reduced fear of humans? Boldness, metabolism and serotonin levels in divergently selected red junglefowl (*Gallus gallus*). *Biology Letters*, *11*(9), 10–13. https://doi.org/10.1098/rsbl.2015.0509

Albuquerque, N., Guo, K., Wilkinson, A., Savalli, C., Otta, E., & Mills, D. (2016). Dogs recognize dog and human emotions. *Biology Letters*, *12*, 20150883. http://dx.doi.org/10.1098/rsbl.2015.0883

Allritz, M., Call, J., & Borkenau, P. (2016). How chimpanzees (*Pan troglodytes*) perform in a modified emotional Stroop task. *Animal Cognition*, *19*, 435–449. doi: 10.1007/s10071-015-0944-3

Amici, F. (2019). Memories of emotional expressions in horses. *Learning and Behavior*, *47*, 191–192. https://doi.org/10.3758/s13420-018-0363-9

Amici, F., Waterman, J., Kellermann, M., Karimullah, K. & Brauer, J. (2019). The ability to recognize dog emotions depends on the cultural milieu in which we grow up. *Scientific Reports*, *9*, 16414. https://doi.org/10.1038/s41598-019-52938-4

Asher, L., Friel, M., Griffin, K., & Collins, L. M. (2016). Mood and personality interact to determine cognitive biases. *Biology Letters*, *12*(11), 20160402.

Baldwin, J. D., & Baldwin, J. I. (1976). Effects of food energy ecology on social play: A laboratory simulation. *Zeitschrift für Tierpsychologie*, *40*(1), 1–14. http://dx.doi.org/10.1111/j.1439-0310.1976.tb00922.x

Baracchi, D., Lihoreau, M., & Giurfa, M. (2017). Do insects have emotions? Some insights from bumble bees. *Frontiers in Behavioral Neuroscience*, *11*, 157. doi: 10.3389/fnbeh.2017.00157

Bekoff, M. (2002). *Minding animals: Awareness, emotions and heart.* Oxford University Press.

Bennett, M., & Gillingham, K. (1991). The role of self-focused attention in children's attributions of social emotions to the self. *Journal of Genetic Psychology*, *152*, 303–309.

Bennet, V., Gourkow, N., & Mills, D. S. (2017). Facial correlates of emotional behaviour in the domestic cat (*Felis catus*). *Behavioural Processes, 141*, 342–350. doi: 10.1016/j.beproc.2017.03.011

Bethell, E. J., Cassidy, L. C., Brockhausen, R. R., & Pfefferle, D. (2019). Toward a standardized test of fearful temperament in primates: A sensitive alternative to the human intruder task for laboratory-housed rhesus macaques (*macaca mulatta*). *Frontiers in Psychology, 10*, 17. http://dx.doi.org/10.3389/fpsyg.2019.01051

Bloom, T. & Friedman, H. (2013). Classifying dogs' (*Canis familiaris*) facial expressions from photographs. *Behavioural Processes, 96*, 1–10. https://doi.org/10.1016/j.beproc.2013.02.010

Blum, M. S. (1969). Alarm pheromones. *Annual Review of Entomology, 14*, 57–80. http://doi. 10.1146/annurev.en.14.010169.000421

Boileau, A., Farish, M., Turner, S. P., & Camerlink, I. (2019). Infrared thermography of agonistic behaviour in pigs. *Physiology & Behavior, 210*, 112637. http://dx.doi.org/10.1016/j.physbeh.2019.112637

Boissy, A. & Bouissou, M. F. (1995). Assessment of individual differences in behavioural reactions of heifers exposed to various fear-eliciting situations. *Applied Animal Behaviour Science, 46*(1–2), 17–31. doi: 10.1016/0168-1591(95)00633-8

Boissy, A., Fisher, A. D., Bouix, J., Hinch, G. N., & Le Neindre, P. (2005). Genetics of fear in ruminant livestock. *Livestock Production Science, 93*(1), 23–32. https://doi.org/10.1016/j.livprodsci.2004.11.003

Boissy, A., Manteuffel, G., Jensen, M. B., Moe, R. O., Spruijt, B., Keeling, L. J., Winckler, C., Forkman, B., Dimitrov, I., Langbein, J., Bakken, M., Veissier, I., & Aubert, A. (2007). Assessment of positive emotions in animals to improve their welfare. *Physiology & Behavior, 92*, 375–397. doi: 10.1016/j.physbeh.2007.02.003

Boissy, A., Terlouw, C., & Le Neindre, P. (1998). Presence of cues from stressed conspecifics increases reactivity to aversive events in cattle: Evidence for the existence of alarm substances in urine. *Physiology & Behavior, 63*(4), 489–495. https://doi.org/10.1016/s0031-9384(97)00466-6

Bowler, D. E., Buyung-Ali, L. M., Knight, T. M., & Pullin, A. S. (2010). A systematic review of evidence for the added benefits to health of exposure to natural environments. *BMC Public Health, 10*, 456. https://doi.org/10.1186/1471-2458-10-456

Brajon, S., Laforest, J. P., Bergeron, R., Tallet, C., Hötzel, M. J., & Devillers, N. (2015). Persistency of the piglet's reactivity to the handler following a previous positive or negative experience. *Applied Animal Behaviour Science, 162*, 9–19. doi: 10.1016/j.applanim.2014.11.009

Briefer, E., Linhart, P., Policht, R., Špinka, M., Leliveld, L., Düpjan, S., Puppe, B., Padilla de la Torre, M., Janczak, A., Bourguet, C., Deiss, V., Boissy, A., Guérin, C., Read, E., Coulon, M., Hillmann, E., & Tallet, C. (2019). Vocal expression of emotional valence in pigs across multiple call types and contexts. *PeerJ*, 27934-1. https://doi.org/10.7287/peerj.preprints.27934

Briefer, E. F., Tettamanti, F., & McElligott, A. G. (2015). Emotions in goats: Mapping physiological, behavioural and vocal profiles. *Animal Behaviour, 99*, 131–143. https://doi.org/10.1016/j.anbehav.2014.11.002

Brosnan, S. F. & Vonk, J. (2019). Nonhuman primate responses to death. In T. K. Shackelford and V. Zeigler-Hill (Eds.), *Evolutionary perspectives on death* (pp. 77–107). Springer.

Brown, J. S., Laundré, J. W., & Gurung, M. (1999). The ecology of fear: Optimal foraging, game theory, and trophic interactions. *Journal of Mammalogy, 80*(2), 385–399.

Bubier, N. E. (1996). The behavioural priorities of laying hens: The effect of cost/no cost multi-choice tests on time budgets. *Behavioural Processes, 37*(2–3), 225–238. https://doi.org/10.1016/0376-6357(96)00019-8

Buck, R. (1999). The biology of affects: A typology. *Psychological Review, 106*, 301–336.

Burghardt, G. M. (2019). A place for emotions in behavior systems research. *Behavioural Processes, 166*, 7. http://dx.doi.org/10.1016/j.beproc.2019.06.004

Burghardt, G. M., Dinets, V., & Murphy, J. B. (2015). Highly repetitive object play in a cichlid fish (*tropheus duboisi*). *Ethology, 121*(1), 38–44. http://dx.doi.org/10.1111/eth.12312

Burghardt, G. M., Ward, B., & Rosscoe, R. (1996). Problem of reptile play: Environmental enrichment and play behavior in a captive Nile soft-shelled turtle *Trionyx triunguis*. *Zoo Biology, 15*(3), 223–238. http://dx.doi.org/10.1002/(SICI)1098-2361(1996)15:3<223::AID-ZOO3>3.0.CO;2-D

Buttelmann, D., Call, J., & Tomasello, M. (2009). Do great apes use emotional expressions to infer desires? *Developmental Science, 12*(5), 688–698. http://dx.doi.org/10.1111/j.1467-7687.2008.00802.x

Buttelmann, D., & Tomasello, M. (2013). Can domestic dogs (*Canis familiaris*) use referential emotional expressions to locate hidden food? *Animal Cognition, 16*(1), 137–145. http://dx.doi.org/10.1007/s10071-012-0560-4

Cabanac, M., & Aizawa, S. (2000). Fever and tachycardia in a bird (*Gallus domesticus*) after simple handling. *Physiology and Behavior, 69*(4–5), 541–545. https://doi.org/10.1016/S0031-9384(00)00227-4

Cabanac, M., & Bernieri, C. (2000). Behavioral rise in body temperature and tachycardia by handling of a turtle (*Clemmys insculpta*). *Behavioural Processes, 49*(2), 61–68. https://doi.org/10.1016/S0376-6357(00)00067-X

Cabanac, A. & Cabanac, M. (2000). Heart rate response to gentle handling of frog and lizard. *Behavioural Processes, 52*(2–3), 89–95. doi: 10.1016/S0376-6357(00)00108-X

Caeiro, C. C., Burrows, A. M., Waller, B. M. (2017). Development and application of CatFACS: Are human cat adopters influenced by cat facial expressions? *Applied Animal Behaviour Science, 189*, 66–78.

Caeiro, C. C., Waller, B. M., Burrows, A. M., Zimmermann, E., Davila-Ross, M. (2013). OrangFACS: A muscle-based coding system for orangutan facial movements. *International Journal of Primatology, 34*(1), 115–129.

Cannas, S., Mattiello, S., Battini, M., Ingraffia, S. I., Cadoni, D., & Palestrini, C. (2020). Evaluation of Maine Coon cat behavior during three different management situations. *Journal of Veterinary Behavior, 37*, 93–100. doi: 10.1016/j.jveb.2019.12.004

Capps, L., Yirmiya, N., & Sigman, M. (1992). Understanding of simple and complex emotions in non-retarded children with autism. *Journal of Child Psychology and Psychiatry, 33*, 1169–1182.

Carlson, N. V., Healy, S. D., & Templeton, C. N. (2020). What makes a "community informant"? Reliability and anti-predator signal eavesdropping across mixed-species flocks of tits. *Animal Behavior and Cognition, 7*(2), 214–246. https://doi.org/10.26451/abc.07.02.13.2020

Cassill, D., Ford, K., Huynh, L., Shiffman, D., Vinson, S. B. (2016). A study on abdominal wagging in the fire ant, *Solenopsis invicta*, with speculation on its meaning. *Journal of Bioeconomics, 18*, 159–167. doi: 10.1007/s10818-016-9226-7

Chandroo, K. P., Duncan, I. J. H., & Moccia, R. D. (2004). Can fish suffer?: Perspectives on sentience, pain, fear and stress. *Applied Animal Behaviour Science, 86*(3–4), 225–250. doi: 10.1016/j.applanim.2004.02.004

Chapman, C. A., & Huffman, M. A. (2018). Why do we want to think humans are different? *Animal Sentience, 163*, 1–8.

Chen, C., Rainnie, D. G., Greene, R. W., & Tonegawa, S. (1994). Abnormal fear response and aggressive behavior in mutant mice deficient for alpha-calcium-calmodulin kinase II. Science, 266(5183), 291–294.

Chijiiwa, H., Takagi, S., Arahori, M., Anderson, J. R., Fujita, K., & Kuroshima, H. (2021). Cats (*Felis catus*) show no avoidance of people who behave negatively to their owner. *Animal Behavior and Cognition, 8*(1), 23–35. https://doi.org/10.26451/abc.08.01.05.2020

Chotard, H., Ioannou, S., & Davila-Ross, M. (2018). Infrared thermal imaging: Positive and negative emotions modify the skin temperatures of monkey and ape faces. *American Journal of Primatology, 80*(5), e22863. doi: 10.1002/ajp.22863

Chung, M., & Harris, C. R. (2018). Jealousy as a specific emotion: The dynamic functional model. *Emotion Review, 10*(4), 272–287. http://dx.doi.org/10.1177/1754073918795257

Clinchy, M., Sheriff, M. J., & Zanette, L. Y. (2013). Predator-induced stress and the ecology of fear. *Functional Ecology, 27*(1), 56–65. https://doi.org/10.1111/1365-2435.12007

Cohen-Charash, Y. (2009). Episodic envy. *Journal of Applied Social Psychology, 39*, 2128–2173. https://doi.org/10.1111/j.1559-1816.2009.00519.x

Cook, P., Prichard, A., Spivak, M. & Berns, G. S. (2018). Jealousy in dogs? Evidence from brain imaging. *Animal Sentience, 22*(1). https://doi.org/10.51291/2377-7478.1319

Correia-Caeiro, C., Guo, K., & Mills, D. S. (2020). Perception of dynamic facial expressions of emotion between dogs and humans. *Animal Cognition, 23*(3), 465–476. http://dx.doi.org/10.1007/s10071-020-01348-5

Cronin, K. A., Bethell, E. J., Jacobson, S. L., Egelkamp, C., Hopper, L. M., & Ross, S. R. (2018). Evaluating mood changes in response to anthropogenic noise with a response-slowing task in three species of zoo-housed primates. *Animal Behavior and Cognition, 5*(2), 209–221. https://doi.org/10.26451/abc.05.02.03.2018

Czycholl, I., Hauschild, E., Büttner, K., Krugmann, K., Burfeind, O., & Krieter, J. (2020). Tail and ear postures of growing pigs in two different housing conditions. *Behavioural Processes, 176*, 104138. https://doi.org/10.1016/j.beproc.2020.104138

Dai, F., Cogi, N. H., Heinzl, E. U. L., Dalla Costa, E., Canali, E., & Minero, M. (2015). Validation of a fear test in sport horses using infrared thermography. *Journal of Veterinary Behavior: Clinical Applications and Research, 10*(2), 128–136. http://dx.doi.org/10.1016/j.jveb.2014.12.001

Daros, R. R., Costa, J. H., von Keyserlingk, M. A., Hotzel, M. J., & Weary, D. M. (2014). Separation from the dam causes negative judgment bias in dairy calves. *PloS ONE, 9*(5), e98429. doi: 10.1371/journal.pone.0098429

Darwin, C. (1872). *The expression of emotions in man and animals*. Philosophical Library.

Davila-Ross, M., Allcock, B., Thomas, C., & Bard, K. A. (2011). Aping expressions? Chimpanzees produce distinct laugh types when responding to laughter of others. *Emotion, 11*(5), 1013–1020. https://doi.org/10.1037/a0022594

Davila-Ross, M., Jesus, G., Osborne, J., & Bard, K. A. (2015). Chimpanzees (*Pan troglodytes*) produce the same types of "laugh faces" when they emit laughter and when they are silent. *PLoS ONE, 10*(6), e0127337. doi: 10.1371/journal.pone.0127337

Davis, K. L., & Montag, C. (2019). Selected principles of Pankseppian affective neuroscience. *Frontiers in Neuroscience, 13*, 1–11. https://doi.org/10.3389/fnins.2018.01025

Dawkins, M. S. (2006). Through animal eyes: What behaviour tells us. *Applied Animal Behaviour Science, 100*(1–2), 4–10. doi: 10.1016/j.applanim.2006.04.010

Deakin, A., Browne, W. J., Hodge, J. J. L., Paul, E. S., & Mendl, M. (2016). A screen-peck task for investigating cognitive bias in laying hens. *PloS ONE, 11*(7), 1–13. doi: 10.1371/journal.pone.0158222

D'Eath, R. B., Roehe, R., Turner, S. P., Ison, S. H., Farish, M., Jack, M. C., & Lawrence, A. B. (2009). Genetics of animal temperament: Aggressive behaviour at mixing is genetically associated with the response to handling in pigs. *Animal, 3*(11), 1544–1554. https://doi.org/10.1017/S1751731109990528

De Catanzaro, D. A. (1999). *Motivation and emotion: Evolutionary, physiological, developmental, and social perspectives.* Prentice-Hall.

Dellinge-Ness, L. A. & Handler, L. (2006). Self-injurious behavior in human and non-human primates. *Clinical Psychology Review, 26*(5), 503–514. doi: 10.1016/j.cpr.2006.03.004

del Toro, C. J., Mondragón-Ceballos, R., & Gutiérrez-García, G. (2020). Potential food availability influences social interactions of young individuals in a neotropical primate (*alouatta palliata*). *Folia Primatologica, 91*(1), 31–47.

Désiré, L., Boissy, A., & Veissier, I. (2002). Emotions in farm animals: A new approach to animal welfare in applied ethology. *Behavioural Processes, 60*(2), 165–180. https://doi.org/10.1016/S0376-6357(02)00081-5

d'Ettorre, P., Carere, C., Demora, L., Le Quinquis, P., Signorotti, L., & Bovet, D. (2017). Individual differences in exploratory activity relate to cognitive judgement bias in carpenter ants. *Behavioural Processes, 134*, 63–69. doi: 10.1016/j.beproc.2016.09.008

de Waal, F. B. M. (1986). The integration of dominance and social bonding in primates. *Quarterly Review of Biology, 61*, 459–479.

de Waal, F. B. M. (1988). The reconciled hierarchy. In M. R. A. Chance (Ed.), *Social fabrics of the mind* (pp. 105–136). Lawrence Erlbaum Associates.

Diamond, J., & Bond, A. B. (2003). A comparative analysis of social play in birds. *Behaviour, 140*, 1091–1115.

Douglas, C., Bateson, M., Walsh, C., Bédué, A., & Edwards, S. A. (2012). Environmental enrichment induces optimistic cognitive biases in pigs. *Applied Animal Behaviour Science, 139*(1), 65–73. https://doi.org/10.1016/j.applanim.2012.02.018

Døving, K. B. & Lastein, S. (2009). The alarm reaction in fishes: Odorants, modulations of responses, neural pathways. *Annals of the New York Academy of Sciences, 1170*, 413–423. doi: 10.1111/j.1749-6632.2009.04111.x

Driscoll, C. A., Macdonald, D. W., & O'Brien, S. J. (2009). From wild animals to domestic pets, an evolutionary view of domestication. *Proceedings of the National Academy of Sciences, 106*, 9971–9978. https://doi.org/10.1073/pnas.0901586106

Düpjan, S., Ramp, C., Kanitz, E., Tuchscherer, A., & Puppe, B. (2013). A design for studies on cognitive bias in the domestic pig. *Journal of Veterinary Behavior, 8*(6), 485–489. doi: 10.1016/j.jveb.2013.05.007

Edgar, J. L., Mullan, S. M., Pritchard, J. C., McFarlane, U. J. C., & Main, D. C. J. (2013). Towards a "good life" for farm animals: Development of a resource tier framework to achieve positive welfare for laying hens. *Animals, 3*(3), 584–605. https://doi.org/10.3390/ani3030584

Ekman, P. (1972). Universals and cultural differences in facial expressions of emotion. In J. Cole (Ed.), *Nebraska Symposium on Motivation* (pp. 207–283). University of Nebraska Press.

Ekman, P. (1992). An argument for basic emotions. *Cognition and Emotion, 6*, 169–200.

Ekman, P. (1993). Facial expression and emotion. *American Psychologist, 48*, 384–392.

Ekman, P., & Friesen, W. V. (1978). *Facial action coding system.* Environmental Psychology & Nonverbal Behavior. https://doi.org/10.1037/t27734-000

Ekman, P., Friesen, W. V., & Hager, J. C. (2002). *Facial action coding system.* Research Nexus.

Faraji, J., & Metz, G. A. S. (2020). Infrared thermography reveals sex-specific responses to stress in mice. *Frontiers in Behavioral Neuroscience, 14*, 1. doi:http://dx.doi.org/10.3389/fnbeh.2020.00079

Favreau-Peigné, A., Calandreau, L., Constantin, P., Bertin, A., Arnould, C., Laurence, A., Richard-Yris, M. A., Houdelier, C., Lumineau, S., Boissy, A., & Leterrier, C. (2016). Unpredictable and repeated negative stimuli increased emotional reactivity in male quail. *Applied Animal Behaviour Science, 183*, 86–94. doi: 10.1016/j.applanim.2016.07.010

Fernández-Carriba, S., Loeches, A., Morcillo, A., & Hopkins, W. D. (2002). Functional asymmetry of emotions in primates: New findings in chimpanzees. *Brain Research Bulletin, 57*(3–4), 561–564. doi: 10.1016/S0361-9230(01)00685-2

Forkman, B., Boissy, A., Meunier-Salaün, M. C., Canali, E., & Jones, R. B. (2007). A critical review of fear tests used on cattle, pigs, sheep, poultry and horses. *Physiology & Behavior, 92*(3), 340–374. doi: 10.1016/j.physbeh.2007.03.016

Friel, M., Kunc, H. P., Griffin, K., Asher, L., & Collins, L. M. (2019). Positive and negative contexts predict duration of pig vocalisations. *Scientific Reports, 9*(1), 1–7. https://doi.org/10.1038/s41598-019-38514-w

Frumin, I., Perl, O., Endevelt-Shapira, Y., Eisen, A., Eshel, N., Heller, I, Shemesh, M., Ravia, A., Sela, L., Arzi, A., & Sobel, N. (2015). A social chemosignaling function for human handshaking. *Elife, 4,* e05154.

Fujisawa, R., Dobata, S., Kubota, D., Imamura, H., & Matsuno, F. (2008). Dependency by concentration of pheromone trail for multiple robots. In *Ant Colony Optimization and Swarm Intelligence: 6th International Conference, ANTS 2008, Brussels, Belgium, September 22-24, 2008. Proceedings 6* (pp. 283–290). Springer. doi: 10.1007/978-3-540-87527-7_28

Galvan, M., & Vonk, J. (2016). Man's other best friend: Domestic cats (*F. silvestris catus*) and their understanding of human emotion cues. *Animal Cognition, 19,* 193–205. doi: 10.1007/s10071-015-0927-4.

Gartland, N., O'Connor, D. B., Lawton, R., & Bristow, M. (2014). Exploring day-to-day dynamics of daily stressor appraisals, physical symptoms and the cortisol awakening response. *Psychoneuroendocrinology, 50,* 130–138. doi: 10.1016/j.psyneun.2014.08.006

Gjendal, K., Franco, N. H., Ottesen, J. L., Sørensen, D. B., & Olsson, I. A. (2018). Eye, body or tail? thermography as a measure of stress in mice. *Physiology & Behavior, 196,* 135–143. http://dx.doi.org/10.1016/j.physbeh.2018.08.022

Gonçalves, A. & Carvalho, S. (2019). Death among primates: A critical review of non-human primate interactions towards their dead and dying. *Biological Reviews, 94,* 1502–1529. doi: 10.1111/brv.12512

Gruenewald, T. L., Dickerson, S. S., & Kemeny, M. E. (2007). A social function for self-conscious emotions: The social self preservation theory. In J. L. Tracy, R. W. Robins, & J. P. Tangney (Eds.), *The self-conscious emotions: Theory and research* (pp. 68–87). Guilford Press.

Hagen, K., & Broom, D. M. (2004). Emotional reactions to learning in cattle. *Applied Animal Behavioral Science, 85*(3–4), 203–213. https://doi: 10.1016/j.applanim.2003.11.00

Hanics, J., Teleki, G., Alpár, A., Székely, A. D., & Csillag, A. (2017). Multiple amygdaloid divisions of arcopallium send convergent projections to the nucleus accumbens and neighboring subpallial amygdala regions in the domestic chicken: A selective pathway tracing and reconstruction study. *Brain Structure & Function, 222*(1), 301–315. doi: 10.1007/s00429-016-1219-8

Hara, K., & Myers, R. E. (1973). Role of forebrain structures in emotional expression in opossum. *Brain Research, 52,* 131–144.

Harmon-Jones, E., Peterson, C. K., & Harris, C. R. (2009). Jealousy: Novel methods and neural correlates. *Emotion, 9*(1), 113–117. http://dx.doi.org/10.1002/9781444323542.ch23

Harris, C. R., & Prouvost, C. (2014). Jealousy in dogs. *PLoS ONE, 9*(7), e94597. doi: 10.1371/journal.pone.0094597

Hart, S. L. (2016). Proximal foundations of jealousy: Expectations of exclusivity in the infant's first year of life. *Emotion Review, 8*(4), 358–366. http://dx.doi.org/10.1177/1754073915615431

Haskell, M. J., Simm, G., & Turner, S. P. (2014). Genetic selection for temperament traits in dairy and beef cattle. *Frontiers in Genetics, 5*(Oct), 1–18. https://doi.org/10.3389/fgene.2014.00368

Hecht, J., Miklósi, Á., & Gácsi, M. (2012). Behavioral assessment and owner perceptions of behaviors associated with guilt in dogs. *Applied Animal Behaviour Science, 139*(1–2), 134–142. http://dx.doi.org/10.1016/j.applanim.2012.02.015

Heintz, M. R., Fuller, G., & Allard, S. (2019). Exploratory investigation of infrared thermography for measuring gorilla emotional responses to interactions with familiar humans. *Animals, 9*(9), 604.

Held, S. D. E., & Špinka, M. (2011). Animal play and animal welfare. *Animal Behaviour, 81*(5), 891–899. doi: 10.1016/j.anbehav.2011.01.007

Hemsworth, P. H., Barnett, J. L., Hansen, C., & Gonyou, H. W. (1986). The influence of early contact with humans on subsequent behavioural response of pigs to humans. *Applied Animal Behaviour Science, 15*(1), 55–63. http://dx.doi.org/10.1016/0168-1591(86)90022-5

Herborn, K. A., Jerem, P., Nager, R. G., McKeegan, D. E. F., & McCafferty, D. J. (2018). Surface temperature elevated by chronic and intermittent stress. *Physiology & Behavior, 191,* 47–55. http://dx.doi.org/10.1016/j.physbeh.2018.04.004

Hessing, M. J. C., Hagelsø, A. M., Van Beek, J. A., Wiepkema, P. R., Schouten, W. G. P., & Krukow, R. (1993). Individual behavioural characteristics in pigs. *Applied Animal Behaviour Science, 37*(4), 285–295. http://dx.doi.org/10.1016/0168-1591(93)90118-9

Hopper, L. M., Freeman, H. D., & Ross, S. R. (2016). Reconsidering coprophagy as an indicator of negative welfare for captive chimpanzees. *Applied Animal Behaviour Science, 176,* 112–119. doi: 10.1016/j.applanim.2016.01.002

Horowitz, A. (2009). Disambiguating the "guilty look": Salient prompts to a familiar dog behaviour. *Behavioural Processes, 81,* 447–452.

Hötzel, M. J., Vieira, M. C., & Leme, D. P. (2019). Exploring horse owners' and caretakers' perceptions of emotions and associated behaviors in horses. *Journal of Veterinary Behavior: Clinical Applications and Research, 29,* 18–24. http://dx.doi.org/10.1016/j.jveb.2018.10.002

Huber, A., Barber, A. L. A., Faragó, T., Müller, C. A., & Huber, L. (2017). Investigating emotional contagion in dogs (*Canis familiaris*) to emotional sounds of humans and conspecifics. *Animal Cognition, 20*(4), 703–715. http://dx.doi.org/10.1007/s10071-017-1092-8

Hussein, N. J. (2019). Using eye and nasal temperatures to measure positive emotions in free-range Hamdani Sheep. *Basrah Journal of Agricultural Sciences, 31*(2), 24–30. https://doi.org/10.37077/25200860.2018.96

Jack, R. E., Garrod, O. G. B., & Schyns, P. G. (2014). Dynamic facial expressions of emotion transmit an evolving hierarchy of signals over time. *Current Biology, 24*(2), 187–192. https://doi.org/10.1016/j.cub.2013.11.064

Jovanovic, T., Phifer, J. E., Sicking, K., Weiss, T., Norrholm, S. D., Bradley, B., & Ressler, K. J. (2011). Cortisol suppression by dexamethasone reduces exaggerated fear responses in posttraumatic stress disorder. *Psychoneuroendocrinology, 36*(10), 1540–1552. doi: 10.1016/j.psyneuen.2011.04.008

Kaas, J. H. (2011). Neocortex in early mammals and its subsequent variations. *Annals of the New York Academy of Sciences, 1225*, 28–36. doi: 10.1111/j.1749-6632.2011.05981.x

Kalin, N. H., Larson, C., Shelton, S. E., & Davidson, R. J. (1998). Asymmetric frontal brain activity, cortisol, and behavior associated with fearful temperament in rhesus monkeys. *Behavioral Neuroscience, 112*(2), 286–292. https://doi.org/10.1037/0735-7044.112.2.286

Kaminski, J., Waller, B. M., Diogo, R., Hartstone-Rose, A., & Burrows, A. M. (2019). Evolution of facial muscle anatomy in dogs. *Proceedings of the National Academy of Sciences, 116*(29), 14677–14681. https://doi.org/10.1073/pnas.1820653116

Kanitz, E., Tuchscherer, M., Otten, W., Tuchscherer, A., Zebunke, M., & Puppe, B. (2019). Coping style of pigs is associated with different behavioral, neurobiological and immune responses to stressful challenges. *Frontiers in Behavioral Neuroscience, 13*, 173. https://doi.org/10.3389/fnbeh.2019.00173

Karlson, P. & Lüscher, M. (1959). "Pheromones": A new term for a class of biologically active substances. *Nature, 183*, 55–56. https://doi.org/10.1038/183055a0

Katajamaa, R., Larsson, L. H., Lundberg, P., Sörensen, I., & Jensen, P. (2018). Activity, social and sexual behaviour in red junglefowl selected for divergent levels of fear of humans. *PLoS ONE, 13*(9), 1–14. https://doi.org/10.1371/journal.pone.0204303

Keen, H. A., Nelson, O. L., Robbins, C. T., Evans, M., Sheperdson, D. J., & Newberry, R. C. (2013). Validation of a novel cognitive bias task based on difference in quantity of reinforcement for assessing environmental enrichment. *Animal Cognition, 17*, 529–541. doi: 10.1007/s10071-013-0684-1

Keltner, D., & Buswell, B. N. (1997). Embarrassment: Its distinct form and appeasement functions. *Psychological Bulletin, 122*(3), 250–270. http://dx.doi.org/10.1037/0033-2909.122.3.250

Khoo, S. Y., Correia, V., & Uhrig, A. (2020). Nesting material enrichment reduces severity of overgrooming-related self-injury in individually housed rats. *Laboratory Animals*. doi: 10.1177/0023677219894356

King, B. J. (2017). The expression of grief in monkeys, apes, and other animals. In A. C. G. M. Robben (Ed.), *Death, mourning, and burial: A cross-cultural reader* (pp. 202–208). Wiley.

Kirkden, R. D., & Pajor, E. A. (2006). Using preference, motivation and aversion tests to ask scientific questions about animals' feelings. *Applied Animal Behaviour Science, 100*(1–2), 29–47. doi: 10.1016/j.applanim.2006.04.009

Kittilsen, S. (2013). Functional aspects of emotions in fish. *Behavioural Processes, 100*, 153–159. doi: 10.1016/j.beproc.2013.09.002

Koboroff, A., Kaplan, G., & Rogers, L. J. (2008). Hemispheric specialization in Australian magpies (*Gymnorhina tibicen*) shown as eye preferences during response to a predator. *Brain Research Bulletin, 76*(3), 304–306. doi: 10.1016/j.brainresbull.2008.02.015

Kolb, B., & Taylor, L. (1990). Neocortical substrates of emotional behavior. In N. L. Stein, B. Leventhal, & T. Trabasso (Eds.), *Psychological and biological approaches to emotion* (pp. 115–144). Psychology Press.

Kops, M. S., de Haas, E. N., Rodenburg, T. B., Ellen, E. D., Korte-Bouws, G. A. H., Olivier, B., Güntürkün, O., Korte, S. M., & Bolhuis, J. E. (2013). Selection for low mortality in laying hens affects catecholamine levels in the arcopallium, a brain area involved in fear and motor regulation. *Behavioural Brain Research, 257*, 54–61. https://doi.org/10.1016/j.bbr.2013.09.035

Laméris, D. W., Verspeek, J., Eens, M., & Stevens, J. M. (2022). Social and nonsocial stimuli alter the performance of bonobos during a pictorial emotional Stroop task. *American Journal of Primatology, 5*, e23356. https://doi.org/10.1002/ajp.23356

Laurence, A., Houdelier, C., Petton, C., Calandreau, L., Arnould, C., Favreau-Peigné, A., Leterrier, C., Boissy, A., Richard-Yris, M. A., & Lumineau, S. (2012). Japanese quail's genetic background modulates effects of chronic stress on emotional reactivity but not spatial learning. *PloS ONE, 7*(10), e47475. doi: 10.1371/journal.pone.0047475

Lazarus, R. S. (1991). *Emotion and adaptation*. Oxford University Press.

Lecorps, B. & Féron, C. (2015). Correlates between ear postures and emotional reactivity in a wild type mouse species. *Behavioural Processes, 120*, 25–29. doi: 10.1016/j.beproc.2015.08.002

Leete, J.A., Vonk, J., Oriani, S., Eaton, T., & Lieb, J. (2020). Domestic cats (*Felis silvestris catus*) do not infer reputation in humans after direct and indirect experience. *Human-Animal Interaction Bulletin, 8*, 35–53.

Leliveld, L. M. C., Düpjan, S., Tuchscherer, A., & Puppe, B. (2017). Vocal correlates of emotional reactivity within and across contexts in domestic pigs (*Sus scrofa*). *Physiology & Behavior, 181*, 117–126. doi: 10.1016/j.physbeh.2017.09.010

Leliveld, L. M. C., Langbein, J., & Puppe, B. (2013). The emergence of emotional lateralization: Evidence in non-human vertebrates and implications for farm animals. *Applied Animal Behaviour Science, 145*(1–2), 1–14. doi: 10.1016/j.applanim.2013.02.002

Lewis, M., Sullivan, M. W., Stanger, C., & Weiss, M. (1989). Self development and self-conscious emotions. *Child Development, 60*(1), 146–156. https://doi.org/10.2307/1131080

Lindell, A. K. (2013). Continuities in emotion lateralization in human and non-human primates. *Frontiers in Human Neuroscience, 7*, 9. http://dx.doi.org/10.3389/fnhum.2013.00464

Lyons, D. M., & Price, E. O. (1987). Relationships between heart rates and behavior of goats in encounters with people. *Applied Animal Behaviour Science, 18*(3–4), 363–369. doi: 10.1016/0168-1591(87)90230-9

Macbeth, B. J., Cattet, M. R. L., Stenhouse, G. B., Gibeau, M. L., & Janz, D.M. (2010). Hair cortisol concentration as a noninvasive measure of long-term stress in free-ranging grizzly bears (*Ursus arctos*): Considerations with implications for other wildlife. *Canadian Journal of Zoology, 88*(10), 935–949. doi: 10.1139/Z10-057

Makowska, I. J. & Weary, D. M. (2013). Assessing the emotions of laboratory rats. *Applied Animal Behaviour Science, 148*(1–2), 1–12. doi: 10.1016/j.applanim.2013.07.017

Man, M. S., Mikheenko, Y., Braesicke, K., Cockcroft, G., & Roberts, A. C. (2012). Serotonin at the level of the amygdala and orbitofrontal cortex modulates distinct aspects of positive emotion in primates. *International Journal of Neuropsychopharmacology, 15*, 91–105. doi: 10.1017/S1461145711000587

Maninger, N., Mendoza, S. P., Williams, D. R., Mason, W. A., Cherry, S. R., Rowland, D. J., Schaefer, T., & Bales, K. L. (2017). Imaging, behavior and endocrine analysis of "jealousy" in a monogamous primate. *Frontiers in Ecology and Evolution, 5*(119), 1–14. https://doi.org/10.3389/fevo.2017.00119

Manning, A., & Dawkins, M. (1992). *An introduction to animal behavior*. Cambridge University Press.

Manteuffel, G., Puppe, B., & Schön, P. (2004). Vocalization of farm animals as a measure of welfare. *Applied Animal Behavior Science, 88*, 163–82. doi: 10.1016/j.applanim.2004.02.012

Masson, J. M., & McCarthy, S. (1995). *When elephants weep: The emotional lives of animals*. Wheeler.

Mathes, E. W., & Deuger, D.J. (1982). Jealousy, a creation of human culture. *Psychological Reports, 51*, 351–354. https://doi.org/10.2466/pr0.1982.51.2.351

Mathuru, A. S., Kibat, C., Cheong, W. F., Shui, G., Wenk, M. R., Friedrich, R. W., & Jesuthasan, S. (2012). Chondroitin fragments are odorants that trigger fear behavior in fish. *Current Biology, 22*(6), 538–544. doi: 10.1016/j.cub.2012.01.061

McGuire, M. C., & Vonk, J. (2018). Gorillas (*Gorilla gorilla gorilla*) fail to learn abstract cues of differential outcomes in a novel cognitive bias test. *Animal Behavior and Cognition, 5*, 103–117. doi.org/10.26451/abc.05.01.08.2018

McGuire, M.C., & Vonk, J. (2020). In or out: Response slowing across housing conditions as a measure of affect in three western lowland gorillas (*Gorilla gorilla gorilla*). *PeerJ, 8*, e9525. doi: 10.7717/peerj.9525

McGuire, M. C., Vonk, J., Fuller, G., & Allard, S. (2017). Using an ambiguous cue paradigm to assess cognitive bias in gorillas (*Gorilla gorilla gorilla*) during a forage manipulation. *Animal Behavior & Cognition, 4*(1), 70–83. doi: 10.12966/abc.06.02.2017

McGuire, M. C., Vonk, J., & Johnson-Ulrich, Z. (2017). Ambiguous results when using the ambiguous-cue paradigm to assess learning and cognitive bias in gorillas and a black bear. *Behavioral Sciences, 7*, 51. doi: 10.3390/bs7030051

McKillup, S. C., & McKillup, R. V. (1995). The responses of intertidal scavengers to damaged conspecifics in the field. *Marine and Freshwater Behaviour and Physiology, 27*(1), 49–57. http://dx.doi.org/10.1080/10236249509378953

Mellor, D. J. (2016). Updating animal welfare thinking: Moving beyond the "five freedoms" towards "a life worth living." *Animals (Basel), 6*(3). https://doi.org/10.3390/ani6030021

Mendl, M., Burman, O. H. P., Parker, R. M. A., & Paul, E. S. (2009). Cognitive bias as an indicator of animal emotion and welfare: Emerging evidence and underlying mechanisms. *Applied Animal Behaviour Science, 118*(3–4), 161–181. doi: 10.1016/j.applanim.2009.02.023

Mendl, M., Burman, O. H. P., & Paul, E. S. (2010). An integrative and functional framework for the study of animal emotion and mood. *Proceedings of the Royal Society B: Biological Sciences, 277*(1696), 2895–2904. doi: 10.1098/rspb.2010.0303

Merola, I., Lazzaroni, M., Marshall-Pescini, S., & Prato-Previde, E. (2015). Social referencing and cat–human communication. *Animal Cognition, 18*(3), 639–648. http://dx.doi.org/10.1007/s10071-014-0832-2

Merola, I., Prato-Previde, E., Lazzaroni, M., & Marshall-Pescini, S. (2014). Dogs' comprehension of referential emotional expressions: Familiar people and familiar emotions are easier. *Animal Cognition, 17*(2), 373–385. http://dx.doi.org/10.1007/s10071-013-0668-1

Merola, I., Prato-Previde, E., & Marshall-Pescini, S. (2012). Social referencing in dog-owner dyads? *Animal Cognition, 15*(2), 175–185. http://dx.doi.org/10.1007/s10071-011-0443-0

Miller, R. S., & Leary, M. R. (1992). Social sources and interactive functions of embarrassment. In M. Clark (Ed.), *Emotion and social behavior* (pp. 322–339). Russell Sage Foundation

Mitchell, R. W., & Hamm, M. (1997). The interpretation of animal psychology: Anthropomorphism or behavior reading? *Behaviour, 134*(3–4), 173–204. http://dx.doi.org/10.1163/156853997X00449

Moe, R. O., Bohlin, J., Flø, A., Vasdal, G., & Stubsjøen, S. M. (2017). Hot chicks, cold feet. *Physiology & Behavior, 179*, 42–48. http://dx.doi.org/10.1016/j.physbeh.2017.05.025

Moe, R. O., Stubsjøen, S. M., Bohlin, J., Flø, A., & Bakken, M. (2012). Peripheral temperature drop in response to anticipation and consumption of a signaled palatable reward in laying hens (*Gallus domesticus*). *Physiology and Behavior, 106*(4), 527–533. https://doi.org/10.1016/j.physbeh.2012.03.032

Møller, A. P. (2010). Interspecific variation in fear responses predicts urbanization in birds. *Behavioral Ecology, 21*(2), 365–371. https://doi.org/10.1093/beheco/arp199

Morimoto, Y. & Fujita, K. (2012). Capuchin monkeys (*Cebus apella*) use conspecifics' emotional expressions to evaluate emotional valence of objects. *Animal Cognition, 15*, 341–347. doi: 10.1007/s10071-011-0458-6

Morris, P., Doe, C., & Godsell, E. (2008). Secondary emotions in nonprimate species? Behavioral reports and subjective claims by animal owners. *Cognition and Emotion, 22*, 3–20. https://doi.org/10.1080/02699930701273716

Neave, H. W., Daros, R. R., Costa, J. H. C., Von Keyserlingk, M. A. G., & Weary, D. M. (2013). Pain and pessimism: Dairy calves exhibit negative judgement bias following hot-iron disbudding. *PLoS ONE, 8*(12). https://doi.org/10.1371/journal.pone.0080556

Oka, T. (2015). Psychogenic fever: How psychological stress affects body temperature in the clinical population. *Temperature, 2*(3), 368–378. https://doi.org/10.1080/23328940.2015.1056907

Ostojić, L., Tkalčić, M., & Clayton, N. S. (2015). Are owners' reports of their dogs' "guilty look" influenced by the dogs' action and evidence of the misdeed? *Behavioural Processes, 111*, 97–100. http://dx.doi.org/10.1016/j.beproc.2014.12.010

Palagi, E., Marchi, E., Cavicchio, P., & Bandoli, F. (2019). Sharing playful mood: Rapid facial mimicry in *Suricata suricatta*. *Animal Cognition, 22*, 719–732. doi: 10.1007/s10071-019-01269-y

Palmer, M. S., & Gross, A. (2018). Eavesdropping in an African large mammal community: Antipredator responses vary according to signaller reliability. *Animal Behaviour, 137*, 1–9. http://dx.doi.org/10.1016/j.anbehav.2017.12.018

Panksepp, J. (1994). Evolution constructed the potential for subjective experience within the neurodynamics of the mammalian brain. In P. Eckman & R. J. Davidson (Eds.), *The nature of emotion: Fundamental questions* (pp. 336–399). Oxford University Press.

Panksepp, J. (1998). *Affective neuroscience: The foundations of human and animal*. Oxford University Press.

Panksepp, J. (2011). The basic emotional circuits of mammalian brains: Do animals have affective lives? *Neuroscience and Biobehavioral Reviews, 35*(9), 1791–1804. https://doi.org/10.1016/j.neubiorev.2011.08.003

Panksepp, J. & Burgdorf, J. (2003). "Laughing" rats and the evolutionary antecedents of human joy? *Physiology & Behavior, 79*, 533–547. doi: 10.1016/S0031-9384(03)00159-8

Parr, L. A., Hopkins, W. D., & de Waal, F. B. (1998). The perception of facial expressions by chimpanzees, Pan troglodytes. *Evolution of Communication, 2*(1), 1–23.

Parr, L. A., Waller, B. M., Burrows, A. M., Gothard, K. M., & Vick, S. J. (2010). Brief communication: MaqFACS: A muscle-based facial movement coding system for the rhesus macaque. *American Journal of Physical Anthropology, 143*(4), 625–630. https://doi.org/10.1002/ajpa.21401

Paul, E. S., Harding, E. J., & Mendl, M. (2005). Measuring emotional processes in animals: The utility of a cognitive approach. *Neuroscience & Biobehavioral Reviews, 29*(3), 469–491. doi: 10.1016/j.neubiorev.2005.01.002

Pavlova, E. K., Alekseeva, G. S., Erofeeva, M. N., Vasilieva, N. A., Tchabovsky, A. V., & Naidenko, S. V. (2018). The method matters: The effect of handling time on cortisol level and blood parameters in wild cats. *JEZ-A Ecological and Integrative Physiology, 329*(3), 112–119. doi: 10.1002/jez.2191

Perdue, B. M. (2017). Mechanisms underlying cognitive bias in nonhuman primates. *Animal Behavior and Cognition, 4*(1), 105–118. https://doi.org/10.12966/abc.08.02.2017

Phillips, R. E., & Youngren, O. M. (1986). Unilateral kainic acid lesions reveal dominance of right archistriatum in avian fear behavior. *Brain Research, 377*(2), 216–220. doi: 10.1016/0006-8993(86)90861-9

Pollock, M. S., Chivers, D. P., Mirza, R. S., & Wisenden, B. D. (2003). Fathead Minnows, *Pimephales promelas*, learn to recognize chemical alarm cues of introduced Brook Stickleback, *Culaea inconstans*. *Environmental Biology of Fishes, 66*, 313–319.

Portavella, M., Torres, B., & Salas, C. (2004). Avoidance response in goldfish: Emotional and temporal involvement of medial and lateral telencephalic pallium. *Journal of Neuroscience, 24*(9), 2335–2342. doi: 10.1523/JNEUROSCI.4930-03.2004

Povinelli, D.J. (2020). Can comparative psychology crack its toughest nut? *Animal Behavior and Cognition, 7*(4), 589–652. https://doi.org/10.26451/abc.07.04.09.2020

Prato-Previde, E., Nicotra, V., Fusar Poli, S., Pelosi, A., & Valsecchi, P. (2018). Do dogs exhibit jealous behaviors when their owner attends to their companion dog? *Animal Cognition, 21*(21), 703–713. doi: 10.1007/s10071-018-1204-0

Prato-Previde, E., Nicotra, V., Pelosi, A., & Valsecchi, P. (2018). Pet dogs' behavior when the owner and an unfamiliar person attend to a faux rival. *PLoS ONE, 13*(4), 1–17. https://doi.org/10.1371/journal.pone.0194577

Pribac, T. B. (2013). Animal grief. *Animal Studies Journal, 2*(2), 67–90.

Price, E. O., & Thos, J. (1980). Behavioral responses to short-term social isolation in sheep and goats. *Applied Animal Ethology, 6*(4), 331–339. doi: 10.1016/0304-3762(80)90133-9

Proctor, H. S., & Carder, G. (2014). Can ear postures reliably measure the positive emotional state of cows? *Applied Animal Behaviour Science, 161*(1), 20–27. https://doi.org/10.1016/j.applanim.2014.09.015

Proctor, H. S., & Carder, G. (2015a). Nasal temperatures in dairy cows are influenced by positive emotional state. *Physiology and Behavior, 138*, 340–344. https://doi.org/10.1016/j.physbeh.2014.11.011

Proctor, H. S., & Carder, G. (2015b) Measuring positive emotions in cows: Do visible eye whites tell us anything? *Physiology & Behavior, 147*(1), 1–6. doi:10.1016/j.physbeh.2015.04.011.

Proctor, H., & Carder, G. (2016). Can changes in nasal temperature be used as an indicator of emotional state in cows? *Applied Animal Behavior Science, 184*, 1–6. https://doi.org/10.1016/j.applanim.2016.07.013

Proops, L., Grounds, K., Smith, A. V., & McComb, K. (2018). Animals remember previous facial expressions that specific humans have exhibited. *Current Biology, 28*(9), 1428–1432. https://doi.org/10.1016/j.cub.2018.03.035

Quaranta, A., d'Ingeo, S., Amoruso, R. & Siniscalchi, M. (2020). Emotion recognition in cats. *Animals, 10*(7), 1107. https://doi.org/10.3390/ani10071107.

Reefmann, N., Kaszàs, F. B., Wechsler, B., & Gygax, L. (2009). Ear and tail postures as indicators of emotional valence in sheep. *Applied Animal Behaviour Science, 118*(3–4), 199–207. doi: 10.1016/j.applanim.2009.02.013

Reimert, I., Bolhuis, J. E., Kemp, B., & Rodenburg, T. B. (2013). Indicators of positive and negative emotions and emotional contagion in pigs. *Physiology & Behavior, 109*, 42–50. https://doi.org/10.1016/j.physbeh.2012.11.002

Reimert, I., Bolhuis, J. E., Kemp, B., & Rodenburg, T. B. (2015). Emotions on the loose: Emotional contagion and the role of oxytocin in pigs. *Animal Cognition, 18*(2), 517–532. https://doi.org/10.1007/s10071-014-0820-6

Reimert, I., Fong, S., Rodenburg, T. B., & Bolhuis, J. E. (2017). Emotional states and emotional contagion in pigs after exposure to a positive and negative treatment. *Applied Animal Behaviour Science, 193*, 37–42. http://dx.doi.org/10.1016/j.applanim.2017.03.009

Rilling, J. K., Winslow, J. T., & Kilts, C. D. (2004). The neural correlates of mate competition in dominant male rhesus macaques. *Biological Psychiatry, 56*(5), 364–367.

Rose, J. D. (2002). The neurobehavioral nature of fishes and the question of awareness and pain. *Reviews in Fisheries Science, 1*, 1–38. doi: 10.1080/20026491051668

Rottman, S. J., & Snowdon, C. T. (1973). Demonstration and analysis of an alarm pheromone in mice. *Journal of Comparative and Physiological Psychology, 81*(3), 483–490. doi: 10.1037/h0033703

Saint-Dizier, H., Constantin, P., Davies, D. C., Leterrier, C., Lévy, F., & Richard, S. (2009). Subdivisions of the arcopallium/posterior pallial amygdala complex are differentially involved in the control of fear behaviour in the Japanese quail. *Brain Research Bulletin, 79*(5), 288–295. doi: 10.1016/j.brainresbull.2009.03.004

Sánchez, M. J., Bartolomé, E., & Valera, M. (2016). Genetic study of stress assessed with infrared thermography during dressage competitions in the *pura raza español* horse. *Applied Animal Behaviour Science, 174*, 58–65. http://dx.doi.org/10.1016/j.applanim.2015.11.006

Sandem, A. I., & Braastad, B. O. (2005). Effects of cow-calf separation on visible eye white and behaviour in dairy cows: A brief report. *Applied Animal Behaviour Science, 95*(3), 233–239. https://doi.org/10.1016/j.applanim.2005.04.01

Sandem, A. I., Braastad, B. O., & Bakken, M. (2006). Behaviour and percentage eye-white in cows waiting to be fed concentrate: A brief report. *Applied Animal Behaviour Science, 97*(2–4), 145–151. https://doi.org/10.1016/j.applanim.2005.08.003

Sandem, A. I., Braastad, B. O., & Bøe, K. E. (2002). Eye white may indicate emotional state on a frustration-contentedness axis in dairy cows. *Applied Animal Behaviour Science, 79*(1), 1–10. doi:10.1016/S0168-1591(02)00029-1.

Sandem, A. I., Janczak, A. M., Salte, R., & Braastad, B. O. (2006). The use of diazepam as a pharmacological validation of eye white as an indicator of emotional state in dairy cows. *Applied Animal Behaviour Science, 96*(3–4), 177–183. https://doi.org/10.1016/j.applanim.2005.06.008

Schehka, S. & Zimmermann, E. (2012). Affect intensity in voice recognized by tree shrews (*Tupaia belangeri*). *Emotion, 12*(3), 632–639. doi: 10.1037/a0026893

Schlosberg, H. (1954). Three dimensions of emotion. *Psychological Review, 61*(2), 81–88. https://doi.org/10.1037/h0054570

Schlüns, H., Welling, H., Federici, J. R., & Lewejohann, L. (2017). The glass is not yet half empty: Agitation but not *Varroa* treatment causes cognitive bias in honey bees. *Animal Cognition, 20*, 233–241. doi: 10.1007/s10071-016-1042-x

Schmoll, T. (2016). Can horses read emotional cues from human faces? Re-analysis of Smith et al. (2016). *Biology Letters, 12*(9), 20160201. https://doi.org/10.1098/rsbl.2016.0201

Silberman, E. K. & Weingartner, H. (1986). Hemispheric lateralization of functions related to emotion. *Brain and Cognition, 5*(3), 322–353. doi: 10.1016/0278-2626(86)90035-7

Siniscalchi, M., d'Ingeo, S., & Quaranta, A. (2018). Orienting asymmetries and physiological reactivity in dogs' response to human emotional faces. *Learning & Behavior, 46*(4), 574–585. doi:http://dx.doi.org/10.3758/s13420-018-0325-2

Smith, A. V., Proops, L., Grounds, K., Wathan, J., & McComb, K. (2016). Functionally relevant responses to human facial expressions of emotion in the domestic horse (*Equus caballus*). *Biology Letters, 12*(2), 20150907. doi: 10.1098/rsbl.2015.0907

Smith, A. V., Proops, L., Grounds, K., Wathan, J., Scott, S. K., & McComb, K. (2018). Domestic horses (*Equus caballus*) discriminate between negative and positive human nonverbal vocalisations. *Scientific Reports, 8*, 13052.

Sotocinal, S. G., Sorge, R. E., Zaloum, A., Tuttle, A. H., Martin, L. J., Wieskopf, J. S., Mapplebeck, J. C., Wei, P., Zhan, S., Zhang, S., McDougall, J. J., King, O. D., & Mogil, J. S. (2011). The Rat Grimace Scale: A partially automated method for quantifying pain in the laboratory rat via facial expressions. *Molecular Pain, 7*, 55. https://doi.org/10.1186/1744-8069-7-55

Spruijt, B. M., van Hooff, J. A., & Gispen, W. H. (1992). Ethology and neurobiology of grooming behavior. *Physiological Reviews, 72*(3), 825–852. doi: 10.1152/physrev.1992.72.3.825

Stewart, M., Webster, J. R., Verkerk, G. A., Schaefer, A. L., Colyn, J. J., & Stafford, K. J. (2007). Non-invasive measurement of stress in dairy cows using infrared thermography. *Physiology & Behavior, 92*(3), 520–525. http://dx.doi.org/10.1016/j.physbeh.2007.04.034

Stubsjøen, S. M., Flø, A. S., Moe, R. O., Janczak, A. M., Skjerve, E., Valle, P. S., & Zanella, A. J. (2009). Exploring non-invasive methods to assess pain in sheep. *Physiology & Behavior, 98*(5), 640–648. http://dx.doi.org/10.1016/j.physbeh.2009.09.019

Su, B., Koda, N., & Martens, P. (2018). How Japanese companion dog and cat owners' degree of attachment relates to the attribution of emotions to their animals. *PLoS ONE, 13*(1), 14. http://dx.doi.org/10.1371/journal.pone.0190781

Suraci, J. P., Clinchy, M., Dill, L. M., Roberts, D., & Zanette, L. Y. (2016). Fear of large carnivores causes a trophic cascade. *Nature Communications, 7*(1), 10698. https://doi.org/10.1038/ncomms10698

Tallentire, C. W., Leinonen, I., & Kyriazakis, I. (2016). Breeding for efficiency in the broiler chicken: A review. *Agronomy for Sustainable Development, 36*(4), 1–16. https://doi.org/10.1007/s13593-016-0398-2.

Tangney, J. P., Miller, R. S., Flicker, L., & Barlow, D. H. (1996). Are shame, guilt, and embarrassment distinct emotions?. *Journal of Personality and Social Psychology, 70*(6), 1256.

Tangney, J. P., & Fischer, K. W. (1995). *Self-conscious emotions: The psychology of shame, guilt, embarrassment, and pride*. Guilford Press.

Taylor, D., Hartmann, D., Dezecache, G., Wong, S. T., & Davila-Ross, M. (2019). Facial complexity in sun bears: Exact facial mimicry and social sensitivity. *Scientific Reports, 9*, 4961. https://doi.org/10.1038/s41598-019-39932-6

Teletchea, F. (2019). Animal domestication: A brief overview. *Intech Open*

Travain, T., Colombo, E. S., Grandi, L. C., Heinzl, E., Pelosi, A., Prato Previde, E., & Valsecchi, P. (2016). How good is this food? A study on dogs' emotional responses to a potentially pleasant event using infrared thermography. *Physiology & Behavior, 159*, 80–87. http://dx.doi.org/10.1016/j.physbeh.2016.03.019

Turpeinen, U., & Hämäläinen, E. (2013). Determination of cortisol in serum, saliva and urine. *Best Practice & Research Clinical Endocrinology & Metabolism, 27*(6), 795–801. doi: 10.1016/j.beem.2013.10.008

Van Bourg, J., Patterson, J. E., & Wynne, C. D. L. (2020). Pet dogs (*canis lupus familiaris*) release their trapped and distressed owners: Individual variation and evidence of emotional contagion. *PLoS ONE, 15*(4), 23. http://dx.doi.org/10.1371/journal.pone.0231742

van der Staay, F. J., van Zutphen, J. A., de Ridder, M. M., & Nordquist, R. E. (2017). Effects of environmental enrichment on decision-making behavior in pigs. *Applied Animal Behaviour Science, 194*, 14–23. https://doi.org/10.1016/j.applanim.2017.05.006

Verduyn, P., Mechelen, I. V., & Tuerlnckx, F. (2011). The relation between event processing and the duration of emotional experience. *Emotion, 11*(1), 20–28. doi: 10.1037/a0021239

Verheggen, F. J., Haubruge, E., & Mescher, M. C. (2010). Alarm pheromones: Chemical signaling in response to danger. *Vitamins and Hormones, 83*, 215–239. doi: 10.1016/S0083-6729(10)83009-2

Vick, S. J., Waller, B. M., Parr, L. A., Smith Pasaqualini, M. C., & Bard, K. A. (2007). A cross-species comparison of facial morphology and movement in humans and chimpanzees using the facial action coding system (FACS). *Journal of Nonverbal Behaviour, 31*(1), 1–20.

Volodin, I. A., Sibiryakova, O. V., Vasilieva, N. A., Volodina, E. V., Matrosova, V. A., Garcia, A. J., Pérez-Barbería, F. J., Gallego, L., & Landete-Castillejos, T. (2018). Old and young female voices: Effects of body weight, condition and social discomfort on the vocal aging in red deer hinds (*Cervus elaphus*). *Behaviour, 155*, 915–939. doi: 10.1163/1568539X-00003513

Von Eugen, K., Nordquist, R. E., Zeinstra, E., & van der Staay, F. J. (2019). Stocking density affects stress and anxious behavior in the laying hen chick during rearing. *Animals, 9*(2). https://doi.org/10.3390/ani9020053

Vonk, J. (2018). Researchers, not dogs, lack control in an experiment on jealousy. Commentary on Cook et al. on jealousy in dogs. *Animal Sentience, 121*(2).

Vonk, J. (2019). Emotional contagion or sensitivity to behavior in ravens? *Proceedings of the National Academy of Sciences, 116*(37), 18168. http://dx.doi.org/10.1073/pnas.1909864116

Vonk, J., McGuire, M., & Leete, J. A. (2022). Testing for the "blues": Using the modified emotional Stroop task to assess the emotional response of gorillas. *Animals, 12*, 1188. https://doi.org/10.3390/ani12091188

Vonk, J., McGuire, M. C., & Johnson-Ulrich, Z. (2021). Bearing fruit: Piloting a novel judgement bias task in an American black bear. *Zoo Biology, 40*(2), 89–97. https://doi.org/10.1002/zoo.21584

Waller, B. M., Lembeck M., Kuchenbuch, P., Burrows, A. M., & Liebal, K. (2012). GibbonFACS: A muscle-based facial movement coding system for hylobatids. *International Journal of Primatology, 33*(4), 809–821.

Waller, B. M., & Micheletta, J. (2013). Facial expression in nonhuman animals. *Emotion Review, 5*(1), 54–59. https://doi.org/10.1177/1754073912451503

Waller, B. M., Peirce, K., Caeiro, C. C., Scheider, L., Burrows, A. M., McCune, S., & Kaminski, J. (2013). Paedomorphic facial expressions give dogs a selective advantage. *PloS ONE, 8*(12), e82686. https://doi.org/10.1007/s10764-012-9611-6

Waller, B. M., Whitehouse, J., & Micheletta, J. (2016). Macaques can predict social outcomes from facial expressions. *Animal Cognition, 19*(5), 1031–1036. http://dx.doi.org/10.1007/s10071-016-0992-3

Wathan, J., Burrows, A. M., Waller, B. M., & McComb, K. (2015). EquiFACS: The Equine Facial Action Coding System. *PLoS ONE, 10*, e0131738. https://doi.org/10.1371/journal.pone.0131738

Webb, C. E., Kolff, K., Du, X., & de Waal, F. (2020). Jealous behavior in chimpanzees elicited by social intruders. *Affective Science, 1*, 199–207. https://doi.org/10.1007/s42761-020-00019-5

Weeks, C., & Nicol, C. (2006). Behavioural needs, priorities and preferences of laying hens. *World's Poultry Science Journal, 62*(2), 296–307. doi:10.1079/WPS200598

Weisfeld, G. E., & Goetz, S. M. M. (2013). Applying evolutionary thinking to the study of emotion. *Behavioral Sciences, 3*(3), 388–407. https://doi.org/10.3390/bs303038

Wiepkema, P. R. (1987). Behavioural aspects of stress. In P. R. Wiepkema, & P. W. M. Van Adrichem (Eds.), *Biology of stress in farm animals: An integrative approach*. Current Topics in Veterinary Medicine and Animal Science, 42. Springer. https://doi.org/10.1007/978-94-009-3339-2_9

Wyatt, T. D. (2020). Reproducible research into human chemical communication by cues and pheromones: Learning from psychology's renaissance. *Philosophical Transactions of the Royal Society B: Biological Sciences, 375*(1800), 20190262 doi: 10.1098/rstb.2019.0262

Yong, M. H., & Ruffman, T. (2014). Emotional contagion: Dogs and humans show a similar physiological response to human infant crying. *Behavioural Processes, 108*, 155–165. http://dx.doi.org/10.1016/j.beproc.2014.10.006

Yong, M. H., & Ruffman, T. (2015). Is that fear? Domestic dogs' use of social referencing signals from an unfamiliar person. *Behavioural Processes, 110*, 74–81. http://dx.doi.org/10.1016/j.beproc.2014.09.018

Yong, M. H., & Ruffman, T. (2016). Domestic dogs and human infants look more at happy and angry faces than sad faces. *Multisensory Research, 29*(8), 749–771. http://dx.doi.org/10.1163/22134808-00002535

CHAPTER 41

Emotion and Empathy in Great Apes

Zanna Clay and Diane A. Austry

Abstract

Humans and other great apes have evolved rich social and emotional capacities that enable them to navigate their complex social worlds. These include sophisticated ways to produce, perceive, and express affective states, as well as to respond effectively to the states of others. A distinctive feature of human emotional functioning is empathy, the capacity to share and understand others' states. Far from being uniquely human, empathy has a deep evolutionary history and may be found across diverse animal species in both mammals and birds. This chapter examines some of the continuities between the emotional processes, including empathy of humans and our closest ape relatives. Chimpanzees (*Pan troglodytes*) and bonobos (*P. paniscus*) are our closest cousins and show numerous overlaps in their socio-affective and cognitive capacities, social structures, and life histories. Studying their emotional and empathic capacities reveals many overlaps, highlighting a deep evolutionary basis of hominid emotionality.

Key Words: consolation, empathy, primate, bonobo, chimpanzee, emotion contagion, mimicry

A Comparative Approach to Emotion and Empathy

In his seminal work, *The Expression of the Emotions in Man and Animals* (1872), Darwin argued for the evolutionary principle of continuity, whereby closely related species should be expected to share similar emotional expressions as well as similar underlying mechanisms. In this vein, our closest living primate relatives should show the greatest overlaps in their emotional expressions and capacities to those of our own, given their close phylogenetic relationship to us. Indeed, although the emotional lives of great apes and other animals are difficult to access and have been relatively under-studied, research highlights apparent similarities in both form and function of their emotional expressions with those of humans, suggesting a shared evolutionary basis (Kret et al., 2020). For instance, during socially tense situations, great apes and other primates produce the "bared teeth facial expression," a facial expression that is thought to function to signal appeasement and social affiliation (de Waal, 1988; Parr et al., 2007; Pritsch et al., 2017; van Hooff, 1967, 1971). The bared teeth display is also produced by humans and is thought to represent the evolutionary basis of the human smile (Preuschoft & van Hooff, 1995; van Hooff, 1967). Although the human smile has taken on much greater diversity in both form and function (Hess & Fischer, 2013), it appears to have retained some of its original evolutionary function as a mediator of social uncertainty.

From a Darwinian perspective (Darwin, 1872), emotion expressions are considered to be external manifestations of internal states. A key question is: What internal emotional states might such communicative signals be expressing in animals? Moreover, can we assume that closely related species that share similar emotional expressions also share similar underlying emotional states governing those expressions? Such a question is difficult to answer for a number of reasons. First, while it may be parsimonious to assume that animals that are closely phylogenetically related should experience similar affective states (Bekoff, 2000; de Waal 1999, 2016), external behaviors might also be driven by different underlying mechanisms and reflect distinct functions that vary across species (Williams et al., 2020; Wynne, 2004). When comparing the emotions of humans and other primates, some researchers have also criticized an anthropomorphic approach, based on the view that human emotions are socially or culturally constructed, and thus not comparable to those of other animals (Barrett, 2013, 2017a, 2017b; Boiger & Mesquita, 2012). Overall, while of continued interest to scientists and non-scientists alike, animal emotions have historically been disregarded as being inaccessible to scientific study, and some might even say scientifically taboo (see de Waal, 2011; Panksepp, 2011).

A major reason for this relates to the inaccessibility of the subjective component of the emotional experience, which largely depends on verbal self-report in human emotion research. In this regard, the absence of language in other animals represents the most substantial challenge in comparative research on emotion (Paul et al., 2005). Given the challenges of studying animal emotion, research on animal emotion has historically taken a back seat, in favor of comparative research on behavior and cognition. This is consistent with a more general bias toward studying behavior cognition across the human and evolutionary sciences, shaped by the influential eras of behaviorism and cognitivism (Dukes et al., 2021).

Nevertheless, the tides are starting to turn. There has recently been a shift toward the view that animal emotions, and their link to behavior, can be systematically studied and compared by examining their measurable behavioral or physiological components (Davila Ross et al., 2008; Heesen et al., 2022; Kret et al., 2020; Massen et al., 2019). This view is buttressed by the advent of new technologies in psychophysiological methods and behavioral experimental paradigms, discussed further below (see also Adriaense et al., 2020). This intellectual shift toward studying emotion extends beyond comparative research, with increasing recognition of the role that emotion plays in shaping and understanding human cognition, and psychology more generally. Additionally, some evolutionary theories of emotions place emotions at center-stage, arguing that emotions effectively coordinate and regulate human cognition, physiology, and behavior (Al-Shawaf et al., 2016; Al-Shawaf & Lewis, 2017; Cosmides & Tooby, 2000). The increasing acknowledgment of the role that emotion plays in psychological and bodily processes has led some scholars to even argue that, from the era of cognitivism, we might now be entering a period of "affectivism" (Dukes et al., 2021).

At this point, while a full definition of emotion goes beyond the scope of this chapter, it is relevant to briefly note our own approach to the definition of emotions within a comparative lens. To enable more meaningful and evolutionarily grounded comparisons, we use the terms "emotion" and "affect" interchangeably to refer to multi-componential phenomena (Anderson & Adolphs, 2014; Sander, 2013) that display variation in behavioral, cognitive, and physiological components. In this respect, emotions may be viewed as a two-step process that involve emotion-elicitation mechanisms that trigger emotional responses (Mendl et al., 2010; Paul et al., 2005). Mechanistically, emotional responses may encompass a variety of aspects, including action tendencies, feelings, expressions, percepts, memory, attention, and decision-making (Sander, 2013).

One of the most fruitful frameworks in the study of animal emotion is the *dimensional* approach, in particular as this framework does not require assumptions about the more subjective components (Mendl et al., 2010). According to the dimensional approach, affect can be viewed along two principal dimensions of *arousal* (from lower to higher intensity) and *valence* (positive or negative; Barrett and Wager, 2006). By conceptualizing emotions in terms of universal core valence and arousal dimensions, the *dimensional approach* can include the study of a fuller scope of emotional states—as compared to the *discrete emotion approach*, which may be more limited in this respect (see Mendl et al., 2010). Nevertheless, the dimensional approach has its limitations, particularly as much of the fundamental nuance of different emotions cannot be easily identified using this method of characterization. For instance, the emotions of anger and fear are both high arousal and negatively valenced emotions. In this respect, while the dimensional approach can provide a useful starting point to enable comparisons across species, it is limited in the degree of resolution it can provide to differentiate between emotions that lie within the same region of valence and arousal.

Emotion and Empathy in Our Closest Living Relatives: The Great Apes

Having briefly introduced the comparative approach and the challenges encountered by the field, we now introduce the great apes to explore their emotional capacities. Humans are part of the *Hominidae* family, along with four other extant great apes: bonobos, chimpanzees, gorillas (*Gorilla gorilla*), and orangutans (*Pongo pygmaeus*). Although humans show many distinctive traits, including in our cognition, behavior, and linguistic communication, comparative research is increasingly revealing that the similarities we share with other great apes far outweigh the differences. This overlap appears to extend into the domain of emotional capacities.

As well as being long-lived species, with some captive apes living into their 70s, a characteristic life-history trait of great apes includes extended periods of parental care and slow periods of offspring development, spanning five years or more (Robson & Wood, 2008); this long period of offspring dependency allows for strong and differentiated social relationships to develop across time, as well as extensive opportunities for both individual and social learning. Regarding their social life, although all great apes show sophisticated social and cognitive skills, there are notable differences across ape species in social structures, cooperative tendencies, and degrees of sociality, with chimpanzees and bonobos being the most social compared to gorillas or orangutans (Pradhan et al., 2012). Compared to humans, chimpanzees and bonobos appear to show many similarities in their social and cooperative tendencies and social organization, making them particularly good models for identifying the evolutionary basis of hominid emotion and social awareness (Furuichi, 2019).

Bonobos and chimpanzees live in complex multi-male, multi-female societies that are characterized by complex fission-fusion dynamics and highly differentiated social relationships with rich forms of cooperation (Gruber & Clay, 2016). It has been argued that the computational challenges of fission-fusion societies, which involve maintaining and monitoring social relationships across highly variable temporal and spatial landscapes, place adaptive pressures on species to evolve more sophisticated socio-cognitive and affective capacities (Amici et al., 2008).

Although group size and habitat vary considerably across communities, chimpanzee and bonobo communities typically average around 30–40 members in territories covering about 20–60 km^2 of dense rainforest (Mitani & Watts, 2005). In both species, males are philopatric, with group composition punctuated by the periodic immigration of females, who typically arrive into new communities during adolescence. Despite their fission-fusion structure, both chimpanzees and bonobos maintain long-term social relationships with other members of their communities, with whom they extensively cooperate and affiliate, including with both kin and non-kin individuals. This includes sharing food, hunting, grooming, supporting one another in social alliances and defending territories (see Gruber & Clay, 2016, for a review). The capacity both to effectively communicate and perceive other's emotional states thus forms a crucial component of how great apes navigate their social environments, enabling them to simultaneously cooperate and compete with other conspecifics within and across their communities.

There is evidence that great apes have remarkably sophisticated socio-cognitive skills, including in the recognition of others' emotional and cognitive states. Great apes can perceive others as intentional agents and attribute mental states to them (Krupenye et al., 2018; Lewis & Krupenye, 2021; Schleidgen et al., 2011). Experimental studies have also established that chimpanzees recognize the emotions of their peers (Izumi & Kojima, 2004; Kano et al., 2008; Kret et al., 2014; Parr, 2003), with attention being biased toward conspecifics' emotional signals (Kret et al., 2016). Great apes are also known to be sensitive to human emotional expressions (Buttelmann et al., 2009). In naturalistic settings, this sensitivity has been detected primarily by observing great apes consoling distressed conspecifics following conflicts, something we discuss further below (Clay & de Waal, 2013a; de Waal & van Roosmalen, 1979).

Thus far, most research on great ape emotions has been conducted with chimpanzees and bonobos, particularly chimpanzees. Although both chimpanzees and bonobos show highly developed cognitive and socio-emotional skills, bonobos appear to have stronger socio-emotional orientation and emotional sensitivity than chimpanzees. For instance, an eye-tracking experiment showed that bonobos make more eye contact than chimpanzees (Kano et al., 2015), have more risk-aversion than chimpanzees in a risky decision task (Haun et al., 2011), and pay more attention to emotional information (Kano et al., 2015). Bonobos also outperform chimpanzees in social cognition tasks involving cooperation, social monitoring, and social tolerance, whereas chimpanzees show more advanced capacities in physical cognition tasks (Herrmann et al., 2010), including tool use. By comparison, while their emotional capacities have thus been relatively unexplored, orangutans and gorillas also show sophisticated socio-cognitive skills, highlighting clear evolutionary continuities in socio-cognitive processes.

Neuro-anatomical research has thus far supported observed behavioral differences in the socio-emotional orientations of chimpanzees and bonobos. One imaging study comparing the neural structure of bonobo and chimpanzee brains revealed that bonobos have more gray matter in the dorsal amygdala compared to chimpanzees (Rilling et al., 2012). This area's activity is linked to the hypothalamic-pituitary-adrenal axis and autonomic nervous system (ANS; Davis, 1997), and therefore constitutes a key aspect of a network that controls negative emotions like distress and anxiety, as well as sexual behaviors (Breedlove & Watson, 2013). This suggests that the bigger amygdala of bonobos could trigger distress, while also motivating sexual behavior that helps alleviate tensions in bonobo communities (de Waal, 1987; Hohmann et al., 2009; Parish, 1996; Rilling et al., 2012).

Compared to chimpanzees, bonobos have a larger pathway linking the amygdala with the ventromedial prefrontal cortex (Rilling et al., 2012). This pathway is implicated in emotion perception (Blair, 2008) and regulation. Therefore, it might be implicated in the higher control of aggressive impulses in bonobos compared to chimpanzees (Davidson et al., 2000; Meyer-Lindenberg et al., 2006). Species differences in pathway size may be amplified by higher testosterone levels in male chimpanzees that inhibit this pathway's functionality (Sannen et al., 2004; van Wingen et al., 2010; Wobber et al., 2010). Finally, bonobos have more gray matter in the anterior insula than chimpanzees (Rilling et al., 2012), a region linked to socio-emotional processing (Allman et al., 2010; Kurth et al., 2010) and risk-taking (Bossaerts, 2010; Kuhnen & Knutson, 2005), and which coactivates with the amygdala (Mutschler et al., 2009). This is consistent with bonobos being more risk-averse and emotionally sensitive than chimpanzees (Heilbronner et al., 2008).

Studying Emotion in Great Apes

Thus far, most experimental research investigating great ape emotion has focused on emotion perception, with data coming from a relatively small number of studies conducted in captivity (e.g., Kano & Tomonaga, 2010; Kret et al., 2016; Kret et al., 2018; Kret & van Berlo, 2020; Parr, 2003; Parr et al., 2002; Tomonaga, 1999a, 1999b, 2007; Wilson & Tomonaga 2018). Such studies have typically depended on computerized touchscreen tasks using match-to-sample paradigms, as well as noninvasive methods such as eye-tracking and dot-probe tasks to investigate attentional biases (e.g., Hopper et al. 2021; Kano et al., 2015; Kret et al. 2016; Kret & van Berlo, 2020). Computerized systems enable researchers to present a variety of visual and acoustic stimuli in controlled and ethical ways that apes can engage with voluntarily (Egelkamp & Ross, 2019). Such research has revealed that great apes possess sophisticated emotional recognition capacities, including abilities to categorize affective displays of varying valence (Parr, 2003) and to match them with relevant contextual cues (Parr, 2001).

Other experimental studies have investigated the effects of affective stimuli on attention. For example, using a dot-probe task, subjects learn to select a large dot on a screen. Kret et al. (2016) found that bonobos' attention was biased toward affective stimuli: bonobos touched a dot more quickly when it flashed up in the location where a social or emotional scene had previously been, as compared with a neutral scene. Overall, touchscreens represent a promising and versatile system that can be employed for a range of tasks to examine emotion and cognitive processes in apes.

Research into the *production* of emotional states in great apes is evidently more challenging. Unlike humans, nonhuman great apes lack language to express their inner thoughts and feelings; thus we have no direct means to access their minds. Moreover, while emotional expressions can provide approximate external indicators of underlying emotional states, it cannot be assumed that such expressions reflect the same functions or mechanisms across species. Additional research is needed to identify the underlying cognitive and physiological basis for such expressions.

The "cognitive judgment bias" paradigm represents another promising approach to investigate animals' affective experience, including that of great apes (Adriaense et al., 2020). The cognitive judgment bias paradigm was first employed by Harding et al. (2004) in a study that showed that rats living in unpredictable circumstances showed reduced performance in a decision-making test. This reduced performance as a result of uncertainty suggests that a negative affective state induces negative cognitive biases or pessimistic expectations. In most cognitive bias test paradigms, animals first undergo discrimination training in which they learn that two cues are associated with either positive or negative outcomes. During the test phase, the animal is then presented with both the positive and negative cues, as well as a novel, ambiguous cue. If the animal's response to the ambiguous cue is similar to that of the positive response, it suggests that the animal "optimistically" perceives the ambiguous cue to be positive. By contract, if their response is more similar to the negative response, it suggests that the animal "pessimistically" anticipates a negative outcome, i.e., a negative cognitive bias. The cognitive bias test has already been applied widely across a variety of species, experimental conditions, and disciplines to examine affective states in animals (for reviews, see Baciadonna & McElligott, 2015; Mendl et al., 2009). Among great apes, the cognitive bias test has only been conducted with a small sample of captive chimpanzees, with somewhat mixed results (Bateson & Nettle, 2015). However, its wide application across other species suggests that this paradigm is a useful avenue to examine the nature of ape affect.

The advent of noninvasive approaches to measure psychophysiology also provides promising opportunities to explore emotion in great apes and other animals. For instance, variation in pupillary dilation correlates with changes in arousal in response to affective triggers and mental activity (Sirois & Brisson, 2014). As changes to pupil dilation happen quickly, pupillometry can be an effective technique to examine the rapid time course of cognitive and affective responses to stimuli. Pupillometry research requires individuals to still relatively still in front of a monitor so that their eyes can be noninvasively tracked using an eye-tracker. Fortunately, comparative researchers have found that apes are willing to do this voluntarily in return for sucking on a small tube that dispenses diluted fruit juice. This setup ensures that pupillometry is an ethical and viable method that can be applied in a range of captive settings. Pupillometry has already been used to detect affiliative mimicry of conspecific pupil size in humans and chimpanzees (Aktar et al., 2020; Kret et al., 2014) as well as chimpanzee arousal in pro-social contexts (Hepach et al., 2012; Hepach et al., 2021).

Infrared thermography (IRT) represents another emerging technique for measuring affect in a wide range of species, including great apes (Sato et al., 2018). IRT uses an infrared camera to record the surface skin temperature of subjects in experimental situations. Similar to pupillometry, IRT is noninvasive and contact-free, making it suitable for diverse use in captivity and the wild. IRT works by measuring changes in body surface temperature that result from changes in blood pressure controlled by the autonomic nervous system (Ioannou et al., 2014; Rubinstein & Sessler, 1990). Variation in internal states leads to variability in vasoconstriction and dilation, which results in changes in surface skin temperature (Ioannou et al., 2014). Research with captive and wild chimpanzees has shown that a drop in nasal skin temperature relative to baseline is associated with negative affective states induced through exposure to negatively valenced vocalizations (Dezecache et al. 2016; Kano et al., 2016). Excitingly, this thermal profile may be dissociable from one produced by positive affect, which appears to be associated with an *increase* in nasal temperature in both humans (Hahn et al., 2012) and other primates (Chotard et al., 2018). This technique is still in its infancy, but it offers exciting potential for examining the affective basis of great ape experiences.

Together, noninvasive measures such as pupillometry, infrared thermal imaging, and gaze-tracking offer exciting and ethical techniques for investigating affect in great apes and other animals.

Empathy in Great Apes
Evidence of great apes' rich socio-emotional capacities is consistent with the evidence of their empathic tendencies. Following social conflicts, great apes (bonobos: Palagi et al., 2004; Clay and de Waal, 2013a, 2013b; chimpanzees: de Waal and van Roosmalen, 1979; Romero & de Waal, 2010; gorillas: Cordoni et al., 2006) have been shown to spontaneously approach distressed peers to offer them comforting contact. This behavior—known as *consolation*—appears to primarily function to reduce the distressed state of the recipient, in the absence of obvious benefits to the actor (Fraser et al. 2008). For this reason, consolation is considered as a behavioral marker of sympathetic concern, which is thought to involve an understanding of the other's state as well as a pro-social motivation to improve that state (de Waal, 2008; de Waal & Preston, 2017; Fraser et al., 2008; Romero et al., 2010).

Comparative research suggests that rather than being restricted to hominids, empathy may be relatively widespread across mammalian species, including other primates (reviewed in Clay et al., 2018; Brooker et al. 2021), elephants (e.g., Plotnik & de Waal, 2014), canids, and small rodent species (e.g., Burkett et al., 2016), as well as in some social avian species, such as ravens (*Corvus corax*; Fraser & Bugnyar, 2010; but see Hooper et al., 2021). The diversity of species exhibiting forms of empathy suggests that empathy may have multiple evolutionary origins, emerging in species where social attachment, cooperation, and/or parental care are key (MacLean, 1985).

Although consolation is the most widely recognized expression of empathy in both humans and animals, other emotion-related behaviors are thought to underpin empathic responding (Clay et al., 2018), which we discuss below. These include automatic forms of affective mirroring, such as rapid facial mimicry, contagion, and behavioral synchrony, as well more specific behavioral responses, such as "targeted helping," which refers to tailored pro-social responses toward another's specific need (de Waal & Preston, 2017). Before discussing these, we first introduce the concept of empathy in more detail in order to set the scene.

The Concept of Empathy

While there are many definitions of empathy in the literature (see Adriaense et al., 2020; Batson, 2009; Cuff et al., 2016), most definitions consider empathy a multidimensional *other-oriented* capacity that includes both affective and cognitive components (de Waal & Preston, 2017; Preston & de Waal, 2002). The affective components broadly refer to the sharing of others' emotional states (Mehrabian & Epstein, 1972; Soto & Levenson, 2009), such as through emotional contagion and mimicry (de Waal & Preston, 2017). By comparison, the *cognitive* components of empathy include the ability to understand others' emotional states and experiences (Hogan, 1969), as well as the capacity to appraise the reasons for those states. Taken together, these affective and cognitive components result in the *other-oriented quality* of empathy. In contrast, personal distress is a self-oriented response that occurs when the individual gets (personally) distressed by someone else's distress, which renders them unable to provide support.

Neurobiological and developmental research support the distinction between the affective and cognitive components of empathy (Decety, 2011). Findings suggest that affective empathy is facilitated by bottom-up, evolutionarily ancient neural processes, whereas cognitive empathy involves top-down neural processes (Decety, 2011; Singer, 2006; Stone, 2006) involved in cognitive perspective-taking, cognitive appraisal, and emotion regulation (Jankowiak-Siuda et al., 2011). In this respect, empathy is thought to involve interacting and particularly overlapping neural processes (Decety, 2011).

Relatedly, empathy relies on various other cognitive processes, including self–other differentiation, self-reflection, and integration of individual experiences to appropriately recognize and respond to others' emotional and mental states (Reniers et al., 2011). The process of self–other differentiation is crucial for the empathy response to be truly other-oriented, where the empathizer is able to correctly perceive and/or attribute the emotional states to the other rather than to their own state. Such self-other differentiation typically works in tandem with emotion-regulation capacities, whereby a personal distress response can be effectively inhibited (Batson et al., 1997; Decety & Lamm, 2006).

Behaviorally, empathy is detected via observing the occurrence of pro-social *responding toward others' emotional states*, which refers to actions that benefit the other without any obvious direct benefit to the actor (Decety et al., 2016). It is worth noting that while empathic responding is ultimately pro-social, not all pro-social behaviors are affectively based or indeed empathic. For instance, in some cases, pro-sociality in primates seems also to be explained as a response to requests for help by recipients (de Waal & Suchak, 2010; Tennie et al., 2016; Yamamoto & Takimoto, 2012). Such a response may not require any affective or empathic resonance toward the other's state of need, but instead may be a behavioral response to a request or even perceived disturbance. This would differ from empathy, which is considered a "receiver-driven behavior" that is internally motivated by an individual's orientation toward the other's state, and typically a motivation to improve that state. Future research pinpointing the underlying mechanisms of pro-social responding is needed to elucidate the degree to which such pro-social behaviors are empathically based.

From an evolutionary perspective, empathy is thought to have evolved within the context of parental care and/or highly dependent social bonds, which has expanded into an adaptation to social group living (MacLean, 1985; Preston, 2013). Indeed, offspring elicit emotional responses from their caregivers by displaying their affective states, with offspring distress often resulting in emotional contagion and corresponding parental distress (MacLean, 1985). The evolutionary importance of this kind of affiliative bond is thought to explain the social bias effects found in empathy. Specifically, empathy and attention toward another's emotional states are often biased toward socially close individuals (see Preston & de Waal 2002), where empathy is predicted by perceived affiliation, similarity, and familiarity (de Waal & Preston, 2017). This social bias extends to consolation, which is preferentially offered to socially close individuals in great apes (Clay & de Waal, 2013a; Palagi & Norscia, 2013; Romero et al., 2010) and some species of monkeys (Demaria & Thierry, 2001). In the human literature, there are robust empirical effects of similarity, familiarity, past experiences, explicit teaching, and salience for empathy as well as emotional attention (see Preston & de Waal, 2002, for a review). These findings suggest shared evolutionary roots in the patterns of empathy among humans and great apes.

One of the leading models of empathy, frequently adopted by comparative researchers, is the Perception-Action Model (PAM; Preston & de Waal, 2002). According to the PAM, the perception of another's mental/emotional state or action elicits one's own representations of this state and/or action, which elicits spontaneous and physiological responses (de Waal & Preston, 2017). The synchronized actions and expressions implicit in the PAM are considered crucial for the development of emotion regulation (Field, 2008; Malatesta & Haviland, 1982), which is crucial for effective empathy. The PAM can further explain certain core components of empathy, including the social biases for similarity and familiarity, which relate to the entrainment of shared emotional components of self and other representations. Mirror neurons have been suggested to support the PAM at the neurological level (de Waal & Preston, 2017; Gallese et al., 1996; Rizzolatti et al., 1996; but see Rizzolatti & Caruana, 2017), however, the function of mirror neurons and their involvement in empathy is still debated (Lamm & Majdandžić, 2015).

Building on the PAM is the Russian Doll Model of empathy (de Waal, 2003). This model rests on the notion that empathy involves increasing layers of complexity, starting from an automatic affective core and expanding to more advanced forms of cognitive appraisal and perspective-taking. This model is based on the principle that "the old always remains present in the new" (de Waal, 2007). Accordingly, the PAM (de Waal & Preston, 2017; Preston & de Waal, 2002) forms the core of the Russian doll, which generates the basic phenomenon of emotional contagion. More complex processes of empathy, such as cognitive appraisal and perspective-taking, are then assumed to rest upon this simpler automatic mechanism. At this stage, the individual not only shares the emotional state of the other, but also seeks to appraise the reason for the distress. Such an ability is considered essential for a more complex behavioral response like targeted helping, where the needs of the other are identified and considered (de Waal & Preston, 2017).

According to the Russian Doll Model, the affective core is essential to initiate the subsequent empathic response, which involves the addition of cognition. Although the Russian Doll Model offers a valuable platform to explain the mechanisms of empathy, the linearity of the model's structure has been debated and challenged (Adriaense et al., 2020). Indeed, the Russian Doll Model asserts that the inner affective components (i.e., emotional contagion) are required for the development of the outer layers (e.g., cognitive empathy; Yamamoto, 2017). However, this dependency is not confirmed by behavioral data (for example, perspective-taking can occur without helping in chimpanzees; Yamamoto et al., 2009). Furthermore, although emotional contagion is often considered a preliminary building block of empathy, its role in forms of empathic responding, including consolation, remain unclear and untested. At present, insufficient data are available to determine the extent to which emotion contagion is implicated in the empathic responding of great apes and other animals (see Adriaense et al., 2020, for discussion).

Nevertheless, despite some unanswered questions, the Russian Doll Model provides a useful framework from which empathy in animals can be operationalized and addressed. Based on the notion of affective and cognitive components, comparative researchers have sought to investigate the various components of empathy described in the Russian Doll Model, from more automatic affective processes, such as yawn contagion and rapid facial mimicry, through consolation and targeted helping. Evidence for these capacities in great apes are discussed below.

Yawn Contagion

Yawn contagion—or the tendency to yawn in response to someone else yawning—is considered to be an automatic and rudimentary form of state-matching that has been proposed by some to be related to empathy (Campbell & de Waal, 2011; Haker et al., 2013; Norscia & Palagi, 2011; Palagi et al., 2009; Platek et al., 2003; Romero et al., 2010). This is because both sex/gender and social closeness effects are found in yawn contagion as well (e.g., Norscia et al., 2016; Norscia & Palagi, 2011; but see Gallo et al., 2021).

Although contagious yawning has been found in chimpanzees (Campbell & Cox, 2019; Campbell & de Waal, 2011), bonobos (Demuru & Palagi, 2012; Palagi et al., 2014), and humans (Provine, 2005), even as young as 2.5 years (Cordoni et al., 2021), it does not appear to be present in gorillas (Palagi et al., 2019). While further replications are required, this potential discontinuity implies that phylogenetic closeness does not automatically predict the presence of yawn contagion (Palagi et al., 2020). Moreover, the developmental profile of yawn contagion also raises questions about its relation to empathy. For instance, although human fetuses spontaneously yawn in the womb (Reissland et al., 2012), children only start to show yawn contagion by the age of 4–5 years (Helt et al., 2010; Millen & Anderson, 2011) which is much later than empathy, which is evidenced even in the first year of life (Davidov et al., 2013; Davidov et al., 2020). Therefore, the link between yawn contagion and empathy remains controversial.

Rapid Facial Mimicry

Rapid facial mimicry (RFM) is another behavioral expression thought to relate to empathy and more general socio-emotional orientation. RFM is a rapid and automatic behavioral response in which individuals spontaneously mimic another's facial expression, typically a play face or smile (Mancini et al., 2013). According to the PAM (Preston & de Waal, 2002), the mirror neuron system generates shared representations during the perception of another's facial expression. As such, RFM is considered a pillar of synchronization between individuals and a potential predictor of emotional contagion (Dimberg et al., 2000). RFM has been widely observed in multiple nonhuman primate species, including great apes (chimpanzees and gorillas: Palagi et al., 2018; bonobos: Palagi et al., 2020; orangutans: Davila-Ross et al., 2008; macaques: Scopa & Palagi, 2016; geladas: Mancini et al., 2013), mainly in the context of play, but also during sexual contact (Palagi et al., 2020).

Consolation

Great apes are known to console conspecifics in emotional distress by offering them friendly contact, such as bystanders approaching victims following a social conflict to offer them gentle contact. Consolation, while outwardly behaviorally similar to other forms of third-party affiliation, appears to differ on its pro-social basis, where its assumed motivation appears to be to reduce the other's distress rather than to offer purely selfish benefits. By comparison, other third-party affiliation behaviors that outwardly resemble consolation—e.g., substituted reconciliation, where the bystander approaches the victim to reconcile on behalf of the aggressor, or self-protection, where the bystander approaches to reduce risk of redirected aggression—might be driven by different proximate mechanisms serving selfish adaptive functions (e.g., Call et al., 2002; Palagi & Cordoni, 2009; Schino & Marini, 2012) such as reducing self-distress, risk of redirected aggression, or establishing reciprocity for future events (Batson, 2011; Palagi et al., 2006; Watts, 2002).

The behavior was termed *consolation* because of its apparent closeness to the behavior observed in humans (de Waal & van Roosmalen, 1979). The first evidence for consolation came from research with chimpanzees (de Waal & van Roosmalen, 1979; Fraser et al., 2008; Romero & de Waal, 2010), and systematic comparisons among primates have since been reported in human children (Hastings et al., 2006; Zahn-Waxler & Radke-Yarrow, 1990), bonobos (Clay & de Waal, 2013a, 2013b; Palagi & Norscia, 2013; Palagi et al., 2004), gorillas (Cordoni et al., 2006), and the Tonkean macaque (*Macaca tonkeana*; Palagi et al., 2014), a monkey species known for its high levels of social tolerance. Thus far, evidence of consolation from other monkeys has remained inconclusive (de Waal & Aureli, 1996; Watts et al., 2000). Importantly, all the primate species demonstrating consolation are known for their high degree of social tolerance and/or cooperation (Ciani et al., 2012; Matsumura, 1999).

Consolation has also been observed in non-primate species, including dogs (Quervel-Chaumette et al., 2016), prairie voles (Burkett et al., 2016), elephants, and corvids (*Corvus corax*; Fraser & Bugnyar, 2010; but see Hooper et al., 2021). However, the psychological mechanisms underlying these pro-social behaviors are unclear. More investigation is required to establish whether the mechanisms of consolation are equivalent across species and ages (Adriaense et al., 2020).

As noted, a hallmark feature of consolation is its social bias: it is strongly predicted by social closeness, being strongest among kin, followed by socially close partners (Clay & de Waal, 2013a; Fraser et al., 2008; Palagi & Norscia, 2013; Romero et al., 2010). More than a direct emotional response to the recipient's distress, consolation is thought to reflect the bystander's understanding of the victim's state and an attempt to ameliorate their distress (de Waal & Preston, 2017). Indeed, consolation has been shown to function to reduce the distress of the recipient—based on rates of self-scratching behaviors, a marker of social anxiety—without immediate or obvious benefits to the actor (Clay & de Waal, 2013a; Fraser et al., 2008; Palagi & Norscia, 2013; Romero et al., 2010). Offering comfort suggests that bystanders can perceive the emotional state of the other and know how to provide the appropriate response to reduce their distress (Fraser et al., 2008; Palagi & Norscia, 2013; Romero et al., 2010).

Although the proposed involvement of perspective-taking suggests that consolation may reflect more cognitively advanced processes, consolation is performed by immature great apes (Clay & de Waal, 2013a, 2013b; Webb et al., 2017) suggesting that it may also reflect simpler mechanisms. Further research is needed to examine patterns of consolation across the life span and the extent to which consolation by younger individuals is mechanistically and functionally comparable to that observed in adults.

Targeted Helping

Targeted helping—also known as "instrumental helping" (Warneken, 2006; Warneken et al., 2007)—refers to offering targeted or tailored help that is based on the cognitive appreciation of another's specific need in a given situation (de Waal, 1996; 2008). It assumes that the actor must understand the situation in order to provide a suitable solution that is tailored to an individual's specific situation or need (Pérez-Manrique & Gomila, 2018). The capacity for targeted helping seems to appear early in human development, with evidence that children before their second year actively help others to achieve their goals in various situations (Warneken, 2006) and understand others' needs as young as nine months (Koester et al., 2016). Several cases of targeted helping have been observed or suggested in animals, including in great apes (chimpanzees: de Waal, 2010; Melis et al., 2011; Yamamoto et al., 2012, although contested by Liebal et al., 2014; Stevens 2004; Tennie et al., 2016), cetaceans (Bearzi et al., 2017), and elephants (Byrne et al., 2008; Douglas-Hamilton et al., 2006). However, detecting whether and to what extent an animal can understand another's goal and offer appropriate help remains challenging, with alternative explanations often difficult to refute. This is because the same external behavior can be triggered by different underlying motivations and therefore different underlying mechanisms. Consequently, it is essential to investigate the underlying processes, such as via the methods described earlier, to explain the observed behaviors.

Overall, conducting naturalistic observations of how great apes and other animals respond to others in distress provides a relevant degree of ecological validity that cannot be achieved by experiments in order to identify the evolutionary drivers shaping empathy. It also provides valuable information on the function of empathy, how it develops (Webb et al., 2017), and its phylogenetic history by investigating it across closely related species (e.g., Palagi et al., 2014). However, observing animals in their natural settings precludes control of external variables, making it difficult to determine the underlying mechanisms. Combining behavioral observations with experimental approaches and corresponding physiological measures are essential in gaining a fuller understanding of empathy and its underlying mechanisms.

Conclusion

In sum, there is strong evidence that great apes exhibit rich emotional lives that are underpinned by a sophisticated social awareness. While it remains difficult to access the inner experiences of nonverbal animals, comparative studies have revealed complex and nuanced capacities in the perception, awareness, and production of emotions, as well as sophisticated socio-emotional and cognitive capacities. For instance, great apes are able to recognize the emotional states of conspecifics as well as humans, they can relate those states to associated contextual cues, and moreover show strong socio-emotional orientation, which likely underpins their sophisticated skills in communication and social cognition. There is also evidence that great apes, along with some other animals, show empathic concern to the emotional states and needs of others, and are able to effectively orient themselves to meet those needs, such as by offering comfort or support.

While research has thus far been limited by methodological constraints, the advent of new technologies and experimental approaches, like IRT, eye tracking, and the cognitive bias test, offer exciting opportunities to further enhance our understanding of animal emotions and their mechanistic bases. Integrating across multiple methods is necessary in order to capture the complexity of such multi-componential phenomena as empathy, and indeed emotions more generally. Moreover, measuring different types of emotional capacities within the same species or study system can yield deeper insights into which components of emotion and empathy may manifest independently and are proximately or functionally linked. Overall, examining comparative evidence for emotion and empathy is crucial to illuminate the social and ecological conditions promoting their evolution, which can shed light on the evolutionary origins of our own social and emotional nature.

References

Adriaense, J. E. C., Koski, S. E., Huber, L., & Lamm, C. (2020). Challenges in the comparative study of empathy and related phenomena in animals. *Neuroscience & Biobehavioral Reviews*, *112*, 62–82.

Aktar, E., Raijmakers, M. E., & Kret, M. E. (2020). Pupil mimicry in infants and parents. *Cognition and Emotion*, *34*(6), 1160–1170.

Allman, J. M., Tetreault, N. A., Hakeem, A. Y., Manaye, K. F., Semendeferi, K., Erwin, J. M., Park, S., Goubert, V., & Hof, P. R. (2010). The von Economo neurons in frontoinsular and anterior cingulate cortex in great apes and humans. *Brain Structure and Function*, *214*(5), 495–517.

Al-Shawaf, L., Conroy-Beam, D., Asao, K., & Buss, D. M. (2016). Human emotions: An evolutionary psychological perspective. *Emotion Review*, *8*(2), 173–186.

Al-Shawaf, L., & Lewis, D. M. G. (2017). Evolutionary psychology and the emotions. In V. Zeigler-Hill & T. Shackelford (Eds.), *Encyclopedia of personality and individual differences* (pp. 173–186). Springer.

Amici, F., Aureli, F., & Call, J. (2008). Fission-fusion dynamics, behavioral flexibility, and inhibitory control in primates. *Current Biology*, *18*(18), 1415–1419.

Anderson, D. J., & Adolphs, R. (2014). A framework for studying emotions across species. *Cell*, *157*(1), 187–200.

Baciadonna, L., & McElligott, A. G. (2015). The use of judgement bias to assess welfare in farm livestock. *Animal Welfare*, *24*, 81–91.

Barrett, L. F., & Wager, T. D. (2006). The structure of emotion: Evidence from neuroimaging studies. *Current Directions in Psychological Science*, *15*(2), 79–83.

Barrett, L. F. (2013). Psychological construction: The Darwinian approach to the science of emotion. *Emotion Review*, *5*, 379–389.

Barrett, L. F. (2017a). *How emotions are made: The secret life of the brain*. Houghton Mifflin Harcourt.

Barrett, L. F. (2017b). The theory of constructed emotion: An active inference account of interoception and categorization. *Social Cognitive and Affective Neuroscience*, *12*(1), 1–23.

Bateson, M., & Nettle, D. (2015). Development of a cognitive bias methodology for measuring low mood in chimpanzees. *PeerJ*, *3*, e998.

Batson, C. D. (2009). These things called empathy: Eight related but distinct phenomena. In J. Decety & W. Ickes (Eds.), *The social neuroscience of empathy* (pp. 3–15). MIT Press.

Batson, C. D. (2011). Empathy-induced altruism: Friend or foe of the common good? In D. R. Forsyth & C. L. Hoyt (Eds.), *For the greater good of all: Perspectives on individualism, society, and leadership* (pp. 29–47). Palgrave Macmillan.

Batson, C. D., Early, S., & Salvarani, G. (1997). Perspective taking: Imagining how another feels versus imaging how you would feel. *Personality and Social Psychology Bulletin*, *23*(7), 751–758.

Bearzi, G., Eddy, L., Piwetz, S., Reggente, M. A. L., & Cozzi, B. (2017). Cetacean behavior toward the dead and dying. In J. Vonk & T. Shackelford (Eds.), *Encyclopedia of animal cognition and behavior* (pp. 1–8). Springer International.

Bekoff, M. (2000). Animal emotions: Exploring passionate natures. *Bioscience*, *50*, 861–870.

Blair, R. J. R. (2008). The amygdala and ventromedial prefrontal cortex: Functional contributions and dysfunction in psychopathy. *Philosophical Transactions of the Royal Society B: Biological Sciences*, *363*(1503), 2557–2565.

Boiger, M., & Mesquita, B., 2012. The construction of emotion in interactions, relationships, and cultures. *Emotion Review*, *4*, 221–229

Bossaerts, P. (2010). Risk and risk prediction error signals in anterior insula. *Brain Structure and Function*, *214*(5–6), 645–653.

Breedlove, S. M., & Watson, N. V. (2013). *Biological psychology: An introduction to behavioral, cognitive, and clinical neuroscience* (7th ed.). Sinauer Associates.

Brooker, J. S., Webb, C. E., & Clay, Z. (2022). Primate empathy: A flexible and multi-componential phenomenon. In B. L. Schwartz, & M. J. Beran (Eds.), *Primate cognitive studies* (pp. 505–531). Cambridge University Press.

Burkett, J. P., Andari, E., Johnson, Z. V., Curry, D. C., de Waal, F. B. M., & Young, L. J. (2016). Oxytocin-dependent consolation behavior in rodents. *Science, 351*(6271), 375–378.

Buttelmann, D., Call, J., & Tomasello, M. (2009). Do great apes use emotional expressions to infer desires? *Developmental Science, 12*(5), 688–698.

Byrne, R., Lee, P. C., Njiraini, N., Poole, J. H., Sayialel, K., Sayialel, S., Bates, L. & Moss, C. J. (2008). Do elephants show empathy?. *Journal of Consciousness Studies, 15*(10–11), 204–225.

Call, J., Aureli, F., & de Waal, F. B. M. (2002). Postconflict third-party affiliation in stumptailed macaques. *Animal Behaviour, 63*(2), 209–216.

Campbell, M. W., & Cox, C. R. (2019). Observational data reveal evidence and parameters of contagious yawning in the behavioral repertoire of captive-reared chimpanzees (*Pan troglodytes*). *Scientific Reports, 9*(1), 13271.

Campbell, M. W., & de Waal, F. B. M. (2011). Ingroup-outgroup bias in contagious yawning by chimpanzees supports link to empathy. *PLoS ONE, 6*(4), e18283.

Chotard, H., Ioannou, S., & Davila-Ross, M. (2018). Infrared thermal imaging: Positive and negative emotions modify the skin temperatures of monkey and ape faces. *American Journal of Primatology, 80*(5), e22863.

Ciani, F., Dall'Olio, S., Stanyon, R., & Palagi, E. (2012). Social tolerance and adult play in macaque societies: A comparison with different human cultures. *Animal Behaviour, 84*(6), 1313–1322.

Clay, Z., & de Waal, F. B. M. (2013a). Bonobos respond to distress in others: Consolation across the age spectrum. *PLoS ONE, 8*(1), e55206.

Clay, Z., & de Waal, F. B. M. (2013b). Development of socio-emotional competence in bonobos. *Proceedings of the National Academy of Sciences, 110*(45), 18121–18126.

Clay, Z., Palagi, E., & de Waal, F. B. M. (2018). Ethological approaches to empathy in primates. In K. Z. Meyza, & E. Knapska (Eds.), *Neuronal correlates of empathy: From rodent to human* (pp. 53–66). Academic Press.

Cordoni, G., Favilli, E., & Palagi, E. (2021). Earlier than previously thought: Yawn contagion in preschool children. *Developmental Psychobiology, 63*(5), 931–944.

Cordoni, G., Palagi, E., & Tarli, S. B. (2006). Reconciliation and consolation in captive western gorillas. *International Journal of Primatology, 27*(5), 1365–1382.

Cosmides, L., & Tooby, J. (2000). Evolutionary psychology and the emotions. In M. Lewis & J. M. Haviland-Jones (Eds.), *Handbook of emotions* (pp. 91–115). Guilford.

Cuff, B. M. P., Brown, S. J., Taylor, L., & Howat, D. J. (2016). Empathy: A review of the concept. *Emotion Review, 8*(2), 144–153.

Davidov, M., Paz, Y., Roth-Hanania, R., Uzefovsky, F., Orlitsky, T., Mankuta, D., & Zahn-Waxler, C. (2020). Caring babies: Concern for others in distress during infancy. *Developmental Science, 24*(2), e13016.

Davidov, M., Zahn-Waxler, C., Roth-Hanania, R., & Knafo, A. (2013). Concern for others in the first year of life: Theory, evidence, and avenues for research. *Child Development Perspectives, 7*(2), 126–131.

Davidson, R. J., Putnam, K. M., & Larson, C. L. (2000). Dysfunction in the neural circuitry of emotion regulation: A possible prelude to violence. *Science, 289*(5479), 591–594.

Davila Ross, M., Menzler, S., & Zimmermann, E. (2008). Rapid facial mimicry in orangutan play. *Biology Letters, 4*(1), 27–30.

Darwin, C. (1872). *The expression of the emotions in man and animals*. Murray.

Davis, M. (1997). Neurobiology of fear responses: The role of the amygdala. *The Journal of Neuropsychiatry and Clinical Neurosciences, 9*(3), 382–402.

Decety, J. (2011). The neuroevolution of empathy. *Annals of the New York Academy of Sciences, 1231*(1), 35–45.

Decety, J., Bartal, I. B.-A., Uzefovsky, F., & Knafo-Noam, A. (2016). Empathy as a driver of prosocial behaviour: Highly conserved neurobehavioural mechanisms across species. *Philosophical Transactions of the Royal Society B: Biological Sciences, 371*(1686), 20150077.

Decety, J., & Lamm, C. (2006). Human empathy through the lens of social neuroscience. *The Scientific World Journal, 6*, 1146–1163.

Demaria, C., & Thierry, B. (2001). A comparative study of reconciliation in rhesus and Tonkean macaques. *Behaviour, 138*(3), 397–410.

Demuru, E., & Palagi, E. (2012). In bonobos yawn contagion is higher among kin and friends. *PLoS ONE, 7*(11), e49613.

de Waal, F. B. M. (1987). Tension regulation and nonreproductive functions of sex in captive bonobos (Pan paniscus). *National Geographic Research, 3*(3), 318–335.

de Waal, F. B. M. (1988). The communicative repertoire of captive bonobos (*Pan paniscus*), compared to that of chimpanzees. *Behaviour, 106*(3–4), 183–251.

de Waal, F. B. M. (1996). *Good Natured: The Origins of Right and Wrong in Humans and Other Animals*. Harvard Univ. Press.

de Waal, F. B. M. (1999). Anthropomorphism and anthropodenial. *Philosophical Topics, 27*, 255–280.

de Waal, F. B. M. (2003). On the possibility of animal empathy. In A. A. Manstead, N. Frijda, & A. Fischer (Eds.), *Feelings and emotions: The Amsterdam symposium* (Vol. 381). Cambridge University Press.

de Waal, F. B. M. (2007). The "Russian doll" model of empathy and imitation. In S. Braten (Ed.), *On being moved: From mirror neurons to empathy* (pp. 35–48), John Benjamins.

de Waal, F. B. M. (2008). Putting the altruism back into altruism: The evolution of empathy. *Annual Review of Psychology, 59*(1), 279–300.

de Waal, F. B. M. (2010). *The age of empathy: Nature's lessons for a kinder society*. Broadway Books.

de Waal, F. B. M. (2011). What is an animal emotion? *Annals of the New York Academy of Sciences, 1224*(1), 191–206.

de Waal, F. B. M. (2016). *Are we smart enough to know how smart animals are?* W. W. Norton.

de Waal, F. B. M., & Aureli, F. (1996). Consolation, reconciliation and a possible cognitive difference between macaques and chimpanzees. In A. E. Russon, K. A. Bard, & S. Taylor Parker (Eds.), *Reaching into thought: The minds of great apes* (pp. 80–110). Cambridge University Press.

de Waal, F. B. M., & Preston, S. D. (2017). Mammalian empathy: Behavioural manifestations and neural basis. *Nature Reviews Neuroscience, 18*(8), 498–509.

de Waal, F. B. M., & Suchak, M. (2010). Prosocial primates: Selfish and unselfish motivations. *Philosophical Transactions of the Royal Society B: Biological Sciences, 365*(1553), 2711–2722.

de Waal, F. B. M., & van Roosmalen, A. (1979). Reconciliation and consolation among chimpanzees. *Behavioral Ecology and Sociobiology, 5*(1), 55–66.

Dezecache, G., Zuberbühler, K., Davila-Ross, M., & Dahl, C. D. (2016). Skin temperature changes in wild chimpanzees upon hearing vocalizations of conspecifics. *Royal Society Open Science, 4*(1), 160816.

Dimberg, U., Thunberg, M., & Elmehed, K. (2000). Unconscious facial reactions to emotional facial expressions. *Psychological Science, 11*(1), 86–89.

Douglas-Hamilton, I., Bhalla, S., Wittemyer, G., & Vollrath, F. (2006). Behavioural reactions of elephants towards a dying and deceased matriarch. *Applied Animal Behaviour Science, 100*(1), 87–102.

Dukes, D., Abrams, K., Adolphs, R., Ahmed, M. E., Beatty, A., Berridge, K. C., Broomhall, S., Brosch, T., Campos, J. J., Clay, Z., Clément, F., Cunningham, W. A., Damasio, A., Damasio, H., D'Arms, J., Davidson, J. W., de Gelder, B., Deonna, J., de Sousa, R., . . . & Sander, D. (2021). The rise of affectivism. *Nature Human Behaviour, 5*(7), 816–820.

Egelkamp, C. L., & Ross, S. R. (2019). A review of zoo-based cognitive research using touchscreen interfaces. *Zoo Biology, 38*(2), 220–235.

Field, T. (2008). The effects of mother's physical and emotional unavailability on emotion regulation. *Monographs of the Society for Research in Child Development, 59*(2–3), 208–227.

Fraser, O. N., & Bugnyar, T. (2010). Do ravens show consolation? Responses to distressed others. *PLoS ONE, 5*(5), e10605.

Fraser, O. N., Stahl, D., & Aureli, F. (2008). Stress reduction through consolation in chimpanzees. *Proceedings of the National Academy of Sciences, 105*(25), 8557–8562.

Furuichi, T. (2019). *Bonobo and chimpanzee* (R. Matsuda Goodwin, Trans.) Springer.

Gallese, V., Fadiga, L., Fogassi, L., & Rizzolatti, G. (1996). Action recognition in the premotor cortex. *Brain, 119*(2), 593–609.

Gallo, A., Zanoli, A., Caselli, M., Palagi, E., & Norscia, I. (2021). First evidence of yawn contagion in a wild monkey species. *Scientific Reports, 11*(1), 17957.

Gruber, T., & Clay, Z. (2016). A comparison between bonobos and chimpanzees: A review and update. *Evolutionary Anthropology: Issues, News, and Reviews, 25*(5), 239–252.

Hahn, A. C., Whitehead, R. D., Albrecht, M., Lefevre, C. E., & Perret, D. I. (2012). Hot or not? Thermal reactions to social contact. *Biology Letters, Physiology, 8*, 1–4.

Haker, H., Kawohl, W., Herwig, U., & Rössler, W. (2013). Mirror neuron activity during contagious yawning: An fMRI study. *Brain Imaging and Behavior, 7*(1), 28–34.

Harding, E. J., Paul, E. S., & Mendl, M., 2004. Animal behaviour: Cognitive bias and affective state. *Nature, 427*(6972), 312–312.

Hastings, P. D., Zahn-Waxler, C., & McShane, K. (2006). We are, by nature, moral creatures: Biological bases of concern for others. In M. Killen & J. G. Smetana (Eds.), *Handbook of moral development* (pp. 483–516). Psychology Press.

Haun, D. B. M., Nawroth, C., & Call, J. (2011). Great apes' risk-taking strategies in a decision making task. *PLoS ONE, 6*(12), e28801.

Heesen R., Austry, D. A., Upton, Z., & Clay, Z. (2022). Flexible signalling strategies by victims mediate post-conflict interactions in bonobos. *Philosophical Transactions of the Royal Society B*, 377(1860), 20210310.

Heilbronner, S. R., Rosati, A. G., Stevens, J. R., Hare, B., & Hauser, M. D. (2008). A fruit in the hand or two in the bush? Divergent risk preferences in chimpanzees and bonobos. *Biology Letters*, 4(3), 246–249.

Helt, M. S., Eigsti, I.-M., Snyder, P. J., & Fein, D. A. (2010). Contagious yawning in autistic and typical development. *Child Development*, 81(5), 1620–1631.

Hepach, R., Vaish, A., Kano, F., Albiach-Serrano, A., Benziad, L., Call, J., & Tomasello, M. (2021). Chimpanzees' (*Pan troglodytes*) internal arousal remains elevated if they cannot themselves help a conspecific. *Journal of Comparative Psychology*, 135(2), 196–207.

Hepach, R., Vaish, A., & Tomasello, M. (2012). Young children are intrinsically motivated to see others helped. *Psychological Science*, 23(9), 967–972.

Herrmann, E., Hare, B., Call, J., & Tomasello, M. (2010). Differences in the cognitive skills of bonobos and chimpanzees. *PLoS ONE*, 5(8), e12438.

Hess, U., & Fischer, A. (2013). Emotional mimicry as social regulation. *Personality and Social Psychology Review*, 17(2), 142–157.

Hogan, R. (1969). Development of an empathy scale. *Journal of Consulting and Clinical Psychology*, 33(3), 307–316.

Hohmann, G., Mundry, R., & Deschner, T. (2009). The relationship between socio-sexual behavior and salivary cortisol in bonobos: Tests of the tension regulation hypothesis. *American Journal of Primatology*, 71(3), 223–232.

Hooper, R., Meekins, E., McIvor, G. E., & Thornton, A. (2021). Wild jackdaws respond to their partner's distress, but not with consolation. *Royal Society Open Science*, 8(6), 210253.

Hopper, L. M., Gulli, R. A., Howard, L. H., Kano, F., Krupenye, C., Ryan, A. M., & Paukner, A. (2021). The application of noninvasive, restraint-free eye-tracking methods for use with nonhuman primates. *Behavior Research Methods*, 53(3), 1003–1030.

Ioannou, S., Morris, P., Mercer, H., Baker, M., Gallese, V., & Reddy, V. (2014). Proximity and gaze influences facial temperature: A thermal infrared imaging study. *Frontiers in Psychology*, 5(845), 1–12.

Izumi, A., & Kojima, S. (2004). Matching vocalizations to vocalizing faces in a chimpanzee (*Pan troglodytes*). *Animal Cognition*, 7(3), 179–184.

Jankowiak-Siuda, K., Rymarczyk, K., & Grabowska, A. (2011). How we empathize with others: A neurobiological perspective. *Medical Science Monitor*, 17(1), RA18–RA24.

Kano, F., Hirata, S., & Call, J. (2015). Social attention in the two species of pan: Bonobos make more eye contact than chimpanzees. *PLoS ONE*, 10(6), e0129684.

Kano, F., Hirata, S., Deschner, T., Behringer, V., & Call, J. (2016). Nasal temperature drops in response to a playback of conspecific fights in chimpanzees: A thermo-imaging study. *Physiology & Behavior*, 155, 83–94.

Kano, F., Tanaka, M., & Tomonaga, M. (2008). Enhanced recognition of emotional stimuli in the chimpanzee (*Pan troglodytes*). *Animal Cognition*, 11(3), 517–524.

Kano, F., & Tomonaga, M. (2010). Attention to emotional scenes including whole-body expressions in chimpanzees (*Pan troglodytes*). *Journal of Comparative Psychology*, 124(3), 287–294.

Köster, M., Ohmer, X., Nguyen, T. D., & Kärtner, J. (2016). Infants understand others' needs. *Psychological Science*, 27(4), 542–548.

Kret, M. E., Jaasma, L., Bionda, T., & Wijnen, J. G. (2016). Bonobos (*Pan paniscus*) show an attentional bias toward conspecifics' emotions. *Proceedings of the National Academy of Sciences*, 113(14), 3761–3766.

Kret, M. E., Muramatsu, A., & Matsuzawa, T. (2018). Emotion processing across and within species: A comparison between humans (*Homo sapiens*) and chimpanzees (*Pan troglodytes*). *Journal of Comparative Psychology*, 132(4), 395–409.

Kret, M. E., Prochazkova, E., Sterck, E. H., & Clay, Z. (2020). Emotional expressions in human and non-human great apes. *Neuroscience & Biobehavioral Reviews*, 115, 378–395.

Kret, M. E., Tomonaga, M., & Matsuzawa, T. (2014). Chimpanzees and humans mimic pupil-size of conspecifics. *PLoS ONE*, 9(8), e104886.

Kret, M. E., & van Berlo, E. (2020). Attentional bias in humans toward human and bonobo expressions of emotion. *Evolutionary Psychology*, 19(3), 14747049211032816.

Krupenye, C., MacLean, E. L., & Hare, B. (2018). *Does the bonobo have a (chimpanzee-like) theory of mind?* (Vol. 1). Oxford University Press.

Kuhnen, C. M., & Knutson, B. (2005). The neural basis of financial risk taking. *Neuron*, 47(5), 763–770.

Kurth, F., Zilles, K., Fox, P. T., Laird, A. R., & Eickhoff, S. B. (2010). A link between the systems: Functional differentiation and integration within the human insula revealed by meta-analysis. *Brain Structure and Function*, 214(5–6), 519–534.

Lamm, C., & Majdandžić, J. (2015). The role of shared neural activations, mirror neurons, and morality in empathy: A critical comment. *Neuroscience Research, 90*, 15–24.

Lewis, L., & Krupenye, C. (2021). *Theory of mind in nonhuman primates*. In B. L. Schwartz & M. J. Beran (Eds.), *Primate Cognitive Studies* (pp. 439–482). Cambridge University Press.

Liebal, K., Vaish, A., Haun, D., Tomasello, M. (2014). Does sympathy motivate prosocial behaviour in great apes? *PLoS ONE, 9*(1), e84299.

MacLean, P. D. (1985). Brain evolution relating to family, play, and the separation call. *Archives of General Psychiatry, 42*(4), 405–417.

Malatesta, C. Z., & Haviland, J. M. (1982). Learning display rules: The socialization of emotion expression in infancy. *Child Development, 53*(4), 991.

Mancini, G., Ferrari, P. F., & Palagi, E. (2013). Rapid facial mimicry in geladas. *Scientific Reports, 3*, 1527.

Massen, J. J. M., Behrens, F., Martin, J. S., Stocker, M., & Brosnan, S. F. (2019). A comparative approach to affect and cooperation. *Neuroscience & Biobehavioral Reviews, 107*, 370–387.

Matsumura, S. (1999). The evolution of "egalitarian" and "despotic" social systems among macaques. *Primates, 40*(1), 23–31.

Mehrabian, A., & Epstein, N. (1972). A measure of emotional empathy. *Journal of Personality, 40*(4), 525–543.

Melis, A. P., Warneken, F., Jensen, K., Schneider, A.-C., Call, J., & Tomasello, M. (2011). Chimpanzees help conspecifics obtain food and non-food items. *Proceedings of the Royal Society B: Biological Sciences, 278*(1710), 1405–1413.

Mendl, M., Burman, O. H. P., Parker, R. M. A., & Paul, E. S. (2009). Cognitive bias as an indicator of animal emotion and welfare: Emerging evidence and underlying mechanisms. *Applied Animal Behaviour Science, 118*(3), 161–181.

Mendl, M., Burman, O. H. P., & Paul, E. S. (2010). An integrative and functional framework for the study of animal emotion and mood. *Proceedings of the Royal Society B: Biological Sciences, 277*(1696), 2895–2904.

Meyer-Lindenberg, A., Buckholtz, J. W., Kolachana, B., Hariri, A. R., Pezawas, L., Blasi, G., Wabnitz, A., Honea, R., Verchinski, B., Callicott, J. H., Egan, M., Mattay, V., & Weinberger, D. R. (2006). Neural mechanisms of genetic risk for impulsivity and violence in humans. *Proceedings of the National Academy of Sciences, 103*(16), 6269–6274.

Millen, A., & Anderson, J. R. (2011). Neither infants nor toddlers catch yawns from their mothers. *Biology Letters, 7*(3), 440–442.

Mitani, J. C., & Watts, D. P. (2005). Correlates of territorial boundary patrol behaviour in wild chimpanzees. *Animal Behaviour, 70*(5), 1079–1086.

Mutschler, I., Wieckhorst, B., Kowalevski, S., Derix, J., Wentlandt, J., Schulze-Bonhage, A., & Ball, T. (2009). Functional organization of the human anterior insular cortex. *Neuroscience Letters, 457*(2), 66–70.

Norscia, I., Demuru, E., & Palagi, E. (2016). She more than he: Gender bias supports the empathic nature of yawn contagion in *Homo sapiens*. *Royal Society Open Science, 3*(2), 150459.

Norscia, I., & Palagi, E. (2011). Yawn contagion and empathy in *Homo sapiens*. *PLoS ONE, 6*(12), e28472.

Palagi, E., Bertini, M., Annicchiarico, G., & Cordoni, G. (2020). Mirror replication of sexual facial expressions increases the success of sexual contacts in bonobos. *Scientific Reports, 10*(1), 18979.

Palagi, E., Celeghin, A., Tamietto, M., Winkielman, P., & Norscia, I. (2020). The neuroethology of spontaneous mimicry and emotional contagion in human and non-human animals. *Neuroscience & Biobehavioral Reviews, 111*, 149–165.

Palagi, E., & Cordoni, G. (2009). Postconflict third-party affiliation in *Canis lupus*: Do wolves share similarities with the great apes? *Animal Behaviour, 78*(4), 979–986.

Palagi, E., Cordoni, G., & Tarli, S. B. (2006). Possible roles of consolation in captive chimpanzees (*Pan troglodytes*). *American Journal of Physical Anthropology, 129*(1), 105–111.

Palagi, E., Dall'Olio, S., Demuru, E., & Stanyon, R. (2014). Exploring the evolutionary foundations of empathy: Consolation in monkeys. *Evolution and Human Behavior, 35*(4), 341–349.

Palagi, E., Leone, A., Mancini, G., & Ferrari, P. F. (2009). Contagious yawning in gelada baboons as a possible expression of empathy. *Proceedings of the National Academy of Sciences, 106*(46), 19262–19267.

Palagi, E., & Norscia, I. (2013). Bonobos protect and console friends and kin. *PLoS ONE, 8*(11), e79290.

Palagi, E., Norscia, I., & Cordoni, G. (2019). Lowland gorillas (*Gorilla gorilla gorilla*) failed to respond to others' yawn: Experimental and naturalistic evidence. *Journal of Comparative Psychology, 133*(3), 406–416.

Palagi, E., Norscia, I., & Demuru, E. (2014). Yawn contagion in humans and bonobos: Emotional affinity matters more than species. *PeerJ, 2*(1), e519.

Palagi, E., Norscia, I., Pressi, S., & Cordoni, G. (2018). Facial mimicry and play: A comparative study in chimpanzees and gorillas. *Emotion, 19*(4), 665–681.

Palagi, E., Paoli, T., & Tarli, S. B. (2004). Reconciliation and consolation in captive bonobos (*Pan paniscus*). *American Journal of Primatology, 62*(1), 15–30.

Panksepp, J. (2011). Cross-species affective neuroscience decoding of the primal affective experiences of humans and related animals. *PLoS ONE, 6*(9), e21236.

Parish, A. R. (1996). Female relationships in bonobos (*Pan paniscus*). *Human Nature, 7*(1), 61–96.

Parr, L. A. (2001). Cognitive and physiological markers of emotional awareness in chimpanzees (*Pan troglodytes*). *Animal Cognition, 4*, 223–229.

Parr, L. A. (2003). The discrimination of faces and their emotional content by chimpanzees (*Pan troglodytes*). In P. Ekman (Ed.), *Emotions inside out: 130 years after Darwin's The expression of the emotions in man and animals* (pp. 56–78). New York Academy of Sciences.

Parr, L. A., Preuschoft, S., & de Waal, F. B. M. (2002). Afterword: Research on facial emotion in chimpanzees, 75 years since Kohts. In N. N. Ladygina-Kohts & F. B. M. de Waal (Eds.), *Infant chimpanzee and human child: A classic 1935 comparative study of ape emotions and intelligence* (pp. 411–452). Oxford University Press.

Parr, L. A., Waller, B. M., Vick, S. J., & Bard, K. A. (2007). Classifying chimpanzee facial expressions using muscle action. *Emotion, 7*(1), 172–181.

Paul, E. S., Harding, E. J., & Mendl, M. (2005). Measuring emotional processes in animals: The utility of a cognitive approach. *Neuroscience & Biobehavioral Reviews, 29*(3), 469–491.

Pérez-Manrique, A., & Gomila, A. (2018). The comparative study of empathy: Sympathetic concern and empathic perspective-taking in non-human animals. *Biological Reviews, 93*(1), 248–269.

Platek, S. M., Critton, S. R., Myers, T. E., & Gallup, G. G. (2003). Contagious yawning: The role of self-awareness and mental state attribution. *Cognitive Brain Research, 17*(2), 223–227.

Plotnik, J. M., & de Waal, F. B. (2014). Asian elephants (*Elephas maximus*) reassure others in distress. *PeerJ, 2*, e278.

Pradhan, G. R., Tennie, C., & van Schaik, C. P. (2012). Social organization and the evolution of cumulative technology in apes and hominins. *Journal of Human Evolution, 63*(1), 180–190.

Preston, S. D. (2013). The origins of altruism in offspring care. *Psychological Bulletin, 139*(6), 1305–1341.

Preston, S. D., & de Waal, F. B. M. (2002). Empathy: Its ultimate and proximate bases. *Behavioral and Brain Sciences, 25*(01), 1–20.

Pritsch, C., Telkemeyer, S., Mühlenbeck, C., & Liebal, K. (2017). Perception of facial expressions reveals selective affect-biased attention in humans and orangutans. *Scientific Reports, 7*(1), 7782.

Provine, R. (2005). Yawning: The yawn is primal, unstoppable and contagious, revealing the evolutionary and neural basis of empathy and unconscious behavior. *American Scientist, 93*(6), 532–539.

Preuschoft, S., & van Hooff, J. A. (1995). Homologizing primate facial displays: A critical review of methods. *Folia primatologica, 65*(3), 121–137.

Quervel-Chaumette, M., Faerber, V., Faragó, T., Marshall-Pescini, S., & Range, F. (2016). Investigating empathy-like responding to conspecifics' distress in pet dogs. *PLoS ONE, 11*(4), e0152920.

Reissland, N., Francis, B., & Mason, J. (2012). Development of fetal yawn compared with non-yawn mouth openings from 24–36 weeks gestation. *PLoS ONE, 7*(11), e50569.

Reniers, R. L. E. P., Corcoran, R., Drake, R., Shryane, N. M., & Völlm, B. A. (2011). The QCAE: A questionnaire of cognitive and affective empathy. *Journal of Personality Assessment, 93*(1), 84–95.

Rilling, J. K., Scholz, J., Preuss, T. M., Glasser, M. F., Errangi, B. K., & Behrens, T. E. (2012). Differences between chimpanzees and bonobos in neural systems supporting social cognition. *Social Cognitive and Affective Neuroscience, 7*(4), 369–379.

Rizzolatti, G., & Caruana, F. (2017). Some considerations on de Waal and Preston review. *Nature Reviews Neuroscience, 18*(12), 769–769.

Rizzolatti, G., Fadiga, L., Gallese, V., & Fogassi, L. (1996). Premotor cortex and the recognition of motor actions. *Cognitive Brain Research, 3*(2), 131–141.

Robson, S. L., & Wood, B. (2008). Hominin life history: Reconstruction and evolution. *Journal of Anatomy, 212*(4), 394–425.

Romero, T., Castellanos, M. A., & de Waal, F. B. M. (2010). Consolation as possible expression of sympathetic concern among chimpanzees. *Proceedings of the National Academy of Sciences, 107*(27), 12110–12115.

Romero, T., & de Waal, F. B. M. (2010). Chimpanzee (*Pan troglodytes*) consolation: Third-party identity as a window on possible function. *Journal of Comparative Psychology, 124*(3), 278–286.

Rubinstein, E. H., & Sessler, D. I. (1990). Skin-surface temperature gradients correlate with fingertip blood flow in humans. *Anesthesiology, 73*(3), 541–545.

Sander, D. (2013). Models of emotion: The affective neuroscience approach. In J. Armony & P. Vuilleumier (Eds.), *The Cambridge handbook of human affective neuroscience* (pp. 5–53). Cambridge University Press.

Sannen, A., Van Elsacker, L., Heistermann, M., & Eens, M. (2004). Urinary testosterone-metabolite levels and dominance rank in male and female bonobos (*Pan paniscus*). *Primates, 45*(2), 89–96.

Sato, Y., Hirata, S., & Kano, F. (2018). Spontaneous attention and psycho-physiological responses to others' injury in chimpanzees. *Animal Cognition, 22*(5), 807–823.

Call, J., & Tomasello, M. (2011). Does the chimpanzee have a theory of mind? 30 years later. In S. Schleidgen, M. Jungert, R. Bauer, & V. Sandow (Eds.), *Human nature and self design*. (pp. 83–96). Mentis.

Schino, G., & Marini, C. (2012). Self-protective function of post-conflict bystander affiliation in mandrills. *PLoS ONE, 7*(6), e38936.

Scopa, C., & Palagi, E. (2016). Mimic me while playing! Social tolerance and rapid facial mimicry in macaques (*Macaca tonkeana* and *Macaca fuscata*). *Journal of Comparative Psychology, 130*(2), 153–161.

Singer, T. (2006). The neuronal basis and ontogeny of empathy and mind reading: Review of literature and implications for future research. *Neuroscience & Biobehavioral Reviews, 30*(6), 855–863.

Sirois, S., & Brisson, J. (2014). Pupillometry. *Wiley Interdisciplinary Reviews: Cognitive Science, 5*(6), 679–692.

Soto, J. A., & Levenson, R. W. (2009). Emotion recognition across cultures: The influence of ethnicity on empathic accuracy and physiological linkage. *Emotion, 9*(6), 874–884.

Stevens, J. R. (2004). The selfish nature of generosity: Harassment and food sharing in primates. *Proceedings of the Royal Society B: Biological Sciences, 271*(1538), 451–456.

Stone, V. (2006). The moral dimensions of human social intelligence: Domain-specific and domain-general mechanisms. *Philosophical Explorations, 9*(1), 55–68.

Tennie, C., Jensen, K., & Call, J. (2016). The nature of prosociality in chimpanzees. *Nature Communications, 7*(1), 13915.

Tomonaga, M. (1999a). Inversion effect in perception of human faces in a chimpanzee (*Pan troglodytes*). *Primates, 40*(3), 417–438.

Tomonaga, M. (1999b). Visual search for the orientations of faces by a chimpanzee (*Pan troglodytes*). *Primate Research, 15*(2), 215–229.

Tomonaga, M. (2007). Visual search for orientation of faces by a chimpanzee (*Pan troglodytes*): Face-specific upright superiority and the role of facial configural properties. *Primates, 48*(1), 1–12.

van Hooff, J. (1967). The facial displays of the catarrhine monkeys and apes. In D. Morris (Ed.), *Primate ethology* (pp. 7–68). Aldine.

van Hooff, J. (1971). A comparative approach to the phylogeny of laughter and smiling. In R. A. Hinde (Ed.), *Non-verbal communication* (pp. 209–241). Cambridge University Press..

van Wingen, G., Mattern, C., Verkes, R. J., Buitelaar, J., & Fernández, G. (2010). Testosterone reduces amygdala–orbitofrontal cortex coupling. *Psychoneuroendocrinology, 35*(1), 105–113.

Warneken, F. (2006). Altruistic helping in human infants and young chimpanzees. *Science, 311*(5765), 1301–1303.

Warneken, F., Hare, B., Melis, A. P., Hanus, D., & Tomasello, M. (2007). Spontaneous altruism by chimpanzees and young children. *PLOS Biology, 5*(7), e184.

Watts, D. (2002). Reciprocity and interchange in the social relationships of wild male chimpanzees. *Behaviour, 139*(2), 343–370.

Watts, D. P., Colmenares, F., & Arnold, K. (2000). Redirection, consolation and male policing: How targets of aggression interact with bystanders. In F. Aureli & F. B. M. de Waal (Eds.), *Natural conflict resolution* (pp. 281–301), University of California Press.

Webb, C. E., Romero, T., Franks, B., & Waal, F. B. M. de. (2017). Long-term consistency in chimpanzee consolation behaviour reflects empathetic personalities. *Nature Communications, 8*(1), 1–8.

Williams, L. A., Brosnan, S. F., & Clay, Z. (2020). Anthropomorphism in comparative affective science: Advocating a mindful approach. *Neuroscience & Biobehavioral Reviews, 115*, 299–307.

Wilson, D. A., & Tomonaga, M. (2018). Exploring attentional bias towards threatening faces in chimpanzees using the dot probe task. *PLoS ONE, 13*(11), e0207378.

Wobber, V., Hare, B., Maboto, J., Lipson, S., Wrangham, R., & Ellison, P. T. (2010). Differential changes in steroid hormones before competition in bonobos and chimpanzees. *Proceedings of the National Academy of Sciences, 107*(28), 12457–12462.

Wynne, C. D. L. (2004). The perils of anthropomorphism. *Nature, 428*, 606–606.

Yamamoto, S. (2017). Primate empathy: Three factors and their combinations for empathy-related phenomena. *Wiley Interdisciplinary Reviews: Cognitive Science*, 8(3), e1431.

Yamamoto, S., Humle, T., & Tanaka, M. (2009). Chimpanzees help each other upon request. *PLoS ONE, 4*(10), e7416.

Yamamoto, S., Humle, T., & Tanaka, M. (2012). Chimpanzees' flexible targeted helping based on an understanding of conspecifics' goals. *Proceedings of the National Academy of Sciences, 109*(9), 3588–3592.

Yamamoto, S., & Takimoto, A. (2012). Empathy and fairness: Psychological mechanisms for eliciting and maintaining prosociality and cooperation in primates. *Social Justice Research, 25*(3), 233–255.

Zahn-Waxler, C., & Radke-Yarrow, M. (1990). The origins of empathic concern. *Motivation and Emotion, 14*(2), 107–130.

CHAPTER 42

Emotions in Dogs: Neuroscientific, Behavioral, and Comparative Perspectives

Miiamaaria V. Kujala and Juliane Bräuer

Abstract

Domestic dog, *Canis familiaris*, is called "human's best friend": dogs are everywhere in the Western societies, and over 470 million dogs are kept as pets worldwide. But what are the social and emotional properties of dogs that enable such an affectionate friendship bond across species? During their domestication 14,000–30,000 years ago, dogs have undergone selective changes and developed behavioral skills that enable them to better function in human social groups. Humans and dogs share some basic emotional functionality of the nervous systems, which aids in interspecies interaction. Dogs have positive and negative affective states, with most research conducted on fear, anger/aggressiveness, reward-processing and joy. Still, dogs are not four-legged, nonverbal humans. In the light of scientific results, canine capability for social emotions such as guilt or jealousy appears limited. Dogs understand human behavior from a dog's point of view, and humans understand dogs from a human's point of view.

Key Words: domestic dog, *Canis familiaris*, animal cognition, behavior, affective neuroscience

Emotions in Humans and Dogs: An Evolutionary Viewpoint

Domestic dog, *Canis familiaris*, is often called "man's best friend." This suggests a close relationship, shared emotions, and mutual companionship between the seemingly odd pair. Both humans and dogs are mammals, which gives a common biological framework for the neural machinery of emotions and social sharing. However, this is where the biological common grounds end: humans belong to the taxonomical order of Primates, whereas dogs belong to the order of Carnivora. When we examine the emotionality and sociality of the two, and attempt to track the evolutionary paths of their emotional development, we must keep this difference of viewpoints in mind. The way dogs see and experience the world is affected by their own evolutionary path, and it is conducted from a carnivore's perspective.

Today, there are over 470 million pet dogs worldwide (Bedford, 2020). Dogs' ancestors were domesticated 14,000–30,000 years ago, earlier than any other animal (e.g., Larson & Bradley, 2014; Thalmann et al., 2013), although the origins of their domestication—when and where the domestication began—are debated. What is agreed upon is that dogs have undergone selective changes during the domestication period. Compared to wolves, dogs have acquired behavioral skills that enable them to better function in human social groups (for a recent review, see Bräuer & Vidal Orga, 2023). These adaptive behavioral skills include socio-emotional features such as attending to and "reading" human behavior and bodily cues, communication, and creating affiliative bonds. Of course, the existence of emotions and being able to signal or share emotions across species are separate issues; but dog prehistory and domestication appear to afford the prerequisites for both. This has likely affected the unique relationship of dogs and humans.

Furthermore, humans have deliberately affected dog qualities through breeding. Although the basic emotional functions remain similar within species, breeding for different purposes has affected skull and brain formation in dogs (Roberts et al., 2010), and consequently, also some behavioral and emotional features (Gnanadesikan et al., 2020; Hecht et al., 2019; McGreevy et al., 2013). The genetic research conducted on dog phenotypes indicates breed differences in predispositions for emotional reactivity, for example in fearfulness (Hakanen et al., 2020; Sarviaho et al., 2020). Narrowing down from the framework set by biology and breeding practices, dogs are individuals, as are humans; knowing one's own pet dog does not mean they all are alike. Dogs have different personalities (for review, Miklósi et al., 2014) just like humans, and this gives rise to individual differences in emotional reactivity and sensitivity.

Basic Emotions, Valence, and Arousal

Basic emotional states, also called primary emotions—such as anger, happiness, and fear—function as the individual's immediate reactive interface with the world. Emotions provide motivations for behavior: fight or flight, approach or avoid. Basic emotions likely improve the chances of survival in many contexts, thus representing an adaptive driving force (Adolphs & Anderson, 2018; de Waal, 2019; Ekman, 1992; Izard, 1992; Panksepp, 1998). Regarding basic emotions, dogs share some of the biological commonalities with other mammals; for example, basic emotions are associated with certain chemical neuroendocrine balance in the brain and are linked to functioning in certain brain regions (Panksepp, 1998). Without going into the theoretical discrete vs. dimensional emotions debate, we will adopt the view that these represent different levels of analysis (Panksepp & Watt, 2011). Basic emotions can also be characterized in humans by their valence and arousal, where valence refers to the negative-positive dimension and arousal refers to the level of alertness and vigilance (Russell, 1980). The same dimensions can be used in describing dogs' positive and negative states, either evaluated by human observers (Farago et al., 2014; Kujala et al., 2017) or detected by machine-learning algorithms (Espinosa et al., 2017).

Emotional arousal can be connected, at least partially, to the functioning of the autonomic nervous system (ANS): heightened arousal is connected to the sympathetic nervous system preparing the animal for a behavioral reaction (Bradley & Lang, 2000). Activation of the sympathetic nervous system causes accelerating heart rate, enhanced blood pressure and skin conductance, as well as hormonal secretion of catecholamines (for review, Gordan et al., 2015). Cortisol may also have a modulatory effect on arousal and vigilance (Bakvis et al., 2009; van Peer et al., 2007). In dogs, increased heart rate and cortisol levels have been detected in both negative (Väisänen et al., 2005; Yong & Ruffman, 2014) and positive (Handlin et al., 2011) contexts. Despite the similar mammalian function of the ANS, the responses of humans and dogs are not always similar within the same context; for example, in positive interaction, human cortisol levels decrease, whereas dog cortisol levels may not do so (Handlin et al., 2011; Odendaal & Meintjes, 2003). This may be interpreted as reflecting different affective content of the situation for dogs and humans, connected to behavior-hormonal response modulation (Petersson et al., 2017).

As opposed to arousal, emotional valence is more difficult to connect to physiology. In the following, we will first review the neuroscientific basis for dog emotions within the context of mammalian physiology, and compare the dog emotional brain with that of humans. Thereafter, we will consider the negative and positive facets of emotional valence separately, before discussing current research on social emotions in dogs.

Brain Processing Underlying Emotions in Dogs vs. Humans

We know much about the brain chemistry and neuronal circuits underlying emotional behavior, and some of the research applied to humans has been conducted with nonhuman mammals. Basic emotional states are associated with neural structures in the limbic system, especially the amygdaloid complex, and they are affected by connections between the limbic system and the cerebral cortex (see Damasio, 1994; LeDoux, 1996; Rolls, 1999). Dogs are no exception to this, and the canine brain includes major structures that underlie basic emotions (for reviews, Evans & de Lahunta, 2013; Jensen, 2007; Kujala, 2017). Human children born without a cerebral cortex exhibit emotions (Merker, 2007), as do carnivores and rodents with decortication (for review, Berridge, 2003); thus the cortex may not be necessary for the existence of basic emotions. However, cortical processing adds re-representation, inhibition, and modulation of basic emotions with both feedback and feedforward mechanisms (for reviews, Dixon et al., 2017; Lane & Nadel, 2002; Ochsner et al., 2012).

When comparing human emotions to the emotions of dogs, the differences between human and dog brains are important to comprehend, as they form the basis for emotional processing capabilities. Dog encephalization quotient, the brain-to-body ratio, is typical for a mammal of its size (for review, Roth & Dicke, 2005). As such, this does not represent emotional capabilities, but together with the connectedness between the subcortical regions and the cerebral cortex, it affects re-representing and processing emotions. Compared with dogs, humans have higher encephalization and abundant connectivity between cortical and subcortical regions (see Berridge, 2003). In the future, the similarity of human and dog brain processes may be clarified with the use of functional connectivity measures (as in Thompkins et al., 2018). The majority (85%) of the cerebral cortex in humans represents association areas not primarily processing sensory information, whereas the proportion of association cortices in dogs is 20% (Evans & de Lahunta, 2013). However, the ratio of phylogenetically older portions of the cortex associated with olfactory processing to the rest of the cerebral cortex is higher in dogs than in humans (see Bolon, 2000).

Now, what do the differences in brain processing hardware mean for emotions in dogs? The obvious effect is the proportional importance of the olfactory world for dogs. The connections between olfactory and limbic areas likely affect dog emotions in ways that humans have a difficult time relating to. The difference in neocortex proportions between human and dog brains means that after the initial reception of an emotional stimulus, there are likely fewer further representations and re-representations in the dog than in human brains. This may cause differences between species, especially regarding social emotions (discussed in detail later in the chapter).

Survival Instincts: Anger/Aggression and Fear

To date, research is more abundant regarding the negatively than positively valenced canine emotions, although the same applies across species. This highlights the ultimate role of these emotions as reactions to life-threatening elements of the environment, but regarding dogs, the studies on aggression and fear also answer the needs of caretaker humans and their problems with dog behavior. Dog fear and aggression are closely linked, as aggressive behavior is often caused by fear (e.g., Galac & Knol, 1997; van den Berg et al., 2003). In behavioral studies testing aggression or fear, certain dog behaviors or objective measures (e.g., time to approach an object) have been quantified under mild provocation. Aggressive reactions of dogs have been provoked with threatening stimuli, such as an unfamiliar barking dog or an approaching, threatening human or other potentially dangerous stimulus (Klausz et al., 2014; Kroll et al., 2004; Netto & Planta, 1997; Sforzini et al., 2009; van den Berg et al., 2003; van der Borg et al., 2010). Behavioral tests provoking fear in dogs have included a loud noise or an object emerging suddenly, or a novel object (Beerda et al., 1998; Hydbring-Sandberg et al., 2004; King et al., 2003; Ley et al., 2007; Melzack, 1952; Morrow et al., 2015).

Behavioral markers of aggression include growling, barking, baring of teeth, direct staring, and stiffening of the body (van den Berg et al., 2003), whereas the markers of fear include panting, salivation, trembling, licking the snout, restless pacing, and vocalization (Palestrini, 2009; van den Berg et al., 2003). Both fearful and aggressive behaviors in dogs are associated with certain physiological responses, both in the nervous system and hormonal levels. Although the neural sources of aggressive and fearful behavior in mammals can be partially different, ANS effects can be overlapping. The brain areas and circuitries associated with fear and anger/aggression/rage are subcortical nuclei within the amygdaloid complex, hypothalamus, and periaqueductal grey (see Panksepp, 1998). Fear-inducing stimuli can increase dog heart rate (Hydbring-Sandberg et al., 2004; King et al., 2003; Ogata et al., 2006), body temperature (Ogata et al., 2006), and levels of cortisol (Beerda et al., 1998; Dreschel & Granger, 2005; Hydbring-Sandberg et al., 2004; King et al., 2003; Morrow et al., 2015) and progesterone (Hydbring-Sandberg et al., 2004). Apart from connections to testosterone, aggressive behaviors are associated with reduced serotonergic function (Reisner, 1997). Canine fearful and aggressive behaviors have been connected with genes abundantly expressed within the above-mentioned brain regions, e.g. amygdala (Zapata et al., 2016). Furthermore, canine aggression is strongly heritable (MacLean et al., 2019).

Being Positive: Reward, Happiness, Joy, and Love

What do we know about the positive emotions of a dog, except that for many owners, a dog's love appears infinite? How can we understand and share joy across species, between a primate and a carnivore? The positively valenced emotions of happiness, joy, and love or attachment counterbalance the ones discussed in the previous section; reward, although not directly seen as a discrete emotion, creates a positively valenced state. Also their evolutionary benefits are quite clear across mammals: something good and beneficial to be drawn to, functioning in both individual and population levels. Positive motivation and reward-related behavior are associated with the neurotransmitter dopamine and the subcortical areas of nucleus accumbens, ventral tegmental area, and caudate nucleus (see, e.g., Panksepp, 1998; Posner et al., 2005). In dogs, reward-related brain activation has occurred in response to food, praise, and the odor of a familiar human, unpacking the value of human attachment for dogs (Berns et al., 2015; Cook et al., 2016).

The subcortical brain regions underlying happiness and joy include dorsomedial diencephalon, periaqueductal gray, and parafascicular area, while the key neurochemicals involved are the opioids and cannabinoids (see Panksepp, 1998). Serotonin also influences happiness, but its effects extend to a wide variety of emotions, behaviors, and more general functions of the central nervous system (Canli & Lesch, 2007). These systems can be applied to dogs as to other mammals, but little research on happiness *as such* exists specifically in dogs. Nonetheless, play behavior is associated with positive, joyful emotional states across species through the effects of opioids and cannabinoids (see Panksepp, 1998), and long-studied play behavior in dogs can be mentioned in this context. Play behavior of dogs follow certain social rules and reciprocity (see Smuts, 2014) as in humans, and there is no reason to assume it provokes any less joy. Play behaviors in dogs are also modulated by the hormones cortisol and oxytocin, at least regarding cross-species play behavior (Horvath et al., 2008; Rossi et al., 2018).

The effects of oxytocin in social interaction are studied widely across species. Oxytocin is known to enhance positive affective states like love and joy. The areas processing attachment and love in dog brains, e.g., anterior cingulate cortex, ventral tegmental area, periaqueductal gray, and stria terminalis, exist in mammals also more generally, as do the modulating neurochemicals oxytocin, dopamine, and opioids (see Panksepp, 1998). Affiliative interaction such as peacefully petting a dog, or just a friendly eye gaze without threat, can cause physiological synchronization across species, increasing oxytocin and dopamine levels and simultaneously lowering cortisol levels in dogs and their owners (Handlin et al., 2011; Miller et al., 2009; Nagasawa et al., 2009; Nagasawa et al., 2015; Odendaal & Meintjes, 2003). However, the type of interaction may be differently perceived by dogs and humans: activating touch (scratching or patting) may increase and petting may decrease dog stress or vigilance as indicated by cortisol levels (Petersson et al., 2017). These similar physiological and hormonal mechanisms may give the possibility for emotional contagion across species, and enhance the friendship between the primate and the carnivore.

Social Emotions: What We Know of Dogs So Far (and How They Differ from Humans)

Social emotions are more complex than basic emotions, as they require modification of emotions through representation of thoughts and feelings of self and others (Burnett & Blakemore, 2009; Hareli & Parkinson, 2008; Lamm & Singer, 2010). Neural processing underlying the social emotions in humans have been identified in functional magnetic resonance studies, involving the medial orbitofrontal cortex, the temporal pole, the superior temporal sulcus, and insula (Burnett & Blakemore, 2009; Lamm & Singer, 2010; Moll et al., 2002). These regions fall into cortical association areas, which we can locate also in dogs—with the ratio of 85% in human and 20% in canine cortices (Evans & de Lahunta, 2013). Currently, we lack detailed knowledge on the functions of the possible homologues of these regions in canine brains. As the human studies on social emotions often include language, clever and ecologically relevant setups are needed to study the equivalent in nonhuman animals.

Requirements of Social Emotions: A Minimal Concept of Self and Others

When we raise the question whether dogs possess social emotions, we should first ask whether they show the neural processing capacity and the behavioral skills that are required for social emotions. So what do dogs know about themselves and about others? Dogs are highly sensitive to humans (for a review, Bräuer, 2014). They constantly monitor humans (Merola et al., 2012a, 2012b) and they are sensitive to what humans can see and hear—both in cooperative and in competitive situations (Bräuer et al., 2013; Call et al., 2003; Gacsi et al., 2004; Kaminski, Bräuer, et al., 2009; Kaminski et al., 2013). However, it is not clear whether dogs understand that seeing leads to knowing (Catala et al., 2017; Kaminski, Bräuer, et al., 2009), or whether they can infer humans' goals and intentions (Bräuer, 2014; Kaminski et al., 2011; Petter et al., 2009; Range et al., 2007). Mainly, dogs seem to be able to understand human intentions in communicative situations, for example by reading communicative intentions (Kaminski et al., 2012; Kaminski, Tempelmann, et al., 2009) or in a situation when the dog could help a human (Bräuer et al., 2013). These findings can be summarized as follows—as

Udell and Wynne (2011) have stated: dogs are not mind readers, but they are excellent readers of human behaviors.

But for the question whether dogs have social emotions, it is relevant to know what dogs understand about their own mental processes (see Leary, 2003). There is no evidence that they recognize themselves in a mirror, although they may be aware of their own odor (Horowitz, 2017). However, in some cases, dogs know what they don't know, or at least may choose an action based on their lack of knowledge. In an information-seeking behavioral paradigm, dogs needed to fetch a hidden reward without immediately available information of its location, thus having to seek additional cues from humans (McMahon et al., 2010). Dogs chose a human informant more often than a non-informant, which suggests that dogs seek additional information when they need it (McMahon et al., 2010). Similarly, Belger and Bräuer (2018) investigated whether dogs were sensitive to the information that they either had or did not have: dogs either saw the baiting of a reward or not. As a result, dogs looked more often for additional information when they had not seen where the reward was hidden (Belger & Bräuer, 2018). Thus, dogs have access to what they have seen and can choose their actions accordingly, but their metacognitive skills are less flexible than those of other species (i.e., Call, 2010, 2012).

We currently do not know whether a full-blown theory of mind is needed for social emotions (Tangney & Salovey, 1999; Udell & Wynne, 2011), but the above-mentioned skills in behavior reading and metacognition might not be sufficient. As we will point out next, dogs might lack other important prerequisites (Bräuer & Amici, 2018) for guilt, jealousy, and sense of fairness.

Guilt, Jealousy, and Fairness: Why Not?
The following findings might be surprising for dog owners, as they contrast with what people typically think. Many owners are sure that their dog "feels guilty as she has stolen food from the table" or that "he is jealous because I pet the neighbor's dog" (Morris et al., 2008). A partial reason for owners' certainty is in the way the human social mind works. The behavior of dogs often looks to us as if they feel guilty or jealous, so that these behaviors are often over-interpreted or misinterpreted. However, experimental research from the last 15 years has addressed the question why dogs show guilt-like or jealousy-like behaviors.

The typical situation for a "guilty" dog is when the owner arrives at home, the dog has done something wrong—at least in the view of the owner—and looks guilty, and the owner gets angry. This situation was mimicked in three different experimental studies. Dogs did something forbidden—or not—and owners thought that dogs did something forbidden—or not. In the study by Horowitz (2009), dogs were forbidden to eat a treat while the owner was out of the room. Dogs either had or did not have the opportunity to disobey the command "do not touch" and the owners were told that their dog either did or did not disobey. From the video recordings of the situation, dog behavior was analyzed to see when dogs showed elements that correspond to an owner-identified "guilty look" (see Figure 42.1). This included behaviors like avoiding to look at the owner, offering the paw, slinking back in a submissive way, ears pressed back on the neck, and lowering the tail between the legs. As a result, dogs did not show more behaviors associated with the "guilty look" when they were "guilty," i.e., when they did not obey the command. However, dogs showed more of such behaviors when owners scolded their dogs. Thus, a better description of the so-called guilty look is that it is a response to owner cues, rather than showing an understanding of a misdeed (Horowitz, 2009). Similarly in another study, no difference was found between obedient and disobedient dogs in their display of associated behaviors of guilt after having the opportunity to disobey a command in the absence of their owners (Hecht et al., 2012).

Figure 42.1. An example of the so-called guilty look in dogs. If dogs are scolded after a possible misdeed, they may show submissive gestures, such as slinking back and pressing their ears backward. These appeasing gestures are more connected to the owner's behavior rather than the dog's, and are present even if the owner mistakenly believes that the dog behaved badly (Hecht et al., 2012; Horowitz, 2009; Ostojíc et al. 2015). When dogs show the "guilty look" as soon as the owner enters the room, this suggests that they have learned to anticipate the owner's behavior and are attempting to pacify the owner in advance. Photo courtesy of Anja Ullrich.

However, sometimes dogs may show "guilty look" behaviors in the absence of being scolded. In a study by Ostojíc and colleagues (2015), dogs could again eat a forbidden treat, but the treat was either visible or not visible upon the owners' return. Based on their dogs' greeting behavior, owners stated that their dog had eaten the food no more than expected by chance. Again, dogs' greeting behaviors were unaffected by their own action or the presence or absence of the food. Thus, Ostojíc et al. (2015) also concluded that the "guilty look" of dogs is not a consequence of dogs' feeling guilty, but of the negative reaction of their owners. It is likely that dogs are able to make causal associations of previous similar incidents, and the "guilty look" may become a preventive appeasing behavior directed at the owner at home—without requiring guilt. Guilt is a self-regulatory emotion that appears unique to humans, as it requires cultural norms and moral rules of what is wrong and what is right, and a sense of responsibility for one's actions (see Amodio et al., 2007; Gilbert, 2003; Zahn-Waxler & Robinson, 1995).

The experimental findings for social emotions such as jealousy or envy are less clear. Envy can be defined as a set of negative emotional and behavioral responses when a rival receives something one wants for oneself, and jealousy involves possessive feelings of another within inter-individual relationships (Salovey, 1991). Thus, envy is a two-minds issue, whereas jealousy is a three-minds issue: one can be jealous of a cherished person, when the person gives a prize to a rival, but at the same time, one can be envious for the prize the rival got. In the studies conducted to investigate the possibility of jealousy in dogs, these two are usually not distinguishable, which makes the results difficult to interpret. In the following, we use the terminology of the authors, but the reader should keep the above in mind—that it is not clear how the experimental situations are perceived and experienced by the dog.

Jealousy in dogs has been studied by confronting a subject with a situation in which a rival receives something positive from a human. Harris and Prouvost (2014) had dogs observe their caregivers praising and interacting with a realistic animatronic dog as well as with socially irrelevant inanimate objects. When their caregivers interacted with the fake dog, dogs had increased behavioral arousal and showed aggression toward the fake dog, but not toward the socially irrelevant objects. In a similar setup, dogs watched their caregiver giving food to a realistic fake dog, which caused an amygdala response, especially in the more aggressive dogs (Cook et al., 2017, 2018). Finally, Prato-Previde et al. (2018) placed dogs in a situation in which their owner and a stranger ignored them while directing positive attention toward three different objects: a book, a puppet, and a fake dog. The authors found no evidence that the behavioral responses of these dogs were triggered by jealousy (Prato-Previde, Nicotra, Pelosi, et al., 2018).

None of these studies provides evidence that the fake dogs were perceived as real, acting as social rivals. It is quite unlikely that dogs—with their social sensitivity and their excellent sense of smell—perceive a fake dog as a real one (Bräuer & Amici, 2018; Vonk, 2018). Dogs are excellent in distinguishing between fake (or unnatural) and real situations (Bräuer et al., 2013; Marshall-Pescini et al., 2014), for example when someone fakes a heart attack (Macpherson & Roberts, 2006). However, perceiving the fake dog as a real conspecific in the previous studies would be a necessary prerequisite for either envy or jealousy. This was deliberately tested with dyads of dogs who lived together (Prato-Previde, Nicotra, Fusar Poli, et al., 2018). Owners either ignored both dogs while reading a magazine (control episode) or petted and praised one of the dogs while ignoring the other, and vice versa (experimental episodes). The only difference between experimental and control episodes was that subject dogs monitored the owner more when he or she praised and petted the rival dog, but subjects were not aggressive toward the conspecific. Although there was variability in the dogs' behavior, they behaved consistently—no matter whether one or both of them were ignored (Prato-Previde, Nicotra, Fusar Poli, et al., 2018).

It appears that the situation with the perspectives of three individuals—the human, the rival receiving something good from the human, and the subject dog—might be too complex for dogs to comprehend. Dogs can learn whether a human has done something good for them, and they prefer that human in subsequent situations (Nitzschner et al., 2012). Dogs can even evaluate which one of two humans is more reliable based on the presence or visual experience of these humans in previous situations (Catala et al., 2017; Maginnity & Grace,

2014). However, these situations present direct experience of the dogs, but circumstances that may provoke jealousy involve three individuals. The subject dog only witnesses how the human is treating the rival, without a direct interaction with the human by the subject dog. In a situation involving similar indirect experience, dogs could not evaluate humans correctly (Nitzschner et al., 2012). When they observed the "nice" or "ignoring" human interacting with another dog, they were unable to establish a preference between the two humans based on this indirect experience.

Still, there are situations involving three individuals in which dogs are at least attentive to what happens to a rival. One question that has received recent attention is whether dogs and other nonhuman animals have a sense of fairness. This sense would allow them to compare their own efforts and subsequent outcomes with those of others, and thus to evaluate and react to inequity. A growing number of studies have investigated how subjects react to unequal situations that humans would perceive as "unfair" (for reviews, Bräuer & Hanus, 2012; Brosnan & de Waal, 2014; McGetrick & Range, 2018).

Sense of fairness is often examined in a setup in which a subject and a rival participate in a task, but receive rewards of different value. The question is whether the subject refuses to continue the task if he or she witnesses the rival obtaining a more attractive reward for the same effort. In a situation where dogs had to give their paw to an experimenter, the dogs did not react to differences in the quality of food that the rival and they themselves received (Range et al., 2009). However, dog subjects showed sensitivity toward the inequity of rewards when they did not receive a reward at all. They were also more sensitive to situations in which the partner was rewarded compared to an asocial control situation, showing an effect different from behavior extinction (Hartley & Phelps, 2012) and suggesting that dogs may have a primitive version of inequity aversion (Range et al., 2009). The subject dogs also avoided their rivals and the experimenter more during the free interaction time following unequal vs. equal treatment (Brucks et al., 2016), which might indicate that they perceived the situation with the unequal treatment as a negative experience.

In sum, it appears that social emotions, requiring mental representation from the point of view of multiple individuals, are limited in dogs. What humans often perceive as "guilt" is submissive behavior as a possibly learned and preventive reaction to certain human behaviors. For aversion of inequity the situation is less clear. When dogs do not receive a reward, they distinguish between a social situation when a rival receives something and a non-social situation. Nevertheless, it might be difficult for them to evaluate a situation in which a human is behaving positively or negatively toward another dog.

Still, dog owners often experience a situation in which they are engaged with the neighbor's dog and their own dog is approaching them. Their own dog may even try to squeeze in between them and the neighbor's dog. This looks like jealousy or envy, as it involves a negative emotional and behavioral response when the rival receives something the dog wants for himself—but simpler explanations for the dog's behavior include at least resource competition (see Cook et al., 2017; Kujala, 2017) and reacting to human cues. It is likely that the owner not only pets the neighbor's dog, but also communicates with him using the so-called ostensive cues that dogs prefer and react to (Ben-Aderet et al., 2017; Benjamin & Slocombe, 2018; Topál, 2014). These consist of a set of nonverbal cues like eye contact and body position, but also verbal cues providing evidence of the communicator's intention to convey information (Topál, 2014). Humans at least in Western cultures produce a special speech register when talking to their dogs. Similar to motherese, this dog-directed speech has some special acoustic features, including elevated pitch and exaggerated affect—compared to normal adult-directed speech (Ben-Aderet et al., 2017; Benjamin & Slocombe, 2018; Mitchell, 2004). When playing with an unfamiliar dog, people use even more praise and are more attentive in order to appear friendly (Mitchell, 2004). Thus, in the described situation, a dog owner probably uses ostensive cues to attract the neighbor's dog, and her/his dog is simply reacting to these cues, perceiving the situation as "it is petting time."

Unless new studies indicate otherwise, simpler explanations for dog behavior are more likely than ascriptions of human-like jealousy or envy. Social emotions may be an example where dogs are often misinterpreted—in particular, as their behavior appears like what we as humans would expect from a conspecific feeling guilty or jealous. Humans should have these alternative explanations in mind, being ready to accept which emotions dogs can have—and which not. Further studies should continue investigating situations of unfairness, envy, and jealousy.

Dog-Human Relationship
Dogs and humans have a special relationship—not only because of dogs' long and special domestication process (Bräuer & Vidal Orga, 2023; Hare & Tomasello, 2005; Kaminski & Marshall-Pescini, 2014), but also because of their ability to develop a close relationship. Generally, dogs prefer humans to other dogs as social partners (Gacsi et al., 2005; Miklosi et al., 2003; Topál et al., 2005), and the dog-human bond is comparable to the attachment between human infants and their mothers (for review, Prato Previde & Valsecchi, 2014). This interspecies bond is maintained at a hormonal level, mediated by oxytocin (see above discussion). Thus, one might expect that both partners of this mutualistic relationship are sensitive to the other's emotions. We will examine this in the following sections.

How Do Dogs Understand Human or Conspecific Emotions?
The question of whether, and to what extent, dogs understand human emotions has received a lot of attention in recent years. Dog owners often claim "my dog knows what I feel." In the long domestication process, this skill may have developed in dogs, as it has been adaptive to perceive negative or positive emotions of humans in order to avoid or to approach them. A related skill has also been suggested to exist already in dogs' ancestors—wolves. Wolves must decide which individuals in a herd of prey to hunt, and it is adaptive for them to perceive which are sick or especially fearful (Bräuer et al., 2017; Gadbois & Reeve, 2014). Emotion recognition in dogs has been recently studied by measuring dogs' reactions to emotional states of humans or other dogs, using stimuli varying from photographs to audio recordings, pretended situations, and emotions induced by the owners (for a review, Kujala, 2017).

One experimental approach allowing control over the details is the use of facial expressions of emotion as stimuli. Faces convey a great deal of communicative information and serve as a source of information for the focus of attention or the individual's current emotion (e.g., Bruce & Young, 1998). Face processing also appears widely across vertebrates (Leopold & Rhodes, 2010; Tate et al., 2006), and domestic dogs readily refer to human faces for information (Gacsi et al., 2005; Miklosi et al., 2003). There is no doubt that dogs can identify their owner or other familiar humans by using visual information from the face, and they also distinguish the faces of familiar persons (Huber et al., 2013; Somppi et al., 2014). Similarly, they can use visual information to identify familiar and unfamiliar dogs (Racca et al., 2010; Somppi et al., 2014).

Importantly, dogs also distinguish negative and positive emotional expressions in human and dog faces (Albuquerque et al., 2016; Barber et al., 2016; Müller et al., 2015; Nagasawa et al., 2011; Somppi et al., 2016). Dogs learned to distinguish pictures of different human facial expressions, and it appeared that dogs used their memories of real emotional human faces to accomplish the task, as associating an angry human face with a reward was difficult for them (Müller et al., 2015). Dogs can also distinguish between smiling or neutral human faces (Nagasawa et al., 2011). One question that arises is *how* dogs are able to discriminate facial expressions from photographs. To investigate this, Somppi et al. (2016) used eye tracking. They examined the gaze fixation of dogs on photographs of conspecifics and human faces. These faces had three emotional expressions (threatening/aggressive, pleasant/happy, and neutral). While dogs' gaze fixations spread systematically among all facial features, the eyes were the most probable target of the first fixations. Dogs evaluated social threat rapidly, but they reacted differently to the depicted species: threatening conspecifics' faces evoked heightened vigilance, but threatening human faces evoked an avoidance response instead (Somppi et al., 2016). Indeed, threatening expressions appear to provoke an early subcortical brain response in dogs, most pronounced for conspecific faces (Kujala et al., 2020). The dogs' responsiveness for threatening/aggressive expressions may be diminished by oxytocin, as it decreases dogs' gaze to the human threatening/angry facial expressions (Kis et al., 2017)—especially the eye region (Somppi et al., 2017).

In an attempt to produce a situation closer to real life, dogs have been set in a situation where their owners or strangers either pretended to cry or hummed: as a result, dogs oriented toward a person more often when the person was pretending to cry (Custance & Mayer, 2012). Dogs also approached differently owners vs. strangers pretending to cry; when approaching the owners they behaved submissively, while they sniffed, nuzzled, and licked the stranger in that condition (Custance & Mayer, 2012). Dogs have treated owners and strangers alike regarding their realistic cues for help (Bräuer et al., 2013), yet failed to help even their owners with a feigned heart attack (Macpherson & Roberts, 2006). As dogs constantly monitor us, they are often able to distinguish between fake and real situations (Bräuer, 2015; Bräuer et al., 2013; Bräuer et al., 2017; Marshall-Pescini et al., 2014). Thus, to test how dogs perceive human emotions, these emotions should be realistic.

To solve this problem, a number of studies used sounds of real emotional situations. When dogs were presented with either sounds of a human infant crying, babbling, or computer-generated "white noise," the dogs reacted to the infant crying behaviorally, combining submissiveness with alertness, exhibiting simultaneously increased cortisol levels (Yong & Ruffman, 2014). In a similar setup combining positive and negative sounds, dogs behaved differently after hearing control sounds compared to emotional sounds, responding similarly to human and conspecific sounds (Huber et al., 2017; see also Quervel-Chaumette et al., 2016). Albuquerque et al. (2016) presented dog subjects with pictures of facial expressions paired with voices, either in congruent (e.g., angry voice and angry facial expression) or incongruent fashion (e.g., angry voice and happy facial expression). Dogs looked longer at the face whose expression was congruent to the valence of vocalization, for both conspecifics and humans. This suggests that dogs can extract and integrate bimodal sensory emotional information, and associate emotional sounds to enacted facial expressions (Albuquerque et al., 2016).

As dogs have an excellent olfactory sense and they rely on olfaction when exploring the environment or recognizing individuals (as in Bräuer & Belger, 2018), transmission of emotional information via chemosignals is also likely. D'Aniello and colleagues (2018) collected odor samples from male donors who watched videos inducing happiness or fear. These olfactory stimuli, together with a neutral no-sweat control, were presented for dogs while they were accompanied by both the owner and a stranger. The authors measured the dogs' heart rate as well as approaching, interacting, and gazing behaviors directed to the owner, stranger, and the sweat dispenser. Presentation of "happy odor" caused fewer and shorter owner-directed behaviors and more stranger-directed behaviors as compared to the fear and to the control conditions. In the fear condition, dogs also displayed more stressful behaviors and higher heart rates. Thus, dogs respond differently to the smell of differing human emotions.

Most studies have investigated only a single aspect or modality of the detection of human emotion by dogs. The perceived emotions were either not "real" but only acted, or the emotional situation was "preserved" as recorded stimuli or in an odor dispenser. Future studies should find a balance in using multiple approaches, both holistic approaches—where humans or conspecifics would be manipulated to experience the emotion during the actual experiment (Bräuer et al., 2017)—and step by step, where carefully controlled experiments from different modalities may rule out alternative interpretations (Kujala, 2018). With the opportunity to use the visual, auditory, and olfactory modalities, dogs may prove to be much more accurate in detecting human emotions, and at least the stimuli used should be realistic—to which extent, we currently don't know. Indeed, dogs do react to induced emotions of their owners: dogs gazed longer at their owners when they watched a cheerful movie compared to a sad movie (Morisaki et al., 2009).

Thus, although the field is still in its infancy, there is direct evidence that dogs are able to distinguish human as well as conspecific emotions. Also, indirect evidence from other studies suggests that dogs are sensitive to human emotions (see Bräuer, 2014). This unique sensitivity might be adaptive, both for dogs and humans. For example, dogs can use emotional information to find food: in a study where the human reacted emotionally (happy, neutral, or disgusted) to the hidden contents of two boxes, dogs chose the boxes that the human pretended to be happy about (Buttelmann & Tomasello, 2013). Dogs can also use their sensitivity toward humans to learn about a potentially dangerous object by social referencing (Merola et al., 2012a, 2012b). Similar to children, they seek information about an object from the owner, to guide their actions. If owners show concern, dogs inhibit their movements toward the object, but if owners show positivity, dogs move toward the object and interact with it sooner (Merola et al., 2012a, 2012b).

Humans, on the other hand, can also take advantage from dogs' monitoring behavior and their sensitivity. As mentioned above, dogs are motivated to help when humans show signs of needing support desperately and when dogs are able to understand how they can help (for review, Bräuer, 2015). Moreover, dogs may alert humans to patient epilepsy and diabetes seizures, and might even be able to predict them, even when they were not trained to do so (Catala et al., 2019; Dalziel et al., 2003; Lim et al., 1992).

But what happens when dogs react to human emotions, helplessness, and even seizures—are they showing empathy? Empathy has several definitions, but most researchers separate the emotional (feeling what the other is feeling) and cognitive (understanding the other's perspective) parts of empathy (for review, Decety & Ickes, 2011). Many researchers consider the roots of empathy to be evolutionarily ancient and shared (see, e.g., Buck & Ginsburg, 1997; Decety et al., 2012), and to explain the underlying processes, Preston and de Waal introduced the Perception Action Model (PAM; Preston & de Waal, 2002). PAM includes five different classification terms: *emotional contagion, sympathy, empathy, cognitive empathy*, and *pro-social behaviors*. The categories differ in (1) the ability to distinguish between self and other, (2) to be in a matching state, and (3) to actually help the other individual. Emotional contagion is the transference of emotions, which appears likely in dogs: in the above experimental conditions, dogs showed submissiveness, alertness, increased cortisol levels, more stressful behaviors, and higher heart rates when confronted with a negative emotion of a human or another dog. However, in the framework of Preston and de Waal (2002), dogs' cognitive *sympathy*, i.e., "feeling sorry" for the other individual, seems unlikely.

Current research does not answer whether dogs experience full-blown *empathy*, as it would require distinguishing between self and other and the possibility of *reacting* to the situation by, for example, helping the emotional individual (Preston & de Waal, 2002). The complexity of empathy is clear from human studies, where the distress caused by emotional contagion is connected to prosocial behavior within an upside-down U-curve: both lack of distress and too much of it hinder helping behavior (Eisenberg & Miller, 1987). Future studies have to clarify the level of empathic capabilities in dogs by using multiple approaches, both by examining parts of empathy separately and creating realistic experimental situations in which real emotions are induced to familiar and unfamiliar persons.

How Do Humans Understand Dog Emotions, and Why Does It Matter?

When dealing with experiences of nonhuman species such as emotions of dogs, we should remind ourselves that the human mind is biologically tuned to social perception. Humans easily attribute intentionality to other living or nonliving things: we seek intentionality in our surroundings (for reviews, Blythe et al., 1999; Kujala, 2017; Scholl & Tremoulet, 2000; Urquiza-Haas & Kotrschal, 2015). Humans also project their views of themselves onto dogs, and their perception of dogs is affected by, e.g., empathy or stereotypes (Kujala et al., 2017; Kwan et al., 2008; Meyer et al., 2014; Westbury Ingham et al., 2015). Additionally, human interpretation of dog emotionality is associated with our cultural environment (Amici et al., 2019). Expertise and training in dog behavior, together with responsibility for a dog, also may affect the interpretation of canine behavior (Kujala et al., 2012; Meyer et al., 2014; Wan et al., 2012), although the effects of experience are sometimes not detectable (Donnier et al., 2020). Thus, there is a need for more future research on how humans acquire understanding about dog emotional experience.

Despite the factors influencing our perception, dog emotional signals are consistently interpreted across humans in many cases (Bloom & Friedman, 2013; Buckland et al., 2014; Farago et al., 2014; Lakestani et al., 2014; Pongracz et al., 2005; Schirmer et al., 2013; Tami & Gallagher, 2009; Walker et al., 2010). Human brain responses to dogs and human conspecifics can also be similar (Desmet et al., 2017; Franklin et al., 2013; Kujala et al., 2012; Spunt et al., 2016). This likely points to the shared basic emotionality in dogs and humans, as well as similar attribution of agency, and it can make it harder for us as humans to comprehend that there may be differences in the emotionality between the two species.

Today, as dogs are such widespread companions among humans, both species would benefit from humans better understanding dog emotionality. Human children appear to misinterpret dog behavior and expressions often (Lakestani et al., 2014; Meints et al., 2010), and dog bites may result from misinterpreting dog behavior (Reisner & Shofer, 2008). In trying to decipher dog emotions and mental processes, the presupposition of the human mind for intentionality concerns researchers and dog owners alike. We should not deny dogs their emotional capabilities, yet we should attempt to evaluate whether our perception of dog behavior is purely observational, or whether it is biased by our own, species-typical psychological attribution. Regarding dogs and other pets, this is important so that we do not demand them to behave and comprehend life as our own conspecifics do, but treat and appreciate them for who they really are.

References

Adolphs, R., & Anderson, D. J. (2018). *The neuroscience of emotion: A new synthesis*. Princeton University Press.

Albuquerque, N., Guo, K., Wilkinson, A., Savalli, C., Otta, E., & Mills, D. (2016). Dogs recognize dog and human emotions. *Biology Letters, 12*(1), 20150883. https://doi.org/10.1098/rsbl.2015.0883

Amici, F., Waterman, J., Kellermann, C. M., Karimullah, K., & Brauer, J. (2019). The ability to recognize dog emotions depends on the cultural milieu in which we grow up. *Scientific Reports*, *9*(1), 16414. https://doi.org/10.1038/s41598-019-52938-4

Amodio, D. M., Devine, P. G., & Harmon-Jones, E. (2007). A dynamic model of guilt: Implications for motivation and self-regulation in the context of prejudice. *Psychological Science*, *18*(6), 524–530. https://doi.org/10.1111/j.1467-9280.2007.01933.x

Bakvis, P., Spinhoven, P., & Roelofs, K. (2009). Basal cortisol is positively correlated to threat vigilance in patients with psychogenic nonepileptic seizures. *Epilepsy & Behavior*, *16*(3), 558–560. https://doi.org/https://doi.org/10.1016/j.yebeh.2009.09.006

Barber, A. L., Randi, D., Müller, C. A., & Huber, L. (2016). The processing of human emotional faces by pet and lab dogs: Evidence for lateralization and experience effects. *PLoS ONE*, *11*(4), e0152393. https://doi.org/10.1371/journal.pone.0152393

Bedford, E. (2020). *Global dog and cat pet population 2018*. Accessed November 15, 2020. https://www.statista.com/statistics/1044386/dog-and-cat-pet-population-worldwide/

Beerda, B., Schilder, M. B. H., van Hooff, J. A. R. A. M., de Vries, H. W., & Mol, J. A. (1998). Behavioural, saliva cortisol and heart rate responses to different types of stimuli in dogs. *Applied Animal Behaviour Science*, *58*, 365–381.

Belger, J., & Bräuer, J. (2018). Metacognition in dogs: Do dogs know they could be wrong? *Learning & Behavior*, *46*(4), 398–413. https://doi.org/10.3758/s13420-018-0367-5

Ben-Aderet, T., Gallego-Abenza, M., Reby, D., & Mathevon, N. (2017). Dog-directed speech: Why do we use it and do dogs pay attention to it? *Proceedings of the Royal Society B: Biological Sciences*, *284*(1846), 20162429. https://doi.org/10.1098/rspb.2016.2429

Benjamin, A., & Slocombe, K. (2018). "Who's a good boy?!" Dogs prefer naturalistic dog-directed speech. *Animal Cognition*, *21*(3), 353–364. https://doi.org/10.1007/s10071-018-1172-4

Berns, G. S., Brooks, A. M., & Spivak, M. (2015). Scent of the familiar: An fMRI study of canine brain responses to familiar and unfamiliar human and dog odors. *Behavioural Processes*, *110*, 37–46. https://doi.org/10.1016/j.beproc.2014.02.011

Berridge, K. C. (2003). Comparing the emotional brains of humans and other animals. In R. J. Davidson, K. R. Scherer, & H. H. Goldsmith (Eds.), *Handbook of affective sciences* (pp. 25–51). Oxford University Press.

Bloom, T., & Friedman, H. (2013). Classifying dogs' (*Canis familiaris*) facial expressions from photographs. *Behavioural Processes*, *96*, 1–10. https://doi.org/10.1016/j.beproc.2013.02.010

Blythe, P. W., Todd, P. M., & Miller, G. F. (1999). How motion reveals intention: Categorizing social interactions. In G. Gigerenzer, P. M. Todd, & ABC Research Group (Eds.), *Simple heuristics that make us smart* (pp. 257–285). Oxford University Press.

Bolon, B. (2000). Comparative and correlative neuroanatomy for the toxicologic pathologist. *Toxicologic Pathology*, *28*(1), 6–27. https://doi.org/10.1177/019262330002800103

Bradley, M. M., & Lang, P. J. (2000). Measuring emotion: Behavior, feeling, and physiology. In R. D. Lane & L. Nadel (Eds.), *Cognitive neuroscience of emotion* (pp. 242–276). Oxford University Press.

Bräuer, J. (2014). What dogs understand about humans. In J. Kaminski & S. Mashall-Pescini (Eds.), *The social dog: Behaviour and cognition* (pp. 295–317). Elsevier.

Bräuer, J. (2015). I do not understand but I care: The prosocial dog. *Interaction Studies*, *16*, 341–360. https://doi.org/10.1075/is.16.3.01bra

Bräuer, J., & Amici, F. (2018). Fake or not: Two prerequisites for jealousy. *Animal Sentience: An Interdisciplinary Journal on Animal Feeling*, *3*(22), 18.

Bräuer, J., & Belger, J. (2018). A ball is not a Kong: Odor representation and search behavior in domestic dogs (*Canis familiaris*) of different education. *Journal of Comparative Psychology*, *132*(2), 189.

Bräuer, J., & Hanus, D. (2012). Fairness in non-human primates? *Social Justice Research*, *25*(3), 256–276.

Bräuer, J., Schönefeld, K., & Call, J. (2013). When do dogs help humans? *Applied Animal Behaviour Science*, *148*(1), 138–149. https://doi.org/https://doi.org/10.1016/j.applanim.2013.07.009

Bräuer, J., Silva, K., & Schweinberger, S. R. (2017). Communicating canine and human emotions. *Animal Sentience: An Interdisciplinary Journal on Animal Feeling*, *2*(14), 7.

Bräuer, J., & Vidal Orga, B. (2023). Why wolves became dogs: Interdisciplinary questions on domestication. In I. Fiore & F. Lugli (Eds.), *Dogs, past and present: An interdisciplinary perspective* (pp. 72–81). Archaeopress Publishing Ltd.

Brosnan, S. F., & de Waal, F. B. M. (2014). Evolution of responses to (un) fairness. *Science*, *346*(6207), 1251776.

Bruce, V., & Young, A. W. (1998). *In the eye of the beholder: The science of face perception*. Oxford University Press.

Brucks, D., Essler, J. L., Marshall-Pescini, S., & Range, F. (2016). Inequity aversion negatively affects tolerance and contact-seeking behaviours towards partner and experimenter. *PLoS ONE, 11*(4), e0153799. https://doi.org/10.1371/journal.pone.0153799

Buck, R., & Ginsburg, B. (1997). Communicative genes and the evolution of empathy. In W. Ickes (Ed.), *Empathic accuracy* (pp. 17–43). Guilford Press.

Buckland, E. L., Volk, H. A., Burn, C. C., & Abeyesinghe, S. M. (2014). Owner perceptions of companion dog expressions of positive emotional states and the contexts in which they occur. *Animal Welfare, 23*, 287–296.

Burnett, S., & Blakemore, S. J. (2009). Functional connectivity during a social emotion task in adolescents and in adults. *European Journal of Neuroscience, 29*(6), 1294–1301. https://doi.org/10.1111/j.1460-9568.2009.06674.x

Buttelmann, D., & Tomasello, M. (2013). Can domestic dogs (*Canis familiaris*) use referential emotional expressions to locate hidden food? *Animal Cognition, 16*(1), 137–145.

Call, J. (2010). Do apes know that they could be wrong? *Animal Cognition, 13*(5), 689–700. https://doi.org/10.1007/s10071-010-0317-x

Call, J. (2012). Seeking information in non-human animals: Weaving a metacognitive web. In M. J. Beran, J. Brandl, J. Perner, & J. Proust (Eds.), *Foundations of metacognition* (pp. 62–75). Oxford University Press.

Call, J., Bräuer, J., Kaminski, J., & Tomasello, M. (2003). Domestic dogs (*Canis familiaris*) are sensitive to the attentional state of humans. *Journal of Comparative Psychology, 117*(3), 257–263. https://doi.org/10.1037/0735-7036.117.3.257

Canli, T., & Lesch, K.-P. (2007). Long story short: The serotonin transporter in emotion regulation and social cognition. *Nature Neuroscience, 10*(9), 1103–1109. https://doi.org/10.1038/nn1964

Catala, A., Grandgeorge, M., Schaff, J.-L., Cousillas, H., Hausberger, M., & Cattet, J. (2019). Dogs demonstrate the existence of an epileptic seizure odour in humans. *Scientific Reports, 9*(1), 1–7.

Catala, A., Mang, B., Wallis, L., & Huber, L. (2017). Dogs demonstrate perspective taking based on geometrical gaze following in a Guesser–Knower task. *Animal Cognition, 20*(4), 581–589. https://doi.org/10.1007/s10071-017-1082-x

Cook, P. F., Prichard, A., Spivak, M., & Berns, G. S. (2016). Awake canine fMRI predicts dogs' preference for praise vs food. *Social Cognitive and Affective Neuroscience, 11*(12), 1853–1862. https://doi.org/10.1093/scan/nsw102

Cook, P., Prichard, A., Spivak, M., & Berns, G. S. (2017). Awake fMRI reveals covert arousal in aggressive dogs under social resource threat. *bioRxiv*, 1–13, 203323. https://doi.org/10.1101/203323

Cook, P., Prichard, A., Spivak, M., & Berns, G. S. (2018). Jealousy in dogs? Evidence from brain imaging. *Animal Sentience: An Interdisciplinary Journal on Animal Feeling, 3*(22), 1.

Custance, D., & Mayer, J. (2012). Empathic-like responding by domestic dogs (*Canis familiaris*) to distress in humans: an exploratory study. *Animal Cognition, 15*(5), 851–859. https://doi.org/10.1007/s10071-012-0510-1

D'Aniello, B., Semin, G. R., Alterisio, A., Aria, M., & Scandurra, A. (2018). Interspecies transmission of emotional information via chemosignals: from humans to dogs (*Canis lupus familiaris*). *Animal Cognition, 21*(1), 67–78.

Dalziel, D. J., Uthman, B. M., Mcgorray, S. P., & Reep, R. L. (2003). Seizure-alert dogs: A review and preliminary study. *Seizure, 12*(2), 115–120.

Damasio, A. R. (1994). *Descartes' error: Emotion, reason, and the human brain*. Avon Books.

Decety, J., & Ickes, W. J. (2011). *The social neuroscience of empathy*. MIT Press.

Decety, J., Norman, G. J., Berntson, G. G., & Cacioppo, J. T. (2012). A neurobehavioral evolutionary perspective on the mechanisms underlying empathy. *Progress in Neurobiology, 98*(1), 38–48. https://doi.org/https://doi.org/10.1016/j.pneurobio.2012.05.001

Desmet, C., van der Wiel, A., & Brass, M. (2017). Brain regions involved in observing and trying to interpret dog behaviour. *PLoS ONE, 12*(9), e0182721. https://doi.org/https://doi.org/10.1371/journal.pone.0182721

de Waal, F. (2019). *Mama's last hug: Animal emotions and what they tell us about ourselves*. W. W. Norton.

Dixon, M. L., Thiruchselvam, R., Todd, R., & Christoff, K. (2017). Emotion and the prefrontal cortex: An integrative review. *Psychological Bulletin, 143*(10), 1033–1081. https://doi.org/10.1037/bul0000096

Donnier, S., Kovács, G., Oña, L. S., Bräuer, J., & Amici, F. (2020). Experience has a limited effect on humans' ability to predict the outcome of social interactions in children, dogs and macaques. *Scientific Reports, 10*(1), 21240. https://doi.org/10.1038/s41598-020-78275-5

Dreschel, N. A., & Granger, D. A. (2005). Physiological and behavioral reactivity to stress in thunderstorm-phobic dogs and their caregivers. *Applied Animal Behaviour Science, 95*(3–4), 153–168. https://doi.org/10.1016/j.applanim.2005.04.009

Eisenberg, N., & Miller, P. A. (1987). The relation of empathy to prosocial and related behaviors. *Psychological Bulletin, 101*(1), 91–119.

Ekman, P. (1992). Are there basic emotions? *Psychological Review, 99*(3), 550–553.

Espinosa, H., Reyes-Meza, V., Arteaga-Castañeda, M. D. L., Espinosa-Curiel, I. E., Bautista, A., & Martínez-Miranda, J. (2017). Assessment of the emotional state in domestic dogs using a bi-dimensional model of emotions and a machine learning approach for the analysis of its vocalizations. *Research in Computing Science*, *144*, 53–65.

Evans, H. E., & de Lahunta, A. (2013). *Miller's anatomy of the dog* (4th ed.). Saunders, Elsevier.

Farago, T., Andics, A., Devecseri, V., Kis, A., Gacsi, M., & Miklosi, A. (2014). Humans rely on the same rules to assess emotional valence and intensity in conspecific and dog vocalizations. *Biology Letters*, *10*(1), 20130926. https://doi.org/10.1098/rsbl.2013.0926

Franklin, R. G., Jr., Nelson, A. J., Baker, M., Beeney, J. E., Vescio, T. K., Lenz-Watson, A., & Adams, R. B., Jr. (2013). Neural responses to perceiving suffering in humans and animals. *Social Neuroscience*, *8*(3), 217–227. https://doi.org/10.1080/17470919.2013.763852

Gacsi, M., Gyori, B., Miklosi, A., Viranyi, Z., Kubinyi, E., Topal, J., & Csanyi, V. (2005). Species-specific differences and similarities in the behavior of hand-raised dog and wolf pups in social situations with humans. *Developmental Psychobiology*, *47*(2), 111–122. https://doi.org/10.1002/dev.20082

Gacsi, M., Miklosi, A., Varga, O., Topal, J., & Csanyi, V. (2004). Are readers of our face readers of our minds? Dogs (*Canis familiaris*) show situation-dependent recognition of human's attention. *Animal Cognition*, *7*(3), 144–153. https://doi.org/10.1007/s10071-003-0205-8

Gadbois, S., & Reeve, C. (2014). Canine olfaction: Scent, sign, and situation. In A. Horowitz (Ed.), *Domestic dog cognition and behavior* (pp. 3–29). Springer.

Galac, S., & Knol, B. (1997). Fear-motivated aggression in dogs: Patient characteristics, diagnosis and therapy. *Animal Welfare*, *6*(1), 9–15.

Gilbert, P. (2003). Evolution, social roles, and the differences in shame and guilt. *Social Research*, *70*(4), 1205–1230. http://www.jstor.org/stable/40971967

Gnanadesikan, G. E., Hare, B., Snyder-Mackler, N., Call, J., Kaminski, J., Miklósi, Á., & MacLean, E. (2020). Breed differences in dog cognition associated with brain-expressed genes and neurological functions. *Integrative and Comparative Biology*, *60*(4), 976–990. https://doi.org/10.1093/icb/icaa112

Gordan, R., Gwathmey, J. K., & Xie, L.-H. (2015). Autonomic and endocrine control of cardiovascular function. *World Journal of Cardiology*, *7*(4), 204–214. https://doi.org/10.4330/wjc.v7.i4.204

Hakanen, E., Mikkola, S., Salonen, M., Puurunen, J., Sulkama, S., Araujo, C., & Lohi, H. (2020). Active and social life is associated with lower non-social fearfulness in pet dogs. *Scientific Reports*, *10*(1), 13774. https://doi.org/10.1038/s41598-020-70722-7

Handlin, L., Hydbring-Sandberg, E., Nilsson, A., Ejdeback, M., Jansson, A., & Uvnas-Moberg, K. (2011). Short-term interaction between dogs and their owners: Effects on oxytocin, cortisol, insulin and heart rate—an exploratory study. *Anthrozoos*, *24*(3), 301–315. https://doi.org/10.2752/175303711x13045914865385

Hare, B., & Tomasello, M. (2005). Human-like social skills in dogs? *Trends in Cognitive Sciences*, *9*(9), 439–444. https://doi.org/https://doi.org/10.1016/j.tics.2005.07.003

Hareli, S., & Parkinson, B. (2008). What's social about social emotions? *Journal for the Theory of Social Behaviour*, *38*(2), 131–156. https://doi.org/10.1111/j.1468-5914.2008.00363.x

Harris, C. R., & Prouvost, C. (2014). Jealousy in dogs. *PLoS ONE*, *9*(7), e94597. https://doi.org/10.1371/journal.pone.0094597

Hartley, C. A., & Phelps, E. A. (2012). Extinction learning. In N. M. Seel (Ed.), *Encyclopedia of the sciences of learning* (pp. 1252–1253). Springer. https://doi.org/10.1007/978-1-4419-1428-6_306

Hecht, E. E., Smaers, J. B., Dunn, W. D., Kent, M., Preuss, T. M., & Gutman, D. A. (2019). Significant neuroanatomical variation among domestic dog breeds. *Journal of Neuroscience*, *39*(39), 7748–7758. https://doi.org/10.1523/JNEUROSCI.0303-19.2019

Hecht, J., Miklósi, A., & Gácsi, M. (2012). Behavioral assessment and owner perceptions of behaviors associated with guilt in dogs. *Applied Animal Behaviour Science*, *139*, 134–142.

Horowitz, A. (2009). Disambiguating the "guilty look": Salient prompts to a familiar dog behaviour. *Behavoural Processes*, *81*(3), 447–452. https://doi.org/10.1016/j.beproc.2009.03.014

Horowitz, A. (2017). Smelling themselves: Dogs investigate their own odours longer when modified in an "olfactory mirror" test. *Behavioural Processes*, *143*, 17–24. https://doi.org/https://doi.org/10.1016/j.beproc.2017.08.001

Horvath, Z., Doka, A., & Miklosi, A. (2008). Affiliative and disciplinary behavior of human handlers during play with their dog affects cortisol concentrations in opposite directions. *Hormones and Behavior*, *54*(1), 107–114. https://doi.org/10.1016/j.yhbeh.2008.02.002

Huber, A., Barber, A. L. A., Farago, T., Muller, C. A., & Huber, L. (2017). Investigating emotional contagion in dogs (*Canis familiaris*) to emotional sounds of humans and conspecifics. *Animal Cognition*, *20*(4), 703–715. https://doi.org/10.1007/s10071-017-1092-8

Huber, L., Racca, A., Scaf, B., Viranyi, Z., & Range, F. (2013). Discrimination of familiar human faces in dogs (*Canis familiaris*). *Learning and Motivation*, *44*(4), 258–269. https://doi.org/10.1016/j.lmot.2013.04.005

Hydbring-Sandberg, E., von Walter, L. W., Hoglund, K., Svartberg, K., Swenson, L., & Forkman, B. (2004). Physiological reactions to fear provocation in dogs. *Journal of Endocrinology*, *180*(3), 439–448. https://doi.org/https://doi.org/10.1677/joe.0.1800439

Izard, C. E. (1992). Basic emotions, relations among emotions, and emotion-cognition relations. *Psychological Review*, *99*(3), 561–565. https://doi.org/https://doi.org/10.1037/0033-295X.99.3.561

Jensen, P. (2007). Mechanisms and function in dog behaviour. In P. Jensen (Ed.), *The behavioural biology of dogs* (pp. 61–75). CABI.

Kaminski, J., Bräuer, J., Call, J., & Tomasello, M. (2009). Domestic dogs are sensitive to a human's perspective. *Behaviour*, *146*(7), 979–998. http://www.jstor.org/stable/40296109

Kaminski, J., & Marshall-Pescini, S. (2014). *The social dog: Behaviour and cognition*. Elsevier.

Kaminski, J., Nitzschner, M., Wobber, V., Tennie, C., Bräuer, J., Call, J., & Tomasello, M. (2011). Do dogs distinguish rational from irrational acts? *Animal Behaviour*, *81*(1), 195–203. https://doi.org/https://doi.org/10.1016/j.anbehav.2010.10.001

Kaminski, J., Pitsch, A., & Tomasello, M. (2013). Dogs steal in the dark. *Animal Cognition*, *16*(3), 385–394. https://doi.org/10.1007/s10071-012-0579-6

Kaminski, J., Schulz, L., & Tomasello, M. (2012). How dogs know when communication is intended for them. *Developmental Science*, *15*(2), 222–232. https://doi.org/10.1111/j.1467-7687.2011.01120.x

Kaminski, J., Tempelmann, S., Call, J., & Tomasello, M. (2009). Domestic dogs comprehend human communication with iconic signs. *Developmental Science*, *12*(6), 831–837. https://doi.org/10.1111/j.1467-7687.2009.00815.x

King, T., Hemsworth, P. H., & Coleman, G. J. (2003). Fear of novel and startling stimuli in domestic dogs. *Applied Animal Behaviour Science*, *82*(1), 45–64. https://doi.org/10.1016/S0168-1591(03)00040-6

Kis, A., Hernádi, A., Miklósi, B., Kanizsár, O., & Topál, J. (2017). The way dogs (*Canis familiaris*) look at human emotional faces is modulated by oxytocin: An eye-tracking study. *Frontiers in Behavioral Neuroscience*, *11*, 210.

Klausz, B., Kis, A., Persa, E., Miklósi, Á., & Gácsi, M. (2014). A quick assessment tool for human-directed aggression in pet dogs. *Aggressive Behavior*, *40*(2), 178–188.

Kroll, T. L., Houpt, K. A., & Erb, H. N. (2004). The use of novel stimuli as indicators of aggressive behavior in dogs. *Journal of the American Animal Hospital Association*, *40*(1), 13–19. https://doi.org/10.5326/0400013

Kujala, M. V. (2017). Canine emotions as seen through human social cognition. *Animal Sentience*, *14*(1). https://www.wellbeingintlstudiesrepository.org/animsent/vol2/iss14/1/

Kujala, M. V. (2018). Canine emotions: Guidelines for research. *Animal Sentience*, *2*(14), 18. https://www.wellbeingintlstudiesrepository.org/animsent/vol2/iss14/18/

Kujala, M. V., Kauppi, J.-P., Törnqvist, H., Helle, L., Vainio, O., Kujala, J., & Parkkonen, L. (2020). Time-resolved classification of dog brain signals reveals early processing of faces, species and emotion. *Scientific Reports*, *10*(1), 19846. https://doi.org/10.1038/s41598-020-76806-8

Kujala, M. V., Kujala, J., Carlson, S., & Hari, R. (2012). Dog experts' brains distinguish socially relevant body postures similarly in dogs and humans. *PLoS ONE*, *7*(6), e39145. https://doi.org/10.1371/journal.pone.0039145

Kujala, M. V., Somppi, S., Jokela, M., Vainio, O., & Parkkonen, L. (2017). Human empathy, personality and experience affect the emotion ratings of dog and human facial expressions. *PLoS ONE*, *12*(1), e0170730. https://doi.org/10.1371/journal.pone.0170730

Kwan, V. S. Y., Gosling, S. D., & John, O. P. (2008). Anthropomorphism as a special case of social perception: A cross-species social relations model analysis of humans and dogs. *Social Cognition*, *26*(2), 129–142. https://doi.org/https://doi.org/10.1521/soco.2008.26.2.129

Lakestani, N. N., Donaldson, M., & Waran, N. (2014). Interpretation of dog behaviour by children and young adults. *Anthrozoos*, *27*, 65–80.

Lamm, C., & Singer, T. (2010). The role of anterior insular cortex in social emotions. *Brain Structure and Function*, *214*(5), 579–591. https://doi.org/10.1007/s00429-010-0251-3

Lane, R. D., & Nadel, L. (2002). *Cognitive neuroscience of emotion*. Oxford University Press.

Larson, G., & Bradley, D. G. (2014). How much is that in dog years? The advent of canine population genomics. *PLoS Genetics*, *10*(1), e1004093. https://doi.org/10.1371/journal.pgen.1004093

Leary, M. R. (2003). The self and emotion: The role of self-reflection in the generation and regulation of affective experience. In R. J. Davidson, K. R. Scherer, & H. H. Goldsmith (Eds.), *Handbook of affective sciences* (pp. 773–786). Oxford University Press.

LeDoux, J. E. (1996). *The emotional brain: The mysterious underpinnings of emotional life*. Simon & Schuster.

Leopold, D. A., & Rhodes, G. (2010). A comparative view of face perception. *Journal of Comparative Psychology*, *124*(3), 233–251. https://doi.org/10.1037/a0019460

Ley, J., Coleman, G. J., Holmes, R., & Hemsworth, P. H. (2007). Assessing fear of novel and startling stimuli in domestic dogs. *Applied Animal Behaviour Science, 104*(1), 71–84. https://doi.org/https://doi.org/10.1016/j.applanim.2006.03.021

Lim, K., Wilcox, A., Fisher, M., & Burns-Cox, C. I. (1992). Type 1 diabetics and their pets. *Diabetic Medicine, 9*(2), S3–S4.

MacLean, E. L., Snyder-Mackler, N., von Holdt, B. M., & Serpell, J. A. (2019). Highly heritable and functionally relevant breed differences in dog behaviour. *Proceedings of the Royal Society B: Biological Sciences, 286*(1912), 20190716. https://doi.org/doi:10.1098/rspb.2019.0716

Macpherson, K., & Roberts, W. A. (2006). Do dogs (*Canis familiaris*) seek help in an emergency? *Journal of Comparative Psychology, 120*(2), 113–119. https://doi.org/10.1037/0735-7036.120.2.113

Maginnity, M. E., & Grace, R. C. (2014). Visual perspective taking by dogs (*Canis familiaris*) in a Guesser-Knower task: Evidence for a canine theory of mind? *Animal Cognition, 17*(6), 1375–1392. https://doi.org/10.1007/s10071-014-0773-9

Marshall-Pescini, S., Ceretta, M., & Prato-Previde, E. (2014). Do domestic dogs understand human actions as goal-directed? *PLoS ONE, 9*(9), e106530. https://doi.org/10.1371/journal.pone.0106530

McGetrick, J., & Range, F. (2018). Inequity aversion in dogs: A review. *Learning & Behavior, 46*(4), 479–500.

McGreevy, P. D., Georgevsky, D., Carrasco, J., Valenzuela, M., Duffy, D. L., & Serpell, J. A. (2013). Dog behavior co-varies with height, bodyweight and skull shape. *PLoS ONE, 8*(12), e80529. https://doi.org/10.1371/journal.pone.0080529

McMahon, S., Macpherson, K., & Roberts, W. A. (2010). Dogs choose a human informant: Metacognition in canines. *Behavioural Processes, 85*(3), 293–298. https://doi.org/https://doi.org/10.1016/j.beproc.2010.07.014

Meints, K., Racca, A., & Hickey, N. (2010). How to prevent dog bite injuries? Children misinterpret dogs facial expressions. *Injury Prevention, 16 (suppl. 1)*, A68. https://doi.org/10.1136/ip.2010.029215.0246

Melzack, R. (1952). Irrational Fears in the Dog. *Canadian Journal of Psychology, 6*(3), 141–147. https://doi.org/10.1037/H0083562

Merker, B. (2007). Consciousness without a cerebral cortex: A challenge for neuroscience and medicine. *Behavioral and Brain Sciences, 30*(1), 63–81; discussion 81–134. https://doi.org/10.1017/s0140525x07000891

Merola, I., Prato-Previde, E., & Marshall-Pescini, S. (2012a). Dogs' social referencing towards owners and strangers. *PLoS ONE, 7*(10), e47653. https://doi.org/10.1371/journal.pone.0047653

Merola, I., Prato-Previde, E., & Marshall-Pescini, S. (2012b). Social referencing in dog-owner dyads? *Animal Cognition, 15*(2), 175–185. https://doi.org/10.1007/s10071-011-0443-0

Meyer, I., Forkman, B., & Paul, E. S. (2014). Factors affecting the human interpretation of dog behavior. *Anthrozoos, 27*(1), 127–140. https://doi.org/10.2752/175303714x13837396326576

Miklósi, A., Kubinyi, E., Topal, J., Gacsi, M., Viranyi, Z., & Csanyi, V. (2003). A simple reason for a big difference: Wolves do not look back at humans, but dogs do. *Current Biology, 13*(9), 763–766. https://doi.org/https://doi.org/10.1016/S0960-9822(03)00263-X

Miklósi, Á., Turcsán, B., & Kubinyi, E. (2014). The personality of dogs. In J. Kaminski & S. Marshall-Pescini (Eds.), *The social dog: Behavior and cognition* (pp. 191–222). Elsevier.

Miller, S. C., Kennedy, C., Devoe, D., Hickey, M., Nelson, T., & Kogan, L. (2009). An examination of changes in oxytocin levels in men and women before and after interaction with a bonded dog. *Anthrozoos, 22*(1), 31–42. https://doi.org/10.2752/175303708x390455

Mitchell, R. W. (2004). Controlling the dog, pretending to have a conversation, or just being friendly? Influences of sex and familiarity on Americans' talk to dogs during play. *Interaction Studies, 5*(1), 99–129.

Moll, J., de Oliveira-Souza, R., Bramati, I. E., & Grafman, J. (2002). Functional networks in emotional moral and nonmoral social judgments. *Neuroimage, 16*(3 Pt 1), 696–703. https://doi.org/S1053811902911183

Morisaki, A., Takaoka, A., & Fujita, K. (2009). Are dogs sensitive to the emotional state of humans? *Journal of Veterinary Behavior: Clinical Applications and Research, 4*(2), 49.

Morris, P. H., Doe, C., & Godsell, E. (2008). Secondary emotions in non-primate species? Behavioural reports and subjective claims by animal owners. *Cognition and Emotion, 22*, 3–20.

Morrow, M., Ottobre, J., Ottobre, A., Neville, P., St-Pierre, N., Dreschel, N., & Pate, J. L. (2015). Breed-dependent differences in the onset of fear-related avoidance behavior in puppies. *Journal of Veterinary Behavior: Clinical Applications and Research, 10*(4), 286–294. https://doi.org/10.1016/j.jveb.2015.03.002

Müller, C. A., Schmitt, K., Barber, A. L., & Huber, L. (2015). Dogs can discriminate emotional expressions of human faces. *Current Biology, 25*(5), 601–605. https://doi.org/10.1016/j.cub.2014.12.055

Nagasawa, M., Kikusui, T., Onaka, T., & Ohta, M. (2009). Dog's gaze at its owner increases owner's urinary oxytocin during social interaction. *Hormones and Behavior, 55*(3), 434–441. https://doi.org/10.1016/j.yhbeh.2008.12.002

Nagasawa, M., Mitsui, S., En, S., Ohtani, N., Ohta, M., Sakuma, Y., Onaka, T., Mogi, K., & Kikusui, T. (2015). Social evolution: Oxytocin-gaze positive loop and the coevolution of human-dog bonds. *Science*, *348*(6232), 333–336. https://doi.org/10.1126/science.1261022

Nagasawa, M., Murai, K., Mogi, K., & Kikusui, T. (2011). Dogs can discriminate human smiling faces from blank expressions. *Animal Cognition*, *14*(4), 525–533. https://doi.org/10.1007/s10071-011-0386-5

Netto, W. J., & Planta, D. J. U. (1997). Behavioural testing for aggression in the domestic dog. *Applied Animal Behaviour Science*, *52*(3–4), 243–263. https://doi.org/Doi 10.1016/S0168-1591(96)01126-4

Nitzschner, M., Melis, A. P., Kaminski, J., & Tomasello, M. (2012). Dogs (*Canis familiaris*) evaluate humans on the basis of direct experiences only. *PLoS ONE*, *7*(10), e46880. https://doi.org/10.1371/journal.pone.0046880

Ochsner, K. N., Silvers, J. A., & Buhle, J. T. (2012). Functional imaging studies of emotion regulation: A synthetic review and evolving model of the cognitive control of emotion. *Annals of the New York Academy of Sciences*, *1251*, E1–E24. https://doi.org/10.1111/j.1749-6632.2012.06751.x

Odendaal, J. S. J., & Meintjes, R. A. (2003). Neurophysiological correlates of affiliative behaviour between humans and dogs. *The Veterinary Journal*, *165*(3), 296–301. https://doi.org/10.1016/S1090-0233(02)00237-X

Ogata, N., Kikusui, T., Takeuchi, Y., & Mori, Y. (2006). Objective measurement of fear-associated learning in dogs. *Journal of Veterinary Behavior: Clinical Applications and Research*, *1*(2), 55–61. https://doi.org/10.1016/j.jveb.2006.06.002

Ostojíc, L., Tkalčić, M., & Clayton, N. (2015). Are owners' reports of their dogs' 'guilty look' influenced by the dogs' action and evidence of the misdeed? *Behavioural Processes*, *111*, 97–100.

Palestrini, C. (2009). Situational sensitivities. In D. F. Horwitz & D. S. Mills (Eds.), *BSAVA Manual of Canine and Feline Behavioural Medicine* (pp. 169–181). British Small Animal Veterinary Association. https://doi.org/doi:https://doi.org/10.22233/9781905319879.16

Panksepp, J. (1998). *Affective neuroscience: The foundations of human and animal emotions*. Oxford University Press.

Panksepp, J., & Watt, D. (2011). What is basic about basic emotions? Lasting lessons from affective neuroscience. *Emotion Review*, *3*(4), 387–396. https://doi.org/10.1177/1754073911410741

Petersson, M., Uvnäs-Moberg, K., Nilsson, A., Gustafson, L.-L., Hydbring-Sandberg, E., & Handlin, L. (2017). Oxytocin and cortisol levels in dog owners and their dogs are associated with behavioral patterns: An exploratory study. *Frontiers in Psychology*, *8*, 1796. https://doi.org/10.3389/fpsyg.2017.01796

Petter, M., Musolino, E., Roberts, W. A., & Cole, M. (2009). Can dogs (*Canis familiaris*) detect human deception? *Behavioral Processes*, *82*(2), 109–118. https://doi.org/https://doi.org/10.1016/j.beproc.2009.07.002

Pongracz, P., Molnar, C., Miklosi, A., & Csanyi, V. (2005). Human listeners are able to classify dog (*Canis familiaris*) barks recorded in different situations. *Journal of Comparative Psychology*, *119*(2), 136–144. https://doi.org/https://doi.org/10.1037/0735-7036.119.2.136

Posner, J., Russell, J. A., & Peterson, B. S. (2005). The circumplex model of affect: An integrative approach to affective neuroscience, cognitive development, and psychopathology. *Development and Psychopathology*, *17*(3), 715–734. https://doi.org/10.1017/S0954579405050340

Prato-Previde, E., Nicotra, V., Fusar Poli, S., Pelosi, A., & Valsecchi, P. (2018). Do dogs exhibit jealous behaviors when their owner attends to their companion dog? *Animal Cognition*, *21*(5), 703–713. https://doi.org/10.1007/s10071-018-1204-0

Prato-Previde, E., Nicotra, V., Pelosi, A., & Valsecchi, P. (2018). Pet dogs' behavior when the owner and an unfamiliar person attend to a faux rival. *PLoS ONE*, *13*(4), e0194577. https://doi.org/10.1371/journal.pone.0194577

Prato Previde, E., & Valsecchi, P. (2014). The immaterial cord: The dog–human attachment bond. In J. Kaminski & S. Marshall-Pescini (Eds.), *The social dog: Behavior and cognition* (pp. 165–189). Elsevier. https://doi.org/10.1016/B978-0-12-407818-5.00006-1

Preston, S. D., & de Waal, F. B. (2002). Empathy: Its ultimate and proximate bases. *Behavioral and Brain Sciences*, *25*(1), 1–20; discussion 20–71. https://doi.org/https://doi.org/10.1017/S0140525X02000018

Quervel-Chaumette, M., Faerber, V., Farago, T., Marshall-Pescini, S., & Range, F. (2016). Investigating empathy-like responding to conspecifics' distress in pet dogs. *PLoS ONE*, *11*(4), e0152920. https://doi.org/10.1371/journal.pone.0152920

Racca, A., Amadei, E., Ligout, S., Guo, K., Meints, K., & Mills, D. (2010). Discrimination of human and dog faces and inversion responses in domestic dogs (*Canis familiaris*). *Animal Cognition*, *13*(3), 525–533. https://doi.org/10.1007/s10071-009-0303-3

Range, F., Horn, L., Viranyi, Z., & Huber, L. (2009). The absence of reward induces inequity aversion in dogs [Research Support, Non-U.S. Gov't]. *Proceedings of the National Academy of Sciences*, *106*(1), 340–345. https://doi.org/10.1073/pnas.0810957105

Range, F., Viranyi, Z., & Huber, L. (2007). Selective imitation in domestic dogs. *Current Biology*, *17*(10), 868–872. https://doi.org/https://doi.org/10.1016/j.cub.2007.04.026

Reisner, I. R. (1997). Assessment, management, and prognosis of canine dominance-related aggression. *Veterinary Clinics of North America-Small Animal Practice*, *27*(3), 479–495–. https://doi.org/10.1016/s0195-5616(97)50050-7

Reisner, I. R., & Shofer, F. S. (2008). Effects of gender and parental status on knowledge and attitudes of dog owners regarding dog aggression toward children. *Journal of the American Veterinary Medical Association*, *233*(9), 1412–1419. https://doi.org/10.2460/javma.233.9.1412

Roberts, T., McGreevy, P., & Valenzuela, M. (2010). Human induced rotation and reorganization of the brain of domestic dogs. *PLoS ONE*, *5*(7), e11946. https://doi.org/10.1371/journal.pone.0011946

Rolls, E. T. (1999). *The brain and emotion*. Oxford University Press.

Rossi, A., Parada, F. J., Stewart, R., Barwell, C., Demas, G., & Allen, C. (2018). Hormonal correlates of exploratory and play-soliciting behavior in domestic dogs. *Frontiers in Psychology*, *9*, 1559. https://doi.org/10.3389/fpsyg.2018.01559

Roth, G., & Dicke, U. (2005). Evolution of the brain and intelligence. *Trends in Cognitive Sciences*, *9*(5), 250–257. https://doi.org/https://doi.org/10.1016/j.tics.2005.03.005

Russell, J. A. (1980). A circumplex model of affect. *Journal of Personality and Social Psychology*, *39*(6), 1161–1178 .

Salovey, P. (1991). *The psychology of jealousy and envy*. Guilford Press.

Sarviaho, R., Hakosalo, O., Tiira, K., Sulkama, S., Niskanen, J. E., Hytönen, M. K., Sillanpää, M. J., & Lohi, H. (2020). A novel genomic region on chromosome 11 associated with fearfulness in dogs. *Translational Psychiatry*, *10*(1), 169. https://doi.org/10.1038/s41398-020-0849-z

Schirmer, A., Seow, C. S., & Penney, T. B. (2013). Humans process dog and human facial affect in similar ways. *PLoS ONE*, *8*(9), e74591. https://doi.org/10.1371/journal.pone.0074591

Scholl, B. J., & Tremoulet, P. D. (2000). Perceptual causality and animacy. *Trends in Cognitive Sciences*, *4*(8), 299–309. https://doi.org/S1364-6613(00)01506-0 [pii]

Sforzini, E., Michelazzi, M., Spada, E., Ricci, C., Carenzi, C., Milani, S., Luzi, F., & Verga, M. (2009). Evaluation of young and adult dogs' reactivity. *Journal of Veterinary Behavior-Clinical Applications and Research*, *4*(1), 3–10. https://doi.org/10.1016/j.jveb.2008.09.035

Smuts, B. (2014). Social behaviour among companion dogs with an emphasis on play. In J. Kaminski & S. Marshall-Pescini (Eds.), *The social dog: Behaviour and cognition* (pp. 105–130). Elsevier.

Somppi, S., Törnqvist, H., Hänninen, L., Krause, C. M., & Vainio, O. (2014). How dogs scan familiar and inverted faces: An eye movement study. *Animal Cognition*, *17*(3), 793–803. https://doi.org/10.1007/s10071-013-0713-0

Somppi, S., Törnqvist, H., Kujala, M. V., Hänninen, L., Krause, C. M., & Vainio, O. (2016). Dogs evaluate threatening facial expressions by their biological validity: Evidence from gazing patterns. *PLoS ONE*, *11*(1), e0143047. https://doi.org/10.1371/journal.pone.0143047

Somppi, S., Törnqvist, H., Topal, J., Koskela, A., Hänninen, L., Krause, C. M., & Vainio, O. (2017). Nasal oxytocin treatment biases dogs' visual attention and emotional response toward positive human facial expressions. *Frontiers in Psychology*, *8*, 1854. https://doi.org/10.3389/fpsyg.2017.01854

Spunt, R. P., Ellsworth, E., & Adolphs, R. (2016). The neural basis of understanding the expression of the emotions in man and animals. *Social Cognitive and Affective Neuroscience*, *12*(1), 95–105. https://doi.org/10.1093/scan/nsw161

Tami, G., & Gallagher, A. (2009). Description of the behaviour of domestic dog (*Canis familiaris*) by experienced and inexperienced people. *Applied Animal Behaviour Science*, *120*, 159–169.

Tangney, J. P., & Salovey, P. (1999). Problematic social emotions: Shame, guilt, jealousy, and envy. In R. M. Kowalski & M. R. Leary (Eds.), *The social psychology of emotional and behavioral problems: Interfaces of social and clinical psychology* (pp. 167–195). American Psychological Association. https://doi.org/10.1037/10320-006

Tate, A. J., Fischer, H., Leigh, A. E., & Kendrick, K. M. (2006). Behavioural and neurophysiological evidence for face identity and face emotion processing in animals. *Philosophical Transactions of the Royal Society B: Biological Sciences*, *361*(1476), 2155–2172. https://doi.org/10.1098/rstb.2006.1937

Thalmann, O., Shapiro, B., Cui, P., Schuenemann, V. J., Sawyer, S. K., Greenfield, D. L., Germonpre, M. B., Sablin, M. V., Lopez-Giraldez, F., Domingo-Roura, X., Napierala, H., Uerpmann, H. P., Loponte, D. M., Acosta, A. A., Giemsch, L., Schmitz, R. W., Worthington, B., Buikstra, J. E., Druzhkova, A., . . . Wayne, R. K. (2013). Complete mitochondrial genomes of ancient canids suggest a European origin of domestic dogs. *Science*, *342*(6160), 871–874. https://doi.org/10.1126/science.1243650

Thompkins, A. M., Ramaiahgari, B., Zhao, S., Gotoor, S. S. R., Waggoner, P., Denney, T. S., Deshpande, G., & Katz, J. S. (2018). Separate brain areas for processing human and dog faces as revealed by awake fMRI in dogs (*Canis familiaris*). *Learning & Behavior*, *46*(4), 561–573. https://doi.org/10.3758/s13420-018-0352-z

Topál, J. (2014). Dogs' sensitivity to human ostensive cues: A unique adaptation? In J. Kaminski & S. Mashall-Pescini (Eds.), *The social dog: Behaviour and cognition* (pp. 319–346). Elsevier.

Topál, J., Gácsi, M., Miklósi, Á., Virányi, Z., Kubinyi, E., & Csányi, V. (2005). Attachment to humans: A comparative study on hand-reared wolves and differently socialized dog puppies. *Animal Behaviour, 70*(6), 1367–1375. https://doi.org/https://doi.org/10.1016/j.anbehav.2005.03.025

Udell, M. A. R., & Wynne, C. D. L. (2011). Reevaluating canine perspective-taking behavior. *Learning & Behavior, 39*(4), 318–323. https://doi.org/10.3758/s13420-011-0043-5

Urquiza-Haas, E. G., & Kotrschal, K. (2015). The mind behind anthropomorphic thinking: attribution of mental states to other species. *Animal Behaviour, 109*, 167–176. https://doi.org/https://doi.org/10.1016/j.anbehav.2015.08.011

Väisänen, M. A., Valros, A. E., Hakaoja, E., Raekallio, M. R., & Vainio, O. M. (2005). Pre-operative stress in dogs: A preliminary investigation of behavior and heart rate variability in healthy hospitalized dogs. *Veterinary Anaesthesia and Analgesia, 32*(3), 158–167. https://doi.org/10.1111/j.1467-2995.2005.00188.x

van den Berg, L., Schilder, M. B. H., & Knol, B. W. (2003). Behavior genetics of canine aggression: Behavioral phenotyping of golden retrievers by means of an aggression test. *Behavior Genetics, 33*(5), 469–483. https://doi.org/https://doi.org/10.1023/A:1025714431089

van der Borg, J. A. M., Beerda, B., Ooms, M., de Souza, A. S., van Hagen, M., & Kemp, B. (2010). Evaluation of behaviour testing for human directed aggression in dogs. *Applied Animal Behaviour Science, 128*(1-4), 78–90. https://doi.org/10.1016/j.applanim.2010.09.016

van Peer, J. M., Roelofs, K., Rotteveel, M., van Dijk, J. G., Spinhoven, P., & Ridderinkhof, K. R. (2007). The effects of cortisol administration on approach–avoidance behavior: An event-related potential study. *Biological Psychology, 76*(3), 135–146. https://doi.org/https://doi.org/10.1016/j.biopsycho.2007.07.003

Vonk, J. (2018). Researchers, not dogs, lack control in an experiment on jealousy. *Animal Sentience: An Interdisciplinary Journal on Animal Feeling, 3*(22), 2.

Walker, J., Dale, A., Waran, N., Clarke, N., Farnworth, M., & Wemelsfelder, F. (2010). The assessment of emotional expression in dogs using a Free Choice Profiling methodology. *Animal Welfare, 19*, 75–84.

Wan, M., Bolger, N., & Champagne, F. A. (2012). Human perception of fear in dogs varies according to experience with dogs. *PLoS ONE, 7*(12), e51775. https://doi.org/10.1371/journal.pone.0051775

Westbury Ingham, H., Neumann, D., & Waters, A. (2015). Empathy-related ratings to still images of human and nonhuman animal groups in negative contexts graded for phylogenetic similarity. *Anthrozoos, 28*(1), 113–130.

Yong, M. H., & Ruffman, T. (2014). Emotional contagion: Dogs and humans show a similar physiological response to human infant crying. *Behavioural Processes, 108*, 155–165.

Zahn-Waxler, C., & Robinson, J. (1995). Empathy and guilt: Early origins of feelings of responsibility. In J. P. Tangney & K. W. Fischer (Eds.), *Self-conscious emotions: The psychology of shame, guilt, embarrassment, and pride* (pp. 143–173). Guilford Press.

Zapata, I., Serpell, J. A., & Alvarez, C. E. (2016). Genetic mapping of canine fear and aggression. *BMC Genomics, 17*(1), 572. https://doi.org/10.1186/s12864-016-2936-3

CHAPTER 43

Comparative Psychology of Frustrative Nonreward

Carmen Torres and Mauricio R. Papini

Abstract

Research with mammals, including humans, shows that unexpected reward downshifts (omissions or reductions) can induce a negative emotional state, called frustrative nonreward, with behavioral, physiological, neurochemical, and molecular consequences. The successive negative contrast (SNC) task has been extensively used to study the effects of reward downshift. In SNC, a downshift from large to small rewards leads to a transient suppression of behavior compared to controls always exposed to small rewards. Behavioral suppression is accompanied by the release of stress hormones, ameliorated by anxiolytics and analgesics, reduced by lesions of the amygdala, and enhanced by lesions to the anterior cingulate cortex. Unlike mammals, other vertebrates exposed to reward downshifts tend to exhibit a gradual adjustment to the small reward, an effect called reversed SNC. This research is leading to a deeper understanding of the mechanisms and consequences of frustrative nonreward, including its effects on health and well-being in humans.

Key Words: frustrative nonreward, successive negative contrast, incentive disengagement, benzodiazepine, opioid, amygdala

Introduction

Frustration, disappointment, loss, psychological pain, and similar terms are commonly used to describe the negative emotional state induced by unexpected situations involving omitted, reduced, or inaccessible rewards. Examples of lost rewards include food, water, sex, social support, health, love, money, care, and others. These events often trigger what is scientifically called frustrative nonreward, a negative emotional state induced by worse-than-expected reward conditions (Papini et al., 2015). The health impact in humans has been recognized by the Research Domain Criteria (RDoC) initiative introduced by the National Institute of Mental Health, in which frustrative nonreward and loss are included as part of the Negative Valence System (Anderzhanova et al., 2017; Carcone & Ruocco, 2017). A variety of experimental paradigms have been developed to study frustrative nonreward under rigorous laboratory conditions, with successive negative contrast (SNC) being a commonly used procedure to induce frustration. SNC consists of a transient reduction in responding for a small reward after previous exposure to a larger reward under the same conditions (the downshift condition), in comparison to the behavior observed in a control group always exposed to the small reward (the unshift condition; Flaherty, 1996). The comparison of appetitive behavior in groups of participants exposed to downshifted vs. unshifted reward conditions has been applied to a variety of species, including humans and other mammals, birds, reptiles, amphibians, and fish. These studies illustrate the commonalities and differences in the behavior of these animals to cope with unexpected reward failures. Pharmacological, endocrine, psychogenetic, neurobiological, and molecular studies reviewed below provide evidence of the involvement of negative emotions in these situations, especially in rodents and humans. The study of SNC is opening an avenue to identify the brain mechanisms underlying frustration, their evolution in early mammals, the adaptive significance of frustrative nonreward, and its impact on human health and disease.

Frustrative Nonreward in Daily Experience
Receiving less reward than expected is a common experience. Our reaction and adjustment to such situations reflects the personal significance of the lost reward. For example, people asked whether losing $1,000 in a bet is devastating would probably answer, "It depends on how much money one has." We judge such situations in relative terms and feel distressed only when we assess the loss to be unexpected and significant. We are writing this chapter in the midst of a global COVID-19 pandemic (World Health Organization, 2020). One consequence of this pandemic involved an unexpected and sudden loss of significant sources of reward that interfere with daily routines: social distancing, stay-at-home directives, use of protective personal equipment, etc. (Mediouni et al., 2020). However, many have also gone through a serious health risk and still others have suffered the loss of loved ones.

The negative impact of loss derived from the COVID-19 outbreak in terms of mental health is gradually emerging and is being recorded by psychological and social scientists. Stress, anxiety, depression, irritability, isolation, uncertainty, addiction, and violence are some of the psychological consequences of the pandemic in the general population (Brooks et al., 2020; Serafini et al., 2020). Daily news organizations have also reported some of the consequences of the pandemic, for example, violent behavior in protest against lockdown measures in the Netherlands (Corder & Dejong, 2021) and death by drug overdose in the United States resulting from a confluence of factors, including social isolation derived from the COVID-19 pandemic (Horsley, 2021). Understanding the neurobehavioral basis of frustrative nonreward may have important implications for basic research and clinical management (e.g., Abler et al., 2005; Papini et al., 2015; Sukhodolsky et al., 2016). But perhaps a subtler point is that research on frustrative nonreward published over the past decades makes events such as violent behavior and excessive drug consumption, among others, predictable effects of the loss of rewards experienced during the pandemic (Amsel, 1992; Bitterman, 1944; Dollar et al., 1939; Gray, 1987; Panksepp, 2010; Torres & Papini, 2016).

This chapter reviews a small fraction of the research on this topic by focusing on the SNC effect, a widely used experimental paradigm to induce frustrative nonreward in the animal laboratory. Examples of the behavioral adjustments to unexpected reward downshift across species will illustrate the diversity of strategies that have evolved to cope with the absence and devaluation of reward. Among such diversity, only the behavior of mammals in these situations seems to exhibit negative emotional activation (Papini, 2003, 2014, 2022).

The Successive Negative Contrast Effect
The experimental study of frustrative nonreward (including reward omission and devaluation) has a long tradition in the psychology of learning as a field. Frustrative nonreward is a psychological construct that refers to the emotional response activated when individuals receive an incentive of lesser value than expected on the basis of prior experience under similar conditions (Amsel, 1992; Flaherty, 1996; Papini & Dudley, 1997; Papini et al., 2015). In SNC situations,

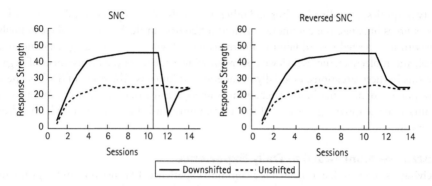

Figure 43.1. A representation of the successive negative contrast (SNC) effect (on the left) and the reversed SNC effect (on the right). Notice that in both cases, downshifted and unshifted groups differ during preshift sessions, thus indicating that the reward magnitudes had differential control over behavior. However, reward downshift leads to a transient rejection of the reward in the case of SNC, but to a gradual adjustment of behavior in the case of the reversed SNC effect. The SNC effect is observed in experiments with mammals, whereas the reversed SNC effect has been the common outcome in experiments with fish, amphibians, and reptiles. Both effects have been observed with birds.

a consummatory (cSNC), instrumental (iSNC), or Pavlovian response (pSNC) is reinforced with a large reward for a number of sessions during a "preshift" phase. Preshift experience is designed to induce a learned expectation of the reward. After this training, the magnitude or quality of the reward is surprisingly devalued during the "postshift" phase, an event aimed at violating that expectation previously acquired under the same conditions. This unexpected reward devaluation induces a transient behavioral suppression or impairment in the downshifted group that surpasses the behavioral level exhibited by a control group always exposed to the small reward. Demonstrations of this effect involved a rejection of a piece of lettuce when banana was expected in a choice situation by monkeys (Tinklepaugh, 1928); the disruption of an instrumental running response in rats by the unexpected finding of sunflower seeds, when a more appealing bran mash reward was expected (Elliott, 1928); the rejection of a 4% sucrose solution by rats, when a sweeter 32% sucrose reward was expected in a consummatory-response situation (Vogel et al., 1968); and a switch to a lever always paired with 2 pellets, when a second lever was downshifted from 12 to 2 pellets in a Pavlovian autoshaping situation (Conrad & Papini, 2018). In all these cases, animals facing the same reward conditions (access to a small or less preferred reward) behave differently as a function of their previous experience with the same reward (unshifted) vs. experience with a more preferred reward (downshifted). SNC is shown in Figure 43.1 (left panel). The SNC effect illustrates the concept of incentive relativity, a distortion in the absolute value of an incentive when this incentive occurs in the context of an inflated reward expectancy based on prior experience (Flaherty, 1996; Papini, 2022; Torres & Papini, 2017).

Comparative Research

Behavioral, psychogenetic, pharmacological, hormonal, and neurobiological studies in rodents and humans described below support the hypothesis that incentives of lesser value than expected activate negative emotion. However, comparative research suggests that non-mammalian vertebrates respond to downshifts in reward magnitude or quality without showing signs of negative emotion, even when the loss is significant (Bitterman, 1975; Papini, 2014; Papini & Torres, 2017). For example, goldfish (*Carassius auratus*) trained under either instrumental (Bitterman, 1984; Gonzalez et al., 1974; Lowes & Bitterman, 1967; Mackintosh, 1971) or consummatory (Couvillon & Bitterman, 1985) conditions showed either a gradual adjustment to reward devaluation or no behavioral change after the downshift, without exhibiting an SNC effect. The fact that these animals demonstrated differential control of behavior by the different reward magnitudes suggests that the absence of SNC was not due to the use of nondiscriminable rewards. The gradual adjustment of behavior or absence of behavioral change following reward downshift has been labeled as *reversed SNC effect* (Papini, 2014). The reversed SNC effect is illustrated in Figure 43.1 (right panel). Similar reversed SNC effects have been reported in several vertebrate species.

Turtles (*Chrysemys picta*, *Geoclemys reevesii*) also exhibited a gradual decrement in performance after an abrupt reduction in the magnitude of a reward, but no evidence of SNC (Papini & Ishida, 1994; Pert & Bitterman, 1970; Pert & Gonzalez, 1974). Similarly, terrestrial toads (*Rhinella arenarum*) respond to reward magnitude by acquiring a runway response faster under large rather than small amounts of water absorption (Schmajuk et al., 1980). However, reward downshift (involving a reduction in the amount of water or in time of access to water) led to a response adjustment without behavioral impairment (Papini et al., 1995; Schmajuk et al., 1981). Toads are extremely sensitive to dehydration as they depend on constant maintenance of water balance for survival. As a result, manipulating the sodium concentration of the water as the reward offers an alternative reward manipulation. Toads exposed to a downshift from distilled water (more preferred) to a slightly hypertonic sodium solution that causes minor dehydration (less preferred) exhibit a reversed SNC effect (Muzio et al., 2011). From an evolutionary perspective (Papini, 2021), goldfish (bony fish), turtles (reptiles), and toads (amphibians) belong to more conservative lineages of vertebrates that, according to fossil evidence, have diverged during the Paleozoic era, more than 250 million years ago. Compared to mammals and birds, they exhibit relatively smaller brains, but experience the same dependence on food, water, and other resources to survive and reproduce. Reversed SNC effects in these animals suggest that they must be using different behavioral strategies to adjust to the unexpected loss in rewards. But what about birds? Evolutionary and neuroscience evidence shows that birds have evolved during the Mesozoic era (at least 200 million years ago, during the Jurassic period) and exhibit relatively large brains, two features that they share with mammals (Papini, 2021).

When exposed to situations involving unexpected reward devaluation and omission, birds show a complex set of results. Reversed SNC effect have been found in pigeons (*Columba livia*). For example, animals trained in a Skinner box to peck at a key under spaced-training conditions (one trial per day) show faster acquisition with a large food reward (15 pigeon pellets) than with a small one (1 pigeon pellet). However, a 15-to-1 pellet downshift induced a gradual behavioral adjustment (Papini, 1997). There is also evidence that pigeons exposed to different magnitudes of reward downshift in an autoshaping key-peck task respond according to the preshift incentive value and independently of the postshift/preshift ratio, as is the case with rats (Pellegrini et al., 2008). Similar results were obtained with male quails (*Coturnix japonica*) rewarded by sexual access to either several (preshift) or just one (postshift) female (Baquero et al., 2009) and with pigeons in a runway situation exposed to appetitive extinction after acquisition with a large vs. small reward (Thomas & Papini, 2003). But not all avian species respond in similar fashion. For example, evidence of SNC (measured in terms of food consumption, but not in terms of feeder switching) has been reported in starlings (*Sturnus vulgaris*) receiving rewards varying in quality (from mealworms to Turkey crumbs; Freidin et al., 2009). Therefore, whether birds exhibit behavioral flexibility and negative emotion activation in reward downshift situations remains unclear (Papini et al., 2019).

Mammalian behavior seems to be controlled by both absolute and relative reward value (Papini, 2022). In mammalian species (including rodents and humans), adjustments to nonreward involve extensive (albeit transient) behavioral deterioration indicative of powerful emotional responses that break the attachment to a resource or associated site (i.e., incentive disengagement), thus promoting the adaptive redirection of behavior to other sources of reward (Papini, 2003; Papini et al., 2022; Stout et al., 2002). One of the most commonly used experimental paradigms to analyze frustrative nonreward involves giving animals access to sucrose solutions at different concentrations while assessing their consummatory behavior. In this cSNC task, animals receive free access for 5 minutes to a high-value sucrose solution (usually 32% sucrose) during several daily sessions, followed by several sessions of access to a low-value sucrose solution (usually 4% sucrose). Performance of downshifted animals is compared to the consummatory behavior of animals that have always received access to 4% sucrose—unshifted controls. The cSNC effect involves a suppression of consummatory behavior after the 32%-to-4% sucrose downshift followed by a recovery to the level of unshifted controls. The initial suppression (typically observed during the first devaluation session) and the recovery that follows (normally starting during the second devaluation session) are dissociable stages of the cSNC effect (Flaherty, 1996; Jiménez-García et al., 2019). Using this procedure, evidence of frustrative nonreward effects has been found in rats (Vogel et al., 1968), mice (Mustaca, Bentosela, et al., 2000), newborn babies (Kobre & Lipsitt, 1972), and didelphid marsupials (Papini et al., 1988). Changes in reward quality have been in turn used to collect evidence of similar cSNC effects in Mongolian gerbils (*Meriones unguiculatus*; Perez-Acosta et al., 2016) and monkeys (Tinklepaugh, 1928).

Behavioral Evidence of Negative Emotion
There is behavioral evidence of negative emotional activation under SNC conditions (Papini et al., 2015). Mammals (including humans) react to reward downshift by showing (during or after the loss event) responses similar to those observed in threatening situations, including performance disruption (Morillo-Rivero et al., 2020; Weinstein, 1981), escape (Daly, 1974), aggression (Azrin et al., 1966), potentiated startle reflex (Wagner, 1963), jumping (Adelman & Maatsch, 1956), distress vocalizations (Amsel, 1992), increased ambulation (Flaherty et al., 1978), sexual inhibition (Freiding & Mustaca, 2004), reduced dominant and aggressive responses (Mustaca & Martínez, 2000; Mustaca, Martínez, et al., 2000), odor emissions (Ludvigson, 1999), increased voluntary consumption of anxiolytic solutions (Manzo et al., 2015), and hypoalgesia (Jiménez-García et al., 2016; Mustaca & Papini, 2005). Behavioral reaction to nonreward seems to be augmented in animals selectively bred for high anxiety/emotional reactivity (Torres & Sabariego, 2014), including Roman Low-Avoidance (Gómez et al., 2009), Syracuse Low-Avoidance (Flaherty & Rowan, 1989), Lewis (Freet et al., 2006), and Spontaneously Hypertensive rats (Bentosela & Mustaca, 2005; Serafini et al., 2020). The fact that animals selectively bred on the basis of differences in their recovery rates from cSNC exhibit differences in response to mother-infant separation also support the connection between reward downshift and negative emotion (Ortega, Norris, et al., 2014).

Physiological Evidence of Negative Emotion
The available physiological evidence is also consistent with the emotional activation that follows reward downshifts described previously. For example, frustrative nonreward activates the hypothalamic-pituitary-adrenal axis, increasing plasma levels of stress hormones such as adrenocorticotropic hormone and corticosterone (Flaherty et al., 1985; Kawasaki & Iwasaki, 1997; Mitchell & Flaherty, 1998; Pecoraro et al., 2009). Moreover, exogenous administration

of corticosterone modulates emotional memory and behavior, increasing consummatory suppression when injected immediately after the first downshift session (Bentosela et al., 2006; Ruetti et al., 2008). As with other stressors, there is evidence suggesting that surprising reward omissions impair immune and autonomic system functioning, reducing lymphoblast proliferation (Mustaca, 1999), increasing values of skin conductance and blood pressure, and decreasing heart rate (Larche et al., 2017; Papini & Dudley, 1997; Scheirer et al., 2002).

Pharmacological Evidence of Negative Emotion

An additional source of evidence suggesting the involvement of negative emotion in nonreward situations is provided by pharmacological studies showing the selective sensitivity of the SNC effects, as measured in terms of consummatory and instrumental behavior, to the actions of anti-anxiety, opioid, and cannabinoid drugs (for an extended review of the pharmacology of cSNC, see Ortega et al., 2017; Papini et al., 2015).

GABAergic anxiolytic drugs consistently attenuate the behavioral impact of frustrative nonreward (Flaherty, 1996; Gray, 1987). Benzodiazepine anxiolytics (including chlordiazepoxide, flurazepam, and midazolam) and alcohol dose-dependently reduce consummatory suppression induced by reward downshift when administered before the second postshift session, but not when injected before the first downshift session (e.g., Becker & Flaherty, 1982; Flaherty et al., 1990; Flaherty et al., 1986; Liao & Chang, 2003; Ortega, Glueck, et al., 2014). Both chlordiazepoxide and ethanol have reducing effects on reward downshift during the initial session after several devaluation cycles (Flaherty, 1996; Flaherty et al., 1996). An increase in time of access to the downshifted reward during the initial postshift session (from 5 to 20 min) also facilitates the anxiolytic effects of chlordiazepoxide during the initial downshift event (Flaherty et al., 1986). Overall, these results suggest that these drugs facilitate recovery from SNC by reducing negative emotion activated after detecting and having some experience with the downshifted reward (Flaherty, 1996; Ortega et al., 2017). Post-trial administration of chlordiazepoxide seems to interfere with memory consolidation of the downshifted reward, promoting the maintenance of the discrepancy between the current (postshift) and the memorized (preshift) incentive, thus delaying the recovery from cSNC (Ortega, Glueck, et al., 2014). By contrast, barbiturates reduce cSNC when administered before either the first or the second downshift session (Flaherty et al., 1982). Barbiturates also facilitate GABAergic neurotransmission by acting on the $GABA_A$ receptor, but at a location different from that of the benzodiazepine site.

There is also evidence indicating that cSNC bidirectionally responds to the action of opioid drugs. For example, the nonselective opioid-receptor agonist morphine has small but reliable reducing effects on cSNC administered on the first or second postshift session (Rowan & Flaherty, 1987). Both effects are abolished by naloxone, a nonselective opioid-receptor antagonist. Naloxone also increases the consummatory suppression induced by the reward-downshift event (Daniel et al., 2009; Pellegrini et al., 2005).

Agonists and antagonists selective for specific opioid receptors seem to differentially modulate the initial reaction vs. the recovery from reward devaluation, while leaving intact the consummatory response itself. The selective delta opioid-receptor agonist DPDPE (D-Penicillamine2-D-Penicillamine5-enkephalin) and the antagonist naltrindole reduced and enhanced, respectively, the cSNC effect only when administered before the first downshift session (Pellegrini et al., 2005; Wood et al., 2005). Alternatively, U50,488H (a kappa opioid receptor agonist) promotes recovery from consummatory suppression starting on the second postshift session, without affecting the initial reaction to the reward devaluation (Wood et al., 2008). Overall, these results show the involvement of the opioid system in the onset (delta receptor) and recovery (kappa receptors) stages of the cSNC effect, suggesting a relationship between the evolution of the opioid system and the evolution of adjustment mechanisms to frustrative nonreward in vertebrates (Papini, 2009).

Studies with cannabinoid drugs merit consideration, as the cannabinoid system also has a relevant role in the modulation of emotion and pain processing (Valverde, 2005; Woodhams et al., 2017). Agonists selective for the type-1 cannabinoid (CB_1) receptors, such as CP-55,940, abolished the cSNC effect (Genn, Tucci, et al., 2004). Alternative CB_1 agonists (WIN 55-212,2) injected into the basolateral amygdala blocked the negative impact of an aversive experience (open space exposure) on iSNC (Ramot & Akirav, 2012). Chronic WIN 55,212-2 administration also increased resistance to change after reward downshift (Conrad et al., 2022). Studies showing significant effects of delta-9-tetrahydrocannabinol (an active analgesic component in marijuana) in reward omission situations also support an involvement of the cannabinoid system in frustrative nonreward (Drewnowski & Gray, 1975; Gonzalez et al., 1971; Mason, 1983).

In summary, the pharmacological studies reviewed here show the predictive validity of cSNC to detect drugs with attenuating effects on emotional activation derived from reward devaluation. These drugs include GABAergic anxiolytics, and opioid and cannabinoid analgesics. The effects of these analgesics support the conceptualization of frustrative nonreward as psychological pain (Papini et al., 2006; Papini et al., 2015).

Neurobiological Evidence of Negative Emotion

The effects of psychopharmacological manipulations of the cSNC effect reviewed previously are consistent with the view that this is a dynamic process with sequential components of detection, evaluation, conflict, and resolution. It seems, then, that different mechanisms selectively acting on each postshift stage regulate the behavioral strategies used by animals to cope with reward devaluation. Neural manipulation and recording studies also indicate that the violation of reward expectancies elicits prediction error signals affecting brain processes in a hierarchical manner, via top-down and bottom-up flow of information (Korka et al., 2020). A variety of brain mechanisms regulate the adjustment to nonreward, including taste processing, reward-downshift detection, reward comparison, negative emotion, and memory update, among others. Some of this complexity is captured by a two-level neural circuitry hypothesized to be involved in the initial response to reward devaluation in the consummatory situation (Ortega et al., 2017). The first level governs the taste-licking modal action pattern, which involves the detection and then consumption of sucrose (Jones et al., 2006). The taste of sucrose generates impulses that travel from the sensory receptors located in the tongue along cranial nerves to brainstem nuclei, including the nucleus of the solitary tract (Lundy & Norgren, 2004a), that in turn project to brainstem nuclei organizing the licking response via motor cranial nerves. While signal transmission can independently produce the licking response at the brainstem level (Flynn & Grill, 1988), taste information also reaches a second level involving several forebrain structures that modulate negative emotion, reward comparison, and motor control. Brain areas in this second level are specialized in detecting the discrepancy between current and expected reward values, assigning a negative valence to the current reward, and suppressing consummatory behavior (Ortega et al., 2017).

Studies involving neural manipulation procedures have proposed a critical role of the amygdala in the cSNC effect, including modulation of gustatory information (Lundy & Norgren, 2004b), reward comparison (Becker et al., 1984; Kawasaki et al., 2017), and negative emotion (Kawasaki et al., 2015; Liao & Chuang, 2003). For example, excitotoxic lesions of the basolateral amygdala (BLA) eliminated the effects of reward devaluation in two procedures dependent on reward comparison: cSNC and anticipatory negative contrast (ANC). ANC involves exposure to the same sucrose solutions, but in a different order. In every session, the animal receives access to 4% sucrose for a few minutes, followed immediately by access to 32% sucrose. ANC involves suppression of licking for 4% sucrose relative to an unshifted group in which the second solution is also 4% sucrose (4% consumption is more suppressed before 32% than before 4% sucrose). ANC is not sensitive to treatment with benzodiazepine anxiolytics, suggesting that it does not involve a significant negative emotional component (Flaherty, 1996). The fact that BLA lesions eliminate both cSNC and ANC suggests that the lesion affected a common feature of these situations, namely, reward comparisons: contrasting the current reward with the memory (retrospective or prospective) of a more preferred reward. However, the BLA lesion did not affect exploratory activity in the open field, an animal test known to induce negative emotion as rats find it threatening to move about an open space (Kawasaki et al., 2017). Consistent with the reward comparison function, c-Fos (a gene-transcription factor activated by neuron depolarizations) and phosphorylated cyclic adenosine monophosphate responsive element-binding protein (pCREB, a molecular marker of synaptic plasticity) expression were both heightened after the devaluation event (Pecoraro & Dallman, 2005; Glueck et al., 2015). The reward-comparison mechanism seems to be partially dependent on converging inputs into the BLA coming from the gustatory thalamus and from the insular cortex. Evidence indicates that lesions of the gustatory thalamus and insular cortex eliminate the cSNC effect (Lin et al., 2009; Reilly & Trifunovic, 2003). One hypothesis (Kawasaki et al., 2017) suggests that the BLA receives information from the gustatory thalamus about the current reward (i.e., the downshift, 4% sucrose) and from the insular cortex about the remembered reward (i.e., the preshift, 32% sucrose). The BLA would then compare these inputs and somehow decide whether to suppress consummatory behavior and reject the downshifted reward, or promote consummatory behavior.

When the comparison process detects a significant negative discrepancy between the current and the expected rewards, neural signals traveling from the BLA to the central amygdala (CeA) would activate a negative emotional circuit (Ortega et al., 2017). Consistent with this view, downshifted rats with lesions in the CeA exhibited a reduced cSNC relative to unshifted animals with lesions and to sham controls (Becker et al., 1984). Additionally, Kawasaki et al. (2015) found that transient inactivation of the CeA (via lidocaine microinfusion) before the first downshift session led to an attenuated cSNC effect, along with signs of anxiolysis as registered in a lighted open field (increased locomotor activity in the central area). Moreover, chemogenetic inhibition of the CeA on sessions involving reward downshift also eliminated the cSNC effect relative to unshifted controls also receiving the chemogenetic inhibition treatment (Guarino et al., 2020). Finally, local CeA infusion of the benzodiazepine diazepam similarly abolished consummatory suppression induced by reward devaluation, while leaving intact the consummatory response of unshifted subjects (Liao & Chuang, 2003). The fact that the anti-contrast effect of diazepam was more profound with drug administration on the second postshift session (see above) suggests that recovery from reward downshift might require the inhibition of CeA neurons and thus release from their suppressing effect on consummatory behavior.

The nucleus accumbens (NAc) is another brain region that receives neural signals from the BLA. There is evidence suggesting that the NAc is involved in the processing of reward omissions (Biesdorf et al., 2015; Judice-Daher & Bueno, 2013). With respect to reward devaluation, even though NAc lesions did not affect cSNC performance (Eagle et al., 1999; Leszczuk & Flaherty, 2000), a microdialysis study found evidence of a significant drop in dopamine release by NAc neurons during the first reward devaluation event, relative to unshifted controls receiving a similar reward, 4% sucrose (Genn, Ahn, et al., 2004). c-Fos activation has also been detected in the NAc following reward devaluation (Pecoraro & Dallman, 2005) and chemogenetic excitation of the NAc increased consummatory suppression after reward downshift (Guarino et al., 2023). Overall, these results suggest the involvement in the NAc not only in the processing of the reward, but also in the frustration response induced by the failure to obtain the expected incentive (Ortega et al., 2017). This role could be partially dependent on the inhibitory function that the lateral habenula (LHb) exerts on ventral tegmental area (VTA) neurons projecting to the NAc (Kimura et al., 2007). In fact, the LHb has been proposed to detect negative prediction errors in situations involving reward omissions (Donaire et al., 2019; Friedman et al., 2010; Friedman et al., 2011). The LHb also regulates behavior in a variety of aversive paradigms (Hu et al., 2020), and its involvement in cSNC situations is suggested by increased c-Fos expression after reward downshift (Agüera et al., 2023). The role of the dorsomedial striatum in reward downshift situations is also controversial. Whereas increased pCREB expression and c-Fos activation have been reported following reward devaluation (Glueck et al., 2015; Pecoraro & Dallman, 2005), its lesion did not affect the cSNC effect, although it did reduce Pavlovian lever pressing under conditions of reward uncertainty (Torres et al., 2016).

In addition to the CeA and the NAc, the BLA also sends information to the anterior cingulate cortex (ACC), a part of the brain's limbic system specialized in integrating inputs from various sources, including motivation, error evaluation, and representations from cognitive and emotional networks (Bush et al., 2000). Its involvement in the control of behavior induced by reward devaluation is supported by studies showing reduced pCREB expression and c-Fos activation in animals exposed to reward downshift in the cSNC situation (Glueck et al., 2015; Pecoraro & Dallman, 2005). In the same vein, lesion studies reported retarded recovery from reward downshift in the cSNC task, relative to unshifted animals with ACC lesion and to downshifted and unshifted animals with sham surgery (Ortega et al., 2011). These results were interpreted as indicating a role of the ACC in coping with frustrative nonreward by promoting learning of the new incentive conditions. Although speculative, an inhibitory influence of the ACC on CeA neurons has been proposed as responsible for this memory update function (Ortega et al., 2017).

Molecular (c-Fos activation) and lesion studies also suggest a role of the orbitofrontal cortex (OFC) in the regulation of the behavioral adjustment to reward downshift (Ortega et al., 2013; Pecoraro & Dallman, 2005). For example, animals receiving electrolytic lesions in the ventrolateral portion of the OFC exhibited a reduced suppression of the consummatory behavior during the first postshift session of a cSNC task. Similar to lesions of the dorsomedial striatum, animals with OFC lesions also showed reduced activation of Pavlovian lever pressing. None of these effects was observed in animals with lesions in the medial prefrontal cortex (mPFC), which just showed decreased consumption of the lowest, 4% sucrose reward under unshifted conditions (Ortega et al., 2013). By contrast, Pecoraro et al. (2008) found evidence of faster recovery from reward downshift after lesions of the mPFC, although the lack of appropriate unshifted controls in this study made the interpretation of these results difficult. Enhanced c-Fos and pCREB expression in the prelimbic section of the mPFC following reward devaluation in the cSNC task have also been reported (Glueck et al., 2015; Pecoraro & Dallman, 2005).

The studies reviewed in this section have identified some of the key components of the neural circuit governing mammalian behavior during reward downshift in the cSNC task. These components are organized into two distinct levels that ultimately control and modulate licking behavior during events involving reward downshift. A brainstem circuit controls the taste-licking modal action pattern, whereas several telencephalic (BLA, CeA, NAc, ACC, insular cortex, and possibly OFC) and diencephalic areas (gustatory thalamus and LHb) modulate the activity of that modal action pattern, enhancing or attenuating the behavioral suppression that follows reward downshift. These areas are in charge of motor control, reward processing, reward comparison, negative emotion, and decision-making involved in the behavioral adjustment to incentive relativity (Ortega et al., 2017). Still unidentified are the specific pathways involved in the two major components of the cSNC effect, namely, the initial suppression of appetitive behavior once the downshift is detected (hypothesized above to involve the BLA-CeA pathway) and the recovery of normal levels of appetitive behavior that follows the cumulative experience with the new reward conditions (hypothesized above to involve the BLA-NAc pathway).

Concluding Remarks

This review has focused on the variety of behavioral adjustments that animals display when dealing with surprising nonreward, with attention to studies conducted with mammals (mainly rats) involving reward downshift manipulations. The factors affecting SNC and the consequences of SNC are summarized in Figure 43.2. Mammals, including humans, consistently react to these manipulations by exhibiting signs of emotional activation and frustration, including behavioral disruption, rejection of the downshifted reward, activation of the hypothalamic-pituitary-adrenal axis, changes in aggressive, sexual, and pain-related responses, and increased voluntary consumption of anti-anxiety drugs (Papini & Dudley, 1997; Papini et al., 2015; Torres & Papini, 2016). Pharmacological and neurobiological studies reviewed here suggest the existence of unique brain circuits that allow mammals to disengage from sources of reinforcement that are no longer available. In this view, negative emotions promote behavioral flexibility via an incentive disengagement process, leading the animal to search for alternative sources of reward (Papini, 2003; Papini et al., 2022). Future experiments will

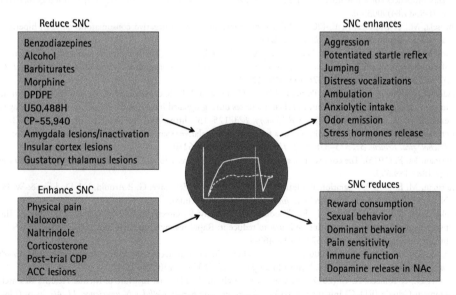

Figure 43.2. Some of the factors that affect SNC and some of the consequences of exposure to reward downshift in the SNC situation. For a more complete list, see Papini et al. (2015) and Ortega et al. (2017).

extend our understanding of the neurobiology of mammalian frustration and identify the equivalent circuit in non-mammalian vertebrates that respond to unexpected reward downshifts on the basis of their absolute values (Papini, 2014, 2022).

As mammals, we humans are also familiar with the emotional consequences of frustrative nonreward as a major source of psychological pain, negative affect, and conflict. This is validated by evidence showing increased risk of psychopathology after having experienced reward loss (e.g., anxiety, depression, post-traumatic stress, drug abuse, etc.; Huston et al., 2013; Papini et al., 2015). The pervasive influence of reward loss in our daily life during the COVID-19 outbreak brings into focus research on the properties, conditions, mechanisms, and health consequences of frustrative nonreward.

References

Abler, B., Walter, H., & Erk, S. (2005). Neural correlates of frustration. *Neuroreport, 16*, 669–672. https://doi.org/10.1097/00001756-200505120-00003.

Adelman, H. M., & Maatsch, J. L. (1956). Learning and extinction based upon frustration, food reward, and exploratory tendency. *Journal of Experimental Psychology, 52*, 311–315. https://doi.org/10.1037/h0045947.

Agüera, A. D. R., Espósito, A. N., Zafra, D., Sabariego, M., Papini, M. R., & Torres, C. (2023). *Surprising reward downshift activates the lateral habenula, but not the medial habenula, as measured in terms of c-Fos.* IBRO World Congress of Neuroscience, Granada, Spain, September, 2023.

Amsel, A. (1992). *Frustration theory: An analysis of dispositional learning and memory.* Cambridge University Press.

Anderzhanova, E., Kirmeier, T., & Wotjak, C. T. (2017). Animal models in psychiatric research: The RDoC system as a new framework for endophenotype-oriented translational neuroscience. *Neurobiology of Stress, 7*, 47–56. https://doi.org/10.1016/j.ynstr.2017.03.003.

Azrin, N. H., Hutchinson, R. R., & Hake, D. F. (1966). Extinction-induced aggression 1. *Journal of the Experimental Analysis of Behavior, 9*, 191–204. https://doi.org/10.1901/jeab.1966.9-191.

Baquero, A., Puerta, A., & Gutiérrez, G. (2009). Magnitude effects of sexual reinforcement in Japanese quail (*Coturnix japonica*). *International Journal of Comparative Psychology, 22*, 113–126.

Becker, H. C., & Flaherty, C. F. (1982). Influence of ethanol on contrast in consummatory behavior. *Psychopharmacology, 77*, 253–258. https://doi.org/10.1007/BF00464576.

Becker, H. C., Jarvis, M. F., Wagner, G. C., & Flaherty, C. F. (1984). Medial and lateral amygdalectomy differentially influences consummatory negative contrast. *Physiology & Behavior, 33*, 707–712. https://doi.org/10.1016/0031-9384(84)90035-0.

Bentosela, M., & Mustaca, A. E. (2005). Efectos del contraste sucesivo negativo consumatorio en ratas hipertensas: ¿Una cuestión de memoria? *Suma Psicológica, 12*, 87–100.

Bentosela, M., Ruetti, E., Muzio, R. N., Mustaca, A. E., & Papini, M. R. (2006). Administration of corticosterone after the first downshift trial enhances consummatory successive negative contrast. *Behavioral Neuroscience, 120*, 371–376. https://doi.org/10.1037/0735-7044.120.2.371.

Biesdorf, C., Wang, A. L., Topic, B., Petri, D., Milani, H., Huston, J. P., & de Souza Silva, M. A. (2015). Dopamine in the nucleus accumbens core, but not shell, increases during signaled food reward and decreases during delayed extinction. *Neurobiology of Learning and Memory, 123*, 125–139. https://doi.org/10.1016/j.nlm.2015.06.002.

Bitterman, M. E. (1944). Behavior disorder as a function of the relative strength of antagonistic response-tendencies. *Psychological Review, 51*, 375–378. https://doi.org/10.1037/h0062108

Bitterman, M. E. (1975). The comparative analysis of learning. *Science, 188*, 699–709. https://doi.org/10.1126/science.188.4189.699.

Bitterman, M. E. (1984). Migration and learning in fishes. In J. D. McCleave, G. P. Arnold, J. J. Dodson, & W. H. Neill (Eds.), *Mechanisms of migration in fishes* (pp. 394–420). Plenum.

Brooks, S. K., Webster, R., Smith, L. E., Woodland, L., Wessely, S., Greenberg, N., & Rubin, G. J. (2020). The psychological impact of quarantine and how to reduce it: Rapid review of the evidence. *Lancet, 395*, 912–920. https://doi.org/10.1016/S0140-6736(20)30460-8.

Bush, G., Luu, P., & Posner, M. (2000). Cognitive and emotional influences in the anterior cingulate cortex. *Trends in Cognitive Sciences, 4*, 215–222. https://doi.org/10.1016/S1364-6613(00)01483-2.

Carcone, D., & Ruocco, A. C. (2017). Six years of research on the National Institute of Mental Health's Research Domain Criteria (RDoC) initiative: A systematic review. *Frontiers in Cellular Neuroscience, 11*, 46. https://doi.org/10.3389/fncel.2017.00046.

Conrad, S. E., Davis, D., Vilcek, N., Thompson, J. B., Guarino, S., Papini, S., & Papini, M. R. (2022). Frustrative nonreward and cannabinoid receptors: Chronic (but not acute) WIN 55,212-2 treatment increased resistance to change in two reward downshift tasks. *Pharmacology Biochemistry & Behavior, 213*, 173320. https://doi.org/10.1016/j.pbb.2021.173320

Conrad, S., & Papini, M. R. (2018). Reward shifts in forced-choice and free-choice autoshaping with rats. *Journal of Experimental Psychology: Animal Learning and Cognition, 44*, 422–440. https://doi.org/10.1037/xan0000187.

Corder, M., & Dejong, P. (2021, January 24). Dutch police clash with anti-lockdown protesters in 2 cities. *AP News*. Retrieved from https://apnews.com/article/netherlands-health-coronavirus-pandemic-riots-amsterdam-550ce0c260d45131181727fbf41e8340.

Couvillon, P. A., & Bitterman, M. E. (1985). Effect of experience with a preferred food on consummatory responding for a less preferred food in goldfish. *Animal Learning & Behavior, 13*, 433–438. https://doi.org/10.3758/BF03208020.

Daly, H. B. (1974). Reinforcing properties of escape from frustration aroused in various learning situations. *Psychology of Learning and Motivation, 8*, 187–231. https://doi.org/10.1016/S0079-7421(08)60455-7.

Daniel, A. M., Ortega, L. A., & Papini, M. R. (2009). Role of the opioid system in incentive downshift situations. *Neurobiology of Learning & Memory, 92*, 439–450. https://doi.org/10.1016/j.nlm.2009.06.003.

Dollard, J., Doob, L. W., Miller, N. E., Mowrer, O. H., & Sears, R. R. (1939). *Frustration and aggression*. Yale University Press.

Donaire, R., Morón, I., Blanco, S., Villatoro, A., Gámiz, F., Papini, M. R., & Torres, C. (2019). Lateral habenula lesions disrupt appetitive extinction, but do not affect voluntary alcohol consumption. *Neuroscience Letters, 703*, 184–190. https://doi.org/10.1016/j.neulet.2019.03.044 .

Drewnowski, A., & Gray, J. A. (1975). Influence of delta9-tetrahydrocannabinol on partial reinforcement effects. *Psychopharmacologia, 43*, 233–237. https://doi.org/10.1007/bf00429256.

Eagle, D. M., Humby, T., Howman, M., Reid-Henry, A., Dunnett, S. B., & Robbins, T. W. (1999). Differential effects of ventral and regional dorsal striatal lesions on sucrose drinking and positive and negative contrast in rats. *Psychobiology, 27*, 267–276.

Elliott, M. H. (1928). The effect of change of reward on the maze performance of rats. *University of California Publications in Psychology, 4*, 19–30.

Flaherty, C. F. (1996). *Incentive relativity*. Cambridge University Press.

Flaherty, C. F., Becker, H. C., & Driscoll, C. (1982). Conditions under which amobarbital sodium influences contrast in consummatory behavior. *Physiological Psychology, 10*, 122–128. https://doi.org/10.3758/BF03327016.

Flaherty, C. F., Becker, H. C., & Pohorecky, L. (1985). Correlation of corticosterone elevation and negative contrast varies as a function of postshift day. *Animal Learning and Behavior, 13*(3), 309–314. https://doi.org/10.3758/BF03200025.

Flaherty, C. F., Blitzer, R., & Collier, G. H. (1978). Open-field behaviors elicited by reward reduction. *American Journal of Psychology, 91*, 429–443. https://doi.org/10.2307/1421690.

Flaherty, C. F., Clark, S., & Coppotelli, C. (1996). Lack of tolerance to the contrast-reducing actions of chlordiazepoxide with repeated reward reductions. *Physiology & Behavior, 60*, 645–652. https://doi.org/10.1016/S0031-9384(96)80043-6.

Flaherty, C. F., Grigson, P. S., & Lind, S. (1990). Chlordiazepoxide and the moderation of the initial response to reward reduction. *Quarterly Journal of Experimental Psychology, 42B*, 87–105. https://doi.org/10.1080/14640749008401873.

Flaherty, C. F., Grigson, P. S., & Rowan, G. A. (1986). Chlordiazepoxide and the determinants of contrast. *Animal Learning & Behavior, 14*, 315–321. https://doi.org/10.3758/BF03200073.

Flaherty, C. F., & Rowan, G. A. (1989). Rats (*Rattus norvegicus*) selectively bred to differ in avoidance behavior also differ in response to novelty stress, in glycemic conditioning, and in reward contrast. *Behavioral & Neural Biology, 51*, 145–164. https://doi.org/10.1016/S0163-1047(89)90782-6.

Flynn, F. W., & Grill, H. J. (1988). Intraoral intake and taste reactivity responses elicited by sucrose and sodium chloride in chronic decerebrate rats. *Behavioral Neuroscience, 102*, 934–941. https://doi.org/10.1037//0735-7044.102.6.934.

Freet, C. S., Tesche, J. D., Tompers, D. M., Riegel, K. E., & Grigson, P. S. (2006). Lewis rats are more sensitive than Fischer rats to successive negative contrast, but less sensitive to the anxiolytic and appetite-stimulating effects of chlordiazepoxide. *Pharmacology, Biochemistry, and Behavior, 85*, 378–384. https://doi.org/10.1016/j.pbb.2006.09.005.

Freidin, E., Cuello, M. I., & Kacelnik, A. (2009). Successive negative contrast in a bird: Starlings' behavior after unpredictable negative changes in food quality. *Animal Behaviour, 77*, 857–865. https://doi.org/10.1016/j.anbehav.2008.12.010.

Freidin, E., & Mustaca, A. E. (2004). Frustration and sexual behavior in male rats. *Animal Learning and Behavior, 32*, 311–320. https://doi.org/10.3758/BF03196030.

Friedman, A., Lax, E., Dikshtein, Y., Abraham, L., Flaumenhaft, Y., Sudai, E., Tzion, M. B., Ami-Ad, L., Rami, Y., & Yadid, G. (2010). Electrical stimulation of the lateral habenula produces enduring inhibitory effect on cocaine seeking behavior. *Neuropharmacology, 59*, 452–459. https://doi.org/10.1016/j.neuropharm.2010.06.008.

Friedman, A., Lax, E., Dikshtein, Y., Abraham, L., Flaumenhaft, Y., Sudai, E., Tzion, B. M., & Yadid, G. (2011). Electrical stimulation of the lateral habenula produces an inhibitory effect on sucrose self-administration. *Neuropharmacology, 60*, 381–387. https://doi.org/10.1016/j.neuropharm.2010.10.006.

Genn, R. F., Ahn, S., & Phillips, A. G. (2004). Attenuated dopamine efflux in the rat nucleus accumbens during successive negative contrast. *Behavioral Neuroscience, 118*, 869–973. https://doi.org/10.1037/0735-7044.118.4.869.

Genn, R.F., Tucci, S., Parikh, S., & File, S.E. (2004). Effects of nicotine and a cannabinoid receptor agonist on negative contrast: Distinction between anxiety and disappointment? *Psychopharmacology, 177*, 93–99. https://doi.org/10.1007/s00213-004-1932-5.

Glueck, A. C., Dennis, T. S., Perrotti, L. I., Torres, C., & Papini, M. R. (2015). Brain expression of pCREB in rats exposed to consummatory successive negative contrast. *Neuroscience Letters, 587*, 93–97. https://doi.org/10.1016/j.neulet.2014.12.036.

Gómez, M. J., Escarabajal, M. D., de la Torre, L., Tobeña, A., Fernández-Teruel, A., & Torres, C. (2009). Consummatory successive negative and anticipatory contrast effects in inbred Roman rats. *Physiology & Behavior, 97*, 374–380. https://doi.org/10.1016/j.physbeh.2009.03.003.

Gonzalez, R. C., Ferry, M., & Powers, A.S. (1974). The adjustment of goldfish to reduction in magnitude of reward in massed trials. *Animal Learning & Behavior, 2*, 23–26. https://doi.org/10.3758/BF03199111

Gonzalez, S. C., Matsudo, V. K. R., & Carlini, E. A. (1971). Effects of marihuana compounds on the fighting behaviour of Siamese fighting fish (*Betta splendens*). *Pharmacology, 6*, 186–190. https://doi.org/10.1159/000136241.

Gray, J. A. (1987). *The psychology of fear and stress* (2nd ed.). Cambridge University Press.

Guarino, S., Conrad, S. E., & Papini, M. R. (2020). Frustrative nonreward: Chemogenetic inactivation of the central amygdala abolishes the effect of reward downshift without affecting alcohol intake. *Neurobiology of Learning and Memory, 169*, 1–7. https://doi.org/10.1016/j.nlm.2020.107173.

Guarino, S., Hagen, C., Nguyen, Q., & Papini, M. R. (2023). Frustrative nonreward and the basal ganglia: Chemogenetic inhibition and excitation of the nucleus accumbens and globus pallidus externus during reward downshift. *Neurobiology of Learning and Memory, 200*, 107736. https://doi.org/10.1016/j.nlm.2023.107736

Horsley, S. (2021, January 28). They lost sons to drug overdoses: How the pandemic may be fueling deaths of despair. *National Public Radio*. Retrieved from https://apnews.com/article/netherlands-health-coronavirus-pandemic-riots-amsterdam-550ce0c260d45131181727fbf41e8340).

Hu, H., Cui, Y., & Yang, Y. (2020). Circuits and functions of the lateral habenula in health and in disease. *Nature Reviews Neuroscience, 21*, 277–295. https://doi.org/10.1038/s41583-020-0292-4.

Huston, J. P., de Souza Silva, M. A., Komorowski, M., Schulz, D., & Topic, B. (2013). Animal models of extinction-induced depression: loss of reward and its consequences. *Neuroscience and Biobehavioral Reviews, 37*, 2059–2070. https://doi.org/10.1016/j.neubiorev.2013.02.016.

Jiménez-Garcia, A. M., Ruiz-Leyva, L., Cendán, C. M., Torres, C., Papini, M. R., & Morón, I. (2016). Hypoalgesia induced by reward devaluation in rats. *PLoS ONE, 11*, e0164331. https://doi.org/10.1371/journal.pone.0164331.

Jiménez-García, A. M., Ruiz-Leyva, L., Vázquez-Agredos, A., Torres, C., Papini, M. R., Cendán, C. M., & Morón, I. (2019). Consummatory successive negative contrast. *Bio-protocol, 9*, e3201. https://doi.org/10.21769/BioProtoc.3201.

Jones, L. M., Fontanini, A., & Katz, D. B. (2006). Gustatory processing: A dynamic systems approach. *Current Opinion in Neurobiology, 16*, 420–428. https://doi.org/10.1016/j.conb.2006.06.011.

Judice-Daher, D. M., & Bueno, J. L. O. (2013). Lesions of the nucleus accumbens disrupt reinforcement omission effects in rats. *Behavioural Brain Research, 252*, 439–443. https://doi.org/10.1016/j.bbr.2013.06.028.

Kawasaki, K., Annicchiarico, I., Glueck, A. C., Morón, I., & Papini, M. R. (2017). Reward loss and the basolateral amygdala: A function in reward comparisons. *Behavioural Brain Research, 331*, 205–213. https://doi.org/10.1016/j.bbr.2017.05.036.

Kawasaki, K., Glueck, A. C., Annicchiarico, I., & Papini, M. R. (2015). Function of the centromedial amygdala in reward devaluation and open-field activity. *Neuroscience, 303*, 73–81. https://doi.org/10.1016/j.neuroscience.2015.06.053.

Kawasaki, K., & Iwasaki, T. (1997). Corticosterone levels during extinction of runway responses in rats. *Life Sciences, 61*, 1721–1728. https://doi.org/10.1016/S0024-3205(97)00778-9.

Kimura, M., Satoh, T., & Matsumoto N. (2007). What does the habenula tell dopamine neurons? *Nature Neuroscience, 10*, 677–678. https://doi.org/10.1038/nn0607-677.

Kobre, K. R., & Lipsitt, L. P. (1972). A negative contrast effect in newborns. *Journal of Experimental Child Psychology, 14,* 81–91. https://doi.org/10.1016/0022-0965(72)90033-1

Korka, B., Schröger, E., & Widmann, A. (2020). What exactly is missing here? The sensory processing of unpredictable omissions is modulated by the specificity of expected action-effects. *European Journal of Neuroscience, 52,* 4667–4683. https://doi.org/10.1111/ejn.14899.

Larche, C. J., Musielak, N., & Dixon, M. J. (2017). The Candy Crush sweet tooth: How "near- misses" in Candy Crush increase frustration, and the urge to continue gameplay. *Journal of Gambling Studies, 33,* 599–615. https://doi.org/10.1007/s10899-016-9633-7.

Leszczuk, M. H., & Flaherty, C. F. (2000). Lesions of nucleus accumbens reduce instrumental but not consummatory negative contrast in rats. *Behavioural Brain Research, 116,* 61–79. https://doi.org/10.1016/s0166-4328(00)00265-5.

Liao, R. M., & Chuang, F. J. (2003). Differential effects of diazepam infused into the amygdala and hippocampus on negative contrast. *Pharmacology, Biochemistry & Behavior, 74,* 953–960. https://doi.org/10.1016/s0091-3057(03)00023-6.

Lin, J. Y., Roman, C., & Reilly, S. (2009). Insular cortex and consummatory successive negative contrast in the rat. *Behavioral Neuroscience, 123,* 810–814. https://doi.org/10.1037/a0016460.

Lowes, G., & Bitterman, M. E. (1967). Reward and learning in the goldfish. *Science, 157,* 455–457. https://doi.org/10.1126/science.157.3787.455.

Ludvigson, H. W. (1999). General introduction to the special issue: Odorous episodes and episodic odors. *Psychological Record, 49,* 371–378. https://doi.org/10.1007/BF03395939.

Lundy, R. F., & Norgren, R. (2004a). Gustatory system. In *The Rat Nervous System* (pp. 891–921). Elsevier. https://doi.org/10.1016/B978-012547638-6/50029-8

Lundy, R. F., & Norgren, R. (2004b). Activity in the hypothalamus, amygdala, and cortex generates bilateral and convergent modulation of pontine gustatory neurons. *Journal of Neurophysiology, 91,* 1143–1157. https://doi.org/10.1152/jn.00840.2003.

Mackintosh, N. J. (1971). Reward and aftereffects of reward in the learning of goldfish. *Journal of Comparative and Physiological Psychology, 76,* 225–232. https://doi.org/10.1037/h0031405.

Manzo, L., Donaire, R., Sabariego, M., Papini, M. R., & Torres, C. (2015). Anti-anxiety self-medication in rats: Oral consumption of chlordiazepoxide and ethanol after reward devaluation. *Behavioural Brain Research, 278,* 90–97. https://doi.org/10.1016/j.bbr.2014.09.017.

Mason, S. T. (1983). The neurochemistry and pharmacology of extinction behavior. *Neuroscience & Biobehavioral Reviews, 7,* 325–347. https://doi.org/10.1016/0149-7634(83)90036-2.

Mediouni, M., Madiouni, R., & Kaczor-Urbanowicz, K. E. (2020). COVID-19: How the quarantine could lead to the depreobesity. *Obesity Medicine, 19,* 100255. https://doi.org/10.1016/j.obmed.2020.100255.

Mitchell, C., & Flaherty, C. F. (1998). Temporal dynamics of corticosterone elevation in successive negative contrast. *Physiology and Behavior, 64,* 287–292. https://doi.org/10.1016/S0031-9384(98)00072-9.

Morillo-Rivero, L. E., Ibáñez-Molina, A. J., & Torres, C. (2020). Successive negative contrast in humans: Dissociation between behavioral and affective measures of frustration. *Learning and Motivation, 70,* 101634. https://doi.org/10.1016/j.lmot.2020.101634.

Mustaca, A. E. (1999). Respuestas rápidas bifásicas del sistema inmune por frustración y euforia. *Revista Latinoamericana de Psicología, 31,* 133–149.

Mustaca, A. E., Bentosela, M., & Papini, M. R. (2000). Consummatory successive negative contrast in mice. *Learning and Motivation, 31,* 272–282. https://doi.org/10.1006/lmot.2000.1055.

Mustaca, A. E., & Martínez, C. (2000). Respuestas agonísticas en ratas sometidas a frustración [Agonistic responses in rats submitted to frustration]. *Revista Latinoamericana de Psicología, 32,* 485–504.

Mustaca, A. E., Martínez, C., & Papini, M. R. (2000). Surprising nonreward reduces aggressive behavior in rats. *International Journal of Comparative Psychology, 13,* 91–100.

Mustaca, A. E., & Papini, M. R. (2005). Consummatory successive contrast induces hypoalgesia. *International Journal of Comparative Psychology, 18,* 333–339.

Muzio, R. N., Pistone-Creydt, V., Iurman, M., Rinaldi, M. A., Sirani, B., & Papini, M. R. (2011). Incentive or habit learning in amphibians? *PLoS ONE, 6,* 1–12. https://doi.org/10.1371/journal.pone.0025798.

Ortega, L. A., Glueck, A. C., Daniel, A. M., Prado-Rivera, M. A., White, M. M., & Papini, M. R. (2014). Memory interfering effects of chlordiazepoxide on consummatory successive negative contrast. *Pharmacology, Biochemistry, and Behavior, 116,* 96–106. https://doi.org/10.1016/j.pbb.2013.11.031.

Ortega, L. A., Glueck, A. C., Uhelski, M., Fuchs, P. N., & Papini, M. R. (2013). Role of the ventrolateral orbital cortex and medial prefrontal cortex in incentive downshift situations. *Behavioural Brain Research, 244,* 120–129. https://doi.org/10.1016/j.bbr.2013.01.029.

Ortega, L. A., Norris, J. N., López-Seal, M. F., Ramos, T., & Papini, M. R. (2014). Correlates of recovery from incentive downshift: A preliminary selective breeding study. *International Journal of Comparative Psychology, 27,* 18–44.

Ortega, L. A., Solano, J. L., Torres, C., & Papini, M. R. (2017). Reward loss and addiction: Opportunities for cross-pollination. *Pharmacology, Biochemistry and Behavior, 154,* 39–52. https://doi.org/10.1016/j.pbb.2017.02.001.

Ortega, L. A., Uhelski, M., Fuchs, P. N., & Papini, M. R. (2011). Impairment of recovery from incentive downshift after lesions of the anterior cingulate cortex: Emotional or cognitive deficits? *Behavioral Neuroscience, 6,* 988–995. https://doi.org/10.1037/a0025769.

Panksepp, J. (2010). The neurobiology of social loss in animals: Some keys to the puzzle of psychic pain in humans. In L. A. Jensen-Campbell & G. MacDonald (Eds.), *Social pain: Neuropsychological and health implications of loss and exclusion* (pp. 11–52). American Psychological Association.

Papini, M. R. (1997). Role of reinforcement in spaced-trial operant learning in pigeons (*Columba livia*). *Journal of Comparative Psychology, 111,* 275–285. https://psycnet.apa.org/doi/10.1037/0735-7036.111.3.275.

Papini, M. R. (2003). Comparative psychology of surprising nonreward. *Brain, Behavior and Evolution, 62,* 83–95. https://doi.org/10.1159/000072439.

Papini, M. R. (2009). Role of opioid receptors in incentive contrast. *International Journal of Comparative Psychology, 22,* 170–187.

Papini, M. R. (2014). Diversity of adjustments to reward downshifts in vertebrates. *International Journal of Comparative Psychology, 27,* 420–445.

Papini, M. R. (2021). *Comparative psychology: Evolution and development of brain and behavior. Third Edition.* Taylor & Francis.

Papini, M. R. (2022). Mechanisms underlying absolute and relative reward value in vertebrates. In M. Krause, K. H. Hollis, & M. R. Papini (Eds.), *Evolution of learning and memory mechanisms* (pp. 176–192). Cambridge University Press.

Papini, M. R., & Dudley, R. T. (1997). Consequences of surprising reward omissions. *Review of General Psychology, 1,* 175–197. https://doi.org/10.1037/1089-2680.1.2.175.

Papini, M. R., Fuchs, P. N., & Torres, C. (2015). Behavioral neuroscience of psychological pain. *Neuroscience and Biobehavioral Reviews, 48,* 53–69. https://doi.org/10.1016/j.neubiorev.2014.11.012.

Papini, M. R., Guarino, S., Hagen, C., & Torres, C. (2022). Incentive disengagement and the adaptive significance of frustrative nonreward. *Learning & Behavior, 50,* 372–388. https://doi.org/10.3758/s13420-022-00519-3

Papini, M. R., & Ishida, M. (1994). Role of magnitude of reinforcement in spaced-trial instrumental learning in turtles (*Geoclemys reevesii*). *Quarterly Journal of Experimental Psychology, 47B,* 1–13. https://doi.org/10.1080%2F14640749408401344.

Papini, M. R., Mustaca, A. E., & Bitterman, M. E. (1988). Successive negative contrast in the consummatory behavior of didelphid marsupials. *Animal Learning and Behavior, 16,* 53–57. https://doi.org/10.3758/BF03209043.

Papini, M. R., Muzio, R. N., & Segura, E. T. (1995). Instrumental learning in toads (*Bufo arenarum*): Reinforcer magnitude and the medial pallium. *Brain, Behavior, and Evolution, 46,* 61–71. https://doi.org/10.1159/000113259.

Papini, M. R., Penagos-Corzo, J. C., & Pérez-Acosta, A. M. (2019). Avian emotions: Comparative perspectives on fear and frustration. *Frontiers in Psychology, 9,* 2707. https://doi.org/10.3389/fpsyg.2018.02707.

Papini, M. R., & Torres, C. (2017). Comparative learning and evolution: Reward loss. In J. Call (Ed.), *APA handbook of comparative psychology* (Vol. II, pp. 267–286). American Psychological Association.

Papini, M. R., Wood, M., Daniel, A. M., & Norris, J. N. (2006). Reward loss as psychological pain. *International Journal of Psychology & Psychological Therapy, 6,* 189–213.

Pecoraro, N., & Dallman, M. F. (2005). c-Fos after incentive shifts: Expectancy, incredulity, and recovery. *Behavioral Neuroscience, 119,* 366–387. https://doi.org/10.1037/0735-7044.119.2.366.

Pecoraro, N., de Jong, H., & Dallman, M. F. (2009). An unexpected reduction in sucrose concentration activates the HPA axis on successive post shift days without attenuation by discriminative contextual stimuli. *Physiology and Behavior, 96,* 651–661. https://doi.org/10.1016/j.physbeh.2008.12.018.

Pecoraro, N., de Jong, H., Ginsberg, A. B., & Dallman, M. F. (2008). Lesions of the medial prefrontal cortex enhance the early phase of psychogenic fever to unexpected sucrose concentration reductions, promote recovery from negative contrast and enhance spontaneous recovery of sucrose-entrained anticipatory activity. *Neuroscience, 153,* 901–917. https://doi.org/10.1016/j.neuroscience.2008.03.043.

Pellegrini, S., Lopez-Seal, F., & Papini, M. R. (2008). Scaling relative incentive value: Different adjustments to incentive downshift in pigeons and rats. *Behavioural Processes, 79,* 182–188. https://doi.org/10.1016/j.beproc.2008.07.008.

Pellegrini, S., Wood, M., Daniel, A. M., & Papini, M. R. (2005). Opioid receptors modulate recovery from consummatory successive negative contrast. *Behavioural Brain Research*, *164*, 239–249. https://doi.org/10.1016/j.bbr.2005.06.035.

Pérez-Acosta, A. M., Martínez, G. S., Corredor, K. E., Vargas, C., & Méndez, L. F. (2016). Consummatory successive negative contrast in Mongolian gerbil (*Meriones unguiculatus*). *International Journal of Psychological Research*, *9*, 52–60. http://dx.doi.org/10.21500/20112084.2425.

Pert, A., & Bitterman, M. E. (1970). Reward and learning in the turtle. *Learning & Motivation*, *1*, 121–128. https://doi.org/10.1016/0023-9690(70)90134-7.

Pert, A., & Gonzalez, R. C. (1974). Behavior of the turtle (*Chrysemys picta picta*) in simultaneous, successive, and behavioral contrast situations. *Journal of Comparative and Physiological Psychology*, *87*, 526–538. https://doi.org/10.1037/h0036995.

Ramot, A., & Akirav, I. (2012). Cannabinoid receptors activation and glucocorticoid receptors deactivation in the amygdala prevent the stress-induced enhancement of a negative learning experience. *Neurobiology of Learning and Memory*, *97*, 393–401. https://doi.org/10.1016/j.nlm.2012.03.003.

Reilly, S., & Trifunovic, R. (2003). Gustatory thalamus lesions eliminate successive negative contrast in rats: Evidence against a memory deficit. *Behavioral Neuroscience*, *117*, 606–615. https://doi.org/10.1037/0735-7044.117.3.606.

Rowan, G. A., & Flaherty, C. F. (1987). The effects of morphine in the consummatory contrast paradigm. *Psychopharmacology*, *93*, 51–58. https://doi.org/10.1007/bf02439586.

Ruetti, E., Mustaca, A., & Bentosela, M. (2008). Memoria emocional: Efectos de la corticosterona sobre los recuerdos. *Revista Latinoamericana de Psicología*, *40*, 461–474.

Scheirer, J., Fernandez, R., Klein, J., & Picard, R. W. (2002). Frustrating the user on purpose: A step toward building an affective computer. *Interacting with Computers*, *14*, 93–118. https://doi.org/10.1016/S0953-5438(01)00059-5.

Schmajuk, N. A., Segura, E. T., & Reboreda, J. C. (1980). Appetitive conditioning and discriminatory learning in toads. *Behavioral and Neural Biology*, *28*, 392–397. https://doi.org/10.1016/s0163-1047(80)91698-2.

Schmajuk, N. A., Segura, E. T., & Ruidiaz, A. C. (1981). Reward downshift in the toad. *Behavioral and Neural Biology*, *33*, 519–523. https://doi.org/10.1016/S0163-1047(81)91959-2.

Serafini, M., Ifran, M. C., Kamenetzky, G., & Cuenya, L. (2020). Diferencias fenotípicas ante la devaluación y omisión de una recompensa esperada. *Revista de Psicología*, *29*, 1–12.

Serafini, G., Parmigiani, B., Amerio, A., Aguglia, A., Sher, L., & Amore, M. (2020). The psychological impact of COVID-19 on the mental health in the general population. *QJM: An International Journal of Medicine*, *113*, 531–537. https://doi.org/10.1093/qjmed/hcaa201.

Stout, S. C., Muzio, R. N., Boughner, R. L., & Papini, M. R. (2002). Aftereffects of the surprising presentation and omission of appetitive reinforcers on key pecking performance in pigeons. *Journal of Experimental Psychology: Animal Behavior Processes*, *28*, 242–256.

Sukhodolsky, D. G., Vander Wyk, B. C., Eilbott, J. A., Spencer, A., McCauley, S. A., Ibrahim, K., Crowley, M. J., & Pelphrey, K. A. (2016). Neural mechanisms of cognitive-behavioral therapy for aggression in children and adolescents: Design of a randomized controlled trial within the National Institute for Mental Health Research Domain Criteria construct of Frustrative Non-Reward. *Journal of Child and Adolescent Psychopharmacology*, *26*, 38–48. https://doi.org/10.1089/cap.2015.0164.

Thomas, B., & Papini, M. R. (2003). Mechanism of spaced-trial runway extinction in pigeons. *Learning and Motivation*, *34*, 104–126. https://doi.org/10.1016/S0023-9690(02)00506-4.

Tinklepaugh, O. L. (1928). An experimental study of representative factors in monkeys. *Journal of Comparative Psychology*, *8*, 197–236. https://doi.org/10.1037/h0075798.

Torres, C., Glueck, A. C., Conrad, S. E., Moron, I., & Papini, M. R. (2016). Dorsomedial striatum lesions affect adjustment to reward uncertainty, but not to reward devaluation or omission. *Neuroscience*, *332*, 13–25. https://doi.org/10.1016/j.neuroscience.2016.06.041.

Torres, C., & Papini, M. R. (2016). Emotional self-medication and addiction. In V. R. Preedy (Ed.), *The neuropathology of drug addictions and substance misuse* (Vol. 1, pp. 71–81). Elsevier.

Torres, C., & Papini, M. R. (2017). Incentive relativity. In J. Vonk & T. K. Shackelford (Eds.), *Encyclopedia of comparative cognition and behavior* (pp. 1–13). Springer International.

Torres, C., & Sabariego, M. (2014). Incentive relativity: Gene-environment interactions. *International Journal of Comparative Psychology*, *27*, 446–458.

Valverde, O. (2005). Participation of the cannabinoid system in the regulation of emotional-like behaviour. *Current Pharmaceutical Design*, *11*, 3421–3429. https://doi.org/10.2174/138161205774370780.

Vogel, J. R., Mikulka, P. J., & Spear, N. E. (1968). Effects of shifts in sucrose and saccharine concentrations on licking behavior in the rat. *Journal of Comparative and Physiological Psychology*, *66*, 661–666. https://doi.org/10.1037/h0026556.

Wagner, A. R. (1963). Conditioned frustration as a learned drive. *Journal of Experimental Psychology, 66*, 142–148. https://doi.org/10.1037/h0047714.

Weinstein, L. (1981). Incentive contrast effects in humans with monetary reinforcement and reaction time. *Acta Psychologica, 47*, 83–87. https://doi.org/10.1016/00016918(81)90040-8.

Wood, M. D., Daniel, A. M., & Papini, M. R. (2005). Selective effects of the δ-opioid receptor agonist DPDPE on consummatory successive negative contrast. *Behavioral Neuroscience, 119*, 446–454. https://doi.org/10.1037/0735-7044.119.2.446.

Wood, M. D., Norris, J. N., Daniel, A. M., & Papini, M. R. (2008). Trial-selective effects of U50,488H, a κ-opioid receptor agonist, on consummatory successive negative contrast. *Behavioural Brain Research, 193*, 28–36. https://doi.org/10.1016/j.bbr.2008.04.016.

Woodhams, S. G., Chapman, V., Finn, D. P., Hohmann, A. G., & Neugebauer, V. (2017). The cannabinoid system and pain. *Neuropharmacology, 124*, 105–120. https://doi.org/10.1016/j.neuropharm.2017.06.015.

World Health Organization (2020). Coronavirus disease (COVID-19). September 28, 2020. https://apps.who.int/iris/handle/10665/335725.

CHAPTER 44

Emotional Vigilance

Guillaume Dezecache and Hugo Mercier

Abstract
Although emotional displays have long been considered mere read-outs of the affective state of agents, recent studies and modern evolutionary thinking instead suggest that they should be characterized as proper communicative signals. This implies that emotional displays have evolved to be used strategically, to serve the senders' interests. However, for these signals to be stable, they must also benefit receivers. What guarantees that emotional signals are beneficial for both emitters and observers? In this chapter, the authors review evidence showing that humans are equipped with mechanisms that evolved to evaluate emotional displays and their sources, so as to minimize the risk of being fooled. They term these mechanisms "emotional vigilance," following the "epistemic vigilance" mechanisms used in ostensive communication. Emotional vigilance, the authors argue, is part of the human cognitive makeup, and they outline empirical avenues to best elucidate its features.

Key Words: emotional display, signaling, emotional vigilance, communication, epistemic vigilance

Introduction

Far from being incidental to human communication, emotional displays (which can be tentatively defined as bodily movements that seem to be associated with our momentary affective states) are ubiquitous in human affairs. The production of emotional displays radically alters the meaning of verbal utterances in conversation. For example, specific facial configurations may convey irony (Attardo et al., 2003), uncertainty (Bitti et al., 2014), or boredom (Bevilacqua et al., 2018). They can also be used to indicate commitment (Reed et al., 2014; Reed & DeScioli, 2017). Emotional displays may also, on their own, express joy, anger, or fear (among others) (Ekman, 1999). In fact, the absence of emotional displays may be detrimental to the success of many social activities, as suggested by the social disruption suffered by people experiencing impairment in the use of body musculature, as in facial paralysis (Bogart et al., 2012; Bogart & Matsumoto, 2010). The invention and use of emoticons is another sign of the centrality of emotional displays in human communication (Cherbonnier & Michinov, 2021).

Because of their tight link with affective experience (they appear to co-occur with affective experience, hence their name), so-called emotional displays are assumed to be causally linked to corresponding affective states. It has been proposed that the production of, for instance, fear displays necessarily accompanies the experience of fear. As such, emotional displays are considered read-outs of emotional experience (Ekman, 1999, 2007). This view entails that people cannot easily fake emotional displays (e.g., making a full-blown and likely authentic so-called fear display in the complete absence of the affective experience of fear); this also entails that people cannot completely inhibit emotional displays when experiencing a given affect. The major assumption that there exists a tight, causal link between emotional displays and affective experience pervades the scientific literature on emotions (Ekman, 2007).

A second traditional assumption in the emotion literature is that the perception of emotional displays automatically leads to a corresponding and similar affective experience in perceivers. This corresponds to the phenomenon of "emotional contagion" or the automatic and unconscious mimicry of muscular configuration momentarily observed in others, which in turn leads to convergence in emotional experience in observers via afferent muscular feedback (Hatfield et al., 1992, 1993; Hatfield et al., 2014).

We believe that these two traditional assumptions are no longer tenable. After a brief introduction to the many types of emotional displays, we review existing criticism of these assumptions, before proposing an alternative paradigm, grounded in the theory of the evolution of communication.

The Many Facets of Emotional Displays

Emotional displays can take a great variety of forms in humans. For obvious reasons of visual accessibility in close-range social interactions, the facial musculature has received a great deal of attention in the literature (Ekman, 2007). Much academic research has been dedicated to the identification of discrete facial configurations linked with the experience of specific affects, with highly debated findings of associations between basic sets of configurations of facial muscular activity and affective experience (Barrett, 2006; Barrett et al., 2019; Crivelli & Fridlund, 2018, 2019; Ekman, 2007; Fridlund, 2014; Jack et al., 2014; Jack & Schyns, 2015).

Besides the facial musculature itself, the voice and its quality (such as prosodic alterations of speech) also are recognized as a major source of emotional displays in humans (Sauter, Eisner, Ekman, et al., 2010). As in the case of facial configurations, there have been debates on whether there are vocal displays specific to particular affective experiences (Anderson et al., 2018; Sauter, Eisner, Calder, et al., 2010; Sauter, Eisner, Ekman, et al., 2010; Simon-Thomas et al., 2009).

Work by de Gelder, Grèzes, and colleagues also suggests that bodily postures can play an important role in emotional perception (de Gelder, 2006; de Gelder et al., 2015; Grèzes et al., 2007; Pichon et al., 2008), with discussions about potential associations between particular bodily muscular configurations (here: the face being excluded) and the experience of certain affects (Atkinson et al., 2004; Veld et al., 2014; Watson & de Gelder, 2020).

Because it has been the focus of most research, and because of its centrality in close-range social interactions, facial displays of emotion will remain the major focus in this chapter, although we believe our conclusions would hold for all emotional displays.

Emotional Displays or Emotional Signals?

As mentioned earlier, one assumption regarding emotional displays is that they are reliable read-outs of the displayers' internal states. In fact, and according to the Basic Emotions Theory (Ekman, 1999, 2007; Keltner et al., 2019), facial displays (or at least, a subset of them) would have been evolutionarily preserved thanks to their status as reliable indicators of the affective state of the agent displaying them. As such, there would be a correspondence between internal affective states and specific muscular configurations (a set of "facial affect programs"), the former causing the latter in an automatic fashion. This theory makes the following two predictions: (a) There is uniformity in production, and universality in recognition, revealing a one-to-one mapping between basic affective experience and basic emotional facial displays in all cultures; (b) people cannot fake facial emotional displays.

Regarding (a), pioneering cross-cultural work with populations of the United States, Brazil, Japan, New Guinea, and Borneo showed that populations across sites are capable (above-chance level) of matching some facial displays with corresponding affective states, strongly suggesting that facial displays of emotion are universally recognized, and likely universally produced (Ekman, 1973; Ekman et al., 1969).

Regarding (b), it was found that one particular variant of smiling behavior (the so-called Duchenne smile; Ekman et al., 1990; Gunnery et al., 2013; Gunnery & Ruben, 2016) could only be produced under the genuine experience of joy and is recognized as genuine. This variant would contrast with the polite smile, associated with non-genuine happiness. Furthermore, it has been argued that, in general, we experience difficulties producing facial displays at will.

More recent research has cast doubt on these two claims:

With respect to (a), a number of methodological problems have been identified that threaten the claim that emotional facial displays are universally produced and recognized (Gendron et al., 2018; Jack et al., 2009; Nelson & Russell, 2013; Russell, 1994). For example, Crivelli and colleagues (2016) showed that gasping facial displays (recognized as "fear" in the Western world) were identified as expressing anger and threatening intent by the Trobrianders of Papua New Guinea. This study (and many others; see Gendron et al., 2018, for a recent review) suggest that facial displays do not possess a distinct meaning in all cultures.

With respect to (b), Gosselin and colleagues (2010) examined the capacity of adults to control volitionally 20 facial action units linked with so-called basic emotions. Most action units (18/20) could be activated voluntarily (Gosselin et al., 2010). This suggests that, in principle, the bulk of facial configurations can actually be produced at will, and that humans could potentially "fake" them.

In fact, in natural situations, facial emotional displays (even those hard to voluntarily produce) are only loosely related to emotional experience. For instance, it is known that smiles (including Duchenne smiles) are loosely related to one's internal state (e.g., success at a bowling alley: Kraut & Johnston, 1979; success at a judo competition: Crivelli et al., 2015). Discrepancies between the actual use of facial emotional displays and the theory of basic emotions led to the birth of the so-called Behavioral Ecology View of facial displays (Crivelli & Fridlund, 2018, 2019; Fridlund, 2014). This view argues that facial displays (including so-called facial emotional displays) are tools for social influence, rather than read-outs of one's internal states. In fact (and we will explain below in greater detail), Fridlund noted that evolution cannot select for behaviors that are detrimental to their bearers (Fridlund, 2014). For example, the automatic expression of, say, fear in situations requiring a neutral look would be selected against. Facial display works in the interests of the displayer, rather than in the interests of their inner uncontrollable states: we should expect context-dependent inhibition of facial displays to serve the interests of signalers (Al-Shawaf et al., 2015; Al-Shawaf & Lewis, 2017).

The Behavioral Ecology View of facial displays has contributed to a renewed theory of the proximate mechanisms at the basis of facial emotional displays. First, facial displays do not "express" anything. They are signals of one's behavioral intention. Our facial displays are not about people, or what is inside them; rather, they are about what one is about to do, or how one is trying to influence others. In other words, facial emotional displays serve as tools to impact and influence others, behaviors that are produced to make others do what one wants them to do (Crivelli & Fridlund, 2018; Krebs & Dawkins, 1984).

Emotional Contagion or Emotional Communication?

As outlined above, another common conception in the emotion literature is that the perception of emotional facial displays causes mimicry and convergence in the emotional states of observers (Hatfield et al., 1993). This is in line with the classical framework of "primitive emotional contagion" (Hatfield et al., 1992). This framework states that the perception of muscular movements in others cause automatic mimicry in ourselves, which in turn momentarily affects our own affective state through muscular feedback. In their very influential book dedicated to emotional contagion, Hatfield, Rapson, and Cacioppo (1994) provide evidence for the existence of the two steps mentioned above: first, that we tend to converge in musculature with others, notably their facial movements, through a process called "facial mimicry" (Dimberg et al., 2000; Hatfield et al., 1994); second, that the adoption of a given facial configuration tends to make agents converge in their emotional states—a smile makes them happy, as the sender was (Larsen et al., 1992; Soussignan, 2002; Strack et al., 1988).

Although popular, this framework suffers from a number of limitations. Mechanistically, there is no evidence of a causal link between the two steps, and the seminal protocol used to demonstrate the facial feedback hypothesis (adopting part of the facial configuration of a smile using a pen in the mouth positively affects funniness rating of cartoons) has not been successfully replicated (Wagenmakers et al., 2016). Another serious problem for this theory is that facial mimicry is in fact far from being an automatic process: as we will see below, studies have shown that facial mimicry is heavily influenced by contextual features, such as one's attitudes toward the emitter. Besides mimicry, we do not automatically and spontaneously share the emotions we see others exhibit. For example, Zillman and Cantor (1977) studied affective responses to emotions seen in an actor. The actor was malevolent, benevolent, or neutral, and they expressed either euphoria or dysphoria at the end of the video clips. Emotional contagion (convergence of affect between the actor and viewer) only occurred when the actor was either benevolent or neutral. When the actor was malevolent, there was a discordance in emotions between actor and viewer.

Another relevant study found that competition (that is, a conflict in the interests of the agents involved) causes "counter-contagion" in participants (Lanzetta & Englis, 1989). As such, our attitudes toward others shape the way we respond to their emotional displays.

The idea that emotions are contagious is popular but incorrect. Conceptually, the process of contagion by pathogens does not apply to emotional convergence between agents, and the mechanisms behind the two are vastly different (Dezecache et al., 2015; Dezecache et al., 2016; Warren & Power, 2015). In fact, "emotional contagion" may be best conceptualized as instances of accidental match between the emotions of two or more persons. No emotion is "transferred" from one individual to another individual. Instead, we react to others' emotional signals, in a way which may or may not be somewhat congruent (and which will never be perfectly congruent) with them (Dezecache et al., 2015; Dezecache et al., 2016).

An Evolutionary Approach to Communication

From an evolutionary perspective, the two traditional assumptions that emotions are a read-out of affective states, and that they provoke mandatory reactions in observers, are not tenable. Rejecting these assumptions paints a picture of emotional displays that is much better aligned with the theory of the evolution of communication (Maynard Smith & Harper, 2004). For emotional displays to be a stable form of communication, they should, on average, benefit both displayers and observers (Maynard Smith & Harper, 2004; Scott-Phillips, 2008; for the case of emotional displays, see Dezecache et al., 2013). Against the first traditional assumption, emotional displays cannot be mere read-outs of emotional experience. If they were, they would often betray affective states that the displayer would be better off hiding (Fridlund, 2014). They would thus often be detrimental to their displayer, and selected against. Eventually, displayers would stop displaying.

Against the second traditional assumption, emotional displays cannot mandatorily cause emotional convergence (or, indeed, any emotional reaction) in observers. If they did, they would often cause reactions that are not in the interest of the observers, leading them to stop attending to emotional displays, making such displays useless (Dezecache et al., 2013). Evolutionarily, we should expect context-dependence in the way we produce and/or respond to facial displays, so as to make sure they serve our best interests, on average (Al-Shawaf et al., 2015).

A radical shift in our thinking about emotional displays, inspired by modern evolutionary treatment of communicative systems, means we should revise our understanding of what emotional displays are, what their perception causes in observers, and what keeps the production and reception of emotional displays evolutionarily stable. This endeavor has been pursued by ourselves (Dezecache et al., 2013; Mercier et al., 2017) and others (e.g., Al-Shawaf et al., 2015; Al-Shawaf & Lewis, 2017). In this chapter, we focus on the latter point: how an evolutionary perspective can cast a new light on the reception of emotional displays. We will argue that mechanisms of *emotional vigilance* determine how emotional displays influence us. Before delving into these mechanisms, we introduce the analogous concept of *epistemic vigilance*, which will illustrate the functioning of these mechanisms.

Epistemic Vigilance

The general logic of the evolution of communication doesn't apply only to emotional displays: for any form of communication to be evolutionarily stable, it has to benefit, on average, both senders and receivers. Unless their interests are almost perfectly aligned (e.g., cells in a body), senders often have incentives to send signals that would be beneficial to them but harmful to the receivers, turning the signals into manipulation and deception. For communication to persist, there must be mechanisms that stop senders from abusing receivers (again, on average). Some signals might be produced in such a way that only individuals with certain traits can emit them (indices). For instance, Thomson's gazelles stot when they see some predators, jumping in place in a way that doesn't help them escape at all. This behavior is thought to display the gazelle's physical fitness, such that only very fit gazelles can stot convincingly, sending an honest signal to the predator that chasing them would be futile (e.g., Al-Shawaf & Lewis, 2018; Caro, 1986; Zahavi & Zahavi, 1999).

Clearly, human ostensive communication is not an index of anything (with rare exceptions, such as saying, "I am not a mute"). Instead, it has been argued that human ostensive communication remains stable thanks to cognitive mechanisms of epistemic vigilance (Mercier, 2020; Sperber et al., 2010). These mechanisms allow receivers to reject most harmful messages, while accepting beneficial messages. They do so by putting different weights on messages as a function of a variety of cues related to the content of the message (Is it plausible? Is it supported by good arguments?) and to its source (Are they competent? Do they have our interests at heart?).

There is a wealth of data showing that mechanisms of epistemic vigilance function efficiently, and that they start developing very early in childhood (some can be observed in infants) (for reviews, see Harris et al., 2018; Mercier, 2020). This evidence comes not only from laboratory experiments, but also from studies on the limited persuasive power of advertising, propaganda, political campaigns, and other mass-persuasion attempts (Mercier, 2020).

In the rest of the chapter, we outline the evolutionary logic justifying the need for mechanisms of emotional vigilance, before reviewing laboratory and observational evidence that demonstrate its workings.

Why We Need Emotional Vigilance

Epistemic vigilance is important because ostensive communication appears to be "cheap talk": with a few exceptions, there is nothing intrinsic in an ostensive signal (e.g., saying, "I love you") that guarantees its veracity. It has been argued, however, that emotional displays do not suffer from the same potential weakness, and that this is precisely what makes them such a useful communicative device (Frank, 1988). This argument rests on the first traditional assumption, that emotional displays are honest read-outs of affective states (i.e., only someone who is genuinely angry could convincingly display anger). As we have seen, however, this traditional assumption has been largely debunked (Al-Shawaf et al., 2015; Crivelli et al., 2016; Crivelli & Fridlund, 2018). Emotional signals are not indices. Evolution cannot make an unfit gazelle stot convincingly, but nothing stops evolution from making individuals send emotional displays decoupled from their underlying affective states—or from affecting the underlying affective states themselves, so that they are felt when displaying the emotion would be strategically useful. As it stands, emotional displays may be used manipulatively and exploitatively (Al-Shawaf et al., 2015).

Since emotional signals are not intrinsically honest, there must exist some other mechanism that keeps them (mostly) honest. By analogy with epistemic vigilance, we suggest that mechanisms of emotional vigilance serve this function (for a related proposal on empathy more specifically, see Weisz & Cikara, 2021).

Emotional Vigilance

Emotional displays are signals, that is, means that others use to influence us. A display of fear encourages us to prepare for swift defensive actions. A display of happiness encourages us to approach, and to preserve the positive interaction. Unlike in spoken communication, our reaction to the emotional displays we perceive may come so fast (a few hundreds of milliseconds) that one may be tempted to say they are "automatic" or at least outside of our control. In fact, they may just not be under our *conscious* control. This does not mean that we lack evolved structures that could control our reactions, or at least adjust them so that, on average, they serve our best interests. Like epistemic vigilance mechanisms (see, e.g. Mercier, 2020), emotional vigilance mechanisms may help put different weights on emotional signals as a function of different contextual cues, in particular the benevolence of the emitters (i.e., whether their fitness interests are aligned with ours) and their competence (i.e., whether their displays are appropriate given background information).

Assessment of Benevolence

There is much evidence showing that we react to others' emotional displays based on whether we perceive their interests to be aligned with ours (benevolence). As discussed above, Zillman and Cantor (1977), as well as Lanzetta and Englis (1989), have shown that emotional convergence with the emotions seen in others is modulated by whether the others were observed acting in malevolent, benevolent, or neutral ways, as well as whether the observers have a competitive or cooperative relationship with the actors. More recently, Likowski and colleagues (2008) have examined the impact of attitudes toward emitters on the facial responses of observers. They found that emitters perceived positively were mimicked more than those perceived negatively when they displayed either happy or sad faces. Using group membership (which provides a crude but important cue of alignment of interests), van der Schalk and colleagues (2011) examined the mimicry of fear and anger seen in emitters. They found that mimicry was higher when exposed to in-group as opposed to out-group emitters. When members of the out-group exhibited anger, this evoked fear in participants, whereas out-group displays of fear evoked aversion in participants. Relatedly, Paulus and Wentura (2015) found that reactions to displays of fear and happiness were a function of the group of the emitter, with in-group emitters eliciting "concordant" behavior (avoidance for fear and approach for happiness) and out-group emitters activating the reverse pattern. Rauchbauer and colleagues (2016) found that anger was mimicked more when displayed by angry out-group members as compared to angry in-group members—showing that, ironically, a reaction closer to mimicry is elicited by out-groups than by in-groups, but only when it is appropriate. Finally, Paulus and colleagues (2016) used a reverse-correlation technique to study the representation of smiles of in-group vs. out-group individuals, demonstrating that in-group smiles are represented with more benevolence than those of out-groups.

Further evidence comes from more explicit situations of misaligned interests, such as those created in Lanzetta and Englis (1989). Participants in the study of Likowski and colleagues (2011) played dice with an avatar with whom they were either engaged in a cooperative, competitive, or neutral interaction. Upon receiving the results of the dice game, avatars produced happy, sad, angry, or neutral displays. In competitive situations, participants reacted with less congruence to happy, sad, and angry avatars (see Seibt et al., 2015; Weyers et al., 2009, for further evidence).

Much of the research covered above is related to the phenomenon of so-called facial mimicry, that is, the adoption of a muscular configuration that bears correspondence (or at least similarity) to the facial muscular configuration seen in others. Less has been done with respect to affective responses to others' *bodily* configuration as a function of their perceived benevolence and overlap in fitness interests (or lack thereof). Future research looking at mechanisms of emotional vigilance could profitably attend to this gap.

Assessment of Competence

Besides the benevolence of the emitter (i.e., overlap in fitness interests between emitter and receiver), emotional vigilance is also attuned to the emitter's competence, that is, whether their emotional displays appear apt given the context in which they are expressed. For example, in a recent study, Kastendieck and colleagues (2021) revealed a top-down influence of judgment of appropriateness on our responses to perceived facial displays, such that smiles in an inappropriate context (funerals) were only mimicked when there was closeness between observers and emitters.

Modulation of reactions according to perceived competence seems to develop early in ontogeny. In a 2012 study, Hepach and colleagues (2012) showed that, when provided with contextual information, 3-year-olds reacted to the distress seen in adults as a function of how warranted the distress was, showing more concern when the distress was justified as opposed to when it was a clear overreaction. Chiarella and Poulin-Dubois (2013) examined 15- and 18-month-old infants' reactions to actors experiencing a positive or a negative emotion, after a justified or an unjustified event. When exposed to unjustified emotional displays, 18-month-old infants looked for more information, presumably in an attempt to make sense of the situation. They also showed less concern for the emitters when the sad displays were unjustified. These results are consistent with a later study by Walle and Campos (2014) that examined 16- and 19-month-old infants' sensitivity to inauthentic emotions, i.e., emotion displays that were exaggerated, inappropriate, or unclear. Nineteen-month-old infants reacted in ways suggesting they were able to identify the non-authentic displays.

Beyond Dyadic Emotional Communication: The Role and Impact of Emotional Vigilance

So far, we have relied on laboratory experiments to show that reactions to emotional displays are modulated in sensible ways by the perceived benevolence and competence of the emitter of the displays, taking these results as evidence that humans possess well-functioning mechanisms of emotional vigilance. However, this conclusion might seem to be belied by real-world phenomena, from panicking crowds to "mass psychogenic illness," when a strong emotion appears to spread uncontrollably in a population. In fact, we briefly argue here that accurate descriptions of both phenomena make them fit well with the current framework (see Mercier, 2020).

Regarding crowds, it is now well established that the naïve view of crowds as being uniform, prone to irrational behavior, and easily influenced by leaders is misguided. Crowds are heterogeneous: they are composed of individuals having different goals and behaving in different ways—they do not blindly imitate the emotions or the behaviors of other crowd members or of leaders (Schweingruber & Wohlstein, 2005). If crowd members influence each other, it is within small groups of people who know each other, who have joined the crowd together, and who thus likely meet the benevolence and competence conditions that characterize emotional vigilance (Aveni, 1977; Drury, 2018; Drury et al., 2020; Johnson et al., 1994; McPhail & Wohlstein, 1983; Stott et al., 2018; Templeton et al., 2018). Instead of crowds being subject to irrational panic or bloodlust, we consistently observe that (1) if anything, people do not panic enough (Dezecache, 2015); (2) even under terrible circumstances, people often engage in prosocial behavior instead of panicking (Dezecache, 2015; Dezecache et al., 2021; Drury, 2018; Drury et al., 2009a, 2009b; Johnson, 1987; Mawson, 2005, 2017); and (3) violent crowds tend to be quite discerning in how they exert violence, in a way that fits with the prior goals of at least some crowd members (e.g., Barrows, 1981; Rudé, 1967). Although much remains to be understood about the behavior of crowds, what we know of them is consistent with the idea that humans are endowed with mechanisms of emotional vigilance, mechanisms which preclude the "contagious transports, irresistible currents of passion, epidemics of credulity" feared by nineteenth-century crowd psychologists (Taine, 1876, p. 241).

What of "mass psychogenic illness," such as the "epidemic of laughter" that affected schoolchildren in Tanganyika (what would become Tanzania; Rankin, 1963)? Children started laughing uncontrollably, and this behavior appeared to spread to hundreds of their schoolmates. Even though we are certainly faced with an extreme behavior, we still observe broad patterns that fit with the current framework. First, and most strikingly, these strong emotions are never passed on to out-group members. In this example, none of the parents, schoolteachers, or other observers were ever affected, with the transmission being restricted to children who knew each other well. In other words, the benevolence condition of emotional vigilance was met: responsive parties (i.e., those showing "contagious" laughter) showed aligned interests with the signalers. Second, the people affected typically find themselves in a particularly stressful situation, and their bizarre behavior allows them at least a temporary reprieve (e.g., they do not have to go to school anymore). Their reaction might thus be less maladaptive than it first seems. As in the case of crowds, mass psychogenic illnesses thus do not directly contradict the current framework, on the contrary, they fit within it—although, admittedly, they remain poorly understood and not very well documented (and potentially largely anecdotal).

Emotional Vigilance: A Research Agenda

As discussed above, evidence suggests that we react to emotional displays based on the emitter's benevolence and competence (or at least the aptness if the display). That said, not all emotional displays are created equal. The costs of reacting when one shouldn't have, and failing to react when one should have, vary as a function of the affect being displayed. *Reacting* to a fake display of pain by feeling pain oneself and potentially helping the emitter might be costlier than failing to feel that pain (which doesn't preclude helping, but makes it non-mandatory); *failing to react* with fear to the fear of others might be costlier than reacting with fear—an unpleasant but not particularly costly feeling that can be extinguished promptly if we ascertain there was no real need for it. In this respect, the "better safe than sorry" principle in ecology and animal behavior states that a mis-calibrated response to any sign of danger is possibly less detrimental than failure to react to actual danger (Haftorn, 2000) (for similar discussion in the evolutionary psychology literature more specifically, see Haselton & Buss, 2000; Nesse, 2005). One should map the diversity of emotions and the costs involved if recipients wrongly react or fail to react to them in a manner consistent with what is expected by the emitter. Moreover, people might learn to adjust their emotional reactions to changing costs and benefits. For example, throughout their curriculum, medical students adjust their reactions to the pain observed in their patients (Smith et al., 2017).

The distribution of emotional vigilance mechanisms in phylogeny is another promising avenue for research. For instance, in some primate species, alarm calls are not innate in form and/or function (Dezecache et al., 2019; Seyfarth & Cheney, 1980), and it is possible that immature individuals call in nonspecific or unreliable ways (Ramakrishnan & Coss, 2000; Seyfarth & Cheney, 1980). In other mammals, the signals (notably: alarm calls) of unreliable individuals may be discounted (Blumstein et al., 2004; Hare & Atkins, 2001). Exciting research avenues lie in examining the extent to which animal receivers transfer reliability across contextual domains (e.g., unreliable alarm callers may also be unreliable food callers), and/or whether they respond to callers in a way that reflects not only assessment of competence but also assessment of benevolence.

Other promising avenues in human research more specifically are individual differences in emotional vigilance, and the question of how emotional vigilance develops in ontogeny, and whether some emotional vigilance mechanisms could emerge earlier than others, based on when they are needed (for example, based on when, on average, relevant adaptive problems are encountered). In cultural contexts where infants are surrounded by mature individuals (rather than peers), benevolence might appear as a more urgent issue than competence, for instance.

Finally, the evolutionary history of emotional vigilance with respect to epistemic vigilance is a question worthy of further investigation. Our thought is that emotional vigilance might have evolved prior to epistemic vigilance, for the type of signals it deals with (emotional displays) are more widely distributed (phylogenetically speaking) than the ostensive signals typically dealt with by epistemic vigilance.

Conclusion

Although emotional displays have been studied within an evolutionary framework since Darwin (1872), we have argued that the traditional understanding of emotional displays in psychology is largely at odds with an evolutionary perspective. An evolutionary approach to communication shows that for communication to be stable, it has to benefit both senders and receivers (in the case of emotional displays, emitters and observers). This means that (1) emotional displays would likely be maladaptive if they mandatorily followed some affect, given that we are often better off not revealing our affects to others; (2) that the reactions to emotional displays would likely be maladaptive if they were mandatory, given that emitters could then influence observers into feeling whatever emotion best serves their own ends, instead of the ends of observers.

Here, we have focused on point (2), suggesting that instead of reactions to emotional displays being mandatory, they are modulated by mechanisms of emotional vigilance. These mechanisms serve the interests of the observer by using cues of benevolence (is the emitter likely to have my interests at heart?), and competence (is the display appropriate in the context?) to adjust the observer's reaction to the displays. This way, the observer resists being purposely or inadvertently duped into experiencing an emotion that would not serve their interests. Much remains to be studied about these defense mechanisms, and the adaptiveness of our reactions to emotional displays more generally. We believe that the current framework may constitute a fertile ground for new hypotheses and research.

Acknowledgments

GD acknowledges the support received from the Agence Nationale de la Recherche of the French government through the program "Investissements d'Avenir" (16-IDEX-0001 CAP 20-25). HM's work is supported by two ANR grants, to FrontCog ANR-17-EURE-0017 and to PSL ANR-10-IDEX-0001-02.

References

Al-Shawaf, L., Conroy-Beam, D., Asao, K., & Buss, D. (2015). Human emotions: An evolutionary psychological perspective. *Emotion Review*. 8(2), 173–186. https://doi.org/10.1177/1754073914565518

Al-Shawaf, L., & Lewis, D. (2018). The handicap principle. In T. K. Shackelford & V. A. Weekes-Shackelford (Eds.), *Encyclopedia of evolutionary psychological science* (pp. 3624–3628). Springer International. https://doi.org/10.1007/978-3-319-16999-6_2100-1

Al-Shawaf, L., & Lewis, D. M. (2017). Evolutionary psychology and the emotions. In V. Zeigler-Hill & T. K. Shackelford (Eds.), *Encyclopedia of personality and individual differences* (pp. 1452–1461). Springer International.

Anderson, C. L., Monroy, M., & Keltner, D. (2018). Emotion in the wilds of nature: The coherence and contagion of fear during threatening group-based outdoors experiences. *Emotion*, 18(3), 355–368. https://doi.org/10.1037/emo0000378

Atkinson, A. P., Dittrich, W. H., Gemmell, A. J., & Young, A. W. (2004). Emotion perception from dynamic and static body expressions in point-light and full-light displays. *Perception*, 33(6), 717–746. https://doi.org/10.1068/p5096

Attardo, S., Eisterhold, J., Hay, J., & Poggi, I. (2003). Multimodal markers of irony and sarcasm. *Humor*, 16(2), 243–260.

Aveni, A. F. (1977). The not-so-lonely crowd: Friendship groups in collective behavior. *Sociometry*, 40(1), 96–99.

Barrett, L. F. (2006). Solving the emotion paradox: Categorization and the experience of emotion. *Personality and Social Psychology Review*, 10(1), 20–46.

Barrett, L. F., Adolphs, R., Marsella, S., Martinez, A. M., & Pollak, S. D. (2019). Emotional expressions reconsidered: Challenges to inferring emotion from human facial movements. *Psychological Science in the Public Interest*, 20(1), 1–68. https://doi.org/10.1177/1529100619832930

Barrows, S. (1981). *Distorting mirrors: Visions of the crowd in late nineteenth-century france*. Yale University Press.

Bevilacqua, F., Engström, H., & Backlund, P. (2018). Changes in heart rate and facial actions during a gaming session with provoked boredom and stress. *Entertainment Computing*, 24, 10–20.

Bitti, P. E. R., Bonfiglioli, L., Melani, P., Caterina, R., & Garotti, P. (2014). Expression and communication of doubt/uncertainty through facial expression. *Ricerche Di Pedagogia e Didattica: Journal of Theories and Research in Education*, 9(1), 159–177.

Blumstein, D. T., Verneyre, L., & Daniel, J. C. (2004). Reliability and the adaptive utility of discrimination among alarm callers. *Proceedings of the Royal Society B: Biological Sciences*, 271(1550), 1851–1857.

Bogart, K., & Matsumoto, D. (2010). Living with moebius syndrome: Adjustment, social competence, and satisfaction with life. *The Cleft Palate-Craniofacial Journal*, 47(2), 134–142. https://doi.org/10.1597/08-257_1

Bogart, K., Tickle-Degnen, L., & Joffe, M. S. (2012). Social interaction experiences of adults with moebius syndrome: A focus group. *Journal of Health Psychology*, 17(8), 1212–1222. https://doi.org/10.1177/1359105311432491

Caro, T. M. (1986). The functions of stotting: A review of the hypotheses. *Animal Behaviour*, 34(3), 649–662.

Cherbonnier, A., & Michinov, N. (2021). The recognition of emotions beyond facial expressions: Comparing emoticons specifically designed to convey basic emotions with other modes of expression. *Computers in Human Behavior*, 118, 106689. https://doi.org/10.1016/j.chb.2021.106689

Chiarella, S. S., & Poulin-Dubois, D. (2013). Cry babies and pollyannas: Infants can detect unjustified emotional reactions. *Infancy: The Official Journal of the International Society on Infant Studies, 18*(Suppl 1), E81–E96. https://doi.org/10.1111/infa.12028

Crivelli, C., Carrera, P., & Fernández-Dols, J.-M. (2015). Are smiles a sign of happiness? Spontaneous expressions of judo winners. *Evolution and Human Behavior, 36*(1), 52–58. https://doi.org/10.1016/j.evolhumbehav.2014.08.009

Crivelli, C., & Fridlund, A. J. (2018). Facial displays are tools for social influence. *Trends in Cognitive Sciences, 22*(5), 388–399. https://doi.org/10.1016/j.tics.2018.02.006

Crivelli, C., & Fridlund, A. J. (2019). Inside-out: From basic emotions theory to the behavioral ecology view. *Journal of Nonverbal Behavior, 43*(2), 161–194. https://doi.org/10.1007/s10919-019-00294-2

Crivelli, C., Russell, J. A., Jarillo, S., & Fernández-Dols, J.-M. (2016). The fear gasping face as a threat display in a Melanesian society. *Proceedings of the National Academy of Sciences, 113*(44), 12403–12407.

Darwin, C. (1872). *The expression of the emotions in man and animals*. Murray.

de Gelder, B. (2006). Towards the neurobiology of emotional body language. *Nature Reviews Neuroscience, 7*(3), 242–249.

de Gelder, B., de Borst, A. W., & Watson, R. (2015). The perception of emotion in body expressions. *WIREs Cognitive Science, 6*(2), 149–158. https://doi.org/10.1002/wcs.1335

Dezecache, G. (2015). Human collective reactions to threat. *WIREs Cognitive Science, 6*(3), 209–219. https://doi.org/10.1002/wcs.1344

Dezecache, G., Crockford, C., & Zuberbühler, K. (2019). The development of communication in alarm contexts in wild chimpanzees. *Behavioral Ecology and Sociobiology, 73*(8), 1–9. https://doi.org/10.1007/s00265-019-2716-6

Dezecache, G., Eskenazi, T., & Grèzes, J. (2016). Emotional convergence: A case of contagion? In S. S. Obhi & E. S. Cross (Eds.), *Shared representations: Sensorimotor foundations of social life* (pp. 417–436). Cambridge University Press. https://doi.org/10.1017/CBO9781107279353.021

Dezecache, G., Jacob, P., & Grezes, J. (2015). Emotional contagion: Its scope and limits. *Trends in Cognitive Sciences, 19*(6), 297–299.

Dezecache, G., Martin, J.-R., Tessier, C., Safra, L., Pitron, V., Nuss, P., & Grèzes, J. (2021). Nature and determinants of social actions during a mass shooting. *PLoS ONE, 16*(12), e0260392.

Dezecache, G., Mercier, H., & Scott-Phillips, T. C. (2013). An evolutionary approach to emotional communication. *Journal of Pragmatics, 59*, 221–233.

Dimberg, U., Thunberg, M., & Elmehed, K. (2000). Unconscious facial reactions to emotional facial expressions. *Psychological Science, 11*(1), 86–89.

Drury, J. (2018). The role of social identity processes in mass emergency behaviour: An integrative review. *European Review of Social Psychology, 29*(1), 38–81.

Drury, J., Cocking, C., & Reicher, S. (2009a). Everyone for themselves? A comparative study of crowd solidarity among emergency survivors. *British Journal of Social Psychology, 48*(3), 487–506.

Drury, J., Cocking, C., & Reicher, S. (2009b). The nature of collective resilience: Survivor reactions to the 2005 London bombings. *International Journal of Mass Emergencies and Disasters, 27*(1), 66–95.

Drury, J., Stott, C., Ball, R., Reicher, S., Neville, F., Bell, L., Biddlestone, M., Choudhury, S., Lovell, M., & Ryan, C. (2020). A social identity model of riot diffusion: From injustice to empowerment in the 2011 London riots. *European Journal of Social Psychology*, ( ). *50*(3), 646–661. https://doi.org/10.1002/ejsp.2650

Ekman, P. (1973). Cross-cultural studies of facial expression. In P. Ekman (Ed.), *Darwin and facial expression: A century of research in review* (pp. 169–222). Academic Press.

Ekman, P. (1999). Basic emotions. In T. Dalgleish & M. J. Power (Eds.), *Handbook of cognition and emotion* (pp. 45–60). John Wiley & Sons Ltd. https://doi.org/10.1002/0470013494.ch3.

Ekman, P. (2007). *Emotions revealed: Recognizing faces and feelings to improve communication and emotional life* (reprint ed.). Holt McDougal.

Ekman, P., Davidson, R. J., & Friesen, W. V. (1990). The Duchenne smile: Emotional expression and brain physiology: II. *Journal of Personality and Social Psychology, 58*(2), 342.

Ekman, P., Sorenson, E. R., & Friesen, W. V. (1969). Pan-cultural elements in facial displays of emotion. *Science, 164*(3875), 86–88.

Frank, R. H. (1988). *Passions within reason: The strategic role of emotions*. W. W. Norton.

Fridlund, A. J. (2014). *Human facial expression: An evolutionary view*. Academic Press.

Gendron, M., Crivelli, C., & Barrett, L. F. (2018). Universality reconsidered: Diversity in making meaning of facial expressions. *Current Directions in Psychological Science, 27*(4), 211–219. https://doi.org/10.1177/0963721417746794

Gosselin, P., Perron, M., & Beaupré, M. (2010). The voluntary control of facial action units in adults. *Emotion, 10*(2), 266–271. https://doi.org/10.1037/a0017748

Grèzes, J., Pichon, S., & de Gelder, B. (2007). Perceiving fear in dynamic body expressions. *Neuroimage, 35*(2), 959–967.
Gunnery, S. D., Hall, J. A., & Ruben, M. A. (2013). The deliberate Duchenne smile: Individual differences in expressive control. *Journal of Nonverbal Behavior, 37*(1), 29–41. https://doi.org/10.1007/s10919-012-0139-4
Gunnery, S. D., & Ruben, M. A. (2016). Perceptions of Duchenne and non-Duchenne smiles: A meta-analysis. *Cognition and Emotion, 30*(3), 501–515. https://doi.org/10.1080/02699931.2015.1018817
Haftorn, S. (2000). Contexts and possible functions of alarm calling in the willow tit, *Parus montanus*: The principle of "better safe than sorry." *Behaviour, 137*(4), 437–449. https://doi.org/10.1163/156853900502169
Hare, J. F., & Atkins, B. A. (2001). The squirrel that cried wolf: Reliability detection by juvenile Richardson's ground squirrels (*Spermophilus richardsonii*). *Behavioral Ecology and Sociobiology, 51*(1), 108–112.
Harris, P. L., Koenig, M. A., Corriveau, K. H., & Jaswal, V. K. (2018). Cognitive foundations of learning from testimony. *Annual Review of Psychology, 69*, 251–273. https://doi.org/10.1146/annurev-psych-122216-011710
Haselton, M. G., & Buss, D. M. (2000). Error management theory: A new perspective on biases in cross-sex mind reading. *Journal of Personality and Social Psychology, 78*(1), 81–91. https://doi.org/10.1037/0022-3514.78.1.81
Hatfield, E., Bensman, L., Thornton, P. D., & Rapson, R. L. (2014). *New perspectives on emotional contagion: A review of classic and recent research on facial mimicry and contagion. Interpersona: An International Journal on Personal Relationships, 8*(2). https://doi.org/10.23668/psycharchives.2195
Hatfield, E., Cacioppo, J. T., & Rapson, R. L. (1992). Primitive emotional contagion. *Review of Personality and Social Psychology, 14*, 151–177.
Hatfield, E., Cacioppo, J. T., & Rapson, R. L. (1993). Emotional contagion. *Current Directions in Psychological Science, 2*(3), 96–100.
Hatfield, E., Cacioppo, J. T., & Rapson, R. L. (1994). *Emotional contagion*. Cambridge University Press.
Hepach, R., Vaish, A., & Tomasello, M. (2012). Young children sympathize less in response to unjustified emotional distress. *Developmental Psychology, 49*(6), 1132–1138. https://doi.org/10.1037/a0029501
Jack, R. E., Blais, C., Scheepers, C., Schyns, P. G., & Caldara, R. (2009). Cultural confusions show that facial expressions are not universal. *Current Biology, 19*(18), 1543–1548.
Jack, R. E., Garrod, O. G. B., & Schyns, P. G. (2014). Dynamic facial expressions of emotion transmit an evolving hierarchy of signals over time. *Current Biology, 24*(2), 187–192. https://doi.org/10.1016/j.cub.2013.11.064
Jack, R. E., & Schyns, P. G. (2015). The human face as a dynamic tool for social communication. *Current Biology, 25*(14), R621–R634. https://doi.org/10.1016/j.cub.2015.05.052
Johnson, N. R., Feinberg, W. E., & Johnston, D. M. (1994). Microstructure and panic: The impact of social bonds on individual action in collective flight from the Beverly Hills Supper Club fire. In R. R. Dynes & K. J. Tierney (Eds.), *Disasters, collective behavior and social organizations* (pp. 168–189). University of Delaware Press.
Johnson, R. N. (1987). Panic and the breakdown of social order: Popular myth, social theory, empirical evidence. *Sociological Focus, 20*(3), 171–183.
Kastendieck, T., Mauersberger, H., Blaison, C., Ghalib, J., & Hess, U. (2021). Laughing at funerals and frowning at weddings: Top-down influences of context-driven social judgments on emotional mimicry. *Acta Psychologica, 212*, 103195. https://doi.org/10.1016/j.actpsy.2020.103195
Keltner, D., Sauter, D., Tracy, J., & Cowen, A. (2019). Emotional expression: Advances in Basic Emotion Theory. *Journal of Nonverbal Behavior, 43*(2), 133–160. https://doi.org/10.1007/s10919-019-00293-3
Kraut, R. E., & Johnston, R. E. (1979). Social and emotional messages of smiling: An ethological approach. *Journal of Personality and Social Psychology, 37*(9), 1539–1553. https://doi.org/10.1037/0022-3514.37.9.1539
Krebs, J. R., & Dawkins, R. (1984). Animal signals: Mind-reading and manipulation. In J. R. Krebs & N. B. Davies (Eds.), *Behavioural ecology: An evolutionary approach* (pp. 380–402). Blackwell Scientific Publications.
Lanzetta, J. T., & Englis, B. G. (1989). Expectations of cooperation and competition and their effects on observers' vicarious emotional responses. *Journal of Personality and Social Psychology, 56*(4), 543–554. https://doi.org/10.1037/0022-3514.56.4.543
Larsen, R. J., Kasimatis, M., & Frey, K. (1992). Facilitating the furrowed brow: An unobtrusive test of the facial feedback hypothesis applied to unpleasant affect. *Cognition and Emotion, 6*(5), 321–338. https://doi.org/10.1080/02699939208409689
Likowski, K. U., Mühlberger, A., Seibt, B., Pauli, P., & Weyers, P. (2008). Modulation of facial mimicry by attitudes. *Journal of Experimental Social Psychology, 44*(4), 1065–1072. https://doi.org/10.1016/j.jesp.2007.10.007
Likowski, K. U., Mühlberger, A., Seibt, B., Pauli, P., & Weyers, P. (2011). Processes underlying congruent and incongruent facial reactions to emotional facial expressions. *Emotion (Washington, D.C.), 11*(3), 457–467. https://doi.org/10.1037/a0023162
Mawson, A. R. (2005). Understanding mass panic and other collective responses to threat and disaster. *Psychiatry: Interpersonal and Biological Processes, 68*(2), 95–113.

Mawson, A. R. (2017). *Mass panic and social attachment: The dynamics of human behavior*. Routledge.

McPhail, C., & Wohlstein, R. T. (1983). Individual and collective behaviors within gatherings, demonstrations, and riots. *Annual Review of Sociology, 9*(1), 579–600.

Mercier, H. (2020). *Not born yesterday: The science of who we trust and what we believe*. Princeton University Press.

Mercier, H., Dezecache, G., & Scott-Phillips, T. (2017). Strategically communicating minds. *Current Directions in Psychological Science, 26*(5), 411–416.

Nelson, N. L., & Russell, J. A. (2013). Universality revisited. *Emotion Review, 5*(1), 8–15.

Nesse, R. M. (2005). Natural selection and the regulation of defenses: A signal detection analysis of the smoke detector principle. *Evolution and Human Behavior, 26*(1), 88–105. https://doi.org/10.1016/j.evolhumbehav.2004.08.002

Paulus, A, & Wentura, D. (2015). It depends: Approach and avoidance reactions to emotional expressions are influenced by the contrast emotions presented in the task. *Journal of Experimental Psychology. Human Perception and Performance, 42*(2), 197–212. https://doi.org/10.1037/xhp0000130

Paulus, Andrea, Rohr, M., Dotsch, R., & Wentura, D. (2016). Positive feeling, negative meaning: Visualizing the mental representations of in-group and out-group smiles. *PLoS ONE, 11*(3), e0151230. https://doi.org/10.1371/journal.pone.0151230

Pichon, S., de Gelder, B., & Grezes, J. (2008). Emotional modulation of visual and motor areas by dynamic body expressions of anger. *Social Neuroscience, 3*(3–4), 199–212.

Ramakrishnan, U., & Coss, R. G. (2000). Age differences in the responses to adult and juvenile alarm calls by bonnet macaques (*Macaca radiata*). *Ethology, 106*(2), 131–144. https://doi.org/10.1046/j.1439-0310.2000.00501.x

Rankin, P. J. (1963). An epidemic of laughing in the Bukoba district of Tanganyika. *Central African Journal of Medicine, 9*(5), 167–170.

Rauchbauer, B., Majdandžić, J., Stieger, S., & Lamm, C. (2016). The modulation of mimicry by ethnic group-membership and emotional expressions. *PloS ONE, 11*(8), e0161064. https://doi.org/10.1371/journal.pone.0161064

Reed, L. I., & DeScioli, P. (2017). Watch out! How a fearful face adds credibility to warnings of danger. *Evolution and Human Behavior, 38*(4), 490–495. https://doi.org/10.1016/j.evolhumbehav.2017.03.003

Reed, L. I., DeScioli, P., & Pinker, S. A. (2014). The commitment function of angry facial expressions. *Psychological Science, 25*(8), 1511–1517.

Rudé, G. F. E. (1967). *The Crowd in the French Revolution*. Oxford University Press.

Russell, J. A. (1994). Is there universal recognition of emotion from facial expression? A review of the cross-cultural studies. *Psychological Bulletin, 115*(1), 102.

Sauter, D. A., Eisner, F., Calder, A. J., & Scott, S. K. (2010). Perceptual cues in nonverbal vocal expressions of emotion. *Quarterly Journal of Experimental Psychology, 63*(11), 2251–2272.

Sauter, D. A., Eisner, F., Ekman, P., & Scott, S. K. (2010). Cross-cultural recognition of basic emotions through nonverbal emotional vocalizations. *Proceedings of the National Academy of Sciences, 107*(6), 2408–2412. https://doi.org/10.1073/pnas.0908239106

Schweingruber, D., & Wohlstein, R. T. (2005). The madding crowd goes to school: Myths about crowds in introductory sociology textbooks. *Teaching Sociology, 33*(2), 136–153. https://doi.org/10.1177/0092055X0503300202

Scott-Phillips, T. C. (2008). Defining biological communication. *Journal of Evolutionary Biology, 21*(2), 387–395.

Seibt, B., Mühlberger, A., Likowski, K. U., & Weyers, P. (2015). Facial mimicry in its social setting. *Frontiers in Psychology, 6*, 1122. https://doi.org/10.3389/fpsyg.2015.01122

Seyfarth, R. M., & Cheney, D. L. (1980). The ontogeny of vervet monkey alarm calling behavior: A preliminary report. *Zeitschrift Für Tierpsychologie, 54*(1), 37–56.

Simon-Thomas, E. R., Keltner, D. J., Sauter, D., Sinicropi-Yao, L., & Abramson, A. (2009). The voice conveys specific emotions: Evidence from vocal burst displays. *Emotion, 9*(6), 838–846.

Smith, J. M., & Harper, D. (2004). *Animal signals*. Oxford University Press.

Smith, K. E., Norman, G. J., & Decety, J. (2017). The complexity of empathy during medical school training: Evidence for positive changes. *Medical Education, 51*(11), 1146–1159.

Soussignan, R. (2002). Duchenne smile, emotional experience, and autonomic reactivity: A test of the facial feedback hypothesis. *Emotion, 2*(1), 52–74. https://doi.org/10.1037/1528-3542.2.1.52

Sperber, D., Clément, F., Heintz, C., Mascaro, O., Mercier, H., Origgi, G., & Wilson, D. (2010). Epistemic vigilance. *Mind & Language, 25*(4), 359–393.

Stott, C., Ball, R., Drury, J., Neville, F., Reicher, S., Boardman, A., & Choudhury, S. (2018). The evolving normative dimensions of "riot": Towards an elaborated social identity explanation. *European Journal of Social Psychology, 48*(6), 834–849.

Strack, F., Martin, L. L., & Stepper, S. (1988). Inhibiting and facilitating conditions of the human smile: A nonobtrusive test of the facial feedback hypothesis. *Journal of Personality and Social Psychology, 54*(5), 768–777. https://doi.org/10.1037//0022-3514.54.5.768

Taine, H. (1876). *The origins of contemporary France* (Vol. 1). New York: H. Holt.
Templeton, A., Drury, J., & Philippides, A. (2018). Walking together: Behavioural signatures of psychological crowds. *Royal Society Open Science, 5*(7), 180172.
van der Schalk, J., Fischer, A., Doosje, B., Wigboldus, D., Hawk, S., Rotteveel, M., & Hess, U. (2011). Convergent and divergent responses to emotional displays of ingroup and outgroup. *Emotion, 11*(2), 286–298. https://doi.org/10.1037/a0022582
Huis in 't Veld, E. M., Boxtel, G. J. M. V., & de Gelder, B. (2014). The Body Action Coding System I: Muscle activations during the perception and expression of emotion. *Social Neuroscience, 9*(3), 249–264. https://doi.org/10.1080/17470919.2014.890668
Wagenmakers, E.-J., Beek, T., Dijkhoff, L., Gronau, Q. F., Acosta, A., Adams Jr, R. B., Albohn, D. N., Allard, E. S., Benning, S. D., & Blouin-Hudon, E.-M. (2016). Registered replication report: Strack, Martin, & Stepper (1988). *Perspectives on Psychological Science, 11*(6), 917–928.
Walle, E. A., & Campos, J. J. (2014). The development of infant detection of inauthentic emotion. *Emotion (Washington, D.C.), 14*(3), 488–503. https://doi.org/10.1037/a0035305
Warren, Z. J., & Power, S. A. (2015). It's contagious: Rethinking a metaphor dialogically. *Culture & Psychology, 21*(3), 359–379.
Watson, R., & de Gelder, B. (2020). The representation and plasticity of body emotion expression. *Psychological Research, 84*(5), 1400–1406. https://doi.org/10.1007/s00426-018-1133-1
Weisz, E., & Cikara, M. (2021). Strategic regulation of empathy. *Trends in Cognitive Sciences, 25*(3), 213–227. https://doi.org/10.1016/j.tics.2020.12.002
Weyers, P., Mühlberger, A., Kund, A., Hess, U., & Pauli, P. (2009). Modulation of facial reactions to avatar emotional faces by nonconscious competition priming. *Psychophysiology, 46*(2), 328–335. https://doi.org/10.1111/j.1469-8986.2008.00771.x
Zahavi, A., & Zahavi, A. (1999). *The handicap principle: A missing piece of Darwin's puzzle*. Oxford University Press.
Zillman, D., & Cantor, J. R. (1977). Affective responses to the emotions of a protagonist. *Journal of Experimental Social Psychology, 13*(2), 155–165. https://doi.org/10.1016/S0022-1031(77)80008-5

CHAPTER 45

More than PMS: The Influence of Hormones on Emotion

Lisa L. M. Welling, Virginia E. Mitchell, Jenna Lunge, and Mercedes Hughes

Abstract

Perimenstrual syndrome (PMS) is but one of several noted relationships between hormonal profile and emotion. Hormones play a moderating role in nearly all focal emotions, including negative (i.e., anger, disgust, fear, sadness) and positive (i.e., happiness) emotions. Associations between hormones and emotions are documented in both men and women, although most work has focused on women. For example, severe depression often presents with hypothalamic-pituitary-adrenal (HPA) axis dysfunction, including elevated cortisol and impaired negative feedback control, and this dysfunction has been observed prior to the development of depression in high-risk populations. This chapter explains basic hormonal processes and reviews the literature on the role of hormones in emotions. The authors review evidence that anger and dominant/aggressive behavior and feelings of disgust are related to steroid hormone levels. Finally, they examine associations between hormones and depression and anxiety disorders. They conclude with recommendations for future research.

Key Words: hormones, emotion, perimenstrual syndrome, PMS, anger, disgust, depression, anxiety

In addition to governing important bodily functions such as reproduction, hormones impact human emotion. Most research on the hormone-emotion relationship focuses on women, often by examining hormonal fluctuations across the menstrual cycle. The menstrual (or ovulatory) cycle consists of two phases. The follicular phase begins at the onset of menses and ends with the release of a mature follicle from the ovary (reviewed by Goodman, 2009). The luteal phase begins at ovulation and ends just prior to the next menstrual onset. This cyclical process is coordinated via the hypothalamic-pituitary-gonadal (HPG) axis. During the follicular phase, the HPG axis promotes the growth of ovarian follicles through the release of neuropeptides (i.e., gonadotropin-releasing hormones [GnRH]), which signal the pituitary to release luteinizing hormone (LH) and follicle-stimulating hormone (FSH) from the anterior pituitary (Levine, 1997). These hormones travel through the blood to the ovaries to stimulate the development of ovarian follicles and the release of estrogen. As the dominant follicle develops, granulosa cells in the follicle secrete increasing quantities of estradiol, and thecal cells secrete androgens (Hillier et al., 1981). In the late follicular phase, estradiol triggers a surge of LH from the anterior pituitary, which in turn triggers ovulation within the next 24–48 hours. Following ovulation, the ruptured follicle develops into the corpus luteum, a temporary structure that secretes progesterone (and some estradiol) to prepare the body for possible pregnancy

(Wuttke et al., 1998). Progesterone levels reach their cyclical peak during the mid-luteal phase. If conception does not occur, the corpus luteum regresses and production of estrogen and progesterone decline sharply, triggering menstruation.

The predictability of the menstrual cycle allows for investigation into how fluctuations in certain hormones impact emotion. Emotions are varied and can be complex, but the basic emotions are fear, disgust, anger, happiness, sadness, and surprise (e.g., Ekman & Friesen, 1971, 1976). The relationships between certain hormones and emotions have been documented in clinical populations. For example, high testosterone combined with low cortisol is associated with externalizing behavior, but only among those who score high on measures of emotional instability and disagreeableness (Tackett et al., 2014). Similarly, perinatal androgen exposure (approximated using digit ratio measurement) is negatively associated with affective borderline personality disorder symptoms in both sexes (Evardone et al., 2008), and women with borderline personality disorder are at higher risk for emotional symptoms of PMS (Eisenlohr-Moul et al., 2018). This association between hormones and emotions extends beyond clinical populations and to most basic emotions.

In this chapter, we provide a cursory overview of the relationship between hormones and emotions. We review evidence for relationships between hormones and anger, disgust, sadness (i.e., depressive disorders), and fear (i.e., anxiety disorders). We include research on PMS with research on depressive disorders because of the strong associations between PMS and mood. We conclude with a few suggestions for future research.

Anger and Aggression

Research on anger has primarily measured the expression of anger through aggressive behavior and related constructs like dominance. Aggression refers to any behavior intended to cause harm or be aversive to others (Baron & Richardson, 1994). In contrast to other emotions, research into anger/aggression and dominance has focused more on males than females. A substance produced by the testes has been implicated in aggressive behavior since the mid-19th century when Berthold removed both testes from developing male chickens and their aggressive behavior was reduced (Berthold & Quiring, 1944). Other nonhuman studies have also implicated testosterone, showing that castration reduces aggression (e.g., mice, Beeman, 1947; macaques, Takeshita et al., 2017). In humans, groups known to be more aggressive, such as young males, have higher levels of testosterone than less aggressive groups, such as women or older males (e.g., Handelsman et al., 2016; Wilson & Daly, 1985). Investigating groups that differ markedly in violence, such as violent or delinquent criminals versus controls or nonviolent criminals, yields mixed results, with some studies supporting the link between violence and testosterone (e.g., Banks & Dabbs, 1996) and others not (e.g., Bain et al., 1987). Experimental work using exogenous testosterone has also shown inconsistent results, but meta-analyses find a significant, albeit weak, association between testosterone and aggression in men (see Archer et al., 2005; Geniole et al., 2020).

The mixed or weak relationship reported across studies could be due to methodological differences, such as using different measures (Strang et al., 2013). Moreover, many studies only measured trait or stable aggression and baseline concentrations of testosterone, which is problematic because aggression is context-dependent and testosterone levels fluctuate (see Groves & Anderson, 2018). Current models and theories on the testosterone-aggression link focus on its context-dependent nature. The Challenge Hypothesis (Archer, 2006; Wingfield et al., 1990) contends that testosterone levels change when cues in the environment signal challenges to fitness or competition. A potential challenge causes an increase in testosterone to enable behavioral changes that maintain or enhance fitness, which can include aggressive behaviors for the purpose of protecting resources or status. Indeed, testosterone changes during competitions correlate with changes in aggression (e.g., Carré et al., 2013; Geniole et al., 2011). Carré, Putnam, and McCormick (2009) found that when participants competed against each other in a rigged game, men, but not women, who showed greater increases in testosterone were more aggressive on subsequent tasks, especially those men in the losing condition. Overall, testosterone fluctuations induced by competition promote aggressive behaviors in men, and are better predictors of aggressive behavior than baseline testosterone, but other factors, such as personality, context, and provocation, can moderate this relationship (e.g., Carré et al., 2017; Geniole et al., 2019; Welker et al., 2017).

Building on the Challenge Hypothesis, the Biosocial Model of Status (Mazur, 1985, 2015) asserts that testosterone surges in response to a challenge and fluctuates in response to the outcome of that challenge. Winners experience an increase in testosterone to promote further aggressive behaviors that maintain or gain status. Conversely, losers experience a decrease in testosterone, which may discourage further challenges and subsequent loss of status. Therefore, the change in aggressive behaviors linked to testosterone may function to promote a status hierarchy (e.g., Cheng et al., 2013), whereby individuals with high testosterone will exhibit more dominant behaviors and also show increasing testosterone levels as a result of status gained, which will promote further status gain. In contrast, individuals with low testosterone are expected to exhibit more submissive behaviors, and when status is lost their testosterone levels should fall further (see Geniole et al., 2017). Support for this idea has been documented in animals through the so-called Winner Effect (reviewed in Hsu et al., 2006), which is the observation that past winning experiences increase the likelihood of future competitive success. There is also evidence supporting the Biosocial Model of Status in humans. Baseline testosterone is positively correlated with taking a dominant position during a decision-making task (Mehta et al., 2017). Individuals with high basal testosterone respond negatively to a decrease in status, whereas those with low basal testosterone levels respond neutrally or negatively to an increase in status (e.g., Josephs et al., 2006; Mehta et al., 2008). Similarly, trait or baseline dominance has been shown to moderate the relationship between testosterone and aggressive or dominant behavior (see Carré & Archer, 2017).

Cortisol, which is released in times of stress and may suppress testosterone secretion (Chen et al., 1997), also plays a role in the link between testosterone and dominant/aggressive behaviors. The Dual-Hormone Hypothesis (Mehta & Josephs, 2010) argues that high levels of testosterone only promote increased status when cortisol levels are low. Testosterone predicts dominant behaviors, but only when an individual has low cortisol (Mehta & Josephs, 2010). Likewise, cortisol moderates the relationship between testosterone and overt aggression (Popma et al., 2007; but see Mazur & Booth, 2014) and testosterone and the severity of violent crimes (Dabbs et al., 1991). A recent meta-analysis supported the Dual-Hormone Hypothesis, although the reported testosterone-cortisol interaction was small (Dekkers et al., 2019). Although research supports a link between testosterone, cortisol, and aggression or dominance in men (see Archer et al., 2005; Dekkers et al., 2019; Geniole et al., 2020), these links in women are weaker or nonexistent (e.g., Carré et al., 2009; Carré et al., 2013; Geniole et al., 2013). These weak findings in women may be due to differences in sensitivities of methods used to determine testosterone levels (Geniole & Carré, 2019), variability due to menstrual cycle changes or use of hormonal contraceptives (e.g., Geniole et al., 2013), or because testosterone may promote different functions in men and women. Importantly, women tend to use indirect forms of aggression (e.g., ostracism, gossiping) rather than physical aggression, and so indirect aggression may better measure female dominance (e.g., Archer, 2009; Hess & Hagen, 2006). Testosterone has been implicated as an important hormone involved in both male (Archer, 2006; Mazur & Booth, 1998) and female intrasexual competition (Hahn et al., 2016; Maner & McNulty, 2013; Welling, Jones, et al., 2007). Future research should further parse the hormonal correlates of specific forms of aggression in women.

Disgust

Disgust is a universal emotion (Curtis & Biran, 2001; Ekman & Friesen, 1971) within the disease-avoidance system that likely evolved to protect one from pathogen threats (Fessler & Navarrete, 2003) and which functions to motivate withdrawal and avoidance of contagion (e.g., Curtis & Biran, 2001; Gangestad & Buss, 1993), thereby providing a fitness advantage that improves individuals' chances of selecting healthy mates and having healthy offspring (Oaten et al., 2009). The facial expression associated with disgust (e.g., wrinkling of the nose and brows; Curtis et al., 2004) communicates information to viewers about the potential presence of contagions (Conway et al., 2007) and is recognized across cultures (Mesquita & Frijda, 1992). Although contamination threats such as bodily secretions and rotting food are the most frequently reported sources of disgust (Oaten et al., 2009), violations of social norms (e.g., stealing) and behaviors that threaten reproductive success (e.g., infidelity) can provoke moral and sexual disgust, respectively (Fessler & Navarrete, 2003; Tybur et al., 2009).

Individual differences in disgust are well documented; individuals who score higher in neuroticism (e.g., Druschel & Sherman, 1999), anxiety (Thorpe et al., 2003), perceived vulnerability to disease (Duncan et al., 2009; Welling, Conway, et al., 2007), and harm avoidance (Sparks et al., 2018) report greater disgust sensitivity. Disgust sensitivity is also associated with contamination fear (e.g., Olatunji et al., 2004; Olatunji et al., 2011) and behavioral avoidance of potential contamination threat (e.g., a bedpan filled with water; Deacon & Olatunji, 2007). Women experience disgust more readily and more intensely than do men (e.g., Al-Shawaf & Lewis, 2013; Sparks et al., 2018), are more accurate in recognizing disgusted facial expressions (Rotter & Rotter, 1988), and attend to disgusted expressions longer (Kraines et al., 2016). These sex differences may account for higher rates of psychopathologies among women that include fear of contamination as a core symptom, such as obsessive-compulsive disorder (OCD; Weissman et al., 1994). Sex differences in disgust sensitivity are not present in childhood (Stevenson et al., 2010), however, suggesting that the differences in adult men and women develop during puberty and are related to reproduction (reviewed in Fleischman, 2014).

Women's disgust sensitivity varies alongside their reproductive hormone profile (e.g., Fessler et al., 2005; Fleischman & Fessler, 2011; but see Jones et al., 2018; Olatunji et al., 2020). Naturally ovulating women (i.e., reproductive aged women who are not using hormonal contraceptives) report greater preference for faces perceived as healthy over faces altered to appear less healthy (i.e., a contamination-related cue) during the luteal (when progesterone is relatively high and conception risk is low) compared to the late-follicular phase (when estrogen and conception risk are relatively high; Jones et al., 2005). Women also perceive disgusted facial expressions with averted gazes as more intense when measured during the luteal versus the follicular phase (Conway et al., 2007). An averted disgust gaze indicates that something near the perceiver may be pathogenic (high contagion risk), whereas a direct disgust gaze indicates the perceiver is prompting the disgust response (low contagion risk). Ovulatory phase is not associated with changes in the perception of happy faces with direct or averted gaze, however, indicating that progesterone primarily influences sensitivity to facial cues that signal nearby threat (Conway et al., 2007).

Progesterone level, specifically, not necessarily cycle phase, however, is associated with disgust sensitivity. After ovulation, progesterone reaches its peak in the mid-luteal phase in naturally ovulating women and continues to rise if pregnancy occurs. Progesterone has adaptive immunosuppressant effects, which downregulate the immune system during pregnancy to prevent an immune response against a developing embryo (reviewed in Fessler, 2001, 2002). According to the Compensatory Prophylaxis Hypothesis, when progesterone is high and the immune system is downregulated, women increase avoidance of potential sources of contagion to decrease their own infection risk (Fessler & Navarrete, 2003). Increases in progesterone are associated with women's self-reported disgust sensitivity (Żelaźniewicz et al., 2016), including grooming behaviors and avoidance of public restrooms (Fleischman & Fessler, 2011). Furthermore, disgust sensitivity is greater among women in the first trimester of pregnancy (when contagion can most easily lead to spontaneous abortion) compared to the second or third, particularly toward sources of contagion like food and bodily secretions (Fessler et al., 2005).

Recent research has not replicated the relationship between self-reported disgust and progesterone level (Jones et al., 2018) or ovulatory cycle phase (Olatunji et al., 2020). Furthermore, to date, only one published study (Jones et al., 2005) has investigated how hormonal contraceptives, which supply artificial progesterone (often in combination with artificial estrogen), influence disgust sensitivity and behavioral avoidance of contamination, finding that hormonally contracepted women report greater attraction to healthy faces compared to naturally ovulating women. This study, however, analyzed all hormonal contraceptive users as a single group, rather than controlling for the unique ratio of artificial progesterone to artificial estrogen contained within participants' contraception. More work is needed to determine how progesterone-induced immunosuppression influences women's disgust sensitivity and behavioral avoidance of contamination threat. Additional research should also investigate hormonal correlates of disgust sensitivity in men.

Depressive Disorders

Depressive disorders are characterized by prolonged sadness and decreased interest in daily life. Disruptions in hormonal systems have been implicated in depressive disorders, and understanding these disruptions, particularly during early development, may be key to developing prevention and treatment options. Next, we review the hormonal underpinnings of various depressive disorders, with a particular focus on major depressive disorder (MDD), premenstrual syndrome (PMS), premenstrual dysphoric disorder (PMDD), and peripartum depression. We also discuss the transition to menopause.

Major Depressive Disorder

MDD is defined by depressed mood and loss of interest in activities previously considered rewarding (i.e., anhedonia) that persists for at least two weeks and that last for most of the day, nearly every day. To be diagnosed, individuals must have experienced anhedonia and at least four of the following symptoms to a severe degree: changes in sleep quality, depressed mood, changes in weight, psychomotor changes, fatigue, feelings of excessive and inappropriate guilt or worthlessness, inability to concentrate, and/or recurrent thoughts of death or suicidal ideation. Approximately 16% of adults in the United States will suffer from MDD during their life span, with another 10% experiencing minor forms of depression (Kessler et al., 2003). MDD also carries with it a substantial risk of recurrence (up to 80%; Kessler et al., 2003). Comparably, subclinical depression has consequences for an individual's quality of life and is a predictor of later being diagnosed with clinical depression (e.g., Cuijpers et al., 2014).

Multiple hormonal systems have been linked to depressive disorders and associated developmental trajectories. The HPA axis, involved in the mammalian stress response, is controlled by a complex system, consisting of the serotonergic (Lowry, 2002), GABAergic (Cullinan et al., 2008), and the noradrenergic systems (Pacak & Palkovits, 2001), and circadian control from the suprachiasmatic nucleus (reviewed by Kudielka & Kirschbaum, 2005). Cortical and limbic structures also provide feedback that modulates the activity of the HPA axis per stimuli that are perceived as threatening and are based on contextual factors (Pacak & Palkovits, 2001). When a stressor is present, the following reactions occur to initiate HPA axis activity: (1) activity in the prefrontal cortex, hippocampus, amygdala, hypothalamus, and septum begins in response to stressful stimuli; (2) sustained activation of the amygdala activates the hypothalamus, which begins to secrete corticotropin-releasing hormone (CRH) and arginine vasopressin in the paraventricular nuclei; (3) CRH activates the anterior pituitary and induces release of adrenocorticotropic hormone (ACTH); (4) ACTH reaches the adrenal glands and promotes the production of glucocorticoids; and (5) glucocorticoid activity prepares the body to cope with prolonged stressors by increasing the availability of glucose, promoting lipid and carbohydrate metabolism, and reducing immune system activity (Bateman et al., 1989).

The HPA axis is overactive in depressed individuals, with elevated cortisol levels found in patients with depression compared to healthy controls (e.g., Brown et al., 2004). This may be caused by a lack of inhibitory control of glucocorticoids on paraventricular nucleus and pituitary gland activity, which results in an abundance of CRH and ACTH secretion (Pariante & Lightman, 2008). In patients with depression, administration of an exogenous agonist of the glucocorticoid receptor, dexamethasone, fails to provide negative feedback to the HPA axis, causing high levels of cortisol following a CRH administrative test (e.g., Heuser et al., 1994). Abnormalities in the functionality of the glucocorticoid receptor (GR) likely cause poor HPA inhibition in these scenarios; experimentally reducing the presence of GRs in animals induces depressive-like behaviors (e.g., Chourbaji et al., 2007), anti-depressant treatment in humans restores GR functionality (Pariante, 2006), and failure of GR activity to regulate in response to treatment is a predictor of depression relapse (e.g., Zobel et al., 2001).

Although dysregulation of the HPA axis is a marker of depression, it is unclear if this is a cause or an effect of depression. There is evidence documenting long-term changes in HPA axis activity that are associated with developmental events, such that experiencing developmental challenges (e.g., abuse) attunes the activity of the HPA axis later in life (e.g., Guerry & Hastings, 2011). These experiences may predispose individuals to developing the pattern of HPA axis activity and reactivity characteristic of those with depression (e.g., Frodl & O'Keane, 2013). The Glucocorticoid Cascade Hypothesis (Sapolsky et al., 1986) posits that prolonged stressors modulate neuroactivity and cause damage to brain structure (e.g., hippocampal neurogenesis) and function (e.g., HPA axis control). Recent reappraisals of this theory (e.g., Frodl & O'Keane, 2013) focus on functional changes in the HPA axis that occur as a result of prolonged and/or severe stressors during development that predispose individuals to different patterns of HPA inhibition. Support for this idea comes from research on youth at higher risk for developing a depressive disorder (e.g., children with high trait neuroticism; Vinkers et al., 2014). Children of parents with bipolar disorder have higher daytime cortisol levels than do controls (Ellenbogen et al., 2006), and this pattern persists during puberty (Ellenbogen et al., 2010) and young adulthood (Ostiguy et al., 2011). Also, REM sleep disturbances and increased HPA axis activity occur before the onset of depression among high-risk individuals (Rao et al., 2009). However, the patterns of expression for specific genes involved in HPA axis control are influenced by lifetime experience, such that increased expression of these genes was predictive of developing MDD across adolescence and young-adulthood, even after controlling for familial risk (Humphreys et al., 2019), suggesting an important environmental role on gene expression.

Sex differences in diagnoses of MDD and differences in symptom experience (e.g., greater agitation in men; Altemus et al., 2014) point to differential effects that sex-typical steroid hormones may have on depression (see Naninck et al., 2011). Relative to men, women are at greater risk of MDD (e.g., Altemus et al., 2014), at least until menopause (Payne, 2003). These sex differences in depression emerge in adolescence and are linked to pubertal transition in girls (e.g., Bennett et al., 2005). Hormonal changes during adolescence may coalesce with social expectations and gender norms to increase the likelihood that girls will experience depression (e.g., Marcotte et al., 2002; Phares et al., 2004). Girls report more stressors that contribute to depression and may also be more likely to experience depression in response to stressors than boys (e.g., Hankin et al., 2007; Shih et al., 2006). One hormone that differs markedly between the sexes from puberty onward is testosterone. Testosterone is an androgen that is responsible for the development of male secondary sexual characteristics (e.g., facial and body hair, deepening of voice) and reproductive tissues. It likely influences mood via its effects on neuropeptide and neurotransmitter systems and their effects on neurogenesis in the hippocampus, which are both dysregulated in MDD patients (Ebinger et al., 2009). Testosterone influences the monoamine system (e.g., Robichaud & Debonnel, 2005), as well as dopaminergic and serotonergic activity (e.g., de Souza Silva et al., 2009), and dysregulation in all three of these neurotransmitter systems has been implicated in depression (Werner & Covenas, 2010). Testosterone supports neuroplasticity, activates the serotonin system, and may also downregulate the activity of the HPA axis, all of which may contribute to its mood effects (Walther et al., 2019).

Men with low levels of testosterone may be at a greater risk for depression (McIntyre et al., 2006; Zarrouf et al., 2009). In a study of approximately 3,000 men who were followed over 10 years, men with low testosterone were diagnosed with depression more than men with higher testosterone (Ford et al., 2016). Testosterone administration treatment for men whose depression is associated with reduced testosterone production may be a viable antidepressant treatment or a supplement to other regiments (Amiaz & Seidman, 2008). However, exogenous testosterone treatment carries serious potential side effects (e.g., increased rates of prostate cancer and cardiovascular disease; Surampudi et al., 2012). In contrast, research investigating the effects of testosterone on depression in women has been inconclusive or contradictory (e.g., Bromberger et al., 2010; Kische et al., 2018), although some evidence suggests testosterone supplementation improves mood in premenopausal women with low sex drive (Goldstat et al., 2003) and may augment treatments for depressed women (Miller et al., 2009; but see Dichtel et al., 2020).

Premenstrual Syndrome and Premenstrual Dysphoric Disorder

Both premenstrual syndrome (PMS) and the more severe and clinically recognized (Reed et al., 2019) premenstrual dysphoric disorder (PMDD; Halbreich et al., 2003) are characterized by the onset of symptoms of depression, anxiety, mood swings, and various physical symptoms (e.g., headaches, breast pain) during the luteal phase, which lessen or are alleviated after the onset of menstruation (see Braverman, 2007; Yonkers et al., 2008). By some estimates, most women experience at least one (usually mild) symptom of PMS during a typical menstrual cycle (e.g., Tschudin et al., 2010), although these estimates vary by study (likely due to variation in method of PMS symptomology assessment; Tschudin et al., 2010) and by cultural context (e.g., Takeda et al., 2006). For example, research has found that 5.3% of

Japanese women (Takeda et al., 2006), 10.3% of Swiss women (Tschudin et al., 2010), 12% of French women (Potter et al., 2009), and 21% of Chinese women (Qiao et al., 2012) experience moderate to severe PMS. The prevalence of PMDD, on the other hand, consistently falls between ~5% and 10% of menstruating women (reviewed in Halbreich et al., 2003). The diagnostic criteria for PMDD require that symptoms onset within the week before menses and improve drastically within a few days of menstrual onset (American Psychiatric Association, 2013). Individuals must also report at least five of the following symptoms: marked change in depressed mood and negative affect, decrease in mood stability, increased anxiety and tension, anhedonia, difficulty concentrating, decreased energy, change in appetite, changes in sleep quantity or amount, a sense of loss of control, and/or physical symptoms (e.g., breast tenderness, headache, joint pain).

Evidence linking PMS and PMDD to steroid hormones is plentiful. Although most of the symptoms of PMDD peak approximately two days prior to menstrual onset, there is variation in the timing of initial symptom onset and intensity prior to menstruation, as well as differences in symptom onset between women and between-cycle variation for the same women (e.g., Pearlstein et al., 2005). Symptom onset is linked to changes in progesterone levels that occur following ovulation at the beginning of the luteal phase (Bäckström et al., 2003), such that progesterone (and estrogen) levels are positively correlated with the intensity of anxiety and depression during the beginning of the luteal phase, but after progesterone levels plateau and begin to drop, symptoms continue to increase until a few days following menstruation, when they decrease. Hysterectomies including bilateral oophorectomy (removal of both ovaries) improve PMS symptoms in women with severe PMS (e.g., Casper & Hearn, 1990), whereas hysterectomies without oophorectomy do not (e.g., Bäckström et al., 1981), reinforcing the idea that PMS symptoms are caused by changes in ovarian steroid hormones. Additionally, GnRH antagonists and gonadotropin hormone blockers, which reduce circulating sex steroid levels, relieve PMS and PMDD symptoms (e.g., Muse et al., 1984; Schmidt et al., 1998). The reintroduction of estradiol or progesterone causes symptoms of PMS to reappear, although these manipulations have no effect on women who do not suffer from PMS, suggesting that women with PMS display a unique response to physiological levels of steroid hormones (Schmidt et al., 1998).

Hormonal contraceptives reduce the production of endogenous steroid hormones and replace endogenous hormones with a steady regimen of synthetic versions of progesterone or progesterone and estrogen. If changes in these steroid hormone levels are part of the etiology of PMS and PMDD, then we expect that hormonal contraceptives would relieve symptoms because they prevent cyclical changes in steroid hormones across the menstrual cycle. However, research in this area has been mixed (reviewed in Lete & Lapuente, 2016); some synthetic progestin compounds show efficacy (e.g., drospirenone), while others show mixed or no effect on PMS symptoms (e.g., levonorgestrel). Contraceptives containing drospirenone (e.g., Yonkers et al., 2005) and monocyclic contraceptives (Bäckström et al., 1992), which contain a consistent hormonal dosage across the active pills, are effectively used to treat PMDD.

The above results do not indicate the underlying physiological differences that predispose some women, but not others, to experiencing PMS or PMDD. Absolute differences in hormone levels (Bäckström et al., 2003) and patterns of hormonal secretion (Lewis et al., 1995) do not differ between women with PMS or PMDD and healthy controls, and progesterone and estrogen levels do not correlate with symptom severity in women with PMDD (e.g., Hsiao, Liu, et al., 2004). Rather, women with PMS and PMDD are more sensitive to changes in ovarian steroid hormone levels (e.g., Schmidt et al., 2017). One potential explanation relates to the activity of and sensitivity to the neurosteroid metabolite of progesterone, allopregnanolone (ALLO). ALLO is one of the main metabolites of progesterone and is a strong positive modulator of the $GABA_a$ receptor (Hantsoo & Epperson, 2020). GABA is the most important inhibitory neurotransmitter in the mammalian central nervous system (CNS), and chemicals and drugs that interact with the GABA system have anxiolytic, depressive effects on the CNS. However, similar to the prevalence of PMDD, 3%–8% of the general population have a paradoxical reaction to positive $GABA_a$ modulators (e.g., benzodiazepines, alcohol), such that exposure to low concentrations produces anxiety, aggression, and unstable mood states. There is evidence linking ALLO activity to PMS and PMDD via its effects on GABAergic functionality (see Bäckström et al., 2014; Hantsoo & Epperson, 2020). For example, in rat models of hormone-withdrawal-induced depression, preventing the conversion of progesterone to ALLO causes withdrawal symptoms, although the apparent levels of progesterone are still high (e.g., Costa et al., 1995) and progesterone blockers do not improve PMS symptoms (Chan et al., 1994). Women who have PMDD or PMS display different sensitivity to ALLO via unique reactivity of the $GABA_a$ receptor, whereby the nervous system of women with PMDD has a reduced ability to appropriately alter GABA subunit composition in accordance with changing levels of ALLO across the menstrual cycle, resulting in poor emotion regulation and experience of negative mood states (Hantsoo & Epperson, 2020).

There is also some evidence that levels of estrogen and estrogen withdrawal may contribute to onset of symptoms. Although absolute levels of estrogen (or progesterone) are not linked to depressive or anxiety symptoms during the late luteal phase (e.g., Hsiao, Liu, et al., 2004), women who have a specific variant of the estrogen receptor alpha gene are more likely to receive a PMDD diagnosis (e.g., Miller et al., 2010). The effects of estrogen on PMS and PMDD may be occurring via the modulatory role that estrogens have on the serotonin system (reviewed in Borrow & Cameron, 2014), which is dysregulated in women with PMS and PMDD (Rapkin & Akopians, 2012). The link between depressive mood states and hormones is further demonstrated by mood disorders that are linked to changes in reproductive states in women across the life span (e.g., postpartum depression).

Peripartum Depression

Pregnancy and postpartum periods are marked by rapid, substantial changes in several hormones. Estrogen and progesterone rise considerably during pregnancy (reviewed in Brett & Baxendale, 2001) and then drop precipitously following birth (e.g., Willcox et al., 1985). Antenatal depression can occur during pregnancy, and postpartum depression (PPD) occurs after birth. Antenatal depression and PPD occur at similar prevalence rates as MDD (ranging 12%–20%; Bennett et al., 2004; Halbreich & Karkun, 2006). PPD typically presents in the first six weeks following parturition with symptoms similar to other depressive disorders (e.g., anhedonia, changes in appetite and sleep, inability to focus, poor memory and concentration, suicidal ideation), but may include a focus on infant-based concerns (e.g., excessive worry about the infant's health; Phillips et al., 2009). A number of factors predispose women to developing peripartum depression. These include neuroticism, lack of social support, financial hardship, an unwanted pregnancy, lack of a partner, and difficult infant temperament (e.g., O'Hara & McCabe, 2013). A prior diagnosis of MDD is one of the strongest risk factors for developing PPD (e.g., Silverman et al., 2017), and women who have a history of MDD are likely to experience a relapse during pregnancy, even when antidepressant medication is congruous before and during pregnancy (e.g., Cohen, Altshuler, et al., 2006). This suggests that not only are the hormonal changes that occur during pregnancy a risk-factor for MDD recurrence, but that treatment for MDD symptoms is not as protective against MDD during pregnancy for some women.

Similar to theories connecting hormone withdrawal to PMDD and PMS symptoms, there are theories describing links between hormonal fluctuations and peripartum depression (Workman et al., 2012). That euthymic women and those with peripartum depression do not vary in absolute levels of sex steroids in the postpartum period (e.g., Bloch et al., 2003) suggests that sensitivity to hormonal change, rather than differences in absolute hormone levels, is associated with developing depressive mood disorders related to reproductive transition. Bloch et al. (2000) induced hypogonadal levels of hormone production in a group of women who had previously experienced PPD and a group of euthymic women using a GnRH antagonist. After GnRH-induced hormonal withdrawal, five of the eight women who had a history of PPD developed changes in mood symptoms, whereas none of the euthymic women did. These results support the argument that some women are more sensitive to hormonal changes. One potential mechanism explaining this difference in hormonal sensitivity suggests that variation in the estrogen receptor gene (*ESR1*; Pinsonneault et al., 2013; although see Tan et al., 2018) and different patterns of estrogen-induced epigenetic changes (Mehta et al., 2019) alter serotonergic system signaling in women with peripartum depression. Women with a specific serotonin transporter gene variant are susceptible to changes in estradiol levels following parturition (Hu et al., 2019), implicating an interaction between genetic variants in both the estrogen and serotonin systems in peripartum depression. Additionally, ALLO levels and subsequent GABAergic modifications have been implicated in the development of peripartum depression (e.g., Walton & Maguire, 2019). For instance, lower levels of ALLO during pregnancy positively predict peripartum depression (Osborne et al., 2017) and self-reported depression (Hellgren et al., 2014), and medications that increase ALLO levels are effective at treating peripartum depression (Walton & Maguire, 2019).

Transition to Menopause
During the menopausal transition, the female reproductive system begins to cease regular monthly menstrual cycles, and production of follicle cells in the ovaries begins to subside. This stage is marked by periods of low and high estrogen levels caused by great variability in FSH concentrations. Rates of MDD and depressive symptoms during this time increase substantially (Bromberger et al., 2011; Cohen, Soares, et al., 2006), and women who have a history of MDD are much more likely to experience MDD during the menopausal transition than euthymic women (Freeman, 2010). Similar to PMDD and peripartum depression, it is unclear whether absolute differences in hormone levels between women undergoing menopause with and without depression are substantially different (Freeman, 2010). Some studies have found that higher testosterone, but not estradiol, levels may contribute to higher depressive symptoms across the menopausal transition (e.g., Bromberger et al., 2010). Others have found that the vasomotor symptoms caused by low estradiol levels (e.g., hot flashes) are associated with depression during menopause, but absolute levels of estradiol are not (Avis et al., 2001).

Estrogen withdrawal sensitivity may help explain why some women develop depression during menopause and others do not. Schmidt et al. (2015) tested whether women with a history of perimenopausal depression were more sensitive to estrogen withdrawal than women who had no history of perimenopausal depression. Participants in each group were administered transdermal estradiol for three weeks, followed by one half of each group being switched to a placebo patch to induce estrogen withdrawal. Women who had a history of perimenopausal depression who were transitioned to the placebo patch had a significant increase in depression severity following transition, whereas women with no history of perimenopausal depression in the transition group showed no changes in depressive symptoms.

Anxiety Disorders

Anxiety disorders are common, with the 12-month prevalence of anxiety disorders reaching nearly 20% in the United States (Kessler et al., 2009), and 31% of Americans and 16% of the worldwide population being diagnosed with an anxiety disorder within their lifetime (Kessler et al., 2009; for similar estimates, see Kessler et al., 2012). Beginning at puberty (e.g., Paus et al., 2008), anxiety disorders become much more common among females, who are nearly twice as likely to develop fear-based psychopathologies such as generalized anxiety disorder (GAD), social anxiety disorder (SAD), post-traumatic stress disorder (PTSD), and panic disorder (PD; e.g., Kessler et al., 2005; Kessler et al., 2012; McLean et al., 2011). Women also report more intense symptoms compared to men (Pigott, 2003). For example, women with PTSD report worse quality of life outcomes (Holbrook et al., 2002) and women with PD report a greater frequency of panic attacks compared to men (Reed & Wittchen, 1998).

Similar to depressive disorders, changes in women's anxiety coincide with fluctuations in their steroid reproductive hormone profile (e.g., at pubertal onset, postpartum, at menopause). The most common age of onset for anxiety disorders in women is their mid- to late-20s (Pigott, 2003), which corresponds with peak reproductive fertility (e.g., Dunson et al., 2002). Pregnancy also influences women's anxiety, with postpartum women reporting higher rates of obsessive-compulsive disorder (OCD) and GAD compared to the general population (reviewed in Ross & McLean, 2006). Within-women differences in anxiety disorders are also prevalent, such that naturally ovulating women report greater anxiety in their luteal phase compared to their follicular phase (Gonda et al., 2008; Nillni et al., 2012).

Steroid reproductive hormones such as progesterone and estrogen may be powerful CNS modulators (reviewed in McEwen & Parsons, 1982) and are likely candidates for influencing the onset, progression, and severity of anxiety disorders among women. Differences in steroid reproductive hormones likely follow two pathways to influence women's susceptibility to anxiety disorders by (1) increasing women's vulnerability to factors that promote disorder development, and (2) promoting maintenance of the disorders after development (reviewed in Li & Graham, 2017). Women with higher trait progesterone, for example, report greater anxiety compared to women with lower trait progesterone (Reynolds et al., 2018). Additionally, progesterone administration during the follicular phase increases women's amygdalar reactivity to angry and fearful faces, suggesting that progesterone may indirectly increase emotional reactions of fear and anxiety and increase women's susceptibility to anxiety when their progesterone levels are high (van Wingen et al., 2007). Here, we briefly outline the influence of steroid reproductive hormones on GAD (lifetime prevalence of 4.3%–5.7%), SAD (lifetime prevalence of 10.7%–12.1%), PTSD (lifetime prevalence rate of 5.7%–6.8%), PD (lifetime prevalence of 3.8%–4.7%), and OCD (lifetime prevalence of 1.6%; Kessler et al., 2005; Kessler et al., 2012).

Generalized Anxiety Disorder
GAD is a chronic anxiety disorder characterized by intense, long-lasting, and excessive worrying or fear (Brown & Barlow, 1992) that causes distress and impairment (Maier et al., 2000). Women appear to have an earlier age of onset (Yonkers et al., 2003; but see McLean et al., 2011), are more likely to report physical symptomology such as fatigue (Vesga-López, Blanco, et al., 2008), and are more likely to have a chronic diagnosis without remission (e.g., Yonkers et al., 2003) compared to men. Women's steroid reproductive hormones appear to influence the severity of GAD, such that women report worsening of GAD symptomology in the premenstrual period (Hsiao, Hsiao, et al., 2004; but see McLeod et al., 1993), experience higher rates during pregnancy (Misri et al., 2015), worsened symptomology during the first and

third trimesters (e.g., Teixeira et al., 2009), and higher rates postpartum (Ross & McLean, 2006). The increase in pregnant women's symptoms of GAD is important, not only because they themselves experience poorer outcomes (e.g., Misri et al., 2015; Teixeira et al., 2009), but also because newborn children of women with GAD have half the levels of brain-derived neurotrophic factor (a growth factor related to brain development; Bernd, 2008), and this association increases accordingly with the length of time of mothers' GAD diagnosis (Uguz et al., 2013).

Social Anxiety Disorder
SAD (also known as social phobia) is characterized by fear and avoidance of situations that may result in scrutiny by others and embarrassment or humiliation (Stein & Stein, 2008). Age of onset for SAD is early compared to other anxiety disorders, with half of cases diagnosed by age 11 and 80% by age 20 (Stein & Stein, 2008). Women are 1.2–1.5 times more likely to develop SAD compared to men (Kessler et al., 2012) and report different triggers for SAD. For example, women are more likely to report fears related to public eating, writing while being watched, and attending social events, whereas men are more likely to report fears related to using public restrooms and returning items to a store (Turk et al., 1998). The effects of reproductive hormones on SAD are inconsistent, with studies finding increased rates of SAD among pregnant women (Adewuya et al., 2006), similar rates between pregnant and nonpregnant women, lower prevalence among postpartum than nonpregnant women (Vesga-López, Schneider, et al., 2008), and improved symptoms among those who experienced symptom change during pregnancy, which then returned to pre-pregnancy levels in the postpartum period (Van Veen et al., 2009).

Post-Traumatic Stress Disorder
PTSD, characterized by fear and helplessness after experiencing a traumatic event, is the most common anxiety disorder to occur after a trauma (Galovski et al., 2012). Though the risk for developing PTSD after experiencing a traumatic event is only ~25% (Kessler et al., 1995), and overall rates of trauma exposure do not vary between men and women (reviewed in Piggott et al., 2019; but see Tolin & Foa, 2006), women are twice as likely to be diagnosed with PTSD (e.g., Kessler et al., 2017; Tolin & Foa, 2006). Sex differences exist in the types of trauma that cause PTSD. For example, girls are more likely than boys to develop PTSD from trauma experienced before the age of 15 (Kessler et al., 1995) and women are more likely to experience sexual violence, whereas men are more likely to experience combat trauma and physical assault (Kessler et al., 2017). Nonetheless, women are at a greater risk of developing PTSD even after accounting for these differences (Blanco et al., 2018). Changes in steroid reproductive hormones appear to influence PTSD; women pregnant with their first child experience PTSD rates twice that of a comparison group (Seng et al., 2010), although this increased risk may be confined to late pregnancy (Adewuya et al., 2006). Among nonclinical populations, women in the early-luteal phase report greater intrusive memories of a stressful film compared to women in the late-luteal or mid-follicular phase (Soni et al., 2013), suggesting a role specifically of the ratio between estrogen and progesterone in women's vulnerability to psychological distress. Additionally, women diagnosed with PTSD are likely to experience fluctuations in the severity of their symptomology. For example, women with PTSD experience poorer recall of fear extinction during their mid-luteal phase compared to their follicular phase (Pineles et al., 2016). In other words, when progesterone reaches its per-cycle peak and estrogen is in

its secondary peak, women with PTSD are more likely to relive fear toward a stimulus where fear had already been unlearned (see also Soni et al., 2013). Ultimately, steroid reproductive hormones may have the capacity to alter women's vulnerability to and the severity of women's experiences of PTSD symptomology.

Panic Disorder

Panic disorder (PD) is characterized by frequent, recurring, and unexpected panic attacks, combined with fear of panic attacks (Piggott et al., 2019), and is 2.5 times more prevalent among women than men (e.g., McLean et al., 2011). PD rarely occurs before puberty or after menopause, with most diagnoses occurring in young adulthood (e.g., Eaton, 1995). Women report greater anxiety sensitivity (i.e., susceptibility to fear of anxiety-provoking situations; Bernstein et al., 2006), which may contribute to greater rates of PD among women. There are, however, marked hormonal influences on women's PD symptomology. The late luteal (or premenstrual) phase is a time of increased risk for panic attacks in women (e.g., Sigmon et al., 2000). Although pregnancy is not reliably associated with worsening of PD symptoms (Goodman et al., 2014), women consistently report worsening of their PD symptoms in the postpartum period. After giving birth, postpartum women experience a rapid decrease in levels of hormones, such as progesterone and ALLO, leading to hormonal withdrawal. ALLO withdrawal and decreased neural inhibition during the postpartum period may thus increase the risk of new or recurrent diagnoses of PD (reviewed in Altemus et al., 2014). However, women diagnosed with PD have higher levels of ALLO compared to nonclinical controls after psychological challenge (Ströhle et al., 2002), possibly because increased ALLO may act as a preventive mechanism against panic attacks (e.g., Rupprecht, 2003).

Obsessive-Compulsive Disorder

OCD is categorized by recurrent, intrusive thoughts (i.e., obsessions) combined with ritualistic behaviors (i.e., compulsions) aimed to relieve the obsessions (Julien et al., 2007). Sex differences in prevalence rates of OCD are inconsistent, but most research (including a recent meta-analysis; Fawcett et al., 2020) suggests that OCD is 1.5–2 times more prevalent in women compared to men (e.g., Kessler et al., 2012). Men and women differ in the types of obsessions and compulsions they report; men are more likely to report sexual or religious obsessions and compulsions, whereas women are more likely to report obsessions and compulsions related to contamination and cleaning (e.g., Labad et al., 2008). This difference may be due, in part, to women's greater susceptibility to experiencing disgust. Women score higher on self-report and behavioral measures of disgust sensitivity (e.g., Al-Shawaf & Lewis, 2013). The strength of women's disgust sensitivity is related to progesterone level (e.g., Żelaźniewicz et al., 2016), suggesting that steroid reproductive hormone levels may also influence OCD vulnerability. Indeed, reports suggest that women's OCD symptomology onset occurs within critical periods of major hormonal fluctuation, such as during the same year as menarche (Labad et al., 2005), during pregnancy, or early within the postpartum period (Forray et al., 2010). The postpartum period also acts as a time of worsened symptomology for women already diagnosed with OCD (Labad et al., 2005; Williams & Koran, 1997). Like other anxiety disorders (e.g., PD; Sigmon et al., 2000), OCD symptomology can worsen in the late-luteal (or premenstrual) phase of the menstrual cycle among naturally cycling women (e.g., Labad et al., 2005; Williams & Koran, 1997). Thus, between-individual differences in steroid reproductive hormones may contribute to one's vulnerability to an initial diagnosis of OCD, whereas within-individual fluctuations in hormone profile may predispose women to worsening of their OCD symptomology.

Conclusion

The word "hormonal" is sometimes applied in an unfounded and sexist way to describe irrational and emotional behavior and to question women's abilities (see Chrisler & Caplan, 2002). For example, premenstrual syndrome (PMS, also called perimenstrual syndrome) emerged in the medical literature in 1931 as a rare hormonal imbalance referred to as premenstrual tension (Frank, 1931), but, in reaction to advances women made in the workforce, it surfaced into public discourse in the 1980s and was construed as a social problem rooted in biology that brought women's competencies into question (Rittenhouse, 1991). However, opinions on hormonal changes are often inaccurate (e.g., Epting & Overman, 1998), ignore positive effects of hormonal fluctuations (e.g., boosts in creativity; Chrisler, 1991), and frequently fail to consider how hormones impact emotion in men. Nonetheless, there is a great deal of evidence that hormones impact emotions in both sexes.

Here we have provided an overview of research linking within-person hormonal fluctuations and between-person hormonal profile differences with emotional states. The fluctuations of mood in congruence with hormonal shifts across the lifetime (e.g., during a menstrual cycle, or during reproductive transitions such as pregnancy and menopause, and, in men, andropause) highlight the modulatory role that hormones play in mood regulatory systems in humans. Emotions are adaptive internal states that encourage fitness-enhancing behaviors (e.g., communal living) and discourage fitness-reducing ones (e.g., high-risk activities), but any emotional state becomes maladaptive in the extreme (e.g., mania, depression, anxiety). Although substantial research exists on hormonal influences on emotions, much remains to be investigated. For starters, a lot of research has focused on one sex or the other, or has focused on specific hormones to the exclusion of others. For example, with few exceptions (e.g., Olsson et al., 2016), little research investigates the influence of estrogens on men's psychology. Understandably, some situations warrant investigation in only one sex or the other (e.g., PMDD). Otherwise, researchers should broaden their research questions to include more hormonal mechanisms and investigate these questions in both sexes.

Women are much more likely to be diagnosed with an anxiety disorder, suggesting that women may be more susceptible to negative outcomes after stressful or traumatic experiences (reviewed in Maeng & Milad, 2015), but more research is needed in this area. The positive association between progesterone level and anxiety in women (e.g., Reynolds et al., 2018) is likely adaptive because it would discourage risk-taking during pregnancy when progesterone is high, but a better understanding of when this relationship becomes dysfunctional may be beneficial to clinical patients. To that end, more research is necessary to understand how hormonal systems contribute to subclinical levels of anxiety and depression. Similarly, differences in sensitivity to hormone withdrawal impacts various types of depression and anxiety in women. Future research should continue to identify the sources of individual differences (e.g., additional genetic variants) that lead to such sensitivity so that these mental health concerns can be prevented or better treated. This research could shed light on inconsistent findings in the literature. For example, findings on the influence of reproductive hormones on SAD find increased (Adewuya et al., 2006), similar (Vesga-López, Schneider, et al., 2008), and decreased (Van Veen et al., 2009) SAD symptoms during pregnancy compared to other times. The reason for this discrepancy is not clear and would be a fruitful area for future investigation. Research could also look at sensitivity to hormone withdrawal in men; men experiencing age-related testosterone decline are at greater risk for depression (Zarrouf et al., 2009), yet there is little by way of explanation behind why age-related testosterone decline impacts some men in this way but not others. Future research opportunities involving the impact of hormones on various emotional states are plentiful.

References

Adewuya, A. O., Ola, B. A., Aloba, O. O., & Mapayi, B. M. (2006). Anxiety disorders among Nigerian women in late pregnancy: A controlled study. *Archives of Women's Mental Health*, *9*(6), 325–328.

Al-Shawaf, L., & Lewis, D.M.G. (2013). Exposed intestines and contaminated cooks: Sex, stress, & satiation predict disgust sensitivity. *Personality and Individual Differences*, *54*(6), 698–702.

Altemus, M., Sarvaiya, N., & Epperson, C.N. (2014). Sex differences in anxiety and depression clinical perspectives. *Frontiers in Neuroendocrinology*, *35*(3), 320–330.

American Psychiatric Association. (2013). *Diagnostic and statistical manual of mental disorders* (5th ed.). APA.

Amiaz, R., & Seidman, S. N. (2008). Testosterone and depression in men. *Current Opinion in Endocrinology, Diabetes and Obesity*, *15*(3), 278–283.

Archer, J. (2006). Testosterone and human aggression: An evaluation of the challenge hypothesis. *Neuroscience & Biobehavioral Reviews*, *30*(3), 319–345.

Archer, J. (2009). Does sexual selection explain human sex differences in aggression? *Behavioral and Brain Sciences*, *32*(3–4), 249–311.

Archer, J., Graham-Kevan, N., & Davies, M. (2005). Testosterone and aggression: A reanalysis of Book, Starzyk, and Quinsey's (2001) study. *Aggression and Violent Behavior*, *10*(2), 241–261.

Avis, N. E., Crawford, S., Stellato, R., & Longcope, C. (2001). Longitudinal study of hormone levels and depression among women transitioning through menopause. *Climacteric*, *4*(3), 243–249.

Bäckström, T., Andreen, L., Birzniece, V., Björn, I., Johansson, I. M., Nordenstam-Haghjo, M., Nyberg, S., Sundström-Poromaa, I., Wahlström, G., Wang, M., & Zhu, D. (2003). The role of hormones and hormonal treatments in premenstrual syndrome. *CNS Drugs*, *17*(5), 325–342.

Bäckström, C. T., Boyle, H., & Baird, D. T. (1981). Persistence of symptoms of premenstrual tension in hysterectomized women. *British Journal of Obstetrics and Gynaecology*, *88*(5), 530.

Bäckström, T., Bixo, M., Johansson, M., Nyberg, S., Ossewaarde, L., Ragagnin, G., Savic, I., Strömberg, J., Timby, E., van Broekhoven, F., & van Wingen, G. (2014). Allopregnanolone and mood disorders. *Progress in Neurobiology*, *113*, 88–94.

Bäckström, T., Hansson-Malmström, Y., Lindhe, B. Å., Cavalli-Björkman, B., & Nordenström, S. (1992). Oral contraceptives in premenstrual syndrome: A randomized comparison of triphasic and monophasic preparations. *Contraception*, *46*(3), 253–268.

Bain, J., Langevin, R., Dickey, R., & Ben-Aron, M. (1987). Sex hormones in murderers and assaulters. *Behavioral Sciences & the Law*, *5*(1), 95–101.

Banks, T., & Dabbs, J. M., Jr. (1996). Salivary testosterone and cortisol in a delinquent and violent urban subculture. *The Journal of Social Psychology*, *136*(1), 49–56.

Baron, R. A., & Richardson, D. R. (1994). *Human aggression* (2nd ed.). Plenum Press.

Bateman, A., Singh, A., Kral, T., & Solomon, S. (1989). The immune-hypothalamic-pituitary sadrenal axis. *Endocrine Reviews*, *10*(1), 92–112.

Beeman, E. A. (1947). The effect of male hormone on aggressive behavior in mice. *Physiological Zoology*, *20*(4), 373–405.

Bennett, D. S., Ambrosini, P. J., Kudes, D., Metz, C., & Rabinovich, H. (2005). Gender differences in adolescent depression: do symptoms differ for boys and girls? *Journal of Affective Disorders*, *89*(1–3), 35–44.

Bennett, H. A., Einarson, A., Taddio, A., Koren, G., & Einarson, T. R. (2004). Prevalence of depression during pregnancy: Systematic review. *Obstetrics & Gynecology*, *103*(4), 698–709.

Bernd, P. (2008). The role of neurotrophins during early development. *The Journal of Liver Research*, *14*, 241–250.

Bernstein, A., Zvolensky, M. J., Stewart, S. H., Comeau, M. N., & Leen-Feldner, E. W. (2006). Anxiety sensitivity taxonicity across gender among youth. *Behaviour Research and Therapy*, *44*, 679–698.

Berthold, A. A., & Quiring, D. P. (1944). The transplantation of testes. *Bulletin of the History of Medicine*, *16*(4), 399–401.

Blanco, C., Hoertel, N., Wall, M. M., Franco, S., Peyre, H., Neria, Y., Helpman, L., & Limosin, F. (2018). Toward understanding sex differences in the prevalence of posttraumatic stress disorder: Results from the National Epidemiologic Survey on Alcohol and Related Conditions. *The Journal of Clinical Psychiatry*, *79*, 16m11364.

Bloch, M., Daly, R. C., & Rubinow, D. R. (2003). Endocrine factors in the etiology of postpartum depression. *Comprehensive Psychiatry*, *44*(3), 234–246.

Bloch, M., Schmidt, P. J., Danaceau, M., Murphy, J., Nieman, L., & Rubinow, D. R. (2000). Effects of gonadal steroids in women with a history of postpartum depression. *American Journal of Psychiatry*, *157*(6), 924–930.

Borrow, A. P., & Cameron, N. M. (2014). Estrogenic mediation of serotonergic and neurotrophic systems: Implications for female mood disorders. *Progress in Neuro-Psychopharmacology and Biological Psychiatry*, *54*, 13–25.

Braverman, P. K. (2007). Premenstrual syndrome and premenstrual dysphoric disorder. *Journal of Pediatric and Adolescent Gynecology, 20*(1), 3–12.

Brett, M., & Baxendale, S. (2001). Motherhood and memory: A review. *Psychoneuroendocrinology, 26*(4), 339–362.

Bromberger, J. T., Kravitz, H. M., Chang, Y. F., Cyranowski, J. M., Brown, C., & Matthews, K. A. (2011). Major depression during and after the menopausal transition: Study of Women's Health Across the Nation (SWAN). *Psychological Medicine, 41*(9), 1879–1888.

Bromberger, J. T., Schott, L. L., Kravitz, H. M., Sowers, M., Avis, N. E., Gold, E. B., Randolph, G. F., & Matthews, K. A. (2010). Longitudinal change in reproductive hormones and depressive symptoms across the menopausal transition: Results from the Study of Women's Health Across the Nation (SWAN). *Archives of General Psychiatry, 67*(6), 598–607.

Brown, E. S., Varghese, F. P., & McEwen, B. S. (2004). Association of depression with medical illness: Does cortisol play a role? *Biological Psychiatry, 55*(1), 1–9.

Brown, T. A., & Barlow, D. H. (1992). Comorbidity among anxiety disorders: Implications for treatment and DSM-IV. *Journal of Consulting and Clinical Psychology, 60*, 835–844.

Carré, J. M., & Archer, J. (2017). Testosterone and human behavior: The role of individual and contextual variables. *Current Opinion in Psychology, 19*, 149–153.

Carré, J. M., Campbell, J. A., Lozoya, E., Goetz, S. M. M., & Welker, K. M. (2013). Changes in testosterone mediate the effect of winning on subsequent aggressive behaviour. *Psychoneuroendocrinology, 38*, 2034–2041.

Carré, J. M., Geniole, S. N., Ortiz, T. L., Bird, B. M., Videto, A., & Bonin, P. L. (2017). Exogenous testosterone rapidly increases aggressive behavior in dominant and impulsive men. *Biological Psychiatry, 82*(4), 249–256.

Carré, J. M., Putnam, S. K., & McCormick, C. M. (2009). Testosterone responses to competition predict future aggressive behaviour at a cost to reward in men. *Psychoneuroendocrinology, 34*(4), 561–570.

Casper, R. F., & Hearn, M. T. (1990). The effect of hysterectomy and bilateral oophorectomy in women with severe premenstrual syndrome. *American Journal of Obstetrics and Gynecology, 162*(1), 105–109.

Chan, A. F., Mortola, J. F., Wood, S. H., & Yen, S. S. (1994). Persistence of premenstrual syndrome during low-dose administration of the progesterone antagonist RU 486. *Obstetrics and Gynecology, 84*(6), 1001–1005.

Chen, S., Wang, J., Yu, G., Liu, W., & Pearce, D. (1997). Androgen and glucocorticoid receptor heterodimer formation: A possible mechanism for mutual inhibition of transcriptional activity. *Journal of Biological Chemistry, 272*, 14087–14092.

Cheng, J. T., Tracy, J. L., Foulsham, T., Kingstone, A., & Henrich, J. (2013). Two ways to the top: Evidence that dominance and prestige are distinct yet viable avenues to social rank and influence. *Journal of Personality and Social Psychology, 104*(1), 103–125.

Chourbaji, S., Vogt, M. A., & Gass, P. (2007). Mice that under-or overexpress glucocorticoid M receptors as models for depression or posttraumatic stress disorder. *Progress in Brain Research, 167*, 65–77.

Chrisler, J. C. (1991). The effect of premenstrual symptoms on creative thinking. In D. Taylor & N. F. Woods (Eds.) *Menstruation, health, and illness* (pp. 73–83). Hemisphere.

Chrisler, J. C., & Caplan, P. J. (2002). The strange case of Dr. Jekyll and Ms. Hyde: How PMS became a cultural phenomenon and a psychiatric disorder. *Annual Review of Sex Research, 13*, 274–306.

Cohen, L. S., Altshuler, L. L., Harlow, B. L., Nonacs, R., Newport, D. J., Viguera, A.C., Suri, R., Burt, V. K., Hendrick, V., Reminick, A. M., Loughead, A., Vitonis, A. F., & Loughead, A. (2006). Relapse of major depression during pregnancy in women who maintain or discontinue antidepressant treatment. *JAMA, 295*(5), 499–507.

Cohen, L. S., Soares, C. N., Vitonis, A. F., Otto, M. W., & Harlow, B. L. (2006). Risk for new onset of depression during the menopausal transition: The Harvard study of moods and cycles. *Archives of General Psychiatry, 63*(4), 385–390.

Conway, C. A., Jones, B. C., DeBruine, L. M., Welling, L. L. M., Law-Smith, M. J., Perrett, D. I., Sharp, M. A., & Al-Dujaili, E. A. (2007). Salience of emotional displays of danger and contagion in faces in enhanced when progesterone levels are raised. *Hormones and Behavior, 51*, 202–206.

Costa, A. M. N., Spence, K. T., Smith, S. S., & French-Mullen, J. M. (1995). Withdrawal from the endogenous steroid progesterone results in GABAA currents insensitive to benzodiazepine modulation in rat CA1 hippocampus. *Journal of Neurophysiology, 74*(1), 464–469.

Cuijpers, P., Koole, S. L., van Dijke, A., Roca, M., Li, J., & Reynolds, C. F. (2014). Psychotherapy for subclinical depression: meta-analysis. *The British Journal of Psychiatry, 205*(4), 268–274.

Cullinan, W. E., Ziegler, D. R., & Herman, J. P. (2008). Functional role of local GABAergic influences on the HPA axis. *Brain Structure and Function, 213*(1–2), 63.

Curtis, V., Aunger, R., & Rabie, T. (2004). Evidence that disgust evolved to protect from risk of disease. *Proceedings of the Royal Society B: Biological Sciences, 21*, S131–133.

Curtis, V., & Biran, A. (2001). Dirt, disgust, and disease: Is hygiene in our genes? *Perspectives in Biology and Medicine, 44*, 17–31.

Dabbs, J. M., Jurkovic, G. J., & Frady, R. L. (1991). Salivary testosterone and cortisol among late adolescent male offenders. *Journal of Abnormal Child Psychology, 19*(4), 469–478.

Deacon, B., & Olatunji, B. O. (2007). Specificity of disgust sensitivity in the prediction of behavioral avoidance in contamination fear. *Behaviour Research and Therapy, 45*, 2110–2120.

Dekkers, T. J., van Rentergem, J. A. A., Meijer, B., Popma, A., Wagemaker, E., & Huizenga, H. M. (2019). A meta-analytical evaluation of the dual-hormone hypothesis: Does cortisol moderate the relationship between testosterone and status, dominance, risk taking, aggression, and psychopathy? *Neuroscience & Biobehavioral Reviews, 96*, 250–271.

de Souza Silva, M. A., Mattern, C., Topic, B., Buddenberg, T. E., & Huston, J. P. (2009). Dopaminergic and serotonergic activity in neostriatum and nucleus accumbens enhanced by intranasal administration of testosterone. *European Neuropsychopharmacology, 19*(1), 53–63.

Dichtel, L. E., Carpenter, L. L., Nyer, M., Mischoulon, D., Kimball, A., Deckersbach, T., Dougherty, D. D., Schoenfeld, D. A., Fisher, L., Cusin, C., Dording, C., Trinh, N., Pedrelli, P., Yeung, A., Farabaugh, A., Papakostas, G. I., Chang, T., Shapero, B. G., Chen, J.,, & Dording, C. (2020). Low-dose testosterone augmentation for antidepressant-resistant major depressive disorder in women: An 8-week randomized placebo-controlled study. *American Journal of Psychiatry, 177*(10), 965–973.

Druschel, B. A., & Sherman, M. F. (1999). Disgust sensitivity as a function of the Big Five and gender. *Personality and Individual Differences, 26*, 739–748.

Duncan, L. A., Schaller, M., & Park, J. H. (2009). Perceived vulnerability to disease: Development and validation of a 15-item self-report instrument. *Personality and Individual Differences, 47*(6), 541–546.

Dunson, D. B., Colombo, B., & Baird, D. (2002). Changes with age in the level and duration of fertility in the menstrual cycle. *Human Reproduction, 17*, 1399–1403.

Eaton, W. W. (1995). Progress in the epidemiology of anxiety disorders. *Epidemiologic Reviews, 17*, 32–38.

Ebinger, M., Sievers, C., Ivan, D., Schneider, H. J., & Stalla, G. K. (2009). Is there a neuroendocrinological rationale for testosterone as a therapeutic option in depression? *Journal of Psychopharmacology, 23*(7), 841–853.

Eisenlohr-Moul, T. A., Schmalenberger, K. M., Owens, S. A., Peters, J. R., Dawson, D. N., & Girdler, S. S. (2018). Perimenstrual exacerbation of symptoms in borderline personality disorder: Evidence from multilevel models and the Carolina premenstrual assessment scoring system. *Psychological Medicine, 48*(12), 2085–2095.

Ekman, P., & Friesen, W. V. (1971). Constants across cultures in the face and emotion. *Journal of Personality and Social Psychology, 17*(2), 124–129.

Ekman, P., & Friesen, W. (1976). *Pictures of facial affect*. Consulting Psychologists Press.

Ellenbogen, M. A., Hodgins, S., Walker, C. D., Couture, S., & Adam, S. (2006). Daytime cortisol and stress reactivity in the offspring of parents with bipolar disorder. *Psychoneuroendocrinology, 31*(10), 1164–1180.

Ellenbogen, M. A., Santo, J. B., Linnen, A. M., Walker, C. D., & Hodgins, S. (2010). High cortisol levels in the offspring of parents with bipolar disorder during two weeks of daily sampling. *Bipolar Disorders, 12*(1), 77–86.

Epting, L. K., & Overman, W. H. (1998). Sex-sensitive tasks in men and women: A search for performance fluctuations across the menstrual cycle. *Behavioral Neuroscience, 112*(6), 1304–1317.

Evardone, M., Alexander, G. M., & Morey, L. C. (2008). Hormones and borderline personality features. *Personality and Individual Differences, 44*(1), 278–287.

Fawcett, E. J., Power, H., & Fawcett, J. M. (2020). Women are at greater risk of OCD than men: A meta-analytic review of OCD prevalence worldwide. *Journal of Clinical Psychiatry, 81*(4), 19r13085.

Fessler, D. M. T. (2001). Luteal phase immunosuppression and meat eating. *Rivista di Biologia (Biology Forum), 94*(3), 407–430.

Fessler, D. M. T. (2002). Reproductive immunosuppression and diet: An evolutionary perspective on pregnancy sickness and meat consumption. *Current Anthropology, 43*(1), 19–61.

Fessler, D. M. T., Eng, S. J., & Navarrete, C. D. (2005). Elevated disgust sensitivity in the first trimester of pregnancy: Evidence supporting the compensatory prophylaxis hypothesis. *Evolution and Human Behavior, 26*(4), 344–351.

Fessler, D. M. T., & Navarrete, C. D. (2003). Domain-specific variation in disgust sensitivity across the menstrual cycle. *Evolution and Human Behavior, 24*(6), 406–417.

Fleischman, D. S. (2014). Women's disgust adaptations. In V. A. Weekes-Shackelford & T. K. Shackelford (Eds.), *Evolutionary perspectives on human sexual psychology and behavior* (pp. 277–296). Springer.

Fleischman, D. S., & Fessler, D. M. T. (2011). Progesterone's effects on the psychology of disease avoidance: Support for the compensatory behavioral prophylaxis hypothesis. *Hormones and Behavior, 59*(2), 271–275.

Ford, A. H., Yeap, B. B., Flicker, L., Hankey, G. J., Chubb, S. P., Handelsman, D. J., Golledge, J., & Almeida, O. P. (2016). Prospective longitudinal study of testosterone and incident depression in older men: The Health in Men Study. *Psychoneuroendocrinology, 64,* 57–65.

Forray, A., Focseneanu, M., Pittman, B., McDougle, C. J., & Epperson, C. N. (2010). Onset and exacerbation of obsessive-compulsive disorder in pregnancy and the postpartum period. *Journal of Clinical Psychiatry, 71,* 1061–1068.

Frank, R. (1931). Hormonal causes of premenstrual tension. *Archives of Neurology and Psychiatry, 26,* 1053–1057.

Freeman, E. W. (2010). Associations of depression with the transition to menopause. *Menopause, 17*(4), 823–827.

Frodl, T., & O'Keane, V. (2013). How does the brain deal with cumulative stress? A review with focus on developmental stress, HPA axis function and hippocampal structure in humans. *Neurobiology of Disease, 52,* 24–37.

Galovski, T. E., Blain, L. M., Mott, J. M., Elwood, L., & Houle, T. (2012). Manualized therapy for PTSD: Flexing the structure of cognitive processing therapy. *Journal of Consulting and Clinical Psychology, 80,* 968.

Gangestad, S. W., & Buss, D. M. (1993). Pathogen prevalence and human mate preference. *Ethology and Sociobiology, 14,* 89–96.

Geniole, S. N., Bird, B. M., McVittie, J .S., Purcell, R. B., Archer, J., & Carré, J. M. (2020). Is testosterone linked to human aggression? A meta-analytic examination of the relationship between baseline, dynamic, and manipulated testosterone on human aggression. *Hormones and Behavior, 123,* 1–11.

Geniole, S. N., Bird, B. M., Ruddick, E. L., & Carré, J. M. (2017). Effects of competition outcome on testosterone concentrations in humans: An updated meta-analysis. *Hormones and Behavior, 92,* 37–50.

Geniole, S. N., Busseri, M. A., & McCormick, C. M. (2013). Testosterone dynamics and psychopathic personality traits independently predict antagonistic behavior towards the perceived loser of a competitive interaction. *Hormones and Behavior, 64,* 790–798.

Geniole, S. N., & Carré, J. M. (2019). Hierarchy and testosterone. In L. L. M. Welling & T. K. Shackelford (Eds.), *The Oxford handbook of evolutionary psychology and behavioral endocrinology* (pp. 281–293). Oxford University Press.

Geniole, S. N., Carré, J. M., & McCormick, C. M. (2011). State, not trait, neuroendocrine function predicts costly reactive aggression in men after social exclusion and inclusion. *Biological Psychology, 87*(1), 137–145.

Goldstat, R., Briganti, E., Tran, J., Wolfe, R., & Davis, S. R. (2003). Transdermal testosterone therapy improves well-being, mood, and sexual function in premenopausal women. *Menopause, 10*(5), 390–398.

Gonda, X., Telek, T., Lazary, J., Vargha, A., & Bagdy, G. (2008). Patterns of mood changes throughout the reproductive cycle in healthy women without premenstrual dysphoric disorders. *Progress in Neuro-Psychopharmacology and Biological Psychiatry, 32,* 1782–1788.

Goodman, H. M. (2009). Hormonal control of reproduction in the female: The menstrual cycle. In H. M. Goodman (Ed.), *Essential Medical Physiology* (pp. 257–275). Academic Press.

Goodman, J. H., Chenausky, K. L., & Freeman, M. P. (2014). Anxiety disorders during pregnancy: A systematic review. *Journal of Clinical Psychiatry, 75,* e1153–e1184.

Groves, C. L., & Anderson, C. A. (2018). Aversive events and aggression. *Current Opinion in Psychology, 19,* 144–148.

Guerry, J. D., & Hastings, P. D. (2011). In search of HPA axis dysregulation in child and adolescent depression. *Clinical Child and Family Psychology Review, 14*(2), 135–160.

Hahn, A. C., Fisher, C. I., Cobey, K. D., DeBruine, L. M., & Jones, B. C. (2016). A longitudinal analysis of women's salivary testosterone and intrasexual competitiveness. *Psychoneuroendocrinology, 64,* 117–122.

Halbreich, U., Borenstein, J., Pearlstein, T., & Kahn, L. S. (2003). The prevalence, impairment, impact, and burden of premenstrual dysphoric disorder (PMS/PMDD). *Psychoneuroendocrinology, 28,* 1–23.

Halbreich, U., & Karkun, S. (2006). Cross-cultural and social diversity of prevalence of postpartum depression and depressive symptoms. *Journal of Affective Disorders, 91*(2–3), 97–111.

Handelsman, D. J., Sikaris, K., & Ly, L. P. (2016). Estimating age-specific trends in circulating testosterone and sex hormone-binding globulin in males and females across the lifespan. *Annals of Clinical Biochemistry, 53*(3), 377–384.

Hankin, B. L., Mermelstein, R., & Roesch, L. (2007). Sex differences in adolescent depression: Stress exposure and reactivity models. *Child Development, 78*(1), 279–295.

Hantsoo, L., & Epperson, C. N. (2020). Allopregnanolone in premenstrual dysphoric disorder (PMDD): Evidence for dysregulated sensitivity to GABA-A receptor modulating neuroactive steroids across the menstrual cycle. *Neurobiology of Stress, 12,* 100213.

Hellgren, C., Åkerud, H., Skalkidou, A., Bäckström, T., & Sundström-Poromaa, I. (2014). Low serum allopregnanolone is associated with symptoms of depression in late pregnancy. *Neuropsychobiology, 69*(3), 147–153.

Hess, N. H., & Hagen, E. H. (2006). Sex differences in indirect aggression: Psychological evidence from young adults. *Evolution and Human Behavior, 27*(3), 231–245.

Heuser, I., Yassouridis, A., & Holsboer, F. (1994). The combined dexamethasone/CRH test: A refined laboratory test for psychiatric disorders. *Journal of Psychiatric Research, 28*(4), 341–356.

Hillier, S. G., Reichert, L. E., & Van Hall, E. V. (1981). Control of preovulatory follicular estrogen biosynthesis in the human ovary. *Journal of Clinical Endocrinology & Metabolism, 52*(5), 847–856.

Holbrook, T. L., Hoyt, D. B., Stein, M. B., & Sieber, W. J. (2002). Gender differences in long-term posttraumatic stress disorder outcomes after major trauma: Women are at higher risk of adverse outcomes than men. *Journal of Trauma and Acute Care Surgery, 53*, 882–888.

Hsiao, C. C., Liu, C. Y., & Hsiao, M. C. (2004). No correlation of depression and anxiety to plasma estrogen and progesterone levels in patients with premenstrual dysphoric disorder. *Psychiatry and Clinical Neurosciences, 58*(6), 593.

Hsiao, M. C., Hsiao, C. C., & Liu, C. Y. (2004). Premenstrual symptoms and premenstrual exacerbation in patients with psychiatric disorders. *Psychiatry and Clinical Neurosciences, 58*, 186–190.

Hsu, Y. Y., Earley, R. L., & Wolf, L. L. (2006). Modulation of aggressive behaviour by fighting experience: Mechanisms and contest outcomes. *Biological Reviews, 81*, 33–74.

Hu, J., Zhou, B., Li, Y., Deng, Y., He, Q., Ye, J., & Ning, Y. (2019). The interaction between estradiol change and the serotonin transporter gene (5-HTTLPR) polymorphism is associated with postpartum depressive symptoms. *Psychiatric Genetics, 29*(4), 97–102.

Humphreys, K. L., Moore, S. R., Davis, E. G., MacIsaac, J. L., Lin, D. T., Kobor, M. S., & Gotlib, I. H. (2019). DNA methylation of HPA-axis genes and the onset of major depressive disorder in adolescent girls: a prospective analysis. *Translational Psychiatry, 9*(1), 1–10.

Jones, B.C., Hahn, A. C., Fisher, C. I., Wang, H., Kandrik, M., Lee, A.J., Tybur, J. M., & DeBruine, L. M. (2018). Hormonal correlates of pathogen disgust: Testing the compensatory prophylaxis hypothesis. *Evolution and Human Behavior, 39*(2), 166–169.

Jones, B. C., Perrett, D. I., Little, A. C., Boothroyd, L., Cornwell, R. E., Feinberg, D. R., Tiddeman, B. P., Whiten, S., Pitman, R. M., Hillier, S. G., Burt, D. M., Stirrat, M. R., Law Smith, M. J., & Moore, F. R. (2005). Menstrual cycle, pregnancy and oral contraceptive use alter attraction to apparent health in faces. *Proceedings of the Royal Society B: Biological Sciences, 272*(1561), 347–354.

Josephs, R. A., Sellers, J. G., Newman, M. L., & Mehta, P. H. (2006). The mismatch effect: When testosterone and status are at odds. *Journal of Personality and Social Psychology, 90*(6), 999–1013.

Julien, D., O'Connor, K. P., & Aardema, F. (2007). Intrusive thoughts, obsessions, and appraisals in obsessive-compulsive disorder: A critical review. *Clinical Psychology Review, 27*, 366–383.

Kessler, R. C., Aguilar-Gaxiola, S., Alonso, J., Benjet, C., Bromet, E. J., Cardoso, G., Degenhardt, L., de Girolamo,G., Dinolova, R. V., Ferry, F., Florescu, S., Gureje, O., Haro, J. M., Huang, Y., Karam, E. G., Kawakami, N., Lee, S., Lepine, J., Levinson. D., & Koenen, K. C. (2017). Trauma and PTSD in the WHO World Mental Health Surveys. *European Journal of Psychotraumatology, 8*(5), 1353383.

Kessler, R. C., Aguilar-Gaxiola, S., Alonso, J., Chatterji, S., Lee, S., Ormel, L., Üstün, T. B., & Wang, P. (2009). The global burden of mental disorders: An update from the WHO World Mental Health (WMH) surveys. *Epidemiologia e Psichiatria Sociale, 18*, 23–33.

Kessler, R. C., Berglund, P., Demler, O., Jin, R., Koretz, D., Merikangas, K., Rush, A. J., Walters, E. E., & Wang, P. S. (2003). The epidemiology of major depressive disorder: Results from the National Comorbidity Survey Replication (NCS-R). *JAMA, 289*(23), 3095–3105.

Kessler, R. C., Berglund, P., Demler, O., Jin, R., Merikangas, K. R., & Walters, E. E. (2005). Lifetime prevalence and age-of-onset distributions of DSM-IV disorders in the National Comorbidity Survey Replication. *Archives of General Psychiatry, 62*, 617–627.

Kessler, R. C., Petukhova, M., Sampson, N. A., Zaslavsky, A. M., & Wittchen, H. U. (2012). Twelve-month and lifetime prevalence and lifetime morbid risk of anxiety and mood disorders in the United States. *International Journal of Methods in Psychiatric Research, 21*, 169–184.

Kessler, R. C., Sonnega, A., Bromet, E., Hughes, M., & Nelson, C. B. (1995). Posttraumatic stress disorder in the National Comorbidity Survey. *Archives of General Psychiatry, 52*, 1048–1060.

Kische, H., Pieper, L., Venz, J., Klotsche, J., März, W., Koch-Gromus, U., Pittrow, D., Lehnert, H., Silber, S., Stalla, G. K., Zeiher, A. M., Wittchen, H., & Zeiher, A. M. (2018). Longitudinal change instead of baseline testosterone predicts depressive symptoms. *Psychoneuroendocrinology, 89*, 7–12.

Kraines, M. A., Kelberer, L. J. A., & Wells, T. T. (2016). Sex differences in attention to disgust facial expressions. *Cognition and Emotion, 31*(8), 1692–1697.

Kudielka, B. M., & Kirschbaum, C. (2005). Sex differences in HPA axis responses to stress: A review. *Biological Psychology, 69*(1), 113–132.

Labad, J., Menchón, J. M., Alonso, P., Segalas, C., Jiménez, S., Juarrieta, N., Leckman, J. F., & Vallejo, J. (2008). Gender differences in obsessive-compulsive symptom dimensions. *Depression and Anxiety, 25*, 832–838.

Labad, J., Menchón, J. M., Alonso, P., Segalas, C., Jiménez, S., & Vallejo, J. (2005). Female reproductive cycle and obsessive-compulsive disorder. *Journal of Clinical Psychiatry, 66*, 428–435.

Lete, I., & Lapuente, O. (2016). Contraceptive options for women with premenstrual dysphoric disorder: current insights and a narrative review. *Open Access Journal of Contraception, 7*, 117.

Levine, J. E. (1997). New concepts of the neuroendocrine regulation of gonadotropin surges in rats. *Biology of Reproduction, 56*(2), 293–302.

Lewis, L. L., Greenblatt, E. M., Rittenhouse, C. A., Veldhuis, J. D., & Jaffe, R. B. (1995). Pulsatile release patterns of luteinizing hormone and progesterone in relation to symptom onset in women with premenstrual syndrome. *Fertility and Sterility, 64*(2), 288–292.

Li, S. H., & Graham, B. M. (2017). Why are women so vulnerable to anxiety, trauma-related and stress-related disorders? The potential role of sex hormones. *Lancet Psychiatry, 4*, 73–82.

Lowry, C. A. (2002). Functional subsets of serotonergic neurones: Implications for control of the hypothalamic-pituitary-adrenal axis. *Journal of Neuroendocrinology, 14*(11), 911–923.

Maeng, L. Y., & Milad, M. R. (2015). Sex differences in anxiety disorder: Interactions between fear, stress, and gonadal hormones. *Hormones and Behavior, 76*, 106–117.

Maier, W., Gansicke, M., Freybergerr, H. J., Linz, M., Huen, R., & Lecrubier, Y. (2000). Generalized anxiety disorder (ICD-10) in primary care from a cross-cultural perspective: A valid diagnostic entity? *Acta Psychiatrica Scandinavica, 101*, 29–36.

Maner, J. K., & McNulty, J. K. (2013). Attunement to the fertility status of same-sex rivals: Women's testosterone responses to olfactory ovulation cues. *Evolution and Human Behavior, 34*(6), 412–418.

Marcotte, D., Fortin, L., Potvin, P., & Papillon, M. (2002). Gender differences in depressive symptoms during adolescence: Role of gender-typed characteristics, self-esteem, body image, stressful life events, and pubertal status. *Journal of Emotional and Behavioral Disorders, 10*(1), 29–42.

Mazur, A. (1985). A biosocial model of status in face-to-face primate groups. *Social Forces, 64*(2), 377–402.

Mazur, A. (2015). A biosocial model of status in face-to-face groups. In V. Zeigler-Hill, L. L. M. Welling, & T. K. Shackelford (Eds.), *Evolutionary perspectives on social psychology* (pp. 303–315). Springer International.

Mazur, A., & Booth, A. (1998). Testosterone and dominance in men. *Behavioral and Brain Sciences, 21*(3), 353–363.

Mazur, A., & Booth, A. (2014). Testosterone is related to deviance in male army veterans, but relationships are not moderated by cortisol. *Biological Psychology, 96*, 72–76.

McEwen, B. S., & Parsons, B. (1982). Gonadal steroid action on the brain: Neurochemistry and neuropharmacology. *Annual Review of Pharmacology and Toxicology, 22*, 555–598.

McIntyre, R. S., Mancini, D., Eisfeld, B. S., Soczynska, J. K., Grupp, L., Konarski, J. Z., & Kennedy, S. H. (2006). Calculated bioavailable testosterone levels and depression in middle-aged men. *Psychoneuroendocrinology, 31*(9), 1029–1035.

McLean, C. P., Asnaani, A., Litz, B. T., & Hofmann, S. G. (2011). Gender differences in anxiety disorders: Prevalence, course of illness, comorbidity and burden of illness. *Journal of Psychiatric Research, 45*, 1027–1035.

McLeod, D. R., Hoehn-Saric, R., Foster, G. V., & Hipsley, P. A. (1993). The influence of premenstrual syndrome on ratings of anxiety in women with generalized anxiety disorder. *Acta Psychiatrica Scandinavica, 88*, 248–251.

Mehta, D., Rex-Haffner, M., Søndergaard, H. B., Pinborg, A., Binder, E. B., & Frokjaer, V. G. (2019). Evidence for oestrogen sensitivity in perinatal depression: Pharmacological sex hormone manipulation study. *The British Journal of Psychiatry, 215*(3), 519–527.

Mehta, P. H., DesJardins, N. M. L., van Vugt, M., & Josephs, R. A. (2017). Hormonal underpinnings of status conflict: Testosterone and cortisol are related to decisions and satisfaction in the hawk-dove game. *Hormones and Behavior, 92*, 141–154.

Mehta, P. H., Jones, A. C., & Josephs, R. A. (2008). The social endocrinology of dominance: Basal testosterone predicts cortisol changes and behavior following victory and defeat. *Journal of Personality and Social Psychology, 94*, 1078–1093.

Mehta, P. H., & Josephs, R. A. (2010). Testosterone and cortisol jointly regulate dominance: Evidence for a dual-hormone hypothesis. *Hormones and Behavior, 58*(5), 898–906.

Mesquita, B., & Frijda, N. H. (1992). Cultural variation in emotions: A review. *Psychological Bulletin, 112*, 179–204.

Miller, A., Vo, H., Huo, L., Roca, C., Schmidt, P.J., & Rubinow, D.R. (2010). Estrogen receptor alpha (ESR-1) associations with psychological traits in women with PMDD and controls. *Journal of Psychiatric Research, 44*(12), 788–794.

Miller, K. K., Perlis, R. H., Papakostas, G. I., Mischoulon, D., Iosifescu, D. V., Brick, D. J., & Fava, M. (2009). Low-dose transdermal testosterone augmentation therapy improves depression severity in women. *CNS Spectrums, 14*(12), 688.

Misri, S., Abizadeh, J., Sanders, S., & Swift, E. (2015). Perinatal generalized anxiety disorder: Assessment and treatment. *Journal of Women's Health, 24*, 762–770.

Muse, K. N., Cetel, N. S., Futterman, L. A., & Yen, S. S. (1984). The premenstrual syndrome: Effects of medical ovariectomy. *New England Journal of Medicine, 311*(21), 1345–1349.

Naninck, E. F. G., Lucassen, P. J., & Bakker, J. (2011). Sex differences in adolescent depression: Do sex hormones determine vulnerability? *Journal of Neuroendocrinology, 23*(5), 383–392.

Nillni, Y. I., Rohan, K. J., & Zvolensky, M. J. (2012). The role of menstrual cycle phase and anxiety sensitivity in catastrophic misinterpretation of physical symptoms during a CO_2 challenge. *Archives of Women's Mental Health, 15*, 413–422.

Oaten, M., Stevenson, R. J., & Case, T.I. (2009). Disgust as a disease-avoidance mechanism. *Psychological Bulletin, 135*(2), 303–321.

O'Hara, M. W., & McCabe, J. E. (2013). Postpartum depression: Current status and future directions. *Annual Review of Clinical Psychology, 9*, 379–407.

Olatunji, B. O., Cox, R. C., & Li, I. (2020). Disgust regulation between menstrual cycle phases: Differential effects of emotional suppression and reappraisal. *Journal of Behavior Therapy and Experimental Psychiatry, 68*, 101543.

Olatunji, B. O., Ebesutani, C., David, B., Fan, Q., & McGrath, P. B. (2011). Disgust proneness and obsessive-compulsive symptoms in a clinical sample: Structural differentiation from negative affect. *Journal of Anxiety Disorders, 25*(7), 932–938.

Olatunji, B. O., Sawchuk, C. N., Lohr, J. M., & de Jong, P. J. (2004). Disgust domains in the prediction of contamination fear. *Behaviour Research and Therapy, 42*(1), 93–104.

Olsson, A., Kopsida, E., Sorjonen, K., & Savic, I. (2016). Testosterone and estrogen impact social evaluations and vicarious emotions: A double-blind placebo-controlled study. *Emotion, 16*(4), 515–523.

Osborne, L. M., Gispen, F., Sanyal, A., Yenokyan, G., Meilman, S., & Payne, J. L. (2017). Lower allopregnanolone during pregnancy predicts postpartum depression: An exploratory study. *Psychoneuroendocrinology, 79*, 116–121.

Ostiguy, C. S., Ellenbogen, M. A., Walker, C.D ., Walker, E. F., & Hodgins, S. (2011). Sensitivity to stress among the offspring of parents with bipolar disorder: A study of daytime cortisol levels. *Psychological Medicine, 41*(11), 2447.

Pacak, K., & Palkovits, M. (2001). Stressor specificity of central neuroendocrine responses: implications for stress-related disorders. *Endocrine Reviews, 22*(4), 502–548.

Pariante, C. M. (2006). The glucocorticoid receptor: Part of the solution or part of the problem? *Journal of Psychopharmacology, 20*(4), 79–84.

Pariante, C. M., & Lightman, S. L. (2008). The HPA axis in major depression: Classical theories and new developments. *Trends in Neurosciences, 31*(9), 464–468.

Paus, T., Keshavan, M., & Giedd, J. N. (2008). Why do many psychiatric disorders emerge during adolescence? *Nature Reviews Neuroscience, 9*, 947–957.

Payne, J. L. (2003). The role of estrogen in mood disorders in women. *International Review of Psychiatry, 15*(3), 280–290.

Pearlstein, T. B., Bachmann, G. A., Zacur, H. A., & Yonkers, K. A. (2005). Treatment of premenstrual dysphoric disorder with a new drospirenone-containing oral contraceptive formulation. *Contraception, 72*(6), 414–421.

Phares, V., Steinberg, A. R., & Thompson, J. K. (2004). Gender differences in peer and parental influences: Body image disturbance, self-worth, and psychological functioning in preadolescent children. *Journal of Youth and Adolescence, 33*(5), 421–429.

Phillips, J., Sharpe, L., Matthey, S., & Charles, M. (2009). Maternally focused worry. *Archives of Women's Mental Health, 12*(6), 409–418.

Pigott, T. A. (2003). Anxiety disorders in women. *Psychiatric Clinics of North America, 26*, 621–672.

Piggott, T. A., Duran, A. N., Jalnapurkar, I., Kimm, T., Linscheid, S., & Allen, M. K. (2019). Sex differences in anxiety disorders. In L. L. M. Welling & T. K. Shackelford (Eds.), *The Oxford handbook of evolutionary psychology and behavioral endocrinology* (pp. 405–432). Oxford University Press.

Pineles, S. L., Nillni, Y. I., King, M. W., Patton, S. C., Bauer, M. R., Mostoufi, S. M., Gerber, M. R., Hauger, R., Resick, P. A., Rasmusson, A. M., & Orr, S. P. (2016). Extinction retention and the menstrual cycle: Different associations for women with posttraumatic stress disorder. *Journal of Abnormal Psychology, 125*, 349–355.

Pinsonneault, J. K., Sullivan, D., Sadee, W., Soares, C. N., Hampson, E., & Steiner, M. (2013). Association study of the estrogen receptor gene ESR1 with postpartum depression: A pilot study. *Archives of Women's Mental Health, 16*(6), 499–509.

Popma, A., Vermeiren, R., Geluk, C. A., Rinne, T., van den Brink, W., Knol, D.L., Jansen, L. M. C., van Engeland, H., & Doreleijers, T. A. (2007). Cortisol moderates the relationship between testosterone and aggression in delinquent male adolescents. *Biological Psychiatry, 61*(3), 405–411.

Potter, J., Bouyer, J., Trussell, J., & Moreau, C. (2009). Premenstrual syndrome prevalence and fluctuation over time: Results from a French population-based survey. *Journal of Women's Health, 18*(1), 31–39.

Qiao, M., Zhang, H., Liu, H., Luo, S., Wang, T., Zhang, J., & Ji, L. (2012). Prevalence of premenstrual syndrome and premenstrual dysphoric disorder in a population-based sample in China. *European Journal of Obstetrics & Gynecology and Reproductive Biology*, *162*(1), 83–86.

Rao, U., Hammen, C. L., & Poland, R. E. (2009). Risk markers for depression in adolescents: Sleep and HPA measures. *Neuropsychopharmacology*, *34*(8), 1936–1945.

Rapkin, A. J., & Akopians, A. L. (2012). Pathophysiology of premenstrual syndrome and premenstrual dysphoric disorder. *Menopause International*, *18*(2), 52–59.

Reed, G. M., First, M. B., Kogan, C. S., Hyman, S. E., Gureje, O., Gaebel, W., Maj, M., Stein, D. J., Maercker, A., Tyrer, P., Claudino, A., Garralda, E., Salvador-Carulla, L., Ray, R., Saunders, J. B., Dua, T., Poznyak, V., Medina-Mora, M. E., Pike, K. M., & Claudino, A. (2019). Innovations and changes in the ICD-11 classification of mental, behavioural and neurodevelopmental disorders. *World Psychiatry*, *18*(1), 3–19.

Reed, V., & Wittchen, H. U. (1998). DSM-IV panic attacks and panic disorder in a community sample of adolescents and young adults: How specific are panic attacks? *Journal of Psychiatric Research*, *32*, 335–345.

Reynolds, T. A., Makhanova, A., Marcinkowska, U. M., Jasienska, G., McNulty, J. K., Eckel, L. A., Nikonova, L., & Maner, J. K. (2018). Progesterone and women's anxiety across the menstrual cycle. *Hormones and Behavior*, *102*, 34–40.

Rittenhouse, C. A. (1991). The emergence of premenstrual syndrome as a social problem. *Social Problems*, *38*(3), 412–425.

Robichaud, M., & Debonnel, G. (2005). Oestrogen and testosterone modulate the firing activity of dorsal raphe nucleus serotonergic neurones in both male and female rats. *Journal of Neuroendocrinology*, *17*(3), 179–185.

Ross, L. E., & McLean, L. M. (2006). Anxiety disorders during pregnancy and the postpartum period: A systematic review. *The Journal of Clinical Psychiatry*, *67*, 1285–1298.

Rotter, N. G., & Rotter, G. S. (1988). Sex differences in the encoding and decoding of negative facial emotions. *Journal of Nonverbal Behavior*, *12*(2), 139–148.

Rupprecht, R. (2003). Neuroactive steroids: Mechanisms of action and neuropsychopharmacological properties. *Psychoneuroendocrinology*, *28*, 139–168.

Sapolsky, R. M., Krey, L. C., & McEwen, B. S. (1986). The neuroendocrinology of stress and aging: the glucocorticoid cascade hypothesis. *Endocrine Reviews*, *7*(3), 284–301.

Schmidt, P. J., Dor, R. B., Martinez, P. E., Guerrieri, G. M., Harsh, V. L., Thompson, K., Koziol, D. E., Nieman, L. K., & Rubinow, D. R. (2015). Effects of estradiol withdrawal on mood in women with past perimenopausal depression: A randomized clinical trial. *JAMA Psychiatry*, *72*(7), 714–726.

Schmidt, P. J., Martinez, P. E., Nieman, L. K., Koziol, D. E., Thompson, K. D., Schenkel, L., Wakim, G., & Rubinow, D. R. (2017). Premenstrual dysphoric disorder symptoms following ovarian suppression: Triggered by change in ovarian steroid levels but not continuous stable levels. *American Journal of Psychiatry*, *174*(10), 980–989.

Schmidt, P. J., Nieman, L. K., Danaceau, M. A., Adams, L. F., & Rubinow, D. R. (1998). Differential behavioral effects of gonadal steroids in women with and in those without premenstrual syndrome. *New England Journal of Medicine*, *338*(4), 209–216.

Seng, J. S., Rauch, S. A. M., Resnick, H., Reed, C. D., King, A., Low, L. K., McPherson, M., Muzik, M., Abelson, J., & Liberzon, I. (2010). Exploring posttraumatic stress disorder symptom profile among pregnant women. *Journal of Psychosomatic Obstetrics & Gynecology*, *31*, 176–187.

Shih, J. H., Eberhart, N. K., Hammen, C. L., & Brennan, P. A. (2006). Differential exposure and reactivity to interpersonal stress predict sex differences in adolescent depression. *Journal of Clinical Child and Adolescent Psychology*, *35*(1), 103–115.

Sigmon, S. T., Dorhofer, D. M., Rohan, K. J., Hotovy, L. A., Boulard, N. E., & Fink, C. M. (2000). Psychophysiological, somatic, and affective changes across the menstrual cycle in women with panic disorder. *Journal of Consulting and Clinical Psychology*, *68*, 425–431.

Silverman, M. E., Reichenberg, A., Savitz, D.A., Cnattingius, S., Lichtenstein, P., Hultman, C. M., Larsson, H., & Sandin, S. (2017). The risk factors for postpartum depression: A population-based study. *Depression and Anxiety*, *34*(2), 178–187.

Soni, M., Curran, V. H., & Kamboj, S. K. (2013). Identification of a narrow post-ovulatory window of vulnerability to distressing involuntary memories in healthy women. *Neurobiology of Learning and Memory*, *104*, 32–38.

Sparks, A. M., Fessler, D. M. T., Chan, K. Q., Ashokkumar, A., & Holbrook, C. (2018). Disgust as a mechanism for decision making under risk: Illuminating sex differences and individual risk-taking correlates disgust propensity. *Emotion*, *18*(7), 942–958.

Stein, M. B., & Stein, D. J. (2008). Social anxiety disorder. *Lancet*, *371*, 1115–1125.

Stevenson, R. J., Oaten, M. J., Case, T. I., Repacholi, B. M., & Wagland, P. (2010). Children's response to adult disgust elicitors: Development and acquisition. *Developmental Psychology*, *46*, 165177.

Strang, E., Peterson, Z. D., Hill, Y. N., & Heiman, J. R. (2013). Discrepant responding across self-report measures of men's coercive and aggressive sexual strategies. *Journal of Sex Research, 50*(5), 458–469.

Ströhle, A., Romeo, E., di Michele, F., Pasini, A., Yassouridis, A., Holsboer, F., & Rupprecht, R. (2002). GABAA receptor-modulating neuroactive steroid composition in patients with panic disorder before and during paroxetine treatment. *The American Journal of Psychiatry, 159*, 145–147.

Surampudi, P. N., Wang, C., & Swerdloff, R. (2012). Hypogonadism in the aging male diagnosis, potential benefits, and risks of testosterone replacement therapy. *International Journal of Endocrinology, 2012*, 1–20.

Tackett, J. L., Herzhoff, K., Harden, K. P., Page-Gould, E., & Josephs, R. A. (2014). Personality × hormone interactions in adolescent externalizing psychopathology. *Personality Disorders: Theory, Research, and Treatment, 5*(3), 235–246.

Takeda, T., Tasaka, K., Sakata, M., & Murata, Y. (2006). Prevalence of premenstrual syndrome and premenstrual dysphoric disorder in Japanese women. *Archives of Women's Mental Health, 9*(4), 209–212.

Takeshita, R. S., Huffman, M. A., Kinoshita, K., & Bercovitch, F. B. (2017). Effect of castration on social behavior and hormones in male Japanese macaques (*Macaca fuscata*). *Physiology & Behavior, 181*, 43–50.

Tan, E. C., Lim, H. W., Chua, T. E., Tan, H. S., Lee, T. M., & Chen, H. Y. (2018). Investigation of variants in estrogen receptor genes and perinatal depression. *Neuropsychiatric Disease and Treatment, 14*, 919.

Teixeira, C., Figueiredo, B., Conde, A., Pacheco, A., & Costa, R. (2009). Anxiety and depression during pregnancy in women and men. *Journal of Affective Disorders, 119*, 142–148.

Thorpe, S. J., Patel, S. P., & Simonds, L. M. (2003). The relationship between disgust sensitivity, anxiety and obsessions. *Behaviour Research and Therapy, 41*(12), 1397–1409.

Tolin, D. F., & Foa, E. B. (2006). Sex differences in trauma and posttraumatic stress disorder: A quantitative review of 25 years of research. *Psychological Bulletin, 132*, 959–992.

Tschudin, S., Bertea, P. C., & Zemp, E. (2010). Prevalence and predictors of premenstrual syndrome and premenstrual dysphoric disorder in a population-based sample. *Archives of Women's Mental Health, 13*(6), 485–494.

Turk, C. L., Heimberg, R. G., Orsillo, S. M., Holt, C. S., Gitow, A., Street, L. L., Schneier, F. R., & Liebowitz, M. R. (1998). An investigation of gender differences in social phobia. *Journal of Anxiety Disorders, 12*, 209–223.

Tybur, J. M., Lieberman, D., & Griskevicius, V. (2009). Microbes, mating, and morality: Individual differences in three functional domains of disgust. *Journal of Personality and Social Psychology, 97*(1), 103–122.

Uguz, F., Sonmez, E. O., Sahingoz, M., Gokmen, Z., Basaran, M., Gezginc, K., Sonmez, G., Kaya, N., Erdem, S. S., Cicekler, H., & Tasyurek, E. (2013). Maternal generalized anxiety disorder during pregnancy and fetal brain development: A comparative study on cord blood brain-derived neurotrophic factor levels. *Journal of Psychosomatic Research, 75*, 346–350.

Van Veen, J. F., Jonker, B. W., Van Vliet, I. M., & Zitman, F. G. (2009). The effects of female reproductive hormones in generalized social anxiety disorder. *The International Journal of Psychiatry in Medicine, 39*, 283–295.

van Wingen, G. A., van Broekhoven, F., Verkes, R. J., Petersson, K. M., Bäckström, T., Buitelaar, J. K., & Fernández, G. (2007). Progesterone selectively increases amygdala reactivity in women. *Molecular Psychiatry, 13*, 325–333.

Vesga-López, O., Blanco, C., Keyes, K., Olfson, M., Grant, B. F., Hasin, D. H. (2008). Psychiatric disorders in pregnant and postpartum women in the United States. *Archives of General Psychiatry, 65*, 805–815.

Vesga-López, O., Schneider, F., Wang, S., Heimberg, R., Liu, S., Hasin, D. S., & Blanco, C. (2008). Gender differences in generalized anxiety disorder: Results from the National Epidemiologic Survey on Alcohol and Related Conditions (NESARC). *Journal of Clinical Psychiatry, 69*, 1606–1616.

Vinkers, C. H., Joëls, M., Milaneschi, Y., Kahn, R. S., Penninx, B. W., & Boks, M. P. (2014). Stress exposure across the life span cumulatively increases depression risk and is moderated by neuroticism. *Depression and Anxiety, 31*(9), 737–745.

Walther, A., Wasielewska, J. M., & Leiter, O. (2019). The antidepressant effect of testosterone: An effect of neuroplasticity? *Neurology, Psychiatry and Brain Research, 32*, 104–110.

Walton, N., & Maguire, J. (2019). Allopregnanolone-based treatments for postpartum depression: Why/how do they work? *Neurobiology of Stress, 11*, 100198.

Weissman, M. M., Bland, R. C., Canino, G. J., Greenwald, S., Hwu, H. G., Lee, C. K., Newman, S. C., Oakley-Browne, M. A., Rubio-Stipec, M., & Wickramaratne, P. J. (1994). The cross national epidemiology of obsessive compulsive disorder: The Cross National Collaborative Group. *The Journal of Clinical Psychiatry, 55*, 5–10.

Welker, K. M., Norman, R. E., Goetz, S., Moreau, B. J. P., Kitayama, S., & Carré, J. M. (2017). Preliminary evidence that testosterone's association with aggression depends on self-construal. *Hormones and Behavior, 92*, 117–127.

Welling, L. L. M., Conway, C. A., DeBruine, L. M., & Jones, B. C. (2007). Perceived vulnerability to disease is positively related to the strength of preferences for apparent health in faces. *Journal of Cultural and Evolutionary Psychology, 5*, 131–139.

Welling, L. L. M., Jones, B. C., DeBruine, L. M., Conway, C. A., Law Smith, M. J., Little, A. C., Feinberg, D. R., Sharp, M. A., & Al-Dujaili, E. A. (2007). Raised salivary testosterone in women is associated with increased attraction to masculine faces. *Hormones and Behavior, 52*, 156–161.

Werner, F. M., & Covenas, R. (2010). Classical neurotransmitters and neuropeptides involved in major depression: A review. *International Journal of Neuroscience, 120*(7), 455–470.

Willcox, D. L., Yovich, J. L., McColm, S. C., & Schmitt, L. H. (1985). Changes in total and free concentrations of steroid hormones in the plasma of women throughout pregnancy: Effects of medroxyprogesterone acetate in the first trimester. *Journal of Endocrinology, 107*(2), 293–300.

Williams, K. E., & Koran, L. M. (1997). Obsessive-compulsive disorder in pregnancy, the puerperium, and the premenstruum. *The Journal of Clinical Psychiatry, 58*, 330–334.

Wilson, M., & Daly, M. (1985). Competitiveness, risk taking, and violence: The young male syndrome. *Ethology and Sociobiology, 6*(1), 59–73.

Wingfield, J. C., Hegner, R. E., Dufty, A. M., & Ball, G. F. (1990). The "challenge hypothesis": Theoretical implications for patterns of testosterone secretion, mating systems, and breeding strategies. *American Naturalist, 136*(6), 829–846.

Workman, J. L., Barha, C. K., & Galea, L. A. (2012). Endocrine substrates of cognitive and affective changes during pregnancy and postpartum. *Behavioral Neuroscience, 126*(1), 54.

Wuttke, W., Theiling, K., Hinney, B., & Pitzel, L. (1998). Regulation of steroid production and its function within the corpus luteum. *Steroids, 63*(5–6), 299–305.

Yonkers, K. A., Brown, C., Pearlstein, T. B., Foegh, M., Sampson-Landers, C., & Rapkin, A. (2005). Efficacy of a new low-dose oral contraceptive with drospirenone in premenstrual dysphoric disorder. *Obstetrics & Gynecology, 106*(3), 492–501.

Yonkers, K. A., Bruce, S. E., Dyck, I. R., & Keller, M. B. (2003). Chronicity, relapse, and illness – Course of panic disorder, social phobia, and generalized anxiety disorder: Findings in men and women from 8 years of follow-up. *Depression and Anxiety, 17*, 173–179.

Yonkers, K. A., O'Brien, P. S., & Eriksson, E. (2008). Premenstrual syndrome. *Lancet, 371*(9619), 1200–1210.

Zarrouf, F. A., Artz, S., Griffith, J., Sirbu, C., & Kommor, M. (2009). Testosterone and depression: systematic review and meta-analysis. *Journal of Psychiatric Practice, 15*(4), 289–305.

Żelaźniewicz, A., Barkowka, B., Nowak, J., & Pawlowki, B. (2016). The progesterone level, leukocyte count and disgust sensitivity across the menstrual cycle. *Physiology & Behavior, 161*(1), 60–65.

Zobel, A. W., Nickel, T., Sonntag, A., Uhr, M., Holsboer, F., & Ising, M. (2001). Cortisol response in the combined dexamethasone/CRH test as predictor of relapse in patients with remitted depression: A prospective study. *Journal of Psychiatric Research, 35*(2), 83–94.

CHAPTER 46

Defect or Design Feature? Toward an Evolutionary Psychology of the Role of Emotion in Motivated Reasoning

Timothy Ketelaar

Abstract

This chapter describes motivated reasoning from an evolutionary perspective. A central premise is that when two individuals arrive at strikingly different interpretations of the same evidence, these different perceptions might not reflect a mere difference of opinions but may instead represent the operation of fundamentally different worldviews. Kant's transcendental psychology offers a philosophical framework for understanding how two individuals—or even the same person in different contexts—will often perceive the same physical reality in markedly different ways. Finally, the chapter draws upon evolutionary insights regarding cognitive bias to review the literature on emotion and motivated reasoning. Equipped with these evolutionary and philosophical insights, this chapter shows how the "Affect-as-Information" model from social cognition can illuminate how many instances of cognitive bias, such as motivated reasoning, may be more accurately interpreted, not as "bugs" in our "mental software," but as possible "design features" of the human mind.

Key Words: emotion, motivated reason, worldview, Kant, evolutionary psychology

In their classic 1954 monograph, "They Saw a Game," Albert Hastorf and Hadley Cantril asked Princeton and Dartmouth students to watch a motion picture of the 1951 football game between these two Ivy League rivals. Undergraduates from both institutions were given identical instructions: watch the game film, record any penalties (taking care to categorize each infraction as either flagrant or mild), and identify which team was responsible. Newspaper accounts depicted a brutal contest with numerous penalties and several players leaving the field with injuries, including Dick Kazmaier, Princeton's Heisman trophy–winning quarterback who left the game in the second quarter with a broken nose. Although the final score of the game was undisputed (Princeton defeated Dartmouth 13–0), students' perceptions of the infractions committed by each squad varied across the two Ivy League institutions.

Despite the fact that students from both schools had watched the same game film, the number and quality of infractions they "observed" differed substantially. These disparate perceptions were not random, but varied as a function of whether the infractions were ostensibly committed by their own team or by their rival. Hastorf and Cantril (1954) observed, for example, that Dartmouth students characterized only 50% of their own team's infractions as "flagrant," whereas Princeton students categorized the vast majority of these same penalties as "flagrant." Similarly, Princeton undergraduates categorized the vast majority of their own team's penalties as "mild," whereas Dartmouth students categorized far fewer of Princeton's infractions as "mild." These striking discrepancies in students' perceptions of the same football game—perceptions of the same "objective" evidence—led Hastorf and Cantril (1954, p. 133) to conclude: "the data here indicate that there is no such 'thing' as a 'game' existing 'out there' in its own right which people merely 'observe.'" Instead, they argued, "The game 'exists' for a person and is experienced by him only insofar as certain happenings have significances in terms of his purpose."

Today we recognize the selective and distorted perceptions of these Ivy League students as a classic example of *motivated reasoning*, a form of cognitive bias in which an actor's perceptions of the world appear to reflect a desired, often self-serving, set of conclusions, rather than an accurate account of the evidence (Kunda, 1990).

Motivated Reasoning

Hastorf and Cantril (1954) also recounted the story of a Dartmouth alumnus who had received a copy of the same game film shortly after it had been reviewed by the Princeton students. The alumnus watched the game film, but could not identify many of the flagrant penalties observed by the Princeton students. He wired his Dartmouth colleagues, concerned that this footage (of the Dartmouth player's infractions) may have been edited out of the version of the film that had been mailed to him: "Preview of Princeton movies indicates considerable cutting of important part please wire explanation and possibly air mail missing part before showing scheduled for January 25 we have splicing equipment."

In other words, having failed to locate the flagrant Dartmouth penalties "observed" by the Princeton students, this Dartmouth alumnus assumed that these events must have been cut from the film. What he did not realize was that the film had not been altered. The striking differences between his own observations and the perceptions of students from a rival institution were not a reflection of different content depicted in two differently edited versions of the same game film (they viewed the same recording), but instead reflected markedly different perceptions of the same recorded images. Given these striking findings, Hastorf and Cantril's (1954) paper has become one of the most widely recognized illustrations of *motivated reasoning*.

The motivation to arrive at a particular set of inferences—including the formation of conclusions that appear to be at odds with the available evidence—is not limited to biased observations of sporting contests or perceptual errors generated while viewing ambiguous stimuli in a psychology laboratory (Balcetis & Dunning, 2006); there are now numerous studies documenting blinkered interpretations of scientific data and "legally significant" facts, including biased interpretations of scientific evidence (Ditto et al., 2003; Stanovich et al., 2013). In one well-known demonstration of how motivated reasoning can creep into the evaluation of scientific evidence, Kunda (1987) asked undergraduates to read and evaluate a scientific paper concerning the effects of caffeine consumption on the risk of a female developing painful lumps in her breast. This "scientific paper" was a fiction created by Kunda and her colleagues, but the results were compelling evidence for motivated reasoning—demonstrating that female students who were also heavy coffee drinkers found more "flaws" in this research paper than did their male counterparts, or less caffeinated women.

In another series of studies, Kahan and colleagues (Kahan, Peters, et al., 2017) demonstrated how easy it is for individuals to draw conclusions that are at odds with the scientific evidence, especially when it is possible to construct an alternative interpretation that is more in line with one's preexisting political beliefs. In a series of experiments, Kahan, Peters, and colleagues (2017) first presented participants with the results of a hypothetical clinical trial of a new experimental skin cream for treating rashes. In this fictious experiment, one group of patients was described as having been treated with the skin cream for two weeks, whereas a second (control) group did not receive the treatment. The researchers created a contingency table (see Figure 46.1) to display the number of patients (treatment vs. no treatment) whose rash got better or worse.[1] The researchers purposefully constructed the data to make arriving at a correct conclusion challenging—i.e., the contingency table depicted a large number of patients whose rash got better in the treatment condition (see Table A in Figure 46.1); but this particular finding was misleading because the percentage of improved cases was higher (84% versus 75%) among patients who did *not* receive the skin cream treatment, thus demonstrating that the skin cream was *not more effective* (compared to doing nothing; see Table A in Figure 46.1). Before testing for motivated reasoning, Kahan, Peters, and colleagues (2017) first established that participants were capable of drawing correct conclusions from contingency table data, regardless of their political ideology. Consistent with this assumption, participants previously identified as scoring higher on a measure of numeracy (the ability to draw correct inferences from numeric data) were—unsurprisingly—*much more likely to generate correct inferences* from the contingency table compared to their less numerate counterparts, *regardless of their political affiliation*. However, when the topic of the study was dramatically switched in a second experiment—by simply changing the labels in the contingency table—to reflect a much more politically charged topic (i.e., the *effectiveness of gun control policy in reducing crime*)—motivated reasoning was clearly present in participants' interpretations of the same contingency tables with switched labels (see Tables C and D in Figure 46.1).

More specifically, when asked to interpret a contingency table displaying data on the effectiveness of a "concealed firearms ban," participants who scored highest in numeracy were more likely to supply the correct conclusion, *but only when the data supported their political views*. By contrast, when the data in the contingency table directly contradicted their political views, these same highly numerate participants *were less likely to generate the correct conclusion from the data*. In short, across several studies, Kahan and colleagues (2017) found that individuals *are more likely to display motivated reasoning* when interpreting evidence that is relevant to their political beliefs compared to when they are asked to interpret the same data presented as reflecting a much less politically charged topic (e.g., evaluating the effectiveness of a skin cream).

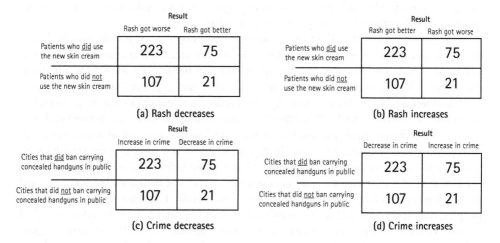

Figure 46.1. Treatment condition. Adapted from Kahan et al. (2017).

In summary, the tendency to defend an identity-relevant worldview with biased reasoning has been conceptually replicated many times (see Ditto & Lopez, 1992; Ditto et al, 1998; Ditto et al., 2003; Haidt, 2012; Kahan, Landram, et al., 2017; Klein & Harris, 2009; Kunda, 1990, 2001; McKenna, 2021; Schaller, 1992; Taber & Lodge 2006) and is a central feature of the phenomenon of *motivated reasoning*, or what is sometimes called "my-side bias" (Stanovich et al., 2013).

Overview

This chapter applies an evolutionary lens to motivated reasoning and other forms of identity-protective cognition. A central assumption is that our understanding of *cognitive bias* and *dysrationalia* is incomplete without an appreciation of the role that emotions play in these processes. Moreover, this focus on emotion aligns well with a common interpretation of Hastorf and Cantril's (1954) classic study of motivated reasoning:

> The students' *emotional stake in affirming their loyalty to their institutions* . . . had unconsciously *shaped what they had seen* when viewing events captured on film. This study is now recognized as a classic demonstration of "motivated cognition," the ubiquitous tendency of people to form perceptions, and to process factual information generally, in a manner congenial to their values and desires. (Kahan, Hoffman, et al., 2012, p. 853, emphasis added)

After introducing several philosophical caveats from Kant's transcendental psychology that cast doubt upon the claim that all members of a species will necessarily have access to the same "shared reality," I review evolutionary insights into the utility of cognitive biases (i.e., the smoke detector principle), including the argument that *argumentation* itself evolved, not for locating truth, but for achieving consensus (Mercier & Sperber, 2011, 2017). Equipped with these evolutionary and philosophical insights, and adopting an "Affect-as-Information" framework, I summarize the scientific literature on emotion and motivated reasoning.

Kantian Idealism and Evolutionary Psychology

Motivated reasoning is typically employed as a strategy to promote or defend a cherished set of beliefs (i.e., a worldview). Before we explore the role of emotion in this biased form of reasoning, it will be helpful to first consider how we acquire our basic assumptions about the social and physical world. In his *Critique of Pure Reason*, Kant (1781) argued that any discussion of metaphysical reality should begin by acknowledging that our perceptions of "reality" are constructed, even determined, by our psychological faculties.

I am not claiming that Kant was arguing for philosophical relativism, postmodernist social constructivism, or epistemic nihilism. Kant was not arguing that it was meaningless to talk about a "real" world existing independent of our own minds. Instead, Kant was pointing out that even if we assume—as most scientists do—that such a physical world exists, it may be philosophically intractable to accurately characterize its existence (a view often referred to as *idealism*; see Kitcher, 1990). This difficulty in establishing the nature of metaphysical reality arises, according to Kant, because our ability to understand the physical world, or to even conceptualize its existence, is ineluctably dependent upon the psychological faculties with which we perceive that same world. It follows that any two individuals with somewhat different mental faculties, or who are experiencing different states of their own faculties, can (and often do) generate different perceptions of the external world. Consider, for example, a neurotypical individual who readily distinguishes the colors pink and blue. When this individual encounters a florist's decorative arrangement of *forget-me-nots*, the difference between pink and blue flowers is literally "self-evident." Yet, for approximately 4% of the human population

(8% of men) who have a form of color blindness (Caufield, 2021), this "self-evident" perception is not possible without special aids. From the perspective of a congenitally color blind observer, their initial exposure to the poetic couplet "Roses are red, Violets are blue" can be a non sequitur in the same sense that judging the "appropriate amount of eye contact" during informal conversation is a daunting social judgment task for the approximately 5.4 million individuals in the United States who have the same visual acuity of their compatriots, but find themselves located in the extreme tail of a distribution of a psychological trait known as systematizing-empathizing (also referred to as autism spectrum disorder; see Baron-Cohen, 2003; Silberman, 2015). In short, what is in our heads (our specific mental faculties) can both enable and constrain the "reality" that we perceive "in the world."[2]

Far from being a pedantic philosophical exercise, these Kantian insights continue to generate coherent debates regarding the metaphysics of perception (e.g., for contemporary debates regarding whether colors are an objective property of the world, see Thompson et al., 1991; for a larger discussion of the *qualia* debate, see Dennett, 1991). Although Kant believed that a metaphysics was possible, he cautioned that any rigorous study of the mind (i.e., any scrupulous science of psychology) should take into account this fundamental recognition that our understanding of the world—including our own minds and the "self-evident" perceptions they generate—is not achieved via a *pure, unbiased faculty of reasoning*. After all, Kant's most influential treatise was not titled *Approbation for the Perfection, Breadth, and Potency of Human Reasoning*, but rather the far more modest *Critique of Pure Reason*.

Kant's transcendental psychology (see Kitcher, 1990, for an accessible overview) is quite consistent with evolutionary psychology. Both frameworks allow us to appreciate how different members of the same species can (and often do) encounter different "realities" by virtue of possessing reliably developing,[3] individually different, evolved psychological faculties. To illustrate the compatibility between Kantian idealism and evolutionary psychology, let's consider several examples from the domain of olfactory and gustatory perception. Many species, including humans, possess a vast repertoire of context-sensitive ingestive behaviors (eating, drinking) that enable members of that species to solve a wide range of adaptive problems centering around the more general problem of maintaining metabolic homeostasis (i.e., efficiently regulating the intake, processing, and storage of potential energy, etc.). To surmount these adaptive challenges, many species have evolved a variety of *bio-mechanical* devices and strategies such as chewing, swallowing, and digesting for regulating their nutrient intake. More relevant to Kantian transcendental psychology, a number of species—including humans—possess specialized *cognitive* (information-processing) systems that appear to be "designed" to generate subjective psychological states corresponding to the organism's current metabolic state (e.g., hunger, thirst, smell, taste, etc.; see Berridge, 1991; Kringelbach, & Berridge, 2017). These specialized information-processing devices appear to generate an adaptively patterned "augmented reality" that the organism deploys while foraging for nutrients. Consider, for example, the reliably emerging changes observed in the subjective sense of smell and taste of certain foods for women in the first trimester of their pregnancy. This temporary shift in perceptions (compared to later trimesters) appears to be well-suited to the avoidance of teratogens when the fetus is most vulnerable to birth defects (see Lieberman & Carlton, 2018, for a review). To take a more familiar example, consider the reliable finding that the subjective "pleasantness" of the smell and taste of a favorite food (e.g., a slice of pizza) will differ dramatically dependent upon whether the individual is in a metabolic state of caloric need (i.e., hungry) compared to when that same individual is sated (i.e., after consuming three slices), a well-documented phenomenon known as *allesthesia* (Cabanac, 1971). Nor should it be surprising that certain species which—in their ancestral environments—evolved to ingest a limited range of dietary substances will often assign different, largely species-specific, subjective "values" to certain edible substances. For example, if the ancestral diet of koalas and panda bears consisted almost exclusively of eucalyptus leaves and bamboo (respectively), an evolutionary biologist might not be surprised to discover that the subjective value assigned to these two substances—i.e., how "good" these foods taste—might differ systematically between the two species, suggesting that the degree of concordance between the adaptive "benefits" of consuming a particular food in ancestral environments and the current psychological "value" assigned to that food is not accidental. To entertain a more striking example, consider that the subjective "taste" of dung surely varies much less as a function of whether you are hungry or sated than upon whether you are a member of the species *Homo sapiens* or *Scarabaeoidea* (i.e., the dung beetle, for whom animal feces is a dietary staple). From an evolutionary perspective, it is not surprising to observe that these subjective psychological states—referred to as "qualia"—can differ substantially from one species to the next. Moreover, it is not surprising that our evolved "psychological software" generates these subjective states in a context-sensitive (and therefore individually different) manner, producing perceptual representations of the environment that are attuned to specific changes in the organism's momentary physiological state (see Berridge, 1999) and uniquely shaped to the historical fitness affordance landscape for that particular species (Buss, 1991; Dangles et al., 2009; Tooby & Cosmides, 1990b).

Because different species possess distinct perceptual faculties uniquely suited to the invariant features of their ancestral environments, different species can, in principle, experience different perceptual worlds—a supposition famously explored by the philosopher Thomas Nagel in his (1974) essay "What is it like to be a bat?" Although Nagel came to the conclusion that it would be impossible to know the mind of other species, over the past half century philosophers of mind, comparative psychologists, and animal cognition researchers have cast doubt upon Nagel's pessimistic assertion. Philosophers have demonstrated that although it is challenging to understand how another organism perceives the world, it is not impossible (see Dennett, 1991; Dennett & Hofstadter, 2000). Moreover, animal cognition researchers and comparative psychologists have studied the "metaphysics" of numerous species, both in the lab as well as in their natural environments, and several researchers have spent much of their careers developing and testing hypotheses regarding how several primate species perceive and represent their social and physical environments (Cheney & Seyfarth, 1990, 2007; Povinelli, 2003). Evolutionary biologists have even coined the term *umwelt* precisely for the purpose of describing these species-specific perceptual worlds anticipated by Kant (see Baggs & Chemero, 2021; Burnett, 2011):

> This *umwelt* differs for each organism, which means that it is difficult for us to truly understand how another organism perceives the world. . . . It should also be noted that it is common for sensory systems to change with development of an animal, meaning that the *umwelt* that organism inhabits can often change over the course of its life (Dangles et al., 2009). . . . This perceptual world is highly dependent upon the senses that a particular organism possesses, although it is also affected by the internal workings of an animal's nervous system at any given time. (Burnett, 2011, p. 75)

From an evolutionary perspective it is not surprising to observe that the *umwelt* for humans does not include an ability to perceive the electrical fields generated by other organisms, even though this perceptual ability is an important feature of the physical world experienced by sharks. This is the case because many cartilaginous fish, including sharks, have evolved specialized perceptual organs, known as *Lorenzini ampullae*, which allow them to detect the electric fields of their prey (Camperi et al., 2007). Thus, if one accepts this evolutionary-Kantian insight (that an organism's perceptions of the world are actively constructed by their evolved senses), it is easier to appreciate that different species—by virtue of possessing different mental faculties tailored to the unique adaptive challenges faced by that species—will not experience identical perceptual worlds. Similarly, it follows that different members of the same species encountering the same physical environment, and even the same individual experiencing the same environment in different contexts (e.g., while hungry vs. sated), will not experience the same *umwelt*. In this light, the observation that our evolved reasoning mechanisms often generate perceptual worlds that appear biased or flawed—especially when compared to a single objective standard—may not be so mysterious. Several evolutionary scholars have suggested that evolved psychological mechanisms capable of generating context-sensitive representations of the world, including systematically self-serving representations, might be better understood as evolved design features rather than defects (Haselton & Nettle, 2006; Nesse, 2001a, 2005).

The Evolution of Adaptive Biases: The Smoke Detector Principle

The software engineer's response, "that's not a bug, it's a feature," captures the evolutionary logic underlying why certain "design features" can appear to be avoidable errors or unnecessary biases (Nesse, 2001a, 2005). Natural and sexual selection are not teleological processes and thus one should not expect that evolution will invariably lead to adaptive solutions optimally attuned to all relevant features of the environment; this is especially the case for novel aspects of current environments that differ substantially from the environments in which a psychological mechanism evolved (Nesse & Williams, 1994, 2019). Moreover, in regard to any attempt to reverse-engineer the mental software that humans evolved for perceiving their physical and social world, is it not reasonable to begin by acknowledging Kant's arguments about the intractability of determining what an "objective" (as opposed to subjective) map of the world would even look like? Thus, a Kantian approach to evolutionary psychology reminds us that the computational task of generating an effective "mental map" of the specific threats and opportunities in an organism's environment—i.e., the fitness affordance landscape for that particular member of that particular species at that particular point in its life history—will ineluctably depend upon on the nature and conditional state of the specific mental faculties that the organism evolved for perceiving the invariant statistical properties of that world (Gibson, 1979).

Change the operating conditions for any particular mental faculty that an organism employs to perceive its physical or social milieu, and you will likely change—if only temporarily—that individual's mental map of the world. Consider, for example, how the mental map of a chimpanzee's social network might change after the death of an important ally (de Waal, 1982), or how humans might perceive their political leaders differently while experiencing an irrelevant happy mood as compared to when they are experiencing an irrelevant sad mood (see Forgas & Moylan, 1982). Similarly, if you switch your focus to the mind of a different species, you may suddenly find that this new species operates with a different mental map of the world, perhaps even a map that is incompatible with the perceptual world experienced by other species. It is well established, for example, that adult humans reliably perceive a pile of dung as a dangerous opportunity to contract disease (Lieberman & Carlton, 2018), whereas a mature dung beetle will invariably interpret the same stimulus as a propitious opportunity to ingest its favorite meal. These observations are not evidence that one species has somehow generated a more accurate map of the world. Instead, these examples illustrate how the trade-offs associated with employing a "highly accurate" map of the world versus constructing a subjective, yet "accurate enough" map are species-specific and uniquely tailored to the ecological niche occupied by that species in its ancestral environments (Haselton & Nettle, 2006; Todd & Gigerenzer, 2012).

The past several decades of research in evolutionary-developmental psychology reveal that humans are endowed with a wide variety of perceptual faculties that reliably unfold over the course of development in a context-sensitive fashion (Boyce & Ellis, 2005). Accordingly, different members of the same species can—by dint of their having different developmental histories, or finding themselves in different environments—experience different perceptual worlds systematically calibrated to their developmental trajectory or their current circumstances. From the perspective of Kantian idealism and evolutionary psychology, the cost-benefit calculus associated with possessing such specialized and environmentally sensitive psychological faculties—evolved for reasoning about the social and physical world—is not predicated on these faculties generating precisely accurate representations of the world. It turns out, for example, that some organisms can prevail in the grand Darwinian steeplechase of life by possessing reasoning mechanisms that place their bets in accord with an adaptationist interpretation of Pascal's Wager—an evolutionary gamble in which it becomes "rational" to "overestimate" the probability of extremely improbable events if the costs associated with failing to predict these events would be catastrophic[4] (Nesse, 2019; see also Taleb, 2010, 2014). Regardless of whether these "black swan" events result in catastrophic losses or windfall profits, what matters is that the organism is able to translate its predictive success into greater reproductive success (i.e., greater success at passing on the genetic basis for these risk-sensitive perceptual systems; see Nesse, 2001a, 2005). When the metric for evaluating "success" is evolutionary fitness (rather than accuracy), the benefits associated with an information-processing system "designed" to grossly overestimate the likelihood of a highly improbable event can be worth the metabolic costs associated with the organism's hypersensitivity to environmental cues that were reliable predictors of rare but catastrophic outcomes in ancestral environments. Appreciating the evolutionary trade-offs between "highly accurate performance" and "good enough performance" has been of such significance to Darwinian medicine and evolutionary psychiatry that these disciplines have developed a special nomenclature to capture this insight: the *smoke detector principle* (Nesse, 2001a, 2005). According to this principle, it can be evolutionarily beneficial to "over-spend" resources in preparing for a rare—but catastrophic—event, such as an attack by a dangerous predator, simply because:

> [t]he costs of such responses tend to be low compared to the benefits of avoiding danger. So when danger may or may not be present, the small cost of a response ensures protection against a much larger harm. That is why we put up with false alarms from smoke detectors. (Nesse, 2019, pp. 73–74)

An understanding of the role of trade-offs can also help us to appreciate the evolutionary origins of perceptual organs with design flaws, such as the optical "blind spot" in the vertebrate eye, the result of a lack of light-sensitive receptors where the optic nerve attaches to the retina (Nesse, 2019). In this case, a more "optimally" designed eye—i.e., one without a blind spot—has been precluded by the vagaries of evolutionary history, including path dependencies associated with epigenetic processes and gene expression. Simply put, once natural selection went down the path of connecting the optic nerve to the back of the vertebrate retina, this made the evolution of a vertebrate eye without a blind spot improbable. Appreciating these evolutionary trade-offs allows us to understand how the costs associated with a flawed perceptual organ—an eye with a blind spot—can be offset by the fact that even a somewhat poorly designed perceptual organ provides greater benefits than an even more poorly designed organ, or no eye at all. Similarly, we might appreciate how the costs associated with a reasoning mechanism that generates cognitive biases can be offset by fact that even a somewhat "inaccurate" reasoning mechanism can provide greater benefits than an even more poorly designed reasoning mechanism, or no reasoning ability at all.

Motivated Reasoning as a Tool for Persuasion: The Argumentative Theory of Reasoning

Despite considerable evidence suggesting that humans routinely engage in flawed and biased reasoning strategies (Gilovich, 1991; Griffin & Kahneman, 2002; Kahneman et al., 1982), it is still widely assumed that bolstering our capacity for reasoning will necessarily lead to improved knowledge and better decision-making. By contrast, Mercier and Sperber (2011, 2017) suggest that efforts aimed at promoting more sophisticated forms of reasoning in pursuit of increased rationality might backfire if our capacity for reasoning evolved not for truth-seeking, but for other purposes. More specifically, their Argumentative Theory of Reasoning (Mercier & Sperber 2011, 2017) contends that human reasoning evolved not primarily for the purpose of locating "truths" about the world (a point that Kant might appreciate), but to win arguments and achieve consensus. As Brockman (2011) notes:

> The idea here is that the confirmation bias is not a flaw of reasoning, it's actually a feature. It is something that is built into reasoning; not because reasoning is flawed or because people are stupid, but because actually people are very good at reasoning—but they're very good at reasoning for arguing.

If our capacity for sophisticated reasoning evolved for purposes other than truth-seeking, might this explain the pervasiveness—perhaps even the utility—of many common forms of cognitive bias? According to Mercier and Sperber(2011, 2017), our intuitive capacities for reasoning so frequently lead to outcomes that are irrational (Gilovich et al., 2002) not because humans are incapable of sound reasoning, but because reasoning evolved to aid us in intuitively and systematically looking for arguments to justify our beliefs and actions. As many experienced attorneys and politicians know, it is not surprising to observe that strategies employed to win arguments or achieve consensus sometimes fall short when compared to more objective standards of truth-seeking. Seen in this light, many examples of "poor reasoning," such as confirmation bias (see Nickerson, 1998, for a review) and other forms of motivated reasoning, appear to function to serve an identity-protective function, rather than a truth-seeking function (see Kahan, Hoffman, et al., 2012; Kahan, Peters, et al., 2012; Kahan, Peters, et al., 2017; McKenna, 2021). Examples of common argumentative biases include: (1) the tendency to spend more effort evaluating arguments that one disagrees with (Edwards & Smith, 1996; Taber & Lodge, 2006); (2), the tendency to search for counterarguments when one disagrees with an argument (Petty & Cacioppo, 1979; Eagly et al., 2000); and (3) the tendency to search for flaws in an opposing argument, stopping when the search has uncovered a specific shortcoming (i.e., problems with the experimental design, concerns regarding statistical reasoning, or a flawed inference somewhere in the model; see Klaczynski, 1997; Klaczynski & Robinson, 2000; Perkins, 1985; Perkins et al., 1991). In short, Mercier and Sperber (2011, p. 72, emphasis added) argue that:

> *motivated reasoning* leads to a biased assessment: Arguments with unfavored conclusions are rated as less sound and less persuasive than arguments with favored conclusions.

If our capacity for reasoning functions as a tool for argumentation (see Haidt, 2001, 2012, and Harris, 2010, for similar views of moral reasoning), sophisticated argumentative skills may not always be deployed in the service of "objectively" evaluating competing arguments; they can also be employed in the defense of a weak, but self-serving, line of reasoning:

> [W]here does reason come into the picture? It is an attempt to justify the choice after it has been made. And it is, after all, the only way we have to try to explain to other people why we made a particular decision. But given our lack of access to the brain processes involved, our justification is often spurious: A post-hoc rationalization, or even a confabulation. (Frith, 2008, p. 45)

Consistent with the view that reasoning is a *tool for persuasion* rather than *truth-seeking*, etymologists have noted that the word "sophisticated" derives from the Greek *sophistēs*, which has a positive connotation as "wise man" or "expert," but is also the root of the word "sophistry." Along these lines, several studies have found that individuals with greater knowledge of science and superior technical reasoning skills ironically arrive at *more* (not less) polarized conclusions when confronted with evidence pertaining to culturally controversial issues (Drummond & Fischhoff, 2017; Kahan, Peters, et al., 2012; Kahan, Landrum, et al., 2017). These findings are in line with what some scholars have referred to as the "Intelligence Trap,"[5] a phenomenon in which cognitive bias—including confirmation bias, over-confidence bias, and motivated reasoning—is *more (not less) common* among participants with ostensibly *superior reasoning ability* (see Heuer, 1999, 2019; Robson, 2019). These findings have prompted some social scientists to suggest that the association between *greater scientific acumen* and *more polarized opinions* is a plausible explanation for the ironic finding that individuals in more secular postindustrial societies often are *more* (not less) skeptical of science than individuals in less secular societies:

> Indeed, the more secular postindustrial societies, exemplified by the Netherlands, Norway, and Denmark, prove most skeptical toward the impact of science and technology, and this is in accordance with the countries where the strongest public disquiet has been expressed about certain contemporary scientific developments such as the use of genetically modified food, biotechnological cloning, and nuclear power. (Norris & Inglehart, 2009, p. 67)

Although such findings run contrary to the common belief that science skepticism is associated with low levels of scientific literacy or poor reasoning abilities (see Kahan, Peters, et al., 2012), these results are consistent with the argumentative theory of reasoning. The consistent evidence that motivated reasoning is common, even among skilled reasoners, when they are debating contentious issues has prompted some researchers to conclude that:

> divisions over climate change stem not from the public's incomprehension of science *but from a distinctive conflict of interest*: between the *personal interest* individuals have in forming *beliefs in line with those held by others* with whom they share close ties and the *collective* one they all share in *making use of the best available science to promote common welfare*. (Kahan, Peters et al., 2012, p. 2, emphasis added)

An uncharitable conclusion one might draw from the motivated reasoning literature is that human reasoning is so biased that neither scientists nor science-based arguments can be trusted. However, a more nuanced—and arguably more accurate—conclusion is that while rhetorical skill can be an effective tool for promoting rational discourse and truth-seeking, these same argumentative talents can sometimes create more discord than insight when they are employed for self-serving purposes.

Affect-as-Information

To illustrate how research at the intersection of emotions and motivating reasoning is amenable to an adaptationist analysis, I utilize the "affect-as-information" model as a framework for appreciating the evolutionary trade-offs associated with emotional influences on human reasoning. The affect-as-information model (see Schwarz & Clore, 1983, 2003) views the feeling states (i.e., affective experiences) that accompany each emotion as important sources of information that systematically influence a wide variety of thought processes, including many forms of reasoning once conceptualized as purely "cold" cognitive processes. Research in the affect-as-information tradition has shown that many forms of reasoning, from judgments of life satisfaction to perceptions of political leaders, are easily influenced by emotions (even incidental emotions).

When seen through the lens of an evolutionary perspective, an affect-as-information framework is particularly helpful in identifying aspects of emotional information-processing that are good candidates for evolved "design features." For example, the aversive feeling state that accompanies the experience of guilt has been shown to reliably exert a motivating influence on cooperative behavior by virtue of "disincentivizing" self-interested behavior (Ketelaar & Au, 2003). Along these lines, I have suggested that our capacity to produce "guilty feelings" may have evolved, in part, to provide us with "information" about the "costs" of not cooperating in situations that resemble indefinitely repeated social bargaining games (Ketelaar, 2004, 2006). This interpretation harkens back to Adam Smith's (1759) view that certain emotions operate as "moral sentiments" that "commit" us to pursuing a more virtuous course of action, in part, by enabling us—like Odysseus strapped to the mast—to overcome the immediate attraction of less virtuous courses of action. Consistent with Adam Smith's view, evolutionary interpretations of guilt have converged on the idea that this emotion evolved as a "commitment device" that, when activated, provides the agent with a powerful incentive to stay the "cooperative" course, especially when we are exposed to spuriously attractive immediate incentives that run contrary to our long-term interests (see Frank, 1988, 2001; Hirschleifer, 1987, 2001; Ketelaar, 2004, 2006; Nesse, 2001b). Consider, for example, how strong feelings of guilt can commit a person to a long-term goal of losing weight by enabling them to overcome the immediate attraction of a second piece of cake. In this manner, emotional commitment devices, such as guilt,

> [c]an and do compete with feelings that spring from rational calculations about material pay offs . . . consider, for example, a person capable of strong guilt feelings. This person will not cheat even when it is in her material interest to do so. The reason is not that she fears getting caught but that she simply does not *want* to cheat. Her aversion to feelings of guilt affectively alters the pay offs she faces. (Frank, 1988, p. 53, emphasis in the original)

An affect-as-information framework can also help us to understand why a "well-designed" emotion mechanism might generate responses that appear wasteful or even irrational in modern environments. After all, if the "affective information" associated with our emotional feelings is calibrated to the cost-benefit calculus of ancestral environments, it would not be surprising to observe that our experience of positive affect (pleasant feelings) and negative affect (unpleasant feelings) in modern environments does not always correspond to a rational mapping of the cost-benefit structure of our contemporary circumstances.

To illustrate how a psychological mechanism might generate behavior that makes little sense in modern environments, despite the fact that it is "well designed" to operate in ancestral environments, it may be helpful to consider the example of a hypothetical "snake fear" mechanism. In the environments in which this "snake fear" mechanism evolved, the "costs" associated with a hypersensitive fear response may have been relatively low compared to the "cost" of failing to detect and respond appropriately to environmental cues (i.e., snake-shaped objects) reliably associated with catastrophic outcomes (i.e., injury or possible death). Consider, for example, the small costs—in both modern and ancestral environments—associated with being compelled—by your fear—to avoid walking down a particular path when confronted with a distant object that resembles either a harmless tree branch or a poisonous snake. In modern environments with health insurance, Medivac helicopters, and emergency rooms stocked with venom antiserum, the benefits of occasionally avoiding a poisonous snake might not be worth the costs of experiencing numerous false alarms (e.g., responding to tree branches, garden hoses, and other snake-like objects). By contrast, in ancestral environments, the benefits of avoiding even a single snake bite—with an accompanying high probability of significant injury or death—might make a hyper-reactive snake-fear mechanism worth the costs of numerous false alarms.

Thus armed with a better understanding of the notion of evolutionary cost-benefit trade-offs (Nesse & Williams, 1994), it is easier to appreciate why evolution by natural and sexual selection does not invariably lead to perceptual mechanisms that generate accurate (unbiased) representations of the physical and social world. In this light, we turn now to a review of the literature on emotions and motivated reasoning, with the aim of investigating whether these processes might be more accurately seen not as "bugs" in our "mental software," but as "design features" of the human mind.

Emotions and Identity-Protective Cognition

US senator Daniel Patrick Moynihan allegedly once said: "You are entitled to your own opinions. But you are not entitled to your own facts." Moynihan's aphorism may be clever, but it is not a viable guide to understanding ideological debates in which an attack on your opinions can seem like an attack on your social identity. This is the case because ideological disputes frequently go beyond minor differences of opinion and are often characterized as sincere disagreements concerning competing "truths" about the world as seen through the eyes of the disputants (Shweder & Levine, 1984). Consider, for example, how often ideological debates evolve into passionate disputes in which one side of the argument claims that the other side can't be serious, or that their ideological opponent can't believe what they are asserting because such beliefs are so "obviously" false from their perspective. It stands to reason, however, that in many instances in which different individuals have reviewed the same evidence, but sincerely claim to have observed different "facts" (e.g., "they saw a game") or earnestly claim to have "rationally" arrived at contradictory conclusions from the same evidence, we are not witnessing a mere difference of opinions, but a clash of identity-relevant worldviews. Even combatants in a rhetorical skirmish between incompatible visions of the world sometimes find themselves exiting a debate reeling with unpleasant emotions and finding themselves in an intellectually vulnerable position, having encountered evidence or arguments that, if true, would undermine some of their fundamental assumptions about the world:

> To the extent that one has become emotionally committed to, or publicly identified with, a particular theory, its failure in the face of evidence imposes psychic costs that can be painful. (Sowell, 2007, p. 240)

In this regard, social science research has found that merely activating an individual's group identity or threatening their cultural values is enough to generate strong emotions which can influence the individual's subsequent evaluation of "legally significant" facts (see Flynn et al., 2017; Kahan & Nussbaum, 1996). Munro et al. (2012), for example, presented participants in two experiments with scientific evidence that disconfirmed their preexisting beliefs. Borrowing from Schwarz and Clore's (1983) classic mood misattribution paradigm, the experimenters gave half of the participants the opportunity to misattribute any negative affect (that they experienced while reading the belief-disconfirming evidence) to an irrelevant source (poor room conditions or caffeinated water). The other half (control group) were not given this opportunity to misattribute their unpleasant feelings. Consistent with an affect-as-information interpretation, Munro and colleagues (2012) observed that participants in the misattribution condition—who could easily dismiss their feelings of discomfort as being due to an irrelevant source—perceived the methodological rigor of the studies to be much stronger compared to participants in the control condition who were given no such opportunity to dismiss their feelings of discomfort. In a similar study, Klein and Harris (2009) asked women to read an article that linked alcohol consumption to breast cancer. Consistent with the claim that threats to identity-relevant worldviews reliably generate emotional responses that can bias the processing of threatening information, women who were moderate-to-heavy drinkers showed an attentional bias towards *ignoring* threatening words in the article. Consistent with an affect-as-information framework, this bias was reduced for those women who were randomly assigned to receive a positive "self-affirmation" message just prior to reading the article. In sum, numerous studies of motivated reasoning have demonstrated that emotions can be an important driver of motivated reasoning, especially when an individual is evaluating evidence that is relevant to highly politicized, identity-relevant issues such as climate change or human papillomavirus (HPV) vaccines (Kahan, Peters, et al., 2012; Kahan, Peters, et al., 2017; McKenna, 2021). In characterizing the role that emotional processes play in identity-protective cognition, Munro and colleagues (2012, p. 11) argue:

> Belief-disconfirming scientific studies elicit negative affect, which mobilizes an expenditure of cognitive resources to reconcile the inconsistency between one's pre-existing beliefs and the scientific evidence. The increased cognitive processing often results in an unfavorable critique of the scientific evidence.

Most individuals are motivated to reduce these feelings of discomfort that arise whenever they perceive an inconsistency (dissonance) between their commitment to an important set of beliefs and their recognition that strong evidence exists which contradicts those beliefs. When an individual experiences strong emotions (e.g., fear, anger, etc.) upon encountering evidence contradicting the fundamental tenets of an important belief system, this heightened emotional state is often a sign that they have interpreted this attack as a serious threat to their social identity (Festinger, 1957; Harmon-Jones, 2019; Young, 1995). Social scientists refer to this state of psychological discomfort as *cognitive dissonance* (Festinger, 1957; Harmon-Jones, 2019). Interestingly, serious threats to an individual's worldview, including threats that produce cognitive dissonance, do not invariably result in the individual abandoning their belief system. In fact, in many cases, encountering overwhelmingly contradictory evidence will lead to a renewed sense of commitment to that worldview, rather than a search for an alternative system of meaning. The classic example is Festinger's study of a "Doomsday cult" whose members had to cope with the cognitive dissonance experienced when the world did not come to an end on December 21, 1954, as predicted by their cult leader (Festinger et al., [1956] 2009). Rather than reject their leader's prophecy as false, and their belief system as problematic, Festinger observed that cult members engaged in increased proselytizing and affirmations of faith in the immediate aftermath of the failed prediction upon which their cult was based.

Holding ideological ground, or even defending it with renewed vigor, makes sense, however, when the individual (whose worldview has been attacked) is a rhetorically sophisticated advocate armed with a coherent, well-integrated set of functionally interdependent facts and arguments—much like a skilled and ethical defense attorney arguing on behalf of an innocent client by introducing exonerating evidence and relevant case law. Nevertheless, there are at least two conditions, as detailed in the following, in which even a rhetorically skilled advocate might find themselves ill-equipped to defend their worldview, and both circumstances are likely to produce a considerable amount of cognitive dissonance in any defendant whose identity is tied to the belief system they are defending.

In the first condition, an *ideologically bereft worldview*, an advocate who is rhetorically skilled will still have trouble producing a strong (logical and evidence-based) defense of their worldview if that worldview is not founded upon clear evidence and sound reasoning, or lacks a stable, coherent, and internally consistent set of foundational tenets.

For example, it would be easier for a sophisticated scientist to successfully defend the claim that "Newton's theory anticipated the existence of the planet Neptune (before its discovery)" than the claim "the Moon is made out of spirit essence looted from Terror Demons." The first case involves defending a claim that references a coherent set of assumptions supported by solid evidence and sound reasoning; the second case does not.

The second condition is a *poorly defended worldview*. Even in cases where a worldview is founded upon supportive evidence and sound reasoning, and can be characterized as a stable, coherent, and internally consistent set of foundational tenets, a rhetorically skilled advocate will still have trouble producing a strong defense of this worldview if they do not have access to the supportive data and sound reasons that support this belief system. In this regard, political scientists have argued that much of the early research on ideology and mass belief systems (e.g., Converse, 1964) overestimated the extent to which even ideological "elites" possess sophisticated belief systems that would enable them to access the best evidence and most compelling reasons when called upon to defend their ideological commitments (see Kalmoe, 2020; Kuklinski & Peyton, 2007, for reviews).

For example, it would be easier for a well-trained attorney to successfully defend (in a court of law) a legal claim (e.g., "Parody and satire are protected forms of speech") if this attorney is familiar with the relevant case law (e.g., *Hustler v. Falwell*, 485 U.S. 46, 1988) compared to a similarly well-trained attorney who is not familiar with the relevant case law. The attorney in the first case has access to the relevant evidence and lines of reasoning needed to successfully defend the claim. The second attorney may have the same litigation skills but, lacking access to the most relevant evidence and lines of reasoning, has little hope of prevailing against a more fully prepared adversary.

Although these two conditions represent somewhat different pathways to the employment of "less-than-rational" strategies—such as motivated reasoning—that may be called upon to defend one's ideological commitments, *bereft worldviews* and *poorly defended worldviews* share two things in common. In particular, they share an element of hypocrisy, a sense of disconnect between the effort that an advocate spends in promoting or defending their worldview and their knowledge of its core tenets. In the case of a *bereft worldview*, this "false advertising" is in regard to the ideology being promoted: a type of "virtue signaling" whereby the substance of what is communicated appears to matter much less than the simple fact that the individual has successfully signaled which ideological team they are on, and which moral and ethical virtues they endorse (see Miller, 2007, for review of the possible evolutionary benefits of virtue signaling). In these circumstances, the advocate has less resemblance to a well-informed defense attorney, and appears more like a politically correct journalist (see Taibbi, 2019) who is more concerned with being *directionally* correct than *technically* accurate, perhaps as a result of "navigating newsrooms where they were being discouraged, sometimes openly, from pursuing true stories with the 'wrong' message," and knowing that their allies will forgive them if they flub the details of the worldviews that they promote, so long as they're supporting the "right" talking points (Taibbi, March 1, 2021, n.p.). In the case of a *poorly defended worldview*, the hypocrisy is in regard to the qualifications of the promoter, not the ideology: simply put, the advocate "does not know what they are talking about" and their ignorance makes them a poor representative of that worldview. How common are these circumstances? Some social scientists have argued that when one conducts a rigorous investigation of political ideologies, for example, one finds that a substantial number of pundits (the so-called political elites) do not know many of the basic tenets of the ideologies they promote or defend (Kalmoe, 2020; see also Kurzban, 2010; Kurzban & Weeden, 2014, for discussion of the prevalence of hypocrisy in public discourse). In both cases, the *cognitive dissonance* generated in response to the inconsistency between their strong allegiance to their worldview, and their recognition that they are ill-prepared to rationally defend it, could motivate them to defend their worldviews through more expedient means[6]—including motivated reasoning.

Emotions and Moral Reasoning, Including Perceptions of Justice

What happens when our ancient emotions find themselves ensconced in contemporary courtrooms and legal proceedings? If modern environments contain many of the same invariant statistical properties that our emotion mechanisms evolved to react to, then we should not be surprised to observe ourselves occasionally generating emotional responses that make little sense in these situations, even if these same emotional proclivities were an effective means of responding to threats and challenges in ancestral environments. One arena in which these reliably activated emotional responses may have unintended, and perhaps unwanted, consequences is in the realm of moral and legal decision-making. The modern criminal justice system, for example, is ostensibly a bastion of reason and evidence, yet there is substantial evidence that emotions (including irrelevant emotions) regularly intrude upon our reasoning about moral, ethical, and legal issues. Moreover, our capacity to instinctively experience emotions when certain environmental cues are present could be exploited by sophists with less than noble intentions. In his book *Against Empathy,* psychologist Paul Bloom (2016) identifies several concerns regarding the "weaponizing" of emotional empathy in persuasive arguments employed in legal settings.

One example of the potential for emotional bias in the courtroom, according to Bloom (2016), is the use of victim impact statements during sentencing or at parole hearings. Victim impact statements consist of written or oral statements which provide crime victims with an opportunity to describe the emotional, physical, and financial harm that they or others have suffered as a direct result of a crime. These statements are permitted in the sentencing phase of trials in 44 US states. Bloom [2019, cf. Illing (2019), January 16, 2019, 8:52 a.m. EST] notes:

> I could not imagine a better recipe for bias and unfair sentencing decisions than this. . . . You suddenly turn the deep questions of how to punish criminals into a question of *how much do I feel for this person in front of me*? So the bias would be incredibly powerful.

One might counter, however, that a high degree of bias is unlikely to occur in a courtroom because the jury is given the opportunity to "see with their own eyes" the evidence that is most relevant to the guilt or innocence of the accused. As reasonable as this counterargument might appear to be, research on motivated reasoning suggests that this view may be perilously naïve (Braman & Kahan, 2003; Kahan et al., 2009).

In a conceptual replication of Hastorf and Cantril's (1954) "They Saw a Game" study, psychologist and legal scholar Daniel Kahan explored the influence of motivated reasoning in a hypothetical courtroom setting in which research participants (the "jury") were asked to interpret "legally significant" facts (Kahan, Hoffman, et al., 2012). In a study titled, "They Saw a Protest," Kahan and colleagues (2012) showed participants a videotape of a political demonstration and asked them to judge whether law enforcement had over-reacted in their efforts to disperse protestors allegedly obstructing or intimidating people from using a public facility. Participants were told to imagine themselves as jurors in a court case that focused on the lawfulness of the police's actions.

Because the identities of the demonstrators could not be easily discerned from the videotape, Kahan was able to experimentally manipulate the "affiliation" of the protestors. Rather than pitting Dartmouth undergraduates against Princeton students as Hastorf and Cantril (1954) had done, Kahan, Hoffman, et al. (2012) created two distinct ideologically motivated groups of demonstrators: (1) Ideologically Conservative Protestors, and (2) Ideologically Progressive Protestors.[7] Half of the "jury" (the participants) were randomly assigned to the *Ideologically Conservative Protest condition* in which they were told that they were watching a demonstration that had occurred outside of an abortion clinic, a scenario in which demonstrators were protesting legalized abortion (i.e., *implying that the protesters were ideologically conservative*). The other half of the participants were told that they were watching a demonstration that occurred at a military recruiting event on a college campus, an event where the demonstrators were protesting the military's ban on service by openly gay and lesbian soldiers ("Don't Ask, Don't Tell"), *implying that the protesters were ideologically progressive*.

Importantly, Kahan also asked participants to rate themselves as ideologically conservative or progressive. Consistent with motivated reasoning, Kahan found that participants who adopted a conservative worldview saw the police as *behaving violently toward the protesters, but only when the protesters were identified as fellow conservatives*. By contrast, when the protestors were labeled as progressives, conservative participants viewed the police as behaving less violently (i.e., more peacefully).

Conversely, individuals adopting a progressive worldview saw the police as *behaving violently towards the protesters, but only when the protesters were their fellow progressives*. Similarly, progressive participants viewed the police as acting peacefully *when the protestors were conservatives*. In short, motivated reasoning appears to be commonplace, occurring in circumstances ranging from interpreting numbers in a contingency table to interpreting legal evidence (a video of police interacting with protestors) that you can "see with your own eyes."

Moreover, emotional influences on perceptions of social justice and morality can be observed beyond the courtroom (see Lukianoff & Haidt, 2018; Kahan & Nussbaum, 1996; Posner, 2008). In this regard, the science of emotion and morality has recently undergone a radical reconceptualization in which the traditional view—portraying moral judgment as primarily reflecting the application of moral "reasoning" (e.g., Kohlberg, 1981)—has been challenged by a new perspective that emphasizes the role of moral sentiments (such as sympathy/empathy) in judgments of moral approbation or disapproval (see Haidt's [2001, 2007] Social Intuitionist Model; also Greene, 2013). In a typical study of emotional influences on moral judgment, Lerner, Goldberg, and Tetlock (1998) observed that individuals experimentally placed in an angry mood subsequently made harsher attributions of blame toward a hypothetical coworker whose negligence had caused them harm. Moreover, these same individuals also ascribed more severe punishments to the same coworker, but only when they were primed with an angry mood (and not when they were placed in a neutral mood). Another study found that research participants provoked to feel disgust, sadness, or fear were observed to require less evidence to make a strong negative moral trait attribution (i.e., uncharitable, unfriendly) compared to individuals placed into a sanguine mood (Trafimow et al., 2005). In short, emotional influences appear to be a fundamental part of many forms of moral "reasoning" that have traditionally been conceptualized as processes of rational decision-making (Bloom, 2016; Greene, 2013; Haidt, 2001; Ketelaar, 2004, 2006; Ketelaar & Koenig, 2007).

Barsky and Kaplan (2007) conducted a meta-analysis (45 studies, 57 distinct samples) on the association between affective states and perceptions of justice. Their analysis revealed a reliable association between measures of state and trait positive and negative affect and perceptions of distributive, procedural, and interactional justice. These relationships were in the predicted directions, with mean population-level correlations (between emotion and perceptions of justice) ranging in absolute magnitude from 0.09 to 0.43. The typical finding was that participants in more a negative mood viewed the social world as less just, compared to participants in a more positive mood (Barsky & Kaplan, 2007). This association between strong emotions and perceptions of social justice has been observed not only in the laboratory but also in the workplace. Lang, Bliese, Lang, and Adler (2011), for example, explored the relationship between social justice in organizations and the emotional health of employees. In this context, the phrase *organizational justice* referred to at least two kinds of perceptions: (1) perceptions of fair and respectful treatment by their supervisors or other authorities, and (2) perceptions of how clearly resource allocations were explained by their superiors.

Interestingly, previous research in organizational settings had often interpreted the correlation between social justice in the workplace and employee psychological health as evidence that unfair treatment in the workplace led to reduced psychological health. However, most of these field studies were correlational in design, and thus did not allow for a test of causal direction (see Lang et al., 2011, for a review). To explore the association between emotion and social justice in a more controlled setting, Lang, Bliese, Lang, and Adler (2011) created three longitudinal data sets in applied field settings (military organizations) that would allow them to test whether (a) organizational justice perceptions influence depressive symptoms over time, and (b) depressive symptoms have a lagged relation with perceptions of organizational justice. Their study revealed evidence that negative affect (depressive symptoms) did lead to perceptions of organizational injustice. Moreover, they observed no effect of organizational injustice perceptions on depressive symptoms. One explanation for these emotional influences on perceptions of justice entails an "affect-as-information" interpretation, as van den Bos (2003, p. 482) explains:

> It is not uncommon for people forming justice judgments to lack information that is most relevant in the particular situation. In information-uncertain conditions, people may therefore construct judgments by relying on how they feel about the events they have encountered and justice judgments may hence be strongly influenced by affect information.

Van den Bos (2003) tested this claim in several experiments in which participants completed a series of simple cognitive tasks (e.g., counting the number of squares inside a pattern presented on a computer screen) and were later rewarded with lottery tickets in proportion to the number of tasks they successfully completed. Across three experiments, van den Bos (2003) observed that individuals experimentally placed into a negative mood subsequently judged that they had been treated in a *less just* manner compared to individuals placed into a more positive mood. Consistent with an "affect-as-information" interpretation, the effects of an experimentally produced mood state had an effect on judgments of justice only when participants were uncertain about how they (and other participants) were going to be rewarded. Van den Bos (2003, p. 482) noted:

> These findings thus reveal that in situations of information uncertainty, people's judgments of justice can be very subjective, susceptible to affective states that have no logical relationship with the justice judgments they are constructing.

Emotions and Reasoning about Risk

Psychological scientists studying risk perception have reached essentially the same conclusion—about our ability to reason accurately about risk—that Hastorf and Cantril (1954) reached in their studies of motivated reasoning in college football fans. Just as Hastorf and Cantril argued that "there is no such thing as a 'game' existing 'out there,'" modern-day cognitive scientists (Slovic, 1999, p. 690) recently concluded that

> risk is inherently subjective. In this view, risk does not exist "out there," independent of our minds and cultures, waiting to be measured. Instead, human beings have invented the concept risk to help them understand and cope with the dangers and uncertainties of life. Although these dangers are real, there is no such thing as "real risk" or "objective risk."

Consistent with this Kantian view, Johnson and Tversky (1983, p. 26) observed that the negative affect generated while participants read news accounts of various tragic causes of deaths (ranging from natural disasters and automobile accidents to homicides and heart attacks) led to "pervasive global effects on their estimates of fatalities" regardless of the specific cause of death that they were asked to estimate. In other words, the negative affect associated with reading a news report of a depressing death from stomach cancer routinely generalized to increased perceptions of mortality risk from toxic chemical spills, terrorism, and auto accidents. Similar effects were demonstrated when participants were asked to read pleasant (non-tragic) news stories, which produced increases in positive affect and corresponding decreases in estimates of risk of death across a wide range of causes (e.g. airplane accidents, leukemia, electrocution, etc.). Although much of the research on risk perception does not adopt an evolutionary perspective (see Barrett & Fiddick, 1999; Elmer et al., 2008, for notable exceptions), most risk researchers acknowledge the important role that "affect-as-information" and "affect heuristic" processes play in guiding judgments and decision-making regarding risk (Slovic, 1999; Slovic et al., 2005; Slovic et al., 2016; Pachur et al., 2012).

Naturalistic experiments examining emotion and risk perception are consistent with these laboratory findings. For example, in the months following the September 11, 2001, terrorist airplane attacks in the United States, many Americans avoided the smaller death risk associated with terrorist attacks by avoiding travel by airplane. Instead, they assumed a much larger death risk (by automobile accident) when they opted for travel via the roadways. Gigerenzer (2004) examined air travel, highway traffic, and fatal traffic accidents for the three months following September 11, and his analysis revealed not only that air travel decreased and highway traffic increased, but that an additional 350 people died in traffic accidents during this period, more than the approximately 250 people who died in airplanes on September 11, 2001. Similar findings were observed by Lopez-Rousseau (2005), who tracked people's transportation choices following the March 2004 terrorist train bombing in Spain which killed approximately 200 people. Lopez-Rousseau (2005) found similar decreases in the mode of transportation associated with a terrorist act (railway travel decreased after the train bombing), although he did not observe an increase in automobile fatalities. In fact, he observed that the Spanish reduced both forms of travel (automobile and train) in the immediate aftermath of the bombing. Both studies (Gigerenzer, 2004; Lopez-Rousseau, 2005; see also Myers, 2001) are consistent with the claim that witnessing or reading about distressing events can influence estimates of risk outside of the social science laboratory.

In sum, research on decision-making regarding risk suggests that risk perception is a product of cognitive and emotional processes capable of generating context-sensitive representations of the world. Consistent with the smoke detector principle, these risk perceptions generate "false alarms" that overestimate the likelihood of improbable catastrophic events in precisely those circumstances in which the costs of these hyper-sensitive responses (a minor inconvenience in one's daily commute) seem infinitesimally small in relation to the much larger costs (serious injury or death) that these mechanisms help us to avoid. Ironically, these emotional mechanisms, which likely evolved to assess risks relevant to ancestral environments—such as estimating the probability of an attack by a dangerous predator—can also lead to ironic and sometimes tragic outcomes (i.e., increases in automobile fatalities; Gigerenzer, 2004) when these same mechanisms are activated outside of the environments in which they evolved to operate (lions, tigers, and bears, as opposed to planes, trains, and automobiles). Nonetheless, these emotional biases are not necessarily evidence that our minds are poorly designed for assessing risk:

> The public is not irrational. Their judgments about risk are influenced by emotion and affect in a way that is both simple and sophisticated. The same holds true for scientists. Public views are also influenced by worldviews, ideologies, and values; so are scientists' views, particularly when they are working at the limits of their expertise. (Slovic, 1999, p. 689)

Final Conclusions

When psychological scientists study the intersection of cognitive bias and human emotion, these phenomena are often lumped together as "defective" aspects of human nature that undermine our otherwise sophisticated capacity for rational thought (Ketelaar & Clore, 1997). Software engineers encounter a similar challenge in explaining why their ostensibly well-designed software programs regularly generate odd behaviors that seem—to the non-engineer—like pointless mistakes or easily avoidable errors. This chapter is offered as a demonstration that the application of evolutionary and philosophical insights, including the well-established "affect-as-information" framework, can provide a powerful set of tools for distinguishing aspects of human emotion that might be referred to as "design features" from those aspects that appear to be more accurately characterized as non-adaptive byproducts, or noise (Haselton & Ketelaar, 2006; Haselton & Nettle, 2006; Nesse, 2019). So, what adaptive function(s) might emotions serve that could also explain how these "design features" of the human mind are so often characterized as bugs in our mental software?

If we are to believe Kant and hence assume that access to a single metaphysical reality is difficult or impossible for members of any species to achieve, then a fitness advantage could be conferred upon the members of a group-living species who were able to more successfully navigate (relative to their competitors) their social and physical world by virtue of possessing a psychological adaptation that reliably "constructed" a "shareable"[8] representation of their environment around which they could coordinate their behavior with conspecifics. To consider one speculative example of a plausible adaptive problem that our consciously accessible emotions (i.e., our affective feeling states) may have evolved to solve, there are a variety of indefinitely repeated social exchange relationships that would have been routinely encountered in ancestral environments (which can be modeled, with the help of behavioral economic and game theoretic methods, as indefinitely repeated social bargaining games) in which locating and coordinating on a specific equilibrium strategy would have afforded a fitness advantage over competitors who were less capable of locating and coordinating upon these strategies (see Ketelaar, 2004, 2006). One way that this adaptive challenge could be addressed would be through the evolution of cognitive and emotional mechanisms capable of constructing a stable "mental map" of the fitness affordance[9] landscape for members of a particular species. This "shared reality" would then enable conspecifics to coordinate their thoughts and behaviors around their shared perceptual and cognitive experiences, as illustrated by a non-emotional example from our visual system which allows two individuals to "experience" the same bird flying in the same sky, even though the visual input these two individuals receive is, by definition, not identical because any two individuals occupying two different locations in space will necessary encounter different visual inputs. Although the details of how this model of emotions as mechanisms for creating a "shared" mental map of the fitness affordance landscape are speculative and beyond the scope of this chapter, this brief discussion is offered with the aim of demonstrating that it is possible to identify plausible adaptive problems—e.g., the challenge of generating a shared cognitive-emotional reality that social organisms could employ to coordinate their actions—in which emotions and motivated reasoning might play a central role. Moreover, the "shared reality" generated by these evolved psychological mechanisms could have been adaptive in ancestral environments, even if the "mental maps" they generated could sometimes be categorized as "biased" when compared to a single, objective standard.

In other words, perhaps our evolved emotional "software" is, in part, responsible for generating the shared worldviews that we routinely and tacitly employ as "mental maps" of our physical and social worlds. At their best, these emotion-based worldviews can provide us with a stable, coherent, and internally consistent set of foundational assumptions upon which we can construct a useful understanding of the social world and our place in it. And precisely because we are so dependent on these guiding frameworks, endowed by our evolved emotions, these worldviews can become a core part of our social identities—identities (and worldviews) that we are motivated to defend. As a result, the same worldviews that bring us comfort and guide us in finding meaning and a sense of purpose, can also be the source of some of our most biased and self-serving interpretations. In this light, it may be reasonable to consider that some of our emotional reasoning processes may be more accurately seen not as "bugs" in our "mental software" but as "design features" of the human mind.

Notes

1. Kahan and colleagues (2017) counter-balanced whether the clinical trial was a success or failure across participants (as seen in Tables A & B in Figure 46.1).
2. Kant's *idealism* can appear to be the polar opposite of Gibson's (1979) *ecological psychology* because Gibson (1979) focused much less on the question of "What is inside your head" (i.e., mental faculties) and more on the question of "What is your head inside of?" However, Gibson (1979) recognized that the affordances of an organism's environment (i.e., its *umwelt*) are the result of an interaction between the historically recurrent invariant properties of the organism's ancestral environments and the specific evolved perceptual and psychological faculties—that arose over the organism's evolutionary history—to exploit/respond to those affordances.
3. Consistent with Kant's transcendental psychology, the past half century of evolutionary-developmental science has identified a plethora of reliably developing, often highly environmentally sensitive, neurologically based traits capable of generating adaptively patterned, individually calibrated, perceptions and representations of the physical and social world (Barkow et al., 1992; Boyce & Ellis, 2005; Tooby & Cosmides, 1990a). Examples of reliably developing and individually tailored evolved psychological faculties include relatively well understood perceptual-cognitive systems, such as *depth perception* (calibrated to reliably appearing interoceptive cues of self-propelled locomotion; Dahl et al., 2013), language acquisition devices (with distinct epigenetic activating conditions; Pinker, 1994, 1999), and episodic memory (tailored to the physical constraints of the world, thus making it difficult or impossible to recall or recollect "physically impossible objects and motions" (Schacter et al., 1991; Shiffar & Freyd, 1991).
4. For example, the annual cost savings accrued by several US cities that chose to prepare for a rare 100-year flood event—in lieu of preparing for a much less probable, but even more devasting 500-year flood event—was irrelevant once the much less probable event occurred (an unfortunate set of circumstances experienced by residents of New Orleans [Hurricane Katrina] and Houston [which experienced three 500-year floods between 2015 and 2017]). See Taleb, 2010, 2014, for a more detailed account of this point.
5. Several scholars have recently argued that rational/analytical ability is independent of general intelligence (for a review, see Stanovich et al., 2016, 2018). In this light, individuals with greater analytical ability may find themselves caught in an "Intelligence Trap" whereby their increased argumentative skill is problematically associated

with an increasingly sophisticated ability to "rationalize," a cognitive tendency that may operate at the expense of other more valid inference-making strategies (see Mercier & Sperber, 2017; Robson, 2019, for reviews).
6. By referring to motivated reasoning as an "expedient" strategy for defending one's worldview, I do not mean to imply that the deployment of motivated reasoning is necessarily a conscious deliberative process. In fact, several lines of research suggest that motivating reasoning is often a tacit process (see Balcetis & Dunning, 2006; Kahan, Hoffman, et al., 2012).
7. *Ideologically conservative*s and *ideologically progressives* were defined as Hierarchical Communitarians and Egalitarian Individualists, respectively; see Kahan, Hoffman, et al. (2012) for details.
8. The cognitive and emotional mechanisms that generate a "shareable" mental map would have to effectively balance the costs and benefits associated with two distinct computational problems: (a) the problem of effectively representing the moment-to-moment changes in *species-specific* threats and opportunities (i.e., corresponding to the specific ecological niche occupied by a particular species in its ancestral environments), and (b) the problem of effectively representing the moment-to-moment changes in the *individual-specific* threats and opportunities (i.e., highly attuned to the characteristics of each particular individual's unique developmental history and phenotypic traits). In this regard, Freyd's (1983, 1990) description of "consciousness" as "shareability" would be one way to think about how human perceptual experiences are typically "conscious" precisely because they are shareable.
9. The term "fitness affordance" was first introduced by evolutionary psychologist Geoffrey Miller in the 1990s as an adaptationist extension of James Gibson's (1979) affordance concept. In the current context, the term "fitness affordance landscape" refers to the specific threats (negative affordances) and opportunities (positive affordances) in an organism's current environment, defined in terms of the specific environmental cues that would have been associated, in ancestral environments, with evolutionary relevant fitness costs and benefits (see Miller, 2007).

References

Baggs, E., & Chemero, A. (2021). Radical embodiment in two directions. *Synthese, 198*, 2175–2190 . https://doi.org/10.1007/s11229-018-02020-9

Balcetis, E. and Dunning, D. (2006). See what you want to see: Motivational influences on visual perception. *Journal of Personality and Social Psychology, 91*, 612–625.

Barkow, J. H., Cosmides, L., & Tooby, J. (Eds.). (1992). *The adapted mind: Evolutionary psychology and the generation of culture*. Oxford University Press.

Baron-Cohen, S. (2003). *The essential difference*. Basic Books.

Barrett, H. C., & Fiddick, L. (1999). Evolution and risky decisions. *Trends in Cognitive Sciences, 4*, 251–252.

Barsky, A., & Kaplan. S. A. (2007). If you feel bad, it's unfair: A quantitative synthesis of affect and organizational justice perceptions. *Journal of Applied Psychology, 92*, 286–295.

Berridge, K. C. (1991). Modulation of taste affect by hunger, caloric satiety, and sensory-specific satiety in the rat. *Appetite, 16*, 103–120.

Berridge, K. (1999). Pleasure, pain, desire, and dread: Hidden core processes of emotion. In D. Kahneman, E. Diener, & N. Schwarz (Eds.), *Well-being: Foundations of hedonic psychology* (pp. 525–557). Russell Sage Foundation.

Bloom, P. (2016). *Against empathy: The case for rational compassion*. HarperCollins Books.

Bloom, P. (2019). cf. Illing (January 16, 2019 8:52 a.m. EST). The case against empathy: Why this Yale psychologist thinks you should be compassionate, not empathetic. https://www.vox.com/conversations/2017/1/19/14266230/empathy-morality-ethics-psychology-compassion-paul-bloom

Boyce, W. T., & Ellis, B.J. (2005). Biological sensitivity to context: I. An evolutionary-developmental theory of the origins and functions of stress reactivity. *Development and Psychopathology, 17*, 271–301.

Braman, D. & Kahan, D. M., (2003). More statistics, less persuasion: A cultural theory of gun-risk perceptions. *University of Pennsylvania Law Review, 151*, Yale Law School, Public Law Research Paper No. 05, Available at SSRN: https://ssrn.com/abstract=286205 or http://dx.doi.org/10.2139/ssrn.286205

Brockman, J. (2011). The argumentative theory: A conversation with Hugo Mercier [4.27.11]. Edge.org. https://www.edge.org/conversation/hugo_mercier-the-argumentative-theory

Burnett, S. (2011). Perceptual worlds and sensory ecology. *Nature Education Knowledge, 3*, 75.

Buss, D. M. (1991). Evolutionary personality psychology *Annual Review of Psychology, 42*, 459–491.

Cabanac, M. (1971). Physiological role of pleasure. *Science, 173*, 1103–1107.

Camperi, M., Tricas, T. C., & Brown, B. R. (2007). From morphology to neural information: The electric sense of the skate. *PLoS Computational Biology, 3*, e113. doi: 10.1371/journal. pcbi.0030113

Caufield, J. (2021, February 11). Color blindness. Color Blindness Awareness. https://www.colourblindawareness.org/colour-blindness/.

Cheney, D. L., & Seyfarth, R. M. (1990). *How monkeys see the world: Inside the mind of another species*. University of Chicago Press.

Cheney, D. L., & Seyfarth, R. M. (2007). *Baboon metaphysics: The evolution of a social mind.* University of Chicago Press.
Converse, P. E. ([1964] 2006). The nature of belief systems in mass publics. *Critical Review, 18,* 1–74.
Dahl, A., Campos, J., Anderson, D., Uchiyama, I., Witherington, D., Ueno, M., Poutrain-Lejeune, L., & Barbu-Roth, M. (2013). The epigenesis of wariness of heights. *Psychological Science, 24,* 1361–1367.
Dangles, O., Irschick, D., Chittka, L. & Casas, J. (2009). Variability in sensory ecology: Expanding the bridge between physiology and evolutionary biology. *Quarterly Review of Biology, 84,* 51–74.
Dennett, D. C. (1991). *Consciousness explained.* Little, Brown.
Dennett, D. C., & Hofstadter, D. R. (2000). *The mind's I: Fantasies and reflections on self and soul.* Perseus Books Group.
de Waal, F. B. M. (1982). *Chimpanzee politics: Power and sex among apes.* Jonathan Cape.
Ditto, P. H., & Lopez, D. F. (1992). Motivated skepticism: Use of differential decision criteria for preferred and non-preferred conclusions. *Journal of Personality and Social Psychology, 63,* 568–584.
Ditto, P. H., Munro, G. D., Apanovitch, A. M., Scepansky, J. A. & Lockhart, L. K. (2003). Spontaneous skepticism: The interplay of motivation and expectation in responses to favorable and unfavorable medical diagnoses. *Personality and Social Psychology Bulletin, 29,* 1120–1132.
Ditto, P. H., Scepansky, J. A., Munro, G. D., Apanovitch, A. M., & Lockhart, L. K. (1998). Motivated sensitivity to preference-inconsistent information. *Journal of Personality and Social Psychology, 75,* 53–69.
Drummond, C., & Fischhoff, B. (2017). Individuals with greater science literacy and education have more polarized beliefs on controversial science topics. *Proceedings of the National Academy of Sciences, 114,* 9587–9592.
Eagly, A. H., Kulesa, P., Brannon, L. A., Shaw, K., & Hutson-Comeaux, S. (2000). Why counter attitudinal messages are as memorable as proattitudinal messages: The importance of active defense against attack. *Personality and Social Psychology Bulletin, 26,* 1392–1408.
Edwards, K., & Smith, E. E. (1996). A disconfirmation bias in the evaluation of arguments. *Journal of Personality and Social Psychology, 71,* 5–24.
Elmer, E. Cosmides, L. & Tooby, T. (2008). Relative status regulates risky decision-making about resources in men: Evidence for the co-evolution of motivation and cognition, *Evolution and Human Behavior, 29,* 106–118.
Festinger, L. (1957). *Cognitive dissonance.* Stanford University Press.
Festinger, L., Riecken, H., & Schacter, S. ([1956] 2009). *When prophecy fails.* Martino Fine Books.
Flynn, D. J., Nyhan, B., & Reifler, J. (2017). The nature and origins of misperceptions: Understanding false and unsupported beliefs about politics. *Advances in Political Psychology, 38,* 127–150.
Forgas, J. P., & Moylan, S. (1982). After the movies: Transient mood and social judgments. *Personality and Social Psychology Bulletin, 13,* 467–477.
Frank, R. H. (1988). *Passions within reason.* W. W. Norton.
Frank, R. H. (2001). Cooperation through emotional commitment. In R. M. Nesse (Ed.), *Evolution and the capacity for commitment* (pp. 57–76). Russell Sage Foundation.
Freyd, J. (1983). Shareability: The social psychology of epistemology. *Cognitive Science, 7,* 191–210.
Freyd, J. (1990). Natural selection or shareability? [commentary] *Behavior and Brain Sciences, 13,* 732–734.
Frith, C. (2008). Reason 2: No one really uses reason. *The New Scientist, 199,* 45.
Gibson, J. J. (1979). *The ecological approach to visual perception.* Taylor & Francis Group.
Gigerenzer, G. (2004). Dread risk, September 11, and fatal traffic accidents. *Psychological Science, 15,* 286–287.
Gilovich, T. (1991). *How we know what isn't so: The fallibility of human reason in everyday life.* The Free Press.
Gilovich, T., Griffin, D., & Kahneman, D. (2002). *Heuristics and biases: The psychology of intuitive judgement.* Cambridge University Press.
Greene, J. (2013). *Moral tribes: Emotion, reason, and the gap between us and them.* Penguin Press.
Haidt, J. (2001). The emotional dog and its rational tail: A social intuitionist approach to moral judgment. *Psychological Review, 108,* 814–834.
Haidt, J. (2007). The new synthesis in moral psychology. *Science, 316,* 998.
Haidt, J. (2012). *The righteous mind: Why good people are divided by politics and religion.* Pantheon.
Harmon-Jones, E. (Ed). (2019). *Cognitive dissonance: Reexamining a pivotal theory in psychology* (2nd ed.). American Psychological Association.
Harris, S. (2010). *The moral landscape: How science can determine human values.* Free Press.
Haselton, M. & Ketelaar, T. (2006). Irrational emotions or emotional wisdom: The evolutionary psychology of affect and behavior. In J. Forgas (Ed.), *Affect in social thinking and behavior* (pp. 21–39). Psychology Press.
Haselton, M. G., & Nettle, D. (2006). The paranoid optimist: An integrative evolutionary model of cognitive biases. *Personality and Social Psychology Review, 10,* 47–66.
Hastorf, A. H., & Cantril, H. (1954). They saw a game: A case study. *The Journal of Abnormal and Social Psychology, 49,* 129–134.

Heuer, R. J., Jr. (1999). Perception: Why can't we see what is there to be seen? In *Psychology of intelligence analysis*. History Staff, Center for the Study of Intelligence, Central Intelligence Agency. Retrieved October 29, 2007.

Heuer, R. J., Jr. (2019). *Psychology of intelligence analysis*. Martino Fine Books.

Hirshleifer, J. (1987). On emotions as guarantors of threats and promises. In J. Dupré (Ed.), *The latest on the best: Essays on evolution and optimality* (pp. 307–326). MIT Press.

Hirshleifer, J. (2001). Game-theoretic interpretations of commitment. In R. M. Nesse (Ed.), *Evolution and the capacity for commitment* (pp. 77–94). Russell Sage Foundation.

Illing, S. (2019, January 16). The case against empathy: Why this Yale psychologist thinks you should be compassionate, not empathetic. *Vox*. https://www.vox.com/conversations/2017/1/19/14266230/empathy-morality-ethics-psychology-compassion-paul-bloom

Johnson, E. J., & Tversky, A. (1983). Affect, generalization, and the perception of risk. *Journal of Personality and Social Psychology, 45*, 20–31.

Kahan, D. M., Hoffman, D. A., & Braman, D. (2009). Whose eyes are you going to believe? Scott v. Harris and the perils of cognitive illiberalism. *Harvard Law Review, 122*, 837–906.

Kahan, D. M., Hoffman, D. A., Braman, D., Evans, D., & Rachlinkski, J. J. (2012). "They saw a protest": Cognitive illiberalism and the speech-conduct distinction. *Stanford Law Review, 64*, 851–906.

Kahan D. M., Landrum, A., Carpenter, K. Helft, L. & Jamieson, K. H. (2017). Science curiosity and political information processing. *Advances in Political Psychology, 38*, 179–199.

Kahan, D. M., & Nussbaum, M. C. (1996). Two conceptions of emotion in law. *Columbia Law Review, 96*, 269–374.

Kahan, D. M., Peters, E., Cantrell Dawson, E. & Slovic, P. (2017). Motivated numeracy and enlightened self-government. *Behavioural Public Policy, 1*, 54–86.

Kahan, D. M., Peters, E., Wittlin, M., Slovic, P., Larrimore Ouellette, L., Braman, D. & Mandel, G. (2012). The polarizing impact of science literacy and numeracy on perceived climate change risks, *Nature Climate Change, 2*, 732–735.

Kahneman, D., Slovic, P., & Tversky, A. (1982). *Judgment under uncertainty: Heuristics and biases*. Cambridge University Press.

Kalmoe, N. P. (2020). Uses and abuses of ideology in political psychology. *Political Psychology, 41*, 771–793.

Kant, I. ([1781] 2007). *Critique of pure reason*. Penguin Books.

Ketelaar, T. (2004). Ancestral emotions, current decisions: Using evolutionary game theory to explore the role of emotions in decision-making. In C. Crawford & C. Salmon (Eds.), *Evolutionary psychology, public policy and personal decisions* (pp. 145–168). Lawrence Erlbaum Associates.

Ketelaar. T. (2006). The role of moral sentiments in economic decision making. In D. DeCremer, M. Zeelenberg, & K. Murnighan (Eds.), *Social psychology and economics* (pp. 97–113). Lawrence Erlbaum Associates.

Ketelaar, T., & Au, W. T. (2003). The effects of feelings of guilt on the behavior of uncooperative individuals in repeated social bargaining games: An affect-as-information interpretation of the role of emotion in social interaction. *Cognition and Emotion, 17*, 429–453.

Ketelaar, T., & Clore, G. L. (1997). Emotions and reason: The proximate effects and ultimate functions of emotions. In G. Matthews (Ed.), *Personality, emotion, and cognitive science* (pp. 355–396). Advances in Psychology Series. Elsevier Science.

Ketelaar, T., & Koenig, B. (2007). Justice, fairness, and strategic emotional commitments. In D. de Cremer (Ed.), *Justice and emotions: Current developments* (pp. 133–154). Lawrence Erlbaum Associates.

Kitcher, P. (1990). *Kant's transcendental psychology*. Oxford University Press.

Klaczynski, P. A. (1997). Bias in adolescents' everyday reasoning and its relationship with intellectual ability, personal theories, and self-serving motivation. *Developmental Psychology, 33*, 273–283.

Klaczynski, P. A., & Robinson, B. (2000). Personal theories, intellectual ability, and epistemological beliefs: Adult age differences in everyday reasoning biases. *Psychology and Aging*, 15, 400–416.

Klein, W. M. P., & Harris, P. R. (2009). Self-affirmation enhances attentional bias towards toward threatening components of a persuasive message. *Psychological Science, 12*, 1463–1467.

Kohlberg, L. (1981). *The philosophy of moral development: Moral stages and the idea of justice*. Harper & Row.

Kringelbach, M. L., & Berridge, K. C. (2017). The affective core of emotion linking pleasure, subjective well-being, and optimal metastability in the brain. *Emotion Review, 9*, 191–199.

Kuklinski, J. H. & Peyton, B. (2007). Belief systems and political decision making. In R. J. Dalton & H-S. Klingemann (Eds.), *The Oxford handbook of political behavior* (pp. 45–64). Oxford University Press.

Kunda, Z. (1987). Motivated inference: Self-serving generation and evaluation of causal theories. *Journal of Personality and Social Psychology, 53*(4), 636–647.

Kunda, Z. (1990). The case for motivated reasoning, *Psychological Bulletin, 108*, 480–498.

Kunda, Z. (2001). *Social cognition: Making sense of people*. MIT Press.

Kurzban, R. (2010). *Why everyone (else) is a hypocrite*. Princeton University Press.
Kurzban, R., & Weeden, J. (2014). *The hidden agenda of the political mind*. Princeton University Press.
Lang, J., Bliese, P. D., Lang, J. W. B., & Adler, A. B. (2011). Work gets unfair for the depressed: Cross-lagged relations between organizational justice perceptions and depressive symptoms. *Journal of Applied Psychology, 96*, 602–618.
Lerner, J. S., Goldberg, J. H., & Tetlock, P. E. (1998). Sober second thought: The effects of accountability, anger, and authoritarianism on attributions of responsibility. *Personality and Social Psychology Bulletin, 24*, 563–574.
Lieberman, D., & Carlton, P. (2018). *Objection: Disgust, morality, and the law*. Oxford University Press.
Lopez-Rousseau, A. (2005). Avoiding the death risk of avoiding a dread risk: The aftermath of March 11 in Spain. *Psychological Science, 16*, 426–428.
Lukianoff, G., & Haidt, J. (2018). *The coddling of the American mind*. Penguin Press.
McKenna, R. (2021). Asymmetrical irrationality: Are only other people stupid? In J. de Ridder and M. Hannon (Eds.), *Routledge handbook of political epistemology* (pp. 285–296). Taylor & Francis Group.
Mercier, H., & Sperber, D. (2011). Why do humans reason? Arguments for an argumentative theory. *Behavioral and Brain Sciences, 34*, 57–111.
Mercier, H., & Sperber, D. (2017). *The enigma of reasoning*. Harvard University Press.
Miller, G. F. (2007). Reconciling evolutionary psychology and ecological psychology: How to perceive fitness affordances. *Acta Psychologica Sinica, 39*, 546–555.
Munro, G. D., Stansbury, J. A., & Tsai, J. (2012). Causal role for negative affect: Misattribution in biased evaluations of scientific information. *Self and Identity, 11*, 1–15.
Myers, D. G. (December 2001). Do we fear the right things? *Observer, 14*, 3.
Nagel, T. (1974). What is it like to be a bat? *Philosophical Review, 83*, 435–450.
Nesse, R. M. (2001a). The smoke detector principle: Natural selection and the regulation of defenses, *Annals of the New York Academy of Sciences, 935*, 75–85.
Nesse, R. M. (2001b). *Evolution and the capacity for commitment*. Russell Sage Foundation.
Nesse, R. M. (2005). Natural selection and the regulation of defenses: A signal detection analysis of the smoke detector principle. *Evolution and Human Behavior, 26*, 88–105.
Nesse, R. M. (2019). *Good reasons for bad feelings: Insights from the frontier of evolutionary psychiatry*. Penguin Random House.
Nesse, R. M., & Williams, G. C. (1994). *Why we get sick: The new science of Darwinian medicine*. Random House.
Nickerson, R. S. (1998). Confirmation bias: A ubiquitous phenomenon in many guises. *Review of General Psychology, 2*, 175–220.
Norris, P., & Inglehart, R. (2009). *Sacred and secular: Religion and politics worldwide*. Cambridge University Press.
Pachur, T., Hertwig, R. & Steinman, F. (2012). How do people judge risks: Availability heuristic, affect heuristic, or both? *Journal of Experimental Psychology: Applied, 18*, 314–330.
Perkins, D. N. (1985). Post-primary education has little impact on informal reasoning. *Journal of Educational Psychology, 77*, 562–571.
Perkins, D. N., Farady, M., & Bushey, B. (1991). Everyday reasoning and the roots of intelligence. In J. Voss, D. Perkins, & J. Segal (Eds.), *Informal reasoning and education* (pp. 83–105). Lawrence Erlbaum Associates.
Petty, R. E. & Cacioppo, J. T. (1979) Issue involvement can increase or decrease persuasion by enhancing message-relevant cognitive responses. *Journal of Personality and Social Psychology, 37*, 1915–1926.
Pinker, S. (1994). *The language instinct*. Allen Lane.
Pinker, S. (1999). *Words and rules: The ingredients of language*. Basic Books,
Povinelli, D. J. (2003). *Folk physics for apes: The chimpanzee's theory of how the world works*. Oxford University Press.
Robson, D. (2019). *The intelligence trap*. W. W. Norton.
Schacter, D. L., Cooper, L. A., Delaney, S. M., Peterson, M. A., & Tharan, M. (1991). Implicit memory for possible and impossible objects: Constraints on the construction of structural descriptions. *Journal of Experimental Psychology: Learning, Memory, and Cognition, 17*, 3–19.
Schaller, M. (1992). In-group favoritism and statistical reasoning in social inference: Implications for formation and maintenance of group stereotypes. *Journal of Personality and Social Psychology, 63*, 61–74.
Schwarz, N., & Clore, G. L. (1983). Mood, misattribution, and judgments of well-being: Informative and directive functions of affective states. *Journal of Personality and Social Psychology, 45*, 513–523.
Schwarz, N., & Clore, G. L. (2003). Mood as information: 20 years later. *Psychological Inquiry, 14*, 296–303.
Shiffar, M., & Freyd, J. (1991). Apparent motion of the human body. *Psychological Science, 1*, 257–264.
Shweder, R. A., & Levine, R. A. (1984). *Culture theory: Essays on mind, self and emotion*. Cambridge University Press.
Silberman, S. (2015). *Neurotribes: The legacy of autism and the future of neurodiversity*. Penguin Random House.
Slovic, P. (1999). Trust, emotion, sex, politics, and science: Surveying the risk-assessment battlefield. *Risk Analysis, 19*, 689–701.

Slovic, P., Finucane, M. L., Peters, R., & MacGregor, D. G. (2016). The affect heuristic. *European Journal of Operational Research, 177,* 1333–1352.

Slovic, P., Peters, R., Finucane, M. L., & MacGregor, D. G. (2005). Affect, risk, and decision making, *Health Psychology, 24,* S35–S40.

Smith, A. (1759). *The theory of moral sentiments.* Printed for A. Millar, and A. Kincaid and J. Bell.

Sowell, T. (2007). *A conflict of visions: Ideological origins of political struggles.* Basic Books.

Stanovich, K. E., West, R. F., & Toplak, M. (2013). Myside bias, rational thinking, and intelligence. *Current Directions in Psychological Science, 22,* 259–264.

Stanovich, K. E., West, R. F., & Toplak, M. (2018). *The rationality quotient: Toward a test of rational thinking.* MIT Press.

Taber, C. S., & Lodge, M. (2006). Motivated skepticism in the evaluation of political beliefs. *American Journal of Political Science, 50,* 755–769.

Taibbi, M. (2019). *Hate, Inc.: Why today's media makes us despise one another.* OR Books.

Taibbi, M. (March 1, 2021) In defense of Substack: UCLA professor Sarah T. Roberts mourns the good old days of gatekeeping and credential-worship. *TK News by Matt Taibbi.* https://taibbi.substack.com/p/in-defense-of-substack.

Taleb, N. N. (2010). *The black swan: The impact of the highly improbable* (2nd ed.). Random House.

Taleb, N. N. (2014). *Antifragile: Things that gain from disorder.* Random House.

Thompson, E., Palacios, A. & Varela, F. J. (1991). Ways of coloring: Comparative color vision as a case study for cognitive science. *Behavioral and Brain Sciences, 15,* 1–26.

Todd, P. M., & Gigerenzer, G. (Eds.). (2012). *Ecological rationality: Intelligence in the world.* Oxford University Press.

Tooby, J., & Cosmides, L. (1990a). On the universality of human nature and the uniqueness of the individual: The role of genetics and adaptation. *Journal of Personality, 58,* 17–67.

Tooby, J., & Cosmides, L. (1990b). The past explains the present: Emotional adaptations and the structure of ancestral environments. *Ethology and Sociobiology, 11,* 375–424.

Trafimow, D. Bromgard, I. K., Finlay, K. A., & Ketelaar, T. (2005). The role of affect in trait attributions from violations of perfect and imperfect duties. *Personality and Social Psychology Bulletin, 31,* 935–948.

van den Bos, K. (2003). On the subjective quality of social justice: The role of affect as information in the psychology of justice judgments. *Journal of Personality and Social Psychology, 85,* 482–498.

Young, A. (1995). *The harmony of illusions: Inventing post-traumatic stress disorder.* Princeton University Press.

CHAPTER 47

The Emergence of Emotionally Modern Humans: Implications for Language and Learning

Sarah Blaffer Hrdy and Judith M. Burkart

Abstract

According to the Cooperative Breeding Hypothesis, apes with the life history attributes of those in the line leading to the genus *Homo* could not have evolved unless male and female allomothers had begun to help mothers care for and provision offspring. As proposed elsewhere, the unusual way hominins reared their young generated novel phenotypes subsequently subjected to Darwinian social selection, favoring those young apes best at monitoring the intentions, mental states, and preferences of others and most motivated to attract and appeal to caretakers. Not only were youngsters acquiring information in different social contexts than other apes, but they would also have been emotionally and neurophysiologically different from them in ways that are relevant to how humans learn. Contingently delivered rewards to dependents who attracted and ingratiated themselves with allomothers shaped their behaviors and vocalizations and transformed the way developing youngsters learned from others and internalized their preferences.

Key Words: cooperative breeding, ingratiating impulses, learning, language, concern for reputation, inter-subjectivity, conscience

Setting the Plio-Pleistocene Stage

Apes with the life history attributes of *Homo sapiens* could not have evolved unless male and female allomothers had helped mothers care for and provision offspring. We refer to this as the "Cooperative Breeding Hypothesis" (Hrdy, 2009, 2016a). Across the animal world, breeding systems characterized by group members other than parents (alloparents) helping parents to care for and provision offspring have evolved many times in social insects, in 9% of 10,000 species of birds (Cockburn, 2006), and in perhaps 3% of 4,500 species of mammals. The prevalence of allomaternal care tends to be higher among social carnivores (Clutton-Brock, 2016), and higher still among primates, where females or males other than the mother care for and *at least minimally provision* offspring in more than 30% of species (Isler & van Schaik, 2012a; Perry, 2020). Extensive alloparental in addition to parental provisioning, however, is only found among humans and in a distantly related subfamily of New World monkeys, the Callitrichidae, containing marmosets and tamarins.

Various circumstances conducive to the evolution of cooperative breeding pertained among hominins in Plio-Pleistocene Africa (Meindl et al., 2018). These included cohesive social groups containing close relatives; production of increasingly costly, slower maturing young; increasing reliance on hunting and extractive foraging such that immatures began to depend on adults to acquire or process food for them and to facilitate their learning appropriate skills(Clutton-Brock, 2016; Emlen, 1991; Hawkes, 2020; Hrdy, 2009; Jaeggi & van Schaik, 2011; Langen, 2000; O'Connell et al., 2002), and importantly, ecological instability (Burkhart et al., 2017; Jetz & Rubenstein, 2011).

Unpredictable rainfall against a background of increasing aridity almost certainly figured in the emergence of shared provisioning among early hominins (Antón et al., 2014; Langen, 2000; Magill et al., 2013; Morgan et al., 2020; Richerson & Boyd, 2020). In spite of recurring periods of food shortage accompanied by high child mortality, hominin mothers in the line of bipedal apes leading to *Homo sapiens* were producing slower maturing, increasingly large-brained, energetically more costly offspring, yet also were beginning to produce infants after shorter intervals. How? Along with others, we hypothesize that by two million years ago with *Homo erectus*, hominin mothers increasingly relied on assistance from other group members to supplement offspring who even after weaning remained years from nutritional independence (Burkart et al., 2009; Hawkes, 2020; Hawkes et al., 1998; Hrdy, 1999; Konner, 2010; Meehan & Crittenden, 2016). Earlier weaning meant mothers could resume cycling, conceive again, and reproduce faster. This is a conservative interpretation. Others propose the emergence of allomaternal assistance as early as *Australopithecus* (DeSilva, 2011) or *Ardipithecus* (Raghanti et al., 2018).

Over time, stacking of closely spaced dependent offspring would further intensify reliance on allomaternal provisioning. By the Pleistocene we suspect that hominins were adopting even more flexible residence patterns than those found in the other great apes (Koenig & Borries, 2012) with "multi-local" residence patterns beginning to resemble those typical of 20th-century hunter-gatherers (Hill et al., 2011; Marlowe, 2010). Greater female autonomy of movement and the emergence of pair-bonds (why they emerged being a topic still debated) would increase chances that probable fathers and matrilineal kin resided nearby (Behar et al., 2008).

Greater postpartum tolerance on the part of ordinarily possessive ape mothers coevolved with increasing, albeit still facultative, neurophysiological responsiveness on the part of fathers and other allomothers increasingly motivated to care for immatures (Abraham et al., 2014; Numan, 2015; Raghanti et al., 2018). The more dependent upon allomaternal assistance primate mothers are, the more sensitive they become to cues of social support, especially postpartum (Hrdy, 1999, 2016b). Compared with the reflexive protectiveness and possessiveness typical of all but the most stressed or inexperienced great ape mothers, who carry comatose or even dead infants for days, postpartum commitment of these hominins would likely have been more conditional. Across traditional societies, mothers are known to abandon at birth infants considered defective, as well as adjust parental investment in line with social and ecological circumstances (Hrdy, 1999, chapters 12 and 13; Konner, 1972; Scrimshaw, 1984).

Infants who could no longer count on being the sole priority of a single-mindedly dedicated mother had to elicit and maintain maternal commitment while also attracting, and increasingly ingratiating themselves with, others. Rewarded when they succeeded, over the course of development infants learned to express otherwise latent sociocognitive potentials. We use the term "ingratiating behaviors" to refer to anything an infant does to increase his or her chances of being chosen as the object of beneficent attention (including provisioning), where offspring best at ingratiating themselves with others would be most likely to survive. Over the course of development, these youngsters learned to monitor and be interested in the intentions, thoughts, and feelings of others, and even to internalize their preferences. Over

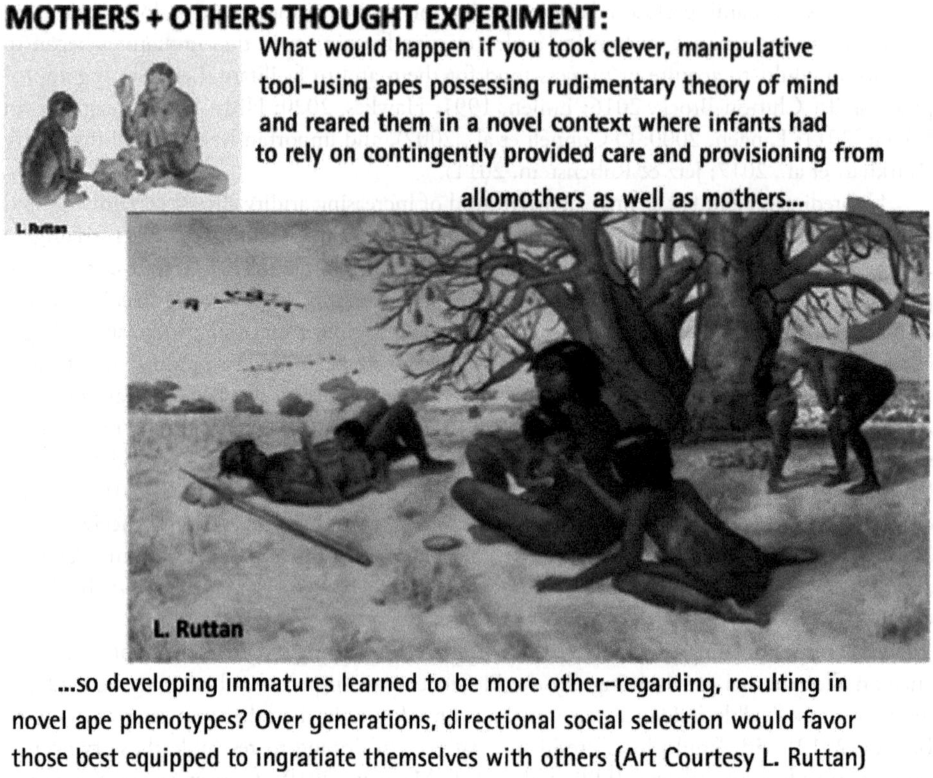

MOTHERS + OTHERS THOUGHT EXPERIMENT:
What would happen if you took clever, manipulative tool-using apes possessing rudimentary theory of mind and reared them in a novel context where infants had to rely on contingently provided care and provisioning from allomothers as well as mothers...

...so developing immatures learned to be more other-regarding, resulting in novel ape phenotypes? Over generations, directional social selection would favor those best equipped to ingratiate themselves with others (Art Courtesy L. Ruttan)

Figure 47.1. This thought experiment traces dual ontogenetic and evolutionary processes set in motion when mothers in the line leading to the genus *Homo* began to rely on alloparental care and provisioning to rear increasingly costly, sometimes more closely spaced, offspring. Intermittent behavioral conditioning would encourage youngsters to repeat and refine facial expressions, attitudes, and vocalizations most likely to appeal to potential caretakers. This would lead to the expression of otherwise latent potentials and the formation of novel neural networks. Over generations, these quite novel ape phenotypes would be exposed to directional social selection favoring youngsters best at ingratiating themselves with others, setting in motion a causal chain of adaptive evolution that began with development (West-Eberhard 2003). <Note: for final submissions, a separate, high resolution, figure file will be uploaded.>

generations, youngsters best at doing so would be more likely to survive, resulting in populations of apes emotionally very different from their ancestors (Figure 47.1).

In this chapter, we reconstruct how growing up in such a social environment may have impacted dependent immatures, along with the cascading consequences this would have had on uniquely human forms of learning and language. We start by asking: How would dependent immatures respond to the challenges of eliciting vital, but facultatively proffered, maternal and allomaternal attentions? What would this little ape need to do? Since none of us can go back in time to observe how early hominin infants would have behaved, we draw on evidence for how nonhuman ape and modern human babies responded in "virtual "experiments with and without allomaternal care to test assumptions made here about how hominin infants would have behaved with it (Hrdy, 2016a), as well as on evidence from callitrichid monkey infants reared in a cooperative context.

Although inevitably speculative, this reconstruction is informed by both comparative evidence and a growing understanding of the survival challenges hominin infants confronted.

As our point of departure, though, we begin with callitrichid monkeys, the only extant primates besides humans with extensive alloparental in addition to parental care and provisioning of infants. Callitrichids face similar challenges to those hominin infants would have faced, although they do so endowed with far smaller brains. Callitrichid mothers customarily give birth to twins, and due to postpartum estrus are immediately pregnant again (Erb & Porter, 2017; Garber, 1997). They are thus lactating and gestating at the same time, and the new set of offspring is born before the previous one is fully independent. This costly reproduction is only possible because other group members act as allomothers and help by carrying infants, protecting them, and substantially provisioning them (Guerreiro Martins et al., 2019). Like human mothers, callitrichid mothers are highly tolerant toward other group members interested in carrying their babies, and they adjust their maternal investment relative to how much help is available (Bardi et al., 2001; Hrdy, 1999). Helpers provisioning immatures exhibit highly prosocial motivations (Brügger et al., 2018; Guerreiro Martins et al., 2019). Within the social group, all members are characterized by high levels of tolerance and pro-sociality compared with independently breeding primates (Burkart et al., 2014). Youngsters born to hominin mothers who, when conditions permitted, similarly produced more closely spaced young (in "as-if" litters) confronted challenges similar to those the callitrichid twins faced. Thus did infants in distantly related species converge upon similar modes of eliciting succor from allomothers as well as mothers. But how might such solutions be extended and transformed if dependent immatures were endowed with much more powerful ape cognitive systems to begin with?

The Hominin Infant's To-Do List
First Order of Business: Appeal to Mother
Although born with open eyes, able to blurrily seek the eyes of someone else, newborn apes are otherwise altricial, utterly dependent on others for warmth, protection, locomotion, and food (Bard, 2012; Tomonaga et al., 2004). Fortunately, apes enjoy the built-in mammalian advantage of being born to a mother who during gestation was suffused by hormones lowering her threshold for responding to sounds and smells of a warm, wriggling, fluid-covered baby. If only the newborn can make it to maternal nipples, root, suck, and stimulate lactation, ensuing surges in oxytocin and prolactin further enhance her nurturing impulses. With lactation underway, even an inexperienced first-time ape mother becomes increasingly bonded to this newcomer. But over the course of hominin evolution, increasing maternal reliance on allomaternal assistance would have rendered mothers increasingly sensitive to cues of available social support. In the absence of social support, the commitment of even the most experienced human mother falters <[see especially 21, 32, 43]>(Bugos & McCarthy, 1984; Hrdy, 1999, 2016b).

Over evolutionary time, more contingent commitment preadapted human mothers to become more discriminating than other apes. In addition to their parity, prior experience, physical condition, and likely social support, mothers began to respond to specific physical attributes of each infant. Consciously or not, each costly infant was in competition not only with still nutritionally dependent older siblings, but also with subsequent infants a mother might bear under ecologically more opportune conditions if only she retrenched upon investment in this one, or bailed out altogether, and resumed cycling sooner. Over the course of the Pleistocene (perhaps earlier?), hominin babies came under increasing pressure to look good and sound vigorous right at birth, advertising that they were full-term, robust, good bets for survival, worth further investment. This challenge may help explain why, over the course of hominin evolution, fetuses began to stockpile adipose tissue at an unlikely time, just prior to squeezing through what were becoming increasingly narrow birth canals. By now, human neonates are born much fatter than other apes (ca. 10%–14% body fat, contrasted with 3%–4% for chimpanzees). No doubt, an extra dollop of energy was initially beneficial for thermoregulation and fueling fast-growing brains, contributing to the emergence in mothers of sensory biases favoring plump babies (Kuzawa et al., 2014). Over time, plumpness may also have come to serve as an infantile equivalent of sex appeal, seducing mothers into embarking on a long, exorbitantly costly, endeavor (Hrdy, 1999, chapter 21).

Once increasingly discriminating hominin mothers began to notice associations between birth weight and later outcomes, one of evolution's more consequential self-reinforcing feedback loops would be underway. With runaway social selection (*sensu* West-Eberhard) for neonatal plumpness underway, extra energy stores became available for brain development, in turn rendering allomaternal provisioning even more essential. Over generations, allomothers as well became attuned to cues of neonatal viability, adjusting levels of commitment accordingly (Hrdy, 2016b).

This brings us to the hominin infant's second order of business.

Attract Others

Because hominin mothers as well benefited from allomaternal assistance, it behoved females to reside near trusted others, matrilineal kin and/or adult males who were probable fathers. Unlike exceedingly possessive great ape mothers, mothers in traditional human societies not only tolerate, but often encourage postpartum contact with infants. Whether this shift was due to innately more tolerant temperaments, to greater autonomy in selecting whom to live among, or both, is not clear. In any event, maternal tolerance facilitated intimate exposure of trusted group members to infantile smells and sounds, generating maternal-like affiliation-promoting neurophysiological transformations in male and female allomothers alike (Abraham et al., 2017; Bales et al., 2004; Carter & Perkeybile, 2018; Hrdy, 2009). Among humans, only a few hours of intimate contact with grandparents are sufficient to produce surges in oxytocin and rearrange priorities (Hrdy, 2019). (Among marmosets, similar oxytocin increases not only in mothers, but in all group members after the birth of new babies; Finkenwirth et al., 2016.)

But other factors also enter in, including the allomother's own physical condition and past caretaking experiences, alternatives available, as well as the infant's vulnerability and level of need. Facing this uncertainty, cues from infants themselves to elicit allomaternal involvement would again be paramount. Over time, human allomothers become sensitive to the same viability cues that mothers respond to. Magnetic resonance images of the brains of modern humans reveal that even nulliparous women find the faces of plump, healthy-looking (read full-term) babies "cuter" and more rewarding to look at (Glocker et al., 2009). Not only physical viability cues, but also behavioral interactions will attract caregivers. Humans are born with neurological capacities comparable to those of other apes, but differences soon emerge (Lonsdorf et al., 2010). At birth, both chimpanzee and human newborns seek out eyes, are capable of mutual gazing, and caught just right, may imitate someone else's outstretched tongue or other facial expressions (Myowa-Yamakoshi, 2010). Both species exhibit reflexive "fairy smiles," soon to be replaced by more open-eyed "social smiles" in response to someone else. Among newborn chimpanzees, however, that someone else would always be their own mother (Matsuzawa, 2010). In traditional human societies, however, blearily gazing newborns engage a wider audience (Konner, 1972, 2010). Over time, as infants grow accustomed to and learn to trust specific allomothers, the sort of emotional bonds primate infants forge with mothers prove sufficiently elastic to encompass multiple attachment figures, an average of six attachment figures among the Central African Aka hunter-gatherers studied by Courtney Meehan (Meehan & Hawks, 2013). It is not known whether human infants are more prone to forge multiple attachments than are other apes if cared for by both mothers and others because the latter virtually never are.

A challenge unique to immatures of cooperatively breeding primates is that they are not in continuous contact with their caregiver. This can be buffered by proactive caregiving motivations by adults, as in callitrichids where group members check babies on carriers, eager to take over when necessary (Yamamoto & Box, 1997), or proactively announce that they have found food and are ready to share it. Such provisioning is different from food sharing patterns in other primates, where at most, immatures are passively tolerated when taking their mother's food (Brown et al., 2004; Jaeggi et al., 2010). Nevertheless, without being in constant body contact with a single caregiver, cooperatively breeding immatures face the chronic risk of being overlooked.

Among apes such as chimpanzees, gorillas, or orangutans, newborns constantly held by mothers in direct skin-to-skin contact have less need to smile or vocalize. Calling would only be useful if separated, or later, at weaning, as youngsters object to maternal rejections. Otherwise, low, scarcely audible sounds make more sense than loudly advertising to predators "vulnerable baby here!" Among primates with shared care, life tends to be noisier. Infants need to stay "in touch without touch" and may complain to prompt maternal retrievals. Infant langur monkeys spend up to 50% of their first day of life being held and carried by females-other-than-mothers, calling incessantly (Hrdy, 1977).

Life is even noisier in animals with biparental and alloparental provisioning, where babies beg for treats. This correlation is best documented in birds (Leighton, 2017), but it also holds for callitrichids and humans, who fall among the most voluble of primates (Burkart, Martins, et al., 2018). Vocalizing starts early in marmosets and tamarins, becoming more frequent and specialized over the course of development. Begging calls spike around weaning, when allomaternal provisioning is most critical (Brown et al., 2004; Rapaport & Brown, 2008). But these infants not only are noisy beggars, but also engage in babbling-like behaviors, by producing repetitive, random-sounding streams of elements of adult vocalizations that can last for more than a minute. This babbling-like behavior comes with likely cost because it is noisy and makes infants conspicuous to predators. It peaks around weaning, when allomaternal provisioning is most critical, and turns out to be an effective attention getter, as adults are more likely to approach and interact with immatures that are babbling (Elowson et al., 1998).

Something similar goes on in humans, with the onset of babbling around the time (in hunter-gatherers at least) when allomothers begin providing edible treats (discussed below). Within weeks of birth, human infants emit engaging noises. Learning progresses more rapidly if infants notice others reacting. By 10 weeks, some actually take turns vocalizing. The sound of a baby laughing generates an especially powerful stimulus, audible at some distance and signaling emotional engagement (Parsons et al., 2013; Riem Madelon et al., 2017). As babies put two and two together, conditioning plus early glimmerings of intersubjectivity (Trevarthen, 1993) lead them to incorporate sensory biases and preferences of potential caretakers into their own expanding repertoires for ingratiating themselves with others (Gopnik, 2020). By nine months, little humans go out of their way to be helpful. Human youngsters clearly care about what others think of their performance (Warneken & Tomasello, 2006).

Vocal Control and More Flexible Vocalizing
Old World monkeys and apes are sophisticated communicators. Vervet monkeys, for example, emit one kind of call to alert group-mates of raptors, a different alarm call for terrestrial enemies. They are also sensitive to context, taking into account who is listening and who

is out of range, modifying calls accordingly (Cheney & Seyfarth, 1990). Apes, particularly chimpanzees and bonobos, also make extensive use of hands and arms to communicate what they want, extending an arm palm up when requesting something. Even so, their vocal repertoires never achieve the richness, sophistication, and flexibility of their gesturing (Pollick & de Waal, 2007). Rather, nonhuman apes seem surprisingly limited in the kinds of vocalizations they emit (Slocombe & Zuberbühler, 2010), a marked contrast with humans, who early in development increase vocal control and start to build larger and more flexible vocal repertoires (Zuberbühler, 2012). So how did this get started?

One important element developed elsewhere concerns the challenges that adults, rather than the immatures of cooperative breeders, are confronted with (Burkart, Martins, et al., 2018; Snowdon, 2001). They face increasing necessity to coordinate their activities with others, such as for infant transfers, and their prosociality motivates them to not only share food with others, but also information that is useful for them. Vocal communication is a prime candidate to provide a solution to exactly these type of challenges, and accordingly, the large vocal repertoires of cooperatively breeding birds is driven by an increase in contact and alarm calls (Leighton, 2017). But a critical element is added by immatures, who grow up in an increasingly voluble environment.

From a comparative perspective, it seems clear that shared care, with babies carried by others, increases vocalization frequency. Allomaternal provisioning and contingent reinforcement raise the stakes, with begging leading to more calling, especially if immatures have to compete for rewarding attentions (Goldstein et al., 2003; Leighton, 2017). Through the expression of otherwise latent capacities and their subsequent shaping, attention-getting and begging set the stage for selection to favor enhanced vocal control accompanied by goal-oriented shaping of acoustic structure. Indeed, as in marmosets, vocal development in humans occurs earlier than motor development (Gustison et al., 2019). By contrast, infants in constant close contact with single-mindedly dedicated mothers (as in independently breeding species such as chimpanzees) would more often be called upon to cling than to cry.

Experiments with marmosets undertaken by Asif Ghazanfar and his team demonstrate how contingent responsiveness by caretakers generates turn-taking and also speeds development of specialized, more mature-sounding calls (Takahashi et al., 2016). For 40 minutes a day during the first two months of life, each of a pair of marmoset twins was separated from their parents and allowed to call. Whereas one twin was provided consistent feedback from taped parental calls, the other twin received less consistent feedback. The more reliable the feedback, the more rapidly infants progressed from the coarse, random-sounding vocalizations typical of immatures to cleaner, more tonal, adult-like *phee* calls (Takahashi et al., 2016, 2017). By two to three months of age, their utterances resembled the turn-taking "conversations" human babies engage in with their caretakers. Chow et al. (2015) further showed that parents actively intervene when immatures make typical mistakes while learning to engage in turn-taking. If immatures get timing wrong and "interrupt" their parents, parents add an extra break before responding. When immatures respond with a wrong call type, the parents themselves interrupt them with the correct *phee* call. In another example of convergent evolution between human cooperative breeders and these tiny-brained, distantly related New World monkeys, Takahashi and colleagues (2017) noted that infant marmosets responding to contingent reinforcement rely on one of the same circuits to guide their *phee* calls that humans use in speech. The patterning of FoxP2 expression in marmosets' cortico-striatal circuit turns out to be analogous to that in both humans and songbirds. Moreover, a role of oxytocin has recently been proposed for the social motivation and evolution of vocal learning and language (Theofanopoulou et al., 2017), which is consistent with the increase of oxytocin in all group members after the birth of marmoset immatures (Finkenwirth et al., 2016) and its link with pro-sociality among group members (Finkenwirth & Burkart, 2017).

Observations of golden lion tamarins (*Leontopithecus rosalia*) in Brazil illustrate how these increasingly complex, two-way conversations function in natural habitats (Rapaport, 2011). Solitary adults traverse the treetops hunting for spiders, insects, and small frogs, prying prey from inside holes or tangled foliage. Youngsters learn to locate, stalk, and dexterously extract and dispatch struggling, sometimes biting or stinging, prey. Learning takes time and practice as immatures grow more adept at responding to adults volunteering prey. Deliveries peak near the end of weaning, when up to 90% of their diets are provided by (mostly male) allomothers (Rapaport, 2011). Food transfers are often initiated by youngsters begging. But when adults locate food, provisioners too emit staccato "food-offering calls." Mothers, probable fathers, and other helpers extract the food and call the infant to come and get the food out of their hands. As prey-catching efficiency improves, but before youngsters reach adult proficiency, mentors switch from "come and get it" calls, to "hey, look here." Adult calls direct older immatures' attention to a particular patch of substrate where prey have been detected. The finder then waits nearby while the young locate and extract it for themselves. Such adjustment of adults to immature skill levels has also been found in other callitrichids in captive studies (cotton-top tamarins: Humle & Snowdon, 2008; common marmosets: Chow et al., 2015; Dell'Mour et al., 2009). As infants increasingly associate an allomother's particular call with a particular reward, they register regularities in how others respond to particular sounds they themselves make.

Opportunities to link own vocal productions to regularities in how others respond to them are particularly evident for babbling (humans) or babbling-like behaviors (callitrichids). In humans, babbling emerges spontaneously at around 5–7 months, about the same time as the emergence of milk teeth, which among hunter-gatherers often coincides with allomothers beginning to offer premasticated and other (sometimes "kiss-fed") treats to infants (Hrdy, 2009). At some level (consciously or not), children recognize that babbling attracts rewarding attention. This may help explain why older children revert to "baby talk" after the birth of a younger sibling (Sarah Blaffer Hrdy, personal observation). Interestingly, babbling in marmosets not only attracts caregivers, but also speeds up the acquisition of adult-like forms of vocalizations. Moreover, babbling similarly can resume and spike among juvenile marmosets following the birth of new infants in their group (Snowdon & Elowson, 2001). Apparently the same message is being conveyed: "pay attention to *me*!"

"If babbling changes adult behavior in predictable, infant-oriented ways," as Goldstein and colleagues propose, "infants should be able to recognize changes in others' actions as a result of their vocalizations" (Goldstein et al., 2003, p. 8034), launching more goal-oriented vocal control. As with other apes, humans are born with limited motor control over articulation, but beginning around 6 months, humans gain increased vocal control, including more tongue involvement, with vocal tracts continuing to develop over the first 15 months, contributing to greater vocal flexibility and larger vocal repertoires in humans than other apes (Zuberbühler, 2012). Impressed by the coincidence in timing between increased vocal control and the transition from baby-calls to babbling-like streams of consonants and vowels, Klaus Zuberbühler makes a compelling case that increased control derived from hominin infants' need to attract allomaternal attentions (Zuberbühler, 2012, pp. 71, 77–79). Although "babbling" is widely assumed to have first emerged in human children in preparation for the acquisition of spoken language, akin to Mother Nature adding training wheels on a bicycle, it makes more sense (and is far less teleological) to consider the initial emergence of traits like babbling as byproducts of infantile needs to attract caregivers. A key innovation here was increased motor control over articulation. Once vocalizations become subject to voluntary control, they can be shaped via conditional reinforcement, critical pre-adaptations for the eventual evolution of spoken language.

Incorporate Others' Preferences

These novel capacities emerged within broader sociocognitive contexts where apes were already endowed with rudimentary Theory of Mind (Hermann et al., 2007; Krupenye et al., 2016; Tomasello, 2019), already utilizing rich gestural repertoires (Pollick & de Waal, 2007), employing tools, and devising new modes of extracting food. By the Late Pleistocene, selection pressures from a range of new subsistence and socioecological challenges also favored greater inter-individual coordination (Boehm, 2012; Guerreiro Martins et al., 2019; Tomasello, 2018; Tomasello et al., 1993). It is within this broader context that recent proposals linking cooperative breeding not only to the evolution of enhanced capacities for joint attention (Ben Mocha et al., 2019), but also for language, need to be understood (Burkart, Martins, et al., 2018; Knight, 2016; Zuberbühler, 2012).

Social selection favoring more flexible communication coincided with other coevolving feedback loops. But by themselves, neither larger brains nor increased uses for cooperation are sufficient to explain the evolution of language. As psychiatrist Peter Hobson reminds us, "before language there [had to be] something else . . . that could evolve in tiny steps . . . that something else was *social engagement with each other*. The links that can join one person's mind with the mind of someone else are, especially to begin with, emotional links" (2004, p. 2, emphasis in original). But what about the foundational steps? Klaus Zuberbühler's speculations point us in a promising direction: "Once vocal control has evolved to help infants secure care, it is only a small step to producing utterances in context-specific ways" (2012, p. 80). But, Zuberbühler adds, such a transformation "may only be possible against a background of other psychological skills, such as the ability to share intentions and attention (Tomasello, 2008), and well-developed comprehension" (Zuberbühler, 2012, p. 80). He expands on Tomasello's insight regarding a "major difference" (Tomasello, 1999) between humans and other primates, involving (as Tomasello would later phrase it) capacities for "intersubjective sharing" (Tomasello & Carpenter, 2007, pp. 121–122).

Eagerness to ingratiate themselves with others would be enhanced by allomaternal care, an interpretation consistent with observations of captive chimpanzees who, when co-reared by responsive human caretakers (allomothers of a different species) as well as their mothers, become more eager than wild chimpanzees are to engage in targeted helping of others (Bard, 2012; Yamamoto et al., 2012; reviewed in Hrdy, 2016a). Even though human-tended chimpanzees do not acquire spoken language and other distinctively human traits, they nevertheless develop greater concern for the intentions and goals of others, learning the power that particular gestures, facial expressions, and utterances exert on others. For example, human-reared chimpanzees point to what they want in ways that wild apes almost never do (Tomasello, 2019). The expression of such interactive potentials in ape phenotypes would increase opportunities to share and increase effectiveness of helping. Over the course of human evolution, such opportunities may have increased selection favoring neuroendocrine systems conducive to pro-social responses, including the increasingly "dopamine dominated" striatal systems being documented by paleontologists working in concert with neuroscientists (Raghanti et al., 2018). Interactions with processes that opened parental neural care systems to a wider range of social stimuli might have resulted in more unsolicited food sharing and general prosociality (Numan, 2015). Apes who needed to be more interested in the preferences of others would also find it more emotionally rewarding to do so. This chain of admittedly speculative reasoning brings us to a key component to the hominin infant's to-do list.

Add Psychological Dimensions to Kindchenschema
Like all other catarrhine primates, apes in the line leading to the genus *Homo* would grow up keenly aware of kin ties, alliances, statuses, and friendships, as well as competencies and reliability of group-mates (Cheney & Seyfarth, 2007; Perry, 2020). The quantitative skills and manipulative capabilities of a chimpanzee or orangutan fall in the same ballpark as those of two-and-a-half-year-old humans. They too exhibit rudimentary capacities for theorizing about what others know (Hermann et al., 2007; Krupenye et al., 2016; Teomasells, 2020). Our last common ancestors with these apes were already beginning to register what others intended or wanted.

So imagine such an ape growing up reliant on the competencies and motivations of others. If contingent reinforcement from allomothers encourages turn-taking and speeds up acquisition of adult vocalizations in tiny-brained marmosets with only minimal awareness of what another marmoset knows (Burkart & Heschl, 2007; Burkart, Martins, et al., 2018), how much more sensitive to the thoughts and preferences of others would apes already attuned to the thoughts and intentions of others become? Contingent allomaternal responses generate new psychological dimensions to *Kindchenschema*, as apes growing up this way are conditioned to become more aware that others have preferences worth appealing to.

Youngsters would be conditioned to not only monitor the intentions of others, but increasingly to probe their thoughts and feelings so as to better conform to their preferences. Over time, learning which facial expressions, sounds, or conversational rhythms result in solicitude would mature into more sophisticated understanding of how others perceived their own intentions, behaviors, and thoughts and to begin to care about their "reputations."

New Dimensions to Social Learning
Expanded Avenues
All apes are endowed with inordinate behavioral flexibility, along with aptitudes for manipulating objects and imitating others. In the case of chimpanzees and orangutans, knowledge about what to eat, where to find and how to process it, is transmitted vertically during 5–8 years of intimate association with one other trusted individual, their mother. Mothers set the stage for socially induced independent practice (Jaeggi et al., 2010; Schuppli et al., 2016; Whiten, 1999) or, as in the case of chimpanzee nut-cracking, very occasionally make helpful adjustments (Boesch, 2012; Matsuzawa, 2010). The processes by which little apes copy and learn from others are, however, primarily self-initiated (Humle et al., 2009). Provisioning and shared care broaden this initial context for social learning.

From an early age, youngsters with shared care observe a wider range of role models. For example, cooperatively breeding magpie jays with many helpers become more adept at harvesting arthropods than jays growing up with few (Langen & Vehrencamp, 1998). Furthermore, demonstrators among cooperative breeders tend to be more pro-social, even deliberately helpful (Burkart et al., 2009; Burkart & van Schaik, 2012). Recall that golden lion tamarin allomothers (often probable or possible progenitors) provide the majority of food for nearly weaned infants. At first, adults call when they have food to offer, but with older immatures, they call them to places where prey is hidden and the immatures have to do the extraction themselves. As performance levels plateau, food calls cease. Rapaport (2011, p. 746) compares the progressive, developmentally sensitive behaviors and vocalizations tracking the needs and skills of youngsters that allomothers use to provide foraging assistance, to "teaching-like" behavior (cf. Thornton & McAuliffe, 2006, for cooperatively breeding meerkats).

Incorporating situation-dependent vocalizations enhances effectiveness of demonstrations, while contingently delivered food rewards rivets the attention of mentees. Anyone who has ever tried to habituate wild creatures, or even skittish domestic ones, knows that food rewards provide the quickest short-cut to taming or training them. Now add to this pro-social-provisioning-vocalizing mix mentalizing mentees eager to accommodate their mentors. Possibilities for information transfer expand exponentially.

Emotionally Modern and Mentalizing Mentees
Even in the absence of detectable Theory of Mind, tiny-brained marmosets prove remarkably pro-social, sharing food or rushing to assist others. Marmosets coordinate with others to crack open tough fruits. They take babies from mothers, then voluntarily return them for nursing (Burkart et al., 2009, 2014; Garber, 1997). Tamarins even use guided demonstrations accentuated by vocalizations to transmit age-appropriate information (Rapaport, 2011). In this respect, tiny-brained callitrichids converge on something close to what ethnographers studying hunter-gatherers term "natural pedagogy" (Hewlett et al., 2011). Yet even as tamarins adjust demonstrations to the skill level of pupils, they do so without mentalizing what another knows. Marmosets who readily follow the gaze of another individual do so without registering *what* that individual is seeing (Burkart & Heschl, 2007).

So what would happen if instead of the reflexive responsiveness of marmosets, the primates undertaking shared care and provisioning of young were already larger-bodied, bipedal, tool-users possessed of rudimentary Theory of Mind, with brains in the process of doubling from the 400 cc of chimpanzees or australopiths to the more expansive brains typical of *Homo erectus*? And what if novel contexts for social development coincided with new foraging tactics, more valuable food packets, and with these, a raised "gray ceiling" so that over time whenever—and for whatever reasons—they became favored, even costlier brains could evolve? (Isler & van Schaik, 2012a, 2012b). Little hominins growing up as cooperative breeders would have opportunities to observe group members of different ages and sexes (Deffner & McElreath, 2020; Gurven et al., 2020; Hawkes, 2020, trust them as their mothers do, gauge their competencies and intentions, decide who was likely to be helpful or not—something modern humans begin to do from as early as three months old (Hamlin et al., 2007, 2010). And what if, at the same time, these infants were beginning to monitor the intentions of others, seeking to conform to their preferences, even beginning to internalize their preferences and at the same time also developing larger and more flexible vocal repertoires?

Many factors were involved in the evolution of language. Some clearly had to do with the unusual way apes in the line leading to *Homo sapiens* were reared. Learning language is a highly social endeavor. Anyone who has ever spent time with babies knows that their mother is not the only person who speaks to them in high-pitched "motherese." It is from eagerly listening to others that youngsters acquire new phonemes and words. Immatures learn new sounds better in the presence of someone else than if by themselves. As young as nine months, babies watching instructive videos more readily discriminate sounds and learn foreign phonemes when another child is present (Lytle et al., 2018).

Not only current interactions, but also past experiences with others influence children's readiness to mentalize what someone else knows. When experimenters set up a computer game where five-year-olds must explain to someone else where to collect a digital prize, they were told that the unseen other (really the experimenters' confederate) was either a toddler or another five-year-old. Subjects adjusted instructions accordingly. When told their partner was a toddler, subjects spent longer explaining the game than when they assumed the other child was older. The more days between birth and age four that the subject had spent with others in daycare, the readier that child was to take the other's level of understanding into account, mentalizing what they were likely to already know (Stolk et al., 2013).

Concern for Reputation and Learning
Within the first year of life, hominins approaching this emotional modernity would, like behaviorally modern humans today, actively seek to become the object of someone else's attention, feel at least a glimmer of pride when approved of, and shame when disapproved of (Reddy, 2003; Trevarthen, 1993). After a year or so, these youngsters may have already been disposed to spontaneously offer something interesting or desirable to someone else, the way 14-month-old behaviorally modern humans do today, even proffering an item differing from their own preference (Repacholi & Gopnik, 1997). Today's behaviorally modern Western children readily absorb and follow normative rules (Gopnik, 2010, pp. 224–225), expect others to do so, and care desperately about their own reputations (Englemann et al., 2012). When someone is trying to teach them something, they not only feel pride at success, but want others to know: "I did it!" Equipped with sophisticated language, these same children, as early as three or four years of age, employ flattery to cultivate the goodwill of others (Fu & Lee, 2007). By early adulthood, behaviorally modern humans find it so pleasurable to talk about themselves that among contemporary Westerners, it stimulates the same neural regions as anticipating something delicious to eat would (Tamir & Mitchell, 2012. This concern with presentation of self, reputation, and impressing others may fuel tendencies to register the intentions and preferences of others who are modeling behavior and then conform. This may explain why human children, but not other apes, don't just imitate demonstrators, but sometimes "over-imitate" them, adding all the same ritualized bells and whistles, even if these exceed procedures needed to accomplish a task (Gopnik, 2010; Nielsen & Tomaselli, 2010; Whiten et al., 2009). Acute sensitivity to the intentions, thoughts, and preferences of others, eagerness for their approval, and a rush of dopamine and other neurochemical rewards when sensing approval add new dimensions to social learning.

Primate-wide, youngsters learn to conform to social rules while growing up, for example internalizing proper etiquette for approaching a dominant group member. But human children display special eagerness to ingratiate themselves with others and internalize their preferences, adding subjective dimensions to this quest. Evolutionary psychiatrist Randolph Nesse hypothesizes that runaway social selection favoring self-consciousness and concern with reputation, in creatures already interested in mentalizing what others think, explains why our ancestors evolved the internal self-monitoring known as "a conscience" (Nesse, 2007, 2019).

Whether or not such ingratiating tendencies encourage humans to behave in fair, generous, or civic-minded rather than more self-serving ways probably depends more on socioecological contexts and immediate goals than on what are sometimes taken to be hard-wired moral sensibilities (Bloom, 2013; Hamlin et al., 2010; Hamlin & Wynn, 2011). As early as six months, long before language, infants exhibit preferences for helpful versus hurtful others (Hamlin & Wynn, 2011). However, it is unclear how pro-social versus self-interested such preferences are. In experiments simulating *voir dire* in an imaginary courtroom, Melnikoff and Bailey (2018) asked adult subjects whom they would prefer in the jury, depending on whether they served as lawyer for the defense or for the prosecution. The researchers were struck by how conditional on people's current goals their preferences for moral vs. immoral actors could be. Whatever standards prevail, quests to demonstrate mental and behavioral responses conforming to others' preferences pave the way for internalizing group norms (Gavriletes &

Richerson, 2017) and for behavior that others consider "moral" (Boehm, 2012; Tomasello, 2016). It is exactly this third-party perspective which is strikingly lacking in nonhuman primates (Burkart, Brügger, et al., 2018) who otherwise exhibit various building blocks of morality (de Waal, 2006; Silk & House, 2016). Other primates may conform to local traditions, but they don't seem to care if *others* do so or not, and even unusually pro-social primates such as marmosets do not manage their reputations by increasing helping efforts when observed by others (Burkart, Brügger et al., 2018). Humans, being able to represent how their behavior appears to others (perhaps as a result of their great ape cognitive heritage) (Krupenye et al., 2016), appear distinctively motivated to care about their reputations. The same would be advantageous for marmosets, too, but they may simply not be able to cognitively represent how they appear to others.

Conclusions

Across taxa, longer spans of post-weaning or post-fledging dependence are predictable corollaries of cooperative breeding. In the case of the cooperatively breeding apes in the line leading to the genus *Homo*, reliance on care and provisioning from alloparents as well as parents conditioned dependent immatures to develop un-ape-like eagerness to monitor and care about the intentions of others, mentalize what they were thinking and feeling, and seek to ingratiate themselves with them, leading to the expression and refinement of otherwise latent ape potentials. This novel context for development and social learning coincided with directional social selection (West-Eberhard, 1983, 2003) favoring youngsters best at ingratiating themselves with protectors, mentors, and providers. By two million years ago, this combined process of development-plus-social selection was already contributing toward the emergence of apes' cognitive and emotional phenotypes very different from those among our last common ancestors with chimpanzees and other apes.

Without any foresight on Mother Nature's part concerning how important questing for intersubjective engagement and escalating concerns with reputations would eventually turn out to be, *Homo erectus* infants would have been conditioned to monitor and care about what others were thinking, including thinking about them, and were rewarded for internalizing their preferences in ways others apes were not. Reputational concerns make having a conscience increasingly useful. Long before the emergence of *anatomically modern* big-brained humans by 300,000 years ago (Hublin et al., 2017), or before behaviorally modern humans with symbolic thought and language, these emotionally different apes were already eager to appeal to and help others. Furthermore, observation of humans today suggests that these tendencies emerge early and in both sexes, with girls if anything better able to interpret others' expressions and feelings than boys (Geary, 2018).

By the Late Pleistocene, when cooperative hunting of big game, division of labor, and sharing of food became important, hominins of both sexes must *already* have become predisposed to read the intentions of others in order to coordinate with and perhaps help them (Hawkes, 2014; Hrdy, 2009, 2016a; Tomasello & Gonzalez-Cabrera, 2017). By the time coordinated hunting of large animals was established in the human repertoire—whether by 400,000 years ago as in Tomasello & Gonzalez-Cabrera's (2017) reconstruction, or closer to Chris Boehm's "magic number" (2012, p. 313) of 250,000 years ago—it was probably accompanied by "punitive social selection" against stingy or overly domineering men, as documented for most well-studied hunter-gatherer societies (2012, p. 164; Tomasello, 2016, 2018). If so, these members of the genus *Homo* would have already become motivationally very different from their more self-centered, solipsistic ape ancestors. In Boehm's account, sanctions against bullies could extend to exile or even execution, pressuring group members to conform and adopt normative "moral" behavior. But with internalization of norms already underway, archaic humans were, from an early age, already sensitive to what others felt and thought about them, concerned about personal reputations, and eager to cooperate. They were pre-adapted to internalize ways of behaving and expressing themselves that others preferred.

With higher-quality food sources and with multiple provisioners continuing to buffer weanlings from recurring shortages, the gray ceiling limiting energy available for brains was raised. The stage was set for these *emotionally modern* early humans to meet Late Pleistocene social and ecological challenges in ways that would favor the evolution of even more costly, anatomically modern, brains. Accompanying motivations would also lead to the emergence of more sophisticated modes of vocal communication that would vastly expand the ability to learn from multiple others (via gossip and teaching) and expand the reach and importance of both normative ways of doing things (Richerson & Boyd, 2020) and of reputations. Such processes would stress conformity and further favor the internalization of group norms and human indoctrinability, hallmarks of *behaviorally modern* humans.

Acknowledgments

We are indebted to Asif Ghazanfar, Kristen Hawkes, and Klaus Zuberbühler for inspiration, and to Camilla Hrdy for valuable comments. JB was supported by SNF grant 31003A_172979.

An earlier version of this essay, titled "The Emergence of Emotionally Modern Humans: Implications for Language and Learning," was published in 2020 in a special issue of the *Philosophical Transactions of the Royal Society*, edited by Alison Gopnik, Michael Tomasello, and Willem Frankenhuis. The essay is reprinted here with permission.

References

Abraham, E., Gilam, G., Kanat-Maymon, Y., Jacob, Y., Zagoory-Sharon, O., Hendler, T., & Feldman, R. (2017). The human coparental bond implicates distinct corticostriatal pathways: Longitudinal impact on family formation and child well-being. *Neuropsychopharmacology, 42*, 2301–2313.

Abraham, E., Hendler, T., Shapira-Lichter, I., Kanat-Maymon, Y., Zagoory-Sharon, O., & Feldman, R. (2014). Father's brain is sensitive to childcare experiences. *Proceedings of the National Academy of Sciences, 111*, 9792–9797.

Antón, S., Potts, R., & Aiello, L. C. (2014). Evolution of early Homo: An integrated ecological perspective. *Science, 345*, 1236828.

Bales, K., Kim, A. J., Lewis-Reese, A. D., & Carter, C. S. (2004). Both oxytocin and vasopressin may influence alloparental behavior in male prairie voles. *Hormones and Behavior, 45*, 354–361.

Bard, K. (2012). Emotional engagement: How chimpanzee minds develop. In F. de Waal & P. F. Ferrari (Eds.), *The primate mind* (pp. 224–245). Harvard University Press.

Bardi, M., Petto, A. J., & Lee-Parritz, D. E. (2001). Parental failure in captive cotton-top tamarins *(Saguinus oedipus)*. *American Journal of Primatology, 54*, 159–169.

Behar, D., Villems, R., Soodyal, H., Blue-Smith, J., Pereira, L., Metspalu, E., Scozzari, R., Makkan, H., Tzur, S., Comas, D., Bertranpetiti, J., Quinatan-Murci, L., Tyler-Smith, C., Spencer Wells, R., Rosset, S., & Geographic Consortium. (2008). The dawn of matrilineal diversity. *American Journal of Human Genetics, 82*, 1–11.

Ben Mocha, Y., Mundry, R., & Pika, S. (2019). Joint attention skills in wild Arabian babblers (*Turdoides squamiceps*): A consequence of cooperative breeding? *Proceedings of the Royal Society B: Biological Sciences, 286*.http://doi.org/10.1098/rspb.2019.0147.

Bloom, P. (2013). *Just babies: The origins of good and evil*. Crown.

Boehm, C. (2012). *Moral origins: The evolution of virtue, altruism and shame*. Basic Books.

Boesch, C. (2012). *Wild cultures: A comparison between chimpanzee and human cultures*. Cambridge University Press.

Brown, G. R., Almond, R. E., & Bergen, Y. V. (2004). Begging, stealing, and offering: food transfer in nonhuman primates. *Advances in the Study of Behavior, 34*, e295.

Brügger, R. K., Kappeler-Schmalzriedt, T., & Burkart, J. M. (2018). Reverse audience effects on helping in cooperatively breeding marmoset monkeys. *Biology Letters, 14*, 20180030.

Bugos, P. E., & McCarthy, M. L. (1984). Ayoreo infanticide: A case study. In G. Hausfater & S. Hrdy (Eds.), *Comparative and evolutionary perspectives on infanticide* (pp. 503–520). Aldine.

Burkart, J. M., Allon, O., Amici, F., Fichtel, C., Finkenwirth, D., Heschl A., Huber, J., Isler, K., Kosonen, Z. K., Martins, E., Meulman, E. J., Richiger, R., Rueth, K., Spillmann, B., Wiesendanger, S., & van Schaik, C. P. (2014). The evolutionary origins of human hyper-cooperation. *Nature Communications, 5*, 4747.

Burkart, J. M., Brügger, R. K., & van Schaik, C. P. (2018). Evolutionary origins of morality: Insights from nonhuman primates. *Frontiers in Sociology, 3*, 17.

Burkart, J. M., & Heschl, A. (2007). Perspective taking or behaviour reading? Understanding of visual access in common marmosets *(Callithrix jacchus). Animal Behaviour, 73*, 457–469.

Burkart, J. M., Hrdy, S. B., & van Schaik, C. P. (2009). Cooperative breeding and human cognitive evolution. *Evolutionary Anthropology, 18*, 175–186.

Burkart, J. M., Martins, E. G., Miss, F., & Zuercher, Y. (2018). From sharing food to sharing information: Cooperative breeding and language evolution. *Interaction Studies, 19*, 136–150.

Burkart, J. M., & van Schaik, C. P. (2012). Group service in macaques, capuchins and marmosets: A comparative approach to identifying proactive prosocial motivations. *Journal of Comparative Psychology, 127*, 212–225.

Burkart, J. M., van Schaik, C. P., & Griesser, M. (2017). Looking for unity in diversity: Human cooperative childcare in comparative perspective. *Proceedings of the Royal Society B: Biological Sciences, 284*, 20171184.

Carter, C. S., & Perkeybile, A. (2018). The monogamy paradox: What do love and sex have to do with it? *Frontiers in Ecology and Evolution, 8*, 202. doi: 10.3389/fevo.2018.00202

Cheney, D., & Seyfarth, R. (1990). *How monkeys see the world: Inside the mind of another species*. University of Chicago Press.

Cheney, D., & Seyfarth, R. (2007). *Baboon metaphysics: The evolution of the social mind*. University of Chicago Press.

Chow, C. P., Mitchell, J. F., & Miller, C. T. (2015). Vocal turn-taking in a non-human primate is learned during ontogeny. *Proceedings of the Royal Society B: Biological Sciences, 282*, 20150069.

Clutton-Brock, T. H. (2016). *Mammal societies*. Wiley.

Cockburn, A. (2006). Prevalence of different modes of parental care in birds. *Proceedings of the Royal Society B: Biological Sciences, 273*, 1375–1383.

Deffner, D., & McElreath, R. (2020). The importance of life history and population regulation for the evolution of social learning. Philosophical Transactions of the Royal Society B, *375*, 20190492. http://dx.doi.org/10.1098/rstb.2019.0492

Dell'Mour, V., Range, F., & Huber, L. (2009). Social learning and mother's behavior in manipulative tasks in infant marmosets. *American Journal of Primatology, 71*, 503–509.

De Silva, J. M. (2011). A shift toward birthing relatively large infants early in human evolution. *Proceedings of the National Academy of Sciences, 108*, 1022–1027.

de Waal, F. (2006). *Primates and philosophers: How morality evolved*. Princeton University Press.

Elowson, A. M., Snowdon, C. T., & Lazaro-Perea, C. (1998). Babbling and social context in infant monkeys: parallels to human infants. *Trends in Cognitive Sciences, 2*, 31–37.

Emlen, S. (1991). Evolution of cooperative breeding in birds and mammals. In J. Krebs & N. B. Davies (Eds.), *Behavioral ecology* (3rd ed., pp. 301–337). Blackwell Scientific.

Englemann, J. M., Herrmann, E., & Tomasello, M. (2012). Five-year olds, but not chimpanzees, attempt to manage their reputations. *PLoS ONE, 7*, e48433.

Erb, W. M., & Porter, L. M. (2017). Mother's little helpers: What we know (and don't know) about cooperative infant care in callitrichines. *Evolutionary Anthropology, 26*, 25–37.

Finkenwirth, C., & Burkart, J. M. (2017). Long-term-stability of relationship structure in family groups of common marmosets, and its link to proactive prosociality. *Physiology & Behavior, 173*, 79–86.

Finkenwirth, C., Martins, E., Deschner, T., & Burkart, J. M. (2016). Oxytocin is associated with infant-care behavior and motivation in cooperatively breeding marmoset monkeys. *Hormones and Behavior, 80*, 10–18.

Fu, G., & Lee, K. (2007). Social grooming in the kindergarten: The emergence of flattery behavior. *Developmental Science, 10*, 255–265.

Garber, P. (1997). One for all and breeding for one. *Evolutionary Anthropology, 7*, 187–199.

Gavriletes, S., & Richerson, P. J. (2017). Collective action and the evolution of social norm internalization. *Proceedings of the National Academy of Sciences, 114*(23), 6068–6073. https://doi.org/10.1073/pnas.1703857114

Geary, D. C. (2018). Autism in the broader context of cognitive sex differences. *Proceedings of the National Academy of Sciences, 115*, 12089–12091.

Glocker, M. L, Langleben, D. D., Ruparel, K., Loughead, J. W., Valdez, J. N., Griffin, M. D., Gur, R. C., & Sachser, N. (2009). Baby schema modulates the reward system in nulliparous women. *Proceedings of the National Academy of Sciences, 106*, 9115–9119.

Goldstein, M. H., King, A. P., & West, M. J. (2003). Social interaction shapes babbling: Testing parallels between birdsong and speech. *Proceedings of the National Academy of Sciences, 100*, 8030–8035.

Gopnik, A. (2010). *The philosophical baby: What children's minds tell us about truth, love, and the meaning of life.* Farrar, Straus, and Giroux.

Gopnik, A. (2020). Childhood as a solution to explore–exploit tensions. *Philosophical Transactions of the Royal Society B, 375*, 20190502. http://dx.doi.org/10.1098/rstb.2019.0502

Guerreiro Martins, E. M., Moura, A. C. A., Finkenwirth, C., Griesser, M., & Burkart, J. M. (2019). Food sharing patterns in three species of callitrichid monkeys (*Callithrix jacchus, Leontopithecus chrysomelas, Saguinus midas*): Individual and species differences. *Journal of Comparative Psychology, 133*, 474–487. doi: 10.1037/com0000169.

Gurven, M. D., Davison, R. J., & Kraft, T. S. (2020). The optimal timing of teaching and learning across the life course. *Philosophical Transactions of the Royal Society B, 375*, 20190500. http://dx.doi.org/10.1098/rstb.2019.0500

Gustison, M. L., Borjon, J. I., Takahashi, D. Y., & Ghazanfar, A. A. (2019). Vocal and locomotor coordination develops in association with the autonomic nervous system. *eLife, 8*, e41853.

Hamlin, J. K., & Wynn, K. (2011). Young infants prefer prosocial to antisocial others. *Cognitive Development, 26*, 30–39.

Hamlin, J. K., Wynn, K., & Bloom, P. (2007). Social evaluation by preverbal infants. *Nature, 450*, 557–559.

Hamlin, J. K., Wynn, K., & Bloom, P. (2010). Three-month-olds show a negativity bias in their social evaluations. *Developmental Science, 13*, 923–929.

Hawkes, K. (2014). Primate sociality to human cooperation: Why us and not them? *Human Nature, 25*, 28–48.

Hawkes, K. (2020). Cognitive consequences of our grandmothering life history: Cultural learning begins in infancy. *Philosophical Transactions of the Royal Society B, 375*, 20190501. http://dx.doi.org/10.1098/rstb.2019.0501

Hawkes, K., O'Connell, J. F., Blurton Jones, N. G., Alvarez, H., & Charnov, E. L. (1998). Grandmothering, menopause and the evolution of human life histories. *Proceedings of the National Academy of Sciences, 95*, 1336–1339.

Hermann, E. A., Call, J., Hernandez-Loreda, M. V., Hare, B., & Tomasello, M. (2007). Humans have evolved specialized skills of social cognition: The cultural intelligence hypothesis. *Science, 317*, 1360–1366.

Hewlett, B. S., Fouts, H. N., & Boyette, A. H. (2011). Social learning among Congo Basin hunter-gatherers. *Proceedings of the Royal Society B: Biological Sciences, 366*, 1168–1178.

Hill, K., Walker, R. S., Bozicevic, M., Eder, J., Headland, T., Hewlett, B., Hurtado, A. M., Marlowe, F., Wiessner, P., & Wood, B. (2011). Co-residence patterns in hunter-gatherer societies show unique human social structure. *Science, 331*, 1286–1289.

Hobson, P. (2004). *The cradle of thought: Exploring the origins of thinking.* Oxford University Press.

Hrdy, S. B. (1977). *The Langurs of Abu: Female and male strategies of reproduction.* Harvard University Press.

Hrdy, S. B. (1999). *Mother Nature.* Pantheon.

Hrdy, S. B. (2009). *Mothers and others: The evolutionary origins of mutual understanding.* The Belknap Press of Harvard University Press.

Hrdy, S. B. (2016a). Development plus social selection in the emergence of "emotionally modern" humans. In C. L. Meehan & A. N. Crittenden (Eds.), *Childhood: Origins, evolution and implications* (pp. 11–44). School for Advanced Research and University of New Mexico Press.

Hrdy, S. B. (2016b). Variable postpartum responsiveness among humans and other primates with "cooperative breeding": A comparative and evolutionary perspective. *Hormones and Behavior, 77*, 272–283.

Hrdy, S. B. (2019). The transformative power of nurturing. In T. Singer & M. Ricard (Eds.), *Power and care* (pp. 15–27). MIT Press.

Hublin, J.-J., Ben-Ncer, A., Bailey, S. E., Freidline, S. E., Neubauer, S., Skinner, M. M., Bergmann, I., Le Cabec, A., Benazzi, S., Harvati, K., & Gunz, P. (2017). New fossils from Jebel Irhoud, Morocco and the pan-African origin of Homo sapiens. *Nature, 546*, 289–292.

Humle, T., & Snowdon, C. T. (2008). Socially biased learning in the acquisition of a complex foraging task in juvenile cottontop tamarins, *Saguinus oedipus*. *Animal Behaviour, 75*, 267–277.

Humle, T., Snowdon, C. T., & Matsuzawa, T. (2009). Social influences on ant-dipping acquisition in the wild chimpanzees *(Pan troglodytes verus)* of Bossou, Guinea, West Africa. *Animal Cognition, 12*(1), 37–48.

Isler, K., & van Schaik, C. P. (2012a). Allomaternal care, life history and brain size evolution in mammals. *Journal of Human Evolution, 63*, 52–63.

Isler, K., & van Schaik, C. P. (2012b). How our ancestors broke through the gray ceiling: Comparative evidence for cooperative breeding in early Homo. *Current Anthropology, 53*, S453–S465.

Jaeggi, A. V., Dunkel, L. P., van Noordwijk, M. A., Wich, S. W., Sura, A. A. L., & van Schaik, C. P. (2010). Social learning of diet and foraging skills by wild immature Bornean orangutans: Implications for culture. *American Journal of Physical Anthropology, 72*, 62–71.

Jaeggi, A., & van Schaik, C. P. (2011). The evolution of food-sharing in primates. *Behavioral Ecology and Sociobiology, 65*, 2125–2140.

Jetz, W., & Rubenstein, D. (2011). Environmental uncertainty and the global biogeography of cooperative breeding in birds. *Current Biology, 21*, 72–78.

Knight, C. (2016). *Decoding Chomsky*. Yale University Press.

Koenig, A., & Borries, C. (2012). Hominoid dispersal patterns and human evolution. *Evolutionary Anthropology, 21*, 108–112.

Konner, M. (1972). Aspects of the foraging ecology of a foraging people. In N. Blurton-Jones (Ed.), *Ethological studies of child behavior* (pp. 285–304). Cambridge University Press.

Konner, M. (2010). *The evolution of childhood: Relationships, emotion, mind*. Belknap Press of Harvard University Press.

Krupenye, C., Kano, F., Hirata, S., Call, J., & Tomasello, M. (2016). Great apes anticipate that other individuals will act according to false beliefs. *Science, 354*, 110–114.

Kuzawa, C. W., Chugani, H. T., Grosman, L. I., Lipovich, L., Musik, O., Hof, P. R., Wildman, D. E., Sherwood, C. C., Leonard, W. R., & Lange, N. (2014). Metabolic costs and evolutionary implications of human brain development. *Proceedings of the National Academy of Sciences, 111*, 13010–13015.

Langen, T. A. (2000). Prolonged offspring dependence and cooperative breeding in birds. *Behavioral Ecology, 11*, 367–377.

Langen, T. A., & Vehrencamp, S. L. (1998). Ecological factors affecting group and territory size in white-throated magpie-jays. *Auk, 115*, 327–339.

Leighton, G. M. (2017). Cooperative breeding influences the number and type of vocalizations in avian lineages, *Proceedings of the Royal Society B: Biological Sciences, 284*, 20171508.

Lonsdorf, E. V., Ross, S. R., & Matsuzawa, T. (Eds.). (2010). *The mind of the chimpanzee: Ecological and experimental perspectives*. University of Chicago Press.

Lytle, S. R., Garcia-Sierra, A., & Kuhl, P. K. (2018). Two are better than one: Infant language learning from video improves in the presence of peers. *Proceedings of the National Academy of Sciences, 115*, 9859–9866.

Magill, C., Ashley, G. M., & Freeman, K. (2013). Ecosystem variability and early human habitats in eastern Africa. *Proceedings of the National Academy of Sciences, 110*, 1167–1174.

Marlowe, F. (2010). *The Hadza hunter-gatherers of Tanzania*. University of California Press.

Matsuzawa, T. (2010). The chimpanzee mind: Bridging fieldwork and laboratory work. In Lonsdorf, E. V., Ross, S. R., & Matsuzawa, T. (Eds.), *The mind of the chimpanzee: Ecological and experimental perspectives* (pp. 1–19). University of Chicago Press.

Meehan, C., & Crittenden, A. (Eds.). (2016). *Childhood: Origins, evolution and implications*. School for Advanced Research and University of New Mexico Press.

Meehan, C. L., & Hawks, S. (2013). Cooperative breeding and attachment among Aka foragers. In N. Quinn and J. M. Mageo (Eds.), *Attachment reconsidered: Cultural perspectives on a western theory* (pp. 85–114). Palgrave Macmillan.

Meindl, R. S., Chaney, M. E., & Lovejoy, C. O. (2018). Early hominids may have been a weed species. *Proceedings of the National Academy of Sciences, 115*, 1244–1249.

Melnikoff, D. E., & Bailey, A. H. (2018). Preferences for moral vs. immoral traits in others are conditional. *Proceedings of the National Academy of Sciences, 115*, e592–e600. doi: 10.1073/pnas.1714945115.

Morgan, T. J. H., Suchow, J. W., & Griffiths, T. L. (2020). Experimental evolutionary simulations of learning, memory and life history. *Philosophical Transactions of the Royal Society B, 375*, 20190504. http://dx.doi.org/10.1098/rstb.2019.0504

Myowa-Yamakoshi, M. (2010). Early social cognition in chimpanzees. In E. V. Lonsdorf, S. R. Ross, & T. Matsuzawa (Eds.), *The mind of the chimpanzee: Ecological and experimental perspectives* (pp. 23–31). University of Chicago Press.

Nesse, R. (2019). *Good reasons for bad feelings: Insights from the frontier of evolutionary psychiatry*. Penguin/Random House.

Nesse, R. M. (2007). Runaway social selection for displays of partner value and altruism. *Biological Theory, 2*(2), 143–155.

Nielsen, M., & Tomaselli, K. (2010). Overimitation in Kalahari Bushman children and the origins of human cultural cognition. *Psychological Science, 21*, 729–736.

Numan, M. (2015). *Neurobiology of social behavior: Toward an understanding of the prosocial and antisocial brain*. Elsevier/Academic Press.

O'Connell, J. F., Hawkes, K., Lupo, K. D., & Blurton Jones, K. G. (2002). Male strategies and Plio-Pleistocene archaeology. *Journal of Human Evolution, 43*, 461–485.

Parsons, C. E., Young, K. S., Bhandari, R., van IJzendoorn, M. H., Bakermans-Kranenburg, M. I., Stein, A., & Kringelbach, M. L. (2013). The bonnie baby: Experimentally manipulated temperament affects perceived cuteness and motivation to view infant faces. *Developmental Science, 17*, 257–269.

Perry, S. (2020). Behavioural variation and learning across the lifespan in wild white-faced capuchin monkeys. *Philosophical Transactions of the Royal Society B*, 375, 20190494. http://dx.doi.org/10.1098/rstb.2019.0494

Pollick, A. S., & de Waal, F. (2007). Ape gestures and language evolution. *Proceedings of the National Academy of Sciences, 104*, 8184–8189.

Raghanti, M.-A., Edler, M. K., Stephenson, A. R., Munger, E. L., Jacobs, B., Hof, P. R., Sherwood, C. C., Holloway, R. L., & Lovejoy, C. O. (2018). A neurochemical hypothesis for the origin of hominids. *Proceedings of the National Academy of Sciences, 115*, e1108–e1116.

Rapaport, L., & Brown, G. (2008). Social influences on foraging behavior in young nonhuman primates: Learning what, where and how to eat. *Evolutionary Anthropology, 17*, 189–201.

Rapaport, L. G. (2011). Progressive parenting in wild golden lion tamarins. *Behavioral Ecology, 22*, 745–754.

Reddy, V. (2003). On being the object of attention: Implications for self-other consciousness. *Trends in Cognitive Science, 7*, 97–402.

Repacholi, B. M., & Gopnik, A. (1997). Early reasoning about desires: Evidence from 14- and 18-month-olds. *Developmental Psychology, 33*, 12–21.

Richerson, P. J., & Boyd, R. (2020). The human life history is adapted to exploit the adaptive advantages of culture. Philosophical Transactions of the Royal Society B, *375*, 20190498. http://dx.doi.org/10.1098/rstb.2019.0498

Riem Madelon, M. E., van IJzendoorn, M. H., Parsons, C. E., Young, K. S., De Carli, P., Kringelbach, M. L., & Bakermans-Kranenburg, M. J. (2017). Experimental manipulation of infant temperament affects amygdala functional connectivity. *Cognitive, Affective, and Behavioral Neuroscience, 71*, 858–868.

Schuppli, C., Forss, S. I., Meulman, E. J., Zweifel, N., Lee, K. C., Rukmana, E., Vogel, E. R., van Noordwijk, M., & van Schaik, C. P. (2016). Development of foraging skills in two orangutan populations: Needing to learn or needing to grow? *Frontiers in Zoology, 13*, 43. http://dx.doi.org/10.1186/s12983-016-0178-5

Scrimshaw, S. (1984). Infanticide in human populations: Social and individual concerns. In G. Hausfater & S. B. Hrdy (Eds.), *Infanticide: Comparative and evolutionary perspectives* (pp. 419–462). Aldine de Gruyter.

Silk, J. B., & House, B. R. (2016). The evolution of altruistic social preferences in human groups. *Philosophical Transactions of the Royal Society B, 371*(1687), 20150097. doi: 10.1098/rstb.2015.0097.

Slocombe, K., & Zuberbühler, K. (2010). Vocal communication in the chimpanzee. In E. V. Lonsdorf, S. R. Ross, & T. Matsuzawa (Eds.), *The mind of the chimpanzee: Ecological and experimental perspectives* (pp. 192–207). University of Chicago Press.

Snowdon, C., & Elowson, A. M. (2001). "Babbling" in pygmy marmosets: Development after infancy. *Behaviour, 138*(10), 1235–1248.

Snowdon, C. T. (2001). Social processes in communication and cognition in callitrichid monkeys: A review. *Animal Cognition, 4*, 247–257.

Stolk, A., Hunnius, S., Bekkering, H., & Toni, I. (2013). Early social experience predicts referential communicative adjustments in five-year-old children. *PLoS ONE, 8*, e72667.

Takahashi, D. Y., Fenley, A. R., & Ghazanfar, A. A. (2016). Early development of turn-taking with parents shape focal acoustics in infant marmoset monkeys. *Philosophical Transactions of the Royal Society B, 37*, 20150370.

Takahashi, D. Y., Liao, D. A., & Ghazanfar, A. A. (2017). Vocal learning via social reinforcement by infant marmoset monkeys. *Current Biology, 27*, 1844–1852.

Tamir, D., & Mitchell, J. (2012). Disclosing information about the self is intrinsically rewarding. *Proceedings of the National Academy of Sciences, 109*, 8038–8043.

Theofanopoulou, C., Boeckx, C., & Jarvis, E. D. (2017). A hypothesis on a role of oxytocin in the social mechanisms of speech and vocal learning. *Proceedings of the Royal Society B: Biological Sciences, 284*, 20170988.

Thornton, A., & McAuliffe, L. (2006). Teaching in wild meerkats. *Science, 313*, 227–229.

Tomasello, M. (1999). *The cultural origins of human cognition*. Harvard University Press.

Tomasello, M. (2008). *Origins of human communication*. MIT Press.

Tomasello, M. (2016). *A natural history of human morality*. Harvard University Press.

Tomasello, M. (2018). How we learned to put our fate in one another's hands: The origins of morality. *Scientific American, 319*(3), 70–75. doi:10.1038/scientificamerican0918-70

Tomasello, M. (2019). *Becoming human: A theory of ontogeny*. Harvard University Press.

Tomasello, M., & Carpenter, M. (2007). Shared intentionality. *Developmental Science, 10*, 121–125.

Tomasello, M., & Gonzalez-Cabrera, I. (2017). The role of ontogeny in the evolution of human cooperation. *Human Nature, 28*, 274–288.

Tomasello, M., Kruger, A. C., & Ratner, H. H. (1993). Cultural Learning. *Behavioral and Brain Sciences, 16,* 495–552.

Tomonaga, M., Tanaka, M., Matsuzawa, T., Myowa-Yamakoshi, M., Kosugil, M., Mizuno, Y., Okamoto, S., Yamaguchi, M. K., & Bard, K. A. (2004). Development of social cognition in infant chimpanzees (*Pan troglodytes*): Face recognition, smiling, gaze, and the lack of triadic interactions. *Japanese Psychological Research, 46,* 227–235.

Trevarthen, C. (1993). The self born in intersubjectivity. In U. Neisser (Ed.), *The perceived self: Ecological and interpersonal sources of self-knowledge* (pp. 121–173). Emory Symposia in Cognition 5. Cambridge University Press.

Warneken, F., & Tomasello, M. (2006). Altruistic helping in human infants and young chimpanzees. *Science, 311,* 1301–1303.

West-Eberhard, M. J. (1983). Sexual selection, social competition, and speciation. *Quarterly Review of Biology, 58,* 155–183.

West-Eberhard, M. J. (2003). *Development, plasticity and evolution.* Oxford University Press.

Whiten A. (1999). Parental encouragement in Gorilla in comparative perspective: implications for social cognition and the evolution of teaching. In S. Taylor Parker, R. W. Mitchell, & H. L. Miles (Eds.), *The mentalities of gorillas and orangutans: Comparative perspective* (pp. 342–366). Cambridge University Press.

Whiten, A., McGuigan, N., Marshall-Pescini, S., & Hopper, L. M. (2009). Emulation, imitation, over-imitation and the scope of culture for child and chimpanzee. *Philosophical Transactions of the Royal Society B, 364,* 2417–2428.

Yamamoto, M. E., & Box, H. O. (1997). The role of non-reproductive helpers in infant care in captive *Callithrix jacchus. Ethology, 103,* 760–771.

Yamamoto, S., Tatyana, H., & Tanaka, M. (2012). Chimpanzees' flexible targeted helping based on an understanding of conspecific goals. *Proceedings of the National Academy of Sciences, 109,* 3588–3592.

Zuberbühler, K. (2012). Cooperative breeding and the evolution of vocal flexibility. In M. Tellerman & K. Gibson (Eds.), *The Oxford handbook of language evolution* (pp. 71–81). Oxford University Press.

CHAPTER 48

Positive Evolutionary Psychology: The New Science of Psychological Growth

Nicole A. Wedberg, Glenn Geher, Brianna McQuade, and Dayna M. Thomas

Abstract

To this point in the history of the behavioral sciences, the fields of evolutionary psychology and positive psychology have progressed independently. Evolutionary psychology holds the basic scientific goal of illuminating causes of behavior by using evolutionary concepts. Positive psychology holds the applied scientific goal of shedding light on processes that cultivate positive growth at both the individual and community levels. This chapter discusses the new field of positive evolutionary psychology, which seeks to synergize these fields by carving out an approach to researching questions that bear on advancing the goals of positive psychology by relying on concepts and research from the field of evolutionary psychology. Using an evolutionarily informed framework holds the key to best understanding such positive psychological issues as happiness, love, and the psychology of cooperation.

Key Words: positive psychology, evolution, emotion, growth, evolutionary psychology

Introduction

How do we achieve happiness? And how important should happiness be in our pursuits? What exactly is love? Why does it exist and how do we find it? How do we know whom we can trust in our social worlds to provide us the support that we need as we navigate the difficulties of life? What are the ingredients of a flourishing community—a community in which trust and cooperation outweigh envy and treachery? The new field of positive evolutionary psychology was designed to address such foundational questions of the human experience by utilizing Charles Darwin's profound insights related to principles of evolution (see Geher & Wedberg, 2020).

In this chapter, we explore the connection of two fields: positive psychology and evolutionary psychology. Specifically, we examine how the merging of these two fields might give us a better understanding of human emotions (Cosmides & Tooby, 2000; see also Al-Shawaf et al., 2015), and how, from an evolutionary perspective, emotional experiences might contribute to growth on both an individual and community scale.

Joy, happiness, regret, anger, grief, pride, and other emotions make up part of the human condition. Here, we focus on the more positive parts of the human experience. Emotions, characteristic traits, and themes like growth, community, gratitude, love, resilience, and, of course, happiness are examined through a Darwinian lens so that we might hope to (a) better understand the function of these emotions, and, along the way, (b) explore the application of these findings about the positive aspects of human functioning.

The field of positive psychology—and the bodies of work studied to date therein—is a relatively young one within psychology (see Conoley & Conoley, 2009). But the thought that our emotions have evolved by natural selection, like any other human trait, is not new. In *The Expression of the Emotions in Man and Animals* (1872), Darwin argued that, like our biological traits, emotion has an evolutionary lineage that can be seen universally across cultures (Al-Shawaf et al., 2018).

When we think about what *growth* means, similar terms that may come to mind might include *flourish, potential,* and *fulfill*. Examined closely, all examples we might think of for *growth* involve learning and/or change. Looking toward evolutionary psychology, we have a grasp of the functions of human emotions in that they can increase the likelihood of survival or reproduction (Guitar et al., 2018). Looking toward positive psychology, we also know that the experience of positive emotions discussed later in this chapter may contribute to individual growth (Fredrickson, 2001). Learning from our own behavior and making an effort to change it—to grow—takes effort and humility (Cohn & Fredrickson, 2010). Further, as noted from the points above, what growth means in terms of evolutionary principles (such as achieving reproductive success) does not always map onto what growth means in terms of the principles of positive psychology.

Further, growth is not exclusive to the individual. Enduring change and subsequent growth is an experience that can be shared in a community (Lehman et al., 2004). Over the course of our evolutionary history, humans have formed communities and groups that extend beyond kin (Bingham & Souza, 2009), and this has contributed to our being a socially communal ape.

Evolutionary Psychology and Positive Psychology: Points of Complementarity

Picture a Venn diagram with evolutionary psychology in one bubble, positive psychology in another bubble, and hearty overlap in the middle. To date, in terms of content areas, the evolutionary psychology bubble has encompassed such domains as mating behavior, evolutionary mismatch, parental investment, human emotions, altruism, and morality, to name a few (see Geher, 2014). Evolutionary psychology often tackles basic, scientific questions as they relate to noticeable patterns in life. This includes questions such as: Why are many men attracted to women with an "hourglass" figure (Buss, 1989)? Why do many people find sugary and fatty foods so much more appealing than healthy alternatives (Rozin & Todd, 2015)? What adaptive benefits might traits like narcissism or anxiety provide, if any (Crysel et al., 2013)? Why would negative feelings or traits have been sexually selected (Marks & Nesse, 1994; Hofmann et al., 2002)? These are important questions that can provide a lens on our ancestral history while explaining modern human behavior. This said, many of the questions studied by evolutionary psychologists do not focus on the more heartwarming parts of the human experience.

In the positive psychology bubble, to date, we have seen domains studied that are more encompassing of positive emotions—gratitude, happiness, joy, resilience, etc. Further, positive psychologists focus on the topic of whether we can experience meaning in life (King et al., 2006). How can we find purpose, come together as a community, or cultivate a life full of gratitude (Cunha et al., 2019)? These are application questions. They follow a pattern of exploration toward human growth, both on an individual level and within a broader community. It is the more heartwarming bubble, to be sure.

So, what does that leave us with in the center of our Venn diagram? In terms of finding a complementary middle ground, basic (theoretically scientific) questions can often help to give us a clearer approach to the kinds of applied questions that serve as the focus of positive psychology. When it comes to emotional experiences, we can ask why the human emotion system evolved as it has, and how this evolutionary history of human emotions might shed light on what we should be striving for during our time on this planet (Geher & Wedberg, 2020).

Let's start with an example to illustrate positive evolutionary psychology—an example that integrates both emotional and social processes. Why be kind? From an evolutionary perspective, we might ask why kindness would exist when it is an inherently selfless act. Put another way, we might ask what benefit kindness might have provided our ancestors. Further, our evolutionist lens might encourage us to ask if kindness is a human universal seen across cultures. To tackle these *why* questions from an evolutionary perspective, we need not look further than the work of Robert Trivers (1971). In his now-classic paper, he first explicated the notion of reciprocal altruism. Reciprocal altruism is the act of doing something positive for another that would seem inherently against self-interest. The theory behind *why* we do such things (scratch someone's back, let's say) is because there is an understanding that our kindness will be reciprocated. One day, our backs will be scratched in return.

But like many social-emotional phenomena, kindness has multiple evolutionary underpinnings. Another angle to understand the evolution of kindness is found in the work of David Buss (2017). He found that kindness is romantically attractive. Across cultures and across sexes, kindness is a trait that humans look for in one another. Kindness lends itself to more success in the mating domain. And in terms of Darwin's bottom-line currency of reproductive success, anything that leads to benefits in the mating domain will be selected and come to characterize a species following generations of selection.

As the great ethologist Niko Tinbergen (1963) taught years ago, behavioral phenomena have both *ultimate* and *proximate* causes. Further, these evolved mechanisms of human behavior are heavily dependent on context (Al-Shawaf et al., 2019). Ultimate causes of behavior focus on the big picture from an evolutionary perspective: Why did this behavior evolve? How does it cultivate survival and/or reproductive success? Proximate causes of behavior include more immediate factors, such as the content of specific affective states or particular classes of physiological activity. Positive psychologists focus more on proximate causes of behavior than do evolutionary psychologists. In understanding something like the emotional facets of kindness, positive psychologists are more likely to seek to understand immediate causes and effects of kindness experiences.

Positive psychologists, thus, are more likely to focus on the fact that performing acts of kindness can work wonders in one's daily life. Those who behave altruistically toward others are more accepted by peers, and they receive a boost in their overall well-being (Layous et al., 2012). Jenkinson and colleagues (2013) also found that volunteering for a cause you believe in can improve overall well-being, increase life satisfaction, and reduce depressive symptoms.

Of course, kindness is but one idea in an entire field of complementarity between the bubbles of evolutionary and positive psychology. When conceptualized in this Venn diagram manner, we can think of many social-emotional phenomena that belong closely to both evolutionary and positive psychology. Such phenomena include gratitude, love, forgiveness, outrage, pride, shame, and more. So many of the complex and moral emotions (see Trivers, 1985) are relevant from both the evolutionary and positive psychological approaches.

Using Evolutionary Principles to Better Understand Individual Growth
When Martin Seligman gave his now-famous speech on positive psychology at the 1998 convention of the American Psychological Association, he called for a large-scale change in how the field of psychology, both in science and in practice, approaches the human experience. To that point, psychology was focused on the negatives associated with people's psychological experiences. Topics related to adverse mental health issues, such as depression, anxiety, and personality disorders, had come to take center stage in the field.

Seligman's 1998 call to action to scientists and practitioners in the field had a simple and singular focus: to get professionals in the field to focus on the positives of the human psychological experience. Sure, people get depressed, angry, and anxious. But they also get happy, inspired, and full of love for others. They build bridges and rocket ships. They write symphonies and choreograph amazing dances. There is a lot of positivity associated with what humans do, and the foundation of positive psychology is to understand, harness, and cultivate this positive side of what it means to be human.

In developing the idea of positive evolutionary psychology, we conceptualized two ways that evolutionary psychology dovetails with the goals of positive psychology. These include the cultivation of positive growth at the individual level and the cultivation of positive growth at the community level. This section focuses on growth at the individual level. A goal of positive psychology is to better understand factors associated with individual growth (see Seligman, 2011).

Much work in the field of positive psychology focuses on emotional growth and the cultivation of positive affect, such as advancing ways to inspire happiness (see McMahan & Choi, et al., 2016; Watkins, 2014). Happiness studies have become a major part of the field of positive psychology, with a goal of advancing happiness in its many forms.

To understand the basics of an evolutionary approach to individual psychological growth, we need to go back to a basic understanding of the evolutionary approach, in general, and from there to understand the concept of "an individual" from an evolutionary perspective. A Darwinian approach to an organism can be well-conceptualized by thinking about Dawkins's (1976) notion of *the selfish gene*. Dawkins's recapitulation of the basic idea of natural selection presents all organisms, including humans, as vehicles for replicating their own particular sets of genes. While this view of a human, as a replicator shaped by natural selection over eons of evolutionary time, may be seen as cold to some, it is powerful in that it puts every facet of the human experience into a natural and scientific context.

When we see human behavior, then, as a result of evolutionary forces over deep time (see Geher, 2014), we can use the arsenal of tools found in evolutionary science to uncover human nature. From this vantage point, any approach to best understanding the factors that lead to positive growth in the human individual experience needs to take evolutionary principles into account. This section dissects this process of thinking about such positive individual growth via such evolutionary principles.

While there are many ways that evolutionary psychology has the capacity to advance the positive psychological goal of individual growth, here we focus on three specifics: increasing positive affect, understanding the evolutionary roots of psychological relativism, and working toward transcendence (see Kaufman, 2020) from an evolutionary perspective.

As addressed in the later section pertaining to human emotions, cultivating positive affect is a major goal of positive psychology. From an evolutionary perspective, the cultivation of positive affective states, such as happiness, should not be done in a vacuum (see Nesse & Ellsworth, 2009). Happiness, like any product of natural selection, evolved because it serves the function of advancing survival and/or reproduction of an individual. Under ancestral conditions, when the human emotion system was evolving, our ancestors experienced happiness as a response to stimuli that had the capacity to facilitate survival and/or reproduction. Such stimuli would have included a large and nutritious meal, securing a loving and attractive mate, advancing one's status in a group, the healthy birth of a child, and so forth. In fact, these same outcomes bring joy to us today (see Acevedo et al., 2012).

The emotions evolved for highly adaptive reasons (see Guitar et al., 2018). While happiness evolved to help us seek outcomes that, on average, would have given our ancestors increased chances at survival and reproduction, emotions that we consider negative, such as sadness, also evolved for adaptive reasons (see Keller & Nesse, 2006). Sadness and worry on the heels of failure, for instance, serve the function of helping people process mistakes they may have made so as to be more successful in the future. From an evolutionary perspective, negatively charged emotions have their place.

A positive evolutionary psychological approach to individual growth regarding happiness, then, focuses on the evolutionary context in which happiness evolved. Happiness evolved to bring people closer toward stimuli and outcomes that facilitated survival and reproduction (Guitar et al., 2018). Getting people to carve out specific steps to achieve such evolutionarily relevant outcomes in today's world should, then, go a long way toward cultivating happiness in the modern human experience.

Humans did not evolve in a vacuum. Our ancestors evolved in small-scale groups where they were surrounded by others with whom they had long-standing social connections (see Dunbar, 1992). Under such conditions, one's success was measured not in absolute terms, but in relativistic terms (see Hill & Buss, 2010). It was better to have four spears if all the other hunters had two spears, compared to a situation in which you had six spears but all the other hunters had nine spears. The human mind evolved to calibrate our emotional states on a relativistic basis, because if you were doing worse than others in your circle (regardless of how you were doing in an absolute sense), this was a signal of failure, which could have negative implications for your survival and reproduction.

Given the fact that we evolved with complex emotion systems, it is useful to think about individual growth today from such a relativistic perspective. Motivating people to be happy with their lot and inspired to thrive can likely be done more effectively by catalyzing relative success rather than absolute success. This is likely part of the reason that people in nomadic groups from around the world who would be considered impoverished by modern Westernized standards often are reported as being happy and satisfied with life (see Montgomery, 2010). Individual growth is not about *absolute success*. Rather, it is about *relativistic success* in the confines of small-scale social groups that parallel the kinds of groups that our ancestors evolved to experience.

A final point of individual growth that can be elucidated by an evolutionary perspective worth mentioning here pertains to transcendence (see Kaufman, 2020). Scott Barry Kaufman's take on psychological transcendence can be thought of as a modern investigation into Maslow's hierarchy of needs (Maslow, 1943). This model of human needs suggests that needs vary from basic, foundational needs, such as the physiological needs for oxygen and water, to more advanced, abstract needs, such as the need for belonging and love. Kaufman's reformation of Maslow's model focuses on transcending oneself as a sort of higher order need that people are motivated to pursue as they develop in life.

This idea of transcendence speaks to a point at which one is less focused on lower needs, and more focused on achieving authenticity, as well as integrating in a positive way into desired communities. Humans are a highly communal ape, and transcendence from an individual to a communal focus can be thought of as an evolutionarily based way to understand human growth and flourishing. Our ancestors who were able to focus on their communities rather than on their own particular needs were able to thrive. Succeeding as a pillar of one's community not only is individually rewarding and satisfying (in a proximate sense), but also has the effect of making the environment a better place. And long-term benefits to oneself and one's kin are sure to follow. From an evolutionary perspective, transcending the self can generate a cascade of benefits. It is the idea of understanding community growth from an evolutionary perspective that we turn to next.

Using Evolutionary Principles to Better Understand Positive Growth in Human Communities

A critical piece of the evolutionary psychological puzzle pertains to the nature of evolutionary mismatch in our social experiences. Under modern conditions, we are often surrounded by hundreds or even thousands of strangers. Under ancestral conditions, for much of our evolutionary history, humans only experienced small-scale societies. And much evidence suggests that our minds evolved for such small-scale living (see Dunbar, 1992; Giphart & Van Vugt, 2018). Given this extraordinary mismatch, it is no wonder that such outcomes as crime, mental health problems, and psychopathic behavior are more common in large cities across the world than in small communities (see Figueredo et al., 2008).

With an evolutionarily informed understanding of human societies, we can think about improving life at the community level by modeling groups after the kinds of groups that we evolved in. Within large organizations or large cities, it is possible to create smaller subgroups that comprise communities that better map onto the ecological details of ancestral human groups. Research that has taken this approach in such cities as Binghamton, New York, has found great success in such outcomes as increasing feelings of efficacy, trust in one's community, altruism, and cooperation in adolescents from a broad array of socioeconomic backgrounds (see Wilson, 2011). An evolutionary perspective, in this way, can be used to cultivate thriving at the community level, a goal of the positive psychology movement.

Another way that an evolutionary approach can be used to elucidate and address modern issues at the community level pertains to the problems associated with the large-scale use of social media and devices across the world. Under ancestral conditions, the only way to communicate with another person was face to face. These days, only a fraction of communication is face to face. And, further, much communication is either anonymous or de-individuated, downplaying the identity of the person with whom one is communicating. A landslide of research on de-individuated communication has found that antisocial behavior increases as communication becomes de-individuated (see Zimbardo, 2007). It is no wonder, then, that rates of cyberbullying map onto rates of social media usage all around the world (Comparitech.com, 2020).

These days, it is easy to get wrapped up in social-related technological advances. However, an evolutionary perspective with a focus on mismatch warns us about the pitfalls of such advances. Communities thrive when people are accountable to one another, and this fact has been true for much of human evolutionary history (see Wilson, 2002). The large-scale trend toward increases in the size of communities, along with increases in de-individuated communication, represents a dangerous combination for the human experience. Thinking about and addressing issues of mismatch when it comes to human social ecological factors can go a long way toward helping human communities thrive and not fissure.

The Emotions Through the Lens of Positive Evolutionary Psychology
Basic Human Emotions

As humans, each with our own unique lived experiences, we actively process an abundance of emotions. We yearn to live lives filled with "positive" emotions and feelings, rather than to experience negative emotions through bad experiences. If we were to be presented with circumstances that were easily overcome and emotionally homogenous all of the time, life would become mundane and uninteresting. Without sadness, happiness loses its meaning. Further, from an evolutionary perspective, the "negative" emotions evolved for evolution-based functions.

Psychology has studied a broad array of negative emotions such as depression and anxiety (see Nesse & Williams, 1994). People are quick to conclude that it focuses on problems that we struggle with internally, and fixates on topics such as mental disorders, and how one's nervous system processes trauma. However, when we step back to take an evolutionary perspective on human emotions, we can understand what we should be striving for, and just why our emotional system has evolved in the way that it has (Geher & Wedberg, 2020).

Modern conditions, which are in many ways mismatched to ancestral conditions, can often provoke feelings of anxiety (Geher, 2014). Uncertainty, deadlines, and new situations are aspects of life that we have to confront—often coupled with anxiety. Symptoms of anxiety have functional significance, aiding in our defense against potential threats. In ancestral conditions, symptoms of generalized anxiety disorder, such as experiencing sleep difficulties, tension, and poor concentration, can be helpful to an extent; although if these symptoms spiral out of control, almost any information perceived from your external environment can become significant enough to provoke an anxious response (Bateson et al., 2011). Anxiety, in the right situation, can be transformed into a motivational factor. Anxiety can work to motivate people to take actions in their lives that are adaptive (Geher & Wedberg, 2020).

Love is quite the opposite to the grief and emotional pain that we feel in our lives. It is complicated in that it contains the most fulfilling, positive emotions, as well as the most negative ones. Love is as simple as holding a baby in your arms for the first time and can be seen as a part of life that fills you with exuberance. Love is also as complicated as having to let someone in your life go, to watch them grow. Love is a strong emotion that serves as an evolutionary function and can be seen through both psychological and physiological markers. Altogether, it is a product of the high levels of parental investment that have evolved in humans, and their relationships with their offspring (see Fisher, 1993). It can also be used as a motivational factor in tending to offspring. This concept is exemplified through parental care. Children with biparental care are at an advantage in comparison to offspring of only one investing adult. This is, in part, due to the social pair bond of love that keeps these altricial beings close and helps parents to successfully raise a family (Geher & Wedberg, 2020). Not only that, but love also drives many decisions that are supported by positive evolutionary psychology, such as forgiveness, having an other-oriented approach to life, and being empathetic toward both kin and non-kin.

HAPPINESS

This seemingly uncomplicated emotion poses an evolutionary benefit largely in a proximate manner. Happiness can be seen as an affective state that motivates us (Guitar et al., 2018). Aspects of our life that are intertwined with happiness also happen to match beneficial outcomes from an evolutionary perspective. Being successful socially, our food intake, and engaging in sex are a few things that make us happy, while also functioning in a way that makes us engage in varied behaviors. These then lead to evolutionarily adaptive outcomes under ancestral conditions (Geher & Wedberg, 2020). Just like anxiety, lessening our exposure to experiencing happiness *fully* can be maladaptive and counterproductive. Finding a balance between hyper-exposure and lack of exposure to happiness is integral in motivating ourselves toward behaviors that benefit us.

Higher-Order Human Emotions

Complex emotions, such as shame, pride, and gratitude, have important roles in our relationships with others. Such complex emotions are socially oriented and are often morally laden. The constant struggle of our morality and human judgment "must bear on the interests or welfare either of society as a whole or at least of persons other than the judge or agent" (Gewirth, 1984, p. 276). This approach has the potential to be seen within ourselves and can be applied to the daily functioning of the collective. Many of the everyday social experiences that affect us emotionally can be thought of in terms of the evolutionary underpinnings of complex human emotions. Some of our most complex emotions are attributable to humans' history of reciprocal altruism (see Geher et al., 2019). Take, for example, feeling trust in someone. Trust is fragile and can quickly devolve into betrayal (see DeJesus et al., 2021). This can be explained in evolutionary terms through reciprocal altruism. If someone you trust does not follow through with a favor you ask them to do for you—then the trust you had in them could *potentially* dissolve rather quickly. This leads you to feel betrayed, and you may pin them as a selfish individual. On the contrary, the person who was not altruistic toward the other may feel guilty. We are more likely to feel guilty when we have behaved selfishly when we might have behaved altruistically (Geher & Wedberg, 2020).

Resilience and gratitude can be interpreted through the evolutionary psychology of disasters. Being resilient through hardship and exhibiting selflessness and gratitude while surviving a disaster can be admirable. Take Hurricane Katrina as an example. Katrina occurred in 2005 and was the most expensive natural and technological disaster in US history. The post-impact period was long lasting and mentally and physically draining for all parties involved, including survivors, Disaster Mental Health staff, and first responders. Often, disasters allow the good in human nature to emerge. This might include racial unity, unexpected acts of kindness, an increase in tolerance, displays of courage, concern for others, or a sense of goodwill. Contrary to straight-out reciprocal altruism, selfless acts connected with resilience go a long way. Resilience is being able to adapt and overcome in the face of an unexpected challenge (Geher & Wedberg, 2020).

The capacity for resilience is seen across species, and this idea can be applied to understanding the post-disaster mentality of the collective, due to our desire and need to belong to groups (Baumeister & Leary, 1995). Persevering through hardships and moving forward through uncontrollable failures can be seen as a prerequisite for success later in life. Such resilience, which is often studied under the purview of positive psychology, can be elucidated using an evolutionary lens (see Geher & Wedberg, 2020). Coupled with resilience, major unprecedented events often prompt both gratitude and selflessness. Reconstruction of communities from the damage of Hurricane Katrina presented people with a choice. Survivors who chose to help their community with no expectations for anything in return were able to maintain family cohesion and preserve the psychological community. Such survivors are also able to contribute to the recovery and reconstruction of their community through selfless acts (Dass-Brailsford, 2008). Selflessness is an important aspect of our evolutionary history. Doing something altruistic with no expectation of a favor in return is seen positively through a small-scale lens, as well as within a broader-scale community. Being generous helps people develop a positive reputation in their community as an altruist, or a reliable source (Geher & Wedberg, 2020). Being proactive and making time to give selflessly is adaptive and often leads to both short- and long-term positive outcomes for that individual (Geher & Wedberg, 2020). Simply put, paying it forward has evolutionary roots.

Human emotion is complex and includes intertwined compilations of different life experiences. The beautiful thing about positive evolutionary psychology is that most emotions we feel can be understood through this lens—even emotions such as stress that might be viewed as "bad" on the surface. Earlier, we explored anxiety and the motivational function that it serves in people's work or school lives. Anxiety in optimal doses can drive us toward success. Positive evolutionary psychology and its relationship with human emotion can even be applied to challenges and uncontrollable disasters we may have to overcome. It is important to understand as well that the "good" emotions are more than just "being good." Humans experience a slew of emotions daily, and sometimes are placed in situations that may make them feel overwhelmed with one emotion or another. These emotions are deeply rooted in evolutionary history and serve important functions in terms of our evolutionary fitness and our adaptive skills. People who appreciate complex emotions and promote meaningful relationships with the power that these emotions bring them may benefit from having more meaningful relationships (see Umberson & Montez, 2010).

Human Community Building and Positive Evolutionary Psychology

As addressed in the prior section about using principles of evolutionary psychology to advance the goals of building positive communities, an evolutionary approach has implications that can guide the development of positive and productive human communities. This section focuses on three specific evolutionary concepts that have positive community-based implications. The three specific community-based goals connected with evolutionary principles addressed are: (1) understanding the foundational human conflict of balancing our own self-interest against the interest of our community (Atkins et al., 2019); (2) appreciating the human environment of evolutionary adaptedness as it relates to modern conditions (see Dunbar, 1992); and (3) catalyzing our natural social organizing tendencies (see Bingham & Souza, 2009).

In a restatement of his ideas on multilevel selection, David Wilson (2019) has noted that a multilevel selection understanding of human evolution can help us understand the foundational human conflict. To understand this conflict, we need to consider the facts that (a) humans are individuals, and that (b) humans evolved to live in stable, social conditions. With these two factors in mind, we can think of mixed evolutionary pressures that have applied to the human experience across large periods of evolutionary time. Essentially, humans, like all organisms, evolved to optimize their own lots, so there has been selection pressure to succeed as an individual within groups. We can think of this as within-group selection pressure.

Yet as a group-ish species, humans also evolved to help their own group succeed over other groups. Human groups have been competing with other human groups for scarce resources across the entirety of human evolutionary history. As such, pressures to sacrifice one's own selfish needs for the benefit of one's group have been a major part of the human evolutionary experience. We can conceptualize this as between-group selection pressure. Humans have experienced a combination of within-group and between-group pressures across our evolutionary history, and navigating this fundamental conflict has been an important feature of human evolution. This feature of our humanity has implications for the building of positively functioning communities. Communities with a high proportion of selfish-acting individuals, who are responding to within-group pressures, will not fare well compared with communities that have a relatively high proportion of other-oriented individuals who are primarily responding to between-group pressures.

A simple way to think about this issue in terms of the modern world pertains to video games. In many popular video games, such as Fortnite, game options include *solo mode* versus *squad mode*. In solo mode, it is every player for himself or herself, whereas in squad mode, teams compete against other teams. Players are more likely to display within-group prosocial behavior in squad mode versus in solo mode. An implication for the cultivation of positively functioning communities is this: the more that the parameters of the community cultivate other-oriented acts as opposed to selfish acts, the more the community will thrive compared with competing communities, and the more that individuals within the group will focus on and take pleasure in helping others in support of their shared goals.

A second concept from evolutionary psychology that speaks to the goal of positive community building is found in an appreciation of the fact that our primary environment of evolutionary adaptedness was a nomadic one, in which individuals lived in small-scale societies alongside kin and other individuals with whom they had long-standing relationships (see Dunbar, 1992). The human mind evolved anticipating small-scale societies, and large-scale societal living often leads to adverse outcomes associated with evolutionarily mismatched conditions. Such adverse outcomes include increases in such psychological problems as mental health disorders (see Srivastava, 2009) and psychopathic behavior (see Figueredo et al., 2008). Adverse physical outcomes, such as obesity and type II diabetes, have also been implicated as outcomes associated with modern large-scale living (see Geher & Wedberg, 2020). Communities that are modeled after small-scale ancestral human conditions better match our evolved psychology and, as such, are less likely to lead to adverse psychological outcomes associated with life in evolutionarily mismatched conditions.

A final set of ideas that are rooted in evolutionary principles and that have implications for the building of positive communities is found in the work of Bingham and Souza (2009). In a unique synthesis of human evolutionary research, these scholars point out that human unique throwing ability, coupled with our proclivity to form groups beyond lines of kinship, comprises a foundational feature of our unique evolved psychology. In short, Bingham and Souza argue that these two aspects of humans, which seemed to have coevolved thousands of generations ago, allowed humans to form powerful alliances, with the capacity for such alliances to hold and exert power. In many primate species, one large dominant male holds all the power and holds primary access to necessary resources. However, in humans, the concomitant abilities to accurately throw projectiles and to form social groups with shared goals allowed for individuals to hold power regardless of physical prowess. In short, four small guys who are loaded with sticks and stones and who are well coordinated can easily defeat one large, aggressive, power-hungry guy who is trying to control them. In humans, the ability to organize goes back deep into our history and it relates to our ability to throw rocks with speed and precision (and potentially fatal consequences).

This conception of the evolution of human uniqueness allows us to consider implications for the building of positive and well-functioning communities. Egalitarianism emerged as a dominant form of structuring human societies as a result of the factors that Bingham and Souza (2009) underscore. One implication for the building of positively functioning human societies pertains to the importance of distributing power across the many. Humans evolved with power distributed in such a way, and people do not tend to do well when they find themselves in powerless situations (see Maier & Seligman, 1976). If you want people in your community to be motivated to contribute positively to the greater good, give the people power. We evolved this way, and it is what works best on many levels.

Research Directions in Positive Evolutionary Psychology
To help better understand the interface between evolutionary psychology and positive psychology, it is important to include some guidance for researchers who are interested in conducting work that fits with the idea of this field. The topics included in this section jump out as areas of inquiry that will likely emerge as particularly fruitful.

The Evolutionary Psychology of the Moral Emotions
The research that our lab has conducted on the moral emotions and how people respond to transgressions has been fascinating. Framing questions related to the moral emotions and social outcomes from an evolutionary psychological perspective helps to focus the nature of research on these topics. Starting with the idea of evolutionary mismatch and Dunbar's number, and integrating ideas related to reciprocal altruism, this research asks questions about human morality, emotions, and social outcomes—all of which connect with the field of positive psychology. Future research can delve further into such questions as: (a) How do reciprocated altruistic acts affect the emotional states of the altruist and the target of the altruist? (b) How do moral emotions such as guilt, shame, and forgiveness play out in a cross-cultural context? And (c) How do social contexts relate to such evolutionarily relevant factors as the tendency to reciprocate altruism?

The Evolutionary Psychology of Happiness and Well-Being
Positive psychologists are sometimes criticized for focusing too much on factors associated with happiness—in spite of relevant contextual factors. The positive evolutionary psychological perspective has much to contribute in this regard. Adding evolutionary concepts allows for an assessment of happiness and well-being in a broader context. Thus, an evolutionary psychologist will not simply ask how we can make people happier—an evolutionary psychologist will first consider the evolutionary origins of emotions such as happiness and will then think about how advancing human happiness now connects with the evolutionary function of happiness. Before starting an all-out program to increase human happiness, the evolutionist asks if unlimited happiness makes sense as a goal, given that all of the negative emotions, such as fear and anxiety, evolved for good evolutionary reasons. The evolutionary perspective gives an important and biologically derived framework for thinking about human emotions and human well-being. Research on this topic can examine such questions as: (a) What factors are universally associated with happiness in humans? (b) What are the physical, social, and psychological effects of increasing positive affect to potentially abnormal levels? And (c) Is there a natural ratio of positive and negative emotions to one another that can be understood in terms of human evolution?

The Evolutionary Psychology of Religion and Spirituality
Thanks to the work of scholars such as Wilson (2002), the conversation about evolution and religion has moved beyond different perspectives on the origins of life. Scholars in evolutionary religious studies have shed light on the nature of humanity by exploring the evolutionary underpinnings of religion. And work in this area connects with the field of positive psychology. Religions across time and place seek to provide guidance on living the good life—and an evolutionary perspective has provided insights into the function of religion. With this in mind, work on the evolutionary functions of religion connects with goals of positive psychology. Research into the evolutionary origins of religion that explicitly takes the goals of positive psychology into account can help address questions of human nature. Sample research questions include: (a) Are there themes that cut across religions that pertain to the pursuit of happiness? (b) What are the proximate goals of religious experiences when it comes to well-being? And (c) What is the role of religion in cultivating healthy organizations?

The Evolutionary Psychology of Community
One of the goals of positive psychology is to shed light on the factors that go into building healthy and effective human communities. An individual exists in multiple communities at different levels at any given time, and taking steps to help increase trust, collaboration, and effectiveness within communities has the capacity to benefit people. You might find yourself in the following communities: your neighborhood; your church; your local volunteer organization (e.g., the Rotary Club), your department at work, a local political action group, etc. Given how communal we are as a species, it is important to understand the factors that lead to well-functioning communities. An evolutionary perspective has much to offer when it comes to the nature of community, including ideas on the origins of our tendency to organize and connect with others beyond kinship. From this perspective, evolutionarily informed research on the topic of community might address such questions as: (a) Are there factors that underlie successful community organization that cut across time and space? (b) Do religious communities differ from non-religious communities in important ways? And can an evolutionary perspective on religion help inform this question? And (c) Based on the work of Robin Dunbar and the idea of small-scale societies, do small-scale community map better onto our psychology compared with large-scale communities?

Positive Evolutionary Psychology and the Broader Human Experience
Positive evolutionary psychology remains a field with many uncharted waters, and we look forward to continuing this approach to the study of human social behaviors. It is important, too, to explore the application of any findings to the broader human experience. We know that people can benefit from dedicating time to cultivating meaningful friendships (Demir & Weitekamp, 2007). For humans, reciprocal altruism is a basic feature of our social ecologies (Trivers, 1985). In such a world, developing genuine friendships is an essential part of our evolutionary heritage. We have evolved to help one another, and we have evolved to have expectations of lasting, reciprocating relationships.

Under modern conditions, we are often surrounded by strangers we've never seen before and will likely never see again (think of being on a train in a foreign country). Under ancestral conditions that typified hominid evolution for thousands and thousands of generations, humans rarely encountered *any* individuals outside their own clan. These clans were stable groups, including both kin and individuals with long-standing relationships with clan members, typically totaling about 150 individuals or fewer (Dunbar, 1992). We know that friendship, love, and connectedness to those around us have always been a part of our lifestyle. Studies across a broad array of platforms have shown that maintaining a loving and connected circle of relationships contributes to greater happiness and better memory into later age when compared to more isolated individuals (Yeh & Liu, 2003). In short, research into the effects of relationship quality and life satisfaction has found that good relationships with others are what keep us happier and healthier. Treating others with kindness, and in a way in which we would hope to be treated ourselves, is a long-standing golden rule that holds merit across cultures.

Another application from the findings of positive evolutionary psychology comes from the outdoors—humans evolved outside in nature. We have an inclination toward things found in nature (McMahan & Cloud, et al., 2016). There is evidence that people are attracted to natural environments that typify the African savanna that our ancestors evolved in (Orions & Heerwagen, 1992). We like to look at trees, animals, and water; of course, all these things had implications for the survival and reproduction of our ancestors, so it makes good sense that we would have evolved to pay attention to these environmental features.

Bottom Line

Positive evolutionary psychology uses Darwinian principles to shed light on the positive emotions and experiences humans have, including the capacity for growth. Like any biological part or function of the human body that has undergone centuries of natural selection, so too have our psychology and the entirety of our emotions. Evolution is nonjudgmental. To discern that it strictly applies to our physical makeup would be both short-sighted and would do a disservice to the human experience.

One of the most tangible examples of human growth from an evolutionary perspective is experienced in the form of resilience. There have been multiple longitudinal studies that show human perseverance and healing after hardship (Werner, 2012). Resilience has a function in human development in that it helps us survive, cope, and move forward (Masten, 2013) on both an individual scale and as a community. Starting new relationships, recovering from trauma, and broad perseverance in life after hardship are ways in which we experience resilience and growth. Similarly, coming together as a collective to restore balance after a natural disaster, or even a pandemic, are examples of experiencing community resilience and growth.

When we reflect back on what our basic scientific goals are—in this case, gaining a better understanding of human behavior and emotions—we can be sure that exploring our own ancestral history provides a solid framework from which to start our research. The pace at which anything in this world evolves is slow enough that we can gain a better understanding of our emotional makeup today by exploring how it came to be. The benefits that our positive socio-emotional makeup may have offered our ancestors can help to inform why our complex range of emotions have remained part of our emotional lexicon. Our understanding of human emotions and growth under modern conditions is better understood using such a bird's-eye, evolutionary approach. And our understanding of the factors that cultivate positive emotional growth, at both the individual and community levels, benefits from applying an evolutionary lens.

Authors' NoteNote that the contributions of the third and fourth author are equal, and the order of appearance was determined alphabetically by last name. Sections of this chapter were adapted from our book *Positive Evolutionary Psychology: Darwin's Guide to Living a Richer Life* (published by Oxford University Press in 2020; used with permission).

References

Acevedo, B. P., Aron, A., Fisher, H. E., & Brown, L. L. (2012). Neural correlates of marital satisfaction and well-being: Reward, empathy, and affect. *Clinical Neuropsychiatry, 9,* 20–31.

Al-Shawaf, L., Conroy-Beam, D., Asao, K., & Buss, D.M. (2015). Human emotions: Anevolutionary psychological perspective. *Emotion Review, 8*(2), 1–14.

Al-Shawaf, L., Lewis, D. M. G., & Buss, D. M. (2018). Sex differences in disgust: Why are women more easily disgusted than men? *Emotion Review, 10*(2), 149–160. https://doi.org/10.1177/1754073917709940

Al-Shawaf, L., Lewis, D. M., Ghossainy, M. E., & Buss, D. M. (2019). Experimentally inducing disgust reduces desire for short-term mating. *Evolutionary Psychological Science, 5,* 267–275. https://doi.org/10.1007/s40806-018-0179-z

Atkins, P. W., Wilson, D. S., Hayes, S. C. (2019). *Prosocial: Using evolutionary science to build productive, equitable, and collaborative groups.* Context Press.

Bateson, M., Brilot, B., & Nettle, D. (2011). Anxiety: An evolutionary approach. *The Canadian Journal of Psychiatry, 56*(12), 707–715.

Baumeister, R. F., & Leary, M. R. (1995). The need to belong: Desire for interpersonal attachments as a fundamental human motivation. *Psychological Bulletin, 117,* 497–529.

Bingham, P. M., & Souza, J. (2009). *Death from a distance and the birth of a humane universe,* BookSurge.

Buss, D. (1989). Sex differences in human mate preferences: Evolutionary hypotheses tested in 37 cultures. *Behavioral and Brain Sciences, 12*(1), 1–14. doi: 10.1017/S0140525X00023992

Buss, D. M. (2017). *The evolution of desire: Strategies of human mating*. New York: Basic Books.
Comparitech.com. (2020). Cyberbullying facts and statistics for 2020. www.comparitech.com/internet-providers/cyberbullying-statistics/
Cohn, M. A., & Fredrickson, B. L. (2010). In search of durable positive psychology interventions: Predictors and consequences of long-term positive behavior change. *The Journal of Positive Psychology, 5*(5), 355–366. doi: 10.1080/17439760.2010.508883
Conoley, C. W., & Conoley, J. C. (2009). *Positive psychology and family therapy*. Wiley.
Cosmides, L., & Tooby, J. (2000). Evolutionary psychology and the emotions. *Handbook of emotions, 2*(2), 91–115.
Crysel, L. C., Crosier, B. S., & Webster, G. D. (2013). The dark triad and risk behavior. *Personality and Individual Differences, 54*(1), 35–40.
Cunha, L. F., Pellanda, L. C., & Tozzi, C. R. (2019). Positive psychology and gratitude interventions: A randomized clinical trial. *Frontiers in Psychology, 10*, 584. doi: 10.3389/fpsyg.2019.00584
Darwin, C. (1872). *The expression of the emotions in man and animals*. Murray.
Dass-Brailsford, P. (2008). After the storm: Recognition, recovery, and reconstruction. *Professional Psychology: Research and Practice, 39*(1), 24–30.
Dawkins, R. ([1976] 1989). *The selfish gene*. Oxford University Press.
De'Jesús, A. R., Cristo, M., Ruel, M., Kruchowy, D., Geher, G., Nolan, K., Santos, A., Wojszynski, C., Alijaj, N., DeBonis, A., Elyukin, N., Huppert, S., Maurer, E., Spackman, B. C., Villegas, A., Widrick, K., & Zezula, V. (2021). Betrayal, outrage, guilt, and forgiveness: The Four Horsemen of the human social-emotional experience. *The Journal of the Evolutionary Studies Consortium, 9*(1), 1–13.
Demır, M., & Weitekamp, L. A. (2007). I am so happy 'cause today I found my friend: Friendship and personality as predictors of happiness. *Journal of Happiness Studies, 8*, 181–211. https://doi.org/10.1007/s10902-006-9012-7
Dunbar, R. I. M. (1992). Neocortex size as a constraint on group size in primates. *Journal of Human Evolution, 22*(6), 469–493.
Figueredo, A. J., Brumbach, B. H., Jones, D. N., Sefcek, J. A., Vasquez, G., & Jacobs, W. J. (2008). Ecological constraints on mating tactics. In G. Geher & G. Miller (Eds.), *Mating intelligence: Sex, relationships, and the mind's reproductive system* (pp. 337–365). Lawrence Erlbaum Associates.
Fisher, H. (1993). *Anatomy of love: A natural history of mating and why we stray*. Ballantine Books.
Fredrickson, B. L. (2001). The role of positive emotions in positive psychology: The broaden-and-build theory of positive emotions. *American Psychologist, 56*(3), 218–226. https://doi.org/10.1037/0003-066X.56.3.218
Geher, G. (2014). *Evolutionary psychology 101*. Springer.
Geher, G., Rolon, V., Holler, R., Baroni, A., Gleason, M., Nitza, E., Sullivan, G., Thomson, G., & Di Santo, J. M. (2019). You're dead to me! The evolutionary psychology of social estrangements and social transgressions. *Current Psychology, 40*, 4516–4530.
Geher, G., & Wedberg, N. (2020). *Positive evolutionary psychology: Darwin's guide to living a richer life*. Oxford University Press.
Gewirth, A. (1984). Rights and virtues. *Analyse & Kritik, 6*(1), 28–48.
Giphart, R., & Van Vugt, M. (2018). *Mismatch*. Robinson.
Guitar, A. E., Glass, D. J., Geher, G., & Suvak, M. K. (2018). Situation-specific emotional states: Testing Nesse and Ellsworth's (2009) model of emotions for situations that arise in goal pursuit using virtual world software. *Current Psychology, 39*, 1245–1259.
Hill, S. E., & Buss, D. M. (2010). Risk and relative social rank: Positional concerns and risky shifts in probabilistic decision-making. *Evolution and Human Behavior, 31*, 219–226.
Hofmann, S. G., Moscovitch, D. A., & Heinrichs, N. (2002). Evolutionary mechanisms of fear and anxiety. *Journal of Cognitive Psychotherapy, 16*(3), 317–330.
Jenkinson, C. E., Dickens, A. P., Jones, K., Thompson-Coon, J., Taylor, R. S., Rogers, M., Bambra, C. L., Lang, I., & Richards, S. H. (2013). Is volunteering a public health intervention? A systematic review and meta-analysis of the health and survival of volunteers. *BMC Public Health, 13*(1), 1–10.
Keller, M. C., & Nesse, R. M. (2006). The evolutionary significance of depressive symptoms: Different life events lead to different depressive symptom patterns. *Journal of Personality and Social Psychology, 91*, 316–330.
Kaufman, S. B. (2020). *Transcend: The new science of self-actualization*. Tarcherperigree.
King, L. A., Hicks, J. A., Krull, J. L., & Del Gaiso, A. K. (2006). Positive affect and the experience of meaning in life. *Journal of Personality and Social Psychology, 90*(1), 179–196. https://doi.org/10.1037/0022-3514.90.1.179
Layous, K., Nelson, S. K., Oberle, E., Schonert-Reichl, K. A., & Lyubomirsky, S. (2012). Kindness counts: Prompting prosocial behavior in preadolescents boosts peer acceptance and well-being. *PLoS ONE, 7*(12), e51380. https://doi.org/10.1371/journal.pone.0051380

Lehman, D. R., Chiu, C.-Y., & Schaller, M. (2004). Psychology and culture. *Annual Review of Psychology, 55*, 689–714.

Maier, S. F., & Seligman, M. E. (1976). Learned helplessness: Theory and evidence. *Journal of Experimental Psychology: General, 105*(1), 3–46.

Marks, I., & Nesse, R. M. (1994). Fear and fitness: An evolutionary analysis of anxiety disorders. *Ethology and Sociobiology, 15*(5–6), 247–261.

Maslow, A. H. (1943). A theory of human motivation. *Psychological Review, 50*(4), 370–396.

Masten, A. S. (2013). Risk and resilience in development. In P. D. Zelazo (Ed.), *The Oxford handbook of developmental psychology*, Vol. 2: *Self and other* (pp. 579–607). Oxford University Press.

McMahan, E. A., Choi, I., Kwon, Y., Choi, J., Fuller, J., & Josh, P. (2016). Some implications of believing that happiness involves the absence of pain: Negative hedonic beliefs exacerbate the effects of stress on well-being. *Journal of Happiness Studies. 17*, 2569–2593.

McMahan, E. A., Cloud, J. M., Josh, P., & Scott, M. (2016). Nature with a human touch: Knowledge of human-induced alteration impacts perceived naturalness and preferences for natural environments. *Ecopsychology, 8*, 54–63.

Montgomery, J. (2010). *The answer model: A new path to healing*. TAM Books.

Nesse, R. M., & Ellsworth, P. C. (2009). Evolution, emotions, and emotional disorders. *American Psychologist, 64*, 129–139.

Nesse, R. M., & Williams, G. C. (1994). *Why we get sick : The new science of Darwinian medicine* (1st ed.). Times Books.

Orians, G., & Heerwagen, J.H. (1992). Evolved responses to landscapes. In J. Barkow, L. Cosmides, & J. Tooby (Eds.), *The adapted mind: Evolutionary psychology and the generation of culture* (pp. 555–579). Oxford University Press.

Rozin, P., & Todd, P. M. (2015). The evolutionary psychology of food intake and choice. In D. M. Buss (Ed.), *The Handbook of evolutionary psychology* (pp. 1–23). Wiley.

Seligman, M. E. P. (2011). *Flourish: A visionary new understanding of happiness and well-being*. Atria Books.

Srivastava, K. (2009). Urbanization and mental health. *Industrial Psychiatry Journal, 18*, 75–76.

Tinbergen, N. (1963) On aims and methods of ethology. *Zeitschrift für Tierpsychologie, 20*, 410–433.

Trivers, R. L. (1971). The evolution of reciprocal altruism. *Quarterly Review of Biology, 46*, 35–57.

Trivers, R. (1985). *Social evolution*. Benjamin/Cummings.

Umberson, D., & Montez, J. K. (2010). Social relationships and health: A flashpoint for health policy. *Journal of Health and Social Behavior, 51* (Suppl), S54–S66.

Watkins, P. (2014). *Positive psychology 101*. Springer.

Werner, E. E. (2012). *What can we learn about resilience from large-scale longitudinal studies?* Springer.

Wilson, D. S. (2002). *Darwin's cathedral: Evolution, religion and the nature of society*. University of Chicago Press.

Wilson, D. S. (2011). *The neighborhood project: Using evolution to improve my city, one block at a time*. Little, Brown.

Yeh, S. C. J., & Liu, Y. Y. (2003). Influence of social support on cognitive function in the elderly. *BMC Health services research, 3*, 1–9.

Zimbardo, P. (2007). The Lucifer effect: Understanding how good people turn evil. *The Journal of The American Medical Association, 298*(11), 1338–1340.

CHAPTER 49

Are There Really So Many Moral Emotions? Carving Morality at Its Functional Joints

Léo Fitouchi, Jean-Baptiste André, and Nicolas Baumard

Abstract

What role do emotions play in moral cognition? Leading accounts argue that a multiplicity of emotions, including guilt, outrage, shame, empathy, and even disgust, play an essential role in moral psychology. Here, this chapter argues that many of these emotions are only superficially associated with moral cognitive contents and adaptive challenges, and that only outrage and guilt rigorously qualify as moral emotions—that is, as computational systems that process distinctively moral representations. Outrage functions to reclaim benefits to which one is rightfully entitled; and guilt to compensate others for violations of one's duties. Shame, by contrast, tracks representations of one's social status, not representations of one's moral obligations. Empathy, similarly, tracks cues of fitness-interdependence—an adaptive challenge that differs from, and in fact often contradicts, the respect of moral obligations. This chapter argues, finally, that both evolutionary rationales and psychological evidence for a role of disgust in moral cognition remain inconclusive for now.

Key Words: morality, emotion, evolutionary psychology, anger, guilt, shame, empathy, moral disgust, cooperation

Introduction: The Messy Landscape of "Moral" Emotions

Evolutionary approaches to psychology have proven fruitful in considering emotions as cognitive adaptations, evolved to coordinate the activity of multiple (e.g., physiological, attentional, motivational) systems in the solution of specific adaptive problems (Al-Shawaf et al., 2016; Al-Shawaf & Lewis, 2017). Fear functions to protect organisms from fitness-costly dangers (Cosmides & Tooby, 2000). Sexual jealousy decreases the probability of infidelity (Buss, 2003), and romantic love facilitates pair-bonding (Fletcher et al., 2015). What about morality?

Morality, too, is undoubtedly emotional: we feel outraged in the face of others' immoral acts, and experience genuine guilt about our own moral shortcomings. Accordingly, moral psychology has departed from its "rationalist" origins (Kohlberg & Kramer, 1969; Piaget, [1932] 1997) to embrace an "affective" perspective stressing the importance of emotional processes in moral cognition (Greene, 2013; Haidt, 2012, 2001, 2007). In this general movement, a large number of emotions have been proposed to play an essential role in moral cognition, as varied as guilt, anger, empathy, contempt, shame, and disgust (Fessler & Haley, 2003; Haidt, 2003; Hutcherson & Gross, 2011; Rozin et al., 1999; Tangney et al., 2007).

This leaves us with an heterogenous bundle of emotions, loosely labeled "moral" because of their co-occurrence with social phenomena we vaguely refer to as "moral." Because it motivates pro-social acts, for example, empathy is often deemed a key component of moral cognition (Flack & De Waal, 2000; Haidt, 2003; Price Tangney et al., 2007). But as many have noted, empathy-driven behavior can be at odds with moral intuitions, such as when we unfairly favor people with whom we empathize more (e.g., kin, friends) in situations where they do not morally deserve more than other individuals (Batson & Ahmad, 2009; Baumard, 2016; Bloom, 2017). This may be because empathy tracks something different than our moral obligations toward others, something that overlaps only partially with behaviors approved by our moral sense. Similarly, while shame is often triggered by a moral violation made public, it sometimes motivates people to further violate moral obligations, such as by lying or hiding their crime, rather than to repair the original violation that triggered shame. Why? Again, this would easily be explained if shame didn't track, by design, the respect of moral obligations, but something else that simply happened to covary with moral behavior. What if, then, many emotions commonly deemed "moral" in fact serve non-moral functions? And, if so, how are these functions distinct from morality?

These examples illustrate the two intertwined problems faced by any attempt to systematize moral emotions:

1. A problem of classification: How to distinguish, in a non-arbitrary and fruitful way, properly moral emotions from merely social ones?
2. A problem of functional specification: What is the specific functional role each emotion plays in moral (or social) cognition?

An evolutionary approach to emotions allows to jointly solve these two problems, as it provides non-arbitrary criteria for classifying emotions that are precisely based on the evolved functional role that each emotion plays in the general cognitive architecture (Al-Shawaf et al., 2016; Al-Shawaf & Lewis, 2017).

The corollary is that a functional picture of moral emotions requires an evolutionary and cognitive theory of morality in general. Here, we build on characterizations of (1) the specific cognitive *content* of moral representations, based on the notion of moral *obligation* (Stanford, 2018; Tomasello, 2020), and (2) the distinctive ultimate *function* of moral representations, rooted in the evolution of human cooperation (André et al., 2022; Baumard et al., 2013b). These specifications allow us to more clearly distinguish, among the emotions seemingly involved in human moral life (e.g., empathy, shame, disgust, guilt, anger), those that serve a properly moral function from those that are merely social.

In particular, we make the somewhat deflationary argument that only guilt and indignation ("moral anger") can be rigorously characterized as moral emotion. They indeed, by design, manipulate distinctively moral representations of individuals' *duties* and *rights* in the context of cooperative interactions, and adjust behavior in accordance to what cooperative partners "owe each other." By contrast, shame functions to manipulate representations of one's *social status*, and empathy to motivate pro-social behavior toward individuals with whom one's fitness is *interdependent*, which is different from respecting moral obligations. Finally, while disgust has often been proposed as a generator of, or emotional reaction to moral representations, we argue that both evolutionary rationales and psychological evidence for this claim remain inconclusive for now.

Situating Emotions in Human Morality
The Cognitive Specificity of Moral Representations

In psychological research, morality is often conflated with pro-social, other-regarding preferences or with the disapproval of harm and selfishness (e.g., Haidt, 2012; Schein & Gray, 2018). This leads researchers to define moral emotions as psychological mechanisms that simply motivate pro-social behavior or condemn selfishness. Haidt (2003), for example, defines moral emotions as "those emotions that are linked to the interests or welfare either of society as a whole or at least of persons other than the judge or agent" (p. 853). Evolutionary psychologists, similarly, seem to define moral emotions as cognitive mechanisms that recalibrate people's "welfare trade-off ratio"—that is, the value that people place on the welfare of other individuals relative to their own welfare, thus determining their disposition for pro-social behavior toward the target (Tooby et al., 2008).

While morality is manifestly about providing others with benefits, and avoiding imposing costs on them, it is characterized, at the cognitive level, by a distinctive type of mental representation that is not well captured in terms of pro-social desires, other-regarding preferences, or welfare trade-off ratios.

Moral representations are, strictly speaking, not about *desires* or *preferences*—however pro-social they may be—but about *obligations* or *duties*. Moral representations are *prescriptive* mental states, representing certain behaviors as what people *ought* to do, even if they don't *desire* to do so. In other words, the content of moral representations is a kind of desire-independent, self-imposed *obligation* that one has toward someone else (Tomasello, 2020), and which exists in virtue of a higher, preference-independent moral demand (Stanford, 2018). This intuitive notion of obligation represents a precise quantity of benefits that we *ought* to provide others because they *deserve* it, or, equivalently, because they are *rightfully* entitled to it. A common set of terms in natural moral language points toward this precise quantity of benefits that constitutes the content of moral obligations: people *deserve* X; i.e., I *owe* them X; i.e., they have a *right* to X; i.e., I have the *duty* to provide them X.

Moral representations, moreover, have the puzzling specificity of depicting obligations independently of my immediate incentives or my current bargaining position: even if I don't want to give them X, because, for example, I am not immediately incentivized to do so, the obligation to do so remains. Even if I actually *refuse* to provide these benefits, the obligation remains: I simply *violated* it, and my behavior is accordingly tagged as morally *wrong* (see Darwall, 2010).

Importantly, morality so understood—as the cognitive calculation of, and behavioral conformity to, "what we owe to each other" (Scanlon, 2000)—is different from the mere motivation for being pro-social, the latter of which can emerge from psychological mechanisms whose function does not involve moral obligations. We can *desire* to provide benefits to some individuals (e.g., kin, friends) without this being aligned with moral obligations, as in the case of morally condemned nepotism (see Baumard, 2016; Boehm, 2012).

The Ultimate Function of Moral Representations

Where, then, do these specific representations of moral obligations ultimately come from? What fitness-relevant regularities do they encode?

Researchers have long argued that morality likely evolved as a cognitive adaptation to the challenges of cooperation recurrent in human social life (Alexander, 1987; Baumard et al.,

2013b; Boehm, 2012; Curry et al., 2019; Haidt, 2012; Tomasello, 2016; Trivers, 1971). Many have proposed that the ultimate function of moral behavior is to secure a good reputation as a cooperator, in order to attract cooperative partners (Alexander, 1987; André & Baumard, 2011; Baumard et al., 2013b; Debove, André, et al., 2015; Debove, Baumard, et al., 2015), or to avoid the costs of the punishment and social control imposed on uncooperative individuals (Boehm, 2012; Wrangham, 2019).

Integrating the above logics, a more general way of phrasing it is the following (see André et al., 2022). In a positive-sum world offering the opportunity of many cooperative interactions (in resource production, collective defense, parental investment, limitations of interpersonal conflict, communication of reliable information, etc.), individuals face two selective pressures. The first is to ensure that I invest only in cooperative interactions that *pay off*, i.e., that provide me more benefits than they cost (including opportunity costs)—otherwise, I would have been better off doing something else (e.g., forage alone, choose other partners, extort benefits by force).

The second selective pressure results from the first: because others only invest in cooperative interactions that pay off, in order to *attract* their cooperation, I have to ensure that cooperation pays more than it costs for them as well. As with any investment, the costliness of a cooperative investment depends critically on its opportunity costs. This means that I have to make sure that, for my partners, investing in a cooperative interaction with me pays more than *the best alternative option* they could have adopted instead of cooperating with me (André et al., 2022). If it does not, people are simply better off doing something else. And this includes *lots* of alternative options they could have adopted instead of cooperating with me, such as not cooperating at all (e.g., forage alone), defecting in the same interaction (Axelrod & Hamilton, 1981; Trivers, 1971), choosing other partners (Baumard et al., 2013b), ostracizing me (Boehm, 1999), or extorting benefits by force at a cost to me (Boehm, 1999, 2012; Clutton-Brock & Parker, 1995; Wrangham, 2019).

As a result, these two symmetrical selective pressures constrain cooperative interactions to be *mutually beneficial*—as if regulated by a *contract* agreed upon with others: in order to enjoy the benefits generated by cooperative surpluses, I should both ensure than my cooperative investments are more beneficial than they are costly for me, *and simultaneously* ensure that my partners, too, do not afterward "regret" having cooperated with me (André et al., 2022). In other words, I must ensure that cooperation offers a net benefit for them, too.

A likely possibility is thus that, in the human mind, a dedicated information-processing mechanism flexibly calculates, based on the costs (including opportunity costs) invested by each partner in each particular cooperative interaction, the *rights* and *duties* of each individual (i.e., the "terms of the contract"). The resulting representations should specify what I *deserve*, but also what I *owe* to others. In other words, they should specify, as moral representations actually do, "what we owe to each other" (Scanlon, 2000) for cooperation to be mutually beneficial. Moreover, even if people don't have an immediate incentive to honor these duties, for example because they enjoy a temporary strategic advantage on a resource, they should, in order to further attract others' cooperative investments, feel *obligated* to respect their partners' interests despite the temptation to exploit them. In other words, this mechanism leads to the distinctive phenomenology of moral obligation (see Tomasello, 2020).

This enables us to give a precise functional content to moral obligations, beyond vague formulations such as "behaving cooperatively," "being fair," "not being selfish," or "not harming others." The precise amount of benefits morally owed to others should at least compensate the total cost they invested in the cooperative interaction, including the opportunity cost of having renounced their best alternative behavioral option (André et al., 2022).

This fits the actual way in which the mind computes moral obligations. For example, children and adults intuit, across cultures, that the amount of benefits owed to others is proportional to the effort they invested in the cooperative interaction (i.e., direct costs) and their talent or skills (i.e., their opportunity costs; André et al., 2022; Baumard et al., 2011, 2013b; Starmans et al., 2017) . More generally, most moral wrongs condemned across cultures appear as unfair advancements of one's interest at the expense of mutual net benefit. For example, adultery, in the context of the cooperative interaction constituting pair-bonding (Gurven et al., 2009), amounts to enjoying the benefits of one's partner's reproductive resources and parental investment, while not repaying, by oneself remaining faithful and parentally investing, the opportunity costs they paid through their fidelity. Betrayal of one's in-group amounts to failing to repay to others, through the benefits brought by my own loyalty, the costs they have paid by not betraying me, that is, by forgoing the opportunity of cooperation with rival coalitions (Fitouchi et al., 2023b). Regarding duties of deference to authority, recent research suggest that leadership is fundamentally about a mutually beneficial division of labor in which leaders provide computational, decision-making services to followers (Hagen & Garfield, 2019). Accordingly, authority appears as morally *legitimate* only when it works for the common good: if leaders take advantage of followers' obedience to selfishly advance their interests at others' expense, people do not feel any duty to obey them (e.g., Boehm, 1999; Saxe, 2022) and withdraw their cooperative investment from the relationship, such as by not obeying, choosing another leader, or imposing reputational or material sanctions (e.g., Boehm, 1999; Hagen & Garfield, 2019).

Moral Emotions in this Context

This detour through the evolution of morality allows us to more clearly articulate the role of emotional systems in the general economy of moral cognition.

WHAT DO MORAL EMOTIONS DO?

A first question pertains to the role of emotions in general in moral cognition. It has often been argued that emotions have a *constitutive* role in morality, i.e., that some behaviors are intuited as morally right or wrong *because* of the emotional processes accompanying their perception (Frank, 1988; Greene, 2013; Haidt, 2001; Nichols, 2002).

The very existence of moral emotions, however, seems dependent on a capacity for moral *judgment* in the first place. What makes an emotion moral is the moral character of the representational content it manipulates: indignation is anger *at injustice*; guilt is regret *of one's immoral behavior*. In other words, something must tag a behavior as unjust or immoral for "moral" emotions to be triggered in the first place. In line with this idea, the overall empirical

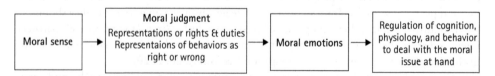

Figure 49.1. Hypothesized general structure of moral cognition. In this perspective, the moral emotions are not the cause of moral representations. Moral representations are instead generated by a mechanism of moral judgment (the "moral sense"), evolved to calculate what cooperative partners owe each other in the context of cooperative interactions. The function of moral emotions is then to orchestrate cognition, physiology, and behavior in accordance with the content of these moral representations.

evidence for an essential role of emotions in moral judgment is weak (Avramova & Inbar, 2013; Landy & Goodwin, 2015; McAuliffe, 2019).

Accordingly, we posit that there is a cognitive system that first generates moral representations, which moral emotions then *process* rather than secrete in the first place (see Figure 49.1). In the evolutionary perspective sketched above, this system of moral judgment (the "moral sense") evolved as a barometer of what each partner *owes* and *deserves* in the context of cooperative interactions. It calculates, based on the costs (including opportunity costs) invested by each partner in entering the interaction, what each partner should receive for cooperation to provide a mutual net benefit.

This is where moral emotions enter the picture: these representations of moral rights and duties, generated by the moral sense, must then be processed by computational systems that orchestrate physiology, cognition, and behavior adaptively in accordance with the specific information conveyed by moral representations—that is, by moral emotions (see Figure 49.1).

WHICH EMOTIONS SERVE A MORAL FUNCTION?

This functional definition of moral emotions provides a principled way to distinguish between properly moral and merely social emotions. In the remainder of this chapter, we argue that only indignation and guilt satisfy the above conditions. While shame has often been considered, alongside guilt, as a key self-conscious moral emotion, only guilt appears to manipulate distinctively moral representations of rights and duties, to adjust behavior to fit moral contracts (see the following section). We then consider the case of empathy, arguing that its interdependence-based pro-social motivation operates independently of moral representations, excluding it from a strictly defined set of moral emotions. We finally turn to other-condemning emotions, arguing that only indignation ("moral anger"), and not disgust, functions to orchestrate cognition and behavior in the face of others' moral violations.

Protecting One's Social Status vs. Doing One's Duty: Guilt (Not Shame) as the Main Self-Conscious Moral Emotion

An often-mentioned class of moral emotions is the *self-conscious* emotions, i.e., emotions that react to moral violations that one has committed. Shame and guilt have been widely considered as the key self-conscious moral emotions (e.g., Haidt, 2003; Prinz & Nichols, 2010; Sheikh & Janoff-Bulman, 2010; Tangney et al., 2007). However, while guilt computes distinctively moral representations of obligations, by disincentivizing (ex ante), and motivating to compensate (ex post), the violation of a moral obligation, shame seems to serve a different function. Shame works to prevent losses of social status (or "social devaluation") (Sznycer, 2019), a function that does not necessarily overlap with, and sometimes even directly contradicts, the fulfilment of moral contracts.

In many species, including humans, status hierarchies define individuals' relative access to contested resources (e.g., food, mates), so that gaining status and avoiding status losses is a key adaptive problem (von Rueden et al., 2011; von Rueden & Jaeggi, 2016). Traits contributing to social status mainly pertain to abilities to inflict costs (e.g., physical or coalition-derived formidability) and to confer benefits (e.g., competence, intelligence, knowledge, attractiveness, generosity; Durkee et al., 2019; von Rueden & Jaeggi, 2016). In this context, adaptations for avoiding losses of social status are particularly beneficial to secure the benefits contingent on one's social value. Recent work strongly suggests that shame precisely functions to limit social devaluation by others, by disincentivizing behaviors that lead to social devaluation, limiting the spread of socially devaluing information, and mitigating the costs of status loss (e.g., by motivating hiding from others, denial of the socially devaluing action, or displays of remorse or submission; Durkee et al., 2019; Sznycer et al., 2016; Szyncer et al., 2018).

This social function is different from the properly moral function of guilt, as suggested by their respective cognitive features.

First, avoiding status devaluation requires being sensitive to others' perceptions of many more traits of the self than merely moral ones. The disposition to repay others' cooperative investments, as component of the willingness to confer them benefits, is indeed only one trait, *among many non-moral others*, that brings social status. In line with this idea, guilt is mainly triggered by moral transgressions, but not by non-moral threats to one's social status (e.g., incompetence, unattractiveness) (Smith et al., 2002). By contrast, in line with a status-management, non-moral function of shame, shame tracks *all types* of threats of social devaluation across cultures: it is typically activated by behaviors that are morally irrelevant yet indicate a low potential to impose costs on or to benefit others, such as being dumb, unattractive, incompetent, physically weak, or not socially influential (Durkee et al., 2019; Sznycer et al., 2016; Tracy & Matsumoto, 2008).

Second, an important reason for the confusion over the moral status of shame is that shame and guilt sometimes co-occur. Acting immorally (which elicits guilt) is one path, among others, to social devaluation (which elicits shame). As a result, immoral actions often generate not only guilt, but also shame, leading to the understandable inference that shame is a moral emotion. But a crucial point here is that *even in these cases, shame is sensitive to what is socially devaluing in immoral actions, whereas guilt is sensitive to what is properly immoral in immoral actions*, namely the gap between what one owed to others and the benefits one actually provided them (or the costs one imposed on them).

In other words, shame processes representations of one's *social value* in the eyes of others, rather than properly moral representations of one's *obligations* toward others. In line with this idea, experimental evidence shows that wrongdoing in itself (i.e., a gap between one's moral obligations and one's actual behavior) is neither necessary nor sufficient to elicit shame: the simple detection that others *falsely believe* that we behaved immorally, when we know we are innocent, is sufficient to elicit shame (Robertson et al., 2018). And conversely, low contributions to a public good on one's part do not independently predict the intensity of shame: only cues that others have devalued us (e.g., through social exclusion) do (Robertson et al., 2018).

Third, regarding their respective outputs, consistent with a properly moral function of guilt, guilt-proneness predicts a greater likelihood of honoring cooperative obligations (Cohen et al., 2013) and a lower likelihood of criminal recidivism (Tangney et al., 2014). After a moral failure, guilt motivates reparative actions, such as apology, confession, acceptance of responsibility, and compensation for the harm done (de Hooge et al., 2007; de Hooge et al., 2011; Ketelaar & Au, 2003; Tangney et al., 2007). These outcomes are all well-suited to reduce the gap between one's actual behavior and what others deserve. By contrast, shame is only contingently associated to cooperative behavior (de Hooge et al., 2007) and can even lead to immoral behaviors, such as aggression, lying, or hiding our crime (e.g., Elison et al., 2014; Gausel et al., 2016). These behaviors are geared toward minimizing status loss, not toward reducing the gap between what we owe others and what we actually offered them.

And this, importantly, seems to be a feature rather than a bug, due to the following logic. There are several paths to social status. Sometimes, when we depend on others' cooperation, rehabilitating one's social value can be done through cooperative behaviors (e.g., compensation, apologies, submissive displays), upregulating others' valuation of ourselves *as a cooperative*

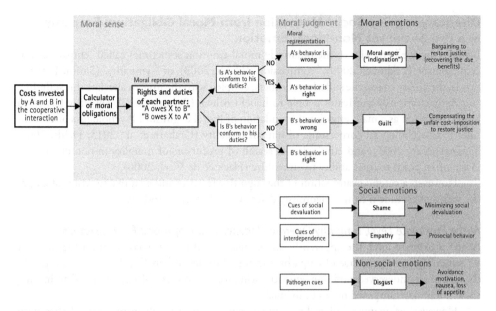

Figure 49.2. Distinction between moral and non-moral emotions based on the different types of representation they process. Moral emotions process moral representations, produced by the moral sense. The moral sense calculates the rights and duties of each cooperative partner, on the basis of the costs that each has invested in the cooperative interaction. These costs must be reimbursed for cooperation to be mutually net beneficial. If A provides B with fewer benefits than he owes her, his behavior is tagged as morally wrong, and triggers in B the emotion of moral anger. Moral anger orchestrates physiology, cognition, and behavior to bargain with A, in order to regain the benefits to which she is rightfully entitled. If B provides A with less benefits than she owes him, she feels guilt. Guilt functions to motivate B to provide A with more benefits, in order to compensate the gap between her initial behavior and what she morally owed to A. By contrast, non-moral emotions such as shame, empathy, or disgust do not compute distinctively moral representations, but rather, respectively, cues of social devaluation, interdependence, or pathogenic content.

partner. Accordingly, in such cases, shame seems to motivate compensation and cooperation (de Hooge et al., 2008; de Hooge et al., 2010; Tangney et al., 2014). In other cases, however, the most effective way to regain social status will be the competitive bargaining, cost-imposing route. Accordingly, in these cases, shame adaptively switches motivations toward competitive tendencies (e.g., anger; Sell, 2017), incentivizing others to value one's welfare through aggressive means that signal one's bargaining power (see, e.g., Elison et al., 2014).

In other words, even when shame leads us to conform to moral obligations, it does this not because it tracks moral obligations per se, but because it tracks one's social value, which *sometimes happens to be conditioned on one's disposition to act morally*. Stated differently, when it motivates pro-social behavior, shame does so not out of a genuinely moral sense of obligation, as guilt does ("It was my duty to do X, and I failed"), but out of an extrinsic, Machiavellian motivation for the social valuation that the moral behavior will bring ("I should do X because otherwise others won't respect me") (Sperber & Baumard, 2012).

In sum, while guilt and shame are widely considered the two key moral self-conscious emotions, it seems that only guilt, and not shame, operates on distinctively moral representations of obligations (see Figure 49.2). Guilt, but not shame, orchestrates cognition and behavior in the solution of a distinctively moral challenge—compensating one's violations of others' rights.

Disentangling Pro-Social Motivation from Moral Obligation: Empathy as a Pro-Social yet Non-Moral Emotion

By empathy, we here refer to the putatively moral emotion sometimes called "empathic concern" (Batson & Ahmad, 2009), "compassion" (Haidt, 2003), or "sympathy" (Smith, 1759)—that is, the ability to feel the suffering of others, coupled with the urge to alleviate this suffering.

As it vicariously motivates people to benefit others (Batson, 2017), empathy has often been considered as a main emotional foundation of moral cognition. Psychologists often consider it a psychological cornerstone of human morality (Graham et al., 2013; Haidt, 2003; Tangney et al., 2007), and ethologists in search of precursors of morality in nonhuman primates often point to their ability to empathize (Flack & de Waal, 2000).

However, a careful examination of the cognitive features and adaptive function of empathy seems to exclude it from a rigorously defined set of moral emotions.

At the Proximate Level, Empathy Operates Independently of Moral Representations

At the proximate level, the apparently moral character of empathy comes from the frequent yet superficial co-occurrence of empathy and moral duties to benefit others. For example, in the face of an undeserved suffering, empathy will motivate pro-social actions aimed at limiting these unfair costs imposed on an individual.

However, as many scholars have noted, empathy-driven altruism often clashes with human moral intuitions (Batson & Ahmad, 2009; Baumard, 2016; Bloom, 2017; A. Smith, 1822). In particular, empathy-induced altruism can lead to actions judged as immoral, often by introducing unfair partiality. For example, participants who were induced to feel empathy for a terminally ill child were more likely to give him priority in the allocation of end-of-life care over children who needed such care more urgently. Participants themselves judged that this decision was less fair and less moral than allocation decisions not biased by their empathy-induced altruism (Batson et al., 1995; for similar results in other settings, see Batson et al., 1999; Batson & Ahmad, 2009). Such dissociations suggest that empathy-driven pro-social motivation is independent, at the cognitive level, from the calculations produced by people's moral sense.

Similarly, in economic games where participants are asked to compensate other individuals for their bad outcomes, empathic concern is a better predictor than moral outrage of helping behaviors directed toward individuals who did *not* suffer an injustice. By contrast, in conditions where the target's bad outcome was due to an injustice (e.g., a partner's refusal to reciprocate), and was thus *undeserved*, moral outrage was a better predictor than empathic concern of directing help toward the cheated person (Thulin & Bicchieri, 2016). Here again, empathy appears sensitive to people's suffering *regardless of the deservingness of that suffering*—that is, regardless of the representations of rights and duties generated by the moral sense. By contrast, the above examples suggest that moral outrage is sensitive to individuals' suffering only when that suffering is undeserved.

Empathy thus appears functionally different from properly moral emotions, in the sense that it does not operate on moral representational content: it motivates pro-social behavior independently of, and sometimes even *contrary* to, the representation of moral rights and obligations generated by the moral sense. The perception of signs of suffering and distress in other individuals seems to directly generate an urge to care for their welfare, without resorting to the representation of a moral duty to do so, underpinned by the intuition that they *deserve* this help (see Figure 49.2).

But if empathy is not a moral emotion, what is it for?

Empathy and Fitness Interdependence
Many scholars have argued that the evolutionary origins of empathy lie in the parental care of offspring, based in kin selection (Decety et al., 2016; Tomasello, 2016). In some species, especially humans, empathic concern extends beyond the circle of genetic relatives to friends and collaborative partners (de Waal, 2008). This suggests that empathy evolved not only for kin-altruism, but for the more general adaptive challenge of fitness interdependence, of which genetic relatedness is just a particular instance (Tomasello, 2016).

Two organisms are (positively) interdependent if an increase in the fitness of one generates an increase in the fitness of the other (Aktipis et al., 2018; Roberts, 2005). In such a context, individuals have a "stake" in the fitness of their partners, which makes cooperative behaviors adaptive when their costs are outweighed by the cooperator's stake in the recipient's benefits (Roberts, 2005). One particular way of generating fitness interdependence is genetic relatedness. But on top of that, cooperative interactions between non-kin generate another type of interdependence: if A and B are, say, hunting partners, and B breaks her leg, A has an interest in helping B to recover quickly, as his fitness depends on B's efficiency in their future cooperative interactions. As a result, it is advantageous for emotions to promote caring for the welfare of individuals with whom one is interdependent, as caring for their welfare leads to increases in one's own fitness.

Several lines of evidence suggest that empathy is one such mechanism. The intensity of empathic feelings is typically modulated by cues of fitness interdependence. In humans and other primates, empathy is amplified by familiarity and social closeness (Preston & de Waal, 2002). For example, children display more empathy-related behaviors toward their mother than toward an unfamiliar individual, and feel more empathy toward in-group rather than out-group members (Davidov et al., 2013; Masten et al., 2010). Activity in the pain neural network is enhanced when individuals view or imagine their loved ones in pain compared with strangers (Cikara et al., 2011). And studies report a modulation of empathic response as a function of racial group membership (Xu et al., 2009), which the mind may consider a proxy of coalitional affiliation (Kurzban et al., 2001).

DISENTANGLING MORALITY FROM FITNESS INTERDEPENDENCE
How is interdependence-based empathy different from the adaptive challenges linked to moral rights and duties, to *obligations* to benefit others and ideas of *deservingness* of receiving benefits?

Crucially, morality functions to ensure the mutually beneficial character of cooperation when the latter is not guaranteed, that is, when individuals have a short-term incentive to cheat by benefiting from others' cooperative investment without repaying it in the future—hence the need for mental representations of an implicit "contract" (André et al., 2022). In other words, representations of moral rights and obligations function to regulate interactions in which I benefit from cooperation only *conditionally on my partners' response* to my cooperative behavior (André et al., 2022). They regulate interactions in which reaping the surplus benefits of cooperation requires the individual to willingly weaken his strategic position, by putting himself in a situation of vulnerability to exploitation, and trust that his partner will not succumb to the short-term temptation to take advantage of this vulnerability—that is, trust that his partner will respect the implicit "contract."

By contrast, the fitness benefits of prosocial behaviors based on interdependence are *not* conditioned on the recipient's responses to the actor's cooperative behavior (Roberts, 2005; Tomasello, 2016). When individuals protect their mates, friends, or children—at least when they do so in proportion to the fitness-stake they have in them—they *automatically* benefit from this pro-social behavior. As there is no short-term incentive to cheat, there is no need for representations encoding a morally legitimate quantity of benefits that each individual ought to receive independently of people's spontaneous desires. And accordingly, empathy does not feel like a "constraint" imposed on us, demanding us to go against our selfish will: instead, it feels like a spontaneous urge to help (see Tomasello, 2020).

As an illustration, consider two individuals, A (a female) and B (a male), who are in a committed long-term pair-bond. Generally, their fitness interdependence is high: if A is hurt, B does not benefit by letting his partner incur damage to her embodied capital on which his own reproductive success depends. Accordingly, high levels of empathy-driven spontaneous pro-sociality will motivate him to care for her welfare. The fitness payoff of B's helping is to a large extent *not conditioned* on A's response to the benefits he provides her—fitness interdependence does the job.

By contrast, in other respects, A's and B's interests are not totally aligned. In particular, they both have a short-term interest to cheat their partner by engaging in extra-pair mating. By mutually guaranteeing sexual fidelity to each other, they both pay the short-term opportunity costs of forgoing alternative, extra-pair reproductive encounters (see Gangestad & Simpson, 2000). They do this in order to reap the larger, future benefits of sustained cooperation in committed pair-bonds (see Gurven et al., 2009). Yet, in order to reap this long-term cooperative benefit by remaining faithful, they place themselves in a situation of vulnerability to exploitation: the benefits of B's sexual fidelity are largely conditioned on A repaying this investment by also not cheating. It is precisely this kind of cooperation dilemma, we argue, that the moral sense is designed to deal with (André et al., 2022). It does so by representing individuals' moral *rights* (here, to fidelity), that individuals *deserve* because of the costs they invested for the *common good* (here, the long-term mutual benefits of committed pair-bonds), that other individuals thus have a *duty* to honor, and that it would be morally *wrong* to violate (here, through adultery).

This allows us to grasp why emotions that promote interdependence-based pro-sociality, such as empathy, and properly moral emotions are functionally distinct mechanisms. The function of respecting moral obligations is not to benefit others to the extent that their welfare immediately makes positive contributions to *my* fitness, but rather to the extent necessary to make *them* better off cooperating with me rather than doing something else (e.g., defecting, choosing another partner, using a power struggle to their benefit). By respecting my partners' rights in such a way, I am both incentivizing them to continue investing in our cooperative relationship and securing a good moral reputation, which attracts cooperative investments from other partners.

Accordingly, interdependence-based pro-sociality and cooperative behavior out of moral obligation do not necessarily overlap: in the same way as my personal, selfish interest can conflict with moral obligations, my interdependence-mediated "selfish" desires to see my kin and friends favored over equally deserving individuals can conflict with moral obligations (see Batson & Ahmad, 2009).

Moral Indignation (Not Disgust) as the Main Other-Condemning Moral Emotion
Moral Indignation Is for Enforcing Moral Contracts
Whereas morality is about the mutually beneficial management of cooperative interactions, anger probably initially evolved in the context of competitive, zero-sum interactions, as a bargaining mechanism for deterring future aggression through retaliation (Fessler, 2009; McCullough et al., 2013), or resolving conflicts of interests in favor of the angry individual, by coercing others to give the angry person more benefits (Sell, 2017; Sell et al., 2009).

Anger is indeed typically triggered by an insufficient delivery of benefits to the self *relative to its bargaining power*: across cultures, anger's intensity is predicted by the perception that the target does not value the angry individual's welfare enough relative to his own (Sell et al., 2017), and individuals with greater bargaining power (e.g., physical strength, coalition support, attractiveness) are more prone to anger (Sell et al., 2009). Its outputs typically instantiate two bargaining tactics: threatening to inflict costs (e.g., through physical or coalition-derived formidability) or withhold benefits (Fessler, 2009; Sell et al., 2009; Sell et al., 2017).

In the human species, a peculiar form of anger appears in moral life, variously called "moral outrage," "indignation," or "righteous anger." Accordingly, anger has widely been considered one of the main moral emotions (Fessler & Haley, 2003; Haidt, 2003; Hutcherson & Gross, 2011; Rozin et al., 1999; Tangney et al., 2007). A likely possibility is that moral indignation evolved by recycling useful design features of "competitive" anger for use in moral situations in which considerations of people's rights and duties in cooperative interactions are paramount.

EVOLVING MORAL INDIGNATION FROM COMPETITIVE ANGER

In cooperative interactions, there is always the possibility that cooperative partners will not respect cooperative obligations—that is, provide me with fewer benefits than the costs I invested in the interaction. This would violate the requirement of mutual beneficence. In this situation, an emotion motivating the recruitment of bargaining mechanisms to regain the deserved-but-missing benefits would be useful, and there is manifest fit between this requirement and the bargaining-oriented design of anger.

An emotion solving this moral problem should be slightly distinct from "raw" competitive anger with respect to some of its computational features. Regarding its triggers, it should be sensitive to the *wrong* or *injustice* that I have suffered, i.e., to the gap between benefits actually provided by others and the benefits they morally *owe* me. This should correspond, at the ultimate level, to the quantity of benefits I should receive to repay the costs I invested in the cooperative interaction. This "fairness gap" is distinct from the gap to which "competitive anger" is sensitive, namely the gap between the benefits actually received and the benefits that my *bargaining power* (e.g., formidability) could allow me to *extort* from others by brute power struggle or cost infliction. The two emotions should also have distinct outputs: competitive anger motivates me to obtain as many benefits as I can within the constraints of my ability to impose costs on others. By contrast, moral indignation should only motivate me to take back the *limited* quantity of benefits that I morally deserve and have been denied. Demanding more than these due benefits would lead *me* to appear as a cheater, with negative consequences for my reputation.

However, in existing empirical studies, it is difficult to precisely distinguish indignation as a moral emotion from competitive anger functioning for raw power struggle (i.e., without concern for partners' rights). Economic games experiments, for example, consistently report "anger" as a key emotional response to unfair distributions of benefits, motivating the punishment of free-riders (Dawes et al., 2007; Fehr & Gächter, 2002; Molleman et al., 2019; Nelissen & Zeelenberg, 2009). But it is unclear whether these negative emotional reactions to unfairness emerge from a moral motivation to restore justice, or instead from non-moral, competitive retaliation aimed at deterring future cost infliction (McCullough et al., 2013; O'Mara Kunz et al., 2011).

Still, some evidence suggests that anger operates on moral representations of rights and duties in the context of cooperative interactions, and at least partly seeks the satisfaction of the moral rights of the harmed individual, rather than a raw retaliation without concern for what each party deserves.

First, in developmental studies where a child takes more than his fair share, or inefficiently plays his role in a cooperative interaction, other children's resentful protest is expressed through the *normative* language typically deriving from moral representations (e.g., "One must do X"; "It's not fair"), rather than in terms of personal preferences or desires (e.g., "I don't like when you do X") (Kachel et al., 2018; Rakoczy et al., 2016). In other words, children's protest seem aimed at "mak[ing] (the partner) sensible, that the person whom he injured did not deserve to be treated in that manner" (Engelmann & Tomasello, 2019, p. 458, quoting Adam Smith, 1759, pp. 95–96). Moreover, this does not seem to trigger a competitive dynamic: the wronged child then trusts her partner to decide to do the right thing, which he often does by re-equalizing the payoffs (Engelmann & Tomasello, 2019).

Second, people's intuitions about punishment, emotionally underpinned by indignation, include a strong requirement of retributive *justice*, that fits the design expected from a system functioning to ensure a fair distribution of the costs and benefits between cooperative partners. When assigning punishment, people want it to conform to "*just deserts*": the costs imposed on the culprit should be *proportionate* to the harm done to the victim, in order to restore a fair balance of the interests between individuals (Baumard, 2010; Baumard et al., 2013b; Carlsmith & Darley, 2008; Darley & Pittman, 2003; Fitouchi & Singh, 2023; Osgood, 2017). Tellingly, the developmental trajectory of childrens' retributive justice intuitions parallels the trajectory of their symmetrical *distributive* justice intuitions, prescribing the fair way to share collectively produced goods (Smith & Warneken, 2016), which are clearly impregnated with moral intuitions about what each partner deserves (Corbit et al., 2017; Engelmann & Tomasello, 2019).

IS THERE SUCH A THING AS THIRD-PARTY MORAL OUTRAGE?

A third key element put forward for the moral character of anger is its capacity to be triggered by a moral violation of which one is not the direct victim—often called "third party moral outrage" (e.g., Haidt, 2003; Fessler & Haley, 2003; Tangney et al., 2007). Various functions have been ascribed to this emotional reaction and the "third-party" punishment that flows from it, such as an evolutionarily altruistic enforcement of cooperation favored by group selection (Henrich & Boyd, 2001) or individual-level reputational fitness benefits from a credible signal of one's cooperative quality (Barclay, 2005; Jordan et al., 2016).

While the existence of such a moral emotion is often taken for granted, we note that it is unclear if there really is such a thing as a truly *third*-party moral outrage—that is, an anger-like emotional reaction to an immoral action whose cost to oneself is *really totally zero*. Surely, there exists such a thing as a moral *judgment* of actions that do not affect us at all, i.e., a representation of that action as violating a moral obligation. The function of such a third-party moral judgment would likely be to encode that future cooperation with the moral violator should be avoided. But are the bargaining-oriented physiological, cognitive, and behavioral mechanisms of anger really triggered by third-party moral violations?

Ethnographic evidence suggests that in many small-scale societies, in the context of which human cognition is often assumed to have evolved, third parties are often indifferent to moral violations toward an unrelated individual: when outrage and punishment are directed toward moral violators, it is typically administered by the aggrieved parties themselves (Baumard, 2010; Black, 2000; Evans-Pritchard, 1969; Fitouchi & Singh, 2023; Wiessner, 2005).

A first possibility is that what sometimes appears as third-party outrage is in fact only anger at costs imposed on an individual with whom one is interdependent (e.g., kin, friends), so that the fitness cost toward oneself is real, albeit indirect. In line with this idea, psychological evidence from modern populations suggests that people do not punish and feel limited outrage toward violations harming individuals with whom they are not interdependent (Pedersen et al., 2018; Pederson et al., 2020), or with whom they have not been induced to empathize (Batson et al., 2007).

Another possibility is that outraged individuals often misleadingly appear as third parties when they are in fact second parties, involved in a larger cooperative interaction in which the moral violation took place. For example, a moral violation such as knocking down a pedestrian in the street can misleadingly appear as wronging only one person (this particular pedestrian), while it probably also constitutes a cheating behavior in a more general contract involving all members of the society. There is indeed, in modern societies, a moral contract whereby people cooperate by paying attention to pedestrians *in general* while driving, so that everyone mutually benefits from safely walking in the street. In this context, injuring a pedestrian because of unsafe driving amounts to violating a more general moral obligation toward all other members of the society, potentially explaining the moral outrage of apparently "third" but in fact second parties. In line with this idea, when people are collectively outraged and punish deviants in small-scale societies, they seem to do so because the target's behavior, even if apparently harming only some individuals, is perceived as dangerous or harmful for themselves too (Baumard & Liénard, 2011; Boehm, 1999, 2012).

Disgust Is (Probably) Not a Moral Emotion

In recent decades, disgust has received enormous attention in moral psychology. The idea that disgust could be a moral emotion emerged from seminal studies in which participants were found to morally condemn harmless yet disgusting actions, such as masturbating in a dead chicken before eating it (e.g., Haidt, 2001; Haidt et al., 1993; Haidt & Hersh, 2001). This generated investigations of two distinct ways by which disgust could be a moral emotion.

The first hypothesis proposes that disgust is a *moralizing* emotion, i.e., that the emotional experience of disgust *itself generates* moral representations of right and wrong. In other words, some actions would be intuited as morally wrong *because* they are disgusting. This hypothesis is often intertwined with another one, according to which disgust is responsible for moral judgments of a specific part of the moral domain, often related to sexuality, purity, and piety (Graham et al., 2013; Haidt, 2012; Rozin et al., 1999).

The second, weaker hypothesis is that disgust does not cause moral condemnation, but is *elicited* by moral violations in general—just as, for example, moral indignation is (Chapman & Anderson, 2013; Hutcherson & Gross, 2011). This weaker and more probable claim is generally associated with another one, according to which this role of disgust in moral cognition is not restricted to a particular domain of morality (e.g., purity), but is observed for violations across the entire moral domain (Chapman & Anderson, 2014; Molho et al., 2017).

In the following, we consider these two families of hypotheses.

DISGUST IS NOT A *MORALIZING* EMOTION

From an evolutionary-functional perspective, it is unclear why merely perceiving an action as disgusting should generate a representation of this action as morally wrong. Indeed, pathogen-related behaviors have no reason to be represented as morally bad if they don't unfairly harm, in some way, the interests of cooperative partners. And indeed, in many cases, disgusting behaviors (e.g., picking one's nose in private), when harmless, are simply disgusting, and not immoral (Pizarro et al., 2011).

Rather than generating moral representations, disgust might, however, play the less important role of an *input* to the moral sense (see also Tybur et al., 2013; Baumard et al., 2013a).

Specifically, disgust could encode some of the costs imposed on some individuals, thereby influencing the moral evaluation of the interaction at hand. For example, farting during a meal can in some contexts be perceived as both disgusting and immoral. Does this mean that the mere disgusting character of farting *moralizes* it? Probably not: what may be intuited as immoral is unfairly *causing* disgust, as a negative psychological experience, in other people who don't deserve to feel this way while eating. To take a less trivial example, acting in a way that endangers other people's lives by exposing them to pathogens (e.g., by spreading an infected substance on them) is likely to be both perceived as immoral and disgusting. But again, this will be probably intuited as immoral only insofar at the pathogens at hand constitute an undeserved cost imposition on others. In other words, to be immoral, disgusting actions should have to be somehow unfair, in the sense of imposing illegitimate costs on other people in the context of cooperative interactions.

In line with these suspicions, experimental evidence for a moralizing role of disgust is overall weak (Piazza et al., 2018, for an extensive review; Landy & Goodwin, 2015, for a meta-analysis). Here, we focus on the following important empirical points.

First, consistent with the above ideas, when participants are asked to judge disgusting actions (e.g., spitting into a napkin while at a dinner party), it is the perception that the action negatively affected the welfare of other people, and not the disgust elicited by the action per se, that significantly predicts people's moralization (Royzman et al., 2009). Relatedly, correlations between disgust-sensitivity and moralizations of purity and sexual behaviors (e.g., Horberg et al., 2009; Inbar, Pizarro, & Bloom, 2009; Inbar, Pizarro, Knobe, et al., 2009) appear largely mediated by perceptions of harm and feelings of anger, and disappear when the latter are controlled for (Schein et al., 2016).

Second, in many (most?) cases, the association between disgust and moral judgments seems merely coincidental: some unfairly harmful actions, naturally judged immoral, also *happen* to have pathogen-related properties, so that they also trigger disgust (e.g., forbidden sex can include sexual fluids, violence can include blood) (Kayyal et al., 2015). Conversely, actions that have *positive* cooperation-related properties, yet also contain disgusting pathogen cues (e.g., a nurse changing an elderly patient's feces-covered sheets), are not morally condemned, but morally *praised* (Kayyal et al., 2015). This suggests that disgust (tracking pathogen cues) and moral judgment (tracking unfair cost imposition or benefit-providing) mostly operate independently, and simply sometimes co-occur in the case of immoral actions that also happen to be disgusting.

Third, and relatedly, even sex- and religion-related violations of so-called purity/sanctity moral concerns, the apparently harmless character of which initially justified the idea of a moralizing disgust, increasingly appear as tied to perceptions of unfair harm (Gray et al., 2014; Royzman et al., 2015; Schein et al., 2016). For example, the famous, intrinsically harmless scenario of "Julie's and Mark's" sibling incest (Haidt, 2001) often taken as evidence that harmless actions are moralized because they are disgusting, in fact fails to convince participants that the action they are judging is really harmless (Royzman et al., 2015). This suggests that moralizations of "purity," too, may be underpinned by computations unrelated to disgust (Fitouchi et al., 2023a, 2023b), and have been mistakenly causally associated with disgust because of the coincidentally disgusting character of some of these behaviors (e.g., sibling incest). In line with this idea, studies that address the confounding effect of pathogen cues find that pathogen-free violations of the morality of purity/sanctity (e.g., stepping on the Quran) are not associated with disgust-related phenomenology or action tendencies, but rather with moral anger, an emotion commonly associated with cooperation-related moral judgments (Royzman et al., 2014).

Fourth, while a range of studies find that experimentally induced disgust amplifies moral judgment (e.g., Horberg et al., 2009; Schnall et al., 2008; Wheatley & Haidt, 2005), a recent meta-analysis of 50 published and unpublished studies found no overall effect of incidental disgust after accounting for a probable publication bias (Landy & Goodwin, 2015; see also Johnson et al., 2016).

Putting these pieces of evidence together suggests the following picture:

1. In many cases, the co-occurrence of disgust and moral representations is merely coincidental (e.g., adulterous sexual pleasure involves sexual fluids, but is not immoral *because of that*) (Kayyal et al., 2015).
2. When this is not the case, disgusting actions are judged immoral only insofar as they are perceived to unjustly impose costs on other people (Royzman et al., 2009; Schein et al., 2016). In other words, it is not disgust per se that produces moralization, but perceptions of unfair cost imposition, to which disgusting behaviors can contribute. In this case, disgust would only play the role of an input informing the moral sense of the costs imposed on other people—just as, say, perceptions of people's pain influence our moral judgments.
3. Moral anger seems to be the predominant emotional response to moral violations *across moral domains*, even when it comes to "purity" violations (Kayyal et al., 2015; Piazza et al., 2018; Royzman et al., 2014; Schein et al., 2016), consistent with the idea that moral indignation is the main other-condemning emotion processing moral representations.

Overall, consistent with the idea that human moral cognition is mostly designed to ensure mutually beneficial cooperation, there is little conclusive evidence for pathogen-avoidance mechanisms playing a strong role in moral representations or moral condemnation.

IS IMMORALITY DISGUSTING?

A weaker hypothesis has been put forward, according to which disgust does not *generate* moral condemnation, but the reverse: immoral behavior generates a reaction of disgust (Chapman & Anderson, 2013). In support for this view, researchers have noted that people report feeling "disgusted" or "morally disgusted" in response to immoral behaviors (e.g., lying, cheating, stealing) (Hutcherson & Gross, 2011), choose facial expressions of disgust as corresponding to their reaction to immoral behaviors (Molho et al., 2017; Rozin et al., 1999), and express disgust-related facial expressions in response to unfair offers in economic games and moral violations (Cannon et al., 2011; Chapman et al., 2009).

From a functional perspective, the theoretical grounding of such "moral disgust" is, however, unclear. A possibility would be that the typical design features of disgust, mainly its avoidance motivation, have been co-opted over evolutionary time to serve the secondary function of avoiding immoral individuals with whom cooperation results in net costs (Curtis & Biran, 2001; Hutcherson & Gross, 2011). Relatedly, it has been suggested that, as opposed to the directly punitive function of anger, moral disgust could function to motivate less costly "indirect" punishments of immoral behavior (e.g., through ostracism or reputational sanctioning) (Mohlo et al., 2017). In a similar vein, scholars have also proposed that moral disgust allows people to facilitate, through the communicative function of disgust's typical facial expression, the coordination of moral condemnation with surrounding individuals, by signaling one's disapproval of a moral violation (Tybur et al., 2013).

In solving each of these adaptive problems, however, it is not clear where the added value of disgust's design features lies. For one thing, why would humans need "moral disgust" to avoid or ostracize immoral individuals, when they already have *contempt*? Contempt seems to unambiguously function for social valuation and partner choice: it is triggered by cues of low relational value (e.g., incompetence, norm transgression), and generates action tendencies of avoidance, exclusion, and relationship dissolution (Gervais & Fessler, 2017). Moreover, both in the lab (Molleman et al., 2019) and in the wild (Boehm, 1999, 2012), moral anger appears to readily motivate the coordination of punishment, condemnation, and ostracism of moral violators—consistent with the bargaining-oriented design of anger. Relatedly, a specific communicative payoff of disgust's facial expression is not obvious when linguistic communication (in the form of gossip) is an efficient and widely used mean for indirect reputational punishment and social valuation coordination (Boehm, 2012; Wiessner, 2005). In other words, is there a place, and a need, for such a thing as a "moral disgust" when we already have moral anger, contempt, and gossip serving these key functions?

These theoretical issues are consistent with widely noted methodological questions regarding the measurement of "moral disgust" (Nabi, 2002; Piazza et al., 2018). The most common operationalizations of moral disgust are difficult to distinguish from moral anger, contempt, or moral disapproval more generally. First, as long noted, it is not clear that studies in which participants self-report being "disgusted" by moral violations imply that the cognitive system of disgust is really triggered. Indeed, the lay meaning of "disgust," when applied to moral transgressions, has been found to largely overlap with reports of "anger," "moral anger," "contempt," and "moral contempt" (Nabi, 2002; Russell & Giner-Sorolla, 2013).

Second, more implicit measures of facial expressions of disgust, initially used to overcome these limitations (e.g., Chapman et al., 2009), appear to face similar problems. Indeed, the "standard" disgust face has been found to potentially express, and be associated with, more emotions than disgust: in particular, again, with anger and contempt (Gervais & Fessler, 2017; Widen & Russell, 2008; Widen et al., 2013). Moreover, even if participants select or express a truly disgust-related face in response to a moral violation, this can be a metaphorical way of communicating their disapproval, not associated to an actual *experience* of disgust—just as we sometimes say we are "hungry" for knowledge without the cognitive and physiological mechanisms of hunger really being triggered (Royzman & Kurzban, 2011; Royzman & Sabini, 2001).

Future research using more discriminant measures of disgust's typical physiological, cognitive, and phenomenological signatures (e.g., nausea, gagging, loss of appetite), as done by Royzman et al. (2014), could probably help settle these issues with more clarity.

Conclusion

In this chapter, we have suggested that a specification of the form and function of moral representations leads to a clearer picture of moral emotions. In particular, it enables a principled distinction between moral and non-moral emotions, based on the particular types of cognitive representations that each type of emotions processes.

Moral representations have a specific content: they represent a precise quantity of benefits that cooperative partners owe each other, a legitimate allocation of costs and benefits that *ought to be*, irrespective of whether it is achieved by people's actual behaviors. Humans intuit that they have a *duty* not to betray their coalition, that innocent people do not *deserve* to be harmed, that their partner has a *right* not to be cheated on. Moral emotions can thus be defined as superordinate programs orchestrating cognition, physiology, and behavior in accordance with the specific information encoded in these moral representations.

On this basis, indignation and guilt appear as the prototypical moral emotions. Indignation ("moral anger") is activated when one receives fewer benefits than one deserves, and recruits bargaining mechanisms to enforce the violated moral contract. Guilt, symmetrically, is sensitive to one's failure to honor one's own obligations toward cooperative partners, and motivates compensation to provide them the missing benefits they deserve. By contrast, often-proposed "moral" emotions—shame, empathy, disgust—seem not to function to compute distinctively moral representations of cooperative obligations, but to serve other, non-moral functions—social status management, interdependence, and pathogen avoidance (Figure 49.2).

Acknowledgments

We thank Laith Al-Shawaf for his thoughtful feedback and corrections. This work was supported by the EUR FrontCog grant ANR-17-EURE-0017.

References

Aktipis, A., Cronk, L., Alcock, J., Ayers, J. D., Baciu, C., Balliet, D., Boddy, A. M., Curry, O. S., Krems, J. A., Muñoz, A., Sullivan, D., Sznycer, D., Wilkinson, G. S., & Winfrey, P. (2018). Understanding cooperation through fitness interdependence. *Nature Human Behaviour*, *2*(7), 429–431. https://doi.org/10.1038/s41562-018-0378-4
Alexander, R. D. (1987). *The biology of moral systems*. A. de Gruyter.
Al-Shawaf, L., Conroy-Beam, D., Asao, K., & Buss, D. M. (2016). Human emotions: An evolutionary psychological perspective. *Emotion Review*, *8*(2), 173–186. https://doi.org/10.1177/1754073914565518
Al-Shawaf, L., & Lewis, D. (2017). Encyclopedia of personality and individual differences. In V. Zeigler-Hill & T. K. Shackelford (Eds.), *Evolutionary psychology and the emotions*. Springer International Publishing AG. https://doi.org/10.1007/978-3-319-28099-8_516-1
André, J.-B., & Baumard, N. (2011). The evolution of fairness in a biological market. *Evolution: International Journal of Organic Evolution*, *65*(5), 1447–1456.
André, J. B., Fitouchi, L., Debove, S., & Baumard, N. (2022). An evolutionary contractualist theory of morality [preprint]. *PsyArxiv*. https://doi.org/10.31234/ osf.io/2hxgu
Avramova, Y. R., & Inbar, Y. (2013). Emotion and moral judgment: Emotion and moral judgment. *Wiley Interdisciplinary Reviews: Cognitive Science*, *4*(2), 169–178. https://doi.org/10.1002/wcs.1216
Axelrod, R., & Hamilton, W. D. (1981). The evolution of cooperation. *Science*, *211*(4489), 1390–1396.
Barclay, P. (2005). Reputational benefits for altruistic punishment. *Evolution and Human Behavior*, *27*(5), 325–344.
Batson, C., & Ahmad, N. (2009). Empathy-induced altruism: A threat to the collective good. *Advances in Group Processes*, *26*, 1–23. https://doi.org/10.1108/S0882-6145(2009)0000026004
Batson, C. D. (2017). The empathy-altruism hypothesis: What and so what. In *The Oxford handbook of compassion science* (pp. 27–40). Oxford University Press. https://doi.org/10.1093/oxfordhb/9780190464684.013.3
Batson, C. D., Ahmad, N., Yin, J., Bedell, S. J., Johnson, J. W., & Templin, C. M. (1999). Two threats to the common good: Self-interested egoism and empathy-induced altruism. *Personality and Social Psychology Bulletin*, *25*(1), 3–16. https://doi.org/10.1177/0146167299025001001
Batson, C. D., Kennedy, C. L., Nord, L.-A., Stocks, E. L., Fleming, D. A., Marzette, C. M., Lishner, D. A., Hayes, R. E., Kolchinsky, L. M., & Zerger, T. (2007). Anger at unfairness: Is it moral outrage? *European Journal of Social Psychology*, *37*(6), 1272–1285. https://doi.org/10.1002/ejsp.434
Batson, C. D., Klein, T. R., Highberger, L., & Shaw, L. L. (1995). Immorality from empathy-induced altruism: When compassion and justice conflict. *Journal of Personality and Social Psychology*, *68*(6), 1042.
Baumard, N. (2016). *The origins of fairness: How evolution explains our moral nature*. Oxford University Press.
Baumard, N. (2010). Punishment is not a group adaptation: Humans punish to restore fairness rather than to support group cooperation. *Mind & Society*, *10*(1), 1–26. https://doi.org/10.1007/s11299-010-0080-3
Baumard, N., André, J.-B., & Sperber, D. (2013a). Partner choice, fairness, and the extension of morality. *Behavioral and Brain Sciences*, *36*(1), 102.
Baumard, N., André, J.-B., & Sperber, D. (2013b). A mutualistic approach to morality: The evolution of fairness by partner choice. *Behavioral and Brain Sciences*, *36*(01), 59–78. https://doi.org/10.1017/S0140525X11002202
Baumard, N., & Liénard, P. (2011). Second-or third-party punishment? When self-interest hides behind apparent functional interventions. *Proceedings of the National Academy of Sciences*, *108*(39), E753–E753.
Baumard, N., Mascaro, O., & Chevallier, C. P. (2011). Preschoolers are able to take merit into account when distributing goods. *Developmental Psychology*, *48*(2), 492–498. https://doi.org/10.1037/a0026598
Black, D. (2000). On the origin of morality. *Journal of Consciousness Studies*, *7*, 107–119.

Bloom, P. (2017). *Against empathy: The case for rational compassion*. Random House.
Boehm, C. (1999). *Hierarchy in the forest: The evolution of egalitarian behavior*. Harvard University Press.
Boehm, C. (2012). *Moral origins: The evolution of virtue, altruism, and shame*. Basic Books.
Buss, D. M. (2003). *The evolution of desire: Strategies of human mating* (rev. ed). Basic Books.
Cannon, P. R., Schnall, S., & White, M. (2011). Transgressions and expressions: Affective facial muscle activity predicts moral judgments. *Social Psychological and Personality Science, 2*(3), 325–331. https://doi.org/10.1177/1948550610390525
Carlsmith, K. M., & Darley, J. M. (2008). Psychological aspects of retributive justice. In M. P. Zanna (Ed.), *Advances in experimental social psychology* (Vol. 40, pp. 193–236). Elsevier. https://doi.org/10.1016/S0065-2601(07)00004-4
Chapman, H. A., & Anderson, A. K. (2013). Things rank and gross in nature: A review and synthesis of moral disgust. *Psychological Bulletin, 139*(2), 300–327. https://doi.org/10.1037/a0030964
Chapman, H. A., & Anderson, A. K. (2014). Trait physical disgust is related to moral judgments outside of the purity domain. *Emotion, 14*(2), 341–348. https://doi.org/10.1037/a0035120
Chapman, H. A., Kim, D. A., Susskind, J. M., & Anderson, A. K. (2009). In bad taste: Evidence for the oral origins of moral disgust. *Science, 323*(5918), 1222–1226. https://doi.org/10.1126/science.1165565
Cikara, M., Botvinick, M. M., & Fiske, S. T. (2011). Us versus them: Social identity shapes neural responses to intergroup competition and harm. *Psychological Science, 22*(3), 306–313. https://doi.org/10.1177/0956797610397667
Clutton-Brock, T. H., & Parker, G. A. (1995). Punishment in animal societies. *Nature, 373*(6511), 209–216. https://doi.org/10.1038/373209a0
Cohen, T. R., Panter, A. T., & Turan, N. (2013). Predicting counterproductive work behavior from guilt proneness. *Journal of Business Ethics, 114*(1), 45–53. https://doi.org/10.1007/s10551-012-1326-2
Corbit, J., McAuliffe, K., Callaghan, T. C., Blake, P. R., & Warneken, F. (2017). Children's collaboration induces fairness rather than generosity. *Cognition, 168*, 344–356. https://doi.org/10.1016/j.cognition.2017.07.006
Cosmides, L., & Tooby, J. (2000). Evolutionary psychology and the emotions. In M. Lewis & J. M. Haviland-Jones (Eds.), *Handbook of emotions* (2(2), pp. 91–115). The Guilford Press.
Curry, O. S., Jones Chesters, M., & Van Lissa, C. J. (2019). Mapping morality with a compass: Testing the theory of 'morality-as-cooperation' with a new questionnaire. *Journal of Research in Personality, 78*, 106–124. https://doi.org/10.1016/j.jrp.2018.10.008
Curry, O. S., Mullins, D. A., & Whitehouse, H. (2019). Is it good to cooperate? Testing the theory of morality-as-cooperation in 60 societies. *Current Anthropology, 60*(1), 47–69. https://doi.org/10.1086/701478
Curtis, V., & Biran, A. (2001). Dirt, disgust, and disease: Is hygiene in our genes? *Perspectives in Biology and Medicine, 44*, 17–31. https://doi.org/10.1353/pbm.2001.0001
Darley, J. M., & Pittman, T. S. (2003). The psychology of compensatory and retributive justice. *Personality and Social Psychology Review, 7*(4), 324–336. https://doi.org/10.1207/S15327957PSPR0704_05
Darwall, S. (2010). III-Moral obligation: Form and substance. *Proceedings of the Aristotelian Society (Hardback), 110*(pt 1), 31–46. https://doi.org/10.1111/j.1467-9264.2010.00278.x
Davidov, M., Zahn-Waxler, C., Roth-Hanania, R., & Knafo, A. (2013). Concern for others in the first year of life: Theory, evidence, and avenues for research. *Child Development Perspectives, 7*(2), 126–131.
Dawes, C. T., Fowler, J. H., Johnson, T., McElreath, R., & Smirnov, O. (2007). Egalitarian motives in humans. *Nature, 446*(7137), 794–796. https://doi.org/10.1038/nature05651
Debove, S., André, J.-B., & Baumard, N. (2015). Partner choice creates fairness in humans. *Proceedings of the Royal Society B: Biological Sciences, 282*(1808), 1–7, 20150392. https://doi.org/10.1098/rspb.2015.0392
Debove, S., Baumard, N., & André, J.-B. (2015). Evolution of equal division among unequal partners: Brief communication. *Evolution, 69*(2), 561–569. https://doi.org/10.1111/evo.12583
Decety, J., Bartal, I., Uzefovsky, F., & Knafo-Noam, A. (2016). Empathy as a driver of prosocial behaviour: Highly conserved neurobehavioural mechanisms across species. *Philosophical Transactions of the Royal Society B: Biological Sciences, 371*, 20150077. https://doi.org/10.1098/rstb.2015.0077
de Hooge, I. E., Breugelmans, S. M., & Zeelenberg, M. (2008). Not so ugly after all: When shame acts as a commitment device. *Journal of Personality and Social Psychology, 95*(4), 933–943. https://doi.org/10.1037/a0011991
de Hooge, I. E., Nelissen, R. M. A., Breugelmans, S. M., & Zeelenberg, M. (2011). What is moral about guilt? Acting "prosocially" at the disadvantage of others. *Journal of Personality and Social Psychology, 100*(3), 462–473. https://doi.org/10.1037/a0021459
de Hooge, I. E., Zeelenberg, M., & Breugelmans, S. M. (2007). Moral sentiments and cooperation: Differential influences of shame and guilt. *Cognition and Emotion, 21*(5), 1025–1042. https://doi.org/10.1080/02699930600980874

de Hooge, I. E., Zeelenberg, M., & Breugelmans, S. M. (2010). Restore and protect motivations following shame. *Cognition and Emotion, 24*(1), 111–127. https://doi.org/10.1080/02699930802584466

de Waal, F. B. M. (2008). Putting the altruism back into altruism: The evolution of empathy. *Annual Review of Psychology, 59*(1), 279–300. https://doi.org/10.1146/annurev.psych.59.103006.093625

Durkee, P. K., Lukaszewski, A. W., & Buss, D. M. (2019). Pride and shame: Key components of a culturally universal status management system. *Evolution and Human Behavior, 40*(5), 470–478. https://doi.org/10.1016/j.evolhumbehav.2019.06.004

Elison, J., Garofalo, C., & Velotti, P. (2014). Shame and aggression: Theoretical considerations. *Aggression and Violent Behavior, 19*(4), 447–453. https://doi.org/10.1016/j.avb.2014.05.002

Engelmann, J. M., & Tomasello, M. (2019). Children's sense of fairness as equal respect. *Trends in Cognitive Sciences, 23*(6), 454–463. https://doi.org/10.1016/j.tics.2019.03.001

Evans-Pritchard, E. E. (1969). *The Nuer: A description of the modes of livelihood and political institutions of a Nilotic people*. Oxford University Press.

Fehr, E., & Gächter, S. (2002). Altruistic punishment in humans. *Nature, 415*, 5.

Fessler, D. M., & Haley, K. J. (2003). The strategy of affect: Emotions in human cooperation. In P. Hammerstein (Ed.), *The genetic and cultural evolution of cooperation* (pp. 7–36). MIT Press.

Fessler, D. M. T. (2009). Madmen: An evolutionary perspective on anger and men's violent responses to transgression. In M. Potegal, G. Stemmler, & C. Spielberger (Eds.), *International handbook of anger: Constituent and concomitant biological, psychological, and social processes* (pp. 361–381). Springer New York.

Fitouchi, L., André, J., & Baumard, N. (2023a). Moral disciplining: The cognitive and evolutionary foundations of puritanical morality. *Behavioral and Brain Sciences, 46*, e293, 1–74. doi:10.1017/ S0140525X22002047

Fitouchi, L., André, J., & Baumard, N. (2023b). The puritanical moral contract: Purity, cooperation, and the architecture of the moral mind. *Behavioral and Brain Sciences, 46*, E322. doi:10.1017/S0140525X23001188

Fitouchi, L., & Singh, M. (2023). Punitive justice serves to restore reciprocal cooperation in three small-scale societies. *Evolution and Human Behavior, 44*(5), 502–514. https://doi.org/10.1016/j.evolhumbehav.2023.03.001

Flack, J. C., & De Waal, F. B. (2000). "Any animal whatever": Darwinian building blocks of morality in monkeys and apes. *Journal of Consciousness Studies, 7*(1–2), 1–29.

Fletcher, G., Simpson, J., Campbell, L., & Overall, N. C. (2015). Pair-bonding, romantic love, and evolution: The curious case of Homo sapiens. *Perspectives on Psychological Science, 10*(1), 20–36. https://doi.org/10.1177/1745691614561683

Frank, R. H. (1988). *Passions within reason: The strategic role of the emotions*. W. W. Norton.

Gangestad, S. W., & Simpson, J. A. (2000). The evolution of human mating: Trade-offs and strategic pluralism. *Behavioral and Brain Sciences, 23*(4), 573–587. https://doi.org/10.1017/S0140525X0000337X

Gausel, N., Vignoles, V. L., & Leach, C. W. (2016). Resolving the paradox of shame: Differentiating among specific appraisal-feeling combinations explains pro-social and self-defensive motivation. *Motivation and Emotion, 40*(1), 118–139. https://doi.org/10.1007/s11031-015-9513-y

Gauthier, D. (1986). *Morals by agreement*. Oxford University Press.

Gervais, M. M., & Fessler, D. M. T. (2017). On the deep structure of social affect: Attitudes, emotions, sentiments, and the case of "contempt." *Behavioral and Brain Sciences, 40*, e225. https://doi.org/10.1017/S0140525X16000352

Graham, J., Haidt, J., Koleva, S., Motyl, M., Iyer, R., Wojcik, S. P., & Ditto, P. H. (2013). Moral foundations theory. In P. Devine & A. Plant (Eds.), *Advances in experimental social psychology* (Vol. 47, pp. 55–130). Elsevier. https://doi.org/10.1016/B978-0-12-407236-7.00002-4

Gray, K., Schein, C., & Ward, A. F. (2014). The myth of harmless wrongs in moral cognition: Automatic dyadic completion from sin to suffering. *Journal of Experimental Psychology: General, 143*(4), 1600–1615. https://doi.org/10.1037/a0036149

Greene, J. (2013). *Moral tribes: Emotion, reason, and the gap between us and them*. Penguin.

Gurven, M., Winking, J., Kaplan, H., von Rueden, C., & McAllister, L. (2009). A bioeconomic approach to marriage and the sexual division of labor. *Human Nature, 20*(2), 151–183. https://doi.org/10.1007/s12110-009-9062-8

Hagen, E. H., & Garfield, Z. (2019). *Leadership and prestige, mothering, sexual selection, and encephalization: The computational services model*. Open Science Framework. https://doi.org/10.31219/osf.io/9bcdk

Haidt, J. (2001). The emotional dog and its rational tail: A social intuitionist approach to moral judgment. *Psychological Review, 108*(4), 814.

Haidt, J. (2003). The moral emotions. In R. J. Davidson, K. R. Scherer, & H. H. Goldsmith (Eds.), *Handbook of affective sciences* (pp. 852–870). Oxford University Press.

Haidt, J. (2007). The new synthesis in moral psychology. *Science, 316*(5827), 998–1002. https://doi.org/10.1126/science.1137651

Haidt, J. (2012). *The righteous mind: Why good people are divided by politics and religion.* Knopf Doubleday.
Haidt, J., & Hersh, M. A. (2001). Sexual morality: The cultures and emotions of conservatives and liberals. *Journal of Applied Social Psychology, 31*(1), 191–221.
Haidt, J., Koller, S. H., & Dias, M. G. (1993). Affect, culture, and morality, or is it wrong to eat your dog?. *Journal of Personality and Social Psychology, 65*(4), 613.
Henrich, J., & Boyd, R. (2001). Why people punish defectors. *Journal of Theoretical Biology, 208*(1), 79–89. https://doi.org/10.1006/jtbi.2000.2202
Horberg, E. J., Oveis, C., Keltner, D., & Cohen, A. B. (2009). Disgust and the moralization of purity. *Journal of Personality and Social Psychology, 97*(6), 963–976. https://doi.org/10.1037/a0017423
Hutcherson, C. A., & Gross, J. J. (2011). The moral emotions: A social-functionalist account of anger, disgust, and contempt. *Journal of Personality and Social Psychology, 100*(4), 719–737. https://doi.org/10.1037/a0022408
Inbar, Y., Pizarro, D. A., & Bloom, P. (2009). Conservatives are more easily disgusted than liberals. *Cognition & Emotion, 23*(4), 714–725. https://doi.org/10.1080/02699930802110007
Inbar, Y., Pizarro, D. A., Knobe, J., & Bloom, P. (2009). Disgust sensitivity predicts intuitive disapproval of gays. *Emotion, 9*(3), 435–439. https://doi.org/10.1037/a0015960
Johnson, D. J., Wortman, J., Cheung, F., Hein, M., Lucas, R. E., Donnellan, M. B., Ebersole, C. R., & Narr, R. K. (2016). The effects of disgust on moral judgments: Testing moderators. *Social Psychological and Personality Science, 7*(7), 640–647. https://doi.org/10.1177/1948550616654211
Jordan, J. J., Hoffman, M., Bloom, P., & Rand, D. G. (2016). Third-party punishment as a costly signal of trustworthiness. *Nature, 530*(7591), 473–476. https://doi.org/10.1038/nature16981
Kachel, U., Svetlova, M., & Tomasello, M. (2018). Three-year-olds' reactions to a partner's failure to perform her role in a joint commitment. *Child Development, 89*(5), 1691–1703. https://doi.org/10.1111/cdev.12816
Kayyal, M. H., Pochedly, J., McCarthy, A., & Russell, J. A. (2015). On the limits of the relation of disgust to judgments of immorality. *Frontiers in Psychology, 6,* 1–7. https://doi.org/10.3389/fpsyg.2015.00951
Ketelaar, T., & Au, W. T. (2003). The effects of feelings of guilt on the behaviour of uncooperative individuals in repeated social bargaining games: An affect-as-information interpretation of the role of emotion in social interaction. Cognition and Emotion, 17(3), 429–453..
Kohlberg, L., & Kramer, R. (1969). Continuities and discontinuities in childhood and adult moral development. *Human Development, 12*(2), 93–120.
Kurzban, R., Tooby, J., & Cosmides, L. (2001). Can race be erased? Coalitional computation and social categorization. *Proceedings of the National Academy of Sciences, 98*(26), 15387–15392.
Landy, J. F., & Goodwin, G. P. (2015). Does incidental disgust amplify moral judgment? A meta-analytic review of experimental evidence. *Perspectives on Psychological Science, 10*(4), 518–536. https://doi.org/10.1177/1745691615583128
Masten, C. L., Gillen-O'Neel, C., & Brown, C. S. (2010). Children's intergroup empathic processing: The roles of novel ingroup identification, situational distress, and social anxiety. *Journal of Experimental Child Psychology, 106*(2–3), 115–128. https://doi.org/10.1016/j.jecp.2010.01.002
McAuliffe, W. H. (2019). Do emotions play an essential role in moral judgments? *Thinking & Reasoning, 25*(2), 207–230. https://doi.org/10.31234/osf.io/ajbc9
McCullough, M. E., Kurzban, R., & Tabak, B. A. (2013). Cognitive systems for revenge and forgiveness. *Behavioral and Brain Sciences, 36*(1), 1–15. https://doi.org/10.1017/S0140525X11002160
Molho, C., Tybur, J. M., Güler, E., Balliet, D., & Hofmann, W. (2017). Disgust and anger relate to different aggressive responses to moral violations. *Psychological Science, 28*(5), 609–619. https://doi.org/10.1177/0956797617692000
Molleman, L., Kölle, F., Starmer, C., & Gächter, S. (2019). People prefer coordinated punishment in cooperative interactions. *Nature Human Behaviour, 3*(11), 1145–1153. https://doi.org/10.1038/s41562-019-0707-2
Nabi, R. L. (2002). The theoretical versus the lay meaning of disgust: Implications for emotion research. *Cognition & Emotion, 16*(5), 695–703. https://doi.org/10.1080/02699930143000437
Nelissen, R. M. A., & Zeelenberg, M. (2009). Moral emotions as determinants of third-party punishment: Anger, guilt, and the functions of altruistic sanctions. *Judgment and Decision Making, 4*(7), 543–553.
Nichols, S. (2002). Norms with feeling: Towards a psychological account of moral judgment. *Cognition, 84*(2), 221–236. https://doi.org/10.1016/S0010-0277(02)00048-3
O'Mara Kunz, E., Eckstein, L., Batson, C., & Gaertner, L. (2011). Will moral outrage stand up? Distinguishing among emotional reactions to a moral violation. *European Journal of Social Psychology, 41,* 173–179. https://doi.org/10.1002/ejsp.754
Osgood, J. M. (2017). Is revenge about retributive justice, deterring harm, or both? Justice, deterrence, or both? *Social and Personality Psychology Compass, 11*(1), e12296. https://doi.org/10.1111/spc3.12296

Pedersen, E. J., McAuliffe, W. H. B., & McCullough, M. E. (2018). The unresponsive avenger: More evidence that disinterested third parties do not punish altruistically. *Journal of Experimental Psychology: General, 147*(4), 514–544. https://doi.org/10.1037/xge0000410

Pedersen, E. J., McAuliffe, W. H. B., Shah, Y., Tanaka, H., Ohtsubo, Y., & McCullough, M. E. (2020). When and why do third parties punish outside of the lab? A cross-cultural recall study. *Social Psychological and Personality Science, 11*(6), 846–853. https://doi.org/10.1177/1948550619884565

Piaget, J. (1997). *The moral judgement of the child*. Simon & Schuster.

Piazza, J., Landy, J. F., Chakroff, A., Young, L., & Wasserman, E. (2018). What disgust does and does not do for moral cognition. In N. Strohminger & V. Kumar (Eds.), *The moral psychology of disgust* (pp. 53–81). Rowman & Littlefield.

Pizarro, D., Inbar, Y., & Helion, C. (2011). On disgust and moral judgment. *Emotion Review, 3*(3), 267–268.

Preston, S. D., & de Waal, F. B. M. (2002). Empathy: Its ultimate and proximate bases. *Behavioral and Brain Sciences, 25*(1), 1–20. https://doi.org/10.1017/S0140525X02000018

Prinz, J. J., & Nichols, S. B. (2010). Moral emotions. In J. M. Doris & Moral Psychology Research Group (Eds.), *The moral psychology handbook* (pp. 111–146). OUP Oxford.

Rakoczy, H., Kaufmann, M., & Lohse, K. (2016). Young children understand the normative force of standards of equal resource distribution. *Journal of Experimental Child Psychology, 150*, 396–403. https://doi.org/10.1016/j.jecp.2016.05.015

Rand, D. G., & Nowak, M. A. (2013). Human cooperation. *Trends in Cognitive Sciences, 17*(8), 413–425. https://doi.org/10.1016/j.tics.2013.06.003

Rawls, J. (2001). *A theory of justice*. Harvard University Press.

Roberts, G. (2005). Cooperation through interdependence. *Animal Behaviour, 70*(4), 901–908. https://doi.org/10.1016/j.anbehav.2005.02.006

Robertson, T. E., Sznycer, D., Delton, A. W., Tooby, J., & Cosmides, L. (2018). The true trigger of shame: Social devaluation is sufficient, wrongdoing is unnecessary. *Evolution and Human Behavior, 39*(5), 566–573. https://doi.org/10.1016/j.evolhumbehav.2018.05.010

Royzman, E., Atanasov, P., Landy, J. F., Parks, A., & Gepty, A. (2014). CAD or MAD? Anger (not disgust) as the predominant response to pathogen-free violations of the divinity code. *Emotion, 14*(5), 892–907. https://doi.org/10.1037/a0036829

Royzman, E., & Kurzban, R. (2011). Minding the metaphor: The elusive character of moral disgust. *Emotion Review, 3*(3), 269–271. https://doi.org/10.1177/1754073911402371

Royzman, E. B., Kim, K., & Leeman, R. F. (2015). The curious tale of Julie and Mark: Unraveling the moral dumbfounding effect. *Judgment and Decision Making, 10*(4), 296–313.

Royzman, E. B., Leeman, R. F., & Baron, J. (2009). Unsentimental ethics: Towards a content-specific account of the moral–conventional distinction. *Cognition, 112*(1), 159–174. https://doi.org/10.1016/j.cognition.2009.04.004

Royzman, E. B., & Sabini, J. (2001). Something it takes to be an emotion: The interesting case of disgust. *Journal for the Theory of Social Behaviour, 31*(1), 29–59. https://doi.org/10.1111/1468-5914.00145

Rozin, P., Lowery, L., Haidt, J., & Imada, S. (1999). The CAD Triad Hypothesis: A mapping between three moral emotions (contempt, anger, disgust) and three moral codes (community, autonomy, divinity). *Journal of Personality and Social Psychology, 76*(4), 574–586.

Russell, P. S., & Giner-Sorolla, R. (2013). Bodily moral disgust: What it is, how it is different from anger, and why it is an unreasoned emotion. *Psychological Bulletin, 139*(2), 328–351. https://doi.org/10.1037/a0029319

Saxe, R. (2022). Perceiving and pursuing legitimate power. *Trends in Cognitive Sciences*. Advanced online publication.

Scanlon, T. (2000). *What we owe to each other*. Belknap Press.

Schein, C., & Gray, K. (2018). The theory of dyadic morality: Reinventing moral judgment by redefining harm. *Personality and Social Psychology Review, 22*(1), 32–70. https://doi.org/10.1177/1088868317698288

Schein, C., Ritter, R. S., & Gray, K. (2016). Harm mediates the disgust-immorality link. *Emotion, 16*(6), 862–876. https://doi.org/10.1037/emo0000167

Schnall, S., Haidt, J., Clore, G. L., & Jordan, A. H. (2008). Disgust as embodied moral judgment. *Personality and Social Psychology Bulletin, 34*(8), 1096–1109. https://doi.org/10.1177/0146167208317771

Sell, A. (2017). Recalibration theory of anger. In T. K. Shackelford & V. A. Weekes-Shackelford (Eds.), *Encyclopedia of evolutionary psychological science* (pp. 1–14). Springer International. https://doi.org/10.1007/978-3-319-16999-6_1687-1

Sell, A., Sznycer, D., Al-Shawaf, L., Lim, J., Krauss, A., Aneta, F., Rascanu, R., Sugiyama, L., Cosmides, L., & Tooby, J. (2017). The grammar of anger: Mapping the computational architecture of a recalibrational emotion. *Cognition, 168*, 110–128. https://doi.org/10.1016/j.cognition.2017.06.002

Sell, A., Tooby, J., & Cosmides, L. (2009). Formidability and the logic of human anger. *Proceedings of the National Academy of Sciences, 106*(35), 15073–15078. https://doi.org/10.1073/pnas.0904312106

Sheikh, S., & Janoff-Bulman, R. (2010). The "shoulds" and "should nots" of moral emotions: A self-regulatory perspective on shame and guilt. *Personality and Social Psychology Bulletin, 36*(2), 213–224.

Smith, A. (1822). *The theory of moral sentiments* (Vol. 1). J. Richardson.

Smith, C. E., & Warneken, F. (2016). Children's reasoning about distributive and retributive justice across development. *Developmental Psychology, 52*(4), 613–628. https://doi.org/10.1037/a0040069

Smith, R. H., Webster, J. M., Parrott, W. G., & Eyre, H. L. (2002). The role of public exposure in moral and nonmoral shame and guilt. *Journal of Personality and Social Psychology, 83*(1), 138–159. https://doi.org/10.1037/0022-3514.83.1.138

Sperber, D., & Baumard, N. (2012). Moral reputation: An evolutionary and cognitive perspective: Moral reputation. *Mind & Language, 27*(5), 495–518. https://doi.org/10.1111/mila.12000

Stanford, P. K. (2018). The difference between ice cream and Nazis: Moral externalization and the evolution of human cooperation. *Behavioral and Brain Sciences, 41*, e95. https://doi.org/10.1017/S0140525X17001911

Starmans, C., Sheskin, M., & Bloom, P. (2017). Why people prefer unequal societies. *Nature Human Behaviour, 1*(4), 1–7. https://doi.org/10.1038/s41562-017-0082

Sznycer, D. (2019). Forms and functions of the self-conscious emotions. *Trends in Cognitive Sciences, 23*(2), 143–157.

Sznycer, D., Tooby, J., Cosmides, L., Porat, R., Shalvi, S., & Halperin, E. (2016). Shame closely tracks the threat of devaluation by others, even across cultures. *Proceedings of the National Academy of Sciences, 113*(10), 2625–2630. https://doi.org/10.1073/pnas.1514699113

Sznycer, D., Xygalatas, D., Agey, E., Alami, S., An, X.-F., Ananyeva, K. I., Atkinson, Q. D., Broitman, B. R., Conte, T. J., Flores, C., Fukushima, S., Hitokoto, H., Kharitonov, A. N., Onyishi, C. N., Onyishi, I. E., Romero, P. P., Schrock, J. M., Snodgrass, J. J., Sugiyama, L. S., . . . Tooby, J. (2018). Cross-cultural invariances in the architecture of shame. *Proceedings of the National Academy of Sciences, 115*(39), 9702–9707. https://doi.org/10.1073/pnas.1805016115

Tangney, J. P., Stuewig, J., & Martinez, A. G. (2014). Two faces of shame: The roles of shame and guilt in predicting recidivism. *Psychological Science, 25*(3), 799–805. https://doi.org/10.1177/0956797613508790

Tangney, J. P., Stuewig, J., & Mashek, D. J. (2007). Moral emotions and moral behavior. *Annual Review of Psychology, 58*, 345–372.

Thulin, E. W., & Bicchieri, C. (2016). I'm so angry I could help you: Moral outrage as a driver of victim compensation. *Social Philosophy and Policy, 32*(2), 146–160. https://doi.org/10.1017/S0265052516000145

Tomasello, M. (2016). *A natural history of human morality*. Harvard University Press.

Tomasello, M. (2020). The moral psychology of obligation. *Behavioral and Brain Sciences, 43*, e56. https://doi.org/10.1017/S0140525X19001742

Tooby, J., Cosmides, L., Sell, A., Lieberman, D., & Sznycer, D. (2008). Internal regulatory variables and the design of human motivation: A computational and evolutionary approach. In *Handbook of approach and avoidance motivation* (pp. 251–271). Routledge, Taylor & Francis Group.

Tracy, J. L., & Matsumoto, D. (2008). The spontaneous expression of pride and shame: Evidence for biologically innate nonverbal displays. *Proceedings of the National Academy of Sciences, 105*(33), 11655–11660.

Trivers, R. (1971). The evolution of reciprocal altruism. *The Quarterly Review of Biology, 46*(1), 35–57.

Tybur, J. M., Lieberman, D., Kurzban, R., & DeScioli, P. (2013). Disgust: Evolved function and structure. *Psychological Review, 120*(1), 65–84. https://doi.org/10.1037/a0030778

von Rueden, C., Gurven, M., & Kaplan, H. (2011). Why do men seek status? Fitness payoffs to dominance and prestige. *Proceedings of the Royal Society B: Biological Sciences, 278*(1715), 2223–2232. https://doi.org/10.1098/rspb.2010.2145

von Rueden, C., & Jaeggi, A. (2016). Men's status and reproductive success in 33 nonindustrial societies: Effects of subsistence, marriage system, and reproductive strategy. *Proceedings of the National Academy of Sciences, 113*(39), 10824–10829. https://doi.org/10.1073/pnas.1606800113

Wheatley, T., & Haidt, J. (2005). Hypnotic disgust makes moral judgments more severe. *Psychological Science, 16*(10), 780–784. https://doi.org/10.1111/j.1467-9280.2005.01614.x

Widen, S. C., Pochedly, J. T., Pieloch, K., & Russell, J. A. (2013). Introducing the sick face. *Motivation and Emotion, 37*(3), 550–557. https://doi.org/10.1007/s11031-013-9353-6

Widen, S., & Russell, J. (2008). Children's and adults' understanding of the "disgust face." *Cognition and Emotion, 22*(8), 1513–1541. https://doi.org/10.1080/02699930801906744

Wiessner, P. (2005). Norm enforcement among the Ju/'hoansi Bushmen: A case of strong reciprocity? *Human Nature*, *16*(2), 115–145. https://doi.org/10.1007/s12110-005-1000-9

Wrangham, R. (2019). *The goodness paradox: The strange relationship between virtue and violence in human evolution*. Vintage.

Xu, X., Zuo, X., Wang, X., & Han, S. (2009). Do you feel my pain? Racial group membership modulates empathic neural responses. *Journal of Neuroscience*, *29*(26), 8525–8529. https://doi.org/10.1523/JNEUROSCI.2418-09.2009

CHAPTER 50

Emotion and Women's Intrasexual Mating Competition

Maryanne L. Fisher

Abstract
Women compete with each other for access to mates who possess desirable qualities. This chapter addresses the emotional underpinnings of women's intrasexual mating competition, and links emotional experiences with specific competitive situations. The emotional side of women's intrasexual competition has rarely been studied, and consequently, much of this chapter is about setting the stage to explore what emotions are presumably experienced. The existing work focuses on experiences of anger, jealousy, and envy, usually within the context of imagining interactions with rivals, and thus, they are individually presented in light of past work. After reviewing the framework of competition, in terms of why women intrasexually compete for mates and the goal of this form of competition, the discussion moves to indirect aggression and then addresses each of these emotions in turn. The chapter ends with concrete suggestions for future research.

Key Words: jealousy, envy, anger, self-esteem, social comparison, intrasexual competition

Introduction

Well love's not a competition, but I'm winning. Or at least I thought I was, but there's no way of knowing.

—Kaiser Chefs

Imagine two friends casually meeting for a coffee to catch up on each other's lives. The friends, whom we will call Charles and Emma, have known each other for a few months and met at work. They discuss a variety of topics, including other people in their social circle. What makes this situation interesting is that while chatting, Emma is trying to figure out how to signal her romantic interest in Charles. She is worried that if he is not similarly interested in her, the friendship will become awkward. If she uses a direct approach, he might rebuff her, which will cause her to feel embarrassed. Emma feels apprehensive and finds it hard to focus on the conversation. These feelings are amplified because she believes Charles might be romantically interested in another woman they both know. She decides to signal her interest covertly, to reduce risk. She knows that Charles is really only interested in forming a long-term relationship, so Emma highlights that she is seeking the same type of relationship and points out that the other person Charles might like (i.e., Emma's potential rival) is promiscuous, dishonest, unkind, and not sexually faithful. In effect, Emma is manipulating Charles so that he excludes the rival from consideration, and consequently, Emma may become the more viable option. They continue to exchange some more information about their social circle, and at every opportunity, Emma displays that her values and preferences align with those expressed by Charles, and how the rival is a really poor choice.

These decisions are complex and dynamic; they rely on reading the emotional state of others, such as a potential mate, and adjusting one's competitive strategy immediately. Just as the quote above from the Kaiser Chefs indicates, competing for love (and mating, more generally) may also not result in clear wins or losses. There is an array of emotions involved, which are closely intertwined with the constructs of self-worth, popularity, and social status, as well as feelings more directly related to winning a competition, such as pride and happiness, or losing a competition, such as sadness and envy. In this chapter, I focus on the constructs that lead to emotional experiences, rather than what is actually felt from winning or losing a mating competition. Understanding how an emotional experience arises (and the ultimate-level explanation for why it is an experience at all) is more important than studying the transitory feelings that accompany a particular outcome.

I aim to unite the work on women's intrasexual competition with emotions primarily for the purposes of acquiring and retaining mates. I focus on women for a few reasons. First, there has been an explosion of research on women's competition in the past two decades (see Fisher, 2017), whereas previously, psychology tended to be dominated by studies on men's competition. Second, the area of men's intrasexual competition will be addressed elsewhere in this volume (see Betzig, Chapter 55). Third, due to specific experiences over human evolutionary history, the sexes often behave in a distinct manner and have sex-specific cognitions, motivations, and emotions. It is outside the scope of this chapter to discuss the emotions experienced by both sexes in conjunction with their intrasexual competition. I also focus on heterosexual women, given that the bulk of research pertains to mating competition for this group, and note that there needs to be further investigation into populations who define themselves in ways other than "straight" (see, e.g., Semenyna et al., 2019, for important steps in this direction).

The majority of literature on women's intrasexual competition pertains to the realm of mating. The use of information for mating competition is crucial to comprehend, as strategies of information sharing are an effective way to reduce the mating value of same-sex rivals (Wyckoff et al., 2019). Further, the ways that one presents oneself, relative to others, is also important to understand. Thus, I begin by reviewing what women are competing for, followed by *how* they compete for mates. Then I review the larger literature on aggression, followed by that on emotions. I next address specific emotions, with the goal of showing how they can be related not just to mating competition, but also to other forms of competitive situations that women face.

What Do Women Compete For?

Females of many species, including humans, compete with other females to gain access to scarce or limited resources that directly impinge upon survival and reproductive success. Stockley and Campbell (2013) review how competition is usually greater among members of the same sex, given that they most often compete for the same resources, including mates. The enduring need to compete intrasexually for limited goods means that it is a significant evolutionary pressure and should be viewed as an undercurrent of female behavior.

Females compete for access to preferred mates (see Fisher, 2013, for a review of research addressing humans), as well as for resources that may influence their reproductive outcomes, such as food, nest-sites, protection, territories, and by interfering with the reproduction of other females (Stockley & Bro-Jørgensen, 2011). Women compete in many arenas, just like females of many species. They compete to be seen as attractive relative to other women (Fisher,

2004), to be in the center of social groups (Liesen, 2013), and in terms of their mothering (e.g., Benoit & Fisher, 2019).

Differences in human physiology necessitate that women are obligated to invest significantly more in reproduction than men. This disproportionate care is seen at numerous developmental levels, including those related to anisogamy, gestation, and lactation, which leads women to have a decreased reproductive potential relative to men, who have a far smaller obligatory investment (see Trivers, 1972). Further, female fitness is typically less associated with access to mates, compared with male fitness, because males must seek fecund females. This difference means that females do not need to compete as much as males for mating *access*, but do need to compete for access to *preferred* mates. This emphasis is important, as it indicates that females must use selection criteria in choosing mates.

Across species, females compete intrasexually when there are high levels of maternal investment, when paternal investment in offspring is beneficial, and where there are large groups of individuals living together, which increases competition for proximal resources (Apicella & Dreber, 2015). Humans display all three of these features. Mothers invest enormously in their children (Hrdy, 1999). Men provide paternal care at higher rates than seen in males of other species (Clutton-Brock, 1991). Humans also aggregate in social groups, resulting in opportunities to be in proximity to others, including not only mating rivals, but also other mothers with children. The presence of the latter may lead to competition for scarce resources that affect the survival of themselves, their current children, and the likelihood of conceiving in the future. For example, socially dominant women inflict stress on subordinates, leading to reproductive suppression (Salmon et al., 2009).

Universally, women intrasexually compete to gain access to mates who possess phenotypic characteristics that may indicate high genetic quality. For example, low voice (Hodges-Simeon et al., 2015), facial symmetry (Thornhill & Møller 1997), low bodily fat and high muscle mass (Lassek & Gaulin, 2009), and smell (Herz & Cahill, 1997) are thought to serve as proxies of genetic quality (see Scheyd et al., 2008, for a review). Indeed, there is considerable advantage to having a mate who possesses the physical ability to serve as a protector, such that he can protect against "infanticide, sexual harassment, theft of valued resources, and general coercion" (Rodseth & Novak, 2006, p. 196).

These traits are in addition to preferences related to an interest in (and ability to provide) paternal care (Gray & Anderson, 2015), social status (Pérusse, 1994), and an ability to accrue material resources (see Fisher, 2013, for a review; Heath & Hadley, 1998, for a case study in Utah). All of these features show variation. For example, men's paternal care varies substantially within and between cultures, which has been typified as following a "cad" or "dad" strategy (see Apicella & Marlowe, 2007, for a review). Moreover, these characteristics can intertwine. Roney and colleagues (2006) report that women are able to detect men's affinity for children when evaluating the former's facial attractiveness, as well as their genetic quality. Testosterone, which signals immunocompetence and hence is directly related to genotype, predicted women's evaluations of male facial masculinity, and was related to women's short-term attractiveness judgments. Simultaneously, men's actual and perceived affinity toward infants predicted women's long-term attractiveness judgments.

Women's competition does not occur in a vacuum. While women seek to improve their fitness via accessing limited resources, including mates, they must also consider the local environmental context. This context includes information about the current mating market, which may be conceptualized as the number of potential rivals and mates in the local area. Women rely on information about rivals in their local environment to determine their own and potential rivals' mate value, alongside the value of potential mates (Fisher & Fernandez, 2017).

Further, factors such as a scarcity of quality mates lead to increased intensity in competition (Dillon et al., 2017).

In addition to mating competition, evolutionary perspectives dictate that one considers other aspects of life that are key to women's fitness, such as their competition as mothers for limited resources that influence the survival of their children. However, this topic remains neglected (although see Fisher et al., 2017), which is curious given that such competition has direct outcomes on individual fitness. There are significant links between mothers and mating that are worthy of empirical research. While mothers have found and potentially secured a mate, they still need to ensure that mates provide care, time, and resources to herself and any resulting children. Also, once a woman becomes a mother, she does not necessarily stop reproducing, and indeed, she may engage in behaviors to remove the current child via abandonment or infanticide to increase her chances of reproduction or securing a higher-quality mate (Hrdy, 1999). Consequently, locating, obtaining access to, and retaining a quality mate are critical to a woman's reproductive success in that it will lead to healthy children who will survive and reproduce.

However, there are other areas independent of mating that impact on a mother and her children, such as competition within kin networks (Karthikeyan & Fisher, 2023), social dominance, relational status, and independently obtaining sufficient resources (Fisher & Moule, 2013). The latter vital resources improve child longevity, and include clean drinking water and medicines, given that the most common cause of mortality for children under five years of age is infectious disease (68%; Black et al., 2010). Women, like all mammals, invest substantially, from the gamete stage throughout pregnancy, lactation, and childcare. To reap benefits from this investment, they must ensure that their children survive, which dictates that they compete to support themselves and their children (Stockley & Bro-Jørgensen, 2011). The importance of this competition must be emphasized; Clutton-Brock (2009) suggests that females in many species may even compete more intensely for reproductive resources than access to mating opportunities.

In summary, while women compete in many arenas, the focus here is on their mating competition. This decision is based on the current corpus of existing research. In the future, there needs to be more attention paid to other ways in which women intrasexually compete that influence their fitness.

How Do Women Compete?

Recently, research has started to show that females in many species can be as aggressive, or even more so, in competitive interactions when compared to males (see Stockley & Campbell, 2013, for a review). However, female competition rarely involves escalating contests or exaggerated secondary sexual characteristics (Clutton-Brock & Huchard, 2013).

Darwin (1871) proposed that intrasexual competition evolved as a behavioral adaptation for attracting mates and for gathering resources necessary for reproduction. Strategies used for intrasexual competition may be overt, such as physically fighting with a known rival, or they may be covert and subtle, such as applying cosmetics to enhance attractiveness, where the rival may not be known. In this chapter, competition must be seen as rivalry, meaning that there are two or more individuals in pursuit of the same resource and that resource is perceived to be in limited quantity. The individuals do not have to be conscious of the rivalry, or be even aware of the identity of their competitors, but they must be partaking in an activity that draws them closer to attaining their desired resource (Hrdy, 1999), which includes high-quality or preferred mates.

Women (and girls') intrasexual competition is argued to rely on indirect aggression. Indirect aggression occurs when a perpetrator attempts to cause harm, but simultaneously hopes to make it seem as though there is no harmful intention (Björkqvist et al., 1992). Women use indirect aggression when they engage in behaviors such as disclosing others' secrets, breaking confidences, criticizing others' appearances, excluding others from the group, or spreading gossip (Björkqvist, 1994; Owens et al., 2000). Moreover, social networks are often used such that the aggression is diffused among many individuals, or at least is perceived to come from multiple sources. It also further obscures a particular individual's intentions to cause harm and thereby reduces the possibility of retaliation and counter-aggression (Björkqvist et al., 1992). Aggressive acts are performed from within a tightly woven group of allies, thereby intensifying the damage to the victim (Simmons, 2002), as more aggressors are involved.

While women tend toward using indirect aggression, it would be remiss to say that they entirely avoid direct aggression. Direct aggression refers to behaviors that are overt, face to face, typically accompanied by an intention to physically harm, verbally harm, or threaten another person, including the use of a weapon, or insulting, yelling, pushing, or hitting (e.g., Richardson & Green, 2006). Women engage in intrasexual direct aggression when they are in environments where they perceive resources to be scarce. For example, archival data on Zambian women indicate that when women lost their rights to own land and other resources due to colonization, intrasexual aggression via direct confrontation and aggression increased (Burbank, 1987). Moreover, crime statistics show that women sometimes engage in direct aggression. A report from Statistics Canada using 2017 data about female offenders (Savage, 2019) shows that assault is the most common violent crime committed by women (i.e., 70% of all violent crime). However, assault level 1 was the most frequent, at 76%; this level of assault includes pushing, slapping, punching, and face-to-face verbal threats such that there is minor physical injury or no injury to the victim. Resource scarcity also seems to be an issue, as the rates of women offending are highest where resources are scarcest in Canada, which is in the north: the territories of Nunavut, Northwest Territories, and Yukon.

However, compared to men, women's rates of direct aggression are lower, indicating their reluctance to escalate to more dangerous forms of conflict. For example, men's rate of aggravated assault (assault level 3) is over three times greater than that for women. An important caveat is that it is the least common type of assault (and most severe) in Canada and involves wounding, maiming, disfiguring, or endangering the life of someone.

Why do women often forgo direct aggression? Perhaps women have evolved alternative methods of competing due to their lower physical strength than men, , and thereby have developed unique strategies (Björkqvist, 1994). Or, possibly, it is linked to women's need to avoid physical harm, given they are the primary caretakers of children (Campbell, 1999). Campbell (1999) suggests that using indirect aggression is a successful adaptation of women over evolutionary time, as it resulted in increased benefits in terms of reproductive success. Mothers must remain alive for their children, because of the level of care and protection the latter require, which means that women (as mothers) use risk-avoidant, indirect strategies for conflict, competition, and resolving disputes. Taylor et al. (2000) extend the importance of mothers, as they propose that women rarely enter into situations that demand direct confrontation. They argue that women do not have a "fight or flight" response because a fight response might cause them to "put themselves and their offspring in jeopardy, and the flight response . . . may be compromised by pregnancy or the need to care for immature offspring" (p. 412). Instead, they contend that women have evolved a "tend or befriend" response to stress, with tending being the quieting and caring for children and blending into the environment, while befriending is the creation of networks of associations with individuals who may provide resources and protection for the woman and her children.

Nevertheless, there are other views. There is debate about how much women rely on indirect aggression (see the next section). Others propose alternative reasons for competition; for example, Liesen (2013) proposes that girls and women use direct and indirect strategies, pursuing dominance and status not only to gain access to material resources (e.g., food, space, mates), but also to reduce harassment by other women and to establish strong alliances. She argues that for women, the goal is not to be at the top of a hierarchy, but rather at the center of attention, where the maximum social, material, and reproductive benefits are located.

Emotions in Relation to Aggression

Decades ago, researchers proposed the frustration-aggression hypothesis to explain why individuals experience frustration when they are thwarted with respect to attaining their goals. This frustration may then cause them to display aggression (Dollard et al., 1939). The aggression is not necessarily overt, as a lack of displayed aggression may be due to one purposely curtailing their behavior for fear of punishment. Later, Berkowitz (1988) refined this hypothesis to clarify that frustration only resulted from obstacles that were perceived to be unjust or intentional. Further, Berkowitz (1988) proposed that negative experiences of pain, whether physical, psychological, or emotional, may lead to aggression as a form of retaliation against those inflicting the harm. Individuals may experience anger or sadness, triggering fight-or-flight responses resulting in an individual behaving aggressively. Aggression has also been viewed as a way to expel emotion, which brings cathartic relief; by being aggressive, an individual rids oneself of the emotion because it has been expressed outside the body (Bushman et al., 2001). In addition, social pressures lead one to avoid behaving aggressively or violently toward others when there is an absence of justification.

Perceived Threat Leading to Competition

This theory of aggression and how it ties to retaliation are important in light of people's responses to feeling threatened by a potential rival. Mating competition is thought to trigger jealousy, which results in mate-guarding behaviors (Buunk, 1991; Shackelford & Buss, 2000). Mate guarding as a response to one feeling a relationship is threatened is dependent on many characteristics of the individuals involved, such as whether one perceives their mate to be desirable, or the rival to be a formidable competitor for their mate.

Men cross-culturally place high importance on potential mates' attractiveness (at least for longer-term relationships; Buss & Schmitt, 1993), which means that women compete via their appearance (Fisher, 2004). Women feel jealousy toward rivals they think are attractive, feel more threatened by attractive rivals, and engage in more mate guarding when rivals are attractive (Dijkstra & Buunk, 1998; Fink et al., 2014; Hurst et al., 2017; Krems et al., 2016). When women are shown photographs of attractive women who may be mating rivals, they report more jealous feelings (Dijkstra & Buunk, 1998). This effect is strong; when women are primed to think about potential threats to their relationships, they derogate women who are external to the situation (Fisher & Archibald, 2019). Similarly, the more a woman rates another woman's facial femininity, facial attractiveness, and breast size as attractive, the more she perceive her to be a mating competitor (Fink et al., 2014). Likewise, the higher potential rivals are rated on facial attractiveness, the greater women's intentions to guard their romantic partners from them (Hurst et al., 2017; Krems et al., 2016).

There are other reasons women may feel threatened by a potential rival. For example, if a woman believes a rival is sexually available or promiscuous, she feels more threatened than if a rival does not appear to be sexually available. Leenaars and colleagues (2008) report that among adolescent girls, as their number of recent sexual partners increased, reports of other girls derogating them correspondingly increased. Trustworthiness also matters; women engage in more mate guarding when they perceive a rival's trustworthiness to be low, especially if they believe their mate to be of high quality (Hurst et al., 2017; Krems et al., 2016). Women with mates they consider high value perceive ovulating rivals as untrustworthy, which led them to have less desire to befriend them (Krems et al., 2016), accompanied by a stronger need to mate guard (Hurst et al., 2017).

The effects of finding a rival threatening include shifts in circulating hormones. Women's testosterone, a hormone linked to aggression, increases after exposure to an ovulating rival (i.e., higher probability of conception), as compared to a non-ovulating rival (Bateup et al., 2002; Maner & McNulty, 2013; Woodward et al., 2015). This finding may indicate that women's physiology is attuned to mating competition, and specifically, the current fecundity of potential rivals.

Social Rejection and Self-Worth

A particular issue that warrants special attention is social rejection, as it is related to aggression and feelings of self-worth. Social rejection has been documented as causing aggression and increasing unpleasant affect. Individuals feel rejected when they perceive others are not valuing them, and specifically when they feel they are not valued as a potential relationship partner (Leary et al., 2006). Rejection leads some individuals to turn to aggression, perhaps as a way to regain control (Gerber & Wheeler, 2009), and results in the experience of negative emotions such as hurt feelings, sadness, anger, and loneliness (Leary, 2010). Simultaneously, other individuals may instead experience an emotional numbing after rejection, whereby one does not feel negative or positive (Blackhart et al., 2009). Given that we are a social species whereby individuals rely extensively on one another, social pain from rejection appears to "piggyback" onto the physical pain system; that is, the body's pain-response system may become activated by either social exclusion or physical pain (Eisenberger et al., 2003).

At face value, one would expect that social rejection would have a negative impact on self-esteem. Indeed, many studies have supported this conclusion (e.g., Bernstein et al., 2010; Bernstein et al., 2008; Gerber & Wheeler, 2009; Williams et al., 2000; Zadro et al., 2004). Rejection may lead individuals to feel bad about themselves, worthless, and incompetent (Gerber & Wheeler, 2009; but see Blackhart et al., 2009).

Wyckoff (2016) explores a different perspective on the evolutionary underpinnings of social rejection and aggression. She argues that during our evolutionary history, we faced aggressive individuals, which was potentially accompanied by the cost of being harmed or a loss of resources, if a contest was lost. One would also not want to be identified as an "easy target" for aggression, and hence, there would be pressure to defend oneself. Deterring aggression would have been advantageous, in that it reduces these potential costs. Wykoff (and others; see Buss & Shackelford, 1997) argues that aggression may be used to deter *future* aggressors, and hence, is a tactic for social manipulation. Therefore, when someone perceives that they are being devalued, rather than walk away, they experience anger, which leads them to be aggressive. This aggression then signals to others, whether observers or the original person who inflicted the rejection, that one is not to be treated in such a manner and is valuable.

Self-esteem presumably underlies feelings of being valuable; if someone has low self-esteem, they will not recognize that they are being undervalued or should not be the target of social rejection. As reviewed, self-esteem may also be lowered due to rejection, so assessments by others play an important role in how people value themselves. Social comparison (Buunk

& Gibbons, 2007) occurs when we learn of our abilities, characteristics, skills, and social status by comparing ourselves with others. Individuals pay particular attention to those they view as similar, and make the strongest social comparisons to these people. Self-esteem is linked with social comparison because when people compare themselves to others and the outcome is favorable (i.e., downward social comparison), self-esteem increases. However, when the outcome indicates that others are better than themselves (upward social comparison), self-esteem decreases. This relationship of upward social comparison and lowered self-esteem is strong (Buunk et al., 1997).

Lowered self-esteem was long thought to be associated with increased aggression, but newer research shows that the relationship is inconsistent (see Wyckoff & Kirkpatrick, 2016, for a review). One reason for the inconsistency is because previous researchers viewed self-esteem as a unitary construct. However, Kirkpatrick and Ellis (2001) argued that social relationships vary and involve distinct types of criteria, and consequently, self-esteem should also vary. This domain-specific approach to self-esteem accounts for much of the inconsistency in prior findings.

One last point to raise is the issue of mate value, the way that we perceive our worth on the mating market, because it is tied with self-esteem. As Brase and Guy (2004) review, according to the sociometer hypothesis, self-esteem functions to gauge an individual's standing relative to others on multiple criteria, one of which is mate value. Mate value, and efforts to increase mate value, are tightly connected with age, sex, and marital status. Mate value and these efforts, as well as marital satisfaction, predict self-esteem. Further, in a cross-cultural study of mate value and self-esteem, Goodwin and colleagues (2012) found a correlation between the two concepts, but noted that there are sex differences in the traits emphasized by participants that underscore this relationship. For example, women emphasize their caring, supportive, and passionate side, which impacts on their mate value, and consequently their self-esteem.

Highlight on Specific Emotions

It is challenging to divide a chapter on emotions and women's intrasexual mating competition into distinct emotions. Often, emotions overlap, or a situation may lead to the simultaneous experience of several emotions. For example, women who were asked to view photographs of attractive versus unattractive women reported more anger, jealousy, and sadness when exposed to the attractive versus unattractive woman (Massar & Buunk, 2010). Further, Little and Mannion (2006) found that exposure to attractive women resulted in decreases in self-perceived attractiveness, while exposure to unattractive women led to increases in self-perceived attractiveness. These changes in perception are undoubtedly tied to various emotions that overlap or that may be transient. Thus, the next sections may provide the inaccurate illusion that emotions involved in women's intrasexual mating competition are distinct, but the division is useful because it allows a more in-depth focus on specific emotions.

Anger

The recalibration theory of anger maintains that anger evolved to motivate the resolution of interpersonal conflict in favor of the person experiencing anger (Sell et al., 2009). When someone is devalued or treated improperly, they respond with anger, which then motivates them to inflict costs or withhold benefits from the offending party. The result is that the offending individual recalibrates how much they value the other person according to their relative position. Consequently, individuals who are physically strong, which signals their ability to inflict harm, or physically attractive, an indicator of their ability to withhold benefits, are more prone to anger than individuals who are not as strong or attractive. Sell and colleagues (2009) contend that because strong and physically attractive individuals are more likely to win conflicts, they feel more entitled to superior treatment from others.

Using this model, higher self-perceived mate value leads to increased aggression (see Wyckoff & Kirkpatrick, 2016). Using the recalibration theory of anger, one may examine the interplay of status and the costs and benefits associated with aggression. The core concept here is that those with high status face lower likelihood of retaliation and injury, and are more likely to gain benefits from inflicting costs or withholding benefits, than those with lower status. Thus, Wyckoff and Kirkpatrick (2016) contend that high-status individuals more often use direct aggression, while indirect aggression is favored as a retaliatory method by those with low status. Direct aggression more often has an audience, so it may signal to others that one has high status, and it more readily deters future mistreatment. Men who report lower mate value use more indirect aggression than those with higher mate value, while women with higher mate value use more direct aggression than those with lower mate value (Wyckoff & Kirkpatrick, 2016). Anger, therefore, acts as a motivation and leads to aggression, which allows individuals to maintain their reputation, gain benefits, and reduce costs, and causes others to recalibrate their treatment.

Further, anger plays an important role in mediating the relationship between mate value and aggression. Wyckoff (2016) found that anger (but not other emotions, including embarrassment/humiliation, fear/nervousness, or depression/sadness) mediates the relationship between self-perceived mate value and self-reported direct aggression. Those who were attractive were more likely to report using direct aggression than unattractive individuals, which was mediated by anger. Stronger individuals also report wanting to use direct aggression more than weaker individuals, which was again mediated by anger. Anger also mediated the relationship between relative mate value and indirect aggression, especially for men. Collectively, her findings show that anger—but not other aversive emotions—leads to aggression.

These theories lead to specific predictions. It may be the case that women who perceive themselves as more attractive rely on direct aggression more than women who perceive themselves as less attractive, and compete accordingly. Attractive women, or at least women who perceive themselves to be attractive, may also experience anger more than less attractive women, such that they feel more anger if thwarted by mating rivals.

Jealousy

Buss and Haselton (2005) discuss jealousy as an adaptation that, as an emotion, functions to alert individuals to potential threats to a valued relationship. They review how it is activated by the presence of available and desirable same-sex rivals, and works to motivate individuals to deter a partner's abandonment or infidelity. For reasons already explained, women are especially distressed by physically attractive rivals, and further, women paired with wealthy men often exhibit more mate guarding, presumably out of jealousy and concerns about loss of their mate. Similar findings come from Kennair and colleagues (2011), who showed that women are most concerned about rivals who are more kind and understanding than themselves, and who have more attractive faces and bodies.

Dijkstra and Buunk (2002) frame jealousy as a reaction to a threat to, or the actual loss of, a valued relationship with another person, to an actual or imagined rival for one's partner's attention. The assumption is that it involves social comparison, where one compares one's own characteristics with those of a rival. The premise of this work is that jealously occurs only when individuals observe that their rival surpasses them on particular qualities (i.e., upward social comparison). Consequently, they may perceive the rival as a threat to the existing relationship.

Following the logic as already presented, due to sex differences in mate preferences, men and women differ in the characteristics that evoke jealousy. For example, Dijkstra and Buunk (2002) report that women experience more jealousy when a rival is highly physically attractive, whereas men experience more jealousy when a rival is high in social and physical dominance, and social status. Indeed, this pattern has been replicated several times (Dijkstra & Buunk, 2001; see, for review, Buunk et al., 2007; Buunk et al., 2011).

Envy
Envy has been proposed to be an emotion that evolved to promote compensatory behavior as a response to unfavorable social comparisons (Arnocky et al., 2016). It is a negative, unpleasant response to others whom one perceives as having better qualities than oneself, and further, that one wishes a rival would lack (Hill & Buss, 2006).

However, given its role in social comparison, envy might *motivate* an individual to increase their mate value. That is, the function of envy may be to cause someone to focus on its source and then serve to motivate change (Hill & Buss, 2006). Envy also maps onto rival characteristics in a way that parallels that already discussed for jealousy; women experience envy most often when a rival is more physically attractive (Hill & Buss, 2006).

The fact that envy can motivate one toward self-improvement makes it distinct from other emotions experienced during intrasexual competition. Past research shows that envy toward other women's attractiveness leads women to express more positivity and openness toward cosmetic surgery, cosmetics, skin tanning, and dieting (e.g., Arnocky et al., 2016).

Discussion
Women intrasexually compete for mates who are desirable. Intrasexual mating competition is critical to women's reproductive success, and often (but not always) relies on strategies related to indirect aggression to reduce potential retaliation or physical harm. Although there are various theories about why women use indirect aggression, what matters most is that they do so, and that it has the consequence of being effective, as reviewed.

My goal in this chapter has been to explore the emotional underpinnings of women's mating competition. I have reviewed how certain characteristics of rivals, and feeling threatened within one's romantic relationship, may be particularly important to one's emotional experiences. Further, I discussed self-worth, and how it links with various emotions. For experiences related to feeling threatened and circumstances that influence self-worth, I focused the arguments around aggression, which effectively makes the connection between these constructs with one's emotions; that is, aggression may result from feeling threatened or having low self-worth, and in this chapter, I have investigated the various emotional states involved in those situations.

The emotional side of women's intrasexual competition has rarely been examined, as compared to the plethora of papers on *how* women compete for mates, and *why* they do so (e.g., Fisher, 2013, for a review). The existing work focuses on experiences of anger, jealousy, and envy, and usually within the framework of feeling distress about losing a mate to a potential rival, rather than one's direct experience with competition per se. This review highlights the need to understand women's emotional experiences with competitors, especially if the mating rival is someone who is otherwise trusted, such as a close friend, a sister, or other genetic kin.

Cooperativeness
Related to how one might experience emotions when confronted by a mating rival who is a friend or sister, for example, is how one decides to cooperate or compete with others, more

generally. Feelings related to being helpful, cooperative, and altruistic toward others need to be included when discussing mating competition between women. Friends and other women with whom one cooperates are most likely to be around the same age, with similar personality characteristics, values, and mate value (see Fisher & Fernandez, 2017, for a review). However, these same individuals are the most likely rivals for mates.

Maintaining cooperative relationships with other women is critical from an evolutionary perspective: male partners can be absent, noncommittal, unable to help, or abusive, and if a woman is a mother, these issues are particularly problematic (see Sokol-Chang et al., 2017, for a review). In fact, circles of supportive women are at times called "survival networks" (Dominguez & Watkins, 2003; Högnas, 2010). As women proceed through their life span and gain experiences (e.g., have children, experience increases or decreases in their mate value and reproductive potential), they encounter situations where they are required to decide if it is best to cooperate or compete with other women (see Fisher et al., 2017). Thus, women's relationships rest on an interesting foundation, as all parties must decide between providing cooperative support, or being competitors with the goal of maximizing their own success.

To further demonstrate the complexity in decision-making about cooperating versus competing, even from moment to moment, one must consider the dynamic nature of emotions. There is some support for the idea that one's emotions may influence cooperativeness, but it is not a straightforward relationship (see, for a review, Hertel et al., 2000), and indeed, the literature remains mixed as to how emotions and cooperativeness interrelate. Instead, emotions influence one's decision-making, such that a positive mood or feeling secure leads one to more heuristic use, while a negative mood such as sadness or insecurity leads to more rational, systematic processing of information (Hertel et al., 2000). How this decision-making plays out in scenarios involving intrasexual mating competition remains to be determined.

Future Work
Aside from the potential avenues already mentioned, there remain several lines of inquiry that are worth exploring. Two of these are reviewed here. To start, anger, jealousy, and envy are not pleasant emotions, but they do not necessarily adequately capture the experiences people have within intrasexual competition. Is it possible that individuals who lose a competitive interaction have positive emotions that motivate them to improve and return to compete better, later? Morris et al. (2017) review the potential positive outcomes surrounding relationship dissolution, under the hypothesis that negative emotions at the time of breakup lead one to make advantageous changes. Some of the changes might lead to personal growth, or the ability to avoid a similar mate loss in the future. Likewise, when one loses a competition, one might step back, reassess strategies and reconsider one's mate value, and then return to the next competition as a stronger candidate. The emotional underpinnings of losing to a rival may not be consistently negative over the long term, if a loss is viewed from the standpoint of being at least somewhat beneficial.

Along the same lines, what do individuals feel when they *win* a competition against a formidable rival? Surely, they experience happiness in relation to being closer to opportunities to increase their individual fitness, via being in an advantageous situation (Nesse, 1990). The emotional experience, whether transitory or long term, of winning a mating competition for women remains unexamined.

Another area that needs attention from researchers is how women experience emotions outside of the young adulthood age range. The majority of research findings are based on single, young women from Western cultures. Past work has overlooked women who are married, above the age of the average college student, or mothers (Fisher, 2017). What emotions do older women experience in the face of intrasexual competition, given that their reproductive value is different from that of younger women? Perhaps these older women have experienced past reproductive success and have children already in their households, or may be grandmothers themselves. Their emotions from competition are likely distinct from those of younger women, given their life history thus far, their more limited prospects of having future children, and so on.

Conclusion

Women's intrasexual competition has been examined within the context of mating, and in particular, how and why women do engage in intrasexual competition in the mating domain. How emotions are involved in mating competition has only begun to be studied, with researchers focusing on anger, jealousy, and envy, often within the context of feeling threatened by a potential rival, or experiencing the sense of not being as desirable as other women. Self-worth, as well as related topics such as social comparison to rivals, is also critical for understanding what emotions may be experienced in mating competition. While important steps have been made, there remains much work to be done, particularly in terms of how one may experience emotions when competing against someone who is otherwise an ally, or how competition may also lead to positive emotions.

References

Apicella, C. L., & Dreber, A. (2015). Sex differences in competitiveness: Hunter-gatherer women and girls compete less in gender-neutral and male-centric tasks. *Adaptive Human Behavior and Physiology*, *1*(3), 247–269.

Apicella, C. L., & Marlowe, F. W. (2007). Men's reproductive investment decisions: Mating, parenting, and self-perceived mate value. *Human Nature*, *18*(1), 22–34.

Arnocky, S., Perilloux, C., Cloud, J. M., Bird, B. M., & Thomas, K. (2016). Envy mediates the link between social comparison and appearance enhancement in women. *Evolutionary Psychological Science*, *2*, 71–83. https://doi.org/10.1007/s40806-015-0037-1

Bateup, H. S., Booth, A., Shirtcliff, E. A., & Granger, D. A. (2002). Testosterone, cortisol, and women's competition. *Evolution and Human Behavior*, *23*, 181–192. doi: 10.1016/S1090- 5138(01)00100-3

Benoit, T., & Fisher, M. (2019). Intrasexual competition and mothers: Perceptions of those who self-promote and derogate their rivals. *EvoS Journal: The Journal of the Evolutionary Studies Consortium, NEEPS, XII*, 67–77.

Berkowitz, L. (1988). Frustrations, appraisals, and aversively stimulated aggression. *Aggressive Behavior*, *14*(1), 3–11.

Bernstein, M. J., Sacco, D. F., Brown, C. M., Young, S. G., & Claypool, H. M. (2010). A preference for genuine smiles following social exclusion. *Journal of Experimental Social Psychology*, *46*(1), 196–199.

Bernstein, M. J., Young, S. G., Brown, C. M., Sacco, D. F., & Claypool, H. M. (2008). Adaptive responses to social exclusion social rejection improves detection of real and fake smiles. *Psychological Science*, *19*(10), 981–983.

Björkqvist, K. (1994). Sex differences in physical, verbal, and indirect aggression: A review of recent research. *Sex Roles*, *30*, 177–188.

Björkqvist, K., Lagerspetz, I. M., & Kaukiainen, A. (1992). Do girls manipulate and boys fight? Developmental trends in regard to direct and indirect aggression. *Aggressive Behavior*, *1*(8), 117–127.

Black, R. E., Cousens, S., Johnson, H. L., Lawn, J. E., Rudan, I., Bassani, D. G., Jha, P., Campbell, H., Walker, C. F., Cibulskis, R., Eisele, T., Liu, L., Mathers, C.; Child Health Epidemiology Reference Group of WHO and UNICEF. (2010). Global, regional, and national causes of child mortality in 2008: A systematic analysis. *Lancet*, *375*, 1969–1987.

Blackhart, G. C., Nelson, B. C., Knowles, M. L., & Baumeister, R. F. (2009). Rejection elicits emotional reactions but neither causes immediate distress nor lowers self-esteem: A meta-analytic review of 192 studies on social exclusion. *Personality and Social Psychology Review*, *13*(4), 269–309. doi: 10.1177/1088868309346065. Erratum in (2010), *Personality and Social Psychology Review*, *14*(2), 259.

Brase, G. L., & Guy, E. C. (2004). The demographics of mate value and self-esteem. *Personality and Individual Differences*, *36*(2), 471–484.

Burbank, V. K. (1987). Female aggression in cross-cultural perspective. *Behavioral Science Research*, *21*, 70–100.

Bushman, B. J., Baumeister, R. F., & Phillips, C. M. (2001). Do people aggress to improve their mood? Catharsis beliefs, affect regulation opportunity, and aggressive responding. *Journal of Personality and Social Psychology, 81*(1), 17–32.
Buss, D. M., & Haselton, M. (2005). The evolution of jealousy. *Trends in Cognitive Science, 9*(11), 508–510.
Buss, D. M., & Schmitt, D. P. (1993). Sexual strategies theory: An evolutionary perspective on human mating. *Psychological Review, 100,* 204–232.
Buss, D. M., & Shackelford, T. K. (1997). Human aggression in evolutionary psychological perspective. *Clinical Psychology Review, 17*(6), 605–619.
Buunk, A. P., & Gibbons, F. X. (2007). Social comparison: The end of a theory and the emergence of a field. *Organizational Behavior and Human Decision Processes, 102*(1), 3–21.
Buunk, A. P., Massar, K., & Dijkstra, P. (2007). A social cognitive evolutionary approach to jealousy: The automatic evaluation of one's romantic rivals. In J. P. Forgas, M. G. Haselton, & W. von Hippel (Eds.), *Sydney symposium of social psychology: Evolution and the social mind: Evolutionary psychology and social cognition* (pp. 213–228). Routledge/Taylor & Francis Group.
Buunk, A. P., Solano, A. C., Zurriaga, R., & González, P. (2011). Gender differences in the jealousy-evoking effect of rival characteristics: A study in Spain and Argentina. *Journal of Cross-Cultural Psychology, 42*(3), 323–339. https://doi.org/10.1177/0022022111403664
Buunk, B. P. (1991). Jealousy in close relationships: An exchange theoretical perspective. In P. Salovey (Ed.), *Psychological perspectives on jealousy and envy* (pp. 148–177). Guilford Press.
Buunk, B. P., Gibbons, F. X., & Buunk, A. P. (1997). *Health, coping and well-being: Perspectives from social comparison theory.* Psychology Press.
Campbell, A. (1999). Staying alive: Evolution, culture, and women's intrasexual aggression. *Behavioral and Brain Sciences, 22,* 203–252.
Clutton-Brock, T. H. (1991). *The evolution of parental care.* Princeton University Press.
Clutton-Brock, T. (2009). Sexual selection in females. *Animal Behaviour, 77*(1), 3–11. https://doi.org/10.1016/j.anbehav.2008.08.026
Clutton-Brock, T., & Huchard, E. (2013). Social competition and its consequences in female mammals. *Journal of Zoology, 289*(3), 151–171.
Darwin, C. (1871). *The descent of man and selection in relation to sex.* Murray.
Dijkstra, P., & Buunk, B. P. (1998). Jealousy as a function of rival characteristics: An evolutionary perspective. *Personality and Social Psychology Bulletin, 24*(11), 1158–1166. https://doi.org/10.1177/01461672982411003
Dijkstra, P., & Buunk, B. P. (2001). Sex differences in the jealousy-evoking nature of a rival's body build. *Evolution and Human Behavior, 22,* 335–341. doi: 10.1016/S1090-5138(01)00070-8
Dijkstra, P., & Buunk, B. P. (2002). Sex differences in the jealousy-evoking effect of rival characteristics. *European Journal of Social Psychology, 32*(6), 829–852.
Dillon, H., Adair, L., & Brase, G. (2017). Operational sex ratio and female competition: Scarcity breeds intensity. In M. Fisher (Ed.), *The Oxford handbook of women and competition* (pp. 265–280). Oxford University Press.
Dollard, J., Miller, N. E., Doob, L. W., Mowrer, O. H., & Sears, R. R. (1939). *Frustration and aggression.* Yale University Press.
Dominguez, S., & Watkins, C. (2003). Creating networks for survival and mobility: Social capital among African-American and Latin-American low-income mothers. *Social Problems, 50*(1), 111–135.
Eisenberger, N. I., Lieberman, M. D., & Williams, K. D. (2003). Does rejection hurt? An fMRI study of social exclusion. *Science, 302*(5643), 290–292.
Fink, B., Klappauf, D., Brewer, G., & Shackelford, T. K. (2014). Female physical characteristics and intra-sexual competition in women. *Personality and Individual Differences, 58,* 138–141. doi: 10.1016/j.paid.2013.10.015
Fisher, M. L. (2004). Female intrasexual competition decreases female facial attractiveness. *Proceedings of the Royal Society of London, Series B (Supplemental), 271,* S283–S285.
Fisher, M. L. (2013). Women's intrasexual competition for mates. In M. L. Fisher, J. Garcia, & R. Sokol-Chang (Eds.), *Evolution's empress: Darwinian perspectives on the nature of women* (pp. 19–42). Oxford University Press.
Fisher, M. L. (Ed.). (2017). *The Oxford handbook of women and competition.* Oxford University Press.
Fisher, M. L., & Archibald, N. (2019). A thousand times more beautiful: Priming competitor derogation in women. *Current Psychology, 41*(1), 338–346. doi: 10.1007/s12144-019-00551-z
Fisher, M. L., Burch, R., & Sokol-Chang, R. (2017). A theoretical proposal for examining the integration of cooperative and competitive mothering behavior. *Human Ethology Bulletin, 32,* 6–16.
Fisher, M. L., & Fernández, A. M. (2017). The influence of women's mate value on intrasexual competition. In M. L. Fisher (Ed.), *The Oxford handbook of women and competition* (pp. 281–299). Oxford University Press.

Fisher, M. L., & Moule, K. (2013). A new direction for intrasexual competition research: Cooperative versus competitive motherhood. *Journal of Social, Evolutionary, and Cultural Psychology, 7*(4), 318–325.

Gerber, J., & Wheeler, L. (2009). On being rejected: A meta-analysis of experimental research on rejection. *Perspectives on Psychological Science, 4*(5), 468–488.

Goodwin, R., Marshall, T., Fülöp, M., Adonu, J., Spiewak, D., Neto, F., & Plaza, S. H. (2012). Mate value and self-esteem: Evidence from eight cultural groups. *PLoS ONE, 7*(4), e36106. doi: 10.1371/journal.pone.0036106

Gray, P. B., & Anderson, K. G. (2015). The impact of fathers on children. In R. E. Tremblay, M. Boivin, RDeV. Peters (Eds.); J. L. Roopnarine (topic Ed.), *Encyclopedia of early childhood development* [online]. Retrieved from https://www.child-encyclopedia.com/father-paternity/according-experts/impact-fathers-children

Heath, K. M., & Hadley, C. (1998). Dichotomous male reproductive strategies in a polygynous human society: Mating versus parental effort. *Current Anthropology, 39*, 269–374.

Hertel, G., Neuhof, J., Theuer, T., & Kerr, N. L. (2000). Mood effects on cooperation in small groups: Does positive mood simply lead to more cooperation? *Cognition and Emotion, 14*(4), 441–472.

Herz, R. S., & Cahill, E. D. (1997). Differential use of sensory information in sexual behavior as a function of gender. *Human Nature, 8*(3), 275–286. https://doi.org/10.1007/BF02912495

Hill, S. E., & Buss, D. M. (2006). Envy and positional bias in the evolutionary psychology of management. *Managerial and Decision Economics, 27*(2–3), 131–143. https://doi.org/10.1002/mde.1288

Hodges-Simeon, C. R., Gurven, M., & Gaulin, S. J. (2015). The low male voice is a costly signal of phenotypic quality among Bolivian adolescents. *Evolution and Human Behavior, 36*(4), 294–302.

Högnas, R. (2010). A mechanism describing how low-income women exchange support in their personal networks. *Sociological Focus, 43*(4), 330–348.

Hrdy, S. B. (1999). *Mother nature: A history of mothers, infants and natural selection*. Ballantine.

Hurst, A. C., Alquist, J. L., & Puts, D. A. (2017). Women's fertility status alters other women's jealousy and mate guarding. *Personality and Social Psychology Bulletin, 43*, 191–203. doi: 10.1177/0146167216678859

Karthikeyan, S., & Fisher, M. L. (2023). A case study of a historical matrilineal community from an evolutionary perspective. *Evolutionary Behavioral Sciences, 17*(1), 61–81. https://doi.org/10.1037/ebs0000293.

Kennair, L. E. O., Nordeide, J., Andreassen, S., Strønen, J., & Pallesen, S. (2011). Sex differences in jealousy: A study from Norway. *Nordic Psychology, 63*(1), 20–34. https://doi.org/10.1027/1901-2276/a000025

Kirkpatrick, L. A., & Ellis, B. J. (2001). An evolutionary-psychological approach to self-esteem: Multiple domains and multiple functions. In G. J. O. Fletcher & M. S. Clark (Eds.), *Blavkwell handbook of social psychology: Interpersonal processes* (pp. 411–436). Blackwell Publishers.

Krems, J. A., Neel, R., Neuberg, S. L., Puts, D. A., & Kenrick, D. T. (2016). Women selectively guard their (desirable) mates from ovulating women. *Journal of Personality and Social Psychology, 110*, 551–573. doi: 10.1037/pspi0000044

Lassek, W. G., & Gaulin, S. J. C. (2009). Costs and benefits of fat-free mass in men: relationship to mating success, dietary requirements, and native immunity. *Evolution and Human Behavior, 30*, 322–328.

Leary, M. R. (2010). Affiliation, acceptance, and belonging: The pursuit of interpersonal connection. In S. T. Fiske, D. T. Gilbert, & G. Lindzey (Eds.), *Handbook of social psychology* (pp. 864–897). Wiley. https://doi.org/10.1002/9780470561119.socpsy002024

Leary, M. R., Twenge, J. M., & Quinlivan, E. (2006). Interpersonal rejection as a determinant of anger and aggression. *Personality and Social Psychology Review, 10*(2), 111–132.

Leenaars, L. S., Dane, A. V., & Marini, Z. A. (2008). Evolutionary perspective on indirect victimization in adolescence: The role of attractiveness, dating and sexual behavior. *Aggressive Behavior, 34*, 404–415.

Liesen, L. (2013). The tangled web she weaves. In M. Fisher, J. Garcia, & R. Sokol-Chang (Eds.), *Evolution's empress: Darwinian perspectives on the nature of women* (pp. 43–62). Oxford University Press.

Little, A. C., & Mannion, H. (2006). Viewing attractive or unattractive same-sex individuals changes self-rated attractiveness and face preferences in women. *Animal Behavior, 72*(5), 981–987.

Maner, J. K., & McNulty, J. K. (2013). Attunement to the fertility status of same-sex rivals: Women's testosterone responses to olfactory ovulation cues. *Evolution and Human Behavior, 34*, 412–418. doi: 10.1016/j.evolhumbehav.2013.07.005

Massar, K., & Buunk, A. P. (2010). Judging a book by its cover: Jealousy after subliminal priming with attractive and unattractive faces. *Personality and Individual Differences, 49*(6), 634–638. doi: 10.1016/j.paid.2010.05.037

Morris, C., Beaussart, M. L., Reiber, C., & Krajewski, L. S. (2017). Intrasexual mate competition and breakups: Who really wins? In M. L. Fisher (Ed.), *The Oxford handbook of women and competition* (pp. 337–351). Oxford University Press.

Nesse, R. M. (1990). Evolutionary explanations of emotions. *Human Nature, 1*(3), 261–289.

Owens, L., Shute, R., & Slee, P. (2000). "Guess what I just heard!": Indirect aggression among teenage girls in Australia. *Aggressive Behaviour, 26*, 67–83.

Pérusse, D. (1994). Mate choice in modern societies: Testing evolutionary hypotheses with behavioral data. *Human Nature, 5*, 255–278.

Richardson, D. S., & Green, L. R. (2006). Direct and indirect aggression: Relationships as social context. *Journal of Applied Social Psychology, 36*(10), 2492–2508.

Rodseth, L., & Novak, S. (2006). The impact of primatology on the study of human society. In J. Barkow (Ed.), *Missing the revolution: Darwinism for social scientists* (pp. 187–220). Oxford University Press.

Roney, J. R., Hanson, K. N., Durante, K. M., & Maestripieri, D. (2006). Reading men's faces: Women's mate attractiveness judgments track men's testosterone and interest in infants. *Proceedings of the Royal Society of London (Series B), 273,* 2169–2175.

Salmon, C., Figueredo, A., & Woodburn, L. (2009). Life history strategy and disordered eating behavior. *Evolutionary Psychology, 7,* 585–600.

Savage, L. (2019). Female offenders in Canada, 2017. Retrieved December 23, 2020, from https://www150.statcan.gc.ca/n1/pub/85-002-x/2019001/article/00001-eng.htm

Scheyd, G. J., Garver-Apgar, C. E., & Gangestad, S. W. (2008). Physical attractiveness: Signals of phenotypic quality and beyond. In C. Crawford & D. Krebs (Eds.), *Foundations of evolutionary psychology* (pp. 239–259). Taylor & Francis Group/Lawrence Erlbaum Associates.

Sell, A., Tooby, J., & Cosmides, L. (2009). Formidability and the logic of human anger. *Proceedings of the National Academy of Sciences, 106*(35), 15073–15078.

Semenyna, S. W., Vasey, P. L., & Honey, P. L. (2019). Replicating the relationships between Dark Triad traits and female mate-competition tactics in undergraduate women. *Personality and Individual Differences, 147,* 73–78.

Shackelford, T. K., & Buss, D. M. (2000). Marital satisfaction and spousal cost-infliction. *Personality and Individual Differences, 28,* 917–928.

Simmons, R. (2002). *Odd girl out: The hidden culture of aggression in girls.* Harcourt.

Sokol-Chang, R., Burch, R. L., & Fisher, M. L. (2017). Cooperative versus competitive mothers. In M. L. Fisher (Ed.), *The Oxford handbook of women and competition* (pp. 505–528). Oxford University Press.

Stockley, P., & Bro-Jørgensen, J. (2011). Female competition and its evolutionary consequences in mammals. *Biological Reviews, 86,* 341–366.

Stockley, P., & Campbell, A. (2013). Female competition and aggression: Interdisciplinary perspectives. *Philosophical Transactions of the Royal Society B: Biological Sciences, 368*(1631), 1–11.

Taylor, S., Klein, L., Lewis, B., Gruenewald, T., Gurung, R., & Updegraff, J. (2000). Biobehavioral responses to stress in females: Tend-and-befriend, not fight-or-flight. *Psychological Review, 107,* 411–429.

Thornhill, R., & Möller, A. (1997). Developmental stability, disease and medicine. *Biological Reviews, 72,* 497–548.

Trivers, R. (1972). Parental investment and sexual selection. In B. Campbell (Ed.), *Sexual selection and the descent of man 1871–1971* (pp. 139–179). Aldine Press.

Williams, K. D., Cheung, C. K., & Choi, W. (2000). Cyberostracism: Effects of being ignored over the Internet. *Journal of Personality and Social Psychology, 79*(5), 748–762. https://doi.org/10.1037/0022-3514.79.5.748

Woodward, S. L., Thompson, M. E., & Gangestad, S. W. (2015). Women exposed to the scents of fertile-phase and luteal-phase women: Evaluative, competitive, and endocrine responses. *Adaptive Human Behavior and Physiology, 1,* 434–448. doi: 10.1007/s40750-014-0019-8

Wyckoff, J. (2016). Aggression and emotion: Anger, not general negative affect, predicts desire to aggress. *Personality and Individual Differences, 101,* 220–226.

Wyckoff, J. P., Asao, K., & Buss, D. M. (2019). Gossip as an intrasexual competition strategy: Predicting information sharing from potential mate versus competitor mating strategies. *Evolution and Human Behavior, 40*(1), 96–104. doi: 10.1016/j.evolhumbehav.2018.08.006

Wyckoff, J. P. & Kirkpatrick, L. A. (2016). Direct and indirect aggression tactics as a function of domain-specific self-esteem. *Personality and Individual Differences, 92,* 135–142.

Zadro, L., Williams, K. D., & Richardson, R. (2004). How low can you go? Ostracism by a computer is sufficient to lower self-reported levels of belonging, control, self esteem, and meaningful existence. *Journal of Experimental Social Psychology, 40*(4), 560–567.

CHAPTER 51
Emotions across Cultures

Roza G. Kamiloğlu, YongQi Cong, Rui Sun, and Disa A. Sauter

Abstract

What can evolutionary theories reveal about emotions, and how can research on emotions inform evolutionary theories? This chapter discusses links between evolutionary theories of emotion and the cross-cultural study of emotion. In particular, the authors emphasize the notion that evolved psychological mechanisms result in cultural differences instantiated as variations on common themes of human universals. They focus on two components of emotions: emotion experience and nonverbal expressions. Several case studies from emotion science are outlined to illustrate this framework empirically. In the domain of emotion experience, they highlight shame as an illustration of the idea of variations occurring across cultures around a common theme. In the domain of nonverbal expression of emotion, this idea is illustrated by the in-group advantage, that is, superior recognition of emotional expressions produced by members of one's own group. Lastly, they review three different theoretical accounts of how to conceptualize cross-culturally shared themes underlying emotions.

Key Words: culture, emotion, emotion experience, evolutionary psychology, nonverbal expression, theory, universals

Introduction

What can evolutionary psychology tell us about consistency and variability in human emotion across cultures? A growing body of research provides cross-cultural data on numerous features of emotion, including expressions (e.g., Elfenbein et al., 2007; Tracy & Matsumoto, 2008), perception (e.g., Cordaro et al., 2016; Crivelli et al., 2017; Laukka et al., 2013), regulation (e.g., Liddell & Williams, 2019; Pauw et al., 2020), and experience (e.g., Sun et al., 2023). This work underscores the interests in empirical tests of the extent to which components of emotions vary across cultures. Evolutionary psychology can offer a useful framework for such endeavors. Cross-cultural differences are consistent with an evolutionary psychological approach to emotions. Despite common belief to the contrary, evolved mechanisms do not imply strict uniformity (Apicella & Barrett, 2016; Tooby & Cosmides, 1992). Evolved mechanisms are expected to produce culturally variable output (e.g., physiological or behavioral changes) in response to variable input in terms of the local environment and culture (e.g., Al-Shawaf & Lewis, 2017). Interaction of evolved psychological mechanisms with a wide range of human environmental and cultural conditions might thus be expected to produce variability in psychological output between human populations. Here, we argue that evolutionary psychology can offer a lens to view the ways through which evolved systems give rise to universal and culturally variable outcomes in the domain of human emotion.

In this chapter, we examine the intersection between evolutionary theories and the study of emotions across cultures. We examine what predictions can be derived from evolutionary theories about cross-cultural consistency and variability of emotion, and highlight the benefits that can be gleaned from their integration. To do so, we first explicate the notion that evolved psychological mechanisms result in cultural differences instantiated as variations around common themes of human universals. Next, we consider this idea in relation to two different components of emotion: experience and nonverbal expressions. We do not comprehensively review the available empirical evidence, but instead provide case studies as illustrative examples, and point readers to resources for further reading. Finally, we discuss three frameworks of emotion theory in terms of their proposals for what constitutes the evolved, cross-culturally shared themes underlying emotions.

Evolved Psychological Mechanisms Can Yield Consistency and Variability

An evolutionary psychological approach posits species-typical psychological mechanisms (Lewis et al, 2017). Influential conceptions of evolutionary psychology hold that the human mind is a product of mechanisms that evolved by natural selection to solve particular adaptive problems faced in ancestral environments over long periods of time (Tooby & Cosmides, 1990, 1992). Adaptive problems refer to conditions that would have had a recurrent impact on an organism's chances of survival and reproductive success, such as avoiding predators, kin detection, attracting a mate, finding nutritious food, and protecting offspring. On this view, the presence of recurrent yet varied adaptive problems would have favored the evolution of functionally specialized mechanisms (but see L. F. Barrett, 2011). Such mechanisms might include sensory, perceptual, affective, and behavioral features that work together to facilitate rapid and effective responses to solving specific kinds of challenges (Barrett & Kurzban, 2006; Cosmides & Tooby, 1994; but see Anderson & Finlay, 2014; Stephen, 2014; Zerilli, 2017).

Evolutionary psychology has tended to emphasize the universality of human psychology (Tooby & Cosmides, 1992). The idea of a universal human nature can easily be taken to mean that specific behaviors must be universal: while universality claims based on evolutionary theorizing imply biological underpinnings, any systematic variation in human psychology and behavior is assumed to be evidence for cultural differences that are not evolved (see Apicella & Barrett, 2016). However, evolution does not necessarily yield uniform results across contexts; evolutionary processes have resulted in highly diverse cultural repertoires of human populations. Human cultural capacities are part of evolved psychological mechanisms (e.g., Heyes, 2020; Richerson & Boyd, 2005). Culture is a human universal, yet culture is obviously a source of variability in human psychology and behavior (Kline et al., 2018). Variation is thus not equivalent to a lack of universality, nor does universality imply a lack of cultural influence. Debates around universality are often framed as competing explanations set up as dichotomies: innate–learned, nature–nurture, or biological–cultural. However, elaborating on the relationship between evolution and culture first requires recognizing that evolutionarily prepared and culturally learned processes are not incompatible but rather complementary. Only then can we begin to understand how evolved psychological mechanisms can create psychological and behavioral variation as well as consistency across populations (H. C. Barrett, 2014).

Evolutionarily prepared and culturally learned mechanisms are thus not mutually exclusive explanations of consistency and variability. Individuals are endowed with the inclination to be easily conditioned to some type of stimuli, or to learn some things more easily than others; these are considered innate prepared mechanisms (e.g., Al-Shawaf et al., 2020; Al-Shawaf et al., 2019; Tooby & Cosmides, 1992). Such underlying mechanisms underlie some nonverbal expressions, such as infants across cultures smiling in response to a familiar voice or to tickling (Eibl-Eibesfeldt, 1973). In addition to these prepared mechanisms, nonverbal expressions can also be learned in a manner that is culturally variable. For instance, tongue protrusion is considered a sign of a culturally specific emotional state, *lajya* (roughly translated as "shame") in the Indian Orissa culture (Menon & Shweder, 1994). Evolutionarily prepared and social learning mechanisms thus together shape human behavior.

While evolutionary theorizing does not propose universal manifest behavior, it does posit species-typical evolved psychological mechanisms (e.g., Lewis et al., 2017). These mechanisms evolved to process cues from our ancestral cultural environments, and mesh with statistical regularities in the specific contemporary environment of the organism (Brown, 1991; Tooby & Cosmides, 1992). Evolved psychological mechanisms allow humans to learn from features that are culturally and ecologically variable by interacting with recurrent structures present in their environment. Consequently, systematic variability across cultural environments can lead to systematically variable psychological output. The operation of a psychological mechanism can be conceptualized as three stages of information-processing in general: environmental and cultural cues are processed as input in evolved information-processing mechanisms, which are then operated upon by computational procedures, and subsequently turn into variable output (e.g., Al-Shawaf & Lewis, 2017). Universality is not predicted at the level of output, but rather at the level of computational design. Variable output is a sign that the contextual proximate inputs differ across cultural environments. Evolutionary approach thus offers a comprehensive framework that links proximate mechanisms to the distal origins of those mechanisms (see Lewis et al., 2017, for a discussion on proximate and ultimate level of analysis). For instance, strong evidence has been found for prelinguistic color categories in infants (Skelton et al., 2017), pointing to universal color categories that are present before color word learning. However, although infant color perception has a universal foundation, learning language changes color perception (Forbes & Plunkett, 2018). Indeed, color perception reflects not only universal tendencies, but also variation based on local linguistic convention (e.g., Reiger & Kay, 2009; Roberson et al., 2009; Roberson et al., 2008). Language and culture thus shape how evolved psychological mechanisms are instantiated.

Human Emotions as Variations on Themes

In understanding evolved and learned mechanisms, cultural differences can be conceptualized as variations around common themes of human universals. Depending on environmental circumstances, species-typical traits may develop differently (H. C. Barrett, 2020). For instance, people who forage daily develop more sophisticated odor categorization skills than city-dwellers, reflecting a biological potential that only develops fully when utilized (Majid & Kruspe, 2018). Evolutionary hypotheses posit that evolved mechanisms respond adaptively to environmental conditions. For instance, cross-cultural research on mate choice has shown varying preferences. The male preference for low waist-to-hip ratio and slimness is universal, but it varies with ecology in response to changes in the local cue structure (e.g., Swami, 2015; Yu & Shepard, 1998). Similarly, the preference for average faces is universal, but the average face shape in a population is determined by faces in the local environment, resulting in variability across groups in which faces are preferred (Apicella et al., 2007). Shared human traits thus develop differently in response to environmental conditions.

Like other psychological mechanisms, human emotions can be positioned within the framework of universal variations on a theme. On this view, emotions would be expected to exist across cultures, but cross-cultural differences should occur in a manner that reflects differences in ecology and culture across groups. However, there is no consensus on how to conceptualize emotions, which makes this proposal challenging to evaluate (Sauter & Russell, 2020). Yet, most scholars of emotion agree that it is useful to distinguish between different components of emotion, including felt experience, cognitive appraisals (i.e., evaluations), nonverbal expressions, and physiological changes (Moors, 2014; Russell, 2009; Scarantino, 2016). These distinctions are particularly pertinent in discussions of cross-cultural similarities and variations, since the extent to which culture modulates different components of emotion is inconsistent across emotion components (see Manokara & Sauter, 2021). Specifically, it has been proposed that culture strongly influences subjective emotion experiences, but weakly influences nonverbal expressions (Levenson et al., 2007). Next, we therefore turn to discussing cross-cultural similarities and variations for these two key emotion components: emotion experience and nonverbal expressions.

Emotion Experience

Cultural differences in emotion experience can be thought of as variations on themes that reflect prototypical "scripts" related to a type of emotion experience (Lazarus, 1991). Elements of such themes include elicitors (causes), appraisals, and tendencies to take different actions. Integration of these elements into a coherent script links a type of situation to the subjective emotion experience. For instance, prototypical scripts for experiencing sadness include an irrevocable loss, while fear involves facing an immediate danger. In an evolutionary psychological framework, the themes would be expected to be universal, yet may predict divergent emotional responses across cultures, which in turn would mean cross-culturally variable emotion experiences.

In the discussion of emotion in relation to culture, a commonly used concept is *individualism–collectivism*, which denotes the extent to which a cultural group values individual needs, wishes, and goals over those of the group or collective (Hofstede, 1983, 2001). Cultures that are more individualistic (e.g., North America and Western Europe), emphasize autonomy and personal goals. In contrast, cultures that are less individualistic and more collectivistic (e.g., East Asia and South America) place more emphasis on relationships with others and social harmony. Much of the research on emotion and culture draws on this distinction.

In the context of emotional experience across cultures, shame is an illustrative example for the notion of cross-cultural variation on a common theme. Shame is an emotion that, across cultures, involves a negative evaluation of the self (Tangney, 1995; Tracy & Robins, 2006). Shame arises when one's shortcomings are exposed to others, and results from a real or imagined negative evaluation by others (Wong & Tsai, 2007). Shame fulfills several functions, including reflecting our concern for others (Lebra, 1988) and preserving our sense of personal identity (Hultberg, 1988; Scheff, 1988). It is believed that people experience shame in all societies; indeed, that it is so important for social control that it is unlikely that a society could be maintained without it (Creighton, 1990). Field experiments including small communities around the world have found that, despite widely varying languages, cultures, and subsistence modes, shame is closely related with devaluation of local audiences (Sznycer et al., 2018). Complementing this cross-cultural consistency, there are important differences in how shame manifests in different cultures, and how different groups see shame. In fact, shame experiences can be considered as variations on a relational theme in at least three ways.

First, there is a difference across cultures in how socially desirable shame is considered to be. In individualistic cultures, shame is considered highly undesirable, as it signals incompetence, inferiority, or weakness (Goffman, 1967), and undermines positive self-regard (Kitayama et al., 2006). In contrast, in collectivistic cultures, shame is not perceived as particularly unpleasant (Romney et al., 1997), possibly because it is seen as conducive to self-improvement and perspective-taking (Heine et al., 1999). In collectivistic cultures, being aware of one's shortcomings and actively correcting them helps individuals realign with social norms and expectations.

Second, the antecedents of shame can be different across cultures (e.g., Boiger et al., 2014). For example, for Americans, situations in which their personal flaws are revealed to others, like getting sick during a team game, are seen as more shameful. For Japanese people, situations that imply a loss of public face to the protagonists themselves, like getting caught during self-talk by a stranger, are perceived as more shameful (Boiger et al., 2013). In American culture, maintaining dignity is defined by an independent, autonomous self, while in Japanese culture, maintaining face is defined by an interdependent, relational self.

Third, cross-cultural variability can illuminate the manner in which cultures differentially highlight, ignore, or group various facets of emotional experience (Fessler, 2004). Shame fails to achieve the central tasks of an independent self (Kitayama et al., 1995), and consequently shame is less salient and indeed made relatively invisible in individualistic, compared to collectivistic, cultures (Scheff, 1988). In individualistic cultures, shame is unarticulated in early child development, and the development of shame instead takes place relatively late in development (Miake & Yamazaki, 1995). Moreover, shame representations are less elaborate in individualistic cultures as compared to other cultural contexts (Mascolo et al., 2003; Shaver et al., 1992). Notably, the difference between *shame* and *guilt* varies across cultures. In individualistic cultures such as the United States, shame is often used synonymously with guilt, but shame arises when one's shortcomings are attributed to oneself, while guilt comes when one's focus is on a particular negative act or circumstance (Robertson et al., 2018; Wong & Tsai, 2007). In fact, exactly because shame may be "overshadowed" by guilt in individualistic cultures, a fuller understanding of shame experiences can only be arrived at by studying shame across cultures (Fessler, 2004).

Shame thus illustrates the notion of emotion experience being organized as variations on a shared theme. Even though clear cross-cultural similarities exist in terms of the basic construct (Sznycer et al., 2018), the experience of shame is diverse across cultures in terms of antecedents, as well as how shame experiences relate to other emotions. A full understanding of shame requires the study of societies that vary on many dimensions, including individualism and collectivism.

Nonverbal Expression

Nonverbal expression of emotion includes facial and bodily expressions like frowns, smiles, and raised fists, as well as vocalizations like laughs and screams. There is evidence for evolved mechanisms underlying the production and perception of such expressions. For instance, we more easily learn to associate certain stimuli with particular nonverbal expressions, like the acquisition of fear response to snakes (e.g., Öhman & Mineka, 2003). Associations between stimuli and expression can also be learned from ecological and environmental input that varies across cultural groups. In addition to associations with stimuli, nonverbal expressions of emotion themselves can develop differently depending on the context, leading to variations on common themes across cultures. Below, we examine how nonverbal expressions of emotions vary across cultures in terms of both perception and production.

Variation in Perception and Production of Emotional Expressions across Cultures

In the domain of nonverbal expressions, cultural differences can be thought of as variations around common themes of human universals, with evolutionarily prepared capacities shaped by environmental factors like culture-specific learning. This is well illustrated by the so-called in-group advantage, which refers to the superior recognition of emotions from nonverbal expressions produced by members of one's own group. Even though reliable emotional information can be inferred across cultural groups from nonverbal cues, research has consistently shown that emotional communication is enhanced when it occurs within, as compared to between, cultural groups (Elfenbein & Ambady, 2002; Laukka & Elfenbein, 2020). Specifically, emotional expressions are better recognized via both facial and verbal cues when the expresser and perceiver share the same cultural background (e.g., Elfenbein et al., 2007; Laukka et al., 2016; Paulmann & Uskul, 2014). This discrepancy in recognition accuracy reflects the fact that culturally specific factors help shape the outcomes of evolutionarily prepared mechanisms.

One explanation for the in-group advantage is that there are systematic differences between groups in terms of expressive styles. This view is articulated in dialect theory, which uses a linguistic metaphor to describe emotion as a universal language with different dialects (Elfenbein, 2013; Elfenbein et al., 2007). An American English speaker can communicate with a British English speaker reasonably well, but not quite as easily as with another American English speaker. Just like linguistic dialects, differences in expressive styles are shaped by culture-specific learning. Individuals learn the expressive behaviors that are prevalent in the environment that they grow up in. As a result, members of the same group share the same "emotion dialect" and are therefore better able to recognize each other's expressions.

There is empirical support for this account from studies that have directly examined nonverbal expressions in different cultures. For example, Elfenbein and colleagues (2007) asked participants from Canada and Gabon to pose a range of emotions using facial expressions. These expressions were then analyzed using the Facial Action Coding System (FACS; Ekman & Friesen, 1978), which objectively codes facial muscle movements. These muscle movements (or combination of muscle movements) are called action units (AUs). When examining the AUs associated with 10 different emotions, there was great convergence between the two cultures. For example, for the emotion surprise, 50% of the Canadian and 60% of the Gabonese encoders showed the prototypical expression (AU1 + AU2 + AU5 with mouth open). At the same time, reliable cultural differences were observed, demonstrating culture-specific variations around the universal facial expressions. For example, when expressing sadness, while individuals from both cultures showed the prototypical expression involving AU1 (27% and 13%) and AU4 (67% and 33%), 43% of Gabonese encoders showed AU 56 (head tilt), while none of the Canadian encoders did. Interestingly, there were greater cross-cultural differences for expressions of emotions that are typically elicited in social interactions (e.g., anger and shame) than for those that are often elicited by non-social events (e.g., fear and disgust).

A recent study of expressive behaviors associated with 22 different emotions across five different cultures found further evidence for culture-specific variations around universal themes (Cordaro et al., 2018). The researchers identified what they called International Core Patterns (ICPs), denoting patterns of expressive behaviors that were conserved across cultures. On average, about half of any participant's expressions of any emotion involved movements from the ICPs. At the same time, unique cultural accents were observed that differed across cultures. Similar patterns were observed for posed and spontaneous expressions of emotions. These findings point to culture-specific expressions around universally shared core expression patterns; these differences in the production of expressions likely contribute to the challenges occurring when interpreting expressions by members of other groups.

Culture-specific learning can thus shape some aspects of the ways in which emotions are expressed. In addition, cultural learning is an important determinant of cultural identity. It has been suggested that the extent to which a perceiver identifies with an expresser determines their motivation to decode signals from the expresser (Thibault et al., 2006). According to this view, the more the perceiver judges the expresser to be a member of their own group, the more motivated the perceiver will be to attempt to interpret the emotional expression. This in turn can lead to higher decoding accuracy. The motivational view thus provides a complementary explanatory framework in which the in-group advantage arises from cultural identity, which is also an outcome of environmental factors.

The motivational view aligns with evolutionary accounts which highlight that investing more resources in members of one's own group contributes to maximizing inclusive fitness (Abbot et al., 2011; Hamilton, 1964). There is empirical support for this view. Superior processing strategies are used when processing in-group, as compared to out-group, expressions. For example, when judging in-group faces, perceivers engage in more configural processing (i.e., processing the interdependence and spatial relationship between face parts) as opposed to analytical processing (i.e., processing the different facial components separately; Hugenberg & Corneille, 2009). Configural processing has been shown to be beneficial for the decoding of emotional facial expressions (Calder et al., 2000). However, the enhanced decoding of emotional expressions from in-group members only occurs during longer presentation times, suggesting that the higher recognition accuracy for in-group signals requires additional processing time (Young & Hugenberg, 2010).

Nonverbal expression can also vary across cultures due to differences in display rules, that is, norms about how appropriate it is to display emotional expressions in a particular context (Friesen, 1972; Manokara et al., 2023; Matsumoto, 1990). Though there are norms regarding the expression of emotion in certain situations in every culture, considerable variations exist in these social rules across cultural groups. Specifically, display rules vary along with important cultural dimensions, including individualism–collectivism (Hofstede, 1983, 2001).

People from more collectivistic cultures have been shown to be less expressive overall (Matsumoto et al., 2008). While there is no evidence that individuals in collectivistic cultures experience fewer or less intense emotions, they are under more social pressure to regulate their emotion displays. This may reflect the fact that a typical goal of individuals in individualistic cultures is to be independent of others, and attending to and expressing one's own attributes such as personal feelings can help distinguish oneself from others (Markus & Kitayama, 1991). In contrast, collectivistic cultures prioritize self-control and accommodating the needs of others over personal desires (Tamis-LeMonda et al., 2008; Triandis, 1995), which might result in less expression of personal feelings. Cultural differences in the degree of individualism–collectivism have been found to map onto the strength of norms for expressing emotions (Matsumoto et al., 2008).

Display rules again illustrate how nonverbal expression can be thought of as variations on a common theme across cultures: evolutionarily prepared nonverbal expressions are shaped by culturally learned display rules. While all cultures have norms dictating how and when one should express their emotions, display rules differ systematically across cultures. These rules are influenced by broader norms and values within a culture, for example those that correspond to individualism–collectivism. These patterns of behavior are self-enforcing within a group and are acquired through culture-specific learning. From an evolutionary perspective, conforming to group norms serves an important signaling function and can confer prestige and better evaluations of fitness by in-group members (Cheng et al., 2013; Henrich & Gil-White, 2001; Wenegrat et al., 1996).

How to Conceptualize Common Themes Underlying Emotions?
Approaching emotion components as variations around universal themes raises the question of how best to characterize those themes. Next, we outline three accounts of emotions with different implications for how to understand the cross-culturally shared themes underlying emotions. We sketch three views on emotion in terms of what each theory considers to be evolutionarily prepared and what is thought to be culturally learned: the Basic Emotion Theory, Appraisal Theory, and psychological constructionism. We do not advocate for one account over the others, but outline their views on how best to conceptualize emotions.

Affect Programs: The Basic Emotion Theory
According to Basic Emotion Theory, emotions are distinct, brief states that were selected for over evolutionary time for their adaptive value in dealing with important ancestral situations (e.g., Ekman, 1992). Basic emotions thus aided organisms in dealing with recurring challenges and opportunities over the course of evolution (e.g., Tooby & Cosmides, 2008). Examples include fear for natural predators, disgust for rotten or toxic food, and joy for playful interactions. All humans are posited to have a biologically innate, latent *affect program* for each basic emotion. What these emotions are varies across theorists, but frequently cited basic emotions are anger, fear, disgust, sadness, surprise, and joy (but see Keltner & Cordaro, 2017, for a more extensive list). The basic emotion framework thus postulates a specialized affect program for each emotion, which can be conceptualized as superordinate programs for coordinating functionally specialized mechanisms, including physiological changes and behavior (e.g., Al-Shawaf et al., 2016; Al-Shawaf & Lewis, 2017; Tooby & Cosmides, 2008). These superordinate programs direct the processing of environmental or somatic cues to aid the organism's reaction to a recurring type of adaptive problem.

Affect programs can be triggered by distinct universal antecedents, like being chased by a predator and smelling rotten food. In addition to universal antecedents, learned elicitors can also trigger affect programs. Regardless of the trigger, affect programs activate the same cascade of emotion components, including physiological, expressive, and subjective responses. On this view, emotions are thus domain-specific modules that facilitate adaptive reactions to particular kinds of ancestral situations. However, emotions can still be shaped by cultural learning, including higher-order cognition (Izard, 2007). The Basic Emotion Theory thus posits evolved mechanisms for discrete emotions, and modulation of emotion processes by cultural learning.

Appraisals: Appraisal Theory
The appraisal approach argues that emotional experiences are triggered by immediate and intuitive evaluations (appraisals) of our environment (e.g., Ellsworth, 2013). Commonly proposed appraisal dimensions are novelty, valence, goal relevance, certainty, and agency. Appraisal theorists do not focus on specific types of situations (e.g., the presence of a snake), but rather on a small set of appraisal dimensions. These dimensions specify constituent elements of emotional experience. While some theorists argue that appraisals trigger a system similar to affect programs posited in the basic emotion approach (Ekman, 1992; Keltner et al., 2006; Roseman, 1991), others propose that different appraisal dimensions influence emotion components separately (Moors, 2014; Scherer, 2001). In this second view, specific changes in emotion episodes (e.g., facial muscle movements, vocal changes) are explained by specific combinations of appraisal dimensions triggered by the event, not by a categorical emotion mechanism.

According to the appraisal approach, appraisals are evolutionarily prepared and constitute the core of emotion. Some appraisal theorists (e.g., Scherer & Moors, 2019) suggest that certain patterns of individual appraisal dimensions were more common throughout human evolutionary history. Those patterns would have resulted an increased temporal synchronization and coherence among several appraisal dimensions. The appraisal framework thus proposes preparedness for appraisals, which result in emotion episodes when the components of episodes are sufficiently synchronized. However, depending on the culture, people might evaluate emotion-eliciting situations differently, resulting in culturally variable emotional experiences and expressions (Ellsworth, 2013; Scherer, 1997).

General-Purpose Mechanisms: Psychological Constructivism
In the psychological constructionist framework, emotions are shaped by proximal socio-contextual factors and not by specialized evolved adaptations (Russell, 2009). From this perspective, emotions are produced by general-purpose mechanisms (L. F. Barrett, 2014). A central feature is core affect, which refers to bodily sensations along the dimensions of arousal (energized or enervated) and valence (good or bad). Core affect is, however, not specific to emotions; bodily sensations are always in some state of arousal and valence. A range of additional processes, such as sensory-perceptual-cognitive processing, respondent behaviors, and instrumental actions, are included in the suite of general-purpose mechanisms thought to underlie emotions according to psychological constructionism.

According to psychological constructionism, the general-purpose mechanisms (but not specific emotion categories or appraisal dimensions) are prepared and consequently universal. In contrast, subjective experience is thought to reflect culturally specific learning processes (Mesquita et al., 2010). Psychological constructivism thus posits cultural variability in emotions, but universality of domain-general mechanisms including core affect.

Conclusions

Can evolutionary psychology inform our understanding of cross-cultural consistency and variability in human emotion? We have discussed this question in the context of the notion that evolved psychological mechanisms led to human universals that are instantiated as variations around cross-culturally shared themes (H. C. Barrett, 2020). According to this idea, specific traits develop differently depending on environmental circumstances, leading to variations on that trait. We have proposed that human emotions can be placed in the framework of cultural differences as variations on a universal theme. For instance, evidence for cross-cultural differences in the experience of shame and emotion recognition from nonverbal expressions reflect variability on universally shared themes. These examples highlight how evolutionarily prepared mechanisms produce outcomes that are shaped by environmental factors like cultural learning. Although there is no consensus on how to best conceptualize the themes, we have outlined the perspectives of three major emotion theories to illustrate some alternative views on this issue.

From an evolutionary psychological perspective, cross-cultural variation in emotion should reflect key differences in ecology and cultural context. However, cross-cultural research on emotion has primarily tended to focus on testing the degree of consistency or variability, while less attention has been given to the factors driving the variability. Nevertheless, recent research points to aspects of cultural variation in emotionally expressive behavior being shaped by historical heterogeneity, that is, the extent to which the present-day population in a country descended from many versus few source countries (Rychlowska et al., 2015). This approach of establishing potential driving forces of cross-cultural differences from ecology and culture has the potential to open up a rich avenue for cross-cultural research. To explain findings regarding cultural variation in human emotion, future research might also more explicitly contrast predictions based the three emotion theories we outlined, in terms of how they explain cross-cultural variability. All in all, the idea of cultural differences as variations on a theme around universals provides an opportunity for testing evolutionary hypotheses regarding cross-cultural variation in human emotion.

References

Abbot, P., Abe, J., Alcock, J., Alizon, S., Alpedrinha, J. A. C., Andersson, M., Andre, J.-B., van Baalen, M., Balloux, F., Balshine, S., Barton, N., Beukeboom, L. W., Biernaskie, J. M., Bilde, T., Borgia, G., Breed, M., Brown, S., Bshary, R., Buckling, A., . . . Zink, A. (2011).Inclusive fitness theory and eusociality. *Nature, 471,* E1–E4. https://doi.org/10.1038/nature09831

Al-Shawaf, L., Conroy-Beam, D., Asao, K., & Buss, D. M. (2016). Human emotions: An evolutionary psychological perspective. *Emotion Review, 8,* 173–186. https://doi.org/10.1177/1754073914565518

Al-Shawaf, L., & Lewis, D. M. (2017). Evolutionary psychology and the emotions. In V. Zeigler-Hill & T. K. Shackelford (Eds.), *Encyclopedia of personality and individual differences* (pp. 1–10). Springer. https://doi.org/10.1007/978-3-319-28099-8_516-1

Al-Shawaf, L., Lewis, D. M., Barbaro, N., & Wehbe, Y. S. (2020). The products of evolution: Conceptual distinctions, evidentiary criteria, and empirical examples. In T. K. Shackelford (Ed.), *The Sage handbook of evolutionary psychology* (pp. 70–95). Sage.

Al-Shawaf, L., Lewis, D. M. G., Wehbe, Y., & Buss, D. M. (2019). Context, environment, and learning in evolutionary psychology. In T. K. Shackelford, & V. A. Weekes-Shackelford (Eds.). *Encyclopedia of evolutionary psychological science* (pp. 1–12). Springer.

Anderson, M. L., & Finlay, B. L. (2014). Allocating structure to function: The strong links between neuroplasticity and natural selection. *Frontiers in Human Neuroscience, 7,* 918. https://doi.org/10.3389/fnhum.2013.00918

Apicella, C. L., & Barrett, H. C. (2016). Cross-cultural evolutionary psychology. *Current Opinion in Psychology, 7,* 92–97. https://doi.org/10.1016/j.copsyc.2015.08.015

Apicella, C. L., Little, A. C., & Marlowe, F. W. (2007). Facial averageness and attractiveness in an isolated population of hunter-gatherers. *Perception, 36,* 1813–1820. https://doi.org/10.1068/p5601

Barrett, H. C. (2014). *The shape of thought.* Oxford University Press.

Barrett, H. C. (2020). Towards a cognitive science of the human: cross-cultural approaches and their urgency. *Trends in Cognitive Sciences, 24*(8), 620–638. https://doi.org/10.1016/j.tics.2020.05.007

Barrett, H. C., & Kurzban, R. (2006). Modularity in cognition: Framing the debate. *Psychological Review, 113,* 628–647. https://doi.org/10.1037/0033-295X.113.3.628

Barrett, L. F. (2011). Was Darwin wrong about emotional expressions? *Current Directions in Psychological Science, 20,* 400–406. https://doi.org/10.1177/0963721411429125

Barrett, L. F. (2014). The conceptual act theory: A précis. *Emotion Review, 6,* 292–297. https://doi.org/10.1177/1754073914534479

Boiger, M., Güngör, D., Karasawa, M., & Mesquita, B. (2014). Defending honour, keeping face: Interpersonal affordances of anger and shame in Turkey and Japan. *Cognition and Emotion, 28,* 1255–1269. https://doi.org/10.1080/02699931.2014.881324

Boiger, M., Mesquita, B., Uchida, Y., & Barrett, L. F. (2013). Condoned or condemned: The situational affordance of anger and shame in the United States and Japan. *Personality and Social Psychology Bulletin, 39,* 540–553. https://doi.org/10.1177/0146167213478201

Brown, D. E. (1991). *Human universals.* Temple University Press.

Calder, A. J., Young, A. W., Keane, J., & Dean, M. (2000). Configural information in facial expression perception. *Journal of Experimental Psychology: Human Perception and Performance, 26,* 527–551. https://doi.org/10.1037/0096-1523.26.2.527

Cheng, J. T., Tracy, J. L., Foulsham, T., Kingstone, A., & Henrich, J. (2013). Two ways to the top: Evidence that dominance and prestige are distinct yet viable avenues to social rank and influence. *Journal of Personality and Social Psychology, 104*(1), 103–125. https://doi.org/10.1037/a0030398

Cordaro, D. T., Keltner, D., Tshering, S., Wangchuk, D., & Flynn, L. M. (2016). The voice conveys emotion in ten globalized cultures and one remote village in Bhutan. *Emotion, 16,* 117–128. https://doi.org/10.1177/0956797618778235

Cordaro, D. T., Sun, R., Keltner, D., Kamble, S., Huddar, N., & McNeil, G. (2018). Universals and cultural variations in 22 emotional expressions across five cultures. *Emotion, 18,* 75–93. https://doi.org/10.1037/emo0000302

Cosmides, L., & Tooby, J. (1994). Origins of domain specificity: The evolution of functional organization. In L. Hirschfeld & S. Gelman (Eds.), *Mapping the mind: Domain specificity in cognition and culture* (pp. 85–116). Cambridge University Press. https://doi.org/10.1017/CBO9780511752902.005

Cosmides, L., & Tooby, J. (2000). Evolutionary psychology and the emotions. In M. Lewis & J. M. Haviland-Jones (Eds.), *Handbook of emotions* (2nd ed., pp. 91–115). Guilford Press.

Creighton, M. (1990). Revisiting shame and guilt cultures: A forty-year pilgrimage. *Ethos, 18*(3), 279–307. Retrieved November 24, 2020, from http://www.jstor.org/stable/640338

Crivelli, C., Russell, J. A., Jarillo, S., & Fernández-Dols, J. M. (2017). Recognizing spontaneous facial expressions of emotion in a small-scale society of Papua New Guinea. *Emotion, 17*, 337–347. https://doi.org/10.1037/emo 0000236

Eibl-Eibesfeldt, I. (1973). Expressive behaviour of the deaf and blind born. In M. von Cranach & I. Vine (Eds.), *Social communication and movement* (pp. 163–194). Academic Press.

Ekman, P. (1992). An argument for basic emotions. *Cognition and Emotion, 6*, 169–200. https://doi.org/10.1080/02699939208411068

Ekman, P., & Friesen, W. V. (1978). *Facial Action Coding System: Investigator's guide*. Consulting Psychologists. https://doi.org/10.1037/t27734-000

Elfenbein, H. A. (2013). Nonverbal dialects and accents in facial expressions of emotion. *Emotion Review, 5*, 90–96. https://doi.org/10.1177/1754073912451332

Elfenbein, H. A., & Ambady, N. (2002). On the universality and cultural specificity of emotion recognition: A meta-analysis. *Psychological Bulletin, 128*, 203–235. https://doi.org/10.1037/0033-2909.128.2.203

Elfenbein, H. A., Beaupré, M., Lévesque, M., & Hess, U. (2007). Toward a dialect theory: Cultural differences in the expression and recognition of posed facial expressions. *Emotion, 7*, 131–146. https://doi.org/10.1037/1528-3542.7.1.131

Ellsworth, P. C. (2013). Appraisal theory: Old and new questions. *Emotion Review, 5*, 125–131. https://doi.org/10.1177/1754073912463617

Fessler, D. (2004). Shame in two cultures: Implications for evolutionary approaches. *Journal of Cognition and Culture, 4*, 207–262. https://doi.org/10.1163/1568537041725097

Forbes, S. H., & Plunkett, K. (2020). Linguistic and cultural variation in early color word learning. *Child Development, 91*, 28–42. https://doi.org/10.1111/cdev.13164

Friesen, W. V. (1972). *Cultural differences in facial expressions in a social situation: An experimental test of the concept of display rules*. Unpublished doctoral dissertation, University of California, San Francisco.

Goffman, E. (1967). *Interaction ritual: Essays on face-to-face interaction*. Aldine.

Hamilton, W. D. (1964). The genetical evolution of social behaviour. II. *Journal of Theoretical Biology, 7*, 17–52. https://doi.org/10.1016/0022-5193(64)90039-6

Heine, S. J., Lehman, D. R., Markus, H. R., & Kitayama, S. (1999). Is there a universal need for positive self-regard? *Psychological Review, 106*, 766–794. https://doi.org/10.1037/0033-295X.106.4.766

Henrich, J., & Gil-White, F. J. (2001). The evolution of prestige: Freely conferred deference as a mechanism for enhancing the benefits of cultural transmission. *Evolution and Human Behavior, 22*, 165–196. https://doi.org/10.1016/S1090-5138(00)00071-4

Heyes, C. (2020). Psychological mechanisms forged by cultural evolution. *Current Directions in Psychological Science, 29*, 399–404. https://doi.org/10.1177/0963721420917736

Hofstede, G. (1983). Dimensions of national cultures in fifty countries and three regions. In J. Deregowski, S. Dziurawiec, & R. Annis (Eds.), *Explications in cross-cultural psychology* (pp. 335–355). Swets & Zeitlinger.

Hofstede, G. (2001). *Culture's consequences: Comparing values, behaviors, institutions and organizations across nations*. Sage Publications.

Hugenberg, K., & Corneille, O. (2009). Holistic processing is tuned for ingroup faces. *Cognitive Science, 33*, 1173–1181. https://doi.org/10.1111/j.1551-6709.2009.01048.x

Hultberg, P. (1988). Shame: A hidden emotion. *Journal of Analytical Psychology, 33*, 109–126. https://doi.org/10.1111/j.1465-5922.1988.00109.x

Izard, C. E. (2007). Basic emotions, natural kinds, emotion schemas, and a new paradigm. *Perspectives on Psychological Science, 2*, 260–280. https://doi.org/10.1111/j.1745-6916.2007.00044.x

Keltner, D., & Cordaro, D. T. (2017). Understanding multimodal emotional expressions: Recent advances in Basic Emotion Theory. In J.-M. Fernandez-Dols & J. A. Russell (Eds.), *The science of facial expression* (pp. 57–76). Oxford University Press. https://doi.org/10.1093/acprof:oso/9780190613501.003.0004

Keltner, D., Horberg, E. J., & Oveis, C. (2006). Emotions as moral intuitions. In J. P. Forgas (Ed.), *Affect in social thinking and behavior* (pp. 161–175). Psychology Press.

Kitayama, S., Markus, H. R., & Matsumoto, H. (1995). Culture, self, and emotion: A cultural perspective on "self-conscious" emotions. In J. P. Tangney & K. W. Fischer (Eds.), *Self-conscious emotions: The psychology of shame, guilt, embarrassment, and pride* (pp. 439–464). Guilford Press.

Kitayama, S., Mesquita, B., & Karasawa, M. (2006). Cultural affordances and emotional experience: Socially engaging and disengaging emotions in Japan and the United States. *Journal of Personality and Social Psychology, 91*, 890–903. https://doi.org/10.1037/0022-3514.91.5.890

Kline, M. A., Shamsudheen, R., & Broesch, T. (2018). Variation is the universal: Making cultural evolution work in developmental psychology. *Philosophical Transactions of the Royal Society B: Biological Sciences, 373*, 20170059. https://doi.org/10.1098/rstb.2017.0059

Laukka, P., & Elfenbein, H. A. (2020). Cross-cultural emotion recognition and in-group advantage in vocal expression: A meta-analysis. *Emotion Review, 13*, 3–11. https://doi.org/10.1177/1754073919897295

Laukka, P., Elfenbein, H. A., Söder, N., Nordström, H., Althoff, J., Iraki, F. K. E., & Thingujam, N. S. (2013). Cross-cultural decoding of positive and negative non- linguistic emotion vocalizations. *Frontiers in Psychology, 4*, 353. https://doi.org/10.3389/fpsyg.2013.00353

Laukka, P., Elfenbein, H. A., Thingujam, N. S., Rockstuhl, T., Iraki, F. K., Chui, W., & Althoff, J. (2016). The expression and recognition of emotions in the voice across five nations: A lens model analysis based on acoustic features. *Journal of Personality and Social Psychology, 111*, 686–705. https://doi.org/10.1037/pspi0000066

Lazarus, R. S. (1991). *Emotion and adaptation*. Oxford University Press.

Lebra, T. S. (1973). Compensative justice and moral investment among Japanese, Chinese, and Koreans. *The Journal of Nervous and Mental Disease, 157*, 278–291.

Levenson, R. W., Soto, J., & Pole, N. (2007). Emotion, biology, and culture. In S. Kitayama & D. Cohen (Eds.), *Handbook of cultural psychology* (pp. 780–796). Guilford Press.

Lewis, D. M., Al-Shawaf, L., Conroy-Beam, D., Asao, K., & Buss, D. M. (2017). Evolutionary psychology: A how-to guide. *American Psychologist, 72*, 353–373. https://doi.org/10.1037/a0040409

Liddell, B. J., & Williams, E. N. (2019). Cultural differences in interpersonal emotion regulation. *Frontiers in Psychology, 10*, 999. https://doi.org/10.3389/fpsyg.2019.00999

Majid, A., & Kruspe, N. (2018). Hunter-gatherer olfaction is special. *Current Biology, 28*, 409–413. https://doi.org/10.1016/j.cub.2017.12.014

Manokara, K., Fischer, A., & Sauter, D. (2023). Display rules differ between positive emotions: Not all that feels good looks good. *Emotion, 23*, 243–260. https://doi.org/10.1037/emo0001078

Manokara, K., & Sauter, D. A. (2021). Emotion universals: The foundation from which cultural variability of emotion emerges. In J. De Leersnyder (Ed.), *The socio-cultural shaping of emotion*. Cambridge University Press.

Markus, H., & Kitayama, S. (1991). Culture and the self: Implications for cognition, emotion, and motivation. *Psychological Review, 98*, 224–253.

Mascolo, M. J., Fischer, K. W., & Li, J. (2003). Dynamic development of component systems of emotions: Pride, shame, and guilt in China and the United States. In R. J. Davidson, K. Scherer, & H. H. Goldsmith (Eds.), *Handbook of affective science* (pp. 375–408). Oxford University Press.

Matsumoto, D. (1990). Cultural similarities and differences in display rules. *Motivation and Emotion, 14*, 195–214. https://doi.org/10.1007/BF00995569

Matsumoto, D., Yoo, S. H., & Fontaine, J. (2008). Mapping expressive differences around the world: The relationship between emotional display rules and individualism versus collectivism. *Journal of Cross-Cultural Psychology, 39*(1), 55–74.

Mesquita, B., Barrett, L. F., & Smith, E. R. (Eds.). (2010). *The mind in context*. Guilford Press.

Menon, U., & Shweder, R. A. (1994). Kali's tongue: Cultural psychology and the power of "shame" in Orissa, India. In S. Kitayama & H. Markus (Eds), *Emotion and culture: Empirical studies of mutual influence* (pp. 241–284). APA Books.

Miake, K., & Yamazaki, K. (1995). Self-conscious emotions, child rearing, and psychopathology in Japanese culture. In J. P. Tangney & K. W. Fischer (Eds.), *Self-conscious emotions* (pp. 488–504). Guilford Press.

Moors, A. (2014). Flavors of appraisal theories of emotion. *Emotion Review, 6*, 303–307. https://doi.org/10.1177/1754073914534477

Öhman, A., & Mineka, S. (2003). The malicious serpent: Snakes as a prototypical stimulus for an evolved module of fear. *Current Directions in Psychological Science, 12*, 5–9. https://doi.org/10.1111/1467-8721 .01211

Paulmann, S., & Uskul, A. K. (2014). Cross-cultural emotional prosody recognition: Evidence from Chinese and British listeners. *Cognition and Emotion, 28*, 230–244. https://doi.org/0.1080/02699931.2013.812033

Pauw, L. S., Vu, T., Sun, R., Vuillier, L., Milek, A., & Sauter, D. (2020, October 19). Emotion regulation and wellbeing: A cross-cultural study during the COVID-19 outbreak. https://doi.org/10.31234/osf.io/9qrw5

Regier, T., & Kay, P. (2009). Language, thought, and color: Whorf was half right. *Trends in Cognitive Sciences, 13*, 439–446. https://doi.org/10.1016/j.tics.2009.07.001

Richerson, P. J., & Boyd, R. 2005 *Not by genes alone: How culture transformed human evolution*. University of Chicago Press. https://doi.org/10.7208/chicago/9780226712130.001.0001

Roberson, D., Hanley, J. R., & Pak, H. (2009). Thresholds for color discrimination in English and Korean speakers. *Cognition, 112*, 482–487. https://doi.org/10.1016/j.cognition.2009.06.008

Roberson, D., Pak, H., & Hanley, J. R. (2008). Categorical perception of colour in the left and right visual field is verbally mediated: Evidence from Korean. *Cognition, 107*, 752–762. https://doi.org/10.1016/j.cognition.2007.09.001

Robertson, T. E., Sznycer, D., Delton, A. W., Tooby, J., & Cosmides, L. (2018). The true trigger of shame: Social devaluation is sufficient, wrongdoing is unnecessary. *Evolution and Human Behavior, 39*, 566–573. https://doi.org/10.1016/j.evolhumbehav.2018.05.010

Romney, A. K., Moore, C. C., & Rusch, C. D. (1997). Cultural universals: Measuring the semantic structure of emotion terms in English and Japanese. *Proceedings of the National Academy of Sciences, 94*, 5489–5494. https://doi.org/10.1073/pnas.94.10.5489

Roseman, I. J. (1991). Appraisal determinants of discrete emotions. *Cognition and Emotion, 5*, 161–200. https://doi.org/10.1080/02699939108411034

Russell, J. A. (2009). Emotion, core affect, and psychological construction. *Cognition and Emotion, 23*, 1259–1283. https://doi.org/10.1080/02699930902809375

Rychlowska, M., Miyamoto, Y., Matsumoto, D., Hess, U., Gilboa-Schechtman, E., Kamble, S., Muluk, H., Masuda, T., & Niedenthal, P. M. (2015). Heterogeneity of long-history migration explains cultural differences in reports of emotional expressivity and the functions of smiles. *Proceedings of the National Academy of Sciences, 112*, E2429–E2436. https://doi.org/10.1073/pnas.1413661112

Sauter, D. A., & Russell, J. A. (in press). What do nonverbal expressions tell us about emotion? In A. Scarantino (Ed.), *Handbook of emotion theory*. Taylor & Francis.

Scheff, T. J. (1988). Shame and conformity: The deference-emotion system. *American Sociological Review, 53*, 395–406. https://doi.org/10.2307/2095647

Scherer, K. R. (1997). The role of culture in emotion-antecedent appraisal. *Journal of Personality and Social Psychology, 73*(5), 902–922.

Scherer, K. R. (2001). *Appraisal considered as a process of multilevel sequential checking: Appraisal processes in emotion: Theory, methods, research*. Oxford University Press.

Scherer, K. R., & Moors, A. (2019). The emotion process: Event appraisal and component differentiation. *Annual Review of Psychology, 70*, 719–745. https://doi.org/10.1146/annurev-psych-122216-011854

Shaver, P. R., Wu, S., & Schwartz, J. C. (1992). Cross-cultural similarities and differences in emotion and its representation. In M. S. Clark (Ed.), *Emotion: Review of personality and social psychology* (pp. 175–213). Sage Publications.

Skelton, A. E., Catchpole, G., Abbott, J. T., Bosten, J. M., & Franklin, A. (2017). Biological origins of color categorization. *Proceedings of the National Academy of Sciences, 114*, 5545–5550. https://doi.org/10.1073/pnas.1612881114

Stephen, I. D. (2014). Putting the theory before the data: Is "massive modularity" a necessary foundation of evolutionary psychology? *Frontiers in Psychology, 5*, 1158. https://doi.org/10.3389/fpsyg.2014.01158

Sun, R., Balabanova, A., Bajada, C. J., Liu, Y., Kriuchok, M., Voolma, S.-R., Đurić, M., Mayer, C.-H., Constantinou, M., Chichua, M., Li, C., Foster-Estwick, A., Borg, K., Hill, C., Kaushal, R., Diwan, K., Vitale, V., Engels, T., Aminudin, R., . . . Sauter, D. (2023). Emotional experiences and psychological well-being in 51 countries during the COVID-19 pandemic. Emotion. Advance online publication. https://doi.org/10.1037/emo0001235

Swami, V. (2015). Cultural influences on body size ideals. *European Psychologist, 20*, 44–51. https://doi.org/10.1027/1016-9040/a000150

Sznycer, D., Xygalatas, D., Agey, E., Alami, S., An, X.-F., Ananyeva, K. I., Atkinson, Q. D., Broitman, B. R., Conte, T. J., Flores, C., Fukushima, S., Hitokoto, H., Kharitonov, A. N., Onyishi, C. N., Onyishi, I. E., Romero, P. P., Schrock, J. M., Snodgrass, J. J., Sugiyama, L. S., . . . Tooby, J. (2018). Cross-cultural invariances in the architecture of shame. *Proceedings of the National Academy of Sciences, 115*, 9702–9707. https://doi.org/10.1073/pnas.1805016115

Tamis-LeMonda, C., Way, N., Hughes, D., Yoshikawa, H., Kalman, R. K., & Niwa, E. Y. (2008). Parents' goals for children: The dynamic coexistence of individualism and collectivism in cultures and individuals. *Social Development, 17*(1), 183–209.

Tangney, J. P. (1995). Recent advances in the empirical study of shame and guilt. *American Behavioral Scientist, 38*, 1132–1145. https://doi.org/10.1177/0002764295038008008

Thibault, P., Bourgeois, P., & Hess, U. (2006). The effect of group-identification on emotion recognition: The case of cats and basketball players. *Journal of Experimental Social Psychology, 42*(5), 676–683. https://doi.org/10.1016/j.jesp.2005.10.006

Tooby, J., & Cosmides, L. (1990). On the universality of human nature and the uniqueness of the individual: The role of genetics and adaptation. *Journal of Personality, 58*, 17–67. https://doi.org/10.1111/j.1467-6494.1990.tb00907.x

Tooby, J., & Cosmides, L. (1992). Psychological foundations of culture. In J. Barkow, L. Cosmides, & J. Tooby (Eds.), *The adapted mind: Evolutionary psychology and the generation of culture* (pp. 19–136). Oxford University Press.

Tooby, J., & Cosmides, L. (2008). The evolutionary psychology of the emotions and their relationship to internal regulatory variables. In M. Lewis, J. M. Haviland-Jones, & L. F. Barrett (Eds.), *Handbook of emotions* (pp. 114–137). Guilford Press.

Tracy, J. L., & Matsumoto, D. (2008). The spontaneous expression of pride and shame: Evidence for biologically innate nonverbal displays. *Proceedings of the National Academy of Sciences, 105*, 11655–11660. https://doi.org/10.1073/pnas.0802686105

Tracy, J. L., & Robins, R. W. (2006). Appraisal antecedents of shame and guilt: Support for a theoretical model. *Personality and Social Psychology Bulletin, 32*, 1339–1351. https://doi.org/10.1177/0146167206290212

Triandis, H. C. (1995). *Individualism and collectivism*. Westview Press.

Wenegrat, B., Abrams, L., Castillo-Yee, E., & Romine, I. J. (1996). Social norm compliance as a signaling system. I. Studies of fitness-related attributions consequent on everyday norm violations. *Ethology and Sociobiology, 17*, 403–416. https://doi.org/10.1016/S0162-3095(97)82225-X

Wong, Y., & Tsai, J. (2007). Cultural models of shame and guilt. In J. L. Tracy, R. W. Robins, & J. P. Tangney (Eds.), *The self-conscious emotions: Theory and research* (pp. 209–223). Guilford Press.

Young, S. G., & Hugenberg, K. (2010). Mere social categorization modulates identification of facial expressions of emotion. *Journal of Personality and Social Psychology, 99*, 964–977. https://doi.org/10.1037/a0020400

Yu, D. W., & Shepard Jr., G. H. (1998). Is beauty in the eye of the beholder?. *Nature, 396*(6709), 321–322. https://doi.org/10.1038/24512

Zerilli, J. (2017). Against the "system" module. *Philosophical Psychology, 30*, 231–246. https://doi.org/10.1080/09515089.2017.1280145

CHAPTER 52

The Role of Emotion in Second- and Third-Party Punishment

Julia Marshall and Katherine McAuliffe

Abstract

Punishment plays a key role in sustaining cooperation by promoting adherence to social norms. Forms of punishment can be organized into two categories: second-party punishment, wherein the punisher is the victim of a transgression; and third-party punishment, wherein the punisher is an uninvolved bystander who witnesses a transgression against someone else. Although empirical work has focused on punishment behavior across these contexts, such work has focused less on the emotional mechanisms supporting both types of punishment. In this chapter, the authors review work that has explored the emotional antecedents of both second- and third-party punishment. For example, the chapter reviews research finding that negative emotions, most notably anger, promote both forms of punishment. This review combines work from a range of methodological approaches, including behavioral studies and physiological methods, providing an integrative overview of the role of emotion in punishment.

Key Words: punishment, emotion, cooperation, evolution, second-party punishment, third-party punishment

Imagine you are writing in a café. You get up to order a coffee and someone runs over, steals your laptop, and runs away. How would you react? Would you sit back down and do nothing, or would you chase down and punish the thief? How would you feel? Now imagine the same scenario, but this time you are not the victim. Instead, the thief steals the laptop belonging to the person sitting next to you. How would you react this time? How would you feel? A growing body of research that spans diverse disciplines, including psychology, economics, and evolutionary biology, suggests that humans will readily punish in both contexts, both when they are the *victims* of a transgression (second-party punishment [2PP]; e.g., Güth et al., 1982) as well as when they are unaffected observers of a transgression (third-party punishment [3PP]; e.g., Fehr & Fischbacher, 2004a).

Theoretical models suggest that both forms of punishment play a key role in supporting social norms in human societies by deterring bad behavior and promoting good behavior (Balliet et al., 2011; Boyd et al., 2003; Mathew & Boyd, 2011). The logic is that people, on average, are less likely to break norms if doing so could potentially result in punishment. The presence of punishment then serves as a way to ensure that people abide by moral and social norms. Consistent with the view that punishment is foundational to human social life, both second- and third-party punishment are seen across diverse societies (Henrich et al., 2006; House et al., 2020; Oosterbeek et al., 2004) and emerge relatively early in child development (e.g., Marshall & McAuliffe, 2020; Sally & Hill, 2006; Sutter, 2007); second-party punishment, at least, is seen in our closest living relatives, chimpanzees (*Pan troglodytes*; Reidl et al., 2012).

On the proximate level of analysis, research has examined the mechanisms which undergird people's decisions to punish. We address this here by reviewing a large body of research investigating the emotional foundations of punitive behavior. We first review how researchers measure punitive behavior in the lab. We then examine how researchers leverage such experimental paradigms to assess what emotions underlie punitive behavior. We discuss a wide variety of findings that link anger, disgust, and other negative emotions with second-party and third-party punishment. Following this, we discuss how positive emotions, such as compassion and affective empathy, have been tied to third-party punishment specifically. We end by briefly discussing how emotions motivate a desire to compensate victims (versus punish transgressors). A key take-away from our review of work on the emotional antecedents of punishment is that both second-party punishment and third-party punishment are proximally motivated by negative emotional responses, most notably anger, in response to moral and social transgressions.

How Researchers Measure Punishment

While definitions of punishment vary somewhat across disciplines (Fehr & Fischbacher, 2004a; Raihani et al., 2012; Vidmar & Miller, 1980), a theme that unites its operationalization is that punishment is the imposition of a cost in response to an uncooperative other. Punitive behavior in the real world can take many forms. For example, punishment may involve sending a child to "time-out," shaming someone on social media, or spreading a rumor about a friend. Punishment can also take harsher forms both outside of and within the criminal justice system. For instance, on the milder side, individuals in the justice system are often fined for breaking laws. On the harsher side, individuals may be sent to prison and even killed for their misdeeds. These sorts of actions are characterized as punitive because they inflict emotional or physical damage on the transgressor. For example, in the case of shaming someone on social media, the transgressor suffers embarrassment at the hands of the shamer. In the case of being sent to prison, the transgressor loses their freedom.

Punitive behaviors are often contrasted with alternative responses, such as forgiveness (e.g., McCullough, 2008), partner choice (e.g., Martin & Cushman, 2015), or—of particular interest here—compensation of the victim (FeldmanHall et al., 2014; Heffner & FeldmanHall, 2019). For example, if someone steals another person's laptop, a witness could punish the transgressor, or they could simply provide the victim with another computer, thereby compensating the victim for their loss. These sorts of actions do not inflict harm on the transgressor in any way and are therefore not considered punitive. These sorts of actions, however, are relevant to how humans respond to injustice and, as a result, are often studied in the psychological literature.

While real-world examples of punishment are important to understand, they are difficult to reconstruct under laboratory settings. Consequently, researchers have devised ways to measure punitive behavior in adults and in children in more controlled contexts. These measures provide useful proxies for how people in the real world would respond to transgressions and can shed light on the cognitive and emotional mechanisms that support their responses.

One way in which researchers have successfully captured people's punitive behavior under controlled conditions is through incentivized economic game paradigms. These games are particularly useful measures of punishment because they involve responses to transgressions with real consequences for participants and frequently require that participants "put their money where their mouths are" and sacrifice personal gain to punish. Two economic games in particular—the Ultimatum Game (Güth et al., 1982; which measures 2PP)—and the Third-Party Punishment Game (Fehr & Fischbacher, 2004a; which measures 3PP), have generated a wealth of information about the contexts in which people engage in punishment and why.

In the Ultimatum Game (Güth et al., 1982) (see Figure 52.1), participants are assigned to one of two roles: the proposer or the responder. An experimenter endows the proposer with an allotment of money that they can divide between themselves and the responder. For example, the proposer may receive $4 (USD) and can divide the money fairly by allocating $2 to the responder, or unfairly, by allocating only $1 to the responder. The responder then has the opportunity to respond to the offer. If the responder *accepts* the offer, the allotment is enacted. If—on the other hand—the responder *rejects* the offer, no one receives any money. Rejection in this game is considered punitive behavior because the responder is imposing a

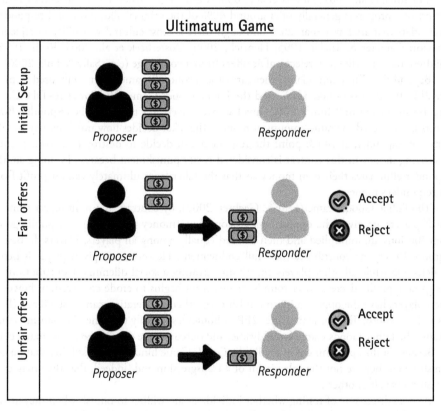

Figure 52.1. Visualization of the Ultimatum Game. This game involves two individuals: the proposer and the responder. In the initial setup, the proposer is endowed with money (in this case, $4). The responder is not allocated any money in the initial setup. The proposer then decides how much, if any, money to offer to the responder. The responder can then accept or reject the offer. If the responder accepts, the division of money is enacted. If the responder rejects, no one receives money. Rejection in this experimental design has been characterized as "irrational" because having any money should be better than having none. However, responders frequently reject non-zero offers, typically refusing splits below 20% of the original allotment (although there is cross-cultural variability in rejection behavior). The emojis portrayed in this figure were designed by Freepik (people, arrow, and accept/reject), Goodware (dollar), and Pixel Perfect (anger) at FlatIcon.com.

cost on the proposer and is considered costly because the responder must sacrifice potential gain in order to reject.

This Ultimatum Game is fascinating from a psychological perspective for many reasons. For one, as mentioned above, punishment is costly to the responder. If the responder rejects the proposer's offer, the responder does not receive any money, although they would stand to (if they accepted the offer). Second, the interactions are one-shot, meaning that the proposer and responder only interact once (Hertwig & Ortmann, 2001). There is also no possibility of future interaction, and the interactions are also generally anonymous. Because of this, the responder's decisions—at least in an immediate sense—cannot be explained by appealing to the proposer's desire to teach the responder a lesson to potentially result in fairer offers in later rounds. As a result of these considerations, rejection is generally characterized as "irrational" because having some money is better than having no money (Camerer, 2003).

Despite this, research utilizing this paradigm has readily found that responders will reject unfair offers from proposers (Bolton & Zwick, 1995; Güth et al., 1982; Güth & Kocher, 2014; Henrich et al., 2001; Nowak et al., 2000; Roth, 1995; Thaler, 1988). Specifically, studies find that proposers generally offer around 40% of the original allocation, and responders reject offers that are lower than 20% (although there is cross-cultural variability in rejection behavior; Camerer & Thaler, 1995; Henrich, 2000; Oosterbeek et al., 2004; Roth, 1995). Children, too, are willing to reject unfair offers from a young age (e.g., Sally & Hill, 2006).

Beyond the Ultimatum Game, there are other economic games commonly used to measure 2PP: the Power-to-Take Game and the Public Goods Game. The Power-to-Take Game (e.g., Bosman and van Winden, 2002) involves two players: the taker and the responder. Both players are allocated the same amount of money. The taker decides how much money to take from the responder, at which point the responder can decide to destroy their own money. Destroying money in this context is considered costly punishment because, in doing so, the responder eliminates their own money so that the taker from ultimately cannot profit from the responder's money.

The Public Goods Game (Fehr & Gachter, 2002), by contrast, is a multiplayer game in which players are given the opportunity to contribute money (or points) to a public good. Contributions are multiplied and then divided equally among all players. Players do best as a group if everyone contributes their full endowment. However, any given player is better off defecting while all other players contribute, creating a social dilemma. Contributions in this game typically decrease over rounds, as defection begins to erode cooperation; however, when players have the opportunity to punish each other, cooperation can be stabilized (Fehr & Gachter, 2000). This game measures 2PP, although less cleanly than the Ultimatum Game, because the Public Goods Game is not dyadic, and outcomes are distributed across many players. Because of this, punishment in the Public Goods Game hints at the possibility that people punish when they are not the sole victim of a transgression and, indeed, that they may even punish on behalf of others.

A more direct way of testing whether individuals are willing to punish when they are an unaffected bystander is the Third-Party Punishment Game (Figure 52.2). This game involves three players: a divider, a receiver, and a bystander. In the game (like in the Ultimatum Game), the experimenter endows the divider with an allotment of money (or points) that the divider can then distribute between themselves and a receiver, who is a passive player in the game. The divider can transfer any proportion of the original allotment to the receiver. After the division is made, the bystander can choose to spend money from their own allocation to punish the divider. In most cases, these situations are one-shot interactions, meaning that the participants involved in the exchange will only interact with each other once, with no possibility of future

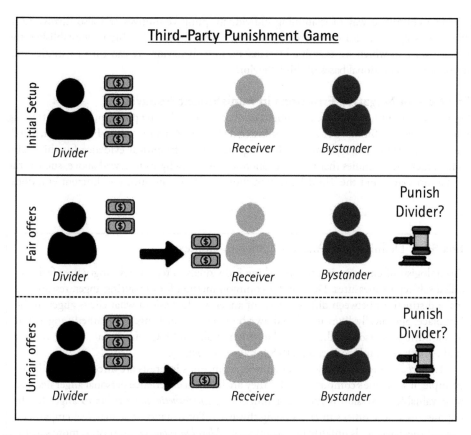

Figure 52.2. Visualization of the Third-Party Punishment Game. This game involves three individuals: the divider, the receiver, and the bystander. The participant is usually assigned to the bystander role. In the initial setup, the divider is endowed with money (in this case, $4). The receiver is not allocated any money in the initial set-up. The divider then has to make a decision about whether to give any money to the receiver. The bystander then has to make a decision whether to spend some of their own money to reduce the payout of the divider. Despite this, bystanders generally punish selfish dividers, even though the bystander is not affected by the divider's selfish behavior. The emojis portrayed in this figure were designed by Freepik (people, arrow, accept/reject, and gavel), Goodware (dollar), and Pixel Perfect (anger) at FlatIcon.com.

interaction (e.g., Hertwig & Ortmann, 2001). Interactions are also generally anonymous, meaning that the individuals do not know one another. Similar to the Ultimatum Game, punishment in the Third-Party Punishment game is costly because the punisher has to give up their own resources to punish the transgressor.

Despite these costs, bystanders routinely punish selfish dividers, even though they are not directly affected by the divider's behavior. For example, in Fehr and Fischbacher's (2004a) original experiment, bystanders punished dividers approximately 70%–80% of the time when the divider gave the receiver 0%–30% of the pie. This type of third-party punishment behavior—like second-party punishment—also appears across different societies (Henrich et al., 2006; House et al., 2020) and early in childhood (McAuliffe et al., 2015).

The incentivized economic games described in this section form the foundation of the majority of the research examining the emotional bases of punitive behavior that we will review in the following sections. They provide a critical test of whether we are willing to punish anonymous others, even when doing so requires sacrifice. Specifically, economic games provide a controlled way of examining individuals' punitive motives and also involve individuals making real decisions where actual money is on the line. Having now established the primary ways in which we examine humans' punitive behavior, we can turn to studies that investigate the emotional bases of this behavior.

The Role of Negative Emotions in Punishment Behavior

Negative emotions have long been thought to play a role in driving punishment or motivating punitive behavior (Binmore et al., 1985; Elster, 1989, 1998; Frank, 1988; Hirschleifer, 1987; Loewenstein, 1996, 2000; Straub & Murnigahn, 1995). Empirical evidence for this claim comes largely from studies that rely on economic game paradigms reviewed above, such as the Ultimatum Game and the Third-Party Punishment Game, and measure different emotions,

---

Box 52.1 Definitions of Anger in Different Contexts

Psychologists often measure anger by asking individuals to report how angry they feel—so called self-report measures. Despite this common method for measuring anger, researchers make distinctions between different *types* of anger on the basis of what elicits anger in the first place. Specifically, lines are often drawn between personal anger, empathetic anger, and moral outrage (Batson et al., 2007; Hartsough et al., 2020; O'Mara et al., 2011; Tetlock et al., 2000; see van Doorn et al., 2018 for a useful review).

Personal anger refers to anger elicited when someone's interests are directly harmed. For example, if someone's computer breaks, they are likely to experience personal anger because their valuable possession is no longer functional. *Empathetic anger* refers to anger felt in response to a close other's interests being thwarted. For instance, one may feel empathetic anger if their partner is unfairly fired from a job. *Moral outrage*, in contrast, is more specifically meant to refer to anger elicited when a stranger's interests are compromised (see Box 52.2, for a greater discussion of moral outrage). For example, one might become angry if they see an authority figure act unfairly toward an unknown peer; such an action would elicit principled moral outrage.

The distinctions between personal anger, empathetic anger, and moral outrage are related to broader theoretical conversations about moral emotions more generally (Haidt, 2003; Prinz & Nichols, 2010; Tangney et al., 2007). According to Haidt (2003) in *Handbook of Affective Sciences*, moral emotions are considered to be "linked to the interests or welfare of society as a whole or at least of persons other than the judge or the agent" (p. 853). The quintessential moral emotion, according to Haidt (2003), is anger. But he, like Batson and colleagues (2007), distinguishes between disinterested anger—anger elicited by a transgression directed toward another person—and less disinterested anger—anger elicited by a transgression directed toward the self. While Haidt (2003) contends that individuals may experience moral anger in response to both self-directed and other-directed transgressions, anger at other-directed transgressions is more characteristically moral than other forms of anger because it is more principled and is elicited in more disinterested contexts.

In the present chapter, we focus on whether anger, broadly construed, promotes punitive behavior. In other words, we look at instances of personal anger, empathetic anger, and moral outrage. Regardless of these distinctions, however, we are most concerned with understanding the emotional foundations of punitive behavior in general and therefore review all studies that link anger in any sense with punitive behavior.

including anger and disgust, in a variety of ways ranging from self-reported emotions to neuronal activity.

Here, we review research linking (a) anger, (b) other negative emotions, such as disgust and sadness, (c) measures of automatic emotional arousal, most notably galvanic skin response, and (d) activation of brain regions associated with negative emotion and emotional regulation to punitive behavior across 2PP and 3PP contexts. Together, evidence from these complementary approaches suggests that negative emotions play a pivotal role in motivating punitive behavior in both second-party and third-party contexts.

Anger as an Antecedent to Punitive Behavior

Most of us are familiar with the experience of anger—we feel it in our everyday lives when our roommate fails to clean the dishes, when a business partner does not close a deal, or when a spouse forgets an anniversary. Anger is generally thought of as a negative emotion because it is often elicited by unpleasant circumstances (Harmon-Jones, 2003). For example, anger can occur as a result of one's goal being thwarted or because one has the experience of being slighted or hurt by another person (Frijda, 1986; see Carver & Harmon-Jones, 2009, for a review). Anger, in general, is often thought of as a strong feeling of displeasure that prompts approach-related behavior (i.e., aggression). Importantly, anger can be elicited in different contexts and is, as a result, sometimes called different names depending on the situation (e.g., personal anger, empathetic anger, moral outrage); see Box 52.1, "Definitions of Anger in Different Contexts," for further discussion of these distinctions.

A prominent idea in the literature on the emotional antecedents of punishment is that anger plays a causal role in punishment behavior. Specifically, individuals punish transgressors because they feel anger when someone treats them unfairly or harms them directly, and that emotional experience in turn motivates approach-related behavior, such as punishment (although it can take other forms, which we review later in the chapter). This hypothesis has received ample empirical support. Here, we provide an overview of this literature, focusing in particular on correlational and causal evidence linking self-reported anger with punitive behavior across 2PP and 3PP.

First, in the context of 2PP, several studies have reported correlations between anger and punitive behavior in second-party situations. For example, a study by Pillutla and Murnighan (1996) found that self-reported anger correlated with rejection decisions in the Ultimatum Game. This finding has also been directly replicated by Bosman, Sonnemans, and Zeelenberg (2001) and conceptually replicated in other economic game paradigms, such as the Power-to-Take game (Ben-Shakhar et al., 2007) and in other economic games that test 2PP (Hopfensitz & Reuben, 2009). This relationship coheres with other work finding that bystanders generally infer that punishment is motivated out of anger (Eriksson et al., 2016).

A similar relationship between anger and punishment has been documented with respect to 3PP. For example, in a study by Fehr and Fischbacher (2004b), participants had the opportunity to engage in 3PP and also reported their anticipated emotions in different situations. The researchers found, in line with previous studies, that participants report greater negative emotions, most notably anger, when the divider allocates resources selfishly than when the divider allocates resources equally. Further supporting the link between 3PP and anger, Jordan and colleagues (2016) found that 3PP was associated with feelings of anger but not feelings of envy. Work by Vitaglione and Barnett (2003) found that empathetic anger (anger on behalf of a victimized person; see Box 52.1 for definitional clarity) predicted punitive responses toward a transgressor. Additionally, Rodrigues and colleagues (2020) found that trait anger—a person's general disposition to be angry across time rather than their momentary anger—predicted 3PP (see also Rodrigues et al., 2018). Nelissen and Zeelenberg (2009) manipulated whether unfair offers were made intentionally or unintentionally under the assumption that intentional selfish offers should elicit greater anger than unintentional ones (Blount, 1995). They found that participants were more inclined to punish as third parties when unfair offers were intentional, providing indirect support for the idea that anger drives 3PP.[1] And, finally, recent work by Molho and colleagues (2020) found that anger predicted third-party punishment in the real world (i.e., self-reported experiences rather than economic games).

This research is correlational, not causal. Follow-up experiments have tested whether self-reported anger mediates the relationship between offer types and punitive behavior. In doing so, we can begin to generate evidence in favor of the possibility that anger causes punitive behavior, although it does not directly demonstrate a causal relationship. Specifically, Srivastava, Espinoza, and Fedorikhin (2009) had participants engage in an Ultimatum Game task (2PP) and also self-report their experienced anger. They found that anger mediated the influence of offer size on rejection rates.[2] Gummerum and colleagues (2020) conceptually replicated this finding: they had children (9-year-olds), adolescents (13-year-olds), and adults participate in an Ultimatum Game experiment. They found that participants tended to punish unfair offers and that negative emotions mediated the link between offer and punishment for all three age groups (children, adolescents, and adults).

Similar results have been documented with respect to 3PP. For example, Gummerum and colleagues (2020) found that self-reported anger mediated the link between offer size and rejection behavior in the Third-Party Punishment Game for adults, but not for children or adolescents. This finding suggests that the link between offer type and rejection behavior via emotional responses may develop throughout childhood and adolescence. Regardless, similar evidence has also been documented with respect to behavior in the Public Goods Game. In this context, participants are given the opportunity to punish non-cooperators. Research has found—like Gummerum and colleagues (2020)—that individuals tend to punish non-contributors more than contributors in the Public Goods Game, and this relationship is mediated by self-reported anger (Fehr & Gachter, 2002; Seip et al., 2014). Finally, similar mediation effects have been found in research that does not rely on economic games, but instead has participants act as mock jurors and make punishment decisions as if they were in a criminal justice system. This research has demonstrated that presenting participants with emotionally evocative materials (such as gruesome crime photos) accentuates anger and other negative emotions toward defendants, which in turn results in participants recommending harsher punishments (Bright & Goodman-Delahunty, 2006; Goldberg et al., 1999; Salerno & Bottoms, 2009; Treadway at al., 2014).

While mediation analyses suggest that anger may cause punitive behavior, these studies do not concretely demonstrate a causal link. For this link to be established, direct experimental manipulations of anger are required (Bullock et al., 2010). As a step in this direction, researchers have manipulated the time between a transgression and a punishment decision as a proxy for an anger manipulation. The logic here is that, as more time passes, individuals' anger may diminish, thereby reducing punitive behavior. In line with this, research by Wang and colleagues (2011) found that time delays did generally reduce punitive behavior in Ultimatum Game contexts (2PP) because it reduced self-reported anger, but only if individuals did not ruminate on the offer. If participants ruminated, they showed a heightened tendency to punish, most likely because they maintained a sense of anger about the economic interaction. Other research also finds that participants—when given the opportunity to reappraise their emotions in response to unfairness—reject offers less often than when they do not regulate their emotions or when they are instructed to suppress their emotions[3] (van't Wout et al.,

2010; also see Grecucci et al., 2013). These findings collectively point toward the possibility that anger is causally related to punitive behavior, although these specific studies only speak to the role of emotion in 2PP, not 3PP.

The most convincing demonstration of anger playing a causal role in punishment comes from research that directly manipulates anger. With respect to 2PP, Andrande and Ariely (2009) manipulated whether participants experienced anger or happiness because of an incidental event (e.g., a happy or sad event)—not as a result of the fair or unfair transgression. They found that individuals who were angry (versus happy) were more inclined to reject an unfair offer in the Ultimatum Game.

Gummerum and colleagues (2016) conducted a similar experiment but for 3PP. They instructed participants to either think about a neutral event (eating dinner the night before) or about a situation that made the participant feel furious. They found that experiencing anger as a result of an incidental event results in greater 3PP than in the neutral condition, but only when participants are given the opportunity to ruminate on their anger (rather than complete a distraction task). Rodrigues and colleagues (2020) conducted a similar study where they induced participants to feel angry, happy, or neutral by having them watch different movie clips. They found some evidence for a causal role of anger in 3PP: participants who watched the anger movie were more likely to punish, even on fair trials.

Box 52.2 Conceptualizing Moral Outrage and Its Consequences

What exactly is *moral outrage*? Scholars' definitions of moral outrage range in scope from narrow to broad. For instance, moral outrage is characterized by some as anger in response to a transgression directed *toward a stranger* (Batson et al., 2007). Under this definition, it is possible to argue that 3PP is motivated by moral outrage because 3PP involves responding to a transgression directed toward an unknown other. However, it would be, by definition, impossible to argue that 2PP is ever motivated by moral outrage because 2PP always involves responding to a transgression directed toward the self. In this way, defining moral outrage as exclusively anger elicited by transgressions directed toward strangers denies the possibility that one may ever experience moral outrage in response to a self-directed transgression, such as being unfairly fired from a job or being cheated on by a partner.

In light of this, others have defined moral outrage more broadly as a *suite of emotions* (i.e., anger and disgust) that are tethered to a desire to shame and punish others (Salerno & Peter-Hagene, 2013; Skitka et al., 2004). For example, sample items of moral outrage from this perspective include questions like, "I feel a compelling need to punish [a transgressor]" or "I feel a desire to hurt [a transgressor]." Under this definition, moral outrage could theoretically motivate either 2PP or 3PP.

Using this broader definition, scholars have debated the normative value of moral outrage: Is moral outrage good or bad? While we cannot adjudicate this debate in the limited space we have here, we can point interested readers to the variety of arguments that have been offered on both sides. Some have argued that moral outrage has important moral value because it can motivate collective action against injustices (e.g., Spring et al., 2019), whereas others have argued that moral outrage has a dark side that is outweighed by any benefits (Brady & Crockett, 2019; Crockett, 2017). This argument is supported by research finding that moral outrage can promote dehumanization and escalating aggression, especially in the digital age (e.g., Bastion et al., 2013; Sawaoka & Monin, 2018). Ultimately, these discussions about the nature of moral outrage and its value in society deserve additional attention in the future and present interesting avenues for additional investigation.

Together, this research links anger with punitive behavior in second-party and third-party contexts in both correlational and experimental paradigms. Evidence from these complementary approaches supports the possibility that anger serves as a key proximate motivator of punitive behavior across both second-party and third-party contexts.

Disgust and Other Negative Emotions as Antecedents to Punitive Behavior
A handful of studies have investigated whether other negative emotions, such as disgust, sadness, and contempt, also provide an impetus for individuals to engage in 2PP and 3PP. This research is motivated by the theoretical argument that "moral outrage" (see Box 52.2, "Conceptualizing Moral Outrage and Its Consequences") is not strictly akin to anger and instead also involves other emotional states, such as disgust (Darley & Pittman, 2003; Jensen & Petersen, 2011; Mullen & Skitka, 2006). Indeed, research by Salerno and Peter-Hagene (2013) found that anger predicts moral outrage only if it is accompanied by experiences of moderate disgust as well, suggesting that measuring anger alone is insufficient to fully capture the emotional profile of "moral outrage."

Research in this vein has examined whether self-reported disgust promotes punitive behavior. For example, Moretti and di Pellegrino (2010) manipulated whether participants experienced negative emotions (sadness or disgust) by viewing images that were either disgusting (such as vomit) or saddening (such as people at a funeral); they also included a neutral condition. Participants were then asked to make a series of decisions in an Ultimatum Game (2PP). They found that individuals who experienced incidental disgust were far more inclined to punish unfair offers in the Ultimatum Game than those in the sad or neutral condition, and this effect only occurred when humans made offers and not when computers did. Relatedly, Molho and colleagues (2020) found that disgust predicted indirect punishment (e.g., gossip and social exclusion) in 2PP and 3PP contexts, but did not predict other forms of punishment, such as direct confrontation. This work, though, focused on real-world experiences of punishment—not punishment in economic games. To our knowledge, there is no other work linking disgust to punishment in third-party contexts, and so the possibility that disgust plays a role in punishment behavior is mostly limited to second-party contexts.

Beyond disgust, some research has linked sadness with punitive behavior in second-party punishment (Harle & Sanfey, 2007). In this work, participants were induced to feel either happiness or sadness by watching a movie clip. They found that those who watched a sad movie clip were more likely to reject unfair offers than those who watched a happy movie clip. Similarly, Dimitroff and colleagues (2020) found that being upset with a transgressor was more predictive of punitive behavior than being sad on behalf of victims.

Other research has linked negative emotional states—such as irritation and contempt—to punitive behavior in the Power-to-Take Game (2PP), although this work is purely correlational (Bosman & van Winden, 2002). And, relatedly, Xiao and Houser (2005) found that participants, when given the opportunity to express their emotions to the divider in an Ultimatum Game, were less likely to reject selfish offers than those who are not given the opportunity to express emotions. The authors argue that perhaps individuals use punishment as a way to express negative emotion, and that—when alternative ways of expressing such emotion are available—punishment is diminished. With respect to 3PP, Lotz et al. (2011) found that self-reported moral outrage (a combination of anger, shock, hostility, distress, and aggravation; Box 52.2) predicted punitive behavior, as did Ginter and colleagues (2021).

Together, these findings suggest that—similar to incidental emotional manipulations of anger—incidental emotional manipulations of disgust and sadness impact social decision-making with respect to 2PP. There is less work experimentally linking negative emotions beyond anger to 3PP. Interestingly, though, there is research relating a broad array of negative emotional states, such as irritation, contempt, and hostility (among others) to 2PP and 3PP in correlational studies. In the next section, we turn to research linking general emotional arousal to punitive behavior in both 2PP and 3PP.

General Arousal as an Antecedent to Punitive Behavior

Related to questions about whether negative emotions, such as anger and disgust, motivate punitive behavior, researchers have also examined whether *arousal*—measured via galvanic skin response (GSR)—relates to punitive behavior. GSR is an index of autonomic nervous system arousal (Bouscein, 2012; Phelps, 2009), and has been linked to self-reported anger (Ben-Shakhar et al., 2007).

The rationale for using this method in the context of punishment is that selfish offers are thought to potentially elicit arousal that can then be measured via GSR. Indeed, many studies have linked GSR to rejections in the Ultimatum Game, suggesting that arousal plays a role in 2PP. Specifically, van't Wout and colleagues (2006) found that GSR was higher for unfair offers than fair ones and was correlated with rejection of unfair offers. This pattern only held true for offers made by humans and not offers made by computers. The general finding that GSR correlates with punitive behavior has been conceptually replicated by Civai and colleagues (2010) and Ben-Shakhar et al. (2007) in different economic game setups, although it is worth noting that Osumi and Ohiri (2009) fail to find a relationship between GSR and unfair offers in the Ultimatum Game. And, importantly, Gummerum and colleagues (2020) also measured GSR and examined whether this arousal response mediated the relationship between offer type (fair, unfair) and rejection behavior. Conceptually replicating van't Wout et al. (2006), they found evidence in favor of the mediating role of anger in rejection behavior in adults. They did not find this relationship in children (9-year-olds) or adolescents (13-year-olds).

With respect to 3PP, skin conductance findings reveal a different story about how emotions may play a role in punitive behavior. Specifically, Civai and colleagues (2010) measured GSR in a 3PP game paradigm and found null results in adults. Similarly, Gummerum and colleagues (2020) failed to find a mediating role of anger in adults. They also did not find an effect when examining whether GSR mediates the relationship between offer type (fair, unfair) and punishment decisions. Both sets of authors interpret their findings to mean that, when it comes to 3PP (which is not directly relevant to the self), automatic emotional responses are not tied to punitive behavior, as had been previously argued.

Why might this be the case? Up until this point, 2PP and 3PP emotional bases appear to overlap across many dimensions. For example, both 2PP and 3PP are correlated with negative emotional states, negative emotional states appear to mediate the relationship between offer behavior and rejection behavior, and punishment behavior in second-party and third-party contexts appears to increase when negative emotions are directly manipulated. The answer here appears to lie in discussions about the nature of GSR. Specifically, GSR and self-reported emotion may represent different levels and stages of processing (Scherer, 2009). It is possible that GSR is more closely tied with automatic emotional appraisals, whereas self-reported emotions represent a compilation of several different inputs (perhaps including cognitive appraisals or other bodily states). Gummerum and colleagues (2020) explain why this may in turn impact differential findings across 2PP and 3PP contexts. Specifically, they write: "In situations where unfairness does not affect the self, more controlled processes, both explicit emotional appraisals and other social-cognitive processes (e.g., affective perspective-taking), might be necessary to bridge this self-relevance gap for third parties to engage in costly punishment" (p. 13).

Together, this research suggests that automatic arousal (measured via GSR) may promote punitive behavior in second-party but not third-party contexts. It seems that this difference may emerge because transgressions affecting other individuals do not directly elicit arousal because they are not relevant to the self, although further empirical investigation into this is necessary.

Neural Basis of Punitive Behavior

Research in neuroscience has investigated whether activation in areas of the brain associated with emotions, such as anger and disgust, relate to and predict social decision-making (see Phelps, 2009, for a review). This work has largely corroborated the link between negative emotional states and punishment in second-party and third-party contexts.

The first key study on this issue was conducted by Sanfey and colleagues (2003). They had participants play several iterations of the Ultimatum Game (2PP) with either a human partner or a computer partner, and found that, when presented with unfair offers, participants exhibited greater neural activity in brain regions typically associated with negative emotion (anterior insula), such as anger and disgust (Calder et al., 2001; Phillips et al., 1997), and also cognition (dorsolateral prefrontal cortex; Miller & Cohen, 2001). This pattern of activation only held for interactions with a human partner, but not a computer one. Neural activity associated with negative emotions also predicted subsequent behavior, further suggesting that emotional response to unfair offers plays a role in shaping decision-making in cooperative games. Similarly, other research has documented greater activation in the ventrolateral prefrontal cortex—a region associated with emotion regulation—in response to selfish offers relative to fair ones (Ciaramelli et al., 2013; Tabibnia et al., 2008).

This work is mostly correlational, linking brain activation with behavioral responses. Critically, follow-up work provides more causal evidence in favor of emotions' role in 2PP. For instance, research by Koenigs and Tranel (2007) found that patients with lesions to the ventromedial prefrontal cortex (vmPFC) are more inclined to reject unfair offers in the Ultimatum Game than people without lesions. Similarly, Crockett and colleagues (2008) found that the depletion of serotonin—a neurotransmitter associated with emotion regulation—tends to lead to increased rejection behavior in the Ultimatum Game. And work by Grecucci and colleagues (2013) yielded conceptually similar results, showing that participants who reappraised the divider's intentions as more negative (versus positive) were more likely to reject (than accept) offers. Together, this work implicates negative emotional states in promoting punitive behavior in second-party contexts.

Similar relationships have been documented for 3PP. Specifically, Buckholtz and colleagues (2008) found that a variety of neurological networks were recruited when participants made punishment decisions about other peoples' misdeeds. Regions of the brain associated with affective processing, including the amygdala, medial prefrontal cortex, and posterior cingulate cortex were associated with punitive decisions. It is important to note, however, that this work is correlational and therefore cannot offer causal conclusions about the neural mechanisms underlying 3PP. A possible causal link between affective processing and 3PP was supported in recent work by Asp and colleagues (2019). Like Koenigs and Tranel (2007), they tested participants with lesions to the vmPFC—an area associated with affective regulation—and found that such participants punished transgressors more leniently for violent crimes (presumably more emotionally evocative crimes) than counterparts who did not have lesions to the vmPFC. Additionally, they did not find a difference in how participants with lesions to the vmPFC punished in comparison to healthy controls for non-emotionally evocative crimes.

Together, work on the relationship between brain areas associated with emotion and punishment finds that such areas are causally implicated in the promotion of punitive behavior across both 2PP and 3PP (e.g., Belluci et al., 2020; Buckholtz & Marois, 2012; Civai et al., 2019; Krueger & Hoffman, 2016). The strongest causal evidence comes from lesion studies where individuals with damage to the vmPFC express systematic variation in the punitive behavior in both second-party and third-party contexts. However, the behavioral outcomes of this damage appear to differ depending on whether 2PP or 3PP is being elicited. For example, Koenigs and Tranel (2007) found that participants with lesions to the vmPFC show greater levels of 2PP. By contrast, Asp et al. (2019) found that participants with lesions to vmPFC showed lower levels of punishment for emotionally evocative crimes specifically—this time in the context of 3PP. Asp and colleagues (2019) argued that, unlike neurotypical individuals, participants with vmPFC lesions do not experience an automatic negative emotional reaction to the abstract violent crimes presented in the vignettes, although they do in response to second-party situations when the transgression directly affects the punisher (note that the 3PP results varied depending on the emotional valence of the situation; see Asp et al., 2019). It is possible, then, that the experience of negative emotional arousal interacts with emotion-regulation capacities to give rise to different punitive responses in different situations, but greater attention to this possibility is required. Together, the work reviewed here suggests that brain areas associated with emotion and emotional regulation are involved in punitive behavior across both second-party and third-party contexts.

Interim Summary
This research on the emotional foundations of punitive behavior in both second-party and third-party contexts has yielded a number of key findings. To summarize what we have reviewed here: (a) self-reported negative emotions, most notably anger, correlate with punitive behavior for both 2PP and 3PP; (b) such emotional reactions often mediate the relationship between offer size and rejection behavior for both 2PP and 3PP; (c) direct manipulation of negative emotions—generally done via incidental event manipulations—increased punitive behavior for both 2PP and 3PP; and (d) areas of the brain associated with negative emotion are often recruited (among other areas) during punitive decision-making in both 2PP and 3PP.

The main area where findings appear to vary as a function of 2PP and 3PP is with respect to emotional arousal (measured by GSR): it seems that automatic emotional arousal measured via GSR is more strongly related to 2PP and not at all related to 3PP (e.g., Civai et al., 2010). It is also possible that this lack of automatic emotional response differentially interacts with those who have lesions to brain areas associated with emotional regulation (vmPFC; Asp et al., 2019), although this possibility requires further investigation. There is also work linking other emotions, such as disgust and sadness, to punitive behavior in 2PP, but virtually no work assessing these links in 3PP. Despite this, the preponderance of evidence ranging from correlational work to causal manipulations to neurological evidence suggests that negative emotions, most notably anger, are core to punitive behavior in both 2PP and 3PP contexts.

The Role of Positive Emotions in Punishment Behavior

Until this point, we have reviewed work suggesting an important link between negative emotions, such as anger, with punitive behavior. However, theorists have argued that *positive emotions* also play a key role in the promotion of cooperative behavior. For instance, classical philosophical discussions of "moral sentiments" posited that feeling others' emotions (affective empathy and sympathy) promotes other-benefiting behavior, such as helping others or perhaps punishing transgressors on behalf of victims (e.g., Hume, 1739; Smith, 1759). More recently, researchers have specifically speculated that "other-suffering" emotions (such as compassion) and "other-praising" emotions (such as gratitude) may play a role in punitive behavior (Haidt, 2003). In this section, we will briefly review literature linking positive emotions, notably compassion, empathy, and gratitude, to 3PP. We also discuss other how other positive emotions, such as satisfaction and Schadenfreude, may reinforce punitive behavior in Box 52.3, "Punishment as Reward-Seeking Behavior." Importantly, this section specifically focuses exclusively on 3PP—not 2PP—for reasons we will describe shortly.

To start, we will focus on *compassion*. Compassion is characterized as "being moved by another's suffering" (Lazarus, 1991), and it can motivate individuals to help suffering others (e.g., Batson et al., 1983). This argument has been advanced to ground the idea that compassionate individuals may be especially punitive. The logic here is that when someone witnesses a transgression, the victim's pain resonates with the witness, which in a sense blurs the line between 2PP and 3PP. In this way then, individuals who are especially compassionate may be more inclined to punish in third-party contexts than their less compassionate counterparts. Because punishment is a response to a transgression, it stands to reason that individuals who are more sensitive to the suffering of others may be more inclined to respond to such suffering with punishment.

Box 52.3 Punishment as Reward-Seeking Behavior

Most of this chapter has focused on the emotions elicited *before* punishment: i.e., immediately after witnessing a transgression but before a punishment decision has been enacted. But this focus neglects the emotions one might experience *after* punishment, experiences which may play a role in promoting punitive behavior in the long term. Specifically, one might experience pleasurable emotions, such as satisfaction or Schadenfreude, after enacting punishment or learning that a criminal who harmed them (or someone else) has suffered retribution.

Evidence in favor of this possibility comes from neuroscientific research. In a key study, de Quervain and colleagues (2004) had participants engage in a 3PP task where they were given the opportunity to either symbolically punish (which did not actually reduce the transgressor's payoff) or effectively punish (which actually reduced the transgressor's payoff). The researchers also measured neural activity utilizing positron emission tomography (PET)—a neuroscientific technique that uses radioactive substances to visualize changes in neural activity. Using this setup, they found that effective punishment (but not symbolic punishment) was associated with enhanced activation of the dorsal striatum—an area of the brain associated with the processing of rewards as a result of goal-directed behaviors. They also found that greater activation in this area of the brain was associated with a heightened willingness to invest in costly 3PP.

Similar findings have been documented in second-party contexts with both adults (Singer et al., 2006) and children (Mendes et al., 2018). Ultimately, these findings are consistent with the possibility that people derive satisfaction from punishing transgressors in second-party and third-party contexts. It may be this experience of derived satisfaction that, over time, reinforces punishment as a valuable behavior and promotes punitive behavior in the long run. Together, this research sheds light on another proximate motive for punishment, beyond experiencing anger or compassion as a result of witnessing a transgression.

This possibility has been most robustly studied by Pfattheicher and colleagues (2019). Specifically, they tested whether compassion relates to punitive behavior. They stipulated that heightened compassion may lead individuals to punish because compassionate individuals are especially concerned about the plight of victims. Indeed, the researchers found such a relationship between compassion and punitive behavior across several experiments involving participants self-reporting their tendency to feel compassion for others (i.e., "I feel quite touched by the people suffering from . . ."). In additional studies, Pfattheicher et al. (2019) also manipulated compassion by encouraging participants to consider how their decisions impact others and found that 3PP increased when participants were induced to think in this way. Related to the previous section on the role of negative emotions in punitive behavior, they also documented that moral outrage (i.e., how angry, sad, fearful, surprised, happy, and disgusted participants were; Box 52.2) mediated the effect of compassion on third-party punishment, suggesting that compassion magnifies 3PP because it increases moral outrage in response to moral transgressions.

Developmental research, too, has documented evidence in favor of the possibility that empathy[4] plays a role in punitive behavior, even in children. Specifically, in work by Will and colleagues (2013), participants witnessed other individuals play a game called Cyberball, where individuals engaged in reciprocal interaction but, at a certain point, one individual excludes one of the players. Participants were asked to report their mood and also the mood of the victim at various points in the experiment. The researchers defined momentary affective perspective-taking as the discrimination between their own mood and the mood of the victim. They found that this measure predicted punitive behavior, suggesting that detecting negative emotions in the victim plays a role in the enactment of 3PP in children as young as nine. This work, alongside work by Pfattheicher and colleagues (2019), points toward the possibility that positive emotional states—such as compassion and affective empathy—play a role in 3PP, although this area is relatively understudied and should be further investigated in future research.

Beyond "other-suffering" emotions, moral emotions scholars have also discussed "other-praising" emotions (Haidt, 2003). These sorts of emotions, most notably *gratitude*, are experienced in response to others' good deeds or moral successes. We experience gratitude in our everyday lives—we may feel appreciative when a friend calls on our birthday, thankful for a kind gift from a colleague, or grateful for the opportunity to take a particularly insightful college course. Gratitude in particular has an important moral motivation underlying pro-social behavior (see McCullough et al., 2001, for a full review). Researchers have recently leveraged the notion that gratitude can motivate pro-social behavior to investigate whether such an emotion may promote 3PP in particular. To do so, Vayness and colleagues (2020) manipulated whether participants experienced gratitude, happiness, or neutrality by asking them to recall an experience in their life when they felt either grateful, happy, or neutral. They also measured how grateful, appreciative, and thankful they were as a result of writing the instructed passage. The researchers hypothesized that, because gratitude is linked to reduced temporal discounting (the tendency to diminish the value of future rewards; DeSteno et al., 2014; Dickens & DeSteno, 2016; Laibson, 1997), grateful participants may be more willing to pay a larger immediate cost via punishment to promote better, more cooperative interactions in the future. Indeed, this is what they found: individuals who were asked to reflect on a situation in which they felt grateful (compared to those who were asked to reflect on a situation in which they felt happy or neutral) exhibited a greater tendency to engage in 3PP.

Interim Summary
While the literature on the emotional antecedents of punishment has tended to focus on negative emotions—and principally on anger—new data suggest that other-oriented emotions, such as compassion and gratitude, may play an important role in motivating punitive behavior. In contrast to negative emotions, other-oriented emotions are thought to mostly involve focusing on the pain or suffering of victims. In this way, other-oriented emotions mark an important contrast with the mechanisms by which negative emotions are believed to exert their influence.

In other ways, however, negative emotions and other-oriented emotions may be aligned in their influence. Specifically, Pfattheicher et al. (2019) found that experiences of moral outrage mediate the link between compassion and punishment, such that those who were more compassionate experienced greater moral outrage, which resulted in greater punishment. These findings then align with the stipulation that negative emotions play a key role in punitive behavior, even if positive emotions also promote punitive behavior. Together, it seems like anger, which is more closely tied to the behaviors of the transgressor, and compassion, which is more closely tied to the feelings of the victim, both play a role in 3PP.

Note that work on other-oriented emotions and punishment has focused exclusively on 3PP. This stands to reason because these emotional responses involve focusing on the person affected by a transgression. In the context of 2PP, the person affected by the transgression is also the punisher, and these other-oriented emotions are less relevant. Nevertheless, future work could more thoroughly examine whether 2PP is motivated by concerns related to positive emotions, such as Schadenfreude, pleasure, or satisfaction.

The Role of Emotions in Selecting between Punitive and Compensatory Behavior

Up until this point, we have focused on punishment behavior. As mentioned earlier, however, there are other ways in which we can intervene in response to a transgressor; for example, we could compensate the victim (FeldmanHall et al., 2014; Heffner & FeldmanHall, 2019), terminate the relationship with the transgressor (Martin & Cushman, 2015), or forgive the transgressor (McCullough, 2008). In the real world, too, it is not uncommon for individuals (or criminal justice systems) to pursue other options outside of punishment to restore justice, such as compensating victims when they have been wronged. Given that individuals can pursue different avenues to restore justice, researchers have examined which emotions promote punishment versus compensation. For the most part, this research has examined how the presence of other options impacts 3PP, and less so 2PP. We review this literature here first with respect to anger and then with respect to affective empathy.

With respect to anger, it stands to reason that anger is more closely tied to a desire to punish because anger is generally elicited by the transgressor's misdeeds, and punishment is a way to directly harm the transgressor. Research motivated by this possibility has yielded mixed results, with some studies showing that anger promotes punishment only, compensation only, or both.

For example, a recent study by Rodrigues and colleagues (2020) induced anger, happiness, or neutral emotions in participants, presented participants with a transgressor, and then gave participants the opportunity to punish or to compensate the transgressor. Participants who were induced to experience anger were more likely to punish the transgressor than to compensate the victim. This finding aligns with research by Gummerum and colleagues (2016): specifically, they manipulated incidental anger and measured compensatory behavior. They found that angry participants were less likely to compensate than those in a neutral condition, suggesting that anger potentially attenuates one's interest in compensating victims.[5] Together, this work suggests that anger is more closely associated with a desire to engage with the transgressor than with the victim.

However, another study found evidence suggesting that anger promotes only compensatory behavior and not punitive behavior when both options are present (van Doorn et al., 2018). Specifically, the researchers instructed participants to describe a situation in which they felt anger (angry condition) or to describe an ordinary day (control condition). They found that participants in the angry condition invested more in compensating the victim than in punishment in both hypothetical situations and incentivized decision-making situations.

To complicate matters further, there is some evidence to suggest that negative emotions, such as anger, promote both compensatory and punitive behavior. Specifically, a study by Lotz and colleagues (2011) presented participants with different options when faced with a transgression: the participant could compensate the victim, punish the transgressor, or both. The researchers measured participants' "offender-focused" emotions, such as anger, shock, or hostility, in addition to "self-focused" emotions, such as anxiety, nervousness, and guilt. They found that offender-focused emotions predicted *both* punitive and compensatory behavior, whereas self-focused emotions only predicted compensatory behavior. In contrast to Rodrigues et al. (2020), Gummerum et al. (2016), and van Doorn et al. (2018), Lotz et al.'s study suggests that anger plays a role in not only punishment decisions but also compensatory ones.

Together, this research paints a complicated picture of how anger relates to punitive versus compensatory behavior. Greater investigation into these questions is required before we can more fully understand whether anger promotes punishment behavior, compensatory behavior, or both, when a wide array of options is provided to participants as means to restore justice.

Beyond anger, other work has examined whether affective empathy promotes intervention via punishment, compensation, or both. It is possible that positive emotions, such as affective empathy, are more closely tethered to a desire to compensate victims because such emotions are elicited by suffering victims, and compensation is a way to directly help such victims. Like with anger, research motivated by this possibility has also yielded mixed results, with some studies finding that affective empathy promotes compensatory behavior and others finding that it promotes both compensatory and punitive behavior depending on the situation.

For instance, Leliveld and researchers (2012) found that in third-party cases, empathy correlates positively with compensatory behavior such that more empathetic individuals are willing to incur a personal cost to compensate the victim of a crime. Interestingly, though, they found empathy to correlate negatively with punitive behavior, such that more empathetic individuals are *less* willing to incur a personal cost to punish someone who commits a crime. This particular finding seems to run contrary to Pfattheicher and colleagues' (2019) finding that compassion promotes punitive behavior in third-party contexts.

Fortunately, other work can shed light on why these studies find inconsistent effects. Specifically, work by Hu and colleagues (2020) finds—like Leliveld and colleagues (2012)—that those with greater empathetic concern are more likely to compensate victims of transgressions than to punish transgressors, but this is only the case when participants are not given specific instructions about what aspects of the situation to focus on. When participants were asked to focus on the norm violation (versus focusing on the victim's feelings), highly empathetic individuals were more likely to punish the transgressor than less empathetic individuals. On the whole, then, it appears that empathetic individuals are more inclined to intervene in response to norm violations—either via punishment or compensation. Whether such individuals pursue compensation (versus punishment) appears to depend on what component of the situation they focus on when making a decision.

Overall Summary, Future Directions, and Concluding Remarks

In this chapter, we have reviewed the empirical literature linking emotions to punitive behavior in both second- and third-party punishment contexts. The clearest message from the existing empirical literature on the emotional antecedents of punishment is that anger and other negative emotions are important drivers of punitive behavior in both second- and third-party contexts (see Figure 52.3). Evidence supporting this claim comes from an integration of work that has used different methodological approaches, including (a) correlational research that has linked anger with punitive behavior in both 2PP and 3PP; (b) mediation analyses that have found negative emotions to mediate the relationship between offer type (e.g., unfair, fair) and punitive behavior; and (c) experimental studies that have directly manipulated anger and measured associated changes in punitive behavior. Additionally, work at the physiological and neural levels has generated support for the link between negative emotional states and punishment, finding that automatic emotional arousal and brain areas associated with negative emotions and emotional regulation play a role in punitive behavior. On the whole, when it comes to understanding the proximate motives underlying punitive behavior, the evidence suggests that anger is a key ingredient in facilitating punitive behavior.

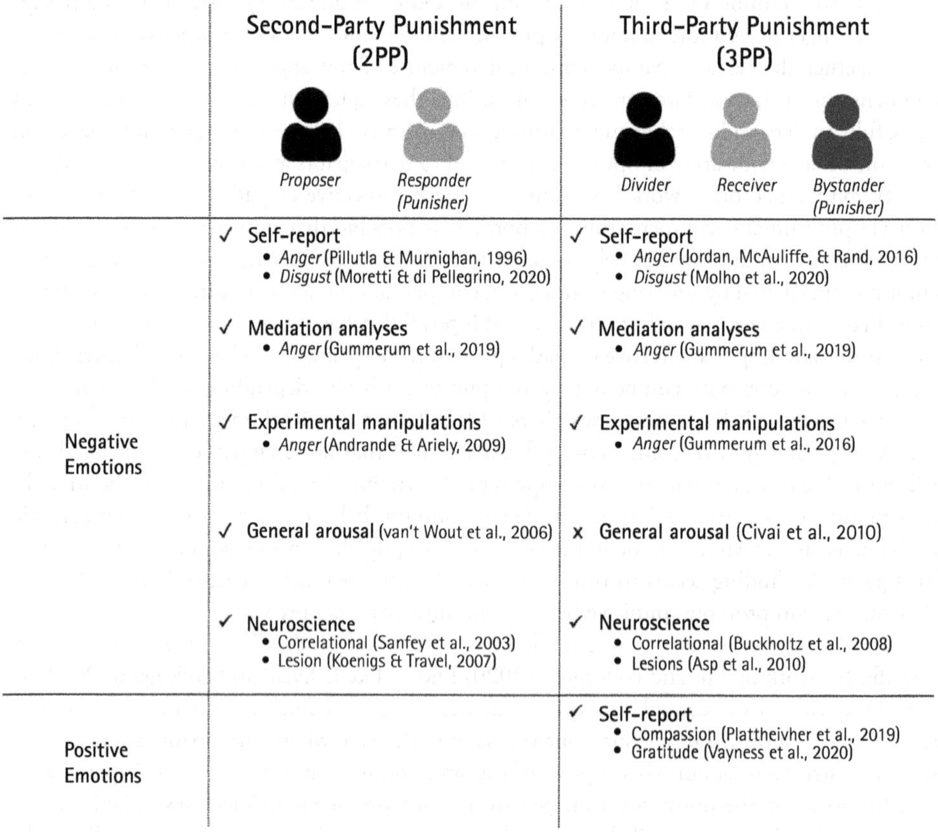

	Second-Party Punishment (2PP) Proposer / Responder (Punisher)	Third-Party Punishment (3PP) Divider / Receiver / Bystander (Punisher)
Negative Emotions	✓ Self-report • *Anger* (Pillutla & Murnighan, 1996) • *Disgust* (Moretti & di Pellegrino, 2020) ✓ Mediation analyses • *Anger* (Gummerum et al., 2019) ✓ Experimental manipulations • *Anger* (Andrande & Ariely, 2009) ✓ General arousal (van't Wout et al., 2006) ✓ Neuroscience • Correlational (Sanfey et al., 2003) • Lesion (Koenigs & Travel, 2007)	✓ Self-report • *Anger* (Jordan, McAuliffe, & Rand, 2016) • *Disgust* (Molho et al., 2020) ✓ Mediation analyses • *Anger* (Gummerum et al., 2019) ✓ Experimental manipulations • *Anger* (Gummerum et al., 2016) x General arousal (Civai et al., 2010) ✓ Neuroscience • Correlational (Buckholtz et al., 2008) • Lesions (Asp et al., 2010)
Positive Emotions		✓ Self-report • Compassion (Plattheivher et al., 2019) • Gratitude (Vayness et al., 2020)

Figure 52.3. Visualization of research linking negative emotions (such as anger and disgust) and positive emotions (such as compassion and gratitude) to second-party (2PP) and third-party (3PP) punishment. Check marks indicate positive evidence in favor of a link between the emotion in question (i.e., anger, disgust, compassion, gratitude) and punishment (either 2PP or 3PP depending on the column). References are not intended to be exhaustive and instead indicate a representative publication. The emojis portrayed in this figure were designed by Freepik at FlatIcon.com.

Still, there are several outstanding questions with respect to the emotional bases of punishment behavior. First, why does automatic emotional arousal relate to punishment in second-party contexts but not third-party contexts? Relatedly, what role does affective empathy play in the relationship between automatic emotional arousal and punitive behavior in third-party contexts? As discussed in detail above, a majority of studies have linked self-reported emotions to punitive behavior in both 2PP and 3PP, but the relationship between physiological measures of arousal (i.e., galvanic skin response; Civai et al., 2010; Gummerum et al., 2020) and punishment appear nonexistent. This discrepancy has received some attention (which we discuss above; Gummerum et al., 2020), but greater investigation into this question would help explain variation in the proximate motives of punishment across 2PP and 3PP contexts.

Second, although negative emotions play a role in both 2PP and 3PP, it seems unlikely that people feel similar levels of negative emotions in response to 2PP and 3PP. Research has found that individuals often feel much more personal anger in response to 2PP than in response to 3PP, but greater moral outrage in response to 3PP than in response to 2PP (see Boxes 52.1 and 52.2; Batson et al., 2007; Hartsough et al., 2020; O'Mara et al., 2011). These findings do not deny the possibility that anger plays a role in both 2PP and 3PP, but do raise the possibility that individuals feel considerably angrier about self-directed transgressions in comparison to other-directed ones. There may be other factors—such as empathy, compassion, or gratitude—that bridge the emotional gap between 2PP and 3PP, although future research should investigate this.

Third, the findings about whether anger promotes compensatory behavior rather than punitive behavior when both options are available are mixed. Some studies find that, even when compensation is available, anger still motivates punitive behavior (Lotz et al., 2011; Rodrigues et al., 2020), whereas other studies find that, when compensation is available, anger motivates compensatory behavior only (van Doorn et al., 2018). In light of this, further research is necessary to better understand the complex relationships between emotions and justice-oriented behavior, whether it be punishment, compensation, or some other response (such as forgiveness, which has received considerably less psychological attention).

Fourth, much of the research to date has focused on negative emotions, such as anger and moral outrage more broadly, with a recent focus on positive emotions, such as compassion and affective empathy. Even still, other emotions, such as guilt (Battigalli & Dufwenberg, 2007; Nelissen & Zeelenberg, 2009), regret (Martinez et al., 2011), shame (de Hooge et al., 2007), or frustration (Aina et al., 2020), may be at play in punitive behavior, despite such emotions' comparative lack of attention in the empirical literature.

Fifth, and finally, much of the research to date focuses on adults, but some work has attempted to better understand the developmental bases of punitive behavior. For example, Gummerum et al. (2020) found that self-reported anger mediates the link between offer amount and punitive behavior in children as young as nine for second-party situations but not for third-party ones. Additionally, work by Marshall, Yudkin, and Crockett (2020) failed to find any correlational relationships between anger or sadness and punitive behavior in 3PP contexts in children as young as five. In light of this, additional research needs to be done to better understand how emotions play a role in motivating punitive behavior over the course of early to middle childhood.

In sum, work on the emotional antecedents of punishment points to a constellation of emotions that play a role in motivating people's decisions to punish others in both second- and third-party contexts. Most notably, anger is a key driver of both forms of punishment. More recently, a spotlight has been shone on other-suffering emotions such as compassion and their role in motivating punishment. Together, the work reviewed here has begun to paint a picture of the emotions that work in concert to promote second- and third-party punishment.

Notes

1. Although see O'Mara and colleagues (2011); they do not find a relationship between anger and punitive behavior.
2. They also find that anger is strongly tied to perceptions of unfairness and propose that cognitive factors also play a large role in punishment behavior.
3. This may seem counterintuitive, considering that one may hypothesize that suppression of emotions may lead to less rejection behavior as a result of feeling less angry. The authors argue that suppression (in comparison to reappraisal) is less effective at combating negative emotions and can even have detrimental social consequences (van't Wout et al., 2010).
4. Some scholars consider empathy not as an emotion but as an ability or capacity to experience the emotions of another person (see Haidt, 2003, p. 862, for a review).
5. In follow-up studies, Gummerum et al. (2016) distinguished between self-focused anger and other-focused anger. They found that self-focused anger reduces compensatory behavior, whereas other-focused anger promotes compensatory behavior. These studies, though, did not compare a desire to engage in compensation versus punishment like the other studies reviewed in this section.

References

Aina, C., Battigalli, P., & Gamba, A. (2020). Frustration and anger in the ultimatum game: An Experiment. *Games and Economic Behavior, 122*, 150–167.
Andrade, E. B., & Ariely, D. (2009). The enduring impact of transient emotions on decision making. *Organizational Behavior and Human Decision Processes, 109*, 1–8.
Asp, E. W., Gullickson, J. T., Warner, K. A., Koscik, T. R., Denburg, N. L., & Tranel, D. (2019). Soft on crime: Patients with ventromedial prefrontal cortex damage allocate reduced third-party punishment to violent criminals. *Cortex, 119*, 33–45.
Balliet, D., Mulder, L. B., & Van Lange, P. A. (2011). Reward, punishment, and cooperation: A meta-analysis. *Psychological Bulletin, 137*, 594–615.
Bastian, B., Denson, T. F., & Haslam, N. (2013). The roles of dehumanization and moral outrage in retributive justice. *PloS ONE, 8*, e61842.
Batson, C. D., Kennedy, C. L., Nord, L. A., Stocks, E. L., Fleming, D. Y. A., Marzette, C. M., Lishner, D. A., Hayes, R. E., Kolchinsky, L. M., & Zerger, T. (2007). Anger at unfairness: Is it moral outrage? *European Journal of Social Psychology, 37*, 1272–1285.
Batson, C. D., O'Quin, K., Fultz, J., Vanderplas, M., & Isen, A. M. (1983). Influence of self-reported distress and empathy on egoistic versus altruistic motivation to help. *Journal of Personality and Social Psychology, 45*, 706–718.
Battigalli, P., & Dufwenberg, M. (2007). Guilt in games. *American Economic Review, 97*, 170–176.
Bellucci, G., Camilleri, J. A., Iyengar, V., Eickhoff, S. B., & Krueger, F. (2020). The emerging neuroscience of social punishment: Meta-analytic evidence. *Neuroscience & Biobehavioral Reviews, 113*, 426–439.
Ben-Shakhar, G., Bornstein, G., Hopfensitz, A., & Van Winden, F. (2007). Reciprocity and emotions in bargaining using physiological and self-report measures. *Journal of Economic Psychology, 28*, 314–323.
Binmore, K., Shaked, A., & Sutton, J. (1985). Testing noncooperative bargaining theory: A preliminary study. *The American Economic Review, 75*, 1178–1180.
Blount, S. (1995). When social outcomes aren't fair: The effect of causal attributions on preferences. *Organizational Behavior and Human Decision Processes, 63*, 131–144.
Bolton, G. E., & Zwick, R. (1995). Anonymity versus punishment in ultimatum bargaining. *Games and Economic Behavior, 10*, 95–121.
Bosman, R., Sonnemans, J., & Zeelenberg, M. (2001). Emotions, rejections, and cooling off in the ultimatum game. Unpublished manuscript.
Bosman, R., & Van Winden, F. (2002). Emotional hazard in a power-to-take experiment. *The Economic Journal, 112*, 147–169.
Boucsein, W. (2012). *Electrodermal activity*. Springer Science & Business Media.
Boyd, R., Gintis, H., Bowles, S., & Richerson, P. J. (2003). The evolution of altruistic punishment. *Proceedings of the National Academy of Sciences, 100*, 3531–3535.
Bright, D. A., & Goodman-Delahunty, J. (2006). Gruesome evidence and emotion: Anger, blame, and jury decision-making. *Law and Human Behavior, 30*, 183–202.

Buckholtz, J. W., Asplund, C. L., Dux, P. E., Zald, D. H., Gore, J. C., Jones, O. D., & Marois, R. (2008). The neural correlates of third-party punishment. *Neuron, 60*, 930–940.

Buckholtz, J. W., & Marois, R. (2012). The roots of modern justice: Cognitive and neural foundations of social norms and their enforcement. *Nature Neuroscience, 15*, 655–661.

Bullock, J. G., Green, D. P., & Ha, S. E. (2010). Yes, but what's the mechanism? (don't expect an easy answer). *Journal of Personality and Social Psychology, 98*, 550–558.

Calder, A. J., Lawrence, A. D., & Young, A. W. (2001). Neuropsychology of fear and loathing. *Nature Reviews Neuroscience, 2*, 352–363.

Camerer, C. F. (2003). *Behavioral game theory: Experiments in strategic interaction*. Princeton University Press.

Camerer, C. F., & Thaler, R. H. (1995). Anomalies: Ultimatums, dictators and manners. *Journal of Economic Perspectives, 9*, 209–219.

Carver, C. S., & Harmon-Jones, E. (2009). Anger is an approach-related affect: Evidence and implications. *Psychological Bulletin, 135*, 183–204.

Ciaramelli, E., Sperotto, R. G., Mattioli, F., & di Pellegrino, G. (2013). Damage to the ventromedial prefrontal cortex reduces interpersonal disgust. *Social Cognitive and Affective Neuroscience, 8*, 171–180.

Civai, C., Corradi-Dell'Acqua, C., Gamer, M., & Rumiati, R. I. (2010). Are irrational reactions to unfairness truly emotionally-driven? Dissociated behavioural and emotional responses in the Ultimatum Game task. *Cognition, 114*, 89–95.

Civai, C., Huijsmans, I., & Sanfey, A. G. (2019). Neurocognitive mechanisms of reactions to second-and third-party justice violations. *Scientific Reports, 9*(1), 9271.

Crockett, M. J. (2017). Moral outrage in the digital age. *Nature Human Behaviour, 1*, 769–771.

Crockett, M. J., Clark, L., Tabibnia, G., Lieberman, M. D., & Robbins, T. W. (2008). Serotonin modulates behavioral reactions to unfairness. *Science, 320*, 1739–1739.

Darley, J. M., & Pittman, T. S. (2003). The psychology of compensatory and retributive justice. *Personality and Social Psychology Review, 7*, 324–336.

de Hooge, I. E., Zeelenberg, M., & Breugelmans, S. M. (2007). Moral sentiments and cooperation: Differential influences of shame and guilt. *Cognition and Emotion, 21*, 1025–1042.

de Quervain, D. J., Fischbacher, U., Treyer, V., & Schellhammer, M. (2004). The neural basis of altruistic punishment. *Science, 305*, 1254.

DeSteno, D., Li, Y., Dickens, L., & Lerner, J. S. (2014). Gratitude: A tool for reducing economic impatience. *Psychological Science, 25*, 1262–1267.

Dickens, L., & DeSteno, D. (2016). The grateful are patient: Heightened daily gratitude is associated with attenuated temporal discounting. *Emotion, 16*, 421–425.

Dimitroff, S. J., Harrod, E. G., Smith, K. E., Faig, K. E., Decety, J., & Norman, G. J. (2020). Third-party punishment following observed social rejection. *Emotion, 20*, 713–720.

Elster, J. (1989). *The cement of society: A survey of social order*. Cambridge University Press.

Elster, J. (1998). Emotions and economic theory. *Journal of Economic Literature, 36*, 47–74.

Eriksson, K., Andersson, P. A., & Strimling, P. (2016). Moderators of the disapproval of peer punishment. *Group Processes & Intergroup Relations, 19*, 152–168.

Fehr, E., & Fischbacher, U. (2004a). Third-party punishment and social norms. *Evolution and Human Behavior, 25*, 63–87.

Fehr, E., & Fischbacher, U. (2004b). Third-party punishment and social norms (Working Paper No. 106). University of Zürich, Institute for Empirical Research in Economics.

Fehr, E., & Gächter, S. (2000). Cooperation and punishment in public goods experiments. *American Economic Review, 90*, 980–994.

Fehr, E., & Gächter, S. (2002). Altruistic punishment in humans. *Nature, 415*, 137–140.

FeldmanHall, O., Sokol-Hessner, P., Van Bavel, J. J., & Phelps, E. A. (2014). Fairness violations elicit greater punishment on behalf of another than for oneself. *Nature Communications, 5*, 1–6.

Frank, R. H. (1988). *Passions within reason: The strategic role of the emotions*. W. W. Norton.

Frijda, N. H. (1986). *The emotions*. Cambridge University Press.

Ginther, M. R., Hartsough, L. E., & Marois, R. (2021). Moral outrage drives the interaction of harm and culpable intent in third-party punishment decisions. *Emotion, 22*, 795–804.

Goldberg, J. H., Lerner, J. S., & Tetlock, P. E. (1999). Rage and reason: The psychology of the intuitive prosecutor. *European Journal of Social Psychology, 29*, 781–795.

Grecucci, A., Giorgetta, C., van't Wout, M., Bonini, N., & Sanfey, A. G. (2013). Reappraising the ultimatum: An fMRI study of emotion regulation and decision making. *Cerebral Cortex, 23*, 399–410.

Gummerum, M., López-Pérez, B., Van Dijk, E., & Van Dillen, L. F. (2020). When punishment is emotion-driven: Children's, adolescents', and adults' costly punishment of unfair allocations. *Social Development, 29*, 126–142.

Gummerum, M., Van Dillen, L. F., Van Dijk, E., & López-Pérez, B. (2016). Costly third-party interventions: The role of incidental anger and attention focus in punishment of the perpetrator and compensation of the victim. *Journal of Experimental Social Psychology, 65*, 94–104.

Güth, W., & Kocher, M. G. (2014). More than thirty years of ultimatum bargaining experiments: Motives, variations, and a survey of the recent literature. *Journal of Economic Behavior & Organization, 108*, 396–409.

Güth, W., Schmittberger, R., & Schwarze, B. (1982). An experimental analysis of ultimatum bargaining. *Journal of Economic Behavior & Organization, 3*, 367–388.

Haidt, J. (2003). The moral emotions. In R. J. Davidson, K. R. Scherer, & H. H. Goldsmith (Eds.), *Handbook of affective sciences*, (Vol. 11, (pp. 852–870). Oxford University Press.

Harlé, K. M., & Sanfey, A. G. (2007). Incidental sadness biases social economic decisions in the Ultimatum Game. *Emotion, 7*, 876–881.

Harmon-Jones, E. (2003). Anger and the behavioral approach system. *Personality and Individual Differences, 35*(5), 995–1005.

Hartsough, L. E., Ginther, M. R., & Marois, R. (2020). Distinct affective responses to second-and third-party norm violations. *Acta Psychologica, 205*, 103060.

Heffner, J., & FeldmanHall, O. (2019). Why we don't always punish: Preferences for non-punitive responses to moral violations. *Scientific Reports, 9*, 1–13.

Henrich, J. (2000). Does culture matter in economic behavior? Ultimatum game bargaining among the Machiguenga of the Peruvian Amazon. *American Economic Review, 90*, 973–979.

Henrich, J., Boyd, R., Bowles, S., Camerer, C., Fehr, E., Gintis, H., & McElreath, R. (2001). In search of *Homo economicus*: Behavioral experiments in 15 small-scale societies. *American Economic Review, 91*, 73–78.

Henrich, J., McElreath, R., Barr, A., Ensminger, J., Barrett, C., Bolyanatz, A., Cardenas, J. C., Gurven, M., Gwako, E., Henrich, N., . . . & Lesorogol, C. (2006). Costly punishment across human societies. *Science, 312*, 1767–1770.

Hertwig, R., & Ortmann, A. (2001). Experimental practices in economics: A methodological challenge for psychologists? *Behavioral and Brain Sciences, 24*, 383–403.

Hirshleifer, J. (1987). On the emotions as guarantors of threats and promises. In J. Duprè (Ed.), *The latest on the best: Essays on evolution and optimality* (pp. 307–326). MIT Press.

Hopfensitz, A., & Reuben, E. (2009). The importance of emotions for the effectiveness of social punishment. *The Economic Journal, 119*, 1534–1559.

House, B. R., Kanngiesser, P., Barrett, H. C., Yilmaz, S., Smith, A. M., Sebastian-Enesco, C., A. Erut, & Silk, J. B. (2020). Social norms and cultural diversity in the development of third-party punishment. *Proceedings of the Royal Society B: Biological Sciences, 287*, 20192794.

Hu, Y., Fiedler, S., & Weber, B. (2020). What drives the (un) empathic bystander to intervene? Insights from eye tracking. *British Journal of Social Psychology, 59*, 733–751.

Hume, D. (1739/1969). *A treatise of human nature*. London: Penguin.

Jensen, N. H., & Petersen, M. B. (2011). To defer or to stand up? How offender formidability affects third party moral outrage. *Evolutionary Psychology, 9*, 147470491100900113.

Jordan, J., McAuliffe, K., & Rand, D. (2016). The effects of endowment size and strategy method on third party punishment. *Experimental Economics, 19*, 741–763.

Koenigs, M., & Tranel, D. (2007). Irrational economic decision-making after ventromedial prefrontal damage: evidence from the Ultimatum Game. *Journal of Neuroscience, 27*, 951–956.

Krueger, F., & Hoffman, M. (2016). The emerging neuroscience of third-party punishment. *Trends in Neurosciences, 39*, 499–501.

Laibson, D. (1997). Golden eggs and hyperbolic discounting. *The Quarterly Journal of Economics, 112*, 443–478.

Lazarus, R. S. (1991). *Emotion and adaptation*. Oxford University Press.

Leliveld, M. C., van Dijk, E., & van Beest, I. (2012). Punishing and compensating others at your own expense: The role of empathic concern on reactions to distributive injustice. *European Journal of Social Psychology, 42*, 135–140.

Loewenstein, G. (1996). Out of control: Visceral influences on behavior. *Organizational Behavior and Human Decision Processes, 65*, 272–292.

Loewenstein, G. (2000). Emotions in economic theory and economic behavior. *American Economic Review, 90*, 426–432.

Lotz, S., Okimoto, T. G., Schlösser, T., & Fetchenhauer, D. (2011). Punitive versus compensatory reactions to injustice: Emotional antecedents to third-party interventions. *Journal of Experimental Social Psychology, 47*, 477–480.

Marshall, J., & McAuliffe, K. (2022). Children as assessors and agents of third-party punishment. *Nature Reviews Psychology*, 1(6), 334–344.

Marshall, J., Yudkin, D. A., & Crockett, M. J. (2020). Children punish third parties to satisfy both consequentialist and retributive motives. *Nature Human Behaviour, 5*, 1–8.

Martin, J. W., & Cushman, F. (2015). To punish or to leave: Distinct cognitive processes underlie partner control and partner choice behaviors. *PloS ONE, 10*, e0125193.

Martinez, L. M., Zeelenberg, M., & Rijsman, J. B. (2011). Behavioural consequences of regret and disappointment in social bargaining games. *Cognition and Emotion, 25*, 351–359.

Mathew, S., & Boyd, R. (2011). Punishment sustains large-scale cooperation in prestate warfare. *Proceedings of the National Academy of Sciences, 108*, 11375–11380.

McAuliffe, K., Jordan, J. J., & Warneken, F. (2015). Costly third-party punishment in young children. *Cognition, 134*, 1–10.

McCullough, M. E. (2008). *Beyond revenge: The evolution of the forgiveness instinct*. Wiley.

McCullough, M. E., Kilpatrick, S. D., Emmons, R. A., & Larson, D. B. (2001). Is gratitude a moral affect? *Psychological Bulletin, 127*, 249–266.

Mendes, N., Steinbeis, N., Bueno-Guerra, N., Call, J., & Singer, T. (2018). Preschool children and chimpanzees incur costs to watch punishment of antisocial others. *Nature Human Behaviour, 2*, 45–51.

Miller, E. K., & Cohen, J. D. (2001). An integrative theory of prefrontal cortex function. *Annual Review of Neuroscience, 24*, 167–202.

Molho, C., Tybur, J. M., Van Lange, P. A., & Balliet, D. (2020). Direct and indirect punishment of norm violations in daily life. *Nature Communications, 11*, 1–9.

Moretti, L., & di Pellegrino, G. (2010). Disgust selectively modulates reciprocal fairness in economic interactions. *Emotion, 10*, 169–180.

Mullen, E., & Skitka, L. J. (2006). Exploring the psychological underpinnings of the moral mandate effect: Motivated reasoning, group differentiation, or anger? *Journal of Personality and Social Psychology, 90*, 629–643.

Nelissen, R. M., & Zeelenberg, M. (2009). Moral emotions as determinants of third-party punishment: Anger, guilt and the functions of altruistic sanctions. *Judgment and Decision Making, 4*, 543–553.

Nowak, M. A., Page, K. M., & Sigmund, K. (2000). Fairness versus reason in the ultimatum game. *Science, 289*, 1773–1775.

O'Mara, E. M., Jackson, L. E., Batson, C. D., & Gaertner, L. (2011). Will moral outrage stand up? Distinguishing among emotional reactions to a moral violation. *European Journal of Social Psychology, 41*, 173–179.

Oosterbeek, H., Sloof, R., & Van De Kuilen, G. (2004). Cultural differences in ultimatum game experiments: Evidence from a meta-analysis. *Experimental Economics, 7*, 171–188.

Osumi, T., & Ohira, H. (2009). Cardiac responses predict decisions: An investigation of the relation between orienting response and decisions in the ultimatum game. *International Journal of Psychophysiology, 74*, 74–79.

Pfattheicher, S., Sassenrath, C., & Keller, J. (2019). Compassion magnifies third-party punishment. *Journal of Personality and Social Psychology, 117*, 124–141.

Phelps, E. A. (2009). The study of emotion in neuroeconomics. In P. W. Glimcher, C. F. Camerer, E. Fehr, & R. A. Poldrack (Eds.), *Neuroeconomics* (pp. 233–250). Academic Press.

Phillips, M. L., Young, A. W., Senior, C., Brammer, M., Andrew, C., Calder, A. J., Bullmore, E. T., Perrett, D. I., Rowland, D., Williams, S. C., & Gray, J. A. (1997). A specific neural substrate for perceiving facial expressions of disgust. *Nature, 389*, 495–498.

Pillutla, M. M., & Murnighan, J. K. (1996). Unfairness, anger, and spite: Emotional rejections of ultimatum offers. *Organizational Behavior and Human Decision Processes, 68*, 208–224.

Prinz, J. J., & Nichols, S. B. (2010). Moral emotions. In J. M. Doris (Ed.), *The moral psychology handbook* (pp. 111–146). Oxford University Press.

Raihani, N. J., Thornton, A., & Bshary, R. (2012). Punishment and cooperation in nature. *Trends in Ecology & Evolution, 27*, 288–295.

Riedl, K., Jensen, K., Call, J., & Tomasello, M. (2012). No third-party punishment in chimpanzees. *Proceedings of the National Academy of Sciences, 109*, 14824–14829.

Rodrigues, J., Liesner, M., Reutter, M., Mussel, P., & Hewig, J. (2020). It's costly punishment, not altruistic: Low midfrontal theta and state anger predict punishment. *Psychophysiology, 57*, e13557.

Rodrigues, J., Nagowski, N., Mussel, P., & Hewig, J. (2018). Altruistic punishment is connected to trait anger, not trait altruism, if compensation is available. *Heliyon, 4*(11), e00962.

Roth, A. E. (1995). Bargaining experiments. In J. H. Kagel & A. E. Roth (Eds.), *Handbook of experimental economics* (pp. 253–348). Princeton University Press.

Salerno, J. M., & Bottoms, B. L. (2009). Emotional evidence and jurors' judgments: The promise of neuroscience for informing psychology and law. *Behavioral Sciences & the Law, 27*, 273–296.

Salerno, J. M., & Peter-Hagene, L. C. (2013). The interactive effect of anger and disgust on moral outrage and judgments. *Psychological Science, 24*, 2069–2078.

Sally, D., & Hill, E. (2006). The development of interpersonal strategy: Autism, theory-of-mind, cooperation and fairness. *Journal of Economic Psychology, 27*, 73–97.

Sanfey, A. G., Rilling, J. K., Aronson, J. A., Nystrom, L. E., & Cohen, J. D. (2003). The neural basis of economic decision-making in the ultimatum game. *Science, 300*, 1755–1758.

Sawaoka, T., & Monin, B. (2018). The paradox of viral outrage. *Psychological Science, 29*, 1665–1678.

Scherer, K. R. (2009). The dynamic architecture of emotion: Evidence for the component process model. *Cognition and Emotion, 23*, 1307–1351.

Seip, E. C., Van Dijk, W. W., & Rotteveel, M. (2014). Anger motivates costly punishment of unfair behavior. *Motivation and Emotion, 38*, 578–588.

Singer, T., Seymour, B., O'Doherty, J. P., Stephan, K. E., Dolan, R. J., & Frith, C. D. (2006). Empathic neural responses are modulated by the perceived fairness of others. *Nature, 439*, 466–469.

Skitka, L. J., Bauman, C. J., & Mullen, E. (2004). Political tolerance and coming to psychological closure following the September 11, 2001, terrorist attacks: An integrative approach. *Personality and Social Psychology Bulletin, 30*, 743–756.

Smith, A. ([1759] 1976). *The theory of moral sentiments*. Clarendon Press.

Srivastava, J., Espinoza, F., & Fedorikhin, A. (2009). Coupling and decoupling of unfairness and anger in ultimatum bargaining. *Journal of Behavioral Decision Making, 22*, 475–489.

Straub, P. G., & Murnighan, J. K. (1995). An experimental investigation of ultimatum games: Information, fairness, expectations, and lowest acceptable offers. *Journal of Economic Behavior & Organization, 27*, 345–364.

Sutter, M. (2007). Outcomes versus intentions: On the nature of fair behavior and its development with age. *Journal of Economic Psychology, 28*, 69–78.

Tabibnia, G., Satpute, A. B., & Lieberman, M. D. (2008). The sunny side of fairness: Preference for fairness activates reward circuitry (and disregarding unfairness activates self-control circuitry). *Psychological Science, 19*, 339–347.

Tangney, J. P., Stuewig, J., & Mashek, D. J. (2007). Moral emotions and moral behavior. *Annual Review of Psychology, 58*, 345–372.

Tetlock, P. E., Kristel, O. V., Elson, S. B., Green, M. C., & Lerner, J. S. (2000). The psychology of the unthinkable: taboo trade-offs, forbidden base rates, and heretical counterfactuals. *Journal of Personality and Social Psychology, 78*, 853–870.

Thaler, R. H. (1988). Anomalies: The ultimatum game. *Journal of Economic Perspectives, 2*, 195–206.

Treadway, M. T., Buckholtz, J. W., Martin, J. W., Jan, K., Asplund, C. L., Ginther, M. R., Jones, O. D., & Marois, R. (2014). Corticolimbic gating of emotion-driven punishment. *Nature Neuroscience, 17*, 1270–1275.

van Doorn, J., Zeelenberg, M., & Breugelmans, S. M. (2018). An exploration of third parties' preference for compensation over punishment: six experimental demonstrations. *Theory and Decision, 85*, 333–351.

van't Wout, M., Chang, L. J., & Sanfey, A. G. (2010). The influence of emotion regulation on social interactive decision-making. *Emotion, 10*, 815–821.

van't Wout, M., Kahn, R. S., Sanfey, A. G., & Aleman, A. (2006). Affective state and decision-making in the ultimatum game. *Experimental Brain Research, 169*, 564–568.

Vayness, J., Duong, F., & DeSteno, D. (2020). Gratitude increases third-party punishment. *Cognition and Emotion, 34*, 1020–1027.

Vidmar, N., & Miller, D. T. (1980). Social psychological processes underlying attitudes toward legal punishment. *Law and Society Review, 14*, 565–602.

Vitaglione, G. D., & Barnett, M. A. (2003). Assessing a new dimension of empathy: Empathic anger as a predictor of helping and punishing desires. *Motivation and Emotion, 27*, 301–325.

Wang, C. S., Sivanathan, N., Narayanan, J., Ganegoda, D. B., Bauer, M., Bodenhausen, G. V., & Murnighan, K. (2011). Retribution and emotional regulation: The effects of time delay in angry economic interactions. *Organizational Behavior and Human Decision Processes, 116*, 46–54.

Will, G. J., Crone, E. A., van den Bos, W., & Güroğlu, B. (2013). Acting on observed social exclusion: Developmental perspectives on punishment of excluders and compensation of victims. *Developmental Psychology, 49*, 2236–2244.

Xiao, E., & Houser, D. (2005). Emotion expression in human punishment behavior. *Proceedings of the National Academy of Sciences, 102*, 7398–7401.

CHAPTER 53

Leadership as an Emotional Process: An Evolutionarily Informed Perspective

Sirio Lonati, Zachary H. Garfield, Nicolas Bastardoz, and Christopher von Rueden

Abstract

A growing literature has recently focused on evolutionary perspectives on both leadership and followership. Distinct from traditional approaches—rooted especially in organizational psychology and management—this body of work has mainly concentrated on the adaptive value and the phylogeny of leadership, while generally neglecting the role of emotions in structuring the emergence and effectiveness of leader-follower relationships. This chapter reviews theoretical and empirical results from both organizational and evolutionarily informed approaches to leadership and emotions, with the aim of bridging these literature streams. Ultimately, the authors ask, can we better understand leadership and followership in small groups or large organizations by studying jointly the evolutionary and emotional processes underpinning them? Within a multidisciplinary framework touching upon psychology, biology, and anthropology, they highlight how these fields can increasingly intersect in future research, discussing especially (but not only) the illustrative example of charismatic leadership.

Key Words: leadership, followership, emotion, evolution, charisma

Evolutionary approaches to leadership have proliferated in the past decade, often involving interdisciplinary collaborations of anthropologists, biologists, economists, political scientists, and psychologists (e.g., Garfield, von Rueden, et al., 2019; Hooper et al., 2010; Lonati, 2020; J. E. Smith et al., 2016; Van Vugt, 2006; Van Vugt, Hogan, et al., 2008). A key focus of this field has been identifying inter-individual variation in leadership characteristics across social contexts, societies, and species, as well as classifying the socioecological conditions favoring distinct leadership styles. Significant advances have been made (see Van Vugt & von Rueden, 2020), yet these recent evolutionary approaches have discussed only marginally a critical component of the leadership process: emotions.

This initial lack of attention can be attributed to the novelty of this research program and its focus on ultimate questions (cf., Tinbergen, 1963). However, in the organizational literature—the field with the strongest focus on leadership and followership (Gardner et al., 2020)—emotions and affect play a critical role (Gooty et al., 2010). Some scholars have even argued that leadership is essentially an emotional process (Pescosolido, 2002; Van Knippenberg & Van Kleef, 2016). Thus, integrating evolutionary and organizational perspectives could provide important insights to understand and explain leadership and followership.

We explore potential pathways for incorporating evolutionary and organizational viewpoints in the study of leadership and emotions. We first review leadership literature across organizational and evolutionary approaches. We then turn to the literature on emotions and leadership, covering, again, both perspectives. We close by discussing future directions for studying leadership and emotions in a multidisciplinary framework. To substantiate our suggestions, we concentrate especially on charismatic leadership, which represents an interesting "case study" for linking emotions and leadership with an evolutionary logic. Charisma has been recently studied through biological and evolutionary lenses (e.g., Grabo et al., 2017; Grabo & Van Vugt, 2016), and has been conceptualized as an emotional process in the organizational sciences (Antonakis et al., 2016; Shamir et al., 1993).

Our review is exploratory and preliminary, yet we aim to make three novel contributions. First, we begin to integrate organizational and evolutionary perspectives on emotions and leadership. This communication across fields is important, especially now that multidisciplinary approaches to social sciences are blooming (Al-Shawaf et al., 2016; Buyalskaya et al., 2021) and calls for more unified theories have been made in the field of leadership (Antonakis, 2017). While organizational researchers have already examined leadership as an emotional process, and there are numerous evolutionary studies on the role of emotions in status navigation (see, e.g., Cheng et al., 2010; Durkee, Chapter 30 in this volume; Durkee et al., 2019; Steckler & Tracy, 2014), leadership and status are distinct constructs (see Cheng & Tracy, 2020; Van Vugt & Smith, 2019), and much remains to be done to combine organizational and evolutionary perspectives on leadership and emotions.

Second, an evolutionarily informed study of leadership and emotions allows us to better bridge ultimate and proximate levels of analysis (cf. Tinbergen, 1963), sketching a research agenda focused on the interplays between leadership, followership, emotions, and their coevolution (cf. Al-Shawaf et al., 2021; Spisak, 2020). Employing evolutionary principles may allow researchers to derive new testable predictions on the relationship between leadership and emotions at both the proximate and ultimate levels. Moreover, whereas several evolved psychological mechanisms related to leadership and followership have been theorized (e.g., "when in danger, follow the orders of a leader"), research on emotions offers a useful starting point to identify theoretically and empirically the proximate building blocks of these mechanisms (Pietraszewski, 2020).

Third, we contribute to the literature on charismatic leadership, discussing especially the role of emotional displays from a signaling perspective, as well as the links between charisma, emotions, and their evolution in groups of varying dimensions and across different cultures. Beyond proposing new research directions, we also argue that bridging different disciplinary perspectives around topics like leadership, charisma, evolution, and emotions—all of which tend to be studied in isolation—provides a more comprehensive picture of them all, fostering clarity on definitions, conceptualizations, and methods used to study constructs of interest for various disciplines.

Leadership and Followership
Leadership and Followership in Organization Studies
The study of leadership has a long history, but its systematic examination in organization studies—the primary field for many leadership scholars—started about a century ago with the "great man" approach, which focused on identifying the individual characteristics that differentiate leaders from nonleaders (Antonakis & Day, 2018). This stream of research aimed at uncovering personality traits predicting leader emergence and effectiveness (Zaccaro et al., 2018). This approach, however, was largely abandoned when two influential pieces (Mann,

1959; Stogdill, 1948)—together with the emergence of a post–World War II context opposed to the "great man" assumption—shifted leadership research toward leader behaviors (a change that also coincided with the emergence of behaviorism in psychology; Day, 2012). Researchers at Ohio State (e.g., Halpin & Winer, 1957) and at the University of Michigan (e.g., Taylor & Bowers, 1972) uncovered two broad classes of effective leader behaviors: one that focused on tasks (i.e., initiating structure or production-oriented), and one that focused on people (i.e., consideration or employee-oriented). This line of research also proliferated due to the emergence and wide acceptance of questionnaires to measure leader behaviors, which became available with the advance of statistical techniques and psychometrics (e.g., Stogdill, 1963). Acknowledging the conceptual and empirical limitations of behavioral theories of leadership, however, the contextual (or contingency) school also emerged in the 1960s (Fiedler, 1964). In its contemporary and simplified version (Oc, 2018), this school suggests that different contexts or situations have different requirements and that leaders need to adapt their behaviors to the context in which they operate.

In the 1970s and 1980s, leadership studies faced an important turning point. Survey studies and self-reported measures—the most common method to measure leadership and its effects—were heavily criticized, because leadership ratings were found to be driven also by the cognitive representations of ideal leader traits and behaviors held by raters (Rush et al., 1977). Also, the "romance of leadership" school argued that leadership is only a social construction, a mere way for individuals to make sense of the complexity of their lives (Meindl & Ehrlich, 1987). This school claimed that leaders do not matter, with some scholars arguing even that "the concept of leadership has outlived its usefulness" (Miner, 1975, p. 200).

Countering this idea, House (1977) published a pivotal manuscript on charismatic leadership. House argued that charismatic leaders, through a combination of traits, behaviors, and contextual variables, can have powerful effects on followers' motivation. This publication provided the theoretical basis for transformational leadership theory (Bass, 1985; Bass & Riggio, 2006). This theory, which became extremely influential in the past decades (Antonakis, Bastardoz, et al., 2014), contrasts a transactional leadership style (based on contingent rewards and sanctions) with a transformational leadership style (based on values and inspiration). Transformational leaders induce followers to perform beyond expectations (Bass, 1985) by relying on four main sub-styles: idealized influence, inspirational motivation, individualized consideration, and intellectual stimulation (Bass & Riggio, 2006). Although not without flaws (see Antonakis et al., 2016; Van Knippenberg & Sitkin, 2013; Yukl, 1999), this theory remains highly influential (Gardner et al., 2020) and overlaps significantly with more recent theories, such as visionary leadership (Van Knippenberg & Stam, 2013), authentic leadership (Alvesson & Einola, 2019), and ethical leadership (Hoch et al., 2018).

Leadership and Followership from an Evolutionary Lens

Over the past decade, a relatively new leadership field—sometimes labeled "biology and evolution of leadership" or "evolutionary leadership theory"—emerged. Whereas an evolutionary approach to leadership was novel from a traditional organizational perspective, the study of leadership, followership, and hierarchies has been present for decades in biology, anthropology, and sociology (Allee, 1938; Morgan, 1877; Mumford, 1906). Indeed, anthropological evidence indicates that leadership is present in all human societies (Garfield et al., 2020; H. S. Lewis, 1974; Murdock, 1967).

Literature in political and evolutionary anthropology has historically suggested that community and political leadership evolved in a "U-shaped" dynamic (Gintis et al., 2015; Knauft et al., 1991; Mattison et al., 2016; von Rueden, 2020). Throughout hominin evolution, there was a general and global transition from primarily dominance-based, despotic social hierarchies among apes and early human ancestors to more egalitarian social hierarchies among mobile human hunter-gatherers, with the ultimate emergence of pronounced social stratification following the agricultural revolution. In this view, hunter-gatherer societies typical of the Pleistocene (i.e., 2.5 million years ago to 10,000 years ago) were largely egalitarian. Still, these mobile, kin-based societies exhibited social hierarchies, as some particularly skilled or experienced "first among equals" managed to exert differential influence over group outcomes (see the ethnographic portrait of the "Big Men" in New Guinea by Sahlins, 1963). Community leadership among mobile hunter-gatherers was probably mainly participatory and situational, non-hereditary, and characterized by little material differences between followers and leaders (cf. Boehm, 1993; R. L. Kelly, 2013; E. A. Smith et al., 2010; Woodburn, 1982). Nonagricultural populations, however, can and in many cases did develop highly stratified societies in some ecological conditions; these societies sometimes had multilevel social structures and complex, nested leadership systems (R. L. Kelly, 2013; Wengrow & Graeber, 2015). Notwithstanding, the agricultural revolution and other shifts in economic systems are thought to be responsible for a widespread reduction in egalitarianism and a transition to more rigid and institutionalized hierarchies across human societies (A. W. Johnson & Earle, 2000; Mattison et al., 2016; E. A. Smith & Choi, 2007).

Bridging the Two Fields

In an attempt to bridge organizational and evolutionary literature streams on leadership, Van Vugt and colleagues developed a new line of research suggesting that our leader and follower psychologies are characterized by a modular set of adaptive cognitive and emotional mechanisms that helped solve recurrent adaptive problems faced in the social and ecological environments of hunter-gatherer bands in the Pleistocene (Van Vugt, 2006; Van Vugt, Hogan, et al., 2008; Van Vugt, Johnson, et al., 2008; Van Vugt & Kurzban, 2007). Rooted in evolutionary psychology (Barkow et al., 1992; Buss, 1995), this approach suggests that leader and follower psychologies evolved as neurocognitive decision rules fostering coordination and motivation of group members in collective actions (e.g., "follow a physically strong leader during conflict situations"; "avoid dominant leader if not experiencing conflict"; cf. Bøggild & Laustsen, 2016). This work has been fruitful and has gained some traction in organizational-focused outlets (see Van Vugt & von Rueden, 2020).

This line of research is still relatively nascent and will benefit from deeper integrations with the organization studies field. To facilitate cross-disciplinary interactions, however, conceptual clarity is required, especially around the definition of leadership. In that regard, the fact that even researchers in organization studies fail to agree on a common conceptualization does not provide a helpful starting point (Ashford & Sitkin, 2019; Bastardoz & Day, 2022; Bedeian & Hunt, 2006). Nonetheless, a generally accepted definition of leadership is that of a process of social influence toward the achievement of common goals (Antonakis & Day, 2018; Yukl, 2002). This definition has two important ramifications (Bastardoz & Day, 2022). First, leadership requires social influence. Without influence, there is no leadership. Second, leadership requires shared goals between leader(s) and follower(s), distinguishing it from similar constructs like power and authority.

In the evolutionarily informed literature, leadership is frequently conceptualized as the coordination of followers' activities (Garfield, Hubbard, et al., 2019; Glowacki & von Rueden, 2015; Lonati, 2020; Pietraszewski, 2020; Powers & Lehmann, 2014; J. E. Smith et al., 2016). In this process, leaders are defined as individuals with some influence on group activities, and followers are individuals who accept the influence and goal of the leader (Bastardoz & Van

Vugt, 2019). Relatedly, in the evolutionary literature, various versions of the dual-strategy theory (described in greater detail later) argue that achieving and maintaining social influence generally follow either a prestige-based or dominance-based strategy (Cheng et al., 2013; Henrich & Gil-White, 2001; Maner, 2017; Maner & Case, 2016). These two strategies have been identified as antecedents of status hierarchy and leadership.

Although correlated, status hierarchy and leadership are nonetheless distinct and should be differentiated. For instance, the most prestigious individuals in a group may be high status but are not necessarily leaders (Van Vugt & Smith, 2019). Also, a dominance-based strategy can lead to leadership when dominant individuals increase group coordination or collective action (e.g., by punishing free-riders; see Redhead et al., 2021). However, the exercise of a dominance strategy over targets who have no other options is not leadership per se (because of the lack of common goals), but rather authority or coercion (Bastardoz & Day, 2022; Bastardoz & Van Vugt, 2019).

Moreover, even though dual-strategy approaches have been influential in the human evolutionary sciences of leadership, scholars have recently begun to focus on various forms of capital (i.e., social, material, embodied) that allow individuals to bestow benefits or impose costs (Durkee et al., 2020; von Rueden, 2014). To this extent, prestige and dominance can overlap (e.g., physical strength can enhance economic productivity, earning respect, while also allowing physical coercion and instilling fear; see Garfield et al., 2020). Furthermore, exercising dominance can generate prestige: leaders' dominance may dissuade would-be free-riders, benefiting the group at large and thus begetting praise (Glowacki & von Rueden, 2015). Prestigious individuals can also draw on their following to enact dominance-based strategies. Thus, it is not uncommon for individual leaders to score highly on both dominance and prestige. For example, elected male leaders in a relatively egalitarian, forager-horticulturist society were found to score higher than nonleaders on peer ratings of both dominance—which included being feared by others—and prestige, which included respect and intelligence (Garfield & Hagen, 2020).

Emotions and Leadership
Emotions
Evolutionary views of emotions have developed substantially over the years. Drawing on Darwin, early evolutionary perspectives focused on putative universal "basic" human emotions, presumed to be broadly conserved across social mammals given their utility in solving recurrent adaptive problems. The universality and phylogeny of emotions such as "fear" of a threat, "anger" toward a rival, and "love" of a social partner are suggested to emerge from species-typical (across many species) adaptations produced by natural selection, because they increased survival or reproduction (Ekman, 1973, 1999). Following the modern synthesis (e.g., Dobzhansky, 1974; Mayr, 1961; Williams, 2018), evolutionary psychologists began to view emotions as evolved, function-specific information-processing mechanisms. These mechanisms rely on environmental inputs in the context of a wide range of adaptive problems and facilitate the coordination of physiological processes and behavioral responses (Cosmides & Tooby, 2000; Tooby & Cosmides, 1990).

More recently, greater emphasis has been placed on the coordinating role of emotions as the "superordinate mechanism" activating, deactivating, and managing programs and systems within the phenotype (Al-Shawaf et al., 2016). This view expands the range of emotions considered and the range of adaptive problems they may have evolved to solve to include a variety of domains, possibly also embracing leader-follower dynamics (see Al-Shawaf et al., 2016). One might thus speculate that emotions simultaneously coordinate systems within the phenotype, while also serving to coordinate multiple phenotypes, facilitating leadership and followership, and possibly even promoting a variety of group-beneficial outcomes. Related to this idea, some literature has already focused on the links between emotions and hierarchies, a topic that is different, but certainly related to leadership. We turn now to a review of some key concepts.

Emotions and Leadership: Evolutionary Perspective

Dominance-based strategies—that is, coercive capacities based on force (Henrich & Gil-White, 2001)—are a feature of human sociality and of leadership across cultures and social contexts (Van Vugt & Smith, 2019). Still, the emotions related to dominance-based strategies are likely distinct from the ones invoked by other strategies (e.g., prestige) used to navigate social hierarchies (Garfield, von Rueden, et al., 2019; von Rueden, 2014). Individuals who regularly use a dominance strategy tend to be aggressive, narcissistic, and Machiavellian compared to those who use a prestige strategy, that is, status gained thanks to respected skills, abilities, or knowledge (Henrich & Gil-White, 2001). Individuals using a prestige strategy tend to be socially accepted, agreeable, and conscientious, and have high self-esteem (Cheng et al., 2010; R. T. Johnson et al., 2007). Prestige is, thus, associated with respect, reverence, and other positive emotional responses (Cheng et al., 2010; Henrich & Gil-White, 2001). High-prestige individuals, like group heads, teachers, or other influential group members, can evoke admiration and awe (Keltner et al., 2006).

A recent line of work also suggests that pride and shame, that is, positive or negative emotional responses to one's own accomplishments or lack thereof, might serve an adaptive function promoting the pursuit or maintenance of social status (Cohen et al., 2020; Durkee et al., 2019; Sznycer et al., 2012; Tracy et al., 2010; Tracy et al., 2013). Dominance is associated with feelings of arrogance, superiority, and conceit (i.e., hubristic pride), whereas prestige is associated with feelings of achievement, but without a sense of superiority or arrogance (i.e., authentic pride; see Cheng et al., 2010; Liu et al., 2016). As previously mentioned, the degree to which dominance and prestige are best described as distinct leadership styles or behavioral strategies has been debated, in part because the ability to dominate others can be a source of prestige when it generates benefits for followers (Durkee et al., 2020; Glowacki & von Rueden, 2015). Nevertheless, the distinction between dominance- and prestige-based strategies may be most observable in terms of both the emotions demonstrated by leaders and the emotional reactions of followers.

Emotions and Leadership: Organizational Perspective

The past 20 years have witnessed the emergence of a so-called affective revolution in the organizational literature (Ashkanasy & Dorris, 2017; Barsade & Gibson, 2007). Although early work discussed the importance of emotions in the leadership process (e.g., House, 1977; Wasielewski, 1985), scholars started to examine leadership as an emotion-laden process in a systematic fashion only at the turn of the 21st century (e.g., George, 2000). Pescosolido (2002) first conceptualized leaders as managers of group emotions, that is, individuals who can convey appropriate emotional responses across contexts and situations to create shared emotional experiences and allow group members to bond. This idea is rooted in an emotional contagion argument (Hatfield et al., 1992), which implies that leaders' emotional displays can spread to different members of a collective. Followers may consciously or unconsciously mimic leaders' emotional expressions, such as body language or facial expressions (cf. Hatfield et al., 1992). Emotional contagion—as well as related mechanisms outlined by alternative theories such as Emotions as Social Information (Van Kleef, 2009)—is thought to be a key mechanism for leaders to generate and diffuse norms in a group (J. R. Kelly & Barsade, 2001; Sy et al., 2005).

Several leadership behaviors and traits have been linked to emotions, but this connection is especially visible in theories of charismatic leadership, that is, a construct rooted in the inspirational communication of values and emotions (Bass, 1990; House, 1977). Charismatic leaders use specific communication tactics to impart their vision (Emrich et al., 2001; Holladay & Coombs, 1994), which tap into the emotions and the self-esteem of their followers (Shamir et al., 1993). In turn, charismatic leaders are mainly associated with the expression of positive emotions and with followers' positive feelings, such as enthusiasm (Bono & Ilies, 2006; Cherulnik et al., 2001).

Charismatic leadership represents a powerful case study for taking stock of the literature on emotions and leadership and for integrating it with an evolutionary perspective. We do so in the next section, where we also discuss issues related to emotional valence, context, and culture in leadership and followership, briefly exploring additionally the coevolution of leadership, followership, and emotions.

Discussion
Charisma Signaling
Recent work on charisma and charismatic leadership has defined charisma as a signal that includes emotions, values, and symbols (Antonakis et al., 2016; Bastardoz, 2020). Grabo and colleagues (2016, 2017) suggested that charismatic leadership evolved given its functional role in facilitating the coordination of autonomous agents in ancestral environments (see also Bastardoz & Van Vugt, 2019). According to this framework, charisma—proxied by specific verbal tactics (e.g., metaphors, rhetorical questions, expression of the group's sentiments) and nonverbal expressions (i.e., animated voice, facial expressions, and gestures; Antonakis et al., 2011)—expresses leader's emotions and signals either the personal cognitive abilities of a potential leader or the willingness of an individual to lead based on specific values (Bastardoz, 2020), especially in the context of urgent cooperation and coordination problems (see Grabo & Van Vugt, 2016; McDermott, 2020).

According to signaling theory (e.g., Bliege Bird & Smith, 2005; B. L. Connelly et al., 2011; Spence, 1973; Zahavi, 1975), signals are communicative acts that convey a message about certain hidden characteristics of the signaler (e.g., traits, abilities, intents). Acting on the signal, recipients may adjust their behaviors in a way that ultimately results in a fitness increase for both the signaler and recipients. In these interactions, the cost of the signal is key. Signals that can be produced at low cost by individuals who do not possess the hidden characteristic (referred to as "cheap signals") are unlikely to evolve, because they convey little to no information and cause no fitness benefits to the signaler and the receiver (Al-Shawaf & Lewis, 2021).

Communicating in a charismatic way involves various emotional displays that might provide information to the followers. From a signaling theory viewpoint, however, it is not clear whether charisma could ever be a credible (i.e., costly) signal of a leader's felt emotions. Research suggests that certain emotions can sometimes be displayed at will by leaders. For instance, business or political leaders frequently conceal their emotions, diluting the credibility of the emotional signals they send. Along these lines, organization studies have long focused on the concept of "emotional labor," that is, the active management of emotions through bodily displays (e.g., Hochschild, 2012). Thus, if leaders can manipulatively send fake emotional signals to their followers, how could charisma signaling have evolved?

We speculate that faking some emotional displays—charisma signaling included—may be cheap in the short run or in one-shot interactions, but might be costly for the sender in the long run or in repeated interactions. When individuals (e.g., leaders and followers) interact over multiple interactions—thus mimicking the conditions that were most likely present in ancestral hunter-gatherer bands—they may learn if any individual (particularly a leader) is faking some emotional displays. Over time, leaders who fake their emotions often will lose their credibility, and followers will start to disregard the signals such leaders send. For instance, an individual who expresses emotions noticeably, employs an animated voice, and uses specific facial expressions (i.e., a strong charisma signal) might clearly signal a specific intent (e.g., to go against the status quo), and might become a leader. The same leader might lose her or his influence—without being able to recoup it later—once s/he starts showing incoherent emotions or if s/he fails to act based on the emotions initially expressed. Additionally, faking a charisma signal might even cause a direct fitness cost to a potential leader. Constantly faking emotional displays without experiencing them (commonly referred to as "surface acting") may create stress, exhaustion, and ultimately decrease well-being (Gardner et al., 2009; Lennard et al., 2019). Similarly, emotional labor in actual organizations is correlated with mental and physical disorders (e.g., Ashforth & Humphrey, 1993; Näring et al., 2006). In a recent review, Hofstee, Jansen, De Lange, Spisak, and Swinkels (2021) show that emotion regulation can also have adverse effects on cognitive performance.

Certainly, an argument based on the potential "long-term credibility" of charisma leaves followers vulnerable to fake leaders' emotional signals in the short term or in unusual situations (Bastardoz, 2020). For instance, the infrequent, indirect, or very short interactions between leaders and followers typical of contemporary organizations or political systems provide leaders with many opportunities for faking emotional signals with little reputation costs. Moreover, the recent COVID-19 crisis has disrupted many leader-follower relations in the workplace, leaving millions of people navigating organizational hierarchies in new and unprecedented modes (Kniffin et al., 2021). Following these systemic shifts, we hope future research will gain a more thorough understanding of how leaders and followers manage emotions and emotional displays (such as charisma signaling) in any novel environment. This topic is especially important for followers who must protect themselves from manipulative leaders (McDermott, 2020).

Assuming that charisma is rooted in a genuine emotional display, some scholars have hypothesized that charisma could have been recruited by natural or cultural selection as a signal of cooperative intents of the leader (see Grabo et al., 2017; Grabo & Van Vugt, 2016). Indeed, emotional displays such as Duchenne smiles or angry expressions can be costly signals of one's intentions or states (e.g., a cooperator or a defector; cf. De Melo et al., 2014; Feinberg et al., 2012; Shariff & Tracy, 2011), especially because emotional displays are often conceptualized as automatic or involuntary responses (e.g., embarrassment, excitement, happiness, anger; see Cosmides & Tooby, 2000; Keltner & Haidt, 1999). Moreover, nonverbal expressivity has been conceptualized as a sign of trustworthiness and cooperation (Boone & Buck, 2003; Centorrino et al., 2015; Schug et al., 2010). In turn, charismatic leadership appears to be linked to an enthusiastic and expressive communication style (e.g., Friedman et al., 1988; Venus et al., 2013).

Future research may benefit from investigating if and how the specific proxies of charisma can serve as credible signals. For instance, researchers could explore if verbal forms of expressivity can be faked, especially in the long run or in repeated interactions, and whether charisma signaling can persuade followers more easily in cooperative rather than competitive situations. As we have argued, a mechanism for keeping charisma signaling honest might be that the detection of fake emotional displays results in a leader's reputation loss or even direct punishment, at least in the long run. This latter kind of signal enforcement is present in nonhumans

(Tibbetts & Izzo, 2010), and empirical tests in the context of charismatic leadership might be interesting. Moreover, future work could also consider alternative explanations. For instance, charisma might be a simple byproduct (and, thus, not a signal per se) of other leader qualities; that is, the verbal and nonverbal tactics identified by the leadership literature might merely correlate with the personal qualities or intents that characterize certain leaders (e.g., intelligence, extraversion, courage, self-sacrifice; cf. Bastardoz, 2020; Garfield & Hagen, 2020; McDermott et al., 2016; von Rueden, 2014).

CHARISMA AND AWE

Rudolph Sohm first introduced charismatic leadership in the context of religious leadership and spiritual experiences (Haley, 1980), implying a possible link with awe, veneration, and astonishment. Some organizational approaches have also conceptualized charisma as part of transformational leadership (Bass, 1990), fostering an intuitive link to the study of prestige and awe (Keltner & Haidt, 2003; Quesnel & Riecke, 2018). Empirical evidence suggests that followers of charismatic leaders may even become "awestruck" by the leader's communication (Menges et al., 2015). This prospect seems particularly interesting, especially considering recent approaches to awe as an evolved emotion (Stellar et al., 2017). We invite future research to systematically theorize and empirically test the link between awe and charismatic leadership.

Context, Leadership, and Emotions
GROUP SIZE

The context of leader-follower interactions can greatly influence leadership and followership (Antonakis & Atwater, 2002; Garfield et al., 2020; Oc, 2018). For instance, an important contextual element related to the effectiveness of charismatic leadership is group size. Group size introduces logistical considerations for leaders because a leader might be less visible and audible in a very large group. In addition, large group size can exacerbate coordination and free-rider problems for group members (Glowacki & von Rueden, 2015). Even though leadership might be less effective as group size increases, a leader signaling charisma might still be effective in large groups (due to emotion contagion; Bono & Ilies, 2006; Cherulnik et al., 2001) because any given follower might have positive expectations regarding how other followers will coordinate their actions in line with the leader's message (cf. Hermalin, 1998) or because the emotional reactions of other followers might serve as credible signals of coordination or cooperation intent (cf. Van Kleef, 2009).

Teasing out the exact mechanisms through which charisma affects coordination and cooperation in groups and exploring whether this effect is moderated by contextual variables like group size are important questions for future research (cf. Al-Shawaf et al., 2021). For instance, researchers could experimentally manipulate the context in which followers receive the charisma signal (e.g., alone vs. in a group; see Antonakis et al., 2022). Using a virtual reality setting, another research idea may be to manipulate the emotional response of followers to a given leader's action (e.g., a charismatic speech) and study its effect on a focal individual. Finally, as neither the mechanism nor the ultimate explanation behind the mood contagion effect is *prima facie* clear, future research could explore this topic in more detail, theorizing clearly about the (fitness) costs and benefits of the mood contagion mechanism, and illuminating its adaptive value also with analytic models and simulations (cf. D. M. G. Lewis et al., 2017).

CULTURE

A naïve reading of the central tenets of evolutionary psychology may imply that the relationship between leaders' emotional displays and followers' emotional reactions—being shaped by natural selection—should be universal. This theoretical prediction is nonetheless overly simplistic: an evolutionary psychological approach does not stipulate the strict universality of outputs (e.g., behaviors, emotional reactions), but rather of psychological mechanisms (Al-Shawaf & Lewis, 2017; Buss, 1990). That is, universal psychological mechanisms can interact with contextually variant inputs to produce heterogeneous outputs.

Such a lens might be beneficial for understanding how different leadership styles are enacted and endorsed across societies, and for studying how differences in emotional displays and felt emotions explain these differences (S. Connelly & Gooty, 2015; Rajah et al., 2011). For instance, cross-national evidence suggests the universality of inspirational and visionary behaviors typical of charismatic leadership (House et al., 2004). However, the actual enactment of the charisma signal is variable across societies (see also Garfield et al., 2020). For instance, American leaders are famous for displaying aggressive and colorful oratory, whereas the rhetoric and expressivity of political, business, and religious leaders in other areas of the world are often more discreet (Bligh & Robinson, 2010; Den Hartog et al., 1999; Den Hartog & Verburg, 1997).

Why do we observe these differences? More research is needed to answer this question, but one possibility is that different emotional signals may have evolved culturally (cf. Mesoudi, 2016). Indeed, cross-cultural differences in expressivity might be related to historical factors. Rychlowska et al. (2015) show that historical migrations (particularly whether current countries' populations descend from few or from many other countries) predict different functions of smiles and emotional expressivity. We do not yet know if cross-cultural variability in the verbal and nonverbal components of charisma is also explained by historical factors, even though recent evidence suggests that followers' preferences for another leadership style are predicted by socio-ecological characteristics of the past. Specifically, the traditional use of intensive agricultural practices (which is, in turn, predicted by different ecological conditions) correlates with the contemporary endorsement of a directive leadership style across different countries (Lonati, 2020). Future research could explore if and how historical factors shape other leadership styles, leaders' emotional expressions, or charisma.

Researchers interested specifically in the cross-cultural heterogeneity of charisma face, however, some important methodological difficulties. For instance, cross-cultural analyses of leaders' verbal communication require comparing speeches given in different languages. Ensuring cross-cultural equivalence when translating such speeches might be complex and even inappropriate (cf. Brislin, 1980). Methodological difficulties could be reduced if one were to study nonverbal displays. Still, observed differences in any emotional display across societies may also be due to observable or unobservable confounds different from culture per se (e.g., economic development, history, ecological conditions), which might be, in turn, the real drivers of the observed difference. A possible solution to this problem is employing migrants' data (for details, see Fernández, 2011), leveraging the fact that migrants and their children share the same context, yet differ in their cultures compared both to natives and to migrants from other regions or countries (for an example applied to leadership literature, see Lonati, 2021).

Emotion Valence in Context

A different question concerns the importance of negative emotional displays in leader-follower interactions. The evolutionarily informed literature suggests that prestige is associated with positive emotions and dominance with negative emotions. In organization studies, leadership had initially been associated with positive emotions (Gooty et al., 2010). Based on a "symmetrical assumption" (Lindebaum & Jordan, 2014, p. 1038), this literature has mainly linked positive emotions with positive outcomes, and negative emotions with negative outcomes (Elfenbein, 2007). For instance, in line with Fredrickson's (2001) Broaden-and-Build Theory, McColl-Kennedy and Anderson (2002) found that transformational leaders were associated with more optimism and less frustration, and ultimately better group performance. A leader's positive mood is also related to a more positive group affective tone, which is associated with better group coordination (Sy et al., 2005).

Recent empirical evidence has taken a more balanced and context-sensitive approach, arguing for the positive effects of negative emotions such as anger, anxiety, or fear in specific situations (Geddes et al., 2020). In fact, leaders' negative emotional displays can provide important informational signals for followers (Fitness, 2000; Van Kleef, 2014). For instance, Wang, Restubog, Shao, Lu, and Van Kleef (2018) found that the effect of anger on perceived leader effectiveness depends on the situation (i.e., the type of violation in performance by followers) and the person (i.e., the type of leader who expresses anger). Also, the effectiveness of a leader's anger expression depends on the type of inferences that followers draw, such that a leader's display of anger attributed to a problematic situation is more effective than a leader's display of anger attributed to the disposition of the leader (Shao et al., 2018). Based on a dual threshold model (Geddes & Callister, 2007), Staw, DeCelles, and de Goey (2019) also found an inverted U-shape relationship between a leader's anger expression and team performance, so that a moderate amount of anger expression is appropriate and more effective than a low or high amount of anger expression.

The complex interplay between a leader's emotional expressions and context is particularly visible in threatening situations. For instance, we tend to be drawn to enthusiastic leaders who portray a bright vision for the future when the context is uncertain or in time of crisis (Conger & Kanungo, 1998; Weber, 1968), that is, in times where fear and anxiety might be natural responses (cf. Nesse, 1994). Similarly, in threat conditions, followers might also seek leaders who challenge the status quo (cf. Spisak et al., 2014). Still, factors like economic harshness and other crises can also favor the emergence of autocratic leaders (Hamblin, 1958; Harms et al., 2018; Huang et al., 2015; Kakkar & Sivanathan, 2017). When group members perceive threats from other groups or experience heightened intra-group conflict, they may also show an increased preference for leaders whose physical formidability suggests a capacity to coordinate and motivate followers via intimidation or fear (Bøggild & Laustsen, 2016).

How can we reconcile these apparently opposing patterns? Future research will need to explore this question in more detail, especially because emotions like fear and outrage are potent coordination devices that leaders can use to build coalitions (McDermott, 2020; Tooby & Cosmides, 2010). A possibility is that fear, anxiety, or stress might be triggers that make followers more receptive to either leadership style, but that specific combinations of threats, leader characteristics, and followers' characteristics might favor the emergence of and the support for either autocratic or charismatic leaders. Still, one needs to consider that these two styles are not necessarily mutually exclusive and that a charismatic leader might also be autocratic. Future empirical studies could investigate why, when, and how similar contextual pressures can give rise to different leadership styles, and how the emotions felt by the followers might mediate these relationships. Moreover, the links between followers' negative emotions, leaders' emotional displays, and other leadership styles need to be explored more in detail, studying, for instance, if and how negative emotional displays can ever serve as charisma signals for potential leaders.

Bridging Emotions and the Evolution of Leadership
Our discussion points to several emotional facets that could have played a role in the evolution of leadership and followership. Concomitantly, pressures for individuals to coordinate their behaviors, as well as variation in the distribution of information across group members—that is, demands and opportunities for leadership—could have played a role in the evolution of human emotions. Conceptualizing leadership and followership as solutions to coordination and cooperation problems in humans and other social mammals (Bastardoz & Van Vugt, 2019; J. E. Smith et al., 2016), one might speculate that leadership would present strong selective pressures on emotionality, whereas emotionality would offer proximate mechanisms for facilitating leadership and followership processes (e.g., group identity, expression of shared values). Just as emotions are now viewed as superordinate mechanisms that evolved to solve problems of multi-mechanism coordination *within individual phenotypes* (Al-Shawaf et al., 2016), we propose that emotions could also be viewed as playing a critical role in the coordination of multiple *individuals within groups*.

In this view, human emotionality may have coevolved alongside human leadership as a coordinating mechanism. The communication of emotions, both consciously and subconsciously, could function as an interface between individuals (alongside language) to facilitate group-level organization. The communication of emotions, which can be done rapidly and independent of language, can encode threats of imposing costs and pledges to provide benefits for individuals potentially in conflict or facing coordination challenges. For example, with a series of distinct glances, gestures, and choice words, a mother, hunt leader, shift supervisor, or board chairperson can signal affective states to distinct group members, communicating approval or disapproval, suggesting and influencing behavioral change or stability. Emotional communication between individuals, and particularly from leaders to followers, may be in some contexts a more salient proximate mechanism for group coordination as opposed to verbal communication, status dynamics, informational asymmetries, or differences in physical formidability.

The dynamics between emotions and leadership raise several questions regarding selective pressures and causality. Some emotions could be evolved features that emerged to govern hierarchical relationships and, perhaps, leadership and followership (Cheng et al., 2010; Durkee et al., 2019; Henrich & Gil-White, 2001). For instance, the ability to detect hubristic pride or other "emotional markers" of dominance might be an important ability to defend oneself from dominant and aggressive leaders in contexts where dominance is not advantageous for followers.

A complementary and likely possibility is that these emotions were first selected for in other domains of social interaction and were then co-opted for leader-follower relations. For instance, anger toward despotic leadership might be a byproduct of similar angry reactions to generic "unfair treatments" documented in emotion science and neurosciences (see, e.g., Gabay et al., 2014; Seip et al., 2014) or evidence of insufficient welfare trade-off ratios, where followers react to perceptions of systematic inequality in leader decision-making (see Bøggild & Petersen, 2016; Sell et al., 2009). For instance, the work of Price and Van Vugt (2014) suggests that followers will exhibit punitive sentiments toward "disrespectful" followers or toward dominant leaders providing no material benefits to their followers. Such punitive sentiment may have first evolved in the context of dyadic relationships to enforce reciprocity.

Conclusion

The literature on evolutionary studies of emotions has grown significantly, as this volume testifies. Similarly, evolutionary approaches to leadership have gained traction. We have aimed to link these two approaches, intersecting them with organizational perspectives on emotions and leadership. Our review and discussion offer more questions than answers, yet provide important bridges to reconcile different disciplines studying similar questions. We hope our suggestions will help researchers interested in leadership and followership, evolutionary psychology, evolutionary anthropology, cultural transmission, and organization studies tackle this broad topic, fostering a novel understanding of the functions and mechanisms of leadership, followership, and emotions.

Acknowledgments

We thank the editors for their careful review of the chapter and helpful comments. Zachary H. Garfield acknowledges IAST funding from the French National Research Agency (ANR) under the Investments for the Future (Investissements d'Avenir) program, grant ANR-17-EURE-0010.

References

Al-Shawaf, L., Conroy-Beam, D., Asao, K., & Buss, D. M. (2016). Human emotions: An evolutionary psychological perspective. *Emotion Review, 8*(2), 173–186.

Al-Shawaf, L., & Lewis, D. M. G. (2017). Evolutionary psychology and the emotions. In V. Zeigler-Hill & T. K. Shackelford (Eds.), *Encyclopedia of personality and individual differences* (pp. 1–10). Springer.

Al-Shawaf, L., & Lewis, D. M. G. (2021). The handicap principle. In T. K. Shackelford & V. Weekes-Shackelfor (Eds.), *Encyclopedia of evolutionary psychological science*. Springer International.

Al-Shawaf, L., Lewis, D. M. G., Wehbe, Y. S., & Buss, D. M. (2021). Context, environment, and learning in evolutionary psychology. In T. K. Shackelford & V. A. Weekes-Shackelford (Eds.), *Encyclopedia of evolutionary psychological science* (pp. 1–12). Springer International.

Allee, W. C. (1938). *The social life of animals*. W. W. Norton.

Alvesson, M., & Einola, K. (2019). Warning for excessive positivity: Authentic leadership and other traps in leadership studies. *The Leadership Quarterly, 30*(4), 383–395.

Antonakis, J. (2017). On doing better science: From thrill of discovery to policy implications. *The Leadership Quarterly, 28*(1), 5–21.

Antonakis, J., & Atwater, L. (2002). Leader distance: A review and a proposed theory. *The Leadership Quarterly, 13*(6), 673–704.

Antonakis, J., Bastardoz, N., Jacquart, P., & Shamir, B. (2016). Charisma: An ill-defined and ill-measured gift. *Annual Review of Organizational Psychology and Organizational Behavior, 3*(1), 293–319.

Antonakis, J., Bastardoz, N., Liu, Y., & Schriesheim, C. A. (2014). What makes articles highly cited? *The Leadership Quarterly, 25*(1), 152–179.

Antonakis, J., d'Adda, G., Weber, R., & Zehnder, C. (2022). "Just words? Just speeches?" On the economic value of charismatic leadership. *Management Science, 68*(9), 6355–6381.

Antonakis, J., & Day, D. V. (2018). *The nature of leadership* (3rd ed.). Sage Publications.

Antonakis, J., Fenley, M., & Liechti, S. (2011). Can charisma be taught? Tests of two interventions. *Academy of Management Learning & Education, 10*(3), 374–396.

Ashford, S. J., & Sitkin, S. B. (2019). From problems to progress: A dialogue on prevailing issues in leadership research. *The Leadership Quarterly, 30*(4), 454–460.

Ashforth, B. E., & Humphrey, R. H. (1993). Emotional labor in service roles: The influence of identity. *Academy of Management Review, 18*(1), 88–115.

Ashkanasy, N. M., & Dorris, A. D. (2017). Emotions in the workplace. *Annual Review of Organizational Psychology and Organizational Behavior, 4*(1), 67–90.

Barkow, J. H., Cosmides, L., & Tooby, J. (1992). *The adapted mind: Evolutionary psychology and the generation of culture*: Oxford University Press.

Barsade, S. G., & Gibson, D. E. (2007). Why does affect matter in organizations? *Academy of Management Perspectives, 21*(1), 36–59.

Bass, B. M. (1985). *Leadership and performance beyond expectations*. Collier Macmillan.

Bass, B. M. (1990). From transactional to transformational leadership: Learning to share the vision. *Organizational Dynamics, 18*(3), 19–31.

Bass, B. M., & Riggio, R. E. (2006). *Transformational leadership*. Psychology Press.

Bastardoz, N. (2020). Signaling charisma. In J. P. Zuquete (Ed.), *Routledge international handbook of charisma* (1st ed., pp. 313–323). Routledge.

Bastardoz, N., & Day, D. V. (2022). Integrating leadership and power: A micro process model. In D. L. Stone & J. H. Dulebohn (Eds.), *Research in human resource management* (pp. 289–330). Information Age.

Bastardoz, N., & Van Vugt, M. (2019). The nature of followership: Evolutionary analysis and review. *The Leadership Quarterly*, *30*(1), 81–95.

Bedeian, A. G., & Hunt, J. G. (2006). Academic amnesia and vestigial assumptions of our forefathers. *The Leadership Quarterly*, *17*(2), 190–205.

Bliege Bird, R., & Smith, E. A. (2005). Signaling theory, strategic interaction, and symbolic capital. *Current Anthropology*, *46*(2), 221–248.

Bligh, M. C., & Robinson, J. L. (2010). Was Gandhi "charismatic"? Exploring the rhetorical leadership of Mahatma Gandhi. *The Leadership Quarterly*, *21*(5), 844–855.

Boehm, C. (1993). Egalitarian behavior and reverse dominance hierarchy. *Current Anthropology*, *34*(3), 227–254.

Bøggild, T., & Laustsen, L. (2016). An intra-group perspective on leader preferences: Different risks of exploitation shape preferences for leader facial dominance. *The Leadership Quarterly*, *27*(6), 820–837.

Bøggild, T., & Petersen, M. B. (2016). The evolved functions of procedural fairness: An adaptation for politics. In T. K. Shackelford & R. D. Hansen (Eds.), *The evolution of morality* (pp. 247–276). Springer International.

Bono, J. E., & Ilies, R. (2006). Charisma, positive emotions and mood contagion. *The Leadership Quarterly*, *17*(4), 317–334.

Boone, R. T., & Buck, R. (2003). Emotional expressivity and trustworthiness: The role of nonverbal behavior in the evolution of cooperation. *Journal of Nonverbal Behavior*, *27*(3), 163–182.

Brislin, R. W. (1980). Translation and content analysis of oral and written materials. In H. C. Triandis & J. W. Berry (Eds.), *Handbook of cross-cultural psychology: Methodology* (pp. 89–102). Allyn and Bacon.

Buss, D. M. (1990). Evolutionary social psychology: Prospects and pitfalls. *Motivation and Emotion*, *14*(4), 265–286.

Buss, D. M. (1995). Evolutionary psychology: A new paradigm for psychological science. *Psychological Inquiry*, *6*(1), 1–30.

Buyalskaya, A., Gallo, M., & Camerer, C. F. (2021). The golden age of social science. *Proceedings of the National Academy of Sciences*, *118*(5), e2002923118.

Centorrino, S., Djemai, E., Hopfensitz, A., Milinski, M., & Seabright, P. (2015). Honest signaling in trust interactions: Smiles rated as genuine induce trust and signal higher earning opportunities. *Evolution and Human Behavior*, *36*(1), 8–16.

Cheng, J. T., & Tracy, J. L. (2020). Why social status is essential (but sometimes insufficient) for leadership. *Trends in Cognitive Sciences*, *24*(4), 261–263.

Cheng, J. T., Tracy, J. L., Foulsham, T., Kingstone, A., & Henrich, J. (2013). Two ways to the top: Evidence that dominance and prestige are distinct yet viable avenues to social rank and influence. *Journal of Personality and Social Psychology*, *104*(1), 103–125.

Cheng, J. T., Tracy, J. L., & Henrich, J. (2010). Pride, personality, and the evolutionary foundations of human social status. *Evolution and Human Behavior*, *31*(5), 334–347.

Cherulnik, P. D., Donley, K. A., Wiewel, T. S. R., & Miller, S. R. (2001). Charisma is contagious: The effect of leaders' charisma on observers' affect. *Journal of Applied Social Psychology*, *31*(10), 2149–2159.

Cohen, A. S., Chun, R., & Sznycer, D. (2020). Do pride and shame track the evaluative psychology of audiences? Preregistered replications of Sznycer et al. (2016, 2017). *Royal Society Open Science*, *7*(5), 191922.

Conger, J. A., & Kanungo, R. N. (1998). *Charismatic leadership in organizations*: Sage Publications.

Connelly, B. L., Certo, S. T., Ireland, R. D., & Reutzel, C. R. (2011). Signaling theory: A review and assessment. *Journal of Management*, *37*(1), 39–67.

Connelly, S., & Gooty, J. (2015). Leading with emotion: An overview of the special issue on leadership and emotions. *The Leadership Quarterly*, *25*(4), 485–488.

Cosmides, L., & Tooby, J. (2000). Evolutionary psychology and the emotions. In M. Lewis & J. M. Haviland-Jones (Eds.), *Handbook of emotions* (2nd ed., pp. 91–115). Guilford Press.

Day, D. V. (2012). Leadership. In S. W. Kozlowski (Ed.), *The Oxford handbook of organizational psychology* (Vol. 1, pp. 696–729). Oxford University Press.

De Melo, C. M., Carnevale, P. J., Read, S. J., & Gratch, J. (2014). Reading people's minds from emotion expressions in interdependent decision making. *Journal of Personality and Social Psychology*, *106*(1), 73.

Den Hartog, D. N., House, R. J., Hanges, P. J., Ruiz-Quintanilla, S. A., Dorfman, P. W., Abdalla, I. A., Adetoun, B. S., Aditya, R. N., Agourram, H., Akande, A., Akande, B. E., Akerblom, S., Altschul, C., Alvarez-Backus, E., Andrews, J., Arias, M. E., Arif, M. S., Ashkanasy, N. M., Asllani, A., . . . Akande, A. (1999). Culture specific and cross-culturally generalizable implicit leadership theories: are attributes of charismatic/transformational leadership universally endorsed? *The Leadership Quarterly, 10*(2), 219–256.

Den Hartog, D. N., & Verburg, R. M. (1997). Charisma and rhetoric: Communicative techniques of international business leaders. *The Leadership Quarterly, 8*(4), 355–391.

Dobzhansky, T. (1974). Chance and creativity in evolution. In F. J. Ayala, & T. G. Dobzhansky (Eds.), *Studies in the philosophy of biology: Reduction and related problems* (pp. 307–338). University of California Press.

Durkee, P. K., Lukaszewski, A. W., & Buss, D. M. (2019). Pride and shame: Key components of a culturally universal status management system. *Evolution and Human Behavior, 40*(5), 470–478.

Durkee, P. K., Lukaszewski, A. W., & Buss, D. M. (2020). Psychological foundations of human status allocation. *Proceedings of the National Academy of Sciences, 117*(35), 21235–21241.

Ekman, P. (1973). *Darwin and facial expression: A century of research in review*. Academic Press.

Ekman, P. (1999). Basic emotions. In T. Dalgleish & M. Power (Eds.), *Handbook of cognition and emotion* (pp. 45–60). Wiley.

Elfenbein, H. A. (2007). Emotion in organizations: A review and theoretical integration. *Academy of Management Annals, 1*(1), 315–386.

Emrich, C. G., Brower, H. H., Feldman, J. M., & Garland, H. (2001). Images in words: Presidential rhetoric, charisma, and greatness. *Administrative Science Quarterly, 46*(3), 527–557.

Feinberg, M., Willer, R., & Keltner, D. (2012). Flustered and faithful: Embarrassment as a signal of prosociality. *Journal of Personality and Social Psychology, 102*(1), 81–97.

Fernández, R. (2011). Does culture matter? In J. Benhabib, A. Bisin, & M. O. Jackson (Eds.), *Handbook of social economics* (Vol. 1, pp. 481–510). Elsevier.

Fiedler, F. E. (1964). A contingency model of leadership effectiveness. In L. Berkowitz (Ed.), *Advances in experimental social psychology* (Vol. 1, pp. 149–190). Elsevier.

Fitness, J. (2000). Anger in the workplace: An emotion script approach to anger episodes between workers and their superiors, co-workers and subordinates. *Journal of Organizational Behavior, 21*(2), 147–162.

Fredrickson, B. L. (2001). The role of positive emotions in positive psychology: The broaden-and-build theory of positive emotions. *American Psychologist, 56*(3), 218–226.

Friedman, H. S., Riggio, R. E., & Casella, D. F. (1988). Nonverbal skill, personal charisma, and initial attraction. *Personality and Social Psychology Bulletin, 14*(1), 203–211.

Gabay, A. S., Radua, J., Kempton, M. J., & Mehta, M. A. (2014). The Ultimatum Game and the brain: A meta-analysis of neuroimaging studies. *Neuroscience & Biobehavioral Reviews, 47*, 549–558.

Gardner, W. L., Fischer, D., & Hunt, J. G. J. (2009). Emotional labor and leadership: A threat to authenticity? *The Leadership Quarterly, 20*(3), 466–482.

Gardner, W. L., Lowe, K. B., Meuser, J. D., Noghani, F., Gullifor, D. P., & Cogliser, C. C. (2020). The leadership trilogy: A review of the third decade of *The Leadership Quarterly*. *The Leadership Quarterly, 31*(1), 101379.

Garfield, Z. H., & Hagen, E. H. (2020). Investigating evolutionary models of leadership among recently settled Ethiopian hunter-gatherers. *The Leadership Quarterly, 31*(2), 101290.

Garfield, Z. H., Hubbard, R. L., & Hagen, E. H. (2019). Evolutionary models of leadership. *Human Nature, 30*(1), 23–58.

Garfield, Z. H., Syme, K. L., & Hagen, E. H. (2020). Universal and variable leadership dimensions across human societies. *Evolution and Human Behavior, 41*(5), 397–414.

Garfield, Z. H., von Rueden, C., & Hagen, E. H. (2019). The evolutionary anthropology of political leadership. *The Leadership Quarterly, 30*(1), 59–80.

Geddes, D., & Callister, R. R. (2007). Crossing the line (s): A dual threshold model of anger in organizations. *Academy of Management Review, 32*(3), 721–746.

Geddes, D., Callister, R. R., & Gibson, D. E. (2020). A message in the madness: Functions of workplace anger in organizational life. *Academy of Management Perspectives, 34*(1), 28–47.

George, J. M. (2000). Emotions and leadership: The role of emotional intelligence. *Human Relations, 53*(8), 1027–1055.

Gintis, H., Van Schaik, C., & Boehm, C. (2015). Zoon politikon: The evolutionary origins of human political systems. *Current Anthropology, 56*(3), 340–341.

Glowacki, L., & von Rueden, C. (2015). Leadership solves collective action problems in small-scale societies. *Philosophical Transactions of the Royal Society B: Biological Sciences, 370*(1683), 20150010.

Gooty, J., Connelly, S., Griffith, J., & Gupta, A. (2010). Leadership, affect and emotions: A state of the science review. *The Leadership Quarterly, 21*(6), 979–1004.

Grabo, A., Spisak, B. R., & Van Vugt, M. (2017). Charisma as signal: An evolutionary perspective on charismatic leadership. *The Leadership Quarterly, 28*(4), 473–485.

Grabo, A., & Van Vugt, M. (2016). Charismatic leadership and the evolution of cooperation. *Evolution and Human Behavior, 37*(5), 399–406.

Haley, P. (1980). Rudolph Sohm on charisma. *The Journal of Religion, 60*(2), 185–197.

Halpin, A. W., & Winer, B. J. (1957). A factorial study of the leader behavior descriptions. In R. M. Stogdil & A. E. Coons (Eds.), *Leader behavior: Its description and measurement* (pp. 39–51) Ohio State University, Bureau of Business.

Hamblin, R. L. (1958). Leadership and crises. *Sociometry, 21*(4), 322–335.

Harms, P. D., Wood, D., Landay, K., Lester, P. B., & Lester, G. V. (2018). Autocratic leaders and authoritarian followers revisited: A review and agenda for the future. *The Leadership Quarterly, 29*(1), 105–122.

Hatfield, E., Cacioppo, J. T., & Rapson, R. L. (1992). Primitive emotional contagion. *Review of Personality and Social Psychology, 14*, 151–177.

Henrich, J., & Gil-White, F. J. (2001). The evolution of prestige: Freely conferred deference as a mechanism for enhancing the benefits of cultural transmission. *Evolution and Human Behavior, 22*(3), 165–196.

Hermalin, B. E. (1998). Toward an economic theory of leadership: Leading by example. *American Economic Review, 8*(5), 1188–1206.

Hoch, J. E., Bommer, W. H., Dulebohn, J. H., & Wu, D. (2018). Do ethical, authentic, and servant leadership explain variance above and beyond transformational leadership? A meta-analysis. *Journal of Management, 44*(2), 501–529.

Hochschild, A. R. (2012). *The managed heart: Commercialization of human feeling*: University of California Press.

Hofstee, G., Jansen, P. G. W., De Lange, A. H., Spisak, B. R., & Swinkels, M. (2021). The cognitive costs of managing emotions: A systematic review of the impact of emotional requirements on cognitive performance. *Work & Stress, 35*(3), 301–326.

Holladay, S. J., & Coombs, W. T. (1994). Speaking of visions and visions being spoken: An exploration of the effects of content and delivery on perceptions of leader charisma. *Management Communication Quarterly, 8*(2), 165–189.

Hooper, P. L., Kaplan, H. S., & Boone, J. L. (2010). A theory of leadership in human cooperative groups. *Journal of Theoretical Biology, 265*(4), 633–646.

House, R. J. (1977). A 1976 theory of charismatic leadership effectiveness. In J. Hunt & L. Larson (Eds.), *Leadership: The cutting edge* (pp. 189–207). Southern Illinois University Press.

House, R. J., Hanges, P. J., Javidan, M., Dorfman, P. W., & Gupta, V. (2004). *Culture, leadership, and organizations: The GLOBE study of 62 societies*. Sage Publications.

Huang, X., Xu, E., Chiu, W., Lam, C., & Farh, J.-L. (2015). When authoritarian leaders outperform transformational leaders: Firm performance in a harsh economic environment. *Academy of Management Discoveries, 1*(2), 180–200.

Johnson, A. W., & Earle, T. K. (2000). *The evolution of human societies: From foraging group to agrarian state*. Stanford University Press.

Johnson, R. T., Burk, J. A., & Kirkpatrick, L. A. (2007). Dominance and prestige as differential predictors of aggression and testosterone levels in men. *Evolution and Human Behavior, 28*(5), 345–351.

Kakkar, H., & Sivanathan, N. (2017). When the appeal of a dominant leader is greater than a prestige leader. *Proceedings of the National Academy of Sciences, 114*(26), 6734–6739.

Kelly, J. R., & Barsade, S. G. (2001). Mood and emotions in small groups and work teams. *Organizational Behavior and Human Decision Processes, 86*(1), 99–130.

Kelly, R. L. (2013). *The lifeways of hunter-gatherers: The foraging spectrum*. Cambridge University Press.

Keltner, D., & Haidt, J. (1999). Social functions of emotions at four levels of analysis. *Cognition & Emotion, 13*(5), 505–521.

Keltner, D., & Haidt, J. (2003). Approaching awe, a moral, spiritual, and aesthetic emotion. *Cognition and Emotion, 17*(2), 297–314.

Keltner, D., Haidt, J., & Shiota, M. N. (2006). Social functionalism and the evolution of emotions. In M. Schaller, J. A. Simpson, & D. T. Kenrick (Eds.), *Evolution and social psychology* (pp. 115–142). Psychosocial Press.

Knauft, B. M., Abler, T. S., Betzig, L., Boehm, C., Dentan, R. K., Kiefer, T. M., Otterbein, K. F., Paddock, J., & Rodseth, L. (1991). Violence and sociality in human evolution [and comments and replies]. *Current Anthropology, 32*(4), 391–428.

Kniffin, K. M., Narayanan, J., Anseel, F., Antonakis, J., Ashford, S. P., Bakker, A. B., Bamberger, P., Bapuji, H., Bhave, D. P., Choi, V. K., Creary, S. J., Demerouti, E., Flynn, F. J., Gelfand, M. J., Greer, L. L., Johns, G., Kesebir, S., Klein, P. G., Lee, S. Y., . . . Choi, V. K. (2021). COVID-19 and the workplace: Implications, issues, and insights for future research and action. *American Psychologist, 76*(1), 63–67.

Lennard, A. C., Scott, B. A., & Johnson, R. E. (2019). Turning frowns (and smiles) upside down: A multilevel examination of surface acting positive and negative emotions on well-being. *Journal of Applied Psychology, 104*(9), 1164–1180.

Lewis, D. M. G., Al-Shawaf, L., Conroy-Beam, D., Asao, K., & Buss, D. M. (2017). Evolutionary psychology: A how-to guide. *American Psychologist, 72*(4), 353–373.

Lewis, H. S. (1974). *Leaders and followers: Some anthropological perspectives*: Addison-Wesley.

Lindebaum, D., & Jordan, P. J. (2014). When it can be good to feel bad and bad to feel good: Exploring asymmetries in workplace emotional outcomes. *Human Relations, 67*(9), 1037–1050.

Liu, C., Yuan, L., Chen, C., & Yu, G. (2016). Authentic and hubristic pride as assessed by self, friends, and strangers. *Social Psychological and Personality Science, 7*(7), 690–696.

Lonati, S. (2020). What explains cultural differences in leadership styles? On the agricultural origins of participative and directive leadership. *The Leadership Quarterly, 31*(2), 101305.

Lonati, S. (2021). Support for autocratic leadership: Context, culture, and transmission. *Academy of Management Proceedings, 2021*(1), 12876.

Maner, J. K. (2017). Dominance and prestige: A tale of two hierarchies. *Current Directions in Psychological Science, 26*(6), 526–531.

Maner, J. K., & Case, C. (2016). Dominance and prestige: Dual strategies for navigating social hierarchies. In J. M. Olson & M. P. Zanna (Eds.), *Advances in experimental social psychology* (Vol. 54, pp. 129–180). Elsevier.

Mann, R. D. (1959). A review of the relationships between personality and performance in small groups. *Psychological Bulletin, 56*(4), 241–270.

Mattison, S. M., Smith, E. A., Shenk, M. K., & Cochrane, E. E. (2016). The evolution of inequality. *Evolutionary Anthropology: Issues, News, and Reviews, 25*(4), 184–199.

Mayr, E. (1961). Cause and effect in biology. *Science, 134*(3489), 1501–1506.

McColl-Kennedy, J. R., & Anderson, R. D. (2002). Impact of leadership style and emotions on subordinate performance. *The Leadership Quarterly, 13*(5), 545–559.

McDermott, R. (2020). Leadership and the strategic emotional manipulation of political identity: An evolutionary perspective. *The Leadership Quarterly, 31*(2), 101275.

McDermott, R., Lopez, A. C., & Hatemi, P. K. (2016). An evolutionary approach to political leadership. *Security Studies, 25*(4), 677–698.

Meindl, J. R., & Ehrlich, S. B. (1987). The romance of leadership and the evaluation of organizational performance. *Academy of Management Journal, 30*(1), 91–109.

Menges, J. I., Kilduff, M., Kern, S., & Bruch, H. (2015). The awestruck effect: Followers suppress emotion expression in response to charismatic but not individually considerate leadership. *The Leadership Quarterly, 26*(4), 626–640.

Mesoudi, A. (2016). Cultural evolution: A review of theory, findings and controversies. *Evolutionary Biology, 43*(4), 481–497.

Miner, J. B. (1975). The uncertain future of the leadership concept: An overview. In J. G. Hunt & L. L. Larson (Eds.), *Leadership frontiers* (pp. 197–208). Kent State University Press.

Morgan, L. H. (1877). *Ancient society, or researches in the lines of human progress from savagery, through barbarism, to civilization*. Macmillan.

Mumford, E. (1906). The origins of leadership. *American Journal of Sociology, 12*(2), 216–240.

Murdock, G. P. (1967). Ethnographic atlas: A summary. *Ethnology, 6*(2), 109–236.

Näring, G., Briët, M., & Brouwers, A. (2006). Beyond demand–control: Emotional labour and symptoms of burnout in teachers. *Work & Stress, 20*(4), 303–315.

Nesse, R. M. (1994). Fear and fitness: An evolutionary analysis of anxiety disorders. *Ethology and Sociobiology, 15*(5–6), 247–261.

Oc, B. (2018). Contextual leadership: A systematic review of how contextual factors shape leadership and its outcomes. *The Leadership Quarterly, 29*(1), 218–235.

Pescosolido, A. T. (2002). Emergent leaders as managers of group emotion. *The Leadership Quarterly, 13*(5), 583–599.

Pietraszewski, D. (2020). The evolution of leadership: Leadership and followership as a solution to the problem of creating and executing successful coordination and cooperation enterprises. *The Leadership Quarterly, 31*(2), 101299.

Powers, S. T., & Lehmann, L. (2014). An evolutionary model explaining the Neolithic transition from egalitarianism to leadership and despotism. *Proceedings of the Royal Society B: Biological Sciences, 281*(1791), 20141349.

Price, M. E., & Van Vugt, M. (2014). The evolution of leader–follower reciprocity: The theory of service-for-prestige. *Frontiers in Human Neuroscience, 8*, 363.

Quesnel, D., & Riecke, B. E. (2018). Are you awed yet? How virtual reality gives us awe and goose bumps. *Frontiers in Psychology, 9*, 2158.

Rajah, R., Song, Z., & Arvey, R. D. (2011). Emotionality and leadership: Taking stock of the past decade of research. *The Leadership Quarterly, 22*(6), 1107–1119.

Redhead, D., Dhaliwal, N., & Cheng, J. T. (2021). Taking charge and stepping in: Individuals who punish are rewarded with prestige and dominance. *Social and Personality Psychology Compass, 15*(2), e12581.

Rush, M. C., Thomas, J. C., & Lord, R. G. (1977). Implicit leadership theory: A potential threat to the internal validity of leader behavior questionnaires. *Organizational Behavior and Human Performance, 20*(1), 93–110.

Rychlowska, M., Miyamoto, Y., Matsumoto, D., Hess, U., Gilboa-Schechtman, E., Kamble, S., Muluk, H., Masuda, T., & Niedenthal, P. M. (2015). Heterogeneity of long-history migration explains cultural differences in reports of emotional expressivity and the functions of smiles. *Proceedings of the National Academy of Sciences, 112*(19), E2429–E2436.

Sahlins, M. D. (1963). Poor man, rich man, big-man, chief: political types in Melanesia and Polynesia. *Comparative Studies in Society and History, 5*(3), 285–303.

Schug, J., Matsumoto, D., Horita, Y., Yamagishi, T., & Bonnet, K. (2010). Emotional expressivity as a signal of cooperation. *Evolution and Human Behavior, 31*(2), 87–94.

Seip, E. C., Van Dijk, W. W., & Rotteveel, M. (2014). Anger motivates costly punishment of unfair behavior. *Motivation and Emotion, 38*(4), 578–588.

Sell, A., Tooby, J., & Cosmides, L. (2009). Formidability and the logic of human anger. *Proceedings of the National Academy of Sciences, 106*(35), 15073–15078.

Shamir, B., House, R. J., & Arthur, M. B. (1993). The motivational effects of charismatic leadership: A self-concept based theory. *Organization Science, 4*(4), 577–594.

Shao, B., Wang, L., & Tse, H. H. M. (2018). Motivational or dispositional? The type of inference shapes the effectiveness of leader anger expressions. *The Leadership Quarterly, 29*(6), 709–723.

Shariff, A. F., & Tracy, J. L. (2011). What are emotion expressions for? *Current Directions in Psychological Science, 20*(6), 395–399.

Smith, E. A., & Choi, J.-K. (2007). The emergence of inequality in small-scale societies: Simple scenarios and agent-based simulations. In T. Kohler & S. van der Leeuw (Eds.), *The model-based archaeology of socionatural systems* (pp. 105–120). School for Advanced Research Press.

Smith, E. A., Hill, K., Marlowe, F. W., Nolin, D., Wiessner, P., Gurven, M., Bowles, S., Borgerhoff Mulder, M., Hertz, T., & Bell, A. (2010). Wealth transmission and inequality among hunter-gatherers. *Current Anthropology, 51*(1), 19–34.

Smith, J. E., Gavrilets, S., Mulder, M. B., Hooper, P. L., Mouden, C. E., Nettle, D., Hauert, C., Hill, K., Perry, S., Pusey, A. E., Van Vugt, M., & Smith, E. A. (2016). Leadership in mammalian societies: Emergence, distribution, power, and payoff. *Trends in Ecology & Evolution, 31*(1), 54–66.

Spence, M. (1973). Job market signaling. *The Quarterly Journal of Economics, 87*(3): 355–374.

Spisak, B. R. (2020). Tinbergen's take on the evolution of leadership: A framework for clarifying and integrating contributions. *The Leadership Quarterly, 31*(2), 101401.

Spisak, B. R., Grabo, A. E., Arvey, R. D., & Van Vugt, M. (2014). The age of exploration and exploitation: Younger-looking leaders endorsed for change and older-looking leaders endorsed for stability. *The Leadership Quarterly, 25*(5), 805–816.

Staw, B. M., DeCelles, K. A., & de Goey, P. (2019). Leadership in the locker room: How the intensity of leaders' unpleasant affective displays shapes team performance. *Journal of Applied Psychology, 104*(12), 1547–1557.

Steckler, C. M., & Tracy, J. L. (2014). The emotional underpinnings of social status. In J. Cheng, J. Tracy, & C. Anderson (Eds.), *The psychology of social status* (pp. 201–224). Springer.

Stellar, J. E., Gordon, A. M., Piff, P. K., Cordaro, D., Anderson, C. L., Bai, Y., Maruskin, L. A., & Keltner, D. (2017). Self-transcendent emotions and their social functions: Compassion, gratitude, and awe bind us to others through prosociality. *Emotion Review, 9*(3), 200–207.

Stogdill, R. M. (1948). Personal factors associated with leadership: A survey of the literature. *The Journal of Psychology, 25*(1), 35–71.

Stogdill, R. M. (1963). *Manual for the leader behavior description questionnaire-Form XII: An experimental revision*. Bureau of Business Research, College of Commerce and Administration, Ohio State University.

Sy, T., Côté, S., & Saavedra, R. (2005). The contagious leader: Impact of the leader's mood on the mood of group members, group affective tone, and group processes. *Journal of Applied Psychology, 90*(2), 295–305.

Sznycer, D., Takemura, K., Delton, A. W., Sato, K., Robertson, T., Cosmides, L., & Tooby, J. (2012). Cross-cultural differences and similarities in proneness to shame: An adaptationist and ecological approach. *Evolutionary Psychology, 10*(2), 147470491201000213. https://doi.org/10.1177/147470491201000213

Taylor, J. C., & Bowers, D. G. (1972). *Survey of organizations: A machine-scored standardized questionnaire instrument*. University of Michigan.

Tibbetts, E. A., & Izzo, A. (2010). Social punishment of dishonest signalers caused by mismatch between signal and behavior. *Current Biology, 20*(18), 1637–1640.

Tinbergen, N. (1963). On aims and methods of ethology. *Zeitschrift für tierpsychologie, 20*(4), 410–433.

Tooby, J., & Cosmides, L. (1990). The past explains the present: Emotional adaptations and the structure of ancestral environments. *Ethology and Sociobiology, 11*(4–5), 375–424.

Tooby, J., & Cosmides, L. (2010). Groups in mind: The coalitional roots of war and morality. In H. Høgh-Olesen (Ed.), *Human morality and sociality: Evolutionary and comparative perspectives* (pp. 91–234). Palgrave-Macmillan.

Tracy, J. L., Shariff, A. F., & Cheng, J. T. (2010). A naturalist's view of pride. *Emotion Review, 2*(2), 163–177.

Tracy, J. L., Shariff, A. F., Zhao, W., & Henrich, J. (2013). Cross-cultural evidence that the nonverbal expression of pride is an automatic status signal. *Journal of Experimental Psychology: General, 142*(1), 163–180.

Van Kleef, G. A. (2009). How emotions regulate social life: The emotions as social information (EASI) model. *Current Directions in Psychological Science, 18*(3), 184–188.

Van Kleef, G. A. (2014). Understanding the positive and negative effects of emotional expressions in organizations: EASI does it. *Human Relations, 67*(9), 1145–1164.

Van Knippenberg, D., & Sitkin, S. B. (2013). A critical assessment of charismatic-transformational leadership research: Back to the drawing board? *The Academy of Management Annals, 7*(1), 1–60.

Van Knippenberg, D., & Stam, D. (2013). Visionary leadership. In D. V. Day (Ed.), *The Oxford handbook of leadership and organizations* (pp. 241–259). Oxford University Press.

Van Knippenberg, D., & Van Kleef, G. A. (2016). Leadership and affect: Moving the hearts and minds of followers. *Academy of Management Annals, 10*(1), 799–840.

Van Vugt, M. (2006). Evolutionary origins of leadership and followership. *Personality and Social Psychology Review, 10*(4), 354–371.

Van Vugt, M., Hogan, R., & Kaiser, R. B. (2008). Leadership, followership, and evolution: Some lessons from the past. *American Psychologist, 63*(3), 182–196.

Van Vugt, M., Johnson, D. D., Kaiser, R., & O'Gorman, R. (2008). Evolution and the social psychology of leadership: The mismatch hypothesis. In C. Hoyt, D. Forsyth, & A. Goethals (Eds.), *Social psychology and leadership* (pp. 267–282). Praeger Perspectives.

Van Vugt, M., & Kurzban, R. (2007). Cognitive and social adaptations for leadership and followership. In J. P. Forgas, M. G. Haselton, & W. von Hippel (Eds.), *Evolution and the social mind: Evolutionary psychology and social cognition* (pp. 229–243). Routledge/Taylor & Francis Group.

Van Vugt, M., & Smith, J. E. (2019). A dual model of leadership and hierarchy: Evolutionary synthesis. *Trends in Cognitive Sciences, 23*(11), 952–967.

Van Vugt, M., & von Rueden, C. R. (2020). From genes to minds to cultures: Evolutionary approaches to leadership. *The Leadership Quarterly, 31*(2), 101404.

Venus, M., Stam, D., & Van Knippenberg, D. (2013). Leader emotion as a catalyst of effective leader communication of visions, value-laden messages, and goals. *Organizational Behavior and Human Decision Processes, 122*(1), 53–68.

von Rueden, C. (2014). The roots and fruits of social status in small-scale human societies. In J. T. Cheng, J. L. Tracy, & C. Anderson (Eds.), *The psychology of social status* (pp. 179–200). Springer.

von Rueden, C. (2020). Making and unmaking egalitarianism in small-scale human societies. *Current Opinion in Psychology, 33*, 167–171.

Wang, L., Restubog, S., Shao, B., Lu, V., & Van Kleef, G. A. (2018). Does anger expression help or harm leader effectiveness? The role of competence-based versus integrity-based violations and abusive supervision. *Academy of Management Journal, 61*(3), 1050–1072.

Wasielewski, P. L. (1985). The emotional basis of charisma. *Symbolic Interaction, 8*(2), 207–222.

Weber, M. (1968). *On charisma and institution building*. University of Chicago Press.

Wengrow, D., & Graeber, D. (2015). Farewell to the "childhood of man": Ritual, seasonality, and the origins of inequality. *Journal of the Royal Anthropological Institute, 21*(3), 597–619.

Williams, G. C. (2018). *Adaptation and natural selection: A critique of some current evolutionary thought* (Vol. 75). Princeton University Press.

Woodburn, J. (1982). Egalitarian societies. *Man, 17*(3), 431–451.

Yukl, G. A. (1999). An evaluation of conceptual weaknesses in transformational and charismatic leadership theories. *The Leadership Quarterly, 10*(2), 285–305.

Yukl, G. A. (2002). *Leadership in organizations* (5th ed.). Prentice Hall.

Zaccaro, S. J., Green, J. P., Dubrow, S., & Kolze, M. (2018). Leader individual differences, situational parameters, and leadership outcomes: A comprehensive review and integration. *The Leadership Quarterly, 29*(1), 2–43.

Zahavi, A. (1975). Mate selection: A selection for a handicap. *Journal of Theoretical Biology, 53*(1), 205–214.

CHAPTER 54

The Negative Effect of Ostracism and Other Forms of Social Exclusion on Emotions

Eric D. Wesselmann, Michaela Pfundmair, Jennifer R. Spoor, and Wesley G. Moons

Abstract

Ostracism, a form of social exclusion primarily characterized by being ignored, is a pancultural phenomenon that has been used historically to punish wayward and burdensome group members. Often, an individual would be ostracized briefly to encourage conformity to the group. If the wayward individual either would not or could not conform, the ostracism could become indefinite. For humans, whose survival and reproductive ability are enhanced by group living, indefinite ostracism would essentially be a death sentence. Thus, researchers have argued that the human species likely evolved to detect any hint of potential ostracism or social exclusion, immediately experiencing these cues as painful. Ostracism also elicits negative emotions such as sadness, anger, and shame. This chapter summarizes ostracism research, focusing on both the social and evolutionary underpinnings. It then highlights the research on emotional outcomes of ostracism and closes by providing suggestions for future research.

Key Words: ostracism, rejection, social exclusion, emotion, evolutionary theory

Humans are social animals, with an inherent motivation to establish and maintain relationships with other people. Data from various disciplines and theoretical approaches suggest that this social orientation evolved, with the necessary neural architecture and behavioral dispositions present at birth (Lieberman, 2013). Strong, consistent relationships provide individuals with a host of benefits throughout life. Individuals who can satisfy this need experience positive physical and psychological outcomes, whereas those who are impoverished in their social relationships develop various health problems, reducing their overall well-being and longevity (Baumeister & Leary, 1995; Cacioppo & Patrick, 2008).

There are various ways in which individuals can experience threats to their social relationships. The experience of *social exclusion* involves a situation in which someone feels physically or emotionally isolated (Riva & Eck, 2016). This concept covers a range of negative social experiences, from being told explicitly that one is unwanted to being given the silent treatment by family or friends. Most research on social exclusion focuses on interpersonal interactions, but the experience of feeling isolated can be systemic as well, such as when experiencing institutionalized discrimination or stigmatization (Smart Richman & Leary, 2009). Regardless of the context and form by which exclusion occurs, excluded individuals experience a host of negative consequences, such as feelings of pain, negative emotions, threats to key psychological needs (e.g., belonging, meaning), and they may even question their sense of humanity (see Wesselmann et al., 2016, for review).

In this chapter, we first unpack the phenomenon of social exclusion within the context of social psychological research, focusing on a particular form of exclusion called *ostracism*. We then discuss the evolutionary context within which many researchers study ostracism. Next, we highlight research on the emotional effects of ostracism, drawing connections between specific emotions and behavioral outcomes. We close by discussing future research directions that will broaden the psychological study of ostracism in theoretical scope and detail.

The Dynamics of Social Exclusion

Some types of social exclusion involve receiving explicit negative attention, like being directly insulted (Twenge et al., 2001) or being the target of an offensive joke (Ford et al., 2020), being laughed at in a mean-spirited way (Klages & Wirth, 2014), or receiving negative feedback on social media posts (e.g., "dislike"; Lutz & Schneider, 2020). Other types of exclusion, however, involve inattention—being treated as if one is invisible or unworthy of attention. For example, someone may be given the "silent treatment" by a friend or family member; no matter what the excluded person says, the other person refuses to respond or to acknowledge them (Williams, 2001). People also can feel ignored when they do not receive an answer to a text message (Smith & Williams, 2004) or acknowledgment on their social media posts (Wolf et al., 2015), or when a conversation partner checks their smartphone during the middle of a conversation (Hales et al., 2018).

There is little agreement among researchers on how best to taxonomize these different forms of social exclusion. One way is to examine the phenomena (and the paradigms used to study them experimentally) and categorize them by theoretically meaningful characteristics. Kipling Williams (e.g., 2001, 2009), one of the leading ostracism researchers, has posited that it is the *lack of* attention (i.e., being ignored) that makes ostracism distinct from other forms of social exclusion because it conveys a sense of social invisibility and a lack of value to others. In a similar fashion, early psychologist Williams James famously wrote that "no more fiendish punishment could be devised . . . than that one should be turned loose in society and remain absolutely unnoticed" and that individuals who found themselves in such an unenviable position would welcome any other type of torture because it would mean that they "had not sunk to such a depth as to be unworthy of attention at all" ([1890] 1950; pp. 293–294). These arguments fit the colloquialism that "bad attention is better than no attention at all." Thus, social exclusion experiences can be sorted into phenomena that involve direct negative attention (*rejection*-focused) and those that involve a lack of attention (*ostracism*-focused; Wesselmann et al., 2016).

A few studies have compared experimental paradigms involving exclusion based on direct negative attention with experimental paradigms involving being ignored and have found different effects (e.g., Lutz & Schneider, 2020; Rudert et al., 2017; Zadro et al., 2005). These studies have found that although both types of experiences have negative psychological effects, ostracism-focused exclusion seems to be worse than rejection-focused exclusion. For the remainder of this chapter, we will focus on research that uses ostracism-focused exclusion paradigms and, as such, we will use the term *ostracism* when referring to individuals' experiences. We occasionally reference studies that may be more accurately described as addressing *rejection*-focused forms of exclusion, but for simplicity we use the term *ostracism* unless the conceptual distinction between direct negative attention and a lack of attention is relevant to understanding outcomes.

Ostracism: "Social Death" for Social Animals

Psychologists and other social scientists have long been interested in ostracism in humans, but systematic empirical studies of the psychological effects of this phenomenon began in earnest in the 1990s (see Wesselmann & Williams, 2017; Williams, 1997, for reviews). Psychologists often use Cyberball—a virtual ball-tossing game—to examine the psychological effects of ostracism (Williams et al., 2000). In the general form of this game, participants are told they are playing with other players over the experimenter's computer network. Further, participants are told the goal of the game is for the group to toss the ball around and use it as an experience in mental visualization—they are to focus less on the tossing and instead visualize what the environment might look like in a face-to-face interaction. In reality, the other players are programmed by the experimenter either to include every player in the game equally or to ostracize the participant. Even though Cyberball presents minimal social information and participants are told they are playing with strangers (whom they will presumably never meet again), the negative effects of being ostracized are powerful and robust (Williams, 2009). Cyberball has become a popular paradigm to examine various dynamics of ostracism and inclusion, and researchers have published over 240 publications using the manipulation in different countries (Williams, 2018).

The phenomenon of ostracism is not limited to simulated games of ball-toss. There is evidence of ostracism occurring not only throughout human history, but also across various species of social animals (see Gruters & Masters, 1986; Söderberg & Fry, 2017; and Williams, 1997, for reviews), and some researchers have argued that it was evolutionarily adaptive to both ostracize others (e.g., Kurzban & Leary, 2001) and rapidly detect threats to inclusion, including ostracism (e.g., Spoor & Williams, 2007; Williams, 2009). Ostracism is commonly used as a punitive measure for dealing with group members who pose a threat to the group's survival, or might otherwise be a hindrance to the group's goals and functioning. Punishing harmful, burdensome, or deviant group members with ostracism (in small doses) can be used to communicate to the targeted group members that their behavior is unacceptable and that they should rehabilitate or risk being ostracized indefinitely. Using ostracism in this way also signals to other group members what the group's expectations are and what behaviors are considered beyond the pale (see relevant reviews by Hales et al., 2017; Wirth & Wesselmann, 2018; and Zadro & Gonsalkorale, 2014).

Assuming that humans have depended on groups for survival and reproduction (Buss & Kenrick, 1998; Spoor & Kelly, 2004), the adaptive response for ostracized targets is to quickly notice and respond to potential ostracism and other threats to inclusion (Spoor & Williams, 2007; Williams, 2009). Indeed, researchers have argued that ostracism is an existential threat, a type of *social death* (e.g., Hales, 2018; Williams, 2007). Whereas ostracism may not present the direct threat to someone's survival that it once had over the course of human evolutionary history, natural selection likely favored those individuals who could detect and respond to cues of ostracism to safeguard their inclusionary status. Thus, any cognitive architecture necessary for detection and response has likely been transmitted through subsequent generations to our current time (Pickett & Gardner, 2005; Spoor & Williams, 2007; Wesselmann et al., 2012).

Many researchers have been inspired by the potential evolutionary underpinnings of how people respond to ostracism. Early studies found that individuals often described ostracism (and their experiences of other social threats) using words related to physical pain (e.g., *hurt* feelings; Leary et al., 1998; see also Williams, 2001). Researchers who were inspired by evolutionary theories in biology and psychology argued that the experience of pain serves as an alarm function for organisms; it cues them to attend to an injury that may threaten their survival. Thus, social species such as humans likely evolved overlapping or shared neural architecture to detect threats to their social health as well as to their physical health, as both were germane to survival (i.e., social pain; Eisenberger & Lieberman, 2005; Ferris, 2019; MacDonald & Leary, 2005). Inspired by this argument, many researchers have found that ostracized individuals report feeling pain on self-report measures commonly used in the medical field (e.g., Chen et al., 2008) and exhibit neural activity in brain regions linked to experiencing physical pain (e.g., Eisenberger et al., 2003; Kross et al., 2011).

Other researchers have investigated the overlap between physical pain and social pain by studying parallels for analgesic effects. Several studies have found that ostracized individuals who have ingested substances with pain-numbing properties, such as acetaminophen, marijuana, or alcohol, experience dampened negative reactions compared to ostracized individuals who have not taken these substances (or in some cases have taken a placebo; Deckman et al, 2014; DeWall et al., 2010; Hales et al., 2015). Other studies have found that noninvasive stimulation of brain regions associated with pain regulation also can reduce the negative effects of ostracism (Riva et al., 2012; Riva et al., 2015). Taken together, the studies provide evidence for the theoretical argument that humans evolved a neural system for detecting cues of ostracism and other threats to their social inclusion.

Upon experiencing the pain triggered by ostracism, the target may respond in any number of ways. Given the importance of group membership, one adaptive response may be to engage in affiliative and cooperative behaviors to demonstrate worthiness and potentially regain group membership, which can be referred to as social servility (Williams, 2009). Examples of social servility include greater unconscious mimicry of ingroup members (Lakin et al., 2008) or conversation partners (Sommer & Bernieri, 2015), compliance with various influence tactics (Carter-Sowell et al., 2008), and greater interest in potential new group memberships (Maner et al., 2007; Wheaton, 2001), including groups endorsing extremist or radical beliefs (Hales & Williams, 2018). In one of the earliest laboratory studies of ostracism, Williams and Sommer (1997) found that women who had been ostracized by strangers in a ball-toss game subsequently exerted more effort on a collective task than when working alone. The same effect was not observed for men, which could be explained in terms of social status (Bozin & Yoder, 2008). From an evolutionary perspective, however, women's greater sociality compared to men in this context could reflect that group membership had greater reproductive benefits for women due to their greater parental investment (Symons, 1979). In other words, in most situations women could provide better care for their offspring in a group rather than alone, and it was therefore more adaptive for them to respond to ostracism (and other forms of stress) in an affiliative manner (Taylor, 2012).

Despite the benefits of affiliative behavior in response to ostracism, there is also an extensive body of research demonstrating negative, anti-social, and avoidant responses to ostracism, including aggression (e.g., Gaertner et al., 2008; Warburton et al., 2006), suicidal thoughts (Chen et al., 2020), and social withdrawal (Ren et al., 2016). These negative responses may be predicted by the pattern of appraisals and emotions associated with the ostracism. For example, Chow et al. (2008) observed more aggressive responses to ostracism when it was perceived to be unfair (see also Tuscherer et al., 2016), and Chen et al. (2020) found that the increase in suicidal thoughts after ostracism was mediated by perceptions that life was meaningless. We discuss the emotional responses to ostracism, and their link to both affiliative and antisocial behaviors, in the following section.

The Role of Emotions in Predicting the Aftermath of Ostracism

Emotions can be considered superordinate programs that coordinate a person's physiological, behavioral, and psychological responses to a situation (Cosmides & Tooby, 2000; Keltner &

Haidt, 2001; Levenson, 1999; Nesse 1990; Rossano, 2003; but also see Barrett, 2006). Thus, *fear* after noticing a predator approaching reduces responses that are irrelevant or unhelpful in the moment (e.g., hunger and fatigue temporarily wane) but amplifies other responses (e.g., attention narrows to finding an escape route or weapon and ensuring that offspring are protected). From this perspective, emotions evolved as solutions to recurrent reproductive and survival challenges. Consistent with this reasoning, people can quickly develop a fear response to environmental dangers that have existed throughout evolutionary history but pose relatively little threat today (e.g., snakes, spiders; Haselton & Ketelaar, 2006). Ostracism likely is another example of this—humans no longer must rely on close social relationships to meet their basic survival needs (i.e., food, shelter, and safety), yet they still suffer physically and psychologically if this social need is not met (Baumeister & Leary, 1995).

Given the survival and reproductive advantages of inclusion in groups, ostracism should activate specific emotions (Shilling & Brown, 2016). In ancestral environments, groups were likely to be based on extended kin or ongoing exchange relationships (Caporael, 2001; Caporael & Brewer, 1991). When ostracism was used to punish the target for specific transgressions (and when the target was aware of their transgressions), the adaptive emotion would likely be *guilt*, activating self-focused attention and corrective actions by the target (e.g., Baumeister et al., 1994). These affiliative responses would increase likelihood of re-inclusion in the group. When ostracism was used in a more arbitrary fashion, or where the target felt the ostracism was not justified, *anger* would be a more likely emotion, activating other-focused attention and increasing the likelihood of aggressive or antisocial responses. When ostracism is more enduring, *sadness* may result, potentially leading to social withdrawal.

In contemporary environments, with complex social and task networks and looser ties to a larger number of groups, ostracized targets may find it difficult to identify the reasons for their apparent exclusion. The inability to identify the reason for ostracism may be one reason why both anger and sadness are commonly observed in laboratory studies (e.g., Chow et al., 2008). Indeed, the ambiguity in being ignored may contribute to ostracism's severe effects (Williams, 2009). Moreover, groups may unintentionally ostracize someone by failing to give them sufficient attention. In this case, the pain of ostracism is in the eye of the beholder. Regardless of whether the ostracism is intentional, the person who feels ostracized likely searches for any attributional information to understand their experience, whether internal or external (e.g., Wirth & Williams, 2009), to ascertain a way to recover from their experience. Theorizing in social psychology to understand which behavioral path an ostracized person will use to recover has focused on motivational factors (e.g., which needs are more important to satisfy, or which opportunities are available; Shilling & Brown, 2016; Wesselmann et al., 2015). The consensus is that if social connection (either with the original group or a new group) is possible and preferred, then the ostracized person will likely respond in pro-social/affiliative ways. If the ostracized person is more interested in asserting control or receiving attention than re-inclusion, or if they believe future inclusion is impossible, then they will likely respond in antisocial ways such as aggression or social withdrawal.

Thus far, theorizing about behavioral responses to ostracism has neglected emotional factors. However, the variety of behavioral outcomes of ostracism are likely attributable to the specific emotion induced by feeling ostracized. Specific emotions are determined by the cognitive appraisals a person makes regarding their emotional situation (Lerner & Keltner, 2000). Multiple appraisals shape the specific negative emotion a person experiences after being ostracized. Among them, appraisals of *certainty*, *control*, and *injustice* can lead to different emotional implications (Lazarus, 1991; Lerner & Keltner, 2001; Tiedens & Linton, 2001).

Certainty in how an emotional situation came about or the consequences of that emotional situation will determine which emotion is experienced. For example, if a person is unaware of why they are being ostracized, they may feel unable to address the causes of the ostracism, hence the increased likelihood to make *both* internal and external attributions (Wirth & Williams, 2009). Appraisals of low certainty are characteristic of emotions like anxiety and fear. Uncovering the factors that led to the ostracism introduces the possibility of remediation by addressing those factors. Unfortunately, identifying the causes of ostracism can be hindered by being denied insights from the individuals inflicting the ostracism because of their silence. Consequently, an ostracized person can suffer a prolonged period of anxiety or fear because of not understanding why they are excluded. Extended periods of anxiety and fear may be part of what leads to the severe negative outcomes experienced by those who are chronically ostracized, such as depression and feelings of helplessness (Riva et al., 2017; Williams, 2009).

Appraisals of control also factor into which specific emotion will result from being ostracized. Even if the causes of the ostracism are certain and understood, an inability to control those causes leaves an ostracized person few options. Some causes of ostracism, such as breaking a group norm, may be addressed by apologizing, paying compensation, or suffering retribution. When an ostracized person makes a high-control appraisal, they are aware that they can take steps to mitigate the ostracism. In such cases, they are likely to experience feelings of guilt and an associated motivation to make reparations (Baumeister et al., 1994). However, some causes of ostracism lie outside of the victim's control (e.g., Wesselmann et al., 2014). Many social group memberships are automatic and immutable. Group memberships that are stigmatized within the larger society or culture are often subjected to systematic ostracism (Kurzban & Leary, 2001). In cases where such group memberships can be concealed, people may choose to "stay in the closet" as a protective measure. When group memberships are conspicuous, a person has no option to rectify or hide their group membership, and therefore they may experience feelings of *shame*. Unlike guilt, shame is evoked when someone feels that there is something morally wrong with their identity, rather than just their actions (Haidt, 2003). Shame and guilt also differ in their impact on immune function and consequent health outcomes (Dickerson et al., 2004). Shame's other pernicious effects include an avoidance motivation, which can amplify external ostracism by inducing self-withdrawal, perhaps putting the person in a never-ending cycle of ostracism (Wesselmann et al., 2021).

Fortunately, people are not just casualties of low certainty and low control. Humans will also appraise whether a situation is just or unjust. Injustice appraisals moderate how other appraisals contribute to specific emotional reactions. For example, the combination of a high-certainty appraisal (i.e., cause is known) and low-control appraisal (i.e., immutable), as might be seen in cases of racial discrimination, can be appraised as unjust. Consequently, rather than experiencing guilt or shame, individuals may be more likely to experience anger. Anger motivates action to redress the perceived injustice by repudiating those who ostracize others. Righteous anger may lead to attempts to improve the situation (Leonard et al., 2011), but it can also lead to destructive behaviors. Some research has found higher levels of anger, and aggressive responses, when the ostracized person perceives their treatment as unjust (Chow et al., 2008; Tuscherer et al., 2016). Indeed, a systematic analysis of mass-shooting events (Leary et al., 2003) found that many perpetrators cited ostracism and other forms of exclusion as their primary motive—they *believed* that they were the victims. These extreme situations were more complicated than simply explaining it with an ostracism-leads-to-mass-violence conclusion, but the data suggest that perceived (unjust) ostracism is a key component in each of these cases.

Experimental Paradigm Considerations

Contemporary ostracism and social exclusion paradigms strip the target of cues that would have triggered different emotion and behavioral patterns for our ancestors. Each paradigm limits the target's attributions of control, certainty, and fairness over their exclusionary status. For example, the life-alone paradigm suggests that everyone will eventually reject the person, no matter what they do (Twenge et al., 2001). The get-acquainted paradigm involves telling participants that no one wanted to work with them on a future task, but participants are not provided with any reason for the decision (Twenge et al., 2001; Wesselmann et al., 2010). In the ball-toss paradigms (face-to-face: Williams & Sommer, 1997; Cyberball: Williams et al., 2000), the target usually has no past or ongoing relationship with the other "players," and cultural expectations of fairness and equal treatment may amplify an attribution that any form of ostracism in that context is unjustified (Wesselmann et al., 2013; but see Rudert & Greifeneder, 2016). Even Cyberball variations that demonstrate ostracized participants are upset even when they know they are playing with a computer programmed to ostracize them (Zadro et al., 2004) are embedded in a cultural belief that the programmers and algorithms should be fair (and probably coupled with a misunderstanding of probability).

These paradigm types, with their strengths and limitations, likely have different effects on emotional outcomes. However, at this point most paradigms have been treated as equivalent and have not been compared directly in terms of psychological outcomes, except for life-alone paradigm and Cyberball. The former is treated as a chronic form of ostracism, whereas the latter is an acute form—the acute form shows the expected increased negative affect and threat to psychological needs, and the chronic-based paradigm leads to a numbing to these outcomes (Bernstein & Claypool, 2012a, 2012b). The life-alone paradigm is unique in that it is the only experimental paradigm that involves chronic (albeit prospective) ostracism; all other experimental paradigms involve either acute real-time experiences of ostracism or retrospective accounts of a single instance of ostracism (Wirth, 2016). It is important for future research to examine how these different acute/retrospective manipulations of ostracism affect participants, both in terms of their threat to psychological needs and the specific emotions they provoke.

Looking to the Future of Ostracism Research

Given the research we have reviewed, there is evidence demonstrating that cues of ostracism activate an "alarm system" that causes feelings of pain and evokes negative emotions such as anger and sadness. There have been numerous studies using a variety of methods demonstrating these links, with participants of various ages and cultural backgrounds. However, there remain questions that researchers should investigate to advance the theoretical understanding of ostracism.

Reconciling Paradoxical Responses

As previously noted, there are two main ways in which people respond to ostracism in laboratory settings: pro-social and antisocial. Whereas a pro-social response is approach-focused, an antisocial response pattern can be either approach-focused (i.e., aggression) or avoidance-focused (i.e., withdrawal). The ostracism literature includes speculations as to how these conflicting responses might coexist, but few studies have provided direct evidence (see Wesselmann et al., 2015, for review).

One way of reconciling these conflicting responses may be to examine the specific characteristics of the paradigms. Contemporary ostracism paradigms strip the person of any sense of control over the situation. By reducing ostracism to its minimal conditions, paradigms such as Cyberball may be amplifying its sting (and the potential for antisocial reactions) precisely because the context and cues that would have been present for our ancestors are stripped away. Moreover, most of these paradigms fail to offer the target any opportunity or expectation that they can or should attempt to affiliate with the sources of ostracism. Thus, these paradigms may bias the literature to overestimate negative, antisocial, and withdrawal behaviors, as these were the only apparent recourse to unfair ostracism. If a social servility response is available and viable in the social context, one might expect ostracized people to favor this option over an antisocial option (see also Spoor & Williams, 2007; Williams, 2009). Further, these paradigms may have different effects that make certain emotional patterns (and thus behavioral responses) more likely. If this is the case, researchers will need to keep this in mind when choosing which paradigms are most appropriate.

Cross-Cultural Considerationsx

Even though there is research demonstrating the negative effects of ostracism across cultures, there is room for cultural variability in terms of these effects. For example, it is possible that certain psychological needs are more important in some cultures, at least in terms of how those needs are met by interpersonal relationships. As such, the patterns of need threat may depend on cultural context. The same may be true of the patterns of negative emotions evoked by ostracism. Further, the identity of the ostracizers also may matter. Laboratory manipulations of ostracism typically involve participants interacting with strangers, either face to face or on virtual platforms (see Williams, 2009; and Wirth, 2016, for reviews; but see Arriaga et al., 2014, for an example of cover stories using romantic partners as the source of ostracism). Does ostracism by strangers hurt more or less in cultures that encourage stronger ties among members of society than in cultures that focus more on individual agency?

These questions are related to *self-construal*, which focuses on the ways individuals define their self-concepts, and how culture influences this process. Individuals classified as having an *independent* self-concept are striving for uniqueness, autonomy, and satisfying individual goals. Individuals characterized as having an *interdependent* self-concept, on the other hand, aim for connectedness with important others and, thus, emphasize maintaining harmony and fitting in (Markus & Kitayama, 1991). An independent self-concept is common among individuals in individualistic cultures (e.g., North America and Western Europe), whereas an interdependent self-concept is widespread in collectivistic cultures (e.g., Asia, Africa, and South America; Hofstede et al., 2010). Notably, all cultures include individualistic and collectivistic aspects, and thus individuals in these cultures incorporate both independent and interdependent aspects into their self-concepts. However, the dichotomy of individualism vs. collectivism is often used because of the tendency for individuals in each culture to favor one aspect over the other.

Since independence and interdependence are related to a need to maintain positive relationships with others (Baumeister & Leary, 1995), it is plausible that individualistic and collectivistic cultures differ in their reactions to ostracism. Research has shown that people in collectivistic cultures are more sensitive to rejection-focused forms of exclusion than people in individualistic cultures (Garris et al., 2011; Hashimoto & Yamagishi, 2013; Yamaguchi et al., 1995). However, at the same time, they show less intense reactions to concrete instances of ostracism. These involve a less steep decline of basic needs (Pfundmair, Aydin, et al., 2015) and a faster recovery of needs for belonging and meaningful existence (Ren et al., 2013). Moreover, people from collectivistic cultures show less pronounced behavioral reactions to instances of ostracism. For example, unlike people from individualistic cultures, they did not lower their impressions about an unknown partner who ostracized them (Fiske & Yamamoto, 2005). Further, whereas participants from individualistic cultures indicated more antisocial and avoidant behavioral intentions in response to ostracism (vs. inclusion), the responses of participants from collectivistic cultures were similar after ostracism and inclusion (Pfundmair, Graupmann, et al., 2015).

Two explanations have been put forward to explain this collectivistic advantage. First, people with more interdependent self-concepts may have greater cognitive accessibility to social resources because they perceive themselves as inherently connected to others, compared with independent-focused people (Gardner et al., 2005). These chronically accessible social representations, in turn, may serve as a natural buffer on which to draw in times of social threat (e.g., an ostracism experience). A second explanatory approach assumes that people from collectivistic cultures are not as vulnerable to ostracism directed at the individual because the individual aspects of the self are not core to their sense of self-integrity (Pfundmair, Aydin, et al., 2015; Pfundmair, Graupmann, et al., 2015). In other words, a self-construal that is characterized by "goals that are larger than the self" (Crocker & Park, 2004, p. 16) may be more favorable in the face of ostracism than having a self-construal focused on one's uniqueness. Thus, previous research suggests that collectivists might be better equipped to cope with ostracism because their sense of self is connected to close interpersonal ties and group-level affiliations. However, some research shows that although collectivists are less bothered than individualists when ostracizers are strangers, when the ostracism is coming from important in-group members, collectivists and individuals are similarly harmed (Uskul & Over, 2014; Yaakobi & Williams, 2016).

Based on these findings, we can expect cross-cultural differences in emotional reactions to ostracism. One might assume that people from individualistic cultures would show stronger emotional reactions to ostracism than people from collectivistic cultures, because they are more affected by it. However, even when ostracized by their in-group (and thus affected similarly), collectivists might still be more moderate in their expressions of either emotions or behaviors, as free expression of emotions is less important to them, and their desire to fit into the interpersonal context requires stronger regulation of emotion and expressive behavior (Matsumoto et al., 2008). Furthermore, self-construal may affect the patterns of negative emotions evoked by ostracism. For example, individualists might show more anger to ostracism and collectivists more sadness or even guilt. Why might that be? Emotional expressions accommodate the meanings and practices of individuals' sociocultural context (Bruner, 2003; see also Al-Shawaf et al., 2016). Specifically, emotions in individualistic contexts seem to help individuals to express autonomy, whereas emotions in collectivistic contexts appear to help strengthen interpersonal bonds (Markus & Kitayama, 1991). Research has found that people with individualistic cultural backgrounds experience more socially disengaging emotions like pride and anger, whereas people with collectivistic cultural backgrounds often experience socially engaging emotions like friendly feelings and guilt (Kitayama et al., 2006). Thus, people with different cultural backgrounds not only may differ in whether they are threatened by a specific ostracism experience, but also their affective experiences may vary in intensity and shape. These ideas scratch the surface of myriad questions about ostracism that could be investigated from a cross-cultural perspective (Schaafsma, 2017). It is imperative that ostracism researchers consider cultural variables as they develop research programs, so that they can obtain a more nuanced understanding of the negative cognitive, emotional, and behavioral effects of ostracism (Henrich et al., 2010).

Ostracism, Extremism, and Emotions
Researchers have long argued that perceived ostracism, whether it occurs at the interpersonal or cultural level, might allow terrorism and other forms of extremism to flourish (e.g., Hales,

Wesselmann, et al., 2020; Weight-Neville & Halafoff, 2010). Much of this work involves qualitative interviews with individuals who either have been captured or have defected from extremist movements, and insights from this qualitative research has been merged theoretically with survey and laboratory-based data on low-level forms of interpersonal aggression, thus limiting the scope and confidence of these connections. These limitations are inherent to studying the psychology of extremist groups (Ginges et al., 2011). However, recent empirical research (predominantly using the Cyberball paradigm) has supported the theoretical connection between ostracism and extremism in laboratory studies using attitudinal measures of extremism. For example, ostracized participants subsequently expressed greater willingness to attend a meeting of an activist campus organization and greater openness toward gang membership than included participants (Hales & Williams, 2018). In another set of studies, ostracized participants adapted their attitude more strongly to a radical group's ideology, particularly when they were high in rejection sensitivity (Bäck et al., 2018). Ostracism also led people to moralize their own group, which translated into endorsement of fight-and-die behaviors, particularly among people high in need to belong (Pfundmair & Wetherell, 2019). In a set of studies which investigated the terrorism concept more directly, ostracized participants, compared to included participants, favored more extreme options to support a pro-democracy terrorist organization and expressed greater willingness to destroy property on behalf of an animal protection terrorist organization (Pfundmair, 2019). Thus, recent experimental work suggests that ostracism might be one of several reasons to adopt extremist ideas or causes.

Ostracized individuals may show increased reception to extremism because of the paradoxical tendencies for aggressive responses (e.g., Warburton et al., 2006) and receptivity to social influence and potential sources of affiliation (e.g., Carter-Sowell et al., 2008; Maner et al., 2007); indeed, both motives could be working in tandem (Knapton, 2004). As we discussed earlier, extant theories of ostracism focus on the cognitive and motivational effects rather than the emotional effects. The work on ostracism and extremism is no exception. However, some have argued that anger is related to normative political action (such as participating in peaceful protests), whereas contempt is related to non-normative political action (such as violence and terrorism; Tausch et al., 2011). Thus, although anger may be a key emotion in understanding why ostracism can prompt low levels of interpersonal aggression (e.g., Chow et al., 2008), it may not be sufficient for prompting extreme forms of aggression. The latter may require an ostracized individual to (also) feel contempt. If so, researchers need to determine the process by which both emotions are provoked. Are they separate but correlated emotions, needing specific situational characteristics to prompt contempt? If so, what might those characteristics be? Research on contempt suggests that it is a moral emotion, evoked when individuals perceive themselves as morally superior to another person or group, and individuals can be motivated to ostracize the object of their contempt (Fischer & Ginger-Sorolla, 2016). However, this definition of contempt suggests that it should provoke a "flight" rather than a "fight" reaction. Perhaps contempt needs to facilitate the development of hatred to provoke extreme violence toward others (Fischer & Ginger-Sorolla, 2016). Perceptions of moral superiority are a key factor in understanding how individuals develop feelings of hate toward out-groups, leading to conflict (Brewer, 1999), so such a connection to violence and terrorism is plausible. As such, future research should examine the degree to which ostracized individuals express contempt for those who ostracize them. It also is likely that contempt (and hatred) is something that develops over repeated ostracism experiences, especially if ostracized individuals believe that the ostracizers' behavior toward them will not change, regardless of what they do. Thus, they may perceive extreme measures as the only viable path to satisfy their chronically threatened needs.

Finally, extremism may result from social situations that make one feel *humiliated* because it provides a way to re-establish a sense of meaning and control (e.g., Webber et al., 2018). Studies directly manipulating ostracism or other forms of social exclusion have found that these experiences increase participants' feelings of humiliation (Hales, McIntyre, et al., 2020; Furukawa et al., 2019). However, research comparing humiliation to other related feelings such as anger and shame suggest that the experience of humiliation involves negative affect directed toward the source of the social threat (an approach response, like anger), yet also a perception of powerlessness (an avoidance response, like shame; Leidner et al., 2012). How can feelings of humiliation involve both an avoidant and approach response? Perhaps chronic humiliation (whether brought on by ostracism or some other form of social exclusion) leads one to believe that extremism is the last, best hope for breaking out of a situation that makes them feel chronically threatened. Regardless, future research needs to reconcile these paradoxical findings.

Conclusion

Ostracism, a form of social exclusion characterized by being ignored, is a common and painful experience. Data from various academic disciplines suggest that humans evolved the ability to detect cues of ostracism or other forms of social exclusion, immediately experiencing them as painful. This pain experience would then orient individuals to respond in ways that safeguard their inclusionary status, and thus their survival. Most ostracism research focuses on cognitive and behavioral outcomes rather than emotional outcomes, acknowledging negative effects but not elucidating further. In this chapter, we have reviewed the ostracism literature and have highlighted the emotion-relevant aspects, framing them within both evolutionary and cultural considerations. We then posited several directions for research that would extend both the theoretical and applied aspects of ostracism research.

References

Al-Shawaf, L., Conroy-Beam, D., Asao, K., & Buss, D. M. (2016). Human emotions: An evolutionary psychology perspective. *Emotion Review, 8*(2), 173–186.

Arriaga, X. B., Capezza, N. M., Reed, J. T., Wesselmann, E. D., & Williams, K. D. (2014). With partners like you, who needs strangers? Ostracism involving a romantic partner. *Personal Relationships, 21*(4), 557–569.

Bäck, E. A., Bäck, H., Altermark, N., & Knapton, H. (2018). The quest for significance: Attitude adaption to a radical group following social exclusion. *International Journal of Developmental Science, 12*(1–2), 25–36.

Barrett, L. F. (2006). Are emotions natural kinds? *Perspectives on Psychological Science, 1*(1), 28–58.

Baumeister, R. F., & Leary, M. R. (1995). The need to belong: Desire for interpersonal attachments as a fundamental human motivation. *Psychological Bulletin, 117*(3), 497–529.

Baumeister, R. F., Stillwell, A. M., & Heatherton, T. F. (1994). Guilt: An interpersonal approach. *Psychological Bulletin, 115*(2), 243–267.

Bernstein, M. J., & Claypool, H. M. (2012a). Social exclusion and pain sensitivity: Why exclusion sometimes hurts and sometimes numbs. *Personality & Social Psychology Bulletin, 38*(2), 185–196.

Bernstein, M. J., & Claypool, H. M. (2012b). Not all social exclusions are created equal: Emotional distress following social exclusion is moderated by exclusion paradigm. *Social Influence, 7*(2), 113–130.

Bozin, M. A., & Yoder, J. D. (2008). Social status, not gender alone, is implicated in different reactions by women and men to social ostracism. *Sex Roles, 58*, 713–720.

Buss, D. M., & Kenrick, D. T. (1998). Evolutionary social psychology. In D. T. Gilbert, S. T. Fiske, & G. Lindzey (Eds.), The Handbook of Social Psychology (pp. 982–1026). McGraw-Hill.

Brewer, M. B. (1999). The psychology of prejudice: Ingroup love and outgroup hate? *Journal of Social Issues, 55*(3), 429–444.

Bruner, J. (2003). The narrative construction of reality. In P. Sengers & M. Mateas (Eds.), *Narrative intelligence* (Vol. 46, pp. 41–62). John Benjamins.

Cacioppo, J. T., & Patrick, W. (2008). *Loneliness*. W. W. Norton.

Caporael, L. R. (2001). Evolutionary psychology: Toward a unifying theory and a hybrid science. *Annual Review of Psychology, 52,* 607–628.

Caporael, L. R., & Brewer, M. B. (1991). Reviving evolutionary psychology: Biology meets society. *Journal of Social Issues, 47*(3), 187–195.

Carter-Sowell, A. R., Chen, Z., & Williams, K. D. (2008). Ostracism increases social susceptibility. *Social Influence, 3*(3), 143–153.

Chen, Z., Poon, K.-T., DeWall, C. N., & Jiang, T. (2020). Life lacks meaning without acceptance: Ostracism triggers suicidal thoughts. *Journal of Personality & Social Psychology, 119*(6), 1423–1443.

Chen, Z., Williams, K. D., Fitness, J., & Newton, N. C. (2008). When hurt will not heal: Exploring the capacity to relive social and physical pain. *Psychological Science, 19*(8), 789–795.

Chow, R. M., Tiedens, L. Z., & Govan, C. L. (2008). Excluded emotions: The role of anger in antisocial responses to ostracism. *Journal of Experimental Social Psychology, 44*(3), 896–903.

Cosmides, L., & Tooby, J. (2000). Evolutionary psychology and the emotions. In M. Lewis & J. M. Haviland-Jones (Eds.), *Handbook of emotions* (2nd ed.; pp. 91–115). Guilford.

Crocker, J., & Park, L. E. (2004). The costly pursuit of self-esteem. *Psychological Bulletin, 130*(3), 392–414.

Deckman, T., DeWall, C. N., Way, B., Gilman, R., & Richman, S. (2014). Can marijuana reduce social pain? *Social Psychological & Personality Science, 5*(2), 131–139.

DeWall, C. N., MacDonald, G., Webster, G. D., Masten, C. L., Baumeister, R. F., Powell, C., Combs, D., Schurtz, D. R., Stillman, T. F., Tice, D. M., & Eisenberger, N. I. (2010). Acetaminophen reduces social pain: Behavioral and neural evidence. *Psychological Science, 21*(7), 931–937.

Dickerson, S. S., Kemeney, M. E., Aziz, N., Kim, K. H., & Fahey, J. L. (2004). Immunological effects of induced shame and guilt. *Psychosomatic Medicine, 66*(1), 124–131.

Eisenberger, N. I., & Lieberman, M. D. (2005). Why it hurts to be left out: The neurocognitive overlap between physical and social pain. In K. D. Williams, J. P. Forgas, & W. von Hippel (Eds.), *The social outcast: Ostracism, social exclusion, rejection, and bullying* (pp. 109–130). Psychology Press.

Eisenberger, N. I., Lieberman, M. D., & Williams, K. D. (2003). Does rejection hurt? An fMRI study of social exclusion. *Science, 302*(5643), 290–292.

Ferris, L. J. (2019). Hurt feelings: Physical pain, social exclusion, and the psychology of pain overlap. In S. C. Rudert, R. Greifeneder, & K. D. Williams (Eds.), *Current directions in ostracism, social exclusion, and rejection research* (pp. 100–119). Routledge.

Fischer, A., & Giner-Sorolla, R. (2016). Contempt: Derogating others while keeping calm. *Emotion Review, 8*(4), 346–357.

Fiske, S. T., & Yamamoto, M. (2005). Coping with rejection: Core social motives, across cultures. In K. D. Williams, J. P. Forgas & W. von Hippel (Eds.), *The social outcast: Ostracism, social exclusion, rejection, and bullying* (pp. 185–198). Psychology Press.

Ford, T. E., Buie, H. S., Mason, S. D., Olah, A. R., Breeden, C. J., & Ferguson, M. A. (2020). Diminished self-concept and social exclusion: Disparagement humor from the target's perspective. *Self & Identity, 19*(6), 698–718.

Furukawa, Y., Nakashima, K. I., & Morinaga, Y. (2019). Guilt signals a crisis of rejection: Two types of individual differences related to social rejection have dissimilar effects on guilt and compensatory behavior. *Japanese Psychological Research, 61*(1), 1–11.

Gaertner, L., Iuzzini, J., & O'Mara, E. M. (2008). When rejection by one fosters aggression against many: Multiple-victim aggression as a consequence of social rejection and perceived groupness. *Journal of Experimental Social Psychology, 44,* 958–970.

Gardner, W., Pickett, C. L., & Knowles, M. (2005). Social snacking and shielding: Using social symbols, selves, and surrogates in the service of belonging needs. In K. D. Williams, J. P. Forgas, & W. von Hippel (Eds.), *The Social Outcast: Ostracism, Social Exclusion, Rejection, and Bullying* (pp. 227–242). Psychology Press.

Garris, C. P., Ohbuchi, K. I., Oikawa, H., & Harris, M. J. (2011). Consequences of interpersonal rejection: A cross-cultural experimental study. *Journal of Cross-Cultural Psychology, 42*(6), 1066–1083.

Ginges, J., Atran, S., Sachdeva, S., & Medin, D. (2011). Psychology out of the laboratory: The challenge of violent extremism. *American Psychologist, 66*(6), 507–519.

Gruters, M., & Masters, R. D. (Eds.). (1986). Ostracism: A social and biological phenomenon. *Ethology & Sociobiology, 7*(3–4), 149–395.

Haidt, J. (2003). The moral emotions. In R. J. Davidson, K. R. Scherer, & H. H. Goldsmith (Eds.), *Handbook of affective sciences* (pp. 852–870). Oxford University Press.

Hales, A. (2018). Death as a metaphor for ostracism: Social invincibility, autopsy, necromancy, and resurrection. *Mortality, 23*(4), 366–380.

Hales, A. H., Dvir, M., Wesselmann, E. D., Kruger, D. J., & Finkenauer, C. (2018). Cell phone-induced ostracism threatens fundamental needs. *The Journal of Social Psychology, 158*(4), 460–473.

Hales, A. H., McIntyre, M. M., Rudert, S. C., Williams, K. D., & Thomas, H. (2020). Ostracized and observed: The presence of an audience affects the experience of being excluded. *Self & Identity, 20*(1) 94–115. https://doi.org/10.1080/15298868.2020.1807403

Hales, A. H., Ren, D., & Williams, K. D. (2017). Protect, correct, and eject: Ostracism as a social influence tool. In S. G. Harkins, K. D. Williams, & J. Burger (Eds.), *The Oxford handbook of social influence* (pp. 205–217). Oxford University Press.

Hales, A. H., Wesselmann, E. D., & Williams, K. D. (2020). Social ostracism, religion, and existential concerns. In K. Vail & C. Routledge (Eds.), *The science of religion, spirituality, and existentialism* (pp. 153–166). Elsevier.

Hales, A. H., & Williams, K. D. (2018). Marginalized individuals and extremism: The role of ostracism in openness to extreme groups. *Journal of Social Issues, 74*(1), 75–92.

Hales, A. H., Williams, K. D., & Eckhardt, C. I. (2015). A participant walks into a bar . . . : Subjective intoxication buffers ostracism's negative effects. *Social Psychology, 46*(3), 157–166.

Haselton, M. G., & Ketelaar, T. (2006). Irrational emotions or emotional wisdom? The evolutionary psychology of emotions and behavior. In J. P. Forgas (Ed.), *Hearts and minds: Affective influences on social cognition and behavior* (pp. 21–40). Psychology Press.

Hashimoto, H., & Yamagishi, T. (2013). Two faces of interdependence: Harmony seeking and rejection avoidance. *Asian Journal of Social Psychology, 16*(2), 142–151.

Henrich, J., Heine, S. J., & Norenzayan, A. (2010). The weirdest people in the world? *Behavioral & Brain Sciences, 33*(2–3), 61–83.

Hofstede, G., Hofstede, G. J., & Minkov, M. (2010). *Cultures and organizations: Software of the mind* (3rd ed.). McGraw-Hill.

James, W. ([1890] 1950). *Principles of psychology* (Vol. 1). Dover.

Keltner, D., & Haidt, J. (2001). Social functions of emotions. In T. J. Mayne & G. A. Bonanno (Eds.), *Emotions: Currrent issues and future directions* (pp. 192–213). The Guilford Press.

Kitayama, S., Mesquita, B., & Karasawa, M. (2006). Cultural affordances and emotional experience: socially engaging and disengaging emotions in Japan and the United States. *Journal of Personality & Social Psychology, 91*(5), 890–903.

Klages, S. V., & Wirth, J. H. (2014). Excluded by laughter: Laughing until it hurts someone else. *The Journal of Social Psychology, 154*(1), 8–13.

Knapton, H. (2014). The recruitment and radicalisation of Western citizens: Does ostracism have a role in home-grown terrorism?. *Journal of European Psychology Students, 5*(1), 38–48.

Kross, E., Berman, M. G., Mischel, W., Smith, E. E., & Wager, T. D. (2011). Social rejection shares somatosensory representations with physical pain. *Proceedings of the National Academy of Sciences, 108*(15), 6270–6275.

Kurzban, R., & Leary, M. R. (2001). Evolutionary origins of stigmatization: The functions of social exclusion. *Psychological Bulletin, 127*(2), 187–208.

Lakin, J. L., Chartrand, T. L., & Arkin, R. M. (2008). I am too just like you: Nonconscious mimicry as an automatic behavioral response to social exclusion. *Psychological Science, 19*(8), 816–822.

Lazarus, R. S. (1991). *Emotion and adaptation*. Oxford University Press.

Leary, M. R., Kowalski, R. M., Smith, L., & Phillips, S. (2003). Teasing, rejection, and violence: Case studies of the school shootings. *Aggressive Behavior, 29*(3), 202–214.

Leary, M. R., Springer, C., Negel, L., Ansell, E., & Evans, K. (1998). The causes, phenomenology, and consequences of hurt feelings. *Journal of Personality & Social Psychology, 74*(5), 1225–1237.

Leidner, B., Sheikh, H., & Ginges, J. (2012). Affective dimensions of intergroup humiliation. *PLoS ONE, 7*(9), e46375. https://doi.org/10.1371/journal.pone.0046375

Leonard, D. J., Moons, W. G., Mackie, D. M., & Smith, E. R. (2011). "We're mad as hell and we're not going to take it anymore": Anger self-stereotyping and collective action. *Group Processes & Intergroup Relations, 14*(1), 99–111.

Lerner, J. S., & Keltner, D. (2000). Beyond valence: Toward a model of emotion-specific influences on judgement and choice. *Cognition & Emotion, 14*(4), 473–493.

Lerner J. S., & Keltner, D. (2001). Fear, anger, and risk. *Journal of Personality & Social Psychology, 81*(1), 146–159.

Levenson, R. W. (1999). The intrapersonal functions of emotion. *Cognition & Emotion, 13*(5), 481–504.

Lieberman, M. D. (2013). *Social: Why our brains are wired to connect*. Crown.

Lutz, S., & Schneider, F. M. (2020). Is receiving dislikes in social media still better than being ignored? The effects of ostracism and rejection on need threat and coping responses online. *Media Psychology, 24*(6), 741–765. https://doi.org/10.1080/15213269.2020.1799409

MacDonald, G., & Leary, M. R. (2005). Why does social exclusion hurt? The relationship between social and physical pain. *Psychological Bulletin, 131*(2), 202–223.

Maner, J. K., DeWall, C. N., Baumeister, R. F., & Schaller, M. (2007). Does social exclusion motivate interpersonal reconnection? Resolving the "porcupine problem." *Journal of Personality & Social Psychology, 92*(1), 42–55.

Markus, H. R., & Kitayama, S. (1991). Culture and the self: Implications for cognition, emotion, and motivation. *Psychological Review, 98*(2), 224–253.

Matsumoto, D., Yoo, S. H., Fontaine, J., Anguas-Wong, A. M., Arriola, M., Ataca, B., Bond, M. H., Broatav, H. B., Breugelmans, S., Cabecinhas, R., Chae, J., Chin, W. H., Comunian, A. L., Degere, D. N., Djunaidi, A., Fok, H. K., Friedlmeier, W., Ghosh, A., Glamcevski, M., . . . Grossi, E. (2008). Mapping expressive differences around the world: The relationship between emotional display rules and individualism versus collectivism. *Journal of Cross-Cultural Psychology, 39*(1), 55–74.

Nesse, R. M. (1990). Evolutionary explanations of emotions. *Human Nature, 1*, 261–289.

Pfundmair, M. (2019). Ostracism promotes a terroristic mindset. *Behavioral Sciences of Terrorism & Political Aggression, 11*(2), 134–148.

Pfundmair, M., Aydin, N., Du, H., Yeung, S., Frey, D., & Graupmann, V. (2015a). Exclude me if you can: Cultural effects on the outcomes of social exclusion. *Journal of Cross-Cultural Psychology, 46*(4), 579–596.

Pfundmair, M., Graupmann, V., Frey, D., & Aydin, N. (2015b). The different behavioral intentions of collectivists and individualists in response to social exclusion. *Personality & Social Psychology Bulletin, 41*(3), 363–378.

Pfundmair, M., & Wetherell, G. (2019). Ostracism drives group moralization and endorsement of extreme actions for the group. *The Journal of Social Psychology, 159*(5), 518–530.

Pickett, C. L., & Gardner, W. L. (2005). The social monitoring system: Enhanced sensitivity to social cues as an adaptive response to social exclusion. In K. D. Williams, J. P. Forgas, & W. von Hippel (Eds.), *The social outcast: Ostracism, social exclusion, rejection, and bullying* (pp. 213–226). Psychology Press.

Ren, D., Wesselmann, E. D., & Williams, K. D. (2013). Interdependent self-construal moderates coping with (but not the initial pain of) ostracism. *Asian Journal of Social Psychology, 16*(4), 320–326.

Ren, D., Wesselmann, E., & Williams, K. D. (2016). Evidence for another response to ostracism: Solitude seeking. *Social Psychological & Personality Science, 7*(3), 204–212.

Riva, P., & Eck, J. (2016). The many faces of social exclusion. In P. Riva & J. Eck (Eds.), *Social exclusion: Psychological approaches to understanding and reducing its impact* (pp. ix–xv). Springer International.

Riva, P., Montali, L., Wirth, J. H., Curioni, S., & Williams, K. D. (2017). Chronic social exclusion and evidence for the resignation stage: An empirical investigation. *Journal of Social & Personal Relationships, 34*(4), 541–564.

Riva, P., Romero Lauro, L. J., DeWall, C. N., & Bushman, B. J. (2012). Buffer the pain away: Stimulating the right ventrolateral prefrontal cortex reduces pain following social exclusion. *Psychological Science, 23*(12), 1473–1475.

Riva, P., Romero Lauro, L. J., DeWall, C. N., Chester, D. S., & Bushman, B. J. (2015). Reducing aggressive responses to social exclusion using transcranial direct current stimulation. *Social Cognitive & Affective Neuroscience, 10*(3), 352–356.

Rossano, M. J. (2003). Expertise and the evolution of consciousness. *Cognition, 89*(3), 207–236.

Rudert, S. C., & Greifeneder, R. (2016). When it's okay that I don't play: Social norms and the situated construal of social exclusion. *Personality & Social Psychology Bulletin, 42*(7), 955–969.

Rudert, S. C., Hales, A. H., Greifeneder, R., & Williams, K. D. (2017). When silence is not golden: Why acknowledgment matters even when being excluded. *Personality & Social Psychology Bulletin, 43*(5), 678–692.

Schaafsma, J. (2017). Ostracism from a cross-cultural perspective. In K. D. Williams & S. A. Nida (Eds.), *Ostracism, social exclusion, and rejection* (pp. 177–191). Psychology Press.

Shilling, A. A., & Brown, C. M. (2016). Goal-driven resource redistribution: An adaptive response to social exclusion. *Evolutionary Behavioral Sciences, 10*(3), 149–167.

Smart Richman, L., & Leary, M. R. (2009). Reactions to discrimination, stigmatization, ostracism, and other forms of interpersonal rejection: A multimotive model. *Psychological Review, 116*(2), 365–383.

Smith, A., & Williams, K. D. (2004). RU there? Ostracism by cell phone text messages. *Group Dynamics: Theory, Research, & Practice, 8*(4), 291–301.

Söderberg, P., & Fry, D. P. (2017). Anthropological aspects of ostracism. In K. D. Williams & S. A. Nida (Eds.), *Ostracism, exclusion, and rejection* (pp. 258–272). Routledge.

Sommer, K. L., & Bernieri, F. (2015). Minimizing the pain and probability of rejection: Evidence for relational distancing and proximity seeking within face-to-face interactions. *Social Psychological & Personality Science, 6*(2), 131–139.

Spoor, J. R., & Kelly, J. R. (2004). The evolutionary significance of affect in groups: Communication and group bonding. *Group Processes & Intergroup Relations, 7*(4), 398–412.

Spoor, J., & Williams, K. D. (2007). The evolution of an ostracism detection system. In J. P. Forgas, M. Haselton, & W. von Hippel (Eds.), *The evolution of the social mind: Evolutionary psychology and social cognition* (pp. 279–292). Psychology Press.

Symons, D. (1979). *The evolution of human sexuality*. Oxford University Press.

Tausch, N., Becker, J., Spears, R., Christ, O., Saab, R., Singh, P., & Siddiqui, R. N. (2011). Explaining radical group behaviour: Developing emotion and efficacy routes to normative and non-normative collective action. *Journal of Personality & Social Psychology, 101*(1), 129–148.

Taylor, S. E. (2012). Tend and befriend theory. In P. A. M. Van Lange, A. W. Kruglanski, & E. T. Higgins (Eds.), *Handbook of theories of social psychology* (pp. 32–49). Sage Publications.

Tiedens, L. Z., & Linton, S. (2001). Judgment under emotional certainty and uncertainty: The effects of specific emotions on information processing. *Journal of Personality & Social Psychology, 81*(6), 973–988.

Tuscherer, T., Sacco, D. F., Wirth, J. H., Claypool, H. M., Hugenberg, K., & Wesselmann, E. D. (2016). Responses to exclusion are moderated by its perceived fairness. *European Journal of Social Psychology, 46*(3), 280–293.

Twenge, J. M., Baumeister, R. F., Tice, D. M., & Stucke, T. S. (2001). If you can't join them, beat them: Effects of social exclusion on aggressive behavior. *Journal of Personality & Social Psychology, 81*(6), 1058–1069.

Uskul, A. K., & Over, H. (2014). Responses to social exclusion in cultural context: Evidence from farming and herding communities. *Journal of Personality & Social Psychology, 106*(5), 752–771.

Warburton, W. A., Williams, K. D., & Cairns, D. R. (2006). When ostracism leads to aggression: The moderating effects of control deprivation. *Journal of Experimental Social Psychology, 42*(2), 213–220.

Webber, D., Babush, M., Schori-Eyal, N., Vazeou-Nieuwenhuis, A., Hettiarachchi, M., Bélanger, J. J., Moyano, M., Trujillo, H. M., Gunaratna, R., Kruglanski, A. W., & Gelfand, M. J. (2018). The road to extremism: Field and experimental evidence that significance loss-induced need for closure fosters radicalization. *Journal of Personality & Social Psychology, 114*(2), 270–285.

Weight-Neville, D., & Halafoff, A. (2010). *Terrorism and social exclusion: Misplaced risk-common security*. Edward Elgar.

Wesselmann, E. D., Butler, F. A., Williams, K. D., & Pickett, C. L. (2010). Adding injury to insult: Unexpected rejection leads to more aggressive responses. *Aggressive Behavior, 36*(4), 232–237.

Wesselmann, E. D., Grzybowski, M. R., Steakley-Freeman, D. M., DeSouza, E. R., Nezlek. J. B., & Williams. K. D. (2016). Social exclusion in everyday life. In P. Riva & J. Eck (Eds.) *Social exclusion: Psychological approaches to understanding and reducing its impact* (pp. 3–23). Springer International.

Wesselmann, E. D., Nairne, J. S., & Williams, K. D. (2012). An evolutionary social psychological approach to studying the effects of ostracism. *Journal of Social, Evolutionary, & Cultural Psychology, 6*(3), 309–328.

Wesselmann, E. D., Ren, D., & Williams, K. D. (2015). Motivations for responses to ostracism. *Frontiers in Psychology, 6*, 40. https://doi.org/10.3389/fpsyg.2015.00040

Wesselmann, E. D., & Williams, K. D. (2017). Social life and social death: Inclusion, ostracism, and rejection in groups. *Group Processes & Intergroup Relations, 20*(5), 693–706.

Wesselmann, E. D., Williams, K. D., Ren, D., & Hales, A. H. (2021). Ostracism and solitude. In R. J. Coplan & J. Bowker (Eds.), *A handbook of solitude: Psychological perspectives on social isolation, social withdrawal, and being alone* (2nd ed.; pp. 209–223). Wiley-Blackwell. .

Wesselmann, E. D., Williams, K. D., & Wirth, J. H. (2014). Ostracizing group members who can (or cannot) control being burdensome. *Human Ethology Bulletin, 29*, 82–103.

Wesselmann, E. D., Wirth, J. H., Pryor, J. B., Reeder, G. D., & Williams, K. D. (2013). When do we ostracize? *Social Psychological & Personality Science, 4*(1), 108–115.

Wheaton, A. (2001). *Ostracism and susceptibility to the overtures of socially deviant groups and individuals*. Unpublished honors thesis, Macquarie University, Sydney, NSW.

Williams, K. D. (1997). Social ostracism. In R. M. Kowalski (Ed.), *Aversive interpersonal behaviors* (pp. 133–170). Plenum Press.

Williams, K. D. (2001). *Ostracism: The power of silence*. Guilford Press.

Williams, K. D. (2007). Ostracism: The kiss of social death. *Social & Personality Psychology Compass, 1*(1), 236–247.

Williams, K. D. (2009). Ostracism: Effects of being excluded and ignored. In M. P. Zanna (Ed.), *Advances in experimental social psychology* (Vol. 41, pp. 275–314). Academic Press.

Williams, K. D. (2018, March 28). *List of Cyberball publications*. Retrieved from http://www1.psych.purdue.edu/~willia55/Announce/Cyberball_Articles.htm

Williams, K. D., Cheung, C. K. T., & Choi, W. (2000). Cyberostracism: Effects of being ignored over the Internet. *Journal of Personality & Social Psychology, 79*(5), 748–762.

Williams, K. D., & Sommer, K. L. (1997). Social ostracism by coworkers: Does rejection lead to loafing or compensation? *Personality & Social Psychology Bulletin, 23*(7), 693–706.

Wirth, J. H. (2016). Methods for investigating social exclusion. In P. Riva & J. Eck (Eds.) *Social exclusion: Psychological approaches to understanding and reducing its impact* (pp. 25–47). Springer International.

Wirth, J. H., & Wesselmann, E. D. (2018). Investigating how ostracizing others affects one's self-concept. *Self & Identity, 17*(4), 394–406.

Wolf, W., Levordashka, A., Ruff, J. R., Kraaijeveld, S., Lueckmann, J. M., & Williams, K. D. (2015). Ostracism online: A social media ostracism paradigm. *Behavior Research Methods, 47*, 361–373.

Yaakobi, E., & Williams, K. D. (2016). Ostracism and attachment orientation: Avoidants are less affected in both individualistic and collectivistic cultures. *British Journal of Social Psychology, 55*(1), 162–181.

Yamaguchi, S., Kuhlman, D. M., & Sugimori, S. (1995). Personality correlates of allocentric tendencies in individualist and collectivist cultures. *Journal of Cross-Cultural Psychology, 26*(6), 658–672.

Zadro, L., & Gonsalkorale, K. (2014). Sources of ostracism: The nature and consequences of excluding and ignoring others. *Current Directions in Psychological Science, 23*(2), 93–97.

Zadro, L., Williams, K. D., & Richardson, R. (2004). How low can you go? Ostracism by a computer is sufficient to lower self-reported levels of belonging, control, self-esteem, and meaningful existence. *Journal of Experimental Social Psychology, 40*(4), 560–567.

Zadro, L., Williams, K. D., & Richardson, R. (2005). Riding the "O" train: Comparing the effects of ostracism and verbal dispute on targets and sources. *Group Processes & Intergroup Relations, 8*(2), 125–143.

CHAPTER 55

Natural Selection and Human Emotions

Laura Betzig

Abstract

Natural selection is differential reproduction. Demographic and ethnographic, historical and genetic evidence suggest that, over the course of our evolutionary past, members of *H. sapiens* varied in reproductive success. Selection for emotions and other adaptations underlying intrasexual and intersexual competition should have been strong. In foragers across continents, from Africa to Australia, reproductive variance among women often was limited to single digits, though reproductive variance occasionally reached double digits among men. Those numbers were higher in more sedentary societies. In the first empires, from Asia to the Americas, emperors consistently left behind hundreds of sons; and genetic evidence suggests that the effective breeding population of women was greater than the effective breeding population of men, by a factor of 17 to 1. Adaptations have developed, and have been put to use, in order to promote reproductive success.

Key Words: sexual selection, human evolution, mate choice, differential reproduction, natural selection

All of 13 years after *The Origin of Species* came out, a year after *Sexual Selection and the Descent of Man* went to print, and 33 years after he started to look into the subject, Darwin published his *Expression of the Emotions in Man and Animals*. He compared emotions in animals, aborigines, infants and works of art. And he used those comparisons to argue that, because of their common ancestry, various species, genera, and larger taxonomic groups shared behaviors, as well as morphological traits.

Roughly a century after Darwin, Paul Ekman and his collaborators looked across seven cultures—the United States, Brazil, Argentina, Chile, Japan, the Sadong of Borneo, and the Fore of New Guinea—and found that they shared facial recognition of six human emotions: happiness, surprise, fear, sadness, anger and disgust (Ekman, 1992, 1999; Ekman & Friesen, 1971; Ekman et al., 1983).

Ekman's contemporary, Carroll Izard showed 32 photographs of faces to subjects across another seven societies—American, English, German, Swedish, French, Greek, and Japanese—and found consensus on eight emotional dimensions: interest-excitement, enjoyment-joy, surprise-startle, distress-anguish, disgust-contempt, anger-rage, shame-humiliation, fear-terror (Izard, 1968, 1971; see too Plutchik, 1980, 2002; Cowen & Keltner, 2017). As Darwin argued, feelings are often common across cultures.

A number of emotions have demonstrated social functions (Al-Shawaf et al. 2021; Sznycer et al., 2021). Pride and anger, shame and gratitude are heightened, or lessened, to the extent that a relationship is considered important. Anger cues that one partner doesn't value another enough; gratitude signals that he or she does. Shame lessens the likelihood of being undervalued by partners; pride raises the odds of being valued highly (Sznycer, Xygalatas, Agey, 2018; Sznycer, Xygalatas, Alami, 2018; Sznycer & Lukaszewski, 2019). Envy and jealousy make competitors try harder (Hill & Buss, 2008; Ramachandran & Jalal, 2017). And interactions with partners may be monitored for imbalances: evidence of cheater-detection mechanisms suggests that they are (Cosmides & Tooby, 2015; Delton et al., 2012).

Other emotions directly affect reproduction. They include sexual attraction (Buss 2016), sexual jealousy (Buss 2000), sexual regret (Galperin et al., 2013) and sexual disgust (Al-Shawaf, Lewis, et al., 2015). They include a number of mechanisms promoting maternal-child, or paternal-child, bonding (Hrdy, 1999, 2024). And they include mechanisms promoting kin recognition. Across cultures, association with the same mother, and co-residence with brothers and sisters, help us to decide who our relatives are (Lieberman et al., 2007; Sznycer & Lieberman 2021).

It's been taken for granted that selection for adaptations promoting survival has been, and continues to be, strong. But it's often been assumed that selection for adaptations for finding mates, or for raising descendants, has been less important in the recent past. That assumption is faulty. Genetic, archaeological, ethnographic, and historical evidence suggests that since the end of the Pleistocene, into the current era, differential reproduction has continued across continents, and in some cases has dramatically increased.

Over the past several centuries, as caravans swept across the Silk Road and caravels sailed across the Atlantic, intrepid explorers met brave indigines and described them. Demographers collected censuses of hunters and gatherers in Africa; geneticists tested global DNA samples; ethnographers told stories about families from the Americas to Australia; historians described harems from the first civilizations in Africa and Asia. And it turned out that men with more status almost always had access to more women, and fathered more children (Betzig 1986, 1997, 2012, 2020a, 2020b).

Africa

Humanity began in Africa. Across most of the continent, for hundreds of thousands of years, people wandered around with no more than they could carry, as they foraged in search of food. Exceptions would have included coastal caves, like the ones at South Africa's Pinnacle Point, where food supplies were relatively rich, and it was easier to live a sedentary life (Kelly, 2013; Marean et al., 2007).

Over the past few decades, quantitative data have been collected on hunter-gatherer demography. Fieldworkers have put together censuses in the deserts of Southern Africa, or in the rainforests of Central Africa, or in East Africa, with the Hadza of Lake Eyasi. Few mothers, and few fathers, in those societies had more than 10 children. But variances in completed fertility were consistently smaller for women than for men.

Barry Hewlett first visited the Aka in the middle of Africa in 1973, and revisited more than 20 times over more than 40 years. He found out that the behaviors of Aka men and women overlapped. Aka women, like Aka men, spent all day, almost every day, tracking and trapping game; and both parents fed, cleaned, caressed, kissed, carried, and played with their daughters and sons. But Aka leaders were invariably male. Elephant killers, or *tuma*, were more likely to become authorities, or *kombeti*; and *kombeti* had more wives, and fathered more children, than other men. Sex differences in reproductive success reflected that. The most reproductively successful Aka father had 14 children; the most successful mother had 11. And reproductive variance among women (5.20) was less than reproductive variance among men (8.64) (Hewlett, 1988, 1991, p. 18).

Nick Blurton Jones and Frank Marlowe came to live with the Hadza of Africa's Rift Valley near the Serengeti, in the 1980s and 1990s. Those foragers had a strong egalitarian ethic; but some Hadza hunters had bigger families than others. No man had more than two wives at a time; and fewer than one in 20 had two at once. But men with reputations as better hunters—those who brought in more food every hour, and brought in more food overall—ended up with more wives. "Hunters get more women," was the Hadza consensus. And they fathered more children. The most reproductively successful mothers had 12 children; the most reproductively successful fathers had 16. And reproductive variance among men (14.31) was roughly twice the reproductive variance among women (7.70) (Blurton Jones, 2016, p. 264; Marlowe, 2010).

When Nancy Howell and Richard Lee rode into the Kalahari in the 1960s, they met Ju/'hoan mothers and fathers who chose husbands for their daughters. Candidates who were good with their spears were preferred (Lee, 1979). Poorer hunters were unmarried; better hunters had wives. But nobody over 40 had never been married, and most men over 50 had been married more than twice. The most reproductively successful man in Howell's sample was the father of 12 children, and the most reproductively successful woman had 9. Reproductive variance was low among both women (4.69) and men (8.60) (Howell, 2000; with Cashdan, 1980, and Wiessner, 2002, 2009 on hunting success).

Genetic evidence is consistent. Across contemporary populations, estimates of the breeding sex ratio are consistently biased in favor of women. Autosomal, Y chromosomal, and mitochondrial DNA samples from across continents suggest that fewer males than females have contributed genes to ancestral generations. There seem to have been on the order of two ancestor mothers for every ancestor father. Over most of our evolutionary history as humans, the ratio of breeding women to breeding men has been on the order of 2:1 (Hammer et al. 2008; Lippold et al. 2014).

The Pacific

From one end of the Pacific to the other, islanders lived under chiefs. On smaller islands, with smaller populations, differences in status and family size were limited; on bigger islands, with bigger populations, differences in rank and reproduction were relatively large.

When James Cook stopped at Botany Bay in the spring of 1770, his assessment of the natives was benign. "They live in a Tranquility which is not disturbed by the Inequality of Condition; the Earth and sea of their own accord furnishes them with all things necessary for life" (Cook, [1768–1780] 1955, p. 92). But as it turned out, some Australians were more equal than others. By the time that the anthropologists Merton Hart and Arnold Pilling showed up on Bathurst and Melville Islands off the northern coast, large numbers of women were hoarded by a small number of husbands. Turimpi, born in the 1830s, had sons in the prime of life when Hart came to visit, and had collected a number of spouses. "A complete list of Turimpi's wives, not all of them, living in his household at the same time or necessarily alive at the same time, contains more than 20 women." Other men of Turimpi's generation married 22, 25, or 29 times. "A successful Tiwi, having had no resident wife at all until his late thirties, would accumulate perhaps half a dozen between his late thirties and late forties as his various betrothed wives reached the age of puberty and joined his household, and from then on he was practically certain to accumulate still more" (Hart et al., 1960, p. 20; Goodale, 1971).

At the other end of the Pacific, when Captain Cook sailed into the American Northwest on *HMS Resolution* in the spring of 1788, trades were made with strict honesty on both sides;

but soon afterward, John Jewitt, the 19-year-old armorer from England who followed Cook to Vancouver on the Massachusetts ship *Boston*, saw most of his crew members slaughtered. Jewitt survived and spent better than two years, from March 1803 to July 1805, as the slave of Maquinna, a Nuu-chah-nulth chief. He noted that chiefs hoarded captives in their cedar plank houses, "spoils of war being understood as appertaining to the king," regardless of who captured them. And they hoarded wives. "Chiefs frequently purchase their wives at the age of 8 or 10, to prevent their being engaged by others, though they do not take them from their parents until they are 16" (Jewitt 1815, pp. 172, 177; Cook, [1768–1780] 1955, p. 310; see too Niblack, 1888, and Driver, 1969).

On islands in the middle of the ocean, there were more chiefs. George Turner was sent to Samoa by the London Missionary Society in 1840; *Samoa: A Hundred Years Ago and Long Before* was published a generation later, in 1884. Over the course of more than 40 years, the missionary discovered that Samoan brides brought along a brother's daughter or maid of honor when they went to live with their husbands. "As a matter of etiquette, she must be attended by her complement of one or more young women." A dozen or more wives and concubines could be collected in short order. "In this way a chief, in the course of his lifetime, might be married well on to fifty times" (Turner, 1884, pp. 96–97, 176; Stair, 1897).

Mary Davis Wallis and her husband, a trader in dried sea cucumbers, and a rough contemporary of the missionary George Turner, sailed from Massachusetts to Fiji earlier in the 19th century. Ms. Wallis's journal, *Life in Feejee, or Five Years among the Cannibals*, was printed in 1851. When she first met Ranu Seru, the chief otherwise known as Cakobau, the "Destroyer of Bau," he showed up with a principal wife and several of her woman attendants. Ranu Tanoa, the father of Ranu Seru, was remembered as a collector of women: "He had many wives and much property." He'd once asked Mr. Wallis if Ms. Wallis was his only wife, and was sorry to hear that she was. "He said, 'That is bad, Mr. Wallis, you should have more.' He then became quite animated while enumerating the advantages of polygamy, said that he had one hundred wives, and ended by advising my husband to get an immediate supply'" (Wallis, 1851, pp. 79–80; Toganivalu, 1912, p. 2).

The Americas

Up and down the Americas, hunters and gatherers wandered about in search of animals and plants. Most lived in small groups, with low reproductive variance (Chagnon, 1979, 1988, 2012; Hill & Hurtado, 1996; Hill & Kaplan, 1988; Kramer, 2005). But where resources were consistent and rich—along rivers, lakes, or coasts—reproductive differentials increased. By the 16th century, when conquistadors sailed across the Atlantic from Spain, first to the Valley of Mexico, then to Peru, the emperors they found there had thousands of women, and had fathered hundreds of daughters and sons.

In the Valley of Mexico, on Lake Texcoco, Nezahualcoyotl, or "Fasting Coyote"—poet, architect, and friend of the *tlatoani*, or ruler of the Aztec empire, Moctezuma I—had 300 rooms in his palace, where his women raised 60 sons and 57 daughters. Nezahualpilli, or "Fasting Boy," his successor, kept 2,000 concubines (Alva Ixtlilxóchitl [1979], *Nezahualcoyotl Acolmitztli*, 4.2). Generations later, when Hernán Cortés came to Tenochtitlán, the Spanish remembered that the Aztecs were keen to fight against Moctezuma II—a great-grandson of Moctezuma I—because so many of his tribute collectors had carried off their daughters and wives. "In Moctezuma's own palaces very fine cloths were woven by those chieftains' daughters whom he kept as mistresses" (Díaz [2003] *Discovery*, p. 60). Emperors collected maize and other staples, raw cotton and textiles, or were offered women: "Provinces that lacked foods and clothing paid in maidens" (Durán [1994], *History*, p. 25; see too Sahagún [1954], *Florentine Codex*, p. 8).

After Francisco Pizarro took Peru in 1532, some of the Jesuits remembered how consorts were collected as tribute: "A judge or commissioner named by the Inka was dispatched to each province, and his only responsibility was this matter of collecting girls" (Cobo [1979], *History*, 2.34). Others, conquistadores, wrote about houses of virgins set up all over the empire: "For none of these lords who did not have more than 700 women for the service of their house and for their pleasure, so that they all had many children" (Cieza de León [1959], *Incas*, 2.10). Garcilaso de la Vega, the son of a Spanish lord and an Inca noble, remembered that Pachacuti, the "World Changer," left 300 or 400 children behind; that his follower Yupanqui left 250 or 300; that Huaina Cápac left 200 or 300 daughters and sons (Garcilaso [1987] *Royal Commentaries*, 6.34, 7.26, 9.15, with Betanzos [1996], *Narrative*, 1.2). And Huamán Poma de Ayala, another Inca noble, added that access to women was strictly prescribed by law. Principal persons got 50, *hunu kurakas* (heads of 10,000 households) got 30, *waranqa kurakas* (heads of 1,000) got 15, *pachaka kurakas* (heads of 100) got 8, *chunka kamayuqs* (heads of 10) got 5, and the "poor Indian" took whatever was left (Poma de Ayala [2009], *Chronicle*, 134).

Asia

Oral histories were passed down for generations before they were written into the Torah. Some told the story of Abraham, his ancestors, and his descendants. Others told stories about judges, or stories about kings. They remembered how the patriarchs, who had three or four women, were followed by judges, who had dozens of them, who were followed by kings, who collected as many as a thousand. Contemporary kings of Egypt, Assyria, Babylon, and Persia did the same (Betzig, 2005, 2009).

To be fruitful and multiply was the lord's order. "Fill the earth and subdue it," he told Adam (Genesis 1:28). "Bring forth abundantly," he told Noah and his sons (Genesis 9:1, 7). "I will make of you a great nation," he told Abraham (Genesis 12:2). Their descendants would be like the dust of the earth, or as the stars of heaven, too many to count (Genesis 13:16, 15:5, 16:10, 17:2–6).

Abraham, a "Father of Multitudes," had sons by three women. There was Isaac, his only heir, by Sarah, his half-sister (Genesis 20:12, 21:3, 25:5–6). There were six sons—Zimran, Jokshan, Medan, Mid'ian, Ishbak and Shuah—by Keturah, married after Sarah had died (Genesis 25:1–2, 1 Chronicles 1:32). And there was Ishmael, his first son, by Hagar, who was Sarah's Egyptian maid (Genesis 16:1–2, 11–16). There would have been other servants. No fewer than 318 trained warriors were born in Abraham's house (Genesis 12:16, 14:14).

Sarah's son Isaac took just one wife. He picked Rebekah, the granddaughter of his father's brother, and she gave him twin sons (Genesis 25:20–26). Esau came first, then his brother Jacob stole his birthright from him (Genesis 25:21–34).

And Jacob went on to father children by four women. Rachel, who was Jacob's mother's brother's daughter, the love of his life, was the mother of two of his sons, Joseph and Benjamin. Leah, who was Rachel's older sister, was the mother of a daughter, Dinah, and of another six sons: Reuben, Simeon, Levi, Judah, Is'sachar and Zeb'ulun. Bilhah, who was Rachel's maid, was the mother of Dan and Naphtali. And Zilpah, who was Leah's servant, was the mother of Gad and Asher. So Jacob had 12 sons in all (Genesis 29:17, 30:21, 35:22–26).

Jacob's son Joseph led his family into Egypt, where they stayed for generations; then Moses led them back to the Jordan, where the lord raised up judges. Gideon had 70 sons by his wives, and at least one son, Abim'elech, by a concubine (Judges 8:30–31, 9:2–18). He was followed by Jair, who had 30 sons (Judges 10:3–4); and by Ibzan, who fathered 30 sons and

30 daughters (Judges 12:8–9); and by Abdon, who had 40 sons and 30 grandsons (Judges 12:13–14). Samson came next, "and the Lord blessed him," but we don't know how much (Judges 13:24).

David, who ruled over a united kingdom, collected more women. There were Ahinoam, Abigail, and Michal—who was a daughter of Saul; there were Maacah, Haggith, Abital, Elgah, and Bathsheba—who was the wife of Uriah. There was just one named daughter, Tamar, but there were 19 named sons (2 Samuel 5:14–16, 1 Chronicles 3:1–9, 14:3–7). And there would have been other children. David lived in an ivory palace, wrapped in myrrh- and cassia-scented garments, entertained by stringed instruments, surrounded by virgin companions and ladies of honor (Psalms 45). He loved to uncover himself and dance in front of his servants (2 Samuel 6:20). He collected concubines from Hebron, then from Jerusalem (2 Samuel 5:13, 20:3). And he was provided with girls to the day he died. When David was advanced in years, a virgin was brought to him. "Let her lie in your bosom, that my lord the king may be warm" (1 Kings 1:1–4).

David's son, Solomon, put up a Hall of Pillars, a Hall of the Throne, a House of the Forest of Lebanon, and a bronze and cedar palace of his own (1 Kings 5–7). Then he filled that palace with women. Solomon took just one wife from Egypt, who got her own house; but he added 699 Moabites, Ammonites, Edomites, Sidonians, Hittites, and so on, "far more precious than jewels" (Proverbs 31:10). Then he added 300 concubines, and he probably added a few chattels. "I bought male and female slaves, and had slaves who were born in my house" (1 Kings 11:1–3; Proverbs 31:10; Ecclesiastes 2:7–8).

Solomon's son, Rehobo'am, who became king of Judah, had 18 wives and 60 concubines, who bore 60 daughters and 28 sons (2 Chronicles 11:21). And Ahab, who later became Israel's king, made Jezebel his queen, and had 70 sons in Samaria alone (2 Kings 10:1–7).

There were other kings across North Africa and the Near East. When, in the 13th century, the 19th-dynasty pharaoh, Ramesses II, took a Hittite bride, the last of his eight or more wives, he added her limitless slaves. And they bore a number of sons. In tomb KV5 in the Valley of the Kings at Thebes, there are chambers for dozens of them. And on reliefs and ostraca and scarabs from all over his empire, the names of dozens of "king's sons of his body" survive from his 67-year reign. There would have been roughly as many daughters (Fisher, 2001; Weeks, 2006).

More than four centuries later, when the Assyrian king Sennacherib laid siege to the fortified cities of Judah, Hezekiah stripped gold off the temple doorposts, and found silver in the treasuries of his house; then he sent 300 talents of silver with 30 talents of gold, and threw in "his daughters, his harem, his male and female musicians," to a palace on the Tigris (2 Kings 18:13–19:36, 2 Chronicles 32:1–22, Isaiah 36:1–37:37; Sennacherib [1989], *Annals*, 3rd campaign). Esarhaddon, who was Sennacherib's son, raided a harem from the king of Egypt (Esarhaddon [1927], *Senjirli Stele*). And Ashurbanipal, who was Esarhaddon's son, brought home chariots, coaches, palanquins, and concubines when he made war on his brother Shamash-shum-ukin, the Babylonian king (Ashurbanipal [1927], *Rassam Cylinder*, 6th campaign).

In the same way, and at around the same time, when Nebuchadnezzar II of Babylon set siege to Jerusalem in 597, he carried off the treasures of the palace and the treasures of the temple, with all the princes and all the craftsmen, and captured "the king's mother, the king's wives, his officials, and the chief men of the land" from Judah's king Jehoi'achin (2 Kings 24:13–15; Jeremiah 28:14). And when Nebuchadnezzar laid siege to Jerusalem again, he took metal vessels from the temple, "and all your wives and your sons" from King Zedeki'ah, and burned Jerusalem with fire. "Behold, all the women left in the house of the king of Judah were being led out to the princes of the king of Babylon" (2 Kings 25:15; Jeremiah 38:22–33).

In the story of Esther, the Persian ruler Ahasuerus, probably the 5th-century Xerxes I, issued an order to "let beautiful young virgins be sought out for the king," to be basted for six months with myrrh and another six months with spices, then herded into the palace. "In the evening she went, and in the morning she came back to the second harem in custody of Sha-ash'gaz the king's eunuch who was in charge of the concubines." Esther wasn't to go in to the king again, unless Ahasuerus delighted in her, and summoned her by name (Esther 2:2, 12–14). This Xerxes's great-grandson, Artaxerxes II, is supposed to have fathered 115 illegitimate *sons*, besides three legitimate ones (Justin [1996], *Epitome*, 10.1–3). And when this Artaxerxes's grand-nephew, Darius III, went to war with Alexander the Great, he took 200 *propinquorum* (close kin) and 15,000 *cognati* (remoter kin) along, with the queen mother, the queen, and 365 female companions (Diodorus [1970], *Library* 17.77.6–7; Curtius [1971], *History* 3.3.23, 6.6.8).

Autochthonous cultures east of Alexander's conquests had always been polygynous. Mauyra emperors, followed by Gupta emperors, supported hundreds or thousands of women, in palaces stocked with peacocks to eat poisonous snakes, on the Ganges and Indus. And in China, emperors counted Honored, Gracious, Worthy, Pure, Wholesome, and Reverent Consorts by the thousands, or tens of thousands, or hundreds of thousands, and left behind dozens of known sons (Betzig, 2020a, 2020b, 2021b, 2024).

Genetic evidence is consistent again. Y chromosome and mitochondrial DNA sequences collected on every inhabited continent suggest a human population bottleneck, at around 8,000 to 4,000 years ago, around the origin of farming, in and around the Near East. More or less at the origins of civilization, more or less as the first words were written, the effective breeding population among women became as high as *17 times* the effective breeding population among men (Karmin et al., 2015; Poznik et al., 2016; see too Zerjal et al., 2003).

Discussion

For the benefit of his children and grandchildren, toward the end of his life, Darwin put together a short memoir. It included a few thoughts about human emotions. Darwin conceded that the world was full of unpleasantness, but contended that happiness prevailed. "If all the individuals of any species were habitually to suffer to an extreme degree, they would neglect to propagate their kind." Negative sensations—pain, hunger, thirst, fear—might help individuals compete with each other, and increase in number. Positive sensations—associated eating and drinking and propagation of the species—might accomplish the same ends. But as far as the autobiographer was concerned: "Pain or suffering of any kind, if long continued, causes depression and lessens the power of action; yet it is well adapted to make a creature guard itself against any great or sudden evil. Pleasurable sensations, on the other hand may be long continued without any depressing effect; on the contrary they stimulate the whole system to increased action" (Darwin [1876] 1983, pp. 51–52).

Most evidence suggests that in *Homo sapiens*, as in other species, adaptations develop in present environments much as they did in the past, and that adaptive behavior is the result (Clutton-Brock, 1988; Ellis, 1995). Emotions and other mechanisms take shape in response to familiar environmental prompts; and they function, as they did in the evolutionary past, to promote not just survival, but reproductive success (Tinbergen, 1963; Betzig, 1989).

Demographic and ethnographic, historical, and genetic evidence suggests that, for most of the 200,000 or more years since *H. sapiens* first walked on earth, individuals have competed to reproduce. In forager societies, in sub-Saharan Africa and beyond, family sizes were usually small, though reproductive variance among women was consistently lower than reproductive variance among men. In more sedentary groups, where resources were continuous and rich, differences in status, resource access, and reproductive success increased. And in the first states, where abundance was surrounded by dearth, the subjected were reproductively suppressed, but emperors collected hundreds or thousands of women and fathered hundreds of sons. None of that changed anytime soon. Sexual access in the Roman empire, across the European Middle Ages, and into the early modern period, remained a prerogative of the rich. It only eroded over the past few centuries, with the Age of Exploration and rise of the Commons (Betzig, 1992, 1995, 2002, 2024).

Selection for underlying adaptations should have been strong (Cosmides & Tooby, 2000; Tooby & Cosmides, 2008). Emotions across contemporary cultures—from anger to gratitude to grief to pride, from sexual attraction to sexual jealousy to sexual disgust, from maternal to paternal affection for children and grandchildren and other relatives—should be designed to solve problems related to survival *and* reproductive success (Al-Sharaf, Conroy-Beam, et al., 2015; Al-Shawaf & Lewis, 2017). Until remarkably recently, they seem to have been.

Differential reproduction didn't end with the Pleistocene. Autosomal, Y chromosome, and mitochondrial DNA samples collected across continents suggest that breeding sex ratios in *H. sapiens* have been consistently biased in favor of women. Across most of our evolutionary history as humans, that ratio has probably been on the order of 2:1. And reproductive differentials dramatically *increased* after we settled down. A population bottleneck shows up at around 4,000–8,000 years ago, in sedentary societies, at the origin of farming, in and around the Near East. Thousands of years after the Pleistocene ended, after the Holocene began, the effective breeding population among women was as high as *17 times* the effective breeding population among men.

Reproductive competition in *H. sapiens* has continued into contemporary times. Successful hunters and gatherers, and horticulturalists, and farmers—in the ethnographic, archaeological, and historical records—have collected more and better partners, and brought up more descendants. In Africa—from the Ju/'hoansi on the Kalahari, to the Aka of the Congo Basin, to the Hadza of Lake Eyasi—good hunters competed to collect on the order of 10 women, and fathered on the order of 10 children. Big men on Pacific Islands—from the people James Cook came across in the American Northwest, to people who were friendly with missionaries in Samoa and Fiji, to the people anthropologists studied on Bathurst and Melville Islands off the north Australian coast—hoarded as many as 50 or 100 women, and probably fathered dozens of children. And emperors—from the Andean Incas, to the Aztecs of Lake Texcoco; from Ramesses II in Egypt, to David's son Solomon in Israel; to Sennacherib and his sons and grandsons on the Tigris and beyond—had sexual access to hundreds of thousands of women, and fathered hundreds of daughters and sons.

Human emotions, and an unfathomable number of other adaptations, should have been shaped over the course of generations by natural selection. Where the conditions under which they have evolved are enough like the conditions under which they are expressed, adaptations should promote staying alive and raising descendants. Up to the past few centuries at least, that seems to have been the case.

References

Al-Shawaf, L., Conroy-Beam, D., Asao, K. & Buss, D. (2015). Human emotions: An evolutionary psychological perspective. *Emotion Review, 8*, 173–186.

Al-Shawaf, L. & Lewis, D. (2017). Evolutionary psychology and the emotions. In V. Ziegler-Hill & T. Shackelford (Eds.), *Encyclopedia of personality and individual differences* (pp. 1–10). Sage Publications.

Al-Shawaf, L., Lewis, D., Barbaro, N. & Wehbe, Y. S. (2021). The products of evolution: Conceptual distinctions, evolutionary criteria, critical examples. In T. Shackelford (Ed.), *SAGE handbook of evolutionary psychology* (pp. 1–40). Sage Publications.

Al-Shawaf, L., Lewis, D. & Buss, D. (2015). Disgust and mating strategy. *Evolution & Human Behavior, 36*, 199–205.

Alva Ixtlilxóchitl, F. de. (1979). *Nezahualcoyotl Acolmitztli: Selección de textos*. Estado de México.

Ashurbanipal. (1927). *Rassam Cylinder*. In *Ancient records of Assyria and Babylon*, (D. Luckenbill, Trans.). University of Chicago Press.

Betanzos, J. de. (1996). *Narrative of the Incas* (R. Hamilton & D. Buchanan, Trans.). University of Texas Press.

Betzig, L. L. (1986). *Despotism and differential reproduction: A Darwinian view of history*. Aldine de Gruyter.

Betzig, L. L. (1989). Rethinking human ethology: A response to some recent critiques. *Ethology and Sociobiology, 10*, 315–324.

Betzig, L. L. (1992). Roman polygyny. *Ethology & Sociobiology, 13*, 309–349.

Betzig, L. L. (1995). Medieval monogamy. *Journal of Family History, 20*, 181–215.

Betzig, L. L. (1997). People are animals. In L. Betzig (Ed.), *Human nature: A critical reader* (pp. 1–17). Oxford University Press.

Betzig, L. L. (2002). British polygyny. In M. Smith (Ed.), *Human biology and history* (pp. 30–97). Taylor and Francis.

Betzig, L. L. (2005). Politics as sex: The Old Testament case. *Evolutionary Psychology, 3*, 326–346.

Betzig, L. L. (2009). The Bible as history and natural history. In R. Goldberg (Ed.), *Judaism in biological perspective* (pp. 42–61). Paradigm Press.

Betzig, L. L. (2012). Means, variances and ranges in reproductive success: Comparative evidence. *Evolution and Human Behavior, 33*, 309–317.

Betzig, L. L. (2014). Eusociality in history. *Human Nature, 25*, 80–99.

Betzig, L. L. (2016). Mating systems. In T. Shackelford & V. Weeks-Shackelford (Eds.), *Encyclopedia of evolutionary social science* (pp. 1–11). Springer.

Betzig, L. L. (2020a). Eusociality in humans. In L. Workman, W. Reader, & J. Barkow (Eds.), *Cambridge handbook of evolutionary perspectives on human behavior* (pp. 37–46). Cambridge University Press.

Betzig, L. L. (2020b). The future is the past. In S. Kanazawa and Y-T. Lee (Eds.), *What's the next big question in evolutionary psychology? Evolutionary behavioral sciences* (Vol. 14, pp. 311–315). Evolutionary Behavioral Sciences. [special issue]

Betzig, L. L. (2021a). Differential reproduction. In T. Shackelford (Ed.), *Sage handbook of evolutionary psychology* (pp. 56–69). Sage Publications.

Betzig, L. L. (2021b). Evolution and history. In T. Shackelford (Ed.), *Sage handbook of evolutionary psychology* (pp. 443–459). London: Sage Publications.

Betzig, L. L. (2024). *The badge of lost innocence: A history of the West*, in preparation.

Blurton Jones, N. B. (2016). *Demography and evolutionary ecology of Hadza hunter-gatherers*. Cambridge University Press.

Buss, D. (2000). *The dangerous passion: Why jealousy is as necessary as love and sex*. Free Press.

Buss, D. (2016). *The evolution of desire: Strategies of human mating* (rev. ed.). Basic Books.

Cashdan, E. (1980). Egalitarianism among hunters and gatherers. *American Anthropologist, 82*, 116–120.

Chagnon, N. A. (1979). Is reproductive success equal in egalitarian societies? In N. Chagnon & W. Irons (Eds.), *Evolutionary biology and human social behavior* (pp. 85–132). Duxbury Press.

Chagnon, N. A. (1988). Life histories, blood revenge, and warfare in a tribal population. *Science, 238*, 985–992.

Chagnon, N. (2012). *Yanomamö: The fierce people* (6th ed.). Holt Rinehart and Winston.

Cieza de León, P. (1959). *The Incas* (H. de Onis, Trans.). University of Oklahoma Press.

Clutton-Brock, T. H. (1988). *Reproductive success*. Cambridge University Press.

Cobo, Bernabé. (1979). *History of the Inca Empire* (R. Hamilton, Trans.). University of Texas Press.

Cook, James. ([1768–1780] 1955). *The journals of Captain James Cook on his voyages of discovery* (J. C. Beaglehole, Ed.). Hakluyt Society.

Cosmides, L., & Tooby, J. (2000). Evolutionary psychology and the emotions. In M. Lewis & J. M. Haviland-Jones (Eds.), *Handbook of emotions* (2nd ed., pp. 91–115). Guilford.

Cosmides, L., & Tooby, J. (2015). Adaptations for reasoning about social exchange. In D. Buss (Ed.), *Handbook for evolutionary psychology* (2nd ed., pp. 625–668). Wiley.

Cowan, A. S., & Keltner, D. (2017). Self-report captures 27 distinct categories of emotion bridged by continuous gradients. *Proceedings of the National Academy of Sciences, 114*, E7900–E7909.

Curtius, Q. (1971). *History of Alexander* (J. C. Rolfe, Trans.). Heinemann.

Darwin, C. R. (1872). *The expression of the emotions in man and animals*. Murray.

Darwin, C. R. ([1876] 1958). *Autobiography* (N. Barlow, Ed.). Collins.

Delton, A. W., Cosmides, L., Guemo, M., Robertson, T. E., & Tooby, J. (2012). The psychosematics of free riding: Dissecting the architecture of a moral concept. *Journal of Personality and Social Psychology, 102*, 1252–1270.
Díaz, B. (2003). *The discovery and conquest of Mexico, 1517–1521* (A. P. Maudslay, Trans.). Da Capo Press.
Diodorus Siculus. (1970). *Library of history* (C. H. Oldfather, Trans.). Heinemann.
Driver, H. (1969). *Indians of North America* (2nd ed.). University of Chicago Press.
Dúran, D. (1994). *History of the Indians of New Spain* (D. Heyden, Trans.). University of Oklahoma Press.
Ekman, P. (1992). Are there basic emotions? *Psychologoical Review, 99*, 550–553.
Ekman, P. (1999). Basic emotions. In T. Dalgleish & M. Power (Eds.), *Handbook of cognition and emotion* (pp. 45–60). Wiley.
Ekman, P., & Friesen, W. (1971). Constants across cultures in the face and emotion. *Journal of Personality & Social Psychology, 17*, 124–129.
Ekman, P., Levenson, R., & Friesen, W. (1983). Autonomic nervous system activity distinguishes between emotions. *Science, 221*, 1208–1210.
Ellis, L. (1995). Dominance and reproductive success among nonhuman animals: A cross-species comparison. *Ethology & Sociobiology, 16*, 257–333.
Esarhaddon. (1927). *Senjirli stele*. In *Ancient records of Assyria and Babylon* (D. Luckenbill, Trans.) (Vol. 2, pp. 224–228). University of Chicago Press.
Fisher, M. (2001). *The sons of Ramesses II*. Harrassowitz.
Galperin, A., Haselton, M. G., Frederick, D. A., Poore, J., von Hippel, W., Buss, D. M., & Gonzaga, G. C. (2013). Sexual regret: Evidence for evolved sex differences. *Archives of Sexual Behavior, 42*, 1145–1161.
Garcilaso de la Vega. (1987). *Royal commentaries of the Incas* (H. Livermore, Trans.). University of Texas Press.
Goodale, J. C. (1971). *Tiwi wives*. University of Washington Press.
Hammer, M. F., Mendez, F. L., Cox, M. P., Woerner, A. E., & Wall, J. D. (2008). Sex-biased evolutionary forces shape genomic patterns of human diversity. *PLoS Genetics, 4*(9), e1000202.
Hart, C. W. M., Pilling, A. R., & Goodale, J. C. (1960). *The Tiwi of North Australia*. Holt, Rinehart and Winston.
Hewlett, B. S. (1988). Sexual selection and paternal investment among Aka pygmies. In L. Betzig, M. Borgerhoff Mulder, & P. W. Turke (Eds.), *Human reproductive behavior* (pp. 263–276). Cambridge University Press.
Hewlett, B. S. (1991). *Intimate fathers: The nature and context of Aka Pygmy paternal infant care*. University of Michigan Press.
Hill, K., & Hurtado, A. M. (1996). *Ache life history*. Aldine.
Hill, K., & Kaplan, H. (1988). Tradeoffs in male and female reproductive strategies among the Ache. In L. Betzig, M. Borgerhoff Mulder, & P. W. Turke (Eds.), *Human reproductive behavior* (pp. 277–306). Cambridge University Press.
Hill, S. E., & Buss, D. M. (2008). The evolutionary psychology of envy. In R. H. Smith (Ed.), *Envy: Theory and research* (pp. 60–70). Oxford University Press.
Howell, N. (2000). *Demography of the Dobe !Kung*. Aldine-de Gruyter.
Hrdy, S. B. (1999). *Mother nature: A history of mothers, infants, and natural selection*. Pantheon.
Hrdy, S. B. (2024). *Father Time*. Princeton University Press.
Izard, C. (1968). *The emotions as a culture-common framework of motivational experiences and communicative cues*. Office of Naval Research.
Izard, C. (1971). *The face of emotion*. Appleton.
Jewitt, J. R. (1815). *A narrative of adventures and sufferings*. Seth Richards.
Justin. (1996). *Epitome of the Philippic history* (J. Yardley, Trans.). Scholars Press.
Karmin, M., Saag, L., Vicente, M., Wilson, M. A., Jarve, M., Talas, U. G., Rootsi, S., Ilumae, A-M., Magi, R., Mitt, M., Pagani, L., Puurand, T., Faltyskova, Z., Clemente, F., Cardona, A., Metspalu, E., Sahakayan, H., Yunusbayev, B., Hudjashov, G., . . . Kivisild, T. (2015). A recent bottleneck of Y chromosome diversity coincides with a global change in culture. *Genome Research, 25*, 459–466.
Kelly, R. L. (2013). *The lifeways of hunter-gatherers: The foraging spectrum*. Cambridge University Press.
Kramer, K. L. (2005). *Mayan children: Helpers at the farm*. Harvard University Press.
Lee, R. B. (1979). *The !Kung San*. Cambridge University Press.
Lieberman, D., Tooby, J., & Cosmides, L. (2007). The architecture of human kin detection. *Nature, 445*, 727–731.
Lippold, S., Xu, H., Ko, A., Li, M., Renaud, G., Butthof, A., Schroder, R. & Stoneking, M. (2014). Human paternal and maternal demographic histories: Insights from high-resolution Y chromosome and mtDNA sequences. *Investigative Genetics, 5*, 13–30.
Marean, C. W. Bar-Matthews, M., Bernatchez, J., Fisher, E., Goldberg, P., Herries, A. I. R., Jacobs, Z., Jerardino, A., Karkanas, P., Minichillo, T., Nilssen, P. J., Thompson, E., Watts, I., & Williams, H. M. (2007). Early human use of marine resources and pigment in South Africa during the Middle Pleistocene. *Nature, 449*, 905–908.

Marlowe, F. W. (2010). *The Hadza hunter-gatherers of Tanzania*. University of California Press.
Niblack, A. P. (1888). *The Coast Indians of Southern Alaska and Northern British Columbia*. National Museum.
Plutchik, R. (1980). A psychoevolutionary theory of emotions. *Social Science Information, 21*, 529–553.
Plutchik, R. (2002). *Emotions and life: Perspectives from psychology, biology and evolution*. APA.
Poma de Ayala, F. (2009). *The first new chronicle of good government* (R. Hamilton, Trans.). University of Texas Press.
Poznik, G. Xue, Y., Mendez, F. L., Willems, T. F., Massaia, A., Wilson, M. A., Ayub, Q., McCarthy, S. A., Narechania, A., Kashin, S., Chen, Y., Banerjee, R., Rodriguez-Flores, J. L., Cerezo, M., Shao, H., Gymerk, M., Malhotra, A., Louzada, S., Desalle, R., . . . Tyler-Smith, C. (2016). Punctuated bursts in human male demography inferred from 1,244 worldwide Y-chromosome sequences. *Nature Genetics, 48*, 593–601.
Ramachandran, V. S., & Jalal, B. (2017). The evolutionary psychology of envy and jealousy. *Frontiers in Psychology, 8*, 1619. doi: 10.3389/fpsyg.2017.01619
Sahagún, B. de. (1954). *Florentine codex* (A. Anderson & C. Dibble, Eds.). School of American Research.
Sennacherib. (1989). *Annals*. In *Ancient records of Assyria and Babylon*. (D. Luckenbill, Trans.) (Vol. 2, pp. 115–128). University of Chicago Press.
Sznycer, D., Xygalatas, D., Agey, E., & Tooby, J. (2018). Cross-cultural invariances in the architecture of shame. *Proceedings of the National Academy of Sciences, 115*, 9702–9707.
Sznycer, D., Xygalatas, D., Alami, S., & Tooby, J. (2018). Invariances in the architecture of pride across small-scale societies. *Proceedings of the National Academy of Sciences, 115*, 8322–8327.
Sznycer, D., & Lukaszewski, A. W. (2019). The emotion-valuation constellation: Multiple emotions are governed by a common grammar of social valuation. *Evolution and Human Behavior, 40*, 395–404.
Sznycer, D., Sell, A. & Lieberman, D. (2021). Forms and functions of the social emotions. *Current Directions in Psychological Sciences, 30*(4). https://mail.google.com/mail/u/0/?tab=wm&ogbl#sent/FMfcgzGwJmFWtFhQPgthzbWpRllsSVjw
Stair, J. B. (1897). *Old Samoa*. The Religious Tract Society.
Tinbergen, N. (1963). On aims and methods of ethology. *Zeitscrift fur Tierpsychologie, 20*, 410–433.
Toganivalu, D. (1912). Ratu Cakobau, translated by G. Beauclerc. *Transactions of the Fijian Society, 1*, 1–12.
Tooby, J., & Cosmides, L. (2008). The evolutionary psychology of the emotions and their relationship to internal regulatory variables. In M. Lewis, J. M. Haviland-Jones, & L. F. Barrett (Eds.), *Handbook of the emotions* (3rd ed., pp. 114–137). Guilford Press.
Turner, G. (1884). *Samoa, a hundred years ago and long before*. Macmillan.
Vatsayana. (1964). *Kamasutra* (R. Burton, Trans.). Penguin.
Wallis, M. D. (1851). *Life in Feejee, or five years among the cannibals*. Heath.
Weeks, K. (2006). *KV5: A preliminary report on the excavation of the tomb of the sons of Rameses II in the Valley of the Kings*. American University in Cairo Press.
Wiessner, P. (2002). Hunting, healing, and Hxaro exchange: A long term perspective on !Kung (Ju/'hoansi) large-game hunting. *Evolution and Human Behavior, 23*, 1–30.
Wiessner, P. (2009). Parent-offspring conflict in marriage: Implications for social evolution and material culture among the Ju/'hoansi bushmen. In S. Shennan (Ed.), *Pattern and process in cultural evolution* (pp. 251–264). University of California Press.
Zerjal, T. Xue, Y., Bertorelle, G., Spencer Wells, R., Bao, W., Zhu, S., Qamar, R., Ayub, Q., Mohyuddin, A., Fu, S., Li, P., Yuldasheva, N., Ruzibakiev, R., Xu, J., Shu, Q., Du, R., Yang, H., Hurles, M. E., Robinson, E., Gerelsaikhan, T., Dashnyam, B., Qasim Medhi, S., & Tyler-Smith, C. (2003). The genetic legacy of the Mongols. *American Journal of Human Genetics, 72*, 717–721.

CHAPTER 56

Evolution, Emotions, and the American Legal System

Keelah E. G. Williams and Carlton Patrick

Abstract

Emotions are embedded in the law—explicitly in statutes, legal opinions, and jury instructions, as well as implicitly in the minds of legal actors. The aim of the law is to regulate behavior; to do so, the law relies on behavioral models and assumptions about the human mind. This chapter introduces an evolutionary approach to emotions in the law, highlighting its descriptive and normative utility in three legal contexts: determining how one's own emotions shape legal decision-making; evaluating how the emotional experiences of others influences their behavior and legal culpability; and the legislative translation of emotions into legal and social policy. Within the legal sphere, an evolutionary approach provides a coherent framework for understanding the causal influences and cognitive mechanics of emotions. In doing so, an evolutionary perspective provides descriptive clarity, highlights novel explanations for legally relevant behavior, and provides insights that may inform normative debates in the law.

Key Words: evolutionary psychology, emotion, law, legal system, behavior

---

Let not warm hearts betray heads that should be cool.
—Herman Melville, *Billy Bud, Sailor*, 1924

Emotional responses can be strong, but reason should underlie a verdict.
—United States v. Bonds, US Court of Appeals for the Seventh Circuit, 2019

Emotions—once thought antithetical to rational, reasoned legal discourse—are engrained in the law. Emotions are explicitly present in statutes, legal opinions, and jury instructions, as well as implicitly in the minds of legal actors: offenders, victims, judges, jurors, lawyers, and legislators. Consider murder, the crime in which a defendant intentionally caused the death of another person. Emotions can aggravate a murder (as when animosity toward a member of a protected group spurred a "hate" crime, or when the defendant's actions were so "vile" as to merit the death penalty). But emotions can also mitigate a murder (as when the defendant acted in the "heat of passion"), excuse murder (as under certain insanity standards, wherein "extreme emotional disturbance" resulted in a total loss of self-control), or even justify it (as when "fear" for one's life drove the defendant to defend themselves using deadly force). Even the most famous of legal phrases—*guilty*—references an emotion.

Yet the law's relationship with emotions has historically been somewhat antagonistic, largely due to a misunderstanding of what emotions are and how they affect cognition and behavior. It is only relatively recently that the law has come to embrace, rather than reject, emotion, and to begin to incorporate knowledge from psychological science in its understanding of emotion. Despite these inroads, significant room exists for legal scholars to integrate the theoretically coherent and generative framework of evolutionary psychological science in pursuit of a better understanding of emotions and the law. There is much to be gained in doing so: in order to successfully regulate human behavior, the law must rely on behavioral models grounded in science rather than folk psychology and intuition (e.g., Jones, 1999). To the extent that the law is based on faulty or incomplete premises, it risks promulgating rules that are inefficient, ineffective, or potentially delegitimizing in the eyes of society (Patrick, 2016). An evolutionary perspective on emotions is therefore useful to the law for its ability to provide deep, theoretically grounded insights into the causes of human behavior, as well as the role that emotions play in producing and shaping behavior.

The aim of this chapter is not to provide a comprehensive review of the (somewhat limited) literature that touches on evolution, emotions, and the law. Rather, we focus on specific examples that demonstrate the power of an evolutionary perspective for understanding the causes and effects of emotions in legal contexts. We begin by providing a brief review of the history of emotions in law and the shifting attitudes toward understanding and embracing emotions. We then articulate the broader role of emotions in law—i.e., why the law cares about emotions and stands to benefit from greater knowledge of their catalysts and consequences. We introduce an evolutionary approach to emotions in law, highlighting its descriptive and normative utility in three legal contexts: determining how one's own emotions shape legal decision-making; evaluating how the emotional experiences of others influences their behavior and legal culpability; and the legislative translation of emotions into legal and social policy. Finally, we conclude with a summative comment on the benefits of adopting an evolutionary approach to understanding emotions and the law.

History of Law and Emotions

Much of the law is formed through an iterative process in which previous discourse constrains or shapes later doctrine. As such, an understanding of the history of law and emotions is helpful for grasping the contemporary state of affairs—in particular, recognizing vestiges of outmoded thinking despite significant advances in our scientific understanding of emotions. Put simply, the law is often resistant and slow to change. This is especially the case for long-standing misconceptions such as the artificial dichotomization of reason and emotion.

Historically, legal philosophers have conceptualized reason and emotion as two separate and sometimes competing forces. Reason, referring to rational thought, was linked to the mind, whereas emotion, referring to intuition and physiological reactions, was linked to the body or the otherworldly "psyche" (Descartes, [1641] 2008). Plato was a proponent of this view, conceptualizing reason as the charioteer attempting to control two horses (representing noble and destructive passions, respectively; Plato, 1997). Similarly, Immanuel Kant viewed rationality as the exercise of reason in service of controlling one's "pathological" emotions (Kant, [1797] 1983). David Hume also partitioned emotions and reason, although he gave the controlling reins to emotions—arguing that we act on our emotions and then use reason post hoc to judge and justify our actions (Hume, [1739] 1969).

Law, which favors legal discourse and logical inference from premise to conclusion, historically cast emotions as an interruptive and undesirable intruder to this process. Patrick (2015) argues that one reason why this perceived dichotomy persisted for so long is because thinking and feeling are associated with different levels of awareness. Thinking is often conscious and controlled, whereas we have little conscious control over the initiation or experience of emotions. Because we are frequently consciously aware of our reasoning process, but not our emotional processes, we tend to view emotion as the interloper to our reasoning, rather than the opposite.

Today, legal scholars recognize that emotion "has an irreducibly mental component" (Posner, 2000, p. 3)—emotions are, in part, cognitive, and reasoning is partly emotive (Bandes, 1996); the two act in concert to shape our perceptions and behavior. Further, distinctions between cognition and emotion fall away at the level of computation; both thinking and feeling can be described in information-processing terms. Emotions, like cognition, are neurally mediated computations executed by the brain. Indeed, as neuroscientific efforts have advanced, new evidence suggests that both thinking and feeling are integrated in the lateral prefrontal cortex (Nowak & Sigmund, 2005; Pessoa, 2008). Reason does not "control" emotion; emotionality is more phylogenetically ancient than rationality, and when the two conflict, emotion typically triumphs (Massey, 2002; Verweij et al., 2015). Rather than artificially separating emotion and reason, current scholars are instead more interested in exploring the interaction between the two. In particular, the law stands to benefit from a scientific understanding of the ways in which emotion can both impede and enhance reasoning, depending on context. This is because the cognitive aspects of emotion—including their automaticity—bear on important legal questions of, for example, culpability and deterrability.

The Role of Emotions in Law

We hold people responsible for volitional failures to adhere to their legal duty—for example, a failure to maintain an appropriate speed when driving on the highway, or a failure to avoid causing serious injury to others. The law imposes costs on proscribed behavior—for example, a ticket or a period of incarceration—as either an act of retribution or in an effort to deter people from future offending. Through a system of prohibitions and sanctions, the law disincentivizes certain behaviors and incentivizes others in an effort to enhance social welfare.

Much of human behavior, including behavior the law seeks to regulate, occurs under the influence of emotion. Emotions therefore bear on the law to the extent that emotions impair volition or affect the manner in which individuals respond to incentives. For example, if emotions diminish one's capacity for or opportunity to exercise self-control, volition—and thus culpability—is reduced. Similarly, if emotions diminish one's ability to weigh the costs and benefits of an action, the proscriptive power of deterrence is weakened. The role of emotion in driving behaviors is therefore inherently relevant to the law. Through a better understanding of emotions, the law can revise legal doctrine to reflect behavioral realities, as well as reconsider policy objectives and the law's ability to implement them (Bandes & Blumenthal, 2012).

If the goal, then, is to understand and predict whether or not an emotion is likely to produce a particular behavior, this goal can be served by understanding the emotion's evolved function. An evolutionary psychological approach not only illuminates questions about the form and function of emotions (i.e., what they are and what they evolved to do), but also provides a coherent framework for predicting how emotions will shape behavior in a given context. In the following sections, we provide a brief overview of an evolutionary approach to emotions and demonstrate its utility for the law across a number of legal contexts.

An Evolutionary Approach to Emotions and Law

Through the process of natural and sexual selection, mental adaptations evolve to address recurrent challenges and opportunities linked to reproductive fitness. The brain can therefore be conceptualized as an information processor designed to produce cognition and behavior that, on average, gave our human ancestors a reproductive advantage compared to available alternatives.

Against this background, emotions act as superordinate cognitive mechanisms that coordinate and guide other information processing programs—such as attention, perception, memory, and physiology—in the service of addressing the relevant adaptive challenge at hand (Al-Shawaf et al., 2016; Al-Shawaf & Lewis, 2017; Cosmides & Tooby, 2000). The emotion that is activated is triggered by cues in the environment or body suggesting that the organism is facing a particular adaptive challenge. Because emotions evolved to address distinct adaptive challenges, the profile of cognitive, physiological, and behavioral effects produced by emotions are also largely distinct. For example, both anger and disgust are "negative" emotions that evolved to improve one's fitness outcomes, but are associated with very different physiological and behavioral responses (e.g., increased heart rate and approach motivation versus nausea and avoidance motivation, respectively). This is not to say that multiple emotions do not share common properties, or that multiple emotions cannot be experienced simultaneously, merely that they are individually calibrated for distinct sets of adaptive challenges. The cognitive responses orchestrated by emotions are also distinct: for example, whereas angry people tend to perceive fewer risks and become more risk tolerant, disgusted people are highly attuned to risk and become particularly risk averse (e.g., Lerner & Keltner, 2001; Lerner & Tiedens, 2006; Sparks et al., 2018). Further, these responses are moderated by features of the individual. For example, men with greater upper body strength (an ancestrally relevant indicator of general physical formidability) are quicker to experience and express anger than their physically weaker counterparts (Sell et al., 2009), whereas individuals who are immunocompromised are quicker to experience and express disgust than their healthier counterparts (Navarette & Fessler, 2006; Navarette et al., 2007).

An evolutionary approach to emotions therefore offers a number of valuable insights into how emotions ultimately affect behavior. First, it suggests which external stimuli are likely to evoke which emotional responses (i.e., those cues suggesting that the individual is facing a specific adaptive challenge). Second, it provides insight into the mechanisms mobilized by a particular emotion (i.e., how a particular emotional response is likely to influence an individual's physiology and cognition). Finally, it suggests which particular actions are likely to be facilitated by the emotional response (i.e., which behavioral responses are likely to occur, why, and what individual and environmental features might modulate the response). Evolutionary psychology thereby helps explain the causes and consequences of emotions, which can then be fruitfully applied to legal contexts. To illustrate this point, we next consider three such contexts. First, how does *feeling* particular emotions affect one's decision-making and actions in legal contexts? Second, how does our *evaluation of the emotions of others* influence our determinations of their culpability and blameworthiness? Third and finally, how do emotions affect the *legislation* of social and legal policy?

Feeling Emotions
The law implicitly and explicitly recognizes that people's decision-making is affected by their emotions. For example, courts can find gory crime scene evidence so potentially prejudicial against defendants that they will prohibit its admission regardless of its probative value (see, e.g., Federal Rules of Evidence 403). Similarly, the Supreme Court once barred victims from reading impact statements during the sentencing phase of death penalty trials, claiming that such events "inflame the passions" of the jury and make it impossible for jurors to "decid[e] the case on the relevant evidence" (*Booth v. Maryland*, 1987). Indeed, jurors may be explicitly instructed to control their emotions: in *California v. Brown*, the Supreme Court found it constitutional for jury instructions to require that jurors "not be swayed by mere sentiment, conjecture, sympathy, passion, prejudice, public opinion or public feeling" (1987, p. 541).

Evolutionary psychological research supports the underlying premise that emotional states shift the information we attend to—and our subsequent behavioral responses—in predictable ways. The emotions that manifest when people respond to crime are part of an evolved suite of mechanisms designed to defend against exploitation by others (Petersen et al., 2010). These counter-exploitative strategies include both punitive and reparative approaches (Petersen et al., 2012), which are reflected in the lay judgments of study participants and in the law itself (Sznycer & Patrick, 2020). Here, we focus on one such emotion, anger, and its relevance for people's decision-making in inflicting punishment or promoting reconciliation toward others.

AN EVOLUTIONARY APPROACH TO ANGER

Anger evolved to solve a specific adaptive problem: alerting us when others place insufficient weight on our welfare, thereby motivating a cascade of cognitive and behavioral responses aimed toward resolving conflicts of interest in the angry individual's favor (Sell et al., 2009). This view of anger is referred to as the *welfare trade-off theory* of anger, based on the notion that everyday life involves decisions in which we make trade-offs between our own welfare and the welfare of others (Petersen et al., 2010). Such weighting can range from skewing selfishly in favor of ourselves, to equating the self and other, to altruistically placing others' interests above our own. In order to make these decisions in fitness-enhancing ways, an internal regulatory variable (welfare trade-off ratio; WTR) indexes the degree to which an actor is willing to impose a cost on a target in order to secure a benefit for the actor (Tooby et al., 2008).

Exploitative acts, such as crimes, indicate a low WTR in the minds of perpetrators—not only toward the victim, but potentially also toward the victim's group members. This is because as highly interdependent, social animals, the costs imposed on one group member may have negative fitness consequences for the rest of the group (Brewer, 2001; Neuberg & Cottrell, 2008; Richerson & Boyd, 1995). Further, exploitative acts against one's fellow group member(s) raise the concern that the perpetrator may commit exploitative acts against oneself in the future.

In response to transgressions against the group or the self, the anger program motivates behaviors designed to increase the weight the target places on the angry person's welfare (Petersen et al., 2010; Sell et al., 2009). The anger program has two primary means through which to incite WTR recalibration: the threat of imposing costs (e.g., physical aggression toward the target) or the threat of withholding or withdrawing benefits (e.g., ending a cooperative relationship with the target). Adopting one or both of these tools ideally leads the target of anger to recalibrate their WTR in a way that benefits the angry individual. Whether the target in fact upregulates their WTR toward the angry person depends on the relative fitness costs of recalibration versus failing to recalibrate. All else being equal, the greater the threatened cost (or withheld benefit), and the greater the angry person's capacity to carry out the threat, the more likely the target is to recalibrate. On the other hand, targets are less likely to recalibrate if the angry individual possesses little capacity for imposing costs, or if the target perceives few benefits to be gained from recalibrating. Depending on the target's response, the angry individual may in turn upregulate or downregulate their own WTR toward the target as a calculation of whether the target is likely to place greater welfare on the angry person in the future.

In sum, the function of anger is to increase the target's valuation of the angry individual's welfare in an attempt to secure better treatment in the future. If the target recalibrates, this could be because the target has reweighted the intrinsic value of the angry person's welfare (their *intrinsic* WTR), or it could reflect a temporary adjustment in an effort to avoid negative fitness consequences so long as the target is observed (their *monitored* WTR). Monitored WTRs guide people's behavior when the recipient or others can observe the behavior—i.e., when the target's behavior is directly monitored by the angry person or the angry person's allies (Petersen et al., 2010). Put simply, monitored WTRs are those that are maintained due to external pressure rather than one's true valuation of the angry person. Intrinsic WTRs, on the other hand, exist even in the absence of the angry person. The distinction between monitored and intrinsic WTRs has implications for the manner and efficacy with which responses to exploitation are carried out. One manner of upregulating a target's monitored WTR is through punishment: the external imposition of costs that reduce the benefits of exploitative behavior (e.g., prison time). Although the punished target may recalibrate in order to avoid further costs, the recalibration may last only so long as the realistic threat of punishment exists. For example, research using economic games shows that punishment may reduce free-riding in early rounds of a game, but if the possibility of punishment is removed in later rounds then free-riding quickly returns (Fehr & Gatcher 2000, 2002).

Alternatively, one may attempt to upregulate a target's intrinsic WTR toward the actor, thereby eliminating the target's motivation to harm the actor even when there is no threat of punishment (Petersen et al., 2010). To do this, the actor might attempt to convince the target that their own welfare is interdependently connected with the welfare of the target and thus the target has underestimated the value of the relationship. Alternatively, or in addition, the actor could demonstrate that the target has underestimated the amount of harm inflicted or overestimated the amount of benefit obtained by the exploitation (Tooby & Cosmides, 1996). If successful, these reparative strategies should lead the target to increase their valuation of the relationship. Such reparative strategies are beneficial because they uphold and promote cooperation between the actor and the target, as compared to punishment strategies, which strain or sever the existing relationship and may lead to hostility between the parties (Petersen et al., 2012).

Literature on anger and punishment commonly focuses on how anger increases punitive tendencies toward offenders (e.g., Goldberg et al., 1999; Petty & Cacioppo, 1986; Pilluta & Murnighan, 1996). However, one important insight from an evolutionary, recalibrational theory of punishment is that anger, itself, does not inherently lead to punishment or an unwillingness to reconcile (Petersen et al., 2012). Rather, the anger program alerts the actor that a particular magnitude of harm has occurred and that the target places too little weight on the welfare of the actor. Whether or not this program leads to punishment is not merely a function of the extent of felt anger, as existing research might suggest (e.g., Georges et al., 2013). Nor is our response to exploitation to unilaterally punish, and punish as severely as possible. Instead, the mind calculates both the seriousness of the crime, which dictates *how much* we react, as well as the benefits and costs of upregulating the target's WTR toward us, which dictates *how* we react (Petersen et al., 2012). We are thus attuned to the "social value" of the target and employ different strategies to upregulate monitored versus intrinsic WTRs.

APPLYING THE EVOLUTIONARY-RECALIBRATIONAL THEORY OF ANGER TO THE LAW

A functional, welfare trade-off approach to anger can be applied to explain existing phenomena in the law, and to improve it in practice. First, reconsider the insight regarding third-party anger toward a transgressor. Because the costs imposed on one group member may (1) have negative fitness consequences for the rest of the group, and (2) signal that the perpetrator may impose costs against oneself in the future, exploitative acts toward one's group may engender a recalibrational response (i.e., anger) from an individual, even when they are not personally harmed or exploited. This insight helps explain why crimes can anger third parties who have no relationship to the victim (Darley & Pittman, 2003), or why the various third-party actors of the legal system (judges, jurors, law enforcement, etc.) would punish perpetrators in proportion to the anger they feel (cf. Gummerum et al., 2016; Nelissen & Zeelenberg, 2009). It further helps account for why legally prescribed punishments depend not just on the amount of harm inflicted, but also on the intention of the perpetrator. If, all else being equal, the mind is calibrating anger and potential punishment in proportion to the amount that the perpetrator has undervalued welfare, intentionally causing harm shows a greater disregard for another's welfare than ignoring the risk that it will occur, which in turn shows a greater disregard for another's welfare than failing to perceive the risk in the first place. The law reflects this exact hierarchy through its categories of purposefulness, recklessness, and negligence (e.g., Model Penal Code § 2.02). Generally speaking, when the amount of harm is held constant, purposefulness is punished more severely than recklessness, and recklessness more severely than negligence (e.g., Model Penal Code § 210).

A welfare trade-off approach to anger can also be used to help improve the law in practice. Consider mediation—a form of alternative dispute resolution in which a neutral third party facilitates an agreement between disputants. The conflicts giving rise to court-ordered mediation often involve two parties, each of whom sees the other as presenting an obstacle to achieving a goal. In other words, each party believes that the other party has insufficiently weighted their welfare (Williams & Hinshaw, 2018): The landlord believes the tenant has threatened the landlord's financial interests by refusing to pay rent; the tenant believes the landlord has infringed on the tenant's right to quiet enjoyment of their rental property by failing to fix the faulty plumbing. It is therefore unsurprising that mediations are fertile grounds for anger. Indeed, anger is one of the most commonly occurring emotions in mediation (Jones, 2001), and skilled mediators must manage anger-laden responses in order to keep discussions productive and moving toward resolution (Moore, 2014; Sinaceur et al., 2013). An evolutionary approach provides insight into numerous questions relevant to succeeding in this endeavor: What precipitates anger? What modulates anger? What reduces anger (e.g., see Sell et al., 2017)?

As described above, from a welfare trade-off framework, anger is evoked when one party believes the other is insufficiently weighting their welfare, motivating the angry party to threaten to inflict costs or withhold benefits if the other party fails to recalibrate their WTR toward the angry party (Sell et al., 2009). To the extent that a party is better positioned to inflict costs or withhold benefits (e.g., as when there is an imbalance of power between the parties), they are more likely to experience anger as a recalibration tool (Overbeck et al., 2010; Williams & Hinshaw, 2018). Evidence suggests that anger-proneness tracks ancestral cues of formidability—i.e., individual differences in anger are predicted by individual differences in the features associated with greater capacity for inflicting costs or withholding benefits in ancestral environments (e.g., greater physical strength or attractiveness, higher status in the group) (Sell et al., 2009). These features also appear to affect how successful anger is: studies find that expressions of anger enhance negotiation outcomes for high-power negotiators but backfire for low-power negotiators (van Kleef & Côté, 2007). This may be because when low-power negotiators express anger, high-power negotiators might perceive low-power negotiators as ill-positioned (and therefore unlikely) to successfully impose costs or withhold benefits. Further, recalibrating is unlikely to produce significant fitness benefits; as a result, high-power negotiators are unlikely to increase the weight they place on low-power negotiators' welfare (Williams & Hinshaw, 2018).

A welfare trade-off framework also has important implications for how mediators might reduce anger and facilitate resolution between angry parties. A welfare trade-off framework suggests that resolution between parties is most likely to occur when each party acknowledges the other's interests, concedes having underestimated the harm they may have caused and/or the value of the relationship, and displays their intention to avoid inflicting damage in the future (i.e., a shift in intrinsic valuation). Further, mediators can potentially move parties from a punitive focus toward a reparative focus by making clear the value or benefits each party may bring to the other in the presence of continued cooperation. Parties are unlikely to be motivated to continue relationships in the absence of evidence of welfare recalibration; the fitness costs of cooperating with people who do not care about your welfare are likely to outweigh the benefits of cooperation (Petersen et al., 2010).

Evaluating Emotions

Law not only regulates human behavior but also is, itself, human behavior—the behavior of judges, lawyers, jurors, legislators, and so forth (Jones & Goldsmith, 2005). In certain contexts, these legal actors must make fact-specific appraisals of the emotions of others. For example, the distinction between first-degree and second-degree murder can hinge on the state of mind of the defendant at the time of the act (was the killing committed "in cold blood" or was the defendant acting "in the heat of passion"?) (e.g., *Maher v. People*, 1862). Certain versions of the insanity defense require legal decision-makers to consider whether experiencing strong emotions can result in the total loss of one's self-control (Finkel & Parrot, 2006; see also *Parsons v. State*, 1886). Judges frequently rely on their assessments of the defendant's "remorsefulness" when determining sentence length (Bandes, 2016). As these examples show, the law treats emotions as important psychological states that bear on questions of motive, intent, and volition, and ultimately on people's culpability and blameworthiness. In this section, we use the provocation doctrine as an example of this process to demonstrate how an evolutionary approach—one that addresses both the function and mechanisms of emotions—can help provide a clearer answer to these questions.

ASSESSING ACTS COMMITTED IN THE "HEAT OF PASSION": MOTIVE

The provocation doctrine holds that those who commit homicides under significant emotional disturbance are less blameworthy than those who commit killings with deliberative intent (Clavel, 2012; Fontaine, 2009). Also known as the "heat of passion" doctrine, provocation is based on the premise that those who committed murder in a highly emotional state did not act out of any "wickedness of heart" but instead temporarily lost control of their reason and acted in poor judgment (e.g., *People v. Beltran*, 2013; Patrick & Lieberman, 2017).

In the United States, there are two primary formulations of the provocation doctrine. The common law standard, developed over time through judges' disposition of relevant cases, requires that the defendant show:

(1) that a reasonable person in the defendant's situation would have been adequately provoked,
(2) that the defendant was in fact provoked and became emotionally charged to an extent that

he lost self-control, (3) that a reasonable person in the defendant's situation would not have had sufficient time to "cool off" between provocation and killing, and (4) that the defendant did not, in fact, cool off before killing his victim. (Patrick & Lieberman, 2017, p. 37)

Alternatively, the Model Penal Code's version of the provocation doctrine requires decision-makers to assess whether the act was "committed under the influence of extreme mental or emotional disturbance" and that the circumstances experienced by the actor would cause "an ordinary person of average disposition to act from passion rather than judgment" (Model Penal Code § 210.3(1)(b), 1980). Under either standard, a finding of provocation results in a mitigated sentencing scheme (for example, manslaughter rather than murder, which can translate to a difference of decades in prison time).

Historically, the law provided a number of specific contexts deemed to give rise to adequate provocation and "compel a response," the most paradigmatic of which is infidelity: a man returns home to discover his wife in bed with another man, flies into a rage, and kills his wife, his wife's lover, or both (Patrick & Lieberman, 2017). Indeed, early applications of the doctrine noted that "[a] man cannot receive a higher provocation" than adultery (*Regina v. Mawgridge*, 1707; see also *Rowland v. State*, 1904). An evolutionary perspective provides novel insight into why infidelity, specifically, might inspire sufficient emotional disturbance as to incite murder—and for whom, exactly, this is likely to be true.

Throughout much of evolutionary history, internal fertilization and gestation meant that women could be certain that their offspring were biologically related to them, whereas men never had 100% certainty (a problem succinctly summarized by the old quip, "mama's baby, papa's maybe"). Investing resources into raising another man's offspring would have been extremely costly to one's reproductive fitness; given this unique challenge, men, more so than women, were highly motivated to ensure the fidelity of their romantic partners. Due to the risk of investing resources in another person's offspring, it may have been adaptive under some circumstances for males to kill spouses who had been unfaithful. Although such an action carries heavy costs (e.g., the loss of a cooperation partner and current or future reproductive opportunities with that spouse), the benefits might outweigh the costs under some circumstances—perhaps by preventing reputational damage and/or loss of resources to a rival's offspring (Patrick & Lieberman, 2017). As a result, in cases where infidelity is certain, an adaptation for jealousy-induced homicide may have evolved in men (e.g., Shackelford et al., 2000; but see Daly & Wilson, 1988, for an opposing byproduct view). This is not to suggest any normative conclusions about spousal killings—explanation is not justification—but it does provide insight into certain patterns of data that exist across time and space. For example, because paternity uncertainty affects men but not women, we should expect that it is far more common for men to kill their wives than for wives to kill their husbands (Patrick & Lieberman, 2017). Indeed, one recent study found that, in the United States, male-on-female spousal homicide was roughly four times more prevalent than female-on-male spousal homicide (Roberts, 2015). Global data echo this ratio (Aldridge & Brown, 2003). And, among uxoricide cases reported by the FBI from 1976 to 1994, 41% of the murders involved suspected or discovered infidelity (Shackelford et al., 2003). Further, if infidelity-inspired wife killings are connected to paternity concerns, one would expect a connection between a woman's fertility and her likelihood of being killed by her husband (Patrick, 2015). Indeed, Todd Shackelford and colleagues (2003) find that the probability of a woman being murdered by a jealous husband increases as the wife approaches peak fertility and then declines with age. Moreover, these results are specific to the age of the wives; husbands' age did not predict the likelihood of wife-killings (Shackelford et al., 2003).

These findings demonstrate the utility of an evolutionary perspective for providing novel insights into who is likely to lose themselves in the "heat of passion," under what circumstances, and why, by focusing on the cognitive mechanisms underlying the behavior. In addition, the perspective identifies asymmetric risk probabilities in victimhood, which can in turn influence the incentive structures the law uses to deter socially undesirable behavior.

ASSESSING ACTS COMMITTED IN THE "HEAT OF PASSION": INTENT AND VOLITION

An evolutionary framework also bears on questions pertaining to "loss of reason." As Patrick and Lieberman (2017) point out, an underlying assumption of the provocation doctrine is that people experiencing highly emotional states will act in ways that they otherwise feel are morally unacceptable. Put another way, the doctrine assumes that anger (the typical emotion considered by the provocation doctrine) can—and does—override one's "moral conscience."

Relying on evolutionarily informed work, Patrick and Lieberman (2017) propose a multidimensional relationship between emotions and our moral conscience. Consider the relationship between a person's behavior and their moral intuitions as to the acceptability of that behavior (i.e., their moral conscience). Patrick and Lieberman (2017) assert that, on the one hand, some emotions, such as guilt and shame, may function to incline behavior toward moral intuitions of right or wrong where the costs of committing wrongdoing (e.g., social devaluation by others) exceed the benefits to be gained from the morally questionable act (Sznycer et al., 2016). However, other emotions in other contexts might instead incline behavior *away* from morally acceptable behavior when the benefits of doing so exceed the potential costs. For example, infidelity-induced anger might shift the mental calculus of payoffs to be gained from "doing the right thing."

To test this possibility, Patrick and Lieberman (2017) gathered a sample of adult men in the United States who had discovered a romantic partner's infidelity in either a previous or current relationship. Participants then responded to two open-ended questions in which they described the circumstances around the infidelity, what the partner did, how the participants discovered the infidelity, and how the incident made them feel. Participants then rated how angry the discovery made them and completed items measuring their motivational and moral responses to the infidelity. All responses were reported using Likert-type scales. The motivation questions presented participants with six retaliatory behaviors, three of which were related to the function of anger (i.e., recalibrating the value paced on the participants' welfare), such as "yell at my partner" and "hit or slap my partner." The other three behaviors were also retaliatory in the sense that they would cause harm to the participant, but were not expected to increase the value placed on the participants' welfare (e.g., "steal money from my partner" and "gossip about my partner to ruin her reputation"). Participants were asked to rate how much they wanted to engage in each of these behaviors at the time they discovered the infidelity. Finally, the moral section asked participants to rate the same six retaliatory behaviors in terms of how justified they would have been in engaging in those behaviors.

The researchers then correlated participants' reported anger with their responses to the motivation items and corresponding moral judgment items. Results indicated that higher levels of anger were associated with increased motivation and increased judgments of moral acceptability across all six behaviors, but the correlations between anger and motivation were stronger for the three behaviors related to the ultimate function of anger (welfare recalibration). Further, anger accounted for variation in motivation beyond what was accounted for by judgments of moral acceptability, but these effects were also specific to the behaviors related to welfare recalibration. Taken together, Patrick and Lieberman's (2017) findings suggest that a heightened state of anger might lead people to behave in ways that they normally feel are morally unacceptable. This accords with the provocation doctrine's assumption that people in highly emotional states may behave uncharacteristically. However, it does not necessarily follow that such actions reflect a "loss of reason." As Patrick and Lieberman (2017) point out, participants' anger did not lead to random, unpredictable behavior; instead, participants' anger activated specific motivational systems consistent with the ultimate function of anger (recalibrating the target's WTR). In other words, anger does not lead to irrationality, as per the provocation doctrine, but instead engages a sophisticated cost-benefit analysis that (unconsciously) weighs the benefits and consequences of potential actions (Patrick & Lieberman 2017).

Thus, an evolutionary framework can help inform questions of *why* and *how* for those legal actors (e.g., jurors) charged with evaluating the actions of an impassioned killer. But more than that, an evolutionary account also helps sharpen the normative questions that lawmakers should be asking with regard to the provocation doctrine. Instead of asking whether the punishment for murder should be mitigated when the killing happens "beyond the bounds of reason," lawmakers might ask whether the punishment for murder should be mitigated when the killing is motivated by a subconsciously formed intent, as opposed to a consciously formed intent. Instead of asking whether the killer has any "wickedness of heart," lawmakers might instead ask how much weight should be attached to a moral conscience versus other inputs our information-processing mechanisms take into account when producing behavior. Further, it may be that certain evolutionarily recurrent situations (here, infidelity) were so high-stakes from a fitness perspective as to occasionally incline a violent reaction. Perhaps the question lawmakers should be asking is whether those who commit crimes in response to these evolutionarily salient triggers are less culpable, or less deterrable, than those who commit the same crime in a different context. And if so, why?

Legislating Emotions

In the previous sections we described how emotions are infused into the law by motivating our punishment decisions and affecting the way that we evaluate the culpability and blameworthiness of others. But emotions also permeate the contents of the law in two ways. First, emotions can drive our support for different legal and social policies. Second, emotions can give rise to moral intuitions that then become codified as law. In this section, we consider an illustration of each process.

EMOTIONS DRIVE SUPPORT FOR LEGAL POLICIES

From an evolutionary perspective, emotions reflect coordinated responses to discrete threats and opportunities. For example, we have evolved inclinations to feel fear (and not sexual arousal) toward a predator, because the predator poses a threat to survival (and not a potential mating opportunity). The emotional response then motivates behaviors specific to countering the threat, such as running away (and not attempting a pick-up line). Cottrell and colleagues (2010) suggest that a similar logic applies to understanding why people support legal policies directed toward particular groups. Namely, in the United States, some White Americans perceive different outgroups (e.g., Mexican Americans; gay and lesbian people) as posing qualitatively distinct threats (e.g., free-riding; moral contamination), which in turn elicits qualitatively distinct emotional responses (e.g., anger; disgust). These emotions, in turn, motivate qualitatively distinct policy attitudes (e.g., restricting immigration; opposition to gay marriage).

To test this hypothesis, Cottrell and colleagues (2010) measured participants' support for four legal policies (immigration policies, gay rights, homeland security policies, and hurricane relief policies), as well as participants' specific affective responses (anger, disgust, fear, pity) toward four groups (Mexican Americans, gay and lesbian people, Arab Muslims, and Black Americans). The researchers also measured whether participants believed each target group posed different kinds of threats to "people like me"; these threats included an unwillingness to reciprocate, inconsistent values, and endangering physical safety. Cottrell and colleagues (2010) predicted that each threat would be associated with a particular emotion, and each emotion associated with support for the corresponding legal policy. For example, opposition to gay rights would be associated with increased disgust toward gay and lesbian people, emerging from a perceived moral contamination threat. In this way, emotional response should mediate the relationship between perceived threat and support for relevant legal policy.

Cottrell and colleagues (2010) found consistent support for the mediating role of affect. Specific perceived threats evoked corresponding emotions, which in turn predicted policy attitudes. For example, anger partially mediated the relationship between the perception that Mexican immigrants and Black Americans willfully violate reciprocity and support for policies limiting immigration and Hurricane Katrina relief measures. Further, disgust toward gays and lesbians partially mediated the relationship between perceived values threat and opposition to gay rights.

These results suggest that emotions play a critical role in forming people's attitudes toward specific legislative aims. In turn, these findings have direct implications for attempts to increase support for socially desirable legal policies: to the extent that perceptions of threats are reduced, corresponding affective reactions should abate and result in less hostility toward the desired legal policies (Cottrell et al., 2010).

The work by Cottrell and colleagues (2010) demonstrates that our emotions can play a role in whether we support particular legislation (and, therefore, in shaping the form and continued existence of said legislation). But our emotions *themselves* can also become codified, as most clearly demonstrated with the conversion from feelings of what is "gross" to determinations of what is "wrong."

HOW DISGUST BECOMES LAW

The emotion of disgust is deeply linked to our moral intuitions and decision-making, such that acts that engender disgust are often consequently branded as immoral (Lieberman & Patrick, 2018). The most straightforward legal example of this is obscenity law, in which a communication is deemed so offensive that it is not protected under First Amendment freedom of expression (see, e.g., *Miller v. California*, 1962). The Supreme Court has struggled mightily with delineating what counts as obscene (as demonstrated by the infamous "I know it when I see it" proclamation), ultimately relying in many instances on definitions that include disgust. For example, in the *Miller v. California* case, the Supreme Court cites a number of dictionary definitions that include phrases such as "disgusting to the senses" and ". . . disgusting, repulsive, filthy, foul, abominable, loathsome" (*Miller v. California*, 1962, fn. 2). After *Miller* was decided, several lower courts opined that disgustingness was indeed the criterion one should use to determine whether the *Miller* test was met (Patrick & Lieberman, 2018). According to the United States Court of Appeals for the Fourth Circuit, obscenity laws are in fact laws about regulating that which elicits disgust ("[a]s the offensiveness requirement in the *Miller* test is more than minimally met . . . the greater the number of people who would react to the material with revulsion and disgust") (*United States v. Guglielmi*, 1987, p. 455).

Laws regarding incest are similarly grounded in disgust. Consider that the logic often adduced in support of incest laws rests on preventing children from the increased likelihood of genetic defect. How, then, does one square this logic with the fact that no laws exist preventing those carrying serious genetic diseases (such as Huntington's disease) from having biological children (Lieberman & Patrick, 2018)? Less reason-defying, and far more parsimonious, is the explanation that humans share an evolved aversion to incest, which is expressed cross-culturally in the forms of norms and laws. This helps to illuminate why anthropologists call incest "the universal taboo" given its ubiquitous prohibited status across space and time (Patrick & Lieberman, 2018; Rosman et al., 2009). Indeed, when Haidt (2001) conducted his moral dumbfounding studies, participants gave up on attempted logical arguments to explain their aversion to the incest vignette and instead fell back on the explanation, "I just know it's wrong, even though I can't explain why" (Patrick & Lieberman, 2018).

To understand how this *gross-to-wrong* pathway came to exist, it is useful to first consider the ultimate function of disgust. Disgust evolved to solve three ancestral challenges recurrently faced by our human ancestors: what to eat, what to touch, and with whom to mate (Lieberman & Patrick, 2018). Disgust integrates input from the social and physical world to generate estimates of the expected fitness value of consuming or contacting a particular substance, as well as mating with a particular individual. If this program computes low expected contact, consumption, or mating values, feelings of disgust are elicited, which, in turn, initiate behavioral avoidance of the disgusting thing (Lieberman & Patrick, 2018; Tybur et al., 2013).

In addition to shaping personal choices about what to eat, touch, and with whom to mate, disgust has also come to operate in the socio-moral domain through its communicative features. Essentially, the disgust program serves as handy scaffolding for a moral system, which can infiltrate and take advantage of the avoidance and elimination motivational systems natively associated with protecting oneself against contamination. When one communicates disgust over a particular person or action, one is in effect communicating a low expected value of that particular person or action. Further, these disgust utterances can signal that one is likely to support condemnation of the targets of disgust. Thus, when one expresses that incest is morally wrong, it is in effect suggesting that the people who engage in incest are of low social value and facilitates the formation of alliances against those who commit the immoral act. Forming such alliances helps individuals and groups to defend existing resources and, more importantly, exploit or marginalize low-power groups in order to acquire their resources. To the extent that a group of individuals finds a particular behavior disgusting, and they have leverage (via formidability or sheer numbers) over the targets engaging in the behavior, those targets are at risk of exploitation. Disgust therefore links to morality by indexing the kinds of actions one finds personally distasteful and the normative proscriptions one might support. Others' expressions of disgust allow us to infer which normative proscriptions they might support or which groups they might target. Through this process, morality (vis-à-vis disgust) can motivate individuals to form alliances and fuel social coordination (DeScioli & Kurzban, 2009; Lieberman & Patrick, 2018).

Although an evolutionary approach provides deep explanatory power for understanding how disgust becomes linked to morality and codified into law, the framework does not—and cannot—address whether society *should* proscribe behaviors that inspire disgust. Evolutionary psychology seeks to describe, explain, and predict (i.e., to understand what *is*)—but cannot prescribe or justify particular states or actions (i.e., determine what *ought to be*). Some scholars, such as bioethicist Leon Kass, have argued that moral disgust remains an important barometer for determining and promoting social good (as Kass famously claimed, "[s]hallow are the souls that have forgotten how to shudder"; 1997, p. 20). Others, such as philosopher and legal scholar Martha Nussbaum, argue that disgust has no place in the law, if only because disgust has a history of being used as a tool to marginalize, ostracize, and discriminate against others

(Nussbaum, 2001). This coheres with the view of disgust as a mechanism designed to mobilize coalitional exploitation, described above (Lieberman & Patrick, 2018; Patrick, 2021). Lieberman and Patrick (2018) argue that our disgust-linked moral judgments should not be granted any sort of privileged status simply because they are generated by an evolved system. The fact that we intuitively "feel" disgust toward a particular action or behavior should not be the guidepost for identifying what the law should proscribe. Instead, whether or not disgust should play a role in legal affairs should ultimately hinge on whether disgust's evolved function promotes a goal of the legal system, and whether the mechanics of disgust are sound enough to be relied on in pursuit of that goal.

Conclusion

In this chapter we have reviewed the manifold connections between emotions and the law, and we have explored how an evolutionary approach to the emotions adds explanatory power to the behavioral models used by the law. Rather than relying on implicit and often outdated assumptions about the mind, we can use a scientific approach to human behavior in order to design effective and efficient legal systems that further our social values and goals (Jones, 1999). Within the legal sphere, an evolutionary approach provides us with a coherent framework for understanding the causal influences, cognitive mechanics, and behavioral outcomes of emotions. In doing so, an evolutionary perspective provides descriptive clarity, generates novel predictions for legally relevant behavior, and provides insights that may inform normative debates in the law.

References

Aldridge, M. L., & Browne, K. D. (2003). Perpetrators of spousal homicide: A review. *Trauma, Violence, & Abuse, 4*(3), 265–276.

Al-Shawaf, L., Conroy-Beam, D., Asao, K., & Buss, D. M. (2016). Human emotions: An evolutionary psychological perspective. *Emotion Review, 8*(2), 173–186.

Al-Shawaf, L., & Lewis, D. M. G. (2017). Evolutionary psychology and the emotions. In V. Zeigler-Hill & T. K. Shackelford (Eds.), *Encyclopedia of personality and individual differences* (pp. 1–10). Springer.

Bandes, S. A. (1996). Empathy, narrative, and victim impact statements. *The University of Chicago Law Review, 63*, 361–412.

Bandes, S. A. (2016) Remorse and criminal justice. *Emotion Review, 8*, 14–19.

Bandes, S. A., & Blumenthal, J. A. (2012). Emotion and the law. *Annual Review of Law and Social Science, 8*, 161–181.

Booth v. Maryland, 482 U.S. 496 (1987).

Brewer, M. B. (2001). Ingroup identification and intergroup conflict: When does ingroup love become outgroup hate? In R. Ashmore, L. Jussim, & D. Wilder (Eds.), *Social identity, intergroup conflict, and conflict reduction* (pp. 17–41). Oxford University Press.

California v. Brown, 479 U.S. 538 (1987).

Clavel, N. Y. (2012). Righting the wrong and seeing red: Heat of passion, the model penal code, and domestic violence. *New England Law Review, 46*, 329–352.

Cottrell, C. A., Richards, D. A. R., & Nichols, A. L. (2010). Predicting policy attitudes from general prejudice versus specific intergroup emotions. *Journal of Experimental Social Psychology, 46*, 247–254.

Cosmides, L., & Tooby, J. (2000). Evolutionary psychology and the emotions. In J. Tooby & L. Cosmides (Eds.), *Handbook of emotions* (Vol. 2, pp. 91–115). Guilford.

Daly, M., & Wilson, M. (1988). *Homicide*. Aldine de Gruyter.

Darley, J. M., & Pittman, T. S. (2003). The psychology of compensatory and retributive justice. *Personality and Social Psychology Review, 7*(4), 324–336.

Descartes, R. ([1641] 2008). *Meditations on first philosophy*. Hackett.

DeScioli, P., & Kurzban, R. (2009). Mysteries of morality. *Cognition, 112*, 281–299.

Fehr, E., & Gächter, S. (2000). Cooperation and punishment in public goods experiments. *The American Economic Review, 90*(4), 980–994.

Fehr, E., & Gächter, S. (2002). Altruistic punishment in humans. *Nature, 415*(6868), 137–140.

Finkel, N. J., & Parrott, W. G. (2006). *Emotions and culpability: How the law is at odds with psychology, jurors, and itself.* American Psychological Association.

Fontaine, R. G. (2009). Adequate (non) provocation and heat of passion as excuse not justification. *University of Michigan Journal of Law Reform, 43,* 27–51.

Goldberg, S., Grusec, J. E., & Jenkins, J. M. (1999). Confidence in protection: Arguments for a narrow definition of attachment. *Journal of Family Psychology, 13*(4), 475–483.

Gummerum, M., Van Dillen, L. F., Van Dijk, E., & López-Pérez, B. (2016). Costly third-party interventions: The role of incidental anger and attention focus in punishment of the perpetrator and compensation of the victim. *Journal of Experimental Social Psychology, 65,* 94–104.

Haidt, J. (2001). The emotional dog and its rational tail: A social intuitionist approach to moral judgment. *Psychological Review, 108,* 814–834.

Hume, D. ([1739] 1969). *A treatise of human nature.* Penguin Books.

Jones, O. D. (1999). Law, emotions, and behavioral biology. *Jurimetrics, 39,* 283–289.

Jones, O. D., & Goldsmith, T. H. (2005). Law and behavioral biology. *Columbia Law Review, 105,* 405–502.

Jones, T. S. (2001). Mediating with heart in mind: Addressing emotion in mediation practice. *Negotiation Journal, 17,* 219–244.

Kant, I. (1993). *Grounding for the metaphysics of morals; with "On a supposed right to live because of philanthropic concerns"* (Trans. J. W. Ellington). Hackett. (Original work published 1785).

Kass, L. R. (1997, June 2). The wisdom of repugnance. *The New Republic,* 17–26.

Lerner, J. S., & Keltner, D. (2001). Fear, anger, and risk. *Journal of Personality and Social Psychology, 81*(1), 146–159.

Lerner, J. S., & Tiedens, L. Z. (2006). Portrait of the angry decision maker: How appraisal tendencies shape anger's influence on cognition. *Journal of Behavioral Decision Making, 19*(2), 115–137.

Lieberman, D., & Patrick, C. (2018). *Objection: Disgust, morality, and the law.* Oxford University Press.

Maher v. People, 10 Mich. 212 (1862).

Massey, D. (2002). A brief history of human society: The origin and role of emotion in social life. *American Sociological Review, 67,* 1–29.

Miller v. California, 413 U.S. 15 (1973).

Model Penal Code (Official Draft and Revised Comments 1980).

Moore, C. W. (2014). *The mediation process: Practical strategies for resolving conflict.* Wiley.

Navarette, C. D., & Fessler, D. M. T. (2006). Disease avoidance and ethnocentrism: The effects of disease vulnerability and disgust sensitivity on intergroup attitudes. *Evolution and Human Behavior, 27,* 270–282.

Navarette, C. D., Fessler, D. M. T., & Eng, S. J. (2007). Elevated ethnocentrism in the first trimester of pregnancy. *Evolution and Human Behavior, 28,* 60–65.

Nelissen, R. M., & Zeelenberg, M. (2009). Moral emotions as determinants of third-party punishment: Anger, guilt and the functions of altruistic sanctions. *Judgment and Decision making, 4*(7), 543–553.

Neuberg, S. L., & Cottrell, C. A. (2008). Managing the threats and opportunities afforded by human sociality. *Group Dynamics: Theory, Research, and Practice, 12*(1), 63–72.

Nowak, M., & Sigmund, K. (2005). Evolution of indirect reciprocity. *Nature, 437*(7063), 1291–1298.

Nussbaum, M. C. (2001). *Upheavals of thought: The intelligence of emotions.* Cambridge University Press.

Overbeck, J. R., Neale, M. A., & Govan, C. L. (2010). I feel, therefore you act: Intrapersonal and interpersonal effects of emotion on negotiation as a function of social power. *Organizational Behavior and Human Decision Processes, 112*(2), 126–139.

Parsons v. State, 81 Ala. 577 (1886).

Patrick, C. (2015). A new synthesis for law and emotions: Insights from the behavioral sciences. *Arizona State Law Journal, 47,* 1239–1287.

Patrick, C. (2016). The long-term promise of evolutionary psychology for the law. *Arizona State Law Journal, 48,* 995–1012.

Patrick, C. (2021). When souls shudder: A brief history of disgust and the law. In S. Bandes, J. L. Madeira, K. Temple, & E. K. White (Eds.), *Research handbook on law and emotions* (pp. 80–93). Edward Elgar.

Patrick, C., & Lieberman D. (2017). Not from a wicked heart: Testing the assumptions of the provocation doctrine. *Nevada Law Journal, 18,* 33–60.

Patrick, C., & Lieberman, D. (2018). How disgust becomes law. In N. Strohminger & V. Kumar (Eds), *The moral psychology of disgust* (pp. 121–138). Rowman & Littlefield.

Pessoa, L. (2008). On the relationship between emotion and cognition. *Nature Neuroscience, 9,* 148–158.

People v. Beltran, 301 P.3d 1120 (Cal. 2013).

Petersen, M. B., Sell, A., Tooby, J., & Cosmides, L. (2012). To punish or repair? Evolutionary psychology and lay intuitions about modern criminal justice. *Evolution and Human Behavior, 33,* 682–695.

Petersen, M. B., Sell, A., Tooby, J., & Cosmides, L. (2010). Evolutionary psychology and criminal justice: A recalibrational theory of punishment and reconciliation. In H. Høgh-Oleson (Ed.), *Human morality & sociality: Evolutionary & comparative perspectives*, (pp. 72–131). Palgrave MacMillan.

Petty, R. E., & Cacioppo, J. T. (1986). The elaboration likelihood model of persuasion. *Advances in Experimental Social Psychology*, *19*, 123–205.

Pillutla, M. M., & Murnighan, J. K. (1996). Unfairness, anger, and spite: Emotional rejections of ultimatum offers. *Organizational Behavior and Human Decision Processes*, *68*(3), 208–224.

Plato (1997). Phaedrus. In J. M. Cooper (Ed.), *Plato: Complete works* (pp. 246a–246b). Hackett.

Posner, E. A. (2000). Law and the emotions. *Georgetown Law Journal*, *89*, 1977–2012.

Regina v. Mawgridge, Kell 119 (1707).

Richerson, P., & Boyd, R. (1995, January). *The evolution of human hypersociality*. Paper presented at the Ringberg Castle Symposium on Ideology, Warfare and Indoctrinability.

Roberts, J. M., Jr. (2015). US spousal homicide rates by racial composition of marriage. *Annals of Epidemiology*, *25*(9), 668–673.

Rosman, A., Rubel, P. G., & Weisgrau, M. (2009). *The tapestry of culture: An introduction to cultural anthropology*. Rowman Altamira.

Rowland v. State, 35 So. 826 (Miss. 1904).

Saint-Georges, C., Chetouani, M., Cassel, R., Apicella, F., Mahdhaoui, A., Muratori, F., Laznik, M., & Cohen, D. (2013). Motherese in interaction: At the cross-road of emotion and cognition? (A systematic review). *PloS ONE*, *8*(10), e78103.

Sell, A., Sznycer, D., Al-Shawaf, L., Lim, J., Krauss, A., Feldman, A., Rascanu, R., Sugiyama, L., Cosmides, L., & Tooby, J. (2017). The grammar of anger: Mapping the computational architecture of a recalibrational emotion. *Cognition*, *168*, 110–128.

Sell, A., Tooby, J. & Cosmides, L. (2009). Formidability and the logic of human anger. *Proceedings of the National Academy of Sciences*, *106*, 15073–15078.

Shackelford, T. K., Buss, D. M., & Peters, J. (2000). Wife killing: Risk to women as a function of age. *Violence and Victims*, *15*(3), 273–282.

Shackelford, T. K., Buss, D. M., & Weekes-Shackelford, V. A. (2003). Wife killings committed in the context of a lovers triangle. *Basic and Applied Social Psychology*, *25*(2), 137–143.

Sinaceur, M., Maddux, W. W., Vasiljevic, D., Nückel, R. P., & Galinsky, A. D. (2013). Good things come to those who wait: Late first offers facilitate creative agreements in negotiation. *Personality and Social Psychology Bulletin*, *39*(6), 814–825.

Sparks, A. M., Fessler, D. M., Chan, K. Q., Ashokkumar, A., & Holbrook, C. (2018). Disgust as a mechanism for decision making under risk: Illuminating sex differences and individual risk-taking correlates of disgust propensity. *Emotion*, *18*(7), 942–958.

Sznycer, D., & Patrick, C. (2020). The origins of criminal law. *Nature Human Behaviour*, *4*(5), 506–516.

Sznycer, D., Tooby, J., Cosmides, L., Porat, R., Shalvi, S., & Halperin, E. (2016). Shame closely tracks the threat of devaluation by others, even across cultures. *Proceedings of the National Academy of Sciences*, *113*(10), 2625–2630.

Tooby, J. & Cosmides, L. (1996). Friendship and the Banker's Paradox: Other pathways to the evolution of adaptations for altruism. In W. G. Runciman, J. Maynard Smith, & R. I. M. Dunbar (Eds.), *Evolution of Social Behaviour Patterns in Primates and Man: Proceedings of the British Academy*, *88*, 119–143.

Tooby, J., Cosmides, L., Sell, A., Lieberman, D. & Sznycer, D. (2008). Internal regulatory variables and the design of human motivation: A computational and evolutionary approach. In A. Elliot (Ed.), *Handbook of approach and avoidance motivation* (pp. 251–271). Lawrence Erlbaum Associates.

Tybur, J. M., Lieberman, D., Kurzban, R., & DeScioli, P. (2013). Disgust: evolved function and structure. *Psychological Review*, *120*(1), 65–84.

United Nations Office on Drugs and Crime (2014). *Global study on homicide 2013*. Available at http://www.unodc.org/documents/gsh/pdfs/2014_GLOBAL_HOMICIDE_BOOK_web.pdf.

United States v. Bonds, 922 F.3d 343, 344 (7th Cir. 2019).

United States v. Guglielmi, 819 F.2d 451 (4th Cir. 1987).

Van Kleef, G. A., & Côté, S. (2007). Expressing anger in conflict: When it helps and when it hurts. *Journal of Applied Psychology*, *92*(6), 1557–1569.

Verweij, M., Senior, T., Dominquez, J., & Turner, R. (2015). Emotion, rationality, and decision-making: How to link affective and social neuroscience with social theory. *Frontiers in Neuroscience*, *9*, 1–13.

Williams, K. E., & Hinshaw, A. (2018). Outbursts: An evolutionary approach to emotions in the mediation context. *Negotiation Journal*, *34*(2), 165–186.

PART IV

Emotions in Psychopathology

CHAPTER 57

The Harmful Dysfunction Analysis: An Evolutionary Approach to Emotional Disorders

Jerome C. Wakefield and Jordan A. Conrad

Abstract

This chapter explores the concept of an emotional disorder from the perspective of Jerome Wakefield's harmful dysfunction analysis (HDA) of mental disorder. According to the HDA, a disorder is the failure of a mechanism to perform its evolved function, in a way that is harmful to the organism. The distinction between disorder and nondisorder is the foundation of medical, including psychiatric, nosology, yet the concept remains much debated. After surveying competing views of mental disorder and arguing for the conceptual advantages of the HDA, this chapter considers some of the challenges that arise in applying the HDA to distinguish disordered versus normal emotional functioning. Reviewing various analyses of the sources of possible diagnostic errors including the cliff-edge and smoke-detector principles, as well as the most prominent evolutionary theory of emotion, the superordinate-program theory of emotion, the authors provide an overview of the unique difficulties emotional disorders pose to diagnostic psychiatry.

Key Words: harmful dysfunction analysis, harmful dysfunction analysis; HDA; emotional disorder; disorder; dysfunction; evolutionary medicine; smoke-detector principle; cliff-edge, superordinate theory of emotion

Introduction: The Problem of Distinguishing Emotional Disorder from Normal Emotional Distress

This chapter considers conceptual and theoretical issues concerning emotional disorders and their nature, including some of the diagnostic challenges in distinguishing emotional disorder from normal emotion. In one sense, the concept of emotional disorder may seem obvious. Anything biologically designed—like anything humanly designed—is capable of going wrong and not performing the function that it was designed to perform. With regard to emotion, when functioning goes wrong, it can be particularly distressing both to the individuals suffering the disorder and to those around them. The fact is that for every one of the many normal human emotions considered in this *Handbook*—anger, shame, hatred, disgust, pride, love, regret, guilt, gratitude, lassitude, boredom, curiosity, elation, jealousy, fear, grief, sadness, and the rest—one can, without too much difficulty, imagine a set of symptoms that would constitute a pathology of that emotional system. This would typically be either because an individual's emotional reaction is extreme in intensity given the triggering circumstances, or the individual lacks a normal-range capacity to experience the emotion even when the triggering circumstances are appropriate, or the emotion is experienced but is misdirected at inappropriate objects. These types of disorder correspond roughly to the classic division of medical disorders into "hyper-" (above normal), "hypo-" (below normal), and "perverse" (misdirected) functional reactions. However, emotions being as complex as they are, this simple classification does not adequately describe all the possible manifestations of emotional disorder, as we shall see.

Of course, emotions are often unwanted or distressing without being disordered. Just as there are many undesirable psychological conditions, from illiteracy and ignorance to lack of talent and lack of a pleasing personality, that are not mental disorders, so as well there are many negative emotions, such as grief, fear, shame, sadness, hatred, and anger, that may be undesirable but are not considered disorders. So, for emotions as well as psychological conditions in general, the question arises: When are negative mental conditions justifiably considered mental disorders rather than other kinds of problems? Although some categories and judgments about disorder versus normality are controversial, especially when they pertain to the emotions, there is an impressive degree of professional and lay consensus about such classificatory judgments regarding what is a disorder versus a nondisorder that requires explanation by an account of the concept of disorder. Such an account may also help us understand what is at stake in controversies over whether specific conditions are or are not disorders, and may even guide us in resolving some such disputes.

Emotions are omnipresent in psychological reactions in general, so emotional problems of various kinds are intimately involved in the majority of mental disorders (Kring, 2008). Some of these emotional issues are not themselves emotional disorders. Instead, they are consequences of a more basic primary dysfunction. For example, a paranoid individual may become intensely hostile or fearful secondarily due to the primary cognitive dysfunction that creates the individual's distorted perception that there is dangerous plotting against the individual; or a schizophrenic individual may develop a defensive fear of engaging socially or even of watching television because in the past such activities have triggered aversive hallucinatory episodes.

The specific locus of a psychological dysfunction is not always obvious and is often a matter of debate. It may even vary from condition to condition within a category. For example, is the central problem in a case of body dysmorphic disorder a distorted perception of the magnitude of a flaw in appearance or a pathologically exaggerated emotion of shame in reaction to the perceived flaw, or both? Because emotions are triggered by cognitions, there is often this sort of ambiguity about whether the source of an intense reaction lies in the cognitive monitoring system or the affect generation system.

However, many mental disorders are plausibly considered to be primarily or partly disorders of specific emotions, and this will be our focus here. For example, the American Psychiatric Association's official diagnostic manual, the *Diagnostic and Statistical Manual of Mental Disorders*, fifth edition (DSM-5; American Psychiatric Association, 2013), includes a variety of categories of mental disorder that either are emotional disorders or are presumed to involve a significant emotional component, such as the following: These encompass, for example, disorders of fear (e.g., specific phobias of everything from snakes to traveling in airplanes, hypochondriasis or illness anxiety disorder; social anxiety disorder), disorders of anxiety (e.g., panic disorder, generalized anxiety disorder, separation anxiety disorder), disorders of sadness (e.g., major depressive disorder, dysthymia), disorders of grief (e.g., prolonged grief disorder), disorders of elation (e.g., mania in bipolar disorder), disorders of love and jealousy (e.g., certain delusional disorders of the erotomanic and jealousy types), disorders of anger (e.g., intermittent explosive disorder), disorders of boredom and need for pleasurable novelty (e.g., some forms of attention-deficit hyperactivity disorders [ADHD]), and other emotion-driven disorders such as body dysmorphic disorder and hoarding disorder.

The *Manual* also includes a listing of an enormous number of problematic conditions that, like the disorders just listed, often involve strong painful emotions and are often presenting problems confronted by mental health professionals, yet are not classified as mental disorders by DSM-5. Instead, they appear in a list of "Other Conditions That May Be a Focus of Clinical Attention." According to DSM's text describing this section, "The conditions and problems listed in this chapter are not mental disorders" but are "additional issues that may be encountered in routine clinical practice" (p. 715). Consider, for example, the following random and partial list of examples: sibling relational problem, relationship distress with spouse or intimate partner, high expressed emotion level within family, uncomplicated bereavement, discord with neighbor, lodger, or landlord, victim of crime, social exclusion or rejection, phase of life problem, acculturation difficulty, target of (perceived) adverse discrimination or persecution, problems related to unwanted pregnancy, adult antisocial behavior, victim of terrorism or torture, parent-child relational problems, religious or spiritual problem, spouse or partner abuse, extreme poverty, and homelessness, among others.

All of the above conditions, both the disorders and the nondisorders, are apparently negative conditions that involve negative emotions. What we need to understand from a conceptual perspective, to guide us in addressing more ambiguous cases, is what makes some of these conditions disorders and others problematic and distressing nondisorders? The answer may not be immediately obvious, and conceptual analysis—the philosophical technique of analyzing the internal conceptual representation that explains such agreement—has been used to attempt to find an answer.

So, the first step in considering the particular difficulties encountered in understanding the nature of emotional disorders is to have some principled way to distinguish disorders from nondisorders (see also, e.g., Conrad & Wakefield, Chapter 63 in this volume; Horwitz & Wakefield, 2007, 2012). For this we need an account of the broader concept of medical disorder. We thus start by examining various approaches to the concept of "disorder" and arguing for the necessity of anchoring it to evolutionary considerations, after some brief comments on why clarity about the concept of disorder is important.

The Need for an Analysis of the Concept of Disorder to Address the Antipsychiatric Critique and Limit False Positive Diagnoses

Because much is at stake intellectually and often personally in whether or not a condition is classified as a disorder, many categories of disorder have become battlegrounds over whether the concept of disorder is being misapplied. The key conceptual challenge is what might be called the "false positives problem" of how to distinguish genuine mental disorders from problematic normal-range disvalued conditions that may superficially resemble mental disorders due to shared symptoms (Wakefield, 2016b). Such nondisorders (e.g., normal child levels of activity misinterpreted as ADHD; illiteracy misinterpreted as dyslexia; self-defensive gang activity in a difficult neighborhood misinterpreted as conduct disorder; normal intense sadness misinterpreted as depressive disorder; normal sibling rivalry misinterpreted as oppositional-defiant disorder) may be genuinely harmful in our social environment due to the social context, but may be treated inappropriately if misinterpreted as disorders. Concern about increasing such false positive diagnoses was the major issue in the intense disputes surrounding the publication of DSM-5 (American Psychiatric Association, 2013), as expressed vividly by Allen Frances, the editor of an earlier DSM edition:

DSM-5 will turn temper tantrums into a mental disorder. . . . Normal grief will become Major Depressive Disorder. . . . The everyday forgetting characteristic of old age will now be misdiagnosed . . . creating a huge false positive population of people. . . . Excessive eating 12 times in 3 months is no longer just a manifestation of gluttony and the easy availability of really great tasting food. DSM-5 has instead turned it into a psychiatric illness. . . . Many millions of people with normal grief, gluttony, distractibility, worries, reactions to stress, the temper tantrums of childhood, the forgetting of old age, and "behavioral addictions" will soon be mislabeled as psychiatrically sick. (Frances, 2012, n.p.)

"Emotional disorders," considered as a subdomain of "mental disorders," which is itself a subdomain of "medical disorders," present acute difficulties to any account of disorder in eliminating false positives in virtue of their wide range of expression, individual and cultural plasticity, the fuzzy relationship between emotion and cognition, and the degree to which sensitivity to context matters. As psychiatry has increasingly expanded from institutional care into the community with all its stressors and the resulting normal distress that can easily be mistaken for disorder, the problem of distinguishing disorder from nondisorder has become critical. The distinction between disorder and other forms of distress and socially stigmatized behavior is important for treatment and hospitalization decisions, policy and funding opportunities, forensic purposes (ranging from the "insanity" defense to sexual predator laws that allow indefinite incarceration for those with certain mental disorders), prognostic projections, practical and judicial decision-making (e.g., ranging from life insurance issuance decisions and removal of children from a family's home to awarding of custody of children in divorce actions) and in social attitudes expressed in everyday life. It also helps in directing funding to those who need it most and allows for the selection of more homogeneous research samples in treatment trials and thus facilitates scientific progress.

The motivation for considering the boundaries of normal versus disordered emotion also reflects an ongoing broader discussion of the concept of disorder. Over the past several decades, there has been a lively multidisciplinary debate about the concept of mental disorder. This debate took center stage when, in the 1960s and 1970s, a movement known as "antipsychiatry" challenged the legitimacy of psychiatry by arguing that the concept of "mental disorder" is conceptually incoherent and relies on a metaphorical use of "disorder" designed to illegitimately align it with medicine. These arguments ranged from Thomas Szasz's (1974) critique of the "myth of mental illness" and R. D. Laing's (1967) argument that schizophrenia is a normal reaction to abnormal family environments (both of whom were psychiatrists themselves) to sociologist Thomas Scheff's (1966) "social labeling" theory of psychiatric diagnosis and historian-of-ideas Michel Foucault's (1965) "history of madness" portraying mental disorder as a socially constructed category that, in response to the Enlightenment's worship of reason, medicalized and treated forms of non-reason as types of medical disorder. However, for many of us who have experienced such conditions either within ourselves or in loved ones, the claim that there is no such thing as mental disorder appears absurd and irresponsible.

The challenge, therefore, is to provide an analysis of the concept of "disorder" that evades the antipsychiatric critique by (1) providing a principled method to demarcate disorder from mere problems of living or social deviance and which is (2) identical with the concept employed by physical medicine. In the next several sections, we critically review some of the more important of the many attempts to define disorder before elaborating what is widely considered thus far to be the most successful account of "disorder," the harmful dysfunction analysis (HDA; First & Wakefield 2010, 2013; Faucher & Forest, 2021; Wakefield 1992a,

1992b, 1999a, 2007, 2014, 2016a, 2021; Wakefield & First 2003, 2012). We then turn to various challenges and complexities the HDA faces, particularly in identifying emotional disorders as evolutionary dysfunctions.

Accounting for Disorder: Facts, Values, Dimensions, and Hybrids

As we discuss the attempts to account for the concept of disorder, the reader ought to keep in mind that "disorder" should not be equated with appropriateness for treatment by mental health professionals. In fact, some analyses do equate disorder with whatever is judged to warrant treatment by a mental health professional. However, the broader domain of appropriate treatment is an obvious everyday reality to anyone who practices in the mental health field, and is formally recognized by the psychiatry's list of diagnostic "Z Codes," which explicitly identify psychological conditions that "are not mental disorders" but that "may be a focus of clinical attention"—like those nondisorders listed earlier. As Robert Spitzer (1998), who designed the modern psychiatric diagnostic system, succinctly put it, "Diagnosis and need for treatment are not the same" (p. 120). Klerman and Schechter (1981) distinguish mental disorders as the core target of psychiatry from a much larger domain of nondisorders that psychiatrists also address, including dealing with life stressors and realization of human potential. However, the classification of a condition as a disorder biases prognosis and treatment decisions and has personal and social consequences, so that even where treatment is warranted, the distinction between disorder and nondisorder remains important. Perhaps this is a good place to emphasize, in keeping with Klerman and Schechter's analysis, that although the distinction between disorder and nondisorder is crucial for many reasons, and is intricately interwoven with our social institutions and concepts, nondisordered individuals who are distressed deserve psychotherapeutic support without having to be spuriously classified as having a mental disorder (and hopefully our insurance system will work toward this humane goal).

Accounts of mental disorder have traditionally fallen into two camps: value-based and fact-based accounts. As the eminent Welsh psychiatrist, Robert Kendell, aptly put the problem:

> The most fundamental issue, and also the most contentious one, is whether disease and illness are normative concepts based on value judgments, or whether they are value-free scientific terms; in other words, whether they are biomedical terms or sociopolitical ones. (1986, p. 25)

Although this distinction remains at the heart of the debate, another account has gained in popularity: the dimensional account, which claims that disorders are nothing but the extreme or severe end of a distribution of symptoms. We start by examining these three accounts, focusing on the particular truth that they each identify in the concept of "disorder," as well as their fatal drawbacks that prevent them from accurately representing the concept as it is used within medicine. We then turn to Jerome Wakefield's harmful dysfunction analysis, which is currently the most widely cited account in the clinical literature, being used to identify false-positive diagnosis in everything from sexual paraphilias (Rind & Yuill, 2012) to psychopathology (Krupp et al., 2012, 2013), and has received endorsement from leading nosologists (First, 2007; Klein, 1999; Spitzer, 1997, 1999).

Pure-Value Accounts of Disorder

Traditional value accounts claim that a condition is a mental disorder if and only if it is considered harmful according to the society in which the patient is situated and therefore at least potentially warranting medical attention. If, as we shall argue later, disorder judgments involve judgments of evolutionary biological dysfunction, it remains the case that evolutionary design and human values often do not coincide so that, if disorder requires harm, evolutionary dysfunction in itself would not be sufficient for a judgment of disorder.

For example, an individual with a focal lesion in the corpus collosum that limits information transfer between brain hemispheres and thus causes dyslexia, an inability to learn to read, is certainly harmed and has a disorder in our reading-dependent society. However, if the same individual lived in mid-Paleolithic times a few thousand years before writing and reading were invented, the same lesion, although still technically a biological dysfunction of the relevant tissues, would have no harmful impact whatever, and so it would be inappropriate to say the individual has a medical disorder. Similarly, if one walks out into the sun, many cells in the skin of the nose suffer genetic mutations that are generally harmless and mostly eventually corrected. Even though those mutations are technically dysfunctions of the relevant genetic loci, no one considers that a medical disorder. The value view reflects the fact that the conditions we identify as medical disorders are limited to those that we consider to be negative in some way, and thus potentially the appropriate target of treatment. So, it would make sense if medicine's central concept—"disorder"—is value-laden. As values-view proponent Peter Sedgwick (1982) explains, "A diagnosis of diabetes, or paresis, includes the recognition of norms or values" (p. 38).

But aren't there disorders that are not negative? For example, some genetic anomalies are clearly deviations from normality but don't actually harm the individual, such as fused small toes (see the next section for further examples). However, it is arguable that in such cases, unless there is some reason such as a cosmetic issue for being concerned about the anomaly, it is not in fact considered a medical disorder, even if it is a form of abnormality. Even a condition that might be considered a disorder based on its biological features that involve a clear deviation from biologically designed functioning may be excluded from the disorder category if the society sees no significant harm in the condition. For example, moderate caffeine addiction—not involving acute caffeine intoxication or caffeine withdrawal symptoms—is not classified as a disorder, and "caffeine use disorder" was specifically excluded as a category of disorder from DSM-5 because our culture approves of the exploitation of the biological effects of caffeine for increasing alertness and work productivity, and we even have admired commercial enterprises that encourage and cater to this mild addition. However, harm is of course a malleable and debatable concept, and so this issue will no doubt come up again.

However, the "pure-value" approach does not stop at incorporating a value component into the concept of disorder. Instead, in an attempt to focus on the social nature of medical judgments, this view makes value judgments the entirety of a disorder judgment. In some respects reminiscent of the antipsychiatric view described earlier, pure-value theorists argue that labeling a condition as a disorder is just expressing a value judgment about it. Sedgwick (1982) offers vivid examples, arguing that there is nothing objective distinguishing disorders from other natural processes, leaving the sole identifying characteristic to be how the condition is valued:

> There are no illnesses or diseases in nature. . . . The fracture of a septuagenarian's femur has, within the world of nature, no more significance than the snapping of an autumn leaf from its twig; . . . . Out of his anthropocentric self-interest, man has chosen to consider as "illnesses" or "diseases". . . the failure to function according to certain values. (p. 30)

This is an interesting argument because in fact the value difference to which Sedgwick points is *not* the only difference between his examples of disorder and nondisorder. There is also a relevant factual difference between the cracking of a femur and the snapping off of an autumn leaf: the leaf is biologically designed to fall off at a certain stage of the tree's life cycle and is not required for the tree's continued functioning, whereas human beings are evolved to function with an intact femur. This points in the direction of a possible factual component that Sedgwick is ignoring.

Indeed, the most basic objection to pure-value accounts is the unlimited scope it would give to medicine due to the enormous number of undesirable physical and mental conditions that are not classified as disorders. Lack of skill or talent, unattractiveness, low confidence, criminality, weakness of will, cowardice, and many others are all disvalued conditions but are not considered disorders. Note as well that some negative conditions (e.g., grief, illiteracy, low intelligence) are clinically significant in that they can cause distress or role impairment but are not considered disorders either. Psychiatry itself is unfortunately replete with historical examples of socially undesirable conditions that were considered disordered (e.g., draepetomania, sluggish schizophrenia, childhood masturbation disorder), and which we now recognize to be erroneous disorder categories reflecting the need for a more objective, fact-based criterion upon which a diagnosis of disorder must rest for psychiatry not merely to be a mechanism of social control. Finally, people with shared value judgments about a condition (e.g., the problematic school behaviors associated with ADHD) can disagree about whether it is a disorder or normal-range functioning, suggesting that undesirability is not sufficient for disorder. The question is, of all the many disvalued conditions, what makes some of them disorders and others not disorders.

It is easy to see that the pure-value view would have devastating effects on how we understand emotional disorder. There are few areas in which we tend to apply value judgments more frequently and vehemently than in our reactions to people's emotions. No doubt there would be debates about whether shame, guilt, embarrassment, moral disgust, resentment, anger at one's partner, and other negative emotions should be pathologized. Transforming socially disapproved emotions into disorders would play into the hands of the antipsychiatrists and make a mess of psychiatric nosology, aside from being manifestly oppressive.

It should be noted that some writers who fundamentally take a pure-value view do recognize that many interactional problems, even if they are distressing, are not true disorders. Thus, they add the very minimal factual requirement that the cause must be internal to the person, and in some cases they also add that it must be treatable, rather than in the environment. The latter idea that treatability equals disorder obviously has no merit given that through most of history most true disorders were not actually treatable, and many remain so to this day. As to the idea that a disorder is any condition that we disvalue that is caused by an internal state, this too does not escape virtually any of the counterexamples we considered above. For example, lack of talent and lack of skill, or for that matter, illiteracy, are all negative conditions that have internal causes (and, for that matter, lack of skill and illiteracy are treatable). This minimal factual addition simply does not help to resolve the problems with the pure-value view. Some deeper scientific factual criterion seems required to explain what we intuitively express by the notion that "something has gone wrong" with an organism's functioning.

Pure-Fact Accounts of Disorder

The other side of Kendell's dichotomy, the pure-factual approach, is appealing from a scientific perspective and can be developed in various ways depending on one's views of which facts are relevant to a disorder judgment. Even discussion of the HDA view, to be considered later, tends to focus on the factual part, the evolutionary dysfunction criterion, because that is usually what is at issue in judging disorder versus normality. Indeed, the most dominant variant at present of a pure-factual view is that a disorder exists simply when something "goes wrong" inside the organism. What it means for something to "go wrong" and even what it is to be a "biological dysfunction" are a matter of dispute which will be examined in the next section. However, the most prominent approach is similar to the HDA's, namely, that there is a biological dysfunction. However, Boorse's (1977) rival "biostatistical" analysis interprets this in statistical terms linked to homeostatic goal-directed functioning aimed at reproduction and survival, rather than directly in evolutionary design terms.

Pure-fact accounts—and any accounts that have a factual component—have the advantage that, if the factual basis for disorder attribution can be identified, it may solve the puzzle we saw above with pure-value accounts of why so many socially disvalued conditions are not considered medical disorders. Both professionals and laypersons regularly distinguish between conditions that share similar negatively valued phenotypes. Consider, for example, illiteracy and dyslexia: illiteracy is not considered a disorder even though it is disvalued and harmful in our society, whereas dyslexia, which is equally disvalued and harmful but is thought to be caused by a lesion in the corpus callosum that interferes with the demanding communication between brain hemispheres necessary for reading, is accepted as a disorder. Similar pairs of nondisordered and disordered conditions sharing disvalued symptoms and distinguished solely by some factual consideration about the disvalued trait's etiology are not difficult to find, for example, grief/depression, high neuroticism/panic disorder, irritability/intermittent explosive disorder, difficulty sleeping/insomnia, and religious experience/psychosis.

These examples strongly support that the factual criterion of something going wrong with the organism is an important component of the disorder concept. However, even a strong factual criterion based on failure of evolved functions is not sufficient to distinguish disorder from nondisorder status. In addition to examples given earlier, one might consider benign angiomas, for example, which are small blood vessels that terminate at the skin rather than connecting to another blood vessel, leaving a small red dot. Though something has clearly "gone wrong" biologically in the development and growth of the blood vessel, they are not harmful and so most people do not consider minor skin blemishes disorders. Examples of this sort are frequent in the medical literature. Everything from invisible skin cell genetic damage upon sun exposure or fused toes to *situs inversus totalis* (a condition which systematically inverts the position of internal organs with no decrease in functioning) are generally precluded from disorder attribution on the grounds that, despite some obvious biological dysfunction, no harm is done to the possessor of these conditions.

The pure-fact view divorces judgments of disorder from any practical relationship to the individual's current social environment. Thus, a genetic mutation that has no impact on an individual whatsoever given current social-environmental conditions—or, for that matter, the mid-Neolithic pseudo-dyslexic, and the mildly caffeine addicted in our Starbucks-dominated culture, would all have medical disorders and a diminution of health. To be speculative, this could lead to puzzling disputes and oppressive judgments about whether emotional dysfunctions that yield socially desirable outcomes are in fact disorders, even though they are harmless and may even make the individual happier. For example, if a dysfunction causes a lack of sexual desire for individuals other than one's partner in a strongly monogamous society, that would still be a disorder. If a dysfunction causes lack of guilt in a hedonistic society, or lack of embarrassment in an expressionist society, or lack of shyness in a mass culture dependent on free public expression, these may cause no harm or even be beneficial and presumably would not in fact be considered disorders in those societies, but the pure-fact view insists that they are disorders nonetheless. As well, a dysfunction that causes true joy when anyone (even a rival) experiences a positive achievement or which causes an elevated dopamine rush during orgasm would, as a dysfunction, be considered a disorder, when most people would consider it a stroke of luck.

Dimensional Models of Disorder

More recently, an account of "disorder" has bootstrapped from dimensional and factor analytic explorations of the psychometric structure of symptoms of mental disorders (e.g., Kotov et al., 2017). In its strongest form, this view argues that syndromes may be decomposed into a hierarchy of factor-analytically determined dimensions covering the full range of each relevant variable, yielding a fully dimensionalized classification system that might replace preexisting diagnostic categories. Because the dimensions would each measure severity on that dimension, this would allow us to identify disorders on the basis of their severity of expression. In fact, some members of the DSM-5 Task Force entertained replacing the entire categorical system with a system of dimensions of various types of symptoms that are applied to the entire population and would yield a unique "diagnosis" for each individual, consisting of a point in the multidimensional symptom severity grid.

One of the supposed benefits of the dimensional approach is that it recognizes the continuity of psychiatric disorder with nondisorder. No doubt the boundary is fuzzy, and a major criticism of the diagnostic criteria used by psychiatry is that they impose "scientifically arbitrary diagnostic cut-offs" (Lilienfeld & Treadway, 2016, p. 439) or "arbitrary boundaries between psychopathology and normality" (Kotov et al., 2017 p. 454).

However, the dimensional view has the problem that it offers no grounds for any sort of natural division point and so makes the boundary between disorder and nondisorder arbitrary, as dimensionalists admit (Clark et al., 2017). It is true that there is a degree of arbitrariness in disorder attribution, and there will always be such when precise boundaries must be drawn for social and institutional reasons. However, by eschewing any further grounding, the dimensionalist view elevates that degree of ambiguity into an entire theory. Thus, this view in effect does away with any clear notion of disorder.

The reality is that boundaries may be fuzzy for all sorts of reasons, but there still may be clear cases on both sides of a distinction that determine the proper zone in which the boundary should be drawn. It is true that the distinctions between child and adult, night and day, orange and red, are fuzzy, but in each case there are genuine distinctions that cover a large range of cases. The purely dimensional view simply avoids the challenge of explaining what makes a condition a disorder. It cannot be simply the property of being extreme on a dimension because many such extremes are positive or neutral. If precise lines need to be drawn, then there will be a degree of arbitrariness, but not the total arbitrariness of the dimensional view. This view would be a welcome development to antipsychiatrists, for what is social deviance other than being an extreme on some socially defined dimension?

Here again, given the wide range of the natural intensities of human emotional expression, a dimensional approach without any constraints other than an arbitrarily sliding scale of being "extreme" could yield socially oppressive disorder judgments that are, as the antipsychiatrists claimed, a means to enforce social control rather than to provide genuine medical treatment. Both positive and negative emotions that reached an arbitrarily determined above-threshold or below-threshold level that was considered socially undesirable could be deemed disordered, further constricting the acceptable range of normal human experience. To some degree this is already happening without the dimensional view. Young people report anecdotally that workplaces are intolerant of grief or sadness responses to life events that cause withdrawal from work for any extended period, and individuals suffering such often normal-range human emotions are pressured to think that something is wrong and they should see a physician for antidepressants. A dimensional view of emotional disorder could accelerate such approaches and narrow the scope of what is accepted as normal human emotion to better conform to social demands.

The Harmful Dysfunction Analysis

As we have seen, each of the three approaches to understanding disorder outlined above suffers from serious drawbacks and counterexamples. The HDA avoids these deficits by providing a "hybrid" account that has two key components. First, its fact-based "dysfunction" component refers to the failure of a feature of the organism to perform the function for which it was biologically designed by natural selection, thus firmly anchoring this view in evolutionary psychology and providing a factual scientific basis for judging that conditions are or are not disorders. Second, it has a value-based "harm" component which refers to the dysfunction's harmfulness to the individual, as judged by social values in the human case. The HDA holds that an attribution of disorder requires both components to be satisfied. By combining both fact and value components, the HDA possesses the discriminatory abilities of pure-fact accounts while remaining sensitive to the problem that there are many harmless dysfunctions that no one considers medical disorders on the grounds of their harmlessness (Wakefield, 2014). The evolutionary component also offers a nonrelativistic "place to stand" from which psychiatric diagnostic criteria can be challenged as scientifically mistaken. In effect, the HDA holds that evolutionary biological dysfunction defines the space of possible medical disorders, and each culture can select from that space a set of conditions it disvalues to be the medical disorders within that culture. However, given the dysfunction component, disorder categories cannot be legitimately manufactured only from social value considerations, blocking the social control tactics that were the target of the antipsychiatrists.

The HDA builds on and is consistent with the DSM's attempts to define the concept of mental disorder, and was in part designed to provide a conceptual underpinning for the DSM. However, it goes beyond the DSM's own attempts by providing a more scientific account of disorder that is anchored in evolutionary medicine. A glance at the DSM reveals that the categories of disorders do seem to capture what are prima facie failures of biological design, consistent with the HDA; that is, the categories tend to correspond to domains in which it is plausible that there are biologically designed mechanisms with evolved functions, and the described pathological conditions appear to be ways in which those mechanisms have gone awry. For example, human developmental processes, thought, appetite, sexuality, and of course, emotions such as anxiety, depression, anger, and elation are all areas covered by the DSM and are areas in which one would expect that complex adaptive psychological mechanisms have been naturally selected, with the corollary that failures of these mechanisms' evolved functions are dysfunctions.

Although the HDA is an explicitly evolutionary view, one technically must distinguish the conceptual analysis of disorder as harmful dysfunction from the scientific evolutionary theory of dysfunction, which together comprise the HDA view of dysfunction. This is because neither the HDA nor any other view can successfully argue that "medical disorder" literally means something evolutionary, simply because the analysis of medical disorder aims to capture what we mean by a widely shared, intuitive medical and lay concept that existed long before evolutionary theory and is shared by many who are ignorant of or who reject evolutionary theory. Simply put, you do not have to understand or accept evolution to possess the concept of disorder. However, throughout history and across various views, it is agreed that disorders represent something going wrong with how human beings are naturally supposed to function. It is a momentous scientific discovery by Darwin, not a matter of definition of the original concept, that natural selection is the essential process that explains what are traditionally known as natural functions and dysfunctions. So, harmful dysfunction is the meaning of "disorder," and evolution is the most incisive scientific theory of the nature of functions and dysfunctions, so that disorder is harmful evolutionary dysfunction.

So, the HDA can be thought of as arriving at the evolutionary account in three steps. First, it recognizes that a disorder relies upon the presence of a dysfunction, specifically in the sense that some mechanism is incapable of performing one of its natural functions. At this stage of the analysis, "natural function" is used in an intuitive sense that has existed for millennia, not in a technical evolutionary sense, based on prototypical instances of the puzzling design-like characteristics of the human mind and body, such as hands grasping, eyes seeing, thirst causing us to get needed water, and fear and pain taking us away from danger or damage. The second step is an inference from the fact that natural functions, like artifact functions, cannot be accidental or irrelevant to the explanation of why the mechanisms that carry these beneficial functions exist in the first place, starting with Aristotle's notion of "final cause" and proceeding through deistic explanations. These two steps then unavoidably lead to the scientific question of what kind of underlying process could be responsible for this apparent design in organic systems. Evolutionary theory provides the only plausible scientific account that exists of how the natural functions of a mechanism can explain the existence and function of the mechanism. This third step leads to the conclusion that disorders entail the failures of some mechanism to perform the function for which it was naturally selected.

The HDA thus links to a broader Darwinian view of medicine. Biological design has been the central puzzle of biology since its beginnings. Medicine exploits the baseline provided by biological design to provide a profession that has as its primary mission the understanding and treatment of harmful failures of biological design, that is, medical disorders. The resulting medical model and its central concept, medical disorder, is arguably one of the most beneficial pieces of "conceptual engineering" in human history, if benefit is measured in terms of lives saved, suffering relieved, and knowledge gained. One way to think about the medical model that results is as a *trouble-shooting* approach to human health, and the DSM—the psychiatric manual with its categories and diagnostic criteria—as a trouble-shooting manual for the mind. The background of assumed design is what makes a focused trouble-shooting approach possible and useful. You often don't need to know how a designed system works, but only what it is designed to do, in order to correct it when something goes wrong and it is malfunctioning. Rather than understanding the system in all its complexity, you just have to figure out what is stopping the system from functioning as designed, although this is of course a tall order in itself. That, thankfully, is often much easier than figuring out how a complexly designed system works when it is working. This might be called the "wrench in the gears" account of the medical model, like seeing that there is a wrench stuck in the gears of a machine that is stopping the gears from turning and the machine from operating, but where you have no idea what the machine does or how it works overall. Yet, you still know that if you simply pull the wrench out of the gears the machine may start doing what it is supposed to do again. What makes medicine so potentially powerful is that we can focus on what is causing a system to go wrong without necessarily understanding the assumed background of designed functioning to which ideally we aim to return the organism.

If one accepts the HDA concept of disorder, then one, by implication, has an analysis of emotional disorders. An emotion is disordered when it is a harmful failure of biologically designed emotional functioning. As noted, this means that one cannot manufacture emotional disorder from social values. For example, there was a time one of us experienced in Berkeley in the 1970s when it was a common and fervently held belief in a subculture that all sexual jealousy was due to pathologically low self-esteem and was a mental disorder. Although the anti-jealousy open-relationship group-living values of that time and subculture implied a negative attitude about sexual jealousy, it is a fact that humans are designed to feel jealousy and so that disorder judgment was simply wrong. (And, it might be added, this mistaken belief system led to a lot of emotional pain and broken relationships.) Conversely, the mere fact of there being a dysfunctional system is not enough to attribute to the individual a disorder status. For example, in our society someone even pathologically low in aggression or high in familial love would perhaps not be harmed sufficiently to warrant a diagnosis of a disorder.

The deeper problems occur not in the in-principle conceptual distinction which the HDA may get right, but when it comes to actual diagnostic practices and the need to make judgments about emotional disorder versus nondisorder in all their complexity and variation. In subsequent sections, we initially reconnoiter some of the ways that biologically designed systems, including emotional systems, offer complexities that lead to misconceptions or potential challenges in applying the HDA in recognizing emotional disorders.

Two Misconceptions about an Evolutionary Account of Disorder

We now turn to consideration of two common misconceptions about an evolutionary psychological approach to disorder. The first is perhaps the most common misunderstanding of selectionist accounts of dysfunction, the so-called mismatch hypothesis. A mismatch in this sense refers to a trait that has been selected for in the environment of evolutionary adaptedness (EEA) but which is maladaptive in the current environment. The mismatch hypothesis holds that a disorder consists of or includes mismatches between traits designed for and adaptive in the EEA's very different environment but problematic in our radically altered current environment. Such mismatches are common. For instance, humans have evolved a desire for high-sugar, high-fat, high-salt foods due to their relative scarcity in our evolutionary history. Now that these are readily available and produced at much higher concentrations than would be found in nature, humans are subject to a host of nutritional and cardiovascular disorders. Some have argued that the same is true for mental disorder as well. For instance, Justin Garson (2021) poses the issue as follows:

> What if some of our devastating psychiatric ailments, such as major depression, anxiety disorders, psychopathy, and so on, actually *benefited* our Pleistocene ancestors? What if, moreover, the *fact* that they benefited those ancestors partly explains why they are around today? Then, if we accept the selected effects theory of function, we would have to say that those disorders do not arise from "dysfunctions." They would be adaptations. [. . .] It seems to me that depression, particularly when severe enough to lead to hospitalization or suicide attempts, constitutes a paradigmatic mental disorder, regardless of how it happened to evolve. (p. 337)

More schematically, the mismatch argument argues: it is empirically plausible that some mental disorders represent mismatches, not dysfunctions. Therefore, it is logically possible that the same is true. But the HDA implies that this claim is logically impossible. So, the HDA is wrong.

The HDA reply is that the argument that a mismatch between individual features and current social and environmental demands is a medical or mental disorder is conceptually confused. Mismatches are problems, and they are problems for which we ought to provide help, especially because they sometimes result from social arrangements (Wakefield, 2015), but they are not disorders and are not so classified. Moreover, routine classification of mismatches as disorders would inevitably lead to the use of psychiatry for social control purposes and a failure to address antipsychiatric challenges because social deviance can always be considered a mismatch between an individual and the social environment.

Here is another way of arguing the point, one that Wakefield sometimes opts for. To the extent that the HDA is a conceptual analysis of clinical usage, then Wakefield is committed to the following prediction: if researchers and clinicians were to generally accept that a certain condition (say, psychopathy) represents an evolved condition mismatched to our current environment, then they would stop labeling it a "disorder." Wakefield uses the example of fever to bolster his point. Medical researchers once considered fever to be a "disorder" that was caused by toxic substances in the blood; when they came to grasp that fever is a biologically designed defensive and regulated process with adaptive significance, even if not always helpful and even on balance harmful in our current environment, they stopped calling it a disorder (Wakefield, 2000, p. 260; also see Wakefield, 1999b, p. 468).

This is a testable hypothesis, and psychopathy, a commonly mentioned example, provides an interesting test case. As we discuss elsewhere (Conrad & Wakefield, Chapter 63 in this volume), and analogous to what happened with fever, when convincing evidence emerged that psychopathy, previously viewed as a paradigm disorder, may be a designed variant and does not entail that anything has gone wrong with the organism to realize that phenotype, psychopathy researchers argued that the condition ought to be depathologized and no longer seen as a disorder, but rather as an evolutionarily designed phenotype problematically mismatched with the demands and constraints of the current social environment. Kinner (2003), for example, writes that "from an evolutionary perspective psychopathy seems to be an adaptation rather than a disease" (p. 67); Reimer (2008) explains: "On any such 'selectionist' model, psychopaths are certainly different than the rest of us, biologically speaking. However, they are not, in any biological sense, disordered" (p. 187); and Krupp et al. (2012) explain: "Although their behavior is objectionable, psychopaths appear to pursue a nepotistic strategy that could have helped to advance their reproductive interests in ancestral environments" (p. 5).

Another such mismatch between evolutionarily selected-for traits and the current environment may exist between genes selected for encouraging exploration and a search for novel stimuli that were adaptive for nomadic individuals (e.g., Eisenberg et al., 2008) but pose difficulties in our constrictive school environments. It also appears that some normal variations of developmental rate cause problems in classroom discipline and are mistaken for disorders (Elder, 2010; Evans et al., 2010; Schwartz, 2012; Zoëga et al., 2012). The evidence is that this is leading to large numbers of normal children being misdiagnosed with ADHD. In conformity with Wakefield's prediction about how we deploy our concepts, those who think that some cases of ADHD are due to a mismatch between a naturally selected variation in intolerance of boredom and our school system tend to argue that such cases of ADHD are not disorders (e.g., Friedman, 2014), even though there is general agreement that in our environment such features are harmful to educational achievement to the point that parents may even seek treatment although believing their children are not disordered.

Mismatches are a legitimate concern and may dispose individuals to the development of a disorder, but, contrary to Garson's (2021) implication, they are not themselves considered disorders once it becomes evident that they originated as naturally selected parts of human nature. The best evidence against such a conceptual mismatch thesis is our actual disorder judgments. One must distinguish the question of whether a mismatch between an evolved trait and the environment is itself a disorder from the different question of whether it increases the risk of disorder or disposes one to disorder. Thus, taste for high-fat food is not considered a disorder in itself, but of course in our environment with high-fat foods so readily available and aggressively marketed, this taste can lead to a risk of cardiovascular disease, which is a genuine disorder. As in this example, mismatches often increase risk of disorder, but they are not themselves disorders.

Moreover, given our rapidly changing social structures, significant mismatches often occur between our evolved biology and our social environmental circumstances, such as the early age of puberty that is mismatched to the age of social maturity and the evolved age of optimal female fertility that is mismatched to social pressures for later childbearing to meet demands for lengthy education and establishment of a career prior to childbearing. Yet, these evolved traits mismatched to our current environment are not considered disorders. Similarly, the tendency toward a sedentary lifestyle and an aversiveness to exercise when there is no immediate demand for activity is thought to have evolved to conserve energy, but is maladaptive in our current environment in which there are few demands for vigorous physical activity that is needed for optimal health, yet it is not generally considered a disorder. The mismatch hypothesis fails to track our judgments about disorders, and it may particularly fail when applied to emotions because many of our intense emotional reactions, such as rage at perceived violations, ethnocentrism, and other aggression- and fear-based responses to various stimuli may have an evolved function but may no longer be adaptive in our modern more controlled and complexly interactive environments.

In addition to mistaking mismatches for disorders, a second common error in evolutionary accounts of disorder is to claim that a disorder does not have to result from a dysfunction but can be actively selected for because it confers an adaptive advantage. The argument seems to arise from two premises:

P1: Evolution by natural selection explains which genes persist.
P2: Many disorder types and the underlying genes that give rise to them have persisted.
C: These disorder types reveal that some disorders are naturally selected.

A clear expression of this view is found in Rachael Cooper (2007), who states that it is not necessary for a condition to result from a dysfunction for it to be considered a disorder:

> This is because in some cases the genetic bases of disorders may confer a biological advantage and thus be selected. In such a situation, from a biological point of view, there is maybe no dysfunction when cases of the disorder occur. This may well be the case with several types of mental disorder. Conditions including manic-depression, sociopathy, obsessive-compulsivity, anxiety, drug abuse and some personality disorders seem to have a genetic basis and yet occur at prevalence rates that are too high to be solely the result of mutations. This has led evolutionary psychologists to suggest that the genetic bases of these mental disorders must be adaptive in some way or other. (p. 33)

This argument is based on a misunderstanding of natural selection. The fact that certain elements of the genetic basis of a disorder have been naturally selected does not entail that the disorder itself has been selected. Consider, for example, the heterozygote advantage conferred by single copies of the genes underlying the genetic disorders of sickle cell anemia and cystic fibrosis. It is thought that having one copy of the genes was selected for to protect against certain pathogens, but when an individual by chance inherits two copies of that gene, that constitutes a dysfunction and a disorder. Neither the resulting disorder nor its specific genetic basis of two copies of the gene was naturally selected. The fact that one copy of the gene confers advantages and was selected for explains the higher-than-expected rate of the disorder. However, even if some genes underlying a disorder were naturally selected, either individually or in specific configurations because of benefits they confer when they appear in those configurations, it may still be the case that there is a specific configuration of the same genes that is a dysfunction and was selected against.

For example, a recent study of the genetics of autism (Polimanti & Gelernter, 2017) found that individual genes that confer a risk for autism are associated with cognitive advantages and were positively selected: "Using genome-wide data, we observed that common alleles associated with increased risk for ASD present a signature of positive selection. . . . ASD risk alleles could positively affect these [cognitive] mechanisms, causing better cognitive ability in carriers as a consequence" (pp. 4, 8). However, certain polygenic combinations to the contrary yielded autism: "However, an excessive burden of these risk variants is correlated with the onset of the developmental disorders included in the autism spectrum as the evolutionary cost" (p. 8). Thus, "[a]ccording to our interpretation of our data, such small-effect alleles were accumulated across the genome (polygenic adaptation) to the benefit of most but to the detriment of some" (p. 9). Cooper's (2007) objection is based on a simple misunderstanding of the difference between, for example, single-gene function versus polygenic dysfunction. To take one more example, it may well be that various genes for high aggressiveness, anxiety tolerance, lack of guilt inhibition, and others were each independently naturally selected as advantageous for niche subpopulations, but when all of them are inherited by one individual, a severe antisocial personality disorder results from the polygenic combination. If so, that does *not* mean that the severe antisocial personality disorder was naturally selected.

Understanding the Evolutionary Sources of Possible Diagnostic Errors in Judging Emotional Disorders

We now turn to two ways that the attribution of disorder versus normality can become confusing. These are expressed in what Randolph Nesse calls the "cliff-edge principle" (2004) and the "smoke detector principle" (2001).

The cliff-edge phenomenon concerns how we understand the likely distribution of normal phenotypes based on underlying genotypes or endophenotypes. For most continuously varying traits such as height or strength, the fitness distribution is a normal curve in which the optimal level of fitness occurs at the mean of the distribution and the fitness levels fall off continuously on either side. Thus, one expects a normal distribution of functional normality as well. However, for some traits, especially complex polygenic traits of the kind likely underlying emotional systems, the optimal fitness level may not be at the mean for the curve, and the fitness may fall off precipitously on one side of the mean, resulting in catastrophic failure (Vercken et al., 2012).

A physical example of a cliff-edge phenomenon is the trade-off linked to what is known as the "obstetrical dilemma." Increasing fetal skull size is advantageous in a roughly continuous way because as pre-birth skull size gets larger, the child's brain development prior to birth can proceed further, yielding adaptive advantages. However, there is a trade-off between that advantage and difficulty of the birth process and potential harm to the mother. These advantages and disadvantages may be considered roughly dimensional up to a point. But, at a certain skull size relative to the mother's birth canal size, there is a sudden extreme danger of impacted childbirth that can lead to the death of mother and child, a discontinuous threat. One question has been why birth canal size has not simply evolved to be larger, but birth canal size appears to be limited by the need to support the viscera during pregnancy (Pavličev et al., 2020). There is some evidence that the cliff-edge itself might be somewhat mitigated by a compensatory mechanism designed to increase correlation of fetal skull size with the mother's skull size and thus indirectly with her birth canal diameter, yielding a covariation between maternal and fetal skull size that reduces the threat to childbirth (Kaneko & Morimoto, 2020). However, in many domains, the cost of producing such protective mechanisms is sufficiently high that the sudden drop-off in adaptation along what otherwise might be considered a continuous phenotypic dimension with continuously varying fitness is left intact.

The cliff-edge view has also been applied to explain certain mental disorders. For example, as Nesse's (2004) comment on Burns's (2004) argument details, traits for social cognition increase the ability to predict how others may behave, but after a point may have radically negative psychological effects:

> [S]trong tendencies to use metarepresentations and [theory of mind] increase the ability to predict other people's behaviors, how they might be influenced, and how they might be trying to

manipulate you. It is only one step further, over the cliff's edge of psychotic cognition, as it were, to finding secret meanings and evidence for conspiracies in other people's most casual gestures, to believing idiosyncratic grand theories and religions, and to thinking that others are controlling your thoughts. (Nesse, 2004, p. 862)

In general, we are used to navigating the social environment with our emotions changing frequently but always staying within certain parameters that are coordinated with other people's level of emotion to yield socially constructive interactions. It is difficult to be aware of how limited the range of such socially constructive emotions may be. Love at first sight once or twice in a lifetime is one thing, but 10 times a day is quite another; fear is an essential emotion, but when the triggering mechanism is off by only a little bit one falls into phobia, hypochondria, panic disorder, and other panful and debilitating disorders. Another emotional example of the cliff-edge phenomenon may be found in suicidality. Suicide runs directly counter to what natural selection would predict, so one may question why the behavior would persist despite the strong natural selective pressure against it. A possible answer is that suicide is the result of multiple traits that increase fitness up to a point but then lead to a catastrophic failure. For example, and to be entirely speculative, an appreciation of one's relative contribution to societal affairs and appreciation by others via a self-esteem function may be advantageous to social cohesion, social coordination, organizing productive behavior, and encouragement to improve where one is lacking. However, too much awareness of a negative self-evaluation may result in going over a threshold which results in a miscalibrated view that everything one does is bad or useless and everyone views you as bad or useless, leading to self-destructive behavior. Similarly, the ability to judge and act decisively and quickly may be adaptive and increase productivity, but beyond a point it may result in impulsiveness. If these traits are combined in an individual, they may result in impulsive suicidality. In fact, the cliff-edge phenomenon is more general than anything having to do with asymmetric tail ends of a distribution. It may be that out of an overall distribution of on-average desirable genes there may be certain idiosyncratic combinations that cause disorder. This may the case with autism, where some combinations of genes that each are cognition-enhancing interact with each other to yield a disastrous drop in fitness.

A second phenomenon that can confuse diagnostic theory is known as the smoke detector principle. Disproportionate emotional responses to triggers are often thought to be an indicator of emotional disorder. The smoke detector principle calls this commonsense criterion into question.

It is often the case that emotions are biologically designed to be triggered at an intensity level that is roughly proportionate to the magnitude of the detected circumstantial trigger that poses the relevant adaptive challenge. For example, fear varies from slight concern or anxiety to terror depending on the imminence and magnitude of the threat. Similarly, the intensity of sadness tends to vary with the magnitude of the loss, the intensity of anger tends to vary with the magnitude of the perceived violation of one's rights, and the intensity of joy tends to vary with the magnitude of the triumph or accomplishment. However, this principle is not universal and is often violated. This is especially so when calibrating the level of emotional response to the nature of the trigger is too demanding of information-processing resources or defeats the need for rapid response. For example, fear of snakes often operates on all snakes and is not necessarily calibrated to the level of dangerousness of a given snake.

That disproportionate reactions often can be biologically designed normal responses in order to avoid a highly negative outcome at all cost has long been embraced by evolutionary-minded theorists and is consistent with common intuitions. Nesse (2001) has even dubbed this kind of defensive "overkill" due to the need to avoid a fatal mistake the "smoke detector principle." The name derives from the fact that, although having the purpose of warning of fires, a smoke detector alarm often all-too-irritatingly goes off when there is no fire due to all sorts of other smoky stimuli (e.g., in one of our apartments, when cooking fish). This nuisance is not considered a malfunction of the smoke detector, but rather a reflection of the fact that the detector is set to be on the sensitive side to detect smoke and is set to allow false positives in order to avoid false negatives because just one real fire that is missed can be fatal. Similar overly sensitive reactions occur in the emotions; for example, beavers display fear and thump their tails as a warning at the least sign that perhaps there is a predator nearby, giving rise to mostly mistaken warnings, yet the behavior is selected because just one mistake in the other direction can be fatal. This is true as well of physical defenses such as fever, which is one reason we often can treat fever and lessen its discomforts without substantially worsening the illness it is fighting, because fever is designed for a worst-case scenario and generally is an overreaction to what is actually needed in a given case of illness.

Of course, smoke detectors do break, either going off incessantly or randomly without a relationship to ambient smoke of the kind and level they are designed to detect, or not going off at all despite smoke. Yet, virtually everyone intuitively understands the distinction between a normally functioning but disproportionately reacting-to-fish-cooking smoke detector and a broken smoke detector on the basis of how it is designed to function, which includes the designed disproportionality to the trigger within its normality, not within malfunction. Perhaps a person unfamiliar with the design of smoke detectors might ask whether the fact that its alarm goes off while cooking fish means it is broken. Similarly, emotions pose a challenge to judgments of malfunction versus designed disproportional reaction because we do not have an independent understanding yet of the nuances of emotional design. However, it is clear that many emotions could be designed to trigger disproportionate reactions given the urgent adaptive challenges that they are often designed to address—as in the earlier example of fear of snakes. Yet, as with a smoke detector, if an emotion is chronically triggered by an irrelevant stimuli, or is disproportionately intense or weak, it provides a prima facie reason to suspect that there is some dysfunction and, given the often-harmful effects of miscalibrated emotions, plausibly an emotional disorder. For example, generalized anxiety disorder involves a persistent undirected anxiety that goes well beyond any kind of adaptive "vigilance" explanation that would fall under the smoke detector principle. As with a smoke detector whose alarm goes off incessantly, such generalized anxiety does not distinguish threatening situations from others and so fails to perform its designed function. Similarly, although there is controversy about when sadness and grief reach levels of disproportionality that indicate dysfunction, the case that is clearly a dysfunction to almost all medical observers is the classic "prototype" case of "out of the blue" sadness unrelated to any actual loss, which is so deep with such severe symptoms (e.g., psychotic ideation, psychomotor retardation), and is so enduring (e.g., continuing unresponsively to positive changes in the triggering situation), that no plausible false-positive protective tactical explanation seems capable of explaining the relationship between the trigger and the reaction (Horwitz & Wakefield, 2007). Similarly, there is no plausible normal-function account of seemingly random panic disorder unrelated to any fearful triggering event (Horwitz & Wakefield, 2012).

Beyond such clear cases, the smoke detector principle poses a major challenge to diagnostic discriminations. If naturally selected emotional mechanisms evolved to react to minor signals in a disproportionate way to avoid unlikely but costly disasters, then this makes it challenging to know when to diagnose emotions that are "over-reactive" to their environment as disorders. For example, although intense jealousy may be harmful to the individual and destructive of a relationship, even if successful a small number of times it might have been adaptive in the EEA where partner choice would have been paramount. Similarly, intense social anxiety may seem irrationally inappropriate in modern contexts but in the EEA, where even a small chance of being rejected by the group could be fatal, a smoke-detector-type oversensitivity to the possibility of social ostracization seems possible, rendering many of our current diagnoses of social anxiety disorder false positives.

The Superordinate Program Theory of Emotion
One reason emotional disorders are so difficult to define is that emotions are so complicated, with so many moving parts that can interact in unexpected ways. Thus, they may yield unusual outcomes that are sometimes normal but sometimes become pathological. To understand the potential range of emotional dysfunction from an evolutionary perspective, we now consider the most prominent current evolutionary psychological perspective on the natural biological functioning of emotions, the Superordinate Program Theory (Tooby & Cosmides, 2008). After some preliminary material, we discuss the theory and its implications, followed by a discussion of some limitations.

To recognize what is novel in the superordinate view, it is useful to understand that traditional theories of emotion have tended to analyze emotions as functionally singular entities, with different theorists each taking a stand on one particular type of feature as being the real essence of emotion. For example, folk psychology understands an emotion almost exclusively as a subjective feeling or pure affectual state; cognitive-behavioral therapists view emotions as essentially responses to certain kinds of cognitions; many psychologists and philosophers analyze emotion as a certain kind of evaluation of a situation, or a certain kind of belief, or a certain kind of desire; behaviorists have considered emotions to be behavioral response dispositions; and yet others have focused on physiological activation as the essence of emotion. Theorists in each of these camps have engaged in protracted debates about the true purpose and essence of emotions.

While these singular-function theories of the emotions were hotly debated, certain figures in the history of philosophy have recognized that such approaches are too simplistic and anticipated a more complex view that has affinities to the kind of polysystemic view that, we will see below, has become the standard evolutionary psychological approach. In order to appreciate the evolutionary turn in understanding the emotions from another angle, we prepare the way by taking a quick look at one of the philosophical views that tried to transcend more limited perspectives.

In approaching the evolutionary theory of emotions, we detour momentarily to comment on a favorite topic of ours, the French philosopher Maurice Merleau-Ponty's (1908–1961) phenomenological approach to emotion and meaning. Continental philosophers such as Merleau-Ponty ([1945] 2012) tend to argue that emotions are a transformation of one's world, and one of us (Wakefield) has long referred to emotions in this spirit as *global transformations*. At the risk of putting off those less interested in philosophy, Merleau-Ponty's theory is anchored in the Gestalt psychological notion that one's conscious "foreground" experiences are, much like a sculptural relief, only apparent and experienced against the form- and context-giving "background." Thus, rather than seeing emotions only as conscious foreground experiences, Merleau-Ponty conceptualizes emotions as involving a background that reshapes all of one's experiences that are formed within that background (Dreyfus & Wakefield, 1988). To the degree that both the foreground and the background against which one's foreground takes shape and gains meaning are reconfigured in an emotional experience, an emotion constitutes a global transformation of one's experience of the world.

Some of Merleau-Ponty's accounts of specific emotions and how the background works are fascinating. For example, grief often involves a feeling that the world is emptied of meaning and possibility. He argues that this is in part because lovers see the world through a joint background that makes everything implicitly appear through each other's eyes as well as their own. The loss of the loved one then removes that layer of background that gave everything part of its meaning and renders the world different and emptier of meaning.

We now turn to the very different global-transformational approach to emotion of the superordinate theory in evolutionary psychology. This theory begins from the premise, supported by both theoretical deductions and empirical evidence, that "the human mental architecture is crowded with evolved, functionally specialized programs" (Tooby & Cosmides, 2008, p. 116) that are each biologically designed to address a certain problem of adaptation confronted in the EEA. However, most adaptive challenges can be optimally confronted when a large number of organismic features are coordinated. When one is in a potentially aggressive confrontation, one's attention, perceptual sensitivities, and alertness are altered, one's muscles and viscera and heart alter their functioning, one's affective experience may be intensely activated, and one's cognitions change. All of these and other changes must be coordinated with each other and proportional to the precise nature of the environmental challenge, as well as responsive in a coordinated fashion to changes over time as the nature of the adaptive challenge alters. For example: "Because sexual rivals could be advantageously driven off by violence or its threat in a substantial fraction of the trillions of ancestral cases of mate competition, sexual jealousy is engineered to prepare the body physiologically for combat, and (when the rival is weak or unwary) motivates the individual to behave violently" (Tooby & Cosmides, 2008, p. 117).

This point can be illustrated by the example of how one sometimes reacts during a heated argument with a romantic partner. In the middle of the argument, one may feel not only physiologically activated and have intense affective experiences, but one's cognitions may change as well. The partner may look less desirable, and one may be thinking that overall the relationship is not worthwhile and perhaps should come to an end. But, as soon as one calms down, one sees the issue in proportion and sees that one was not looking at the evidence in a balanced way, and that despite the problems the relationship is overall a worthwhile one that one would not want to give up. This illustrates the important fact that even one's rational faculty of weighing evidence is altered during an emotional episode, giving rise to the classic view of there being a conflict between emotion and reason—although in fact reason is being adjusted to be more adaptive in the triggering circumstance. Moreover, as the biologically programmed terminators of emotional episodes fail to occur—for example, an apology is not forthcoming when one is angry at someone who, one feels, has violated one's rights or territory in an unjustifiable way—some emotions can cycle up to higher levels in order to force the desired response from a target individual, so if one is frustrated by lack of response, one may get frustrated and angrier and, say, yell and feel indignantly enraged.

The many different facets of the emotional reaction have to be coordinated because divergences in different aspects could undermine the adaptive response. Evolutionary psychologists list as many as 14 different aspects of functioning that might fall under a superordinate emotional regulation program: (1) perceptual mechanisms, (2) attention, (3) memory, (4) categorization, (5) motivational priorities, (6) current goals, (7) information-gathering adaptations, (8) specialized inference mechanisms, (9) communication and expression, (10) learning mechanisms, (11) reflexes, (12) energy level, mood, and effort allocation, (13) physiology, and (14) behavior (Al-Shawaf, 2016; Al-Shawaf et al., 2016,;Tooby & Cosmides, 1990, 2008; Cosmides & Tooby, 2000).

Moreover, the stimuli that might activate any particular program may simultaneously and potentially problematically activate other programs, thereby delivering "outputs that conflict with one another, interfering with or nullifying each other's functional products. For example, sleep and flight from a predator require mutually inconsistent actions, computations, and physiological states" (Tooby & Cosmides, 2008, p. 116). In order not only to coordinate all the subprograms of a given emotional response but also to avoid conflicting outputs resulting from a singular environmental stimuli, Tooby and Cosmides (2008) argue that we must have evolved superordinate programs that override some programs while others are active and coordinate many subprograms: "Each emotion entrains various other adaptive programs—deactivating some, activating others, and adjusting the modifiable parameters of still others—so that the whole system operates in a particularly harmonious and efficacious way when the individual is confronting certain kinds of triggering conditions or situations" (p. 117).

The theory thus states that an emotion is a superordinate program evolved for the purpose of orchestrating lower-level, stimuli-responsive programs such that two (or more) conflicting activities (e.g., sleep and flight from a predator) do not occur. One might argue that this aligns remarkably well to Merleau-Ponty's account of the emotions in the sense that what it means to say that emotions "[entrain] various other adaptive programs [by] deactivating some, activating others, and adjusting the modifiable parameters of still others" is just to say that it regiments the "background" such that one's foreground experience is realized within a world appropriate for its expression.

Some Concerns about the Superordinate Program Theory of Emotion

Although the superordinate view certainly reflects the nature of emotions better than monotheoretical views, there are several concerns one might have about it specifically as a proposed theory of emotion, as opposed to a description of one aspect of emotion. Perhaps the main problem is that it is too general. Although the superordinate view is a helpful corrective to one-dimensional thinking about emotion, the idea that emotions are superordinate programs tells very little about what is distinctive about emotions. The considerations emphasized by superordinate-program theorists—for example, that multiple evolved programs require coordination in many situations in order not to get in each other's way, that emotions have many subcomponents that must be coordinated, and that emotional components need real-time tweaking to respond optimally to environmental challenges—apply to many evolved processes. There is nothing distinctively "emotional" about emotions in this regard. Surely sleep, heart rate, and many other designed systems also require superordinate coordinating functions but are not emotions. Thus, for all its helpful illumination, the superordinate view fails to address classic problems such as what distinguishes emotions from other psychological systems such as drives. Laith Al-Shawaf (2016) argues persuasively that hunger has all the same properties as a superordinate emotional program in influencing the 14 variables cited above, and it certainly seems true that when one is very hungry one's cognition, affect, perceptual vigilance, attention, motivation, and so on, all are altered to address the adaptive challenge. As Al-Shawaf observes: "Indeed, the original authors of this idea suggest that, on their view, there may be no principled, non-arbitrary distinction between drive states and other emotion programs (Cosmides & Tooby, 2000)" (Al-Shawaf, 2016, p. 591, n. 1). If there is no distinction between emotion and other evolved superordinate programs, this is a useful finding, but this in effect denies that the category of emotion has something distinctive about it, and that is something that ironically would suggest that books like this one are misguided in relying on this category to organize an intellectual endeavor. We fail to be convinced that this traditional folk and scientific concept will go so easily into the night, and this point requires critical examination before dismantling the emotion category due to its sharing some salient features with other systems. Of course, as Al-Shawaf argues, it may be that a superordinate category encompassing superordinate programs of various kinds—hunger, sleep, emotions—can be usefully defined and explored, and that emotions could still be studied as one distinct subcategory of this higher-order conceptualization.

A second potentially problematic feature of conceptualizing emotions as superordinate programs is that this conception describes emotions strictly in information-processing computational terms, a common approach in evolutionary psychology. It thereby offers no insight into what most people take to be the most salient property of emotions, the role or nature of subjective emotional feelings or affects. Feelings of love, joy, pride, pity, rage, grief, or terror, for example, are for many people the most important and distinctive feature of emotions, and the feature most to be sought or avoided. We are not claiming, as has often been suggested, that these varying affective feelings are the essences of each of the emotions. However, they do seem to have a central role at least in folk thinking and they play a major role in identification of emotional disorders, and this is an area that the superordinate view fails to address in an illuminating way. Indeed, in the clinic, it is often these subjective feelings that are the source of distress and the indicator of an emotional disorder, as in chronic undirected anxiety in generalized anxiety disorder.

Note that we are not saying that the superordinate view totally ignores subjective experience. In fact, it is listed as one of the 14 subfeatures and as an important component of emotion. Rather, the superordinate view offers no distinctive insight into, and perhaps insufficient emphasis on, what is often considered, in life and in the psychiatric clinic, to be the most salient and even defining aspect of emotional experience. We acknowledge, however, that no theory at present adequately addresses the role of conscious experience in evolved mechanisms. These are profound issues for which no solution is currently in sight. The problem is that in proceeding from a "programming" model of the mind, the superordinate view inherently tends to sideline conscious experience in a conceptual-experiential sense, even if it is on the list of subprograms.

This brings us to a third issue, that, pending future neuroscientific research, the very name of the "superordinate program" view may be substantively misleading about the structure of emotions. The idea that there is a superordinate program coordinating all the components of a given emotional response—let alone the idea that there is a super-superordinate program regulating multiple such superordinate programs to prevent their maladaptive conflicting responses—could to some degree or in some instances be an adaptationist fantasy of how evolution would deal with such coordination challenges. It is common for organisms to lack internal mechanisms to do things that can instead be done by relying on environmental constraints. Most adaptive challenges at which emotions are directed have environmental triggers, and those environmental triggers could be relied upon to provoke multiple consistent mechanism responses without the intercession of a superordinate program. This is not a conceptual issue, but rather a scientific substantive issue of how mechanism coordination works. For example, in the area of anxiety, Le Doux and Pine (2016) propose that, rather than the traditional view that there is one overarching coordinating brain circuit corresponding to an overarching superordinate coordinating program that yields multiple aspects of anxiety, including behavioral and physiological arousal on the one hand and subjective affect on the other, in fact there are independent circuits that address each of these facets of an anxiety response. This view challenges current assumptions and remains controversial (e.g., Fanselow & Pennington, 2017; Pine & Le Dux, 2017). However, if these differing circuits underlying facets of the anxiety response do possess a degree of independence, then this has profound implications both for identifying anxiety disorders and for treating them, for "anxiety disorder" might in fact be referring to two quasi-independent loci of dysfunction. Moreover, if, as LeDoux and Pine suggest, even at the programming level conscious affect is not an epiphenomenon of behavioral and physiological activation, this brings more to the fore the issue raised earlier of the role of subjective experience that is ignored or downplayed as just one function among many in the standard superordinate account.

A final concern is that the intrinsic evolutionary plausibility of the superordinate view of emotion may obscure real differences among the emotions. The detailed analyses of individual emotions provided in this volume illustrate the challenges of elucidating what is unique about each emotion. This differentiation should extend to the superordinate structure of the emotion as well. Some emotions, such as fear and love, clearly involve complex reactions to ongoing environmental circumstances that present a coordination problem. For others, such as, say, nostalgia or regret, it is not so clear. It is possible that the superordinate theory of emotion is to some degree a result of having in mind certain emotions that are prototypical cases of requiring submechanism coordination, but that in fact the emotional universe is more diverse than the theory envisions. If so, then correspondingly, the nosologist's challenge of distinguishing emotional normality from emotional disorder is that much more complicated.

Conclusion

We have seen that, although one can argue that the concept of emotional disorder has a clear meaning as harmful emotional dysfunction, where dysfunction refers to failure of biologically designed function, the actual judgment as to what is and is not an emotional disorder can be extraordinarily complex and subject to many potential errors. It is important to recognize that access to treatment of problematic emotions should not be limited to emotional disorders. Society's demands may not correlate with our biologically designed emotional natures and cause emotional distress that deserves social support and attempts at remediation. Regarding emotional disorder itself, the difficulties we have surveyed perhaps partially explain why emotional disorders such as depressive and anxiety disorders are some of the most controversial categories in the DSM, with intense debates about whether we are overdiagnosing or underdiagnosing emotional disorders. A greater understanding of how human beings are biologically designed to function emotionally within each emotion category is needed in order to clarify the basic distinctions underlying psychiatric intervention. The detailed chapters on specific emotions and emotional issues in this volume are a step in the right direction toward a more sophisticated understanding of the nuances of difference between emotional disorder and our remarkably flexible and often intense emotional normality.

References

Al-Shawaf, L. (2016). The evolutionary psychology of hunger. *Appetite, 105*, 591–595.
Al-Shawaf, L., Conroy-Beam, D., Asao, K., & Buss, D. M. (2016). Human emotions: An evolutionary psychological perspective. *Emotion Review, 8*(2), 173–186.
American Psychiatric Association. (2013). *Diagnostic and statistical manual of mental disorders* (5th ed.: DSM-5). APA.
Boorse, C. (1977). Health as a theoretical concept. *Philosophy of Science, 44*, 542–573.
Burns, J. K. (2004). An evolutionary theory of schizophrenia: Cortical connectivity, metarepresentation, and the social brain. *The Behavioral and Brain Sciences, 27*(6), 831–885.
Clark, L. A., Cuthbert, B., Lewis-Fernández, R., Narrow, W. E., & Reed, G. M. (2017). Three approaches to understanding and classifying mental disorder: ICD-11, DSM-5, and the National Institute of Mental Health's Research Domain Criteria (RDoC). *Psychological Science in the Public Interest: A Journal of the American Psychological Society, 18*(2), 72–145.
Cooper, R. (2007). *Psychiatry and philosophy of science*. Routledge.
Cosmides, L., & Tooby, J. (2000). Evolutionary psychology and the emotions. In M. Lewis & J. M. Haviland-Jones (Eds.), *Handbook of emotions* (2nd ed., pp. 91–115). Guilford Press.
Dreyfus, H. L., & Wakefield, J. C. (1988). From depth psychology to breadth psychology: A phenomenological approach to psychopathology. In S. Messer, L. Sass, & R. Woolfolk (eds.), *Hermeneutics and psychological theory: Interpretive approaches to personality, psychotherapy, and psychopathology* (pp. 272–288). Rutgers University Press.
Eisenberg, D. T., Campbell, B., Gray, P. B, Sorenson, M. (2008). Dopamine receptor genetic polymorphisms and body composition in undernourished pastoralists: An exploration of nutrition indices among nomadic and recently settled Ariaal men of northern Kenya. *BMC Evolutionary Biology, 8*, 173. https://doi.org/10.1186/1471-2148-8-173.

Elder, T. E. (2010). The importance of relative standards in ADHD diagnoses: Evidence based on exact birth dates. *Journal of Health Economics, 29*, 641–656.

Evans, W. N., Morril, M. S., & Parente, S. T. (2010). Measuring inappropriate medical diagnosis and treatment in survey data: The case of ADHD among school-age children. *Journal of Health Economics, 29*, 657–673.

Fanselow, M. S., & Pennington, Z. T. (2017). The danger of LeDoux and Pine's two-system framework for fear. *American Journal of Psychiatry, 174*(11), 1120–1121.

Faucher, L., & Forest, D. (Eds.). (2021). *Defining mental disorder: Jerome Wakefield and his critics*. MIT Press.

First, M. (2007). Potential implications of the harmful dysfunction analysis for the development of DSM-V and ICD-11. *World Psychiatry, 6*(3), 158–159.

First, M. B., & Wakefield, J. C. (2010). Defining "mental disorder" in DSM-V. *Psychological Medicine, 40*(11), 1779–1782.

First, M. B., & Wakefield, J. C. (2013). Diagnostic criteria as dysfunction indicators: Bridging the chasm between the definition of mental disorder and diagnostic criteria for specific disorders. *Canadian Journal of Psychiatry, 58*(12), 663–669.

Foucault, M. (1965). *Madness and civilization: A history of insanity in the Age of Reason* (R. Howard, Trans.). Pantheon.

Frances, A. (2012). DSM-5 is a guide, not a bible: Simply ignore its 10 worst changes. *HuffPost Science Blog*. Available at http://www.huffingtonpost.com/allen-frances/dsm-5_b_2227626.html. Accessed November 23, 2013.

Friedman, R. A. (2014). A natural fix for A.D.H.D. *New York Times*, October 31, 2014. https://www.nytimes.com/2014/11/02/opinion/Sunday/a-natural-fix-for-adhd.html. Accessed February 9, 2022.

Garson, J. (2021). The developmental plasticity challenge to Wakefield's view. In L. Faucher & D. Forest (Eds.), *Defining mental disorder: Jerome Wakefield and his critics* (pp. 335–351). MIT Press.

Horwitz, A. V., & Wakefield, J. C. (2007) *The loss of sadness: How psychiatry transformed normal sorrow into depressive disorder*. Oxford University Press.

Horwitz, A. V., & Wakefield, J. C. (2012). *All we have to fear: Psychiatry's transformation of natural anxieties into mental disorders*. Oxford University Press.

Kaneko, A., & Morimoto, N. (2020). Covariation of fetal skull and maternal pelvis during the perinatal period in rhesus macaques and evolution of childbirth in primates. *Proceedings of the National Academy of Sciences, 117*(35), 21251–21257.

Kinner, S. (2003). Psychopathy as an adaptation: Implications for society and social policy. In R. W. Bloom & N. Dess (Eds.), *Psychological dimensions to war and peace. Evolutionary psychology and violence: A primer for policymakers and public policy advocates* (pp. 57–81). Praeger/Greenwood.

Klein, D. F. (1999). Harmful dysfunction, disorder, disease, illness, and evolution. *Journal of Abnormal Psychology, 108*(3), 421–429.

Klerman, G., & Schechter, G. (1981). Ethical aspects of drug treatment. In S. Bloch & P. Chodof (Eds.), *Psychiatric ethics* (pp. 117–130). Oxford University Press.

Kotov, R., Krueger, R. F., Watson, D., Achenbach, T. M., Althoff, R. R., Bagby, R. M., Brown, T. A., Carpenter, W. T., Caspi, A., Clark, L. A., Eaton, N. R., Forbes, M. K., Forbush, K. T., Goldberg, D., Hasin, D., Hyman, S. E., Ivanova, M. Y., Lynam, D. R., Markon, K. . . . Zimmerman, M. (2017). The hierarchical taxonomy of psychopathology (HiTOP): A dimensional alternative to traditional nosologies. *Journal of Abnormal Psychology, 126*(4), 454–477.

Kring, A. M. (2008). Emotion disturbances and transdiagnostic processes in psychopathology. In M. Lewis, J. M. Havoland-Jones, & L. F. Barrett (Eds.), *Handbook of emotions* (3rd ed., pp. 691–705). Guilford Press.

Krupp, D. B., Sewall, L. A., Lalumière, M. L., Sheriff, C., & Harris, G. T. (2012). Nepotistic patterns of violent psychopathy: Evidence for adaption? *Frontiers in Psychology, 3*, 1–8.

Krupp, D. B., Sewall, L. A., Lalumière, M. L., Sheriff, C., & Harris, G. T. (2013). Psychopathy, adaption, and disorder. *Frontiers in Psychology, 4*, 1–5.

Laing, R. D. (1967). *The politics of experience*. Penguin Books.

LeDoux, J. E., & Pine, D. S. (2016). Using neuroscience to help understand fear and anxiety: A two-system framework. *American Journal of Psychiatry, 173*(11), 1083–1093.

Lilienfeld, S. O., & Treadway, M. T. (2016). Clashing diagnostic approaches: DSM-ICD versus RDoC. *Annual Review of Clinical Psychology, 12*, 435–463.

Merleau-Ponty, M. ([1945] 2012). *Phenomenology of perception* (D. A. Landy, Trans.). Routledge.

Nesse, R. M. (2001). The smoke detector principle: Natural selection and the regulation of defensive responses. *Annals of the New York Academy of Sciences, 935*(1), 75–85.

Nesse, R. M. (2004). Cliff-edge fitness functions and the persistence of schizophrenia. *Behavioral and Brain Sciences, 27*(6), 862–863.

Pavličev, M., Romero, R., & Mitteroecker, P. (2020). Evolution of the human pelvis and obstructed labor: New explanations of an old obstetrical dilemma. *American Journal of Obstetrics and Gynecology, 222*(1), 3–16.

Pine, D. S., & LeDoux, J. E. (2017). Elevating the role of subjective experience in the clinic: Response to Fanselow and Pennington. *American Journal of Psychiatry, 174*(11), 1121–1122.

Polimanti, R., & J. Gelernter. (2017). Widespread signatures of positive selection in common risk alleles associated to autism spectrum disorder. *PLoS Genetics, 13*(2), e1006618.

Reimer, M. (2008). Psychopathy without (the language of) disorder. *Neuroethics, 1*(3), 185–198.

Rind, B. & Yuill, R. (2012). Hebephilia as mental disorder? A historical, cross-cultural, sociological, cross-species, non-clinical empirical, and evolutionary review. *Archives of Sexual Behavior, 41*(4), 797–829.

Scheff, T. J. (1966). *Being mentally ill: A sociological theory*. Aldine.

Schwartz, A. (2012, October 9). Attention disorder or not, pills to help in school. *New York Times*. https://www.nytimes.com/2012/10/09/health/attention-disorder-or-not-children-prescribed-pills-to-help-in-school.html

Sedgwick, P. (1982). *Psycho politics*. Harper & Row.

Spitzer, R. L. (1997). Brief comments from a psychiatric nosologist weary from his own attempts to define mental disorder: Why Ossorio's definition muddles and Wakefield's "harmful dysfunction" illuminates the issues. *Clinical Psychology: Science and Practice, 4*(3), 259–261.

Spitzer, R. L. (1998). Diagnosis and need for treatment are not the same. *Archives of General Psychiatry, 55*, 120.

Spitzer, R. L. (1999). Harmful dysfunction and the DSM definition of mental disorder. *Journal of Abnormal Psychology, 108*(3), 430–432.

Szasz, T. S. (1974). *The myth of mental illness: Foundations of a theory of personal conduct* (Rev. ed.). Harper & Row.

Tooby, J. & Cosmides, L. (1990). The past explains the present: Emotional adaptations and the structure of ancestral environments. *Ethology and Sociobiology, 11*, 375–424.

Tooby, J., & Cosmides, L. (2008). The evolutionary psychology of the emotions and their relationship to internal regulatory variables. In M. Lewis, J. M. Havoland-Jones, & L. F. Barrett (Eds.), *Handbook of emotions* (3rd ed., pp. 114–137). Guilford Press.

Vercken, E., Wellenreuther, M., Svensson, E. I., & Mauroy, B. (2012). Don't fall off the adaptation cliff: when asymmetrical fitness selects for suboptimal traits. *PLoS ONE, 7*(4), e34889.

Wakefield, J. C. (1992a). The concept of mental disorder: On the boundary between biological facts and social values. *American Psychologist, 47*, 373–388.

Wakefield, J. C. (1992b). Disorder as harmful dysfunction: A conceptual critique of DSM-III-R's definition of mental disorder. *Psychological Review, 99*, 232–247.

Wakefield, J. C. (1999a). Evolutionary versus prototype analyses of the concept of disorder. *Journal of Abnormal Psychology, 108*, 374–399.

Wakefield, J. C. (1999b). Mental disorder as a black box essentialist concept. *Journal of Abnormal Psychology, 108*, 465–472.

Wakefield, J. C. (2000). Spandrels, vestigial organs, and such: Reply to Murphy and Woolfolk's "The harmful dysfunction analysis of mental disorder." *Philosophy, Psychiatry, and Psychology, 7*, 253–269.

Wakefield, J. C. (2007). The concept of mental disorder: Diagnostic implications of the harmful dysfunction analysis. *World Psychiatry, 6*, 149–156.

Wakefield, J. C. (2014). The biostatistical theory versus the harmful dysfunction analysis, part 1: Is part-dysfunction a sufficient condition for medical disorder? *Journal of Medicine and Philosophy, 39*, 648–682.

Wakefield, J. C. (2015). Psychological justice: DSM-5, false positive diagnosis, and fair equality of opportunity. *Public Affairs Quarterly, 29*, 32–75.

Wakefield, J. C. (2016a). The concepts of biological function and dysfunction: Toward a conceptual foundation for evolutionary psychopathology. In D. Buss (Ed.), *Handbook of evolutionary psychology* (2nd ed., Vol 2., pp. 988–1006). Oxford University Press.

Wakefield, J. C. (2016b). Diagnostic issues and controversies in DSM-5: Return of the false positives problem. *Annual Review of Clinical Psychology, 12*, 105–132.

Wakefield, J. C. (2021). Are there naturally selected disorders? Supplementary reply to Rachel Cooper. In L. Faucher and D. Forest (Eds.), *Defining mental disorder: Jerome Wakefield and his critics* (pp. 577–591). MIT Press.

Wakefield, J. C., & First, M. B. (2003). Clarifying the distinction between disorder and nondisorder: Confronting the overdiagnosis ("false positives") problem in DSM-V. In K. A. Phillips, M. B. First, and H. A. Pincus (Eds.), *Advancing DSM: Dilemmas in psychiatric diagnosis* (pp. 23–56). American Psychiatric Press.

Wakefield, J. C., & First, M. B. (2012). Placing symptoms in context: The role of contextual criteria in reducing false positives in DSM diagnosis. *Comprehensive Psychiatry, 53*, 130–139.

Zoëga, H., Valdimarsdóttir, U. A., & Hernández-Díaz, S. (2012). Age, academic performance, and stimulant prescribing for ADHD: a nationwide cohort study. *Pediatrics, 130*, 1012–1018.

CHAPTER 58

Anxiety and Phobias

Leif Edward Ottesen Kennair, Miriam Lindner, Kristen Hagen, and Simen Mjøen Larsen

> **Abstract**
> Anxiety is an exaggerated fear-like response to experienced threat. Several different subtypes of anxiety disorders exist, with emphasis on the specific triggers, stimuli, and situations that the patient will avoid and typical safety behaviors that are employed to reduce the experienced threat. The development of anxiety, once considered to be best described by associative theories, has a clear non-associative element. Over the years, efficient treatment of anxiety has developed from exposure and response-prevention interventions, to encompass more cognitive and metacognitive methods. While several adaptive and evolutionary-based explanations for anxiety disorders have been proposed, this chapter suggests that none of these current theories is convincing: fear of actual danger or threats is adaptive, anxiety disorders are probably not. The chapter discusses evolutionary approaches to the development of different anxiety disorders and their maintenance, considers existing evidence for the potential adaptive value of anxiety disorders, and presents new research from the treatment of specific anxiety disorders.
>
> **Key Words:** fear, phobia, anxiety disorder, adaptation, evolutionary clinical psychology

Introduction

Some people search every room, especially the nooks and crannies, for spiders. Others will take the stairs of high-rise buildings despite fully operational elevators. Many people fret about how other people might perceive them as weird, weak, or awkward for blushing or sweating at social gatherings. Then there are those who feel like they will have a heart attack every time they get excited. Finally, some people live their lives as if they were horror movie directors—considering every bad thing that might happen to them in almost any situation. None of these behaviors needs to be problematic, of course. Maybe the individual in the first example is a biologist, studying arachnids. The second person may be an athlete or someone in dire need of more daily exercise. However, these behaviors are typically displayed by people suffering from anxiety disorders and phobias, attempting to keep danger at bay while simultaneously coping the best they can with the aversive bodily symptoms of fear.

Fear is one of the most prominent examples of a functional emotion. In his functional approach to fear, Cannon (1915) identified the fight-or-flight aspect of fear and how physiological activation solved these problems (later expanded with another typical defense behavior, freeze). The functional nature of fear is well established. As Darwin (1872) noted, across species, we find fear-like emotions and behaviors. If animals did not fear recurring and real threats, they would have produced fewer offspring, resulting in reduced fitness (Kennair, 2007). This is generally understood by most researchers, clinicians, and patients alike.

While fear is a normal and appropriate emotional response to actual and present danger, anxiety and phobias encompass many specific mental disorders, characterized by a disproportionate response in the absence of such danger. Fear motivates avoidance of dangers that may otherwise result in harm or death. Fear also triggers adaptive species-specific defense behaviors, selected by natural selection because of their ability to reduce the likelihood of harm or loss in threatening situations (Bolles, 1970). Anxiety disorders mirror this by motivating safety behaviors and avoidance. However, in the case of anxiety disorders, the fear response is exaggerated; the safety behaviors will most often maintain the disorder and/or increase symptoms, rather than providing a solution to an actual problem. As such, a fundamental understanding of the underlying adaptive emotions and their evolutionary functions is helpful for clinicians and anxiety researchers.

The current chapter considers anxiety disorders and phobias from this functional perspective. While we do not consider these exaggerated conditions adaptive, an evolutionary psychological approach reveals design features and other aspects of these emotional states. We will also consider the current status of both anxiety acquisition and treatment, highlighting their evolutionary aspects, while also critically discussing these approaches from a clinical perspective.

What Are Anxiety Disorders?

Occasional bouts of anxiety, worry, and fear are common, normal, and to be expected. However, when bouts of anxiety or worry become strong or pervasive enough to interfere with daily activities, we enter the domain of psychopathology. An anxiety disorder is a mental health disorder characterized by intense feelings of worry, anxiety, or fear; a stress response disproportionate to an event's impact; the inability to set aside a worry; and restlessness, among others. Several types of anxiety disorders exist, including social anxiety disorder, generalized anxiety disorder, panic disorder, and various specific phobias. Anxiety disorders are very common, with a conservative 12-month prevalence estimate of approximately 18% of the population, with social anxiety disorder and phobias being the two most common specific disorders. Anxiety disorders exhibit a high degree of comorbidity, especially among the more severe cases (Kessler et al., 2005).

Two basic underlying emotions are dysregulated or overactive in anxiety disorders and phobias: fear and disgust. While many symptoms of anxiety disorders are borne out of exaggerated fear reactions, in some cases, the aversive emotional reaction is primarily disgust. For example, some patients with obsessive-compulsive disorder experience high levels of disgust as the most prominent reaction, and many phobias—including phobias for snakes, insects, rodents, spiders, and even of small holes (trypophobia)—are primarily rooted in a disgust response. Clinicians need to understand the difference between the functions of fear and disgust in anxiety disorders and specific phobias—and the cognitions and metacognitions engaged in each of them—to best accommodate the patient and to properly devise relevant exposure, behavioral, and cognitive therapy interventions.

Individuals suffering from anxiety disorders experience increased physiological, sympathetic activation. Physical symptoms may therefore include, but are not limited to, shortness of breath, tensioning of striatal musculature, increased flow of blood to the large muscle groups resulting in paleness, sweating, and other bodily changes that aid preparation for fight or flight. With disgust, one may also experience feelings of repulsion and nausea, which motivates avoidance. Cognitively, there will be increased worry and apprehension, and disorder-typical hypervigilance, and danger monitoring directed toward the disorder-defining stimuli or situations. Behaviorally, anxiety will motivate avoidance of the stimulus or situation that elicits the emotional response as well as safety behaviors intended to reduce the perceived danger. These are specific to each disorder and will be described in detail below. In treatment, therefore, one needs to approach all anxiety disorders with an exposure and response-prevention approach: one wishes to increase the patient's ability to approach the aversive stimulus or situation without avoidance, while simultaneously discontinuing the safety behaviors—some of which may be cognitive (Kennair, 2007; Kennair & Kleppestø, 2018; Kennair & Lindner, 2017).

Evolutionary Approaches to Specific Anxiety Disorders
Why We Need to Consider Specific Anxiety Disorders
Different anxiety disorders are functionally defined by the specific avoidance and safety behaviors that patients typically display. As such, two disorders that may look similar on the surface—such as social anxiety disorder and agoraphobia—will differ in, for example, why different patients get nervous in a queue at the supermarket. Whereas individuals suffering from social anxiety disorder primarily consider negative evaluations from peers based upon their interoceptive experience of how their symptoms are perceived by others (Clark & Wells, 1995), individuals suffering from agoraphobia are primarily mostly distressed about being unable to run home should they experience a panic attack (Clark, 1986). To fully understand the specific disorders, we need to consider current diagnostic criteria (which are ever-evolving) and the most influential cognitive-behavioral clinical models. The latter identifies the most relevant functional features (e.g., safety behaviors, information processing, and stimulus avoidance (Kennair, 2007, 2014). Correct diagnosis, therefore, also has consequences for the choice of treatment approaches.

Many different evolutionary psychological accounts of specific disorders exist (Kennair, 2007); while they account for aspects of underlying mechanisms that might have been adaptive, they also describe the disorders as harmful dysfunctions (Wakefield, 1999). We will discuss some major subtypes of anxiety disorders, along with prominent evolutionary psychological theories that aim to explain their etiology.

Specific Phobias
It seems that only human imagination sets the limit for what kinds of objects can trigger a phobic reaction. However, clinical experience tells us that fear of evolutionarily relevant threats is more common. From an evolutionary perspective, it is unsurprising that objects thought to have signaled threats to fitness and reproductive success in the environment of evolutionary adaptedness (EEA) are prevalent triggers (Öhman & Mineka, 2001). Heights, darkness, water, snakes, spiders, rodents, insects, strangers, and "monsters" are among the common triggers. Typically these stimuli are classical features of horror movies (Clasen, 2017). Although less dangerous in modern times, avoidance protected our ancestors from physical injury, disease, violence, and predation. Acquisition of fear for those things that were dangerous in our evolutionary past is much easier than for evolutionary novel phenomena, such as driving too fast or not wearing seatbelts (Kennair & Lindner, 2017; Öhman et al., 1976; Öhman & Mineka, 2001). This proclivity has consequences for modern governmental health campaigns; most people do not fear excessive amounts of sugar, fat, alcohol, drugs, nicotine, unprotected sex, sunbathing without applying sunscreen, or speeding beyond the limit. Health campaigns attempting to induce fear are often unsuccessful (Ruiter et al., 2001). Rather than scaring people, these stimuli often engage reward circuits—and because we have evolved to seek rather

than avoid them, they often result in lifestyle disorders (Zheng et al., 2009). Rather than being horror ingredients, these are the makings of a happy holiday in Ibiza, Palm Beach, or Phuket.

Specific phobias are common and widespread among the general population. Estimated cross-national lifetime and 12-month prevalence rates of specific phobia are 7.4% and 5.5%, respectively (Harvard Medical School, 2007), and about 12% will endure some kind of phobic symptoms at some time in their lives (Seim & Spates, 2009). Because many fear-inducing stimuli bear evolutionary relevance, it is no surprise that evolutionary psychologists have begun to address their origins, patterns of expression, and avenues for intervention. In explaining specific phobias, they have divided explanatory questions into two broad categories: those concerning ultimate evolutionary function, on the one hand, and those concerning proximate mechanisms, on the other. There is growing recognition that we need to understand the proximal mechanisms that underlie disorders and the more distal, evolutionary mechanisms that give rise to pathology in the first place (Nesse & Williams, 1996). While Darwin himself argued that anxiety served an adaptive function (1872), recent theories in the field of evolutionary psychology have highlighted the importance of threat-detection mechanisms (Marks & Nesse, 1994) and how biases in such threat-detection mechanisms may be relevant to the psychopathology of specific phobias. Here, we review prominent theoretical approaches in evolutionary psychology that explain specific phobias, followed by an overview of empirical studies by the domain of specific phobias.

PREPAREDNESS

Originally proposed as a reformulation of the conditioning model, the perspective of preparedness posits that certain stimuli have such evolutionary relevance that they are more likely to evoke fear. Because fearing these stimuli has benefited survival, the most common fears are more stable, more easily acquired, or both. The distribution of fears mirrors the distribution of phobias, as the more commonly feared stimuli in specific phobias are usually evolutionarily old threats (Marks & Nesse, 1994).

FEAR MODULE THEORY

Discounting the notion of purely non-associative fear acquisition, Öhman and Mineka (2001) and Mineka and Öhman (2002a) suggested the concept of a fear module, a system specifically adjusted to solve adaptive problems provoked by life-threatening situations in our ancestral past. Based on Razran (1971), the authors argued that the acquisition of fears (and, by extension, phobias) involves an interplay between the almost-automatic, involuntary detection of threatening stimuli (governed by the amygdala, which contains associative pathways that collect and store information about reliable cues-and-consequences relationships) and higher modes of cognition (governed by the hippocampus). The latter enables expectations that allow avoidance of threats in the absence of explicit cues that signal danger (Mineka & Öhman, 2002b). Cognitions result from these responses because of the need to give meaning to an experience and justification for the fear (Foa et al., 1989). The fear module includes four characteristics: relative selectivity to stimuli (not all stimuli will be equally effective in activating the module); automaticity in response; encapsulation (once initiated, the fear response remains out of cognitive control); and a specific neuronal circuit (the amygdala). Effectiveness refers to the faster acquisition and more resistance to extinction of associations between the stimulus and fear (Mineka & Öhman, 2002b).

Certain fears and phobias, such as fear of strangers, separation, and darkness, occur as part of different stages in human development and follow a stable pattern (Boyer & Bergstrom, 2011). An example is a normal apprehension of heights that emerges in development simultaneous with the ability to crawl (Gibson & Walk, 1960). Cognitive machinery dedicated to approach/avoidance evaluations regarding height could trigger activation of the fear module if conditions are met (e.g., appraisal of lack of control). The probability of activating the fear module depends on species-typical adaptations (e.g., tree-dwelling monkeys seldom develop a fear of heights, but humans do), within-species variation in those adaptations (e.g., prepared connectivity between cognitive machinery dedicated to evaluations of heights and the fear module), and context (e.g., appraisal of control). Learning through conditioning would then skew evaluations toward avoidance of heights.

DISGUST SENSITIVITY

According to the disgust-sensitivity hypothesis, certain fears and phobias are born out of disease- and contamination-avoidance. Disgust sensitivity can therefore explain why people might be phobic of animals, which, rather than being predatory, are associated with disease (e.g., cockroaches and maggots).

While these theoretical accounts differ concerning the role of innateness, learning, and conditioning of fear responses—and the acquisition of phobias—they share the underlying notion that major phobias constitute exacerbated responses to evolutionarily relevant threats. When considered from this perspective, many phobias are not as irrational as often assumed. We are more likely to fear events, situations, and objects that posed threats to the survival of our ancestors (e.g., deadly predators, darkness, heights, wide-open spaces) than the most frequently encountered potentially deadly objects in our modern environment, such as guns, cars, or motorcycles (Marks, 1969; Seligman, 1971). Further, these recent accounts of phobias openly admit to the divergent etiologies possessed by different types of phobias. In contrast with phobic responses to fitness-relevant stimuli, such as height phobia, water phobia, snake phobia, and spider phobia (Menzies & Clarke, 1993; Murray & Foote, 1979), they acknowledge that the onset of evolutionary-neutral fears—which make up a relatively small proportion of phobias—may stem from conditioning (e.g., dental phobias, dog phobia, accident phobia, choking phobia (Di Nardo et al., 1988; Greenberg et al., 1988; Kuch, 1997; Oosterink et al., 2009).

BLOOD-INJECTION-INJURY PHOBIAS

A special case of a simple phobia is blood-injection-injury (BII) phobia. Affected individuals experience automatic and uncontrollable fear when exposed; however, they do not typically experience the elevated heart rate that is associated with the fight or flight response (Kennair, 2007; Marks, 1988). Instead, they experience a decrease in blood pressure, making it the only anxiety disorder that causes people to faint. This might be adaptive; lying down with a steep drop in blood pressure might be more helpful than having high blood pressure and moving around after sustaining severe injury and bleeding profusely.

Panic Disorder and Agoraphobia

Panic disorder is defined by sudden, intense, and recurring feelings of terror and fear in the absence of real danger. These feelings are commonly not limited to specific situations or circumstances, making them unpredictable (producing episodic paroxysmal anxiety; APA, 2013). As a result of suffering a panic attack in a particular place or location, individuals will often develop agoraphobia, defined by a fear of leaving home or fear of being unable to return to safety when they experience a panic attack. While clinicians consider them as distinct mental disorders, the comorbidity between the two conditions is so high that they are usually considered together: indeed, about a fifth of those who satisfy the criteria for panic disorder in their life also meet the criteria for agoraphobia, and over half of those with agoraphobia also have panic disorder (Kessler et al., 2005). In a cross-national analysis, De Jonge et al. (2016) report a DSM-5 lifetime prevalence for panic disorder of 1.7% (in the United States, the prevalence is higher, 4.8%) and a projected lifetime risk at age 75 years of 2.7%. Panic attacks are common in the general population, with a reported lifetime prevalence of 13.2% and a projected risk of 23.0% at age 75.

The paroxysmal anxiety experienced in panic disorder is thought to be an acute stress response evoked by the perception of immediate danger, and the symptoms seem to be preparation for or execution of the flight response (Bracha et al., 2004; Cannon, 1915). However, this will not solve the misperceived threat of choking or suffering a heart attack. In panic disorder, the threats are not real; instead, they are misinterpretations of bodily symptoms of anxiety. The four most common catastrophes that anxiety symptoms are misinterpreted to signal are falling into madness ("going crazy"), suffering a heart attack, choking, or fainting. This is because symptoms of anxiety can mimic these outcomes. The acuteness of the symptoms and the perceived distressing consequences commonly lead to the avoidance of situations or places associated with a panic attack. Such avoidance then develops into agoraphobia.

Traditionally, learning theorists have viewed panic attacks as an unconditioned response that spreads to new stimuli through stimulus generalization (Jansson & Öst, 1982; Watson & Marks, 1971) However, patients will rarely be able to identify the trigger of the unconditioned stimulus. Recent theories posit that the capacity for panic serves to facilitate escape from mortal danger (and preparing the body to engage in flight), but that the brain "misinterprets" bodily sensations to mean that such danger is indeed present. As such, our vulnerability to experience panic constitutes a byproduct of our capacity for understanding abstract concepts and metacognitive abilities. However, patients with panic disorder will more often lay down than run when having an attack, and attacks are often triggered by the slightest physical exertion and activation—and these symptoms of bodily activation are interpreted as a heart attack.

Sometimes, panic attacks will occur in a designated safe place. In such cases, fleeing does not prevent the panic itself; rather, panic occurs in a place where the perceived likelihood of getting help for the possible catastrophe is more likely. Ancestrally, this direction of flight toward home and trusted kin could have been beneficial since these were quintessential for protection. Yet again, in panic disorder, there is no real danger to escape. Thus, while the underlying mechanisms might serve an ultimate function, panic disorder's safety behaviors merely maintain the false and catastrophic interpretation of the activated fight-or-flight response (Clark, 1986).

The understanding that panic is not life-threatening or that one will not faint from panic attacks—which one attempts to accomplish in treatment—makes it unlikely that panic disorder is an evolved adaptation. Panic simply does not solve any fitness-relevant problem. In addition, panic is a culturally defined misconception disorder: in Western cultures, anxiety symptoms are mistaken to be the onset of a heart attack; in Arabic cultures, the same symptoms may be interpreted as a *djinn* sitting on one's chest (Bragazzi & Del Puente, 2012). Panic disorder exists because anxiety causes symptoms, and due to being catastrophically misinterpreted as bodily or mental or spiritual catastrophes, thereby elicit safety behaviors that further maintain the problem (Clark, 1986).

Social Anxiety Disorder
Social anxiety disorder is characterized by intense fear and avoidance of one or more social situations that signal potential evaluation by and scrutiny of others (APA, 2013; Kennair & Kleppestø, 2018). Individuals suffering from social anxiety disorder will experience debilitating

anxiety around social interactions, fearing self-consciousness, embarrassment, and judgment. First recognized as a separate diagnosis in 1980, it has since been divided into subtypes, depending on the generalizability of social triggers and combinations of symptoms (Hofmann et al., 2004). Social anxiety disorder is the most common anxiety disorder outside the specific phobias, with a lifetime prevalence of about 12% (Kessler et al., 2005).

Early comprehensive evolutionary models of social anxiety (Öhman, 1986) viewed social anxiety of dominant and aggressive conspecifics in light of preparedness. Angry faces are salient social markers indicating the threat of ostracism and non-acceptance by others. Hence, social anxiety might be a functional part of adaptations designed to ensure submissiveness toward those who can impose fitness-relevant costs.

Humans have a fundamental need to belong to social groups since they offer support, especially in times of hardship (Baumeister & Leary, 1995). From an evolutionary perspective, ostracism presented an enormous hazard to fitness in the hunter-gatherer ecology. However, group membership is not given but earned. To receive others' investment and care, one must be a valuable member of said social group. Naturally, this introduces competition: individuals will perform behaviors commonly seen as beneficial to the group, leaving some at the higher and some at the lower end of a group hierarchy. At the lower end, individuals will attempt to improve their status, attractiveness, and value to the group; at the higher end, individuals will attempt to defend their social standing. To enhance their social standing, low-status individuals will engage in a range behaviors—such as placating dominant others, monitoring their own actions, and avoiding direct eye gaze—to signal deference and subordination (Gilbert, 2001). This theoretical account is in line with social anxiety constituting an appeasement strategy (Trower & Gilbert, 1989), rather than a prepared phobic response to ancestrally relevant social stimuli. In line with this, social anxiety upregulates perceptions of hostility and the perceived probability of negative evaluations from others, and downregulates others' perceived affiliative motives.

While these adaptations for social maneuvering enabled humans to navigate social interactions in our ancestral past—after all, solving these problems was essential to successfully attract mates and coalition partners (Buss et al., 1990)—social phobics will experience dysfunctions in a modern world that requires them to navigate large, anonymous, and complex encounters with others. Later evolutionary psychological models of social anxiety focus on the misinterpretation of interoceptive signals such as blushing (Stein & Bouwer, 1997) in social encounters. People suffering from social anxiety disorder perceive bodily signals indicating stress as evidence for the presence of social threat. Importantly, people usually do not harbor aggressive reactions toward those displaying symptoms of anxiety; it is more likely that people will forgive rather than despise a blusher after a social faux pas.

Other, recent theoretical developments incorporate self-presentation theory into an evolutionary framework (Leary & Jongman-Sereno, 2014). On this account, feelings of low confidence in impression management elicit social anxiety, and relational value mediates the anxiety response—that is, social anxiety about making good impressions increases when others are valuable to the individual. A strength of this line of reasoning is that it addresses the maneuvering of social hierarchies beyond submission toward dominant and hostile others.

Öhman, Dimberg, and Öst (1985) proposed that social fears and social phobia originated from a second evolved behavioral system related to conspecific attack and self-defense (see Blanchard & Blanchard, 1988). This system controls the interaction among individuals in a group by defining which group members to boss or yield to. The resulting dominance hierarchy provides a vehicle for bringing order to the group and minimizing further aggressive encounters. Öhman et al. (1985) related social fear and anxiety to excessive social submissiveness. Facial expressions of threat and submissiveness provide an essential channel of communication in dominance contests among primates, which makes threatening facial features a powerful fear stimulus (Dimberg & Öhman, 1996; Öhman & Dimberg, 1984).

While Öhman et al. (1985) invoked differential evolutionary backgrounds to understand differences between animal and social phobias, both inter- and intra-specific defenses appear to rely on the same neural system (Blanchard & Blanchard, 1988). Like animal stimuli, facial stimuli suggesting threat (in the form of aggression, anger, potential devaluation, etc.) are powerful attention catchers in humans. Similar to visual detection paradigms in the processing of animal-type stimuli, non-anxious participants were quicker to detect a discrepant threatening face among neutral and friendly distractors (vs. a friendly face against neutral or threatening distractors) (Öhman, Lundqvist, et al., 2001). Similarly, Lundqvist, Esteves, and Öhman (1999) reported that frowned eyebrows composed of diagonal V-shaped lines provided decisive information for the negative evaluation of schematic faces and that such faces were rapidly and accurately detected among distractor faces in visual search tasks (Öhman, Lundqvist, et al., 2001). Further work to identify features or configurations of features that can activate the fear module is crucial because it would promote understanding of the psychological information-processing mechanisms that control the fear module.

Overall, the same fear module may serve different behavioral contexts provided by the predatory defense and the social submissiveness systems (and for the much less studied nature-type fears). For example, anti-predator strategies tend to rely on active defenses that tax metabolic resources, thus prompting cardiac accelerations (Öhman & Wiens, 2003). In contrast, social submissiveness may rest on behavioral immobility and prolonged risk assessment (Blanchard & Blanchard, 1988), thereby putting less demand on the cardiovascular system. The relative balance between these two types of defenses (active, such as fight-flight, vs. passive, such as immobility) is also related to the imminence of the threat.

While an evolutionary perspective suggests that a healthy dose of social anxiety helps people ensure an adequate level of social acceptance, it also helps identify the triggers commonly seen in social anxiety disorder. Fear of negative evaluation by the group is common, especially when feeling insecure about one's social standing and status in the group or when exposing oneself to increased attention from the community. Evolutionary theories do suggest why people might be vulnerable to developing social anxiety disorder. Nevertheless, an explanation of social anxiety disorder needs to address how common the fear of negative social evaluation contrasts with how relatively rare satisfying the diagnostic criteria of social anxiety disorder is (despite being the most frequent anxiety disorder).

While the different models presented above attempt to highlight some adaptive element of social anxiety and fear of negative social evaluation, one of the major problems of this approach is that the safety behaviors and social avoidance employed by the socially anxious patient ensure a large degree of social ostracism: they drop out of education earlier, they marry less, they receive fewer job promotions (Kennair & Kleppestø, 2018). One may criticize the idea that a modicum of social intelligence requires a necessary and healthy degree of social anxiety, as people tend to find extroversion most socially and sexually attractive (Kennair, 2007; Kennair & Kleppestø, 2018; Nettle, 2005). However, social assertiveness also increases the potential for conflict (Nettle, 2011). Still, it is paradoxical how theories of social anxiety disorder fail to consider the clinical presentation and consequences of social anxiety.

Generalized Anxiety Disorder

Generalized anxiety disorder is a disorder that involves persistent and excessive worry (Wells & Papageorgiou, 1995). Akin to panic disorder, the anxiety is not specific to certain situations or circumstances, and there is a wide range of issues that causes the individual to feel anxious.

However, unlike panic disorder, the bad outcome is not perceived as an acute danger of bodily or mental harm, but rather an apprehension, the anticipation of tragedy and disaster in the near future. In generalized anxiety disorder, common worries involve accidents or sickness that could afflict the patient or their loved ones, and general worries about money, family, work, or even international politics or the environment. Because the danger is not present in the moment, patients will not exhibit paroxysmal attacks with the characteristic flight response that defines panic disorder. Instead, control is sought through worry as a cognitive safety behavior and avoidance. An estimated 2.7% of US adults suffer from generalized anxiety disorder, and an estimated 5.7% of US adults experience generalized anxiety disorder at some time in their lives, with women suffering from generalized anxiety disorder more often than men (Harvard Medical School, 2007).

Worrying refers to the uncontrollable verbal process of catastrophic anticipation of future events (Borkovec et al., 1983). Unique to humans, worry has been found to inhibit emotional processing and can be understood as cognitive avoidance from the anxious experience (Borkovec et al., 1998). Although people who worry a lot often wish to worry less, patients report that worrying could help them in some way (Cartwright-Hatton & Wells, 1997). From an evolutionary perspective, positive metacognitions about worry in patients with generalized anxiety disorder might be important—if worrying had beneficial consequences on fitness, it could be an evolved adaptation. Similar lines of reasoning have been put forward for depressive rumination (Andrews & Thomson, 2009); however, similar to how discontinuing rumination has lasting effects on depression (Solem et al., 2019), discontinuing worry is effective for treating generalized anxiety disorder (Nordahl et al., 2018). Worrying is part of the human experience—indeed, members of demographics that are known to worry less (i.e., young men) have a higher probability of death than those who tend to worry more (i.e., older men or women; Kruger & Nesse, 2004), presumably partly because they experience less anxiety about real dangers (Kruger & Nesse, 2006). Thus, while women worry more (i.e., are more hyperphobic) than men, young men may be considered hypophobic—they have less fear than the situation might demand (Marks & Nesse, 1994). Hypophobia is worth considering as both maladaptive to many individuals the succumb to the poor odds, while at the same time increasing the fitness of those individuals who take the risk and reap the benefits (thus genes for hypophobia will spread): hypophobia is probably adaptive in warfare (Tooby & Cosmides, 1988) and is a feature of young male syndrome (Wilson & Daly, 1985), but it is not considered a mental disorder, revealing one problem with current nosological taxonomy, despite increasing mortality risk (Kruger & Nesse, 2004).

It has not been established whether normal, nondisruptive levels of worry have beneficial effects, and evolutionary psychological theories about the adaptive value of repetitive thinking have been challenged (Kennair et al., 2017). Worry does not imply clairvoyance, and it is impossible to prepare for every possible future. Cognitive resources spent on worrying about the future cannot be utilized in a helpful way in the present. Further, even if one should happen to worry about an issue that materializes into a real threat, worrying is only helpful if it motivates preparation. It seems that the return on investment of cognitive resources on excessive worry diminishes with frequency and duration. In fact, challenging the positive metacognitions about worry is part of effective treatment of generalized anxiety disorder (Nordahl et al., 2018; Wells, 2009).

Obsessive-Compulsive Disorder

Although no longer classified as an anxiety disorder in the DSM-5, obsessive-compulsive disorder is traditionally viewed as an anxiety disorder, and anxiety is perhaps the most prominent emotional component of obsessive-compulsive disorder. Obsessive-compulsive disorder is a relatively prevalent condition and is heterogeneous in thought content (Solem, Hagen, Hansen, et al., 2015), insight (Solem, Hagen, Wenaas, et al., 2015), and clinical presentation (Leckman & Bloch, 2008). Obsessive-compulsive disorder is characterized by the presence of obsessive thoughts followed by compulsions. In addition to underlying mechanisms, including fear and disgust mechanisms, we also see mechanisms involved in fundamental religious psychology and magical thinking, such as thought-object and thought-event fusions. Obsessions are persistent, recurring, and unwanted intrusive thoughts, images, or doubts that evoke substantial anxiety and distress in the individual. The obsessions are typically accompanied by compulsions, the repetitive or ritualistic mental or physical actions performed deliberately to avoid negative consequences or reduce anxiety evoked by the obsessions (APA, 2013). The compulsion is linked to the obsession through some idiosyncratic logic, but is experienced by the individual as ineffective in reducing actual threats. The individuals' insight into the abnormality of the obsessions and the ineffectiveness of the compulsive strategy in controlling the obsession (Abramowitz, 2006; Feygin et al., 2006) makes obsessive-compulsive disorder an especially debilitating condition (Eisen et al., 2006) with a poor prognosis if not treated (Skoog & Skoog, 1999; Wells et al., 2017).

Perhaps it is the heterogeneity of the disorder combined with the often-bizarre (but not delusional) nature of the obsessions and compulsions that makes evolutionary approaches numerous yet diverging. Most evolutionary theories about obsessive-compulsive disorder view the disorder as maladaptive (Marks & Nesse, 1994; Rapoport, 1991). Suggestions that pediatric autoimmune neuropsychological disorders associated with streptococcal infections (PANDAS) cause obsessive-compulsive disorder (Leonard & Swedo, 2001) are challenged by the fact that most patients with obsessive-compulsive disorder show symptom reduction after few sessions of exposure with response prevention (Solem et al., 2009) or very brief treatment programs (Hansen et al., 2018; Hansen et al., 2019). This is not the case with perseverations typically seen in patients suffering brain damage. Others have conceptualized obsessive-compulsive disorder as a psychological immune system gone awry (Abed & de Pauw, 1998; Taylor et al., 2005).

Del Giudice (2014) uses a life-history framework to propose subgroups of obsessive-compulsive disorder, including an impulsive type, but their nosological value has been challenged (Kennair, 2014). Nevertheless, some form of subcategorization of the phenomena included in obsessive-compulsive disorder may yield benefits. From an evolutionary psychological perspective, there are differences between normal to extreme hygiene and grooming, hoarding, and ritualistic behavior. A conceptual division between harm prevention and "just right" experiences has recently been explored within a life-history framework (Del Giudice, 2018).

Boyer and Liénard (2006) explain routines and obsessive thoughts with reference to the commonality of ritualized behaviors in children (Evans et al., 1999) and adults (Leckman et al., 2004). On this theory, ritualized behaviors serve as a vigilance-precaution system designed to scan the environment for potential threats (e.g., contamination). If a threat is detected, the appraisal system is sated and will be quiet; however, if the level of concern about a dangerous outcome cannot be dismissed, the precautionary systems will remain engaged. This view posits that ritualized behaviors seen in obsessive-compulsive disorder patients are an exaggerated deviation from the norm and not an aberration per se (Leckman et al., 2005).

While disgust is seen as an adaption (Al-Shawaf et al., 2016; Darwin, 1872; Tybur et al., 2009), few theories view the phenotypes seen in obsessive-compulsive disorder as adaptations. The obsessive-compulsive disorder patient is often engaged in reducing or controlling uncomfortable inner states through behavior that is often seen as bizarre and maladaptive. But even if the goal of feeling "good" or "right" could be achieved through compulsions, it would hardly result in any adaptive advantage.

Post-Traumatic Stress Disorder

Acute threats to survival continued to pose an adaptive problem to be solved for contemporary humans and were probably ubiquitous not only to our ancestors, but to life on earth in general (Buss, 2015; Pinker, 2012). Post-traumatic stress disorder is defined as a delayed or prolonged reaction to (i.e., difficulty recovering from) a terrifying event, such as violent personal assault, sexual assault, natural or human-made disasters, accidents, emotional and/or physical abuse, and combat. Symptoms cluster around four factors; re-experiencing, avoidance, numbing, and hyperarousal (APA, 2013). Post-traumatic stress disorder is unique among psychiatric diagnoses in that it requires exposure to and the witnessing of a horrifying event to be elicited. As such, it is classified as an adjustment disorder rather than an anxiety disorder. From an evolutionary perspective, it is interesting that most symptoms of post-traumatic stress disorder are normal and appropriate reactions to an acute threat (Grubaugh, 2014). However, prolonged and inappropriate use of fearful defenses and safety behaviors warrants a functional analysis that overlaps with the other anxiety disorders. An estimated 3.6% of US adults suffer from post-traumatic stress disorder, with a lifetime prevalence of 6.8% (Harvard Medical School, 2007).

Cantor (2005) has put forth a theory of post-traumatic stress disorder as a manifestation of evolved defenses, both those that have an evolutionary history at least as old as our common ancestor with reptiles (e.g., startle reflex) and uniquely mammalian defenses (e.g., appeasement strategies). In humans, defenses are hierarchically organized, with avoidance (i.e., refuge-seeking) being the primary defense strategy. If this defense strategy is deemed unsatisfactory in bringing about safety (e.g., refuge is denied due to insufficient food storage), the individual will move on to subsequent avoidance strategies, such as engaging attentive immobility (i.e., threat monitoring) when interacting with the environment. Further, if signals of threat appear, classic flight response is activated. If escape to refuge is denied, the fight response will be activated next. If the threat is evoked by a conspecific and is perceived to be inescapable or undefeatable, mammals tend to engage in subordinate behavior and various appeasement strategies. If continuous harassment is perceived to be unavoidable, tonic immobility is the last resort. Signaling a lack of responsiveness might make the aggressor inflict less damage until the situation changes.

These defenses and their coordination have been proposed as evolved adaptations (e.g., (Bracha, 2004; Marks & Nesse, 1994). Cantor (2005) theorizes that post-traumatic stress disorder is the result of an "agonic switch" to a more hypervigilant mode of processing, where cost–benefit evaluations shift away from favoring somatic effort toward threat-monitoring and defense displays when threats are perceived as uncontrollable (Del Giudice, 2018).

Wells (2000) developed the metacognitive model of post-traumatic stress disorder. While this clinical model is not based on evolutionary thinking, it does consider a reflexive adaptation process (based in the here and now, rather than in the evolutionary past) as the normal and automatic response to intrusive cognitions, and as such describes a mental adaptation for handling intrusions and processing trauma. Wells argues that although stress symptoms are normal in the immediate aftermath of a traumatic event, most people have a built-in capacity to adapt following trauma and therefore do not develop post-traumatic stress disorder. Although anxiety symptoms are an evident response to a traumatic episode and may be adaptive for the first period, the anxiety naturally subsides over time. However, the natural process of overcoming a traumatic episode may be disturbed by the activation of a specific pattern of cognition and coping called the cognitive-attentional syndrome (CAS). The CAS consists of rumination, worrying, threat monitoring, and maladaptive coping patterns (Wells & Colbear, 2012). As a result of these patterns, the individual struggles to downregulate and adapt to a threat-free environment. According to the metacognitive model, activation of the CAS is the reason why some interventions delivered soon after the traumatic episode may increase the likelihood of developing post-traumatic stress disorder.

Recent Developments in Evolutionary Research on Anxiety

Recent evolutionary research largely remains inspired by the pioneering work of Öhman and Mineka (2001). In producing empirical evidence supporting their theory, much experimental work has focused on the automaticity of detecting evolutionarily relevant, fear-inducing stimuli, both among the general population and in patients suffering from specific phobias. In the following, we review some of these pivotal findings, with a focus on the involuntary, automatic perceptual processes involved in responding to fitness-relevant threats in two domains: animal-type phobias and the fear of darkness (nyctophobia). A major tool in the investigation of these specific phobias is the use of visual detection paradigms. Central to the visual detection paradigms are perceptual processes that automatically scan and analyze the perceptual field for threatening stimuli. While experimental approaches in the study of these two types of phobias focus on the same perceptual processes, they reveal key insights concerning the roles of fear and disgust.

Animal-Type Phobias

The sight of a snake, spider, or rodent strikes terror in the hearts of millions of people. While few of these critters pose a significant threat to humans in the modern environment, encountering dangerous animals could have severely compromised our ancestors' fitness. Of all animal-type phobias, spider phobias are among the most common, with a prevalence rate of 3.5% in the population (Jacobi et al., 2004). Since all spiders are predators and must subdue their prey with poison, some have suggested that fear of spiders might be an evolutionary adaptation, and various strands of empirical research support this preparedness account.

Empirical work in developmental psychology has demonstrated that visual attention in infants and young children is prioritized for potentially dangerous stimuli resembling the ancestral hazard of spiders, well before they acquire any threat-relevant fears. Infants are quicker to detect the presence of spiders than various categories of harmless biological distractor stimuli (LoBue, 2010), such as flowers or fish. Using a preferential looking and habituation paradigm, Rakison and Derringer (2008) demonstrated a perceptual template for spiders that generalizes to real-world images of spiders, but not for other non-threatening biological stimuli, in infants as young as five months old.

However, spiders are not the only group of arthropods that could have been hazardous to our ancestors—other groups, including bees and wasps, can sting people and kill them through envenomation. Recent experimental work suggests that the human aversion of arthropods is indeed spider-specific: spiders elicit significantly greater fear and disgust (emotional and cognitive responses, respectively) than any other arthropod group (e.g., bees/wasps; beetles, butterflies, and moths), and spiders were rated as more dangerous. Respondents with arachnophobia showed a similar but elevated response pattern compared with nonphobic participants (Gerdes et al., 2009; New & German, 2015). These findings mirror other studies reporting a pre-attentively controlled bias for picking out threatening animals (snakes and spiders) from complex visual displays. This bias is particularly pronounced among those phobic of the relevant animal category (Öhman, Flykt, et al., 2001).

Some studies have focused on perceptions of disgust, especially on how a gradual increase in general disgust sensitivity can exacerbate fear of animal-type stimuli. For example, laboratory-based studies have indicated that experimentally increasing general disgust sensitivity levels causes respondents to report higher levels of fear toward common, fear-relevant animals (Davey et al., 1993), suggesting that increases in nonspecific disgust sensitivity exacerbate aversive evaluations of disgust-relevant outcomes associated with these animals (Davey et al., 2003).

People might be apprehensive of spiders (but not butterflies and bees, for example) because they find the rapid and uncontrollable movement of spiders threatening. They may be simple, such as when stimuli exhibit a rapid onset (Yantis & Johnson, 1990) or directed movements (Bernstein et al., 1971). In visual search tasks, respondents located evolutionarily relevant and animate objects faster and with the least impact of high perceptual load, compared to evolutionarily novel and inanimate objects that were located slower and with the highest impact of perceptual load (Jackson & Calvillo, 2013).

However, they may also include more complex characteristics, such as sinusoidal shapes related to snakes or hairy bodies with many protruding legs, such as in spiders. For example, Aronoff, Barclay, and Stevenson (1988) reported that participants rated curved lines converging on a joint point (which suggest the legs and body of a spider) as more negative and active than when the same curved lines were regularly arranged in parallel with no point of convergence. Further evidence stems from research on a surprisingly common phobia, trypophobia, in which images of holes instill fear. This is because fear-inducing stimuli had a spectral composition typically associated with a range of potentially dangerous animals (Cole & Wilkins, 2013).

Öhman et al. (1985) suggested that the predatory defense system has its evolutionary origin in a prototypical fear of reptiles in early mammals who were targets for predation by the then-dominant dinosaurs. Thus, contemporary snakes and lizards remain powerful actual fear stimuli (Agras et al., 1969; Costello, 1982).

Darkness

Throughout human evolution, darkness has been associated with danger. Long before the advent of modern technology, humans were exposed to predators that would overwhelmingly hunt at night. Paired with relatively poor eyesight in low-lit conditions, we were therefore particularly vulnerable at nighttime. While fear of darkness can persist throughout development and strengthen in magnitude (King et al., 2005), accounts of nyctophobia are generally consistent with error management theory: when it is dark, it is better to err on the side of caution (i.e., wrongfully assuming that it harbors danger vs. wrongfully assuming that it does not). Many studies have demonstrated that humans are afraid of the dark (Grillon et al., 1997; Nasar & Jones, 1997) and that the lack of visual stimuli increases anxiety, uncertainty, and tension in people, to the extent that darkness facilitates a startle response in the brain that increases anxiety, especially among those suffering from post-traumatic stress disorder (Nasar & Jones, 1997).

People believe that being on the lookout for potential threats might save them in case an actual threat might be present (Nasar & Jones, 1997). Nasar and Jones showed that aspects of concealment, hiding places, and dark spots influenced how people viewed fear of crime in the dark, such that numerous potential hiding places (shrubs, parked cars) increased said fear. The knowledge that the stranger might be present is enough to induce fear (Nasar & Jones, 1997).

This tendency appears to be more pronounced when the stranger belongs to an outgroup—in one study, a dark environment strengthened the stereotypical association between African Americans and danger among White respondents, but only for people with a chronic belief that our world is a dangerous place (Schaller et al., 2003).

Cross-cultural findings pertaining to fear of darkness suggest that the fear response varies across cultures. Cultural variation in folk tales can shape how people perceive darkness to affect an individual, and studies suggest that children from the Middle East and West Indies show a much higher rate of fear of the dark than most White American children.

Etiology, Risk Factors, and Maintenance of Anxiety Disorders

One of the much-debated questions regarding anxiety and phobia is the issue of pathways of acquisition. One of the most influential theories was Mowrer (1947) two-factor theory. On this approach, one first acquires the phobia through classical (Pavlovian) conditioning, after which it is maintained through avoidance (i.e., operant conditioning) (Rachman, 1977). A central contribution of Mowrer's theory lies in explaining how avoidance maintains the disorder, with exposure being an important counter to this behavior, and in most cases, a curative intervention. Nevertheless, the two-factor theory is not able to predict or explain who develops an anxiety disorder, or how this occurs. One can test this in virtually any large group: ask how many people have been stung by a wasp and how many people are phobic of wasps. One will not need to run the chi-square test: the small percentage of people with strong fears of bees will not all have been stung; the large percentage of people who have been stung are not overly phobic of bees.

Non-Associative Theories

Poulton, Menzies, and colleagues (Poulton & Menzies, 2002a, 2002b; Poulton et al., 1999; Poulton et al., 2001) proposed the non-associative model, which posits the existence of a range of innate, species-typical, and evolutionary-relevant fears that manifest without critical and aversive learning experiences with the stimulus—that is, phobias might be acquired without any exposure at all. This perspective holds that clinical phobias appear later in life and are a result of biologically relevant fears failing to habituate. This account is based on two strands of evidence: first, a lack of supportive evidence for simple conditioning (or learning) in the etiologies of several prevalent phobias; and second, a lack of evidence for a learning component that supports the view that the existence of these prevalent phobias is innate. Indeed, many patients state that they can trace back the origins of their phobia to their very first experience with a given stimulus. Notably, the non-associative account primarily concerns an ultimate explanation, such that it attempts to explain the existence of prevalent phobias in terms of the adaptive and protective function that these predispositions may have served.

Motivation to Unlearn Phobias: The Role of Risky Play

Sandseter and Kennair (2011) address one possible mechanism that might explain how anxiety disorders may be unlearned through risky play. Children find several different types of risky play thrilling. Importantly, they seek this motivational aspect by expanding the limits of their mastery of different environmental features in ways that are relatively safe (Kennair et al., 2018), without being too simple and boring. As the children mature, they continuously engage in play with more autonomy, speed, height, and total risk, and are thereby motivated to learn to cope with both their matured anxiety (as mapped by Poulton and colleagues above) and to master their environment. Risky play thereby increases exposure, training, and coping, and thereby reduces the children's anxiety adaptively.

While anxiety symptoms in a normal population may diminish across time (Kessler et al., 2005), half of those who had a diagnosis of an emotional or mental disorder early in life will have an anxiety disorder later in life (Gregory et al., 2007). This finding suggests a need to provide efficient treatment early.

Treatment Approaches: How Clinical Work with Anxiety Elucidates the Mechanism and Function of Anxiety

Traditional Behavioral and Cognitive Therapy

In traditional behavioral approaches, the key element of the treatment of anxiety was gradual exposure to what was considered conditioned stimuli (CS) to elicit the conditioned response (CR), without avoidance or safety behaviors ("response prevention"). Initial activation followed by a gradual reduction in distress ("habituation") was considered the central indication of the weakening of the dysfunctional CS-CR association. In this tradition, studies were often conducted with animals and a brief induction of phobia-like stimuli. This line of research addresses two important aspects: the motivation for safety behaviors—species-specific defense responses of fight or freeze and avoidance/flight that the functional approach to fear has informed us of. Through removing safety behaviors and increasing exposure, the treatment has been efficient. However, the discussion has focused on what makes the treatment work. Also, as noted above, the notion that the disorder is conditioned is no longer hegemonic or even considered the best explanation of etiology (Kendler et al., 2002; Kennair et al., 2018; Poulton & Menzies, 2002b; Sandseter & Kennair, 2011).

With the development of cognitive therapy, thoughts and appraisals were considered to be the primary cause of emotions and behaviors (Beck, 1979). The cognitive model for anxiety disorders stipulates that danger-related beliefs lead to an attentional bias toward threats, which leads to safety biases and influences information processing and interpretations of ambiguous stimuli (Beck, 2005). Based on this, it was assumed that anxiety disorders could be treated by helping patients to recognize dysfunctional reasoning and to challenge the content of the beliefs and assumptions that lead to anxiety and distress (Beck, 1993). A series of different techniques were developed, like Socratic questioning or strategies to question the evidence underlying assumptions of beliefs. Most cognitive therapy approaches include strategies to identify logical implications of beliefs and assistance to empirically test or conduct "behavioral experiments" to challenge the validity of those beliefs (Bennett-Levy, 2003).

Emotional Processing Model

Foa and Kozak (1986) introduced a model that combines the main elements of traditional behavioral models and cognitive therapy. According to their model, emotional responses like anxiety disorders are represented by information structures in memory, containing both CS-CR associations and information that supports these associations. Modification of such underlying memory structures ("fear structures") was described as emotional processing (Deacon et al., 2013). It was argued that gradual exposure to feared situations activate the fear structure and facilitate the integration of corrective information. According to Foa and Kozak (1986), physiological activation and habituation within and across exposure sessions were considered to be the main indicators of emotional processing. Theoretical inconsistencies of this model (and empirical studies failing to support its predictions) have led to several revisions and refinements (e.g. Foa et al., 2006; Foa & McLean, 2016).

The Inhibitory Learning Model
According to behavioral models, treatment gains are the result of weakening and eliminating the dysfunctional CS-CR associations. One of the most influential new developments within this tradition is the Inhibitory Learning Model (ILM; Craske et al., 2014), which highlights inhibitory learning as central to extinction. However, habituation is still considered to be involved in the process. This model challenges some basic assumptions about how the brain learns and remembers fear-related information. In line with both clinical observations and experimental studies, successful treatment of anxiety disorders does not seem to be dependent on erasing old memories, but rather on forming new ones. This is more in line with the non-associative approaches to phobia acquisition. Treatment success is a function of how well these new memories can inhibit the old memories. As a comparison, when constructing a new highway, resources are spent to make it efficient and to lead the traffic to it, rather than erasing every trace of old and less efficient roads.

The ILM challenges traditional models that emphasize the importance of in- and between-session habituation (Craske et al., 2008). Experimental studies and reports from clinical work indicate that habituation is less correlated to treatment success than previously assumed. Rather than unlearning or erasing, treatment success seems to result from learning new information about safety that competes with and inhibits the existing memories (Craske, 2015). In line with this model, several strategies have been proposed to enhance such learning (Craske et al., 2014).

Instead of habituation, treatment should focus on tolerance of anxiety and distress. The goal is to maximize situation-specific safety learning and form new memories that such feelings or reactions are not proof of real danger or in themselves dangerous. Distress and anxiety are usually related to expectations about unwanted outcomes (Baker et al., 2010; Deacon et al., 2013). Therefore, it is recommended that exposure is conducted in a way that provides information that disconfirms such expectations. According to the ILM, the treatment outcome is enhanced when the information provided during exposure violates expectations consistent with the "old memories" (Craske, 2015). The element of surprise also enhances learning; in line with ILM, it is recommended that the treatment is planned and conducted to increase the likelihood of such experiences. Further, combining fear cues is assumed to increase safety learning that inhibits existing fear-related memories. To maximize generalization of safety learning, variation in location and over aspects of where, how, and when the exposure is conducted might enhance inhibitory learning and increase long-term treatment effects (Craske et al., 2014).

While several experimental studies lend supportive evidence to the ILM, evidence from clinical studies remains limited. Since the approach suggests several ways to enhance Exposure and Response Prevention (ERP) treatment effects, it is challenging to conduct rigorous clinical studies both isolating the relative (positive or negative) impact of each of these strategies and possible interactions. The lack of a clear distinction between the proposed procedures and "traditional" ERP and cognitive behavioral therapy (CBT) also adds to these challenges. Hopefully, further research will focus on experimental studies, clinical studies evaluating each of the components, and randomized controlled trials comparing ILM protocols with traditional ERP manuals.

Disorder-Specific Models
The models described are general and trans-diagnostic models. From the mid-1980s, several disorder-specific models have been presented. Clark (1986) and Barlow et al. (1989) independently developed highly similar models and treatment procedures for panic disorder. The key

element of their approaches was the misinterpretation of normal and benign bodily sensations or symptoms as a sign of illness associated with an acute risk of serious consequences. They further suggested that such appraisals increase anxiety, leading to an increase in bodily arousal and activation. This activation would, in turn, lead to an even stronger assumption and appraisal of danger. This description of a vicious circle is often referred to as "the panic circle." Treatment manuals have been developed to target the specific appraisals and regulation of symptoms specified by the model (Clark et al., 1999). A number of studies have demonstrated the effectiveness of this approach and support for the model (Pompoli et al., 2016).

Third Wave: A Shift to Process over Content

A number of such disorder-specific models have been developed, and another example is the Clark and Wells (1995) model for social anxiety disorder. In addition to disorder-specific appraisals, the model specifies the negative effect of attentional strategies such as self-focused attention. The model builds on traditional CBT elements and focuses on exposure and behavior experiments to provide disconfirmation of beliefs assumed to underlie and maintain the disorder. The emphasis on attentional strategies represented a shift from traditional behavior models or cognitive models mainly focusing on disconfirmation of beliefs.

In recent years a series of new models have been developed that challenge traditional behavior and cognitive models and their focus on modifying thoughts and emotions. Instead, these models focus on how such thoughts and emotions are appraised and the efforts to modify or control these (Brown et al., 2011). Instead of strategies to alter internal events, these approaches emphasize the importance of acceptance, mindfulness, or detached mindfulness. Steve Hayes has categorized these approaches as a the "third wave" of psychotherapy approaches (Hayes, 2004), including models like mindfulness-based cognitive therapy (MBCT; Segal & Teasdale, 2018), acceptance and commitment therapy (ACT; Hayes et al., 2009), metacognitive therapy (Wells, 2008), and dialectical behavior therapy (DBT; Linehan, 2018). Despite differences in theoretical understanding, treatment focus, and interventions, controversy surrounds whether these approaches are best understood as revised or extended versions of CBT or a "new wave" (Arch & Craske, 2008; Hofmann & Asmundson, 2008). The maintaining mechanisms that these new approaches specify, especially when shown to be relevant processes in clinical studies, should receive attention from evolutionary researchers interested in the mental mechanisms involved in anxiety disorders (Kennair, 2014).

Treatment Approaches and Evolutionary Perspectives

The smoke-detector principle explains why we are predisposed to err on the side of safety and may have a lowered threshold for responding to danger cues (Nesse, 2001). A lowered threshold for threats, however, does not fully explain the nature of anxiety disorders, as anxiety tends to be chronic, even in the absence of actual danger (Brosschot et al., 2016). Although the initial underlying emotional reactions to danger may have been adaptive, having an anxiety disorder is related to distress both for individuals and their relatives (Mendlowicz & Stein, 2000). One evolutionary approach that does not presuppose initial learning of anxiety, but is based on the non-associative approach, suggests that we increase the threshold adaptively through play and other interactions with our ecology, learning new behaviors and unlearning fear of harmless stimuli, but respect of potentially harmful stimuli (Kennair et al., 2018; Sandseter & Kennair, 2011). There is a need for clinical approaches to better integrate basic research and for academic evolutionary approaches to better integrate clinical theory and models (Kennair, 2011, 2014; Kennair et al., 2020). The best clinical models improve treatment and address the underlying dysregulated or malfunctioning mechanisms in anxiety disorders.

Anxiety: Disorder or Adaptation?

One of the most controversial issues within evolutionary psychopathology is the question of whether or not a disorder is an adaptation. While evolutionary psychology is generally wary of panadaptationism (Kennair, 2002), there are novel and interesting theories that may be formulated and tested. In them, the pathology itself can be considered from an adaptive perspective. This has been the case with suicidal ideation (de Catanzaro, 1995); it has been posited that suicide might harbor fitness-relevant benefits which can be extended to kin, by removing a fitness cost to close kin in case of poor health. However, we still lack longitudinal predictive studies to test this hypothesis. It is also the case with major depression, where depressive rumination is considered an evolved adaptive response to solving complex social problems (Andrews & Thomson, 2009; Bartoskova et al., 2018). However, there is little consensus that brooding, which is the relevant cognitive process, solves any problems per se—rather, *not* brooding often is more conducive to mastering life and social problems (Nettle, 2004). Further, most clinically trained evolutionary psychopathologists are highly skeptical of this approach (Kennair et al., 2017; Nesse, 2019). Finally, clinical research suggests that discontinuing rumination reduces suffering and increases life quality over extended periods of time (Solem et al., 2019).

In his recent book, Nesse (2019) addresses the pitfalls of considering disorders as adaptations. He asserts that disorders themselves are not adaptations and should therefore not be explained in evolutionary terms. According to Nesse, the tendency to view disorders as adaptations is the most significant problem and mistake within evolutionary medicine (including evolutionary psychopathology). Nesse is clear in his recommendation: an evolutionary approach to mental disorders needs to consider why we have evolved to become vulnerable to mental disorders, rather than how the disorder itself has evolved. Many of the evolutionary theories discussed in this chapter provide at least some functional explanation. Still, at their best, they specify possible testable features of underlying normal psychological evolved mental mechanisms that may increase our likelihood of developing a mental disorder.

We do not argue that disorders are functional. Conversely, though, there is also the danger of creating a false sense that biological malfunctions cause mental disorder, a view that is too simplistic and often wrong (Kennair & Kleppestø, 2018; Kennair et al., 2020; Troisi & McGuire, 2002). The speed and effect of exposure therapy for phobias and obsessive-compulsive disorder, or the effects of psychotherapy for depression with modern treatments mentioned above, suggest that the brain disorder approach is incorrect. We recommend an exploration of how underlying mechanisms may be adaptations and how evolutionary psychological analyses and methods focusing on emotions and cognitive structures can elucidate them (Al-Shawaf et al., 2016; Tooby & Cosmides, 1995). Instead of asking how the minds of those with mental disorders are fundamentally different from those not affected by mental disorder, clinical evolutionary psychology should address what proclivities of our normal, evolved human nature make our species so vulnerable to developing mental disorders (Nesse, 2019).

This is mostly the case with modern evolutionary-oriented studies into the underlying mechanisms involved in arachnophobia that we have reviewed above (Kennair & Lindner, 2017). These mechanisms will identify specific ecological threats that might make us hyperaware or trigger perceptual mechanisms in feature-specific manners. We learn dangers and specific features of evolutionary relevant danger stimuli more efficiently than other phenomena (Garcia & Koelling, 1966; Öhman et al., 1976; Öhman & Mineka, 2001), and fear these in a more maturational than associative manner (Poulton & Menzies, 2002a). And unlearning these threats as we develop and become more competent is also adaptive (Kennair et al., 2018; Sandseter & Kennair, 2011). All these underlying structures of disordered anxiety are adaptations that make up the context-specific aspects of functional fear. Evolutionary analyses of the specific contexts and stimuli that may, at some point in development, be threatening will theoretically reduce the design space, and suggest features which one may map from a normal, evolutionary psychology approach, thus informing an evolutionary psychopathology approach about the malfunctioning mental mechanisms that might be involved in the specific anxiety disorder.

For example, arachnophobia may be simplistically considered adaptive in some geographic areas where venomous spiders that may harm people are common (most spiders are venomous, but many cannot pierce the human skin). However, this misses the central point of a phobia and how engaging with one's ecology makes one adapted to it: reducing fear of previously dangerous or predisposed stimuli (Sandseter & Kennair, 2011). Even in these areas, a phobic response will constitute a dysfunctional, exaggerated fear. Fearing venomous and dangerous spiders, mastering how to dispose of or avoid them, and simultaneously acquiring knowledge of which arachnids are *not* dangerous are what makes it adaptive. The same is true of all other hazardous and phobic stimuli. Some, but not all, snakes are dangerous and should be avoided; others should be eaten or ignored altogether. Phobic responses to snakes, in general, are probably not adaptive. Being respectful of ecological features such as the dark, heights, or water is sensible, but being phobic would reduce overall fitness. An adaptive level of fear, coupled with approach behavior that makes it possible to learn, cope, and master, is desirable and adaptive (Kennair et al., 2018).

Anxiety disorders, considered from an evolutionary perspective, are probably among the best-understood disorders. The evolutionary, functional approach to fear is likely shared by virtually all anxiety researchers and treatment specialists, providing both better descriptions of the specific disorders and a deeper understanding of both avoidance and safety behaviors (Kennair, 2007). Nevertheless, several examples of adaptive reasoning get close to considering the adaptive benefits of the disorder itself. As addressed above, social phobia does not defend against social ostracism; it motivates patients to socially self-exclude, leads to lower aspirations, and makes individuals forgo romantic relationships (Kennair & Kleppestø, 2018). Thus, to conclude, it is not the specific disorder that is the adaptation; nevertheless, the underlying adaptations that cause and maintain anxiety disorders and phobias may be understood from an evolutionary and adaptive perspective. Thus, the underlying mechanisms involved in the detection and perception of specific stimuli, such as arachnids (Kennair & Lindner, 2017), are probably adaptations, while a phobic response to spiders in general would not be adaptive.

Conclusion

Fear and the fight, flight, and freeze responses are best understood from an evolutionary perspective; if you do not defend against or avoid real and present dangers, you will have reduced fitness. This functional approach to fear informs our understanding of exaggerated and maladaptive fear responses—anxiety and phobias—and has influenced both treatment and theories about specific disorders. It has also guided research into the underlying mechanisms that make us more vulnerable to anxiety disorders and phobias. While the anxiety disorders and phobias themselves are not adaptations, the functional, evolutionary approach to fear of specific evolutionary relevant dangers elucidates why we are prepared to fear particular stimuli, including arachnids or negative social evaluation.

References

Abed, R. T., & de Pauw, K. W. (1998). An evolutionary hypothesis for obsessive compulsive disorder: a~ psychological immune system? *Behavioural Neurology*, *11*(4), 245–250.

Abramowitz, J. S. (2006). The psychological treatment of obsessive-compulsive disorder. *Canadian Journal of Psychiatry*, *51*(7), 407–416. doi: 10.1177/070674370605100702

Agras, S., Sylvester, D., & Oliveau, D. (1969). The epidemiology of common fears and phobia. *Comprehensive Psychiatry*, *10*(2), 151–156.

Al-Shawaf, L., Conroy-Beam, D., Asao, K., & Buss, D. M. (2016). Human emotions: An evolutionary psychological perspective. *Emotion Review*, *8*(2), 173–186.

Andrews, P. W., & Thomson, J. A., Jr. (2009). The bright side of being blue: Depression as an adaptation for analyzing complex problems. *Psychological Review*, *116*(3), 620.

APA. (2013). *Diagnostic and statistical manual of mental disorders (DSM-5)*. American Psychiatric Association.

Arch, J. J., & Craske, M. G. (2008). Acceptance and commitment therapy and cognitive behavioral therapy for anxiety disorders: Different treatments, similar mechanisms? *Clinical Psychology: Science and Practice*, *15*(4), 263–279.

Aronoff, J., Barclay, A. M., & Stevenson, L. A. (1988). The recognition of threatening facial stimuli. *Journal of Personality and Social Psychology*, *54*(4), 647–655.

Baker, A., Mystkowski, J., Culver, N., Yi, R., Mortazavi, A., & Craske, M. G. (2010). Does habituation matter? Emotional processing theory and exposure therapy for acrophobia. *Behaviour Research and Therapy*, *48*(11), 1139–1143. https://doi.org/10.1016/j.brat.2010.07.009

Barlow, D. H., Craske, M. G., Cerny, J. A., & Klosko, J. S. (1989). Behavioral treatment of panic disorder. *Behavior Therapy*, *20*(2), 261–282. doi:10.1016/S0005-7894(89)80073-5

Bartoskova, M., Sevcikova, M., Durisko, Z., Maslej, M. M., Barbic, S. P., Preiss, M., & Andrews, P. W. (2018). The form and function of depressive rumination. *Evolution and Human Behavior*, *39*(3), 277–289.

Baumeister, R. F., & Leary, M. R. (1995). The need to belong: Desire for interpersonal attachments as a fundamental human motivation. *Psychological Bulletin*, *117*(3), 497–529.

Beck, A. T. (1979). *Cognitive therapy and the emotional disorders*. Penguin.

Beck, A. T. (1993). Cognitive therapy: past, present, and future. *Journal of Consulting and Clinical Psychology*, *61*(2), 194–198.

Beck, A. T. (2005). The current state of cognitive therapy: A 40-year retrospective. *Archives of General Psychiatry*, *62*(9), 953–959. doi: 10.1001/archpsyc.62.9.953 %J

Bennett-Levy, J. (2003). Mechanisms of change in cognitive therapy: The case of automatic thought records and behavioural experiments. *Behavioural and Cognitive Psychotherapy*, *31*(3), 261–277. doi: 10.1017/S1352465803003035

Bernstein, A. S., Taylor, K., Austen, B. G., Nathanson, M., & Scarpelli, A. (1971). Orienting response and apparent movement toward or away from the observer. *Journal of Experimental Psychology*, *87*(1), 37–45.

Blanchard, D. C., & Blanchard, R. J. (1988). Ethoexperimental approaches to the biology of emotion. *Annual Review of Psychology*, *39*(1), 43–68.

Bolles, R. C. (1970). Species-specific defense reactions and avoidance learning. *Psychological Review*, *77*(1), 32–48. doi: 10.1037/h0028589

Borkovec, T. D., Ray, W. J., & Stober, J. (1998). Worry: A cognitive phenomenon intimately linked to affective, physiological, and interpersonal behavioral processes. *Cognitive Therapy and Research*, *22*(6), 561–576.

Borkovec, T. D., Robinson, E., Pruzinsky, T., & DePree, J. A. (1983). Preliminary exploration of worry: Some characteristics and processes. *Behaviour Research and Therapy*, *21*(1), 9–16.

Boyer, P., & Bergstrom, B. (2011). Threat-detection in child development: An evolutionary perspective. *Neuroscience & Biobehavioral Reviews*, *35*(4), 1034–1041. http://dx.doi.org/10.1016/j.neubiorev.2010.08.010

Boyer, P., & Liénard, P. (2006). Why ritualized behavior? Precaution systems and action parsing in developmental, pathological and cultural rituals. *Behavioral and Brain Sciences*, *29*(6), 595–613.

Bracha, H. S. (2004). Freeze, flight, fight, fright, faint: Adaptationist perspectives on the acute stress response spectrum. *CNS Spectrums*, *9*(9), 679–685.

Bracha, H. S., Williams, A. E., Haynes, S. N., Kubany, E. S., Ralston, T. C., & Yamashita, J. M. (2004). The STRS (shortness of breath, tremulousness, racing heart, and sweating): a brief checklist for acute distress with panic-like autonomic indicators; development and factor structure. *Annals of General Hospital Psychiatry*, *3*(1), 8.

Bragazzi, N. L., & Del Puente, G. (2012). Panic attacks and possession by djinns: Lessons from ethnopsychiatry. *Psychology Research and Behavior Management*, *5*, 185–190. doi: 10.2147/prbm.s37714

Brosschot, J. F., Verkuil, B., & Thayer, J. (2016). The default response to uncertainty and the importance of perceived safety in anxiety and stress: An evolution-theoretical perspective. *Journal of Anxiety Disorders*, *41*, 22–34.

Brown, L. A., Gaudiano, B. A., & Miller, I. W. (2011). Investigating the similarities and differences between practitioners of second- and third-wave cognitive-behavioral therapies. *Behavior Modification, 35*(2), 187–200. doi: 10.1177/0145445510393730

Buss, D. M. (2015). *Evolutionary psychology: The new science of the mind.* Psychology Press.

Buss, D. M., Abbott, M., Angleitner, A., Asherian, A., Biaggio, A., Blanco-Villasenor, A., Bruchon-Schweitzer, M., Ch'U, H.-Y., Czapinski, J., Deraad, B., Ekehammar, B., El Lohamy, N., Fioravanti, M., Georgas, J., Gjerde, P., Guttman, R., Hazan, F., Iwawaki, S., Janakiramaiah, N., . . . Yang, K.-S. (1990). International preferences in selecting mates: A study of 37 cultures. *Journal of Cross-Cultural Psychology, 21*(1), 5–47.

Cannon, W. B. (1915). *Bodily changes in pain, hunger, fear, and rage.* D. Appleton.

Cantor, C. (2005). *Evolution and posttraumatic stress: Disorders of vigilance and defence.* Routledge.

Cartwright-Hatton, S., & Wells, A. (1997). Beliefs about worry and intrusions: The Meta-Cognitions Questionnaire and its correlates. *Journal of Anxiety Disorders, 11*(3), 279–296.

Clark, D. M. (1986). A cognitive approach to panic. *Behaviour Research and Therapy, 24*(4), 461–470. https://doi.org/10.1016/0005-7967(86)90011-2

Clark, D. M., Salkovskis, P. M., Hackmann, A., Wells, A., Ludgate, J., & Gelder, M. (1999). Brief cognitive therapy for panic disorder: A randomized controlled trial. *Journal of Consulting and Clinical Psychology, 67*(4), 583–589.

Clark, D. M., & Wells, A. (1995). A cognitive model of social phobia. In R. G. Heimberg, M. R. Liebowitz, D. A. Hope, & F. R. Schneier (Eds.), *Social phobia: Diagnosis, assessment, and treatment* (pp. 69–93). Guilford Press.

Clasen, M. (2017). *Why horror seduces.* Oxford University Press.

Cole, G. G., & Wilkins, A. J. (2013). Fear of holes. *Psychological Science, 24*(10), 1980–1985.

Costello, C. G. (1982). Fears and phobias in women: A community study. *Journal of Abnormal Psychology, 91*(4), 280–286.

Craske, M. G. (2015). Optimizing exposure therapy for anxiety disorders: An inhibitory learning and inhibitory regulation approach. *Verhaltenstherapie, 25*(2), 134–143. doi: 10.1159/000381574

Craske, M. G., Kircanski, K., Zelikowsky, M., Mystkowski, J., Chowdhury, N., & Baker, A. (2008). Optimizing inhibitory learning during exposure therapy. *Behaviour Research and Therapy, 46*(1), 5–27. https://doi.org/10.1016/j.brat.2007.10.003

Craske, M. G., Treanor, M., Conway, C. C., Zbozinek, T., & Vervliet, B. (2014). Maximizing exposure therapy: An inhibitory learning approach. *Behaviour Research and Therapy, 58*, 10–23. doi:10.1016/j.brat.2014.04.006

Darwin, C. (1872). *The expression of the emotions in man and animals.* Murray.

Davey, G. C., Cavanagh, K., & Lamb, A. (2003). Differential aversive outcome expectancies for high-and low-predation fear-relevant animals. *Journal of Behavior Therapy and Experimental Psychiatry, 34*(2), 117–128.

Davey, G. C., Forster, L., & Mayhew, G. (1993). Familial resemblances in disgust sensitivity and animal phobias. *Behaviour Research and Therapy, 31*(1), 41–50.

de Catanzaro, D. (1995). Reproductive status, family interactions, and suicidal ideation: Surveys of the general public and high-risk groups. *Ethology and Sociobiology, 16*(5), 385–394. http://dx.doi.org/10.1016/0162-3095(95)00055-0

De Jonge, P., Roest, A. M., Lim, C. C., Florescu, S. E., Bromet, E. J., Stein, D. J., Harris, M., Nakov, V., Caldas-de-Almeida, J. M., Levinson, D., Al-Hamzawi, A. O., Haro, J. M., Viana, M. C., Borges, G., O'Neill, S., de Girolamo, G., Demyttenaere, K., Gureje, O., Iwata, N., . . . Scott, K. M. (2016). Cross-national epidemiology of panic disorder and panic attacks in the world mental health surveys. *Depression and Anxiety, 33*(12), 1155–1177.

Deacon, B., Kemp, J. J., Dixon, L. J., Sy, J. T., Farrell, N. R., & Zhang, A. R. (2013). Maximizing the efficacy of interoceptive exposure by optimizing inhibitory learning: A randomized controlled trial. *Behaviour Research and Therapy, 51*(9), 588–596. https://doi.org/10.1016/j.brat.2013.06.006

Del Giudice, M. (2014). An evolutionary life history framework for psychopathology. *Psychological Inquiry, 25*(3–4), 261–300. doi:10.1080/1047840X.2014.884918

Del Giudice, M. (2018). *Evolutionary psychopathology: A unified approach.* Oxford University Press.

Di Nardo, P. A., Guzy, L. T., Jenkins, J. A., Bak, R. M., Tomasi, S. F., & Copland, M. (1988). Etiology and maintenance of dog fears. *Behaviour Research and Therapy, 26*(3), 241–244.

Dimberg, U., & Öhman, A. (1996). Behold the wrath: Psychophysiological responses to facial stimuli. *Motivation and Emotion, 20*(2), 149–182.

Eisen, J. L., Mancebo, M. A., Pinto, A., Coles, M. E., Pagano, M. E., Stout, R., & Rasmussen, S. A. (2006). Impact of obsessive-compulsive disorder on quality of life. *Comprehensive Psychiatry, 47*(4), 270–275. https://doi.org/10.1016/j.comppsych.2005.11.006

Evans, D. W., Gray, F. L., & Leckman, J. F. (1999). The rituals, fears and phobias of young children: Insights from development, psychopathology and neurobiology. *Child Psychiatry and Human Development, 29*(4), 261–276.

Feygin, D. L., Swain, J. E., & Leckman, J. F. (2006). The normalcy of neurosis: Evolutionary origins of obsessive–compulsive disorder and related behaviors. *Progress in Neuro-Psychopharmacology and Biological Psychiatry, 30*(5), 854–864. https://doi.org/10.1016/j.pnpbp.2006.01.009

Foa, E. B., Huppert, J. D., & Cahill, S. P. (2006). Emotional Processing Theory: An update. In B. O. Rothbaum (Ed.), *Pathological anxiety: Emotional processing in etiology and treatment.* (pp. 3–24). Guilford Press.

Foa, E. B., & Kozak, M. J. (1986). Emotional processing of fear: Exposure to corrective information. *Psychological Bulletin, 99*(1), 20–35. doi: 10.1037/0033-2909.99.1.20

Foa, E. B., & McLean, C. P. (2016). The efficacy of exposure therapy for anxiety-related disorders and its underlying mechanisms: The case of OCD and PTSD. *Annual Review of Clinical Psychology, 12*(1), 1–28. doi: 10.1146/annurev-clinpsy-021815-093533

Foa, E. B., Steketee, G., & Rothbaum, B. O. (1989). Behavioral/cognitive conceptualizations of post-traumatic stress disorder. *Behavior Therapy, 20*(2), 155–176.

Garcia, J., & Koelling, R. A. (1966). Relation of cue to consequence in avoidance learning. *Psychonomic Science, 4*(1), 123–124.

Gerdes, A. B., Uhl, G., & Alpers, G. W. (2009). Spiders are special: Fear and disgust evoked by pictures of arthropods. *Evolution and Human Behavior, 30*(1), 66–73.

Gibson, E. J., & Walk, R. D. (1960). The "visual cliff." *Scientific American, 202*(4), 64–71.

Gilbert, P. (2001). Evolution and social anxiety: The role of attraction, social competition, and social hierarchies. *Psychiatric Clinics, 24*(4), 723–751.

Greenberg, D. B., Stern, T. A., & Weilburg, J. B. (1988). The fear of choking: Three successfully treated cases. *Psychosomatics, 29*(1), 126–129. https://doi.org/10.1016/S0033-3182(88)72435-4

Gregory, A. M., Caspi, A., Moffitt, T. E., Koenen, K., Eley, T. C., & Poulton, R. (2007). Juvenile mental health histories of adults with anxiety disorders. *American Journal of Psychiatry, 164*(2), 301–308.

Grillon, C., Pellowski, M., Merikangas, K. R., & Davis, M. (1997). Darkness facilitates the acoustic startle reflex in humans. *Biological Psychiatry, 42*(6), 453–460.

Grubaugh, A. L. (2014). Trauma and stressor-related disorders. In D. C. Beidel, B. C. Frueh, & M. Hersen (Eds.), *Adult psychopathology and diagnosis* (pp. 387–406). John Wiley & Sons, Inc.

Hansen, B., Hagen, K., Öst, L. G., Solem, S., & Kvale, G. (2018). The Bergen 4-Day OCD treatment delivered in a group setting: 12-month follow-up. *Frontiers in Psychology, 9*, 639. doi: 10.3389/fpsyg.2018.00639

Hansen, B., Kvale, G., Hagen, K., Havnen, A., & Öst, L. G. (2019). The Bergen 4-day treatment for OCD: Four years follow-up of concentrated ERP in a clinical mental health setting. *Cognitive Behaviour Therapy, 48*(2), 89–105. doi: 10.1080/16506073.2018.1478447

Harvard Medical School. (2007). National Comorbidity Survey (NCS). Retrieved from https://www.hcp.med.harvard.edu/ncs/index.php

Hayes, S. C. (2004). Acceptance and commitment therapy, relational frame theory, and the third wave of behavioral and cognitive therapies. *Behavior Therapy, 35*(4), 639–665. doi: 10.1016/S0005-7894(04)80013-3

Hayes, S. C., Strosahl, K. D., & Wilson, K. G. (2009). *Acceptance and commitment therapy.* American Psychological Association.

Hofmann, S. G., & Asmundson, G. (2008). Acceptance and mindfulness-based therapy: New wave or old hat? *Clinical Psychology Review, 28*(1), 1–16.

Hofmann, S. G., Heinrichs, N., & Moscovitch, D. A. (2004). The nature and expression of social phobia: Toward a new classification. *Clinical Psychology Review, 24*(7), 769–797.

Jackson, R. E., & Calvillo, D. P. (2013). Evolutionary relevance facilitates visual information processing. *Evolutionary Psychology, 11*(5), 1011–1026. 147470491301100506.

Jacobi, F., Wittchen, H.-U., Hölting, C., Höfler, M., Pfister, H., Müller, N., & Lieb, R. (2004). Prevalence, comorbidity and correlates of mental disorders in the general population: results from the German Health Interview and Examination Survey (GHS). *Psychological Medicine, 34*(4), 597.

Jansson, L., & Öst, L.-G. (1982). Behavioral treatments for agoraphobia: An evaluative review. *Clinical Psychology Review, 2*(3), 311–336.

Kendler, K. S., Myers, J., & Prescott, C. A. (2002). The etiology of phobias: An evaluation of the stress-diathesis model. *Archives of General Psychiatry, 59*(3), 242–248.

Kennair, L. E. O. (2002). Evolutionary psychology: An emerging integrative perspective within the science and practice of psychology. *Human Nature Review, 2*, 17–61.

Kennair, L. E. O. (2007). Fear and fitness revisited. *Journal of Evolutionary Psychology, 5*(1), 105–117. doi: 10.1556/JEP.2007.1020

Kennair, L. E. O. (2011). The problem of defining psychopathology and challenges to evolutionary psychology theory. In D. M. Buss & P. H. Hawley (Eds.), *The evolution of personality and individual differences* (pp. 451–479). Oxford University Press.

Kennair, L. E. O. (2014). Evolutionary psychopathology and life history: A clinician's perspective. *Psychological Inquiry, 25*(3–4), 346–351. doi: 10.1080/1047840X.2014.915707

Kennair, L. E. O., & Kleppestø, T. H. (2018). Social anxiety. In T. K. Shackelford & V. A. Weekes-Shackelford (Eds.), *Encyclopedia of Evolutionary Psychological Science* (pp. 1–3). Springer International Publishing.

Kennair, L. E. O., Kleppestø, T. H., Larsen, S. M., & Jørgensen, B. E. G. (2017). Depression: is rumination really adaptive? In T. K. Shackelford & V. Zeigler-Hill (Eds.), *The evolution of psychopathology* (pp. 73–92). Springer.

Kennair, L. E. O., Larsen, S. M., & Kleppestø, T. H. (2020). Evolutionary clinical psychology. In T. K. Shackelford (Ed.), *Sage handbook of evolutionary psychology* (Vol. 2; pp. 152–171). Sage Publications.

Kennair, L. E. O., & Lindner, M. (2017). Fears and phobias. In T. K. Shackelford & V. A. Weekes-Shackelford (Eds.), *Encyclopedia of evolutionary psychological science* (pp. 1–4). Springer International.

Kennair, L. E. O., Sandseter, E. B. H., & Ball, D. (2018). Risky play and growing up: How to understand the overprotection of the next generation. In Kaufman & Kaufman (Eds.), *Pseudoscience: The conspiracy against science* (p. 171–194). MIT Press.

Kessler, R., Chiu, W., Demler, O., Merikangas, K., & Walters, E. (2005). Prevalence, severity, and comorbidity of 12-month DSM-IV disorders in the national comorbidity survey replication. *Archives of General Psychiatry, 62*(7), 709–709.

King, N. J., Muris, P., & Ollendick, T. H. (2005). Childhood fears and phobias: Assessment and treatment. *Child and Adolescent Mental Health, 10*: 50-56. https://doi.org/10.1111/j.1475-3588.2005.00118.x

Kruger, D. J., & Nesse, R. M. (2004). Sexual selection and the male: Female mortality ratio. *Evolutionary Psychology, 2*(1), 147470490400200112.

Kruger, D. J., & Nesse, R. M. (2006). An evolutionary life-history framework for understanding sex differences in human mortality rates. *Human Nature, 17*(1), 74–97.

Kuch, K. (1997). Accident phobia. In G. C. Davey (Ed.), *Phobias: A handbook of theory, research and treatment* (pp. 153–162). Wiley.

Leary, M. R., & Jongman-Sereno, K. P. (2014). Social anxiety as an early warning system: A refinement and extension of the self-presentation theory of social anxiety. In S. G. Hofmann & P. M. DiBartolo (Eds.), *Social anxiety* (pp. 579–597). Elsevier.

Leckman, J. F., & Bloch, M. H. (2008). A developmental and evolutionary perspective on obsessive-compulsive disorder: Whence and whither compulsive hoarding? *American Psychiatric Association, 165*(10), 1229–1233. doi: 10.1176/appi.ajp.2008.08060891

Leckman, J. F., Feldman, R., Swain, J. E., Eicher, V., Thompson, N., & Mayes, L. (2004). Primary parental preoccupation: Circuits, genes, and the crucial role of the environment. *Journal of Neural Transmission, 111*(7), 753–771.

Leckman, J. F., Mataix-Cols, D., & Rosario-Campos, M. C. d. (2005). Symptom dimensions in OCD: Developmental and evolutionary perspectives. In J. S. Abramowitz & A. C. Houts (Eds.), *Concepts and controversies in obsessive-compulsive disorder* (pp. 3–25). Springer.

Leonard, H. L., & Swedo, S. E. (2001). Paediatric autoimmune neuropsychiatric disorders associated with streptococcal infection (PANDAS). *International Journal of Neuropsychopharmacology, 4*(2), 191–198.

Linehan, M. M. (2018). *Cognitive-behavioral treatment of borderline personality disorder*: Guilford Press.

LoBue, V. (2010). And along came a spider: An attentional bias for the detection of spiders in young children and adults. *Journal of Experimental Child Psychology, 107*(1), 59–66. http://dx.doi.org/10.1016/j.jecp.2010.04.005

Lundqvist, D., Esteves, F., & Öhman, A. (1999). The face of wrath: Critical features for conveying facial threat. *Cognition & Emotion, 13*(6), 691–711.

Marks, I. M. (1969). *Fears and phobias*. Heinemann.

Marks, I. M. (1988). Blood-injury phobia: A review. *The American Journal of Psychiatry, 145*(10), 1207–1213. doi: 10.1176/ajp.145.10.1207

Marks, I. M., & Nesse, R. M. (1994). Fear and fitness: An evolutionary analysis of anxiety disorders. *Ethology and Sociobiology, 15*(5–6), 247–261.

Mendlowicz, M. V., & Stein, M. B. (2000). Quality of life in individuals with anxiety disorders. *American Journal of Psychiatry, 157*(5), 669–682.

Menzies, R. G., & Clarke, J. C. (1993). The etiology of fear of heights and its relationship to severity and individual response patterns. *Behaviour Research and Therapy, 31*(4), 355–365.

Mineka, S., & Öhman, A. (2002a). Born to fear: Non-associative vs associative factors in the etiology of phobias. *Behaviour Research and Therapy, 40*(2), 173–184.

Mineka, S., & Öhman, A. (2002b). Learning and unlearning fears: Preparedness, neural pathways, and patients. *Biological Psychology, 52*, 927–937.

Mowrer, O. H. (1947). On the dual nature of learning: A re-interpretation of "conditioning" and "problem-solving." *Harvard Educational Review, 17*, 102–148.

Murray, E. J., & Foote, F. (1979). The origins of fear of snakes. *Behaviour Research and Therapy, 17*(5), 489–493.
Nasar, J. L., & Jones, K. M. (1997). Landscapes of fear and stress. *Environment and Behavior, 29*(3), 291–323.
Nesse, R. M. (2001). The smoke detector principle. *Annals of the New York Academy of Sciences, 935*(1), 75–85. doi: 10.1111/j.1749-6632.2001.tb03472.x
Nesse, R. M. (2019). *Good reasons for bad feelings: Insights from the frontier of evolutionary psychiatry.* Penguin.
Nesse, R. M., & Williams, G. C. (1996). *Why we get sick: The new science of Darwinian medicine.* Vintage.
Nettle, D. (2004). Evolutionary origins of depression: A review and reformulation. *Journal of Affective Disorders, 81*(2), 91–102.
Nettle, D. (2005). An evolutionary approach to the extraversion continuum. *Evolution and Human Behavior, 26*(4), 363–373. doi: 10.1016/j.evolhumbehav.2004.12.004
Nettle, D. (2011). Evolutionary perspectives on the Five-Factor Model of personality. In D. M. Buss & P. H. Hawley (Eds.), *The evolution of personality and individual differences* (pp. 5–28). Oxford University Press.
New, J. J., & German, T. C. (2015). Spiders at the cocktail party: An ancestral threat that surmounts inattentional blindness. *Evolution and Human Behavior, 36*(3), 165–173.
Nordahl, H. M., Borkovec, T. D., Hagen, R., Kennair, L. E. O., Hjemdal, O., Solem, S., Hansen, B., Haseth, S., & Wells, A. (2018). Metacognitive therapy versus cognitive–behavioural therapy in adults with generalised anxiety disorder. *BJPsych Open, 4*(5), 393–400. doi: 10.1192/bjo.2018.54
Öhman, A. (1986). Face the beast and fear the face: Animal and social fears as prototypes for evolutionary analyses of emotion. *Psychophysiology, 23*(2), 123–145. doi: 10.1111/j.1469-8986.1986.tb00608.x
Öhman, A., & Dimberg, U. (1984). An evolutionary perspective on human social behavior. In W. M. Waid (Eds.), *Sociophysiology* (pp. 47–86). Springer.
Öhman, A., Dimberg, U., & Öst, L. (1985). Animal and social phobias: Biological constraints on learned fear responses. In S. Reiss & R. R. Bootzin (Eds.), *Theoretical issues in behavior therapy* (pp. 123–175). Academic Press.
Öhman, A., Flykt, A., & Esteves, F. (2001). Emotion drives attention: Detecting the snake in the grass. *Journal of Experimental Psychology: General, 130*(3), 466–478.
Öhman, A., Fredrikson, M., Hugdahl, K., & Rimmö, P.-A. (1976). The premise of equipotentiality in human classical conditioning: Conditioned electrodermal responses to potentially phobic stimuli. *Journal of Experimental Psychology: General, 105*(4), 313–337.
Öhman, A., Lundqvist, D., & Esteves, F. (2001). The face in the crowd revisited: A threat advantage with schematic stimuli. *Journal of Personality and Social Psychology, 80*(3), 381–396.
Öhman, A., & Mineka, S. (2001). Fears, phobias, and preparedness: Toward an evolved module of fear and fear learning. *Psychological Review, 108*(3), 483–522.
Öhman, A., & Wiens, S. (2003). On the automaticity of autonomic responses in emotion: An evolutionary perspective.
Oosterink, F. M., De Jongh, A., & Hoogstraten, J. (2009). Prevalence of dental fear and phobia relative to other fear and phobia subtypes. *European Journal of Oral Sciences, 117*(2), 135–143.
Pinker, S. (2012). *The better angels of our nature: Why violence has declined.* Penguin Group USA.
Pompoli, A., Furukawa, T. A., Imai, H., Tajika, A., Efthimiou, O., & Salanti, G. (2016). Psychological therapies for panic disorder with or without agoraphobia in adults: A network meta-analysis. *Cochrane Database of Systematic Reviews* (4). doi: 10.1002/14651858.CD011004.pub2
Poulton, R., & Menzies, R. G. (2002a). Fears born and bred: Toward a more inclusive theory of fear acquisition. *Behaviour Research and Therapy, 40*(2), 197–208. doi: 10.1016/S0005-7967(01)00052-3
Poulton, R., & Menzies, R. G. (2002b). Non-associative fear acquisition: A review of the evidence from retrospective and longitudinal research. *Behaviour Research and Therapy, 40*(2), 127–149. doi: 10.1016/S0005-7967(01)0004-6
Poulton, R., Menzies, R. G., Craske, M. G., Langley, J. D., & Silva, P. A. (1999). Water trauma and swimming experiences up to age 9 and fear of water at age 18: A longitudinal study. *Behaviour Research and Therapy, 37*(1), 39–48.
Poulton, R., Milne, B. J., Craske, M. G., & Menzies, R. G. (2001). A longitudinal study of the etiology of separation anxiety. *Behaviour Research and Therapy, 39*(12), 1395–1410.
Rachman, S. (1977). The conditioning theory of fear acquisition: A critical examination. *Behaviour Research and Therapy, 15*(5), 375–387.
Rakison, D. H., & Derringer, J. (2008). Do infants possess an evolved spider-detection mechanism? *Cognition, 107*(1), 381–393.
Rapoport, J. L. (1991). *The boy who couldn't stop washing: The experience and treatment of obsessive-compulsive disorder.* Penguin.
Razran, G. (1971). *Mind in evolution: An East-West synthesis of learned behavior and cognition.* Houghton Mifflin.
Ruiter, R. A., Abraham, C., & Kok, G. (2001). Scary warnings and rational precautions: A review of the psychology of fear appeals. *Psychology and Health, 16*(6), 613–630.
Sandseter, E. B. H., & Kennair, L. E. O. (2011). Children's risky play from an evolutionary perspective: The antiphobic effects of thrilling experiences. *Evolutionary Psychology, 9*(2), 257–284.

Schaller, M., Park, J. H., & Mueller, A. (2003). Fear of the dark: Interactive effects of beliefs about danger and ambient darkness on ethnic stereotypes. *Personality and Social Psychology Bulletin, 29*(5), 637–649.

Segal, Z. V., & Teasdale, J. (2018). *Mindfulness-based cognitive therapy for depression*. Guilford Press.

Seim, R. W., & Spates, C. R. (2009). The prevalence and comorbidity of specific phobias in college students and their interest in receiving treatment. *Journal of College Student Psychotherapy, 24*(1), 49–58.

Seligman, M. E. (1971). Phobias and preparedness. *Behavior Therapy, 2*(3), 307–320.

Skoog, G., & Skoog, I. (1999). A 40-year follow-up of patients with obsessive-compulsive disorder. *Archives of General Psychiatry, 56*(2), 121–127. doi: 10.1001/archpsyc.56.2.121

Solem, S., Hagen, K., Hansen, B., Håland, A. T., Launes, G., Lewin, A. B., Storch, E. A., & Vogel, P. A. (2015). Thought Content and Appraisals in Cognitive Behavioral Therapy for Obsessive-Compulsive Disorder. *Journal of Cognitive Psychotherapy, 29*(2), 106–115. doi: 10.1891/0889-8391.29.2.106

Solem, S., Hagen, K., Wenaas, C., Haland, A. T., Launes, G., Vogel, P. A., Hansen, B., & Himle, J. A. (2015). Psychotic and schizotypal symptoms in non-psychotic patients with obsessive-compulsive disorder. *BMC Psychiatry, 15*(1), 121. doi: 10.1186/s12888-015-0502-1

Solem, S., Hansen, B., Vogel, P. A., & Kennair, L. E. O. (2009). The efficacy of teaching psychology students exposure and response prevention for obsessive-compulsive disorder. *Scandinavian Journal of Psychology, 50*(3), 245–250. https://doi.org/10.1111/j.1467-9450.2008.00703.x

Solem, S., Kennair, L. E. O., Hagen, R., Havnen, A., Nordahl, H. M., Wells, A., & Hjemdal, O. (2019). Metacognitive therapy for depression: A 3-year follow-up study assessing recovery, relapse, work force participation, and quality of life. *Frontiers in Psychology, 10*, 2908.

Stein, D. J., & Bouwer, C. (1997). A neuro-evolutionary approach to the anxiety disorders. *Journal of Anxiety Disorders, 11*(4), 409–429. http://dx.doi.org/10.1016/S0887-6185(97)00019-4

Taylor, S., McKay, D., & Abramowitz, J. S. (2005). Hierarchical structure of dysfunctional beliefs in obsessive-compulsive disorder. *Cognitive Behaviour Therapy, 34*(4), 216–228.

Tooby, J., & Cosmides, L. (1988). *The Evolution of War and its Cognitive Foundations*. Institute for Evolutionary Studies Technical Report 88-1.

Tooby, J., & Cosmides, L. (1995). Mapping the evolved functional organization of mind and brain. In M. S. Gazzaniga (Ed.), *The cognitive neurosciences* (pp. 1185–1197). MIT Press.

Troisi, A., & McGuire, M. T. (2002). Darwinian psychiatry and the concept of mental disorder. *Neuroendocrinology Letters, 23*(Suppl 4), 31–38.

Trower, P., & Gilbert, P. (1989). New theoretical conceptions of social anxiety and social phobia. *Clinical Psychology Review, 9*(1), 19–35. http://dx.doi.org/10.1016/0272-7358(89)90044-5

Tybur, J. M., Lieberman, D., & Griskevicius, V. (2009). Microbes, mating, and morality: individual differences in three functional domains of disgust. *Journal of Personality and Social Psychology, 97*(1), 103–122.

Wakefield, J. C. (1999). Evolutionary versus prototype analyses of the concept of disorder. *Journal of Abnormal Psychology, 108*(3), 374–399. doi: 10.1037/0021-843X.108.3.374

Watson, J., & Marks, I. (1971). Relevant and irrelevant fear in flooding: A crossover study of phobic patients. *Behavior Therapy, 2*(3), 275–293.

Wells, A. (2000). *Emotional disorders and metacognition: Innovative cognitive therapy*. Wiley.

Wells, A. (2008). Metacognitive therapy: Cognition applied to regulating cognition. *Behavioural and Cognitive Psychotherapy, 36*(6), 651–658. doi: 10.1017/S1352465808004803

Wells, A. (2009). *Metacognitive therapy for anxiety and depression*. Guilford Press.

Wells, A., & Colbear, J. S. (2012). Treating posttraumatic stress disorder with metacognitive therapy: A preliminary controlled trial. *Journal of Clinical Psychology, 68*(4), 373–381.

Wells, A., Myers, S., Simons, M., & Fisher, P. (2017). Metacognitive model and treatment of OCD. In J. S. Abramowitz, D. McKay, E. A. Storch (Eds.), *The Wiley handbook of obsessive compulsive disorders* (Vol. 1, pp. 644–662). Wiley.

Wells, A., & Papageorgiou, C. (1995). Worry and the incubation of intrusive images following stress. *Behaviour Research and Therapy, 33*(5), 579–583.

Wilson, M., & Daly, M. (1985). Competitiveness, risk taking, and violence: the young male syndrome. *Ethology and Sociobiology, 6*(1), 59–73. doi:10.1016/0162-3095(85)90041-X

Yantis, S., & Johnson, D. N. (1990). Mechanisms of attentional priority. *Journal of Experimental Psychology: Human Perception and Performance, 16*(4), 812–825.

Zheng, H., Lenard, N. R., Shin, A. C., & Berthoud, H. R. (2009). Appetite control and energy balance regulation in the modern world: Reward-driven brain overrides repletion signals. *International Journal of Obesity, 33*(2), S8–S13. doi:

CHAPTER 59

Credible Sadness, Coercive Sadness: Depression as a Functional Response to Adversity and Strife

Edward H. Hagen and Kristen L. Syme

Abstract
Evolutionary medicine offers the insight that many unpleasant conditions such as physical pain are not harmful in themselves, but are evolved mechanisms to mitigate harm. A major goal of the field is to distinguish illnesses from aversive conditions that are evolved defenses. There are numerous evolutionary theories of depression, but many fail to account for the central role of conflict and cannot explain suicidality. This chapter reviews evidence from Western and non-Western societies that depression is caused by adversity, conflict, and powerlessness. The most parsimonious theory is that depression evolved, in part, as a form of psychological pain that functions to mitigate harm, credibly signal need, and coerce help when the powerless are in conflicts with powerful others.

Key Words: depression, suicide, mental health, cross-cultural, evolutionary medicine

> *For of men one can, in general, say this: They are ungrateful, fickle, deceptive and deceiving, avoiders of danger, eager to gain. As long as you serve their interests, they are devoted to you. They promise you their blood, their possessions, their lives, and their children, as I said before, so long as you seem to have no need of them. But as soon as you need help, they turn against you.*
> —Machiavelli, *The Prince* (D. Wootten, Ed., 1995, p. 52)

Introduction

Many of life's problems cannot be solved alone. Sadness and grief therefore are expressed in the face, posture, gait, tone of voice, and by crying (Grosbras et al., 2018; Sebe et al., 2006), all of which likely evolved to signal need to family, friends, and other important social partners, who in turn provided essential assistance. As we will describe here, depression, too, involves distinctive behavioral patterns, including reduced activity, eye gaze, tone of voice, posture, and gait, which readily communicate dysphoria. This suggests that depression might also involve signals of need. Yet depression alienates others (Coyne, 1976a, 1976b; Segrin &

Dillard, 1992) and is stigmatized in some societies (Larkings & Brown, 2018). How, then, could it possibly elicit help?

In examining emotions under the lens of evolution, we confront the discomforting specter that emotions sometimes motivate socially undesirable behaviors. Emotions solve a wide range of adaptive problems (Tooby & Cosmides 1990; Al-Shawaf et al., 2016), many of which involve conflicts with social partners over, for instance, the distribution of resources and access to mates. Anger is aversive to the self and others, yet likely evolved to garner concessions from social partners when there were conflicts of interest (Sell et al., 2009). Men probably evolved to angrily threaten their wives when paternity was at stake, for example, or when wives diverted resources to offspring of other men (Buss & Duntley, 2011; Wilson & Daly, 1998). Similarly, mothers did not evolve to distribute resources equally among their offspring and probably evolved to not form attachments to newborn infants under poor environmental conditions (Hagen, 1999). Many social institutions such as police forces and courts have culturally evolved to reduce these socially undesirable behaviors, e.g., by punishing norm violators. But as Cosmides and Tooby (1999) observed, ". . . what is desirable or harmful are rarely matters of harmonious consensus or intersubjective agreement, much less matters of fact" (p. 456). This applies to individuals within society and across societies. Wife-beating is a punishable offense in Western society, but it is an acceptable, if not normative, practice in many societies (Rauchholz, 2016; Uthman et al., 2009). Indeed, institutions of social control in these societies sanction women who complain or attempt to escape (Jolly et al., 2012). Many critics have argued that psychiatry is, in part, an institution designed to control certain socially undesirable behaviors by labeling them as illnesses (see Syme & Hagen, 2020, for review).

Our approach to depression, which emphasizes its ability to elicit and coerce benefits from others by imposing, or threatening to impose, aversive costs on them, similar to anger, has been criticized for exactly this reason by other experts in evolutionary approaches to mental illness (Allen & Badcock, 2003; Nesse, 2006; Nettle, 2004). If one needed help from others, would not "normal" low mood, sadness, and grief suffice, leaving depression as a pathological extreme (Wolpert, 1999)? We hope to convince you that the answer is *no*, that although sadness and grief work well when there is little conflict with family, friends, coworkers, or employers, they will not work when there is substantial conflict. The difference between depression and "normal" sadness or grief is not psychopathology, we will argue, but is instead the degree of conflict in one's key relationships. Psychiatry might classify depression as a mental illness not because it is a brain dysfunction, but because it is aversive to all involved.

What Is Major Depression?

A diagnosis of major depression (MD), according to the *Diagnostic and Statistical Manual of Mental Disorders* (fifth edition, DSM-5), requires that an individual experience five or more of nine symptoms in a two-week period. Symptom criteria include: subjective feelings of sadness, hopelessness, or emptiness; diminished interest in activities; sleep changes; fatigue; inability to concentrate; weight changes; feelings of guilt; suicidal thoughts; and psychomotor agitation or retardation (APA, 2013). Most researchers regard these symptoms, taken individually, as normal responses to adversity, at least to some degree (suicidality would be the exception). Under the DSM-5, when the number and duration of symptoms exceed the above threshold, however, depression is considered to be a dysfunction regardless of environmental conditions.

Most MD and Suicidality Are Caused by Adversity

Ordinary sadness and grief are caused by adverse events. A common view about MD is that it is fundamentally different, striking without cause. Contrary to this common view, there is

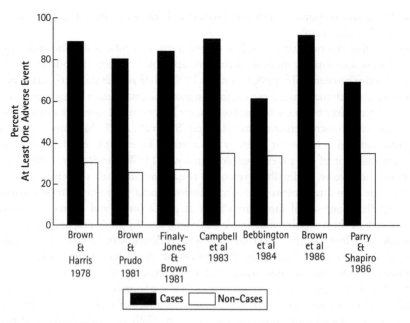

Figure 59.1. Life events and onset of major depression. Figure and caption from Mazure (1998).

a consensus that MD is caused in large part by adverse events, and that more severe events increase the risk and severity of MD. Many early studies found that about 80% of cases of MD had evidence of at least one adverse event, compared to a much lower rate among non-cases (Mazure, 1998) (see Figure 59.1).

Kendler et al. (1999) investigated if stressful life events *cause* MD by assessing the dates of stressful life events and the dates of onset of depression (if any) in a large sample of US female twins. Stressful life events were categorized as either dependent on participants' behavior (e.g., divorce) or independent of participants' behavior (e.g., death of a loved one). A close temporal association of an independent stressful life event with depression onset was taken as strong evidence of a causal effect of the former on the latter. Kendler et al. (1999) conclude that "[s]tressful life events have a substantial causal relationship with the onset of episodes of major depression. However, about one-third of the association between stressful life events and onsets of depression is non-causal, since individuals predisposed to major depression select themselves into high-risk environments" (p. 837) (see Table 59.1).

Non-Western Evidence

Findings from non-Western samples further support that various forms of adversity are strongly associated with, and likely cause, depression, anxiety, and post-traumatic stress disorder (PTSD). An estimated one in five people suffers from depression, PTSD, anxiety disorders, and related disorders in conflict-affected countries, compared to one in 14 worldwide (Charlson et al., 2019). In a study of individual-level data from 160 countries, Elgar et al. (2021) analyzed the association of relative and absolute food insecurity with the number of mental health symptoms: physical pain, worry, sadness, stress, and anger. Higher levels of both relative and absolute food insecurity were associated with higher numbers of mental health

Table 59.1 Odds Ratios for the Onset of DSM-III-R Major Depression in 1,898 Female Twins in the Month of, and 1–3 Months after, Stressful Life Events Rated as Probably or Definitely Independent of Respondent Behavior.

Life Event	Odds Ratio for Onset of Major Depression [a]			
	In Month of Event	1 Month After Event	2 Months After Event	3 Months After Event
Personal Assault	25.36***	4.31	—[b]	—[b]
Divorce/separation	5.22	—[b]	—[b]	—[b]
Financial problems	5.85***	2.75	4.31**	2.36
Serious housing problems	7.24***	2.71	1.25	1.26
Serious illness or injury	3.10**	0.70	0.76	0.43
Job loss	3.95*	—[b]	—[b]	—[b]
Legal problems	3.81	—[b]	4.55	10.81**
Loss of confidant	3.17*	1.05	3.19*	1.28
Serious marital problems	8.39*	14.26***	—[b]	4.29
Being robbed	2.74	1.40	1.42	5.01**
Serious work problems	2.44	1.82	1.87	2.74
In subject's social network				
Serious trouble getting along with an individual	5.04***	2.46	1.79	2.23
Serious personal crisis	2.32***	0.65	0.78	0.74
Death	6.29***	0.81	0.86	1.00
Serious illness	2.50***	1.12	0.98	0.43

[a] Odds ratios are calculated from logistic regression of person-months (N ≈ 24,648), and their significance is determined by Wald chi-square test (df = 1).

[b] Not estimable because of small cell sizes.

* $p < 0.05$; ** $p < 0.01$; *** $p < 0.001$.

Source: Kendler et al. (1999).

symptoms. There were stronger associations for relative vs. absolute food insecurity, indicating the importance of social comparisons in experiences of distress.

Suicidality, an important symptom of depression, is also associated with adversity across populations. Multi-country studies show that violence against women is a strong predictor of emotional distress and suicidality (Devries et al., 2011; Ellsberg et al., 2008). Bullying from peers is another risk factor for suicidality in geographically diverse populations (Alavi et al., 2017; Butler et al., 2019; Ford et al., 2017; Wang et al., 2020). In a Norwegian adolescent sample that included indigenous Sami and non-Sami age 15–16 years, suicide attempters reported more than twice as many adversities compared to non-attempters (Reigstad & Kvernmo, 2017). A comprehensive review of the ethnographic record found that discussions of suicidality commonly described threats to the victim's fitness (i.e., adversity), such as forced or thwarted marriages and physical abuse (Syme et al., 2016).

The Weak Evidence That MD in Community Populations Is a Brain Dysfunction

Almost all research on MD uses either the DSM criteria or the *International Classification of Diseases* (IDC) criteria, which is informed by the DSM. The current DSM-5 criteria are basically the same as those in DSM-III, which ushered in the modern era of depression research. These criteria are listed in the right-most column in Table 59.2.

Everyone will experience at least one of these symptoms at some point in their lives, and the majority of people will probably experience most of them. Prima facie, none of these symptoms indicates a brain dysfunction.

Table 59.2 Historical Origins of the Symptomatic Criteria for MD: Criteria Proposed 1950–1980.

Stone and Burris 1950	Cassidy et al. 1957	Feighner et al., 1972	Research Diagnostic Criteria, 1975	DSM-III criteria, 1980
Feeling depressed	Depressed mood	Dysphoric mood	Dysphoric mood	Dysphoric mood
Sleeplessness	Insomnia	Sleep difficulty (insomnia or hypersomnia)	Sleep difficulty or sleeping too much	Insomnia or hypersomnia
Appetite loss	Anorexia	Poor appetite or weight loss	Poor appetite or weight loss; or increased appetite and weight gain	Poor appetite or weight loss; or increased appetite and weight gain
Weight loss	Weight loss			
Agitation	Wringing hands, pacing	Agitation or retardation	Psychomotor agitation or retardation	Psychomotor agitation or retardation
Self-deprecation		Self-reproach, guilt	Self-reproach or guilt	Worthlessness, self-reproach or guilt
Psychomotor retardation	Slowed thinking			
	Loss of concentration	Diminished ability to think or concentrate	Diminished ability to think or concentrate	Diminished ability to think or concentrate
Suicidal thoughts	Suicidal ideation	Thoughts of death, suicide	Thoughts of death of suicide	Thoughts of death or suicidal ideation
	Constipation			
	Fatigue	Loss of energy	Loss of energy, fatigue	Loss of energy, fatigue
	Decreased sex interest	Loss of interest or decreased sex drive	Loss of interest or pleasure	Loss of interest or pleasure

Source: Kendler et al. (2010).

Depression criteria come from studies dating back to the 1950s conducted among groups of individuals determined to suffer from a variety of severe psychiatric disturbances (or physical illnesses). The goal of these studies was to develop criteria that would enable different psychiatrists to reliably provide the same patient with the same diagnosis, such as bipolar disorder or schizophrenia. Importantly, these studies were *not* designed to distinguish the mentally ill from the healthy.

The DSM-III criteria for MD can be traced to Stone and Burris (1950), a clinical study of 50 selected cases; Cassidy et al. (1957), a quantitative study of 100 manic-depressive patients compared to 50 medically sick controls; Feighner et al. (1972), a study of 314 psychiatric emergency room patients and 87 psychiatric inpatients; and Spitzer et al. (1975), which tested the reliability of the Research Diagnostic Criteria (RDC) with 218 psychiatric inpatients (see Table 59.2).

None of the studies that defined MD as we understand it today included any healthy participants, nor any identified as experiencing only ordinary sorrow, sadness, or grief. There is thus no reason to believe that, when applied to the general population, the criteria developed in these studies would effectively distinguish the small minority of individuals with a genuine brain dysfunction from the much larger number of individuals who were suffering ordinary low mood, sadness, or grief in response to adversity (see also Horwitz et al., 2016). Yet they are widely used for this purpose.

The Implausibly High Prevalence of Putatively Disordered Affect

It is no surprise, then, that when DSM criteria were first applied to the general population in the Epidemiologic Catchment Area (ECA) program, they generated implausibly high prevalence rates of mental illness. Over a quarter of the population (28.5%) was identified as suffering a mental illness in the past year, and nearly half the population (48%) was identified as having suffered a mental illness in their lifetimes. For MD, up to 10% were identified to have suffered an episode in the past year, and 17% to have suffered MD in their lifetime (Regier et al., 1998).

If MD were a genuine brain disorder, its epidemiology might resemble that of other genuine brain disorders, such as developmental brain disorders, which occur early in life, or the brain disorders related to aging, i.e., those that occur late in life. To compare MD with three common developmental brain disorders, we use data from the 2017 Global Burden of Disease Study (see Figure 59.2).

New cases of MD are common starting in adolescence and throughout adulthood and, as we discuss in more detail below, most individuals fully recover within several months to a year. In comparison, autism spectrum disorders are lifelong conditions that are relatively rare and present at birth (hence prevalence, rather than incidence, is reported). Bipolar disorder and schizophrenia are also lifelong and relatively rare, with peaks in incidence rates in late adolescence and early adulthood. Similarly, although incidence of MD increases with age, it does not resemble other brain disorders related to aging, such as dementias and Parkinson's disease (which do not remit), or stroke, all of which are rare until after the age of 40 or 50 years (see Figure 59.3).

Starting in adolescence, the incidence of MD is about an order of magnitude higher than other mental illnesses. Regier et al. (1998, p. 114) acknowledged that these high rates call into question the validity of "diagnoses" based on DSM criteria in community populations (Reiger initiated the ECA and was vice-chair of the DSM-5 task force):

> Although it is possible that all of these community-based disorders are simply milder cases of essentially the same disorders seen in clinical settings, there are other possibilities as well. Based on

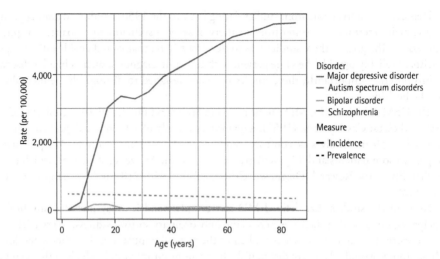

Figure 59.2. Major depression incidence compared to epidemiology of brain disorders that appear to be due to developmental disruption. X-axis: age (0–100 years). Y-axis: incidence/prevalence (rate per 100,000).

Data from Global Burden of Disease (2017) and healthdata.org.

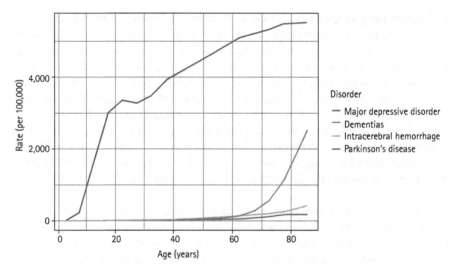

Figure 59.3. Major depression incidence compared to epidemiology of brain disorders that appear to be due to aging. X-axis: age (0–100 years). Y-axis: incidence (rate per 100,000).

Data from Global Burden of Disease (2017).

the high prevalence rates identified in both the ECA and the NCS, it is reasonable to hypothesize that some syndromes in the community represent transient homeostatic responses to internal or external stimuli that do not represent true psychopathologic disorders. The human organism has a limited repertoire of response patterns to various physical, biological, and emotional stresses. Transient changes in blood pressure, pulse rate, body temperature, anxiety, or mood are not always indicators of pathology but of appropriate adaptive responses. It is possible that many people with currently defined mental syndromes (*in particular among the affective and anxiety disorders*) not brought to clinical attention may be having appropriate homeostatic responses that are neither pathologic nor in need of treatment—e.g., other equivalents of grief reactions that meet clinical criteria but are not considered pathologic if they are time-limited. (emphasis added)

Spitzer, leader of the DSM-III effort, expressed similar concern for the potential of high false positive rates for MD (Spitzer & Wakefield, 1999).

No Evidence That MD Is Caused by a Chemical Imbalance

The first two drugs found to decrease depression symptoms both acted on monoamine pathways to increase monoamine concentrations, which motivated the "chemical imbalance theory"[1] of depression. Although depression, like all mental states, has a biological basis, decades of research have found no evidence that depression is caused by a simple imbalance of serotonin or any other neurotransmitter (Ruhé et al., 2007). The chemical action of antidepressants is a weak foundation for the "chemical imbalance" model. After all, aspirin reduces headaches, but headaches are not caused by an aspirin imbalance. Further, antidepressant effects appear after several weeks even though these drugs increase monoamines within minutes after ingestion (Frazer & Benmansour, 2002; Harmer et al., 2009).

Importantly, antidepressant drugs are only modestly efficacious at best (e.g., Kirsch & Sapirstein, 1999). Adjusting for unreported studies, effect sizes indicated a modest advantage of treatment over placebo (Cohen's d = .31 to.32) corresponding to less than 2 points on the Hamilton Depression Scale (HAM-D), which ranges from 0 to 52 (Cipriani et al., 2018; Kirsch, 2008; Turner et al., 2008). A 3-point difference on the HAM-D is a criterion for clinical significance for depression treatment (Kirsch, 2014).

Depression Symptoms Occur on a Continuum

Depression symptomatology exists on a continuum, with little evidence for discrete nondepressed vs. depressed states (Prisciandaro & Roberts, 2005) (see Figure 59.4). A recent meta-analysis of studies that compared categorical (e.g., depressed vs. nondepressed) with dimensional (i.e., continuous) approaches to psychological traits supported the dimensional over the categorical approach by a factor of 5 to 1 (Haslam et al., 2020). Putatively dysfunctional MD is continuous with normality. Moreover, the severity and frequency of the stressors

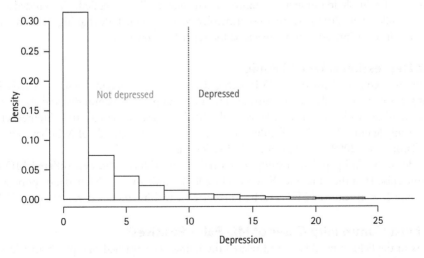

Figure 59.4. Distribution of depression scores from the Patient Health Questionnaire (PHQ-9), with a conventional threshold of 10 to diagnose MD. Nationally representative US data from NHANES 2011–2012.

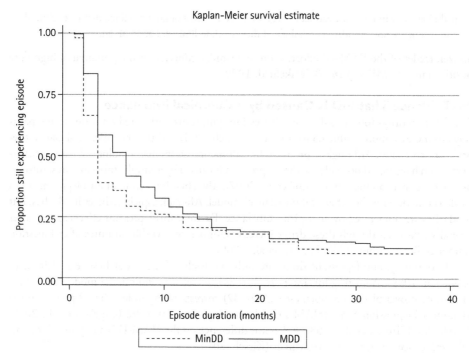

Figure 59.5. Survival curves of a cohort (n = 393) with newly originated (first or recurrent) depressive episodes in the general population. MinDD: minor depressive disorder. MDD: major depressive disorder.

Figure and caption from ten Have et al. (2017).

that cause depression predict the severity of the depression, in a dose-response relationship (Bustamante et al., 2020; Jenness et al., 2019; Tennant, 2002), albeit with possible differences due to age and sex (e.g., Ge et al., 1994; Kendler et al., 2004). When Cassidy, developer of one of the historical antecedents to the DSM-III MD criteria (see Table 59.2), was asked how he decided on the threshold number of symptoms to diagnose MD, he replied, "It sounded about right" (Kendler et al., 2010). There is no principled reason to conclude that higher scores indicate brain disorder instead of more severe sadness, grief, or low mood.

Most Depression Is Not Chronic

Despite the frequent claim that MD is a chronic disease, the median duration of MD in a recent study of a nationally representative community sample was six months, and about 75% of cases remitted within a year (ten Have et al., 2017; see also Richards, 2011; Steinert et al., 2014). Only about 12%–15% of individuals with at least one episode of MD have chronic MD (Eaton et al., 2008; ten Have et al., 2018) (see Figure 59.5).

Indeed, in a US population study, about half of individuals who ever suffered MD had only one episode in their lifetime (Eaton et al., 2008). Similarly, in a Netherlands population study, only 27% of remitted MD cases had a recurrence within 20 years (ten Have et al. 2018).

Are Most Community Cases of MD False Positives?

Leaders in the field of psychiatry and related disciplines have warned that psychiatry, in general, and the DSM, in particular, increasingly medicalize normal, healthy conditions. Allen

Frances, chair of the DSM-IV effort, has criticized an excess of diagnostic labels for variations of normal behavior (Frances, 2013). If depression, anxiety, and PTSD are adaptive responses to adversity, then labeling them as disorders is a problem of conceptual validity (Wakefield, 1992, 2013). On this view, most cases of MD in community populations are false positives.

The DSM-III and DSM-IV included a *bereavement exclusion*: a diagnosis for depressive symptoms occurring within two months following the loss of a loved one was excluded (unless symptoms of worthlessness and suicidality were also present). Depression in this circumstance was seen to be a normal grief response (Wakefield, 2013). Critics proposed that the bereavement exclusion should be expanded to include other forms of adversity that often cause depression, such as interpersonal conflicts, job loss, and physical or sexual abuse (Kendler & Gardner, 2016; Mazure, 1998).

Members of the DSM-5 depression workgroup instead wanted to remove the bereavement exclusion because MD caused by the death of a loved one is similar to cases of MD caused by other stressors (Kendler et al., 2008; Wakefield et al., 2007). Their proposal sparked one of the most contentious debates over the medicalization of normal human experience in recent years (see Wakefield, 2013).

Ultimately, the bereavement exclusion was removed in the DSM-5, largely because bereaved individuals are at increased risk of suicidality, relative to individuals who have not recently experienced a stressful event, and therefore need treatment (Zisook, 2013). (As Wakefield, 2013, noted, however, the bereavement exclusion never applied to suicidal individuals.) Nevertheless, because most cases of MD in the general population are caused by recent adversity, involve common symptoms like sadness, loss of interest, and changes to appetite and sleep, and resolve within several months to a year, it is unlikely that they represent brain dysfunctions.

Because any evolved function can dysfunction, some cases of MD, such as those seen among psychiatric inpatients, might reflect genuine disorders. Spitzer and Wakefield (1999, p. 1863) suggested that to identify genuinely disordered MD, DSM criteria should be altered to something like the following:

> The symptoms are not better accounted for by a normal reaction to a psychosocial stressor (e.g., loss of a loved one, terminal medical illness in self or loved one, loss of relationship); i.e., *the disturbance is judged to be markedly excessive in intensity or duration relative to the nature of the stressor*. (emphasis added)

The Real Mysteries of Depression

The primary scientific questions about MD are not what causes it. Adversity causes MD. The primary questions are, first, why, after experiencing what would seem to be the same degree of adversity, do different individuals experience widely varying levels of negative affect, some of which exceed the threshold for MD diagnosis? (see Figure 59.4). Few studies consider adversity from an evolutionary perspective. Divorce is a stressful life event, for example, but it might represent a benefit to individuals with good mating prospects and a severe adversity to individuals with poor mating prospects. Physical assault could be very adverse for weak individuals but might be much less adverse for formidable individuals. Death of a child might be more adverse for mothers than fathers (e.g., due to paternity uncertainty and/or the shorter female reproductive life span). Circumstances that inflicted fitness costs over much of human evolution, on the other hand, such as late or delayed reproduction, small family size, and failure to form a long-term mateship, might not be experienced as adversities by many people and therefore are not included on life event questionnaires, yet may be extremely adverse for some. Thus, some differences in depression levels for similar adversities could be attributable to the fact that the degree of adversity depends on difficult-to-assess individual circumstances.

The second primary question is: What are the evolved functions of depressed mood, if any, and especially of mysterious depression symptoms like suicidality and profound loss of interest in virtually all activities?

Many Studies of Depression Are Poorly Designed to Resolve Its Mysteries

Studies of MD commonly employ the following, fatally flawed case-control design: a group of participants that meet diagnostic criteria for MD—cases—are compared to a group of "healthy" controls, i.e., individuals without MD. Most of the individuals diagnosed with MD are (1) experiencing sadness or low mood (one of two necessary symptoms according to the DSM), and (2) have suffered recent adversity. Most members of the control group, in contrast, are not experiencing sadness or low mood, and have not suffered recent adversity. Hence, MD is almost completely confounded with sadness and recent adversity. Thus, any differences between the cases and controls could be due to differences in adversity or differences in ordinary sadness, rather than the presence or absence of putatively pathological MD.

Studies of "vulnerability" and "resilience" are an important exception to the foregoing in that these studies often recruit individuals who have suffered a common adversity, such as a particular severe physical illness (e.g., spinal cord injury) or loss (death of a loved one), and then investigate why some individuals suffer lower or higher levels of depression, anxiety, and/or PTSD than others, i.e., are vulnerable or resilient (e.g., Bonanno et al., 2012; Maccallum et al., 2015; for review, see Galatzer-Levy et al., 2018; Kalisch et al., 2019; for critique of high rates of resilience, see Infurna & Luthar, 2018).

The gold standard criteria for studies of vulnerability and resilience include a prospective design in which a large sample is assessed at baseline (T1) on the outcome measure (e.g., depression levels), as well as on a number of sociodemographic, psychosocial, or other factors that are thought to confer vulnerability or resilience, and is then exposed to a stressor at T2. The key term to estimate is the moderation effect of the putative vulnerability or resilience factors on the relationship between stressor levels and outcome. Kalisch et al. (2017) identified only 13 such resilience studies that met these criteria (albeit in a non-systematic review), many of which investigated the extent to which various factors moderated the effect of war zone deployment on subsequent PTSD in soldiers. Effect sizes were generally small, with several null results.

Two factors that have been consistently associated with higher vulnerability to MD in response to adversity are neuroticism and female sex (see Figure 59.6). We address the evolutionary significance of neuroticism and the sex difference later.

Toward a Comprehensive Evolutionary Model of Depression

Adaptations are traits that evolved because they had positive effects on the fitness of an organism's ancestors. To identify psychological adaptations, evolutionary theorists consider the following: (1) evidence of a long-standing computational problem in past environments; (2) evidence that solving this computational problem would have increased the biological fitness of ancestors with the trait relative to those without it; (3) evidence that humans maintain the computational ability to solve this problem; and (4) evidence that the computational ability reliably develops in nearly all humans of one or both sexes during one or more stages of development, absent any disruptive environmental mismatches (Tooby & Cosmides, 1990; Williams, 1966).

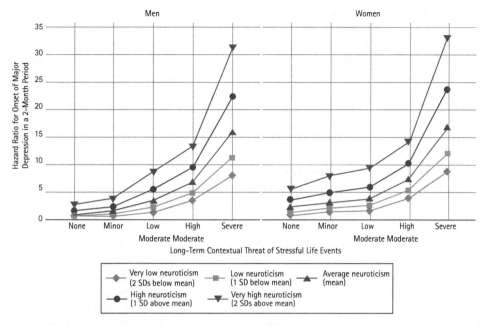

Figure 59.6. Hazard ratios indicating risk of onset of major depression for a population-based sample ($n = 7,517$) classified by sex, neuroticism, and stressful life events. Figure and caption from Kendler et al. (2004).

Evolutionary models of MD take as their starting point that MD is caused by adversity, proposing that it is either (1) mostly a functional response to adversity continuous with sadness and low mood (with only a minority of cases representing genuine dysfunction), or (2) dysregulated sadness and low mood (for reviews, see Allen & Badcock, 2006; Del Giudice 2018; Durisko et al., 2015; Hagen, 2011; Nesse, 2000, 2019; Nettle, 2004). Thus, the correct evolutionary account of MD requires understanding the evolved functions of sadness and low mood, to wit, if and how the latter increased fitness in the wake of adversity. (For simplicity, we will use the term "negative affect" to refer to the entire range of low mood, sadness, grief, and depressive symptoms, but excluding other negative emotions such as anger, anxiety, and jealousy. We will use the term "depression" to refer to a range of sub- and supra-threshold depression symptoms. We will reserve the term MD for major depression as defined in DSM-5).

Before continuing, it is critical to reiterate that nothing in DSM-5 (and almost nothing in DSM-III and DSM-IV) predicates a diagnosis of MD on the experience or lack of experience of adversity (the exception is the bereavement exclusion in DSM-III and DSM-IV). Many studies of MD therefore do not measure adversity. Consequently, it is difficult to relate many facts about MD to the nature of the adverse circumstances that cause it. This makes it difficult to evaluate evolutionary models of depression, most of which incorporate adversity. One evolutionary model, for instance, defines depression as inactivity even when environmental conditions are good (Trimmer et al., 2015). But it is unknown how many, if any, individuals with MD fit that description.

The evolutionary significance of adversity is that it reduced fitness, and any psychological adaptations to adversity would function to mitigate these costs and avoid future costs from similar adverse events. There are many hypotheses for the fitness benefits that negative affect provides to victims of adversity, including energy conservation (Anders et al., 2013; Kinney & Tanaka, 2009; Raison et al., 2006; Raison & Miller, 2013, 2017), submission (Gilbert &

Allan, 1998; Price et al., 1994), risk reduction (Allen & Badcock, 2003, 2006; Badcock et al., 2017), and goal disengagement (Nesse, 2000, 2006).

Hypothesized functions of depression can be divided into two major categories. Some focus on the emotional and cognitive features, such as sadness and rumination, without specifying particular types of adversity or behavioral response to adversity. Others attempt to link specific behavioral features of depression, such as reduced activity, to specific types of adversity, such as loss of resources. Although there is considerable overlap between the two categories, the most general and promising approach to the evolution of depression belongs to the first category.

The Psychological Pain Hypothesis

Alexander (1986) argued that "mental pain" serves a function similar to physical pain, i.e., it evolved to help solve the problem that caused the pain. Building on this suggestion, Thornhill and Thornhill (1989, p. 78) developed their *psychological pain* hypothesis:

> Our hypothesis is that humans will have evolved to experience mental distress in direct relation to the actual or potential occurrence of circumstances, especially social, that historically would have reduced inclusive [citations omitted]. This hypothesis views the evolutionary function of mental pain as analogous to the evolutionary function of physical pain. Physical pain serves to draw an individual's attention to some aspect of anatomy that needs tending and can be fixed by the individual's attention. Mental pain seems to focus an individual's attention on the significant social events causing the pain and the evaluation of future courses of action.

Psychological pain, like physical pain, signals fitness threats, and functions by way of being aversive (Thornhill & Thornhill, 1989; Tooby & Cosmides, 1990).

The psychological pain hypothesis is not specific to MD, nor does it address the claim that MD is an adaptation. Instead, it is a general model that applies to a wide spectrum of low mood and negative affect. As we reviewed above, however, MD is caused by adversity, is characterized by psychological pain, and the most common and most depressogenic forms of adversity were probably experienced by most individuals for most of human evolutionary history, and plausibly inflicted inclusive fitness costs. These include assault, loss of one's mate, loss of resources, serious illness or injury, and death of a loved one (see Figure 59.5). It would be remarkable if humans had not evolved psychological mechanisms to mitigate the negative fitness consequences of adversity.

Given that most cases of MD are not pathological, and that symptoms occur on a continuum, the psychological pain hypothesis is a compelling account of depression, including MD. The psychological pain hypothesis does not single out specific types of adversity, nor does it specify a particular behavioral response to adversity, because different types of adversity and different individual circumstances will require different behaviors to mitigate costs.

There are few direct tests of the psychological pain hypothesis. Thornhill and Furlow (1998) and Hagen (1999) independently evaluated postpartum depression (PPD) as a case study, finding that PPD was strongly associated with circumstances that would have inflicted fitness costs on ancestral mothers of newborns, including low paternal and social support, lack of resources, and poor infant and maternal health, and in some circumstances motivated disinvestment in the newborn (see also Hagen, 2002; Hagen & Barrett, 2007; Hagen & Thornhill, 2017). Thornhill and Thornhill also evaluated the hypothesis in the case of rape victims (Thornhill & Thornhill, 1990a, 1990b, 1990c, 1991).

Divorce is a good test case for adaptive theories of depression because loss of a mate could have a profound impact on biological fitness. Rosenström et al. (2017) developed mathematical models of four competing causal, mechanistic theories of the relationship between divorce and depression: an adaptationist model similar to the psychological pain hypothesis (in which the risk of divorce triggers depression, which yields benefits by decreasing the risk of divorce, but increases the risk of death, e.g., from suicide), and three stress-diathesis models (e.g., a stress-relief model in which the period before divorce is depressogenic and the period afterward is not). These models were used to generate four quantitative predicted temporal distributions of depressive symptoms relative to divorce. Rosenström et al. then tested this model using national registry data on 304,111 Finns that examined the association of divorce with antidepressant use as a proxy for depression (Metsä-Simola & Martikainen, 2013). Their study afforded an unprecedented temporal resolution of one depression prevalence estimate every three months for 10 years with no bias from attrition or repeated interactions with researchers. Rosenström et al. quantitatively assessed how well each predicted distribution of depression relative to divorce fit the empirical distribution, finding that the adaptationist model best fit the data.

Analytical Rumination Hypothesis
One of the most important extensions of the psychological pain hypothesis, the analytical rumination hypothesis (ARH), was developed by Paul Andrews and colleagues. Depressed individuals commonly ruminate about the problems that triggered their depression, which they perceive to be complex, severe, and difficult to solve. Their rumination is intrusive, persistent, resistant to distraction, and difficult to suppress, yet, as the psychological pain hypothesis predicts, depressed people believe it gives them insight into their problems (Andrews & Thomson, 2009).

Because depressive rumination decreases performance on other cognitive tasks, mainstream researchers have interpreted it as a cognitive dysfunction (e.g., Nolen-Hoeksema, 1991). Andrews and Thomson (2009) instead argue that there is a necessary trade-off: because cognitive resources are limited, individuals experiencing challenging problems should concentrate on solving them, rather than allocating attention to solving unrelated problems in laboratory experiments. The more complex and intractable the problem, the more intense the rumination should be.

There is a small but growing literature testing the ARH (Barbic et al., 2014; Bartoskova et al., 2018; Maslej et al., 2019). A recent study by Sevcikiova et al. (2020) that included depressed inpatients and community controls found that depressed patients reported a greater number of problems of greater complexity relative to controls, and engaged in more causal analysis but not in more problem-solving analysis. Depressed inpatients who engaged in more problem-solving analyses relative to other depressed inpatients at the start of hospitalization showed a decrease in symptoms at the end of hospitalization; however, there was no relationship with the likelihood of remission or a decrease in symptoms at follow-up.

There is a critique of the ARH from within evolutionary medicine and psychiatry that cites evidence that interventions to suppress rumination produce positive outcomes for patients (Kennair et al., 2017). Another limitation of the current formulation is that rumination is only moderately associated with depression, and is also moderately associated with anxiety (Olatunji et al., 2013). Rumination, worry, and repetitive negative thinking are similar experiences that follow "emotionally evocative" experiences (McEvoy et al., 2013). Thus, the ARH might not be specific to depression but instead might apply to a broad range of difficult situations that could inflict costs or yield benefits, and therefore it is probably associated with a range of negative and positive emotions (e.g., Li et al., 2017).

The Association of Depression and Suicidality with Strife and Anger

The psychological pain and analytical rumination hypotheses do not account for all the important symptoms of depression, such as suicidality and profound loss of interest in virtually all activities. In the remainder of this chapter we argue that these mysterious symptoms are best explained as strategic responses to adversity *under strife*.

Much adversity does not involve social conflict. The death of a young child from an infectious disease is a tragedy that requires painful rumination to promote understanding that can help prevent the deaths of other children, but it does not necessarily involve conflict. Although Thornhill and Thornhill (1989), in their development of the psychological pain hypothesis, emphasize the negative fitness consequences of adversities that involve conflict, such as loss of status and sexual assault, and Andrews and Thomson's (2009) ARH similarly notes that solving social dilemmas often requires considerable reflection, psychological pain and rumination function to mitigate adversity regardless of conflict, and thus are expected to operate in a broad range of conflictual and non-conflictual conditions.

It is an empirically well-supported but poorly recognized fact, however, that MD is closely associated with social conflict and anger (Cassiello-Robbins & Barlow, 2016). Many of the most potent risk factors for MD, such as physical and sexual assault, serious marital problems, legal problems, robbery, and job loss, are prima facie instances of social conflict (see Table 59.1). Many studies of MD confirm that sufferers are often embroiled in interpersonal conflict. In a study of a large nationally representative US sample (n = 4,688), Bertera (2005) found strong and consistent support for the association of social negativity, as measured by items such as "How frequently do you argue with friends (spouse or relatives)?" and "How often do friends (spouse or relatives) make you feel tense," with the number of mood disorders. Whisman and Uebelacker (2009), in a two-year prospective study of an English population-based sample (n = 1,869 couples), found that baseline marital discord predicted subsequent depression, and that baseline depression predicted subsequent marital discord, i.e., there is a bidirectional relationship between conflict and depression. Among the Tsimane, Amazonian horticulturalists, depression was significantly associated with social conflicts, especially with non-kin (Stieglitz et al., 2015). A meta-analysis of 165 studies of the relationship between bullying in children and adolescents and mental health outcomes that included samples from high-, middle-, and low-income countries indicated a causal relationship between bullying victimization and anxiety, depression, poor general and mental health, non-suicidal self-injury, suicide attempts, and suicide ideation (Moore et al., 2017, p. 72). In a probability sample from 11 European countries (n = 4,779 couples), marital conflict was associated with both self-reported and partner-reported depressive symptoms in both sexes (albeit with a weaker association for women in Northern Europe compared to women elsewhere) (Salinger et al., 2020). A longitudinal study of a representative sample of German couples (n = 1,273 couples), comprising three age cohorts, found that for both sexes, financial conflict and depressive symptoms were related initially and over time, that depression in one partner predicted future perceptions of conflict in the other partner, and that men's perception of financial conflict was associated with increasing depression in their partners over time (Morgan & Lim, 2020).

Fatal and non-fatal suicidal behavior also commonly occurs in the wake of social conflict, particularly with family members or spouses. Firth (1961) characterized acts of suicidal behavior among the Tikopia as a form of protest. In many Muslim-majority countries, suicidal behavior among women is regarded as recourse against oppressive kin or restrictive social structures (Billaud, 2012; Canetto, 2015), and the anthropological literature abounds with comparable models of suicide as a form of protest, revenge, and/or appeal (e.g., Malinowski, 1926; Niehaus, 2012). Among the Toraja, Hollan (1990, p. 371) reported that suicide is rooted in "intense feelings of injustice and mistreatment" when, for instance, adolescents "feel their own legitimate needs and desires have been neglected by their parents and relatives." Staples and Widger (2012) highlighted protest as a central theme of the ethnographic literature on suicide. Syme, Garfield, and Hagen (2016) and Syme and Hagen (2019), in studies of suicide across 53 traditional cultures, found that conflict was a central theme.

Death of a loved one, one of the most common causes of MD and suicidality, does not at first glance seem to involve social conflict. There are solid theoretical reasons, however, backed by accumulating empirical evidence, to believe that loss of an important social partner often does cause conflict with others and probably did so over human evolution. Social partners provide critical benefits, such as food, protection, information, and assistance with childrearing and other tasks. Individuals who lose these benefits due to the death of a social partner must acquire them from other social partners. Ethnographic research on grief among children and adolescent farmers and foragers in the Congo Basin, for example, shows that the death of a parent or other close family member is tied to the loss of vital resources (e.g., food, clothes), and life can be challenging for bereaved youths. Hewlett (2017) reported that living kin members would console them by offering clothes, money, and other resources, which relieved some of their painful sadness and made it possible for them to grow up and have children of their own. Social network research has found that deaths of family members and confidants can result in profound changes in social networks (Cornwell & Laumann, 2018; Wrzus et al., 2013). But social partners, who have other relationships, cannot always easily compensate for one individual's loss of benefits. A study of 156 Australian families that had suffered the death of a parent found that about one-third of families were characterized by conflict six weeks after the death, one-quarter at six months, and 15% at 13 months (Kissane et al., 1996). A systematic review found that, after a loss, family conflict was a major risk factor for complicated grief (Delalibera et al., 2015).

The association between inflammation and depression (Maes, 1999; Stieglitz et al., 2015) also supports the role of social conflict in depression. Although researchers have proposed that depressive symptoms might, e.g., conserve energy for the immune system or reduce appetite to avoid exposure to pathogens (Anders et al., 2013; Kinney & Tanaka, 2009; Raison & Miller, 2013, 2017; Raison et al., 2006), there is considerable evidence that social threats activate the immune system (Slavich & Irwin, 2014). Social conflict, no doubt, frequently led to physical harm throughout human evolutionary history, as it does today. For instance, one study reported that 85% of Tsimane endured physical abuse from their spouses (Stieglitz et al., 2011), and another in the same population found associations between depression and immune biomarkers (Stielglitz et al., 2015). Further, assault is a potent risk factor for depression (Kendler et al., 1999). It is likely that increased immune activation in the depressed is a consequence of either their elevated risk of suffering physical attack due to severe conflicts, or prior or ongoing physical abuse.

There is an equally clear association of depression with anger. Riley et al. (1989) found that depressed subjects experienced moderately abnormal levels of anger and tended to suppress instead of express their anger. A study of patients with MD ($n = 73$), anxiety disorders ($n = 67$), somatoform disorders ($n = 47$), and healthy controls ($n = 215$) found that patients with MD were more likely to have higher anger, hostility, and aggression than the other groups (Koh et al. 2002). Gilbert et al. (2004) conducted interviews with 50 depressed inpatients and outpatients and found that 82% reported suppressing anger (the researchers did not ask about expressed anger) and 88% reported feelings of entrapment. Nearly all reported reasons for suppressing anger involved avoiding losing social standing or harming important relationships. Similarly, participants commonly reported feeling trapped for social reasons, e.g., losing a relationship that would be hard to replace. A study of a nationally representative sample of Australians (n = 8,841) found that, controlling for demographics and comorbidity, several mood, anxiety, and substance use disorders were independently associated with symptoms of anger (E. L. Barrett et al., 2013) Among US patients with MD at intake (n = 536), overt expression of irritability/anger was associated with greater severity and longer duration of the MD episode (Judd et al., 2013). Bodner et al. (2018), in a laboratory study of interactions between parents and their adolescent children (the latter either depressed or nondepressed), found that families of depressed adolescents expressed more anger than families of nondepressed adolescents during the interaction, and expressions of anger co-occurred and interacted more, potentially creating a self-sustaining network of angry negative affect. Ou and Hall (2018), in a systematic review of the literature on postpartum depression and anger, found that anger and depression were often linked, with anger elevated in depressed vs. nondepressed mothers, and that anger was associated with powerlessness. In a large study of psychiatric outpatients (n = 3,800), anger and overt aggression were common, particularly among those diagnosed with MD, intermittent explosive disorder, and cluster B personality disorders (e.g., antisocial, borderline, histrionic) (Genovese et al., 2017). In a 25-year longitudinal study of depression and anger among Canadians (n = 944), Galambos et al. (2018) found a stable relationship between higher anger and higher depression both between individuals, and within individuals over time. In a meta-analysis of 491 studies (n = 235,085) examining the associations of depression, anger, anxiety, and negative affect among employees, Ng et al. (2019) found that these emotions strongly correlated with each other (weighted average correlation = 0.69), and that they were similarly associated with job-related stressors. A study investigating personality traits among suicide attempters and non-attempters among the Idu Mishmi ethnic group in India found that attempters scored significantly higher on aggression and impulsivity than non-attempters (Singh & Rao, 2018). In summary, those who have suffered adversity are often embroiled in conflict and are angry, depressed, and sometimes suicidal.

Some Non-Western Concepts Incorporate Elements of Depression, Conflict, and Anger

DSM criteria for major depression are a good index of the clinical syndrome of depression. But . . . this depressive syndrome is not entirely constituted by the DSM criteria.

—Kendler et al. (2016, p. 780)

There is a direct line of descent from Hippocrates's writings on melancholia, a condition characterized by extreme sadness, to the modern psychiatric model of depression (see Jackson, 1986). It is noteworthy that many languages do not have direct translations of "depression" (Littlewood, 2002). There are, however, many terms in non-Western languages that overlap with depression, and in addition to sadness or anhedonia, these terms often denote conflict and anger. In rural Trinidad, the term *tabanka* refers to a state of lassitude accompanied by feelings of low self-worth, anger, anhedonia, appetite loss, and suicidal behavior. Unlike depression, this state is specific to males who have recently lost a spouse or romantic partner to a competitor (Littlewood, 1985). Among Chon Chuuk Micronesians, the term *amwunumwun* denotes a state of anger and despondency that usually arises when one, often an adolescent or young adult, is rebuffed by an elder kinsmen who is both loved and respected. *Amwunumwun* is associated with behavioral withdrawal, including avoidance, refusal to eat or speak, running away, and suicide (Hezel, 1987). The Hopi word *qövisti* is a state of moodiness and sullenness in young women facing intractable conflicts with parents and other elders and can end in a "willful death" (Titiev, 1944).

Powerlessness

Resolving conflicts in one's favor typically requires some advantage over adversaries. Depression, though, is associated with feeling powerless (Gilbert, 1992; Gilbert et al., 2004; Gilbert & Allan, 1998; Price et al., 1994). The depressed perceive themselves as unable to unilaterally change things for the better. There is robust evidence of an association between depression and defeat (Gilbert & Allan, 1998), hopelessness (Abramson & Metalsky, 1989; Abramson et al., 1978), external locus of control (Rotter, 1966), and entrapment (Brown et al., 1995). A meta-analysis found that external locus-of-control and depression were significantly related, that the relation was moderately strong, and that it was consistent across studies; in addition, a belief that events were controlled by powerful others and by chance was associated with higher levels of depression (Benassi et al., 1988). A meta-analysis of the helplessness models found that attribution of positive events to external causes (i.e., those not under one's control) was associated with depression (Sweeney et al., 1986). A study of 7,322 adult twins found that higher ratings of loss and humiliation predicted onset of MD and mixed MD-generalized anxiety syndrome (MD-GAS), and high ratings of entrapment predicted onset of MD-GAS (Kendler et al., 2003).

Although it could be the case that feelings of powerlessness are illusory, there is substantial variation in physical and social formidability in humans and other animals. One interpretation of the association between depression and powerlessness, which draws on comparative evidence from nonhuman primates and other nonhuman animals, is that depression is an *involuntary subordinate strategy* following aggressive contests between competitors. According to this *social competition hypothesis*, depression is caused by a specific type of adversity—social defeat—and involves specific behavioral responses that signal de-escalation and submission. Specifically, these models focus on the behavioral signs of depression, such as slumped posture, lowered eye gaze, and social withdrawal, noting that these resemble submission strategies exhibited by a diverse range of species (Price et al., 1994; Price et al., 2007).

The social risk hypothesis similarly sees the social withdrawal of depression as a harm-reduction strategy. Using a model analogous to risk-sensitive foraging, Allen and Badcock (2003) proposed that individuals with a robust social network can afford to take risks, whereas individuals with a weak social network risk ostracism and cannot take social risks. A more recent version of the model incorporates the free-energy principle into their model, but the emphasis on reducing social risk remains (Badcock et al., 2017).

There are many types of adversity that cause depression, however, such as death of a loved one or an ill newborn, that are not losses of social competitions. Submission is also not a universally beneficial response to all types of adversity that cause depression, nor even to all types of social competitions, even when engaged with a formidable adversary. Finally, the social competition hypothesis does not make sense of all the symptoms of depression, such as suicidality. Nevertheless, powerlessness appears to be an important characteristic of depressed individuals. As we explain next, the powerless do have the means to change others who are reluctant to change, but sad expressions and crying are not enough—the powerless often have to pay a cost.

Bargaining: Credibly Signaling Need under Conflict

Suicidality, one of the DSM diagnostic criteria for MD, is not well explained by most evolutionary theories of depression, nor is pronounced loss of interest in virtually all activities, one of the defining features of MD. In our view, these perplexing symptoms are best explained by considering the confluence of adversity, conflict, and powerlessness. In these circumstances, individuals are in need, but conflict with social partners and powerlessness prevent their needs from being met. We argue that depression, like other emotions, involves characteristic signals, specifically *credible* signals of need.

Signals are necessary if the signaler's state is unknown to receivers, i.e., if the signaler's state is *private information*. Signals thus function to reveal private information to receivers.

Signaling between organisms is ubiquitous across the tree of life: bacteria coordinate via molecular quorum sensing signals (Jayaraman & Wood, 2008); plants signal pollinators and the natural enemies of insect herbivores, and possibly communicate with each other (Karban, 2015; Woźniak & Sicard, 2018); and animals send and receive signals from offspring, mates, and competitors (Godfray, 1991; Skyrms, 2010). In humans, characteristic facial expressions signal emotions such as anger and sadness, albeit with some variation across cultures (Darwin, 1916; Ekman & Cordaro, 2011; cf. Barrett et al., 2019). In a study of 6 million online videos, for example, Cowen et al. (2020) found that 16 types of facial expressions, including anger, pain, and sadness, systematically covaried with specific social contexts across 144 countries. A study across 12 countries that highlighted variation in the facial recognition of seven emotion categories, such as sadness and anger, nevertheless found that most participants accurately classified facial expressions into emotion categories (the primary exception was that fear was often misclassified as surprise; Quesque et al., 2022).

Tears and crying by infants, children, and adults have long been interpreted as signals of need (Balsters et al., 2013; Lummaa et al., 1998; Trivers, 1974). An eye-tracking study found that tears were a magnet for visual attention, and a single tear running down a cheek was associated with increased emotional inference and greater perception of sincerity (Picó et al., 2020). It has been proposed that infected individuals experience the emotion of lassitude, which generates protective sickness behavior, including signals of need (Schrock et al., 2020; see also Steinkopf, 2015; Tiokhin, 2016).[2]

Deceptive signaling is also rife in nature (Mokkonen & Lindstedt, 2016). When there are conflicts of interest between signalers and receivers, signalers can benefit by sending deceptive signals that exploit receivers. Mimicry and crypsis are widespread across taxonomic groups (Starrett, 1993). Morphological and behavioral mimicry of ants has evolved independently at least 70 times, for example, and is known in 2,000 species belonging to 200 genera in 54 families (McIver & Stonedahl, 1993).

Highly cooperative species are vulnerable to social parasites who mimic cooperative signals to receive benefits. To defend against social parasites, ants have evolved a sophisticated chemical recognition system enabling them to behave altruistically toward nestmates and to reject non-nestmates (Lenoir et al., 2001). Despite their recognition system, ant species are parasitized by a number of arthropods, including butterflies, beetles, and even other ants. In fact, of the 10,000 or so known ant species, more than 200, or about 2%, parasitize other, often closely related, species, and in the unusually well-characterized ant fauna of Switzerland, about 1/3 of the species are parasitic (Buschinger, 1986). Social parasites are known in a wide variety of other invertebrate and vertebrate species. In vertebrates, well-studied examples include avian brood parasites, such as cuckoos and cowbirds, that lay eggs in the nests of other species to avoid the costs of brood care (Rothstein & Robinson, 1998). Deception is also widespread in primates (Bryne & Corp 2004).

Humans who have recently suffered adversity and are in need, but who also have conflicts with important social partners, face the formidable challenge of convincing them their need is genuine. A wife whose husband has died, for instance, might need assistance with childcare from her sister, or she might instead have enough money to hire help—her true level of need is private information. Because assistance from her sister would be beneficial, she has an incentive to send a signal of need whether or not she is genuinely needy. Providing regular childcare is time consuming, so the sister would only want to provide it if the need is genuine. If the sisters had a history of conflict, one might be skeptical of the other's level of need.

Theorists have devoted considerable attention to mechanisms that can ensure signal credibility despite conflicts of interest. "Costly" signals are one well-studied mechanism to ensure the credible signaling of private information (Grafen, 1990; Spence, 1973; Zahavi, 1975). In brief, if the benefits of sending a signal necessarily outweigh the costs for signalers in (private) state A but not signalers in state B (e.g., because the benefits are the same for both but the costs are necessarily lower for signalers in state A), then agents can evolve to send the signal when in state A but not when in state B, and receivers can evolve to infer that the signaler is in state A, and respond to the signal in a way that benefits them both.

Hagen and colleagues have proposed that depression (Hagen, 1999, 2002, 2003, 2011; Hagen & Barrett, 2007; Watson & Andrews, 2002), self-harm (Hagen et al., 2008), and suicidality (Andrews, 2006; Nock et al., 2008; Rosenthal, 1993; Syme et al., 2016; Syme & Hagen, 2019) are costly signals that can credibly reveal the true level of need when conflicts with social partners render cheap signals (such as verbal requests, sad faces, or crying) unreliable. The basic logic is that for individuals whose fitness prospects are poor due to, e.g., loss of a mate, important social partner, or job, a dramatic reduction in productivity or putting one's life at risk, as seen in MD, is relatively low cost, whereas for individuals whose fitness prospects are good, these behaviors are quite costly. Thus, only individuals with poor fitness prospects can afford to send the signal, and skeptical social partners will only help those who send the signal.

A further consideration is that humans evolved in small, highly interdependent groups that included close kin, affines, and non-kin, and individuals had both shared and competing interests (e.g., Hagen 2003; Hill et al., 2011; Tomasello et al., 2012). Group members cooperated to raise their children and to provide food and protection. Individuals who reduced their productivity, or put their own lives at risk, imposed costs on the rest of the group (Hagen 1999, 2002, 2003). Theoretical models of bargaining show that if need is public information, such as clear indicators of physical injury, then interdependent social partners should immediately provide care (Rubinstein, 1982). If need is private information, however, and there are conflicts of interest that incentivize exaggerating need, costly signals are required to reveal the genuine level of need before social partners will help. Labor strikes provide an analogy: workers who forgo their salaries during a labor strike are honestly signaling that their salary is too low. For workers making good salaries, a strike is too costly. But for workers whose salaries are genuinely insufficient, a strike has low costs because forgoing a poor salary has little cost. At the same time, the strike imposes costs on employers, who therefore have an incentive to increase wages (Kennan & Wilson, 1993). Similarly, depression and suicidality, by putting one's ability to provide benefits to others at risk, incentivize interdependent social partners to provide support that they might not otherwise provide. See Hagen (2003) for a thorough discussion of the bargaining model of depression.

The bargaining model is not a comprehensive model of MD or depressive states. Our comprehensive model of depressive states combines the psychological pain hypothesis with credible signals of need (bargaining). Most individuals experiencing adversity would experience a degree of psychological pain, but not all of them would need to send credible signals of need to social partners. Credible signals of need are only required when (1) individuals need help from social partners, but (2) have severe conflicts of interest with social partners that prevent cheap signals, such as verbal requests, sad expressions, or crying, from being believed or eliciting the necessary help.

Suicidality as a Credible Signal of Need

Killing oneself is unlikely to be an adaptive strategy, especially for young and healthy individuals. Most suicidal thoughts and behaviors, though, do not result in death. In 2013, the US adolescent suicide rate was about 8 per 100,000 (0.008%) per year, yet about 1,500 times as many adolescents (12%) reported suicidal ideation (Nock et al., 2013). In low- and middle-income countries, as many as 17% of adolescents report suicidal ideation in a 12-month period (Uddin et al., 2019). In the United States, the ratios of suicide attempts to suicide deaths are approximately 100:1 and 10:1 among young adult women and men, respectively (Syme et al., 2016). This high survival rate is likely not entirely a product of advances in life-saving technologies. Among the Bimin-Kuskusmin of Papua New Guinea, where as many as 10% of deaths over six generations were due to suicide, Poole (1985) reported that females attempted suicide twice as often as they died by suicide. In one Pacific island community, a local clergyman estimated that as many as 30%–50% of the adult male population had attempted suicide (Rubinstein, 1995), whereas the rate of suicide deaths was about 40 per 100,000 per year (Hezel, 1989).

If suicidal behavior is a credible signal, it must only arise when less costly signals such as verbal communication are ineffective. Specifically, (1) the victim faces a fitness threat (adversity) prior to suicidal behavior; (2) there is a conflict of interest between the victim and invested social partners such that the social partners are not otherwise willing to provide support based on less costly signals alone (e.g., verbal communication, sad expressions, crying); (3) the victim is otherwise powerless to single-handedly mitigate the fitness threat; (4) the suicidal behavior involves a low but non-zero risk of death; (5) social partners interpret suicidality as the victim being truly in need; and (6) the social partners assist the victim in mitigating the fitness threat.

In our research investigating suicidal behavior in 53 cultures using the Human Relations Area Files (Syme et al., 2016; Syme & Hagen, 2019), we found substantial cross-cultural support for each of the foregoing predictions: those who turned to suicidal behavior had suffered adversity such as abuse, forced and thwarted marriages, and status loss; were relatively powerless individuals caught in intractable conflicts with more powerful others or groups; and who, if they survived, received important benefits, including social pressure against an abuser, avoidance of an unwanted marriage, or forgiveness for violating a taboo. The non-zero risk of death is an honest signal of the low value that victims place on their current circumstances. From this perspective, suicidal behavior is a last resort of the truly powerless.

Loss of Interest in Virtually All Activities as a Credible Signal of Need

If depression has an essence, it is loss of interest in virtually everything. To diagnose MD according to DSM criteria, one symptom must be either loss of interest in virtually all activities, or depressed mood. "Virtually all activities" could include one's job, relationships with friends, spouses, and children, as well as the basics of living, such as eating, grooming, bathing, and sex. In concert with other symptoms of depression, like fatigue, loss of energy, hypersomnia, and psychomotor retardation, loss of interest should have a substantial impact on one's ability to be productive and to contribute to cooperative ventures.

One way to assess the effects of these symptoms is to estimate the impact of depression on economic productivity. Using a variety of methods, several studies have found that depression has a significant, negative impact on unemployment, absenteeism (missed days of work), and presenteeism (reduced productivity at work, usually measured in missed day equivalents). In a large, cross-cultural study, for instance, Ormel et al. (1999) found that depression was associated with a twofold increase in days of disability. Stewart et al. (2003) found that, compared to the mean 1.5 hours per week of lost productive time among the general population of

US workers, depressed workers reported 5.6 hours per week of lost productive time, 81% of which was due to reduced productivity at work. In a nationally representative sample of US adults, Kessler et al. (2006) found that depression accounted for 8.7 days of absenteeism and 18.2 days of presenteeism per year, for a total of 27.2 days of lost productivity per depressed worker per year. Beck et al. (2011) found that, among 771 depressed individuals, each 1-point increase in depression scores was associated with a 1.65% loss of productivity, from approximately a total 30% loss of productivity at the lower range of depression scores to about a 50% loss at the upper range. Khansa et al. (2020), in a random proportionate sample of Lebanese workers, found a strong positive association between depression scores and impairment in work and activity. In a global systematic review and meta-analysis of studies of the monetary cost of depression, König et al. (2020) found that the mean cost of reduced or lost productivity was 128% higher in the depressed compared to nondepressed group (the later included both healthy controls and individuals with, e.g., physical disorders).

A recent review of these and similar studies concluded that presenteeism rather than absenteeism accounted for more lost productivity, with more severe depression symptoms increasing the loss. The predominance of preseentism's negative impact on productivity shows that depression is costly not only to the sufferer, but also to coworkers and employers. In the United States, the estimated value of this lost productivity exceeds $84 billion/year (Evans-Lacko & Knapp, 2016). Evidence indicates that risk factors for workplace depression include job strain, low decision latitude, and bullying (Theorell et al., 2015). These results are consistent with the hypothesis that, under adverse conditions, depression serves as a bargaining strategy by imposing costs on the signaler as well his or her social partners to compel them to make concessions.

Because depression hurts companies and not just individuals, much of the research on depression and work productivity has aimed to make a "business case" for depression treatment, arguing that the benefit of increased worker productivity would outweigh employers' cost of treatment (Donohue & Pincus, 2007). If depression is a genuine disease, this makes sense: treating it is in everyone's interest. If depression is not a disease, however, then treatment raises an important ethical issue. What if an employee were depressed because she was exploited by her employer, as the evidence suggests? In this case, chemically treating the employee's depression symptoms without improving her work environment would simply allow her employer to more effectively exploit her.

Sex Differences in Depression and Bargaining
Females are at higher risk of depression than males (Kuehner, 2017). Hagen (2003) proposed that physical aggression and depression were complementary strategies to resolve conflicts. Physical formidability, in the form of upper body strength, provides an advantage in conflict, as does having social allies (Sell et al., 2012). Upper body strength is positively associated with propensity to anger, a history of physical fighting, and feelings of entitled access to resources (Hess et al., 2010; Sell et al., 2009; Sell et al., 2012). Men in many cultures use violence against their wives in service of their own fitness interests (Stieglitz et al., 2011; Stieglitz et al., 2012).

Hagen and Rosenström (2016) hypothesized that the dramatic sex difference in physical formidability helps explain the dramatic sex difference in depression. Specifically, the physically formidable (often men) are able to resolve conflicts in their favor with physical threats, whereas the unformidable (often women) must more often resolve conflicts with depressive signaling that imposes costs on others by imposing costs on oneself. They found that in a nationally representative US sample of adults, grip strength (an index of formidability) was negatively associated with depression and that sex differences in grip strength explained a substantial fraction of the sex difference in depression, a result that was replicated by Smith et al. (2022). Kerry and Murray (2018) similarly found that, in a sample of US undergraduates, grip strength was negatively correlated with neuroticism, an important risk factor for depression, and that the sex difference in grip strength accounted for the sex difference in neuroticism.

Social Partners Interpret Depression as an Aversive Signal of Need
Several evolutionary researchers have questioned the bargaining model of depression because depressive behaviors are aversive to social partners (Allen & Badcock, 2003; Nesse, 2019, 2000; Nettle, 2004; Myers et al., 2016). These researchers have failed to appreciate the central role of conflict in the bargaining model. Anger, an adaptive emotion, is also aversive to social targets because it threatens to impose costs on them, and that is precisely its evolved function (Sell et al., 2009). Under the bargaining model, depression and suicidality, like anger, function in part to impose costs on interdependent social partners so as to resolve conflicts in the signaler's interest; aversiveness is an evolved feature.

Stereotypical behaviors in depression and suicidality are stereotypical because they are signals that must be correctly interpreted by social partners. After confirming Coyne's (1976a, 1976b) finding that depression alienates others, including strangers in brief interactions (for a meta-analysis, see Segrin & Dillard, 1992), researchers began to explore what it is that depressed people do or fail to do that leads to others' hostility and rejection. A large literature has since accumulated documenting differences in interpersonal interactions by depressed and nondepressed individuals. Findings include differences in communication "style," such as vocal characteristics, eye gaze, and gestures, and differences in "content," such as preferred topics and themes of conversation (Segrin & Abramson, 1994;Segrin, 2000).

With regard to style (e.g., paralinguistic qualities like low rate, low volume, and low monotone pitch), depressed people appear to be "very 'skilled' at communicating sadness and despair" (Segrin, 2000, p. 385). With regard to content, depressed individuals are eager to self-disclose personally relevant negative issues, often at what are judged to be inappropriate times, and they view such topics as more appropriate for discussion than do the nondepressed (Segrin, 2000). Such self-disclosures have been shown to be a key ingredient in the rejection of depressed persons by others, and "may appropriately be understood as an attempt to elicit social support from targets" (Segrin & Abramson, 1994, p. 657). In interactions with spouses, depressed individuals express anger and aggression, and make frequent demands for help. Segrin & Abramson (1994) speculate that

> [t]he discussion of negative well-being, dysphoric feelings, and frequent demands for help may impose on other people, making them feel either responsible or obligated to offer assistance or find out the cause of the depression. This feeling of obligation or responsibility could potentially prove to be aversive and motivate withdrawal and rejection of the depressed person. (p. 660)

Excessive reassurance seeking (ERS) is another well-studied factor implicated in depression and rejection by others. ERS is defined as repeatedly requesting reassurance that one is lovable and worthy despite previous attempts by others to provide such reassurance. According to Joiner et al. (1999):

> The key idea is that the aversive properties of depression are not interpersonally aversive unless clearly and repeatedly signaled to other people and, further, signaled in such a way that others are both implicated in the development of the problem (e.g., "you don't really love me anymore, do you?"), as well as overwhelmed by demands, whether implicit or stated, to solve the problem. (p. 272)

Our view is that excessive reassurance-seeking predisposes people to the development of depressive symptoms. Initially, this may occur as a function of growing demoralization of the high reassurance-seeking person, who has struggled to gain—but has been disappointed with—others' responsiveness. (p. 273)

A meta-analysis of 38 studies found ERS to be moderately associated with depression ($r = .32$) and weakly but significantly associated with rejection ($r = .14$), although the relationship with rejection could be stronger when the seeker is depressed (Starr & Davila, 2008).

Because depression alienates others, however, differences in the style and content of interpersonal interactions of the depressed vs. nondepressed, rather than being seen as an aversive signal of need, are interpreted as *deficits*, such as social skill deficits or "excessive" reassurance-seeking (Segrin & Abramson, 1994; Joiner et al., 1999). Yet infant cries, clear signals of need, motivate caregiving, in part by being so aversive that caregivers work to terminate the cries. The noxiousness of these cries can also evoke abuse or avoidance by caregivers (Owings & Zeifman, 2004).

Normal sadness can also alienate others. Young children, for instance, find sad people to be rather unlikable (Glasberg & Aboud, 1981, 1982), and report controlling their own sadness, especially around peers, because they fear negative interpersonal consequences (Zeman & Garber, 1996). Adults commonly regulate their emotions, too, including sadness, in part because there are negative social consequences to emotional expression, in addition to positive ones (for reviews, see Gross, 1998, 2002; Ochsner & Gross, 2005).

Why would others respond negatively to signals of need? From an evolutionary perspective, the real question is: Why would others respond *positively* to signals of need? As Machiavelli recognized 500 years ago, self-interested agents frequently turn against those in need because helping them means paying a cost with no guarantee of a compensating benefit. Needless to say, people do help the needy, at least some of the time, and have done so over the course of human evolutionary history (otherwise signals of need, like infant cries and universal facial expressions of sadness and grief, would probably not have evolved), but social partners will only provide help when it is in their fitness interests to do so. If there are few conflicts among social partners, and relationships are valuable, then each will see it in their benefit to provide help to a child, spouse, relative, friend, or coworker when he or she is in need. In this case, cries, sadness, grief, and simple verbal requests should work well to signal need. But like aggression, signals of need do not always end in an outcome in the signaler's favor.

A reasonable summary of results to date is that depressed people have a distinctive style of communication that is easily recognized by others and is effective at expressing sadness and despair (but not other emotions), and that the style and content of their conversations and interactions signal, correctly in our view, that they have problems and needs and want to talk about them and gain reassurance and support.

Evidence That Depression Elicits Benefits

If depression functions to signal need and to bargain for more care from social partners, then it should elicit increased help and other benefits from them, at least some of the time. Because depression is almost universally regarded as an illness, very few studies have explored possible benefits of depression. Nevertheless, several studies have shown that they exist.

The literature on depression and family dynamics shows that depression elicits benefits from others, so much so that many researchers worry that these benefits "reinforce" the depression. An advantage of several of these studies, compared to most interpersonal studies of depression, is that they observe depressed individuals interacting with social partners in real time, sometimes in their own homes, coding the temporal sequence of depressive behaviors, such as complaints, downcast eyes, and crying; aggressive behaviors, such as threats and angry gestures; facilitative behaviors, such as approval, smiles, and a warm voice; and so forth.

Biglan et al. (1985), for instance, asked couples to discuss two important marital problems for 10 minutes each. For couples in which the wife was depressed, a good deal of the discussion focused on her and her complaints, with the husband proposing most of the solutions, whereas in couples without depression, husbands and wives proposed about the same number of solutions. For those couples experiencing marital distress, the wife's depressive behavior reduced her husband's subsequent aggressive behavior. His facilitative behavior, in turn, reduced his wife's subsequent depressive behavior (as did his aggressive behavior). Hops et al. (1987), in one-hour observations of this same sample in their homes, confirmed that mothers' dysphoric behavior reduced subsequent aggressive behavior by fathers and children. Caring behavior on the part of children and fathers, in turn, reduced mothers' dysphoric behavior. Responses by third parties to both written and video depictions of dysphoric and distressed behavior provide further evidence that although these induce negative feelings in others, such behaviors also prompt others to be solicitous and to refrain from aggression (Biglan et al., 1989).

These results have been extended to depression in children and adolescents. Behavioral observations of depressed juveniles interacting with their parents found that depression elicited sympathetic, facilitative, and problem-solving behaviors from parents and suppressed parental aggression, which in some cases depended on the sex of the parent (Dadds et al., 1992; Sheeber et al., 1997).

To experimentally control the depressive behaviors thought to be responsible for interpersonal effects, Stephens et al. (1987) trained confederates to enact depressive, anxious, and normal roles. A sample of female college students then interacted with one of the confederates in a 15-minute conversation before completing questionnaires about the experience. As expected, subjects viewed the "depressed" confederates more negatively than they did the "anxious" or "normal" subjects. Despite their aversive impact, depressed confederates elicited more verbal support and advice and less negative feedback than the other confederates. Subjects appeared to feel obligated to help the depressed and to withhold negative reactions.

In another study of college students, Hokanson et al. (1986) compared roommate relationships in which one roommate was dysphoric to relationships with two nondepressed roommates. They found that dysphoric students initiated the roommate relationship with relatively dependent behaviors, which increased over the three months of the study, and that the roommates showed some evidence of progressive increases in caretaking behaviors. In a 25-year longitudinal study of depression and anger among Canadians (n = 944), Galambos et al. (2018) found that higher anger at ages 18 and 20 years predicted increased social support one and two years later; and that higher depression at age 19 years predicted greater social support one year later (but somewhat older men with higher depression experienced subsequent decreases in social support a few to many years later).

Finally, an experimental vignette study in which fictional victims of adversity (e.g., physical or sexual assault) had incentives to deceptively express need, found that compared to verbal requests and crying, victims' depression and suicidality significantly increased participants' beliefs that the victim was telling the truth and their willingness to help them (Gaffney et al. 2022).

In summary, this research found that depression in naturalistic and laboratory settings elicits attention, concern, potential solutions to problems, and other facilitative behaviors, and care, at least some of the time, and suppresses aggression in situations that frequently involve conflict. Privately, people are alienated by depression, but their actual behavior, at least over the short-to-medium term, aims to help the dysphoric and distressed.

Many researchers have expressed concern that these positive effects of depression could reinforce depressive behavior (e.g., Biglan et al., 1985; Biglan et al., 1989; Hops et al., 1987; Sheeber et al., 1997; Sheeber et al., 2001). Given that the depressed almost always have serious, genuine problems, however, a fact strangely missing from much of the literature on interpersonal relations and depression, eliciting problem-solving behavior and care from social partners is, in our view, a valuable function of depression. Reducing aggression in families plagued by conflict, furthermore, strikes us as a good thing.

The alienating qualities of depression could diminish the enthusiasm of social partners to continue their relationship with the depressed. In situations where switching partners is relatively easy, the depression strategy will therefore frequently fail. Switching partners, however, is often difficult. A father of a newborn with a depressed mother can't simply find a different, nondepressed mother to help care for the newborn. Parents of a depressed adolescent can't simply decide to have another child to replace the unhappy one sitting at their dinner table. Even college students are "stuck" with their depressed roommates for at least a few months, and feel obligated to offer care.

Consider the screaming infant. It is the very aversiveness of the screaming that motivates rapid attention to the infant's needs by parents who can't exchange it for an infant that doesn't scream. In fact, there are several game theory models of begging by juvenile animals that are conceptually similar to our model of depression. In these models, juveniles want more food from parents than parents are inclined to provide. To increase feeding, juveniles threaten their own survival by crying loudly, potentially attracting predators to the nest or expending excessive energy, thereby blackmailing or credibly signaling their parents to increase feeding (Bergstrom & Bergstrom, 1999; Eshel & Feldman, 1991; Godfray, 1991, 1995; Godfray & Johnstone, 2000; Royle et al., 2002; Soltis, 2004; Zahavi, 1977; empirical evidence for begging costs is mixed; for review, see Moreno-Rueda, 2007).

Unlike screaming infants, however, whose needs for food, attention, or a diaper change are, in most cases, easily met, the depressed often have serious problems whose solution might require substantial restructuring of existing social arrangements, leaving social partners expending more effort and/or accepting less return. If depression were not burdensome and aversive to social partners, they would have little incentive to make these changes.

Improved Conditions Are Associated with Remission

If the bargaining model is correct, depression should lead to long-term life improvements, at least some of the time, after which depression would cease. In support, there is increasing evidence that *positive* life events closely precede, and may well cause, recovery from depression. In a study of depression in working-class women, for instance, Brown et al. (1988) found that a reduction in life difficulties, presence of difficulty-reducing events, and the occurrence of "fresh start" events were correlated with recovery. Fresh starts are events, such as getting a job after months of unemployment or starting a new relationship after many months of being single, that seem to promise new hope against a background of deprivation (Harris, 2001). Similarly, Brown et al. (1992) found that women's recovery from depression was associated with a prior positive event. These events were characterized by one or more of three dimensions: anchoring, involving increased security; fresh start, involving increased hope arising from a lessening of a difficulty or deprivation; and relief, involving amelioration of a difficulty without a fresh start. Fresh starts were particularly associated with recovery from depression.

In primary care patients with anxiety or depression, Leenstra et al. (1995) found a twofold excess of positive life changes in the three months prior to recovery compared to base rates, with difficulty reduction as the most important recovery-enhancing factor. They conclude that positive life change facilitates recovery but is neither a necessary nor sufficient condition for remission. In an analysis of a sample that overlapped with the previous study, but was restricted to those with depression, Oldehinkel et al. (2000) explored whether positive life change interacted with sex, neuroticism, self-esteem, coping style, and other factors to facilitate remission. They found that positive life change reduced time to remission most for women and those with high levels of neuroticism. In yet another analysis of the data from Leenstra et al. (1995), Neeleman et al. (2003) found that irrespective of diagnosis and symptom intensity, positive life change increased remission rates 2.9-fold. Remission rates were higher in patients with larger social networks and who sought more help, and this was partly because such persons experienced more positive life change earlier during episodes. In a naturalistic, six-month prospective study of adult patients in general practice with depressive, anxiety, or panic disorder, Ronalds et al. (1997) found that at follow-up the most important predictor of improvement was reduction in marked difficulties over the prior six months. In a nine-year longitudinal study of 2,052 participants with anxiety or depression, or healthy controls, Hovenkamp-Hermelink et al. (2019) found that more positive life events at T2, T4, and T9 (but not at T6) predicted a subsequent decrease in depression severity.

Our model of depression requires that sufficiently improved circumstances cause depression to remit. These studies provide evidence that they do. In some cases, the improvement came about because the depressed individuals themselves initiated positive life changes, such as starting school after years as a housewife (Harris, 2001). This is consistent with the adaptive rumination hypothesis, which proposes that depression engenders a sustained focus on solving one's problems. In other cases, however, the positive life changes were the result of a new development not under the direct control of the depressed subject's agency or control, which, in one study, was true of 76% of the instances of fresh starts and difficulty reductions (Brown et al., 2009). Of the latter, it was sometimes obvious that the subject's depression played no role in the positive event, such as learning that a cancer diagnosis was incorrect. Other times, however, such as starting to work in a boyfriend's shop, it seems possible that depression might have beneficially influenced the social network.

The high fraction of positive events not under direct control of the depressed subject, combined with the finding that more positive life changes occurred to depressed subjects with larger social networks (Neeleman et al., 2003), could mean, speculatively, that depression causes social partners to make changes beneficial to the depressed. On current evidence it is also possible, of course, that depression has no effect or even decreases the probability that a positive life change will occur. However, we have already seen that depression does elicit short-term helping behavior from social partners, so it might also elicit behavior from social partners that provides long-term benefits involving reduction of difficulties or fresh starts, which, as these studies strongly suggest, then lead to remission.

Concluding Remarks

The adversities that cause MD, such as death of a loved one, loss of a mate, loss of resources, and physical attack, were ubiquitous over the course of human evolution. Successfully responding to adversity required a properly functioning nervous system, and brain dysfunctions during common adverse events would have been strongly selected against. Mainstream psychiatry's claim that common adversities cause brain dysfunctions in a sizable fraction of the population is remarkable and very unlikely to be true.

Adversity can unfavorably tip life's balance of effort vs. reward, often causing low mood, sadness, or grief. This aversive psychological pain motivates a search for a solution that will favorably rebalance reward vs. effort. Many individuals in such circumstances can unilaterally redress imbalances by rearranging their lives. Some individuals, though, lack sufficient options, resources, or physical or political power to solve their problems by themselves, and need help from relatives, friends, and other social partners, which they obtain by asking or by signaling need with facial expressions, crying, and other behaviors. Yet if key relationships are marked by anger and conflict and their partners do not hold them in high esteem, it is difficult to solve these problems because social partners either are skeptical that the needs are real or do not want to provide additional help. Without their help, however, the problems might be impossible to solve. Folks in this situation feel helpless, hopeless, and trapped. Instead of responding with "normal" sadness, they become depressed.

Depression, we propose, is in part a credible signal of need, involving distinctive behaviors and reduced effort in collective enterprises such as work and parenting. This signal is credible because reduced effort is more costly to those whose lives are going well than it is to those whose lives are not going well—only the genuinely needy can afford this signal. This dysphoric behavior is easily recognized by social partners, and the message is clear: the depressed have problems, want to talk about them, and need help. Privately, social partners react negatively to this signal of need, probably because it entails reduced benefits from the depressed person and the redirection of more time and effort toward the depressed person.

Nevertheless, social partners do try to help, suppressing their anger and aggression, and offering attention, care, potential solutions to problems, and other facilitative behaviors. Perhaps, despite conflict in the relationship, the depression has convinced them that the needs are genuine. Yet in the short term this help rarely leads to immediate recovery from depression. It is the depressed's lack of response to offers of help, in fact, that many researchers believe is one of the most aversive qualities of depression. Just as workers will not end a strike until their employer offers a significant increase in salary, most initial offers of help do not lead to recovery from depression because the depressed have serious problems and the initial offers of help are "too small" to solve them. The depressed need to compel substantially better offers from reluctant social partners.

In our model, depression facilitates positive developments that eventually lead to recovery. Perhaps intense rumination has uncovered a solution to a social dilemma or makes the depressed more attentive to new opportunities, for instance, or prolonged anhedonia or suicidality has extracted substantial concessions from social partners. When difficulties are reduced or new profitable opportunities arise, the depressed recover.

We have not proved our case—far from it. Serious limitations in our argument include that although most of the correlations we cite are well established, the causal relationships we assume are less so. The causal relationships we assume, however, are usually the ones for which depression researchers have found supporting evidence. The primary missing piece in our argument is whether depression brings about reductions in difficulties or other positive life events that are thought to lead to recovery. Given that depression does elicit help from others, however, it is reasonable to hypothesize that, in many cases, it elicits enough help to change one's life for the better.

Our main point is not that depression must be an adaptation; it is that there is little reason to believe most cases of MD are brain dysfunctions, and we can account for most of the facts about MD, including its aversiveness and undeniable costs such as suicidality and reduced productivity, with a relatively parsimonious theory that makes four simple, intuitive assumptions: (1) psychological pain is an aversive but functional response to many forms of adversity; (2) in many situations, problems cannot be solved alone; (3) there are conflicts with social partners; and (4) need is private information. In these circumstances, depression as credible sadness emerges as a functional, not pathological, response to adversity.

Notes

1. The chemical imbalance model is also known as the catecholamine, monoamine, or serotonin deficiency hypothesis.
2. It is important to distinguish cues from signals. Cues provide information about an organism's state to others, but did not evolve to provide that information. Vomiting, for instance, is a cue of illness but not a signal of illness. Crying after stubbing one's toe, on the other hand, is probably a signal because the tears do not serve to heal the injured toe. Reliable cues of organism state can evolve into signals if sending that information increases the fitness of the signaler by changing the behavior of the receiver (e.g., Maynard Smith & Harper 2003; Tiokhin 2016).

References

Abramson, L. Y., Metalsky, G. I., & Alloy, L. B. (1989). Hopelessness depression: A theory-based subtype of depression. *Psychological Review, 96*(2), 358–372.
Abramson, L. Y., Seligman, M. E. P., & Teasdale, J. D. (1978). Learned helplessness in humans: Critique and reformulation. *Journal of Abnormal Psychology, 87*(1), 49–74.
Alavi, N., Reshetukha, T., Prost, E., Antoniak, K., Patel, C., Sajid, S., & Groll, D. (2017). Relationship between bullying and suicidal behaviour in youth presenting to the emergency department. *Journal of the Canadian Academy of Child and Adolescent Psychiatry, 26*(2), 70–77.
Alexander, R. D. (1986). Ostracism and indirect reciprocity: The reproductive significance of humor. *Ethology and Sociobiology, 7*(3–4), 253–270.
Allen, N., & Badcock, P. (2003). The social risk hypothesis of depressed mood: Evolutionary, psychosocial, and neurobiological perspectives. *Psychological Bulletin, 129*, 887–913.
Allen, N. B., & Badcock, P. B. T. (2006). Darwinian models of depression: A review of evolutionary accounts of mood and mood disorders. *Progress in Neuro-Psychopharmacology and Biological Psychiatry, 30*(5), 815–826.
Al-Shawaf, L., Conroy-Beam, D., Asao, K., & Buss, D. M. (2016). Human emotions: An evolutionary psychological perspective. *Emotion Review, 8*(2), 173–186.
Anders, S., Tanaka, M., & Kinney, D. K. (2013). Depression as an evolutionary strategy for defense against infection. *Brain, Behavior, and Immunity, 31*, 9–22.
Andrews, P. W. (2006). Parent-offspring conflict and cost-benefit analysis in adolescent suicidal behavior. *Human Nature, 17*(2), 190–211.
Andrews, P. W., & Thomson Jr., J. A. (2009). The bright side of being blue: depression as an adaptation for analyzing complex problems. Psychological Review, *116*(3), 620–654.
American Psychiatric Association (2013). *Diagnostic and Statistical Manual of Mental Disorders* (5th ed.). APA.
Badcock, P. B., Davey, C. G., Whittle, S., Allen, N. B., & Friston, K. J. (2017). The depressed brain: an evolutionary systems theory. *Trends in Cognitive Sciences, 21*(3), 182–194.
Balsters, M. J. H., Krahmer, E. J., Swerts, M. G. J., & Vingerhoets, A. J. J. M. (2013). Emotional tears facilitate the recognition of sadness and the perceived need for social support. *Evolutionary Psychology, 11*(1), https://doi.org/10.1177/147470491301100114
Barbic, S. P., Durisko, Z., & Andrews, P. W. (2014). Measuring the bright side of being blue: A new tool for assessing analytical rumination in depression. *PloS ONE, 9*(11), e112077.
Barrett, E. L., Mills, K. L., & Teesson, M. (2013). Mental health correlates of anger in the general population: Findings from the 2007 National Survey of Mental Health and Wellbeing. *Australian & New Zealand Journal of Psychiatry, 47*(5), 470–476.
Barrett, L. F., Adolphs, R., Marsella, S., Martinez, A. M., & Pollak, S. D. (2019). Emotional expressions reconsidered: Challenges to inferring emotion from human facial movements. *Psychological Science in the Public Interest, 20*(1), 1–68.
Bartoskova, M., Sevcikova, M., Durisko, Z., Maslej, M. M., Barbic, S. P., Preiss, M., & Andrews, P. W. (2018). The form and function of depressive rumination. *Evolution and Human Behavior, 39*(3), 277–289.
Beck, A., Crain, A. L., Solberg, L. I., Unützer, J., Glasgow, R. E., Maciosek, M. V., & Whitebird, R. (2011). Severity of depression and magnitude of productivity loss. *The Annals of Family Medicine, 9*(4), 305–311.

Benassi, V. A., Sweeney, P. D., & Dufour, C. L. (1988). Is there a relation between locus of control orientation and depression? *Journal of Abnormal Psychology, 97*(3), 357–367.

Bergstrom, C. T., & Bergstrom, T. C. (1999). Does mother nature punish rotten kids? *Journal of Bioeconomics, 1*(1), 47–72.

Bertera, E. M. (2005). Mental health in U.S. adults: The role of positive social support and social negativity in personal relationships. *Journal of Social and Personal Relationships, 22*(1), 33–48.

Biglan, A., Hops, H., Sherman, L., Friedman, L. S., Arthur, J., & Osteen, V. (1985). Problem-solving interactions of depressed women and their husbands. *Behavior Therapy, 16*(5), 431–451.

Biglan, A., Rothlind, J., Hops, H., & Sherman, L. (1989). Impact of distressed and aggressive behavior. *Journal of Abnormal Psychology, 98*(3), 218–228.

Billaud, J. (2012). Suicidal performances: Voicing discontent in a girls' dormitory in Kabul. *Culture, Medicine, and Psychiatry, 36*(2), 264–285.

Bodner, N., Kuppens, P., Allen, N. B., Sheeber, L. B., & Ceulemans, E. (2018). Affective family interactions and their associations with adolescent depression: a dynamic network approach. *Development and Psychopathology, 30*(4), 1459–1473.

Bonanno, G. A., Kennedy, P., Galatzer-Levy, I. R., Lude, P., & Elfström, M. L. (2012). Trajectories of resilience, depression, and anxiety following spinal cord injury. *Rehabilitation Psychology, 57*(3), 236–247.

Brown, G. W., Adler, Z., & Bifulco, A. (1988). Life events, difficulties and recovery from chronic depression. *British Journal of Psychiatry, 152*, 487–498.

Brown, G. W., Harris, T. O., & Hepworth, C. (1995). Loss, humiliation and entrapment among women developing depression: A patient and non-patient comparison. *Psychological Medicine, 25*(1), 7–21.

Brown, G. W., Harris, T. O., Kendrick, T., Chatwin, J., Craig, T. K. J., Kelly, V., Mander, H., Ring, A., Wallace, V., & Uher, R. (2009). Antidepressants, social adversity and outcome of depression in general practice. *Journal of Affective Disorders, 121*(3), 239–246.

Brown, G. W., Lemyre, L., & Bifulco, A. (1992). Social factors and recovery from anxiety and depressive disorders. A test of specificity. *The British Journal of Psychiatry, 161*(1), 44–54.

Buschinger, A. (1986). Evolution of social parasitism in ants. *Trends in Ecology & Evolution, 1*(6), 155–160.

Buss, D. M., & Duntley, J. D. (2011). The evolution of intimate partner violence. *Aggression and Violent Behavior, 16*(5), 411–419.

Bustamante, C. M. V., Rodman, A. M., Dennison, M. J., Flournoy, J. C., Mair, P., & McLaughlin, K. A. (2020). Within-person fluctuations in stressful life events, sleep, and anxiety and depression symptoms during adolescence: A multiwave prospective study. *Journal of Child Psychology and Psychiatry, 61*(10), 1116–1125.

Butler, C., Joiner, R., Bradley, R., Bowles, M., Bowes, A., Russell, C., & Roberts, V. (2019). Self-harm prevalence and ideation in a community sample of cis, trans and other youth. *International Journal of Transgenderism, 20*(4), 447–458.

Byrne, R. W., & Corp, N. (2004). Neocortex size predicts deception rate in primates. *Proceedings of the Royal Society of London. Series B: Biological Sciences, 271*(1549), 1693–1699.

Canetto, S. S. (2015). Suicidal behaviors among Muslim women: Patterns, Pathways, meanings, and prevention. *Crisis, 36*(6), 447–458.

Cassidy, W. L., Flanagan, N. B., Spellman, M., & Cohen, M. E. (1957). Clinical observations in manic-depressive disease: A quantitative study of one hundred manic-depressive patients and fifty medically sick controls. *Journal of the American Medical Association, 164*(14), 1535–1546.

Cassiello-Robbins, C., & Barlow, D. H. (2016). Anger: I unrecognized emotion in emotional disorders. *Clinical Psychology: Science and Practice, 23*(1), 66–85.

Charlson, F., van Ommeren, M., Flaxman, A., Cornett, J., Whiteford, H., & Saxena, S. (2019). New WHO prevalence estimates of mental disorders in conflict settings: A systematic review and meta-analysis. *Lancet, 394*(10194), 240–248.

Cipriani, A., Furukawa, T. A., Salanti, G., Chaimani, A., Atkinson, L. Z., Ogawa, Y., Leucht, S., Ruhe, H. G., Turner, E. H., Higgins, J. P. T., Egger, M., Takeshima, N., Hayasaka, Y., Imai, H., Shinohara, K., Tajika, A., Ioannidis, J. P. A., & Geddes, J. R. (2018). Comparative efficacy and acceptability of 21 antidepressant drugs for the acute treatment of adults with major depressive disorder: A systematic review and network meta-analysis. *Focus, 16*(4), 420–429.

Cornwell, B., & Laumann, E. O. (2018). Structure by death: Social network replenishment in the wake of confidant loss. In D. F. Alwin, D. H. Felmlee, & D. A. Kreager (Eds.), *Social networks and the life course: Integrating the development of human lives and social relational networks* (pp. 343–365). Springer International.

Cosmides, L., & Tooby, J. (1999). Toward a taxonomy of treatable conditions. *Journal of Abnormal Psychology, 108*, 453–464.

Cowen, A. S., Keltner, D., Schroff, F., Jou, B., Adam, H., & Prasad, G. (2020). Sixteen facial expressions occur in similar contexts worldwide. *Nature, 589*, 251–257.

Coyne, J. C. (1976a). Depression and the response of others. *Journal of Abnormal Psychology, 85*(2), 186–193.

Coyne, J. C. (1976b). Toward an interactional description of depression. *Psychiatry, 39*(1), 28–40.

Dadds, M. R., Sanders, M. R., Morrison, M., & Rebgetz, M. (1992). Childhood depression and conduct disorder: II. An analysis of family interaction patterns in the home. *Journal of Abnormal Psychology, 101*(3), 505–513.

Darwin, C. (1916). *The expression of the emotions in man and animals*. Appleton.

Delalibera, M., Presa, J., Coelho, A., Barbosa, A., & Franco, M. H. P. (2015). Family dynamics during the grieving process: A systematic literature review. *Ciencia & Saude Coletiva, 20*, 1119–1134.

Del Giudice, M. (2018). *Evolutionary psychopathology: A unified approach*. Oxford University Press.

Devries, K., Watts, C., Yoshihama, M., Kiss, L., Schraiber, L. B., Deyessa, N., Heise, L., Durand, J., Mbwambo, J., Jansen, H., Berhane, Y., Ellsberg, M., & Garcia-Moreno, C. (2011). Violence against women is strongly associated with suicide attempts: Evidence from the WHO multi-country study on women's health and domestic violence against women. *Social Science & Medicine, 73*(1), 79–86.

Donohue, J. M., & Pincus, H. A. (2007). Reducing the societal burden of depression: A review of economic costs, quality of care and effects of treatment. *Pharmacoeconomics, 25*, 7–24.

Durisko, Z., Mulsant, B. H., & Andrews, P. W. (2015). An adaptationist perspective on the etiology of depression. *Journal of Affective Disorders, 172*, 315–323.

Eaton, W. W., Shao, H., Nestadt, G., Lee, B. H., Bienvenu, O. J., & Zandi, P. (2008). Population-based study of first onset and chronicity in major depressive disorder. *Archives of General Psychiatry, 65*(5), 513–520.

Ekman, P., & Cordaro, D. (2011). What is meant by calling emotions basic? *Emotion Review, 3*(4), 364–370.

Elgar, F. J., Pickett, W., Pförtner, T.-K., Gariépy, G., Gordon, D., Georgiades, K., Davison, C., Hammami, N., MacNeil, A. H., Da Silva, M. A., & Melgar-Quiñonez, H. R. (2021). Relative food insecurity, mental health and wellbeing in 160 countries. *Social Science & Medicine, 268*, https://doi.org/10.1016/j.socscimed.2020.113556.

Ellsberg, M., Jansen, H. A., Heise, L., Watts, C. H., & Garcia-Moreno, C. (2008). Intimate partner violence and women's physical and mental health in the WHO multi-country study on women's health and domestic violence: An observational study. *Lancet, 371*(9619), 1165–1172.

Eshel, I., & Feldman, M. W. (1991). The handicap principle in parent-offspring conflict: Comparison of optimality and population-genetic analyses. *The American Naturalist, 137*(2), 167–185.

Evans-Lacko, S., & Knapp, M. (2016). Global patterns of workplace productivity for people with depression: Absenteeism and presenteeism costs across eight diverse countries. *Social Psychiatry and Psychiatric Epidemiology, 51*(11), 1525–1537.

Feighner, J. P., Robins, E., Guze, S. B., Woodruff, R. A., Jr., Winokur, G., & Munoz, R. (1972). Diagnostic criteria for use in psychiatric research. *Archives of General Psychiatry, 26*(1), 57–63.

Firth, R. (1961). Suicide and risk-taking in Tikopia society. *Psychiatry, 24*(1), 1–17.

Ford, R., King, T., Priest, N., & Kavanagh, A. (2017). Bullying and mental health and suicidal behaviour among 14- to 15-year-olds in a representative sample of Australian children. *Australian & New Zealand Journal of Psychiatry, 51*(9), 897–908.

Frances, A. (2013). The past, present and future of psychiatric diagnosis. *World Psychiatry, 12*(2), 111–112.

Frazer, A., & Benmansour, S. (2002). Delayed pharmacological effects of antidepressants. *Molecular Psychiatry, 7*(1), S23–S28.

Gaffney, M. R., Adams, K. H., Syme, K. L., & Hagen, E. H. (2022). Depression and suicidality as evolved credible signals of need in social conflicts. *Evolution and Human Behavior, 43*(3), 242–256.

Galambos, N. L., Johnson, M. D., & Krahn, H. J. (2018). The anger–depression connection: Between-persons and within-person associations from late adolescence to midlife. *Developmental Psychology, 54*(10), 1940–1953.

Galatzer-Levy, I. R., Huang, S. H., & Bonanno, G. A. (2018). Trajectories of resilience and dysfunction following potential trauma: A review and statistical evaluation. *Clinical Psychology Review, 63*, 41–55.

Ge, X., Lorenz, F. O., Conger, R. D., Elder, G. H., & Simons, R. L. (1994). Trajectories of stressful life events and depressive symptoms during adolescence. *Developmental Psychology, 30*(4), 467–483.

Genovese, T., Dalrymple, K., Chelminski, I., & Zimmerman, M. (2017). Subjective anger and overt aggression in psychiatric outpatients. *Comprehensive Psychiatry, 73*, 23–30.

Gilbert, P. (1992). *Depression: The evolution of powerlessness*. Guildford Press.

Gilbert, P., & Allan, S. (1998). The role of defeat and entrapment (arrested flight) in depression: An exploration of an evolutionary view. *Psychological Medicine, 28*(3), 585–598.

Gilbert, P., Gilbert, J., & Irons, C. (2004). Life events, entrapments and arrested anger in depression. *Journal of Affective Disorders, 79*(1), 149–160.

Glasberg, R., & Aboud, F. (1982). Keeping one's distance from sadness: Children's self-reports of emotional experience. *Developmental Psychology, 18*(2), 287–293.

Glasberg, R., & Aboud, F. E. (1981). A developmental perspective on the study of depression: Children's evaluative reactions to sadness. *Developmental Psychology, 17*(2), 195–202.

Global Burden of Disease Study 2017 (GBD) (2017). Results. Seattle, United States: Institute for Health Metrics and Evaluation (IHME), 2018. Available from http://ghdx.healthdata.org/gbd-results-tool.

Godfray, H. C., & Johnstone, R. A. (2000). Begging and bleatiIThe evolution of parent offspring signalling. *Philosophical Transactions of the Royal Society B: Biological Sciences, 355*(1403), 1581–1591.

Godfray, H. C. J. (1991). Signalling of need by offspring to their parents. *Nature, 352*(6333), 328–330.

Godfray, H. C. J. (1995). Signaling of need between parents and young: Parent-offspring conflict and sibling rivalry. *The American Naturalist, 146*(1), 1–24.

Grafen, A. (1990). Biological signals as handicaps. *Journal of Theoretical Biology, 144*(4), 517–546.

Grosbras, M.-H., Ross, P. D., & Belin, P. (2018). Categorical emotion recognition from voice improves during childhood and adolescence. *Scientific Reports, 8*(1), 14791. https://doi.org/10.1038/s41598-018-32868-3

Gross, J. J. (1998). The emerging field of emotion regulation: An integrative review. *Review of General Psychology, 2*, 271–299.

Gross, J. J. (2002). Emotion regulation: Affective, cognitive, and social consequences. *Psychophysiology, 39*(03), 281–291.

Hagen, E. H. (1999). The functions of postpartum depression. *Evolution and Human Behavior, 20*(5), 325–359.

Hagen, E. H. (2002). Depression as bargaining: The case postpartum. *Evolution and Human Behavior, 23*(5), 323–336.

Hagen, E. H. (2003). The bargaining model of depression. In P. Hammerstein (Ed.), *Genetic and Cultural Evolution of Cooperation* (pp. 95–123). MIT Press.

Hagen, E. H. (2011). Evolutionary theories of depression: A critical review. *The Canadian Journal of Psychiatry, 56*(12), 716–726.

Hagen, E. H., & Barrett, H. C. (2007). Perinatal sadness among Shuar women: Support for an evolutionary theory of psychic pain. *Medical Anthropology Quarterly, 21*(1), 22–40.

Hagen, E. H., & Thornhill, R. (2017). Testing the psychological pain hypothesis for postnatal depression: Reproductive success versus evidence of design. *Evolution, Medicine, and Public Health, 2017* (1), 17–23.

Hagen, E. H., Watson, P. J., & Hammerstein, P. (2008). Gestures of despair and hope: A view on deliberate self-harm from economics and evolutionary biology. *Biological Theory, 3*(2), 123–138.

Hagen, E. H., & Rosenström, T. (2016). Explaining the sex difference in depression with a unified bargaining model of anger and depression. *Evolution, Medicine, and Public Health, 2016*(1), 117–132.

Harmer, C. J., Goodwin, G. M., & Cowen, P. J. (2009). Why do antidepressants take so long to work? A cognitive neuropsychological model of antidepressant drug action. *The British Journal of Psychiatry, 195*(2), 102–108.

Harris, T. (2001). Recent developments in understanding the psychosocial aspects of depression. *British Medical Bulletin, 57*(1), 17–32.

Haslam, N., McGrath, M., Viechtbauer, W., & Kuppens, P. (2020). Dimensions over categories: A meta-analysis of taxometric research. *Psychological Medicine, 50*, 1–15.

Hess, N., Helfrecht, C., Hagen, E., Sell, A., & Hewlett, B. (2010). Interpersonal aggression among Aka huntergatherers of the Central African Republic: Assessing the effects of sex, strength, and anger. *Human Nature, 21*(3), 330–354.

Hewlett, B. L. (2017). Vulnerable lives. In B. S. Hewlett & M. E. Lamb (Eds.), *Hunter-gatherer child^oods* (1st ed., pp. 322–342). Routledge.

Hezel, F. X. (1987). Truk suicide epidemic and social change. *Human Organization, 46*(4), 283–291.

Hezel, F. X. (1989). Suicide and the Micronesian family. *The Contemporary Pacific, 1*(1–2), 43–74.

Hill, K. R., Walker, R. S., Božičević, M., Eder, J., Headland, T., Hewlett, B., Hurtado, A. M., Marlowe, F., Wiessner, P., & Wood, B.. (2011). Co-residence patterns in hunter-gatherer societies show unique human social structure. *Science, 331*(6022), 1286–1289.

Hollan, D. (1990). Indignant suicide in the Pacific: An example from the Toraja highlands of Indonesia. *Culture, Medicine and Psychiatry, 14*(3), 365–379.

Hokanson, J. E., Loewenstein, D. A., Hedeen, C., & Howes, M. J. (1986). Dysphoric college students and roommates: A study of social behaviors over a three-month period. *Personality and Social Psychology Bulletin, 12*(3), 311–324.

Hops, H., Biglan, A., Sherman, L., Arthur, J., Friedman, L., & Osteen, V. (1987). Home observations of family interactions of depressed women. *Journal of Consulting and Clinical Psychology, 55*(3), 341–346.

Horwitz, A., Wakefield, J., & Lorenzo-Luaces, L. (2016). History of depression. In R. J. DeRubeis & D. R. Strunk (Eds.), *The Oxford handbook of mood disorders* (pp. 1–24). Oxford University Press.

Hovenkamp-Hermelink, J. H., Jeronimus, B. F., Spinhoven, P., Penninx, B. W., Schoevers, R. A., & Riese, H. (2019). Differential associations of locus of control with anxiety, depression and life-events: A five-wave, nine-year study to test stability and change. *Journal of Affective Disorders, 253*, 26–34.

Infurna, F. J., & Luthar, S. S. (2018). Re-evaluating the notion that resilience is commonplace: A review and distillation of directions for future research, practice, and policy. *Clinical Psychology Review, 65*, 43–56.

Jackson, S. W. (1986). *Melancholia and depression: From Hippocratic times to modern times.* Yale University Press.

Jayaraman, A., & Wood, T. K. (2008). Bacterial quorum sensing: Signals, circuits, and implications for biofilms and disease. *Annual Review of Biomedical Engineering, 10*(1), 145–167.

Jenness, J. L., Peverill, M., King, K. M., Hankin, B. L., & McLaughlin, K. A. (2019). Dynamic associations between stressful life events and adolescent internalizing psychopathology in a multiwave longitudinal study. *Journal of Abnormal Psychology, 128*(6), 596–609.

Joiner, T. E., Metalsky, G. I., Katz, J., & Beach, S. R. H. (1999). Depression and excessive reassurance-seeking. *Psychological Inquiry, 10*(3), 269–278.

Jolly, M., Brewer, C., & Stewart, C. (2012). *Engendering violence in Papua New Guinea* (1st ed.). Canberra: ANU E Press.

Judd, L. L., Schettler, P. J., Coryell, W., Akiskal, H. S., & Fiedorowicz, J. G. (2013). Overt irritability/anger in unipolar major depressive episodes: Past and current characteristics and implications for long-term course. *JAMA Psychiatry, 70*(11), 1171–1180.

Kalisch, R., Baker, D. G., Basten, U., Boks, M. P., Bonanno, G. A., Brummelman, E., Chmitorz, A., Fernàndez, G., Fiebach, C. J., Galatzer-Levy, I., Geuze, E., Groppa, S., Helmreich, I., Hendler, T., Hermans, E. J., Jovanovic, T., Kubiak, T., Lieb, K., Lutz, B., ... Kleim, B. (2017). The resilience framework as a strategy to combat stress-related disorders. *Nature Human Behaviour, 1*(11), 784–790.

Kalisch, R., Cramer, A. O. J., Binder, H., Fritz, J., Leertouwer, Ij., Lunansky, G., Meyer, B., Timmer, J., Veer, I. M., & van Harmelen, A.-L. (2019). Deconstructing and reconstructing resilience: A dynamic network approach. *Perspectives on Psychological Science, 14*(5), 765–777.

Karban, R. (2015). *Plant sensing and communication.* University of Chicago Press.

Kendler, K. S., & Gardner, C. O. (2016). Depressive vulnerability, stressful life events and episode onset of major depression: A longitudinal model. *Psychological Medicine, 46*(9), 1865–1874.

Kendler, K. S., Hettema, J. M., Butera, F., Gardner, C. O., & Prescott, C. A. (2003). Life event dimensions of loss, humiliation, entrapment, and danger in the prediction of onsets of major depression and generalized anxiety. *Archives of General Psychiatry, 60*(8), 789–796.

Kendler, K. S., Karkowski, L. M., & Prescott, C. A. (1999). Causal relationship between stressful life events and the onset of major depression. *American Journal of Psychiatry, 156*(6), 837–841.

Kendler, K. S., Kuhn, J., & Prescott, C. A. (2004). The interrelationship of neuroticism, sex, and stressful life events in the prediction of episodes of major depression. *American Journal of Psychiatry, 161*(4), 631–636.

Kendler, K. S., Muñoz, R. A., & Murphy, G. (2010). The development of the Feighner criteria: A historical perspective. *American Journal of Psychiatry, 167*(2), 134–142.

Kendler, K. S., Myers, J., & Zisook, S. (2008). Does bereavement-related major depression differ from major depression associated with other stressful life events? *American Journal of Psychiatry, 165*(11), 1449–1455.

Kennair, L. E. O., Kleppestø, T. H., Larsen, S. M., & Jørgensen, B. E. G. (2017). Depression: Is rumination really adaptive? In T. K. Shackelford & V. Zeigler-Hill (Eds.), *The evolution of psychopathology* (pp. 73–92). Springer International.

Kennan, J., & Wilson, R. (1993). Bargaining with private information. *Journal of Economic Literature, 31*(1), 45–104.

Kerry, N., & Murray, D. R. (2018). Strong personalities: Investigating the relationships between grip strength, self-perceived formidability, and Big Five personality traits. *Personality and Individual Differences, 131*, 216–221.

Kessler, R. C., Akiskal, H. S., Ames, M., Birnbaum, H., Greenberg, P., Hirschfeld, R. M. A., Jin, R., Merikangas, K. R., Simon, G. E., & Wang, P.S., (2006). Prevalence and effects of mood disorders on work performance in a nationally representative sample of US workers. *American Journal of Psychiatry, 163*(9), 1561–1568.

Khansa, W., Haddad, C., Hallit, R., Akel, M., Obeid, S., Haddad, G., Soufia, M., Kheir, N., Hallit, C. A. E., Khoury, R., Salameh, P., & Hallit, S. (2020). Interaction between anxiety and depression on suicidal ideation, quality of life, and work productivity impairment: Results from a representative sample of the Lebanese population. *Perspectives in Psychiatric Care, 56*(2), 270–279.

Kinney, D. K., & Tanaka, M. (2009). An evolutionary hypothesis of depression and its symptoms, adaptive value, and risk factors. *The Journal of Nervous and Mental Disease, 197*(8), 561–567.

Kirsch, I. (2008). Challenging received wisdom: Antidepressants and the placebo effect. *McGill Journal of Medicine: MJM, 11*(2), 219–222.

Kirsch, I. (2014). Antidepressants and the placebo effect. *Zeitschrift für Psychologie, 222*(3), 128–134.

Kirsch, I., & Sapirstein, G. (1998). Listening to prozac but hearing placebo: A meta-analysis of antidepressant medication. *Prevention & Treatment, 1*(2). https://doi.org/10.1037/1522-3736.1.1.12a

Kissane, D. W., Bloch, S., Dowe, D. L., Snyder, R. D., Onghena, P., McKenzie, D. P., & Wallace, C. S. (1996). The Melbourne family grief study, I: Perceptions of family functioning in bereavement. *American Journal of Psychiatry, 153*(5), 650–658.

Koh, K. B., Kim, C. H., & Park, J. K. (2002). Predominance of anger in depressive disorders compared with anxiety disorders and somatoform disorders. *Journal of Clinical Psychiatry, 63*(6), 486–492.

König, H., König, H.-H., & Konnopka, A. (2020). The excess costs of depression: A systematic review and meta-analysis. *Epidemiology and Psychiatric Sciences, 29*, e30.

Kuehner, C. (2017). Why is depression more common among women than among men? *Lancet Psychiatry, 4*(2), 146–158.

Larkings, J. S., & Brown, P. M. (2018). Do biogenetic causal beliefs reduce mental illness stigma in people with mental illness and in mental health professionals? A systematic review. *International Journal of Mental Health Nursing, 27*(3), 928–941.

Leenstra, A. S., Ormel, J., & Giel, R. (1995). Positive life change and recovery from depression and anxiety. A three-stage longitudinal study of primary care attenders. *The British Journal of Psychiatry, 166*(3), 333–343.

Lenoir, A., d'Ettorre, P., Errard, C., & Hefetz, A. (2001). Chemical ecology and social parasitism in ants. *Annual Review of Entomology, 46*(1), 573–599.

Li, Y. I., Starr, L. R., & Hershenberg, R. (2017). Responses to positive affect in daily life: positive rumination and dampening moderate the association between daily events and depressive symptoms. *Journal of Psychopathology and Behavioral Assessment, 39*(3), 412–425.

Littlewood, R. (1985). An indigenous conceptualization of reactive depression in Trinidad. *Psychological Medicine, 15*(2), 275–281.

Littlewood, R. (2002). *Pathologies of the West: An anthropology of mental illness in Europe and America*. Cornell University Press.

Lummaa, V., Vuorisalo, T., Barr, R. G., & Lehtonen, L. (1998). Why cry? Adaptive significance of intensive crying in human infants. *Evolution and Human Behavior, 19*(3), 193–202.

Maccallum, F., Galatzer-Levy, I. R., & Bonanno, G. A. (2015). Trajectories of depression following spousal and child bereavement: A comparison of the heterogeneity in outcomes. *Journal of Psychiatric Research, 69*, 72–79.

Machiavelli, N. (1995). *The Prince* (D. Wootton, Ed.). Hackett.

Maes, M. (1999). Major depression and activation of the inflammatory response system. In R. Dantzer, E. E. Wollman, & R. Yirmiya (Eds.), *Cytokines, stress, and depression* (pp. 25–46). Springer.

Malinowski, B. (1926). *Crime and custom in savage society*. Routledge & Kegan Paul.

Maslej, M., Rheaume, A. R., Schmidt, L. A., & Andrews, P. W. (2019). Using expressive writing to test an evolutionary hypothesis about depressive rumination: Sadness coincides with causal analysis of a personal problem, not problem-solving analysis. *Evolutionary Psychological Science, 6*, 119–135.

Mazure, C. M. (1998). Life stressors as risk factors in depression. *Clinical Psychology: Science and Practice, 5*(3), 291–313.

McEvoy, P. M., Watson, H., Watkins, E. R., & Nathan, P. (2013). The relationship between worry, rumination, and comorbidity: Evidence for repetitive negative thinking as a transdiagnostic construct. *Journal of Affective Disorders, 151*(1), 313–320.

McIver, J. D., & Stonedahl, G. (1993). Myrmecomorphy: Morphological and behavioral mimicry of ants. *Annual Review of Entomology, 38*(1), 351–377.

Metsä-Simola, N., & Martikainen, P. (2013). Divorce and changes in the prevalence of psychotropic medication use: A register-based longitudinal study among middle-aged Finns. *Social Science & Medicine, 94*, 71–80.

Mokkonen, M., & Lindstedt, C. (2016). The evolutionary ecology of deception. *Biological Reviews, 91*(4), 1020–1035.

Moore, S. E., Norman, R. E., Suetani, S., Thomas, H. J., Sly, P. D., & Scott, J. G. (2017). Consequences of bullying victimization in childhood and adolescence: A systematic review and meta-analysis. *World Journal of Psychiatry, 7*(1), 60–76.

Moreno-Rueda, G. (2007). Is there empirical evidence for the cost of begging? *Journal of Ethology, 25*(3), 215–222.

Morgan, P., & Lim, H. (2020). Depressive symptom and financial conflict relate over time among couples. *Journal of Family and Economic Issues, 41*(3), 391–404.

Myers, S., Burger, O., & Johns, S. E. (2016). Postnatal depression and reproductive success in modern, low-fertility contexts. *Evolution, Medicine, and Public Health, 2016* (1), 71–84.

Neeleman, J., Oldehinkel, A. J., & Ormel, J. (2003). Positive life change and remission of non-psychotic mental illness: A competing outcomes approach. *Journal of Affective Disorders, 76*(1–3), 69–78.

Nesse, R. M. (2000). Is depression an adaptation? *Archives of General Psychiatry, 57*(1), 14–20.

Nesse, R. M. (2006). Evolutionary explanations for mood and mood disorders. In D. J. Stein, D. J. Kupfer, & A. F. Schatzberg (Eds.), *The American Psychiatric Publishing textbook of mood disorders* (pp. 159–175). American Psychiatric Publishing.

Nesse, R. M. (2019). *Good reasons for bad feelings: Insights from the frontier of evolutionary psychiatry*. Penguin.

Nettle, D. (2004). Evolutionary origins of depression: A review and reformulation. *Journal of Affective Disorders*, 81(2), 91–102.

Ng, T. W. H., Sorensen, K. L., Zhang, Y., & Yim, F. H. K. (2019). Anger, anxiety, depression, and negative affect: Convergent or divergent? *Journal of Vocational Behavior*, 110, 186–202.

Niehaus, I. (2012). Gendered endings: Narratives of male and female suicides in the South African Lowveld. *Culture, Medicine, and Psychiatry*, 36(2), 327–347.

Nock, M. K., Borges, G., Bromet, E. J., Cha, C. B., Kessler, R. C., & Lee, S. (2008). Suicide and suicidal behavior. *Epidemiologic Reviews*, 30(1), 133–154.

Nock, M. K., Green, J. G., Hwang, I., McLaughlin, K. A., Sampson, N. A., Zaslavsky, A. M., & Kessler, R. C. (2013). Prevalence, correlates, and treatment of lifetime suicidal behavior among adolescents: Results from the national comorbidity survey replication adolescent supplement. *JAMA Psychiatry*, 70(3), 300–310.

Nolen-Hoeksema, S. (1991). Responses to depression and their effects on the duration of depressive episodes. *Journal of Abnormal Psychology*, 100(4), 569–582.

Ochsner, K. N. & Gross, J. J. (2005). The cognitive control of emotion. *Trends in Cognitive Sciences*, 9(5), 242–249.

Olatunji, B. O., Naragon-Gainey, K., & Wolitzky-Taylor, K. B. (2013). Specificity of rumination in anxiety and depression: A multimodal meta-analysis. *Clinical Psychology: Science and Practice*, 20(3), 225–257.

Oldehinkel, A. J., Ormel, J., & Neeleman, J. (2000). Predictors of time to remission from depression in primary care patients: Do some people benefit more from positive life change than others? *Journal of Abnormal Psychology*, 109(2), 299–307.

Ormel, J., Vonkorff, M., Oldehinkel, A. J., Simon, G., Tiemens, B. G., & Üstün, T. B. (1999). Onset of disability in depressed and non-depressed primary care patients. *Psychological Medicine*, 29(4), 847–853.

Ou, C. H., & Hall, W. A. (2018). Anger in the context of postnatal depression: An integrative review. *Birth*, 45(4), 336–346.

Owings, D. H. & Zeifman, D. M. (2004). Human infant crying as an animal communication system: Insights from an assessment/management approach. In Oller, D. K. & Griebel, U. (Eds.), *Evolution of communication systems: A comparative approach* (pp. 151–170). MIT Press.

Picó, A., Espert, R., & Gadea, M. (2020). How our gaze reacts to another person's tears? Experimental insights into eye tracking technology. *Frontiers in Psychology*, 11, https://doi.org/10.3389/fpsyg.2020.02134.

Poole, F. J. P. (1985). Among the boughs of the hanging tree: Male suicide among the Bimin-Kuskusmin of Papua New Guinea. In F. X. Hezel, D. H. Rubinstein, & G. W. White (Eds.), *Culture, youth and suicide in the Pacific: Papers from an East-West Center Conference*. Honolulu: Pacific Islands Studies Program Working Papers, University of Hawaii.

Price, J., Sloman, L., Gardner, R., Gilbert, P., & Rohde, P. (1994). The social competition hypothesis of depression. *British Journal of Psychiatry*, 164(3), 309–315.

Price, J. S., Gardner, R., Jr., Wilson, D. R., Sloman, L., Rohde, P., & Erickson, M. (2007). Territory, rank and mental health: The history of an idea. *Evolutionary Psychology*, 5(3), 147470490700500320.

Prisciandaro, J. J., & Roberts, J. E. (2005). A taxometric investigation of unipolar depression in the National Comorbidity Survey. *Journal of Abnormal Psychology*, 114(4), 718–728.

Quesque, F., Coutrot, A., Cox, S., de Souza, L. C., Baez, S., Cardona, J. F., Mulet-Perreault, H., Flanagan, E., Neely-Prado, A., Clarens, M. F., Cassimiro, L., Musa, G., Kemp, J., Botzung, A., Philippi, N., Cosseddu, M., Trujillo-Llano, C., Grisales-Cardenas, J. S., Fittipaldi, S., . . . Bertoux, M. (2022). Does culture shape our understanding of others' thoughts and emotions? An investigation across 12 countries. *Neuropsychology*, 36(7), 664–682. https://doi.org/10.1037/neu0000817.

Raison, C. L., Capuron, L., & Miller, A. H. (2006). Cytokines sing the blues: Inflammation and the pathogenesis of depression. *Trends in Immunology*, 27(1), 24–31.

Raison, C. L., & Miller, A. H. (2013). Malaise, melancholia and madness: The evolutionary legacy of an inflammatory bias. *Brain, Behavior, and Immunity*, 31, 1–8.

Raison, C. L., & Miller, A. H. (2017). Pathogen–host defense in the evolution of depression: Insights into epidemiology, genetics, bioregional differences and female Preponderance. *Neuropsychopharmacology*, 42(1), 5–27.

Rauchholz, M. (2016). Masculine sexuality, violence and sexual exploitation in Micronesia. *The Asia Pacific Journal of Anthropology*, 17(3–4), 342–358.

Regier, D. A., Kaelber, C. T., Rae, D. S., Farmer, M. E., Knauper, B., Kessler, R. C., & Norquist, G. S. (1998). Limitations of diagnostic criteria and assessment instruments for mental disorders: Implications for research and policy. *Archives of General Psychiatry*, 55(2), 109–115.

Reigstad, B., & Kvernmo, S. (2017). Concurrent adversities and suicide attempts among Sami and non-Sami adolescents: the Norwegian Arctic Adolescent Study (NAAHS). *Nordic Journal of Psychiatry, 71*(6), 425-432.

Richards, D. (2011). Prevalence and clinical course of depression: A review. *Clinical Psychology Review, 31*(7), 1117–1125.

Riley, W. T., Treiber, F. A., & Woods, M. G. (1989). Anger and hostility in depression. *Journal of Nervous and Mental Disease, 177*(11), 668–674.

Ronalds, C., Creed, F., Stone, K., Webb, S., & Tomenson, B. (1997). Outcome of anxiety and depressive disorders in primary care. *The British Journal of Psychiatry, 171*(5), 427–433.

Rosenström, T., Fawcett, T. W., Higginson, A. D., Metsä-Simola, N., Hagen, E. H., Houston, A. I., & Martikainen, P. (2017). Adaptive and non-adaptive models of depression: A comparison using register data on antidepressant medication during divorce. *PLoS ONE, 12*(6), e0179495.

Rosenthal, R. W. (1993). Suicide attempts and signalling games. *Mathematical Social Sciences, 26*(1), 25–33.

Rothstein, S. I., & Robinson, S. K. (1998). *Parasitic birds and their hosts*. Oxford University Press.

Rotter, J. B. (1966). Generalized expectancies for internal versus external control of reinforcement. *Psychological Monographs: General and Applied, 80*(1), 1–28.

Royle, N. J., Hartley, I. R., & Parker, G. A. (2002). Begging for control: When are offspring solicitation behaviours honest? *Trends in Ecology & Evolution, 17*(9), 434–440.

Rubinstein, A. (1982). Perfect equilibrium in a bargaining model. *Econometrica: Journal of the Econometric Society, 50*(1), 97–109.

Rubinstein, D. H. (1995). Love and suffering: Adolescent socialization and suicide in Micronesia. *The Contemporary Pacific, 7*(1), 21–53.

Ruhé, H. G., Mason, N. S., & Schene, A. H. (2007). Mood is indirectly related to serotonin, norepinephrine and dopamine levels in humans: A meta-analysis of monoamine depletion studies. *Molecular Psychiatry, 12*(4), 331–359.

Salinger, J. M., Whisman, M. A., Randall, A. K., & Hilpert, P. (2020). Associations between marital discord and depressive symptoms: A cross-cultural analysis. *Family Process, 57*(3), 649–661.

Schrock, J. M., Snodgrass, J. J., & Sugiyama, L. S. (2020). Lassitude: The emotion of being sick. *Evolution and Human Behavior, 41*(1), 44–57.

Sebe, N., Cohen, I., Gevers, T., & Huang, T. S. (2006). Emotion Recognition Based on Joint Visual and Audio Cues. *18th International Conference on Pattern Recognition (ICPR'06), 1*, 1136–1139. https://doi.org/10.1109/ICPR.2006.489

Segrin, C. (2000). Social skills deficits associated with depression. *Clinical Psychology Review, 20*(3), 379–403.

Segrin, C., & Abramson, L. Y. (1994). Negative reactions to depressive behaviors: A communication theories analysis. *Journal of Abnormal Psychology, 103*, 655–655.

Segrin, C., & Dillard, J. P. (1992). The interactional theory of depression: A meta-analysis of the research literature. *Journal of Social and Clinical Psychology, 11*(1), 43–70.

Sell, A., Hone, L. S. E., & Pound, N. (2012). The importance of physical strength to human males. *Human Nature, 23*(1), 30–44.

Sell, A., Tooby, J., & Cosmides, L. (2009). Formidability and the logic of human anger. *Proceedings of the National Academy of Sciences, 106*(35), 15073–15078.

Sevcikova, M., Maslej, M. M., Stipl, J., Andrews, P. W., Pastrnak, M., Vechetova, G., Bartoskova, M., & Preiss, M. (2020). Testing the analytical rumination hypothesis: exploring the longitudinal effects of problem solving analysis on depression. *Frontiers in Psychology, 11,* https://doi.org/10.3389/fpsyg.2020.01344.

Sheeber, L., Hops, H., Alpert, A., Davis, B., & Andrews, J. (1997). Family support and conflict: Prospective relations to adolescent depression. *Journal of Abnormal Child Psychology, 25*(4), 333–344.

Sheeber, L., Hops, H., & Davis, B. (2001). Family processes in adolescent depression. *Clinical Child and Family Psychology Review, 4*(1), 19–35.

Singh, P. K., & Rao, V. R. (2018). Explaining suicide attempt with personality traits of aggression and impulsivity in a high risk tribal population of India. *PLoS ONE, 13*(2), e0192969.

Skyrms, B. (2010). *Signals: Evolution, learning, and information*. Oxford University Press.

Slavich, G. M., & Irwin, M. R. (2014). From stress to inflammation and major depressive disorder: a social signal transduction theory of depression. *Psychological Bulletin, 140*(3), 774–815.

Smith, C. B., Rosenström, T., & Hagen, E. H. (2022). Strength is negatively associated with depression and accounts for some of the sex difference: A replication and extension. *Evolution, Medicine, and Public Health, 10*(1), 130–141.

Soltis, J. (2004). The signal functions of early infant crying. *Behavioral and Brain Sciences, 27,* 443–490.

Spence, M. (1973). Job Market Signaling. *The Quarterly Journal of Economics, 87*(3), 355–374. Spitzer, R. L., Endicott, J., & Robins, E. (1975). Clinical criteria for psychiatric diagnosis and DSM-III. *The American Journal of Psychiatry, 132*(11), 1187–1192.

Spitzer, R. L., & Wakefield, J. C. (1999). DSM-IV Diagnostic criterion for clinical significance: Does it help solve the false positives problem? *American Journal of Psychiatry, 156*(12), 1856–1864.

Staples, J., & Widger, T. (2012). Situating suicide as an anthropological problem: Ethnographic approaches to understanding self-harm and self-inflicted death. *Culture, Medicine, and Psychiatry, 36*(2), 183–203.

Starr, L. R., & Davila, J. (2008). Excessive reassurance seeking, depression, and interpersonal rejection: A meta-analytic review. *Journal of Abnormal Psychology, 117*(4), 762.

Starrett, A. (1993). Adaptive resemblance: A unifying concept for mimicry and crypsis. *Biological Journal of the Linnean Society, 48*(4), 299–317.

Steinert, C., Hofmann, M., Kruse, J., & Leichsenring, F. (2014). The prospective long-term course of adult depression in general practice and the community. A systematic literature review. *Journal of Affective Disorders, 152–154*, 65–75.

Steinkopf, L. (2015). The signaling theory of symptoms: An evolutionary explanation of the placebo effect. *Evolutionary Psychology, 13*(3), https://doi.org/10.1177/1474704915600559.

Stephens, R. S., Hokanson, J. E., & Welker, R. (1987). Responses to depressed interpersonal behavior: Mixed reactions in a helping role. *Journal of Personality and Social Psychology, 52*(6), 1274–1282.

Stewart, W. F., Ricci, J. A., Chee, E., Hahn, S. R., & Morganstein, D. (2003). Cost of lost productive work time among US workers with depression. *JAMA, 289*(23), 3135–3144.

Stieglitz, J., Gurven, M., Kaplan, H., & Winking, J. (2012). Infidelity, jealousy, and wife abuse among Tsimane forager-farmers: Testing evolutionary hypotheses of marital conflict. *Evolution and Human Behavior, 33*(5), 438–448.

Stieglitz, J., Kaplan, H. S., Gurven, M. D., Winking, J., & Tayo, B. V. (2011). Spousal violence and paternal disinvestment among Tsimane' forager-horticulturalists. *American Journal of Human Biology, 23*(4), 445–457.

Stieglitz, J., Trumble, B. C., Thompson, M. E., Blackwell, A. D., Kaplan, H., & Gurven, M. (2015). Depression as sickness behavior? A test of the host defense hypothesis in a high pathogen population. *Brain, Behavior, and Immunity, 49*, 130–139.

Stone, T. T., & Burris, B. C. (1950). Melancholia: Clinical study of fifty selected cases. *Journal of the American Medical Association, 142*(3), 165–168.

Sweeney, P. D., Anderson, K., & Bailey, S. (1986). Attributional style in depression: A meta-analytic review. *Journal of Personality and Social Psychology, 50*(5), 974–991.

Syme, K. L., Garfield, Z. H., & Hagen, E. H. (2016). Testing the bargaining vs. inclusive fitness models of suicidal behavior against the ethnographic record. *Evolution and Human Behavior, 37*(3), 179–192.

Syme, K. L., & Hagen, E. H. (2019). When saying "sorry" isn't enough: Is some suicidal behavior a costly signal of apology? *Human Nature, 30*(1), 117–141.

Syme, K. L., & Hagen, E. H. (2020). Mental health is biological health: Why tackling "diseases of the mind" is an imperative for biological anthropology in the 21st century. *American Journal of Physical Anthropology, 171*, 87–117.

Syme, K. L., & Hagen, E. H. (2023). Bargaining and interdependence: Common parent-offspring conflict resolution strategies among Chon Chuuk and their implications for suicidal behavior. *American Anthropologist, 125*, 262–282.

ten Have, M., Graaf, R. de, Dorsselaer, S. van, Tuithof, M., Kleinjan, M., & Penninx, B. W. J. H. (2018). Recurrence and chronicity of major depressive disorder and their risk indicators in a population cohort. *Acta Psychiatrica Scandinavica, 137*(6), 503–515.

ten Have, M., Penninx, B. W. J. H., Tuithof, M., Dorsselaer, S. van, Kleinjan, M., Spijker, J., & Graaf, R. de. (2017). Duration of major and minor depressive episodes and associated risk indicators in a psychiatric epidemiological cohort study of the general population. *Acta Psychiatrica Scandinavica, 136*(3), 300–312.

Tennant, C. (2002). Life events, stress and depression: A review of recent findings. *Australian & New Zealand Journal of Psychiatry, 36*(2), 173–182.

Theorell, T., Hammarström, A., Aronsson, G., Träskman Bendz, L., Grape, T., Hogstedt, C., Marteinsdottir, I., Skoog, I., & Hall, C. (2015). A systematic review including meta-analysis of work environment and depressive symptoms. *BMC Public Health, 15*(1), 738. https://doi.org/10.1186/s12889-015-1954-4

Thornhill, N. W., & Thornhill, R. (1991). An evolutionary analysis of psychological pain following human (*Homo sapiens*) rape: IV. The effect of the nature of the sexual assault. *Journal of Comparative Psychology, 105*(3), 243–252.

Thornhill, N. W., & Thornhill, R. (1990a). An evolutionary analysis of psychological pain following rape. III: Effects of force and violence. *Aggressive Behavior, 16*(5), 297–320.

Thornhill, N. W., & Thornhill, R. (1990b). An evolutionary analysis of psychological pain following rape: I. The effects of victim's age and marital status. *Ethology and Sociobiology, 11*(3), 155–176.

Thornhill, N. W., & Thornhill, R. (1990c). An evolutionary analysis of psychological pain following rape: II. The effects of stranger, friend, and family-member offenders. *Ethology and Sociobiology, 11*(3), 177–193.

Thornhill, R., & Furlow, F. B. (1998). Stress and human behavior: Attractiveness, women's sexual development, postpartum depression, and baby's cry. In Anders Pape Møller, Manfred Milinski, Peter J.B. Slater (Eds.), *Advances in the study of behavior* (Vol. 27, pp. 319–369). Academic Press.

Thornhill, R., & Thornhill, N. W. (1989). The evolution of psychological pain. In R. W. Bell & N. J. Bell (Eds) *Sociobiology and the social sciences* (pp. 73–103). Texas Tech University Press.

Tiokhin, L. (2016). Do symptoms of illness serve signaling functions? (hint: yes). *The Quarterly Review of Biology, 91*(2), 177–195.

Titiev, M. (1944). *Old Oraibi: A study of the Hopi Indians of Third Mesa*. Published by the Museum.

Tomasello, M., Melis, A. P., Tennie, C., Wyman, E., & Herrmann, E. (2012). Two key steps in the evolution of human cooperation: The interdependence hypothesis. *Current Anthropology, 53*(6), 673–692.

Tooby, J., & Cosmides, L. (1990). The past explains the present. *Ethology and Sociobiology, 11*(4–5), 375–424.

Trimmer, P. C., Higginson, A. D., Fawcett, T. W., McNamara, J. M., & Houston, A. I. (2015). Adaptive learning can result in a failure to profit from good conditions: Implications for understanding depression. *Evolution, Medicine, and Public Health, 2015* (1), 123–135.

Trivers, R. L. (1974). Parent-offspring conflict. *Integrative and Comparative Biology, 14*(1), 249–264.

Turner, E. H., Matthews, A. M., Linardatos, E., Tell, R. A., & Rosenthal, R. (2008). Selective publication of antidepressant trials and its influence on apparent efficacy. *New England Journal of Medicine, 358*(3), 252–260.

Uddin, R., Burton, N. W., Maple, M., Khan, S. R., & Khan, A. (2019). Suicidal ideation, suicide planning, and suicide attempts among adolescents in 59 low-income and middle-income countries: A population-based study. *The Lancet Child & Adolescent Health, 3*(4), 223–233.

Uthman, O. A., Lawoko, S., & Moradi, T. (2009). Factors associated with attitudes towards intimate partner violence against women: A comparative analysis of 17 sub-Saharan countries. *BMC International Health and Human Rights, 9*(1), 14, https://doi.org/10.1186/1472-698X-9-14 .

Wakefield, J. C. (1992). The concept of mental disorder: On the boundary between biological facts and social values. *American Psychologist, 47*(3), 373–388. https://doi.org/10.1037/0003-066X.47.3.373Wakefield, J. C. (2013). The DSM-5 debate over the bereavement exclusion: Psychiatric diagnosis and the future of empirically supported treatment. *Clinical Psychology Review, 33*(7), 825–845.

Wakefield, J. C., Schmitz, M. F., First, M. B., & Horwitz, A. V. (2007). Extending the bereavement exclusion for major depression to other losses: Evidence from the National Comorbidity Survey. *Archives of General Psychiatry, 64*(4), 433–440.

Wang, G.-F., Han, A.-Z., Zhang, G.-B., Xu, N., Xie, G.-D., Chen, L.-R., Yuan, M.-Y., & Su, P.-Y. (2020). Sensitive periods for the effect of bullying victimization on suicidal behaviors among university students in China: The roles of timing and chronicity. *Journal of Affective Disorders, 268*, 12–19.

Watson, P. J., & Andrews, P. W. (2002). Toward a revised evolutionary adaptationist analysis of depression: The social navigation hypothesis. *Journal of Affective Disorders, 72*(1), 1–14.

Whisman, M. A., & Uebelacker, L. A. (2009). Prospective associations between marital discord and depressive symptoms in middle-aged and older adults. *Psychology and Aging, 24*(1), 184–189.

Williams, G. C. (1966). *Adaptation and natural selection: A critique of some current evolutionary thought*. Princeton University Press.

Wilson, M., & Daly, M. (1998). Lethal and nonlethal violence against wives and the evolutionary psychology of male sexual proprietariness. In R. E. Dobash & R. P. Dobash (Eds.), *Rethinking Violence against women* (pp. 199–230). SAGE Publications.

Wolpert, L. (1999). *Malignant sadness: the anatomy of depression*. Faber & Faber.

Woźniak, N. J., & Sicard, A. (2018). Evolvability of flower geometry: Convergence in pollinator-driven morphological evolution of flowers. *Seminars in Cell & Developmental Biology, 79*, 3–15.

Wrzus, C., Hänel, M., Wagner, J., & Neyer, F. J. (2013). Social network changes and life events across the life span: A meta-analysis. *Psychological Bulletin, 139*(1), 53–80.

Zahavi, A. (1975). Mate selection: A selection for a handicap. *Journal of Theoretical Biology, 53*(1), 205–214.

Zahavi, A. (1977). Reliability in communication systems and the evolution of altruism. In B. Stonehouse & C. M. Perrins (Eds.), *Evolutionary ecology* (pp. 253–259). Macmillan.

Zeman, J., & Garber, J. (1996). Display rules for anger, sadness, and pain: It depends on who is watching. *Child Development, 67*(3), 957–973.

Zisook, S. (2013, February 25). Getting past the grief over grief. *Scientific American Blog Network*. https://blogs.scientificamerican.com/guest-blog/getting-past-the-grief-over-grief/. Accessed October 15, 2020.

CHAPTER 60

Evolutionary Perspectives on Eating Disorders

Riadh Abed

Abstract

Eating disorders (primarily anorexia and bulimia nervosa) are of particular interest to evolutionists for a number of reasons. These include the claim that they are evolutionarily novel, that they have increased in prevalence in developed countries in recent decades, their large female preponderance, and the fact that they have the highest risk of mortality of any psychiatric disorder. These, have led to a proliferation of theoretical etiological models. Some of these features increase the possibility that evolutionary approaches dealing with ultimate causation may facilitate our understanding of proximate causes. A review of the current evolutionary literature suggests that the sexual competition hypothesis has, so far, had the strongest empirical support from clinical and nonclinical studies. While other evolutionary theories focus on anorexia nervosa, the sexual competition hypothesis offers an explanation for both anorexia nervosa and bulimia nervosa and also explains the specific presentations of eating disorders in males.

Key Words: evolution, female competition, eating disorders, anorexia nervosa, bulimia nervosa

Introduction

The classification of eating disorders (EDs) was revised in the fifth edition of the *Diagnostic and Statistical Manual of Mental Disorders* (DSM-5; American Psychiatric Association, 2013) and now includes: anorexia nervosa (AN), bulimia nervosa (BN), and binge eating disorder (BED). The previous category of EDNOS (eating disorder not otherwise specified) which was used in DSM-IV for individuals with partial syndromes of eating disorders was renamed OSFED (other specified feeding or eating disorder) in the DSM-5. The DSM-5 OSFED includes: atypical AN, subthreshold BN, subthreshold BED, purging disorder, and night eating syndrome. The focus of this chapter will primarily be on AN and BN, as these are the main categories of eating disorders that have been discussed in the current evolutionary literature.

The DSM-5 criteria for AN and BN are outlined in Boxes 60.1 and 60.2. AN and BN share core features of morbid fear of fatness, distorted body image, and a pattern of behavior aimed at weight reduction, including purging, restriction of food intake, or excessive exercise—and this is also true for ICD-10 classification (World Health Organization, 1993; American Psychiatric Association, 2013). AN is characterized by low body weight, whereas BN is associated with binge eating and a normal body weight. The DSM-5 classifies AN into the restricting (AN-R) and binge eating/purging subtypes (AN-BP) (Box 60.1). Previously, female preponderance of EDs had been reported to be around 10:1 (Gordon, 1990). However,

> **Box 60.1** DSM-5 Criteria for Anorexia Nervosa
>
> A. Restriction of energy intake relative to requirements, leading to a significantly low body weight in the context of age, sex, developmental trajectory, and physical health. Significantly low weight is defined as a weight that is less than minimally normal or, for children and adolescents, less than that minimally expected.
> B. Intense fear of gaining weight or of becoming fat, or persistent behavior that interferes with weight gain, even though at a significantly low weight.
> C. Disturbance in the way in which one's body weight or shape is experienced, undue influence of body weight or shape on self-evaluation, or persistent lack of recognition of the seriousness of the current low body weight.
>
> AN Restricting type (AN-R): During the last 3 months, the individual has not engaged in recurrent episodes of binge eating or purging behavior (i.e., self-induced vomiting or the misuse of laxatives, diuretics, or enemas). This subtype describes presentations in which weight loss is accomplished primarily through dieting, fasting, and/or excessive exercise.
>
> AN Binge-eating/purging type (AN-BP): During the last 3 months, the individual has engaged in recurrent episodes of binge eating or purging behavior (i.e., self-induced vomiting or the misuse of laxatives, diuretics, or enemas).

> **Box 60.2** DSM-5 Criteria for Bulimia Nervosa
>
> A. Recurrent episodes of binge eating. An episode of binge eating is characterized by both of the following:
>   1. Eating, in a discrete period of time (e.g., within any 2-hour period), an amount of food that is definitely larger than what most individuals would eat in a similar period of time under similar circumstances.
>   2. A sense of lack of control over eating during the episode (e.g., a feeling that one cannot stop eating or control what or how much one is eating).
> B. Recurrent inappropriate compensatory behaviors in order to prevent weight gain, such as self-induced vomiting; misuse of laxatives, diuretics, or other medications; fasting; or excessive exercise.
> C. The binge eating and inappropriate compensatory behaviors both occur, on average, at least once a week for 3 months.
> D. Self-evaluation is unduly influenced by body shape and weight.
> E. The disturbance does not occur exclusively during episodes of anorexia nervosa.

more recent lifetime prevalence estimates have suggested a female preponderance of around 3:1 for both AN and BN. BN is more common than AN in both females and males, with lifetime prevalence rates for AN of 0.9% in women and 0.3% in men, whereas BN has a lifetime prevalence of 1.5% for women and 0.5% for men (Hudson et al., 2007). Nevertheless, those presenting for treatment are overwhelmingly female, with males accounting for only 1%–5% of patients with AN and 5%–10% of patients with BN (National Centre for Eating Disorders, 2020).

AN is known to run a more chronic course and has a poorer prognosis compared to BN (Keel et al., 2012; Steinhausen, 2002). AN is also associated with lower remission rates (50% for AN as opposed to 75% for BN) at 10-year follow-up (Keel & Brown, 2010). Both AN and BN can be associated with severe and debilitating symptoms, including thinning of the bones (osteoporosis), infertility, muscle wasting, worn tooth enamel, damage to the structure and function of the heart, brain damage, and multiorgan failure (NIMH, 2020; Sugermeyer, 2020). However, it is important to note that these serious symptoms are the consequences of the primary symptoms of AN and BN listed in Boxes 60.1 and 60.2 and are not the core symptoms of these disorders. Hence, a distinction between the primary and secondary symptoms of EDs is necessary for their proper understanding, as confusing them can lead to flawed theories and models. It is of particular concern that EDs have the highest mortality of any mental disorder, of around 5.9%–10% (Fichter & Quadflieg, 2016; Insel, 2012). In addition, evidence suggests significant heritability (Bulik et al., 2016; Yilmaz et al., 2015), with estimates of 33%–84% for AN and 28%–83% for BN (Zerwas & Bulik, 2011).

EDs show a number of unique and notable epidemiological features. Besides the marked female preponderance, these include the fact that both AN and BN are vastly more prevalent in developed, Western countries compared to developing countries, particularly when considering sub-threshold phenotypes (Katzman et al., 2004), and the evidence that there has been a significant increase in all EDs in recent decades (Russell, 2000). Furthermore, there are claims that this increase is spreading to developing countries in association with industrialization, urbanization, and Westernization (Erskine et al., 2016; Pike et al., 2014; Sugermeyer, 2020). Hence, a major paradox of EDs is that their incidence and prevalence are much higher in sociocultural environments where high-energy nutrition abounds (Nesse, 2017).

These rather puzzling features, together with the claim of their recent emergence, make EDs of particular interest to evolutionary scholars. The aim of the present chapter is to survey current medical/psychological thinking on EDs, with particular emphasis on extant evolutionary models. The evolutionary theories/hypotheses on EDs provide explanations at the ultimate or evolutionary level, which can be compatible with a range of proximate non-evolutionary theories (Abed, 1998). Hence, following Tinbergen (1963), the chapter will explore the evolutionary roots of EDs through an examination of both the phylogenetics and function of the presumed evolved psychological mechanisms involved in these disorders. To achieve this end, a raft of data from animal and anthropological studies will be considered in some depth and should help set the scene for a better understanding of the thinking behind many of the evolutionary models discussed and briefly evaluated later in the chapter.

Non-Evolutionary Theories of Eating Disorders

There is a wide range of non-evolutionary theories for EDs, perhaps reflecting our ignorance of their etiology. The theories can be classified broadly into biomedical and psychosocial theories (Russell, 2000). An incomplete list of such theories and models includes: Onset of Puberty Model (Bruch, 1978), Psychosomatic Families Model (Minuchin et al., 1978), thin ideal of Western culture (the cult of thinness) (Keel & Klump, 2003), the role of the media (e.g., Grabe et al., 2008), Peer Influence Model (e.g., Levine et al., 1994), Interpersonal Formulation Model (Rieger et al., 2010), Culture-Bound Syndrome Model (e.g., Gordon, 1990), Cognitive Biases Model (e.g., Fairburn et al., 1998), Emotional Regulation Model (Hawkins & Clement, 1984), Escape Model (Heatherton & Baumeister, 1991), biological and genetic theories (e.g., Klump et al., 2006; Klump et al., 2012), childhood sexual abuse, the role of personality disorders, the role of anxiety and depression, and the role of self-esteem (Li et al., 2014; Russell, 2000). A detailed review of the voluminous non-evolutionary literature is beyond the scope of the present chapter, and the interested reader should refer to the numerous standard texts on the subject.

It is of interest that despite the immense diversity of the non-evolutionary theories and the sheer volume of biological, psychological, and social research data on various aspects of EDs, none of the extant theories/models has gained wide acceptance, and neither have they yielded particularly effective treatments (Murray et al., 2019). As a result, the "multi-factorial model" remains popular among specialists in the field despite being recognized by authoritative opinion as having "little explanatory value" (Campbell, 1995; Russell, 2000).

By their nature, non-evolutionary theories focus on proximate causation and, therefore, fail to explain core features of these disorders, including: Why are females disproportionately affected? Why do they primarily affect females of reproductive age? Why are they much more prevalent in Western and Westernized countries? And why have they emerged/increased in recent decades? (Abed, 1998).

It is now widely accepted that many proximate causes are likely to be involved in the onset and maintenance of disordered eating. In addition, biological research, including the results of various behavioral genetics studies, suggests a significant genetic component. However, identifying specific genes with significant effects has remained elusive (Li et al., 2014).

Evolutionary Theories of Eating Disorders

There are a variety of evolutionary theoretical models for EDs (see Table 60.1 at the end of this section for a summary of evolutionary theories reviewed in this chapter). Unlike the non-evolutionary approaches, these deal with ultimate or evolutionary causation, attempting to answer the "why" question. Evolutionary psychologists/psychiatrists assume that all human thoughts, feelings, and behavior arise from evolved psychological mechanisms and the interaction of these mechanisms with environmental input (Buss, 1995). For example, while an evolutionary approach recognizes that food restriction can be harmful and even deadly, the motivation to restrict food intake may be adaptive under certain circumstances and for limited periods. Hence, evolutionary authors have attempted to explore possible evolved mechanisms underlying such motivations and the circumstances in which they can become overactivated and/or dysfunctional.

Most evolutionary theories have focused on AN; the exceptions are the Sexual Competition Hypothesis (Abed, 1998) and the more recent Mismatch Theories (Ayton & Ibrahim, 2020; Rantala et al., 2019). Two major evolutionary themes emerge from a review of the evolutionary literature on EDs: female competition and environmental mismatch. Given the importance of these two concepts in understanding the thinking behind most extant evolutionary models, a brief discussion of female competition and mismatch is warranted before tackling individual theories.

The Human Mating System and the Evolutionary Roots of Female Intrasexual Competition

Despite the wide variation in human mating practices cross-culturally, there are recurring features found in nearly all human societies. One core feature is the pair-bond between a male and female. Marriage, the distinctively human form of long-term mateship, is common to all human societies and forms the public acknowledgment of who has sexual access to whom, with divorce often resulting from extramarital relationships (Irons, 1983; Kramer & Greaves, 2011; Marlowe, 2003). However, typical of the range of behavioral variation expressed by humans, many exceptions exist, and sex is found outside of marriage both cross-culturally and among individuals within a society (Schacht & Kramer, 2019). Although data from a representative global sample of primarily pre-industrial societies indicates that polygynous

Table 60.1 Summary of Main Characteristics of Selected Evolutionary Theories on Eating Disorders

	Mismatch	Female Competition	Relevant to AN	Relevant to BN	Relevant to other EDs	Relevant to Male Syndromes	Supported by Empirical Evidence
Reproductive Suppression Hypothesis	Yes	Yes	Yes	No	No	No	Yes Non-clinical studies
Adapted to Flee Famine Hypothesis	Yes	Possibly	Yes	No	No	No	No
Parental Manipulation Hypothesis	No	No	Yes	No	No	No	No
Insurance Hypothesis	Yes	No	Yes	No	Yes (Obesity)	No	No
Social Threat Hypothesis	Yes	Possibly	Yes	No	No	No	No
Sexual Competition Hypothesis	Yes	Yes	Yes	Yes	Possibly	Yes	Yes Clinical and nonclinical studies
Extended Mismatch Hypothesis	Yes	Yes	Yes	Yes	Yes	Yes	No

marriage is sanctioned in nearly 85% of societies, upon closer inspection the majority of marriages in foraging societies are monogamous (Binford, 2001; Flinn & Low, 1986; Murdock & White, 1969). However, while most marriages are monogamous at any one point in time, over the life course, individuals may re-enter the marriage market more than once (Schacht & Kramer, 2019).

Chapais (2017) proposes that our hominid ancestors moved from a promiscuous mating system that likely characterized the last common ancestor of chimps and humans, to a pair-bonding system (that is frequently monogamous) via an intermediate, polygynous phase. Be that as it may, however, it is important to note that the human mating system is distinctive and peculiar compared to all other great apes and has resulted in the evolution of a suite of psychological mechanisms to manage the challenges that it presented. The distinctive feature of this pair-bonded mating system was the evolution of paternal investment and provisioning. This is unusual among primates and mammals generally. Also, an important byproduct of the establishment of stable breeding bonds is the transformative impact it has had on kinship structures in the human lineage (Chapais, 2017). Whereas paternity remained unknown among the promiscuous chimpanzees and bonobos, knowledge of paternity in the human mating system resulted in the evolution and the emergence of patrilineal kinship that has no counterpart in nonhuman primates. Hence, rather than dominance, rank, physical condition, and genetic quality being the main determinants of male mate value, as is the case in the majority of mammals, in humans, male willingness and ability to provision the female and her young became an important, even crucial, determinant of male mate value. This is due to the extraordinarily heavy burdens of pregnancy, lactation, and childcare through an extended childhood and juvenile dependence, which is compounded by reduced inter-birth intervals (compared to chimpanzees; Muller, 2017). This resulted in the need to simultaneously support multiple dependent offspring (e.g., Kaplan et al., 2000) which, in ancestral environments, could rarely be achieved by a lone mother and required biparental care and/or support from kin.

Paternal investment is ubiquitous in human societies and is rare among apes (Alger et al., 2020). Studies have found that, among foragers, men provide 85% of the protein and 65% of the total calories (Cordain et al., 2000; Kaplan et al., 2000; Marlowe, 2001), with positive effects on female fecundity and offspring immune function, health, and survival (Gurven & Hill, 2009). Further evidence of fitness benefits of male provisioning comes from reports that Ache juveniles with a living father had a one-third lower mortality than those whose fathers had died (Hill & Hurtado, 1996), although it should be noted that the effects of fathers on correlates of offspring fitness can vary across social and ecological contexts (e.g., Bribiescas et al., 2012; Hewlett & Macfarlan, 2010; Marlowe, 1999, 2001, 2005; Sear & Mace, 2008). Such conditions in our evolutionary past have shaped female psychology so that when assessing prospective long-term mates, cues of willingness and ability to invest in offspring are assessed, such as kindness, industriousness, and ability to acquire resources (Buss & Schmitt, 1993). Consistent with these findings, women find men's ability to provide resources attractive (Wang et al., 2018). It is unlikely that any of these attributes carry much importance to female chimpanzees or bonobos when seeking a mate. Why is this important? It is important because through tracing the phylogenetic roots of the human mating system we come to realize that aspects of human psychology related to mate attraction, retention, and mate choice, as well as the existence of long-term mateships, are evolutionarily novel and have emerged distinctively and uniquely within the human lineage and are not shared by our closest relatives (chimpanzees and bonobos), let alone other mammals. This is particularly important when animal models are considered. However, it is worth remembering that conditions such as EDs involve complex interactions of numerous systems, some more phylogenetically ancient than others.

Similarly, female mate value is shaped by the demands of the novel human pair-bond and high male investing mating system. In the promiscuous mating system of the chimpanzees and bonobos, any ovulating female (estrus is advertised by a conspicuous pink/red genital swelling) is worth copulating with, from a male's point of view, regardless of her age and condition, as the male invests no more than the time and energy involved in copulating and depositing sperm into the female. Hence, a female chimpanzee can mate with two dozen males in a single day, averaging five per hour (Muller & Pilbeam, 2017). As a result, the female chimpanzee appears to aim to mate with as many males in the troop as possible, probably as a strategy to confuse paternity and reduce the risk of infanticide (Muller et al., 2011). The female chimpanzee can often expect to mate with all the adult and adolescent males in her troop during a single ovarian cycle (Muller & Pilbeam, 2017; Wrangham, 2002). In contrast to chimpanzees and bonobos, who have no equivalent of human long-term mating strategies and for which males have no discernible bond with or investment in offspring, human males show much more involvement in provisioning and protection of the female and her offspring. The basis of the human mating system is the exchange of male investment in return for paternity assurance. Hence, within this pair-bonded mating system, a man's fitness became dependent on his female mate's fertility and fidelity. This does not mean, of course, that extra-pair copulations do not take place in humans. Studies suggest that men may be cuckolded around 3% of the time, perhaps slightly less often in some contexts and more often in others (Anderson, 2006; Bellis et al., 2005). However, non-paternity rates in human societies remain relatively low compared to other monogamous species and range from 0% to 11% across societies (Anderson, 2006; Simmons et al., 2004), with median values falling between 1.7% and 3.3%, while among monogamous birds these rates regularly exceed 20% (Griffith et al., 2002; Schacht & Kramer, 2019).

As a result, female reproductive potential became a crucial indicator of female mate value in humans, as the longer a man can monopolize a given woman's reproductive years, the greater are his fitness returns. Hence, men evolved particular sensitivity to cues of high reproductive potential (number of fertile years remaining), which involve primarily cues of youth and good health. In ancestral human environments these constituted the hour-glass nubile shape with evidence of fat deposits in the breasts, thighs, and buttocks, each of which is associated with increased fertility (Jasienska et al., 2004). These are the evolutionary roots of male visual sensitivity to cues of female physical attractiveness and also of women's motivation to display, preserve, and improve their physical attractiveness (signs of youth and good health) and thus increase their mate value (Abed, 1998; Sugiyama, 2016; Symons, 1979, 1995). It is worth noting that in ancestral human environments with relatively small population sizes, the task of finding and mating with a fecund female was no easy task. For example, Symons (1995) estimated that a Yanomamo (an indigenous South American tribe) woman would only be able to conceive on 78 out of the 8,030 days of her total reproductive life span if the time spent pregnant and lactating were taken into account. Sugiyama (2016) gave a similar estimate using hunter-gatherer data from other sources. Another important reason for the significance of youth in relation to fertility in women is the fact that women cease to reproduce many years before the end of their life span. Menopause is rare in other great apes but ubiquitous in humans. Among Ache women, the average age of last birth is 42 years and the mean age at last birth for women in 10 foraging societies is 34.9 years (Sugiyama, 2005). Therefore, it is likely that some ancestral females survived far beyond their reproductive years and continued to invest in their offspring well into adulthood (Sugiyama, 2016).

Hence, as a result of the pair-bonding mating system, psychological mechanisms adapted for long-term mating evolved and, unlike many nonhuman animals, human mate choice became almost invariably bidirectional (Adair et al., 2017). This means that both females and males must compete with members of the same sex for access to high-quality and high-investing mates; poor long-term mate choice is associated with high fitness costs for both men and women. This has resulted in the shaping of a mating psychology of choosiness in both males and females, which is strikingly different from the relatively indiscriminate mating behavior of chimpanzees and bonobos, where female competition for mates and male choosiness are either weak or largely absent (Parker, 1983).

While female competition in humans is subtler and more covert compared to males (Campbell, 2004), research suggests that ancestral women who were good intrasexual competitors experienced greater reproductive success than women who were less accomplished competitors (Fisher, Chapter 50 in this volume; Salmon, 2017).

So, in short, the evolution of pair-bonding and long-term mating strategies have had a direct and powerful impact on shaping intrasexual competition in both males and females. Whereas in chimpanzees and bonobos, females have little need to compete intrasexually for mates (although they still compete vigorously for rank and resources), humans of both sexes must also compete for long-term mates. Hence, men who paid close attention to the female's age, health, and other signs of fertility such as the nubile shape and were able to monopolize the reproductive years of a female of high reproductive potential would have left more progeny than their rivals. Similarly, women who correctly evaluated men for their ability and willingness to acquire and provide resources and who successfully attracted and retained such men in long-term mateships (marriages) would have had greater reproductive success than their rivals.

It should be added that while in the discussion thus far the emphasis has been on the evolution of psychological mechanisms governing the pair-bonded, long-term human mating system, both men and women may simultaneously pursue a complementary strategy of short-term mating which can yield sex-specific fitness payoffs (Buss & Schmitt, 1993; Pillsworth & Haselton, 2006).

Evolutionary Mismatch and the Emergence of Eating Disorders

There are claims that all EDs are novel conditions that have arisen in recent times within modern, industrialized, Western societies (Rantala et al., 2019). Others have asserted that BN is a new disorder that had arisen in the second half of the 20th century in developed, Western countries, and have also drawn attention to a significant rise in the incidence of both AN and BN across the Western world over recent decades (Russell, 2000). As a result, EDs may be considered prime examples of "Western disease" or "diseases of civilization" (Pollard, 2008) where evolutionary mismatch may have played a significant role. For these reasons, EDs have been of particular interest to evolutionary thinkers, and many of them have included aspects of mismatch in their models.

Evolutionary mismatch is arguably one of the most important Darwinian insights into the causation of novel diseases and disorders in the modern environment (Nesse & Williams, 1994). Mismatch is based on the fact that adaptations are shaped by selection to solve recurring problems of survival and reproduction in a given environment. If the environment changes too rapidly, this can result in an "adaptive lag" and can lead to dysfunctional or maladaptive outcomes (Crawford, 1995; Tooby & Cosmides, 1990). To understand mismatch, we should note that the human lineage lived for 99% of its evolutionary history in relatively small, mobile, foraging, kin-based groups. It is under these conditions that human psychological mechanisms were shaped by selection. The seeds for mismatch were sown with the advent of agriculture, which resulted in permanently settled living around 10,000–12,000 years ago (Li et al., 2018). There are numerous aspects of the modern environment that have attracted the attention of evolutionists, but mismatches within the sociocultural and nutritional domains have been of particular interest in relation to EDs.

One of the major strengths of evolutionary psychology relevant to mismatch is the introduction of the concept of evolved psychological mechanisms. These are specialized neurobiological systems shaped by selection to solve recurrent problems of survival and reproduction faced by humans over their evolutionary history (Tooby & Cosmides, 1992). An understanding of the function of evolved mechanisms provides unique insights into how and why these mechanisms can misfire, leading to maladaptive responses. An illustrative example of the derailing of an evolved mechanism is the way that the cuckoo exploits the innate parental feeding mechanism of certain bird species. The hatching cuckoo chick provides a supernormal stimulus that triggers a feeding response with a huge gaping beak in the nest of a different species (such as a great reed warbler) that induces the warbler to feed the cuckoo chick to the detriment of its own offspring (e.g., Tanaka et al., 2011). Mismatch can similarly lead to the derailment of evolved psychological mechanisms in humans when presented with an array of novel environmental conditions. The modern human environment diverges from the ancestral environment in a number of important ways. These include: living in much higher population densities (especially in urban settings), living among many strangers, reduced levels of kin support, constant abundance of food, exposure to mass media images, and many others. Hence, taking the effects of mass media in the modern environment as an example, it is suggested that women may respond to stimuli which are not of real female competitors but instead represent *supernormal stimuli* of virtual, hyper-attractive females, leading to maladaptive competitive responses in some women (Yong et al., 2017).

The Reproductive Suppression Hypothesis (RSH)

The Reproductive Suppression Hypothesis (RSH) for AN considers eating restriction a strategy to delay reproduction in times of disadvantageous environmental conditions by lowering the amount of body fat to a level incompatible with ovulation (Surbey, 1987; Voland & Voland, 1989; Wasser & Barash, 1983). This hypothesis rests on the assumption that not all conditions are equally favorable for reproduction (Wasser & Barash, 1983). For example, poor mental and physical health, lack of social support, and the existence of other environmental stressors can trigger the suppression of reproduction in the expectation that future conditions would become more favorable (Wasser & Barash 1983). Hence, the RSH proposes that AN is not itself an adaptation and that what was selected for is the ability of females to alter the timing of reproduction, with AN being a byproduct of this process that arises through mismatch by the unnaturally prolonged engagement of the reproductive suppression mechanisms as a result of novel environmental conditions (Locke & Arnocky, 2020; Salmon et al., 2008). Consistent with the RSH, women who perceive low levels of support from romantic partners and family are prone to dieting and do not feel ready for parenthood, suggesting that poor environmental conditions may be causal in the development of AN (Juda et al., 2004).

Salmon et al. (2008) conducted a study to test the RSH. They hypothesized that two main cues in the modern environment signaled unfavorable reproductive conditions: female-female social competition and unwanted sexual attention from males. They hypothesized that given women's reliance on cooperation with other females in childrearing, an environment characterized by intense female competition would signal low levels of support and lead to delaying reproduction. Unwanted male attention referred to conditions of the modern urban environment where population density is high and with large numbers of males, signaling the risk of compromised female choice (Salmon et al., 2008). Their findings offered some support for their hypotheses and hence for RSH, but the authors noted that other, more neutral kinds of stress also had the potential of increasing concern and dissatisfaction over weight and body shape (Salmon et al., 2008). Hence, the RSH suggests that whereas in ancestral environments such cues would have signaled the need for temporary postponement of reproduction, in the modern environment the intensity and duration of such experiences can lead to a concern with body image and fatness that escalates to anorexic-type behaviors and symptoms. Therefore, mismatch is a critical element of the RSH, where the perception of large numbers of high-quality female competitors may signal a poor reproductive environment, triggering an evolved mechanism to suppress ovulation, and this leads to excessive weight loss and maladaptive outcomes. The emphasis of the RSH on the pivotal role of the abnormally intense female competition in the modern environment creating a mismatch scenario leading to dysfunction shows an overlap with the Sexual Competition Hypothesis (SCH) and, hence, the two hypotheses are not necessarily mutually exclusive. However, unlike SCH, the explanatory scope for RSH is limited to AN given it is the only variant of EDs that involves suppression of ovulation.

A variant of the RSH was proposed by Linda Mealey (2000). Unlike the original RSH, which hypothesized the occurrence of reproductive self-suppression, Mealey's hypothesis suggested reproductive suppression is imposed upon subordinate females by dominant females, leading to AN, which was described as a "losing strategy." This hypothesis is also based on the idea of intense female competition that results in AN for the losers. While Mealey's hypothesis remains untested, the evidence suggests that AN patients are frequently high achievers and frequently have a high-status background, both of which, at least on the face of it, seem to go against AN being a subordinate or losing strategy (Abed et al., 2012).

Although plausible, the RSH has some limitations (Li et al., 2014). Aside from its exclusive focus on AN, the RSH does not directly explain the function of distorted body image or why some men are also afflicted. Also, it is of interest that amenorrhea is no longer considered to be a useful indicator of AN and has been deleted as a criterion for AN in DSM-5 (American Psychiatric Association, 2013).

Parental Manipulation Model
Parental manipulation is a variant of the RSH in which dominant parents, who are highly involved in controlling resources, induce reproductive suppression in their daughter(s) (Voland & Voland, 1989). Demaret (1991) suggested that AN may be an analogue to the phenomenon of the "helper at the nest" found in a number of species. This model draws on kin selection theory (Hamilton, 1964) and asserts that AN may be adaptive insofar as it increases the helping behavior of an individual with AN toward her own kin and thus aids their survival and reproduction while suppressing her own reproductive activity. Such a kin selection–based mechanism would have been particularly beneficial in large family units, which were prevalent in human history until recently (Li et al., 2014).

Males have greater reproductive potential than females in families with high status, because an abundance of resources contributes to male mate value more than female mate value (Trivers, 1972; Trivers & Willard, 1973). Thus, this model contends that by favoring the reproduction of male offspring over that of females, greater inclusive fitness will be achieved (Li et al., 2014).

Correlational studies have shown that AN individuals worry about the well-being of their families, and it is noted that family members possess mutually overprotective attitudes (Minuchin et al., 1975). Also, it is claimed that AN development is correlated with having dominant and overprotective mothers (Steiger et al., 2003) as well as overly controlling parents (Bruch, 1988). Moreover, studies conducted in pre-industrial societies have found that daughters born early (thus able to provide a greater contribution to the care of younger siblings) tend to increase their parents' reproductive success (Turke, 1989). In addition, the prevalence of arranged marriages over human evolutionary history (Apostoulou, 2007) suggests that parental interference in reproductive decisions of their offspring has been consequential and adds a degree of plausibility to this model. The parental manipulation model, however, does not account for the drive for thinness or AN behaviors that derive from sources external to the family. Nor does this model explain the recent increase in the incidence of AN and EDs generally, precisely in societies where overall fertility and parental influence have plummeted. Finally, no studies to date have demonstrated increased fertility in parents of AN patients.

Adapted-to-Flee-Famine Hypothesis (AFFH)
Guisinger (2003) proposed an evolutionary hypothesis that states that symptoms of AN evolved to cope with famine, whereby food restriction, denial of starvation, and hyperactivity represent an adaptive behavior that helped ancestral nomadic foragers to migrate from depleted environments to more promising surroundings in times of food shortages. The AFFH was prompted by curious features of AN that include self-starvation associated with heightened levels of activity. Li et al. (2014) suggest that the hypothesis is supported by data from both animal and human studies. They propose that the findings from a range of studies are consistent with the possibility that there are adaptations to deactivate desires for eating and activate traveling and suggest that AN may be an adaptive mechanism that benefited our ancestors faced with food shortages, motivating them to overcome the pain of hunger and energize them to migrate to more food-abundant locations.

Nevertheless, this model is problematic in a number of ways. First is the fact that prolonged food restriction is dangerous and potentially deadly (contributing to AN's high mortality) (Del Giudice, 2018; NIMH, 2020). Moreover, it is likely that food restriction in ancestral environments would have been even more hazardous than it is in the modern environment. Also, if the function of the adaptation is to move away from an area of food scarcity, the AFFH fails to explain why individuals with AN resist eating food when it is readily available (Del Giudice, 2018; Li et al., 2014). A further major weakness is the fact that the AFFH appears to confound consequences with causation (or primary with secondary symptoms) as the features of "fleeing famine" (e.g., restlessness and hyperactivity) represent the consequences of starvation that arise in AN as a result of self-imposed restriction of food intake (Nettersheim et al., 2018). Also, Guisinger's explanation for the sex difference in AN is unsatisfactory (Del Giudice, 2018), as it relies on ancestral humans' assumed patrilocality that involved females leaving their natal group to join their husband's group and, hence, that it would have been safer for females to travel further from home in search of food. However, contrary to AFFH, the anthropological record shows that men have a much larger exploration range than women and that, in contrast to the assumption of universal patrilocality, marital residence patterns in foragers are quite flexible (Alvarez, 2004; Del Giudice, 2018; Geary, 2010; Marlowe, 2004). Finally, there is the crucial question of what triggers the primary AN symptoms in the first place. Guisinger's explanation for the onset of AN appears to rely on female competition to attract mates: "In monogamous species females compete for good quality males. To this end, she tries to make herself as attractive as possible" and goes on to explain: "The current epidemic of eating disorders is a result of girls and women attempting to diet below their normal body weight to look more attractive by modern standards" (Guisinger, 2003, p. 754). These explanations render the AFFH more or less indistinguishable from the Sexual Competition Hypothesis (see below).

The Insurance Hypothesis (IH)
Although this hypothesis is primarily concerned with obesity, it makes specific predictions regarding AN. The IH proposes that the function of storing fat is to provide a buffer against shortfall in the food supply (Nettle et al., 2017). Thus, individuals should store more fat when they receive cues that access to food is uncertain. Nettle et al. (2017) suggest that IH is relevant to AN in two ways. First, the hypothesis predicts that AN will occur when the individual's estimate of their food security is unusually high. That is, if an individual has the perception that shortfalls will never occur, he or she should favor an extremely lean body and be motivated to maintain it. Support for this prediction comes from the evidence that AN risk, in contrast to obesity risk, is highest in families of relatively high socioeconomic position (Goodman et al., 2014). This prediction is also supported by the data that show higher rates of AN in high-income countries and in conditions in which there are high levels of food security. A second area of relevance to AN is treatment. If the abnormally high level of food security is causally significant in AN, then inducing some food insecurity, for example, by randomly varying feeding routines, might be useful in combating low body weight (Nettle et al., 2017). The authors concede that this is a contentious proposal, because AN patients are at considerable risk of starving themselves to death. However, they suggest that given that AN tends to run a chronic and disabling course, the food-insecurity perspective deserves further, if cautious, exploration.

The IH's primary focus is explaining obesity, and the explanation of AN is a useful byproduct. The hypothesis suggests that the perception of absolute food security (arising from mismatch) leads to the "shutdown" of food-consumption mechanisms, which in turn lead to AN. The model has echoes of an evolutionary model for the placebo effect in which the assurance of high levels of safety leads to the "shutting down" of other defenses, allowing the natural bodily healing mechanisms to be "switched on" (Humphrey & Skoyles, 2012) but with opposite valency. Nevertheless, the model has considerable face validity but also suffers from limitations. First, it is only relevant to AN and has no relevance to BN or other EDs. Also, it offers little explanation for AN's large female preponderance or for AN's major clinical features, such as the distorted body image.

The Social Threat Hypothesis for AN
Gatward (2007) proposed that AN is the outcome of competition for status within the group. As social animals, an individual's survival depends on group membership and acceptance by others, as exclusion from the group was risky, even potentially fatal in the ancestral past. Maintaining or improving status is thus of paramount importance, as status is an indicator of one's worth to the group and is strongly linked with access to reproductive resources. The argument is that, unlike in pre-industrial environments where fatness or at least plumpness was a sign of status, in modern Western environments where there is abundance of food, status becomes linked to self-control. Gatward's hypothesis relies on Guisinger's (2003) AFFH (see above), the RSH, and to a lesser extent Mealey's (2000) "losing strategy" hypothesis for AN. The Social Threat Hypothesis for AN closely resembles the Social Risk Hypothesis for depression (Allen and Badcock, 2003), where the risk of social exclusion results in a dysfunctional response (AN in the former and depression in the latter). The hypothesis shares a number of weaknesses with the AFFH, is difficult to test, and does not rule out alternatives (Li et al., 2014).

The Sexual Competition Hypothesis (SCH)
The Sexual Competition Hypothesis (SCH) attempts to explain both AN and BN, as well as the phenomenon of the drive for thinness that includes a spectrum of subclinical states (Abed,

1998). As we have seen, intrasexual competition occurs in both males and females, but some of the behavioral manifestations are sex-specific. The importance of physical attractiveness and nubile shape as a marker and visual cue for high reproductive potential in females has already been noted. Also, we saw that the significance of female reproductive potential relates specifically to the human mating system characterized by pair-bonding and high male investment. Uniquely, this system has given rise to the distinctive female intrasexual competition *for mates*. However, female strategies for intrasexual competition in humans evolved in small-scale foraging societies, a setting far removed from the modern, densely populated, urban, Western environments, with their ubiquitous mass media images of attractive females and abundance of nutrients. This creates a plethora of mismatches that crucially includes abnormally intense and persistent female intrasexual competition.

The SCH proposes that intense female intrasexual competition is the biological root for the drive for thinness, an adaptive response originally suited to small-scale, ancestral environments, and that the extreme version of this manifests itself in what we now recognize as EDs. Hence, the SCH proposes that a range of EDs (AN, BN, partial syndromes of both, as well as the drive for thinness) are manifestations of abnormally intense female intrasexual competition whereby females of reproductive age compete with each other in the novel environment of modern (Western and Westernized) cities through a strategy of "the pursuit of thinness" as a signal of youth (see below). This is claimed to lead to a state of "runaway female intrasexual competition," the extreme versions of which are EDs (Abed, 1998).

The SCH is based on the fact that throughout human evolutionary history, the female shape has been a reliable indicator of the female's reproductive history and, consequently, her reproductive potential (Bovet & Raymond, 2015; Singh, 1994). The same is not true for men, where physical appearance is still relevant, but provides less useful information about reproductive history or reproductive potential. Youth, good health, and nulliparity have always been the major determinants of female mate value as a result of the human mating system (see section on female competition above) and also because of the finite reproductive window in women that abruptly ends with menopause. The visual signal for a female's peak reproductive potential in ancestral environments was the female's nubile shape, which was generally short-lived and declined with the repeated cycles of gestation and lactation (Symons, 1979, 1995).

As good health has become ubiquitous in Western societies, it has declined in importance as a competitive signal. Therefore, according to SCH, signaling a youthful appearance became the primary means of female intrasexual competition (Abed, 1998). Studies have found that thinness in females (especially in Western societies) is consistently associated with youthfulness (Singh, 1994). Hence, according to SCH, female intrasexual competition in Western societies became focused on the preservation and/or the recreation of the nubile shape through the pursuit of thinness to display signs of youth. The SCH further proposes that other important socio-ecological factors serve to upregulate the intensity of female intrasexual competition in modern societies. These include the following (Abed et al., 2012; Nettersheim et al., 2018):

1. Female autonomy, which refers to the freedom of individual females to make mating decisions with relatively little interference from kin. This contrasts markedly with the situation during the majority of human evolutionary history (as well as in present-day traditional societies), where most of the important female mating decisions were made by parents and elders (Apostolou, 2007). This means that in a modern, Western environment, females must compete with other autonomous females in the mating market largely through their own efforts (Abed, 1998).

2. Living in modern cities, where females coexist in close proximity to and encounter abnormally high densities of other autonomous females.
3. Reduced fertility (birth rates) (Vining, 1986) has meant that females have increasingly managed to preserve their nubile shape beyond the age of nubility, thus creating the novel phenomena of the older but still nubile-looking woman, which further intensifies female intrasexual competition (Abed, 1998).
4. The particular Western brand of socially sanctioned monogamy, which, in contrast to polygamy, creates a shortage of eligible men in the marriage market (Henrich, 2020) and thus increases female intrasexual competition.
5. The ubiquity of abnormally attractive youthful nubile female images in the media that are mistaken for competitors (Ferguson et al., 2011; Li et al., 2018).

Therefore, the SCH is based on the idea that there is a mismatch between the design of the female's psychological adaptations for mate attraction and retention and for competing with rival females on the one hand, and the novel circumstances of the modern, Westernized urban environment on the other.

The SCH's claim for a common origin of AN and BN is based on the common features that include, besides female preponderance, the core psychopathological features of preoccupation with body shape and weight and a persistent pattern of behavior aimed at weight reduction (see Boxes 60.1 and 60.2). In addition, the line of demarcation between these two conditions can be clinically hazy, as many patients move between the diagnostic categories over time, with estimates of 15% moving from BN to AN and about 30% moving from AN to BN (Eddy et al., 2008).

Therefore, the explanatory value the SCH claims to offer goes beyond AN and extends to BN, partial syndromes of both, and also provides an explanation for the drive for thinness, the female preponderance, and the fact that these disorders affect primarily females of reproductive age, as well as their geographical distribution.

However, if both AN and BN are associated with abnormally intense female intrasexual competition as the SCH proposes, what factors determine who succumbs to one rather than the other? The SCH in its original form had no answer to this important question. Life history factors have been proposed as a promising avenue to explore (Abed et al., 2012).

LIFE HISTORY THEORY (LHT)

Life History Theory (LHT) posits that organisms allocate resources to either somatic effort or reproduction (Ellis et al., 2009; Stearns, 1992). Somatic effort includes growth and body maintenance/defense, whereas reproductive effort includes mating, parenting, and nepotistic effort, each of which can be offset or delayed in favor of the other (Del Giudice, 2018; Nettersheim et al., 2018). The trade-offs generate a spectrum of life-history strategies, with differences between and within species that are not functionally independent of one another, but that form a pattern of trait covariation that can be aligned on a one-dimensional scale ranging from slow to fast life-history patterns (Del Giudice, 2018; Ellis et al., 2009). Individuals who pursue a fast strategy invest more in reproductive than in somatic effort, and more in mating than parenting effort, while individuals who pursue slow strategies follow the reverse pattern (Figueredo et al., 2007). The trade-offs are between quality and quantity of offspring, the present and the future, and parental as opposed to mating effort. Fast strategies are associated with behavioral traits such as "impulsivity, short-term thinking, promiscuity, low female parental investment, little or no male parental investment, little social support, disregard for social rules, and extensive risk-taking" (Figueredo et al., 2006, p. 246). By contrast, slow strategies correlate with behavioral traits such as "long-term thinking, monogamy, high levels of parental investment, substantial social support structures, adherence to social rules (e.g., cooperation and altruism), and careful consideration of risks" (Figueredo et al., 2006, p. 245).

According to this view, one may argue that within the spectrum of EDs, individuals with BN are more likely to pursue fast life-history strategies, whereas individuals with AN are more likely to pursue slow life-history strategies (Abed et al., 2012; Nettersheim et al., 2018). Support for this contention comes from BN's association with heightened impulsivity, sensation seeking, novelty seeking, and borderline personality disorder (Cassin & von Ranson, 2005), as well as with early menarche and early sexual experiences (Kaltiala-Heino et al., 2001). Also consistent with this view is AN's association with low impulsivity, at least in AN-R (Waxman, 2009).

The application of LHT suggests that the risk of BN increases under conditions of intense female intrasexual competition associated with a fast life-history strategy, where competition is for short-term mates through the display of immediate fecundity, whereas the risk of AN increases with intrasexual competition combined with a slow life-history strategy, where females compete for long-term mates through the display of thinness and hence reproductive potential (Del Giudice, 2018). Therefore, the LHT version of SCH proposes that BN individuals are engaged in future discounting and immediate reproductive effort, whereas AN individuals are forgoing current reproduction in favor of doing so in the future (Nettersheim et al., 2018).

STUDIES TESTING SCH IN CLINICAL AND NONCLINICAL POPULATIONS

Predictions of SCH and LHT have been examined in a few nonclinical studies and in one explorative clinical study. Faer et al. (2005) were the first to explore the connection between female intrasexual competition and disordered eating behavior through studying questionnaire responses of American female undergraduates. The prediction was that intrasexual competition for mates would play a major role in BN, and intrasexual competition for status a major role in AN. The main findings of this study were that intrasexual competition for mates was the determining factor for both anorexic and bulimic tendencies, and intrasexual competition for status in those with anorexic tendencies was mediated through the influence of perfectionism. Hence, the findings of this study were supportive of the SCH.

Another study of American female undergraduate students measured indicators of a slow life-history strategy, disordered eating behavior, executive functions, and female intrasexual competitiveness for mates and for status (Salmon et al., 2009). This work found an inhibitory effect of a slow life-history strategy on disordered eating behavior, as well as on female intrasexual competitiveness via executive functions as mediator. No direct effect emerged of female intrasexual competition for mates or status on disordered eating behavior. Instead, the model predicted that the correlation between female intrasexual competitiveness and disordered eating behavior was attributable to the common causal influence of executive functions.

In a more recent study of female undergraduates in the United Kingdom testing the relationship between intrasexual competition, LHT, and abnormal eating behavior, a slow life-history strategy was negatively correlated with disordered eating behavior (Abed et al., 2012). Moreover, in line with Faer et al. (2005), this work reported that intrasexual competition was related to disordered eating behavior (Abed et al., 2012). It is important to note that both studies relied on nonclinical college student samples, in which AN and BN could not be adequately distinguished. Also, it is noteworthy that BN-related behaviors typically have a higher prevalence in such nonclinical populations.

In another study of undergraduate students in the United States by Li et al. (2010), male and female participants were exposed to profiles of individuals of average attractiveness with either high or low intrasexual competition cues. The high intrasexual competition cues led to more restrictive eating attitudes and body image concerns in heterosexual women and homosexual men, whereas homosexual women and heterosexual men showed no differences between the two sets of conditions. In addition, an investigation into the relationship between intrasexual competition for status and disordered eating behavior showed that exposure to thin, successful women resulted in greater body dissatisfaction in the participating women who scored high on status aspiration than in the participating women who scored low on status aspiration (Smith et al., 2011). This suggests that intrasexual competition for status may play a role in the development of eating disorders independent of intrasexual competition for mates.

There has, so far, been one small explorative study of a clinical population of AN and BN patients testing predictions of SCH and LHT (Nettersheim et al., 2018). The study included 20 patients with each diagnosis and 30 age-matched controls. The predictions were that patients with AN and BN will score higher than controls on measures of competition for mates and that patients with AN will score higher than BN and controls on measures of competition for status. Also, it was predicted that BN patients will show evidence of faster life-history strategy compared to both AN and controls.

These predictions were partially confirmed. BN was associated with several measures typical of a fast life-history strategy, whereas AN did not significantly differ from controls (age-matched female college students), which suggests that individuals with AN lie on the slow end of the life-history continuum. However, there was no direct relationship between disordered eating behavior and life-history strategies. This finding is in partial contrast to previous studies examining life-history strategies in connection with disordered eating behavior, which reported an inhibitory effect of a slow life-history strategy on disordered eating behavior, suggesting that EDs are associated with a fast life-history strategy (Abed et al., 2012; Salmon et al., 2009). The explanation for this result could be that neither of the two previous studies could differentiate between AN and BN due to their reliance on nonclinical samples. This interpretation is consistent with the higher prevalence of BN in community surveys (Hoek & van Hoeken, 2003) and also the higher levels of bulimic behavior scores in previous nonclinical studies (Nettersheim et al., 2018).

The significance of this study is that it is the first to test an evolutionary theory of EDs in clinical populations. The study found evidence of high levels of intrasexual competition in BN but not AN. The negative finding regarding intrasexual competition in AN is problematic for the SCH. However, when taking the whole sample of eating disorder patients together (AN and BN combined), there was evidence of increased intrasexual competition for mates with higher scores of abnormal eating behavior, thus lending partial support to the SCH in a clinical population with EDs. A major limitation of this study was that it was small and underpowered, which might explain the negative finding regarding intrasexual competition in the AN group. Also, the age ranges in this study were 18–30 years and thus would have excluded some cases of AN, which commonly has an earlier onset.

SCH, MALE INTRASEXUAL COMPETITION, AND THE DRIVE FOR MUSCULARITY

The existence of EDs in males has been a problem for a number of evolutionary formulations, especially those based on reproductive suppression and female competition. Interestingly, unlike females who present with the female-typical "drive for thinness" disorders that include AN and BN, males present (though less frequently) with two variants of body dissatisfaction.

In addition to "drive for thinness" variant that afflicts a proportion of males and is known to be associated with homosexuality (Abed, 1998; Calzo et al., 2017; Li et al., 2010), there is a second, newly recognized, male-typical variant of body dissatisfaction where young men focus on their upper body musculature, feeling it to be too small (Karazsia et al., 2017; Murray et al., 2016a; Pope et al., 2002). A particular strength of SCH is that it is the only evolutionary theory that can claim to explain both these variants. In the case of the drive for thinness in males (AN and BN), SCH's explanation is a partial one, as it can account for the existence of these disorders in homosexual men, who, like heterosexual women, aim to attract men and hence rely heavily on physical attractiveness (Abed, 1998), but the SCH has trouble accounting for male heterosexual patients who exhibit drive for thinness (Rantala et al., 2019). However, the drive for muscularity fits well into the SCH framework. It is argued that this particular variant of body dissatisfaction has evolutionary roots in male intrasexual competition, where intense competition between males is influenced by some of the same socio-ecological factors that affect female competition in the modern environment, but with a sex-specific bias. Although the influence of the modern Western environment on male competition appears to run in both directions, with socially sanctioned monogamy tending to reduce male competition (compared to polygynous societies) (Henrich, 2020), other factors may have the effect of increasing competition. These include living in urban environments with high population densities, as well as the influence of media images of high-status muscular men.

To understand the evolutionary roots of the drive for muscularity in males, it is necessary to explore the role of sexual selection in the evolution of human sexual dimorphism. Humans are moderately sexually dimorphic, with men, on average, around 20% heavier than women (Puts et al., 2016). This is below the threshold of dimorphism for polygynous species (60%) but above that for monogamous species (10%) (Archer, 2009; Clutton-Brock & Harvey, 1984; Marlowe & Berbesque, 2012). However, it has been argued that examining differences in weight alone in humans can be misleading, as females store much greater body fat than do other great apes, most probably to support the higher encephalization of the human fetus (Lassek & Gaulin, 2008). The fat-free sexual dimorphism in humans is significantly higher at 31%–43% (Lassek & Gaulin, 2009), and men possess 61% more lean muscle mass than women, including 50% more lower body muscle mass and 75% more arm muscle mass (Lassek & Gaulin, 2009). In addition, men show 90% greater upper-body strength, so that the average man is stronger than most women (Abe et al., 2003; Lassek & Gaulin, 2009)—not only due to higher lean body mass, but also because their muscles have shorter fibers and greater angles of pennation (Chow et al., 2000). It has been suggested that these sex differences in muscularity are comparable to those of gorillas, a highly sexually dimorphic, polygynous species (Puts et al., 2016; Zihlman & MacFarland, 2000). Furthermore, sex differences in aggression and violent behavior are evident cross-culturally, and this is particularly the case when examining the data on extreme violence resulting in homicide. Male-male homicide accounts for about 95% of all homicides (Daly & Wilson, 1988) and if war killings are included, the proportions of same-sex killings perpetrated by men would approach 100%. Across all 70 preliterate societies surveyed by Whyte (1978), men were vastly more likely than women to engage in warfare. Furthermore, there is evidence from at least one indigenous, preliterate South American society (the Yanomamo), where men who have killed other men acquire a special designation and have greater reproductive success compared to men who have not killed other men (Chagnon, 1988). No similar fitness advantage has been claimed for same-sex female homicides or other extreme violence.

Taken together, this evidence points to the importance of physical strength and specifically upper body strength in males for use in male intrasexual competition both for direct physical contests, as well as a visual signal of formidability to intimidate male rivals, over human evolutionary history (Puts et al., 2016). Importantly, upper body musculature would have also acted as a physical attractor to females (e.g. Fredrick & Haselton, 2007). Hence, the SCH uniquely provides a parsimonious explanation for the ultimate causation for the phenomenon of the "drive for muscularity" that can afflict some young men.

The Extended Mismatch Models of Eating Disorders

A number of authors have suggested that despite the explanatory power of the SCH, it remains incomplete. These evolutionists accept that intense female intrasexual competition is a pivotal and necessary factor in the causation of EDs including AN and BN, but argue that it is not sufficient (Ayton & Ibrahim, 2020; Rantala et al., 2019). Ayton and Ibrahim (2020) propose that nutritional mismatch focusing specifically on ultra-processed foods, prevalent in developed countries, with their potential pro-inflammatory and other deleterious effects, is a necessary additional ingredient in the causation of EDs, whereas Rantala et al. (2019) have proposed a multifaceted mismatch theory that includes modern nutrition but also incorporates the effects of stress and stress hormones, immune responses and pro-inflammatory cytokines, disruption in the composition of the microbiota, as well as the additional effects of a range of comorbidities. The explanatory scope of these evolutionary mismatch hypotheses goes well beyond AN and BN and includes binge eating disorder (BED), obesity, and other eating disorders, and extends to a range of medical conditions such as type 2 diabetes, coronary heart disease, and many other health problems prevalent in the modern environment (Li et al., 2018; Rantala et al., 2019).

Rantala et al.'s mismatch hypothesis for EDs proposes that the modern environment has led to an "adaptive metaproblem" (Al-Shawaf, 2016) through creating a fundamental conflict between the evolved psychological mechanisms for food consumption and those for mating. They propose that evolved psychological mechanisms responsible for food intake (Al-Shawaf, 2016; King, 2013; Love & Sulikowski, 2018; Rolls, 2017) and those responsible for mating (Weekes-Shackelford & Shackelford, 2014) that functioned harmoniously in ancestral environments became conflicted in the conditions of the modern environment. The novel conditions of the abundance of calorically dense nutrients creates a novel situation where the previously co-adapted mechanisms of food intake and mating become antagonistic and where individuals become torn between food rewards and mating rewards. This antagonism, they suggest, drives the adaptive metaproblem in contemporary humans, manifesting ultimately in various forms of EDs (Rantala et al., 2019).

These theories attempt to integrate a range of well-known mismatches, together with data on proximate factors, into a unified model that explains the existence of these novel disorders, accounts for individual differences, and also explains the shifts from one presentation or variant to another (Rantala et al., 2019). They propose that their model shows that rather than being clinically separate conditions, EDs lie on a continuum, with binge eating disorder at one end, AN-Restrictive at the other end, and BN and AN-bingeing/purging located in between. They suggest that our improved understanding of the role of stress, neuroinflammation, and gut dysbiosis in the etiology of eating disorders lends support to this continuum model.

These recently proposed mismatch models build on the SCH and integrate a wide range of data that improve the original SCH's explanatory power. The models are an important addition to the evolutionary literature on EDs and show considerable promise in terms of furthering our understanding of both proximate and ultimate causation of EDs, as well as for future therapeutic interventions.

Conclusion and Future Directions

An evolutionary analysis of EDs illustrates the relevance of ultimate causation to the understanding of disease and dysfunction. It shows how the consideration of the phylogenetics and function of evolved psychological mechanisms can help identify potential proximate causal mechanisms and complement existing explanations by supplying missing ultimate considerations. Table 60.1 shows that mismatch is an important element in the majority of the evolutionary models surveyed, despite their diverse underlying assumptions. The idea of mismatch provides conceptual tools to understand why previously adaptive strategies/mechanisms can become maladaptive, even destructive, when environmental conditions change radically and rapidly. The mistake by some in the field of EDs of dismissing evolutionary explanations because of AN's damaging effect on fitness is to misunderstand some of the basic tenets of evolutionary medicine (e.g., Murray et al., 2016b). Mismatch is one of an array of evolutionary explanations for the existence and persistence of disease and disorder (Nesse & Williams, 1994) that remain poorly understood (Abed & St John-Smith, 2021). It should be evident from the present review that non-evolutionary explanations that focus exclusively on proximate causation and neglect ultimate causation remain necessarily incomplete.

Like all models, evolutionary models and hypotheses may not be correct, but they must be testable, even if indirectly, and it is clear that some of the evolutionary theories on EDs discussed in this chapter are testable and refutable. This should help dispel accusations of being "just so stories."

Currently, the SCH is the evolutionary model for EDs with the greatest theoretical consistency and empirical support (Li et al., 2014; Locke & Arnocky, 2020; Rantala et al, 2019), whereas the extended mismatch hypothesis (an extension of the SCH) is the model that shows the greatest explanatory scope and promise for the future (but other evolutionary theories reviewed in this chapter may well prove to be relevant to AN).

Nevertheless, evolutionary models of EDs have a long way to go to prove their worth to clinical practitioners. Evolutionary approaches remain underappreciated in psychiatry and medicine generally, and this is not limited to the field of EDs (Abed & St John-Smith, 2021). The reasons for this are many and varied, but it falls to evolutionists to demonstrate the value and utility of the application of Darwinian principles to the understanding of disease and disorder. Thus far, evolutionary psychiatry has largely been a theoretical enterprise generating interesting models and drawing attention to Darwinian dynamics affecting health and disease. This is undoubtedly valuable, even essential, but it is not enough.

The field of EDs may particularly lend itself to the promotion of evolutionary thinking in the psychiatric and medical communities given their unique set of characteristics. However, if an evolutionary approach is to make inroads into mainstream psychiatric and medical thinking, large-scale clinical studies of promising evolutionary models of EDs will be required, both to test their predictions and to rigorously evaluate possible interventions arising from them.

Acknowledgment

I am grateful to Paul St John-Smith and to the editors for their valuable comments on previous drafts of this chapter.

References

Abe, T., Kearns, C. F., & Fukunaga, T. (2003). Sex differences in whole body skeletal muscle mass measured by magnetic resonance imaging and its distribution in young Japanese adults. *British Journal of Sports Medicine, 37*, 436–440.

Abed, R., Mehta, S., Figueredo, A. J., Aldridge, S., Balson, H., Meyer, C. & Palmer, R. (2012). Eating disorders and intrasexual competition: Testing an evolutionary hypothesis among young women. *The Scientific World Journal*, 290813. doi: 10.1100/2012/ 290813

Abed, R., & St John-Smith, P. (2021). Evolutionary psychology and psychiatry. In T. K. Shackelford (Ed.), *The Sage handbook of evolutionary psychology* (pp 24–50). Sage Publications.

Abed, R. T. (1998). The sexual competition hypothesis for eating disorders. *British Journal of Medical Psychology, 71*, 525–547. doi: 10.1111/j.2044-8341.1998.tb01007.x

Adair, L. E., Dillon, H. M., & Brase, G. L. (2017). I'll have who she's having: Mate copying, mate poaching, and mate retention. In M. L. Fisher-MacDonnell (Ed.), *Handbook on women and competition* (pp. 319–336). Oxford University Press. http://dx.doi.org/10.1093/oxfordhb/9780199376377.013.2

Alger, I., Hooper, P. L., Cox, D., Stieglitz, J. & Kaplan, H. S. (2020). Paternal provisioning results from ecological change. *PNAS, 117*(20), 10746–10754. doi:10.1073/pnas.1917166117

Allen, N. B. & Badcock, P. B. (2003). The social risk hypothesis of depressed mood: Evolutionary, psychosocial and neurobiological perspectives. *Psychological Bulletin, 129*, 887–913.

Al-Shawaf, L. (2016). The evolutionary psychology of hunger. *Appetite 105*, 591–595. doi: 10.1016/j.appet.2016.06.021

Alvarez, H. P. (2004). Residence groups among hunter-gatherers: A view of the claims and evidence for patrilocal bands. In B. Chapais & C. Berman (Eds.), *Kinship and behavior in primates* (pp. 420–442). Oxford University Press.

American Psychiatric Association. (2013). *Diagnostic and statistical manual of mental disorders* (5th ed.). APA. doi: 10.1176/appi.books. 9780890425596

Anderson, K. (2006). How well does paternity confidence match actual paternity? Evidence from worldwide nonpaternity rates. *Current Anthropology, 47*, 513–520. doi: 10.1086/504167

Apostolou, M. (2007). Sexual selection under parental choice: The role of parents in the evolution of human mating. *Evolution and Human Behavior, 28*, 403–409. doi: 10.1016/j. evolhumbehav.2007.05.007

Archer, J. (2009). Does sexual selection explain human sex differences in aggression? *Behavioral and Brain Sciences, 32*, 249–266.

Ayton, A. & Ibrahim, A. (2020). The Western diet: A blind spot of eating disorder research? A narrative review and recommendations for treatment and research. *Nutrition Reviews, 78*(7), 579–596. https://doi.org/10.1093/nutrit/nuz089

Bellis, M. A., Hughes, K., Hughes, S., & Ashton, J. R. (2005) Measuring paternal discrepancy and its public health consequences. *Journal of Epidemiology and Community Health, 59*(9), 749–754. doi: 10.1136/jech.2005.036517

Binford, L. R. (2001). *Constructing frames of reference: An analytical method for archaeological theory building using ethnographic and environmental data sets*. University of California Press.

Bovet, J., & Raymond, M. (2015). Preferred women's waist-to-hip ratio variation over the last 2,500 years. *PLoS ONE, 10*, e0123284. doi: 10.1371/journal.pone. 0123284

Bribiescas, R. G., Ellison, P. T., & Gray, P. B. (2012) Male life history, reproductive effort, and the evolution of the genus Homo: New directions and perspectives. *Current Anthropology, 53*(6), 424–435. doi: 10.1086/667538

Bruch, H. (1978). *The golden cage: The enigma of anorexia nervosa*. Harvard University Press.

Bruch, H. (1988). *Conversations with anorexics*. Aronson.

Bulik, C. M., Kleiman, S. C., & Yilmaz, Z. (2016). Genetic epidemiology of eating disorders. *Current Opinion in Psychiatry, 29*, 383–388. doi: 10.1097/YCO. 0000000000000275

Buss, D. M. (1995). Evolutionary psychology: A new paradigm for psychological science. *Psychological Inquiry, 6*(1), 1–30. https://doi.org/10.1207/s15327965pli0601_1

Buss, D. M., & Schmitt, D. P. (1993). Sexual strategies theory: An evolutionary perspective on human mating. *Psychological Review, 100*(2), 204–232. https://doi.org/10.1037/0033-295X.100.2.204

Calzo, J. P., Blashill, A. J., Brown, T. A., & Argenal, R. L. (2017). Eating disorders and disordered weight and shape control behaviors in sexual minority populations. *Current Psychiatry Reports, 19*(8), 49. doi: 10.1007/s11920-017-0801-y

Campbell, A. (2004). Female competition: Causes, constraints, content, and contexts. *Journal of Sex Research, 41*, 16–26.

Campbell, P. G. (1995) What would a causal explanation of the eating disorders look like? In G. Szmukler, C. Dare & J. Treasure (Eds.), *Handbook of eating disorders: Theory, treatment and research* (pp 49–64). Wiley.

Cassin, S. E., & von Ranson, K. M. (2005). Personality and eating disorders: A decade in review. *Clinical Psychology Review, 25*, 895–916. doi: 10.1016/j.cpr.2005.04.012

Chagnon, N. A. (1988). Life histories, blood revenge, and warfare in a tribal population. *Science, 239*, 985–992.

Chapais, B. (2017) From chimpanzee society to human society: Bridging the kinship gap. In M. N. Muller, R. W. Wrangham, & D. R. Pilbeam (Eds.), *Chimpanzee and human evolution* (pp. 427–463). Belknap Press of Harvard University Press.

Chow, R. S., Medri, M. K., Martin, D. C., Leekam, R. N., Agur, A. M., & McKee, N. H. (2000). Sonographic studies of human soleus and gastrocnemius muscle architecture: Gender variability. *European Journal of Applied Physiology, 82*, 236–244.

Clutton-Brock, T. H., & Harvey, P. H. (1984). Comparative approaches to investigating adaptation. In J. R. Krebs & N. B. Davies (Eds.), *Behavioral ecology: An evolutionary approach* (2nd ed., pp. 7–29). Blackwell.

Cordain, L., Brand Miller, J., Boyd Eaton, S., Mann, N., Holt, S. H. A. & Speth, J. D. (2000). Plant-animal subsistence ratios and macronutrient energy estimations in worldwide hunter-gatherer diets. *The American Journal of Clinical Nutrition, 71*(3), 682–692. https://doi.org/10.1093/ajcn/71.3.682

Crawford, C. (1995). Environments and adaptations: Then and now. In C. Crawford & D. L. Krebs (Eds.), *Handbook of evolutionary psychology: Ideas, issues, and applications* (pp. 275–302). Lawrence Erlbaum Associates.

Daly, M., & Wilson, M. (1988). *Homicide*. Aldine de Gruyter.

Del Giudice, M. (2018). *Evolutionary psychopathology: A unified approach*. Oxford University Press.

Demaret, A. (1991). De la grossesse nerveuse a l'anorexie mentale. *Acta Psychiatrica Belgica, 91*, 11–22.

Eddy, K. T., Dorer, D. J., Franko, D. L., Tahilani, K., Thompson-Brenner, H., & Herzog, D. B. (2008). Diagnostic crossover of in anorexia and bulimia nervosa: implications for DSM-V. *American Journal of Psychiatry, 165*, 245–250. doi: 10.1176/appi.ajp. 2007.07060951

Ellis, B. J., Figueredo, A. J., Brumbach, B. H., & Schlomer, G. L. (2009). Fundamental dimensions of environmental risk: The impact of harsh versus unpredictable environments on the evolution and development of life history strategies. *Human Nature, 20*, 204–268. doi: 10.1007/s12110-009-9063-7

Erskine, H. E., Whiteford, H. A., & Pike, K. M. (2016). The global burden of eating disorders. *Current Opinion in Psychiatry, 29*, 346–353. doi: 10.1097/YCO. 0000000000000276

Faer, L. M., Hendriks, A., Abed, R. T., & Figueredo, A. J. (2005). The evolutionary psychology of eating disorders: Female competition for mates or for status? *Psychology and Psychotherapy: Theory, Research and Practice, 78*, 397–417.

Fairburn, C. G., Shafran, R., & Cooper, Z. (1998). A cognitive behavioral theory of anorexia nervosa. *Behavior Research and Therapy, 37*, 1–13.

Ferguson, C. J., Winegard, B., & Winegard, B. M. (2011). Who is the fairest one of all? How evolution guides peer and media influences on female body dissatisfaction. *Review of General Psychology, 15*(1), 11–28. https://doi.org/10.1037/a0022607

Fichter, M. M., & Quadflieg, N. (2016). Mortality in eating disorders: Results of a large prospective clinical longitudinal study. *International Journal of Eating Disorders, 49*, 391–401. doi: 10.1002/eat.22501

Figueredo, A. J., Vásquez, G., Brumbach, B. H., & Schneider, S. M. R. (2007). The K-factor, covitality, and personality: A psychometric test of life history theory. *Human Nature, 18*, 47–73. doi: 10.1007/BF02820846

Figueredo, A. J., Vásquez, G., Brumbach, B. H., Schneider, S. M. R., Sefcek, J. A., Tal, I. R., Hill, D., Wenner, C. J., & Jacobs, W. J. (2006) Consilience and life history theory: From genes to brain to reproductive strategy. *Developmental Review, 26*, 243–275. doi: 10.1016/j.dr.2006.02.002

Flinn, M. V., & Low, B. S. (1986). Resource distribution, social competition, and mating patterns in human societies. *Ecological Aspects of Social Evolution., 14*, 217–243.

Frederick, D. A., & Haselton, M. G. (2007) Why is muscularity sexy? Tests of the fitness indicator hypothesis. *Personality and Social Psychology Bulletin, 33*(8),1167–1183. doi: 10.1177/0146167207303022

Gatward, N. (2007). Anorexia nervosa: An evolutionary puzzle. *European Eating Disorders Review, 15*, 1–12. https://doi.org/10.1002/erv.718

Geary, D. C. (2010). *Male, female: The evolution of human sex differences* (2nd ed). APA Press.

Goodman, A., Heshmati, A. & Koupil, I. (2014) Family history of education predicts eating disorders across multiple generations among 2 million Swedish males and females. *PLoS ONE, 9*(8), e106475. http://doi.org/10.1371/journal.pone.0106475

Gordon, R. A. (1990). *Anorexia and bulimia: Anatomy of a social epidemic*. Wiley-Blackwell.

Grabe, S., Ward, L. M., & Hyde, J. S. (2008). The role of the media in body image concerns among women: A meta-analysis of experimental and correlational studies. *Psychological Bulletin, 134*(3), 460–476.

Griffith, S. C., Owens, I. P., & Thuman, K. A. (2002). Extra pair paternity in birds: A review of interspecific variation and adaptive function. *Molecular Ecology, 11*, 2195–2212. doi: 10.1046/j.1365-294X.2002.01613.x

Guisinger, S. (2003). Adapted to flee famine: Adding an evolutionary perspective on anorexia nervosa. *Psychological Review, 110*, 745–761. doi: 10.1037/0033-295X.110. 4.745

Gurven, M., & Hill, K. (2009). Why do men hunt? A reevaluation of "man the hunter" and the sexual division of labor. *Current Anthropology, 50*(1), 51–62.

Hamilton, W. D. (1964). The genetical evolution of social behavior. II. *Journal of Theoretical Biology, 7*, 17–52.

Hawkins, R. C., & Clement, P. F. (1984). Binge eating: Measurement problems and a conceptual model. In R. C. Hawkins, W. J. Fremouw, & P. F. Clement (Eds.), *The binge purge syndrome: Diagnosis, treatment, and research* (pp. 229–251). Springer.

Heatherton, T. F., & Baumeister, R. F. (1991). Binge eating as escape from self-awareness. *Psychological Bulletin, 110*, 86–108.

Henrich, J. (2020) *The weirdest people in the world: How the West became psychologically peculiar and particularly prosperous.* Allen Lane.

Hewlett, B., & Macfarlan, S. (2010) Fathers' roles in hunter-gatherer and other small-scale cultures. In M.E. Lamb (Ed.), *The role of the father in child development* (pp. 413–434). Wiley.

Hill, K., & Hurtado, M. (1996). *Ache life history*. Aldine.

Hoek, H. W., & van Hoeken, D. (2003). Review of the prevalence and incidence of eating disorders. *International Journal of Eating Disorders, 34*, 383–396. doi: 10.1002/eat.10222

Hudson, J. I., Hiripi, E., Pope, H. G., Jr., & Kessler, R. C. (2007). The prevalence and correlates of eating disorders in the national comorbidity survey replication. *Biological Psychiatry, 61*, 348–358. doi: 10.1016/j.biopsych.2006.03.040

Humphrey, N., & Skoyles, J. (2012). The evolutionary psychology of healing: A human success story. *Current Biology, 22*(17), R695–R698.

Insel, T. (2012). National Institute of Mental Health (NIMH): Spot-light on eating disorders. https://www.nimh.nih.gov/about/directors/thomas-insel/blog/2012/spotlight- on-eating-disorders.shtml. Accessed August 29, 2020.

Irons, W. (1983). Human female reproductive strategies. In S. K. Wasser (Ed.), *Social behavior of female vertebrates* (pp. 169–213). Academic Press.

Jasieńska, G., Ziomkiewicz, A., Ellison, P. T., Lipson, S. F., & Thune, I. (2004) Large breasts and narrow waists indicate high reproductive potential in women. *Proceedings of the Royal Society B: Biological Sciences, 271*(1545), 1213–1217. doi: 10.1098/rspb.2004.2712.

Juda, M. N., Campbell, L., & Crawford, C. B. (2004). Dieting symptomatology in women and perceptions of social support: An evolutionary approach. *Evolution and Human Behavior, 25*, 200–208. https://doi.org/ 10.1016/j.evolhumbehav.2004.02.001.

Kaltiala-Heino, R., Rimpelä, M., Rissanen, A., & Rantanen, P. (2001). Early puberty and early sexual activity are associated with bulimic-type eating pathology in middle adolescence. *Journal of Adolescent Health, 28*, 346–352. doi: 10.1016/ S1054- 139X(01)00195- 1

Kaplan, H. S., Hill, K. R., Lancaster, J. B., & Hurtado, A. M. (2000). A theory of life history evolution: Diet intelligence and longevity. *Evolutionary Anthropology, 9*, 156–185.

Karazsia, B. T., Murnen, S. K., & Tylka, T. L. (2017). Is body dissatisfaction changing across time? A cross-temporal meta-analysis. *Psychological Bulletin, 143*(3), 293–320. https://doi.org/10.1037/bul0000081

Katzman, M. A., Hermans, K. M. E., van Hoeken, D., & Hoek, H. W. (2004). Not your "typical island woman": Anorexia nervosa is reported only in subcultures in Curaçao. *Culture, Medicine, and Psychiatry, 28*, 463–492. doi: 10.1007/s11013-004-1065-7

Keel, P. K., & Brown, T. A. (2010). Update on course and outcome in eating disorders. *International Journal of Eating Disorders, 43*, 195–204. doi: 10.1002/eat.20810

Keel, P. K., Brown, T. A., Holland, L. A., & Bodell, L. P. (2012) Empirical classification of eating disorders. *Annual Review of Clinical Psychology, 8*, 381–404. doi: 10.1146/annurev-clinpsy-032511-143111

Keel, P. K., & Klump, K. L. (2003). Are eating disorders culture-bound syndromes? Implications for conceptualizing their etiology. *Psychological Bulletin, 129*, 747–769.

King, B. M. (2013). The modern obesity epidemic, ancestral hunter-gatherers, and the sensory/reward control of food intake. *American Psychologist, 68*, 88–96. doi: 10.1037/a0030684

Klump, K. L., Culbert, K. M., Slane, J. D., Burt, S. A., Sisk, C. L., & Nigg, J. T. (2012). The effects of puberty on genetic risk for disordered eating: Evidence for a sex difference. *Psychological Medicine, 42*, 627–637.

Klump, K. L., Gobrogge, K. L., Perkins, P. S., Thorne, D., Sisk, C. L., & Breedlove, S. (2006). Preliminary evidence that gonadal hormones organize and activate disordered eating. *Psychological Medicine, 36*, 539–546.

Kramer, K. L., & Greaves, R. D. (2011). Postmarital residence and bilateral kin associations among hunter-gatherers. *Human Nature, 22*, 41. doi: 10.1007/s12110-011-9115-7

Lassek, W. D., & Gaulin, S. (2008). Waist-hip ratio and cognitive ability: Is gluteofemoral fat a privileged store of neurodevelopmental resources? *Evolution and Human Behavior, 29*, 26–34.

Lassek, W. D., & Gaulin, S. J. C. (2009). Costs and benefits of fat-free muscle mass in men: Relationship to mating success, dietary requirements, and natural immunity. *Evolution and Human Behavior, 30*, 322–328.

Levine, M. P., Smolak, L., & Hayden, H. (1994). The relation of sociocultural factors to eating attitudes and behaviors among middle school girls. *Journal of Early Adolescence, 14*, 471–490.

Li, N. P., Smith, A. R., Griskevicius, V., Cason, M. J., & Bryan, A. (2010). Intrasexual competition and eating restriction in heterosexual and homosexual individuals. *Evolution and Human Behavior, 31*, 365–372. doi: 10.1016/j.evolhumbehav.2010. 05.004

Li, N. P., Smith, A. R., Yong, J. C., & Brown, T. A. (2014). Intrasexual competition and other theories of eating restriction. In V. Weekes-Shackelford & T. Shackelford (Eds.), *Evolutionary perspectives on human sexual psychology and behavior* (pp. 323–346). Springer. https://doi.org/10.1007/978-1-4939-0314-6_17

Li, N. P., van Vugt, M., & Colarelli, S. M. (2018) The evolutionary mismatch hypothesis: Implications for psychological science. *Current Directions in Psychological Science, 27*(1), 38–44. doi:10.1177/0963721417731378

Locke, A., & Arnocky, S. (2020) Eating disorders. In T. K. Shackelford & V. A. Weekes-Shackelford (Eds.), *Encyclopedia of evolutionary psychological science*. Springer. https://doi.org/10.1007/978-3-319-16999-6_696-1

Love, H., & Sulikowski, D. (2018). Of meat and men: Sex differences in implicit and explicit attitudes towards meat. *Frontiers in Psychology, 9*, 559. doi: 10.3389/fpsyg. 2018.00559

Marlowe, F. (2001). Male contribution to diet and female reproductive success among foragers. *Current Anthropology, 42*, 755–760.

Marlowe, F. (2004). Martial residence among foragers. *Current Anthropology, 45*, 277–284.

Marlowe, F. W. (1999). Showoffs or providers? The parenting effort of Hadza men. *Evolution and Human Behavior, 20*, 391–404.

Marlowe, F. W. (2003). The mating system of foragers in the Standard Cross-Cultural Sample. *Cross-Cultural Research: The Journal of Comparative Social Science, 37*(3), 282–306. https://doi.org/10.1177/1069397103254008

Marlowe, F. W. (2005). Hunter-gatherers and human evolution. *Evolutionary Anthropology, 14*, 54–67.

Marlowe, F. W., & Berbesque, J. C. (2012). The human operational sex ratio: Effects of marriage, concealed ovulation, and menopause on mate competition. *Journal of Human Evolution, 63*, 834–842.

Mealey, L. (2000). Anorexia: A "losing" strategy? *Human Nature, 11*, 105–116. https://doi.org/10.1007/s12 110-000-1005-3

Minuchin, S., Baker, L., Rosman, B. L., Liebman, R., Milman, L., & Todd, T. C. (1975). A conceptual model of psychosomatic illness in children. *Archives of General Psychiatry, 32*, 1031–1038.

Minuchin, S., Rosman, B. L., & Baker, L. (1978). *Psychosomatic families: Anorexia nervosa in context*. Harvard University Press.

Muller, M. N. (2017). Introduction. In M. N. Muller, R. W. Wrangham, & D. R. Pilbeam (Eds.), *Chimpanzee and human evolution* (pp. 3–21). Belknap Press of Harvard University Press.

Muller, M. N. & Pilbeam, D.R. (2017). The evolution of the human mating system. In M. N. Muller, R. W. Wrangham, & D. R. Pilbeam (Eds.), *Chimpanzee and human evolution* (pp. 427–463). Belknap Press of Harvard University Press.

Muller, M. N., Thompson, M. E., Kahlenberg, S. M., & Wrangham, R. W. (2011). Sexual coercion by male chimpanzees shows that female choice may be more apparent than real. *Behavioral Ecology and Sociobiology, 65*(5), 921–933.

Murdock, G. P., & White, D. R. (1969). Standard cross-cultural sample. *Ethnology, 8*, 329–369. doi: 10.2307/3772907

Murray, S., Griffiths, S., & Mond, J. (2016a). Evolving eating disorder psychopathology: Conceptualising muscularity-oriented disordered eating. *British Journal of Psychiatry, 208*(5), 414–415. doi:10.1192/bjp.bp.115.168427

Murray, S., Griffiths, S., & Mond, J. (2016b). Evolutionary theories in eating disorders (Authors' reply). *British Journal of Psychiatry, 209*(4), 352. https://doi.org/10.1192/bjp.209.4.352

Murray, S. B., Quintana, D. S., Loeb, K. L., Griffiths, S., & Le Grange, D. (2019). Treatment outcomes for anorexia nervosa: A systematic review and meta-analysis of randomized controlled trials. *Psychological Medicine, 49*, 535–544. https://doi.org/10.1017/S0033291718002088

National Centre for Eating Disorders. (2020). https://eating-disorders.org.uk/information/eating-disorders-in-males/). Accessed August 29, 2020.

National Institute of Mental Health (NIMH). (2020). Eating disorders. https://www.nimh.nih.gov/health/publications/eating-disorders/index.shtml. Accessed August 29, 2020.

Nesse, R. M. (2017). Anorexia: A perverse effect of attempting to control the starvation response. *Behavioral and Brain Sciences, 40*, 31–32. doi: 10.1017/ S0140525X16001503

Nesse, R. M., & Williams, G. (1994). *Why we get sick: The new science of Darwinian Medicine*. Times Books.

Nettersheim, J., Gerlach, G., Herpertz, S., Abed, R., Figueredo, A., & Brüne, M. (2018). Evolutionary psychology of eating disorders: An explorative study in patients with anorexia nervosa and bulimia nervosa. *Frontiers in Psychology, 9*, 2122. doi: 10.3389/fpsyg.2018.02122

Nettle, D., Andrews, C., & Bateson, M. (2017) Food insecurity as a driver of obesity in humans: The insurance hypothesis. *Behavioral and Brain Sciences, 40*, E105. doi: 10.1017/S0140525X16000947.

Parker, G. A. (1983). Mate quality and mating decisions. In P. Bateson (Ed.), *Mate choice* (pp. 141–164).: Cambridge University Press.

Pike, K. M., Hoek, H. W., & Dunne, P. E. (2014). Cultural trends and eating disorders. *Current Opinion in Psychiatry, 27*, 436–442. doi: 10.1097/YCO. 0000000000000100

Pillsworth, E. G., & Haselton, M. (2006). Women's sexual strategies: The evolution of long-term bonds and extrapair sex. *Annual Review of Sex Research, 17*, 100–159.

Pollard, T. (2008). *Western diseases: An evolutionary perspective*. Cambridge University Press. doi: 10.1017/CBO9780511841118

Pope, H. G., Phillips, K. A., & Olivardia, R. (2002). *The Adonis complex: How to identify, treat, and prevent body obsession in men and boys*. Free Press.

Puts, D. A., Bailey, D. H., & Reno, P. L. (2016). Contest competition in men. In D. M. Buss (Ed.), *The handbook of evolutionary psychology* (pp. 385–402). Wiley.

Rantala, M. J., Luoto, S., Krama, T., & Krams, I. (2019) Eating disorders: An evolutionary psychoneuroimmunological approach. *Frontiers in Psychology, 10*, 2200. doi: 10.3389/fpsyg.2019.02200

Rieger, E., Van Buren, D. J., Bishop, M., Tanofsky-Kraff, M., Welch, R., & Wilfley, D. E. (2010). An eating disorder-specific model of interpersonal psychotherapy (IPT-ED): Causal pathways and treatment implications. *Clinical Psychology Review, 30*, 400–410.

Rolls, B. J. (2017). Dietary energy density: Applying behavioral science to weight management. *Nutrition Bulletin, 42*, 246–253. doi: 10.1111/nbu.12280

Russell, G. (2000) Disorders of eating. In M. G. Gelder, J. J. Lopez-Ibor, Jr., & N. C. Andreasen (Eds.), *New Oxford textbook of psychiatry* (Vol. 1, pp. 835–855). Oxford University Press.

Salmon, C. (2017). Is female competition at the heart of reproductive suppression and eating disorders? In M. L. Fisher (Ed.), *The Oxford handbook of women and competition* (pp. 764–796). Oxford University Press. doi: 10.1093/oxfordhb/9780199376377.013.26

Salmon, C., Crawford, C., Dane, L., & Zuberbier, O. (2008). Ancestral mechanisms in modern environments: Impact of competition and stressors on body image and dieting behavior. *Human Nature, 19*, 103–117. doi: 10.1007/s12110- 008- 9030- 8

Salmon, C., Figueredo, A. J., & Woodburn, L. (2009). Life history strategy and disordered eating behavior. *Evolutionary Psychology, 7*, 585–600. doi: 10.1177/ 147470490900700408

Schacht, R., & Kramer K. L. (2019). Are we monogamous? A review of the evolution of pair-bonding in humans and its contemporary variation cross-culturally. *Frontiers in Ecology and Evolution, 7*, 230. doi: 10.3389/fevo.2019.00230

Sear, R., & Mace, R. (2008). Who keeps children alive? A review of the effect of kin on child survival. *Evolution and Human Behavior, 29*, 1–18.

Simmons, L. W., Firman, R. C., & Rhodes, G. (2004). Human sperm competition: Testis size, sperm production and rates of extrapair copulations. *Animal Behavior, 68*, 297–302. doi: 10.1016/j.anbehav.2003.11.013

Singh, D. (1994). Ideal body shape: Role of body weight and waist-to-hip ratio. *International Journal of Eating Disorders, 16*, 283–288.

Smith, A. R., Li, N. P., & Joiner, T. E. (2011). The pursuit of success: Can status aspirations negatively affect body satisfaction? *Journal of Social and Clinical Psychology, 30*, 531–547. doi: 10.1521/jscp.2011.30.5.531

Stearns, S. C. (1992). *The evolution of life histories*. Oxford University Press.

Steiger, H., Bruce, K., & Israel, M. (2003). Eating disorders. In G. Stricker, T. A. Widiger, & I. B. Weiner (Eds.), *Handbook of psychology* (Vol. 8, pp. 173–194). Wiley.

Steinhausen, H. C. (2002). The outcome of anorexia nervosa in the 20th century. *American Journal of Psychiatry, 159*(8), 1284–1293. doi: 10.1176/appi.ajp.159.8.1284.

Sugermeyer, J. (2020) Eating disorders (ED), a global epidemic: De-stigmatizing ED to save lives. In S. Okpaku (Ed.), *Innovations in global mental health*. Springer. https://doi.org/10.1007/978-3-319-70134-9_107-1

Sugiyama, L. S. (2005). Physical attractiveness in adaptationist perspective. In D. M. Buss (Ed.), *The handbook of evolutionary psychology* (pp. 292–343). Wiley.

Sugiyama, L. A. (2016). Physical attractiveness: An adaptational perspective. In D. Buss (Ed.), *The handbook of evolutionary psychology* (pp. 317–384). Wiley.

Surbey, M. K. (1987). Anorexia nervosa, amenorrhea and adaptation. *Ethology and Sociobiology, 8*, 47–62.

Symons, D. (1979). *The evolution of human sexuality*. Oxford University Press.

Symons, D. (1995). Beauty is in the adaptations of the beholder. In P. R. Abramson & S. D. Pinkerson (Eds.), *Sexual nature, sexual culture* (pp. 80–118). University of Chicago Press.

Tanaka, K. D., Morimoto, G., Stevens, M., & Ueda, K. (2011) Rethinking visual supernormal stimuli in cuckoos: Visual modeling of host and parasite signals, *Behavioral Ecology, 22*(5), 1012–1019. https://doi.org/10.1093/beheco/arr084

Tinbergen, N. (1963). On the aims and methods of ethology. *Zeitschrift fur Tierpsychologie, 20*, 410–433.
Tooby, J., & Cosmides, L. (1990). The past explains the present: Emotional adaptations and the structure of ancestral environments. *Ethology and Sociobiology, 11*, 375–424.
Tooby, J., & Cosmides, L. (1992). The psychological foundations of culture. In J. H. Barkow, L. Cosmides, & J. Tooby (Eds.), *The adapted mind: Evolutionary psychology and the generation of culture* (pp. 19–136). Oxford University Press.
Trivers, R. L. (1972). Parental investment and sexual selection. In B. Campbell (Ed.), *Sexual selection and the descent of man 1871–1971* (pp. 136–179). Aldine.
Trivers, R. L., & Willard, D. E. (1973). Natural selection of parental ability to vary the sex ratio of offspring. *Science, 179*, 90–92. doi: 10.1126/science.179.4068.90
Turke, P. (1989). Evolution and the demand for children. *Population and Development Review, 15*(1), 61–90. doi: 10.2307/1973405
Vining, D. R. (1986). Social versus reproductive success: The central theoretical problem of human sociobiology. *Behavioral and Brain Science, 9*, 167–216.
Voland, E., & Voland, R. (1989). Evolutionary biology and psychiatry: The case for anorexia nervosa. *Ethology and Sociobiology, 10*, 223–240.
Wang, G., Cao, M., Sauciuvenaite, J., Bissland, R., Hacker, M., Hambly, C., Vaanholt, L. M., Niu, C., Faries, M. D., & Speakman, J. R. (2018). Different impacts of resources on opposite sex ratings of physical attractiveness by males and females. *Evolution and Human Behavior, 39*(2), 220–225. https://doi.org/10.1016/j.evolhumbehav.2017.12.008
Wasser, S. K., & Barash, D. P. (1983). Reproductive suppression among female animals: Implications for biomedicine and sexual selection theory. *Quarterly Review of Biology, 58*, 513–538.
Waxman, S. E. (2009). A systematic review of impulsivity in eating disorders. *European Eating Disorders Review, 17*, 408–425. doi: 10.1002/erv.952
Weekes-Shackelford, V. A., & Shackelford, T. K. (Eds). (2014). *Evolutionary perspectives on human sexual psychology and behavior*. Springer.
Whyte, M. K. (1978). *The status of women in preindustrial societies*. Princeton University Press.
Wrangham, R. (2002). The cost of sexual attraction: Is there a trade-off in female Pan between sex appeal and received coercion? In L. Marchant, C. Boesch, & G. Hohmann (Eds.), *Behavioral diversity in chimpanzees and bonobos* (pp. 204–216). Cambridge University Press. doi: 10.1017/CBO9780511606397.020
World Health Organization. (1993). *The ICD-10 classification of mental and behavioral disorders*. WHO.
Yilmaz, Z., Hardaway, J. A., & Bulik, C. M. (2015). Genetics and epigenetics of eating disorders. *Advances in Genomics and Genetics, 5*, 131–150. doi: 10.2147/AGG.S55776
Yong, J. C., Li, N. P., Valentine, K. A., & Smith, A. R. (2017). Female virtual intrasexual competition and its consequences: An evolutionary mismatch perspective. In M. L. Fisher (Ed.), *The Oxford handbook of women and competition* (pp. 657–680). Oxford University Press. doi: 10.1093/oxfordhb/9780199376377.013.38
Zerwas, S., & Bulik, C. M. (2011). Genetics and epigenetics of eating disorders. *Psychiatric Annals, 41*, 532–538.
Zihlman, A. L., & MacFarland, R. K. (2000). Body mass in lowland gorillas: A quantitative analysis. *American Journal of Physical Anthropology, 113*, 61–78.

CHAPTER 61

Narcissism and Narcissistic Personality Disorder: Evolutionary Roots and Emotional Profiles

Anna Z. Czarna, Monika Wróbel, Logan F. Folger, Nicholas S. Holtzman, Jennifer R. Daley, and Joshua D. Foster

Abstract

This chapter introduces the construct of narcissism, reviews its evolutionary origins, and explores its relationship with emotions. Narcissism is presented as a personality trait with grandiose and vulnerable expressions, as well as a personality disorder characterized by extreme levels of narcissism combined with impairment. Some discussion surrounds whether grandiose and vulnerable expressions of narcissism should be conceptualized as distinct, stable traits versus oscillating narcissistic states. Evolutionary topics include the heritability of narcissism, the genetic foundations of narcissism, evolutionarily grounded strategies, including mating and survival strategies, that may have facilitated sexual and natural selection of narcissistic traits, as well as critiques of existing theory in this literature. The emotion section focuses on the emotional experiences of narcissists, paying particular attention to how these experiences contrast, depending on whether narcissism is more grandiose or vulnerable. Attempts are made throughout the chapter to identify connections between the conceptual, evolutionary, and emotion literatures.

Key Words: narcissism, grandiose narcissism, vulnerable narcissism, evolution, emotion

Introduction

The goals of this chapter are threefold. First, we will introduce readers to the construct of narcissism, beginning with its literary roots and continuing with its clinical and general personality manifestations. We will mostly adhere to a trait-theory perspective when describing narcissism; that is, we will present narcissism as a constellation of interrelated traits that have the potential to create intrapersonal and interpersonal dysfunction, potentially leading to a diagnosis of narcissistic personality disorder (NPD; American Psychiatric Association, 2013). Thus, although we highlight research that focuses on NPD specifically, we assert that research focusing on the more general personality traits that comprise narcissism (e.g., grandiosity, vulnerability, antagonism) provides a solid framework for understanding narcissism as a personality trait as well as a personality disorder (Crowe et al., in press).

Next, we provide an overview of the literature that discusses the evolutionary origins of narcissism. This section focuses on topics such as heritability, genetic foundations (or lack thereof), evolutionarily grounded strategies including mating strategies and survival strategies, and critiques of existing theory in this literature.

We will then conclude by reviewing the literature on the emotional experiences of narcissists. This section focuses on emotions that are central and recurrent in the lives of narcissists and focuses on the evolutionary relevance of these experiences. Although the conceptual, evolutionary, and emotion literatures pertaining to narcissism have been largely distinct from one another—with the exception of Joey Cheng's work (Cheng et al., 2010; Tracy et al., 2011), which brings the three literatures together—whenever possible, we highlight connections among these literatures.

Origins of the Construct

The term "narcissism" has ancient mythological roots; specifically, Ovid's poem *Echo and Narcissus* tells the story of unrequited love between Narcissus, a dashing but self-absorbed and cruel hunter, and Echo, a mountain nymph who falls hopelessly in love with him (Ovidius Naso & Raeburn, 2004). In the 1,200 years since the story of Narcissus famously gazing longingly at his own reflection in a pond, the term "narcissism" still retains some of its original meaning, although it has also morphed into a complex constellation of personality traits and a psychological disorder.

Contemporary discussion of narcissism dates to the work of Havelock Ellis (1898), who described it as a pathological sexual disorder, and Sigmund Freud (1914), who described it as a normal stage of child development. Heinz Kohut (1977) and Otto Kernberg (1975) played important roles in continuing to define narcissism as a pathological syndrome and were integral in making narcissism an official diagnosis with the inclusion of NPD in the third edition of the *Diagnostic and Statistical Manual of Mental Disorders* (American Psychiatric Association [APA], 1980). NPD continues to appear in the current, fifth edition of the DSM (DSM-5; APA, 2013).

NPD, Narcissistic Personality, and Grandiose versus Vulnerable Narcissism

The DSM-5 description of NPD includes the following nine criteria (a total of five or more are required to receive a diagnosis): (1) grandiose self-importance, (2) preoccupation with fantasies of unlimited power, brilliance, etc., (3) belief that one is special and unique, (4) need for excessive admiration, (5) sense of entitlement, (6) being interpersonally exploitative, (7) lacking empathy, (8) envious of others, and (9) arrogant and superior attitude and behavior (APA, 2013). These symptoms mostly reflect grandiose content (e.g., grandiose self-importance), and largely exclude vulnerable expressions of narcissism, although not entirely (e.g., being envious of others is a vulnerable quality; Krizan & Johar, 2012). This asymmetry has led to criticism, as some scholars assert that the DSM definition of NPD fails to adequately capture the more vulnerable side of the disorder, such as feelings of insecurity and shame (Skodol et al., 2014).

The grandiosity and vulnerability schism that pervades the NPD literature is also found in the more general narcissistic personality literature. NPD is a disorder of personality—the personality trait of narcissism. A straightforward way to think about NPD is that it is a pathological form of narcissistic personality. That is, narcissistic personality (or narcissism, for short) becomes NPD when the constellation of traits that comprise narcissism create significant impairment or distress (Miller, Lynam, Hyatt, et al., 2017). There are myriad ways in which narcissistic traits can create impairment or distress. To some degree, though, the type of impairment or distress experienced depends on whether narcissism is characterized by higher levels of grandiosity versus vulnerability. For example, vulnerable narcissism is linked to a variety of negative emotions, such as anxiety and depression (Kaufman et al., 2020; Weiss & Miller, 2018), whereas grandiose narcissism is unrelated to these types of negative emotions (although this becomes more complicated in older age groups; Hill & Roberts, 2011), but more so connected to interpersonal dysfunction, such as romantic game-playing and infidelity (Campbell et al., 2002; Foster & Brunell, 2018).

According to several prominent and current theoretical accounts of narcissism, it is useful to conceptualize narcissism as three interrelated dimensions (Ackerman et al., 2019; Crowe et al., 2019). Using the language of the trifurcated model (Crowe et al., 2019), grandiose and vulnerable narcissism share a "core" dimension called self-centered antagonism. In addition to this core, grandiose narcissism possesses an additional "specifier" dimension called agentic extraversion, and vulnerable narcissism possesses an additional specifier dimension called narcissistic neuroticism. In short, both grandiose and vulnerable narcissism are characterized by self-centeredness and interpersonal conflict. However, whereas grandiose narcissism is further characterized by an egocentric brand of extraversion, vulnerable narcissism is characterized by subjective distress stemming from perceived lack of respect. In terms of the Five Factor Model or the Big Five Model of personality (Anglim & O'Connor, 2019; Widiger, 2015), grandiose and vulnerable narcissism share low levels of agreeableness and, whereas grandiose narcissism is also associated with high levels of extraversion, vulnerable narcissism is also associated with high levels of neuroticism (Miller et al., 2011).

Stable Trait or Dynamic State?
Although the consensus in the research literature is that narcissism comes in two principal forms, grandiose and vulnerable, which resemble the description provided by the trifurcated model (Crowe et al., 2019), there is controversy over whether grandiose and vulnerable narcissism are best conceptualized as stable and relatively separable traits or dynamic expressions of narcissism that vary across time within persons (Wright & Edershile, 2018). For example, according to the dynamic perspective, people with narcissistic personalities may oscillate between grandiose and vulnerable expressions of narcissism. Because the hypothesized oscillations happen within persons and relatively quickly, detecting them requires advanced statistics and methods including multilevel modeling (Nezlek, 2008) and ecological momentary assessment (Shiffman et al., 2008). State-level measures of narcissistic grandiosity and vulnerability did not exist until recently (Crowe et al., 2016; Crowe et al., 2018; Edershile et al., 2019), suggesting that this literature may accelerate soon.

Of these few studies that have tested the oscillation hypothesis, some could be characterized as indirect tests, such as asking people who are classified as primarily grandiose or vulnerable narcissists whether they experience the complimentary variant (Gore & Widiger, 2016; Hyatt et al., 2018). Findings suggest that primarily grandiose narcissists may experience bouts of narcissistic vulnerability; however, vulnerable narcissists do not appear to experience bouts of narcissistic grandiosity as frequently. To our knowledge, there has been one published study that has tested the oscillation hypothesis directly using ecological momentary assessment (Edershile & Wright, 2021). Like the previous indirect tests, this study found evidence that participants who were primarily grandiose in terms of their narcissism experienced bouts of vulnerability, but found no evidence that participants who were primarily vulnerable experienced moments of grandiosity. Thus, although research testing the oscillation hypothesis is still emerging, some evidence suggests that grandiose narcissists experience periodic states of vulnerable narcissism.

Summary
NPD is a personality disorder characterized by extreme levels of narcissistic personality combined with impairment. The impairment can be intrapersonal or interpersonal, as is true for all personality disorders. Regarding the underlying personality trait of narcissism, the consensus

is that narcissism comes in grandiose and vulnerable expressions. Both share a common theme of interpersonal antagonism. Whereas grandiose narcissism is further characterized by agentic extraversion, vulnerable narcissism is characterized by narcissistic neuroticism. There is debate over whether vulnerable narcissism, in particular, is sufficiently represented in the DSM-5 description of NPD. Furthermore, there is debate over whether grandiose and vulnerable narcissism should be conceptualized as relatively stable and separable traits versus oscillating narcissistic states (Weiss & Miller, 2018).

Evolution of Narcissism

The first section of this chapter provided a general overview of narcissism, including several key concepts; this next section examines the evolutionary origins of narcissism. Specifically, we will examine whether narcissism is at least partly genetically grounded, as well as the means by which narcissism might get selected—in particular, sexual and natural selection.

Narcissism and Genes

The evolutionary literature on narcissism focuses mostly on its grandiose form and how it has been selected (e.g., Holtzman & Strube, 2011; Holtzman, 2018; Jonason et al., 2010; Buss & Schmitt et al., 2017; Tracy et al., 2011). Therefore, when we use the term "narcissism" in this section, we will be referring to grandiose narcissism unless otherwise specified. The evolutionary literature views narcissism as an evolved personality trait. An essential element of an evolutionary theory is the genetic basis for traits, as genes are the main unit of selection (Dawkins, 1976). Behavioral genetics has established a heritability component for narcissism (Vernon et al., 2008). While this does not imply that specific genes are associated with narcissism (because heritability does not signify a genetic substrate; Jackson et al., 2011), this finding is a necessary (yet insufficient) condition for showing that narcissism has a genetic basis (Livesley et al., 1993).

Evidence in search of specific genes that reflect narcissism is lacking. There is scant research evidence on the molecular genetics of narcissism, so it is difficult to draw conclusions regarding putative gene-narcissism associations. Some research has examined polymorphisms in the *5-HTTLPR* gene, which codes for serotonin transporters. This genetic variant has been linked to a variety of psychiatric disorders and symptoms, including several personality traits associated with psychopathy and narcissism (Brammer et al., 2016; Luo & Cai, 2018; Sadeh et al., 2010). Still, this research is in its infancy, and it is not yet known what genes or combinations of genes might play a role in the development of narcissism.

Indirect evidence of a genetic basis for narcissism comes from genetic associations with antagonism and extraversion, and the corresponding biological psychology literature pertaining to these broad-band personality traits. As noted earlier, both grandiose and vulnerable narcissism are antagonistic traits at their core (Crowe et al., 2019; Vize et al. 2020). Consistent with this view, grandiose narcissism (as well as vulnerable narcissism) involves disagreeableness (Miller et al., 2011; Paulhus & Williams, 2002; Vazire et al., 2008). Neighboring research has shown that narcissism—particularly the grandiose variant—is strongly positively correlated with extraversion (Lee & Ashton, 2005; Paulhus & Williams, 2002), which is indeed evident across different measures of the Big Five ($r = .46$ on the Big Five; $r = .49$ on the HEXACO; Lee & Ashton, 2005). Most research in this literature, including both self-report and behavioral measures, is consistent with Paulhus's (2002) minimalist assertion that grandiose narcissists are "disagreeable extraverts."

Because grandiose narcissism manifests as disagreeable extraversion (Paulhus, 2001), any genetic basis for agreeableness and extraversion could be taken as indirect evidence of a genetic basis for narcissism. Multiple studies have provided evidence of specific genes associated with extraversion and agreeableness (Kim et al., 2015; see Sanchez-Roige et al., 2018, for review), although there is stronger such evidence for extraversion than agreeableness (Luo et al., 2017; Sanchez-Roige, 2018). These genetic factors account for approximately 1%–20% of the variance in extraversion and agreeableness in genome-wide association studies and polygenic studies (Luo et al., 2017; Sanchez-Roige et al., 2018). We will use a round number percentage (10%) as a heuristic for the genetic basis for narcissism, recognizing that the confidence interval is large. We assert that the genetic components for these two traits are approximately 10%, which—albeit lower than the common heuristic of 50% heritability for personality traits based on behavior genetic research—indirectly suggests a genetic basis for narcissism. Because narcissism appears to be partly genetically inherited, next we consider two primary pathways (perhaps somewhat positively intertwined) that may help explain the evolution of narcissism and how it was selected—sexual and natural selection.

Narcissism and Sexual Selection

Based on pioneering work of many scholars (Buss & Chiodo, 1991; Buss & Schmitt, 1993; Foster et al., 2006; Jonason et al., 2009; Mealey, 1995), Holtzman and Strube (2011) proposed that narcissism was selected to facilitate a short-term mating (STM) strategy, which is arguably a frequency-dependent phenomenon (Lewontin, 1958), where frequency-dependent selection is consistent with good genes sexual selection models (Martinossi-Allibert et al., 2019a; see also Gangestad et al., 2007). These models do not posit unidirectional selection for narcissism overall, but rather posit that narcissistic individuals coexist at the population level with non-narcissistic individuals (indeed, non-narcissistic qualities may coevolve); both can have evolutionary advantages according to frequency-dependence models. If this is true, then according to Holtzman and Strube (2011), there should be evidence that narcissism (a) is associated with traits (e.g., attractiveness) and proclivities (e.g., social boldness) that facilitate STM strategies; (b) is associated with coercive behavior; and (c) manifests in developmental specificity for the trait (i.e., it should peak in adolescence). All considered, nature should consolidate these positively inter-correlated features into a physically attractive and coercive constellation of traits that peaks in adolescence. The consolidated result would manifest as narcissism. Here, we review this literature and provide an update regarding these key criteria with respect to sexual selection.

If narcissism was selected to facilitate STM, then narcissism should positively correlate with qualities that are differentially adaptive for STM, such as physical attractiveness. The evidence regarding physical attractiveness is mixed (see Holtzman, 2018, for review). Early meta-analytic evidence showed a positive relationship between narcissism and physical attractiveness (Holtzman & Strube, 2010). Some evidence suggests that narcissists are more attractive as potential mates and are more successful in STM (Dufner et al., 2013), at least insofar as it concerns soliciting dates from strangers. Other research suggests that narcissistic individuals may not be especially physically attractive, however: when narcissists could not self-regulate their appearance, they were rated merely comparable in attractiveness to non-narcissists (Holtzman & Strube, 2013). Thus, narcissists do not appear to be innately (i.e., in their unadorned state) more attractive than non-narcissists, but their attractiveness may be bolstered by self-regulation, which is arguably a dynamic, complex, non-genetic, and high-level cognitive process that is presumably less susceptible to selection pressures.

Perplexingly, ongoing research in one of our labs (Burchette et al., in progress) suggests that narcissistic men are *not* significantly more likely than non-narcissistic men to actively pursue STM. This suggests that narcissism is not about internally motivated STM pursuits.

However, even if it is true that narcissists are not internally motivated to pursue STM, narcissists may nevertheless engage more frequently in STM because of the dynamic features of their personality. Narcissists may possess personality traits that allow them to present themselves to others as more viable candidates for STM (Dufner et al., 2013; Wurst et al., 2017). Their high confidence and self-perceived attractiveness may be appealing to potential short-term mates (Back et al., 2011; Murphy et al., 2015).

Specifically, the agentic self-enhancement, dominance, and social boldness of narcissists may help to explain the increased mate appeal in narcissists (Dufner et al., 2013; Gangestad et al., 2007; Wurst et al., 2017). All these characteristics are encapsulated by narcissistic admiration, one of two positively correlated dimensions of (grandiose) narcissism according to the narcissistic admiration and rivalry concept (NARC; Back et al., 2013). The NARC model is a two-dimensional conceptualization of grandiose narcissism consisting of an admiration dimension and a rivalry dimension. The narcissistic admiration dimension is characterized by the tendency to promote one's self in social situations (using self-enhancement), while narcissistic rivalry is the tendency to defend oneself from social failure (driven by self-protection). The NARC shares much in common with the trifurcated model's conceptualization of grandiose narcissism (Crowe et al., 2019), with admiration being similar to agentic extraversion and rivalry being similar to interpersonal antagonism. Wurst et al. (2017) proposed that the increased mate appeal associated with narcissism in STM is mostly attributable to narcissistic admiration, which is characterized by charm, social boldness, and self-confidence. In their research, they found that people high in narcissistic admiration were rated as more attractive in video and face-to-face encounters, reported higher self-perceived attractiveness as potential mates, reported being more likely to approach the opposite sex, and had a higher preference for casual sex (Wurst et al., 2017).

By way of interim summary, narcissists do not appear to be more physically attractive, at least not in the unadorned state. However, they may do more than others to control their physical appearance, such as pay increased attention to dress and grooming. Second, recent research suggests that narcissists may not actively pursue STM, although they may possess personality traits and characteristics that make them more likely to engage in STM, such as charming personalities and dominant interpersonal styles—both of which may attract potential mates.

A more controversial and disturbing possibility is that narcissism was sexually selected, not so much because of narcissists' attractiveness and ability to attract others for STM, but rather because of narcissists' proclivity to engage in sexual coercion and rape (which is morally abhorrent, but evolutionarily possible). For example, according to the narcissistic reactance model of rape and sexual coercion, narcissism should be linked to sexual coercion because narcissists feel entitled to sex and feel it is their right to demand sex when rejected by others (Baumeister et al., 2002; Bushman et al., 2003). In general, narcissists are more likely to express anger and aggression and less likely to internalize the negative emotions associated with social rejection (Twenge & Campbell, 2003). More specifically, Bushman et al. (2003) observed that when put in a situation in which they experienced a sexual refusal by a female research confederate, male narcissists reacted more aggressively toward the female confederate.

With regard to general models of narcissistic personality, this cognition and behavior is most closely associated with the NARC model's rivalry dimension of grandiose narcissism (Back et al., 2013). Indeed, narcissistic rivalry predicts endorsement of coercive sexual behavior when individuals are reminded of social rejection (Lamarche & Seery, 2019). Additionally, narcissists self-report that they engage in more coercive sexual behavior and fantasize more about coercion and sadistic acts (Mouilso & Calhoun, 2012; Williams et al., 2009). Moreover, narcissists appear to be less empathic to victims of sexual assault and tend to blame the victims

(Bushman et al., 2003; see also Jonason et al., 2017; Long, 2018; Willis et al., 2017). This suggests that narcissists might have emotional and motivational profiles that are reactive to rejection and potentially make them prone to engaging in acts of sexual coercion and violence.

Most of this literature on narcissism and sexual coercion focuses on male perpetrators. The most common form of sexual coercion is men pressuring women into unwanted sexual experiences (30% of men self-report having physically forced or verbally coerced women into unwanted sexual acts; Zeigler-Hill, Enjaian, et al., 2013; cf. Blinkhorn et al., 2015, 2016; Lyons et al., 2022), so this focal point makes sense. However, some research suggests that narcissistic women are also prone to sexual coercion (Blinkhorn et al., 2015). Different facets of narcissism may be correlated with sexual coercion in women compared to men. Some studies suggest that sexual coercion by women is best predicted by narcissistic traits of exploitativeness and entitlement (Blinkhorn et al., 2019; Lyons et al., 2022; Ryan et al., 2008), whereas leadership/authority and grandiose exhibitionism are more strongly associated with sexual coercion by men (Blinkhorn, 2018).

The final point about sexual selection, echoing Holtzman and Strube (2011), is that it would make evolutionary sense if narcissism peaked in adolescence precisely when a STM strategy is likely to pay off; this is termed *developmental specificity* (see Andrews et al., 2002, for review). Some evidence points to this being the case (e.g., Carlson & Gjerde, 2009; Foster et al., 2003), with narcissism levels being highest in young adults and gradually declining in older age groups. Narcissism in young adulthood may enhance the enactment of the sexual strategy for which narcissists were theoretically sexually selected. However, it is important to acknowledge the complexity of human mating, including sex differences (e.g., women prefer older mates than men prefer; Conroy-Beam & Buss, 2018).

Narcissism and Natural Selection

Sexual selection is just one route to evolutionary success. Another possibility is that narcissism was *naturally* selected in part because it facilitates the attainment of status (Tracy et al., 2011), which confers resources that enable one to navigate the problems of life. Status attainment can be achieved through either prestige or dominance (Henrich & Gil-White, 2001). The prestige path refers to status that is obtained by being recognized and respected by others for skills, success, or knowledge. The dominance path refers to status attained through the use of fear and intimidation (e.g., threatening to withhold resources). Dominance is strongly associated with narcissism (Bradlee & Emmons, 1992) and narcissistic individuals are more likely to use the dominance strategy than the prestige strategy to achieve status (Cheng et al., 2010). Narcissists' dominant behavior can make them appear more competent and allow them to gain influence over others (Anderson & Kilduff, 2009). Thus, it is not surprising that narcissistic individuals would have an advantage in the pursuit of status in some contexts (Carlson & DesJardins, 2015; Mahadevan et al., 2019).

The two-dimensional conceptualization of grandiose narcissism proposed by the NARC model (Back et al., 2013) can be used to explain narcissists' success in obtaining status, especially in early acquaintanceships. Narcissistic admiration accounts for the enactment of dominant behaviors, which can appear assertive and thereby increase the perception of competence (Carlson & DesJardins, 2015; Leckelt et al., 2015). However, narcissists often fail to maintain this status over the long term (Carlson & DesJardins, 2015; Paulhus, 1998). Narcissistic rivalry may account for declining popularity and status over time, which evidently results from narcissistic expressions of antagonistic and aggressive behaviors (Leckelt et al., 2015); this may lead to a revolving door of interpersonal relationships such that narcissists are perpetually in the relationship "emerging zone"—a stage in which relationships are new and relatively shallow

(Campbell & Campbell, 2009). An endless stream of new relationships may allow narcissists to use interpersonal charm and similar traits to their advantage in extracting resources from others (Back et al., 2010).

Although narcissists often do not maintain their popularity and status over the long term, frequently they do manage to achieve and maintain high leadership positions, such as in the workplace (Rauthmann & Kolar, 2012). They do this by creating self-enhancing opportunities consistent with the narcissistic admiration dimension (Back et al., 2013). Grijalva and colleagues (2015) found that while narcissism is associated with leadership emergence, people who are high in narcissism are not particularly effective leaders, and the positive association between narcissism and leadership emergence is a function of extraversion, central to the narcissistic admiration dimension. Moreover, similar to what was discussed above, although narcissists frequently achieve popularity and status in the workplace and other organizations, and they even rise to positions of leadership due to their extraverted and dominant personalities, this advantage is usually brief, as the antagonistic side emerges over time (Grijalva et al., 2015; Paulhus, 1998). Narcissistic rivalry may also be used to explain the negative emotional and motivational effects that narcissistic leaders have on followers, especially when traits associated with narcissistic rivalry (e.g., derogatory attitudes) are expressed as observable behaviors (Fehn & Schütz, 2021).

Summary
In this section, we discussed evolutionary pathways that might have allowed narcissism and narcissistic traits to be selected and maintained in the population. Genetics research suggests that at least some small portion of narcissistic personality is regulated by genes. This is important because it is genetic code that is shaped by evolutionary forces, such as sexual and natural selection. With regard to sexual selection mechanisms, the most heavily studied hypothesis is that some of the genes that comprise narcissism confer advantages in STM. We noted that narcissists do not appear to be more physically attractive, at least when in the unadorned state. However, they may possess traits and proclivities (e.g., flashier dress, bold and extraverted interpersonal style) that make them more noticeable and appealing to others looking for STM partners. Narcissists tend to engage in sexually coercive behavior, which (although morally repugnant) could be sexually selected. Finally, we observed that narcissism appears to peak in young adults, which would be expected for a trait that confers advantages through sexual selection of STM. As for natural selection, narcissism may offer advantages for attaining status and power. We noted that traits associated with narcissistic admiration may help narcissists attain status and emerge as leaders. Consistent with the duality of narcissism, however, whereas traits associated with narcissistic admiration may help narcissists attain status, traits associated with narcissistic rivalry may undermine their ability to maintain status. Thus, narcissism would appear to be particularly useful in turbulent social situations that provide frequent opportunities for narcissists to engage in shallow interpersonal acquaintanceships rather than deeper and longer-term relationships.

Narcissism and Emotions
Now that we have discussed what narcissism is and its possible evolutionary origins, we turn to the emotions of narcissists. Depending on whether narcissism takes on a grandiose or vulnerable form (Pincus et al., 2009), it can be associated with emotional experiences of different valence, strength, dynamics, and expression. In this section, we outline plausible functional links between the two forms of narcissism and describe characteristic aspects of their emotional

lives. We also briefly discuss these emotional profiles in the context of evolutionary functions of emotions.

Self-regulatory models of narcissism hold that narcissists desire status and admiration from other people to "convince themselves" of their own superiority (Grapsas et al., 2020; Morf & Rhodewalt, 2001). Some models even compare the relentless pursuit of esteem by narcissists to addiction (Baumeister & Vohs, 2001). According to these models, the motivation is so strong and toxic, and the goal of building and maintaining a grandiose self based entirely on receiving endless proofs of appreciation from others so unattainable, that narcissists' attempts to fulfill this motivation can be self-defeating. Trying to elicit continual admiration, they ruin the relationships on which they rely for the admiration they seek. Not unlike addictions, narcissism thus involves a pattern of yielding to inner urges in a way that proves costly and self-destructive. In consequence, a narcissist's life may be characterized not by a stable sense of inflated self-regard, but rather likely by periods of self-aggrandizing inflation, leading to destructive consequences that may cause the person to revert to a more "moderate" view of self or even to a sense of inferiority and a phase of depression (especially later in life; Hill & Roberts, 2011). Thus, when we describe the emotional profiles of grandiose and vulnerable narcissism below, we do so as if the two constituted semi-independent personality traits. However, as described in the first section, periods of grandiosity filled with intense positive emotions and an accompanying sense of superiority, punctuated by phases of increased vulnerability, have been observed and may even be typical in narcissists (Edershile & Wright, 2021). Thus, the emotional profiles we present for grandiose and vulnerable narcissism may manifest at different times in the same person.

Emotional Profile of Grandiose Narcissists

Grandiose narcissists are approach-oriented and sensitive to rewards (Foster & Brennan, 2012; Pincus et al., 2009). They tend to be in an energetic, upbeat, and optimistic mood (Sedikides et al., 2004) and rarely experience sadness, loneliness, anxiety, and other negative states (e.g., Miller et al., 2011; Sedikides et al., 2004). Grandiose narcissists have therefore been described as "successful narcissists," and their high emotional well-being has been attributed to their high self-esteem (Sedikides et al., 2004). This implies, however, that any factor that lowers narcissists' self-esteem is also likely to reduce their well-being. And, indeed, the well-being of grandiose narcissists is far from stable: grandiose narcissism is characterized by strong mood variability, which is thought to be due to their contingent self-esteem and sensitivity to social comparisons (Bogart et al., 2004; Geukes et al., 2017; Krizan & Bushman, 2011; Rhodewalt & Morf, 1998). For instance, narcissists' state self-esteem decreases substantially on days with more negative achievement events, leading to rapidly changing emotions (Zeigler-Hill et al., 2010).

It is likely that grandiose narcissists' desire to maintain an overly positive self-image leads them to experience hubristic pride (Tracy et al., 2011; Tracy et al., 2009). In contrast to authentic pride, which is based on actual achievements and leads to the development of genuine self-esteem, hubristic pride stems not from actual accomplishments but from generalized, distorted positive self-views (Tracy & Robins, 2007b). Whereas authentic pride results from attributions to internal, unstable, but controllable causes, hubristic pride results from attributions to internal, stable, and uncontrollable causes (i.e., the self; Tracy & Robins, 2007a). Although it has been suggested that in both forms of narcissism, hubristic pride constitutes a response to chronic excessive shame (Tracy et al., 2009), recent studies indicate that grandiose narcissists are not particularly prone to shame (Di Sarno et al., 2020). Similarly, unlike vulnerable narcissists, grandiose narcissists do not generally experience excessive envy (Krizan &

Johar, 2012; Neufeld & Johnson, 2016). Indeed, grandiose narcissists tend not to hold negative self-opinions of any sort (Campbell et al., 2004). A grandiose form of narcissism (or possibly, this "phase" in the narcissism "cycle") is better characterized by successful self-regulatory efforts that ward off negative emotions, such as shame and envy (Campbell et al., 2004).

In a related vein, research has also established differences in the triggers and use of aggression by grandiose and vulnerable narcissists. Grandiose narcissists seem to use aggression in a cold, instrumental manner to defend and assert their position of dominance in the face of a threat. This route does not necessarily include the intermediary of shame (Campbell et al., 2004). An important factor that protects grandiose narcissists from experiencing anger and hostility is likely their low neuroticism (Czarna et al., 2019). Accordingly, grandiose narcissists do not respond aggressively to minor provocations but resort to aggression mostly when faced with strong direct threats to their agentic self or status (Bettencourt et al., 2006; Krizan & Johar, 2015; Rasmussen, 2016). Their aggressive responses might thus be calculated tactics aimed at restoring their superiority, rather than outbursts of unrestrained, uncontrollable rage fueled by shame and anger (Barry et al., 2007; Fossati et al., 2010; Krizan & Johar, 2015). This view, known as the threatened egotism model, assumes that acts of aggression by grandiose narcissists are motivated by inflated self-esteem and entitlement rather than shame (Bushman & Baumeister, 1998; Morf & Rhodewalt, 2001).

Still, narcissistic self-esteem contingency and sensitivity to social comparison might result in affective lability (e.g., Hart et al., 2019). Grandiose narcissists use other people to regulate their self-esteem, producing a typical dynamic of initial excitement, "seduction," and later disappointment, altogether generating interpersonal turmoil (Campbell & Campbell, 2009; Morf & Rhodewalt, 2001; Paulhus, 1998). They also display substantial emotional volatility in response to agentic failure (e.g., Besser & Priel, 2010; Rhodewalt & Morf, 1998). Yet, some researchers point to few emotion-regulation difficulties among grandiose narcissists (Zhang et al., 2015). For instance, grandiose narcissists report high levels of positive emotions and resilience, even when facing failure (Wallace et al., 2009). They also flexibly regulate their emotions by promptly withdrawing from tasks when easier paths to success are provided, but persistently performing tasks when no other paths to self-enhancement are available. Although narcissists show high resilience to stress and an ability to maintain positive mood, there may be considerable physiological costs to narcissism in the form of heightened reactivity observed on hormonal, cardiovascular, and neurological levels (Cheng et al., 2013; Edelstein et al., 2010; Reinhard et al., 2012; Sommer et al., 2009; Zhang et al., 2015).

Perhaps the most important emotional characteristic of grandiose narcissists is their reduced empathy and low susceptibility to resonate with others' emotions (Czarna et al., 2015; Giammarco & Vernon, 2014; Vonk et al., 2013). Nonetheless, evidence regarding grandiose narcissists' ability to accurately process emotion-related information has been mixed. Some studies report deficits and biases (Czarna et al., 2023; Tardif et al., 2014; Wai & Tiliopoulos, 2012), while others report intact or even superior abilities (Konrath et al., 2014; Ritter et al., 2011). Meta-analyses show that grandiose narcissism is negatively associated with self-reported cognitive and affective empathy. Yet, when empathy is measured behaviorally, grandiose narcissism is significantly associated only with affective empathy (negatively) but not cognitive empathy (Urbonaviciute & Hepper, 2020). This suggests that empathic limitations in narcissism may not be due to inability to empathize, but rather due to lacking motivation for understanding others' emotional states and needs (Aradhye & Vonk, 2014; Stietz et al., 2019).

Emotional Profile of Vulnerable Narcissists

In contrast to grandiose narcissists, vulnerable narcissists have been described as "struggling" or "failed" narcissists (Campbell et al., 2004). Vulnerable narcissists are avoidance oriented and sensitive to threats (Foster & Trimm, 2008). They tend to experience anxiety, depression, hostility, and other negative states (Miller et al., 2011; Tracy et al., 2011). Vulnerable narcissism is almost entirely reducible to neuroticism (the remaining variance being antagonism and hostility; Miller, Lynam, Vize, et al., 2017), which is a strong negative predictor of subjective well-being (Diener & Lucas, 1999). Some researchers propose that vulnerable narcissism reflects general personality pathology (Wright & Edershile, 2018). Similar to grandiose narcissists, vulnerable narcissists experience high mood variability, which is likely due to their contingent self-esteem. When confronted with shameful interpersonal experiences, such as relational rejections, vulnerable narcissists react with a sudden and substantial drop in state self-esteem and rapidly changing emotions (Besser & Priel, 2010; Sommer et al., 2009; Thomaes et al., 2008).

Vulnerable narcissists' emotional lability may manifest in a tendency to experience overwhelming shame and hubristic pride (Krizan & Johar, 2015; Tracy et al., 2011). In their case, hubristic pride often serves as a defense from chronic excessive shame. It has been suggested that this dynamic results from a structural split in the self-representational system—an unstable and conflicting situation of implicit feelings of global shame and inadequacy coexisting with explicit feelings of grandiosity (Kuchynka & Bosson, 2018). Hubristic pride has been linked to antisocial emotions and behaviors such as anger, hostility, and aggression (Cheng et al., 2010; Tracy et al., 2009): According to the "authentic versus hubristic" model of pride, externalizing blame and experiencing anger might be a viable strategy for coping with chronic shame. Aggressive responses in vulnerable narcissists are therefore a part of a "shame-rage" spiral (Scheff, 1987; Tracy et al., 2011): they serve an ego-protective function and provide relief from the pain of shame (Tangney & Dearing, 2003).

Another source of emotional misery and aggression of vulnerable narcissists is their propensity for envy. This painful emotion plays a central role in their lives: They resent higher-status peers and revel in the misfortune of others (Krizan & Johar, 2012; Nicholls & Stukas, 2011). The envious impulses are likely elicited by a deep-seated feeling of inferiority and, together with vulnerable narcissists' poor regulation abilities, may contribute to hostility (Czarna et al., 2019). Emotion-regulation difficulties are evident in vulnerable narcissists' nonacceptance of their own emotional responses, poor impulse control, limited access to regulation strategies, and a lack of emotional clarity (Zhang et al., 2015). They all may result in high affect volatility induced by self-esteem contingency, inclination for incessant social comparison, and a deeply rooted sense of worthlessness. Their hypersensitivity and disappointment stemming from unmet expectations lead to social withdrawal and avoidance in a futile attempt to regulate self-esteem. Indeed, interpersonal rejection remains the most painful trigger for vulnerable narcissists (Besser & Priel, 2010), generating shame, depression, anger, and hostility (Dickinson & Pincus, 2003; Krizan & Johar, 2015). Narcissistic vulnerability rather than grandiosity has therefore been identified as a key source of narcissistic rage, as its necessary conditions include a fragile sense of self, an explosive mixture of shame, hostility, and extreme anger (Krizan & Johar, 2015). The resultant outburst of aggression is disproportionate, dysfunctional, and often misdirected.

Although the lack of empathy is a core part of narcissism, research focusing on empathy of vulnerable narcissists has been scarce and the findings are inconsistent (Urbonaviciute & Hepper, 2020). Some studies found vulnerable narcissism to be negatively associated with cognitive empathy, but unrelated to affective empathy (Aradhye & Vonk, 2014; Böckler et al., 2017). However, the distinction between self-report and behavioral measures is crucial: vulnerable narcissism is significantly negatively associated with self-reported cognitive and affective empathy, but it is not significantly associated with behaviorally measured cognitive empathy. Because a common component of both variants of narcissism is antagonism, it seems likely that empathy deficits manifest in the same way in grandiose and vulnerable narcissists (Urbonaviciute & Hepper, 2020), but evidence for this claim is limited. To date, there have been no studies employing behavioral measures of affective empathy among vulnerable narcissists.

Evolutionary Relevance of Narcissists' Emotionality

An evolutionary hypothesis for why narcissism persists suggests that narcissism serves as a frequency-dependent variant of behavioral dominance that promotes successful STM (Holtzman & Strube, 2011). We propose that the emotionality of narcissists, in particular of grandiose narcissists, facilitates their reproduction and survival, thus reflecting sexual and natural selection. In evolutionary psychology, emotions are strategies for achieving goals that increase the probability of desired outcomes (e.g., maintaining high status and self-esteem), or that reduce the probability of negative outcomes (e.g., preventing decreases in status and self-esteem; Al-Shawaf et al., 2015). For example, anger and pride (both hubristic and authentic), like inflated self-esteem, facilitate attainment of evolutionarily relevant objectives (e.g., Beall & Tracy, 2020; Cheng et al., 2010) via several routes. The emotion of pride seems to play a major role in the mechanisms that promote status-seeking efforts, allocate psychological rewards, and adjust psychological systems to maintain achieved status, as well as provide the medium that signals status achievements or self-perceived status (Cheng et al., 2010). Pride and high self-esteem reinforce self-confidence and entitlement, promote assertive behavior, "advertise" high mate value, and communicate high status to group members (the broadcasting function of self-esteem; e.g., Zeigler-Hill, Besser, et al., 2013). Empirical evidence confirms that narcissists are often perceived as having high self-esteem and thus are liked (Giacomin & Jordan, 2018). Hubristic pride may also facilitate dominance in narcissistic individuals through feelings of superiority and arrogance, which can help individuals psychologically prepare to exert the necessary force and intimidation needed to achieve a dominant reputation (Cheng et al., 2010). Anger can also contribute to increasing status as it enables narcissists to act aggressively and "recalibrate" others so that they put a high value on the narcissist's welfare (Sell et al., 2009). High status has direct evolutionary implications as it is an important factor in sexual selection and, by definition, implies preferential access to mates and resources.

Narcissists also seek access to resources and mates via less socially desirable means, and their emotional profiles facilitate these efforts. For instance, low affective empathy with intact capacity for cognitive empathy (as indicated by emotion-recognition abilities) supports effective lying, cheating, and even stealing without experiencing a lot of guilt in multiple social settings, including academic, occupational, and intimate relationship contexts (O'Reilly & Doerr, 2020; Schröder-Abé & Fatfouta, 2019; Shimberg et al., 2016). It also enables narcissists to enjoy cheating (Lobbestael et al., 2014), to exploit fellow humans, and to apply coercive tactics, including rape (Hart et al., 2018; Willis et al., 2017). To the extent that it is linked to low emotional attachment, low commitment, dishonesty, ease of abandoning a mate, and a "ludus" love style, it also aids in executing an STM strategy (Holtzman & Strube, 2011).

Altogether, narcissism brings benefits and costs, but from an evolutionary perspective, the costs may not outweigh the benefits. For instance, the fact that the popularity and status benefits of narcissism are short-lived (Leckelt et al., 2015) does not diminish their evolutionary relevance. Narcissists are judged attractive and popular at first sight (Back et al., 2010; Dufner et al., 2013; Sedikides & Campbell, 2017) and this advantage and its associated support for mating success might be sufficient to "keep it in the population's genetic pool." Furthermore, growing evidence shows that grandiose narcissism comes with a physical and mental health cost. For example, narcissists' disproportionate physiological reactivity may be a cost of protecting their grandiosity (Cascio et al., 2015; Edelstein et al., 2010; Reinhard et al., 2012). Similarly, the episodes of vulnerability with associated suffering might be considered costs of excessive narcissistic grandiosity. In conclusion, despite the costs, traits like narcissism can confer reproductive and survival benefits for the individual (Jonason et al., 2012).

Summary
Overall, the emotional profile of grandiose narcissists partly explains why they have been referred to as "successful narcissists" (Campbell et al., 2004). Due to their high self-esteem and tendency to overestimate their own capabilities, they often experience strong positive emotions and rarely experience negative ones, including shame and envy. Their self-enhancement goes together with hubristic (rather than authentic) pride. They might use aggression to assert their dominance. However, in certain circumstances (e.g., when faced with acute threats to their ego or status), grandiose narcissists' emotional experiences might become qualitatively different. In such circumstances, grandiose narcissists may exhibit episodes of vulnerability, and this vulnerability may be present for a substantial portion of the time in their lives (Hyatt et al., 2018). In contrast to grandiose narcissists, their vulnerable counterparts are low in subjective well-being and high in negative emotionality. They too tend to experience hubristic pride and may resort to aggression, but in their case, these responses occur as a result of overwhelming shame. Their intense anger and hostility occasionally lead to outbursts of uncontrollable rage. Research suggests that both forms of narcissism are associated with reduced affective empathy. From the evolutionary point of view, the emotional profiles of narcissists may facilitate STM and may support the attainment of status-related goals.

Chapter Summary
We have discussed narcissism/NPD in general, its possible evolutionary origins, and the emotional experiences of narcissists. In the first section, we saw that narcissism is both a personality trait and a personality disorder (i.e., NPD). One way to think about NPD is that it is present when narcissistic personality becomes a problem. Thus, people can be exceptionally high narcissists but not have NPD if they do not also experience significant intrapersonal and interpersonal impairment. As a personality trait, narcissism is probably best conceptualized as two superordinate dimensions, labeled as grandiose and vulnerable narcissism. Both expressions of narcissism share a common theme of interpersonal antagonism, low agreeableness, and narcissistic rivalry (the specific labels vary depending on the model). However, whereas grandiose narcissism is also characterized by agentic extraversion or narcissistic admiration, vulnerable narcissism is characterized by narcissistic neuroticism. As was discussed in the first section as well as the section on narcissism and emotions, there is some evidence that people may oscillate between grandiose and vulnerable narcissistic states. In particular, there is evidence that grandiose narcissists experience moments of vulnerable narcissism. More research is needed, however, to firmly establish how much this occurs and what prompts it.

The second section focused on the possible evolutionary origins of narcissism. Narcissistic personality is partially heritable, and our best guess is that it has a small (perhaps 10%) component that is genetic. Through sexual and natural selection, narcissism is likely to comprise a constellation of qualities that serve reproductive and survival functions. There is evidence that narcissism, in particular, grandiose narcissism, may confer some reproductive advantages by facilitating STM. Although not necessarily more physically attractive than their non-narcissistic counterparts, narcissists may dress and act in ways that make them more visible and attractive to STM partners. More disturbingly, narcissists may also be more likely than others to engage in sexually coercive behavior. With regard to natural selection, narcissism—again, particularly, grandiose narcissism—is linked to short-term popularity, status, and leadership emergence. Narcissists have domineering personalities, which may give them some advantages when competing with others and allow them access to more abundant resources.

The third and final section focused on the emotional profiles of narcissists. Although it is debatable whether grandiose and vulnerable narcissism are stable and distinct versus dynamic traits, they are considerably different regarding emotions. The extent to which grandiose and vulnerable narcissists are seen as "successful" versus "failed" narcissists, respectively, may be attributable to their emotional profiles. Grandiose narcissism is linked with mostly positive emotional experiences, and grandiose narcissists appear to be relatively well-defended psychologically from threats to the self. It has been said that narcissism is like a disease where everyone around the narcissist suffers (Campbell, 2016). Although even grandiose narcissists probably have their vulnerable moments, to the extent that this description of narcissism is correct, it is clearly a more apt description of grandiose narcissism. Vulnerable narcissism, on the other hand, is linked almost exclusively to negative emotional experiences. Vulnerable narcissists are not nearly as psychologically well-defended as their grandiose counterparts. They are prone to excessive feelings of shame, doubt, and jealousy. Unlike grandiose narcissists, vulnerable narcissists suffer greatly, and vulnerable narcissism is most likely the source of much of the intrapersonal dysfunction associated with NPD. This section concluded by discussing how these emotional profiles, in particular, that associated with grandiose narcissism, may have been shaped through sexual and natural selection. As discussed in the earlier section on evolution, status-signaling traits (e.g., pride, high self-esteem) associated with grandiose narcissism may confer mating and survival advantages.

Acknowledgment

Portions of this work were supported by grant no. 2016/23/G/HS6/01397 from the National Science Center, Poland, awarded to AZC.

References

Ackerman, R. A., Donnellan, M. B., & Wright, A. G. C. (2019). Current conceptualizations of narcissism. *Current Opinion in Psychiatry*, *32*(1), 32–37. https://doi.org/10.1097/YCO.0000000000000463

Al-Shawaf, L., Conroy-Beam, D., Asao, K., & Buss, D.M. (2015). Human emotions: An Evolutionary psychological perspective. *Emotion Review*, *8*(2), 173–186. https://doi.org/10.1177/1754073914565518

American Psychiatric Association. (1980). *Diagnostic and statistical manual of mental disorders* (3rd ed.). American Psychiatric Association. https://doi.org/10.1176/appi.books.9780890425596

American Psychiatric Association. (2013). *Diagnostic and statistical manual of mental disorders* (5th ed.). American Psychiatric Association. https://doi.org/10.1176/appi.books.9780890425596

Anderson, C., & Kilduff, G. J. (2009). Why do dominant personalities attain influence in face-to-face groups? The competence-signaling effects of trait dominance. *Journal of Personality and Social Psychology*, *96*(2), 491–503. https://doi.org/10.1037/a0014201

Andrews, P. W., Gangestad, S. W., Matthews, D. (2002). Adaptationism: How to carry out an exaptationist program. *Behavioral and Brain Sciences*, *25*, 489–553.

Anglim, J., & O'Connor, P. (2019). Measurement and research using the Big Five, HEXACO, and narrow traits: A primer for researchers and practitioners. *Australian Journal of Psychology*, *71*(1), 16–25. https://doi.org/10.1111/ajpy.12202

Aradhye, C. & Vonk, J. (2014). Theory of mind in grandiose and vulnerable facets of narcissism. In A. Besser. (Ed.), *Handbook of the psychology of narcissism: Diverse perspectives* (pp. 347–363). Nova.

Back, M. D., Küfner, A. C. P., Dufner, M., Gerlach, T. M., Rauthmann, J. F., & Denissen, J. J. A. (2013). Narcissistic admiration and rivalry: Disentangling the bright and dark sides of narcissism. *Journal of Personality and Social Psychology*, *105*(6), 1013–1037. https://doi.org/10.1037/a0034431

Back, M. D., Penke, L., Schmukle, S. C., Sachse, K., Borkenau, P., & Asendorpf, J. B. (2011). Why mate choices are not as reciprocal as we assume: The role of personality, flirting and physical attractiveness. *European Journal of Personality, 25*(2), 120–132. https://doi.org/10.1002/per.806

Back, M. D., Schmukle, S. C., & Egloff, B. (2010). Why are narcissists so charming at first sight? Decoding the narcissism-popularity link at zero acquaintance. *Journal of Personality and Social Psychology, 98*(1), 132–145. https://doi.org/10.1037/a0016338

Barry, T. D., Thompson, A., Barry, C. T., Lochman, J. E., Adler, K., & Hill, K. (2007). The importance of narcissism in predicting proactive and reactive aggression in moderately to highly aggressive children. *Aggressive Behavior, 33*(3), 185–197. https://doi.org/10.1002/ab.20198

Baumeister, R. F., Catanese, K. R., & Wallace, H. M. (2002). Conquest by force: A narcissistic reactance theory of rape and sexual coercion. *Review of General Psychology, 6*(1), 92–135. https://doi.org/10.1037/1089-2680.6.1.92

Baumeister, R. F., & Vohs, K. D. (2001). Narcissism as addiction to esteem. *Psychological Inquiry, 12*(4), 206–210.

Beall, A. T., & Tracy, J. L. (2020). Evolution of pride and shame. In L. Workman, W. Reader, & J. H. Barkow (Eds.), *Cambridge handbook of evolutionary perspectives on human behavior* (pp. 179–193). Cambridge University Press.

Besser, A., & Priel, B. (2010). Grandiose narcissism versus vulnerable narcissism in threatening situations: Emotional reactions to achievement failure and interpersonal rejection. *Journal of Social and Clinical Psychology, 29*(8), 874–902. https://doi.org/10.1521/jscp.2010.29.8.874

Bettencourt, B. A., Talley, A., Benjamin, A. J., & Valentine, J. (2006). Personality and aggressive behavior under provoking and neutral conditions: A meta-analytic review. *Psychological Bulletin, 132*(5), 751–777. https://doi.org/10.1037/0033-2909.132.5.751

Blinkhorn, V. J. (2018). *Narcissism in females: Relationships to attitudes towards violence, sexual coercion, and offending behaviour in a non-forensic sample* (Publication Number 28018456). PhD dissertation, University of Liverpool.

Blinkhorn, V., Lyons, M., & Almond, L. (2015). The ultimate femme fatale? Narcissism predicts serious and aggressive sexually coercive behaviour in females. *Personality and Individual Differences, 87*, 219–223. https://doi.org/https://doi.org/10.1016/j.paid.2015.08.001

Blinkhorn, V., Lyons, M., & Almond, L. (2016). Drop the bad attitude! Narcissism predicts acceptance of violent behaviour. *Personality and Individual Differences, 98*, 157–161. https://doi.org/https://doi.org/10.1016/j.paid.2016.04.025

Blinkhorn, V., Lyons, M., & Almond, L. (2019). Criminal minds: Narcissism predicts offending behavior in a non-forensic sample. *Deviant Behavior, 40*(3), 353–360. https://doi.org/10.1080/01639625.2017.1422458

Böckler, A., Sharifi, M., Kanske, P., Dziobek, I., & Singer, T. (2017). Social decision making in narcissism: Reduced generosity and increased retaliation are driven by alterations in perspective-taking and anger. *Personality and Individual Differences, 104*, 1–7. https://doi.org/10.1016/j.paid.2016.07.020

Bogart, L. M., Benotsch, E. G., & Pavlovic, J. D. P. (2004). Feeling superior but threatened: The relation of narcissism to social comparison. *Basic and Applied Social Psychology, 26*(1), 35–44. https://doi.org/10.1207/s15324834basp2601_4

Bradlee, P. M., & Emmons, R. A. (1992). Locating narcissism within the interpersonal circumplex and the five-factor model. *Personality and Individual Differences, 13*(7), 821–830. https://doi.org/https://doi.org/10.1016/0191-8869(92)90056-U

Brammer, W. A., Jezior, K. L., & Lee, S. S. (2016). Psychopathic traits mediate the association of serotonin transporter genotype and child externalizing behavior: Psychopathic traits mediation. *Aggressive Behavior, 42*(5), 455–470. https://doi.org/10.1002/ab.21642

Burchette, R., Lasko, E., & Holtzman, N. S. (in progress). Do narcissistic men pursue short-term mating?

Bushman, B. J., & Baumeister, R. F. (1998). Threatened egotism, narcissism, self-esteem, and direct and displaced aggression: Does self-love or self-hate lead to violence? *Journal of Personality and Social Psychology, 75*(1), 219–229.

Bushman, B. J., Bonacci, A. M., van Dijk, M., & Baumeister, R. F. (2003). Narcissism, sexual refusal, and aggression: Testing a narcissistic reactance model of sexual coercion. *Journal of Personality and Social Psychology, 84*(5), 1027–1040. https://doi.org/10.1037/0022-3514.84.5.1027

Buss, D. M., & Chiodo, L. M. (1991). Narcissistic acts in everyday life. *Journal of Personality, 59*(2), 179–215.

Buss, D. M., & Schmitt, D. P. (1993). Sexual strategies theory: An evolutionary perspective on human mating. *Psychological Review, 100*(2), 204–232. https://doi.org/10.1037/0033-295X.100.2.204

Buss, D. M., & Schmitt, D. P. (2017). Sexual strategies theory: An evolutionary perspective on human mating. In *Interpersonal Development* (pp. 297–325). Routledge.

Campbell, W. K. (2016, February). *The psychology of narcissism* [Video]. TED Ed. https://www.ted.com/talks/w_keith_campbell_the_psychology_of_narcissism

Campbell, W. K., & Campbell, S. M. (2009). On the self-regulatory dynamics created by the peculiar benefits and costs of narcissism: A contextual reinforcement model and examination of leadership. *Self and Identity*, *8*(2–3), 214–232. https://doi.org/10.1080/15298860802505129

Campbell, W. K., Foster, C. A., & Finkel, E. J. (2002). Does self-love lead to love for others? A story of narcissistic game playing. *Journal of Personality and Social Psychology*, *83*(2), 340–354. https://doi.org/10.1037/0022-3514.83.2.340

Campbell, W. K., Foster, J. D., & Brunell, A. B. (2004). Running from shame or reveling in pride? Narcissism and the regulation of self-conscious emotions. *Psychological Inquiry*, *15*(2), 150–153.

Carlson, E. N., & DesJardins, N. M. L. (2015). Do mean guys always finish first or just say that they do? Narcissists' awareness of their social status and popularity over time. *Personality and Social Psychology Bulletin*, *41*(7), 901–917. https://doi.org/10.1177/0146167215581712

Carlson, K. S., & Gjerde, P. F. (2009). Preschool personality antecedents of narcissism in adolescence and young adulthood: A 20-year longitudinal study. Journal of Research in Personality, 43(4), 570–578.

Cascio, C. N., Konrath, S. H., & Falk, E. B. (2015). Narcissists' social pain seen only in the brain. *Social Cognitive and Affective Neuroscience*, *10*(3), 335–341. https://doi.org/10.1093/scan/nsu072

Cheng, J.T., Tracy, J.L., & Henrich, J. (2010). Pride, personality, and the evolutionary foundations of human social status. *Evolution and Human Behavior*, *31*(5), 334–347. https://doi.org/10.1016/j.evolhumbehav.2010.02.004

Cheng, J. T., Tracy, J. L., & Miller, G. E. (2013). Are narcissists hardy or vulnerable? The role of narcissism in the production of stress-related biomarkers in response to emotional distress. *Emotion*, *13*(6), 1004–1011. https://doi.org/10.1037/a0034410

Conroy-Beam, D., & Buss. D. M. (2018). Why is age so important in human mating? Evolved age preferences and their influences on multiple mating behaviors. *Evolutionary Behavioral Sciences*, *13*, 127–157. http://dx.doi.org/10.1037/ebs0000127

Crowe, M. L., Carter, N. T., Campbell, W. K., & Miller, J. D. (2016). Validation of the Narcissistic Grandiosity Scale and creation of reduced item variants. *Psychological Assessment*, *28*(12), 1550–1560. https://doi.org/10.1037/pas0000281

Crowe, M. L., Edershile, E. A., Wright, A. G. C., Campbell, W. K., Lynam, D. R., & Miller, J. D. (2018). Development and validation of the Narcissistic Vulnerability Scale: An adjective rating scale. *Psychological Assessment*, *30*(7), 978–983. https://doi.org/10.1037/pas0000578

Crowe, M. L., Lynam, D. R., Campbell, W. K., & Miller, J. D. (2019). Exploring the structure of narcissism: Toward an integrated solution. *Journal of Personality*, *87*(6), 1151–1169.

Czarna, A. Z., Mauersberger, H., Kastendieck, T., Zdunek, R. R., Sedikides, C. & Hess, U. (2023). Narcissism predicts noise perception but not signal decoding in emotion. *Scientific Reports*. doi: 10.1038/s41598-023-41792-0

Czarna, A. Z., Wróbel, M., Dufner, M., & Zeigler-Hill, V. (2015). Narcissism and emotional contagion: Do narcissists "catch" the emotions of others? *Social Psychological and Personality Science*, *6*(3), 318–324. https://doi.org/10.1177/1948550614559652

Czarna, A. Z., Zajenkowski, M., Maciantowicz, O., & Szymaniak, K. (2019). The relationship of narcissism with tendency to react with anger and hostility: The role of neuroticism and emotion regulation ability. *Current Psychology*, *40*(11), 5499–5514. https://doi.org/10.1007/s12144-019-00504-6

Dawkins, R. (1976). The Selfish Gene. Oxford University Press.

Dickinson, K. A., & Pincus, A. L. (2003). Interpersonal analysis of grandiose and vulnerable narcissism. *Journal of Personality Disorders*, *17*(3), 188–207. https://doi.org/10.1521/pedi.17.3.188.22146

Diener, E., & Lucas, R. (1999). Personality and subjective well-being. In D. Kahneman, E. Diener & N. Schwarz (Eds.), *Well-being: The foundations of hedonic psychology* (pp. 213–230). Russell Sage Foundation.

Di Sarno, M., Zimmermann, J., Madeddu, F., Casini, E., & Di Pierro, R. (2020). Shame behind the corner? A daily diary investigation of pathological narcissism. *Journal of Research in Personality*, *85*, 103924. https://doi.org/10.1016/j.jrp.2020.103924

Dufner, M., Rauthmann, J. F., Czarna, A. Z., & Denissen, J. J. (2013). Are narcissists sexy? Zeroing in on the effect of narcissism on short-term mate appeal. *Personality and Social Psychology Bulletin*, *39*(7), 870–882. https://doi.org/10.1177/0146167213483580

Edelstein, R. S., Yim, I. S., & Quas, J. A. (2010). Narcissism predicts heightened cortisol reactivity to a psychosocial stressor in men. *Journal of Research in Personality*, *44*(5), 565–572. https://doi.org/10.1016/j.jrp.2010.06.008

Edershile, E. A., Woods, W. C., Sharpe, B. M., Crowe, M. L., Miller, J. D., & Wright, A. G. C. (2019). A day in the life of Narcissus: Measuring narcissistic grandiosity and vulnerability in daily life. *Psychological Assessment*, *31*(7), 913–924. https://doi.org/10.1037/pas0000717

Edershile, E. A., & Wright, A. G. C. (2021). Fluctuations in grandiose and vulnerable narcissistic states: A momentary perspective. *Journal of Personality and Social Psychology*. 120(5), 1386–1414. https://doi.org/10.1037/pspp0000370

Ellis, H. (1898). Auto-eroticism: A psychological study. *Alienist and Neurologist*, 19, 260–299.

Fehn, T., & Schütz, A. (2021). What you get is what you see: Other-rated but not self-rated leaders' narcissistic rivalry affects followers negatively. *Journal of Business Ethics*, 174, 549–566. https://doi.org/10.1007/s10551-020-04604-3

Fossati, A., Borroni, S., Eisenberg, N., & Maffei, C. (2010). Relations of proactive and reactive dimensions of aggression to overt and covert narcissism in nonclinical adolescents. *Aggressive Behavior*, 36(1), 21–27. https://doi.org/10.1002/ab.20332

Foster, J. D., & Brennan, J. C. (2012). Narcissism, the agency model, and approach-avoidance motivation. In W. K. Campbell & J. D. Miller (Eds.), *The handbook of narcissism and narcissistic personality disorder* (pp. 89–100). Wiley. https://doi.org/10.1002/9781118093108.ch8

Foster, J. D., & Brunell, A. B. (2018). Narcissism and romantic relationships. In A. D. Hermann, A. B. Brunell, & J. D. Foster (Eds.), *Handbook of trait narcissism: Key advances, research methods, and controversies* (pp. 317–326). Springer International. https://doi.org/10.1007/978-3-319-92171-6_34

Foster, J. D., Campbell, W. K., & Twenge, J. M. (2003). Individual differences in narcissism: Inflated self-views across the lifespan and around the world. *Journal of Research in Personality*, 37(6), 469-486.

Foster, J. D., Shrira, I., & Campbell, W. K. (2006). Theoretical models of narcissism, sexuality, and relationship commitment. *Journal of social and Personal Relationships*, 23(3), 367–386.

Foster, J. D., & Trimm, R. F. (2008). On being eager and uninhibited: Narcissism and approach–avoidance motivation. *Personality and Social Psychology Bulletin*, 34(7), 1004–1017. https://doi.org/10.1177/0146167208316688

Freud, S. (1914). On narcissism: An introduction. In J. Strachey (Ed.), *The standard edition of the complete psychological works of Sigmund Freud* (pp. 73–102). Hogarth.

Gangestad, S. W., Garver-Apgar, C. E., Simpson, J. A., & Cousins, A. J. (2007). Changes in women's mate preferences across the ovulatory cycle. *Journal of Personality and Social Psychology*, 92(1), 151–163. https://doi.org/10.1037/0022-3514.92.1.151

Geukes, K., Nestler, S., Hutteman, R., Dufner, M., Küfner, A. C. P., Egloff, B., Denissen, J. J. A., & Back, M. D. (2017). Puffed-up but shaky selves: State self-esteem level and variability in narcissists. *Journal of Personality and Social Psychology*, 112(5), 769–786. https://doi.org/10.1037/pspp0000093

Giacomin, M., & Jordan, C. H. (2018). Misperceiving grandiose narcissism as self-esteem: Why narcissists are well liked at zero acquaintance. *Journal of Personality*, 87(4), 827–842. https://doi.org/10.1111/jopy.12436

Giammarco, E. A., & Vernon, P. A. (2014). Vengeance and the Dark Triad: The role of empathy and perspective taking in trait forgivingness. *Personality and Individual Differences*, 67, 23–29. https://doi.org/10.1016/j.paid.2014.02.010

Gore, W. L., & Widiger, T. A. (2016). Fluctuation between grandiose and vulnerable narcissism. *Personality Disorders: Theory, Research, and Treatment*, 7(4), 363–371. https://doi.org/10.1037/per0000181

Grapsas, S., Brummelman, E., Back, M. D., & Denissen, J. J. (2020). The "why" and "how" of narcissism: A process model of narcissistic status pursuit. *Perspectives on Psychological Science*, 15(1), 150–172. https://doi.org/10.1177/1745691619873350

Grijalva, E., Harms, P. D., Newman, D. A., Gaddis, B. H., & Fraley, R. C. (2015). Narcissism and leadership: A meta-analytic review of linear and nonlinear relationships. *Personnel Psychology*, 68(1), 1–47. https://doi.org/10.1111/peps.12072

Hart, W., Tortoriello, G. K., Richardson, K., & Adams, J. (2018). "S/he's taken": Effects of grandiose and vulnerable narcissism on responses to relationship threats from rivals. *Journal of Individual Differences*, 39(4), 212–219. https://doi.org/10.1027/1614-0001/a000266

Hart, W., Tortoriello, G. K., Richardson, K., & Adams, J. M. (2019). Detecting the elusive narcissistic reactivity phenomenon: The case for a mechanistic focus. *Self and Identity*, 20(2), 311–322. https://doi.org/10.1080/15298868.2019.1634144

Henrich, J., & Gil-White, F. J. (2001). The evolution of prestige: freely conferred deference as a mechanism for enhancing the benefits of cultural transmission. *Evolution and Human Behavior*, 22(3), 165–196. https://doi.org/https://doi.org/10.1016/S1090-5138(00)00071-4

Hill, P. L., & Roberts, B. W. (2011). Examining 'Developmental Me'. In W. K. Campbell & J. D. Miller (Eds.), *The handbook of narcissism and narcissistic personality disorder: Theoretical approaches, empirical findings, and treatments* (pp. 191–201). John Wiley & Sons, Inc.

Hill, P. L., & Roberts, B. W. (2012). Narcissism, well-being, and observer-rated personality across the lifespan. *Social Psychological and Personality Science*, 3(2), 216–223. doi: 10.1177/1948550611415867

Holtzman, N. S. (2018). Did narcissism evolve? In A. D. Hermann, A. B. Brunell, and J. Foster (Eds.), *The handbook of trait narcissism* (pp. 173–181). Springer. https://doi.org/10.1007/978-3-319-92171-6_19

Holtzman, N. S., & Strube, M. J. (2010). Narcissism and attractiveness. *Journal of Research in Personality, 44*(1), 133–136. https://doi.org/10.1016/j.jrp.2009.10.004

Holtzman, N. S., & Strube, M. J. (2011). The intertwined evolution of narcissism and short-term mating. In W. K. Campbell & J. D. Miller (Eds.), *The handbook of narcissism and narcissistic personality disorder: Theoretical approaches, empirical findings, and treatments* (pp. 210–220). Wiley. https://doi.org/10.1002/9781118093108.ch19

Holtzman, N. S., & Strube, M. J. (2013). People with dark personalities tend to create a physically attractive veneer. *Social Psychological and Personality Science, 4*(4), 461–467. https://doi.org/10.1177/1948550612461284

Hyatt, C. S., Sleep, C. E., Lynam, D. R., Widiger, T. A., Campbell, W. K., & Miller, J. D. (2018). Ratings of affective and interpersonal tendencies differ for grandiose and vulnerable narcissism: A replication and extension of Gore and Widiger (2016), *Journal of Personality, 86*(3), 422–434. https://doi.org/10.1111/jopy.12325

Jackson, J. J., Hill, P. L., & Robert, B. W. (2011). Sociogenomic theory as an answer to the heritability problem. [Online forum comment]. Message posted to https://journals.sagepub.com/doi/10.1002/per.834

Jonason, P. K., Girgis, M., & Milne-Home, J. (2017). The exploitive mating strategy of the Dark Triad traits: Tests of rape-enabling attitudes. *Archives of Sexual Behavior, 46*(3), 697–706. https://doi.org/10.1007/s10508-017-0937-1

Jonason, P. K., Koenig, B.L., & Tost, J. (2010). Living a fast life. *Human Nature, 21*(4), 428–442. https://doi.org/10.1007/s12110-010-9102-4

Jonason, P. K., Li, N. P., Webster, G. D., & Schmitt, D. P. (2009). The dark triad: Facilitating a short-term mating strategy in men. *European Journal of Personality: Published for the European Association of Personality Psychology, 23*(1), 5–18.

Jonason, P. K., Webster, G. D., Schmitt, D. P., Li, N. P., & Crysel, L. (2012). The antihero in popular culture: Life history theory and the Dark Triad personality traits. *Review of General Psychology, 16*(2), 192–199. https://doi.org/10.1037/a0027914

Kaufman, S. B., Weiss, B., Miller, J. D., & Campbell, W. K. (2020). Clinical correlates of vulnerable and grandiose narcissism: A personality perspective. *Journal of Personality Disorders, 34*(1), 107–130. https://doi.org/10.1521/pedi_2018_32_384

Kernberg, O. (1975). *Borderline conditions and pathological narcissism*. Jason Aronson.

Kim, B.-H., Kim, H.-N., Roh, S.-J., Lee, M. K., Yang, S., Lee, S. K., Sung, Y.-A., Chung, H. W., Cho, N. H., Shin, C., Sung, J., & Kim, H.-L. (2015). GWA meta-analysis of personality in Korean cohorts. *Journal of Human Genetics, 60*(8), 455–460. https://doi.org/10.1038/jhg.2015.52

Kohut, H. (1977). *The restoration of the self*. International Universities Press.

Konrath, S., Corneille, O., Bushman, B. J., & Luminet, O. (2014). The relationship between narcissistic exploitativeness, dispositional empathy, and emotion recognition abilities. *Journal of Nonverbal Behavior, 38*(1), 129–143. https://doi.org/10.1007/s10919-013-0164-y

Krizan, Z., & Bushman, B. J. (2011). Better than my loved ones: Social comparison tendencies among narcissists. *Personality and Individual Differences, 50*(2), 212–216. https://doi.org/10.1016/j.paid.2010.09.031

Krizan, Z., & Johar, O. (2012). Envy divides the two faces of narcissism. *Journal of Personality, 80*(5), 1415–1451. https://doi.org/10.1111/j.1467-6494.2012.00767.x

Krizan, Z., & Johar, O. (2015). Narcissistic rage revisited. *Journal of Personality and Social Psychology, 108*(5), 784–801. https://doi.org/10.1037/pspp0000013

Kuchynka, S. L., & Bosson, J. K. (2018). The psychodynamic mask model of narcissism: Where is it now? In A. Hermann, A. Brunell, & J. Foster (Eds.) *The handbook of trait narcissism: Key advances, research methods, and controversies* (pp. 89–95). Springer International.

Lamarche, V. M., & Seery, M. D. (2019). Come on, give it to me baby: Self-esteem, narcissism, and endorsing sexual coercion following social rejection. *Personality and Individual Differences, 149*, 315–325. https://doi.org/https://doi.org/10.1016/j.paid.2019.05.060

Leckelt, M., Küfner, A. C. P., Nestler, S., & Back, M. D. (2015). Behavioral processes underlying the decline of narcissists' popularity over time. *Journal of Personality and Social Psychology, 109*(5), 856–871. https://doi.org/10.1037/pspp0000057

Lee, K., & Ashton, M. C. (2005). Psychopathy, Machiavellianism, and narcissism in the Five-Factor Model and the HEXACO model of personality structure. *Personality and Individual Differences, 38*(7), 1571–1582. https://doi.org/https://doi.org/10.1016/j.paid.2004.09.016

Lewontin, R. C. (1958). A general method for investigating the equilibrium of gene frequency in a population. *Genetics, 43*(3), 419-434.

Livesley, W. J., Jang, K. L., Jackson, D. N., & Vernon, P. A. (1993). Genetic and environmental contributions to dimensions of personality disorder. *The American Journal of Psychiatry, 150*(12), 1826–1831. https://doi.org/10.1176/ajp.150.12.1826

Lobbestael, J., Baumeister, R. F., Fiebig, T., & Eckel, L. A. (2014). The role of grandiose and vulnerable narcissism in self-reported and laboratory aggression and testosterone reactivity. *Personality and Individual Differences, 69*, 22–27. https://doi.org/10.1016/j.paid.2014.05.007

Long, A.D. (2018). *An empathy prime study of narcissism and rape myth acceptance among heterosexual college males* (Publication Number 10812604). M.A. thesis, American University.

Luo, J., Derringer, J., Briley, D. A., & Roberts, B. W. (2017). Genetic and environmental pathways underlying personality traits and perceived stress: Concurrent and longitudinal twin studies. *European Journal of Personality, 31*(6), 614–629. https://doi.org/10.1002/per.2127

Luo, Y. L. L., & Cai, H. (2018). The etiology of narcissism: A review of behavioral genetic studies. In A. D. Hermann, A. B. Brunell, & J. D. Foster (Eds.), *Handbook of trait narcissism: Key advances, research methods, and controversies* (pp. 149–156). Springer International. https://doi.org/10.1007/978-3-319-92171-6_16

Lyons, M., Houghton, E., Brewer, G., & O'Brien, F. (2020). The Dark Triad and sexual assertiveness predict sexual coercion differently in men and women. *Journal of Interpersonal Violence, 37*(7–8), NP4889–NP4904, 088626052092234. https://doi.org/10.1177/0886260520922346

Mahadevan, N., Gregg, A. P., & Sedikides, C. (2019). Is self-regard a sociometer or a hierometer? Self-esteem tracks status and inclusion, narcissism tracks status. *Journal of Personality and Social Psychology, 116*(3), 444–466. https://doi.org/10.1037/pspp0000189

Martinossi-Allibert, I., Rueffler, C., Arnqvist, G., & Berger, D. (2019a). The efficacy of good genes sexual selection under environmental change. *Proceedings of the Royal Society B: Biological Sciences, 286*(1896), 20182313.

Mealey, L. (1995). The sociobiology of sociopathy: An integrated evolutionary model. *Behavioral and Brain Sciences, 18*(3), 523–599.

Miller, J. D., Hoffman, B. J., Gaughan, E. T., Gentile, B., Maples, J., & Keith Campbell, W. (2011). Grandiose and vulnerable narcissism: A nomological network analysis. *Journal of Personality, 79*(5), 1013–1042. https://doi.org/10.1111/j.1467-6494.2010.00711.x

Miller, J. D., Lynam, D. R., Hyatt, C. S., & Campbell, W. K. (2017). Controversies in narcissism. *Annual Review of Clinical Psychology, 13*(1), 291–315. https://doi.org/10.1146/annurev-clinpsy-032816-045244

Miller, J. D., Lynam, D. R., Vize, C., Crowe, M., Sleep, C., Maples-Keller, J. L., Few, L. R., & Campbell, W. K. (2017). Vulnerable narcissism is (mostly) a disorder of neuroticism. *Journal of Personality, 86*(2), 1467–1494. https://doi.org/10.1111/jopy.12303

Morf, C. C., & Rhodewalt, F. (2001). Unraveling the paradoxes of narcissism: A dynamic self-regulatory processing model. *Psychological Inquiry, 12*(4), 177–196. https://doi.org/10.1207/S15327965PLI1204_1

Mouilso, E. R., & Calhoun, K. S. (2012). Narcissism, psychopathy and five-factor model in sexual assault perpetration. *Personality and Mental Health, 6*(3), 228–241. https://doi.org/10.1002/pmh.1188

Murphy, S. C., von Hippel, W., Dubbs, S. L., Angilletta, M. J., Wilson, R. S., Trivers, R., & Barlow, F. K. (2015). The role of overconfidence in romantic desirability and competition. *Personality and Social Psychology Bulletin, 41*(8), 1036–1052. https://doi.org/10.1177/0146167215588754

Neufeld, D. C., & Johnson, E. A. (2016). Burning with envy? Dispositional and situational influences on envy in grandiose and vulnerable narcissism. *Journal of Personality, 84*(5), 685–696. https://doi.org/10.1111/jopy.12192

Nezlek, J. B. (2008). An introduction to multilevel modeling for social and personality psychology. *Social and Personality Psychology Compass, 2*(2), 842–860. https://doi.org/10.1111/j.1751-9004.2007.00059.x

Nicholls, E., & Stukas, A. A. (2011). Narcissism and the self-evaluation maintenance model: Effects of social comparison threats on relationship closeness. *The Journal of Social Psychology, 151*(2), 201–212. https://doi.org/10.1080/00224540903510852

O'Reilly, C.A., III, & Doerr, B. (2020). Conceit and deceit: Lying, cheating, and stealing among grandiose narcissists. *Personality and Individual Differences, 154*, 109627. https://doi.org/10.1016/j.paid.2019.109627

Ovidius Naso, P., & Raeburn, D. (2004). *Metamorphoses: A new verse translation*. Penguin Books.

Paulhus, D. L. (2001). Normal narcissism: Two minimalist accounts. *Psychological Inquiry, 12*(4), 228–230.

Paulhus, D. L. (1998). Interpersonal and intrapsychic adaptiveness of trait self-enhancement: A mixed blessing? *Journal of Personality and Social Psychology, 74*(5), 1197–1208. https://doi.org/10.1037/0022-3514.74.5.1197

Paulhus, D. L., & Williams, K. M. (2002). The Dark Triad of personality: Narcissism, Machiavellianism, and psychopathy. *Journal of Research in Personality, 36*(6), 556–563. https://doi.org/https://doi.org/10.1016/S0092-6566(02)00505-6

Pincus, A. L., Ansell, E. B., Pimentel, C. A., Cain, N. M., Wright, A. G. C., & Levy, K. N. (2009). Initial construction and validation of the Pathological Narcissism Inventory. *Psychological Assessment*, *21*(3), 365–379. https://doi.org/10.1037/a0016530

Rasmussen, K. (2016). Entitled vengeance: A meta-analysis relating narcissism to provoked aggression. *Aggressive Behavior*, *42*(4), 362–379. https://doi.org/10.1002/ab.21632

Rauthmann, J. F., & Kolar, G. P. (2012). How "dark" are the Dark Triad traits? Examining the perceived darkness of narcissism, Machiavellianism, and psychopathy. *Personality and Individual Differences*, *53*(7), 884–889. https://doi.org/https://doi.org/10.1016/j.paid.2012.06.020

Reinhard, D. A., Konrath, S. H., Lopez, W. D., & Cameron, H. G. (2012). Expensive egos: Narcissistic males have higher cortisol. *PLoS ONE*, *7*(7), e30858. https://doi.org/10.1371/journal.pone.0030858

Rhodewalt, F., & Morf, C. C. (1998). On self-aggrandizement and anger: A temporal analysis of narcissism and affective reactions to success and failure. *Journal of Personality and Social Psychology*, *74*(3), 672–685. https://doi.org/10.1037/0022-3514.74.3.672

Ritter, K., Dziobek, I., Preißler, S., Rüter, A., Vater, A., Fydrich, T., Lammers, C.-H., Heekeren, H. R., & Roepke, S. (2011). Lack of empathy in patients with narcissistic personality disorder. *Psychiatry Research*, *187*(1–2), 241–247. https://doi.org/10.1016/j.psychres.2010.09.013

Ryan, K. M., Weikel, K., & Sprechini, G. (2008). Gender differences in narcissism and courtship violence in dating couples. *Sex Roles: A Journal of Research*, *58*(11–12), 802–813. https://doi.org/10.1007/s11199-008-9403-9

Sadeh, N., Javdani, S., Jackson, J. J., Reynolds, E. K., Potenza, M. N., Gelernter, J., Lejuez, C. W., & Verona, E. (2010). Serotonin transporter gene associations with psychopathic traits in youth vary as a function of socioeconomic resources. *Journal of Abnormal Psychology*, *119*(3), 604–609. https://doi.org/10.1037/a0019709

Sanchez-Roige, S., Gray, J. C., MacKillop, J., Chen, C. H., & Palmer, A. A. (2018). The genetics of human personality. *Genes, Brain and Behavior*, *17*(3), e12439.

Scheff, T. J. (1987). The shame-rage spiral: A case study of an interminable quarrel. In H. B. Lewis (Ed.), *The role of shame in symptom formation* (pp. 109–149). Lawrence Erlbaum Associates.

Schröder-Abé, M., & Fatfouta, R. (2019). Shades of narcissistic dishonesty: Grandiose versus vulnerable narcissism and the role of self-conscious emotions. *Journal of Economic Psychology*, *71*, 148–158. https://doi.org/10.1016/j.joep.2018.06.003

Sedikides, C., & Campbell, W. K. (2017). Narcissistic force meets systemic resistance: The energy clash model. *Perspectives on Psychological Science*, *12*(3), 400–421.

Sedikides, C., Rudich, E. A., Gregg, A. P., Kumashiro, M., & Rusbult, C. (2004). Are normal narcissists psychologically healthy? Self-esteem matters. *Journal of Personality and Social Psychology*, *87*(3), 400–416. https://doi.org/10.1037/0022-3514.87.3.400

Sell, A., Tooby, J., & Cosmides, L. (2009). Formidability and the logic of human anger. *Proceedings of the National Academy of Sciences*, *106*(35), 15073–15078. https://doi.org/10.1073/pnas.0904312106

Shiffman, S., Stone, A. A., & Hufford, M. R. (2008). Ecological momentary assessment. *Annual Review of Clinical Psychology*, *4*(1), 1–32. https://doi.org/10.1146/annurev.clinpsy.3.022806.091415

Shimberg, J., Josephs, L., & Grace, L. (2016). Empathy as a mediator of attitudes toward infidelity among college students. *Journal of Sex & Marital Therapy*, *42*(4), 353–368. https://doi.org/10.1080/0092623X.2015.1053019

Skodol, A. E., Bender, D. S., & Morey, L. C. (2014). Narcissistic personality disorder in DSM-5. *Personality Disorders: Theory, Research, and Treatment*, *5*(4), 422–427. https://doi.org/10.1037/per0000023

Sommer, K. L., Kirkland, K. L., Newman, S. R., Estrella, P., & Andreassi, J. L. (2009). Narcissism and cardiovascular reactivity to rejection imagery. *Journal of Applied Social Psychology*, *39*(5), 1083–1115. https://doi.org/10.1111/j.1559-1816.2009.00473.x

Stietz, J., Jauk, E., Krach, S., & Kanske, P. (2019). Dissociating empathy from perspective-taking: Evidence from intra-and inter-individual differences research. *Frontiers in Psychiatry*, *10*, 126. https://doi.org/10.3389/fpsyt.2019.00126

Tangney, J. P., & Dearing, R. L. (2003). *Shame and guilt*. Guilford Press.

Tardif, J., Fiset, D., & Blais, C. (2014). Narcissistic personality differences in facial emotional expression categorization. *Journal of Vision*, *14*(10), 1444.–1444. https://doi.org/10.1167/14.10.1444

Thomaes, S., Bushman, B. J., Stegge, H., & Olthof, T. (2008). Trumping shame by blasts of noise: Narcissism, self-esteem, shame, and aggression in young adolescents. *Child Development*, *79*(6), 1792–1801. https://doi.org/10.1111/j.1467-8624.2008.01226.x

Tracy, J. L., & Robins, R. W. (2007a). The nature of pride. In J. L. Tracy, R. W. Robins, & J. P. Tangney (Eds.), *The self-conscious emotions: Theory and research* (pp. 263–282). Guilford Press.

Tracy, J. L., & Robins, R. W. (2007b). The psychological structure of pride: A tale of two facets. *Journal of Personality and Social Psychology*, *92*(3), 506–525. https://doi.org/10.1037/0022-3514.92.3.506

Tracy, J. L., Cheng, J. T., Martens, J. P., & Robins, R. W. (2011). The emotional dynamics of narcissism: Inflated by pride, deflated by shame. In W. K. Campbell & J. D. Miller (Eds.), *The handbook of narcissism and narcissistic personality disorder* (pp. 330–343). Wiley. https://doi.org/10.1002/9781118093108.ch29

Tracy, J. L., Cheng, J. T., Robins, R. W., & Trzesniewski, K. H. (2009). Authentic and hubristic pride: The affective core of self-esteem and narcissism. *Self and Identity, 8*(2–3), 196–213. https://doi.org/10.1080/15298860802505053

Twenge, J. M., & Campbell, W. K. (2003). "Isn't it fun to get the respect that we're going to deserve?" Narcissism, social rejection, and aggression. *Personality and Social Psychology Bulletin, 29*(2), 261–272. https://doi.org/10.1177/0146167202239051

Urbonaviciute, G., & Hepper, E.G. (2020). When is narcissism associated with low empathy? A meta-analytic review. *Journal of Research in Personality, 89,* 104036. https://doi.org/10.1016/j.jrp.2020.104036

Vazire, S., Naumann, L. P., Rentfrow, P. J., & Gosling, S. D. (2008). Portrait of a narcissist: Manifestations of narcissism in physical appearance. *Journal of Research in Personality, 42*(6), 1439–1447. https://doi.org/https://doi.org/10.1016/j.jrp.2008.06.007

Vernon, P. A., Villani, V. C., Vickers, L. C., & Harris, J. A. (2008). A behavioral genetic investigation of the Dark Triad and the Big 5. *Personality and Individual Differences, 44*(2), 445–452. https://doi.org/10.1016/j.paid.2007.09.007

Vize, C. E., Collison, K. L., Miller, J. D., & Lynam, D. R. (2020). The "core" of the Dark Triad: A test of competing hypotheses. *Personality Disorders: Theory, Research, and Treatment, 11,* 91–99. doi: 10.1037/per0000386

Vonk, J., Zeigler-Hill, V., Mayhew, P., & Mercer, S. (2013). Mirror, mirror on the wall, which form of narcissist knows self and others best of all? *Personality and Individual Differences, 54*(3), 396–401. https://doi.org/10.1016/j.paid.2012.10.010

Wai, M., & Tiliopoulos, N. (2012). The affective and cognitive empathic nature of the Dark Triad of personality. *Personality and Individual Differences, 52*(7), 794–799. https://doi.org/10.1016/j.paid.2012.01.008

Wallace, H. M., Ready, C. B., & Weitenhagen, E. (2009). Narcissism and task persistence. *Self and Identity, 8*(1), 78–93. https://doi.org/10.1080/15298860802194346

Weiss, B., & Miller, J. D. (2018). Distinguishing between grandiose narcissism, vulnerable narcissism, and narcissistic personality disorder. In A. D. Hermann, A. B. Brunell, & J. D. Foster (Eds.), *Handbook of trait narcissism* (pp. 3–13). Springer International. https://doi.org/10.1007/978-3-319-92171-6_1

Widiger, T. A. (Ed.). (2015). *The Oxford handbook of the Five Factor Model* (Vol. 1). Oxford University Press. https://doi.org/10.1093/oxfordhb/9780199352487.001.0001

Williams, K .M., Cooper, B. S., Howell, T. M., Yuille, J. C., & Paulhus, D. L. (2009). Inferring sexually deviant behavior from corresponding fantasies: The role of personality and pornography consumption. *Criminal Justice and Behavior, 36*(2), 198–222. https://doi.org/10.1177/0093854808327277

Willis, M., Birthrong, A., King, J. S., Nelson-Gray, R. O., & Latzman, R. D. (2017). Are infidelity tolerance and rape myth acceptance related constructs? An association moderated by psychopathy and narcissism. *Personality and Individual Differences, 117,* 230–235. https://doi.org/10.1016/j.paid.2017.06.015

Wright, A. G., & Edershile, E. A. (2018). Issues resolved and unresolved in pathological narcissism. *Current Opinion in Psychology, 21,* 74–79. https://doi.org/10.1016/j.copsyc.2017.10.001

Wurst, S. N., Gerlach, T. M., Dufner, M., Rauthmann, J. F., Grosz, M. P., Küfner, A. C. P., Denissen, J. J. A., & Back, M. D. (2017). Narcissism and romantic relationships: The differential impact of narcissistic admiration and rivalry. *Journal of Personality and Social Psychology, 112*(2), 280–306. https://doi.org/10.1037/pspp0000113

Zeigler-Hill, V., Besser, A., Myers, E. M., Southard, A. C., & Malkin, M. L. (2013). The status-signaling property of self-esteem: The role of self-reported self-esteem and perceived self-esteem in personality judgments. *Journal of Personality, 81*(2), 209–220. https://doi.org/10.1111/j.1467-6494.2012.00790.x

Zeigler-Hill, V., Enjaian, B., & Essa, L. (2013). The role of narcissistic personality features in sexual aggression. *Journal of Social and Clinical Psychology, 32*(2), 186–199. https://doi.org/10.1521/jscp.2013.32.2.186

Zeigler-Hill, V., Myers, E. M., & Clark, C. B. (2010). Narcissism and self-esteem reactivity: The role of negative achievement events. *Journal of Research in Personality, 44*(2), 285–292. https://doi.org/10.1016/j.jrp.2010.02.005

Zhang, H., Wang, Z., You, X., Lü, W., & Luo, Y. (2015). Associations between narcissism and emotion regulation difficulties: Respiratory sinus arrhythmia reactivity as a moderator. *Biological Psychology, 110,* 1–11. https://doi.org/10.1016/j.biopsycho.2015.06.014

CHAPTER 62

Addiction and Substance Use

Russil Durrant

Abstract

A number of evolutionary explanations for substance use and addiction have been advanced, with much of the debate centered on whether humans have evolved specific adaptations for drug use, or whether it is better to conceptualize the human attraction to psychoactive substances as reflecting their action on more domain-general motivational and emotional systems that have evolved for other purposes. This chapter reviews evolutionary approaches to understanding drug use and addiction, arguing that extant approaches fail to fully account for the heterogenous nature of substance use and the range of effects that drugs have on users. To more clearly conceptualize substance-using behavior, the author argues that one needs to consider how drugs affect different motivational and emotional systems. This approach can account for the diverse nature of drug-using experiences, and can also provide insights into how drug use and addiction varies by age, gender, and other individual characteristics.

Key Words: addiction, drug use, evolutionary psychology, fundamental motive, emotion

Introduction

Why are humans so attracted to drugs? The use of psychoactive substances is a ubiquitous feature of human societies (Durrant & Thakker, 2002) and, if we recognize that caffeine, tobacco, and alcohol are all substances that can alter cognition, emotion, and behavior, then many people consume drugs on a daily basis. Drug use occurs in a diverse range of contexts, from the ritual-religious use of ayahuasca among the Matsigenka (Shepard, 1998) to the widespread social recreational use of alcohol in Western societies. As such, drugs can deliver putative benefits to users: caffeine promotes alertness and reduces fatigue; alcohol can reduce anxiety and facilitate sociality; opiates are highly effective in suppressing pain; and hallucinogen use generates alternative states of consciousness that many users find attractive and which mesh with religious worldviews (Courtwright, 2001; Durrant & Thakker, 2002). However, at an aggregate level, the use of psychoactive substances causes a significant amount of harm in society. And, although many people use psychoactive substances with few if any problems, some individuals will experience problems with drug use, leading to the development of substance use disorders (SUDs) (American Psychiatric Association, 2013).

The relationships among drug use, SUDs, and emotion are recognized by many scholars (e.g., Kassel et al., 2013). Perhaps most straightforwardly, people use—and become addicted to—drugs because they have the capacity to generate positive, and alleviate negative, emotional states. In short, from a folk-psychological perspective, people use drugs (in part) because drugs make them feel good, whether through their capacity to generate positive affect or to alleviate or diminish negative affect. The critical task from an evolutionary perspective is to account for *why* drugs have this capacity to alter emotional states in ways that promote their use, and how an understanding of the evolutionary origins of drug use and addiction may contribute to reducing overall drug-related harm.

In this chapter I first outline key features of drug use and SUDs, with a focus on the role of motivation and emotion. Many proximal explanations for substance use and SUDs focus on the way that drugs act on reward systems in the brain (e.g., Berridge & Robinson, 2016) in ways that result in pathological "wanting," and how emotional dysregulation is related to problem drug use as individuals turn to psychoactive substances to alleviate negative emotional states (Garland et al., 2018). I then review evolutionary approaches to understanding substance use and addiction, focusing in turn on three main perspectives that highlight the role of distal causal processes in facilitating drug use and addiction. Although it is widely recognized that addiction can be conceptualized as a disorder of motivation, I suggest that an evolutionary approach that highlights the plurality of evolved motivational systems offers a more nuanced framework for considering drug use and addiction. Drawing from Kenrick et al.'s (2010) revised "pyramid of needs," I elaborate how substance use and substance use problems can be understood in light these fundamental human motives. I conclude by briefly teasing out some of the implications of this approach for reducing drug-related harm.

Drug Use, Substance Use Disorders, and Emotion

There is no widely agreed-upon definition of what the term *drug* encompasses. Nutt (2012, p. 4) defines a drug as "a substance that comes from outside the body, crosses the blood/brain barrier, and has an effect similar to our natural neurotransmitters." For Durrant & Thakker (2003, p. 14), a drug is "any substance, whether natural or artificial in origin, which, when taken into the body in sufficient quantities, exerts a non-negligible effect on a user's perception, cognition, emotion, and/or behavior." Although these definitions are inclusive in scope, encompassing hundreds of different substances, the literature focuses on a small set of psychoactive drugs—those used in recreational contexts and whose use can result in harm to users. These can be broadly—albeit somewhat imperfectly—classified into four main classes, based on their characteristic psychopharmacological effects: opioids (e.g., opium, heroin, methadone); stimulants (e.g., caffeine, cocaine, qat); depressants (e.g., alcohol, barbiturates); and hallucinogens (e.g., LSD, psilocybin mushrooms) (Julien, 1998; Nutt, 2012). Some drugs, like cannabis, ecstasy, and ketamine, imperfectly fit into this rubric, and it is important to keep in mind that the effect of a drug depends not just on its chemical properties, but also on the quantity consumed, the mode of use, the psychological characteristics of the user (e.g., personality, expectancies), and the situation or context of use (Zinberg, 1984). The diversity of drugs that humans consume, their different psychoactive properties, and the different contexts of use all point to the importance of recognizing the heterogeneity of drug-using behavior and hence the varied etiological pathways that might account for their use.

Although most episodes of drug use likely entail little harm to users or to others, it is clear that, in aggregate, the use of drugs imposes significant costs on society. For example, globally the use of tobacco is responsible for approximately 7 million deaths each year (World Health Organization, 2017), a further 3 million deaths each year result from alcohol use (World Health Organization, 2018), and over half a million deaths arise from the use of illicit drugs (United Nations Office of Drugs and Crime, 2019). Although a significant minority of drug-related deaths arise from the acute effects of drug use—for example, there are approximately 100,000 deaths from opioid overdoses annually (Degenhardt et al., 2019)—it is patterns of chronic drug use over time that largely account for the global burden of drug-related harm (Degenhardt et al., 2014). The natural focus for public health is, therefore, on *problem drug users*, especially those that meet the criteria for a substance use disorder (SUD). According to the DSM-5, "The essential feature of substance use disorder is a cluster of cognitive, behavioral, and physiological symptoms indicating that the individual continues using the substance despite significant substance-related problems" (American Psychiatric Association, 2013, p. 483). The diagnostic criteria for SUDs in the DSM-5 recognizes four key clusters of problems (MacCoun, 2013): (1) impaired control over drug use, characterized by drug cravings and difficulties in regulating substance-using behaviors; (2) social impairment as substance use impacts on normal social functioning; (3) risky use, highlighted by continued use of substances despite problems arising from use; and (4) pharmacological indicators as indicated by tolerance to the effect of the drug and characteristic withdrawal symptoms on cessation of drug use. There remains a vigorous debate in the literature about whether addiction (which I use here as a rough synonym for SUD) is best characterized as a disease (or, typically, a *brain* disease), but regardless of how this dispute resolves (see Leshner, 1997; Lewis, 2017; Volkow & Koomb, 2015) it is clear that the use and abuse of psychoactive substances cause significant harm to users and to society. It is important, therefore, to develop clear etiological accounts of why individuals use drugs and why drug use can sometimes lead to SUDs.

A useful starting point for theoretical endeavors is to consider how substance use and substance-related problems are patterned. Although there is some variation by drug type and population sampled, one consistent finding is that men are more likely to use drugs, more likely to have drug-related problems, and are more likely to develop SUDs, compared to women. For example, in England and Wales, over twice as many males age 16–59 (12.3%) had taken an illicit drug in the past year, compared to females in the same age group (6.3%) (NHS digital, 2019). Men are also more likely to meet the criteria for SUD (Vasilenko et al., 2017), and are more likely to experience drug-related mortality compared to women. For example, in the United States, Glei and Preston (2020) estimated that between 1999 and 2016, drug use cost men an average of 1.4 years of life expectancy compared to 0.7 for women. Substance use and substance-use problems are also more common among adolescents and young adults than among older age groups, while being married and having children are protective factors against problem drug use (Skewes & Gonzalez, 2013). Risk factors for substance use problems have also been widely studied and include a raft of psychological (impulsivity, delayed reward discounting, emotional dysregulation, sensation seeking), social (economic adversity, peer drug use), and developmental (childhood adversity, family conflict) factors (Garland et al., 2018; Halpern et al., 2018; Owens et al., 2019; Skewes & Gonzalez, 2013). For example, in a meta-analysis of longitudinal studies on the relationship between maltreatment and illicit substance abuse, Halpern et al. (2018) found that individuals with a history of physical abuse during childhood were 74% more likely to develop substance use problems compared to those without a history of abuse. The experience of SUDs is also highly correlated with the experience of other mental disorders, with an international review by Mills and Marvel (2013, p. 486) concluding that ". . . between one-third and one-half of individuals with SUDs meet criteria for a comorbid mental disorder at some in their lives, and 20%–25% will experience these comorbid disorders in any 12-month period."

There is no shortage of theories developed to explain why individuals use drugs, and why some individuals develop substance use problems (West & Brown, 2013). A comprehensive review of etiological theories is beyond the scope of this chapter, so here I focus on theoretical approaches that emphasize the core role of motivational and emotional processes, while recognizing that a comprehensive account of substance use and addiction will entail integrating a range of explanations at different levels of analysis, from genetics to culture (Durrant & Thakker, 2002; Ouzir & Errami, 2016; Skewes & Gonzalez, 2013).

The importance of emotion or affect is recognized in a number of theoretical perspectives. Broadly, two main theoretical approaches have drawn on affective responses to account for substance use and addiction: positive-reinforcement models and negative-reinforcement models (Kassel et al., 2013). According to the positive-reinforcement model, people use drugs because they generate positive emotional experiences (Meyer & Quenzer, 2005), a finding that is supported by research that has explored users' subjective experiences of drug use. There is some variation in the nature of these positive affective experiences depending on the drug, user, and context of use, but in understanding the ongoing attraction of psychoactive substances to individuals it is impossible to ignore the fact that drugs often generate positive hedonic experiences. Different drugs act on different neurotransmitter systems, but one important finding is that most drugs of abuse—directly, or indirectly—elevate levels of the neurotransmitter dopamine in mesocorticolimbic dopamine systems (Piciotto, 1998; Wise & Robble, 2020). According to one prominent perspective on addiction, the chronic use of drugs results in a downregulation of dopamine receptors, raising reward thresholds and leading to greater dependence on drugs to generate positive emotional states (Koob, 2006; Wise & Robble, 2020).

The specific role of dopamine in the generation of positive emotional responses to drug use, however, has been challenged by other researchers who highlight a more important role for other neurotransmitter systems, such as the opioid system, in generating the subjectively pleasurable aspects of drug use (Berridge & Robison, 2016; Nutt et al., 2015). Problem drug use is also often characterized by a *decrease* in the pleasurable response to drug ingestion over time, while drug craving and the motivation to use drugs increase. According to the incentive-sensitization model of drug addiction, it is essential to distinguish between "liking" and "wanting" in their role in initiating and maintaining problem drug use (Berridge & Kringelbach, 2015; Berridge & Robinson, 2016). Research by Berridge and colleagues suggests that the "liking" component of drug use—the aspect that generates positive emotional states—is mediated by hedonic "hot spots" that are distributed across the wider limbic system in the brain and that are sensitive to endogenous opioids and endocannabinoids (Berridge & Kringelbach, 2015; Berridge & Robinson, 2016). In contrast, "wanting" refers to the motivational salience of drug rewards and is mediated by the mesocorticolimbic dopamine system. Compulsive drug use—addiction—arises, according to this model, when this wanting system becomes sensitized, and drugs and drug cues take on elevated motivational properties.

A second broad perspective on the etiology of drug use and addiction focuses on the ability of drugs to alleviate negative emotional states. According to the self-medication hypothesis, first developed by Khantzian (1997), individuals use drugs to deal with stress, negative experiences, and the adverse emotional states that these engender (Gil-Rivas & McWhorter, 2013). As patterns of drug use become problematic, they are maintained via negative reinforcement as drugs effectively relieve the negative emotional states related to withdrawal (Kassel et al., 2013) and key neurobiological systems underlying emotion become dysregulated (Koob, 2015). The role of emotional dysregulation in drug use and addiction finds support from the high comorbidity of SUDs with depression and anxiety disorders. It is also consistent with the finding that adverse developmental experiences such as child abuse are risk factors for later problem drug use. However, although the use of drugs to ameliorate negative emotional states is well supported, establishing causality remains a pressing issue for future research, as it is unclear, as Garland et al. (2018, p. 321) highlight, whether "emotional dysregulation is a cause, correlate, or consequence of addictive behavior."

This brief overview of substance use and addiction highlights a number of important characteristics of drug use. First, the use of psychoactive substances is a common feature of all human societies, although some individuals are more likely to use drugs than are others. Second, some individuals engage in problematic patterns of use that result in SUDs. Again, some individuals are more prone to the development of SUDs than are others. Third, although there are a large number of etiological theories of drug use and addiction, the role of motivation and emotion is central to many accounts. In short, people use drugs because they have the capacity to generative positive, and alleviate negative, emotional states. As such, individuals are motivated to use drugs and, with repeated use, motivational and emotional systems in the brain are changed in ways that promote addiction and create vulnerability to relapse on cessation of drug use. The focus of these etiological accounts has been on the proximate mechanisms that underly drug use and maintain drug addiction. However, for a complete explanatory account we also need to consider distal explanations based on the evolutionary function and evolutionary history of these mechanisms (Tinbergen, 1963). Just *why* are humans (and other animals) vulnerable to the psychopharmacological properties of certain substances which—in some cases—can result in harmful and destructive patterns of behavior? An evolutionary perspective can help to address this question.

Evolutionary Approaches to Understanding Substance Use and Addiction

In his class monograph on *Plant Intoxicants*, published in 1855, Baron Ernst von Bibra ([1855] 1995), musing on the apparent ubiquity of drug use, reflects that ". . . since there exist no people on the Earth that fails to consume one or another of these dainties, which I have subsumed under the name 'pleasure drugs' . . . there must therefore exist a deeper motive, and the notion of fashion or the passion for imitation cannot be applied here." Although published four years prior to Darwin's *On the Origin of Species*, the "deeper motive" alluded to in this passage intimates that there is something fundamental about *human nature* that can account for our attraction to psychoactive substances. Over the past 30 or so years a relatively small, but quite diverse evolutionary literature has emerged that has attempted to address the *distal* causes of drug use and addiction (e.g., Calvey, 2017; Davis, 2014; Durrant & Thakker, 2002; Durrant et al., 2009; Hill, 2013; Nesse & Berridge, 1997; Orsolini et al., 2018; Panksepp et al., 2002; Sullivan & Hagen, 2002).

Hill (2013) proposes that three main evolutionary approaches to understanding drug use and addiction can be discerned in the literature. Although these are referred to in somewhat different terms by different authors, I shall label these three approaches here as: (1) the byproduct or "hijack" approach; (2) the life history approach; and (3) the drug use as adaptation approach. The first two of these approaches suggests that drug use and addiction are essentially byproducts of evolved motivational and emotional systems which have evolved for other reasons. The third approach differs in that it makes the case that certain types of drug use might have been specifically selected for.

According to advocates of the byproduct or "hijack" account, it is unlikely that drug use of any kind has been specifically selected for. In other words, humans do not possess mind/brain adaptations *for* drug use (Durrant et al., 2009; Nesse & Berridge, 1997; Panksepp et al., 2002). Rather, the widespread attraction of drugs and the human propensity for problem drug use arise because psychoactive substances act on motivational-emotional systems that have evolved for other reasons. More specifically, drugs often generate positive emotional states because they act on mesocorticolimbic reward systems that have evolved to generate positive hedonic responses to stimuli which have evolutionary significance (e.g., food, sex, positive social relationships). These systems evolved to signal to organisms stimuli that are linked to reproductive fitness (those that generate positive affective responses) and to motivate actions that are likely to realize fitness benefits (the desire and pursuit of those stimuli). As Nesse and Berridge (1997, p. 64) summarize:

> Drugs of abuse create a signal in the brain that indicates, falsely, the arrival of huge fitness benefit. This changes behavioral propensities so that drug-seeking increase[s] in frequency and displaces adaptive behaviors.

Addiction to drugs occurs when repeated use alters these motivational-emotional systems in ways that promote the motivational salience of drugs and—via learning processes—drug-related stimuli, in ways that lead to compulsive drug use. As highlighted in the DSM-5 criteria for SUD, one feature of addiction is the tendency for individuals to pursue drugs at the expense of other, normally rewarding, activities despite the harmful consequences that arise (Durrant et al., 2009). The capacity for drugs—at least in the short term—to alleviate negative emotional states such as anxiety and depression can also promote drug use, as the removal of these states (which likely evolved to signal and deal with threats and loss, respectively) is rewarding (Nesse & Berridge, 1997). However, although there may be a role for psychotropic drugs in relieving the symptoms of certain mental disorders (e.g., Nesse & Stein, 2019), problems can arise as the underlying source of the negative emotional states are not addressed.

Many other animal species also consume psychoactive substances if given the opportunity, either in the context of their natural environment or within the laboratory (Calvey, 2017). Indeed, animal "models" of addiction have played an important role in understanding the brain mechanisms that underpin drug use and suggest that motivational-emotional systems that drugs act on are remarkably conserved across species (Berridge & Kringelbach, 2015). As noted earlier, drug use is also extremely widespread among diverse human cultural groups, suggesting that the use of psychoactive substances may well have been a relatively enduring feature of our evolutionary history. This raises an important question: If drugs have been a recurrent feature of our selection environment and have the capacity to cause significant harm to users, why haven't we evolved mechanisms to limit their negative effects, just as we have evolved physiological mechanisms that serve to control the pursuit of other rewarding substances, like food (Hill, 2013; see Davis, 2014; Wiss et al., 2018)? For proponents of the byproduct approach, the main reason why addiction is so prominent in contemporary environments is that although humans may have a deep history of drug use, the ready availability of novel, potent psychoactive substances and effective mechanisms for their delivery (e.g., hypodermic syringes) means that there is a *mismatch* between evolved mechanisms and modern environments (Nesse & Berridge, 1997).

The idea of evolutionary mismatch has played a prominent role in evolutionary psychology (Li et al., 2018). As Li et al. (2018) outline, mismatch can arise in a number of different ways and results in a range of different consequences for individuals. Drug use in largely unproblematic ways probably best reflects a mismatch between naturally occurring stimuli (plant alkaloids) and motivational-emotional systems that have evolved for other purposes, as outlined above. In this respect, the outcomes have negligible impacts on reproductive fitness as drug use does not impair normal functioning in any significant way. Problematic patterns of drug use (as characterized in SUDs), however, best reflect the result of human-induced changes (the ready availability of purified, high-potentcy drugs like distilled alcohol, cocaine, methamphetamines, and heroin) and evolved emotional-motivational systems. This results in changes in the intensity of inputs (drugs are readily available and highly potent) that replace the importance of reproductively relevant stimuli, resulting in significant harms to users (see

Figures 62.1a and 62.1b for a schematic overview of the mismatch hypothesis as applied to problem drug use). Arguably, other potential addictions, such as those that relate to gambling, pornography, and perhaps food (e.g., sugar), reflect similar processes (e.g., Davis, 2014; Wiss et al., 2018), although as Durrant et al. (2009) note, it is difficult to ignore the fact that drugs, by virtue of their psychopharmacological properties, may pose a greater liability for addiction.

Although the "byproduct" evolutionary account can help us to understand the ubiquity of drug use cross-culturally and historically, and the human vulnerability to SUDs, it does not, by itself, account for the way that substance use and substance use problems are *patterned*. As noted above, illicit drug use and substance use problems, more generally, are more prevalent among men, younger individuals (adolescents, young adults), and those from lower socioeconomic backgrounds. In addition, substance use problems are more prevalent among single and childless individuals, and are related to a range of other risky behaviors such as crime, dangerous driving, and problem gambling. A number of scholars have noted that these patterns are broadly consistent with the idea that the use and abuse of psychoactive substances can understood in the context of life-history theory (Durrant et al., 2009; Hill & Chow, 2002; Richardson et al., 2016; Richardson et al., 2017).

Life-history theory is a "middle-level" evolutionary theory (see Buss, 1995) which is centrally concerned with how organisms optimally allocate resources across the course of their life span (Del Guidice et al., 2005). In short, three key trade-offs frame this optimal allocation: (1) current reproduction vs. future reproduction; (2) offspring quality vs. offspring quantity; and (3) mating vs. parenting. How organisms negotiate these trade-offs will depend on the species, sex, age, and aspects of the local environment. Between-species differences in the allocation of resources based on these trade-offs can be broadly captured along a fast (higher mortality, shorter life span, earlier maturation, offspring quantity, limited parental care), slow (lower

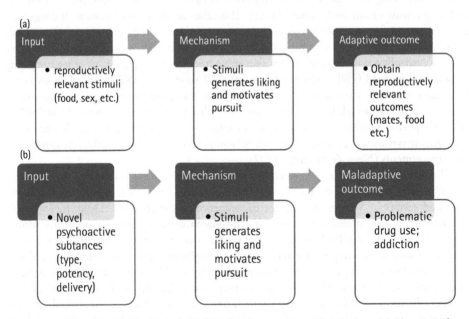

Figure 62.1. a. The action of evolved motivational/emotional systems in natural environments. b. The action of evolved motivational/emotional systems in modern environments.

Source: Adapted from Li et al. (2018).

mortality, longer life span, later maturation, offspring quality, more parent care) continuum. Evolutionary psychologists have employed this fast-slow continuum to explain individual differences in traits and characteristics *within* species, with a focus on humans (Del Guidice, 2020). In brief, fast life-history traits such as greater risk-taking, a focus on present rewards, and unrestricted socio-sexuality should be more likely to emerge in harsh or unstable environments because these traits are more likely to promote reproductive success in uncertain environments (Ellis et al., 2009). Life-history theory also predicts that young men should also be more prone to risk-taking because men, compared to women, have more to gain and less to lose (in evolutionary terms) from risky but rewarding behaviors, a difference heightened during late adolescence and early adulthood as competition for mates, status, and resources intensifies (Ellis et al., 2012). At the neurobiological level, these differences are manifest in age, sex, and individual differences in the activity of reward mechanisms in the brain which, arguably, are calibrated in ways that promote adaptive behavior (Steinberg, 2014). The logic here for understanding some of the main patterns in drug use and abuse are clear: if drug use entails the pursuit of potentially risky rewards with a focus on immediate gratification, then it is unsurprising that risk for drug use is higher for young, unmarried males, from socially and economically disadvantaged backgrounds. In this respect, the patterns in drug use are a byproduct of the mechanisms that promote the pursuit of rewards, and are reflected in other related correlates of problem drug use like crime and antisocial behavior (Durrant & Ward, 2015).

Most accounts, as outlined above, have linked drug use—including problem drug use—to fast life-history strategies. Does this relationship also hold for substance use *disorders*, as they are articulated in the DSM-5? In a recent evolutionary framework—the Fast-Slow-Defense (FSD) model—for understanding and organizing psychopathology, Del Guidice (2018; Del Guidice & Haltigan, 2020) argues that psychopathologies can be broadly categorized into three main types of disorder: fast spectrum (F-type) disorders, slow spectrum (S-type) disorders, and defense activation (D-type) disorders. These categories are largely self-explanatory. F-type disorders are related to fast life-history traits like impulsivity, sensation seeking, and unrestricted socio-sexuality. Examples include conduct disorder, antisocial personality disorder, and most cases of schizophrenia spectrum disorder. S-type disorders, in contrast, are related to slow life-history traits such as conscientiousness and high self-control, and examples include a subtype of autism spectrum disorder, obsessive-compulsive disorder, and a subtype of eating disorder. Finally, D-type disorders are linked to evolved defense mechanisms, and include depression, social anxiety disorder, and post-traumatic stress disorder. In addition to providing a much-needed evolutionary framework for conceptualizing mental disorders, the FSD model has the added advantage of recognizing heterogenous subtypes within DSM diagnostic categories, thus opening up scope for the consideration of multiple etiological pathways. For example, the model recognizes two subtypes of eating disorder—an F-type characterized by high impulsivity and bulimic symptoms, and a S-type which is linked to high conscientiousness (Del Guidice, 2018).

Substance use disorders have yet to be explicitly considered within the FSD model (Del Guidice & Haltigan, 2020), but based on our understanding of these disorders and their relationship to other behavioral and psychological traits, it is possible to sketch out some preliminary suggestions. Given the relationship between substance use problems and traits such as impulsivity, risk-taking, sensation seeking, and delayed discounting and the role of adverse developmental experiences as risk factors for substance use problems, it seems most straightforward to conceptualize SUDs as F-type disorders. This would also be consistent with the substantial comorbidity between SUDs and mental disorders like antisocial personality disorder, bipolar disorder, and schizophrenia spectrum disorders (Mills & Marel, 2013). However, there is also a significant relationship between SUDs and D-type disorders such as depression, various anxiety disorders, and post-traumatic stress disorder (Mills & Marel, 2013). This opens up the possibility that there may be subtypes of SUDs, with different etiological pathways: first, an F-type SUD linked to impulsivity, risk-taking, and sensation seeking, and driven—initially at least—by the positive affective states that drug use generates; second, a D-type SUD that is primarily related to negative affect (anxiety, depression, and panic). Although there has been some work on etiological subtypes, particularly as they relate to alcohol use disorder (e.g., see Cloninger et al., 1996), there is scope for future research to explore this possibility within an explicitly evolutionary framework and to consider how these subtypes might be related to gender (perhaps F-type more male biased; D-type more female biased), age of onset, specific drug of abuse, and course of the disorder (see Becker & Chartoff, 2019).

The two evolutionary perspectives considered to this point conceptualize drug use and addiction as byproducts of mechanisms that have evolved for other reasons. A third perspective challenges this idea and, instead, suggests that at least the use of some psychoactive substances might have been specifically selected for due to their benefits in promoting survival and reproductive success. Sullivan, Hagen, and colleagues (Hagen et al., 2009; Hagen et al., 2013; Hagen et al., 2018; Sullivan & Hagen, 2002; Sullivan et al., 2008) have championed the idea that the long coevolutionary relationship between humans and plants has led to the capacity of humans (and other animals) to exploit certain plant toxins (such as those that have psychoactive effects) for self-medication purposes. In direct contrast to the hijack or mismatch hypothesis, Hagen et al. (2013, p. 3) propose that:

> . . . the brain might not accidentally reward or reinforce consumption of nicotine and other addictive drugs, as the hijack model proposes, nor generate purely aversive reactions, as drug toxicity would suggest, but instead has evolved specialized mechanisms to precisely *regulate* drug consumption to minimize cost and maximize benefits. (italics in original)

According to their neurotoxin regulation hypothesis, humans have evolved the capacity to utilize otherwise toxic substances such as nicotine, caffeine, and cannabis in ways that can promote reproductive success. Most importantly, the use of these substance can help to alleviate the negative impacts of macro-parasites such as helminths, which plague hunter-gatherer populations. Support for this model comes from a cluster of studies with Aka foragers of the Congo basin which demonstrate that the use of nicotine (Roulette et al., 2014), and cannabis (Roulette et al., 2016) have a protective effect against helminth infection. Age differences in substance use can be explained in the model due to the greater risk for harms arising from plant toxin ingestion among children, and alternative mechanisms for regulating toxin consumption (e.g., neophobia, and a stronger aversion to the characteristically bitter taste of plant toxins), while sex differences are partly explained due to the negative impact of plant toxins on fetuses and nursing infants (Hagen et al., 2013; Roulette et al., 2016; although see Placek et al., 2019).

In a similar fashion, Dudley (2002) proposes that the consumption of alcohol may have been selected for in humans (and other species) as cues to ethanol would have guided hominins to a potentially valuable food source, rich in calories: fermenting fruit. Given the long exposure of hominins and our primate ancestors to fermenting fruit, it is plausible to suggest that we have evolved specific olfactory and gustatory mechanisms to detect low levels of ethanol, which would have guided humans to this useful source of nutrition, with subsequent effects on our preferences for alcoholic beverages with greater ethanol concentrations.

Summary
There is still a lack of specific empirical research which allows us to evaluate the three broad evolutionary perspectives presented here, although there are some promising lines of research. Although the models are often pitched as alternatives, they are potentially compatible rather than competing perspectives, and it is possible to draw them together in an integrated evolutionary model of substance use (e.g., Durrant & Thakker, 2003). For instance, it is plausible that humans have evolved gustatory and olfactory preferences which have guided the use of certain plants, which have psychoactive properties (e.g., those that contain nicotine, THC, arecoline, and alcohol) because they led to better reproductive outcomes (i.e., reduced parasite load, nutrition). These substances *also* generate positive emotional states because of their action on mesocorticolimbic reward pathways, which may have guided foragers to these particular plants, which were then incorporated into folk pharmacopeia, much as other plants were. Over time, those plants that were particularly effective in improving health outcomes might have selected for gustatory and olfactory processes that promoted their use, much as the neurotoxin regulation model suggests, in a culture-gene coevolutionary process. Our attraction to the full range of psychoactive substances probably better reflects their specific action on evolved motivational-emotional systems, and to understand how use of these substances can lead to addiction we need to recognize the substantial mismatch between the current array of drugs that are available to humans and the sparser selection that would have featured in our ancestral pasts. Ultimately, understanding why humans use drugs and why this use can sometimes lead to SUDs requires us to understand the motivations that underpin drug-using behavior in more detail.

The Fundamental Motives Framework

The idea that addiction is fundamentally a disorder of *motivation* is central to many etiological explanations for problem drug use (West & Brown, 2013). For example, West and Brown (2013, p. 7) suggest that "[a]ddiction involves a chronic condition of the *motivational system* . . . in which there is an abnormally and damagingly high priority given to a particular activity" (italics in original). An evolutionary perspective, however, recognizes that there are *multiple* human motives and hence an array of domain-specific motivational-emotional systems that have evolved to realize these motives. Here, I outline how a framework that focuses on fundamental motives can help us to understand drug use and addiction. This framework draws heavily from recent evolutionary work on fundamental motives (Kenrick et al., 2010; Schaller et al., 2017), evolved motivational (Aunger & Curtis, 2013, 2015; Del Guidice, 2018), and emotional (Beall & Tracy, 2017) systems, and how these might be applied to specific domains (e.g., Ward & Carter, 2019) (see Table 62.1).

A case can be made for the primacy of motivation in any account of psychological phenomena (Baumesiter, 2016; Kruglanski et al., 2016). For organisms to act in ways that promote their inclusive fitness, they must be *motivated* to engage in certain behaviors, balance and prioritize conflicting motivational demands, and adjust motivational priorities depending on critical life-history and contextual variables. The first key point is the recognition that humans (and other organisms) have a *number* of fundamental motives that reflect and map onto the specific problems that they were designed to solve (Kenrick et al., 2010). In their revised pyramid of needs, Kenrick et al. (2010) delineate seven fundamental motives or needs: immediate physiological needs, self-protection, affiliation, status/esteem, mate acquisition, mate retention, and parenting. Each of these fundamental motives are realized via distinct motivational systems.

Table 62.1 Fundamental Motives, Emotions, Substance Use, and Addiction

Fundamental Motives[a]	Main Motivational-Emotional Systems[b] and (Characteristic Emotions/Feeling States)[c]	Evolutionary Functions[b]	Example implications for Substance Use, Substance Use Problems, and Addiction (Role of Specific Drugs)
Immediate physiological needs	Food/water acquisition, pain avoidance (hunger, thirst, pain)	To ensure survival by acquiring metabolic resources and maintaining bodily integrity	Use of drugs for their caloric/medicinal/thirst quenching properties (nicotine, caffeine, alcohol); use of drugs to alleviate physical pain (opiates, alcohol)
Self-protection	Fear system (fear)	To avoid, escape, or otherwise respond to immediate threats	Use of drugs to dampen fear and anxiety (opiates, alcohol, benzodiazepines); use of drugs associated with low disgust sensitivity; paranoia/hyper-vigilance related to chronic use of stimulant drugs (amphetamines/cocaine/other psychostimulants)
	Disgust system (disgust)	To avoid contact with harmful pathogens	
	Security system (fear, anxiety)	To detect and respond to potential threats	
Affiliation	Affiliation system Happiness (depression)	To form and maintain relationships with group members (kin and non-kin)	Use of a wide variety of substances to generate positive (and alleviate negative) emotional states (especially opioids, alcohol); role of certain drugs (e.g., ecstasy) in generating feelings of empathy and compassion.
	Reciprocity system Happiness (anger)	To find, select, and maintain cooperative partners	
Status/Esteem	Status system (pride, shame)	To obtain and maintain a favorable position in social hierarchies (dominant and/or prestige)	Stimulants such as cocaine promote confidence, power, feelings of high self-esteem/grandiosity
Mate acquisition	Mating system (lust)	To find and attract sexual partners	Drug use related to more general risk-taking behavior; intra-sexually competitive drug use (e.g., binge drinking, drug experimentation); Drug use as display (e.g., binge drinking, drug experimentation); drug use and unrestricted socio-sexuality
Mate retention	Pair-bonding system (romantic love)	To form and maintain long-term relationships with sexual partners	Mechanisms of addiction may share overlapping pathways with those that mediate feelings of romantic love. Opioids, in particular, can hijack this system and act as substitute for a pair-bond. Marriage as a potential protective factor against problem drugs use
Parenting	Attachment system (parental love)	To maintain close relationship with caregivers	Parenting as protective factor against problem drug use
	Caregiving system (tenderness)	To protect and nurture offspring	
Other motivational systems	Aggression system	To leverage advantage for self, kin, and group	Certain substances may increase (e.g., alcohol, cocaine, methamphetamine) or decrease (e.g., alcohol, opiates) anger/aggression, although this is strongly influenced by individual and contextual factors.
	Play system		The use of many substances is linked to curiosity, and sensation seeking. This may be particularly the case for hallucinogens.

Sources: [a] Kenrick et al. (2010); [b] Del Guidice (2018, p. 39), Aunger & Curtis (2013, p. 53); [c] Beall & Tracy (2017).

Just how many motivational systems humans possess, and how best to characterize these systems, is a matter of some debate. One critical issue concerns the relationship between motivation and emotion. For Baumeister (2016), emotions represent the subjective experiences that provide information to organisms about motivationally salient events. The standard evolutionary psychological account of emotions, however, outlines a broader role, one that overlaps substantially with evolutionary conceptualizations of motivation (Al-Shawaf et al., 2016; Sznycer et al., 2017). Thus, Al-Shawaf et al. (2016, p. 173) argue that emotions "evolved as superordinate mechanisms responsible for coordinating suites of other information-processing programs." As Beall & Tracy (2017) note, fundamental motives and specific emotions are closely related, and it may in fact be more useful to characterize these as *motivational-emotional* systems to recognize the tight coupling between motivational and emotional processes. Just how many different motivational systems humans possess is a matter of dispute, with different authors providing different lists. In Table 62.1, I have mapped the more widely recognized motivational systems as listed by Del Guidice (2018) and Aunger and Curtis (2013, 2015) onto the seven fundamental motives presented by Kenrick et al. (2010), noting the most salient emotions associated with these systems (Beall & Tracy, 2017). We should also recognize that there are motivational systems (e.g., the aggression system) that are less domain specific and that may be recruited to realize a range of fundamental motives depending on the context (e.g., self-protection, status, mate retention). Finally, a comprehensive framework for understanding human motivation and how it is translated into behavior will need to recognize the other key systems that play a pivotal role in managing trade-offs among competing motivational needs given specific social and ecological contexts. These will include systems underlying self-regulation and decision-making, mentalizing/perspective taking, and more domain-general reward/salience systems.

How might this framework for understanding evolved motivational-emotional systems help us to understand substance use and addiction? Two points can be made. First, because most drugs of abuse act on evolutionarily conserved, domain-general reward/salience systems, as discussed in the byproduct account of evolution presented in the previous section, we can expect that drug use and, especially, drug addiction reflect a re-routing of motivational priorities to the pursuit and use of psychoactive substances. In this respect, "the use of drugs" is artificially "inserted" into Kenrick et al.'s (2010) revised pyramid of needs and may—in cases of addiction—come to supplant other motivational needs. This is certainly consistent with the literature on the nature of addiction (Lewis, 2015) and the DSM-5 diagnostic criteria for SUDs (American Psychiatric Association, 2013) that highlight how drugs continue to be used, despite negative impacts on individual health (immediate physiological needs), occupational functioning (status/esteem needs), and social relations (affiliation, mate retention, parenting needs). Second, by recognizing the potential role of multiple motivational-emotional systems, the framework presented in Table 62.1 can provide a more fine-grained evolutionary analysis that is able to help understand different aspects of drug use and addiction, and how these might manifest in different individuals and for different types of psychoactive substances.

Humans, like all other animals, are motivated to meet *immediate physiological needs* for food, water, and pain avoidance, and possess physiological systems that respond to the negative affective states (hunger, thirst, pain) in ways that meet these needs. There are some clear implications here for substance use and substance use problems. Drugs like nicotine, caffeine, cannabis, and arecoline are employed among foraging societies to medicate against helminth infections, as the neurotoxin regulation hypothesis suggests (Roulette et al., 2014; Roulette et al., 2016). Alcohol is consumed for its nutritional properties (in addition to its other effects), and is considered a "food" in many cultures (Heath, 2000). The widespread consumption of alcohol, historically, has also been an important source of fluids given the lack of clean drinking water in many societies (Courtwright, 2001), and many drugs (e.g., coca leaves, nicotine) are used to partly alleviate hunger (Courtwright, 2001; Durrant & Thakker, 2003). In addition, drugs—especially alcohol and opiates—have played, and continue to play, an important role in alleviating both physical and psychological pain, as the self-medication hypothesis suggests. Drug use is maintained, therefore, due its positive effect on relieving the negative subjective states that relate to hunger, thirst, and pain. The role of drugs in addressing immediate physiological needs, of course, depends on the broader social and ecological context of use (e.g., risk of parasite infection, availability of food and water, exposure to physical and psychological trauma).

Humans, like other animals, also have motivational-emotional systems that function to provide *self-protection* against harms. The fear system functions to avoid, escape, or otherwise respond to immediate threats. Fear is an aversive emotion, but is important in facilitating protection against social and physical harms. Various drugs have the capacity to dampen fear and anxiety, especially depressants such as alcohol and benzodiazepines and opioids, both natural and synthetic (Nutt, 2012). Recent work on alcohol suggest that the anxiolytic effects of alcohol are related to the capacity of alcohol to reduce activity in the salience network, which plays a key role in the experience of anxious emotional states (Gorka et al., 2018). Indeed, consistent with the self-medication hypothesis, the problem use of these substances may relate in part to their anxiolytic effects, and there is some evidence that individuals who drink to "relax" may consume larger quantities of alcohol (Linden-Carmichael et al., 2020). Because drug use involves the ingestion of substances, the disgust system (Curtis et al., 2011; Neuberg et al., 2011) and subjective experiences of disgust should play a role in influencing drug-using behavior because, like other ingested substances, drug consumption entails potential risks relating to ingestion of harmful microorganisms and plant toxins (Lieberman et al., 2018). In short, we should expect that individuals with high disgust sensitivity are less likely to consume psychoactive substances and are more likely to be morally opposed to the use of drugs. Various lines of evidence support these links between disgust sensitivity and drug use, and may account for age and gender differences in drug use. Finally, it is worth pointing out how the use of some drugs (especially stimulants such as cocaine and methamphetamine) may adversely affect the security system, resulting in states of paranoia and hypervigilance which, in turn, increase the risk for aggression and violence (McKetin et al., 2014).

Humans have a fundamental need to belong (Baumeister & Leary, 1995). In other words, we—like other social species—have a strong need for *affiliation*, that is realized through the affiliation and reciprocity motivational-emotional systems and is related to the emotion of happiness. Feelings of depression or low mood arguably act as indicators that this motivational need is not being fulfilled and may contribute to the pursuit of behaviors that can generate positive emotional responses. The implications for drug use and addiction are reasonably clear here. As noted above, the acute use of a wide variety of drugs is related to their capacity to generate positive emotional states, such as feelings of euphoria. Relatedly, drugs can temporarily alleviate negative emotional states such as depression (e.g., Blum et al., 2013). There is likely a particularly important role for the use of opiates in promoting feelings of social bonding with others, and opiate use may serve as an effective proxy or substitute for affiliative relationships for some individuals. According to the brain opioid theory of social attachment (Kyte et al., 2020; Machin & Dunbar, 2011), experiences of physical and social pain are instantiated in the same regions of the brain and are served by the endogenous opiate system. Humans may, therefore, turn to *exogenous* opiates (heroin, morphine, oxycodone, etc.) as a way of assuaging feelings of social pain, particularly as they arise from social rejection, loneliness, and/or feelings of insecure attachment (Hill et al., 2017; Kyte et al., 2020). It is also worth noting that the capacity for certain psychoactive substances, such as MDMA (ecstasy), to generate feelings of intimacy, trust, social connectedness, compassion, and empathy likely play an important role in their use by facilitating the human motive of affiliation (e.g., Sumnall et al., 2006; Wardle et al., 2014).

There is agreement that humans—despite our relatively egalitarian evolutionary history—have a fundamental need for *status/esteem* (Anderson et al., 2015). The status motivational-emotional system and feelings of pride and shame are functionally related to obtaining and maintaining favorable positions in social hierarchies (Tracy et al., 2020). Relatively little work has explicitly explored the potential role of the status system in promoting drug use. However, stimulant drugs have the capacity to promote feelings of confidence, high self-esteem, and power that arguably are attractive subjective states because of their role in signaling high social status. Indeed, in a study by Seecoff and Tenant (1986) of participants' experiences of a cocaine rush, the two most common experiences for males were "excitement" and "power." Interestingly, for female participants "power" was much less likely to be mentioned, perhaps reflecting sex differences in the motivational importance of social status (although see Neel et al., 2016).

Mate acquisition and *mate retention* are important motivational needs and are underpinned by the mating (lust), and pair-bonding (love), motivational-emotional systems, respectively. As noted above, the demographic pattern of drug use and substance use problems (more prevalent for males/young adults) is consistent with a life-history evolutionary perspective that highlights the role of the mating system in problem drug use. This approach suggests that risky drug use reflects more general mechanisms underlying risk-taking, which is more prevalent among young males because they have more to gain in evolutionary terms from such behavior (Hill & Chow, 2002; Wilson & Daly, 1985). Drugs may also play a role more directly in intra-sexual competitions among young males—for example, competitive drinking among young men is common in a variety of cultures (Heath, 2000), and drug use is a cross-culturally common feature of coming-of-age rituals (Grob & Dobkin de Rios, 1992). Drug use is related to a relatively unrestricted sociosexual orientation (e.g., Cavazos-Rehg et al., 2011), and thus might facilitate a short-term mating strategy, especially among young males.

Unlike our closest genetic relative, the chimpanzee, pair-bonding is an important feature of our mating systems, and is underpinned by the pair-bonding motivational-emotional system and the experience of romantic love (Fletcher et al., 2015). On the face of it, romantic love shares many psychological and behavioral similarities with the phenomenon of drug addiction (Fisher et al., 2002; Fisher et al., 2016). As Fisher et al. (2016, para 1) summarize: "Individuals in the early stage of intense romantic love show many symptoms of substance and non-substance or behavioral addictions, including euphoria, craving, tolerance, emotional and physical dependence, withdrawal and relapse." This similarity between drug addiction and romantic love arises, according to Fisher et al. (2002, 2006), because the neurobiological systems underpinning the experience of romantic love overlap with those that are involved in drug addiction. Problem drug use may then, in part, arise because of the absence of romantic relationships, and the experience of romantic love might serve as a "reward replacement" for problem drug users. The final fundamental motive outlined in Table 62.1 relates to *parenting*, and is underpinned by attachment and caregiving systems. There are similar implications here to those outlined for mate retention and affiliation, and it is recognized that parenthood is a protective factor against problem drug use.

Summary and Implications
Although many of the links between fundamental motives, motivational-emotional systems, and drug use and addiction are relatively tentative at this stage, I suggest that this approach encourages a more nuanced perspective on drug-using behavior that reflects the role of multiple pathways to drug use that might differ based on gender, age, and other life-history variables. This may, in turn, encourage approaches to intervention that are more tailored in ways that recognize the varied motivational underpinnings of drug use and addiction. Space precludes anything like a thorough presentation of implications for drug prevention, but some initial ideas can be sketched for reducing drug-related problems.

First, it is important to recognize that it is unlikely that we can eliminate substance use or substance use problems. Given the capacity for a wide variety of psychoactive drugs to generate positive, and alleviate negative emotional states, the embeddedness of drug use in a diverse range of cultural contexts, and the way that drug use is linked to fundamental motives, it seems unrealistic to assume that the use of drugs will be eliminated. Moreover, given the role of many psychoactive substances in meeting fundamental motives (e.g., the suppression of pain; the reduction of anxiety), the eradication of all drugs for all people is not desirable. Where possible, however, we should recognize that, in many cases, there is a "motivational mismatch" (Curtis & Aunger, 2011) between the nature and availability of drugs in contemporary society, and evolved motivational mechanisms. This mismatch contributes to the development of SUDs and the significant costs that drug use has on users and society. Public policy initiatives that limit the availability and potency of drugs therefore have an important role to play, although care needs to be taken that certain policies (e.g., drug prohibition) do not generate more harm than the harms they are designed to limit, and genuine harm-reduction initiatives (e.g., needle exchange, opioid substitution programs) have an important role to play given that humans are going to continue to use (and become addicted to) psychoactive substances.

Although SUDs have a high rate of relapse, there is good evidence that a diverse range of treatment approaches—from 12-step programs, to cognitive behavioral therapy (CBT), to mindfulness meditation, to motivational interviewing—can be effective in reducing problem drug use (Miller et al., 2001; Prendegast et al., 2002). Indeed, the success of such a diverse range of programs suggests that they may be successful by addressing different motivational systems. For instance, the value in group-based therapies may lie, in part, in the affiliative networks and social support that they provide for users for whom affiliative needs have been met previously through drug use. Various other techniques—e.g., motivational interviewing, CBT—may exert their positive effects, in part, through their capacity to highlight the way that problem drug use may ultimately result in the long-term failure to meet fundamental motives (e.g., status, self-protection, mate retention, parenting) and to make the fulfillment of these motives without drug use a priority. Weak evidence for the efficacy of compulsory drug treatment (e.g., Werb et al., 2016) emphasizes the importance of individuals recognizing for themselves the negative impacts of their substance-using behaviors and how their motivational needs can be met through other channels.

As outlined above, the role of emotions in the etiology of substance use disorders is clear. Research supports the idea that the use of substances to cope with negative emotional states and—perhaps to a lesser extent—promote positive emotions plays an important role in the maintenance and relapse to substance use problems (Cooper et al., 1995; Koob, 2015). This suggests that interventions designed to address emotional dysregulation have an important role to play in treating individuals with substance use disorders. Indeed, in a recent meta-analysis of the effect of substance use interventions on emotion outcomes, Kang et al. (2019) found that a diverse range of interventions for substance use disorders significantly reduce negative emotions, which potentially plays a role in the efficacy of these treatments. The approach presented in this section suggests the need to take a more fine-grained approach to the way that problem drug use is maintained via a diverse range of both positive and negative emotional states and how these can be met in a non-harmful way.

Conclusion

Despite the vigorous efforts to control the global supply of illegal substances through crop eradication programs, interdiction of drugs at borders, law enforcement efforts, and—in many places—punitive criminal justice responses, there is little evidence that the cultivation and production of illegal drugs have declined in recent years and, in fact, the prevalence of substance use and substance use disorders appears to be increasing (United Nations Office of Drugs and Crime, 2020). The persistence of drug use and substance use disorders, the diverse range of drugs that are currently available, and the constant flow of new psychoactive substances emerging from clandestine laboratories (Reuter & Pardo, 2017) speak to the enduring attraction these substances have to humans. As argued in this chapter, this attraction can be understood in terms of how evolution has shaped our fundamental motivational-emotional systems.

By taking a pluralistic approach to human fundamental motives, it is possible to provide a fine-grained analysis of drug use and addiction that recognizes diverse etiological pathways. For some individuals, problem drug use is likely to be related to the positive, rewarding characteristics of drug experience as they act on reward pathways that have evolved to signal the gratification of fundamental motives relating to immediate physiological needs or social status. For others, problem drug use reflects a desire to ameliorate the aversive experiences of negative emotions as they relate to self-protection (fear and anxiety), affiliation (social rejection), or romantic love (or its absence). Recognizing the ways that drugs become motivational priorities for individuals offers opportunities for intervention and the need to provide resources that enable individuals to realize fundamental motives in ways that are less harmful.

The framework presented in this chapter is speculative in many respects, and there is scope to explore in more detail how drug use may be related to evolved motivational-emotional systems and how this relationship might vary depending on the characteristics of drug users and the substances that are employed. Providing a balanced approach to substance use and substance use problems remains a challenge for policymakers. An evolutionary perspective does not provide any simple solutions to alleviating the global burden of drug-related harm, but by providing a more complete account of why people use drugs and why this use can sometimes result in substance use problems, it can provide valuable guidance.

References

Al-Shawaf, L., Conroy-Beam, D., Asao, K., & Buss, D. M. (2016). Human emotions: An evolutionary psychological perspective. *Emotion Review*, 8(2), 173–186. doi: 10.1177/1754073914566518.

American Psychiatric Association. (2013). *Diagnostic and statistical manual of mental disorders* (5th ed.). American Psychiatric Association.

Anderson, C., Hildreth, J. A. D., & Howland, L. (2015). Is the desire for status a fundamental human motive? A review of the empirical literature. *Psychological Bulletin*, 141(3), 574–601.

Aunger, R., & Curtis, V. (2013). The anatomy of motivation: An evolutionary-ecological approach. *Biological Theory*, 8, 49–63. doi: 10.1007/s13752-013-0101-7

Aunger, R., & Curtis, V. (2015). *Gaining control: How human behavior evolved*. Oxford University Press.

Baumeister, R. F. (2016). Toward a general theory of motivation: Problems, challenges, opportunities, and the big picture. *Motivation and Emotion*, 40(1), 1–10. doi: 10.1007/s11031-015-9521-y

Baumeister, R. F., & Leary, M. R. (1995). The need to belong: desire for interpersonal attachments as a fundamental human motivation. *Psychological Bulletin*, 117(3), 497–529.

Beall, A. T., & Tracy, J. L. (2017). Emotivational psychology: How distinct emotions facilitate fundamental motives. *Social and Personality Psychology Compass, 11*(2), e12303. doi: 10.1111/spc3.12303

Becker, J. B., & Chartoff, E. (2019). Sex differences in neural mechanisms mediating reward and addiction. *Neuropsychopharmacology, 44*(1), 166–183.

Berridge, K. C., & Kringelbach, M. L. (2015). Pleasure systems in the brain. *Neuron, 86*(3), 646–664.

Berridge, K. C., & Robinson, T. E. (2016). Liking, wanting and the incentive-sensitization theory of addiction. *American Psychologist, 71*, 670–679. doi: 10.1037/amp0000059.

Blum, J., Gerber, H., Gerhard, U., Schmid, O., Petitjean, S., Riecher-Rössler, A., Wiesbeck, G. A., Borgwardt, S. J., & Walter, M. (2013). Acute effects of heroin on emotions in heroin-dependent patients. *The American Journal on Addictions, 22*(6), 598–604.

Buss, D. M. (1995). Evolutionary psychology: A new paradigm for psychological science. *Psychological Inquiry, 6*(1), 1–30.

Calvey, T. (2017). The extended evolutionary synthesis and addiction: The price we pay for adaptability. *Progress in Brain Research, 235*, 1–18. doi: 10.1016/bs.pbr.2017.07.004

Cavazos-Rehg, P. A., Krauss, M. J., Spitznagel, E. L., Schootman, M., Cottler, L. B., & Bierut, L. J. (2011). Number of sexual partners and associations with initiation and intensity of substance use. *AIDS and Behavior, 15*(4), 869–874.

Cloninger, C. R., Sigvardsson, S., & Bohman, M. (1996). Type I and type II alcoholism: An update. *Alcohol Health and Research World, 20*, 18–23.

Cooper, M. L., Frone, M. R., Russell, M., & Mudar, P. (1995). Drinking to regulate positive and negative emotions: A motivational model of alcohol use. *Journal of Personality and Social Psychology, 69*, 990–1005.

Courtwright, D. T. (2001). *Force of habit: Drugs and the making of the modern world.* Harvard University Press.

Curtis, V., & Aunger, R. (2011). Motivational mismatch: Evolved motives as the source of–and solution to–global public health problems. In S. C. Roberts (Ed.), *Applied Evolutionary Psychology* (pp. 259–275). Oxford University Press.

Curtis, V., De Barra, M., & Aunger, R. (2011). Disgust as an adaptive system for disease avoidance behaviour. *Philosophical Transactions of the Royal Society B: Biological Sciences, 366*(1563), 389–401.

Davis, C. (2014). Evolutionary and neuropsychological perspectives on addictive behaviors and addictive substances: Relevance to the "food addiction" construct. *Substance Abuse and Rehabilitation, 5*, 129–137. doi: 10.2147/sar.s56835

Degenhardt, L., Greberly, J., Stone, J., Hickman, M., Vickerman, P., Marshall, B. D. L., Bruneau, J., Altice, F. L., Henderson, G., Rahmimi-Movaghar, A., & Larney, S. (2019). Global patterns of opioid use and dependence: Harms to populations, interventions, and future action. *Lancet, 394*, 1560–1579. doi: 10.1016/S0140-6763-6(19)32229-9.

Del Giudice, M. (2018). *Evolutionary psychopathology: A unified approach.* Oxford University Press.

Del Giudice, M., Gangestad, S. W., & Kaplan, H. S. (2015). Life history theory and evolutionary psychology. In D. M. Buss (Ed.), *The handbook of evolutionary psychology* (pp. 68–95) Wiley.

Del Giudice, M., & Haltigan, J. D. (2023). An integrative evolutionary framework for psychopathology. *Development and Psychopathology, 35*, 1–11

Dudley, R. (2002). Fermenting fruit and the historical ecology of ethanol ingestion: Is alcoholism in modern human an evolutionary hangover? *Addiction, 97*, 381–388.

Durrant, R., Adamson, S., Todd, F., & Sellman, D. (2009). Drug use and addiction: An evolutionary perspective. *Australian and New Zealand Journal of Psychiatry, 43*, 1049–1056.

Durrant, R., & Thakker, J. (2003). *Substance use and abuse: Cultural and historical perspectives.* Sage Publications.

Durrant, R., & Ward, T. (2015). *Evolutionary criminology: Towards a comprehensive explanation of crime.* Academic Press.

Ellis, B. J., Figueredo, A. J., Brumbach, B. H., & Schlomer, G. L. (2009). Fundamental dimensions of environmental risk. *Human Nature, 20*(2), 204–268.

Ellis, B. J., Del Giudice, M., Dishion, T. J., Figueredo, A. J., Gray, P., Griskevicius, V., Hawley, P. H., Jacobs, W. J., Jenee, J., Volk, A. A., & Wilson, D. S. (2012). The evolutionary basis of risky adolescent behavior: Implications for science, policy, and practice. *Developmental Psychology, 48*(3), 598–623.

Fisher, H. E., Aron, A., Mashek, D., Li, H., & Brown, L. L. (2002). Defining the brain systems of lust, romantic attraction, and attachment. *Archives of Sexual Behavior, 31*(5), 413–419.

Fisher, H. E., Xu, X., Aron, A., & Brown, L. L. (2016). Intense, passionate, romantic love: A natural addiction? How the fields that investigate romance and substance abuse can inform each other. *Frontiers in Psychology, 7*, 687. doi: 10.3389/fpsyg.2016.00687

Fletcher, G. J., Simpson, J. A., Campbell, L., & Overall, N. C. (2015). Pair-bonding, romantic love, and evolution: The curious case of *Homo sapiens*. *Perspectives on Psychological Science, 10*(1), 20–36.

Garland, E. L., Bell, S., Atchley, R. M., & Froeliger, B. (2018). Emotional dysregulation in addiction. In T. P. Beauchaine & S. E. Crowell (Eds.), *The Oxford handbook of emotion dysregulation* (pp. 313–326). Oxford University Press.

Gill-Rivas, V., & McWhorter, L. (2013). Self-medication. In P. M. Miller (Ed.), *Principles of addiction* (Vol. 1, pp. 235–488). Elsevier.

Glei, D. A., & Preston, S. H. (2020). Estimating the impact of drug use on US mortality, 1999–2016. *PloS ONE, 15*(1), e0226732.

Gorka, S. M., Phan, K. L., & Childs, E. (2018). Acute calming effects of alcohol are associated with disruption of the salience network. *Addiction Biology, 23*(3), 921–930.

Grob, C., & Dobkin de Rios, M. (1992). Adolescent drug use in cross-cultural perspective. *Journal of Drug Issues, 22*, 121–138.

Hagen, E. H., Roulette, C. J., & Sullivan, R. J. (2013). Explaining human recreational use of "pesticides": The neurotoxin regulation model of substance use vs. the hijack model and implications for age and sex differences in drug consumption. *Frontiers in Psychiatry, 4*, 1-21.

Hagen, E. H., Sullivan, R. J., Ahmed, S., & Pickard, H. (2018). The evolutionary significance of drug toxicity over reward. In H. Pickard & S. H. Ahmed (Eds.), *Routledge handbook of philosophy and science of addiction* (pp. 102–120). Routledge.

Hagen, E. H., Sullivan, R. J., Schmidt, R., Morris, G., Kempter, R., & Hammerstein, P. (2009). Ecology and neurobiology of toxin avoidance and the paradox of drug reward. *Neuroscience, 160*, 69–84.

Halpern, S. C., Schuch, F. B., Scherer, J. N., Sordi, A. O., Pachado, M., Dalbosco, C., Fara, L., Pechansky, F., Kessler, F., & Von Diemen, L. (2018). Child maltreatment and illicit substance abuse: A systematic review and meta-analysis of longitudinal studies. *Child Abuse Review, 27*, 344–360. doi: 10.1002/car.2534.

Heath, D. B. (2000). *Drinking occasions: Comparative perspectives on alcohol and culture*. Sheridan Books.

Hill, E. M. (2013). An evolutionary perspective on addiction. In P. Miller (Ed.), *Principles of addiction: Comprehensive addictive behaviors and disorders* (pp. 41–50). Academic Press.

Hill, E. M., & Chow, K. (2002). Life-history theory and risky drinking. *Addiction, 97*, 401–413.

Hill, E. M., Hunt, L., & Duryea, D. G. (2017). Evolved vulnerability to addiction: The problem of opiates. In T. K. Shackelford & V. Zeigler-Hill (Eds.), *The evolution of psychopathology* (pp. 141–169). Springer.

Julien, R. M. (1998). *A primer of drug action* (8th edition). W. H. Freeman.

Kang, D., Fairbairn, C. E., & Ariss, T. A. (2019). A meta-analysis of the effect of substance use interventions on emotion outcomes. *Journal of Consulting and Clinical Psychology, 87*(12), 1106-1123. doi: 10.1037/ccp0000450

Kassel, J. D., Veilleux, J. C., Heinz, A. J., Braun, A. R., & Conrad, M. (2013). Emotions and addictive processes. In P. Miller (Ed.), *Principles of addiction* (Vol. 1, pp. 213–222). Elsevier.

Kenrick, D. T., Griskevicius, V., Neuberg, S. L., & Schaller, M. (2010). Renovating the pyramid of needs: Contemporary extensions built upon ancient foundations. *Perspectives on Psychological Science, 5*(3), 292–314. doi: 10.1177/1745691610369469.

Khantzian, E. J. (1997). The self-medication hypothesis of substance use disorders: A reconsideration and recent applications. *Harvard Review of Psychiatry, 4*(5), 231–244.

Koob, G. F. (2006). The neurobiology of addiction: A neuroadaptational view relevant for diagnosis. *Addiction, 101*, 23–30.

Koob, G. F. (2015). The dark side of emotion: The addiction perspective. *European Journal of Pharmacology, 753*, 73–87. doi: 10.1016/j.ejphar.2014.11.044

Kruglanski, A. W., Chernikova, M., & Jasko, K. (2016). Aspects of motivation: Reflections on Roy Baumeister's essay. *Motivation and Emotion, 40*(1), 11–15. doi: 10.1007/s11031-015-9534-6.

Kyte, D., Jerram, M., & DiBiase, R. (2020). Brain opioid theory of social attachment: A review of evidence for approach motivation to harm. *Motivation Science, 6*(1), 12–20.

Leshner, A. (1997). Addiction is a brain disease, and it matters. *Science, 278*(5335), 45–47. doi: 10.1126/science.278.5335.45

Lewis, M. (2015). *The biology of desire: Why addiction is not a disease*. Public Affairs.

Lewis, M. (2017). Addiction and the brain: Development, not disease. *Neuroethics, 10*, 7–18. Doi: 10.1007/s12152-016-9289-0

Li, N. P., van Vugt, M., & Colarelli, S. M. (2018). The evolutionary mismatch hypothesis: Implications for psychological science. *Current Directions in Psychological Science, 27*, 38–44. doi: 10.1177/0963721417731378

Lieberman, D., Billingsley, J., & Patrick, C. (2018). Consumption, contact and copulation: How pathogens have shaped human psychological adaptations. *Philosophical Transactions of the Royal Society B: Biological Sciences, 373*(1751), 20170203.

Linden-Carmichael, A. N., Allen, H. K., & Lanza, S. T. (2020). The language of subjective alcohol effects: Do young adults vary in their feelings of intoxication? *Experimental and Clinical Psychopharmacology,* 670–678..

MacCoun, R. J. (2013). The puzzling unidimensionality of DSM-5 substance use disorder diagnoses. *Frontiers in Psychiatry, 4,* 1–5..

Machin, A. J., & Dunbar, R. I. (2011). The brain opioid theory of social attachment: A review of the evidence. *Behaviour, 148*(9–10), 985–1025.

McKetin, R., Lubman, D. I., Najman, J. M., Dawe, S., Butterworth, P., & Baker, A. L. (2014). Does methamphetamine use increase violent behaviour? Evidence from a prospective longitudinal study. *Addiction, 109*(5), 798–806.

Meyer, J. S., & Quenzer, L. F. (2005). *Psychopharmacology. Drugs, the brain and behaviour.* Sineaur Associates.

Miller, W. R., Walters, S. T., & Bennett, M. E. (2001). How effective is alcoholism treatment in the United States? *Journal of Studies on Alcohol, 62*(2), 211–220.

Mills, K. L., & Marel, C. (2013). International data on the prevalence and correlates of comorbid substance use and psychiatric disorders. In P. Miller (Ed.), *Principles of addiction* (Vol. 1, pp. 481–488). Elsevier.

Neel, R., Kenrick, D. T., White, A. E., & Neuberg, S. L. (2016). Individual differences in fundamental social motives. *Journal of Personality and Social Psychology, 110*(6), 887–907.

Nesse, R. M., & Berridge, K. C. (1997). Psychoactive drug use in evolutionary perspective. *Science, 278,* 63–66. doi: 10.1126/science.278.5335.63

Nesse, R. M., & Stein, D. J. (2019). How evolutionary psychiatry can advance psychopharmacology. *Dialogues in Clinical Neuroscience, 21,* 167–175. doi: 10.31887/DCNS.2019.2/rmnesse

Neuberg, S. L., Kenrick, D. T., & Schaller, M. (2011). Human threat management systems: Self-protection and disease avoidance. *Neuroscience & Biobehavioral Reviews, 35*(4), 1042–1051.

NHS digital (2019). Statistics on drug misuse. England 2019. Retrieved from https://digital.nhs.uk/data-and-information/publications/statistical/statistics-on-drug-misuse/2019

Nutt, D. (2012). *Drugs without the hot air: Minimising the harms of legal and illegal drugs.* UIT Cambridge Press.

Nutt, D. J., Lingford-Hughes, A., Erritzoe, D., & Stokes, P. R. (2015). The dopamine theory of addiction: 40 years of highs and lows. *Nature Reviews Neuroscience, 16*(5), 305–312.

Orsolini, L., St John-Smith, P., McQueen, D., & Schifano, F. (2018). Evolutionary and dual inheritance models of initiation and use of psychoactive substances, including novel psychoactive substances. *Research and Advances in Psychiatry, 5,* 63–74.

Ouzir, M., & Errami, M. (2016). Etiological theories of addiction: A comprehensive update on neurobiological, genetic, and behavioural vulnerability. *Pharmacology, Biochemistry and Behavior, 148,* 59–68. doi: 10.1016/j.pbb.2016.06.005.

Owens, M. M., Syan, S. K., Amlung, M., Beach, S. R. H., Sweet, L. H., & MacKillop, J. (2019). Functional and structural neuroimaging studies of delayed reward discounting in addiction: A systematic review. *Psychological Bulletin, 145,* 141–164. doi: 10.1037/bul0000181

Panksepp, J., Knutson, B., & Burgdorf, J. (2002). The role of brain emotional systems in addictions: a neuro-evolutionary perspective and new "self-report" animal model. *Addiction, 97,* 459–469.

Picciotto, M. R. (1998). Common aspects of the action of nicotine and other drugs of abuse. *Drug and Alcohol Dependence, 51,* 165–172.

Placek, C., Roulette, C., Hudanick, N., Khan, A., Ravi, K., Jayakrishna, P., Srinivas, P., & Madhivanan, P. (2019). Exploring biocultural models of chewing tobacco and paan among reproductive-aged women: Self-medication, protection, or gender inequality? *American Journal of Human Biology, 31*(5), e23281. doi: 10.1002/ajhb.23281

Prendergast, M. L., Podus, D., Chang, E., & Urada, D. (2002). The effectiveness of drug abuse treatment: A meta-analysis of comparison group studies. *Drug and Alcohol Dependence, 67*(1), 53–72.

Reuter, P., & Pardo, B. (2017). New psychoactive substances: Are there any good options for regulating new psychoactive substances? *International Journal of Drug Policy, 40,* 117–122.

Richardson, G. B., Chen, C. C., Dai, C. L., Swoboda, C. M., Nedelec, J. L., & Chen, W. W. (2017). Substance use and mating success. *Evolution and Human Behavior, 38*(1), 48–57.

Richardson, G. B., Dai, C. L., Chen, C. C., Nedelec, J. L., Swoboda, C. M., & Chen, W. W. (2016). Adolescent life history strategy in the intergenerational transmission and developmental stability of substance use. *Journal of Drug Issues, 46*(2), 102–121. doi: 10.1177/002042615623986

Roulette, C. J., Kazanji, M., Breurec, S., & Hagen, E. H. (2016). High prevalence of cannabis use among Aka foragers of the Congo Basin and its possible relationship to helminthiasis. *American Journal of Human Biology, 28*(1), 5–15. doi: 10.1002/ajhb.22740

Roulette, C. J., Mann, H., Kemp, B. M., Remiker, M., Roulette, J. W., Hewlett, B. S., Kazanji, M., Breurec, S., Monchy, D., Sullivan, R. J., & Hagen, E. H. (2014). Tobacco use vs. helminths in Congo basin hunter-gatherers: Self-medication in humans? *Evolution and Human Behavior, 35*(5), 397–407. doi: 10.1016/j.evolhumbehav.2014.05.005

Schaller, M., Kenrick, D. T., Neel, R., & Neuberg, S. L. (2017). Evolution and human motivation: A fundamental motives framework. *Social and Personality Psychology Compass, 11*(6), e12319. doi: 10.1111/spc3.12319

Seecof, R., & Tennant, F. S. (1986). Subjective perceptions to the intravenous "rush" of heroin and cocaine in opioid addicts. *The American Journal of Drug and Alcohol Abuse, 12*(1–2), 79–87.

Shepard, G. H. (1998). Psychoactive plants and ethnopsychiatric medicines of the Matsigenka. *Journal of Psychoactive Drugs, 30*, 321–332.

Skewes, M. C., & Gonzalez, V. M. (2013). The biopsychosocial model of addiction. In P. Miller (Ed.), *Principles of addiction* (Vol. 1, pp. 61–70). Elsevier.

Steinberg, L. (2014). *Age of opportunity: Lessons from the new science of adolescence.* Houghton Mifflin Harcourt.

Sullivan, R. J., & Hagen, E. H. (2002). Psychotropic substance-seeking: evolutionary pathology or adaptation? *Addiction, 97*(4), 389–400.

Sullivan, R. J., Hagen, E. H., & Hammerstein, P. (2008). Revealing the paradox of drug reward in human evolution. *Proceedings of the Royal Society B: Biological Sciences, 275*(1640), 1231–1241.

Sumnall, H. R., Cole, J. C., & Jerome, L. (2006). The varieties of ecstatic experience: An exploration of the subjective experiences of ecstasy. *Journal of Psychopharmacology, 20*(5), 670–682.

Sznycer, D., Cosmides, L., & Tooby, J. (2017). Adaptationism carves emotions at their functional joints. *Psychological Inquiry, 28*(1), 56–62.

Tinbergen, N. (1963). On aims and methods of ethology. *Zeitschrift für tierpsychologie, 20*(4), 410–433.

Tracy, J. L., Mercadante, E., Witkower, Z., & Cheng, J. T. (2020). The evolution of pride and social hierarchy. *Advances in Experimental Social Psychology, 62*, 51–114. doi: 10.1016/bs.aesp.2020.04.002

United Nations Office of Drugs and Crime. (2019). *Global Study on Homicide, 2019.* United Nations.

United Nations Office of Drugs and Crime (2020). World drug report, 2020. Retrieved from https://wdr.unodc.org/wdr2020/index.html

Vasilenko, S. A., Evans-Polce, R. J., & Lanza, S. T. (2017). Age trends in rates of substance use disorders across ages 18–90: Differences by gender and race/ethnicity. *Drug and Alcohol Dependence, 180*, 260–264.

Volkow, N. D., & Koob, G. (2015). Brain disease model of addiction: Why is it so controversial? *Lancet, Psychiatry, 2*, 677–679. doi: 10.1016/S2215-0366(15)00236-9.

Von Bibra, E. (1855/1995). *Plant intoxicants.* Healing Art Press.

Ward, T., & Carter, E. (2019). The classification of offending and crime related problems: A functional perspective. *Psychology, Crime & Law, 25*, 542–560. doi: 10.1080/1068316X.2018.1557182

Wardle, M. C., & de Wit, H. (2014). MDMA alters emotional processing and facilitates positive social interaction. *Psychopharmacology, 231*(21), 4219–4229.

Werb, D., Kamarulzaman, A., Meacham, M. C., Rafful, C., Fischer, B., Strathdee, S. A., & Wood, E. (2016). The effectiveness of compulsory drug treatment: A systematic review. *International Journal of Drug Policy, 28*, 1–9.

West, R., & Brown, J. (2013). *Theories of addiction* (2nd ed.). Wiley.

Wilson, M., & Daly, M. (1985). Competitiveness, risk taking, and violence: The young male syndrome. *Ethology and Sociobiology, 6*(1), 59–73.

Wise, R. A., & Robble, M. A. (2020). Dopamine and addiction. *Annual Review of Psychology, 71*, 79–106. doi: 10.1146/annurev-psych-010418-103337.

Wiss, D. A., Avena, N., & Rada, P. (2018). Sugar addiction: From evolution to revolution. *Frontiers in Psychiatry, 9*, 545. doi: 10.3389/fpsyt.2018.00545

World Health Organization. (2017). *WHO report on the global tobacco epidemic, 2017: Monitoring tobacco use and prevention policies.* World Health Organization.

World Health Organization. (2018). *Global status report on alcohol and health, 2018.* World Health Organization.

Zinberg, N. E. (1984). *Drug, set, and setting: The basis for controlled intoxicant use.* Yale University Press.

CHAPTER 63

Rethinking the Neurodiversity Debate from the Harmful Dysfunction Perspective: The Implications of DSM Category Evolutionary Heterogeneity

Jordan A. Conrad and Jerome C. Wakefield

Abstract

Neurodiversity advocates argue that psychiatry mistakenly classifies certain normal psychological variations as mental disorders. These arguments raise fundamental issues about psychiatric diagnosis and classification and tend to be broadly revisionist in claiming that entire DSM categories are in fact normal "neurodiverse" conditions. This chapter evaluates these arguments within the framework of Jerome Wakefield's evolutionary "harmful dysfunction analysis" of mental disorder and with a focus on disorders involving the expression of emotion. The authors argue that the considerable heterogeneity of most DSM categories suggests the likelihood that each category is a mix of true disorders caused by dysfunctions and miscategorized normal neurodiversity. They explore several standard DSM categories, each of which has implications for emotional processes, including psychopathy, premenstrual dysphoric disorder, attention-deficit hyperactivity disorder, and autistic spectrum disorder, to illustrate how heterogeneity can both warrant and limit neurodiversity claims.

Key Words: harmful dysfunction analysis, neurodiversity, psychopathy, antisocial personality disorder, autistic spectrum disorder, premenstrual dysphoric disorder, attention-deficit hyperactivity disorder, mental disorder

After its perceived successes in World War II, psychiatry in the mid-20th century was coming into its own and achieving a new level of authority and credibility, especially with the advent of what seemed to be very promising psychopharmacological interventions. Indeed, as captured in the Rolling Stones song *Mother's Little Helper*, psychotropic medications became widely used for emotional regulation unrelated to mental disorder and more related to the stresses of modern life, triggering concern that psychiatry was being used more broadly for social control. As a result, and reflecting the anti-establishment tenor of the times, a multifaceted challenge to psychiatric authority arose in the 1960s that came to be known as the antipsychiatry movement. Antipsychiatrists argued that psychiatry illegitimately extended the concept of "medical disorder" to the mental domain and that psychiatric treatment was in fact simply a mechanism to control socially deviant behavior (Foucault, 1965; Laing, 1967; Rosenhan, 1973; Sarbin, 1967; Scheff, 1966, 1975; Szasz, 1961). These critiques were supported by extensive evidence of the unreliability of psychiatric diagnosis (Professional Staff of the United States–United

Kingdom Cross-National Project, 1974; Strauss et al., 1974). It was only after the radical third revision of the American Psychiatric Association's official *Diagnostic and Statistical Manual of Mental Disorders* (DSM-III; American Psychiatric Association, 1980), which specified symptom-based diagnostic criteria that increased the reliability of psychodiagnosis and limited diagnostic categories to a medically defined domain of dysfunctions that cause harms, such as distress or impairment in social functioning, that psychiatry was able to put to rest the antipsychiatric critique.

With the issue of the legitimacy of the concept of mental disorder more or less behind us, a new and subtler challenge to psychiatry has recently been issued by a new social movement. The neurodiversity movement encompasses a great variety of different positions, but its most basic argument, on which its other views are often predicated, is that certain neurocognitive conditions are illegitimately pathologized by psychiatric nosology when in fact they represent mere normal-range differences in thinking and emoting. The neurodiversity movement thus reproduces elements of the earlier antipsychiatric critique, but in a more focused way that does not challenge the legitimacy of the concept of disorder, but only its application to certain categories.

Of course, "neurodiversity" in a literal, sheerly descriptive sense of neurological differences between individuals and groups, does not in itself imply anything about disorder versus nondisordered normal-range variation. Every variation in psychological condition, whether normal or disordered, corresponds to a neurological condition, and thus "neurodiversity" in the literal sense is omnipresent. However, neurodiversity at its core is not merely a claim about difference. It puts forward the more radical substantive claim that certain conditions are being mistakenly pathologized by psychiatry, and that these conditions are not true disorders but are rather normal variations in brain functioning that may be socially disfavored (Hughes, 2019; Wakefield et al., 2020).

In this chapter, we will be considering this central claim by examining various DSM-defined disorder categories that at one time or another have been claimed by critics of the DSM to be, or to include, nondisorders, and which are therefore relevant to neurodiversity's goal of depathologizing conditions that are erroneously labeled disordered. Specifically, we will examine psychopathy (or "antisocial personality disorder" in the DSM), premenstrual dysphoric disorder (PMDD), and attention-deficit hyperactivity disorder (ADHD), as well as autism, now labeled "autism spectrum disorder," which is a major focus of neurodiversity depathologization. In each case, we will consider whether a neurodiversity perspective may have some validity in pointing to invalid pathologization of human psychological variation, and whether heterogeneity of the category may limit or modify any sweeping neurodiversity generalizations about the category.

Disorder as Harmful Dysfunction: An Evolutionary Approach to the Concept of Disorder

In order to address the question of normal range vs. disordered human functioning and thus whether certain conditions are genuine disorders or not, some account of disorder must be assumed. Such an account must explain common intuitions, but must also offer a principled way to demarcate between disorder and nondisorder that provides a basis for the judgments of the medical community. In psychiatry and clinical psychology, the most widely cited definition of mental disorder that is often used to guide discussion about whether a given condition is a disorder is Jerome Wakefield's harmful dysfunction account (HDA) of medical, including mental, disorder (Faucher & Forest, 2021; First & Wakefield 2010; Wakefield 1992a, 1992b, 1993, 1999a, 1999b, 2001, 2007, 2011, 2013, 2015, 2016a; Wakefield & First 2003). The

HDA builds on and is consistent with the DSM's attempts to define the concept of mental disorder, but provides a more scientific account that is anchored in the contemporary movement to understand human psychological functioning from an evolutionary perspective. The HDA posits that "disorder" has two key components: a fact-based "dysfunction" component that refers to the failure of a feature of the organism to perform the function for which it was biologically designed by evolution and natural selection, and a value-based "harm" component which refers to that dysfunction's harmfulness to the individual, as judged by social values.

A glance at the DSM reveals that the categories of disorders do seem to capture what are prima facie failures of biological design; that is, the categories tend to correspond to domains in which it is plausible that there are biologically designed mechanisms with evolved functions, and the described pathological conditions appear to be ways in which those mechanisms have gone awry. For example, human developmental processes, thought, emotions, appetite, and sexuality are all areas in which one would expect that complex adaptive psychological mechanisms have been naturally selected, with the corollary that failures of these mechanisms' evolved functions are dysfunctions.

Neurodiversity advocates are correct about at least one fundamental point: there is enormous normal-range variation in neurological structure and consequent psychological functioning. The degree of normal psychological variation in human populations in personality and cognitive variables has many potential explanations, although the correct explanation remains a matter of scientific controversy (Penke et al., 2007). This degree of normal variation means that "disorder" cannot simply be equated with deviation from statistically normal behavior, a point emphasized in the DSM's introduction as well. However, as the proponents of neurodiversity emphasize, the heterogeneity of normal human functioning can easily be confused with disorder, yielding a potential false-positives problem in which we pathologize perfectly normal functioning that is atypical or socially disvalued. In effect, evolutionary considerations thus yield two contrary pulls in responding to neurodiversity claims. On the one hand, evolutionary theory predicts or allows high levels of normal variation. On the other hand, biological design in the form of the many naturally selected psychological mechanisms imparted to us by evolution is subject to the general principle that complexly designed mechanisms can and inevitably will fail in multiple ways. The HDA, by grounding judgments of disorder versus nondisorder in evolution, offers a way to transcend disorder judgments based solely on statistical deviation. By relying on a deeper understanding of the evolutionary origins of various behaviors and emotions, the HDA allows for a reasoned mediation between the two evolutionary pulls of accepting normal variation and recognizing failures of design.

Neurodiversity arguments tend to take one of two approaches to depathologization. The first is to examine whether the conditions currently labeled disordered are in fact harmful, or if the harm associated with the condition is merely a result of societal and personal prejudices against the condition in question, as was the case in regard to homosexuality, which was eventually eliminated from categories of disorder. The second approach focuses on whether the condition is the result of a dysfunction or normal variation. In this chapter, we will focus on the second approach, which disputes whether a category of disorder is in fact composed of conditions that are caused by evolutionary dysfunctions. However, harm sometimes factors into the dysfunction arguments as a heuristic for revealing likely dysfunction—this can happen, for example, when the harm seems to be impairing in a way that suggests evolutionary disadvantage.

One argument we will encounter is the idea that certain conditions are not dysfunctions, but rather are associated with harms only because of a mismatch between the environment in which the trait evolved and the modern environment. In this way, certain disorder classes may be argued to be mislabeled on the grounds that they do not arise from dysfunctions, but rather from perfectly functioning features that are mismatched to modern life. Examples of such evolutionary mismatches are common: it is not a disorder to prefer fatty, sweet, and calorie-dense foods in an environment where the easy availability of these foods are problematic for long-term health, or to desire multiple sexual partners in an environment where monogamous fidelity is valued and such desires are punished.

Neurodiversity advocates generally mount their arguments, including the mismatch argument, against entire DSM categories. However, DSM categories are likely etiologically heterogeneous, so it is typically difficult to apply such arguments to an entire category. Rather, the category must be closely examined for potentially etiologically heterogeneous subtypes that may not share an evolutionary history—this may lead to the realization that the same category may contain both genuine disorders and invalidly pathologized normal variation. To understand why DSM categories may be heterogenous, it is useful to understand the distinction between conceptual and construct validity, and the envisioned process of validation for DSM categories.

Disorder categories are initially developed by formulating symptom syndromes that may provisionally define a class of conditions that share some symptomatic features and that point to an inferred dysfunction. Such DSM diagnostic categories are not initially assumed to be etiologically homogeneous. Rather than identifying homogenous etiological groupings, this initial categorization is designed only to achieve *conceptual validity*, which refers to the category being defined in such a way that it includes only disordered conditions (Wakefield, 1992b).

Conceptual validity is a much more limited initial goal than the more demanding ultimate goal of *construct validity*, which requires that the category include only disorders with a homogeneous etiology based on the same type of underlying dysfunction. Each conceptually valid category, such as schizophrenia or major depression, might include several different etiological types that must be differentiated in order to achieve construct validity. Etiological homogeneity of a given category cannot simply be assumed; it has to be demonstrated through etiological research or else accomplished by breaking up the original heterogeneous category into multiple subtypes or subcategories that are themselves homogeneous.

DSM syndromal diagnostic criteria sets are designed to achieve conceptual validity, the easier of the two. Every feature of the diagnostic criteria sets, including duration requirements, symptom thresholds, the symptoms that are specified, the frequency, intensity and persistence of the symptoms, and contextual exclusions, are all attempts to operationalize the notion that something has gone wrong and allow an inference about dysfunction versus normal-range distress or problems of living (First & Wakefield, 2013; Wakefield, 2016b; Wakefield & First, 2012). Construct validity requires identifying etiologies, which is an ambitious scientific goal that psychiatry has yet to achieve (Robins & Guze, 1970). It is thus a mistake to "reify" current syndromally defined categories into individuated disorders, treating the conceptual validity we have achieved as if it were true construct validity (Hyman, 2010).

However, careful conceptual examination of a DSM category can suggest heterogeneities that plausibly represent distinct subgroups within the overall category. Thus, heterogeneity of this kind can be used to draw distinctions within DSM categories, enabling us to identify subgroups to which neurodiversity arguments may apply and those to which such arguments are unlikely to apply.

Psychopathy or "Antisocial Personality Disorder"

Although neurodiversity arguments are most frequently brought to bear on intellectual and developmental disabilities such as autism, ADHD, and dyslexia (Jaarsma & Welin, 2012), some have extended these arguments to other standard categories of psychiatric disorders, such as bipolar disorder (Antonetta, 2007), schizophrenia (Chapman, 2019), and sociopathy (Anton, 2013).

Psychopathy (or, alternatively, sociopathy) is listed in the DSM-5 (American Psychiatric Association, 2013) as *antisocial personality disorder* and is characterized by a sustained pattern of disvaluing others' rights, interests, and feelings, as manifested in criminal behavior; lying, using aliases, and conning others; impulsivity; irritability, and aggressiveness; recklessness; irresponsibility and a disregard for commitments or promises; and a lack of remorse. Though often charming and sociable, psychopaths tend not to form lasting relationships due to their egocentrism and deficits in experiencing social emotions such as love, shame, remorse and guilt, and empathy. Antisocial personality disorder is the only personality disorder that is not diagnosable in childhood; before the age of 18, the child must be diagnosed with *conduct disorder*, which takes a very similar form but is measured by a frequent pattern of bullying, possessing dangerous weapons, being physically violent to people or animals, stealing, sexual assault, property destruction, lying, and violating rules (e.g., curfew, school attendance, running away from home). These criteria have been criticized for being excessively behaviorally oriented, and so a subtype specifier was added in the DSM-5 that encompasses those with limited pro-social emotions.

Other prominent measures of psychopathy include Robert Hare's (1991, 2003) Psychopathy Checklist–Revised (PCL-R) and Scott Lilienfeld and Brian Andrews's (1996; Lilienfeld et al., 2005) Psychopathy Personality Inventory–Revised (PPI-R). The PCL-R is a 20-question checklist focusing on two primary symptom domains: interpersonal affective symptoms (e.g., lack of empathy, manipulativeness) and antisocial symptoms (e.g., impulsivity, aggression). Each question is scored on a 3-point scale from 0 to 2, with a score of 30 generally considered the diagnostic threshold for psychopathy (Hare et al., 1991), although a threshold of 25 is sometimes used (e.g., Krupp et al., 2012). The PPI-R is a 154-item scale frequently used to test for the presence of psychopathic traits in noncriminal populations. It uses a 4-point Likert scale to measure the constructs of Fearless Dominance (FD), which includes subscales for Social Potency, Stress Immunity, and Fearlessness, and Self-Centered Impulsivity (SCI), consisting of subscales measuring Carefree Nonplanfulness, Impulsive Nonconformity, Machiavellian Egocentricity, and Blame Externalization.

As should be clear from these descriptions, the construct of psychopathy as measured by DSM criteria, the PCL-R, and the PPI-R represents what is in fact a large range of heterogeneous phenotypes from, for example, heartless serial killers and impulsive self-centered individuals who cannot function socially, to individuals who are unusually fearless, unempathetic, and instrumental in their behavior but quite capable of functioning successfully, and sometimes outstandingly, in social contexts.

Phenotypic heterogeneity has been an issue in the development of various scales. The DSM-III transitioned from the DSM-II's psychological notion of *psychopathy* to a more behavioral characterization of *antisocial personality disorder* that was intended to be a more reliable measure by focusing on descriptive features rather than on inferred motivations. However, researchers then argued that antisocial personality disorder does not equate to psychopathy for the very reason that it encompasses a heterogeneous mix of motivations that can lead to the antisocial behaviors, some of which are not truly disordered or at least are not the same condition as psychopathy: "Most psychopaths (with the exception of those who somehow manage to plow their way through life without coming into formal or prolonged contact with the criminal justice system) meet the criteria for ASPD, *but most individuals with ASPD are not psychopaths*" (Hare, 1996).

Similarly, the PCL-R is believed to be particularly effective in measuring psychopathy among forensic populations who have engaged in criminal behavior, but researchers have expressed concern that it may not be as effective in noncriminal settings in which psychopathic personality traits may not involve overt criminal behaviors (Benning et al., 2003; Skeem & Cooke, 2010). By contrast, the PPI-R was designed with a greater focus on personality than behaviors in order to measure the prevalence of psychopathy in noncriminal populations. If the two scales are measuring a similar construct, one would expect their scores to be correlated. However, although total scores are reasonably highly correlated (Copestake et al., 2011; Kruh et al., 2005; Poythress et al., 1998; Poythress et al., 2010), there is only a weak association among subfactors (Copestake et al., 2011), suggesting that the PPI-R and PCL-R may be tapping distinct conceptualizations of psychopathy (Copestake et al., 2011; Marcus et al., 2012). Moreover, it is unclear whether the PPI-R assesses a single underlying condition. For example, among prison populations, those that score high on the PPI-R subscale of "fearless dominance" are no more or less likely to score high on "self-centered impulsivity" (Marcus et al., 2012), suggesting that convergence of both traits is merely coincidental and not occasioned by a single underlying dysfunction.

The difficulties that these various accounts and measures of psychopathy encounter is illustrative of the general problem of phenotypic, and likely etiological, heterogeneity. From Cleckley's (1955) initial account of the disorder, which seems to capture paradigm cases of coldhearted, impulsive, and violent people who are incapable of controlling their sadistic impulses and thus destroy their own lives through wanton violence that has no relationship to instrumental gain, to modern accounts which attempt to capture psychopathy among corporate executives in which the presence of certain psychopathy-related traits such as fearlessness, boldness, and coldheartedness may be advantageous (Fritzon et al., 2013), psychopathy as a construct has radically expanded. This is not an unusual situation in which an initial rather narrow conception of a form of psychopathology is theorized in various ways that extend the category to a heterogeneous mix of individuals, many of whom may not have the original disorder (or perhaps any disorder at all), but simply evidence a point on the dimensions used by theoreticians to express the essence of the original disorder construct.

How do the heterogeneity and expansion of the category of psychopathy fit with the neurodiversity claim that psychiatry may be mistaking normal but socially problematic human variation with mental disorder? We provide two examples, one addressing psychopathy itself and the other addressing the adolescent or childhood form of psychopathy that falls under the DSM category of conduct disorder.

We start by examining Terrie Moffit's (1993) seminal work on conduct disorder. Recall that this child and adolescent disorder is defined by certain antisocial behaviors (except for one subtype added in the DSM-5 that refers to limited pro-social emotions) and is considered an early developmental version of adult psychopathy. In examining this large category for heterogeneity that might reflect multiple constructs hidden within the similar behavioral outcomes, Moffitt started with the observation that although there is considerable continuity in antisocial behavior from adolescence into adulthood, it is also true that antisocial behavior increases dramatically—almost 10-fold—during adolescence. Moffitt arrived at a distinction between two patterns of child and adolescent antisocial behavior that both fell under the DSM diagnostic criteria for conduct disorder. The first was early-onset (i.e., in childhood before adolescence) problems of social functioning that solidify into an enduring lifelong pattern of antisocial behavior. She theorizes that this personality formation may be caused in part by an interaction of early personal, family, and social variables (potentially including some neurocognitive deficits) that yield a full-blown personality disorder. The second group consists of adolescents who develop antisocial behavior in a manner more reflective of the traditional notion of "delinquency," in which the antisocial behavior arises in early adolescence and continues for some time until receding prior to full adulthood, and does not re-emerge in later life. Moffitt theorizes that this adolescent-limited form of antisocial behavior is caused not by a psychological or neurological dysfunction, but by a mismatch between the physical maturity of adolescents and the restricted freedom, power, and esteem that they can achieve due to our society's delay in conferring responsibility until later adulthood. Moffitt thus comes to the conclusion that life-course persistent antisocial behavior is a genuine mental disorder, whereas adolescence-limited antisocial behavior is not, thus dividing the category of conduct disorder into two constructs, summarized as follows:

> *Life-Course-Persistent Antisocial Behavior as Psychopathology.* The life-course-persistent antisocial syndrome, as described here, has many characteristics that, taken together, suggest psychopathology. . . . The syndrome of life-course-persistent antisocial behavior described here has a biological basis in subtle dysfunctions of the nervous system. (Moffitt, 1993, p. 685)

> *Adolescence-Limited Antisocial Behavior Is Not Pathological Behavior* . . . . Instead of a biological basis in the nervous system, the origins of adolescence-limited delinquency lie in youngsters' best efforts to cope with the widening gap between biological and social maturity. (Moffitt, 1993, p. 692)

Moffitt's account suggests that a condition which displays even a high degree of syndromal uniformity may result from diverse etiologies. As she elaborated in a paper written over two decades later, the pathological version "emerges from inherited or acquired neurophysiological variation" which initially manifests "as subtle cognitive deficits, difficult temperament, or hyperactivity," ultimately manifesting in "hallmark features of physical aggression and antisocial behavior" which "will infiltrate multiple adult life domains: illegal activities, problems with employment, and victimization of intimate partners and children" (Moffit, 2006, p. 571). In contrast, the nonpathological version "emerges alongside puberty, when otherwise ordinary healthy youngsters experience psychological discomfort during the relatively role-less years" and "experience dissatisfaction with their dependent status as a child and impatience for what they anticipate are the privileges and rights of adulthood" (p. 571). She explains that among this latter group "it is virtually normative for them to find the delinquent style appealing and to mimic it as a way to demonstrate autonomy from parents, win affiliation with peers, and hasten social maturation," noting as well that "because their predelinquent development was normal" this latter group tend not to remain antisocial into adulthood (pp. 571–572). In carefully distinguishing two etiological pathways that yield nearly identical syndromal presentations during adolescence but involve different neurological substrates, and arguing persuasively that one is likely a disorder due to dysfunction while the other is not, Moffitt has in effect made a neurodiversity-type case that psychiatry has failed to recognize normal behavior for what it is and has pathologized individuals who likely do not have a dysfunction but are simply mismatched to the current social environment.

Turning now to an equally provocative analysis of adult psychopathy, Linda Mealey (1995a) used a game-theoretic evolutionary analysis to argue that there are two distinct etiological pathways present in psychopathy: one in which psychopathic personality traits are programmed to express themselves uniformly across a wide range of situations independent of instrumental value, and the other in which psychopathic traits must be reinforced throughout development by situational factors to become stable features of personality. In other words, the type of "cheating" behavior evidenced in psychopaths in one case results directly from one's genotype which has encoded that strategy to perform in a variety of contexts, and in the other case it results from an "environmentally contingent, facultative cheating strategy not as clearly tied to genotype" (p. 539). Arguing against standard wisdom, she concluded that the former "primary" genetic form represents a "frequency-dependent adaptation" that confers advantages when it occurs rarely and among a nonpsychopathic majority. Making a similar kind of intra-category distinction as Moffit, Mealey explains that if there is an evolutionary basis to certain forms of psychopathy, those forms should not be considered a truly "disordered" class: "If sociopaths are not a type designed by natural selection to fill a particular niche, then we could probably agree that they do not function normally; but if they are a type, then . . . the medical model is no longer appropriate" (Mealey, 1995b, p. 584).

As one of us has noted elsewhere (Wakefield, 2021), other medical researchers have followed suit in depathologizing some indefinite range of psychopathy in response to Mealey's research. Richard Machalek (1995), for instance, comments on the incompatibility of a condition being both a medical disorder and naturally selected (note that Machalek uses "pathogen" synonymously with "dysfunction"):

> As the term itself suggests, the medical model attributes sociopathy to a "pathogen," in this case an emotional deficit that may be genetically rooted and physiologically expressed. . . . [E]volutionary theory takes us beyond mere diagnostic descriptors and prompts us to ask whether such antisocial behaviors may, in some fundamental sense, be advantageous to those who express them. . . . Framing sociopathy in evolutionary terms accordingly frees us from the explanatory constraints imposed by the medical model that would have us attribute its causes to some "pathogen," when it is not at all clear that the sorts of genetic and physiological processes attributed to sociopathy are necessarily pathological. (Machalek, 1995, p. 564)

Subsequent research in this area has since echoed this view. Kinner (2003), for example, writes that "from an evolutionary perspective psychopathy seems to be an adaptation rather than a disease" (p. 67), and Reimer (2008) explains: "On any such 'selectionist' model, psychopaths are certainly different than the rest of us, biologically speaking. However, they are not, in any biological sense, disordered" (p. 187).

Finally, Krupp et al. (2012) have devised a clever test of the adaptiveness of psychopathy by examining the degree to which violent offenders harm genetic relatives. They argue that "individuals executing well-designed strategies, a necessary feature of psychological adaptations, should tend to be nepotistic—providing aid to close genealogical kin and/or sparing them from harm" (Krupp 2012, p. 2). Controlling for geographic proximity between the (psychopathic) perpetrator and victim (as family members might naturally be more nearby), Krupp et al. found that in a sample of 289 violent offenders receiving a diagnosis of psychopathy by the PCL-R, psychopaths are more likely to victimize a non-family-member; in fact, "as PCL-R score increased, victim-offender relatedness decreased" (Krupp et al., 2012, p. 3). Despite heightened aggression, sexual assault frequency, and impulsivity, psychopathic violent offenders thus appear to spare genetic conspecifics even when they are proximally easier targets: "Although their behavior is objectionable, psychopaths appear to pursue a nepotistic strategy that could have helped to advance their reproductive interests in ancestral environments" (2012, p. 5).

Krupp et al.'s (2012) comments reveal how the distinction between selection and disorder can factor into testable hypotheses:

> Psychopaths routinely disregard social norms by engaging in selfish, antisocial, often violent behavior. Commonly characterized as mentally disordered, recent evidence suggests that psychopaths are executing a well-functioning, if unscrupulous strategy that historically increased

reproductive success at the expense of others. Natural selection ought to have favored strategies that spared close kin from harm, however, because actions affecting the fitness of genetic relatives contribute to an individual's inclusive fitness. Conversely, there is evidence that mental disorders can disrupt psychological mechanisms designed to protect relatives. Thus, mental disorder and adaptation accounts of psychopathy generate opposing hypotheses: psychopathy should be associated with an increase in the victimization of kin in the former account but not in the latter. . . . These results stand in contrast to models positing psychopathy as a pathology, and provide support for the hypothesis that psychopathy reflects an evolutionary strategy. . . . (p. 1)

In a later paper responding to critics, Krupp et al. (2013) explain why, even if psychopathy is an adaptive personality type, there may be brain differences between psychopaths and others and that these brain differences do not imply pathology:

We take it as given that the brains of psychopaths differ from those of nonpsychopaths in systematic ways. Without such differences, psychopaths could not be reliably set apart in their cognition and behavior from nonpsychopaths. But difference is not isomorphic with dysfunction. For instance, although the brains of men and women have much in common, they must also be different on average, as must the brains of young and old, married and single, androphile and gynephile, Anglophone and Francophone, and so on, even if these brain differences are solely the result of differences of experience. While the life sciences have begun to recognize that such differences do not inherently reflect disorder, the relationship between difference and disorder nevertheless continues to bedevil the study of mental health.

An argument for dysfunction must marshal supporting evidence, and this must be distinguishable from evidence of difference. (2013, p. 1)

Krupp et al.'s (2013) lucid explanation of how difference, even at the level of brain biology, does not necessarily suggest disorder supports the neurodiversity claim that phenotypic differences between neuroatypical and neurotypical individuals need not imply disorder. The recent psychopathy research illustrates how balancing selection of emotional dispositions can produce people with very different emotional natures who are nevertheless functionally normal despite being mismatched to our current social conditions. Such mismatches may be problematic both personally and societally, but they are not therefore disorders. Understanding that nondisordered people can be very different even in these seemingly fundamental ways presents the neurodiversity argument in a new and powerful light.

Premenstrual Syndrome and Premenstrual Dysphoric Disorder

Premenstrual syndrome (PMS) is a condition, generally considered normal and nondisordered although varying in severity and sometimes treated, that most women experience to some degree prior to the onset of menses. PMS is characterized by physical symptoms such as headache, fatigue, joint and muscle pain, and breast tenderness, as well as emotional and psychological symptoms including irritability, anxiety, difficulty concentrating, sleep disturbance, and sadness. Premenstrual dysphoric disorder (PMDD), in contrast, is a stand-alone criterial disorder category in the DSM-5's depressive disorders chapter. Despite the important distinction between PMS as normal variation and PMDD as a disorder, there is no obvious dividing line in the distribution of PMS/PMDD symptoms in the population, and so the distinction has traditionally been based on intuitions about excessive severity. The diagnosis of PMDD is based largely on symptoms also characterizing PMS, but at a more severe level and with an emphasis on emotional symptoms, especially depression. Specifically, for diagnosis of PMDD, the DSM-5 requires that one possess at least one of the following emotional symptoms: affective lability (i.e., mood swings), irritability and anger, depressed mood and hopelessness, and anxiety or a feeling of being on edge; as well as at least one of the following psychological symptoms: decreased interest in typical activities, difficulty concentrating, fatigue, change in appetite, sleep disturbances, a sense of being overwhelmed, or physical symptoms found in PMS, with a total of five symptoms altogether. These symptoms, particularly the emotional symptoms of sadness and irritability, are required to be so severe that they impair the ability to carry out everyday activities associated with social roles.

PMDD was accepted as a criterial disorder and listed in the main part of the manual only in 2013 in the DSM-5. Prior to that, PMDD was listed in the DSM-IV's (American Psychiatric Association, 1994) Appendix B of "Criteria sets ... provided for further study." Experts among the DSM-5 Mood Disorders Work Group eventually concluded that the move was justified by empirical evidence (Epperson, 2012; Epperson et al., 2012), but many expressed concern that the conceptual basis for PMDD's inclusion was simply the fact of its being on the extreme end of the symptom severity dimension. The problem that many feminist and psychiatric critics identified was that if PMDD is simply an extreme level of a normal-range female condition without any distinct underlying dysfunction, and thus due to etiologically homogeneous processes that differed only in severity, the use of an arbitrary threshold for disorder would open the door to increased pathologizing of women whose symptoms are lower on the severity dimension (Vargas-Cooper, 2012). Given the arbitrary threshold on the severity dimension, the question could then be raised as to whether the entire PMS spectrum, from mild to severe, should be classified as a disorder or nondisorder. This issue had practical implications for the FDA's process of approving medications to treat presumptive disorders and was in fact debated on FDA panels (Food and Drug Administration, 1999). The primary theory that suggested a categorical difference between PMS and PMDD was that women with PMDD suffered from a dysfunction that caused much higher levels of circulating hormones during their cycle. However, research had disproven this theory; measures of hormone levels in women with PMDD were no different from the levels in women with PMS. Given that the severity dimension seemed otherwise etiologically homogeneous in nature, the neurodiversity view applied here might hold that the entire PMS and PMDD spectrum is merely a neurodiverse condition relative to the male lack of menstruation and should not be pathologized.

The disorder status of PMDD was resolved when scientific advances revealed an underlying etiological heterogeneity along the PMS/PMDD dimension that was not apparent at the symptomatic level, demonstrating that PMDD was not simply the extreme end of the severity dimension of PMS after all. Given the previous disconfirmation of the higher-hormone-level theory, the most plausible alternative theory of PMDD as a distinct condition was that there exists a difference in women's reactions to rapidly changing hormone levels even when the hormones themselves are at the same levels. To test this idea, researchers performed suppression and add-back studies in which they administered drugs that reduced circulating menstruation-related hormones to virtually zero in groups of women, some of whom complained of PMDD and others of whom had less severe PMS. They then reintroduced the depleted hormones, mimicking the upsurge in hormone levels that occurs during the late luteal phase of the menstrual cycle, and compared the reactions of women with a PMDD history versus those with no such history. Although the changes in hormone levels were the same, the PMDD sample had a pronounced symptomatic response that was not experienced by the control groups. These studies (e.g., Baller et al., 2013; Schmidt et al., 1998) demonstrated significant differences in both subjective and behavioral reactions as well as brain-level reactions by the PMDD sample to changing hormone levels, suggesting some kind of qualitative dysfunction concealed within the severity dimension. Such a qualitative difference was established when specific genetic mutations that appear to be associated with these anomalous reactions were identified (Dubey et al., 2017) and later confirmed in animal models of PMDD (Marroco et al., 2020) and shown to yield anomalous over-expression of some cellular-level reactions and under-expression of others in processing hormone variation.

The case of PMDD is particularly helpful in illustrating a misconception about the nature of "disorder." Disorder is not simply the extreme end of the severity dimension of a condition. Nondisordered conditions can in fact be far more severe than disordered ones (Wakefield, 2022). What matters to psychiatric judgments about disorder status is whether the condition results from a dysfunction, which scientists were able to demonstrate in the case of PMDD. The phenotypic similarities between PMS and PMDD obscured the fact of etiological heterogeneity. Once this etiological heterogeneity was recognized, it became apparent that in fact one part of the PMS/PMDD spectrum is a disorder and not merely normal neuronal diversity, whereas the rest of the PMS spectrum appears to be a matter of normal neurodiversity. Discovery of etiological dysfunction within a segment of an otherwise symptomatically continuous condition provides a principled reason to carve out that section as disordered, and of course the same applies in reverse: if a segment of a continuum of symptom presentations is discovered to be adaptive and merely mismatched to the present environment, that segment ought to be depathologized according to the HDA, consistent with the neurodiversity perspective. The crucial issue is to look under the hood of continuous phenotypic variation to see if the underlying causes are heterogeneous or homogeneous.

Attention-Deficit Hyperactivity Disorder

Attention-deficit hyperactivity disorder (ADHD), a disorder that until recently was diagnosed primarily in children due to problems in school, has generally been conceptualized as having two essential symptoms, hyperactivity-impulsivity and distractibility. Depending on the way the symptoms manifest, the DSM-5 recognizes three different forms of ADHD: one that is primarily distracted, one that is primarily hyperactive and impulsive, and one that is a combination of both. ADHD is by far the most prevalently diagnosed childhood psychiatric disorder. As of 2011, 11% of all children age 4–17—and a remarkable one out of five teenage boys in American schools—had received an ADHD diagnosis, of which over two-thirds (over 6% of all US children) were currently taking ADHD medication (Visser et al., 2014). The sheer magnitude of the rates, as well as their rapid increase over recent decades, suggests possible diagnostic validity problems. While there are unquestionably genuine disorders of emotional regulation and attentional and impulse-control mechanisms fitting the criteria for ADHD, the category has been one of the most controversial in the DSM due to the suspicion that normal child variation in rambunctiousness is being pathologized to fit our constrictive school environments.

Although the DSM criteria focus on attention problems and impulse control, understandings of the disorder prior to the DSM-III (e.g., Douglas & Peters, 1979; Still, 1902; Wender, 1971) generally included emotional dysregulation as a constitutive feature of the disorder. Recent research and clinical theory tend to support this perspective. For example, Russell Barkley, a leading ADHD researcher, argues that emotional impulsivity and deficient emotional self-regulation are essential to properly understanding the disorder. He argues that excessive focus on behavioral symptoms has led to neglect of "a deficiency in both the effortful (executive or cognitive) inhibition and the top-down self-control of emotions in general and particularly those pertaining to the self regulation of frustration, impatience, and anger" and a "striking propensity for failure to inhibit emotions, or emotional impulsivity," so that the child with ADHD will more quickly "react with primary (particularly negative) emotions in response to events compared to others of the same developmental level or age" (Barkley, 2015,

p. 81). Similarly, Shaw et al. (2014) emphasize deficits in emotional regulation that include "emotional expressions and experiences that are excessive in relation to social norms and context-inappropriate; rapid, poorly controlled shifts in emotion ('lability'); and the anomalous allocation of attention and to emotional stimuli" (Shaw et al., 2014, p. 2). Again, Nigg and Casey (2005) argue that a dysfunction in the frontal-limbic-amygdala circuit creates affective impairments including demotivation, emotional reactivity, and difficulty in self-regulating emotions. And Sagvolden et al. (2005) theorize that the impulsivity and low tolerance for frustration found in many with ADHD result from hypodopaminergic activation. These researchers treat the emotionality of ADHD—including boredom, novelty-seeking, impulsivity, frustration, and excitability—as central to the disorder itself.

While ADHD has in the past been considered a childhood disorder, more recently it is being recognized in adulthood, with some estimates claiming prevalence rates of 3%–5% of the US adult population (Dopheide & Pliszka, 2009). While it was thought initially that childhood ADHD continued and explained adult ADHD, it turns out that most children exit from the diagnosis prior to adulthood (Beiderman et al., 2010; Hill & Schoener, 1996; Klein, 2011; Moffit et al., 2015; Shaw et al, 2013), so the two phenomena are likely distinct to some extent. DSM symptom descriptions have been modified for adults, and include, for the attentional type, for example, such criteria as: difficulty sustaining focused attention during lectures; being easily sidetracked from workplace duties; failure to meet deadlines; difficulty keeping materials in order; disliking preparing reports; often losing things such as tools, wallets, keys, paperwork, eyeglasses, or mobile telephones; and often being forgetful about returning calls, paying bills, or keeping appointments. The question can certainly be raised as to whether these conditions may sometimes consist of normal personality variation that is mismatched with the demands of our society. However, we focus here on childhood ADHD.

There are several lines of compelling evidence that the high reported prevalence of ADHD results in part from massive overdiagnosis, and that some ADHD represents a mismatch between normal-range human predispositions and modern social and environmental demands. Perhaps the simplest and most compelling support for the overdiagnosis hypothesis comes from recent studies in school systems that determine grade by month of birth, so that within a grade, children may vary in age by up to one year. The studies show that within a given school grade, the younger students have a much higher rate of diagnosis (as much as 50% greater) than the older kids in that grade, making age within grade one of the most potent risk factors for diagnosis (Elder, 2010; Evans et al., 2010; Zoega et al., 2012). The best explanation is that younger children have less-developed inhibitory controls and thus are more disruptive. They are diagnosed to help them perform better in school and to allow the class to perform more effectively (Schwartz, 2012). This is a paradigm case of environmental mismatch, rather than disorder stemming from a dysfunction in evolved attentional and impulse-control mechanisms, and suggests that the ADHD category subsumes heterogeneous groups, only some of which have genuine attentional disorders.

Consistent with the suspicion of heterogeneity and possible false positive diagnoses, studies of brain development in children diagnosed with ADHD versus controls tend to reveal differences in rates of maturation of various brain areas. However, these differences tend to disappear over time, yielding a brain maturation delay hypothesis (Hoogman et al., 2017; Shaw et al., 2007) that may indicate normal variation in some cases and disorder in others. Shaw et al. (2007), observing that "it is unclear whether the disorder results from a delay in brain maturation or whether it represents a complete deviation from the template of typical development," studied brain development in ADHD children versus controls and "found maturation to progress in a similar manner regionally in both children with and without

ADHD" (p. 19649), with delay in the ADHD children most prominent in areas that control attention and motor planning, and with faster development in motoric regions. The NIMH press release described the results as follows: "Brain Matures a Few Years Late in ADHD, But Follows Normal Pattern" (National Institute of Mental Health, 2007). Similar delay phenomena (rather than enduring abnormalities) have emerged in more recent studies (Hoogman et al., 2017). Although these researchers persist in labeling the studied conditions "disorders," the fact is that variations in developmental timing of the observed magnitude are common across developmental domains. For example, normal age of brain development that precipitates the beginning of walking varies between 8 months and 18 months (WHO Multicentre Growth Reference Study Group, 2006), and such variations are of course considered entirely within the normal human range.

In addition to confusions of ADHD with normal variation in age-related maturation or rate of brain development, there is persuasive evidence of naturally selected subtypes of ADHD that are not disordered, but are mismatched to the modern school environment. A multifaceted research program concerns the "seven repeat" polymorphism of the *DRD4* gene, *DRD4-7R*, which codes for aspects of the structure of the brain's dopamine receptor and is known to be disproportionately common among ADHD children and may represent about 20%–30% of such children (Faraone et al., 2001; Grady et al., 2003; Grady et al., 2005; Rapoport, 2007). Relative to other repeat levels, *DRD4-7R* slows the uptake and metabolism of dopamine, thus decreasing experience of reward and heightening response to negative stimuli, supporting the emotional interpretation of ADHD-related experiences (Gehricke et al., 2015; Volkow et al., 2009; Volkow et al., 2011). ADHD in this group can thus be seen as inattention and impulsive activity due to lessened reward and consequent boredom when sedentary, and the search for novel sources of reward. This fits with the fact that stimulants used to successfully treat ADHD enhance dopamine metabolism.

Rather than these discoveries implying that *DRD4-7R*-related ADHD is a genetic disorder, research indicates just the opposite. The occurrences of *7R* variants of *DRD4* in the general population are too common to be random mutations, and there is strong evidence from genetic analysis that *7R* was naturally selected (Ding et al., 2002; Grady et al., 2013; Wang et al., 2004). The claim that *DRD4-7R* is a naturally selected normal variation gained support from field research that studied those with this gene in nomadic human tribes and sedentary settled human populations from within the same gene pool, and established that *DRD4-7R* correlates with an increased fitness advantage in the nomadic situation but decreased fitness in a sedentary culture, with fitness measured by indices of health such as body mass index (BMI) (Eisenberg et al., 2008). The gene has higher incidence in populations that resulted from geographic dispersal and is associated with risk-taking, and appears to yield a longevity benefit as well (Dreber et al., 2009; Grady et al., 2013). This polymorphism seems to adaptively promote exploratory behavior by creating the need for more intense dopamine responses that come with novel stimuli. However, for students in modern school systems that demand long periods of focused and sedentary behavior, this naturally selected gene is problematic. Rather than revealing a genetic disorder, the research on *DRD4-7R* has revealed a likely naturally selected normal variation in dopamine metabolism that is being treated as a disorder due to a mismatch between the environment in which it evolved and the demands of our society.

From an HDA perspective, the false-positive problem in ADHD diagnosis results from the DSM-5's failure to reflect what clinicians and researchers already know: that although there are genuine dysfunctions of impulse-control and attentional mechanisms (and thus legitimate cases of ADHD), a substantial percentage of those diagnosed with ADHD are false positives; they do not have a disorder. The case is thus strong that DSM-diagnosed ADHD is a genuinely neurodiverse category in which some individuals who happen to have a different normal variant in brain function are being misdiagnosed as disordered.

Autism Spectrum Disorders

Of the conditions explored in this chapter, autism spectrum disorder (ASD) is the one that is most closely associated with the neurodiversity movement (Graby, 2015). The neurodiversity perspective was originally introduced by autists (Blume, 1998; Meyerding, 1998; Sinclair, 1993; Singer, 1999) and its central claims have been defended by prominent autism scholars (Armstrong, 2015; Chapman, 2019; Jaarsma & Welin, 2012; Ortega, 2009).

Initially, autism was identified by Leo Kanner (1943) based on a triad of severe social, communicational, and behavioral impairments. Diagnosis of DSM-5 autism spectrum disorder (ASD) was revised to require deficits in two areas: first, social communication and interaction, and second, rigid/repetitive behavior and interests. The symptoms may manifest, for example, in deficits in nonverbal communication, stereotyped and repetitive movements, narrow interests pursued with unusual intensity, inflexibility with routines, and either a hyper- or hypo-reactivity to sensory inputs. Additionally, ASD symptoms include a strong and multifaceted emotional component. For example, autists typically struggle to express appropriate social emotions or connect empathically with others. They have difficulty intuiting what others are thinking or feeling without explicit instruction to that effect (Baron-Cohen, 1990). They are also prone to "meltdowns" when frustrated or experiencing other negative emotions (Bennie, 2016).

In conceptualizing autism as a spectrum, the DSM-5 allowed for less and more severe variants, giving rise to the notion of what has come to be called "high-functioning" autism—a condition that satisfies symptom criteria for falling on the autism spectrum, but in which intelligence and communicative abilities are not substantially impaired. Indeed, many on this portion of the spectrum live and work independently and, despite having some symptoms, are not greatly debilitated by the condition. This heterogeneity of the ASD category has supported arguments that the category mistakenly pathologizes a condition that is in fact a mere difference in brain functioning that is a normal variation but that is being oppressed by our society. With regard to high-functioning autism, this argument has some plausibility. It is more challenging when it comes to classic severe autism.

The transition from the DSM-IV's "autistic disorder" to the DSM-5's reconceptualization of the condition as a "spectrum" naturally expanded the condition to include markedly differing presentations. However, "autism" continues to be extended in further ways, and the category's heterogeneity has increased markedly even beyond the confines of DSM criteria. First, a milder but similar former disorder category, Asperger's syndrome, has now been largely encompassed within ASD. Second, there is provision within the DSM-5 to diagnose subthreshold cases that do not meet full ASD criteria and may manifest only one of the two required dimensions but may still be diagnosed under the DSM-5's "other specified neurodevelopmental disorder" category. More radically expansive still, some researchers have measured the presence of mild nonclinical levels of autistic-like personality traits in the general population, referred to as the "broader autism phenotype" (BAP). For example, someone who eats at the same restaurant every week or walks the same path to work might be considered to have rigid/repetitive-like behavior. Despite the mildness of these symptoms and the cautions of the scale developers that the BAP scale is not aimed at diagnosing disorder, these measures have nonetheless been used to identify those with autistic traits who are loosely described as autistic (e.g., Fitzgerald, 2018; Hurley et al., 2007; Landry & Chouinard, 2016; Nishiyama & Kanne, 2014; Nishiyama et al., 2014; Ruzich et al., 2015; Skylark & Baron-Cohen, 2017).

As one might expect, the expansion from severe classic autism as described by Kanner to "high-functioning" autism and the BAP has resulted in vast increases in the number of people formally or informally labeled as autistic (Baio et al., 2018; Dave & Fernandez, 2015). A majority of the rise in diagnosis is among children with average or above-average intelligence (Baio et al., 2018; Lord & Bishop, 2015). Researchers at times conflate differing points on the spectrum, reporting findings that purport to discuss ASD in general but that are in fact about high-functioning autism (e.g., Schriber et al., 2014), or alternatively they generalize findings about severe autism to the entire category, thus in one direction or the other conflating properties of a subset of autists with the nature of the entire heterogeneous category.

Neurodiversity advocates argue that not only are there autists who are not significantly impaired by the condition, but that many ASD-related traits are in fact advantageous, which may suggest that autism itself has been positively selected for. For example, while autists are frequently less interested in emotionally interacting with others and may prefer to focus on physical systems and objects such as computers rather than people (Attwood, 1998; Baron-Cohen, 2000), such interests are not necessarily negative. As Temple Grandin, a leading neurodiversity advocate, puts it: "The Asperger's brain is interested in things rather than people, and people who are interested in things have given us the computer you're working on right now" (Grandin quoted in Mayor, 2008, p. 2). Similarly, a lack of context sensitivity, often referred to as "weak central coherence," that is found in autism is sometimes argued to provide an advantage by promoting a focus on detail without distraction and providing creative insights that are sometimes unavailable to neurotypical people who are overly influenced by context. The argument that the emphasis on autistic traits as negative or pathological obscures the benefits they possess is supported as well by the presence of surprising savant abilities among some autists (Happé, 2018). Neurodiversity advocates argue that when these traits are not pathologized on the basis of their mere divergence from the neurotypical baseline, their benefits become more apparent and the argument appears more plausible that these traits and autism as a whole represent a naturally selected "cognitive style" (Happé, 1999) rather than a dysfunction.

Although the claim that useful traits are present in an autistic condition does provide a prima facie reason to consider whether the condition might be nondisordered, many other considerations are relevant as well. The presence of beneficial traits—assuming that they can be shown to be beneficial—is only the beginning of an evolutionary argument. For one thing, any harmful traits associated with ASD must also be explained. Evolutionary trade-off arguments regarding autism face the challenge of showing a reliable connection and favorable balance between advantageous and disadvantageous symptoms, either for the category in general or for some specific subgroup. Savant abilities, for instance, occur in only a minority of autists (between 10% and 25%; Happé, 2018). With regard to weak central coherence and its lack of sensitivity to context, there is no evidence that it was naturally selected or conferred an overall advantage in human ancestral environments. Sensitivity to context and the ability to form Gestalts routinely develop in the course of normal maturation, suggesting that this is a species-typical developmental achievement. The claimed advantage of weak central coherence is sometimes said to be demonstrated by the fact that autistic individuals are less prone to experience standard optical illusions. However, young children are also more resistant to optical illusions than neurotypical adults (Doherty et al., 2010), and this fades as children develop, suggesting that optical illusions are a normal side effect of the way normal-range evolved perceptual systems develop.

Even if a specific feature is useful, that does not necessarily imply that the entire condition of which it is a part, which may include some negative features, is on balance advantageous. For example, savant musical abilities such as possessing perfect pitch and a heightened accuracy in identifying and remembering musical notes are remarkable indeed, but these advantages when they occur by themselves do not constitute a form of autism. Within the context of autism, they often occur in autists who also have language difficulties (Bonnel et al., 2010; Heaton et al., 2008; Jones et al., 2009) and in those for whom sound is over-arousing and who may even have hyperacusis (a hearing disorder where everyday sounds are experienced as distressing) (Gomes et al., 2008), making practical use of these gifts difficult. Indeed, it is claimed that some autistic children's "meltdowns" result from such sensory overload: "A tantrum in a young child typically stems from frustration from not getting what they want in that moment. . . . An autistic meltdown on the other hand is all about being overwhelmed . . . when they reach the point of sensory, emotional, and information overload" (Bennie, 2016). For severe classic autists who lack robust cooperative, communicative, and flexibility skills, the possession of savant abilities may confer little or no advantage and is likely to be insufficient to explain their overall condition as advantageous or naturally selected. For higher functioning autists, it is more likely that such an explanation could apply.

There is a possible explanation that might account for the prevalence of some ASD-related traits as naturally selected but still imply that severe classic autism is a disorder. Unlike many traits with normal-range variations in which fitness effects follow a normal distribution that falls off gradually on either side of the mean, the fitness advantage of some mental traits fits a pattern that has been characterized as a cliff-edge (Nesse & Williams, 1994). For such traits, there is increasing advantage up to a point, after which the advantage drops off precipitously and becomes a liability. Potentially suggesting this pattern, a recent study found that individual risk genes for autism are associated with cognitive advantage and have been positively selected (Polimanti & Gelernter, 2017), but that certain polygenic combinations of these individually selected genes resulted in autism. They concluded that "according to our interpretation of our data, such small-effect alleles were accumulated across the genome (polygenic adaptation) to the benefit of most but to the detriment of some" (p. 9). It is thus possible that multiple genetic factors that are in themselves often positive (e.g., attention to detail, attraction to the mechanical causation) may through some cliff-edge combinatory effect yield the negative traits of autism (e.g., weak central coherence, difficulty relating).

Finally, in considering possible evolutionary roots of a global category such as autism, one must establish whether the target traits are constitutive of a condition with a single etiology. If these traits result from multiple etiologies, then their functional status may vary, such that some have been selected for, but others not. Phenotypic and syndromal presentations may provide an initial reason to suspect etiological homogeneity, but these superficial similarities are defeasible. For example, normal sadness, depression, and grief may share a common characteristic of intense sadness, but the intensity of sadness is not a good indication of pathology, as we know from comparisons of grief (which often involves sadness that is intense but not the result of an underlying dysfunction) and dysthymia (a disordered condition characterized by chronic non-severe sadness). Indeed, researchers have found that at a certain level of neurofunctioning, major depression and normal sadness are identical, presumably because both involve intense sadness (Mayberg et al., 1999). However, normal sadness and major depressive disorder have divergent deeper etiologies, with one being a normal evolved emotional response and the other a disorder of that response. Similarly, whether or not all autists evince weak central coherence (Frith, 1989) or mind-blindness (Baron-Cohen, 1990) does not resolve whether all people who have those traits are non-disordered or disordered because those traits may derive from a variety of etiologies.

As a result of the autism category's apparent heterogeneity, a growing number of autism researchers are coming to reject single-factor etiological accounts. Boucher (1975), for instance, explains that "[t]here is no a priori reason to suppose that all the presenting symptoms of autism stem from a single primary impairment of behavior" (p. 68), and suggests dissecting the large ASD category into homogeneous subgroups including "prototypical autism" (Boucher, 2011). After surveying the evidence in favor of the dissociability of groupings of ASD-related traits, she concludes: "It appears, therefore, that the concept of autism as a unitary disorder resulting from a single common cause at some or other level of explanation may be at the point of being abandoned, to give way to a model of the routes to ASD-related behaviors as both multiple and independent" (2011, p. 472). Similarly, Happé, Ronald, and Plomin's (2006) paper, entitled "Time to give up on a single explanation for autism," not only argued that the triad of ASD-related traits often occurred independently of one another, suggesting different etiologies, but that single-factor explanations have failed. They find that "the degrees of social difficulty, communicative impairment and rigid/repetitive behavior are only modestly related" and conclude: "In light of the above research, we suggest that it is time to give up on the search for a monolithic cause or explanation for the three core aspects of autism, at the genetic, neural and cognitive levels" (2006, pp. 1218–1219). Schaaf and Zoghbi (2011) write, "It is well established that the ASDs represent a heterogeneous group of disorders" (p. 806); Amaral (2011) explains, "A hallmark of virtually every biological parameter assayed in individuals with autism is the enormous heterogeneity—far greater than in the general population" (p. 6); and Fletcher-Watson and Happé (2019) suggest that "[h]eterogeneity of etiology may be one reason why progress has been slow; many people now talk of 'the autisms' to reflect the belief that different individuals have different biological paths to autism" (p. 52).

Excessive belief in diagnostic homogeneity is common for two reasons. First, because theoreticians interested in the diagnostic category attempt to theorize about the underlying essential theoretical nature of the category in a general way that encompasses everybody in the category, heterogeneity may be ignored and homogeneity assumed where it does not exist. Second, psychologists often want to gain greater understanding of a category by studying features that are intrinsic to the category but also extend beyond the category to gain a broader view. This can confusingly suggest that the broader group is homogeneous not just with respect to the property being studied, but also with regard to the disordered nature of the condition. This, for example, appears to be what has happened with the BAP. Clearly, heterogeneity is being ignored in a way that yields confusion in the neurodiversity argument.

Conclusion

Neurodiversity arguments pose a provocative and legitimate challenge to psychiatric nosology, for in fact the current diagnostic system has too often overextended diagnostic labels to normally but atypically functioning individuals. The enormous normal range of variation in psychological and neurological structure and emotional expression indicates that the pathologization of those that are merely statistically atypical is a mistake and an abuse of medical power. Neurodiversity advocates are correct to question this type of diagnostic overreach.

However, although neurodiversity advocates correctly emphasize phenotypic heterogeneity and appropriately contend that rare, unusual, or socially disvalued traits do not necessarily constitute disorders, they often fail to appreciate the etiological heterogeneity from which these traits arise. Oddly enough, they also often fail to appreciate that DSM categories are not necessarily theoretically homogeneous groups. Failing to draw careful distinctions among different subgroups that fall within a category of interest, philosophers and advocates can make the mistake of assuming intra-category homogeneity, leading to fallaciously overgeneralized arguments about who is and who is not disordered. It is important to look under the phenotypic hood, so to speak, to assess whether the underlying etiology in a category is homogeneous or heterogeneous.

A central motive of the neurodiversity movement is to achieve diagnostic justice in which individuals who have conditions that are normal variations are not misclassified as disordered and treated unfairly as a result. However, in a society that offers special help and support to the disordered, it is also unjust to mislabel disordered and thereby disadvantaged individuals as nondisordered, potentially depriving them of the help they need. Both errors must be avoided, for the sake of both scientific accuracy and minimizing harm to people. This is why there was an outcry when the DSM-5 reduced the scope of autism.

There is also a danger of creating too strong a link between nondisorder status and civil rights. The relationship between justice and disorder is a complex one. When Robert Spitzer originally advocated for the elimination of homosexuality from the DSM as a category of mental disorder, he explained that "homosexuals have been denied civil rights in many areas of life on the ground that . . . they suffer from a 'mental illness'" (1973, p. 1216), and he claimed that depathologizing the condition would remove "one of the justifications for the denial of civil rights" (p. 1216). However, Spitzer hastened to add the clarification that he was not implying that the presence of disorder justifies a curtailment of rights: "By linking the removal of homosexuality from the diagnostic nomenclature with an affirmation of the civil rights of homosexuals, no implication is intended justifying the irrational denial of civil rights to individuals who do suffer from true psychiatric disorders" (p. 1216). The important point to draw from this is that issues of justice and issues of diagnosis are largely separable. Neurodiversity advocates who link depathologization with justice too closely thus run the risk of implying that those individuals who have a genuine disorder may justifiably be denied certain rights. After the real progress that has been made in achieving civil rights for the mentally disordered, that would be a terrible and unjustified conclusion to draw from neurodiversity arguments. The ultimate goal is to treat all humans with justice, and to accord them all their human and civil rights, regardless of whether they have a disorder or not.

References

Amaral, D. G. (2011). The promise and the pitfalls of autism research: An introductory note for new autism researchers. *Brain Research*, *1380*, 3–9.

American Psychiatric Association. (1980). *Diagnostic and statistical manual of mental disorders* (3rd ed.; DSM-III). APA.

American Psychiatric Association. (1994). *Diagnostic and statistical manual of mental disorders* (4th ed.; DSM-IV). APA.

American Psychiatric Association. (2013). *Diagnostic and statistical manual of mental disorders* (5th ed.; DSM-5). APA.

Anton, A. L. (2013). The virtue of sociopaths: How to appreciate the neurodiversity of sociopathy without becoming a victim. In C. D. Herrera & A. Perry (Eds.), *Ethics and neurodiversity* (pp. 111–130). Cambridge Scholars.

Antonetta, S. (2007). *A mind apart: Travels in a neurodiverse world*. Penguin.

Armstrong, T. (2010). *Neurodiversity: Discovering the extraordinary gifts of autism, ADHD, dyslexia, and other brain differences*. De Capo Press.

Attwood, T. (1998). *Asperger's syndrome: A guide for parents and professionals*. Jessica Kingsley.

Baio, J., Wiggins, L., Christensen, D. L., Maenner, M. J., Daniels, J., Warren, Z., Kurzius-Spencer, M., Zahorodny, W., Rosenberg, C. R., White, T., Durkin, M. S., Imm, P., Nikolaou, L., Yeargin-Allsopp, M., Lee, L.-C., Harrington, R., Lopez, M., Fitzgerald, R. T., Hewitt, A., . . . Dowling, F. N. (2018). Prevalence of autism spectrum disorder among children aged 8 years: Autism and developmental disabilities monitoring network, 11 sites, United States, 2014. *Morbidity and Mortality Weekly Report—Surveillance Summaries*, *67*(6), 1–23.

Baller, E. B., Wei, S-M., Kohn, P. D., Rubinow, D. R., Alarcón, G., Schmidt, P. J., & Berman, K. F. (2013). Abnormalities of dorsolateral prefrontal function in women with premenstrual dysphoric disorder: A multimodal neuroimaging study. *American Journal of Psychiatry*, *170*, 305–314.

Barkley, R. A. (2015). Emotional dysregulation is a core component of ADHD. In R. A. Barkley (Ed.), *Attention-deficit hyperactivity disorder: A handbook for diagnosis and treatment* (pp. 81–115). Guilford Press.

Baron-Cohen, S. (1989). The autistic child's theory of mind: A case of specific developmental delay. *Journal of Child Psychology and Psychiatry, 30*(2), 285–297.

Baron-Cohen, S. (1990). Autism: A specific cognitive disorder of "mind-blindness." *International Review of Psychiatry, 2*, 81–90.

Bennie, M. (2016, Feb 2). Tantrum vs. autistic meltdown: What is the difference? *Autism Awareness Centre*. Retrieved at https://autismawarenesscentre.com/what-is-the-difference-between-a-tantrum-and-an-autistic-meltdown/

Benning, S. D., Patrick, C. J., Hicks, B. M., Blonigen, D. M., & Krueger, R. F. (2003). Factor structure of the psychopathic personality inventory: Validity and implications for clinical assessment. *Psychological Assessment, 15*(3), 340–350.

Biederman, J., Petty, C. R., Evans, M. Small, J., & Faraone, S. V. (2010). How persistent is ADHD? A controlled 10-year follow-up study of boys with ADHD. *Psychiatry Research, 177*, 299–304.

Blume, H. (1998, September). Neurodiversity. *The Atlantic*. Retrieved from https://www.theatlantic.com/magazine/archive/1998/09/neurodiversity/305909/

Bonnel, A., McAdams, S., Smith, B., Berthiaume, C., Bertone, A., Ciocca, V., Burack, J. A., & Mottron, L. (2010). Enhanced pure-tone pitch discrimination among persons with autism but not Asperger syndrome. *Neuropsychologia, 48*(9), 2465–2475.

Boucher, J. (1975). *A neuropsychological approach to the study of autism: Two exploratory hypothesis*. Unpublished doctoral dissertation, University of Birmingham, UK.

Boucher, J. (2011). Redefining the concept of autism as a unitary disorder: Multiple causal deficits of a single kind? In D. Fein (Ed.), *The neuropsychology of autism* (pp. 469–482). Oxford University Press.

Brownlow, C. (2010). Re-presenting autism: The construction of NT syndrome. *Journal of Medical Humanities, 31*(3), 243–256.

Burgoine, E., & Wing, L. (1983). Identical triplets with Asperger's syndrome. *British Journal of Psychiatry, 143*, 261–265.

Chapman, R. (2019). Neurodiversity theory and its discontents: Autism, schizophrenia, and the social model of disability. In S. Tekin & R. Bluhm (Eds.), *The Bloomsbury companion to philosophy of psychiatry* (pp. 371–389). Bloomsbury.

Cleckley, H. M. (1955). *The mask of sanity* (3rd ed.). C. V. Mosby.

Conrad, J. A. (2018). On intellectual and developmental disabilities in the United States: A historical perspective. *Journal of Intellectual Disabilities, 24*(1), 85–101.

Copestake, S., Gray, N. S., & Snowden, R. J. (2011). A comparison of a self-report measure of psychopathy with the Psychopathy Checklist-Revised in a UK sample of offenders. *Journal of Forensic Psychiatry & Psychology, 22*, 169–182.

Dave, D. M., & Fernandez, J. M. (2015). Rising autism prevalence: Real or displacing other mental disorders? Evidence from demand for auxiliary healthcare workers in California. *Economic Inquiry, 53*(1), 448–468.

Ding, Y.-C., Chi, H.-C., Grady, D. L., Morishima, A., Kidd, J. R., Kidd, K. K., Flodman, P., Spence, M. A., Schuck, S., Swanson, J. M., Zhang, Y.-P., & Moyzis, R. K. (2002). Evidence of positive selection acting at the human dopamine receptor D4 gene locus. *Proceedings of the National Academy of Science, 99*, 309–314.

Doherty, M. J., Campbell, N. M., Tsuji, H., & Phillips, W. A. (2010). The Ebbinghaus illusion deceives adults but not young children. *Developmental Science, 13*(5), 714–721.

Dopheide, J. A., & Pliszka, S. R. (2009). Attention-deficit-hyperactivity disorder: An update. *Pharmacotherapy, 29*(6), 656–679.

Douglas, V. I., & Peters, K. G. (1979). Toward a clearer definition of the attentional deficit of hyperactive children. In G. A. Hale & G. Lewis (Eds.), *Attention and the developments of cognitive skills* (pp. 173–248). Plenum Press.

Dreber, A., Apicella, C. L., Eisenberg, D. T. A., Garcia, J. R., Zamore, R. S., Lum, J. K., & Campbell, B. (2009). The 7R polymorphism in the dopamine receptor D4 gene (DRD4) is associated with financial risk taking in men. *Evolution and Human Behavior, 30*, 85–92.

Dubey, N., Hoffman, J. F., Schuebel, K., Yuan, Q., Martinex, P. E., Nieman, L. K., Rubinow, D. R., Schmidt, P. J., & Goldman, D. (2017). The ESC/E(Z) complex, an effector of response to ovarian steroids, manifests an intrinsic difference in cells from women with premenstrual dysphoric disorder. *Molecular Psychiatry, 22*(8), 1172–1184.

Eisenberg, D. T., Campbell, B., Gray, P. B, & Sorenson, M. (2008). Dopamine receptor genetic polymorphisms and body composition in undernourished pastoralists: An exploration of nutrition indices among nomadic and recently settled Ariaal men of northern Kenya. *BMC Evolutionary Biology, 8*, 173.

Elder, T. E. (2010). The importance of relative standards in ADHD diagnoses: Evidence based on exact birth dates. *Journal of Health Economics, 29*, 641–656.

Epperson, C. N. (2013). Premenstrual dysphoric disorder and the brain. *American Journal of Psychiatry, 170*, 248–252.
Epperson, C. N., Steiner, M., Hartlage, S. A., Eriksson, E., Schmidt, P. J., Jones, I., & Yonkers, K. A. (2012). Premenstrual dysphoric disorder: Evidence for a new category for DSM-5. *American Journal of Psychiatry, 169*, 465–475.
Evans, W. N., Morril, M. S., & Parente, S. T. (2010). Measuring inappropriate medical diagnosis and treatment in survey data: The case of ADHD among school-age children. *Journal of Health Economics, 29*, 657–673.
Faraone, S. V., Doyle, A. E, Mick, E., & Biederman, J. (2001). Meta-analysis of the association between the 7-repeat allele of the dopamine D4 receptor gene and attention deficit hyperactivity disorder. *American Journal of Psychiatry, 158*, 1052–1057.
Faucher, L., & Forest, D. (2021). *Defining mental disorder: Jerome Wakefield and his critics*. MIT Press.
First, M. B., & Wakefield, J. C. (2010). Defining "mental disorder" in DSM-V. *Psychological Medicine, 40*(11), 1779–1782.
First, M. B., & Wakefield, J. C. (2013). Diagnostic criteria as dysfunction indicators: Bridging the chasm between the definition of mental disorder and diagnostic criteria for specific disorders. *Canadian Journal of Psychiatry, 58*(12), 663–669.
Fitzgerald, M. (2018). The broader autism phenotype: Expanding the clinical Gestalt of autism and broadening DSM V criteria of autism spectrum disorder. *Journal of Psychology and Clinical Psychiatry, 9*(3), 316–324.
Fletcher-Watson, S., & Happé, F. (2019). *Autism: A new introduction to psychological theory and current debate*. Routledge.
Fombonne, E. (2002). Epidemiological trends in rates of autism. *Molecular Psychiatry, 7*, s4–s6.
Food and Drug Administration. (1999, November 3). Minutes of the meeting of the Psychopharmacologic Drugs Advisory Committee of the Food and Drug Administration Center for Drug Evaluation and Research, Hearing on NDA 18-936(S), Prozac (fluoxetine hydrochloride), Ely Lilly and Company, Indicated for the Treatment of Premenstrual Dyshporic Disorder. Gaithersburg, MD.
Foucault, M. (1965). *Madness and civilization: A history of insanity in the Age of Reason*. Pantheon.
Frith, U. (1989). *Autism: Explaining the enigma*. Blackwell.
Fritzon, K., Croom, S., Brooks, N., & Bailey, C. (2013). The Corporate Personality Inventory. Unpublished.
Gehricke, J.-G., Swanson, J., Duong, S., Nguyen, J., Wigal, T., Fallon, J., Caburian, C., Muftuler, L. T., & Moyzis, R. (2015). Increased brain activity to unpleasant stimuli in individuals with the 7R allele of the DRD4 gene. *Psychiatry Research, 231*, 58–63.
Gomes, E., Pedroso, F. S., & Wagner, M. B. (2008). Auditory hypersensitivity in the autistic spectrum disorder. *Pró-fono: Revista de Atualização Cientifica, 20*(4), 279–284.
Graby, S. (2015). Neurodiversity: Bridging the gap between the disabled people's movement and the mental health system survivors' movement? In H. Spandler, J. Anderson, & B. Sapey (Eds.), *Madness, distress and the politics of disablement* (pp. 231–244). Policy Press.
Grady, D. L., Chi, H.-C., Ding, Y.-C., Smith, M., Wang, E., Schuck, S., Flodman, P., Spence, M. A., Swanson, J. M., & Moyzis, R. K. (2003). High prevalence of rare dopamine receptor D4 alleles in children diagnosed with attention-deficit hyperactivity disorder. *Molecular Psychiatry, 8*, 536–545.
Grady, D. L., Harxi, A., Smith, M., Flodman, P., Spence, M. A., Swanson, J. M., & Moyzis, R. K. (2005). Sequence variants of the DRD4 gene in autism: Further evidence that rare DRD4 7R haplotypes are ADHD specific. *American Journal of Medical Genetics, 136B*, 33–35.
Grady, D. L., Thanos, P. K., Corrada, M. M., Barnett Jr., J. C., Ciobanu, V., Shustarovich, D., Napoli, A., Moyzis, A. G., Grandy, D., Rubinstein, M., Wang, G.-J., Kawas, C. H., Chen, C., Dong, Q., Wang, E., Volkow, N. D., & Moyzis, R. K. (2013). DRD4 genotype predicts longevity in mouse and human. *The Journal of Neuroscience, 33*(1), 286–291.
Grandin, T., & Panek, R. (2013). *The autistic brain: Thinking across the spectrum*. Houghton Mifflin Harcourt.
Happé, F. (1999). Autism: Cognitive deficit or cognitive style? *Trends in Cognitive Science, 3*(6), 216–222.
Happé, F. (2018). Why are savant skills and special talents associated with autism. *World Psychiatry, 17*(3), 280–281.
Happé, F., Ronald, A., & Plomin, R. (2006). Time to give up on a single explanation for autism. *Nature Neuroscience, 9*, 1218–1220.
Hare, R. D. (1991). *The Hare Psychopathy Checklist-Revised*. Multi-Health Systems.
Hare, R. D. (1996). Psychopathy and antisocial personality disorder: A case of diagnostic confusion. *Psychiatric Times, 13*(2). Retrieved from https://www.psychiatrictimes.com/view/psychopathy-and-antisocial-personality-disorder-case-diagnostic-confusion
Hare, R. D. (2003). *The Hare Psychopathy Checklist-Revised* (2nd ed.). Multi-Health Systems.

Hare, R. D., Hart, S. D., & Harpur, T. J. (1991). Psychopathy and the DSM-IV criteria for antisocial personality disorder. *Journal of Abnormal Psychology, 100*(3), 391–398.

Heaton, P., Williams, K., Cummins, O., & Happé, F. (2008). Autism and pitch processing splinter skills: A group and subgroup analysis. Autism: *The International Journal of Research and Practice, 12*(2), 203–219.

Hill, J. C., & Schoener, E. P. (1996). Age-dependent decline of attention deficit hyperactivity disorder. *American Journal of Psychiatry, 153*, 1143–1146.

Hoogman, M., Bralten, J., Hibar, D. P., Mennes, M., Zwiers, M. P., Schweren, L. S. J., van Hulzen, K. J. E., Medland, S. E., Shumskaya, E., Jahanshad, N., de Zeeuw, P., Szekely, E., Sudre, G., Wolfers, T., Onnink, A. M. H., Dammers, J. T., Mostert, J. C., Vives-Gilabert, Y., Kohls, G., . . . & Franke, B.(2017). Subcortical brain volume differences in participants with attention deficit hyperactivity disorder in children and adults: A cross-sectional mega-analysis. *Lancet Psychiatry, 4*, 310–319.

Hughes, J. A. (2021). Does the heterogeneity of autism undermine the neurodiversity paradigm? *Bioethics, 35*, 47–60.

Hurley, R. S., Losh, M., Parlier, M., Reznick, J. S., & Piven, J. (2007). The Broad Autism Phenotype Questionnaire. *Journal of Autism and Developmental Disorders, 37*(9), 1679–1690.

Hyman, S. E. (2010). The diagnosis of mental disorders: The problem of reification. *Annual Review of Clinical Psychology, 6*, 155–179.

Jaarsma, P., & Welin, S. (2012). Autism as a natural human variation: Reflections on the claims of the neurodiversity movement. *Health Care Analysis, 20*, 20–30.

Jones, C. R. G., Happé, F., Baird, G., Simonoff, E., Marsden, A. J. S., Tregay, J., Phillips, R. J., Goswami, U., Thomson, J. M., & Charman, T. (2009). Auditory discrimination and auditory sensory behaviours in autism spectrum disorders. *Neuropsychologia, 47*(13), 2850–2858

Kanner, L. (1943). Autistic disturbances of affective contact. *Nervous Child, 2*, 217–250.

Kinner, S. (2003). Psychopathy as an adaptation: Implications for society and social policy. In R. W. Bloom & N. Dess (Eds.), *Psychological dimensions to war and peace: Evolutionary psychology and violence: A primer for policymakers and public policy advocates* (pp. 57–81). Praeger/Greenwood.

Kirk, S. A., Wakefield, J. C., Hsieh, D. K., & Pottick, K. J. (1999). Social context and social workers' judgments of mental disorder. *Social Service Review, 73*(1), 82–104.

Klein, R. G. (2011). Thinning of the cerebral cortex during development: A dimension of ADHD. *American Journal of Psychiatry, 168*, 111–113.

Kruh, I. P., Whittemore, K., Arnaut, G. L. Y., Manley, J., Gage, B., & Gagliardi, G. J. (2005). The concurrent validity of the Psychopathic Personality Inventory and its relative association with past violence in a sample of insanity acquittees. *International Journal of Forensic Mental Health, 4*, 135–145.

Krupp, D. B., Sewall, L. A., Lalumière, M. L., Sheriff, C., & Harris, G. T. (2012). Nepotistic patterns of violent psychopathy: Evidence for adaption? *Frontiers in Psychology, 3*, 1–8.

Krupp, D. B., Sewall, L. A., Lalumière, M. L., Sheriff, C., & Harris, G. T. (2013). Psychopathy, adaption, and disorder. *Frontiers in Psychology, 4*, 1–5.

Laing, R. D. (1967). *The politics of experience*. Penguin Books.

Landry, O., & Chouinard, P. (2016). Why we should study the broader autism phenotype in typically developing populations. *Journal of Cognition and Development, 17*, 584–595.

Lilienfeld, S. O., & Andrews, B. P. (1996) Development and preliminary validation of a self-report measure of psychopathic personality traits in noncriminal populations. *Journal of Personality Assessment, 66*, 488–524.

Lilienfeld, S. O., Widows, M. R., & Staff, P. A. R. (2005). *Psychopathic Personality Inventory™-Revised*. Psychological Assessment Resources, Inc..

Lord, C., & Bishop, S. L. (2015). Recent advances in autism research as reflected in DSM-5 criteria for autism spectrum disorder. *Annual Review of Clinical Psychology, 11*, 53–70.

Machalek, R. (1995). Sociobiology, sociopathy, and social policy. *Behavioral and Brain Sciences, 18*(3), 564.

Marcus, D. K., Fulton, J. J., & Edens, J. F. (2012). The two-factor model of psychopathic personality: Evidence from the Psychopathic Personality Inventory. *Personality Disorders: Theory, Research, and Treatment, 3*, 140–154.

Marrocco, J., Einhorn, N. R., Petty, G. H., Li, H., Dubey, N., Hoffman, J., Berman, K. F., Goldman, D., Lee, F. S., Schmidt, P. J., & McEwen, B. S. (2020). Epigenetic intersection of BDNF Val66Met genotype with premenstrual dysphoric disorder transcriptome in cross-species model of estradiol add-back. *Molecular Psychiatry, 25*, 572–583.

Mayberg, H. S., Liotti, M., Brannan, S. K., McGinnis, S., Mahurin, R. K., Jerabek, P. A., Silva, J. A., Tekell, J. L., Martin, C. C., Lancaster, J. L., & Fox, P. T. (1999). Reciprocal limbic-cortical function and negative mood: Converging PET findings in depression and normal sadness. *American Journal of Psychiatry, 156*(5), 675–682.

Mayor, T. (2008). Asperger's and IT: Dark secret or open secret? *Computer World.* Retrieved from http://www.computerworld.com/action/article.do?command=viewArticleBasic&ta xonomyId=10&articleId=9072119&intsrc=hm_topic

Mealey, L. (1995a). The sociobiology of sociopathy: An integrated evolutionary model. *Behavioral and Brain Sciences, 18*(3), 523–541.

Mealey, L. (1995b). Primary sociopathy (psychopathy) is a type, secondary is not. *Behavioral and Brain Sciences, 18*(3), 579–599.

Meyerding, J. (1998). Thoughts on finding myself differently brained. *Autonomy: The Critical Journal of Interdisciplinary Autism Studies, 1*(2), 1–9. https://www.inlv.org/subm-brain.jane.eng.html

Moffitt, T. E., Houts, R., Asherson, P., Belsky, D. W., Corcoran, D. L., Hammerle, M., Harrington, H., Hogan, S., Meier, M. H., Polanczyk, G. V., Poulton, R., Ramrakha, S., Sugden, K., Williams, B., Rohde, L. A., & Caspi, A.. (2015). Is adult ADHD a childhood-onset neurodevelopmental disorder? Evidence from a four-decade longitudinal cohort study. *American Journal of Psychiatry, 172*, 967–977.

Moffitt, T. E. (1993). Adolescence-limited and life-course-persistent antisocial behavior: A developmental taxonomy. *Psychological Review, 100*(4), 674–701.

Moffitt, T. E. (2006). Life-course-persistent versus adolescence-limited antisocial behavior. In D. Cicchetti & D. J. Cohen (Eds.), *Developmental psychopathology: Risk, disorder, and adaptation* (pp. 570–598). Wiley.

National Institute of Mental Health. (2007). Brain matures a few years late in ADHD, but follows a normal pattern. *NIMH News Releases.* Retrieved from https://www.nih.gov/news-events/news-releases/brain-matures-few-years-late-adhd-follows-normal-pattern#:~:text=In%20youth%20with%20attention%20deficit,of%20Mental%20Health%20(NIMH)%20has

Nigg, J. T., & Casey, B. J. (2005). An integrative theory of attention-deficit/hyperactivity disorder based on the cognitive and affective neurosciences. *Development and Psychology, 17*, 765–806.

Nishiyama, T., & Kanne, S. M. (2014). On the misapplication of the BAPQ in a study of autism. *Journal of Autism and Developmental Disorders, 44*, 2079–2080.

Ortega, F. (2009). The cerebral subject and the challenge of neurodiversity. *BioSocieties, 4*, 425–445.

Penke, L., Denissen, J. J. A., & Miller, G. F. (2007). The evolutionary genetics of personality. *European Journal of Personality, 21*, 549–587.

Polimanti, R., & Gelernter, J. (2017). Widespread signatures of positive selection in common risk alleles associated to autism spectrum disorder. *PLoS Genetics, 13*(2), e1006618. https://doi.org/10.1371/journal.pgen.1006618

Poythress, N. G., Hoge, S. K., Bonnie, R. J., Monahan, J., Eisenberg, M., & Feucht-Haviar, T. (1998). The competence-related abilities of women criminal defendants. *Journal of the American Academy of Psychiatry and the Law, 26*, 215–222.

Poythress, N. G., Lilienfeld, S. O., Skeem, J. L., Douglas, K. S., Edens, J. F., Epstein, M., & Patrick, C. J. (2010). Using the PCL-R to help estimate the validity of two self-report measures of psychopathy with offenders. *Assessment, 17*, 206–219.

Professional Staff of the United States–United Kingdom Cross-National Project. (1974). The diagnosis and psychopathology of schizophrenia in New York and London. *Schizophrenia Bulletin, 1*, 80–102.

Rapoport, J. L. (2007). Association of the dopamine receptor D4 (DRD4) gene 7-repeat allele with children with attention-deficit/hyperactivity disorder (ADHD): An update. *American Journal of Medical Genetics, 144B*, 379–382.

Reimer, M. (2008). Psychopathy without (the language of) disorder. *Neuroethics, 1*(3), 185–198.

Robins, E., & Guze, S. B. (1970). Establishment of diagnostic validity in psychiatric illness: Its application to schizophrenia. *American Journal of Psychiatry, 126*, 107–111.

Rosenhan, D. (1973). On being sane in insane places. *Science, 179*, 250–258.

Ruzich, E., Allison, C., Smith, P., Watson, P., Auyeung, B., Ring, H., & Baron-Cohen, S. (2015). Measuring autistic traits in the general population: A systematic review of the autism spectrum quotient (AQ) in a nonclinical population sample of 6,900 typical adult males and females. *Molecular Autism, 6*, 2.

Sagvolden, T., Johansen, E. B., Aase, H., & Russell, V. A. (2005). A dynamic developmental theory of attention-deficit/hyperactivity disorder (ADHD) predominantly hyperactive/impulsive and combined subtypes. *Behavioral and Brain Sciences, 25*, 397–468.

Sarbin, T. (1967). On the futility of the proposition that some people be labeled "mentally ill." *Journal of Consulting and Clinical Psychology, 31*, 447–453.

Schaff, C. P. & Zoghbi, H. Y. (2011). Solving the autism puzzle a few pieces at a time. *Neuron, 70*, 806–808.

Scheff, T. J. (1966). *Being mentally ill: A sociological theory.* Aldine.

Scheff, T. J. (1975). *Labeling madness.* Prentice Hall.

Schmidt, P. J., Nieman, L. K., Danaceau, M. A., Adams, L. F. & Rubinow, D. R. (1998). Differential behavioral effects of gonadal steroids in women with and in those without premenstrual syndrome. *New England Journal of Medicine, 338*, 209–216.

Schriber, R. A., Robins, R. W., & Solomon, M. (2014). Personality and self-insight in individuals with autism spectrum disorder. *Journal of Personality and Social Psychology, 106*(1), 112–130.

Schwartz, A. (2012, October 9). Attention disorder or not, pills to help in school. *New York Times*. Retrieved from https://www.nytimes.com/2012/10/09/health/attention-disorder-or-not-children-prescribed-pills-to-help-in-school.html

Shaw, P., Eckstrand, K., Sharp, W., Blumenthal, J., Lerch, J. P., Greenstein, D., Clasen, L., Evans, A., Gledd, J., & Rapoport, J. L. (2007). Attention-deficit/hyperactivity disorder is characterized by a delay in cortical maturation. *Proceedings of the National Academy of Sciences, 104*(49), 19649–19654.

Shaw, P., Malek, M., Watson, B., Greenstein, D., de Rossi, P., & Sharp, W. (2013). Trajectories of cerebral cortical development in childhood and adolescent and adult attention-deficit/hyperactivity disorder. *Biological Psychiatry, 74*, 599–606.

Shaw, P., Stringaris, A., Nigg, J., & Leibenluft, E. (2014). Emotional dysregulation and attention-deficit/hyperactivity disorder. *American Journal of Psychiatry, 171*(3), 276–293.

Sinclair, J. (1993). Don't mourn for us. *Autonomy: The Critical Journal for Interdisciplinary Autism Studies, 1*, 1–4.

Singer, J. (1999). Why can't you be normal for once in your life? From a "problem with no name" to the emergence of a new category of difference. In M. Corker & S. French (Eds.), *Disability discourse* (pp. 59–67). Open University Press.

Skeem, J. L., & Cooke, D. J. (2010). Is criminal behavior a central component of psychopathy? Conceptual directions for resolving the debate. *Psychological Assessment, 22*, 433–445.

Skylark, W. J., & Baron-Cohen, S. (2017). Initial evidence that non-clinical autistic traits are associated with lower income. *Molecular Autism, 8*, 61. doi:10.1186/

Spitzer, R. (1973). A proposal about homosexuality and the APA nomenclature: Homosexuality as an irregular form of sexual behavior and sexual orientation disturbance is a psychiatric disorder. *American Journal of Psychiatry, 130*(11), 1214–1216.

Still, G. F. (1902). Some abnormal psychical conditions in children. *Lancet, 1*, 1008–1012, 1077–1082, 1163–1168.

Strauss, J. S., Carpenter, W. T., & Bartko, J. J. (1974). The diagnosis and understanding of schizophrenia: Summary and conclusions. *Schizophrenia Bulletin, 1*, 70–80.

Szasz, T. S. (1961). *The myth of mental illness: Foundations of a theory of personal conduct*. Hoeber-Harper.

Vargas-Cooper, N. (2012). The billion dollar battle over premenstrual disorder. *Salon*. Retrieved from https://www.salon.com/2012/02/26/the_billion_dollar_battle_over_premenstrual_disorder/

Visser, S. N., Danielson, M. L., Bitsko, R. H., Holbrook, J. R., Kogan, M. D., Ghandour, R. M., Perou, R., & Blumberg, S. J. (2014). Trends in the parent-report of health care provider-diagnosed and medicated attention-deficit/hyperactivity disorder: United States, 2003–2011. *Journal of the American Academy of Child and Adolescent Psychiatry, 53*(1), 34–46.

Volkow, N. D., Wang, G.-J., Kollins, S. H., Wigal, T. L., Newcorn, J. H., Telang, F., Fowler, J. S., Zhu, W., Logan, J., Ma, Y., Pradhan, K., Wong, C., & Swanson, J. M. . (2009). Evaluating dopamine reward pathway in ADHD. *JAMA, 302*, 1084–1091.

Volkow, N. D., Wang, G.-J., Newcorn, J. H., Kollins, S. H., Wigal, T. L., Telang, F., Fowler, J. S., Goldstein, R. Z., Klein, N., Logan, J., Wong, C., & Swanson, J. M. . (2011). Motivation deficit in ADHD is associated with dysfunction of the dopamine reward pathway. *Molecular Psychiatry, 16*, 1147–1154.

Wakefield, J. C. (1992a). The concept of mental disorder: On the boundary between biological facts and social values. *American Psychologist, 47*, 373–388.

Wakefield, J. C. (1992b). Disorder as harmful dysfunction: A conceptual critique of DSM-III-R's definition of mental disorder. *Psychological Review, 99*, 232–247.

Wakefield, J. C. (1993). Limits of operationalization: A critique of Spitzer and Endicott's (1978) proposed operational criteria of mental disorder. *Journal of Abnormal Psychology, 102*, 160–172.

Wakefield, J. C. (1999a). Evolutionary versus prototype analyses of the concept of disorder. *Journal of Abnormal Psychology, 108*, 374–399.

Wakefield, J. C. (1999b). Mental disorder as a black box essentialist concept. *Journal of Abnormal Psychology, 108*, 465–472.

Wakefield, J. C. (2001). Evolutionary history versus current causal role in the definition of disorder: Reply to McNally. *Behaviour Research and Therapy, 39*, 347–366.

Wakefield, J. C. (2007). The concept of mental disorder: Diagnostic implications of the harmful dysfunction analysis. *World Psychiatry, 6*, 149–156.
Wakefield, J. C. (2011). Darwin, functional explanation, and the philosophy of psychiatry. In P. R. Adriaens and A. De Block (Eds.), *Maladapting minds: Philosophy, psychiatry, and evolutionary theory* (pp. 143–172). Oxford University Press.
Wakefield, J. C. (2013). DSM-5 grief scorecard: Assessment and outcomes of proposals to pathologize grief. *World Psychiatry, 12*(2), 171–173.
Wakefield, J. C. (2015). DSM-5, psychiatric epidemiology and the false positives problem. *Epidemiology and Psychiatric Sciences, 24*(3), 188–196.
Wakefield, J. C. (2016a). The concepts of biological function and dysfunction: Toward a conceptual foundation for evolutionary psychopathology. In D. Buss (Ed.), *Handbook of evolutionary psychology* (2nd ed., Vol 2., pp. 988–1006). Oxford University Press.
Wakefield, J. C. (2016b). Diagnostic issues and controversies in DSM-5: Return of the false positives problem. *Annual Review of Clinical Psychology, 12*, 105–132.
Wakefield, J. C. (2021). Are there naturally selected disorders? Supplementary reply to Rachel Cooper. In L. Faucher & D. Forest (Eds.), *Defining mental disorder: Jerome Wakefield and his critics* (pp. 577–591). MIT Press.
Wakefield, J. C. (2022). Klerman's "credo" reconsidered: Neo-Kraepelinianism, Spitzer's views, and what we can learn from the past. *World Psychiatry, 21*(1), 4–25.
Wakefield, J. C., & First, M. B. (2003). Clarifying the distinction between disorder and nondisorder: Confronting the overdiagnosis ("false positives") problem in DSM-V. In K. A. Phillips, M. B. First, & H. A. Pincus (Eds.), *Advancing DSM: Dilemmas in psychiatric diagnosis* (pp. 23–56). American Psychiatric Press.
Wakefield, J. C., & First, M. B. (2012). Placing symptoms in context: The role of contextual criteria in reducing false positives in DSM diagnosis. *Comprehensive Psychiatry, 53*, 130–139.
Wakefield, J. C., Wasserman, D. T, & Conrad, J. A. (2020). In A. Cureton & D. T. Wasserman (Eds.) *The Oxford handbook of philosophy and disability* (pp. 501–521). Oxford University Press.
Wang, E., Ding, Y.-C., Flodman, P., Kidd, J. R., Kidd, K. K., Grady, D. L., Ryder, O. A., Spence, M. A., Swanson, J. M., & Moyzis, R. K. (2004). The genetic architecture of selection at the human dopamine receptor D4 (DRD4) gene locus. *American Journal of Human Genetics, 74*, 931–944.
Wender, P. H. (1971). *Minimal brain dysfunction in children*. Wiley.
World Health Organization. (2006, November 11). WHO child growth standards: Length/height-for-age, weight-for-age, weight-for-length, weight-for-height and body mass index-for-age: Methods and development. *WHO Publications*. Retrieved from: https://www.who.int/publications/i/item/924154693X
Zoëga, H., Valdimarsdóttir, U. A., & Hernández-Díaz, S. (2012). Age, academic performance, and stimulant prescribing for ADHD: A nationwide cohort study. *Pediatrics, 130*, 1012–1018.

CHAPTER 64

Post-Traumatic Stress Disorder and Post-Combat Reintegration: An Evolutionary Model

Hector A. Garcia

Abstract

The medical model and mental health stigma frame post-traumatic stress disorder (PTSD) as an essential malfunction. However, in this chapter the author argues that what are regarded as PTSD sequelae exist today because they are based on survival adaptations, helping human ancestors avoid predation, cope with aggressive in-group members, and survive violent inter-group conflicts. While distressing to the experiencer, PTSD-related interpersonal difficulties, as well as behavioral, cognitive, and comorbid symptomology, have ancestral survival utility. In particular, combat-related PTSD and the associated difficulties soldiers face reintegrating into civilian life are illuminated by an evolutionary framing of PTSD, evolved male coalitionary psychology, and the mismatch between the evolutionary past and life in modern, peacetime, civilian environments. Evolutionary explanations of PTSD can help reduce mental health stigma, and increase rates of engagement and completion of evidence-based psychotherapies.

Key Words: evolutionary psychology, post-traumatic stress disorder, combat, veterans, fitness, stigma

Introduction

What is post-traumatic stress disorder (PTSD)? To begin, it is an emotionally anguishing mental health condition experienced across the globe. For this reason, it is also a set of clinical sequelae outlined in the diagnostic manuals used to assess psychiatric conditions (such as the DSM-5; American Psychiatric Association, 2013). Following the field of medicine more generally, psychiatry is conceptually grounded in the disease model. That model emphasizes disease entities, phenomena regarded as system failures that cause harm to the individual. While the disease model is invaluable—for rendering diagnoses and prognoses, for delivering treatment, and for disease prevention—it overlooks the possibility that certain psychiatric conditions may be rooted in adaptations that aided the survival and reproduction of our ancestors. PTSD is among these conditions, and an evolutionary framing of the disorder can offer insights not only into the disorder's origins, but also for improving treatment outcome and treatment retention efforts.

While *evolutionary psychiatry* is a common term for the nascent field that is beginning to uncover this framing, the discipline draws from much more than neurochemistry and the classification and treatment of diseases (where psychiatry maintains its greatest focus), including fields such as evolutionary biology and psychology, clinical psychology, ethology, neuropsychology, and biological anthropology, among others. For this reason, I will use the classic term *evolutionary psychopathology* throughout this chapter to describe the model.

Pathogenesis

Evolutionary psychopathology rests on the understanding that, as a species, we spent 99% of our history as hunter-gatherers living in drastically different environments than those in which most of us currently live. Given the recency of our modernized world, human brains are still equipped with adaptations that aided the survival and reproduction of our ancestors. As such, even some of our psychopathologies may reflect evolved responses to ancient survival pressures. Since psychiatric conditions sometimes generate profound emotional distress, any utility may seem counterintuitive. But while psychiatric conditions are often undesirable for the individual experiencing them, in some cases they can benefit the individual's genes by aiding survival and reproduction—nature favoring *survival over quality of life* (Diamond & Zoladz, 2016).

These adaptive responses differ from those diagnoses that represent true system failures. For example, dementias are malfunctions in normal cognitive processes caused by damaged or diseased neurons that impair functioning and sometimes lead to death. By contrast, phobic fears of snakes may represent utility. Base rates of snake phobias are unusually high, far disproportionate to phobic fears of real dangers of the modern world, such as driving, even in places were the probability of encountering a venomous snake is near zero (Agras et al., 1969). Fearing venomous snakes in our ancestral past, when the threat was far more prevalent, had clear adaptive value—it prevented our ancestors from getting envenomed. In short, the threat was present long enough to establish a prominent place among our evolved fears, whereas the threat of getting killed in a motor vehicle accident has not. Similar evolutionary processes may account for PTSD.

The disease model has dominated conceptualizations of PTSD, including a focus on neuropathology—e.g., the hypothesis that trauma experiences resulting in excessive glucocorticoid production damage the hippocampus (McEwan et al., 1992). Although a growing body of evidence points to the adaptive origins of PTSD symptoms, cautions have been voiced for how we frame evolutionary medicine. For example, Randy Nesse argues that "[t]hey [diseases] are not adaptations shaped by natural selection. Genes or traits associated with some disease provide advantages or disadvantages that influence natural selection. . . . The correct question is why did natural selection shape traits that make us vulnerable to diseases" (2019, p. 41).

Another possibility is that PTSD represents extreme variants of adaptive traits. Consistent with this idea, low rates of PTSD are found globally. Across a 24-nation sample, World Mental Health (WMH) researchers found a lifetime trauma prevalence rate of 70.4% (Kessler et al., 2017). However, only a small minority of trauma survivors develop PTSD; WMH surveys revealed rates ranging from only 1.3% (Japan; Kawakami et al., 2014) to 8.8% (Northern Ireland; Ferry et al., 2014). Whether adaptive in some proportion, too much of any trait can impinge on fitness. Excessive fear may prevent engagement in necessary risks to acquire food and mates, or other fitness-critical behaviors. Too little fear, and impetuous risks procure untimely and expectable removal from the gene pool. In nonhuman animals, intense vigilance is associated with less feeding behavior, poorer parental care, and even fewer offspring (Lima & Dill, 1990; Zanette et al., 2011). Nevertheless, even behaviors that come at a cost to fitness can be adaptive. As Lima and Dill succinctly put it, "Few failures . . . are as unforgiving as the failure to avoid a predator: being killed greatly decreases future fitness" (1990, p. 619). An alternative to PTSD reflecting a system failure, or a tail of the normal curve, is that it represents an evolutionary mismatch.

Is PTSD a Mismatch Disease?

An *evolutionary mismatch* occurs when an adaptation becomes disadvantageous because it no longer fits the environment, for example as a function of temporal change (e.g., environmental change over time) or spatial change (e.g., migrations). Humans are unique in that with our technology we have affected drastic and rapid environmental change, faster than our genomes could keep pace. This has created numerous mismatch health disorders. As hunter-gatherers, our ancestral lifestyles were marked by high physical activity and punctuated by periods of scarcity. Binging on high-calorie foods, rich in fat and sugar, was advantageous. But advances in our ability to produce and modify food has made fat and sugar available in far higher concentrations and far easier to acquire. With intense cravings paired with easy access (along with sedentary lifestyles), industrialized nations are plagued with type II diabetes, morbid obesity, and heart disease.

Evolutionary scholars argue that to substantiate a mismatch, the function of an evolved mechanism must be established, along with discrepancies in the "quantity, intensity, or constitution" of "input cues" between the current and ancestral environments being processed by that mechanism (Norman et al., 2017 p. 40). In the case of PTSD, the proposed function is straightforward—a set of defensive responses "intended" to help our ancestors survive danger. The proposed discrepancy lies in the prevalence of danger. Our ancestral environments presented far higher frequencies of mortal dangers not commonly encountered in the industrialized world, such as large predators, (greater vulnerability to) environmental calamities, venomous or poisonous fauna, and mortal inter-group conflict. PTSD has been described as a disorder of fear extinction (Kearns et al., 2012). However, while in the natural world failing to habituate in the absence of threat can exact fitness costs, when danger is ubiquitous, down-regulation can be fatal.

DSM-5

Criterion A

In the case of PTSD, the proposed mismatch discrepancy corresponds to a criterion necessary for a diagnosis—a dangerous event or "trauma." Per DSM-5, "criterion A" reads: "The person was exposed to: death, threatened death, actual or threatened serious injury, or actual or threatened sexual violence" (APA, 2013, p. 271). In the modern world, PTSD can arise from traumatic experiences as varied as child abuse, domestic violence, assault, rape, natural disasters, motor vehicle or occupational accidents, animal attacks, or combat.

While such criterion A stressors can all result in a PTSD diagnosis, predation is nearly as old as life itself, as are evolved predation-defense responses. Much of the neurobiology of our fear responses is therefore rooted in predator avoidance (Cantor, 2005). However, our recent positioning at the top of the food chain has made animal attacks relatively rare and thus difficult to study. Greater prevalence of war-related trauma (along with a larger research base) and our predisposition to fear conspecific violence make combat-related PTSD a pertinent focus of evolutionary psychopathology. Although the tragedy of war is that it destroys and traumatizes across demographics, war is predominately a male occupation, predominately kills men, and has likely selected for adaptations specifically in men that have unique relevance for combat-related PTSD. For this reason, the focus here will prioritize male psychology.

Evidence suggests that an important selective pressure across our species' history was (male) human-on-human violence. Massacre sites regularly unearthed by archaeologists reveal crushed skulls, broken bones, and embedded spear points (Teschler-Nicola et al., 1999). Moreover, homicides among contemporary hunter-gatherers, who live reasonably similar lifestyles to our ancestors, are remarkably high (Mirazón Lahr et al., 2016; Pinker, 2007)—in some societies, lethal violence rates (among males, in particular) reach 30% (Keeley, 2014). The decline in violence since our days as hunter-gatherers has been precipitous, and today we are inordinately less likely to be killed by other humans (Pinker, 2007).

Yet, such a prominent pressure has selected for a persistent and predispositional fear of other humans. Across its 24-nation sample, WMH research found that the unexpected death of loved ones and motor vehicle accidents were the most common trauma types (Kessler et al., 2017). However, interpersonal traumas (in particular, recurrent violence and sexual assault) were the best predictors of PTSD.

Other studies also reveal our sensitivity to dangerous humans. By pairing mild electric shocks with certain stimuli (such as photos), researchers can examine the rate of acquisition and extinction of fear responses. Fast acquisition and slow extinction suggest evolutionary loading. In one study (Olsson et al., 2005), researchers paired mild shock with photos of birds and butterflies, or snakes and spiders. When photos were shown without the shock, subjects quickly habituated to the photos of birds and butterflies, but failed to habituate fully to the photos of snakes and spiders. Birds and butterflies were not the killers of humans, as were snakes and spiders, so our brains easily relinquish fear of the former, but not of the latter.

The researchers then repeated the experiment with Black and White subjects, but instead of animal photos, subjects were shown photos of unfamiliar Black or White people. In this experiment, Black people habituated fully to Black faces in the absence of mild shock, and vice versa for White subjects, but not to the photos of the other race. That we are predisposed to fearing groups of humans perceived as outsiders suggests that a history of inter-group violence was prevalent enough to shape our fears.

Another study extended the procedures. Black and White subjects were shown photos of Black and White men and women. During the non-shock phase, subjects habituated to photos of women regardless of their in-group or out-group status. The only photos to which subjects failed to habituate were of *out-group men* (Navarrete et al., 2010). Results suggest that *men* from outside groups were a prominent threat across our species' history, that our brains "know" this, and that consequently we are slow to relinquish fears of out-group males. Other research points to an early, prepared fear of men; across cultures, infants show fear of strangers, and they exhibit greater fear of unfamiliar males (Skarin, 1977). These results echo epidemiological research finding that among trauma types, combat exposure is associated with the greatest persistence of PTSD symptoms after the occurrence of trauma (Kessler et al., 2017)—notably, combat-related trauma is almost exclusively caused by aggression from out-group men. The starkly higher prevalence of male inter-group violence in our past, along with the persistence of our fear responses, implicate combat-related PTSD as an evolutionary mismatch designed to help us survive inter-group hostility.

Other evidence is anecdotal, but telling. As a clinical psychologist specializing in combat-related PTSD, my veteran patients often describe not even noticing symptoms until after their combat deployment, when they attempt to reintegrate into in the peacetime, civilian world where they felt mismatched (e.g., in their level of anger, vigilance, mistrust)—much as we would expect if PTSD is an evolved response to combat in ancestral environments, and not to suburbia. Many veterans with multiple combat deployments report that between deployments they couldn't wait return to combat because that was the only place they felt "normal." After separating from the military, many veterans take high-risk employment as police or corrections officers, or with private defense contractors, for the same reason—"to feel normal."

Intrusive Symptoms

This symptom cluster includes experiences such as: recurrent distressing trauma memories, nightmares, flashbacks, and memory triggers or cues that elicit strong emotional and physiological responses (e.g., increased heart rate, perspiration). In the absence of danger, intrusive symptoms inject daily experience with distressing levels of physiological arousal and negative emotions, and they distract from normal experiences, such as work, school, or family life. In the case of nightmares, they disrupt sleep, which causes fatigue and concentration difficulties. The subjective experiences can be dreadful.

All criteria in this cluster, however, suggest enhanced memory for danger. Chris Cantor (2005) proposes that nightmares help consolidate danger information into long-term memory, to preserve potentially lifesaving information. While forgetting dangerous events could be fatal, the retention of strong, enduring, and even recurrent intrusive memories of them has survival value, particularly when facilitating the avoidance of future danger (Clinchy et al., 2013; Zanette et al., 2011). Two brain pathways to processing danger memories have been identified. One pathway is subcortical, involving the limbic system, which enables fast-acting, reflexive defensive responses to danger, and another involving the neocortex, which is slower, and facilitates making finer discriminations between types of stimuli to assess level of danger (LeDoux, 1994; Silove, 1998). We see these pathways represented in intrusive symptoms, alternately as conscious memories, or as reflexive physiological responses to trauma cues.

From an evolutionary perspective, sensitization to such cues has similar utility, by eliciting a cascade of defensive, excitatory physiological processes which effectively chambers fight-or-flight responses for rapid enaction. In other words, if I hear a noise that reminds me of a prior attack, I experience adrenal responses that ready me to fight off or run from a potential attacker. Indeed, research on nonhuman animals finds that individuals previously injured by predators will initiate defensive behavioral sequences faster than uninjured individuals (Staudinger et al., 2011), and that sensitization to danger cues are long-lasting (Walters, 1994), as in PTSD. These responses are essential in unpredictable natural environments where danger is prevalent.

As one of many examples from war, in recent fields of operation in Iraq and Afghanistan, US and allied forces are targeted with improvised explosive devices (IEDs), bombs hidden in roadside trash, roadkill, potholes, etc. Troops returning from these campaigns are sensitized to these types of stimuli, which trigger intense arousal (i.e., preparatory physiological responses) and evasion—suddenly swerving, changing lanes, or speeding. In a peacetime environment, these physiological and behavioral sequences are problematic, causing unnecessary distress (or traffic violations, fender-benders, terrified wives). But in the combat theater they are critical for survival. Sensitizing to stimuli such as the language or phenotype of the enemy, smells, landscapes, or crowds of strangers, causes similar problems in peacetime, but produces similar advantages in war (or in our ancestral environments).

Avoidance

The second PTSD symptom cluster involves avoiding trauma memories, or external reminders of the trauma memories (places, situations) that cause distressing arousal. The irony of avoiding cognitive material such as memories (i.e., *thought suppression*) is that it often elicits a *rebound effect*—an involuntary *increase* in the target thought or memory (Wegner, 1989). The reasons for this response are not well understood, and more research is needed to identify any adaptive functions. It is hypothesized that cognitive avoidance facilitates behavioral avoidance (Baumeister et al., 1994). One study found that when subjects were instructed to avoid thoughts of skinheads, they chose to sit further away from skinheads than subjects who did not engage in thought suppression (McCrae et al., 1994).

Avoiding places or situations to prevent overarousal in the absence of danger is problematic. Many avoided stimuli—restaurants, movies, family gatherings, and so on—are otherwise pleasurable people, places, or activities that inoculate against depression. Avoiding them limits interaction and strains relationships with friends and family, or causes problems in educational or occupational goal attainment. In more severe cases, PTSD sufferers rarely leave home.

The survival utility of avoiding places or situational reminders of the trauma is obvious; if the last time I walked by a certain cave entrance a large predator rushed out and nearly killed me, it serves my survival to avoid that cave in the future. Avoidance, evasion, and refuging/sheltering are common predator-avoidance strategies across the animal kingdom, and increase with greater predation (Lima, 1998). For veterans, what is regarded as pathological avoidance in the civilian world is a tactical necessity in theater; open spaces without cover, crowds, traffic, and of course, the enemy, are imminently dangerous and therefore avoided.

Negative Alterations in Mood, or Cognitions about Oneself or Others or the World

Three criteria for PTSD in the current DSM have significant overlap with depressive sequelae, and will be explored more fully below in the context of depression. Among them, emotional numbing merits discussion here.

NUMBING

The experience and expression of emotions is essential for healthy relationships. Many veterans complain (or report that their spouses complain) about being emotionally cold or unable to feel love or empathy. A common experience is that when a family member dies, amid a room full of mourners a veteran is dry-eyed and emotionless, which draws understandable confusion or disapproval.

While socially problematic in peacetime, the ability to suppress emotion, particularly fear, helps combatants perform under the intense stressors of war. Across endless scenarios, panicking on the battlefield can threaten the life of the individual panicking, as well as everyone else relying on him/her to perform under pressure. The value of fear suppression is exemplified by a long history of warfare in which cowardice or desertion have resulted in execution. Suppressing sadness has similar utility; excessively mourning a dead comrade can be fatally distracting in war. Likewise, empathy can compromise enemy engagement. In light of research on high misfire rates (or actually not aiming for the enemy) on the battlefield, along with intense guilt about wartime killing, it has been proposed that humans have some emotional disinclination to kill conspecifics. Often deliberate cognitive strategies are taken to circumvent empathy—such as by imputing genetic distance, framing enemies as subhuman, animals, or monsters. (Grossman, 1995). Suppressing empathy, then, is essential for war's central task—killing. Similarly, suppressing positive emotions such as happiness can help soldiers avoid potentially life-ending complacency, and to stay emotionally prepared for traumatic loss. For these reasons, emotional numbing is so valuable a commodity in combat that it is expected between soldiers as a show of in-group commitment (Garcia, 2016).

Further support emerges from the fact that men, who have most often engaged in combat across our history as a species, experience less empathy than women *more generally*. From as early as one year of age, boys show less empathy to others' suffering than girls (Volbrecht et al., 2007). Women also score higher on measures of empathy (Davis, 1996). Further, less empathy among men is associated with larger testes (Mascaro et al., 2013), and in autism, a condition that has been described as an *extreme form of the male brain* (afflicting males to females at a ratio of 10:1), empathy is usually impaired (Baron-Cohen, 2002). Greater empathy in women may be linked to the demands of childrearing. However, the historical prevalence of tribal warfare, along with the liabilities of empathy in combat, implicate intergroup violence as a selective pressure for sex differences, giving men the ability to kill their competitors with greater facility. In keeping with this hypothesis, studies have also found sex differences in PTSD symptom expression, with men reporting greater emotional numbing than women (King et al., 2013; Peters et al., 2006; Tekin et al., 2016).

Other explanations for emotional numbing have been proposed. Litz and Gray (2002) suggest that it is an output of preferential allocation of attention to potential threat, which reduces focus on non-threatening or positive stimuli—e.g., benign social interaction and its associated emotions. Another is that numbing is related to the tonic immobility response (freezing) when cornered by a more dominant individual, which may facilitate appeasement (Cantor, 2005). Numbing may also facilitate withdrawal from unwinnable conflicts, as described below.

Cognitive "Errors"
Trust
Disruption in cognitive processing is another PTSD symptom. In PTSD, cognitive distortions involving trust are prevalent, a criterion in the DSM-5, and a central target of evidence-based psychotherapies (EBPs; Resick et al., 2007). Ostensibly, little trust between ancestral humans and wild animals was assumed, which points to conspecific violence as a selective pressure for PTSD-related mistrust. Mistrust would have utility when dealing with violent or unpredictable in-group members, or a murderous neighboring tribe. Put simply, mistrust facilitates both avoidance and vigilance.

Costly Signaling and Group Size
Mistrust's centrality to combat-related PTSD requires elaboration. Because genes build traits that ensure more copies of themselves get replicated over time, including those that reside in other individuals, genetic relatives have an incentive to help one another, even at a cost to themselves (Dawkins, 1976). Humans are adept at extending cooperation beyond genetic kin through *reciprocal altruism* (Trivers, 1971), helping non-kin with the expectation that fitness-enhancing help will later be reciprocated.

But there are fitness advantages to cheating on reciprocal exchanges—e.g., the hunter who enjoys a split of his tribemates' kills but secretly hoards his own, or the warrior who refuses to take risks to protect his comrades. Nature has responded by creating sensitive cheater-detection systems in the brains of species that cooperate. In turn, humans tend to be extremely wary of cheaters, and exert great effort defining in-group membership.

Exchanging signals of commitment is one way to deter free-riders. William Irons (2001, p. 298) reminds us that "for such signals of commitment to be successful they must be hard to fake. Other things being equal, the costlier the signal the less likely it is to be false" (2001, p. 298). "Costly signals" often come in the form of bans, behaviors, and badges (Sosis, 2006). *Bans* can be placed on things like alcohol or tobacco or foods. *Behaviors* can be harsh initiation rites, such as feats of endurance or bravery, or ritualistic scarring or branding, as we see across tribal societies. Cheaters are much less likely to endure these painful rituals, whereas completing them assures the tribe of sincerity.

Some costly signals of the modernized world are virtually indistinguishable from those of hunter-gatherers. Fraternity brothers, for example, will brand their respective Greek symbols into their arms. In the military, unit tattoos, grueling training regimens, or extremely harsh qualification procedures also assure commitment. *Badges* can be tribal regalia, the scars themselves, or uniforms. Many harsh military qualification hurdles come with actual insignia, which engender respect and trust. In war, costly signals hold the ultimate importance. War requires the commitment to push past any pain, fear, or risk to help one's comrade fight other men to the death, as he will you. Failure or refusal to do so can be fatal.

Inter-group conflict has been a unique selective pressure for men. Across the history of conflict, from tribal skirmishes to organized warfare, massacres have been common in which all males are killed, and females kept as the spoils of war (Garcia, 2015, 2019). Understandably, these forces have shaped male in-group/out-group psychology (Van Vugt et al., 2007). Research finds that men tend to be more xenophobic than women, more often believe that their group should hold a dominant position over other groups (Sidanius et al., 1995), and characterize outsiders as nonhuman with greater ease (Van Vugt, 2009). Out-group hostility is matched by in-group trust. Men tend to have stronger kinship ties than women (Wrangham & Peterson, 1996), and men identify and cooperate with others more when researchers posit an outside threat, a response largely not seen among women (Van Vugt et al., 2007). Indeed, fighting men have reported having closer emotional connections to each other than to their own wives (Grossman, 1995).

In addition, hunter-gatherer groups top off at around 150 members, and evidence suggests that our brains are built to operate most effectively in groups of that size (Dunbar, 1992). Modern group size has been identified as an evolutionary mismatch (Cosmides & Tooby, 1997). Accordingly, the sizes of fighting units among modern militaries settle on the psychologically familiar sizes of early hominid groups (Cantor, 2005).

In sum, when men go off to war, they eat, sleep, and fight together, in small groups much as we did in our evolutionary past, and their ancient tribalistic psychology, including their need for costly signals, gets activated with high emotional valence (Junger, 2016). In small, tight-knit combat units, just as it in small tribes, trust is easier to monitor, behavioral signals of commitment are near constant, and similar uniforms, national flags, and unit insignia have made badges of commitment easy to detect. But post-deployment, trusted members of fighting units disperse, and veterans often return to megalopolises filled with people only distally cooperating, none distinguishable through tribal colors, few offering overt signals of commitment, much less one of the most important signals possible—*one's fighting history*. Combined, these mismatch factors explain why war veterans with PTSD so often have difficulties trusting anyone outside their tribe of brothers-in-arms, and why civilians so often hear the refrain, "If you were never there, you could never understand" (Garcia, 2016).

Overgeneralizing
"Overgeneralizing" negative events is interpreted as a cognitive error, and is a target of EBPs for PTSD. As one example, for decades before treatment, many of my Vietnam veteran patients apprehensively avoided anyone with Asian features, including, for example, people of Japanese ancestry (e.g., refusing to enter a Japanese restaurant). Japan was not an enemy of the United States in Vietnam (in fact, Japan was a staging ground for US operations in Vietnam). Yet distressing hyperarousal was elicited among veterans denying any animosity toward the Japanese people, and even with the understanding that such fear responses were irrational (recalling subcortical fear-learning pathways mentioned above). Similarly, my younger veteran patients from the wars in Afghanistan and Iraq will overgeneralize fear responses to people from India, or even to Americans of Mexican descent, due to phenotypes similar to their former enemies overseas. Many of these men vehemently deny racist attitudes toward the people they anxiously monitor for danger, reporting, "I just can't seem to help it."

Although there may be moral implications of heuristics of this kind, generalizing danger cues is an evolved survival reaction. Fear conditioning occurs when a stimulus associated with danger elicits a defensive response. Over-specificity would constrain responses in complex environments where mortal threats rarely assume the identical form (Dunsmoor & Murphy, 2015), and would be selected against. As with the utility of false-positive-leaning defense systems in general, in times of conflict viewing anyone who resembles the enemy with suspicion is useful, as would being wary of animals with phenotypes similar to previously encountered predators.

All-or-None Thinking

All-or-none (or "black and white") thinking is interpreted to reflect a failure to incorporate a range of negative and positive qualities of self, other people, or the environment into a cohesive whole; for example, summarily placing someone into a "good person" or "bad person" category, or seeing one's performance as either a total success or a total failure. To address the associated relationship difficulties and problems in mood, EBPs for PTSD systematically recalibrate cognitive rigidities of this kind in favor of greater integrative complexity.

In a similar vein, intolerance for ambiguity would be useful in dangerous environments, such as combat. For instance, seeing a rival group as possibly dangerous, depending on the context, would potentially get men killed more often than those thinking in strictly categorical terms. The same can be said for categorizing performance as either a total success or failure—in combat, mistakes are fatal at a far higher frequency than in peacetime. In other words, when the stakes are life and death, it makes more sense to think in all-or-none terms. It may seem counterintuitive that errors in thinking could be adaptive, but as succinctly noted by Paul Gilbert, "information processing has evolved to minimize the cost of mistakes, but not mistakes themselves" (1998, p. 450).

Mindreading

It has been proposed that the costs of mistakes involving violence have resulted in a bias in overestimating the aggressive intent of others (Haselton & Buss, 2000). This idea has been tested. In one study, subjects were asked to estimate the likelihood of committing murder under certain conditions (e.g., if paid a million dollars) versus how likely they were to be killed by others with the same contingency. Subjects estimated a vastly higher likelihood of getting murdered (80%) than of committing murder (10%; Duntley & Buss, 1998). While adaptive amid treacherous conspecifics, in safe environments imputing negative intentions to others is socially problematic, and is regarded as a cognitive error called *mindreading* that is systematically targeted in EBPs (Resick et al., 2007).

Alterations in Arousal

Hypervigilance

In public, combat veterans often sit with their backs to the wall to monitor traffic in and out of a room, and to size up potential (male) threats. Often tactical scenarios are mentally rehearsed, including routes of egress and ingress, defensive actions, and potential weapons of opportunity. In a restaurant, these behaviors amount to PTSD symptoms that distract from social interaction and drain pleasure away from normal activities. Because the behaviors are excessive, and therefore mismatched for the current environment, they are considered *hyper*-vigilance. But in a combat environment, or on our ancestral savannas, these same vigilance behaviors are adaptive. Vigilance behavior is prevalent across the animal kingdom (Blanchard et al., 1991), and is a face-valid means to prevent predation or attack by conspecifics.

Sleep Disturbance

Anyone who has experienced sleep deprivation can attest how miserable it feels. However, in dangerous environments, deep, long, and uninterrupted sleep patterns are a potential liability, making individuals more vulnerable to predation. Accordingly, in nonhuman animals, sleep duration is negatively correlated with predation risk (Lesku et al., 2008). Many predators that our ancestors faced on the African savannas hunt at night, and threats from conspecifics also emerge under cover of darkness; to gain tactical advantages, raids among hunter-gatherers (as with modern-day combatants) are often conducted at nighttime. For this reason, sleep disturbance among combat veterans often involves not just lack of sleep, but hypersensitivity to noises, checking behaviors, or patrolling the perimeter of their homes. A long ancestral history of nighttime attacks appears to have had an enduring impact; even in economically developed nations, insomnia is strongly associated with perceived danger from crime (Hill et al., 2016).

Anger

Excessive anger in safe, predictable, peacetime environments causes expectable strain in relationships, and occupational or even legal problems. But in dangerous environments, anger facilitates aggression, the half of the fight-or-flight responses that allows us to dispatch predators or kill an enemy. The fitness-enhancing uses of aggression, particularly in dangerous, harsh, or unpredictable environments, are numerous, including: ". . . expropriating resources, defending against incursions, establishing encroachment-deterring reputations, inflicting costs on rivals, ascending dominance hierarchies," and some aid in violent male mate competition, "dissuading partner defection, eliminating fitness draining offspring, and obtaining new mates" (Buss, 2009, p. 271).

Comorbidity

PTSD's most commonly comorbid condition is major depressive disorder, occurring in up to 52% of PTSD cases (Rytiwnski et al., 2013), and comorbid depression of lesser severity is also common. Further insight into PTSD's purposive nature is gleaned from this comorbidity; depression likely evolved as a means of regulating violent competition for rank, and the resources rank confers, such as food and sex (Price et al., 1994).

Low self-esteem is a principal symptom of depression. An important related concept is *resource holding potential* (RHP), the probability than an animal will win in an all-out confrontation (Parker, 1974). When presented with confrontation, individuals estimate their own RHP against rivals, a calculation with clear fitness implications; challenging more powerful individuals (or groups) can be fatal. Self-esteem is seen as the subjective experience of this gauge, which motivates evolved responses (Gilbert et al., 1995); lower RHP estimates and lower self-esteem motivate yielding and avoidance behaviors. Perhaps unsurprisingly, low self-esteem is a criterion for PTSD, "negative beliefs about oneself," and a central target of EBPs (Resick et al., 2007). In a dangerous environment, low self-esteem may be useful at preventing overconfident engagement in unwinnable conflicts, and may facilitate avoidance, withdrawal, and sheltering.

Related to emotional numbing, in particular the reduced ability to experience *positive* emotions, is depressive anhedonia. Defined as the loss of ability to experience pleasure, anhedonia commonly affects the appetitive drives for eating, sex, and affiliation. Symptoms are evinced across species, often following social defeats (some of them violent/traumatic), and facilitate surrendering food, sex, or territory to more powerful individuals (Koolhaas et al., 1990). Anhedonia is a common experience in PTSD (Nawijin et al., 2015) and spans several PTSD criteria—"the persistent ability to experience positive emotions; markedly diminished interest or participation in significant activities; and feelings of detachment or estrangement from others" (APA, 2013, p. 272). Like low self-esteem, a drop in appetitive drives can also facilitate potentially lifesaving avoidance.

Mate Competition

If intergroup conflict was a selective pressure that produced an adaptive propensity for PTSD, then understanding the *purpose* of conflict can provide insights into the disorder's clinical course. Proximate reasons for war abound, but conflict among men parallels conflict among other male animals—that is, it is ultimately grounded in male-mate competition.

Massacre sites unearthed by archaeologists reveal a notable absence of bones of reproductive aged females, suggesting that those women were not killed, but taken captive (Teschler-Nicola et al., 1999). In raids, hunter-gatherers often kidnap women from the rival group to keep as wives (Chagnon, 1983). Today soldiers may not go to war with the conscious intention of sequestering mates. However, wartime rape has been staggeringly common throughout history, and mitigated only when sternly punished. ISIS and Boko Haram are contemporary examples of men making war with the *explicit* intention of killing their rivals and taking their women as the sexual spoils of war. One journalist documented how ISIS targeted not only men, but also boys who began to show secondary sex characteristics. In evolutionary terms, the boys had transitioned from children to *male sexual competitors*:

> Adolescent boys were told to lift up their shirts, and if they had armpit hair they were directed to join their older brothers and fathers, where they were forced to lie down in the dirt and sprayed with automatic fire. (Callimachi, 2015)

In an evolutionary context, temporarily abandoning mate competition can be adaptive as an act of concession to a more powerful individual or group (i.e., live to reproduce another day), which depressive low mood, poor self-esteem, and anhedonia facilitate, all of which are mediated by our endocrine systems. Research finds that high testosterone (T) is associated with better mood (Almeida et al., 2008), winning competitions (Mazur & Lamb, 1980), and higher sex drive (O'Carroll & Bancroft, 1984), whereas low T is associated with depressed mood (Almeida et al., 2008), withdrawal from competition (Mehta & Josephs, 2006), and lower sex drive (O'Carroll & Bancroft, 1984). Because throughout our history, male mate competition has involved mortal violence, withdrawing from potentially life-ending contests can be adaptative. Perhaps unsurprisingly, sexual dysfunction has been found in up to 89% of male combat veterans with PTSD, including loss of interest in sex (Yehuda et al., 2015).

There is more consistency in the literature on the relationship of low T to depression (e.g., Hintikka et al., 2009; Shores et al., 2005). Studies of T and PTSD have been mixed. High T has anxiolytic effects (Handa & Weiser, 2014), and increased anxiety has been observed in men following chemical castration for the purposes of cancer treatment (Almeida et al., 2004). Decreases in T have been found following acute stress, for example after intense survival or combat training (Bernton et al., 1995; Gomez-Merino et al., 2005; Morgan et al., 2000), and lower cerebrospinal fluid T concentrations have been found in PTSD patients (Mulchahey et al., 2001). However, higher serum (Mason et al., 1990) and plasma T levels (Reijnen et al., 2015) have also been found in PTSD patients, which supports what is known as the *challenge hypothesis*—the notion that T levels increase in anticipation of a challenge (Archer, 2006). Given these mixed results, scholars have called for more research on potential mediators, such as personality and trauma type (Reijnen et al., 2015). More research is also needed to determine whether alternating endocrine responses, either increased or decreased T in the aftermath of trauma, reflect differing assessments of RHP; research finds that in some competitors T *rises* after losing competitions, which predicts re-engaging in competition (Mehta & Josephs, 2006).

Social Support

Another clue to the adaptive origins of PTSD lies in one of its most significant predictors—low social support (Brewin et al., 2000). Though the relationship between social support and PTSD severity, and even PTSD treatment response (Price et al., 2018), is widely discussed in the clinical literature, the reasons *why* its absence predicts PTSD severity remains understudied. However, from an adaptive framework of PTSD, the connection is intuitive—in dangerous environments we are more vulnerable alone, but safer among our allies, and social support in the modern day may signal protective alliance. From this perspective, an increase in PTSD safety-related behaviors in the absence of social support—such as sheltering, or avoidance—along with greater anxiety, serves an adaptive function. Venturing from our ancestral camps without the protection of one's tribemates (just as venturing from one's forward operating base in the combat theater) must have exponentiated potential threat. The link between social support and protection is illustrated by many of my veteran patients who report high PTSD symptoms in public places with their untrained wives and children, but that their anxiety quickly attenuates when accompanied by their brothers-in-arms. Similarly, women who perceive low social support are more susceptible to developing PTSD following rape (Chivers-Wilson, 2006). According to David Buss, social support may translate to having "bodyguards" to help protect rape survivors against future revictimization, and perceived lack of support may reflect a realistic appraisal of threat (Buss, 2021).

Treatment

That we may have evolved a propensity for PTSD in certain circumstances does not mean that trauma survivors are condemned to a lifetime of symptoms. Most combat veterans return home without PTSD. In the United States, political, bureaucratic, and methodological issues have likely inflated base rates of PTSD among newly returning veterans (McNally & Frue, 2013). Still, even liberal estimates such as the Institute of Medicine's estimate of 13%–20% (IOM, 2012) suggest that a majority of veterans adapt well to peacetime.

Moreover, our signature adaptation as humans is outsmarting our genes. Every piece of technology, from stone tools to supercomputers, is evidence of this. Relatedly, decades of clinical research, including randomized controlled trials, have produced effective treatments for PTSD—prolonged exposure (PE; Powers et al., 2010) and cognitive processing therapy (CPT; Resick et al., 2007).

While adaptive when danger is present, avoidance maintains PTSD by preventing corrective learning in the absence of danger. PE is a nine-week training protocol in which patients are exposed to avoided memories and safe situations or places (such as grocery stores or restaurants) until the fight-or-flight response extinguishes. Reflecting the two pathways of fear learning mentioned above, many patients will report a conscious understanding that restaurants are not dangerous, but (before treatment) experience distressing physiological arousal in those environments nevertheless. When treatment is completed, nightmares dissipate, trauma memories no longer generate distress, and crowded places are not only tolerated, but enjoyed, without the intense perturbations of limbic system engagement.

CPT is a 12-week protocol that systematically corrects erroneous cognitions that arise in response to trauma, with a focus on mistrust and safety concerns. In the case of combat-related PTSD, often those cognitions are "stuck" on the survival rules and danger probabilities of the combat theater. Similarly, threat appraisals are useful when danger is present, but socially problematic in its absence. Once cortical control over limbic system activation is gained, new lives are possible.

Given that PE and CPT recalibrate ancient responses designed to help us survive in ancestral environments—where inter-group killing was normative, and groups were smaller, familiar, and trusted—so that veterans can function effectively in the modernized, peacetime, civilian world, the treatments serve to reverse evolutionary mismatches. Most who receive the treatments no longer meet full criteria for the disorder upon treatment completion.

However, a treatment is only as effective as the patient's ability to access and complete it. Many veterans avoid treatment altogether, and dropout rates are high among those who make it into the therapy office (Garcia et al., 2011). Stigma about help-seeking, particularly among men, has been identified as a key factor constraining access to mental healthcare. While mental health stigma impacts women as well, adherence to masculine gender role norms, such as an emphasis on psychological toughness (Jakupcak et al., 2013), or emotional suppression (Mahalik et al., 2003), is associated with less help-seeking (Addis & Mahalik, 2003). For many men, admitting psychological distress is seen as effeminate or implying weakness (Hoge et al., 2004; Sileo & Kershaw, 2020), and having a PTSD diagnosis, much less seeking treatment for it, is seen as a personal failure (Lorber & Garcia, 2010). These social pressures are concentrated in military settings, and among men, more generally. But they are not exclusive to men. When women are granted combat roles, they join highly masculinized cultures and are often expected to abide by male gender-role norms surrounding emotional restriction and treatment seeking.

Those norms often prevent PTSD sufferers from accessing life-altering care, sometimes for decades. But, from an evolutionary perspective, PTSD symptoms are not personal failures. They are evolved survival mechanisms that kept our ancestors alive, that are responsible for us being here today, but that do not extinguish without proper training. Evidence-based psychotherapies are those trainings, which help people adapt to the here and now, to the worlds of relative safety and predictability that we humans have created for ourselves.

While evolutionary psychology has been criticized for a lack of practical application, in my practice I have found immense value in sharing the evolutionary basis of PTSD as a tool for targeting self-stigma and enhancing motivation for treatment. Many patients report feeling less "broken" when they come to understand PTSD as an evolutionary mismatch. Many report that reframing the "narrative of failing" through an evolutionary lens is what shifted their ambivalence about care, and indeed what prevented them from dropping out. Given that treatments such as prolonged exposure necessitate the experience of a degree of anxiety, enhancing motivation is a critical task for clinicians. The task is made more difficult when that anxiety is paired with guilt. Because of the strong affiliative bonds demanded by combat, soldiers often report that their greatest fear in going to war is not getting killed—rather, it is making a mistake that gets their *comrades* killed (Junger, 2016). Whereas supporting one's comrades in war requires suppressing emotion, psychotherapy requires understanding, experiencing, and expressing emotion. Often the emotive processes required by treatment can feel like violations of an ancient social contract to not feel.

So ancient are these rules, that they can fly under the radar of conscious awareness, generating intense guilt about treatment, without understanding why. The insights gained by an explanation of costly signaling theory can also be profound, as with the functionality of each PTSD symptom. They reframe cognitions such as "I am broken" or "I am betraying" to "my survival instincts have not yet shifted." The differences in perspective afforded by an evolutionary understanding of PTSD are immense and numerous. And they allow PTSD patients to have greater compassion for themselves.

References

Addis, M. E., & Mahalik, J. R. (2003). Men, masculinity, and the contexts of help seeking. *American Psychologist, 58*, 5–14.

Agras, S., Sylvester, D., & Oliveau, D. (1969). The epidemiology of common fears and phobia. *Comprehensive Psychiatry, 10*, 151–156. http://dx.doi .org/10.1016/0010-440X(69)90022-4

Almeida, O. P., Waterreus, A., Spry, N., Flicker, L., & Martins, R. N. (2004). One year follow-up study of the association between chemical castration, sex hormones, beta-amyloid, memory and depression in men. *Psychoneuroendocrinology, 29*, 1071–1081.

Almeida O. P., Yeap, B. B., Hankey, G. J., Jamrozik, K., & Flicker, L. (2008). Low free testosterone concentration as a potentially treatable cause of depressive symptoms in older men. *Archives of General Psychiatry, 65*(3), 283–289. doi: 10.1001/archgenpsychiatry.2007.33

American Psychiatric Association. (2013). *Diagnostic and statistical manual of mental disorders* (5th ed.). APA.

Archer, J., (2006). Testosterone and human aggression: An evaluation of the challenge hypothesis. *Neuroscience & Biobehavioral Reviews, 30*, 319–345.

Baron-Cohen, S. (2002) The extreme male brain theory of autism. *Trends in Cognitive Sciences, 6*(6), 248–254.

Baumeister, R. F., Heatherton, T. F. & Tice, D. M. (1994). *Losing control: How and why people fail at self-regulation*. Academic Press.

Bernton, E., Hoover, D., Galloway, R., & Popp, K. (1995). Adaptation to chronic stress in military trainees. *Annals of the NY Academy of Sciences, 774*, 217–231.

Blanchard, D. C., Blanchard, R. J., & Rodgers, R. J. (1991). Risk assessment and animal models of anxiety. In B. Olivier, J. Mos, & J. L. Slangen (Eds.), *Animal models in psychopharmacology* (pp. 117–134). APS: Advances in Pharmacological Sciences. Birkhäuser. https://doi.org/10.1007/978-3-0348-6419-0_13

Brewin, C. R., Andrews, B., & Valentine, J. D. (2000). Meta-analysis of risk factors for posttraumatic stress disorder in trauma-exposed adults. *Journal of Consulting and Clinical Psychology, 68*(5), 748–766. https://doi.org/10.

Buss, D. M. (2009). The multiple adaptive problems solved by human aggression. *Behavior and Brain Science, 32*(3–4), 271. [This article is a commentary on Archer, Does sexual selection explain human sex differences in aggression?].

Buss, D. M. (2021). *When men behave badly: The hidden roots of sexual deception, harassment, and assault*. Little, Brown & Spark.

Callimachi, R. (2015). ISIS enshrines a theology of rape. *New York Times*, August 13, 2015, https://www.nytimes.com/2015/08/14/world/middleeast/isis-enshrines-a-theology -of-rape.html.

Cantor, C. (2005). *Evolution and posttraumatic stress: Disorders of vigilance and stress*. Routledge.

Chagnon, N. A. (1983) *Yąnomamö: The fierce people* (3rd ed.). Holt, Rinehart & Winston.

Chivers-Wilson, K. (2006). Sexual assault and posttraumatic stress disorder: A review of the biological, psychological and sociological factors and treatments. *McGill Journal of Medicine: MJM, 9*, 111–118.

Clinchy, M., Sheriff, M. J., & Zanette, L. Y. (2013) Predator-induced stress and the ecology of fear. *Functional Ecology, 27*, 56–65.

Cosmides, L., & Tooby, J. (1997, January). Evolutionary psychology: A primer. Retrieved from http://www.psych.ucsb.edu/research/cep/primer .html

Davis, M. H. (1996), *Empathy: A social psychological approach*. Westview Press.

Dawkins, R. (1976). *The selfish gene*. Oxford University Press.

Diamond, D. D., & Zoladz, P. R. (2016). Dysfunctional or hyperfunctional? The amygdala in posttraumatic stress disorder is the bull in the evolutionary china shop. *Journal of Neuroscience Research, 94*, 437–444.

Dunbar, R. I. M. (1992). Neocortex size as a constraint on group size in primates. *Journal of Human Evolution, 22*, 469–493.

Dunsmoor, J. E., & Murphy, G. L. (2015). Categories, concepts, and conditioning: How humans generalize fear. *Trends in Cognitive Sciences, 19*(2), 73–77. https://doi.org/10.1016/j.tics.2014.12.003

Duntley, J., & Buss, D. M. (1998, July). *Evolved anti-homicide modules*. Paper presented at the annual meeting of the Human Behavior and Evolution Society Conference, Davis, CA.

Ferry, F., Bunting, B., Murphy, S., O'Neill, S., Stein, D., & Koenen, K. (2014). Traumatic events and their relative PTSD burden in Northern Ireland: a consideration of the impact of the "Troubles." *Social Psychiatry and Psychiatric Epidemiology, 49*(3), 435–446. doi: 10.1007/s00127-013-0757-0. PMID: 23959590.

Garcia, H. A. (2015). *Alpha God: The psychology of religious violence and oppression*. Prometheus Books.

Garcia, H. A. (2016). If you've never been there you wouldn't understand: The evolutionary reasons for veteran mistrust. *Evolutionary Behavioral Sciences, 11*(1), 53–62.

Garcia, H. A. (2019). *Sex, power, and partisanship: How evolutionary science makes sense of our political divide*. Prometheus Books.

Garcia, H. A., Kelley, L. P., Rentz, T. O., & Lee, S. (2011). Pretreatment predictors of dropout from cognitive behavioral therapy for PTSD in Afghanistan and Iraq War veterans. *Psychological Services, 8*(1), 1–11.

Gilbert P. (1998). The evolved basis and adaptive functions of cognitive distortions. *British Journal of Medical Psychology, 71*(4), 447–463. doi: 10.1111/j.2044-8341.1998.tb01002.x. PMID: 9875955.

Gilbert, P., Price, J., & Allan, S. (1995). Social comparison, social attractiveness, and evolution: How might they be related? *New Ideas in Psychology, 13*, 149–165.

Gomez-Merino, D., Drogou, C., Chenaoui, M., Tiollier, E., Mathieu, J., & Guezennec, C. Y. (2005). Effects of combined stress during intense training on cellular immunity, hormones and respiratory infections. *Neuroimmunomodulation, 12*, 164–172.

Grossman, D. (1995). *On killing: The psychological cost of learning to kill in war and society.* Bay Back.

Handa, R. J., & Weiser, M. J. (2014). Gonadal steroid hormones and the hypothalamo-pituitary-adrenal axis. *Frontiers in Neuroendocrinology, 35*, 197–220.

Haselton, M. G., & Buss, D. M. (2000). Error management theory: A new perspective on biases in cross-sex mind reading. *Journal of Personality and Social Psychology, 78*, 81–91.

Hill, T. D., Trinh, H. N., Wen, M., & Hale, L. (2016). Perceived neighborhood safety and sleep quality: a global analysis of six countries. *Sleep Medicine, 18*, 56–60. https://doi.org/10.1016/j.sleep.2014.12.003

Hintikka, J., Niskanen, L., Koivumaa-Honkanen, H., Tolmunen, T., Honkalampi, K., Lehto, S. M., & Viinamäki, H. (2009). Hypogonadism, decreased sexual desire, and long-term depression in middle-aged men. *Journal of Sexual Medicine, 6*, 2049–2057.

Hoge, C. W., Castro, C. A., Messer, S. C., McGurk, D., Cotting, D. I., & Koffman, R. L. (2004). Combat duty in Iraq and Afghanistan, mental health problems, and barriers to care. *New England Journal of Medicine, 351*, 13–22.

IOM (Institute of Medicine). (2012). *Treatment for posttraumatic stress disorder in military and veteran populations: Initial assessment.* National Academies Press.

Irons, W. (2001). Religion as a hard-to-fake sign of commitment. In R. M. Nesse (Ed.), *Evolution and the capacity for commitment* (p. 298). Russell Sage Foundation.

Jakupcak, M., Blais, R. K., Grossbard, J., Garcia, H. A., & Okiishi, J. (2013) Toughness and its association with psychiatric symptoms and perceived barriers to care among Iraq and Afghanistan War veterans. *Psychology of Men and Masculinity, 15*(1), 100–104. doi: 10.1037/a0031508

Junger, S. (2016). *Tribe: On homecoming and belonging.* Hatchette Book Group.

Kawakami, N., Tsuchiya, M., Umeda, M., Koenen K. C., & Kessler, R. C. (2014). World Mental Health Survey Japan. Trauma and posttraumatic stress disorder in Japan: Results from the World Mental Health Japan Survey. *Journal of Psychiatric Research, 53*, 157–165. doi: 10.1016/j.jpsychires.2014.01.015.

Kearns, M. C., Ressler, K. J., Zatzick, D., & Rothbaum, B. O. (2012). Early interventions for PTSD: A review. *Depression and Anxiety, 29*(10), 833–842. https://doi.org/10.1002/da.21997

Keeley, L. H. (2014). War before civilization—15 years on. In T. K. Shackelford & R. D. Hansen (Eds.), *The evolution of violence* (pp. 23–31). Springer. https://doi.org/10.1007/978-1-4614-9314-3_2.

Kessler, R. C., Aguilar-Gaxiola, S., Alonso, J., Benjet, C., Bromet, E. J., Cardoso, G., Degenhardt, L., de Girolamo, G., Dinolova, R. V., Ferry, F., Florescu, S., Gureje, O., Haro, J. M., Huang, Y., Karam, E. G., Kawakami, N., Lee, S., Lepine, J. P., Levinson, D., Navarro-Mateu, F., . . . Koenen, K. C. (2017). Trauma and PTSD in the WHO World Mental Health Surveys. *European Journal of Psychotraumatology, 8*(Suppl 5), 1353383. https://doi.org/10.1080/20008198.2017.1353383

King, M. W., Street A. E., Gradus J. L., Vogt D. S., & Resick P. A. (2013) Gender differences in posttraumatic stress symptoms among OEF/OIF veterans: An item response theory analysis. *Journal of Traumatic Stress, 26*(2), 175–183. doi: 10.1002/jts.21802.

Koolhaas, J., Hermann, P., Kemperman, C., Bohus, B., Vandenhoofdakker, R., & Beersma, D. (1990). Single social defeat in male rats induces a gradual but long lasting behavior change: A model of depression. *Neuroscience Research Communications, 7*, 35–41.

LeDoux, J. E. (1994). Emotion, memory and the brain. *Scientific American, 270*(6), 32–39.

Lesku, J. A., Roth, T. C., Rattenborg, N. C., Amlaner, C. J., & Lima, S. L. (2008). Phylogenetics and the correlates of mammalian sleep: A reappraisal. *Sleep Medicine Reviews, 12*(3), 229–244. https://doi.org/10.1016/j.smrv.2007.10.003

Lima, S. L. (1998). Nonlethal effects in the ecology of predator-prey interactions. *BioScience, 48*, 25–34.

Lima, S. L., & Dill, L. M. (1990). Behavioral decisions made under the risk of predation: A review and prospectus. *Canadian Journal of Zoology, 68*, 619–640.

Litz, B. T., & Gray, M. J (2002) Emotional numbing in posttraumatic stress disorder: Current and future. *Research Directions, 36*(2) 198–204. https://doi.org/10.1046/j.1440-1614.2002.01002.x

Lorber, W., & Garcia, H. A. (2010) Not supposed to feel this: Traditional masculinity in psychotherapy with male veterans returning from Afghanistan and Iraq. *Psychotherapy Theory Research Practice and Training, 47*(3), 296–305.

Macrae, C. N., Bodenhausen, G. V., Milne, A. B., & Jetten, J. (1994). Out of mind but back in sight: Stereotypes on the rebound. *Journal of Personality and Social Psychology, 67*, 808–817.

Mahalik, J. R., Locke, B., Ludlow, L., Diemer, M., Scott, R., Gottfried, M., & Freitas, G. (2003). Development of the conformity to masculine norms inventory. *Psychology of Men & Masculinity, 4*, 3–25.

Mascaro, J. S., Hackett, P. D., & Rilling, J. K. (2013). Testicular volume is inversely correlated with nurturing-related brain activity in human fathers. *Proceedings of the National Academy of Sciences, 110*(39), 15746–15751. https://doi.org/10.1073/pnas.1305579110

Mason, J. W., Giller, E. L., Jr., Kosten, T. R., & Wahby, V. S. (1990). Serum testosterone levels in post-traumatic stress disorder inpatients. *Journal of Traumatic Stress, 3*, 449–457.

Mazur, A., & Lamb, T. (1980). Testosterone, status, and mood in human males. *Hormones and Behavior, 14*, 236–246.

McEwan, B. S., Gould, E. A., & Sakai, R. R. (1992). The vulnerability of the hippocampus to protective and destructive effects of glucocorticoids in relation to stress. *British Journal of Psychiatry, 160*, 18–24.

McNally, R. J., & Frueh, B. C. (2013). Why are Iraq and Afghanistan War veterans seeking PTSD disability compensation at unprecedented rates? *Journal of Anxiety Disorders, 27*, 520–526. http://dx.doi.org/10.1016/j.janxdis.2013.07.002

Mehta, P. H. & Josephs, R. A. (2006). Testosterone change after losing predicts the decision to compete again. *Hormones and Behavior, 50*(5), 684–692.

Mirazón Lahr, M., Rivera, F., Power, R. K., Mounier, A., Copsey, B., Crivellaro, F., Edung, J. E., Mallio Fernandez, J. M., Kiarie, C., Lawrence, J., Leakey, A., Mbua, E., Miller, H., Muigai, A., Mukhongo, D. M., Van Baelen, A., Wood, R., Schwenninger, J. L., Grün, R., . . . Foley, R. A. (2016). Inter-group violence among early Holocene hunter-gatherers of West Turkana, Kenya. *Nature, 529*, 394–398.

Morgan, C. A., Wang, S., Mason, J., Southwick, S. M., Fox, P., Hazlett, G., Charney, D. S., & Greenfield, G., (2000). Hormone profiles in humans experiencing military survival training. *Biological Psychiatry, 47*, 891–901.

Mulchahey, J. J., Ekhator, N. N., Zhang, H., Kasckow, J. W., Baker, D. G., & Geracioti, T. D., Jr. (2001). Cerebrospinal fluid and plasma testosterone levels in post-traumatic stress disorder and tobacco dependence. *Psychoneuroendocrinology, 26*, 273–285.

Navarrete, C. D., McDonald, M. M., Molina, L. E., & Sidanius, J. (2010). Prejudice at the nexus of race and gender: An outgroup male target hypothesis. *Journal of Personality and Social Psychology, 98*(6), 933–945. https://doi.org/10.1037/a0017931

Nawijn, L., van Zuiden, M., Frijling, J. L., Koch, S. B., Veltman, D. J., & Olff, M. (2015). Reward functioning in PTSD: a systematic review exploring the mechanisms underlying anhedonia. *Neuroscience & Biobehavioral Reviews, 51*, 189–204. doi: 10.1016/j.neubiorev.2015.01.019.

Nesse, R. M. (2019). *Good reasons for bad feelings: Insights from the frontier of evolutionary psychiatry*. Dutton.

Norman, P. L., van Vugt, M., & Colarelli, S. M. (2017). The evolutionary mismatch hypothesis: Implications for psychological science. *Current Directions in Psychological Science, 27*(1), 38–44.

O'Carroll, R., & Bancroft, J. (1984). Testosterone therapy for low sexual interest and erectile dysfunction in men: A controlled study. *British Journal of Psychiatry, 145*, 146–151. doi: 10.1192/bjp.145.2.146. PMID: 6380630.

Olsson, A., Ebert, J. P., Banaji, M. R., & Phelps, E. A. (2005). The role of social groups in the persistence of learned fear. *Science (New York, N.Y.), 309*(5735), 785–787. https://doi.org/10.1126/science.1113551

Parker, G. A. (1974). Assessment strategy and the evolution of fighting behaviour. *Journal of Theoretical Biology, 47*(1), 223–243.

Peters, L., Issakidis, C., Slade, T., & Andrews, G. (2006). Gender differences in the prevalence of DSM-IV and ICD-10 PTSD. *Psychological Medicine, 36*, 81–89. doi: 10.1017/S003329170500591X

Pinker, S. (2007). *The better angels of our nature: Why violence has declined*. Penguin.

Powers, M. B., Halpern, J. M., Ferenschak, M. P., Gillihan, S. J., & Foa, E. B. (2010). A meta-analytic review of prolonged exposure for post-traumatic stress disorder. *Clinical Psychology Review, 30*, 635–641. http://dx.doi.org/10.1016/j.cpr.2010.04.007

Price, J., Sloman, L., Gardner R., Jr., Gilbert, P., & Rohde, P. (1994). The social competition hypothesis of depression. *British Journal of Psychiatry, 164*(3), 309–315. doi: 10.1192/bjp.164.3.309. PMID: 8199784.

Price, M., Lancaster, C. L., Gros, D. F., Legrand, A. C., van Stolk-Cooke, K., & Acierno, R. (2018). An examination of social support and PTSD treatment response during prolonged exposure. *Psychiatry, 81*(3), 258–270. https://doi.org/10.1080/00332747.2017.1402569

Reijnen, A., Rademaker, A. R., Vermetten, E., & Geuze, E., (2015). Prevalence of mental health symptoms in Dutch Military personnel returning from deployment to Afghanistan: A 2-year longitudinal analysis. *European Psychiatry, 30*(2), 341–346.

Resick, P. A., Monson, C. M., & Chard, K. M. (2007). *Cognitive processing therapy: Veteran/military version.* Department of Veterans Affairs.

Rytwinski, N. K., Scur, M. D., Feeny, N. C., & Youngstrom, E. A. (2013) The co-occurrence of major depressive disorder among individuals with posttraumatic stress disorder: A meta-analysis. *Journal of Traumatic Stress, 26*(3), 299–309.

Shores, M. M., Moceri, V. M., Sloan, K. L., Matsumoto, A. M., & Kivlahan, D. R. (2005). Low testosterone levels predict incident depressive illness in older men: effects of age and medical morbidity. *Journal of Clinical Psychiatry, 66*, 7–14.

Sidanius, J., Pratto, F., & Brief, D. (1995). Group dominance and the political psychology of gender: A cross-cultural comparison. *Political Psychology, 16*, 381–396. http://dx.doi.org/10.2307/3791836

Sileo, K. M., & Kershaw, T. S. (2020). Dimensions of masculine norms, depression, and mental health service utilization: Results from a prospective cohort study among emerging adult men in the United States. *American Journal of Men's Health, 14*(1), 1557988320906980. https://doi.org/10.1177/1557988320906980

Silove, D. (1998) Is posttraumatic stress disorder an overlearned survival response? An evolutionary-learning hypothesis. *Psychiatry, 61*(2), 181–190. doi: 10.1080/00332747.1998.11024830

Skarin, K. (1977). Cognitive and contextual determinants of stranger fear in six- and eleven-month old infants. *Child Development, 48*, 537–544.

Sosis, R. (2006). Religious behaviors, badges and bans: Signaling theory and the evolution of religion. In P. McNamara (Ed.), *Where god and science meet* (pp. 61–86). Praeger.

Staudinger, M. D., Hanlon, R. T., & Juanes, F. (2011). Primary and secondary defences of squid to cruising and ambush fish predators: Variable tactics and their survival value. *Animal Behavior, 81*, 585–594.

Tekin, A., Karadağ, H., Süleymanoğlu, M., Tekin, M., Kayran, Y., Alpak, G., & Şar, V. (2016). Prevalence and gender differences in symptomatology of posttraumatic stress disorder and depression among Iraqi Yazidis displaced into Turkey. *European Journal of Psychotraumatology, 7*, 28556. https://doi.org/10.3402/ejpt.v7.28556

Teschler-Nicola, M., Gerold, F., Bujatti-Narbeshuber, M., Prohaska, T., Latkoczy, C., Stingeder, G., & Watkins, M. (1999). Evidence of genocide 7000 BP: Neolithic paradigm and geo-climatic reality. *Collegium Antropolicum, 23*(2), 437–450.

Trivers, R. (1971). The evolution of reciprocal altruism. *The Quarterly Review of Biology, 46*, 35–57.

Van Vugt, M. (2009). Sex differences in intergroup competition, aggression, and warfare: The male warrior hypothesis. *Annals of the New York Academy of Sciences, 1167*, 124–134. http://dx.doi.org/10.1111/j.1749-6632.2009.04539.x

Van Vugt, M., De Cremer, D., & Janssen, D. P. (2007). Gender differences in cooperation and competition: The male-warrior hypothesis. *Psychological Science, 18*, 19–23. http://dx.doi.org/10.1111/j.1467-9280.2007.01842.x

Volbrecht, M. M., Lemery-Chalfant, K., Aksan, N., Zahn-Waxler, C., & Goldsmith, H. H. (2007). Examining the familial link between positive affect and empathy development in the second year. *The Journal of Genetic Psychology, 168*(2), 105–129. https://doi.org/10.3200/GNTP.168.2.105-130

Walters, E. T. (1994). Injury-related behavior and neuronal plasticity: An evolutionary perspective on sensitization, hyperalgesia, and analgesia. *International Review of Neurobiology, 36*, 325–427.

Wegner, D. M. (1989). *White bears and other unwanted thoughts.* Viking/Penguin.

Wrangham, R. W., & Peterson, D. (1996). *Demonic males: Apes and the origins of human violence.* Houghton Mifflin.

Yehuda, R., Lehrner, A., & Rosenbaum, T. (2015). PTSD and sexual dysfunction in men and women. *Journal of Sexual Medicine, 12*(5), 1107–1119. http://dx.doi.org/10.1111/jsm.12856.

Zanette, L. Y., White, A. F., Allen, M. C. & Clinchy, M. (2011) Perceived predation risk reduces the number of offspring songbirds produce per year. *Science, 334*, 1398–1401.

CHAPTER 65

An Evolutionary Approach to Emotional Difficulties in Borderline Personality Disorder

Lawrence Ian Reed, Cameryn Cooley, and Sara Okun

Abstract

Borderline personality disorder (BPD) represents a pervasive personality pathology characterized by emotional dysregulation leading to signs and symptoms such as impulsivity, behavioral dysregulation, and interpersonal hypersensitivity. This chapter describes how emotions and emotional processes are central to borderline pathology and how current evolutionary accounts of emotions can shed light on the disorder. First, the authors provide a definition of BPD and its diagnostic criteria as reflected in the DSM-5, emphasizing the centrality of emotion, followed by an evolutionary explanation of emotions that contextualize evolutionary approaches to the emotional vulnerability and dysregulation characteristic of BPD. They then present attachment theory and life history theory as two middle-level explanations of BPD within the context of the DSM-5 definition and clinical formulations of borderline pathology. The chapter concludes with a summary of each approach and the potential they bring toward a clearer understanding of BPD and psychopathology in general.

Key Words: borderline personality disorder, emotion, evolution, attachment theory, life history theory

Borderline Personality Disorder

Borderline personality disorder (BPD) is among the most prevalent and widely studied of the personality disorders. Despite this wide reach, BPD remains an esoteric disorder that is difficult to diagnose and treat. The term "borderline" was coined by Stern (1938) to describe patients who fell somewhere between neurosis and psychosis. The term survived among object relations theorists who characterize a "borderline personality organization" as one defined by immaturity, identity diffusion, and the use of specific defense mechanisms such as splitting and projective identification without breaking from reality (Kernberg, 1976; Kernberg et al., 1989).Currently, BPD is primarily conceptualized as a disorder defined by difficulties in emotion (Linehan, 1993), cognitive assumptions (Beck et al., 2004), and interpersonal difficulties (Gunderson, 2001).

According to the fifth edition of the *Diagnostic and Statistical Manual of Mental Disorders* (American Psychiatric Association, 2013), a personality disorder is defined as "an enduring pattern of inner experience and behavior that deviates markedly from the expectation of the individual's culture, is pervasive and inflexible, has an onset in adolescence or early adulthood, is stable over time, and leads to distress or impairment" (p. 645). BPD is defined as "a pervasive pattern of instability of interpersonal relationships, self-image, and affects, and marked impulsivity, beginning by early adulthood and present in a variety of contexts, as indicated by five (or more) of the following" (p. 663):

1. Frantic efforts to avoid real or imagined abandonment;
2. A pattern of unstable and intense interpersonal relationships characterized by alternating between extremes of idealization and devaluation;
3. Identity disturbance: markedly and persistently unstable self-image or sense of self;
4. Impulsivity in at least two areas that are potentially self-damaging (e.g., spending, sex, substance abuse, reckless driving, binge eating);
5. Recurrent suicidal behavior, gestures, or threats, or self-mutilating behavior;
6. Affective instability due to a marked reactivity of mood (e.g., intense episodic dysphoria, irritability, or anxiety usually lasting a few hours and only rarely more than a few days);
7. Chronic feelings of emptiness;
8. Inappropriate intense anger or difficulty controlling anger (e.g., frequent displays of temper, constant anger, recurrent physical fights);
9. Transient, stress-related paranoid ideation or severe dissociative symptoms.

Some have argued that the fear of abandonment (criterion 1) is a central feature of BPD (Masterson, 1972) in that it contextualizes both the etiology and treatment of BPD (Gunderson, 2001). It has also been argued that the fear of abandonment leads to dysfunctional emotion regulation strategies that are characteristic of the remaining criteria (Peters et al., 2015). Interestingly, abandonment elicits a similar response (e.g., poor anger control and destructive behavior) within nonclinical populations (Twenge et al., 2003). The differences, however, might be how easily those with BPD interpret interpersonal events as abandonment. Lysaker and colleagues (2017) found that those with BPD had difficulties understanding others' motivations and how their motivations might be related to their behavior. This is consistent with difficulties in mentalization described by Fonagy and Bateman (2007).

Unstable and intense interpersonal relationships (criterion 2) are also thought to be a core feature of BPD in part because of their relationship to the other diagnostic criteria. Suicidal behavior, non-suicidal self-injury (NSSI), inappropriate anger, and affective instability all typically occur within interpersonal contexts (Brodsky et al., 2006; Stiglymayr et al., 2005). Interpersonal difficulties may also precede substance abuse (Welch & Linehan, 2002), which is often an impulsive behavior.

Specific difficulties in interpersonal relationships have been examined in social dilemmas, demonstrating that those with BPD are less trusting and less cooperative. King-Casas et al. (2008) examined the cooperative behavior of a group of individuals diagnosed with BPD using an iterated trust game (Berg et al., 1995; Weigelt & Camerer, 1988). In comparison to a group of control participants (i.e., without psychopathology), those with BPD showed a failure to cooperate across iterated exchanges. A similar study using a single trust game, conducted by Unoka, Seres, Aspan, Bodi, and Keri (2009), found that individuals with BPD gave smaller investments to trustees in comparison to control participants. Studies using social dilemmas have also demonstrated that an online sample of participants behave less cooperatively (Reed et al., 2018), bargain more competitively (Reed et al., 2019), and are less trustworthy (Reed et al., 2020) when interacting with confederates described as having borderline personality pathology.

Identity disturbance (criterion 3) is the subject of relatively more theoretical (Kernberg, 1975, 1984) (Kernberg O., 1984; Kernberg O., 1975)than empirical work. This is in part because the criterion comes from a psychoanalytic tradition. Furthermore, it is difficult to operationally define because it is internal and unobservable. However, an empirical investigation conducted by Wilkinson-Ryan and Westen (2000) found that the construct includes four factors: role absorption, painful incoherence, inconsistency, and a lack of commitment. Furthermore, it was found that each of these factors is characteristic of BPD.

Impulsivity (criterion 4), seen in many psychological disorders, can be conceptualized as a lack of reflection and planning, as well as quick action without forethought (Hochhausen et al., 2002). Impulsivity is thought to be a central diagnostic criterion of BPD (American Psychiatric Association, 2013) and it has been argued that BPD is best conceptualized as an impulse spectrum disorder (Zanarini, 1993). The characteristic impulsive behaviors associated with BPD include disordered eating, suicidal behavior, non-suicidal self-injury, substance abuse, promiscuous sexual behavior, and reckless driving (American Psychiatric Association, 2013; Doughterty et al., 2004; Rosval et al., 2006; Soloff et al., 2000; Trull et al., 2000).

Several research findings point to the centrality of impulsivity in BPD. First, impulsive behaviors were found to be the most consistent predictor of BPD at a 7-year follow-up (Links et al., 1999). Second, impulsivity remains an independent and separate factor in cluster analyses of BPD symptoms. Finally, antisocial personality disorder and substance abuse disorders are the most frequent diagnoses among first-degree relatives of BPD probands (White et al., 2003). Similarly, there is a strong relationship between other impulse disorders and BPD (Zanarini, 1993).

Recurrent suicidal behavior and non-suicidal self-injury (NSSI) (criterion 5) have also been argued to be defining characteristics of BPD (Soloff et al., 2000). A recent review conducted by Klonsky (2007) suggests that NSSI serves to regulate negative affect. It is estimated that those suffering from BPD represent 9%–33% of all suicides (Runeson & Beskow, 1991; Kullgren et al., 1986). Among those with BPD, 46%–92% attempt suicide (Black et al., 2004), with 3%–10% going on to complete suicide (Dingman & McGlashan, 1986; Kullgren et al., 1986; Paris & Zweig-Frank, 2001). One study found a mean of 3.4 suicide attempts across the lifetime among those with BPD (Soloff et al., 1994).

NSSI has been defined as the deliberate and direct destruction of bodily tissue without suicidal intent (Nock, 2010; Nock & Favazza, 2009; Nock et al., 2008). Methods of NSSI vary, and they may include but are not limited to drug overdoses, wrist cutting, headbanging, and burning. Although these behaviors occur in the absence of suicidal intent, they are nevertheless dangerous. NSSI can lead to permanent disability and can escalate into suicidal behavior (Klonsky, 2011). NSSI occurs in 50%–80% of patients with BPD (Snir et al., 2015; Soloff et al., 1994)and the average number of lifetime instances of NSSI range from 3.4 (Soloff et al., 1994) to 50 (Favazza & Conterio, 1989).

Affective instability (criterion 6) in BPD is not well understood (Dick & Suvak, 2018). This could be because the construct is vaguely defined (Koenigsberg, 2010; Benazzi, 2008) and because it has not been extensively empirically investigated (Ebner-Priemer, Kuo, et al., 2007). Affective instability includes the following types of emotion dysregulation: frequent categorical shifts, high affect intensity, rapid emotion rise-times, slow rates of return to emotional baseline, excessive reactivity to psychosocial cues, random, chaotic, or rapid fluctuation in affect, and histrionic reporting of affective experiences (Koenigsberg, 2010). Empirical studies using ecological momentary assessment and imaging have converged on the finding that patients with BPD experience a greater amount of variability in positive and negative affect and are more likely to report experiencing extreme levels of positive or negative affect in comparison to non-borderline controls (Ebner-Premier, Kuo, et al., 2007; Ebner-Premier, Welch, et al., 2007; Schulze et al., 2011; Trull et al., 2008).

Chronic feelings of emptiness (criterion 7) have been reported in 71%–73% of patients with BPD, in contrast to 26%–34% of patients without BPD (Grilo et al., 2001; Johansen et al., 2004). Like affective instability and identity disturbance, emptiness has not seen extensive empirical investigation (Klonsky, 2008). Feelings of emptiness are difficult to define, even among those who experience them (Lamprell, 1994). However, results of a review by Klonsky (2008) suggest that the experience is closely related to feelings of hopelessness, loneliness, and isolation. Feelings of emptiness also have been related to the physical experiences of woodenness (LaFarge, 1989), numbness (Fuchs, 2007), as well as nothingness and deadness (Cary, 1972).

Chronic feelings of emptiness have been linked to poor psychosocial functioning and suicidal behavior. Ellison and colleagues (2016) found a relationship between feelings of emptiness and each of several measures of psychosocial morbidity, including suicidality, history of suicide attempts, hospitalizations, social and work dysfunction, comorbidity with Axis I disorders, and global functioning. The review by Klonsky (2008) found a stronger relationship between suicidal ideation and emptiness than with any other criterion of BPD. Similarly, Miller and colleagues (2020) found that feelings of emptiness in patients with BPD was associated with NSSI, suicidality, and lower social and vocational functioning.

Inappropriate anger (criterion 8) is, in part, subsumed within affective instability. However, Koenigsberg and colleagues (2002) found that labile anger predicted BPD with an accuracy of 72% in a discriminant functional analysis. As such, it is suggested that inappropriate anger specifically, and not affective instability generally, sufficiently describes BPD (Koenigsberg et al., 2002). In addition to the portion of the criterion relating to unstable anger, those with BPD also show high levels of trait anger (Gardner et al., 1991; Linehan et al., 1994). Not surprisingly, the feelings and displays of anger cause difficulties in interpersonal relationships (Clarkin et al., 1983; Gardner et al., 1991; Koenigsberg et al., 2001; Tritt et al, 2005) and are thus a primary focus in treating individuals with BPD (Linehan, 1993; Kernberg et al., 1989).

The DSM-5 defines dissociation (criterion 9) as "disruption of and/or discontinuity in the normal integration of consciousness, memory, identity, emotion, perception, body representation, motor control, and behavior" (American Psychiatric Association [APA], 2013, p. 291). This is a broad definition of a phenomenon that occurs not only in BPD, but also in the dissociative disorders (e.g., dissociative amnesia, dissociative identity disorder, depersonalization/derealization disorder, other specified dissociative disorder, and unspecific dissociative disorder). Dissociation is not well understood by clinicians (Korzekwa et al., 2009) and has been criticized by others. For example, McHugh (2008) stated that calling a phenomenon dissociative is "merely a description with a professional ring masquerading as an explanation. One really knows no more about a case of amnesia or fugue by saying the patient 'dissociates' than by saying the patient behaved as though he or she couldn't remember" (p. 45).

Despite the difficulty in defining the phenomenon, dissociation is thought to occur in a substantial portion of those with BPD (Korzekwa et al., 2009). Specifically, Zanarini and colleagues (2008) identified three subgroups of those with BPD based on the severity of dissociative symptoms. These included those with low (32%), moderate (42%), and severe (26%) dissociation. Others have posited that the severity of dissociative symptoms among those with BPD might be related to the severity of trauma and/or abuse experienced in their history, as well as their early attachment relationships (Korzekwa et al., 2009).

Epidemiology

Epidemiological studies indicate that the point prevalence (i.e., the prevalence of the disorder at any one point in time) in the general population ranges between 0.5% and 5.9% (Grant et al., 2008; Lenzenweger et al., 2007; Trull et al., 2010). From this rate in the general population, the prevalence of BPD increases along with the level of care. BPD is the most common personality disorder in hospital settings, where it affects 10% of all psychiatric outpatients and 15%–20% of all psychiatric inpatients (Torgersen et al., 2001; Widiger & Weissman, 1991).

Reports of sex differences in BPD are mixed. The DSM-5 states that BPD is diagnosed predominantly (i.e., about 75%) in women. However, several studies report that BPD is equally prevalent in men and women (De Moor et al., 2009; Grant et al., 2008; Torgersen et al., 2001). It is thought that these discrepant reports might be due to women having a higher likelihood of seeking treatment (Holthausen & Habel, 2018).

Course of Illness

Consistent with the DSM-5 description of borderline personality disorder (i.e., beginning by early adulthood), BPD is most likely to be diagnosed in early adulthood (Lenzenweger et al., 2007). However, there is evidence that individual diagnostic symptoms vary in the timing of their appearance and remission. For example, Zanarini and colleagues (2006) found that 30% of patients with BPD engaged in NSSI at or before the age of 12 years, with another 30% of patients engaging in NSSI between the ages of 13 and 17 years. Additionally, longitudinal studies of BPD suggest that although impulsivity seems to remit with age (Stevenson et al., 2003; Zanarini et al., 2007), unstable interpersonal relationships appear to be persistent and chronic (Zanarini et al., 2007).

Most of those suffering from BPD experience remission over time (Zanarini, 2018). This has been found in two prominent longitudinal studies of patients with BPD. The McLean Study of Adult Development (MSAD) found that 99% of patients diagnosed with BPD at baseline no longer met diagnostic criteria for a period of two years or longer at a 16-year follow-up (Zanarini et al., 2012). The Collaborative Longitudinal Personality Disorders Study (CLPS) found that 25% of patients diagnosed with BPD at baseline met fewer than two criteria for a period of two months or longer at a two-year follow-up. A 10-year follow-up found that around 90% of patients diagnosed with BPD at baseline no longer had the diagnosis for 12 months or longer (Gunderson et al., 2011).

Genetic Influence

Psychological traits show a genetic influence (Ebstein et al., 2010; Plomin, 2019), and BPD is no exception. Estimates of the heritability (i.e., the differences between individuals that can be explained by genetic differences rather than environmental differences) of BPD have been examined using twin studies. These studies have consistently estimated the heritability of BPD to be approximately 40% (Amad et al., 2014), with two studies estimating the heritability to be above 60% (Torgersen et al., 2000; Torgersen et al., 2012). These studies suggest that the heritability of BPD is substantial; however, they also suggest that there are important environmental influences that contribute to the expression of the disorder.

Conceptual Accounts of Borderline Personality Disorder

Current conceptual accounts of BPD focus on emotion (Conklin et al., 2006; Gunderson, 2001; Kernberg, 1984; Linehan, 1993; Livesley et al., 1998; McCloskey et al., 2009; Skodol et al., 2002), including specific difficulties in emotional vulnerability and emotion dysregulation (Linehan, 1993). According to Linehan (1993), emotional vulnerability involves an increased sensitivity toward emotional reactions, a high intensity of emotional experiences, and a slow return to baseline after an emotional experience. Emotion dysregulation, on the other hand, refers to an inability to control or modulate emotional experiences. These conceptualizations are consistent with empirical studies suggesting that BPD is associated with a wide range of difficulties related to emotion (Glenn & Klonsky, 2009; Salsman & Linehan, 2012).

As such, emotional vulnerability and emotion dysregulation are captured within the diagnostic criteria for BPD. It has been argued that each of these criteria are either directly related to emotional vulnerability and emotion dysregulation or are a consequence of emotion vulnerability and dysregulation (Linehan, 1993; McMain et al., 2001). Lieb, Zanarini, Schmahl, Linehan, and Bohus (2004) divided the diagnostic criteria into four "sectors" of psychopathology: affective disturbance, disturbed cognition, impulsivity, and intense unstable relationships.

The criteria in the affective disturbance sector (i.e., inappropriate anger, affective instability, and emptiness) are directly related to emotional vulnerability and emotion dysregulation. The criteria in the cognitive sector (i.e., dissociation under stress and identity disturbance) are direct consequences of emotional vulnerability and emotion dysregulation. Dissociation is listed in the criteria as a consequence of stress, which is closely related to emotion and mood. In addition, identity disturbance is a consequence of affective instability. It is difficult to maintain a stable sense of self when one's emotions are fleeting, unexpected, and inconsistent. Several theoretical works suggest that criteria in the behavioral sector (recurrent suicidal behavior and impulsivity) also are a consequence of emotion dysregulation (Kernberg, 1984; Linehan, 1993; McCloskey et al., 2009). Finally, several authors suggest that emotional vulnerability and emotion dysregulation afford pathways toward difficulties in the interpersonal sector (i.e., fear of abandonment and unstable and intense interpersonal relationships; Berenson et al., 2011; Dixon-Gordon et al., 2013; Finkelhor et al., 2009; Sadikaj et al., 2013).

Evolutionary Explanations of Emotions and Emotional Vulnerability and Dysregulation in Borderline Personality Disorder
An Evolutionary Approach to the Emotions

Given that difficulties of emotion are at the core of borderline pathology, we propose that current conceptualizations of the disorder would be improved by understanding (a) the function for which emotions were designed, and (b) the reasons for individual differences in emotional functioning. Many evolutionary theories of emotion focus on the physiological and/or communicative functions of a specific set of culturally universal emotions (Ekman, 1992; Ekman & Cordaro, 2011; Izard, 1992, 1997)(Ekman, 1992; Ekman & Cordaro, 2011; Izard, 1992; Izard, 1997). Often, these emotions are defined by the presence of a distinct set of co-occurring characteristics including, but not limited to, a distinct physiology, a universal signal, and an emotional experience (Dolan, 2002; Ekman, 1992; Izard, 1992, 1994; Scherer, 2000; Tomkins, 1962)(Dolan, 2002; Ekman, 1992; Izard, 1992; Izard, 1994; Scherer, 2000; Tomkins, 1962). Although these theories have generated an impressive amount of theoretical and empirical work, it has been argued that the characteristics they require to identify an emotion might be arbitrary, restrictive, and overgeneralized, leaving out many emotions with important functions (Al-Shawaf & Lewis, 2017; Buss, 2014; Tooby & Cosmides, 1990).

A more nuanced evolutionary approach, introduced by Tooby and Cosmides (1990), suggests that emotions are superordinate programs that coordinate physiological and psychological subprograms to solve recurrent adaptive problems (Al-Shawaf et al., 2016; Sznycer et al., 2017; Tooby & Cosmides, 2008). From this approach, the function of emotions is to coordinate the activation and deactivation of our many subprograms (e.g., perception, attention, physiology, energy level, memory, etc.) to motivate responses that are orchestrated harmoniously, rather than in opposition and resulting in self-defeat. The coordination of subprograms need not include every subprogram that might be activated or deactivated for every other emotion. They need only to be those relevant for the specific emotion and with regard to the specific situation. This approach has been referred to as the coordinating mechanism view of the emotions (Al-Shawaf & Lewis, 2017).

Data from self-report studies suggest that this coordination might be impaired among those with BPD, resulting in undifferentiated or less clearly defined emotional experiences. Emotional granularity (also referred to as emotional differentiation) refers to the ability to make subtle distinctions between similarly valenced emotional states (Barrett, 2004; Feldman, 1995a, 1995b)(Barrett, 2004; Feldman, 1995; Feldman, 1995). Individuals with high emotional granularity represent their emotional states with specificity, while individuals with low emotional granularity represent their emotional states more globally. Viewed within the context of the coordinating mechanism view of emotions, low emotional granularity (i.e., a more global representation of emotional states) may be the result of a lack of successful coordination.

Suvak and colleagues (2011) examined individual differences in emotional granularity in BPD. They found that women with BPD represented emotions with lower granularity in comparison to non-borderline control participants. Specifically, those with BPD overemphasized valence and underemphasized arousal when self-reporting emotional experiences. The authors suggest that this might contribute to the all-or-nothing thinking patterns often characteristic of those with BPD.

These findings are consistent with research demonstrating a lack of granularity/differentiation in BPD. Leible and Snell (2004) found that participants who scored higher on a self-report measure of BPD reported less emotional clarity (i.e., how well they understand their feelings) on the Trait Meta-Mood Scale. Similarly, Levine, Marziali, and Hood (1997) found that participants diagnosed with BPD showed lower levels of emotional awareness and a limited capacity to coordinate mixed valence feelings. Finally, Webb and McMurran (2008) suggest that the difficulty in differentiating emotions in BPD might lead to impairments in emotion regulation.

It is important to note that these are self-reported data. As such, they only represent aspects of the emotional experiences that participants are aware of and can report. Also, these data do not speak directly to coordination of subprograms, but instead to a lack of consolidation or integration of superordinate programs and subprograms in borderline pathology.

Evolutionary Approaches to Emotional Vulnerability and Dysregulation in Borderline Personality Disorder

Within broader evolutionary metatheory are two mid-level explanations (Buss, 1990, 1995; Ketelaar & Ellis, 2000) (Buss, 1990; Buss, 1995; Ketelaar & Ellis, 2000)useful in describing BPD. These mid-level explanations are deductively connected to broader evolutionary metatheory and can be used to generate hypotheses that can be tested to support the mid-level explanation. These two mid-level theories are attachment theory and life history theory.

Attachment Theory
Attachment theory, proposed by John Bowlby ([1969]1982, 1973, 1980)(Bowlby, 1969/1982; Bowlby, 1973; Bowlby, 1980), is a mid-level evolutionary theory of social and personality development. Bowlby noted that newborns are both helpless and highly dependent on their caregivers for survival, presenting recurrent adaptive problem for newborns. That is, how can newborns manage the relationship between themselves and their primary caregivers in ways that promote their survival and further development?

As a solution to this recurrent problem, Bowlby posited that humans evolved an innate psychobiological system that (a) attends to local information that provides clues to the nature and quality of the environmental conditions in which the newborn is raised, and (b) forms attachment bonds between newborns and caregivers depending on these conditions (Ainsworth et al., 1978; Belsky, 1997; Belsky, Fish, et al., 1991; Chisholm, 1996). These attachment bonds are emotional and cognitive strategies that solve the adaptive problem presented by different kinds of environmental conditions during rearing (Belsky, 1997; Chisholm, 1996; Main & Westen, 1981). Emotionally, the attachment bond motivates the newborn to organize their own behavior in ways that maintain proximity to caregivers. Cognitively, the attachment bonds become ingrained in the newborn as internal working models (Ainsworth et al., 1978; Weinfield et al., 1999) that organize beliefs about the child and caregiver and thus guide the child's interpersonal behavior with the caregiver. The content of these internal working models is related to how valuable, lovable, and acceptable the newborn is in the eyes of the caregiver (Agrawal et al., 2004). Attachment bonds provide an evolutionary advantage to helpless and dependent offspring who cannot yet take care of themselves (Simpson & Belsky, 2008).

There are two primary components of attachment theory (Simpson & Belsky, 2008). The first component predicts similarities within species and describes how and why attachment bonds are formed. The second component predicts individual differences within species and describes how and why different patterns of attachment exist.

As mentioned above, the type of attachment bond is dependent upon environmental conditions which are approximated by the caregiver's behavior toward the newborn (Bowlby [1969]1982)(Bowlby, 1969/1982). Variations in attachment bonds, termed attachment styles, are long-lasting relational models of the self and others that begin with the relationship with the caregiver and provide a working model that guides future interpersonal interactions. Ainsworth, Blehar, Waters, and Wall (1978) identified three primary attachment styles in the laboratory using the "strange situation" task. In this task, Ainsworth and colleagues reunited mothers with their 12–18-month-old infants and examined the infant's behavior. The three primary attachment styles (secure, anxious-ambivalent, and anxious-avoidant) each represent a different solution to the adaptive problem presented by the child's specific rearing environment (Belsky, 1997; Chisholm, 1996; Main & Westen, 1981).

In a secure attachment, mothers are available and responsive to the needs of their children (Ainsworth et al., 1978; De Wolff & Van Izjendoorn, 1997). In turn, children use mothers to ameliorate their distress and usually return to normal activities after being calmed down. In this attachment relationship, children need not be concerned about the availability or responsiveness of their caregiver or the security of their environment. It is thought that a secure attachment will result in a stable and positive self-image, feeling worthy of love, and positive expectations of others' behavior toward the self (Agrawal et al., 2004).

In an anxious-ambivalent attachment, mothers sometimes appear to be uninvolved and respond inconsistently to their children's needs (Belsky, 1984; Isabella et al., 1989; Lewis & Feiring, 1989; Scholmerich et al., 1995; Smith & Pederson, 1988; Vondra et al., 1995). Anxious-ambivalent children make inconsistent efforts to elicit comfort from their caregivers, frequently alternating between clinginess at one extreme and angry outbursts at the other (Bowlby, 1973). These children are also characterized as hypervigilant and ruminate about the loss of caregiver support (Cassidy & Berlin, 1994).

Mothers of anxious-avoidant children are described as cold and rejecting, as evidenced by a distaste for close bodily contact (Ainsworth et al., 1978), and are less responsive to their children's distress (Crockenberg, 1981). In response, anxious-avoidant children avoid caregivers upon reunion in the strange situation and are forced into a strategy of independence and self-reliance (Simpson & Belsky, 2008).

Although not originally identified by Ainsworth and colleagues (1978), a fourth attachment style, termed disorganized-disoriented, has been added (Ainsworth & Eichberg, 1991; Hesse & Main, 2000; Main & Solomon, 1986). Whereas the secure, anxious-ambivalent, and anxious-avoidant styles have been conceptualized as adaptive strategies specific to the local environment, the disorganized-disoriented style has been interpreted as a collapse of a behavioral strategy (Levy, 2005). The caregivers of disorganized-disoriented children are thought to experience unresolved trauma (Hesse & Main, 2000) and, in turn, subject their children to maltreatment or frightening behaviors. The caregiver becomes a source of both comfort and fear. As a result, disorganized-disoriented children experience emotional and motivational conflict (e.g., conflicting approach and avoidance behaviors, dissociative states, and sudden aggressive actions) (Hesse & Main, 2006; Lyons-Ruth & Jacobvitz, 1999; Lyons-Ruth et al., 1999).

Bowlby (1979) originally surmised that attachment styles persist "from the cradle to the grave." He also thought of attachment styles as the root of both normal and pathological development, with pathological characteristics including emotional distress (i.e., anxiety, anger, depression, and emotional detachment), marital problems, trouble raising children, and personality disorders (Bowlby, 1977). Accordingly, many theoretical conceptualizations of the emotional difficulties present in BPD focus on impairments in early attachment relationships (Blatt et al., 1997; Fonagy et al., 1996; Gunderson, 1996; Levy & Blatt, 1999). These conceptualizations note that the characteristics of a secure attachment seem to oppose those traits characteristic of BPD. A secure attachment is defined by feelings of acceptance, love, and being worthy of love. In contrast, the affective instability and intense interpersonal relationships common in BPD are the product of malevolent and split representations of the self and others (Kernberg, 1967)(Kernberg O., 1967), neediness and manipulation (Gunderson, 1984; Masterson, 1972), fear of abandonment, and otherwise insecure patterns of attachment (Gunderson, 1996). Similarly, many theorists have specifically stated that disorganized-disoriented attachment styles constitute a risk factor for the development of BPD (Fonagy et al., 2002; Holmes, 2003, 2004; Liotti, 2000).

The relationship between adult attachment and BPD has been examined using measures of adult attachment schemas. One of the most widely used measures is the Adult Attachment Inventory (AII) (George et al., 1985), in which participants respond to questions pertaining to their caregiver relationships with the aim of understanding how their early relationships influence their current relationships.

The AII identifies four attachment styles in adulthood (Hesse, 1999), each corresponding to an attachment style in childhood. The secure-autonomous style is characterized by a coherent and collaborative discourse, a tolerance and acceptance of imperfections in the self and the parent, and a flexible, compassionate, and objective view of others. This style corresponds with a secure attachment in childhood. The dismissing style is characterized by an incoherent discourse. The self is described as strong and independent with little articulation of negative feelings, and their responses are rigidly focused away from attachment characteristics. This style corresponds with an avoidant attachment in childhood. The preoccupied style is dominated by a confused, angry, or passive preoccupation with the attachment figures. This style corresponds to the ambivalent attachment in childhood. Both dismissive and preoccupied styles are considered to be insecure. Finally, the unresolved/disorganized style is indicative of unresolved trauma and presents as momentary lapses in reasoning and discourse. This style corresponds with a disorganized-disoriented attachment in childhood.

Several studies have used the AII (Babcock et al., 2000; Barone, 2003; Diamond et al., 2003; Fonagy et al., 1996), as well as other measures (Salzman et al., 1997), to examine the relationship between adult attachment and BPD. Each shows a strong relationship between BPD and insecure attachment styles, particularly the preoccupied and unresolved/disorganized styles. For detailed reviews, see Agrawal et al. (2004), Levy, (2005), and Levy et al. (2015). The consistency of these results strongly suggests that insecure attachment styles are associated, possibly causally, with BPD.

Life History Theory

Life history theory is a mid-level evolutionary theory that is consistent with attachment theory (Belsky, Steinberg, et al., 1991; Draper & Harpending, 1982) and provides a framework for addressing how individuals expend resources in ways that maximize their fitness across the life span (Charnov, 1993; Del Giudice et al., 2016; Ellis et al., 2009; Hill, 1993; Hill & Kaplan, 1999; Kaplan & Gangestad, 2005).

All individuals face the costs of survival and reproduction under the constraints of a limited budget of resources (i.e., time and energy) afforded by the environment. This presents a recurring adaptive problem; that is, how does an individual allocate a finite amount of resources toward the various traits and behaviors that might differentially increase survival or reproduction?

Any allocation of resources involves a trade-off. Devoting time and energy in one effort must come at the cost of neglecting another (Gadgil & Bossert, 1970; Williams, 1966). The most primary of these trade-offs involves investing in resources that increase either the age/schedule of survival or in resources that increase the age/schedule of fertility. Resources invested in the age/schedule of survival can be further divided into those invested in growth, survival, body maintenance, and developmental activity (Geary, 2002). Resources invested in the age/schedule of reproduction can be further divided into those invested in mating effort, parenting effort, and nepotistic effort (Del Giudice, 2014a).

As a solution to this recurrent problem, nature selected for individuals who, based on their early environmental conditions (Belsky, Steinberg, et al., 1991; DeWitt & Scheiner, 2004), adopted a specific life history strategy. A life history strategy can be defined as an adaptive solution to optimally navigate fitness trade-offs within the constraints of limited resources. Life history strategies are functionally complex phenotypes with cohesive morphological, physiological, and behavioral traits (Braendle et al., 2011). These traits and behaviors covary together (Del Giudice et al., 2016) and include risk-taking, self-regulation, aggression, exploration, mating, and childcare (Reale et al., 2010; Wolf et al., 2007).

Both within and across species, life history strategies fall on a continuum ranging from fast to slow. A fast life history strategy is characterized by an insecure attachment, early maturation and reproduction, fast growth, small body size, high fertility, short life span, and a low investment in offspring quality. In contrast, a slow life history strategy is characterized by a secure attachment, late maturation and reproduction, slow growth, large body size, low fertility, long life span, and high investment in offspring quality (Belsky, Steinberg, et al., 1991; Promislow & Harvey, 1990).

Similar to attachment theory, life history theory makes predictions concerning differences both between and within species. Beginning with Belsky, Steinberg, and Draper (1991), the framework has been applied to individual differences in personality and psychopathology (Del Giudice, 2014a, 2014b; Del Giudice et al., 2016). Regarding personality traits, the Five Factor Model (Costa & McCrae, 1995) traits of conscientiousness and agreeableness have been found to be associated with slow life history strategy indicators such as restricted socio-sexuality, relationship stability, risk aversion, and pro-social behavior. In contrast, extraversion, openness to experience, and neuroticism have been found to be associated with fast life history strategy indicators such as unrestricted socio-sexuality, short-term mating, relationship instability, risk taking, and antisocial behavior (Del Giudice, 2012). Regarding psychopathology, Del Guidice (2014a) distinguishes between fast spectrum disorders (i.e., those that cluster at the fast end of the life history continuum) and slow spectrum disorders (i.e., those that cluster at the slow end of the life history continuum). A provisional life history taxonomy of mental health disorders places schizophrenia, bipolar disorder, obsessive compulsive disorder, and borderline personality disorder as fast spectrum disorders, with autism spectrum, obsessive compulsive disorder, and obsessive-compulsive personality disorder as slow spectrum disorders.

Based on several diagnostic criteria for BPD (e.g., unstable and intense interpersonal relationships, impulsivity, affective instability, and inappropriate and intense anger), it has been hypothesized that BPD represents the pathological extreme of the adaptive fast life history strategy (Brune, 2016; Brune et al., 2010; Del Giudice, 2014a). In addition, Brune (2016) notes that several traits are associated with both BPD and a fast life history strategy. For example, a fast life history strategy is associated with unpredictability and adversity early in life (Belsky, Steinberg, et al., 1991). This is consistent with several traits of BPD, including poor impulse control and inability to delay gratification (Volker et al., 2009), hypersensitivity to cues that might signal abandonment (Linehan, 1993), and distrust of others (Gunderson & Lyons-Ruth, 2008; King-Casas et al., 2008: Unoka et al., 2009). Moreover, a fast life history strategy is associated with an earlier debut of sexual intercourse. This is consistent with studies showing that women with BPD have an earlier debut of sexual intercourse as well as more sexual partners in comparison to non-borderline control participants (Sansone et al., 2008; Sansone et al., 2011). Also consistent is the finding that those with BPD are more likely to experience breakups in comparison to non-borderline controls (Labonte & Paris, 1993). In contrast to this hypothesis, Brune (2016) notes that there is, thus far, no evidence of an association between BPD and an early age of menarche, as would be expected for a fast life history. However, it is noted that a younger age of menarche is associated with an increased risk for psychological disorders, in general (Graber, 2013).

Summary

BPD can be conceptualized as the direct and indirect consequences of emotional vulnerability and emotion dysregulation (Linehan, 1993). In this chapter, we have proposed that conceptualizations of BPD focusing on these emotional difficulties would be improved by understanding the functions for which emotions were designed and the reasons for individual differences in emotional functioning. This proposition is at the heart of evolutionary psychopathology, which is the application of evolutionary theory to the study of mental disorders (Del Giudice, 2014a). Evolutionary psychopathology aims to provide a framework for understanding the etiology, development, and classification of putative mental disorders with the aim of guiding treatments. It suggests that some putative mental disorders might be better conceptualized as evolutionary strategies and/or adaptive responses that may or may not have socially or personally desirable consequences (Del Giudice et al., 2016).

We presented two middle-level evolutionary theories, attachment theory and life history theory, that provide useful frameworks for understanding BPD. Attachment theory suggests that individual differences in both personality and psychopathology might reflect adaptive solutions to insecure local environments that persist throughout the life span. In this framework, BPD might reflect an adaptive strategy to navigate early insecure attachments, albeit one that can overstay its welcome. Similarly, life history theory suggests that strategies along the fast–slow continuum might represent adaptive responses to stable and unstable local environments. In this framework, BPD might represent an extreme of the fast life history strategy (Brune, 2016). Each provides an ultimate explanation for BPD that can be applied to improve the lives of those dealing with the disorder. Moreover, these evolutionary explanations of BPD exemplify the promise that evolutionary psychopathology holds in understanding other disorders related to personality, emotions, and moods.

Acknowledgement
We thank Marco Del Giudice for comments on a previous version of this chapter.

References

Agrawal, H. R., Gunderson, J., Holmes, B. M., & Lyons-Ruth, K. (2004). Attachment studies with borderline patients: A review. *Harvard Review of Psychiatry*, *12*(2), 94–104.

Ainsworth, M., Blehar, M., Waters, E., & Wall, S. (1978). *Patterns of attachment: A psychological study of the Strange Situation*. Lawrence Erlbaum Associates.

Ainsworth, M., & Eichberg, C. (1991). Effects on infant-mother attachment of mother's unresolved loss of an attachment figure or other traumatic experience. In C. Murray & J. Stevenson-Hinde (Eds.), *Attachment across the life cycle* (pp. 160–183). Tavistock/Routledge.

Al-Shawaf, L., Conroy-Beam, D., Asao, K., & Buss, D. M. (2016). Human emotions: An evolutionary psychological perspective. *Emotion Review*, *8*(2), 173–186.

Al-Shawaf, L., & Lewis, D. M. (2017). Evolutionary psychology and the emotions. In V. Zeigler-Hill & T. K. Shackelford (Eds.), *Encyclopedia of personality and individual differences* (pp. 1–10). Springer.

Amad, A., Ramoz, N., Thomas, P., Jardri, R., & Gorwood, P. (2014). Genetics of borderline personality disorder: Systematic review and proposal of an integrative model. *Neuroscience and Biobehavioral Reviews*, *40*, 6–19.

American Psychiatric Association. (2013). *Diagnostic and statistical manual of mental disorders*. APA.

Babcock, J. C., Jacobson, N. S., Gottman, J. M., & Yerington, T. P. (2000). Attachment, emotional regulation, and the function of marital violence: Differences between secure, preoccupied, and dismissing violent and nonviolent husbands. *Journal of Family Violence*, *4*, 391–409.

Barone, L. (2003). Developmental protective and risk factors in borderline personality disorder: A study using the Adult Attachment Interview. *Attachment and Human Development*, *5*, 64–77.

Barrett, L. F. (2004). Feelings or words? Understanding the content in self-report ratings of experienced emotion. *Journal of Personality and Social Psychology*, *87*, 266–281.

Beck, A. T., Freeman, A., David, D. D. (2004). *Cognitive therapy of personality disorders* (2nd ed.). Guilford Press.

Belsky, J. (1984). The determinants of parenting: A process model. *Child Development*, *55*, 83–96.

Belsky, J. (1997). Attachment, mating, and parenting: An evolutionary interpretation. *Human Nature*, *8*, 361–381.

Belsky, J., Fish, M., & Isabella, R. A. (1991). Continuity and discontinuity in infant negative and positive emotionality: Family antecedents and attachment consequences. *Developmental Psychology*, *27*, 421–431.

Belsky, J., Steinberg, L., & Draper, P. (1991). Childhood experience, interpersonal development, and reproductive strategy: An evolutionary theory of socialization. *Child Development*, *62*, 647–670.

Benazzi, F. (2008). A relationship between bipolar II disorder and borderline personality disorder? *Progress in Neuro-Psychopharmacology and Biological Psychiatry*, *32*(4), 1022–1029.

Berenson, K. R., Downey, G., Rafaeli, E., Coifman, K. G., & Paquin, N. L. (2011). The rejection-rage contingency in borderline personality disorder. *Journal of Abnormal Psychology*, *120*(3), 681–690.

Berg, J., Dickhaut, J., & McCabe, K. (1995). Trust, reciprocity, and social history. *Games and Economic Behavior*, *10*(1), 122–142.

Black, D. W., Blum, N., Pfohl, B., & Hale, N. (2004). Suicidal behavior in borderline personality disorder: Prevalence, risk factors, prediction, and prevention. *Journal of Personality Disorders*, *18*(3), 226–239.

Blatt, S. J., Auerbach, J. S., & Levy, K. N. (1997). Mental representations in personality development, psychopathology, and the therapeutic process. *Review of General Psychology*, *1*, 351–374.

Bowlby, J. ([1969] 1982). *Attachment and loss*, Vol. 1: *Attachment*. Basic Books.

Bowlby, J. (1973). *Attachment and loss*, Vol. 2: *Separation*. Basic Books.

Bowlby, J. (1977). The making and breaking of affectional bonds: I. Aetiology and psychopathology in the light of attachment theory. *British Journal of Psychiatry*, *130*, 201–210.

Bowlby, J. (1979). The Bowlby-Ainsworth attachment theory. *Behavioral and Brain Sciences*, *2*(4), 637–638.

Bowlby, J. (1980). *Attachment and loss*. Basic Books.

Braendle, C., Heyland, F., & Flatt, T. (2011). Integrating mechanistic and evolutionary analysis of life history variation. In T. Flatt, & F. Heyland (Eds.), *Mechanisms of life history evolution: The genetics and physiology of life history traits and trade-offs* (pp. 3–10). Oxford University Press.

Brodsky, B. S., Groves, S. A., Oquendo, M. A., Mann, J. J., & Stanley, B. (2006). Interpersonal precipitants and suicide attempts in borderline personality disorder. *Suicide and Life Threatening Behavior, 36*(3), 313–322.

Brune, M. (2016). Borderline personality disorder: Why "fast and furious"? *Evolution, Medicine, and Public Health, 2016*(1), 52–66.

Brune, M., Ghiassi, V., & Ribbert, H. (2010). Does borderline personality reflect the pathological extreme of an adaptive reproduction strategy? Insights and hypotheses from evolutionary life-history theory. *Clinical Neuropsychiatry, 7*, 3–9.

Buss, D. M. (1990). Evolutionary social psychology: Prospects and pitfalls. *Motivation and Emotion, 14*(4), 265–286.

Buss, D. M. (1995). Evolutionary psychology: A new paradigm for psychological science. *Psychological Inquiry, 6*(1), 1–30.

Buss, D. M. (2014). Comment: Evolutionary criteria for considering an emotion "basic." *Emotion Review, 6*(4), 313–315.

Cary, G. L. (1972). The borderline condition: A structural-dynamic viewpoint. *Psychoanalytic Review, 59*(1), 33–54.

Cassidy, J., & Berlin, L. J. (1994). The insecure/ambivalent pattern of attachment: Theory and research. *Child Development, 65*, 971–991.

Charnov, E. L. (1993). *Life history invariants: Some explorations of symmetry in evolutionary ecology*. Oxford University Press.

Chisholm, J. S. (1996). The evolutionary ecology of attachment organization. *Human Nature, 7*(1), 1–38.

Clarkin, J. F., Widiger, T. A., Frances, A., Hurt, S. W., & Gilmore, M. (1983). Prototypic typology and the borderline personality disorder. *Journal of Nervous and Mental Disorders, 179*, 157–161.

Conklin, C. Z., Bradley, R., & Westen, D. (2006). Affect regulation in borderline personality disorder. *The Journal of Nervous and Mental Disease, 194*(2), 69–77.

Costa, P. T., & McCrae, R. R. (1995). Domains and facets: Hierarchical personality assessment using the Revised NEO Personality Inventory. *Journal of Personality Assessment, 64*(1), 21–50.

Crockenberg, S. B. (1981). Infant irritability, mother responsiveness, and social support influences on the security of infant-mother attachment. *Child Development, 52*(3), 857–865.

Del Giudice, M. (2012). Sex ratio dynamics and fluctuating selection on personality. *Journal of Theoretical Biology, 297*, 48–60.

Del Giudice, M. (2014a). An evolutionary life history framework for psychopathology. *Psychological Inquiry, 25*(3–4), 261–300.

Del Giudice, M. (2014b). A tower unto heaven: Toward an expanded framework for psychopathology. *Psychological Inquiry, 24*, 394–413.

Del Giudice, M., Gangestad, S. W., & Kaplan, H. S. (2016). Life history theory and evolutionary psychology. In D. M. Buss (Ed.), *The handbook of evolutionary psychology* (pp. 88–114). Wiley.

De Moor, M. H., Distel, M. A., Trull, T. J., & Boomsma, D. I. (2009). Assessment of borderline personality features in population samples: Is the personality assessment inventory- borderline features scale measurement invariant across sex and age? *Psychological Assessment, 21*(1), 125.

DeWitt, T. J., & Scheiner, S. M. (2004). *Phenotypic plasticity: Functional and conceptual approaches*. Oxford University Press.

De Wolff, M. S., & Van Izjendoorn, M. H. (1997). Sensitivity and attachment: A meta-analysis on parental antecedents of infant attachment. *Child Development, 68*(4), 571–591.

Diamond, D., Stovall-McClough, C., Clarkin, J. F., & Levy, K. N. (2003). Patient-therapist attachment in the treatment of borderline personality disorder. *Bulletin of the Menninger Clinic, 67*, 227–259.

Dick, A. M., & Suvak, M. K. (2018). Borderline personality disorder affective instability: What you know impacts how you feel. *Personality Disorders: Theory, Research, and Treatment, 9*(4), 369–378.

Dingman, C. W., & McGlashan, T. H. (1986). Discriminating characteristics of suicides: Chestnut Lodge follow-up sample including patients with affective disorder, schizophrenia, and schizoaffective disorder. *Acta Psychiatrica Scandinavica, 74*, 91–97.

Dixon-Gordon, K. L., Yiu, A., & Chapman, A. L. (2013). Borderline personality features and emotional reactivity: The mediating role of interpersonal vulnerabilities. *Journal of Behavior Therapy and Experimental Psychiatry, 44*(2), 271–278.

Dolan, R. J. (2002). Emotion, cognition, and behavior. *Science, 298*(5596), 1191–1194.

Doughterty, D. M., Mathias, C. W., Marsh, D. M., Papageorgiou, T. D., Swann, A. C., & Meoller, F. G. (2004). Laboratory measured behavioral impulsivity relates to suicide attempt history. *Suicide and Life Threatening Behavior, 34*, 374–385.

Draper, P., & Harpending, H. (1982). Father absence and reproductive strategy: An evolutionary perspective. *Journal of Anthropological Research, 38,* 255–273.

Ebner-Priemer, U. W., Kuo, J., Kleindienst, N., Welch, S. S., Reisch, T., Reinhard, I., Lieb, K., Linehan, M. M., & Bohus, M. (2007). State affective instability in borderline personality disorder assessed by ambulatory monitoring. *Psychological Medicine, 37*(7), 961–970.

Ebner-Priemer, U. W., Welch, S. S., Grossman, P., Reisch, T., Linehan, M. M., & Bohus, M. (2007). Psychophysiological ambulatory assessment of affective dysregulation in borderline personality disorder. *Psychiatry Research, 150*(3), 265–275.

Ebstein, R. P., Israel, S., Chew, S. H., Zhong, S., & Knafo, A. (2010). Genetics of human social behavior. *Neuron, 65*(6), 831–844.

Ekman, P. (1992). An argument for basic emotions. *Cognition & Emotion, 6*(3–4), 169–200.

Ekman, P., & Cordaro, D. (2011). What is meant by calling emotions basic. *Emotion Review, 3*(4), 364–370.

Ellis, B. J., Figueredo, A. J., Brumbach, B. H., & Schlomer, G. L. (2009). The impact of harsh versus unpredictable environments on the evolution and development of life history strategies. *Human Nature, 20,* 204–268.

Favazza, A. R., & Conterio, K. (1989). Female habitual self-mutilators. *Acta Psychiatrica Scandinavica, 79*(3), 283–289.

Feldman, L. A. (1995a). Valence focus and arousal focus: Individual differences in the structure of affective experience. *Journal of Personality and Social Psychology, 21,* 153–166.

Feldman, L. A. (1995b). Variations in the circumplex structure of mood. *Personality and Social Psychology Bulletin, 21,* 806–817.

Finkelhor, D., Ormrod, R., Turner, H., & Holt, M. (2009). Pathways to poly-victimization. *Child Maltreatment, 14*(4), 316–329.

Fonagy, P., & Bateman, A. W. (2007). Mentalizing and borderline personality disorder. *Journal of Mental Health, 16*(1), 83–101.

Fonagy, P., Gergely, G., Jurist, E. L., & Target, M. (2002). *Affect regulation, mentalization, and the development of the self.* Other Press.

Fonagy, P., Leigh, T., Steele, M., Steele, H., Kennedy, R., Mattoon, G., Target, M., & Gerber, A. (1996). The relation of attachment status, psychiatric classification and response to psychotherapy. *Journal of Consulting and Clinical Psychology, 64*(1), 22–31.

Fuchs, T. (2007). Fragmented selves: Temporality and identity in borderline personality disorder. *Psychopathology, 40*(6), 379–387.

Gadgil, M., & Bossert, W. H. (1970). Life historical consequences of natural selection. *American Naturalist, 104,* 1–24.

Gardner, D. L., Leibenluft, E., O'Leary, K. M., & Cowdry, R. W. (1991). Self-rating of anger and hostility in borderline personality disorder. *Journal of Nervous and Mental Disorders, 179,* 157–161.

Geary, D. C. (2002). Sexual selection and human life history. *Advances in Child Development and Behavior, 30,* 41–101.

George, C., Kaplan, N., & Main, M. (1985). The Berkeley Adult Attachment Interview. Unpublished manuscript.

Glenn, C. R., & Klonsky, E. D. (2009). Emotion dysregulation as a core feature of borderline personality disorder. *Journal of Personality Disorders, 23*(1), 20–28.

Graber, J. A. (2013). Pubertal timing and the development of psychopathology in adolescence and beyond. *Hormones and Behavior, 64*(2), 262–269.

Grant, B. F., Chou, S. P., Goldstein, R. B., Huang, B., Stinson, F. S., Saha, T. D., Smith, S. M., Dawson, D. A., Pulay, A. J., Pickering, R. P., & Ruan, W. J. (2008). Prevalence, correlates, disability, and comorbidity of DSM-IV borderline personality disorder: Results from the Wave 2 National Epidemiologic Survey on Alcohol and Related Conditions. *Journal of Clinical Psychiatry, 69*(4), 533–545.

Grilo, C. M., McGlashan, T. H., Morey, L. C., Gunderson, J. G., Skodol, A. E., & Shea, M. T. (2001). Internal consistency, intercriterion overlap, and diagnostic efficiency of criteria sets for DSM-IV schizotypal, borderline, avoidant, and obsessive-compulsive personality disorders. *Acta Psychiatrica Scandinavica, 104,* 264–272.

Gunderson, J. G. (1984). *Borderline personality disorder: A clinical guide.* American Psychiatric.

Gunderson, J. G. (1996). Borderline patient's intolerance of aloneness: Insecure attachments and therapist availability. *American Journal of Psychiatry, 153,* 752–758.

Gunderson, J. G. (2001). *Borderline personality disorder: A clinical guide.* American Psychiatric Press.

Gunderson, J. G., & Lyons-Ruth, K. (2008). BPD's interpersonal hypersensitivity phenotype: A gene-environment-developmental model. *Journal of Personality Disorders, 22*(1), 22–41.

Gunderson, J. G., Stout, R. L., McGlashan, M., Shea, T. M., Morey, L. C., Grilo, C. M., Zanarini, M. C., Yen, S., Markowitz, J. C., Sanislow, C., & Ansell, E. (2011). Ten-year course of borderline personality disorder: Psychopathology and function from the Collaborative Longitudinal Personality Disorders study. *Archives of General Psychiatry, 68*(8), 827–837.

Hesse, E. (1999). The Adult Attachment Interview: Historical and current perspectives. In P. R. Shaver & J. Cassidy (Eds.), *Handbook of attachment: Theory, research, and clinical applications* (pp. 395–433). Giulford Press.

Hesse, E., & Main, M. (2000). Disorganized infant, child, and adult attachment: Collapse in behavioral and attentional strategies. *Journal of the American Psychoanalytic Association, 48*, 1097–1127.

Hesse, E., & Main, M. (2006). Frightened, threatening, and dissociative parental behavior in low-risk samples: Description, discussion, and interpretations. *Development and Psychopathology, 18*(2), 309–343.

Hill, K. (1993). Life history theory and evolutionary anthropology. *Evolutionary Anthropology, 2*, 78–88.

Hill, K., & Kaplan, H. (1999). Life history traits in humans: Theory and empirical studies. *Annual Review of Anthropology, 28*, 397–430.

Hochhausen, N. M., Lorenz, A. R., & Newman, J. P. (2002). Specifying the impulsivity of female inmates with borderline personality disorder. *Journal of Abnormal Psychology, 111*(3), 495–501.

Holmes, J. (2003). Borderline personality disorder and the search for meaning: An attachment perspective. *Australia-New Zealand Journal of Psychiatry, 37*, 524–531.

Holmes, J. (2004). Disorganized attachment and borderline personality disorder: A clinical perspective. *Attachment and Human Development, 6*, 181–190.

Holthausen, B. S., & Habel, U. (2018). Sex differenes in personality disorders. *Current Psychiatry Reports, 107*, 1–7.

Isabella, R., Belsky, J., & von Eye, A. (1989). Origins of infant-mother attachment: An examination of interactional synchrony during the infant's first year. *Developmental Psychology, 25*, 12–21.

Izard, C. E. (1992). Basic emotions, relations among emotions, and emotion-cognition relations. *Psychological Review, 99*(3), 561–565.

Izard, C. E. (1994). Innate and universal facial expressions: Evidence from developmental and cross-cultural research. *Psychological Bulletin, 115*(2), 288–299.

Izard, C. E. (1997). Emotions and facial expressions: A perspective from differential emotions theory. In J. A. Russell, & J. M. Fernandez-Dols (Eds.), *Studies in emotion and social interaction, 2nd series: The psychology of facial expression* (pp. 57–77). Cambridge University Press.

Johansen, M., Karterud, S., Pedersen, G., Gude, T., & Falkum, E. (2004). An investigation of the prototype validity of the borderline DSM-IV construct. *Acta Psychiatrica Scandinavica, 109*(4), 289–298.

Kaplan, H. S., & Gangestad, S. W. (2005). Life history theory and evolutionary psychology. In D. M. Buss (Ed.), *Handbook of evolutionary psychology* (pp. 68–95). Wiley.

Kernberg, O. (1975). A systems approach to priority setting of interventions in groups. *International Journal of Group Psychotherapy, 25*(3), 251–275.

Kernberg, O. (1976). Technical considerations in the treatment of borderline personality organization. *Journal of the American Psychoanalytic Association, 24*(4), 795–829.

Kernberg, O. F., Selzer, M. A., Koenigsberg, H. W., Carr, A. C., & Applebaum, A. H. (1989). *Psychodynamic psychotherapy for borderline patients*. Basic Books.

Ketelaar, T., & Ellis, B. J. (2000). Are evolutionary explanations unfalsifiable? Evolutionary psychology and the lakatosian philosophy of science. *Psychology Inquiry, 11*(1), 1–21.

King-Casas, B., Sharp, C., Lomax-Bream, L., Lohrenz, T., Fonagy, P., & Montague, P. R. (2008). The rupture and repair of cooperation in borderline personality disorder. *Science, 321*(5890), 806–810.

Klonsky, E. D. (2007). The functions of deliberate self-injury: A review of the evidence. *Clinical Psychology Review, 27*, 226–239.

Klonsky, E. D. (2008). What is emptiness? Clarifying the 7th criterion for borderline personality disorder. *Journal of Personality Disorders, 22*(4), 418–426.

Klonsky, E. D. (2011). Non-suicidal self-injury in United States adults: Prevalence, sociodemographics, topography, and functions. *Psychological Medicine, 41*(9), 1981–1986.

Koenigsberg, H. W. (2010). Affective instability: Toward an integration of neuroscience and psychological perspectives. *Journal of Personality Disorders, 24*, 60–82.

Koenigsberg, H. W., Harvey, P. D., Mitropoulou, V., New, A. S., Goodman, M., Silverman, J., Serby, M., Schopick, F., & Siever, L. J. (2001). Are the interpersonal and identity disturbances in the borderline personality disorder criteria linked to the traits of affective instability and impulsivity? *Journal of Personality Disorders, 15*(4), 358–370.

Koenigsberg, H. W., Harvey, P. D., Mitropoulou, V., Schmeidler, J., New, A. S., Goodman, M., Silverman, J. M., Serby, M., Schopick, F., & Siever, L. J. (2002). Characterizing affective instability in borderline personality disorder. *American Journal of Psychiatry, 159*(5), 784–788.

Korzekwa, M. I., Dell, P. F., & Pain, C. (2009). Dissociation and borderline personality disorder: An update for clinicians. *Current Psychiatry Reports, 11*(1), 82–88.

Kullgren, G., Renberg, E., & Jacobsson, L. (1986). An empirical study of borderline personality disorder and psychiatric suicides. *Journal of Nervous and Mental Disease, 174*(6), 328–331.

Labonte, E., & Paris, J. (1993). Life events in borderline personality disorder. *Canadian Journal of Psychiatry, 38*, 638–640.

LaFarge, L. (1989). Emptiness as defense in severe regressive states. *Journal of the American Psychoanalytic Association, 37*(4), 965–995.

Lamprell, M. (1994). From emptiness to loss: A journey from the intrapersonal to the interpersonal. *British Journal of Psychotherapy, 10*(1), 331–343.

Leible, T., & Snell, W. (2004). Borderline personality disorder and multiple aspects of emotional intelligence. *Personality and Individual Differences, 37*, 393–404.

Lenzenweger, M. F., Lane, M., Loranger, A. W., & Kessler, R. C. (2007). DSM-IV personality disorders in the national comorbidity survey replication (NCS-R). *Biological Psychiatry, 62*, 553–564.

Levine, D., Marziali, E., & Hood, J. (1997). Emotion processing in borderline personality disorders. *Journal of Nervous and Mental Disease, 185*, 240–246.

Levy, K., & Blatt, S. (1999). Attachment theory and psychoanalysis: Further differentiation within insecure attachment patterns. *Psychoanalytic Inquiry, 19*, 541–575.

Levy, K. N. (2005). The implications of attachment theory and research for understanding borderline personality disorder. *Development and Psychopathology, 17*, 959–986.

Levy, K. N., Johnson, B. N., Clouthier, T. L., Scala, J. W., & Temes, C. M. (2015). An attachment theoretical framework for personality disorders. *Canadian Psychology, 56*(2), 197–207.

Lewis, M., & Feiring, C. (1989). Infant, mother, and mother-infant interaction behavior and subsequent attachment. *Child Development, 60*, 831–837.

Lieb, K., Zanarini, M. C., Schmahl, C., Linehan, M. M., & Bohus, M. (2004). Borderline personality disorder. *Lancet, 364*(9432), 453–461.

Linehan, M. M. (1993). *Skills training manual for treating borderline personality disorder*. Guilford Press.

Linehan, M. M., Tutek, D. A., Heard, H. L., & Armstrong, H. E. (1994). Interpersonal outcome of cognitive behavioral treatment for chronically suicidal borderline patients. *American Journal of Psychiatry, 151*(12), 1771–1776.

Links, P. S., Heslegrave, R., & van Reekum, R. (1999). Impulsivity: Core aspect of borderline personality disorder. *Journal of Personality Disorders, 13*, 1–9.

Liotti, G. (2000). Disorganized attachment, models of borderline states and evolutionary psychotherapy. In K. G. Bailey, & P. Gilbert (Eds.), *Genes on the couch: Explorations in evolutionary psychotherapy* (pp. 232–256). Brunner-Routledge.

Livesley, W. J., Jang, K. L., & Vernon, P. A. (1998). Phenotypic and genetic structure of traits delineating personality disorder. *Archives of General Psychiatry, 55*(10), 941–948.

Lyons-Ruth, K., Bronfman, E., & Parsons, E. (1999). Atypical attachment in infancy and early childhood among children at developmental risk. IV. Maternal frightened, frightening, or atypical behavior and disorganized infant attachment patterns. *Monographs of the Society for Research in Child Development, 64*(3), 67–96.

Lyons-Ruth, K., & Jacobvitz, D. (1999). Attachment disorganization: Unresolved loss, relational violence, and lapses in behavioral and attentional strategies. In J. Cassidy, & P. R. Shaver, *Handbook of attachment: Theory, research, and clinical application* (pp. 520–554). Guilford Press.

Main, M., & Solomon, J. (1986). Discovery of an insecure-disorganized/disoriented attachment pattern. In M. W. Yogman, & T. B. Brazelton (Eds.), *Affective development in infancy* (pp. 95–124). Ablex.

Main, M., & Westen, D. R. (1981). The quality of the toddler's relationship to mother and to father: Related to conflict behavior and the readiness to establish new relationships. *Child Development, 52*(3), 932–940.

Masterson, J. F. (1972). *Treatment of the borderline adolescent*. Wiley.

McCloskey, M. S., New, A. S., Siever, L. J., Goodman, M., Koenigsberg, H. W., Flory, J. D., & Coccaro, E. F. (2009). Evaluation of behavioral impulsivity and aggression tasks as endophenotypes for borderline personality disorder. *Journal of Psychiatric Research, 43*(12), 1036–1048.

McHugh, P. R. (2008). *Try to remember*. Dana Press.

McMain, S., Korman, L. M., & Dimeff, L. (2001). Dialectical behavior therapy and the treatment of emotion dysregulation. *Journal of Clinical Psychology, 57*(2), 183–196.

Nock, M. K. (2010). Self-injury. *Annual Review of Clinical Psychology, 6*, 339–363.

Nock, M. K., & Favazza, A. R. (2009). Nonsuicidal self-injury: Definition and classification. In M. K. Nock (Ed.), *Understanding nonsuicidal self-injury: Origins, assessment, and treatment* (pp. 9–18). American Psychological Association.

Nock, M. K., Wedig, M. M., Janis, I. B., & Deliberto, T. L. (2008). Self-injurious thoughts and behaviors. In J. Hunsley, & E. J. Mash (Ed.), *A guide to Assessments that work* (pp. 158–177). Oxford University Press.

Paris, J., & Zweig-Frank, H. (2001). The 27-year follow-up of patients with borderline personality disorder. *Comprehensive Psychiatry, 42*(6), 482–487.

Peters, J. R., Smart, L. M., & Baer, R. A. (2015). Dysfunctional responses to emotion mediate the cross-sectional relationship between rejections sensitivity and borderline personality features. *Journal of Personality Disorders, 29*(2), 231–240.

Plomin, R. (2019). *Blueprint: How DNA makes us who we are.* MIT Press.

Promislow, D., & Harvey, P. (1990). Living fast and dying young: A comparative analysis of life-history variation among mammals. *Journal of the Zoological Society of London, 220*, 417–437.

Reale, D., Grant, D., Humphries, M. M., Bergeron, P., Careau, V., & Montiglio, P. O. (2010). Personality and the emergence of the pace-of-life syndrome concept at the population level. *Philosophical Transactions of the Royal Society B, 365*, 4051–4063.

Reed, L. I., Best, C. K., & Hooley, J. M. (2018). Cooperation with characters: How a partner's personality disorder decreases cooperation in two economic games. *Personality and Individual Differences, 126*, 33–37.

Reed, L. I., Harrison, E. G., Best, C. K., & Hooley, J. M. (2019). Bargaining with characters: How personality pathology affects behavior in the ultimatum and dictator games. *Personality and Individual Differences, 140*, 65–69.

Reed, L. I., Meyer, A. K., Okun, S. J., Best, C. K., & Hooley, J. M. (2020). In smiles we trust? Smiling in the context of antisocial and borderline personality pathology. *PloS ONE, 15*(6), e0234574.

Rosval, L., Steiger, H., Bruce, K., Israel, M., Richardson, J., & Aubut, M. (2006). Impulsivity in women with eating disorders: Problem of response inhibition, planning, or attention? *International Journal of Eating Disorders, 39*, 590–593.

Runeson, B., & Beskow, J. (1991). Borderline personality disorder in young Swedish suicides. *Journal of Nervous and Mental Disease, 179*(3), 153–156.

Sadikaj, G., Moskowitz, D. S., Russell, J. J., Zuroff, D. C., & Paris, J. (2013). Quarrelsome behavior in borderline personality disorder: Influence of behavioral and affective reactivity to perceptions of others. *Journal of Abnormal Psychology, 122*(1), 195–207.

Salsman, N. L., & Linehan, M. M. (2012). An investigation of the relationships among negative affect, difficulties in emotion regulation, and features of borderline personality disorder. *Journal of Psychopathology and Behavioral Assessment, 34*(2), 260–267.

Salzman, J. P., Salzman, C., & Wolfson, A. N. (1997). Relationship of childhood abuse and maternal attachment to the development of borderline personality disorder. In M. Zanarini (Ed.), *Role of sexual abuse in the etiology of borderline persoanlity disorder* (pp. 71–91). American Psychiatric Association.

Sansone, R. A., Barnes, J., Muennich, E., & Wiederman, M. W. (2008). Borderline personality symptomatology and sexual impulsivity. *The International Journal of Psychiatry in Medicine, 38*(1), 53–60.

Sansone, R. A., Chu, J. W., & Wiederman, M. W. (2011). Sexual behaviour and borderline personality disorder among female psychiatric inpatients. *International Journal of Psychiatry in Clinical Practice, 15*(1), 69–73.

Scherer, K. R. (2000). Emotions as episodes of subsystems synchronization driven by nonlinear appraisal processes. In M. D. Lewis, & I. Granic, *Cambridge studies in social and emotional development. Emotion, development, and self-organization: Dynamic systems approaches to emotional development* (pp. 70–99). Cambridge University Press.

Scholmerich, A., Fracasso, M., Lamb, M., & Broberg, A. (1995). Interactional harmony at 7 and 10 months of age predicts security of attachment as measured by Q-sort ratings. *Social Development, 34*, 62–74.

Schulze, L., Domes, G., Kruger, A., Berger, C., Fleischer, M., Prehn, K., Schmahl, C., Grossmann, A., Hauenstein, K., & Herpertz, S. C. (2011). Neuronal correlates of cognitive reappraisal in borderline patients with affective instability. *Biological Psychiatry, 69*(6), 564–573.

Simpson, J. A., & Belsky, J. (2008). Attachment theory within a modern evolutionary framework. In J. Cassidy, & P. R. Shaver (Eds.), *Handbook of attachment: Theory, research, and clinical applications* (pp. 131–157). Guilford Press.

Skodol, A. E., Gunderson, J. G., Pfohl, B., Widiger, T. A., Livesley, W. J., & Siever, L. J. (2002). The borderline diagnosis I: Psychopathology, comorbidity, and personality structure. *Biological Psychiatry, 51*(12), 936–950.

Smith, P. B., & Pederson, D. R. (1988). Maternal sensitivity and patterns of infant-mother attachment. *Child Development, 59*, 1097–1101.

Snir, A., Rafaeli, E., Gadassi, R., Berenson, K., & Downey, G. (2015). Explicit and inferred motives for nonsuicidal self-injurious acts and urges in borderline and avoidant personality disorders. *Personality Disorder: Theory, Research, and Treatment, 6*(3), 267–277.

Soloff, P. H., Lis, J. A., Kelly, T., Cornelius, J., & Ulrich, R. (1994). Self-mutilation and suicidal behavior in borderline personality disorder. *Journal of Personality Disorders, 8*(4), 257–267.

Soloff, P. H., Lunch, K. G., Kelly, T. M., Malone, K. M., & Mann, J. J. (2000). Characteristics of suicide attempts of patietns with major depressive episode and borderline personality disorder: A comparative study. *American Journal of Psychiatry, 157*, 601–608.

Stern, A. (1938). Psychoanalytic investigation of and therapy in the borderline group of neuroses. *Psychoanalytic Quarterly, 7*, 467–489.

Stevenson, J., Meares, R., & Comerford, A. (2003). Diminished impulsivity in older patients with borderline personality disorder. *American Journal of Psychiatry, 160*(1), 165–166.

Stiglmayr, C. E., Grathwol, T., Linehan, M. M., Ihorst, G., Fahrenberg, J., & Bohus, M. (2005). Aversive tension in patients with borderline personality disorder: A computer based controlled field study. *Acta Psychiatrica Scandinavica, 111*(5), 372–379.

Sznycer, D., Cosmides, L., & Tooby, J. (2017). Adaptationism carves emotions at their functional joints. *Psychological Inquiry, 28*(1), 56–62.

Tomkins, S. S. (1962). *Affect, imagery, and consciousness*, Vol 1: *The positive affects*. Springer.

Tooby, J., & Cosmides, L. (1990). The past explains the present: Emotional adaptations and the structure of ancestral environments. *Ethology and Sociobiology, 11*(4–5), 375–424.

Tooby, J., & Cosmides, L. (2008). The evolutionary psychology of the emotions and their relationship to internal regulatory variables. In M. Lewis, J. M. Haviland-Jones, & L. F. Barrett (Eds.), *Handbook of emotions* (pp. 114–137). Guilford Press.

Torgersen, S., Kringlen, E., & Cramer, V. (2001). The prevalence of personality disorders in a community sample. *Archives of General Psychiatry, 58*(6), 590–596.

Torgersen, S., Lygren, S., Oien, P. A., Skre, I., Onstad, S., Edvardsen, J., Tambs, K., & Kringlen, E. (2000). A twin study of personality disorders. *Comprehensive Psychiatry, 41*(6), 416–425.

Torgersen, S., Myers, J., Reichborn-Kjennerud, T., Roysamb, E., Kubarych, T. S., & Kendler, K. S. (2012). The heritability of cluster B personality disorders assessed both by personal interview and questionnaire. *Journal of Personality Disorders, 26*, 848–866.

Tritt, K., Nickel, C., Lahmann, C., Leiberich, P. K., Rother, W. K., Loew, T. H., & Nickel, M. K. (2005). Lamotrigine treatment of aggression in female borderline patients: A randomized, double-blind, placebo-controlled study. *Journal of Psychopharmacology, 19*, 287–291.

Trull, T. J., Jahng, S., Tomko, R. L., Wood, P. K., & Sher, K. J. (2010). Revised NESARC personality disorder diagnoses: Gender, prevalence, and comorbidity with substance dependence disorders. *Journal of Personality Disorders, 24*(4), 412–426.

Trull, T. J., Sher, K. J., Minks-Brown, C., Durbin, J., & Burr, R. (2000). Borderline personality disorder and substance use disorders: A review and integration. *Clinical Psychology Review, 20*(2), 235–253.

Trull, T. J., Solhan, M. B., Tragesser, S. L., Jahng, S., Wood, P. K., Piasecki, T. M., & Watson, D. (2008). Affective instability: Measuring a core feature of borderline personality disorder with ecological momentary assessment. *Journal of Abnormal Psychology, 117*(3), 647.

Twenge, J. M., Catanese, K. R., & Baumeister, R. F. (2003). Social exclusion and the deconstructed state: Time perception, meaninglessness, lethargy, lack of emotion, and self-awareness. *Journal of Personality and Social Psychology, 85*(3), 409–423.

Unoka, Z., Seres, I., Aspan, N., Bodi, N., & Keri, S. (2009). Trust game reveals restricted interpersonal transactions in patients with borderline personality disorder. *Journal of Personality Disorders, 23*(4), 399–409.

Volker, K. A., Spitzer, C., Limberg, A., Grabe, H. J., Freyberger, H. J., & Barnow, S. (2009). Executive dysfunctions in female patietns with borderline personality disorder with regard to impulsiveness and depression. *Psychotherapie, Psychosomatik, Medizinische Psychologie, 59*(7), 264–272.

Vondra, J., Shaw, D., & Kevinides, M. (1995). Predicting infant attachment classification from multiple, contemporaneous measures of maternal care. *Infant Behavior and Development, 18*, 415–425.

Webb, D., & McMurran, M. (2008). Emotional intelligence, alexithymia, and borderline personality disorder traits in young adults. *Personality and Mental Health, 2*, 265–273.

Weigelt, K., & Camerer, C. (1988). Reputation and corporate strategy: A review of recent theory and applications. *Strategic Management Journal, 9*(5), 443–454.

Weinfield, N. S., Sroufe, L. A., Egeland, B., & Carlson, E. A. (1999). The nature of individual differences in infant-caregiver attachment. In J. Cassidy, & P. R. Shaver (Eds.), *Handbook of attachment: Theory, research, and clinical applications* (pp. 68–88). Guilford Press.

Welch, S. S., & Linehan, M. M. (2002). High-risk situations associated with parasuicide and drug use in borderline personality disorder. *Journal of Personality Disorders, 16*(6), 561–569.

White, C. N., Gunderson, J. G., Zanarini, M. C., & Hudson, J. I. (2003). Family studies of borderline personality disorder: A review. *Harvard Review of Psychiatry, 11*(1), 8–19.

Widiger, T. A., & Weissman, M. M. (1991). Epidemiology of borderline personality disorder. *Psychiatric Services, 42*(10), 1015–1021.

Wilkinson-Ryan, T., & Westen, D. (2000). Identity disturbance in borderline personality disorder: An empirical investigation. *American Journal of Psychiatry, 157*(4), 528–541.
Williams, G. C. (1966). *Adaptation and natural selection: A critique of some current evolutionary thought.* Princeton University Press.
Wolf, M., van Doorn, G. S., Leimar, O., & Weissing, F. J. (2007). Life-history trade-offs favour the evolution of animal personalities. *Nature, 447,* 581–585.
Zanarini, M. C. (1993). Borderline personality disorder as an impulse spectrum disorder. In J. Paris (Ed.), *Borderline Personality Disorder: Etiology and Treatment* (pp. 67–85). American Psychiatric Press.
Zanarini, M. C. (2018). *In the fullness of time: Recovery from borderline personality disorder.* Oxford University Press.
Zanarini, M. C., Frankenburg, F. R., Reich, D. B., & Fitzmaurice, G. (2012). Attainment and stability of sustained symptomatic remission and recovery among patients with borderline personality disorder and axis II comparison subjects: A 16-year prospective follow-up study. *American Journal of Psychiatry, 169*(5), 476–483.
Zanarini, M. C., Frankenburg, F. R., Reich, D. B., Silk, K. R., Hudson, J. I., & McSweeney, L. B. (2007). The subsyndromal phenomenology of borderline personality disorder: A 10-year follow-up study. *American Journal of Psychiatry, 164*(6), 929–935.

CHAPTER 66

An Evolutionary Perspective on Psychopathy

Virgil Zeigler-Hill and Gracynn R. Young

> **Abstract**
> Psychopathy refers to a constellation of personality traits that includes a willingness to deceive or manipulate others, impulsiveness, and a lack of empathy and guilt. Further, psychopathy is characterized by the tendency to violate basic social norms by engaging in behaviors that are selfish, aggressive, and harmful to others. There has been considerable debate in the literature concerning whether psychopathy represents a form of psychopathology or if it is better conceptualized as part of an alternative life-history strategy that is evolutionarily adaptive. The purpose of this chapter is to review the evidence and arguments regarding both of these perspectives, and to attempt to integrate these perspectives whenever it is possible to do so. The chapter will conclude with suggestions for future research that may help to resolve this debate.
>
> **Key Words:** psychopathy, empathy, guilt, selfishness, disorder

An Evolutionary Perspective on Psychopathy

Psychopathy is a construct that has important implications for our understanding of human behavior. The modern conceptualization of psychopathy was first described in the classic book *The Mask of Sanity* (Cleckley, [1941] 1976), but similar conditions involving antisocial behaviors have been identified dating as far back as the 1700s (e.g., *manie sans délire*, moral insanity, moral imbecility, degenerate constitution, congenital delinquency, constitutional inferiority, psychopathic taint; see Ogloff, 2006, for an extended discussion). These conditions have led to considerable debate regarding the nature of antisocial behavior and whether these conditions should be considered mental disorders. This issue has emerged again during recent years, with some scholars arguing that psychopathy should not be considered to be a form of psychopathology. These arguments often focus on the idea that psychopathy may actually reflect an alternative life-history strategy that is evolutionarily adaptive, rather than constituting a mental disorder. The purpose of the present chapter is to review the evidence and arguments regarding this issue and attempt to integrate different perspectives whenever it is possible to do so.

What Is Psychopathy?

Psychopathy refers to a complex set of personality traits that are characterized by selfishness, deceitfulness, recklessness, and a lack of concern for the welfare of others (see Patrick, 2018, for a review). Psychopathy is characterized by a disregard for social norms, as evidenced by its associations with a wide variety of aversive attitudes and behaviors, such as those involving physical aggression (e.g., Cornell et al., 1996; Jones & Paulhus, 2010; Reidy et al., 2007), sexual aggression (e.g., Hersh & Gray-Little, 1998; Knight & Guay, 2018; Kosson et al., 1997; Mokros et al., 2011), lying (e.g., DePaulo & Rosenthal, 1979; Hare, 1980; Lykken, 1995), and cheating (e.g., Coyne & Thomas, 2008; Nathanson et al., 2006). Psychopathy has been shown to emerge relatively early during the course of development and to remain relatively stable throughout adulthood (e.g., Kubak & Salekin, 2009; Lee et al., 2010; Lynam et al., 2007; Lynam & Gudonis, 2005).

The connections that psychopathy has with aversive attitudes and behaviors may be explained, at least in part, by the affective abnormalities that characterize it. For example, psychopathy is associated with difficulties in the processing of various sorts of emotional stimuli (e.g., Anderson et al., 2017; Blair et al., 2005; Hare & Neumann, 2008; Hoppenbrouwers et al., 2016; Meloy, 1988; Patrick et al., 2009). The basic idea is that psychopathy may interfere with the ability to experience, recognize, and learn from emotional cues such as fear, stress, and sadness (e.g., Hare, 2003; Lykken, 1995). In addition, psychopathy is characterized by a reduction in the range and depth of other emotional experiences, including social emotions such as guilt, shame, and embarrassment (e.g., Harenski et al., 2014). This is important because these social emotions promote cooperative behaviors and discourage various forms of antisocial behaviors that may have short-term benefits but often involve substantial long-term costs (e.g., reputational damage; Barkow, 1989; Walsh & Wu, 2008). Psychopathy has also been shown to be associated with difficulties in identifying social emotions in others, including less accuracy regarding the likelihood that certain events would lead someone else to experience either guilt or shame (Djeriouat & Trémolière, 2020).

Although it is sometimes argued that psychopathy is characterized by a complete lack of emotion, this view does not appear to be supported by the available evidence. For example, it has been argued that psychopathy may actually be associated with experiencing *higher* levels of negative emotions that are directed toward other individuals (Lynam & Widiger, 2007; Meloy, 1988). Consistent with this possibility, psychopathy has been found to be associated with other-directed emotions such as anger (Hoppenbrouwers et al., 2016; Jackson et al., 2007; Kosson et al., 2016) and contempt (Garofalo et al., 2019). It has also been suggested that issues concerning shame—such as the avoidance of shame—may play an important role in understanding psychopathy (Campbell & Ellison, 2005; Holmqvist, 2008; Morrison & Gilbert, 2001; Nyström & Mikkelsen, 2013). For example, psychopathy has been shown to be associated with responses to potentially shame-inducing events that involve heightened experiences of anger (Morrison & Gilbert, 2001), as well as attempts to attribute the blame for these events to an external source such as another person (Campbell & Elison, 2005).

Another approach for understanding psychopathy has focused on its cognitive features, such as its association with difficulties in focusing attention on the most salient cues for certain events (e.g., Koenigs & Newman, 2013). For example, individuals with high levels of psychopathy tend to have difficulty recognizing certain facial expressions (e.g., fear, sadness) because they often fail to pay attention to the most important areas of the face for detecting these emotions (i.e., regions around the eyes and mouth; Dadds et al., 2006; Dawel et al., 2012). However, the difficulties with associative learning that characterize psychopathy are not limited to affect-related stimuli because these issues also emerge for other types of stimuli (e.g., Larson et al., 2013). It should be noted that these difficulties are significantly reduced when individuals with high levels of psychopathy are directed to attend to the appropriate cues (e.g., Koenigs & Newman, 2013; Larson et al., 2013).

Is Psychopathy a Mental Disorder?
The issue of whether psychopathy should be considered a mental disorder has received considerable attention during recent years (e.g., Jurjako, 2019; Krupp et al., 2012, 2013; Lalumiere et al., 2001; Münch et al., 2020; Nadelhoffer & Sinnott-Armstrong, 2013). This specific debate takes place within the context of broader discussions regarding the nature of mental disorders more generally and how they should be defined (e.g., Boorse, 1976; Gorenstein, 1984; Wakefield, 1992; Widiger & Trull, 1985). Mental disorders are defined in the *Diagnostic and Statistical Manual of Mental Disorders* (DSM-5; American Psychiatric Association [APA], 2013) as:

> a syndrome characterized by clinically significant disturbance in an individual's cognition, emotion regulation, or behavior that reflects a dysfunction in the psychological, biological, or developmental processes underlying mental functioning. Mental disorders are usually associated with significant distress or disability in social, occupational, or other important activities. An expectable or culturally approved response to a common stressor or loss, such as the death of a loved one, is not a mental disorder. Socially deviant behavior (e.g. political, religious, or sexual) and conflicts that are primarily between the individual and society are not mental disorders unless the deviance or conflict results from a dysfunction in the individual, as described above. (p. 20)

As noted by Münch et al. (2020), this definition for mental disorders involves a dysfunction in the psychological processes of the individual that is usually associated with harm for the individual in terms of distress or disability.

The definition for a mental disorder adopted by the DSM-5 is similar to—but distinct from—the highly influential concept of *harmful dysfunction* (Wakefield, 1992), which argues that mental disorders must involve harm to the individual that is produced by a psychological mechanism no longer serving its evolved function. Wakefield (1992) argued that making *both* "harm" (a value term) and "dysfunction" (a scientific and factual term) necessary components of the definition for a mental disorder avoids some definitional problems. For example, other definitions for mental disorders that focus exclusively on harm may be at risk of pathologizing behaviors that are not socially valued, whereas definitions that focus exclusively on dysfunction may be so broad as to include any sort of deviation from the scientifically defined standard, even if these deviations do not involve any actual harm to the individual. However, it is important to note that the DSM-5 definition for mental disorders differs from the harmful dysfunction definition in two important ways. First, the DSM-5 definition says that mental disorders are "usually associated with" harm (i.e., significant distress or disability), which means that harm is not actually *required*. This is a departure from earlier editions of the DSM (i.e., DSM-III-R [APA, 1987], DSM-IV [APA, 1994], and DSM-IV-TR [APA, 2000]), which included harm as a necessary element of the definition (see Amoretti & Lalumera, 2019, for an extended discussion of this issue). Second, the DSM-5 does not specify that the dysfunction has to involve a failure of the psychological process to serve its *evolved function*, which is central to the concept of harmful dysfunction proposed by Wakefield (1992). These definitional distinctions will be important for considering whether psychopathy should be considered a form of psychopathology.

It is important to clarify the actual current standing of psychopathy as a mental disorder before considering whether it *should* be considered a mental disorder. There has been considerable confusion surrounding the term *psychopathy*, which has led to it often being used interchangeably with *antisocial personality disorder* (ASPD).[1] Despite the tendency for scholars to sometimes conflate these terms, they refer to distinct—but related—constructs. This is an important issue because psychopathy is not considered to be a mental disorder in either the

DSM-5, which is the most commonly used diagnostic system in the United States, or the *International Statistical Classification of Diseases and Health Related Problems* (ICD-10; World Health Organization [WHO], 2004), which is the most commonly used diagnostic system outside of the United States. Thus, calls to *remove* psychopathy as a psychiatric diagnosis are somewhat misguided because it is not currently included in diagnostic manuals.

In contrast to psychopathy, ASPD is actually a diagnosis that is included in the DSM-5. More specifically, ASPD is described as "a pervasive pattern of disregard for and violation of the rights of others, occurring since age 15 years" (APA, 2013, p. 659). The DSM-5 relies on a polythetic criteria set and requires individuals to meet three or more of the following criteria in order to be assigned an ASPD diagnosis:

(1) Failure to conform to social norms with respect to lawful behaviors, as indicated by repeatedly performing acts that are grounds for arrest; (2) Deceitfulness, as indicated by repeated lying, use of aliases, or conning others for personal profit or pleasure; (3) Impulsivity or failing to plan ahead; (4) Irritability and aggressiveness, as indicated by repeated physical fights or assaults; (5) Reckless disregard for safety of self or others; (6) Consistent irresponsibility, as indicated by repeated failure to sustain consistent work behavior or honor financial obligations; (7) Lack of remorse, as indicated by being indifferent to or rationalizing having hurt, mistreated, or stolen from another. (APA, 2013, p. 659)

In addition, the DSM-5 specifies that the individual must be at least 18 years old, must have shown evidence of conduct disorder prior to age 15, and the antisocial behaviors must not be occuring exclusively during the course of schizophrenic or bipolar disorder.

Psychopathy clearly has similarities with ASPD, but there are also important distinctions (e.g., Crego & Widiger, 2015). For example, the prevalence estimates for psychopathy and ASPD are subtantially different in incarcerated samples, with about 15%–20% of prisoners meeting the criteria to be classified as "psychopaths" using certain assessment tools, whereas diagnoses of ASPD among prisoners can be as high as 80% (e.g., Hare et al., 1991). This pattern is consistent with the observation that ASPD has much closer ties to criminal behavior than is the case for psychopathy. Also, psychopathy has been found to have clearer links with neurological functioning (especially in the paralimbic system and the prefrontal cortex) than is the case for ASPD (e.g., Blair, 2007, 2008; Kiehl, 2006).

Another issue that distinguishes psychopathy from ASPD is its structure. More specifically, an array of studies and meta-analyses have clearly demonstrated that psychopathy is a *dimensional* construct rather than a *categorical* construct (e.g., Edens et al., 2006; Guay et al., 2007; Hare & Neumann, 2008; Marcus et al., 2004; Walters et al., 2015; Walters, Gray, et al., 2007).[2] This means that psychopathy exists on a continuum, with no clear boundaries separating "psychopaths" from "non-psychopaths" (e.g., Lilienfeld, 2013; Marcus et al., 2011). As a result, any dividing lines are somewhat arbitrary because individuals with high levels of psychopathy differ from other individuals as a matter of *degree* rather than as a matter of *kind* (Knight & Guay, 2018).

It may be tempting to dismiss the dimensional structure of psychopathy as merely being an academic issue that is of limited interest to anyone other than a select group of taxometric experts. However, the fact that psychopathy is a dimensional construct—rather than a categorical construct—has important implications for issues such as its potential causation (e.g., dimensional constructs are more likely to be the product of multiple factors rather than a single all-or-nothing causal factor), strategies for assessing psychopathy (e.g., it is important to use instruments that are sensitive to a broad range of variation when assessing dimensional constructs), sampling issues in research concerning psychopathy (e.g., it is important to include participants who represent a broad range of variation when dealing with dimensional constructs, rather than sampling from the extreme ends of the continuum), and data analytic strategies (e.g., analyzing data as continuous provides greater power than creating artificial groups based on arbitrary cutoffs when dealing with dimensional constructs; see Ruscio, 2011, for an extended discussion).

If psychopathy has a dimensional structure, then what sort of structure characterizes ASPD? ASPD is conceptualized as a categorical construct, which means that it should be similar to all-or-none constructs such as pregnancy (i.e., the condition of pregnancy is either present or absent, rather than being a matter of degree). That is, ASPD should reflect a difference in *kind* rather than *degree*. Although ASPD was intended to be a discrete condition, research has challenged this perspective by consistently showing that it is actually dimensional in nature, rather than possessing the expected categorical structure (Marcus et al., 2006; Marcus et al., 2008; Walters, Diamond, et al., 2007). That is, contrary to initial expectations, there is no clear qualitative shift that separates individuals who receive an ASPD diagnosis from those who do not receive the diagnosis. This issue is not limited to ASPD, as similar concerns have been raised about the broader use of categorical diagnoses that are often found throughout the various editions of the DSM and the ICD (e.g., First, 2005; Kraemer, 2007). These concerns about the categorical nature of many diagnoses—including personality disorders such as ASPD—have contributed to the inclusion of a new dimensional system in Section III ("Emerging Measures and Models") of the DSM-5 for conceptualizing and assessing personality pathology. The ICD-11 (WHO, 2018) also shifted away from its categorical system for personality disorders by including the severity of these disorders (i.e., mild, moderate, or severe) along with the use of particular traits and behaviors as specifiers (e.g., dissociality). The adoption of dimensional systems for understanding personality disorders is consistent with suggestions that have been made by many leading experts in this area of the literature (e.g., Hopwood et al., 2018; Krueger et al., 2011; Widiger & Trull, 2007).

Another issue that separates psychopathy from ASPD is that psychopathy clearly has a multidimensional structure (e.g., Coid et al., 2009; Cooke & Michie, 2001; Harpur et al., 1988; Sellbom et al., 2018; Skeem et al., 2011; Widiger & Lynam, 1998). There is still considerable debate concerning the best way to conceptualize the structure of psychopathy, but there is broad consensus that it is not a unidimensional construct. One of the most influential perspectives concerning the structure of psychopathy during the past decade is that it involves three basic personality traits: *meanness* (predatory exploitativeness, lack of empathy, and contempt for others); *disinhibition* (impulsiveness, difficulties with regulating emotions, and lack of restraint); and *boldness* (confidence, social assertiveness, and emotional resiliency; Patrick et al., 2009, 2012). Despite the appeal of this model, there are still questions regarding the extent to which each of these traits is important for our understanding of psychopathy, or if each trait needs to be present in order to adequately capture psychopathy. For example, it is widely accepted that meanness and disinhibition are likely to be essential elements for many conceptualizations of psychopathy (Crego & Widiger, 2015; Lynam & Miller, 2015; Lynam et al., 2018; Morgan et al., 2011; Poythress & Hall, 2011; Sellbom et al., 2018), but there has been a great deal of debate regarding what role—if any—boldness should have in the conceptualization of psychopathy (Lilienfeld, Smith, Sauvigné, et al., 2016; Lilienfeld, Smith, & Watts, 2016; Lilienfeld et al., 2018; Wall et al., 2015).

Issues concerning the multidimensional structure of psychopathy have important implications for the conceptualization of psychopathy. For example, psychopathy research often focuses on psychopathic traits separately, but it may be beneficial for future research to incorporate models that allow these traits to interact with each other (e.g., Lilienfeld, 1994; Lilienfeld

& Fowler, 2006; Patrick & Drislane, 2015; Sellbom et al., 2018; Skeem et al., 2011). If these psychopathic personality traits are viewed as distinct but synergistic aspects of psychopathy, then configural approaches may reveal that particular combinations of meanness, disinhibition, and boldness reflect different manifestations of psychopathy (e.g., meanness may have particularly aversive outcomes for other individuals when it is combined with disinhibition; Lilienfeld et al., 2018).

Concerns regarding the relative importance of meanness, disinhibition, and boldness for understanding psychopathy also extend to the diagnostic criteria for ASPD. For example, many of the diagnostic criteria in the DSM-5 could be interpreted as behavioral manifestations of either meanness (e.g., lack of remorse) or disinhibition (e.g., failure to plan ahead). Although meanness and disinhibition are both represented to at least some extent in the diagnostic criteria for ASPD, it is important to note that boldness is completely absent. As a consequence, individuals who are mean and disinhibited can easily receive an ASPD diagnosis regardless of whether they are bold or not. The fact that the diagnostic criteria for ASPD do not address boldness at all is one of the issues that clearly separates this diagnosis from the construct of psychopathy (e.g., Lilienfeld et al., 2018; Miller & Lynam, 2012; Murphy et al., 2016; Venables et al., 2014; Wall et al., 2015).

Does Psychopathy Involve Harm for the Individual?

As noted earlier, definitions for what constitutes a mental disorder often involve harm for the individual. The concept of harmful dysfunction proposed by Wakefield (1992) argues that harm is a necessary component for mental disorders, whereas the DSM-5 merely says that mental disorders are "usually associated with" harm in the form of significant distress or disability. This leads to the question of whether psychopathy actually involves harm for the individual. It has been suggested that psychopathy does not involve harm because individuals with elevated levels of psychopathy often report relatively low levels of distress about their condition and they rarely seek out treatment for their symptoms (e.g., Glenn et al., 2013; Hübner & White, 2016; Reid & Gacono, 2000; see Münch et al., 2020, for an extended discussion). In cases where individuals with elevated levels of psychopathy are distressed, it is often attributable to their conflicts with society (e.g., interactions with the criminal justice system) rather than being a direct product of their psychopathy.

It is certainly possible that the lack of a positive association between psychopathy and distress may indicate that psychopathy is not harmful to the individual. However, it is also possible that this lack of distress may actually be a manifestation of the underlying psychopathology since psychopathy is linked with weakened responses to certain types of stressors (e.g., Benning et al., 2005). Further, the idea of harm in the context of mental disorders extends beyond simply whether the individual is actually aware of being harmed (Graham, 2013). For example, individuals with elevated levels of psychopathic personality traits may experience harm in the sense that their ability to form deep and meaningful interpersonal relationships with others is impaired, even if they are unaware or unconcerned about these impairments. Of course, this issue is further complicated by the fact that assumptions regarding how individuals *should* live are almost always based on certain values (e.g., it is better to have deep and meaningful connections with others that involve mutual benefits than to have shallow and superficial relationships in which the goal is to manipulate and exploit others; Münch et al., 2020).

The question of whether psychopathy involves harm for the individual is still open for debate, but it is abundantly clear that psychopathy is harmful for others (see Reidy et al., 2015, for an extended discussion). In addition, nearly all of the diagnostic criteria for ASPD in DSM-5 can be interpreted as involving harm to others, or at least the potential for causing harm to others (APA, 2013). The extent to which a condition such as psychopathy leads to harm for others and creates conflict with society has led to the introduction of the concept of a *dangerous* dysfunction to serve as a complement to the existing concept of a *harmful* dysfunction (Malón, 2012). That is, some diagnoses—such as ASPD and pedophilic disorder—may actually be considered to be mental disorders because they are viewed as dangerous rather than harmful. However, the medical community may often be reluctant to acknowledge the role that perceived dangerousness plays in certain diagnoses because of the history of mental disorders being used to control certain members of society (e.g., Malón, 2012; Reich, 1991; Walker, 1994). If psychopathy is primarily harmful or dangerous to others, then it could be argued that it should be considered as something more akin to a *moral* disorder rather than a *mental* disorder in order to avoid the "medicalization" of vice-laden behaviors (e.g., Münch et al., 2020; Sadler, 2008).

Does Psychopathy Involve Dysfunction?

There are various ways to conceptualize whether a psychological process constitutes a dysfunction (e.g., Schramme, 2010). This is important because the DSM-5 uses the term "dysfunction" in its definition of mental disorders without restricting itself to a particular view of dysfunction. However, scholars involved in the debate concerning whether psychopathy should be considered a mental disorder often rely on the concept of harmful dysfunction, which explicitly argues that mental disorders involve psychological mechanisms that are no longer serving their *evolved* functions. Based on this perspective, psychopathy would not be a mental disorder if it was simply serving its evolved function. Of course, this raises the question: *Does psychopathy actually have an evolved function?* The following sections will review some of the possible evolved functions that have been offered for psychopathy.

Mating

Researchers who consider psychopathy from an evolutionary perspective have sometimes argued that it may actually have benefits with regard to biological fitness (e.g., Glenn et al., 2011; Mealey, 1995); that is, psychopathy may reflect an alternate life-history strategy that may provide individuals with some reproductive benefits—at least in the short term—rather than constituting a dysfunction (e.g., Book et al., 2019; Book & Quinsey, 2004; Glenn et al., 2011; Harris et al., 1994; Mealey, 1995; Seto et al., 1997). This perspective suggests that one possible evolved function of psychopathy is that it may facilitate the use of exploitative short-term mating strategies (Barr & Quinsey, 2004; Crawford & Salmon, 2002; Jonason et al., 2009; Mealey, 1995; Raine, 1993). Consistent with this possibility, psychopathy has been found to be associated with various aspects of sexual behavior, including an earlier onset of sexual activity (Harris et al., 2007; Međedović, 2019), a greater number of sexual partners over the life span (Lalumière & Quinsey, 1996), and a focus on short-term mating that involves a preference for sexual relationships with relatively low levels of commitment (e.g., Jonason & Kavanagh, 2010; Jonason et al., 2009; Jonason et al., 2010; Međedović, 2019; Visser et al., 2015). Further, psychopathy is associated with attitudes and behaviors that are connected with sexual coercion (e.g., Lalumiere & Quinsey, 1996; Rice et al., 1990; Rowe, 1996). These results are certainly consistent with the possibility that psychopathy may promote the use of exploitative short-term mating strategies, but the exact nature of this connection remains unclear. For example, it is possible that shared antecedents—such as exposure to harsh or unpredictable socioecological conditions during the earliest years of life—may account, at least in part, for the connection between psychopathy and the use of exploitative short-term mating strategies.

Research has provided clear and consistent evidence that individuals with high levels of psychopathy invest considerable effort in obtaining short-term mating opportunities (e.g., Jonason et al., 2011). However, relatively few studies have examined whether this heightened mating effort translates into reproductive success in the modern environment as captured by the actual number of offspring produced during the course of a lifetime. The few studies that have directly examined this issue have revealed conflicting results, with some studies finding positive associations between certain psychopathic personality traits and number of offspring (Harris et al., 2007; Međedović et al., 2017; Neumann et al., 2012), whereas other studies have found *negative* associations (Carter et al., 2018; Međedović et al., 2017). The inconsistency of these results across studies may be due to the different conceptualizations of psychopathy that have been employed. For example, Međedović et al. (2017) found that psychopathic traits involving an egocentric focus and the tendency to manipulate others were *positively* associated with number of offspring, whereas psychopathic traits concerning impulsivity and a lack of responsibility were *negatively* associated with number of offspring. This suggests that additional research will be necessary to provide a clearer and more nuanced understanding of the associations that particular psychopathic personality traits have with reproductive success.

One intriguing possibility is that the connections that psychopathic personality traits have with reproductive success may depend on environmental conditions, with certain psychopathic traits being most beneficial when conditions are harsh or unpredictable (e.g., Međedović, 2019; Međedović et al., 2017). This possibility is consistent with life-history theory, which argues that it may be advantageous for individuals to focus on strategies that emphasize risk-taking, instant gratification, and the discounting of future outcomes when they are operating in harsh or unpredictable environments (e.g., Figueredo et al., 2006; Mealey, 1995). Of course, it is also possible that psychopathy may have promoted reproductive success in ancestral environments but that certain aspects of the modern environment disrupt the reproductive benefits of psychopathic personality traits.

Cheating

Another possible evolved function of psychopathy is that it may represent a cheater strategy that involves exploiting the cooperation of others for personal gain (e.g., Book & Quinsey, 2004; Harpending & Sobus, 1987; Mealey, 1995). In essence, individuals with elevated levels of psychopathy may take advantage of the majority of the population who engage in pro-social and cooperative activities. This perspective would be consistent with arguments that individuals with high levels of psychopathy are essentially *social predators* who exploit and manipulate others for their own benefit, using strategies such as deception and coercion (e.g., Meloy et al., 2018). Cheating others by exploiting their cooperative tendencies would have at least short-term benefits since individuals would be reaping the benefits of these social exchanges without incurring the costs that are involved with reciprocation. Research has consistently demonstrated that psychopathy is associated with outcomes connected to cheating, such as the tendency to use deception (Jonason et al., 2014; Seto et al., 1997), the willingness to exploit and manipulate others (Jonason & Webster, 2012; Mealey, 1995), and the tendency to be involved in various forms of antisocial or criminal behaviors (e.g., Skeem & Cooke, 2010).

Many aspects of psychopathy would seem to be beneficial for an evolutionary strategy that is focused on cheating or exploiting others. For example, psychopathic characteristics such as abnormal startle potentiation, reduced autonomic reactions to the distress experienced by others, dampening of neural and hormonal mechanisms involved in social emotions (e.g., guilt, shame), and perseveration of goal-directed activities despite changing circumstances should make it easier for individuals with psychopathic tendencies to pursue strategies that involve cheating, as well as make it more difficult for others to detect these cheating behaviors (e.g., Glenn & Raine, 2009; Mealey, 1995; Walsh & Wu, 2008). Consistent with the possibility that psychopathy may reflect an evolved strategy, it appears that there are some constraints on psychopathic cheating behavior such that individuals with elevated levels of psychopathy often direct most of their aversive behaviors toward non-relatives and minimize their exploitation of genetic relatives (e.g., Krupp et al., 2012).

It is important to note that psychopathy potentially serving an evolved "cheating" function does not necessarily conflict with the possibility that it serves a "short-term mating" function. Rather, it is possible that the exploitative short-term mating strategies that tend to characterize individuals with elevated levels of psychopathy are simply specific examples of a broader tendency to exploit the cooperation of others. This view is consistent with the perspective that the sorts of traits that promote various sorts of cheating behaviors may have actually been selected during the course of evolution *because* of their connection with exploitative short-term mating strategies (e.g., Rowe, 1996).

Cheater-Hawk

The possibility that psychopathy may represent a cheater strategy provides a potential explanation for many of the attitudes and behaviors that characterize psychopathy, but it does not provide a clear explanation for the aggressive behaviors that are often associated with psychopathy. For example, psychopathy has been found to be associated with various forms of aggression (e.g., Cima & Raine, 2009; Flight & Forth, 2007; Reidy et al., 2007) including particularly strong associations with *instrumental aggression*, which refers to the use of aggression to achieve goals such as obtaining resources or gaining status (e.g., Glenn & Raine, 2009; von Borries et al., 2012; Walsh et al., 2009). This pattern suggests that psychopathy may be most closely aligned with the use of aggression for self-benefit, rather than as a reaction to certain forms of provocation. This suggests that psychopathy may be linked to two separate interpersonal strategies (i.e., cheating and aggression) that may both be potentially adaptive. This recognition led to the development of the "cheater-hawk" explanation of psychopathy (Book & Quinsey, 2004), which argues that psychopathy may promote the manipulation and exploitation of others (cheater strategy) as well as the use of violence or aggression to achieve various interpersonal goals (hawk strategy). This basic idea has received support in studies showing that psychopathy is associated with various forms of both cheating and aggression (e.g., Book et al., 2019; Book & Quinsey, 2004; Coyne & Thomas, 2008).

Although there are clearly short-term benefits associated with the cheater-hawk social strategy, it is important to note that this strategy is associated with a number of important long-term costs, including reputational damage, limited opportunities for cooperation with others, loss of future resources (that would stem, in part, from reputational damage and limited interactions with others), and retaliatory physical harm that may result from the use of aggression (see Book et al., 2019, for an extended discussion). This perspective suggests that psychopathic cheater-hawk strategies can be supported as long as the short-term benefits of cheating others and behaving aggressively toward them outweigh the long-term costs of those behaviors. One possibility is that individuals with elevated levels of psychopathic personality features may attempt to avoid the repercussions of their behaviors by remaining highly mobile (e.g., exploiting individuals in one place and then moving to another location before those individuals realize that they have been exploited; Glenn et al., 2011).

Selfishness
The final possibility that we will consider is that the evolved function of psychopathy is to promote selfishness and personal gain in social interactions. In general, selfishness refers to prioritizing one's own welfare without regard for the consequences of others (e.g., Raine & Uh, 2019). Selfishness is often considered in evolutionary explanations of social behavior (e.g., cooperation; Fehr & Gächter, 2002) and there are clear links between psychopathy and selfishness (Raine & Uh, 2019; Sonne & Gash, 2018). For example, individuals with high levels of psychopathy have been found to engage in more selfish behaviors when performing social tasks, which often results in them accruing more resources than others (Mokros et al., 2008; Rilling et al., 2007; cf. Widom, 1976). This suggests that psychopathy may allow individuals to maximize their own benefits in short-term encounters. It is possible that the lack of stable personal relationships that often characterizes psychopathy may tend to facilitate selfishness by preventing their interactions with others from lasting long enough for those individuals to recognize the extent of their selfishness (e.g., Mokros et al., 2008).

The selfish behaviors that characterize psychopathy often focus on maximizing the difference between themselves and others in their immediate social environment (e.g., Mokros et al., 2008). This suggests that psychopathy may be characterized by selfishness as well as *spitefulness*, which concerns the willingness of individuals to incur costs in order to inflict harm on others (Marcus et al., 2014). The tendency to engage in spiteful behaviors can evolve if these costs are imposed on *negative relatives* (i.e., individuals who are unlikely to bear copies of the alleles that are associated with the behavior) because this decreases the reproductive success of rival alleles that are housed in the bodies of those individuals (Gardner & West, 2004; Hamilton, 1970); that is, it is possible for natural selection to favor behavioral patterns such as spitefulness that involve costs to direct fitness as long as the indirect fitness benefits outweigh these costs (e.g., reducing the fitness of rivals; Hamilton, 1964, 1970). This suggests the intriguing possibility that individuals with high levels of psychopathy may behave selfishly when doing so provides them with direct fitness benefits, but they may also behave spitefully in situations where they are able to impose significant harm on others despite incurring some direct costs themselves (see Krupp et al., 2012, for an extended discussion). Consistent with this possibility, there is evidence that psychopathy is associated with spitefulness (e.g., Garofalo et al., 2019; Marcus et al., 2014; Zeigler-Hill et al., 2020) and that it may be associated with an increased likelihood of inflicting harm on non-relatives (Krupp et al., 2012).

How Does Psychopathy Persist in the Population?
Psychopathic personality traits are dimensional such that individuals differ in the extent to which they possess these traits; that is, psychopathic personality traits tend to follow the typical inverted-U distribution, with most individuals having somewhat moderate levels of these traits and relatively few individuals having either extremely high or extremely low levels of these traits. How do evolutionary explanations account for the persistence of heritable variation in these psychopathic traits? Some of the possible explanations include mechanisms such as *balancing selection* (selection actually maintaining variation in psychopathy because it offers fitness advantages in specific environments) and *contingent shifts* (psychopathic traits serving as adaptive responses to specific environmental conditions such as harshness and unpredictability during childhood; e.g., Glenn et al., 2011). One possibility is that psychopathy may be maintained due to a specific form of balancing selection known as *negative frequency-dependent selection*, which refers to certain traits being favored as long as they are rare in frequency. The basic argument is that the benefits connected with psychopathy—such as being selfish and exploiting others—would depend on the prevalence of psychopathy in a population (e.g.,

Mealey, 1995); that is, high levels of psychopathy may be beneficial if the environment consists largely of cooperators, but the benefits of psychopathy would begin to wane if its prevalence rate was too high because there would be fewer cooperators to potentially exploit. This is an interesting potential explanation for the persistence of variability in psychopathy across generations, but there remains little direct evidence to support this possibility at the present time.

Another variant of balancing selection that is due to *environmental heterogeneity* may provide a more likely explanation for the sustained variability in psychopathy. The idea is that variability in traits can be maintained within a population if the trait has different fitness consequences across different contexts, as long as the average fitness consequences are nearly neutral when all relevant contexts are considered (e.g., Bürger, 2000; Penke et al., 2007; Roff, 1997; Turelli & Barton, 2004). This perspective has led to the argument that balancing selection by environmental heterogeneity may be one of the most plausible mechanisms for maintaining genetic variation in personality traits in general (e.g., Penke et al., 2007). This explanation may also apply to psychopathic personality traits in particular because these traits may provide a net fitness benefit to individuals in harsh or unpredictable environments where it may pay to exploit others, but the same traits may actually lead to long-term fitness costs in safer and more stable environments where cooperation with recurring social partners provides greater dividends over time. However, more research is needed to understand the role that environmental heterogeneity may play in sustaining the variability in psychopathic traits.

The contingent shift explanation for psychopathy involves the possibility that psychopathic personality traits may be adaptive responses to particular environmental conditions (e.g., Glenn et al., 2011). This explanation is consistent with the observation that organisms often possess mechanisms that allow them to adjust their strategies for resolving particular trade-offs (e.g., mating effort vs. parental effort) based on environmental cues during the course of development (e.g., a safe and stable environment vs. a harsh and unpredictable environment; Belsky et al., 1991; Del Guidice et al., 2011; Ellis et al., 2006; West-Eberhard, 2003). In essence, psychopathy may serve as a conditional adaptation that alters the course of development in order to prepare the individual for living in a particular environment (e.g., Del Guidice et al., 2011). For example, it is possible that exposure to highly stressful environments during the earliest years of life may contribute to increased levels of psychopathy (e.g., Del Giudice et al., 2013; Glenn et al., 2011; Patch & Figueredo, 2017).

The contingent shift explanation is supported by various studies showing that harsh or unpredictable conditions during childhood are often associated with the development of psychopathic personality traits (e.g., Auty et al., 2015; Gao et al., 2010; McCrory et al., 2012; Mealey, 1995; Salekin & Lochman, 2008). The basic argument is that psychopathy may promote behaviors that are beneficial in harsh and upredictable environments, such as increased risk-taking, a focus on short-term benefits, and the prioritization of mating effort over parental effort (e.g., Ellis & Del Giudice, 2019; Glenn et al., 2011; Jonason et al., 2016; Mealey, 1995; Neumann et al., 2012; Patch & Figueredo, 2017). Further, the lack of concern for the welfare for others and lower stress reactivity may increase both the resilience and perceived formidability of individuals with psychopathic personality traits (e.g., da Silva et al., 2015; Del Giudice et al., 2011). To put it another way, psychopathic personality traits may be viewed as a strategy that allows individuals to "survive and thrive" in harsh and unpredictable environments (e.g., da Silva et al., 2019; Ellis & Del Giudice, 2019).

Should Psychopathy Be Considered a Mental Disorder?

Our perspective is that there are reasonable concerns about whether psychopathy should be considered a form of psychopathology. However, we believe there are still so many unanswered questions regarding psychopathy that it may be premature to draw any firm conclusions. For example, it is quite possible that psychopathy may only involve harm to others, but not to the individual. If that is the case, then it certainly weakens the argument that psychopathy should be considered a form of psychopathology. However, it is important to note that the absence of observed distress among those with elevated levels of psychopathy does not necessarily indicate they are not experiencing any sort of harm. Rather, their lack of concern about certain impairments (e.g., difficulties in forming deep and meaningful connections with others) could potentially be interpreted as a manifestation of their psychopathology, depending on how issues surrounding harm and subjective distress are incorporated into the definition of psychopathology. Additional research concerning the potential harm experienced by those with elevated levels of psychopathy is needed in order to gain a better understanding of this issue.

We are also uncertain as to whether psychopathy constitutes a dysfunction. There has been a great deal of theorizing concerning the possible evolved function of psychopathy. These potential functions include exploitative short-term mating, cheating, a blend of cheating and aggression, and selfishness. Although this speculation is certainly intriguing, the existing evidence is still too weak to draw any firm conclusions about whether psychopathy actually has an evolved function, or what that evolved function may be.

The harmful dysfunction concept proposed by Wakefield (1992) has been influential when considering how to define mental disorders, but this approach has also received considerable criticism (e.g., Fulford & Thornton, 2007; Lilienfeld & Marino, 1995; Murphy & Woolfolk, 2001a, 2001b; Schramme, 2010). Perhaps the most important criticism is that it is often exceptionally challenging to clearly establish whether a psychological process actually has an evolved function. This is an important issue because it is often quite difficult to determine whether a psychological process is a direct adaptation or may be better understood as a *spandrel* (i.e., a byproduct of other adaptations) or an *exaptation* (i.e., a process that originally evolved for one function but was then co-opted by natural selection for a new one). For example, Leedom and Almas (2012) argue that it is actually dominance that confers an adaptive advantage for individuals, and that variation in psychopathic personality traits merely arises as a consequence of selection for social dominance. The unfortunate reality is that we simply do not have enough information at the present time to draw a definitive conclusion about whether psychopathy has an evolutionary function, or what that function may be. As a result, it is imperative for researchers to continue developing and testing hypotheses that address the potential evolved function of psychopathy.

Conclusion

Psychopathy is characterized by a range of affective abnormalities. For example, psychopathy is associated with restrictions in the range and depth of emotional experiences (e.g., relative lack of guilt), as well as difficulties with recognizing and learning from emotional cues. These affective abnormalities have contributed to the perspective that psychopathy is pathological. However, it has also been argued that psychopathy may actually reflect an alternative life-history strategy that is evolutionarily adaptive rather than reflecting a form of psychopathology. For example, the lack of guilt that often characterizes psychopathy may facilitate interpersonal strategies that involve the exploitation and manipulation of others. Our review of the existing literature did not allow us to draw any firm conclusions regarding whether psychopathy should be considered to be a form of psychopathology, but we believe this issue warrants additional consideration. One suggestion that we would offer for future research and debate regarding this issue is that it may be beneficial to reframe the basic question; that is, it may be helpful to transition away from simple all-or-none questions concerning whether psychopathy is pathological. Instead, we suggest a slightly different set of questions that acknowledge the dimensional nature of psychopathy. For example, instead of asking *whether* psychopathy is pathological, it may be better to ask questions such as: *At what level*—if any—do psychopathic personality traits become pathological? Do similar patterns emerge for the different psychopathic personality traits of meanness, disinhibition, and boldness? Or do the patterns diverge for these traits such that meanness and disinhibition become pathological at lower levels than is the case for boldness? Are certain *combinations* of these psychopathic traits particularly pathological? We believe that addressing these sorts of questions may provide a deeper and more nuanced understanding of psychopathy.[2]

Notes

1. It should also be noted that distinctions have been sometimes drawn between *psychopathy* and *sociopathy*. The primary distinction concerns the roles that biological predispoitions and environmental conditions are believed to play in the development of these conditions. For example, Lykken (1995) argued that psychopathy stems from genetically influenced temperamental characteristics (e.g., fearlessness) that make individuals exceptionally difficult to socialize, whereas sociopathy involves poor socialization interacting with weaker biological predispositions.
2. There are some studies that have asserted that psychopathy is categorical rather than continuous (Harris et al., 1994, 2007; Vasey et al., 2005) but those studies have been criticized for methodological issues (Guay et al., 2007; Marcus et al., 2011; Murrie et al., 2007; Walters et al., 2011).

References

American Psychiatric Association. (1987). *Diagnostic and statistical manual of mental disorders* (3rd ed., revised). APA.
American Psychiatric Association. (1994). *Diagnostic and statistical manual of mental disorders* (4th ed.). APA.
American Psychiatric Association. (2000). *Diagnostic and statistical manual of mental disorders* (4th ed., text revision). APA.
American Psychiatric Association. (2013). *Diagnostic and statistical manual of mental disorders* (5th ed.). APA.
Amoretti, M. C., & Lalumera, E. (2019). A potential tension in DSM-5: The general definition of mental disorder versus some specific diagnostic criteria. *Journal of Medicine and Philosophy, 44*(1), 85–108.
Anderson, N. E., Steele, V. R., Maurer, J. M., Rao, V., Koenigs, M. R., Decety, J., Kosson, D. S., Calhoun, V. D., & Kiehl, K. A. (2017). Differentiating emotional processing and attention in psychopathy with functional neuroimaging. *Cognitive, Affective, and Behavioral Neuroscience, 17*(3), 491–515.
Auty, K. M., Farrington, D. P., & Coid, J. W. (2015). Intergenerational transmission of psychopathy and mediation via psychosocial risk factors. *The British Journal of Psychiatry, 206*(1), 26–31.
Barkow, J. H. (1989). *Darwin, sex, and status*. University of Toronto Press.
Barr, K. N., & Quinsey, V. L. (2004). Is psychopathy a pathology or a life strategy? Implications for social policy. In C. Crawford & C. Salmon (Eds.), *Evolutionary psychology, public policy, and personal decisions* (pp. 293–317). Lawrence Erlbaum Associates.
Belsky, J., Steinberg, L., & Draper, P. (1991). Childhood experience, interpersonal development, and reproductive strategy: An evolutionary theory of socialization. *Child Development, 62*(4), 647–670.
Benning, S. D., Patrick, C. J., & Iacono, W. G. (2005). Psychopathy, startle blink modulation, and electrodermal reactivity in twin men. *Psychophysiology, 42*(6), 753–762.
Blair, R. J. R. (2007). The amygdala and ventromedial prefrontal cortex in morality and psychopathy. *Trends in Cognitive Sciences, 11*(9), 387–392.
Blair, R. J. R. (2008). The amygdala and ventromedial prefrontal cortex: functional contributions and dysfunction in psychopathy. *Philosophical Transactions of the Royal Society B: Biological Sciences, 363*(1503), 2557–2565.
Blair, R. J. R., Mitchell, D. G. V., & Blair, K. S. (2005). *The psychopath: Emotion and the brain*. Blackwell.
Book, A., Methot-Jones, T., Blais, J., Hosker-Field, A., Volk, A., Visser, B. A., Gauthier, N., Holden, R. R., & D'Agata, M. T. (2019). Psychopathic traits and the cheater-hawk hypothesis. *Journal of Interpersonal Violence, 34*(15), 3229–3251.
Book, A. S., & Quinsey, V. L. (2004). Psychopaths: cheaters or warrior-hawks? *Personality and Individual Differences, 36*(1), 33–45.
Boorse, C. (1976). What a theory of mental health should be. *Journal for the Theory of Social Behavior, 6*, 61–84.
Bürger, R. (2000). *The mathematical theory of selection, recombination, and mutation*. Wiley.

Campbell, J. S., & Ellison, J. (2005). Shame coping styles and psychopathic personality traits. *Journal of Personality Assessment, 84*(1), 96–104.

Carter, G. L., Lyons, M., & Brewer, G. (2018). Lifetime offspring and the Dark Triad. *Personality and Individual Differences, 132*, 79–83.

Cima, M., & Raine, A. (2009). Distinct characteristics of psychopathy relate to different subtypes of aggression. *Personality and Individual Differences, 47*(8), 835–840.

Cleckley, H. ([1941] 1976). *The mask of sanity* (5th ed.). Mosby.

Coid, J., Yang, M., Ullrich, S., Roberts, A., & Hare, R. D. (2009). Prevalence and correlates of psychopathic traits in the household population of Great Britain. *International Journal of Law and Psychiatry, 32*(2), 65–73.

Cooke, D. J., & Michie, C. (2001). Refining the construct of psychopathy: Towards a hierarchical model. *Psychological Assessment, 13*(2), 171–188.

Cornell, D. G., Warren, J., Hawk, G., Stafford, E., Oram, G., & Pine, D. (1996). Psychopathy in instrumental and reactive violent offenders. *Journal of Consulting and Clinical Psychology, 64*(4), 783–790.

Coyne, S. M., & Thomas, T. J. (2008). Psychopathy, aggression, and cheating behavior: A test of the Cheater-Hawk hypothesis. *Personality and Individual Differences, 44*(5), 1105–1115.

Crawford, C., & Salmon, C. (2002). Psychopathology or adaptation? Genetic and evolutionary perspectives on individual differences and psychopathology. *Neuroendocrinology Letters, 23*(Suppl 4), 39–45.

Crego, C., & Widiger, T. A. (2015). Psychopathy and the *DSM. Journal of Personality, 83*(6), 665–677.

Dadds, M. R., Perry, Y., Hawes, D. J., Merz, S., Riddell, A. C., Haines, D. J., Solak, E., & Abeygunawardane, A. I. (2006). Attention to the eyes and fear-recognition deficits in child psychopathy. *The British Journal of Psychiatry, 189*(3), 280–281.

da Silva, D. R., Rijo, D., & Salekin, R. T. (2015). The evolutionary roots of psychopathy. *Aggression and Violent Behavior, 21*, 85–96.

da Silva, D. R., Vagos, P., & Rijo, D. (2019). An evolutionary model to conceptualize psychopathic traits across community and forensic male youth. *International Journal of Offender Therapy and Comparative Criminology, 63*(4), 574–596.

Dawel, A., O'Kearney, R., McKone, E., & Palermo, R. (2012). Not just fear and sadness: Meta-analytic evidence of pervasive emotion recognition deficits for facial and vocal expressions in psychopathy. *Neuroscience & Biobehavioral Reviews, 36*(10), 2288–2304.

Del Giudice, M., Ellis, B .J., & Shirtcliff, E. A. (2011). The adaptive calibration model of stress responsivity. *Neuroscience and Biobehavioral Reviews, 35*, 1562–1592.

Del Giudice, M., Ellis, B. J., & Shirtcliff, E. A. (2013). Making sense of stress: An evolutionary- developmental framework. In G. Laviola, & S. Macrì (Eds.), *Adaptive and maladaptive aspects of developmental stress* (pp. 23–43). Springer.

DePaulo, B. M., & Rosenthal, R. (1979). Telling lies. *Journal of Personality and Social Psychology, 37*(10), 1713–1722.

Djeriouat, H., & Trémolière, B. (2020). Shame and guilt situational identification in subclinical primary psychopaths. *Current Psychology, 39*, 238–245.

Edens, J. F., Marcus, D. K., Lilienfeld, S. O., & Poythress, N. G. (2006). Psychopathic, not psychopath: Taxometric evidence for the dimensional structure of psychopathy. *Journal of Abnormal Psychology, 115*(1), 131–144.

Ellis, B. J., & Del Giudice, M. (2019). Developmental adaptation to stress: An evolutionary perspective. *Annual Review of Psychology, 70*, 111–139.

Ellis, B. J., Jackson, J. J., & Boyce, W. T. (2006). The stress response systems: Universality and adaptive individual differences. *Developmental Review, 26*(2), 175–212.

Fehr, E., & Gächter, S. (2002). Altruistic punishment in humans. *Nature, 415*(6868), 137–140.

Figueredo, A. J., Vásquez, G., Brumbach, B. H., Schneider, S. M., Sefcek, J. A., Tal, I. R., Hill, D., Wenner, C. J., & Jacobs, W. J. (2006). Consilience and life history theory: From genes to brain to reproductive strategy. *Developmental Review, 26*(2), 243–275.

First, M. B. (2005). Clinical utility: A prerequisite for the adoption of a dimensional approach in *DSM. Journal of Abnormal Psychology, 114*(4), 560–564.

Flight, J. I., & Forth, A. E. (2007). Instrumentally violent youths: The roles of psychopathic traits, empathy, and attachment. *Criminal Justice and Behavior, 34*(6), 739–751.

Fulford, K. M., & Thornton, T. (2007). Fanatical about "harmful dysfunction." *World Psychiatry, 6*(3), 161–162.

Gao, Y., Raine, A., Chan, F., Venables, P. H., & Mednick, S. A. (2010). Early maternal and paternal bonding, childhood physical abuse and adult psychopathic personality. *Psychological Medicine, 40*(6), 1007–1016.

Gardner, A., & West, S. A. (2004). Cooperation and punishment, especially in humans. *The American Naturalist, 164*(6), 753–764.

Garofalo, C., Neumann, C. S., Zeigler-Hill, V., & Meloy, J. R. (2019). Spiteful and contemptuous: A new look at the emotional experiences related to psychopathy. *Personality Disorders: Theory, Research, and Treatment, 10*(2), 173–184.

Glenn, A. L., Johnson, A. K., & Raine, A. (2013). Antisocial personality disorder: A current review. *Current Psychiatry Reports, 15*(12), 427–434.

Glenn, A. L., Kurzban, R., & Raine, A. (2011). Evolutionary theory and psychopathy. *Aggression and Violent Behavior, 16*(5), 371–380.

Glenn, A. L., & Raine, A. (2009). Psychopathy and instrumental aggression: Evolutionary, neurobiological, and legal perspectives. *International Journal of Law and Psychiatry, 32*(4), 253–258.

Gorenstein, E. E. (1984). Debating mental illness: Implications for science, medicine, and social policy. *American Psychologist, 39*, 50–56.

Graham, G. (2013). *The disordered mind: An introduction to philosophy of mind and mental illness* (2nd ed.). Routledge.

Guay, J. P., Ruscio, J., Knight, R. A., & Hare, R. D. (2007). A taxometric analysis of the latent structure of psychopathy: Evidence for dimensionality. *Journal of Abnormal Psychology, 116*(4), 701–716.

Hamilton, W. D. (1964). The genetic theory of social behavior: I and II. *Journal of Theoretical Biology, 7*, 1–52.

Hamilton, W. D. (1970). Selfish and spiteful behaviour in an evolutionary model. *Nature, 228*(5277), 1218–1220.

Hare, R. D. (1980). A research scale for the assessment of psychopathy in criminal populations. *Personality and Individual Differences, 1*, 111–119.

Hare, R. D. (2003). *The Hare Psychopathy Checklist–Revised (PCL-R) manual* (2nd ed.). Multi-Health Systems.

Hare, R. D., Hart, S. D., & Harpur, T. J. (1991). Psychopathy and the DSM-IV criteria for antisocial personality disorder. *Journal of Abnormal Psychology, 100*(3), 391–398.

Hare, R. D., & Neumann, C. S. (2008). Psychopathy as a clinical and empirical construct. *Annual Review of Clinical Psychology, 4*, 217–246.

Harenski, C. L., Edwards, B. G., Harenski, K. A., & Kiehl, K. A. (2014). Neural correlates of moral and non-moral emotion in female psychopathy. *Frontiers in Human Neuroscience, 8*, 741.

Harpending, H. C., & Sobus, J. (1987). Sociopathy as an adaptation. *Ethology and Sociobiology, 8*, 63–72.

Harpur, T. J., Hakstian, A. R., & Hare, R. D. (1988). Factor structure of the Psychopathy Checklist. *Journal of Consulting and Clinical Psychology, 56*(5), 741–747.

Harris, G. T., Rice, M. E., Hilton, N. Z., Lalumiere, M. L., & Quinsey, V. L. (2007). Coercive and precocious sexuality as a fundamental aspect of psychopathy. *Journal of Personality Disorders, 21*(1), 1–27.

Harris, G. T., Rice, M. E., & Quinsey, V. L. (1994). Psychopathy as a taxon: Evidence that psychopaths are a discrete class. *Journal of Consulting and Clinical Psychology, 62*(2), 387–397.

Hersh, K., & Gray-Little, B. (1998). Psychopathic traits and attitudes associated with self-reported sexual aggression in college men. *Journal of Interpersonal Violence, 13*(4), 456–471.

Holmqvist, R. (2008). Psychopathy and affect consciousness in young criminal offenders. *Journal of Interpersonal Violence, 23*, 209–224.

Hoppenbrouwers, S. S., Bulten, B. H., & Brazil, I. A. (2016). Parsing fear: A reassessment of the evidence for fear deficits in psychopathy. *Psychological Bulletin, 142*(6), 573–600.

Hopwood, C. J., Kotov, R., Krueger, R. F., Watson, D., Widiger, T. A., Althoff, R. R., Ansell, E. B., Bach, B., Bagby, R. M., Blais, M. A., Bornovalova, M. A., Chmielewski, M., Cicero, D. C., Conway, C., De Clercq, B., De Fruyt, F., Docherty, A. R., Eaton, N. R., Edens, J. F., . . . Zimmerman, J. (2018). The time has come for dimensional personality disorder diagnosis. *Personality and Mental Health, 12*(1), 82–86.

Hübner, D., & White, L. (2016). Neurosurgery for psychopaths? An ethical analysis. *AJOB Neuroscience, 7*(3), 140–149.

Jackson, R. L., Neumann, C. S., & Vitacco, M. J. (2007). Impulsivity, anger, and psychopathy: The moderating effect of ethnicity. *Journal of Personality Disorders, 21*(3), 289–304.

Jonason, P. K., Icho, A., & Ireland, K. (2016). Resources, harshness, and unpredictability: The socioeconomic conditions associated with the Dark Triad traits. *Evolutionary Psychology, 14*(1), 1–11.

Jonason, P. K., & Kavanagh, P. (2010). The dark side of love: Love styles and the Dark Triad. *Personality and Individual Differences, 49*(6), 606–610.

Jonason, P. K., Koenig, B. L., & Tost, J. (2010). Living a fast life. *Human Nature, 21*(4), 428–442.

Jonason, P. K., Li, N. P., Webster, G. D., & Schmitt, D. P. (2009). The Dark Triad: Facilitating a short-term mating strategy in men. *European Journal of Personality, 23*(1), 5–18.

Jonason, P. K., Lyons, M., Baughman, H. M., & Vernon, P. A. (2014). What a tangled web we weave: The Dark Triad traits and deception. *Personality and Individual Differences, 70*, 117–119.

Jonason, P. K., Valentine, K. A., Li, N. P., & Harbeson, C. L. (2011). Mate-selection and the Dark Triad: Facilitating a short-term mating strategy and creating a volatile environment. *Personality and Individual Differences, 51*(6), 759–763.

Jonason, P. K., & Webster, G. D. (2012). A protean approach to social influence: Dark Triad personalities and social influence tactics. *Personality and Individual Differences, 52*(4), 521–526.

Jones, D. N., & Paulhus, D. L. (2010). Different provocations trigger aggression in narcissists and psychopaths. *Social Psychological and Personality Science, 1*(1), 12–18.

Jurjako, M. (2019). Is psychopathy a harmful dysfunction? *Biology and Philosophy, 34*(1), 5.

Kiehl, K. A. (2006). A cognitive neuroscience perspective on psychopathy: Evidence for paralimbic system dysfunction. *Psychiatry Research, 142*(2–3), 107–128.

Knight, R. A., & Guay, J. P. (2018). The role of psychopathy in sexual coercion against women: An update and expansion. In C. J. Patrick (Ed.), *Handbook of psychopathy* (Vol. 2, pp. 662–681). Guilford Press.

Koenigs, M., & Newman, J. P. (2013). The decision making impairment in psychopathy: Psychological and neurobiological mechanisms. In W. P. Sinnott-Armstrong & K. A. Kiehl (Eds.), *Handbook on psychopathy and law* (pp. 93–106). Oxford University Press.

Kosson, D. S., Kelly, J. C., & White, J. W. (1997). Psychopathy-related traits predict self-reported sexual aggression among college men. *Journal of Interpersonal Violence, 12*(2), 241–254.

Kosson, D. S., Vitacco, M. J., Swogger, M. T., & Steuerwald, B. L. (2016). Emotional experiences of the psychopath. In C. B. Gacono (Ed.), *The clinical and forensic assessment of psychopathy: A practitioner's guide* (2nd ed., pp. 111–135). Routledge.

Kraemer, H. C. (2007). DSM categories and dimensions in clinical and research contexts. *International Journal of Methods in Psychiatric Research, 16*(S1), S8–S15.

Krueger, R. F., Eaton, N. R., Derringer, J., Markon, K. E., Watson, D., & Skodol, A. E. (2011). Personality in DSM-5: Helping delineate personality disorder content and framing the metastructure. *Journal of Personality Assessment, 93*(4), 325–331.

Krupp, D. B., Sewall, L. A., Lalumière, M. L., Sheriff, C., & Harris, G. T. (2012). Nepotistic patterns of violent psychopathy: Evidence for adaptation? *Frontiers in Psychology, 3*, 305.

Krupp, D. B., Sewall, L. A., Lalumière, M. L., Sheriff, C., & Harris, G. (2013). Psychopathy, adaptation, and disorder. *Frontiers in Psychology, 4*, 139.

Kubak, F. A., & Salekin, R. T. (2009). Psychopathy and anxiety in children and adolescents: New insights on developmental pathways to offending. *Journal of Psychopathology and Behavioral Assessment, 31*(4), 271–284.

Lalumière, M. L., Harris, G. T., & Rice, M. E. (2001). Psychopathy and developmental instability. *Evolution and Human Behavior, 22*(2), 75–92.

Lalumière, M. L., & Quinsey, V. L. (1996). Sexual deviance, antisociality, mating effort, and the use of sexually coercive behaviors. *Personality and Individual Differences, 21*(1), 33–48.

Larson, C. L., Baskin-Sommers, A. R., Stout, D. M., Balderston, N. L., Curtin, J. J., Schultz, D. H., Kiehl, K. A., & Newman, J. P. (2013). The interplay of attention and emotion: Top-down attention modulates amygdala activation in psychopathy. *Cognitive, Affective, and Behavioral Neuroscience, 13*(4), 757–770.

Lee, Z., Salekin, R. T., & Iselin, A. M. R. (2010). Psychopathic traits in youth: Is there evidence for primary and secondary subtypes? *Journal of Abnormal Child Psychology, 38*(3), 381–393.

Leedom, L., & Almas, L. H. (2012). Is psychopathy a disorder or an adaptation? *Frontiers in Psychology, 3*, 549.

Lilienfeld, S. O. (1994). Conceptual problems in the assessment of psychopathy. *Clinical Psychology Review, 14*(1), 17–38.

Lilienfeld, S. O. (2013). Is psychopathy a syndrome? Commentary on Marcus, Fulton, and Edens. *Personality Disorders: Theory, Research, and Treatment, 4*, 85–86.

Lilienfeld, S. O., & Fowler, K. A. (2006). The self-report assessment of psychopathy. In C. J. Patrick (Ed.), *Handbook of psychopathy* (pp. 107–142). Guilford Press.

Lilienfeld, S. O., & Marino, L. (1995). Mental disorder as a Roschian concept: A critique of Wakefield's "harmful dysfunction" analysis. *Journal of Abnormal Psychology, 104*, 411–420.

Lilienfeld, S. O., Smith, S. F., Sauvigné, K. C., Patrick, C. J., Drislane, L. E., Latzman, R. D., & Krueger, R. F. (2016). Is boldness relevant to psychopathic personality? Meta-analytic relations with non-Psychopathy Checklist-based measures of psychopathy. *Psychological Assessment, 28*(10), 1172–1185.

Lilienfeld, S. O., Smith, S. F., & Watts, A. L. (2016). Fearless dominance and its implications for psychopathy: Are the right stuff and the wrong stuff flip sides of the same coin? In V. Zeigler-Hill & D. K. Marcus (Eds.), *The dark side of personality: Science and practice in social, personality, and clinical psychology* (pp. 65–86). American Psychological Association.

Lilienfeld, S. O., Watts, A. L., Smith, S. F., & Latzman, R. D. (2018). Boldness: Conceptual and methodological issues. In C. J. Patrick (Ed.), *Handbook of psychopathy* (2nd ed., pp. 165–186). Guilford Press.

Lykken, D. T. (1995). *The antisocial personalities*. Lawrence Erlbaum Associates.

Lynam, D. R., Caspi, A., Moffitt, T. E., Loeber, R., & Stouthamer-Loeber, M. (2007). Longitudinal evidence that psychopathy scores in early adolescence predict adult psychopathy. *Journal of Abnormal Psychology, 116*(1), 155–165.

Lynam, D. R., & Gudonis, L. (2005). The development of psychopathy. *Annual Review of Clinical Psychology, 1*, 381–407.

Lynam, D. R., & Miller, J. D. (2015). Psychopathy from a basic trait perspective: The utility of a five-factor model approach. *Journal of Personality, 83*(6), 611–626.

Lynam, D. R., Miller, J. D., & Derefinko, K. J. (2018). Psychopathy and personality: An articulation of the benefits of a trait-based approach. In C. Patrick (Ed.), *Handbook of psychopathy* (pp. 259–280). Guildford Press.

Lynam, D. R., & Widiger, T. A. (2007). Using a general model of personality to identify the basic elements of psychopathy. *Journal of Personality Disorders, 21*(2), 160–178.

Malón, A. (2012). Pedophilia: A diagnosis in search of a disorder. *Archives of Sexual Behavior, 41*(5), 1083–1097.

Marcus, D. K., John, S. L., & Edens, J. F. (2004). A taxometric analysis of psychopathic personality. *Journal of Abnormal Psychology, 113*(4), 626–635.

Marcus, D. K., Lilienfeld, S. O., Edens, J. F., & Poythress, N. G. (2006). Is antisocial personality disorder continuous or categorical? A taxometric analysis. *Psychological Medicine, 36*(11), 1571–1581.

Marcus, D. K., Ruscio, J., Lilienfeld, S. O., & Hughes, K. T. (2008). Converging evidence for the latent structure of antisocial personality disorder: Consistency of taxometric and latent class analyses. *Criminal Justice and Behavior, 35*(3), 284–293.

Marcus, D. K., Sanford, G. M., Edens, J. F., Knight, R. A., & Walters, G. D. (2011). Taxometrics and evolutionary theory: The case of the psychopathic sexuality taxon. *Scientific Review of Mental Health Practice, 8*(1), 6–16.

Marcus, D. K., Zeigler-Hill, V., Mercer, S. H., & Norris, A. L. (2014). The psychology of spite and the measurement of spitefulness. *Psychological Assessment, 26*(2), 563–574.

McCrory, E., De Brito, S. A., & Viding, E. (2012). The link between child abuse and psychopathology: A review of neurobiological and genetic research. *Journal of the Royal Society of Medicine, 105*(4), 151–156.

Mealey, L. (1995). The sociobiology of sociopathy: An integrated evolutionary model. *Behavioral and Brain Sciences, 18*, 523–599.

Međedović, J. (2019). Harsh environment facilitates psychopathy's involvement in mating-parenting trade-off. *Personality and Individual Differences, 139*, 235–240.

Međedović, J., Petrović, B., Želeskov-Đorić, J., & Savić, M. (2017). Interpersonal and affective psychopathy traits can enhance human fitness. *Evolutionary Psychological Science, 3*(4), 306–315.

Meloy, J. R. (1988). *The psychopathic mind: Origins, dynamics, and treatment*. Aronson.

Meloy, J. R., Book, A., Hosker-Field, A., Methot-Jones, T., & Roters, J. (2018). Social, sexual, and violent predation: Are psychopathic traits evolutionarily adaptive? *Violence and Gender, 5*(3), 153–165.

Miller, J. D., & Lynam, D. R. (2012). An examination of the Psychopathic Personality Inventory's nomological network: A meta-analytic review. *Personality Disorders: Theory, Research, and Treatment, 3*, 305–326.

Mokros, A., Menner, B., Eisenbarth, H., Alpers, G. W., Lange, K. W., & Osterheider, M. (2008). Diminished cooperativeness of psychopaths in a prisoner's dilemma game yields higher rewards. *Journal of Abnormal Psychology, 117*(2), 406–413.

Mokros, A., Osterheider, M., Hucker, S. J., & Nitschke, J. (2011). Psychopathy and sexual sadism. *Law and Human Behavior, 35*(3), 188–199.

Morgan, J. E., Gray, N. S., & Snowden, R. J. (2011). The relationship between psychopathy and impulsivity: A multi-impulsivity measurement approach. *Personality and Individual Differences, 51*(4), 429–434.

Morrison, D., & Gilbert, P. (2001). Social rank, shame and anger in primary and secondary psychopaths. *Journal of Forensic Psychiatry and Psychology, 12*, 330–356.

Münch, R., Walter, H., & Müller, S. (2020). Should behavior harmful to others be a sufficient criterion of mental disorders? Conceptual problems of the diagnoses of antisocial personality disorder and pedophilic disorder. *Frontiers in Psychiatry, 11*, 954.

Murphy, B., Lilienfeld, S. O., Skeem, J., & Edens, J. F. (2016). Are fearless dominance traits superfluous in operationalizing psychopathy? Incremental validity and sex differences. *Psychological Assessment, 28*, 1597–1607.

Murphy, D., & Woolfolk, R. L. (2001a). The harmful dysfunction analysis of mental disorder. *Philosophy, Psychiatry, and Psychology, 7*, 241–252.

Murphy, D., & Woolfolk, R. L. (2001b). Conceptual analysis versus scientific understanding: An assessment of Wakefield's folk psychiatry. *Philosophy, Psychiatry, and Psychology, 7*, 271–292.

Murrie, D. C., Marcus, D. K., Douglas, K. S., Salekin, R. S., Lee, Z., & Vincent, G. (2007). Youth with psychopathy features are not a discrete class: A taxometric analysis. *Journal of Child Psychology and Psychiatry, 48*, 714–723.

Nadelhoffer, T., & Sinnott-Armstrong, W. P. (2013). Is psychopathy a mental disease? In N. A. Vincent (Ed.), *Neuroscience and legal responsibility* (pp. 229–255). Oxford University Press.

Nathanson, C., Paulhus, D. L., & Williams, K. M. (2006). Predictors of a behavioral measure of scholastic cheating: Personality and competence but not demographics. *Contemporary Educational Psychology, 31*(1), 97–122.

Neumann, C. S., Schmitt, D. S., Carter, R., Embley, I., & Hare, R. D. (2012). Psychopathic traits in females and males across the globe. *Behavioral Sciences and the Law, 30*(5), 557–574.

Nyström, M. B. T., & Mikkelsen, F. (2013). Psychopathy-related personality traits and shame management strategies in adolescents. *Journal of Interpersonal Violence, 28*(3), 519–537.

Ogloff, J. R. (2006). Psychopathy/antisocial personality disorder conundrum. *Australian and New Zealand Journal of Psychiatry, 40*(6–7), 519–528.

Patch, E. A., & Figueredo, A. J. (2017). Childhood stress, life history, psychopathy, and sociosexuality. *Personality and Individual Differences, 115*, 108–113.

Patrick, C. J. (2018). Psychopathy as masked pathology. In C. J. Patrick (Ed.), *Handbook of psychopathy* (pp. 3–21). Guilford Press.

Patrick, C. J., & Drislane, L. E. (2015). Triarchic model of psychopathy: Origins, operationalizations, and observed linkages with personality and general psychopathology. *Journal of Personality, 83*(6), 627–643.

Patrick, C., Drislane, L. E., & Strickland, C. (2012). Conceptualizing psychopathy in triarchic terms: Implications for treatment. *International Journal of Forensic Mental Health, 11*(4), 253–266.

Patrick, C. J., Fowles, D. C., & Krueger, R. F. (2009). Triarchic conceptualization of psychopathy: Developmental origins of disinhibition, boldness, and meanness. *Development and Psychopathology, 21*, 913–938.

Penke, L., Denissen, J. J., & Miller, G. F. (2007). The evolutionary genetics of personality. *European Journal of Personality, 21*(5), 549–587.

Poythress, N. G., & Hall, J. R. (2011). Psychopathy and impulsivity reconsidered. *Aggression and Violent Behavior, 16*(2), 120–134.

Raine, A. (1993). *The psychopathology of crime: Criminal behavior as a clinical disorder*. Academic Press.

Raine, A., & Uh, S. (2019). The selfishness questionnaire: Egocentric, adaptive, and pathological forms of selfishness. *Journal of Personality Assessment, 101*(5), 503–514.

Reich, W. (1991). Psychiatric diagnosis as an ethical problem. In S. Bloch & P. Chodoff (Eds.), *Psychiatric ethics* (pp.101–133). Oxford University Press.

Reid, W. H., & Gacono, C. (2000). Treatment of antisocial personality, psychopathy, and other characterologic antisocial syndromes. *Behavioral Sciences and the Law, 18*(5), 647–662.

Reidy, D. E., Kearns, M. C., DeGue, S., Lilienfeld, S. O., Massetti, G., & Kiehl, K. A. (2015). Why psychopathy matters: Implications for public health and violence prevention. *Aggression and Violent Behavior, 24*, 214–225.

Reidy, D. E., Zeichner, A., Miller, J. D., & Martinez, M. A. (2007). Psychopathy and aggression: Examining the role of psychopathy factors in predicting laboratory aggression under hostile and instrumental conditions. *Journal of Research in Personality, 41*(6), 1244–1251.

Rice, M. E., Harris, G. T., & Quinsey, V. L. (1990). A follow-up of rapists assessed in a maximum-security psychiatric facility. *Journal of Interpersonal Violence, 5*(4), 435–448.

Rilling, J. K., Glenn, A. L., Jairam, M. R., Pagnoni, G., Goldsmith, D. R., Elfenbein, H. A., & Lilienfeld, S. O. (2007). Neural correlates of social cooperation and non-cooperation as a function of psychopathy. *Biological Psychiatry, 61*(11), 1260–1271.

Roff, D. A. (1997). *Evolutionary quantitative genetics*. Chapman and Hall.

Rowe, D. C. (1996). An adaptive strategy of crime and delinquency. In J. D. Hawkins (Ed.), *Delinquency and crime: Current theories* (pp. 268–314). Cambridge University Press.

Ruscio, J. (2011). Why and how should we classify individuals? Introduction to the special section on categories and dimensions. *Scientific Review of Mental Health Practice, 8*(1), 3–5.

Sadler, J. Z. (2008). Vice and the diagnostic classification of mental disorders: A philosophical case conference. *Philosophy, Psychiatry, and Psychology, 15*(1), 1–17.

Salekin, R. T., & Lochman, J. E. (2008). Child and adolescent psychopathy: The search for protective factors. *Criminal Justice and Behavior, 35*(2), 159–172.

Schramme, T. (2010). Can we define mental disorder by using the criterion of mental dysfunction? *Theoretical Medicine and Bioethics, 31*(1), 35–47.

Sellbom, M., Lilienfeld, S. O., Fowler, K. A., & McCrary, K. L. (2018). The self-report assessment of psychopathy: Challenges, pitfalls, and promises. In C. J. Patrick (Ed.), *Handbook of psychopathy* (pp. 211–258). Guilford Press.

Seto, M. C., Khattar, N. A., Lalumière, M. L., & Quinsey, V. L. (1997). Deception and sexual strategy in psychopathy. *Personality and Individual Differences, 22*(3), 301–307.

Skeem, J. L., & Cooke, D. J. (2010). Is criminal behavior a central component of psychopathy? Conceptual directions for resolving the debate. *Psychological Assessment, 22*(2), 433–445.

Skeem, J. L., Polaschek, D. L., Patrick, C. J., & Lilienfeld, S. O. (2011). Psychopathic personality: Bridging the gap between scientific evidence and public policy. *Psychological Science in the Public Interest, 12*(3), 95–162.

Sonne, J. W., & Gash, D. M. (2018). Psychopathy to altruism: Neurobiology of the selfish–selfless spectrum. *Frontiers in Psychology, 9*, 575.

Turelli, M., & Barton, N. H. (2004). Polygenic variation maintained by balancing selection: Pleiotropy, sex-dependent allelic effects and G×E interactions. *Genetics, 166*, 1053–1079.

Vasey, M. W., Kotov, R., Frick, P. J., & Loney, B. R. (2005). The latent structure of psychopathy in youth: A taxometric investigation. *Journal of Abnormal Child Psychology, 33*, 411–429.

Venables, N. C., Hall, J. R., & Patrick, C. J. (2014). Differentiating psychopathy from antisocial personality disorder: A triarchic model perspective. *Psychological Medicine, 44*, 1005–1013.

Visser, B. A., DeBow, V., Pozzebon, J. A., Bogaert, A. F., & Book, A. (2015). Psychopathic sexuality: The thin line between fantasy and reality. *Journal of Personality, 83*(4), 376–388.

von Borries, A. K. L., Volman, I., de Bruijn, E. R. A., Bulten, B. H., Verkes, R. J., & Roelofs, K. (2012). Psychopaths lack the automatic avoidance of social threat: Relation to instrumental aggression. *Psychiatry Research, 200*(2–3), 761–766.

Wakefield, J. C. (1992). Disorder as harmful dysfunction: A conceptual critique of *DSM-III-R*'s definition of mental disorder. *Psychological Review, 99*, 232–247.

Walker, N. (1994). Dangerousness and mental disorder. In A. G. Phillips (Ed.), *Philosophy, psychology and psychiatry* (pp. 179–190). Cambridge University Press.

Wall, T. D., Wygant, D. B., & Sellbom, M. (2015). Boldness explains a key difference between psychopathy and antisocial personality disorder. *Psychiatry, Psychology and Law, 22*, 94–105.

Walsh, A., & Wu, H. H. (2008). Differentiating antisocial personality disorder, psychopathy, and sociopathy: Evolutionary, genetic, neurological, and sociological considerations. *Criminal Justice Studies, 21*(2), 135–152.

Walsh, Z., Swogger, M. T., & Kosson, D. S. (2009). Psychopathy and instrumental violence: Facet level relationships. *Journal of Personality Disorders, 23*(4), 416–424.

Walters, G. D., Diamond, P. M., Magaletta, P. R., Geyer, M. D., & Duncan, S. A. (2007). Taxometric analysis of the Antisocial Features Scale of the Personality Assessment Inventory in federal prison inmates. *Assessment, 14*(4), 351–360.

Walters, G. D., Ermer, E., Knight, R. A., & Kiehl, K. A. (2015). Paralimbic biomarkers in taxometric analyses of psychopathy: Does changing the indicators change the conclusion? *Personality Disorders: Theory, Research, and Treatment, 6*(1), 41–52.

Walters, G. D., Gray, N. S., Jackson, R. L., Sewell, K. W., Rogers, R., Taylor, J., & Snowden, R. J. (2007). A taxometric analysis of the Psychopathy Checklist: Screening Version (PCL: SV): Further evidence of dimensionality. *Psychological Assessment, 19*(3), 330–339.

Walters, G. D., Marcus, D. K., Edens, J. F., Knight, R. A., & Sanford, G. M. (2011). In search of the psychopathic sexuality taxon: Indicator size does matter. *Behavioral Sciences and the Law, 29*(1), 23–39.

West-Eberhard, M. J. (2003). *Developmental plasticity and evolution*. Oxford University Press.

Widiger, T. A., & Lynam, D. R. (1998). Psychopathy and the five-factor model of personality. In T. Millon, E. Simonson, M. Birket-Smith, & R. D. Davis (Eds.), *Psychopathy: Antisocial, criminal, and violent Behavior* (pp. 171–187). Guilford Press.

Widiger, T. A., & Trull, T. J. (1985). The empty debate over the existence of mental illness: Comments on Gorenstein. *American Psychologist, 40*, 468–471.

Widiger, T. A., & Trull, T. J. (2007). Plate tectonics in the classification of personality disorder: Shifting to a dimensional model. *American Psychologist, 62*(2), 71–83.

Widom, C. S. (1976). Interpersonal conflict and cooperation in psychopaths. *Journal of Abnormal Psychology, 85*(3), 330–334.

World Health Organization. (2004). *International statistical classification of diseases and related health problems* (10th revision). WHO.

World Health Organization. (2018). *International statistical classification of diseases and related health problems* (11th revision). WHO.

Zeigler-Hill, V., Martinez, J. L., Vrabel, J. K., Ezenwa, M. O., Oraetue, H., Nweze, T., Andrews, D., & Kenny, B. (2020). The darker angels of our nature: Do social worldviews mediate the associations that dark personality features have with ideological attitudes? *Personality and Individual Differences, 160*, 109920.

CHAPTER 67

Obsessive-Compulsive and Related Disorders, Hypochondriasis, and Behavioral Addictions

Vlasios Brakoulias

Abstract

Obsessive-compulsive and related disorders are characterized by obsessions (recurrent and intrusive thoughts, images, or impulses) and/or compulsions (repetitive behaviors or mental acts). Hypochondriasis is characterized by repetitive concerns regarding one's health and repetitive checks and investigations. Behavioral addictions are characterized by excessive repetitive actions. This chapter aims to explore the symptoms of obsessive-compulsive and related disorders, hypochondriasis, and behavioral addictions from an evolutionary perspective. The repetition associated with many of these disorders has been linked to protection from harm and reward in a way that supported ancestral survival. An evolutionary perspective may assist people suffering from these disorders in forming an alternative conceptualization for the origin of their symptoms and has potential to enhance outcomes from psychological therapies. Such conceptualizations may be of particular benefit for those sufferers who wish to gain understanding and who may be embarrassed by the seemingly senseless nature of their symptoms.

Key Words: obsessive-compulsive disorder, evolution, behavioral addiction, hypochondriasis, obsession

Introduction

Obsessive-compulsive disorder (OCD) is characterized by maladaptive repetition of thought or behavior, as are the other obsessive-compulsive-related disorders such as hoarding disorder, body dysmorphic disorder, trichotillomania, dermatillomania, onychophagia, olfactory reference syndrome, and other related disorders such as hypochondriasis (or illness anxiety disorder or somatic symptom disorder), and the proposed behavioral addictions such as problematic internet use, internet gaming disorder, pathological gambling, sex addiction, and compulsive buying. There is debate regarding the diagnostic classification of these symptom clusters. It is uncertain whether behavioral addictions are more closely related to obsessive-compulsive-related disorders or substance use disorders (Starcevic & Khazaal, 2017). Similarly, hoarding disorder, dermatillomania, trichotillomania, and body dysmorphic disorder have been viewed by some as behavioral addictions (Demetrovics & Griffiths, 2012). From a symptom perspective, the disorders are similar in the sense that they are characterized by repetitive thoughts and/or behaviors that the sufferer finds challenging to resist and, therefore, they are grouped together in this chapter.

This chapter describes common symptoms related to these groups of disorders, their associated emotions, and how an evolutionary perspective may assist in enhancing our understanding of these repetitive symptoms. This chapter also will explore how an evolutionary perspective may assist with the alleviation of these symptoms.

Obsessive-Compulsive Disorder

Obsessive-compulsive disorder is characterized by recurrent and intrusive thoughts, images, and impulses associated with strong emotions and repetitive behavior and mental acts. The emotions associated with obsessive-compulsive symptoms are anxiety, fear, discomfort, and distress, and a common associated behavior is avoidance. An evolutionary perspective can assist us in understanding the emotions and behaviors associated with obsessive-compulsive symptoms. The fear response and its associated avoidance, withdrawal, and actions to prevent harm are often used to aid in explaining symptoms to patients suffering from such symptoms. However, not all symptoms arise in the context of anxiety. Contamination fears can arise secondary to the emotion of disgust. Disgust leads to distancing from a pungent odor or avoiding eating something that may cause illness, and so such a reaction is likely to have a protective function in a manner similar to the fight-or-flight response.

Although there are many potential symptoms of OCD, studies have repeatedly demonstrated five common clusters of symptoms (Brakoulias, Starcevic, Berle et al., 2013): hoarding, contamination and cleaning, symmetry and ordering, doubt and checking compulsions, and unacceptable/taboo thoughts. Unacceptable/taboo thoughts have traditionally been called "Pure O" or "pure obsessional," as sufferers of these symptoms were thought to only experience obsessions with no compulsions. We have since documented that sufferers often engage in covert compulsions such as mental rituals in an attempt to neutralize their distressing obsessions (Brakoulias, Starcevic, Berle et al., 2013). There are other obsessive-compulsive-related disorders such as body dysmorphic disorder (characterized by excessive preoccupation with one's appearance or a part of their body, e.g., their nose, and excessive checking), trichotillomania (hair-pulling disorder), onychophagia (nail-biting disorder), and dermatillomania (skin-picking disorder). However, evolutionary models for these disorders have not been described.

Contamination/Cleaning

Instances in history during which water supplies have become contaminated or diseases have spread through communities due to poor hygiene have conferred an evolutionary advantage to people who give importance to thoughts of contamination and cleaning (Leckman et al., 1999; Leckman & Bloch, 2008). Examples include the cholera epidemic spread by contaminated water and, more recently, the COVID-19 pandemic. An evolutionary perspective proposes that contamination/cleaning symptoms associated with OCD evolved because they increased survival rates in the context of contamination or infectious disease (Leckman et al., 2007). In clinical practice, some sufferers with excessive avoidance of potential contaminants and excessive cleaning and disinfecting of surfaces have resisted changing their behaviors as they see their reduced rate of viral infections as justification that their excessive behaviors work.

Using an evolutionary model to explain contamination/cleaning symptoms can validate sufferers and reduce distress related to the perception that this is senseless and bizarre behavior and from the uncertainty as to why this behavior is occurring. An evolutionary perspective emphasizes the need to take care more wisely and more efficiently, rather than excessively. A health professional can explain how skin loses its protective barrier with excessive washing, scrubbing, and the associated dryness and erythema. Conversely, good hand hygiene is promoted to reduce the transmission of disease. The concept of striking a healthy balance is not overly emphasized in cognitive behavioral models, yet an evolutionary model offers useful insights that are more likely to be acceptable to the sufferer (Hoffman, 2011).

Symmetry/Ordering

Evolutionary explanations for symmetry/ordering symptoms center around a need for certainty and the reassurance that an object is in "just the right" position. Several authors have speculated that heightened attention to the placement of specific objects in the environment has a role in improving one's sense of security (Leckman et al., 2007; Leckman & Bloch, 2008). The symptoms could also be viewed as a way of ensuring that "everything is in its place" in case it needs to be taken quickly in an emergency. Symmetry/ordering and arranging objects into a correct position can be associated with a feeling of being "just right," whereas checking that an object is still in the position that it has been left in is more often associated with a desire for certainty (Coles et al., 2003).

An analogy that may be useful in therapy for people with symmetry and ordering symptoms is the need to put things in their place after a storm or earthquake. There is a natural tendency to straighten moved objects and to correctly position items that have moved as a result of a disruptive event. These actions are useful in restoring a sense of normality (feeling things are "right" again) and being able to work and to function normally within an environment. Using an evolutionary perspective, we can illustrate how symmetry and ordering can be useful in the right circumstances, but unhelpful when it is excessive and time consuming. It can be useful to reorient the sufferer to an evolutionary purpose for interest in symmetry and ordering, i.e., to enable people to function more efficiently within their environments, and hence any excessive obsessions or compulsions involving these symptoms place this efficiency at risk. The energy and drive associated with these symptoms need to be redirected toward being able to locate items in an efficient manner when they are needed, rather than being wasted on repetitive actions that cause inefficiency.

Checking Compulsions

Checking compulsions may be related to thoughts and behaviors that solve the adaptive problem of preventing harm (Leckman et al., 2007). Checking achieves this by providing the individual with certainty that the threatening event will not occur. Examples of such threats include the risk of fire, rising flood waters, predatory animals, and thieves. Checking that a campfire is out can prevent loss of lives and property; however, a campfire that may appear to have been put out can start up again, so it might be useful to check several times. Checking is not only of benefit to the individual, as families and groups of people require cautious individuals who check things repeatedly for the benefit of the group.

When working with people who suffer from excessive checking, it is important to recognize that the person's checking can be useful in preventing harm to themselves and others. This sense of validation assists in engagement with the individual, in relieving associated distress, and in the reorientation of the sufferer's motivation and energy onto the goal of preventing harm, rather than the need to check (Moretz & McKay, 2009).

Unacceptable/Taboo Thoughts

Evolutionary conceptualizations of unacceptable/taboo thoughts alone have not been well described. Obsessions relating to threat of embarrassment, performing taboo sexual acts, or immoral acts may serve a protective function by preventing a person from performing these actions. Aggressive, sexual, and religious obsessions might help to improve social cohesion, order, and harmony (Leckman et al., 2007).

In accordance with the literature (Bogetto et al., 1999; Labad et al., 2008; Tukel et al., 2004), higher scores on the unacceptable/taboo thoughts symptom dimension were more likely in males. Despite two decades of research in this area, there are no clear explanations for sex differences in OCD symptoms. It is possible that evolutionary, environmental, and cultural factors have led to men and women giving varying levels of importance to different aspects of life, with men having to focus on controlling their aggressive and sexual impulses more than women. The positive findings in regard to increased hostility and past substance abuse may also play a role in explaining the increased likelihood of individuals with unacceptable/taboo thoughts being male, with both being more prevalent in males (Lemogne et al., 2011; Weiss et al., 2011; Williams et al., 2011). From a biological perspective, one could hypothesize that testosterone increases hostility; however, studies have not shown any significant association between testosterone and hostility (King et al., 2005; Sluyter et al., 2000).

Individuals who suffer with unacceptable/taboo thoughts may receive some comfort in knowing that they represent a natural means of preventing horrible events from occurring, for the obsessions are experienced as repulsive and ego dystonic. The thoughts quickly remind the individual of what they would not want to do. However, the "reminder system" is excessive. In keeping with the concept of reorienting drive and energy toward a more constructive outcome, it may be helpful for the sufferer to look toward the core values that are associated with the obsessions that they are suffering from. For example, an aggressive obsession that has the purpose of preventing harm to others could be redirected toward the value of kindness and being respectful toward others, rather than avoiding people for fear of harming them.

Hoarding Disorder

Evolutionary perspectives can help explain similarities between human and animal behavior. Examples of animals that collect food or objects include the squirrel collecting acorns for the winter and the male bowerbird (see Figure 67.1) that collects blue items to decorate its nest and attract a mate. From an evolutionary perspective, hoarding can be thought of as enhancing survival and of being beneficial in times of drought or famine, as the person who hoards is likely to have saved a good supply of food (Brune, 2006). In contrast, other symptoms of OCD have evolved to deal with different threats (Leckman et al., 2011; Leckman et al., 1999). A common belief reported by people with hoarding disorder is that they will need these items in the future (Brakoulias et al., 2018). Their beliefs are strengthened when a time arises when they do indeed use an item that they have kept.

An evolutionary perspective can be useful in acknowledging the benefits of hoarding and illustrating how hoarding disorder is inefficient and unnecessary. Hoarding disorder is not defined by functional impairment of the individual, but rather the inability to effectively use spaces within one's home. For example, collecting a room full of old printers and not making use of them for several years would not only represent an inefficient use of space, but could mean that the room can no longer be used to receive visitors, to sleep in, or to eat or cook in. Therapeutic suggestions could then include trying to make use of the printers now, by selling parts or fixing them to make some money that would be more useful, or clearing the room so that it could be used to store something that would be more valuable to collect and more helpful at a time of need.

Hypochondriasis

Newer conceptualizations of hypochondriasis have renamed this disorder as *illness anxiety* disorder and/or *somatic symptom disorder*, depending on whether the preoccupation is related primarily to an illness (such as developing cancer) or a somatic complaint (such as epigastric discomfort). Either way, the disorder is characterized by an overemphasis on the threat of illness or of the significance of a somatic complaint, and usually there is repetitive checking in the form of medical investigations and consultations to gain reassurance that they are not unwell or that they do not have a serious illness. Some researchers also refer to hypochondriasis as *health anxiety*. From an evolutionary perspective, we again see similar themes in that the behaviors may prevent premature death from a serious health issue. It can be somewhat of a surprise for the clinician, yet validating for the patient, when occasionally patients who have been diagnosed as suffering from hypochondriasis are later diagnosed with a serious medical illness. In some of these situations, clinicians can retrospectively realize that the individual must have had some symptom that triggered their concern, but that it was too early to have identified an issue by physical examination or medical investigations. This provided some impetus for the diagnosis of somatic symptom disorder, in that there is an acknowledgment that a medical diagnosis may be made at some point in the future, but is not possible at this point in time (Brakoulias, 2014). Accepting this uncertainty is much easier for the clinician than the patient, and hence tolerating uncertainty is a common theme in cognitive approaches to psychological therapy.

Obsessive-Compulsive Personality Disorder

Although obsessive-compulsive personality disorder is not regarded as an obsessive-compulsive-related disorder in DSM-5, it has common symptoms to OCD and is frequently co-occurring (Starcevic, Berle & Brakoulias et al, 2013). Estimates of rates of obsessive-compulsive personality disorder in patients with OCD are between 25% and 50% (Starcevic & Brakoulias, 2014). At times, the symptoms can be difficult to distinguish, and the key differences are that although repetitive checking, washing, arranging, etc., may be seen as distressing to an observer, they are not distressing to the individual with obsessive-compulsive personality disorder, i.e., they are *ego-syntonic* as opposed to the ego-dystonic nature of obsessions and compulsions in OCD. Additionally, the person with obsessive-compulsive personality disorder is seen as rigid and perfectionistic. The individual has often had these characteristics their entire adult life and often has the belief that their obsessional nature is integral to their existence. This is of key significance from an evolutionary perspective, as many of their recurrent cognitions and core values arise from a need to complete things perfectly and to prevent mistakes or failure. Some professions in which perfectionism and some degree of obsessive-compulsive personality are valued include those of doctor, pilot, and schoolteacher. These are the very professions where a mistake is much more likely to lead to death than in other professions, and where one could argue that individuals in these professions with these qualities have an evolutionary advantage when it comes to responsible and high-risk situations.

Problematic Internet Use

Problematic internet use refers to excessive use of the internet to the extent that this behavior impacts one's ability to function. It does not include excessive gaming, but includes excessive use of social media, internet search engines ("web surfing" or "googling"), and excessive use of images or video (e.g., YouTube). When exploring the underlying cognitions regarding this excessive behavior, it can resemble obsessive-compulsive disorder, but at other times, patients can describe the experience as pleasurable or even as an "escape from reality." When patients are able to articulate a rationale, there may be a "need to know," and this has been identified as a miscellaneous obsession within the Yale Brown Obsessive-Compulsive Symptom Scale (Y-BOCS) symptom checklist (Goodman et al., 1989). Others may be engaging in excessive use of the internet to compare their physical attributes to those of others, and this may be related to body dysmorphic disorder, while others may be excessively reading medical information as a result of their hypochondriacal concerns in a behavior that has been termed *cyberchondria* (Starcevic & Berle, 2013).

Sex Addiction

As the name suggests, sex addiction or compulsive sexual behavior disorder refers to excessive sexual behaviors. People suffering from this disorder often present wanting help to cease their excessive sexual habits due to the impact it has on their ability to function and the detrimental effects on their relationships and on their health when exposed to sexually transmitted diseases (Carnes & Adams, 2019). It may seem obvious that an evolutionary perspective would suggest that sexual activity is important; however, the consequences for those presenting for treatment usually far outweigh the advantages. There are obvious similarities to addiction to substances, but the level of preoccupation and the difficulty resisting the strong urges to engage in sexual activity also share similarities to OCD. An evolutionary perspective may be useful in conceptualizing how "animal instincts" need to be tamed to live in a civilized manner in modern society, where parallels may be drawn with violence and aggression. These parallels may be useful in the clinical setting and may be used to illustrate techniques used to control aggressive and sexual urges.

Compulsive Buying

Compulsive buying shares similarities with compulsive acquisition associated with hoarding disorder. We again see the need to purchase items in case a need arises for them in the future. In some cases, the buying may be precipitated by a sale or discounted prices and the perception that the individual is getting a bargain; however, often the items are not needed and are seen by others as a wasteful purchase. In compulsive buying, there may be an additional degree of impulsivity triggered by a special or an item that is perceived to be of value or use, and there may not be compulsive hoarding to the extent that the house is cluttered and full of items. An evolutionary perspective may be useful in reminding the sufferer to curtail their compulsive buying that may be fueled by instinctual drives to gather and not miss out, and to spend more wisely.

It is also important to note that mood may play a role in some of these disorders, including compulsive buying (Kyrios et al., 2013). The term "retail therapy" has been used in marketing to promote the positive effects of shopping on mood. There may be some evolutionary explanation for the apparent reward of having acquired an object. An example may be the happiness associated with the gathering of an abundant crop of food, in comparison to the misery associated with having no food to hunt or gather.

Pathological Gambling

In a similar manner to compulsive buying, pathological gambling may be also seen as a method of acquiring wealth. Unfortunately, the reality is far from this, in that the excessive spending in pursuit of a win can lead to financial ruin, and unlike compulsive buying, pathological gambling is associated with significant risk-taking. Spinella (2003) argues that gambling involves an evolutionary mismatch. According to this theory, traditional hunter-gatherer lifestyles were associated with surges of dopamine as a result of a quick win or successful pursuit of an animal, and this has led to deeply ingrained neural pathways that promote the pursuit of activities that will lead to similar dopamine surges. In this case, the dopamine surges arise from the pursuit of a win from gambling in those so predisposed. Explaining such theories to patients may assist in encouraging patients to find less detrimental ways of pursuing the reward sensation associated with dopamine surges, such as sporting games or exercise.

Internet Gaming Disorder

Internet gaming disorder shares similarities to pathological gambling in that the gamer is constantly pursuing a win and on occasion there are some financial rewards, but again the detrimental financial and functional outcomes are far outweighed by this remote possibility. Internet gaming disorder is associated with a most extreme level of preoccupation and need for absolute attention to the task. The level of commitment is so severe and prolonged in some cases that sufferers have been known to wear diapers to avoid toileting and have asked relatives to bring them food and water so that they remain uninterrupted. In a real world of violence and wars, such individuals may have been the ultimate warriors, but in today's society sufferers often live in fantasy worlds with significant neglect of their self-care and the real world. An evolutionary perspective may present some creative avenues to allow the individual to refocus on more useful and less detrimental activities; it also reminds us to take care when attempting to reduce internet gaming in individuals whose neural reward pathways are likely to be dependent on such activities for the generation of adequate levels of dopamine.

Evolutionary Perspectives in Therapy

An evolutionary perspective can be helpful in conceptualizing and making sense of symptoms that can be difficult to understand. Just as the fight-or-flight model is useful for sufferers of anxiety to understand how their symptoms arise, applying an evolutionary perspective for each obsession and/or compulsion may be useful for sufferers of obsessive-compulsive and related disorders and their family members.

An evolutionary perspective may also be useful in placing symptoms on a spectrum from normal obsessions and compulsions to pathological. The recent COVID-19 pandemic has placed contamination fears and hand-washing compulsions into perspective. Sufferers of OCD with contamination and cleaning compulsions have reported feeling less anxious and much more justified within the context of the pandemic (Perkes et al., 2020).

The therapeutic benefit of assisting a sufferer with an understanding of how their symptoms may have been of benefit in certain circumstance may be of benefit in enhancing insight and cognitive restructuring aiming at correcting maladaptive cognitions, and in acknowledging the sufferer's context, while setting more realistic treatment goals. Another recurrent theme is the reorientation of the excessive activity, drive, and energy associated with the pathological behavior toward the evolutionary intention of the behavior. It can be useful for the sufferer to see themselves as valuable from an evolutionary perspective and to refocus on the reasons why these symptoms could be seen as useful and on the values that underpin them.

Conclusions

An evolutionary perspective on obsessive-compulsive and other repetitive and difficult to control behaviors can be useful for individuals suffering from these debilitating disorders. The potential to feel understood, acknowledged, and reassured can be valuable for a sufferer. Furthermore, the therapeutic value of using an evolutionary perspective to assist sufferers of obsessive-compulsive disorder and other related disorders, particularly behavioral addictions, to reorient some of their drives and energy in a constructive manner is worthy of further systematic evaluation.

References

Bogetto, F., Venturello, S., Albert, U., Maina, G., & Ravizza, L. (1999). Gender-related clinical differences in obsessive-compulsive disorder. *European Psychiatry, 14*(8), 434–441.

Brakoulias, V. (2014). DSM-5 bids farewell to hypochondriasis and welcomes somatic symptom disorder and illness anxiety disorder. *Australian and New Zealand Journal of Psychiatry, 48*(7), 688–688.

Brakoulias, V., Starcevic, V., Berle, D., Milicevic, D., Moses, K., Hannan, A., Sammut, P., & Martin, A. (2013). The characteristics of unacceptable/taboo thoughts in obsessive-compulsive disorder. *Comprehensive Psychiatry, 54*(7), 750–757.

Brakoulias, V., Starcevic, V., Berle, D., Sammut, P., Milicevic, D., Moses, K., Hannan, A., & Martin, A. (2013). Further support for five dimensions of obsessive-compulsive symptoms. *The Journal of Nervous and Mental Disease, 201*(6), 452–459.

Brakoulias, V., Starcevic, V., Milicevic, D., Hannan, A., Viswasam, K., & Brown, C., (2018). The Nepean belief scale: Preliminary reliability and validity in obsessive–compulsive disorder. *International Journal of Psychiatry in Clinical Practice, 22*(2), 84–88.

Brune, M. (2006). The evolutionary psychology of obsessive-compulsive disorder: The role of cognitive metarepresentation. *Perspectives in Biology and Medicine, 49*(3), 317–329.

Carnes, P. J., & Adams, K. M. (Eds.). (2019). *Clinical management of sex addiction*. Routledge.

Coles, M. E., Frost, R. O., Heimberg, R. G., & Rhéaume, J., (2003). "Not just right experiences": Perfectionism, obsessive-compulsive features and general psychopathology. *Behaviour Research and Therapy, 41*(6), 681–700.

Demetrovics, Z., & Griffiths, M. D. (2012). Behavioral addictions: Past, present and future. *Journal of Behavioral Addictions, 1*, 1–2.

Goodman, W. K., Price, L. H., Rasmussen, S. A., Mazure, C., Fleischmann, R. L., Hill, C. L., Heninger, G. R., & Charney, D. S. (1989). The Yale-Brown obsessive compulsive scale: I. Development, use, and reliability. *Archives of General Psychiatry, 46*(11), 1006–1011.

Hofmann, S. G. (2011). *An introduction to modern CBT: Psychological solutions to mental health problems*. Wiley.

King, J. A., Rosal, M. C., Ma, Y., & Reed, G. W. (2005). Association of stress, hostility and plasma testosterone levels. *Neuroendocrinology Letters, 26*(4), 355–360.

Kyrios, M., McQueen, P., & Moulding, R. (2013). Experimental analysis of the relationship between depressed mood and compulsive buying. *Journal of Behavior Therapy and Experimental Psychiatry, 44*(2), 194–200.

Labad, J., Menchon, J. M., Alonso, P., Segalas, C., Jimenez, S., Jaurrieta, N., Leckman, J.F., & Vallejo, J. (2008). Gender differences in obsessive-compulsive symptom dimensions. *Depression and Anxiety, 25*(10), 832–838.

Leckman, J., Mayes, L., Feldman, R., Evans, D., King, R., & Cohen, D. (1999). Early parental preoccupations and behaviors and their possible relationship to the symptoms of obsessive-compulsive disorder. *Acta Psychiatrica Scandinavica Supplementum, 100*(Suppl 396), 1–26.

Leckman, J. F., & Bloch, M. H. (2008). A developmental and evolutionary perspective on obsessive-compulsive disorder: Whence and whither compulsive hoarding? *American Journal of Psychiatry, 165*(10), 1229–1233.

Leckman, J. F., Rauch, S. L., & Mataix-Cols, D. (2007). Symptom dimensions in obsessive-compulsive disorder: Implications for the DSM-V. *CNS Spectrums, 12*(5), 376–387.

Leckman, J. F., Rauch, S. L., & Mataix-Cols, D. (2011). Symptom dimensions in obsessive-compulsive disorder: Implications for DSM-V. In Hollander, E., Zohar, J., Sirovatka, P. J., & Regier, D. A. *Obsessive-compulsive spectrum disorders: Refining the research agenda for DSM-V* (pp. 117–140). American Psychiatric Association.

Lemogne, C., Fossati, P., Limosin, F., Nabi, H., Encrenaz, G., Bonenfant, S., & Consoli, S. M. (2011) Cognitive hostility and suicide. *Acta Psychiatrica Scandinavica, 124*(1), 62–69.

Moretz, M. W., McKay, D. (2009). The role of perfectionism in obsessive–compulsive symptoms: "Not just right" experiences and checking compulsions. *Journal of Anxiety Disorders, 23*(5): 640–644.

Perkes, I. E., Brakoulias, V., Lam-Po-Tang, J., Castle, D. J., & Fontenelle, L. F. (2020). Contamination compulsions and obsessive-compulsive disorder during COVID-19. *Australian & New Zealand Journal of Psychiatry, 54*(11), 1137–1138.

Sluyter, F., Keijser, J. N., Boomsma, D. I., van Doornen, L. J., van den Oord, E. J., & Snieder, H. (2000). Genetics of testosterone and the aggression-hostility-anger (AHA) syndrome: A study of middle-aged male twins. *Twin Research, 3*(4), 266–276.

Spinella, M. (2003). Evolutionary mismatch, neural reward circuits, and pathological gambling. *International Journal of Neuroscience, 113*(4), 503–512.

Starcevic, V., & Berle, D. (2013). Cyberchondria: Towards a better understanding of excessive health-related Internet use. *Expert Review of Neurotherapeutics, 13*(2), 205–213.

Starcevic, V., Berle, D., Brakoulias, V., Sammut, P., Moses, K., Milicevic, D., & Hannan, A. (2013). Obsessive-compulsive personality disorder co-occurring with obsessive-compulsive disorder: Conceptual and clinical implications. *Australian & New Zealand Journal of Psychiatry, 47*(1), 65–73.

Starcevic, V., & Brakoulias, V. (2014). New diagnostic perspectives on obsessive-compulsive personality disorder and its links with other conditions. *Current Opinion in Psychiatry, 27*(1), 62–67.

Tukel, R., Polat, A., Genc, A., Bozkurt, O., & Atli, H. (2004). Gender-related differences among Turkish patients with obsessive-compulsive disorder. *Comprehensive Psychiatry, 45*(5), 362–366.

Weiss, J. W., Mouttapa, M., Cen, S., Johnson, C. A., & Unger, J. (2011). Longitudinal effects of hostility, depression, and bullying on adolescent smoking initiation. *Journal of Adolescent Health, 48*(6), 591–596.

Williams, E. D., Steptoe, A., Chambers, J. C., & Kooner, J. S. (2011). Ethnic and gender differences in the relationship between hostility and metabolic and autonomic risk factors for coronary heart disease. *Psychosomatic Medicine, 73*(1), 53–58.

AFTERWORD: EVOLUTIONARY EMOTION RESEARCH AT THE CROSSROADS

Marco Del Giudice

This is an exciting book. Not just in the sense that it is a fine volume, full of sophisticated and up-to-date contributions. (Compared with my memories when I first got interested in emotion research as a student, the field has been transformed almost beyond recognition; it is amazing how much progress has been made in this relatively short time.) Not just because the coverage of specific emotions and domains is exceptionally broad and fine-grained (from love and grief to *kama muta*, from conflict and reconciliation to care for the sick), or because so many chapters display that unique combination of explanatory power and trueness to life that is the hallmark of the evolutionary behavioral sciences (Pinker, 2015). To me, the book as a whole transmits a palpable excitement, not only for what it already contains, but also for what it foreshadows—a truly integrated theory of emotions, in which a set of shared functional principles link together the myriad particulars of our affective lives, with their phenomenal richness and subtlety.

Although this vision is still unrealized, and there remain many loose threads and gaps to fill, I believe that this volume marks an important step in the right direction. A clear tension toward integration runs through the book—as if the chapters were magnetic pieces, ready to snap into place and self-assemble into a unified construction. But before this can happen, evolutionary scholars will have to do some important conceptual groundwork to clarify the terms on which integration will take place. Evolutionary emotion research is at a crossroads—and we are lucky to be here in what promise to be very exciting times. Having been given the honor of writing this concluding chapter, I want to use the opportunity to review and critically discuss what I see as the most pressing theoretical issues in the field, then propose a research agenda for addressing them. While the items in the agenda lend themselves to a variety of approaches, I will argue that they can be tackled most effectively from an explicitly motivational perspective—a perspective already adopted by several authors of this *Handbook*, and presented somewhat more formally in my earlier chapter (Del Giudice, Chapter 5 in this volume).

Key Theoretical Issues
Specialized Mechanisms and the Great Bifurcation
The differences and similarities between emotion theories can be parsed using a number of different criteria (see, e.g., Scarantino, 2018). Without doubt, the most significant contrast in the evolutionary study of emotions is between theories that postulate the existence of multiple *specialized mechanisms* (or *programs*) dedicated

to emotions and theories that deny it. The mechanism-rich camp includes the various incarnations of Basic Emotions Theory (BET; see Cordaro, Chapter 1 in this volume), the coordination approach synthesized by Tooby, Cosmides, and others (see Tooby & Cosmides, Chapter 2 in this volume; Al-Shawaf et al., 2016; Nesse, 1990), and LeDoux's theory of "survival circuits" (e.g., LeDoux & Brown, 2017). The main representatives of the mechanism-free camp are the constructionist theories advanced by L. F. Barrett (2006, 2017) and Russell (2003); Fridlund and Russell (Chapter 3 in this volume) also argue that the Behavioral Ecology View (BECV) of facial displays aligns with a constructivist, mechanism-free stance that denies the existence of central coordination machinery.

With a few notable exceptions (e.g., Lin & Westgate, Chapter 17 in this volume), the authors of this *Handbook* adopt one version or another of the mechanism-rich perspective. On the one hand, this probably has something to do with the theoretical preferences of the editors; on the other hand, I suspect that the assumption of specialized mechanisms is more empirically generative, as it encourages researchers to focus on particular emotions and their possible adaptive functions. Be as it may, it is important to acknowledge that constructionist, mechanism-free theories are becoming increasingly popular in emotion research, especially outside the circle of scholars with an explicitly evolutionary perspective.

While I believe that constructionists have made hugely important contributions—not least by sharpening the methodological tools of emotion research, and successfully challenging some untenable assumptions of classical BET—I also believe that their arguments against specialized mechanisms are much weaker than they look on the surface. As others have noted, the evidence offered in support is perfectly compatible with the (mechanism-rich) coordination approach, and with revisions of BET that integrate the same functional principles (e.g., Faucher, 2013; Nesse, 2020; Scarantino, 2012a, 2015; Sznycer & Cohen, 2021).

Take the finding that episodes of "the same emotion" (e.g., anger) within and between individuals are heterogeneous, with relatively low coherence among different components of the response (subjective feelings, facial expressions, autonomic patterns, etc.). In the constructivist literature, this is regarded as evidence that emotions arise from the action of multiple independent processes without a central program, even if they are subjectively *categorized* as unitary phenomena. There are several problems with this inference. To begin, folk emotion labels like "anger" likely refer to the outputs of multiple mechanisms, each with its own specific rules of operation; thus, relying on folk categories is going to inflate the apparent variability of emotional responses (Scarantino, 2012a, 2015; Sznycer et al., 2017). Even more importantly, dealing effectively with fitness-critical situations requires emotion programs to be sensitive to context and produce open-ended response tendencies, rather than rigid and reflex-like behaviors (Al-Shawaf & Lewis, 2017; Al-Shawaf et al., 2016; Scarantino, 2015). Invariance is expected at the level of the function and information-processing structure of the mechanism, but not at that of the mechanism's output, which should display systematic variability across persons and situations. As noted by Sznycer and Cohen (2021), "adaptive orchestration may call for response coherence in some contexts and for low coherence or discoherence in other contexts" (p. 3).

Finally, one has to factor in the existence of pervasive individual differences (partly caused by genetic variation), both in the emotion mechanisms themselves and in the cognitive and physiological mechanisms they coordinate (Nesse, 2020). Clearly, response variability does not militate against the existence of (context-sensitive) emotion mechanisms; on the contrary, it may signal the need to postulate *more* mechanisms than would be suggested by folk emotion categories like "anger," "sadness," and "fear." The inference from response variability to the absence of specialized mechanisms is an unwarranted move, buttressed by rhetorical devices such as charges of "essentialism"—a term that by now has very little meaning, except as name-calling—and invocations of Mayr's authoritative-sounding but nebulous concept of "population thinking" (e.g., L. F. Barrett, 2017; on population thinking, see Hey, 2011; Witteveen, 2015, 2016, 2018).

In the constructivist literature, neurobiological evidence of "degeneracy" (i.e., many brain regions or networks can be mapped to one emotion category) and "neural reuse" (i.e., a single region or network can be mapped to many emotion categories) are used to argue that there are no specialized brain centers that coordinate emotional responses (see L. F. Barrett, 2017). But in fact, degeneracy and reuse are exactly what one expects if the overarching function of emotions is to orchestrate the activity of multiple mechanisms across the entire brain. If emotions work as coordination programs, the corresponding patterns of brain activity are inevitably going to look highly distributed and to overlap substantially with one another, as different emotions recruit many if not most of the same mechanisms (e.g., De Gelder & Vandenbulcke, 2012; Scarantino, 2012b). Likewise, findings of "reuse" are expected if emotions are not neatly separated neural mechanisms that evolved independently from one another, but partially differentiated adaptations that evolved from common precursors and may share substantial portions of their neural machinery (Nesse, 2004, 2020).[1]

The constructivist interpretation of the neuroscientific data is further vitiated by what I have called the *prediction-explanation fallacy*, or the uncritical use of prediction-optimized models for explanatory purposes (Del Giudice, 2021). For example, Barrett (2017) stated:

> Ironically, perhaps the strongest evidence to date for the theory [of constructed emotions] comes from studies that use pattern classification to distinguish categories of emotion—a finding that is routinely construed as providing the long awaited support for the classical view [. . .]. However, patterns that distinguish among the categories in one study do not replicate in the other studies. (p. 15)

The problem is that, in many applications of machine-learning techniques, prediction-optimized models deliberately introduce biases to improve predictive performance, at the expense of accurate explanation (see James et al., 2021; Shmueli, 2010; Yarkoni & Westfall, 2017). And because different models tend to be biased in different ways, they may suggest conflicting explanations of the same phenomenon—even when they are trained on the same or very similar data, and achieve similar levels of predictive accuracy (Breiman, 2001). Hence, it is a fallacy to interpret discordances between prediction-optimized models as straightforward evidence that the underlying phenomenon lacks consistency (for details see Del Giudice, 2021).

Fridlund and Russell (Chapter 3 in this volume) argue that facial behaviors (and presumably other behavioral and physiological phenomena that are usually regarded as components of emotional responses) evolved "in granular fashion" with no central coordination machinery, so that there are no "emotion centers in the brain." But this is a non sequitur, based on the unsubstantiated assertion that specialized computational mechanisms are somehow problematic from an evolutionary standpoint.

While adaptations *can* evolve as mosaics (and bipedalism seems a fitting example), this does not mean that all or even most of them do; in reality, organisms are packed with regulation and coordination mechanisms that control functionally related suites of traits and behaviors, and can be targets of selection in their own respect. Hormonal systems (and their regulatory centers in the hypothalamus) are obvious examples (Cox et al., 2016). Another striking illustration comes from the medial preoptic area (MPOA) in rodents, whose function is increasingly well understood thanks to progress in cellular and molecular neuroscience. This region of the hypothalamus collects and integrates parenting-relevant information from the environment (tactile, auditory, and chemical signals from pups, cues of nearby predators, etc.) and coordinates parental behaviors in a modular fashion by projecting to multiple regions of the brain (Kohl & Dulac, 2018; Kohl et al., 2018). This is as clear a counterexample as any to the idea that complex behavioral adaptations must evolve as mosaics, without specialized coordination centers. Even highly composite, multifaceted, delocalized adaptations like the immune system have shared regulatory nodes that coordinate their activity on a broad scale (Kitano & Oda, 2006). The ubiquitous logic of bow-tie architectures (Csete & Doyle, 2004; Doyle & Csete, 2011; see Del Giudice, Chapter 5 in this volume) shows that "outside-in" granularity and "inside-out" centralized coordination are not mutually exclusive, and instead can effectively complement each other.

The Readout Problem

Another important contrast that runs through the pages of this *Handbook* concerns the evolutionary plausibility of "readouts"—nonverbal displays that reliably signal the internal state of the individual in an involuntary fashion. Both BET and the coordination approach assume that displays *can* function as involuntary expressions of emotional states, at least for certain emotions and in certain contexts (Al-Shawaf et al., 2016; Tooby & Cosmides, Chapter 2 in this volume). BECV decisively rejects this assumption, in favor of the idea that nonverbal displays evolve as "social tools" designed to influence the behavior of other individuals (e.g., eliciting affiliation or prompting retreat), without expressing anything about the signaler's internal states (Fridlund, 1994, 2017; Fridlund & Russell, Chapter 3 in this volume).

Without question, BECV has had a salutary effect on the field by pushing scholars beyond naïve conceptions of uniformity and automaticity in the expression of emotions, thanks to its emphasis on the fitness costs and benefits of signals and on the role of contextual factors (e.g., audience effects; see Keltner et al., 2019; Scarantino, 2017a). That said, the wholesale rejection of "readouts" (and, by extension, expressions of internal states) turns out to be another non sequitur: BECV begins an important evolutionary argument about the costs and benefits of communicative signals, but stops before considering its implications in full. The argument starts from the assumptions that (a) signals evolve to serve the biological interest of signalers; and that (b) involuntary readouts of internal states would benefit receivers, thus imposing a potential fitness cost on the signaler. While these premises are both true, it is wrong to conclude that readouts are inevitably selected against "in the service of deception, economy, and privacy" (Fridlund, 1994, p. 109).

The first corrective is that, *pace* Fridlund, expressions need not be *entirely* automatic and reflex-like; instead, they can lie on continua of flexibility–inflexibility and voluntariness–involuntariness, thus allowing a degree of strategic control and cost mitigation (e.g., Scarantino, 2017a). In the BECV literature, this is ruled out by fiat because "expressions" are defined from the start as fully involuntary, reflex-like displays with no sensitivity to context; however, this is a way to avoid the issue rather than confronting it. Displays can be statistically reliable without being always and perfectly truthful, and can have an involuntary quality without being a hundred percent automatic and inflexible (Scarantino, 2017a, 2017b).

Even more importantly, honest signaling of one's state *can* be fitness-enhancing when there is common interest between signalers and receivers: this may happen when the receiver is genetically related to the signaler, or when transmitting reliable information about internal states permits coordination and reciprocity with one's cooperation partners (see Svetieva, Chapter 35 in this volume; Al-Shawaf et al., 2016; Bergstrom & Lachmann, 1997, 1998; Keltner et al., 2019; Krebs & Dawkins, 1984; Planer & Godfrey-Smith, 2021). More generally, it is crucial to realize that receivers can drive the evolution of reliable signals—including signals that carry fitness costs—as long as they are in a position to impose even larger costs on the signalers (e.g., by ostracizing or otherwise punishing them), and/or provide them with benefits that outweigh the costs (e.g., by choosing them as social or sexual partners). The fact that readouts have disadvantages is not a particular obstacle to their evolution, as long as their *net* effect on the signaler's fitness is positive. Indeed, social and sexual selection can favor the evolution of high levels of cooperativeness and altruism that benefit other group members at a significant cost to the individual (Aktipis, 2011; Nesse, 2007), and can lead individuals to produce credible, often expensive displays that reveal their internal condition and genetic quality (Biernaskie et al., 2018; Clutton-Brock & Huchard, 2013). Why should emotion expressions be an exception? By rejecting social partners who fail to provide legible information about their emotions, or who provide it in ways that turn out to be too confusing or misleading (and hence not predictive), receivers can select for the evolution of emotional readouts despite their potential costs.

On this count, there is intriguing evidence that emotional expressivity—not just for positive, but also for negative emotions—increases affiliation, cooperation, and trust (Boone & Buck, 2003; Feinberg et al., 2012; Schug et al., 2010; Wubben et al., 2011). Trust and likeability also increase when a person's emotional expressions are predictable (i.e., they match the observer's expectations based on contextual information; Chanes et al., 2018). The flip side is that we tend to avoid and mistrust people who come across as emotionally opaque or whose emotional responses are hard to predict. When receivers equipped with mind-reading adaptations can respond to differences in signaling behavior with affiliation or ostracism, excessive restraint in revealing one's inner states can be as damaging as excessive transparency; this demands a careful consideration of the payoff structures associated with social interactions, rather than a blanket rejection of the idea of readouts/expressions.

On a related point, Dezecache and Mercier (Chapter 44 in this volume) suggest that mechanisms of *emotional vigilance* in receivers may play a critical role in maintaining the (average) honesty of emotional displays, which is not guaranteed by their intrinsic features (e.g., metabolic costs). At various points in their fascinating chapter, the authors seem to embrace the BECV postulate that displays cannot function as readouts of emotional states; I find this somewhat ironic, because emotional vigilance is precisely the kind of receiver adaptation that *could* drive the evolution of credible readouts (see also McCullough & Reed, 2016).

Another questionable assumption of BECV is that displays benefit receivers mainly by allowing them to predict the signaler's actions in the immediate future; for example, a scowling, bared-teeth display might indicate that a person is more likely to start behaving aggressively. From this perspective, emotional states (to the extent that they can be said to actually exist; see Fridlund & Russell, Chapter 3 in this volume) would add nothing of value to the receiver, because they would fail to predict future behavior with any precision (for extended discussion of this point, see Scarantino, 2017a). This strikes me as a surprisingly narrow view of prediction: we build models of other people to anticipate their behavior on timescales that extend far beyond the immediate future—and not just in response to the present state of reality, but also in hypothetical future scenarios. Granted, knowing that someone is angry says little about what *exactly* they are going to do the next minute (though it remains predictive in a statistical sense); but, combined with contextual knowledge about the cause of anger, it can provide many other kinds of information that are invaluable in the long run—information about their goals and priorities, perception of that situation (and possibly similar ones), self-perceptions and self-evaluations, expectations from others, sensitivity to specific "triggers," regulation abilities, broader personality, and so forth. Indeed, people routinely use others' emotional reactions to "reverse-engineer" the appraisal process and draw inferences about their goals, values, motivations, and other traits of interest, and hence predict their future decisions more accurately (Gratch & de Melo, 2019: Hareli & Hess, 2010, 2019; Keltner et al., 2019). Emotional readouts can be hugely valuable to mind-reading receivers, setting the stage for social selection favoring displays that signal emotions with some degree of reliability.

Whither Basic Emotions?

It is hard to overstate the importance of BET in the history of emotion research. Over the years, the initial list of six basic emotions has been expanded to include more than twenty; Cordaro (Chapter 1 in this volume) lists 26 candidates, ranked at various levels of evidentiary support. In recent years, researchers working in the BET tradition have started to collect very large data sets of expressions and self-reports (Cowen & Keltner, 2020; Cowen et al., 2019); analyses usually yield about 25–30 dimensions of variation, which overlap largely—but not completely—across different studies and with the criteria-based lists offered by Cordaro (Chapter 1 in this volume), Keltner et al. (2019), and others. These and similar findings are quite impressive (see Keltner et al., 2019), but the edifice of BET is increasingly showing its cracks, which are largely conceptual rather than empirical in nature.

The first and most pressing issue with BET is that the criteria used to classify emotions as basic are not grounded in a functional and computational analysis of each emotion, but reflect the researchers' somewhat arbitrary intuitions of what an evolved emotion should look like. The three criteria of *brief duration* (usually specified as "less than a minute"), *universal signals*, and *primate homologies* (sometimes extended more broadly to mammals; e.g., Keltner et al., 2019) are particularly problematic and lack any coherent functional rationale. To give just an example, jealousy fails the first two criteria and possibly all three,[2] despite very strong evidence of adaptive design (Al-Shawaf et al., 2016; Buss, 2014). More generally, two evolved emotions may easily match different subsets of the "basic" criteria because of their specific functions and phylogenetic histories. Consider two hypothetical emotions A and B. Emotion A has clear homologues in other primates and occurs in brief episodes; whereas B has evolved more recently, and tends to manifest itself in longer-lasting episodes because its function unfolds on a longer timescale (e.g., by promoting certain forms of sustained cognitive processing). In the framework of BET, functional differences of this kind would be misinterpreted as mere differences in evidentiary support, so that emotion A would be classified as a "strong" candidate while B would be regarded as a "weak" contender for the title of basic emotion (see Table 1.2 in Cordaro, Chapter 1 in this volume). The deeper problem is that BET relies on a fixed set of criteria that are supposed to apply across the board; this use of checklists is arguably the original sin of BET, and at this point is holding back the theory rather than providing useful heuristic guidance.

A related problem—which also highlights the need for deeper functional thinking—is that BET tends to take folk emotional categories at face value, raising doubts about whether the "basic" emotions identified by researchers correspond to specific evolved mechanisms (see also Ortony, 2022). For example, different emotion programs may well elicit similar nonverbal displays—there is no reason to expect a strict one-to-one correspondence between emotions and expressions. As I noted in my earlier chapter, the reduction methods used to extract emotional dimensions from empirical data sets (PCA and such) do not help in this regard, because they are simply not capable of identifying the underlying mechanisms, except in unrealistic special cases (Del Giudice, Chapter 5 in this volume). The only way out of this quandary is through functional and computational analysis. This is the focus of the "New BET" (NBET) formulated by Scarantino (2015); in this important revision of the theory, folk categories are regarded as potentially heterogeneous, so that a single category like "fear" may comprise more than one basic emotion; an emotion is not regarded as basic because it fulfills a list of preset criteria, but because it can be shown to correspond to a specific evolved mechanism. Also, NBET answers the question of response variability by postulating that at least some emotional programs are "output-flexible," in the sense that they produce context-sensitive response *tendencies* instead of the mandatory, "output-rigid" responses of classical BET. Clearly, NBET goes a long way toward bridging the gap between the basic emotions tradition and the coordination model (e.g., Sznycer et al. 2017). In my view, the confluence of these approaches into a unified mechanism-rich theory is inevitable in the long run—and the sooner it happens, the better.

A Big-Picture Agenda

The theoretical issues I just surveyed have implications for all the major debates in emotion research; they need to be addressed and resolved, before an integrated evolutionary theory of emotions can emerge from the competing approaches that dominate the scene today. To this end, I would like to propose an agenda for evolutionary scholars who wish to tackle the big questions in the field. I formulate my suggestions as a member of the mechanism-rich team; but of course, many of the same points are just as relevant when viewed from the perspective of mechanism-free approaches.

Mechanisms and Variability

One of the main obstacles to the functional analysis of emotions is the fact that folk emotion categories may not identify specific adaptations, but rather collections of superficially similar mechanisms, with different purposes and rules of operation. While this is not a new insight (e.g., Cosmides & Tooby, 2000; Scarantino, 2012a), I note that many chapters in this *Handbook* still take folk categories at face value, and do not probe them for the possible existence of multiple underlying mechanisms. This should be a top research priority for mechanism-rich approaches, including BET. In the crucial task of "carving nature at its joints," functional and computational analyses can be usefully complemented by the fine-grained neurobiological dissection of brain regions and pathways (e.g., Panksepp, 1998, 2011).

Other important contributions in this sense can come from comparative and phylogenetic data, which are surprisingly under-utilized in the evolutionary study of emotion (but see Clay & Austry, Chapter 41 in this volume; Habecker & Flinn, Chapter 12 in this volume; Kujala & Braüer, Chapter 42 in this volume; O'Connell et al., Chapter 26 in this volume; Torres & Papini, Chapter 43 in this volume; Vonk et al., Chapter 40 in this volume). The view of emotions as partially differentiated mechanisms that evolve via reuse, duplication, and modification (Nesse, 2004, 2020; see also H. C. Barrett, 2012; Holbrook & Fessler, 2015; West-Eberhard, 2003) opens up many interesting questions about the phylogeny of emotions and corresponding neural mechanisms, from early animals to humans via the common ancestors of mammals and primates. Crucially, scholars need to abandon the preconception that evolved emotion mechanisms must be highly conserved, and instead expect a mixture of stability, novelty, and species-specific variation. The interplay between "granular" and "centralized" modes of evolution during phylogeny could be usefully tackled with simulations; for example, agent-based models could be used to explore the evolution of emotional mechanisms and their components under different conditions. The concept of bow-tie architectures (Csete & Doyle, 2004) could inform the design of these simulations and help interpret their results.

The problem of response coherence vs. variability is particularly tricky, because even if virtually all scholars agree that perfect coherence is not a reasonable expectation, it remains unclear how much variability is predicted by different theoretical models (and hence what amount of variability should count as supporting vs. disconfirming evidence). On this turf, constructivist models play with a tactical advantage: since they deny the existence of specialized mechanism, they have no grounds to expect a particular degree of coherence, and any evidence of variability can be loosely counted in their favor. From a mechanism-rich perspective, the solution is to start building explicit computational models of emotional responses, and—once the models become sufficiently realistic—to use their predictions as benchmarks to evaluate the empirical data. Models of this kind would also allow researchers to formulate predictions about *qualitative* patterns of variability (e.g., which components of a response are going to be the most/least variable), and about the individual and contextual factors that influence the coherence of emotional responses. Given the current lack of information and the fact that both sides of the debate rely on intuitions, even drastically simplified models are likely to provide useful insights. As far as I know, this research direction has remained virtually unexplored in the literature; the recent paper by Sznycer and Cohen (2021) is a step in the right direction, but still a long way from the explicit formal models that would be needed to adequately meet the constructivist challenge.

Eventually, computational models of emotions will need to explicitly integrate the physiological dimensions of the response (including, but not limited to, patterns of autonomic activation; see Tooby & Cosmides, Chapter 2 in this volume). Physiological changes modulate the internal state of the organism, but also have a range of perceptible effects that may function as signals (e.g., eyeblinks, blushing, changes in pupil size; Kret, 2015); also, physiological measures are often used in empirical studies of response coherence (e.g., Mauss et al., 2005; Rattel et al., 2020). In principle, then, physiology plays an important role in the coordination approach. However, current computational models of anger (Sell & Sznycer, Chapter 6 in this volume), shame (Landers et al., Chapter 7 in this volume), and many other emotions are still largely silent about the interplay between physiology and the cognitive/behavioral components on which they mainly focus. To include physiology in their models, evolutionary psychologists will have to get out of their "comfort zone" and cross the borders of evolutionary neurobiology and endocrinology; this is a vital but challenging task, which is made even more challenging by our very limited understanding of individual differences in physiological parameters and their functional meaning (see, e.g., Ellis & Del Giudice, 2019; Ellis et al., 2021; Gangestad & Grebe, 2017). At the same time, a computational mindset can greatly enrich the study of physiology and hormones—for example by underscoring the information-processing aspects of neurobiological mechanisms, framing individual differences in terms of internal regulatory variables (Tooby & Cosmides, 2008), and generally helping researchers ask important "why" questions in addition to the "how" questions of the standard mechanistic approach.

Readouts and Inferences

As I discussed earlier, BECV's negative argument against readouts does not follow from its premises, and readouts—in the sense of statistically reliable, at least partially involuntary signals of internal states—can certainly evolve, even if they have some costs and drawbacks. But this does not mean that emotional readouts *will* evolve in practice. To properly answer the critique from BECV, proponents of mechanism-rich models should clarify the conditions in which readouts are more or less likely to evolve, and identify the factors that tend to increase or decrease their "honesty" and credibility. These and similar questions could be usefully tackled with evolutionary simulations in which signaler and receiver strategies are free to coevolve (for an interesting but still rudimentary example, see Lowe et al., 2004); and when the models become sufficiently realistic, they could be tested against comparative data from animals with different ecologies and social structures.

Simulations are also an ideal way to formalize existing theories of emotional inference (Hareli & Hess, 2019), and refine them with the addition of mechanisms of emotional vigilance (Dezecache & Mercier, Chapter 44 in this volume). More generally, an evolutionary perspective would add specificity and depth to our understanding of inferential processes; the range of potential inferences that an observer could draw is almost limitless, but some aspects of the signaler's internal state are likely to be much more informative and/or fitness-relevant than others. The focus of emotional inferences may also shift depending on the specific social relationship between signaler and receiver—for example, the kind of information we seek can be quite different if we are dealing with a friend, an enemy, a relative, an attractive stranger, or a romantic partner.

Integration between Basic Emotions Theory and the Coordination Approach

I believe that the future will see a convergence between BET and the coordination approach, and would like to propose some ways to help the process along. First, coordination theorists should pay more attention to the large-scale empirical findings by researchers such as Cowen, Keltner, and others (e.g., Cowen & Keltner, 2020; Cowen et al., 2019). Patterns of perceived similarity can suggest ways to refine existing hypotheses; for example, emotion concepts form a continuum from anger and hate to sadness and despair, and while "righteous indignation" and "feeling oppressed" lie close to anger, "feeling let down" and "feeling betrayed" are much closer to sadness (Fig. 2 in Cowen et al., 2019). This seems potentially relevant to the recalibration theory of anger (Sell & Sznycer, Chapter 6 in this volume), and may point to a deep functional link between anger and sadness that has not been discussed in the recalibration literature (e.g., certain forms of sadness may reflect the recalibration of one's overly optimistic estimates of other people's welfare trade-off ratios).

From a different perspective, a crucial test of the coordination approach will be its ability to reproduce the observed patterns of correlation among emotional concepts, experiences, and/or expressions—not inductively, but starting from well-defined mechanisms and their functional relations with one another. The recent work on valuation as the common grammar of social emotions (Scrivner et al., Chapter 4 in this volume) is the beginning of a much-needed shift from a narrow, analytical focus on single emotions to a more synthetic perspective. An important next step would be to reproduce the broad structure of people's emotion-related concepts and perceptions, starting from a model of the underlying mechanisms. Of note, any discrepancies between the actual and predicted structure would provide invaluable information about gaps and inconsistencies in the model.

Finally, even though the BET criteria for basic emotions are blunt tools when it comes to identifying adaptations, they can suggest interesting questions about the reasons why different emotions show different patterns of correlates. For example, what are the main exceptions to the criterion of "brief duration"? What do those emotions have in common? What are the cognitive and neurobiological processes that sustain emotions for longer periods of time, and what is their design logic? Other potentially fruitful questions concern the degree of universality vs. cross-cultural variability of different emotions, and the functional meaning of differences in expression modalities: What are the relative strengths and weaknesses of visual, auditory, tactile, and olfactory cues (e.g., Bradbury & Vehrencamp, 2011)? Are different nonverbal modalities better suited to different purposes and social relationships? So far, these questions have been addressed only piecemeal in the BET literature; an integrated approach would have the tools to formulate and answer them in a systematic fashion.

The Advantages of a Motivational Perspective

The motivational perspective I synthesized in my earlier chapter (Del Giudice, Chapter 5 in this volume) is the antithesis of the mechanism-free approach—it takes an already rich model of emotions and extends it by adding *more* layers of specialized mechanisms (second-order motivational systems and third-order mood programs). Here I wish to briefly make the case that the resulting increase in complexity is worth the price, and that a focus on motivational systems can help with many of the items in the research agenda I just sketched—starting with the task of looking for multiple mechanisms within folk categories such as "anger" or "sadness." Carving nature at its joints gets much easier when the analysis can be guided by well-grounded functional distinctions; the distinctions between motivational domains can be used to generate plausible hypotheses about, say, various kinds of "anger" and their adaptive purposes.

From a neurobiological standpoint, the neural substrates of motivational systems may be easier to identify and study than those of specific emotions; for instance, the MPOA is a very promising candidate as the control hub of the parenting/caregiving motivational system. Also, the logic of bow-tie architectures suggests that motivational systems should be phylogenetically more conserved than emotions, and hence easier to study and compare across species. When it comes to integrating physiology in current models of emotions, the literature on motivational systems provides some useful computational principles, including control-theoretic ideas about feedback and feedforward regulation. The concept of internal regulatory variables has parallels and precursors in attachment theory ("internal working models"; Bowlby, 1969) and other classical theories of motivation, which I believe can still be mined for fresh insights.

A motivational perspective also helps frame the issue of readouts and emotional inferences: the functional parameters of motivational systems (e.g., their relative priorities and activation sensitivities) bridge emotions with personality, and can be extremely useful for predicting behavior in the long run. Because of this, people should often use emotions as indicators of the underlying motivational processes, which I suggested work as a privileged level of analysis for inference and prediction. Not least, motivational systems may offer a parsimonious way to organize the high-dimensional maps of "emotion spaces" that are emerging from the large descriptive studies carried out by BET scholars. Indeed, motivational states can be thought of as attractors of the more complex dynamics of emotions and moods; as such, they should help make sense of the increasingly rich, detailed, but also potentially overwhelming data on specific emotions by revealing their underlying functional structure.

Conclusion

I am grateful to the authors and editors of this *Handbook* for their contribution to what I think will become a landmark for the discipline. Researchers are already busy extending the reach of evolutionary approaches to more and more emotions, domains, and areas of application. To complement this enterprise and bring it to full fruition, they will have to address the most pressing conceptual issues head-on, and find convincing answers to some long-standing questions in the study of emotion. The call is not just for bigger and better data, but for a major investment in good theory, which—as per Kurt Lewin's maxim—is really the most practical of things. The day is young; let's get to work.

Acknowledgments

I am indebted to Laith Al-Shawaf, Andrea Scarantino, and Daniel Sznycer for their many insightful comments and suggestions.

Notes

1. On a side note, the predictive Bayesian models of the brain that inform Barrett's current *theory of constructed emotions* (L. F. Barrett, 2017) offer powerful explanations of perception and (perhaps) action control, but struggle to provide a realistic, tractable account of motivation (Colombo, 2016; Klein, 2018; Sun & Firestone, 2020a, 2020b). In light of the deep connections between motivation and emotion, I see this as more reason to be skeptical about the conceptual adequacy of this framework.
2. The jury is still out on the existence of proto-jealousy in other primates; see, e.g., Maninger et al. (2017).

References

Aktipis, C. A. (2011). Is cooperation viable in mobile organisms? Simple Walk Away rule favors the evolution of cooperation in groups. *Evolution and Human Behavior, 32*, 263–276.

Al-Shawaf, L., Conroy-Beam, D., Asao, K., & Buss, D. M. (2016). Human emotions: An evolutionary psychological perspective. *Emotion Review, 8*, 173–186.

Al-Shawaf, L., & Lewis, D. M. G. (2017). Evolutionary psychology and the emotions. In V. Zeigler-Hill & T.K. Shackelford (Eds.), *Encyclopedia of personality and individual differences* (pp. 1452–1461). Springer.

Barrett, H. C. (2012). A hierarchical model of the evolution of human brain specializations. *Proceedings of the National Academy of Sciences, 109*, 10733–10740.

Barrett, L. F. (2006). Are emotions natural kinds? *Perspectives on Psychological Science, 1*, 28–58.

Barrett, L. F. (2017). The theory of constructed emotion: An active inference account of interoception and categorization. *Social Cognitive and Affective Neuroscience, 12*, 1–23.

Bergstrom, C. T., & Lachmann, M. (1997). Signalling among relatives. I. Is costly signalling too costly? *Philosophical Transactions of the Royal Society B: Biological Sciences, 352*, 609–617.

Bergstrom, C. T., & Lachmann, M. (1998). Signaling among relatives. III. Talk is cheap. *Proceedings of the National Academy of Sciences, 95*, 5100–5105.

Biernaskie, J. M., Perry, J. C., & Grafen, A. (2018). A general model of biological signals, from cues to handicaps. *Evolution Letters, 2*, 201–209.

Boone, R. T., & Buck, R. (2003). Emotional expressivity and trustworthiness: The role of nonverbal behavior in the evolution of cooperation. *Journal of Nonverbal Behavior, 27*, 163–182.

Bowlby, J. (1969). *Attachment and loss*, Vol. I: *Attachment*. Basic Books.

Bradbury, J. W., & Vehrencamp, S. L. (2011). *Principles of animal communication* (2nd ed.). Sinauer.

Breiman, L. (2001). Statistical modeling: The two cultures. *Statistical Science, 16*, 199–231.

Buss, D. M. (2014). Comment: Evolutionary criteria for considering an emotion "basic": Jealousy as an illustration. *Emotion Review, 6*, 313–315.

Chanes, L., Wormwood, J. B., Betz, N., & Barrett, L. F. (2018). Facial expression predictions as drivers of social perception. *Journal of Personality and Social Psychology, 114*, 380–396.

Clutton-Brock, T. H., & Huchard, E. (2013). Social competition and selection in males and females. *Philosophical Transactions of the Royal Society B: Biological Sciences, 368*, 20130074.

Colombo, M. (2016). Social motivation in computational neuroscience (Or, if brains are prediction machines, then the Humean theory of motivation is false). In J. Kiverstein (Ed.), *The Routledge handbook of philosophy of the social mind* (pp. 336–356). Routledge.

Cosmides, L., & Tooby, J. (2000). Evolutionary psychology and the emotions. In M. Lewis & J. M. Haviland-Jones (Eds.), *Handbook of emotions* (2nd ed., pp. 91–115). Guilford Press.

Cowen, A. S., & Keltner, D. (2020). What the face displays: Mapping 28 emotions conveyed by naturalistic expression. *American Psychologist, 75*, 349–364.

Cowen, A., Sauter, D., Tracy, J. L., & Keltner, D. (2019). Mapping the passions: Toward a high-dimensional taxonomy of emotional experience and expression. *Psychological Science in the Public Interest, 20*, 69–90.

Cox, R. M., McGlothlin, J. W., & Bonier, F. (2016). Hormones as mediators of phenotypic and genetic integration: An evolutionary genetics approach. *Integrative and Comparative Biology, 56*, 126–137.

Csete, M., & Doyle, J. (2004). Bow ties, metabolism and disease. *Trends in Biotechnology, 22*, 446–450.

De Gelder, B., & Vandenbulcke, M. (2012). Emotions as mind organs. *Behavioral and Brain Sciences, 35*, 147–148.

Del Giudice, M. (2021). The prediction-explanation fallacy: A pervasive problem in scientific applications of machine learning. *PsyArXiv*. https://doi.org/10.31234/osf.io/4vq8f

Doyle, J. C., & Csete, M. (2011). Architecture, constraints, and behavior. *Proceedings of the National Academy of Sciences, 108*, 15624–15630.

Ellis, B. J., & Del Giudice, M. (2019). Developmental adaptation to stress: An evolutionary perspective. *Annual Review of Psychology, 70*, 111–139.

Ellis, B. J., Horn, A. J., Carter, C. S., van IJzendoorn, M. H., & Bakermans-Kranenburg, M. J. (2021). Developmental programming of oxytocin through variation in early-life stress: Four meta-analyses and a theoretical reinterpretation. *Clinical Psychology Review, 86*, 101985.

Faucher, L. (2013). Comment: Constructionisms? *Emotion Review, 5*, 374–378.

Feinberg, M., Willer, R., & Keltner, D. (2012). Flustered and faithful: Embarrassment as a signal of prosociality. *Journal of Personality and Social Psychology, 102*, 81–97.

Fridlund, A. J. (1994). *Human facial expression: An evolutionary view.* Academic Press.

Fridlund, A. J. (2017). The behavioral ecology view of facial displays, 25 years later. In J. M. Fernández-Dols & J. A. Russell (Eds.), *The science of facial expression* (pp. 77–92). Oxford University Press.

Gangestad, S. W., & Grebe, N. M. (2017). Hormonal systems, human social bonding, and affiliation. *Hormones and Behavior, 91*, 122–135.

Gratch, J., & de Melo, C. (2019). Inferring intentions from emotion expressions in social decision making. In U. Hess & S. Hareli (Eds.), *The social nature of emotion expression: What emotions can tell us about the world* (pp. 141–160). Springer.

Hareli, S., & Hess, U. (2010). What emotional reactions can tell us about the nature of others: An appraisal perspective on person perception. *Cognition and Emotion, 24*, 128–140.

Hareli, S., & Hess, U. (2019). The reverse engineering of emotions: Observers of others' emotions as naïve personality psychologists. In U. Hess & S. Hareli (Eds.), *The social nature of emotion expression: What emotions can tell us about the world* (pp. 103–118). Springer.

Hey, J. (2011). Regarding the confusion between the population concept and Mayr's "population thinking." *Quarterly Review of Biology, 86*, 253–264.

Holbrook, C., & Fessler, D. M. (2015). The same, only different: Threat management systems as homologues in the tree of life. In P. J. Carroll, R. M. Arkin, & A L. Wichman (Eds.), *Handbook of personal security* (pp. 95–110). Psychology Press.

James, G., Witten, D., Hastie, T., & Tibshirani, R. (2021). *An introduction to statistical learning with applications in R* (2nd ed.). Springer.

Keltner, D., Sauter, D., Tracy, J., & Cowen, A. (2019). Emotional expression: Advances in basic emotion theory. *Journal of Nonverbal Behavior, 43*, 133–160.

Kitano, H., & Oda, K. (2006). Robustness trade-offs and host–microbial symbiosis in the immune system. *Molecular Systems Biology, 2*, 2006.0022.

Klein, C. (2018). What do predictive coders want? *Synthese, 195*, 2541–2557.

Kohl, J., Babayan, B. M., Rubinstein, N. D., Autry, A. E., Marin-Rodriguez, B., Kapoor, V., Miyamishi, K., Zweifel, L. S., Luo, L., Uchida, N., & Dulac, C. (2018). Functional circuit architecture underlying parental behaviour. *Nature, 556*, 326–331.

Kohl, J., & Dulac, C. (2018). Neural control of parental behaviors. *Current Opinion in Neurobiology, 49*, 116–122.

Krebs, J. R., & Dawkins, R. (1984). Animal signals: Mind-reading and manipulation. In J. R. Krebs & N. B. Davies (Eds.), *Behavioural ecology: An evolutionary approach* (2nd ed., pp. 380–402). Blackwell.

Kret, M. E. (2015). Emotional expressions beyond facial muscle actions. A call for studying autonomic signals and their impact on social perception. *Frontiers in Psychology, 6*, 711.

LeDoux, J. E., & Brown, R. (2017). A higher-order theory of emotional consciousness. *Proceedings of the National Academy of Sciences, 114*, E2016–E2025.

Lowe, R., Cañamero, L., Nehaniv, C. L., & Polani, D. (2004). The evolution of affect-related displays, recognition and related strategies. In J Pollack, M. Bedau, P. Husbands, T. Ikegami, & R. A. Watson (Eds.), *Artificial life IX: Proceedings of the Ninth International Conference on the Simulation and Synthesis of Living Systems* (pp. 176–181). MIT Press.

Maninger, N., Mendoza, S. P., Williams, D. R., Mason, W. A., Cherry, S. R., Rowland, D. J., Schaefer, T., & Bales, K. L. (2017). Imaging, behavior and endocrine analysis of "jealousy" in a monogamous primate. *Frontiers in Ecology and Evolution, 5*, 119.

Mauss, I. B., Levenson, R. W., McCarter, L., Wilhelm, F. H., & Gross, J. J. (2005). The tie that binds? Coherence among emotion experience, behavior, and physiology. *Emotion, 5*, 175–190.

McCullough, M. E., & Reed, L. I. (2016). What the face communicates: Clearing the conceptual ground. *Current Opinion in Psychology, 7*, 110–114.

Nesse, R. M. (1990). Evolutionary explanations of emotions. *Human Nature, 1*, 261–289.

Nesse, R. M. (2004). Natural selection and the elusiveness of happiness. *Philosophical Transactions of the Royal Society B: Biological Sciences, 359*, 1333–1347.

Nesse, R. M. (2007). Runaway social selection for displays of partner value and altruism. *Biological Theory, 2*, 143–155.

Nesse, R. M. (2020). Tacit creationism in emotion research. In C. Price & E. Walle (Eds.), *Emotion researcher: ISRE's sourcebook for research on emotion and affect*. International Society for Research on Emotion. https://emotionresearcher.com/tacit-creationism-in-emotion-research

Ortony, A. (2022). Are all "basic emotions" emotions? A problem for the (basic) emotions construct. *Perspectives on Psychological Science, 17,* 41–61.

Panksepp, J. (1998). *Affective neuroscience: The foundations of human and animal emotions*. Oxford University Press.

Panksepp, J. (2011). Cross-species affective neuroscience decoding of the primal affective experiences of humans and related animals. *PLoS ONE, 6,* e21236.

Pinker, S. (2015). Foreword. In D. M. Buss (Ed.), *The handbook of evolutionary psychology* (2nd ed., pp. ix–xvi). Wiley.

Planer, R. J., & Godfrey-Smith, P. (2021). Communication and representation understood as sender–receiver coordination. *Mind & Language, 36,* 750–770.

Rattel, J. A., Mauss, I. B., Liedlgruber, M., & Wilhelm, F. H. (2020). Sex differences in emotional concordance. *Biological Psychology, 151,* 107845.

Russell, J. A. (2003). Core affect and the psychological construction of emotion. *Psychological Review, 110,* 145–172.

Scarantino, A. (2012a). How to define emotions scientifically. *Emotion Review, 4,* 358–368.

Scarantino, A. (2012b). Functional specialization does not require a one-to-one mapping between brain regions and emotions. *Behavioral and Brain Sciences, 35,* 161–162.

Scarantino, A. (2015). Basic emotions, psychological construction, and the problem of variability. In L. F. Barrett & J. A. Russell (Eds.), *The psychological construction of emotion* (pp. 334–376). Guilford Press.

Scarantino, A. (2017a). How to do things with emotional expressions: The theory of affective pragmatics. *Psychological Inquiry, 28,* 165–185.

Scarantino, A. (2017b). Twelve questions for the theory of affective pragmatics. *Psychological Inquiry, 28,* 217–232.

Scarantino, A. (2018). The philosophy of emotions and its impact on affective science. In L. F. Barrett, M. Lewis, & J. M. Haviland-Jones (Eds.), *Handbook of emotions* (4th ed., pp. 3–48). Guilford Press.

Schug, J., Matsumoto, D., Horita, Y., Yamagishi, T., & Bonnet, K. (2010). Emotional expressivity as a signal of cooperation. *Evolution and Human Behavior, 31,* 87–94.

Shmueli, G. (2010). To explain or to predict? *Statistical Science, 25,* 289–310.

Sun, Z., & Firestone, C. (2020a). The dark room problem. *Trends in Cognitive Sciences, 24,* 346–348.

Sun, Z., & Firestone, C. (2020b). Optimism and pessimism in the predictive brain. *Trends in Cognitive Sciences, 24,* 683–685.

Sznycer, D., & Cohen, A. S. (2021). Are emotions natural kinds after all? Rethinking the issue of response coherence. *Evolutionary Psychology, 19,* 14747049211016009.

Sznycer, D., Cosmides, L., & Tooby, J. (2017). Adaptationism carves emotions at their functional joints. *Psychological Inquiry, 28,* 56–62.

Tooby, J., & Cosmides, L. (2008). The evolutionary psychology of the emotions and their relationship to internal regulatory variables. In M. Lewis, J. M. Haviland-Jones, & L. F. Barrett (Eds.), *Handbook of emotions* (3rd ed., pp. 114–137). Guilford Press.

West-Eberhard, M. J. (2003). *Developmental plasticity and evolution*. Oxford University Press.

Witteveen, J. (2015). "A temporary oversimplification": Mayr, Simpson, Dobzhansky, and the origins of the typology/population dichotomy (part 1 of 2). *Studies in History and Philosophy of Science C: Studies in History and Philosophy of Biological and Biomedical Sciences, 54,* 20–33.

Witteveen, J. (2016). "A temporary oversimplification": Mayr, Simpson, Dobzhansky, and the origins of the typology/population dichotomy (part 2 of 2). *Studies in History and Philosophy of Science C: Studies in History and Philosophy of Biological and Biomedical Sciences, 57,* 96–105.

Witteveen, J. (2018). Typological thinking: Then and now. *Journal of Experimental Zoology B: Molecular and Developmental Evolution, 330,* 123–131.

Wubben, M. J., De Cremer, D., & van Dijk, E. (2011). The communication of anger and disappointment helps to establish cooperation through indirect reciprocity. *Journal of Economic Psychology, 32,* 489–501.

Yarkoni, T., & Westfall, J. (2017). Choosing prediction over explanation in psychology: Lessons from machine learning. *Perspectives on Psychological Science, 12,* 1100–1122.

INDEX

For the benefit of digital users, indexed terms that span two pages (e.g., 52–53) may, on occasion, appear on only one of those pages.

Note: Tables, figures, and boxes are indicated by *t, f,* and *b* following the page number. Notes are indicated by an *n,* followed by the note number

A

abandonment
    fear of, in borderline personality disorder, 1280
    by romantic partner, 392, 394
Abed, Riadh, 1172–90
Abraham (biblical patriarch), and his descendants, 1060–61
absenteeism, depression and, 1154–55
ACC. *See* anterior cingulate cortex
acceptance and commitment therapy, 1125
Ache of Paraguay, 191
    food-sharing among, 623
acquisition (motivational) system, 104, 105*f*, 111
ACT. *See* acceptance and commitment therapy
ACTH. *See* adrenocorticotropic hormone
adaptation(s), 145, 469–70, 682, 1062. *See also* environment of evolutionary adaptedness; functional analysis of adaptation(s)
    versus artifacts, 51n.7
    characteristics of, 27, 35, 1144
    complex, 32–33
    concomitants or byproducts of, 26–27
    Darwinism and, 24, 26–27
    disorders versus, 1126–27
    evolution as mosaics, 1329–30
    and facial action, 67–71
    functions of, 164–65
    genetic variation and, 32–33, 51n.6
    ongoing, 23–24
    versus phenotypic properties, 35, 51n.7
    as population-typical, 32–33, 51n.6
    as record of past, 31–32, 49–50
    as recurrent design, 33, 34, 35
    search for, 24–25, 50n.2
    as species-typical, 32–33, 35, 51n.6
    variability in expression versus uniformity in design, 33–34
adaptationism, 72n.2, 164–65, 393
    and emotion-personality constellation, 87
adaptationist program, 21–22
    and analysis of behavior, 27–29
    and causal explanations, 25–26
    versus correspondence program, 22–24
Adapted to Flee Famine Hypothesis, and anorexia nervosa, 1176*t*, 1182
adaptive choice switching, 248
adaptive immune system, maturity, and disgust sensitivity in children, 193
adaptiveness, 21. *See also* correspondence/correspondence program; hyperadaptiveness
    definition of, 51n.9
    and "feasible alternatives," 36–37, 51n.9
    search for, 24–25, 50n.2
adaptive problem(s), 27, 29, 145, 265–66, 298, 406, 748–49, 984
    adaptations that solve, characterization of, 35
    complexity of, 32–33
    hierarchy negotiation and, 589–93
    and human motivational systems, 104–12, 105*f*
    identification of, 43
    of social valuation, 80
    strategies for solving, 614–15, 1135
adaptive rumination hypothesis, 254–55, 1147, 1148
    and depression, 1147, 1148, 1160
addiction, 255, 1218–19. *See also* behavioral addiction; sex addiction; substance use disorder(s)
    as disease, 1219–20
    evolutionary perspective on, 1222–27
    fundamental motives framework for, 1227–33, 1228*t*
    incentive-sensitization model of, 1221
    motivational-emotional systems and, 1220–33, 1228*t*
    recovery, contentment and, 454
    romantic love and, 228
ADHD. *See* attention-deficit hyperactivity disorder
admiration
    kama muta and, 348
    narcissistic, 1202, 1204 (*see also* narcissistic admiration and rivalry concept)
    versus respect, 597
    and status hierarchies, 587, 593, 594*t*, 597
adolescence
    antisocial behavior in, 1243–44
    emotional development in, 466
    humor in, functions of, 549, 554
    loss in, 492
    major depression in, 1139
    narcissism in, 1203
    suicidality in, 1154
    suicide rate in, 1154
adolescents, depression in, interpersonal effects of, 1158, 1159

adrenocorticotropic hormone
   in depression, 866
   fear and, 505
   frustrative nonreward and, 834–35
Adult Attachment Inventory,
   1287–88
adultery, 948
adulthood
   crying in, 467
   emotional development in, 466
adversity, 1146
   and brain dysfunction, 1160
   evolutionary significance of,
      1145–46
   and major depression, 1135–36,
      1136f, 1137t, 1145–46, 1161–62
   responses to, 1135
   and reward vs. benefit
      balance, 1161
   under strife, depression and
      suicidality associated with,
      1148–50
   and suicidality, 1135–36
affect(s), 463–64, 520–21, 544. *See
   also* core affect; negative affect;
   positive affect
   cognitive effects of, 374–77
   conservation across
      species, 325–26
   definition of, 374
   and emotional disorders, 1105
   and emotions, 319–20
   empirical study of, 521
   evolution of, 464–65
   facial expression of, 60, 73n.10
   functions of, 323, 521, 538
   as information, 319–21
   informational or content effect
      of, 523–25
   and learning, 465
   limbic structures and, 468–69
   and memory, 469
   memory-based, 524
   neural function and, 464–65
   primary, 60–61
   as primitive and
      dangerous, 520–21
   processing effects of, 523–
      24, 527–29
   and social stimuli, 521
   universal, 463–64, 471–72
affect-as-information, 524–25, 894–
   97, 901, 902, 903
Affect as Information
   Hypothesis, 374
affect infusion, 524, 525
   in judgments, 525–26

   in memory, 525–26
   negative, benefits of, 525–27
   in social behaviors, 526–27
Affect Infusion Model, 374, 525,
   526, 527
affection, parent–child, olfaction
   and, 670–71, 673f
affective empathy, 566, 575–76, 633,
   797, 820. *See also* emotional
   empathy
   and compensatory versus punitive
      behaviors, 1013
   and forgiveness, 725–26
   in narcissism, 1206, 1207–8
   and punitive behaviors, 1015
affective experience(s),
   categorization of, 12–13
affective instability, in borderline
   personality disorder, 1280,
   1281–82
affective neuroscience, 764, 766
affective resonance, emotional
   contagion and, 740
affective science, evolutionary. *See
   also* emotion science
   English-language constructs
      and, 382
   research recommendations
      for, 381–83
affectivism, 792
affect priming, 524
affect program, 990
AFFH. *See* Adapted to Flee Famine
   Hypothesis
affiliation
   attachment love and, 373t
   display of, in animals, 791
   emotional expressivity and, 1331
   third-party, 800
affiliation (motivational) system,
   102, 103–4, 105f, 110, 1227,
   1228t
   and drug use/addiction, 1228t,
      1230–31
affiliative behaviors, in
   animals, 770
affirmation and negation, gestures
   of, 72n.3
affordance(s), 905n.9
   environmental, 698–99,
      711, 904n.2
   negative, 905n.9
   positive, 905n.9
Africa, differential reproduction in,
   ethnographic and historical
   perspective on, 1057–58
agape, 220–21

agency
   as appraisal dimension, 990
   and happiness, 476
   pride and, 208
aggression, 1227, 1228t. *See also* cute
   aggression; defensive aggression
   system; predatory aggression;
   ritualized aggression
   adaptive problems solved by, 139
   affective, 107
   anger-based, bargaining function
      of, 138–39
   bargaining, 138–39
   as cathartic, 973
   defensive, 107–8
   definition of, 862
   depression and, 1156
   direct, high-status individuals
      and, 976
   direct, women's use of, 972–73
   in dogs, 811–12
   dominance competition
      and, 108–9
   drug use and, 1230
   ear movement signaling of, in
      animals, 771
   emotional, 107
   emotions in relation to, 973–75
   expression in animals, 770–71, 812
   in female intrasexual competition,
      972–75, 977–79
   fitness-enhancing uses of, 1271
   frustration and, 973
   hatred-based, 173
   hormones and, 862–64
   humor and, 550
   indirect, low-status individuals
      and, 976
   indirect, women's use of, 972–
      73, 977
   inhibition of, 285
   instrumental, 107, 1306
   and mate retention, 399
   in men, 972
   as motivation, 104, 107–8
   narcissism and, 1206, 1207
   and olfactory communication,
      668, 673f
   ostracism and, 1043
   pain and, 973
   physical, psychopathy and, 1298–99
   predatory, 107
   proactive, 107–8
   psychopathy and, 1306
   reactive, 107
   reduction, in response to
      depressed persons, 1157–59

regulation of, 285
self-perceived mate value and, 976
sex differences in, 1188
sexual, psychopathy and, 1298–99
shame and, 147–48, 154–55
social rejection and, 974–75
and suicidality, 1149–50
in women, 863–64
agoraphobia, 1111, 1113–14
agreeableness
    anger and, 122–23
    emotion-personality constellation and, 87
    genetic basis for, 1200–1
    gratitude and, 264–65
    and life-history strategies, 1288–89
    motivational analysis of, 122–23, 124n.7
    olfactory performance and, 672
    pride and, 206–8, 207t
agriculture, 1179–80
AIM. *See* Affect Infusion Model
Ainsworth, M. D. S., 485–87
Aka Pygmies
    attachment figures among, 914–15
    differential reproduction in, ethnographic and historical perspective on, 1057–58
    male, helminth infection, and nicotine consumption, 140
Aktipis, Athena, 622–42
alarm calls, context and, 915–16
alarm signals
    chemical, in animals, 767
    nonvocal, 507–8, 683
    reliable versus unreliable, 855
    social functions of, 508
    ultrasonic, 507–8
    vocal, 507–8
alcohol, and effects of frustrative nonreward, 835
alcohol use, 1218, 1229–30
    as adaptation, 1226
    anxiolytic effects of, 1228t, 1230
    mortality caused by, 1219–20
Alexander, R. D., 1146
allergy(ies), 182, 187, 191
allesthesia, 889–90
alliance formation, 102
allodynia, 418
alloparenting, 287, 306, 910, 922
    evolutionary perspective on, 910–13, 912f
allopregnanolone
    and panic disorder, 873
    and peripartum depression, 870
    and PMS/PMDD, 868–69

all-or-none thinking
    in borderline personality disorder, 1285
    in post-traumatic stress disorder, 1270
allostasis, 116–17
    definition of, 443
allostatic load, 443–46
    perception of, and contentment, 443–46
Allport, Floyd, 59, 60–61, 64, 67, 73n.12
Al-Shawaf, Laith, xxi–xxii, 62, 79–90, 145–57, 391–409, 1104, 1229
altruism, 284
    definition of, 421
    empathy-driven, 952
    guilt and, 289
    inhibition of, 292f, 286–87, 292
    kin, 286–87
    offspring care and, 567–68
    pain of, 418
    reciprocal, 287, 463, 474, 549–50, 568, 634, 683
    romantic love and, 227
altruistic motivational system, 100
amae, 382
ambiguity, intolerance for, benefits of, 1270
amenorrhea, 1181
Americas, differential reproduction in, ethnographic and historical perspective on, 1059–60
amusement
    and affiliative connections, 379
    evolutionary origins of, evidence for, 10t, 11
amwunumwun, 1150
amygdala, 766, 1112
    and anxiety, 506–7
    basolateral area of, 237–38, 238f, 239–40
    and behavioral adjustment to frustrative nonreward, 836–39
    in bonobos, 794–95
    in dogs, 812
    and emotion processing, 237–38, 238f
    and emotions, 468–69
    and fear responding/fear learning, 503–10, 509f
    and laughter, 557
    long-term depression in, 238, 240f, 240
    long-term potentiation in, 238, 240f, 240–41
    in olfactory processing, 665, 666f

oxytocin and, 238–42
    and punitive behavior, 1008
    and threat avoidance in illness, 307
AN. *See* anorexia nervosa
analytical rumination hypothesis. *See* adaptive rumination hypothesis
ancestral conditions. *See* environment of evolutionary adaptedness
ancestral cues, central role of, 39–40
André, Jean-Baptiste, 944–61
Andrews, Brian, 1242
Andrews, Paul, 1147
androgen secretion, conditioning and, 465
androstadienone, 669–70
androstanol, 669
androstenone, 669–70
Angelman syndrome, and laughter, 557
anger, xiii, 155, 437–38, 742–43, 944–45. *See also* social emotions; welfare trade-off ratio
    activation in response to low WTR, 137–38, 170, 176, 393, 1071
    adaptive functions of, 521–22, 1071
    apologies and, 141–42
    bargaining function of, 140–41, 173, 954–55, 960
    as basic emotion, 4, 103, 990
    behavioral outputs of, 393
    behaviors associated with, in animals, 768
    in borderline personality disorder, 1280, 1282
    characteristics of, 135, 142n.1
    and choice of cooperative partner, 624t292f
    co-activation with jealousy, 404–5
    and compensatory versus punitive behaviors, 1012–13, 1016n.5
    competitive, evolution of moral indignation from, 955–56
    computational model of, 1334
    contexts and, 1002b, 1003
    and cooperation, 624t, 636, 639–40
    deactivation of, 393, 464
    and decision-making/actions in legal contexts, 1071–72
    defensive aggression and, 117–18
    defusion of, 137
    depression and, 1149–50, 1156

anger *(cont.)*
   and detection of negative association value, 167
   disinterested versus less disinterested, 1002*b*
   disorders of, 1086–87
   downregulation, and saving behavioral resources, 754
   empathetic, 1002*b*, 1003
   evolutionary origins of, evidence for, 10*t*, 11
   evolutionary perspective on, 371–72, 1071–72
   evolved function of, 135–36
   expression of, and relative status, 599
   facial expression of, 598, 685
   and female intrasexual competition, 975–76
   functionally distinct variants of, 122–23
   function of, 148–49, 464, 501, 502*f*, 598, 975–76, 1056–57, 1072, 1135, 1156
   and hatred, 170, 176
   hormones and, 862–64
   individual differences in, and relative status, 599
   infidelity-induced, 1075, 1076–77
   information-processing and, 393
   insults and, 137–38
   intensity of, variations of, 598, 1100
   intentionality in, 137
   in intergroup context, 698–99, 700, 704, 705
   interpersonal functions of, 624*t*, 636, 639–40
   versus jealousy, 404–5
   in leader–follower interactions, 1031, 1032
   and mate value–aggression relationship, 976
   and mediation, 1073–74
   moral, 956–57, 1002*b*
   and moral conscience, 1076–77
   and moral life, 955
   motivational systems and, 102–3, 122–23
   in narcissism, 1208
   as negative emotion, 1003
   in negotiation about entitlement, 610
   negotiation process of, 142
   neuroscience of, 1008
   non-Western concepts related to, 1150
   ostracism and, 1044, 1045
   personal, 1002*b*, 1003
   and political judgment and behavior, 608–9, 610, 1049
   in post-traumatic stress disorder, 1271
   as primary emotion, 764
   primate expression of, 685
   psychopathy and, 1299
   and punishment, 1003–06, 1009, 1014–16, 1014*f*, 1016n.1, 1072
   recalibrational theory of, 117–18, 135, 172–73, 598, 610, 975–76, 1071–72, 1073–74, 1076–77, 1335
   research on, 318
   righteous, 955
   self-relevant events and, 8
   shame and, 155
   shared, 742–43
   as social emotion, 80–81, 82–83, 84–85, 85*f*, 86*f*
   and status hierarchies, 593, 594*t*, 598–99, 600–1
   subroutines and adaptations in, 142
   "switching off," 402
   task analytical approach to, 393
   tendency to feel, and political attitudes, 613
   and terminating costly relationships, 624*t*, 640–41
   thresholds for, bargaining power and, 141
   trait, and third-party punishment, 1003–04
   triggers of, 137, 138, 178n.4, 464
   unfairness perceptions and, 1004, 1016n.2
   upregulation of, and instrumental outcomes, 751–52
   vulnerability and, 117–18
anger face, 173
   universal human, 139–40
anhedonia, 468, 477, 865
   definition of, 1271–72
   depressive, 1271–72
   in post-traumatic stress disorder, 1271–72
animal(s). *See also* animal emotions; domestication of animals; ethology; great apes; mammals; primate homologues of basic emotions
   affect in, 317
   affiliative behaviors in, 770
   appeasement displays in, 776
   assessment of emotion capacities in, 765–67
   boredom in, 325–27
   captive, negative behaviors of, 768
   chemical signals used by, 767
   cognitive bias tests in, 773–74
   conspecific, jealousy in, 777–78
   curiosity-like behaviors in, 359–60, 365
   cuteness response evoked by, 340–41
   debilitation in, 418
   discrimination of facial expressions by, 771–73
   dominance displays, 212
   emotional contagion in, 769, 775
   emotional reactivity in, 768–69
   emotional responses in, 371
   emotional Stroop test in, 774
   emotion discrimination by, 772
   and emotion regulation, 757–58
   empathy in, 797, 799
   and envy, 776–78
   facial expressions in, 770–73, 791
   fear in, 778–79
   frustrative nonreward in, 830–40
   grief in, 487–89, 768
   group-living, reconciliation in, 720
   habituation in, 464
   happiness in, 770
   harm avoidance in, 284–85
   hemispheric lateralization of emotion processing in, 767
   hormonal assessment of, 765–66
   infrared thermography in, 766
   and jealousy, 776–78
   judgment bias test in, 773–74
   laughter expression in, 544
   love in, 488–89
   negative behaviors of, 768–69
   nociception in, 418–19, 429
   nonverbal status signals used by, 212
   olfactory cues and mate choice in, 667
   ostracism in, 1042
   pain in, 417, 418–20, 429–30, 502–3
   physiological assessment of, 765
   play behavior in, 770–71
   positive behaviors in, 769–73
   psychoactive substance use in, 1223
   reconciliation in, 720–23, 731
   response to threat, 464

reversed SNC effect in, 832–33
ritualized aggression in, 139–40
second-party punishment
 in, 997–98
self-grooming in, 770
separation reactions in, 493
signaling and behavior of, 67–
 68, 686–87
signs of self-control in, 758
sleep duration, predation risk
 and, 1271
speeded response tests in, 774
status hierarchies among, 588
successive negative contrast effects
 in, 830–40
targeted helping in, 801
use of cues/information, 40–42
vocal signals used by, 685, 768
animal communication, as form of
 manipulation, 688
animal emotions, 4, 325–27. *See also*
 dogs, emotions in
behavioral variables associated
 with, 768–69, 792
cognitive measures
 and, 773–74
dimensional approach to,
 764, 793
discrete emotion approach to, 793
ear movement and, 771
expression of, 685, 686–87, 763–
 65, 767, 792
humans' recognition of, 773
neurological underpinnings
 of, 766–67
physiological component of,
 763–64, 792
research on, approaches and
 techniques, 765–67, 795–
 96, 801–2
secondary, 774–78
subjective component of, 763–
 64, 792
animal-type phobia(s), evolutionary
 research on, recent
 developments in, 1120–21
anorexia nervosa, 1172. *See also*
 eating disorder(s)
Adapted to Flee Famine
 Hypothesis and, 1176*t*, 1182
atypical, 1172
binge-eating/purging type, 1172–
 73, 1173*b*
clinical and nonclinical studies of,
 1186–87
DSM criteria for, 1172–73,
 1173*b*, 1185

epidemiology of, 1172–73,
 1174, 1185
evolutionary perspective on, 1175–
 89, 1176*t*, 1190
heritability of, 1174
Insurance Hypothesis and,
 1176*t*, 1183
life-history strategies and, 1185–87
losing strategy hypothesis for,
 1181, 1183
mismatch hypotheses for, 1189
parental manipulation hypothesis
 and, 1176*t*, 1181–82
Reproductive Suppression
 Hypothesis for, 1176*t*, 1180–81
restricting type, 1172–73, 1173*b*
Sexual Competition Hypothesis
 for, 1176*t*, 1180–81, 1183–
 89, 1190
Social Threat Hypothesis for,
 1176*t*, 1183
anosmia, 665–66
and emotional reactions, 672
and olfactory experience of close
 relationships, 671
and sexuality, 670–71
antagonism, interpersonal, in
 narcissism, 1199, 1202, 1204
anterior cingulate cortex, 241, 468
and behavioral adjustment to
 frustrative nonreward, 838
anthropoid evolution, 71, 74n.21
anticipatory negative
 contrast, 836–37
antidepressants, 1141
antipsychiatry, 1087–89, 1093, 1094,
 1238–39
antisocial behavior, 1298
in adolescence, 1243–44
adolescence-limited, 1243–44
life-course-persistent, as
 psychopathology, 1243–44
antisocial personality disorder. *See
 also* psychopathy
and borderline personality
 disorder, 1281
as categorical construct, 1302
and criminality, 1301
as dimensional construct, 1302
DSM diagnostic criteria for, 1242,
 1301, 1303
and emotional dysregulation, 1086
and harm for others, 1303–4
polygenic basis of, 1098–99
versus psychopathy, 1242, 1300–2
and substance use disorders,
 comorbidity, 1225–26

antithesis, 72n.3
ants
caring for sick/injured among, 288
chemical recognition system
 of, 1152
mimicry of, 1152
parasitic, 1152
anxiety, 935, 937
disorders of, 510–11
as disorder versus adaptation,
 1126–27
and drug use/addiction, 1223, 1228*t*,
 1230
evolutionary research on, recent
 developments in, 1120–22
versus fear, 501
functions of, 1123–25
illness and, 307
infidelity and, 405
with injury/illness, 649
mechanism of, 1123–25
menstrual cycle and, 871
neural circuitry in, 506–7
non-Western findings on, 1136–37
and obsessive-compulsive
 symptoms, 1318
ostracism and, 1045
post-conflict, 721–22
reduction, contentment and, 454
relational, 721–22, 731
response, components of, 1105
romantic love and, 227
subclinical, 874
trauma-related, 1119–20
anxiety disorder(s), 1086–87, 1105,
 1110. *See also* generalized
 anxiety disorder; illness anxiety
 disorder; phobia(s); separation
 anxiety disorder; social anxiety
 disorder
behavioral manifestations of,
 1110–11
behavioral therapy for, 1123
characteristics of, 1110
cognitive model of, 1123
cognitive response in, 1110–11
cognitive therapy for, 1123
definition of, 1110–11
disorder-specific models, 1124–25
emotional processing model, 1123
emotions underlying, 1110
epidemiology of, 1110
etiology of, 1122–23
evolutionary perspective on, 1111–
 20, 1125
functional features of, 1110–11
hormones and, 871–73

anxiety disorder(s) (*cont.*)
  inhibitory learning model and, 1124
  maintenance of, 1122–23
  non-associative model, 1122
  physical symptoms of, 1110–11
  physiological manifestations of, 1110–11
  prevalence of, 871
  risk factors for, 1122–23
  sex differences in, 871
  treatment of, 1110–11, 1123–25
  two-factor theory of, 1122
  types of, 1110
  unlearning of, risk play and, 1122–23
  in women, 871, 874
anxiolytics, and effects of frustrative nonreward, 835–36
apes
  communication by, 915–16
  maternal–infant bonding, 913
  mating systems, 1175–79
  and newborns' vocalizations, 915
  and new psychological dimensions of *Kindchenschema*, 919
  social learning in, 919
Aplysia, pain phases in, 419
apology(ies), 176, 727–31
  and anger, 141–42
  components of, 727
  cost-free, 728
  costly, 728–30
  definition of, 727
  embarrassment and, 730–31
  and forgiveness, 727–28, 731
  guilt and, 730, 731
  and perceived exploitation risk, 727–28
  and perceived sincerity, 729
  proximate emotions and, 730–31
  and relationship value, 727–28
  shame and, 730–31
  as signal of benign intent, 727–30, 731
appeasement displays, in animals, 776, 791
appraisal theories, 320, 764–65. *See also* emotional appraisal theory
Appraisal Theory, 990–91
approach motivation, 121, 124n.6
  positive emotion and, 375–76
aprosodia, 237
arachnophobia, 1126–27
  evolutionary research on, recent developments in, 1120–21

arecoline, protective effect against helminth infection, 1229–30
arena test, 768–69
argumentation, and consensus, 888, 893–94
Argumentative Theory of Reasoning, 893–94
arguments, anger-based, welfare trade-off ratio "grammar" in, 138
ARH. *See* adaptive rumination hypothesis
Aristotle, 473–74, 549
arousal
  alterations, in post-traumatic stress disorder, 1270
  as antecedent to punitive behavior, 1007–08, 1009
  basic emotions and, 810
  and core affect, 991
  definition of, 810
  emotions in animals and, 764, 793
  measurement of, 1007
Artaxerxes II, 1062
arthropods, human fear of, 1120–21
artificial selection, and emotions in animals, 778–79
ASD. *See* autism/autism spectrum disorder(s)
Ashtanga Yoga, 439
Asia, differential reproduction in, ethnographic and historical perspective on, 1060–62
ASPD. *See* antisocial personality disorder
Asperger's syndrome, 1251
assault, 972
association value, 165, 166–67. *See also* toxic individuals
  misperceived, correction of, 176
  negative, detection of, 166–67, 168–72
asthma, 191
attachment, 289–90
  in bonded couples, 221
  and grief, 485–87
  in infancy, 914–15
  insecure, 490
  loss and, 490
  as motivation, 104
  neuroendocrinology of, 235–42, 236f
  oxytocin and, 238–42
  physiological effects of, 377
  reward systems and, 239, 241
  and separation, 493
attachment love, 379

and affiliation, 373t
and mate retention, 373t
attachment style(s), 752, 1286–88
  adult, 455, 1287–88
  anxious, 752, 756
  anxious, and psychological illness, 455
  anxious-ambivalent, 485–87, 486t, 1286
  anxious-avoidant, 1286–87
  avoidant, 485–87, 486t, 752, 756
  and borderline personality disorder, 1287–88
  dismissing, 1287
  disorganized, 485–87, 486t
  disorganized-disoriented, 1287
  and emotion regulation, 756
  and grief characteristics, 485–87, 486t
  insecure, 486t, 1287–88
  loss and, 490
  preoccupied, 1287
  and psychological illness, 455
  secure, 485–87, 486t, 1286, 1287
  secure-autonomous, 1287
  unresolved/disorganized, 1287
attachment system, 102–3, 105f, 109
attachment theory, 1285–88, 1336
  and grief, 484–87
attention
  affective influence on, 527–29
  allocation, emotion regulation and, 753–54
  and boredom, 320–21, 329
  cuteness and, 343
  emotions and, 44
  lack of, in social exclusion, 1041
  negative, in social exclusion, 1041
  positive emotion and, 375–76
attentional deployment, 748, 749–50
attention bias, in infancy, 362
attention-deficit hyperactivity disorder, 1239
  in adulthood, 1249
  brain maturation delay hypothesis of, 1249–50
  depathologization of, neurodiversity movement and, 1248–51
  and *DRD4-7R*, 1250
  DSM classification of, 1248–49
  DSM diagnostic criteria, for adults, 1249
  and emotional dysregulation, 1248–49
  false-positive diagnoses of, 1250–51
  misdiagnosis of, 1097

neuroendocrinology of, 1248–49
overdiagnosis of, 1249
prevalence of, 1248, 1249
attention deficits, and
boredom, 320–21
attentive immobility, 107
attract, as motive, 104, 105–6
attractiveness
and allocation of attention to
potential mates, 754
emotion regulation and, 755–56
and negotiation about
entitlement, 610–11
attunement, physiological synchrony
and, 741–42
Auden, W. H., "Funeral Blues," 483
audience
effective, 150–52
evolved concept of, 150–52
firsthand, 150–52
perceived, 150–52
shame and, 150–52
audience devaluation, shame and,
149–50, 151f
audience effects, 65, 68, 691
Aunger, R., 104, 105–6, 107–8,
111, 1229
Austry, Diane A., 791–802
authority, morally
legitimate, 948
autism/autism spectrum disorder(s),
888–89, 1239. See also broader
autism phenotype
beneficial traits in, 1252
characteristics of, 1251
cliff-edge principle and, 1100, 1253
as cognitive style, 1252
depathologization, neurodiversity
movement and, 1251–54
DSM conceptualization of, 1251
and embarrassment, 775
empathy impairment in, 1267–68
evolutionary perspective on,
1252–53
genetics of, 1098–99
heterogeneity of, 1254
high-functioning, 1251, 1252
life-history perspective on,
1288–89
"meltdowns" in, 1251, 1252–53
prevalence of, 1139, 1140f
weak central coherence in (lack of
context sensitivity), 1252, 1253
autoimmunity, 182, 187, 191
autonomic nervous system, 6, 9, 56,
66–67, 72, 446–48, 494, 812
and arousal, 810

and attachment, 239
and emotional responses, 236–
38, 236f
and fear responding/fear
learning, 504–5
frustrative nonreward and, 834–35
positive emotions and, 377
and threat detection, 284
AV. See association value
aversion, behaviors associated with,
in animals, 768
avoidance, 631–32
cognitive, 1266–67
as defense, 1119, 1123
disgust response and, 183
experiential, 749
hatred and, 176
and maintenance of anxiety
disorders, 1122–23
neurochemistry of, 468
obsessive-compulsive symptoms
and, 1318
in post-traumatic stress disorder,
1266–67
avoidance motive, 121, 124n.6
avoidant personality disorder, and
emotional dysregulation, 1086
awe, 348
charisma and, 1029
cognitive effects of, 376–77
evolutionary origins of, evidence
for, 10t, 12
lexical concept for, conflation
with scientific construct, 382
physiological effects of, 377
aww, 346
ayahuasca, 1218
Ayton, A., 1189

B

babbling, 917–18
in human infants, 915
babbling-like behavior, 917
immature animals' use of, 915
baboons
laughter expression in, 544
low-cost conciliatory signaling
in, 723
baby schema, 340–41, 342, 349–50
back test, 768–69
badges, as costly signals, 1268–69
Bąk, Halszka, 62–63
balancing selection, 1307–8
by environmental
heterogeneity, 1308
ball-toss paradigms, for
ostracism, 1046

bans, as costly signals, 1268
BAP. See broader autism phenotype
barbiturates, and effects of
frustrative nonreward, 835
bared teeth facial expression, 791
bargaining
conflict and, 1156–57
and credibly signaling need,
1151–53
sex differences in, 1155–56
shame and, 950–51
theoretical models of, 1153
bargaining model, of depression,
1152–53
Barkley, Russell, 1248–49
Barlow, D. H., 1124–25
Barrett, L. F., 1327–28, 1329,
1337n.1
BAS. See Behavioral
Activation System
basal ganglia, and emotional
responses, 236–37
basic emotion(s), 103, 319, 609, 810–
13, 935–36, 1025–26, 1332–33.
See also anger; Basic Emotion
Theory; disgust; fear; joy;
sadness; surprise
appraisal mechanism and, 6, 8, 8t
and arousal, 810
automatic occurrence of, 5–6,
7–8, 8t
and behavioral tendencies, 8, 8t
biologically native patterns in, 14
brief duration of, 7–8, 8t, 1332
candidate (see candidate basic
emotion(s))
categorization of, 12–13
and cognition, 8, 8t
and coordination of response
systems, 7–8, 8t, 1025–26
as cross-cultural universals, 9–11,
10t, 13–15, 61–63
as cross-species universals, 9, 103
culturally native patterns in, 14
cultural variability and, 13–15
culture and, 13–16
definition of, 4–5, 544
differentiating criteria, 7–9, 8t, 63,
437–38, 437t
discrete features of, 5, 7–8, 16
empirical criteria for, 7–9, 8t,
12–13, 437–38, 437t, 1332
environment and, 6–7
evidence for, 9–13
evolutionary features of, 5, 7–8, 16
functions of, 4–5
genetic basis of, 5

basic emotion(s) (*cont.*)
   individually native patterns in, 14
   initial studies of, 4
   language and, 13, 15–16
   mechanism of action, 5–7
   neurobiology of, 5–6, 8t, 9–11, 10t
   and nonverbal communication, 8t, 9–11, 10t, 685–86
   number of, 1332
   as open programs, 6–7, 15
   physiological patterns produced by, 8t, 9–11, 10t, 16
   primary features of, 5
   primate homologues of, 1332 (*see also* primate homologues of basic emotions)
   "pure," 6–7
   rapid onset of, 7–8, 8t
   self-relevant events and, 8, 8t
   shared criteria, 7–9, 8t, 437–38, 437t
   and subjective experience, 8, 8t
   universal signals produced by, 8t, 9–11, 10t, 1332
   valence of, 810
Basic Emotion Theory, 3, 16, 55, 59–67, 99–100, 685–86, 687, 688, 848–49, 990, 1327–28, 1330, 1332–33
   challenges to, 62–63
   and coordination approach, integration of, 1335
   culture and individual experience in, 13–16
   empirical criteria in, 7–9, 8t, 12–13, 437–38, 437t, 1332
   and facial behaviors, 68–70, 69t
   history of, 3–4
   origins of, 3–4
   reformed version, 99–100 (*see also* New BET)
   research, directions for, 12–13
Bastardoz, Nicolas, 1021–33
Baumard, Nicolas, 944–61
Baumeister, R. F., 1229
Beall, A. T., 100, 104, 1229
BECV. *See* Behavioral Ecology View
bed nucleus of stria terminalis
   and compassion, 574–75
   and fear responding/fear learning, 503–4, 506–7
behavior(s). *See also* emotion-related behavior(s); maladaptive behavior; political behavior
   as adaptation, 36
   adaptationist analysis of, 27–29
   adaptive, versus adaptation, 36

   adaptive value of, 358–59
   biological perspective on, 358–59
   as costly signals, 1268
   cues and, 40–42
   developmental/ontogenetic aspect of, 358–59
   deviant, humor and, 549
   emancipated, 67–68
   emotion regulation and, 754
   emotions and, 45
   and fitness maximization, 25
   genetics and, 72n.6
   innate, Darwin's account of, 56–57
   versus mechanism, 36
   as output of adaptations, 50
   phylogenetic aspects of, 358–59
   prediction, 1331–32
   proximate cause of, 358–59
   proximate explanations of, 28, 358–59, 370, 376
   regret and, 247–48, 253–56
   successive negative contrast and, 834
   ultimate explanations of, 358–59, 370
behavioral activation system, 124n.6
Behavioral Activation System, 375–76
behavioral addiction, romantic love as, 228
behavioral ecology, 33–34, 67, 68
   and nonverbal communication, 686–87
Behavioral Ecology View, 55–56, 67, 68–69, 69t, 71–72, 74n.20, 74n.22, 849, 1327–28, 1330–32, 1334
   and evolution of facial behavior, 70–71
behavioral fever, 303
behavioral immune system, 618n.1, 655–56
   disgust response as, 183
   sensitivity of, 656
behavioral inhibition system, 124n.6
Behavioral Inhibition System, 375–76
behavioral system(s), 101. *See also* motivational system(s)
   emotions and, 102, 124n.2
behavioral therapy, for anxiety disorders, 1123
behaviorism, 101, 124n.1, 792
   and leadership studies, 1022–23
behavior modification, open versus closed genetic programs and, 6

Bell, Charles, 58, 59
Beltran, Diego Guevera, 622–42
Bendixen, Mons, 246–59
benevolence, assessment of, 852–53
benign intent hypothesis, for reconciliation, 722–23
benign intent signal(s)
   in animals, 722–23
   apologies as, 727–30, 731
Bentham, Jeremy, 470, 521
Benton, Bridget, 763–79
benzodiazepines, frustrative nonreward and, 835
bereavement, 485
   adult, behaviors in, 486t
   and suicidality, 1143
bereavement exclusion, for depressive symptoms, 1143
Berlyne, Daniel, 357–58, 361, 362–63
BET. *See* Basic Emotion Theory
Betzig, Laura, 1056–63
Bhagavad Gita, 439–40
bias
   in emotional responding, 470
   intergroup (*see* intergroup conflict)
Big Five personality traits, 87
   and emotional thresholds, 466
   gratitude and, 264–65
   individual differences in, motivational reaction norms and, 120
   and life-history strategies, 1288–89
   and narcissism, 1199, 1200
   pride and, 206–8, 207t
Big Six personality traits, 87
   behavioral traits linked to, 120
binge eating, boredom and, 322
binge eating disorder, 1172
   mismatch hypotheses for, 1189
   subthreshold, 1172
Bingham, P. M., 938
biomarkers
   collection of, 192
   in disgust research, 192, 194–95
biopsychosocial model(s), 689–90
Biosocial Model of Status, 863
biparental investment, 630
bipedalism, in hominins, evolution of, 71, 74n.21
bipolar disorder, 1086
   life-history perspective on, 1288–89
   neurodiversity and, 1241–42
   prevalence of, 1139, 1140f
birds
   alarm calls of, 507–8

alloparenting in, 910
babies' vocalizations, 915
empathy in, 423, 797
fear response in, 766–67
flight initiation distance in, 506
frustrative nonreward in, 833
juvenile, innovative and
 exploratory behavior, 363
neurological underpinnings of
 emotions in, 766–67
and reconciliation, 720
reversed SNC effect in, 833
social behaviors of, 67–68
Birdwhistell, Ray, 73n.14
BIS. *See* Behavioral
 Inhibition System
black swan events, preparation
 for, cost–benefit analysis of,
 892, 904n.4
blood-brain barrier, 300
blood-injection-injury phobia, 1113
blood pressure, 446, 810
Bloom, Paul, *Against Empathy,* 899
blushing, 688–89, 1115
BN. *See* bulimia nervosa
BNST. *See* bed nucleus of stria
 terminalis
body dysmorphic disorder, 1086,
 1317, 1318
body odor
 and attractiveness
  perception, 668–69
 child's, and parental relationship
  with child, 671
 constituents of, 668–69
 emotional intensity and, 667–68
 emotional state communicated
  via, 667–68
 infants', maternal responses
  to, 671
 maternal, infants' responses
  to, 670–71
 as social communication, 667–68
body temperature
 in animals, and emotional
  state, 766
 in dogs, 812
Boehm, Chris, 922–23
boldness, in psychopathy, 1302–3,
 1309–10
bonding
 maternal–offspring,
  neuroendocrinology of, 239
 neuroendocrinology of, 235–38,
  236f, 239
 parent–child, 1057
bonobos. *See also* great apes

attention in, affective stimuli
 and, 795
communication by, 915–16
consolation behaviors in, 800
cooperation in, 793–94
emotions in, 794
mating systems, 1175–79
neuroanatomy of, 794–95
social characteristics of, 793–94
socio-cognitive skills of, 794
Boorse, C., 1091–92
Booth v. Maryland, 1071
borderline [term], 1279
borderline personality disorder,
 1279–82
 affective disturbance in, 1284
 attachment and, 1287–88
 conceptual accounts of, 1283–84
 course of, 1283
 diagnostic criteria for, 1283–
  84, 1289
 DSM features of, 1279–82
 and emotional dysregulation, 1086
 emotional dysregulation in, 1280,
  1281–82, 1283–84
 emotional granularity/
  differentiation in, 1285
 epidemiology of, 1283
 genetics and, 1283
 heritability of, 1283
 hormones and, 862
 impulsivity in, 1280, 1281, 1283
 life-history perspective on,
  1288–89
 non-suicidal self-injury in, 1280,
  1281, 1282, 1283
 remission, 1283
 sex differences in, 1283
 suicidality in, 1280, 1281, 1282
boredom
 and academic outcomes, 328–29
 and action versus inaction, 328
 as adaptive, 327–29
 in animals, 325–27
 attention component of, 320–
  21, 329
 attention deficits and, 320–21
 beliefs about, and boredom
  outcomes, 327
 benefits of, 323, 327
 causes of, 320–21
 in children, 326–27
 choice availability and, 328–29
 in classrooms, 331
 definition of, 320
 disorders of, 1086–87
 environmental mismatch and, 329

evolutionary origins of, evidence
 for, 10t, 12
evolutionary perspective on,
 323, 329
experience of, 321
and exploration, 324–25
as feedback, 323
functions of, 318–19
as information, 319–21
maladaptive responses to, 318–
 19, 322–23
and maximization of learning, 324
meaning component of, 320–
 21, 329
meaning deficits and, 321
and mental health risks, 322
and minimization of opportunity
 costs, 324
in modernity, 329–31
and novelty seeking, 324–25, 328
and other negative emotions, 322
outcomes, as function of boredom
 causes, 328
person–environment fit
 and, 327–29
and physical health risks, 322
prevalence of, 318, 319f
in prisons, 331
and reduction of prediction
 error, 325
research on, 318, 318f
risks of, 321–23
and self-regulation failure, 322
societal costs of, reduction, 331
socioecological views of, 331
state, 322
technology and, 330–31
trait, 322
Borgia, G., 38
bottlenose dolphins, and
 reconciliation, 720
Bowlby, John, 102, 103, 124n.2, 484–
 87, 493, 494, 1285
bow-tie architecture, 100–1, 113f, 114,
 1329–30, 1333, 1336
BPD. *See* borderline personality
 disorder
brain/brain activity. *See also* reward
 systems
 in animals, 765
 and behavioral adjustment to
  frustrative nonreward, 836–39
 canine, and emotions, 811
 in compassion, 576–77
 and curiosity, 363–64
 in cuteness response, 341, 342
 degeneracy and, 1329

brain/brain activity (cont.)
  differences, versus disorder, 1246
  disorders/damage, and humor/
    laughter abnormalities, 557–58
  and emotions, in dogs versus
    humans, 811
  emotions and, 236–38, 236f, 238f
  and fear responding/fear
    learning, 503–10
  in humor appreciation, 556–57
  in humor comprehension, 556
  and jealousy, in animals, 777
  and laughter, 557
  neural reuse and, 1329
  in offspring care, 574–77
  in olfaction, 665
  pleasure centers of, 468
  pro-inflammatory signals
    and, 300
  in punitive behavior, 1008–09
  reward-related, in dogs, 812
  in romantic love, 223, 225
  subcortical structures, and
    emotions, 5, 8t, 9, 10t, 11–12, 16,
    60, 103, 437t, 504, 508–9, 777,
    811, 812–13, 818–19, 1266, 1269
brain development, in ADHD,
  1249–50
brain region(s), as command systems
  in animals, 764
brainstem
  and emotional responses, 236–
    38, 236f
  and fear responding/fear learning,
    503–4, 506
Brakoulias, Vlasios, 1317–23
Bräuer, Juliane, 809–21
breast odor, infants' responses
  to, 670
breeding sex ratio(s), human,
  1058, 1063
Broaden-and-Build Theory, 371–72,
  375–76, 445, 1030–31
broader autism phenotype, 1251–
  52, 1254
Broca, Paul, 237
Brooks Pribac, T., 487–88
Brumbaugh, Claudia C., 219–30
Buddhism
  and compassion, 571
  contentment in, 440–41
Bugental, D. B., 102, 107
bulbar palsy, 557
bulimia nervosa, 1172. See also eating
  disorder(s)
  clinical and nonclinical studies of,
    1186–87

DSM criteria for, 1172–73,
  1173b, 1185
epidemiology of, 1172–73,
  1174, 1185
heritability of, 1174
life-history strategies and, 1185–87
mismatch hypotheses for,
  1189, 1190
Sexual Competition Hypothesis
  for, 1176t, 1180–81, 1183–
  89, 1190
subthreshold, 1172
bullshit receptivity, affective
  influence on, 532–33, 534f
bullying, emotional distress caused
  by, 1137, 1148
Burkart, Judith M., 910–23
Burke, Edmund, 382
burnout, 475, 654
  gratitude intervention and, 265
  prevention, in healthcare
    workers, 265
Burns, J. K., 1099
Buss, David M., 38, 62, 88, 393,
  394, 395–97, 398, 400–1,
  931, 1273
Byrd-Craven, Jennifer, 737–43

C
caffeine, 1218
  moderate addition to, 1090
  protective effect against helminth
    infection, 1229–30
Cakobau, 1059
California mouse, 241–42
California v. Brown, 1071
callitrichid monkeys
  alloparental and parental
    provisioning in, 910, 912–13
  infants' vocalizations, 915
  natural pedagogy in, 920
callousness, 285–86, 289–90, 291
  versus cruelty, 285–86
  definition of, 285
calm, 437–38
Calvi, Jessica L., 737–43
candidate basic emotion(s), 7,
  448, 1332
  as cross-cultural universals,
    evidence for, 9–11, 10t
  emerging, 10t, 12
  evolutionary origins of, evidence
    for, 9–11, 10t
  moderate, 10t, 11
  nascent, 10t, 12
  neural correlates, evidence for,
    9–11, 10t

signals of, evidence for, 9–11, 10t
strong, 10t, 11
universality, evidence for, 9–
  11, 10t
weak, 10t, 12
Canis familiaris. See dogs
cannabinoids
  in dogs, 812–13
  and effects of frustrative
    nonreward, 836
cannabis, protective effect against
  helminth infection, 1226,
  1229–30
cannibalism, inhibition of, 284
Cannon, Walter, 72, 1109–10
Cantor, Christopher H., 415–30,
  1119, 1266
Cantril, Hadley. See Hastorf, Albert,
  and Hadley Cantril
capuchin monkeys, emotion
  discrimination by, 772
cardiometabolic conditions, 309
  chronic, and carbohydrate
    intake, 141
care/caring, 103, 282–83, 293. See also
  healthcare
  and awareness/inhibition of
    harming, 284–88
  compassion and, 567–68
  depression and, 1157–59
  evolution of, 283–84
  evolved behaviors for, 288
  and guilt, 287–88, 292
  for ill/injured, 654
  infant–parent dyad and, 283–84
  kama muta and, 349
  for kin, 654
  maturation of, 289–90
  neuroendocrinology of, 287
  reward systems and, 575
  for sick and injured, 288
  and social responsibility, 287–88
care eliciting, 102
careful behavior, cuteness and, 343
caregiving, 427
  cooperation and, 423–24
  empathy and, 423–24
  pain-related, 422
caregiving (motivational) system,
  102, 103, 104, 105f, 109–10
care-seeking, lassitude and, 301,
  301f, 307–8
carnivores
  social, allomaternal care
    in, 910
  social, caregiving in, 423–24
  social, moral behavior in, 422

CAS. *See* cognitive-attentional syndrome
casual sex. *See also* short-term mating
　emotions related to, 249–51
　prevalence of, 249
　and regret, 251–56
catecholamines, 810
categorical imperative, 472
caterpillars, fear responding/fear learning in, 500, 504
cats
　adaptive emotional expression in, 771
　emotion discrimination by, 772–73
　facial expressions in, 770
　fear learning in, 510
　and jealousy, 776–77
　pain behaviors in, 419–20
　postural expressions of fear, 508
　purring in, 770
　recuperation after surgery, 429
　social referencing by, 772
cattle
　chemical signals in, 767
　ear movement, emotions and, 771
　emotional state in, 764, 765
　infrared thermal imaging of, 766
　nasal temperatures in, 766
　pain behaviors in, 420
　temperament of, selection for, 779
causation
　functional, 487
　immediate, 487
　integration, in evolutionary perspective, 689–90
　levels of, 363–64, 370, 484–85
　ontogenetic, 487
　phylogenetic, 487
　proximate levels, 358–59, 484–85, 689, 931, 985
　ultimate levels, 484–85, 689, 931, 985
CBT. *See* cognitive behavioral therapy
Cepon-Robins, Tara J., 181–95
cerebellum, and emotional responses, 236–37
cerebral cortex, 811
　and emotions, 237, 469
certainty, as appraisal dimension, 990, 1044–45
cetaceans
　caregiving in, 423–24
　moral behavior in, 422
　targeted helping in, 801

CGD. *See* complicated grief disorder
Challenge Hypothesis, 862–63
　and testosterone, 1272–73
chameleon effect, 740
Chapais, B., 1177
charisma, 1022
　and awe, 1029
　cross-cultural heterogeneity of, 1030
　definition of, 1027
charisma signaling, 1027–29
　honest versus faked, 1027–29
charismatic leadership, 1022, 1023
　context and, 1031
　cross-cultural comparisons of, 1030
　emotions and, 1027
　evolutionary perspective on, 1027
　and group coordination/cooperation, 1029
　group size and, 1029
cheater-detection mechanisms, 428, 630, 1056
cheater-hawk, 1306
cheating, 1268
　psychopathy and, 1298–99, 1305–6
checking compulsions, obsessive-compulsive disorder and, 1318, 1319
chemosensation, phylogenetics of, 664–65
chemosignals, 667–68
　in animals, 767
　dogs' use of, 819–20
　in humans, 767
　and mother–child relationship, 670–71
Cheng, Joey, 1198
chickens
　in battery cages, 770
　empathy in, 423
　infrared thermal imaging of, 766
　temperament of, selection for, 779
child abuse, 169
　and substance use, 1220, 1221
childhood
　emotional development in, 466
　and exploration, 324
　extended, functions of, 363
children
　boredom in, 326–27
　consolation behaviors in, 800
　depression in, interpersonal effects of, 1158, 1159
　distributive justice intuitions in, 956

loss/grief in, Piaget's theory and, 489–92
　mentalizing by, 920–21
　and normative rules, 921–22
　not having, regret about, 258
　peacemaking behaviors in, 723–24
　punitive behavior in, 1015
　retributive justice intuitions in, 956
　sensitivity to inauthentic emotions, 853
　targeted helping in, 801
chimpanzees, 235–36. *See also* great apes
　altruistic cooperation in, 423
　caregiving in, 423–24
　cognitive bias testing in, 795–96
　communication by, 915–16
　conflict among, 290
　consolation behaviors in, 800
　cooperation among, 421
　cooperation in, 793–94
　emotion discrimination by, 772–73
　emotion regulation in, 758
　emotions in, 794
　facial expressions in, 770
　grief in, 488
　human-reared, incorporation of others' preferences, 918–19
　humans' recognition of emotions in, 773
　humor in, 544–45
　infrared thermography of, 796
　jealousy in, 777–78
　laughter expression in, 544, 770–71
　mating system, 1175–79
　neuroanatomy of, 794–95
　and newborns' vocalizations, 915
　orphaned, 488
　and post-conflict reconciliation, 720
　second-party punishment in, 997–98
　social characteristics of, 793–94
　social learning in, 919
　socio-cognitive skills of, 794
China, polygamy in, 1062
chisoku, 444t
chlordiazepoxide, and effects of frustrative nonreward, 835
Choekey language, 15
Chog shes, 444t
chokkshay (emotion), 15
Christian philosophy, contentment in, 442

chronic pain
   as adaptive, 416, 427
   communicative function of, 416, 429
   and debilitation, 418
   emotional components of, 427
   environmental mismatch and, 416
   and family functioning, 424
   and marital functioning, 424
   protective function of, 416
   and recuperation, 417–18, 427
   research, future directions for, 429–30
   stigmatic attitudes toward, 427–28
cingulate cortex, and empathy, 469
civil rights, disorder versus nondisorder status and, 1255
Clark, D. M., 1124–25
CLAS. *See* Contentment with Life Assessment Scale
class–compassion gap, 570
Clay, Zanna, 791–802
cleaner fish *(Labroides dimidiata)*, 34
Cleckley, H., *The Mask of Sanity*, 1298
cliff-edge principle, 1099–100, 1253
coalitional group system, 102
Coalitional Mate Retention Inventory, 401
co-brooding, 737–38
coevolution, signaling theory and, 426–27
cognition
   and emotion, 1069, 1070
   in fear module theory, 1112
   identity-protective, emotions and, 896–99
   positive mood/emotion and, 374–77
   romantic love and, 226–27
   sadness and, 523, 524–25, 527–29
cognitive appraisal, and empathy, 798–99
cognitive-attentional syndrome, 1119–20
cognitive behavioral therapy, 1124, 1125
cognitive bias, 888, 893, 894. *See also* motivated reasoning
cognitive bias tests, 795–96
   in animals, 773–74
cognitive dissonance, 897, 898–99
cognitive empathy, 566, 571–72, 575–76, 740, 797, 820
   and forgiveness, 725–26
   in narcissism, 1206, 1207–8

cognitive processing therapy, for treatment of post-traumatic stress disorder, 1273–74
cognitive reappraisal, 119–20, 748, 749–50, 752, 754–55
cognitive therapy, for anxiety disorders, 1123
cognitivism, 792
Cohen, A. S., 1328, 1333–34
Cohn, J. F., 70
collectivist culture
   and display rules, 989
   and emotion experience, 986–87
   and ostracism, 1047–48
color perception
   language and culture in, 985
   universal foundation of, 985
comedians, health and longevity of, 551
comfort, 104
communal sharing, 345–46, 347, 348–51. *See also kama muta*
communication. *See also* vocal communication
   charismatic, 1027–29
   de-individuated, 934
   emotions and, 44–45
   evolutionary perspective on, 850–51, 855
   verbal, sadness and, 534–38
communication content, depression and, 1156–57
communication style, depression and, 1156–57
communion, pride and, 208
community(ies)
   evolutionary psychology of, research on, future directions for, 940
   growth in, 930, 934
   power distribution in, 938
   small-scale, and psychological outcomes, 938
community building, positive evolutionary psychology and, 937–38
community health behaviors, in healthcare, 656
compassion, 290, 293. *See also* empathy; sympathy
   antecedents of, 568–72
   appraisal model of, 568–72
   appraisal of target's deservedness and, 570–71
   in attribution-compassion-helping pathway, 570–71

biological systems involved in, 574–77
and choice of cooperative partner, 624t, 632–33
and cooperation, 632–33, 637
as core motive, 566–67
cost–benefit appraisals and, 568–71, 575–76
costliness of, 569
as cultivated attitude, 566–67
cuteness and, 343–44
decoding of, 572–73
definition of, 565–66, 653–54
and disgust, integration in healthcare, 656–57
as dispositional trait, 566–67
as emotion, 566–67
emotion regulation and, 571–72
empathy and, 575–76
encoding of, 572–73
evolutionary perspective on, 567–68, 570–71, 574, 654–55
expression of, 572–73
functions of, 568, 574
genetic relationship and, 569–71
in healthcare, 649, 653–54, 657
individual differences in, 571–72
interpersonal functions of, 624t, 632–33, 637
kama muta and, 348
for kin versus non-kin, 569–70
versus love, 568
magnitude of suffering/need and, 569, 571
in negotiation about entitlement, 610, 611
neuroscience of, 575–77
nonverbal communication of, 572–73
numeracy bias and, 571–72
offspring care and, 567–68
outcomes of, 574
perception of, 572–73
and perception of ability to help, 571–72
and perception of benefits of help, 569–71
in political judgment and behavior, 608–9
and punitive behavior, 1010–11, 1014–16, 1014f
relationship type and, 569–71
research on, 565, 566f
responsibility attributions and, 570–71
reward systems and, 577
versus sadness, 568

self-efficacy and, 571–72
social class and, 570
touch as signal of, 572–73
as unpleasant and effortful, 569
vagal tone and, 575
vocal communication of, 572–73
compassion collapse, 569
compassion training, 289, 571, 575, 576–77
compensation
emotions and, 1012–13, 1016n.5
versus punishment, emotions and, 1012–13, 1015
shame and, 950–51
Compensatory Behavioral Prophylaxis Hypothesis, 188, 864–65
competence, assessment of, 853
competition. *See also* female intrasexual competition; sexual competition
humor and, 549–50
perceived threat leading to, 973–74
shame and, 950–51
Complementarity Theory, 346
complicated grief disorder, 495
component process model, 682
Comprehensive Satisfaction Index, 453
compulsion(s), 1117–18, 1318
ego-syntonic versus ego-dystonic, 1321
evolutionary perspective on, 1323
compulsive buying, 1317, 1322
ComSI. *See* Comprehensive Satisfaction Index
conation, 468
conceptual analysis, 1087
conceptual frameworks, emotions and, 44
conceptual validity, 1142–43, 1241
concrete operational stage, 489
loss for children in, 491–92
concurrent values, 468
conditioning, and anxiety disorders, 1122–25
conduct disorder, 1242, 1243–44
configural processing, in decoding of facial expressions, 989
confirmation bias, 893, 894
conflict. *See also* financial conflict; intergroup conflict
bargaining and, 1156–57
in chimpanzees, 290
and depression, 1135, 1137t, 1148–50

group living and, 717
intractable, 700
non-Western concepts related to, 1150
Conformation Theory, 346
confusion, 465
and energy level/effort allocation, 46
evolutionary origins of, evidence for, 10t, 12
Cong, YongQi, 983–92
Conrad, Jordan A., 1085–106, 1238–55
conscience, 921, 922
conscientiousness
and life-history strategies, 1288–89
pride and, 206–8, 207t
consciousness, as shareability, 905n.8
conscious self-awareness, 290
conservation, Piagetian concept of, and jokes, 553
conservative political attitudes
emotions and, 612–13
threat perception and, 613–15
consolation behavior, 422
in great apes, 796, 800–1
social bias in, 798, 800
constructionist/constructivist view, 1333–34
of emotions, 62, 72, 320, 325–26, 687–88, 1137n.1, 1327–29
construct validity, 1241
consumption, lassitude and, 138–39, 301, 301f
consumptive model, 473
contamination/cleaning, obsessive-compulsive disorder and, 1318–19
contamination sensitivity, 184
contempt, xiii, 944–45, 960
definition of, 1049
evolutionary origins of, evidence for, 10t, 12
in intergroup context, 704
nonverbal communication of, 597–98, 601n.5
ostracism and, 1049
and political judgment and behavior, 1049
psychopathy and, 1299
and punitive behavior, 1006
as sentiment, 601n.5
and status hierarchies, 587, 593, 594t, 597–98
and terminating costly relationships, 624t, 641
contentare, 442–43, 444t

contentment, 456–57
affective space of, 455, 456f
allostatic load and, 443–46
as barometer, 445–46
as basic emotion, 436–37, 438, 456–57
in Buddhist philosophy, 440–41
in Christian philosophy, 442
in *contentare* lineage, 442–43, 444t
cross-cultural expression/recognition of, 449–52
in Daoist philosophy, 441
default state of, 443–45
definition of, 436–37
differentiation from other emotions, 455
as discrete emotion, 455
dispositional, benefits of, 455–56
divine, 442
elicitation of, 443–45
etymology of, 444t
evolutionary origins of, evidence for, 10t, 12
evolutionary perspective on, 454
evolution of, 443–46
expression of, 448–52
facial/bodily expressions of, 451–52
functions of, 436–37
versus happiness, 439
history of, 438–43
and homeostasis, 443–45
in Islamic and Sufi philosophy, 442
in Judaic philosophy, 441–42
linguistic traditions of, 438–43, 444t
measurement of, 452–54
and physical health, 445–46, 448, 454
physiological correlates of, 446–48
positivity offset and, 445–46
and prosocial behavior, 454
and psychological health, 445–46
psychophysiology of, 446–48, 450t
research, future directions for, 448, 456–57
in *santosha* traditions, 438–41
in S-L-M lineage, 441–42
and social bonding, 445
universal expressions of, 448–52
in Vedic philosophy, 438–40
vocalizations of, 449–52
and well-being, 454–56
in yogic philosophy, 439–40

Contentment with Life Assessment Scale, 452–53
contingency table interpretation, numeracy and, 887
contingent shifts, 1307–8
continuity principle, 791
contrition, 719–20
control, appraisals of, 1045
control theory, 117, 118
conversational competence, affective influence on, 534, 535f
Cook, James, 1058–59
Cooley, Cameryn, 1279–90
Cooper, Rachel, 1098–99
cooperation, 427, 641–42. *See also* cooperative ties
  altruistic, 421, 422–23
  benefits of, 378
  and caregiving, 423–24
  challenges of, 622
  definition of, 421
  emotional expressivity and, 632, 1331
  emotions and, 630–31
  evolutionary perspective on, 421–22, 718
  and inclusive fitness, 421–22
  moral behavior and, 946–48
  morality and, 422
  as mutually beneficial, 947
  nonverbal communication and, 683–84
  positive emotions and, 378, 380
  proximate emotions and, 631–32
  punishment and, 639–40
  selective pressure and, 947
  shame and, 154–55, 950–51
  social emotions and, 624t, 631–42
  society-level, 378
  types of, 631–32
  ultimate interpersonal functions of, 631–32
cooperative breeding, 109–10, 623, 922
  evolutionary perspective on, 910–13, 912f
  and vocal communication, 916
cooperative guilt, 287–88
cooperativeness, female intrasexual competition and, 977–78
cooperative relationships, building and maintaining, social emotions and, 624t, 637–40
cooperative ties, compassion and, 568, 570
coordination approach to emotions, 99–100, 309, 361, 1025–26,
1284–85, 1327–28, 1329, 1330, 1334. *See also* coordination mechanisms/coordination programs, emotions as; coordination problem
  and Basic Emotion Theory, integration of, 1335
  motivational systems and, 100–1, 104, 112–18
coordination mechanisms/coordination programs, emotions as, 99–100, 112–18, 113f, 298, 309, 361, 609
coordination problem, 99, 309
coppery Titi monkey, jealousy in, 777–78
coprophagy, in captive animals, 768
Cordaro, Daniel, 3–16, 73n.13, 436–57, 1332
core affect, 991
Core Affect Theory, 374
co-reflection, 737–38
co-regulation, 741–42
correspondence/correspondence program, 21
  versus adaptationist program, 22–24
  and causal explanations, 25–26
  teleological metaphors in, 24–25
  and transient properties versus design properties, 33–34
  and universals versus variability, 32
correspondence bias, 529
Cortés, Hernán, 1059–60
corticosterone, frustrative nonreward and, 834–35
corticotropin-releasing factor, fear and, 505
corticotropin-releasing hormone, in depression, 866
cortisol, 810, 862
  and animals' emotional state, 765–66
  contentment and, 447–48, 450t
  in depression, 866
  in dogs, 810, 812–13
  fear and, 765–66
  mediation of testosterone's link to dominant/aggressive behaviors, 863–64
  and romantic love, 222–23, 224–25
  in separation distress, 493
  stress and, 765–66
co-rumination
  costs versus benefits of, 743

defining features of, 737
  developmental perspective on, 738–39
  evolutionary perspective on, 742–43
  female same-sex friendships and, 737–43
  and internalizing symptoms, 738–39
  negative affect and, 738–39
  physiological effects of, 739
  sex differences in, 738–40, 741
  as social process, 739–40
corvids, consolation behaviors in, 800
Cosmides, Leda, 21–50, 62–63, 271, 273, 298, 325–26, 1103–4, 1135, 1284–85, 1327–28
costly signaling
  and post-traumatic stress disorder, 1268–69, 1274
  types of, 1268
  in war, 1268–69
counterfactual reasoning, 166, 169
courage, guilt and, 291
Cousins, Norman, 550
COVID-19 pandemic, 1323
  and guilt, 291
  loss and grief in, 497
  loss resulting from, 831
  psychological effects of, 831
Cowen, Alan, 1056, 1335
cows. *See* cattle
coyness, evolutionary origins of, evidence for, 10t, 12
CPM. *See* component process model
CPT. *See* cognitive processing therapy
crabs, fear responding/fear learning in, 504
Craig, Kenneth D., 415–30
create, as motive, 104
creativity, and problem-solving, 615
CRF. *See* corticotropin-releasing factor
CRH. *See* corticotropin-releasing hormone
criminal justice system
  emotions and, 899–901
  shame and, 156–57
  social valuation and, 89–90, 156–57
criticism, corrective effect of, 549
Crivelli, C., 55–56, 61, 62, 64–65, 66, 67
crowds, behavior of, 854
Croy, Ilona, 663–73

cruelty, 285–86, 290, 291
  versus callousness, 285–86
  definition of, 285–86
crying. *See also* infants' crying;
    screaming
  in adulthood, 467
  cultural display rules and, 66
  cultural diversity in, 57, 59–60
  dogs' responsiveness to, 819
  grief and, 485
  joy and, 467–68
  sadness and, 467
  as signal of need, 1152
crypsis, 1152
CTFT. *See* tit-for-tat, contrite
cuckoo, 1180
cue(s), 1070. *See also* ancestral cues
  and decision rules, 39–42
  identification of, 43, 51n.10
  ostensive, dogs and, 817–18
  and outcomes, 39–40, 39*t*
  relational, 41–42
  versus signals, 425, 1162n.2
  situation, emotions elicited
    by, 42–43
  uniformity of, 41–42
cultural display rules, 64, 65–66
cultural identity, 988–89
cultural learning, 988–89, 991
culture. *See also* collectivist culture;
    individualistic culture
  and adaptiveness, 38
  and basic emotions, 13–16
  and components of
    emotion, 985–86
  and emotion regulation, 757
  and emotions, 320, 346–47,
    370, 371
  evolutionary perspective on, 242
  and gratitude, 268–70
  as human universal, 984
  and humor, 554
  and leadership, 1030
  and medical disorders, 1094
  and nonverbal
    communication, 987–89
  and nyctophobia, 1122
  and ostracism, 1047–48
  and pride, 382–83
  and romantic love, 220–21
  and sensitivity to fear cues, 510
  and social emotions, 85–86
  and variation of psychology and
    behavior, 984
curiosity, 465
  in animals, 359–60, 365
  backward, 365

behavioral biology framework for,
    358–59, 365
  bottom-up, 365
  brain regions involved in, 363–64
  definition of, 359
  deprivation-based, 361, 365
  developmental perspective
    on, 362–63
  dimensions of, 361, 365
  disorders of, 1086–87
  diversive, 357–58, 361, 365
  dopamine system and, 363–64
  epistemic, 357, 361, 365
  ethological perspective on, 359
  evolutionary perspective on,
    358–59, 365
  and exploitation, 363
  and exploration, 363
  forward, 365
  functional (adaptive) perspective
    on, 360–62, 365
  functions of, 358, 360–61, 364
  information-gap theory of, 357–
    58, 362–63
  as information-seeking, 357, 364
  interest-based, 361, 365
  as knowledge emotion, 358, 360–
    61, 364
  and learning, 324
  mechanistic perspective on, 363–
    64, 365
  morbid, 361–62
  novelty-seeking, 357, 360–61, 365
  perceptual, 357, 361, 365
  phylogenetic perspective
    on, 359–60
  and play, 362–63
  research on, 365
  scientific, 357, 361, 365
  social, 361, 362
  specific, 357–58, 361, 365
  state, 358
  taxonomy of, 361, 365
  theoretical frameworks for, 357–58
  top-down, 365
  trait, 358
  types of, 357
  as uncertainty reduction, 360, 364
curiosity (motivational) system, 104,
    105*f*, 111
Curtis, V., 104, 105–6, 107–8,
    111, 1229
cute-affect, 346
cute aggression, 345, 349–50
cute-emotion, 346
cuteness/cuteness response, 339–40.
  See also kama muta; kawaii

as aesthetic, 339–40, 345
  age and, 342
  brain areas involved in, 341, 342
  and caretaking, 343, 379
  as culture-general and
    universal, 341–42
  definition of, 339–40
  and dimorphous emotional
    expression, 345
  emotions involved in, 342,
    372, 373
  and empathic concern, 343–44
  evolutionary perspective
    on, 340–41
  factors affecting, 341
  individual differences in, 342
  and morality, 343–44
  motivational aspects of, 349, 379
  and prosocial behavior, 343–44
  protection and caregiving
    in, 340–41
  as psychological response, 339–40
  research on, 345–46
  sex differences in, 342, 379
  and social engagement, 343
Cyberball, 1011, 1042, 1046
cyberchondria, 1321–22
cybernetics, 101
cytokines, pro-inflammatory,
    300, 301*f*
Czarna, Anna Z., 1197–210

D

damage-associated molecular
    patterns, 300, 301*f*
DAMPs. *See* damage-associated
    molecular patterns
danger, cues, overgeneralizing of,
    1269–70
Daoism, contentment in, 441
Darius III, 1062
darkness, fear of. *See* nyctophobia
Dark Room Problem, 325
Darwin, Charles, 72n.3, 437–38,
    467–68, 1094
  on continuity principle, 791
  Descent of Man, 57, 58, 72n.5, 1056
  on disgust, 181
  on emotions, 1062
  on expression of emotions, 616
  *The Expression of the Emotions in
    Man and Animals*, 3–4, 56–58,
    67, 68, 72n.5, 73n.8, 685, 763,
    791, 930, 1056
  face-reading study, 59
  on facial behavior, 70
  on fear, 1109–10

Darwin, Charles (*cont.*)
  on grief, 485
  hypotheses about emotions, 4
  on infants' features, 340
  on intrasexual competition, 971
  and nonverbal
    communication, 681–82
  Origin of Species, 56, 67,
    72n.5, 1056
  *Principle of Serviceable Associated
    Habits*, 56, 72n.3
  on sexual selection, 67
  study of laughter, 543
  on tickling, 546
  views on emotions, 56
Darwinism
  and adaptations, 24, 26–27
  misinterpretations of, 23, 56–58
  and ontogenetic
    environment, 30–31
David (biblical king), 1061
Davis, K. L., 121
Dawkins, R., 932
DBT. *See* dialectical behavior
    therapy
death
  of child, and depression, 1143–44
  children's perception of, 490–92
  of family member, 1149
  of parent, 1149
  of social partner, 1149
deception, 154–55, 687, 1152
  detection of, 62
  detection of, affective influence
    on, 531, 531*f*, 532*f*
  facial expressions and, 69–70
  predatory aggression and, 173
  psychopathy and, 1305
decision rules
  cues/information and, 39–42
  recalibration, emotions
    and, 46–47
defensive aggression system, 105*f*,
    107–8, 117–18
defensive motivational
    system, 102
Del Giudice, Marco, 99–124, 309,
    1118, 1225, 1229, 1288–89,
    1327–36
delinquency, 1243–44
dementia, 1263
  and laughter, 557
  prevalence of, 1139, 1140*f*
depressants (drugs), 1219
depression, 476–77, 1157–59. *See
    also* major depression/major
    depressive disorder; peripartum
depression; postpartum
    depression
  adaptive rumination hypothesis
    and, 1147, 1148, 1160
  age-related testosterone decline
    and, 874
  and anger, 1149–50
  in animals, after loss, 488
  antepartum, hormones
    and, 869–70
  as aversive signal of need, 1156–57
  bargaining model of, 1152–53
  behavioral manifestations of,
    1134–35, 1151, 1156, 1161
  benefits of, evidence for, 1157–59
  bereavement exclusion for, 1143
  communication style associated
    with, 1156–57
  and conflict, 1135, 1137*t*, 1148–50
  as continuum of symptoms, 1141–
    42, 1141*f*
  as credible signal of need, 1151–
    53, 1161
  decreased, gratitude and, 264–65
  diagnostic criteria for, 1138–
    39, 1138*t*
  differences in levels of, with
    similar adversities, 1143–44
  divorce and, 1137*t*, 1143–44,
    1146–47
  and drug use, 1223, 1228*t*,
    1230–31
  and economic productivity,
    1154–55
  and energy level/effort
    allocation, 46
  entrapment and, 1149–50, 1151
  epidemiology of, 865
  evolutionary perspective on, 254–
    55, 476, 1144–46
  and excessive reassurance seeking,
    1156–57
  external locus of control
    and, 1151
  fresh start and, 1159
  functions of, 1144, 1146
  helplessness and, 1151
  illness and, 308
  inflammation and, 1149
  with injury/illness, 649
  interpersonal effects of, 1157–59
  and interpersonal interactions,
    1156, 1161
  and investment from social
    allies, 308
  as involuntary subordinate
    strategy, 1151
  loss of interest in virtually all
    activities in, 1154–55
  menopausal transition and, 870
  negative valence of, 46
  neuroticism and, 1144, 1145*f*, 1160
  non-Western concepts related
    to, 1150
  non-Western findings on, 1136–37
  and normal grief, 1143
  in orphaned apes, 488
  ostracism and, 1045
  persistent, disease and, 299–300
  positive life change and, 1159–
    60, 1161
  and post-traumatic stress disorder,
    1271–72
  and powerlessness, 1151
  psychological pain hypothesis
    and, 1146–47, 1153
  recovery from, 1159–60
  remission of, 1142, 1159–60
  resilience and, 1144
  sex differences in, 1144, 1145*f*,
    1155–56, 1160
  and sickness behavior, 651–52
  social competition hypothesis
    of, 1151
  social partners' response to, 1156–
    59, 1161
  social risk and, 1151
  Social Risk Hypothesis for, 1183
  studies of, shortcomings, 1144
  subclinical, 865, 874
  and substance use disorders,
    comorbidity, 1225–26
  and testosterone, 1272–73
  treatment, "business case" for, 1155
  vulnerability and, 1144
depression contagion, 739, 741–42
depressive disorders, hormones
    and, 865–67
depth perception, 904n.3
dermatillomania, 1317, 1318
descent with modification, 56, 105
desire, evolutionary origins of,
    evidence for, 10*t*, 11
detached reappraisal, and
    physiological resources, 754–55
development
  emotional changes during, 466
  and fears/phobias, 1112–13
  Piaget's theory of, 489–90
  and sense of humor, 553–55
developmental specificity, 1203
Dewey, John, 58, 67
Dezecache, Guillaume, 847–56, 1331
dhṛti, 449

Diagnostic and Statistical Manual of Mental Disorders (DSM), 1093, 1238–39
- antisocial personality disorder in, 1301
- autism/autism spectrum disorder(s) in, 1251
- bereavement exclusion for depressive symptoms, 1143
- borderline personality disorder in, 1279–82
- categories of mental disorders, 1086, 1094
- classification of eating disorders, 1172
- conceptually valid categories in, 1241
- construct validity in, 1241
- definition of mental disorders, 1300
- diagnostic criteria sets in, 1241
- dimensional system in, 1302
- disorder categories in, 1240, 1241
- disputes about, 1087–88
- and harmful dysfunction analysis, 1094
- heterogeneous etiological subtypes of disorders, 1241
- and major depression, 1135, 1138–39, 1138*t*, 1145
- narcissistic personality disorder in, 1198, 1199–200
- other conditions that may be a focus of clinical attention, 1087
- personality disorder in, 1279–80
- post-traumatic stress disorder in, 1264–68
- premenstrual dysphoric disorder in, 1246–47
- substance use disorder in, 1219–20
- as trouble-shooting manual, 1095

dialectical behavior therapy, 1125
dialect theory, 988
dictator game, 537–38
diet
- human, 623
- hunter-gatherer, 623

differential reproduction, 305, 1057, 1063
- in Africa, ethnographic, genetic, and historical perspective on, 1057–58
- in Americas, ethnographic, genetic, and historical perspective on, 1059–60
- among Aka Pygmies, ethnographic and historical perspective on, 1057–58
- among Hadza, ethnographic and historical perspective on, 1057, 1058
- among Ju/'hoansi, ethnographic and historical perspective on, 1057, 1058
- in Asia, ethnographic, genetic, and historical perspective on, 1060–62
- in Pacific region, ethnographic, genetic, and historical perspective on, 1058–59

Dill, L. M., 1263–64
discomfort, and obsessive-compulsive symptoms, 1318
discrete emotions theory, 463, 468–69, 471
disease
- chronic, evolutionary mismatch and, 309
- natural selection and, 1263

disease avoidance, 103–4
disease avoidance threat-management system, 703. *See also* behavioral immune system
- and intergroup conflict, 707–8

disease environment, and disgust sensitivity, 184–86
disease model, 1262
diseases of despair, 474
disgust, xiii, 155, 254, 256, 343, 437–38, 618n.1, 944–45
- adaptive problems related to, 182–83, 1079
- altruistic, 656
- in ancestral environments, 182
- and anxiety disorders, 1110
- avoidance, 655–56, 756–57
- as basic emotion, 4, 990
- and body odor, 668
- brain activity and, 468–69
- categories of, 183–84
- communicative features of, 1079
- context sensitivity of, 655–56
- and cooperation, 624*t*, 637
- definition of, 655–56
- and drug use/addiction, 1228*t*, 1230
- and empathy, integration in healthcare, 656–57
- evolutionary perspective on, 10*t*, 11, 181, 182, 195, 371–72
- evolutionary psychology and, 181–82, 191–92
- expression of, 685
- facial expression of, 960
- functions of, 181, 195, 521–22, 656, 864, 1079
- and hatred, 171
- hormones and, 864–65
- human population biology and, 181–82, 191–92
- immorality and, 959–60
- individual differences in, 864
- with injury/illness, 649, 653, 655–56
- in intergroup context, 704, 707–8
- interpersonal functions of, 624*t*, 637
- and legal system, 1078–80
- and morality, 957–60, 1079–80 (*see also* moral disgust)
- as moralizing emotion, 957–59
- as motive, 104
- neuroscience of, 1008
- as non-moral emotion, 949, 951*f*
- obsessive-compulsive symptoms and, 1318
- olfaction and, 666
- pathogen, 108, 182–83, 864
- as pathogen-avoidance mechanism, evolution of, 182–84
- pathogen specificity of, 183–84
- and political attitudes, 612–13
- as primary emotion, 764
- in primates, 184
- and punitive behavior, 1006, 1009, 1014–16, 1014*f*
- regulation of, 656
- sex differences in, 864
- sexual, 108, 182–83, 864
- universality of, 184
- utility of, evidence for, 190–91
- in WEIRD populations, 182, 195n.1

disgust research
- biomarkers in, 192, 194–95
- cross-cultural, 183–84
- hypotheses, testing outside WEIRD environments, 192–95
- multidisciplinary approaches for, 191–92
- in non-WEIRD populations, 191–95
- in subsistence-based, natural fertility populations, 182, 188–89, 191–95
- in understudied populations, 182
- in WEIRD populations, 182, 193–94, 195

disgust sensitivity, 1113
  age-related variation in, 186–87, 193–94
  and animal-type phobias, 1121
  in children, adaptive immune system and, 193
  definition of, 184
  disease environment and, 184–86
  environmental calibration and, 191–92
  exposure-related desensitization and, 187
  factors affecting, 183–84, 864
  food-related, age and, 187
  and gut microbiota, 191
  habituation and, 187, 193–94
  in high-pathogen environments, and pathogen avoidance, 193
  hygiene-related, age and, 187
  immune status and, 189–90, 194
  individual variation in, complexity of, 190
  infection history and, 184–86, 193, 194–95
  lassitude and, 141
  lifestyle change and, 186, 191–92
  market integration and, 186, 191–92, 193–94
  measurement of, 191–92
  nutritional stress and, 189–90, 194
  pathogen exposure and, 184–86, 193
  and reproductive immunomodulation, 188–89
  reproductive status-related variation in, 187–89
  sex differences in, 187–89, 864
  utility of, evidence for, 190–91
  variation in, 184–90, 192–95
disgust system, 105f, 108
disinhibition
  in antisocial personality disorder, 1303
  in psychopathy, 1302–3, 1309–10
disorder(s), 1248. *See also* dysfunction; medical disorder(s); mental disorder(s)
  versus adaptations, 1126–27
  antipsychiatric critique of, 1087–89
  as biological dysfunction, 1091–92
  concept of, 1087–89
  versus disvalued conditions, 1091, 1092
  dysfunction in, 1094–95, 1239–40
  versus dysfunctions, 1098
  erroneous categories of, 1091
  evolutionary perspective on, 1239–41
  genetic basis of, and natural selection, 1098–99
  in harmful dysfunction analysis, 1094, 1095
  as harmful evolutionary dysfunction, 1094, 1239–41
  versus mismatches, 1096–99
  versus normality, 1085–89
  versus treatability, 1089, 1091
  types of, 1085–86
  versus undesirable conditions, 1091
  value-based harm component of, 1239–40
display rules, 687, 989. *See also* cultural display rules
Dispositional Positive Emotion Scale, 452–53
dissociation
  in borderline personality disorder, 1280, 1282, 1284
  definition of, 1282
distraction, in motivation regulation, 119
distress. *See also* empathic distress (personal distress)
  disengagement from, 285, 291
  lack of, in psychopathy, 1303, 1308–9
  and obsessive-compulsive symptoms, 1318
  personal, 797
  response to, 285, 289
  romantic love and, 227
distributive justice, 956
divorce, 1175–77
  and depression, 1137t, 1143–44, 1146–47
dog–human relationship, 809, 818–21
  emotional contagion in, 813
dogs
  aggression in, 811–12
  behavior of, human interpretation of, 818, 821
  behavior reading skills of, 813–14, 816–17
  breeds, and emotional reactivity, 810
  chemosignaling and, 819–20
  consolation behaviors in, 800
  cross-species empathy in, 769
  and crying, 819
  domestication of, 809–10
  and emotional vocalizations, 819
  emotion discrimination by, 772–73
  emotion recognition in, 818
  emotions in, 809–10
  and empathy, 820–21
  encephalization quotient in, 811
  eyebrow movement in, 771
  face processing in, 818–19
  facial expressions in, 770
  and fairness, 817
  fear in, 811–12
  fear responding/fear learning in, 504
  and guilt, 814–18
  guilty look in, 814–16, 815f
  happiness in, 812–13
  helping behaviors in, 820–21
  humans' recognition of emotions in, 773
  humans' understanding of, 821
  identification of other dogs, 818
  individual differences in, 810
  and inequity aversion, 817
  infrared thermal imaging of, 766
  and jealousy, 776–77, 814–18
  joy in, 812–13
  love in, 812–13
  metacognition and, 814
  misinterpretation of, 818, 821
  negative emotions in, 811–12
  neurobiology of jealousy in, 777
  neuroscience of emotions in, 811
  olfaction in, 811, 819–20
  ostensive cues and, 817–18
  pain behaviors in, 419–20
  physiological response to negative affect, 812
  play behavior in, 812–13
  positive emotions in, 812–13
  postural expressions of fear, 508
  recuperation after surgery, 429
  reward-related brain activation in, 812
  reward systems in, 812–13
  secondary emotions in, 776
  selective breeding of, 810
  sensitivity to human emotions, 820
  shame/guilt behavior in, 775–76
  and social emotions, 813–18
  social referencing by, 772
  speech directed to, characteristics of, 817–18
  threat responsiveness in, 818–19
  understanding of human or conspecific emotions, 818–21
Doherty, Jaclyn K., 219–30

dolphins, grief in, 488
domestication of animals
   and animal emotions, 778–79
   commensal pathway, 779
   directed pathway, 779
   and ecology of fear, 778–79
   pathways of, 779
   prey pathway, 779
domestic dogs. *See* dogs
dominance, 103, 472
   animals' displays of, 212
   in cuteness response, 345
   definition of, 210
   emotional markers of, 1032
   hormones and, 862–64
   humor and, 548, 549–50, 555
   and leadership, 1025, 1026
   and narcissism, 1203
   nonverbal communication of, 214
   and pride, 213–14, 380
   psychopathy and, 1309
   and rank attainment, 210, 1024–25
   and status attainment, 1203
dominance hierarchy(ies), in social groups, 1115–16
dominance motivational system, 108–9
Doomsday cult, 897
dopamine system, 468. *See also* reward systems
   and attachment, 239, 241
   in attention-deficit hyperactivity disorder, 1250
   and curiosity, 363–64
   in dogs, 812, 813
   and gambling, 1322–23
   and prediction error, 364
   and romantic love, 222–23
   substance use and, 1221
Doucet, Jeff, 163, 165, 168–72
DPES. *See* Dispositional Positive Emotion Scale
Draper, P., 36–37
DRD4-7R, and attention-deficit hyperactivity disorder, 1250
drive(s), 361
   versus emotions, 1104
drug(s)
   definition of, 1219
   euphoriant, 468
   psychoactive, classification of, 1219
drug use, 1218–19. *See also* addiction; substance use
   as adaptation, 1222, 1226, 1227
   byproduct ("hijack") approach to, 1222–24

emotional dysregulation and, 1221, 1232–33
   and emotional states, 1218–19
   epidemiology of, 1220
   heterogeneity of, 1219
   life-history approach to, 1222, 1224–26
   "liking" versus "wanting" component of, 1221
   mortality caused by, 1219–20
   motivational-emotional systems and, 1220–33, 1228*t*
   prevention of, 1232–33
   social costs of, 1219–20
DSM. *See Diagnostic and Statistical Manual of Mental Disorders* (DSM)
DSM-5. *See Diagnostic and Statistical Manual of Mental Disorders* (DSM)
DSM-IV. *See Diagnostic and Statistical Manual of Mental Disorders* (DSM)
Dual-Hormone Hypothesis, 863–64
dual inheritance theories, 346–47
Dual Process Model of Grief, 484
Dubey, R., 360–61, 364
Duchenne de Boulogne, 59
Duchenne laughter. *See* laughter, genuine (Duchenne)
Duchenne smiles. *See* smile(s)/smiling
Dunbar, Robin, 22
Durkee, Patrick, 587–601
Durrant, Russil, 1218–33
dysfunction. *See also* disorder(s); harmful dysfunction; harmful dysfunction analysis
   dangerous, 1303–4
   definition of, 1106
   versus disorder, 1098
   in disorders, 1094–95, 1300
   in harmful dysfunction analysis, 1094
   in mental disorders, 1304
   psychopathy and, 1304–7
dyslexia, 1090, 1092
   neurodiversity and, 1241–42
dysphoria, mild. *See* sadness
dysrationalia, 888
dysthymia, 1253

E

Easterlin paradox, 475
eating disorder(s). *See also* anorexia nervosa; bulimia nervosa
   biomedical models of, 1174–75

   clinical and nonclinical studies of, 1186–87
   continuum of, 1189
   DSM classification of, 1172
   epidemiology of, 1172–73, 1174
   etiology of, 1189
   evolutionary perspective on, 1174, 1175–89, 1176*t*, 1190
   extended mismatch models of, 1176*t*, 1189, 1190
   Fast-Slow-Defense model and, 1225
   female competition and, 1175–79, 1176*t*
   genetics of, 1175
   life-history strategies and, 1185–87
   in males, 1187–89
   mismatch hypotheses for, 1175, 1176*t*, 1179–80, 1189, 1190
   mortality rate for, 1174
   multi-factorial model of, 1175
   non-evolutionary theories of, 1174–75
   primary symptoms of, 1173*b*, 1174
   proximate causes of, 1175
   psychosocial models of, 1174–75
   secondary symptoms of, 1174
   Sexual Competition Hypothesis and, 1176*t*, 1180–81, 1183–89, 1190
   as Western disease (diseases pf civilization), 1179
EBP. *See* evidence-based psychotherapy
ECA. *See* Epidemiologic Catchment Area
ecological psychology, 904n.2
economic games. *See also* Third-Party Punishment Game; Ultimatum Game
   incentivized, as proxy for punitive behavior, 998–1001
economy, social valuation and, 90
ecstasy (drug). *See* MDMA (ecstasy)
EDs. *See* eating disorder(s)
EEA. *See* environment of evolutionary adaptedness
Efe men, honey intake, infection and, 140
effort allocation, emotions and, 46
egalitarianism, 329, 614–15, 688–89, 938, 1023–24, 1058, 1231
eiréné, 442, 444*t*
Ekman, Paul, 57, 60–63, 64–66, 69–70, 73n.11, 73n.13, 73n.14, 73–74n.15, 382, 449, 501–2, 544, 572, 685–86, 687, 688, 1056

elation, disorders of, 1086–87
elder abuse, 169
elderly
  emotional development in, 466
  and humor, 554–55
electric shock, and fear responding/fear learning, 503–4
electrodermal activity, 446
  contentment and, 450t
electroencephalography, 446
elephants
  consolation behaviors in, 800
  empathy in, 797
  grief in, 488
  moral behavior in, 422
  targeted helping in, 801
Ellis, G. E., 107
Ellis, Havelock, 1198
embarrassment, 320
  animals and, 775–76
  and apology-making, 730–31
  and choice of cooperative partner, 624t
  and cooperation, 635
  evolutionary origins of, evidence for, 10t, 12
  expression of, 731
  interpersonal functions of, 624t, 635
  nonverbal communication of, 380
  psychopathy and, 1299
  as self-conscious emotion, 764
  social functions of, 380
emojis, 693
emoticons, 847
emotion(s). *See also* negative emotion(s); positive emotion(s); secondary emotions; self-conscious emotions; social emotions; superordinate theory of emotions
  as adaptations to recurring situations, 40–42, 698–99
  adaptive functions of, 369, 370–71, 462–63, 682, 764–65, 903–4, 1070, 1135
  in animals (*see* animal emotions)
  automatic occurrence of, 5–6, 7–8, 8t
  aversive-but-adaptive, 155
  basic (*see* basic emotion(s))
  behavioral response to, neuroendocrine systems and, 236f, 236–38

broad individual differences in, navigation of status hierarchies and, 600–1
categorization of, 12–13
characterization of, 43–48
classic view of, 319
coevolution with leadership, 1032
and cognition, 1069, 1070
cognitive/computational procedures and, 48–49, 1069
comparative psychology of, 763, 791–93
complex, 936–37
components of, 763–64, 792, 985–86, 1103
computational architecture of, 112–18, 113f, 1333–34
conscious experience and, 1105
constructionist view of, 62, 72, 320, 325–26, 687–88
in contemporary culture, 1063
and cooperation, 630–31
coordination approach to (*see* coordination approach to emotions)
coordination function of, 99, 112–18, 113f, 298, 309, 361, 792, 1025–26
and coordination of individuals in groups, 1032
criteria for, xiii, 7–9, 8t, 12–13, 14
cross-culturally shared themes underlying, 990–91
cross-cultural variation in, 983–92
culture and, 320, 346–47, 370, 371
Darwin's treatment of, 56
definition of, 72n.1, 372, 501–3, 544, 609, 630–31, 664, 792
developmental changes in, 466
discrete, affective space of, 455, 456f
as distinct events, 4
versus drives, 1104
evolutionary perspective on, 320, 369, 370–72, 383–84, 930, 945, 1025–26, 1284–85
evolution of, 235–36
and evolution of leadership, 1032
experience and, 13–16
as feedback, 323
feeling (*see* emotional responses; emotion experience)
and fitness contingencies of situations, 48
as functional adaptations, 47–48
functions of, 164–65, 370, 464, 609, 1056, 1062, 1284–85

global-transformational approach to, 1102–3
and goal pursuit, 609
and healthcare, 653–57
higher-order, 936–37
high- versus low-activation, 437–38, 455, 501
human conduct affected by, xiii–xiv
and identity-protective cognition, 896–99
imaginary experience of, 469
individual differences in, 466
individual tendency to feel, and political attitudes, 612–13
inherent relationship to politics, 615–17
injury/illness and, 649, 650–53
integrated theory of, 1327, 1335
intensity of, measurement, 471–72
interaction with reason, 1069
language of, 13, 15–16
language-related, neuroscience of, 237
and law (*see* law and emotion)
lexical concepts for, conflation with scientific constructs, 382
and long-term political goals, 617
versus moods, 115–16, 523–24
and motivation/motivational systems, 100, 102–3, 323, 1336
motor responses to, neuroendocrine systems and, 236–38, 236f
narcissism and, 1198, 1204–9
neuroscience of, 235–38, 236f
normal versus disordered, 1085–89
objects of, 7
olfaction and, 663–64, 666–67
other-oriented, and punitive behavior, 1009–11, 1012
other-praising, and punitive behavior, 1009–10, 1011
other-suffering, and punitive behavior, 1009–11
and personality, motivation as bridge between, 122–23
phylogeny of, 1333
physiology of, neuroendocrine systems and, 236f, 236–38
and planning, 40
and political coordination, 616–17
and political judgment and behavior, 608–11
and political negotiation, 612–15
in politics, 607
postcoital, 249–51

primary, 764 (*see also* basic emotion(s))
proximate causes of, 363–64, 370
in romantic love, 225–26, 227, 228
self-report of, 502–3, 741, 792
sex differences in, 466
singular-function theories of, 1102
situation cues and, 42–43
social functions of, 1056–57
socially constructive, 1100
and social relationships, 235–36
sociocultural perspective on, 370–71
specific, importance of, 463–64
specificity of, 463–64
and status hierarchies, 587–88, 593–600, 594*t*, 601n.3
subjective experience of, 237, 502–3
subject of, 7
theories of, 369, 371
types of, xiii
ultimate causes, 370
universality, 4, 62, 320, 463–64
as variations on themes, 985–89
vicarious, 469
vocalizations of, 449–52
emotional appraisal theory, 704
emotional communication, culture and, 987–89
emotional contagion, 422, 566, 688, 739–40, 848
in animals, 769, 775
in dog–human relationship, 813
emotional displays and, 850
and empathy, 422, 769, 798–99, 821
leadership and, 1026–27
olfactory communication and, 668, 673*f*
primitive, 850
social media and, 693
emotional disorder(s). *See also* disorder(s); mental disorder(s)
cliff-edge principle and, 1099–100
definition of, 1106
versus normal emotional distress, 1085–89, 1106
smoke-detector principle and, 1099, 1100–2, 1125
subjective experience and, 1105
types of, 1085–86
emotional displays, 847. *See also* facial expression(s)
affective experience and, causal linkage, 847–48

benevolence of emitter, assessment of, 852–53
competence of emitter, assessment of, 853
definition of, 847
and emotional communication, 850
and emotional contagion, 850
versus emotional signals, 848–49
evolutionary perspective on, 850–51, 855
failing to react to, 854–55
faked, 1027–28
functions of, 847
inauthentic, children's sensitivity to, 853
leadership and, 1027–28
reacting to, when display is fake, 854–55
reactions to, cost–benefit analysis of, 854–55
as signals, 852
traditional assumptions about, 847–48, 850–51, 852
variety of, 848
emotional dysregulation
and attention-deficit hyperactivity disorder, 1248–49
in borderline personality disorder, 1280, 1281–82, 1283–84
definition of, 1283–84
and drug use/addictive behavior, 1221, 1232–33
and personality disorders, 1086
emotional empathy, 740. *See also* affective empathy
emotional granularity
in borderline personality disorder, 1285
definition of, 1285
emotional inference, 1335, 1336
emotional labor, 1027–28
emotional modernity, 920–22
and behavioral modernity, 923
and learning, 921–22
and reputation, 921–22
emotional numbing, in post-traumatic stress disorder, 1267–68
emotional processing model, of anxiety disorders, 1123
emotional reactivity, tests, in animals, 768–69
emotional responses
behavioral outcomes of, 1077
coherence of, 1328–29, 1333–34
computational models of, 1333–34

neuroscience of, 236–38, 236*f*
to ostracism, 1043–46
variability of, 1328–29, 1332–34
to vulnerability, 372–73 (*see also* nurturant love; tenderness)
emotional stability, pride and, 206–8, 207*t*
emotional tolerance, 242
emotional vigilance, 851, 1331, 1335
and benevolence assessment, 852–53
and competence assessment, 853
and crowd behavior, 854
development of, 853, 855
evolutionary perspective on, 855
functions of, 852
importance of, 852
individual differences in, 855
and mass psychogenic illness, 854
mechanisms, 852
phylogenetic studies of, 855
research on, future directions for, 854–55
emotional vulnerability
in borderline personality disorder, 1283–84
definition of, 1283–84
emotion experience
cross-cultural similarities and variations in, 986–87
and decision-making/actions in legal contexts, 1071–74
emotion frequency(ies)
definition of, 595
navigation of status hierarchies and, 595, 596, 597, 598, 599–600
emotion mechanisms, 381–82, 1327–34
and coordination programs, 112–18, 113*f*
as if–then algorithms, 382–83
interactions with ecology and culture, 382–83
numerosity of, 114, 124n.5
and prioritizing algorithms, 112–18, 113*f*
second-order coordination problem, 114, 309
and situation-detecting algorithms, 112–18, 113*f*
third-order coordination problem, 114–15, 309
universality of, 382–83
emotion misregulation, 756
emotion program, 682

emotion psychology
  development of, 437–38
  high-activation bias in, 437–38
emotion recognition, 59
emotion regulation, 708
  adaptive functions of, 748–49
  adaptive problems solved
    by, 751–55
  animals and, 757–58
  an prosocial behavior, 571–72
  antecedent-focused, 749–50
  appraisal-based framework
    for, 708–10
  and attentional resources, 753–54
  and behavioral resources, 754
  and compassion, 571–72
  culture and, 757
  definition of, 748
  in developmental plasticity, 752
  versus emotional response, 750–51
  and empathy, 571–72
  and energy economics, 753–55
  evolutionary perspective
    on, 748–49
  explicit, 750
  extrinsic, 750
  and flexible adjustment
    to social environmental
    conditions, 752–53
  implicit, 750
  instrumental outcomes of, 751–52
  in intergroup context, 708–10
  intrinsic (self-regulation), 750
  maladaptive, 749, 756–57
  menstrual cycle and, 756
  mindfulness-based, and
    reproductive outcomes, 751–52
  and motivation regulation, 118–19
  motives for, sex differences
    in, 755–56
  online, 710–11
  and physiological
    resources, 754–55
  process model of, 749–50
  pro-hedonic, 756–57
  prospective, 710–11
  proximate outcomes of, 751
  and punitive behavior, 1004–05,
    1008, 1009
  and reproductive success, 749,
    751–52, 755–56, 758
  response-focused, 749–50
  sex differences and, 755–56, 758
  and situation
    modification, 749–50
  and situation selection, 749–50
  strategies, 119–20, 748, 749–51

  universality of, 757
  voluntary, 749–51
  and well-being, 756
emotion-related behavior(s), 55
  as communication, Darwin
    on, 73n.8
  cultural diversity in, 57
  Darwin's treatment of, 56, 72n.3
  evolution of, 70–71
  as habits, 57–58, 73n.8
  universality, 62
  willful, for Darwin, 58, 73n.8
Emotions as Social Information
  theory, 1026–27
emotion science, 7. See also affective
  science, evolutionary
  future of, 12–13
  origin of, 4
  progress in, xiii–xiv
emotion spaces, 1336
emotion suppression
  and punitive behavior, 1004–05
  in war, 1267
emotion threshold(s)
  definition of, 595
  differences in, 466
  navigation of status hierarchies
    and, 595, 596, 597, 598, 599–600
  personality traits and, 466
empathic accuracy, 566
empathic concern, 565–66
  cuteness and, 343–44
  kama muta and, 348
empathic distress (personal distress),
  565–66, 571–72
empathic sharing, 566
empathy, 264–65, 287, 422–23, 428,
  469, 565–66, 739–40, 775, 944–
  45. See also affective empathy;
  cognitive empathy
  affective components of, 797
  in animals, 797
  for apologetic offenders, 727–
    28, 731
  behaviors associated with, in
    animals, 797
  benefits of, 654
  and caregiving, 423–24
  and choice of cooperative
    partner, 632–33
  cognitive components of, 797, 952
  comparative psychology
    of, 791–93
  and compassion, 575–76
  and consoling behaviors, 422
  and cooperation, 624t, 632–
    33, 637

  costs versus benefits of, 743
  cuteness and, 343–44
  definition of, 565–66, 653–54,
    797, 952
  disengagement, and
    callousness, 285
  and disgust, integration in
    healthcare, 656–57
  dogs and, 820–21
  emotional contagion and, 422,
    769, 798–99, 821
  and emotion regulation, 571–72,
    797, 798
  evolutionary perspective on, 423,
    654–55, 797, 798, 820, 953
  expression of, 797
  and fitness
    interdependence, 953–54
  and forgiveness, 725–26, 731
  and friendship, 474
  functions of, 742–43
  in grandiose narcissism, 1206
  in great apes, 796–97, 799
  and guilt, 288–89
  and healthcare, 653–54
  and helping behavior, 569–70
  in intergroup context, 709–10
  interpersonal functions of, 632–
    33, 637
  kama muta and, 348
  lack of, 167–68
  and moral behavior, 945
  morality and, 422
  neurophysiology of, 289, 797
  offspring care and, 567–68
  olfactory performance and, 672
  other-oriented quality of, 797
  pain and, 422
  Perception-Action Model and,
    798–99, 820
  and perspective-taking, 422
  perspective-taking and, 633
  positive, 637
  and prosocial responding, 797–
    98, 952, 953–54
  as prosocial yet non-moral
    emotion, 945–46, 949,
    951f, 952–54
  at proximate level, and
    morality, 952
  and punitive behavior, 1011,
    1016n.4
  rapid facial mimicry and, 799–800
  and reconciliation in intergroup
    context, 709–10
  research on, in naturalistic
    settings, 801

Russian Doll Model of, 798–99
self–other differentiation and, 797
sex differences in, 741, 1267–68
social bias in, 798
as social emotion, 951f
spectrum of, 422
suppression, in war, 1267
in vulnerable narcissism, 1207–8
yawn contagion and, 799
emptiness, chronic feelings of, in borderline personality disorder, 1280, 1282
encephalization quotient, in dogs versus humans, 811
endocrine system. *See also* hormones
and fear responding/fear learning, 504–5
endorphins, actions of, 468
energy economics
chronic pain and, 418
emotion regulation and, 753–55
of immune response, 649
energy level, emotions and, 46
enthusiasm, physiological effects of, 377
entrapment, feeling of, and depression, 1149–50, 1151
environment
as decisionally opaque, 40–41
and emotions, 6–7, 13
modern, versus ancestral, 1180
present (ontogenetic environment), 28–29, 30–31
environmental mismatch
and attention-deficit hyperactivity disorder, 1249, 1250
and chronic pain, 416
and expression of emotion, 692–93
environment of evolutionary adaptedness, 27, 29
as adaptation-specific, 30
definition of, 29–30
as evolutionary change-specific, 30
invariances in, 31
for species, 30
as statistical composite, 29–30
and statistical regularities, 31
time depth of, 30
envy, 169, 320, 472. *See also* social emotions
animals and, 774–75
benign, 601n.4
and choice of cooperative partner, 624t
and cooperation, 636

definition of, 816
and detection of negative association value, 167
evolutionary origins of, evidence for, 10t, 12
evolutionary perspective on, 170
and female intrasexual competition, 977
function of, 977, 1056–57
and hatred, 170
interpersonal functions of, 624t, 636
versus jealousy, 776, 816
malicious, 601n.4
narcissism and, 1205–6, 1207
in negotiation about entitlement, 610, 611
outputs of, 596–97
in political judgment and behavior, 608–9, 615
as secondary emotion, 764–65
as self-conscious emotion, 764
and self-improvement motive, 977
as social emotion, 81–83
and status hierarchies, 587, 593, 594t, 596–97
unitary versus dual models of, 601n.4
Epidemiologic Catchment Area, 1139–41
epigenetics, 66
parental care and, 283–84
epilepsy
gelastic, 557
psychomotor, 469
epistemic vigilance, 612, 851–52
evolutionary perspective on, 855
importance of, 852
ERBs. *See* emotion-related behavior(s)
eros, 220–21
ERP. *See* Exposure and Response Prevention
error management theory, 416
nyctophobia and, 1121
ERS. *See* excessive reassurance seeking
ESS, senescence-like processes and, 50–51n.5
essentialism, 1328–29
Esther, 1062
estradiol, 669
and depression in menopausal transition, 870
estrogen
and anxiety disorders, 871

and depression in menopausal transition, 870
and peripartum depression, 870
and PMS/PMDD, 868–69
and PTSD symptoms, 872–73
ethanol, and effects of frustrative nonreward, 835
ethology, 67–68, 101–2, 463, 686
eusociality, 421–22
Evans, Kortnee C., 391–409
evidence-based psychotherapy. *See also* cognitive processing therapy; prolonged exposure
for post-traumatic stress disorder, 1268, 1269, 1270, 1271, 1274
evolutionary emotion research, 1327
big picture agenda for, 1333–35
comparative, 1333–35
future directions for, 1333–35
key theoretical issues and, 1327–33
on mechanisms and variability, 1333–34
motivational perspective, advantages of, 1336
and readout problem, 1330–32
on readouts and inferences, 1334–35
and specialized mechanisms, 1327–33
evolutionary functionalism. *See* function/functionalism, in evolutionary biology
evolutionary game theory, 717, 723. *See also* prisoner's dilemma; tit-for-tat
evolutionary mismatch, 1240–41. *See also* mismatch hypothesis
and chronic disease, 309
definition of, 1264
modern group size as, 1269
and post-traumatic stress disorder, 1264
evolutionary psychiatry, 1262–63
evolutionary psychology, 27, 181–82, 930, 944, 983–84, 1030, 1070
content areas and questions in, 930
context and, 400
and disgust system, 181–82, 191–92
Kantian idealism and, 888–91, 904n.2
and positive psychology, connection/complementarity of, 929, 930–31, 932
and "post hoc" theorizing problem, 381–82
research recommendations for, 381–83
theoretical bases in, 381–82

evolutionary psychopathology, 1262–63
evolved psychological mechanism(s), 492–93, 494, 1180
　and consistency, 984–85
　functional specialization of, 984
　and leadership, 1022
　operation of, and information-processing, 985
　and variation of psychology and behavior, 984–85
exaptation, 1309
excessive reassurance seeking, depression and, 1156–57
excitation. *See also* arousal
　emotions in animals and, 764
exclusion, 631–32
experience
　and emotions, 13–16
　words and, 15
experience sharing. *See* affective empathy
experiential avoidance, 749
exploitation, 423
　curiosity and, 363
　responses to, 1072 (*see also* anger)
exploration
　boredom and, 324–25
　childhood and, 324
　curiosity and, 363
exploration/competence motivational system, 102
Exposure and Response Prevention, 1124
expression [term], 58, 72n.1
expression of emotion(s), 13–15, 44–45, 72n.1, 448–52, 544, 572, 682. *See also* facial expression(s); nonverbal communication; tactile signals; vocal signals
　context and, 687, 690–92
　and cooperation, 632
　cultural variation, historical heterogeneity and, 991–92, 1030
　culture and, 685–86, 690–92, 987–89
　Darwin's term, criticisms of, 58
　decoding hypothesis, 448, 451–52
　dimorphous, 345
　encoding hypothesis, 448, 451–52
　evolutionary perspective on, 466–68
　flexibility–inflexibility of, 1330
　flexibility of, 490
　functions of, 463
　and group living, 683

as honest signaling, 70, 1330–31, 1334
mismatch and, 692–93
modern communication technology and, 692–93
multimodal, 686
in *Nayasastra*, 449
neuroscience of, 236–38, 236f, 685–86
and political coordination, 616–17
sex differences in, 689–90
as social communication, 686–87
social construction of, 687–88
social functional account of, 688–89
social situations and, 690–92
socioecological context and, 490
socioeconomic context and, 490
unintentional, 688–89
voluntariness–involuntariness of, 1330
without emotion experience, 682, 687
expressive suppression, 749–50, 753, 754–55
　in animals, 758
　culture and, 757
externality management, 79–80
external locus of control, depression and, 1151
extraversion
　agentic, in narcissism, 1199–200, 1202
　genetic basis for, 1200–1
　grandiose narcissism and, 1200–1
　gratitude and, 264–65
　humor styles and, 548
　and life-history strategies, 1288–89
　pride and, 206–8, 207t
extremism, ostracism and, 1048–50
eyewitness memory, affective influence on, 527–29, 529f

F

face-reading, 59. *See also* pose(s)
　context dependency of, 59
　posed, decline of, 67
facetiousness, 557
facial action, adaptation and, 67–71
Facial Action Coding System, 14–15, 770, 988
facial action units, 501–2, 770, 849, 988
Facial Affect Coding System, 573
facial affect program, 61, 64
facial behaviors. *See* facial expression(s)

facial expression(s), 55, 72n.1, 320, 451–52, 465, 501–2, 572, 616, 684, 848, 1056, 1152, 1329. *See also* anger face; Behavioral Ecology View; emotional displays; rapid facial mimicry
and affect, 464–65
of anger, 685, 705
in animals, 770–73, 791
and attractiveness, 755–56
audience effects and, 65
bared teeth display, 791
Basic Emotion Theory and, 68–70, 69t, 848–49
Behavioral Ecology View of, 68–70, 69t, 74n.20, 849
and candidate basic emotions, 9, 10t, 11–12
of compassion, 572–73
consistency in, 686, 848–49
of contempt, 597–98
context and, 686
culture and, 57, 63–66, 685–86, 849
culture-specific variations in, 988
Darwin's account of, 56–58
and deception, 69–70
decoding, sex differences in, 741
difficulty recognizing, in psychopathy, 1299
discrimination of, in animals, 771–73
of disgust, 685, 864, 960
emotions without, 609, 616, 664
evolution of, 70–71
eye region and, 741
of fear, 74n.22, 508–10, 599, 685
hiding, by chimpanzees, 758
as honest signaling, 70
inauthentic, 69–70, 849
as intention movements, 68–69, 69t, 74n.20
in intergroup context, 705
interpretation, mood bias and, 531, 532f
micromomentary, 70
neuroscience of, 237, 685–86
in pain display, 419, 423, 425
perception, configural processing and, 989
and political coordination, 616–17
private versus public, 65
processing of, odor perceptions and, 671–72
of sadness, 522
as signals, 849
as social influence tools, 849

social processing of, multisensory
  input and, 671–72
species-specificity of, 773
of sympathy, 572
of threat, 1115–16
universality and, 59–67, 73n.14,
  686, 848–49
facial lies, 69–70
facial mimicry, 770–71, 850, 853. *See
  also* rapid facial mimicry
  and emotional contagion, 769
facial muscles, 73n.10
facial paresis, 237, 847
FACS. *See* Facial Affect
  Coding System
factor analysis, 106–7, 124n.3, 1093
Faer, L. M., 1186
fairness
  affective influence on, 537–38, 538f
  appraisals of, 1045
  dogs and, 817
  and moral obligation, 948
  sense of, 817
faithfulness, 474
false-positives problem, 1240
family, 89
family relationships, human. *See
  also* attachment; bonding; pair-
  bonding; parental behavior
  emotional response in, evolution
    of, 242
FAP. *See* facial affect program; fixed
  action patterns
Fast-Slow-Defense model, 1225
fatigue, 465
  persistent, disease and, 299–300
fear, xiii, 437–38, 500. *See also*
  anxiety disorder(s); phobia(s)
  acquisition, 1265
  adaptive perspective and, 1126–27
  in animals, 778–79
  as anticipatory, 501, 502f
  versus anxiety, 501
  and anxiety disorders, 1110
  appraisal mechanism and, 8
  and auditory signaling, 507–10
  aversive quality of, 510–11
  as basic emotion, 4, 103, 990
  behavioral aspects of, 506–7
  behaviors associated with, in
    animals, 768
  biochemical aspects of, 504–10
  in birds, neurology of, 766–67
  bottom-up response, 240
  brain activity and, 468–69
  chemical signals of, in
    animals, 767

chemosensory signals of, 507–10
cliff-edge principle and, 1100
communication of, 507–10
conditioning, 1269–70
of darkness (*see* nyctophobia)
and defensive aggression, 107
definition of, 501–3
disorders of, 510–11, 1086–87
in dogs, 811–12
and drug use/addiction, 1228t,
  1230
and energy level/effort
  allocation, 46
evolutionary origins of, evidence
  for, 10t, 11, 503–4
evolutionary perspective
  on, 371–72
expression in animals, 770–71, 812
expression of, 467, 508–10,
  599, 683
extinction, 1264, 1265
facial expression of, 74n.22, 501–
  2, 599, 685
in fish, neurology of, 766–67
functions of, 254, 319, 521–22,
  748–49, 944, 1043–44, 1109–10,
  1126–27
and harm avoidance, 282–83
and hatred, 171
with injury/illness, 649
intensity of, variations of, 1100
in intergroup context, 698–99,
  704, 709
and leadership, 1031
maladaptive (*see* anxiety; anxiety
  disorder(s); phobia(s))
as motive, 104
neural circuitry and, 503–10, 509f
neuroendocrinology of, 237–38,
  238f, 239–40, 240f, 504–5
and nonvocal alarm calls, 507–
  10, 683
objects of, 7
and obsessive-compulsive
  symptoms, 1318
and odor emission, 507–10
and olfactory communication,
  507–10, 668, 673f
ostracism and, 1045
out-groups and, 1265
pain and, 417
personality and, 87
physiologic effects of, in dogs, 812
and political negotiation, 612
postural expressions of, 508, 509–10
versus precaution system, 108
as primary emotion, 764

research on, 318
retention in moths, through
  metamorphosis, 500
self-report of, 502–3
and social communicative
  responses, 507–10
and status hierarchies, 593, 594t,
  599–600
subject of, 7
suppression, in war, 1267
tendency to feel, and political
  attitudes, 613
top-down response, 239–40, 240f
and visual signaling, 507–10
and vocalizations, 507–10, 683
fear cues
  interpretation of, 508–10
  perception of, 508–9
  sensitivity to, 510
  social functions of, 507–10
fear learning, 503–4
  neural mechanisms in, 510
fear module theory, 1112–13, 1116
fear system, 105f, 107
feedback regulation, 116–17, 1336
feedforward regulation, 116–17, 1336
feeding behavior, 299b
feeding niche, human, 623, 641–42
feeling sick, 651–53
Fehr, B., 62–63
female intrasexual competition,
  968–69, 1175–79, 1176t, 1183–
    84, 1186–87
  for access to preferred mates, 970
  aggression in, 972–73, 977–79
  anger and, 975–76
  appearance and, 973
  areas of, 969–71
  and cooperativeness, 977–78
  emotions and, 968–69, 975–79
  environmental context and, 970–71
  envy and, 977
  jealousy and, 976–77
  and mating, 969–71
  in modern societies, 1183–89
  in older women, future research
    on, 978–79
  perceived threat leading
    to, 973–74
  research on, future directions
    for, 978–79
  for resources, 970–71, 972–73
  as rivalry, 971
  strategies for, 971–73
  when rival is friend or
    sister, 977–78
  winning, future research on, 978

INDEX   1365

female same-sex friendships, and co-rumination, 737–43
Fernandez-Dols, José-Miguel, 55–56
fertility
   female human, 1178
   natural, and disgust sensitivity, 188–89
   natural, and immunomodulation, 188–89
Festinger, L., 897
fever, 302–3, 1096–97, 1100–1. *See also* behavioral fever
   adaptive value of, 463
   emotional, in animals, 766
fight-flight-freeze system, 107, 124n.6, 506–7, 1109–10
fight or flight, 107, 1056
   in panic disorder, 1114
financial conflict, in couples, and depression, 1148
fire ants, abdominal wagging by, 770
fish
   chemical alarm signals, 767
   fear response in, 766–67
   neurological underpinnings of emotions in, 766–67
   nociception in, 415, 418–19
Fisher, Helen, 221
Fisher, Maryanne L., 968–79
Fisher, Ronald, 56–57
fission-fusion dynamics, 728, 793–94
fitness, 22–24, 33. *See also* inclusive fitness
   as outcome of design, 26, 50n.4
   and social valuation, 79–80
   striving for, 50
fitness affordance, 889–90, 891, 903–4, 905n.9
fitness contingencies, of actions, emotions and, 48
fitness interdependence, 641–42
   definition of, 953
   empathy and, 953–54
   genetic relatedness and, 953
   and morality, 953–54
   non-kin and, 953
   sources of, 623–30
fitness maximization, 38, 50
   all-purpose, 38–39
   Lamarckianism and, 37–39
   transient phenomena and, 33–34
Fitouchi, Léo, 944–61
fixed action patterns, 61
flight initiation, fear/threat and, 506
Flinn, Mark V., 235–42
Foa, E. B., 1123
Folger, Logan F., 1197–210

folk categories of emotions, 99–100, 106, 1328–29, 1332–33, 1336
followership, 1021, 1022–25, 1032
   evolutionary perspective on, 1023–24
   organizational perspective on, 1022–23
foodborne infection, prevention of, 141
food insecurity, and mental health symptoms, 1136–37
food intake
   and energy costs of digestion, 140
   during infection, metabolic state and, 139–40
   lassitude and, 138–39
   and mating, as modern adaptive metaproblem, 1189
   nutrient preferences in, infection and, 140–41
food-sharing, 623, 630
Fore tribe, 60–61, 73–74n.15
   endocannibalism, 73–74n.15
Forgas, Joseph P., 520–39
forgiveness, 724–27. *See also* tit-for-tat
   apologies and, 727–28, 731
   belief in, in couples, sex differences in, 257
   conscious cost–benefit analysis and, 725, 726
   costly apologies and, 728–30
   definition of, 724–27
   empathy and, 725–26, 731
   gratitude and, 269
   health benefits of, 725
   mediation by proximate emotions, 725–26
   perceived exploitation risk and, 726–27, 727f
   psychological mechanisms of, 724–25
   remorse expressions and, 287–88
   similarity to animal reconciliation, 693, 724
   valuable relationship hypothesis and, 724–26
formal operational stage, 489
   loss for children in, 492
formidability
   anger face and, 139–40
   and anger-proneness, 1073–74
   and predatory aggression, 174
   ritualized aggression and, 139
   and sex differences in depression, 1155–56
   upper body strength and, 1155

welfare trade-off ratio and, 139
Foster, Joshua D., 1197–210
Foucault, Michel, 1088
Four Pillars of Well-Being, 454–55
Four Questions (Tinbergen), 358, 484–85, 487, 543–44
Frances, Allen, 1087–88, 1142–43
Frank, Robert, 70
Fredrickson, Barbara, 371–72, 375, 377–78
free-rider problem, 630, 1268
   and altruistic punishment, 428
Freud, Sigmund, 484, 520–21, 1198
Freyd, J., 905n.8
Fridlund, Alan J., 55–72, 72n.3, 72–73n.7, 686–87, 1327–28, 1329, 1330
friendship(s), 270, 940. *See also* female same-sex friendships
   best, versus other friendships, 406–7
   dynamics of, sex differences in, 738
   evolutionary perspective on, 742–43
   and happiness, 473–74
   implicit social contract of, 406–7
   and infidelity, 406
   self-disclosure in, 738–39
friendship jealousy, 392, 405–8, 409. *See also* jealousy
"friends with benefits," infidelity and, 407–8
Friesen, Wallace, 60–61, 62, 64, 66, 69–70
Frijda, N. H., 382
frontal lobe
   and emotional responses, 236–37
   and humor comprehension, 556
   and laughter, 557
fruit fly
   fear responding/fear learning in, 503–4
   response to threat, 464
frustration, 437. *See also* frustrative nonreward
   behaviors associated with, in animals, 768
   expression in animals, 770–71
   and punitive behavior, 1015
frustration-aggression hypothesis, 973
frustrative nonreward, 830–31
   and behavioral evidence of negative emotion, 834
   comparative research on, 832–34
   in daily experience, 831

definition of, 831–32
experimental study of, 831–32
and neurolobiological evidence of negative emotion, 836–39
and pharmacological evidence of negative emotion, 835–36
and physiological evidence of negative emotion, 834–35
FSD. *See* Fast-Slow-Defense model
function/functionalism, in evolutionary biology, 22–24
functional analysis of adaptation(s), 35
rules for, 34–35
task analysis/computational theory phase of, 29, 31
fundamental attribution error, 529–30
fundamental motive(s), 103–4
definition of, 372
and drug use/addiction, 1227–33, 1228*t*
and emotions, 1228*t*, 1229
list of, 1227
positive emotions and, 372–73, 373*t*
fundamental social motives. *See* fundamental motive(s)

G

GABAergic system
actions of, 868–69
and effects of frustrative nonreward, 835–36
and peripartum depression, 870
and PMS/PMDD, 868–69
GAD. *See* generalized anxiety disorder
Gadjusek, Carlton, 73–74n.15
galvanic skin response, as measurement of arousal, 1007–08
gambling, pathological. *See* pathological gambling
Garcia, Hector A., 1262–74
Garcia effect, 184–85
Garcilaso de la Vega, 1060
Garfield, Zachary H., 1021–33
Garson, Justin, 1096, 1097
gateway groups, 710–11
Gatward, N., 1183
gay rights, support for, emotions and, 1077–78
gazelles, stotting in, 425–26, 851
Geher, Glenn, 929–41
gelatophobia, 558
gene(s)
and behavioral phenotypes, 72n.6
and complex adaptations, 32–33
and morphological phenotypes, 72n.6
and narcissism, 1200
sexual recombination of, 32–33, 50–51n.5
generalized anxiety disorder, 1086, 1105, 1110, 1116–17. *See also* major depression and generalized anxiety syndrome, mixed
epidemiology of, 1116–17
hormones and, 871–72
maternal, and neonatal brain development, 871–72
prevalence of, 871
sex differences in, 871–72
smoke-detector principle and, 1101
in women, 871–72
worry in, 1116–17
genetic program(s), open versus closed, 6
genetics, and evolutionary theory, 56–57, 72n.6
genetic switch(es), 50–51n.5, 51n.6
genocide, 707–8
gerbils, frustrative nonreward in, 834
Gere, Richard, 175–76
Gervais, M., 548, 551
get-acquainted paradigm, for ostracism, 1046
gibbons, facial expressions in, 770
Gibson, J. J., 904n.2
Gibson, James, 905n.9
Gilbert, P., 102, 105–6
Gilbert, Paul, 282–93, 1270
Gillespie, Joseph, 545–46
giving. *See* cooperation
global transformations, emotions as, 1102–3
Glucocorticoid Cascade Hypothesis, 866–67
glucocorticoid receptors, in depression, 866
glucocorticoids
and animals' emotional state, 765–66
fear and, 505
glutamatergic system, in attachment, 239–40
goal(s)
emotions and, 43–44
instrumental, and emotion regulation, 749
long-term, emotions and, 617
motivational, 112–18, 113*f*
pro-hedonic, and emotion regulation, 749
goal pursuit. *See also* cooperation
emotions and, 609
goal pursuit/evaluation algorithms in motivational systems, 112–18, 113*f*
pride and, 207*t*, 208, 210
goal relevance, as appraisal dimension, 990
goal-seeking, 25
goal-setting
competition and, 470
and happiness, 469–71
realistic, 470
goats, and reconciliation, 720
Goetz, Jennifer L., 565–78
Goetz, Stefan M. M., 462–77
Goffman, Erving, 73n.8
golden lion tamarins
allomothers, teaching-like behaviors of, 919–20
infant, development of vocal control and flexible vocalizing, 917
goldfish, reversed SNC effect in, 832–33
Goldilocks ("just right") principle, jealousy and, 394–95
Goodall, J., 488
Gopnik, Alison, 363
gorillas *(Gorilla gorilla). See also* great apes
consolation behaviors in, 800
humor in, 544–45
and newborns' vocalizations, 915
orphaned, 488
socio-cognitive skills of, 794
gossip, functions of, 960
GQ-6. *See* Gratitude Questionnaire Six-Item Form
Grandin, Temple, 1252
gratitude, xiii, 474, 936. *See also* social emotions
affective benefits of, 264–65
and choice of cooperative partner, 624*t*, 631, 634
communicative function of, 273–75
and cooperation, 624*t*, 634, 637–38
and cooperative relationships, 263–64, 265–66, 270, 274–75
costs and benefits related to, 276–77
cross-cultural commonalities and differences in, 268–70

gratitude (*cont.*)
   crying and, 467–68
   definition of, 380
   as discrete emotion/natural kind, 277
   evolutionary origins of, evidence for, 10t, 12
   evolutionary perspective on, 270–76
   expression of, cross-cultural studies of, 268–69
   and forgiveness, 269
   functional structure of, 277
   function of, 148–49, 742–43, 1056–57
   and helping behaviors, 266
   importance of, 263–64
   and indebtedness, 269
   and indirect reciprocity, 276–77
   information-processing structure of, 270
   interpersonal functions of, 624t, 631, 634
   and intimate bonds, 267
   kama muta and, 348
   in negotiation about entitlement, 611
   and personality traits, 264–65
   in political judgment and behavior, 611
   and positive affect, 264
   and prosociality, 264–67
   and punitive behavior, 1011, 1014f, 1014–16
   qualia of, 277
   relationship closeness and, 266–67
   research on, 263–64, 276–77
   science of, 264–70
   as social emotion, 80, 82–83, 84–85, 85f, 86f
   as social exchange barometer, 266
   social functions of, 380
   state, 264
   trait, 264–65
   and welfare trade-off ratios, 270–75, 277
   and well-being, 264, 265, 269, 277
gratitude interventions, and well-being, 265, 269, 277
Gratitude Questionnaire Six-Item Form, 269
graylag geese, 67, 488
great apes. *See also* bonobos; chimpanzees; gorillas; orangutans; primates
   bared teeth facial expression in, 791
   cognitive bias testing in, 795–96
   consolation behavior in, 796, 800–1
   emotion in, 793–95, 801–2
   emotion recognition in, 795
   empathy in, 796–97, 799
   expression of emotions in, 795
   gaze-tracking in, 796
   infrared thermography of, 796
   juvenile period in, 793
   life-history characteristics of, 793
   pupillometry in, 796
   rapid facial mimicry in, 799–800
   sociality in, 793
   socio-cognitive skills of, 794
   socio-emotional skills of, 794
   studying emotion in, 795–96
   targeted helping in, 801
   yawn contagion in, 799
great man, 1022–23
greed, pride and, 209
grief, xiii, 496–97, 1253. *See also* prolonged grief disorder
   adult behaviors in, 486t
   adversity and, 1135–36
   in animals, 487–89, 768
   attachment and, 485–87
   attachment theory and, 484–85
   biochemical correlates of, 493–94
   childhood behaviors in, 486t
   complicated, 495–96
   COVID-19 pandemic and, 497
   and crying, 485
   definition of, 485–87
   disorders of, 495–96, 1086–87
   Dual Process Model of, 484
   expression of, 1134–35
   functional aspects of, 494–95
   functions of, 1135
   as idiosyncratic, 487
   immediate causes of, 492–94
   insecure attachment and, 485–87
   intensity of, predictors, 492–93, 494–95
   Kübler-Ross stage theory of, 484
   mechanisms of, 492–94
   neuroendocrinology of, 487–88
   ontogenetic aspects of, 489–92
   Parkes-Bowlby theory of, 484–87
   phylogenetic aspects of, 487–89
   physiologic effects of, 487–88, 492–94, 495
   smoke-detector principle and, 1101
   theories of, 484
   universality of, 484
grief therapy, 495–96
Griffiths, T. L., 360–61, 364
grip strength, 1155–56
Grøntvedt, Trond Viggo, 246–59
group conflict. *See also* intergroup conflict
   proactive aggression and, 107–8
group hierarchy(ies), adaptive problems posed by, 589–93
group selection, in eusocial communities, 421–22
group size
   and charismatic leadership, 1029
   modern, as evolutionary mismatch, 1269
growth. *See also* resilience
   in communities, 930, 934
   definition of, 930
   evolutionary perspective on, 930
   individual, evolutionary perspective on, 932–34
   learning and/or change in, 930
   positive psychology and, 930
guilt, 152–53, 936, 944–45, 948–49, 960–61. *See also* social emotions; survivor guilt
   and altruistic behavior, 289
   animals and, 775–76
   and apology-making, 730, 731
   brain functions necessary for, 288–92
   and cooperation, 624t, 638
   and cooperative relationships, 287–88
   and courage, 291
   definition of, 290–91
   dimensions of, 290–91
   dogs and, 814–18
   emotions associated with, 291, 292
   empathy and, 288–89
   evolutionary origins of, evidence for, 10t, 12
   evolutionary perspective on, 282, 292f, 292–93, 895
   expression of, and punishment, 287–88
   facilitators of, 293
   from failure to prevent harm, 282–83, 292, 292f
   from failure to rescue, 291
   forensic, 290
   function of, 148–49, 282, 287–88, 292–93, 742–43
   inhibition of, 289–90, 293
   and intended harm, 290
   interpersonal functions of, 638

mechanisms for, 283–84
and moral conscience, 1076
as moral emotion, 945–46, 949–51, 951*f*
and moral principles, 291
motivational model of, 292*f*, 292–93
in negotiation about entitlement, 611
ostracism and, 1044, 1045
in political judgment and behavior, 611
in post-traumatic stress disorder, 1274
and prosocial behavior, 291, 293
psychological aspects of, 290–91
psychopathy and, 1299, 1309–10
and punitive behavior, 1015
and recalibration, 46–47, 946
and regret, 256
and reparation, 286, 290, 950
as secondary emotion, 764–65
as self-conscious emotion, 764, 949–51
self-conscious phenomenology of, 152–54
and self-punishment, 730
and shame, 149, 282–83, 291–92, 950
versus shame, 987
as social emotion, 81, 82, 84–85, 85*f*, 86*f*
and unintentional harm, 292, 292*f*
guilty look, in dogs, 814–16, 815*f*
guinea pigs, pain behaviors in, 420
Guisinger, S., 1182, 1183
gullibility, reduced, negative affect and, 532
gut microbiota, disgust sensitivity and, 191

H

Habecker, Heather, 235–42
habit(s)
  Darwin's account of, 57
  emotion-related behaviors as, 57–58, 73n.8
habitat, versus environment of evolutionary adaptedness, 29–30
habituation, 469–70, 750, 1123, 1124
  in animals, 464
  and disgust sensitivity, 187, 193–94
  pain and, 417
Hadza, differential reproduction in, ethnographic and historical perspective on, 1057, 1058

Hagen, Edward H., 308, 1134–62, 1226
Hagen, Kristen, 1109–27
Haidt, J., 946, 1002*b*
hair-pulling disorder. *See* trichotillomania
Haldane, J. B. S., 56–57
hallucinogen(s), 1218, 1219
halo effects, 530*f*, 530
Hamilton's rule, 46
handicap principle of biological signaling theory, 426, 428
happiness, 235–36, 436, 452, 502*f*
  affective space of, 455, 456*f*
  age and, 476
  in animals, 770
  disorders of, 476–77
  in dogs, 812–13
  evolutionary origins of, evidence for, 10*t*, 11
  evolutionary perspective on, 932–33, 935–36
  evolutionary psychology of, 939
  evolutionary significance of, 462–63
  expressions of, 466–68
  facial/bodily expressions of, 451–52
  friendship and, 473–74
  functions of, 474
  as general emotion, 466–68
  and goal-setting, 469–71
  hedonistic conceptions of, 471
  heritability of, 472
  income and, 475
  individual versus collective, 463
  leisure and, 475
  and longevity, 471
  lottery winners and, 475
  marriage and, 473
  measurement of, 471–72
  and mental health, 471
  national differences in, 476
  neurochemical basis of, 468–69
  olfaction and, 666
  and olfactory communication, 668, 673*f*
  parenthood and, 473
  personality factors and, 472–73
  and physical health, 471
  as primary emotion, 764
  pursuit of, 521
  religion and, 475–76
  research on, 471
  retirement and, 476
  self-relevant events and, 8
  sex differences in, 476

social support and, 473
stability of, 473
upregulation of, 751–52, 756–57
work and, 474–75
Hare, Robert, 1242
harm, causing, avoidance of. *See* harm avoidance
harm avoidance, 282–83, 293
  in animals, 284–85
  fear-based, 282–83
  guilt and, 282–83, 292, 292*f*
  parental care and, 284–88
  shame-based, 282–83
harmful dysfunction, 1303–4, 1309
  definition of, 1300
  intentional versus unintentional, 169
harmful dysfunction analysis, 1088–89, 1091–92, 1094–96, 1239–40
  disorders in, 1094, 1095
  and DSM, 1094
  dysfunction in, 1094
  misconceptions or potential challenges in applying, 1096–99
Hart, Merton, 1058
Harvard Bereavement Study, 485–87, 486*t*
hasham, 380
Hastorf, Albert, and Hadley Cantril, "They Saw a Game," 885–86, 888
hatred. *See also* neutralization theory of hatred
  versus anger, 163
  anger and, 170, 176
  and attentional direction, 175–76
  and avoidance, 176
  behavioral strategies related to, 163–64, 167–68, 173, 177–78
  cognitive responses to, 166–67, 169–70, 175–76, 177–78
  computational structure of, 172–73
  as contagious, 170, 175
  contempt and, 1049
  costs of, outweighing benefits, 177
  disgust and, 171
  envy and, 170
  and fear, 171
  and homicide, 174
  and information gathering, 175–76
  and information warfare, 174–75
  in intergroup context, 700, 704, 709–11
  jealousy and, 170–71

hatred (cont.)
  mutual/reciprocal, 171–72, 177
  neutralization theory of, 163–64, 173, 174
  new alliances and, 177
  new cooperation and, 177
  ostracism and, 1049
  and predatory aggression, 173–74
  shame and, 171, 178n.3
  social learning of, 169–70
  terminating conditions for, 176–77
  triggers of, 168–72
  unjust harm and, 171–72
Hayes, Steve, 1125
HDA. *See* harmful dysfunction analysis
health anxiety, 1320–21. *See also* hypochondriasis
healthcare
  community health behaviors in, 656
  compassion in, 649, 653–54, 657
  emotions associated with, 653–57
  and empathy, 653–54
  evolutionary perspective on, 654–55, 657
  integration of empathy and disgust in, 656–57
  motivations for, 655
  prosocial behavior in, 648–49
  racial discrimination in, 655
  social care in, 656
healthcare workers, and status, 654
heart rate, 446, 810
  in animals, 765, 766
  contentment and, 447, 450*t*
  in dogs, 810, 812
  fear and, 504–5
heart rate variability, 446
  contentment and, 447, 450*t*
  fear and, 505
hedonic adaptation, 469–70
hedonic assumption, 118–19
hedonic principle, 521
hedonic values, emotions and, 45
hedonism, 471
Heinroth, Magdalena, 74n.19
Heinroth, Oskar, 67–68, 74n.19
helminth infection
  and disgust sensitivity, 189, 194–95
  substances protective against, 1226, 1229–30
helper role, 649
helping behavior(s). *See also* targeted helping

benefits of, perception of, and compassion, 569–71
in children, 286–87
cross-species, 421
gratitude and, 266
with kin versus non-kin, 567–68, 569–70
offspring care and, 567–68
relationship type and, 567–68, 569–71
self-efficacy and, 571–72
helping behaviors, in dogs, 820–21
helplessness
  depression and, 1151
  ostracism and, 1045
hemisphere(s), cerebral
  and humor comprehension, 556
  and lateralization of emotion processing in animals, 767
hermaphrodite, protogynous sequential, 34
Hewlett, Barry, 1057–58
HEXACO personality traits. *See* Big Six personality traits
hierarchical power system, 102
Hinde, Robert, 68, 73n.9
hippocampus, 1112
  in olfactory processing, 665, 666*f*
Hitchens, Christopher, 178n.3
HLA. *See* human leukocyte antigen system
hoard, as motive, 104
hoarding, obsessive-compulsive disorder and, 1318
hoarding disorder, 1086, 1317, 1320
Hobbes, Thomas, 549
Hobson, Peter, 918
Holtzman, Nicholas S., 1197–210
homeland security policies, support for, emotions and, 1077–78
homeostasis, 116–17
  contentment and, 443–45
  definition of, 443
  maintenance of, 443
homicidal fantasy(ies), 174
homicide, 1264–65
  hatred and, 174
  infidelity and, 1075, 1076–77
  in Ju/'hoansi, 1058
  and provocation doctrine, 1074–77
  sex differences in, 1188
  spousal, 1075
hominin infant(s)
  alloparenting of, 911–13, 912*f*
  appeal to mother, 913–14
  attraction of potential caregivers, 914–15

development-plus-social selection in, 922
incorporation of others' preferences, 918–19
and maternal bonding, 913–14
and new psychological dimensions of *Kindchenschema*, 919
survival challenges faced by, 913–19
homology. *See also* primate homologues of basic emotions
versus homoplasy, 72–73n.7
homophily, 474
homoplasy, 72–73n.7
homosexuality
  depathologization of, 1255
  and male eating disorders, 1187–88
honey, intake, infection and, 140
Honnold, Alex, 500, 511
hookups. *See* casual sex; short-term mating
hope, in intergroup context, 709
hormonal contraceptives
  and disgust sensitivity, 865
  and PMS/PMDD, 868
hormones
  and aggression, 862–64
  and anger, 862–64
  and animals' emotional state, 765–66
  and anxiety disorders, 871–73
  and borderline personality, 862
  and depressive disorders, 865–67
  and disgust, 864–65
  and emotions, 862, 874
  and generalized anxiety disorder, 871–72
  and major depressive disorder, 865–67
  and menopausal transition, 870
  in menstrual cycle, 861–62
  and obsessive-compulsive disorder, 873
  and panic disorder, 873
  and peripartum depression, 869–70
  and post-traumatic stress disorder, 872–73
  and premenstrual dysphoric disorder, 867–69
  and premenstrual syndrome, 867–69
  research on, future directions for, 874
  and romantic love, 222–25
  and social anxiety disorder, 871, 872

horses
  emotion discrimination by, 773
  facial expressions in, 770
  infrared thermal imaging of, 766
  pain behaviors in, 420
  pain display in, 419, 425
  secondary emotions in, 776
Howell, Nancy, 1058
HPA. *See* hypothalamic–pituitary–adrenal axis
Hrdy, Sarah Blaffer, 910–23
HRV. *See* heart rate variability
5-*HTTLPR* gene, 1200
Huaina Cápac, 1060
hubris, 152–53, 635
Hughes, Austin, 22
Hughes, Mercedes, 861–74
human adaptive complex, 622–30
human approach test, 768–69
human leukocyte antigen system, 669
human population biology, and disgust system, 181–82, 191–92
Hume, David, 521, 1068–69
humiliation
  and extremism, 1050
  ostracism and, 1050
humor, 543. *See also* laughter; mirth
  and affiliative connections, 379, 547–48, 550
  analgesic effects of, 550
  appreciation, neural basis of, 556–57
  benefits to humorist, 547–48
  benefits to recipient, 546–47
  and competition, 549–50
  comprehension, neural basis of, 556
  contagion effect of, 545, 547–48, 551
  as corrective, 549
  in courtship, 552
  culture and, 554
  developmental perspective on, 553–55
  and dominance, 548, 549–50, 555
  elderly people and, 554–55
  as emotion, 544, 558
  evolutionary perspective on, 543–44, 546–48, 556
  evolved basis of, 544–45
  expressions of, 545
  functional explanations of, 546, 549–53, 558
  and group solidarity, 550
  health effects of, 550–51

  incongruity in, 547, 548, 549, 550, 553–54, 555, 556
  individual differences and, 555
  and intelligence, 552
  ironic, 554
  and learning, 551
  and marital satisfaction, 552–53
  and mate selection, 552
  neuroscience of, 556–57
  pathology affecting, 557–58
  and play, 555–56
  psychological benefits of, 551
  as resistance, 616–17
  sex differences in, 555
  theories of, 545–46
  in workplace, 551
humor style(s), 548
  affiliative, 548, 550, 551, 553
  aggressive, 548, 549, 550, 551, 553
  self-defeating, 548, 551, 553
  self-enhancing, 548, 551
hunger, 104, 299b, 361
  conditioning and, 465
  deactivation of, 402
  and disgust sensitivity, 189, 194
  and drug use, 1228t, 1229–30
  and satiety, 468
  as superordinate regulatory program, 1104
hunter-gatherers, of Pleistocene, and leadership, 1023–24
hunter-gatherers in Africa, differential reproduction in, ethnographic and historical perspective on, 1060–62
hurricane recovery, emotions and, 936–37
hurricane relief policies, support for, emotions and, 1077–78
Hussein, Saddam, 178n.3
Hutterites, 36–37
Huxley, Julian, 67–68
H-Y antigen, 50–51n.5
hyenas, juvenile, innovative and exploratory behavior, 363
Hygiene Hypothesis, 187
hyperacusis, 1252–53
hyperadaptiveness, and Lamarckianism, 37–39
hyperalgesia, 418
hypercapnia, and fear responding/fear learning, 503–4
hypervigilance, in post-traumatic stress disorder, 416, 1270
hypochondriasis, 1317, 1320–21
hypocrisy, 898–99
hypomania, 225–26

hypophobia, 1117
hyposmia, 665–66
  and emotional reactions, 672
  and olfactory experience of close relationships, 671
  and sexuality, 670–71
hypothalamic–pituitary–adrenal axis
  and attachment, 239
  in depression, 866–67
  fear and, 505
  frustrative nonreward and, 834–35
  romantic love and, 224
  in stress response, 865–67
hypothalamus, 468, 469
  and compassion, 574–75
  and emotional responses, 236–38, 236f
  and fear responding/fear learning, 504–5
  oxytocin synthesis in, 238–39

I

Ibrahim, A., 1189
ICPs. *See* International Core Patterns
idealism, Kantian, and evolutionary psychology, 888–91, 904n.2
identifiable victim effect, 472
identity disturbance, in borderline personality disorder, 1280, 1281
IH. *See* Insurance Hypothesis
illicit drug use, mortality caused by, 1219–20
illiteracy, 1092
illness. *See* sickness
illness anxiety disorder, 1086. *See also* hypochondriasis
illness behavior. *See* sickness behavior
ILM. *See* inhibitory learning model
imagery, and planning, 46–47
imagination, of future, affective component of, 617
immediate physiological needs, 103–4, 1227, 1228t
  and drug use/addiction, 1228t, 1229–30
immigrant paradox, 476
immigration, attitudes toward
  disease avoidance threat management and, 707–8
  emotions and, 1077–78
  pathogen disgust sensitivity and, 613
immobility
  attentive, 107
  tonic, 107, 1119

immorality, as disgusting, 959–60
immune function, 297
　behaviors supporting, 297–98
　biomarkers of, 192
　disgust response and, 183, 192
　factors affecting, 297–98
　frustrative nonreward and, 834–35
　positive affect and, 377
　reproductive hormones and, 188
　vertebrate, conservation of, 297
immune system, 648, 649
　acquired, 299
　activation, energy costs of, 301–2
　acute phase response, 299–300, 301–3, 308
　development, and disgust sensitivity, 186–87
　and disgust sensitivity, 186, 189–90
　innate, 299–300
　social conflict and, 1149
immunosuppression, and disgust sensitivity, 189–90, 194
improbable events, preparation for, cost–benefit analysis of, 892, 904n.4
impulse control, 383
impulse disorders, and borderline personality disorder, 1281
impulsivity, 470–71
　in borderline personality disorder, 1280, 1281, 1283, 1284
　and suicidality, 1149–50
inbreeding, selection pressures against, 28–29, 155–56
incentive relativity, 831–32
incest, laws regarding, disgust and, 1078–79
incest avoidance, 28–29, 30–31
inclusive fitness, 22, 50, 427, 691
　cooperation and, 421–22
　maximization, 38–39
inclusive fitness theory, 567–68, 569–70
income, and happiness, 475
income inequality, 475
incongruity, in humor, 547, 548, 549, 550, 553–54, 555, 556
incredulity, 465
indebtedness, gratitude and, 269
indices, signaling and, 851, 852
Indigenous populations
　disgust sensitivity research in, 186, 191, 193
　personality research in, 191
indignation, 948–49, 960–61

and enforcement of moral contracts, 954–57
evolution from competitive anger, 955–56
as moral emotion, 945–46, 949, 951f, 954–60
moral violations and, 957–59
as other-condemning emotion, 954–60
indirect reciprocity
　gratitude and, 276–77
　upstream, 276–77
individualistic culture, 986
　and display rules, 989
　and emotion experience, 986–87
　and ostracism, 1047–48
inequality
　left- versus right-wing views on, 614, 615
　political judgments about, emotions and, 610–11
inequity, 472
infancy
　emotional development in, 466
　olfaction in, 670–71
infant(s). See also hominin infant(s)
　development of vocal control and flexible vocalizing, 917–18
　ingratiating behaviors of, 911–12, 912f, 915
　pain behavior in, 428
　pain in, 502–3
　plumpness, evolutionary perspective on, 913–14
　reaction to separation from parent, 485, 493
　vocal control, 915–18
　vocalizations by, 915
infants' crying, 467
　behaviors elicited by, 1157, 1159
　contagion, 422
infection(s), 297. See also pathogen(s)
　acute, signs of, 300
　biomarkers of, and disgust, 192, 194–95
　calorie restriction in, 138–39
　disgust sensitivity and, 184–86, 190–91, 194–95
　immune response to (see immune function; lassitude)
　weight loss in, 138–39
inference, specialized, emotions and, 45
infidelity, 229
　adaptive problems related to, 394

aspects of rival in, information acquisition about, 397–98
cause of, subtle interrogation about, 397–98
certainty of, and jealousy deactivation, 402–3
circumstances of, information acquisition about, 397–98
in consensually non-monogamous relationships, 407
cues to, 393, 394, 401
direct interrogation of partner about, 396
emotional versus sexual, 257, 395–97, 398–99, 403
and expressed forgiveness, 257
friendship and, 406
"friends with benefits" and, 407–8
and guilt, 291–92
and homicide, 1075, 1076–77
and jealousy, 392
in long-term monogamous relationships, 407, 409
and shame, 291–92
short-term mating and, 408
in short-term uncommitted relationships, 407–8
termination vs. maintenance of relationship after, 402–4
type of, and forgiveness, 403–4
infidelity threat(s). See also relationship threat
　appraisal of, 395–99
　contextual factors affecting, 400
　defense against, 399–401
　direct interrogation of partner about, 396–97
　inferences under uncertainty and, 398–99
　information acquisition about, 396–99, 400
　low mate value and, 400–1
　mate value discrepancy and, 400–1
　resolution, and jealousy deactivation, 402–4
　and resource provisioning, 399
　sequential response to, 393–94
　surreptitious information acquisition about, 398
　types of, 394
inflammation, 300
　chronic, 141, 299–300
　and depression, 1149
information, neural representation of, 364
informational vigilance, 612

information-processing
  accommodative, affective influence on, 527–29
  affect and, 523–29
  assimilative, affective influence on, 527–29
  in operation of psychological mechanisms, 985
information processing, positive mood/emotion and, 374–77
information-processing
  sadness and, 523–25, 527–29
  styles, affective influence on, 527–29
information-seeking, 111
information threat theory, of shame, 146–49, 153
information warfare, and damage to hated other, 174–75
infrared thermography, 766, 796
ingratiation, affective influence on, 536–37, 537f
in-group advantage, 987–89
in-group/out-group psychology
  and dehumanization of outgroups, 637, 707–8
  disgust and, 637
  and emotional expression perception/production, 987–89
  and emotional vigilance, 852–53
  male, 1269
in-group versus out-group. *See also* gateway groups
  and activation of self-protection, 705
  and disease avoidance, 707–8
  and recognition of emotion expressions, 692, 705
inhibitory learning model, and anxiety disorders, 1124
injury. *See* sickness
injustice, appraisals of, 1045
innovation, and problem-solving, 615
insanity defense, 1074
insect(s)
  cognitive bias testing in, 773–74
  habituation in, 464
  response to threat, 464
  social, alloparenting in, 910
  social, chemical alarm signals, 767
insecurity, infidelity and, 405
insight, and guilt, 288–92
instinct(s), 101. *See also* behavior(s), innate
  emotions associated with, 101
  hierarchical structure of, 101
  primary, 101
instinct blindness, 164–65
instinct theory, 101, 103, 105, 124n.1
instrumental helping. *See* targeted helping
insula, 468–69
  and empathy, 469
insult(s), and anger, 137–38
Insurance Hypothesis, and eating disorders, 1176t, 1183
intelligence
  and analytical ability, 904–5n.5
  correlation in spouses, 552
  humor and, 552
Intelligence Trap, 894, 904–5n.5
intensity of emotion, variations of, 1100
intentionality, and guilt, 290, 293
intention movements, 67
  facial expressions as, 68–69, 69t, 74n.20
interest, evolutionary origins of, evidence for, 10t, 12
intergroup conflict, 698–703, 711. *See also* war/warfare
  appraisals and emotional regulation in, 708–10
  benefits of, 701–2
  current examples of, 699
  de-escalation of, 709
  disease avoidance threat-management system and, 707–8
  in early humans, 699–700
  emotion-focused interventions in, 708–11
  emotion regulation in, appraisal-based framework for, 708–10
  female psychology of, 701–2
  gateway groups and, 710–11
  historical perspective on, 699–700
  male psychology of, 702–3
  and mate competition, 1272–73
  and men, 1269
  men as instigators of, 702
  men as targets of, 702–3
  modern, 699, 700
  mortality from, 699
  motivation for, 700
  and reproductive fitness, 701, 702
  resource disputes and, 700–1
  revenge and, 700
  sex differences in, 701–3
  threat-management systems for, 703–8
  threats posed by, 698–99
intergroup relationships, development of, 242
intermittent explosive disorder, 1086
internal regulatory variable, 100
International Classification of Diseases and Health-Related Problems, 1300–1
  and major depression, 1138
International Core Patterns, 988
internet gaming disorder, 1317, 1323. *See also* problematic internet use
Interpersonal Circumplex, pride and, 208
interpersonal relationships, in borderline personality disorder, 1280, 1283, 1284
intersubjectivity, 918, 922, 1135
intrinsic welfare trade-off ratio, 167–68, 178n.1, 1072
  negative, 167–68, 172–73
invariances, in environment of evolutionary adaptedness, 31
invertebrates, fear responding in, 503–4
Irons, William, 1268
irony, 554
irritation, and punitive behavior, 1006
IRT. *See* infrared thermography
Islam, 442
iWTR. *See* intrinsic welfare trade-off ratio
Izard, Carroll, 73n.11, 1056

J

Jacobsen organ. *See* vomeronasal organ
James, William, 59–60, 72, 164–65
  on curiosity, 357, 361
  on social exclusion, 1041
jealousy, 110, 169, 1101–2, 1332. *See also* friendship jealousy; sexual jealousy
  across relationship types, 405–8
  activation of, 392, 393, 394
  adaptive problem related to, 392
  versus anger, 404–5
  animals and, 774–75, 776–78
  behavioral outputs related to, 392, 393–95
  in best friendship, 407
  between-individual differences in, 408–9
  co-activation with anger, 404–5

jealousy (cont.)
  deactivation when infidelity is certain, 402–3
  deactivation when threat is successfully thwarted, 402
  definition of, 816
  differential operation, mating strategy and, 407–8
  disorders of, 1086–87
  dogs and, 814–18
  versus envy, 776, 816
  and female intrasexual competition, 976–77
  "friends with benefits" and, 407–8
  functions of, 229, 742–43, 776, 976–77, 1056–57
  Goldilocks ("just right") principle and, 394–95
  and hatred, 170–71
  and information acquisition, 396–98, 401, 409
  information-processing and, 393–94, 401
  input–output mappings of, 400, 401
  knowledge about, 391–92
  in long-term monogamous relationships, 407, 409
  in mating relationships, 392, 405–6, 407
  neurobiology of, in animals, 777
  quantitative variation in, 408–9
  romantic love and, 227, 229
  sequential behavioral response in, 393–94
  sex differences in, 257, 393, 395–97, 402, 409, 977
  sibling, 392, 405–6, 409
  sociosexual orientation and, 408, 409
  task analytic approach to, 391–92, 393, 394–401
  and termination vs. maintenance of relationship after infidelity, 402–4, 405, 409
  in uncommitted relationships, 407–8
  within-individual shifts in, 408–9
jealousy research, 393
  adaptationist, 393
  future directions for, 394, 408, 409
Jesus of Nazareth, 442
Jewitt, John, 1058–59
Johnson-Laird, P. N., 62–63
jokes
  cognitive consistency (cognitive congruity) and, 553

cultural differences in, 554
joke telling, 546
  benefits to humorist, 547–48
  benefits to recipient, 546–47
  sex differences in, 555
  and status, 547
Jones, Nick Blurton, 1058
joy, xiii, 437–38
  as basic emotion, 4, 990
  and crying, 467–68
  in dogs, 812–13
  intensity of, variations of, 1100
Judaic philosophy, contentment in, 441–42
judgment(s). *See also* political judgment
  affect infusion in, 525–26
  affective influence on, 529–33
  positive emotions and, 374–75, 376–77
judgment bias test, 795–96
  in animals, 773–74
Ju/'hoansi, differential reproduction in, ethnographic and historical perspective on, 1057, 1058
jury instruction, re emotions, 1071
justice. *See also* distributive justice; organizational justice; restorative justice; retributive justice; social justice
  disorder versus nondisorder status and, 1255
  emotion-valuation constellation and, 90
  morality and, 422
  as motive, 104
  perceptions of, emotions and, 899–901
juvenile period
  biparental investment and, 630
  energy economy of, 623
  extended, functions of, 363
  in great apes, 793

K

Kahan, Daniel, 886–87, 899–900, 904n.1
Kaiser Chefs, 968, 969
kama muta, xiii, 345–51
  biological evolution of, 346–47
  cultural evolution of, 346–47
  as cuteness emotion, empirical evidence for, 350–51
  evocation of, 345–46, 347
  evolutionary perspective on, 346–47
  experience of, 347

motivational aspects of, 348–50
  relation to other emotions, 348
  theory of, 346–47
Kamiloğlu, Roza G., 983–92
Kanner, Leo, 1251
Kant, Immanuel, 472, 1068–69
  Critique of Pure Reason, 888, 889
  idealism, and evolutionary psychology, 888–91, 904n.2
  transcendental psychology of, 889–90, 904n.3
Kass, Leon, 1079–80
Kaufman, Scott Barry, 933
kawaii, 341–42, 344–45, 346, 349–50
Keltner, Dacher, 57, 61, 1056, 1332, 1335
Kendell, Robert, 1089, 1091–92
Kennair, Leif Edward Ottesen, 246–59, 1109–27
Kenrick, D. T., 103–4, 105–6, 107, 121, 1219, 1227, 1229
Kernberg, Otto, 1198
Ketelaar, Timothy, 885–904
Khoisan, breeding sex ratio in, 1058
kibbutzim, and mate choice, 28–29, 30–31
killer whales, grief in, 488
killing. *See also* homicide
  hatred-based, 173, 174
Kimchi-Palmer Task, 375, 376
kin altruism, 286–87
kin care, 103–4
  nurturant love and, 373, 373t
Kindchenschema, 339–40, 346, 919
kindness
  evolutionary perspective on, 931
  in positive evolutionary psychology, 931
Kinner, S., 1097
kin recognition, 1057
  olfaction and, 670–71, 673f
kin selection, 79–80, 155–56, 1181
kinship, human, 1177
kinship index, 100
kinship networks, evolutionary perspective on, 242
Kirsch, Amanda P., 369–84
Kisley, Michael A., 118–19, 748–58
Klineberg, O., 64
Kohut, Heinz, 1198
Kotoye, Christian, 698–711
Kozak, M. J., 1123
Krupp, D. B., 1097
k-selection, 283
Kübler-Ross, E., stage theory of grief, 484
Kujala, Miiamaaria V., 809–21

kuru, 73–74n.15

L
labor pain, 420, 650
lactase, 30
Laing, R. D., 1088
lajya, 984–85
Lamarckism/Lamarckianism, 56, 58
  hyperadaptiveness and, 37–39
Landers, Mitchell, 145–57, 163–78
Langfeld, Herbert, 59
language
  acquisition, 904n.3
  and basic emotions, 13, 15–16
  of emotions, 13, 15–16
  evolution of, 918, 920
  learning, by youngsters, 920
language processing, affective influence on, 534–35, 536*f*
langur monkeys, and newborns' vocalizations, 915
Laozi, 441
Larsen, Simen Mjøen, 1109–27
lassitude, xiii, 361, 651–53, 657, 1152
  activation, situation-defining cues and, 298–300, 301*f*, 309–10
  and care-seeking, 301, 301*f*, 307–8
  characteristics of, 299*b*
  chronic, 299–300
  cognitive mechanisms and, 310
  conservation across species, 309
  and consumption, 138–39, 301, 301*f*
  definition of, 299*b*
  and disgust sensitivity, 141
  as emotion versus mood, 116
  evolutionary perspective on, 310
  functional outputs, context sensitivity of, 310
  in humans, research needs, 310
  and mating, 301, 301*f*, 305–6
  motivational variables regulated by, 301–10, 301*f*
  and movement/rest, 301, 301*f*, 302
  and parental effort, 301, 301*f*, 306–7
  and sexual motivation, sex differences in, 306
  and signaling vulnerability, 301, 301*f*, 308–9
  as superordinate program, 298, 299*b*, 309, 310
  and threat avoidance, 301, 301*f*, 307
  and warmth-seeking, 301, 301*f*, 302–3
laughter, 543–44, 545. *See also* humor

in animals, 770–71
benefits of, 546
brain activity in, 557
as contagious, 545, 557, 558, 632, 854
elicitors of, 545
excessive, pathology causing, 557–58
feigned, 545
functions of, 545, 556, 616–17
genuine (Duchenne), 545
hysterical, epidemic, 558
phylogenetic origins of, 544
and play, 546
sham, 557
universality of, 544
law. *See also* criminal justice system; law and emotion
  ancient, emotion-valuation constellation and, 90
  codification, emotions and, 1077–80
  criminal, 89, 90
  dichotomization of reason and emotion in, 1068–69
  disgust and, 1078–80
  recalibrational theory of anger and, 1073–74
law and emotion, 1067–68
  behavioral aspects of, 1069–70
  and evaluation of emotions, 1074–77
  evolutionary perspective on, 1070–80
  historical perspective on, 1068–69
  and insanity defense, 1074
  and intent, 1076–77
  and motive, 1074–76
  and provocation doctrine, 1074–77
  and volition, 1076–77
law of economy, 465
leadership, 1022–25. *See also* charismatic leadership; transformational leadership
  authentic, 1023
  autocratic, 1031
  behavioral perspective on, 1022–23
  coevolution with emotions, 1032
  contextual perspective on, 1022–23, 1029–30
  culture and, 1030
  definition of, 1024–25
  directive, agricultural origins of, 1030
  dominance and, 1025

dominance-based strategies and, 1026
  as emotional process, 1021–22, 1026–27
  emotions and, 1026–27
  and emotion valence in context, 1030–31
  ethical, 1023
  evolutionary perspective on, 1021–22, 1023–24, 1026
  evolution of, emotions and, 1032
  and fear, 1031
  and group coordination/cooperation, 1029
  group size and, 1029
  morally legitimate, 948
  multidisciplinary study of, 1021
  and negative emotions, 1030–31
  organizational perspective on, 1021–23, 1026–27
  and positive emotions, 1030–31
  prestige and, 1025
  prestige-based strategies and, 1026
  and shared goals with followers, 1024
  as social construction, 1023
  and social influence, 1024–25
  and status hierarchies, 1024–25
  threatening context and, 1031
  visionary, 1023
leadership style
  contextual pressures and, 1031
  historical factors and, 1030
  transactional, 1023
learning, 111. *See also* inhibitory learning model
  affect and, 465
  and anxiety disorders, 1122–23
  concern for, modern humans', 921–22
  curiosity and, 324
  emotions and, 45
  humor and, 551
  in infancy, 362–63
  maximization, boredom and, 324
  observational, 469
LeBrun, Charles, 58, 59
LeDoux, J. E., 1105, 1327–28
Lee, Richard, 1058
left ventricular ejection time, 446
  contentment and, 447, 450*t*
left-wing ideology
  threat perception and, 613–15
  worries associated with, 613–15
legal evidence, interpretation, motivated reasoning and, 899–900, 905n.7

legal policy(ies), support for, emotions and, 1077–78
legislation, support for, emotions and, 1077–80
leisure, and happiness, 475
Leontopithecus rosalia. *See* golden lion tamarins
lethargy
  chronic pain and, 418
  in illness, 302
  pathogen-induced, 310
Levy, Robert, 15
Lewis, David M. G., 391–409
Leys, Ruth, 66, 70, 74n.16
Li, N. P., 1182, 1187, 1223–24
Lichtenberg, J. D., 102
Lieberman, Debra, 263–78, 1076–77, 1079–80
life-alone paradigm, for ostracism, 1046
life history, human, 623
life-history strategy(ies), 1288–89
  definition of, 1288
life-history theory, 305, 1185–87, 1224–25, 1288–89
  and borderline personality disorder, 1288–89
  and eating disorders, 1185–87
  and psychopathy, 1298, 1305, 1309–10
  and substance use, 1222, 1224–26
life satisfaction, 471
  gratitude and, 264–65, 269
  parenthood and, 473
lifestyle. *See also* market integration
  measurement of, 192
liking, versus wanting, 468
Lilienfeld, Scott, 1242
Lima, S. L., 1263–64
limbic system, 238–39, 464–65, 468–69, 811
  and danger memories, 1266
  and emotion processing, 237
  and laughter, 557
  and mirth, 556–57
  and olfaction, 664
Lin, Yijun, 317–32
Lincoln, Abraham, 545–46
Lindner, Miriam, 1109–27
linguistics. *See* language
lipopolysaccharide, 300
  use in humans, 310
lizards
  behavioral fever in, 303
  as fear stimuli, 1121
Loewenstein, G., 358, 362–63
Lonati, Sirio, 1021–33

longevity
  happiness and, 471
  human, evolution of, 654
long-tailed macaques, conflict and reconciliation in, 721, 722
Lopez, Anthony C., 163–78
Lorenz, Konrad, 61, 68, 340–41, 346, 349, 488
Lorenzini ampullae, 890–91
Loria, Riley N., 263–78
losing strategy hypothesis, 1181, 1183
loss
  biochemical correlates of, 493–94
  children's perception of, 490–92
  concept of, 490
  COVID-19 pandemic and, 497
  cultural context and, 522
  genetic relatedness and, 492–93
  Piaget's theory of, 489–92
  spousal, 493
loss aversion, sadness and, 624t, 634
loss of interest (in virtually all activities), as signal of need, 1154–55
lottery winners, and happiness, 475
love, 110, 935. *See also* nurturant love; romantic love
  in animals, 488–89
  cliff-edge principle and, 1100
  companionate, 230
  versus compassion, 568
  disorders of, 1086–87
  in dogs, 812–13
  evolutionary origins of, evidence for, 101t, 12
  functional analysis of, 382
  as motive, 104, 105–6
  as opposite of hatred, 178n.2
  as scripted sequence, 382
  as sentiment, 382
LPS. *See* lipopolysaccharide
ludus, 220–21
Lukaszewski, Aaron W., 79–90
Lunge, Jenna, 861–74
lust, 221
  as basic emotion, 103
  as motive, 104, 105–6
LVET. *See* left ventricular ejection time
lying, psychopathy and, 1298–99
Lykken, D. T., 1310n.1
Lyshol, Johanna Katarina Blomster, 339–51

M

Maasai herders, cooperation among, 623–30

MAC. *See* Meaning and Attention Components model
macaques. *See also* long-tailed macaques; rhesus monkey; Tonkean macaque
  facial expressions in, 770–71
Machalek, Richard, 1245
Machiavelli, 1157
  The Prince, 1134
Machiavellianism, emotion-personality constellation and, 87
MacLean, Paul D., 237
magpie jays, social learning in, 919–20
Mahabarata, 439–40
major depression/major depressive disorder, 1086, 1253. *See also* depression
  adaptive perspective and, 1126, 1161–62
  in adolescents, 1139
  adversity and, 1135–36, 1136f, 1137t, 1145–46, 1161–62
  and anger, 1149–50
  and brain dysfunction, weak evidence related to, 1138–39, 1160
  cause of, 1135–36, 1136f, 1137t, 1145, 1161–62
  chemical imbalance theory of, 1141, 1162n.1
  chronic, 1142
  as continuum of symptoms, 1141–42, 1141f
  definition of, 1135
  diagnostic criteria for, 865
  DSM criteria for, 1135, 1138–39, 1138t, 1141–42, 1143, 1145, 1150
  duration of, 1142, 1142f
  epidemiology of, 865, 1139–41, 1140f
  false-positives, 1141, 1142–43
  hormones and, 865–67
  menopausal transition and, 870
  onset, stressful life events and, 1135–36, 1136f, 1137t
  and post-traumatic stress disorder, 1271–72
  in pregnancy, 869
  prevalence of, 1139–41, 1140f
  psychological pain hypothesis and, 1146–47, 1153, 1161–62
  recurrence of, 865
  remission of, 1142, 1159–60
  risk factors for, 1137t, 1148
  and risk for postpartum depression, 869

sex differences in, 867
social conflict and, 1137t, 1148–50
major depression and generalized anxiety syndrome, mixed, 1151
maladaptive behavior
  information value of, 36–37
  modern warfare as, 51n.8
malaise, 651–53
  chronic pain and, 418
  with injury/illness, 649
male intrasexual competition, 1187–89
  in Africa, 1057–58
  in Americas, 1059–60
  in Asia, 1060–62
  in modernity, 1063
  in Pacific region, 1058–59
males. *See also* men
  body dissatisfaction in, 1187–88
  drive for muscularity in, 1187–89
  eating disorders in, 1187–89
male-warrior psychology, 702
malingering, 429, 650–51
malnutrition. *See also* nutritional stress
  and disgust sensitivity, 194
mammals. *See also* primate homologues of basic emotions
  alloparenting in, 910
  chemical signals in, 767
  curiosity in, 359–60
  defense strategies used by, 1119
  emotional responses in, 371
  facial expressions in, 770–71
  frustrative nonreward in, 834
  laughter expression in, 544
  mating systems, 1175–79
  motives in, 103
  neurological underpinnings of emotions in, 766
  nociception in, 415
  playful motivation in, 111–12
  SEEKING system in, 364
mania, 1086
  and laughter, 557
mania (love), 220–21
manic depression, 476
marginal value theorem, 35
marital couples, with depressed partner, behaviors elicited in, 1158
marital discord, and depression, 1148
marital satisfaction, parenthood and, 473
market integration
  assessment of, 192
  and disgust sensitivity, 186, 191–92

and gut microbiota diversity, 191
markets, 89
Marler, Peter, 68
Marlowe, Frank, 1058
marmoset(s), 241–42
  alloparental and parental provisioning in, 910
  babbling-like behavior in, 917
  infant, development of vocal control and flexible vocalizing, 916–17
  infants' vocalizations, 915
  natural pedagogy in, 920
marriage, 1175–77
  and happiness, 473
  humor in, 552–53
Marsh, Abigail A., 500–11
marsupials, frustrative nonreward in, 834
Martin, Heidi, 483–97
Maslow, A. H., 103–4, 471–72, 933
massacres, 1272
mass psychogenic illness, 854
mass shootings, perceived unjust exclusion and, 1045
mate acquisition, 103–4, 105–6, 1227, 1228t
  and drug use/addiction, 1228t, 1231
  and sexual desire, 373t
mate attraction, 105–6
mate choice, cross-cultural variation in, 985
mate competition
  and hatred, 170–71
  intergroup conflict and, 1272–73
  male, 1272–73
  violent male, 1271
mate guarding, 973–74, 976
mate retention, 103–4, 105–6, 1227, 1228t
  and attachment love, 373t
  and drug use/addiction, 1228t, 1231
Mate Retention Inventory, 393–94, 399, 401
mate-retention tactics, 399–401
  coalitional, 398
  differential deployment of, 400–1, 409
  efficacy of, context and, 400
  surreptitious information acquisition and, 398
  in uncommitted relationships, 408
Material Style of Life survey, 192, 193–94

maternal behavior, neuroendocrinology of, 239
mate selection
  olfaction and, 668–69, 673f
  romantic love and, 222
mate value
  discrepancy, and infidelity threat, 400–1
  female human, 1178, 1184
  low, and infidelity threat, 400–1
  male human, 1177
  self-perceived, and aggression, 976
  self-perceived, and self-esteem, 975
  and termination versus restoration of relationship after infidelity, 403–4, 405
mating. *See also* pair-bonding (motivational system); short-term mating
  food intake and, as modern adaptive metaproblem, 1189
  lassitude and, 301f, 301, 305–6
  as motivation, 104, 105–6
  psychopathy and, 1304–5, 1306
mating strategy, 249. *See also* short-term mating
  and disgust sensitivity, 187–88
  long-term, 249
mating system
  and drug use/addiction, 1228t, 1231
  human, 1175–79
mating (motivational) system, 102, 105f, 109
MBCT. *See* mindfulness-based cognitive therapy
McCarter, R., 60–61, 73n.10
McDonald, Melissa M., 698–711
McDougall, W., 101, 103
McQuade, Brianna, 929–41
MD. *See* major depression
MD-GAS. *See* major depression and generalized anxiety syndrome, mixed
MDMA (ecstasy), 1230–31
Mead, Margaret, 73n.14
Mealey, Linda, 1181, 1183, 1244–45
meaning, and boredom, 320–21, 329
Meaning and Attention Components model, 320, 322
meaning deficits, and boredom, 321
meanness
  in antisocial personality disorder, 1303
  in psychopathy, 1302–3

mechanism(s). *See also* cheater-
detection mechanisms;
coordination mechanisms/
coordination programs,
emotions as; emotion
mechanisms; evolved
psychological mechanism(s)
  versus behavior, 36, 690–91
  correlated, 120–21
  covariation among, 120–21
  definition of, 36
medial forebrain bundle, 468
medial preoptic area, in rodents,
  1329–30, 1336
mediation, 1073–74
medical disorder(s), 1094, 1238–39
  versus abnormality, 1090
  culture and, 1094
  evolutionary biological
    dysfunction and, 1094
  trouble-shooting approach
    to, 1095
  value-based accounts of, 1090
medicine
  Darwinian view of, 1095
  as trouble-shooting, 1095
Meehan, Courtney, 914–15
melancholia, 522, 1150. *See also*
  sadness
Melville, Herman, 1067
memory
  affect and, 469
  affect infusion in, 525–26
  affective component of, 617
  affective influence on, 527–
    29, 528f
  associative network of, affect
    and, 524
  for danger, in post-traumatic
    stress disorder, 1266
  emotions and, 44
  episodic, 904n.3
  romantic love and, 224
  welfare trade-off ratio and, 172
memory(ies), new, in treatment of
  anxiety disorders, 1124
men. *See also* males; out-group men
  affinity for children, women's
    assessment of, 970
  attractiveness of, women's
    judgment of, 970
  cognitive effects of romantic love
    in, 226–27
  and combat-related post-
    traumatic stress disorder, 1264
  depression in, 867, 874
  and drug use, 1220

effective breeding population of,
  1058, 1063
emotion regulation in, 755–56
empathy levels in, 1267–68
facial attractiveness, women's
  assessment of, 970
formidability and welfare trade-
  off ratio for, 139
friendships among, 474
genetic quality of, proxies for, 970
happiness in, 476
hormone withdrawal in, 874
humor in, 555
and intergroup conflict, 701–
  3, 1269
and jealousy-induced
  homicide, 1075
kinship ties of, 1269
and mental health stigma, 1274
narcissistic, and sexual
  coercion, 1203
and negotiation about
  entitlement, 610
obsessive-compulsive disorder
  in, 873
post-traumatic stress disorder
  in, 872–73
smiling by, evolutionary
  perspective on, 689–90
status among, fitness relevance
  of, 589
upper body strength, and
  formidability, 139–40
as warriors, 702
work and happiness relationship
  for, 474–75
menarche
  age at, 1289
  and obsessive-compulsive
    disorder, 873
menopausal transition, hormones
  and, 870
menopause, 1178, 1184
  and reproduction expediting, 258
menstrual cycle, 861–62
  and anxiety, 871
  and disgust sensitivity, 864–65
  and emotion regulation, 756
  hormonal fluctuations in, 861–62
  and obsessive-compulsive
    disorder, 873
  and onset of PMS/PMDD, 868
  and panic symptomatology, 873
  and PTSD symptoms, 872–73
mental disorder(s). *See also*
  disorder(s); emotional
  disorder(s); psychopathology

adaptive basis of, 1098
concept of, 1088, 1238–39
definition of, 1239–40, 1300
diagnostic criteria for, criticisms
  of, 1093
dimensional accounts of, 1089, 1093
drug use and, 1223
DSM categories of, 1086
DSM definition of, 1300
versus emotional problems, 1085–89
evolutionary perspective on, 1126
fact-based (pure-fact) accounts of,
  1089, 1091–92, 1094
factor analytic approach to, 1093
false positives problem, 1087–89
implausible high prevalence of, in
  ECA program, 1139
life-history perspective on,
  1288–89
versus secondary linked
  effects, 1086
and substance use disorders,
  comorbidity, 1220, 1225–26
value-based (pure-value) accounts
  of, 1089–91, 1094
mental health, happiness and, 471
mental illness, affect disorders
  in, 476–77
mentalizing, 566
mental map(s). *See also* worldview(s)
  construction of, 891
  emotion-based, 904
  of fitness affordance landscape,
    903–4, 905n.9
  shareable, 905n.8
mental time travel. *See also*
  imagination; memory
  affective component of, 617
Menzies, R. G., 1122
Mercadante, Eric, 203–14
Mercier, Hugo, 847–56, 1331
Merleau-Ponty, Maurice, 1102–
  3, 1104
metacognitive therapy, 254–55, 1125
mice
  aggression in, 779
  alarm calls of, 507–8
  ear movement, emotions and, 771
  facial expressions in, 464–65
  frustrative nonreward in, 834
  illness and vulnerability display
    in, 308–9
  immune benefits of calorie
    restriction in, 139
  infrared thermal imaging of, 766
  juvenile, innovative and
    exploratory behavior, 363

pain behaviors in, 423
pain display in, 419, 423, 425
pain empathy in, 423
pain face in, 423, 425
and parental care during illness, 307
response to hypercapnia, 503
midbrain, 468, 469
    and fear responding/fear learning, 506
Miller, Geoffrey, 552, 905n.9
Miller v. California, 1078
mimicry, 1152. *See also* rapid facial mimicry
    emotional contagion and, 740
mind-blindness, 1253
mindfulness, 290
    benefits of, 454–55
mindfulness-based cognitive therapy, 1125
mindreading, and post-traumatic stress disorder, 1270
Mineka, S., 1112, 1120
mirror neurons, 289, 557, 798, 799–800
mirth, 544
    brain activity in, 556–57
    evolved basis of, 544–45
mismatch hypothesis, 182, 1096–99. *See also* environmental mismatch; evolutionary mismatch
    and cardiometabolic disease, 309
    and eating disorders, 1175, 1176t, 1179–80, 1189, 1190
    and gambling, 1322–23
    and human social ecology, 934
    and lassitude, 309
    and post-traumatic stress disorder, 1264, 1269, 1274
    and substance use, 1223–24, 1224f
mistrust, in post-traumatic stress disorder, 1268–69
Mitchell, Virginia E., 861–74
mockery, 549
Moctezuma I, 1059–60
Moctezuma II, 1059–60
Moffit, Terrie, 1243–44
monkeys
    alarm calls of, 507–8
    communication by, 915–16
    curiosity in, 359–60
    frustrative nonreward in, 834
    information value for, 364
    juvenile, innovative and exploratory behavior, 363
    pain behaviors in, 420
montane vole, 241–42
mood(s). *See also* negative affect; positive affect
    alterations, in post-traumatic stress disorder, 1267–68
    and bullshit receptivity, 532–33, 534f
    cognitive and behavioral effects of, 523–24
    cognitive effects of, 374–77
    and compulsive buying, 1322
    and conversational competence, 534, 535f
    and deception detection, 531, 531f, 532f
    definition of, 374
    versus emotions, 115–16, 523–24
    functions of, 46, 539
    and goal-directed behavior, 115
    in grandiose narcissists, 1205–6
    and gullibility, 532
    and ingratiation, 536–37, 537f
    and language processing, 534–35, 536f
    low, evolved functions of, 1145
    maintenance, 533
    motivational systems and, 113f, 115–16, 1336
    and persuasion, 535–36, 536f
    regulation of, 120
    repair, 533
    and requesting, 526–27, 526f
    reward/punishment detection/response and, 115
    and self-assessment, 525–26
    and self-disclosure, 526, 528f
    and selfishness vs. fairness, 537–38, 538f
    and social behaviors, 526–27
    as superordinate programs, 113f, 1097
    as third-order coordination programs, 115–16, 120
    and truth judgments, 532, 533f
    in vulnerable narcissists, 1207–8
mood contagion, 741–42
Moons, Wesley G., 1040–50
moral anger. *See* indignation
moral behavior, ultimate function of, 946–47
moral cognition
    disgust and, 957
    emotional processes in, 944–45, 948–49
    structure of, 948f, 949
moral conscience, emotions and, 1076
moral contracts, 953
    enforcement of, indignation and, 954–57
    evolution of, 946–48
moral disgust, 108, 182–83, 613, 618n.1, 864, 959–60, 1079–80
moral duty(ies), 946, 949, 953, 954, 955–56, 960–61
moral emotion(s), 944–46, 951f, 960–61, 1002b
    computational framework of, 946
    definition of, 946
    evolutionary psychology of, 939
    functional specification, 945
    functions of, 948–49, 948f
    non-moral functions of, 945
    versus social emotions, 945, 949
    systematizing of, 945
moral indignation. *See* indignation
morality, 89, 428, 921–23, 944–45, 1079–80
    definition of, 422
    emotions in, 946–49
    evolutionary perspective on, 946–47
    and fitness interdependence, 953–54
    personal qualities and, 422
    species-specific features of, 422
moral judgment, 948–49, 948f
    disgust and, 957–59
    emotions and, 900
    third-party, 956
moral language, 946
moral obligations, 945, 946, 947, 948, 953, 954
    computation of, 948
    fairness and, 948
    functional content of, 947
    and prosocial motivation, differentiation of, 952–54
moral outrage, 955, 1002b, 1003, 1006
    definition of, 1002b
    normative value of, 1002b
    as suite of emotions, 1002b
    third-party, 956–57
    and third-party punishment, 1006
    undeserved suffering and, 952
moral panic, 152
moral reasoning, emotions and, 899–901
moral representations, 951f, 960–61
    cognitive content of, 945
    cognitive specificity of, 946–49
    as prescriptive mental states, 946
    of right and wrong, 946–49
    ultimate function of, 945
    and "what we owe each other," 946, 947

moral rights, 949, 952, 953, 954, 955–56, 960–61
moral sense, 948f, 949, 951f
   disgust as input to, 957–59
mother–child relationship, olfaction and, 670–71, 673f
moths, fear in, 500
motivated reasoning, 886–88. *See also* cognitive bias
   in defense of worldview, 898–99, 905n.6
   in evaluation of scientific evidence, 886–87, 887f
   identity-protective function of, 893
   and interpretation of legal evidence, 899–900, 905n.7
   political beliefs and, 887
   as tacit process, 905n.6
   as tool for persuasion, 893–94
motivation(s), 361
   as bridge between personality and emotion, 122–23
   and emotions, 100, 323, 1137n.1, 1228t, 1229, 1336
   information-gathering, emotions and, 44
   negative affect and, 533–34
   and person perception, 123
   prioritizing, emotions and, 44
   for pursuing status, 590–91, 601n.2
   taxonomy of, 104
motivational-emotional systems, and substance use, 1220–33, 1228t
motivational mismatch, 1232
motivational system(s), 100, 101–4. *See also* behavioral system(s)
   adaptive problems related to, 104–12, 105f
   components of, 103–4
   computational logic of, 118
   conceptual developments about, 102–3
   and coordination of emotion mechanisms, 112–18, 113f
   cross-modulation of, 114–15
   dynamics of, 106–7
   emotions and, 102–3, 104, 118, 1336
   feedback and feedforward processes in, 116–17, 1336
   functions of, 100–1
   goals of, 102–3
   human, map of, 104–12, 105f
   interplay of, 118
   lassitude and, 301–9, 301f

   moods and, 113f, 115–16, 1336
   neural substrate of, 1336
   numerosity of, 105–7
   operational rules and, 102–3
   recent research on, 103–4
   reciprocal potentiation of, 102–3
   and second-order coordination problem, 114, 309
   and sequence integration problem, 116
   set of emotions tied to, 102–3
   taxonomy of, 104–12, 105f
   theory of, origins, 101
   and third-order coordination problem, 114–15, 309
motivation regulation
   emotion regulation and, 118–19
   strategies, 119–20
motive(s). *See also* fundamental motive(s)
   approach, 121, 124n.6
   avoidance, 121, 124n.6
   pan-mammalian, 103
   taxonomy of, 104
motor cortex, and emotional responses, 236–37, 236f
motor neurons, and emotional responses, 236–37, 236f
movement/rest, lassitude and, 301, 301f, 302
Mowrer, O. H., 1122
Moynihan, Daniel Patrick, 896
MPOA. *See* medial preoptic area
M-SOL. *See* Material Style of Life survey
Müller, Johannes, 72n.3
multilevel selection, 421–22
multiple sclerosis, and laughter, 557
muscularity
   drive for, in males, 1187–89
   and sexual dimorphism, 1188
mutualism, 421

N

NAcc. *See* nucleus accumbens
Nagel, Thomas, 890
nail-biting disorder. *See* onychophagia
NARC. *See* narcissistic admiration and rivalry concept
narcissism, 264–65
   in adolescence, 1203
   dynamic perspective on, 1199
   emotionality in, evolutionary relevance of, 1208–9
   and emotions, 1198, 1204–9

   evolutionary perspective on, 1197, 1208–9
   evolution of, 1200–4
   genetics and, 1200–4
   grandiose, 1198–200, 1204–10
   heritability of, 1200
   historical perspective on, 1198–200
   and leadership emergence, 1204
   and natural selection, 1203–4
   oscillation hypothesis of, 1199–200
   personality traits and, 1197, 1199
   and physical attractiveness, 1201–2
   and physiological reactivity, 1206, 1208–9
   pride and, 206–8, 207t
   self-regulatory models of, 1205
   and sexual coercion/rape, 1202–3
   sexual selection and, 1201–3
   and short-term mating, 1201–3, 1208
   as stable trait, 1199
   term, origin of, 1198
   and threatened egotism model, 1206
   trait-theory perspective on, 1197
   trifurcated model of, 1199, 1202
   vulnerable, 1198–200, 1204–10
Narcissism, emotion-personality constellation and, 87
narcissistic admiration and rivalry concept, 1202–4
narcissistic personality disorder, 1197, 1198–200, 1209–10
   DSM criteria for, 1198, 1199–200
   and emotional dysregulation, 1086
natural function, 1094–95
natural selection, 26, 1094. *See also* differential reproduction
   and design, 33
   and disease, 1263
   and diversity, 66, 74n.17
   and genetics of disorders, 1098–99
   narcissism and, 1203–4
nature, human attraction to, evolutionary perspective on, 940
nausea, infection and, 141
Navon Letter Task, 375
Nayasastra, 449
Nebuchadnessar, 1061–62
needs. *See also* immediate physiological needs
   credible signaling of, under conflict, 1151–53
   hierarchy of, 933

as private versus public information, 1152–53
pyramid of, 103–4
revised pyramid of, 1219, 1227, 1229
Neel, R., 121
negative affect, 521, 1145. *See also* mood(s); sadness
 adaptive function of, 520, 527, 539
 and attention, 527–29
 benefits of, 527, 538–39
 cognitive effects, 374
 co-rumination and, 738–39
 deleterious effects of, 539
 differences in levels of, with similar adversities, 1143–44
 evolutionary perspective on, 520
 and eyewitness memory, 527–29, 529f
 and ingratiation, 536–37, 537f
 judgmental benefits of, 529–33
 and memory performance, 527–29, 528f
 and mood repair, 533
 motivational benefits of, 533–34
 and persuasion, 535–36, 536f
 and reduced self-handicapping, 534
 reduction, with jealousy deactivation, 402
 and selfishness vs. fairness, 537–38, 538f
 in victims of adversity, fitness benefit of, 1145–46
negative affect infusion, benefits of, 525–27
negative emotion(s). *See also* anger; boredom; disgust; fear; sadness; worry
 activation by successive negative contrast, 834–36
 in animal conflict resolution, 721–22
 behaviors associated with, in animals, 768–69
 and body odor, 668
 comparative psychology of, 764–65
 of dogs, 811–12
 evolutionary perspective on, 371–72, 467, 933, 935–36
 frustrative nonreward and, 834–39
 functions of, 319, 521–22
 in leader–follower interactions, 1030–31
 neuroscience of, 1008

in punitive behavior, 1002–09, 1012, 1014–16, 1014f
 tendency to feel, and political attitudes, 612–13
Negative Valence System, 830–31
negativity bias, 470, 525–26
negotiation. *See also* cooperation
 anger and, 639
 guilt and, 638
neocortex, 766, 811
 and danger memories, 1266
 and emotions, 469
 and fear responding, 507
nervous system. *See also* autonomic nervous system; parasympathetic nervous system; sympathetic nervous system
 action of, Darwin's account of, 72n.3
 development of, 494
Nesse, Randolph, 46, 115, 416, 484–85, 487, 488, 492–93, 494, 921, 1099, 1100–1, 1126, 1222–23, 1263
Nettle, D., 1183
neurobiology/neurocircuitry, of basic emotions, 5–6, 8t, 9–11, 10t, 16
neurochemistry
 of avoidance, 468
 of happiness, 468–69
 of pleasure, 468
 of romantic love, 228
 of wanting, 468
Neurocultural Theory, 61, 62, 65–66, 73n.13
 challenges to, 62–63
neurodiversity
 difference versus disorder and, 1246
 normal versus dysfunctional sources of, 1239
neurodiversity movement, 1239
 and depathologization of variation, 1239, 1240
neuroendocrinology
 of attachment, 235–42, 236f
 of bonding, 235–38, 236f, 239
 of caring, 287
 of emotions, 235–38, 236f
 of fear, 237–38, 238f, 239–40, 240f, 504–5
 of grief, 487–88
 of maternal behavior, 239
 of pair-bonding, 239
 of sociality, 235–38, 236f, 242

neuropathology, and post-traumatic stress disorder, 1263
neuroscience. *See also* affective neuroscience
 in animals, 766–67
 of compassion, 575–77
 constructivist interpretation of, 1329
 of emotional responses, 236–38, 236f
 of emotions, 235–38, 236f
 of emotions in dogs, 811
 of empathy, 289
 of expression of emotions, 236–38, 236f
 of facial expression, 237
 of fear, 503–10, 509f
 of fear learning, 510
 of humor, 556–57
 of negative emotion activation by frustrative nonreward, 836–39
 of punitive behavior, 1008–09, 1014–16, 1014f
 of romantic love, 222–23
neuroticism
 and depression, 1144, 1145f
 humor styles and, 548
 and life-history strategies, 1288–89
 narcissistic, 1199–200
 and vulnerable narcissism, 1207–8
neurotoxin regulation hypothesis, 1229–30
 of substance use, 1226
neutralization theory of hatred, 163–64, 167–77
 definition of, 167
New BET, 1332–33
newborns
 birthweight, evolutionary perspective on, 913–14
 frustrative nonreward in, 834
 viability cues related to, 913–15
Nezahualcoyotl, 1059–60
Nezahualpilli, 1059–60
NHAs (nonhuman animals). *See* animal(s)
nicotine
 anti-parasitic effects, 140
 protective effect against helminth infection, 1226, 1229–30
night eating syndrome, 1172
nightmares, in post-traumatic stress disorder, 1266
nociception, 415–16
 in animals, 418–19, 429
 physiology of, 418–19
nonhuman animals. *See* animal(s)

INDEX | 1381

non-suicidal self-injury
  in borderline personality disorder, 1280, 1281, 1282, 1283
  definition of, 1281
  methods for, 1281
nonverbal communication. *See also* facial expression(s)
  adaptiveness of, 682
  among strangers, 683–84
  audience effects and, 65, 68, 691
  basic emotions and, 8*t*, 9–11, 10*t*, 685–86
  Basic Emotion Theory and, 685–86, 687, 688
  and behavioral coordination, 632
  behavioral ecology and, 686–87, 1330–32
  of compassion, 572–73
  of contempt, 597–98, 601n.5
  context and, 690–92
  culture and, 685–86, 690–92, 984–85, 987–89
  of dominance, 214
  of embarrassment, 380
  of emotions, 6, 501–2
  evolutionary perspective on, 681–84, 689–92, 984–85
  flexibility of, 490
  in group living, 683
  importance of, 681–82
  in intergroup context, 705
  modalities for, 684
  origins of, 684
  of prestige, 214
  of pride, 204–5, 204*f*, 212–13, 380, 382–83, 595, 635
  in primates, 9 (*see also* primate homologues of basic emotions)
  sex differences in, 689–90
  of shame, 205, 595–96
  social situations and, 690–92
  theories about, 685–89
  universality of, 686
norepinephrine, and romantic love, 222–23, 224
norm(s), 922–23
  children and, 921–22
  definition of, 155–56
  group, and display rules, 989
  punishment and, 997–98
  social, 155–56
normal variation, 1142–43, 1240, 1254
novel object test, 768–69
novelty
  as appraisal dimension, 990
  and humor, 555
  and play, 555

Nowicki, S., 70
NPD. *See* narcissistic personality disorder
NSSI. *See* non-suicidal self-injury
nucleus accumbens, 241, 468, 469
  and behavioral adjustment to frustrative nonreward, 837–39
nucleus ambiguus, and fear responding/fear learning, 504–5
numbing, in post-traumatic stress disorder, 1267–68
numeracy, and contingency table interpretation, 887
numeracy bias, and compassion, 571–72
nurturant love, 343–44, 346, 348, 372, 379
  and kin care, 373, 373*t*
  physiological effects of, 377
  sex differences in, 383
nurture, as motive, 104
Nussbaum, Martha, 1079–80
nutritional stress, and disgust sensitivity, 189–90, 194
nyctophobia, 1120
  culture and, 1122
  error management theory and, 1121

O

Oatley, K., 62–63
obesity
  Insurance Hypothesis and, 1176*t*, 1183
  mismatch hypotheses for, 1189
obscenity law, 1078
obsession(s), 1117–18, 1318, 1319–20
  ego-syntonic versus ego-dystonic, 1321
  evolutionary perspective on, 1323
obsessive-compulsive disorder, 182, 1117–19, 1317, 1318
  evolutionary perspective on, 1118–19
  heterogeneity of, 1117–18
  hormones and, 873
  life-history framework and, 1118
  life-history perspective on, 1288–89
  prevalence of, 871
  related disorders, 1317
  ritualized behaviors in, 1118
  romantic love and, 228
  serotonin in, 224, 228
  sex differences in, 864, 873
  symptoms, 1318–20
  treatment, evolutionary perspective on, 1323
  in women, 871

obsessive-compulsive personality disorder, 1321
  life-history perspective on, 1288–89
obstetrical dilemma, 1099
O'Connell, Katherine, 500–11
octopus, fear responding/fear learning in, 504
odor(s). *See also* body odor
  affective influence of, 663
  behavior responses to, 665, 666
  definition of, 664
  and emotions, 663–64
  localization of, 665
  and memory, 663–64
  pleasant versus unpleasant, 666
offspring care, biological systems in, 574–77
Öhman, A., 1112, 1115–16, 1120, 1121
Ohtsubo, Yohsuke, 717–32
Okun, Sara, 1279–90
Old Friends Hypothesis, 187
olfaction. *See also* smell (sense of)
  anatomical relationship to emotion processing, 664
  and auditory sensation, 671–72
  definition of, 664
  disorders of, 665–66
  in dogs, 811, 819–20
  as emotional sense, 663–64
  and emotions, 663–64, 666–67
  evolutionary perspective on, 664–65
  functional liaison with emotional processing, 664–65, 671–72
  functions of, 664, 666
  hedonicity and, 663–64
  in infancy, 670–71
  integration with other senses, 671–72
  inter- and intra-individual variability in, 667
  and intimate relationships, 668–69, 673*f*
  and mother–child relationship, 670–71, 673*f*
  neuroscience of, 665, 666*f*
  and romantic relationships, 668–69, 673*f*
  and sexuality, 669–71, 673*f*
  and tactile sensation, 671–72
olfactory bulb
  and emotional responses, 238, 238*f*
  in olfactory processing, 665, 666*f*
olfactory epithelium, in olfactory processing, 665, 666*f*
olfactory hallucinations, 666
olfactory reference syndrome, 1317

ontogenetic environment. *See*
    environment, present
    (ontogenetic environment)
onychophagia, 1317, 1318
open-mouth threat display, 768
openness to experience
    and life-history strategies, 1288–89
    pride and, 206–8, 207*t*
    and problem-solving, 615
operant conditioning, 465
opiates, 1218, 1230–31
    endogenous, 1230–31
    exogenous, 1230–31
opioid receptor agonists and
    antagonists, and effects of
    frustrative nonreward, 835–36
opioids, 1219
    in dogs, 812–13
    and effects of frustrative
        nonreward, 835–36
    endogenous, in animal conflict
        resolution, 722
opossums, open-mouth threat
    display in, 768
opportunity cost(s)
    definition of, 324
    minimization, boredom and, 324
oppositional-defiant disorder, 1086
optical illusions, 1252
optimism, gratitude and, 264–65
orangutans. *See also* great apes
    facial expressions in, 770
    and newborns' vocalizations, 915
    social learning in, 919
    socio-cognitive skills of, 794
orbitofrontal cortex, 468–69, 557,
    575, 766
    and behavioral adjustment to
        frustrative nonreward, 838
    and curiosity, 364
    in forgiveness, 724–25
    in olfactory processing, 665, 666*f*
    in relationship valuation, 724–25
organizational justice, perceptions
    of, emotions and, 901
ostracism, 1041. *See also* social exclusion
    acute, 1046
    and aggression, 1049
    and anger, 1044, 1045
    in animals, 1042
    antisocial response to, 1044,
        1046–47
    and anxiety, 1045
    ball-toss paradigms for, 1046 (*see
        also* Cyberball)
    behavioral responses to, 1043–44
    certainty appraisal and, 1045

chronic, 1046
and contempt, 1049
control appraisal and, 1045
cross-cultural considerations with,
    1047–48
and depression, 1045
emotional responses to, 1043–46
evolutionary perspective on,
    1042–43
experimental paradigms applied
    to, 1046
and extremism, 1048–50
and fear, 1045
get-acquainted paradigm for, 1046
and guilt, 1044, 1045
and hatred, 1049
and helplessness, 1045
and humiliation, 1050
injustice appraisals and, 1045
life-alone paradigm for, 1046
and pain, 1042–43
paradoxical responses to,
    reconciliation of, 1046–47
prosocial/affiliative response to,
    1044, 1046–47
psychological effects of, 1042–43
research on, future directions for,
    1046–50
and sadness, 1044
and shame, 1045
as social death for social animals,
    1042–43
uses of, 1042
out-group men
    and attributions of danger, 705
    facial expressions of, and
        self-protection threat
        management, 705
    and fear acquisition, 1265
    potential threat from, processing
        of, 705–7
    as sexual threat, and women's bias
        against them, 705–7
    women's bias against, 705–7
over-confidence bias, 894
OXT. *See* oxytocin
oxytocin
    actions of, 238–39, 575
    and amygdala, 238–42
    and attachment, 238–42, 379
    and caring behavior, 287, 575
    and compassion, 575
    in dogs, 812–13, 818–19
    effects in animals, 767
    intimate contact with newborns
        and, 914
    and pleasure, 468

and romantic love, 222–23, 224
synthesis of, 238–39
and vocal learning, 916–17
oxytocin receptors
    distributions of, 241–42
    in human brain, 241–42

P

Pachacuti, 1060
Pacific region, differential reproduction
    in, ethnographic and historical
    perspective on, 1058–59
Pages, Erika, 369–84
pain, 155. *See also* chronic pain;
    psychological pain hypothesis
    acute, 415, 420, 427
    and aggression, 973
    in animals, 417, 418–20, 429–30
    animals' sense of, 502–3
    assessment of, 415–16
    of childbirth, 650
    communicative functions of, 416–
        17, 425, 428, 650–51
    coping aspects of, 416–17
    definition of, 415–16
    and drug use, 1228*t*, 1229–30
    emotional component of, 416
    and empathy, 422
    evolutionary origins of, evidence
        for, 10*t*, 11
    evolutionary perspective on, 420
    experience of, 417, 465, 502–3
    expression of, 417, 425
    faking of, 650–51
    fear and, 417
    functions of, 417
    gate control model of, 428
    habituation and, 417
    humor and, 550
    and immobility, 417
    infants' sense of, 502–3
    inhibition of, 417
    with injury/illness, 649, 650–51, 657
    mental, 1146
    motivational aspects of, 650
    neuromatrix model of, 428
    ostracism and, 1042–43
    phases of, 417
    physiological correlates of, 10*t*, 11
    research, future directions
        for, 429–30
    sensitization to, 417, 428
    social, and drug use, 1230–31
    social plasticity of, 651
    social rejection and, 974
    as social transaction, 427
    and vocalization, 417

pain behaviors, 416–17
  context and, 419
  evolutionary perspective on, 419
  human, 416–17
  in infants, 428
  interpersonal aspects of, 416–17
  and social functioning, 418
  in social species, 419
  species-specific, 416–17, 418–20
pain communication
  analgesic effect of, 427
  decoding of, 425
  factors affecting, 425
  by newborns, 425
  psychological support and, 424–25
  signaling theory and, 425–27
  social context and, 424–25
pain face, 423
pain of altruism, 418
pair-bonding. *See also* romantic love
  and drug use/addiction, 1228*t*, 1231
  human, 1175–79
  humor and, 379
  neurohormonal systems of, 239
  oxytocin ad, 241–42
  oxytocin and, 224
  romantic love and, 221–22
pair-bonding (motivational system), 103, 104, 105–6, 105*f*, 110
paleontology, 31–32
PAM. *See* Perception-Action Model
PAMPs. *See* pathogen-associated molecular patterns
panic, 103
panic circle, 1124–25
panic disorder, 1101, 1110, 1113–14
  disorder-specific model, 1124–25
  epidemiology of, 873, 1113–14
  hormones and, 873
  prevalence of, 871
  sex differences in, 871, 873
Panksepp, J., 103, 121, 488–89, 544, 764, 766
Pan paniscus. *See* bonobos
Pan troglodytes. *See* chimpanzees
Papez, James, 237
Papini, Mauricio R., 830–40
Papua New Guinea. *See* Fore tribe
parasite infection. *See also* helminth infection
  and disgust sensitivity, 194–95
parasympathetic nervous system, 446–48, 501
  disgust response and, 183
  and fear responding/fear learning, 504–5

parental behavior
  and altruism, 284
  biological systems in, 574–77
  evolution of, 283–84
  oxytocin ad, 241–42
parental effort, lassitude and, 301, 301*f*, 306–7
parental investment, 249, 567–68
  k-selection and, 283
  and nurturant love, 383
parental manipulation hypothesis, and anorexia nervosa, 1176*t*, 1181–82
parenthood, and happiness, 473
parenting, 103–4, 1227, 1228*t*
  and drug use/addiction, 1228*t*, 1231
parietal lobe, and emotional responses, 237
Parkes, C. M., 485–87, 490, 493
Parkinsonism, 477
  and laughter, 557
Parkinson's disease, prevalence of, 1139, 1140*f*
parosmia, 666
partial pressure of carbon dioxide, 446
  contentment and, 447, 450*t*
partner choice, 79–80
  and shame, 148
partner valuation, 630
Pascal, Blaise, 443
past, observation of, 31–32
Patañjali, 439
paternal investment/provisioning, 1177–78
pathogen(s)
  avoidance, and moral concerns, 957–59
  as disgust elicitors, 183–84
  and disgust response, 182–84
  exposure to, and disgust sensitivity, 184–86
  and human behavior, 183
  and human biology, 183
  and human personality, 183
pathogen-associated molecular patterns, 300, 301*f*
pathogen avoidance, disgust and, 182–84
pathogen disgust, 108, 182–83, 618n.1
  and anti-immigration attitudes, 613
  and political attitudes, 613, 618n.2
pathological gambling, 1317, 1322–23
pathology, molecular cues of, 300, 301*f*

Patrick, Carlton, 90, 1067–80
PCA. *See* principal component analysis
PCL-R. *See* Psychopathy Checklist–Revised
PE. *See* prolonged exposure
PEACE scale. *See* Positive Emotion Assessment of Contentment Experience scale
Pedersen, Eric, 263–78
peer contagion, 741–42
perception(s)
  emotions and, 44
  metaphysics of, 888–89, 904n.3
  physiology and, 889–90
  variations in, 889–91
Perception-Action Model, 798–800, 820
periaqueductal gray, and compassion, 574–75
perimenstrual syndrome. *See* premenstrual syndrome
peripartum depression
  hormones and, 869–70
  risk factors for, 869
perplexity, 465
perseverance, sadness and, 533–34
personality
  computational models of, 121
  and emotion, motivation as bridge between, 122–23
  emotional systems and, 121
  emotion-valuation constellation and, 87–89
  motivational basis of, 120–21
  navigation of status hierarchies and, 600–1
  reinforcement sensitivity theory as model of, 124n.6
  variation, niche variation and, 191
personality disorder(s)
  definition of, 1279–80
  dimensional system for, 1302
  and emotional dysregulation, 1086
personality traits
  and adaptive challenges of hierarchy navigation, 600–1
  and happiness, 472–73
  humor styles and, 548
  pride and, 206–8, 207*t*
  pro-social, gratitude and, 264–65
  psychopathic, as dimensional, 1307–8, 1309–10
person perception, motivation and, 123
perspective-taking, 422, 566, 571–72, 575–76

and empathy, 633, 798–99
persuasion
    affective influence on, 535–36, 536f
    emotion-based, 612
    motivated reasoning as tool
        for, 893–94
    resistance to, 612
Petersen, Michael Bang, 607–17
Pfundmair, Michaela, 1040–50
PGD. *See* prolonged grief disorder
phantosmia, 666
phenotype(s)
    description of, role of, 34–35
    heterogeneity of, 1254–55
    observation of, principles
        for, 34–35
    and variability in expression
        versus uniformity in
        design, 33–34
pheromones, 667, 767
Phillips, A., 404–5
phobia(s). *See also* anxiety
        disorder(s); specific phobia(s)
    acquisition of, 1113
    animal-type, 1120–21
    blood-injection-injury, 1113
    disgust sensitivity and, 1113
    emotions underlying, 1110
    etiology of, 1122–23
    evolutionary perspective on, 1263
    evolutionary research on, recent
        developments in, 1120–22
    unlearning of, risk play and,
        1122–23
phylogeny
    of behavior, 358–59
    of chemosensation, 664–65
    of curiosity, 359–60
    of emotional vigilance, 855
    of emotions, 1333
    of grief, 487–89
    of laughter, 544
physical assault, and depression,
        1137t, 1143–44
physical health
    happiness and, 471
    humor and, 550–51
    positive emotions and, 377
physical strength
    and attitudes about
        inequality, 610–11
    and formidability, 139–40
    and negotiation about
        entitlement, 610–11
    and support for war, 610–11
physiological synchrony, and
        coordinated behaviors, 741–42

physiology, 27
    of basic emotions, 8t, 9–11, 10t,
        16, 319–20
    of contentment, 446–48
    emotions and, 44, 1334
    positive emotions and, 377
Piaget, Jean, 489–92
Pieters, R., 247–48
pigeons, frustrative nonreward
    in, 833
pigs
    aggression in, 779
    chemical signals in, 767
    ear movement, emotions and, 771
    emotional contagion in, 769
    infrared thermal imaging of, 766
    pain behaviors in, 420
    vocal signals used by, 770
Pilling, Arnold, 1058
Pine, D. S., 1105
piriform cortex, in olfactory
    processing, 665, 666f
Pizarro, Francisco, 1060
placebo effect, 308, 550, 652
planning
    cues and, 39–40
    emotions and, 40, 46–47
    imagery and, 46–47
Plato, 520–21, 1068–69
Plauché, Leon Gary, 163, 165, 168–72
play, 103, 1227, 1228t
    in animals, 770–71
    curiosity and, 362–63
    in dogs, 812–13
    evolutionary perspective on, 556
    functions of, 111–12
    humor and, 555–56
    and laughter, 546
    and learning, 111
    pretend, 554
    risky, and unlearning of phobias,
        1122–23
play face, 545, 556
play (motivational) system, 104,
    105f, 111–12
pleasurable novelty, longing for,
    disorders of, 1086–87
pleasure, 472
    neurochemistry of, 468
Pleistocene, 30
Plutchik, Robert, 1056
PMDD. *See* premenstrual dysphoric
    disorder
PMS. *See* premenstrual syndrome
political attitudes
    tendency to feel emotions
        and, 612–13

threat perception and, 613–15
political behavior
    adaptations for, 608–9
    emotions and, 608–11
political beliefs, and motivated
    reasoning, 887
political coordination, emotions
    and, 616–17
political judgment
    adaptations for, 608
    affect and, 524
    emotions and, 608–11
political psychology,
    evolutionary, 607–9
politics, 89
    emotions in, 607
    inherent relationship to
        emotions, 615–17
    as negotiation about entitlement/
        resources, 607–9
    offensive strategies and defensive
        counter-strategies in, 608
polygamy
    in Africa, 1057–58
    in Americas, 1059–60
    in Asia, 1060–62
    in Pacific region, 1058–59
polyvagal system, 494, 575
Poma de Ayala, Huamán, 1060
Pongo pygmaeus. See orangutans
population thinking, 1328–29
pose(s), as representing emotions,
    65, 66–67, 74n.16
positive affect, 521, 538–39. *See also*
    mood(s)
    benefits of, 523
    cognitive effects of, 374–77
    and health outcomes, 377
    intrapersonal functions
        of, 374–78
    and lower mortality rates, 377
    and mood maintenance, 533
positive emotion(s)
    in animal conflict resolution, 722
    in animals, 769–73
    and approach motivation, 375–76
    Broaden-and-Build Theory of,
        371–72, 375–76, 445
    cognitive effects of, 374–77
    comparative psychology
        of, 764–65
    of dogs, 812–13
    evolutionary perspective on,
        371–72, 467
    functions of, 319, 370–71, 372
    and fundamental social motives,
        372–73, 373t

positive emotion(s) (*cont.*)
   and heuristic facilitation of information processing, 374–77
   and intervention in intergroup conflict, 709–10
   intrapersonal functions of, 374–78
   leadership and, 1030–31
   and physical health, 377
   physiological effects of, 377
   and punitive behavior, 1009–12, 1014–16, 1014*f*
   regulatory functions of, 377–78
   social functions of, 378–80
Positive Emotion Assessment of Contentment Experience scale, 453–54
positive emotion disposition, benefits of, 455
positive evolutionary psychology, 929, 937, 941
   and community building, 937–38
   and emotions, 935–36
   findings from, and broader human experience, 940
   kindness in, 931
   research in, future directions for, 939–40
positive experiences, sharing, and relationship strength, 637
positive psychology, 543, 930, 932
   domains and applied questions in, 930–31
   and evolutionary psychology, connection/complementarity of, 929, 930–31, 932
positive temperament, 453
positivity offset, 445–46, 448
posterior cingulate cortex, and punitive behavior, 1008
postpartum depression, 1146
   and anger, 1149–50
   hormones and, 869–70
   symptoms of, 869
postpartum period
   and obsessive-compulsive disorder, 873
   and panic disorder, 873
post-traumatic stress disorder, 1119–20, 1262
   all-or-none thinking in, 1270
   anger in, 1271
   anhedonia in, 1271–72
   arousal alterations in, 1270
   avoidance in, 1266–67
   cognitive "errors" in, 1268–69
   combat-related, 1264, 1265
   comorbidity in, 1271–72
   costly signaling and, 1268–69, 1274
   criterion A (DSM) for, 1264–65
   definition of, 1119
   disease model of, 1263
   as disorder of fear extinction, 1264
   DSM features of, 1264–68
   epidemiology of, 1119
   evolutionary perspective on, 1119, 1262
   hormones and, 872–73
   hypervigilance in, 416, 1270
   intrusive symptoms in, 1266
   metacognitive model of, 1119–20
   and mindreading, 1270
   mismatch factors and, 1264, 1269, 1274
   mistrust in, 1268–69
   mood alterations in, 1267–68
   non-Western findings on, 1136–37
   numbing in, 1267–68
   overgeneralizing in, 1269–70
   pathogenesis of, 1263–64
   prevalence of, 871, 1263–64
   in rape survivors, 1273
   sex differences in, 871, 872–73, 1267–68
   and sexual dysfunction, 1272–73
   sleep disturbance in, 1271
   social support and, 1273
   and substance use disorders, comorbidity, 1225–26
   symptoms of, 1119
   and testosterone, 1272–73
   thought suppression in, 1266–67
   treatment of, 1273–74
   types of trauma causing, 1264–65
posture
   animals', with negative emotions, 768
   and emotional display, 848
Poulton, R., 1122
pouting, cultural diversity in, 57
powerlessness, and depression, 1151
Power-to-Take Game, 1000, 1003, 1006
2PP. *See* second-party punishment
3PP. *See* third-party punishment
PPD. *See* postpartum depression
PPI-R. *See* Psychopathy Personality Inventory–Revised
pragma, 220–21
prairie vole, 224, 228, 241–42
   consolation behaviors in, 800
precaution system, 103, 105*f*, 108
predation
   motivational system for, 107–8
   risk, and sleep duration, 1271
predator avoidance, 1263–64, 1267
predatory aggression, 107, 173–74
   characteristics of, 173–74
   hatred and, 173–74
   rapid deployment of, 174
   timing of, 174
predatory defense, 1116
prediction error
   dopaminergic system and, 364
   reduction, boredom and, 325
prediction-explanation fallacy, 1329
prefrontal cortex, 1069
   and compassion, 576–77
   and punitive behavior, 1008–09
pregnancy
   and anxiety, 871, 874
   disgust sensitivity in, 188, 864–65
   and generalized anxiety disorder, 871–72
   and obsessive-compulsive disorder, 873
   and post-traumatic stress disorder, 872–73
   and social anxiety disorder, 872, 874
premenstrual dysphoric disorder, 1239
   depathologization of, neurodiversity movement and, 1246–48
   DSM criteria for, 1246–47
   as dysfunction, 1247–48
   hormones and, 867–69
   prevalence of, 867–68
   symptoms of, 867–68
premenstrual syndrome, 874, 1246–48
   hormones and, 867–69
   prevalence of, 867–68
   symptoms of, 867–68
premotor cortex, and emotional responses, 236–37, 236*f*
preoperational stage, 489
   loss for children in, 490–91
preparedness, 1112
presenteeism, depression and, 1154–55
prestige, 108–9
   definition of, 210
   and leadership, 1025, 1026
   nonverbal communication of, 214
   and pride, 213–14
   and rank, 210, 1024–25
   and status, 1024–25, 1203
pride, xiii, 152–53, 437. *See also* social emotions

achievements motivated
  by, 209–10
authentic, 204f, 205–12, 1026
brain activity and, 468–69
and choice of cooperative partner,
  624t, 631
cognitive appraisals and, 208–9
and cooperation, 635–36
culture and, 382–83
definition of, 372–73
displays of, adaptive benefits
  of, 212–13
and dominance, 213–14, 380
dominance and, 1026
effort/ability attribution and,
  207t, 208–9
evolutionary origins of, evidence
  for, 10t, 11
evolutionary perspective
  on, 209–14
functions of, 148–49, 203–4, 209–
  12, 372–73, 1056–57, 1208
and greed, 209
hubristic, 204f, 205–9, 210–12,
  635, 1026, 1032
hubristic, in narcissism, 1205–6,
  1207, 1208
informational properties of, 210
interpersonal functions of, 624t,
  631, 635–36
and long-term behavioral
  regulation, 617
and mental health
  outcomes, 208
national, and politics, 611
in negotiation about entitlement,
  610, 611
nonverbal expression of, 204–5,
  204f, 212–13, 380, 382–83,
  595, 635
personality correlates of, 206–
  8, 207t
in political judgment and
  behavior, 608–9, 611
and prestige, 213–14
prestige and, 1026
psychological structure of, 205–9
recognition of, 204–5, 204f
research on, directions for, 214
as self-conscious emotion,
  203, 764
social behaviors motivated
  by, 209–10
as social emotion, 80, 82, 83–85,
  85f, 86f
social functions of, 380
and social rank, 203, 209–12, 380

and status, 212–13, 372–73, 373t,
  587, 593, 594t, 595, 635–36
primacy effects, 530
primate homologues of basic
  emotions, 5, 8t, 9–11, 16
  evidence for, 10t, 11–12
  pain and, 11
primates. *See also* great apes
  alarm calls, reliable versus
    unreliable, 855
  alloparenting in, 910
  bared teeth facial expression
    in, 791
  caregiving in, 423–24
  cooperation among, 421
  curiosity in, 359–60
  emotional responses in, 371
  empathy in, 797
  expression of emotions, 685
  grief in, 488–89
  hemispheric lateralization of
    emotion processing in, 767
  infrared thermal imaging of, 766
  laughter expression in, 544, 545
  low-cost conciliatory signaling
    in, 723
  mating systems, 1175–79
  moral behavior in, 422
  pain behaviors in, 420
  parental care in, 284
  pathogen avoidance in, 184
  and post-conflict
    reconciliation, 720
  post-conflict stress in, 721–22
  postural expressions of fear, 508
  prosociality in, 797–98
  proto-jealousy in, 1337n.2
  rapid facial mimicry in, 799–800
  silent bared teeth display
    in, 688–89
  status hierarchies among, 588
principal component analysis, 106–7
prioritizing algorithms, and emotion
  mechanisms, 112–18, 113f
prisoner's dilemma, 718, 721
  iterated, 638, 718
problematic internet use, 1317,
  1321–22
procrastination, 322
progesterone
  and anxiety disorders, 871, 874
  and disgust sensitivity,
    188, 864–65
  in dogs, 812
  and panic disorder, 873
  and PMS/PMDD, 868–69
  and PTSD symptoms, 872–73

prolonged exposure, for treatment of
  post-traumatic stress disorder,
  1273–74
prolonged grief disorder, 495, 1086
propensity(ies), 101
property rights, 89
prosocial behavior
  biological systems and, 575–76
  cuteness and, 343–44
  emotion regulation and, 571–72
  guilt and, 291, 293
  in healthcare, 648–49
prosociality, 753
  empathy and, 797–98, 952, 953–54
  gratitude and, 264–67, 634
  and moral obligation,
    differentiation of, 952–54
  in primates, 797–98
provocation doctrine, 1074–77
pseudobulbar palsy, 557
psychodiagnosis, reliability of,
  1238–39
psychological constructivism, 991
psychological mechanism(s),
  evolved. *See* evolved
    psychological mechanism(s)
psychological pain hypothesis, 1146–
  47, 1148, 1153
psychological support, and pain
  communication, 424–25
psychology, 365. *See also*
  evolutionary psychology
  as science, origin of, 4
psychopathology. *See also* borderline
  personality disorder;
  depression; evolutionary
  psychopathology; mental
  disorder(s); narcissistic
  personality disorder; post-
  traumatic stress disorder
  Fast-Slow-Defense model of, 1225
psychopathy, 289, 1096–97, 1239.
  See also antisocial personality
  disorder
  affective abnormalities in, 1299,
    1309–10
  and aggression, 1298–99, 1306
  versus antisocial personality
    disorder, 1242, 1300–2
  associative learning difficulties
    in, 1299
  aversive attitudes and behaviors
    in, 1298–99
  as categorical construct, 1301,
    1310n.2
  characteristics of, 574–75, 1242,
    1243, 1298–99

psychopathy (cont.)
  cheater-hawk explanation for, 1306
  and cheating, 1298–99, 1305–6
  cognitive features of, 1299
  and criminality, 1243
  definition of, 1298–99
  depathologization of, neurodiversity movement and, 1241–46
  as dimensional construct, 1301–2, 1307–8, 1309–10
  DSM diagnostic criteria for, 1242
  and dysfunction, 1304–7, 1309
  early developmental disorder of (in children and adolescents) (*see* conduct disorder)
  emotion-personality constellation and, 87
  etiological pathways in, 1244–45
  evolutionary perspective on, 1244–46, 1304–7, 1309
  guiltlessness in, 285, 286
  and harm for individual, 1303–4, 1308–9
  and harm for nonrelatives, 1307
  and harm for others, 1303–4, 1307, 1308–9
  lack of distress in, 289, 1303, 1308–9
  life-history perspective on, 1298, 1305, 1309–10
  and mating, 1304–5, 1306
  measures of, 1242–43
  as mental disorder, 1298, 1300–3, 1308–9
  multidimensional structure of, 1302–3
  and nonresponse to distress signals, 285, 289
  persistence in populations, 1307–8
  and personality traits, 1302–3
  phenotypic heterogeneity of, 1242, 1243
  as psychiatric concept, 1300–1
  and reproductive success, 1305
  and selfishness, 1307
  versus sociopathy, 1310n.1
  and spitefulness, 1307
  victim–offender relatedness and, 1245
Psychopathy Checklist–Revised, 1242–43, 1245
Psychopathy Personality Inventory–Revised, 1242–43
psychophysiology, 446–48. *See also* autonomic nervous system; physiology

psychotherapy, "third wave" of, 1125
PTI. *See* Scale of Positive Temperament in Indian Context
PTSD. *See* post-traumatic stress disorder
Public Goods Game, 1000, 1004
punishment, 1072. *See also* second-party punishment; third-party punishment
  alternatives to, 998, 1012–13
  altruistic, 428
  anger and, 1003–06, 1009, 1014–16, 1014f, 1016n.1, 1072
  cognitive aspects of, 1016n.2
  compassion and, 1010–11, 1014–16, 1014f
  versus compensation, emotions and, 1012–13, 1015
  and cooperation, 639–40
  definition of, 631–32, 998
  developmental basis of, 1015
  disgust and, 1006, 1009, 1014f, 1014–16
  emotional antecedents of, 998, 1003, 1006–07
  empathy and, 1011, 1016n.4
  forms of, 998
  frustration and, 1015
  general arousal and, 1007–08, 1009
  gratitude and, 1011, 1014–16, 1014f
  guilt and, 1015
  legal, emotion-valuation constellation and, 90
  legally prescribed, 1073
  negative emotions and, 1002–09, 1014–16, 1014f
  neural basis of, 1008–09, 1014–16, 1014f
  other-oriented emotions and, 1009–11, 1012
  positive emotions and, 1009–12, 1014–16, 1014f
  regret and, 1015
  researchers' measurement of, 998–1002
  as reward-seeking behavior, 1010b
  sadness and, 1006, 1009
  self-reported emotions and, 1003, 1004, 1014f, 1015
  shame and, 1015
  social functions of, 997–98
puns, 547
pupil dilation, fear and, 504–5
pupillometry, 796
purging disorder, 1172

purity/sanctity, morality of, 957–59

Q
qŏvisti, 1150
quail, frustrative nonreward in, 833
qualia
  of gratitude, 277
  interspecies differences, 889–90
  perception of, 56, 72, 72n.1
Qur'an, 442

R
rabbits
  fever in, protective effects, 303
  pain display in, 425
racial discrimination, perceived injustice of, 1045
rage, 103
  defensive aggression and, 117–18
  narcissistic, 1207
Raley, Jennifer R., 1197–210
Ramesses II, 1061
Randles, D., 57
rank attainment
  dominance/prestige account for, 210–12, 1024–25
  pride and, 203, 209–12
Rantala, M. J., 1189
Ranu Seru, 1059
Ranu Tanoa, 1059
rape
  and depression, 1146
  in intergroup context, 700, 701–2
  narcissism and, 1202–3
  survivors, post-traumatic stress disorder in, 1273
  wartime, 1272
rapid facial mimicry, 799–800
RAQ. *See* Retrospective Attachment Questionnaire
rats
  alarm calls of, 507–8
  chemical signals in, 767
  food intake during infection, metabolic state and, 140
  frustrative nonreward in, 833, 834
  laughter expression in, 544
  nutrient preferences, infection and, 140
  pain behaviors in, 420
  pain display in, 425
  pain grimace in, 771
  response to hypercapnia, 503
  sexual motivation during infection, sex differences in, 306

successive negative contrast and negative emotional activation in, 834
vocal signals used by, 768, 770
ravens, empathy in, 797
Razran, G., 1112
Read, S. J., 121
readout problem, 1330–32, 1334–35, 1336
and honesty, 1334
reappraisal(s)
of events, 708–9
online, 708–9
prospective, 709
reason
definition of, 1068–69
versus emotion, 1068–69
interaction with emotion, 1069
reasoning. *See also* motivated reasoning
argumentative theory of, 893–94
and guilt, 288–92
rebound effect, thought suppression and, 1266–67
recalibrational theory
of anger, 135, 1335
of sadness, 1335
reciprocal altruism, 931, 936–37, 940, 1268
research on, future directions for, 939
reciprocation, 79–80
reciprocity. *See also* cooperation; indirect reciprocity
direct, 421, 567
indirect, 421, 427–28, 567, 634
network, 421
reciprocity system, 102, 104, 105f, 110
and drug use/addiction, 1228t, 1230–31
reconciliation, 717. *See also* apology(ies); forgiveness
in animals, 720–23, 731
and appeasement of both sides, 731–32
benign intent hypothesis for, 722–23, 731
evolvability of, 718–20, 731
in group-living animals, 720
human, evolutionary perspective on, 723–32
in intergroup context, 709–10
long- versus short-term benefits of, 722
proximate cause of, 721–22
ultimate cause of, 721

uncertainty-reduction hypothesis for, 721–22
valuable relationship hypothesis for, 721, 722, 731
recuperation, chronic pain and, 417–18
red deer, vocal signals used by, 768
redistribution, 89
red-necked wallabies, and reconciliation, 720
Reed, Lawrence Ian, 1279–90
reflexes, emotions and, 45
regret, xiii. *See also* sexual regret
about not having children, 258
action versus inaction, 251–53, 254, 256–58, 259n.1
anticipatory, 246, 247–48
behavioral implications of, 247–48, 253–56
benefits of, 253
casual sex and, 251–56
as counterfactual cognitive-emotional process, 246, 250, 256
definition of, 246
development of, 248
evolutionary perspective on, 247, 258
functions of, 253, 255–56, 258
metacognitions about, 253, 255
as motivation, 247
psychological function of, 247
and punitive behavior, 1015
research on, future directions for, 258
research on, in psychology, 247–49
romantic relationships and, 256–57
sex differences in, 248–49, 251–53, 256–58
regret regulation
alternative-focused, 247
decision-focused, 247–48
feeling-focused, 247
theory of, 247–48
Reimer, M., 1097
reinforcement sensitivity theory, 124n.6
rejection, excessive reassurance seeking and, 1157
Relational Models Theory, 346, 347, 348–49
relationship dissolution
and positive outcomes, 978
social emotions and, 624t, 640–41

relationships, costly, termination of, social emotions and, 624t, 640–41
relationship threat. *See also* infidelity threat
cues to, jealousy in response to, 394–95
and female intrasexual competition, 973–74
relativity of rewards, 469–70
relaxed open mouth, 770–71
relief, evolutionary origins of, evidence for, 10t, 12
religion, 89
evolutionary perspective on, 475–76
evolutionary psychology of, 939
and happiness, 475–76
remorse, 286, 287–88, 292
and guilt, 291
reparation, guilt and, 286, 290, 950
reproduction
Darwinism and, 26–27, 50n.4
emotions affecting, 1057
energy costs of, sex differences in, 306
lassitude and, 305–6
romantic love and, 222
women's resource-assessment mechanisms and, 36–37
reproduction expediting, menopause and, 258
reproductive competition, in contemporary times, 1063
reproductive hormones
and disgust sensitivity, 188–89, 192
and immune function, 188–89
reproductive status, and disgust sensitivity, 187–89
reproductive strategy(ies), 283
reproductive success, human, 1062–63
Reproductive Suppression Hypothesis, 1176t, 1180–81
reproductive value, residual, 305–6
reptiles, as fear stimuli, 1121
reputation, 79–80
concern for, 921–22
helpful, and social network rewards, 421
moral behavior and, 946–48
requesting, affective influence on, 526–27, 526f
rescue behavior, 419
Research Diagnostic Criteria, 830–31
and major depression, 1138t, 1139

resilience, 936–37, 941
    contentment and, 454
    studies of, 1144
resource(s)
    access to, and intergroup conflict, 700–1
    acquisition of, 111
resource distribution, 1135
resource holding potential, 1271
respect
    versus admiration, 597
    and status hierarchies, 587, 593, 594t, 597
respiratory rate, 446
    in animals, 765
    contentment and, 447, 450t
    fear and, 504–5
rest. *See* movement/rest
restorative justice, 285, 287–88, 640
restraint tests, 768–69
retail therapy, 1322
reticular formation, and emotional responses, 236f, 237
retirement, and happiness, 476
retributive justice, 287–88, 956
Retrospective Attachment Questionnaire, 487
revenge, in intergroup context, 700
rewards, 472
    downshifted versus unshifted conditions for, 830–32
    goal gradient effect and, 470
    lost, 830–31 (*see also* frustrative nonreward)
    propinquity (immediacy) and, 470
    relativity of, 469–70
reward systems, 364, 468, 469, 575
    and attachment, 239, 241
    and caregiving, 575
    and compassion, 577
    cuteness and, 341
    in dogs, 812–13
    and mirth, 556–57
    and punitive behavior, 1010b
    in romantic love, 223, 225
RFM. *See* rapid facial mimicry
rhesus monkey
    emotion regulation in, 758
    fear learning in, 510
    laughter expression in, 544
    neurobiology of jealousy in, 777
    and post-conflict reconciliation, 720, 721
    threat avoidance in illness, 307
Rhoads, Shawn A., 500–11
RHP. *See* resource holding potential

Rida, 442
ridicule, 549
    excessive sensitivity to, 558
right-wing ideology
    threat perception and, 613–15
    worries associated with, 613–15
risk perception, emotions and, 902–3
risk-pooling, 79–80, 623–30
risk-taking, drug use and, 1219–20, 1224–26, 1228t, 1231
ritualization, 67–68, 685
ritualized aggression
    in animals, 139–40
    in humans, 139
    versus predatory aggression, 174
rituals, 89
rivalry. *See also* narcissistic admiration and rivalry concept
    narcissistic, 1202–4
rodents. *See also* mice; rats
    alarm calls of, 507–8
    empathy in, 797
    fear learning in, 510
    fear responding/fear learning in, 503–4
    frustrative nonreward in, 834
    medial preoptic area in, 1329–30, 1336
    moral behavior in, 422
    neural circuitry, and fear responding, 507
    postural expressions of fear, 508
romantic love, 110, 219, 235–36, 320, 944
    and addiction, 228
    and altruism, 227
    benefits of, 225–27
    biological factors affecting, 222–25
    and cognition, 226–27
    commitment dimension of, 222
    cultural differences in, 220–21
    decline of, deterrents to, 229–30
    drawbacks of, 227–29
    and drug addiction, similarities, 1228t, 1231
    emotions in, 225–26, 227, 228
    evolutionary perspective on, 221–22, 227
    falling out of, 229–30
    functions of, 221–22
    health benefits of, 226
    hormones and, 222–25
    and hypothalamic–pituitary–adrenal axis, 224
    and jealousy, 227, 229

    in long-term relationships, 225, 229–30
    and mental health, 228
    as motivational system, 222, 225
    neural correlates of, 222–23
    neurochemistry of, 228
    and obsessive-compulsive disorder, 228
    and pair-bonding, 221–22
    partner benefits of, 227
    partner idealization in, 227
    physical effects of, 226
    physiological effects, 226, 227–28
    and positive feelings, 225–26
    reward systems in, 223, 225
    and sexual desire, 221–22
    and stress, 227–28
    and suicide, 227, 229
    universality of, 220–21
romantic relationships
    gratitude and, 267
    olfaction and, 668–69, 673f
    and regret, 256–57
r-selection, 283
RSH. *See* Reproductive Suppression Hypothesis
rumination, 749. *See also* adaptive rumination hypothesis; co-rumination
    depressive, 254–55, 1117, 1126, 1147
    metacognitions about, 254–55
Russell, James A., 55–72, 1327–28, 1329
Russian Doll Model, of empathy, 798–99

S

SAD. *See* social anxiety disorder
sadism, 167–68
sadness, xiii, 437–38, 521, 523–24. *See also* negative affect; social emotions
    adversity and, 1135–36
    appraisal mechanism and, 8
    and attention, 527–29
    as aversive, 1157
    as basic emotion, 4, 990
    behavioral effects of, 523
    benefits of, 521–22, 538–39
    and bullshit receptivity, 532–33, 534f
    and choice of cooperative partner, 624t, 633–34
    cognitive effects of, 523, 524–25, 527–29
    and conversational competence, 534, 535f

and cooperation, 633–34
and crying, 467
cultural context and, 522
disorders of, 1086–87
elicitors of, 568
evolutionary origins of, evidence for, 10t, 11
evolutionary perspective on, 371–72, 522–24, 933
expression of, 467, 522, 1134–35
and eyewitness memory, 527–29, 529f
functions of, 501, 502f, 520, 522–24, 539, 1135, 1145
as general emotion, 467
and guilt, 291, 292
and halo effects, 530, 530f
informational or content effect of, 523–25
and information-processing, 525–29
and ingratiation, 536–37, 537f
intense, 1253
intensity of, variations of, 1100
internal signaling function of, 522–23
interpersonal functions of, 624t, 633–34
judgmental benefits of, 529–33
kama muta and, 348
and language processing, 534–35, 536f
and loss aversion, 624t, 634
and memory performance, 527–29, 528f
motivational benefits of, 533–34
ostracism and, 1044
and perseverance, 533–34
and persuasion, 535–36, 536f
and primacy effect, 530
as primary emotion, 764
processing (cognitive tuning) function of, 523–24, 527–29
and punishment, 1006, 1009
recalibrational theory of, 1335
and requesting, 526–27, 526f
and self-disclosure, 526, 528f
and selfishness vs. fairness, 537–38, 538f
smoke-detector principle and, 1101
and social behaviors, 526–27
as social emotion, 81, 82, 84–85, 85f, 86f
and stereotyping, 530–31
suppression, in war, 1267
and terminating costly relationships, 624t, 640–41

and verbal communication, 534–38
safety behaviors, anxiety disorders and, 1123
salām, 442, 444t
Salmon, C., 1180–81
same-sex friendship(s), 738. *See also* female same-sex friendships
benefits of, 742–43
evolutionary perspective on, 742–43
santosha, 444t
and contentment, 438–41
definition of, 439
santoso, 444t
sarcasm, 554
satisfaction, and punitive behavior, 1010b
Satisfaction with Life Scale, 452–53
Sauter, Disa A., 983–92
savant ability(ies), 1252–53
Scale of Positive Temperament in Indian Context, 453
Scarantino, A., 99–100, 1332–33
SCH. *See* Sexual Competition Hypothesis
Schadenfreude, xiii, 81–82, 167–68, 285–86, 549–50, 1009–10, 1010b
in intergroup context, 710
Schäfer, Laura, 663–73
Scheff, Thomas, 1088
schizoid personality disorder, and emotional dysregulation, 1086
schizophrenia
life-history perspective on, 1288–89
neurodiversity and, 1241–42
prevalence of, 1139, 1140f
Schmidt, K. L., 70
Schrock, Joshua M., 297–310
Schubert, Thomas, 339–51
Schulkin, J., 416
Schützwohl, A., 392, 396, 397, 402–3
science skepticism
motivated reasoning and, 894
in secular postindustrial societies, 894
scientific acumen, and polarized opinions, 894
scientific evidence, biased interpretation of, 886–87, 896–97
Scott, J. P., 102, 124n.2
screaming, 507–8. *See also* crying
cultural diversity in, 57, 59–60
infants', behaviors elicited by, 1159

Scrivner, Coltan, 79–90, 163–78, 357–65
sea lions, grief in, 488
Searcy, W. A., 70
sea slugs, fear responding/fear learning in, 504
secondary emotions, 764–65
in animals, 774–78
second-party punishment
across societies, 997–98
anger and, 1003–06
in chimpanzees, 997–98
definition of, 997
disgust and, 1014–16, 1014f
emotional antecedents of, 998, 1012, 1014–16, 1014f
general arousal and, 1007–08, 1009
negative emotions and, 1009, 1014–16, 1014f
neuroscience of, 1008–09
sadness and, 1006
security system, 103, 108. *See also* precaution system
drug use and, 1230
as motivation, 104
Sedgwick, Peter, 1090–91
seeking, 103
functions of, 501, 502f
Seibt, Beate, 339–51
selection
balancing, 1307–8
negative frequency-dependent, 1307–8
ongoing, 23–24
sexual recombination and, 32–33, 50–51n.5, 51n.6
selection pressure, 146, 164
between-group, 937
and emotions in animals, 778
and social valuation, 136
and species design, 38
toxic individuals and, 165–67
within-group, 937
selective pressure, and cooperative interactions, 947
selective serotonin reuptake inhibitors, side effects of, 223–24
self-acceptance, unconditional, 455–56
self-assessment
affective influence on, 534
mood and, 525–26
self-awareness, 774–75
conscious, 290
and guilt, 288–92, 293

self-blame, 153–54
self-concept
  independent, 1047–48
  interdependent, 1047–48
self-conscious emotions, 153, 203, 764, 774–75. *See also* embarrassment; guilt; pride; shame
  interpersonal adaptive functions of, 153
  and moral emotions, 949–51
  neurocognitive architecture of, 153
  norm-based theories of, 156
self-construal, 1047
  and emotional response to ostracism, 1047–48
self-control, 617
  in animals, 758
  definition of, 758
self-disclosure. *See also* co-rumination
  affective influence on, 526, 528f
  in co-rumination, 738–39
  in friendships, 738–39
  risks associated with, 743
self-esteem, 146
  domain-specific approach to, 975
  in grandiose narcissists, 1205–6
  and greed, 209
  high, functions of, 1208
  low, in depression, 1271
  low, in post-traumatic stress disorder, 1271
  pride and, 206–8, 207t, 210
  and self-perceived mate value, 975
  as social barometer (sociometer), 210
  social comparison and, 974–75
  social rejection and, 974–75
  vulnerable narcissism and, 1207–8
self-grooming, in animals, 770
self-handicapping, affective influence on, 534
self-harm, as credible signal of need, 1153
self-injury, in captive animals, 768
self-interest
  balanced with interest of community, 937–38
  versus envy, 611
  and evolution of cooperation, 421
selfish gene, 932
selfishness
  affective influence on, 537–38, 538f
  and psychopathy, 1307
self-presentation theory, 921, 1115
self-protection, 103–4, 1227, 1228t

and drug use/addiction, 1228t, 1230
self-punishment, guilt and, 730
self-regulation strategies, 119–20
self-worth. *See* self-esteem
Seligman, Martin, 932
Sell, Aaron, 135, 163–78, 393
semiochemicals, 667
Sennacherib, 1061
sensorimotor stage, 489
  loss for children in, 490
sensory ecology, variability in, 889–90
sensory regulation, and facial displays, 74n.22
sentiment
  contempt as, 601n.5
  definition of, 601n.5
separation
  and attachment, 493
  effects of, 485, 493
separation anxiety disorder, 1086
sequence integration problem, 116
serotonin
  and contentment, 448
  and depression, 1141
  in dogs, 812–13
  in obsessive-compulsive disorder, 224, 228
  and peripartum depression, 870
  and positivity offset, 446
  and punitive behavior, 1008
  and romantic love, 222–24, 228
sex addiction, 1317, 1322
sex differences
  in bargaining, 1155–56
  biopsychosocial model of, 689–90
  in depression, 1155–56
sex steroids, ovarian, and PMS/PMDD, 868–69
sexual activity, emotion regulation and, 755–56
sexual arousal, xiii
  brain activity and, 468–69
  deactivation of, 402
sexual attraction, 1057
sexual behavior
  borderline personality disorder and, 1289
  moralizations of, 957–59
  psychopathy and, 1304–5
sexual coercion
  narcissism and, 1202–3
  psychopathy and, 1304
  women's vulnerability to, and bias against out-group men, 705–7
sexual competition, human, 1175–79, 1176t

Sexual Competition Hypothesis
  clinical and nonclinical studies of, 1186–87
  and eating disorders, 1176t, 1180–81, 1183–89
  and male body dissatisfaction, 1187–88
sexual desire, 105–6, 378–79
  and mate acquisition, 373t, 378–79
sexual dimorphism
  in gorillas, 1188
  human, 1188
sexual disgust, 108, 182–83, 613, 1057
  and political attitudes, 618n.2
sexual dysfunction, in post-traumatic stress disorder, 1272–73
sexuality
  anosmia and, 670–71
  hyposmia and, 670–71
  olfaction and, 669–71, 673f
sexuality motivational system, 102
sexual jealousy, xiii, 32, 42–43, 62, 944, 1057, 1095, 1103. *See also* jealousy
sexual motivational system, 100
sexual over-perception bias, 249
sexual regret, 1057
sexual reproduction, 50n.4
sexual selection, 67, 249. *See also* differential reproduction
  emotion regulation and, 755–56
  and human sexual dimorphism, 1188
  narcissism and, 1201–3
Sexual Strategies Theory, 246, 249–50, 253–54, 255–57
sexual system, 105–6
sexual transgressions, in intergroup context, 700, 701–2
Shackelford, T., 393, 394, 400–1, 403
shalom, 442, 444t
shamanism, 653, 655
shame, xiii, 145–57, 944–45. *See also* social emotions
  and aggression, 147–48, 154–55
  alternative theories of, 152–56
  and anger, 155
  animals and, 775–76
  anticipatory, 149–50
  and apology-making, 730–31
  attributional account of, 154–55
  audience and, 150–52
  and audience devaluation, 149–50, 151f
  and bargaining, 950–51

behavioral outputs of, 88
brain activity and, 468–69
and compensation, 950–51
and competition, 950–51
computational model of, 1334
and cooperation, 154–55, 624t, 638–39, 950–51
and criminal law, 156–57
cross-cultural variation in, 986–87
culture and, 148, 157n.1
elicitors of, 950
evolutionary origins of, evidence for, 10t, 11
evolutionary perspective on, 145, 155
function of, 148–49, 595–96, 949–50, 986, 1056–57
and guilt, 149, 282–83, 291–92, 950
versus guilt, 987
and harm avoidance, 282–83
and hatred, 171, 178n.3
immoral outcomes with, 950
information threat theory of, 146–49, 153
interpersonal functions of, 638–39
as intrapersonal emotion, 152–54
as maladaptive emotion, 154–55
and moral behavior, 945
and moral conscience, 1076
narcissism and, 1205–6, 1207
negative effects of, 1045
in negotiation about entitlement, 610, 611
non-moral function of, 949, 950, 951f
nonverbal expression of, 205, 595–96
norm-based accounts of, 155–56
ostracism and, 1045
over-activation, 149
and partner choice, 148
in political judgment and behavior, 608–9, 611
and prosocial behavior, 951
prospective, 149
psychology of, 282–83
psychopathy and, 1299
and punitive behavior, 1015
reverse-engineering of, 145–46
as secondary emotion, 764–65
self-blaming of, 153–54
as self-conscious emotion, 764, 949
self-conscious phenomenology of, 152–54
self-relevant events and, 8
social devaluation and, 146–48, 153, 154–55, 949–50

as social emotion, 81, 82, 84, 945–46, 951f
and status hierarchies, 587, 593, 594t, 595–96
status-management function of, 950
as ugly emotion, 155
under-activation, 149
variation in, 148
shame display, 147–48
shame-proneness, pride and, 206–8, 207t
shareability, 905n.8
shared reality. See also worldview(s)
access to, 888
Shariff, A. F., 57
sharing, intersubjective, 918
Shaver, P. R., 382
sheep
infrared thermal imaging of, 766
pain behaviors in, 420
Shiota, Michelle N., 369–84, 622–42
Shiva Sutras, 440
shlam, 442, 444t
shooter's bias, 530–31
short-term mating, 249. See also casual sex
and disgust sensitivity, 187–88
drug use and, 1231
emotions related to, 249–51
and infidelity, 408
narcissism and, 1201–3, 1208
psychopathy and, 1304–5, 1306
sex differences in, 249–51
Shuar of Ecuador, disgust sensitivity research in, 186, 190–91, 193
shunning, corrective effect of, 549
sickness
as adaptive problem, 648–49
emotions associated with, 649, 650–53
signs and symptoms of, 652
as test of social status, 653
sickness behavior, 299b, 418, 651–53
evolutionary perspective on, 310
in humans, research needs, 310
sick role, 423–24, 427, 428, 649
Siddartha Gautama, 440–41, 442
signal(s), 848–49. See also readout problem
biological, 425–27
costs of, 425–26, 428
credible, 1151–53
versus cues, 425, 1162n.2
deceptive, 1152
definition of, 426, 1027
functions of, 425–26, 1152
honest, 426, 428, 1330–31, 1334

as indices, 851, 852
signal detection theory, 51n.10
signaling theory, 425–27, 428–29, 1027
biological, 425–27, 428
coevolution and, 426–27
signaling vulnerability, lassitude and, 301, 301f, 308–9
silent treatment, 1041
Simon-Thomas, Emiliana, 565–78
situation(s)
fitness contingencies of, emotions and, 48
identification of, 43
prioritizing, 43
situation-detecting algorithms
and emotion mechanisms, 112–18, 113f
in motivational systems, 112–18, 113f
skepticism, affective influence on, 531–32
skin conductance, 810
as measurement of arousal, 1007–08
skin-picking disorder. See dermatillomania
sleep
duration, predation risk and, 1271
positive affect and, 377
sleep disturbance, in post-traumatic stress disorder, 1271
sleep quality, boredom and, 322
S-L-M *(shalam; Shin-Lamedh-Mem)*, 441–42
Slovic, Paul, 612
smartphones
and boredom, 330–31
displacement-interference-complementary framework for, 330
smell (sense of), 663. See also olfaction
smile(s)/smiling, 466, 545, 684
affiliation, 688–89
and cooperative intent, 378
dominance, 688–89
Duchenne, 69–70, 378, 449, 688, 849
evolutionary perspective on, 791
functions of, 545, 556, 683–84
genuine, 378, 449
inauthentic, 69–70, 378, 449
as manipulative cue, 632
polite, 449, 849
reward, 688–89
sex differences in, 689
social functions of, 378, 688–89

Smith, Adam, 717–32, 895
smoke-detector principle, 416, 427, 891–93, 902–3
  and emotional disorders, 1099, 1100–2, 1125
snakes, as fear stimuli, 895–96, 1121, 1127, 1263
SNC. *See* successive negative contrast
sneering, 57
Snodgrass, J. Josh, 297–310
social anxiety disorder, 1086, 1101–2, 1110, 1111, 1114–16, 1127
  characteristics of, 1114–15
  disorder-specific model, 1125
  evolutionary perspective on, 1115–16
  hormones and, 871, 872, 874
  prevalence of, 871, 1114–15
  sex differences in, 872
social behaviors, affect infusion in, 526–27
social bias, in consolation behavior, 798, 800
social care, in healthcare, 656
social categorization, in intergroup context, 710
social comparison
  and envy, 977
  and jealousy, 976
  and self-esteem, 974–75
social constructionist views, of emotional expression, 62, 72, 320, 325–26, 687–88
social death, ostracism as, 1042–43
social devaluation, 149. *See also* social valuation
  context effects and, 148
  fitness cost of, 146–47
  information-triggered, 146–47
  prevention of, 146–47
  procedures for countering, 153, 154–55
  shame and, 146–48, 153, 154–55, 949–50
  threat of, as trigger of shame, 147–48
social emotions, 148–49, 951*f*
  behavioral outputs of, 88
  and cooperation, 624*t*, 631–41
  culture and, 85–86
  definition of, 80
  dogs and, 813–18
  evolutionary perspective on, 742–43
  functions of, 79–82, 631, 742–43
  imagining and, 83
  individual differences and, 88

intensity of, and social valuation, 82–83
  neural processing underlying, 813
  and partner valuation, 624*t*, 631
  psychopathy and, 1299
  requirements for, 813–14
  self-concept and, 813–14
  social valuation and, 79–83, 949–51
  and termination of costly relationships, 624*t*
social exchange relationships, 270
social exclusion, 1040–41. *See also* ostracism
  dynamics of, 1041
  negative psychological effects of, 1041
  ostracism-focused, 1041
  rejection-focused, 1041
  types of, 1041
social group(s), hierarchical, adaptive problems posed by, 589–93
social hierarchy(ies), evolution of, 1023–24
sociality
  benefits of, 683
  challenges of, 622
  costs of, 683
  neuroendocrine systems and, 235–38, 236*f*, 242
  sex differences in, 1043
socialization, cuteness and, 343
social justice, perceptions of, emotions and, 900–1
social learning, 919–22
  expanded avenues for, 919–20
  of hatred, 169–70
social media
  and boredom, 330–31
  and cyberbullying, 934
  hate following on, 175–76
social norms, and shame, 155–56
social organization, human capacity for, evolutionary perspective on, 938
social parasites, 1152
social partners, depression in, interpersonal effects of, 1156–59
social phobia. *See* social anxiety disorder
social predators, 1305
social rank, 102. *See also* status/esteem
  deservedness of, nonverbal signaling of, 212
  dominance/prestige account for, 210–12, 1024–25

humor styles and, 548
  nonverbal expression of pride as signal of, 212–13
  nonverbal signals of, in nonhuman animals, 212
  pride and, 209–12
social rejection
  and aggression, 974–75
  and self-esteem, 974
Social Risk Hypothesis, for depression, 1183
social selection
  hominin infants and, 922
  punitive, 922–23
social servility, 1043, 1046
social support, 471
  in care of ill/injured, 424, 648–49
  depression and, 1158
  and happiness, 473
  and internalizing symptoms, 741–42
  and pain communication, 424–25
  and post-traumatic stress disorder, 1273
  and recuperation, 418
Social Threat Hypothesis, for anorexia nervosa, 1176*t*, 1183
social valuation. *See also* social devaluation
  adaptive problems of, 80, 146
  assignment of, 136, 146
  and criminal justice system, 89–90, 156–57
  and fitness, 79–80
  grammar of, 82–86, 85*f*, 86*f*, 88, 1335
  neurocognitive mechanisms and, 79–80
  origin of, 79–80
  shame and, 950–51
  and social emotions, 79–83, 949–51
  universal aspects of, 83–86, 85*f*, 86*f*, 88
social welfare, political judgments about, emotions and, 611
social withdrawal, ostracism and, 1043, 1044
society(ies)
  evolutionary perspective on, 934
  small-scale ancestral, versus modern conditions, 938
socioecological context
  and boredom, 331
  and expression of emotion, 490
socioeconomic status
  and disgust sensitivity, 185–86
  and expression of emotion, 490

sociopathy, 1242. *See also* psychopathy
 evolutionary perspective on, 1245
 neurodiversity and, 1241–42
Sohm, Rudolph, 1029
Solomon (biblical King), 1061
somatic symptom disorder. *See* hypochondriasis
Sorenson, E. R., 60–61, 64, 73–74n.15
Souza, J., 938
spandrel, 1309
specific phobia(s), 1086, 1110, 1111–13
 epidemiology of, 1112
 triggers of, 1111
speech, dog-directed, characteristics of, 817–18
speeded response tests, in animals, 774
Spencer, H., 55–56, 72n.3
spider phobias. *See* arachnophobia
spinal cord, and emotional responses, 237
spirituality, evolutionary psychology of, 939
spite, 172
 envious, 81–82
spitefulness
 and negative relatives, 1307
 and psychopathy, 1307
Spitzer, Robert, 1089, 1255
Spoor, Jennifer R., 1040–50
spotted hyena, and reconciliation, 720
spousal killing, 170–71
squirrels, alarm calls of, 507–8
SSRIs. *See* selective serotonin reuptake inhibitors
SST. *See* Sexual Strategies Theory
starlings, frustrative nonreward in, 833
startle response, emotion downregulation and, 754
State Contentment Measure, 452–53
status/esteem, 103–4, 174–75, 1227, 1228t. *See also* status hierarchy(ies)
 allocation of, 592, 594t
 ancestral importance of, 588–89
 attainment of, 590–91, 1203
 dominance/prestige account for, 210–12, 1024–25, 1203
 and drug use/addiction, 1228t, 1231
 evolutionary perspective on, 1208
 fitness relevance of, 589, 601n.1
 of healthcare workers, 654
 in human groups, 588
 humor styles and, 548

leveraging of, 591, 594t
 and long-term behavioral regulation, 617
 loss of, mitigating, 591–92, 594t, 949–50
 maintenance of, 591, 594t
 as motive, 104, 372–73, 373t
 narcissism and, 1203–4
 pathways to, 950–51
 poor choices affecting, and regret, 257–58
 pride and, 372–73, 373t, 380
 relative, among group members, tracking, 592, 594t
 Social Threat Hypothesis and, 1183
 traits contributing to, 949–50
status-decreasing characteristics, avoidance/concealment of, 590, 591
status-enhancing characteristics
 advertisement of, 590
 identification of, 590
status hierarchy(ies), 949–50
 adaptive challenges posed by, 588, 589–93
 among animals, 588
 emotions and, 587–88, 593–600, 594t, 601n.3
 higher-status individuals in, interaction with, 591, 593, 594t
 and leadership, 1024–25
 leveling of, 593, 594t
 restructuring of, 593, 594t
 testosterone and, 863
 ubiquity of, 588–89
status pursuit, 590–91, 601n.2
 emotions and, 594t
 motivations for, 590–91, 601n.2
status system, 102–3, 105f, 108–9. *See also* status hierarchy(ies)
Steckler, C. M., 57
Steinkopf, Lander, 648–57
Steinnes, Kamilla Knutsen, 339–51
stereotyping, affective influence on, 530–31
steroid hormones
 and anxiety, 871
 and obsessive-compulsive disorder, 873
 ovarian, and PMS/PMDD, 868–69
 and PTSD symptoms, 872–73
stickleback, parental behavior in, 283–84
stimulant drugs, 1219
STM. *See* short-term mating
storge, 220–21
stress, 443. *See also* nutritional stress
 appraisal of, 445

conflict-related, relationship value and, 725
 humor and, 551
 management of, 445
 positive emotions and, 377–78
 post-conflict, in primates, 721–22
 psychosocial, and disgust sensitivity, 189
 reduction, contentment and, 454
 romantic love and, 227–28
stress reactivity
 maturation of, 494
 positive social interactions and, 379
stress response
 evolutionary perspective on, 742–43
 female, 739, 742–43
 hormonal changes in, 446
 HPA axis in, 865–67
 male, 742–43
stroke
 impending, and laughter, 557
 prevalence of, 1139, 1140f
Strube, M. J., 1201, 1203
submissiveness
 ear movement signaling of, in animals, 771
 postures for, in animals, 768
 social, 1115–16
substance use. *See also* addiction; drug use
 boredom and, 322
 distal causes of, 1219, 1222
 and dopamine system, 1221
 epidemiology of, 1220, 1224
 evolutionary perspective on, 1222–27
 fundamental motives framework for, 1227–33, 1228t
 mismatch hypothesis applied to, 1223–24, 1224f
 motivational-emotional systems and, 1220–33, 1228t
 negative-reinforcement model of, 1220–21, 1232–33
 neurotoxin regulation hypothesis of, 1226
 patterns of, 1220, 1224–25
 positive-reinforcement model of, 1220–21, 1232–33
 prevalence of, 1218, 1233
 prevention of, 1232–33
 proximate causes of, 1219, 1222
 risk factors for, 1220
 self-medication hypothesis for, 1221, 1229–30

substance use disorder(s), 1218–19
  and borderline personality
    disorder, 1281
  DSM diagnostic criteria for, 1219–
    20, 1229
  DSM features of, 1219–20
  emotional dysregulation and,
    1221, 1232–33
  epidemiology of, 1220, 1224
  Fast-Slow-Defense model and,
    1225–26
  and mental disorders,
    comorbidity, 1220
  patterns of, 1220, 1224
  prevalence of, 1233
  prevention of, 1232–33
  treatment, 1232
successive negative contrast, 830–31
  absolute versus relative, 933
  and behavioral evidence of
    negative emotion, 834
  consequences of, 839–40, 839f
  factors affecting, 839–40, 839f
  and neurobiological evidence of
    negative emotion, 836–39
  and pharmacological evidence of
    negative emotion, 835–36
  and physiological evidence of
    negative emotion, 834–35
successive negative contrast effect,
  831–39, 832f
  reversed, 832–34, 832f
successive negative contrast task
  consummatory (cSNC), 831–32,
    834, 835–39
  instrumental (iSNC), 831–32, 836
  Pavlovian (pSNC), 831–32
SUDs. *See* substance use disorder(s)
Sugiyama, Lawrence S., 297–310
suicidality, 1135, 1151–52
  in adolescence, 1154
  adversity and, 1135–36
  behavioral manifestations of, 1156
  bereavement and, 1143
  in borderline personality disorder,
    1280, 1281, 1282, 1284
  bullying and, 1148
  as credible signal of need,
    1153, 1154
  non-Western findings on, 1137
  ostracism and, 1043
  risk factors for, 1154
  social conflict and, 1148–50
suicide, 476–77
  adaptive perspective and, 1126
  attempts versus deaths by, sex
    differences in, 1154

cliff-edge principle and, 1100
  as protest, 1148–49
  romantic love and, 227, 229
sulking, cultural diversity in,
  57, 59–60
Sullivan, R. J., 1226
sun bears, emotional expression
  in, 770–71
superior temporal sulcus, in
  compassion, 576
supernormal stimuli, 1180
superordinate theory of emotions,
  99, 298, 309, 325–26, 371, 587–
  88, 609–10, 616, 617, 682, 750–
  51, 990, 1025–26, 1070, 1102–4,
  1229, 1284–85
  concerns about, 1104–6
  and functions regulated, 1103
surprise, xiii, 437–38
  as basic emotion, 4, 990
  evolutionary origins of, evidence
    for, 10t, 11
  expression of, culture-specific
    variations in, 988
  as primary emotion, 764
survival, 22
  versus quality of life, 1263
survival circuits, 1327–28
survivor guilt, 291, 292–93
Susskind, J. M., 74n.22
Svetieva, Elena, 681–93
swallow-tailed kite, 166
SWLS. *See* Satisfaction with
  Life Scale
Syme, Kristen L., 308, 1134–62
symmetry/ordering, obsessive-
  compulsive disorder and,
  1318, 1319
sympathetic nervous system, 446–
  48, 501, 810
  emotion regulation and, 754–55
  and fear responding/fear
    learning, 504–5
  romantic love and, 227–28
sympathy, 565–66. *See also*
  compassion; empathy
  cuteness and, 343–44
  elicitors of, 568
  evolutionary origins of, evidence
    for, 10t, 12
  kama muta and, 348
Szasz, Thomas, 1088
Sznycer, Daniel, 79–90, 135, 145–57,
  170, 1328, 1333–34

T

tabanka, 1150

tactile signals
  and candidate basic
    emotions, 9, 10t
  of compassion, 572–73
Tahiti, 15
tamarins. *See also* golden lion
  tamarins
  alloparental and parental
    provisioning in, 910
  infants' vocalizations, 915
  natural pedagogy in, 920
Tao Te Ching, 441
targeted helping, 801
  definition of, 801
task analysis, 361
  evolutionary, 29, 31, 106,
    361, 391–92
  of jealousy, 394–401
teaching, 111
teasing, in flirtation/courtship, 552
technology
  and boredom, 330–31
  and cue–decision rule–outcome
    relationship, 39–40
  and expression of
    emotion, 692–93
teleology, 24–25, 50n.3
temporal lobe, and laughter, 557
temporal parietal junction, in
  compassion, 576
Tend-and-Befriend Theory, 742–43
tenderness, 346, 372, 565–66
  cuteness and, 343–44
  kama muta and, 348
tend or befriend strategy, 972–73
terrorism
  ostracism and, 1048–50
  and risk perception, 902
testosterone, 862, 1320
  age-related decline, and
    depression, 874
  and aggression, 862–63
  and attachment, 239
  challenge hypothesis and,
    1272–73
  competition and, 862–63
  and depression, 867, 1272–73
  and depression in menopausal
    transition, 870
  and disgust sensitivity, 188
  and dominance behaviors, 862–64
  female ovulatory body odor
    and, 669–70
  and mate competition, 1272
  and mating competition in
    females, 974
  mood effects of, 867

and post-traumatic stress disorder, 1272–73
and status hierarchy, 863
success and, 475
and violence, 862
TFT. *See* tit-for-tat
theory(ies). *See also* Basic Emotion Theory
  in emotion science, xiv, 7
theory of mind, 421, 740–41, 775, 814, 918, 920
  and incongruity resolution in humor, 556
  and ironic humor, 554
thinness
  drive for, in males, 1187–88
  pursuit of, 1183–89 (*see also* eating disorder(s))
  and youthfulness, 1184
third-party punishment, 956–57, 1073
  across societies, 997–98
  anger and, 1003–06, 1014–16, 1014f
  compassion and, 1011, 1014–16, 1014f
  definition of, 997
  disgust and, 1014–16, 1014f
  emotional antecedents of, 998, 1012, 1014–16, 1014f
  general arousal and, 1007–08, 1009
  gratitude and, 1011, 1014–16, 1014f
  moral outrage and, 1006
  negative emotions and, 1009, 1014–16, 1014f
  neuroscience of, 1008–09
  positive emotions and, 1014–16, 1014f
Third-Party Punishment Game, 998–99, 1000–01, 1001f, 1002–03, 1004
thirst, and drug use, 1228t, 1229–30
Thomas, Dayna M., 929–41
Thornhill, N. W., 1146–47, 1148
Thornhill, R., 1146–47, 1148
thought suppression
  in post-traumatic stress disorder, 1266–67
  and rebound effect, 1266–67
threat(s). *See also* infidelity threat
  appraisal of, 698–99
  behavioral responses to, 506–7
  coordinated response to, 703–4
  dogs' responsiveness to, 818–19
  emotional appraisals of, 704

emotions associated with, and support for legal policies, 1077–78
facial expressions of, 1115–16
immediate, and fear, 108
in intergroup conflict, 698–99, 701–2
and leadership, 1031
perceived, leading to competition, 973–74
potential, and precautionary system, 108
sensitivity to, factors affecting, 703
unconditioned, and fear responding/fear learning, 503–4
threat avoidance, lassitude and, 301, 301f, 307
threat detection/perception, 284, 698–99
  and political attitudes, 613–15
  and specific phobias, 1112
threatened egotism model, 1206
threat-management system(s)
  basic principles of, 703–4
  and coordination of response to threat, 703–4
  for disease avoidance, 703, 707–8
  emotions elicited by, 703–4
  and false-positives, 703, 708, 711
  for intergroup conflict, 703–8
  and protection of reproductive choice, 705–7
  for self-protection, 703, 705
tickling, 544–45, 546, 555
tidal volume, 446
  contentment and, 447, 450t
TikTok, and boredom, 330–31
Timber Game, 454
Tinbergen, Niko, 61, 67–68, 101, 235, 358, 365, 484–85, 487, 492–93, 494, 543–44, 686, 689, 931, 1021, 1022, 1174
tit-for-tat, 718
  contrite, 719–20, 722–23, 728–29
  generous, 718–19
  noise and, 718–19
toads
  frustrative nonreward in, 833
  reversed SNC effect in, 833
tobacco use, mortality caused by, 1219–20
Tomkins, Silvan, 60–61, 73n.10, 73n.11, 73n.12
tonic immobility, 107, 1268
tonic immobility test, 768–69

Tonkean macaque, consolation behaviors in, 800
Tooby, John, 21–50, 62–63, 271, 273, 298, 325–26, 1103–4, 1135, 1284–85, 1327–28
Torah, 441–42, 1060
Torgerson-White, Lauri, 763–79
Toronchuk, J. A., 107
Torres, Carmen, 830–40
toxic individuals, 165–67
  counterfactual reasoning about, 166, 169
  fitness costs of, minimization, 167
  identification of, 165–67, 169
  killing of, 167
Tracy, Jessica L., tradition, and problemsolving, 57, 100, 104, 203–14, 614–15, 1229
trait(s)
  development, environment and, 985, 991
  fitness distribution of, 1099
  polygenic, fitness distribution of, 1099
  universal, 22
  variability in expression versus uniformity in design, 33–34
transcendence, 933–34
transformational leadership, 1023
  charisma and, 1029
  sub-styles of, 1023
trauma. *See also* post-traumatic stress disorder
  anxiety provokes by, 1119–20
  combat-related, 1265
  interpersonal, and post-traumatic stress disorder, 1265
  prevalence of, 1263–64
  types, and post-traumatic stress disorder, 1264–65
tree shrews, vocal signals used by, 768
trichotillomania, 1317, 1318
triumph, evolutionary origins of, evidence for, 10t, 12
Trivers, Robert, 931
trust, 936
  distortions, in post-traumatic stress disorder, 1268–69
  emotional expressivity and, 1331
  and female intrasexual competition, 973–74
  nonverbal communication and, 683–84
truth judgments, affective influence on, 532, 533f
trypophobia, 1121

Tsimane of Bolivia, 191
  cooperation among, 623–30
  depression in, social conflict and, 1148, 1149
  status and fitness-relevant outcomes in, 589
Turke, Paul, 21, 29–30, 31–32, 36–37
Turner, George, 1059
turtles, frustrative nonreward in, 833
TV watching, and civic behavior, 475

U

Ultimatum Game, 537–38, 538f, 752, 998–1000, 999f, 1002–03, 1004–05, 1006, 1007, 1008
umwelt, 890–91, 904n.2
unacceptable/taboo thoughts, obsessive-compulsive disorder and, 1318, 1319–20
uncertainty-reduction hypothesis, for reconciliation, 721–22
undoing effect, 377–78
unemployment
  depression and, 1154–55
  and unhappiness, 474
United States v. Bonds, 1067
universality, of human psychology, 984
upper body strength, and formidability, 1155
Uruvashi, 438–40
utilitarianism, 472

V

vacation, and happiness, 475
vagal tone, 494
vagus nerve
  and compassion, 575
  and fear responding/fear learning, 504–5
valence
  as appraisal dimension, 990
  of basic emotions, 810, 811
  and core affect, 991
  definition of, 810
  of emotions in animals, 764, 767, 793
valuable relationship hypothesis
  and animal reconciliation, 721, 722
  and forgiveness, 724–26
valuation. *See* social valuation
van Leeuwen, Florian, 607–17
Vaşistha's Yoga, 440
Vedas, 438–40
ventral striatum, 241, 575

ventral tegmental area, 241
vertebrates
  fear responding in, 503–4
  frustrative nonreward in, 832–34
  nociception in, 418–19
  reversed SNC effect in, 832–34
vervet monkeys, communication by, 915–16
vestigial organs/structures, Darwin's treatment of, 56, 72n.4, 72n.5
veterans
  adaptation to peacetime, 1273
  and post-traumatic stress disorder, 1265
  treatment avoidance by, 1274
vicarious experience, 566
victim(s), sympathy for, 472
victim impact statements, 899, 1071
vigilance. *See* emotional vigilance; epistemic vigilance
vigilance behavior, 1270. *See also* hypervigilance
VIM. *See* violence inhibition mechanism
vindictiveness, 43–44
violence
  deaths from, 699–700
  drug use and, 1230
  intergroup, and fear acquisition, 1265
  male human-on-human, 1264–65
  sex differences in, 1188
  against women, emotional distress caused by, 1137
violence inhibition mechanism, 285
virtue signaling, 898–99
visual detection paradigms, 1120
visual strategy(ies), dynamic nature of, 74n.22
VNO. *See* vomeronasal organ
vocal communication
  comparative perspective on, 916
  cooperative breeding and, 916
vocal displays, 848
vocalization
  as pain behavior, 419, 420, 635
  by prey, in predator attacks, 420
vocal signals
  by animals, 685
  and candidate basic emotions, 9, 10t, 11–12
  of compassion, 572–73
  of emotions, 684
vomeronasal organ, 667
von Bibra, Ernst, 1222
Vonk, Jennifer, 763–79
von Rueden, Christopher, 1021–33

Vornlocher, Carley, 369–84
VS. *See* ventral striatum
VTA. *See* ventral tegmental area
vulnerability. *See also* signaling vulnerability
  and anger, 117–18
  and attachment love, 379
  emotional response to, 372–73 (*see also* nurturant love; tenderness)
  studies of, 1144

W

Wakefield, Jerome, 1085–106, 1238–55, 1300, 1303, 1309. *See also* harmful dysfunction analysis
Wallis, Mary Davis, 1059
wanting
  versus liking, 468
  neurochemistry of, 468
Waorani society, intergroup conflict in, 700
war/warfare, 89. *See also* information warfare; intergroup conflict
  costly signaling in, 1268–69
  and emotional numbing, 1267–68
  and male sexual violence, 1272
  and memory for danger, 1266
  modern, as maladaptive behavior, 51n.8
  physical strength and, 610–11
  and post-traumatic stress disorder, 1264
  proactive aggression and, 107–8
  sex differences in, 1188
warmth-seeking, lassitude and, 301, 301f, 302–3
WEIRD populations, 182, 195n.1
  disgust research in, 182, 191
  disgust sensitivity and health-related outcomes in, 191
  gratitude studies in, 268–70
  research beyond, need for, 383
Weisfeld, Carol Cronin, 483–97, 543–58
Weisfeld, Glenn E., 462–77, 543–58
welfare trade-off decisions, 146, 148–49
welfare trade-off ratio, 168–69, 172, 742–43, 946. *See also* intrinsic welfare trade-off ratio
  anger and, 136–42, 170, 172–73, 610, 1071–72, 1073–74
  and anger-based arguments, 138
  apologies and, 727–28
  in cooperative relationships, anger and, 140–41
  definition of, 136

formidability and, 139
gratitude and, 270–75, 277, 611
guilt and, 611
and memory, 172
monitored, 1072
negative, 167–68, 172–73
recalibration, by hated target, 176–77
women and, 137–38
well-being
contentment and, 454–56
emotion regulation and, 756
emotions and, research on, future directions for, 939
gratitude and, 264, 265, 269, 277
positive emotions and, 370–71, 377–78
subjective, 471
Welling, Lisa L. M., 861–74
Wells, A., 1119–20, 1125
Wesselmann, Eric D., 1040–50
Western, educated, industrialized, rich, and democratic populations. *See* WEIRD populations
Westgate, Erin C., 317–32
Westmarck incest-avoidance mechanism. *See* incest avoidance
Williams, Blythe, 74n.21
Williams, George, 22, 33, 49–50, 72n.2
Adaptation and Natural Selection, 23–24
Williams, Keelah E. G., 1067–80
Williams, Kipling, 1041
Wilson, D. S., 548, 551
Wilson, David, 937
Winner Effect, 863
Witkower, Zachary, 203–14
Witzelsucht, 557
wolves, 818
moral behavior in, 422
and reconciliation, 720
women. *See also* female intrasexual competition
access to, and intergroup conflict, 700–2

aggression in, 863–64
anxiety disorders in, 871, 874
with borderline personality disorder, sexual behavior of, 1289
cooperativeness among, 977–78
depression in, 867
disgust sensitivity in, hormones and, 864–65
effective breeding population of, 1058, 1063
emotion regulation in, 755–56
empathy levels in, 1267–68
friendships among, 474
happiness in, 476
humor in, 555
and intergroup conflict, 701–3
and mental health stigma, 1274
narcissistic, and sexual coercion, 1203
and negotiation about entitlement, 610
obsessive-compulsive disorder in, 873
panic disorder in, 873
post-traumatic stress disorder in, 872–73
and protection of reproductive choice, 705–7
recovery from depression, positive events and, 1159–60
resource-assessment mechanisms of, 36–37
response to ostracism, 1043
as sexual spoils of war, 1272
social anxiety disorder in, 872
social smiling by, evolutionary perspective on, 689–90
supportive, as survival networks, 978
violence against, emotional distress caused by, 1137
as warriors, 701, 702
welfare trade-off ratio and, 137–38
work and happiness relationship for, 474–75
work, and happiness, 474–75

work productivity, depression and, 1154–55
worldview(s). *See also* mental map(s)
bereft, 898–99
context-sensitive, 889–91
defense of, motivated reasoning in, 898–99, 905n.6
emotion-based, 904
identity-relevant, and motivated reasoning, 886–88, 896–99
poorly defended, 898–99
worry, 254–55
evolutionary perspective on, 933
in generalized anxiety disorder, 1116–17
metacognitions about, 254–55
Wróbel, Monika, 1197–210
WTR. *See* welfare trade-off ratio
Wundt, Wilhelm, 64

X
Xerxes I, 1062

Y
Yanomamo society, 699–701, 1178, 1188
intergroup conflict in, 700–1
violent death in, 699–700
yawn contagion, 799
Yoga Sutras, 439
youthful appearance, female intrasexual competition and, 1183–89
Yupanqui, 1060

Z
Z Codes, 1089
zebra finches
movement/rest in illness, 302
sickness behavior in, 652
zebrafish, fear responding/fear learning in, 504
Zeelenberg, M., 247–48
Zeigler-Hill, Virgil, 1298–310
Zhao Shixiu, 317–18
zhīzú, 441, 444t
Zickfield, Janis H., 339–51
Zuberbühler, Klaus, 917–18